PREFACE

In writing this book we have been influenced by a tradition of labour law scholarship which, as we explain in Chapter 1, views this branch of the law as indissolubly linked to the goals of social policy. How labour law operates as a mechanism for the expression of those goals involves a consideration of many wider social, economic and philosophical issues than a book such as this can hope adequately to address. Nevertheless, an essential first step in attaining a wider understanding of labour law is to explain its internal conceptual structure. Accordingly, our foremost aim has been to produce a text which, without being encyclopædic, is broadly comprehensive in nature and so can serve as a resource in the teaching of labour law in universities. We have been pleased to find that what we have had to say in previous editions has also been of interest to practitioners of labour law in the legal and other interested professions, and we hope to continue to address this group in future.

We have sought to explain the contemporary law in a way which brings out the dynamic and continuously evolving nature of doctrine in this area, and, in particular, to show how it is shaped by the interaction between the principal sources of labour law (the common law, collective bargaining, social legislation and transnational labour standards). To that end we have attempted to locate the law in its historical context; to make selective use, where appropriate, of comparative and international material; to consider areas of labour market regulation which are closely related to labour law (such as active labour market policy and aspects of tax and social security law); and to discuss, where relevant, theories and accounts of the law's economic and social impact. At various points we have, perhaps, been able to do no more than indicate further lines of inquiry for those who may be interested in considering these dimensions of the subject; but if we are able to whet the appetite of readers in this way, we shall be content.

Our aim throughout has been to integrate our account of legal doctrine with analysis of law and policy. We have attempted to make the text more digestible by the use of numbered paragraphs and sub-headings. We also conclude our analyses of areas of the law with assessment sections, either within or at the end of chapters, whose purpose is to provide a critical evaluation of those areas.

We are grateful for all the support and encouragement we have received from our publishers.

In April 2000 one of us, Gillian Morris, was appointed a deputy chairman of the CAC. This work is written entirely in a personal capacity and its contents should not be taken to represent the views of the CAC unless indicated otherwise in the text.

For the sake of clarity we have used the nomenclature of the Civil Procedure Rules throughout, regardless of whether the case with which we are concerned was subject to these rules. Thus, 'plaintiffs' become 'claimants', 'interlocutory' injunctions are 'interim'. We also refer to 'employment' tribunals throughout. However, we refer to the Supreme Court, which replaced the Appellate Committee of the House of Lords in October 2009, only in relation to decisions made by that specific body.

The law of England and Wales is stated as at 6 April 2012, although it has been possible to include some amendments since that date.

SFD
GSM
28 June 2012.

CONTENTS

Labour Law

Sixth Edition

Simon Deakin
Professor of Law and Fellow of Peterhouse, University of Cambridge

Gillian S Morris
Barrister, Matrix Chambers;
a Deputy Chairman of the Central Arbitration Committee;
Honorary Professor, Warwick Business School, University of Warwick;
and a former Professor of Law at Brunel University

OXFORD AND PORTLAND, OREGON
2012

Published in the United Kingdom by Hart Publishing Ltd
16C Worcester Place, Oxford, OX1 2JW
Telephone: +44 (0)1865 517 530
Fax: +44 (0) 1865 510 710
email: mail@hartpub.co.uk
Website: http://www.hartpub.co.uk

Published in North America (US and Canada) by
Hart Publishing
c/o International Specialized Book Services
920 NE 58th Avenue, Suite 300
Portland, OR 97213-3786
USA
Tel: +1 503 287 3093 or toll-free: (1) 800 944 6190
Fax: +1 503 280 8832
E-mail: orders@isbs.com
Website: www.isbs.com

British Library Cataloguing in Publication Data
Data Available

ISBN: 978-1-84946-341-6

Edited and typeset by Rebecca Forster, in Minion 10/11 pt
Printed and bound in Great Britain by
TJ International Ltd, Padstow, Cornwall

TABLE OF STATUTES

UNITED KINGDOM LEGISLATION

INTERNATIONAL LEGISLATION

Canada

France

LIST OF CASES

H

J

L

N

Q

R

xcii   LIST OF CASES

TABLE OF ABBREVIATIONS

ACAS	Advisory, Conciliation and Arbitration Service
BERR	Department for Business Enterprise and Regulatory Reform
BFOQ	Bona Fide Occupational Qualification
BIS	Department for Business, Innovation and Skills
CA	Court of Appeal
CAC	Central Arbitration Committee
CBI	Confederation of British Industry
CEACR	Committee of Experts on the Application of Conventions and Recommendations
CFREU	Charter of Fundamental Human Rights of the European Union
CIE	Committee of Independent Experts
CJEU	Court of Justice of the European Union
CO	Certification Officer
CPR	Civil Procedure Rules
CRE	Commission for Racial Equality
CROTUM	Commissioner for the Rights of Trade Union Members
CRPD	Convention on the Rights of Persons with Disabilities
DEFRA	Department for Environment, Food and Rural Affairs
DfEE	Department for Education and Employment
DfE	Department for Education
DPP	Director of Public Prosecutions
DRA	Default Retirement Age
DWP	Department of Work and Pensions
DRC	Disability Rights Commission
DTI	Department of Trade and Industry
EAT	Employment Appeal Tribunal
EC	European Community
ECHR	European Convention on Human Rights
ECtHR	European Court of Human Rights
ECJ	European Court of Justice
ECSR	European Committee of Social Rights
EDT	Effective Date of Termination
EEC	European Economic Community
EHRC	Equality and Human Rights Commission
EOC	Equal Opportunities Commission
ESC	European Social Charter

ESOP	Employee Share Ownership Plan
ET	Employment Tribunal
ETOR	Economic, Technical or Organisational Reason
EU	European Union
EWC	European Works Council
GCHQ	Government Communications Headquarters
GMP	Guaranteed Minimum Pension
GOQ	Genuine Occupational Qualification
GOR	Genuine Occupational Requirement
HL	House of Lords
HMCTS	Her Majesty's Courts and Tribunals Service
HMRC	Her Majesty's Revenue and Customs
HSC	Health and Safety Commission
HSE	Health and Safety Executive
ICCPR	International Covenant on Civil and Political Rights
ICESCR	International Covenant on Economic, Social and Cultural Rights
ICO	Information Commissioner's Office
ICP	Information and Consultation Procedure
ILO	International Labour Organisation
I and C	Information and Consultation
JCHR	Joint Committee on Human Rights
JIC	Joint Industrial Council
NEDC	National Economic Development Council
NHS	National Health Service
NI CA	Court of Appeal, Northern Ireland
NIRC	National Industrial Relations Court
NMW	National Minimum Wage
NRA	Normal Retirement Age
ODT	Operative Date of Termination
OMC	Open Method of Coordination
OPB	Occupational Pensions Board
OPRA	Occupational Pensions Regulatory Authority
PEA	Pre-Existing Agreement
PILON	Payment of Wages in Lieu of Notice
QIP	Qualified Independent Person
SSP	State Second Pension
SAYE	Save as You Earn Share Options Scheme
SE	Societas Europaea (European Company)
SERPS	State Earnings-Related Pension Scheme
SDDP	Statutory Dismissal and Disciplinary Procedure
SGP	Statutory Grievance Procedure
SMP	Statutory Maternity Pay
SNB	Special Negotiating Body
SOSR	Some Other Substantial Reason
SSP	Statutory Sick Pay

TEC	Training and Enterprise Council
TEU	Treaty on European Union
TFEU	Treaty on the Functioning of the European Union
TS	Tribunals Service
TUC	Trades Union Congress
UKBA	UK Border Agency
ULR	Union Learning Representative

LEGISLATION

APLR	Additional Paternity Leave Regulations
ASPPR	Additional Statutory Paternity Pay (General) Regulations
AWR	Agency Workers Regulations
CA	Companies Act
CCBMR	Companies (Cross-Border Mergers) Regulations
CJPOA	Criminal Justice and Public Order Act
CPA	Civil Partnership Act
DCOA	Deregulation and Contracting Out Act
DDA	Disability Discrimination Act
DPA	Data Protection Act
DRCA	Disability Rights Commission Act
DTR	Disclosure and Transparency Rules
EA	Employment Act
EADR	Equality Act Disability Regulations
EADRR	Employment Act 2002 (Dispute Resolution) Regulations
ECSIER	European Cooperative Society (Involvement of Employees) Regulations
EE(A)R	Employment Equality (Age) Regulations
EE(RB)R	Employment Equality (Religion or Belief) Regulations
EE(SO)R	Employment Equality (Sexual Orientation) Regulations
EPA	Employment Protection Act
EPCA	Employment Protection (Consolidation) Act
EPLLCEIGBR	European Public Limited-Liability Company (Employee Involvement) (Great Britain) Regulations
EPLLCR	European Public Limited-Liability Company Regulations
EqA	Equality Act
EqPA	Equal Pay Act
ERABR	Employment Relations Act 1999 (Blacklists) Regulations
ERDRA	Employment Rights (Dispute Resolution) Act
ERelA	Employment Relations Act
ETA	Employment Tribunals Act
FTER	Fixed Term Employees (Prevention of Less Favourable Treatment) Regulations
FWER	Flexible Working (Eligibility, Complaints and Remedies) Regulations

FWPR	Flexible Working (Procedural Requirements) Regulations
GRA	Gender Recognition Act
HRA	Human Rights Act
HSWA	Health and Safety at Work etc Act
IA	Insolvency Act
ICER	Information and Consultation of Employees Regulations
ICTA	Income and Corporation Taxes Act
ITEAP	Income Tax (Earnings and Pensions) Act
IRA	Industrial Relations Act
LGA	Local Government Act
MHSW	Management of Health and Safety at Work Regulations
MPLR	Maternity and Parental Leave etc Regulations
NIA	National Insurance Act
NMWA	National Minimum Wage Act
NMWR	National Minimum Wage Regulations
OPPSCER	Occupational and Personal Pension Schemes (Consultation by Employees and Miscellaneous Amendment) Regulations
PA	Pensions Act
PALR	Paternity and Adoption Leave Regulations
PSA	Pension Schemes Act
PTWR	Part-Time Workers (Prevention of Less Favourable Treatment) Regulations
RIPA	Regulation of Investigatory Powers Act
RR(Am)A	Race Relations (Amendment) Act
RRA	Race Relations Act
SDA	Sex Discrimination Act
SMPR	Statutory Maternity Pay (General) Regulations
SPPR	Statutory Paternity Pay and Statutory Adoption Pay (General) Regulations
SSA	Social Security Act
SSAA	Social Security Administration Act
SSCBA	Social Security Contributions and Benefits Act
SSFA	Schools Standards and Framework Act
SSPA	Statutory Sick Pay Act
TCA	Tax Credits Act
TDA	Trade Disputes Act
TICER	Transnational Information and Consultation of Employees Regulations
TUA	Trade Union Act
TULRA	Trade Union and Labour Relations Act
TULRCA	Trade Union and Labour Relations (Consolidation) Act
TUPE	Transfer of Undertakings (Protection of Employment) Regulations
TURERA	Trade Union Reform and Employment Rights Act
UCTA	Unfair Contract Terms Act
WA	Wages Act
WFA	Work and Families Act
WTR	Working Time Regulations

1

INTRODUCTION

LABOUR LAW: THE SCOPE AND NATURE OF THE SUBJECT

Labour law as a discipline

1.1 The discipline of *labour law* is defined in part by its subject-matter, in part by an intellectual tradition. Its immediate subject-matter consists of the rules which govern the employment relationship. However, a broader perspective would see labour law as the normative framework for the existence and operation of all the institutions of the labour market: the business enterprise, trade unions, employers' associations and, in its capacity as regulator and as employer, the state. The starting point for analysis is the existence of the employment relationship as a distinct economic and legal category. Labour law stems from the idea of 'the subordination of the individual worker to the capitalist enterprise';[1] it is above all the law of *dependent labour*, and hence is specific to those categories of economic relationship which in some way involve the exchange of *personal service or services* for remuneration. Labour law is concerned with how these relationships are constituted, a role which in common law systems is accorded primarily to contract, and with how they are regulated, a role shared by the common law and social legislation but also by extra-legal sources such as collective bargaining and workplace custom and practice. Its scope accordingly extends from the individual to the collective, from the contract of employment to relations between the institutions of organised labour and capital, and to the conduct and resolution of conflicts between them.

The intellectual tradition to which we referred sees *labour law* as a unified discipline which has outgrown its diverse origins in the law of obligations and in the regulatory intervention of the state. As a subject with its own doctrinal unity and structure, it spans the divides between common law and legislation and between private law and public law. In Britain, as elsewhere in Europe, it has established itself as one of the principal branches of legal studies.[2] The view that labour law is more than just the sum of its parts is derived initially from the writings of German jurists in the

---

[1] Hepple, 1986a: p 11.

[2] We will from time to time refer to 'labour law in Britain' or 'British labour law', while being fully aware that there is no such thing as 'British law'. The case for referring to 'British labour law' is that while the common law is, of course, the common law of England and Wales, labour legislation (like that of social security) is by and large general to both the legal systems of Great Britain. We do not, however, seek to discuss the distinctive features of the Scottish legal system or those principles of Scottish law which differ from those of the law of England and Wales.

early decades of the twentieth century, who saw the subject as the embodiment of social policy in action. This view, which at its broadest implied that labour law should embrace 'sociology, social policy and the theory of business organisation',[3] came to influence the study of labour law in Britain through the writings of Sir Otto Kahn-Freund who, having been a labour court judge in the Germany of the Weimar Republic, lived and taught in Britain from the 1930s. His conception of the subject stressed the functional inter-dependence of the positive law with extra-legal sources of regulation, in particular collective bargaining: his contribution 'revolutionised the study, the teaching and the very character of labour law in Britain'.[4] This perspective remains valid today, notwithstanding the enormous changes which have taken place in the form and content of labour law since Kahn-Freund elaborated his theory of the subject in writings of the 1950s[5] which were to have a major impact not just on scholarship but also on the courts[6] and on the formulation of public policy in this area.[7]

Although the notion of labour law as the normative framework for the institutions of the labour market has commanded increasing attention in recent years,[8] it should be borne in mind that other, closely-related areas of law are also important determinants of labour market outcomes. For reasons of space, and also because these other areas are dealt with in specialist works in the fields concerned, we do not aim to provide a comprehensive treatment of each of them in this book. However, an understanding of *social security law* is essential to an appreciation of many important aspects of the employment relationship, including the impact of social security contributions on the earnings of the individual employee and the entitlements of the unemployed and those seeking work to the receipt of social security benefits. We have included material on the relevant principles of social security law[9] where their relationship with labour law is particularly close. However, it should be remembered that social security law constitutes a body of principle which is studied in its own right,[10] since it extends far beyond the employment relationship to embrace, in a wider sense, many aspects of the relationship between the citizen and the state in the distribution of economic resources. Very much the same point applies to the *law of taxation*, which also has a major impact on the employment relationship through the incidence of income tax and also on occupational pension rights,[11] but which again extends to a far broader field of public policy issues. From a slightly different perspective, it is also evident that labour law intersects with *company law*, and that some awareness of company law principles is central to an understanding of the legal nature of the business enterprise. Again, where appropriate we highlight the significance of company law and of the increasingly important area of corporate governance,

---

[3] Sinzheimer, 1910–1911, cited in Hepple, 1986a: p 9.

[4] Wedderburn, 1983: p 29. For further analysis of Kahn-Freund's contribution, see para 1.10 below.

[5] Kahn-Freund, 1954a, 1954b, 1959.

[6] *Ford Motor Co Ltd v AUEFW* [1969] 2 QB 303.

[7] Most notably in the *Report of the Royal Commission on Trade Unions and Employers' Associations* (the 'Donovan Report'), Cmnd 3623, 1968.

[8] P Davies and M Freedland, 1984; Szyszczak, 1986; H Collins, 1989; Deakin and Wilkinson, 1991; Mitchell, 1995; H Collins *et al*, 2000; A Davies, 2004; Deakin and Wilkinson, 2005; P Davies and M Freedland, 2007.

[9] See paras 3.16–3.17 (active labour market policy); paras 4.129–4.141 (occupational pension schemes); and paras 11.87–11.89 (industrial action and social security benefits).

[10] See N Harris, 2000; Wikeley, 2002.

[11] See paras 3.19 and 4.132, respectively.

in particular in our discussion of the labour law concept of the 'employer' and its relationship to company law notions of the enterprise and of its constituent elements.[12]

The techniques of *comparative law* have provided one of the most important tools of analysis of national labour law systems, and have greatly enhanced the theory of labour law.[13] The study of comparative labour law has increased in importance in recent years largely because of the growing tendency towards global economic integration, and the development of transnational labour standards which draw on a number of different national traditions and methods. In the case of labour law in Britain, the increasing influence of European Union standards has brought with it a heightened awareness of other European systems. In this work we do not purport to offer systematic comparative analyses of the issues we examine, but we make selective use of comparative material in constructing the framework for our analysis and to indicate, where it is possible to do so, how distinctive legal solutions are possible to what are frequently common problems.

Following the tradition begun by the German *sozialjuristen*, many British labour law scholars have attempted to integrate into their work the insights of other social science disciplines. The influence of industrial sociology has been most widely felt, in large part because of the close links which have long existed between labour law and the study of industrial relations. More recently, growing use has been made of labour economics, feminist legal theory, and political theory.[14] The principal aim of this book is to analyse the conceptual and doctrinal structure of labour law and to examine its application to concrete problems of the kind which frequently arise in practice, rather than to present labour law from the viewpoint of another social science discipline. We have taken this approach in the belief that a thorough explication of labour law doctrine is essential, in order for labour law to be understood both as a *juridical* and as a *social and economic* phenomenon. At the same time, we do not believe that an effective doctrinal account of this area can be provided without close consideration being given to the influence upon the law of ideas drawn from economics and social policy, and we will therefore make reference to those influences wherever appropriate in the text that follows.

The structure of this book

1.2   Certain divisions of the legal material which forms labour law have become generally accepted. A broad division is taken to exist between 'individual labour law', the law relating in a narrow sense to the relationship of employer and employee, and 'collective labour law', or the law which is concerned with collective bargaining, trade union organisation and industrial action. In practice, the 'individual' and 'collective' aspects of the subject are closely interlinked and, we would suggest, cannot be adequately considered in isolation from one another. For example, in analysing the individual employment relationship, it is necessary to take into account the influence of norms which are derived from collective sources, in particular collective bargaining.[15] Conversely, the

---

[12] See paras 3.61–3.65 below.
[13] On the advantages but also the pitfalls of comparative analysis of labour law, see Kahn-Freund, 1972.
[14] For a review, see H Collins, 1997.
[15] See ch 4 below, in particular paras 4.26–4.31.

contract of employment plays a fundamental role in relation to the economic torts and other aspects of the law governing industrial action.[16]

This does not mean that the generally-accepted classifications are not useful for the purposes of organisation and exposition of the subject. Although other sub-divisions of the subject are possible,[17] we believe that there is much to be said for retaining a framework which will be broadly familiar to labour law scholars and practitioners alike. Nevertheless, within this framework, we have attempted to integrate 'individual' and 'collective' aspects of the subject wherever possible in the treatment of particular issues.

We also take the view that an appreciation of the historical development of the labour law system is essential to an understanding of its current form and content. This is particularly so with regard to the inter-relationship between the principal *sources* of labour law, namely the common law, social legislation and non-formal sources including collective bargaining and workplace custom and practice. We therefore preface our analysis of the substantive law with two introductory chapters. The remainder of this chapter examines in historical perspective some core themes of labour law in Britain and concludes by posing the question: what is the rationale of contemporary labour law? Here we analyse two apparently competing conceptions of labour law as promoting economic efficiency, on the one hand, and as protecting fundamental social and economic rights, on the other.

Chapter 2 is concerned with sources and institutions of labour law. Here we examine in greater detail the relationship between formal sources of law, in particular the common law and legislation, and what we term 'voluntary' sources, of which collective bargaining is the most significant. This chapter also explains the nature of institutions which are particular to labour law, including the employment tribunal system and forms of administrative intervention in employment relations. We also outline the role of EU law within labour law and consider the influence of other international labour standards.

The rest of the book is devoted to the study of areas of substantive legal doctrine. Chapter 3 analyses the law governing the formation and constitution of the employment relationship. Chapters 4 and 5 then examine the contents of that relationship: chapter 4 is concerned with the law governing terms and conditions of employment, and chapter 5 with the subject of discipline and termination of employment. Chapter 6 is devoted to the analysis of equal treatment in employment. Chapter 7 provides an overview of the law relating to collective organisation by both workers and employers, and thereby provides a framework for chapters 8 to 10 which examine specific aspects of collective relationships. Chapter 8 examines the law relating to freedom of association, chapter 9 collective representation and the law, and chapter 10 the law relating to trade unions and their members. Finally, in chapter 11 we analyse the legal implications at both collective and individual levels of industrial action.

---

[16] See paras 11.10 *et seq* and 11.64 *et seq.*

[17] For discussion of a treatment of the subject which would see labour law more clearly as a form of regulation of the labour market, see Mitchell, 1995.

Labour law, collective bargaining and labour standards

1.3   A theme to which we will return at numerous points is the role of collective bargaining in relation to social legislation, and it may be useful to clarify at the outset our use of some key terms. By *collective bargaining* we mean the process of negotiation between an employer or group of employers on the one hand and one or more trade unions on the other, designed to produce *collective agreements* which may have a number of functions. Two functions of collective agreements are particularly important: the *procedural* or *contractual* function of regulating the relationship between the collective parties themselves; and the *normative* or *rule-making* function, which consists of the establishment of terms and conditions which are applicable to the contracts of individual workers. Collective agreements may operate on a number of levels. *Sector-level bargaining* refers to a process of negotiation which takes place at the level of a particular trade or industry, normally between an employers' association and one or more trade unions. This form of bargaining, once prevalent in Britain, is now rare. It is more usual for bargaining to take place either at the level of the *company* or *enterprise*, or, within companies, at the level of the *plant* or *establishment*.

The term *social legislation* refers, broadly, to legislation in the field of employment, which may be one of two types.[18] *Regulatory legislation* directly affects employment relationships, typically by laying down statutory norms which override the parties' own agreement. Examples include minimum wage legislation and legislation limiting the power of the employer to terminate the relationship (unfair dismissal legislation). *Auxiliary legislation*, by contrast, consists of legal supports for the process of collective bargaining and other aspects of collective organisation; in this sense its impact on the employment relationship is indirect. Examples of such legislation include laws which may require employers to recognise trade unions for the purpose of collective bargaining, and laws which oblige employers to consult with or give information to representatives of the workforce.

It can be seen from this analysis that *labour standards* – the protective norms which govern the employment relationship – can derive either from legal sources (legislation or, more exceptionally, the common law) or from extra-legal sources, of which collective bargaining is one of the most significant. Moreover, the balance between regulatory and auxiliary legislation is an important determinant of the extent to which the state supports or, alternatively, displaces collective bargaining as a form of regulation.

HISTORICAL DEVELOPMENT

1.4   Our intention here is to offer a brief historical outline of the evolution of labour law which is more thematic than chronological in nature.[19] We consider in turn five central themes in the

---

[18] The distinction between regulatory and auxiliary legislation was developed by Kahn-Freund: see P Davies and M Freedland, 1983: ch 2.

[19] The subject of labour law history is an important and growing field in its own right. On the eighteenth and nineteenth centuries, see Orth, 1991; on wartime labour law, Rubin, 1987; on the development of the contract of employment, Deakin, 1998, 2000, and Deakin and Wilkinson, 2005; on the modern period, P Davies and M Freedland, 1993 and 2007; and for a brief overview, Ewing and Morris, 2000.

development of labour law: collective organisation, and the attitude towards it of the common law; the relationship between collective bargaining and social legislation; the evolution of the employment relationship; the impact on collective bargaining of wider forms of state intervention in and management of the economy, in particular state corporatism; and legal policies aimed at enhancing the flexibility of the labour market.

Collective organisation and the common law

1.5   The common law has traditionally been hostile to the collective self-organisation of workers, and it is only by means of statutory intervention, in the form of 'immunities' from common law liability, that a space has been created within which trade unions, in particular, may operate lawfully for the purposes of collective bargaining and activities associated with it, such as the conduct of industrial action and the regulation of particular trades and occupations. The hostility of the common law to collectivist values is deep-rooted, and has been expressed in a number of different legal doctrines: these include the crime (and later the tort) of conspiracy, the doctrine of restraint of trade as a ground for the invalidation of contracts, and the economic torts which protect the trade and livelihood of individuals and businesses against direct or intentional interference. One of the most remarkable features of this aspect of the common law is that it has been maintained in one form or another practically throughout the modern period, and notwithstanding periodic changes in the attitude of the legislature.

The corporative system and its decline

1.6   As late as the middle of the eighteenth century, the labour market continued to be regulated by a 'corporative' system involving controls over prices, wages, labour mobility and training, the cornerstone of which was the Statute of Artificers of 1562.[20] Wage regulation was still formally the responsibility of the local magistrates in agriculture and of the guilds in the urban trades; related legislation governed poor relief and the right to a parish settlement. The corporative system purported to guarantee workers a certain degree of wage stability and occupational protection, but at the same time restricted labour mobility and effectively outlawed strikes and combinations of workers designed to maintain and improve terms and conditions of employment. Such combinations constituted a criminal conspiracy at common law.[21] In addition, numerous Acts of Parliament from the 1720s onwards outlawed associations of journeymen and apprentices aimed at raising wages or reducing hours. The first of these measures was an Act of 1720 'for regulating the journeymen tailors' in London, which followed the formation of the London Journeymen Tailors' Union and a strike of the preceding year. The Act made agreements for the purpose of advancing wages or reducing hours null and void, and made it an offence subject to two months' imprisonment to enter into such agreements. It was also made an offence for a journeyman tailor

---

[20] This Act, in turn, contained elements derived from the first formal labour statutes of the middle ages, the Ordinance of Labourers of 1349 and the Statute of Labourers of 1351. See Deakin and Wilkinson, 2005: pp 44–61.
[21] *R v Journeymen-Tailors of Cambridge* (1721) 8 Mod 10.

to leave work unfinished or to quit before the end of his agreed term of employment. Similar legislation, dealing with combinations or work discipline or both, followed for individual trades, and a more general anti-combination law was passed in 1749[22] covering several expanding manufacturing trades including cotton and iron. These laws assumed that combinations to raise wages were unlawful at common law – it was 'contrary to law' for the journeymen weavers 'to enter into combinations, and to make by-laws or orders, by which they pretend to regulate the trade and prices of their goods, and to advance their wages unreasonably'[23] – but the Acts had the advantage over the common law of providing for a summary procedure for conviction. In contrast, common law actions for criminal conspiracy were less straightforward to argue and more expensive to bring.[24] The Combination Acts of 1799 and 1800, which imposed a general ban on combinations, went further still by empowering justices to grant a licence to employers to take on labour contrary to the apprenticeship rules of the Statute of Artificers of 1562 and related legislation, in any case where combinations of workmen struck for higher wages or interfered with business, or where:

> ... the qualified journeymen and workmen usually employed in any manufacture, trade or business, shall refuse to work therein for reasonable wages, or to work for any particular person or persons, or to work with any particular persons, or shall, by refusing to work for any cause whatsoever, or by misconducting themselves when employed to work, in any manner impede or obstruct the ordinary course of any manufacture, trade or business, or endeavour to injure the person or persons carrying on the same.[25]

Shortly after, the protective provisions of the corporative system were formally repealed. The wage-regulation provisions of the Statute of Artificers were repealed in 1813 and the repeal of the apprenticeship regulations followed a year later. They had already been eroded by restrictive judicial interpretations,[26] and had fallen into disuse in large parts of agriculture and industry. However, they were not abandoned without a struggle: in 1812–1813 the London artisans' associations mounted a substantial but unsuccessful campaign for the preservation of the regulations, through which they had been able to control entry into the trade and regulate competition and the setting of prices. It was in part as a consequence of these reforms that major employers were prepared to acquiesce in the repeal of the Combination Acts in 1824.[27] However, when this repeal led to (or at least coincided with) a wave of strikes, a second Act was passed in 1825 which reimposed certain criminal sanctions in respect of picketing and activities designed to persuade workers not to work.[28] A further measure, the Molestation of Workmen Act 1859, slightly ameliorated the restraints thereby imposed. For the fifty years or so after 1825 the legal position was, in principle, that freedom of association was permitted, and that collective bargaining could be lawfully pursued; however, strike action remained tightly confined. In practice, there was no effective right

---

[22] 22 Geo II c 27.
[23] 12 Geo I c 34.
[24] Orth, 1991: ch 4.
[25] 39 & 40 Geo III c 106, s 15. For further details on this legislation, see para 7.12 below.
[26] *Raynard v Chase* (1756) 1 Burr 2; *Smith v Company of Armourers* (1792) Peake 199.
[27] 'Such a relaxed view was consistent with them having achieved mastery in their own establishments': Moher, 1989: p 241.
[28] See Orth, 1991: ch 5.

to resist employers who refused to enter into collective bargaining since the main weapon open to trade unions, namely strike action, was regulated by the criminal law. The criminal law also imposed sanctions on individual workers who quit their employment in breach of contract, by virtue of the Master and Servant Act 1823 which was the successor to a number of eighteenth-century statutes which had a similar effect.

The decriminalisation of labour law

1.7   It was not until the 'legislative settlement' of the 1870s that legislation lifted the threat of criminal sanctions from all but violent forms of behaviour associated with industrial action. The first breach in the restrictive labour laws of the early and mid-nineteenth century was the Master and Servant Act of 1867, which was intended to make imprisonment of workers for breach of contract a measure of last resort, available only for 'aggravated' misconduct and for damage to persons or property, with a fine the more normal penalty. At the same time, other aspects of the magistrates' jurisdiction were extended, including the power to award damages for breach of contract and to order specific performance of the obligation to work. Following the 1867 Act prosecutions continued at high levels and magistrates made extensive use of their remaining powers of imprisonment. The more general case for reform of the legal position of trade unions was considered by the 1867 Royal Commission under Sir William Erle, which was set up in the aftermath of disturbances during an industrial dispute which became known as the Sheffield 'outrages'. The Royal Commission was also able to consider the implications of the decision of the Court of Queen's Bench in *Hornby v Close*,[29] which held that trade unions were unlawful associations in so far as their objects included the raising of wages and the control of labour in the trades in which their members worked; such objects and activities amounted to restraint of trade. One effect of *Hornby v Close* was that union property could not necessarily be safeguarded against appropriation.

The majority report of the 1867 Royal Commission declared in favour of placing trade union organisation on a legal footing, but only in return for the removal from union rule books of clauses providing for control of apprenticeships and the prohibition of piecework and sub-contracting; the minority argued for a more complete immunisation of trade unions from the laws of conspiracy and restraint of trade. The Trade Union Act of 1871 went part of the way to meeting the minority's recommendations. Sections 2 and 3 of the Act stipulated that the purposes of trade unions (and by extension, employers' associations) were not to be deemed unlawful in either the criminal or the civil law 'by reason merely that they are in restraint of trade'. This had the effect, among other things, of reversing *Hornby v Close*,[30] so that union funds could be protected; in addition, provision was made for unions to register with the Registrar for Friendly Societies in order to gain certain tax and administrative advantages. The aim of keeping the courts out of union affairs was further reinforced by section 4 of the Act, which provided that none of the internal rules of trade unions were to be enforceable as contracts, so as to prevent unions either suing or being sued for their breach. Although meant primarily for the protection of trade unions, these

---

[29] (1867) 10 Cox CC 393.
[30] (1867) 10 Cox CC 393.

provisions of the 1871 Act also had the effect that collective agreements between trade unions and employers' associations could not be given legal force or implemented by the courts, a view later endorsed by the Royal Commission on Labour of 1891–1894. At that time, this was explained on the alternative grounds, either that unions and associations lacked legal personality under section 6, or that section 4(4) prevented agreements between them being enforced as contracts.

The second measure of 1871, the Criminal Law Amendment Act, made only minor changes to the existing statutory law on molestation and obstruction. The continuing role of the criminal law in restricting trade union action was confirmed in the following year when workers taking part in the London gas stokers' strike were imprisoned for 'aggravated' breach of contract under section 14 of the 1867 Master and Servant Act and their leaders convicted of criminal conspiracy.[31] The trial judge held that the strike leaders committed the crime of conspiracy at common law in addition to conspiracy to induce the criminal act of aggravated misconduct, and imposed sentences in excess of the three months stipulated for unlawful molestation by the Criminal Law Amendment Act. The decision on common law conspiracy was seen as undermining the 1871 legislation, and a further Royal Commission was established by the incoming Conservative government in 1875.

The majority report of the 1875 Commission recommended that collective rights of association should prevail over the common law doctrine of restraint of trade and that breach of the contract of service should not give rise to criminal liability. Two Bills introduced by the Conservative administration in 1875 reflected the recommendations of the Royal Commission; they were amended in the course of their passage as a result of Liberal pressure,[32] with the result that the magistrates' criminal jurisdiction for breach of the employment contract was removed altogether by the Employers and Workmen Act 1875, and the Criminal Law Amendment Act 1871 was repealed and replaced by the more precise criminal provisions of the Conspiracy and Protection of Property Act 1875. These were now confined to the cases of violent or intimidatory picketing, deliberate breach of contract by public utility workers (gas and water), and deliberate breach of contract involving injury to persons or property. The narrowing down of these statutory criminal provisions made the new immunity from conspiracy all the more important; this provided that common law conspiracy should have no application 'to an agreement or combination by two or more persons to do or procure to be done any act in contemplation or furtherance of a trade dispute', if the act in question would not be a crime if committed by a single person. The legislation of the 1870s had thereby laid the basic legal foundations for the voluntary collective bargaining system – the principle of the legal non-enforceability of collective agreements, which emerged from the Trade Union Act, and the *trade dispute formula* of immunity from common law liability for concerted action in protection of workers' economic interests.

The economic torts and trade dispute immunities

1.8 The process begun by the legislation of the 1870s of removing restrictive legal intervention in trade union affairs was not completed until the trade dispute formula was extended to cover tortious liability by the Trade Disputes Act 1906. In the thirty years following the adoption of

---

[31] *R v Bunn* (1872) 12 Cox CC 316.
[32] Spain, 1991.

the Conspiracy and Protection of Property Act 1875, the courts filled the gap left by the removal of criminal liability by expanding the economic torts in a series of innovative decisions. These established that industrial action would normally involve the organisers of strikes in committing one or more of a number of torts. Calling workers out on strike involved the tort of inducing breach of contract, first formulated in a separate context in *Lumley v Gye* in 1853.[33] The courts stopped only just short of accepting the concept of *prima facie* tort liability for the 'malicious' infliction of economic loss by one person on another, the House of Lords insisting in *Allen v Flood*[34] that independently unlawful means were needed. This principle did not extend to the case of concerted action, however: the tort of conspiracy was likely to apply to collective industrial action taken with the aim of persuading an employer not to make use of non-union labour, for example.[35] Most importantly, in *Taff Vale Railway Co v ASRS*[36] the House of Lords held in 1901 that the trade union itself could be sued in damages under its registered name, that is the name adopted for the purposes of registration under the Trade Union Act 1871, an effect which those who drafted the Act of 1871 had neither intended nor anticipated. This opened up union funds to the threat of depletion through actions in tort by employers and others affected by strikes, effectively returning trade unions to the position they occupied prior to 1875.

The position was restored by the Trade Disputes Act 1906, which extended the trade dispute immunity to cover certain of the economic torts, namely conspiracy and the tort of inducing breach of a contract of employment. Those organising strikes were immunised against liability in these torts if they were acting 'in contemplation or furtherance of a trade dispute'; the union had a blanket immunity from being sued for tortious liability of any kind. The Act also conferred a right to take part in peaceful picketing 'merely for the purpose of peacefully persuading or communicating information, or of peacefully persuading any person to work or abstain from working'. The Act contained a wide definition of trade dispute, which extended to 'any dispute between employers and workmen, or between workmen and workmen, which is connected with the employment or non-employment, or the terms of the employment, or with the conditions of labour, of any person'; for this purpose, 'workmen' included 'all persons employed in trade or industry, whether or not in the employment of the employer with whom a trade dispute arises'.[37]

The Act was effective in insulating collective industrial relations from judicial interference for well over half a century. Minor restrictions on the scope of the immunities were introduced in the Trade Disputes and Trade Union Act 1927, but were repealed again in 1946. Moreover, the courts themselves, at least for part of this period, accepted the underlying philosophy of the 1906 Act, namely the protection of the right to strike as a basic element of a system of voluntary collective bargaining. According to Lord Wright, the commercial interest of an employer or worker in his or her trade or livelihood was not unqualified:

> … limitations are inevitable in organised societies, where the rights of individuals may clash. In commercial affairs, each trader's rights are qualified by the right of others to compete. Where the rights of labour are concerned, the rights of the employer are conditioned by the

---

[33] 2 E & B 216 (see Howarth, 2005); *South Wales Miners' Federation v Glamorgan Coal Co Ltd* [1905] AC 239.
[34] [1898] AC 1.
[35] *Quinn v Leathem* [1901] AC 495.
[36] [1901] AC 426.
[37] TDA 1906, s 5. See further our discussion in ch 11 below.

rights of the men to give or withhold their services. The right of workmen to strike is an essential element in the principle of collective bargaining.[38]

In *Crofter*, the common law tort of conspiracy was narrowed down by the expansion of the defence of justification, in essence enabling the collective actors to combine for their own economic self-interest, without fear of incurring liability in tort for having thereby harmed the economic interests of others. In addition to its considerable implications for legal doctrine, *Crofter* also signified an important degree of judicial acceptance of strikes aimed at enforcing the 'closed shop', or the principle of compulsory union membership in certain employments, which in many trades was a fundamental goal of trade union organisation, and which was seen as a prerequisite for the achievement of the objectives of economic security and effective collective bargaining.[39]

However, the decision in *Crofter*, issued at the height of wartime co-operation between labour and capital in 1942, is one of the few occasions on which collective values have permeated the structure of common law liability in this way. Within a further twenty years or so, in *Rookes v Barnard*,[40] a case which was also concerned with the closed shop, the House of Lords was to throw the economic torts into turmoil once again, by giving an expansionist interpretation to the tort of intimidation at the same time as construing the statutory immunities in a highly literal and formalistic way. Although Parliament acted immediately, passing the Trade Disputes Act 1965, to restore the 1906 Act, the longer-term effect of the decision in *Rookes* was to spark off further judicial innovation which resulted in the continual 'outflanking' of the statutory immunities:[41] developments have included the suggestion that 'bare' interference with contractual relations suffices for the purposes of the torts of inducing breach of contract and interference with trade by unlawful means;[42] the possibility of a new remedy in respect of pressure amounting to 'economic duress';[43] and new nominate torts of inducing breach of statutory duty and inducing breach of fiduciary duty.[44] Since 1979 these judicial developments have been over-shadowed to a certain extent by the restrictions placed on the immunities by the legislature itself.[45] However, they serve as a reminder of the continuing presence of the common law in this area and of its powers of self-regeneration.

A second area of persistent judicial intervention and innovation is that of the internal affairs of trade unions. In its judgment in the *Osborne*[46] case in 1909, the House of Lords ruled that political donations by trade unions were unlawful on grounds again related to an unanticipated interpretation of the Trade Union Acts 1871 and 1876 which was concerned, on this occasion, with the statutory definition of a 'trade union'. Parliament responded by passing the Trade Union

---

[38] [1942] AC 435, 463.

[39] McCarthy, 1964.

[40] [1964] AC 1129.

[41] See para 11.14 *et seq* below. The case law in this area now requires reconsideration in the light of the House of Lords decisions in *OBG v Allan; Douglas v Hello! Ltd (No 3) and Mainstream Properties Ltd v Young* [2007] IRLR 608 and *Total Network SL v HMRC (suing as Commissioners of Customs and Excise)* [2008] 1 AC 1174, discussed in ch 11.

[42] *Torquay Hotel Co Ltd v Cousins* [1969] 2 Ch 106; *Dimbleby & Sons Ltd v NUJ* [1984] 1 WLR 427; see para 11.14 below.

[43] *Universe Tankships Inc of Monrovia v ITWF* [1983] 1 AC 366; see para 11.17 below.

[44] *Meade v Haringey London Borough Council* [1979] ICR 494 and *Associated British Ports v TGWU* [1989] 3 All ER 796, CA, and *Prudential Assurance Co v Lorenz* (1971) 11 KIR 78, respectively; see para 11.12 below.

[45] See para 11.30 *et seq* below.

[46] *Amalgamated Society of Railway Servants v Osborne* [1910] AC 87.

Act 1913 which, by making it possible for such donations to be made through the medium of a political fund, effectively saved the young Labour Party from bankruptcy.[47] The courts were also hostile to section 4 of the Trade Union Act 1871, which attempted, albeit somewhat inadequately, to exclude union rule books from the normal process of the judicial construction and enforcement of contracts. Section 4 was given a narrow interpretation which meant that 'within fifty years of the Act being passed, union autonomy was protected within only a very narrow range'.[48] Judicial intervention reached the point at which trade unions were regarded as akin to public or statutory bodies whose decision-making powers were subject to judicial control on grounds of *ultra vires*. The courts implied the right to natural justice into the union rulebook practically as a mandatory term,[49] and also, on occasion, attempted to fashion doctrines such as the 'right to work' which would once more have exposed the union rules to judicial scrutiny on substantive grounds,[50] in an attempt to outflank the immunity granted to unions by statute against the common law doctrine of restraint of trade. The scale of judicial intervention has abated in recent years primarily, it would seem, because this is another area now intensively regulated by legislation restricting the powers of trade unions in respect of their individual members.[51]

Judicial activism in labour law

1.9   How may we account for this attitude of the courts towards trade unions and their activities? If there is bias, it is not conscious, according to Scrutton LJ who wrote in the 1920s that 'the habits you are trained in, the people with whom you mix, lead to your having a certain class of ideas of such a nature that, when you have to deal with other ideas, you do not give as sound and accurate judgments as you would wish'.[52] More generally, there is no doubt that the common law's sceptical attitude towards collectivism is deeply rooted and goes beyond the issue of conflicts between labour and capital. Economic liberalism has been a consistent theme in the common law since at least the start of the seventeenth century, and many of the most influential common law judges, including Coke and Mansfield, were strong proponents of open competition and hostile to monopolies and to associations of workers and producers.[53] The sociology of the legal profession itself may be relevant here: the strong individualism of barristers (notwithstanding the fact that the Bar itself was and is a kind of monopoly or 'closed shop') and their close links with the commercial and mercantile classes may help to explain the persistence of anti-collectivist values.[54]

It is perhaps significant that the judges have chosen particular moments, such as the 1900s or the mid-1960s, to launch new developments within the common law.[55] Both periods saw high inflation, low levels of unemployment and a rapidly-growing trade union movement, within

---

[47] See generally Ewing, 1982. The 1913 Act was extensively amended by the Trade Union Act 1984 and subsequent legislation. The relevant legislation is now contained in TULRCA 1992, Ch VI; see further para 10.18 *et seq* below.
[48] Elias and Ewing, 1987: p 11.
[49] *Lee v Showmen's Guild of Great Britain* [1952] 2 QB 329; see further para 10.3 below.
[50] *Edwards v SOGAT* [1971] Ch 354
[51] See ch 10 below.
[52] Scrutton, 1923: p 8; see generally Wedderburn, 1986: pp 27–47 for discussion of the issue of judicial impartiality.
[53] Atiyah, 1979: p 112 *et seq.*
[54] Atiyah, 1979: p 112 *et seq.*
[55] Cf Wedderburn, 1995: p 80, discussing *Rookes v Barnard* [1964] AC 1129 and *JT Stratford & Sons Ltd v Lindley* [1965] AC 269.

which shopfloor organisation was particularly strong; during both periods there was concern at 'abuses' by trade unions of their economic power, and claims that the statutory immunities placed them above the rule of law. The passage of the Trade Disputes Act 1906 prompted Dicey to write that 'the rule of equal law is in England now exposed to a new peril',[56] while Pollock thought that 'legal science has evidently nothing to do with this violent empirical operation on the body politic'.[57] In 1980 essentially similar comments were made by the members of the House of Lords in *Duport Steels Ltd v Sirs*[58] when reluctantly giving effect to the immunities laid down in succession to the Act of 1906 by the Trade Union and Labour Relations Act 1974. Whatever the origins and legitimacy of such attitudes might be, their persistence would seem to put in doubt the effectiveness of any system of immunities, no matter how widely drafted, in protecting even the most basic collective rights of organised labour.

Collective bargaining and social legislation

(i) The meaning of collective laissez-faire

1.10   The nature of the relationship between collective bargaining and social legislation is in many ways the key to the distinctive form of labour law which has evolved in Britain, in contrast to that which has grown up elsewhere in western Europe. This distinctiveness lies in the relatively limited role played by legislation in directly regulating employment relations, and the greater importance traditionally accorded to voluntary sources, of which collective bargaining has been the most important. In 1954 Kahn-Freund wrote that 'there is, perhaps, no major country in the world in which the law has played a less significant role in the shaping of [labour-management relations] than in Great Britain'.[59] By this he meant that not only was collective bargaining, and not legislation, the principal source of norms governing wages, working time and other terms and conditions of employment for most workers; but also that legislation played little or no role in determining the form which collective bargaining between labour and management should take. The broad statutory immunities of the Trade Disputes Act 1906 created a space within which collective bargaining could develop autonomously from the state. Collective bargaining rested on the state's support for collective institutions over those of individual contract, but the law did not prescribe either the level, the form or the contents of collective agreements, which continued to be regarded as not giving rise to enforceable obligations between employers and trade unions.

Kahn-Freund described the result as 'collective laissez-faire'.[60] However, although the approach of the law at this time has also been called 'abstentionist' or 'voluntarist', the system was not one in which the state was absent, or neutral.[61] The state supported collectivism and the recognition of trade unions for the purposes of collective bargaining, not simply through the statutory immunities for those organising industrial action, but also through various

---

[56] Dicey, [1908] 1979: p 204.
[57] Pollock, 1908: p v.
[58] [1980] ICR 161.
[59] Kahn-Freund, 1954b: p 47.
[60] Kahn-Freund, 1959.
[61] See Wedderburn, 1995: ch 1.

non-legal means at its disposal, including its own policies as an employer and administrative encouragement towards recognition.[62] Nor could it be said that there was only a limited amount of social legislation in place in the 1950s, when Kahn-Freund advanced his notion of collective laissez-faire: there was extensive intervention, at this time, in the form of factories legislation which governed working time and health and safety at work, together with the Wages Councils Acts which provided for statutory minimum rates of pay in certain industries. However, the role of this legislation was rightly seen by Kahn-Freund as subsidiary to that of voluntary collective bargaining: it only applied to groups of workers or to sectors of the economy in which, for various reasons, voluntary collective bargaining had failed to take root; or to areas of regulation, such as health and safety, which collective bargaining between trade unions and management had failed to cover. Social legislation, at least in the field of employment relations (the same did not apply to social security), was 'an adjunct to, a gloss on, collective bargaining'.[63]

(ii) Nineteenth-century attitudes to social legislation and the origins of collective laissez-faire

1.11   The origins of collective laissez-faire are traceable to two related developments of the late nineteenth and early twentieth centuries: on the one hand, there was a failure to extend the Factories Acts model of regulation into a generalised labour code; at the same time, the state made a growing commitment to the *indirect* support of voluntary collective bargaining, expressed through the statutory immunities which were embodied in the legislative settlement of the 1870s (and then of 1906), and in measures of an extra-legal kind which were designed to promote collective bargaining through conciliation and arbitration without involving the state in direct legal compulsion. To put this development in context, we need briefly to consider the nature of the nineteenth-century Factories Acts, which constituted virtually the first industrial legislation of the modern period of any country, and provided a model of regulation which was widely adopted elsewhere in the industrialising economies of that time.[64]

Early factory legislation was concerned with the conditions of employment and working hours of children, and specifically with those of pauper apprentices.[65] The working conditions of women were first the subject of regulation in the early 1840s. The Mines Regulation Act of 1842 barred women from underground working and the Factories Act of 1844 applied to women textile workers the restrictions on working hours which governed the employment of the under-18s. The fact that early industrial regulation took a legislative rather than a voluntary form reflects the weakness of the factory-based unions during the period prior to 1870 and their inability to achieve agreements through collective bargaining; at the same time, the legislature was reluctant to countenance general interference with the freedom of contract of adult males, rejecting a number of Bills to this effect in the 1850s. Male workers indirectly benefited from the controls over the hours of women and children because the working hours of each group were closely integrated; when employers attempted to defeat this effect through the 'relay system', under which the hours

---

[62] See generally Fredman and Morris, 1989.

[63] Kahn-Freund, 1959: p 248. See McCarthy, 1992; P Davies and M Freedland, 1993: ch 1; Wedderburn, 1995: ch 1, 2000; and Brodie, 2003, for further discussion and evaluation of Kahn-Freund's theory of collective laissez-faire.

[64] See Hepple, 1986a.

[65] See Hutchins and Harrison, 1926.

children were permitted to work were spread over a number of separate 'relays' across the different shifts worked by adults, Parliament enacted further legislation in 1850 and 1853 to counter this by requiring common starting and finishing times for all workers in a given factory. However, it stopped short of extending the Acts to cover all adult males.

After the 1870s legislation ceased to be the principal means of reducing working hours. By the early 1900s collective bargaining was already beginning to improve upon the hours set by legislation, and women workers covered by factories legislation frequently worked longer hours than men who had the protection of shop floor or sector-level agreements setting a nine or nine and a half hour day.[66] From this period legislation regulating non-factory employment permitted longer statutory hours than was normal either for core factory employment within the Acts or for employments regulated by collective bargaining. Social legislation of this kind had become a second-best option for groups of workers (predominantly female) unable to secure the benefits of collective bargaining: the law, wrote Hutchins and Harrison in 1903 'is still ostensibly based on the idea of "protection for those who cannot help themselves", instead of openly and avowedly adopting the more fruitful principle of raising the standard of life and health for the common good'.[67]

(iii) The rise of trade union organisation

1.12   After 1870, as the role of factory legislation diminished in importance, trade union membership grew steadily, more than doubling in the period to 1905, as the effects of lifting the legal restrictions on trade union activity came to be felt. At first growth was not continuous, and early gains were reversed with the onset of the Great Depression in 1873, and again between 1889 and 1893. After 1905 the rate of increase once more accelerated, with membership doubling by 1914 and doubling again by 1920, when membership reached the figure of 8.5 million (although this was reduced to 5.5 million by 1924 in the wake of the post-war slump). Union growth took two forms during this period: on the one hand the extension of membership to the less skilled, and to white-collar and women workers, in the already organised trades; and on the other the unionisation of hitherto unorganised industries and firms. Thus, whereas in 1897 three-quarters of union members were employed in mining, construction and manufacturing – with over half employed in the mining, engineering, cotton and construction sectors alone – by 1924 the proportion of total membership in transport, public and private services and general labouring occupations had increased from 25% to 40%.[68] An important feature of union growth during this time was also the consolidation of the Trades Union Congress as the principal confederation of trade unions. Founded in the late 1860s, by the early 1920s the TUC had effectively seen off all its rivals. The strength of the TUC was that it covered unions of different kinds; craft unions organising particular trades, general unions open to a number of trades and occupations; and unions organising particular industries.[69] Unlike in other European systems where separate trade union confererations had been organised on religious or political lines, in Britain there

---

[66] Hutchins and Harrison, 1926: p 98; J Morris, 1985: p 79.
[67] Hutchins and Harrison, 1926: p 209.
[68] Tarling and Wilkinson, 1982.
[69] See further our discussion in ch 7 below.

would henceforth be a single organisation representing the union movement as a whole and with mechanisms for resolving through its own procedures the vast majority of inter-union disputes.

The issue of how far to encourage collective bargaining through legislation, or to seek to regulate it by those means, was extensively debated from the time of the Royal Commission on Labour of 1891–1894. The majority report lent its support to collective bargaining based on 'powerful trade unions on the one hand and powerful associations of employers on the other',[70] but rejected proposals to grant compulsory legal effect to the awards made by the voluntary boards of conciliation which had grown up to regulate terms and conditions of employment in a number of sectors. As a result the Conciliation Act 1896 simply enabled the Board of Trade to conduct inquiries into trade disputes and, on the application of the parties themselves, to arrange arbitration or conciliation. Registration of joint boards of employers and employees with the Board of Trade was voluntary and primarily for the purposes of collecting information. The Board was given the power to conduct inquiries into the establishment of new, voluntary boards in sectors and districts where joint regulation did not exist. The Labour Department of the Board of Trade, which had been established in 1893, became the administrative arm by which the government's policy of promoting joint regulation was implemented; it was the forerunner of the Ministry of Labour, which was established in 1917. Although the direct legal impact of the 1896 Act was minimal, it confirmed the support of the state for the system of joint regulation while affirming the voluntarist ethos of the legislative settlement of the 1870s, and was an essential complement to the Conspiracy and Protection of Property Act 1875 and the Trade Disputes Act of 1906. The government subsequently lent its support to the extension of collective bargaining into sectors where it was vigorously resisted by employers, including the railways and the mines.[71]

(iv) Minimum wages and the regulation of the 'sweated trades'

1.13   The selective character of regulatory legislation was not universally accepted at this time. The larger, general unions, in particular, supported the campaign for a statutory eight-hour day within the TUC and in their evidence to the Royal Commission of 1891–1894. The Commission discovered that 'reduction of the normal standard hours of labour has always been one of the leading objects of trade unions; the aim of the modern movement is the attainment of this end by legislation'.[72] The majority nevertheless rejected a standard set of regulations for all trades as not 'a proposal which bears serious examination',[73] and described an existing measure, the Railway Servants (Hours of Labour) Act of 1893 as exceptional and justified by the threat posed to public safety by the long hours worked by railway employees. The minority trade union members of the Royal Commission argued for statutory intervention and called on the Board of Trade to use its statutory powers to initiate a 48-hour week for railway workers, and for statutory reforms to set a 48-hour week in textiles and extend factories legislation 'to all classes of labour', adult males included.[74] What emerged instead was the much more limited, but potentially significant measure

---

[70] Report of the *Royal Commission on Labour*, Parliamentary Papers (1894) XXXV.9, at para 364.
[71] Clegg, 1985.
[72] Parliamentary Papers (1894) XXXV.9, at para 162.
[73] Parliamentary Papers (1894) XXXV.9, at para 320.
[74] Royal Commission on Labour, Minority Report, Parliamentary Papers (1894) XXXV.9, at p 140.

in section 28 of the Factories and Workshops Act 1895, which authorised 'the making of special rules or requirements prohibiting the employment of, or modifying or limiting the period of employment for, all or any classes of persons in any process or particular description of manual labour which is certified by the Secretary of State... to be dangerous or injurious to health, or dangerous to life and limb'. According to Hutchins and Harrison, 'in these apparently unimportant provisions which at first sight read only like a trifling extension of regulations already enacted, the principle is however, implicitly granted that, cause being shown, the protection of the law can be extended to men as well as to women and children'.[75] However, the section was not subsequently used as a basis for regulating general working time. It was confined in its scope to the specific effect of long hours on health and safety in certain industries.

The debate for and against comprehensive regulation culminated in the campaigns surrounding the passage of the Trade Boards Act in 1909. The House of Commons had earlier passed Fair Wages Resolutions in 1891 and 1909 which required government departments to insist that their commercial suppliers should respect the prevailing wages and terms and conditions in their trades; the obligation to do so would then take effect in the commercial contract agreed between the relevant department and the supplier. The 1909 Resolution referred to 'rates of wages and ... hours of labour not less favourable than those commonly recognised by employers and trade societies (or in the absence of such recognised wages and hours, those which in practice prevail amongst good employers) in the trade in the district where the work is carried out'. The Webbs, among others, made the argument for a more extensive implementation of a 'national minimum' standard of living through legislation, leaving collective bargaining to build a 'living wage' on this foundation.[76] However, the Trade Boards Act reflected a much less ambitious conception of setting up joint wage regulation in selected sweated trades on a statutory basis, with independent members sitting with employers' and employees' representatives in order to bring about agreement; a plan to outlaw the payment of wages in all industries below the line set by the 'national minimum' was rejected.[77]

(v) State support for employee representation and collective bargaining

1.14 The debate over the role the state should play in encouraging and regulating collective bargaining was re-opened by the Whitley Committee Reports of 1917–1919. During the war of 1914–1918 extensive controls were put in place for the regulation and direction of labour; the Munitions Acts of 1916 and 1917 marked a formal departure from voluntarism which was, however, only intended to be temporary. Nevertheless, the Whitley Reports envisaged the establishment of joint representative committees at national, district and workplace level, 'each of the three forms of organisation being linked up with the others so as to constitute an organisation covering the whole of the trade, capable of considering and advising upon matters affecting the welfare of the industry, and giving to labour a definite and enlarged share in the discussion and

[75] 1926: p 203.
[76] S Webb and B Webb, [1898] 1920: p 767.
[77] J Morris, 1985: p 209.

settlement of industrial matters with which employers and employed are jointly concerned'.[78] The Joint Industrial Council was to form the basis for national level bargaining between employers' associations and independent trade unions in the various trades. The Committee came close to recommending legal enforcement of JIC agreements – 'it may be desirable at some later stage for the State to give the sanction of law to agreements made by the Councils, but the initiative in this direction should come from the Councils themselves'.[79] For trades already well organised, government encouragement for the adoption of a standard JIC model was thought sufficient, and for the unorganised trades, it was suggested that the trade boards system should be expanded. The Trade Boards Act of 1918 incorporated many of the Whitley Committee's recommendations and a vast expansion of the trade board system then took place. The trade boards were given legal powers to set minimum rates of pay and, in due course, other terms and conditions of employment in their respective trades; criminal sanctions could be levied against employers who failed to observe the terms of orders. However, in the 1920s there was a period of retrenchment, and the principle of limiting the scope of statutory intervention to unorganised trades was subsequently strictly maintained.[80] The pattern of joint regulation outside the trade board sector in the inter-war period was one in which there was no single model for multi-employer bargaining and legislation played only a marginal role in selected industries in the enforcement of minimum terms. Within the public sector national-level bargaining was established through the Whitley Councils and similar representative institutions, but in the private sector many of the remaining JICs ceased to set national wage rates. Only 20 bodies remained in operation by 1939.[81] Large areas of industry stayed outside the JIC system altogether, including coal, rail, engineering, shipping, iron and steel, and cotton.[82]

The completion of a system of national-level collective bargaining took place as a result of the second extension of governmental powers during the 1939–45 war, and the favourable conditions for trade unionism after the war including low unemployment. National collective bargaining was actively fostered by the Conditions of Employment and National Arbitration Order of 1940 (Order 1305) which banned strikes and lock-outs and established a mechanism for compulsory unilateral arbitration; this was a means by which the terms of national level agreements could be compulsorily applied to the contracts of employment of employers who did not otherwise observe the terms of such agreements. In effect, Order 1305, while amounting to legal compulsion of the kind which had previously been rejected, nevertheless finally prevented the undercutting of established wages and conditions which unions in the inter-war period had fought largely unsuccessfully to limit, by applying the fair wages principle throughout private industry: the Order made agreements 'between organisations of employers and trade unions representative respectively of substantial proportions of the employers and workers engaged in that trade or industry in that district' binding on all such employers. The wartime government also rejected formal controls on wage increases, and concentrated instead on keeping down retail prices and

---

[78] *Ministry of Reconstruction, Final Report of the Committee on Relations between Employers and Employed*, Cd 9153, 1918, at p 2.

[79] *Reconstruction Committee, Report of the Sub-Committee on Relations between Employers and Employed*, Cd 8606, 1918, at p 16.

[80] See *Final Report of the Committee on Industry and Trade* (Balfour Report), Cmd 3282, 1929, at p 90; para 4.42 below.

[81] Fox, 1985: p 297.

[82] Richardson, 1938.

the rationing of essential commodities as means of containing wage inflation. In addition, the war years saw a revival of shopfloor organisation in areas such as mining and engineering where it had earlier been rolled back as a result of the inter-war depression, and its establishment for the first time in newer industries such as aircraft and motor production.

After the war, the Wages Councils Act 1945 was the occasion both for the expansion of the trade boards sectors into the service sector, and for a more general attempt to place institutional wage determination on a secure footing. The 1945 Act facilitated the setting up of new wages councils and the scope of wage regulation orders was widened to cover all questions of wages, hours and holidays (the latter now no longer subject to the one-week limit set by the Holidays with Pay Act 1938), so making the wages councils more like collective bargaining institutions. The result of expansion was to widen the statutory sector to cover one in four of all employees, 3.5 million being covered by wages councils and 0.75 million by agricultural wages boards.[83] In addition to strengthening the wages councils, the 1945 Act renewed Order 1305 for the enforcement of collectively agreed terms and conditions through unilateral arbitration, and in 1946 the House of Commons passed a strengthened version of the Fair Wages Resolution for government contractors. In 1951, following an unsuccessful attempt to use Order 1305 to prosecute gas workers and dockworkers, that Order was repealed and replaced by a new measure, Order 1376, which lifted the ban on strikes and lock-outs and removed penal sanctions but retained the principle of compulsory arbitration over the extension of minimum terms and conditions laid down by sector-level collective agreements; these terms could still be imposed on employers via the contracts of employment of individual employees. Measures of this sort were to remain in place up to 1980.[84] The post-war years also saw a renewal of the voluntary Joint Industrial Councils. By 1946 56 JICs had been either reactivated or newly created, and the Ministry of Labour estimated that almost 90% of workers in industries and services were covered either by joint voluntary collective bargaining or by statutory machinery. By 1960 some 200 JICs were in existence, and union membership had increased to 9.8 million from a figure of 6.1 million in 1938.

(vi) Social legislation and the floor of rights

1.15 By the means just described, a virtually comprehensive system of minimum terms and conditions was established, but without the kind of general legal intervention through a *statutory* floor of rights which characterised other European systems at this time.[85] There was a dual aspect to the system, with the separation into voluntary and statutory sectors, which had no counterpart elsewhere. The voluntary system operated at arm's length from the state through the JICs which were not statutory bodies, but with the qualification that few employers, in practice, had the option of contracting-out of the results of collective bargaining, thanks to Order 1305, Order 1376 and their successors. Non-union firms faced the likelihood of concerted collective pressure to accept the principle of trade union recognition, depending on the economic strength of the trade unions

---

[83] Bayliss, 1962: p 73.

[84] Order 1376 was replaced by the Terms and Conditions of Employment Act 1959, and the procedure was further modified by the IRA 1971 and the EPA 1975, Sch 11. See P Wood, 1978 and Wedderburn, 1995: pp 9–17 for discussion of these changes.

[85] On the evolution of other systems in the direction of comprehensive legislation, see A Jacobs, 1986.

concerned, given that the law placed few restraints on the exercise of that power; and although (at that time) individual firms might nonetheless exercise the right not to engage in collective bargaining, they would normally be bound to respect the minimum wage rates and other terms and conditions laid down at sector level. In the statutorily-regulated sectors, the rates laid down by the wages councils had the force of law and penal sanctions were available against employers; in these sectors the role of the law was more directly interventionist.

The essential distinction between Britain and other systems in western Europe in the immediate post-war period, therefore, was not that there was necessarily a smaller body of law in the British system, but that labour standards in Britain were not given the formal support of legislation which laid down minimum wage levels and maximum working hours for *all* workers. There was no equivalent, for example, to the French laws of 1946, which re-established a 40-hour basic working week, and 1950, which set a statutory minimum wage, in each case providing a universal floor of labour standards under all employments. In Britain, where broadly equivalent standards operated in practice in the voluntary sector (although the basic working week was longer than in France or Germany at this point), they did so without the same direct support of the law; although this was subject to the possibility of compulsory arbitration under Order 1305 and its successors. Moreover, as has been explained, the state offered its general support for collective bargaining through other means, not least by encouraging union membership in the public sector.

The absence of statutory codification for these standards was the result of conscious policy choices at important junctures in the period following the Royal Commission of 1891–1894. In 1894 the trade union members of the Royal Commission predicted that attempts to introduce compulsion into arbitration and conciliation procedures and enforce the terms of collective agreements against trade unions would 'provoke the most embittered resistance from the whole body of Trade Unionists'.[86] Individual trade unions also resisted legal intervention to set general minimum wage rates at the time of the Trade Boards Act 1909, on the grounds that this could be used by the Board of Trade as a pretext for the introduction of compulsory arbitration procedures which would undermine the right to strike.[87] Governments and employers were reluctant, on the whole, to go down a more interventionist route. In the inter-war period, the corporatist experiments of Lloyd George's government after 1918[88] quickly gave way to an official view, expressed in the Cave Report of 1922 on the Trade Boards and in the Report of the Balfour Committee on Trade and Industry in 1929, that extensive wage regulation would be costly and impractical. Even when in 1945, with the return of a Labour government, the wages councils were considerably expanded in terms of the numbers of employees and sectors covered, the principle of a binding floor to wages which they embodied was not extended to the sectors which were considered to be adequately covered by voluntary collective bargaining.

This raises the question of in what sense, if at all, it made any difference to have a dual system of labour market regulation, one part voluntary and the other part directly underpinned by legal sanctions? According to Kahn-Freund, the advantages of collective laissez-faire were the flexibility it accorded to collective agreements, which could evolve 'dynamically' to meet changing industrial and economic conditions, and the democratic value of having strong collective institutions which

[86] Parliamentary Papers (1894) XXXV.9, at p 154.
[87] J Morris, 1985.
[88] See Ewing, 1988.

were autonomous from the state: the absence of legal sanctions stemmed from 'the maturity of collective industrial relations in Britain'.[89] There was also an advantage for the unions in not being directly reliant on the state, since 'what the State has not given, the State cannot take away'.[90] Hence collective laissez-faire was, in Kahn-Freund's account, at least as much prescriptive and ideological in character as it was descriptive.[91]

Less attention was paid then to the disadvantages of viewing legislative intervention as a second-best option, to be limited to under-organised areas of the economy and to areas not touched by collective bargaining, such as health and safety. How far the philosophy of collective laissez-faire gave rise to a form of direct regulation which was less than satisfactory, being partial and 'subsidiary' in nature, is difficult to gauge; but the example of trade union opposition to the introduction of a general minimum wage at the time of the Trade Boards Act and subsequently,[92] a policy which was reversed only as recently as the 1980s,[93] indicates what the effects were of accepting that the regulatory intervention of the law had to be strictly confined, in order not to upset the priority of voluntary procedures. This meant that the standard of protection conferred by statutory bodies could not be set too high, for fear that it would undermine autonomous procedures. Throughout their history, but particularly in the inter-war years, the trade boards and wages councils consistently failed to narrow the gap in terms of earnings between the lowest paid workers and the rest;[94] and the statutory standards contained in the Factories Acts, with regard to working time, lagged behind those of voluntary collective bargaining, and stopped advancing altogether after the 1930s.[95] One aspect of collective laissez-faire was therefore a certain degree of structural inequality between the voluntary and regulated sectors, and the absence of legal guarantees of universal social and economic rights for all employees.

The employment relationship

(i) The master-servant model and its legacy

1.16   In one sense, the modern contract of employment dates from the legislative settlement of the 1870s, which repealed the Master and Servant Acts and removed the last vestiges of the pre-modern system of labour regulation under the Statute of Artificers. Prior to these reforms, the master-servant model of the eighteenth and nineteenth centuries had embodied an extensive conception of the employer's implied powers of direction and discipline, backed up by sanctions administered by the local magistracy. The Act of 1747 gave the local magistrates the power to order payment of wages due, on the one hand, but also to punish the servant or labourer for any 'misdemeanour, miscarriage or ill behaviour' by the abatement of wages or imprisonment for up to a month; they could also discharge the servant from the contract. An Act of 1758 extended this jurisdiction to cover servants in husbandry (agriculture) hired for less than one year and that of

---

[89] Kahn-Freund, 1954b: p 212.
[90] Kahn-Freund, 1959: p 244.
[91] See Wedderburn, 1995: p 27.
[92] See generally Bayliss, 1962, and C Craig et al, 1982, for the evolution of minimum wage policy after 1909.
[93] On the recent adoption of minimum wage legislation in the form of NMWA 1998, see paras 4.46–4.60 below.
[94] C Craig et al, 1982; see also J Morris, 1985.
[95] See below, paras 4.76 and 4.96; Deakin, 1990a.

1766 made it an offence for the servant to quit before the end of the agreed contract term. This last provision was an attempt to bring up to date the similar prohibition in section 15 of the Statute of Artificers of 1562. The Master and Servant Act of 1823 established new crimes of absconding from work and refusing to work, and provided for imprisonment of workers for up to three months. Complementing the Master and Servant Acts were numerous measures passed specifically to deal with theft and embezzlement by servants and outworkers. The use of the criminal law to enforce contractual obligations was readily justified. 'Imprisonment may be viewed as a mode of compelling the performance of contracts', wrote JE Davis in his account of the Master and Servant Act 1867:[96] 'in some cases, damages might recompense a master for the breach of a contract by his servant, but the latter is seldom in a position to pay damages, and therefore, in the absence of any other remedy, he might set his employer at defiance'. Court procedure was streamlined and, generally, beneficial to the employer who would normally be the one to bring the complaint. In complaints of neglect of work, which took the form of proceedings for a summary conviction as opposed to an order of the court for a sum of money to be paid or work to be performed, the servant could not be a witness in his or her own defence.[97]

Following the decision in *Lowther v Earl of Radnor* in 1806,[98] the Master and Servant Acts were applied to all servants and labourers, but not to higher status employees such as managers, agents and clerks. The latter were excluded by implication from the wording of the Acts. The selective effect of the disciplinary provisions of the legislation was clarified further by the Master and Servant Act of 1867, which in section 3 stated that it was only to apply to the classes of servants and labourers. The test adopted for distinguishing between servants and independent contractors was based on the criterion of 'exclusive service'.[99] Most of the leading decisions on the extent of the application of the Acts concerned skilled artisans and intermediaries such as 'butty workers' in the mines; the Acts were also used to enforce the 'pit bond' in the mining industry, a form of long-term contracting not far removed from indentured service. In terms of numbers of prosecutions alone, the material impact of the Acts was considerable, in particular in the mining and metal trades and in certain regions of the country, such as the Potteries. In England and Wales, numbers of prosecutions never fell below 7,000 per year between 1858 and the repeal of the Acts in 1875; a peak of over 17,000 prosecutions was reached in 1872. Prosecutions played an important role in relation to the business cycle, by providing employers with a disciplinary weapon to counter the effects of a tight labour market; prosecutions for absconding or refusing to work rose at times of high levels of economic activity, as workers sought better paid or less dangerous work.[100]

For the bulk of industrial and agricultural workers in the nineteenth century, the imposition of a restrictive disciplinary code supported by legislation and by the criminal jurisdiction of the magistrates' courts makes it impossible to speak of a developed contractual theory of the employment relationship before 1875. A contractual model of employment only began to emerge in the case of middle-class, salaried workers, whose position placed them outside the scope of the Master and Servant Acts. Thus, although a modern-style contract of employment can be seen developing in the nineteenth century, the scope of its application was limited by clear notions of

---

[96] J Davies, 1868: pp 6–7.
[97] J Davies, 1868: p 10.
[98] 8 East 113.
[99] *Lancaster v Greaves* (1829) 9 B & C 628, 631–632 (Parke J).
[100] Simon, 1954; Woods, 1982; Hay and Craven, 2004.

social and economic status. One indication of this is the terminology used by the courts; the terms 'employee' and 'servant' denoted different forms of work relationship at this time.[101]

(ii) The emergence of the contract of employment

1.17 The development of a contractual model based on reciprocity and mutuality of obligation can be observed in cases concerning the rights of higher-status employees to be given work and not to be wrongfully dismissed. Contractual notions were used to limit the employer's right to give orders. The modern contract action for wrongful dismissal was synthesised in 1853 in *Emmens v Elderton*,[102] a case concerning a company solicitor. The basis of the action was the employer's duty to find work for the employee for the duration of the contract, in default of which the employee would be entitled to receive damages for breach of contract. Even in the case of commission agents and others paid on a piece-rate basis, the employer's act of wrongfully preventing the employee from earning his or her commission amounted to an unjustified repudiation of the contract.[103] The status and skills of the professional set a limit to the work he or she could be required to do; if 'hired as a buyer, he was not bound to perform services not properly appertaining to that character';[104] nor would a single act of disobedience or neglect justify the summary dismissal of a manager or a journalist.[105]

The shift which occurred in 1875 was in one sense more formal than real, however.[106] The abolition of the Master and Servant Acts removed the option of criminal sanctions against the employee for breach of contract; henceforth, only civil remedies applied on both sides. However, this apparent parity of remedies did not exclude the use of the magistrates' courts by employers seeking a summary remedy for breach of contract. Under section 3(3) of the Employers and Workmen Act 1875 the court had the power in effect to order specific performance against an employee who was in breach of contract, a right not available under the general law of contract either at that time or since.[107] Damages awards made by the courts under the 1875 Act tended to be in the nature of fines, for the reason that no attempt was usually made to quantify any precise loss flowing to the employer from breach.[108] This was a clear exception to the approach normally followed in the law of contract.

The lingering influence of the master and servant model, given a practical expression in the continuing role of the magistrates as enforcers of discipline, therefore retarded the application of general contractual principles to the service relationship. It is only in decisions of the early twentieth century that the courts can first be seen applying the contractual model, which they had developed for the middle classes, to industrial workers, agricultural labourers and domestic

---

[101] Foster, 1983. To some extent, the distinction between 'servant' and 'employee' was carried on in the distinction between manual and non-manual workers in social legislation between 1880 and 1945. See our discussion of the 'control test' below, at para 3.26.

[102] (1853) 13 CB 495.

[103] See *Turner v Goldsmith* [1891] 1 QB 544.

[104] *Price v Mouat* (1862) 11 CBNS 508; Foster, 1983: p 15.

[105] *Cussons v Skinner* (1843) 11 M & W 161.

[106] See Deakin and Wilkinson, 2005: ch 2.

[107] *De Francesco v Barnum* (1890) 45 Ch D 430.

[108] On the relationship between the 1875 Act and the Truck Acts which regulated deductions from pay at this time, see Deakin, 1992 and below, on statutory wage protection more generally, paras 4.71–4.73.

servants. A first step was to protect the right to payment for completed labour by holding that in the case of piece workers, wages were apportionable to work actually done, and that employers could only make deductions from wages which had accrued if they could show loss flowing from a breach of contract by the employee.[109] Similarly, it was held in *Hanley v Pease & Partners*[110] that an employer had no implied right to suspend the contract of a workman without pay for incompetence or disobedience – in the absence of an express term providing for suspension, the employee had the right to bring a claim for damages for breach of contract – and in *Devonald v Rosser & Sons Ltd*[111] employees recovered damages equivalent to wages for the employer's failure to provide work before and during a period of notice.

(iii) The impact of collective bargaining

1.18   The rise of collective bargaining was also an important factor in the decline of the service model, although this did not, in itself, give rise to the modern form of the contract of employment as we know it today. Collective bargaining led to a shortening of the notice period for most industrial workers. Although this reduced the formal legal right of individual workers to a measure of job and income security under the contract, it also achieved the more important practical effect of nullifying the disciplinary jurisdiction of the magistrates and county courts under the Employers and Workmen Act. As Tillyard noted in 1928, the restrictive provisions of the Act were 'practically a dead letter', principally because 'contracts of service are determinable more and more by short notice, so that powers to rescind and powers to enforce performance for unexpired periods of service are in practice rarely if ever wanted'.[112] The Act continued to be used as a weapon of discipline in the mining industry, and cases arising from its use reached the higher courts as late as 1940 and 1945;[113] however, in most industries it appears to have played a gradually diminishing role, although it was repealed only in the 1970s.[114] Individual sanctions against the employee enforced by law and resting on his or her formal subordination to the employer gave way to collective procedures resting more on a formal equality between the parties: Tillyard argued that:

> ... the inferior status of the worker has disappeared. This is absolutely true as regards the administration of the law, but it is also largely true of other means of settling disputes. On Boards of Conciliation, on Trade Boards, on Courts of Referees, and on other bodies dealing with trade interests, working men and employers meet on an equality.[115]

---

[109] *Parkin v South Hetton Coal Co* (1907) 98 LT 162; *George v Davies* [1911] 2 KB 445 (a case concerning a domestic servant).

[110] [1915] 1 KB 698.

[111] [1906] 2 KB 728.

[112] Tillyard, 1928: pp 328–329.

[113] *Nokes v Doncaster Amalgamated Collieries Ltd* [1940] AC 1014; *Dorman, Long & Co Ltd v Carroll* (1945) 173 LT 141.

[114] See IRA 1971, Sch 9; Statute Law (Repeals) Act 1973, Sch 1.

[115] Tillyard, 1928: pp 17–18.

One effect of collective laissez-faire, then, was that individual litigation over contractual rights declined in significance. As collective bargaining evolved, the individual contract of employment was not completely effaced, but the role of individual agreement became a minimal one. The principal role of the contract of employment was to provide a means by which to express the regulatory or *normative* effect of a collective agreement upon the rights and obligations of the individual parties; terms and conditions of employment contained in a collective agreement were deemed to be incorporated into individual contracts by virtue of an express or implied 'bridging term' at the level of the individual contract.[116] Terms derived from wages orders and, after 1940, from arbitration awards made under Order 1305 and its successors were incorporated into individual contracts as a matter of law. However, other social legislation did not depend on the contract of employment for its effect. The large body of regulations under the Factories Acts which imposed obligations on employers was mainly enforced by criminal sanctions and policed by the factory inspectorate; it owed more to a public law model of statutory regulation than to the private law institution of the contract of employment.[117] Where individual employees sued for compensation for occupational injuries or disease, they did so not in contract but almost exclusively through actions in tort, either in negligence or, where the Factories Acts had been infringed, for breach of statutory duty.[118]

(iv) Employment protection legislation

1.19   It was only with the advent of employment protection legislation in the 1960s and 1970s that the individual contract of employment came to assume the importance which it has in the modern law. Starting with the Contracts of Employment Act 1963, a basic floor of statutory rights was put in place, granting employees certain protections against loss of income and employment. This Act provided for the first time for minimum periods of notice to be given by both employer and employee of their intention to terminate the contract of employment; it also imposed an obligation upon the employer to issue the employee with a written statement of his or her terms and conditions of employment. Although, in principle, the statement merely recorded terms which were agreed separately by the parties or incorporated into the contract on the basis of a bridging term, in practice it had a considerable influence in formalising contract terms and heightening awareness of their role in regulating employment relations. The Redundancy Payments Act 1965 introduced a right to statutory compensation for loss of employment on grounds of redundancy, and the Industrial Relations Act 1971, the right not to be unfairly dismissed. The latter was re-enacted by the Trade Union and Labour Relations Act 1974 and strengthened by the Employment Protection Act 1975, most notably by granting employment tribunals the power to order the reinstatement or re-engagement of an unfairly dismissed employee. The Act of 1975 also introduced a number of measures in the area of income security, including a right to maternity pay and a right to guaranteed minimum pay in the event of lay-off for lack of work. In addition, individual employees, together with certain self-employed workers and applicants for employment, received important protection against discrimination by virtue of the Equal Pay Act

[116] *MacLea v Essex Line Ltd* (1933) 45 Ll L 254.
[117] See below, para 4.10, for further discussion of this point.
[118] See further *Lister v Romford Ice and Cold Storage Co Ltd* [1957] AC 555, discussed below at para 4.108.

1970, the Sex Discrimination Act 1975 and the Race Relations Act 1976. Following a period of relative stagnation, at least in terms of new legislative initiatives (other than deregulatory ones) in the 1980s and 1990s,[119] a further significant strengthening of individual employment law was achieved by the Employment Relations Act 1999, although the Employment Act 2002, in establishing statutory grievance and disciplinary procedures and limiting access to employment tribunals, arguably weakened the protection available to employees while also making the legislation more complex.[120] These statutory procedures were deemed to be a failure and the relevant parts of the 2002 Act were repealed by the Employment Act 2008 and replaced by a more flexible regime.[121]

The employment protection legislation recognised the contract of employment as the basis for the legal regulation of the individual employment relationship, and although it displaced many common law rules, the conceptual structure of the Acts was very heavily dependent on contractual language and reasoning. In this sense it gave the contract of employment a new lease of life. This might seem a contradictory statement; after all, the legislation formally overrode the freedom of contract of the individual parties in numerous respects. On the other hand, by limiting managerial prerogative, and in particular the employer's sanction of dismissal, the legislation limited the otherwise open-ended disciplinary powers which the employer had enjoyed at common law, and which owed as much to the master-servant model of the nineteenth century as it did to general principles of contract. The legislation did not, therefore, represent a straightforward movement from contract to status; on the contrary, in mitigating some aspects of the employee's subordination, it made the relationship in some ways more closely resemble the model of a contract based on reciprocal rights and duties.[122]

Nor did the employment protection legislation, extensive as it was and still is, constitute a comprehensive statutory code governing the employment relationship. Many significant aspects of the employment relationship remain governed by the common law or, indirectly, by collective bargaining. The reforms of the 1960s and 1970s did not touch on areas such as minimum rates of pay and the control of working time, partly on the grounds that these should remain within the scope of voluntary collective bargaining. Direct statutory regulation, through the wages councils and Agricultural Wages Boards, was still regarded as exceptional, and covered only a minority of employees; indeed, the scope of such legislation diminished after 1960, as a number of wages councils were wound up in the belief that statutory intervention was holding back the emergence of voluntary arrangements.[123] It was only in the late 1990s that comprehensive national minimum wage legislation was at last enacted and that working time standards laid down in European Union law were implemented.[124]

Employment protection legislation was, then, only a partial breach of the system of collective laissez-faire. One aspect of its rationale was, nevertheless, a perception that there were limits to what could be achieved through collective bargaining, and that additional legal intervention was needed to fulfil various economic and social policy goals of the state. The Contracts of Employment

---

[119] See below, para 1.26.
[120] On the EA 2002, see Hepple and Morris, 2002.
[121] See below, paras 2.20–2.21 and 5.119 *et seq.*
[122] See further para 3.2 below.
[123] This is prefigured in Bayliss, 1962. See generally C Craig *et al*, 1982; below, para 4.44.
[124] See below, paras 1.34, 4.44 and 4.77.

Act 1963 was a harbinger of a form of labour market intervention which, in various forms, was to call into question the philosophy of collective laissez-faire.

State corporatism, incomes policies and collective bargaining

(i) The concept of corporatism in labour law

1.20   The concept of corporatism is open to a number of interpretations, but in the present context is generally understood to represent the growth of formalised links between the state and autonomous economic groups (in particular organisations representing labour and capital), ranging from consultation to more formal negotiation over economic outcomes. On the one hand the state aims to take a more interventionist role in economic management, limiting the autonomy of the collective parties; on the other hand, the representative institutions of labour and capital are granted access to governmental policy making. The precise forms of these arrangements have differed considerably from one period to another and, in the international context, a great variety of forms may also be found.[125] In some European systems, for example, it is common for tripartite bargaining between government, employers and trade unions to lead to framework collective agreements which are subsequently given the force of law. This has not happened in Britain. However, from the 1940s onwards incomes policies, aimed at curbing wage inflation, have at various times had a highly significant impact on the labour market and on the system of collective bargaining.

(ii) Incomes policies

1.21   Incomes policies relied on a mixture of statutory and voluntary controls. The Labour Government of 1964–1970 was the first to take statutory powers in the area of pay restraint. In 1966 a statutory wage freeze was introduced via the Prices and Incomes Act which set criminal sanctions for firms disobeying the law. Although the freeze was lifted the following year and a policy of voluntary adherence was formally resumed, certain statutory powers were retained for the purpose of referring wage settlements to the National Board for Prices and Incomes, which could delay their implementation for a period of six months. This period was later extended to a year. The Conservative Government of 1970–1974 also took statutory powers to enforce wage freezes and limits on pay during its term of office.

   In a reaction against the use of coercive powers the Labour Government of 1974–1979 left the enforcement of pay norms under the Social Contract to the TUC which in effect became responsible for 'policing' settlements on the Government's behalf. The Social Contract originated in discussions between the TUC and the Labour Party in 1973, when Labour was in opposition. In essence, the agreement committed the Labour Party to introducing a series of statutory measures (including price and rent controls, improved social welfare and employment legislation, industrial

---

[125] See Deakin, Michie and Wilkinson, 1992, on which this discussion is based, and P Davies and M Freedland, 1983: introduction; Deakin and Wilkinson, 2005: pp 243–264.

democracy legislation, public control of investment, and measures for the redistribution of income and wealth through the tax and social security system), in return for voluntary pay restraint on the part of the unions. However, at its 1977 Congress the TUC voted for a return to free collective bargaining, to take effect upon the expiry of the 12-month pay settlements which were then in force. This was, in effect, the end of the Social Contract. In its final year in office the Labour Government proposed a 5% pay norm but took no direct legal measures to enforce it. In the public sector direct government influence was brought to bear, at the cost of provoking widespread strike action by local authority and health service employees during the 'winter of discontent'.

(iii) Growing state intervention in industrial relations

1.22   From a legal point of view the impact of incomes policies was quite marginal; even when statutory powers were taken, every effort was made to separate incomes policies from the normal working of collective labour law and the trade dispute immunities in particular. Thus incomes policies have left no lasting mark on the institutions of labour law. During the 1960s and 1970s it continued to be public policy to maintain and promote collective bargaining, so that 'there was between 1948 and 1979 a dichotomy in government policies: anti-wage inflation policy on the one hand, and traditional labour law, or IR [industrial relations], policy on the other'.[126]

But if the institutional effects of incomes policies were limited, the effects of other forms of state intervention in the industrial relations systems in the 1960s and 1970s proved to be more enduring. A move towards greater emphasis on plant-level bargaining in the private sector was validated by the Report of the Royal Commission on Trade Unions and Employers' Associations, which was completed in 1968 (the 'Donovan Report').[127] On the face of it, Donovan confirmed the continuing relevance of the principles of collective laissez-faire. Most significantly, the Commission rejected proposals for the legal enforcement of collective agreements containing 'peace obligations' taking the form of commitments not to strike until certain procedures were exhausted. On the other hand, the Commission marked a turning point in attitudes towards the voluntary system of collective bargaining, by criticising both employers and trade unions for 'sustaining the facade of industry-wide bargaining'.[128] It favoured the development of greater formality of procedures and processes at plant level as a means of combating what was seen as the 'disorder' of the 'informal system' of industrial relations within individual firms and establishments. Employment protection legislation was to be an important part of this. The Commission recommended the enactment of unfair dismissal legislation, to be administered through a system of 'labour tribunals', one of the functions of which would be to reduce the incidence of wildcat strikes by providing a forum within which disputes over dismissal and discipline could be resolved without resort to industrial action.[129] This proposal was later enacted as part of the Industrial Relations Act 1971, which adopted for this purpose the existing system of employment tribunals, which already had jurisdiction to resolve issues arising out of legislation on training levies and redundancy compensation.

---

[126] Wedderburn, 1985: p 77.
[127] Cmnd 3623. For analyses see R Lewis, 1986; McCarthy, 1992; P Davies and M Freedland, 1993: ch 6.
[128] Cmnd 3623, 1968: para 111.
[129] See ch 5 below.

Donovan's endorsement of abstentionism in the collective sphere was qualified not just by this specific recommendation for legislation in the individual field, but also by its more general call for reform of voluntary processes. As Lewis suggests, 'Donovan's reform strategy ... departed from traditional non-intervention by advocating a series of legislative measures and by strongly emphasising the need for managerial and economic efficiency, a strand of industrial relations policy which was closely linked with the requirements of incomes policy'. However, 'the central issue for Donovan was how to restore order, peace and efficiency to industrial relations and yet to preserve and even extend the voluntarist tradition of collective bargaining'.[130] Donovan's rejection of greater legal compulsion in the field of collective relations was itself rejected by the Conservative government of 1971–1974, whose Industrial Relations Act 1971 introduced a completely new system of collective labour law.[131] The traditional combination of common law liability coupled with statutory immunities for industrial action was replaced by a system of unfair labour practices loosely modelled on the American Taft-Hartley Act of 1947; provision was made for pre-strike ballots and 'cooling-off periods' in emergency disputes, with a prominent role for a new labour court, the National Industrial Relations Court. Statutory controls over the closed shop were introduced for the first time. Protection for trade unions against the large part of civil liabilities was made conditional upon them being registered under the Act, but virtually all refused in order to avoid exposing their rule books to substantive powers of legal review. The Act proved to be a failure, largely thanks to the strength of union resistance; it did nothing to reduce levels of strike activity, and the National Industrial Relations Court was faced with repeated embarrassments in attempting to enforce its orders.[132] But even this measure, which contained what were then unprecedented powers of direct legal compulsion, was not necessarily hostile to the Donovan Report's underlying goal of preserving collective bargaining by reforming it. Unions were offered a range of positive rights, in particular a right to recognition in certain circumstances, in return for submitting themselves to the controls which would stem from registration under the Act. It was a package 'to draw the unions into a regulated and regulatory system'.[133] As it was, although the unions declined this offer, the supporters of the 1971 Act 'always refused to accept that it was an anti-union measure ... it was sometimes argued to be compatible with true underlying intentions of [collective laissez-faire] – if not with its outward form'.[134]

The Labour Government of 1974–1979 repealed the Industrial Relations Act 1971 and restored the 1906 pattern of statutory immunities in a strengthened form in the Trade Union and Labour Relations Act 1974. Nonetheless, certain parts of the 1971 Act were subsequently revived. The unfair dismissal jurisdiction was re-enacted in the Act of 1974, and the Employment Protection Act 1975 contained a modified recognition procedure, under which a union with substantial support in a given workplace might obtain the right to recognition through a procedure operated by the Advisory, Conciliation and Arbitration Service.[135] This procedure, although successful in achieving advances in recognition in areas of professional and managerial employment where it had previously been resisted, was dogged by the intervention of the courts through judicial

---

[130] R Lewis, 1986: p 32.
[131] Wedderburn, [1971] 1995: ch 3; McCarthy, 1992: pp 18–24; P Davies and M Freedland, 1993: ch 7.
[132] See Weekes *et al*, 1975
[133] Wedderburn, 1991b: p 21.
[134] McCarthy, 1992: p 21.
[135] On ACAS, see below, paras 2.23 *et seq*

review,[136] and was repealed in 1980. However, the unfair dismissal legislation, together with the other elements of employment protection law which were significantly strengthened by the Act of 1975, has largely remained in place to this day, and has had a considerable influence in leading management to adopt more formal procedures at plant level, much as the Donovan Report intended.[137] Not all agree that this formalisation of plant-level procedures has necessarily been the principal cause of rising labour productivity and a reduction in the incidence of strikes during the 1980s;[138] but there can be little doubt that the reforms initiated by Donovan have had a substantial impact on personnel practice and employment relations at the level of the workplace.

Labour market flexibility and deregulation

(i) The shift in government policy after 1979

1.23   The Labour Government of 1974–1979, in common with its immediate predecessors, failed to reconcile the tensions between the traditional forms of state support for voluntary collective bargaining and increasing intervention in the economy through incomes policies.[139] The stage was set for a revolution in economic and social policy which would see the abandonment both of collective laissez-faire and of the attempt to manage the economy through state corporatism. The 1979–1997 Conservative governments chose to adopt instead a programme of economic deregulation and liberalisation, designed to promote product-market competition and reduce the size of the public sector. Reform of industrial relations and restructuring of the labour market were central parts of this wider economic programme. Legislation limited the right to strike and subjected trade unions to an unprecedented degree of external regulation and supervision, at the same time as statutory employment rights were qualified and in some instances removed completely, in favour of a return to the common law institution of the individual contract of employment. Incomes policies for the private sector were formally rejected, although in the public sector cash limits on pay were imposed at various times. Unions in the nationalised and public employment sectors suffered demoralising defeats in a series of strikes, most notably in steel and coal. The government consistently claimed a link between these statutory changes and an improved climate in industrial relations, leading to superior economic performance:

> The Government's reforms have led to major and important changes of attitude. The atmosphere of industrial relations today is very different from what it was in the 1970s. Management has regained the freedom to manage, and the incentive and the will to do so.[140]

What was perhaps most remarkable about this programme of reform was the use of labour law not as a means of achieving distributive goals or embodying a notion of industrial justice, but as part

---

[136] See Simpson, 1978.
[137] For further discussion see paras 1.27–1.28 below.
[138] Cf Metcalf, 1989; Nolan and Marginson, 1990.
[139] P Davies and M Freedland, 1993: p 663.
[140] Department of Employment, Employment for the 1990s, Cm 540, 1988, at p 16.

of an economic policy designed to foster competitiveness. This is not to say that considerations of rights played no part at all in the reforms of the 1980s and 1990s. The rights of individual union members, in particular, were advanced as a rationale for legislation regulating internal trade union affairs and the obligation to hold strike ballots, and the reforms to the law governing industrial action were justified in part by the need to protect the rights of third parties adversely affected by industrial disputes (consumers, members of the general public and employers who were not party to disputes).[141] We have also seen that the linking, within governmental policy, of economic and social issues began well in advance of the election of Mrs Thatcher's first administration, being traceable at least to the Donovan Report of 1968 and earlier.[142] In the 1980s, however, the subordination of social policy to a wider economic agenda reached a new level. Any assessment of the legislative reforms of the 1980s and 1990s needs to focus on their economic impact, since that was the *principal* justification offered for the radical changes made to the law.

(ii) The neoliberal critique of collective bargaining and social legislation

1.24   The deregulation of the labour market complemented the Conservative government's adoption of a monetarist macro-economic policy and its formal abandonment of policies of managing demand in the economy in an attempt to maintain full employment.[143] Attention switched from explanations of unemployment which stressed inadequate demand to those which focused on the role of the supply side, and in particular on perceived rigidities stemming from the role of trade unions in regulating workplace practices and setting a floor to wages and conditions through sector-level collective bargaining. This policy received its clearest expression in the 1985 White Paper, *Employment: the Challenge for the Nation*,[144] which was as much a justification and review of policies already in place as a programme for future reforms. The White Paper rejected low demand as the cause of unemployment, in favour of 'the failure of our jobs market, the weak link in our economy'. The substantial increase in unemployment between 1980–1982 appeared 'in large measure [because] the disguised unemployment of earlier years, with overmanning rife, was forced into the open'. A three-fold solution was offered: a 'sound' framework of economic policy based on the control of the money supply; the removal of obstacles to the creation of jobs in the form of labour market regulation; and, in exceptional cases, direct action in the form of training and make-work schemes for the long-term and young unemployed.

Both the arguments of the government and the means by which they sought to implement them were close to the published views of FA Hayek.[145] Although the degree of Hayek's influence over legislative change has been doubted,[146] his work is significant for the way in which it expressly linked demand-management and trade union 'control' of labour markets as the twin causes of unemployment and inflation in the 1960s and 1970s.[147] For Hayek, institutions of collective regulation prevented the price mechanism of the labour market from functioning. The cure he

---

[141] See Fredman, 1992a, for a discussion and critique of these justifications.
[142] See above, para 1.22; P Davies and M Freedland, 1993.
[143] See F Wilkinson, 1987.
[144] Cmnd 9474.
[145] Hayek, 1960, 1973, 1984.
[146] Auerbach, 1990.
[147] See, in particular, Hayek, 1980.

proposed was to limit union power by removing the statutory immunities which protected the right to strike and to organise, so creating a greater scope once again for the common law of tort and contract.[148] Related libertarian arguments focused on restriction of the closed shop as a means of limiting union monopoly power.[149] Social security benefits and employment protection legislation were also identified as sources of rigidities; unemployment benefits were thought to raise the reservation wage – that is, the lowest wage which an unemployed worker would accept – above the market-clearing rate for employment in the non-union sector, so adding to unemployment, and unfair dismissal legislation was said to increase the costs for employers of hiring the unemployed. The solution here involved the wholesale deregulation of protective legislation and the restriction of social security payments.[150] Similar approaches to labour market reform were advocated in other countries at this time, most notably in the USA and Germany, but the degree of legislative change in these systems has proved to be nowhere near as great as in the case of Britain.[151]

(iii) Reform of the law governing industrial relations

1.25   In some ways, the particular features of the British labour law and industrial relations system at the start of the 1980s presented an opportunity but also a difficulty for a strategy of deregulation. By international standards, formal labour law regulation in Britain was comparatively weak, but extra-legal sources of regulation were correspondingly strong, part of the legacy of collective laissez-faire. On the one hand, this made the task of deregulation easier in the sense that legislative regulation, much of it dating only from the 1960s and 1970s, had scarcely had time to take root. On the other hand, the support traditionally given to autonomous collective bargaining through the system of collective laissez-faire also meant that new forms of legal intervention were necessary to address the issue of union power in the labour market, as the sources of union strength lay largely outside formal legal procedures and protections. In collective labour law, then, simple delegalisation, or even a 'return to private law', would not be effective, as the sources of trade union power did not depend on a formal statutory underpinning of positive rights. Some inroads were made by the rescission in the early 1980s of the Fair Wages Resolution and the repeal of the statutory procedure for the extension of minimum terms and conditions laid down in sector-level collective agreements. The bulk of changes in trade union law, however, took the form of expanding, rather than diminishing, the role of the law.

To this end, a series of Acts cut back the scope of the statutory immunities as Hayek had proposed, so increasing the scope of common law regulation of strike activity. After a modest beginning in the Employment Act 1980, a more radical measure was the Employment Act 1982 which removed the blanket immunity of trade unions from liability in tort, narrowed down the 'trade dispute' formula which had previously protected most forms of industrial action, and prohibited industrial action aimed at extending the closed shop and union recognition to third

---

[148] Hayek, 1973: pp 141–142. For a sustained critique of this hypothesis in the context of freedom of association, see Wedderburn, 1989.

[149] Hanson *et al*, 1982.

[150] Minford *et al*, 1986.

[151] For comparative discussion of the impact of deregulation in this period, see Mückenberger and Deakin, 1989; Deakin, 1991.

party employers. The immunities were further narrowed down in the 1988 and 1990 Acts, which among other things imposed a general ban on secondary industrial action (action involving employers who are not immediate parties to the trade dispute) and shut off all means of enforcing the closed shop through industrial action.

In addition, new forms of statutory regulation were introduced to complement the expanded role of the common law. The Trade Union Act 1984, whose provisions were extended in 1988 and 1993, made membership ballots compulsory prior to industrial action for which the union was legally responsible, and imposed regular balloting requirements for the election of certain union officials and for the maintenance of union political funds. The Employment Act 1988 and the Trade Union Reform and Employment Rights Act 1993 provided individual members with a further set of rights against their unions, most notably by limiting the power of unions to discipline those refusing to obey strike calls or similar instructions, and the Employment Act 1990 extended the range of union responsibility for 'unofficial' strikes and increased employers' powers to dismiss strikers. The 1993 Act introduced new procedural requirements, including an obligation upon the union to give employers seven days' notice of the commencement of industrial action.

Changes to employment protection law further increased the difficulties facing unions. Enforcement of the post-entry closed shop[152] through dismissals of non-union members became progressively more difficult after 1980 until, in 1988, it became automatically unfair for an employer to dismiss an employee for reasons related to their non-membership of a union. In 1990 a new statutory civil wrong was established which made it unlawful for an employer to refuse to hire an individual on the grounds of membership and non-membership, thereby hampering enforcement of the pre-entry closed shop.[153] Following the judgment of the House of Lords in the *Wilson* and *Palmer* cases[154] in 1995, the way was opened for employers to offer incentives for employees to accept 'individualised' terms and conditions of employment outside the scope of collective agreements, without falling foul of the statutory obligation not to discriminate between union members and non-members, a change which had already been reflected in somewhat narrower form by an amendment introduced in the 1993 Act as the case was proceeding through the courts.

(iv) Labour market flexibility and the employment relationship

1.26 Within individual labour law, a policy of partial or selective deregulation was adopted, on the grounds that this would promote labour market flexibility. One aspect of this was the removal of legal protections for specific groups, in particular young workers and the low paid. Protective legislation governing the employment of young workers was repealed in the Employment Act 1989.[155] The limited statutory floor to wages was withdrawn, first of all through the placing of

---

[152] The 'post-entry closed shop' refers to an arrangement whereby employees are required, as a condition of continuing in employment, to become or remain a member of a particular trade union. In a 'pre-entry closed shop', the individual must be a member of the relevant union in order to be hired in the first place.

[153] On the pre-entry closed shop, see n 152 above.

[154] *Associated Newspapers Ltd v Wilson, Associated British Ports v Palmer* [1995] 2 AC 454; see below, paras 7.9 and 8.17 et seq.

[155] See Deakin, 1990.

restrictions on the regulatory powers of the wages councils in the Wages Act 1986, and later through their complete abolition in the Trade Union Reform and Employment Rights Act 1993.

At the start of the period of Conservative government, employment protection legislation contained a number of exemptions which had the effect of removing certain part-time workers and fixed-term employees from protection. These exemptions were allowed to remain in place, and further disqualifications were introduced. The minimum period of continuous employment needed to qualify for unfair dismissal protection, which had been six months in 1979, was raised in stages to two years by 1985.[156] The government held back from recommending the complete abolition of employment protection legislation.[157] Nevertheless, for those employees who did qualify for protection, statutory rights which were theoretically available were diminished in value by the imposition of procedural obstacles (including the possibility of being made to pay a pre-hearing deposit as a contribution to the employer's costs, introduced in the Employment Act 1989) and by failing to raise with inflation the statutory upper limit on dismissal compensation awards.[158]

A theoretical basis for this policy of selective deregulation was provided by accounts which were critical of labour law and social security legislation for having introduced 'rigidities' into the labour market. At the micro-level, labour flexibility was argued to be necessary if firms were to deal effectively with increasingly turbulent and competitive conditions in product markets. According to an influential model,[159] firms might seek to do this through *functional flexibility*, breaking down demarcation lines between jobs and trades and encouraging multi-skilling on the part of a 'core' workforce of secure employees, while employing a 'periphery' of less secure labour employed on part-time and/or short-term contracts (*numerical flexibility*), or on contracts under which the fixed element of the wage or salary was reduced in favour of bonus payments and overtime premia which would enable the firm to vary its costs according to shifts in demand (*financial flexibility*). Although the research on which this model was based did not itself offer any particular policy prescription, others, including the Department of Employment,[160] concluded that laws and collective agreements setting minimum terms and conditions and protecting security of employment were hostile to flexibility in the sense of restricting firms' ability to hire and fire, set variable wage rates, move workers around between tasks, vary production levels by modulations in working time, and to employ sub-contract or part-time labour.

At the macro-level, the flexibility debate was concerned with the role of labour standards in slowing down processes of economic adjustment. The idea here was that at a time of high unemployment and reduced labour demand within national economies, wages should fall in order to restore equilibrium in the labour market, and workers should be prepared to move from declining sectors to those which were expanding. It was hypothesised that collective agreements and legislative regulation which imposed a minimum floor of rights within and between sectors could hold up these processes of structural adjustment.[161] In this vein, an influential comparative

---

[156] See below, para 3.48.

[157] See *Department of Employment, Building Businesses ... Not Barriers* Cmnd 9794, 1986, and *Wages Councils: Consultation Document*, 1988.

[158] See below, para 5.153.

[159] See Atkinson, 1985.

[160] Particularly in the 1985 White Paper, Cmnd 9474, above.

[161] Metcalf, 1986.

study[162] argued that even if wholesale deregulation was impractical and undesirable given the disruption it would cause to existing employment relationships, a form of partial deregulation could be used to encourage the hiring of new recruits. Job protection rules should be relaxed and the costs of hiring new recruits reduced, while leaving the acquired rights of existing job holders intact. This is not unlike the policy which emerged in the UK, at least as far as individual employment law was concerned: the large part of employment protection legislation was kept intact, even though protective laws relating to particular sections of the workforce, such as those protecting the low paid, were repealed on the grounds that employers needed to be given incentives to hire workers in these categories.

To a certain extent, these developments were counter-balanced by the growing influence of European Union law. In addition to the impact of rulings of the European Court of Justice which established that European law took priority over domestic law in the event of a conflict, and the acceptance by the British courts that individuals could enforce rights which had direct effect, directives dating from the 1970s which were concerned with equal pay and equal treatment between men and women, on the one hand, and employment protection, on the other, slowly began to take effect.[163] The principle of equal pay for work of equal value was introduced into British labour law in 1983,[164] and further changes followed to the treatment of male and female workers in relation to retirement and pension rights[165]and the rights of part-time workers.[166] One of the most influential provisions was the 1977 Acquired Rights Directive,[167] which was used to protect the rights of employees in certain situations of contracting out or where there was a change in the identity of the employer following privatisation. Nevertheless, Britain was practically alone in western Europe at this time in failing to legislate for a basic statutory floor of rights to terms and conditions,[168] while legislative interference with trade union autonomy led to repeated condemnations of government policy by various supervisory bodies of the International Labour Organisation.[169]

(v) The impact of changes in the law on trade union membership and the coverage of collective bargaining during the 1980s and 1990s

1.27   In contrast to a period of rapid growth in the 1970s, union membership declined rapidly in the 1980s and 1990s. The proportion of union members in workplaces with more than 25 workers fell from 65% in 1980 to 47% in 1990 and 36% in 1998.[170] This still represented a high

---

[162] Emerson, 1988.

[163] See para 2.36 below.

[164] In the form of the Equal Pay (Amendment) Regulations 1983, SI 1983/1794.

[165] A major stimulus to change in this area was the decision of the ECJ in Case C-262/88 *Barber v Guardian Royal Exchange Assurance Group* [1990] IRLR 240.

[166] Following the decision of the House of Lords in *R v Secretary of State for Employment, ex p Equal Opportunities Commission* [1994] IRLR 176 applying the then Art 119 (subsequently 141) of the EC Treaty, now Art 157 TFEU, and Directive 76/307 on equal treatment in employment, the 8- and 16-hour thresholds for certain employment rights were removed by SI 1995/31. See para 3.54 *et seq* below.

[167] Directive 77/187/EEC. See paras 3.66 *et seq* and 5.182 *et seq* below.

[168] Deakin, 1990b.

[169] Ewing, 1994a.

[170] Cully *et al*, 1999: p 235.

figure internationally, although care must be taken in interpreting comparative data in this area as not only do methods of calculating density differ from country to country, but membership itself is not necessarily a good indicator of union strength. Britain remained in the middle order of OECD countries, with a density in terms of the labour force as a whole which was comparable to that of Italy and Germany and far higher than in France or the USA.[171] Explanations for the decline in British trade union membership focused on the cyclical effects of high unemployment and economic recession, rather than the compositional effects associated with the decline of manufacturing industry relative to services.[172] The rapid decline of manufacturing at the start of the 1980s and the resulting loss of full-time, male-dominated jobs certainly had an impact in terms of flows out of membership. However, union density fell in all sectors and not just in manufacturing. At any given time trade unions were recruiting large numbers of members and losing others; what has to be explained is the contrast to the 1970s when density rose rapidly at a time of continuing decline in manufacturing employment and a rise in female employment. From this perspective, the critical factors since 1980 appear to have been the inhibiting effect of high unemployment and the combination of relatively low inflation and the absence of an incomes policy, which produced rising real incomes for most private sector employees, in particular in those areas of the economy where collective bargaining remained strongly embedded.

The role of legislation as a factor separate from the economic cycle and from general government hostility to trade unionism is difficult to assess. An attempt to measure the impact of legal change between 1980 and 1986 by Freeman and Pelletier concluded that 'legal changes caused density to fall by 9.4 percentage points from 1980 to 1986 – effectively the entire decline in UK density in that period'. If the Labour government's legislation of the 1970s had been in force, it is estimated that there would have been a drop of only 1 to 2 percentage points in density.[173] However, other studies have argued that union weakness caused the legislation, rather than the other way around.[174]

Density, which is usually calculated on the basis of membership, is only one measure of union strength and influence; a more meaningful measure of the influence of trade union power in regulating terms and conditions of employment is the coverage of collective bargaining agreements. The coverage of collective agreements will be greater than union membership for a number of reasons. It is normal for terms and conditions laid down in agreements at either plant or sector level to be applied to union members and non-members alike in plants where unions are recognised, while in the past it has also been common for firms not recognising unions to follow sector-level agreements informally; in addition, the impact of statutory wages orders should be considered here as a substitute for collective bargaining which affected large numbers of non-unionised employees. ACAS estimates at the start of the 1980s suggested that the terms and conditions of over two-thirds of full-time employees in employment were affected in some way by a collective agreement,[175] while the extensive influence of collective bargaining in manufacturing industry and the public sector was confirmed by the first Workplace Industrial Relations Survey.[176] More recent research suggests that there was then a considerable decline in collective bargaining

---

[171] W Brown *et al*, 1997.
[172] Kelly, 1990; Disney, 1990.
[173] Freeman and Pelletier, 1990: p 155.
[174] Disney, 1990.
[175] R Lewis, 1986: p 20.
[176] Daniel and Millward, 1984.

coverage which by the late 1990s was only just above 40% of the employed labour force, with the fall particularly marked in the private sector.[177] Here, the difference between the UK and other systems was clear, and can be largely attributed to institutional changes which contributed to the decline in sector-level collective bargaining.[178]

Derecognition and the structure of collective bargaining

1.28   Apart from some *causes célèbres* in the docks and national newspapers, formal derecognition – the withdrawal of collective bargaining rights from recognised unions – was rare throughout the 1980s, despite the fact that there were very few legal obstacles to it.[179] New forms of collective agreements, such as single-union deals and no-strike agreements, were also very rare. Despite the attention which they attracted,[180] they did not cover more than a small number of establishments, almost exclusively on new, 'greenfield' sites. The repeal in 1980 of the rather weak union recognition laws of the 1970s at first appeared to have had little general impact, because most bargaining arrangements pre-dated those laws and had grown up without direct legal support or regulation. Similarly, the removal of legal support for the closed shop did not immediately lead to a substantial decline in union strength in the workplace: 'the demise of the union shops is likely to have had only a marginal impact on the levels of union density, with its effects in practice having been to "top-up" by "compulsory" means levels of membership which were already high'.[181] Pre-entry closed shops had covered a declining number of workers since the 1960s,[182] and many of them were under threat even prior to the Employment Act 1990 which formally prohibited restrictions on the hiring and employment of non-union workers.

However, in the 1990s employers in a wide range of sectors resorted to derecognition, making it clear that the legal regime posed no obstacle to employers undermining longstanding bargaining arrangements, and that trade unions were not always in a strong position to respond to such tactics.[183] Derecognition occurred in companies in printing and publishing, engineering, banking and food processing. Companies sometimes coupled derecognition with offers of enhanced pay and benefits to employees who gave up rights associated with trade union membership, such as the right to trade union representation, and in other cases made unilateral cuts in pay and conditions as part of an anti-union drive. In the Timex dispute at Dundee, tactics used by the employer included the threat of mass dismissal to be followed by the employment of a completely new workforce, the lock-out of employees who refused to accept unilateral cuts in pay and benefits and, eventually, the closure of the plant.[184]

Alongside these changes at firm level, there was the continuing decline of national or sector-level bargaining, and the weakening of union power in the labour market which came with the

[177] In workplaces of 25 or more workers, coverage was 41% in 1998: see Cully *et al*, 1999: p 243. For a historical perspective on the decline in coverage, see Milner, 1995.
[178] See W Brown *et al*, 1997.
[179] ACAS, Annual Report, 1991: pp 11–12.
[180] Basset, 1986.
[181] Ewing, 1990: p 644.
[182] Dunn and Gennard, 1984.
[183] Taylor, 1994: ch 2.
[184] K Miller and C Woolfson, 1994.

enforced decentralisation of bargaining levels.[185] As we have seen,[186] the decline of sector-level bargaining long pre-dated the advent of the Thatcher governments; from the mid-1960s onwards national agreements in manufacturing were increasingly confined to setting a floor of minimum wages and conditions which were only directly relevant for employees without a recognised union to negotiate for them at plant or company level.[187] In the 1980s even this floor was removed, first by the repeal in the early 1980s of 'fair wages legislation' which provided for the extension of sector-level agreements to non-union firms, and later by the break-up of national multi-employer bargaining in a number of sectors. The then Government's attitude to multi-employer bargaining was spelled out in the 1988 White Paper:

> … many existing approaches to pay bargaining, beloved of trade unions and employers alike, will need to change if we are to secure the flexibility essential to employment growth. In particular, 'the going rate', 'comparability' and 'cost of living increases', are all outmoded concepts – they take no account of differences in performance, ability to pay or difficulties of recruitment, retention or motivation. Pay structures too have to change. National agreements which affect the pay of half the workforce all too often give scant regard to differences in individual circumstances or performance.[188]

A number of means, direct and indirect, were used to undermine national bargaining. These included the ending of the statutory system of industry training boards in most sectors in 1982 and the abolition in 1993 of the powers of statutory wages councils which previously determined the pay and conditions of 2.75 million low-paid workers.[189] Changes to strike law also indirectly undermined national bargaining. In some sectors, including merchant shipping and newspapers, laws restricting picketing and secondary action limited the ability of unions to resist employer moves to break up or narrow the scope of national agreements. The 1982 Act made it difficult to conduct national disputes except as the aggregation of local disputes between employers and their own employees. This was partly responsible for the demise of the national engineering agreement in 1990, which followed a series of local settlements to the engineering unions' demands for working-time reductions. Similar moves towards decentralisation of collective bargaining occurred in the public sector, as a consequence of compulsory competitive tendering following the Local Government Act 1988 and the ban on local authorities from using contract compliance to maintain union recognition and minimum terms and conditions for the privatised workforce.[190]

(i) Restriction of industrial action

1.29   The late 1980s and 1990s saw a considerable reduction in strike activity. In terms of working days lost per year, the average of the 1980s was 7.2 million as opposed to 12.9 million in

---

[185] W Brown and J Walsh, 1990; W Brown, 1993; W Brown *et al*, 2000.
[186] See para 1.22 above.
[187] W Brown, 1981.
[188] Cm 540, 1988: pp 23–24.
[189] Minimum wage regulation was restored, in a new form, by NMWA 1998. See below, paras 1.34 and 4.46 *et seq.*
[190] Compulsory competitive tendering has since been replaced by the system of 'best value' (see LGA 1999) and it is once again permissible to use fair wages clauses under certain specified circumstances (SI 2001/909; para 2.6, below).

the 1970s and 3.5 million in the 1960s.[191] The figure for the 1980s was affected by a small number of very large-scale strikes, in particular the miners' strike of 1984–1985. In terms of the number of stoppages, the 1980s showed a reduction as compared with both the 1960s and the 1970s. The incidence of industrial action in the period 1990–1996 was even lower; only 278,000 and 415,000 working days were lost in 1994 and 1995 respectively. In 1996, 1.3 million working days were lost which, although an increase on the years immediately preceding it, was still a very low figure by the standards of the previous three decades.[192] In subsequent years, the incidence of industrial action has continued at what is, by historical standards, a very low level.[193]

The narrowing of the immunities and the ending of the blanket immunity of trade unions from liability in tort provided employers with many more strategic options than they had previously had for breaking strike resistance, and these were put to effective use in particular disputes, such as the Wapping and Messenger disputes in the newspaper printing industry.[194] The imposition of controls on internal union procedures had a more ambiguous effect, at least initially, both upon strike levels and upon union government more generally: as Kelly commented, 'the balloting provisions are a classic example of unintended consequences'.[195] By making unions formally responsible for a wide range of strikes, and by requiring membership ballots in the case of all strikes which were in law the union's responsibility, the Trade Union Act 1984 strengthened the power of central union organisation over the rank and file, reversing a trend towards fragmentation which had weakened unions in some sectors. Although some strikes foundered owing to the failure of unions early on to observe the balloting requirements of the 1984 Act, where they were observed they could be put to good effect to rally support for industrial action and to put pressure on employers in advance of the strike commencing. Brown and Wadwhani suggested that 'while the new procedure may thus reduce the actual occurrence of strikes, it may not commensurately diminish the impact of the strike threat': their research, published in 1990, found that over 90% of strike ballots under the new procedures had resulted in votes for industrial action.[196] Nor was it the case, on the whole, that the provisions of the 1988 Act preventing unions from disciplining members who refused to take part in strikes greatly weakened the strike weapon, given the small numbers of such individuals.

Against the background of criticism that the 1984 balloting laws could lend a 'spurious legitimacy' to industrial action,[197] the Government introduced amendments in the 1988, 1990 and 1993 Acts which sought to diminish the effectiveness of ballots as a source of union negotiating strength; it was this legislation rather more than the original Act of 1984 which was largely responsible for creating a situation in which industrial action could not be undertaken without going through procedures of inordinate complexity.[198] Research found that union officials saw these new procedural requirements as constraining their capacity to respond quickly to changes in circumstances in the run up to a trade dispute.[199]

---

[191] Bird, 1991.
[192] Sweeney, 1997.
[193] See Monger, 2004; W Brown and S Oxenbridge, 2004; Hale, 2010; ch 11, below.
[194] Ewing and Napier, 1986.
[195] Kelly, 1990: p 56.
[196] W Brown and S Wadwhani, 1990: p 62.
[197] Hanson and Mather, 1988: p 77.
[198] See further para 11.32 *et seq* below.
[199] Elgar and Simpson, 1996.

These legal factors were not the only influence on the reduced strike activity of the later 1980s and the 1990s. Higher unemployment and the absence of an incomes policy more clearly distinguish the 1980s from the strike-prone 1970s. Nevertheless, the decline in strike activity in Britain since the late 1970s was greater than the average for OECD countries, and this might suggest some role for factors which were particular to the British experience, one of which may have been the legislation.[200]

(ii) Labour market outcomes: employment, unemployment, wage distribution, and inequality[201]

1.30   Even though the UK economy underwent significant 'flexibilisation' in the 1980s and 1990s, the level of unemployment did not consistently fall during this period, but rather became more volatile than it had been in previous decades. Unemployment swung from 6.4% in 1980 to 12.4% in 1983, down to 6.8% in 1990, up again to 10% in 1993, and then down to below 6% by 2001[202] and below 5% by 2004.[203] During this period unemployment became increasingly concentrated among 'workless households' in which neither adult worked; these amounted to almost 20% of all households by the end of the 1990s. Employment levels rose during the 1980s and 1990s, mainly as a result of growing female participation in paid employment. In part, this was related to a significant decline in full-time, permanent employment and an increase in the use of 'flexible' forms of work since 1980. However, the link between this change and the framework of regulation governing employment is unclear. The growth in part-time work began in the 1960s and 1970s, prior to the general trend towards deregulation in the 1980s. The most significant rise in 'atypical' work after 1979 was the rapid increase in male self-employment, but this was concentrated in the early 1980s. After 1990 the growth in self-employment almost ceased. During the mid-1990s there was an increase in the use of fixed-term contracts especially in public administration, health and education which appears to have been linked to the exclusion of this type of employment from dismissal protection.[204] The tax-benefit system also played a role. The growth of both self-employment and part-time work at low rates of weekly pay in the 1980s can convincingly be linked to features of income tax and social security contributions which, in effect, subsidised these forms of work.[205] However, these effects are waning thanks to more recent regulatory changes. In the mid-1990s, during the period of Conservative government, the Inland Revenue began to take steps to regularise the position of many freelancers and self-employed construction workers, in the process eliminating many of the tax advantages they had formerly enjoyed, and this policy continued following the election of a Labour government in 1997.[206]

There was a growing consensus amongst commentators that increased flexibility and the comparatively low unemployment rate in Britain had been achieved at the price of a deterioration

---

[200] See W Brown *et al*, 1997: p 78.

[201] This part summarises Deakin and Reed, 2000b, to which the reader is referred for a more detailed account.

[202] See *Labour Market Trends*, February 2001, Table A.1. The figures quoted in the text refer to the ILO definition of unemployment which is significantly higher than the claimant count (see *Labour Market Trends*, February 2001, p S2). On the significance of different measures of unemployment, see Nickell, 1999.

[203] *Labour Market Trends*, March 2005, Figure 3.

[204] See Burchell et al, 1999. On the nature of this exclusion, and changes to the law in 1999 and 2002 which limited its impact, see paras 3.49 *et seq*.

[205] M Harvey, 1995.

[206] See para 3.33 below.

in wages, growing insecurity, and increasing poverty.[207] After a long period of wage stability, wage inequality grew sharply in the 1980s and 1990s, resulting in higher differentials than at any other time during the twentieth century.[208] The pay gap between the lowest decile and the highest decile of workers grew consistently, and although the real earnings of workers in the lowest decile rose in real terms during the 1990s, low pay was disproportionately experienced by women in low paying industries or occupations and by members of ethnic minorities. The impact of the decline in collective bargaining on pay and terms and conditions of employment during this period is difficult to assess, because other relevant factors at this time included changes in general labour market conditions and increased competition in product markets. Studies nevertheless suggest that the decline in the coverage of collective bargaining was responsible for between one-eighth and one-quarter of the increase in earnings inequality during this period.[209] The alternative explanation for inequality would place more emphasis upon falling demand for 'unskilled' labour as a result of changes in technology and in the structure of demand for goods and services. However, comparative studies suggest that these factors can only account for a part of the polarisation of earnings in systems such as Britain, the USA and New Zealand which engaged in policies of market liberalisation. These more flexible systems saw the pay of their relatively less skilled workers fall more rapidly than in systems which offered more systematic institutional support for investment in human capital, such as Germany and Sweden, casting doubt on the skills-based explanation.[210]

(iii) Employment policy and work incentives

1.31 An increasingly important form of direct labour market intervention which was used to counter the rise in unemployment in the 1980s and 1990s was employment policy. This consisted of measures aimed at making labour supply more flexible, ranging from direct subsidies paid to employers offering training and/or work experience, to changes to social security and employment law designed to cut employers' hiring costs and encourage the unemployed to enter or re-enter the labour market 'at wages which employers can afford to pay'.[211] Training policy also received a higher profile in the 1980s and 1990s than before, but for most of this time it was subordinated to the wider policy goal of labour market deregulation. As a result, the role of trade unions in the training infrastructure was marginalised, with the abolition of the statutory industrial training boards and the winding up of the Manpower Services Commission, on both of which unions had been represented. Training subsidies, including the Youth Training allowance and payments under various short-lived youth employment schemes,[212] were designed to set a low ceiling of 'more realistic levels of pay' to the wages and income of young workers.[213] To similar effect was the removal after 1988 of access to income support for the under-18s, part of the reforms to social

---

[207] Marx, 1999. On the record of the New Labour government since 1997 in mitigating some of the effects of rising poverty and inequality during the preceding period of Conservative government, see Hills, 2009.
[208] Machin, 1996.
[209] Gosling and Machin, 1995.
[210] Nickell, 1997: p 71.
[211] Cmnd 9474, 1985. See paras 3.16–3.17 below.
[212] See below, paras 3.17 and 3.32.
[213] Cmnd 9474, 1985: Annex 2.

security brought about by the Social Security Act 1986, on the assumption that all those below this age would either be in education or in employment or, failing that, would receive an offer of a training place. It was argued that these policies, by linking training and occupational development to the more general strategy of subsidising low pay, directly contradicted the government's efforts to raise awareness of the importance of training and to improve training quality.[214]

Extensive changes made in social security included the tightening of the qualifying conditions for unemployment benefits; the widening of the grounds for disqualification from benefit; the introduction of greater monitoring of the unemployed by employment officers through the *Restart* programme, a process which was carried a stage further by the introduction of the jobseeker's allowance to replace unemployment benefit with effect from 1997; changes to the system of national insurance contributions, designed to lower contributions in respect of low-paid work; and the introduction of family credit as an addition to the net, after-tax earnings of low-paid employees.[215] The restriction of social security entitlements was influenced by two limited surveys of the unemployed from which the government concluded in 1988 that 'there is evidence that a significant minority of benefit claimants are not actively looking for work'.[216] The size of the fall in unemployment in the mid-1980s and its timing have been ascribed to the tightening of social security administration brought about in 1986 by the *Restart* programme, under which the long-term unemployed were subject to regular monitoring by employment service officials to assess their availability for work.[217]

The assumption that incentives for the unemployed could be improved by these means was widely criticised. Research showed that the greatest disincentive for the unemployed was often the precariousness of work and income in most of the jobs which were on offer to them.[218] Studies of local labour markets in areas of high unemployment demonstrated that over half the jobs taken up by benefit recipients involved non-standard working hours or forms of employment, and that the median level of pay on offer to the unemployed was very low, at less than half the average hourly wage.[219] Disenchantment with the prevailing policy of deregulation led policy-makers to perceive the need to combine work incentives with a basic framework of labour market regulation which would make employment more feasible and attractive for the unemployed, and this fed into the new turn in labour market regulation which accompanied the election of a Labour government in 1997.

Pragmatic reconstruction? Labour law under 'New Labour'

1.32   A number of elements characterised labour law policy following the election of a 'New Labour' government in 1997. In the first place, there was acceptance of the Conservative reforms in the law relating to industrial action, joined with a willingness, nevertheless, to use legal means to encourage trade union recognition at workplace and enterprise level, thereby offering

---

[214] Keep, 1990: p 154.
[215] See generally Deakin and Wilkinson, 1991, 2005; P Davies and M Freedland, 1993: ch 10.
[216] Cm 540, 1988: p 55.
[217] Dicks and Hatch, 1989.
[218] McLaughlin et al, 1989.
[219] Marsh *et al*, 1990.

support to collective bargaining. Second, basic labour standards were strengthened in the areas of minimum wages, working time and employment protection with the aim, in part, of achieving a better balance between working life and family life, albeit within the framework of a continuing commitment to labour market flexibility. This policy switch was consistent with the Labour government's acceptance of the extensions which had made to the competence of the European Community organs to legislate in the area of social policy by the Maastricht Treaty in 1991, which the previous Conservative governments had rejected and from which they had secured an 'opt-out' for the UK. The Amsterdam Treaty of 1997 ended this opt-out, and the influence of the EU on domestic UK labour law increased markedly over the subsequent period.[220] Third, employment policy was used to promote employment opportunities, together with an increasing emphasis on the 'responsibilities' of workers and jobseekers. What linked these developments was less, perhaps, an overarching philosophy of the 'third way'[221] than a series of pragmatic responses to particular issues and to the wider political and economic context of the time. How far the policies of the Labour governments which held office between 1997 and 2010 marked a true break from neoliberalism continues to be contested.[222]

(i) Collective labour law: towards 'partnership'?

1.33   Labour governments after 1997 insisted that there should be 'no going back' to the period, during the 1970s, when industrial action was characterised by secondary action, widespread picketing and strikes without ballots.[223] On this basis, they declined to accept calls for the restoration of the trade-dispute immunities to the position they had occupied at the end of the 1970s. A substantial element of the balloting and notice legislation of the 1980s and 1990s was retained; some procedural reforms were introduced but they did relatively little to make it more straightforward for union officials to conduct industrial action in an effective way.[224] Nor were many changes made to the law governing trade union organisation.

At the same time, the first Labour government elected after 1997 initiated a major change in the law relating to collective bargaining, by re-introducing the principle that a trade union with majority support in a bargaining unit was legally entitled, under particular circumstances, to require the employer to enter into negotiations over pay and certain conditions of employment. A law of this kind had operated for most of the 1970s, without great success. For most of the modern period, trade unions have relied on a combination of organising strength, the protection of the

---

[220] See further our analysis in paras 2.35 *et seq* below.

[221] On the 'third way', see Blair, 1998; Giddens, 1998; and for views of its influence on labour law, see H Collins, 2001b; Novitz and Skidmore, 2001; Kilpatrick, 2004; Fredman, 2004a.

[222] For views critical of New Labour's failure to break with the past, see P Smith and G Morton, 2001, 2006; McIlroy and Daniels, 2009; IER, 2009. P Davies and M Freedland, 2007, discuss the coexistence of elements of continuity and change in New Labour policy after 1997, arguing that while there was a common link with neoliberalism in the emphasis on the market-regulatory function of labour law, there was a reduced emphasis on deregulation as the means of achieving economic goals. For an analysis stressing elements of continuity between the pre- and post-1997 periods, and charting broader trends in labour law since the mid-1960s which include the decline of collective bargaining and the individualisation of dispute resolution, see Wedderburn, 2007. See also our discussion at para 1.37 *et seq*, below.

[223] *Fairness at Work*, Cmnd 3968 (1998), at 4 (Foreword by the Prime Minister). See Novitz and Skidmore, 2001: pp 6–8.

[224] See ch 11 below.

trade-dispute immunities and the (intermittent) support of government to promote recognition; a legal duty to bargain has generally been regarded as impractical and possibly even counter-productive.[225] Nor did the new law, introduced by the Employment Relations Act 1999,[226] mark a complete break with this 'voluntarist' past. In effect, it held statutory recognition in reserve as a threat for employers who failed to enter into voluntary recognition agreements with trade unions. The new procedure was designed principally to operate in respect of bargaining units where, prior to the law's coming into force, there was no recognition agreement, thus leaving most voluntary arrangements untouched. The procedure was designed to encourage employers and unions at any one of a number of stages to make a voluntary agreement which would avert the need for the intervention of the Central Arbitration Committee. Even if an order of statutory recognition was made, this would not necessarily lead to the making of a collective agreement, nor to the incorporation of improved terms and conditions into the contracts of workers in the relevant bargaining unit.

The apparent contradiction in legislating for union recognition while doing little or nothing to restore the collective rights formerly guaranteed by wide statutory immunities in relation to industrial action disappears on closer inspection. Both the new recognition law and the preservation of the Conservative governments' constraints on industrial action reflected the New Labour government's stress on 'partnership at work' as a means of raising productivity and improving economic performance.[227] The idea of partnership implied a process through which unions could achieve a recognised status within the workplace as the means for expressing collective employee 'voice', in return for facilitating organisational changes capable of enhancing performance and productivity. This idea was not new; the pursuit of co-operative labour-management relations had been a principal goal of the industrial relations reforms of the 1960s and 1970s. What was new, by comparison with the 1960s, was the changed economic environment within which the compromise between labour and management was being forged. Both the effectiveness of union sanctions and the scope for redistribution through collective bargaining were now limited, in part by the law, but also by increased product market competition and growing financial pressures on corporate management.[228] Under these circumstances, the partnership agenda could only offer unions a limited role in issues of workplace governance.

Although the New Labour government was committed to partnership at work, its commitment to the delivery of partnership through independent trade unions was much more equivocal.[229] The *Fairness at Work* White Paper stated:

> Collective representation can help achieve important business objectives, including good communication. It can facilitate negotiation on terms and conditions without preventing the recognition of good individual performance. Representatives who are respected by other employees can help employers to explain the company's circumstances and the need for

---

[225] See Simpson, 1991.

[226] The relevant law, contained in Schedule A1 of TULRCA 1992, was amended further by the Employment Relations Act 2004. Bogg, 2009a, discusses the confluence of policies and ideas which informed the passage of the union recognition law contained in the Employment Relations Act 1999, and examines how far the law matches up to conceptions of workplace democracy. See our analysis below, para 9.5 *et seq*.

[227] See W Brown, 2000.

[228] See W Brown *et al*, 2001; W Brown and S Oxenbridge, 2004; Stuart and Martinez-Lucio, 2005.

[229] On the concept of 'independence' in this context, see paras 7.22 *et seq* below.

change. Collective representation can give employees a more effective voice in discussion with employers by drawing on a wide range of expertise and experience in the company.[230]

This passage tellingly makes no reference to independent employee representation, and it was suggested around this time that 'the "partnership" which New Labour sought to encourage within the employment relationship was not one which necessarily involved trade unions'.[231] Legislation significantly expanded the role of employee representatives outside the structure of trade unions in the course of the 1990s and 2000s, building on EU law developments.[232] In workplaces where there was no recognised trade union or no collective agreement in force, the implementation of statutory rights in such areas as fixed-term employment, working time and parental leave could now be achieved through 'workforce agreements' between the employer and employee representatives who may have no link to a union.[233] These employee representatives could also exercise information and consultation rights in relation to redundancies, transfers of undertakings and health and safety issues (although, contrary to the position taken under legislation adopted under a Conservative government in 1995, they could no longer do so where a recognised trade union was already established[234]). . It remained open to trade unions to use information and consultation laws for their own ends, and there was some evidence that they were doing so.[235] However, the government provided little support for such engagement, being reluctant to support European Union proposals aimed at extending information and consultation rights at work over a range of issues previously left untouched by UK legislation.[236] The relevant directive[237] only came into force in the UK in 2005, and even then the UK government took advantage of derogations to limit the impact of the new legislation.[238]

(ii) Labour standards and labour flexibility

1.34 The *Fairness at Work* White Paper committed the government to pursuing the goal of a 'flexible and efficient labour market'[239] and the then Prime Minister's Foreword, warning of 'overburdensome regulation', asserted that '[e]ven after the changes we propose, Britain will have the most lightly regulated labour market of any leading economy in the world'.[240] The changes made to employment protection law by the Employment Relations Act 1999 and related measures were, nevertheless, significant; they included the removal of derogations from unfair dismissal protection for fixed-term contract workers, the shortening of the qualifying period for

[230] Cmnd 3968, para 4.3.
[231] Novitz and Skidmore, 2001: p 14.
[232] Davies, 1994b
[233] See, respectively, paras 3.52, 4.78 and 6.119 below.
[234] See para 9.30 *et seq* below.
[235] See McCarthy, 2000, for discussion of union policy on this issue, and Armour and Deakin, 2003, for case-study evidence of union use of consultation laws in the context of corporate reorganisation.
[236] On the nature of this opposition, see Bercusson, 2001.
[237] Directive 2002/14/EC establishing a general framework for informing and consulting employees within the European Community. See below, para 9.30.
[238] See below, para 9.50 *et seq*; for assessments of the impact of the law, see Hall et al, 2007, 2008; Deakin and Koukiadaki, 2012a.
[239] Cmnd 3968, para 1.8.
[240] Cmnd 3968, p 4.

unfair dismissal from two years to one, and the raising of the upper limit on unfair dismissal compensation awards and its indexing to price inflation for future years. Yet, within a short period the government was persuaded to enact a series of measures which sought to limit access to employment tribunals, on the grounds that rising litigation was imposing an undue burden on employers. These provisions, principally contained in the Employment Act 2002, required employees to institute an internal grievance procedure prior to bringing a tribunal claim in respect of a wide range of statutory employment rights, with provision for a substantial reduction in compensation, if the employee's claim was successful, for non-completion of that procedure.[241] In addition, employees who failed to exhaust an internal disciplinary procedure prior to bringing a tribunal claim risked a substantial reduction in their unfair dismissal compensation,[242] while at the same time the content of procedural standards in relation to unfair dismissal was watered down. These provisions introduced additional layers of complexity into the law and failed in their aim of encouraging the early resolution of disputes. They were repealed with effect from April 2009 and replaced by more flexible provisions.[243]

Two particularly important developments in the area of basic labour standards were the National Minimum Wage Act 1998, which established a comprehensive statutory minimum wage for the first time in Britain, and the Working Time Regulations 1998, which, by finally implementing the Working Time Directive of 1993,[244] introduced comprehensive working time standards. The process by which the national minimum wage was established exemplified the government's pragmatic and consensus-building approach to labour law policy, in particular through the involvement of both trade unions and employers' organisations in the Low Pay Commission which was given responsibility, among other things, for making recommendations on the rate of the minimum wage. Subsequent rises in the minimum wage did something to assuage criticism of the low rate at which it was initially set.[245] The process by which the Working Time Directive was adopted proved to be a more enduring source of controversy, thanks to the wide derogations contained in the 1998 and 1999 Regulations.[246] The exceptions contained in the Regulations exploited to the full, and possibly went beyond, the derogations contained in the Directive. Similarly, the manner in which the EC Directives on Part-Time Work,[247] Parental Leave,[248] Fixed-Term Work[249] and Agency Work[250] were implemented prompted concerns that the government's aim of achieving a more flexible labour market while also providing for a better reconciliation of family time and work time was unlikely to be realised.[251]

---

[241] See para 2.20 below.

[242] See generally Hepple and Morris, 2002.

[243] See paras 2.20–2.21 and 5.119 *et seq*, below.

[244] Directive 93/104/EC (later replaced by Directive 2003/88/EC)

[245] On the law governing the national minimum wage, and the changes which have taken place in its rate over time, see paras 4.46–4.59 below; for an account of its 'minimal' impact on poverty and the structure of employment, see R Dickens and A Manning, 2003. W Brown, 2009, emphasises the extent to which the 1998 Act achieved pay rises for the lowest paid over and above what would otherwise have been the case.

[246] WTR 1998 (SI 1998/1833), as amended. See paras 4.77–4.92 below; Barnard *et al*, 2003.

[247] Directive 97/81/EC, implemented by PTWR 2000 (SI 2000/1551). See para 3.58 below.

[248] Directive 96/34/EC, extended to the UK by Directive 97/75/EC and implemented by ERelA 1999. See para 6.119 below.

[249] Directive 99/70EC, implemented by FTER 2002 (SI 2002/2034). See para 3.52 below.

[250] Directive 2008/104/ EC, implemented by AWR 2010 (SI 2010/93). See para 3.53 below.

[251] For discussion, see McColgan, 2000a, 2000b; Kilpatrick, 2004; A Davies, 2010; and see paras 6.110–6.122 below, for discussion of the complex body of law on work-life balance which has taken shape in this area since the early 2000s.

At the same time, these measures marked a break with the view, which was widely held during the 1980s and 1990s, that mandatory labour standards were inevitably incompatible with labour market flexibility and efficiency. The economic argument for re-regulation of basic standards, although muted in *Fairness at Work*, was more fully acknowledged in less high-profile documents, such as the government's Regulatory Impact Assessment of measures which went on to form part of the Employment Relations Act 1999. This stated that 'employers have shown that establishing decent standards is consistent with, and can contribute to, competitive business' and noted that while 'the main reason for introducing parental leave is to help individuals to balance work and home life', there should also be 'economic benefits to the economy and to individual employers through reduced staff turnover, and improved commitment leading to improved labour productivity'.[252]

(iii) The expansion of equality law

1.35 A major change which occurred during the 2000s and culminated in the passage of the Equality Act 2010 was the expansion and rationalisation of the law governing equality in employment. The initial impetus for this development came from EU law and in particular from the adoption of the Framework Directive on Equal Treatment in 2000.[253] The Framework Directive extended the range of grounds on which discrimination in employment was prohibited beyond sex and race, to cover sexual orientation, religion and belief, disability, and age. A more limited form of disability discrimination legislation had been introduced into the UK in 1995[254] and some protection from discrimination on the grounds of sexual orientation and age had previously been recognised as stemming from the prohibition on sex discrimination.[255] The changes flowing from the introduction of the new heads of discrimination were substantial and had a major impact on UK employment law as they were gradually introduced in the course of the succeeding decade. The Equality Act 2010 completed this process,[256] bringing all the 'protected characteristics' into a single statute, harmonising the scope of the discrimination concept across the different heads of claim, and introducing a number of procedural and remedial reforms. The 2010 Act confirmed the role of the Equality and Human Rights Commission as the single body charged with overseeing the implementation of equality law as a whole,[257] inheriting the functions of bodies which had previously operated in relation to the separate heads of sex, race and disability discrimination. The Act enjoyed broad cross-party support and, although formally enacted in the final days of the Labour government which left office in 2010, was mostly brought into force by the Coalition government which succeded it. However, the new government did not implement certain parts

---

[252] Department of Trade and Industry, *Employment Relations Bill. Regulatory Impact Assessment*, February 1999: paras 15–16. See also para 16, referring to the 'adverse selection' argument for labour market regulation. For an overview of this and related justifications for intervention, see H Collins, 2001a, 2003; Deakin and Wilkinson, 2005. For conflicting views of the role of mandatory labour standards in promoting competitiveness, see H Collins, 2001a, 2001b, 2003; Deakin and Wilkinson, 2005.

[253] Directive 2000/78/EC.

[254] Disability Discrimination Act 1995. See below, paras 6.123 *et seq.*

[255] See below, paras 6.40 and 6.41, respectively.

[256] See para 6.11 below.

[257] This step had previously been taken in EqA 2006. See below, para 6.69. The Coalition government has proposed to remove some of the statutory powers of the EHRC: see GEO, 2011; Hepple, 2011.

of the 2010 Act, including provision for greater disclosure of pay inequalities by private-sector companies[258] (the principle of disclosure had previously been accepted in the public sector[259]), and a modification to the discrimination concept that had been intended to facilitate claims based on multiple protected characteristics.

(iv) 'Rights and responsibilities' in the labour market and corporate governance

1.36   Under New Labour, a point of departure not just from the policies of the 1980s but also from the period of the welfare state which preceded them lay in the development of a language of 'rights and responsibilities' which was coupled with a role for government in terms of the 'enabling state'. The coupling of rights and responsibilities was exemplified by the 'New Deal' for the delivery of training and employment opportunities for the unemployed, which operated alongside the stringent benefit disqualification rules of the Jobseekers Act 1995 and related measures introduced by Conservative governments.[260] As the then Chancellor of the Exchequer explained in his James Meade Memorial Lecture of May 2000, the basis of the New Deal was the notion that government measures should support not just 'new opportunities for employment' but also 'new obligations to seize them'. The government's task of building a 'strong economy and fairer society' implied a 'new, modern understanding of the duties of citizenship and the role and limits of Government'.[261]

On this basis, the provision of government aid designed to find work for the unemployed was symmetrically dependent upon regulations which required the unemployed to take up the opportunities which they are offered, on pain of losing benefit entitlements. More broadly, the idea of 'making work pay' by improving incentives was doubled-edged: the raising of the minimum wage and the subsidisation of low wages through tax credits was conditional upon increasing legal regulation of the process of transition from unemployment into work.[262] The idea that employers might have corresponding duties was less well developed. The then Chancellor's 2000 James Meade Memorial Lecture referred fleetingly to the need for 'a responsible citizenship' whether it be 'individual or corporate responsibility'.[263] However, the more far-reaching 'stakeholder' conception of corporate governance remained marginalised in the context of the government's review of companies legislation,[264] and as late as 2007, shortly before the onset of a financial crisis triggered in part by excessive bank lending and exposure to risk arising from takeovers and mergers in banking and financial services, the former Chancellor, subsequently Prime Minister, referred

---

[258] EqA 2010, s 78.

[259] By virtue of the introduction of the public sector equality duty, now set out in EqA 2010, s. 149, and originating in the context of racial discrimination law in RRA 2000.

[260] See para 3.16 below.

[261] Chancellor of the Exchequer, Gordon Brown MP, James Meade Memorial Lecture at the London School of Economics, 8 May 2000, at p 3.

[262] On this coupling of rights and responsibilities, see S White, 1999.

[263] James Meade Memorial Lecture, 8 May 2000, at 3.

[264] See Department of Trade and Industry, *Modern Company Law for a Competitive Economy. Developing the Framework*, March 2000, at para 2.24, and on the eclipse of stakeholder-related thinking in Labour party policy after the general election of 1997, see Novitz and Skidmore, 2001: p 14; Deakin, 2004; Wedderburn, 2004. For an argument in favour of employee participation which combines labour law and corporate governance perspectives, see Njoya, 2004.

in a City of London speech to the need to maintain a 'light touch regulatory environment'[265] in the corporate sector.

Labour law under the Coalition government

1.37   In 2010 the Labour government left office and was succeeded by a Conservative-Liberal Democrat coalition which set out the essential element of its legislative programme in an agreement made between the two parties prior to the formation of the government. The Coalition Agreement committed the incoming administration to carry out a review of laws affecting employers and employees 'to ensure they maximise flexibility for both parties while protecting fairness and providing the competitive environment required for enterprise to thrive'.[266] The Coalition also undertook in the Agreement to 'examine the balance of the EU's existing competencies and... [to] work to limit the application of the Working Time Directive in the UK'.[267] At the same time, the Agreement reiterated the Coalition's acceptance of the principle of the national minimum wage and its intention to secure effective enforcement of legislation governing equality between women and men.

Consistently with the Coalition Agreement, in the autumn of 2011 the government, through the BIS Department, initiated a review of employment laws as part of a wider initiative aimed at reducing 'red tape'.[268] Proposals subsequently put forward by BIS included extending the qualifying period for unfair dismissal protection from one year to two (implemented with effect from April 2012) and removing statutory wage fixing in agriculture above the floor set by the national minimum wage. Measures which will further discourage claims to employment tribunals have also been introduced.[269] In November 2011 a further review of employment protection laws was announced, following a report commissioned by the Prime Minister's office which referred to 'the terrible impact of the current unfair dismissal rules on the efficiency and hence competitiveness of our businesses'.[270] One of the measures on which BIS undertook to consult was a proposal to remove unfair dismissal protection in micro-firms employing fewer than ten employees, replacing it with a right to 'no-fault dismissal compensation'.[271] At the time of writing, the outcome of these various reviews is unclear, but it seems highly likely that some further deregulation of labour law will take place under the Coalition, which is due to hold office until May 2015.

---

[265] Gordon Brown MP, Mansion House speech, 21 June 2007.

[266] HM Government, *The Coalition: Our Programme for Government* (2011), at p 10.

[267] *Programme for Government*, at p 19.

[268] BIS, *Flexible, Effective and Fair: Promoting Economic Growth through a Strong and Efficient Labour Market* (2011).

[269] BIS and HM Courts and Tribunals Service, *Resolving Workplace Disputes: Government response to the consultation* (2011). See further paras 2.16 *et seq* below.

[270] This report, the 'Beecroft report', was not initially published, but it was leaked to the Daily Telegraph, which reproduced its executive summary on its website. See Ewing and Hendy, 2012.

[271] At the time of writing the Coalition is seeking evidence on this concept: *BIS Dealing with Dismissal and 'Compensated No Fault Dismissal' for Micros Businesses: Call for Evidence*, March 2012.

ASSESSMENT: THE PROSPECTS FOR LABOUR LAW

1.38   The 1979–1997 Conservative administration transformed British labour law, reversing the policies not only of its Labour predecessors but also, in its attack on the principles of collective laissez-faire, undermining the framework which, with varying degrees of enthusiasm, all governments had supported since 1918. Since 1997 there has been no return to the policies and approaches of the pre-1979 period, but rather a continuing emphasis on the role of labour law in regulating the labour market in the interests of promoting and flexible and competitive economy.[272] What are the prospects for labour law at a time of rapid economic and technological change when the nature of legal intervention of the labour market is also being transformed?

The radical reform of labour law instituted by the 1979–1997 Conservative administration raised fundamental questions for labour lawyers as to the legitimate role of the law in industrial relations and, indeed, the very purpose of labour law itself. The nature of the changes introduced made it impossible to continue to see the principal rationale of labour law as the support of voluntary collective bargaining. The abandonment of the policy of collective laissez-faire resolved the tension which had existed in the 1960s and 1970s between voluntary collective bargaining and the state's wider economic goals in favour of the latter. However, it inevitably raised the question: if the principal purpose of labour law is no longer the support of collective bargaining, what is it?

Davies and Freedland have identified the ever-intensifying problem for labour law as being 'how to reconcile the various demands upon governments in relation to industrial society, within a framework of reasonably acceptable, democratic, representative and humane labour law'.[273] Accordingly, the relationship between labour market regulation, economic efficiency and competitiveness is a central issue in labour law today. At the same time, the decline of collective bargaining has led to renewed interest in how far labour law could or should be used to articulate certain fundamental social and economic rights.[274] The degree to which such fundamental rights may be enshrined in law without burdening enterprises with excessive costs, or creating harmful labour-market rigidities, continues to be at the heart of debates over the future development of legislative policy both in Britain and in the European Union. In the remainder of this chapter, we indicate the nature of this debate and the issues which it raises.[275] We also draw upon the themes referred to here in later chapters.

(i) Labour law and economic efficiency

1.39   As we have seen, the debate over labour market flexibility and the efficiency of labour law has, since the late 1970s, stressed the degree to which over-rigid labour laws and excessive social security provision in Britain have been responsible for slowing down processes of labour market adjustment. The 1994 European Commission White Paper, *European Social Policy – A*

---

[272] P Davies and M Freedland, 2007.

[273] P Davies and M Freedland, 1993: p 663.

[274] For discussions of the theme of fundamental rights in labour law, see Wedderburn, 1991, 1995; Ewing, Gearty and Hepple (eds), 1994; Hepple, 1995, 2005a.

[275] For a wide-ranging analysis of contemporary British labour law which takes up the theme of the contrast between rights-based and efficiency-based approaches, drawing on human rights theory and on the economics of law, see A Davies, 2009.

Way Forward for the Union, acknowledged the importance of this issue when it commented that 'the need to alter fundamentally, and update, the structure of incentives which influence the labour market is still not adequately recognised'.[276] At the same time, there has been a growing recognition that the problem of incentive structures will not necessarily be solved by a simple process of deregulation, if that is understood to mean the removal of protective legislation and a return to the unregulated individual contract of employment or employment relationship. As the experience of the United Kingdom in the 1980s shows, 'deregulation' is a complex process which, while it may lead to the removal of regulatory controls in some areas, is compatible with an enlarged role for legislation in others, in particular with regard to the control of collective organisation. The extreme complexity of British legislation dealing with industrial action and with internal trade union affairs is testimony to the continuing importance of the law in this area. More generally, the removal of certain labour law protections during this period did not mean that the state had effectively withdrawn: 'contrary to all appearances, the "activist" state is by no means dismissed ... far from simply rejecting all interference, the state is assigned the task of setting the elementary conditions for a functioning market'.[277] An important implication of this is that so-called deregulation did not, of itself, reverse the process of the 'juridification' of labour relations, or the increasing intervention of the state in economic and social relations.[278] Nor is it at all clear that the aim of enhancing labour market efficiency can most effectively be met by the means of deregulation, given the persistence within 'unregulated markets' of market failures of various kinds.[279]

There is an argument to the effect that the question of efficiency should be approached by seeking to strike a better balance between economic and social policy goals: in the words of the EC White Paper, 'long-run competitiveness is to be sought, not through a dilution of the European model of social protection, but through the adaptation, rationalisation and simplification of regulations, so as to establish a better balance between social protection, competitiveness and employment creation'.[280] Elsewhere, however, the White Paper referred to a view which suggests that there is no *necessary* conflict between economic and social policy: 'the pursuit of high social standards should not be seen only as a cost but also as a key element in the competitive formula. It is for these essential reasons that the Union's social policy cannot be second string to economic development or to the functioning of the internal market'.[281]

Others have questioned whether there is an inevitable trade-off between rights and efficiency in this context. A study published by the UK Employment Department in 1995 found substantial evidence of what it took to be increased flexibility in the labour market which could be ascribed to the legal changes introduced since 1980. At the same time, the author of the study pointed out that 'it is difficult to establish precise linkages between measures of flexibility and labour market outcomes'.[282] The study found evidence of greater micro-level flexibility in the UK in

---

[276] COM (94) 333, at p 11.
[277] Simitis, 1987: p 128.
[278] Simitis, 1987: p 128. For discussion of the juridification thesis in the context of British labour law see Clark and Wedderburn, 1987; and for analysis of labour law as a mechanism of 'reflexive' social and economic regulation, see Rogowski, 1994; Rogowski and Wilthagen, 1994; H Collins, 2003; De Schutter and Deakin, 2005.
[279] Deakin and Wilkinson, 1994, 2000a, 2000b, 2005.
[280] COM (94) 333, at p 11.
[281] COM (94) 333, p 2. See also para 2.6 below.
[282] M Beatson, 1995: p 64.

the form of an increase by firms of part-time, temporary and self-employment, as well as an increase in 'functional flexibility', or the adaptability of workers within enterprises. At the macro-level, by contrast, there was still evidence of substantial wage rigidity, and in particular a lack of responsiveness of wages to changes in levels of unemployment.

The Employment Department's analysis also confirmed a finding of several earlier studies, namely that different countries achieve flexibility by different routes.[283] Thus intensively-regulated systems like Germany, Japan and the Scandinavian countries have succeeded in maintaining a high rate of productivity growth, notwithstanding their continuing commitment to a high level of social protection and respect for employment rights. In this regard, a comprehensive comparative study by Blank found that 'there is little evidence that labour market flexibility is substantially affected by the presence of these social protection programmes, nor is there strong evidence that the speed of labour market adjustment can be increased by limiting these programmes'.[284]

From the mid-1990s onwards the case was made for the positive economic effects of labour standards, as an alternative to deregulation. It was argued that labour standards could help to foster long-termism, encourage firms to invest in labour quality through training and, more generally, to underpin a high-wage, high-productivity strategy for the achievement of economic competitiveness.[285] The very nature of the change in economic competition towards greater stress on innovation, flexibility and responsiveness by firms makes it doubtful that a low-wage strategy will be sufficient: 'ultimately, innovation and dynamism are not derived from making labour resources cheaper, but from making labour more effective, productive and innovative. While enlightened firms may follow this advice independently, commonly agreed and shared standards are needed to diffuse the productive impact of good labour use on a wider scale'.[286]

However, this argument was not taken up by the New Labour government elected in 1997. Instead, there was an emphasis on conceptions of 'flexibility' and 'competitiveness' which emphasised the potentially constraining role of labour standards.[287] In particular after 2001, when the legislative programme set out by Labour in opposition had been largely implemented, there was a move to accommodate business concerns over 'excessive' regulation, above all in the area of dismissal legislation.[288] As it turned out, the changes made in the Employment Act 2002 and associated measures, which were aimed at streamlining the process for dealing with individual employment disputes and reducing the load on tribunals, failed to have this effect, instead introducing extra layers of complexity into both the law and practice of dispute resolution.[289] In other respects, the period after 2001 saw significant new additions to the content of individual employment rights, in particular in the area of work and families legislation and in the growing

---

[283] M Beatson, 1995: p 64.

[284] Blank, 1994: p 181. The United Kingdom continues to have lower productivity growth than similar, developed economies, a point recognised in a book written by the former Director-General of the Confederation of British Industry (A Turner, 2001). See also the review of the literature and comparative empirical analysis of the economic impact of labour law systems, using newly available datasets on the evolution of labour regulation in developed economies, contained in Deakin and Sarkar, 2008.

[285] Deakin and Wilkinson, 1994, 2005.

[286] Sengenberger, 1994: p 10.

[287] See H Collins, 2001a, 2001b. This is also a growing trend in EU law, as a result of the development of free movement jurisprudence and its application to national labour law systems: see Syrpis, 2008; paras 2.38 and 11.52 below.

[288] For the suggestion that 2001 marks a turning point in New Labour policy on labour law, see P Davies and M Freedland, 2007: p 60.

[289] See para 2.20 below.

body of equality law. There was also a tendency to employ flexible or 'reflexive' regulatory techniques which make provision for employers and workers (and/or their representatives) to modify statutory standards by agreement at organisation or workplace level.[290] The effectiveness of reflexive forms of regulation has however been called into question.[291] Following the election of the Coalition government, there has been a move back to the language of the 1980s, with the view that 'much of employment law and regulation impedes the search for efficiency and competitiveness'[292] gaining ground once again.

(ii) Labour law and fundamental rights

1.40   A second major theme of contemporary labour law is that of the use of the law to express and make effective in practice the fundamental civil, social and economic rights of workers. There has been a long-running debate concerning the framework of the statutory immunities for collective labour law, and whether they should be replaced by a system of 'positive rights'.[293] Because any system of positive rights would inevitably have to contain within it derogations and exceptions to the right to strike or the right to freedom of association, for example, the issue of immunities against positive rights does not, in itself, decide the question of what the substance of those rights should be. Nor would the enactment of positive rights necessarily lead to a change in the attitude of the courts, or to any reduction of their role.

The only relevant recent experience in Britain of such a radical development in the law is the period of the Industrial Relations Act 1971. That legislation excluded the common law in favour of a comprehensive framework of statutory controls over unfair labour practices, combining extensive legal compulsion over industrial action and control of the rule books and constitutions of the unions which chose to register under the Act, with significant legal guarantees of collective bargaining and recognition rights for those unions. The attitude of the judges, as expressed in particular through the National Industrial Relations Court, was based not so much on the traditional aim of the defence of the common law against the incursions of legislation,[294] as on a corporatist objective of intervening to reduce the costs of strike action and enhance the effectiveness of collective procedures in the 'public interest'.[295] The Industrial Relations Act failed for a number of reasons,[296] but not least among them was that its enactment coincided with a period of union strength and militancy when unemployment was low and the unions had the option of not co-operating with the new laws. It seems unlikely that legislation would again seek in the foreseeable future to combine collective rights and obligations in the fashion of the 1971 Act. This route to reform would have to face up to the trade unions' justifiable suspicion of any attempt to give the courts a more powerful role in resolving collective disputes.

---

[290] See P Davies and M Freedland, 2007: 240-247.
[291] See Hepple *et al*, 2000; McCrudden, 2007c; Deakin and McLaughlin, 2008, 2012; Hepple, 2011; and Fredman, 2011, discussing 'reflexive' techniques in the equality law area.
[292] The Beecroft report, commissioned by the Prime Minister's Office in 2011; see para 1.37 above.
[293] See, in particular, with regard to the right to strike, Wedderburn, 1985; Ewing, 1986.
[294] See above, para 1.9.
[295] Donaldson, 1975.
[296] Weekes *et al*, 1975.

A wider issue is how far employment rights of both a collective and an individual nature could or should be enshrined in a basic constitutional text, thereby granting them a status superior to that of norms contained in ordinary legislation.[297] This debate, which once seemed far removed from British experience, has been stimulated by the adoption in 1998 of the Human Rights Act. As a consequence of this Act, Convention rights – that is, rights guaranteed by the European Convention on Human Rights – must be taken into account by courts and tribunals when interpreting labour legislation and, in certain contexts, when developing rules of the common law. As we shall explore at various points throughout this book, the discourse of human rights now plays a growing role within labour law. Moreover, the UK's membership of the European Union has also meant that a constitutional status is already accorded to certain rights, including the right to equal pay between men and women, by virtue of the doctrine of direct effect. The British Equality Act, is effectively subject to Article 157 of the TFEU, and courts and employment tribunals are under an obligation to apply the superior norm of European Union law in the event of conflict with it. The potential impact of EU law upon domestic legislation was illustrated in *R v Secretary of State for Employment, ex p Equal Opportunities Commission*,[298] in which the House of Lords removed a central aspect of the legislative treatment of part-time workers by ruling that the exclusion of those working for fewer than 16 and (in some instances) 8 hours per week from employment protection contravened the principle of equality of treatment in European Union law. As the jurisprudence of the CJEU evolves in the direction of recognition for a range of fundamental rights,[299] the impact of European Union law on UK legislation seems set to continue.

The rights which are enshrined in the European Convention on Human Rights refer mainly to civil rights, and not to social rights of the kind which are to be found in the constitutional texts of a number of western European systems. Hence the Italian Constitution of 1947 recognises 'all citizens' right to work',[300] as well as the right to an equitable wage, the right to equal pay for equal work between men and women, the right to social assistance, the right to trade union organisation and the right to strike.[301] The Preamble to the French Constitution of 1946 also refers to the right to work, the right to strike and the principle of trade union freedom. A particularly important development in recent years has been the use by courts in other European systems of more general constitutional provisions to provide basic protections for freedom of expression and personal dignity and autonomy in the context of the employment relationship. Much of the inspiration has come from the Basic Law of the German Federal Republic, which in Article 1 guarantees the 'Protection of human dignity', and which lays down in Article 2(1) that 'Everyone shall have the right to the free development of his personality in so far as he does not violate the rights of others or offend against the constitutional order'. These provisions, together with Article 4 on freedom of opinion, conscience and religion, Article 5 on freedom of expression, and Article 6 on the protection of marriage and the family, have had an extensive influence on German labour law,[302] and also influenced the Spanish Constitution of 1978 and its subsequent

[297] For critical discussion of this concept, see Ewing, 1994b.
[298] [1994] IRLR 176. See below, paras 3.55 and 6.30.
[299] See para 2.39 below.
[300] Constitution of the Italian Republic, 22 December 1947, Art 4.
[301] Constitution of the Italian Republic, 22 December 1947, Arts 35–40.
[302] Daübler, 1991: ch 5; Simitis, 1994.

interpretation by the courts. In short, these systems have experienced what has been described as the 'constitutionalisation' of labour law.[303]

In considering whether the experience of these other European systems has anything of value for Britain, the long-standing issues of the legitimate role of the courts, the degree of effectiveness, in practice, of legal rights, and the proper balance to be struck between legal intervention and self-regulation in industry are once again to the fore.[304] Whatever the prospects for constitutional reform in Britain, the continuing influence of European Union law has already given rise to a situation in which the English and Scottish courts are faced with issues which are phrased in an essentially constitutional form, namely involving conflicts between rights which are expressed in broad terms, on the one hand, and instrumental or efficiency-related factors which are put forward in justification for practices limiting those rights, on the other.[305] The Human Rights Act 1998 also requires certain labour law issues to be determined within a framework of this type of discourse. At present, the discussion, at least in the courts, is somewhat uneven, because notions of what constitutes a fundamental right in legal terms are somewhat more advanced than the notions of efficiency which are set against them.[306] Indeed, it is not always obvious what the normative or legal meaning of economic efficiency might be in this context, or to what extent such a concept should be advanced at the expense of other values or interests. It seems likely that the future of labour law as a form of market intervention will increasingly turn on how successful courts and policy-makers are in finding a language in which to express and reconcile these conflicts of rights and efficiency.

[303]Del Rey Guanter, 1992.

[304] For such an analysis, see Deakin, 1996a.

[305] See in particular *R v Secretary of State for Employment, ex p Equal Opportunities Commission* [1994] IRLR 176, discussed above; see also paras 6.30–6.32 below.

[306] See Deakin, 1994a, for a discussion of this point in the context of the ruling of the House of Lords in *Ex p Equal Opportunities Commission* [1994] IRLR 176, and for contrasting analyses of the role of economic discourse in labour law, see H Collins, 2001b, 2003; Supiot, 2000, 2005; A Davies, 2009; Deakin and Wilkinson, 2005; P Davies and M Freedland, 2007; ch 5.

2

SOURCES AND INSTITUTIONS OF LABOUR LAW

INTRODUCTION

2.1 Unlike some systems labour law in Britain does not take the form of a comprehensive Labour Code; rather it is derived from a multiplicity of sources, both legal and extra-legal, which may interact in complex ways. Determining the law on a particular matter, therefore, may involve examination of a range of sources. In analysing the legal liability of those organising industrial action, for example, there is a need first to decide whether any tort has been committed. This will frequently depend upon whether the industrial action in question constitutes a breach of their employment contract by those participating in it, which may in turn require reference to collective agreements or to custom and practice in the industry or workplace. It may then be necessary to decide whether the action is afforded immunity against tortious liability by statute, which itself involves entry into a legislative maze. To assess an employer's chances of successfully pursuing a legal remedy, knowledge of civil procedure becomes important, particularly where (as is generally the case) an interim injunction is being sought. Moreover, if picketing is undertaken, whether such action infringes the criminal law, and the implications of the HRA 1998, may be at issue. Finally, it is possible that an agreement made by an employer under threat of industrial action may lead to a subsequent claim in restitution based upon the doctrine of 'economic duress'. To take another example, examining the legal consequences of making employees redundant may require not only consideration of the law governing contracts of employment and the relevant statutory rights, both individual and collective, but also EU law to see if the dismissals may be discriminatory on grounds of sex (for example) or contrary to procedures for collective consultation, the terms of any relevant collective agreements if unfair selection is alleged, and potential remedies in public law if the decision in question falls within its reach.

It is sometimes said that labour law in Britain lacks autonomy from the common law, in the sense that the reach of common law doctrines is particularly extensive. Employment rights may be radically affected by common law precedents argued in an entirely different legal context; thus the scope of the freedom to withdraw labour may be curtailed by a decision on the scope of a common law tort in proceedings which have no connection with industrial disputes (such as a commercial dispute between two companies). Whether there should – or can – be an autonomous system of labour law insulated against developments in the common law is a fundamental issue which those who seek to change the present system radically would need to address.[1] The HRA 1998 may now modify the application of the common law in specific contexts, such as picketing, but for the reasons we explain in para 7.9 its implications for collective labour law in general have, to date, been limited.

In this chapter, in order to explain the existing sources of labour law and the relationship between them we have drawn a distinction between formal (legal) sources and 'voluntary' norms created by the conduct of the parties, such as collective agreements and works rules. However, it is important to emphasise at the outset that this does not mean that the formal and voluntary sources are completely separate; on the contrary, autonomous norms will frequently play a vital role in determining the parties' legal rights. Their significance is appropriately emphasised by Hepple when he states that '[t]he interaction between autonomous norms and state law is a central aspect of any study of labour law.'[2] Equally, the ordering of our discussion, which commences with the formal sources, should not be taken as indicative of a particular hierarchy of norms; indeed until the 1970s voluntary norms were by far the more important source of labour law in Britain and it could be argued that even now, despite the vast increase in legislation, it would be equally appropriate to commence with voluntary sources. What is incontrovertible is that consideration only of the formal sources would provide a dangerously misleading picture of the contemporary law.

Having outlined the formal and informal sources of domestic labour law we then examine the nature of the institutions by which it is interpreted and enforced. We begin by examining the judicial mechanisms for dispute settlement, the courts and employment tribunals. We then look at the non-judicial bodies which play a role in this area together with those which have statutory functions in relation to specific areas of labour law such as equality and trade union affairs. It is important to stress at this stage that the allocation of jurisdiction between the judicial and non-judicial bodies in relation to the settlement of disputes is not immutable and, indeed, is an aspect of the contemporary labour law system which has been subject to reform.

Our discussion of domestic sources and institutions is followed by an analysis of the role of international labour standards in UK law. European Union law is, of course, an integral part of national law and should, strictly speaking, be analysed in that context. However, the jurisdictional base and scope of EU social law is a matter of particular significance to labour lawyers, especially given the distinctive procedures which are available for enacting legislation in this field and the many questions which these raise. In view of the importance and complexity of this area we treat it as a separate section of this chapter. We then outline the role of other international labour standards which are not, unless embodied in legislation, incorporated in national law. However, this does not mean that they can thereby be ignored: where national legislation is ambiguous there is a (rebuttable) presumption that Parliament did not intend to legislate in breach of the UK's international obligations and the courts may refer to international treaties when called upon to decide upon the position at common law. Moreover, these labour standards may be relevant when a court or tribunal is interpreting 'Convention rights' under the HRA 1998, particularly where there is no jurisprudence from the Convention organs or a domestic court is being urged to take a wider view of what a right entails. Finally, the UK's obligation in international law to comply

---

[1] See Wedderburn, 1987a; Howarth, 1988; Wedderburn, 1991a and references therein.
[2] Sweet and Maxwell, 1992, as updated: para 1-1019.

with treaties it has ratified may be a powerful influence upon the formulation of domestic legal policy although, as we shall see, its influence upon the 1979–1997 Conservative Governments was not always a significant one, nor did it weigh heavily with their Labour successors and there is no indication that the Coalition Government which came into office in 2010 will take a different approach. Finally, we consider the question of conflicts of law between different national systems of regulation.

The purpose of this chapter is to provide a framework for the remainder of the text. Where areas are dealt with in greater detail in later chapters, we do not, at this stage, provide full references.

FORMAL SOURCES OF LABOUR LAW

The common law

2.2   Despite the volume of legislation now governing the area of labour law, the common law remains at the core of the system at both the individual and collective levels. At the individual level, with the exception of some public service workers, the employment relationship is constituted by a contract which is governed, essentially, by principles emanating from the common law. Moreover the existence, or potential existence, of a contract is the basis of access by workers to the vast majority of statutory employment protection rights. At the collective level the mere existence of trade unions, and the organisation of industrial action, are unlawful at common law, a position which continues to be of paramount importance given the fragility of the protection afforded against this liability by statute.

The dominant effect of the common law links the current system inextricably with the past. In Wedderburn's striking phrase it 'enjoys the curse of exaggerated continuity'.[3] The doctrine of precedent means that judicial decisions remain embedded within the legal culture even though social conditions may have changed radically since they were reached. Thus decisions dating back to the nineteenth century and earlier may still be influential in the contemporary courts. At the individual level the concept of the managerial prerogative, which has its origins in the early law of master and servant, remains a powerful one in several contexts. The fact that the employment relationship is constituted in a contractual form allows the courts considerable discretion to shape it by means of implied terms where a matter is not dealt with by express agreement. The implied duties of employees to obey lawful and reasonable orders of their employer and to co-operate in the running of the enterprise are among the most notable manifestations of this inherent managerial prerogative. Furthermore, as we shall see, 'the archetypal models of master and servant' have also influenced the interpretation of modern employment protection legislation.[4] Thus, in the context of unfair dismissal legislation, for example, employers' interests in restructuring the enterprise, which may necessitate significant changes to the terms and conditions of their workforce, are accorded primary importance to the extent that they may even, in practice, trump employees' contractual rights.

---

[3] Wedderburn, 1993: p 253.
[4] Wedderburn, 1993: p 261, and see generally pp 238–262 for a discussion of the relationship between the common law and 'labour'.

At the collective level the common law is also of fundamental significance. During the nineteenth century the courts found the purposes of most trade unions to be unlawful as being in restraint of trade,[5] and to this day those organising industrial action nearly always commit a common law tort.[6] The lawfulness of trade unions' status and the (now very limited) freedom to take industrial action depend entirely upon statutory immunities from the common law liabilities which would otherwise apply. Reliance upon a system of immunities rather than one of positive statutory rights has had important practical implications: because such immunities constitute exceptions to the common law, historically the courts have tended to construe them narrowly and the overriding discretion of the courts to grant an interim injunction where a common law right is at stake remains, in the final analysis, intact.[7] It also means that the activities of workers' organisations are always vulnerable to the extension of liabilities at common law which are outside the protection of the immunities, a prevailing theme in the context of industrial action (exemplified in the discovery by the courts of the unprotected wrong of inducing breach of a statutory duty). The language of immunities also has important rhetorical significance, enabling opponents to present unions as having unwarranted special 'privileges' which are denied to other bodies,[8] rather than seeing them as repositories of fundamental civil and social rights.

The final area where the common law remains important (although more now in theory than in practice) is the relationship between trade unions and their members.[9] A trade union is, in legal terms, an association of individuals bound together by a contract of membership (contained primarily in the union rules) which regulates the relationship between them. In the past proceedings to enforce this contract have, again, provided judges with the opportunity to mould the relationship of the parties via the mechanism of implied terms. In general the courts have inclined towards an interpretation which protects the interests of the individual union member, although the HRA 1998 has the potential to bring greater respect for trade union autonomy in those areas left untouched by legislation. In recent years, however, the conduct of trade union affairs has become subject to increasingly extensive statutory regulation, leaving only very narrow scope for the unrestricted operation of union rules. For this reason the notion of unions as autonomous bodies whose rules are based upon agreement between their members is now no more than a fiction.

Legislation

2.3   As we saw in chapter 1, legislation played an important but subsidiary role in labour law for many years; for individual workers voluntary collective bargaining was the primary source of protection, with statute being confined to the areas which collective bargaining did not reach: the

---

[5] *Hornby v Close* (1867) LR 2 QB 153.

[6] See ch 11.

[7] See in the context of industrial action Lord Diplock in *NWL Ltd v Woods* [1979] ICR 867, 881–882 (as corrected [1980] ICR 167); Lord Fraser in *Duport Steels Ltd v Sirs* [1980] ICR 161, 187. Cf *RMT v Serco Docklands; ASLEF v London Midland* [2011] IRLR 399, at [9] where the Court of Appeal stated that, in the light of Art 11 of the ECHR, the legislation should now be construed without presumptions one way or the other.

[8] See, for example, Hayek, 1980: p 58: 'there can be no salvation for Britain until the special privileges granted to trade unions three-quarters of a century ago are revoked'.

[9] See generally ch 10.

protection of women and children, some aspects of health and safety, and wage-fixing machinery for particularly vulnerable workers. In relation to collective organisation, the role of legislation was largely confined to affording (limited) protection against liabilities which would otherwise arise at common law. By contrast, the past thirty years or so have witnessed an expansion in the range and scope of legislation covering most areas of labour law; while that relating to the individual employment relationship has, in general, enhanced employment protection, in the collective field the role of legislation has varied much more greatly and in the area of industrial action is now essentially restrictive in its nature.

Perhaps surprisingly, in view of the crucial importance of legislation in guiding the conduct of both workers and employers, it can be extremely difficult to ascertain the relevant provisions governing a particular issue. Frequently they will be scattered among several statutes and possibly also statutory instruments. Even within an individual statute the law may be located in a number of different sections and multi-paragraphed schedules may contain amendments and provisos which may easily be overlooked. Moreover, such legislation is often cast in language which it is difficult for the experienced lawyer, let alone the lay person, to comprehend. In 1981 Browne-Wilkinson J described the provisions relating to maternity leave then in force as being of 'inordinate complexity exceeding the worst excesses of a taxing statute',[10] a criticism endorsed by the Court of Appeal.[11] The same comment could equally be made of many other statutory employment protection rights. It applies with even greater force to the myriad of provisions now governing trade union conduct. The opaque or ambiguous nature of statutory language makes scrutiny of Parliamentary debates a particularly important element of legal research in this area, although the interpretation offered by the relevant minister in Parliament may not ultimately be reflected in the decisions of the courts and the opportunities for invoking parliamentary material in argument are limited.[12] The difficulties of interpretation are exacerbated when major changes are introduced in the form of statutory instruments; here time for Parliamentary debate is very limited, thus precluding detailed examination of their import, and, in general, there is no opportunity for amendments to be proposed.[13] Important provisions introduced as delegated legislation under the European Communities Act 1972 include the Transfer of Undertakings (Protection of Employment) Regulations 1981,[14] and the Working Time Regulations 1998.[15] As this brief summary indicates, even within the confines of legislation, let alone beyond it, predicting accurately the meaning of labour law in Britain can be a hazardous task. Judicial decisions as to

---

[10] *Lavery v Plessey Telecommunications Ltd* [1983] IRLR 180, 182 .

[11] [1983] IRLR 202, 206 (Slade LJ).

[12] See *Pepper v Hart* [1993] AC 593 where the House of Lords held that, in specific circumstances, reference could be made to Hansard. Lord Browne-Wilkinson, who gave the principal opinion, concluded that, subject to the question of House of Commons' privileges, reference should be permitted as an aid to the construction of legislation which is ambiguous or obscure or whose literal meaning leads to an absurdity provided that the parliamentary material clearly discloses the mischief aimed at or the legislative intention underlying the ambiguous or obscure words. He could not foresee that a statement other than that of a minister or other promoter of the Bill was likely to satisfy those criteria. See D Oliver, 1993 for the implications of this decision, and see *R v Secretary of State for the Environment, Transport and the Regions, ex p Spath Holme Ltd* [2001] 1 All ER 195 on the doctrine applicable to the scope of a statutory power. See also *Robinson v Secretary of State for Northern Ireland* [2002] UKHL 32 and *Wilson v Secretary of State for Trade and Industry* [2004] 1 AC 816 and Vogenauer, 2005, Sales, 2006, and P Joseph, 2010.

[13] This can happen only if the parent Act so permits: W McKay, 2004: pp 676–677.

[14] SI 1981/1794 (now repealed). The Regulations currently in force, SI 2006/246, were introduced under the ECA 1972 and ERelA 1999, s 38.

[15] SI 1998/1833.

the interpretation of particular statutory provisions may eventually provide clarification but this is of little help to those who wish to organise their affairs in order to comply with the law from the outset. Moreover, pre-existing interpretations of legislation may require reconsideration in the light of the HRA 1998.[16] In addition, many important statutory concepts are treated as questions of fact for first instance courts or tribunals to adjudicate upon, with limited scope for appeal, so that different tribunals are able legitimately to reach opposite conclusions on identical sets of facts. This situation does little to assist those who are seeking to know their basic legal rights. The decision as to whether a worker is an 'employee', the gateway to many statutory rights, is perhaps the most important casualty of this approach.[17]

The relationship between legislation and the common law may be an intricate one. Legislation will normally prevail in the sense that any agreement between the parties specifically to exclude its operation will be void but to achieve this result it has been necessary, on occasion, to state specifically that statutory norms take precedence over the common law.[18] In the area of individual rights, legislation may be given effect in a variety of ways. In rare cases statutory provisions can displace express contractual terms and are then enforceable through the contract. One example is the sex equality clause which is deemed by the Equality Act 2010 to be included in the terms of the contract of a woman (or man) where specified conditions are satisfied.[19] Another is the award which may be made if an employer refuses to comply with an order to disclose information for collective bargaining purposes as required by statute.[20] More commonly statutory rights stand independent of the contract although they may be set off against contractual rights, for example in the areas of guaranteed and maternity pay.[21] The effect of this is that any contractual payment goes towards discharging statutory liability and vice versa but liability for any greater amount under either head remains. In some cases, however, a right which may appear wholly independent of the contract may not be so in practice; thus the courts have held that access to the statutory right of unfair dismissal rests upon a valid contract with the result that where the contract is tainted with illegality, because, for example, of the employee's 'collusion' in evading tax, access to that right may be lost.[22]

In the area of collective labour law the relationship between common law and statute is particularly intricate as regards industrial action where statute affords very limited immunity against specific, but not all, common law torts. By contrast, in relation to trade union government, as we indicated in para 2.2, statute now directly or in practice overrides union rules in most important areas.

---

[16] Section 3.

[17] See ch 3.

[18] See ERA 1996, s 203(1), but note also s 203(2) which indicates when access to rights may be precluded. The prohibition on exclusion will not necessarily prevent the employment relationship being constructed in such a way that the qualifications necessary to meet a claim are not met, for example by placing the financial risks on the worker to create a self-employed relationship in circumstances where only employees are qualified to bring a claim. The relationship between Convention rights and contract is particularly controversial: see G Morris, 2001a.

[19] EqA 2010, ss 64-70.

[20] TULRCA 1992, s 185(5); see further para 9.24 below.

[21] See paras 4.127 and 6.118, below.

[22] See para 3.25 below.

Codes of Practice

2.4   The Secretary of State for Employment, ACAS and, within their respective areas of jurisdiction, the EHRC and HSE,[23] are empowered by statute to issue Codes of Practice which provide practical guidance on conduct in particular areas.[24] These Codes are not intended merely to codify existing practices but rather actively to promote those which are viewed as desirable, and there is evidence to suggest that they are capable of having a significant impact in the workplace.[25] Breach of a Code of Practice does not of itself render an individual liable to legal proceedings.[26] However, the Codes of Practice issued by ACAS are admissible in evidence in proceedings before an employment tribunal;[27] those by the Secretary of State and EHRC are additionally admissible in proceedings before the courts,[28] and these bodies must take into account any provisions of a Code which seem relevant to an issue before them. Thus, although Codes of Practice are not legally binding as such, compliance or non-compliance with their provisions may influence the outcome of proceedings and, indeed, in some cases their recommendations have, in practice, been elevated almost to the status of legal principles. One notorious example of this practice was the Code of Practice on Picketing which specifies that pickets and their organisers should ensure in general a maximum of six pickets at the entrance to any workplace;[29] this has been reflected in the terms of injunctions ordered by the courts to restrict the conduct of future picketing[30] and in the use of police discretion (although, as we discuss in para 11.53 *et seq*, the HRA 1998 requires reconsideration of this approach). On occasion Codes have contained recommendations which explicitly exceed the requirements of the parent legislation. The Code of Practice on Industrial Action Ballots and Notice to Employers, which we discuss in para 11.45, is a prominent example of this.

---

[23] Until 2008 this power lay with the Health and Safety Commission. The Health and Safety Executive was granted this power with effect from 1 April 2008 when the Commission was abolished.

[24] Codes currently in force issued by the Secretary of State are the Code of Practice on Picketing (revised in 1992); the Code of Practice on Access and Unfair Practices during Recognition and Derecognition Ballots (revised and expanded to include unfair practices in 2005); and the Code of Practice on Industrial Action Ballots and Notice to Employers (revised in 2005). ACAS has, to date, issued Codes of Practice in three areas: Disclosure of Information to Trade Unions for Collective Bargaining Purposes (revised in 1997), Disciplinary and Grievance Procedures (revised in 2009) and Time Off for Trade Union Duties and Activities (revised in 2010). ACAS Codes require the approval of the Secretary of State and Parliament to come into force; the Secretary of State must consult ACAS and also obtain parliamentary approval before issuing a Code: TULRCA 1992, ss 199–206.

[25] See L Dickens et al, 1985: pp 232–234 on the impact of the ACAS Code on Disciplinary Practices and Procedures in Employment initially issued in 1977. The 1980 Workplace Industrial Relations Survey showed that in nine out of ten cases disciplinary procedures contained provision for oral then written warnings as recommended in the Code: Daniel and Millward, 1983: p 165.

[26] See, for example, TULRCA 1992, s 207(1).

[27] TULRCA 1992, s 207(2).

[28] TULRCA 1992, s 207(3) and EqA 2006, s 15(4). Codes of Practice issued or approved by the Health and Safety Executive are admissible in evidence in criminal proceedings: HSWA 1974, ss 16 and 17.

[29] Para 5.1 of the Code; see further para 11.53 below.

[30] *Thomas v NUM (South Wales Area)* [1985] IRLR 136; *News Group Newspapers Ltd v SOGAT '82 (No 2)* [1986] IRLR 337.

Public law and labour law

2.5 It may appear strange that public law should be relevant to the essentially private relationship of worker and employer. In many systems, however, public employment is governed by a wholly separate legal regime from that applicable in the private sector, and in some countries, such as Germany and France, certain public employees (*Beamten* and *fonctionnaires* respectively) are governed by public administrative law. In Britain there is no such formal demarcation between the public and private sectors, although many areas of public service employment have been subject to distinctive laws and internal regulations (special disciplinary codes and restrictions on outside or political activities, for example) to meet the perceived requirements of the individual service.[31] However, public law may have implications for employment rights where the employer is a public body which is subject to the supervisory jurisdiction of the courts through the mechanism of judicial review. An application for judicial review is subject to procedural restrictions which do not apply to claims in private law: the application may be made only with the permission of the court and the time limit within which permission must be sought is short.[32] Despite these procedural obstacles judicial review has proved a popular route for public employees although the circumstances where an application may lie in the employment context are unpredictable and controversial.[33] First, it may extend to situations where there are no remedies available in private law. Thus, when the UK Conservative Government banned membership of national civil service trade unions at Government Communications Headquarters in 1984 without any prior consultation with workers or their unions, despite a long-standing practice of consultation on important issues, a public law claim based upon breach of a legitimate expectation of consultation offered the unions their only possible remedy.[34] Second, it may offer remedies for individual groups of workers who are denied access to claims in private law. For a dismissed member of a police force, who has no contract of employment or access to the statutory remedy of unfair dismissal, judicial review is the only possible avenue to pursue beyond the rights provided in the internal disciplinary procedure. Last, even if a private law action is available the remedies in public law may be superior; for example a quashing order can quash an employer's decision to dismiss, thus securing at least temporary reinstatement in employment, and, unlike private law proceedings, may overturn a decision relating to a group not merely an individual worker.

[31] For a general analysis see Fredman and Morris, 1989; for a critique of the position see G Morris and S Fredman, 1993 and G Morris, 2000 and, on political activities, G Morris, 1998b.

[32] A claim form for judicial review must be filed 'promptly', and in any event not later than three months after the grounds to make the claim first arose: CPR r 54.5. There is a three-month time limit for bringing claims for unfair dismissal, subject to the discretion of the employment tribunal to extend this period: ERA 1996, s 111(2). For an overview of the regime governing judicial review applications since October 2000 see Fordham, 2001; see also Cornford and Sunkin, 2001.

[33] See, in particular, Fredman and Morris, 1991a, and references therein, from which much of what follows is taken; see also Fredman and Morris, 1994; Woolf *et al* 2007, paras 3-066-3-068; T Poole, 2000; SH Bailey, 2007

[34] *Council of Civil Service Unions v Minister for the Civil Service* [1985] AC 374. In the event the duty to consult was trumped by national security considerations.

The courts have taken a restrictive view of when judicial review may properly lie in the employment context.[35] One might have thought that the mere fact that the employer is a public body should suffice on the ground that, although impacting upon private individuals, decisions relating to employment involve the exercise of public power. However, this view has been rejected in favour of a complex (and sometimes conflicting) set of criteria by which the designation of a claim as public or private is decided. None has proved to be satisfactory. Most prominent among these tests has been the existence of a contract. In the leading case of *R v East Berkshire Health Authority, ex p Walsh*[36] the Court of Appeal held that where the application concerns rights arising directly out of a contract, rather than the exercise of statutory duties or powers, then it is properly one of private law. This decision assumes that the pattern of contractual and non-contractual relations in the public services is coherent whereas in reality it is usually the product of ad hoc, historical evolution rather than of principle. In the context of civil service employment it also produced some unseemly contradictory tactical arguments by the Crown as to the existence of a contract of employment, depending upon whether a claim was brought in public or in private law.[37] A second approach to demarcation, developed primarily by Lord Woolf, is based upon the subject-matter of the decision. Taking as its starting-point the premise that the employment relationship is essentially a private one, it acknowledges that there may nevertheless be situations where judicial review may be appropriate, for example where a process of dismissal has a statutory or similar underpinning relating to procedure or a decision is one of policy affecting a group of workers and not merely a single individual.[38] This is equally unsatisfactory; the latter category, for example, immediately prompts questions as to when a sufficiently large group of workers will be deemed to be affected and overlooks the 'precedent' value of a decision which may, ostensibly, only concern a single individual. Third, an application for judicial review may be defeated, even if one of the above two tests is satisfied, if the court considers that there are alternative remedies in private law, such as the right to claim unfair dismissal or breach of contract, even though the remedies may not, in fact, be true equivalents.[39] Moreover, the courts have more recently adopted a further test that asks whether 'the defendant was performing a public duty owed to the claimant in the particular circumstances under consideration.'[40]

As well as being potentially applicable to public employees, judicial review is also important in controlling the exercise of discretion by various statutory bodies which have jurisdiction in the field of labour law. It has been particularly significant in relation to decisions of the Central

---

[35] Prior to the new CPR Part 54 the courts took a rigid view of the public/private divide, holding not only that its predecessor, RSC Order 53, should be used for 'public law' matters (pursuant to the House of Lords decision in *O'Reilly v Mackman* [1983] 2 AC 237) but that an applicant could not use RSC Order 53 if the claim was properly classified as 'private'. Although the decision in *Roy v Kensington and Chelsea and Westminster Family Practitioner Committee* [1992] 1 AC 624 showed signs of greater flexibility it left the divide essentially intact: see Fredman and Morris, 1994: pp 82–83; although cf *Mercury Communications Ltd v Director General of Telecommunications* [1996] 1 All ER 575, HL, noted P Craig, 1996; *Trustees of the Dennis Rye Pension Fund v Sheffield City Council* [1997] 4 All ER 747, 754–756, Lord Woolf MR; *Steed v Secretary of State for the Home Department* [2000] 3 All ER 226. CPR 54 has brought greater flexibility of approach where a case is commenced under the 'wrong' procedure (see Woolf *et al*, 2007: paras 3-103-3.104) but still requires the courts to determine if the matter is amenable to judicial review.

[36] [1985] QB 152.

[37] See Fredman and Morris, 1991b.

[38] See *McLaren v Home Office* [1990] IRLR 338; *R v Derbyshire County Council, ex p Noble* [1990] IRLR 332.

[39] See further para 5.47 below.

[40] *R (on the Application of Tucker) v Director General of the National Crime Squad* [2003] IRLR 439, at [24] (Scott Baker LJ).

Arbitration Committee and also of the Equal Opportunities Commission and Commission for Racial Equality (now replaced by the EHRC). However, it has also been an important weapon in the hands of bodies with statutory functions. In the landmark case of *R v Secretary of State for Employment, ex p EOC*[41] the Equal Opportunities Commission successfully brought judicial review proceedings for a declaration that the (then) 16-hour qualifying threshold for redundancy and unfair dismissal rights under EPCA 1978 was contrary to what is now Article 157 of the TFEU (then Article 119 of the EC Treaty) and to the Equal Treatment Directive.[42] In that case the House of Lords upheld the argument, rejected by the Court of Appeal, that the EOC had standing to bring the application, a decision that meant that the EOC was in a strong position to challenge, before the UK courts, legislation which contravened the principle of gender equality.[43] The Equality Act 2006 makes clear that the EHRC has the capacity to institute or intervene in legal proceedings by judicial review (or otherwise) if it appears to the Commission that the proceedings are relevant to a matter in connection with which it has a function.[44]

Finally it should be noted that, despite the procedural divide, the influence of public law concepts, in particular procedural fairness, has spread in some contexts to proceedings brought in private law although the courts have failed to adopt the suggestion that natural justice should be implied into every contract of employment.[45] We discuss this development further in para 5.53 below. As we shall see in chapter 10 public law values have also been heavily influential in the courts' treatment of the relationship between trade unions and their members and officials, to which the concepts of 'natural justice' have been applied, although in recent years statutory restrictions have rendered this area less significant in practice.

Administrative practices

2.6   In recent years the primary mechanism by which the state has sought to regulate employment practices has been by legislation. Historically, however, its administrative practices also played an important role. For most of the twentieth century the state perceived itself as setting an example to the private sector by virtue of its own employment practices.[46] Thus, collective bargaining was introduced into the civil service in 1919 despite misgivings as to its appropriateness because the government believed that it could not otherwise expect private employers to do the same. Another means by which the state sought to exercise its influence was by means of its extensive power as contractor with the private sector.[47] The use of a 'contract compliance' strategy in Britain dates back to 1891 when the House of Commons passed the first of three Fair Wages Resolutions (the others being in 1909 and 1946).[48] This required government departments to include a term

---

[41] [1994] IRLR 176.

[42] EC Directive 76/207; see further para 3.55 below.

[43] See Deakin, 1994a.

[44] Section 30.

[45] See Woolf LJ in *R v Derbyshire County Council, ex p Noble* [1990] IRLR 332 at 337; Sedley, 1994; Laws, 1997. For a broader discussion of the influence of public law on labour law, see P Davies and M Freedland, 1997.

[46] See generally Fredman and Morris, 1989.

[47] For a useful overview, see Hepple *et al*, 2000, paras 3.61–3.77 and references therein.

[48] For a detailed study of the history and operation of the fair wages policy see Bercusson, 1978; see also para 1.13 above.

in contracts with private sector employers that contractors should pay their workers the generally accepted rate for the job. Subsequent Resolutions extended these requirements to other conditions of employment and to freedom of association. Although not within the terms of the Resolution, from an early stage local authorities also applied fair wages policies and in later years nationalised industries were encouraged by successive governments to implement its terms. In more recent times local authorities also used contract compliance policies to further other purposes such as discouraging reliance on self-employed labour by contractors; promoting equal opportunities, training and the provision of trade union facilities; insisting upon health and safety policies; and encouraging the use of local labour on contracts whenever possible.[49]

The Conservative Government which came to office in 1979 had a very different view of its role as employer, seeking to reverse the traditional model by implementing in the public sector practices which it deemed typical of private sector employers. It perceived the Fair Wages Resolution as a damaging anachronism, impeding competitiveness and destroying jobs, and in 1982 gave notice to rescind it from 1983, a move which necessitated denouncing ILO Convention No 94 on Labour Clauses in Public Contracts which requires contracts between public authorities and employers to include a 'fair wages' clause. Later in the decade the use of contract compliance as a strategy was further undermined when the Local Government Act 1988 made it unlawful for local authorities and several other public bodies to consider 'non-commercial matters' in their choice of, and dealings with, contractors.[50] This prevented consideration of matters such as wages and conditions, employee status, freedom of association or equal opportunities (with a very limited exception for local authorities in the case of race[51]). The Local Government Act 1999 empowers the Secretary of State to provide by order that any of these matters should cease to be a 'non-commercial' matter, either generally or in a specific context, in relation to authorities, including local authorities, that operate according to the 'best value' regime the Act establishes.[52] At the time of writing the terms and conditions of employment of workers; the composition of and opportunities afforded to the workforce; and the conduct of contractors or their workers in industrial disputes, are no longer treated as 'non-commercial', but only so far as necessary or expedient to permit or facilitate compliance with the best value requirements of the Act or where there is a transfer of staff to which TUPE may apply.[53]

Limited steps have been taken to revive contract compliance as a strategy.[54] The Race Relations (Amendment) Act 2000 obliged a wide range of public authorities to promote race equality[55] and public authorities were subsequently required to promote equality of opportunity between disabled and other persons[56] and between men and women.[57] The Equality Act 2010 introduced a single equality duty which brings together the earlier race, disability and sex duties and also covers age, gender reassignment, pregancy and maternity, religion or belief and sexual orientation. Public

[49] Institute of Personnel Management, 1987: ch 2.
[50] LGA 1988, s 17. See further Fredman and Morris, 1989: ch 12.
[51] See s 18(2). This was inserted because of the duty of local authorities under the RRA 1976, s 71 to have regard, inter alia, to the promotion of equality of opportunity. A duty on a broader range of bodies was imposed under s 71 as substituted by the Race Relations (Amendment) Act 2000, s 2 and Sch 1A (now repealed). See now EqA 2010, discussed below..
[52] LGA 1999, s 19. 'Best value' authorities are defined in s 1; see also s 2.
[53] The Local Government Best Value (Exclusion of Non-commercial Considerations) Order 2001, SI 2001/ 909.
[54] See McCrudden, 2012, forthcoming. On the position in Northern Ireland, see Fitzpatrick, 1999.
[55] RRA 1976, s 71 (now repealed).
[56] DDA 1995, ss 49A-D, inserted by the DDA 2005, s 3 (now repealed).
[57] SDA 1975, s 76A-C, inserted by EqA 2006, s 84(1) (now repealed).

authorities are required, in the exercise of their functions, to have due regard to the need, inter alia, to eliminate discrimination, harassment, victimisation and any other conduct prohibited by the Act and to advance equality of opportunity between persons who share a relevant protected characteristic and those who do not.[58] 'Functions' include purchasing of goods and services. In the contemporary 'contract state' contract compliance has considerable potential as a mechanism for disseminating specific employment practices,[59] although reliance upon it now requires close scrutiny of the restrictions imposed by EU Directives on Public Procurement.[60] As we indicate in para 2.43 below, the use of an analogous strategy as a mechanism for securing international labour standards is a current issue of debate.

VOLUNTARY SOURCES

2.7   As we emphasised in para 2.1 voluntary norms have been, and continue to be, a crucial source of labour law in Britain. The lack of legislation governing the employment relationship left largely unrestricted the discretion of employers and workers and/or trade unions to shape it as they chose and despite the extension of statutory regulation this is still true today in many areas. We begin this section by discussing the role of collective agreements as a source of law. As we saw in chapter 1 historically trade unions regarded collective bargaining as preferable to legislation as a means of securing workers' terms and conditions of employment. It was estimated that in 1984 71% of employees were covered by collective agreements.[61] By 1990 this figure had fallen to 54%,[62] and by 2004 to around 35%,[63] although, as we discuss in para 9.2 below, this figure varies greatly between sectors. Despite this, collective agreements still remain a significant source of labour law. The other voluntary sources of labour law we consider much more briefly: works rules and other documents issued by employers to workers and self-regulatory codes of conduct issued by trade unions and other bodies. We conclude by reviewing briefly the relationship between the formal and informal sources of labour law.

Collective agreements

2.8   Collective agreements fulfil two major purposes.[64] First, they regulate relations between employers (and employers' associations) and trade unions (the *procedural* or *contractual* function). These arrangements are usually of a constitutional nature (and are generically called

---

[58] EqA 2010, s 149. See Hepple, 2011: pp 134-143; Henty, 2011; *Report of the Social Clauses Project 2008*, Cabinet Office: Office of the Third Sector, 2008 and para 6.75 below.

[59] The Government Equalities Office estimates that more than £220 billion per year is is spent by the public sector on contracts with external organisations, amounting to over 15% of gross domestic product: *Equality Act 2010: The public sector equality duty: Promoting equality through transparency*, 2010. For a detailed analysis of this area, see McCrudden, 2007a; see also McCrudden, 2007b and 2012, forthcoming

[60] See further Arrowsmith, 2005; Arrowsmith and Kunzlik, 2009.

[61] Millward *et al*, 1992: p 94.

[62] Millward *et al*, 1992: p 94.

[63] Kersley *et al*, 2006: p 185; see generally pp 179-188.

[64] See P Davies and M Freedland, 1983: ch 6.

procedural agreements) and can take a variety of forms. Thus they may, for example, establish permanent joint machinery for the negotiation of terms and conditions of employment or specify the procedural stages to be followed for the resolution of disputes, possibly limiting industrial action until the procedure has been exhausted. The second function of collective agreements is to regulate the terms of individual contracts of employment (the *normative* function). These 'substantive' terms may cover pay scales, working hours, holidays, shift work and overtime, and many other areas. In practice both procedural and substantive terms may frequently be found in the same collective agreement. There may also be terms which cannot be classified in either category, such as an obligation on every employer belonging to an employers' association which is party to an agreement to provide copies of the agreement to its employees. In recent years collective agreements have been accorded a further role in legislation implementing EU standards. Provided that the trade union party to it is 'independent',[65] a collective agreement may exclude or modify specified provisions relating to working time[66] and the successive use of fixed-term contracts,[67] and may determine the terms upon which parental leave is taken.[68]

Collective agreements are an important source of labour law in many systems. Their importance as a source of labour law in Britain is particularly remarkable in view of their independence from the formal legal system. As we explained in chapter 1, in general collective bargaining developed in this country on a voluntary basis, without legal regulation of either its procedures or its outcomes. Although there is now a statutory procedure enabling unions to gain statutory recognition, accompanied by an enforceable collective bargaining 'method', even now there remains no obligation to reach agreement. Moreover, there is no legal requirement that collective agreements cover any specified matters,[69] include any specific terms or are of any minimum or maximum (or even specified) duration,[70] or are in any particular form.[71] There is no requirement for them to be registered with any administrative authority as is the case in some other jurisdictions. Most surprisingly, perhaps, to a student of civil law systems of labour law, their legal status is entirely a matter for the collective parties: although since 1971 the determination of this question has been subject to a statutory presumption relating to enforceability this does not restrict the parties' capacity to choose.

2.9 Before the Industrial Relations Act 1971 there was no provision specifically dealing with the enforceability of collective agreements. The Trade Union Act 1871, section 4(4) (repealed in 1971) prevented the enforcement of agreements between one trade union and another and, because the

---

[65] See para 7.23.
[66] See paras 4.78 and 4.90.
[67] See paras 3.52 and 5.75.
[68] See para 6.119.
[69] The 'method' contained in the statutory model which may be imposed under the statutory recognition procedure provides that an employer may not vary the pay, hours or holidays of workers in the bargaining unit unless it has first discussed its proposals with the union, but this does not impose a duty to provide for such matters in a collective agreement: see further para 9.18.
[70] This does not mean that the terms of a collective agreement will necessarily be able to be applied, however; see, for example, EqA 2010, ss 145-146, 148 (discussed at para 6.68). A 'closed shop' agreement could not be lawfully enforced: see para 8.33 *et seq* below. At times of officially-imposed pay restraint incomes policies may prevent or delay the application of agreements.
[71] *Burke v Royal Liverpool University Hospital NHS Trust* [1997] ICR 730 (collective agreement formed by an exchange of letters between employer and union).

existing definition of 'trade union' probably covered many employers' associations, would thus have prevented collective agreements to which they were a party being enforced directly in the courts.[72] However, this provision did not touch agreements between individual employers and trade unions. In an influential analysis of the prevailing British system in 1954 Kahn-Freund wrote:

> … [i]n the long history of British collective bargaining it does not ever seem to have happened that either a trade union or an employers' association attempted to prevent the violation of a collective agreement by an action for an injunction or to seek compensation by an action for damages. The reason can certainly not be found in the absence of such violations … [73]

He concluded that the explanation lay in the intention of the parties that their agreements should be 'binding in honour' only, and enforceable through 'social … but not through legal sanctions'. The correctness of the assumptions which lay behind this view has been doubted.[74] What is incontrovertible, however, is its influence on modern practice. It was mirrored in evidence presented to, and the findings of, the Donovan Commission,[75] which regarded the intention (and policy) that collective agreements should remain outside the law as 'deeply rooted' in the industrial relations structure.[76] This view, in turn, was also highly influential when the question finally came before the courts in 1969.

In *Ford Motor Co Ltd v AUEFW*[77] the employer sought an injunction against the union on the ground that the union's support for industrial action was in breach of collective agreements between the union and the company. There was no indication in the agreements as to whether the parties had intended to create a contract and the court was forced therefore to ascertain their intention from the surrounding circumstances. The court referred, *inter alia*, to the writings of Kahn-Freund and to the Report of the Donovan Commission which clearly showed that the 'climate of opinion was almost unanimous to the effect that no legally enforceable contracts resulted from … collective agreements',[78] and took the view that the parties to the Ford agreement must be credited with knowledge of these sources which also provided evidence of their state of mind at the time. The court reached the same conclusion applying an objective test, maintaining that 'the fact that the agreements *prima facie* deal with commercial relationships is outweighed by the other considerations, by the wording of the agreements, by the nature of the agreements, and by the climate of opinion voiced and evidenced by the extra-judicial authorities'.[79]

The unions in the *Ford* case argued in addition that the 'vague and aspirational' wording of the agreements provided further evidence that the parties could not have intended to create a contract, a view which was accepted by the court.

---

[72] The Royal Commission on Trade Unions and Employers' Associations 1965–1968, Cmnd 3623, 1968 (the Donovan Commission) took the view (para 470) that such bodies could have made their agreements 'indirectly' enforceable and, for example, obtained from a court a declaration concerning the meaning of an agreement.
[73] Kahn-Freund, 1954: p 57.
[74] See R Lewis, 1979, and references therein.
[75] See note 72 above. It was the unanimous view of the Ministry of Labour, TUC and CBI.
[76] Para 471.
[77] [1969] 2 All ER 481.
[78] At 494.
[79] At 496.

The extra-legal character of the collective bargaining process was also reflected in its dynamic nature; rather than aiming to conclude agreements which remained set in stone for any given period, much collective bargaining took place within a framework which allowed collective agreements to be modified or reinterpreted as the need arose.[80] This in turn meant that labour law in Britain, unlike that in many other jurisdictions, did not recognise a distinction between disputes of right, concerned with interpretation of an existing agreement, and disputes of interest, which concern conflicts over renegotiated terms; all such disputes were equally susceptible to resolution through the collective bargaining process.

In 1971 the Industrial Relations Act, as part of a general strategy of bringing industrial relations within a legal framework, imposed a statutory presumption that collective agreements were intended to be legally enforceable unless they contained a statement to the contrary. In practice nearly all agreements concluded during the currency of the Act contained such a statement; the decision to insert it seems not to have been an issue between the parties,[81] thus demonstrating the strength of the consensus that this was not an appropriate area for legal regulation. Since 1974 the reverse statutory presumption has applied – a 'collective agreement'[82] will only be regarded as legally enforceable at collective level if it is in writing and there is a clear statement indicating the intention that it should be.[83] Evidence suggests that this hardly ever happens (a notable exception was the collective agreement negotiated in 1997 to ensure staff relations are conducted peacefully and without disruption to operations at GCHQ: see further para 7.10). This may on occasion be a mixed blessing for unions; although in the past debate about enforceability revolved around unions reneging on obligations not to take industrial action before exhausting agreed dispute resolution procedures, in more recent years employers, too, have been more ready to flout agreements.

2.10 The general non-enforceability of collective agreements in Britain stands in marked contrast to the position in many other systems. A further contrast is the lack of any automatic or compulsory integration of the norms generated by these agreements into individual employment contracts, even where they result from statutory recognition.[84] The perception of collective agreements as non-enforceable between the collective parties has not prevented them being an important source of terms governing the relationship between individual employers and workers where their wording is sufficiently clear and precise.[85] On the contrary, it has been common practice for workers' individual contracts expressly to incorporate such agreements; where they do not but collectively-agreed terms have been applied in practice incorporation has been readily

---

[80] See further paras 4.38–4.40 below for the effect of modifying a collective agreement upon the individual contract.

[81] Weekes *et al*, 1975: pp 156–161.

[82] Defined by TULRCA 1992, s 178(2); see further para 9.26 below. Note that agreements outside this definition will be governed by the common law.

[83] The notion of making collective agreements enforceable by law was floated and rejected on at least two occasions subsequent to the IRA 1971: see the Green Papers *Trade Union Immunities*, Cmnd 8128, 1981, para 243 and *Industrial Relations in the 1990s* Cm 1602, 1991: ch 8. Proposals to remove the immunities from industrial action in breach of procedure agreements in essential services, contained in the 1983 Conservative Party election manifesto, were also shelved.

[84] For an analysis of the variety of ways in which collective agreements can bind the parties to the employment relationship (and a salutary warning against over-simplification), see Wedderburn, 1992c; 1993: p 225 *et seq*.

[85] However, the courts have sometimes confused the relationship between the two: see *Loman and Henderson v Merseyside Transport Services Ltd* (1968) 3 ITR 108; *Gascol Conversions Ltd v Mercer* [1974] ICR 420. See now, however, *Marley v Forward Trust Group Ltd* [1986] ICR 891, CA; see further para 4.32 below.

implied.[86] However, unlike in other systems, whether such a practice is observed has been a matter entirely for the individual parties, even where collective bargaining follows statutory recognition. In France, for example, the Labour Code provides that where an employer is bound by the terms of a collective agreement those terms apply to its employment contracts, replaceable only by terms more favourable to the employee.[87] This approach is reflected in ILO Recommendation No 91 concerning Collective Agreements, which stipulates that employers and workers bound by collective agreements should not be able to include in contracts of employment terms contrary to those collectively agreed and, moreover, that the terms of the collective agreement should apply to all workers of the relevant descriptions employed by such employers. In Britain, employers cannot be obliged as a matter of law to apply the terms of collective agreements, even those to which they are directly party, to their workers, although where they have so chosen they have generally applied them to all workers within the scope of the agreement irrespective of their union membership. *A fortiori* there is no mechanism by which non-parties to collective agreements can be required to abide by them. In a number of countries, including Belgium, France and Germany, the public authorities have been empowered, after following a variety of complex procedures, to extend the application of a collective agreement to additional employers and their workers by order. This prevents any downward flexibility in the application of sectoral agreements and any consequent competitive advantage to employers who may otherwise be tempted to reward their workers below the collectively-agreed rate. Again this concept of 'extension' is enshrined in ILO Recommendation No 91.[88] Between 1940 and 1980 English law contained a form of extension mechanism which unions or employers within a particular trade or industry could invoke but this was repealed on the ground of its allegedly inflationary effect.[89]

A final consequence of the lack of legal regulation of collective bargaining is that where bargaining takes place at different levels there is no procedure for determining which of two (or possibly more) collective agreements, containing different provisions, should apply. As William Brown explains:

> Any one bargaining unit may be influenced by bargaining at more than one level. An employer on a building site, for example, might augment an industry agreement with a site agreement. Furthermore, any one bargaining level may deal with more than one bargaining unit. A chemicals refinery, for example, might have separate site agreements for the process workers, the maintenance workers and the staff. Finally, an employee may be included in different bargaining units for different aspects of his or her terms and conditions of employment. For example, there may be a company-wide training agreement, a divisional redundancy agreement, and a workplace performance-related pay agreement.[90]

---

[86] The written statement of employment terms which employers are now obliged to give their new employees (or existing employees on request) must contain particulars of any collective agreements which directly affect the terms and conditions of the employment including, where the employer is not a party, the persons by whom they were made: ERA 1996, s 1(4)(j); see further 4.16 below.

[87] Article L 135-2. For a comparative survey of the relationship between collective agreements and individual contracts of employment, see Sewerynski, 2003.

[88] Para 5.

[89] See paras 1.25 above and 7.15 below.

[90] W Brown, 1992: p 297.

The decision as to which agreement should apply in case of conflict has been treated, in our system, as a question for the courts, unlike in systems which prescribe a specific hierarchy of norms.[91] Few, if any, coherent principles have developed in this area.[92] However, this presents less of a practical problem now that single-employer bargaining has superseded the pattern of earlier years, when national industry-wide agreements set basic rates, supplemented by bargaining at company or plant level.[93]

In summary, therefore, to invoke the language of Kahn-Freund, in Britain the collective agreement is neither a contract nor a Code.[94] This has implications at European Union, as well as at domestic, level. Collective agreements are potentially capable of having a multiple role in EU law; first as a source of legal obligations under the terms of the 'social dialogue'; second, as a method of implementing obligations derived from other sources (such as directives); and third, as a mechanism, under controlled circumstances, for derogating from standards laid down in directives.[95] The absence of any mechanism for securing compliance with terms that have been collectively agreed means that, in Britain, the second of these roles is not currently an option.

Workforce agreements

2.11 We referred in para 2.8 above to the novel role accorded to collective agreements in modifying or excluding standards in the area of working time and use of successive fixed-term contracts, and in determining the terms on which parental leave is taken, provided that the trade unions party to the agreement are independent. The legislation in these areas also permits this function to be performed by a 'workforce agreement', an innovative statutory vehicle designed to implement the flexibility in the application of standards permitted by the respective EU Directives where the employer does not recognise a union.[96] We discuss the definition of a 'workforce agreement' in para 4.78, but essentially it means an agreement made either with elected representatives of the workforce or, in certain circumstances, a majority of the workers themselves. Notably, there is no requirement that such representatives meet the criteria of 'independence' required of trade unions, a cause for concern given the significance of their powers.

Works rules, notices and other documents issued by management to employees

2.12 Documents issued by management to their employees take a wide variety of forms, ranging from general rule books and handbooks governing conduct at the workplace to notices on specific matters. Whether these will take effect as terms of the individual contract, or are

---

[91] See further para 4.32 below.

[92] See *Clift v West Riding County Council* (1964) Times, 10 April; *Loman and Henderson v Merseyside Transport Services Ltd* (1968) 3 ITR 108; *Gascol Conversions Ltd v Mercer* [1974] IRLR 155 (criticised Hepple, 1974). In *South Tyneside Metropolitan Borough Council v Graham* UKEAT/0107/03/DA the tribunal was required to decide whether there was a 'local agreement' in existence.

[93] W Brown 1992, 1993.

[94] See, for example, P Davies and M Freedland, 1983: ch 6.

[95] See Bercusson, 1994d and para 2.8 above.

[96] See further paras 3.52, 4.78, 4.90 and 5.75.

merely emanations of the managerial prerogative which can be changed at will, depends upon the application of tests which we discuss in detail in chapter 4. In the past internal disciplinary and grievance procedures have generally been viewed as giving rise to contractual terms, particularly in the light of the employer's obligation to issue a written statement of terms and conditions of employment, although, in *obiter* remarks in *Johnson v Unisys Ltd*, Lord Hoffmann cast doubt on this approach.[97] Irrespective of whether such procedures are contractually binding, they are relevant in unfair dismissal proceedings. As well as formal documents, informal arrangements in the workplace or particular industry, commonly designated 'custom and practice' or 'trade usage', may eventually take effect as terms of the contract if they are deemed 'reasonable, certain and notorious'.[98] However, as we indicate in para 4.33 below, the greater formalisation of contract terms and conditions, and in particular the statutory provision for employees to receive a written statement of their employment terms, is likely to make it much more difficult than in the past to establish that practices which are solely a matter of custom and practice have contractual force.

Self-regulatory codes of conduct

2.13   In para 2.4 above we outlined Codes of Practice which are issued under statutory authority and whose effect is governed by statute. Private organisations may also issue codes of conduct to govern practices within their sphere of operation. The most prominent example is the TUC 'Bridlington' Principles, first promulgated by the TUC[99] in 1939 and most recently revised in 2007.[100] These principles were designed to minimise disputes between unions over membership questions. Although not intended to constitute a legally enforceable contract, they are 'accepted by all affiliated organisations as a binding commitment for their continued affiliation to the TUC'.[101] The primary aim of these procedures is to promote voluntary settlement of disputes between unions but if this avenue fails the matter may be referred to an internal Disputes Committee. Failure to comply with an award of that Committee attracts a variety of sanctions including, ultimately, exclusion from the TUC.

The TUC has also issued other guidance to its members on occasion. Thus in 1984 it issued a 'statement of guidance on political fund arrangements' designed to ensure that union members are informed about and able to exercise their right to contract out from contributing if their union has a 'political fund'. In 1979, during the 'winter of discontent' disputes which preceded the General Election of that year, it issued a Guide to Affiliated Unions on the Conduct of Industrial Disputes, designed to ensure that essential services were maintained. This formalised a practice followed by many unions with members in these services. Observance of such codes was generally conditional on employers exercising reciprocal self-restraint by not seeking to undermine the

---

[97] [2001] IRLR 279, at [63]–[66]; cf *Edwards v Chesterfield Royal Hospital NHS Foundation Trust* [2012] IRLR 129, Lord Dyson at [28]; see further para 5.35.

[98] *Sagar v H Ridehalgh & Son Ltd* [1930] 2 Ch 117.

[99] The TUC, formed in 1868, is a permanent federation of trade unions to which nearly all major unions are affiliated. For its history, see RM Martin, 1980; Taylor, 2000.

[100] TUC Disputes Principles and Procedures, TUC, 2007. For an evaluation of the operation of the principles before the 2000 revision see Elgar and Simpson, 1994, and references therein. See further para 10.11 below.

[101] TUC Disputes Principles and Procedures, Preface.

action in ways considered unacceptable by unions.[102] In the light of a greater willingness on the part of employers to invoke legal sanctions during disputes (and the 'statutory' right of action for consumers created by TURERA 1993) unions may be less likely to follow this course in the future.[103]

Relationship between the formal and informal sources

2.14   The interplay between the formal and the informal sources of labour law is complex. First, as we have seen, collective agreements, while not themselves constituting legally-binding contracts, may be accorded legal force if incorporated into individual contracts of employment. Second, such agreements,[104] together with 'workforce agreements' discussed in para 2.11, may modify or exclude standards in the area of working time and the use of successive fixed-term contracts, and may determine the terms of parental leave. Third, in assessing the rights of trade union officials and members to time off for union duties and activities during working hours, the terms of the agreement between the collective parties will be an important guide to what is 'reasonable'.[105] Finally, internal disciplinary procedures, even if not incorporated directly into the individual contract, may influence a tribunal in assessing whether an employer has acted fairly in deciding to dismiss. The procedural terms of collective agreements may also have indirect legal effect in relation to the granting of injunctions to halt industrial disputes; the Code of Practice issued by the Secretary of State recommends that a ballot should not take place until any agreed procedures which might lead to a resolution of the dispute without the need for industrial action have been completed.[106] Compliance with the terms of a procedural agreement on the part of an employer is also relevant in determining whether the period for which it is automatically unfair to dismiss an employee for taking 'protected industrial action' extends beyond twelve weeks.[107] In many areas, therefore, it is crucial to have regard to standards derived from voluntary sources in order to ascertain individual or collective rights.

THE ROLE OF COURTS AND EMPLOYMENT TRIBUNALS

2.15   Just as there is no Labour Code in England, equally there is no separate labour court system for dealing with all labour law disputes.[108] Rather the judicial determination of labour law matters is divided between tripartite employment tribunals, which, broadly speaking, hear claims involving statutory employment rights as well as certain common law claims, and the common law courts. Issues before the common law courts are most likely to involve matters of contract and

---

[102] See generally G Morris, 1986a: chs 5 and 6.
[103] See further G Morris, 1991 and 1993.
[104] Provided that the trade union party to the agreement is 'independent': see para 2.8.
[105] See further para 8.42 below.
[106] See further para 11.45 below.
[107] See para 11.81.
[108] There is a considerable literature on the issues which the introduction of a Labour Court would raise: see, for example, Wedderburn, 1991a, and references therein. For a brief comparative overview, see Gladstone, 2010.

tort and, for specific groups of workers, public law. The appropriate forum for a common law claim depends upon its value; claims for more than £25,000 can be brought in the High Court (other than for personal injuries, where the minimum is £50,000), those for less than that normally in a locally-based county court.[109] Thus many contractual or minor personal injuries claims will be heard in the county court; employers' claims in tort against trade unions in relation to industrial action are heard in the High Court, together with claims for interim injunctions to halt the action. Claims in public law are always heard in the Administrative Court, subject, as we indicated in para 2.5, to the need for permission. We discuss the procedural aspects of bringing common law claims in greater detail in those contexts, such as dismissal and industrial action, where they have particularly significant implications.

The bifurcation between courts and tribunals means that an employee generally needs to bring separate proceedings in each where both contractual and statutory rights are at issue. One exception to this principle, introduced in 1994, allows employment tribunals to hear claims for money due under the contract, or damages for breach of contract, of up to £25,000 if the claim arises or is outstanding on termination of an employee's employment.[110] This means that an employee who is dismissed with less than the contractually-agreed period of notice, for example, may be able to sue for damages and claim unfair dismissal compensation in the same set of proceedings.[111] However, tribunals may not award an injunction to restrain the termination of a contract; an employee who seeks this remedy will still have to bring an action under common law. The upper limit of £25,000 on common law claims in tribunals appears anomalous given that there is no limit on the compensation which tribunals may award in a variety of contexts, including equality cases[112] and those involving unauthorised deductions from pay contrary to ERA 1996, ss 13–27.[113]

Termination of employment apart, all other contractual claims must be brought in the common law courts.[114] This does not mean that common law concepts are irrelevant in tribunal hearings, however. On the contrary, there is a variety of contexts in which the scope and terms of the contract of employment are material to a statutory claim – whether an employee has been 'constructively dismissed' due to the employer's repudiatory breach, for example – and the status of

---

[109] High Court and County Courts Jurisdiction (Amendment) Order 1991, SI 1991/724, as amended; CPR Part 7 Practice Direction 7A paras 2.1–2.4. In February 2012 the Coalition Government announced that the minimum threshold for non-personal injury claims in the High Court would be raised from £25,000 to £100,000: Ministry of Justice, *Solving disputes in the county courts: creating a simpler, quicker and more proportionate system: The Government response*, 2012.

[110] Employment Tribunals Extension of Jurisdiction (England and Wales) Order 1994, SI 1994/1623; ETA 1996, ss 2, 3. Certain claims are excluded, including damages for personal injuries. There is no jurisdiction if the complaint is presented before the effective date of termination of the contract: *Capek v Lincolnshire County Council* [2000] IRLR 590. The claim must be immediately enforceable at that date: *Peninsula Business Services Ltd v Sweeney* [2004] IRLR 49; see also *Miller Bros and F P Butler Ltd v Johnston* [2002] IRLR 386. It is notable that the Donovan Commission envisaged that the 'labour tribunals' they proposed should cover all cases arising from the contract of employment as well as statutory claims: see Royal Commission on Trade Unions and Employers' Associations 1965–1968: Report, Cmnd 3623, 1968, ch X.

[111] If the employee takes this course it is then open to an employer to bring a counterclaim in contract if grounds for doing so exist. If claimants consider that their contractual claim may exceed £25,000 they should confine their employment tribunal claim to that of unfair dismissal: see *Fraser v HLMAD Ltd* [2006] IRLR 687.

[112] See further para 6.66 below.

[113] See further paras 4.71-4.73 below.

[114] Note, however, that claims under ERA 1996, ss 13–27 may, in practice, involve the determination of contractual matters: see para 4.73 below.

employee, which is crucial to access to many employment rights, is based entirely upon common law tests.[115]

As the discussion which follows makes clear, there are important differences between courts and employment tribunals which make the choice of forum significant for the parties. For example, in employment tribunals applicants can be represented by the person of their choice, such as a union official, whereas in the courts the only alternative to legal representation is self-representation. State-funded legal aid is not available for employment tribunals, unlike for courts[116] and, whereas courts may award costs against the unsuccessful party at their discretion, costs in tribunals have to date been awarded only in exceptional circumstances.[117] Where the applicant is free to make a choice about where to initiate a claim these may be material considerations. However, the differences between the systems become less apparent if the right to appeal is exercised. Appeals can be made from employment tribunals to the Employment Appeal Tribunal (EAT).[118] Although the right to the representative of one's choice remains, legal aid is available for EAT proceedings. Subsequent appeals may be made, with leave, to the Court of Appeal[119] and thence to the Supreme Court. At that point proceedings are subject to the procedural rules which normally apply and in that sense the statutory and common law jurisdictions can be said to converge. It is perhaps ironic that ultimately the most authoritative interpretations of the law come from the non-specialist, appellate courts; for this reason the system of labour courts lacks genuine autonomy unlike that in Germany, for example, where the Federal Labour Court has the final word on issues of interpretation. The general principles of *stare decisis* apply within this area. Thus the employment tribunals are bound by decisions of the EAT which itself is bound by decisions of the higher courts. For the EAT its own previous decisions are of persuasive value. Employment tribunal decisions have no precedent value for other tribunals although in the absence of any other authority they may be regarded as persuasive.

In the following paragraphs we outline the constitution and operation of employment tribunals and the EAT. We then consider the implications of reforms that have recently been made to the tribunal system and to its relationship with other means of dispute settlement. As we discuss in para 2.20 below, the Coalition Government decided in 2011 that in future fees should be charged for access to employment tribunals and the EAT, although at the time of writing the structure of the charging regime has not yet been determined.

---

[115] See further Anderman, 2000.

[116] It is arguable that the failure, in certain circumstances, to make legal aid available for complex cases may contravene Art 6 of the ECHR: see *Airey v Ireland* judgment of 9 October 1979, (1979–80) 2 EHRR 305, paras 20–28; *Steel v UK* judgment of 15 February 2005, (2005) 41 EHRR 22. In addition the CJEU has observed that there may be a right to legal aid to allow EU law rights to be vindicated: see Case C-279/09 *DEB Deutsche Energiehandels-und Beratungsgesellschaft mbH v Germany* judgment of 22 December 2010, paras 59-62. Legal aid for representation in employment tribunals where specified criteria are satisfied has been available in Scotland since January 2001.

[117] In 2010–2011 they were awarded in 487 cases disposed of at hearings (132 to claimants and 355 to respondents): HMCTS, *Employment Tribunals and EAT Statistics , 2010-11*, Table 12. The median award was £1,273.

[118] Note that appeals from the decisions of employment tribunals in their 'non-employment' jurisdiction, such as health and safety at work, lie to the High Court under the provisions of the Tribunals and Inquiries Act 1992, s 11.

[119] ETA 1996, s 37.

Employment tribunals

2.16   Employment tribunals, until ERDRA 1998 called 'industrial tribunals', were established in 1964, initially to deal with appeals by employers against industrial training levies imposed under the Industrial Training Act. In 1965 their jurisdiction was extended to cover claims for the newly-introduced statutory redundancy payments. They were accorded a more central role in labour law disputes with the introduction of protection against unfair dismissal in the Industrial Relations Act 1971 and since then their jurisdiction has been progressively extended to a wide range of employment-related matters.[120] The biggest single category of claim has generally been that of unfair dismissal but there was a greater number of claims relating to unauthorised deductions from pay between 2009 and 2011.[121] Many claims cover more than one statutory right (unfair dismissal and discrimination, for example). Employment tribunals also have jurisdiction over statutory rights which may be exercised against trade unions in relation to discipline or exclusion or expulsion from membership. A further area of their jurisdiction (which lies largely beyond the scope of this work) is in the field of health and safety. Tribunals have no jurisdiction to award injunctions, although in very limited circumstances they can order 'interim relief' to maintain an employee in his or her employment pending the hearing of an unfair dismissal claim.[122] They can order re-instatement or re-engagement of an employee found to have been unfairly dismissed but these orders cannot be enforced; the sanction against an employer who refuses to comply with such an order is additional financial compensation to the claimant.[123] Moreover, they have no power to enforce their money judgments: if an award is not paid enforcement action must be taken through the county court, although since April 2010 a 'fast track' scheme has enabled successful claimants to ask a High Court Enforcement Officer to commence proceedings on their behalf and to seize and sell the employer's goods if payment is not made.[124] In 2010–2011 more than 218,100 claims were accepted by employment tribunals,[125] although a significant proportion did not reach a hearing because they were resolved either through ACAS conciliation; withdrawn, for example, as a result of a private settlement; or struck out.[126] The lack of provision for 'class actions' to be brought on behalf of a group of workers means that the total number of claims may be inflated by multiple claims against the same employer; this commonly occurs in relation to equal pay.[127]

---

[120] Her Majesty's Courts and Tribunals Service ('HMCTS') provides statistical information relating to employment tribunals.

[121] HMCTS, *Employment Tribunals and EAT Statistics, 2010-11*, Table 1.

[122] See para 5.153 below.

[123] ERA 1996, s 117.

[124] The costs of enforcement are added to the employer's debt and the details of any enforcement action are placed on a publicly-available Register of Judgments, Orders, Fines and Tribunal Decisions which may affect an employer's ability to obtain credit. Research published in 2009 (prior to the introduction of the 'fast track' scheme) found that, of 1,002 claimants who had been awarded a monetary payment by an employment tribunal between January 2007 and April 2008, only 53% had been paid in full and 39% had received nothing. Of those who had not received payment only a minority had initiated county court proceedings: L Adams *et al*, 2009.

[125] Above, note 121.

[126] Above, note 121, Tables 1 and 2. There were 382,000 'jurisdictional complaints' (complaints under individual jurisdictions). Table 2, which shows the outcomes of claims, refers to jurisdictional complaints.

[127] Another example is the working time claims in 2010-11, of which 84,000 were resubmitted multiple claims against an employer or small number of employers.

The constitution and procedures of employment tribunals are governed by ETA 1996 and statutory regulations.[128] They sit in a variety of locations around Great Britain.[129] Administrative support for employment tribunals and the EAT is provided by Her Majesty's Courts and Tribunals Service ('HMCTS'), an executive agency of the Ministry of Justice.

Unlike the ordinary courts, employment tribunals are tripartite in their composition (although, as we indicate below, there are an increasing number of jurisdictions where the Employment Judge may sit alone). Each tribunal is chaired by a barrister or solicitor who has been qualified as such for at least seven years, appointed by the Lord Chancellor.[130] Since November 2008 the chairman has been known as an Employment Judge.[131] He or she normally sits with two lay members drawn from separate panels of employer and employee representatives who are appointed by the Lord Chancellor.[132] For cases involving sex discrimination, an attempt is made to include at least one woman on the tribunal, and in race discrimination cases a member with experience and training in race cases in the area of employment. Although the Employment Judge controls the conduct of proceedings the lay members can also intervene and their vote is equal to the Employment Judge's on all matters. However, they do not sit as representatives of their respective organisations and should make an independent judgement. In practice the vast majority of decisions are unanimous.[133] Employment tribunals have sometimes been dubbed by the higher courts 'industrial juries',[134] a description criticised by Wedderburn because, unlike the standard jury system, in this case the legal chair retires with the jury.[135]

Before 1993 tribunal chairmen could sit without the lay members only for very limited purposes such as interlocutory matters. TURERA 1993 extended this power to include, for example, cases on unauthorised deductions from pay, rights on the insolvency of the employer, breach of contract proceedings (where permitted) and those where the parties agree to this course.[136] ERDRA 1998 empowered a chairman to sit alone on a yet wider range of matters, including unauthorised deduction of union subscriptions by employers,[137] non-payment of a guarantee

[128] The Employment Tribunals (Constitution and Rules of Procedure) Regulations 2004, SI 2004/1861, as amended. For a description of tribunal practice and procedure, see Harvey, 1972, as updated, Division P1. For an overview of the role and management of employment tribunals, see Meeran, 2006; on the Employment Tribunal System Taskforce, see Gaymer, 2006.

[129] The number of tribunals to be established is determined by the President of the Employment Tribunals (England and Wales), who is appointed by the Lord Chancellor. The Lord Chancellor has the power to appoint Regional Employment Judges, each of whom is then responsible for the administration of justice by tribunals in the area specified by the President: SI 2004/1861, regs 4–6. The Senior President of Tribunals is the independent leader of the tribunal judiciary as a whole, including employment tribunals and the EAT: Tribunals, Courts and Enforcement Act 2007, s 2.

[130] ETA 1996, s 4(1); SI 2004/1861, regs 8, 9. Special provisions apply in national security cases: regs 10–12.

[131] The Tribunals, Courts and Enforcement Act 2007 (Transitional and Consequential Provisions) Order 2008, SI 2008/2683, reg 6, Sch 1, paras 240-259. Tribunal chairmen were permitted to be referred to as Employment Judges from December 2007: ETA 1996, s 3A, inserted by the Tribunals, Courts and Enforcement Act 2007.

[132] SI 2004/1861, regs 8, 9, as amended by SI 2008/3240 with effect from 6 April 2009. Prior to this, appointments were made by the Secretary of State. See *Smith v Secretary of State for Trade and Industry* [2000] IRLR 6, Morrison P at 9; *Scanfuture UK Ltd v Secretary of State for Trade and Industry* [2001] IRLR 416 for discussion of the compatibility of this position with Art 6 of the ECHR.

[133] Meeran, 2006: p 132; Corby and Latreille, 2011: p 16.

[134] See, for example, Lord Donaldson MR in British Telecommunications plc v Sheridan [1990] IRLR 27, 30.

[135] Wedderburn, 1991a: p 40.

[136] ETA 1996, s 4. Where jurisdiction is based upon the parties' consent, there is no requirement for either party to have received independent advice before agreeing to this course.

[137] See para 8.47 below.

payment or protective award in the context of redundancies,[138] disputes over entitlement to a redundancy payment[139] and, most controversially, complaints relating to the written statement of employment particulars.[140] In April 2009 claims for holiday pay under the Working Time Regulations 1998 were added to the list.[141] In November 2011 the Coalition Government announced that Employment Judges would be permitted to hear unfair dismissal cases alone although (as with the other jurisdictions), they could choose otherwise.[142] The Government justified this decision on grounds of cost despite opposition from many consultees who pointed out that unfair dismissal cases often revolve around factual questions where the experience of lay members may be particularly relevant[143] and evidence that the majority of Employment Judges considered that lay members add value in unfair dismissal cases.[144] At the time of writing the Enterprise and Regulatory Reform Bill makes provision for a 'legal officer' to determine proceedings in respect of which an employment tribunal has jurisdiction if such proceedings are specified in an order made jointly by the Secretary of State and Lord Chancellor and all parties consent in writing.

2.17   The Donovan Commission expressed the view that 'labour tribunals' should provide 'an easily accessible, speedy, informal and inexpensive procedure' for the settlement of disputes.[145] These aims remain the touchstone for assessing the performance of employment tribunals today although it may be questioned whether, in view of the complexity of the law, they are now realistic aims. However they provide a convenient framework within which to discuss the distinctive features of employment tribunals. We discuss more major reforms, designed to assist employment tribunals to deal with the increasing number of applications being made to them and to encourage parties to attempt to resolve problems internally first, in para 2.20 *et seq*. Since April 2001 tribunals have had an overriding statutory objective to deal with cases 'justly', which includes, so far as practicable, ensuring that the parties are on an equal footing; saving expense; dealing with a case in ways that are proportionate to the complexity or importance of the issues; and ensuring that it is dealt with expeditiously and fairly.[146]

In terms of accessibility a claimant who believes that he or she has a claim completes a claim form which requires his or her personal details and those of the respondent, together with details of the claim.[147] Once accepted by the tribunal a copy of the claim is sent to the employer who has 28 days to enter a response stating whether it intends to resist the claim and, if so, on what grounds. These forms are then copied to the Advisory Conciliation and Arbitration Service

---

[138] See paras 4.127 and 9.40 below. Non-payment of an award for failure to consult on a transfer of the undertaking is also included in the power: see para 9.45 below.

[139] See para 5.164 *et seq* below.

[140] See para 4.14 *et seq* below.

[141] The Employment Tribunals Act 1996 (Tribunal Composition) Order 2009, SI 2009/789. See para 4.84 below.

[142] Implemented by The Employment Tribunals Act 1996 (Tribunal Composition) Order 2012, SI 2012/988 with effect from 6 April 2012.

[143] BIS, *Resolving Workplace Disputes: Government response to the consultation*, November 2011,: paras 116-117.

[144] Corby and Latreille, 2011: p 12. See generally Corby and Latreille, 2012. The EAT has in the past expressed disquiet as to the use made by Employment Judges of the power to sit alone in cases where the experience of lay members could be significant: see, for example, *Southwark London Borough Council v O'Brien* [1996] IRLR 420; *Sutcliffe v Big C's Marine* [1998] IRLR 428 at 430–431. On the exercise of the discretion to sit alone, see *Sogbetun v London Borough of Hackney* [1998] IRLR 676; cf. *Post Office v Howell* [2000] IRLR 224; *Morgan v Brith Gof Cyf* [2001] ICR 978.

[145] Royal Commission on Trade Unions and Employers' Associations 1965–1968: Report, Cmnd 3623, 1968, para 578.

[146] SI 2004/1861, reg 3.

[147] See generally on rules of procedure SI 2004/1861, reg 16 and Sch 1. See further para 2.21 on the grievance procedure contained in the ACAS Code of Practice that employees should generally follow before presenting a claim.

(ACAS)[148] whose conciliation officers have a duty for most types of claim[149] to attempt to promote a settlement between the parties without the need for a tribunal hearing. As we indicated earlier, a significant proportion of cases are settled by ACAS conciliation or withdrawn (in 2010-11, 29% and 32% respectively of the jurisdictional claims received by tribunals).[150] Settlements reached under the auspices of a conciliation officer and recorded on the appropriate form may not then proceed to a tribunal hearing.[151] TURERA 1993 also introduced the 'compromise agreement' as a further mechanism by which binding settlements could be reached.[152] To be effective the applicant must have received 'independent' advice as to the meaning of and effect of the agreement[153] from a qualified lawyer[154] insured for loss arising from any subsequent claim on the advice.[155] ERDRA 1998 extended this provision to 'advice from a relevant independent adviser', a category which includes, as well as lawyers, officers, officials, employees or members of an independent trade union[156] whom the union has certified in writing as competent to give advice and has authorised to do so, and those who work at advice centres (whether as employees or volunteers) whom the centre has so certified and authorised.[157] However, any such persons are excluded if they are employed by or acting *in the matter* (our italics) for the employer or an associated employer;[158] if the union or centre giving advice is itself the employer or an associated employer; or, in the case of advice centres, if the worker pays for the advice. The compromise agreement must state that the statutory conditions have been satisfied.[159] At the time of writing the Coalition Government is considering how it can reduce the costs of settling claims by developing a standard text for parties to download and simplifying the coverage of existing and future claims; it also proposes to change the name from 'compromise' to 'settlement' agreements.[160]

The tribunal itself may screen out claims at a 'pre-hearing review', an 'interim hearing' conducted by an Employment Judge alone unless a party otherwise requests not less than ten days before the scheduled date and the Employment Judge considers that a substantive issue of fact is likely to be

---

[148] SI 2004/1861, Sch 1, r 21.

[149] ETA 1996, ss 18, 19. The fixed period for conciliation inserted by EA 2002 was repealed by EA 2008 s 6, with the effect that ACAS's duty to conciliate subsists until the tribunal delivers a decision.

[150] Above, note 121, p 5.

[151] ETA 1996, s 18; ERA 1996, s 203(1)(e). See *Allma Construction Ltd v Bonner* [2011] IRLR 204, EAT. There are provisions equivalent to s 203(1)(e) in other relevant statutes: see for example EqA 2010, s 147.

[152] ERA 1996, s 203(2)(f), (3), (4). A compromise agreement will only cover claims which the parties could not have had in contemplation (for example, claims that as a matter of law did not exist) if they use language that unambiguously indicates that it does so: *BCCI SA (in Compulsory Liquidation) v Ali* [2001] IRLR 292. See also *Hinton v University of East London* [2005] IRLR 552; *McWilliam v Glasgow City Council* [2011] IRLR 568, EAT . In *Industrious Ltd v Horizon Recruitment Ltd (in liquidation)* [2010] IRLR 204 the EAT held that an employment tribunal can determine whether a compromise agreement should be set aside on grounds of misrepresentation, for example.

[153] In *McWilliam v Glasgow City Council*, above, the EAT confirmed that there was no requirement for the employee to have been advised whether the deal on offer was a good one.

[154] A barrister or solicitor who holds a practising certificate: ERA 1996, s 203(4)(a). 'Independent' advice means that it was given by a lawyer who was not acting in the matter for an employer or an associated employer: s 203(4).

[155] ERA 1996, s 203(3)(d).

[156] See para 7.23 below.

[157] The Secretary of State may extend this category by order; see, for example, SI 2004/754. All 'relevant legal advisers' must be covered by a contract of insurance or an indemnity provided for members of a profession or professional body.

[158] See para 3.65 below for the definition of an 'associated employer'.

[159] ERA 1996, s 203(3)(f). A compromise agreement that fails to comply with the statutory conditions may still be valid in respect of non-statutory claims: see *Sutherland v Network Appliance Ltd* [2001] IRLR 12.

[160] BIS, *Resolving Workplace Disputes: Government response to the consultation*, November 2011: paras 32-51. This change of name is contained in the Enterprise and Regulatory Reform Bill.

determined and that a full tribunal would be desirable.[161] Oral or written representations or evidence, as well as the claim form and response, may be considered.[162] Preliminary issues, such as whether the tribunal has jurisdiction to hear a case – for example whether the employee had the requisite period of service – may be determined at a pre-hearing review and, if appropriate, the claim may be struck out at this stage.[163] In addition, if it appears the contentions put forward by a party in relation to a particular matter have 'little reasonable prospect of success' that party may be ordered to pay a deposit of up to £1,000 as a condition of being permitted to continue to take part in the proceedings relating to that matter.[164] In determining whether a deposit should be ordered, and the amount, the tribunal must take account of the party's means.[165] The tribunal should also give a warning that the party may be liable for the other party's costs (if legally represented) or preparation time (if not so represented) if they subsequently lose the case and could lose their deposit[166] (which is set off against a costs or preparation time award).[167] If the required deposit is not paid within 21 days, and no extension of this period has been requested and granted, the claim or response, as appropriate, will be struck out.[168]

Regardless of whether a deposit is required, costs orders may be ordered by an employment tribunal following the proceedings in favour of each legally-represented party[169] if in bringing or conducting the proceedings[170] a party has acted 'vexatiously, abusively, disruptively or otherwise unreasonably' or the bringing or conducting of the proceedings was 'misconceived'[171] (which includes 'having no reasonable prospect of success').[172] When making an order, the tribunal may (but is not required to) have regard to a party's ability to pay.[173] A maximum of £20,000 may be awarded, although the parties may agree a greater sum.[174] The 2004 Regulations also made provision, in similar circumstances, for 'preparation time' orders to be made in favour of non-legally represented parties (including time spent by employees and advisers up to but not including at any hearing),[175] subject to a current maximum of £32 per hour and a total of £10,000.[176] In addition, 'wasted costs' orders may be made against a representative, unless he or she is not acting in pursuit of profit with regard to those proceedings, as a result of any 'improper, unreasonable or negligent act or omission'

---

[161] SI 2004/1861, Sch 1, r 18(1), (3), (4).

[162] SI 2004/1861, Sch 1, r 18(2).

[163] See SI 2004/1861, Sch 1, r 18(7) for the judgments or orders that may be made at a pre-hearing review. See also *Balls v Downham Market High School and College* [2011] IRLR 217, EAT.

[164] SI 2004/1861, Sch 1, r 20(1). This figure stood at £500 until 6 April 2012.

[165] SI 2004/1861, Sch 1, r 20(2).

[166] SI 2004/1861, Sch 1, r 20(3).

[167] SI 2004/1861, Sch 1, r 47(2). Note, however, that in *Gee v Shell UK Ltd* [2003] IRLR 82 the Court of Appeal held that in the circumstances the costs warning constituted unfair pressure on the claimant to withdraw her claim.

[168] SI 2004/1861, Sch 1, r 20(4). A strike-out for non-payment of a deposit is a 'judgment' and, as such, reviewable under r 34: *Sodexho Ltd v Gibbons* [2005] IRLR 836.

[169] SI 2004/1861, Sch 1, r 38(2).

[170] Or his or her representative in conducting them.

[171] SI 2004/1861, Sch 1, r 40(2), (3). Costs orders may also be made against a party who has not complied with an order or practice direction or where on the application of a party the tribunal or Employment Judge has postponed the day or time fixed for or adjourned a hearing or pre-hearing review: Sch 1, r 40(1), (4).

[172] SI 2004/1861, reg 2. See *Scott v Commissioners of Inland Revenue* [2004] IRLR 713; *Nicolson Highlandwear Ltd v Nicolson* [2010] IRLR 859, EAT. In *Barnsley MPC v Yerrakalva* [2012] IRLR 78, where the Court of Appeal substituted a costs order of 50% for one of 100% of costs, the court emphasised the limited circumstances in which an appeal against a costs order would succeed.

[173] SI 2004/1861, Sch 1, r 41(2), overturning the effect of *Kovacs v Queen Mary and Westfield College* [2002] IRLR 414.

[174] SI 2004/1861, Sch 1, r 41. This figure stood at £10,000 until 6 April 2012.

[175] SI 2004/1861, Sch 1, r 42(3).

[176] SI 2004/1861, Sch 1, r 43–45.

by the representative or which, in the light of any such act or omission occurring after the costs were incurred, the tribunal considers it 'unreasonable' to expect a party to pay.[177]

This 'move to strengthen ... [employment] ... tribunal procedures to deter and weed out cases at an early stage'[178] replaced a procedure of 'pre-hearing assessments' introduced in 1980, which did not include a deposit system and which was not, in later years, widely used.[179] The deposit system has the clear potential to discourage applicants with limited means, particularly if unrepresented, from proceeding with a case whose merits may not be apparent without evidence from witnesses or the opportunity to cross-examine those of the other party (there is no requirement on an Employment Judge to hear evidence before ordering a deposit to be paid).[180] Moreover, the very cases which may appear unarguable to Employment Judges may be those which radically change the law.[181] Prior to the 2004 Regulations, a deposit could be required only if there was 'no reasonable prospect of success'; the change to 'little reasonable prospect of success' is a lower hurdle and allows deposits to be ordered in a greater range of cases. As we have seen, the powers of tribunals to award costs have to date been rarely used, and the perception that the system is being used by unmeritorious claimants is based on anecdote rather than research.[182]

As far as the speed of the tribunal process is concerned, the time limit for presenting claims is specified under each head of statutory jurisdiction. It varies between claims but is commonly within three months of the act complained of.[183] If this deadline is not met the tribunal usually has jurisdiction to grant such further period as it considers reasonable if satisfied that it was not 'reasonably practicable' for the complaint to be presented in time.[184] The onus is on the applicant to show this.[185] There is considerable case law on what is meant by 'reasonably practicable', which has been interpreted as 'reasonably feasible', [186] although this is largely a question of fact for the

---

[177] SI 2004/1861, Sch 1, r 48. Regard must be had to the representative's ability to pay: r 48(6). See *Gill v Humanware Europe plc* [2010] IRLR 877, CA.

[178] *Employment Gazette*, October 1994: p 367.

[179] In 1992–1993 and 1993–1994 there were 196 and 185 pre-hearing assessments respectively: *Employment Gazette*, October 1994, table 7A. In the year ending September 1984 there were 3,000: Hepple and Fredman, 1992: para 85.

[180] SI 2004/1861, Sch 1, r 18(2)(c).

[181] See, for example, Case C 152/84 *Marshall v Southampton and South West Hampshire Area Health Authority* [1986] IRLR 140.

[182] A 1998 Survey of Employment Tribunal Applications found that fewer than 4% of cases were 'vexatious' in the sense that the claimant had been advised by a professional adviser that they were likely to lose, and in seven of the 35 cases so classified the applicant went on to win at a tribunal hearing: Findings from the 1998 *Survey of Employment Tribunal Applications*, Employment Relations Research Series 13, DTI, 2002: p 28.

[183] The statutory language varies as to whether the date of the act itself counts for the purposes of computation. The Enterprise and Regulatory Reform Bill provides for time limits to be extended to facilitate conciliation before proceedings are instituted.

[184] See, for example, ERA 1996, s 111(2). Note that under EqA 2010 proceedings must be brought within the specified period or 'such other period as the employment tribunal thinks just and equitable': s 123(1),(2). This discretion is broader than in the context of the unfair dismissal provisions: see (on predecessors of EqA 2010) *Hawkins v Ball and Barclays Bank plc* [1996] IRLR 258; *British Coal Corpn v Keeble* [1997] IRLR 336; *Department of Constitutional Affairs v Jones* [2008] IRLR 128; *Chief Constable of Lincolnshire Police v Caston* [2010] IRLR 327, CA.

[185] *Porter v Bandridge Ltd* [1978] IRLR 271.

[186] *Palmer and Saunders v Southend-on-Sea Borough Council* [1984] IRLR 119. In *Schultz v Esso Petroleum Co Ltd* [1999] 3 All ER 338 the Court of Appeal held that attention would normally focus on the closing rather than the early stages of the period in assessing whether something should have been done. In *Marley (UK) Ltd v Anderson* [1996] IRLR 163 the Court of Appeal held that although an employee's complaint on the initial ground put forward was time-barred, it had jurisdiction to consider the complaint on a different ground which had subsequently come to light and which the employee had raised, by amendment to his existing claim, within a reasonable period after acquiring the relevant knowledge. See also *Cambridge and Peterborough Foundation NHS Trust v Crouchman* [2009] ICR 1306.

tribunal. In the light of this, previous cases are of limited value but afford some general guidance. To show that it was not 'reasonably practicable' to present a claim in time is now a difficult test to satisfy, particularly if the applicant has engaged 'skilled advisers' which include in this context solicitors,[187] trade union officers,[188] and a Citizens Advice Bureau[189] (but not an employee of an employment tribunal).[190] However, tribunals have been warned against treating recourse to a skilled adviser as an absolute bar to extension of the time limit regardless of the circumstances.[191] Because the time limit goes to the tribunal's jurisdiction the employer cannot unilaterally agree to waive it.[192] In 2005/6 more that 75% of cases were brought to a first hearing within 26 weeks.[193] Although any delay is highly undesirable, particularly in cases of dismissal, the speed with which cases are heard by tribunals compares favourably with the ordinary courts.

2.18   Full hearings of tribunals must normally take place in public.[194] However, a government minister may direct that a tribunal should sit in private in the interests of national security for all or part of particular Crown proceedings, and the tribunal itself may decide to do so on this ground[195] or where evidence is likely to consist of information whose disclosure would be contrary to statute, which has been communicated in confidence, or which would cause substantial injury to the employer's undertaking other than any effects it may have on collective bargaining.[196] The Employment Judge may give directions on any matter arising in connection with the proceedings, including requiring a party to give additional information, the provision and exchange of witness statements, and the provision of written answers to questions put by the tribunal. He or she may also grant orders for the disclosure and inspection of documents and require the attendance of witnesses and production of documents.[197] A failure to comply with a direction or requirement may result in the claim or response being struck out, or the respondent debarred from defending the claim altogether.[198] In discrimination cases for which the merits hearing is expected to take three days or more, the Employment Judge will advise the parties of the possibility of judicial

---

[187] *Dedman v British Building and Engineering Appliances Ltd* [1973] IRLR 379.

[188] *Union Cartage Co Ltd v Blunden* [1977] IRLR 139.

[189] *Riley v Tesco Stores Ltd* [1980] IRLR 103, cf, however, *Marks and Spencer plc v Williams-Ryan* [2005] IRLR 562, Lord Phillips MR at [32].

[190] *Jean Sorelle Ltd v Rybak* [1991] IRLR 153.

[191] *London International College Ltd v Sen* [1993] IRLR 333, 336 (Bingham MR). See also *Virdi v Commissioner of Police of the Metropolis* [2007] IRLR 24, [40]: errors of his solicitors should 'not be visited on … [the claimant's] head'; *Bleuse v MBT Transport Ltd* [2008] IRLR 264; cf *Northamptonshire County Council v Entwhistle* [2010] IRLR 740, EAT.

[192] See *Radakovits v Abbey National plc* [2010] IRLR 307, CA.

[193] Employment Tribunals Service, *Annual Report and Accounts 2005–2006*, HC 1303, p 12. This information does not appear in subsequent annual statistics

[194] SI 2004/1861, Sch 1, r 26(3). In *Storer v British Gas Plc* [2000] IRLR 495 the Court of Appeal quashed a tribunal decision where the public had not been afforded unimpeded access to the hearing. The ETA 1996, s 7(3A), 7(3AA) enables regulations to authorise the determination of proceedings without a hearing where all parties consent to this in writing or the respondent has not presented a response or does not contest the case. No such regulations have been issued at the time of writing.

[195] SI 2004/1861, Sch 1, r 54. See *Home Office v Tariq* [2011] IRLR 843, SC.

[196] SI 2004/1861, Sch 1, r 16. See also r 50 and ETA 1996, ss 11, 12 for provisions relating to restricted reporting orders in cases involving allegations of sexual misconduct or complaints relating to disability discrimination and *Chief Constable of West Yorkshire Police v A* [2000] IRLR 465 and *X v Stevens* [2003] IRLR 411.

[197] SI 2004/1861, Sch 1, r 10. This may be done either at the request of one of the parties or at the Employment Judge's own initiative.

[198] SI 2004/1861, Sch 1, r 13.

mediation although research on a judicial mediation pilot conducted between June 2006 and March 2007 showed no statisically significant impact on settlement rates.[199]

The form of employment tribunal proceedings remains adversarial rather than investigatory; each party has to present and prove its case and may cross-examine the witnesses of the other. However, the Employment Judge or tribunal shall ' [s]o far as it appears appropriate ..., seek to avoid formality in his or its proceedings and shall not be bound by any enactment or rule of law relating to the admissibility of evidence in proceedings before the courts'.[200] This means that the hearsay rule of evidence, for example, does not apply. Moreover, the Employment Judge or tribunal 'shall make such enquiries of persons appearing before him or it and witnesses as he or it considers appropriate and shall otherwise conduct the hearing in such manner as he or it considers most appropriate for the clarification of the issues and generally for the just handling of the proceedings'.[201]

Despite the emphasis on informality, appearing at an employment tribunal is likely to be a stressful experience for the non-represented litigant, particularly in the light of the technical nature of much of the contemporary law. As we indicated earlier, parties to tribunal hearings can be represented by the person of their choice. A survey of tribunal cases between February 2007 and the end of January 2008 found that 73% of employers were represented at a full tribunal hearing compared with 34% of claimants. Despite the lack of legal aid, in cases where parties were represented in 60% of cases this took the form of legal representation.[202]

Reasons must be given for all tribunal judgments.[203] These need only be given orally unless a party requests written reasons,[204] or if written reasons are requested by the EAT.[205] Written reasons must contain the issues the tribunal or Employment Judge identified as being relevant to the claim; if some identified issues were not determined, what these were and why they were not determined; findings of fact; a concise statement of the applicable law; how the relevant findings and applicable law have been applied to determine the issues; and where there is provision for compensation or other payment, how this was calculated.[206] Normally a party who wishes to lodge an appeal with the EAT must do so within 42 days of the date on which written reasons were sent to the parties or, where none were requested and written reasons were not reserved, 42 days from the date on which the written record of the judgment was sent to the parties.[207] We consider the implications of this course further below.

---

[199] Boon *et al*, 2011.

[200] SI 2004/1861, Sch 1, r 14(2).

[201] SI 2004/1861, Sch 1, r 14(3).

[202] M Peters *et al*, 2010: ch 5. See Latreille *et al*, 2005, for the impact of lawyer representatives on the stage of resolution of claims and the financial compensation paid in tribunal applications.

[203] SI 2004/1861, Sch 1, r 30(1).

[204] This must be done orally at the hearing, if judgment is issued there, or in writing within 14 days of the judgment being sent to the parties: SI 2004/1861, Sch 1, r 30(3), (5).

[205] SI 2004/1861, Sch 1, r 30(3).

[206] SI 2004/1981, Sch 1, r 30(6).

[207] The Employment Appeal Tribunal Rules 1993, SI 1993/2854, as amended r 3(3). The EAT judge has a discretion to extend the time limit: *Jurkowska v HLMAD Ltd* [2008] IRLR 430.

Employment Appeal Tribunal (EAT)

2.19   Appeals from employment tribunals on points of law are heard by the EAT.[208] The EAT was established by the Employment Protection Act 1975[209] and replaced the National Industrial Relations Court (NIRC) created by the Industrial Relations Act 1971. It also hears appeals from decisions of the Certification Officer relating to trade union matters and from the CAC on information and consultation, again on points of law. The EAT has the same powers as the High Court with regard to the attendance and examination of witnesses, production and inspection of documents and other matters incidental to its jurisdiction. In disposing of an appeal the EAT may either determine the issue itself or remit the case to the same or a differently-constituted employment tribunal to be decided in the light of its ruling on the law.

The EAT has premises in London although it can also sit elsewhere.[210] Like the employment tribunals it has a tripartite composition, consisting of a judge and non-lawyer members who have special knowledge or experience of industrial relations, either as representatives of employers or of workers.[211] At the time of writing an appeal is usually heard by a judge and two lay members[212] although the judge normally sits alone to deal with interim matters and to hear an appeal where the original decision was made by an Employment Judge without lay members. The Coalition Government has recently announced that the default constitution of the EAT will be the judge alone in all cases unless he or she directs that members should sit.[213] This radical departure from the tripartite principle was justified on grounds of cost.[214] In view of research which found that a majority of EAT judges considered that lay members add value in unfair dismissal and discrimination cases[215] it will be interesting to monitor how often they are asked to sit under the new regime.

In contrast to the position with employment tribunals, legal aid is available for EAT hearings, although the parties may still have non-lawyer representation. As in the case of employment tribunals costs are not generally awarded for EAT proceedings, but the court has power to award them if it considers that the proceedings were unnecessary, improper, vexatious or misconceived or that that there has been unreasonable delay or other unreasonable conduct of proceedings by a party.[216] Since 2004, it may also make costs orders in other specified situations (for non-compliance with an order, for example) and can make wasted costs orders against representatives,

---

[208] See para 2.16 for the 'non-employment' jurisdiction of employment tribunals.

[209] See now ETA 1996, s 20 *et seq.*

[210] The EAT has jurisdiction to hear appeals from employment tribunals in Scotland, as well as England and Wales, and tribunals in England are bound by decisions of a Scottish division: see Morison P in *Davidson v City Electrical Factors Ltd* [1998] IRLR 435.

[211] ETA 1996, s 22.

[212] Unless the parties otherwise consent there should be an equal number of employer and worker representatives on any hearing. Exceptionally, the judge may sit with four lay members: see, for example, *GCSF v Certification Officer* [1993] IRLR 260. See ETA 1996, Part II for the provisions as to the membership, sittings, proceedings and powers of the EAT. The EAT's procedure is governed by Rules (Employment Appeal Tribunal Rules 1993, SI 1993/2854, as amended) and Practice Directions. Although appeals are confined to questions of law the lay members can outvote the judge; in practice, this very rarely happens.

[213] BIS, *Resolving Workplace Disputes: Government response to the consultation*, November 2011, para 119. Provision for this is made by the Enterprise and Regulatory Reform Bill. See Corby and Latreille, 2012.

[214] Above. Lay members were estimated to cost around £300,000 per year.

[215] Corby and Latreille, 2011: p 20 *et seq*

[216] On costs in the EAT, see EAT Rules 1993, SI 1993/2854, rules 34 and 34A–34D, inserted by SI 2004/2526.

subject in all cases to a discretion to consider a party's or a representative's ability to pay. There is also now provision for costs to be awarded in favour of a litigant in person.

In 2010-11, 2,048 appeals were made to the EAT but only 363 reached a full hearing, the remainder having been filtered out by the EAT at a preliminary stage or withdrawn. Of those 363, 91 were allowed and 103 were allowed and remitted to the same or another tribunal.[217] All appeals to the EAT are sifted by a judge (or by the registrar with an appeal to a judge) to determine the most effective management of the case.[218] On the sift the judge has four options: an order for a stay (with a final date by which the papers must be restored for further consideration); a strike out if the notice of appeal or any of the grounds in it discloses no reasonable grounds for bringing the appeal, is an abuse of process, or is otherwise likely to obstruct the just disposal of the proceedings;[219] to send the appeal to a Full Hearing; or to list the appeal for a Preliminary Hearing, to be used in cases 'about which, on the sift, a judge feels genuine doubt as to their arguability' or perhaps cases which 'may, on being sorted out, disclose a nugget of argument'.[220] For appeals on points of law fresh evidence which was not before the tribunal will be admitted only in exceptional circumstances.[221]

The distinction between questions of law and of fact, crucial to whether an appeal will lie, is a notoriously difficult one to apply. To succeed in an appeal on a point of law an appellant must establish that the tribunal misdirected itself in law, or misunderstood the law, or misapplied the law; or that there was no evidence to support a particular conclusion or finding of fact; or that the decision was 'perverse' in that it was one which no reasonable tribunal, directing itself properly on the law, could have reached, or alternatively, was one which was obviously wrong.[222] In practice, it will be very difficult to classify as 'perverse' a decision which did not fall within one of the previous two categories.[223]

These criteria do not, in many cases, lend very much assistance. It is clear that, on the one hand, construction of a statute will be a question of law. Conversely, where witnesses' accounts of events conflict, which version is preferred will be a question of fact. However, in many situations the position is much less clear-cut. When does the 'reasonableness' of an employer's action in dismissing an employee become a question of law, for example?[224] What of the definition of an 'employee' and the application of that definition to a given set of circumstances? As we shall see the answers to these questions have not always been consistent over time. On occasion the higher courts have made no secret of their desire to restrict appeals, sometimes in the guise of discouraging undue 'legalism' in employment matters. However, the effect of designating a matter a question of fact is that employment tribunals are then free to make their own decisions which

---

[217] HMCTS, *Employment Tribunals and EAT Statistics, 2010-11*, Tables 13-16.

[218] See now Practice Direction (Employment Appeal Tribunal Procedure) 2008, 9; M Burton, 2005.

[219] Within 28 days the appellant may submit a fresh notice of appeal for further consideration or request an oral hearing before a judge: see further *Haritaki v South East England Development Agency* [2008] IRLR 945.

[220] M Burton, 2005: p 277.

[221] *Jones v Governing Body of Burdett Coutts School* [1998] IRLR 521; *Leicestershire County Council v UNISON* [2006] IRLR 810.

[222] *British Telecommunications plc v Sheridan* [1990] IRLR 27, 30 (Lord Donaldson MR); *Melon v Hector Powe Ltd* [1980] IRLR 477, 479 (Lord Fraser); *Hereford and Worcester County Council v Neale* [1986] IRLR 168, 174 (May LJ); *Piggott Bros & Co Ltd v Jackson* [1991] IRLR 309, 312 (Lord Donaldson MR); *Watling v William Bird & Son (Contractors) Ltd* (1976) 11 ITR 70, 71.

[223] See *Yeboah v Crofton* [2002] IRLR 634.

[224] See *Fuller v London Borough of Brent* [2011] IRLR414, CA.

may be at variance with those of others; that different tribunals have reached differing conclusions on the same or similar facts does not necessarily mean that one of them has made an error of law. When such decisions concern an issue fundamental to an individual's access to the right in question, such as, for many jurisdictions, the definitions of 'employee' and, for the purposes of unfair dismissal, of 'industrial action', this may have very serious consequences.[225]

Reforming the tribunal system

2.20   In 1994 the Employment Department published proposals for reform of the tribunal system 'with a view to identifying any changes which would help … to cope with an increasing volume and complexity of cases with reduced delays, while containing demands on public expenditure'.[226] It pointed to the pressures on the system resulting from the increased workload of tribunals, which had more than doubled from 34,697 applications in 1989–1990 to 71,661 in 1993–1994[227] (figures which now seem modest compared with the 218,100 in 2010–2011 described in para 2.16 above). The Conservative Government was removed from office before its draft Bill could be enacted; reforms were eventually introduced by the Labour Government in the shape of ERDRA 1998 and EA 2002 and amendments to the rules of procedure governing tribunals, although the major reforms introduced by EA 2002 were repealed by EA 2008 and replaced by further changes. The Coalition Government, in turn, has announced additional reforms which we outline below.

These reforms have had a variety of aims which space does not permit us to discuss in full. Here, we focus on the primary policy aim; that of reducing the number of cases going to tribunals by encouraging parties to resolve disputes by alternative means. ERDRA 1998 began this process.[228] First, the Act empowered ACAS to prepare a scheme, for approval by the Secretary of State, for the resolution of unfair dismissal disputes by arbitration.[229] After some delay, this scheme came into effect in May 2001.[230] ACAS appoints the arbitrator from a panel of individuals chosen for their practical knowledge and experience of workplace discipline and dismissal. Recourse to arbitration is voluntary but precludes recourse to an employment tribunal on the matter,[231] and

---

[225] For views of the successive Presidents of the EAT as to its role see Phillips, 1978; Browne-Wilkinson, 1982; Waite, 1986; Popplewell, 1987; Sir John Wood, 1990.

[226] See *Resolving Employment Rights Disputes – Options for Reform*, Employment Department, Cm 2707, 1994: para 1.1. For a commentary on these proposals, see Cockburn, 1995. For earlier recommendations as to how the system could be reformed, see Justice, 1987.

[227] *Resolving Employment Rights Disputes – Options for Reform*, Employment Department, Cm 2707, 1994: table 3.1. This was attributed partly to an expansion in tribunals' jurisdiction.

[228] For an overview of ERDRA 1998, which also contained provisions relating to tribunal procedures and staffing issues, see R Lewis. 1998; see also MacMillan, 1999.

[229] On unfair dismissal generally see ch 5. For the case in support of arbitration in this context see R Lewis and J Clark, 1993; see also J Clark, 1999. There is provision for this scheme to be extended to other statutory rights by statutory instrument approved by a resolution of both Houses of Parliament, and in April 2003 it was extended to cover claims under the flexible working legislation.

[230] For the principles of the arbitration scheme, see SI 2004/753, revoking and replacing SI 2001/1185. ACAS has also produced guidance on the operation of the scheme. See Earnshaw and Hardy, 2001.

[231] Entry to the scheme may be through a settlement reached with the assistance of an ACAS conciliation officer, or through a valid 'compromise agreement': see para 2.17. The agreement must be accompanied by a specified 'Waiver Form'. In the event that different aspects of the same dispute (a claim for unpaid wages, for example) are being heard in the employment tribunal, the arbitrator may decide to postpone the arbitration proceedings pending the tribunal's determination.

the outcome is binding on the parties. The arbitration is confined to the question of whether the dismissal was fair or unfair, and the parties are required to confirm, as a condition of admission to the scheme, that there is no dispute between them on any jurisdictional issue, such as whether the worker is an 'employee' or was 'dismissed'. The procedures to be followed are intended to be non-legalistic and more informal than tribunals,[232] and as far as possible general principles of fairness and good conduct, rather than legal precedent, are expected to be followed. However the arbitrator may request the assistance of an ACAS-appointed legal adviser if a question of EU law or the HRA 1998 is relevant to the matter. The parties are expected to co-operate fully with the arbitration process, including complying without delay with any determination of the arbitrator on procedural or evidential matters such as the provision of documents or attendance of witnesses, and whilst the arbitrator has no power to compel compliance with these requirements, adverse inferences may be drawn from a failure to comply. The process is designed to achieve finality: there is no provision for appeal from the arbitrator's award on a point of law other than EU law and the application of the HRA 1998;[233] otherwise, awards may be challenged only on the grounds of substantive jurisdiction or specified forms of irregularity affecting the tribunal, the proceedings or the award which the court considers has caused or will cause substantial injustice to the claimant.[234] Arbitrations are conducted in private and awards are confidential to the parties, although ACAS may publish general summary information without identifying individual cases. Very little use has been made of the scheme; up to March 2008 a total of 60 cases had been accepted for resolution by this means[235] and ACAS Annual Reports no longer include this information. Other provisions in ERDRA 1998 designed to encourage alternative dispute resolution included extending the range of persons who may conclude 'compromise agreements', which we discussed in para 2.17, and provisions designed to encourage internal appeal procedures in unfair dismissal cases.

The reforms in ERDRA appeared modest in comparison with those introduced by EA 2002; the requirements for claimants in most cases to institute a statutory grievance procedure prior to presenting a tribunal claim and for employers to commence, and both parties to participate in, a statutory disciplinary and dismissal procedure in relation to 'direct' dismissal cases. The statutory grievance procedures (SGPs) themselves were complex: a 'standard' procedure applied in the majority of cases, a 'modified' procedure in limited circumstances, and there were exceptions to the requirement to follow either. The application (or otherwise) of an SGP also had implications for the time limit for presenting a claim to a tribunal. The consequences for an employee who failed to follow the applicable SGP were severe: he or she was debarred from presenting a complaint altogether if the initial step of the SGP had not been followed and a stated period had not expired, or, if the employee began proceedings prior to completion of the SGP and non-completion was (loosely speaking) his or her fault, reduction of any eventual award made by the tribunal by up to

[232] Notably, cross-examination of witnesses is prohibited. The parties may, if they choose, be represented by a person of their choice.

[233] Arbitration Act 1996, s 69, as modified by the ACAS Arbitration Scheme, above, para 164.

[234] Arbitration Act 1996, ss 67 and 68, as modified by the ACAS Arbitration Scheme, above, paras 162 and 163. Applications may be made to the High Court or the Central London County Court.

[235] *ACAS Annual Report and Resource Accounts 2007/08*, HC 696, 2008: p 35. Research published in 2004 showed that there was low awareness of the Scheme among employees, employers and representatives: see *The ACAS Arbitration Scheme: An evaluation of parties' views*, ACAS, 2004.

50% and (exceptional circumstances apart) a minimum of 10%. Awards could be increased by up to 50% (with a minimum of 10%) if non-completion was the employer's fault.[236]

The strength of the Labour Government's case for these reforms, and the specific measures introduced, were highly controversial.[237] The provisions governing the SGPs themselves generated substantial litigation. The Labour Government instituted a review of the new procedures which concluded that they carried 'an unnecessarily high administrative burden for both employers and employees and have had unintended negative consequences which outweigh their benefits'.[238] Rather than encouraging early resolution the procedures had led to the use of formal processes to deal with problems that could have been resolved informally, and the complexity of the procedures and penalties for non-compliance meant that both parties had tended to seek external advice at an earlier stage. The review recommended repeal of the procedures and their replacement by clear, simple non-prescriptive guidelines, although with a discretion for tribunals to take into account reasonableness of behaviour and procedure in making awards and costs orders. The Labour Government consulted on these recommendations and measures to take them forward.[239] Respondents to the consultation exercise generally favoured repeal of the procedures.[240] The majority also supported their replacement by new guidelines on resolving workplace disputes, and a mechanism to encourage parties to follow them, although some, including the Law Society and CBI, thought that incorporating guidelines in a statutory code which would be admissible in evidence would provide a sufficient incentive for compliance. The Labour Government concluded that basic principles should be enshrined in a statutory ACAS Code of Practice and that tribunals should have discretion to adjust awards by up to 25% in the event of non-compliance with the Code, but that there should be no impact on costs in order to avoid a disproportionate impact on employees and less well-informed employers and the risk that 'unscrupulous employers might use the threat of cost orders to intimidate employees into withdrawing' claims.[241] We discuss these provisions, which came into force on 6 April 2009, in para 2.21 below.

In November 2011 the Coalition Government announced its intention to require claimants to submit the details of any potential claim to ACAS prior to making a tribunal claim; they will then be offered the opportunity of early conciliation, although either party will be free to reject this offer.[242] The Government also announced that the former President of the EAT, Underhill J, would undertake a 'fundamental review' of the procedural rules governing tribunals, although some reforms described in paras 2.16 *et seq* above (including increased limits for deposits and costs orders and extension to situations when Employment Judges and judges in the EAT may sit alone) would take effect more quickly. A provision for employment tribunals to be able to levy financial penalties, payable to the Exchequer, of between £100 and £5,000, depending on the total

---

[236] These procedures were analysed in greater detail in paras 2.21–2.26 of the fourth edition of this work.

[237] See generally Hepple and Morris, 2002; *Routes to Resolution*, DTI, 2001; G Morris, 2005; Pollert, 2005.

[238] *Better Dispute Resolution: A Review of Employment Dispute Resolution in Great Britain* (the 'Gibbons Review'), DTI, March 2007: p 8.

[239] *Success at Work: Resolving Disputes in the Workplace: a Consultation*, DTI, March 2007.

[240] *Resolving Disputes in the Workplace Consultation: Government Response*, BERR, May 2008.

[241] Above, para 2.40.

[242] BIS, *Resolving Workplace Disputes: Government response to the consultation*, November 2011, paras 52-70. Provision for this is made in the Enterprise and Regulatory Reform Bill. Since April 2009 ACAS has been empowered to offer a voluntary pre-claim conciliation service which, in 2010-11, dealt with around 16,700 jurisdictional claims, of which nearly 8,000 were resolved: ACAS Annual Report 2010-11: p 41.

amount awarded to the claimant, on employers found to have breached employment rights will also be introduced.[243] Most radically, the Government announced early in 2011 that fees would be introduced to use tribunals and the EAT 'as part of the wider reforms to support and encourage early resolution of workplace disputes and in order to transfer some of the cost burden from the taxpayer to the users of the system'.[244] At the time of writing the Government is consulting on the structure of the fee-charging regime, which is intended to take effect in either 2013 or 2014 depending on which option is adopted. These changes, taken together, will transform access to, and the operation of, employment tribunals.[245]

Grievance procedures and the consequences of failure to follow them

2.21   In accordance with the policy decisions discussed above, EA 2008 repealed the statutory dispute resolution procedures introduced by EA 2002 and replaced them with provision for tribunals to adjust awards in the event of non-compliance with a 'relevant Code of Practice', defined as a Code issued under Chapter III of TULRCA 1992 which 'relates exclusively or primarily to procedure for the resolution of disputes'.[246] Of the codes issued under Chapter III, this definition currently applies to the ACAS Code of Practice on Disciplinary and Grievance Procedures, a revised version of which came into force on 6 April 2009.

The legislation applies the provision for adjustment to a wide range of specified jurisdictions. These include claims about equal pay or discrimination; detriment in relation to union membership or activities, union recognition rights, matters specified in ERA 1996, s 48 or in relation to the national minimum wage; unauthorised deductions from pay; unfair dismissal and redundancy payments; claims of breach of contract on termination of employment; and claims under the WTR 1998.[247] If an *employee* brings a claim in any of these areas and it appears to the tribunal that the claim concerns a matter to which such a Code of Practice applies; that the employee failed to comply with the Code in relation to that matter; and that failure was unreasonable the tribunal *may*, if it considers it just and equitable in all the circumstances to do so, reduce any award it makes to the employee by no more than 25%. There are equivalent provisions permitting the increase of an award by a maximum of 25% if the employer unreasonably fails to comply with the Code.[248] The Code itself excludes dismissals due to redundancy and non-renewal of fixed-term contracts on their expiry from its scope.[249]

---

[243] BIS, above, paras 132-146.Provision for this is made in the Enterprise and Regulatory Reform Bill where a breach of rights has 'one or more aggravating features'.

[244] Ministry of Justice, *Charging Fees in Employment Tribunals and the EAT*, CP 22/2011, 14 December 2011, p 5.

[245] For a robust judicial defence of employment tribunals, see *Gayle v Sandwell and West Birmingham Hospitals NHS Trust* [2011] IRLR 810, CA, Mummery LJ at [9]-[22].

[246] EA 2008, ss 1, 3, inserting TULRCA 1992, s 207A.

[247] See TULRCA 1992, Sch A2, inserted by EA 2008, s 3. The Secretary of State may amend Sch A2 by statutory instrument, subject to approval by each House of Parliament: TULRCA 1992, s 207A(6)-(9).

[248] TULRCA 1992, s 207A(1)-(4).

[249] Code of Practice, para 1.

The provisions of the Code of Practice relating to grievances are relatively brief.[250] Grievances are defined as 'concerns, problems or complaints that employees raise with their employers'.[251] The Code states that rules and procedures should be developed to deal with grievances; these should be set out in writing; and be specific and clear. It recommends that employees and, where appropriate, their representatives should be involved in the development of such rules and procedures and that employees and managers should be helped to understand what the rules and procedures are, where they can be found and how they are to be used.[252] It states that where some form of action is needed, what action is reasonable or justified 'will depend on all the circumstances of the particular case. Employment tribunals will take the size and resources of an employer into account when deciding on relevant cases and it may sometimes not be practicable for all employers to take all of the steps set out in this Code'.[253] However, the need for prompt and consistent action by both employees and employers, and provision for employees to appeal against formal decisions, are emphasised as integral to the generally-applicable principles of fairness.[254] The Code then specifies the 'keys' to handling grievances. If it is not possible to resolve a grievance informally employees should raise the matter formally and 'without unreasonable delay' with a manager who is not the subject of the grievance. This should be done in writing and should set out the nature of the grievance.[255] Employers should arrange for a formal meeting to be held 'without unreasonable delay' after a grievance is received and employers, employees and their companions should make every effort to attend.[256] Employees should be allowed to explain their grievance and how they think it should be resolved. Consideration should be given to adjourning the meeting for any investigation that may be necessary.[257] Following the meeting, the employer should communicate to the

---

[250] See paras 5.125 *et seq* below for the provisions relating to discipline. Unlike the repealed procedure, the Code does not expressly distinguish between 'direct' dismissal, which would be subject to the provisions on discipline, and constructive dismissal, which would seem to require compliance with the grievance provisions of the Code. As we discuss in para 5.68, the line between the two forms of dismissal is not necessarily clear-cut but the need for failure to comply with the Code to be 'unreasonable' offers a safeguard when a party's view of events was explicable. For ACAS's comments on the final version of the Code of Practice, see *Discipline and Grievance Code of Practice – Consultation Outcome*, 2008. Further advice and guidance on dealing with grievances and sample procedures, is contained in *Discipline and grievances at work: the ACAS Guide*, 2009. Unlike the Code, employment tribunals are not required to have regard to this. The definition of 'grievance' in the Code of Practice is wider than that in the repealed provisions ('a complaint by an employee about action which the employer has taken or is contemplating against him': EADRR 2004, reg 2). The 'trigger' event which determined whether the new or the repealed regime applied was the date of the action about which the employee complains. In the case of continuing acts, such as a series of alleged breaches of the implied term of trust and confidence in support of an allegation of constructive dismissal (see para 5.70 below), there may be scope for argument as to the date the 'trigger' event occurred.

[251] Code of Practice, para 1.

[252] Code of Practice, para 2.

[253] Code of Practice, para 3.

[254] Code of Practice, para 4.

[255] Code of Practice, para 31.

[256] Paras 34-37 of the Code of Practice refers to the statutory right of workers under ERelA 1999 to be accompanied at a grievance meeting which deals with a complaint about a duty owed by the employer to the worker, which we discuss in para 5.121 *et seq* below. Curiously, the Code makes no reference to the right of a worker to postpone the hearing if the chosen companion is not available at the time specified by the employer. The ACAS Council was conscious that, by putting guidance on accompaniment in the Code, there was a possibility of employers facing the 'double jeopardy' of the specific penalty provided in ERelA 1999 and an adjustment of the employee's award. It concluded that employment tribunals were sufficiently experienced to take a 'commonsense approach' so as to avoid this being an issue in practice: *Discipline and Grievance Code of Practice – Consultation Outcome*, 2008, para 22.

[257] Code of Practice, paras 32-33.

employee in writing its decision on what action, if any, to take 'without unreasonable delay' and, where appropriate, should set out what action the employer intends to take to resolve the grievance. The employee should be informed that he or she can appeal if not content with the action taken.[258] Employees should be able to appeal if they feel that their grievance has not been satisfactorily resolved and should let the employer know the grounds for their appeal in writing 'without unreasonable delay'. Appeals should be heard 'without unreasonable delay' and at a time and place which should be notified to the employee in advance.[259] The appeal should be dealt with impartially and wherever possible by a manager who has not previously been involved in the case. The outcome of the appeal should be communicated to the employee in writing 'without unreasonable delay'.[260] The Code concludes by dealing with two areas that were specifically addressed in the pre-existing procedures. First, it states that where an employee raises a grievance during a disciplinary process, that process may be temporarily suspended in order to deal with the grievance, although where the two are related it may be appropriate to deal with both issues concurrently.[261] Second, collective grievances, defined as those raised on behalf of two or more employees by a representative or a recognised trade union or other appropriate workplace representative, are excluded from the Code.[262]

It remains to be seen whether these provisions are more successful than their predecessors in encouraging disputes to be resolved at workplace level.[263] It also remains to be seen how much additional litigation they will generate; at the time of writing the extent to which the power to adjust awards is being used is not known. There is obvious potential for factual disputes as to whether the Code itself has been complied with; whether a step has been taken or an appeal heard 'without unreasonable delay', for example. There may also be disputes about whether an acknowledged or proven failure to comply was 'unreasonable'. Unlike the repealed procedures (see para 2.20 above), the tribunal is not obliged to make any adjustment to an award; it is a matter of discretion. However this does not mean that the scope for appeal against its decision will be removed. Tribunals will need, if written reasons are requested, to indicate the reasons for their conclusion that the Code was or was not complied with and this may involve spelling out the interpretation placed on a particular provision within it. Moreover, like the repealed procedures, the provision for adjustment of awards applies only to employees, not the wider category of 'workers'.[264] In the case of claims which may be brought by workers as well as 'employees', such as discrimination claims, it may be necessary, if the claim is upheld,

---

[258] Code of Practice, para 38.

[259] Again, reference is made to the statutory right to be accompanied: see n 256 above.

[260] Code of Practice, paras 39–43. The repealed procedures stated that '[e]ach step and action under the procedure must be taken without unreasonable delay': EA 2002, Sch 2, para 12. In *Selvarajan v Wilmot* [2008] IRLR 824, the Court of Appeal held (contrary to a series of EAT decisions) that this was a procedural standard to be observed in the process rather than a procedural step. Although the current legislation does not make the distinction between completion of, and non-compliance with, procedure, this case may have influenced the decision by ACAS to insert 'without unreasonable delay' specifically into each step and we have therefore replicated the wording in our account.

[261] Code of Practice, para 44.

[262] Code of Practice, para 45.

[263] The foreword to the Code of Practice states that where employers and employees cannot resolve their disputes they should consider using mediation. However this was deliberately omitted from the Code itself to avoid the risk that failure to use mediation could attract a financial penalty. The same concern prompted the reference to using informal, prior to formal, action to be confined to the foreword: *Discipline and Grievance Code of Practice – Consultation Outcome*, 2008, paras 9, 10.

[264] On the distinction between employees and workers, see para 3.33

to determine whether the worker is an 'employee' in order to ascertain whether consideration should be given to adjusting the award (which, in the case of discrimination claims which are not subject to any statutory limit, could involve a substantial sum). This has the potential to lengthen proceedings considerably and to afford an additional potential ground of appeal against an award. In the case of the repealed procedures the EAT in England and Wales took the view that the size of the award itself should not be subject to appeal provided that there were sufficient reasons why a reasonable tribunal might have chosen the percentage which it did.[265] This case law is of continuing relevance. The EAT held that it was 'good practice' for the tribunal to specify the factors influencing its decision.[266] It also held that although in 'routine cases' the tribunal would arrive at the percentage by which an award should be adjusted without regard to the initial size of the award, this did not preclude the tribunal taking size into account where the tribunal considered it just and equitable provided that it explained that it was so doing.[267]

We criticised the repealed procedures on the ground that an employee's rights were in danger of being prejudiced by ignorance of what the legislation obliges him or her to do. The Code urges employers to ensure that employees understand the grievance procedures and where they are located and it is likely to be argued that an employee's failure to comply with the Code was not 'unreasonable' if he or she was not informed about what the Code requires. Nevertheless, it would be desirable if there were greater incentives to close the 'information gap'. Although employers are obliged to include information about grievance (and disciplinary) procedures in the written statement of employment terms, this statement need not be issued until two months after the commencement of employment and there is no requirement for employees to be notified specifically of the consequences of not abiding by the Code (as opposed to any other elements of the procedure), either in the written statement or elsewhere.[268] The financial consequences if an employer fails to comply with its minimal statutory obligations are derisory,[269] particularly when contrasted with the potential consequences for employees if they do not comply with the Code. Moreover, even though the Code requires employees to be informed that they can appeal against an employer's decision following an initial meeting, there is no requirement to indicate that a failure to do so may prejudice their rights. It is to be hoped that in this respect, as in others, tribunals will be astute to discover whether an employee's failure to comply with the Code was based on ignorance and, if so, be slow to find that this failure was 'unreasonable'.

---

[265] *CEX Ltd v Mark Lewis* UKEAT/0013/07/DA, [49]; *Home Office v Khan and King* UKEAT/0257/07/CEA, [39],[40]; cf the decisions of the EAT in Scotland in *Aptuit (Edinburgh) Ltd v Kennedy* UKEATS/0057/06 and *McKindless Group v McLaughlin* [2008] IRLR 678. See also *Wardle v Credit Agricole* [2011] IRLR 819, CA.

[266] *Home Office v Khan and King*, above, at [40].

[267] *Abbey National v Chagger* [2009] IRLR 86, at [135].

[268] ERA 1996, s 1, 3; see further para 4.14 *et seq.*

[269] Between two and four weeks' pay can be awarded for failure to provide an initial statement of particulars or to notify the employee of changes, but only where the employee has been successful in relation to other specified proceedings: EA 2002, s 38, Sch 5. A week's pay is subject to the statutory maximum in ERA 1996, s 227, which as of 1 February 2012 and at the time of writing is £430. TULRCA 1992, s 207A, inserted by EA 2008, s 3, states that where an award is to be adjusted both under s 207A and under EA 2002, s 38, the adjustment under s 207A should be made first.

GOVERNMENTAL INSTITUTIONS RELEVANT TO LABOUR LAW

2.22   In this section we outline the activities of a range of institutions which, although funded by government, operate at a day-to-day level independently from it. They are a heterogeneous collection. The Advisory, Conciliation and Arbitration Service (ACAS) has a broad range of functions across the field of industrial relations. The Central Arbitration Committee (CAC) has an adjudicatory jurisdiction in the field of collective labour law, including statutory recognition and information and consultation, and can also serve as a voluntary arbitral body. The Certification Officer has a wide range of functions in relation to trade unions. Finally, the Equality and Human Rights Commission (EHRC) has extensive powers and duties in relation to equality legislation and human rights. As in the case of statutory bodies generally the decisions of the majority of these bodies are subject to judicial review, a remedy that placed considerable constraints on some investigatory activities of the Equal Opportunities Commission and Commission for Racial Equality (now dissolved and absorbed into the EHRC)[270] and has also been significant in relation to the decisions of the CAC. Decisions of the Certification Officer may be appealed against in the EAT, as may those of the CAC in relation to information and consultation.

The Advisory, Conciliation and Arbitration Service (ACAS)

2.23   State involvement in the processes of conciliation and arbitration dates back to the Conciliation Act 1896.[271] However, for many decades this function was performed by the government department charged with responsibility for employment matters. By the time the Labour Party came into office in 1974 'the conciliation and arbitration services of the Department [of Employment] had become tainted, in the eyes of the labour movement, by the Department's involvement first with prices and incomes policy and then with the operation of the Industrial Relations Act'.[272] There was perceived to be an urgent need to establish an independent body for these purposes and ACAS was set up soon after the Government took office and placed on a statutory basis by the Employment Protection Act 1975.[273] The Service is directed by a tripartite council consisting of a chairman and nine 'ordinary' members, three nominated by the TUC, three by the CBI and three independent members (although it is also open to the Secretary of State to appoint a further two ordinary members and up to three deputy chairmen).[274] In 2010– 2011 it employed an average staff of 859.[275] Its independence from ministerial direction as to the

---

[270] The scope for judicial review of the EHRC's investigatory activities may be less, however: see O'Cinneide, 2007: pp 147–155.

[271] For a summary of the background to the performance of these functions before the establishment of ACAS see Sir John Wood, 1992; Mumford, 1996.

[272] Freedland, 1992: p 282.

[273] It was initially established on a non-statutory basis in September 1974. For the argument that the removal of the conciliation and arbitration function from the Department of Employment had major implications for its perception of future policy formation see Freedland, 1992. See Towers and Brown, 2000 for reflections on the first 25 years of ACAS, and Sisson and Taylor, 2006 for a subsequent review.

[274] TULRCA 1992, s 248.

[275] Annual Report 2010–2011: p 86. This number does not take account of staff who work in the Certification Office or CAC, who are also employed by ACAS.

performance of its functions is specifically enshrined in statute[276] although it submits an annual report to the Secretary of State on its activities each year.[277] It is charged with the general duty of promoting 'the improvement of industrial relations'.[278] Originally its statutory remit also included the extension, development and, where necessary, reform of collective bargaining machinery. However, this aspect of its duties was removed by TURERA 1993, an important symbol of the abandonment of support for collective bargaining by the Conservative Government. Despite a more hospitable environment for collective bargaining under its Labour successor, the specific duty was not reinstated, but activities relating to collective bargaining are almost certainly permissible under its general duty.[279]

Although the industrial relations climate in which ACAS operates has altered radically since its inception it has always worked within a voluntary framework; there is no compulsion on the industrial relations actors to use its services. As the list which follows indicates, the functions it performs range widely.

(i) Conciliation in individual cases

2.24   The process of conciliation involves assisting the parties to clarify their points of disagreement and attempting to promote a settlement, but the terms of any settlement remain the responsibility of the parties. As we saw in para 2.17 the conciliation stage is provided for by statute in relation to the majority of types of claim which are presented to employment tribunals. The Secretary of employment tribunals forwards to ACAS a copy of the claim form, response and any other relevant documents.[280] It will then be for an ACAS conciliation officer to contact the parties to see whether a conciliated settlement is possible, either at the request of one of the parties or on his or her own initiative.[281] Either party can decline to co-operate with the conciliation process. All discussions with the conciliation officer are confidential and nothing said by or to him or her is admissible if the process fails and the matter goes forward to a hearing. This service is free of charge to the parties.[282] As we indicated in para 2.20 above, since April 2009 ACAS has been empowered to offer a voluntary pre-claim conciliation service and the Coalition Government has announced the intention to require that details of all claims are submitted to ACAS for early conciliation prior to being made to a tribunal, although either party will be free to reject this option.

As we saw in para 2.16, a high proportion of cases are either settled or withdrawn at the conciliation stage.[283] There are considerable savings to the Exchequer if a claim is dealt with in this way.[284] Additional benefits of this form of resolution are avoidance of the stress of a tribunal

---

[276] TULRCA 1992, s 247(3).

[277] TULRCA 1992, s 253(1). These reports are published and constitute a useful source of information for researchers.

[278] TULRCA 1992, s 209.

[279] Hepple, 2000a: p 153.

[280] SI 2004/1861, Sch 1, para 21.

[281] ETA 1996, s 18(2).

[282] Curiously the provision of individual conciliation does not fall within ACAS's statutory functions. This is material in that the power to direct it to charge for its statutory functions to which we refer below does not extend to this area.

[283] See generally L Dickens, 2000; Dix, 2000 and ACAS Annual Reports.

[284] In 2010/11 the cost of a successfully cleared individual conciliation case was £238: *ACAS Annual Report 2010–2011*: p 37.

hearing, savings to the parties, confidentiality, ability of the parties to determine the terms of settlement, and benefits in dismissal cases of speedy re-employment if this can be arranged. It may also lead to shortcomings in the employer's procedures or communications systems being addressed, so having wider implications than the instant claim.[285] However, the fact that ACAS does not give advice on the merits of proposed settlements has led to concerns being voiced that the relative inequalities of the parties may be perpetuated by this process.[286] In 1987 the Justice report proposed that advice agencies such as Citizens' Advice Bureaux and Law Centres should be funded to provide advice to applicants at the conciliation stage but this has not been followed up.[287] As the level of applications to tribunals has increased so has the workload of ACAS; in 2010-11 nearly 75,000 cases were received for conciliation from the employment tribunals (excluding multiple equal pay cases in local authorities and the NHS, which also placed significant demands on ACAS resources).[288] As we discuss in para 2.20, only a very modest number of cases have so far been received under the ACAS Arbitration Scheme for unfair dismissal claims and flexible working.

(ii) Conciliation in collective disputes

2.25 ACAS provides facilities for settling existing or apprehended 'trade disputes'[289] by conciliation, either at the request of one of the parties or on its own initiative.[290] However, regardless of how the process starts it remains entirely voluntary and any of the parties is free to withdraw at any stage. As in the area of individual disputes ACAS, when acting as conciliator, does not recommend the terms of settlement. Before offering its services ACAS must have regard to the desirability of encouraging the parties to use their agreed procedures for the negotiation or settlement of disputes, although reference to ACAS may be incorporated in the procedural terms of collective agreements. Research published in 2000 showed that an annual average of 1,300 requests for collective conciliation had been made in recent years, around 40% consisting of joint requests by management and trade unions, and that close to 90% of completed cases resulted in a settlement or progress towards a settlement.[291] In 2010–2011, 1,054 requests for assistance were received, in 91% of which ACAS resolved matters or helped the parties move towards a resolution.[292] Sir John Wood offers an interesting comparison between the 'success rates' of collective and individual conciliation in this respect. 'The parties seeking collective conciliation realise that the alternative is costly strife, whereas the individual still has the opportunity to shun conciliation and seek his remedy before the tribunal.'[293]

---

[285] *ACAS Annual Report 2003–2004*; p 22.

[286] See L Dickens *et al*, 1985: p 180; L Dickens, 2000: pp 75–78.

[287] Justice, 1987: para 2.28.

[288] *ACAS Annual Report 2010–2011*: p 14.

[289] These are defined in TULRCA 1992, s 218 and have a wider meaning than in the context of the industrial action immunities: see s 244(1), analysed in para 11.25 *et seq* below.

[290] TULRCA 1992, s 210. See generally Dix and Oxenbridge, 2004.

[291] J Goodman, 2000: pp 37–47. For a detailed analysis of collective conciliation, see Dawe and Neathey, 2008.

[292] *ACAS Annual Report 2010–2011*: p 12.

[293] Sir John Wood, 1992: p 250.

(iii) References to mediation and arbitration in collective disputes

2.26   If agreed procedures have been exhausted and conciliation has failed or seems unlikely to succeed, ACAS may appoint a mediator to attempt to settle the dispute. However, this can be done only at the request of one or more of the parties and they must all consent to this. Mediation differs from conciliation in that a mediator may make positive recommendations, although the parties themselves retain the responsibility to resolve the details of any settlement. ACAS considers that this process is most suited to dealing with complex issues 'where the parties have to weigh for themselves the impact of the options that may be available'.[294] In practice it is used much less commonly than arbitration,[295] which may be conducted provided that the same conditions are met (as with conciliation this may be incorporated as the final stage of the parties' own procedures). The arbitration may be conducted by a person appointed by ACAS, although independent of the service, or by the CAC.[296] The parties agree on the form of arbitration and the arbitrator's terms of reference. Although the award is not legally binding ACAS makes it clear in advance to the parties that there is a long-established principle that both sides must accept the arbitrator's decision. The cost of conducting the arbitration is borne by ACAS but the parties pay their own expenses and there is no power to award the payment of costs against an 'unsuccessful' party. For that reason legal representation is rare. The award may be published if ACAS so decides and all parties consent to this.[297]

The arbitration caseload has declined sharply from nearly 350 cases in 1979 to an average of below 200 in the early 1980s; in 2010–2011 there were 28 cases.[298] By far the most popular method of third party intervention in disputes is reference to a single arbitrator; in 2010–2011, all but one case was referred for settlement in this way.[299]

(iv) Advisory and information services

2.27   ACAS provides advice on a wide range of industrial relations matters to employers and their associations, workers and trade unions, either by telephone, letter or personal visit.[300] It has also developed a range of electronic resources.[301] In the year 2010–2011 ACAS received around 954,000 calls at its enquiry points;[302] conducted more than 3,500 advisory visits and in-depth phone calls; and helped 220 workplaces with joint working and partnership building.[303] All advice is given on an impartial and confidential basis. Until recently all aspects of this service, like

---

[294] Annual Report 1994: p 49.

[295] There were two requests for dispute mediation in 2010–2011 (one single mediation and one two-tier single mediation/arbitration): *ACAS Annual Report 2007–2008*: p 45.

[296] TULRCA 1992, s 212(1).

[297] TULRCA 1992, s 212(4)(b).

[298] *ACAS Annual Report 2010–2011*: p 45. There was also a two-tier mediation/arbitration case. During the period 1997–2000 the caseload averaged 55: J Goodman, 2000: pp 56–57. See generally Gennard, 2009. For an assessment of ACAS's arbitration work in a historical perspective, see Mumford, 1996.

[299] J Goodman, 2000: pp 56–57; *ACAS Annual Report 2010–2011*: p 45.

[300] TULRCA 1992, s 213.

[301] *ACAS Annual Report 2010–2011*: pp 21–25.

[302] There is a separate government-funded Pay and Work Rights Helpline for queries relating to the NMW, agricultural minimum wage, working time, gangmasters and employment agencies: see Rutherford and Achur, 2010.

[303] *ACAS Annual Report 2010–2011*: pp 19, 37 and 63.

other ACAS services, were free. Since TURERA 1993 it has been empowered to charge a fee for exercising its statutory functions, subject to directions from the Secretary of State, although the latter cannot direct this course without consulting ACAS.[304] ACAS now charges for some of its training activities and advisory publications.[305]

(v) Inquiry

2.28   ACAS has the statutory power, as it thinks fit, to hold inquiries on 'any question relating to industrial relations generally or in a particular industry or undertaking or part thereof'.[306] The findings may be published. This power appears not to have been used since 1983.[307]

(vi) Codes of practice

2.29   ACAS has a general power to issue codes of practice containing practical guidance to promote the improvement of industrial relations, subject to approval by the Secretary of State and Parliament.[308] As we indicated in para 2.4, these Codes are admissible in evidence before employment tribunals and the CAC but not (unlike those issued by the Secretary of State) in courts.[309] ACAS has issued three codes to date: on Disclosure of Information to Trade Unions for Collective Bargaining Purposes (revised in 1997); on Disciplinary and Grievance Procedures (revised in 2009); and on Time Off for Trade Union Duties and Activities (revised in 2010); ACAS has also issued non-statutory guides in a range of areas, including discipline and grievances at work, and a number of advisory booklets on particular matters such as the handling of redundancies.

(vii) Equal pay

2.30   ACAS has the responsibility of designating independent experts to report on claims for equal pay for work of equal value when required to do so by an employment tribunal. It maintains a list of such experts of which, as of March 2011, there were 25.[310]

---

[304] TULRCA 1992, s 251A.

[305] In 2010-11 ACAS traded services and publications brought in over £3.73 million of revenue: *ACAS Annual Report 2010–2011*: p 63.

[306] TULRCA 1992, s 214(1). See also ss 215–216 for provision for the Secretary of State to appoint a court of inquiry in relation to a particular dispute.

[307] Information supplied by ACAS. See Sir John Wood, 1992: pp 262–267 for the use which has been made historically of the inquiry process.

[308] TULRCA 1992, ss 199–202.

[309] TULRCA 1992, s 207(2).

[310] *ACAS Annual Report 2010–2001*: p 16.

(viii) Disclosure of information and information and consultation

2.31   ACAS has specific functions in relation to these procedures which we discuss in paras 9.24 and 9.50 below.

The Central Arbitration Committee

2.32   The Central Arbitration Committee (CAC) was established by the Employment Protection Act 1975 as a permanent and independent industrial relations arbitration body.[311] As such it constitutes a direct descendant to the Industrial Court which was established in 1919 to provide a national government-funded facility for this purpose. It is composed of a chairman, deputy chairmen, and other members appointed by the Secretary of State.[312] All are 'persons experienced in industrial relations', some of whom have experience as representatives of employers, some as representatives of workers.[313] The chairman is currently a High Court judge. The CAC is charged with operating the statutory recognition and derecognition procedures; adjudicating on complaints relating to a failure by employers to disclose information for collective bargaining purposes; and adjudicating on specified matters under TICER 1999, ICER 2004, ECSIER 2006,CCBMR 2007 and EPLLCEIGBR 2009 (provisions formerly contained in EPLLCR 2004.)[314] It can also serve as a voluntary arbitration body on a reference from ACAS, as described above,[315] but last performed this role in 1989.

In all areas of its jurisdiction the CAC seeks to adopt a flexible and problem-solving approach. On receiving a complaint in relation to a failure to disclose information, it is standard practice for the chairman or a deputy, together with an ACAS conciliation officer, to meet the parties and to attempt to encourage a joint, rather than an adversarial, approach to the problem in preference to 'passing judgment on them and leaving aside the question of their continuing relationship'.[316] It has had considerable success in this approach; from 1 February 1977, when the disclosure provisions came into force, until the end of 2011 the Committee had received 573 complaints of which only 13.26% resulted in a formal decision.[317] As Davies and Freedland have remarked, in this area of its jurisdiction the CAC has developed 'a genuinely novel approach to the process of adjudication which may serve as a model in any future proposals for reform'.[318] In performing its functions generally, the CAC is composed of the chairman, or a deputy, and such other members as the chairman may direct; there is also a discretion to call in one or

---

[311] See now TULRCA 1992, s 259. For a discussion of CAC activities up to 2001, see Rideout, 2002; for a later analysis see S Gouldstone and G Morris, 2006. See also the CAC Annual Reports.

[312] TULRCA 1992, s 260. Members are appointed by the Secretary of State after consultation with ACAS.

[313] TULRCA 1992, s 260(3). As of March 2011 there were 10 deputy chairmen and 49 employer and worker members: *CAC Annual Report 2010–2011*: p 4.

[314] See further ch 9. For the CAC's other jurisdictions during the period 1975-1980 (now abolished) see P Davies and M Freedland, 1993: pp 394–396.

[315] The parties may, subject to the agreement of the CAC, nominate a representative from the panel of members and these together with the independent chairman, will form the arbitration committee. Its procedures are entirely flexible, and there is a moral, but not a legal, obligation, to honour the award.

[316] Annual Report 1993: para 2.1.

[317] Information supplied by the CAC.

[318] P Davies and M Freedland, 1993: p 396.

more assessors to assist it.[319] For the purposes of the recognition and derecognition procedures, however, the CAC is required to consist only of a tripartite panel chaired by the chairman or a deputy chairman; a member whose experience is as a representative of employers; and a member whose experience is as a representative of workers.[320] Decisions are reached by a majority; if there is no majority, the chairman of the panel decides.[321] Subject to this, each panel is formally free to regulate its own procedure,[322] although in practice there is a measure of consistency between panels.[323] The CAC is generally required to consider evidence put to it by the union and employer when deciding particular questions, and each side has the opportunity to comment on the other's case and evidence material to it. An application must be supported by such documents as the CAC requires,[324] but beyond that there is no power to order documents to be disclosed. If a hearing is needed to decide a particular matter, it will be conducted in as informal a manner as is consistent with clarity and fairness; the parties may appoint representatives, but there is no obligation to use lawyers and no power to award costs. It is notable that once an application for recognition (and, in some cases, derecognition) has been accepted by the CAC, it is accorded the role both of conciliator and of adjudicator. However, in trying to help the parties the CAC may suggest that they seek assistance from ACAS, a course that may be preferable where a party wishes to communicate confidential information; while the CAC panel would maintain confidentiality at the conciliation stage, if the case goes to a hearing that information may need to be revealed to the other party to enable it to check or challenge it. The caseload of applications to the CAC under these procedures, and their outcomes, are discussed at para 9.18. At the time of writing there have been only a small number of applications under TICER 1999 and ICER 2004 and none under ECSIER 2006, CCBMR 2007, or EPLLCEIGBR 2009 (or its predecessor EPLLCR 2004).

The Certification Officer

2.33   The Certification Officer is an independent officer with statutory responsibility for an extensive range of functions relating to trade unions and employers' associations.[325] He or she is appointed by the Secretary of State after consultation with ACAS. The first Certification Officer was appointed in 1975 and took over the role previously performed by the former Registrar of Friendly Societies under earlier trade union legislation. The functions of the Certification Officer now include maintaining lists of unions and employers' associations and ensuring that they comply with their accounting obligations; determining whether unions meet the statutory test of 'independence'; dealing with complaints relating to trade union elections; ensuring observance of the procedures concerning trade union political funds; and supervising union mergers. In 1993 the Certification Officer was also granted controversial powers of investigation in relation to

---

[319] TULRCA 1992, s 263.
[320] TULRCA 1992, s 263A.
[321] TULRCA 1992, s 263A(5),(6).
[322] TULRCA 1992, s 263A(7).
[323] The procedures that panels can be expected to follow are detailed in *Statutory Recognition – A Guide for the Parties*, obtainable from the CAC.
[324] See TULRCA 1992, Sch A1, para 33, for example.
[325] TULRCA 1992, s 254; see further ch 10 and Cockburn, 2006; Lockwood, 2006.

unions' financial affairs. Prior to ERelA 1999 the Certification Officer's jurisdiction was confined to breaches of specified statutory obligations. However, as we discuss in para 10.5, it has now been extended to cover alleged breaches of union rules in specific areas, giving union members an alternative to seeking redress from the High Court.[326] The procedure for applying to the Certification Officer is relatively simple; details of the application are forwarded by the Office to the union for comment and any comments are then copied to the applicant for observation. The Certification Officer makes such inquiries as he or she thinks fit in relation to an application and is required to give the applicant and union an opportunity to present their case at a hearing. The Certification Office pays expenses by applicants and their witnesses in attending hearings, but does not pay legal costs. If the Certification Officer upholds an application, he or she must grant a declaration and, unless this is considered inappropriate, an 'enforcement order' which requires the union to take specified steps to remedy the declared failure and/or to abstain from specified acts in the future. Enforcement orders may be enforced as if they were orders of the court, so rendering the union liable for contempt in the event of non-compliance. Either party may appeal against a decision of the Certification Officer to the EAT.

The Equality and Human Rights Commission (EHRC)

2.34   The EHRC was established by the Equality Act 2006 and came into being on 1 October 2007. It absorbed the functions of the three previously-existing equality commissions (the Equal Opportunities Commission, Commission for Racial Equality and Disability Rights Commission) which were dissolved, and its role covers the full range of equality and human rights principles.[327] It has a 'general duty' at the time of writing to exercise its functions to encourage and support the development of a society in which people's ability to achieve their potential is not limited by prejudice or discrimination; there is respect for and protection of each individual's human rights; respect for the dignity and worth of each individual; each individual has an equal opportunity to participate in society; and there is mutual respect between groups based on understanding and valuing of diversity and on shared respect for equality and human rights.[328] It also has an extensive range of specific powers and duties.[329] The ECHR consists of up to 15 members (and no fewer than 10) appointed by the Secretary of State, one of whom is (or has been) a disabled person; in addition, two further Commissioners must respectively 'know about conditions' in Scotland and in Wales.[330] Further details of the activities of the EHRC are given in chapter 6.

---

[326] These avenues of complaint are now mutually exclusive. The Certification Officer's jurisdiction was extended following the abolition of the Commissioner for the Rights of Trade Union Members: see para 7.18.

[327] For an overview of the previous Commissions and background to the new Commission see Hepple, 2006 and O'Cinneide, 2007. See also Hepple, 2011: pp 145-154.

[328] Equality Act 2006, s 3. The Enterprise and Regulatory Reform Bill contains a provision repealing this section of the Act.

[329] See O'Cinneide, 2007.

[330] Equalities Act 2006, Sch 1, Part 1.

EUROPEAN UNION LAW

2.35   European Union law has become a major source of UK labour law.[331] As we shall see in subsequent chapters of this book, many of the most significant legislative initiatives of the past decade and a half, including new legislation in relation to working time, the work-life balance, equality of treatment, the treatment of part-time, fixed-term contract and temporary agency workers, and information and consultation of worker representatives, are derived from European directives.[332] EU law in the area of social policy mostly takes the form of Treaty provisions and directives.[333] Directives are in most cases given effect in UK law through delegated legislation derived from powers conferred by the European Communities Act 1972.[334] As we have already noted,[335] this mode of implementation has given rise to a certain number of stand-alone provisions in such areas as transfers of undertakings, which are not well integrated into the wider body of legislation governing those matters.[336] In certain other cases, amending legislation has taken the form of changes to Acts of Parliament, and where this has been done – as, for example, in the case of major alterations to the law governing sex, race and disability discrimination during the 2000s[337] – the fragmentation of the law which often results from the implementation of directives has been alleviated, if not necessarily avoided altogether.

2.36   The Court of Justice of the European Union[338] has also had a pivotal influence on the development of UK labour law in areas which include transfers of undertakings, sex discrimination and occupational pensions, both through references from national courts for preliminary rulings on points of EU law, and through decisions in infringement proceedings brought against the United

---

[331] On European Union law relating to social policy, see P Davies *et al*, 1996; Nielsen and Szyszczak, 1997; Hervey, 1998; Barnard, 2000a; Shaw, 2000; Hervey and Kenner, 2003; De Schutter and Deakin, 2005; Barnard, 2006; Bercusson, 2009; O'Neill, 2011: ch 12. Although it is strictly accurate to refer in this regard to 'European Community law' in certain contexts, including that of social policy, the term 'European Union law' is increasingly used, and we shall follow that practice here.

[332] On working time, see para 4.78 *et seq* below; on work-life balance issues, para 6.119 *et seq*; on part-time, fixed-term and agency working, para 3.49 *et seq*; on information and consultation, para 9.29 *et seq*.

[333] The relevant Treaty provisions are outlined below, para 2.37; relevant directives and other instruments, such as regulations and opinions, are referred to at various points in the detailed account of the law in this book.

[334] ECA 1972, s 2(2). Occasionally, a power is taken to adopt legislation in a field governed by EU law which goes beyond the powers conferred by s 2(2); see, eg, ERelA 1999, s 38, which was relied on to enact part of the revised version of the TUPE Regulations, SI 2006/246; see below, para 3.66.

[335] See para 2.3 above.

[336] The failure to integrate the law governing transfers of undertakings into the general provisions governing employment protection, contained in ERA 1996 and its predecessor statutes, caused some difficulty in respect of the link between the different categories of potentially fair reasons in TUPE 1981 and the 1996 Act. See DTI, *TUPE Draft Revised Regulations Public Consultation Document* (2005), paras 52–53.

[337] Thus major changes were made to sex discrimination legislation by SI 2001/2660, to race discrimination legislation by SI 2003/1626, and to disability discrimination by SI 2003/1673, in each case using powers under ECA 1972, s 2(2). These provisions are now to be found in the EqA 2010, which provides, within a single statute, a systematic treatment of the law governing equality in employment, which integrates provisions deriving from EU law with others which have a domestic law origin. See generally ch 6, below.

[338] This Court, previously known as the European Court of Justice, was renamed following the Lisbon Treaty of 2009, on which see para 2.38 below. For convenience and clarity we retain the term 'ECJ' in relation to judgments issued before the coming into force of the Lisbon Treaty, and 'CJEU' for judgments issued thereafter.

Kingdom by the Commission.[339] Moreover, the principle of the direct effect of certain Treaty provisions and directives has enabled both the Court of Justice and UK courts, where appropriate, to apply certain EU law rules even where they conflict with domestic legislation. This principle has had a major impact, in particular, on the development of the law governing equality of pay between men and women.[340] The principle that UK courts should, as far as possible, interpret UK legislation purporting to implement EU directives in line with the provisions of those directives (so-called 'indirect effect'), has also played a significant role in shaping UK labour law on certain issues, as decisions on sex discrimination law[341] and transfers of undertakings[342] illustrate.

2.37   To begin with, however, social policy occupied a marginal place in the developing European legal order. Article 117 of the Treaty of Rome of 1957 (now, heavily amended, Article 151 TFEU),[343] provided that 'Member States agree upon the need to promote improved working conditions and an improved standard of living for workers, so as to make possible their harmonisation while the improvement is being maintained'. However, this provision did not create any jurisdiction to implement social policy through directives or regulations. Similarly, under Article 118 (now Article 156 TFEU), the European Commission was confined to promoting co-operation between the Member States on a number of matters relating to social policy (including working conditions, social security, occupational health and safety, the right of association and collective bargaining), while under Article 122 (now Article 161 TFEU) it simply had an obligation to make annual reports on social policy to the Parliament. Articles 119 and 120 (now respectively Articles 157 and 158 TFEU) alone placed specific substantive obligations on Member States in relation to labour law. Article 119 laid down the principle of equal pay for equal work between men and women which, as we have just noted, was to form the basis for many of the later interventions of the European Court of Justice; Article 120, which required the Member States to 'endeavour to maintain the existing equivalence between paid holiday schemes', by contrast proved to be insignificant. These two Articles were included in the original treaty on the insistence of the French government which raised the threat of unfair competition from states with less extensive legal protections. Overall, however, 'the social provisions of the Treaty ... turned out to be pretty meagre',[344] and the period of the implementation of the first phase of the common market up to the late 1960s was one of 'benign neglect' as far as social policy was concerned.[345]

---

[339] For the purposes of this book we assume a basic knowledge of the relationship between EU Treaty provisions, directives, regulations and other legal acts, and UK domestic law. A full account of the meaning of the concepts of direct effect and indirect effect, and the process of preliminary references and infringement proceedings, is also beyond the scope of this work. For the background to these concepts, the reader is referred to the relevant standard works on EU law and UK constitutional law.

[340] Landmark judgments of the Court in this area include Case 43/73 *Defrenne v Sabena* [1976] ECR 455, on the direct effect of Art 119 of the EEC Treaty (now Art 157 of the TFEU), and Case C-262/88 *Barber v Guardian Royal Exchange Assurance Group* [1990] IRLR 240, applying that principle to occupational pension schemes. See generally para 6.5 below.

[341] See, in particular, the decision of the HL in *Rhys-Harper v Relaxion Group plc* [2003] IRLR 484.

[342] See, eg, the decision of the Court of Appeal in *ADI (UK) Ltd v Willer* [2001] IRLR 542, in particular the judgment of Dyson LJ.

[343] The Treaty of Amsterdam replaced the EEC Treaty with the Treaty Establishing the European Community (TEC) with effect from 1 May 1999, and the Treaty of Lisbon, which came into force on 1 December 2009, replaced the TEC with the Treaty on the Functioning of the European Union (TFEU). On the Treaty of Lisbon, see para 2.38 below

[344] P Davies, 1992: p 325.

[345] Mosley, 1990.

This changed with the enlargement of the Community to nine states in 1971. The first Social Action Programme was adopted in 1974 and this led eventually to the adoption by the Council of a series of directives relating to equal pay and equality of treatment between the sexes in relation to employment and social security.[346] Less extensive but nevertheless significant measures were also adopted in relation to employment protection, with directives laying down minimum standards of redundancy consultation and protection of employee rights in the event of business transfers and the insolvency of companies. [347] These measures could be adopted without amendment of the Treaty; general provisions empowering the Council to adopt measures for the implementation of the common market and related purposes were used as a jurisdiction base.[348] The difficulty was that these provisions required the Council to be unanimous. The Single European Act of 1986 introduced a new Article 118a (this is now, in an amended form, Article 153 TFEU), allowing qualified majority voting (in this context, overriding the veto of a single Member State) in the area of health and safety. The so-called Social Charter adopted by eleven of the (then twelve) Member States at the Strasbourg summit in November 1989 (the United Kingdom was the exception) did not, however, mark a significant legal advance, being simply a declaration of principle. Continuing dissatisfaction with the lack of progress on social policy led to a number of Treaty amendments being proposed as part of the inter-governmental conference on economic union leading up to the Maastricht summit in November 1991. Treaty amendments require unanimity, and the United Kingdom duly used its veto to block what would have been the 'Social Chapter' of the new Treaty. Under a last-minute political compromise, the other Member States agreed to a procedure for the implementation of the social dimension separately from the United Kingdom, contained in a separate Protocol and Agreement on Social Policy.

The Agreement on Social Policy had three main purposes: to confirm and clarify the legal competence of the Community in regard to social policy; to extend qualified majority voting in the social area; and to give greater institutional priority to the social dialogue between management and labour at transnational level.[349] The Agreement provided for qualified majority voting on matters including health and safety, working conditions, information and consultation of workers, equality between the sexes and integration of excluded groups. For certain other areas, including social security, protection of workers in relation to the termination of employment, 'representation and collective defence' of workers (including co-determination), rights of third-country nationals, and financial measures for the promotion of employment, unanimity was required. Finally, some matters were excluded from the Agreement altogether: these were 'pay, the right of association, the right to strike [and] the right to impose lock-outs'. But the most innovative aspect of the Agreement on Social Policy was the introduction of a mechanism by which European-level legislation could be produced through a process of *social dialogue* between the social partners, that is, the transnational federations of the ETUC (representing trade unions),

---

[346] Directive 75/117/EEC on equal pay; Directive 77/207/EEC on equal treatment in employment; Directive 79/7/EEC on equal treatment in social security; Directive 86/378/EEC on equal treatment in occupational social security.

[347] Directive 75/129/EEC on collective redundancies; Directive 77/187/EEC on acquired rights on transfers of undertakings; Directive 80/987/EEC on protection of employee rights in the event of insolvency.

[348] Arts 100 and 235 of the Treaty (now Arts 115 and 352-3 TFEU).

[349] The Agreement also reproduced in a slightly modified form the equal pay provisions of Art 119 of the old Treaty, with a new provision for limited forms of positive discrimination in favour of women (Art 6(3)).

UNICE and CEEP (representing private-sector and public-sector employers respectively).[350] In particular, the social partners were given the option of concluding framework agreements which could be implemented either according to the procedures and practices of each Member State or by way of a Council 'decision', a term which was taken to include directives.

Following a change of government in 1997, the United Kingdom indicated that it wished to 'opt in' to the Agreement on Social Policy. In part as a consequence of this, the Treaty of Amsterdam made a series of further amendments to the social policy provisions of the EC Treaty. In effect, most of the terms of the Agreement were incorporated into a revised Social Chapter in the main body of the EC Treaty (Articles 136–145 EC, now Articles 151-161 TFEU). The substance of the Agreement was not greatly affected.[351] The solution to the United Kingdom's need to 'opt in' was for the Council to re-adopt a number of directives agreed between 1994 and 1998 under the Agreement, with the United Kingdom now fully bound by their provisions.[352] Since then the social dialogue procedure has produced a further agreement and directive, on fixed-term work,[353] and a number of 'autonomous agreements' which allow for implementation in national law through action by the social partners, the most significant of which is on the subject of teleworking.[354] However, the social partners subsequently failed to agree on the texts of agreements concerning information and consultation and temporary agency work, and directives on these issues were eventually adopted through the more regular procedure involving the Council and the European Parliament.[355]

Another step taken at Amsterdam was the adoption of an Employment Title, heralded by the inclusion in Article 2 TEC of a new task for the Community of promoting 'a high level of employment and of social protection', which has had the effect of placing Community action in the area of active labour market policy on a clearer legal footing.[356] In addition, a new legal basis was given for prohibiting discrimination on the grounds of sex, racial or ethnic origin, religion or belief, disability, age or sexual orientation (Article 13 TEC, now Article 19 TFEU).[357] The Council of Ministers went on to agree two particularly significant directives under this provision, the so-called Framework Directive providing a general framework for equal treatment in employment and occupation in relation to religion or belief, disability, age, and sexual orientation,[358] and the Race Directive on equal treatment irrespective of racial or ethnic origin.[359] These have had a considerable influence in reshaping British equality law.[360] More generally, however, there was a

---

[350] In Case T-135/96 *UEAPME v Council of the European Union* [1998] IRLR 602 an unsuccessful challenge was made to the parental leave directive on grounds of the lack of representativeness of the social partners, by a European association representing the interests of small and medium-sized undertakings.

[351] See Barnard, 1997a for an account of the changes made at Amsterdam.

[352] Directives on European Works Councils (94/45/EC) and Parental Leave (96/34/EC) were readopted in this way in December 1997 (by Directives 97/74/EC and 97/75/EC, respectively); the Part-time Work Directive (97/81/EC) in April 1998 (by Directive 98/23/EC); and the Burden of Proof Directive (97/80/EC) in July 1998 (98/52/EC).

[353] Directive 99/70/EC; see further para 3.52 below.

[354] See below, para 3.34.

[355] Directive 2002/14/EC and Directive 2008/104 EC, respectively; see further paras 9.30 and 3.53 below.

[356] On the history of active labour market policy in the Community, see Freedland, 1996a. The development of a distinctive method of regulation, the 'open method of coordination' or OMC, began in the context of the European employment strategy which grew out of the Employment Title. For reviews of developments in respect of the OMC, see De Schutter and Deakin, 2005; Barnard, 2006: ch 3; Barnard and Deakin, 2012.

[357] See L Waddington, 1999.

[358] Directive 2000/78 EC.

[359] Directive 2000/43 EC.

[360] See generally ch 6 below.

marked slowing of the pace of legislative change in social policy after the turn of the millennium. Repeated attempts to bring about a revision of the Working Time Directive were unsuccessful,[361] and although a Directive on Temporary Agency Work was agreed in late 2008, its scope was limited.[362]   Other recent developments include revisions to the Directives on European Works Councils[363] and Parental Leave.[364]

2.38   In December 2001 the Laeken European Council established the Convention on the Future of Europe and entrusted it with the task of drafting a European Constitution that would replace the existing EU Treaties. The resulting Treaty establishing a Constitution for Europe was agreed in October 2004 but never came into force following 'no' votes in referenda held in France and the Netherlands in the course of the following year. With the failure of the Constitutional Treaty, negotiations began for a Reform Treaty that would have the more modest aim of updating the existing EU Treaty texts. The outcome of this process, the Lisbon Treaty, was ratified in the course of 2008 and 2009, and came into force on 1 December 2009. The principal legal texts are now the Treaty on European Union ('TEU'), which sets out the basic institutional structure of the Union, and the Treaty on the Functioning of the European Union ('TFEU'), which provides in more detail for the operation of the Union's organs and determines their competences.

The Lisbon Treaty, like the Constitutional Treaty before it, made no substantive change to EU competences in the social policy field. Title X of the TFEU, which contains the social policy competences, mostly copies out the provisions of its predecessor, Title XI TEC. The Lisbon Treaty did, however, make at least two changes with potential significance for labour law.[365] These concern, respectively, the relationship between values and objectives of the Union as set out in Articles 2 and 3 TEU, and the granting of legal status to the provisions of the Charter of Fundamental Rights of the European Union ('CFREU') through Article 6 TEU. These developments have implications for the role of fundamental social rights in EU law and for their relationship to the economic freedoms which form the basis for the operation of the single market.

2.39   Human or 'fundamental' rights were recognised by the Court to be part of the EU legal order as 'general principles' from an early stage,[366] and the   Treaty of Amsterdam committed the EU to respect fundamental rights, as guaranteed by the ECHR and 'as they result from the constitutional traditions common to the Member States, as general principles of Community law'.[367] In December 2000 a Charter of Fundamental Rights of the European Union, drafted by a Convention, was proclaimed by the President of the European Parliament, the president of the European Commission, and the President of the Council of Ministers after approval by Member States.[368] The Charter was divided into six chapters: dignity, freedoms, equality, solidarity,

---

[361] See below, para 4.91.

[362] Directive 2008/104/EC, discussed at para 3.53 below.

[363] Directive 2009/38/EC, the recast EWC Directive: see Laulom, 2009; paras 9.60-9.63 below.

[364] Directive 2010/18/EU. See para 6.119 below.

[365] For a wider review of the social policy implications of the Lisbon Treaty, noting its impact on, among other things, subsidiarity, competences, and social dialogue, see Bruun, Lörcher and Schömann (eds), 2012.

[366] Case 11/70 *Internationale Handelsgesellschaft v Einfuhr- und Vorratsstelle fur Getreide* [1970] ECR 1125, 1134; Case 4/73 *Nold v Commission* [1974] ECR 491, para 13.

[367] Art 6 TEU (1999).

[368] See further Lenaerts, 2000; de Burca, 2001; Lenaerts and de Smijter, 2001.

citizens' rights and justice. Most of the rights set out in the Charter, such as the right to life, the prohibition of slavery and forced labour, the right to respect for private life, and freedom of expression, were based on the provisions of the ECHR and other international legal instruments, and were uncontroversial (although some were amplified or updated to take account of more recent societal developments). The inclusion of social rights was more contentious, with some Member States maintaining that these were not fundamental in nature, or that they remained a matter for individual states.[369] Eventually it was agreed that fundamental social rights could be included in a chapter on Solidarity,[370] in addition to a provision on freedom of association which appeared in the Freedoms Chapter,[371] and to provisions on equality in employment which were placed in the Equality Chapter.[372] Rights of particular relevance to labour law included the right of workers and their representatives, at appropriate levels, to information and consultation within the undertaking; the right of workers and employers, or their organisations, to negotiate and conclude collective agreements and, in cases of conflicts of interest, to take collective action, including strike action; and the right of every worker to protection against 'unjustified dismissal'.[373] All of these rights were stated to be exercisable only 'in accordance with Union law and national laws and practices'. There was also an unqualified right for every worker 'to working conditions which respect his or her health, safety and dignity' as well as a right to 'limitation of maximum working hours, to daily and weekly rest periods and to an annual period of paid leave'.[374]

The Charter was not legally binding, and it established no new legal competences. However, it was soon used by the Court to give content to the notion of 'general principles' of EU law.[375] In *Albany*, where the relationship between collective agreements and social policy measures, on the one hand, and EU competition law, on the other, was at issue, the Court emphasised that under Article 3(1)(g) and (j) TEC:

> ... the activities of the Community are to include not only a 'system ensuring that competition in the internal market is not distorted' but also 'a policy in the social sphere'. Article 2 ... [TEC] provides that a particular task of the Community is 'to promote throughout the Community a harmonious and balanced[376] development of economic activities' and 'a high level of employment and of social protection'.[377]

The Court had previously recognised freedom of association as a fundamental right;[378] in *Albany* Advocate General Jacobs considered that the collective right of workers to take action, in addition to the right to form and join a union, had been also been confirmed as such a right.[379]

---

[369] See Hepple, 2001b for the concerns raised by the UK Government. For an analysis of the Charter, see Hervey and Kenner, 2003.
[370] See now CFREU, Arts. 27–34.
[371] This is now CFREU, Art 12.
[372] This is now CFFEU, Arts 20–26.
[373] Now CFREU, Arts 27, 28 and 30.
[374] Now CFREU, Art 31.
[375] See, in particular, Case C-173/99 *BECTU v Secretary of State for Trade and Industry* [2001] ECR I-4881.
[376] This is the wording of the judgment. Art 2 TEC referred to 'harmonious, balanced and sustainable development'.
[377] Case C-67/96 *Albany International BV v Stichting Bedrijfspensioenfonds Textielindustrie* [1999] ECR I-5751, para 54. See further para 7.11.
[378] Case C-415/93 *Union Royale Belge des Sociétés de Football Association ASBL v Jean-Marc Bosman* [1995] ECR I-4921, paras 79 and 80.
[379] Case C-67/96 above, [1999] ECR I-5751, para 139.

In two pivotal cases decided by the Court in December 2007 on the relationship between European Union law on freedom of movement and national laws governing industrial action, *Viking* and *Laval*, the Court held that the right to take collective action, including the right to strike, was a 'fundamental right' which formed 'an integral part of the general principles of Community law'.[380] However, in each case the Court severely qualified this conclusion by ruling that the right to take collective action was subject to restrictions imposed by European Union law and referring, for support for this view, to Article 28 of the CFREU.[381] Contrary to the line taken in *Albany* in the context of competition policy, the Court ruled that the right to strike could not be entirely separated from the impact of the law governing freedom of movement, in particular Article 43 TEC (now Article 49 TFEU) on freedom of establishment (*Viking*) and Article 49 TEC (now Article 56 TFEU) on the freedom to provide services (*Laval*). The *Viking* ruling suggested that in disputes with a transnational element giving rise to a restraint on the freedom of establishment of the employer, the national court had to strike a balance between economic and social interests in a way which, in practice, could narrow the scope for lawful industrial action; it thereby introduced a new element of legal regulation of industrial action into the domestic legal systems of the Member States. In *Laval* the Court itself took a highly interventionist line on the issue of 'balancing', holding that industrial action taken with a view to enforcing collective agreements of the host state which were not capable of being extended to workers employed by foreign service providers under the terms of the Posted Workers Directive[382] was contrary to Article 49 TEC.[383]

The Court's judgments in *Viking* and *Laval*, particularly the latter, surprised many observers[384] and disappointed those who had hoped that the Court would give clearer recognition to the autonomy of national laws on industrial action and collective bargaining, as it had done in *Albany*.[385] However, subsequent decisions made it clear that these were not going to be isolated decisions. In *Rüffert*[386] and *Luxembourg*[387] the Court maintained its narrow interpretation of the Posted Workers Directive in decisions which appeared to undermine the principle of the territorial effect of national labour legislation, and put in doubt the effectiveness of long-standing arrangements in certain member states for the extension of sector-level collective agreements.[388]

In this uncertain legal environment, the first potentially significant change made by the Lisbon Treaty was to realign the relationship between values and objectives in the definition of the basic institutional structure of the Union. The version of the TEU agreed at Amsterdam in 1997 had previously referred to 'objectives', while the Constitutional Treaty had added reference to 'values' of the Union, to which the 'objectives' gave effect. The post-Lisbon version of the TEU

[380] See Case C-438/05 *ITWF v Viking Line* [2008] IRLR 143, para 44. Case C-341/05 *Laval Un Partneri Ltd v Svenska Byggnadsarbetareförbundet* [2008] IRLR 160, para 91, is to broadly similar effect.
[381] *ITWF v Viking Line*, above, para 44.
[382] Directive 96/71/EC; see para 2.48, below.
[383] See below, para 11.52.
[384] See Eklund, 2008, referring to the 'Pandora's box' opened by *Laval*.
[385] See Bercusson, 2007, on the significance of the *Viking* and *Laval* litigation for the European trade union movement.
[386] Case C-346/06 *Dirk Rüffert v Land Niedersachsen* [2008] IRLR 467.
[387] Case C-319/06 *Commission v Luxembourg* [2009] IRLR 388. On the implications of *Laval*, *Rüffert* and *Luxembourg* for the relationship between economic freedoms and social rights, see Deakin, 2008.
[388] The implications of *Viking* and *Laval* for the rights of trade unions and workers to organise and participate in industrial action were addressed by a draft Council Regulation on the exercise of the right to take collective action within the context of the freedom of establishment and the freedom to supply services (the so-called 'Monti II' Regulation), published in March 2012 (COM (2012) 130 final). At the time of writing (May 2012), the prospects of this Regulation being adopted are unclear.

now refers to a number of values on which the Union 'is founded' and which are listed as 'respect for human dignity, freedom, democracy, equality, the rule of law and respect for human rights, including the rights of persons belonging to minorities'. Article 2 then goes on to provide that these values 'are common to the Member States in a society in which pluralism, non-discrimination, tolerance, justice, solidarity and equality between women and men prevail'. It has been suggested that while 'the structure of Article 2 is enigmatic' in separating certain high-ranking values from other institutional features of democratic societies, solidarity should nevertheless be regarded as a value 'which is at the core of the EU and hence an important tool for interpretation'.[389]

Article 3 TEU provides further clues to the relationship between social rights and economic freedoms. In the Constitutional Treaty, the equivalent provision set out the 'objectives' of the Union as ancillary to the more fundamental 'values'. The term 'objectives' does not appear in the new version of Article 3, but the revised drafting seems to reflect the same idea of a distinction between ends (Article 2) and means (Article 3).[390] It is therefore significant that the internal market, set out in Article 3(3), is described not as an end in itself, but as a means to the various ends ('values') contained in Article 2. Article 3(3) also refers to the Union working for, among other things, 'a highly competitive social market economy, aiming at full employment and social progress', combating 'social exclusion and discrimination', and promoting 'social justice and protection, equality between women and men, [and] solidarity between generations'. On this basis, social policy is not clearly subordinated to the operation of the single or internal market.[391]

Article 6 TEU defines the place of human or 'fundamental' rights within the EU legal order. Article 6(1) provides that the rights, freedoms and principles set out in the CFREU 'shall have the same legal value' as the EU Treaties, that is, the TEU and TFEU. However, it goes on to stipulate that the provisions of the CFREU 'shall not extend in any way the competences of the Union as defined in the Treaties'. It then states that the rights, freedoms and principles contained in the Charter 'shall be interpreted in accordance with the general provisions in Title VII of the Charter governing its interpretation and application and with due regard to the explanations referred to in the Charter, that set out the sources of those provisions'.[392] The Charter itself is appended to the body of the TFEU. Its substantive content is little changed from the original draft of 2000. Its Title VII, which is new, expands on Article 6(1) in a number of ways. It provides, among other things, that the provisions of the Charter are addressed to the Member States 'only when they are implementing Union law', and that while the Member States must 'respect the rights, observe the principles and promote the application thereof' they are required to do so 'in accordance with their respective powers and respecting the limits of the powers of the Union'.[393] Rights recognised in the Charter for which provision is also made in the Treaties are to be exercised 'under the conditions and within the limits' set out in the Treaties;[394] while the Charter's principles may be implemented by the EU's institutions and by acts of the Member States 'when they are implementing Union law', principles are to be 'judicially cognisable only in the interpretation of such acts and in the ruling

---

[389] Dorssemont, 2012: pp 47-48.

[390] It may be noted, moreover, that in the context of the European Employment Strategy, Art 145 TFEU continues to refer to the 'objectives' set out in Art 3 TEU. On para 145, see our discussion at para 3.17 below.

[391] Dorssemont, 2012: p 50; Deakin, 2012: p 39. On the meaning of the term 'social market economy' in this context, see Joerges and Roedl, 2012.

[392] On the meaning of the term 'explanations', see below, this para.

[393] CFREU, Art 51(1).

[394] CFREU, Art 52(2).

on their legality'.[395] The Explanations drawn up initially by the Convention which drafted the original version of the Charter prior to its agreement at the Nice Council in 2000 are 'to be given due regard' by the courts of the EU and of the Member States.[396]

The uncertainty created by simultaneously elevating the Charter to the same 'legal value' as the Treaties while excluding it from the main body of the TFEU and setting out specific rules for its interpretation is compounded, in the case of the UK, by Protocol 30 of the TFEU. Reflecting yet another UK opt-out, Protocol 30 states that the Charter does not extend the power of the CJEU or of any national court 'to find that the laws, regulations, or administrative provisions, practices or action... of the United Kingdom are inconsistent with' the Charter;[397] that, 'for the avoidance of doubt', nothing in the Charter's Solidarity Title, Title IV, 'creates justiciable rights' applicable to the United Kingdom, except in so far as such rights already exist in national law;[398] and, finally, to the extent that the Charter refers to national laws and practices, it shall apply to the United Kingdom only 'to the extent that the rights or principles that it contains are recognised' by UK law.[399]

Article 6 TEU goes on to make further changes of significance for the relationship between EU law and European human rights law as set out in the ECHR. It provides, first, that the EU 'shall accede' to the ECHR,[400] and, second, that fundamental rights as guaranteed by the ECHR and as resulting from the constitutional traditions of the Member States 'shall constitute general principles' of EU law.[401]

Where all this leaves the relationship between social rights and economic freedoms under EU law, and with what impact on the domestic labour law systems of the Member States, is far from clear pending the emergence of a more substantial body of case law interpreting the provisions introduced by the Lisbon Treaty. Some possible lines of development are, however, already becoming clear. A first point to make is that the Court had already developed the idea that fundamental rights, including social rights, are part of EU law as 'general principles' which have to be taken into account when interpreting Treaty provisions as well as those of Directives. In this light, the changes made by the Lisbon Treaty are not as far-reaching as they might appear. The substantive provisions of the Charter can be understood as largely clarifying the content of rights which the Court's jurisprudence had already recognised. Thus the repeated attempts in the drafting of the TEU and the Charter itself to ensure that no new justiciable rights would be created by the granting of legal effect to the Charter, culminating in the opt-out provided to the United Kingdom in Protocol 30, should arguably make no difference to the approach to interpretation taken by the courts in social policy cases.[402] Even rights such as the right to strike

---

[395] CFREU, Art 52(5). The meaning of the distinction between 'rights' and 'principles' in the context of the Charter's social policy provisions is far from clear. Kollonay-Lehoczky *et al* (2012: pp 78-79) suggest that 'the core social rights (such as Articles 12 and 27 to 32) are not touched upon by this provision because they are considered to be rights (from the wording and [their] content)'.

[396] CFFEU, Art 52(7). The Explanations were updated, without major amendment, in 2007 (see OJ C/303-17, 14.12.2007). For the most part they simply indicate the source of the provision. Those relevant to labour law and social policy variously originate in the ECHR, the ESC, EU Treaty provisions, and other EU legal instruments, including directives.

[397] TFEU, Protocol 30, Art 1(1). Protocol 30 also applies to Poland.

[398] Art 1(2).

[399] Art 2.

[400] Art 6(2). See further Art 218(8) TFEU. A joint working party of the EU and Council of Europe to negotiate the process of accession was set up in 2010.

[401] Art 6(3).

[402] On this point, see Case C-155/10 *British Airways plc v Williams* [2011] IRLR 948, in which the Court of Justice referred to the right to paid annual leave as provided for in the CFREU, without referring to the UK's opt-out.

contained in Article 28 of the Charter, which at first sight could be problematic for UK law given the restrictions which operate on the exercise of collective action under UK legislation,[403] have already been recognised as general principles of EU law by the Court,[404] and thus already form part of UK law. As far as UK labour law is concerned, Protocol 30 would appear to be of political or symbolic, rather than legal, significance.

A second, related point is that, given the presence in EU law of these general principles, the potential significance of the Lisbon Treaty could be seen as lying not in extending the role played by human rights within EU law, but in limiting it. A close reading of the changes made by the Lisbon Treaty suggests that it has probably not had this effect. For example, a plausible analysis of Article 51 of the Charter is while Member States must have regard to the provisions of the Charter when implementing EU law, they are not prevented from going beyond those provisions when exercising national powers: the Charter 'should be a ceiling for Union-set obligations, but only the floor for national human rights régimes'.[405] Similarly, although Article 52(5) of the Charter restricts judicial cognisance of its provisions to contexts where a court is interpreting an existing provision of EU law, this seems to take nothing away from the obligation of courts to give effect to fundamental rights as general principles of EU law when determining the meaning of a Treaty provision or directive.[406]

A third point to consider is that while the granting of legal effect to the Charter does not extend the competences of the Union in the social policy field, competences already exist in respect of most of the labour law provisions of the Charter.[407] The major exceptions to this are the rights to collective bargaining and collective action in Article 28, which, expressly or by implication, are the subject of a derogation from the power to adopt directives in the social policy field under Article 153 TFEU.[408] The right to a minimum wage, which is also excluded from the competences set out in Article 153,[409] is not mentioned in the Charter either.

The fourth point is that, while the changes made by the Lisbon Treaty can be read as clarifying the role of fundamental rights in the social policy sphere, they do not, at least as so far interpreted, bring us any closer to a rebalancing of social rights and economic freedoms in the aftermath of the Court's rulings in *Viking* and *Laval*. There is no compelling case, yet, for arguing that the granting of legal effect to the Charter has elevated social rights above economic freedoms. In the Constitutional Treaty, the Charter had been placed inside the body of the Treaty in a way which arguably conferred a protected status on fundamental rights.[410] That interpretation has less traction now that the Charter is appended to the TFEU, and, as have seen,[411] the values and objectives clauses of the TEU imply at best a certain degree of parity between social rights and economic freedoms. This leaves the issue where it was before, for the Court to resolve, and they have so far shown no more willingness than they had before the passage of the Lisbon Treaty to

---

[403] See below, ch 11.

[404] This was one of the consequences of the rulings in *Viking* and *Laval* (see above, this para).

[405] Kollonay-Lehoczky *et al*, 2012: p 74.

[406] See Case C-555/07, *Kücükdeveci v Swedex GmbH & Co KG*, judgment of 19.1.2010, and Case C-236/09 *Association belge des Consommateurs Test-Achats ASBL*, judgment of 1 March 2011, both decided after the Lisbon Treaty had come into force.

[407] Lörcher, 2012.

[408] See Art 153(5) TFEU.

[409] As a result of the reference to 'pay' in Art 153(5) TFEU.

[410] See Dorssemont, 2012.

[411] See above, this para.

limit the operation of the free movement principle by reference to social policy considerations.[412] Further evolution of the law on this point could arise from the alignment of EU law with European human rights law under the ECHR implied by Article 6(3) TFEU, but how that process might develop in the future remains to be seen.[413]

The fifth and final point to be made in the context of this discussion is that the future evolution of EU social policy will inevitably take place in the shadow of the sovereign debt crisis that began in the Eurozone in 2010 and has started to have far-reaching effects on the institutional governance of the EU. The so called 'six pack' of measures introduced in the autumn of 2011 envisages a régime of budgetary and macroeconomic surveillance, designed to forestall a future debt crisis and to ensure the alignment of the economies of the Eurozone Member States. While these measures do not directly address social policy issues, their indirect impact on wage fixing mechanism and welfare state institutions could prove to be significant. The Euro Plus Pact of March 2011 more directly addresses social policy at national level, by putting in place a system of central oversight of, among things, wage policy and welfare state expenditure.[414] The UK, as it remains outside the Eurozone, is not immediately affected by these developments, but since they are likely to lead to a recalibration of the wider relationship between EU economic and monetary policy, on the one hand, and social policy at the level of the Member States, on the other, UK labour law is unlikely to remain entirely unaffected by them over the longer term.[415]

OTHER INTERNATIONAL LABOUR STANDARDS

2.40   As well as its obligations deriving from membership of the European Union the United Kingdom is subject to a wide range of other international labour standards which, although not part of domestic law, it is obliged under international law to secure. By far the most numerous and specific standards emanate from the International Labour Organisation (ILO), established in 1919 and based upon a tripartite structure of governments and of employers' and workers' representatives.[416] The constitution of the ILO, revised in 1946, affirms that 'labour is not a commodity', that 'freedom of expression and of association are essential to sustained progress', that 'poverty anywhere constitutes a danger to prosperity everywhere' and that 'all human beings, irrespective of race, creed or sex, have the right to pursue both their material well-being and their spiritual development in conditions of freedom and dignity, of economic security and equal opportunity'.[417] The ILO comprises three main bodies.[418] First is the International Labour Conference which normally meets once a year. It consists of delegations from Member States

---

[412] The case for parity was made by Cruz Villalon AG in Case C-515/08 *Santos Palhota* [2011] CMLR 34, Opinion, paras 51-53, and by Trstenjak AG in Case 271/08 *Commission v. Germany (Occupational Pensions)* [2011] All ER (EC) 912, Opinion, paras 183-90, but in neither case did the Court take up the invitation to reconsider the approach to balancing social and economic rights that was taken in *Laval*.

[413] For discussion see Kollonay-Lehoczky *et al*, 2012: pp 97-98.

[414] See Barnard, 2012, for an account of the 'six pack' and the Euro Plus Pact.

[415] See Deakin, 2012.

[416] For the history of the ILO see Alcock, 1971; and, for a more recent overview, Ewing, 1994a.

[417] Taken from the Declaration of Philadelphia adopted by the International Labour Conference in 1944 and subsequently incorporated into the ILO's Constitution.

[418] See generally; Valticos and von Potobsky, 1995; Bartolemei, von Potobsky and Swepston, 1996; Swepston, 1997; Creighton, 2004b; Novitz and Syrpis, 2006; Swepston, 2010.

containing two government delegates and one employers' and workers' delegate, each nominated in agreement with the most representative organisations of employers and workers within that state. The second is the Governing Body which consists of 56 members, 28 representing governments, the remainder an equal number of employer and worker representatives. Its members are elected every third year at the Conference by their respective groups.[419] The third is the International Labour Office, the permanent secretariat of the Organisation, whose Director-General is appointed by the Governing Body.

The Constitution of the ILO lays down a number of principles, such as freedom of association and non-discrimination, which are regarded as a direct source of law. Other standards are laid down in Conventions and Recommendations. A state which ratifies a Convention is then obliged to 'take such action as may be necessary to make effective' its provisions,[420] although, at certain intervals, it is open to states to denounce a previously ratified Convention. Recommendations aim at providing guidance to policy, legislation and practice and currently are 'used mainly to supplement Conventions, in order to indicate in greater detail the manner of giving effect to their provisions or to advocate the establishment of higher standards'.[421] The adoption of a new Convention or Recommendation requires approval by a two-thirds majority of the delegates at the International Labour Conference, normally after discussion at two successive sessions. Adoption is preceded by what can be a lengthy process[422] which includes the preparation of a preliminary report by the International Labour Office setting out existing law and practice on the question in different countries which is then circulated for comment by governments which in turn are expected to consult the most representative organisations of unions and employers in their respective countries.[423] As of 2011 the ILO had adopted more 180 Conventions and around 200 Recommendations.[424] Eight Conventions (relating to freedom of association and the right to organise; the abolition of forced labour; equality; and the elimination of child labour)[425] are regarded as fundamental, in the dual senses of being applicable irrespective of the level of development of an individual state and of being a precondition for the application of other labour standards.

2.41   The ILO Constitution prescribes that any question or dispute relating to the interpretation of the Constitution or a Convention shall be submitted to the International Court of Justice. This has happened only once, in 1932. However, the International Labour Office is frequently consulted as to the interpretation of Conventions. These opinions are communicated to the Governing Body and published in the *Official Bulletin*. In addition, the various supervisory bodies have built up a body of case law relating to the scope and meaning of various Conventions. Each state is required by the ILO Constitution to supply reports at regular intervals (the period depending on the

---

[419] Ten of the government seats are reserved for states of chief industrial importance, of which the UK is one.

[420] ILO Constitution, Art 19(5)(d).

[421] Swepston, 2007: para 15. They may also be used to deal with subjects that are not yet ripe for a Convention or do not lend themselves to the adoption of Conventions entailing international obligations.

[422] See Ewing, 1994a: paras 3.5–3.6.

[423] For countries which have ratified the Tripartite Consultation (International Labour Standards) Convention 1976 (No 144) such consultation is mandatory.

[424] See the ILO web site www.ilo.org for the text of these Conventions. For an overview see Swepston, 2010; see also Trebilock, 2010. Some Conventions are confined to particular industries, such as coal mining, or particular groups of workers, such as seafarers. For a critique of the number and quality of standards, see Creighton, 2004b: pp 257–259.

[425] Conventions Nos 87, 98, 29, 105, 111, 100, 138 and 182. See Bellace, 2001.

Convention in question)[426] on the measures taken to implement the Conventions it has ratified. These are examined by an independent Committee of Experts whose reports are submitted to a tripartite Committee on the Application of Conventions and Recommendations, established at each session of the International Labour Conference, before which Government representatives may appear. In its report the Committee may draw attention to the most serious violations of ratified Conventions in a 'special paragraph', one of the strongest sanctions which may be taken against a Member State.

As well as these monitoring procedures (which are vulnerable to states failing to meet their reporting obligations)[427] there are also those instigated by complaints. These may be made either by one Member State against another co-signatory to a Convention, or by the Governing Body of its own motion or at the instigation of a delegate to the Conference. In addition employers' or workers' organisations may make representations that a state is not securing the application of a ratified Convention; such representations are considered initially by a three-member committee of the Governing Body and then by the Governing Body itself. The significance of respect for the principles of freedom of association for the effective functioning of the ILO is reflected in the special procedures which have been developed to deal with alleged failures of compliance in this area.[428] Two bodies are concerned with this. First, there is a tripartite Committee on Freedom of Association, composed of nine members appointed by the Governing Body, which has dealt with a large number of individual cases, based mainly on written submissions but sometimes involving oral hearings or visits to the states concerned.[429] In addition there is a Fact-finding and Conciliation Commission, composed of independent persons, which may undertake more extensive investigations, similar to a commission of inquiry, provided that the Member State consents. These procedures can be invoked against governments which have not ratified all or any of the freedom of association Conventions because it is assumed that the very fact of ILO membership carries with it an obligation to respect these principles.[430]

2.42   As of May 2012, the UK had ratified a total of 68 ILO Conventions.[431] Although this is a higher number than many countries, several significant Conventions were omitted;[432] those which have never been ratified include the Hours of Work (Industry) Convention 1919 (No 1); the Holidays with Pay Convention, 1936 (No 52); and the Occupational Safety and Health Convention, 1981 (No 155). Moreover, in furtherance of its deregulatory strategy the UK Conservative administration of 1979–1997 denounced a number of Conventions, including the Minimum

---

[426] In the case of fundamental and 'priority' Conventions (the latter covering tripartite consultation (No 144) labour inspection (Nos 81 and 129) and employment policy (No 122)) alternate years; in the case of other Conventions, every five years.

[427] In 2010 the total number of reports received from Member States within the requisite time limit stood at 67% of those due: see *Conference Committee on the Application of Standards: Extracts from the Record of Proceedings*, ILO, 2011, para 45.

[428] Creighton, 1994: p 2.

[429] See ILO, 2006, for a digest of its decisions to that date.

[430] Creighton, 1993: p 2. See now the ILO Declaration on Fundamental Principles and Rights at Work, 1998 and the ILO Declaration on Social Justice for a Fair Globalization, 2008. Governments that have ratified a freedom of association Convention are also subject to the normal supervisory procedures relating to ratified Conventions.

[431] This figure excludes those previously ratifies and subsequently denounced. For accounts of the relationship between Britain and the ILO see Ewing, 1994a; Creighton, 1993; D Brown and A McColgan, 1992; Mills, 1997; Novitz, 1998, 2000; for an earlier account see Stewart, 1969.

[432] Ewing, 1994a: paras 4.8–4.12.

Wage-Fixing Machinery Convention, 1928 (No 26), the Labour Clauses (Public Contracts) Convention 1949 (No 94) and the Protection of Wages Convention 1949 (No 95); indeed, as of May 2012, 17 Conventions previously ratified had been denounced (although in five cases this was as a result of ratification of later Conventions instead). It is notable that, despite the traditional policy of ratifying ILO Conventions only when domestic law and practice were in compliance with their specifications, the Conservative Government introduced and maintained legislation which breached Conventions Nos 87 and 98 on freedom of association despite 'unprecedented levels of criticism'[433] from ILO supervisory bodies. We discuss the specific nature of these breaches later in this work. The intransigence of the UK Government in the light of the condemnation of its actions demonstrated the limits of a system which relies ultimately upon goodwill and persuasion. As our discussion shows, many of these breaches were not remedied by its Labour successor.[434]

2.43   Standards relevant to labour law are also present in a number of instruments which deal with a wider range of human, civil and political or socio-economic rights. These include the Universal Declaration of Human Rights, adopted by the United Nations General Assembly in 1948, to which effect was given in international law by the International Covenant on Economic Social and Cultural Rights (ICESCR) and International Covenant on Civil and Political Rights (ICCPR), both of 1966. In the case of the UK, compliance with both covenants is monitored by means of reports from signatory states.[435] At European level the European Convention on Human Rights (ECHR) and its economic and social counterpart, the European Social Charter (ESC) both include provisions relating to labour law. The ECHR is enforced by means of state and (more commonly) individual applications;[436] in the field of labour law the provision most relevant to the UK has been Article 11, which guarantees freedom of association, including the right to form and join trade unions. The HRA 1998 enabled the ECHR to be relied upon in domestic courts and tribunals in a much wider range of situations than heretofore, and Convention rights other than Article 11, which we examine in appropriate sections of this book, are also now significant. The ESC contains a much larger number of provisions which are relevant to labour law than the ECHR.[437] Part II of the Charter contains 19 articles, including the right to work (Article 1), the right to just conditions of work (Article 2), the right to safe and healthy working conditions (Article 3), the right to a fair remuneration (Article 4), the right to organise (Article 5), the right to bargain collectively and the right to strike (Article 6); the right of children and young persons to protection (Article 7) and the right of employed women to protection (Article 8). However, signatory states

---

[433] Creighton, 1994: p 4.

[434] See Novitz 1998, 2000, 2003.

[435] In the case of the ICCPR there is an optional inter-state procedure and an individual communications procedure to the Human Rights Committee which the UK has not accepted. On the ICCPR and ICESCR see S Joseph, 2010; on the ICESCR see Craven, 1998; Joint Committee on Human Rights, 21st Report, Session 2003/2004.

[436] On the procedure for bringing a case before the European Court of Human Rights see Reid, 2007, Part I.

[437] A revised ESC was opened for signature on 3 May 1996. The changes made include widening the non-discrimination principle and adding new rights such as the right to protection in cases of termination of employment, the worker's right to dignity and the right of workers with family responsibilities to equal opportunities and equal treatment. The UK signed the revised charter in November 1997, but at the time of writing has not ratified it. See generally Blanpain, 2001.

may choose to be bound by only ten of these articles (or 45 numbered paragraphs).[438] Moreover, unlike the ECHR, there is no avenue for enforcing the Charter open to individuals although in 1995 a Protocol providing for a system of collective complaints by management, labour and non-governmental organisations was introduced.[439] However the general mechanism for enforcement is scrutiny by a committee of nine independent experts, assisted by an ILO representative in a consultative capacity, of reports on law and practice within each signatory state supplied by the respective governments, although unions and employers' organisations have a chance to comment on them. This Committee, now known as the European Committee of Social Rights,[440] draws up a report which is sent to the organs of the Council of Europe. In the last resort the Committee of Ministers can make any necessary recommendations to an individual state. This procedure is open to a number of criticisms, including the fact that evidence of compliance with Charter obligations is produced solely by governments, unless some other body chooses gratuitously to furnish evidence, and that ultimately the role of the Committee of Ministers means that the parties are judges in their own cause.[441]

We shall refer to the relevant provisions of the instruments referred to above as they relate to the particular areas dealt with in this work. Here we confine ourselves to emphasising that the standards they prescribe are, in general, considerably less detailed than those formulated by the ILO. Moreover, they are not rooted in a labour relations framework, a consequence which, as we shall see, has produced significant differences in the interpretation of the freedoms which they guarantee from the standards developed by the ILO. The dangers of such discrepancies are amply demonstrated by the differential treatment of the UK Government's ban on membership of national civil service trade unions in 1984 which we discuss in para 7.10.[442]

2.44   In the UK, international obligations are not, as such, part of domestic law unless enshrined in legislation. This does not mean that they should thereby be ignored, however. Apart from their importance as a benchmark of accepted standards, in interpreting ambiguous legislation the courts act on a (rebuttable) presumption that Parliament intended to legislate in accordance with international obligations. In addition when interpreting the common law the courts may be persuaded to take cognisance of international standards,[443] and they may look beyond decisions of the ECtHR in interpreting the scope of 'Convention rights' pursuant to the HRA 1998. It is also possible that standards drawn from other instruments may enter UK domestic law via EU obligations; the principle of equal pay for work of equal value, incorporated in ILO Convention

---

[438] Art 20. Ironically, because the ESC allows contracting states some discretion as to the articles they accept it was used in the past by the ECtHR to bolster a narrow interpretation of Art 11 of the ECHR: see further *National Union of Belgian Police v Belgium* judgment of 27 October 1975, (1975) 1 EHRR 578 at para 38. There was a break with this approach in *Demir and Baykara v Turkey* judgment of 12 November 2008, [2009] IRLR 766; see further para 7.9 below.

[439] See Brillat, 1996; Cullen, 2000; Evju, 2001a; Churchill and Khaliq, 2004.

[440] Formerly the Committee of Independent Experts. For a useful overview of the Committee's jurisprudence, see Samuel, 1997. Recent ECSR Conclusions are on the ESC web site: www.coe.int.

[441] See D Harris, 1984; O'Higgins, 1991.

[442] For a more detailed critique of the relationship between standards formulated by the ILO and those of other bodies in the area of freedom of association see G Morris, 1994a. For a broader discussion, see O'Higgins, 2002.

[443] See Laws, 1993; Hunt, 1997. For the dangers of exposing ILO instruments to (mis)interpretation by the UK courts see *R v Secretary of State for Foreign and Commonwealth Affairs, ex p Council of Civil Service Unions* [1984] IRLR 353, CA and the trenchant critique by Ewing, 1994a: paras 8.10–8.13.

No 100 on Equal Remuneration, being one prominent example.[444] Moreover, ILO principles may inform the decisions of the ECJ in interpreting existing EU law, as has the ECHR.[445] However, unless specifically enshrined in EU legislation, it could not be argued that the principles contained in ILO Conventions constituted free-standing, enforceable rights under EU law.[446]

A common feature of institutionalised international labour standards generally is the weakness in the mechanisms for enforcing them. An additional mechanism, of potentially great significance, is to make compliance with such standards a condition of international trade agreements, a strategy analogous to that of contract compliance outlined in para 2.6. There are a number of recent examples of 'social clauses' being inserted into trade agreements, although to date a social clause has yet to be adopted by the World Trade Organisation, and opponents have suggested (disingenuously or otherwise) that clauses of this nature may act as a form of protectionism in preserving jobs in rich countries that have the resources to meet such standards rather than promoting economic progress in poorer ones.[447] A further development in recent years has been the adoption of codes by transnational corporations keen to advertise themselves as upholders of ethical business practices, so 'privatising' labour standards, although research has shown that the content of these codes may be highly selective (with few addressing freedom of association, for example), and compliance with them inadequately monitored and enforced.[448] It is unlikely that the economic power of these corporations alone can be relied upon to secure core labour standards in the absence of independent supervision.

LABOUR STANDARDS AND PRIVATE INTERNATIONAL LAW

2.45   With increasing transnational mobility of labour and, in particular, of capital, the issue of conflicts of law between different labour law regimes is a very live one.[449] The relevant issues here include the question of which law governs employment relationships, and what the relationship is between a formal choice of law clause in a contract and the potentially overriding rules of employment legislation.

The applicable law of the contract of employment

2.46   The starting point for analysis is the rules of the conflict of laws applied by English and Scottish courts for ascertaining the applicable law of the contract of employment. Where the parties have made a formal choice of law the courts will generally respect this, although it is thought that

---

[444] For an assessment of the (limited) opportunities for incorporating ILO standards further into EU law see Ewing, 1994a: paras 8.14–8.18.

[445] See, for example, Case C-438/05 *ITWF v Viking Line ABP* [2008] IRLR 143, paras 43 and 44; see further para 11.52.

[446] Ewing, 1994a: p 49.

[447] See generally Hepple, 1997a: pp 360–362; Ewing and Sibley, 2000; Tsogas, 2000; Cullen, 2000b; Murray, 2001; Gibbons, 2004; Hepple, 2005b.

[448] Hepple, 1999a; Arthurs, 2002; Gibbons, 2004; Hepple, 2005b: ch 3; Blanpain, 2010. International framework agreements have the potential to offer a more fruitful means of securing standards: see Drouin, 2010.

[449] For a fuller treatment of this complex subject, see L Collins *et al*, 2008 and supplements: paras 33-058–33-105.

they would disregard a choice of law clause which established as the applicable law one with which the contract had no real connection, and which was manifestly to the employee's disadvantage.[450] In the absence of an express or implied choice, the test of 'closest and most real connection' applies. This has been applied flexibly to cover the differing situations of employees. For senior employees, the applicable law is usually held to be that of the state in which the undertaking is based or from which it is controlled.[451] For lower level employees, the applicable law will normally be the state in which they reside or in which they normally work.[452] The justification for this different treatment is that high-level employees are more closely associated with the central control of the organisation and hence with its base. The place in which the contract is made may also be a relevant factor.

The territorial scope of employment legislation

2.47 By virtue of various provisions contained in UK labour law statutes, a choice of law clause in a contract of employment or other contract does not exclude the provisions of those statutes if their enforcement would otherwise fall within the jurisdiction of the UK courts.[453] While this bar on contracting out sometimes poses a problem for transnational employers with employees working in a number of different jurisdictions, any other approach would run the risk of contracts being framed so as to evade UK legislation, in favour of regulation by the weaker laws of another state.

Until recently many significant employment protection rights were denied to employees who ordinarily worked outside Great Britain.[454] This restriction was abolished by ERelA 1999 in relation to rights protected by ERA 1996,[455] so removing any geographical limitation on its scope from the face of the statute. This change, which was linked to the implementation by the United Kingdom of the Posted Workers Directive[456] but had wider implications for the reach of employment legislation, created considerable uncertainty as to ERA's territorial application. In *Lawson v Serco Ltd*,[457] which concerned the application of the right not to be unfairly dismissed

---

[450] See Kahn-Freund, 1978a; Hepple, 1978; Morse, 1982.

[451] *Re Anglo-Austrian Bank* [1920] 1 Ch 69.

[452] *South African Breweries v King* [1899] 2 Ch 173.

[453] Some statutes contain provisions dealing specifically with the question of the applicable law of the employment contract (TULRCA 1992, s 289; ERA 1996, s 204)as well as more general provisions preventing the use of the contract terms, including, arguably, a choice of law clause, from excluding the protection of the legislation concerned (TULRCA 1992, s 288; ERA, 1996, s 203). Some statutes contain only provisions of the second type (see NMWA 1998, reg 49; WTR 1999, reg 35; PTWR 2000, reg 9; FTER 2002, reg 10; AWR 2010, reg 15 (cross-referring to ERA 1996, s 203)).

[454] ERA 1996, s 196 (now repealed). The terms of the exclusion varied with the right in question. On the application of the Act to offshore employments in the territorial waters of the UK and on the continental shelf, a category which includes employment on North Sea oil platforms, see ERA 1996, s 201 and the Employment Protection (Offshore Employment) Order 1976, SI 1976/766, as amended.

[455] Section 32(3).

[456] See below, para 2.49.

[457] [2006] IRLR 289. This was one of three co-joined appeals, the others being *Crofts v Veta Ltd* and *Botham v Ministry of Defence*. The facts of the respective cases are outlined at [2006] IRLR 289, [2]-[5]. See also *Williams v University of Nottingham* [2007] IRLR 660; *YKK Europe Ltd v Heneghan* [2010] IRLR 563; *Ministry of Defence v Wallis and Grocott* [2011] ICR 617; *Duncombe v Secretary of State for Children, Schools and Families (No 2)* [2011] IRLR 840; *Ravat v Halliburton Manufacturing and Services Ltd* [2012] IRLR 315; Merrett, 2010. In *Pervez v Macquarie Bank Ltd (London Branch)* [2011] IRLR 284 the EAT construed reg 19 of SI 2004/1861 broadly to avoid it depriving a claimant of a forum to enforce a right.

under ERA 1996, s 94(1), Lord Hoffmann, with whose speech the remainder of the House of Lords agreed, stated that it was 'inconceivable that Parliament was intending to confer rights upon employees working in foreign countries and having no connection with Great Britain'.[458] The relevant question concerned the connection between Great Britain and the employment relationship that was required in order to make s 94(1) the applicable law. The answer to this depended upon the construction of the specific statutory provision at issue according to established principles, rather than upon the application of an 'ancillary rule'.[459] In the case of s 94(1), what Parliament must have intended as the 'paradigm case' was the employee who was working in Great Britain. Under the repealed legislation, the decisive question was whether 'under the employee's contract of employment' he or she ordinarily worked outside Great Britain. Lord Hoffmann considered that the 'radical change' in the attitude of Parliament and the courts to the employment relationship since 1971, when that restriction had first been introduced,[460] meant that the application of s 94(1) 'should now depend upon whether the employee was working in Great Britain at the time of his dismissal, rather than upon what was contemplated at the time, perhaps many years earlier, when the contract was made'.[461] Where, however, the employee was a peripatetic worker, such as an airline pilot or international management consultant, who might spend considerable periods working overseas, the employee's 'base' should be treated as the place of employment.[462] In relation to the 'base' test, Lord Hoffmann cited the judgment of Megaw LJ in *Wilson v Maynard Shipbuilding Consultants AB* where he said that in identifying an employee's base, account should be taken of such contract terms:

> ... as expressly define his (sic) headquarters, or which indicate where the travels involved in his employment begin and end; where his private residence – his home – is, or is expected to be; where, and perhaps in what currency, he is expected to be paid; [and] whether he is to be subject to pay national insurance contributions in Great Britain.[463]

On this approach, the fact that employees may spend more time out of the country than in it will not, of itself, exclude them from protection, nor will the fact that pilots who are based in London are employed by a foreign airline.[464] Lord Hoffmann also held that there may be 'unusual' circumstances in which 'expatriate employees' could fall within s 94(1) even though they both work and are based abroad. Although he did not wish to define them, he sought to 'identify the characteristics which such exceptional cases will ordinarily have' by reference to two examples.[465] The first was where the employee was posted abroad by a British employer for the purposes

---

[458] [2006] IRLR 289, [1].

[459] [2006] IRLR 289, [23], [34].

[460] In IRA 1971, s 27(2).

[461] [2006] IRLR 289, [25]–[27]; cf *Carver v Saudi Arabian Airlines* [1999] IRLR 370, which Lord Hoffmann said he would expect to be decided differently today (and which was subsequently not followed in *Saggar v Ministry of Defence* [2005] IRLR 618). Lord Hoffmann considered that the approach outlined in the text would accord with the spirit of the Posted Workers Directive. It should be noted, however, that, as interpreted in Case C-319/06 *Commission v Luxembourg* [2009] IRLR 388, the Posted Workers Directive neither requires nor permits a member state to apply unfair dismissal legislation (among other things) to a posted worker. See para 2.49 below.

[462] [2006] IRLR 289, [28]-[30], approving *Todd v British Midland Airways Ltd* [1978] IRLR 370, 371 (Lord Denning MR).

[463] [1978] ICR 376, 387.

[464] This was the case in *Crofts v Veta Ltd* above, note 457.

[465] [2006] IRLR 289, [36]–[40].

of a business conducted in Britain, such as the foreign correspondent on the staff of a British newspaper who was posted, say, to Rome and lived there for some years but who remained a permanent employee of the newspaper who could be posted to some other country. The second example was that of an employee of a British employer who was operating within what amounted for practical purposes to 'an extra-territorial British enclave in a foreign country'. This was the position of a 'UK-based youth worker' who worked at various Ministry of Defence establishments in Germany[466] and that of the claimant in *Lawson*, an employee of a British company employed to provide security at an RAF base on Ascension Island, which was, in practice, 'a British outpost in the South Atlantic'. He had not taken up employment in a foreign community in the same way as if his employer had been 'providing security services for a hospital in Berlin'.[467]

While *Lawson v Serco* provided welcome clarification to the territorial scope of ERA 1996, s 94(1), which was said to be a question of law,[468] a number of issues still remain.[469] The first relates to the 'paradigm' case. Although Lord Hoffmann stated that an employee who is 'merely on a casual visit' to Britain at the time of dismissal would not be covered, and that the contractual terms and prior history of the relationship may be relevant in determining this,[470] he did not indicate how long such an employee would need to have worked in Britain before he or she was protected. Second, there may be cases which fall between the 'paradigm' and the peripatetic cases – an employee who is recruited in Great Britain but works overseas on an occasional basis and who is dismissed while overseas. Third, when an expatriate employee takes up, or does not take up, 'employment in a foreign community' may not be straightforward to determine. More broadly, the decision leaves open the principles that apply to the many rights other than unfair dismissal that ERA 1996 protects.[471] In *Ravat v Halliburton Manufacturing and Services Ltd* the Supreme Court stated that Lord Hoffmann's indication of the circumstances in which expatriate employees could be covered by s 94(1) of ERA 1996 should not be treated as exhaustive; rather they were examples of a general principle.[472] The starting point of inquiry was that the employment relationship must have a 'stronger connection with Great Britain than with the foreign country where the employee works'.[473] In each case it would be a question of fact and degree whether the connection is 'sufficiently strong' to overcome the general rule that the place of employment is decisive.[474] For those who not only worked but also lived outside Great Britain 'an especially strong connection' with Great Britain and British employment law would need to be shown; for a 'commuter' with a home in Britain the burden would be less onerous.[475]

Express geographical restrictions remain in place in relation to certain other statutory rights. Anti-discrimination legislation was until recently limited in its scope to employment 'at

---

[466] The claimant in *Botham v Ministry of Defence*; see above, note 457.

[467] [2006] IRLR 289, [39].

[468] Above, [34]. Lord Hoffmann also stated, however, that it was 'a question of degree on which the decision of the primary fact-finder is entitled to considerable respect'.

[469] See further Linden, 2006.

[470] [2006] IRLR 289, [27].

[471] On the significance of the Posted Workers Directive in this context, see para 2.49 below.

[472] [2012] IRLR 315.

[473] [2012] IRLR 315, Lord Hope (giving the judgment of the Court) at [27].

[474] [2012] IRLR 315 at [28].

[475] [2012] IRLR 315 at [28], [29].

an establishment in Great Britain',[476] but under EqA 2010 these express restrictions have been repealed, so that '[a]s far as territorial application is concerned, in relation to Part 5 (work) and following the precedent of the Employment Rights Act 1996, the Act leaves it to tribunals to determine whether the law applies, depending on for example the connection between the employment relationship and Great Britain'.[477] The NMWA 1998 requires an individual to be working, or ordinarily working, in the UK under his or her contract in order to qualify for the national minimum wage.[478] Specified rights under TULRCA 1992 – the right not to be denied access to employment, or to suffer a detriment in employment, on grounds relating to trade union membership and activities, and the right to time off for union duties and activities – are excluded where *under* his or her contract of employment 'an employee works, or in the case of a prospective employee, would ordinarily work, outside Great Britain'.[479] In addition, in deciding whether a valid request for recognition may be made against an employer, it may be necessary to determine whether workers employed by an associated employer ordinarily worked in Great Britain during a particular period.[480] The WTR 1998 'extend to Great Britain only'.[481]

As the examples given above make clear, where express 'place of work' restrictions remain in place, they are not framed in a uniform fashion. They commonly refer to where an individual 'ordinarily' works but differ as to whether reference is made to the worker's contract. In cases where no such reference is made, the dicta in *Lawson* are likely to be persuasive. Under the pre-*Lawson* case law it was held that a person ordinarily works either in or outside Great Britain; the argument that he or she could simultaneously work in both was rejected.[482]

Although an express choice of law clause may not have the effect of ousting the jurisdiction of the British courts if it is clearly provided for by statute, it can have the effect of extending that jurisdiction in two cases. The first is where statutory rule in question is derived from EU law. In *Bleuse v MBT Ltd*[483] the employment in question was carried out mostly in Germany and Austria, but the parties' agreement stated that English law was the applicable law of the contract. Elias P held that where 'English law is the proper law of the contract… an English court properly exercising jurisdiction must seek to give effect to directly effective rights derived from an EU Directive by construing the relevant English statute, if possible, in a way which is compatible with the right conferred'.[484] On this basis he held that the claimant could assert the right to paid

---

[476] EqPA 1970, s 1(1); SDA 1975, s 6; RRA 1976, s 4; DDA 1995, s 4(6); EE(SO)R 2003, reg 6; EE(RB)R 2003, reg 9; EE(A)R 2006, reg 7.

[477] Explanatory Notes to the Equality Act 2010, para 15.

[478] Section 1(2).

[479] Section 285. The duty to notify the Secretary of State of collective redundancies is also excluded in relation to such employees. TULRCA 1992, ss 145A–151 do not apply to employment where under his or her contract personally to do work or perform services a worker who is not an employee works outside Great Britain: s 285(1A).

[480] TULRCA 1992, Sch A1, paras 7(3), (4). See also *Skyshare* and *Netjets Management Ltd* TUR1/553 (2012), where the CAC was required to decide whether there were any territorial restrictions relevant to whether the application for recognition should be accepted.

[481] WTR 1998, reg 1(2).

[482] *Wilson v Maynard Shipbuilding Consultants AB* [1978] ICR 376, 384.

[483] [2008] IRLR 264. See also the judgment of the Court of Appeal in *Duncombe v Secretary of State for Children, Schools and Families* [2010] IRLR 331, in which it was suggested that a UK statute deriving from an EU law source could have extra-territorial effect in these circumstances whether or not the right in question was directly effective. In the Supreme Court the case was decided on slightly different grounds (see below, this para).

[484] [2008] IRLR 264, at [55] and [56]. Elias P thought that the same principle applied in a case where English law provided the body of mandatory rules applicable to the employment relationship under Art 6(2) of the Rome Convention (now superseded by Art 8(2) of the Rome I Regulation), on which see para 2.48 below).

annual leave under WTR 1998 in a claim before a British employment tribunal.   The second situation arises where the presence of a choice of law clause can be read, along with other factors, as establishing a sufficiently close connection between the employment in question and British employment law under the *Lawson v Serco* test. In *Duncombe v Secretary of State for Children, Schools and Families (No 2)*[485] claims for unfair dismissal under s 94(1) ERA 1996 were brought by teachers employed by the UK government to teach English at European schools located on the continent and providing education for the children of EU civil servants. Their contracts stated that their employment was governed by English law. According to Baroness Hale, four factors pointed to allowing the claims to proceed before a British employment tribunal: the employer, being the UK government, had the strongest possible connection to Britain; the choice of law clause gave rise to expectations on the part of the claimants that they would be protected by the provisions of British employment legislation; while abroad they were effectively working in UK enclaves in the sense set out in *Lawson v Serco*; and it would have been analmous and unfair to deny their claims on jurisdictional grounds given that teachers of English employed at European schools located in Britain would not have been so barred.

The impact of the Rome I Regulation and the Posted Workers Directive

2.48   The Convention on the Law Applicable to Contractual Obligations 1980 (the 'Rome Convention') was signed by the UK in 1981, and was incorporated into UK law by the Contracts (Applicable Law) Act 1990.[486] The main aim of the Convention was to harmonise different national rules of the conflict of laws, and it made a significant difference to British practice as far as the contract of employment was concerned by limiting the effectiveness of a choice of law clause in the employment context. Under Article 6(1), 'in a contract of employment a choice of law made by the parties shall not have the result of depriving the employee of the protection afforded to him by the mandatory rules of the law which would be applicable ... in the absence of choice', while under Article 6(2), in the absence of choice, a contract of employment was to be governed:

(a)   by the law of the country in which the employee habitually carries out his work in performance of the contract, even if he is temporarily employed in another country; or

(b)   if the employee does not habitually carry out his work in any one country, by the law of the country in which the place of business through which he was engaged is situated;

unless it appears from the circumstances as a whole that the contract is more closely connected with another country, in which case the contract shall be governed by the law of that country.

These provisions only applied for the benefit of the employee.

---

[485] [2011] IRLR 840.
[486] R Smith and V Cromack, 1993.

The Rome Convention has been superseded by the Rome I Regulation.[487] The UK initially opted out of the process for agreeing the Rome I Regulation as it was permitted to do by the Protocol on the position of the United Kingdom and Ireland agreed at the Amsterdam Treaty in 1997 but the Labour Government indicated that it would abide by the Regulation and it came into force in the UK in December 2009.[488] Article 8(1) of the Rome I Regulation retains the rule set out in Article 6(1) of the Rome Convention, while under Article 8(2),

> To the extent that the law applicable to the individual employment contract has not been chosen by the parties, the contract shall be governed by the law of the country in which or, failing that, from which the employee habitually carries out his work in performance of the contract. The country where the work is habitually carried out shall not be deemed to have changed if he is temporarily employed in another country.

A significant change here is the reference to the applicable law of the contract of employment being that of the country 'from which' the employee habitually works. This addition was intended to have the effect of bringing within the Regulation cases involving airline pilots and other transport workers who habitually worked *from* a particular base or location, but who, because they did not habitually work *in* a given country, might not have fallen under Article 6(2);[489] as we have seen, UK law independently takes a flexible view of the territorial reach of unfair dismissal legislation on this point.[490]

In a case involving the temporary posting of a worker from one member state (the 'home state') to another (the 'host state'), the effect of Article 8 is to ensure that the law of the home state applies. This will be the case, first, by virtue of Article 8(1), in a case where the contract of employment states that the law of the home state is the applicable law, and, secondly, by virtue of Article 8(2), which indicates that in the absence of choice the law of the home state applies even if the worker is temporarily employed elsewhere. While a choice of law clause cannot deprive the worker of the protection of the mandatory laws which would apply in the absence of choice according to the 'habitual work' test, the final sentence of Article 8(2) ensures that this law is, in any event, the law of the home state in a posting case. On this basis, a worker temporarily posted to the UK from another member state would not have the protection of UK employment protection legislation, notwithstanding its normal territorial effect as explained by Lord Hoffmann in *Lawson v Serco Ltd*.[491] When the Rome Convention was still in force, there were other provisions of the Convention which could be invoked for the worker's protection in this context. Article 7(2) of the Rome Convention provided that '[n]othing in this Convention shall restrict the application of the rules of the law of the forum in a situation where they are mandatory irrespective of the law otherwise applicable to the contract'. By virtue of the various legislative provisions which gave compulsory effect to statutory employment rights regardless of the choice of law in the contract of employment or other relevant contract,[492] it was arguable that UK labour legislation

[487] Regulation (EC) No 593/2008 on the law applicable to contractual obligations (Rome I).
[488] See Barnard, 2009a; SI 2009/3064.
[489] Although a flexible interpretation of Art 6(2) would probably have caught many such cases: see Case C-29/10 *Koelzsch v Luxembourg* [2011] IRLR 514.
[490] See our discussion of *Lawson v Serco Ltd* [2006] IRLR 289 in para 2.47 above.
[491] [2006] IRLR 289.
[492] See above, para 2.47.

was 'mandatory' in the sense intended by Article 7(2), and so applied to workers posted to the UK from other member states regardless of the choice of law in their contracts of employment. However, this protection has arguably been qualified by the coming into force of the Rome I Regulation with effect from December 2009. This is because Article 9 of the Regulation, the successor to Article 7, is confined in its application to 'overriding mandatory provisions of the law of the forum', and these are defined as 'provisions the respect for which is regarded as crucial by a country for safeguarding its public interests, such as its political, social or economic organisation, to such an extent that they are applicable to any situation falling within their scope, irrespective of the law otherwise applicable to the contract under this Regulation.' As Barnard suggests,[493] it is unlikely that rights set out in employment legislation could be regarded as 'crucial' to its 'public interests' in this sense, in particular in the light of rulings of the European Court of Justice[494] which give a narrow reading to this concept and which provided a reference point in the drafting of Article 9.[495]

2.49   The situation is further complicated by the Posted Workers Directive.[496] The Directive carves out a series of derogations from the rules laid down in the Rome Regulation in a situation of a temporary posting. As we just seen, the normal rule in the Regulation is that the home state law applies to the posting. The Directive makes an exception to this by providing that posted workers must receive the protection of certain minimum labour standards which apply to employment in the host state while they are working there. However, as interpreted by the European Court of Justice in its recent rulings in *Laval*, *Rüffert* and *Luxembourg*,[497] member states may not confer protections on posted workers which go beyond those required or permitted by the Directive.

The Directive applies in the following three situations:[498] where undertakings in the home state and host state agree a contract for the supply of labour services between them; where the posting takes place through administrative arrangements made within a single group of companies (for example, where an employee of a group company based in the home state is seconded to a group company in the host state); and, where the posting takes place in the course of the supply of labour by an employment business/agency in the home state to an employer or agency in the host state.

The host state must then ensure that the workers concerned are covered by basic standards contained in laws, regulations and administrative provisions governing the following matters which are listed in Article 3(1): working hours, holidays, minimum pay, regulation of conditions of supply of labour by agencies, health and safety, protection of pregnancy and maternity, and

---

[493] Barnard, 2009a.

[494] In particular, Joined Cases C-369/96 and C-376/96 *Arblade* [1999] ECR I-8453.

[495] See Commission, *Proposal for a Regulation of the European Parliament and the Council on the law applicable to contractual obligations (Rome I)*, COM(2005)650 final, at p 7.

[496] Directive 96/71/EC concerning the posting of workers in the framework of the provision of services.

[497] Case C-341/05 *Laval Un Partneri Ltd v Svenska Byggnadsarbetareförbundet* [2008] IRLR 160; Case C-446/06 *Dirk Rüffert v Land Niedersachsen* [2008] IRLR 467; Case C-319/06 *Commission v Luxembourg*, judgment of 19 June 2008, [2009] IRLR 388. See also the decision of the EFTA Court in Case E-12/10, *EFTA Surveillance Authority v Iceland* [2011] IRLR 773.

[498] Art 1(3).

equal treatment of men and women and 'other provisions on discrimination'.[499] In respect of the building and construction trades only,[500] the host state must also apply standards derived from collective agreements 'which have been declared universally applicable',[501] that is to say, those agreements or awards 'which must be observed by all undertakings in the geographical area and in the profession or industry concerned'.[502] In *Rüffert*[503] the Court held that a German law which allowed a regional government to give mandatory effect to a sectoral collective agreement governing the performance of public building contracts only did not fall under Article 3(8), because it did not cover all undertakings in the relevant region and industry. In the absence of a system for declaring agreements or awards to be of universal application member states may, if they so decide, adopt for this purpose agreements or awards 'which are generally applicable to all similar undertakings' in the area and sector and/or collective agreements which have been concluded by the 'most representative' employers' and labour organisations at national level and which are applicable throughout national territory.[504] If a member state wishes to take up either of these options, it must do so explicitly; the Court's judgment in *Laval*[505] indicates that alternative methods of enforcement, involving, for example, legal support for or toleration of industrial action in support of collective agreements, fall outside the Directive, and may as a result involve a breach of the employer's rights in respect of the freedom to supply services under Article 56 TFEU (formerly Article 49 TEC).[506]

The Directive also states, in Article 3(10), that host states may enlarge their regulatory competence in two ways. They may apply norms derived from collective agreements (as defined above) to posted workers other than those in the building and construction industries, and they may apply to posted workers 'terms and conditions of employment' on matters other than those contained in the list of mandatory items in Article 3(1) where they are in the nature of 'public policy provisions'. The latter route appears at first sight to give the UK the option of applying unfair dismissal law, for example, to posted workers, and would therefore make it possible to make use, in their case, of the broad territorial effect accorded to ERA 1996 s 94(1) in *Lawson v Serco*.[507] However, this view is probably incompatible with the line taken by the European Court of Justice in *Commission v Luxembourg*.[508] The Court first of all drew on its earlier decision in *Arblade*[509] to argue that the concept of 'public policy provisions' in Article 3(10) refers to 'national provisions compliance with which has been deemed to be so crucial for the protection of the political,

---

[499] An obligation is also imposed upon the home state: its courts will be required to apply the minimum standards of the law of the host state for the period of the posting even if, in other respects, the contract is governed by the law of the home state. However, it is arguable that the relevant minimum standards here are cumulative, so that an employee cannot be made worse off by the application of the laws of the host state. See generally P Davies, 1997. The Directive gives workers the right to have proceedings instituted in the Member State to which they have been posted without prejudice, where applicable, to the right, under existing international conventions on jurisdiction, to institute proceedings in another State: Art 6.

[500] The relevant sectors are defined in the Annex to the Directive.

[501] Art 3(1).

[502] Art 3(8).

[503] Case C-446/06 *Dirk Rüffert v Land Niedersachsen* [2008] IRLR 467.

[504] Art 3(8). Any such arrangements must ensure equality of treatment between posting and national employers by imposing the same obligations with the same effects on each.

[505] Case C-341/05 *Laval Un Partneri Ltd v Svenska Byggnadsarbetareforbundet* [2008] IRLR 160.

[506] See further para 11.52.

[507] [2006] IRLR 289.

[508] Case C-319/06 *Commission v Luxembourg* [2009] IRLR 388.

[509] Joined Cases C-369/96 and C-376/96 *Arblade* [1999] ECR I-8453.

social or economic order in the Member State concerned as to require compliance therewith by all persons present on the national territory of that Member State and all legal relationships within that State'.[510] Later in its judgment the Court said that 'while the Member States are still, in principle, free to determine the requirements of public policy in the light of their national needs, the notion of public policy in the Community context, ... may be relied on only if there is a genuine and sufficiently serious threat to a fundamental interest of society', and added that a member state wishing to invoke Article 3(10) would have to bring forward 'appropriate evidence or ... an analysis of the expediency and proportionality of the restrictive measure adopted by that State, and precise evidence enabling its arguments to be substantiated'.[511] The Court's interpretation of Article 3(10) is an extremely narrow one, and while it may be compatible with the restrictive meaning given to the phrase 'overriding mandatory provisions' of law in Article 9 of the Rome Regulation, the result is to give member states virtually no scope to use this derogation in labour law matters.[512]

A proposal to exempt from the Directive all postings for less than three months, which had been included in an earlier draft, was removed from the final version. Three broad categories of exemptions remain.[513] First, a host state *must* exempt from the minimum pay and paid annual holiday provisions workers involved in cross-border provision of initial assembly and/or installation of goods where this is an integral part of a contract for the supply of goods, necessary for taking the goods supplied into use, and carried out by skilled and/or specialist workers of the supplying undertaking, and the posting does not exceed eight days.[514] Second, in the case of postings for less than one month, the host state, after consulting the social partners, may exempt workers from the provisions of minimum pay provisions, but this does not apply to agency-supplied labour. Third, in the case of postings where 'the amount of work to be done is not significant', exemption from minimum pay and paid leave provisions is allowed, but again this does not apply to agency-supplied labour.

It is open to question whether the Posted Workers Directive can be seen as having the purpose of protecting posted workers. Its 'treaty base' is Article 53 TFEU (formerly Article 47 TEC), which authorises the Council by qualified majority voting to adopt harmonising directives 'in order to make it easier for persons to take up and pursue activities as self-employed persons'; Article 62 TFEU (formerly Article 55 TEC) extends this provision to the freedom to provide services. Protecting posted workers can, in principle, be seen as an indirect way of encouraging the trans-border supply of services: 'as a means of protecting both the established workforce in the higher paying country and the migrant worker, who is ignorant about the general level of costs in the new country, one could argue that the ... full integration of workers from other Member

---

[510] *Commission v Luxembourg*, at para 29.

[511] *Commission v Luxembourg*, at paras 50, 51.

[512] See Barnard, 2009a; Merrett, 2010. There may, nevertheless, be scope to introduce arguments from public procurement law and equality law to limit the exclusion of local collective agreements under the Posted Workers Directive; see Barnard, 2009b, discussing the law relevant to the dispute which occurred at the Lindsey Oil Refinery during 2009.

[513] Art 3(2)–(6).

[514] As P Davies, 1997 points out at p 583 this appears to be an exemption from the obligation on the host state to apply its national provisions to posted workers, but does not state whether the host state is prohibited from imposing these provisions. However, it seems that the exemption must have this effect in order to distinguish this provision from those which give host states a choice. Note that this exemption does not apply to the building trades listed in the Annex to the Directive.

States into the domestic labour regulation of the importing state is the correct policy'.[515] However, in *Laval*, *Rüffert* and *Luxembourg* the Court interpreted the Directive in a very different light, as a measure designed to enhance the rights of service providers.[516] This was the basis for its view that the Directive essentially amplifies or concretises the meaning of Article 56 TFEU on the freedom to provide services, and for its decision to interpret the Directive as providing a ceiling rather than a floor of rights as far as the powers of member states to legislate for the protection of posted workers are concerned.[517]

The effect of *Luxembourg* is that the UK could well be in breach of the Directive. As we have seen,[518] the Directive was implemented in the UK in a rather unusual way, not through the enactment of a new code of rules applying to posted workers, but by the removal of provisions which had previously confined the scope of certain protective statutes to workers who did not ordinary work outside Great Britain. Once these provisions were repealed, the residual and implicit principle of the territorial scope of protective legislation, as subsequently confirmed by the House of Lords in *Lawson v Serco*,[519] came into play. If *Lawson v Serco* were followed in respect of other employment protection rights (it is not entirely clear that it would be as that decision can be seen as turning on the precise scope of unfair dismissal rights under ERA s 94(1)[520]), posted workers would have the benefit of other rights set out in ERA 1996 such as those relating to the written statement, whistleblowing, and redundancy compensation. The same point applies to the rights of part-time workers, fixed-term employees and temporary agency workers under PTWR 2000, FTER 2002 and AWR 2010 respectively. However, *Luxembourg* indicates that only those matters listed in Article 3(1) of the Directive can clearly and unequivocally be applied to posted workers. Although the matter is not free from doubt, then, UK law may well go too far in protecting posted workers.[521]

Exclusive jurisdiction clauses

2.50 The issue of jurisdiction over disputes arising out of the employment relationship is also affected by European Union law. An exclusive jurisdiction clause may purport to require a worker to pursue any claim before the courts of the state where the employer is based; that court might take a different view of the applicable law. As far as statutory rights are concerned, specific legislative provisions ensure that contract terms purporting to oust the jurisdiction of the employment tribunal are invalid.[522] Contractual disputes fall under the Brussels Regulation of 2001,[523] replacing the earlier Brussels Convention of 1968. The basic rule under the Regulation, as it was under the Convention, is that the employee may sue in the courts of the member state in which he or she

---

[515] P Davies, 1997: p 600.

[516] P Davies, 1997: p 600. Note also Case C-165/98 *Belgium v Mazzoleni* [2001] ECR I-2189.

[517] See Deakin, 2008; Barnard, 2009a.

[518] See para 2.46.

[519] [2006] IRLR 289.

[520] See our discussion in para 2.46 above.

[521] See Barnard, 2009a.

[522] See, eg, ERA 1996, s 203.

[523] Regulation (EC) No 44/2001 on jurisdiction and the recognition and enforcement of judgments in civil and commercial matters.

habitually carries out his or her work, or, if there is no such state, in the place where the business which engaged the employee is or was situated.[524] An employer may only sue in the member state where the employee is domiciled.[525] In addition, an exclusive jurisdiction clause in a contract of employment can only have effect, broadly speaking, in the employee's favour or in a case where the agreement conferring jurisdiction was entered into after the dispute arose.[526]

In *Rutten v Cross Medical Ltd*,[527] a decision under the Convention, the European Court of Justice held that where a contract of employment is performed in more than one Contracting State, the 'place where the employee habitually carried out his work' is the place where the employee has established the effective centre of his or her working activities and where, or from which, he or she in fact performs the essential part of his or her duties vis-à-vis the employer. In reaching this decision the court was concerned to protect the employee as the weaker party to the contract and to identify the place where it was least expensive for him or her to bring or defend proceedings. In *Weber v Universal Ogden Services Ltd* the Court held that where an employee performs for his or her employer the same activities in more than one Contracting State, the place where he or she 'habitually works' will be the place where the employee has worked the longest unless, on the facts, the subject-matter of the dispute is more closely connected with a different place of work.[528] The Court went on to hold that if these criteria do not enable the national court to identify the habitual place of work, the employee will have the choice of suing the employer either in the courts of the place where the business which engaged him or her is situated, or in the courts of the Contracting State in whose territory the employer is domiciled.[529] In *Samengo-Turner v JH Marsh & McLennan (Services) Ltd*[530] the Court of Appeal had to consider the effect of an exclusive jurisdiction clause in the context of a dispute over the enforcement of a restrictive covenant contained in a bonus agreement. The employer maintained that the dispute should have been litigated in the New York courts under the terms of the clause. The Court ruled in the claimants' favour, finding, first, that the bonus agreements were part of their contracts of employment, and second, that the English courts had the closest connection to the dispute under the tests set out in the Brussels Regulation. The claimants were employed by a UK-based company within the wider group, and worked in London. The Court issued an anti-suit injunction to restrain New York proceedings begun by the employer.

Conflict of law issues in collective labour law

2.51 The determination of the applicable law may also affect the enforceability and application of collective agreements and the incidence of liability for industrial action. As far as collective agreements are concerned, in the absence of an express choice the conflict of laws test of 'closest and most real connection' applies. In *Monterosso Shipping Co Ltd v ITWF*[531] this led the Court

---

[524] Regulation (EC) No 44/2001, s 5, Art 19.
[525] Regulation (EC) No 44/2001, s 5, Art 20.
[526] Regulation (EC) No 44/2001, s 5, Art 21.
[527] Case C-383/95 [1997] IRLR 249.
[528] Case C-37/00 [2002] IRLR 365, para 58.
[529] Case C-37/00 [2002] IRLR 365, para 58.
[530] [2008] IRLR 237; see also *Duarte v Black and Decker Corpn* [2007] EWHC 2720 (QB).
[531] [1982] ICR 675.

of Appeal to conclude that an agreement entered into in Spain and regulating the recruitment of Spanish seamen was governed by Spanish law, with the effect that the shipowners could sue for damages for its breach; had English law been the applicable law, the action would have been barred by the statutory presumption that collective agreements are not legally binding as contracts between parties to them.[532]

The applicable law in the case of collective industrial action will generally be determined by the rules of the conflicts of laws governing liabilities arising in tort or by virtue of another non-contractual obligation. Under the Rome II Regulation,[533] the basic rule is that where both the claimant and the defendant 'have their habitual residence in the same country at the time when the damage occurs', the law of that country applies.[534] However, without prejudice to this rule, the Regulation states that in cases of liability for damages caused by industrial action, 'the law of the country where the action is to be, or has been taken' shall apply.[535]

---

[532] TULRCA 1992, s 179; see para 9.26 below. See also *Dimskal Shipping Co SA v ITWF* [1992] IRLR 78, in which the identification of English law as the applicable law of a contract meant that the union was held liable to make restitution for economic duress, when under the law of Sweden, where the industrial action took place, no such liability would have been incurred.

[533] Regulation (EC) No 864/2007 on the law applicable to non-contractual obligations (Rome II), implemented in the UK by SI 2008/2986 with effect from 11 January 2009.

[534] Regulation (EC) No 864/2007, Art 4(2).

[535] Regulation (EC) No 864/2007, Art 9.

3

THE EMPLOYMENT RELATIONSHIP

INTRODUCTION

3.1   This chapter is concerned with the law governing the definition and formation of the individual employment relationship. Contractual concepts are central here, a role recognised in Kahn-Freund's striking description of the contract of employment as the 'cornerstone' of the modern labour law system.[1] The existence of the legal relationship of employment presupposes the voluntary consent of the parties to its creation, expressed through the process of hiring. The hiring process itself is the subject of only limited statutory intervention: there are few controls over the form it may take, and the protection of applicants for employment against exclusion by reason of discrimination of various kinds is far from comprehensive. In this area, at least, the common law of contract, and more specifically the principle of freedom of contract, retains much of its force.

The role of freedom of contract is, however, more limited in relation to the contents of the employment relationship and the means by which the relationship may be terminated. Subsequent chapters examine in greater detail the specific norms, deriving from statute, the common law and (indirectly) from collective bargaining, which apply in these areas.[2] In order to delimit the scope of these regulatory norms, it has been necessary for the law to develop criteria by which the subject-matter of labour law regulation, *dependent labour*, may be identified. These criteria have largely been borrowed from the common law, with the result that the category of dependent labour coincides largely, although not completely, with the common law concept of the contract of employment. Only an *employee* who is employed under a contract of employment is capable of qualifying for the majority of the protective rights contained in ERA 1996 and TULRCA 1992; the self-employed worker and independent contractor, whether or not they have a business of their own or employ others, are for the most part excluded from this legislation. Given that the process of identifying the contract of employment is, accordingly, crucial to determining the scope of this legislation, it is both surprising and unfortunate that the statutes themselves have had little or nothing to say about the criteria to be applied, leaving it to the courts to decide this issue according to common law tests which have become notorious for their complexity. Nevertheless, the development by the courts of these notions of employment status in the context of social legislation serves as a reminder that, as the 'cornerstone' of the labour law system, the concept of

---

[1] Kahn-Freund, 1954b: p 47.
[2] See, in particular, chs 4 and 5 below.

the contract of employment has a dual function: while underpinning the managerial power of the employer, it also serves as the gateway to social protection for the employee.[3]

The contract of employment is not the only concept deployed to these ends. In certain areas, which include equal treatment and health and safety legislation, the legislature has extended the normal definition of dependent labour beyond the contract of employment, to include certain categories of the self-employed and individuals whose employment status would otherwise be doubtful. These extensions are an important reminder that self-employment is not altogether excluded from the scope of labour law and, moreover, that statutory intervention can be used to overcome some of the limitations of the common law concept of the employee. It is significant, in this context, that the broader concept of the *worker* forms the basis for the application of the minimum wage, controls over working time, and other statutory labour standards which were introduced in the late 1990s. In addition, section 23 of the Employment Relations Act 1999 introduced a power, as yet unexercised, under which a statutory instrument can be used to extend the scope of employment rights to individuals who would not otherwise be protected by legislation.

Legislation contains additional bases for classifying and sub-dividing employment relationships. Once an individual has achieved employee status, to gain statutory protection it will often be necessary to show that he or she has also crossed certain minimum *qualifying thresholds* relating, in particular, to the length and regularity of their employment. These thresholds are expressed in the statutory concept of *continuity of employment* which is found in ERA 1996 and, in a slightly different form, in parts of SSCBA 1992. Between them, the requirements of employee status and continuity of employment potentially exclude from protection many individuals who either do not work a standard, full-time working week; who are employed on fixed-term contracts or for a short duration; who are employed as trainees or on government-funded employment schemes; who are employed to work at or from home; or who work on the basis that their labour is supplied to an employer by an employment agency or business. As the numbers of those in such 'flexible' or 'atypical' forms of employment have grown as a proportion of the labour force, so have the difficulties of applying to them a conceptual framework for labour law which, for the most part, is still wedded to the notion that the full-time, 'permanent' and regular employment relationship is the norm.

Just as it is essential to determine the legal status of a worker in relation to protective rights, so it is also vital to ascertain the nature and identity of the *employer* upon whom, or which, obligations may be imposed. While only a human person can be an employee, the employer may in principle be either a human person or a legal entity in the form of a partnership, a limited company, or a public authority or similar body. Courts and tribunals may then be faced with the question of which one of several different but related legal entities constitutes the employer for legal purposes. While in general there are few controls over the corporate form in which the owners of a business may choose to constitute it, the employment unit may sometimes be extended to cover associated employers within the same corporate group. In addition, employees may in some cases be able to shift liability from the employer with whom they are in direct contractual privity to a successor or purchaser company or other entity, to which the business in which they are or were employed has been transferred (a 'transfer of employment'). Situations also arise in which the normal functions

---

[3] See Deakin, 1998.

of the employer are divided between different entities. This is the case with agency work, for example. Here, the law has a role to play in determining which obligations will normally attach to the *agency* and which are assumed by the *user* or direct recipient of the worker's services. The principles according to which liability can be redistributed in these various ways are considered in later sections of this chapter. We also analyse concepts which are used, in particular contexts, to determine the form and scope of the *unit of employment*. The most important of these is the *establishment*, a term which is not limited to the physical location of work but which may for some purposes also embrace a managerial, financial or administrative unit.

CONTRACT OR STATUS?

3.2 Although the basic conceptual framework for the individual employment relationship is provided by contract, many have questioned whether it is useful to think of the employment relationship in this way. Kahn-Freund wrote of the employment relationship that '[i]n its inception it is an act of submission, in its operation it is a condition of subordination, no matter how much the submission and the subordination may be concealed by that indispensable figment of the legal mind known as the contract of employment'.[4] Prior to the hiring, there is rarely any parity in the relative bargaining power of employer and worker. This is not just because of the size of many modern employing organisations; few individuals have the independent means to enable them not to work. Thus Adam Smith, for example, recognised that:

> It is not … difficult to see which of the two parties must, upon all occasions, have the advantage in the dispute and force the other into compliance with their terms … Many workmen could not subsist a week, few could subsist a month, and scarce any a year, without employment. In the long run, the workman may be as necessary to his master as his master is to him; but the necessity is not so immediate.[5]

Social security law, while providing an alternative source of income to waged labour, also contains disciplinary mechanisms which may, for example, penalise the unemployed (or 'jobseekers') for not 'actively seeking work' or for refusing offers of employment,[6] and so can only be said partially to mitigate the pre-contractual inequality of employer and worker.

3.3 A second sense in which the employment relationship seems to lack the normal features of a contract is that agreement between the parties plays a relatively minor role in determining the substance of their reciprocal obligations. In part this is because of the inherent power of command which vests in the employer. As Fox has shown, this 'managerial prerogative' does not simply result from the employer's superior bargaining power prior to the agreement; it is also underpinned by certain legal norms, which today tend to take the form of the common law implied terms of the contract of employment. These implied obligations of fidelity, obedience and care which fill in

---

[4] P Davies and M Freedland, 1983: p 8.
[5] A Smith [1776] 1886: pp 27–28.
[6] See para 3.16 below.

the 'empty boxes of the contract'[7] can be traced back in many cases to the master and servant legislation of the nineteenth century and before: the needs of employers 'were met by infusing the employment contract with the traditional law of master and servant, thereby granting them a legal basis for the prerogative they demanded'.[8] The contract may be said to create a form of *status* which, as a source of the norms which govern the relationship of the parties, is separate from their express agreement.

Legal support for managerial powers is only one aspect of status in the modern employment relationship, however. The asymmetrical qualities of the employment relationship have been offset by a second form of status, derived from employment protection legislation and collective bargaining. Employment protection, working time and minimum wage legislation, among others, formally limits freedom of contract by providing rights which in most cases are 'inderogable', in the sense that they cannot be contracted away or made the subject of waiver.[9] This type of legislation has created new forms of status-based classifications, dividing workers, as we shall see, not simply according to whether they are employees or self-employed, but also, within the category of employees, according to the degree of length and regularity of employment, the duration of the normal working week, and the normal weekly wage or salary. These forms of protective regulation are sometimes said to have reversed what Maine described as the movement of 'progressive societies' from status to contract.[10] The application of this description to modern labour law is not straightforward, however. Kahn-Freund pointed out that Maine used the term 'status' to refer to relationships in which rights and obligations were imposed upon a person completely independently of his or her own volition, for example by virtue of their place of birth, nationality, or familial origin; in contrast, the modern usage of the term 'status' refers to relationships such as employment or marriage which although regulated by law are voluntarily entered into by the parties concerned. Although protective labour legislation frequently provides for 'inderogable rights', it also assumes the prior existence of a contract of employment (or, less usually, of another contract of some kind, such as a contract for personal services) which has been voluntarily entered into by the parties.[11] Contract and status (in the modern sense of that term) can be seen as interdependent: the capacity to contract is itself a form of status recognised by law, and the more specific status which attaches to the employment relationship 'operates on an existing contractual relation'.[12]

3.4   However, a wider point is at issue in neo-liberal critiques of labour law which echo Maine by suggesting that modern employment legislation represents a regression to status relations. These see protective regulation as illegitimate on the twin grounds of compromising the autonomy of the contracting parties and of creating unnecessary rigidities, and hence inefficiencies, in the labour market.[13] The contract-status debate persists in large part because it reflects this deeper concern about the legitimacy of statutory regulation of contract. The central issue is whether

---

[7] Fox, 1974: p 183.

[8] Fox, 1974: p 184.

[9] On the notion of 'inderogability' in this sense, see Wedderburn, 1992b.

[10] Maine, [1861] 1927: p 174.

[11] Kahn-Freund, 1967: p 640; cf the definition of an employee in ERA 1996, s 230(1), as 'an individual who has entered into or works under … a contract of employment'.

[12] Kahn-Freund, 1967: p 640.

[13] See Epstein, 1983, 1984.

contract and status are opposites, as the neoliberal critiques imply, or whether, as historical and institutional accounts suggest, they are better viewed as *interdependent* 'layers of regulation'.[14] Some points have already been made about this wider debate within economic and legal theory.[15] For immediate purposes, it may be useful to supplement our earlier analysis by considering some instances of the way in which tensions between contract and social legislation have been managed within the modern law of the employment relationship.

3.5 Summers, writing about the relationship between collective agreements and contract in US labour law, has suggested that the most important question is not whether these agreements are contracts since (in this, US, context) 'no one doubts' that they are:

> … but how much they are unlike other contracts and whether this makes them somehow less contractual in character. More specifically, in what particular respects are [they] unique, and how does their uniqueness affect their contractual character?[16]

Certain of the distinctive features of US collective agreements, as identified by Summers, apply also to contracts of employment; in particular, they are characterised by a high degree of incompleteness and uncertainty in the way the contract terms are defined. Individual bargaining provides, at most, only a general framework of express terms to govern the performance of the contract, which is partly why other sources of contract terms are also important: these range from implicit assumptions of the parties, the parties' own conduct subsequent to the formation of the contract, and custom and practice in the workplace concerned, to formal external sources of regulation, including collective agreements and legislation. Extending Summers' analysis, then, it could be argued that these distinctive features – the incompleteness of the contract and the role of sources subsequent or external to the agreement in completing it – make it inappropriate to apply to the contract of employment those principles of contract law which are designed to govern specific commercial transactions of a *different kind*, such as the sale of goods. As Lord Steyn has put it, whatever the position may have been in the past, '[i]t is no longer right to equate a contract of employment with commercial contracts. One possible way of describing a contract of employment in modern terms is as a relational contract'.[17] This does not necessarily mean that all of the general principles of contract law are irrelevant to the employment relationship. The question is whether these general principles of contract law are sufficiently flexible to be applied to the employment relationship without producing artificial reasoning and unsatisfactory results.

3.6 One area of employment law in which the principles of the common law of contract have undergone a substantial modification concerns the relationship between the collective agreement and the individual contract of employment. Terms from the collective agreement which are designed to regulate individual contracts take legal effect by virtue of the contractual doctrine of incorporation; the terms are incorporated by a 'bridging term' which may be express or

---

[14] Mückenberger and Deakin, 1989: p 192.
[15] See our analysis in ch 1 at paras 1.16–1.19 above.
[16] Summers, 1969: p 528.
[17] *Johnson v Unisys Ltd* [2001] IRLR 279, at [20]. On the employment contract as a relational contract, see Brodie, 2011.

implied into the contract of employment.[18] In this way, a principle of the common law achieves the same end as legislation performs in more highly regulated systems. Whether it does so in a fully effective way is perhaps doubtful. The courts have failed to deal consistently, for example, with the problem of conflicts between separate levels of bargaining, which is approached more systematically in systems which recognise a hierarchical relationship between separate sources of norms.[19] But in general, 'the individual contract has been skilfully refashioned by the courts to take collective bargaining into account while leaving the individual free to negotiate and enforce his own contract, which may be either more or less advantageous to him than the terms of the collective agreement'.[20]

3.7   The relationship between the common law of contract and social legislation is also a complex one.[21] The description given to the systems of law and equity in the decades following the Judicature Acts, namely that 'the two streams of jurisdiction, though they run in the same channel, run side by side, and do not mingle their waters',[22] is to some extent applicable to the relationship between common law and legislation within modern labour law. Statutory rights, for example, are rarely given the form of terms of the contract of employment.[23] Instead they more normally take the form of extra-contractual impositions,[24] which are often administered outside the regular system of the civil courts: the criminal courts were the principal mechanism for the enforcement of the nineteenth century Factory Acts and Truck Acts, as are employment tribunals in the case of modern employment protection legislation.[25] Some of the most difficult and persistent doctrinal questions in labour law have arisen at the point where the two bodies of principle come into contact with each other. There are rules for dealing with *conflicts* between them: it is a basic constitutional principle that legislation prevails over the common law. The precise scope of the statutory norm may not be readily ascertainable, however. A central question here is how far the application of statutory rules can be defeated by the contrary contractual intent of the parties. In part because of the extra-contractual form taken by most statutory rights, courts have in the past allowed parties to derogate from or 'contract out' of statutory rights, arguing that common law rights can only be ousted by clear wording in the statute.[26] In response, statutes have had to be drafted increasingly precisely, so that contractual terms which purport to remove statutory protection are *explicitly* prohibited and the limits of any permissible derogations are set by the legislation itself.[27] A further set of questions concerns what might be called the capacity of the two bodies of principle for *mutual recognition*. An enormous amount of litigation has been devoted to the question of how far regulatory legislation carrying criminal responsibility

---

[18] See ch 4, below, at para 4.29.

[19] See Supiot, 1994: p 30.

[20] Hepple, 1981b: p 56.

[21] Hepple, 2005a: lecture 3; J Beatson, 1997.

[22] Ashburner, 1933: p 18; cf the more modern view of fusion which is that expressed by Lord Diplock in *United Scientific Holdings Ltd v Burnley Borough Council* [1978] AC 904, 925; and see Freedland, 2003: pp 3–4.

[23] A rare example is the implication into contracts of employment and certain contracts for personal services of a 'sex equality clause' under EqA 2010, s 66 (see para 6.102 below).

[24] Hepple, 1981b: p 57.

[25] The difference became less marked with the extension of the jurisdiction of employment tribunals by SI 1994/1623: see para 2.15 above.

[26] For a clear statement of this, see *Valentine v Hyde* [1919] 2 Ch 129, 153 (Astbury J).

[27] Cf ERA 1996, s 203 (on which, see para 3.60 below), and TULRCA 1992, s 288.

also creates implied civil obligations in contract and tort. This concerns issues such as whether minimum wage legislation can be invoked to enable an employee to sue the employer in contract for the wages set by statute,[28] and whether the employer's failure to meet standards set by health and safety legislation can found an action for breach of statutory duty in tort.[29]

In the modern law, we can identify three principal ways in which the relationship between contractual and statutory rights has come to be defined. In the first place, there are areas in which legislation plays no direct regulatory role. Legislation says little or nothing about the formation of the contract of employment, for example, or about the conditions under which wages and salaries are payable by the employer in return for the employee's performance of the contract. In a second set of cases, legislation supplies a *floor of rights*[30] upon which contractual practice, and the common law, have built. In the areas of income and employment security covered by ERA 1996, NMWA 1998 and other statutes, as we have seen, derogation from the statutory norms is generally prohibited, but improvement on the standards set by statute is not prohibited, and is implicitly encouraged. This has created an additional role for contract. Terms may be improved by collective bargaining or by internal company rules, the relevant parts of which may then be incorporated into individual contracts of employment; in addition, contractual terms can be implied at common law, for example in relation to sick pay or lay off, for the protection of the employee.[31] In a third set of cases, legislation has established a further role for contract by explicitly allowing for contractual derogation from the norms it lays down. Thus under Part II of ERA 1996 (formerly the Wages Act 1986), express agreement by the parties to the contract of employment may displace and override statutory standards which would otherwise regulate deductions from wages.[32] Here, the derogation is 'controlled' in the sense of being subject to written formalities. Thus the legislation creates a space within which agreement can operate to make the application of protective standards more flexible, and to some extent moulds the form which that agreement will take.

Even in the areas where it is now accepted that statute has ousted contrary rules of the common law, extensive statutory intervention has, paradoxically, enhanced the importance of contractual principles by borrowing concepts and language from the common law. As Elias has put it, 'far from being cowed by [the] statutory assault, the contract of employment has emerged more resilient, and has proved to be infinitely more relevant than could possibly have been foreseen', largely because 'the statutory rights have been built upon the common law contractual framework, so that whilst the contract is of diminishing importance as a direct independent source of rights, it remains central to the operation of these statutory provisions'.[33]

---

[28] *Gutsell v Reeve* [1936] 1 KB 272 and *Cooner v PS Doal & Sons* [1988] IRLR 338 suggested that the employee can bring a civil claim of this kind even where the statute is silent or unclear. For the position under NMWA 1998, see ch 4, below, at para 4.59.

[29] See G Williams, 1960, and our discussion below, ch 4, para 4.95.

[30] Wedderburn, 1986: p 6; see below, paras 4.9–4.12. More recent, and highly contested, is the idea that in some contexts, social legislation sets a 'ceiling' of rights, in effect pre-empting or ousting the common law where it would have had the effect of conferring additional rights to those set out in statute. This idea was used by the House of Lords to limit the scope for the development of implied contract terms in *Johnson v Unisys Ltd* [2001] IRLR 279, and controversially extended to the case of certain express contract terms by the Supreme Court in *Edwards v Chesterfield Royal Hospital NHS Foundation Trust* [2012] IRLR 129. See our analysis below at para 5.43 *et seq.*

[31] See below, paras 4.4–4.8.

[32] ERA 1996, s 13.

[33] Elias, 1982: p 95. At the same time, it is clear that traditional contract law principles are substantially modified in the context of statutory provisions making use of the concept of the contract of employment: see *Gisda Cyf v Barratt* [2010] IRLR 1073, at [35]-[41] (Lord Kerr).

Statutory borrowing of the common law tests of employee status, the courts' use of the doctrine of illegal contracts of employment and the influence of contractual reasoning on the statutory notion of continuity of employment, each of which is considered later in this chapter,[34] illustrate this process, as do many other examples which are examined in this book. One which may briefly be considered here concerns the statutory definition of 'constructive dismissal' in section 95(1)(c) of ERA 1996. This provides that a dismissal takes place (*inter alia*) in a situation where 'the employee terminates … [the contract of employment] … (with or without notice), in circumstances in which he is entitled to terminate it without notice by reason of the employer's conduct'.[35] In *Western Excavating (ECC) Ltd v Sharp*[36] the Court of Appeal held that the question of when the employee was entitled to terminate the contract was to be settled by reference to principles of the common law of contract, namely the law relating to the right of an innocent party (the employee) to elect to terminate a contract for repudiatory breach by the other (the employer). The decision in *Western Excavating* has been criticised as setting up an unduly complex and restrictive test.[37] Just as important as the decision itself, however, are the developments which it subsequently prompted within the common law: faced with the task of defining the meaning of the employer's repudiatory breach for the purposes of section 95(1)(c) of ERA 1996, courts and tribunals extended the notion of the reciprocal duty of co-operation, in the process imposing certain obligations upon the employer to respect the personal dignity and autonomy of the employee.[38] This is one area in which the common law of contract has evolved in new directions as a consequence of its encounter with social legislation.[39]

3.8   The absence of a comprehensive labour code, the open-ended nature of common law rules, and the fragmented quality of much modern legislation have all contributed to a sharpening of the contract-status divide in British labour law. But, as we have just seen, these conflicts between sources may be thought to mask a deeper, functional interdependence between contract and status as modes of governing the employment relationship. Not only does the common law contain within it elements of status derived in part from the legacy of 'master and servant'; modern legislation, in addition to using contractual concepts, preserves for contract the important functions of building on the statutory 'floor of rights' and providing a method of 'controlled derogation' from certain standards. It is increasingly difficult to view the common law of contract and social legislation as separate streams whose waters 'do not mingle'.

---

[34] See below, paras 3.19, 3.25 and 3.59 respectively. Freedland, 2003: pp 10–11 distinguishes between 'statutory contractual formulae' which borrow straightforwardly from the common law, such as the definition of dismissal in ERA 1996, s 95(1)(c), and 'statutory para-contractual formulae', such as the notion of continuity of employment under ERA 1996, ss 210–219, which adapt or modify common law concepts.
[35] See below, paras 5.69-72.
[36] [1978] QB 761.
[37] Kerr, 1984.
[38] Hepple, 1981b: ch 9; see below, paras 4.100–4.109.
[39] See Deakin, 1997; Anderman, 2000; Freedland, 2003: ch 1; Hepple, 2005a: lecture 3. On the relationship between contract and HRA 1998, see G Morris, 2001a. The decision of the majority of the House of Lords in *Johnson v Unisys Ltd* [2001] IRLR 279 suggested that there might be limits to how far the courts were prepared to allow the common law to evolve in this way, and that the presence of social legislation might, paradoxically, provide a reason for limiting the further development of the common law; see also *Eastwood v Magnox Electric plc; McCabe v Cornwall Council* [2004] IRLR 733 and *Edwards v Chesterfield Royal Hospitals NHS Foundation Trust* [2012] IRLR 129. The view we express in the text accords more closely, however, with Lord Steyn's dissent in *Johnson*, which saw the common law as advancing in response to changes in social legislation. See generally our discussion of these cases at paras 5.43–5.45 below.

THE HIRING PROCESS

3.9   Access to the national labour market of the United Kingdom is governed by the Immigration Rules and by the principle of free of movement of labour within the European Economic Area. A full treatment of this subject lies outside the scope of this book, but the central principles will be noted here, in particular as they relate to the obligations of employers under asylum and immigration legislation. Access to a particular employment is subject for the most part to the principle of freedom of contract, but the law provides for protection against discrimination on a number of grounds including sex, sexual orientation, race, religion or belief, disability, age, and membership or non-membership of a trade union.

Access to the labour market

3.10   Rights of access to the labour market for non-UK citizens are governed by the relevant rules of European Union law for states within the European Economic Area,[40] and by the Immigration Act 1971 and the Immigration Rules for nationals of other countries. The Immigration Rules are promulgated and applied under the authority of the Home Office as an aspect of the prerogative power, although under the Immigration Act 1971 they must be laid before both Houses of Parliament for their approval.[41] If a resolution of either House is passed within forty days disapproving the proposed Rules, the Home Secretary is required to make such changes as he or she thinks fit and to re-submit them to Parliament.

(i) Non-EEA nationals

3.11   The general effect of the Immigration Rules governing employment is to regulate the supply of foreign labour into the UK. With effect from the third quarter of 2008, a new 'points-based' system for classifying migrant workers from outside the EEA came into force. From 2010 onwards the conditions for entry under this scheme were tightened and quotas put in place for certain categories of entry. There are currently three main 'tiers' governing entry for the purposes of employment, covering, respectively, 'high value migrants' with the capability to contribute to UK growth and productivity ('Tier 1'); 'skilled workers' with a job offer from a UK-based employer ('Tier 2'); and 'temporary workers' entering the UK to carry out short-term assignments in the creative industries, sports, religion or a number of related categories ('Tier 5'). Within each of the tiers, individuals will generally qualify for entry only if they can accumulate sufficient points on the basis of their qualifications, skills and experience. Tier 2 roughly corresponds to workers who would previously have required a work permit. Workers in Tier 2 (along with most of those in Tier

---

[40] The European Economic Area (EEA) consists of the Member States of the European Union and of the European Free Trade Area (EFTA). Under UK immigration law and practice, Swiss nationals are treated in the same way as EEA nationals.

[41] The current rules are based on HC Vol 395, Sess 1993–1994, 23 May 1994, as amended. The most recent changes were made in June 2012. A consolidated text is available on the Home Office web site: www.ukba.homeoffice.gov.uk/policyandlaw/immigrationlaw/immigrationrules//.

5) must find a sponsor before they apply for entry to the UK. To be a sponsor, an employer must be licensed as such by the UK Borders Agency ('UKBA'). Only employers with a 'sponsor licence' (which involves compliance with certain record keeping and related requirements) can apply for a certificate of sponsorship in respect of a given migrant worker. A certificate, in turn, may only be issued if a number of conditions are met.   In the case of most Tier 2 entrants, employer must demonstrate compliance with a 'resident labour market test' designed to ensure that the job in question could not have been filled from within the UK. Other limits apply to the number of workers who can be admitted under the Tier 2 general scheme. Thus for fiscal year 2011-12, a limit of 20,700 Tier 2 general entrants earning below £150,000 per annum has been set.   No limit applies in the case of Tier 2 workers earning above the statutory threshold.   Limits are also placed on the numbers who can be admitted under the Tier 1 scheme; for example, no more than 1,000 endorsements may be made in respect of persons of 'exceptional talent' in the sciences and arts.[42]

(ii) Citizens of EEA states

3.12   For citizens of EEA states – that is to say nationals of EU Member States and of other states which are party to the Agreement on the European Economic Area of 1992 – the rights of free movement of labour, as guaranteed by EU law, apply.[43] Article 21 TFEU (ex Article 18 TEC) states that 'every citizen of the Union shall have the right to move and reside freely within the territory of the Member States, subject to the limitations and conditions laid down in the Treaties and by the measures adopted to give them effect'. Under Articles 45 and 46 TFEU (ex Articles 39 and 40 TEC), three rights are established in relation to the free movement of workers: these are the *right to enter* another Member State for the purposes of employment, which includes the right to enter to look for work; a *right to reside* in the Member State where the worker has found work or (for a limited period) is seeking work, which may be lost once employment ends, except in certain cases of retirement and incapacity for work; and *a right to work on equal terms* with the nationals of the Member State concerned.[44] There are a number of general derogations to these rights on the grounds of public policy, public security and public health, which are strictly construed.[45] More detailed rules on entry and residence requirements are set out in Directive 2004/38/EC while the right of a citizen of an EEA state to work on equal terms with the nationals of the Member State is

---

[42] This limit applies between 9 August 2011 and 5 April 2012. See generally the UKBA website, above.

[43] See the Immigration (European Economic Area) Regulations 2006, SI 2006/1003. A separate agreement, made in 1999, between the EC, its Member States and Switzerland governs the access of Swiss nationals to the territories of the Member States, effectively conferring on them the same rights as EU citizens. SI 2006/1003 also implements this agreement.

[44] Arts 45 and 46 have direct effect in national law, following the opinion of the ECJ in Case 41/74 *Van Duyn v Home Office* [1974] ECR 1337.

[45] Case 41/74 *Van Duyn v Home Office* [1974] ECR 1337. Art 45(4) contains an exception for public employment which has also been strictly construed: Case 152/73 *Sotgiu v Deutsche Bundespost* [1974] ECR 153; Case 149/79 *Commission v Belgium* [1980] ECR 3881.

amplified by Regulation 492/2011. Transitional rules currently apply to nationals of Bulgaria and Romania seeking to work in the UK.[46]

(iii) Obligations of employers under immigration and asylum legislation

3.13　The regulatory effect of immigration controls was considerably reinforced by the passage of the Asylum and Immigration Act 1996,[47] which made it an offence punishable by a fine for an employer to employ a person who, under immigration law, did not have the legal right to work in the UK. This part of the 1996 Act has now been superseded by sections 15-26 of the Immigration, Asylum and Nationality Act 2006. These provisions and regulations made under them allow the imposition of a civil penalty of up to £10,000 in each individual case if an employer employs a worker who lacks the relevant legal status.[48] An employer may have a defence if it can show that it took certain steps in advance to establish whether the applicant possessed documentation establishing the right to work, such as a passport, work permit, or immigration status document issued by the UKBA provided that it did not know at any time during the period of employment that the employment was unlawful.[49] If the employer knowingly employs an illegal worker, there is a criminal offence punishable by up to two years' imprisonment and an unlimited fine.

　An employer who refuses to employ an individual because of doubts over his or her right to work may commit racial discrimination under EqA 2010. In *Dhatt v McDonald's Hamburgers Ltd*,[50] a case decided prior to the passage of the Asylum and Immigration Act 1996, the Court of Appeal held that no breach of the Race Relations Act (the predecessor to EqA 2010) had occurred in a case where an employee, who was born in India and held Indian citizenship, was dismissed for failing to convince his employer that he had the right to take up employment in the UK. The evidence offered by the employee, namely his passport stamped with the words 'Given leave to enter the United Kingdom for an indefinite period', was sufficient in principle to establish his right to work, but the employer was not aware of the relevant principles of immigration law. The Court held that the complainant had not been the subject of direct discrimination on the grounds of his *race*, a highly questionable decision since it seems unlikely that the applicant's ethnic origin played no part in the employer's treatment of him. The Court also suggested that if the case has been viewed as one of indirect discrimination, the steps taken by the employer would have provided it with a defence of justification.[51] This second aspect of the judgment also seems questionable. It could reasonably be argued that the employer in this case did not take adequate steps to ascertain the correct legal position.

---

[46] Workers from Bulgaria and Romania must normally apply for a 'worker accession card' from the UKBA (see the Accession (Immigration and Worker Authorisation) Regulations 2006, SI 2006/3317). This scheme is due to remain in force until 2013. For a recent Home Office summary of the relevant rules see www.ukba.homeoffice.gov.uk/eucitizens/bulgaria-romania/. See also Ryan, 2008.

[47] See Ryan, 1997.

[48] Immigration (Employment of Adults Subject to Immigration Control) (Maximum Penalty) Order 2008, SI 2008/132.

[49] These provisions are complex; see further the Immigration (Restrictions on Employment) Order 2007, SI 2007/3290 and the UKBA website: www.ukba.homeoffice.gov.uk/business-sponsors/preventing-illegal-working/.

[50] [1991] IRLR 130. See also below, para 6.19.

[51] On the difference between direct and indirect discrimination, and the role of the justification defence, see below, para 6.13.

If a similar case to *Dhatt* were to arise now, an employer might have a defence against liability under the 2006 Act where the worker had presented, prior to the beginning of the employment, documentation capable of establishing his or her right to take up the employment in question. Given the existence of this defence, it is hard to see how an employer could be justified in refusing to hire an individual on the grounds of their ethnic origin or nationality when they were, *objectively*, entitled to work. The implication of the tightened controls contained in the 2006 Act is that, in order to avoid the risk of incurring liabilities, employers should carry out document checks on all prospective workers, whatever their race or ethnic origin. Home Office advice is to the effect that for an employer to insist on document checks only for applicants of certain racial or ethnic origins, or to dispense with them in selected cases, amounts to racial discrimination.[52]

Access to employment: non-discrimination

3.14   The traditional approach of the common law to the hiring process was based on freedom of contract: the employer was free to refuse to hire a person for any reason, no matter how capricious, or for no reason at all.[53] However, discrimination in hiring is now prohibited by statute in relation to a number of specified criteria. In particular, decisions may not be based on the sex, sexual orientation, race, religion or belief, age or disability of the applicant.[54] A wide range of regulations which formerly excluded women workers from certain jobs on health and safety grounds were repealed in the 1980s,[55] leaving only a few such exclusions in place; a large body of regulations restricting the employment of children below the school leaving age remains in force. These provisions are considered in more detail in a later chapter.[56] Legislation also forbids employers hiring or refusing to hire an individual on the basis of their current membership or non-membership of a trade union (the principal aim of which is to restrict the operation of the pre-entry closed shop), and prohibits the blacklisting of workers on the grounds of their union membership or activities.[57]

3.15   Additionally, an employer may not refuse to hire an individual on the basis of a 'spent conviction' as that is defined by the Rehabilitation of Offenders Act 1974.[58] The Act does not provide any explicit civil remedy for such discriminatory action by an employer; there is no provision for damages to be awarded to a disappointed job applicant, nor for the employer to be required to hire him or her. The Act does provide, however, that the individual is permitted to conceal a spent conviction in answer to a question put to them by a prospective employer, and that 'the person questioned shall not be subjected to any liability or otherwise prejudiced

---

[52] See the UKBA website: http://www.ukba.homeoffice.gov.uk/business-sponsors/preventing-illegal-working/complyingwiththelaw/avoidingdiscrimination/.

[53] As restated in *Allen v Flood* [1898] 1 AC 1, 173 (Lord Davey).

[54] EqA 2010, s. 39(1). See generally our analysis in ch 6 below, in particular at paras 6.35–6.46.

[55] By virtue of SDA 1986 and EA 1989. See Deakin, 1990a.

[56] See ch 4, para 4.91 below.

[57] TULRCA 1992, ss 137–143 and ERABR 2010, respectively; see below, ch 8, at paras 8.33–8.37 and 8.27-8.32.

[58] Rehabilitation of Offenders Act 1974, s 4(3). There are numerous derogations from this principle for particular occupations (see the Rehabilitation of Offenders 1974 (Exceptions) Order 1975, SI 1975/1023, as amended) and the notion of a 'spent conviction' is only applicable to certain offences.

in law by reason of any failure to acknowledge or disclose a spent conviction.[59] In effect, then, those who go on to become employees are protected by the general law relating to dismissal: the employer may not later lawfully dismiss them if it should emerge that they lied about the spent conviction prior to being hired. Such a dismissal would be both a breach of contract at common law and equivalent to being an automatically unfair dismissal for statutory purposes. However, if an individual gives a misleading answer in relation to a conviction which is not spent, he or she commits a misrepresentation which renders the contract voidable at common law. It is also unlikely that an employer who finds out about such a conviction would be regarded as committing an unfair dismissal if it decided to terminate the employment.[60]

Active employment policy

3.16   In the modern period, state direction of labour to particular employments has been implemented only as a temporary measure during periods of national emergency during the two world wars. Regulations providing particular groups with a monopoly in the supply of labour for certain employments, such as the monopoly at one time enjoyed by Registered Dock Workers under the National Dock Labour Scheme, have been repealed.[61] A more persistent form of state intervention is constituted by active employment policy, which consists of measures designed to promote employment opportunities and facilitate the hiring process in various ways. Various subsidy schemes from the 1970s onwards have sought to protect or to promote employment through the payment of direct or indirect subsidies to employers,[62] but from a juridical point of view, the impact of active employment policy has turned out to be negligible. The hiring process is also implicitly shaped by social security benefits which are targeted onto lower paid employment. This is currently done through the system of tax credits which, while in some respects building on initiatives of the 1970s and 1980s, assumed its current form in 1999 with the introduction of the *working family tax credit*. This benefit was 'designed to make work pay for families, guaranteeing them a minimum income, above and beyond the minimum wage'; the government hoped that 'its clear link with employment [would] demonstrate the rewards of work over welfare and help ensure that people move off welfare into work'.[63] From 2003 the principal device has been the *working tax credit* scheme.[64]

The rules governing eligibility for unemployment benefits are another important aspect of state intervention in the hiring process. Social security legislation has contained an element of work discipline from its inception, although the rigour of the tests involved has fluctuated over time. In the 1920s the unemployed had to show that they were 'genuinely seeking whole-time employment' in order to retain benefit, and in the 1980s, when unemployment again reached historically-high levels, a number of similar initiatives were taken with the aim of 'sharpening' work

---

[59] Rehabilitation of Offenders Act 1974, s 4(2).

[60] *Torr v British Railways Board* [1977] IRLR 184; and, more generally on pre-contract misrepresentations and dismissal law, see *O'Brien v Prudential Assurance Co Ltd* [1979] IRLR 140, discussed below, para 5.137.

[61] The National Dock Labour Scheme was repealed by the Docks Work Act 1989.

[62] See generally Freedland, 1980, 1983; Lindley, 1983; Szyszczak, 1990.

[63] HM Treasury, *The Modernisation of Britain's Tax and Benefits System: Number Three. The Working Families Tax Credit and Work Incentives*, April 1998. The principal legislation governing the WFTC was the Tax Credits Act 1999.

[64] The relevant legislation here is the Tax Credits Act 2002. See Wikeley, 2002: ch 10.

incentives.[65] This process was taken a step further by the Jobseekers Act 1995. Disqualification for voluntary unemployment was retained, as were requirements that the individual should be available for work and actively seeking work; the penalties for failure were strengthened to the extent that entitlement could now be completely lost for a period of up to 26 weeks.[66] One of the most significant new provisions was the inclusion of a novel condition for receipt of benefits, namely that the claimant should agree to enter into a 'jobseeker's agreement' which lays out the steps that must be taken to find work. Loss of benefit may follow if the claimant fails to observe the agreement or to comply with directions issued by a local job centre officer.[67]

(i) The European Employment Strategy

3.17   A general framework for the conduct of active employment policy is now provided by the European Employment Strategy. The main legal source for this is the Employment Title of the TFEU, which was originally inserted into the TEC by the Treaty of Amsterdam in 1997. Article 145 TFEU specifies that 'Member States and the Union shall … work towards developing a co-ordinated strategy for employment and particularly for promoting a skilled, trained and adaptable workforce and labour markets responsive to economic change with a view to achieving the objectives defined in Article 3 of the Treaty on European Union'.[68] Article 146 TFEU outlines the more detailed obligations of the Member States. They are called on to co-ordinate their policies for the promotion of employment (which is to be regarded as an issue of 'common concern') within the Council, although, with an eye to social policy, they are also to have regard to 'national practices related to the responsibilities of management and labour', a significant reference to the role of the social partners.[69] At the same time, the Member States are required to act within the framework of the set of policies aimed at economic and monetary union (EMU) and in particular the broad economic guidelines which are issued annually by the Council as part of the process of ensuring economic stability and convergence.[70]

Article 147 TFEU calls on the Union to contribute to a high level of employment by encouraging and supporting the action of the Member States, and by *complementing* their action only 'if necessary' and after respecting 'the competences of the Member States'. The subsidiarity principle thereby carefully circumscribes the Community's role. Under Article 149 TFEU the European Parliament and the Council can act to 'adopt incentive measures designed to encourage co-operation between Member States and to support their action in the field of employment through initiatives aimed at developing exchanges of information and best practices, providing comparative analysis and advice as well as promoting innovative approaches and evaluative experiences, in particular by recourse to pilot projects'. However, these limited measures 'shall not include harmonisation of the laws and regulations of the Member States'. The framework put in place by the Employment Title is therefore facilitative rather than prescriptive. Through

[65] See Wikeley, 1989b; Deakin and Wilkinson, 1991.

[66] Jobseekers Act 1995, s 19; see also the Jobseeker's Allowance Regulations, SI 1996/207 (as amended).

[67] On the changes made by the Coalition government to the jobseeker's allowance and related aspects of social security law through the Welfare Reform Act 2012, see Puttick, 2012.

[68] On Art 3 TEU, see para 2.39 above.

[69] TFEU, Art 146(2).

[70] TFEU, Art 146(1).

the technique of EU-level governance known as the 'open method of coordination', Member States continue to have immediate control over their own employment policies, but these are benchmarked against employment guidelines issued by the Commission.[71]

IDENTIFYING DEPENDENT LABOUR

Classifying labour as 'dependent' or 'independent'

3.18   All systems of labour law draw a fundamental distinction between employment which is categorised as 'dependent' or 'subordinate' and that which is 'independent' or 'autonomous'.[72] In Britain this distinction principally takes the form of the classification of workers as either *employees*, on the one hand, or *self-employed* or *independent contractors* on the other. Employees are subject to the employer's common law powers of direction and control which, if they do not take the form of express contract terms, tend to be read into the contract as implied terms.[73] In return, employees come under the scope of employment protection and social security legislation: they may benefit from statutory rights to wage protection, limits on working time, income maintenance, and compensation for loss of employment.[74] By contrast, fewer of the burdens or benefits of dependent status apply to a relationship in which the worker is self-employed.

This basic picture must, however, be qualified in a number of respects. In the first place there is lack of consensus on the appropriate criteria for identifying dependence or subordination. The English courts have had occasion to use many different and potentially contradictory tests for this purpose, including 'control', 'integration', 'economic reality' and 'mutuality of obligation'.[75] However, this problem is unique neither to English law nor to the common law in general.[76] In most systems there is a conflict or tension between the use of criteria of *formal or personal subordination*, on the one hand, and those of *economic subordination*, on the other, as the principal

---

[71] For assessments of the Employment Strategy and related aspects of the open method of coordination, see Biagi, 1998; Kenner, 1999a; Szyszczak, 2000b; Ashiagbor, 2000; Deakin and Reed, 2000a; De Schutter and Deakin, 2005; Heidenreich and Zeitlin, 2009; and on the wider context and history of active labour market policy at EC level, see Freedland, 1996. The Euro Plus Pact, agreed by the Eurozone states along with a number of other Member States in March 2011, extends the mechanism of the OMC to cover aspects of economic and fiscal policy which have a number of direct implications for labour law and social policy at national level. Although the Pact is of considerable significance for the evolution of EU social policy, it is likely to have little direct impact for the UK, which remains outside the Eurozone and is not a signatory to the Pact. See Barnard, 2012.

[72] Barbagelata, 1986; Hepple, 1986b: p 74; Burchell *et al*, 1999; P Davies and M Freedland, 2000, 2004; Deakin and Wilkinson, 2005: ch 2; Langille and Davidov (eds.) 2006; Freedland, 2006; Deakin, 2007; Barnard and Deakin, 2008; Freedland and Kountouris, 2008. See also *Hall v Lorimer* [1994] IRLR 171, 174, in which Nolan LJ refers to 'the extent to which the individual is dependent or independent of a particular paymaster for the financial exploitation of his talents' as a relevant test of employee status.

[73] See, for example, *Sim v Rotherham Metropolitan Borough Council* [1987] Ch 216, discussed in ch 4, below, at para 4.65.

[74] See generally chs 4 and 5 below.

[75] See below, paras 3.26-3.29.

[76] Couturier, 1988: p 87 refers to a 'long-running debate' in France on the distinguishing features of the contract of employment. See, for comparative perspectives, Pedrazzoli, 1988. On the use of the term 'subordination' to define the scope of the principle of equal pay in EU law, see Case C-256/01 *Allonby v Accrington and Rossendale College* [2004] IRLR 224 at para 68, discussed below, para 3.33.

tests of dependence.[77] The use of 'economic' criteria tends to result in a widening of the scope of statutory protection, encompassing relationships in which the worker retains extensive discretion over the manner and timing of performance of the work but is nevertheless bound to the employer through dependence on wages or salary for subsistence. In English law a move towards the adoption of 'economic' criteria occurred when the courts used the integration test to extend employee status to certain professionals, such as doctors or accountants, who were employed within large organisations,[78] and also when they invoked the 'economic reality' test to extend the scope of protective legislation to include certain part-time workers and homeworkers.[79] But in general it cannot be said that economic criteria have successfully displaced rival tests: although control 'can no longer be regarded as the sole determining factor'[80] it must still be taken into account, and the more modern test of mutuality of obligation has led to a renewed emphasis on formality of commitment between the parties which has placed the status of many casual workers in doubt.[81]

A second problem is that the boundary between dependent and independent labour shifts according to the particular statutory context which is being considered. There is no universal dividing-line of general application between employees, who are protected by legislation, and the rest who are not. Thus while it is the case that only employees may qualify for most rights under ERA 1996, other statutes explicitly cover certain categories of the self-employed. In particular, protective legislation may be applicable to individuals who are not employees but do not have an identifiable business of their own. Some provisions of health and safety legislation apply to this group, as does equality legislation and legislation governing basic labour standards in relation to minimum wages and working time. Moreover, although the self-employed have no protection against dismissal in the context of industrial action, a dispute between self-employed workers and their employer may form the basis for a legitimate trade dispute which may enable the individual organisers of industrial action and their trade union to avoid liability in tort. The precise scope of these statutes in relation to the self-employed is examined in greater detail below;[82] for the moment, it is sufficient to point out that the self-employed are very far from being excluded completely from labour law regulation.[83]

The process of classification is complicated by the lack of a uniform terminology in the different Acts of Parliament which regulate the employment relationship. In ERA 1996 the term 'employee' is used to describe dependent labour but the equivalent term for most of the benefits

---

[77] The contrast is clearly expressed in the decision of the US Supreme Court in *United States v Silk* 331 US 704 (1946) and in the judgment of Cooke J in *Market Investigations Ltd v Minister of Social Security* [1969] 2 QB 173. See also Deakin, 1986.

[78] *Stevenson, Jordan and Harrison Ltd v Macdonald and Evans* [1952] 1 TLR 101; *Beloff v Pressdram Ltd* [1973] 1 All ER 241.

[79] *Market Investigations Ltd v Minister of Social Security* [1969] 2 QB 173; *Airfix Footwear Ltd v Cope* [1978] ICR 1210.

[80] *Market Investigations Ltd v Minister of Social Security* [1969] 2 QB 173, 185 (Cooke J).

[81] The leading modern judgment is *O'Kelly v Trusthouse Forte plc* [1983] IRLR 369, discussed below, paras 3.29 and 3.30.

[82] See para 3.33.

[83] The growing inclusion within protective labour statutes of certain categories of the self-employed, together with the difficulties faced by the courts in applying the distinction between employment and self-employment, led Freedland (2003) to argue for a unified concept of the 'personal employment contract' in place of the existing scheme of classification of employment relationships. See the special issue of the *Industrial Law Journal* published in March 2007, on the theme of 'Reconstructing Employment Contracts', which contains assessments of Freedland's thesis by a number of authors writing from comparative, historical and interdisciplinary perspectives, and see also Freedland and Kountouris (2011), extending Freedland's original hypothesis in the framework of a comparative analysis.

provided by SSCBA 1992 is 'employed earner'. In older statutes and judgments the terms 'servant' and 'workman' were used, but these expressions are not necessarily synonymous with the modern 'employee'. The terms 'employment', which is used in equality legislation, and 'worker', which is used in parts of ERA 1996 (such as Part II, consolidating provisions derived from the Wages Act 1986) and more generally under TULRCA 1992, NMWA 1998 and WTR 1998, offer yet another set of definitions, being wider in scope than 'employee' and therefore encompassing certain of the self-employed. Finally, specific provisions regulate the status of civil servants and certain others employed in the public sector.

Employees and employed earners

3.19   Under ERA 1996, an 'employee' is defined as an 'individual who has entered into or works under ... a contract of employment', and 'contract of employment' is defined, in turn, to mean 'a contract of service or apprenticeship, whether express or implied, and (if it is express) whether oral or in writing'.[84] No further definition is offered: the scope of the legislation, in effect, rests upon the common law tests as developed and applied over time by the courts. The principal rights which are thereby confined to employees concern unfair dismissal protection, redundancy compensation, minimum notice upon termination, guaranteed pay, the right to maternity, paternity and parental leave, and the right to return to work after taking such leave.

European Union directives in the employment protection field are mostly stated to apply to employees: this is the case, for example, with Directive 2001/23 on the protection of acquired rights in relation to transfers of undertakings, and Directive 91/533 on information concerning terms and conditions of employment.[85] The Court of Justice has decided that national courts are entitled to apply their own national definitions of employment status when transposing these employment protection directives, even if this results in some inconsistency in the implementation of directives in the different Member States. In this vein, the Directive of 1991 on information concerning terms and conditions of employment applies to 'every paid employee having a contract or employment relationship defined *by the law in force in a Member State and/or governed by the law in force in a Member State*' (emphasis added),[86] and is stated to be 'without prejudice to national law and practice concerning: the form of the contract or employment relationship, proof as regards the existence and content of a contract or employment relationship, [and] the relevant procedural rules'.[87] By contrast, the Court has insisted on widely-phrased definitions and greater conformity to a single standard throughout the Member States for the term 'worker' set by European Union law in cases concerning freedom of movement and equal opportunities, on the grounds that these

---

[84] ERA 1996, s 230(1), (2).

[85] By contrast, Directive 98/59 on Collective Redundancies uses the term 'worker', but nothing seems to turn on this different terminology. UK legislation transposing this Directive is confined in its scope to protecting 'employees'. See below, para 9.32.

[86] Directive 91/533, Art 1.

[87] Directive 91/533, Art 6. See also Directive 94/33 on the protection of young people at work, which applies (subject to derogations) to 'any person under 18 years of age having an employment contract or an employment relationship defined by the law in force in a Member State and/or governed by the law in force in a Member State' (Art 2(1)).

two areas are concerned with 'fundamental rights' contained in EU law and recognised as such by the jurisprudence of the Court.[88]

Income taxation and social security legislation also divide the labour force into the two principal groups of employees and the self-employed. Income from employment under a contract of service is taxable under Schedule E which means, among other things, that the employer is responsible for making the relevant deduction at source and paying the amounts over to the tax authorities under the PAYE system.[89] Under social security legislation, an 'employed earner' is liable to pay primary Class 1 national insurance contributions on his or her earnings up to the upper earnings limits and their employer, in addition to being under a legal duty to deduct these sums at source, must also pay secondary Class 1 national insurance contributions on the employee's earnings, for the purpose of which no upper limit applies. Under SSCBA 1992, an 'employed earner' is defined as an individual who is 'gainfully employed under a contract of service'.[90] By contrast, workers who are self-employed arrange their own payments of income tax under Schedule D, with the opportunity to set their tax off against a range of expenses, and pay Class 2 and/or Class 4 national insurance contributions without involving their employer in any additional liability to contribute. The adoption of self-employment by the worker may therefore bring significant tax and contribution savings to both parties to the contract.[91] On the other hand, only an employed earner who has paid Class 1 contributions can qualify for the jobseeker's allowance[92] and rights to statutory maternity and paternity pay, and statutory sick pay, are also confined to 'employed earners' in this sense.[93]

It might be thought that since the same concept of the contract of employment or service underlies the definitions used in employment, social security and tax legislation, a common test should be applied which would result in an individual having a single status for these different purposes. This would also seem to accord with the philosophy underlying the division between employees and the self-employed. Employment protection and social security legislation are forms of regulation aimed at protecting the employee against risks arising from loss of income and/or employment. They are designed for relationships characterised by a high degree of personal and economic dependence between employer and worker; they work less satisfactorily in cases of self-employment where the worker is not so highly dependent upon a single employer over a substantial period of time. In determining employee status, courts and tribunals frequently have

---

[88] In the context of free movement see the ruling in Case 53/81 *Levin v Staatssecretaris van Justitie* [1982] ECR 1035 and in relation to equality of opportunity, see Case C-256/01 *Allonby v Accrington and Rossendale College* [2004] IRLR 224, discussed further, below, para 3.33. It should be noted that the term 'worker' does not necessarily bear the same wide meaning in these two different contexts: see *Allonby*, at para 63.

[89] Income Tax (Earnings and Pensions) Act 2003, Part 11.

[90] SSCBA 1992, ss 1(2)(a)(i), 2(1)(a); in addition, primary Class 1 contributions are also payable by individuals employed in an office with emoluments subject to income tax under Schedule E. Under SSCBA 1992, s 122(1), a 'contract of service' is defined as 'any contract of service or apprenticeship whether written or oral and whether express or implied'. On the meaning of 'gainfully employed', see *Vandyk v Minister of Pensions and National Insurance* [1955] 1 QB 29.

[91] For example, in *Hall v Lorimer* [1994] IRLR 171, the respondent had over a period of time received fees of £32,875 in respect of his employment, against which he had incurred expenses of £9,250. It was only by establishing that he was self-employed that he was able to set the latter sum off against the former, so reducing the net sum on which he was liable to pay income tax. See below, para 3.30.

[92] Jobseekers Act 1995, s 2.

[93] See SSCBA 1992, ss 164(1), 171(1) (statutory maternity pay); ss 171ZA(2)(b) and 171ZB(2)(b) (statutory paternity pay; note that in the case of statutory adoption pay, the term 'employee' is used (SSCBA 1992, s 171ZL(1)); and see also ss 151 and 163(1) (statutory sick pay). See further below, paras 6.118, 6.120 and 4.125, respectively, on the more detailed qualifying conditions for these benefits.

recourse to precedents deriving from legislation of a different kind from that which is immediately at issue, as well as from the cases concerning the vicarious liability of the employer at common law.[94]

However, it cannot be assumed as a general rule that a decision from one area of law will necessarily determine the outcome in another, and, indeed, the recent practice of the courts tends to suggest that they will not pay much regard to the tax or social security law status of the worker when deciding on their status for employment law purposes. There may be good reasons for treating each area of law separately. For example, it is arguable that in cases of tax and national insurance, the public interest in ensuring the efficient collection of revenue should weigh strongly against any attempts by the parties to adopt the form of self-employment in order simply to avoid paying the normal incidence of tax. In cases involving vicarious liability, the interests of third parties – tort victims – are at stake. Where, on the other hand, no third party is directly affected by the parties' own determination of the worker's status, as will tend to be the case with regard to employment protection, the courts might be justified in paying greater regard to the parties' expressed wish to adopt self-employment. But to take this view would be to assume that the worker has made a conscious choice to weigh up the costs and benefits of employee status, when, in practice, it may well be the case that he or she has been presented by the employer with a standard form agreement which there has been no effective opportunity to modify. Moreover, fragmenting the status of the worker across different areas of law can produce real hardship. This is the case, for example, where casual workers, who are often treated as dependent labour for tax purposes, and therefore have their income tax deducted at source, fail to qualify as employees for labour law purposes.[95] It can also result in serious conceptual confusion of the kind which arises when workers who are regarded as self-employed in respect of employment law are treated as 'servants' or employees for the purposes of triggering the vicarious liability of their employer in tort.[96] But for the time being at least, it seems that there is no prospect of a unified approach emerging.

Fact or law?

3.20   The lack of a unified approach has arisen partly because consistency in the application of the statutory tests has been sacrificed to a perceived need to defer to the decisions of lower-level tribunals whenever possible. In *O'Kelly v Trusthouse Forte plc*[97] the Court of Appeal decided by a majority (Ackner LJ dissenting) that the application of the legal criteria for identifying a contract of employment was a 'question of mixed law and fact' to which several correct answers are possible. Because appeals may only lie from employment tribunals on a point of law,[98] this means that the appellate courts have no power to interfere with the finding of an employment tribunal unless the tribunal adopts the wrong test, states the law incorrectly, or applies the law in a perverse way, in the sense of reaching a decision which 'no reasonable tribunal would make'. Although in principle it is

---

[94] See, eg, the tax case of *Hall v Lorimer* [1994] IRLR 171, in which the judgment of Nolan LJ refers to cases in social security law (*Market Investigations Ltd v Minister of Social Security* [1969] 2 QB 173) and employment law (*O'Kelly v Trusthouse Forte plc* [1983] IRLR 369 and *Lee Ting Sang v Chung Chi-Keung* [1990] IRLR 236).

[95] This is by no means unusual in practice. See the cases discussed in Burchell *et al*, 1999.

[96] On this point, see the judgment of Sedley LJ in *Dacas v Brook Street Bureau (UK) Ltd* [2004] IRLR 358.

[97] [1983] ICR 728.

[98] ETA 1996, s 21. See further para 2.19, above.

open to the EAT or Court of Appeal to substitute their own decision for that of the tribunal if they decide that the tribunal made an error of law,[99] this will not happen as a matter of course. Under this approach, it is not possible to lay down anything other than the most general of guidelines for tribunals, with the result that the position of casual workers such as the applicants in *O'Kelly* is at best uncertain, at worst one of exclusion from the scope of statutory protection. It also means that tribunals may legitimately decide essentially similar cases in different ways, thereby undermining the regulatory impact of employment protection legislation.

Prior to *O'Kelly* there were numerous decisions in which it was either expressly stated or implicitly assumed that the question of whether a particular contract is a contract of employment or some other kind of contract was a question of law to which there was a right and a wrong answer,[100] and after *O'Kelly* the House of Lords held in *Davies v Presbyterian Church of Wales*[101] that the employment status of a church minister was also a question of law. In *Hellyer Bros v McLeod*,[102] however, the Court of Appeal distinguished *Davies* and preserved the status of *O'Kelly* on the grounds that the former was a decision concerning the construction of a written contract, whereas the latter, involving an arrangement based partly on conduct and partly on writing, fell to be decided as a question of mixed fact and law. In principle there seems to be no good reason for drawing such a distinction, nor can it be inferred from the relevant provisions of the employment protection legislation. On the contrary, the legislation implicitly negates such a distinction, defining a contract of employment as 'a contract of service ... *whether express or implied, and (if it is express) whether oral or in writing*' (emphasis added).[103] However, in *Carmichael v National Power plc*[104] the House of Lords reaffirmed the view laid out in *O'Kelly*. According to the majority opinion of Lord Irvine of Lairg LC, the construction of an employment contract could only be a question of pure law if the parties had intended the written documents passing between them to be the exclusive source of their agreement. In the view of Lord Hoffmann, who gave a concurring opinion, whether the parties had such an intention in a given case was itself a question of fact. In the construction of employment contracts, it would normally be open to a tribunal to take into account the behaviour of the parties after entering into the relationship of employment as well as their subsequent understanding of what the contract required them to do. Cases of completely written contracts of employment would therefore be 'untypical'.[105]

While the flexible approach to construction advanced by Lord Hoffmann has much to commend it in the context of employment contracts, it remains highly undesirable that crucial questions concerning the applicability of employment protection legislation cannot be settled

---

[99] This occurred, for example, in *Hellyer Bros v McLeod* [1987] ICR 526, in favour of the employer, and in *Lee Ting Sang v Chung Chi-Keung* [1990] IRLR 236, in favour of the employee.

[100] See *Young & Woods Ltd v West* [1980] IRLR 201; *Addison v London Philharmonic Orchestra Ltd* [1981] ICR 261; *WHPT Housing Association Ltd v Secretary of State for Social Services* [1981] ICR 737; *President of the Methodist Conference v Parfitt* [1984] IRLR 141.

[101] [1986] ICR 280. On the status of ministers of religion, see below, para 3.36.

[102] [1987] ICR 526, 537.

[103] ERA 1996, s 230(1), (2).

[104] [2000] IRLR 43; see also the Privy Council case of *Lee Ting Sang v Chung Chi-Keung* [1990] IRLR 236, 239 (Lord Griffiths), referring to 'the threat of the appellate courts being crushed by the weight of appeals if the many borderline cases were considered to be questions of law'.

[105] [2000] IRLR 43, 46. A factor which may make such agreements more typical in future is the growing use of 'entire agreements' clauses in standard form contracts, stipulating that the written terms form the entire contract, and may not be varied except by writing. See *Cable & Wireless plc v Muscat* [2006] IRLR 354 and *Consistent Group Ltd v Kalwak* [2008] IRLR 505 for discussion of such clauses; see also, however, para 3.22 below.

according to a clearer framework of principle. In this context, what is of paramount importance is not the artificial and unsatisfactory distinction between completely written and partly oral or implicit agreements, which entered employment law after *Davies* and *Hellyer*, but the need for consistency in the application of the law if the aims of protective legislation are not be frustrated. Notwithstanding *Carmichael*, the appellate tribunal or court is still entitled to intervene in a case where the employment tribunal misconstrues the meaning of contractual documents or fails to apply the correct test for the implication of a contract term, since these errors amount to errors of law. In the end, then, it is for the appellate court itself to define what amounts, in a given case, to an error of law *within* the wider process of determining employment status. Given that this is so, it is far from clear that the decision in *Carmichael* has done anything to reduce the volume of cases on employment status going to appellate tribunals and courts, which, since the early 2000s, has been very considerable.

Parties' own choice: waiving employee status

3.21   There are two parts to the process by which the courts identify dependent labour: 'in order to enter the magic circle of employees, the worker has to solve not only the riddle of "contract" but also that of "employment".'[106] We shall begin our analysis by considering the role of contract before looking in more detail at the principal tests of employment, which to an increasing degree, particularly in the case of the test of 'mutuality of obligation', have become imbued with a contractual logic.

An issue which arises at the outset, given the contractual foundations of the employment relationship, is how far the parties can make their own explicit designation of employment status, in the contract or otherwise. On one view, the status of the worker is a question which only the court can resolve, by looking at all the evidence. If the 'reality' is one of employee status, the parties cannot override this by 'choosing' to adopt self-employment in order to avoid the impact of tax and protective legislation or for any other purpose: a 'statement that … [a worker] supplies [services] as a self-employed worker is not conclusive of his status, since it has been said many times that whether someone is an employee is a matter of analysing all the rights and obligations created by the contract'.[107] Similarly, in the final analysis it is for the court and not for the parties to determine whether a contractual nexus can be inferred from the regular practice of work being carried out in return for payment.

It is possible to go further, and argue that an attempted waiver of this kind should be ignored on public policy grounds. In *Ferguson v John Dawson & Partners (Contractors) Ltd*[108] Megaw LJ said that 'a declaration by the parties, even if it were incorporated in the contract, that the workman was to be, or was to be deemed to be, self-employed, an independent contractor, ought to be wholly disregarded – not merely treated as not being conclusive – if the remainder of the contractual terms, governing the realities of the relationship, showed the relationship of employer

---

[106] Hepple, 1986b: p 71.

[107] *McMeechan v Secretary of State for Employment* [1995] IRLR 461, 463 (Mummery J). See also the judgments of the Court of Appeal, [1997] IRLR 353.

[108] [1976] 1 WLR 1213, 1223. The statement in the text is, on one view, *obiter*, since Megaw LJ decided the case on a separate ground.

and employee'. One reason for taking this view is that any other will fail to accord adequate recognition to the power of statutory regulation to override the common law: hence it should not be open to the parties themselves 'by their own whim, by the use of a verbal formula, unrelated to the reality of the relationship, [to] influence the decision on whom the responsibility for the safety of workmen, as imposed by statutory regulations, should rest'.[109] The full application of health and safety legislation may be thought to be of paramount importance from a public policy perspective. However, similar arguments could also be made in the context of the rights contained in employment legislation, much of which explicitly limits the contractual power of the employer in the interests of protecting the employee, and to tax and national insurance regulations, one purpose of which is to ensure the efficient collection of revenue.[110]

Nevertheless, arguments based on public policy have not won universal approval. In *Calder v H Kitson Vickers & Sons (Engineers) Ltd*[111] Ralph Gibson LJ said that 'a man is without question free under the law to contract to carry out certain work for another without entering into a contract of service. Public policy has nothing to say either way'. This does not mean that the courts will simply validate whatever status the parties choose to confer on themselves, if all the evidence points the other way; but in a finely balanced case, the parties' own view of their relationship may tip the scales in one direction or another: 'since the law looks to substance and not to form, the fact that the parties honestly intend that between themselves the contract shall be a contract for services and not a contract of service is not conclusive but it is a relevant fact, and when parties do deliberately agree for the man [sic] to be self-employed it may afford strong evidence that that is their real relationship'.[112]

The role of standard form agreements in excluding employee status: 'no obligations' and 'substitution' clauses, and 'sham' agreements

3.22   More subtle forms of contracting out may be available. Increasingly, employers use standard forms containing terms which are incompatible with employee status. A term denying that the employer has any obligation to provide work on a continuing basis, sometimes called a 'no obligations clause',[113] may lead a court to conclude that the relationship lacks the necessary

---

[109] [1976] 1 WLR 1213, 1223. See also *Lane v Shire Roofing Co (Oxford) Ltd* [1995] IRLR 493, 496 (Henry LJ).

[110] See, eg, *Rennison v Minister of Social Security* (1970) 10 KIR 65.

[111] [1988] ICR 232, 251.

[112] [1988] ICR 232, 251. For further illustrations of this approach see *Massey v Crown Life Assurance Co Ltd* [1978] ICR 590, 596 and *WHPT Housing Association Ltd v Secretary of State for Social Services* [1981] ICR 737, and, in the context of the definition of 'worker' under WTR 1998, *Redrow Homes (Yorkshire) Ltd v Wright* [2004] IRLR 720, at [21] (Pill LJ); by contrast, clauses providing for workers to be self-employed were ignored in *Young & Woods Ltd v West* [1980] IRLR 201; and in *Catamaran Cruisers Ltd v Williams* [1994] IRLR 386, where other factors pointed strongly to employee status. See also *Thames TV Ltd v Wallis* [1979] IRLR 136 in which the court expressly disapproved attempts to contract out of unfair dismissal legislation by this route, and Case C-256/01 *Allonby v Accrington and Rossendale College* [2004] IRLR 224 for an argument that, in the context of the right to equal pay for equal work under Art 141 of the EC Treaty (now Art 157 TFEU), a worker with a merely 'notional' independence should fall under the scope of protection (at para 71). In more recent decisions, the emphasis has shifted from express 'waivers' of employee or worker status, to the meaning of 'indirect' waivers through 'obligations' and 'substitution' clauses. See para 3.22 below.

[113] See eg *Consistent Group Ltd v Kalwak* [2008] IRLR 505.

'mutuality of obligation' to be a contract of employment.[114] Another example is a term according to which the worker is not required to provide his or her personal service, but can nominate a substitute. In *Express and Echo Publications Ltd v Tanton*[115] the presence of such a term persuaded the Court of Appeal that the applicant was not an employee. The applicant argued in vain that this term was not observed in practice and did not reflect the way in which the parties' relationship had been conducted. *Tanton* was subsequently followed in a line of cases in which courts held that the presence of an effective 'substitution clause' was enough to deflect not only employee status,[116] but also the possibility that the applicant might qualify for certain rights as a self-employed 'worker' under a contract to supply personal services.[117] This was because the substitution clause was said to negative the 'irreducible minimum of obligation' which must be present in any contract, whether for employment or self-employment, which involves the provision of personal service.

The courts have no statutory power to strike out or modify the effects of 'unfair' or terms contained in standard form employment agreements, as they do in consumer contracts.[118] On the face of it there is nothing to prevent an employer using a standard form to set the terms of the agreement in such a way as to resolve the issue of employment status. Where, however, the way in which the contract is performed bears little or no relationship to the terms set out in the agreement, it may be open to a court or tribunal to go beyond the written text when construing the contract. Terms providing for mutuality of obligation and for the 'irreducible minimum' of personal service may be implied on the basis of conduct. In principle, the written agreement should prevail over any contrary implied term. However, entirely orthodox rules of construction allow a court to find that an unusual term in a standard-form agreement does not form part of the contract if the party seeking to rely on it did not bring it to the other's attention prior to the contract being made.[119] In commercial cases applying this approach, the term in question has been contained in a document which was separated from the main part of the agreement;[120] this will not often be the case in the employment context, and, in any event, the employer can easily deal with this potential problem by issuing the contract as a single document.

Alternatively, the court may disregard a term which it concludes to be a 'sham'. In *Consistent Group Ltd v Kalwak* the Court of Appeal took an extremely strict view of what constitutes a 'sham' for this purpose: there must be a finding 'that, at the time of the contract, *both* parties intended [the term] to misrepresent their true contractual relationship' (emphasis added).[121] A more flexible approach was suggested by the EAT in *Redrow Homes (Yorkshire) Ltd v Buckborough*,[122] in which it was held that a contract term (in this case a substitution clause) which the parties never genuinely intended to be effective or to constitute an effective obligation between them could

---

[114] See below, para 3.29. For an empirical study providing evidence of the use of such terms, see Burchell *et al*, 1999: ch 6.

[115] [1999] IRLR 367.

[116] *Staffordshire Sentinel Newspapers Ltd v Potter* [2004] IRLR 752; *Lanksford v Business Post Ltd* [2004] EWCA Civ 1448.

[117] *Tanton* was used in this way in *Commissioners of Inland Revenue v Post Office Ltd* [2003] IRLR 199.

[118] See the Unfair Contract Terms Act 1977 and the Unfair Terms in Consumer Contracts Regulations 1994 and 1999; H Collins, 2007.

[119] See Spencer, 1974.

[120] See *Interfoto Picture Library Ltd v Stiletto Visual Pictures Ltd* [1989] QB 433.

[121] [2008] IRLR 508, at [51] (Rimer LJ). An alternative and looser formulation is that a sham exists where the term 'does not represent the real intentions of the parties objectively ascertained': *Accounttax Marketing Ltd v Halstead*, EAT, 6 November 2003, Appeal No UKEAT/0313/03/ZT, at [18].

[122] [2009] IRLR 34.

be a sham. In *Protectacoat Firthglow Ltd v Szilagyi*[123] the Court of Appeal moved away from the *Kalwak* test in emphasising that where it is asserted that the written document does not accurately describe the relationship, the court or tribunal must decide what that relationship is, regardless of whether there had been a common intention to misrepresent the nature of the relationship This more flexible approach was confirmed by the Supreme Court in *Autoclenz Ltd v Belcher*.[124] In this case, car valeters were employed, in the words of the agreements they had signed, 'from time to time on a sub-contract basis', and given the right to substitute another to carry out their work, subject to requirements for such substitute staff set out by the employer. They brought claims for holiday pay under WTR 1998, arguing that they had 'employee' or, failing that, 'worker' status. The Employment Tribunal found that they were employees: they could not control their own work or working time, they were fully integrated into the employer's business, took orders from supervisors employed by the employer, and were paid at rates set by the employer. On this basis, the Tribunal considered that the 'no obligations' and 'substitution' clauses in the written agreements were shams. The case was appealed all the way to the Supreme Court which held that the Tribunal had adopted the correct approach in this case and confirmed its decision. Lord Clarke rejected the 'common intention to mislead' test as inappropriate for the employment context where 'the relative bargaining power of the parties must be taken into account in deciding whether the terms of any written agreement in truth represent what was agreed and the true agreement will often have to be gleaned from all the circumstances of the case, of which the written agreement is only a part'.[125]

The approach in *Autoclenz* is consistent with the flexible approach to the interpretation of employment contracts laid down by the House of Lords in *Carmichael v National Power plc*,[126] which, as we have seen,[127] gives the courts some leeway to interpret the terms of the contract in the light of the behaviour of the parties during its performance. Clauses which are uncertain in their scope or meaning should carry little weight if the parties never rely upon them in practice.[128] Even in a case where the court is not convinced that a term is a 'sham', it can find that the original, written contract has been varied by a subsequent agreement based on conduct.[129] More generally, it can be argued that even a clearly-worded 'substitution clause' should not defeat employee or worker status, for the reason that a *limited* or *partial* right to substitute another to do part of

---

[123] [2009] IRLR 365: service agreement between the company and a 'partnership' found to be a sham. See A Davies, 2009.

[124] [2011] IRLR 820. A notable feature of Lord Clarke's judgment is its reliance on academic writings (A Davies, 2009; Bogg, 2010a).

[125] [2011] IRLR 820 at [35].

[126] [2000] IRLR 43, in particular the opinion of Lord Hoffmann.

[127] See para 3.20, above.

[128] See, on this point, the judgment of Sedley LJ in the CA in *Autoclenz*, [2010] IRLR 70 at [104], confirmed by Lord Clarke, [2011] IRLR 820 at [37].

[129] 'Entire agreement' clauses, stipulating that the contract is entirely contained in the written agreement and can only be varied in writing, are frequently used in order (among other things) to avoid this outcome; see, for example, the use of such a clause in the *Kalwak* case ([2007] IRLR 560, [2008] IRLR 508). However, if the court was satisfied that the original contract had been dissolved and a new contract entered into, such a clause should have no bearing on the construction of the new contract. For a case in which the EAT took a robust view of an entire agreement clause, see *RNLI v Bushaway* [2005] IRLR 674.

the agreed work may not be incompatible with the existence of a contract of employment;[130] similarly, a 'no obligations clause' which gives the worker the right to refuse work under certain circumstances, will not negative the presence of mutuality of obligation as long as there still a duty to carry out 'some minimum, or at least reasonable, amount of work'.[131] For these various reasons, a number of options remain open to courts and tribunals in addressing the issue of standard form agreements which bear 'no practical relation to the reality of the relationship'.[132]

Statutory control of waivers of employment rights

3.23   Legislation provides that an agreement by an individual to waive protective rights under ERA 1996 or TULRCA 1992, whether or not contained in a standard form, is void[133] (subject to exceptions explicitly provided for in the Acts). These prohibitions on contracting out could, conceivably, be invoked to nullify a contract term which purports to derogate from an individual's status as an employee. However, there is an element of circularity here. Unless the individual can establish, on independent grounds, that he or she is employed as an employee, they cannot invoke the statutory prohibitions on contracting out.[134] If they can establish this, however, the statutory provisions concerning derogations will probably be unnecessary, since any term which is merely a 'sham', as opposed to one which alters the substance of the relationship, will be ignored by the courts in any case.

The use of personal service companies and other intermediaries

3.24   A further route which the parties may adopt in order to deflect employee status is for the worker to contract to supply his or her services through a 'personal service company' set up for this purpose. There may, as a result, be no contract between the worker and the end user of his or her services. There is nothing unlawful, per se, in contracting for labour to be supplied in this way, and from the worker's point of view it was once advantageous to do so for tax reasons, since it was possible, by this route, to avoid paying income tax on the relevant earnings, and pay a much lower rate of corporation tax instead. That route has now been blocked off by reforms to tax law which introduced the so-called 'IR35' status for subcontractors operating through personal

---

[130] See *MacFarlane v Glasgow City Council* [2001] IRLR 7, in which the EAT held that a limited power to delegate was not necessarily incompatible with the contract of employment; *Byrne Bros (Formwork) Ltd v Baird* [2002] IRLR 96, discussing the judgment of McKenna J on this point in *Ready Mixed Concrete (South East) Ltd v Minister for Pensions and National Insurance* [1968] 2 QB 497; and the EAT judgment in *Consistent Group Ltd v Kalwak* [2007] IRLR 560, at [31] (Elias P). The IR35 case of *Usetech Ltd v Young* [2004] EWHC 2248 (Ch), discussing the Privy Council decision in *Narich Pty Ltd v Commissioner of Pay-Roll Tax* [1984] ICR 286, is to similar effect.

[131] *Nethermere (St Neots) Ltd v Taverna and Gardiner* [1984] IRLR 240, 250 (Dillon LJ); *Cotswold Developments Construction Ltd v Williams* [2006] IRLR 181, at [55].

[132] *Autoclenz Ltd v Belcher* [2010] IRLR 70 at [104] (Sedley LJ). See Leighton and Wynn, 2011, for a full review of the case law,which takes into account parallel developments in tax law.

[133] ERA 1996, s 203; TULRCA 1992, s 288.

[134] See *M & P Steelcraft Ltd v Ellis* [2008] IRLR 355, 363.

service companies.[135] In the employment law context, there are examples of the courts 'lifting the corporate veil' to find that, notwithstanding the use of the personal service company, there was a contractual nexus between the two principal parties to the transaction. This is more likely where, prior to entering into this type of arrangement, the worker concerned was previously directly employed as an employee by the same employer,[136] although there are decisions where even this was not enough to persuade the court to lift the veil.[137]

Agency work is another situation in which an intermediary – here, the agency or 'employment business' – comes between the worker and the end 'user'. Again, there are cases in which the courts have held that the user assumes the duties of an employer, either because the user exercises managerial powers in relation to the worker in such a way as to satisfy the common law test of 'control',[138] or because a particular statutory provision allows the user to be treated as if it were the employer for certain purposes.[139] We consider agency work in more detail below.[140]

The effects of illegality on the contract of employment

3.25   If an employee is party to an agreement unlawfully to evade tax or national insurance contributions, or to commit some other unlawful act, the contract may be void on the grounds of illegality. This will have the effect of depriving the employee of any statutory employment rights, since he or she will be unable to show that they were employed 'under a contract of employment' or other contract at the relevant time. The scope of this principle is unclear, however, and its application, in such a way as to defeat otherwise valid claims for employment protection, is highly controversial.   Many cases concerning illegality have arisen out of attempts to defraud the tax authorities, for example by agreeing to a certain payment being made without any deduction of income tax or national insurance contributions. Such an agreement will be void *ab initio* regardless of whether either party was aware that the arrangement in question was illegal as such.[141] However, this situation must be distinguished from one in which the parties made an 'error of categorisation' without there being false representations to the Revenue. The receipt of tax advantages from self-employment does not bar the worker from subsequently claiming employee

---

[135] The core of the IR35 legislation is contained in the Income Tax (Earnings and Pensions) Act 2003, Part II, ch 8 (for income tax) and SSCBA 1992, s 4A, inserted by the Welfare Reform and Pensions Act 1999 (for national insurance). See *R (on the application of the Professional Contractors Group Ltd) v IRC* 2002 STC 165 (in which a challenge to the legislation on human rights grounds was rejected); *Synaptek Ltd v Young* [2003] ICR 1149; *Usetech Ltd v Young* [2004] EWHC 2248 (Ch); *Dragonfly Consultancy Ltd v Revenue and Customs Commissioners* [2008] EWHC 2113 (Ch); *Novasoft Ltd v Revenue and Customs Commissioners* [2010] UKFTT 150. Under the terms of the Coalition Agreement, a review of IR35 was initiated in 2010, but in March 2011 the government accepted a recommendation from the Office of Tax Simplification to the effect that the scheme should be retained, with some relatively minor modifications to its administration.
[136] This was the case in *Catamaran Cruisers Ltd v Williams* [1994] IRLR 386. On intermediary companies and 'lifting the corporate veil' more generally, see below, paras 3.35 and 3.65.
[137] See *Hewlett Packard v O'Murphy* [2002] IRLR 4; *Lanksford v Business Post Ltd* [2004] EWCA Civ 1448.
[138] See *Motorola Ltd v Davidson* [2001] IRLR 4; *Hewlett Packard v O'Murphy* [2002] IRLR 4; *Stephenson v Delphi Diesel Systems Ltd* [2003] ICR 471; *Dacas v Brook Street Bureau (UK) Ltd* [2004] IRLR 358; *Cable & Wireless plc v Muscat* [2006] IRLR 354; cf *James v Greenwich London Borough Council* [2008] IRLR 302; *Tilson v Alstom Transport* [2011] IRLR 169; Leighton and Wynn, 2011. See below, para 3.35.
[139] *Abbey Life Assurance Co Ltd v Tansell* [2000] IRLR 387; see below, para 3.35.
[140] See para 3.35.
[141] *Miller v Karlinski* (1945) 62 TLR 85; *Salvesen v Simons* [1994] IRLR 52. A similar result follows if legislation forbids the formation of a particular contract, as is the case with child protection laws: Mogridge, 1981: p 24.

status on the basis that the nature of the relationship was mischaracterised, as long as he or she acted in good faith.[142] Where it is the employer who takes the initiative in the non-payment of tax, the outcome will depend in part on the employee's state of mind. If he or she did not know that his or her wages were being paid without tax being deducted, or that the employer was attempting to defraud the Revenue, the employee may be able to enforce the contract which is said to be 'tainted by illegality', as opposed to being void *ab initio*. The test of knowledge is subjective – what did the employee actually know or understand? – but a tribunal may be justified in inferring that the employee was, at least, familiar with the normal arrangements for deduction of tax and was put on notice that something was amiss if the normal deductions did not appear in the wage slip or other statement of pay.[143] In a case where both employer and employee were 'in it up to the neck', the employee was held to have forfeited the right to statutory employment protection.[144]

The ground for denying efficacy to the contract of employment in this situation is public policy, and in particular the need to ensure the effectiveness of the revenue collection system. An employee who attempts to cheat the system should not, it is said, be in a position to benefit from the protection provided by employment law. However, in most cases it is the employer who presses for arrangements of this kind to be made, and who benefits most clearly from them. Research has shown that wages of workers in the 'shadow economy' tend to be paid below the level of normal wages, the difference representing the tax and national insurance contributions which the employer is able to avoid paying.[145] It is odd that an employee who does not object to such an arrangement, and who perhaps may be in no position to do so while still retaining that employment, should then be punished by the loss of employment protection rights. The suggestion has therefore been made that tribunals should have regard to the importance, when weighing public policy considerations, of ensuring that statutory employment protection rights are not evaded, and should either enforce employment rights regardless of illegality affecting the contract or pay closer attention to the relative blameworthiness of employer and employee.[146]

Moreover, the line drawn between a case of defrauding the Revenue and one in which the parties legitimately but unsuccessfully attempt to arrange their affairs so as to limit tax liability is often so fine as to be virtually invisible.[147] In *Rennison v Minister of Social Security*[148] Bridge J saw through a scheme to describe weekly paid secretarial workers as self-employed for tax and national insurance purposes, holding that they were employees and liable to pay Class 1 national insurance contributions. There was no suggestion that the contracts they entered into were illegal as such, however. Similarly, in *Young & Woods Ltd v West*[149] the Court of Appeal held that the applicant was entitled to claim unfair dismissal on the grounds that 'in reality' he had a contract of employment, and that an attempt to present him as self-employed was a sham. It could easily, however, have held the arrangement to have been illegal, in which case the employee would have been unable to

[142] *Enfield Technical Services Ltd v Payne* [2008] IRLR 500, 503 (Pill LJ); Pilgerstorfer and Forshaw, 2008.
[143] See *Davidson v Pillay* [1979] IRLR 275; *Corby v Morrison* [1980] IRLR 218; *Colen v Cebrian (UK) Ltd* [2004] IRLR 210; *Soteriou v Ultrachem Ltd* [2004] IRLR 870 (HC), [2004] EWCA Civ 1520, CA.
[144] *Tomlinson v Dick Evans 'U' Drive Ltd* [1978] ICR 639.
[145] S Smith, 1986.
[146] Mogridge, 1981: p 33.
[147] See, eg, *Lightfoot v D & J Sporting Ltd* [1996] IRLR 64.
[148] (1970) 10 KIR 65.
[149] [1980] IRLR 201.

pursue his unfair dismissal claim. These cases are 'not readily distinguishable'[150] from others in which statutory rights have been forfeited on the public policy grounds mentioned above.

The principle of nullity may also apply in cases where overseas workers are employed under circumstances where they do not have the right to work in the United Kingdom. In *Vakante v Addey and Stanhope School*[151] the applicant, a Croatian national who had earlier entered the UK as an asylum seeker, falsely told his employer that he had the right to take up paid employment. He was subsequently dismissed for other reasons, and brought a claim alleging racial discrimination. The EAT and Court of Appeal ruled that the contract, having been entered into in contravention of immigration legislation and on the basis of a fraudulent representation by the applicant, was void from the outset, with the effect that the claim was barred.

Other recent decisions demonstrate a reluctance to exclude employment claims on illegality grounds. In *Leighton v Michael*[152] the EAT, under Mummery J, drew a distinction between a claim for unfair dismissal or redundancy compensation under ERA 1996, which 'is directly founded upon, relies upon and seeks to enforce the contract of employment', and a claim of sex discrimination under SDA 1975 (which would now arise under EqA 2010), which although it 'involves a reference to the contract to determine whether the person is "employed" within the meaning of the statute', is not a claim founded upon contract since it does not require the complainant to show that he or she was dismissed or otherwise deprived of contractual rights.[153] Attractive as this idea might be, as a way of preventing unmeritorious attempts by employers to avoid protective obligations to employees, it seems to be based on a false distinction. Like ERA 1996, EqA 2010, in common with its precedessor statute the SDA 1975, defines 'employment' (other than for Crown employment and parliamentary staff) exclusively in contractual terms.[154]

A sounder basis for the outcome in *Leighton* may be inferred from the later decision of the Court of Appeal in *Hall v Woolston Hall Leisure Ltd*.[155] The Court of Appeal reasserted the view that employment contracts which incorporated an unlawful method of payment, as opposed to an unlawful purpose, were unlikely to be void, at least where it was the employer who instigated the arrangement in question and the employee did not actively participate in the illegality. Mere knowledge of the illegality on the part of the employee would not be enough.[156] This argument would be equally applicable to employment protection cases. The *Hall* judgment is principally significant for the purposive approach taken to the interpretation of employment legislation. The case turned on the interpretation to be given to the Sex Discrimination Act 1975 by reference to the Equal Treatment Directive, 76/207. Mance LJ said: 'construing the 1975 Act in the light of the Directive, I doubt whether it is appropriate … to treat the statutory requirement of a contract as subject to domestic conceptions

---

[150] Mogridge, 1981: p 33.

[151] [2004] EWCA Civ 1065. On the EAT judgment ([2004] ICR 279), see Forshaw and Pilgerstorfer, 2005. *Vakante* was followed in *Hounga v Allen* [2012] EWCA Civ 609.

[152] [1996] IRLR 67.

[153] [1996] IRLR 67, 69.

[154] EqA 2010, s 83(2) (previously SDA 1975, s 82(1)); see below, para 3.33. This aspect of *Leighton* was upheld by the Court of Appeal in *Hall v Woolston Hall Leisure Ltd* [2000] IRLR 578, in part on the grounds that since sex discrimination is a form of 'statutory tort', a clear causal link between the illegality and the loss which forms the basis of the complaint would have to be shown before the doctrine could apply. While this is entirely correct, it still does not get round the problem that if the contract is void for illegality, the complaint falls at the outset since the complainant does not fall under the personal scope of the statute (see the judgment of the EAT in *Hall*, cited at [2000] IRLR 578, 584). *Hall* was approved but distinguished on its facts by the Court of Appeal in *Vakante v Addey and Stanhope School* [2004] EWCA Civ 1065.

[155] [2000] IRLR 578; *Wheeler v Quality Deep Ltd (t/a Thai Royale Restaurant)* [2005] ICR 265; Fraser and Sher, 2006.

[156] See [2000] IRLR 578, 583 (Peter Gibson LJ), 588 (Mance LJ).

of public policy which would prevent an employee from enforcing it in the English courts if she had sued upon it. The Directive contains no such reservation'.[157] It is possible that this approach could also be applied to purely domestic legislation, as a matter of statutory interpretation: even in the absence of a Directive, it is arguably inappropriate to operate the illegality doctrine in a rigid way where the effect of doing so is to defeat the intended application of protective legislation.

It does not follow that the doctrine of illegality would then be irrelevant in every case, but its scope would be limited and, possibly, clarified. It would remain open to a court to disqualify a claim arising under employment or equal treatment legislation where the claim in question was 'inextricably bound up' with the relevant illegality.[158] This would almost certainly be the case where the employment was entered into with a clearly illegal purpose which was known to the employee from the outset. A clearer focus on the issue of the causal link between the illegality and the claim in question would be preferable, in this context, to the somewhat artificial idea that claims arising from illegal employment contracts necessarily fall outside the scope of protective legislation.

Control

3.26   Having considered the role of 'contract' in the contract of employment, we now turn to examine in more detail the tests used by the courts in determining 'employment' or 'service'. A test which has been applied in some form or another since at least the last quarter of the nineteenth century and which retains a certain force today is that of 'control'. The best known expression of the test is that of Bramwell LJ in *Yewens v Noakes*:[159] a 'servant is a person subject to the command of his master as to the manner in which he shall do his work'. This dictum needs to be treated with a good deal of care, however. There is a sense in which 'the "control test" has been misapplied almost from the moment of its emergence'.[160] This is because the concept of 'servant' which Bramwell LJ was addressing was not the same as the modern day notion of 'employee'. The term 'servant' in the middle and late nineteenth century did not simply denote a worker who was wage-dependent as opposed to being self-employed; it was used to draw a distinction *within* the category of wage-dependent workers, namely between mainly manual workers who were classified as 'servants' or 'workmen' on the one hand, and higher-status employees such as professionals and managers on the other. The former group, but not the latter, were subject to the Master and Servant Acts and, after the repeal of those Acts, to the Employers and Workmen Act 1875 under which the magistrates retained a civil law jurisdiction to deal with employment disputes; similarly, early social legislation, such as the Workmen's Compensation Acts and National Insurance Acts, drew

---

[157] [2000] IRLR 578, 589.

[158] On the 'inextricability' test, see the judgment of Peter Gibson LJ in *Hall* ([2000] IRLR 578, at [42]), and for an argument that, contrary to *Hall*, even this test should not apply in the context of EU Directives in the area of equality of treatment, see Forshaw and Pilgerstorfer, 2005.

[159] (1880) 6 QBD 530, 532, 533.

[160] Merritt, 1982: p 113

distinctions between manual and non-manual labour in terms of the scope of statutory coverage.[161] It was in the context of *this* distinction, and not that between dependent and independent labour in the modern sense, that the control test evolved.

Yewens v Noakes itself was a tax case, in which the court decided that a clerk, earning a substantial yearly salary, was not a servant, any more than were 'the manager of a bank, a foreman with high wages, persons almost in the position of gentlemen'.[162] The leading cases which later established Bramwell's dictum as a principal test of status were concerned with the scope of workmen's compensation[163] and national insurance legislation.[164] In this context, control was used to exclude from the scope of regulation those higher-status employees for whom the court considered protective legislation inappropriate,[165] as well as workers who were not in a direct employment relationship with the ultimate employer. This was at a time when the internal contracting system was common in mining, shipbuilding, construction, textiles and iron and steel; foremen or 'butty workers' would be responsible for hiring gangs of workmen and for supplying their services to the employer. The foreman or butty was likely to be classified in law as an independent contractor,[166] while those directly under his command might not, for this reason, be regarded as under the control of the ultimate employer, who was thereby relieved of the legal responsibilities imposed by social legislation.[167]

The notion that a dependent worker is one whose mode of performance is closely monitored and controlled by a superior embodies a strong version of personal or formal subordination, which is not appropriate for many workers whom the modern law regards as employees. Bramwell's test would not classify as 'dependent' those workers who have a high level of occupational or professional training, or who have a substantial degree of discretion as to their hours of work and mode of performance. However, many doctors, lawyers, managers and others who work in large, bureaucratic organisations are self-evidently employed as employees and not as independent contractors. Moreover, the legal distinction between manual and clerical workers now has little or no place in the law; as far as workmen's compensation and social insurance are concerned it was replaced, after 1945, by the more clear-cut division between employees and the self-employed which we are familiar with in the modern law,[168] which as we have seen was subsequently incorporated into employment protection legislation. For these various reasons, the control test as formulated by Bramwell has fallen into disuse.

---

[161] See the definitions of 'workman' and associated concepts in the Employers and Workmen Act 1875, s 10; the Employers Liability Act 1880, s 8; the Workmen's Compensation Act 1897, s 7(2); and the Truck (Amendment) Act 1887, s 2. The National Insurance Act 1911, s 1 and Sch 1, excluded from its provisions non-manual workers earning over £160 a year. The emergence of the 'employee' concept during the first half of the twentieth century is discussed by Deakin, 1998, 2000, and Deakin and Wilkinson, 2005: ch 2; on the same development in Australia, see Howe and Mitchell, 1999.

[162] *Yewens v Noakes* (1880) 6 QBD 530, 538 (Thesiger LJ).

[163] *Simmons v Heath Laundry Co* [1910] 1 KB 543. Cases of vicarious liability appear not to have played a major role in the development of the control test since at this time actions based on vicarious liability were very rare as a consequence of the doctrine of common employment and the operation of the volenti defence.

[164] *Scottish Insurance Comrs v Edinburgh Royal Infirmary* 1913 SC 751; *Hill v Beckett* [1915] 1 KB 578.

[165] *Simpson v Ebbw Vale Steel, Iron & Coal Co* [1905] 1 KB 453.

[166] See, eg, *Vanplew v Parkgate Iron & Steel Co* [1903] 1 KB 851.

[167] See, eg, *Littlejohn v Brown & Co Ltd* 1909 SC 169.

[168] The National Insurance Act 1946, s 1(2), established two main classes of contributors, 'employed earners' (akin to employees) and others, in place of the multiplicity of categories which had operated under the 1911 Act and its successors.

If control is understood as the employer's right to dictate the precise way in which work is done, the test is anachronistic as Kahn-Freund argued: 'the control test postulates a combination of managerial and technical functions in the person of the employer, ie what to modern eyes appears as an imperfect division of labour'.[169] In a wider sense, however, the idea that an employee is one who agrees to *serve*, as opposed to producing finished goods or supplying a specified service, is still retained as one of the tests of employee status, and if control is understood as the employer's right to give orders and direct the general nature of the employee's work it is far from irrelevant in a modern context. According to MacKenna J in *Ready Mixed Concrete (South East) Ltd v Minister for Pensions and National Insurance*,[170] 'control includes the power of deciding the thing to be done, the means to be employed in doing it, the time when and the place where it shall be done. All these aspects of control must be considered in deciding whether the right exists in a sufficient degree to make one party the master and the other his servant'. In the recent Supreme Court case of *Autoclenz Ltd v Belcher*,[171] the absence of control on the part of so-called 'subcontractors' over the content of their own work and over working time was held to be a factor in favour of a finding of employee status, with the contract terms suggesting otherwise disregarded as 'shams'. Similarly, in *McMeechan v Secretary of State for Employment*[172] an agreement under which an agency worker agreed 'to fulfil the normal common law duties which an employee would owe to an employer so far as they are applicable', including duties of fidelity, confidentiality and obedience to instructions, was for that reason held likely to give rise to a contract of employment between himself and the agency. Control has also been invoked to support a finding that the user of an agency worker's labour could be his employer,[173] although this will not be the case unless a contractual nexus can also be implied between these two parties, assuming that one has not been expressed.[174] These decisions demonstrate that while the control which exists under modern labour market conditions may be less personal and more bureaucratic in nature than that identified by the nineteenth century judges,[175] it is arguably no less important as a feature which separates the employment relationship from other forms of the provision of labour.

Integration

3.27 An alternative to control which sees the essence of employment as the employee's subjection to the rules and procedures of an organisation, rather than as subjection to personal command, is the integration test: 'one feature which seems to me to run through the instances is that, under a contract of service, a man is employed as part of the business and his work is done as an integral part of the business; whereas under a contract for services his work, although done for the business, is not integrated into it but is only accessory to it'.[176] When it was first formulated this

---

[169] Kahn-Freund, 1951: p 505.

[170] [1968] 2 QB 497, 515.

[171] [2011] IRLR 820 at [37] (Lord Clarke, referring with approval to the findings of fact by the Employment Tribunal); see above, para 3.21.

[172] [1995] IRLR 461, EAT; affd [1997] IRLR 353, CA; cf *Montgomery v Johnson Underwood Ltd* [2001] IRLR 269.

[173] *Motorola Ltd v Davidson* [2001] IRLR 4.

[174] *Dacas v Brook Street Bureau (UK) Ltd* [2004] IRLR 358; *James v Greenwich London Borough Council* [2008] IRLR 302; *Tilson v Alstom Transport* [2011] IRLR 169. See further below, para 3.35.

[175] Cf H Collins, 1986.

[176] *Stevenson, Jordan & Harrison v MacDonald & Evans* [1952] 1 TLR 101, 111 (Denning LJ).

test was a response to the difficulties, referred to above, in applying Bramwell's test to professional employees, and adequately explains, for example, why a journalist working on a newspaper or nurses and doctors employed by a hospital will normally have contracts of employment. Thus in *Beloff v Pressdram Ltd* a highly-paid journalist was unable to argue that, given her high status, she could not be regarded as having a contract of employment, even though she worked full-time for the newspaper and was treated as an employee for tax and national insurance purposes. According to Ungoed-Thomas J, 'the greater the skill required for an employee's work, the less significant is control in determining whether the employee is under a contract of service'.[177]

The notion of which work is 'integral' to a business is not easily applied, however. The integration test may be useful for explaining the employee status of managerial and professional workers, but it is less effective in explaining the position of outworkers or workers employed by a sub-contractor of the ultimate user of labour: their work may frequently be 'integral' to the user business, without them necessarily being its employees. With the increasing tendency of employers to make use of 'outsourcing' of various kinds and to employ workers with a peripheral or 'marginal' attachment to the firm in order to reduce direct labour costs, the focus of the modern case law has shifted to two tests which often provide divergent answers, namely 'economic reality' and 'mutuality of obligation'.

Economic reality

3.28   The test of business or 'economic' reality essentially asks whether the worker is in business on his or her own account, as an entrepreneur, or works for another who takes the ultimate risk of loss or chance of profit. Casual or irregular workers and others who may have a high degree of personal autonomy in their working arrangements may nevertheless be classified as employees under this test if they are economically dependent on one principal employer. In *Market Investigations Ltd v Minister of Social Security*[178] it was held that a part-time market researcher could be an employee for this reason, notwithstanding that she had 'a limited discretion as to when she should do the work'.

The same approach may be applied to skilled and professional workers who organise their own working schedules and do not come under close personal supervision. They will probably still be employees if the ownership of the relevant tools or equipment vests principally in the employer and if it is the latter who takes the residual risk of the business failing. The method of payment may give some indication as to who bears the residual risk, but this should not be taken too far. If the worker receives a regular salary or a wage based on time rates, there would normally be little doubt that he or she is an employee. Even if, on the other hand, he or she is paid on a piece-rate basis or receives either all of part of the wage in the form of profit-related pay, they may still be an employee. An employer's decision to link pay to performance or profits does not, in itself, imply that the worker

---

[177] [1973] 1 All ER 241, 250; see also *Cassidy v Minister of Health* [1951] 2 KB 343 and for a recent application in the Supreme Court, *Autoclenz Ltd v Belcher* [2011] IRLR 820 at [37] (Lord Clarke, referring to the judgment of the Employment Tribunal) .

[178] [1969] 2 QB 173, applying the US case of *United States v Silk* 331 US 704 (1946), where the term 'economic reality' originated; see also *Airfix Footwear Ltd v Cope* [1978] ICR 1210.

undertakes responsibility for the management and profitability of the business in the sense used here.

As Lord Griffiths put it in *Lee Ting Sang v Chung Chi-Keung*,[179] there is a difference between 'a skilled artisan earning his living by working for more than one employer as an employee and ... a small businessman venturing into business on his own account as an independent contractor with all its attendant risks'. In this case, an appeal from Hong Kong, the Privy Council held that a skilled construction worker was employed as an employee, so as to come within the scope of health and safety regulations. The applicant neither hired his own helpers nor provided his own equipment; moreover, 'he had no responsibility for investment in, or management of, the work on the construction site, he simply turned up for work and chipped off concrete to the required depth upon the beams indicated to him on a plan by the [employer]... It is true that he was not supervised in his work, but this is not surprising, he was a skilled man and he had been told the beams upon which he was to work and the depth to which they were to be cut and the work was measured to see that he achieved that result'.[180]

This does not mean, however, that either a professional or a casual worker *must* be an employee so long as he or she does not have an identifiable business of his own. On the contrary, there is a category of workers who are self-employed without necessarily being entrepreneurs, for the reason that they lack dependence on any particular employer. This was the case in *Hall v Lorimer*,[181] where the respondent was a skilled television technician who worked for around 20 separate companies on a series of short-term engagements. He was held to be self-employed, and therefore chargeable to income tax under Schedule D. According to Nolan LJ:

> ... the question, whether the individual is in business on his own account, though often helpful, may be of little assistance in the case of one carrying on a profession or vocation. A self-employed author working from home or an actor or a singer may earn his living without any of the normal trappings of a business ... the most outstanding feature to my mind is that Mr Lorimer customarily worked for 20 or more production companies and that the vast majority of his assignments ... lasted only for a single day.[182]

This approach makes sense given the context of the decision, namely the assessment of income over an extended period (here, a year) for the purpose of determining the incidence of tax. However, it leaves open the question of how the court should approach the designation of status in a case where it is required to consider the position of a worker during a short-term hiring for a particular employer. In *Lane v Shire Roofing Co (Oxford) Ltd*[183] the claimant was a building worker who was hired by the defendant employer to carry out a re-roofing job for which he was to be paid according to a daily rate. The defendant 'considered it prudent and advantageous to hire for individual jobs'.[184] While carrying out the work, the claimant fell and was injured. It was

---

[179] [1990] ICR 409, 414; see also *Ferguson v John Dawson & Partners (Contractors) Ltd* [1976] 1 WLR 1213.

[180] Lord Griffiths, [1990] ICR 409, 413–414.

[181] [1994] IRLR 171.

[182] [1994] IRLR 171, 175. Cf also *Wickens v Champion Employment Agency* [1984] ICR 365, 371: the common law 'does not include as a necessary element the question whether the individual carries on a separate business. If it did, then it would follow that a casual worker must always be employed under a contract of service unless he has his own business and that, plainly [sic], cannot be the law'.

[183] [1995] IRLR 493.

[184] [1995] IRLR 493, 496 (Henry LJ).

held that he was an employee for the purposes of the job, and so was owed the common law duty of care with regard to his health and safety. According to Henry LJ, applying the test of economic reality, the 'business' involved in the work was that of the defendant, not the claimant. The health and safety context of *Lane* cannot be ignored; the courts appear to take a strict approach to claims that a worker is self-employed in this type of case. Nevertheless, it indicates that there may well be circumstances under which a pattern of successive short-term hirings with different employers is compatible with employee status.

Mutuality of obligation

3.29   Notwithstanding the clarity of the test of 'economic reality', recent decisions of the courts have placed a fresh emphasis on a form of personal control in the form of 'mutuality of obligation'. Mutuality is a necessary feature of all bilateral contracts: without reciprocal promises, the basic element of consideration will be lacking and the arrangement will have no contractual force.[185] In this fundamental sense, mutuality of obligation is a feature not just of contracts of employment, but also of contracts for the supply of personal services;[186] it cannot therefore function as an indicator of employee status.

However, a separate meaning of 'mutuality of obligation' entered employment law in the late 1970s:[187] with specific reference to the contract of employment, this was based on the presence of mutual commitments to maintain the employment relationship in being over a period of time. It was an adaptation of the idea that the contract of employment is more than just a contract to serve in return for wages; in addition, there is a *second tier of obligation* consisting of mutual promises of future performance. Mark Freedland's treatise, *The Contract of Employment*, published in 1976, contained this passage:

> At the first level there is an exchange of work for remuneration. At the second level there is an exchange of mutual promises of future performance. The second level – the promises to employ and to be employed – provides the arrangement with its stability and with its continuity as a contract. The promises to employ and to be employed may be of short duration or may be terminable at short notice; but they still form an integral and most important part

---

[185] A difficult question is whether a 'unilateral' contract – one involving the performance of an act in return for a promise – can constitute a 'contract of employment' or a 'contract for personal services' within the meaning of those terms in modern employment legislation. Recent decisions interpreting the 'worker' concept can be read as indicating that a unilateral contract is outside the scope of this legislation. See our analysis, below, at para 3.33, and the discussion of unilateral employment contracts by Freedland, 2003: p 89–90.

[186] This is recognised in the growing case law concerning the 'worker' concept under NMWA 1998 and WTR 1998, and the concept of 'employment' under equal treatment legislation. See the decision of the Court of Appeal in *Mingeley v Pennock* [2004] IRLR 373, and our discussion at para 3.33 below.

[187] The more recent case law on the 'mutuality of obligation' test dates back to *Airfix Footwear Ltd v Cope* [1978] ICR 1210 (although the EAT, in that case, found that there was sufficient evidence of mutuality to establish a contract of employment in a case concerning an outworker). The test received the approval of the Court of Appeal in *O'Kelly v Trusthouse Forte plc* [1983] ICR 728 and *Nethermere (St Neots) Ltd v Taverna and Gardiner* [1984] IRLR 240 and of the House of Lords in *Carmichael v National Power plc* [2000] IRLR 43.

of the contract. They are the mutual undertakings to maintain the employment relationship in being which are inherent in any contract of employment so called.[188]

One interpretation of Freedland's analysis is that the second tier of obligation, if not the subject of an express term, should normally be implied into the contract as a necessary incident of the employment relationship. However, a different interpretation is that work relationships in which the second tier of obligation is lacking for some reason do not constitute contracts of employment for the purposes of statutory employment protection. The second interpretation has only a tenuous connection, at best, to the first, and is, moreover, contradicted by a large number of older cases in which courts had no difficulty accepting the presence of an express right, on the part of the employer, to suspend work or terminate the employment relationship without notice (or on minimal notice), within the framework of a contract of service or employment.[189] Nor was the duration of the hiring, at this point, regarded as a significant factor pointing away from employee status.[190] But be that as it may, the mutuality test was put forward with increasing frequency from the mid-1980s onwards in cases involving workers hired on a casual, short-term or intermittent basis. Often the result was that work relationships of this kind were classified as falling outside the scope of protective employment legislation. This could be for one of two reasons: either there was no 'global' or 'umbrella' contract of employment linking separate hirings, with the result that applicants lacked the necessary continuity of employment to bring statutory claims for which a minimum period of service was required; or the individual hirings themselves, because of the absence of a commitment to make work available in future (on the part of the employer) and to be available for work (on the part of the worker), could not be classified as contracts of employment.

In the leading case of *O'Kelly v Trusthouse Forte plc*[191] the applicants, who were wine waiters, were employed by a hotel chain as so-called 'regular casuals'. This meant that they were hired periodically to work on a particular catering job and could be relied upon to offer their services at regular intervals; the employer kept a list of their names and gave them preferential treatment in the allocation of any available work. They had no other regular employment and, if they refused work offered to them by the employer, they would be taken off the preferential list. They claimed that they had been dismissed on the grounds of their membership of an independent trade union, a claim which does not depend upon continuity of employment but simply requires employee status at the time of dismissal.[192] There were two possible ways of construing the arrangements so as to find employee status: by interpreting each separate engagement as a contract of employment, or by finding a continuing or 'global' contract of employment which spanned the separate engagements. The employment tribunal held that they had neither a global contract of employment nor a series

---

[188] Freedland, 1976b: pp 21–22. In his 2003 treatise, *The Personal Employment Contract*, which both updates and extends his earlier analysis, Freedland discusses this passage in the light of the intervening case law and the growing use by legislation of the 'worker' concept. See Freedland, 2003: pp 91–92.

[189] See, in particular, *Marshall v English Electric Co Ltd* [1945] 1 All ER 653, discussed in the context of lay-off below, ch 4, at para 4.126.

[190] On this point, see the discussion of Leighton, 1984.

[191] [1983] ICR 728.

[192] The relevant law is now contained in TULRCA 1992, s 152. Note that since 1 October 2004 protection against subjection to a detriment for this reason has applied to the wider category of workers: see para 8.5 below.

of separate ones. The EAT reversed on the second of these two points but the Court of Appeal restored the employment tribunal's decision.

The employment tribunal found against the applicants on the grounds that they were under no *obligation* to offer their services on a regular basis:

> The applicants entered into their relationship with the company in the expectation that they would be provided with any work which was currently available. It was a purely commercial transaction for the supply and purchase of services for specific events, because there was no obligation for the company to provide work and no obligation for the applicants to offer their further services.[193]

They were therefore in the position of independent contractors who simply chose to work for a single client. The tribunal refused to imply a term into the contract on the grounds of 'business efficacy' requiring the employer to provide work, on the basis that the arrangement could work perfectly well without one. This view was confirmed by the Court of Appeal: the judgment of the EAT 'must involve a misdirection of law or every independent contractor who is content or able only to attract one client would be held to work under a contract of employment'. Nor was there clear evidence of a global contract: 'what happened could equally well be attributed to market forces'.[194]

In other decisions, courts have been able to construe working practices in such a way as to discover a legal obligation on the part of the employer to find work for the employee, indicating that there is some leeway in the application of the mutuality test. In *Airfix Footwear Ltd v Cope*[195] and *Nethermere (St Neots) Ltd v Taverna and Gardiner*,[196] cases concerning homeworkers, the courts declined to accept that arrangements for the regular placing of work with the applicants lacked all legal force. In *Nethermere* Dillon LJ found it 'unreal to suppose that the work in fact done by the applicants for the company over the not inconsiderable periods ... was done merely as a result of the pressures of market forces on the applicants and the company and under no contract at all',[197] and Stephenson LJ could not see 'why well-founded expectations of continuing homework should not be hardened or refined into enforceable contracts by regular giving and taking of work over periods of a year or more, and why outworkers should not thereby become employees under contracts of service, like those doing similar work in the factory'.[198] Stephenson LJ also invoked the long-standing authority of *Devonald v Rosser & Sons Ltd*[199] to hold that the obligation on the employee's part to accept work could be used to imply an obligation on the part of the employer to offer it, by way of reciprocity.[200]

By contrast, in *Clark v Oxfordshire Health Authority*[201] the Court of Appeal held that there was no evidence of a global contract of employment in the case of a nurse who, under an arrangement

---

[193] Cited at [1983] ICR 730, 744.
[194] [1983] 730, 763 (Sir John Donaldson MR).
[195] [1978] ICR 1210; although cf *Mailway (Southern) Ltd v Willsher* [1978] ICR 511.
[196] [1984] IRLR 240.
[197] [1984] IRLR 240, 246.
[198] [1984] IRLR 240.
[199] [1906] 2 KB 728; see below, ch 4, at para 4.126.
[200] [1984] IRLR 240, 246.
[201] [1998] IRLR 125.

with the health authority, was offered work as and when the need arose, but who otherwise had no regular working hours. Similarly, in *Carmichael v National Power plc*[202] the House of Lords ruled that tour guides who worked on a 'casual as required basis' had been correctly classified as being employed under arrangements which lacked the mutuality of obligation needed to establish a global contract. These cases suggest that it may be difficult to establish a continuing legal nexus in cases of so-called 'zero hours contracts', where the employer unequivocally refuses to commit itself in advance to make any given quantum of work available.[203] Nevertheless, a vital aspect of *Carmichael* was that, in the view of the tribunal, the applicants were free to refuse to work even when invited to work by the employer. A different outcome is possible in a case where the employee contracts to be on call, that is, to be available to work whenever the employer calls upon him or her to do so. It is then open to a court to infer the existence of the reciprocal obligation on the employer's part to offer work when it becomes available. Where that is the case, there could be sufficient mutuality to establish a global contract of employment.

It is also completely consistent with *Carmichael* for workers who are employed on a 'zero-hours' basis to be employees during the period when they are at work or in respect of particular engagements or hirings. One possible interpretation of *O'Kelly* and the cases which followed it is that very short-term hirings are incompatible with employee status; unless there is a global contract of employment spanning the gaps between jobs, the individual hirings must also take the form of contracts for services. But the better view is that there is no reason why a particular hiring should not take the form of a contract of employment; duration is not a decisive factor. This was the conclusion of the Court of Appeal in *McMeechan v Secretary of State for Employment*:[204] under his terms and conditions, the agency worker in that case might have been employed by the agency as either an employee or as self-employed for the purposes of a particular assignment or 'single engagement'. As we have noted, it will often be necessary for an employee to establish a global contract in order to show that he or she has the necessary continuity of employment to claim certain statutory rights which depend upon length and regularity of service.[205] However, there are numerous employment protection rights which do not depend upon extensive continuity of service, and for the purposes of these provisions, the decision in *McMeechan* is particularly useful.[206]

The emergence of the mutuality test at a particular point in the evolution of modern employment law suggests that it should be seen as an attempt to refute the criterion of 'economic

---

[202] [2000] IRLR 43. See H Collins, 2000b.

[203] It was estimated in 1998 that approximately 200,000 individuals were employed on zero hours contracts. See DTI, *Fairness at Work*, Cm 3968, 1998, at para 3.14. According to data collected as part of the Workplace Employment Relations Survey of 2004, 5% of workplaces with 10 or more employees offered zero hours contracts, an increase from 3% from the same survey in 1998 (Kersley *et al*, 2005).

[204] [1997] IRLR 353; see also *Clark v Oxfordshire Health Authority* [1998] IRLR 125; *Carmichael v National Power plc* [2000] IRLR 43; *Cornwall CC v Prater* [2006] IRLR 362 (discussed by A Davies, 2006b); *James v Redcats (Brands) Ltd* [2007] IRLR 296, at [75]–[93].

[205] See our analysis at para 3.59 below.

[206] For example, of the cases discussed in the text, *McMeechan* concerned employees' rights in the event of the employer's insolvency (ERA 1996, Part XII), and *O'Kelly* was about the right of an employee not to be dismissed for trade-union related reasons (TULRCA 1992, s 152). *Carmichael v National Power plc* concerned the right to a written statement of terms and conditions of employment (ERA 1996, s 1) for which one month's continuity is required; on this aspect of the case, see H Collins, 2000b. It should also be noted that the Court of Appeal in *Clark v Oxfordshire Health Authority* did not decide that there could not be individual contracts of employment in respect of the periods when the applicant was employed to work; this point was remitted to the tribunal. See generally A Davies, 2007.

reality' and to reassert formal subordination as the basis of employment: workers who do not make a formal, long-term commitment to the firm are viewed as having no claim to employment protection from it.[207] For example, it was on this ground that temporary workers employed by an agency were said 'wholly to lack the elements of continuity, and care of the employer for the employee, that one associates with the contract of service'.[208] Yet it may be argued that the strict application of the mutuality test, by making the *duration* of the hiring a central factor in deciding employment status, produces some odd results.[209] If one of the waiters in *O'Kelly* had spilled the contents of a bottle of wine on one of Trusthouse Forte's customers, would a court have denied the customer an action against the company on the grounds that it was not vicariously liable for the negligence of independent contractors?[210] One way out of this difficulty would be to decide that the individual, although not an employee for the purposes of employment protection legislation, could be regarded as such for the different purposes of the employer's vicarious liability in tort.[211] It is arguable that the individual should be bound by the arrangement he or she chooses to make with the employer when it comes to defining the scope of their mutual rights and obligations, but that a third party should not be deprived of the right to sue the employer in tort by a contract to which he or she is not privy. But this is surely to place too much emphasis on an arrangement which was offered to the worker on a 'take it or leave it basis' and was the result of the casualisation of the trade in question, rather than a measured weighing by the workers concerned of the costs and benefits of independent contractor status.

Although there are serious implications for the effectiveness of employment protection legislation of the use by the courts of a test whose origins are contentious and whose effects are potentially highly confusing, the importance of the mutuality test has if anything increased over time. There is now a considerable body of case law concerning the interpretation of standard-form employment agreements which refer to the mutuality issue. A 'no obligations clause', under which the parties agree that the employer shall be under no obligation to offer work beyond a given hiring, and that the worker is free to refuse future offers of work, may have the effect of excluding employee status for the reasons discussed above.[212]

As we have seen,[213] a court can look beyond a 'no obligations clause' if it is convinced that it is a 'sham',[214] or if it can find evidence that the parties, notwithstanding the formal agreement they initially made, subsequently entered into a new employment contract by conduct.[215] Mutual

---

[207] For discussion of the values underlying the mutuality test, see Leighton, 1984; Deakin, 2003. In some recent cases, 'mutuality' and 'control' have often been considered alongside each other, as overlapping criteria for identifying employment status. See, eg, *Stephenson v Delphi Diesel Systems Ltd.* [2003] ICR 471; *Bridges v Industrial Rubber plc*, EAT, 21 September 2004, Appeal No UKEAT/0150/04/DM.

[208] *Wickens v Champion Employment Agency* [1984] ICR 365, 371; see also *Ironmonger v Movefield Ltd* [1988] IRLR 461.

[209] The courts' stress on this particular factor also differs from the emphasis given by Freedland in his formulation of the test, in which 'the promises to employ and to be employed may be of short duration or may be terminable at short notice' (see above).

[210] See the discussion of this point by Sedley LJ in *Dacas v Brook Street Bureau (UK) Ltd* [2004] IRLR 358.

[211] See McKendrick, 1990.

[212] See *Stevedoring and Haulage Services Ltd v Fuller* [2001] IRLR 627 for a clear illustration of this point.

[213] See para 3.22, above.

[214] *Protectacoat Firthglow Ltd v Szigalyi* [2009] IRLR 365; *Autoclenz Ltd v Belcher* [2011] IRLR 820; see para 3.22 above.

[215] For a reminder that a contract of employment can be entered into entirely on the basis of conduct, where that is sufficient to imply an exchange of promises, see *Newnham Farms Ltd v Powell*, EAT, 7 March 2003, Appeal No EAT/0711/01/MAA.

obligations may be implied from a repeated course of dealing. Even if no global contract can implied, a single hiring is highly likely to be regarded as a bilateral legal arrangement, either contract for the supply of personal services or a contract of employment, for as long as work continuing.[216] But for a court or tribunal to imply a contract on the basis of conduct, it must have evidence that the parties possessed the relevant contractual intention, and it must be also able to spell out what the terms of the contract are.[217] In numerous cases, these requirements have proved to be a substantial barrier to a finding of employee status.[218]

A 'multi-factor test'?

3.30   None of the tests considered so far will necessarily be decisive on its own. According to Lord Wright in *Montreal v Montreal Locomotive Works*, 'in many cases the question can only be settled by examining the whole of the various elements which constitute the relationship between the parties'.[219] This open-ended approach is exemplified by the 'multi-factor' or 'multiple' test as stated by MacKenna J in *Ready Mixed Concrete (South East) Ltd v Minister for Pensions and National Insurance*:[220]

> A contract of service exists [when] three conditions are fulfilled. (i) The servant agrees that, in consideration of a wage or other remuneration, he will provide his own work and skill in the performance of some service for his master. (ii) He agrees, expressly or impliedly, that in the performance of that service he will be subject to the other's control in a sufficient degree to make that other master. (iii) The other provisions of the contract are consistent with its being a contract of service.

Although this test has since been cited with approval on numerous occasions, in its first two stages it represents little more than a repetition of the test of personal control. The third stage adds nothing, since it neither indicates what the core features of the contract of service (or employment) are, nor which features are necessarily inconsistent with it. It invites the courts to engage in a balancing act, the outcome of which may be almost impossible to predict in advance. This adds to the uncertainty created by the decision in *O'Kelly v Trusthouse Forte plc*,[221] limiting the scope for appellate guidance and review of tribunals' decisions. In particular, it makes it difficult for the parties to rely on earlier decisions in similar cases; it has been said that 'the process involves painting a picture in each individual case',[222] and that it is 'quite impossible in a field where a very

---

[216] *McMeechan v Secretary of State for Employment* [1997] IRLR 353; *Stevedoring & Haulage Services Ltd v Fuller* [2001] IRLR 627; *Stephenson v Delphi Diesel Systems Ltd* [2003] ICR 471.

[217] *Accounttax Marketing Ltd v Halstead*, EAT, 6 November 2003, Appeal No UKEAT/0313/03/ZT, at [35] and [39].

[218] In the more recent case law, this has been a particular problem in the context of agency workers (*Bunce v Postworth Ltd t/a Skyblue* [2005] IRLR 557; *Cairns v Visteon Ltd* [2007] IRLR 175; *Consistent Group Ltd v Kalwak* [2008] IRLR 505), freelance workers (*PA News Ltd t/a The Press Association v Loveridge*, EAT, 1 September 2003, Appeal No EAT 0135/03/MAA) and homeworkers (*Bridges v Industrial Rubber plc*, EAT, 21 September 2004, Appeal No UKEAT/0150/04/DM). See generally Leighton and Wynn, 2011.

[219] [1947] 1 DLR 161, 169.

[220] [1968] 2 QB 497, 515.

[221] [1983] ICR 728.

[222] *Hall v Lorimer* [1992] 1 WLR 939, 944 (Mummery J); see also the Court of Appeal judgments ([1994] IRLR 171).

large number of factors have to be weighed, to gain any real assistance by looking at the facts of another case and comparing them one by one to see what facts are common, what are different and what particular weight is given by another Tribunal to the common facts'.[223] As a result, courts and advisers often have to resort to what Wedderburn has termed the 'elephant test': the contract of employment has become 'an animal too difficult to define, but easy to recognise when you see it'.[224] Some of the uncertainties to which this gives rise can be illustrated by considering in turn the leading cases of *Ready Mixed Concrete, O'Kelly* and *Hall v Lorimer*.

Ready Mixed Concrete concerned the status, for national insurance contribution purposes, of a lorry driver who delivered cement for the applicants. He was in the process of buying the lorry from them on hire purchase terms and had to paint it in the company's colours, to drive it on the company's business for a certain number of hours per week and to wear the company's uniform when doing so. He was paid according to a rate per mile for a given quantity of delivered cement. If he was unable to work he had to hire a replacement. The contract described him as self-employed but also required him to obey all reasonable orders of the company. MacKenna J held that he was self-employed, because 'these are obligations more consistent, I think, with a contract of carriage than with one of service. The ownership of the assets, the chance of profit and the risk of loss in the business of carriage are his and not the company's'.[225]

The decision is surprising, given the duty to obey orders and the clear identification of the work to be done with the company's own business. It is perhaps begging the question to talk of the 'business of carriage' being the business in relation to which the worker took the risk of loss and the chance of profit; arguably, the relevant business here was the company's cement business. Whatever arguments might be put for or against the outcome, however, *Ready Mixed Concrete* is a good example of the balancing act which courts and tribunals must engage in when applying the 'multiple test' without any clear guidance from the legislation itself or from the appellate courts as to which factors are more important than others.

In *O'Kelly v Trusthouse Forte*[226] the employment tribunal produced a list of no fewer than 18 different relevant factors, some of which were considered consistent with the existence of a contract of employment. These included the lack of any financial investment by the applicants in the company's business; the payment by the company of holiday pay and an incentive bonus based on past service; the presence of control by the company when the waiters were at work; and the fact that they were paid weekly in arrears with tax and national insurance deducted at source. A second category contained factors which were regarded as *not inconsistent* with a contract of employment. The applicants were only paid for work actually performed, but 'the method of calculating entitlement to remuneration is not an essential aspect of the employment relationship'; similarly, it was not fatal that there were no regular weekly working hours, nor that the applicants were not members of the company's sick pay and pension schemes. Finally, the tribunal recognised a category of factors which were inconsistent with employee status. These were: the contracts were terminable without notice on either side; the applicants had the right to refuse work; the company was under no obligation to provide work; the parties themselves took the view that the applicants, as casual workers, were independent contractors; and it was also

---

[223] *Walls v Sinnett* (1987) 60 TC 150, 164 (Vinelott J).
[224] Wedderburn, 1986: p 116.
[225] [1968] 2 QB 497, 526.
[226] [1983] ICR 728.

the recognised custom and practice in the industry to treat casual workers as employed under contracts for services. The tribunal considered that while none of these factors was decisive in its own right, on balance 'it would be irresponsible lightly to disregard the clear evidence of the parties derived from an engagement under custom and practice, because this would have widespread and damaging repercussions throughout the whole industry';[227] this was therefore a case in which the parties' own designation of status tipped the balance.

Self-employment was also the outcome in the tax case of *Hall v Lorimer*.[228] Mr Lorimer was a skilled television technician (a 'vision mixer') who had previously worked as an employee for one particular company, but had then become a freelance worker, building up a clientele of around twenty different production companies. He did not supply or own his own equipment and worked on the premises of the companies concerned; on the other hand, he was paid on a fee basis for each separate engagement and occasionally hired a substitute when he could not carry out certain work. In any one year he had over 100 separate engagements, most of which lasted no more than one day, and he had no continuing or 'global' contract with any one company. The Court of Appeal, dismissing an appeal by the Inland Revenue, found that Mr Lorimer was self-employed.

In both *Ready Mixed Concrete* and *O'Kelly* there was clear evidence of both personal and economic dependence between worker and employer. In each case the worker consistently contracted with the same employer, was required to obey certain orders and was dependent on that employer for continuing work and income. *Lorimer*, by contrast, seems a much clearer case of self-employment. Like the applicants in *O'Kelly*, Lorimer had no business of his own, but this is not necessarily a crucial factor, as we have seen.[229] An essential difference in his case, though, was that he was 'independent of a particular paymaster for the financial exploitation of his talents':[230] he worked for a large number of different businesses without being economically dependent on any one of them. An emphasis on economic dependence, so defined, would arguably produce greater predictability than the open-ended multiple test, in which any one of a number of factors could turn out to be essential in tipping the balance on one side or the other. In *Autoclenz Ltd v Belcher*[231] the issue was whether car valeters who were described in the agreements they signed as 'sub-contract' labour had contracts of employment with the ultimate user of their labour services. Relevant factors in favour of a finding of employee status which was finally upheld in the Supreme Court were the lack of control the valeters exercised over the content of the work and their own working time, their integration into the organisational structure of the respondent, the fixed rates of pay on the basis of which their remuneration was calculated, and the limited opportunity they had to profit from their activities in the way that genuine entrepreneurs would have done. Lord Clarke approved the use by the Employment Tribunal of what he called a 'purposive' approach to classifying the work relationship in this case.[232]

---

[227] [1983] ICR 728, 745 (Ackner LJ, summarising the decision of the employment tribunal).
[228] [1994] IRLR 171.
[229] See para 3.30 above.
[230] [1994] IRLR 171, 175.
[231] [2011] IRLR 820.
[232] [2011] IRLR 820, at [35].

QUASI-DEPENDENT LABOUR

3.31 The uncertainty created by the common law tests for defining employee status has led to a number of extensions of the scope of protective legislation. Those affected include apprentices and trainees; self-employed workers who are economically dependent on the business of another; homeworkers; and agency workers. These individuals are *employed* – they do not have their own businesses – without necessarily being *subordinated* workers according to the criteria examined above. Because of this, and because they are treated as being equivalent to employees only for certain purposes, the term 'quasi-dependent labour' may be used to refer to this group.

Apprentices and trainees

3.32   Apprentices come within the scope of employment protection legislation, the contract of apprenticeship being included within the broad definition of the contract of employment for this purpose.[233] The essence of apprenticeship is that the employer undertakes formally to train and instruct the apprentice in a particular trade or skill; the apprentice, in turn, contracts to serve the employer[234] and to learn from those from whom he or she receives instruction. According to Widgery LJ in *Dunk v George Waller & Son Ltd*,[235] 'a contract of apprenticeship secures three things for the apprentice; it secures him, first, a money payment during the period of apprenticeship; secondly, that he shall be instructed and trained and thereby acquire skills which will be of value to him for the rest of his life; and thirdly it gives him status, because ... once a young man, as here, completes his apprenticeship and can show by certificate that he has completed his time with a well-known employer, this gets him off to a good start in the labour market and gives him a status the loss of which may be of considerable damage to him'. The contract is normally one for a fixed term and cannot be terminated by either party, by the giving of notice, before the term has expired. The grounds on which the employer may dismiss the apprentice for misconduct are also more limited than they would be in the case of an employee. Hence in *Dunk*[236] the employer was not entitled to end the apprenticeship when the apprentice failed a certain examination, and had to pay damages representing not just lost wages but the prospective loss of skills and enhanced earning capacity. Nor can the apprentice normally be dismissed for redundancy during the term of the contract; such a dismissal is only permitted in extreme circumstances, such as the total closure of the employment unit.[237] However, once the agreed period of training comes to an end there is no obligation on the part of the employer to continue employing the now-qualified apprentice, nor does the latter qualify for a redundancy payment if he or she is not re-employed.[238] There is no legal maximum age limit for beginning an apprenticeship; traditionally,

---

[233] ERA 1996, s 230(1), (2).

[234] If the individual does not undertake to serve, the relationship cannot be one of apprenticeship: *Edmonds v Lawson QC* [2000] IRLR 391 (a pupil barrister was not employed under a contract of apprenticeship for the purposes of NMWA 1998).

[235] [1970] 2 QB 163, 169.

[236] [1970] 2 QB 163.

[237] *Wallace v C A Roofing Services Ltd* [1996] IRLR 435; *Flett v Matheson* [2006] IRLR 277.

[238] *North East Coast Shiprepairers v Secretary of State for Employment* [1978] ICR 755; *Ryan v Shipboard Maintenance* [1980] ICR 88.

industrial apprenticeships were invariably begun immediately upon leaving school, but this is no longer an inflexible practice.

The number of apprenticeships has declined considerably since the late 1970s, partly as a consequence of increased government funding for alternative forms of work-related training. The element of state subsidy in supporting the wages of trainees, together with the predominant role played by governmental bodies in setting the framework for the training process, are among the factors distinguishing these forms of training from the traditional apprenticeship. A majority of the EAT in *Daley v Allied Suppliers Ltd*[239] concluded that a trainee under the Youth Training Scheme which was then in force had no contract of any kind. The principal reason given was that the terms of the trainee's placement were set by the rules laid down by a state agency which was responsible for administering the training programme (at that time the Manpower Services Commission) and not by the parties themselves. As was said in the similar case of *Hawley v Fieldcastle & Co Ltd*,[240] 'because of the intervention of the [Manpower Services Commission] by agreement between both the applicant and the respondent and the limitations which that intervention imposes upon the freedom of action of both the parties, the relationship between the parties in [this] case is not that of employer/employee'. This is not a very convincing argument, however; many contracts of employment are subject to regulation by an external source of norms, such as a collective agreement, without losing their character as contracts. A second line of argument in *Daley* was that the applicant had a *contract for training* which was juridically distinct from a contract of employment or apprenticeship, and therefore outside the scope of the relevant legislation: 'the underlying purpose of any contract between [the parties] was not to establish a relationship of an employer and an employee but to enable Miss Daley to acquire certain skills and experience',[241] without the parties having entered into the more specific obligations characteristic of an apprenticeship. So-called 'modern apprenticeships', despite having some similarities to the scheme considered in *Daley*, may give rise to a common law contract of apprenticeship depending on the nature of the employer's obligations under such agreements.[242]

Since the decision in *Daley*, the legislature has acted to grant a partially protected status to trainees who are not accorded employee or apprentice status by their employers: as a result, they are covered by legislation in the areas of health and safety, working time, and equal treatment discrimination,[243] while remaining excluded from most of the protective rights contained in ERA 1996. Apprentices below the age of 19, and apprentices below the age of 26 during their first year of training, are excluded from the coverage of the national minimum wage. All workers below the

[239] [1983] IRLR 14.
[240] [1982] IRLR 223.
[241] *Daley v Allied Suppliers Ltd* [1983] IRLR 14, 17; see also *Wiltshire Police Authority v Wynn* [1980] ICR 649.
[242] See the contrasting decisions of the EAT in *Whitely v Marton Electrical Ltd* [2003] IRLR 197 and *Thorpe v Dul* [2003] ICR 1556, and the decision of the CA, in favour of a contract of apprenticeship, in *Flett v Matheson* [2006] IRLR 277. In the light of *Flett* and the additional common law protections that it conferred on trainees under statutory schemes, the government took the step of inserting a provision into the Apprenticeships, Skills, Children and Learning Act 2009 (s 32) indicating that 'apprenticeship agreeements' under the scheme set up by that Act were not to be treated as giving rise to contracts of apprenticeship, but, instead, to contracts of service and hence to the more limited 'employee' status. See Ryan and Lewis, 2012.
[243] See, for health and safety, SI 1983/1919; for working time, WTR 1998, reg 42; and for equality law, EqA 2010, s 83(2)(a).

age of 16 are excluded; those between 16-17 and 18-21 receive lower minimum rates. A number of more specific exclusions also apply to particular training schemes.[244]

The Employment Act 1988[245] conferred a power on the Secretary of State to designate the status of trainees on youth training programmes by order for particular purposes. An order may state that such persons are to be treated as employed, or not, and that their status may be that of trainees or employees; the legal nature of the payments they receive by way of the training allowance may also be determined by this means. Powers under this section have been exercised on a number of occasions.

'Workers', the self-employed, and those supplying personal services

3.33   In December 2011 the self-employed represented around 14% of the active labour force in the UK.[246] The legal notion of self-employment is, however, not easy to pin down, and the 14% figure given in official statistics represents a highly heterogeneous category.[247] The legal nature of self-employment has achieved a new importance as a result of growing reliance on the 'worker' concept, in preference to the more normal 'employee'. The following definition is the one now widely in use:

> ... "worker"... means an individual who has entered into or works under (or, where the employment has ceased, worked under) -
> (a) a contract of employment, or
> (b) any other contract, whether express or implied and (if it is express) whether oral or in writing, whereby the individual undertakes to do or perform personally any work or services for another party to the contract whose status is not by virtue of the contract that of a client or customer of any profession or undertaking carried on by the individual; and any reference to a worker's contract shall be construed accordingly.[248]

The reason for using this extended definition of dependent status is to be found in the purpose of the particular statutory provisions to which it applies. A first set of such provisions is concerned with the application of basic labour standards in relation to minimum wages, protection against

---

[244] See paras 4.47–4.48 below.

[245] Section 26. The power was extended by the Learning and Skills Act 2000; see the discussion of this provision in *Thorpe v Dul* [2003] ICR 1556.

[246] ONS, Labour Market Statistics, December 2011, Table EMP 01.

[247] See Burchell *et al*, 1999, for a discussion of the statistical definitions of the self-employed used by government, and historical background on the rise of self-employment in the 1980s and 1990s, and Lindsay and Macauley, 2004 for a more recent review of different usages.

[248] ERA 1996, s 230(3) (this definition is used in the ERA 1996 in the context of the right not to have arbitrary deductions made from wages under Part II of the Act (formerly Part I of the Wages Act 1986)). See also similar provisions in NMWA 1998, s 54 (minimum wage); WTR 1998, reg 2 (working time); TULRCA, 1992, s 296(1) (various collective rights); ERelA 1999, s 13 (right to be accompanied in disciplinary hearings). See Davidov, 2005 for discussion of the 'worker' definition. McCrudden, 2012, in a discussion of the recent Supreme Court decision in *Jivraj v Hashwani* [2011] IRLR 827, argues that the modern use of the term 'worker' is descended from the concept of the 'workman' in late nineteenth and early twentieth century social legislation, a view which would justify a narrow reading of the 'worker' notion, but for a different view, arguing that the 'workman' concept referred to what would now be a sub-category of the 'employee' concept, see Deakin, 2007.

arbitrary deductions from pay, and protection from excessive working hours. Here, through its use of the worker definition, the legislature has in essence taken the view that casual workers who would not necessarily fall within 'employee' status should not, for that reason, be denied basic protections which do not depend, for their effective functioning, upon the employment relationship in question being regular or long-term.[249]

Health and safety law has long operated according to a similar principle. The Health and Safety at Work Act 1974 imposes a general duty on employers 'to ensure, so far as is reasonably practicable, the health, safety and welfare at work of all [their] employees', as well as more specific duties including the maintenance of a safe plant and system of work and a safe workplace, the provision of information and training and the maintenance of an adequate working environment as regards facilities and arrangements for welfare.[250] As elsewhere, an 'employee' is defined here as a person employed under a contract of employment or apprenticeship.[251] In addition, the employer is under a duty to conduct his undertaking in such a way as to ensure that, as far as reasonably practicable, 'persons not in his employment who may be affected thereby are not thereby exposed to risks to their health or safety', a phrase which would certainly cover self-employed workers employed on or about the employer's premises.[252]

A second category relates to collective rights, including the provision of immunity from liability in tort for those who organise industrial action and provisions governing the formation and constitution of trade unions. Here, the widened definition of 'worker' means that there may be a lawful trade dispute (a prerequisite of immunity for the organisation of industrial action) in defence of the interests of self-employed 'workers' in the sense described above, and not merely to defend the interests of employees. The legislature also recognises that trade unions recruit and represent the interests of many individuals who are not employees in the legal sense of that term, either because they are seeking employment (this particular definition applies to those looking for employment as either employees or workers) or because their status is in doubt on account of a lack of regular employment or a high degree of autonomy in the way they do their work (while, at the same time, excluding associations of professionals, such as the Law Society, from this definition[253]). Following this logic, the right of the individual not to be dismissed or otherwise discriminated against within employment on grounds related to the statutory trade union recognition procedure applies to workers as well as to employees, as do other aspects of that procedure.[254] In addition, the right to be protected against discrimination on grounds of membership of an independent trade union has been extended to workers.[255] However the right

---

[249] See *Cotswold Developments Construction Ltd. v Williams* [2006] IRLR 181, at [53].

[250] HSWA 1974, s 2(1)–(2).

[251] HSWA 1974, s 53(1).

[252] HSWA 1974, s 3. The phrase 'persons not in his employment' can be read as meaning all those who are not his employees: under s 53(1), '"employee" means an individual who works under a contract of employment, and related expressions shall be construed accordingly' (emphasis added). See also the Framework Directive on Health and Safety, Directive 89/391, Art 3(a)–(b).

[253] *Carter v Law Society* [1973] ICR 113. The definition of 'trade union' is contained in TULRCA 1992, s 1; see para 7.20 below.

[254] For example, under TULRCA 1992, Sch A1, para 1, the union may seek recognition in respect of a 'group or groups of workers'; see *R (on the application of the BBC) v CAC* [2003] IRLR 460. The anti-discrimination provisions are to be found in Sch A1, paras 156–165.

[255] TULRCA 1992, s 146, as amended by ERelA 2004, s 30.

to protection against discrimination for taking part in industrial action continues to apply only to employees.[256]

A third category relates to the principle of equal treatment. Equality legislation extends to employment 'under a contract of employment, a contract of apprenticeship or a contract personally to do work'[257] as well as to applicants for employment, so defined.[258] This wide definition is underpinned by European Union law. In *Allonby v Accrington and Rossendale College*[259] the ECJ held that the term 'worker', in the context of the right to equal pay for equal work in Article 141 EC (now Article 157 TFEU), 'cannot be defined by reference to the legislation of the Member States but has a Community meaning'.[260] Moreover, because the right to equal pay 'forms part of the foundations of the Community',[261] the worker concept 'cannot be interpreted restrictively'.[262] For this purpose, 'there must be considered as a worker a person who, for a certain period of time, performs services for and under the direction of another person in return for which he receives remuneration'.[263] A similarly broad reading of the term 'worker' was given in a subsequent ruling of the Court, *Wippel*, in which it held that a part-time worker employed under a 'framework' contract which did not specify set working hours (in the manner of a 'zero-hours' contract) had to be regarded as a worker covered by the Equal Treatment Directive.[264]

The precise issue before the Court in *Allonby* was whether the exclusion of the applicant from a public sector pension scheme governed by legislation, the Teachers' Superannuation Scheme, on the grounds that she was not an employee – she was an agency worker employed by the agency under a contract for services, and had no contract of any kind with the user to whom she supplied her services – amounted to an infringement of the equal pay principle. The Court held that, in the absence of justification, Mrs Allonby's exclusion from the TSS might amount to indirect discrimination under Article 141 TEC (now Article 157 TFEU), if it could be shown that the relevant rules of the scheme disproportionately affected more female than male workers, and that this could not be justified.[265]

British equality legislation appears to satisfy the *Allonby* test, given the inclusion in that legislation not just of employees but of workers with contracts 'personally to do work'. However, the scope of that legislation has been put in doubt by the Supreme Court decision in *Jivraj v Hashwani*.[266] The issue here was whether a commercial arbitrator could be regarded as in 'employment' for the purposes of triggering legislation on discrimination on the grounds of religion or belief. The Supreme Court held that he was not, as he did not perform his services or earn his fees for and under the direction of the parties; he was an independent provider of services who was not in a relationship of subordination with the parties who received them. According to Lord Clarke, for equality legislation to be applied to a given work relationship, there had to be

---

[256] TULRCA 1992, s 237–238A.

[257] EqA 2010, s. 83(2)(a)).

[258] EqA 2010, s. 39.

[259] Case C-256/01, [2004] IRLR 224.

[260] Case C-256/01, [2004] IRLR 224, at para 66.

[261] Case C-256/01, [2004] IRLR 224, para 65.

[262] Case C-256/01, [2004] IRLR 224, para 66.

[263] Case C-256/01, [2004] IRLR 224, para 67.

[264] Case C-313/02 *Wippel v Peek & Coppenburg GmbH & Co KG* [2005] IRLR 211.

[265] On the concepts of adverse impact and group disadvantage under the test for indirect discrimination, see our analysis in ch 6 below, at paras 6.25 *et seq.*

[266] [2011] IRLR 827; McCrudden, 2012; Freedland and Kountouris, 2012.

not simply a contract 'personally to do work', but also 'employment' under that or another relevant contract.[267] 'Employment', in turn, implied 'subordination' as defined by the ECJ in *Allonby*,[268] which Lord Clarke took to refer to a relationship within which services were performed 'for and under the direction of another person'.[269]

One possible reading of the Court's judgment in *Allonby* is that it used the term 'subordination' in the same sense as that intended by the 'control' test in UK labour law.[270] The *Allonby* judgment contrasted a worker who performs work 'under the direction of another person' with 'independent providers of services who are not in a relationship of subordination with the person who receives the services'.[271] The emphasis in *Allonby* was, however, on ensuring that workers who passed the control test came under the protection of EU law, whether or not they would otherwise have been protected under national legislation. In *Jivraj*, *Allonby* was interpreted as deciding that *only* workers who passed the control test were protected by equality law. This is an implausible reading of *Allonby* given the narrowness of the control test and availability in British labour law of more flexible tests, such as 'integration' and 'business reality', for determing employee status.[272] The wider problem with the Supreme Court's approach in *Jivraj* is that it gets dangerously close to eliding the concept of 'employment' under equality legislation, and, by extension, the 'worker' concept under other labour law statutes, with the more limited 'employee' category. As we have seen,[273] the 'employment' concept in the context of equality law, and the 'worker' concept more generally, were introduced in order to ensure that the personal scope of labour legislation was not confined to 'employees' as narrowly defined by the 'control' test and other common law equivalents to the continental European notion of subordination, such as the mutuality of obligation test.[274] It would be unfortunate if *Jivraj* resulted in an interpretation of the 'worker' and 'employment' concepts that was so plainly at odds with their clear statutory purpose.

Even with the extension of the scope of protective legislation implied by the use of the 'worker' and 'employment' concepts, there must still be a direct contractual nexus of some kind between the provider of labour services and the recipient. It is for this reason that, in a number of recent decisions, tribunals and courts applying the 'worker' concept have insisted on the need for 'mutuality of obligation'.[275] The use of the term 'mutuality' appears to refer here to the basic elements of consideration which must be present in any contract, rather than to the specific sense of 'mutuality' which has been used, in a separate context, to draw a distinction between contracts of employment and contracts giving rise to self-employment.[276] It is, to say the least, confusing to see the phrase 'mutuality of obligation' used in these two distinct senses. When the phrase is used in relation to the 'worker' concept, it is not clear what, if anything, is being added to the requirement of consideration.

---

[267] Thus EqA 2010, s. 83(2)(a) refers to 'employment under a ... contract personally to do work'.

[268] Case C-256/01, [2004] IRLR 224.

[269] [2011] IRLR 827, at [34].

[270] [2004] IRLR 224, at para 68.

[271] Case C-256/01, [2004] IRLR 224, paras 67 and 68.

[272] On the control, integration and business reality tests, see paras 3.26-3.28, above. UK labour law is not fundamentally different, in this respect, from the approaches taken in other EU Member States, which all recognise to some degree the need to supplement the basic test of personal subordination with tests based on economic dependence; see Freedland and Kountouris, 2011, in particular chs. 3 and 10.

[273] See above, this para.

[274] See Freedland and Kountouris, 2012.

[275] See, in particular, *Byrne Brothers (Formwork) Ltd v Baird* [2002] IRLR 96; *Stephenson v Delphi Diesel Systems Ltd* [2003] ICR 471; *Cotswold Developments Construction Ltd v Williams* [2006] IRLR 181.

[276] See para 3.29, above.

One possibility is that, for the 'worker' concept to apply, labour services must be provided under a 'bilateral' contract, that it to say, one in which the parties undertake mutual commitments in advance of performance. A 'unilateral' contract, under which the employer's obligations are triggered only at the point when the work is completed, would be excluded. But there is much to be said for the courts operating according to a presumption in favour of implying a bilateral contract, all other things being equal, when work is carried out in return for remuneration.[277]

A further limitation on the 'worker' and 'employment' concepts relates to those who do not contract to supply *personal* services. One possibility here is that the 'dominant purpose' of an arrangement is for a person to supply an end product or service without necessarily contracting to supply their *own* work and labour. It is partly for this reason that in a series of cases, courts have held that postmasters and postmistresses fall outside the scope of equal treatment and minimum wage legislation.[278] By contrast, in *Loughran and Kelly v Northern Ireland Housing Executive*[279] the House of Lords held that individual solicitors could bring an action for unlawful discrimination against the respondent even though they had applied for employment not in their personal capacity but through the firms through which they worked. This decision turns on the nature of a solicitors' partnership; the partnership or 'firm' is not an entity in its own right which can be regarded as separate from the individual partners. The decision is questionable since, as Lord Clyde commented in his dissent, a more plausible construction of the terms of appointment in question was that the solicitors in question would arrange for the work to be done by one of the members of their respective firms, rather than undertaking to supply their own services. Lords Slynn and Steyn considered that the Act could also confer rights upon the partnership as such as well as upon individuals, but this view was rejected by Lords Griffiths, Lloyd and Clyde.[280]

In respect of both the need for 'mutuality' and the requirement of 'personal services', employers may try to avoid the application of protective statutes through the insertion of standard-form terms and conditions which are designed to exclude the obligation to provide personal services. The decision of the Court of Appeal in *Express & Echo Publications Ltd v Tanton*[281] is just as much in point here as it is in the context of the definition of 'employee' status, and similar arguments will apply. Thus it is open to an applicant to argue that a 'substitution' clause has not been effectively incorporated into the relevant contract,[282] or that the term in question, if it is ambiguous, should be read in the light of the way in which the work was carried out.[283] Following the decision of the

---

[277] See *Stephenson v Delphi Diesel Systems Ltd* [2003] ICR 471, at [13]: [t]he question of mutuality of obligation … poses no difficulties during the period when the individual is actually working. For the period of such employment a contract must, in our view, clearly exist' (Elias J); *James v Redcats (Brands) Ltd* [2007] IRLR 296, at [83]–[84] (Elias P); *Muschett v HM Prison Service* [2010] IRLR 451, at [36] ('mutuality of obligation... is not a condition of a contract for services', Rimer LJ). See also, on the tendency of the courts to construe employment relations as giving rise to bilateral and relational contracts, Freedland, 2003: pp 89–90.

[278] *Tanna v Post Office* [1981] ICR 374; *Mirror Group v Gunning* [1986] ICR 145; *Sheehan v Post Office Counters Ltd* [1999] ICR 73; *Commissioners of Inland Revenue v Post Office Ltd* [2003] IRLR 199. See also *Mingeley v Pennock* [2004] IRLR 373 (a private hire taxi driver did not have a personal work contract with the vehicle operator).

[279] [1998] IRLR 593. This action was brought under the Fair Employment (Northern Ireland) Act 1976 which contains in s 57 a particularly wide definition of 'employment'.

[280] It should be noted that specific rules operate to provide limited protection to individuals who do not clearly benefit from the protection of the 'worker' concept, such as EC Directive 86/653 concerning commercial agents.

[281] See *Express & Echo Publications Ltd v Tanton* [1999] IRLR 367, discussed above at para 3.22.

[282] See *Morris Homes (North) Ltd v Batty*, EAT, 16 June 2004, Appeal No UKEAT/0691/03/DM.

[283] *Redrow Homes (Yorkshire) Ltd v Wright* [2004] IRLR 720.

Supreme Court in *Autoclenz Ltd v Belcher*,[284] substitution clauses are likely to be more carefully scrutinised in future to see if they represent the 'reality' of the work relationship.

Moreover, in a case where a contract cannot be implied because of the presence of a 'substitution' or similar clause, it can be argued, following the judgment of the ECJ in the *Allonby* case, that, in respect of statutory obligations which are underpinned by European Union law on equality of treatment,[285] the precise legal nature of the work relationship should not matter, as long as services are being provided to another under conditions of 'subordination'. This is because of the Court's ruling that '[p]rovided that a person is a worker within the meaning of Article 141(1) EC, the nature of his legal relationship with the other party to the employment relationship is of no consequence in regard to the application of that article'. The Court went on to indicate that '[t]he formal classification of a self-employed worker under national law does not exclude the possibility that a person must be classified as a worker within the meaning of Article 141(1) EC if his independence is merely notional, thereby disguising an employment relationship within the meaning of that Article'.[286] It also stated that, in determining whether agency workers in the position of Mrs. Allonby fell under Article 141 TEC (now Article 157 TFEU), it would be necessary to consider 'the extent of any limitation on their freedom to choose their timetable, and the place and content of their work', while 'the fact that no obligation is imposed on them to accept an assignment is of no consequence in that context'.[287] The Court appears, here, to be leaning towards a test of *factual* rather than purely *legal* subordination, that is to say, one in which the presence of the substantive indicia of the employment relationship – in particular, the provision of personal services in return for remuneration, and an element of subordination to the direction of another – outweighs the absence of a formal, juridical nexus between the parties of the kind required under the 'mutuality of obligation' test.

A further distinction which must be drawn under the 'worker' category is between independent contractors who have a business of their own, and who in that sense can be said to be entrepreneurs who take the risk of losses and the chance of profits, and those, such as the taxpayer in *Hall v Lorimer*,[288] who do not have an identifiable business but who work as professionals or otherwise for a large number of separate employers or clients. An entrepreneur, if the business is incorporated, will most likely be an employee of *that* business; in principle, the individual owner and controller of a business may be an employee of the corporate entity which is the formal legal mechanism through which the business operates.[289] This means that for the purposes of labour law, the most important group of self-employed workers consists of those who do not have a business of their own (or, at least, do not choose to incorporate it), but who are not in a position of subordination or dependence to another such as to make them employees.

What the legislature appears to have in mind, then, is a category of self-employed workers who have neither a regular profession to protect them, nor a business of their own. This group

---

[284] [2011] IRLR 820; see para 3.22 above.

[285] On this point, see our discussion above.

[286] *Allonby*, at paras 70 and 71.

[287] *Allonby*, at para 72.

[288] [1994] IRLR 171.

[289] *Lee v Lee's Air Farming Ltd* [1961] AC 12; *Secretary of State for Trade and Industry v Bottrill* [1998] IRLR 120; *Sellars Arenascene Ltd v Connolly* [2001] IRLR 222; *Clark v Clark Construction Initiatives Ltd.* [2008] IRLR 364; *Secretary of State for Business Enterprise and Regulatory Reform v Neufeld* [2009] IRLR 475; see para 3.64 below.

is sometimes referred to as the 'dependent self-employed'[290] or those with a 'semi-dependent worker's contract'.[291] The logic of this distinction reflects the notion of 'economic dependence' which forms part of the tests for employee status, but seeks to extend protection to those with irregular or intermittent work falling outside the 'employee' concept.[292] This was recognised by the EAT in *Byrne Brothers (Formwork) Ltd v Baird*,[293] a case arising under the WTR 1998:

> The reason why employees are thought to need [working time] protection is that they are in a subordinate and dependent position vis-à-vis their employers: the purpose of the Regulations is to extend protection to workers who are, substantively and economically, in the same position. Thus the essence of the intended distinction must be between, on the one hand, workers whose degree of dependence is essentially the same as that of employees and, on the other, contractors who have a sufficiently arm's-length and independent position to be treated as being able to look after themselves in the relevant respects.

A similarly purposive approach has been adopted in equal treatment legislation as a means of overcoming the problem of 'feigned' self-employment. In *Quinnen v Hovells*[294] the EAT held that the Equal Pay and Sex Discrimination Acts applied to the employment of a temporary sales assistant who had been taken on by his employer as self-employed in order to avoid 'the relationship of employer and employee and the complications that accompany that relationship'. The EAT held that although self-employed, the applicant came within the scope of the Acts: 'a contract for the personal execution of work or labour was intended, in our judgment, on a proper reading of the legislative purpose of the two Acts to enlarge upon (as opposed merely to supplying an instance of) the ordinary connotation of employment, so as to include persons outside the master-servant relationship'.[295] This purposive approach to the interpretation of equality legislation may be contrasted with the more formalist analysis of the 'employment' concept adopted by the Supreme Court in *Jivraj v Hashwani*.[296]

More specific solutions to the problem of 'fake' self-employment have been adopted in certain sectors, in particular the construction industry. In the early 1990s a new scheme for the collection of income tax was instituted in this sector, as part of which tax was to be deducted at source under Schedule E whether or not the worker was an employee. The only workers who were allowed an exemption from this rule were those who had acquired from the Inland Revenue a certificate stating that they are genuinely carrying on their own business.[297] This is one of a number of instances of workers being treated as employees for the purposes of tax and national insurance

---

[290] See Burchell *et al*, 1999.

[291] Freedland, 2003: p 30.

[292] See generally the judgment of Elias P in *James v Redcats (Brands) Ltd* [2007] IRLR 296, at [39]–[70]. The notion of 'economic dependence' may also be relevant in determining whether the individual is a member of a regular 'profession' which can be understood as offering protection and support. See *R (on the application of the BBC) v CAC* [2003] IRLR 460.

[293] [2002] IRLR 96, at [17]; *James v Redcats (Brands) Ltd* [2007] IRLR 296, at [6] (Elias P). For a more sceptical view of the value of a policy perspective, see the judgment of Pill LJ in *Redrow Homes (Yorkshire) Ltd v Wright* [2004] IRLR 720, at [21].

[294] [1984] IRLR 227. See also the discussion of this point by the ECJ in Case C-256/01 *Allonby v Accrington and Rossendale College* [2004] IRLR 224, at para 71.

[295] [1984] IRLR 227, 229.

[296] [2011] IRLR 827.

[297] See M Harvey, 1995.

legislation, even where they do not clearly have the benefit of employment protection law.[298] Such workers do at least now have the possibility of protection of minimum wage and working time legislation; a large proportion of the case law generated by the 'worker' concept refers to self-employed construction workers who pay a proportion of their tax at source under the Revenue rules referred to above. For the most part, tribunals and courts have held that the 'worker' concept does apply in this type of situation, but in the absence of a certification mechanism which could definitively establish the status of the individual for employment law purposes in the manner of the tax law scheme, cases continue to go both ways.[299]

Homeworkers

3.34   Homeworking is a form of work which grew particularly rapidly in the 1970s and 1980s, when it doubled to reach about 3% of the active labour force.[300] Those who work *at home* tend to be women workers; 'freelances' and others who work *from home* tend to be male, and probably should not be considered in the same category although for statistical purposes the two groups are difficult to separate. Homeworking has long been associated with low pay, poor working conditions and lack of access to fringe benefits.[301] While a great deal of attention has been devoted to new technology homeworking and 'teleworking', this form of work still accounts for only a few thousand people; the majority of homeworkers are employed in more traditional occupations.[302]

Homeworkers do not have a clear employment status. The precariousness of their work and in particular the lack of clear mutual commitments to make work available and to be available to do it make it difficult for a court or tribunal to infer the existence of a contract of employment, although the case law has not consistently come down against employee status.[303] However, any homeworker who is able to establish employee status may be unable to go on to prove that he or she has the necessary continuity of employment to claim rights such as statutory sick pay and protection from unfair dismissal.[304]

The difficulty of classifying homeworkers led to attempts in the past to extend protective legislation beyond the categories of 'employee' and 'worker'.[305] There is now a specific definition of 'homeworker' for the purposes of the national minimum wage, according to which a homeworker is one who 'contracts with a person, for the purposes of that person's business,

---

[298] For discussion of this issue, see Burchell *et al*, 1999, in particular chs 6 and 7. The IR35 procedure (see above, para 3.24) for dealing with personal service companies is another indication of the radical solutions which operate in fiscal law and which have no true equivalent in employment law.

[299] In addition to the *Byrne*, *Redrow* and *Morris* cases noted above, contrast *JNJ Bricklaying Ltd v Stacey*, EAT, 8 July 2003, Appeal No EAT/0088/03/ILB and *Redrow Homes (Yorkshire) Ltd. v Buckborough* [2009] IRLR 34, in which construction workers were found to be 'workers' in the statutory sense, with *Bamford v Persimmon Homes NW Ltd*, EAT, 16 June 2004, Appeal No UKEAT/0049/04/DM and *Bacica v Muir* [2006] IRLR 35, reaching the opposite result. In *Staddon v Dent*, EAT, 17 March 2003, Appeal No EAT/0945/02/SM and *McCarthy v Blue Sword Construction Ltd*, EAT, 14 July 2003, Appeal No EAT/0223/03/DM, casual construction workers were found to be employees.

[300] Hakim, 1985. See also Felstead and Jewson, 1995.

[301] Rubery and Wilkinson, 1981.

[302] Stanworth and Stanworth, 1989.

[303] For differing outcomes, see *Airfix Footwear Ltd v Cope* [1978] ICR 1210; *Nethermere (St Neots) Ltd v Taverna and Gardiner* [1984] ICR 612; *Bridges v Industrial Rubber plc*, EAT, 21 September 2004, Appeal No UKEAT/0150/04/DM.

[304] See below, paras 3.59–3.60.

[305] See National Insurance Act 1911, Sch 1, Part 1; SRO 1912/880; SRO 1913/33; Wages Act 1986, s 26(1).

for the execution of work to be done in a place not under the control or management of that person'.[306] This definition, like the 'worker' concept, therefore stresses the criterion of economic dependence (hence the need to show that the homeworker is employed for the purposes of the other contracting party's business, rather than his or her own[307]), at the expense of control (the absence of which, as we have just seen, is explicitly stated to be irrelevant to protected status in this context). Although specific protection for homeworkers remains exceptional, the establishment of standards of good practice for certain categories of homeworkers may also be assisted by the adoption in 2004 of *Telework Guidance*[308] by the CBI, TUC and the UK branch of the European public employers' federation, CEEP. The *Guidance*, which is voluntary, follows on from a non-binding framework agreement on teleworking agreed by UNICE, CEEP and the ETUC under the EU social dialogue process.

Agency employment and other employment through intermediaries

3.35   Estimates of the number of temporary agency workers vary widely but all surveys reveal a substantial increase in their numbers over the past fifteen years or so. In 2003 the government estimated that about 600,000 people, around 3% of the labour force, were employed as temporary agency workers in the UK.[309] This may have been an underestimate;[310] by 2008 it was thought that between 1.1 and 1.5 million workers were employed through agencies.[311] The supply of labour by employment agencies and employment businesses is governed by the Employment Agencies Act 1973[312] and the Conduct of Employment Agencies and Employment Businesses Regulations 2003.[313] However, this legislation says little or nothing about the nature of the contractual relationships to which agency work gives rise, which is one of the most difficult and controversial in contemporary employment law. The difficulty arises, in large part, because the worker has two separate, overlapping relationship: one with the 'agency', which normally arranges work assignments and is responsible for ensuring payment; and the other the 'user', which normally assumes the power to give orders and takes the direct benefit of the services which are being provided.

---

[306] NMWA 1998, s 35; *James v Redcats (Brands) Ltd* [2007] IRLR 296.

[307] In *Commissioners of Inland Revenue v Post Office Ltd* [2003] IRLR 199, postmasters and postmistresses were held to fall outside the definition of 'homeworker' for this reason.

[308] *Telework Guidance*, as agreed by the CBI, TUC and CEEP (2004). For analysis see Deakin and Koukiadaki, 2012b.

[309] See DTI, *Proposal for a Directive of the European Parliament and of the Council on Working Conditions for Temporary Agency Workers – Regulatory Impact Assessment* (2003), p 7.

[310] The DTI figure contrasts with a figure of 1.3 million given by the Recruitment and Employment Confederation around that time.

[311] BIS, *Agency Working in the UK: A Review of the Evidence*, Employment Relations Research Series No. 93 (October 2008).

[312] As amended. For the purposes of these provisions, a distinction is drawn between recruitment agencies which aim to find employment for workers with another employer (these are referred to as 'employment agencies') and suppliers of agency labour (these are referred to as 'employment businesses'). In practice, the term 'employment agency' is commonly used in other contexts (including the case law on the employment status of agency workers) to refer to organisations which would most likely be classified as employment businesses for the 1973 Act, and we therefore retain this general usage in the text. See also the Gangmasters (Licensing) Act 2004 which applies specific requirements in relation to agricultural work, gathering shellfish, and related activities. See further Wynn, 2009.

[313] SI 2003/3319, replacing SI 1976/715. On regulations governing agency work, see generally G Morris, 2004b, and for a comparative survey, Blanpain and Graham (eds), 2004.

Workers hired out by an agency for use by a third party were once thought to have a unique *'sui generis'* status, being neither employees nor self-employed.[314] There was an unsatisfactory, ad hoc air to this approach to classification, suggesting as it did that the courts could invent new categories of employment status at will. A better view is that agency workers will almost certainly have a contract of some kind with the agency; depending on the terms upon which they make themselves available for work, this can either be a contract of employment or a contract providing for self-employment. In addition, it is possible, but less likely, that the worker will have a contractual relationship with the user. Whether or not there is a contract in either case, legislation imposes certain obligations on both agencies and users.

The 2003 Regulations (like their predecessors of 1976) do not specify what the status of temporary workers should be for the purposes of employment legislation, leaving the matter to be decided under the common law tests of status. This is in contrast to income tax and national insurance legislation, each of which treats temporary workers as if they were the employees of the agency for the purposes of determining liability for income tax under Schedule E and Class 1 national insurance contributions.[315] Precisely because it is imposed by statute, the courts tend to take the view that the tax and national insurance treatment of agency workers has no bearing on their employment status for other purposes.[316] The 2003 regulations merely require the agency to issue its temporary workers with a written statement of terms and conditions, which must indicate whether the agency regards them as its employees or as self-employed.[317] This statement will not necessarily determine their status in law: even in cases where temporary workers have been designated as employees in the written statement, courts have disregarded this to hold that they were self-employed, on the grounds that the arrangement between them and the agency lacked the mutuality of obligation needed for a contract of employment.[318] An employment contract may be implied in a case where the agency exercises disciplinary control over the worker and requires him or her to undergo regular retraining.[319] In most cases, however, a 'global' contract will be ruled out by the intermittent nature of most agency work.[320] This may not, however, prevent the courts from finding on occasion either a contract of employment or a contract for personal services in respect of specific hirings or periods of employment.[321] Whether or not they are employees, the agency is under an obligation not to discriminate against agency workers on grounds related to their sex, sexual orientation, race, religion or belief, or age.[322]

---

[314] *Construction Industry Training Board v Labour Force Ltd* [1970] 3 All ER 220.

[315] See Income Tax (Earnings and Pensions) Act 2003, Part 2, Ch 7 (and for case law interpreting earlier, analogous provisions, *Brady v Hart (trading as Jaclyn Model Agency)* [1985] STC 498; *Bhadra v Ellan* [1988] STC 239); Social Security (Categorisation of Earners) Regulations, SI 1978/1689.

[316] *McMeechan v Secretary of State for Employment* [1997] IRLR 353, 358 (Waite LJ).

[317] SI 2003/3319, reg 15(a).

[318] *Wickens v Champion Employment Agency* [1984] ICR 365; *Ironmonger v Movefield Ltd* [1988] IRLR 461. Later decisions have taken a similar line on the need for mutuality and control: see *Montgomery v Johnson Underwood Ltd* [2001] IRLR 269.

[319] *Ncube v 24/7 Support Services* ET/2602005/05 (a case involving the supply of nursing services).

[320] This seemed likely following the overruling by the CA ([2008] IRLR 505) of the EAT decision in *Consistent Group Ltd v Kalwak* [2007] IRLR 560 which had seemed to herald a more flexible approach to the construction of the standard form agreements used by employment agencies but *Kalwak* now requires consideration in the light of the more recent decision in *Protectacoat Firthglow Ltd v Szilagyi* [2009] IRLR 365. See our discussion at para 3.22, above.

[321] See, in particular, *McMeechan v Secretary of State for Employment* [1997] IRLR 353, in which a contract of employment for a specific hiring was found.

[322] EqA 2010, s 55.

It is possible that the user will be regarded as the employer under circumstances where it assumes managerial authority over the performance of the work for a substantial period of time. In *Dacas v Brook Street Bureau (UK) Ltd.*[323] the applicant had worked for the user for several years before she was subject to an allegation of misconduct. Her agency was then informed that her services were no longer required. The employment tribunal found that she had no contract of employment with the agency, following the well-established case law on this issue. The EAT reversed on this point but the Court of Appeal restored the original tribunal decision. However, the Court of Appeal held by a majority (Munby J dissenting) that the tribunal had made an error of law in not giving adequate consideration to the possibility that there was an implied contract of employment between the applicant and the user. Both Mummery and Sedley LJJ also thought that a triangular employment contract, with both the agency and the user sharing the responsibilities of the employer, was, in principle, a possible way of analysing agency relations. This view was confirmed by a later Court of Appeal decision, *Cable & Wireless plc v Muscat.*[324] The essence of this complex case is that the applicant provided his services through a series of agency arrangements which had been entered into at the request of the employer and a predecessor employer. Mr Muscat had originally been employed as an employee. For this reason, the decision is perhaps best thought of as a lifting the veil case, or as one in which the formal arrangements were a sham. Two later Court of Appeal decisions, *James v Greenwich London Borough Council*[325] and *Tilson v Alstom Transport*[326] reasserted the orthodox position that a contract of employment will only be implied between the worker and the user where it is necessary to do so in order to give legal effect to their relationship. As Mummery LJ put it in *James*, 'in many cases agency workers will fall outside the scope of the protection of the 1996 Act because neither the workers nor the end users [are] in any kind of express contractual relationship with each other and it is not necessary to imply one in order to explain the work undertaken by the worker'.[327]

The upshot of *Dacas, Muscat James* and *Tilson* is that while a contract of employment between the worker and the user may be implied from conduct, it is not straightforward to do so. It is necessary for there to be not simply control over the manner in which the work is carried out, but a contractual nexus between the two parties. This will be very difficult to demonstrate in a situation in which the user is not responsible for arranging the payment of remuneration to the worker (this is normally done by the agency). It may be possible to infer a contract with the user in a case where the supplier or agency was only acting as a go-between or recruitment agency, and had no continuing relation with the worker, but, by definition, this is not the paradigm case of agency employment.

However, it is entirely possible, indeed likely, that the user will be fixed with certain duties of an employer with regard to the worker, whether or not there is a contractual nexus between them. In particular, it will be subject to the requirements of equality legislation.[328] The user, described here as the 'principal', must not discriminate on these grounds against 'contract workers'. A 'principal' is one who makes work available for by an individual who is employed by another person who

---

[323] [2004] IRLR 358; to similar effect is another Court of Appeal decision, *Franks v Reuters Ltd* [2003] IRLR 423. See also *Bunce v Postworth Ltd t/a Skyblue* [2005] IRLR 557 (agency worker an employee of neither the agency nor the user).
[324] [2006] IRLR 354; see Wynn and Leighton, 2006.
[325] [2008] IRLR 302. See also the decision of the EAT ([2007] IRLR 168).
[326] [2011] IRLR 169.
[327] [2008] IRLR 302, 307.
[328] EqA 2010, s. 41.

supplies them 'under a contract to which the principal is party whether or not that other person is a party to it)' ; a 'contract worker' is an individual supplied to the principal in furtherance of such a contract.[329] The contract worker need not be an employee of the person who supplies their labour to the user,[330] so an agency worker who has a contract for services with the agency is not, by reason of their self-employed status, excluded from bringing a claim against the end user.

A growing body of case law illustrates how this type of provision applies to a number of situations where employment is arranged through an intermediary or where the normal duties of the employer are divided between separate entities. *Harrods Ltd v Remick*[331] concerned the complex set of commercial and employment arrangements which can arise as a result of franchising arrangements. Employees of companies which were concessionaires (similar to franchisees) of the Harrods department store alleged that they had been subjected to discrimination by Harrods on the grounds of their race. Harrods had withdrawn from the employees, or in one case had refused to grant, 'store approval', as a result of which they were dismissed by their employers (or, in the one case, not employed when they otherwise would have been). Under the contractual arrangements made between Harrods and the concessionaires, the latter undertook to market the goods in question (which were the property of Harrods) and to promote their sale, and to ensure that the relevant department was adequately staffed. The Court of Appeal held that the arrangement fell under the provision in the Act aimed at protecting 'contract workers'. This was so, notwithstanding that the main purpose of the contract in each case was, arguably, for the concessionaire to promote the sale of the goods, and not to supply labour as such; nor was it considered relevant that Harrods did not have immediate powers of direction and control over the staff.[332]

This is a significant decision, but some potential limits must be borne in mind. In particular, it is not clear whether the non-discrimination principle, when applied to contract workers, allows the applicant to compare his or her position to that of a comparable worker in the user's 'regular' employment or simply to that of a fellow contract worker. If the former were the case, the requirement of equal treatment would impose a strict limit on the employer's use of agency work to differentiate between categories of workers in terms of their benefits and treatment. While this could legitimately be taken to have been the intention of the legislature, given the purpose of the Acts in question, such a conclusion has so far been resisted by the courts. This is the effect of the ruling of the ECJ in the *Allonby* case, in which the Court ruled that under Article 141 of the EC Treaty (now Article 157 TFEU), it was not possible for the applicant, who was an agency worker, to compare her employment with that of a comparator who was employed by the user, even though

---

[329] There is a similar but slightly differently worded definition of 'agency worker' for the purposes of the national minimum wage: NMWA 1998, s 34.

[330] The term 'employed' in EqA 2010, s 41(5)(a), should be interpreted consistently with the wide meaning of the term 'employment', in s 83, on which, see Royston, 2011, discussing *Muschett v HM Prison Service* [2010] IRLR 451.

[331] [1997] IRLR 9, EAT; affd [1997] IRLR 583, CA. See also, for applications of the anti-discrimination Acts then in force (see now EqA 2010) to end users of labour, *BP Chemicals Ltd v Gillick* [1995] IRLR 128, *Patefield v Belfast City Council* [2000] IRLR 664, and *Leeds City Council v Woodhouse* [2010] IRLR 625. In *Secretary of State for Education and Employment v Bearman* [1998] IRLR 431, by contrast, a similar claim failed. For discussion of these cases, see Deakin, 2001a; Royston, 2011.

[332] See [1997] IRLR 583, 585–586.

the applicant had previously been directly employed by the user in question, and had only recently been dismissed by it with the aim of limiting its employment law obligations to her.[333]

The second significant case is *Abbey Life Assurance Co Ltd v Tansell*,[334] a decision under the Disability Discrimination Act 1995 for the purposes of which the need to identify a comparator, in the sense just described, did not arise.[335] The applicant had set up his own personal service company for the supply of his services as a computer consultant. His personal service company (Intelligents) contracted with an employment agency (MHC) to supply his services to the end user, Abbey Life. The contract between Intelligents and MHC had the effect of placing the complainant 'under the control of Abbey Life'[336] as part of a team working on the impact of the 'millennium bug' on Abbey Life's computer systems. About five months into this arrangement, Abbey Life terminated its use of the complainant's services, shortly after he had been diagnosed as suffering from diabetes. He brought claims against both MHC and Abbey Life for disability discrimination. The EAT and the Court of Appeal held that Abbey Life, but not MHC, owed the complainant obligations of non-discrimination under the then section 12 (subsequently section 4B) of the Disability Discrimination Act,[337] even though there was no contract between Abbey Life (the alleged 'principal') and Intelligents. According to Mummery LJ, 'the statutory definition only requires the supply of the individual to be "under a contract made with [the principal]". It does not expressly stipulate who is to be the party who contracts with [the principal]'.[338] Under EqA 2010 section 41, the successor to section 12 of the Disability Discrimination Act 1995, it is now expressly stated a 'contract worker' need not be employed by the person who contracts with the principal.[339]

The user is also under a responsibility to ensure the health and safety of temporary workers while they are working on its premises. As an employer, the user will owe a duty under the Health and Safety at Work Act 1974 to persons who are not in its employment 'who may be affected thereby',[340] a category which would appear to cover any temporary workers. It is less clear whether the user will incur obligations to the temporary workers working on its premises by virtue of the employer's common law duty of care in respect of the health and safety of its employees. There is some authority to suggest that this duty is only owed to those employed under a contract of employment, a lower standard being imposed with regard to independent contractors and others.[341] On the other hand, it has been held that the common law duty of care can extend from a main contractor to cover the employees of one of its sub-contractors working on the same site.[342] Temporary workers working on the user's premises are arguably in an analogous position. If they are not, the United Kingdom is potentially in breach of Directive 91/383. This Directive, which is concerned with the health and

---

[333] Case C-256/01 *Allonby v Accrington and Rossendale College* [2004] IRLR 224, discussed further in ch 6, below, at para 6.82. It should be noted that agency workers are specifically excluded from the scope of the requirement of equal treatment between fixed-term and permanent employees under FTER 2002 (see reg 19). However, the question of equal treatment between agency workers and 'permanent' workers of the user has now been addressed by Directive 2008/104/EC on Temporary Agency Work and AWR 2010. See para 3.53 below.

[334] [2000] IRLR 387; see also the judgment of the EAT sub nom *MHC Consulting Ltd v Tansell* [1999] IRLR 677.

[335] On the reasons for this, see para 6.125 below.

[336] [2000] IRLR 387, 388.

[337] See now EqA 2010, s 41.

[338] [2000] IRLR 387, 390.

[339] EqA 2010, s 41(5)(b).

[340] HSWA 1974, s 3(1).

[341] *Jones v Minton Construction Ltd* (1973) 15 KIR 309.

[342] *McArdle v Andmac Roofing Co* [1967] 1 All ER 583; but cf Hepple and Napier, 1978.

safety both of fixed-term contract workers and agency workers, requires Member States to ensure that 'without prejudice to the responsibility of the temporary employment business as laid down in national legislation, the user undertaking and/or establishment is/are responsible, for the duration of the assignment, for the conditions governing performance of the work.'[343] In requiring the user to be responsible for the 'conditions governing performance', the Directive appears to envisage that it could be liable for any breach of health and safety law with regard to the workers assigned to its use. A decision which is highly questionable in the context of the Directive is *Costain Building and Civil Engineering Ltd v Smith*,[344] in which it was held that an agency worker who was elected to be a health and safety representative on the site where he was working did not have the protection of legislation designed to prevent the unlawful dismissal of such representatives, since he was not an employee of the user.

The legislation which we have been considering so far uses the technique of attaching particular obligations to the user and others to the agency. The problem with this approach is that some of the responsibilities which are normally assumed by the employer may fall upon neither of them. Labour standards legislation attempts to deal with this issue by stipulating that the national minimum wage and working time controls must be observed by 'whichever of the agent and the principal [or user] is responsible for paying the agency worker in respect of the work', or, failing that, whichever of them actually pays the agency worker in respect of the work.[345]

The EU Directive on Temporary Agency Work, adopted in 2008[346] and implemented in Britain in 2010 through the Agency Work Regulations,[347] imposes an obligation upon the agency and user (termed the 'hirer' in the Regulations) to observe a principle of equal treatment according to which the basic working and employment conditions of an agency worker must be equivalent to those that would have applied if they been directly recruited by the user undertaking to carry out the work in question. We consider the implications of the Directive and the implementing Regulations (which contain their own, *sui generis* definition of the term 'agency worker'), in our discussion of the law relating to equality between workers employed in 'flexible' and 'regular' employment relationships later in this chapter.[348]

Ministers of religion

3.36 For many years the courts held that persons holding religious office did not normally have a contract of any kind, let alone a contract of employment. A number of reasons were given for this approach. It was argued that the spiritual nature of a religious office made it incompatible with the

---

[343] Directive 91/383, Art 8(1).
[344] [2000] ICR 215.
[345] NMWA 1998, s 34; WTR 1998, reg 36; see generally Deakin, 2001a. See also ERelA 1999, s 13(2)(c), stipulating that in the context of a worker's right to be accompanied at a disciplinary or grievance hearing, either the agency or the user may be designated the employer of an agency worker. It may be noted that, in the context of the common law of tort, the courts have accepted the principle that where an employee is assigned from one employer to work for another, both employers may be vicariously liable for torts committed by the employee in the course of employment: *Viasystems (Tyneside) Ltd v Thermal Transfer Northern Ltd* [2005] EWCA Civ 1151, [2006] QB 510.
[346] Directive 2008/104/EC.
[347] SI 2010/93.
[348] See para 3.53 below.

undertaking of contractual obligations[349] and that there was a presumption against an intention to create legal relations in the context of the 'historic and special pre-existing legal framework of [the] church, of an ecclesiastical hierarchy established by law, of spiritual duties defined by public law rather than by private contract, and of ecclesiastical courts with jurisdiction over the discipline of clergy'.[350] In *Percy v Church of Scotland Board of National Mission*[351] these arguments were given short shrift. The House of Lords (Lord Hoffmann dissenting) held that an associate minister in a Church of Scotland parish was employed within the meaning of section 82 of the Sex Discrimination Act 1975 (now section 83 EqA 2010), which requires a contract personally to execute work and labour (or as it is now put, a contract 'personally to do work'[352]). The terms of the applicant's appointment were set out in writing and contained detailed provision on the expected duration of the employment, remuneration, travelling expenses, holidays and accommodation. The majority held that employment status under the 1975 Act (and, by extension, other anti-discrimination statutes) was not inconsistent with the holding of an ecclesiastical office.[353] In *Percy* the applicant was not claiming employee status (this was not necessary for her to bring a claim of sex discrimination), but in the later case of *New Testament Church of God v Stewart*[354] the EAT applied *Percy* to hold that 'if the relationship between church and minister has many of the characteristics of a contract of employment in terms of rights and obligations, these cannot be ignored simply because the duties are of a religious or pastoral nature'.

The position of clerical office holders in the Church of England has now been clarified by legislation. The Ecclesiastical Offices (Terms of Service) Regulations 2009[355] provide for a range of statutory employment protection rights to apply to these clerical office holders, on the assumption that they not normally employed as employees. The rights extended in this way include the right to a written statement of particulars of office, the right to a minimum stipend, the right to a weekly rest period and to annual leave, the right to maternity, paternity, parental and adoption leave, the right to the protection of capability and grievance procedures, and the right to claim unfair dismissal in the event of the termination of the office. Church of England office holders who do have contracts of employment are excluded from these Regulations, on the basis that they will have normal access, as employees, to the protection of the relevant labour law statutes.

---

[349] *Re Employment of Church of England Curates* [1912] 2 Ch 563; *President of the Methodist Conference v Parfitt* [1984] ICR 176; *Davies v Presbyterian Church of Wales* [1986] IRLR 194; but see Brodin, 1996, for a comprehensive analysis which argues that 'religious or spiritual duties are not incompatible with a contract of employment'.

[350] *Diocese of Southwark v Coker* [1998] ICR 140,147, per Mummery LJ.

[351] [2006] IRLR 195.

[352] EqA 2010, s 83(2)(a).

[353] This was the point of Lord Hoffmann's dissent ('a minister of a church has no employer but holds an office': [2006] IRLR 195, at [56]). In other contexts, the courts have rejected the idea that an office holder is barred, for that reason, from being an employee: see *102 Social Club v Bickerton* [1977] ICR 911.

[354] [2007] IRLR 178, 184; affd [2008] IRLR 134. In *President of the Methodist Conference v Moore* [2012] IRLR 229 the Court of Appeal held that *President of the Methodist Conference v Parfitt* [1984] ICR 176 should be regarded as overruled by *Percy*.

[355] SI 2009/2108. See McLean, 2008.

Voluntary workers

3.37 The position of 'volunteers' or 'voluntary workers' has given rise to a growing body of litigation. In principle, it is open to the parties to a work relationship to make a voluntary arrangement which excludes the possibility of a contract of employment or contract for personal services. A voluntary worker who carries out work for charitable bodies may be entitled, by agreement with the organisation concerned, to receive work-related expenses. However, this arrangement, without more, will most likely lack the mutuality of obligation needed to imply a contract of employment, unless the individual in question also undertakes an obligation to make himself or herself available for work over a given period of time.[356] On the other hand, it would not rule out the possibility of a worker's contract based on the provision of personal services, particularly since the courts have recently made it clear that 'mutuality of obligation... is not a condition of a contract for services',[357] and given their greater willingness to regard contract terms which do not accurately reflect the realities of the employment relationship as 'shams'.[358] Alternatively, the parties to a voluntary arrangement could be described as lacking the intention to create legal relations. It is arguable, nevertheless, that tribunals and courts should be slow to reach such a conclusion. Clear evidence should be required of a joint intention to create a voluntary work relationship. The case law suggests that it is not at all uncommon for employers to present wages as expenses in an attempt to avoid the coverage of protective legislation.[359]

There is an argument to the effect that voluntary workers who supply their labour to an employer on a regular basis, even if they do not have the right to the minimum wage[360] or to the rights to income and job security which are conferred by employment protection legislation, should be entitled to certain other protections which relate to the way in which work is organised. This argument could extend, for example, to health and safety legislation, as well as to legislation ensuring equality of treatment within employment on the grounds of sex, sexual orientation, race, religion or belief, disability or age. However, voluntary workers will not be 'employed persons' within the meaning of British equality legislation unless they can establish that they are employed under, at the very least, a contract to provide personal services in return for remuneration of some kind. In *X v Mid-Sussex Citizens' Advice Bureau*[361] the claimant entered into an arrangement described as a 'volunteer agreement ... binding in honour only ... and not a contract of employment or legally binding'. After the arrangement was terminated, she brought a claim of disability

[356] See *South East Sheffield CAB v Grayson* [2004] IRLR 353; *Bruce v Dial House Chester*, 20 August 2004, Appeal No UKEAT/0555/04/SM; *Melhuish v Redbridge Citizens' Advice Bureau* [2005] IRLR 419.
[357] *Muschett v HM Prison Service* [2010] IRLR 451, at [36] (Rimer LJ).
[358] *Autoclenz Ltd. v Belcher* [2011] IRLR 820.
[359] See D Morris, 1999, discussing case law in which tribunals and courts concluded, on the one hand, that the payment of 'expenses' was a sham and, on the other, in which 'employment' was distinguished from 'membership' of a voluntary organisation. Whether, for an example, an 'intern' has a worker's or employee's contract is a question of fact in each case which will turn on the court's view of the nature of the relationship between the parties. According to an opinion poll carried out in April 2011, around a fifth of British businesses were employing interns 'as a cheap source of labour': *The Guardian*, 28 April 2011.
[360] NMWA 1998, s 44 (as amended by EA 2008, s 14) specifically excludes 'voluntary workers' (who are defined as those working for charities, voluntary organisations, associated fund-raising bodies and certain statutory bodies and not receiving 'monetary payments of any description' aside from expenses) from the coverage of minimum wage legislation, and sets out in some detail the nature of expenses and benefits in kind which they may receive without the employer forfeiting this exemption. See further para 4.48, below.
[361] [2011] IRLR 335.

discrimination. The Employment Tribunal found that there was no contract in this case and, on that basis, held that she was not in 'employment' in the sense relevant to equality legislation. The claimant argued that even if there were no contract in this case, she came within the protection of the Directive since the notions of 'employment' and 'occupation' could be extended to cover such a case, but this argument was rejected in the EAT and Court of Appeal.

The power to confer employment rights on other categories of individuals

3.38   Section 23(1) of the Employment Relations Act 1999 empowers the Secretary of State by order to confer upon 'individuals who are of a specified description' any 'right conferred on an individual against an employer (however defined)' under one of the following provisions: TULRCA 1992, ERA 1996, the 1999 Act itself, and instruments made under section 2(2) of the European Communities Act 1972 (this last category includes TUPE 2006 and WTR 1998). Thus statutory employment rights under these provisions can be extended, by order, to cover individuals who are not currently protected by them. The order can take effect either as a free-standing statutory instrument or as an amendment to primary legislation.[362] The power of extension applies even if the exclusion results from an express provision in the statute in question. One type of case which the Act seems to have in mind, but which is not explicitly mentioned in section 23, is one in which the exclusion arises from a contract term, or from judicial construction of working or commercial arrangements. This is implicit in section 23(4), which states that an order under this section may '(a) provide that individuals are to be treated as parties to workers' contracts or contracts of employment', and '(b) make provision as to who are to be regarded as the employers of individuals'. Under section 23(5), the order can operate in such a way as to modify the application of the right in question. Section 41 NMWA 1998 contains a broadly analogous power to extend the application of the national minimum wage.

The origins of section 23 lie in the *Fairness at Work* White Paper of 1998, which noting that the national minimum wage and working time controls would apply to 'all those who work for another person, not just those employed under a contract of employment', advanced 'the idea of legislation enabling [the government] similarly to extend the coverage of some or all existing employment rights by regulation'.[363] The reference to the minimum wage and working time link what is now section 23 to the 'worker' concept. One possible use of section 23, then, would be to extend protection to those who are not 'employees' but who are 'workers'. However, this does not mean that the 'worker' concept sets limits to the power contained in section 23. On the face of it, the Secretary of State has the power to confer employment rights on individuals who would otherwise be neither employees nor workers, and, for statutory purposes, to deem them to be employed under the relevant contract. An Opposition motion to amend section 23, so as to make it clear that it should only apply to 'an individual who is a worker within the meaning of section [13]' of the Act, together with related changes, was debated and rejected during the House of Commons Committee stage. The minister concerned rejected the motion on the grounds that 'it would place too great a restriction on the flexibility of the new rule-

---

[362] Section 23 was amended by ERelA 2004, s 39 explicitly to allow an order to extend employment rights either by the use of a free-standing provision or by amending the legislation conferring the right.

[363] Cm 3968 (1998), at para 3.18.

making power', and made specific reference to 'members of the clergy, registration officers, share fisherman, merchant seamen, members of the armed forces, and police officers' as categories of individuals who could benefit from the exercise of the new power.[364]

The suggestion that section 23 can be used to extend rights to police officers or registration officials suggests that something in the nature of a tidying up operation is intended. If, because of a statutory oversight or an adverse court decision, an individual in one of these categories falls within neither the 'employee' nor the 'worker' category, they can be brought within protection by means of the new power.[365] The power can also be used to specify which one of several possible parties is the employer of the individual concerned.[366] With the exception of share fishermen (an almost vanished category in any event), all the other groups listed by the minister in his reply consist of employments which largely satisfy the criteria of both formal and economic dependence.[367] For various reasons, however, most of which are ad hoc or the result of historical accident as much as anything, they are not regarded as being employed under a contract of employment. Although there may well be compelling practical considerations for ministers to consider for extending full employment rights to these groups, such extensions would not mark a radical departure from current practice; rather, they would signify the final extension of the predominant legal model of employment to a set of anomalous cases.

A more radical use of section 23 would be to extend further the application of certain labour law rights to the self-employed. References were made during the relevant Parliamentary debates to the need to deal with 'feigned' self-employment,[368] but there is a wider case to be made for extending labour legislation with a human rights dimension (such as rights of expression) and rights which do not depend upon regularity of employment to certain of the self-employed and to agency workers.[369]

PUBLIC SECTOR EMPLOYMENT

3.39 For statistical purposes, the government defines the public sector as covering employment in central government, which includes the civil service, armed forces, and the National Health

---

[364] Mr Willis MP, Hansard, House of Commons Standing Committee E, 2 March 1999, col 237.

[365] For examples of the types of problem which can arise, see *Commissioner of Police of the Metropolis v Lowrey-Nesbitt* [1999] ICR 401, in which the EAT held that a police officer in the Metropolitan Police was not a 'worker' for the purposes of the law governing deductions from wages; *Johnson v Ryan* [2000] ICR 236, in which it held that a rent officer was not an employee of either the chief rent officer or the Secretary of State, but of the relevant local authority; and *Perceval-Price v Department of Economic Development* [2000] IRLR 380, in which the Northern Ireland Court of Appeal held that employment tribunal chairmen were 'workers' for the purposes of European Union sex discrimination law.

[366] See *Johnson v Ryan* [2000] ICR 236.

[367] See above, paras 3.26–3.28

[368] See Lord Simon of Highbury, HL Debs, 10 May 1999, cols 968–969: s 23 will 'empower the Secretary of State to rationalise and update the coverage of the existing body of employment rights by conferring, by order, some or all of those rights on specified categories of individuals who may not or clearly cannot benefit from them at present but who are not genuinely self-employed'; and Mr Phil Hope MP, House of Commons Standing Committee E, 2 March 1999, col 235: 'It is intended that the new powers will not be extended to the genuinely self-employed. The clause deals with the grey zone that has grown up over the past 20 years'.

[369] See Deakin, 2001b. For a suggestion that s 23 should be invoked in the case of agency workers, see *Montgomery v Johnson Underwood Ltd* [2001] IRLR 269, at [43].

Service; local government; the police; maintained educational establishments;[370] and the 'public corporations' such as Royal Mail, London Underground Ltd and (since October 2008) Royal Bank of Scotland and Lloyds Banking Group.[371] An estimated 5.98 million workers (20.6% of total employment) were employed in the UK public sector in autumn 2011.[372] However, these categories do not form a homogeneous group for legal purposes: 'there is no clear legal test for determining what makes employment public'.[373]

In recent years the boundaries of state employment have been further blurred by the introduction of compulsory competitive tendering, market testing and internal contracting in large parts of central and local government. This means that identical jobs may be performed either by those directly employed in the public service, or by those who work for private sector employers which have a contractual relationship with the public body in question. Even before these reforms, however, there was no hard dividing line between the law of public-sector employment and that of private-sector employment, as exists in some other European countries. Public-sector employees are subject, for the most part, to the same basic principles of labour law as apply more generally.[374] There are some specific restrictions in relation to freedom of association for particular groups of public sector workers.[375] In general, however, public and private sector employment share the same conceptual framework.[376]

Civil servants

3.40   Although public sector employment is largely assimilated to the model of the contract of employment, doubts remain about the status of civil servants, who have the Crown as their employer. It was thought at one stage that since the Crown could not fetter its own discretion by contract,[377] it could not be contractually bound by any undertakings it made to those in its employment. In *R v Civil Service Appeal Board, ex p Bruce*,[378] however, the Divisional Court concluded that it was constitutionally possible for civil servants to have a contract of employment, but that there was no contractual nexus in the case before it for the quite separate reason that the parties did not intend to create legal relations. This was the consequence of paragraph 14 of the Civil Service Pay and Conditions Code then in force which stated that 'a civil servant does not have a contract of employment enforceable in the courts'. This last part of the analysis was rejected, however, by the Court of Appeal in *R v Lord Chancellor's Department, ex p Nangle*,[379] on the grounds

---

[370] Note that universities are now treated as part of the private sector in the National Accounts.

[371] Statistics on public sector employment are produced on a quarterly basis by the Office of National Statistics; reports also describe which sectors are included.

[372] Office of National Statistics data.

[373] G Morris and S Fredman, 1993: p 120.

[374] See S Fredman and G Morris, 1989; G Morris and S Fredman, 1993.

[375] See para 8.2 below.

[376] It should nevertheless be noted that HRA 1998 gives a free standing right of action to those who work for certain public authorities to enforce Convention rights against their employer, which is not available to other workers: see G Morris, 1998c: pp 299–303. For a critique of the assimilation of public-sector employment to the wider labour law model, see G Morris, 2000.

[377] *Rederiaktiebolaget Amphitrite v R* [1921] 3 KB 500.

[378] [1988] ICR 649.

[379] [1991] IRLR 343.

that paragraph 14 was merely descriptive of the state of affairs which the parties believed to exist. The test of intention to create legal relations was objective and depended on the view the court took of the terms of the relationship. According to Stuart-Smith LJ, 'the relationship of employer and employee, master and servant, which plainly exists here must of its very nature be one that involves an intention to create legal relations, unless such intention is clearly excluded expressly or by necessary implication'.[380] The decision in *Nangle* can be criticised on the grounds that the notion of 'contractual intention' is a judicial construct, which is capable of being manipulated to suit the particular circumstances of individual cases. The discovery of a contractual nexus in that case, for example, ruled out the possibility of civil servants using judicial review to challenge an exercise of disciplinary power, although there are additional reasons for thinking that this remedy will not normally be available to them.[381] The Constitutional Reform and Governance Act 2010 placed the management of most of the civil service on a statutory basis but regrettably the opportunity to clarify the employment status of civil servants was not taken.[382]

In practice, the precise status of the civil servant has less significance now owing to the scope of statutory protection. The long-standing common law rule that civil servants can be dismissed at will, notwithstanding any agreement to the contrary such as an undertaking to employ them for a fixed term or to operate procedures governing discipline and dismissal,[383] has not been expressly abolished by legislation.[384] However the effect of this rule has been mitigated by the extension to civil servants of most of the protective provisions of TULRCA 1992 and ERA 1996,[385] together with the equality legislation[386] and basic labour standards regulation.[387] Conversely, TULRCA 1992 deems civil servants to have a contract of employment for the purpose of ensuring that the normal incidents of liability in tort attach to those who organise industrial action in the

[380] [1991] ICR 743, 752. Note that in 1994 the Conservative Government resolved that its relationship with senior civil servants should become explicitly contractual: *The Civil Service: Continuity and Change*, Cm 2627, 1994. See Freedland, 1995 for a discussion of the issues raised by this. The Information Note for Personnel Managers on Appointment Letters (www.civilservice.gov.uk/about/resources/pins: PIN 14 Revision 1) refers to the 'contractual terms' applicable to the appointment of civil servants and seems to use the terms 'civil servant' and 'employee' interchangeably.

[381] S Fredman and G Morris, 1991b; see below, paras 5.46–5.52.

[382] Until recently the power to determine the pay and conditions of civil servants apparently derived from the royal prerogative. The Constitutional Reform and Governance Act 2010 gave the Minister for the Civil Service the statutory power to make regulations and give instructions for the management of the Civil Service, including the power to prescribe conditions of service (although security vetting and the management of specified parts of the Civil Service, including the Security Service and GCHQ, are excluded and remain subject to the preregative). The Act also establishes the Civil Service Commission, whose functions include oversight of recruitment, as a body corporate; puts the requirement for a civil service code on a statutory footing; and states that the code forms part of the terms and conditions of service of any civil servant covered by it. Pursuant to the Civil Service (Management Functions) Act 1992, the Minister for the Civil Service has in turn made delegations to Ministers, office holders in charge of departments, the First Minister in the Scottish Executive and the Welsh Assembly Government, to determine certain terms and conditions (who may in turn delegate further, in respect of executive agencies, to Agency Chief Executives); the rules and principles to which they must adhere are set out in the Civil Service Management Code, available only online at www.civilservice.gov.uk/about/resources/civil-service-management-code. The 2010 Act did not define the civil service; for the difficulties in doing so, see Sandberg, 2006.

[383] *Dunn v R* [1896] 1 QB 116; *Rodwell v Thomas* [1944] KB 596; *Riordan v War Office* [1959] 1 WLR 1046.

[384] Although the management of the civil service is now on a statutory basis it is not clear that the principles on which the cases in the note above were decided have thereby ceased to apply.

[385] TULRCA 1992, ss 273–276; ERA 1996, ss 191–193. The main exceptions are the right to a minimum notice period and the right to a statutory redundancy payment under ERA 1996. Provision for compensation on dismissal for redundancy is made in the Civil Service Compensation Scheme: see *R (PCS) v Minister for the Civil Service* [2010] ICR 1198, Adm Ct.

[386] EqA 2010, s 83(2)

[387] See NMWA 1998, s 36; WTR 1998, reg 37.

civil service.[388] Moreover, the courts have held that principles of contract law are applicable for other purposes, even if the precise status of the civil servant remains unclear: thus a civil servant necessarily comes under an implied duty to serve the employer faithfully and with reasonable care and skill and, conversely, has the right to sue for arrears of pay.[389] One area where the absence of a contract of employment might harm civil servants is in relation to the variation of terms: here there is little effective statutory intervention and the protection of terms and conditions depends, as a result, on the application of principles drawn from the common law of contract, which may not be applicable to civil servants if their relationship of employment is not formally classified as contractual in nature.[390] That being said, once it is accepted that the concept of dismissal at will is not incompatible with the existence of a contract of employment, it is conceivable that variation at will may also be viewed in this way, on the basis that it constitutes the exercise of power to terminate a contract followed by the offer of another contract on different terms.[391]

Members of the armed forces

3.41   Members of the armed forces, like civil servants, are subject to the authority of the Crown exercised through the royal prerogative, but unlike civil servants there have been few suggestions that they either have or should have contracts of employment. Long-standing precedents clearly indicate that they cannot claim damages for breach of agreements concerning security of employment.[392] However, in recent years there have been moves to bring their statutory rights more closely into line with civilian workers. They are now protected by the equality legislation, with the exceptions of discrimination on the grounds of age and disability; in addition requirements to be male or not transexual may be applied if shown to be a proportionate means of ensuring 'combat effectiveness'. [393] They are outside the scope of the national minimum wage[394] but, with some modifications, they are protected by working time legislation.[395] At the time of writing they are also excluded from the ERA 1996 but there is provision for certain rights, including protection against unfair dismissal, to be brought into force by order.[396] However, they remain excluded from statutory collective rights:[397] they have no right, as a result, to legal protection

---

[388] TULRCA 1992, s 245.

[389] *Reilly v R* [1934] AC 176; *Riordan v War Office* [1959] 1 WLR 1046.

[390] See below, paras 4.35–4.40. The Civil Service Management Code, above, note 382, Introduction para 6, emphasises that existing rights cannot be altered arbitrarily and that departments and agencies should consult as necessary with their staff and the recognised trade unions.

[391] See Freedland, 1995: p 230.

[392] See *De Dohse v R* (1886) 3 TLR 114; *Grant v Secretary of State for India* (1877) 2 CPD 445.

[393] EqA 2010, s 83; Sch 9, para 4. EC Directive 76/207 on Equality of Treatment in Employment applies to the armed forces: see further *Ministry of Defence v Cannock* [1994] IRLR 509; *R v Ministry of Defence, ex parte Smith and Grady* [1996] IRLR 100; Case C-273-97 *Sirdar v Army Board and Secretary of State for Defence* [2000] IRLR 47. Members of the armed forces are required to make a 'service complaint' under the armed forces internal redress procedures before applying to an employment tribunal: EqA 2010, s 121; see the Armed Forces Act 2006, ss 334-339 and related regulations and JSP 831 (guidance published by the Ministry of Defence which also contains relevant legislation) for details of the current 'service complaints procedure'. The period for bringing complaints under EqA 2010 is extended to six months to allow the internal procedures to be carried out: EqA 2010, s 123(2)

[394] NMWA 1998, s 37.

[395] WTR 1998, reg 38; but note also the effect of reg 18(2)(a), discussed below, para 4.79.

[396] ERA 1996, s 192(1), (2). At the time of writing ERA 1996, Sch 2, para 16 applies.

[397] TULRCA 1992, s 274.

against discrimination on the grounds of trade union membership, nor do they have the right to collective representation in respect of the matters over which employers are normally required to inform and consult representatives of their employees.

Parliamentary staff

3.42   Parliamentary staff are in a distinct position thanks to the doctrine of Parliamentary privilege. Matters internal to the Houses of Parliament are excluded from the jurisdiction of the courts, as a consequence of which it is thought that parliamentary staff do not have contracts of employment;[398] but as in the case of civil servants, not much turns on this.[399] Procedures for the appointment of House of Commons staff and for the establishment of their terms and conditions of employment, which are broadly comparable to those of civil servants, are governed by the House of Commons (Administration) Act 1978. House of Commons staff and House of Lords staff are also covered by equality legislation and by most of the provisions of TULRCA 1992 and ERA 1996,[400] and by labour standards legislation.[401]

Police officers

3.43   The balance of judicial opinion is that police officers do not have contracts of employment.[402] In constitutional terms, police constables are regarded as 'independent officers' capable of exercising legal powers derived from the nature of their office. This is why it was held that for the purpose of vicarious liability in tort they were not the employees of the relevant police authority.[403] In practice, police officers are subject to the managerial control of their superiors, and their scope for individual action is limited by the powers of the chief constable as well as by the Police Regulations. The chief constable exercises powers of promotion, discipline and dismissal and is vicariously liable in respect of any unlawful conduct by constables under his or her direction or control in the performance or purported performance of their functions.[404] Wages and salaries, on the other hand, are the responsibility of the local police authority, although at the time of

---

[398] See Lock, 1983; Fredman and Morris, 1989: pp 73–74.

[399] Note, in particular, TULRCA 1992, ss 277(2) and 278(2A) and ERA 1996, ss 194(4) and 195(4).

[400] EqA 2010, ss 79(6), 83; TULRCA 1992, ss 277, 278; ERA 1996, ss 194, 195.

[401] NMWA 1998, ss 38, 39; WTR 1998, regs 39, 40.

[402] The cases were reviewed and reaffirmed by the EAT in *Commissioner of Police of the Metropolis v Lowrey-Nesbit* [1999] ICR 401.

[403] *Fisher v Oldham Corpn* [1930] 2 KB 364. Possession of the powers of a constable has not been regarded as incompatible with employee status in relation to members of the British Transport Police: *Spence v British Railways Board* [2001] ICR 232. On the status of members of the 'extended police family' see G Morris, 2002

[404] Police Act 1996, ss 10 and 88, as amended by the Police Reform Act 2002. See *White v Chief Constable of South Yorkshire Police* [1999] IRLR 110, where for the purposes of a negligence claim against the Chief Constable, police officers were regarded as being analogous to employees; *Waters v Commissioner of Police of the Metropolis* [2000] IRLR 720; *Lennon v Commissioner of Police of the Metropolis* [2004] IRLR 385.

writing police authorities are due to be abolished in November 2012 when directly-elected Police and Crime Commissioners are introduced.[405]

Police officers are explicitly excluded from most of the protective provisions of ERA 1996.[406] The courts have taken the view that, given the absence of a contractual nexus between a police constable and any putative employer, the police are implicitly excluded from those other rights on which ERA 1996 is silent.[407] Formal exclusions also apply to collective rights: police officers cannot be 'employees' or 'workers' for the purposes of TULRCA 1992, nor can they invoke rights in relation to trade union membership.[408] For these and other reasons, they have no right to take part in industrial action, nor to form or join a trade union.[409] However, all police officers below the rank of superintendent automatically belong to the Police Federation, a body established by legislation whose membership is confined to the police service.[410] The Secretary of State is empowered to determine the conditions of service of police officers, including pay and allowances.[411] However, before making a determination relating to pay and other specified matters the Secretary of State is required to take into consideration recommendations of the Police Negotiating Board, a statutory body of which staff representative bodies, as well as police authorities and specified ministers, are members.[412] There are also statutory consultative bodies for a range of other matters, such as disciplinary procedures, relating to employment.[413]

Although outside the scope of statutory employment protection, police officers are nevertheless covered by equality legislation; these provisions impose obligations on the chief constable or, in an appropriate case, on the responsible authority.[414] Moreover, the police are explicitly covered by working time legislation.[415] Legislation governing the national minimum wage is silent on the matter of police service. As a general rule the right of police officers to invoke judicial review to cure a breach of natural justice or other *ultra vires* act is well recognised and extends to all ranks, including trainee officers;[416] this is so by virtue not simply of the office they occupy but also because of the clear absence of any alternative contractual or statutory remedies for the protection of their employment. However the courts have qualified this position by holding that whether judicial review will lie depends upon whether 'the defendant was performing a public duty owed

---

[405] See the Police Reform and Social Responsibility Act 2011. The PCC model was introduced in London in January 2012.

[406] ERA 1996, s 200. Note, however, the Police (Health and Safety) Act 1997 which provides, *inter alia*, that police constables and cadets have the right not to be unfairly dismissed, or subjected to any detriment, in health and safety cases: see also ERA 1996, s 134A; and ERA 1996, s 43KA, which applies protections against dismissal and other detriment for making a 'protected disclosure' (see para 4.117) to the police, and *Lake v British Transport Police* [2007] 1 ICR 1293.

[407] See *Commissioner of Police of the Metropolis v Lowery-Nesbit* [1999] ICR 401, discussing the meaning, in this context, of ERA 1996, s 200.

[408] TULRCA 1992, s 280(1).

[409] See further paras 7.13 and 11.60, respectively.

[410] The Police Federation was initially established by the Police Act 1919; the relevant provision is now the Police Act 1996.

[411] Police Act 1996, s 50; Police Regulations 2003, SI 2003/527.

[412] Police Act 1996, s 61, 62; see also www.ome.uk.com. A fuller account can be found in *The Staff Side of the Police Negotiating Board v The Secretary of State for the Home Department* [2008] EWHC 1173 (Admin).

[413] Police Act 1996, s 63 (Police Advisory Board for England and Wales and Police Advisory Board for Scotland); see further www.ome.uk.com.

[414] EqA 2010, ss 42, 43, 79.

[415] WTR 1998, reg 41, but see also reg 18(2)(a).

[416] *Chief Constable of North Wales Police v Evans* [1982] 1 WLR 1155.

to the claimant in the particular circumstances under consideration;[417] a development we discuss further in paras 5.48–5.52.

Prison officers

3.44   Prison officers, who were at one time held to be 'in police service' for the purposes of unfair dismissal legislation,[418] had their position clarified by the Criminal Justice and Public Order Act 1994 and are not to be treated as being in police service for the purposes of TULRCA 1992 and ERA 1996;[419] as a result, they may claim employment protection rights and form a trade union. They have no right to take part in industrial action, however, thanks to the establishment by the 1994 Act of a statutory duty not to induce a prison officer to take (or continue to take) any industrial action or to commit a breach of discipline.[420]

Employment in public corporations, local government, education and the NHS

3.45   Those employed in public corporations, local government, the education service and the National Health Service work under normal contracts of employment. Their employers are bodies created by statute, so the uncertainties which attach to the status of civil servants who are employed by the Crown do not apply here. The identity of the employer is not always straightforward, however. In the case of a nationalised corporation it is the relevant corporate body established by statute. Local government workers are employed by the relevant local authority, which means the council and not the councillors who are elected to it.[421] Local councils are empowered by statute to employ such officers as they consider necessary for the discharge of their functions,[422] although no councillor of the authority may serve as an officer[423] and certain posts are 'politically restricted' which means that their holders may not be members, *inter alia*, of any local authority.[424] The discretion of local authorities to employ labour directly was for some years limited by legislation which required certain classes of work to be subjected to periodic competitive tendering and,

---

[417] *R (on the application of Tucker) v Director General of the National Crime Squad* [2003] IRLR 439, [24] (Scott Baker LJ).

[418] *Home Office v Robinson* [1982] ICR 31.

[419] CJPOA 1994, s 126(1)–(2); ERA 1996, s 200(2)(a).

[420] CJPOA 1994, s 127(1)–(2), as amended by the Criminal Justice and Immigration Act 2008, s 138; see further para 11.12 below. See www.ome.uk.com for the role of the Pay Review Body for Prison Officers. See also generally, G Morris, 1994b.

[421] A council can be vicariously liable for an act of a councillor which undermines the obligation of trust and confidence in the employment relationship; for discussion of when, precisely, vicarious liability of this kind may arise, see *Moores v Bude-Stratton Town Council* [2000] IRLR 676.

[422] Local Government Act 1972, s 112.

[423] Local Government Act 1972, ss 80(1).

[424] Local Government and Housing Act 1989, ss 1, 2. The Act, and the Local Government Officers (Political Restrictions) Regulations 1990, SI 1990/851 made thereunder, prohibit a wide range of political activities: see further G Morris, 1998a, 1998b. In *Ahmed v UK* [1999] IRLR 188, the European Court of Human Rights ruled that these restrictions did not violate Arts 10 or 11 of, or Art 3 of Protocol 1 to, the ECHR; see G Morris, 1999b.

under some circumstances, contracted-out to external suppliers of services.[425] This has now been replaced by an obligation to obtain 'best value', measured by reference to economy, efficiency and effectiveness, whether from the public or the private sector.[426]

Teachers in the public sector are employed by the local education authority (LEA),[427] with the exception of those who work in voluntary aided and foundation schools and 'academies', which employ their staff directly.[428] However, as part of a process of devolving powers and responsibilities to individual schools, most of the powers usually exercised by an employer are accorded to the governing body of the school, to the extent that governing bodies have been described as 'employers in practice, even where the formal contract is with the ... [LEA]'.[429] Thus the LEA cannot normally refuse to appoint staff recommended by the governing body,[430] and must terminate the contract of any staff the governing body dismisses where they are employed to work solely at the school or, in any event, require them not to work at the school.[431] Moreover, the governing body is the respondent in specified statutory (but not contractual) proceedings brought by staff consequent upon the exercise of its employment powers.[432] However, the LEA retains the burdens of being the employer in the sense that it must meet any legal costs and statutory compensation payable to an employee,[433] and will only in exceptional circumstances be able to shift all or part of these costs to the governing body.[434]

Like the education service, the National Health Service has been subject to extensive statutory changes designed to encourage the devolution of budgetary controls and the management of personnel and resources. Most hospital staff are employed by self-governing trusts which have the status of autonomous entities for this purpose.[435]

Office holders

3.46   The category of 'office holder' which applies to certain high-ranking public-sector employees confers few if any special privileges or protections. The traditional definition of an office is 'a subsisting, permanent, substantive position which had an existence independent from the person who filled it, which went on and was filled in succession by successive holders'.[436] This definition adequately describes many posts in the public services, some created explicitly

---

[425] Local Government Acts of 1988 and 1992.

[426] Local Government Act 1999.

[427] Education Act 2002, s 35.

[428] Education Act 2002, s 36; School Staffing (England) Regulations 2009, SI 2009/2680; Education Act 1996, s 482

[429] *Teachers: Meeting the challenge of change*, DfEE, 1998, para 172. This process was begun by the 1979–1997 Conservative Government and extended by the Labour Government which took office in 1997. See generally G Morris, 1999d.

[430] SI 2009/2680, Part 2.

[431] SI 2009/2680, reg 20. See *Askew v Governing Body of Clifton Middle School* [1999] IRLR 708.

[432] Education (Modification of Enactments Relating to Employment) Order 2003, SI 2003/1964, reg 6. The Order states that it covers specified sections of SDA 1975, RRA 1976, TULRCA 1992, DDA 1995, ERA 1996, and EA 2002; at the time of writing it has not been updated to refer to EqA 2010. See *Murphy v Slough Borough Council* [2005] ICR 721; *Butt v Bradford Metropolitan District Council* UKEAT/0210/10/ZT.

[433] Education (Modification of Enactments Relating to Employment) Order 2003, SI 2003/1964, reg 6(3).

[434] Education Act 2002, s 37.

[435] See the National Health Service Act 2006, s 25; G Morris, 1999a: pp 73–76.

[436] *Great Western Rly Co v Bater* [1920] 3 KB 266, 274.

by statute,[437] whose holders almost certainly have contracts of employment and will therefore benefit from the protections conferred upon employees by labour legislation.[438] Even if a court takes the view that the holder of a statutory public office may not, as such, be regarded as having a contract of employment, it may nevertheless regard the relationship as 'analogous to contract' and apply contract law principles to determine the common law rights of the parties. This occurred, for example, in *Miles v Wakefield Metropolitan District Council*,[439] a case concerning a claim for payment of salary by a Registrar of Births, Deaths and Marriages. It should also be noted that office holders who are not employees will nevertheless be liable to pay income tax under Schedule E[440] as well as primary Class 1 national insurance contributions.[441] In short, the category of officer holder, like that of civil servant, is gradually losing any distinctive character it once had in relation to the contract of employment,[442] although serious anomalies remain in relation to the statutory employment protection afforded to particular groups.[443]

CONTINUITY OF EMPLOYMENT, QUALIFYING THRESHOLDS, AND EQUALITY OF TREATMENT FOR FIXED-TERM, PART-TIME AND AGENCY WORKERS

3.47 The category of 'employee' contains within it further sub-divisions of employment status. Distinctions which used to exist between manual and non-manual employees have now almost completely disappeared from the law.[444] However, more modern legislation has drawn distinctions between employees according to such criteria as length of service, regularity of employment, the duration of the working week and the amount of weekly pay. These have had the effect of excluding some part-time and temporary workers, who have the status of employees but who lack the necessary continuity of employment, from the coverage of certain employment protection rights under ERA 1996.

The statutory concept of *continuity of employment* is therefore an important filter for employment protection. The two dimensions of continuity are *length* and *regularity* of employment. As far as length is concerned, two years' continuous employment is currently needed for protection against unfair dismissal[445] and the right to redundancy compensation: many temporary and fixed-

---

[437] S Fredman and G Morris, 1989: pp 74–75.

[438] See, however, *Lincolnshire County Council v Hopper* EAT/819/01, 24 May 2002, where the EAT was 'reluctantly driven' to conclude that a Registrar of Births, Marriages and Deaths, along with other substantial groups, was not an employee.

[439] [1987] ICR 368.

[440] Income Tax (Pensions and Earnings) Act 2003, s 5.

[441] SSCBA 1992, s 2(1)(a).

[442] See *Johnson v Ryan* [2000] ICR 236 (a local authority rent officer could be both an employee and an office holder), *Perceval-Price v Department of Economic Development* [2000] IRLR 380 (tribunal chairmen were within employment for the purposes of the EC Equal Treatment Directive 76/207; see now also Directive 2000/78 and Directive 2002/73) and *O'Brien v Ministry of Justice* [2010] IRLR 883, SC (reference to the CJEU for a preliminary ruling on judges); Case C-393/10 *O'Brien v Ministry of Justice* [2012] IRLR 421, CJEU. It should be noted that the category of 'office-holder' no longer seems to be relevant to the availability of the remedy of judicial review if, indeed, it ever truly was.

[443] See *Lincolnshire County Council v Hopper* EAT/819/01, 24 May 2002. The EAT was highly critical of the position and sent a copy of the judgment to the Minister for the Office for National Statistics.

[444] See our discussion in the context of the right to wages, ch 4, at para 4.62 *et seq* below.

[445] ERA 1996, s 108(1) as amended by SI 2012/989. The two-year period applies to those employed from 6 April 2012.

term employees are thereby placed outside the scope of protection. The need for regularity means that employees who are employed on a periodic basis, with frequent spells of non-employment in between periods of work, may also be excluded from protection.

It is not just 'flexible' or 'atypical' employment forms which are affected by the need for continuity. Because continuity must be maintained intact up to the event triggering the legal claim (such as a dismissal),[446] employees of many years' seniority may lose statutory rights by virtue of working on a periodic or irregular basis near the end of their period of service. Continuity is also important for determining the extent as well as the basic entitlement of employees to protection; for example, the length of continuous employment will determine the amount of redundancy compensation to which an employee is entitled.

Qualifying periods of continuous employment

3.48   Continuity is computed in weeks, so that *regularity* of employment must be established from one working week to the next;[447] *length* of employment is calculated in years and months.[448] The two-year qualifying period does not apply to most 'automatically unfair' reasons for dismissal.[449] The qualifying period for redundancy compensation remains two years.[450]

For guarantee payments and payments during suspension on medical grounds the specified period of continuity is one month.[451] The right to receive a minimum period of notice of dismissal is also dependent upon continuous employment of one month. This gives the employee the right to receive one week's notice. After two years of continuous employment this rises to two weeks, and so on for each year of extra service up to a maximum of 12.[452]

In the cases of statutory sick pay (SSP) and statutory maternity pay (SMP), the qualifying conditions reflect the history of these two benefits, which combine elements of social insurance and employment protection.[453] The social insurance origins of SSP can be seen in the rule that employees whose normal weekly earnings fall below the lower earnings limit do not qualify for protection.[454] The intention of this is to exclude employees who do not regularly pay primary Class 1 national insurance contributions, even though the payment of these contributions is no longer, *as such*, a precondition of qualifying.

SMP is available to an employee who has been continuously employed in employed earners' employment for a period of 26 weeks up to the qualifying week, that is to say, the fifteenth week before the expected week of confinement. In addition she must show that she had average weekly earnings above the lower earnings limit for contributions for the period of eight weeks prior to

---

[446] On the 'effective date of termination' in the law of unfair dismissal, see below, paras 5.80–5.84.

[447] ERA 1996, ss 210–219.

[448] ERA 1996, s 210. A 'year' is, for these purposes, twelve calendar months (see s 210(1), (2)) and continuity is computed from the day on which the employee starts work. It follows that an employee whose employment began on 8 April 2002 and was terminated with effect from 7 April 2003 had sufficient continuity: *Pacitti Jones v O'Brien* [2005] IRLR 888.

[449] See generally paras 5.92–5.111 below.

[450] ERA 1996, s 155.

[451] See, respectively, ERA 1996, ss 29, 65.

[452] ERA 1996, s 86.

[453] See below, paras 4.125, 6.118, respectively.

[454] SSCBA 1992, Sch 11, para 2(c).

the qualifying week.[455] Following the implementation of Directive 92/85 in TURERA 1993, the qualifying period of two years for claims for unfair dismissal on the grounds of pregnancy was abolished,[456] and the introduction of a general right to 14 weeks' maternity leave, not dependent upon any continuity of employment, was introduced. Under the work and family reforms put in place by the Employment Relations Act 1999 and related statutory instruments, a right to 'ordinary maternity leave' of 18 weeks, again not dependent on continuity of employment, was established, rising to 26 weeks in 2002.[457] These reforms also established a right to 'additional maternity leave' of a further twenty-six weeks, which required twenty-six weeks' continuous employment up to the qualifying week. At the time of the implementation of the Work and Families Act 2006, the qualifying period for additional maternity leave was abolished.[458]

Certain other employment protection rights, while not dependent upon continuity of employment in the sense required by Part XIV of ERA 1996, nevertheless require service of a certain length. Thus the employer must issue a written statement of terms and conditions to all employees whose employment continues for one month and the statement must be issued within two months of the employment beginning.[459]

As we have already noted, employment protection legislation does not simply require employees to have minimum periods of continuous service; where continuity is required, it must be maintained for the specified period of time ending with the particular event which triggers the legal claim. In the case of SMP, for example, this is the fifteenth week before the expected week of confinement, as explained above.[460] For unfair dismissal, continuity of two years up to the 'effective date of termination'[461] is needed for those employed from 6 April 2012, and for redundancy compensation the same notion is expressed in the concept of the 'relevant date', prior to which two years of continuity are needed.[462] Thus it is only partially true that the continuity requirement is a function of the need for an employee to have accrued a certain degree of seniority before being allowed a claim against his or her employer. In practice, seniority or length of service is only one factor; because of the stress on regularity of employment, employees with years of service may forfeit employment protection benefits in a somewhat arbitrary way by virtue of the operation of the continuity rule.[463]

---

[455] SSCBA 1992, s 164(1)–(2). Parallel provisions apply in the case of statutory paternity and adoption pay (see, respectively, SSCBA 1992, s 171ZA(2)(b)–(c) and PALR 2002, reg 4, and SSCBA 1992, s 171ZL(2)(b)–(d) and PALR 2002, reg 15).

[456] See now ERA 1996, s 99(1)–(3).

[457] SI 2002/2789.

[458] SI 2006/2014, repealing MPLR 1999, reg 5(b), with effect from 1 October 2006. 26 weeks of continuous employment are required for statutory paternity leave and adoption leave following, respectively, the birth or adoption of a child: see PALR 2002, regs 4(2)(a), 8(2)(a) and 15(2)(b). Entitlement to parental leave for the purposes of caring for a child requires one year's continuous employment: MPLR 1999, reg 13(1)(a).

[459] ERA 1996, ss 1(1), (2), 2(6) and 5(1).

[460] SSCBA 1992, s 164(2)(a).

[461] ERA 1996, s 97(1).

[462] ERA 1996, s 155.

[463] See, eg, *Hellyer Bros Ltd v McLeod* [1987] ICR 526, discussed below.

Temporary, fixed-term and agency employment, qualifying service and equality of treatment

3.49   As we have just seen, the qualifying thresholds referred to above have the potential to affect all employees, but they are particularly significant in the case of those employed on fixed-term or temporary contracts.[464] A large proportion of temporary jobs are low paid and there is substantial overlap with part-time work and self-employment.[465] Sectors where this form of work is common include hotel and catering and general services, as well as part of the public sector.[466]

Individuals employed on a fixed-term contract are usually classed as employees for legal purposes. From 1999 they could no longer be required by their employers to waive their rights to unfair dismissal protection upon the expiry of the fixed term,[467] and from 2002 the possibility of them waiving claims to redundancy compensation was also removed.[468]

(i) Challenges to qualifying periods

3.50   The two-year qualifying period for unfair dismissal which operated from 1985 to 1999 was challenged on the grounds of its incompatibility with Article 119 (subsequently Article 141) of the EC Treaty (now Art 157 TFEU) [469] and with the Equal Treatment Directive[470] in *R v Secretary of State, ex p Seymour-Smith and Perez.*[471] Evidence was led which indicated that between 1985 (when the two-year qualifying period was introduced) and 1991, between 72% and 77.4% of male employees working 16 hours or more per week had two years' or more service, compared to between 63.8% and 68.9% of women. On average, the number of women qualifying was around 90% of the number of men. After lengthy litigation, during which a number of questions were referred to the ECJ for a preliminary ruling, the House of Lords concluded (by a bare majority) that a case of adverse impact was made out, but went on to hold that the government was able to show that the qualifying period was capable of being justified on the grounds that it fell within 'the broad margin of discretion afforded to governments when adopting measures of this type'.[472] This decision illustrates the substantial leeway given to governments to make exceptions to the equal treatment principle on grounds related to more general labour market considerations, in this case, 'to encourage recruitment by employers'.[473] Although the two-year qualifying period for

---

[464] The numbers employed on temporary work of various kinds were reported to be between 5% and 6% of the active labour force in the autumn of 2008 (*Economic and Labour Market Review*, December 2008, 'Labour Market Statistics', Table 2.03) but this figure does not count a further category, perhaps constituting as much as 10% of the active labour force, of employees who regard themselves as being in 'permanent' work but are employed under fixed-term contracts. See Burchell *et al*, 1999: ch 5, where the difficulties which arise in arriving at a reliable figure for those employed on fixed-term contracts are discussed. For accounts of employers' reasons for using temporary labour, see Heather *et al*, 1996; Casey *et al*, 1997.

[465] See Sly and Stilwell, 1997.

[466] Sly and Stilwell, 1997: pp 351–352.

[467] ERelA 1999, s 18, amending ERA 1996, s 197.

[468] By virtue of FTER 2002. See further below.

[469] This part of the claim was added at the stage of the Court of Appeal hearing. See [1995] IRLR 464, 467.

[470] Directive 76/107, now replaced by Directive 2000/78.

[471] [1994] IRLR 448, DC (see Freedland, 1994), [1995] IRLR 464, CA; [1997] IRLR 315, HL; Case C-167/97 [1999] IRLR 253 (ECJ); [2000] IRLR 263 (HL) (see Barnard and Hepple, 2000).

[472] [2000] IRLR 263, 271 (Lord Nicholls).

[473] [2000] IRLR 263, 270 (Lord Nicholls). The adverse impact and justification aspects of this decision are considered in greater detail in ch 6, below.

general unfair dismissal protection was reduced to one year with effect from June 1999,[474] the two-year period was restored with effect from 6 April 2012[475] as part of the Coalition Government's deregulatory reforms to employment law.

(ii) Directive 91/383 on protection of the health and safety of temporary workers

3.51 Temporary work has been the subject of several attempts to introduce directives providing for parity of treatment of different forms of employment relationships.[476] The first of these to succeed, Directive 91/383, provides that employees with a fixed-term contract of employment or with a temporary employment relationship with an agency or employment business, as part of which they are assigned to work with a third party user, are entitled to 'the same level of protection as that of other workers in the user undertaking and/or establishment' with regard to health and safety.[477] More specific obligations concern the provision of information and training to temporary workers (and to certain third parties) and medical surveillance of their activities. These provisions were incorporated into British law by the Management of Health and Safety Regulations 1992 (subsequently replaced by MHSW 1999).[478]

(iii) Directive 99/70/EC concerning the Framework Agreement on Fixed-Term Work concluded by ETUC, UNICE, and CEEP, and the Fixed-Term Employees (Prevention of Less Favourable Treatment) Regulations 2002

3.52 This Directive implemented a Framework Agreement made by the social partners under the social dialogue procedure put in place by the Maastricht Treaty.[479] The Agreement is premised on the view that 'contracts of an indefinite duration are, and will continue to be, the general form of employment relationship between employers and workers'.[480] While there is recognition that 'fixed-term employment contracts respond, in certain circumstances, to the needs of both employers and workers',[481] the Agreement aims to control what it regards as abuse by employers of the fixed-term contract option, and imposes a requirement of equal treatment between fixed-term and permanent workers, thereby arguably reinforcing a sense in which the indeterminate-duration contract of employment is the norm against which other employment forms are to be compared.[482]

The Agreement applies to 'fixed-term workers who have an employment contract or employment relationship as defined in law, collective agreements or practice in each Member

---

[474] SI 1999/1436.

[475] SI 2012/989. The two-year period applies to those employed on or after that date

[476] See generally, Hepple, 1990a.

[477] Directive 91/383, Art 2(1).

[478] SI 1992/2051, regs 10 and 13; SI 1999/3242.

[479] See para 2.37 above.

[480] Directive 99/70, Annex (Framework Agreement on Fixed-Term Work concluded by ETUC, UNICE and CEEP), recital 2.

[481] Framework Agreement on Fixed-Term Work, recital 2.

[482] For assessments of the Agreement which discuss its policy orientation, see Murray, 1999; Tiraboschi, 1999; P Lorber, 1999.

State'[483] and defines a fixed-term worker as 'a person having an employment contract or relationship entered into directly between an employer and a worker where the end of the employment relationship is determined by objective conditions' such as reaching a specific date, completing a specific task, or the occurrence of a specific event'.[484] This definition was intended to have the effect, among other things, of excluding agency work from the scope of the Agreement (by virtue of the reference to an employment contract entered into 'directly' by the employer and worker); agency work is the subject of a separate Directive, adopted in 2008.[485]

The Agreement establishes a general principle of equal treatment, according to which 'in respect of employment conditions, fixed-term workers shall not be treated in a less favourable manner than comparable permanent workers solely because they have a fixed-term contract or relation unless different treatment is justified on objective grounds'.[486] The expression 'employment conditions' includes pay and occupational pension benefits, but not payments made under state social security schemes.[487] Equality means equal treatment 'pro rata temporis', that is, taking into account differences in actual length of service, but the Agreement prohibits laws which count continuity of employment differently according to whether employment is fixed term or permanent.[488] The Court of Justice has ruled that 'objective grounds' refers to 'precise and concrete circumstances characterising a given activity, which are therefore capable, in that particular context, of justifying the use of successive fixed-term employment contracts'. Such circumstances may arise 'from the specific nature of the tasks for the performance of which such contracts have been concluded and from the inherent characteristics of those tasks or, as the case may be, from pursuit of a legitimate social policy objective of a Member State'.[489]

The second principal advance made by the Agreement is to require Member States to take measures to 'prevent abuse arising from the use of successive fixed-term contracts or relationships'.[490] Member States are called on to 'introduce in a manner which takes account of the needs of specific sectors and/or categories of workers, one or more of the following measures: (a) objective reasons justifying the renewal of such contracts or relationships; (b) the maximum total duration of successive fixed-term employment contracts or relationships; (c) the number of

---

[483] Framework Agreement on Fixed-Term Work, cl 2(1).

[484] Framework Agreement on Fixed-Term Work, cl 3(1).

[485] See below, para. 3.53.

[486] Framework Agreement on Fixed-Term Work, cl 4(1). In Case C-268/06, *Impact v Minister for Agriculture and Food* [2008] IRLR 552 the Court held that this provision is capable of having direct effect in national law.

[487] Case C-307/05 *Del Cerro Alonso v Osakidetza-Servicio Vasco de Salud* [2007]IRLR 911; Case C-268/06, *Impact v Minister for Agriculture and Food* [2008] IRLR 552.

[488] The Agreement refers to 'period-of-service qualifications'. UK law on continuity of employment arguably complies with the Agreement in this respect: see *Kingston upon Hull City Council v Mountain* [1999] ICR 715, 720.

[489] Case C-307/05 *Del Cerro Alonso v Osakidetza-Servicio Vasco de Salud* [2007] IRLR 911, at para 53; Case C-212/04 *Adeneler v Ellinikos Organismos Galaktos* [2006] IRLR 716, at paras 69–70; Case C-486/08 *Zentralbetriebsrat des Landeskrankenhaüser Tirols v Land Tirol* [2010] IRLR 631, at para 44; Joined Cases C-444/09 and C-456/09 *Gavieiro v Consellería del Educácion e Ordinácion Universitaria de la Xunta de Galícia* [2011] IRLR 504. This formula is also relevant in the interpretation of cl 5 of the Agreement.

[490] Framework Agreement on Fixed-Term Work, cl 5. See Case C-378/07 *Angelidaki v Organismos Nomarchiakis Autodioikisis Rethymnis* [2009] ECR I- 3071, discussed by Peers, 2010, and Kilpatrick, 2010.

renewals of such contracts or relationships'.[491] This provision signifies a radical departure from the traditional position in UK law, which was to impose no restrictions upon the rights of the parties to agree successive fixed-term employment contracts.

The Directive was implemented in the UK by the Fixed-Term Employees (Prevention of Less Favourable Treatment) Regulations which came into effect in 2002.[492] These Regulations have several notable features. Their scope is limited to *employees*;[493] thus they do not confer any protection on fixed-term workers who are unable to establish employee status, for example because of the absence of mutuality of obligation. On the other hand, the relevant definition of 'fixed-term contract' is wider than that which was previously used in the context of 'dismissal' for the purposes of unfair dismissal and statutory redundancy payments (which itself was extended by the Regulations to cover non-renewal of a 'limited-term contract'[494]). For the purposes of the Regulations, 'fixed-term contract' includes contracts which are intended to terminate on the expiry of a 'fixed term' (for the purposes of which, a contract which contains a notice clause is not, for that reason, excluded from the scope of the Regulations[495]), and it also covers task contracts and contracts which are intended to terminate 'on the occurrence or non-occurrence of any other specific event' except the attainment by the employee of any normal and bona fide normal retiring age in the establishment for the position which he or she holds. By contrast, the notion of the 'comparable permanent employee' is narrowly specified: the two employees must be employed by the same employer, engaged in broadly similar work and must normally be based at the same establishment. No comparison can be made if the permanent employee has ceased to be employed by the employer.[496]

The right to equality consists of the right to be treated no less favourably in relation to the terms of the contract of employment and the right not to be subjected to any detriment by the employer; this includes a right to equal treatment in relation to any relevant period of qualifying service, opportunities for training, and opportunities to secure a permanent position in the establishment.[497] The pro-rata principle applies: this means that 'where a comparable permanent employee receives or is entitled to pay or any other benefit, a fixed-term employee is to receive or be entitled to such proportion of that pay or other benefit as is reasonable in the circumstances having regard to the length of his contract or employment and to the terms on which the pay

---

[491] The judgment of the ECJ in Case C-144/-04 *Mangold v Helm* [2006] IRLR 143 focused on the compatibility of German legislation exempting older workers from the protection of fixed-term employment regulations with the prohibition on age discrimination contained in Directive 2000/78. The Court did not express a view on whether the legislation was compatible with cl 5 of the Framework Agreement. See also Case C-109/09 *Deutsche Lufthansa AG v Kumpan* [2011] ICR 1278, ECJ. In Case C-268/06, *Impact v Minister for Agriculture and Food* [2008] IRLR 552 the Court held that cl 5 was not capable of having direct effect in national law.

[492] FTER 2002, SI 2002/2034.

[493] FTER 2002, reg 1(2). Agency workers are explicitly excluded: reg 19.

[494] See ERA 1995, ss 95(1)(b), 136(1)(b), 235(2A), (2B); see further paras 5.75–5.76.

[495] *Allen v National Australia Group Europe Ltd* [2004] IRLR 847.

[496] FTER 2002, reg 2. Comparison with an employee employed at another establishment of the employer is possible if there is no comparable permanent employee in the establishment where the applicant is employed (FTER 2002, reg 2). Definitions of 'fixed-term worker' and 'comparable permanent worker' are contained in cl 3 of the Framework Agreement. The Agreement provides that the comparison must normally be with a permanent worker in the same establishment but if none is available, a comparison can be made by reference to relevant collective agreements or to national law or practice. This is a somewhat broader provision than that contained in FTER 2002 and raises the question of whether the Regulations are fully compliant with the Agreement.

[497] FTWR 2002, reg 3. Refusal to renew or extend a fixed-term contract does not constitute less favourable treatment for the purposes of reg 3: *Department of Work and Pensions v Webley* [2005] IRLR 288.

or other benefit is offered'.[498] However, the right to equality is only infringed if the ground for unequal treatment was the fixed-term status of the applicant; and as we have seen, the right is in any event subject to an open-ended defence of objective justification.[499] Justification will be made out if the employer can show that 'the terms of the fixed-term employee's contract of employment, taken as a whole, are at least as favourable as the terms of the comparable permanent employee's contract of employment'.[500] It is open to question whether this 'package' approach to justification complies with the Directive. The principal remedy for breach of these provisions is a complaint to an employment tribunal which may make a recommendation to the employer and award compensation to the employee.[501]

The most far-reaching change to UK law was brought about by regulation 8. Where an employee is employed under successive fixed-term contracts and has continuity of employment of four years or more from 10 July 2002 (the transposition date of the Directive), the term limiting the duration of the contract of employment is to be of no effect from the date on which the four years of continuous employment were acquired, or from the date on which the contract was most recently renewed, if later. This provision is subject to the possibility of the employer showing that the use of a fixed term is 'justified on objective grounds'. These are not specified, and it remains to be seen how far the courts will be persuaded that objective grounds include factors of the kind which have proved relevant in the context of the law of unfair dismissal, such as the ending of an external grant or commercial contract to which the employment in question was linked.[502] In addition, it is open to the employer to vary the effect of regulation 8 through a collective or workforce agreement. This may specify the maximum total period for which an employee may be employed on fixed-term contracts before they are deemed to be permanent; the maximum number of renewals of fixed-term contracts which may be made; and more detailed objective grounds justifying fixed-term employment.[503]

Regulation 8 was analysed by the Supreme Court in *Duncombe v Secretary of State for Children, Schools and Families (No. 1)*.[504] This case arose from the practice of employing schoolteachers working in European schools, which provided education to the children of EU staff members, on a series of fixed-term contracts, the duration of which could not in total exceed nine years. The rationale for this was a policy of encouraging mobility of teachers between the European school system and the school systems of the individual Member States. In one of the cases decided in *Duncombe*, the claimant argued that his dismissal upon reaching the nine year limit to his employment in the European school system was unfair; he also sought a declaration that he was entitled to a permanent employment contract under regulation 9. The claim failed in the Supreme Court on the basis that the operation of the European schools system, which was beyond the control of the UK government, rendered the use of fixed-term contracts in this

---

[498] FTER 2002, reg 1(2).

[499] FTER 2002, reg 3(3).

[500] FTER 2002, reg 4.

[501] FTER 2002, reg 7. In addition, there is a right to receive from the employer a written statement of the reasons for less favourable treatment (reg 5), and dismissal is automatically unfair if it is for the reason that the employee has, in one or more of a number of ways, asserted his or her rights under the Regulations (reg 6).

[502] *Terry v East Sussex County Council* [1976] ICR 536; see below, para 5.173. Koukiadaki, 2009, reviews recent decisions at tribunal level arising out of employment in the higher education sector.

[503] See further our discussion of regulation 8 in ch 5, below, at paras 5.75–5.76. The relevant definitions of 'collective' and 'workforce' agreements are contained in FTER 2002, Sch 1.

[504] [2011] IRLR 498.

case objectively justifiable. The leading judgment of Baroness Hale is notable for its emphasis on the very limited protection provided by the Regulations. Noting that 'the Fixed-term Directive is not directed against fixed-term contracts as such',[505] she suggested that it could not be read as ruling out the use of fixed-term employment in a given case simply because the employer could be shown to have a need for the work in question to be carried out on a continuing basis. Because the Secretary of State did not need to justify the nine-year limit overall to employment in the European school system, the dismissal of the claimant upon the expiry of his last contract, when that nine-year limit was reached, was objectively justified.

(iv) Directive 2008/104/EC on Temporary Agency Work and the Agency Workers Regulations 2010

3.53 As we have seen,[506] agency work was excluded from the scope of the Framework Agreement on Fixed-Term Work of 1999. Attempts to reach an agreement on a measure governing agency work through the social dialogue process had broken down by the spring of 2001, but the issue re-emerged in the mid-2000s as part of the 'flexicurity' debate.[507] A Directive of the Parliament and Council was adopted on 19 November 2008, to be brought into force in the Member States by 5 December 2011.

Article 5(1) of the Directive sets out a 'principle of equal treatment' in the following terms:

> ... [t]he basic working and employment conditions of temporary agency workers shall be, for the duration of their assignment at a user undertaking, at lease those that would apply if they had been recruited directly by that undertaking to occupy the same job.

The term 'basic working and employment conditions' is narrowly defined: it refers to provisions governing working time and pay which have been 'laid down by legislation, regulations, administrative provisions, collective agreements and/or other binding general provisions in force in the user undertaking'.[508] In addition, the Directive stipulates that the rules in force in the user undertaking on the protection of pregnant women, 'nursing mothers' and children and young people, as well those governing equal treatment on the grounds of sex, race or ethnic origin, religion, beliefs, disabilities, age or sexual orientation, must also be applied equally to agency workers.[509] Thus the equal treatment principle contained in the Directive creates a new right to equality in respect of pay and working time standards set out in collective agreements. As we shall see below, the implementing Regulations go beyond the requirements of the Directive by extending the right to equal treatment to terms and conditions whether or not they are derived from collective agreements or other sources specified in the Directive.

The term 'temporary agency worker' is defined in the Directive as 'a worker with a contract of employment or an employment relationship with a temporary-work agency with a view to being assigned to a user undertaking to work temporarily under its supervision and direction'.[510]

---

[505] [2011] IRLR 498 at [9].
[506] See above, para 3.52.
[507] See Barnard and Deakin, 2008; Countouris, 2009.
[508] Directive 2008/104, Art 3(1)(f).
[509] Directive 2008/104, Art 5(1).
[510] Directive 2008/104, Art 1(3)(c).

For reasons explored earlier in this chapter,[511] agency workers in the UK will rarely have a contract of employment with their agencies, although they will almost certainly have a contract of some kind, possibly a contract for services. Whether this situation fits the notion of 'contract of employment or employment relationship' is far from obvious. Some help is provided by the Directive's definition of 'worker' which refers to 'any person who, in the Member State concerned, is protected as a worker under national employment law'.[512] Arguably, agency workers who are not employees fall within the notion of workers protected by national employment law thanks to the various provisions which protect them as a specific category or as 'workers' in the sense of that term implied by British labour law legislation.

The Directive also sets out a number of possible derogations from the principle of equal treatment. First, Member States may, after consulting the social partners, provide for an exemption from the equal principle treatment as it applies to pay, in situations where agency workers 'who have a permanent contract of employment with a temporary-work agency continue to be paid in the time between assignments'.[513] Second, and more generally, Member States may grant the social partners, 'at the appropriate level' and subject to conditions which the Member States may lay down, the option of making collective agreements which depart from the principle of equal treatment 'while respecting the overall protection of temporary agency workers'.[514] Third, Member States, such as the UK, where 'there is either no system in law for declaring collective agreements universally applicable or ... for extending their provisions to all similar undertakings in a certain sector or geographical area', may 'after consulting the social partners at national level and on the basis of an agreement concluded by them' put in place arrangements which derogate from the principle of equal treatment. Such arrangements may make provision for a qualifying period and shall specify whether occupational social security schemes, including pension schemes, fall within the definition of 'basic working and employment conditions'. They must also ensure that 'an adequate level of protection is provided for temporary agency workers' and that the resulting measures are sufficiently clear and precise for the firms and sectors concerned to be able to identify and comply with their obligations.[515] The UK took up this third option. The CBI and TUC reached agreement in May 2008 on arrangements which included a 12-week qualifying period and the exclusion of occupational social security schemes from the definition of basic working and employment conditions, and this substance of this accord was then incorporated into the Agency Work Regulations 2010.[516]

In addition to providing for equal treatment of agency workers, the Directive stipulates that temporary workers should count towards thresholds governing the rights of worker representatives, with Member States having the choice of applying this principle either to the agency or to the user undertaking, or to both.[517] It provides that temporary workers should be informed of vacant posts in the user undertaking, and encourages social dialogue on the issue of temporary workers' access to training, among other things. [518] It also calls on Member

---

[511] See para 3.35 above.
[512] Directive 2008/104, Art 3(1)(a).
[513] Directive 2008/104, Art 5(2).
[514] Directive 2008/14, Art 5(3).
[515] Directive 2008/104, Art 5(4).
[516] *Agency Workers: Joint Declaration by the Government, the CBI and the TUC*, 20 May 2008.
[517] Directive 2008/104, Art 7.
[518] Directive 2008/104, Art 6(1), (5).

States to take measures to prevent circumvention of the Directive through the use of successive assignments.[519]

The Agency Workers Regulations 2010 implement the Directive, with effect from 1 October 2011. They define an agency worker as an individual 'supplied by a temporary work agency to work temporarily for and under the supervision and direction of a hirer' and who has either a contract of employment with the agency or 'any other contract with the agency to perform work or services personally'.[520] The Regulations go on to exclude cases where either the agency or hirer has a relationship with the worker which is that of a client or customer of a profession or business undertaking carried on by the individual,[521] while, conversely, including a range of cases where the individual is supplied to the hirer via one or more intermediaries.[522] A 'temporary work agency' is defined as a person engaged in the economic activity (which can be public or private, and operating for profit or otherwise) of 'supplying individuals to work temporarily for and under the supervision and direction of hirers' or 'paying for... the services of individuals who are supplied to work temporarily for and under the supervision and direction of hirers'.[523] The effect of this set of provisions is to cast the net widely when defining which of a number of entities engaged in the supply of labour to hirers counts as an agency; if successive intermediaries and others are involved, more than one may be constituted as an agency for the purposes of the Regulations. Finally, a hirer is defined as a person engaged in economic activity 'to whom individuals are supplied, to work temporarily for and under the supervision and direction of that person'.[524] This definition is noteworthy for not requiring a contract to have come into force between the hirer and the agency worker.

The core right provided for in the Regulations is the right of the agency worker to receive the 'basic working and employment conditions' that he or she would have received had they been recruited directly by the hirer at the start of the relevant qualifying period.[525] More precisely, an agency worker is entitled to receive the same terms and conditions as a 'comparable employee' working for and under the direction and supervision of the hirer in the same establishment and 'engaged in the same or broadly similar work having regard, where relevant, to whether they have a similar level of qualification and skills'.[526] If there is no comparable employee in the same establishment, an employee who is otherwise comparable but works or is based at a different establishment of the hirer will become the relevant comparator.[527] In a further set of clarifications, the terms and conditions which the agency worker is entitled to receive are those which would ordinarily be included in the contracts of employees of the hirer, if the agency worker would have been recruited as an employee, or in the contracts of workers of the hirer if the agency worker would have been recruited as a worker,[528] and which relate to a number of matters which are listed as pay, the duration of working time, night work, rest periods, rest breaks, and annual

---

[519] Directive 2008/104, Art 5(5).
[520] AWR 2010, reg 3(1).
[521] AWR 2010, reg 3(2).
[522] AWR 2010, reg 3(3)-(5).
[523] AWR 2010, reg 4.
[524] AWR 2010, reg 2.
[525] AWR 2010, reg 5(1).
[526] AWR 2010, reg 5(3), (4)
[527] AWR 2010, reg 5(4). See para 3.62 below, on the notion of 'establishment'.
[528] AWR 2010, reg 5(2).

leave.[529] Although the Directive's scope is confined to terms and conditions laid down in collective agreements in force in the undertaking of the hirer or derived from other specified sources, the Regulations apply to terms ordinarily included in the contracts of employees or workers employed by the hirer, whether or not they are derived from such sources.[530]

A major restriction on the scope of the Regulations is that the right to the terms and conditions specified do not apply until the agency worker has completed a qualifying period of 12 continuous calendar weeks 'in the same role'.[531] An agency worker is deemed to remain in the same role unless, in the new role, the relevant work or duties 'are substantively different from the work or duties that made up the whole or the main part of the previous role', and the agency has informed the worker in writing of the type of work that is required in the new role.[532] A further exclusion in relation to pay is made for agency workers who have a continuing or 'permanent' contract of employment with the agency and specified conditions are satisfied.[533] Rights in relation to access to collective facilities and amenities and to information about relevant vacancies are not subject to any qualifying period and so are available from 'day one'.[534]

The principal remedy for breach of the Regulations is a claim before an employment tribunal, which can make a declaration, order the payment of compensation, and/or make a recommendation of action to obviate or reduce the adverse impact on the complainant of the breach in question.[535] Compensation is such as the tribunal considers just and equitable having regard to the infringement or breach and any loss attributable to it and there is no limit on the amount which may be awarded. A further amount of up to £5,000 may be awarded where 'anti-avoidance' provisions are found to apply.[536] Liability for breach of 'day one' entitlements lies with the hirer; in relation to infringements relating to working and employment conditions liability lies with the agency or the hirer to the extent that they are responsible for the breach, although the agency can avoid liability where it took specified steps to obtain relevent information from the hirer and acted reasonably in applying it [537] The Regulations also contain procedures by which agency workers can obtain information about possible infringements of their rights; the tribunal may infer that rights have been infringed from a failure to provide information, or an evasive or equivocal response.[538]

The Regulations are complex and likely to be uncertain in their application until such time as a significant body of case law has been established. It remains to be seen how effective they will prove in ensuring equality of treatment for agency workers.

---

[529] AWR 2010, reg 6. 'Pay' means 'any sums payable to a worker of the hirer in connection with the worker's employment' such as bonuses and holiday pay, but specified payments and rewards are excluded: reg 6(2)-(4).

[530] AWR 2010, reg 5(2).

[531] AWR 2010, reg 7. Reg 7 also specifies circumstances in which weeks before and after breaks between assignments or during an assignment will be deemed to be 'continuous'. See also reg 9.

[532] See AWR 2010, reg 7(3).

[533] See AWR 2010, reg 10.

[534] AWR 2010, regs 12 and 13.

[535] AWR 2010, reg 18.

[536] See AWR 2010, reg 9, which, in broad terms, deems the agency worker to have completed the qualifying period but for assignments having been structured with the intention of preventing this.

[537] See AWR 2010, reg 14.

[538] AWR 2010, reg 16.

Part-time work and weekly hours thresholds

3.54   For statistical purposes the UK authorities count those working 30 hours or less as employed part-time: the numbers so employed have grown rapidly in the past 30 years, mainly in services, and currently constitute over 26% of the employed labour force, an increase from 19% in 1990 and 16% in 1979.[539] The 30-hour threshold does not carry any legal significance. However, until 1995, the relevant employment protection legislation contained qualifying thresholds which had the effect of potentially excluding certain part-time employees from the scope of employment protection legislation. The basic rule was that an employee had to be regularly employed for at least 16 hours per week for that week to count towards continuity. An exception was made for employees with five years' continuous employment with their employer, for whom an 8-hour threshold applied. Both the 8-hour and 16-hour thresholds were abolished in 1995,[540] following the decision of the House of Lords in *R v Secretary of State for Employment, ex p Equal Opportunities Commission*[541] that they contravened European Union law concerning equal treatment between male and female employees.

   Another significant threshold operated in social security law, by virtue of the lower earnings limit for national insurance contributions; it was estimated in the early 1990s that as many as 2.5 million part-time workers, or just over 10% of the employed labour force, received weekly earnings below this lower threshold, with the consequence that they were unable to build up the contributions record needed to claim social insurance benefits (including the contribution-based jobseeker's allowance and the state retirement pension).[542] To some extent the problem of part-time earnings outside the social insurance system has been addressed by changes to the structure of national insurance contributions introduced from the late 1990s, which mitigate the effect on net income of earnings rising above the lower earnings level.[543]

(i) Hourly thresholds and sex discrimination

3.55   The vast majority of part-time workers in Britain are women with domestic and family responsibilities, although the numbers of young, single men and women working part-time have increased in recent years. The clear link between part-time work and women's employment is legally significant, since it raises issues of sex discrimination under both domestic and European Union law. Unequal treatment of part-time workers may constitute indirect sex discrimination by virtue of the fact that any exclusion of part-timers is likely to affect far more women than men

---

[539] For data relating to the autumn of 2008, see *Economic and Labour Market Review*, December 2008, 'Labour Market Statistics', Table 2.03; for the earlier periods, see Labour Force Survey figures, reported in Deakin and Reed, 2001b, Table 4; Bell, 2011.

[540] SI 1995/31.

[541] [1994] IRLR 176.

[542] See L Dickens, 1992: p 27; and, for a more recent discussion, Fredman, 2004b.

[543] Because contributions became payable on all earnings including those below the threshold (although at a lower rate) once the lower earnings level was reached, there was a disincentive to raise earnings to that point. From 1999, a new system of national insurance contributions came into force under which contributions were payable only on earnings above the threshold. See Deakin and Wilkinson, 2005: p 189.

within the relevant group. This has been recognised by English courts and by the Court of Justice.[544] Following the *Barber* judgment of the ECJ which extended the concept of 'pay' under what is now Article 157 TFEU to include certain statutory payments made by employers,[545] a challenge to the 8 and 16-hours thresholds under employment protection legislation became possible. The central question was whether the thresholds could be supported by a justification defence of some kind, such a defence in principle being available in claims of indirect discrimination.

In *R v Secretary of State for Employment, ex p Equal Opportunities Commission*[546] the Equal Opportunities Commission launched a challenge to the legislation by way of proceedings for judicial review against the Secretary of State for Employment, and this eventually succeeded in the House of Lords. A declaration was granted to the effect that the thresholds for redundancy were contrary both to Article 119 and to the Equal Treatment Directive (76/207), and that those for unfair dismissal were contrary to the Directive.[547] Both sides in *Ex p EOC* accepted that a *prima facie* case of indirect discrimination arose, by virtue of the fact that the overwhelming proportion of part-time workers in the UK are female. On the issue of justification, Lord Keith accepted that the promotion of job opportunities was an appropriate goal for employment legislation, but concluded that an affidavit from a Department of Employment official did not contain 'anything capable of being regarded as factual evidence' in support of the Department's contentions. Nor had the Secretary of State attempted to argue that the 16-hour threshold was justified by the administrative burden involved with providing protection for part-timers on very short hours. A statutory instrument subsequently repealed all the relevant hours thresholds contained in the Employment Protection (Consolidation) Act 1978 (the predecessor of ERA 1996) and in TULRCA 1992.[548] However, the lower earnings limit for national insurance purposes was unaffected by this process, and it is still the case that qualification for statutory sick pay and statutory maternity pay depends on the employee having had regular weekly earnings at or above this level. As a result, part-time employment continues to be excluded from certain forms of protective legislation.

(ii) Access to occupational pension schemes

3.56   Inequality between part-time work and full-time work is not confined to the issue of statutory hours thresholds; similar thresholds may operate at the level of occupational benefits provided by employers. Benefits provided by occupational pension schemes fall under the definition of 'pay' in Article 157 TFEU (formerly Article 119 of the Treaty of Rome and Article 141 TEC),[549] and the exclusion of part-time workers from access to these schemes may, as a

---

[544] See, in particular, Case 96/80 *Jenkins v Kingsgate (Clothing Productions) Ltd* [1981] ICR 592, ECJ; *Clarke v Eley (IMI) Kynoch Ltd* [1983] ICR 165, EAT; Case 170/84 *Bilka-Kaufhaus GmbH v Weber von Hartz* [1986] IRLR 317; Case 171/88 *Rinner-Kühn v FWW Spezial Gebäudereinigung GmbH & Co Kg* [1989] ECR 2743.

[545] Case C-262/88 *Barber v Guardian Royal Exchange Assurance Group plc* [1990] ECR I-1889.

[546] [1991] IRLR 493, DC; affd [1993] IRLR 10, CA; on appeal [1994] IRLR 176, HL; Deakin, 1994a.

[547] In his judgment in *Ex p EOC*, Lord Keith considered that it was not necessary to decide whether the unfair dismissal threshold infringed Art 119 as well as Directive 76/307, but once the general question of justification was resolved in favour of the EOC his reasoning could be read as extending to Art 119 as well (see *Mediguard Services Ltd v Thame* [1994] IRLR 504).

[548] SI 1995/31.

[549] Case C-262/88 *Barber v Guardian Royal Exchange Assurance Group plc* [1990] ECR I-1889.

consequence, amount to unlawful sex discrimination. In its judgment in *Vroege*,[550] the ECJ ruled that the bar on 'retrospective' claims under the *Barber* judgment did not apply to rights of access to schemes (as opposed to rights to equality in respect of benefits paid out). However, separate time limits applied in *domestic* law by virtue of the Equal Pay Act 1970 and the question of whether these time limits placed a bar on actions being brought in respect of exclusions dating back more than two years gave rise to a highly complex body of case law.[551] In *Magorrian and Cunningham v Eastern Health and Social Services Board*,[552] the Court, on a reference from Northern Ireland, held that such a limitation would be contrary to EU law, on the ground that it would render ineffective, in practice, the exercise of Community law rights under what was then Article 141 EC. Since the Northern Irish legislation was very similar to the equivalent statute governing the rest of the United Kingdom, it was open to the British courts to declare the domestic time limits invalid at that point; however, in *Preston v Wolverhampton Healthcare NHS Trust*[553] the House of Lords decided instead to refer a number of outstanding questions to the ECJ by way of a preliminary ruling. The Court again confirmed that the two-year limitation was contrary to the principle that rights under Article 157 (as it now is) should be effective, but noted that workers applying to join pension schemes with retrospective effect would not have the right to avoid paying contributions for the periods in question.[554]

(iii) Further applications of the principle of non-discrimination on the grounds of sex: equality of pay; seniority; the right to work part-time

3.57 Part-time work is associated with lower than average levels of hourly pay: there is a clear differential across the whole economy between part-time and full-time earnings, even allowing for the existence of a gap between female and male earnings in general.[555] Inequality of pay also arises from the limited access of part-time workers to fringe benefits and from their lack of entitlement to overtime premia, shift rates and paid leave (all of which tend to be calculated on the basis that a full-time working week of between 35 and 40 hours is the norm).[556] To some extent, these forms of differential treatment can be challenged through the means provided by EqA 2010, which enables a female part-time worker to claim equality of hourly pay with a male worker who is an appropriate comparator within the meaning of the 2010 Act, whether full-time or part-time, if she can show that he is employed either on like work, work rated as equivalent, or work of equal value to hers.[557] That she works part-time and he works full-time is unlikely, in itself, to provide grounds for a finding that they are not employed on like work or work of equal value; nor will

---

[550] Case C-57/93 *Vroege v NCIV Instituut voor Volkshuisvesting BV* [1994] IRLR 651. See also Case C-435/93 *Dietz v Stichting Thuiszorg Rotterdam* [1996] IRLR 692.

[551] See *Vroege*, where the relevant cases are discussed.

552 Case C-246/96 [1998] IRLR 86.

[553] [1998] IRLR 197. See further paras 6.100 *et seq* below.

[554] Case C-78/98 [2000] IRLR 506, applied by the HL in *Preston v Wolverhampton Healthcare NHS Trust (No 2)* [2001] IRLR 237. See below, paras 6.103–6.104.

[555] See generally Equal Opportunities Commission, *Facts about Women and Men in Britain* (2005); M Bell, 2011, pp 266-269 and references therein.

[556] See L Dickens, 1992a; Horrell, Rubery and Burchell, 1989.

[557] EqA 2010, s 65. See below, paras 6.88-6.94.

such a difference in itself provide an employer with the defence of material factor.[558] However, the limitations on claims under EqA 2010 should also be borne in mind (particularly the need for an applicant to find a male comparator who is employed by her employer at the same establishment or at an establishment covered by common terms and conditions of employment[559]).

In the context of redundancy, the EAT has held that the selection of part-timers for dismissal ahead of full-timers gave rise to a prima facie case of indirect sex discrimination, which in the circumstances could not be justified.[560] A more difficult question concerns the principle of 'last in, first out' (LIFO) in redundancy selection. This could give rise to adverse impact against women, on the grounds that because women workers are more likely than men to take career breaks for family or related reasons, they may not have comparable seniority to men and so are more likely to be selected for redundancy where LIFO is applied. The EAT left open the possibility that LIFO or a similar seniority principle might provide the basis for a justification defence in these circumstances.[561]

In other respects, the ECJ has strictly applied the equality principle to claims that part-time workers should not be granted equal seniority rights to those working full time. The effect of its rulings in *Kording*[562] and *Gerster*[563] are that periods of part-time employment should be counted equally with periods of full-time employment when computing length of service for the purposes of access to promotion or occupational qualification, unless objective reasons can be found for doing otherwise. *Gerster* concerned civil service regulations which stated that for promotion purposes, periods of employment under half normal working hours were not to be counted at all; hours between a half and two-thirds of normal time were to be counted at the rate of two-thirds; and hours which were two thirds or more of the norm were to be counted in the same way as full-time hours. In *Kording*, the applicant, who was employed for half normal working hours, was required to have fifteen years of service in order to be exempt from an examination in order to qualify as a tax consultant; the employer argued that her periods of employment should only be counted *pro rata* according to the hours she actually worked. In each case, the Court held that because of the association of part-time employment with female work, there was a prima facie case of indirect discrimination, and that the seniority rules could only be defended if the employer was able to show that they were objectively justified. This meant, for example, that the employer would have to demonstrate 'that part-time employees are generally slower than full-time employees in acquiring job-related abilities and skills'.[564]

This effects-orientated approach can be contrasted with the Court's earlier decision in *Stadt Lengerich v Helmig*,[565] where the court rejected an argument to the effect that it was discriminatory for an employer to confine overtime premia to employees working a full-time week. Although such a practice arguably disadvantages part-timers in the same way as the seniority rules in *Kording* and *Gerster*, the Court concluded that 'part-time employees do receive the same overall pay as

[558] Case 96/80 *Jenkins v Kingsgate (Clothing Productions) Ltd* [1981] ICR 592, ECJ.
[559] EqA 2010, s 79; see paras 6.82–6.84 below.
[560] *Clarke v Eley (IMI) Kynoch Ltd* [1983] ICR 165.
[561] *Clarke v Eley (IMI) Kynoch Ltd* [1983] ICR 165. On length of service and age discrimination see para 6.43 below.
[562] Case C-100/95 *Kording v Senator für Finanzen* [1997] IRLR 710.
[563] Case C-1/95 *Gerster v Freistaat Bayern* [1997] IRLR 699.
[564] Case C-1/95 *Gerster v Freistaat Bayern* [1997] IRLR 699, 709; see also Case C-77/02 *Steinicke v Bundesanstalt für Arbeit* [2003] IRLR 892.
[565] Cases C-399, 409, 425/92, 34, 50, 78/93 [1995] IRLR 216.

full-time employees for the same number of hours worked'.[566] By contrast, in *Elsner-Lakeberg v Land Nordrhein-Westfalen*[567] the ECJ held that a practice under which teachers received additional remuneration for extra hours worked above a minimum threshold of three hours per month discriminated against part-time workers, since the threshold was more difficult for them to surmount.

A further question is whether an employee who normally works full-time has the *right* to work part-time if, for reasons related to family or domestic responsibilities or for some other reason, it is impractical for them to work full-time for a period. In general the individual employee has no right to have his or her contract terms varied to suit their changing circumstances, but an issue of sex discrimination can be seen to be involved if women employees, who are more likely than men to have family responsibilities, are not provided with a degree of flexibility in their working time arrangements. A series of decisions which are considered in greater detail in chapter 6 illustrate that it is not necessarily a straightforward matter to establish 'particular disadvantage' or a *prima facie* finding of indirect discrimination, and that even if this can be shown there is still the possibility of the employer invoking a justification defence.[568] To some extent, however, the issue has been resolved in favour of the employee, by the enactment of a statutory right to request flexible working to look after a child for which he or she is responsible.[569]

(iv) Directive 97/81EC Concerning the Framework Agreement on Part-Time Work concluded by ETUC, UNICE and CEEP and the Part-Time Workers (Prevention of Less Favourable Treatment) Regulations 2000

3.58   Numerous proposals have been advanced by the European Commission since the early 1980s for the adoption of measures to ensure greater parity of treatment between part-time and full-time workers. The principle of equal treatment in respect of terms and conditions of employment and the application of statutory employment protection is recognised in most other European systems.[570] However, the embodiment of this principle in an EC directive was for many years prevented by the consistent opposition of the British government, on the grounds that regulation of this kind would add to costs and inhibit job creation.[571]

In 1997 a Directive on part-time work was finally agreed.[572] The Directive incorporates a Framework Agreement between the social partners which was made under the social dialogue procedure of the Maastricht Agreement on Social Policy. The Agreement, while formally adopting a principle of equal treatment between part-time and full-time workers, allows for some significant exceptions, and envisages the use of deregulatory measures to encourage part-time work.

---

[566] [1995] IRLR 216, 223.

[567] Case C-285/02, [2005] IRLR 209.

[568] *Home Office v Holmes* [1984] IRLR 299; *Kidd v DRG (UK) Ltd* [1985] ICR 405; *Clymo v Wandsworth London Borough Council* [1989] IRLR 241; see below, paras 6.25 *et seq.*

[569] ERA 1996, s 80F; see ch 6, below, at para 6.122.

[570] Eg, French Code du Travail, Article L 212-4-2.

[571] See the statement of Secretary of State for Employment, Michael Portillo MP, HC Debs, 6th series, Vol 251, Written Answers, 20 December 1994, at cols 1100–1101. An account of the various draft directives in this area is contained in Hepple, 1990a.

[572] Directive 97/81 on part-time work. See OJ 1998 L14/9.

Under clause 2(1), the Agreement covers part-time workers with an employment contract or employment relationship as defined by the relevant law, collective agreement or practice of the Member State; in addition, the Member State is permitted under clause 2(2) to exclude certain casual workers from the coverage of the Agreement, 'for objective reasons' and after consulting the social partners and acting in accordance with national law, collective agreements or practice. In *Wippel* the ECJ held that, under these provisions, a part-time worker employed under a 'framework contract' with no set hours (akin to a 'zero-hours contract') was covered by the Agreement if she satisfied the requirement of national law for the existence of an employment contract or relationship, and did not fall under a derogation made by the Member State under clause 2(2).[573]

Clause 1 of the Agreement states that it aims 'to provide for the removal of discrimination against part-time workers and to improve the quality of part-time work', and 'to facilitate the development of part-time work on a voluntary basis and to contribute to the flexible organisation of working time in a manner which takes into account the needs of employers and workers'.[574] To achieve these ends, it stipulates in clause 4 that 'in respect of employment conditions, part-time workers shall not be treated in a less favourable manner than comparable full-time workers solely because they work part time unless different treatment is justified on objective grounds'.[575]

For this purpose, a part-time worker is defined as 'an employee whose normal hours of work, calculated on a weekly basis or on average over a period of employment of up to one year, are less than the normal hours of work of a comparable full-time worker', while a comparable full-time worker is 'a full-time worker in the same establishment having the same type of employment contract or relationship, who is engaged in the same or similar work/ occupation, due regard being given to other considerations which may include seniority and qualifications/skills'. Where there is no comparable full-time worker in the establishment, comparison may be made by reference to an applicable collective agreement or, if there is no such agreement, in accordance with national law, collective agreements or practice.[576]

The Agreement goes on to state that in judging whether there is less favourable treatment, 'where appropriate, the principle of *pro rata temporis* shall apply'.[577] As we have just seen in our discussion of the seniority cases, the application of the pro rata principle, in this context, could be seen as having an indirectly discriminatory effect. The Framework Agreement also permits Member States and/or the social partners in appropriate cases to 'make access to particular conditions of employment subject to a period of service, time worked or earnings qualification'.[578] This is conditional upon the exemption being justified by objective grounds.

In *Wippel*[579] the ECJ held that clause 4 of the Agreement did not invalidate national legislation which set a maximum working week for full-timers 'which is by definition greater than that for part-time work',[580] nor did it invalidate an open-ended 'framework' or zero-hours contract which the applicant had entered into with her employer. The main obstacle facing the applicant in this

---

[573] Case C-313/02 *Wippel v Peek & Cloppenburg GmbH & Co KG* [2005] IRLR 211.

[574] Framework Agreement on Part Time Work, cl 1.

[575] Framework Agreement on Part Time Work, cl 4(1). See Case C-486/08 *Zentralbetriebsrat des Landeskrankenhaüser Tirols v Land Tirol* [2010] IRLR 631 and Joined Cases C-395/08 and C-396/08, *INPS v Bruno and Lotti* [2010] IRLR 890, both giving a broad reading to this provision.

[576] Framework Agreement on Part Time Work, cl 3.

[577] Framework Agreement on Part Time Work, cl 4(2).

[578] Framework Agreement on Part Time Work, cl 4(4).

[579] Case C-313/02 *Wippel v Peek & Cloppenburg GmbH & Co KG* [2005] IRLR 211.

[580] *Wippel*, Judgment, at para 49.

case, according to the Court, was that there was no full-time worker, either in or beyond the establishment, whose position was comparable to hers,[581] a ruling which illustrates the limited scope of the Agreement.

The other main substantive provision of the Agreement is concerned with promoting opportunities for part-time work. Clause 5(1) calls on Member States and the social partners to identify and review potential obstacles to part-time work and, where appropriate, to eliminate them. On the face of it, this measure could be used to justify a degree of deregulation, and this is also hinted at by a further provision which states:

> Implementation of the provisions of this Agreement shall not constitute valid grounds for reducing the general level of protection afforded to workers in the field of this agreement. This does not prejudice the right of Member States and/or social partners to develop different legislative, regulatory or contractual provisions, in the light of changing circumstances, and does not prejudice the application of clause 5.1 as long as the principle of non-discrimination in clause 4.1 is complied with.[582]

Much turns, then, on how clauses 5(1) and 4(1) are to be reconciled by the Member States.

The Agreement also provides that a worker's refusal to transfer from full-time to part-time work or vice versa is not in itself to constitute a valid ground for dismissal (although without prejudice to 'other reasons such as may arise from the operational requirements of the establishment concerned');[583] conversely, employers are required to give consideration to a number of matters including requests for such transfers by workers, the provision of information on the availability of part-time and full-time positions in the establishment, facilitating access to part-time work at all levels of the enterprise 'including skilled and managerial positions' where appropriate; facilitating access of part-time workers to 'vocational training to enhance career prospects and occupational mobility'; and providing information about part-time working to workforce representatives.[584]

The Agreement was brought into effect in UK law by the Part-Time Workers (Prevention of Less Favourable Treatment) Regulations 2000.[585] The Regulations address the central issue of comparability between part-time and full-time workers in a highly detailed and complex way.[586] A full-time worker is defined as one who 'is paid wholly or in part by reference to the time he works and, having regard to the custom and practice of the employer in relation to workers employed by the worker's employer under the same type of contract, is identifiable as a full-time worker'. A part-time worker is one who is not identifiable as a 'full-time worker' in the same way.[587] For a

---

[581] *Wippel*, Judgment, at para 66 (and reaching the same conclusion with regard to a claim under Art 5 of the Equal Treatment Directive).

[582] Directive 97/81, Framework Agreement on Part Time Work, clause 6(2). Note also clause 6(1) which states that Member States and/or the social partners 'may maintain or introduce more favourable provisions than set out in this agreement'.

[583] Framework Agreement on Part Time Work, cl 5(2).

[584] Framework Agreement on Part Time Work, cl 5(3).

[585] PTWR 2000: SI 2000/1551. See McColgan, 2000a; M Bell, 2011.

[586] PTWR, 2000 reg 2.

[587] For these purposes, the term 'worker' bears the same meaning as it does under the more general labour law provisions discussed in para 3.33 above. See PTWR 2000, reg 1. In *O'Brien v Ministry of Justice* [2010] IRLR 883 the Supreme Court referred to the CJEU the question of whether a recorder (the holder of a part-time judicial office), who was excluded from the coverage of the Regulations by virtue of PTWR 2000, reg 17, fell under the protection of the Directive. See Case C-393/10 *O'Brien v Ministry of Justice* [2012] IRLR 421, CJEU.

part-time worker to be able to compare his or her position with that of a full-time worker, it must be shown that both workers are employed by the same employer under the same 'type of contract'; that they are engaged 'in the same or broadly similar work having regard, where relevant, to whether they have a similar level of qualification, skills and experience'; and that they work at the same establishment, unless there are no comparable full-time workers employed at the applicant's establishment, in which case employment at another establishment of the employer will suffice. Regulation 2(3) sets out a number of different 'types of contract'. This provision appears to envisage three principal, mutually exclusive contract types, namely a contract of employment, a contract for services, and a contract of apprenticeship,[588] with provision also being made for a residual category consisting of types giving rise to 'any other description of worker that it is reasonable for the employer to treat differently from other workers on the ground that workers of that description have a different type of contract.' In *Matthews v Kent and Medway Towns Fire Authority*[589] the House of Lords held that 'retained' or on-call firefighters were not employed on a different 'type' of contract from their full-time comparators within the meaning of this provision.

The applicant can compare his or her position to that of a hypothetical comparator in only two situations: first, where he or she has moved from full-time to part-time work and, second, where he or she returns to part-time work after absence from work of less than one year. Then, the claim can be made 'as if there were a comparable full-time worker' employed under the terms that applied to the applicant before his or her contract was varied or, in the case of returning to work, under the terms of the contract they had before the period of absence commenced.[590]

The content of the right to equal treatment is described in regulation 5. A part-time worker must not be treated less equally either 'as regards the terms of his contract' or 'by being subjected to any other detriment by any act, or deliberate failure to act, of his employer'. The treatment must be 'on the ground that the worker is a part-time worker'.[591] There is some authority at EAT level to suggest that the employer must 'intend' to discriminate on the basis of part-time work, and that the 'but-for' test which applies elsewhere in employment discrimination cases is not applicable here;[592] but this proposition, for which no authority is present in the Regulations themselves, is yet to receive sustained consideration.[593] The right to equal treatment applies only if the treatment is not justified on objective grounds. The pro-rata principle is to be applied 'unless it is inappropriate'. It is also made clear that part-time workers are not be entitled to receive overtime premia unless they have worked full-time, normal hours.

A part-time worker has the right to receive from the employer a statement of reasons for being treated less favourably. The main remedy for breach of the Regulations is a complaint to an

---

[588] Fixed-term employment contracts were a further, separate category in the initial version of reg 2(3), but were removed by FTER 2002.

[589] [2006] IRLR 367. The House also held that the applicants were employed on 'the same or broadly similar work' to that of their full-time colleagues, allowing a comparison of their terms and conditions of employment to proceed.

[590] PTWR 2000, regs 3 and 4. See *Carl v The University of Sheffield* [2009] IRLR 616, EAT

[591] Part-time status must be a reason, but need not be the only reason, for the employer's action: *Sharma v Manchester City Council* [2008] IRLR 336.

[592] See para 6.19 below.

[593] The principal authority for the view that the employer must intend to discriminate on the grounds of the employee's part-time status is an unreported EAT decision, *Gibson v Scottish Ambulance Service*, EATS/0052/04, which was applied without substantive discussion in *McMenemy v Capita Business Services Ltd* [2007] IRLR 400. Cf *Sharma*, above, note 591 at [58] and the discussion in M Bell, 2011: pp 261-262.

employment tribunal that the worker has suffered a detriment.[594] Workers who are also employees can bring a claim for unfair dismissal under specified circumstances of victimisation, for which no qualifying period is needed.[595]

The requirement of an actual comparator (for all but a few cases) is at odds with the approach under equal treatment law more generally.[596] McColgan suggests that 'the comparator problem is so overwhelming as to render the [Regulations] largely irrelevant to the vast majority of part-time workers'.[597] Figures produced by the government during the consultation process indicated that only one sixth of the 6 million part-time workers in the UK would find a comparator within the meaning of the Regulations, and that only around 400,000 individuals would be likely to benefit directly from the equal treatment principle.[598] Unlike the relevant principles of British and EU equality law, the Regulations do not protect applicants for employment. Nor do they confer any rights on full-time workers, so missing the opportunity to provide for a more extensive right to transfer from full-time to part-time work. For these reasons, and because of limitations in the remedial structure of the Regulations, it seems likely that claims will continue to be brought under the general provisions of sex equality law.[599]

Establishing continuity: the significance of the contract

3.59   Continuity is defined for the purposes of ERA 1996 by Part XIV, Chapter I of that Act, and broadly analogous (although not identical) provisions are contained in other relevant regulations.[600] At least formally, these texts override the contract of employment as the source of continuity.[601] Thus continuity may be maintained across a number of separate contracts, as long as the requirements of the Act are met: 'even though a man may change his job from, say, manual work to clerical work, even though he may change the site of his work from one place to another, even though he may change the terms of his contract of employment and enter into a new contract of employment, as long as he is with the same employer all the way through, then it is continuous employment'.[602] The accumulation of continuity is not a matter for bargaining for employer and employee,[603] and any agreement to waive continuity would be void under section 203 of ERA 1996. There is also a presumption that employment 'during any period' is continuous unless the contrary is shown;[604] in effect the employer has the onus of disproving continuity.

---

[594] If the claim is upheld, the employment tribunal may make a declaration of rights, order compensation, or issue a recommendation to the employer: PTWR 2000, reg 8(7).

[595] PTWR 2000, reg 7.

[596] See ch 6 below.

[597] McColgan, 2000a: p 266.

[598] McColgan, 2000a: p 263.

[599] McColgan, 2000a: p 267.

[600] See, eg, those governing SMP (SI 1986/1960, regs 11–16) and SPP (SI 2002/2822, regs 33–38).

[601] *Collison v BBC* [1998] IRLR 238; *Carrington v Harwich Dock Co Ltd* [1998] IRLR 567; *Sweeney v J & S Henderson (Concessions) Ltd* [1999] IRLR 306 (casting doubt on *Roach v CSB (Moulds) Ltd* [1991] IRLR 200); see Anderman, 2000: pp 235–237.

[602] *Wood v York County Council* [1978] IRLR 228, 229 (Lord Denning MR).

[603] *Hanson v Fashion Industries (Hartlepool) Ltd* [1980] IRLR 393; *Jennings v Salford Community Service Agency* [1981] IRLR 76; *Morris v Walsh Western UK Ltd* [1997] IRLR 562; *Bradford Metropolitan District Council v Dawson* [1999] ICR 312.

[604] ERA 1996, s 210(5).

Nevertheless, the Act defines continuity in such a way that it *is* dependent in practice on the express and implied terms of the contract of employment, and only in exceptional cases can it be acquired and maintained without reference to the contract terms. Under Chapter I of Part XIV, the basic unit of continuous employment is the working week. With one major exception,[605] any week which does not count towards a qualifying period also breaks continuity,[606] so cancelling out accrued periods of continuous employment. In *Booth v United States of America*,[607] the employer sought to avoid the accrual of an employee's continuity of employment by following a practice of inserting regular two-week gaps in between successive fixed-term contracts. The EAT found that continuity had indeed been broken.

As a result of the amendments introduced in 1995 following the judgment of the House of Lords in *Ex p EOC*,[608] the basic rule is that 'any week during the whole or part of which an employee's relations with his employer are governed by a contract of employment counts in computing the employee's period of employment'.[609] This replaces a complex set of provisions which previously required the employee to show that he or she was either actually employed for 16 hours or more in a given week, or employed for any part of it under a contract of employment which normally involved employment for 16 or more hours per week. The courts are no longer required to explore the question of whether a period of work was part of an employee's normal contractual hours.[610]

Pre-1995 case law may still be relevant, however, in a second type of situation which arises where there are periodic gaps in the provision of work by the employer to the employee. Where the work is discontinuous, it may be possible to discover, through construction, a global or umbrella contract of employment. Alternatively, it could be that each separate period of work is carried out under a separate contract of employment, which, following the 1995 amendments, will enable the week in question to be counted. However, it could also be the case that all or some of the separate hirings are for contracts for services, in which case continuity cannot be established.

In *Hellyer Bros Ltd v McLeod*[611] claims for redundancy compensation were made by a number of deep sea trawlermen whose employers had withdrawn their fleets from service following a decline in fishing stocks. In each case the applicant had worked exclusively for the employer over periods amounting to several decades. They were employed on a series of crew agreements which lasted for the duration of each voyage; in between voyages, the men claimed unemployment benefit. They regarded themselves as bound to their respective employers and did not miss a voyage without their permission; the employers also provided equipment and operated holiday pay and pension schemes. As fishing stocks declined the gaps between voyages grew longer until the employers decided not to fish any further.

The employment tribunal found that the men had each been employed under a global contract of employment and that they therefore had sufficient continuity to bring a claim in redundancy,

---

[605] This concerns weeks lost through strikes and lock-outs. Such weeks do not count towards the qualifying period but do not cancel out accrued periods of continuity either: ERA 1996, s 216. Other exceptions are contained in ss 215 and 217.

[606] ERA 1996, s 210(4).

[607] [1999] IRLR 16.

[608] [1994] IRLR 176; SI 1995/31. See above, para 3.55.

[609] ERA 1996, s 212(1).

[610] *Parkes Classic Confectionery v Ashcroft* (1973) 8 ITR 43; *Dean v Eastbourne Fishermen's Society* [1977] ICR 556; *Lake v Essex County Council* [1979] ICR 577; *Letheby & Christopher Ltd v Bond* [1988] ICR 480.

[611] [1987] ICR 526.

but the EAT reversed this ruling, and its judgment was upheld by the Court of Appeal. The Court found insufficient evidence of mutual commitments to offer work and to accept it: 'we do not see how it is possible to infer from the parties' conduct the existence in between crew agreements of a trawlerman's obligation *to serve*, which is part of the "irreducible minimum of obligation" on the part of the employee required to support the existence of a contract of service'.[612]

The decision in *Hellyer* turns on its own rather distinctive facts, but it is unsatisfactory that the issue of redundancy entitlement under statute should have turned on such a narrow and debatable construction of the particular contractual arrangements in that case, not least because mutual obligations were implied by other courts in cases with not dissimilar facts.[613] However, the 1995 amendments at least overcame the situation which arose in *Surrey County Council v Lewis*,[614] whereby an employee with a series of separate but overlapping contracts of employment with the same employer failed to establish continuity for the reason that she could not aggregate the hours worked under the separate arrangements. With the abolition of the hours threshold, it is simply necessary to show that the employee was employed under a contract of employment for any *part* of the week in question. This principle was applied in *Cornwall County Council v Prater*,[615] a decision which suggests that employees with intermittent work relationships may be able to establish continuity of employment even in a situation where they do not have 'global' or 'umbrella' contracts of employment. As long as there is sufficient mutuality of obligation for there to be contracts of employment in place during individual hirings, the periods spent in work will count towards continuity; periods between hirings may then be counted in by virtue of one of the exceptions to the normal rule requiring a contact which are set out in section 212 of the Act.[616]

Establishing continuity outside the contract

3.60 Section 212(3) of ERA 1996 provides for continuity to be preserved in certain limited circumstances where no contract of employment is in force between the parties.[617] These are periods of incapability through sickness or injury, up to a maximum of 26 weeks;[618] absence 'on

---

[612] [1987] ICR 526, 549 (Slade LJ).

[613] *Boyd Line Ltd v Pitts* [1986] ICR 244 (trawler captain); *Nethermere (St Neots) Ltd v Taverna and Gardiner* [1983] ICR 319 (homeworkers).

[614] [1987] 3 All ER 641.

[615] [2006] IRLR 362.

[616] See para 3.60 below.

[617] This is the effect of the heading to the paragraph, 'periods in which there is no contract of employment', as interpreted by Lord Diplock in *Ford v Warwickshire County Council* [1983] IRLR 126. Cf Lord Upjohn in *Fitzgerald v Hall, Russell & Co* [1970] AC 984, 1000: 'Counsel on neither side was able to give it any sensible meaning ... I propose for the purpose of construing the [Act] to ignore that cross-heading'.

[618] ERA 1996, s 212(3)(a), (4). Incapability for work is defined by reference to the work which the employee was employed to do before the period of absence began and, if it is different, to the work which he is employed to do subsequently: *Pearson v Kent County Council* [1993] IRLR 165; *Donnelly v Kelvin International Services* [1992] IRLR 496.

account of a temporary cessation of work';[619] and absence in circumstances such that the worker is regarded as a matter of custom or arrangement as continuing in employment.[620]

Section 212 has no application to a week in which there *is* a contract of employment in force. Until 1995 this posed a problem in cases of job-sharing where two employees would work alternate weeks; the employee's week off would break continuity under the Act since it would prevent him or her from reaching the weekly hours threshold of 8 or 16 as the case might be, but nor could the week be counted under the predecessor of section 212 since the contract of employment had not come to an end.[621] However, with the removal of the 8- and 16-hour thresholds, this problem has been solved: the week off will now count under section 212(1) of ERA 1996, since it is a week in which the employee is employed under a contract of employment.

In the cases where section 212 does apply, it can be read as giving statutory recognition to certain extra-contractual expectations of the employee. Continuity, the foundation of statutory rights, may remain in force notwithstanding the employer's termination of the contract of employment. One effect, as Lord Upjohn put it in *Fitzgerald v Hall, Russell & Co*,[622] is that 'a previous contract of employment which has been terminated may be relevant in computing the period of employment', while in *Ford v Warwickshire County Council*[623] Lord Diplock said that it was among the provisions which take 'the relationship between employer and employee out of the field of contract and into that of status'. It follows that the question of whether there is a 'temporary cessation of work' or a 'customary absence' should not be decided primarily by reference to the contract.

Ford illustrates this principle. The employee was employed as a lecturer on a series of fixed-term contracts spanning the academic year from September to July; for the summer months in between contracts she was not employed by the Council. The House of Lords held that the gaps between work could be counted under the forerunner to section 212(3)(b) on the grounds that the employee's absence was caused by a temporary cessation of work. It was irrelevant that the contracts themselves provided for the absence by setting a fixed term for their duration or that the applicant's expectations of a renewal of her contract 'had never hardened into an enforceable obligation':[624] what mattered was the *substantive reason* for the break, and not the *form* it was given in the contract.[625]

---

[619] ERA 1996, s 212(3)(b); see below.

[620] ERA 1996, s 212(3)(c). This may apply to situations of lay-off for lack of work (*Puttick v John Wright & Sons (Blackwall) Ltd* [1972] ICR 457) and to the lending or secondment of an employee to another employer (*Wishart v National Coal Board* [1974] ICR 460), but its scope is limited; it is not clear whether it could have had any application in *Hellyer Bros Ltd v McLeod* [1987] ICR 526, where it was not argued. In *Booth v United States of America* [1999] IRLR 16 the EAT rejected a suggestion that it could be invoked to deal with regular fortnightly gaps between fixed-term contracts which were adopted by the employer in order to avoid the accrual of continuity of employment, and in *Curr v Marks & Spencer plc* [2003] IRLR 74 it was held not to cover a situation of a 'child break scheme' lasting several years (but cf the opposite outcome in *Unwin v Barclays Bank plc*, EAT, 26 February 2003, Appeal No EAT/0273/02). Quaere whether an 'arrangement' needs to be in place before the gap: see *London Probation Board v Kirkpatrick* [2005] IRLR 443.

[621] The decision to the contrary in *Lloyds Bank Ltd v Secretary of State for Employment* [1979] ICR 258, applying the provision which is now contained in ERA s 212(3)(c), appeared to be wrong in the light of Lord Diplock's opinion in *Ford v Warwickshire County Council* [1983] IRLR 126; see also *Corton House Ltd v Skipper* [1981] IRLR 78, anticipating *Ford*.

[622] [1970] AC 984, 1001.

[623] [1983] IRLR 126, 128.

[624] The phrase used by Stephenson LJ in the Court of Appeal: [1982] ICR 520.

[625] To similar effect is the recent decision of the EAT in *Hussain v Acorn Independent College Ltd.* [2011] IRLR 463.

The court had to examine the substantive reason for the absence, in Lord Diplock's view, since the termination of the fixed-term contract amounted to a dismissal[626] for which the employer would normally have to show a potentially fair reason if it was to avoid a finding of unfair dismissal. This is not a very good argument since there may be cases in which an employee does not, at the time of the dismissal, have the necessary qualifying service to bring an unfair dismissal claim. The better view is probably that there can be a 'cessation of work' within the meaning of section 212(3)(b) whether or not the employer contemplated it at the time of contracting. But whatever the precise reason, it is clear that the form of the contract – whether it is fixed-term or for an indefinite duration – is irrelevant in this context.[627]

It is the *cessation of work* and not the *absence* which must be temporary; this means that continuity will be maintained until such time as the cessation becomes permanent, even if the employment does not resume. Where work is resumed, the question of whether the cessation is temporary or not is to be determined in the first instance by comparing the length of the break to the periods of work on either side of it, as in *Ford*.[628] However, this is only one possible approach, and it may be appropriate in a given case to take a much broader view, looking at the length and number of the breaks in relation to the period of employment as a whole.[629] The application of the test is inevitably somewhat impressionistic.

However, although *Ford* clearly ruled that the terms of the contract are not central to establishing whether there is a *temporary cessation*, the same cannot be said with confidence of the approach the courts will take to the question of whether *work* has temporarily ceased or not. A number of decisions have appeared to 'recontractualise' section 212(3)(b) at this stage of the test.

In *Byrne v Birmingham City District Council*[630] the applicant was employed as a street cleaner under a contract which allowed the employer to allocate work to him as it became available on a 'pool' basis with other employees. The Court of Appeal took the view that there was no global contract of employment in this case as the arrangement lacked the necessary mutuality of obligation; nor could the applicant rely on the predecessor of section 212(3)(b) to bridge the gaps between periods of work. This was because the employer had work available, but, in accordance with the arrangements agreed between the parties, had exercised the right to allocate it to others for the periods in question. According to Purchas LJ, 'the expression "cessation of work" must denote that some "quantum of work" had for the time being ceased to exist, and, therefore, was no longer available for the employer to give to the employee'.[631]

Byrne is a problematic decision since it ignores the limitations which section 212(3)(b) implicitly places on the employer's powers to determine continuity under the Act. It also goes against *dicta* in the earlier House of Lords decision of *Fitzgerald v Hall, Russell & Co*, in which Lord Upjohn held that the correct test was whether work is made available by the employer *to that individual employee*, and not whether there was a wider 'quantum' of work to be shared amongst employees as a group.[632]

---

[626] Under ERA 1996, s 95(1)(b). See below, ch 5, paras 5.75–5.76.
[627] See Lord Brightman in *Ford*, [1983] IRLR 126, 130.
[628] [1983] IRLR 126, 130 (Lord Diplock); *Sillars v Charrington Fuels Ltd* [1988] IRLR 180.
[629] *Flack v Kodak Ltd* [1986] IRLR 255, applying *Fitzgerald v Hall, Russell & Co* [1970] AC 984.
[630] [1987] ICR 519.
[631] [1987] ICR 519, 525. To similar effect is *Letheby and Christopher v Bond* [1988] ICR 480.
[632] [1970] AC 984.

A more flexible approach was taken in *Cornwall County Council v Prater*.[633] Here, the applicant was employed under a series of contracts to teach children who were unable to attend school. Some of the engagements lasted a few months, some several years. It was accepted that she had no 'global' contract of employment, but the employment tribunal found that there was sufficient mutuality for the individual hirings to give rise to contracts of employment. The tribunal then held that the periods between hirings came under the 'temporary cessation of work' exception. Its findings were endorsed on appeal.

Independently of section 212, there may be instances in which a contract term which apparently has the effect of removing accrued continuity of employment will be denied that effect by section 203 of ERA, which (subject to certain exceptions) renders void any contract term to the extent that it purports to 'exclude or limit the operation of any provision of this Act'. In *Secretary of State for Employment v Deary*,[634] section 203 (previously section 140 of EPCA 1978) was applied to a term reducing employees' hours below the statutory threshold for continuity after they had previously acquired the necessary qualifying service, thereby enabling continuity to be preserved. In effect, the term only had validity at common law for the purpose of defining the mutual rights and obligations of the parties under the contract. No distinction was drawn in *Deary* between terms introduced for the purpose of undermining the Act, and terms simply having that effect: in both cases, the court thought that section 203 could be invoked. By contrast, in *Surrey County Council v Lewis*[635] the House of Lords held that contractual documents would be taken at face value unless they were clearly a sham. The predecessor of section 203 was apparently not cited to the courts in *Lewis*; had it been, the outcome might have been different. *Deary* nevertheless remains a somewhat isolated authority as far as the application of section 203 to the concept of continuity is concerned.

IDENTIFYING THE EMPLOYER[636]

3.61   In the vast majority of cases the employer will not be an individual but will instead be a legal entity, that is to say a partnership or company, a statutory body such as a local authority or, in the case of civil servants, the Crown.[637] Freedom of contract means that the employer's identity is essentially a matter for the parties themselves, and one employer cannot normally be substituted for another without the consent of the parties to the original contract and of the third party employer. However, consent may not be needed for certain statutory responsibilities to be shared amongst or shifted between 'associated employers', where, for example, one company controls the other or both are controlled by a third party. These occasions are rare; on the whole, labour law

[633] [2006] IRLR 362.
[634] [1984] ICR 413.
[635] [1987] 3 All ER 641; see also *Booth v United States of America* [1999] IRLR 16.
[636] See Collins, 1990a; Deakin, 2001a; Freedland 2003: ch 1.
[637] Freedland, 2003: p 36 argues that the 'personal' conception of the employment relationship is a legacy of nineteenth century legal attitudes which 'imposes a strongly defined and prescriptive view of the institutional organization of work which is outdated and artificial' and suggests that (at p 39) 'because it is so important to keep it in mind that the employing party is not normally a single (male) human being trading as such, we [should] use the terminology of the "employing entity" instead of that of the "employer" to refer to the human or corporate persons who may constitute the employing party'.

respects the 'corporate veil' which separates the legal entity of the company from its owners and controllers.

Employer, undertaking and establishment

3.62   It is important to separate these concepts. The 'employer' is not the business or undertaking itself, but, in general, the person which is the *owner* of the undertaking. The concept of the 'undertaking', in turn, represents the notion of the business as a *going concern*. It is therefore not constituted simply by the business assets of the employer (machinery, land, intellectual property, and so on); it embraces business goodwill and other non-tangible assets, although not the right to the future services of the employees: their contracts of employment may not be transferred to another employment if they refuse to give consent.[638] As we shall see shortly,[639] for the purposes of the TUPE (Transfer of Undertakings (Protection of Employment)) Regulations 2006 and of the Acquired Rights Directive (77/187; now 2001/23) which they aim to implement, an undertaking, or part of one, must form an 'economic entity' in its own right, and not merely a particular 'activity' of that employer.

Employee rights may also be defined by reference to the establishment, rather than to the employer or undertaking. The concept of 'establishment' is used to delimit the scope of comparisons between male and female employees in equal pay legislation and between agency workers and employees of the hirer in the context of the Agency Work Regulations 2010, and also for the purposes of defining the employer's obligation to consult over proposals for redundancy, although in none of these cases is the term 'establishment' actually defined in the legislation itself.[640] Case law suggests that the establishment concept refers not to the employer's business or undertaking as defined above, but to a sub-unit of the business, such as the place of work of an employee or group of employees.[641]

Employer and company

3.63   The employer need not be, but may well be, a legal entity such as a partnership or company. Whereas equity partners remain personally liable, on a joint and several basis, for the debts of the business, the shareholders of a company limited by share capital are sheltered from personal responsibility for its debts and normally stand to lose only the nominal value of their shares if the business fails.[642] Thus 'among the principal reasons which induce persons to form private companies ... are the desire to avoid the risk of bankruptcy, and the increased facility for borrowing money. By means of a private company ... a trade can be carried on with limited liability, and without exposing the persons interested in it in the event of failure to the harsh provisions of

---

[638] *Nokes v Doncaster Amalgamated Collieries Ltd* [1940] AC 1014; see below, para 3.76.
[639] See below, para 3.66 *et seq.*
[640] See, respectively, EqA 2010, s 79(3)(b); AWR 2010, reg 5(4); TULRCA 1992, s 188(2). See also TULRCA 1992, s 228 which, in the context of strike ballots, refers to a 'workplace' (see s 228(4) for a definition).
[641] See further para 9.32 below.
[642] Insolvency Act 1986, s 74(2).

company law. A company, too, can raise money on debentures, which an ordinary trader cannot do.[643] Although Parliament has sought to 'lift the corporate veil' for various purposes, chiefly in the field of taxation law, the courts themselves are generally reluctant to do so. The fact that one company (a 'subsidiary') is owned or controlled by another company (its 'parent'), or by a certain individual, is not in itself grounds for ignoring the separate legal personality of that company.[644] It has been said that 'where the character of a company, or the nature of the persons who control it, is a relevant feature the court will go behind the mere status of the company as a legal entity, and will consider who are the persons as shareholders or even as agents who direct and control the activities of a company which is incapable of doing anything without human assistance'.[645] But this begs the question of what precisely in the character of a company or its shareholders will suffice for this purpose. A clear case of corporate personality being used in an attempt to deflect a pre-existing legal liability might be enough.[646] But otherwise, the mere presence of cross-shareholdings between companies in a company 'group' will not suffice to confer corporate personality on that 'group' as a separate entity, nor to enable the court to ignore the separate legal personalities of the companies within it. In particular, the court will not lift the corporate veil:

> … merely because the corporate structure has been used so as to ensure that the legal liability (if any) in respect of particular future activities of the group (and correspondingly the risk of enforcement of that liability) will fall on another member of the group rather than the defendant company. Whether or not this is desirable, the right to use a corporate structure in this manner is inherent in our corporate law.[647]

This principle was applied in a labour law context in *Michael Peters Ltd v Farnfield*.[648] Mr Farnfield was chief executive of MPG plc, which was the parent company in a group containing twenty-five subsidiary companies. The parent and its subsidiaries were put into receivership and Mr Farnfield was dismissed for redundancy; four of the subsidiaries were subsequently sold to buyers. For the purposes of the TUPE Regulations 1981,[649] Mr Farnfield argued that he was an employee of one of those subsidiaries, and therefore entitled to continuing employment with that company. The EAT held that the companies concerned did not form a 'single economic unit' and that it would therefore be wrong to lift the corporate veil on this occasion. As Mr Farnfield was not an employee of the subsidiary company, his employment had not been transferred.

Nonetheless, the EAT went on to say that it might be appropriate in a given case to treat a 'single economic unit' of companies as a single employer for employment purposes, where the subsidiaries 'do not have discretion to determine their continued membership of their parent

---

[643] *Salomon v A Salomon & Co Ltd* [1897] AC 22, 52 (Lord Macnaghten).

[644] The suggestions of Lord Denning that it should be (*Littlewoods Mail Order Stores Ltd v IRC* [1969] 1 WLR 1241, 1254; *Wallersteiner v Moir* [1974] 1 WLR 991, 1013) have not been followed.

[645] *Merchandise Transport Ltd v British Transport Commission* [1962] 2 QB 173 (Danckwerts LJ).

[646] *Jones v Lipman* [1962] 1 WLR 832.

[647] *Adams v Cape Industries plc* [1990] Ch 433, 544 (Slade LJ), on which, see the discussion of P Davies and M Freedland, 2004; *Bank of Tokyo Ltd v Karoon* [1987] AC 45n, 64 (Robert Goff LJ); *Chandler v Cape plc* [2011] EWHC 951 (QB), in which the court held that a parent company could owe a duty of care in tort directly to an employee of a subsidiary company, thereby obviating the need to lift the corporate veil.

[648] [1995] IRLR 190. See also *Sunley Turriff Holdings Ltd v Thomson* [1995] IRLR 184; *Colt Group v Couchman* [2000] ICR 327.

[649] Now TUPE 2006. See below, para 3.66 *et seq*.

company'.[650] If this were approach were taken on a regular basis, it would considerably limit the potential of separate corporate personality as a mechanism for delimiting the impact of employment law upon a given business. The scope of the principle adverted to by the EAT is wider than that normally applied in 'lifting the veil' cases. According to the Court of Appeal in *Millam v Print Factory (London) 1991 Ltd.*,[651] lifting the veil should only occur in an employment context where 'it is established that activity x is carried on by company A, but for policy reasons it is sought to show that in reality the activity is the responsibility of the owner of company A, company B', with the result that 'the subsidiary company is a sham or façade'. However, there is some authority[652] for a more extensive use of the notion of the 'economic unit' in interpreting provisions of EU law and related provisions of UK law, such as TUPE.

A flexible approach to defining the employer for the purposes of TUPE is consistent with the recent decision of the Court of Justice in *Albron Catering BV v FNV Bondgenoten*.[653] The Court held that where, within a group of companies, an employee was formally contracted to one company within the group, but was assigned on a permanent basis to work in the undertaking of another company in the same group, he was entitled to the protection of the Acquired Rights Directive in the event of a transfer of the latter undertaking to a third party employer. The Court based its judgment in part on a broad reading of Article 3(1) of the Directive, under which the terms and conditions 'arising from a contract of employment *or from an employment relationship* existing on the date of a transfer' (emphasis added) are to be carried over to the new employment. This meant that 'in the mind of the Union legislature, a contractual link with the transferor is not required in all circumstances for employees to be able to benefit from the protection conferred by' the Directive.[654] Although precedence would normally be given to the contractual employer, in a case such as this the non-contractual employer could be regarded as the transferor where it was responsible for the undertaking in which the employee worked on a continuing basis.

Company directors, partners, shareholders and employees

3.64   One consequence of separate corporate personality is that a company director may be, but need not necessarily be, an employee of that company. If he or she is a managing or executive director with a service contract of some kind, they will be employed by the company, most likely in the capacity of employee according to the tests considered earlier in this chapter. The concept of 'employee' is not in any way restricted to personnel of a particular rank, so that high-level managers may be employees just as much as those below them in the company hierarchy. Nor does holding a directorship, which is an 'office' for the purposes of company law, in any way prevent the person who holds it from also being an employee. Nor, moreover, is a company director who is also the principal shareholder or *de facto* controller of the company, for that reason alone, prevented from being its employee as opposed to the employer. Once the owner has taken the decision

---

[650] [1995] IRLR 190, 192.

[651] [2007] IRLR 526, Buxton LJ at [7]. In this case, the Court decided that a transfer had occurred under TUPE in circumstances where the transferee acted as the new employer, even though the sale of the business had been effected by share transfer and hence was, on the face of it, outside TUPE. See further para 3.74 below.

[652] See [1995] IRLR 190, 192.

[653] Case C-242/09 [2011] IRLR 76.

[654] [2011] IRLR 76, at [24].

to incorporate the business as a limited liability company with a separate legal personality, the company normally becomes the employer. The right to take advantage of incorporation under the Companies Acts in this way is not easily lost and the courts will only rarely lift the corporate veil to impose a personal liability upon the shareholders or controller of the company, or otherwise disregard the company's separate legal personality.[655]

One situation in which the courts might, nevertheless, look sceptically on a claim that a director or controlling shareholder is also an employee of the company, is that of an insolvency or related corporate restructuring. A director or controlling shareholder who would normally rank behind the creditors in the event of the company's insolvency may be able to achieve preferred creditor status in their capacity as an employee. But even here, the courts have tended to maintain the principle of separate corporate personality.[656] In *Clark v Clark Construction Initiatives Ltd*[657] the applicant set up a company in which he was sole shareholder. He was the managing director and declared himself to be an employee, although there was no formal contract of employment and no written statement of terms and conditions was issued. He was paid a low salary (apparently in order to minimise tax obligations) and received substantial loans from the company to cover his living expenses. At a later point he sold his shares to two business associates and began to receive a regular and substantial salary, while remaining managing director. He fell out with his associates, who dismissed him on the grounds of redundancy and transferred the other staff to another company. The applicant's claim for unfair dismissal failed on the grounds that, prior to the point when he sold his majority shareholding, he had not been employed as an employee, and so lacked the necessary continuity of employment. The EAT upheld this ruling. According to Elias P:

> The unease sometimes felt about recognising that controlling shareholders can be employees derives from the feeling that there is an air of unreality in describing the controlling shareholder as under the control of the company when he can, by the exercise of his votes as majority shareholder, ultimately control what the company does. Is the controlling shareholder really in a subordinate economic and social position when he can control the very body that ostensibly has control over him?[658]

A possible argument against such a view would refer to the principle of the division of responsibilities between the different organs of the company: even a controlling shareholder in a private (closely-held) company is not necessarily entitled, by virtue of that position, to intervene directly in management. He or she may replace the board in the event of a disagreement, but this is not the same thing as assuming personal control of the company's business. Whether or not a closer review of the principle of delegation and control in company law is relevant in this context, *Clark* does not decide that a controlling shareholder cannot also be an employee. Elias P set out three grounds on which it would not be legitimate, in such a case, to give effect to

---

[655] *Lee v Lee's Air Farming* [1961] AC 12.
[656] See *Buchan v Secretary of State for Employment* [1997] IRLR 80; *Fleming v Secretary of State for Trade and Industry* [1997] IRLR 682; *Secretary of State for Trade and Industry v Bottrill* [1998] IRLR 120, [1999] IRLR 326, doubting *Buchan*; *Sellars Arenascene Ltd v Connolly* [2001] IRLR 222; *Gladwell v Secretary of State for Trade and Industry* [2007] ICR 264; *Secretary of State for Business, Enterprise and Regulatory Reform v Neufeld* [2009] IRLR 475.
[657] [2008] IRLR 364; cf *Nesbitt v Secretary of State for Trade and Industry* [2007] IRLR 847.
[658] [2008] IRLR 364, 370.

an alleged contract of employment; where the company itself is a sham; where the contract of employment has been entered into for an ulterior purpose, such as circumventing the normal rules of priority of creditors; and 'where the parties do not in fact conduct their relationship in accordance with the contract'.[659] This would be the case where 'the controlling shareholder acts in a manner which suggests that the contract is set at nought, or is treated as no more than an irrelevant piece of paper'. The facts of *Clark* fell into this latter category. In *Secretary of State for Business, Enterprise and Regulatory Reform v Neufeld*[660] the Court of Appeal took a somewhat more cautious view, suggesting that there was nothing in principle to prevent a company director also being an employee, and that the absence of a written agreement would not in itself negative employee status.

It is not uncommon for some individuals to offer their services via companies which they have set up for the purpose, with themselves and another person as directors. Normally, as we have just seen, the individual will be the employee of the company which they have set up in this way, and not the employee of the company or other entity which is the end user of their services. However, in a case of a 'sham' arrangement it is open to the courts to disregard the presence of the intermediary, and find that the true employer is the end user. This occurred in *Catamaran Cruisers Ltd v Williams*.[661] Mr Williams was initially employed as an employee with the appellant and then, when he moved to work of a different kind, was told that he would have to offer his services as an independent contractor. This he agreed to do; however, the Inland Revenue persisted in regarding him as employee for tax purposes. Mr Williams then set up a company, Unicorn Enterprises, with himself and his mother as directors. Unicorn next contracted to supply Mr Williams' services to the appellant, for which it received a fee paid without deduction of income tax. Subsequently, these services were no longer needed and the question arose of Mr Williams' entitlement to compensation for unfair dismissal. The employment tribunal found that apart from the change in the form of payment, 'there was no factual change whatsoever in the terms of Mr Williams' employment',[662] and concluded that he was still an employee of the appellants. This judgment was upheld by the EAT, which considered that 'there is no rule of law that the importation of a limited company into a relationship such as existed in this case prevents the continuation of a contract of employment. If the true relationship is that of employer and employee, it cannot be changed by putting a different label upon it'.[663]

Unlike a director, an equity partner in a partnership such as a firm of solicitors or accountants cannot be an employee of that firm, for the reason that the firm has no legal personality separate from its partners who are, collectively, the employers.[664] Since a person cannot be simultaneously the employer and an employee in relation to the same business, it also follows that the owner of an unincorporated business will be the employer of those who work for him or her, and not one of the employees of that business.

---

[659] [2008] IRLR 364, [94]. See also *Secretary of State for Business, Enterprise and Regulatory Reform v Neufeld* [2009] IRLR 475.

[660] [2009] IRLR 475.

[661] [1994] IRLR 386.

[662] [1994] IRLR 386, 388.

[663] [1994] IRLR 386. See also *Abbey Life Assurance Co Ltd v Tansell* [2000] IRLR 387, discussed above, para 3.35; Deakin, 2001a.

[664] *Cowell v Quilter Goodison & Co Ltd* [1989] IRLR 392. See *Kovats v TFO Management LLP* UKEAT/0357/08/ZT, 21 April 2009; *Tiffin v Lester Aldridge LLP* [2012] IRLR 391, on limited liability partnerships.

The employees of a partnership are employed by *all* the partners at any given time. According to Scott LJ in *Briggs v Oates*,[665] in large partnerships 'common sense' dictates that the contracts of employment of the employees continue in force as partners come and go.[666] The process can be understood as the novation of the contracts concerned,which operates on the implicit consent of all the parties. However, if an employee raises an objection to a particular partner, it is difficult to see how the contract of the employee concerned can then be said to have been novated. There is authority to suggest that under these circumstances the contract is automatically terminated, at least where the change in the identity of the partners affects the nature of the business or the employee's role in it.[667]

Non-executive directors of a company who are not contracted to provide their labour or services to the business will not be employees merely by virtue of their director's office.[668] However, under the Companies Acts and under the principles of fiduciary obligation, all directors necessarily incur duties to the company and, more exceptionally, to the shareholders, whether or not they are employed by the company. As part of their duties to the company, directors were required by section 309 of the Companies Act 1985 to have regard to the interests of 'the company's employees in general' as well as to those of its members (the shareholders). However, section 309 'appear[ed] to make it clear that shareholders' (and creditors') interests prevail in any crunch situation'.[669]

Section 309 has now been subsumed into a wider provision, contained in section 172 of the Companies Act 2006, under which a director must:

> ... act in the way he considers, in good faith, would be most likely to promote the success of the company for the benefit of its members as a whole, and in doing so have regard (amongst other matters) to–
>
> (a) the likely consequences of any decision in the long term,
>
> (b) the interests of the company's employees,
>
> (c) the need to foster the company's business relationships with suppliers, customers and others,
>
> (d) the impact of the company's operations on the community and the environment,
>
> (e) the desirability of the company maintaining a reputation for high standards of business conduct, and
>
> (f) the need to act fairly as between members of the company.[670]

---

[665] [1990] IRLR 472; *Tiffin v Lester Aldridge LLP* [2012] IRLR 391.

[666] This result was achieved in the context of an unincorporated association in *Affleck v Newcastle Mind* [1999] IRLR 405: the employer consisted of the management committee and its members as constituted at any given time.

[667] *Brace v Calder* [1895] 2 QB 253; see further para 3.75 below.

[668] See, eg, *Parsons v Albert J Parsons Ltd* [1979] ICR 271; cf *Folami v Nigerline (UK) Ltd* [1978] ICR 277. In practice a non-executive director may receive written terms of appointment but these will not necessarily be intended to have the result of making him or her an employee of the company.

[669] Wedderburn, 1986: p 102; although cf Prentice, 1981.

[670] CA 2006, s 172(1). CA 1985, s 309 was described as 'obscure and ambiguous' by the Company Law Review Steering Committee (*Modern Company Law for a Competitive Economy: Final Report Volume 1* (2001), at p 352), which argued for its repeal (*Modern Company Law for a Competitive Economy: The Strategic Framework* (1999), at para 5.1.20), a recommendation which anticipated what is now s 172 of the CA 2006. For discussion of this and related aspects of corporate governance reform, see Wedderburn, 2004.

It remains to be seen whether the enactment of section 172 will change the way in which boards conduct their business, or whether it will make any practical difference to the priority accorded to the interests of different corporate constituencies. It is possible that the inclusion of new factors to be taken into account will even reduce the attention given to employees' concerns, but this is to assume that section 309 had been effective in the past in protecting their interests, a proposition for which it is difficult to find any strong evidence.

Associated employers

3.65   Statute provides for what is in effect a limited lifting of the corporate veil in a number of specified instances. For these purposes, two employers are to be treated as associated if '(a) one is a company of which the other (directly or indirectly) has control, or (b) both are companies of which a third person (directly or indirectly) has control'.[671] In practice the most important occasion on which this provision may be invoked relates to continuity of employment. If an employee moves his or her employment from one associated employer to another, their continuity is unbroken and their service from the previous employment is counted towards it.[672]

Other occasions on which the principle of associated employers may be invoked are few in number; nor do they *always* favour the employee, although most do. Certain employment rights only apply if the number of workers employed by the employer is greater than a specified number; for this purpose, workers of an associated employer can normally be added to the total.[673] For the purposes of a claim for equal pay the applicant may choose as a comparator a person employed by the same employer or an associated employer, if they fulfil the other necessary conditions of being employed at the same establishment or in an establishment to which common terms and conditions apply.[674] An employment tribunal may, in the event of unfair dismissal, order re-engagement against an associated employer.[675] But an associated employer may, conversely, make an offer of re-engagement to an employee who has been made redundant, which, if the employee unreasonably refuses, will lead to him or her losing any entitlement to redundancy compensation,[676] and an employee will lose the right to a guarantee payment if he or she is laid off on account of an industrial dispute involving an employee of his employer or an associated employer.[677] The position of an associated employer is also relevant in relation to the right of an employee to return to work after pregnancy. The failure to permit the employee to return to work is regarded as an automatically unfair dismissal unless, *inter alia*, an associated employer makes an offer of suitable alternative employment and this offer is either accepted or unreasonably refused.[678] Finally, in the collective sphere, the obligation to disclose information to a recognised trade union for the purposes of collective bargaining extends to certain information in the possession of either the employer or an associated employer. The employer must disclose information the absence of

---

[671] ERA 1996, s 231; TULRCA 1992, s 297; EqA 2010, s 79(9).
[672] ERA 1996, s 218(6).
[673] See, for example, TULRCA 1992, Sch A1, para 7.
[674] EqA 2010, s 79(3), (4).
[675] ERA 1996, s 115.
[676] ERA 1996, s 146(1).
[677] ERA 1996, s 29(3).
[678] MPLR 1999, reg 20(7).

which would seriously impede collective bargaining between itself and the trade union; however, it is not required to disclose information relevant to collective bargaining between the union and the associated employer.[679] This leaves something of a gap in a situation where the associated employer does not recognise the trade union for collective bargaining purposes and so cannot itself be made subject to the disclosure requirement.

The notion of associated employers provides a useful means of closing off some of the more obvious routes by which the application of statutory rights could be avoided by the adoption of separate corporate personality for different parts of an undertaking. By no means all the possible escape routes are covered, however, and some have been opened up again by legislation. Thus it used to be the case that a shop steward was entitled to paid time off for duties connected with industrial relations not just between his or her employer and its employees, but also for those between an associated employer and its employees. This reference to associated employers was deleted, along with other changes, in the Employment Act 1989.[680]

Moreover, the courts sometimes take the view that by extending the effects of employment legislation to associated employers in certain specific instances, Parliament implicitly rules out action by the courts to lift the corporate veil in other, closely related situations. In *Dimbleby & Sons Ltd v National Union of Journalists*[681] Lord Diplock would not 'wholly exclude the possibility even in the absence of express words stating that one company, although separately incorporated, is to be treated as sharing the same legal personality of another'; such a conclusion could be justified by a purposive interpretation. However, statutory phrases should not be interpreted in this way if, in the same legislation, specific but more limited provision had been made to lift the corporate veil: the more specific provision would then become 'entirely otiose'.[682]

The term 'control' is, however, capable of being interpreted in a flexible way, and is potentially broader than tests based exclusively on the presence of a majority shareholding, which are 'both too narrow, as a majority shareholding need not confer control due to weighted voting, and too wide, as control may be obtained without a majority shareholding'.[683] As a result, the definition of associated employers in terms of control of one company by another, or of the two of them by a third party, is capable of embracing the concept of corporate group liability. A company group can be identified as consisting of inter-linked associated employers, as in *Pinkney v Sandpiper Drilling Co*.[684] Here, companies which had been formed into a 'partnership of companies' were found to be associated employers, so that each one was responsible as employer to the employees of the various different entities. This is a somewhat unusual case, however, and there would seem to be ample scope for more complex corporate arrangements to be put in place which could avoid this outcome.

In some cases the employment law test has shown itself incapable of recognising the realities of control. Although the 'person' who controls two associated employers need not be an individual

---

[679] TULRCA 1992, s 181(2).

[680] The old law was contained in EPCA 1978, s 27, and was amended by EA 1989, s 14 (see Deakin, 1990a: p 16). The relevant provision is now TULRCA 1992, s 168.

[681] [1984] ICR 386, 410.

[682] The case concerned the definition of secondary industrial action, which now makes no reference to associated employers since the relevant provision (EA 1980, s 17(4)) has been repealed (by EA 1990, s 4). See TULRCA 1992, s 224.

[683] Bercusson, 1986: p 149.

[684] [1989] IRLR 425.

but could be a group of individuals acting together,[685] it has been held that they must be the *same* individuals in the case of both companies. In *Poparm Ltd v Weekes*[686] the applicant, prior to her dismissal, had previously been employed by Bamfords International Ltd and claimed that this was an associated employer of Poparm. Poparm was owned 50% by Mr Zabadne and 20% by his wife, the remainder of the shares being owned by a third party. Bamfords was a wholly owned subsidiary of a company, Euranglo Trading Ltd, whose shares were owned 35% by Mr Zabadne, 25% each by two of his brothers and 15% by a third brother. The EAT held that Bamfords and Poparm were not associated employers. Although Mr Zabadne was in a position to control Poparm by acting in concert with his wife and to control Euranglo by acting in concert with his brothers, it could not be said that any one person was in control of both companies. By contrast, control was established in *Payne v Secretary of State for Employment*[687] where a husband and wife together held shares in a company, and the wife was shown to be a nominee of the husband.

It was held in *Gardiner v Merton London Borough Council*[688] that the term 'company' meant a limited company, and did not refer to other forms of body corporate such as a local authority.[689] However, the company in question need not necessarily be incorporated in the United Kingdom; it suffices that it is a company which, in its essentials, may be likened to a limited company incorporated under the UK Companies Acts.[690] In this way, the notion of associated employers may extend to a transnational corporate group, consisting of companies incorporated in different jurisdictions.

Notwithstanding the notion of associated employers, it remains the case that labour law lacks sufficiently flexible conceptual devices for dealing with the liability of groups of interrelated economic entities. Corporate entities can be bound together not just by cross-shareholdings but also through contractual arrangements such as franchises, joint ventures and subcontracting. Collins[691] has suggested that the law 'should continue to respect the general principle that one person should not be held responsible for the actions of another, whilst recognising that the formal separation of legal identities in complex economic organisations may conceal what in reality constitutes a single set of productive relations which should be treated as a united group for the purpose of the ascription of legal responsibility'.

In the light of this suggestion, it is interesting to consider again the decision of the Court of Appeal in *Harrods Ltd v Remick*.[692] The Court accepted that Harrods could (if allegations were proved) be responsible for acts of racial discrimination which arose from the dismissal of the complainants by companies which were, themselves, concessionaires or franchisees of Harrods. The terms of the commercial contracts between Harrods and the franchisees placed Harrods in the perhaps unexpected position of being the 'principal' to whom 'contract workers' were supplied for the purposes of section 7 of the Race Relations Act 1976 (now section 41 of the Equality Act 2010). One effect of these contractual arrangements was that Harrods had the final word over who

---

[685] *Zarb and Samuels v British and Brazilian Produce Co (Sales) Ltd* [1978] IRLR 78.

[686] [1984] IRLR 388.

[687] [1989] IRLR 352.

[688] [1980] IRLR 472.

[689] The decision was reversed on its specific facts by SI 1983/1160, providing for continuity of employment to be preserved on a change of employment from one local authority to another.

[690] *Hancill v Marcon Engineering Ltd* [1990] IRLR 51.

[691] H Collins, 1990a: p 744.

[692] [1997] IRLR 583; see para 3.35 above.

worked in its department store, even in respect of persons who were not its own employees. Here, then, the court can be seen as having identified the true source of the economic power to which the complainants were subject. A similar outcome was achieved in *Abbey Life Assurance Co Ltd v Tansell*,[693] under the parallel provisions of section 12 of the Disability Discrimination Act 1995 (as it then was): here, the end user of the applicant's services, Abbey Life, was bound to respect the principle of equal treatment, even though it had no direct contractual relationship with Mr. Tansell, who was not only contracting through his own personal service company but, in addition, through an employment agency which arranged for his services to be supplied to Abbey Life.

TRANSFERS OF EMPLOYMENT

3.66   The Transfer of Undertakings (Protection of Employment) Regulations 2006 ('TUPE') constitute a major limitation on both the principle of freedom of contract and the power of employers to arrange their commercial and corporate affairs in such a way as to minimise or fragment their employment law liabilities. The main effect of the Regulations is to require the contract of employment of an employee to be transferred to the purchaser of a business in the event of its sale from one employer to another. The Regulations are also capable of applying where work is first contracted out from an employer to a sub-contractor (and vice versa), and when one sub-contractor subsequently succeeds another. Since the effect of the Regulations is not only to preserve the employment relationship but also the pre-existing terms and conditions of the employees affected, it has a direct and potentially substantial impact on the employment costs and liabilities of both the transferor and the transferee.

The Regulations touch on a number of substantive issues which are considered in more detail in later chapters: these include the consequences of a relevant transfer in terms of statutory dismissal rights,[694] the preservation of collective agreements and of union recognition,[695] and the scope of the duty to inform and consult representatives of the workforce.[696] At this point, some of the more salient features of the Regulations will be noted as they relate to the concepts of employer and undertaking and to the effects of a relevant transfer on the employment relationship.

The Regulations were adopted in their original form in 1981[697] by way of implementation of the EC Acquired Rights Directive of 1977; in 1998 the Directive was revised and in 2001 it was consolidated.[698] The 1998 amendments were required to be brought into effect in the UK by July 2001, but the most important changes made in 1998 related to the definition of 'relevant transfer',[699] which had arguably been assimilated into the relevant case law in any event, and to the possibility of derogations from the general principle of the transfer of employees' rights,[700] which were optional. In 2005, the Labour Government issued a public consultation document setting out proposals for the amendment of the Regulations, partly by way of implementation of the 1998

---

[693] [2000] IRLR 387.
[694] See below, paras 5.182 *et seq*.
[695] See below, para 9.27.
[696] See below, paras 9.43–9.45.
[697] SI 1981/1794.
[698] See Directives 77/187, 98/50 and 2001/23, respectively.
[699] See below paras 3.68 *et seq*.
[700] See below, paras 3.82 and 5.188-5.190.

revisions, and partly in order to extend and clarify their scope in the interests of creating a 'level playing field' for contractors bidding for service contracts, 'so that tendering decisions are taken on commercial merit rather than on differing views as to the employment rights of employees, and so that transaction risks and costs are reduced'.[701] These changes were mostly incorporated into the Regulations of 2006.[702] The new Regulations go beyond what the 2001 Directive requires, with the government relying on powers, contained in section 38 of ERelA 1999, to enact secondary legislation setting out more favourable provisions (to employees) than those imposed by EU law. Because many aspects of the Regulations were unaffected, or only minimally affected, by the changes made in 2006, the earlier law remains relevant, although certain points at which it has been superseded by the 2006 revisions will be noted in the analysis which follows.

Scope of the Regulations: 'undertaking' and 'relevant transfer'

(i) 'Undertaking'

3.67 The Regulations apply to relevant transfers of 'undertakings'. An 'undertaking', for this purpose, may be either 'public' or 'private' but, it must be 'engaged in economic activities whether or not [it is] operating for gain'.[703] The ECJ's case law, beginning with its judgment in *Dr Sophie Redmond Stichting v Bartol*,[704] makes it clear that the Directive may apply to transfers of public sector undertakings into the private sector, whether through privatisation involving a change of legal identity and status, or through a process of contracting out work which was previously done in-house. In *Henke*,[705] on the other hand, the Court ruled that the Directive has no application to transfers concerned exclusively with 'activities involving the exercise of public authority',[706] such as the transfer of administrative functions from one public authority to another, or within a single public authority. The *Henke* exclusion is now set out in the amended version of the Directive.[707] However, it has been narrowly construed.   The Court has ruled that the Directive does apply to the transfer of an entity from a non-profit making association governed by private law to a public law organisation,[708] and has reaffirmed that the transfer of industrial undertakings from state ownership into private ownership will normally be caught by the Directive.[709] It has also held that the Directive applies to transfers within the public sector of activities which can be described as

---

[701] DTI, TUPE *Draft Revised Regulations Public Consultation Document* (2005), para 18.

[702] SI 2006/246.

[703] TUPE 2006, reg 3(4)(a); *Law Society of England and Wales v Secretary of State for Justice* [2010] IRLR 407 (ruling that the Law Society's Legal Complaints Service was an 'undertaking' for the purposes of TUPE). The business or undertaking, or part of it, must also be 'situated... in the United Kingdom' immediately before the transfer. On the question of the transnational reach of TUPE, see *Holis Metal Industries Ltd v GMB* [2008] IRLR 187, and for a more general discussion of the territorial scope of employment protection legislation, see para 2.47 above.

[704] Case C-29/91 [1992] IRLR 366.

[705] Case C-298/94 *Henke v Gemeinde Schierke and Verwaltungsgemeinschaft 'Brocken'* [1996] IRLR 701.

[706] [1996] IRLR 701, 710.

[707] Art 1(c). See TUPE, reg. 3(5), discussed in *Law Society of England and Wales v Secretary of State for Justice* [2010] IRLR 470.

[708] Case C-175/99 *Mayeur v APIM* [2000] IRLR 783. See also Case C-234/98 *Allen v Amalgamated Construction Co Ltd* [2000] IRLR 119 in which the Court held that the Directive could apply to a transfer between two companies in the same corporate group.

[709] Case C-343/98 *Collino and Chiappero v Telecom Italia SpA* [2000] IRLR 788.

'economic' in the sense of involving the provision of goods and services in competition with those offered by the private sector.[710]

In the British context, a *Statement of Practice on Staff Transfers in the Public Sector*,[711] issued by the Cabinet Office on 7 January 2000 and revised in 2007,[712] provides that, as a general rule, the provisions of TUPE should be applied to the transfer of functions within the public sector as well as to transfers (in either direction) between the public and private sectors, even where to do so might go beyond the strict terms of the Regulations. Since the statement was first drafted, the extension of the Regulations by virtue of the changes made in 2006, to cover 'service provision' changes beyond the scope of the Directive,[713] has helped to clarify their scope.

(ii) 'Relevant transfer': the 'economic entity' test

3.68   The principal test under the Directive of what is meant by a 'relevant transfer' is that there must be a transfer of an 'economic entity which retains its identity, meaning an organised grouping of resources which has the objective of pursuing an economic activity, whether or not that activity is central or ancillary'.[714] This wording closely follows the so-called 'economic entity' test set out by the ECJ in the decision of *Süzen v Zehnacker Gebäudereinigung GmbH Krankenhausservice*.[715] By way of amplification of this test, the Court in *Süzen* repeated almost word for word a formula used in the earlier decision of *Spijkers v Gebroeders Benedik Abbattoir CV*:[716]

> ... it is necessary to consider whether the business was disposed of as a going concern, as would be indicated, *inter alia*, by the fact that its operation was actually continued or resumed by the new employer, with the same or similar activities. In order to determine whether these conditions are met, it is necessary to consider all the facts characterising the transaction in question, including the type of undertaking or business, whether or not the business's tangible assets, such as building and moveable property, are transferred, the value of its intangible assets at the time of the transfer, whether or not the majority of its employees are taken over by the new employer, whether or not its customers are transferred and the degree of similarity between the activities carried on before and after the transfer and the period, if any, for which those activities were suspended.

The *Süzen* case was regarded at one time as having narrowed the test of 'relevant transfer' by drawing a distinction between an 'economic entity' and an 'activity', particularly where the 'activity' consists only of supplying services under a specific contract. This suggestion closely followed a proposal of the European Commission to the effect that the then version of the Directive should be amended, so that a 'transfer only of an activity of an undertaking, business or part of a business, whether or not it was previously carried out directly, does not in itself constitute a transfer within

---

[710] Case C-108/10, *Scattolon v Ministero dell'Istruzione, dell'Università e della Ricerca* [2011] IRLR 1020.
[711] See www.civiservice.gov.uk/publications/staff_transfers/publications_and_forms/pdf/stafftransfers.pdf.
[712] A Code of Practice on Workforce Matters in Public Sector Service Contracts, (colloquially known as the 'two-tier Code'), first issued in 2005, was withdrawn with immediate effect on 13 December 2010.
[713] See below, para 3.73.
[714] Directive 2001/23, Art 1(b).
[715] Case C-13/95 [1997] IRLR 255, 259.
[716] Case 24/85 [1986] 2 CMLR 296, at para 13.

the meaning of the Directive.[717] In the event, this form of words did not find its way into the 1998 amendments. *Süzen* can be understood as clarifying a tendency which was present in the pre-existing case law of the Court. The British courts did not radically alter their approach to interpreting TUPE after *Süzen*.[718] Regulation 3(1)-(2) of TUPE 2006 now incorporates the revised text of the 2001 Directive, more or less word for word.[719]

Whether the court can identify an 'economic entity which retains its identity' depends on a variety of factors: a 'relevant transfer' is more likely where some employees are taken on by the transferee, some of the work is carried on at the same premises as before, and there is a sale or lease of equipment. However, none of these factors is conclusive in itself, nor is the absence of any one of them inevitably fatal to there being a relevant transfer.[720] The Court of Justice has held that neither the absence of a sale[721] or transfer of any kind[722] of assets, nor the failure to transfer assets for independent commercial use,[723] will necessarily prevent the Directive (and, by extension, the Regulations) applying. Nor does there have to be an agreement by the transferee to take on all or part of the workforce of the transferor.[724] The Regulations specify that there may be a relevant transfer notwithstanding that it is effected through more than one transaction[725] and that no property is transferred.[726] There can be an identifiable 'organised grouping of resources' even if there is an alteration in the organisational structure of the entity, as long as, following the transfer, a 'functional link' remains between the various elements of production and the transferee uses them to pursue 'an identical or analogous economic activity' to that undertaken by the transferor.[727] However, an emerging theme in the case law is the Court's increasing willingness to exclude from the scope of the Directive a range of transactions in which the purchaser does not voluntarily re-employ any of the employees.[728] The exclusion of these so-called 'labour intensive' transfers runs the risk of creating a significant gap in the protection provided by the Directive.

The application of the 'economic entity' test to situations involving privatisation, sub-contracting and other forms of outsourcing has been particularly problematic. In Britain, under legislation beginning with the Local Government Act 1988, local authorities were required to submit large parts of their services to a process of periodic compulsory competitive tendering (CCT), which enables outside suppliers to bid against the direct labour organisation or internal workforce of the authority for the right to carry out the work. A major feature of the 1988 Act

---

[717] COM(94) 300 final, 8.9.94.

[718] See, in particular, the EAT judgment in *ECM (Vehicle Delivery Service) Ltd v Cox* [1999] IRLR 559. The *Cox* line was confirmed by the Court of Appeal, notwithstanding a strong dissent, in *ADI (UK) Ltd v Willer* [2001] IRLR 542 and in *RCO Support Services Ltd v Unison* [2002] IRLR 401; see also *Balfour Beatty Power Networks Ltd. v Wilcox* [2007] IRLR 63.

[719] On the background to this revision, see *TUPE Draft Revised Regulations Public Consultation Document* (2005), at p 39.

[720] See generally Case C-171/94 *Merckx and Neuhuys v Ford Motors Co Belgium SA* [1996] IRLR 467.

[721] Case 324/86 *Foreningen v Daddy's Dance Hall* [1988] IRLR 315; Case 101/87: *P Bork International v Foreningen* [1989] IRLR 41 (both cases of the lease of property)

[722] Case C-209/91 *Rask v ISS Kantineservice* [1993] IRLR 133 at para 15; Case C-458/05 *Jouini v Princess Personal Service GmbH* [2007] IRLR 1005.

[723] Joined Cases C-232/04 and C-233/04 *Güney-Görres v Securicor Aviation* [2006] IRLR 305.

[724] Case C-392/92 *Schmidt v Spar- und Leihkasse der früheren Ämter Bordesholm, Kiel und Cronshagen* [1994] IRLR 302.

[725] TUPE 2006, reg 3(6)(a).

[726] TUPE 2006, reg 3(6)(b).

[727] Case C-466/07 *Klarenberg v Ferrotron Technologies GmbH* [2009] IRLR 301, at para 48.

[728] See in particular Case C-463/09 *Clece v Valor* [2011] IRLR 251, discussed below, para 3.70.

was that it ruled out the stipulation by the local authority of 'non-commercial matters' such as 'fair wages' policies which used to be common in dealings between councils and their suppliers; it became unlawful to insist, as a precondition of a supplier winning the contract, that they should respect generally-applicable terms and conditions of employment, or maintain recognition of an independent trade union. However, if the Directive and Regulations could be shown to apply, there was the chance of reintroducing a degree of fair wages control through this route, since the supplier would then have to respect the pre-existing terms and conditions of the internal workforce, as well as offering employment to those employees. The Labour government elected in 1997 replaced CCT with a duty to obtain 'Best Value', and the Secretary of State was empowered to provide, by order, that a matter should be excluded from the list of 'non-commercial matters'.[729] A number of matters have been excluded under this provision.[730]

TRANSFERS INVOLVING SINGLE-CONTRACT ENTITIES

3.69   A first issue to consider in the application of the Directive and Regulations to cases of outsourcing is the difficult case of 'single-contract entities'. In *Schmidt v Spar- und Leihkasse der früheren Ämter Bordesholm, Kiel und Cronshagen*[731] the employee worked in a bank as a cleaner and was dismissed when her employer wished to contract out the work to a company which was already responsible for cleaning the bank's other branches. She was offered a job with the cleaning company for less pay. The ECJ, on an application for a preliminary ruling, held that the employee's position could constitute 'part of an undertaking' for the purposes of the Directive: 'when an undertaking entrusts by contract the responsibility for operating one of its services, such as cleaning, to another undertaking which thereby assumes the obligations of an employer towards employees assigned to those duties, that operation may come within the scope of the Directive'.[732] The idea that a single employee could constitute a relevant undertaking perhaps sits uneasily with the entity test put forward in *Süzen* and in the revised Directive. However, the British case law suggests that a single employee, or, for that matter, several employees working on a 'single-contract' arrangement for a particular client, could amount to an economic entity under TUPE, if other aspects of the test are satisfied. Hence in *Argyll Training Ltd v Sinclair and Argyll and the Islands Enterprise Ltd*[733] the EAT held that the transfer of a training contract under which a single employee had been employed by the transferor could, in principle, be caught by the Regulations, in the process giving a narrow interpretation to the ECJ's suggestion, in the *Rygaard* case,[734] that a transfer must relate 'to a stable economic entity whose activity is not limited to one specific works contract'.

---

[729] See Local Government Act 1999, s 19; Department of the Environment, Transport and the Regions, *Consultation Paper, Modernising Local Government: Improving Local Services through Best Value* (1997).

[730] See generally para 2.6 above.

[731] Case C-392/92 [1994] IRLR 302; John McMullen, 1994.

[732] [1994] IRLR 302, 304.

[733] [2000] IRLR 630; *Dudley Bower Building Services Ltd v Lowe* [2003] IRLR 260.

[734] Case C-48/94 [1996] IRLR 51, at para 20. See also similar doubts expressed on the application of the Directive to single-contract entitites in *Süzen* itself, [1997] IRLR 255 at para. 21; Joined Cases C-127/96, C-229/96 and C-74/97 *Francisco Hernández Vidal SA v Gomez Pérez, etc* [1999] IRLR 132, at para 32; Joined Cases C-173/96 and C-247/96 *Sánchez Hidalgo v Asociación de Servicios ASER and Sociedad Cooperativa Minerva* [1999] IRLR 136, at para 32. For discussion of the relevance, in the UK context, of the requirement that the economic entity be 'stable', see John McMullen, 2006: p 119.

'LABOUR INTENSIVE' VERSUS 'TANGIBLE ASSET' TRANSFERS

3.70   In *Oy Liikenne Ab v Liskojärvi*[735] the Court of Justice sought to draw a distinction between entities which were 'based mainly on manpower', in which a voluntary transfer of employees would be both necessary and sufficient to establish a transfer,[736] and those in which physical plant and other non-human or 'tangible' assets were essential to the identity of the entity, in which case it would be necessary to show that the transferee took on the relevant physical assets. . By dividing human and non-human assets of the entity in this way, the *Oy Liikenne* judgment opened the way to employers framing commercial transactions so as to avoid the protective purpose of the Directive, either by declining to purchase physical plant or equipment, in a 'tangible assets' case, or by refusing to re-employ the workforce, in a 'labour intensive' case. In *Oy Liikenne* the Court ruled that as physical assets were essential to the operation of a public transport system, the transferee's failure to take on the assets of the transferor in this case pointed to the absence of a relevant transfer under the Directive, even though, in this case, the transferee had agreed to take on the employees. By contrast, in *Clece SA v Valor*[737] it was the failure of the transferee to take on the employees in a 'labour intensive' case that was the critical factor in negativing a relevant transfer. The Court ruled that 'the identity of an economic entity... which is essentially based on manpower, cannot be retained [after the alleged transfer] if the majority of its employees are not taken on by the alleged transferee'.

The British courts have, on the whole, interpreted this line of case law flexibly, using the 'multi-factor' approach,[738] to give TUPE a purposive reading; in the words of the EAT, 'the basic principle of [TUPE] is that employees should be protected where the undertaking in which they work is transferred "over their heads"... if both tenderers bid on a level playing field, that is, one where the terms and conditions of the staff are the same in either case, this provides the necessary protection for the employees, who can have no influence over whether or not the undertaking in which they work changes hands'.[739]   In particular, the British courts have repeatedly declined to take the view that TUPE can be avoided by the transferee simply deciding not to take on either assets or workers. In the *ECM* case,[740] the Court of Appeal declined to interpret *Süzen* as deciding that transfers in which the new employer takes on none of the pre-existing employees must fall outside the Directive and Regulations. This led the EAT in *RCO Support Services and Aintree Hospital Trust v UNISON*[741] formally to reject the claim that 'the absence of movement both of significant assets and of a major part of the workforce must necessarily deny the existence of a relevant transfer',[742] a view later confirmed by the Court of Appeal in the same case[743] and by its

---

[735] Case C-172/99 [2001] IRLR 171, at para 42. See P Davies, 2001.

[736] On the transfer of employees as a sufficient condition, see Case C-458/05 *Jouini v Princess Personal Service GmbH* [2007] IRLR 1005.

[737] Case C-463/09, [2011] IRLR 251, at para 41.

[738] *Cheesman v R Brewer Contracts Ltd* [2001] IRLR 144; *P & O Trans European Ltd v Initial Transport Services Ltd* [2003] IRLR 128; *Balfour Beatty Power Networks Ltd. v Wilcox* [2007] IRLR 63; see John McMullen, 2006: p 121.

[739] *Securicor Guarding Ltd v Fraser Security Services Ltd* [1996] IRLR 552, 556 (Judge Clark); although a rather different view of the implications of the Directive for competition in the supply of services is implied by the remarks of the Advocate General in Case C-13/95 *Süzen* [1997] IRLR 255, Opinion, at para 7.

[740] [1999] IRLR 559.

[741] [2000] IRLR 624.

[742] [2000] IRLR 624, 629.

[743] [2002] IRLR 401.

majority ruling in *ADI (UK) Ltd v Willer*.[744] Likewise, in *Lightways (Contractors) Ltd v Associated Holdings Ltd*[745] the Court of Session ruled that a tribunal was entitled to inquire into the motive of the transferee in declining to take on the employees, and to scrutinise with particular care a transaction deliberately structured with a view to avoiding TUPE altogether. In *Clece* the Advocate General noted the 'methodologically dubious' consequences of deciding that the principal legal consequence of the Directive, namely the transferee's obligation to take on the employees of the undertaking being transferred, should also be the main criterion for its application; she also referred to the danger of creating 'incentives for the new employer to get rid of as many of the employees as possible'.[746] But she then went on to suggest that 'an excessively broad interpretation of the notion of "economic entity"... may lead to a disproportionate restriction of the employer's private autonomy if he is prevented from organising his contractual relationships in accordance with his legitimate interests', while 'an unconditional obligation on the part of the employer to re-employ the previous staff would run counter to the principle of free competition'.[747] These dicta, which are consistent with the judgment of the Court in *Clece*, suggest that there may be increased scope in future to structure commercial transactions so as to avoid the Directive, although whether the British courts will follow the lead of the Court of Justice in this regard remains to be seen.

TRANSFERS FROM ONE SUBCONTRACTOR TO ANOTHER ('SECOND GENERATION' TRANSFERS)

3.71   It has long been clear that the Regulations apply to a situation in which work is contracted out for the first time.[748] However, for a period it was less clear that they applied to a situation in which one subcontractor succeeded another (a so-called 'second-generation transfer'). *Süzen* contains statements which suggested that it was less likely that a there would be a transfer under the Directive in a second-generation case. The Court held that:

> ... the mere fact that the service provided by the old and the new awardees of a contract is similar does not ... support the conclusion that an economic entity has been transferred. An entity cannot be reduced to the activity entrusted to it. Its identity also emerges from other factors, such as its workforce, its management staff, the way in which its work is organised, its operating methods or indeed, where appropriate, the operational resources available to it.
>
> The mere loss of a service contract to a competitor cannot therefore by itself indicate the existence of a transfer within the meaning of the Directive. In those circumstances, the service undertaking previously entrusted with the contract does not, on losing a customer, thereby cease fully to exist, and a business belonging to it cannot be considered to have been transferred to the new awardee of the contract.[749]

---

[744] [2001] IRLR 542. See also the decision of the EAT in *Astle v Cheshire County Council* [2005] IRLR 12, laying out the steps which tribunals should follow in applying the *ECM* case. Notwithstanding the decisions in the *RCO* and *ADI* cases, it clearly remains open to a court to find that there has been no transfer in a case where no assets of any kind have been transferred and no employees taken on, as in *Law Society of England and Wales v Secretary of State for Justice* [2010] IRLR 407.

[745] [2000] IRLR 247; although for a case in which the outcome went the other way, see *Whitewater Leisure Management Ltd v Barnes* [2000] IRLR 456.

[746] Case C-463/09, [2011] IRLR 251, Opinion of Advocate General Trstenjak, at paras 62 and 63. On the issue of perverse incentives, see P Davies, 2001.

[747] At para 65.

[748] See *Kenny v South Manchester College* [1993] IRLR 265; *BSG Property Services v Tuck* [1996] IRLR 134.

[749] [1997] IRLR 255, at paras 15–16.

In *Betts v Brintel Helicopters Ltd and KLM Era Helicopters (UK) Ltd*,[750] a case decided by the Court of Appeal shortly after *Süzen*, Brintel had provided helicopter services for North Sea oil rigs under three separate contracts with Shell (UK) Ltd. When the contracts expired, Shell awarded Brintel two of the contracts, but awarded the third to KLM. KLM did not re-hire any of the employees previously employed by Brintel, and used its own helicopters and infrastructure; it also flew out of a different base. The Court of Appeal decided that there had been no transfer. By contrast, in the pre-*Süzen* case of *Dines v Initial Health Care Services Ltd*,[751] a transfer was established where the new contractor took on most of the employees (at lower rates of pay) of the company which it had just defeated in the process of competitive tendering. *Dines* is by no means incompatable with *Süzen* and the subsequent revisions to the Directive and Regulations. Where the large majority of the pre-existing workforce is retained, this factor weighs in favour of there being a transfer.[752]

'SERVICE PROVISION CHANGES' BEYOND THE SCOPE OF THE DIRECTIVE

3.72   Notwithstanding scope for the courts to take a flexible approach on the issue of second-generation transfer, doubts concerning the scope of the Directive led the UK government, in its March 2005 consultation document, to propose extending the scope of TUPE to cover additional categories of 'service provision changes', in the interests of introducing greater certainty into the law and ensuring employee protection in all appropriate cases.[753] This proposal was incorporated, with some modifications, into the 2006 version of the Regulations.[754] Under TUPE regulation 3, a 'service provision change' (which for this purpose falls within the broader definition of a 'relevant transfer') occurs where immediately before the service provision change 'there is an organised grouping of employees situated in Great Britain which has as its principal purpose the carrying out of the activities concerned on behalf of the client' and 'the client intends that the activities will, following the service provision change, be carried out by the transferee other than in connection with a single specific event or task of short-term duration'.[755] The concept covers the situation of a first-time contracting out of activities from a client to a contractor; a second-generation change from one contractor to another; and the reabsorption of activities into the organisation of the client.[756] It does not apply to a situation in which the purpose of the subcontract was the ' supply of goods for the client's use'.[757]

   In the first case on the interpretation of these provisions to reach the appellate courts, *Kimberley Group Housing Ltd. v Hambley*,[758] the EAT upheld a ruling to the effect that a service provision change had taken place under circumstances where, because of the absence of an asset transfer, there was no transfer within the meaning of the Directive; in this case, the supply of accommodation and rental services to asylum seekers was held to constitute a relevant 'activity'.

---

[750] [1997] IRLR 361.
[751] [1994] IRLR 336.
[752] *Betts v Brintel Helicopters Ltd* [1997] IRLR 361, 366 (Kennedy LJ); *Süzen* [1997] IRLR 255, at para 21. See also the decision of the EFTA Court of Justice in Case E-2/95 *Eidesund v Stavanger Catering A/S* [1996] IRLR 684.
[753] See *TUPE Draft Revised Regulations Public Consultation Document* (2005), at p 39.
[754] See John McMullen, 2006: pp 120-125.
[755] TUPE 2006, reg 3(3)(a).
[756] TUPE 2006, reg 3(1)(b). In *Hunter v McCarrick* [2012] IRLR 274 the EAT held that for there to be a service provision change within reg 3(1)(b)(ii) the activities carried out by different contractors before and after the transfer must be carried out for the same client.
[757] TUPE 2006 reg 3(3)(b). See *Pannu v Geo W King (in liquidation)* [2012] IRLR 193.
[758] [2008] IRLR 682; Wynn-Evans, 2008.

A similarly broad approach to the interpretation of the service provision change concept was taken in *Metropolitan Resources Ltd. v Churchill Dulwich Ltd.*,[759] where the EAT rejected an argument to the effect that a 'multi-factor' test, similar to that developed under the Directive for the purposes of identifying a 'relevant transfer', should be used under regulation 3, preferring instead a 'straightforward and commonsense application'[760] of the statutory formula. Under this approach, 'minor' differences in the specification of tasks before and after the transfer would be unlikely to negative a service provision change, nor would a simple change of location suffice to exclude the Regulations. In *Enterprise Management Services Ltd v Connect-Up Ltd*,[761] however, the EAT supported a more restrictive approach. Here the claimants had been employed by Enterprise on a contract to provide curriculum and administrative support to schools run by Leeds City Council ('LCC'). Enterprise decided not to re-tender for the contract when it expired and the bulk of the work, but not the curriculum work, was taken over by Connect-Up. The EAT held that the employment judge had been entitled to conclude that the omission of the curriculum work, which represented some 15% of the work done by the orgainsed grouping of Enterprise employees dedicated to the LCC schools service, meant that 'the activities carried out by Connect were not essentially or fundamentally the same as those carried on by Enterprise'.[762]

(iii) Transfer of the part of the undertaking to which the employee is assigned

3.73   A difficult issue is how to apply the Regulations in a case where only part of an undertaking is transferred, in circumstances where an employee's duties prior to the transfer related both to that part which was transferred and partly also to other aspects of the work of the transferor which are not the subject of the transfer. In *Botzen v Rotterdamsche Droogdok Maatschappij BV*[763] the ECJ rejected an argument that the relevant test was whether the employee worked full-time in the department or sector which was transferred, 'to the exclusion of those engaged in partial tasks in various businesses or parts of businesses and those who, although working for several businesses or parts of businesses, form part of the remaining staff'. Instead, the relevant test was whether 'a transfer takes place of the department to which they were assigned and which formed the organisational framework within which their employment relationship took effect'.

The basis on which it should be determined whether or not an employee has been assigned to a department for this purpose is not entirely clear. In *Duncan Web Offset (Maidstone) Ltd v Cooper*[764] the EAT declined to give guidance to employment tribunals on this issue because it considered that the facts of cases could vary markedly. The Appeal Tribunal accepted that all of the following factors could be relevant: the amount of time spent on one part of the business or other; the amount of value given to each part by the employee; the terms of the contract showing what the employee could be required to do; and how the cost to the employer of the employee's services had been allocated between the different parts of the business. However, it also held

---

[759] [2009] IRLR 700.
[760] [2009] IRLR 700, at [28].
[761] [2012] IRLR 190. See also *Eddie Stobart Ltd v Moreman* [2012] IRLR 356 on the meaning of 'organised grouping' of employees.
[762] [2012] IRLR 190, HH Judge Peter Clark at [14].
[763] Case 186/83 [1986] 2 CMLR 50, at paras 13–14.
[764] [1995] IRLR 633.

that this was not an exhaustive list. In practice, the application of the test will often be finely balanced; it is perhaps unfortunate that the test of the requisite connection could not be more clearly specified. In *Sunley Turriff Holdings Ltd v Thomson*[765] the EAT applied *Botzen* to a case of a company secretary who was employed by one company but was also company secretary of a subsidiary company in the group and worked part of the time on the subsidiary's affairs. Both companies went into receivership and the subsidiary was sold together with a part of the parent company's undertaking. The EAT held that the employee's employment had been transferred over to the transferees, since his employment related to that part of the parent company which was subject to the transfer.

The amended Regulations apply the principle of novation to those employees who are 'assigned to the organised grouping of resources or employees that is subject to the relevant transfer'.[766] 'Assignment' here means assigned 'other than on a temporary basis'.[767] In *Kimberley Group Housing v Hambley*[768] the EAT was faced with a situation in which the activity in question – the provision of accommodation and retail services to asylum seekers – was divided unequally between two different subcontractors. The employment tribunal held that, since there was no question of the reinstatement of any of the employees, the pre-transfer liabilities of the transferor should be divided between the two transferees according to the proportion of the rental properties that they had taken on. The EAT reversed on the grounds that there was no authority for such an approach, in the light of the clear reference to the assignment test in the case law of the ECJ and the revised Regulations. It substituted a ruling to the effect that the liabilities had been inherited by the employer which had taken on the vast majority of the properties.

(iv) Change of control through share purchase

3.74   An important limitation on the scope of the Regulations is the exclusion of changes of control in a company through share purchase.[769] The rationale for this exclusion is that, in this case, the identity of the employer does not change: the employer is the same company as before, even though there has been a change of controlling interest. Nor, as we have just seen,[770] will the courts normally be prepared to lift the corporate veil to the extent of disregarding the separate legal personality of the company and treating the controller (whether it be an individual or a parent company) as the 'real' employer.[771] This means, on the one hand, that an employee cannot decline to carry on working by virtue of the change of control; on the other hand, although statutory intervention is not necessary to ensure that the contractual nexus between employer

---

[765] [1995] IRLR 184. See also *Securicor Guarding Ltd v Fraser Security Services Ltd* [1996] IRLR 552; *Marcroft v Heartland (Midlands) Ltd.* [2011] IRLR 599

[766] TUPE 2006, reg 4(1).

[767] TUPE 2006, reg 2(1).

[768] [2008] IRLR 682; Wynn-Evans, 2008.

[769] See *SI (Systems and Instrumentation) Ltd v Grist* [1983] IRLR 391; *Brookes v Borough Care Services Ltd and CLS Care Services* [1998] IRLR 636. The revised Regulations refer to the transfer of the undertaking 'to another person' (reg 3(1)(a)).

[770] Para 3.65 above.

[771] *Millam v Print Factory (London) 1991 Ltd* [2006] IRLR 923 (EAT), [2007] IRLR 526 (CA), which nevertheless demonstrates that it is open to an employment tribunal to find that a transfer of assets and resources from the subsidiary to the parent, sufficient to trigger TUPE, can take place following or in conjunction with a share transfer.

and employee is maintained, nor can a recognised trade union (or other relevant body) invoke the provisions of the Regulations concerning the employer's duty to inform and consult with the representatives of the workforce.

The point is not a new one and was raised in the slightly different context of a company reconstruction and amalgamation in *Nokes v Doncaster Amalgamated Collieries Ltd*.[772] There Lord Romer, in a dissenting judgment, argued that it was artificial to suggest that the personal liberty of the employees was at stake in a case where a reconstruction led to a formal change in the identity of the employer, but not in a case where there was a change in control through share transfer:

> … in truth it is an exaggeration to use the word injustice in such a connection as the present. If all or the large majority of the shares in one company are acquired by another, the first company will almost certainly come under the control of new directors and managers carrying out a policy that may differ widely from that of their predecessors. Yet no one could possibly say without gross exaggeration that the landlord, the contractors, or the servants of the first company had suffered an injustice. Their position nevertheless would differ little for any practical purpose from the position they would be in had the first company been amalgamated with the second company by means of [a reconstruction].[773]

The Regulations, conversely, take the view that there *is* a potential injustice to employees in the event of a change of ownership, but if this is so there is a fundamental flaw in their approach: they do not apply to the most common method by which control of a business, as distinct from its formal ownership, is transferred, that is to say by the sale of a controlling shareholding.

Novation of the contract of employment

3.75   At common law, the sale or transfer of a business or undertaking by one employer (the transferor) to another (the transferee) has the effect of terminating the contracts of employment of the employees of the transferor. The effect is generally considered to be that of a wrongful dismissal,[774] although another possibility is that the contract is determined automatically, that is to say, without a breach.[775] The transferee cannot be substituted as a party to any contract of employment without both its consent and the consent of the employee concerned. This need for mutual consent is a clear consequence of the contractual basis of the employment relationship. On the one hand, it preserves the employee's freedom to refuse to serve a new employer, a right which Lord Atkin in *Nokes v Doncaster Amalgamated Collieries Ltd* considered to be 'ingrained in the personal status of a citizen under our laws'.[776] The contracts of employment, being personal

---

[772] [1940] AC 1014. The relevant legislation was CA 1939, s 129.

[773] [1940] AC 1014, 1046–1047.

[774] *Brace v Calder* [1895] 2 QB 253; *Nokes v Doncaster Amalgamated Collieries Ltd* [1940] AC 1014, 1019 (Viscount Simon LC).

[775] A winding up order leading to a company's liquidation was thought to lead to an automatic discharge of the employees' contracts in *Re General Rolling Stock Co, Chapman's Case* (1866) LR 1 Eq 346. See further paras 5.196–5.198 below.

[776] [1940] AC 1014, 1026. For discussion of the appropriateness of this 'personified' view of the employment relationship, see Freedland, 2003: pp 38–39, and for an application of the same principle outside the context of TUPE, see *Bolwell v Redcliffe Homes Ltd and O'Connor* [1999] IRLR 485.

to the employees concerned, cannot be treated in the same way as other business assets of the employer.

On the other hand, *Nokes* denies the employee any right to continuing employment, and frees the transferee to employ a new workforce. TUPE reverses this rule by providing that a 'relevant transfer shall not operate so as to terminate the contract of employment of any person employed by the transferor and assigned to the organised grouping of resources or employees that is subject to the relevant transfer, which would otherwise be terminated by the transfer, but any such contract shall have effect after the transfer as if originally made between the person so employed and the transferee'.[777]

Unlike a common law novation, the statutory novation is automatic in that it does not depend upon the employee receiving notice of the transfer itself, nor of the identity of the transferee.[778] Nor does it depend in any way upon the transferee accepting the transfer.[779] However, the consent of the employee is required. In a judgment under the 1977 version of the Directive, *Katsikas v Konstandinidis*,[780] the ECJ said that the Directive did not require Member States to make provision for compulsion against the employee: 'such an obligation would undermine the fundamental rights of the employee who must be free to choose his employer and cannot be obliged to work for an employer that he has not freely chosen'.[781] Following this ruling, an amendment was made to the 1981 Regulations by TURERA 1993, which has been carried over, with some modifications, to the revised Regulations.[782] These provide that if the employee gives notice of his or her objection to the transfer,[783] the contract of employment is not novated;[784] instead, the transfer terminates the contract of employment, but without the employee being regarded as dismissed by the transferor for any purpose.[785] The effect of this provision is to prevent the employee bringing any claim for unfair dismissal or redundancy against the transferor (or, for that matter, the transferee, where the employee's choice prevents the novation of the contract from taking place[786]). However, the Regulations then go on to state that 'where a relevant transfer involves or would involve a substantial change in working conditions to the material detriment of a person whose contract of employment is or would [otherwise] be transferred…, such an employee may treat the contract of employment as having been terminated, and the employee shall be treated for any purpose as having been dismissed

---

[777] TUPE 2006, reg 4(1).

[778] *Secretary of State for Trade and Industry v Cook* [1997] IRLR 150, EAT, rejecting the conclusion reached by a differently constituted EAT in *Photostatic Copiers (Southern) Ltd v Okuda* [1995] IRLR 11.

[779] Case C-305/94 *Rotsart de Hertaing v J Benoidt (in liquidation) and IGC Housing Service SA* [1997] IRLR 127, ECJ.

[780] Case C-132/91 [1993] IRLR 179. See also Case C-171/94 *Merckx v Ford Motor Co. (Belgium)* [1996] IRLR 467.

[781] [1993] IRLR 179, 183.

[782] TUPE 2006, reg 4(7)-(9).

[783] On the meaning of 'objection', see *Hay v George Hanson (Building Contractors) Ltd* [1996] IRLR 427; *Senior Heat Treatment Ltd v Bell* [1997] IRLR 614; *Celtec Ltd v Astley* [2006] IRLR 635 (in which the HL held that civil servants, who worked on secondment for training and enterprise councils for several years before giving up their right to return to the civil service, were subject to a TUPE transfer at the point where their secondments began even though they could have returned to the civil service after that point, preserving their continuity of employment); *New ISG Ltd v Vernon* [2008] IRLR 115; *Capita Health Solutions v McLean* [2008] IRLR 595. See R Davies, 2004 for an account of the NHS Retention of Employment Model and its implications for employee consent to transfers.

[784] TUPE 2006, reg 4(7).

[785] TUPE 2006, reg 4(8).

[786] On this point, see *University of Oxford v Humphreys and Associated Examining Board* [2000] IRLR 183, 189.

by the employer'.[787] The revisions made to the Regulations in 2006 make it clear that the right to resign and bring a claim for either wrongful or unfair dismissal does not depend on there being a repudiatory breach of contract (as would normally be the case with a constructive dismissal).[788]

The transfer of contractual and statutory rights

(i) Transfer and preservation of contractual rights

3.76   Once a relevant transfer is identified, the Regulations have effect in relation to the contract of employment of a person employed 'immediately before the transfer'.[789] The transfer is deemed to take place, for this purpose, at a given moment in time, that it to say, the point at which the relevant transaction or transactions are effected.[790] The effect of the transfer is to assign to the transferee 'all the transferor's rights, powers, duties and liabilities under or in connection with [the contract of employment]'.[791]

The ECJ has said that the effect of the equivalent provision in the Directive is mandatory, in the sense that it may not be the subject of derogation through bargaining between the employer and the employee.[792] In principle, then, the transferee comes under a duty not just to re-employ the employees, but also not to derogate from their pre-transfer terms and conditions of employment (there is no objection to the parties agreeing improved terms and conditions[793]). However, in many instances the transferee will wish to make changes to terms and conditions of employment, in order to bring the employment contracts of the transferred employees into line with those of other employees. The following question then arises: what impact do the Regulations have on the power of the transferee to effect a variation of this kind?

One way of approaching this issue is by putting it in the context of the overall purpose of the Directive and Regulations, which is to transfer and preserve *existing* rights; they are not intended to confer *additional* rights to those which the employees would have had against the transferor

---

[787] TUPE 2006, reg 4(9); *Tapere v South London and Maudsley NHS Trust* [2009] IRLR 972. See below, paras 5.185–5.187 for further discussion of this point.

[788] The effect of the amendments made in 2006 is to reverse the decision of the CA in *Rossiter v Pendragon plc* [2002] IRLR 483 on this point.

[789] TUPE 2006, reg 4(3). For this purpose, an employee who, at the time of the transfer, has made an internal appeal against a decision by the transferor to dismiss him or her, will be treated as having been employed if the appeal (which, notwithstanding the transfer, must be conducted by the transferor) is later successful: *G4S Justice Services (UK) Ltd. v Anstey* [2006] IRLR 588.

[790] *Secretary of State for Employment v Spence* [1986] IRLR 248; Case C-478/03 *Celtec Ltd v Astley* [2005] IRLR 647 (ECJ), applied by the HL in *Celtec Ltd v Astley* [2006] IRLR 635, which was nevertheless able to find in the claimants' favour (see fn 732, above).

[791] TUPE 2006, reg 4(2)(a). The transfer of rights will be effective even if the transferor fails to provide 'employee liability information' to the transferee as required by the amended regulations (TUPE 2006, reg 11; see Directive 2003/21, reg 3(2)).

[792] Case 324/86 *Foreningen af Arbejdsledere i Danmark v Daddy's Dance Hall A/S* [1988] IRLR 315; Case C-209/91 *Rask v ISS Kantineservice A/S* [1993] IRLR 133; Case C-305/94 *Rotsart de Hertaing v J Benoidt SA* [1997] IRLR 127.

[793] *Power v Regent Security Services Ltd.* [2007] IRLR 226 (EAT), [2008] IRLR 66 (CA).

had they stayed in its employment.[794] On this basis, the answer to the question just posed is reasonably straightforward: the transferee can bring about a valid variation of the contract terms in just the same way as any other employer can. In other words, the variation will be effective if it is individually agreed with the relevant employee. Alternatively, in the event of the contract terms being governed by a 'bridging term' which allows for incorporation from a collective agreement, the transferee can seek to make an amending agreement with the relevant trade union.[795] Such changes should not be rendered ineffective by the anti-waiver provisions of the Directive and Regulations; because the legislation cannot confer any greater rights upon the employees than they had before, what would have been a valid variation pre-transfer will also be effective post-transfer.

This view has much to commend it in terms of logic and clarity, but there are several decisions of the ECJ and of the British courts standing in the way of this conclusion. The most important barrier is a dictum of the ECJ in *Daddy's Dance Hall*,[796] according to which:

> ... employees are not entitled to waive the rights conferred on them by the Directive and ... those rights cannot be restricted even with their consent. This interpretation is not affected by the fact that... the employee obtains new benefits in compensation for the disadvantages resulting from an amendment to his contract of employment, so that, taking the matter as a whole, he is not placed in a worse position than before.[797]

This statement could be read as saying no more than that the employee cannot agree to waive the right to have his or her pre-transfer terms carried over into the new employment. However, the Court went on to formulate a broader principle, according to which any subsequent variation would be ineffective if the reason for it was the transfer itself:

> ... in so far as national law allows the employment relationship to be altered in a manner unfavourable to employees in situations other than the transfer of an undertaking, in particular as regards their protection against dismissal, such an alternative is not precluded merely because the undertaking has been transferred in the meantime and the agreement has therefore been made with the new employer. Since by virtue of Article 3(1) of the Directive the transferee is subrogated to the transferor's rights and obligations under the employment relationship, that relationship may be altered with regard to the transferee to same extent as it could have been with regard to the transferor, *provided that the transfer of the undertaking itself may never constitute the reason for that amendment*.[798] [emphasis added]

---

[794] This view is inherent in Lord Slynn's opinion in *Wilson v St Helen's Borough Council/British Fuels Ltd v Baxendale and Meade* [1998] IRLR 408; see also Upex, 1999 and the decisions of the EAT in *Ralton v Havering College of Further & Higher Education* [2001] IRLR 738 and CA in *Jackson v Computershare Investor Services plc* [2008] IRLR 70.

[795] For a general overview of the principles governing variation of the contract of employment, see below, paras 4.35–4.40.

[796] Case 324/86 [1988] IRLR 315, at paras 14–17. See also *Wilson v St Helen's Borough Council* [1996] IRLR 320, EAT, [1997] IRLR 505, CA, [1998] IRLR 706, 715–16 (dictum of Lord Slynn); *Crédit Suisse First Boston (Europe) Ltd v Lister* [1998] IRLR 700.

[797] *Daddy's Dance Hall*, at para 15.

[798] *Daddy's Dance Hall*, at para 17.

The scope of this principle is unclear. At one time, it seemed that it was linked, in the UK context at least, to the rules concerning dismissal in the event of a transfer. Under regulation 7(1) of TUPE 2006, a dismissal by reason of the transfer or for a reason connected with it is automatically unfair, unless it is for an 'economic, technical or organisational reason entailing changes in the workforce' (an 'ETOR'). The matter was considered under the 1981 Regulations in *Wilson v St Helens Borough Council/British Fuels Ltd v Baxendale and Meade*,[799] two cases in which employees who were dismissed by a transferor prior to a TUPE transfer were then re-employed by the transferee on inferior terms and conditions of employment. The Court of Appeal[800] (reversing, in each case, a ruling of the EAT[801]) had held that the employees in *Wilson* had been dismissed for redundancy which was a potentially fair reason under the ETOR provision then contained in regulation 8(2) (now regulation 7(2)), and that the subsequent variation to their terms and conditions of employment was therefore effective. In *Baxendale and Meade*, by contrast, there was no potentially fair reason for the dismissal. The Court of Appeal concluded that under regulation 8(1) as it then was (now, regulation 7(1)(a)) the purported dismissal was a nullity, that the former contract of employment should be regarded as remaining in force, and that the pre-existing terms and conditions of employment would apply even after the transfer of employment took place. The House of Lords, reversing the result in *Baxendale and Meade*, held that a dismissal which contravened regulation 8(1) was not, for that reason, ineffective. Although an employee dismissed contrary to regulation 8(1) could assert claims for compensation for wrongful and unfair dismissal against the transferee,[802] English law did not accept the idea that such a dismissal was a nullity. Nor was such a conclusion required by the Directive since, as Lord Slynn explained, 'neither the Regulations nor the Directive nor the jurisprudence of the Court create a Community law right to continue in employment which does not exist under national law'.[803]

Lord Slynn's opinion strives to separate the issue of variation from that of dismissal. A clear implication of his approach is that a validly agreed variation should have precisely the same effect in a transfer situation as it would in any other context. However, the dictum of the ECJ in *Daddy's Dance Hall* apparently prevents this. Because the *Wilson* and *Baxendale and Meade* cases all arose from dismissals, Lord Slynn was not required directly to address the question of what happens if there is a variation of the contract terms by consent. He nevertheless commented that, for the purposes of such a variation, 'there must, or at least may, come a time when the link with the transfer is broken or can be treated as no longer effective', and said that if this issue had been raised on the facts of the cases then before him, he would have referred the question to the ECJ.[804]

The consultation document on TUPE which was issued by the DTI in March 2005 attempted to deal with the problem by drawing a distinction between purported variations 'for which the sole or principal reason is the transfer itself or a reason connected with the transfer which is not an ETO reason', and variations for which there is an ETOR. Those falling into the first category were to be 'void – ie ineffective' – while those in the second were to be 'potentially

---

[799] [1998] IRLR 706.

[800] [1997] IRLR 505.

[801] [1996] IRLR 320 (*Wilson*) and 541 (*Meade*).

[802] This is the effect of the decision of the House of Lords in *Litster v Forth Dry Dock & Engineering Co. Ltd* [1989] IRLR 161, discussed at para 5.185–5.187 *et seq* below.

[803] [1998] IRLR 706, 714.

[804] [1998] IRLR 708, 715. The issue did not arise because, on the facts, Lord Slynn found that there had been valid variations in each of the cases.

effective – ie effective, subject to being agreed between the parties (or their representatives)'.[805] According to the consultation document, this change would be consistent with the Directive; without an ETOR exception for variations, given the possibility of a fair dismissal based upon an ETOR, there would be 'a perverse incentive for employers to dismiss employees and then offer to re-engage them (with loss of continuity), or recruit new staff, on different terms and conditions, contrary to the employment protection aims of the legislation'.[806] The solution put forward in the consultation document is that now embodied in the Regulations: under regulation 4(4), a purported variation of a contract subject to the principle of novation shall be void if the sole or principal reason is the transfer itself or a transfer-related reason which is not an ETOR.[807] Conversely, under regulation 4(5), a variation may be effective if it is made for an ETOR or for a reason unconnected with the transfer.[808]

Thus the pre-transfer contract terms are entrenched against even a consensual variation for a certain period of time following the transfer, unless the variation can be understood to take place for a reason other than the transfer itself.[809] Neither the length of time for which this period of preservation might last, nor the test to be applied when determining whether the transfer itself is the reason for the variation, is clear. The law therefore provides little or no guidance to employers or employees (or their representatives) in determining the period for which a contractual variation will be ineffective.

It has been suggested that an employer might try to get round the preservation of pre-transfer terms by dismissing the employee and offering a new contract of employment.[810] One difficulty with this route is that the dismissal will be automatically unfair (under regulation 7(1)) if found to be by reason of the transfer or a reason connected with the transfer that is not an ETOR. The employer might incur substantial liabilities by way of compensation for unfair dismissal and/or redundancy.[811] It is also possible that the employee could be reinstated as a result of a tribunal decision in his or her favour,[812] and, indeed, that he or she could carry on working while still maintaining an unfair dismissal claim which leads to reinstatement.[813] But even if these difficulties are overcome, it is still not clear that the variation would be effective, since there is nothing in the ECJ's ruling in *Daddy's Dance Hall* to suggest that the principle stated in that case can be evaded by these means.

---

[805] *TUPE Draft Revised Regulations Public Consultation Document* (2005), at para 44.

[806] *TUPE Draft Revised Regulations Public Consultation Document* (2005), at para 45.

[807] TUPE 2006, reg 4(4).

[808] TUPE 2006, reg 4(5).

[809] For applications, see *Crédit Suisse First Boston (Europe) Ltd v Lister* [1998] IRLR 700 and *Cross v British Airways plc* [2006] IRLR 804. A variation to the employee's advantage will be valid: *Power v Regent Security Services Ltd.* [2007] IRLR 226.

[810] See John McMullen, 1999a: p 81. Another possibility is that employees who are subject to a transfer can enter into valid 'compromise agreements' with the transferee: see *Solectron Scotland Ltd v Roper* [2004] IRLR 4. In addition, if the transfer takes place from the private to the public sector, the equivalent of a post-transfer variation may be possible according to the ECJ in Case C-425/02 *Boor v Ministre de la Fonction Publique et de la Réforme Administrative* [2005] IRLR 61: here, an exception to the principle of the non-derogability of terms following a transfer arose on the grounds of the mandatory principles of public law of the Member State concerned.

[811] *Cornwall County Care Ltd v Brightman* [1998] IRLR 228; and see below, para 5.154 *et seq.*

[812] See below, paras 5.138 *et seq.*

[813] See below, paras 4.41–4.42.

3.77   A particularly problematic issue concerns the relationship between terms and conditions deriving from a collective agreement in force prior to the transfer, and entrenched for a certain period of time following it by virtue of regulation 4(4), and those laid down by collective agreements applying more generally to employment within the undertaking of the transferee. In principle the transferee has no right to substitute new terms and conditions for those carried over from the transferor, whether or not the new terms have been collectively negotiated.   A variation is permissible, as we have seen, where it can be supported by an ETOR.   However, as it has developed in the context of dismissal law, the ETOR concept is relatively narrow, and cannot be used to justify significant changes to terms and conditions merely because the employer can point to a reasonable business case for them; it is normally necessary for the employer to go further and show that there were business-related reasons for altering the size and structure of the workforce.[814]   If the same approach to defining the ETOR were to be followed in variation cases (and the presumption must be, pending the emergence of significant case law on the variation issue, that it will be), there would be limited scope for using this route to harmonise the terms and conditions of the transferred employees with those of other employees of the transferee.[815]

Article 3(3) of the Directive, however, offers a possible alternative solution, by providing that a Member State may limit the period for which the collective agreement made by the transferor remains in force after the transfer, so long as this is not less than one year. The United Kingdom has not taken up this option. However, Article 3(3) also states that, regardless of whether a Member State takes up the one year option, the previous collective agreement will only apply 'until the date of termination or expiry of the collective agreement or the entry into force or application of another collective agreement'. In *Scattolon v Ministero dell'Istruzione, dell'Universitá e della Ricerca*[816] the Court of Justice ruled that this provision 'must be interpreted as meaning that it is lawful for the transferee to apply, from the date of the transfer, the working conditions laid down by the collective agreement in force with him', as long as this did not have the result of 'imposing on … [the transferred] workers conditions which are, overall, less favourable than those applicable before the transfer'.[817] This approach would seem to give the transferee some leeway in implementing terms and conditions which involve offsetting gains and losses for the employees affected. Further uncertainty attaches to the question of whether post-transfer changes to the collective agreement can take effect in the new employment, if the transferee is not otherwise bound by or a party to that collective agreement. The incorporation of terms and conditions from a collective agreement into individual contracts of employment turns on the presence of an express or implied bridging term in those individual contracts. On the face of it, the effect of the novation of the contract of employment under TUPE is to carry a 'dynamic' bridging term over into the new employment, in just the same way as in the case of other relevant contract terms.[818] If the collective agreement is subsequently modified, it does not matter that the transferee was not a party to that change; the incorporation of the new terms follows automatically from the presence in the individual contract of the employment of the bridging term, which cannot be varied unless there is an ETOR justifying such a change, which, as we have seen, is unlikely.

---

[814] See *Berriman v Delabole Slate* [1985] ICR 546; *Nationwide BS v Benn* [2010] IRLR 922; para 5.183 below.
[815] See John McMullen, 2006.
[816] Case C-108/10, [2011] IRLR 1020.
[817] *Scattolon v Ministero dell'Istruzione, dell'Universitá e della Ricerca* [2011] IRLR 1020, at [75] and [76].
[818] *Whent v T Cartledge Ltd* [1997] IRLR 153.

However, in *Werhof v Freeway Traffic Systems GmbH & Co. KG*[819] the Court of Justice held, in the context of an application for a preliminary ruling from a German labour court, that the Directive could not have the effect of requiring the transferee to observe the terms of a collective agreement which had not been agreed at the time of the transfer. In *Parkwood Leisure Ltd. v Alemo- Herron*[820] the Supreme Court made a further reference to the Court of Justice in order to clarify the implications of the *Werhof* ruling for regulation 4 of TUPE. The Supreme Court ruled that a preliminary ruling was needed because it was not clear that the Court was prevented from interpreting regulation 4 as conferring greater protection than that provided for by the Directive. *Werhof* had turned, in part, on the negative implications for freedom of association (of employers) of a ruling that the transferee was, in effect, bound by a collective agreement to which it was not a signatory. According to Lord Hope, the issue of an employer's freedom to decide which collective agreement it wished to adhere to did not arise in the same way in the UK context, where the effect of collective agreements was resolved at the level of the individual contract of employment.[821] It remains to be see how the Court of Justice will respond to this argument.

3.78 Another problem arising in connection with regulation 4 is that of determining whether certain contractual liabilities are, on their true construction, capable of being transferred from one employer to another. In *Unicorn Consultancy Services Ltd v Westbrook*[822] the transferor operated a profit-related pay scheme according to which the pay of employees was linked to the profits of the corporate group of which it formed part. Following the transfer, the employees claimed that the new employer, which had no contact of any kind with the corporate group of their former employer, was nevertheless obliged to continue to observe the terms of the profit-related pay scheme. This was not simply a claim for any amounts still outstanding under the scheme at the time the transfer took place; the employees' argument was that the terms of the profit-related pay scheme had been incorporated into their contracts of employment prior to the transfer, and continued to apply to them once the transfer had taken place. An employment tribunal allowed the employees' claims and its decision was upheld on appeal. The EAT held that, on a proper construction of the rules of the scheme, the employees were still within its provisions post-transfer; regulation 4 of TUPE (as it now is), under which all contractual liabilities were transferred to the transferee, did the rest. The EAT's decision, taken with full awareness of the practical difficulties of operating the scheme once the transferred undertaking was no longer part of the transferor's group, illustrates the potentially far-reaching effects of regulation 4.[823]

(ii) Transfer and preservation of statutory rights

3.79 The Regulations do not expressly indicate whether accrued statutory rights under ERA 1996 are also transferred over under regulation 4(2)(a). These rights normally do not take the form of contractual terms and conditions, but it is arguable that they nevertheless arise 'under

---

[819] Case C-499/04, [2006] IRLR 400. See further para 9.27 below.
[820] [2011] IRLR 696.
[821] [2011] IRLR 696, at [47].
[822] [2000] IRLR 80.
[823] For a contrasting approach, however, see *Mitie Managed Services Ltd v French* [2002] IRLR 512, EAT.

or in connection with' the contract of employment since, as we have seen,[824] they depend upon the prior existence of such a contract. If this interpretation is correct, accrued continuity of employment would be maintained from one employment to another.[825]

To this extent, the TUPE regulations overlap closely[826] with the continuity provisions of ERA 1996. Under section 218(2), 'if a trade or business or an undertaking ... is transferred from one person to another – (a) the period of employment of an employee in the trade or business or undertaking at the time of the transfer counts as a period of employment with the transferee, and (b) the transfer does not break the continuity of the period of employment'. This provision pre-dated the 1981 Regulations; unlike them, it did not override the common law rule that the sale of the business terminated the contracts of employment of the employees, and so would only apply if both the transferee and the employee concerned agreed to the latter entering the employment of the former. After the introduction of the 1981 and 2006 Regulations, section 218 may now usefully be regarded as spelling out what regulation 4(2)(a) fails to make completely clear, namely that continuity rights are preserved along with the assignment to the transferee of rights and obligations arising directly under the contract. The scope of section 218 largely coincides with that of regulation 4 of TUPE.[827] Thus the employee must be employed by the transferor at the time of the transfer; this has led to problems where there is a gap of a week or more between the end of the employee's employment and the date of the transfer, not least because under the continuity provisions of ERA 1996 the loss of one week normally breaks the employee's continuity.[828] For this purpose it is arguable that the purposive interpretation given to what is now regulation 4 by the House of Lords in the *Litster* case could be applied to section 218, to bridge any such gap;[829] if it could not, direct reliance would have to be placed on regulation 4 in order to ensure that continuity rights were carried over to the new employment, but there are potential problems in this. For one thing, it is not clear that *Litster* has any application to a case where the employee does not have the necessary continuity of employment (now two years for those employed on or after 6 April 2012) to claim unfair dismissal at the time of the transfer.[830] But in practice it seems that the

---

[824] See above, para 3.2 *et seq*.

[825] This was assumed to be the case in the HL decision in *Celtec Ltd v Astley* [2006] IRLR 635. However, while if this argument has been accepted in the context of continuity of employment, its wider application may be limited. For example, it would not have the effect of preserving an equal pay claim against the transferor beyond the normal six month limitation period which begins when the employment ends, which was taken to be point at which the transfer occurred in *Gutridge v Sodexo Ltd.* [2009] IRLR 721.

[826] The two provisions are not integrated because the decision was taken in 1981 to implement the Acquired Rights Directive in the form of regulations under the European Communities Act 1972, rather than by way of primary legislation amending EPCA 1978.

[827] One notable respect in which s 218 may confer greater protection than TUPE concerns the operation of the insolvency derogations under TUPE (see paras 5.188-5.190, below), which do not apply to the statutory concept of continuity of employment under ERA 1996: see *Oakland v Wellswood (Yorkshire) Ltd* [2010] IRLR 82.

[828] ERA 1996, s 210(4); see *Teesside Times Ltd v Drury* [1980] ICR 338; *Brook Line Finance Co Ltd v Bradley* [1988] IRLR 283.

[829] *Macer v Abafast Ltd* [1990] ICR 234. The purposive interpretation given to reg 4 could be extended to ERA 1996, s 218(2), notwithstanding the fact that the predecessors of s 218(2) preceded the adoption of the Acquired Rights Directive, by invoking the broad principle of 'indirect effect' in Case C-106/89 *Marleasing SA v La Comercial Internacional de Alimentación SA* [1990] ECR I-4135.

[830] See below, paras 5.185-5.187.

courts are capable of giving a broad interpretation to section 218 in any event, and that its effect is unlikely to diverge much from that of regulation 4 of TUPE.[831]

(iii) Transfer of other liabilities

3.80   The Regulations provide for any 'act or omission before the transfer is completed, of or in relation to the transferor in respect of that contract or a person assigned to that organised grouping of resources or employees, [to] be deemed to have been an act or omission of or in relation to the transferee'.[832] This reinforces the point that it is not just contractual obligations which may be transferred; liabilities arising out of other acts done by the transferor in relation to the employee, such as (for example) conduct amounting to sex discrimination[833] and liabilities in tort,[834] may also be carried over. The same principle also applies to liabilities which an employer may incur for failure to comply with statutory information and consultation requirements.[835]

(iv) Exclusion of rights of access to occupational pension schemes

3.81   It is provided by regulation 10 of TUPE that regulation 4 should not apply to 'so much of a contract of employment ... as relates to' an occupational pension scheme which is contracted-out of the state pension scheme under the provisions of the Pensions Schemes Act 1993.[836] While this is clear enough, there is a question of its compatibility with the Directive. Article 3(4)(a) of the Directive allows a Member State to exclude from the scope of regulation 'employees' rights to old-age, invalidity or survivors' benefits under supplementary company or inter-company pension

---

[831] This has been done by holding that the notion of the 'time of a transfer' can under certain circumstances, for the purposes of s 218(2), span a gap of more than a week during which work is not done. *A & G Tuck Ltd v Bartlett* [1994] IRLR 162; *Justfern Ltd v D'Ingerthorpe* [1994] IRLR 164; *Clark & Tokeley Ltd v Oakes* [1997] IRLR 564, [1998] IRLR 577. It is unclear whether this flexible approach is compatible with the ECJ's ruling in Case C-478/03 *Celtec Ltd v Astley* [2005] IRLR 647, to the effect that under the Directive, which postdates s 218 but which governs UK law on the issue of the transfer of (among other things) statutory employment rights, the transfer must be understood as taking place at a particular point in time. The Directive can be interpreted as setting out minimum rights which must not be derogated from, but as allowing Member States to set superior protections where they consider them to be appropriate (this is the basis on which the 2006 Regulations were extended to the case of service provision changes beyond the Directive; see para 3.72, above). On that basis, it may still be permissible to give s 218 the flexible reading which it has had up to now (because the effect of that will often be to preserve continuity where this would not otherwise be the case).

[832] TUPE 2006, reg 4(2)(b).

[833] *DJM International Ltd v Nicholas* [1996] IRLR 76.

[834] In *Bernadone v Pall Mall Services Group/Martin v Lancashire County Council* [2000] IRLR 487 the Court of Appeal held that the transferee received the benefit of the transferor employer's liability insurance policy, since without this the employee might be significantly disadvantaged by the transfer (for example, if the transferee became insolvent). To the same end, reg 17(2) of the 2006 Regulations now provides that where the transferor is not obliged to carry employer's insurance under the Employer's Liability (Compulsory Insurance) Act 1969, the transferor and transferee are to be jointly and severally liable in respect of any personal injury claims incurred by the transferor. This is one of only two situations in which the United Kingdom has taken advantage of the option of imposing joint and several liability on the two employers in Art 3(1) of Directive 2001/23 (see John McMullen, 2006: p 137). The other is referred to in the next footnote.

[835] *Kerry Foods Ltd v Creber* [2000] IRLR 10; *Alamo Group (Europe) Ltd v Tucker* [2003] IRLR 266; cf *TGWU v James McKinnon* [2001] IRLR 597. The 2006 Regulations make provision for joint and several liability of transferor and transferee (reg 15(9)). See further paras 5.192 and 9.45 below.

[836] TUPE 2006, reg 10. On pension legislation, see ch 4 below, at para 4.129 *et seq.*

schemes outside the statutory social security schemes in Member States'.[837] It could be argued that a contracted-out, defined benefit scheme under the 1993 Act *is* part of the statutory social security scheme operating in the United Kingdom, since it operates in partial substitution for the state retirement pension and is intensively regulated by statute. However, this argument was rejected by the EAT (in relation to the predecessor of the 1993 Act) in *Walden Engineering Co Ltd v Warrener*[838] on the grounds that schemes of this kind, because they fell under the scope of Article 119 TTEC as it then was (now Article 157 TFEU) for the purposes of equal pay, are for that reason also 'outside the statutory social security schemes in Member States' for the purposes of the Acquired Rights Directive.[839]

Article 3(4)(b) of the Directive provides that if Member States take advantage of the derogation in Article 3(4((a), they 'shall adopt the measures necessary to protect the interests of employees and of persons no longer employed in the transferor's business at the time of the transfer in respect of rights conferring on them immediate or prospective entitlement to old-age benefits, including survivors' benefits' under occupational pension schemes. In *Adams v Lancashire County Council*[840] the Court of Appeal concluded that this provision did not have the effect of requiring a Member State to put in place laws requiring transferees to maintain an occupational pension scheme, to which employees transferred under TUPE could have access on terms equivalent to those they enjoyed when employed by the transferor. Rather, the effect of sub-paragraph b was to require Member States to take steps to protect only those rights of employees which had already *accrued* by virtue of their earlier service.[841] Under the Pensions Act 2004, provision is now made, in a case where the employee was a member of an occupational pension scheme run by the transferor at the time of the transfer,[842] for the transferee to assume one of two obligations: either to provide the employee with membership of another occupational pension scheme, or to provide, and to contribute towards, a 'stakeholder' pension.[843]

---

[837] This formula does not cover benefits paid in the event of premature retirement on grounds of redundancy: Case C-164/00 *Beckmann v Dynamco Whicheloe MacFarlane Ltd* [2000] IRLR 578; Case C-4/01 *Martin v South Bank University* [2004] IRLR 74; Pollard, 2005.

[838] [1993] IRLR 420. See also Case E-2/95 *Eidesund v Stavanger Catering A/S* [1996] IRLR 684.

[839] See also *Perry v Intec Colleges Ltd* [1993] IRLR 56, where an employment tribunal argued for a purposive interpretation to be given to what is now regulation 4 which would have had the effect of transferring over pension rights to the extent necessary to comply with Art 3(4)(b) of the Directive.

[840] [1997] IRLR 436.

[841] This obligation was arguably met by the provisions of occupational pensions legislation: see *Adams v Lancashire County Council* [1997] IRLR 436, 438 (discussing the provisions of Part IV of the Pension Schemes Act 1993 which are now contained in the Pensions Act 2004). See also Hepple and Mumgaard, 1998, for discussion of Art 3(4) and some of the problems which would be encountered if TUPE, reg 4 were to include provision for the transfer of occupational pension rights.

[842] More precisely, the employee must have been either an active member, eligible to become one, or eligible to become one upon completing a further period of service: Pensions Act 2004, s 257(1)–(4). See, generally, Pollard, 2005.

[843] Pensions Act 2004, s 258; SI 2005/649. On occupational and stakeholder pensions, see below, ch 4, at paras 4.132 *et seq*. The obligation to contribute to a stakeholder pension is significant in this context, since normally the employer is only obliged to make such a scheme available to the employee – it is not obliged to contribute to it. However, it may be noted that the Pensions Act 2004, s 258(6) states that it is open to the employer and employee, after the transfer, to make a contract varying or nullifying the transfer of pension obligations. As it goes against the principle of the non-derogability of contract terms following a transfer (see para 3.77 above), this provision presumably reflects the view that the Directive does not require this form of pension protection.

(v) Derogations in the event of the employer's insolvency

3.82   The 1998 amendments to the Acquired Rights Directive allow Member States to put in place derogations from the normal transfer rules for insolvent undertakings, whether or not they are subject to proceedings aimed at the liquidation of the transferor.[844] The 2005 consultation document published by the DTI set out a series of proposals for taking advantage of certain of these derogations, which have now been incorporated into the 2006 version of the Regulations.[845] We discuss these changes in our analysis of TUPE and unfair dismissal in chapter 5, below.[846]

ASSESSMENT

3.83 Labour law has tended to privilege a particular form of the employment relationship, namely employment based on an open-ended or 'permanent' contract, combined with regular and full-time working hours. Other, so-called 'flexible' or 'non-standard' forms of employment have tended to fall outside the core of protection as a result. This problem has been associated with a narrow approach to defining the 'threshold' concepts through which the law filters access to employment protection rights, namely, the common law concept of the contract of employment and the statutory concept of continuity of employment. To a certain extent, this problem has been addressed by legislative changes which began, in the mid-1990s, by liberalising the rules on continuity. The initial basis for this change was the impact of the equal treatment principle, and, above all, the perception that the exclusion of part-time workers from employment protection was contrary to EC law rules prohibiting discrimination on the grounds of sex, following the judgment of the House of Lords in the *Ex p EOC* case.[847] In the late 1990s the legislature addressed the issue of the basic definition of the employment relationship, through greater use of the 'worker' concept and by enacting the power to extend employment rights to individuals in section 23 of the Employment Relations Act 1999.

This last development built on a proposal made by Hepple in the mid-1980s, to the effect that 'the contract of service should be replaced by a broad definition of an "employment relationship" between the worker and the undertaking by which he is employed'.[848] Hepple's proposal involved extending the notion of service or employment to embrace 'both the intermittent exchange of work for remuneration, and the single continuous contract'. This was intended to address the issue of 'mutuality of obligation'; legislation would still exclude the independent contractor who was in business on his or her own account, but would seek to cover economically dependent contractors without a business of their own. In essence, this is the direction in which the law has moved since 1997. Nevertheless, ambiguities remain in the use of the 'worker' concept.[849] It can be seen

---

[844] Directive 2001/23, reg 5. For discussion, see P Davies, 1998; Hardy and Painter, 1999; Armour and Deakin, 2000, 2003.

[845] TUPE 2006, regs 8–9.

[846] See paras 5.188–5.190.

[847] [1994] IRLR 176; para 3.55 above.

[848] Hepple, 1986: p 74.

[849] See P Davies and M Freedland, 2000, 2004; Deakin, 2001b; Freedland, 2003: chs 1 and 2 (proposing the integration of the contract of employment and the 'semi-dependent worker's contract' within a single category of 'personal employment contracts'); Deakin and Wilkinson, 2005: ch 5; Davidov, 2005; McCrudden, 2012; Freedland and Kountouris, 2012.

as essentially clarifying the notion of dependent labour, by in effect displacing the mutuality of obligation test with the rival test of economic dependence which is inherent in the test of 'economic reality'. A more radical interpretation, though, would see in the worker concept the increasing encroachment of labour law regulation on the category of self-employment. This implies that the 'binary divide'[850] between employees and the self-employed, on which the modern forms of employment regulation and taxation have been based, is itself breaking down, in favour of a more complex and variegated form of regulation of the different types of employment relationship.[851]

The other element of Hepple's proposal addressed the notion of the 'employer'. He suggested redefining the employer as 'the company or other person or persons who has control of the undertaking in which the employee is employed ....' An implication of this definition would be that the worker would retain rights [analogous to those preserved by TUPE] on a change of control, eg a change in the share ownership of the controlling company'.[852] Reform in this area has been much slower to arrive. The test for the identification of the employer remains predominantly contractual. The TUPE Regulations mark a significant exception to this, but other qualifications to the employer's right of incorporation, such as the statutory concept of 'associated employers', remain under-developed. Nevertheless, the imaginative use of the 'agency labour' provisions of the discrimination legislation is one sign that statutory solutions may be available to deal with the fragmentation of the traditional functions of the enterprise among several different entities.[853] One implication of decisions such as *Dacas*[854] and *Tansell*[855] is that concepts in this area of law are sufficiently flexible to deal with contractual devices, such as agency work and the supply of labour through intermediaries, which would otherwise have the effect of fragmenting the legal notion of the enterprise in such a way as to deny workers employment protection. In particular, these judgments point the way to a legal analysis of intermediary work which will respect the need for a clearer division of legal responsibilities between the end user of labour and the supplier of workers to be established. The adoption in 2008 of the Directive on Temporary Agency Work is a step in this direction, although its implications for UK law and practice may turn out to be quite modest.[856]

A wider issue is how far labour law should aim to legitimise forms of work other than the open-ended, full-time employment relationship. In principle there is widespread agreement that, as the European Commission has put it, 'in no circumstances can the need for these specific forms of employment relationship be called into question ... What is required is to define a number of basic rules which [have] regard on the one hand to firms' need for flexibility and on the other, the aspirations of a number of workers'.[857] There is less consensus on how such a compromise might be achieved. The need for flexibility can be invoked as an argument for avoiding regulation of part-time and temporary or fixed-term work. However, this option is intrinsically undesirable: the economic benefits to both employers and employees of part-time work appear to be such as to outweigh any

---

[850] See Freedland, 1995.

[851] For further discussion of the prospects for conceptual 'mutations' through which labour law can adapt to changing conditions of work and employment, see Supiot (ed), 1999; Deakin, 2001c.

[852] Hepple, 1986: p 74.

[853] See Deakin, 2001a.

[854] *Dacas v Brook Street Bureau (UK) Ltd* [2004] IRLR 358; although see now *James v Greenwich London Borough Council* [2008] IRLR 302.

[855] *Abbey Life Assurance Co Ltd v Tansell* [2000] IRLR 387.

[856] Directive 2008/104/EC; see above, para 3.53.

[857] European Commission, Explanatory Memorandum COM (90) 228 final: para 4.

disadvantages which might follow from the extension of general principles of employment law to that form of work. Moreover, as a practical possibility the option of discrimination is restricted by Article 157 TFEU and by related provisions in the law of equal treatment, including the provisions introduced with the aim of specifically protecting part-time, fixed-term and agency workers. The aim of integrating non-standard forms of work into the existing framework of labour law is not straightforward, however. It is not enough simply to extend the concept of dependent labour, on the one hand, and to reduce the impact of qualifying thresholds, on the other; changes are also required to the substance of many regulations which are designed with the model of the full-time, indefinite-duration contract in mind. Legislation governing income protection – sick pay and lay-off – is one such example. Many other rights in labour law and social security are based on seniority and will inherently favour those who work on a regular, full-time basis over an extended period of time. This is not to suggest that regulations of this kind do not fulfil important functions of income and employment protection. It is important to recognise here that the model of regular employment, although no longer so clearly the 'norm' in the labour market, still represents the best prospect for most individuals of access to a secure and reliable source of income. Part-time and fixed-term contract jobs are very often thought of as transitory, or as appropriate for particular points in the life-cycle; trainees and workers employed on fixed-term contracts often hope or expect to get a 'permanent' job in due course and women workers tend to be employed part-time during periods when family responsibilities are most demanding. One implication of this is that the legal framework should not seek to undermine full-time employment as such, but should seek to avoid penalising individuals for making particular choices at points in the life-cycle when full-time work or a 'permanent' contract of employment may not be a viable option, and by striking a better overall balance between working time and family time.

4

TERMS OF EMPLOYMENT AND WORKING CONDITIONS

INTRODUCTION

4.1 This chapter examines the law concerning the contents of the individual employment relationship. Although the basic conceptual framework of that relationship is derived from the common law of contract, in practice very few of the parties' rights and obligations are based on express agreement between them. The contract of employment is above all a mechanism for expressing the impact upon the individual relationship of one or more of a number of external sources of governance or regulation. These sources are external to the individual relationship in the sense that they derive not from the parties' own agreement but, for example, from agreements involving third parties, as in the case of collective agreements, or from sources of legal regulation to which, in whole or in part, the relationship is understood to be subject, such as the applicable rules of the common law of employment and those of legislation. The employer's own rule-making power can also be thought of as an external source in this sense, since it goes beyond the scope of the express contract terms agreed with the individual employee. The central legal issues here are how these external forms of regulation are given contractual expression at the level of the individual relationship, and how conflicts between different sources are resolved.

The role of the common law is particularly important. Terms implied at common law loosely define the employee's open-ended obligations of obedience, co-operation and care, and thereby underwrite important aspects of the employer's rule-making power. Conversely, the employer may also be bound without formal consent to maintain the contract during interruptions caused, for example, by the employee's illness or by a lack of available work. These are 'default' terms in the sense that they normally apply only in the absence of any express agreement to the contrary. To what extent there are certain irreducible obligations which apply regardless of the content of the express terms, such as an obligation to maintain the 'mutual trust and confidence' on which the employment relationship is said to rest, is unclear in the present state of the law. In relation to collective bargaining, the 'normative' or regulatory function of collective agreements takes effect within the individual contract through the common law doctrine of the incorporation of terms; rules derived from employer handbooks may also be incorporated in this way. Social legislation has imposed a further set of obligations on the employer with regard to protection of income and employment. These statutory interventions tend to be seen as external impositions which formally constrain freedom of contract, without necessarily taking the form of contract terms themselves. They are nevertheless an important source of rights and obligations of the parties. Moreover, while formally restricting contractual autonomy, they can also be seen as restoring a degree of contractual reciprocity to the employment relationship, by virtue of the limits which they place on managerial prerogative.

The chapter begins by outlining the means by which the contract gives expression to the different sources of regulation and how conflicts between them are resolved. The employer's statutory obligation to issue the employee with a written statement of terms and the common law processes of the construction, incorporation and variation of terms are considered next. The remainder of the chapter is concerned with particular substantive aspects of the employment relationship: the basic terms of the wage-work bargain, governing wages and working time; terms and conditions relating to health and safety and the working environment; the implied obligations of obedience, co-operation and care; employee fidelity, the enforcement of non-competition clauses and the protection of confidential information; protection of income security in the event of interruptions to work; and the law governing occupational employee benefits, in particular those under defined-benefit pension schemes.

SOURCES OF CONTRACTUAL TERMS AND CONDITIONS

4.2   Before examining the substance of the employment relationship in detail, it is necessary to consider the nature of the sources of contractual terms and conditions. An important issue here is how far the law recognises the normative effect of the different sources, and how it deals with conflicts between them. We shall consider, in turn, managerial prerogative; common law implied terms; and regulation through social legislation and collective bargaining.

Express terms and managerial prerogative

4.3   The express terms of the contract of employment are only capable of playing a limited role in defining the agreement made by the parties. The precise degree of effort which the employee must devote to the work in order to earn the agreed wages cannot be stated in advance: 'the contract of employment hardly ever specifies exactly what the employee undertakes to do during each hour or day of his employment'.[1] The contract may lay down formal rules and procedures, such as those governing discipline and dismissal, as well as terms and conditions of employment such as wage or salary rates, working hours, holidays, sick pay and pension rights. Whether these express terms are agreed individually or, as is more usual, incorporated by reference to a collective agreement or other external source, they give rise to legally-binding, reciprocal obligations between the two parties. But 'a vital part of the contract, the content of the work to be done and the quality, intensity and pace of work effort, can neither be specified, nor enforced in the same way'.[2]

One reason for this which is suggested by transaction cost economics is that to specify the precise contents of performance in advance would be too costly. All long-term contracts contain this element of incompleteness, in the sense that limited information prevents the parties from anticipating all future contingencies and specifying the form which performance is to take under

[1] Lupton and Bowey, 1974: p 72.
[2] Pankhurst, 1988: p 5.

those conditions.[3] What is distinctive about the contract of employment is that the problem of incompleteness is addressed by granting one party, the employer, unilateral rights of direction over the other, the employee. The employee agrees to *serve* in return for wages, rather than undertaking to provide a particular service or product within which his or her labour is embodied; hence what the employer buys '*is not an agreed amount of labour, but the power to labour over an agreed period of time*'.[4] The employee undertakes to accept, within limits which are not always clearly defined, the authority of the employer to determine the mode of performance.

The idea that the employer possesses a prerogative power which lies beyond the express terms of the contract, just as the employee owes the employer a 'diffuse obligation of obedience',[5] is recognised by the common law of the contract of employment. The employer has the implied power to lay down certain norms for the performance of work which do not take the form of contract terms; they do not need to be agreed in advance with the employees on an individual or collective basis (through their representatives), and they can be changed unilaterally. This can be seen from cases involving the practice of 'working to rule' as part of industrial action against the employer. The employees may adhere precisely and literally to the work rules, but if these rules are simply an expression of the employer's prerogative power they cannot claim to have exhausted their contractual obligations by doing so. On the contrary, since the aim of the work to rule is to impair the effectiveness of the employer's business or service, the individual employees will be in breach of contract by virtue of not fulfilling their 'duty of co-operation' which, if unstated, is nevertheless regarded by the courts as fundamental to the contract.[6]

There is a lack of clarity about precisely where the express contract terms end and managerial prerogative begins. The employer has no inherent power to vary unilaterally the wage rates, hours of work and other conditions of employment which constitute contract terms.[7] Thus an employee's working hours may not normally be altered without his or her agreement. The precise form taken by a weekly timetable of lessons taught by a schoolteacher has been held, on the other hand, to be subject to the employer's right to specify the mode of performance, subject only to the need for the orders given to be lawful and reasonable in the circumstances.[8] This doctrine, while undoubtedly an important source of flexibility from the employer's point of view, can only be taken so far without undermining the contractual nature of the employment relationship. Obligations which are *specific* in nature will normally be construed as express terms which limit the employee's more open-ended duties of obedience and co-operation.[9] Moreover, although its open-endedness makes it seem to lie 'beyond contract',[10] the employer's residual prerogative power is nevertheless clothed in the form of various implied terms which may be limited in their scope not just by formal agreement between the parties but also by terms incorporated from sources external to the relationship, in particular collective bargaining.

---

[3] O Hart, 1989.

[4] Braverman, 1974: p 54 (emphasis in original). Braverman's analysis is an elaboration of Marx's distinction in Volume 1, chapter 7 of *Capital* between labour and labour power.

[5] Gouldner, 1954: p 152.

[6] *Secretary of State for Employment v ASLEF (No 2)* [1972] 2 QB 455; *Cresswell v Board of Inland Revenue* [1984] ICR 508; *Sim v Rotherham Metropolitan Borough Council* [1987] Ch 216.

[7] *Robertson v British Gas Corpn* [1983] ICR 351.

[8] *Sim v Rotherham Metropolitan Borough Council* [1987] Ch 216.

[9] See below, para 4.7.

[10] Cf Fox, 1974.

Terms implied at common law

4.4   The common law is a highly significant source of regulation of contractual terms and conditions. The 'bridging' term, through which the normative contents of collective agreements are given effect in the contract of employment, is one of the most important examples of a common law implied term.[11] Terms implied at common law underpin managerial prerogative by expressing the employee's duties of obedience, fidelity and care,[12] but also protect certain of the employee's expectations of continuing work and employment. Thus the employer may come under an obligation to compensate the employee for lay-off or suspension of work caused by lack of demand, and to pay sick pay if the employee falls ill.[13] The reciprocal duty of co-operation places both sides under an obligation to take steps to ensure that the contract can be made to work effectively. The scope of this obligation is notoriously unclear. Sometimes it amounts to saying that the employee's first responsibility is to the business, even at the possible cost of their own job security.[14] However, it is also the source of an obligation on the employer's side to avoid action which would be likely to damage or seriously undermine mutual trust and confidence between the parties.[15] The judicial recognition and extension of this implied term are among the most significant developments in employment law of the past two decades.[16]

4.5   The obligations created by implied terms are, by their nature, diffuse and open-ended. They epitomise the merging of contract and status within the contract of employment: 'to the employee, the arrangement is much more like the all-encompassing status agreement than the express limited regime of contract'.[17] Merritt has traced their presence in the modern contract back to nineteenth century master and servant legislation: 'the status-based incidents of the old master-servant relationship, appropriate to domestic and agricultural service, were grafted on to the relationship of principal and independent contractor, producing, by the end of the nineteenth century, the concepts of employer and employee'.[18] Her analysis relates to the employment law of New South Wales, but other studies have found evidence that a similar process took place in other common law jurisdictions in North America and England: 'the merger of master-servant law and contract meant that the law never treated the employment contract as the result of free bargaining and mutual consent, despite dogma that this was indeed the case. Instead, the contract was deemed to include "implied" terms which reserved to the employer the full authority and direction of employees'.[19]

An important finding of Merritt's study is that the concept of the contract of employment developed comparatively recently; until the last quarter of the nineteenth century it was not possible to speak of a contract of employment applying to all categories of wage-dependent labour. Instead,

---

[11] See below, para 4.29.

[12] See below, para 4.98 *et seq.*

[13] See below, para 4.123 *et seq.*

[14] Cf *Cresswell v Board of Inland Revenue* [1984] ICR 508, discussed below, para 4.104.

[15] See, in particular, the opinion of Lord Steyn in *Malik v BCCI SA* [1997] IRLR 462.

[16] See below, paras 4.105–4.107.

[17] Atleson, 1983: p 8.

[18] Merritt, 1982b: p 56; also on the development of the contract of employment in Australia, see Howe and Mitchell, 1999.

[19] Atleson, 1983: p 8; also on the US, see Tomlins, 1993; on Britain, Foster, 1983; Deakin, 1998, 2001; Steinfeld, 2003; Deakin and Wilkinson, 2005; Deakin, 2007.

there were separate categories of *service* and *employment*.[20] In England the notion of service, with its implications of hierarchy and command, applied to relationships coming under the scope of the Master and Servant Acts and, after their repeal, the Employers and Workmen Act 1875. It was only in the case of higher-status workers such as managers and clerks, who were outside the scope of this legislation, that employment was recognisably contractual in the sense of being based on reciprocal obligations. This is not to say that *none* of the features of the service relationship was defined by contract. The doctrine of common employment, whereby the servant bore the risk of negligence by a worker in the same employment, operated through an implied contract term.[21] However, in the case of those classified as servants, contract otherwise played little or no role in defining the limits to managerial prerogative or in providing any degree of income security.

In so far as there was a contractual model of employment in the nineteenth century its application was limited to employees in the professional and managerial classes. The extension of this model to all categories of wage-dependent workers took place alongside the growth of social legislation and of collective bargaining, which regulated the exercise of managerial prerogative.[22] During this time many incidents of the employment relationship were still not conceptualised in contractual terms, but were thought of as duties imposed by the law of tort. The employer's duty to take reasonable care with regard to the health and safety of its employees was formulated as a duty of care in tort in *Wilsons & Clyde Coal Co v English*, decided in 1937.[23] When in 1957 the House of Lords considered the employee's obligation of care and attention in *Lister v Romford Ice and Cold Storage Co Ltd*, Lord Radcliffe commented that 'there is no real distinction between the two sources of obligation. But it is certainly, I think, as much contractual as tortious. Since in modern times the relationship between master and servant, between employer and employed, is inherently one of contract, it seems to me entirely correct to attribute the duties which arise from that relationship to implied contract'.[24]

Today, even though the implied incidents of the employment relationship are generally understood to be contractual in nature, it is only with some difficulty that they can be made to fit into a contractual framework, and they bear evident signs of their origins in statutory regulation and the law of tort. The normal tests for implying a contract term, the 'officious bystander' and 'business efficacy' tests,[25] seek to discover the unstated intentions of the parties; consent remains the rationale for the presence of the term. Implied terms in the contract of employment, on the other hand, are sometimes said to be 'legal incidents' of the relationship; they do not necessarily arise from the presumed intention of the parties but by virtue of the nature of the underlying transaction. In a similar context, Lord Denning has said of this technique, 'these obligations are not founded on the intention of the parties, actual or presumed, but on more general considerations ... the obligation is a legal incident of the relationship which is attached by the law itself and not by reason of any implied term'.[26]

---

[20] Foster, 1983.

[21] Napier, 1986: p 329.

[22] Deakin, 1989: ch 4, 1998, 2000; Howe and Mitchell, 1999; Merritt, 1982b: pp 79–82.

[23] [1938] AC 57.

[24] [1957] AC 555, 587. Lord Simonds referred to *Harmer v Cornelius* (1858) 5 CBNS 236 as authority for the existence of the employee's *contractual* duty to exercise care and attention, but as Merritt points out (1982b: p 59) this case concerned an independent contractor, not a servant or employee.

[25] *Shirlaw v Southern Foundries (1926) Ltd* [1939] 2 KB 206 and *The Moorcock* (1889) 14 PD 64, respectively.

[26] *Shell UK Ltd v Lostock Garage Ltd* [1977] 1 All ER 481, 487.

4.6   The incidents which are implied into the contract of employment are, characteristically, those which reflect the continuing nature of the employment relationship and the mutual dependence to which it gives rise. In *Mears v Safecar Security Ltd*[27] Stephenson LJ referred to obligations which 'the general law will impose and imply, not as satisfying the business efficacy or officious bystander tests applicable to commercial contracts where there is no such relationship, but as legal incidents of those other kinds of contractual relationship'. In this case the Court of Appeal was prepared to imply a term for the payment of sick pay: '[w]e can treat as an agreed term a term which would not have been at once assented to by both parties at the time when they made the contract'.[28] Similarly, a court may imply into a contract of employment the 'bridging term' necessary to give effect to a collective agreement which is applicable to that contract, on the grounds that this aligns the legal contents of the contract with the circumstances governing its operation in practice.[29]

The House of Lords has said that an 'incident' of the relationship must be 'necessary' to give effect to the transaction, and not simply 'reasonable' in the eyes of the court.[30] This is because, in principle, the courts have no power to insert a term at common law on the grounds of 'reasonableness', having the power only to strike out agreed terms on the limited grounds allowed by the doctrine of public policy. The common law courts do not formally draw what Kahn-Freund referred to as 'the distinction between *ius cogens* and *ius dispositivum*, between "imperative" and "optional" norms of the law of contract, [which] is familiar to every practising lawyer in any Continental legal system'.[31] The scope given to the intention of the contracting parties apparently means that common law implied terms can only ever be 'dispositive' or optional, that is to say, terms which the parties are free to depart from if they wish to. An express term should therefore prevail over a potential implied term relating to the same matter.[32] In this vein, the EAT has said that 'if it is not necessary to make the contract work there is no room for such a further implied term. Certainly the court cannot intervene [simply] because it appears reasonable or equitable to do so'.[33]

However, the common law implied terms are not as fragile as the priority of express terms would tend to suggest. This is partly because, being by nature residual, the implied terms occupy the space which the express terms, because of their incompleteness, inevitably leave behind. The implied terms of obedience and care are used to resolve issues of the precise definition of work effort and the scope of the employee's commitment which, as we saw above, cannot be completely specified in advance, since to do so would be too costly. Where, however, an express term has been agreed which deals with the issues in question, it may be regarded as narrowing down or limiting the effect of the relevant implied term: 'if there is a term of the contract which is in general terms (eg a duty to take reasonable care not to injure the employee's health) and another term which is precise and detailed (eg an obligation to work on particular tasks notwithstanding

---

[27] [1982] ICR 626, 650.

[28] [1982] ICR 626, 651.

[29] *Tadd v Eastwood and the Daily Telegraph Ltd* [1983] IRLR 320.

[30] *Liverpool County Council v Irwin* [1977] AC 239; although see *Crossley v Faithful and Gould Holdings Ltd* [2004] IRLR 377 in which Dyson LJ describes the 'necessity' test as 'protean' and 'elusive', and discusses an alternative test based on 'reasonableness, fairness and the balancing of competing policy considerations' (at [34]–[36]). By contrast, the 'necessity' test was relied on in *Rutherford v Seymour Pierce Ltd* [2010] IRLR 606 to reject a term which would have allowed the employer to exclude an employee from a bonus scheme during a period of notice.

[31] Kahn-Freund, 1967: p 641.

[32] See *Reda v Flag Ltd* [2002] IRLR 747.

[33] *Express Lift Co Ltd v Bowles* [1977] ICR 474, 477 (Kilner Brown J).

that they involve an obvious health risk expressly referred to in the contract) the ambit of the employer's duty of care for the employee's health will be narrower than it would be if there were no such express term.[34] Similarly, a job description accorded to a particular employee or an express mobility clause will serve to identify the limits to his or her implied obligation of obedience.[35]

4.7   To what extent is it possible to go further and state that certain implied terms constitute an irreducible core of obligation in the contract of employment, which cannot be removed by express agreement? It is difficult, for example, to envisage a contract of employment which did not contain *some* implied obligation of co-operation and obedience on the employee's part. How far does the contract contain an equivalent implied obligation on the part of the employer to treat the employee with dignity and respect? The courts have found a way of limiting the effect of express terms by requiring the employer to *act reasonably* in exercising the option to invoke the powers such terms confer. An express mobility clause will necessarily prevail over the limits which might have been set by an implied term;[36] but an employer must give the employee reasonable notice of the move to a new place of work.[37] In *Imperial Group Pension Trust Ltd v Imperial Tobacco Ltd* Browne-Wilkinson VC held that the discretion given to an employer, under the terms of an occupational pension scheme, to agree to increases in pensions, was not unqualified: the employer was not obliged to agree to an increase, but it *was* obliged to exercise its powers in good faith and avoid an arbitrary or capricious result.[38]

4.8   The notion that express terms are qualified by an implied obligation to exercise the powers they create in a reasonable way is not without its difficulties, however. It may amount to the same thing as imposing a qualification on the scope of the term itself: 'are not all contractual obligations optional in that they may or may not be exercised by the promisee and compulsory only in that they bind the promisor when they are exercised?'[39] This approach, then, arguably does little to clarify the essential questions of which qualifications might be justifiably imposed, and on what grounds. The issues were considered by the Court of Appeal in *Johnstone v Bloomsbury Health Authority*.[40]

The employee, a junior hospital doctor, sought damages for ill health brought on by working excessive hours, and a declaration that his contract of employment did not require him to work hours beyond the point where his health was put in danger. His contract required him to work a basic 40-hour working week and to be available for a further 48 hours of overtime per week. Leggatt LJ, who would have struck out the claim as disclosing no cause of action, took the view that the express agreement to be available for up to 88 hours a week prevailed over any implied term for the protection of the employee's safety and health.

---

[34] *Johnstone v Bloomsbury Health Authority* [1992] QB 333, 350 (Browne-Wilkinson VC); see also *Johnson v Unisys Ltd* [2001] IRLR 279, at [24] (Lord Steyn); *Reda v Flag Ltd* [2002] IRLR 747 (express power to dismiss without notice qualified implied term).

[35] See below, paras 4.99, 4.109.

[36] *Express Lift Co Ltd v Bowles* [1977] ICR 474.

[37] *United Bank Ltd v Akhtar* [1989] IRLR 507.

[38] [1991] IRLR 66. See also *Scally v Southern Health and Social Services Board* [1991] IRLR 522; *Clark v Nomura International Ltd* [2000] IRLR 766; *Mallone v BPB Industries Ltd* [2002] IRLR 452; see para 4.105 *et seq* below.

[39] McLean, 1992: p 25.

[40] [1992] QB 333.

The two other judges refused to strike out the claim but gave different reasons for their decisions. Stuart-Smith LJ said that the contract terms did not override the duty of the employer in both contract and tort to take reasonable care to ensure the employee's safety and health. Browne-Wilkinson VC, reiterating his analysis in the *Imperial Tobacco* case,[41] argued that the 'express and implied terms of the contract have to be capable of co-existence without conflict'[42] and that the effect of the express term, in this case, was to narrow down the implied obligation of care owed by the employer to the employee. However, the agreement to work overtime simply gave the employer the *option* to call on the employee to perform, and this option had to be exercised reasonably, with regard to the consequences of doing so for the employee's health.

There are a number of reasons for thinking that the judgment of Stuart-Smith LJ is correct in principle, notwithstanding that he found himself in a minority of one in believing that the express term governing working hours was limited by the employer's implied obligations with regard to health and safety. First, it would be odd if the employer's obligation, which is both an implied term in the contract and also a duty of care in tort, could be limited by an express contract term which did not take the form of a formal disclaimer or exclusion clause of the kind which would normally be needed to oust a tort duty of this kind.[43] Second, if the contract term does limit the employer's duty of care in tort, since that duty relates to the physical health and safety of the employee the term might be nullified by section 2(1) of the Unfair Contract Terms Act 1977. Third, it is arguable in this case that the ambit of the express term was limited by public policy,[44] although none of the judgments in *Johnstone* accepted this.

A more general difficulty is that none of the arguments advanced above is of general application to the relationship between implied and express terms. The first argument rests on the rather fortuitous factor that, in this case, the contract term in question was replicated by a duty of care in tort. This will not always be so. In relation to the second argument, the application of the Unfair Contract Terms Act 1977 to cases arising out of the employment relationship is unclear.[45] With regard to the third argument, public policy will only be of assistance, in this context, if the term in question relates to an issue of life and limb.

There is authority, however, for a broader principle which could be invoked to explain the result in *Johnstone* if not the reasoning used in that case. This is that the contract does indeed contain an irreducible obligation on the part of the employer 'not to destroy the mutual trust and confidence on which co-operation rests'.[46] This is not necessarily equivalent to a duty to act reasonably, but it does imply an obligation not unreasonably to prevent the other party from performing the contract, in particular by avoiding action which is completely capricious and

---

[41] [1991] IRLR 66.

[42] [1992] QB 333, 350.

[43] Deakin, Johnston and Markesinis, 2008: pp 919–920.

[44] Weir, 1991: p 399.

[45] More recently the Court of Appeal has held that employment contracts are not necessarily covered by the provisions of UCTA 1977, s 3 concerning exclusion and limitation clauses in contracts based on the written standard terms of the defendant or which involve a business-consumer relationship (*Commerzbank AG v Keen* [2007] IRLR 132); however, this leaves open the possibility that s 2(1) of UCTA, since it relates to claims in tort as opposed to contract, may be relevant in the employment context.

[46] Hepple, 1981: p 134. The leading judicial decision on the duty of mutual trust and co-operation is now the ruling of the House of Lords in *Malik v BCCI SA* [1997] IRLR 462; see Brodie, 1998b. This aspect of Malik is discussed below, paras 4.106–4.107.

arbitrary.[47] In his opinion in the leading case of *Malik v BCCI SA*,[48] Lord Steyn referred to the implied term of mutual trust and confidence as a default term, suggesting that it only applies in the absence of an express agreement on the point in question. This use of the expression 'default term', however, opens up a discussion on the different types of default which may operate in the context of the employment relationship. The *Malik* term of good faith or trust and co-operation could be described as a 'strong' default which can only be qualified by an express term of a very clear and precise nature, in contrast to other types of default term which are more easily waivable.[49] This formulation respects the central place occupied by the *Malik* term within the modern employment contract,[50] without infringing the orthodox view of the relationship between express and implied terms at common law.[51]

Regulation by statute and collective bargaining[52]

4.9   Statutory norms of income and employment protection do not, on the whole, take the form of implied terms of the contract of employment. Minimum wage legislation provides for automatic incorporation into contracts of employment of the rates of pay laid down by statute.[53] A similar approach is taken with regard to minimum periods of notice imposed by statute upon employers and employees. The legislation states that notice 'is not less' than a specified period and lays down that 'any provision for shorter notice ... has effect subject to' these periods.[54] The statute provides that either side retains the right to waive the right to notice or to accept payment in lieu of notice, thereby replicating the common law rules which would apply to a contract term.[55] It also states that failure by the employer to give the requisite notice 'shall be taken into account in assessing his liability for breach of the contract'.[56] Nothing is said explicitly about the *employee's* liability for failing to give minimum statutory notice, but it is probably the case that an employer would have an action for damages for breach of contract in this event.

[47] *Woods v WM Car Services (Peterborough) Ltd* [1982] ICR 693; *White v Reflecting Roadstuds Ltd* [1991] IRLR 331; McLean, 1992.
[48] [1997] IRLR 462, 468; see Brodie, 1998b: pp 82–83.
[49] This is a well-known distinction in the theoretical literature on implied terms and other default rules in contract and company law. See the seminal paper by Ayres and Gertner, 1989, and for an application to part of UK company law, see Deakin and Hughes, 1999.
[50] On this, see Brodie, 1998b.
[51] See also *Johnson v Unisys Ltd* [2001] IRLR 279, at [24] (Lord Steyn) and [37] (Lord Hoffmann). All the opinions in this case concluded that the common law implied term of a duty to act fairly (the term preferred, in the context of termination, to 'mutual trust and confidence') could, in principle, be applied to termination of employment notwithstanding the presence of an express notice clause; there was no necessary conflict between the express and implied terms. However, the majority (Lord Steyn dissenting) ruled that the common law should not be developed in a way which would undermine the separate, statutory jurisdiction of unfair dismissal. See below paras 5.34–5.35 and 5.43–5.45 for further discussion of Johnson and of the related Supreme Court decision in *Edwards v Chesterfield Royal Hospital NHS Foundation Trust* [2012] IRLR 129.
[52] See generally, Anderman, 2000.
[53] For an authority under the now-repealed wages councils legislation, see *Cooner v PS Doal & Sons* [1988] IRLR 338; and on the position under NMWA 1998, see *WA Armstrong & Sons Ltd v Borrill* [2000] ICR 367; *Paggetti v Cobb* [2002] IRLR 861; para 4.59 below.
[54] ERA 1996, s 86(1), (3).
[55] ERA 1996, s 86(3). See para 5.15 below.
[56] ERA 1996, s 91(5). The Court of Appeal recognised the contractual nature of the employee's action for damages by imposing a mitigation requirement in *Westwood v Secretary of State for Employment* [1985] ICR 209.

4.10   The courts traditionally regarded 'protective legislation, such as that imposing standards of health, safety or welfare in factories, mines, etc, or maximum hours of work ... not as operating on a contract but as imposing extra-contractual obligations, enforceable through criminal prosecutions and actions in tort'.[57] The Truck Acts were viewed, for example, as giving rise to a statutory right to sue for the agreed wage and not a right under the contract, so that statutory limitation periods applied.[58] One reason for the failure to achieve a better fit between statute and contract was that, during the period when most of this legislation was passed, the contract of employment as we know it today did not exist; as we have seen, few incidents of the service relationship were clearly rationalised in contractual terms.[59]

Contract plays a central role in defining the scope of modern employment protection legislation since, as we have seen, that legislation adopts the common law concept of the contract of employment for a number of purposes including the classification of employment relationships.[60] However, claims arising under protective legislation are, for the most part, seen as statutory in nature, with individual statutes defining the scope of the relevant remedies. For example, an employer's failure to pay wages when due, in addition to being a breach of contract, also gives rise to a statutory claim.[61] The limitation period for this claim is three months, much shorter than the six year period for breach of contract claims,[62] and it must be asserted before an employment tribunal rather than the County Court or High Court. Although, since 1994, employment tribunals have had the jurisdiction to hear common law claims for damages for breach of contract,[63] there is no parallel provision for the County Court or High Court to hear statutory claims arising out of the employment relationship.

Protective rights originating in statute may nevertheless have an indirect effect on the terms of the contract. In *Barber v RJB Mining*[64] it was held that the 48-hour weekly limit to working time in WTR 1998, regulation 4(1), gave rise to an implied contractual obligation on the part of the employer to observe that limit, enabling the applicants to obtain a declaration of their rights under regulation 4. The decision is striking since the Working Time Regulations are silent on the question of enforcement through the contract of employment, and it might have been supposed that, by providing for other, criminal, remedies in respect of a breach of regulation 4(1),[65] they had implicitly closed this route off. *Barber* is a somewhat isolated decision which has not been followed in other working time cases.[66]

---

[57] Kahn-Freund, 1967: p 641.

[58] *Pratt v Cook, Son & Co (St Pauls) Ltd* [1940] AC 437.

[59] See above, para 4.5.

[60] See above, para 3.18 *et seq*.

[61] ERA 1996, ss 23, 24.

[62] In contrast to the six-year period for breach of contract claims, claims for the statutory rights referred to in the text must be lodged within three months of the relevant event. See eg ERA 1996, s 23.

[63] Their jurisdiction was extended by SI 1994/1623; D Brown, 1994. See para 2.15 *et seq* above.

[64] [1999] IRLR 308.

[65] The remedy provided for a breach of reg 4 is a fine (see WTR, reg 29). The availability of this criminal sanction was one of the factors which led Ramsey J to deny the possibility of a claim in tort for breach of statutory duty under reg 4 in *Sayers v Cambridgeshire County Council* [2007] IRLR 29. See also *Commissioners of Inland Revenue v Ainsworth* [2005] IRLR 465 in which the Court of Appeal held that the right to paid leave under WTR 1998 could not be asserted by way of a claim for unpaid wages under ERA 1996, s 23, but only under WTR, reg 30 (the effect of which was to bar the employee's claim as stricter rules on limitation applied under reg 30).

[66] See, in particular, *Commissioners of Inland Revenue v Ainsworth* [2005] IRLR 465.

4.11   As we saw earlier,[67] employment protection legislation mostly forms a 'floor of rights', setting minimum standards from which derogation is not permitted. Contracting out from rights contained in ERA 1996 and TULRCA 1992 is formally prohibited by statutory rules to the effect that 'any provision in an agreement (whether a contract of employment or not) is void in so far as it purports – (a) to exclude or limit the operation of any provision of this Act or (b) to preclude a person from bringing any proceedings under this Act before an employment tribunal'.[68] Similar provisions apply, for example, to the rights to SSP and SMP under SSCBA 1992.[69] This means that the employee cannot validly contract to receive *inferior* rights and/or benefits to those stipulated by legislation. The few exceptions to this principle are strictly limited by legislation itself.[70]

In principle, the purpose of the statutory floor of rights is to provide a platform on which individual agreement or, more likely, collective bargaining can build to provide more advantageous terms and conditions of employment. This has not been the sole aim of the legislation providing rights to security of income, however. The imposition on employers of the obligations to pay statutory sick pay and guaranteed pay were designed to shift responsibility away from the social security system, which had previously borne the cost of meeting these payments through sickness benefit and unemployment benefit.[71] The shift to payment by the employer resulted in employees being, if anything, worse off. Previously, employees would often receive social security sickness benefit in addition to any contractual entitlement to sick pay under occupational schemes which many employers operated. When statutory sick pay was introduced after 1982, however, provision was made for statutory and contractual rights to be set off against each other.[72]

Floor of rights legislation in Britain has, historically, lacked the comprehensive character of its equivalents in mainland European systems. Instead of entrenching minimum wage rates and maximum working hours which applied throughout the labour force, the practice in Britain was for many decades to legislate only in the case of specific groups of workers, who tended to be those who were not protected by collective agreements of any kind. This was the case, for example, with the working time provisions of the Factories Acts, which did not apply to adult male workers, and with the Trade Boards Acts and Wages Councils Acts, whose application was confined to particular, low-paying sectors of the economy.[73] As long as an effective system of sector-level collective bargaining was in place for most of the labour force, this policy of selective statutory regulation had limited consequences. However, during the 1980s the effectiveness of sector level collective agreements declined rapidly, with the result that the coverage of collective bargaining narrowed from some three-quarters of the labour force to less than half.[74] At the same time, deregulatory legislation removed the remaining controls on minimum wages in the

[67] See para 1.15 above.
[68] ERA 1996, s 203(1); TULRCA 1992, s 288. For discussion of whether contract can be used to exclude Convention rights under HRA 1998, see G Morris, 2001a.
[69] SSCBA 1992, s 151(2) and s 164(6), respectively.
[70] Collective exemptions are possible from the guaranteed pay and unfair dismissal provisions of ERA 1996: see below, paras 4.127 and 5.64. The Working Time Directive makes extensive provision for both collective and individual derogation which is reflected in the provisions adopted to bring it into force in the UK: see below, paras 4.86 *et seq.*
[71] See below, paras 4.125 and 4.127.
[72] SSCBA 1992, Sch 12, para 2(2); see also Sch 13, para 3(2) (SMP). The introduction of guaranteed pay also led to employees being worse off, since at that time unemployment benefit (the forerunner to the jobseeker's allowance) had provided for a higher level of compensation: see below, para 4.127.
[73] See above, para 1.11.
[74] See above, para 1.27.

Wages Councils sectors and the working time provisions of the Factory Acts, leaving only the Agricultural Wages Boards as bodies capable of setting legally-binding minimum terms and conditions of employment.[75] As a result, a situation came into existence in which a large segment of the employed labour force was without statutory or collective protection of any kind in respect of minimum wage levels and maximum hours of work. However, the absence of effective, general regulation has been addressed, in part at least, by the enactment of the National Minimum Wage Act 1998[76] and by the translation into UK law of relevant provisions of the EC Directives on Working Time and Young People at Work.[77]

4.12   Sector level collective bargaining continues in some industries, and collective bargaining at the level of the company or establishment also remains a significant source of regulation of terms and conditions for many employees. Its legal impact on the individual contract of employment is determined by the common law doctrine of incorporation. Incorporation is neither compulsory nor automatic,[78] but rests instead on the presence of an express or implied 'bridging term' in the contract of employment.[79] While the common law is quite effective for most purposes in translating the normative terms of the collective agreement into the individual contract, it has difficulty in resolving conflicts between different external sources of norms, in particular different levels of collective agreements. Nor has the law succeeded in entrenching the normative terms of the collective agreement against attempts by employers to derogate from or vary them. Although the employer cannot unilaterally alter the contract terms, it may destroy their effect by dismissing the employees and offering them new terms. This route is not entirely risk-free: if large numbers of employees are involved, the employer *may* face potentially extensive liability in the form of unfair dismissal or redundancy compensation payments to those who have been dismissed.[80] This may act as something of a disincentive. However, dismissal in breach of contract is not automatically unfair, and is likely to be fair if the employer can demonstrate that it was in the interests of the business. In short, British labour law has no equivalent to the compulsory effect which is accorded to the normative terms of collective agreement by many of the civil law systems.[81]

WRITTEN NOTIFICATION OF TERMS

4.13   No formalities attach to the formation of the contract of employment at common law.[82] This is reflected in the definition of the contract of employment for statutory purposes, which makes it clear that it may be either express or implied and, if it is express, either oral or in writing.[83]

---

[75] See below, para 4.44. At the time of writing the Agricultural Wages Board is due to be abolished.

[76] See below, para 4.46 *et seq.*

[77] See below, para 4.75 *et seq.*

[78] Legislation providing for a form of compulsory incorporation (the EPA 1975, Sch 11) was repealed by the EA 1980, and the Fair Wages Resolution of the House of Commons, which had a broadly similar effect in relation to work performed under public contracts, was rescinded with effect from 1983.

[79] See below, para 4.29.

[80] See below, para 4.41.

[81] See below, para 4.27 *et seq.*

[82] For a decision which stresses the potential informality of the hiring process, see *Stransky v Bristol Rugby Ltd* 2002 WL31914196, High Court, 11 December 2002.

[83] ERA 1996, s 230(2).

However, legislation has superimposed a duty upon the employer to provide the employee with written information concerning particulars of employment, including certain terms of the contract and certain statutory rights.[84]

The scope of the statutory written statement

4.14   The right to the written statement was (along with the right to minimum periods of notice) the first of the modern employment protection rights to be enacted, in the Contracts of Employment Act 1963. Its immediate aims included the reduction of disputes over contract terms and the formalisation of procedures at the level of the individual company or establishment; in these respects it anticipated later developments in the area of employment protection, in particular the unfair dismissal and income protection legislation of the 1970s, into which it was subsumed.[85] The scope of the employer's duty, initially confined to the most basic of the contract terms, was widened by the IRA 1971 and the EPA 1975 to include reference to job title and to disciplinary and grievance procedures. Further modifications were introduced by TURERA 1993, implementing Directive 91/533. The Directive is 'designed to provide employees with improved protection against possible infringements of their rights and to create greater transparency on the labour market'.[86] The TURERA amendments liberalised the relevant qualifying conditions, replacing the 16-hour weekly threshold with one of 8 hours (although this was subsequently repealed in its turn) and shortening the period within which the statement had to be issued from 13 weeks to the present two months. They also imposed for the first time the obligation to give details of collective agreements affecting the employment relationship, and strictly limited the option of referring the employee to another 'reference document'. Under the old section 2(3) of EPCA 1978, the employer could discharge its obligations by reference in the written statement to 'some document which the employee has reasonable opportunities of reading in the course of his employment or which is made reasonably accessible to him in some other way'. After 1993 the right to invoke a reference document was limited to certain specific particulars, namely those concerning illness or incapacity for work, pension rights, length of notice and disciplinary procedures. TURERA 1993 also significantly tightened the obligation to notify the employee of changes to the particulars. Previously, under the old section 4 of EPCA 1978, changes could be notified via the reference document within one month of them taking effect. After TURERA, the changes had to be notified in an additional written statement provided to each employee. At the time the 1993 Act was passed, there were fears that it would give rise to an excess of paperwork.[87]

---

[84] ERA 1996, s 1.

[85] R Lewis, 1986: pp 13, 32; P Davies and M Freedland, 1993: p 145.

[86] Directive 91/533/EC, Recital, para 2. On the Directive, see generally Clark and Hall, 1992; Wedderburn, 1995: pp 4–6; and Joined Cases C-253/96 to C-258/96 *Kampelmann v Landschaftsverband Westfalen-Lippe* [1998] IRLR 333 (discussed by Kenner, 1999b), in which the ECJ held that the provisions of Art 2(2)(c) of the Directive, under which the employer is obliged to notify the employee of his or her job title or to provide a brief description of their duties, are sufficiently unconditional and precise to have direct effect in national law. See also Case C-350/99 *Lange v Georg Schünemann GmbH* [2001] IRLR 244, where the ECJ emphasised that Art 2(2) of the Directive did not reduce the scope of the general requirement under Art 2(1) for the employer to notify employees of the essential aspects of the contract or employment relationship (in that case the obligation to work overtime on request).

[87] See the account of the Parliamentary debates on these provisions in Ewing, 1993a: p 169.

The emphasis on greater certainty and transparency in the employment relationship was, on the other hand, welcomed by several employers' organisations and by the TUC.[88]

(i) Information which must be contained in a single document

4.15   Under ERA 1996, s 1 the employer must issue a 'written statement of particulars of employment' as a single document containing, first, basic information about the employment relationship, that is to say the names of the parties, the date on which employment began and the date on which the employee's continuous employment began, taking into account employment with a previous employer which counts towards that period.[89] Second, the same document must also contain information about certain terms and particulars of employment.[90] These are: the scale or rate of remuneration or the method of calculating it;[91] the intervals at which it is paid (weekly, monthly or other specified interval); any terms relating to hours of work and normal working hours; any terms relating to holidays (including public holidays and holiday pay); the job title;[92] and the employee's place of work or, failing that, the employer's name and address.

(ii) Information which may be contained in a separate document issued to the employee

4.16   A third category of information may be provided in a separate document issued to the employee. This is information concerning the period for which the contract is expected to continue or the date fixed for it to come to an end, in cases where it is not intended to be 'permanent' or indefinite; any collective agreements 'which directly affect the terms and conditions of the employment including, where the employer is not a party, the persons by whom they were made'; and, where the employee is required to work outside the United Kingdom for more than one month, details of the time to be spent working abroad, the currency in which he or she will be paid, any additional payment due for working abroad, and any terms and conditions relating to his or her return to the UK.[93]

---

[88] Clark and Hall, 1992: p 114.

[89] ERA 1996, ss 1(3), 2(3).

[90] ERA 1996, s 1(4).

[91] This includes any minimum rate of remuneration to which the employee becomes entitled by virtue of NMWA 1998. The itemised pay statement which must be issued under ERA 1996, s 8, must also make reference to the details of the wages paid to the employee (see para 4.73 below). NMWA 1998, s 12, confers a power on the Secretary of State to make provision for a minimum wage statement to be issued to all workers (a wider group than the 'employees' covered by ERA 1996, ss 1 and 8), but this power has not yet been exercised. See further para 4.60 below.

[92] More precisely, 'the title of the job which the employee is employed to do or a brief description of the work for which he is employed' (ERA 1996, s 1(4)(f)). In interpreting the equivalent provision of Directive 91/533 (Art 2(2)(c)(ii)), the ECJ held that 'the mere designation of an activity cannot in every case amount to even a brief specification or description of the work done by an employee' so as to comply with the Directive: Joined Cases C-253/96 to C-258/96 *Kampelmann v Landschaftsverband Westfalen-Lippe* [1998] IRLR 333, 342; Kenner, 1999b.

[93] ERA 1996, s 1(4)(g), (j), (k).

(iii) Information which may be contained either in a written statement or in another reasonably accessible document

4.17   A fourth category relates to information which may be notified to the employee either in a written statement or in another document which the employee has a reasonable opportunity to read in the course of employment or which is made reasonably accessible in some way.[94] The relevant particulars are those relating to incapacity for work (including entitlement to sick pay),[95] and occupational pension schemes and benefits (unless the scheme takes effect by or under an Act of Parliament which, independently of ERA 1996, requires such information to be given to the employee).[96] Details of the length of notice which the employee is entitled to receive and which he or she is required to give may be provided by way of reference to the relevant law (contained in sections 86 *et seq* of ERA 1996) or to any relevant collective agreement, which must be accessible to the employee in the sense used above.[97]

(iv) Disciplinary and grievance procedures and contracting-out certificates

4.18   A fifth category concerns disciplinary and grievance procedures (other than those relating to health and safety at work). Any such procedures must be specified to the employee in the written statement; disciplinary rules and procedures may alternatively be specified in another, reasonably accessible document.[98] Details of a person to whom an employee may apply to seek redress of a grievance must also be notified in writing.[99] The statement should also include a note stating whether there is in force a contracting-out certificate for the purposes of the Pensions Schemes Act 1993.

(v) Timing of notification

4.19   The relevant information must be notified to all employees whose employment continues for one month or more,[100] and the statement must be issued within two months of the employment beginning,[101] even if the employment ends at some point in the second month.[102] If the statement is issued in the form of more than one document – that is, the 'written statement' followed by

---

[94] ERA 1996, s 6.
[95] ERA 1996, ss 1(4)(d)(ii), 2(2).
[96] ERA 1996, ss 1(4)(d)(iii), 1(5) and 2(2).
[97] ERA 1996, ss 1(4)(e) and 2(3).
[98] ERA 1996, s 3. EA 2002 repealed provisions excluding the duty to provide a written statement of disciplinary procedures in a case where the employer, together with an associated employer, employed fewer than twenty employees (formerly ERA 1996, s 3(3)–(4)). On the provisions of the ACAS Code of Practice on Disciplinary and Grievance Procedures, and the consequences of failing to comply with them, see paras 2.21 above and 5.125 *et seq* below
[99] ERA 1996, s 3(1)(b)(ii). On grievance procedures and implied terms, see *WA Goold (Pearmak) Ltd v McConnell* [1995] IRLR 516, discussed below, para 4.105; and on the statutory right of a worker to be accompanied at a grievance hearing, see paras 5.121–5.124 below.
[100] ERA 1996, s 198, previously s 5(1) of EPCA 1978 as amended by SI 1995/31, removing the 8-hour threshold. See para 3.55 above.
[101] ERA 1996, ss 1(2).
[102] ERA 1996, s 2(6).

additional 'instalments' – then they must all be issued within this two-month period.[103] The particulars must be those which were in effect on a specified date not more than seven days before the date on which the statement was issued. In general, if there are no particulars in effect in respect of one of the categories listed above, that fact must itself be stated.[104] However this provision does not apply to the matters referred to in para 4.18 above. We discuss the implications of this in para 4.24 below.

(vi) Changes to the particulars

4.20   If there is a change to any of the relevant particulars, section 4 provides that the employer must issue a further written statement 'at the earliest opportunity' and at any event not later than one month after the change took place.[105] This section 4 statement need only detail the relevant changes; it does not need to lay out all the relevant particulars in full, as under section 1. The section 4 statement may, as under section 1, make reference to other documents. A section 4 statement is sufficient if the only change is to the name but not to the identity of the employer, or if the employer's identity changes without the employee losing continuity of employment or any other relevant particulars being affected.[106]

(vii) Use of a written contract of employment or letter of engagement to issue particulars

4.21 In practice, employers frequently issue written documents which purport to be contracts of employment, and they sometimes do not distinguish very carefully between 'contracts' and 'statements'.[107] In principle, the two types of document are distinct: a written contract has normative force in its own right, but a statement is merely declaratory of contract terms whose legal effect is derived from express agreement or from the incorporation or implication of terms. However, by virtue of a change made by the Employment Act 2002,[108] the employer may now satisfy its obligations under the written statement law by issuing 'a document in writing in the form of a contract of employment or letter of engagement' if that document contains all the written particulars which the employer is obliged, by statute, to notify to the employee. These provisions avoid the unnecessary duplication which would arise if the employer had to issue two documents, one a written contract or letter of engagement setting out the contract terms, and the other a written statement simply restating them. At the same time, the changes made by the 2002

---

[103] ERA 1996, s 1(2). This states that '[t]he statement may (subject to s 2(4)) be given in instalments and (whether or not given in instalments) shall be given not later than two months after the beginning of the employment'.

[104] ERA 1996, s 2(1).

[105] ERA 1996, s 4(1), (3). If the change relates to the employee working abroad, the new statement must be issued no later than the time of departure from the United Kingdom: ERA 1996, s 4(3)(b). The equivalent provisions of Directive 91/533 are contained in Art 5.

[106] ERA 1996, s 4(5)–(8).

[107] See Deakin, 1999.

[108] EA 2002, s 37, inserting ERA 1996, ss 7A, 7B (s 7A refers to documents complying with ERA 1996, ss 1-3 and issued after employment begins but within the time limits set out under those provisions; s 7B extends s 7A to documents issued before the start of employment).

Act may make it less straightforward to distinguish between contract and statement in certain situations. We consider this issue further below.[109]

(viii) Remedies

4.22 The remedy for the employer's failure to comply with its obligations under section 1 is by way of a reference to an employment tribunal under section 11, which may 'amend those particulars, or substitute other particulars for them, as [it] may determine to be appropriate'.[110] The tribunal has no general power to award compensation to the employee; nor is the employer's failure to comply with the Act a criminal offence.[111] However, since 1 October 2004, where the employee has been successful in relation to other specified statutory proceedings, between two and four weeks' pay can be awarded for failure to provide an initial statement of particulars or to notify the employee of changes.[112]

The precise scope of the employment tribunal's jurisdiction to hear complaints arising from a breach of the written statement provisions of ERA 1996 was considered in *Southern Cross Healthcare Co Ltd v Perkins*.[113] The argument in this case turned on whether the claimants had been able to establish a contractual entitlement to long service leave in addition to statutory leave entitlements provided for by WTR 1998. The EAT considered that it was the tribunal's task to construe the contract of employment as a necessary step to determining whether the written statement was correct. In the Court of Appeal, Maurice Kay LJ said that this view was right 'to the extent that an employment tribunal will have to identify the terms of the contract in order to see that the statutory statement correctly reflects them'.[114] However he went on to say that the tribunal has no power to interpret the written statement itself, and that 'the only forum with jurisdiction in relation to the construction issue ... is the ordinary civil court'.[115] This aspect of *Southern Cross* is hard to understand.[116] In general, if the tribunal is to arrive at a view on whether the written statement is aligned with the terms of the contract, it logically has to decide what each of them means. More specifically, if, as in the case of *Southern Cross*, the written statement is evidence of the content of the contract terms, the tribunal must interpret it as a necessary step to determining what those terms are. As we shall see shortly, the statement is only an indication of the content

---

[109] See para 4.25.

[110] ERA 1996, s 12(2).

[111] The Contracts of Employment Act 1963 made provision for breach by the employer to be an offence, punishable by fine, but this was repealed in 1965: Wedderburn, 1986: p 139.

[112] EA 2002, s 38; Sch 5. A week's pay is subject to the statutory maximum in ERA 1996, s 227, which as of 1 February 2012 stood at £430. Where an award is to be adjusted under TULRCA 1992, s 207A and under EA 2002, s 38, the adjustment under s 207A is to be made first: TULRCA 1992, s 207A(5), inserted by EA 2008, s 3(2).

[113] [2011] IRLR 247.

[114] [2011] IRLR 247 at [33].

[115] [2011] IRLR 247, at [34].

[116] The outcome, which was that the claims for breach of contract failed for lack of jurisdiction, seems correct, as employment tribunals have no jurisdiction to hear common law claims for breach of contract which do not arise out of, or are not outstanding on, the termination of employment (SI 1994/1623, reg 3; see para 2.16 above). The claims in *Southern Cross* appear to have fallen into this category. The employment tribunal did not consider the issue of the scope of jurisdiction under the written statement law, which was taken up for the first time in the EAT.

of the contract terms; it is not conclusive.[117] But it should not follow that the tribunal has no jurisdiction to interpret it.

Limited normative effect of sections 1–4

4.23   The Act has been interpreted as requiring the employer to notify the employee only of those particulars which have independent contractual force (in addition to the statutory rights to notice and continuity of employment which are also specifically mentioned).[118] This is despite the fact that it is not stated clearly that the 'terms and conditions' which must be notified are those which are *contractual* in nature. It is conceivable that certain particulars could take the form of the work rules considered by the Court of Appeal in *Secretary of State for Employment v ASLEF (No 2)* to be 'in no way terms of the contract of employment'.[119] Whether, if they did, this would affect the employer's obligations under the Act is unclear. The answer is probably that as a matter of construction, any rules concerning the matters listed in sections 1 and 3 are presumed to be contractual in nature, unless the contrary is shown; and that, as such, they trigger the employer's statutory obligations in respect of the written statement.

In *Edwards v Chesterfield Royal Hospital NHS Foundation Trust*[120] Lord Dyson expressed the somewhat heterodox view that, in enacting sections 1 and 3 ERA 1996, Parliament had decided that 'contractual force should be given to [the] rules and procedures' referred to in those provisions of the Act. This view is heterodox because the more conventional understanding is that the parties themselves make the contract subject, in effect, to the relevant common law principles of the construction of contract terms, and that all the legislature did in enacting the written statement law was to impose an obligation of notification on employers. The *practical* effect of the passage of the written statement law may well have been to encourage employers to formalise employment procedures which, as a matter of construction, then came to be regarded as contract terms,[121] but this is very different from saying that the legislature *requires* the courts to interpret disciplinary and other procedures as having contractual effect. Notwithstanding Lord Dyson's dictum, in the unlikely event that it could be shown that disciplinary procedures (for example) did not have contractual force, no obligation of notification under the Act would arise (except to say that no relevant particulars existed); nor would it arise if there were neither contract terms nor particulars of any other kind.

This seems to be the effect, in the first place, of section 2(1), which states that '[i]f, in the case of a statement under section 1, there are no particulars to be entered under any of the heads of paragraph (d) or (k) of subsection (4) of that section, or under any of the other paragraphs of subsection (3) or (4) of that section, that fact shall be stated'. This implies that if there are no agreed terms (or other particulars) relating to a certain matter, there is nothing to notify to the employee, except the fact of their absence.[122] Presumably for the avoidance of doubt, some (but

---

[117] See para 4.25 below.
[118] *Eagland v British Telecommunications plc* [1992] IRLR 323; Morley v Heritage plc [1993] IRLR 400.
[119] [1972] 2 QB 455, 490 (Lord Denning MR); see above, para 4.3.
[120] [2012] IRLR 129, at [28].
[121] See Deakin, 1999.
[122] *Eagland v British Telecommunications plc* [1992] IRLR 323, 327 (Leggatt LJ).

not all) of the paragraphs and heads of section 1 require notification of 'any terms and conditions' on the matters listed there (emphasis added).[123] Under section 3(1)(a) and (aa), the employer is only required to notify the employee of 'any disciplinary rules' and 'any procedure applicable to the taking of disciplinary decisions'; again, if there are no such rules, or procedure, there is nothing on which the statute can bite.[124] However, section 3(1)(b) does not contain the normal qualification, and apparently *requires* the employer to identify a person to whom a complaint may be made if the employee is dissatisfied with a disciplinary decision relating to him or her and the name of a person to whom he or she may present a grievance.[125] In these two cases only does the Act clearly have an effect which is independent of the terms of the contract.

Apart from this, the Act does not prevent there being, for example, a 'zero hours' contract of employment, under which no fixed hours are laid down and employees are called in to work on demand by the employer; nor, at a less extreme level, does the contract necessarily have to contain terms relating to holidays, incapacity or to pension benefits. This absence of any general normative effect would seem at first sight to defeat the purpose of the Act: an employer can avoid the statutory obligation to formalise and record the contract terms by declining to agree to them in the first place. However, this interpretation has been put beyond doubt by two decisions of the Court of Appeal.

In *Eagland v British Telecommunications plc*[126] the Court held that a written statement which contained no reference to holiday pay, sick pay, pension entitlements and disciplinary rules was an accurate record of the employee's contractual entitlements and had therefore not been issued in breach of section 1. According to Parker LJ, although an employment tribunal considering an application to amend the statutory statement would have the power to conclude that 'because the contract turned out to be a contract of employment, it was a necessary legal incident of that contract that the ordinary requirement of such a relationship be included', these requirements 'do not include disciplinary rules, pension, sick pay or holiday pay and in my judgment they have no power to impose upon an employer any such terms if it be the fact... that either it had been agreed that there should be no pension, sick pay, holiday pay or disciplinary rules, or the matter had not been agreed at all. The wording of the section makes it perfectly plain, as indeed must be the case at common law, that there may be no such terms and there is nothing in any section of the Act which empowers or requires the Tribunal to impose upon the parties terms which had not been agreed ...'[127]

In *Morley v Heritage plc*[128] the Court considered the requirement that particulars concerning holidays should be 'sufficient to enable the employee's entitlement, including any entitlement to accrued holiday pay on the termination of employment, to be precisely calculated'.[129] It was held that this did not mean that a term providing for either holidays or holiday pay had to be implied: on the contrary, section 1 'so far from requiring that a contract of employment must give

---

[123] ERA 1996, s 1(4)(c), (d), (j) and (k)(iv).
[124] See, however, paras 5.125 *et seq* for the consequences of a failure to comply with the ACAS Code of Practice on Disciplinary and Grievance Procedures.
[125] See *WA Goold (Pearmak) Ltd v McConnell* [1995] IRLR 516, 517 (Morison J).
[126] [1992] IRLR 323.
[127] [1992] IRLR 323, 326. The statement made by Stephenson LJ in *Mears v Safecar Security Ltd* [1982] IRLR 183, 191, to the effect that s 11 requires the tribunal to 'find the specified terms, and in the last resort invent them for the purposes of literally writing them into the contract', was expressly disapproved.
[128] [1993] IRLR 400.
[129] ERA 1996, s 1(4)(d)(i).

entitlement to pay in lieu of holiday not taken, does no more than recognise that a contract can include such a provision.[130]

In *Eagland*[131] Parker LJ referred to a distinction between 'mandatory' and 'non-mandatory' terms of the contract of employment in the following terms:

> So far as mandatory terms are concerned... [t]here may be a case where there is, for example, no provision as to the length of notice. In such a case the Tribunal would in my view have power to conclude that there must be reasonable notice. It may also have power to decide, as would a court of law, the length of such notice, which would be a question of fact. But I do not consider that even in mandatory cases the Tribunal have power to impose on parties terms which have not been agreed.

The meaning of the phrase 'mandatory term' is not immediately obvious. The only terms which the Act requires the statement to contain are, as we have just seen, those relating to certain aspects of disciplinary and grievance procedures under section 3(1)(b). If it is meant to refer to the statutory minimum period of notice which is imposed upon the parties by statute,[132] this should arguably be notified to the employee by virtue of section 1(3)(e) of the Act, regardless of agreement. One possible interpretation of Parker LJ's remarks is that the employment tribunal has the duty, under a section 11 application, to seek to clarify the nature of those implied terms which are 'necessary legal incidents' of the contract. But what these might be – other than the inevitably diffuse implied obligations such as those of obedience, co-operation and care – is unclear. They could be said to include matters such as the identity of the parties and the rate or method of calculating pay, since it is difficult to envisage there being a contract of employment which did not contain *some* terms on these matters.

4.24   The failure of the Act to impose any general normative effect is easier to understand, if not necessarily to justify, by bearing in mind that the regulatory framework for terms and conditions of employment was far more comprehensive at the time of the Act's inception than it is today. When the Contracts of Employment Act 1963 was enacted, the vast majority of employees were protected either by the minimum terms set by sector-level collective agreements or by the legally-binding provisions of statutory wages orders, in each case incorporated into individual contracts of employment. The statutory notification requirements were therefore underpinned by substantive rights in the case of most employees and they, in turn, contributed to the effectiveness of those rights in practice. Research carried out in the 1970s showed that the practice of issuing written statements became widespread following the passage of the 1963 Act, and that although there was in many cases some confusion between the statements issued by employers and the normative terms laid down by collective agreements, there was also a greater awareness on the part of individual employees of their contractual rights than there had been prior to the passage of the 1963 Act.[133]

---

[130] [1993] IRLR 400, 402 (Rose LJ). On the right to paid annual leave under WTR 1998, see para 4.82.
[131] [1992] IRLR 323, 326.
[132] ERA 1996, s 86.
[133] Leighton and Dunville, 1977.

Since this research was undertaken, the obligations upon employers to adopt the minimum terms of sector-level collective agreements have been abolished and the coverage of collective bargaining has been considerably reduced.[134] It is possible, then, that in respect of employment which is no longer protected by a floor of rights set by collective bargaining, there will *not* be any terms relating to such issues as hours of work, holidays, incapacity, pension benefits and disciplinary procedures, since these are not necessarily matters which the contract of employment is obliged by statute to provide for, either directly or by reference to a collective agreement. This lack of an effective floor of minimum terms and conditions considerably limits the scope, in practice, of the employer's obligations under section 1, although to some extent the situation has now been ameliorated by the enactment of basic labour standards legislation in relation to minimum wages and maximum working hours.[135] There may also be an irreducible minimum of information concerning the 'necessary legal incidents' of the contract, in the sense identified above.[136] But there is evidence to suggest that in workplaces without an effective trade union presence, employees are less likely to receive written statements or may receive documents whose status (contract or statement) is highly ambiguous, thanks in part to employers' ignorance of the law but also to the lack of an effective sanction for its breach.[137]

EC Directive 91/533 is differently worded from the equivalent provisions of ERA 1996. Article 2 of the Directive states that 'an employer shall be obliged to notify an employee to whom this Directive applies ... of the essential aspects of the contract or employment relationship'. These 'essential aspects' are then stated to 'cover at least' a number of listed matters which include, for example, 'the amount of paid leave to which the employee is entitled or, where this cannot be indicated when the information is given, the procedures for allocating and determining such leave',[138] and 'the length of the employee's normal working day or week'.[139] Since the language used here is unqualified, and there is no reference to an obligation to inform the employee of the *absence* of particulars on any point, the Directive could be read as requiring the employer to provide for particulars on the matters which make up the 'essential aspects' of the employment relationship. This interpretation is strengthened by the sixth recital to the Directive, which refers to point 9 of the Community Charter of Fundamental Social Rights for Workers under which '[t]he conditions of employment of every worker of the European Community shall be stipulated in laws, a collective agreement or a contract of employment, according to arrangements applying in each country'. On the other hand, Article 6 of the Directive states that '[t]his Directive shall be without prejudice to national law and practice concerning the form of the contract or employment relationship, proof as regards the existence and content of a contract or employment relationship, [and] the relevant procedural rules'. This can be read as preserving the pre-existing position of British labour law, namely that (with the exceptions identified in para 4.18 above) sections 1 to

---

[134] See above, para 2.7.

[135] See paras 4.41–4.60, on the minimum wage, and 4.75–4.93, on working time. It would seem to follow from the decision of the High Court in *Barber v RJB Mining Ltd* [1999] IRLR 308, holding that working time limits laid down in WTR 1998, reg 4(1) give rise to contractual rights on the part of workers covered by the Regulations, that the employer is obliged to include details of relevant working time limits in the written statement issued under ERA 1996, s 1, although that decision was not followed in *Commissioners of Inland Revenue v Ainsworth* [2005] IRLR 465).

[136] See above, para 4.7.

[137] Empirical studies addressing the recent operation of the written statement law include NACAB, 1990 (see Clark and Hall, 1992: p 116); Deakin, 1999; W Brown *et al*, 2000.

[138] Directive 91/533, Art 2(2)(f).

[139] Directive 91/533, Art 2(2)(i).

4 of the Act do not create an obligation to inform the employee of particulars which have no independent contractual (or other) existence, although the point is far from clear.

Distinguishing contract and statement

4.25   Even if, in principle, contract and statement are conceptually discrete, in practice one or both of the parties may regard the statement as being equivalent to a contract in both form and effect. Particular difficulty arises from the practice of employers of issuing written documents which either purport to be contracts in their own right or which depart in some respect or other from the entitlements which are meant to vest in employees by virtue of incorporation from a collective agreement or some other external source.[140] Since the written statement is merely *declaratory* of the contract terms, it cannot prevail over terms which are expressly or impliedly agreed by the parties, including those which are incorporated from a collective agreement. On the face of it, the statement is only the employer's view of the contract's contents. Although it may be *evidence* of what the parties have agreed, and to this extent may need to be considered alongside other factors, such as their conduct, in construing the agreement, there is a presumption that it cannot be relied on by the employer to derogate from what would otherwise be clear contractual entitlements of the employee: this can only be done if there is clear evidence that the statement represents the contractual intentions of both parties.

An early decision which suggested that the statement might readily be accorded normative effect as an offer of contract terms was *Gascol Conversions Ltd v Mercer*.[141] The employer sent each of its existing employees a document which purported to discharge its obligations to issue a written statement under the IRA 1971 (a predecessor of ERA 1996, section 1), but which was headed 'contract of employment'. The applicant signed and returned to the employer a form which stated: 'I confirm receipt of a new contract of employment ... which sets out as required under the Industrial Relations Act 1971 the terms and conditions of my employment'. The Court of Appeal held that the document constituted an offer of a new contract, which the employee accepted by returning the signed form. Since the contract was in writing, there was a presumption against according contractual force to any other terms which might have been expressed orally or implied by conduct. The employee's acceptance of the statement had amounted to a variation of the original contract terms.

The difficulty in the reasoning in *Mercer* is that a document which purports to discharge the employer's statutory obligations is meant to be a statement of the *existing* contract terms; it cannot, logically, be at the same time an offer of *new* terms. As explained by Browne-Wilkinson J in *System Floors Ltd v Daniel*, this means that 'in the absence of an acknowledgement by the parties that the statement is itself a contract and that the terms are correct, such as that contained in the *Mercer* case, the statutory statement does not itself constitute a contract in writing'.[142]

---

[140] Empirical research suggests that both of these have been widespread practices since the enactment of the legislation. See Leighton and Dunville, 1977; W Brown *et al*, 1998; Deakin, 1999.

[141] [1974] ICR 420.

[142] *System Floors Ltd v Daniel* [1982] ICR 54, 58. See also *Glendale Managed Services v Graham* [2003] IRLR 465, at [5]: 'written particulars of employment supplied by an employer in performance of its statutory duty do not normally constitute the contract of employment itself, but are simply evidence of the terms of the contract and not conclusive evidence' (Keene LJ).

Short of such acknowledgement, the employee cannot be taken to have agreed to a contractual variation; merely carrying on working will not suffice. Moreover, in attempting to introduce new or different terms by means of the written statement the employer will be in breach of its statutory obligations under section 1, and this makes it difficult to argue that the employee is estopped from denying that the contract has been varied: according to the Court of Appeal in *Robertson v British Gas Corp*, the employer will not be allowed to set up its own legal wrong as the basis for such an estoppel.[143]

Although these later decisions have distinguished *Mercer* without actually overruling it, the present position is that an employer will not easily be able to present the statement as evidence of terms which derogate from the terms which would otherwise apply. Far from being equivalent to the contract, under these circumstances the statement is 'not even conclusive evidence of the contract'.[144]

Where, conversely, the statement favours the employee, it has been held to represent 'strong prima facie evidence' of the contract terms. The written particulars 'place a heavy burden on the employer to show that the actual terms of contract are different from those which he has set out in the statutory statement'.[145] This 'heavy burden' does not apply to the employee who wishes to show that the contract terms are different from those in the statement.[146]

In effect, then, the statement is strong evidence in the employee's favour, but weak evidence in favour of the employer. This is appropriate, given that statute has placed the duty of clarifying the contract terms clearly on the employer, without, however, seeking to undermine the effectiveness of terms incorporated from collective agreements or other external sources for the protection and regulation of terms and conditions of employment.[147] Nevertheless, what has just been said does not amount to saying that the employer is conclusively bound by the contents of the written statement; nor does it have the effect of reversing the burden of proof which would normally fall on the employee as applicant or claimant if he or she is seeking to establish the existence of a contract term on a particular matter. Hence, in interpreting the equivalent provisions of Directive 91/533, the ECJ has held that:

> ... the notification referred to in Article 2(1) of the Directive, in so far as it informs an employee of the essential aspects of the contract or employment relationship and, in particular, of the points listed in Article 2(2)(c), enjoys the same presumption as to its correctness as would attach, in domestic law, to any similar document drawn up by the employer and communicated to the employee. The employer must none the less be allowed

---

[143] *Robertson v British Gas Corp* [1983] ICR 351, 355 (Ackner LJ). On variation generally, see below, paras 4.35–4.42.

[144] *Turiff Construction Ltd v Bryant* (1967) 2 KIR 659.

[145] *System Floors (UK) Ltd v Daniel* [1982] ICR 54, 58 (Browne-Wilkinson J).

[146] The Court of Appeal has rejected an argument that 'an equally heavy burden rests on the employee': *Robertson v British Gas Corp* [1983] ICR 351, 355 (Ackner LJ).

[147] What has been said in the text about the effect of s 1 statements also applies to statements of changes to particulars under s 4: this is discussed in the context of the variation of contract terms at para 4.37 below. Note that not all the provisions contained in a written statement may be capable of being incorporated in an employee's contract of employment: see *Bristol City Council v Deadman* [2007] IRLR 888.

to bring any evidence to the contrary, by showing that the information in the notification is either inherently incorrect or has been shown to be so in fact.[148]

As we have seen, since the coming into force of the Employment Act 2002, statute has provided that an employer may satisfy its obligations under the written statement law by providing an employee with a written contract of employment containing the particulars which it would otherwise have to notify to the employee in a separate written statement.[149] Does this mean that if the employer issues a document headed 'contract of employment', and the employee then indicates his or her consent to its terms, the employee can no longer challenge the document using the logic of *System Floors Ltd v Daniel* and *Robertson v British Gas Corp*? Although the point has not been tested, it is arguable that the changes made by the 2002 Act have made no difference to the basic proposition that the contract is one thing and the statutory obligation to notify the employee of its terms in writing is another. Thus where the employer seeks to satisfy its statutory obligations by issuing a written contract of employment, the question of whether that document is an exhaustive account of the contract terms should be approached in the same way as before: because of the statutory context in which the document is issued, and the protective purpose of the Act and of Directive 91/533, the document should be construed as strong evidence of contract terms in the employee's favour, but weak evidence at best, of terms favouring the employer.

CONSTRUCTION, INCORPORATION AND VARIATION OF TERMS

4.26   Subject to what has just been said about the very slight normative effect of sections 1–4 of ERA 1996,[150] the terms of the contract will be determined by techniques of construction derived from the common law. Construing an employment contract is not necessarily straightforward, however, and the approach taken to construing commercial agreements may be of little help or even positively misleading.[151] There may be a formal offer of employment contained in a written document to which the employee is invited to assent, but even then it would be unusual for the document to constitute an *exhaustive* account of the contract terms. It would be usual for some terms, at least, to be implied or incorporated by reference to one of a number of external sources, such as a collective agreement or company handbook. The manner in which the contract is performed is also an important guide to its contents. In principle, the substance of a contract, once made, cannot be modified merely by the parties' subsequent behaviour; contractual obligations can only be varied by mutual agreement. This is to assume, however, that the substance of the original agreement is completely clear; and this will rarely be the case with contracts of employment. Two forms of practice, in particular, will be important in construing the agreement: the 'custom and

---

[148] Joined Cases C-253/96 to C-258/96 *Kampelmann v Landschaftsverband Westfalen-Lippe* [1998] IRLR 333, 342 (see also the opinion of Tesauro AG, [1998] IRLR 333, 337); and see Case C-350/99 *Lange v Georg Schünemann GmbH* [2001] IRLR 244 making, in this respect, much the same point.

[149]   ERA 1996, ss 7A, 7B, inserted by EA 2002, s 37.

[150] See para 4.25 above.

[151] On the need for a flexible approach to the construction of employment contracts, see the opinion of Lord Hoffmann in *Carmichael v National Power plc* [2000] IRLR 43, and for a decision applying Lord Hoffmann's approach to contractual interpretation in *Investors' Compensation Scheme Ltd v West Bromwich Building Society* [1998] 1 WLR 896 to the employment context, see *Birmingham City Council v Wetherill* [2007] IRLR 781.

practice' of the plant or establishment, which the parties may (not must) be assumed to have had in mind when they contracted; and their own conduct subsequent to the agreement, which may be taken to be a guide to what they initially intended.[152]

Incorporation of terms from collective agreements

4.27 Labour law in Britain has played a negligible role in regulating and enforcing collective agreements between trade unions and employers. Section 4 of the Trade Union Act 1871, which denied contractual force to agreements between trade unions, also had this effect with relation to sector-level collective agreements, since an employers' association was deemed to be a 'trade union' for the purpose of that Act.[153] At common law, agreements between a trade union and a single employer were thought to lack contractual force on the twin grounds of uncertainty and the absence of any intention to create legal relations.[154] There is now a statutory presumption that a collective agreement is 'not to have been intended by the parties to be a legally enforceable contract'. This presumption is displaced if the agreement is in writing and contains a provision stating that the parties do intend it to have legal effect, whereupon it is conclusively presumed to be a legally binding contract. Agreements made binding in this way are very rare.[155] However, the non-enforceability of the vast majority of agreements at the collective level does not affect their enforceability as terms of the individual contract of employment.[156] This 'normative' or term-setting function of the collective agreement, as distinct from its 'contractual' function of regulating the relationship of the collective parties, finds legal expression through the incorporation of terms into individual contracts.

In most mainland European systems, legislation specifies the circumstances in which the normative terms of collective agreements take effect, regulating the sectoral scope and level of their application, the extent to which they apply to non-union members and their temporal effect in the case of the lapse or termination of relations between the collective parties. Where the employer is a member of the relevant employers' association for the industry, the effect of a sector-level agreement is generally both *automatic*, in the sense that the terms apply immediately to all contracts of employment whether or not previously agreed by the individual parties, and *compulsory*, in the sense of laying down minimum rights which cannot be derogated from by individual contract. In France, Article L 135-2 of the Labour Code provides that 'where an employer is bound by the terms of a [relevant collective agreement], these terms take effect in the contracts of employment to which he is a party, unless more advantageous terms apply'.[157] The employee cannot waive his or her minimum entitlements under the terms of the collective agreement, and the collective terms are substituted for the individual ones where the latter provide inferior benefits. The effect of the collective agreement does not depend upon incorporation via the individual contract, but upon its own 'regulatory nature', which is similar

---

[152] See *Dunlop Tyres Ltd v Blows* [2001] IRLR 629.
[153] TUA 1871, s 4(4). The Act was repealed by the IRA 1971.
[154] Kahn-Freund, 1959; *Ford Motor Co Ltd v AUEFW* [1969] 2 QB 303.
[155] TULRCA 1992, s 179(1)–(2). See below, para 9.26.
[156] *Marley v Forward Trust Group* [1986] ICR 891.
[157] 'Lorsqu'un employeur est lié par les clauses d'une convention ou d'un accord collectif du travail, ces clauses s'appliquent aux contrats conclus avec lui, sauf dispositions plus favorables'.

to that of legislation.[158] Nor is the trade-union status of the employee relevant: the normative terms apply whether or not he or she is a member of any or a particular trade union. A broadly similar approach is taken in Germany, under the terms of the Collective Agreements Act.[159] In both systems, provision is made for the *extension* of sectoral agreements to cover non-associated employers, in this way ensuring that minimum norms are respected throughout a given industry.[160]

The civil law technique of according collective bargaining regulatory effect over the contract of employment may be contrasted with the approach taken in the North American systems, where plant or company-level collective agreements come close to displacing the individual contract of employment altogether. In the United States, where an employer comes under a duty to bargain with a certified bargaining agent of the workforce, the resulting collective agreement is seen as exhaustively defining the mutual rights and obligations of the parties with regard to terms and conditions of employment. Neither derogation from nor improvement upon terms is allowed, since 'the very purpose of providing by statute for the collective agreement is to supersede the terms of separate agreements by employees with terms which reflect the strength and bargaining power and welfare of the group'.[161] In Canada it has been said that 'the common law as it applies to individual contracts of employment is no longer relevant to employer-employee relationships governed by a collective agreement which ... deals with discharge, termination of employment, severance pay and a host of other matters that have been negotiated between union and company as the principal parties thereto'.[162]

At no point has general legislation in the United Kingdom provided for automatic and compulsory effect to be granted to the normative terms of sector-level collective agreements.[163] The closest British labour law has come to this is the Conditions of Employment and National Arbitration Order of 1940 (Order 1305), which established compulsory unilateral arbitration on terms and conditions as a *quid pro quo* for banning strikes and lock-outs. This made 'recognised terms and conditions', defined as terms deriving from agreements 'between organisations of employers and trade unions representative respectively of substantial proportions of the employers and workers engaged in that trade or industry in that district', generally binding, in the sense that 'all employers in the trade or industry in that district shall observe the recognised terms and conditions or such terms and conditions of employment as are not less favourable than the recognised terms and conditions'.[164] Failure to observe the recognised terms was a criminal offence and the trade union or employers' association in question had the standing to seek arbitration before the National Arbitration Tribunal, which had the power to make an award implying the relevant terms and conditions into the individual contracts of the employees affected. This procedure was continued in force after the end of World War Two, although, from 1951, without

---

[158] See Pelissier, Supiot and Jeammaud, 2008: p 1335 *et seq*.

[159] German Collective Agreements Act 1949, Art 2. Non-union members are not automatically covered by all normative terms; see Weiss, 1992: p 9; Wedderburn, 1992c: p 246.

[160] French Labour Code, Art L 133-8; German Collective Agreements Act, Art 5. See Weiss, 1992: p 23.

[161] *JI Case Co v NLRB* 321 US 332, 338 (1943) (Jackson J).

[162] *McGavin Toastmasters Inc v Ainscough* [1976] 1 SC 718, 725 (Laskin CJ).

[163] This was done, exceptionally, for certain categories of public sector employment (National Health Service Act 1977, Sch 5, para 10(1) and SI 1974/296).

[164] SR & O 1940/1305, reg 5(1); Wages Councils Act 1945, s 19 and Sch 3, para 1(1).

criminal sanctions,[165] and was later merged with the principle of enforcement of the 'general level' of terms and conditions in a given trade, in Schedule 11 of the EPA 1975.[166]

Order 1305 and its successors differed from the mainland European pattern of regulation in two important respects. First, its effect was not automatic. The making of an agreement did not, in itself, confer rights on employees; they acquired the protection of the minimum terms only after an arbitral award had been made by the relevant tribunal.[167] Nor did employees have standing to seek such an award. Second, it did not take the form of an *extension* procedure which was specific to the non-federated firms. The same arbitration procedure applied to *all* employers in the trade, whether they were federated or not. Schedule 11 of the EPA 1975 was repealed in 1980 on the grounds that it had an inflationary effect on pay claims, as well as being part of the Conservative government's rolling programme of labour market deregulation.[168]

In the absence of statutory regulation the issue of incorporation is dealt with by the common law, which knows no principle of automatic and compulsory effect.[169] The legal basis for the normative effect of the collective agreement must rest at the level of the individual contract of employment, because the collective agreement lacks the 'regulatory effect' or force of law accorded to it in other systems. A number of conceptual explanations for incorporation have been offered.

(i) Agency

4.28   One possibility is that the trade union, through one or more of its officials, negotiates with the employer as agent for each individual union member as principal, with the resulting terms forming part of the contract of employment without the need for further agreement. This has been put forward as the most likely explanation in a small number of cases.[170] As a general explanation, though, it is unconvincing. It is unable to account for the incorporation of terms into the contracts of employment of non-members, for example; nor does it deal with the position of employees who either join the employment or, conceivably, the union, after the collective agreement has been concluded. It would also suggest that an individual member can unilaterally revoke his or her authority to the union to negotiate on their behalf, and in this way avoid the normative effect of the collective agreement completely. This is unlikely to reflect the intention of either the trade union or the employer. From the union's point of view, it would be undesirable to allow the effect of the collective agreement to be fragmented by enabling non-unionists to opt out. For the employer, collective bargaining is a way of avoiding the high transaction costs involved in treating union members and non-members differently and being required to negotiate individually with those who are outside the union. In *practice*, terms and conditions of employment are normally applied uniformly, to members and non-members alike. To differentiate between these two groups may,

---

[165] Cf the Industrial Disputes Order, SI 1951/1376; Terms and Conditions of Employment Act 1959, s 8.

[166] The 'general level' principle referred to the level observed in practice, as distinct from that laid down by agreement. See P Davies and M Freedland, 1984: pp 159–163.

[167] *Hulland v William Saunders & Son* [1945] KB 78.

[168] See above, para 1.24.

[169] *Dudfield v Ministry of Works* (1964) 108 Sol Jo 118.

[170] *Holland v London Society of Compositors* (1924) 40 TLR 440; *Edwards v Skyways* [1964] 1 WLR 349; *Singh v British Steel Corpn* [1974] IRLR 131; *Harris v Richard Lawson Autologistics Ltd* [2002] IRLR 476.

depending on the employer's purpose, give rise to a breach of the anti-discrimination provisions of TULRCA 1992.[171]

These points notwithstanding, there is no reason in principle why an agency agreement should not be made between a trade union and an individual member (or, for that matter, between an individual employee and another organisation which undertakes to negotiate on his or her behalf), nor is there any obstacle to an employer negotiating with a trade union on the basis that the final terms will take effect in individual contracts of employment via such agency. However, there would have to be clear evidence that these were the intentions of the parties concerned. The mere existence of the contract of membership between union and member does not authorise the former to act as agent for the latter;[172] something more specific is needed.[173]

(ii) The 'bridge' term

4.29   The most generally accepted basis for incorporation is that it takes place through a 'bridging term' in the contract of employment.[174] The principal function of the 'bridge' is to identify the external source from which the terms of the contract are to be drawn, but it may also perform other functions: it may determine which terms are appropriate for incorporation and resolve conflicts between different sources. Once it is present, incorporation may take effect automatically in the sense that no further authorisation or agreement by either party to the contract of employment is needed, although this will depend to a large degree on practice in the workplace in question.[175]

A bridging term could be expressly agreed by the parties.[176] It is more likely that any express reference will today be found in the written statement of terms and conditions.[177] The written statement is not, as we have seen, the same thing as the contract, but it is evidence of it; hence, a reference to the normative effect of a collective agreement can be regarded as significant evidence of a term which was either previously expressed by the parties or tacitly accepted by them. The chances of finding such a reference have strengthened as a result of the amendments made to section 1 of EPCA 1978 (now section 1 of ERA 1996) in 1993, introducing for the first time the obligation to include details of 'any collective agreements which directly affect the terms and conditions of the employment'.[178]

If there is no express bridging term one may be implied by using the normal common law tests, but its existence cannot be assumed simply from the presence of the collective agreement. A term may be implied on the basis of custom and practice, if it is the regular practice in the plant or establishment in question to observe the terms of a particular agreement.[179] A more modern

---

[171] See further, para 8.13 *et seq*.

[172] *Boxfoldia Ltd v NGA* (1982) [1988] ICR 752: a union has no implied authority to terminate the employment contracts of its members by giving strike notice to their employer.

[173] See *Burton Group v Smith* [1977] IRLR 351; *Lee v GEC Plessey Telecommunications Ltd* [1993] IRLR 383, 391. It is not clear what this more specific element might have been in *Harris v Richard Lawson Autologistics Ltd* [2002] IRLR 476.

[174] Hepple, 1983: p 402.

[175] See *Glendale Managed Services v Graham* [2003] IRLR 465.

[176] *National Coal Board v Galley* [1958] 1 WLR 16.

[177] For an example, see *Edinburgh Council v Brown* [1999] IRLR 208.

[178] EPCA 1978, s 1(3)(j), now contained in ERA 1996, s 1(4)(j).

[179] *MacLea v Essex Line Ltd* (1933) 45 Ll L Rep 254; *Henry v London General Transport Services Ltd* [2002] IRLR 472; *Tees and Hartlepool Port Authority v Bosomworth*, EAT, 10 July 2003, Appeal No EAT/0728/02/SM.

way of achieving this result is to use the 'incidents of employment' test. A bridging term may be 'imposed by law as a necessary incident of the contract, without which that contract would be inefficacious, absurd or futile'.[180] If this approach is taken, it may not matter that the employee had no specific knowledge of the collective agreement in question:[181] the implication is based not so much on his or her tacit consent and understanding, as on the need for the contract to reflect the reality of the parties' relationship. The 'legal incidents' test therefore brings the common law closer to the civilian model of regulation and further away from a consensual model of contract.

This approach may be applied not simply to a plant or company-level agreement but also to one at sector level. In *Howman & Son Ltd v Blyth*[182] the EAT implied a right to sick pay on the basis that 'the relationship between the parties requires that there should be some agreed term which has not in fact been agreed but both parties would have agreed what that term would be if they had been asked'. The fact that sick pay was regularly paid in the *industry* in question was thought to be relevant: 'in an industry where the normal practice is to provide sick pay for a limited period only, the reasonable term to imply is the term normally applicable in that industry'.[183] Here, a term was implied from industry-wide practice without the need even for a 'bridge' as such. This is to stretch the language of contract to the limit: 'the latitude which is asserted is ... a latitude to engage in judicial legislation about the terms of the contract of employment'.[184] In effect, the EAT found a common law route to the insertion into contracts of the 'general level' of protection in an industry, to replace the statutory mechanism which previously had this effect under Schedule 11 of the EPA 1975. This case illustrates the inherent flexibility and wide applicability of these common law techniques.

(iii) Appropriateness of terms for incorporation

4.30   A major limitation on the normative effect of collective agreements is the doctrine of the *appropriateness* of terms for incorporation.[185] Terms intended to regulate the employment of one group of employees will not be incorporated into the contracts of others.[186] It may also be that certain terms are intended to be part of the 'contractual' function of the agreement which governs the collective relationship between employer and trade union, as opposed to regulating the terms and conditions of employees. This question could be dealt with expressly, either in the individual contract or in the collective agreement. Express terms in the collective agreement can take effect in the individual contract via the bridging term. More often, the bridging term will be silent on the matter. Difficulty arises, in particular, if a term which is collective in nature is also capable of conferring rights or imposing obligations upon an individual employee.

One possible basis for addressing the issue of appropriateness is to distinguish between terms which are procedural in nature and those which are substantive. Substantive terms, laying down entitlements in relation to pay, working time and other benefits, are normally incorporated

---

[180] *Tadd v Eastwood and the Daily Telegraph Ltd* [1983] IRLR 320, 327.
[181] Cf the discussion of Hepple, 1981b: p 128.
[182] [1983] ICR 416.
[183] [1983] ICR 416, 420 (Browne-Wilkinson J).
[184] P Davies and M Freedland, 1984: p 306.
[185] *Young v Canadian Northern Rly Co* [1931] AC 83; *Burroughs Machines Ltd v Timmoney* [1977] IRLR 404.
[186] Hepple, 1981b: p 129.

into contracts of employment without difficulty. The terms of a collective agreement concerning employees' entitlements to severance pay would normally be incorporated into their individual contracts, for example.[187] By extension, an employment opportunities policy, stating that employees were not to be discriminated against on a number of grounds including age, was held to be suitable for incorporation by the House of Lords in *Taylor v Secretary of State for Scotland*.[188] By contrast, a 'no compulsory redundancy' agreement was held by the Court of Appeal to be inappropriate for incorporation in *Kaur v MG Rover Group Ltd*, on the grounds that it reflected 'an aspiration rather than a binding contractual term'.[189] While all these decisions turn, in the end, on their own facts, *Kaur* is difficult to reconcile with the previous case law on the incorporation of substantive terms.

Procedural clauses have often been regarded as inappropriate for incorporation. In *British Leyland (UK) Ltd v McQuilken*[190] a collective agreement provided that the employer would interview employees in order to establish whether they wished to take up an option of retraining or accept redundancy. This was held to be 'a long-term plan, dealing with policy rather than the rights of individual employees under their contracts of employment'.[191] In *Alexander v Standard Telephones and Cables Ltd (No 2)*[192] a last-in, first-out agreement, according to which employees would be selected for redundancy according to their length of service with the employer, was also deemed inappropriate for incorporation. As a general guide, this would seem to be highly questionable: the seniority acquired by an individual employee can be seen as an important feature of his or her overall contractual package. In *Alexander v Standard Telephones and Cables Ltd*,[193] Aldous J, considering an application for an injunction which he rejected on separate grounds, was prepared to incorporate the last-in, first-out agreement on the basis that it was 'designed and intended to benefit' individual employees in proportion to their length of service. This approach seems to be preferable to that of drawing a sharp distinction between procedural and substantive terms. In general, 'it may be a mistake to assume that a provision which is procedural in nature necessarily has no impact on the position of individual employees, and therefore wrong to assume that all such provisions should be excluded from incorporation'.[194] Many apparently 'procedural' terms are capable of benefiting employees, and there is no reason in principle why terms relating to disciplinary procedures, for example, should not be incorporated into individual contracts since they are capable of conferring important protections upon employees.[195] In *Adams v British Airways*

---

[187] *Lee v GEC Plessey Telecommunications Ltd* [1993] IRLR 383.

[188] [2000] IRLR 502.

[189] [2005] IRLR 40, at [32] (Keene LJ).

[190] [1978] IRLR 245.

[191] [1978] IRLR 245, 246 (Lord McDonald).

[192] [1991] IRLR 286.

[193] [1990] ICR 291, 303; to similar effect is *Anderson v Pringle of Scotland Ltd* [1998] IRLR 64, in which the Outer House of the Court of Session not only held that a 'first-in, last-out' clause was incorporated into the employee's contract of employment, but granted an interim interdict to restrain his dismissal in breach of that provision. See further para 5.61.

[194] Auerbach, 1993: p 18.

[195] Much of the recent case law of the effect of disciplinary procedures on contractual rights and remedies assumes that they are capable of being incorporated in this way. See below, paras 5.53–5.60. In *Bristol City Council v Deadman* [2007] IRLR 888 Moore-Bick LJ stated at [17] that where an employer has published and implemented with the concurrence of employees' representatives formal procedures providing for the manner in which complaints are to be investigated, it will usually become a term of the contract that those procedures will be followed. See also Lord Dyson's view in *Edwards v Chesterfield Royal Hospital NHS Foundation Trust* [2012] IRLR 129 at [28], that the effect of the written statement law in ERA 1996, ss 1-4 is that disciplinary and grievance procedures will normally have contractual force, on which see our discussion in para 4.23 above.

plc[196] the Court of Appeal seems to have had little difficulty in accepting that provisions governing seniority rights were appropriate for incorporation into individual contracts of employment and in *Keeley v Fosroc International Ltd*[197] a clearly expressed provision in an employer handbook providing for an enhanced redundancy payment was held to be apt for incorporation.

On the other hand, provisions of collective agreements relating to organisational matters, such as the allocation of employees to certain tasks or operations, may not be appropriate for incorporation at the individual level. In *Malone v British Airways plc*[198] the Court of Appeal held that an agreement on the normal complement of cabin crew on long-distance flights was not incorporated into individual contracts, notwithstanding its clear impact on working conditions. The agreement had been intended both to protect crew in general against excessive work demands and to safeguard jobs. However, the Court took the view that the collective parties cannot have intended the rules on crew numbers to be individually enforceable since the effect of that would have been 'disastrous' for the employer, in the sense that 'an individual or a small group of cabin crew members [could have brought] a flight to a halt by refusing to work under complement'.[199] The Court's insistence on the need to interpret the collective agreement in the light of the employer's business needs is a reminder of the limits of the doctrine of incorporation as a device for the protection of employee interests.

The decision of the Court of Appeal in *Camden Exhibition and Display Ltd v Lynott*[200] illustrates the problems which may arise from deciding the issue of incorporation according to whether a term is procedural or substantive in nature. The Court held by a majority that the following term of a national level collective agreement was incorporated into individual contracts of employment: 'overtime required to ensure the due and proper performance of contracts shall not be subject to restriction, but may be worked by mutual agreement and direct arrangement between the employer and the operatives concerned'. The majority construed this as imposing a substantive obligation on the individual employees not to take any action to restrict overtime, such as an overtime ban.[201] This appears to have been a misreading of a term whose intention was to regulate the relationship between the national collective agreement and agreements at company or plant level: the amount of overtime was to be agreed at plant level, without restriction by the national agreement.[202] The essential point, however, was not so much that the term was procedural, as that it was intended to regulate the collective relationship and not that of the individual parties, which was to be free from any national-level 'restriction'.

(iv) 'No legal effect' clauses

4.31   Related to the issue of appropriateness is the question of how far the employer can avoid incorporation by denying that the norms in question were intended to have legal effect at the

---

[196] [1996] IRLR 574.
[197] [2006] IRLR 961.
[198] [2011] IRLR 32.
[199] [2011] IRLR 32, at [62] (Smith LJ).
[200] [1966] 1 QB 555.
[201] As such, it would now be subject to the specific rules governing the incorporation of no-strike or other industrial action clauses into contracts of employment under TULRCA 1992, s 180: see below, para 11.67.
[202] [1966] 1 QB 555, 568, per Russell LJ, dissenting (on this point).

individual level. A statement in a collective agreement that the terms are intended to be 'binding in honour only' is likely to be interpreted as referring only to the collective relationship. It was common in the early 1970s to place TINALEA clauses in collective agreements ('this is not a legally enforceable agreement'), since at that time it was necessary to do so in order to avoid giving them legal effect as contracts under the provisions of the IRA 1971. Now the presumption is reversed, and clear words are necessary to create, rather than to exclude, legal effect.[203] It is conceivable that collective agreements may still contain TINALEA clauses, however, either through inertia or to make the parties' intentions completely clear. There is no reason to infer from such a clause that the collective parties did not intend the normative terms to have effect in individual contracts of employment.[204]

(v) Conflicts between levels of bargaining

4.32   An issue which the courts have not always addressed satisfactorily is that of conflicts between different levels of collective bargaining. If the floor of rights character of regulation is taken into account, resolving these conflicts should not be too problematic: sectoral agreements would be regarded as providing the basic floor on which company or plant-level agreements are permitted to build, but from which they may not derogate.[205] Unfortunately, the matter cannot be approached so straightforwardly. There is no legislative guidance on the issue of derogation from sectoral agreements, following the repeal of Schedule 11 of the EPA 1975. The question falls to be decided at common law as usual, and will be determined by the scope of any express or implied bridging term. If an express term deals clearly with the conflict of levels, there is no difficulty; such a term should be incorporated by reference to one of the relevant collective agreements.[206] If the court, on the other hand, has to operate on the basis of an implied bridging term or one which is silent on this question, the matter is much less clear. No obvious principle emerges from the few cases in which it has been addressed, except to say that the courts have evidently not been guided by the argument that sectoral agreements should be viewed, at least presumptively, as providing a non-derogable floor of rights. In one case, a local agreement providing for inferior benefits was given priority, apparently because it was agreed later in time than the sectoral agreement.[207] In other cases, sectoral agreements setting lower basic working hours prevailed over local agreements providing for longer hours (and hence higher levels of weekly pay).[208] The courts appear to have been worried about the fragmentation of national level agreements,[209] but this is to misunderstand the function of the local agreement in building on the basic floor set nationally. With the decline of national level bargaining in many sectors, the issue has lost some of its salience.

---

[203] TULRCA 1992, s 179; see below, para 9.26.
[204] *Marley v Forward Trust Group* [1986] ICR 891. See also the discussion of 'no legal effect' clauses in the context of employer handbooks in para 4.34 below.
[205] Cf French Labour Code, Art L 132-13.
[206] Eg, *Barrett v National Coal Board* [1978] ICR 1101.
[207] *Clift v West Riding County Council* (1964) Times, 10 April.
[208] *Loman and Henderson v Merseyside Transport Services Ltd* (1968) 3 ITR 108; *Gascol Conversions Ltd v Mercer* [1974] ICR 420.
[209] *Loman and Henderson v Merseyside Transport Services Ltd* (1968) 3 ITR 108, 112 (Lord Denning).

Custom and practice

4.33 Collective agreements are a relatively formal, documentary source of norms governing pay, working hours and similar incidents of employment. Terms may also be incorporated by reference to the less formal 'custom and practice' of the plant or workplace or to a 'trade usage'. This will only be the case, however, if it can be shown that the parties implicitly contracted on the assumption that these informal norms would apply. Custom and practice has been defined as 'those transactional rules of job regulation which arise, not from any explicit and formal negotiation, but from a process whereby managerial error or omission establishes a practice which workers see as legitimate to defend'.[210] Examples are as numerous as the practices of particular workplaces, but a typical illustration from a period when managements were weaker than they are now was the right of engineering piece workers to boycott jobs which could not earn them a satisfactory wage.[211] Custom and practice may also take a form which favours management, such as an alleged implied right of lay off.[212] Whether unwritten practices of this sort should be accorded contractual recognition is doubtful. The importance of custom and practice is less than it was, thanks in part to the very formalisation of contract terms and conditions which employment protection legislation, and in particular the introduction of the statutory written statement, has encouraged.

In principle, a custom can only be incorporated into a contract of employment if it is 'reasonable, certain and notorious'.[213] That this is a more restrictive test than normally applies to the implication of contract terms is justified by the informal nature of custom and practice. A court would not normally decline to imply a term simply on the grounds that it is not 'reasonable' to do so.[214] Certainty, in this context, means that the court can distil a clear and specific term from the practice in question, and notoriety means that the practice is widely known and observed in the plant or trade. It is not, apparently, necessary for the individual employee to know of the custom or practice, however. In *Sagar v H Ridehalgh & Son Ltd*[215] the employer claimed the benefit of a custom of 'making deductions for careless work [which] had been in existence for many years' in its mill. It was also argued that a majority of mills in the district observed a similar practice. The employee 'stated that at the time of his engagement he knew nothing of the system of fines or deductions, and that until much later he did not become aware that there was a system in vogue at the defendants' mill'. He claimed to be entitled to payment according to a list of prices agreed between his trade union and the employers' association of which the employer was a member, and which was posted up as a notice in the mill. Farwell J held against incorporation on the grounds that the usage was not sufficiently general (15% of the Lancashire mills did not observe it) and that 'the practice was not reasonable or certain, because it was precarious, depending on the will of the master'.[216] His decision was reversed by the Court of Appeal. Lawrence LJ, citing the employer's evidence that the practice had been in operation at the mill for over 30 years, held that 'it is clear that the claimant accepted employment in the defendants' mill on the same terms as the other

---

[210] W Brown, 1972: p 61.

[211] W Brown, 1973.

[212] Cf *Bond and Neads v CAV Ltd* [1983] IRLR 360.

[213] *Devonald v Rosser & Sons* [1906] 2 KB 728, 743 (Farwell LJ); *Sagar v H Ridehalgh & Son Ltd* [1930] 2 Ch 117, 133 (Farwell J); *Henry v London General Transport Services Ltd* [2002] IRLR 472.

[214] See above, para 4.6. For a recent application of this principle see *Rutherford v Seymour Pierce Ltd* [2010] IRLR 606.

[215] [1930] 2 Ch 117; revsd [1931] 1 Ch 310.

[216] [1930] 2 Ch 117, 133.

weavers employed at that mill ... it is immaterial whether he knew of it or not, as I am satisfied that he accepted his employment on the same terms as to deductions for bad work as the other weavers at the mill.[217] Nor was the usage either insufficiently general within the trade or unreasonable in the circumstances: 'the deductions are not arbitrary deductions at the will and pleasure of the employers; they are limited to cases where there has been bad work, and they are limited to an amount which does not exceed the actual or estimated damage or loss occasioned to the employer by the act or omission of the workman'.[218]

The same result would not necessarily be achieved today, thanks to the degree of formalisation now imposed upon the employment relationship by legislation. Contract terms of this kind, concerning the method of calculation of pay, should be included in the section 1 written statement.[219] The failure to refer to a term of this kind in the written statement does not have the effect of nullifying that term at common law. However, the absence of any reference to a particular custom or practice in the written statement may well be strong evidence that the parties did not regard it as having normative effect, at least in a case where the alleged term favours the employer.[220] For this reason, it may be said that the existence of the employer's duty to issue the written statement makes it more difficult to invoke custom and practice as a source of contract terms.[221]

The greater formality of collective agreements has also had this effect. In *Bond v CAV Ltd*[222] an alleged implied right to lay off employees without pay was rejected on the grounds that the custom had been overtaken (and implicitly limited) by a national level collective agreement on guaranteed pay.

These caveats notwithstanding, the possibility of implying a term into a contract of employment on the basis of a unilateral managerial practice still exists. In *Garratt v Mirror Group Newspapers Ltd*[223] the employer successfully argued for an implied term to the effect that, in order to qualify for an enhanced redundancy payment under a scheme incorporated into the contract by reference to a collective agreement, an employee had to sign a compromise agreement. The employer argued that such a term represented a long-standing practice in that employment and was also generally understood and implied in the industry. Neither the collective agreement in question nor the employee's written statement of terms and conditions made any reference to such a term. The Court of Appeal, sidestepping the *Sagar v Ridehalgh*[224] test, held that the critical factors in determining whether an employer practice was incorporated into the contract were 'the length of time, frequency and extent to which a practice was followed in every case as a matter of routine'; 'the understanding and knowledge of both employer and employees'; and whether the practice was reduced to writing.[225] On this basis, the term argued for by the employer was implied

---

[217] [1931] 1 Ch 310, 336.

[218] [1931] 1 Ch 310, 338.

[219] ERA 1996, s 1(4)(a).

[220] *System Floors (UK) Ltd v Daniel* [1982] ICR 54, discussed above, at para 4.24.

[221] For a recent example, however, see *Harlow v Artemis International Corporation Ltd* [2008] IRLR 629.

[222] [1983] IRLR 360.

[223] [2011] IRLR 591.

[224] [1930] 2 Ch 117, [1931] 1 Ch 310.

[225] [2011] IRLR 591, at [35] (Leveson LJ). On these points, see also *Albion Automotive Ltd v Walker* [2002] All ER 170,

into the contract. Leveson LJ went on to apply the *Sagar* test[226] and ruled that the outcome was the same. The practice was very widely known and, despite not being written down in the collective agreement or written statement, certain in its effects and application, because it was written down in the compromise agreement offered to the employee in return for the enhanced redundancy payment. Leveson LJ held that the practice was also reasonable, on the basis that the employer had a legitimate interest in seeking finality when making a redundancy payment, and was acting proportionately as the employee had the option of refusing the terms that were on offer.

Works rules and company handbooks

4.34   As we saw above, works rules may not constitute terms of the contract if they are simply a codified form of instructions from the employer, which can be altered unilaterally as part of managerial prerogative.[227] Certain rules are too precise in their effect to be classified in this way, however; in particular, rules concerning discipline, hours of work or the method of calculating pay would normally be contract terms. The mere existence of such rules in a notice or handbook does not, however, confer upon them contractual effect. Their effect depends upon the same principles as we have just been examining: they must either be incorporated through a bridging term in the individual contract,[228] or by way of analogy to custom and practice. A number of old authorities suggest that a notice posted in the workplace can form part of the contract, on the basis that the parties impliedly contracted subject to the general rules of the plant. It was considered irrelevant that the employee might be illiterate or never have read the notice, or even never have had it brought to his or her attention.[229] But these decisions must, again, be read subject to the statutory notification requirements of ERA 1996, section 1, in particular following the 1993 amendments. These limit the use which the employer may make of notices and other 'reference documents' in discharging the duty to issue the statutory written statement. Subject to only a few exceptions, the substance of any notice, and not just a reference to that notice, must be reproduced in the written statement which is issued to the employee.[230] If the statutory statement does not refer to the contents of the notice, this does not in itself deny them contractual effect; but it raises a rebuttable presumption against the employer that the parties did not intend them to form part of the contract of employment. To rebut such a presumption the employer would probably have to produce evidence that the employee was made aware both of the notice and of its contractual force, or alternatively that employees generally were aware of its existence and significance.

[226] At first instance the judge had ruled that *Sagar* was only applicable to cases of alleged customs operating at trade or industry level, as opposed to that of a single organisation, but this point does not form part of the Court of Appeal's reasoning in *Garratt*.

[227] See above, para 4.3; *Secretary of State for Employment v Aslef (No 2)* [1972] 2 QB 455. See also *Wandsworth London Borough Council v D'Silva* [1998] IRLR 193: provisions in an employer's code of practice on staff sickness relating to the level at which absence would be reviewed were not contractually binding on the employer.

[228] Thus in *Attrill v Dresdner Kleinwort Ltd.* [2011] IRLR 613 the contract of employment was set out in a letter of engagement which incorporated terms from the employer handbook, including a term to the effect that bonuses could be notified to employees via the company intranet. The terms of a bonus notified in this way were held held to be contractually binding on the employer.

[229] *Carus v Eastwood* (1875) 32 LT 855; *Petrie v MacFisheries Ltd* [1940] 1 KB 258.

[230] See above, para 4.14.

A company handbook which is given to individual employees on their appointment may serve as the written statement which the employer is required to issue under section 1 as well as a source of contractual terms and conditions in its own right. To satisfy section 1, however, it would have to be adapted to contain certain information which was specific to each employee, such as the date on which their employment began. If a company handbook is general in nature, the employer will not have satisfied section 1 by merely issuing that handbook together with a written statement which refers the employee to its contents. The written statement must itself contain the substance of those particulars which the Act requires to be issued in a 'single document'.[231]

An increasingly important issue with regard to handbooks is the legal meaning of statements denying that particular benefits or provisions are legally binding on the employer. It may be open to a court to regard the terms in question as non-enforceable on the grounds of a lack of intention to create legal relations.[232] If, however, the terms in practice constitute the normative basis for the parties' relationship in the sense of being regularly observed and understood to be binding, a court may treat as irrelevant a statement by the employer that they are not, and conclude that they have contractual effect. This is because it is for the court, and not for the parties alone, to construe the arrangements in question; and the test of whether contractual effect exists is an objective one.[233] In addition, as we have seen,[234] the employer will find it difficult in practice to contradict the contents of the section 1 written statement; thus if reference is made to a particular benefit in the written statement, there would be a strong presumption that the employer intended to be contractually bound by that provision.

It seems increasingly unlikely that an employee can argue that a 'no legal effect' clause of this type is caught by section 3 of the Unfair Contract Terms Act 1977. In *Commerzbank AG v Keen*[235] the Court of Appeal ruled that it was artificial to regard the employee as contracting in the capacity of a 'consumer' in respect of pay for services rendered as an employee ; it also held that a standard-form employment agreement could not be equated with the employer's written standard terms of business, another possible basis for triggering section 3. Even if UCTA were held to apply to employment contracts, its usefulness as a device for regulating 'no legal effect' clauses would be limited. This is because UCTA does not regulate unfair contract terms in general, but only exclusion or limitation clauses in the particular sense prescribed by that Act. For the purposes of section 3, this means terms which enable the employer either: 'when himself in breach of contract, [to] exclude or restrict any liability of his in respect of the breach'; to 'render a contractual performance substantially different from that which was reasonably expected of him'; or to render no performance at all.[236] In *Brigden v American Express Bank Ltd*[237] the High Court

---

[231] Cf ERA 1996, s 1(3)–(4), 2(4).

[232] *Cadoux v Central Regional Council* [1986] IRLR 131; *Quinn v Calder Industrial Materials Ltd* [1996] IRLR 126.

[233] See, in a different context, the judgment of Stuart-Smith LJ in *R v Lord Chancellor's Department, ex p Nangle* [1991] IRLR 343. Several decisions have arisen in which the courts have had to construe the terms of employer handbooks in connection with sickness and disability schemes: see *Briscoe v Lubrizol Ltd* [2002] IRLR 607; *Pioneer Technology (UK) Ltd v Jowitt* [2002] IRLR 190, [2003] IRLR 356; *Scottish Courage Ltd v Guthrie*, 5 February 2004, Appeal No UKEAT/0788/03/MAA.

[234] See para 4.25 above.

[235] [2007] IRLR 132. See also *Brigden v American Express Bank Ltd* [2000] IRLR 94, 95–96. The discussion of the scope of UCTA in *Brigden* was arguably not very complete (see the 4th edition of this book at para 4.33) but following the decision of the Court of Appeal in *Keen* the issue has been more clearly resolved.

[236] UCTA 1977, s 3(2).

[237] [2000] IRLR 94.

ruled that a clause under which the employer's disciplinary procedure did not apply to dismissals in the first two years of employment was not an exclusion clause within the meaning of the Act: the clause 'although expressed in negative terms, is a clause setting out the claimant's entitlement and the limits of his rights'.[238]

Variation of contract terms

4.35 The employer has no implied right unilaterally to vary the contract terms. This is so notwithstanding the existence of a category of 'prerogative' powers to determine the manner in which performance takes place through works rules and instructions which do not have contractual status. The express terms of the contract, by defining the scope of the employee's implied obligations of obedience, co-operation and care, also limit managerial prerogative; although every contract of employment must contain a certain irreducible element of co-operation, including an obligation not to obstruct the introduction of new technology or forms of work organisation,[239] this cannot be invoked to override terms and conditions on such matters as pay, hours and employee benefits which were clearly understood to be mutually binding.

However, nearly all the terms of the contract of employment may be varied at any time by agreement between the individual parties, as in the case of any contract.[240] Legislation is capable of creating non-derogable rights (such as the right to statutory sick pay or the right to unfair dismissal) but until recently it did so, by and large, through non-contractual 'statutory impositions'. Minimum rates of pay, maximum hours of work, overtime and holiday entitlements now form part of a statutory floor of rights under NMWA 1998 and WTR 1998. However, above this floor, terms and conditions generally do not have a statutory underpinning, and the employer can seek to rely on a number of possible legal mechanisms to bring about a contractual variation.

(i) Reliance on an express power of variation

4.36 A first possibility is that the employer may attempt to reserve for itself an express power to vary terms of the contract unilaterally. In *Wandsworth London Borough Council v D'Silva* the Court of Appeal stated, *obiter*, that 'clear language' would be required 'to reserve to one party an unusual power of this sort'.[241] The Court distinguished between 'contractual provisions with which [a] party was required to comply' and those 'giving rights to employees',[242] . Only in the former case would a court be likely to favour a power of unilateral variation. However, the dividing line beteen

---

[238] [2000] IRLR 94, 96. See also *Peninsula Business Services Ltd v Sweeney* [2004] IRLR 49.

[239] *Cresswell v Board of Inland Revenue* [1984] ICR 508; discussed below, para 4.104.

[240] The one exception to this principle arises in the case of certain variations carried out in connection with a transfer of an undertaking: see para 3.76 above.

[241] [1998] IRLR 193, 197, Lord Woolf MR. *Securities and Facilities Division v Hayes* [2001] IRLR 81 also stresses the need for an express term to justify variation of a contractual bonus scheme. From this perspective, *Airlie v City of Edinburgh District Council* [1996] IRLR 516, in which the EAT held that despite the lack of an express power for the employer to alter a bonus scheme in a wholesale and comprehensive way, the scheme as a whole could be construed to afford such a power, seems anomalous.

[242] [1998] IRLR 193, 197.

these categories of terms may be obscure in practice; the employer's obligation is the obverse of the employee's right. In *Bateman v Asda Stores Ltd.*[243] the court gave effect to a contract term enabling the employer to 'revise, amend or replace' terms set out in a company handbook, and in *Malone v British Airways plc*[244] a term referring to the employer's power to make 'reasonable changes to any' term of employment was liberally construed.

These decisions pose a number of issues. As a matter of construction, it is arguable that terms in employer handbooks and similar documents purporting to give employers carte blanche to rewrite terms and conditions of employment should not be regarded as incorporated into individual contracts if they not clearly and explicitly brought to the attention of the employee, and that, if they are incorporated, they should be construed against the party seeking to rely on them, that is to say *contra proferentem*, by analogy with the rules on the interpretation of exclusion and limitation clauses.[245] It can also be argued that any unilateral power of variation should not, on its true meaning, be interpreted as extending to terms incorporated from collective agreements, as a consideration of the 'factual background' of the individual contract[246] should lead the court to conclude that the parties cannot have intended a result which would 'completely undermine the value and integrity of the collective bargaining process'.[247]

An employer may also attempt to reserve to itself a wide power to insist on flexibility by including a wide mobility clause or job classification clause in the employee's conditions of employment, or by stipulating that the terms on which a contractual bonus is paid can be altered by the employer or depend on its discretion. Such clauses may overcome the absence of a general implied power to change the terms and conditions of employment, but they should also be read subject to the implied, reciprocal duty of co-operation. Thus courts have been prepared to hold that certain rights under express mobility clauses must be exercised in good faith and in such a way not to undermine mutual trust and confidence, so that, for example, an employee must be given adequate notice of a change of his or her place of work.[248] Similarly, decisions on bonuses indicate that the courts are reluctant to interpret express contract terms in such a way as to make the payment of a bonus a matter entirely at the employer's discretion, although they may acknowledge a role for the employer's subjective view on whether a bonus is earned.[249] Although there is no implied requirement that an employer should always act reasonably in contexts such as these, a court or tribunal 'may nevertheless be persuaded to intervene where the employer is exercising a discretionary right to impose change in a situation where the implications for the employee are particularly oppressive'.[250]

---

[243] [2010] IRLR 370.

[244] [2010] IRLR 431. This point was not considered in the CA judgment in *Malone* ([2011] IRLR 32; see above, para 4.30).

[245] See Reynold and Hendy, 2012.

[246] On the importance of the context or background of the contract, see the opinion of Lord Hoffmann in *Investors Compensation Scheme Ltd v West Bromwich Building Society Ltd* [1998] 1 WLR 896, 912-913.

[247] Reynold and Hendy, 2012: p 91.

[248] *United Bank Ltd v Akhtar* [1989] IRLR 507; on the implied duty of mutual trust and confidence, see further para 4.100 *et seq*, below.

[249] *GX Networks v Greenland* [2010] IRLR 991; *Khatri v Cooperatieve Centrale Raiffeisen-Boerenleenbank BA* [2010] IRLR 715; *Humphreys v Norilsk Nickel International (UK) Ltd* [2010] IRLR 976.

[250] Auerbach, 1993: p 14. See also *Solectron Scotland Ltd v Roper* [2004] IRLR 4 where at [27] Elias J doubted that a custom could ever vary existing contractual rights, and said that even if it could, it would require a very long established practice before it could be concluded that a party had accepted less favourable rights on this basis.

Sometimes flexibility clauses are drafted in such a way as to make explicit reference to reasonableness. In *Land Securities Trillium Ltd v Thornley*[251] the relevant clause stated, 'You will perform to the best of your ability all the duties of this post and any other post you may subsequently hold and any other duties which may reasonably be required of you and will at all times obey all reasonable instructions given to you'. The EAT, confirming a finding of constructive dismissal following an attempted variation by the employer, held that '[o]nce it is found that the duties required by the appellants were unreasonably required of her, as the tribunal found to be the case, the fact that there may have been valid, commercial grounds, as opposed to a wholly arbitrary basis, for the appellants requiring her to undertake them, cannot in a contract of employment cure the unreasonableness of the requirement in so far as the employee is concerned'.[252]

(ii) Variation through the written statement of particulars of employment

4.37   A *second* possibility is that an employer attempts to vary agreed or incorporated contract terms by reference to the written statutory statement of terms. As we have already seen,[253] the written statement normally cannot be used in this way to derogate from the agreed terms. It has no contractual force in its own right and will not be regarded as strong evidence of the contract if its effect is to deprive the employee of vested contractual rights. Because it purports to be declaratory of the *existing* contract terms, a written statement will not normally be capable of being construed as an offer of *new* terms. This applies both to initial section 1 statements and to statements of changes issued under section 4. A section 4 statement which alters the particulars, without further oral discussion between the parties, 'cannot be compelling evidence of an express oral variation'.[254] Nor will an employee who continues to work without objection necessarily be taken to have consented to the variation. According to the EAT in *Jones v Associated Tunnelling Co Ltd*[255] a court should find a variation only 'with great caution', at least if the term has no 'immediate practical effect'. This is because 'it would be unrealistic of the law to require him to risk a confrontation with his employer on a matter which has no immediate practical impact on the employee'. Nor will an estoppel easily be implied in the employer's favour, given that it has acted in breach of section 1 by issuing a statement which is incorrect: this would be to enable the employer to benefit from its own legal wrong.[256]

(iii) Improvements negotiated through a collective agreement

4.38   A *third* situation to consider is that in which a collective agreement improves upon the terms and conditions which are applicable to a given category of employment, as the result, for example, of annual negotiations between the employer and the trade union. If an employee's contract contains an express or implied bridging term, its effect may be to incorporate the new

---

[251] [2005] IRLR 765.
[252] [2005] IRLR 765, at [55].
[253] Para 4.25 above.
[254] *Jones v Associated Tunnelling Co Ltd* [1981] IRLR 477, 481 (Browne-Wilkinson J).
[255] *Jones v Associated Tunnelling Co Ltd* [1981] IRLR 477; see also *Hogg v Dover College* [1990] ICR 39.
[256] *Robertson v British Gas Corp* [1983] ICR 351, 357 (Ackner LJ).

terms without the need for any further agreement.[257] The outcome may depend on how the bridging term is phrased; if, for example, it states that the employee's terms and conditions will be such as are 'laid down from time to time' in a given collective agreement, that is likely to suffice to incorporate the new terms without the need for anything further from the individual parties. Additional consideration would not then be needed, at this point, for the improved terms to be binding on the employer. Consideration may alternatively be inferred from the avoidance of any dispute over pay: by continuing to work, the employees abandon 'any argument that the increase should have been even greater and [remove] a potential area of dispute between employer and employee'.[258]

More generally, 'if in each individual contract of employment there were incorporated the provisions of relevant collective agreements agreed from time to time, as well as general instructions and notices, the contention that each improvement in the employee's terms requires fresh consideration fails to give proper recognition to the value to be attributed by the employer to the continuation of the same workforce in his employ and/or to the possibility of making adjustments from time to time to the detail of the contracts of employment without having to issue new contracts whenever adjustments are put into effect'.[259] This amounts to saying that in virtually all circumstances involving a bridging term, consideration for the improved terms can easily be implied. But in principle, there is reason to think that the question of consideration is irrelevant, at least if the bridging term expressly or impliedly refers not just to the present agreement of the collective parties but to future agreements between them. As long as the bridge itself is supported by the consideration at the time the initial contract was made, incorporation of the new terms would effectively be automatic. Thus in *Robertson v British Gas Corp*[260] Ackner LJ thought that when 'from time to time the collective scheme modified the bonus which was payable ... that variation became a part of the employer's obligation to pay and the employee's obligation to accept in satisfaction'; similarly, Kerr LJ accepted a submission of counsel that 'when the terms of the collective agreements were varied by consent between the two [collective] sides, then the new terms clearly became incorporated into the individual contracts of employment'.[261] Neither judge appears to have thought that consideration was an issue here.

(iv) Derogations negotiated through a collective agreement

4.39   A *fourth* possible scenario arises where a collective agreement introduces changes which are detrimental to particular employees, as a result, for example, of 'concession bargaining' over pay and conditions. In *Lee v GEC Plessey Telecommunications Ltd*[262] the employer attempted to revoke an agreement it had made with the union in 1985 concerning severance pay, in favour of less generous compensation arrangements. In the 1991 pay round an agreement was reached with recognised trade unions that the 1985 terms would apply up to 31 May 1991; thereafter, terms would be subject to negotiation. At the same time, a pay increase of 4.25% was agreed.

---

[257] *Glendale Managed Services v Graham* [2003] IRLR 465.
[258] *Lee v GEC Plessey Telecommunications Ltd* [1993] IRLR 383, 389.
[259] *Lee v GEC Plessey Telecommunications Ltd* [1993] IRLR 383, 389.
[260] [1983] ICR 351, 356.
[261] [1983] ICR 351, 358.
[262] [1993] IRLR 383.

Employees sought declarations that their contracts of employment included a term entitling them to severance pay at the original, higher rate, in the event of their being made redundant. The employers argued that the new terms had been incorporated by agreement at the time of the 1991 pay round, but this was rejected by Connell J who granted the declarations sought. The agreement to negotiate over severance pay in respect of redundancies after 1991 was, he held, too uncertain to be enforceable and was not appropriate for incorporation, since it related to collective negotiations between the employer and the trade union. The terms of the 1985 agreement, having previously been incorporated into contracts, remained in force at the individual level.

Although, in this case, incorporation of a concession was not achieved, the judgment does not rule out the possibility that it might have been had the employer taken a different approach. Had the employer communicated to the employees at the time of the 1991 pay round that it was ending the 1985 agreement *and* that acceptance of the 1991 pay increase amounted to consent to the change to the terms reducing entitlement to severance pay, that, in the view of the judge, would have been sufficient.[263]

This case suggests therefore that in the event of concession bargaining, an employer may succeed in varying the contract terms if it offers the employees a *quid pro quo*, in the form of a pay increase or some other new benefit, in return for the loss of rights elsewhere. It would be up to each individual employee to decide whether to accept or reject the new offer.

The result could be a fragmentation of contractual terms and conditions as different employees respond in different ways, an outcome which collective bargaining is designed to avoid. There is a case for saying that just as any improvement may be automatically incorporated into contracts by virtue of the bridging term, so will any derogation as long as it is contained in a collective agreement of the kind referred to, implicitly or expressly, by the bridge. This would maintain the uniform application of the agreement. There is some authority for this view.[264] In so far as this matter remains unresolved, it is perhaps because of a reluctance on the part of the courts to subordinate individual consent so completely to the normative effect of the collective agreement. The individual contract of employment remains the legal source of the agreement's effectiveness, unlike the position in other systems where the collective has in varying degrees displaced the individual level of bargaining. Although certain civilian systems allow collective agreements, on occasion, to derogate not just from pre-existing terms but also from certain statutory standards, the circumstances in which this is permitted are strictly controlled, and only unions which achieve a certain level of representation among the workforce are granted this power.[265] These safeguards are lacking in the British system.

(v) Abrogation by the employer of the collective agreement

4.40   A *fifth* situation is that in which an employer either abrogates all or part of a collective agreement or gives notice, under the terms of that agreement, to terminate it. This may happen

---

[263] [1993] IRLR 383, 392.

[264] *Miller v Hamworthy Engineering Ltd* [1986] IRLR 461; *MacBeth v United Counties Omnibuses Ltd* (1988) 350 IRLIB 9. Dicta of Ackner and Kerr LJJ in *Robertson v British Gas Corp* [1983] ICR 351, 356, 358 can also be seen as lending support to this view.

[265] See Wedderburn, 1992c.

if the employer is unsuccessful in achieving concessions, or simply wishes to end the union's collective negotiating rights. Unless recognition has been attained as a result of a request made under the statutory recognition procedure,[266] the employer is under no duty to bargain with any trade union and has the legal right to withdraw recognition. In doing so, it will almost certainly not be liable to the union for breach of contract, since nearly all collective agreements are non-enforceable within the terms of section 179 of TULRCA 1992.[267] However, the lack of collective enforcement does not affect the individual contract. In principle, terms and conditions which have previously been incorporated via the bridging term will remain in force until such time as the individual employee consents to vary them.

In *Robertson v British Gas Corp*[268] a collective agreement provided for a bonus incentive scheme, the results of which were incorporated into the contracts of individual employees. The employer gave notice to the trade union that it was terminating the scheme. No new scheme was agreed and the employer ceased paying bonus payments. The employees brought a claim for arrears of pay based on the old scheme, to which they were held to be entitled. Kerr LJ said that once incorporation has taken place, 'it is only if and when those terms are varied collectively by agreement that the individual contracts of employment will also be varied. If the collective scheme is not varied by agreement, but by some unilateral abrogation or withdrawal or variation to which the other side does not agree, then it seems to me that the individual contracts of employment remain unaffected'. This view was reinforced by the high degree of interdependence between the different terms of the contract: the bonus scheme constituted 'an integrated and general framework for a very large number of the mutual rights and obligations of the parties. Indeed, it becomes virtually impossible to determine what the full terms of these individual contracts of employment are if you once take away the agreed collective scheme for an incentive bonus as an integral part of these contracts'.[269]

The employer's refusal to abide by the agreed contract terms is, then, almost invariably a repudiatory breach of contract, which the employee has the option to accept, bringing the contract to an end; or he or she may, alternatively, affirm the contract by remaining in employment. This, in itself, does not amount to agreement to vary the contract terms in the employer's favour. In particular, if the employee makes his or her disagreement clear, there can be no possibility of variation. The employee can remain in employment and claim wages or salary at the rate provided for in the contract; a claim in debt, for accrued wages, or in damages for the employer's breach of contract, can be made, and a declaration granted with respect to the future performance of the contract.[270] If, on the other hand, the contract of employment has been brought to an end, the employee's rights under the contract will not be kept in force merely because the collective agreement from which they initially derived is still in existence.[271]

---

[266] See further para 9.5 *et seq* below.

[267] See above, para 4.31.

[268] [1983] ICR 351; see also *Ackinclose v Gateshead Metropolitan Borough Council* [2005] IRLR 79.

[269] [1983] ICR 351, 358.

[270] *Morris v CH Bailey Ltd* [1969] 2 Lloyd's Rep 215; *Burdett-Coutts v Hertfordshire County Council* [1984] IRLR 91; *Gibbons v Associated British Ports* [1985] IRLR 376; *Rigby v Ferodo Ltd* [1988] ICR 29; *Lee v GEC Plessey Telecommunications Ltd* [1993] IRLR 383.

[271] *City and Hackney Health Authority v NUPE* [1985] IRLR 252.

(vi) Dismissal and re-engagement on new terms

4.41   *Robertson's* case appears to make the terms incorporated from a collective agreement binding on the employer. This appearance is deceptive, however, as a *sixth* option exists for the employer, namely to dismiss the employees and offer them employment on new terms and conditions. At common law, this may be done without breach of contract by giving the employees notice. If they are summarily dismissed, that would normally amount to a breach of the duty to give notice, but damages would most likely be limited to net wages or salary for the notice period.[272] Such action amounts to a dismissal, whether or not the employees accept the offer of new terms, and it is possible that the employees may be able to bring claims for redundancy compensation and/or compensation for unfair dismissal. If this is the case, the employer may face liabilities which outweigh any savings to be made from abrogating the collective agreement. Formally, incorporated terms are not entrenched against the superior bargaining power of the employer: they can be changed through the route of dismissal and re-employment. They may be entrenched *de facto*, however, if statutory remedies for termination of employment defeat the employer's aim of cutting costs.

On the other hand, it is possible that dismissal in these circumstances will be held to be neither for reasons of redundancy, nor unfair. The issue is perhaps sufficiently unclear to deter an employer, but the statutory remedies cannot necessarily be relied on by the employees. At the outset, the employee will need to have been continuously employed for the requisite period prior to the dismissal.[273] Moreover, if the employer can show that there is a good business reason for seeking to change the contract terms, such as the need to enhance flexibility or efficiency of work organisation or even, simply, to make savings in response to a fall in external funding or in demand for its products, any dismissal flowing from the refusal of the employee to accept the new terms is likely to be potentially fair. It could be for reasons of redundancy, in which case the employee is automatically entitled to receive a statutory redundancy payment.[274] It is more likely, however, that the tribunal will find that it falls into the residual category of 'some other substantial reason',[275] in which case the employee may receive additional compensation for unfair dismissal but may, alternatively, receive nothing if the tribunal finds that the dismissal was fair in the circumstances.[276] This will be determined not simply according to whether the offer of new terms was reasonable from the point of view of the employee, but according to whether a *reasonable employer* would have dismissed the employee for refusing the new terms.[277] This is essentially a question for the tribunal, and tribunals are entitled to reach findings on a case-by-case basis with similar cases resulting in different outcomes.[278] In assessing reasonableness, however, it is largely irrelevant that the employer is seeking unilaterally to alter the agreed contract terms; what matters is the nature of the economic pressure which the business is facing and the reasonableness of the

---

[272] See generally, para 5.20 below.

[273] ERA 1996, s 108(1); see above, para 3.48.

[274] ERA 1996, s 135; see below, para 5.163 *et seq.*

[275] ERA 1996, s 98(1)(b); *Hollister v National Farmers' Union* [1979] ICR 542. If the dismissal is found to be in connection with a transfer of an undertaking, however, it may be more difficult to show that the dismissal is potentially fair under TUPE 2006: see para 5.182 *et seq* below.

[276] This can present employers and their advisers with a dilemma when considering the implications of forcing through a variation to terms and conditions of employment. See *Port of Sheerness Ltd v Brachers* [1997] IRLR 214.

[277] *St John of God (Care Services) Ltd v Brooks* [1992] IRLR 546; *Farrant v Woodroffe School* [1998] IRLR 176.

[278] *Kent County Council v Gilham* [1985] ICR 227.

employer's response to it. Only in rather extreme circumstances have employees succeeded in winning unfair dismissal claims of this kind, as in a case where the new terms gave the employer an apparently unqualified right to call on the employee to work unlimited overtime hours on demand.[279]

The authorities were reviewed by the EAT in *Catamaran Cruisers Ltd v Williams*.[280] A business which had been in financial difficulties was taken over by a new owner, which then negotiated changes to terms and conditions of employment with the recognised trade union. The new terms, which departed from those laid down by a federation of employers for the trade in question, were offered to the employees, most of whom accepted. Those who did not were dismissed. The employment tribunal found that the dismissals were unfair, on the basis of a two-stage test under which they first considered whether the employer had a sound business reason and second, 'whether, in refusing to accept the new terms and conditions, the employees are acting unreasonably, having regard to the necessity which the employer has for proposing the new terms': with regard to the second stage, the tribunal considered that if the new terms are 'much less favourable to the employee than were the old terms, then unless the business reasons are so pressing that it is absolutely vital for the survival of the employer's business that the terms be accepted, then the employee is not ... unreasonable in refusing to accept those terms and, consequently, any dismissal of him for a refusal to accept is unfair'. This view of the law was held to be incorrect by the EAT, which remitted the case for rehearing. Specifically, it was incorrect to say that the employer could only propose less or much less favourable terms if the existence of the business depended on it. The tribunal had to consider the benefit or potential benefit to the employer in balancing the two interests and should also, in a case such as this, consider the relevance of the large majority of employees accepting the new terms.

Catamaran Cruisers tilts the balance in the employer's favour: the tribunal's error was not to have failed to consider the employer's motives and position, but to have apparently accorded this equal weight to the employees' interests in avoiding a serious deterioration in their pay and conditions. The lay members of the EAT in that case felt it necessary to state that 'much of recent employment law has been to protect employees against arbitrary changes of their terms and conditions of employment and ... this, as a principle, must stand'.[281] But the hurdle which the employer must overcome, in demonstrating a business reason for altering terms and conditions, is not a high one after this decision.

Some qualifications should nevertheless be borne in mind. Even though dismissals of this kind may not amount to redundancies for individual purposes, they will almost certainly fall under the expanded definition of redundancy for the purposes of collective consultation rights, namely a dismissal 'for a reason not related to the individual concerned'.[282] An employer's failure adequately to comply with the collective consultation rights would, under this provision, result in liability to pay a protective award to the employees concerned. Another factor which may increase the risk of liability for the employer is the nature of the response from the workforce as a whole.

---

[279] *Evans v Elemeta Holdings Ltd* [1982] IRLR 143.

[280] [1994] IRLR 386.

[281] [1994] IRLR 386, 389.

[282] TULRCA 1992, s 195. This expanded definition was inserted by the TURERA 1993, s 34(1), implementing Directive 75/129, Art 1(a). See para 9.32 below.

If a large majority of employees opposes the change, it may be more difficult for a tribunal to conclude that their dismissal was fair.

In *Catamaran Cruisers*, not only did most of the employees accept the new contracts, but the terms being offered were the result of negotiation with the recognised trade union. This was a very different case, then, from one in which an employer presents its workforce with terms on a 'take-it-or-leave-it basis', or chooses to go down the route of a mass dismissal. The constraints imposed by unfair dismissal law, although they do not provide automatic protection for the agreed contract terms, 'may in practice provide the union more opportunities to engage in the process of negotiation of new terms and conditions'.[283]

(vii) The legal implications of 'working under protest' following a purported variation of terms

4.42 It follows from the analysis we have just provided of the different ways in which a variation may be brought about that where the employer seeks to impose new terms and conditions without first dismissing the employee and offering a new contract, the employee is entitled to regard the existing contract as still in force and to carry on working under it.[284] The employee must nevertheless make it clear to the employer that he or she is not accepting the purported variation. It may be insufficient for the employee to carry on 'working under protest' as this may be taken to signify assent to the new terms and conditions. In *Robinson v Tescom Corporation*[285] the employee refused to accept a change in his job duties (which amounted to a doubling the size of his designated sales region). In a letter to his employer he wrote,

> I will work under the terms of the varied job description... but under protest. I do not accept the terms and I am treating the change as a breach of contract and dismissal from the original contract. I retain the right to seek damages from my employer for a breach of contract and/or declaration from the courts that my employer must abide by the original terms of my contract.

He was subsequently dismissed for refusing to work to the new job description. The employment tribunal ruled that he had been fairly dismissed for disobeying a lawful and reasonable order. On appeal, the EAT ruled that the tribunal had been correct to find that '[t]he contract of employment was extant, the claimant had agreed in writing to continue working under it, and under the varied job description, but then failed and refused to do so'.[286] The difficulty with this analysis is that both the employment tribunal and the EAT took the view that the original contract had not been terminated.[287] If that is so, and the original terms remained in force, it is hard to see how the

---

[283] Auerbach, 1993: p 26. The use of mass dismissal notices as a means of bringing about a change in employment conditions is rare in practice. It was used by Rolls Royce plc in 1991 but the company eventually withdrew the notices and resumed negotiations with the recognised trade union. The case is discussed by Jeremy McMullen and Philippa Kaufman, 1991.

[284] See also, on this point, the recent PC decision, applying the law of Mauritius, in *Adamas Ltd v Cheung* [2011] IRLR 1014, at [25] (Lord Mance).

[285] [2008] IRLR 408; R White, 2008.

[286] [2008] IRLR 408, at [33].

[287] More precisely, they held that the change to the contract was not sufficient to constitute a dismissal under the principle in *Hogg v Dover College* [1990] ICR 39, discussed below, para 5.68.

employer's instruction could have been a lawful and reasonable one. Another way of reading the case is that the employee had agreed to the variation, the references to working 'under protest' and refusing to accept the new terms notwithstanding.[288] The decision illustrates the practical difficulties facing employees in such cases (the employee in this case was following guidance set out in an ACAS leaflet). But even if the employment tribunal was wrong on the variation point, it does not follow that Mr. Robinson would have been successful in his claim. It would still have been open to the tribunal to find that the employer had had a potentially fair reason for requiring the change to his contract, and that the dismissal was reasonable in the circumstances.[289]

PAYMENT OF WAGES AND SALARIES

4.43   Legislative regulation of wages and salaries may perform one or both of two related functions. First, *minimum wage legislation* may regulate basic rates of pay in order to ensure that employees receive a certain minimum level of income in return for their labour. This can be done directly by inserting a stated minimum level of hourly, weekly or monthly pay into contracts of employment, or indirectly by providing for wage-fixing machinery which will then be used to set legally-enforceable basic rates.[290] In Britain, regulation has, traditionally, been indirect in the sense of supplying statutory force to certain wage-fixing machinery. This type of intervention, which was associated with the wages councils which operated in a number of forms between 1909 and 1993, was confined to particular sectors or industries. However, with the passage of the National Minimum Wage Act 1998, a single, statutory minimum wage covering the labour force as a whole is now in force in the UK for the first time.[291]

A second form of regulation is that constituted by *wage protection legislation*. This aims to ensure, among other things, that the employee is paid on a regular basis and receives his or her mandated or agreed wage in full, that is to say, free from arbitrary or excessive deductions by the employer.[292] The employer's power of deduction may be limited by *substantive* controls, such as a requirement that any deduction should be related to an identifiable breach of discipline and should be reasonable in the circumstances, or by controls of a *procedural* kind, such as an obligation to agree relevant rules with a recognised trade union (or equivalent representative body) and to notify employees of their existence. Legislation governing deductions from pay has a long history. The Truck Acts of the nineteenth century, which extended the scope of regulations which had previously applied at the level of individual trades, required wages to be paid in full in the coin

---

[288] This view is perhaps inconsistent with the suggestion of Browne-Wilkinson J in *Jones v Associated Tunnelling Co Ltd* [1981] IRLR 477, 481 that a court should find a valid variation 'only with great caution' but it should be borne in mind that Browne-Wilkinson J was discussing a purported variation made through the written statement of particulars of employment to which special considerations apply (see para 4.36 above) and that he was referring specifically to a variation with 'no immediate practical effect'. See also *Harlow v Artemis International Corporation Ltd* [2008] IRLR 629 (changes in redundancy terms did not immediately impinge on the employee).

[289] As submitted by counsel for the respondent: see [2008] IRLR 408, at [21].

[290] ILO instruments lay down standards for regulation by the latter, indirect route: Convention concerning the Creation of Minimum Wage-Fixing Machinery, No 26, 1928; Convention concerning Minimum Wage-Fixing in Agriculture, No 99, 1951. The UK was a signatory to these Conventions but denounced them in the 1980s.

[291] See below, para 4.46 *et seq*.

[292] ILO Convention concerning the Protection of Wages, No 95, 1949. This Convention was denounced by the UK in 1985.

of the realm (thereby outlawing 'truck' or payment in kind)[293] and regulated disciplinary 'fines' and deductions from pay.[294] However, this legislation was complex and difficult to apply and was never accorded a clear priority over the common law, which continued to determine the scope of the employer's obligation to pay wages in return for service rendered. The Wages Act 1986 (now consolidated in Part II of ERA 1996) repealed the Truck Acts and replaced them with a looser form of statutory regulation, under which substantive limits on deductions are imposed only in relation to cash shortages and stock deficiencies occurring in the course of retail employment. Otherwise, this legislation permits deductions from agreed wages, as long as they are authorised by statute or by a term of the individual's contract; in the latter case, the deduction will be valid if the individual has given his or her prior consent in writing, or if the employer has provided them with written notification of the deduction before it takes place (not necessarily before the event giving rise to it). Outside the retail sector, then, the employer's obligation is at present confined to a procedural one of providing information to an individual whose pay is subjected to a deduction.

Collective bargaining has traditionally been the primary source of regulation of basic rates of pay, the intervals between payment and methods of calculating pay. Payment systems are mostly specific to particular occupations and industries. Industrial workers tend to be paid either on a piece-work basis, that is to say by reference to particular items or quantities of completed work, or on a time-rate, normally by the hour or by the day, or by some combination of the two, with weekly or monthly intervals between payment. Professional, managerial and clerical workers, whether or not they are covered by collective bargaining, normally receive salaries calculated without reference to particular items of completed work or to hours spent in employment, and are normally paid at monthly intervals. With the relative decline in the scope and influence of collective bargaining, payment systems have become less standardised, and in many cases a larger element of an employee's pay is now determined by reference to an individual's performance or to the profitability of the company or group as a whole. The law offers encouragement to the use of profit-related pay by a variety of tax reliefs, but it has so far failed to provide effective protection for employees who may lose valuable share option rights if they are wrongfully dismissed.[295]

Given the decreasing importance of both legislation and collective bargaining in the regulation of pay, the common law has come to assume a pre-eminent role as a source of norms in this area. A number of presumptions have grown up which the courts rely on to interpret the 'wage-work bargain' made by the parties. One issue here is the determination of precisely what the employee must do in order to earn his or her wages: is it the completion of a given quantum of work or labour, or is it being ready and willing to work? The answer depends largely on how the employee's pay is calculated: piece work and hourly-paid workers are less likely to succeed in showing that they are paid for merely being ready to work than salaried workers are.

A related question concerns the scope of the employer's power to make deductions from the agreed wage. At common law, once the employee has shown that he or she has performed the contractual obligation which triggers the employer's obligation of payment, any deduction from or retention of wages or salary must be justified by contractual authority of some kind, such as an express or implied term or an implied right of set-off for breach of contract. It must, in addition, satisfy the obligations imposed by Part II of ERA 1996. The employee's rights in relation

---

[293] Truck Act 1831; see below, para 4.71.
[294] Truck Acts 1887 and 1896; see below, para 4.71.
[295] McLean, 1994; see below, para 4.74.

to payment can be asserted by way of an application to an employment tribunal if they arise under Part II[296] or, if the claim is related to the termination of the employment, at common law.[297]

Statutory minimum rates of pay

(i) Evolution of minimum wage legislation

4.44   A number of different objectives have, at various times, influenced legislative policy in Britain towards minimum wages. The first modern legislation was part of a broader attempt at the end of the nineteenth and start of the twentieth century to curb the insanitary labour conditions and exploitation in the form of very low pay which were associated with 'sweated labour'. The sweated trades were seen as 'parasitic', on the basis that employers who paid wages below what was needed for subsistence were receiving a subsidy from the rest of the community. Hence, 'the enforcement of a common standard throughout the trade not only stops the degradation, but in every sense conduces to efficiency'.[298] State regulation of wages was undertaken in response to this in the form of the Fair Wages Resolutions of 1891, 1909 and 1946, and in the Trade Boards Act 1909 which introduced statutory regulation for the first time but only covered a selected number of very low paying industries. The subsequent history of the wages councils (as the trade boards became) reflects a tension between the original aim of controlling 'sweating' and a second objective, namely that of using legal enforcement of minimum rates to support the wider system of collective bargaining. The Wages Councils Act 1945 'amounted to the use of State power to keep collective bargaining going when economic circumstances tended to destroy it, and was quite different from the simpler, ameliorative purpose of abolishing sweating'.[299] The wages councils system did little to address a third objective, namely the reduction of poverty. The minimum rates set by wages regulation orders tended to follow those separately set by collective agreements, and were not used for the purpose of ensuring a levelling-up of the position of the lower paying sectors relative to the rest.

Between 1960 and 1980 a major retrenchment of the wages council system took place, as 27 councils covering half a million workers were abolished. The pressure for reform came from a perception, shared by trade unions and government, that wages councils were stifling the development of voluntary collective bargaining. In the 1980s a further reduction in the scope of statutory regulation took place, but not with the aim of enhancing voluntary collective bargaining. On the contrary, both wages councils and collective bargaining were now seen as contributing to unemployment by setting minimum wages above the market clearing rate. The Wages Act 1986[300] took the first steps towards complete abolition by excluding workers under the age of 21 from the scope of coverage; restricting the powers of wages councils to setting single minimum wage rates for each sector as a whole (as opposed to a range of rates for workers of different grades within each sector as previously); abolishing their power to regulate paid holidays and

---

[296] ERA 1996, s 23.
[297] SI 1994/1623; D Brown, 1994.
[298] S Webb and B Webb, [1898] 1920: p 767.
[299] Bayliss, 1962: p 56.
[300] WA 1986, Pt II.

other terms and conditions of employment; and requiring wages councils to consider 'the effect that that rate will have on the level of employment among the workers to whom it will apply, and in particular in those areas where the remuneration received by such workers is generally less than the national average for such workers'.[301] The remaining powers of the wages councils were abolished completely in 1993.[302] This move affected around 2.5 million workers, or 10% of the employed labour force, who were covered by wages orders prior to 1993.[303]

(ii) International labour standards and comparative perspectives on minimum wages

4.45   Many European countries either legislate directly for a minimum wage or provide legal support for wage-fixing machinery which secures an effective floor of rights.[304] In France, the SMIC (*salaire minimum interprofessionel de croissance*) applies to all sectors and occupations and may not be the subject of derogation by either individual or collective bargaining.[305] It is expressed as a minimum hourly rate, and further provision is made for workers employed for at least the basic working week to receive a monthly minimum based on this rate. The relevant law contains a mechanism linking the statutory minimum to increases in both wages and prices. The rate must be raised automatically with every 2% increase in the official consumer price index, and must maintain an annual rate of growth of at least 50% of the growth in the purchasing power of the average wage. In other systems with a statutory minimum, provisions for indexation are weaker and exemptions for younger workers tend to be more extensive. An alternative method of regulating minimum pay is through collective agreements at national or sectoral level. In Belgium, for example, national-level collective agreements are concluded annually by representatives of trade unions and employers' associations; the minimum rates thereby established apply to the small minority of employments which are not covered by a separate industry-level agreement. In Germany, on the other hand, basic rates are supplied by sector-level agreements whose terms can be given general legal effect through extension procedures. The vast majority of employees receive a basic legal entitlement by this means. Denmark achieves general protection through a combination of sectoral and company-level collective bargaining, and Ireland has a system of selective statutory regulation, similar to the former wages council model, for sectors lacking voluntary collective bargaining.[306]

Prior to the Wages Act 1986, the then Conservative government took the opportunity to denounce ILO Convention No 26 of 1928 on Machinery for Minimum Wage-Fixing, which had been modelled on the British Trade Boards Acts. A number of other international instruments remain relevant to the question of minimum wages. Article 4(1) of the Council of Europe's Social Charter of 1961 provides that Member States should recognise 'the right of workers to a

---

[301] WA 1986, s 14(6)(a).

[302] TURERA 1993, s 35.

[303] For the policy background to this repeal and assessment of its effects, see Deakin and Wilkinson, 1992; R Dickens *et al*, 1993.

[304] See Deakin, 1990b.

[305] French Labour Code, Art R 141-1 *et seq*.

[306] Italy lacks a formal minimum wage. However, in contrast to the UK, Italian sector-level collective bargaining is an effective mode of regulation in larger firms, and terms and conditions may be extended to non-federated firms using a judicial procedure derived from an activist interpretation of Art 36 of the Italian Constitution. See Deakin, 1990b.

remuneration such as will give them and their families a decent standard of living'.[307] There is no right of individual petition under the Social Charter;[308] instead, periodic reports of the European Committee on Social Rights are made to see how far Member States are complying with their obligations. In interpreting Article 4(1), the Committee of Experts has developed the notion of a 'decency threshold' of 68% of average (mean) earnings as a benchmark level for legal minimum wages.

Article 5 of the European Community Charter of Fundamental Social Rights, adopted by all the Member States except the UK in 1989, states that 'all employment shall be fairly remunerated ... in accordance with the arrangements applying in each country' and goes on to provide, inter alia, that 'workers shall be assured of an equitable wage, ie a wage sufficient to enable them to have a decent standard of living'. The Charter has no legal force in its own right, and there is no prospect of the European Union adopting a legally-binding measure on minimum wages which might give effect to Article 5 in the near future. 'Pay' was one of the issues stated to be outside the scope of the Maastricht Agreement on Social Policy,[309] the text of which was subsequently incorporated into the EC Treaty and is now part of Article 153 TFEU.[310] In September 1993 the European Commission agreed a non-binding Opinion on an Equitable Wage. It noted that 'the persistence of very low wage levels raises problems of equity and social cohesion, which could be harmful to the effectiveness of the economy in the long term', but reiterated the view taken by the Commission in the Social Action Programme of 1989 that 'wage setting is a matter for the Member States and the social partners'.[311] Member States were called on, inter alia, to improve the collection and dissemination of information and to consider legislation 'to ensure that the right to an equitable wage is protected' with particular reference to discrimination, the treatment of homeworkers and 'mechanisms for the establishment of negotiated minima and the strengthening of collective bargaining arrangements'.[312] However, the Opinion, by its nature, does not impose any legal obligation upon Member States; it is advisory only.

(iii) The National Minimum Wage Act 1998[313]

4.46   The introduction of a national statutory minimum wage was a commitment in the Labour Party manifestos of 1992 and 1997, and after the General Election of 1997 the new government made it the first priority of employment law reform. The National Minimum Wage Act 1998

---

[307] This is reiterated in the 1996 Charter which the UK has signed but not ratified. See also UN Universal Declaration of Human Rights, Art 23(3): every worker has the right 'to just and favourable remuneration ensuring for himself and his family an existence worthy of human dignity'. The International Covenant on Economic, Social and Cultural Rights refers to the right of every person to the enjoyment of just and favourable conditions of work (Art 7) and a decent living for workers and their families (Art 7(a)(1)).

[308] A 1995 Protocol makes provision for collective complaints, but this has not been signed by the UK.

[309] Agreement on Social Policy, Art 2(6), now Art 153(5) TFEU. No reference to minimum wages is made in the CFREU (see para. 2.39 above).

[310] See para 2.37.

[311] Commission Opinion on an Equitable Wage, COM (93) 388 final, OJ 1993 C 248/7, recitals 5 and 7 respectively.

[312] Commission Opinion on an Equitable Wage, Art 3.

[313] For a comprehensive account of the legal issues arising from this Act, see Simpson, 1999a, 1999b and for later assessments, Simpson 2004, 2009. EA 2008 ss 8–14 made a number of changes to the Act, mostly designed to improve its enforcement. Useful guidance on the 1998 Act and related Regulations, and on administrative and enforcement matters, is set out on the Businesslink and Directgov websites (www.businesslink.gov.uk and www.direct.gov.uk respectively).

provides for a minimum basic hourly rate of pay for workers of 26 or over, with the possibility of a lower rate (or rates) for younger workers, some of whom may also be completely excluded. The Act has many features of a framework provision, with more detailed aspects of the regulation of the minimum wage being left to the National Minimum Wage Regulations 1999. The Low Pay Commission, a tripartite body, offers advice to the Secretary of State on matters of setting and implementing the minimum wage. This advice has, in some instances, been reflected in the terms of the National Minimum Wage Regulations.[314]

SCOPE

4.47   The Act applies initially to any 'worker' who 'is working, or ordinarily works, in the United Kingdom under his contract', and who is above compulsory school leaving age.[315] A 'worker', for this purpose, means an individual who has entered into or works under either a contract of employment or a contract whereby he or she 'undertakes to do or perform personally any work or services for another party to the contract whose status is not by virtue of the contract that of a client or customer of any profession or business undertaking carried on by the individual'.[316] The Act thereby adopts the wide definition of 'worker' which was previously used under the wages councils legislation and is currently used in a number of other statutory contexts.[317]

Agency workers and homeworkers are also the subject of special treatment. The Act recognises that an 'agency worker' (defined as one who is 'supplied by a person (the 'agent') to do work for another (the 'principal') under a contract or other arrangements made between the agent and the principal') might not be a 'worker' as just defined, because of the absence of the necessary contractual nexus between the individual and either the agency (the 'agent') who supplies them or the client for whom they work (the 'principal'). Under these circumstances, the Act applies as if there were a worker's contract between the agency worker, and whichever one of the agency or client is responsible for paying the individual or, failing that, whichever one actually makes the payment.[318]

Under the Act, a 'homeworker' means an individual who 'contracts with a person, for the purposes of that person's business, for the execution of work to be done in a place not under the

[314] The Low Pay Commission (LPC) was initially set up in a non-statutory form in July 1997. Its members comprise representatives of employers' bodies and trade unions and a number of academics. The Act provided for this 'non-statutory Low Pay Commission' to be put on a more permanent, statutory footing (NMWA 1998, s 8). The Secretary of State was required to consult the LPC when first setting the rate of the minimum wage (see s 5) and has the power to refer other matters concerning the minimum wage to it (ss 6–7). The Commission's first report, *The National Minimum Wage. First Report of the Low Pay Commission*, was published in June 1998, and a number of further reports have since been published. For accounts of the work of the LPC by two of its members, see Metcalf, 1999 and W Brown, 2009. Metcalf, 2008 provides an overview of evidence concerning the economic impact of the NMW.
[315] NMWA 1998, s 1(2). General principles of illegality which may affect the validity of all or part of the contract agreed between the parties apply here as they do in other statutory contexts: see *Blue Chip Trading v Helbawi* [2009] IRLR 128, in which the EAT ruled that a worker employed in excess of twenty hours per week, the limit set by his student visa, could not claim the minimum wage in respect of the hours worked illegally.
[316] NMWA 1998, s 54(3); see *Edmonds v Lawson QC* [2000] IRLR 391, in which the Court of Appeal held that a pupil barrister was neither an apprentice nor, more generally, a worker within the meaning of this provision, essentially because of the apparent absence of a commitment to serve.
[317] See para 3.33 above and the particularly important decision, in the context of NMWA 1998, of *James v Redcats (Brands) Ltd* [2007] IRLR 296, discussed at para 3.33. NMWA 1998 has no application to postmasters and postmistresses who do not contract to provide personal services: *Commissioners of Inland Revenue v Post Office Ltd* [2003] IRLR 199.
[318] NMWA 1998, s 34. On agency workers, see paras 3.35 and 3.53 above.

control or management of that person'. A homeworker, so defined, is capable of coming under the definition of a 'worker' even if he or she does not undertake personally to supply the work or services in question.[319]

The Act applies (with only minor modifications) to Crown employees (but not members of the armed forces), House of Lords and House of Commons staff, and certain workers on board ships registered in the United Kingdom.[320] Additionally, the Secretary of State has a sweeping reserve power to make regulations for the application of the Act to 'any individual of a prescribed description who would not otherwise be a worker', and to identify, for this purpose, their employer.[321]

The scope of the Act is considerably broader, then, than that of employment protection legislation, which is mostly confined to employees employed under a contract of employment.[322] This makes it necessary for the Act to confer certain rights which are normally granted only to employees – such as the right to protection against being subjected to a detriment by the employer – upon workers as well.[323] However, the Act stops short of granting a worker the right not to be unfairly dismissed for asserting his or her rights in respect of the national minimum wage – this form of protection remains confined to employees.[324]

4.48 This extensive coverage of the Act is subject to a number of exceptions. Share fishermen, voluntary workers employed by charities, voluntary organisations, associated fund-raising bodies and certain statutory bodies, prisoners and members of the armed forces are specifically exempted.[325] More broadly, sections 3 and 4 confer specific powers of exclusion and modification on the Secretary of State; certain groups may, by regulation, be excluded from the application of the national minimum wage, and/or made subject to a different minimum rate from that generally in force. However, the Secretary of State may not adopt regulations which provide for different treatment by reference to different areas, sectors of employment, undertakings of different sizes, or different occupations.[326] Under the 1999 Regulations, as amended, the following categories of workers are completely excluded from the minimum wage: workers under compulsory school age;[327] certain workers participating in designated government-run training schemes; and certain

---

[319] NMWA 1998, s 35; *Commissioners of Inland Revenue v Post Office Ltd* [2003] IRLR 199; James v Redcats (Brands) Ltd [2007] IRLR 296. On homeworkers generally, see para 3.34 above.

[320] NMWA 1998, ss 36–40.

[321] NMWA 1998, s 41.

[322] See ch 3, above.

[323] NMWA 1998, ss 23–24. In addition, s 12 empowers the Secretary of State to adopt regulations providing for workers to receive a written statement of their minimum wage entitlements from their employer; however, this power has not been exercised.

[324] NMWA 1998, s 25.

[325] NMWA 1998, ss 43–45, s 37; s 44 (as amended by EA 2008, s 14) sets out in detail the categories of expenses and other payments which 'voluntary workers' (who unlike pure 'volunteers' are contracted to supply their personal service or services) may receive without forfeiting that status. There is no specific exception for 'interns', and in principle they will be covered by the Act if they are employed under a contract to provide personal service or services in return for payment. Note also ss 44A (resident workers in religious and other communities) and 45A (persons discharging fines by unpaid work). volunteers, see para 3.37 above; Simpson, 1999a: pp 6–7; D Morris, 1999; Simpson, 2009: pp 58–60.

[326] See ss 3(3) and 4(2).

[327] See NMWA 1998, s 1(2)(c). The restriction of the NMW to workers over the age of 18 was removed by SI 2004/1930.

workers receiving training at a higher education institution.[328] In addition, the 1999 Regulations added *au pairs* and family workers to the list of those outside the protection of the Act.[329] A further series of groups receives the minimum wage at a lower rate than the adult rate. Those aged 18 or over but less than 21 years receive the minimum wage at a lower 'development rate' which was set at £4.98 per hour from 1 October 2011. The rate is £3.68 per hour (with effect from 1 October 2011) for 16 and 17-year olds and £2.60 per hour for apprentices under the age of 19 or in the first year of their apprenticeship.[330]

DETERMINATION OF THE MINIMUM HOURLY RATE

4.49 The power to set the rate is vested in the Secretary of State for Trade and Industry who, when setting the rate for the *first* time, was required to consult the Low Pay Commission.[331] The Act makes no provision for the automatic uprating of the minimum hourly rate. Whether it is raised in any given year is, therefore, a matter for the discretion of the Secretary of State, who *may* make a reference on this question to the Low Pay Commission,[332] but is not obliged to do so. In June 1998 the Government announced that the rate for those aged 22 or over would be £3.60 an hour from April 1999. By 1 October 2011 this rate, now payable to those aged 21 or over, had risen to £6.08 per hour.[333]

APPLICATION OF THE MINIMUM HOURLY RATE

4.50 After the minimum rate is set, it is necessary to determine how the rate is to be applied to different types of contractual arrangements governing pay and working time. The Act says relatively little about how this is to be done, instead delegating the power to make regulations on these questions to the Secretary of State who, on the adoption of the first regulations, was required to consult the Low Pay Commission (and who *may* consult the LPC when adopting further regulations).

4.51 The Act and the Regulations address these issues through three core legal concepts.[334] The first of these is the *pay reference period*.[335] Payments made during this period must, when averaged out, be such as to ensure that the worker receives the statutory minimum rate in respect of the relevant hours worked. The pay reference period is defined as the interval between the payments normally received by the worker, up to a maximum of one month.[336] For certain

---

[328] NMWR 1999, reg 12, as amended, most recently by SI 2010/1901, which reversed the previous exclusion of apprentices (those on designated government schemes aside).

[329] NMWR 1999, reg 2(2)–(4). Family workers are those who work for a 'family business' as a member of the family in question and reside in the family home of the employer. For discussion, see Simpson, 1999b: pp 174–175.

[330] These rates are set out in NMWR 1999, reg 13, as amended. On the meaning of 'apprenticeship' in this context, see reg 13(6).

[331] NMWA 1998, s 5.

[332] NMWA 1998, s 6.

[333] NMWR 1999, reg 11, as amended . According to W Brown, 2009 the NMW had, by 2007, raised the pay of those affected by 20%, on average, over the level which they would otherwise have received.

[334] See Simpson, 1999a: p 11.

[335] NMWA 1998, s 1(4). The 'payment reference period' is the 'unit of account' by reference to which the wage or salary is paid, in contrast to the 'time' spent working which is 'the amount of time spent on the work (or deemed work)' under the Regulations: see the judgment of Arden LJ in *Walton v Independent Living Organisation Ltd* [2003] IRLR 469, at [37].

[336] NMWR 1999, reg 10.

purposes, a payment made in one pay reference period can be counted towards satisfying the employer's obligation in respect of the immediately preceding one.[337]

4.52   The next step is to determine which payments count towards the *wage* or 'remuneration' of the worker for the purposes of satisfying the employer's obligation to observe the minimum rate.[338] The starting point is the gross wage or salary paid to the worker during the pay reference period. Included in total gross pay for this purpose are incentive pay and bonuses, but not tips paid through the payroll.[339] Certain deductions made by the employer from gross pay also 'count' towards the wage for this purpose.[340] These include: deductions for income tax and national insurance purposes; deductions made under the worker's contract in relation, for example, of a breach of discipline;[341] deductions in respect of an advance of wages; deductions to pay for shares or securities; deductions to recover accidental overpayments of wages; and deductions not made for the employer's use and benefit, such as the worker's pension contribution or union membership dues. Deductions in respect of expenditures which the employee is required to make in connection with the employment, such as expenditures relating to safety equipment, tools or uniforms, do not count towards pay either.[342] Certain payments are outside the scope of statutory remuneration.[343] These include overtime and shift premia, geographical and other allowances,[344] exceptional payments for bad weather, and payments in kind, with an exception made for the provision of living accommodation subject to an upper daily limit.[345]

[337] NMWR 1999, reg 30(b). See Simpson, 1999a: pp 12–13. The pay reference period can also be adjusted to take into account situations where workers submit time sheets some time after the relevant period: see reg 30(c).

[338] NMWR 1999, regs 30–37.

[339] See generally Albin, 2010. In a case decided under wages councils legislation, it was held that tips paid by credit card or cheque were the property of the employer, so that when the employer passed them on to the worker through the payroll, it thereby discharged part of the obligation to pay the minimum wage: *Nerva v RL & G Ltd* [1996] IRLR 461. In *Nerva v United Kingdom* [2002] IRLR 815 the ECtHR held that this practice did not contravene the worker's property rights under Art 1 of Protocol 1 of the European Convention on Human Rights and Freedoms. In *Revenue and Customs Commissioners v Annabel's (Berkeley Square) Ltd* [2008] ICR 1076, on the other hand, the EAT held that the payment of tips to workers by customers or clients or by a 'troncmaster' on the employer's behalf meant that they were not paid by the employer within the meaning of NMWR 1999, reg 30, and so did not discharge the employer's obligation to pay the minimum wage. This decision was upheld on appeal: *Annabel's (Berkeley Square) Ltd v Revenue & Customs Commissioners* [2009] 4 All ER 55. A number of options for law reform were set out in BERR, *The National Minimum Wage: Service Charges, Tips, Gratuities and Cover Charges: A Consultation* (November 2008), and an amendment was subsequently made to NMWR 1999 by SI 2009/1902, reg 5, the effect of which was to exclude tips paid to the worker through the payroll from discharging the employer's obligation to pay the statutory minimum (see NMWR, reg 31(1)(e)).

[340] See reg 33, which must be read in conjunction with regs 31(1)(g) and 32.

[341] See reg 33(a). This regulation makes no reference to the lawfulness of the deduction under ERA 1996, Part II (see below, para 4.69). See Simpson, 1999a: p 15.

[342] NMWR 1999, reg 31(1)(a).

[343] See reg 31.

[344] Thus attendance allowances fall outside the definition of remuneration for this purpose: see *Laird v AK Stoddart Ltd* [2001] IRLR 591.

[345] NMWR 1999, regs 30(d), 31(i) and 36. From October 2011 this was set at £4.73. On the operation of the 'accommodation offset' rules, see *Leisure Employment Services Ltd v Commissioners for HM Revenue and Customs* [2007] IRLR 450.

4.53   The third key concept is that of the *working time* for which the national minimum rate must be paid.[346] Four employment types are identified for this purpose: time work, salaried-hours work, output work, and unmeasured work. These four categories are exhaustive in the sense that between them, they cover all types of employment falling under the Act and Regulations, and also mutually exclusive in the sense that only one of them can apply to a given period of working time; however, it is possible that within a single employment or work relationship, more than one could be relevant for different periods.

4.54   Under regulation 3, *time work* is work that is paid by reference to a set or varying period of time, typically an hour or number of hours.[347] In *British Nursing Association v Inland Revenue (National Minimum Wage Compliance Team)*[348] the Court of Appeal held that duty nurses who worked at home during the night, responding to telephone requests for nursing help, were engaged in 'time work' throughout the period of their shift, and not simply when they were answering the telephone. On similar grounds, a night watchman[349] and a security guard[350] have been able to argue that the entire period of their shifts during counted as time work. Under regulation 15(1), the definition of time work is extended to cover 'time when a worker is available at or near a place of work for the purpose of doing time work' and is required by their contract to be so available. As Buxton LJ put it in the *British Nursing Association* case, this extension 'relates to workers who are, in colloquial terms, "on call".'[351] It is subject to two exceptions: the first applies where the worker in question under their contract spends time on call at home, and their home is at or near their place of work;[352] the second relates to a period when the worker, 'by arrangement', spends part of the on-call time sleeping, using facilities provided by the employer.[353] However, these exceptions only apply to the 'on-call' provisions set out in regulation 15(1) and not to the core definition of time work under regulation 3.[354] Regulation 15 also provides that periods of training and certain periods spent travelling in connection with work (but not travelling to and from home) are within the definition of time work. Various periods of absence from work on account of rest and meal breaks, holidays, maternity or parental leave, industrial action, and periods of sickness or ill health are excluded.

[346] NMWR 1999, regs 15–29A; Simpson, 1999a: pp 16–20, 1999b: pp 176–180; *National Minimum* Wage Guide, pp 51–89. As the EAT pointed out in *South Holland District Council v Stamp*, EAT/1097/02 RN, the phrase 'working time' does not appear in the NMWA 1998 and NMWR 1999, and the concept of 'working time' under WTR 1998 is, on the face of it, a separate one from that contained in the NMWA (see *British Nursing Association v Inland Revenue (National Minimum Wage Compliance Team)* [2002] IRLR 480, at [20] (Buxton LJ)). It has however become conventional to use the expression 'working time' in the context of the NMW to refer to a composite notion based on the four concepts of 'time work', 'salaried work', 'output work' and 'unmeasured work' referred to in the text, below. It is also arguable that, in the interests of consistency and clarity in the application of labour legislation, the NMW legislation should as far as possible be interpreted in line with the WTR. See L Rodgers, 2009.
[347] See also reg 15; Simpson 2004: pp 29–32.
[348] [2002] IRLR 480.
[349] *Scottbridge Construction Ltd v Wright* [2001] IRLR 589, [2003] IRLR 21.
[350] *Burrow Down Support Services Ltd v Rossiter*, UKEAT/0592/07/LA; L Rodgers, 2009.
[351] [2002] IRLR 480, [17].
[352] NMWR 1999, reg 15(1)(a)–(b).
[353] NMWR 1999, reg 15(1A).
[354] *Scottbridge Construction Ltd v Wright* [2003] IRLR 21; *Burrow Down Support Services Ltd v Rossiter* [2008] ICR 1172, discussed by L Rodgers, 2009; *South Manchester Abbeyfield Society Ltd v Hopkins* [2011] IRLR 300.

4.55   *Salaried work* exists where the worker is paid in relation to a set basic number of hours per year, is entitled to an annual salary, and is paid in equal instalments (for example, 12 monthly or 52 weekly payments).[355] The definition of working time essentially mirrors that for a time worker, except that certain periods of absence which are normally remunerated now count as working time. Thus it is customary for salaried workers to be paid in respect of 'absences' such as meal breaks, sick leave, and holidays;[356] in a given case, the definition of working time for this purpose will turn on the relevant terms of the worker's contract. A similar definition of 'on-call' time applies as in the case of time work.[357] Detailed rules govern the situation in which a salaried worker works annual hours in excess of those set out in the contract.[358]

4.56   *Output work* refers to work in respect of which the payment is linked to the number of items or products produced by the worker, as in the case of piece work or commission work, without reference to a given period of time.[359] The Regulations initially made provision for the employer and worker to make a 'fair estimate' agreement setting out the number of hours which the worker was expected to work during the relevant pay reference period. This had to be not less than four fifths of the time an average worker would take to do the same amount of work in the same conditions. The employer was then under an obligation to pay the statutory minimum for the 'fair estimate' hours. With effect from 1 October 2004, this system was replaced by one based on 'fair piece rates'.[360] Now, the employer must either pay the minimum rate for each hour actually worked, or put in place a system for determining the 'mean hourly output rate' for a particular piece or task. This can be done either by measuring the performance of all the workers concerned or of a representative sample. The 'fair piece rate' in a given case must be such as to enable a worker achieving the 'mean hourly output rate' to earn the minimum wage in respect of that hour. From 6 April 2005 the fair piece rate has been calculated by reference to 120% of the time which an average worker would take to earn the minimum wage, in effect increasing its value by a fifth.[361]

4.57   *Unmeasured work* is work which does not fall into one of the other three categories.[362] This would be the case, for example, with a task contract which does not specify times or periods during which the work is to be done. The employer must either pay the minimum rate for each hour actually worked, or come to an agreement in writing with the worker which specifies a 'daily average' of hours to be worked.[363]

4.58   The most difficult issues to have arisen in respect of the definitions of working time in the Act and Regulations are those concerning the treatment of on-call workers. Courts and tribunals

---

[355] NMWR 1999, reg 4.

[356] See below, para 4.62.

[357] NMWR, reg 16; see *Hughes v Jones and Jones t/a Graylyns Residential Home*, UK/EAT/0159/08/MAA (discussed by L Rodgers, 2009); *South Manchester Abbeyfield Society Ltd v Hopkins* [2011] IRLR 300.

[358] NMWR 1999, reg 22.

[359] NMWR 1999, reg 5.

[360] NMWR 1999, regs 24–26A, as amended by SI 2004/1161, reg 2.

[361] See NMWR reg 26, as amended by SI 2004/1161, reg 3.

[362] NMWR 1999, reg 6.

[363] NMWR 1999, regs 18, 27–29; for an example of a 'daily average' agreement under reg 28, see *Walton v Independent Living Organisation Ltd* [2003] IRLR 469.

have tended to find that 'on-call' time counts as working time under one category or another, and in doing so have drawn on decisions interpreting the Working Time Directive and Regulations.[364] Even though these decisions are not directly on point in a minimum wage case, applicants frequently make claims for both minimum wage and working time protection in respect of the same periods of work. Under these circumstances it is not surprising that courts and tribunals should have sought to arrive, as far as possible, at a common definition of working time. However, it is not enough simply to establish that on-call time is working time; in the context of the minimum wage legislation, the outcome of the case may turn on which of the four categories the work in question falls under. In *Walton v Independent Living Organisation Ltd*[365] a carer who was on call for 24 hours three days a week was found to have been engaged in unmeasured work. She was able to carry out her tasks in an average of 6 hours 50 minutes per week. The Court of Appeal held that she had come to an agreement with her employer on what her average hours would be, as provided for by regulation 28. Since, as a result, hours above that figure did not count as working time, her claim for minimum wage protection in respect of those hours failed. By contrast, in *MacCartney v Oversley House Management*[366] a residential manager who was required to be on site or within a three mile radius of a residential home and respond to emergencies for 24 hours a day, four days a week, was held to have been employed on salaried work within the meaning of regulation 4 for the whole of this period (even though much of it was spent at home and for part of it the claimant was asleep). Her claim for minimum wage protection (along with a claim in respect of daily rest periods and rest breaks under the Working Time Regulations) succeeded. A further variation on the range of possible outcomes is illustrated by *Hughes v Jones and Jones t/a Graylyns Residential Home*.[367] A care assistant who worked on a number of tasks for 8 hours per week and who had to be available on call for a further 77 hours per week was held to have been employed on salaried work throughout. The EAT held that the claimant's situation came under the on-call extension to the concept of salaried work set out in regulation 16, with the result that time spent asleep did not count towards her working time.

EFFECT AND ENFORCEMENT[368]

4.59 The right to receive the national minimum wage takes effect as a term in the worker's contract. The Act provides that '[I]f a worker who qualifies for the national minimum wage is remunerated for any pay reference period by his employer at a rate which is less than the national minimum wage, the worker shall... be taken to be entitled under his contract to be paid, as additional remuneration in respect of that period, the amount'[369] to which he is entitled by virtue of the Act.[370] Aside from the possibility of a claim for wages due under the common law or Part

---

[364] See below, paras 4.80.
[365] [2003] IRLR 469.
[366] [2006] IRLR 514.
[367] UK/EAT/0159/08/MAA; L Rodgers, 2009. See also *South Manchester Abbeyfield Society Ltd v Hopkins* [2011] IRLR 300.
[368] See Simpson, 1999a: pp 24–28, and 1999b: pp 180–181, and 2004: pp 35–39 for commentary on these provisions; Skidmore, 1999. Note also the strengthening of enforcement procedures and sanctions in EA 2008, ss 8–12, amending various provisions of NMWA 1998, discussed Simpson, 2009; see also G Morris, 2012: pp 24–25.
[369] NMWA 1998, s 17(1).
[370] NMWA 1998, s 17(2). By virtue of the changes made to s 17 by EA 2008, s 8, the worker may be able to benefit, when calculating arrears, from any increases in the NMW rate which have occurred since the time of the underpayment.

II of ERA 1996[371] which this provision creates, the NMWA 1998 provides additional mechanisms of enforcement. A notice of underpayment may be issued by a government officer[372] against an employer who is failing or who has failed to comply with the law, requiring the employer to make the necessary payments to one or more workers within 28 days of the notice,[373] together (generally) with a financial penalty to the Secretary of State.[374] The penalty is 50% of the total underpayment of the NMW, with a minimum penalty of £100 and a maximum of £5,000. If the employer complies with the notice within 14 days of its service the penalty is reduced by 50%.[375] The employer has the right to appeal to an employment tribunal against the decision to serve the notice or any requirement imposed by it before the end of the 28-day period allowed for payment.[376] If an enforcement notice is not complied with, the officer may present a complaint on behalf of the worker concerned to an employment tribunal under Part II of ERA 1996 or commence proceedings for breach of contract.[377] In addition, an employer who wilfully neglects to pay the national minimum wage is guilty of an offence punishable by an unlimited fine.[378] In the case of corporate entities, both the employer and a corporate officer may be convicted of an offence.[379] Where an employer is convicted of an offence the financial penalty under the notice of underpayment must be withdrawn.[380] There is provision for the officer serving the notice to suspend the penalty where he or she considers that an employer has been, or may be, prosecuted; it can be reactivated if no prosecution occurs or the employer is not convicted. [381]

RELATED OBLIGATIONS OF EMPLOYERS

4.60   In addition to the obligation to pay the national minimum wage, employers must also meet a number of requirements which are designed to facilitate enforcement and to protect workers who assert their rights to the minimum wage. Particularly relevant are the obligations to keep wages records[382] and to allow workers and their representatives to have access to them.[383] As we have already noted, a worker who suffers detriment as a result of asserting his or her rights in relation

---

[371] See below, paras 4.71–4.73.

[372] NMWA 1998, s 13 provides for the Secretary of State to appoint officers for the purposes of performing this and various related functions under the Act, or to arrange for these functions to be carried out by a government department or other body performing functions on behalf of the Crown. This is currently performed by officers of Her Majesty's Revenue and Customs (HMRC).

[373] NMWA 1998, s 19, as substituted by EA 2008, s 9. Arrears are assessed at the current rate rather than the rate applicable at the date of underpayment.

[374] NMWA 1998, s 19A. The Secretary of State may by directions specify circumstances in which a notice of underpayment is not to impose a requirement to pay a financial penalty.

[375] NMWA 1998, s 19A.

[376] NMWA 1998, s 19C.

[377] NMWA 1998, s 19D.

[378] NMWA 1998, s 31 as amended by EA 2008, s 11.

[379] NMWA 1998, s 32; on the definition of a corporate officer, see s 32(3). See also s 48 dealing with 'superior employers'.

[380] NMWA 1998, s 19B(6).

[381] NMWA 1998, s 19B(1)-(5).

[382] NMWA 1998, s 9. The power, under s 12, to make regulations requiring employers to issue a minimum wage statement to all workers entitled to receive the statutory minimum (as opposed to employees who will in any event receive an itemised pay statement under ERA 1996, s 8) has not yet been exercised; although a draft was prepared at an early stage of the process of producing the 1999 Regulations, this did not survive into the final version of the Regulations. See Simpson, 1999b: pp 180–181 on the background to this issue.

[383] NMWA 1998, ss 10–11. Under s 10(4)(b), the worker may be accompanied, for the purposes of inspection, by 'such other person as the worker may think fit'.

to the minimum wage may present a complaint to that effect to an employment tribunal,[384] and an employee who is dismissed in such circumstances may make a claim of unfair dismissal which, if upheld, will be regarded as automatically unfair.[385] Also important from the point of view of enforcement is a general provision to the effect that in proceedings in respect of the minimum wage, the employer has the burden of showing either that an individual is not covered by the Act or that he or she did receive the required minimum payment.[386]

(iv) Statutory wage fixing for agricultural workers

4.61   The pay and conditions of around 150,000[387] agricultural workers are regulated by statutory orders made by the Agricultural Wages Boards for England and Wales and for Scotland under legislation which has been in force, in various forms, since the 1920s.[388] The Agricultural Wages Boards have the power to regulate minimum rates of pay together with holiday entitlements and other terms and conditions of employment. These minimum terms take effect automatically and compulsorily in the contracts of the workers affected, so that an individual may bring a civil claim in debt or damages for the difference between the wages paid to him or her by their employer and those due to them under the relevant statutory order.[389] They may also apply to an employment tribunal to recover arrears of pay.

The Agricultural Wages Board remained in operation after the passage of the National Minimum Wage Act 1998. However, that Act amended the Agricultural Wages Act,[390] so as to ensure that the rate set by the Agricultural Wages Board was not less than the relevant rate set for the national minimum wage. The enforcement provisions of the 1998 Act were also made applicable (with some minor modifications) to the rates set for agricultural workers.[391]

Statutory wage fixing in agriculture in England and Wales, however, seems unlikely to remain in operation for much longer. Shortly after taking office in 2010, the Coalition government announced a review of the Agricultural Wages Board for England and Wales, and the Public Bodies Act 2011[392] makes provision for its abolition. The government's position in the autumn of 2011 was that the operations of the Board 'gold-plate the provisions of the national minimum wage legislation and working time regulations. There is, therefore, a heavy regulatory burden on employers, and we believe that it is hampering the industry from creating jobs and damaging long-term prosperity and sustainability'.[393]

---

[384] NMWA 1998, ss 23–24.
[385] NMWA 1998, s 25, inserting a new s 104A into ERA 1996; see para 5.101 below.
[386] NMWA 1998, s 28. Note also the formal ban on contracting out (s 49).
[387] Figures based on the *June Survey of Agriculture and Horticulture for 2011* as reported by DEFRA and the Scottish Government.
[388] Now the Agricultural Wages Act 1948; Agricultural Wages (Scotland) Act 1949.
[389] *Gutsell v Reeve* [1936] 1 KB 272.
[390] NMWA, 1998, ss 46–47 and Sch 2.
[391] The amendments to NMWA 1998 made by EA 2008, s 9–11 do not have effect in relation to the agricultural minimum wage in Scotland.
[392] Public Bodies Act 2011, Sch 1.
[393] Jim Paice MP, Minister of State at DEFRA, Hansard, 25 October 2011, col 218.

The common law of the wage-work bargain

4.62   The principal mechanism by which an individual may claim his or her wages is by a civil action in debt (or an 'action for the price'); hence, the employee's right to payment depends upon performance of the contractual obligation which corresponds to the employer's obligation to pay. For this purpose, the court seeks to discover, through a process of construction, whether wages are payable in return for finished work, services actually rendered over a period of time, or readiness to work. Where the contract stipulates that wages are to be paid on a piece-work basis, it is self-evident that the right to payment depends upon the relevant work being finished.[394] In relation to time rates of payment, there was at one stage a presumption that hourly-paid employees – that is to say, those paid by reference to an hourly rate of pay – had to complete each hour of work in order to be entitled to their wages.[395] In their case, no work meant no pay: 'the consideration for work is wages, and the consideration for wages is work'.[396] By contrast, salaried employees were regarded as receiving payment in return for a more general commitment of loyalty and 'faithful service' over time.[397] As a result, merely being ready and willing to work sufficed for them to claim payment. What this meant in practice was that salaried employees were entitled to payment in the event of being unable to work for reasons beyond their control, such as illness or lay-off caused by a lack of work,[398] whereas hourly-paid employees were not.[399]

At the time this distinction was most clearly articulated, in the late 1930s,[400] it appears to have been influenced by social insurance legislation, which drew a similar distinction between manual and non-manual employees. It was reasonable to argue at that point that because manual employees were covered by the state social insurance system in relation to loss of income caused by illness and unemployment, they should not also be covered by the contract; but this was not so for salaried employees, most of whom were outside state social insurance at this point.[401] Modern social security legislation no longer draws this distinction. Moreover, many manual or hourly-paid employees benefit from long notice periods and other features of stable, long-term employment relationships such as occupational sick pay and pension rights, to the extent that that they are in a similar position to salaried staff of being paid in return for a general commitment of loyal service. The formal harmonisation of the terms and conditions of manual and non-manual staff is well advanced in some sectors and companies, but is by no means complete.

It is arguable, then, that the approach to construction, whatever it is, should be the same for both groups. This view was taken by the House of Lords in *Miles v Wakefield Metropolitan District Council*,[402] which concerned a claim for salary arising in the context of limited industrial

---

[394] Eg, *Devonald v Rosser & Sons* [1906] 2 KB 728.

[395] This was apparently also the case if the term governing the rate of pay was not agreed but was imposed by statute, as in *Gutsell v Reeve* [1936] 1 KB 272.

[396] *Browning v Crumlin Valley Collieries Ltd* [1926] 1 KB 522, 528 (Greer LJ); see also *Automatic Fire Sprinklers Pty Ltd v Watson* (1946) 72 CLR 435, 465 (Dixon CJ).

[397] Denning, 1939: p 354. It does not follow that a salaried employee cannot claim overtime pay for hours worked beyond his or her normal daily or weekly working time, if there is an agreement to that effect: *Driver v Air India Ltd* [2011] IRLR 992.

[398] Eg, *Orman v Saville Sportswear Ltd* [1960] 1 WLR 1055.

[399] *Hancock v BSA Tools Ltd* [1939] 4 All ER 538, *Petrie v Macfisheries Ltd* [1940] 1 KB 258 (both sick pay cases), *Marshall v English Electric Co Ltd* [1945] 1 All ER 653 (suspension).

[400] See in particular, Denning, 1939, and the sick pay cases cited above.

[401] Denning, 1939: pp 356–357 made this point.

[402] [1987] AC 539. See below, para 4.68.

action. According to Lord Templeman, in this context 'there is no logical distinction between a superintendent registrar who is paid a weekly salary for a 37-hour week and a municipal dustman who is paid a weekly wage for a 37-hour week'.[403] In both cases, the employee would have to show that he was at least willing to work as a *necessary condition* of claiming payment.[404] Although *Miles* does not clearly decide that, in other contexts such as involuntary illness or lay-off, readiness to work is a *sufficient* condition for such a claim, it seems likely that it is.[405] An avoidable absence, such as one arising from the imprisonment of the employee, would however negate a claim for wages based on readiness to work.[406]

The construction of the wage-work bargain, although essential in determining the scope of any claim by the employee in *debt*, is only one aspect of the employer's obligations under the contract. The employer may alternatively be liable for a breach of contract resulting in an award of *damages*, which in some circumstances will offer an alternative form of income protection to the employee. In *Devonald v Rosser & Sons*[407] piece-workers who were laid off without pay were able to claim by way of damages an amount equivalent to their net wages for the contractual period of notice, through an implied term that the employer would ensure that work was made available to them for this period. Similarly, an implied or express term may be the basis for a claim in damages for sick pay, as an alternative to a claim for the agreed wages in debt.[408]

There are some important differences between debt claims and damages claims however. The claim in debt is for a liquidated sum (that is, a sum set by the contract itself) and no duty to mitigate arises on the part of the employee. Damages, by contrast, represent the claimant's loss and are paid as an unliquidated sum assessed by the court. They may be subject to reductions for the employee's failure to mitigate or in respect of their receipt of offsetting gains (such as unemployment compensation). Thus the employee will normally choose the action in debt to enforce the employer's promise to pay a sum of money in return for performance.

The failure to pay wages at the agreed time is, in itself, a breach of contract by the employer giving rise to a claim in damages,[409] although the employee will not be compensated twice over in respect of the same quantum of wages or salary. The principal significance of the employer's failure to pay being a breach of contract is that if the breach is repudiatory at common law, which it may be depending on the circumstances, the employee will be entitled to terminate the contract without notice and bring actions for wrongful and/or unfair dismissal.[410]

---

[403] [1987] AC 539, 556–557. This statement may now have to be read in the light of NMWR 1999, which, as we have seen (paras 4.54–4.55), draws a distinction between time work and salaried work similar to that made by Denning, 1939.

[404] See *Beveridge v KLM (UK) Ltd* [2000] IRLR 765.

[405] *Burns v Santander (UK) plc* [2011] IRLR 639, at [10].

[406] *Burns v Santander (UK) plc* [2011] IRLR 639, at [12].

[407] [1906] 2 KB 728; see below, para 4.126.

[408] *Mears v Safecar Security Ltd* [1982] ICR 626 is a case of an implied term; the earlier sick pay cases, such as *Marrison v Bell* [1939] 2 KB 187 and *Petrie v Macfisheries Ltd* [1940] 1 KB 258 appear to have been argued solely in debt. See *New Century Cleaning Co Ltd v Church* [2000] IRLR 27 for a refusal to imply a term preventing the employer from implementing a unilateral pay cut in response to a fall in profits. The scope of the implied terms relating to income security is considered later in this chapter, at paras 4.124 and 4.126 below.

[409] See, eg, *Rigby v Ferodo Ltd* [1988] ICR 29.

[410] See *Cantor Fitzgerald International v Callaghan* [1999] IRLR 234 on the circumstances under which a failure to pay wages or salary amounts to a repudiatory breach.

Deduction and retention at common law

4.63   The circumstances under which an employer can withhold all or part of the agreed wage are determined, in the first instance, by the common law. The first issue to consider here is the point at which the employee's contractual right to payment accrues. Where payment is governed by a time rate of some kind, an employee who has performed the contract as required becomes entitled to payment in respect of *that* period. There is a distinction to be drawn here between the point at which the right to payment accrues, which is when the performance is completed, and the point at which the wage becomes payable, which may be later. It is standard practice in many employments, for example, to pay wages and salaries a week or month in arrears; there is nothing unlawful about this practice, although it would be normal for it to be supported either by an express contract term or by one implied from a collective agreement or from custom and practice. Notwithstanding this possibility of an interval between accrual and actual payment of the wage, once the right has accrued it cannot be forfeited by anything which the employee does between that point and the time at which payment falls due,[411] except to the extent that the employee may commit a subsequent breach of contract which gives rise to a counterclaim or set-off in damages.

It follows that the right to payment of an hourly-paid worker accrues hour by hour, as the work is carried out (subject to the possibility of an employee showing that mere readiness to work suffices). In the case of a salaried employee for whom no time rate as such is set, the interval between payments – normally a month – becomes important in establishing the point at which the right to payment is earned.[412] In principle, performance must be rendered in full for each month before *any part* of the salary for that month (or other period) becomes due. This was established in a number of nineteenth-century cases concerning employees who either quit or who were dismissed for breach of contract before the expiry of their fixed term of employment: the courts held that they had no claim for work done either in contract or in quantum meruit.[413] The outcome is sometimes seen as an aspect of the common law doctrine of 'entire obligations': the debt, or price, cannot be apportioned except to the extent that the contract itself provides for this. The courts do not normally imply a term allowing for pro rata payment where to do so would contradict an express agreement.[414]

4.64   It is possible, however, that an employee may invoke, in this context, section 2 of the Apportionment Act 1870, which provides that 'all rents, annuities, dividends, and other periodical payments in the nature of income [shall] be considered as accruing from day to day, and shall be apportionable in respect of time accordingly'; for this purpose, the term 'annuities' is expressed to include 'salaries'. Although there is evidence that it was not the intention at the time this Act was passed to apply this part of it to contracts of employment in general,[415] in *Sim v Rotherham Metropolitan Borough Council*[416] Scott J thought that it did apply to the salaries of monthly-paid

---

[411] *George v Davies* [1911] 2 KB 445.

[412] *Sim v Rotherham Metropolitan Borough Council* [1987] Ch 216, 255 (Scott J).

[413] *Turner v Robinson* (1833) 5 B & Ad 789; *Ridgway v Hungerford Market Co* (1835) 3 Ad & El 171; *Saunders v Whittle* (1876) 33 LT 816; *Boston Deep Sea Fishing & Ice Co v Ansell* (1888) 39 Ch D 339.

[414] G Williams, 1941.

[415] Matthews, 1982.

[416] [1987] Ch 216, 255.

schoolteachers which 'may be regarded as accruing day by day'.[417] The term 'wages' is not mentioned in the 1870 Act and it is unclear whether the Act could apply to non-salaried employees. However, the recent tendency of the courts has been to give the Act a general application to contracts of employment.[418]

4.65   The harshness of the common law doctrine of entire performance is also mitigated by the principle that *substantial* performance is sufficient to discharge a contractual obligation, and gives rise to the equivalent obligation on the part of the payor. In the context of employment this has been taken to mean that an employee cannot be prevented from claiming payment in respect of a particular period of employment merely because he or she has committed a minor breach of contract which falls short of being repudiatory.[419] For example, an hourly-paid employee who completes a basic 39-hour week is, *prima facie*, entitled to the normal weekly wage based on the applicable hourly rate; if he or she has, at some point in that week, committed a minor breach of discipline, this would not, *in itself*, entitle the employer to withhold all or part of the payment for that week.[420] Under these circumstances, a deduction would be lawful only if the employer could point either to an express term authorising the deduction, or to an implied right of abatement or set-off.[421]

4.66   Any express term has to have been incorporated into the contract according to the tests considered earlier in this chapter.[422] Even then, the effect of the term is not guaranteed, since it could be struck down in equity as a penalty clause[423] if the court considers that it was inserted *in terrorem* and not by way of a genuine attempt at a pre-estimate of the cost of breach to the employer. The implied right of set-off, conversely, depends upon the employer showing that the employee committed a breach of contract which caused him loss of some kind; that loss can be abated or set off against the wages which are due to the employee.

4.67   In *Sim v Rotherham Metropolitan Borough Council*[424] schoolteachers who were taking part in industrial action refused to cover the classes of absent colleagues as they would normally have done. Their employers deducted a small percentage of their monthly salaries in respect of the hours when they refused to work normally. The teachers' action was held to have been a breach of their contractual duty of trust and co-operation, resulting in damage to the employer which was at least the equivalent of the deductions made from their monthly salaries. According to Scott J:

---

[417] See also, for more recent applications of this Act, *Thames Water Utilities v Reynolds* [1996] IRLR 186; *Taylor v East Midlands Offender Employment* [2000] IRLR 760.

[418] The Divisional Court held that it applied to a case of directors' fees in *Moriarty v Regent's Garage Co Ltd* [1921] 2 KB 766; its decision was reversed on different grounds. In *Item Software (UK) Ltd v Fassihi* [2004] IRLR 928, the Court of Appeal held that the Act applied in a case of a salaried director.

[419] G Williams, 1941. On repudiatory breach of the contract of employment, see paras 5.18–5.19 below.

[420] Freedland, 1976: p 229.

[421] On the need for the employer to be able to point to a contract term authorising deduction once the employee has established that the wages or salary are due in return for performance, see *Davies v MJ Wyatt (Decorators) Ltd* [2000] IRLR 759; *Beveridge v KLM (UK) Ltd* [2000] IRLR 765.

[422] See para 4.26 *et seq* above.

[423] According to the principle in *Dunlop Pneumatic Tyre Co Ltd v New Garage & Motor Co Ltd* [1915] AC 79. See *Giraud (UK) Ltd v Smith* [2000] IRLR 763; *Tullett Prebon Group Ltd v El-Hajjali* [2008] IRLR 760.

[424] [1987] Ch 216.

... the correct approach in cases like the present is to start with the teachers' contractual monthly salary entitlement. If in the course of the month there has been a breach of contract by a teacher, it is necessary to consider what, if any, damages can be claimed by the employer by reason of that breach of contract. If the breach of contract has not given rise to any recoverable loss to the education authority, then ... there is no deduction that can properly be made from the salary on account of the breach. If recoverable loss has been caused to the education authority, it is necessary to consider whether the law allows, by way of abatement or by way of set-off, the deduction of the damages from the monthly salary ...[425]

The principal argument against allowing an *implied* right of set-off in contracts of employment is that it may undermine explicit procedures for dealing with breach of discipline. However, Scott J held that there was no distinction, for this purpose, between contracts of employment and other contracts to which set-off applied; accordingly, the deductions made were lawful.[426]

If the approach in *Sim* is adopted, the employer must prove both breach and damage before any deduction may be made. The result may be described as 'part work, part pay': the partial failure of performance is reflected in the amount deducted by way of set-off. In cases of industrial action involving a deliberate refusal to perform the contract as intended, however, cases decided after *Sim* suggest that the employer may be able to rely on a wider principle to withhold payment completely.

4.68   In *Miles v Wakefield Metropolitan District Council*,[427] as part of industrial action, a local government registrar of births, deaths and marriages refused to conduct weddings on Saturday mornings. He normally worked a 37-hour week. On the Saturdays in question he attended his office for the normal three hours and carried out other duties related to his work. His employer made a deduction of 3/37ths of his salary for the period of the industrial action; his action for the recovery of the full salary was rejected in the House of Lords.

According to Lord Templeman, 'when a worker in breach of contract declines to work in accordance with the contract, but claims payment for his wages, it is unnecessary for the employer to rely on the defences of abatement or equitable set-off. The employer may or may not sustain and be able to prove and recover damages by reason of the breach of contract of each worker. But so far as wages are concerned, the worker can only claim them if he is willing to work'.[428] The employee's claim fails at the outset, then, on the grounds of failure to perform the contract as required; and even though the employer may receive certain benefits from part performance, it does not have to pay for them if it informs the employees that it declines to accept partial performance as equivalent to the whole.

This left open the possibility of an action in restitution for the value of the partial services rendered by the employee. Lords Brightman and Templeman were prepared to entertain this

---

[425] [1987] Ch 216, 255.

[426] Abatement was a doctrine of the common law, set-off one of equity. In the context of employment, *Sim* decides that there is no difference between them. There is some authority, notwithstanding the judgment of Scott J, to suggest that nineteenth-century courts did not accept the application of the doctrines of set-off and abatement to salaries: *Le Loir v Bristow* (1815) 4 Camp 134; *Stimson v Hall* (1857) 1 H & N 831; see Deakin, 1992: p 850.

[427] [1987] AC 539.

[428] [1987] AC 539, 561. See also *British Telecommunications plc v Ticehurst* [1992] ICR 383, discussed further below at para 11.71.

possibility, but Lord Bridge thought it 'contrary to the realities of the situation'[429] and Lords Brandon and Oliver expressly reserved their opinion on the question.

4.69   The full implications of *Miles* became clear in *Wiluszynski v London Borough of Tower Hamlets*.[430] Local government officers taking part in industrial action refused over a period of several weeks to deal with queries from the constituents of councillors. During this period they carried out other duties as normal. After the industrial action was over they were able to deal with the backlog of queries in a matter of a few hours. The employer withheld payment in full for the period of the industrial action and was held to have acted lawfully in doing so.

A deliberate refusal in advance of performance to work under the contract as normal therefore *completely* defeats the employee's contractual claim to wages or salary. This continues for as long as the refusal fully to perform goes on (in practice, the duration of the industrial action) and the employer can defeat any claim to *part* payment by making it clear that it declines to waive its right to receive performance in full. The effect is 'part work, *no pay*'.[431] Nor is the alternative quantum meruit route to partial compensation a particularly feasible one. In principle, if the employer's refusal to waive the right to full performance is regarded as effective in contract, it should operate for the restitutionary claim too. The contract has not been discharged, and so should continue to govern the parties' relationship either way.[432]

It is not clear that the decisions in *Miles* and *Wiluszynski* can readily be justified by contract law doctrine, however. It is odd that the employer can apparently suspend the obligation of payment while other aspects of the contract remain in force. At common law, the employer in these cases could have dismissed the employees for committing repudiatory breaches of contract. That it did not do so suggests that it may have been concerned about legal consequences in the form of actions for unfair dismissal,[433] but also that it did not wish to lose completely the services of valued staff. In either case, the issue is whether the employer should go on receiving the substantial benefit of performance in return for nothing, simply by virtue of a unilateral declaration to the effect that it was not 'accepting' part performance.

Lord Templeman in *Miles* thought that some protection for the employer was necessary in order to avoid a situation in which a worker was protected against 'losing both his job and his wages' in the event of taking industrial action. However, it is not clear that this situation would have arisen. First, it was not then the case that, as his Lordship put it, 'an individual worker is unfairly dismissed if the only reason for his dismissal is that he has taken part in industrial action unless all workers who take part are also dismissed'.[434] Even now, employees are deemed to be unfairly dismissed for taking industrial action only in a relatively restricted range of circumstances.[435]

Second, if *Miles* had been decided differently, the employee would not necessarily have received payment in full; some deduction would have been permissible by way of set-off or abatement, to reflect the employee's breach of contract. As *Sim* shows, in the context of industrial action such a breach can justifiably be seen as causing damage to the employer in the form of the

[429] [1987] AC 539, 552.
[430] [1989] IRLR 259, applied in *Spackman v London Metropolitan University* [2007] IRLR 744.
[431] G Smith, 1989.
[432] Although, for a different point of view on this, see G Mead, 1991.
[433] See *Miles v Wakefield Metropolitan District Council* [1987] AC 539, 559.
[434] [1987] AC 539, 559.
[435] TULRCA 1992, s 237–238A; see below, para 11.73 *et seq*.

loss of a certain proportion of the services of the employee in question. The latter may admittedly be difficult to quantify in a given case. In *Miles* and *Sim* the deductions were calculated by reference to the hours in a given month when less than full performance was rendered.[436] Similarly, in *British Telecommunications plc v Ticehurst*[437] deductions from monthly pay were made in proportion to particular days during which no work was carried out, following a withdrawal of goodwill by the employees. In *Royle v Trafford Borough Council*[438] a deduction was made according to the number of pupils excluded from classes by teachers' industrial action over the issue of class size.

More generally, in so far as *Miles* represents a gloss on the common law notions of what constitutes contractual performance, its effects are probably confined to the specific situation of industrial action involving a deliberate refusal to perform the contract as intended. For the reasons given above, it should have no application to a situation of inadvertent or non-premeditated breach of the duties of care or obedience.[439]

Recovery of overpayments

4.70   If an employee is overpaid on one or more occasions, the employer may be able to recover the overpayment by an action for money had and received. Until fairly recently the courts drew a distinction between payments made under a mistake of fact and those made under a mistake of law, but after the House of Lords decision in *Kleinwort Benson Ltd v Lincoln City Council*[440] there is a general right to recover money paid under a mistake subject to a number of possible defences including change of position. The nature of this defence is illustrated by *Avon County Council v Howlett*,[441] which was brought as a test case following a number of overpayments which arose in the aftermath of local government reorganisations in the 1970s. The employee, who was on leave of absence through illness, was paid at the full rate of pay for the whole of this period. Under his contract he should have received only half his normal pay after six months of leave had elapsed. When the mistake was discovered his employers initiated an action to recover the overpayment of £1,007, which the employee had already spent. The employee was able, however, to invoke the defence of change of position. In general, this will be possible if the employee can show: first, that the employer made a representation of fact leading them to believe that the money was theirs; second, that they changed their position, in good faith, in reliance on the representation; and third, that the overpayment was not caused by their own fault. In *Avon County Council v Howlett*[442] these conditions were satisfied, and the employee kept the entire amount by which he had been overpaid. The Court of Appeal rejected an argument that the principle of estoppel should only apply to that proportion of the overpayment which could clearly be shown to have been spent in

---

[436] The precise basis for making a calculation of this kind may differ according to whether the court accepts the set-off approach of *Sim* or the view, in *Miles*, that the wages are not due as earned: see *Cooper v Isle of Wight College* [2008] IRLR 124.

[437] [1992] ICR 383.

[438] [1984] IRLR 184.

[439] This was the view in *Miles* itself of Lord Brightman ([1987] AC 539, 552) and Lord Templeman ([1987] AC 539, 561).

[440] [1998] 4 All ER 513.

[441] [1983] IRLR 171.

[442] [1983] IRLR 171.

reliance on the employer's representation: it held that this would be to impose an excessive burden on the employee of showing precisely when and how the sums in question were spent.

Statutory wage protection

4.71   The practice of making deductions from pay is a disciplinary device of long standing, which legislation has not been particularly effective in controlling. The Truck Act of 1831, which consolidated and generalised a series of earlier enactments, restricted the payment of wages in kind and was interpreted as also regulating deductions, since 'the truck system, against which the statute was confessedly levelled, was itself a system of stoppage or deduction. Deduct so much for supplies and pay the balance of cash, constituted the evil the statute was passed to remedy; nor is it easy to perceive how there could be a part payment of goods, or otherwise than in the current coin of the realm, without a stoppage or deduction'.[443] Section 3 of the 1831 Act required the payment of 'the entire amount of the wages earned by or payable to' the worker to be made in the current coin of the realm. The courts, however, succeeded in reserving to the common law the question of whether wages were 'earned by or payable to' an individual under their contract. Thus agreed deductions for the 'rent' of the employer's equipment or a part of the cost of heating and lighting the factory were not caught by the Act. These were 'the mode of calculating the amount of wages, and nothing more', so that the wages 'payable to' the worker were the net, and not the gross amount.[444]

The Truck Act 1896 attempted to clarify workers' rights in respect of works rules authorising the abatement of wages for acts of negligence and disobedience, but encountered similar difficulties of statutory interpretation. The Act required any power to levy a disciplinary 'fine' or a deduction for bad workmanship to be notified in advance to the worker in a fixed notice or written contract; to be proportionate to the loss caused to the employer; to be 'fair and reasonable, having regard to all the circumstances of the case'; and, in the case of a fine, to specify the amount to be deducted and the acts and omissions in respect of which the deduction could take place.[445] The courts nevertheless held that these provisions did not regulate contractual terms for the disciplinary suspension without pay of employees, because 'you cannot deduct something from nothing'; 'such a contract is not a contract for any deduction from the sum contracted to be paid since no sum was ever contracted to be paid during a period of suspension'.[446] The aims of the 1896 Act were given clearer effect in *Bristow v City Petroleum*,[447] decided only after the Act had already been repealed.

---

[443] *Archer v James* (1862) 2 B & S 67, 78 (Keating J). In support of this construction, ss 23 and 24 of the 1831 Act specified that certain deductions were to be lawful, a provision which would have been unnecessary if ss 1–3 had been confined to payments in kind.

[444] *Chawner v Cummings* (1846) 8 QB 311, 323 (Denman CJ); Archer v James, above (in which the Court of Exchequer Chamber divided equally on the question); Redgrave v Kelly (1889) 5 TLR 477.

[445] Truck Act 1896, ss 1–2. Section 1 applied to both manual workers and shop assistants; s 2, like the Truck Act 1831, applied only to manual workers ('workmen': see also the Truck (Amendment) Act 1887, s 2). The Lancashire cotton trades sought and won exemption from the Act of 1896: cf *Sagar v H Ridehalgh & Son Ltd* [1931] 1 Ch 310.

[446] *Bird v British Celanese Ltd* [1945] 1 All ER 488, 491 (Scott LJ) and 492–493 (Lawrence LJ).

[447] [1988] ICR 165.

The Truck Acts were once described as 'suffering from an incurable logical disease'[448] and certainly left a great deal to be desired from the point of view of legal clarity. They have now been replaced by Part II of ERA 1996 (formerly Part I of the Wages Act 1986), a measure which on the whole imposes a somewhat looser regime of controls over the practice of disciplinary deductions or fines and payments to the employer. Part II of ERA 1996 applies to all employees, both manual and non-manual, and to some self-employed workers who fall under the definition of 'worker'.[449]

4.72   Section 13 of ERA permits deductions to be made without limit in two situations: where the worker has given his or her prior written agreement to the deduction; and where the employer has some statutory or contractual authority to make it.[450] In the first case, the written agreement must precede the event or conduct of the worker which triggers the deduction.[451] In the second case, however, the employer is simply obliged to pre-notify the worker in writing that it has the required authority before it exercises it – not necessarily before the event occurs which gives it the occasion to do so.[452] If the employer is relying on a written contract term, it must give the worker a copy of it before making the deduction.[453] If it is relying on the 'effect' of a term or upon an implied or oral term, it must give the worker written notification prior to making the deduction.[454] This last provision enables the employer to continue to rely on any common law rights of implied abatement or set-off, as long as it satisfies the pre-notification requirements of the Act as explained above.[455] Only if a contract term is varied after the commencement of employment is there an obligation to notify the worker of the effect of its terms in advance of the conduct or event in question occurring.[456] There is no specific time limit for making deductions under this part of the Act, other than that implied by the general six-year limitation period for actions in contract. Section 15 of the Act applies parallel provisions to the case of payments made to the employer.

4.73   The right to protection against deductions is subject to some exceptions: under sections 14 and 16, these are deductions in respect of overpayments of wages; recovery of sums due in consequence of a statutory disciplinary procedure; sums required by statute to be paid to a public

---

[448] Kahn-Freund, 1949: p 2.

[449] See ERA 1996, s 230(3).

[450] ERA 1996, s 13(1). The question of what is a relevant statutory authorisation was discussed in *McCree v London Borough of Tower Hamlets* [1992] IRLR 56.

[451] ERA 1996, s 13(6).

[452] ERA 1996, s 13(1).

[453] ERA 1996, s 13(2)(a).

[454] ERA 1996, s 13(2)(b), which was overlooked in *Pename Ltd v Paterson* [1989] IRLR 195. According to Potter v Hunt Contracts Ltd [1992] IRLR 108, 109, the notification must take the form of a 'document in writing'. In Kerr v Sweater Shop Ltd [1996] IRLR 424 the EAT held that the display of a notice in a factory did not constitute adequate notification under the Act. On the relationship between notification under s 13 and the requirements of working-time legislation for deductions in respect of 'excess' holiday pay, see *Hill v Chapell* [2003] IRLR 19.

[455] In *Chiltern House v Chambers* [1990] IRLR 88, 90 the EAT confirmed, obiter, that an employer would not be able to avoid the formal requirements of the provision which is now s 13 of the Act by claiming that a deduction was made to meet a future damages claim. For discussion of whether the Act adequately meets the need formally to override the common law, see Deakin, 1992: p 856.

[456] Section 13(5); *York and City District Travel v Smith* [1990] IRLR 213; *Discount Tobacco and Confectionery Ltd v Williamson* [1993] IRLR 327.

authority (such as income tax under Schedule E); sums which the individual has agreed should be paid over to third parties (such as union dues or pension contributions); deductions made or payments received in respect of participation in a strike or industrial action; and sums payable in satisfaction of an order of a court or tribunal.[457]

The provisions of Part II of the Act cut somewhat awkwardly across the employer's separate statutory duty to issue a written statement of terms under section 1 of ERA 1996 to employees, for which the primary remedy is the amendment of the statutory statement by the tribunal.[458] The employer is also under an obligation to give details of any deductions in the itemised pay statement required by section 8 of ERA 1996, on pain of being required to repay the amounts in question,[459] but this statement may be issued on the pay day itself and so does not give the employee any greater protection than Part II of ERA 1996.[460]

The only substantive controls contained in the Act relate to the employment of retail workers.[461] The Act places an upper limit on deductions for cash shortages and stock deficiencies of 10% of a retail worker's gross weekly earnings on a given pay day, and sets a time limit of twelve months from the date on which the shortage could reasonably have been discovered for the deduction (or the first of a series) to be made. The full amount of any shortage can be deducted on the final pay day of the worker's employment.

The remedy for breach of Part II is an application to an employment tribunal for the restitution of the amounts in question; the employer is then precluded from suing for the sums by any other legal means such as a civil action in contract.[462] The employee must lodge an application within three months of the date of the pay day when the deduction took effect.[463] Since 6 April 2009 employment tribunals have also been empowered to order an employer to make a compensatory payment to reflect any financial loss suffered by the worker as a result of the employer's default.[464]

As we have just seen, section 13 of the Act makes reference to the common law rules on the construction of the contract. The tribunal must consider first whether the employer has contractual authority to make a deduction, and second whether it has complied with the formalities imposed by the Act; moreover, the Act applies to a case of complete non-payment as well as to a partial deduction.[465] The Act can be invoked, therefore, to challenge a failure to pay agreed wages in full, in situations where an employer's attempt to effect a unilateral variation of contract terms is

---

[457] ERA 1996, ss 14 and 16. On the scope for deductions in relation to income tax under Schedule E, see *Patel v Marquette Partners (UK) Ltd* [2009] IRLR 425.

[458] See above, para 4.22. Note, however, EA 2002, s 38, Sch 5, which came into force on 1 October 2004; see further para 4.22.

[459] ERA 1996, s 12(4). This jurisdiction was preserved by the WA 1986 (s 6(2)), now contained in ERA 1996, s 26. The applicant may therefore proceed under both Acts, but the total he or she can recover in respect of any one deduction may not be more than the amount of that particular deduction (ERA 1996, s 26). EA 2002, s 38 does not apply to ERA 1996, s 12: see EA 2002, Sch 5.

[460] The European Committee on Social Rights has formed the view that the limited nature of substantive controls over deductions places the UK in breach of Art 4(5) of the European Social Charter (Conclusions XIV, 2, 1999).

[461] ERA 1996, ss 17–21.

[462] ERA 1996, ss 24(1), 25(4); *Potter v Hunt Contracts Ltd* [1992] IRLR 108.

[463] ERA 1996, s 23(2); see *Taylorplan Services Ltd v Jackson* [1996] IRLR 184; *Group 4 Nightspeed Ltd v Gilbert* [1997] IRLR 398.

[464] ERA 1996, s 24(2), inserted by EA 2008, s 7(1).

[465] *Delaney v Staples* [1991] IRLR 112; *Fairfield Ltd v Skinner* [1993] IRLR 4.

ineffective, on the ground that the wages remain due at common law.[466] However, section 13 does not apply to sums payable by way of damages for breach of contract, such as a failure to give the employee due notice of termination. This is the effect of the House of Lords' decision in *Delaney v Staples*.[467] The applicant was summarily dismissed from a recruitment agency, and claimed payment of outstanding commission of £18 and accrued holiday pay at the date of dismissal of £37.50. She also claimed recovery of £82 as wages in lieu of notice, which her employer had refused to pay on the ground that she had broken the contract by removing confidential information. Both her claims failed in the EAT; the Court of Appeal allowed an appeal in relation to the outstanding sums but not the payment in lieu of notice and an appeal on the latter point was rejected by the House of Lords. The Act itself is unclear on the question of notice, although it contains a broad definition of 'wages' which covers 'any sums payable to the worker by his employer in connection with his employment, including (a) any fee, bonus, commission, holiday pay or other emolument referable to his employment, whether payable under his contract or otherwise'.[468] According to Lord Browne-Wilkinson, however, 'the provisions of the Act cannot be made to work if payments in lieu were included in the word "wages"'. Because notice payments take the form of damages for breach of contract there is no fixed date upon which they fall due, thereby making it impossible to calculate the 'occasion' when wages became payable under section 13(3) and the date from which the three-month time limit for bringing an action starts to run under section 23(2).

Thus, apart from payments specifically mentioned in section 27(1), the term 'wages' is confined to payments in respect of work done, or to be done, under a subsisting contract of employment.[469] A lump sum paid to the employee at the start of 'garden leave' would probably be 'wages', even though paid in advance, because the contract is still subsisting, but sums paid or payable in respect of termination are outside the Act whether they are the result of a contract term providing for payment in lieu, a special agreement to that effect or simply damages for breach of contract by the employer. Although not subject to the pre-notification requirements of ERA 1996, from 1994 contractual claims in respect of notice pay could be brought before employment tribunals in their own right.[470] To fall within the statutory protection it is necessary that the sum can be quantified.[471]

---

[466] *Yemm v British Steel plc* [1994] IRLR 117 (a refusal to pay wages as due was not an error of computation under s 13(4)); *Bruce v Wiggins Teape (Stationery) Ltd* [1994] IRLR 536; *Davies v Hotpoint Ltd* [1994] IRLR 538; *International Packaging Corpn (UK) Ltd v Balfour* [2003] IRLR 11; *Elizabeth Claire Care Management Ltd v Francis* [2005] IRLR 858. Conversely, in *Ali v Christian Salvesen Food Services Ltd* [1997] IRLR 17 (overturning [1995] IRLR 624), *Hussman Manufacturing Ltd v Weir* [1998] IRLR 288 and *New Century Cleaning Co Ltd v Church* [2000] IRLR 27 (see Freedland, 1999) claims for unauthorised deduction failed because variations in payments were found to be contractually permissible.

[467] [1992] ICR 483.

[468] ERA 1996, s 27(1). On bonuses see *Farrell Matthews and Weir v Hansen* [2005] IRLR 160 and *Small v Boots Co plc* [2009] IRLR 328; *Tradition Securities and Futures SA v Mouradian* [2009] EWCA Civ 60. Applications to enforce entitlement to holiday pay under WTR 1998 may be made under s 23: *HMRC v Stringer* [2009] IRLR 677. Among the matters excluded from the definition of 'wages' under s 27(2) are work-related expenses: see *Southwark London Borough v O'Brien* [1996] IRLR 420.

[469] In *Robertson v Blackstone Franks Investment Management Ltd* [1998] IRLR 376 the Court of Appeal held that wages for work done before termination may be payable and paid after termination without thereby losing their character as wages.

[470] As a result of SI 1994/1623; D Brown, 1994.

[471] See, for example, *Coors Brewers Ltd v Adcock* [2007] IRLR 440; *Tradition Securities and Futures SA v Mouradian* [2009] EWCA Civ 60.

The scope of the exemptions listed in section 14 has given rise to difficulties of interpretation. In *Home Office v Ayres*[472] the EAT expressed the view that deductions made to recover an overpayment of wages fell within the Act, notwithstanding section 14(1) (formerly section 1(5)(e) of the Wages Act 1986), if the employer could not show that it had lawful authority, contractual or otherwise, to make the deduction. However, the better view is probably that the tribunal has no jurisdiction if, for example, an overpayment, or the employee's participation in industrial action, is the reason for the deduction, whether or not the deduction was permitted at common law.[473] The employment tribunal must nonetheless still satisfy itself that there has in fact been, for example, an overpayment or industrial action, and not simply rely on the employer's assertion to that effect.[474] This issue is less pressing than it was now that the employment tribunals have jurisdiction over common law claims for payment in addition to their jurisdiction under Part II of ERA 1996; however, they only have this jurisdiction in respect of common law claims arising out of termination of employment.

Two significant aspects of wage protection which are not regulated in any way by Part II of ERA 1996 are payments in kind (which were formerly regulated by the Truck Acts[475]) and the length of intervals between payment. These matters are therefore subject only to the terms agreed by the parties or implied into the contract of employment by reference to a collective agreement, custom and practice or some other external source. In relation to intervals, the present state of the law contrasts unfavourably with Article 12(1) of ILO Convention No 95 on the Protection of Wages (1949) which states: '[w]ages shall be paid regularly. Except where other appropriate arrangements exist which ensure the payment of wages at regular intervals, the intervals for the payment of wages shall be prescribed by national laws or regulations or fixed by collective agreement or arbitration award'. The UK government denounced this Convention in anticipation of the passage of the Wages Act 1986.

More generally, Part II of ERA 1996 might well be thought to be an inadequate response to the problems of deductions as a mechanism of discipline. The Act poses few substantive restraints on the power to make deductions and does not limit this power to situations where the individual employee was clearly at fault. Nor does it require the employer to observe minimum procedures before making a deduction. In this way, the failure to regulate deductions undermines the more general protection provided against arbitrary discipline by the law of unfair dismissal.[476]

Share options and related forms of financial participation

4.74 Since the early 1980s, in parallel with the reduction in the extent of institutional regulation of pay through legislation and sector-level collective bargaining, there has been a rise in the use

---

[472] [1992] IRLR 59.

[473] *Sunderland Polytechnic v Evans* [1993] IRLR 196; *SIP (Industrial Products) Ltd v Swinn* [1994] IRLR 323; see also *Scott v Strathclyde Fire Board* EATS/0050/03 26 April 2004.

[474] *Gill v Ford Motor Co* [2004] IRLR 840.

[475] The Truck Acts required payment in cash but they did not apply to salaried employees, for whom payment by cheque or bank transfer was and is normal. The Payment of Wages Act 1960 set up a scheme whose main feature was to enable workers covered by the Truck Acts to opt into payment by way of cheque, bank transfer or postal order by giving written notice to their employer.

[476] See further para 5.125 *et seq* below.

of discretionary or flexible payment systems at company level which are designed to motivate individual employees. This was a change encouraged by the policy of the Conservative governments of that period. According to the Department of Employment in 1988,

> the 'going rate', 'comparability' and 'cost of living increases', are all outmoded concepts – they take no account of differences in performance, ability to pay or difficulties of recruitment, retention or motivation. Pay structures too have to change. National agreements which affect the pay of half the workforce all too often give scant regard to differences in individual circumstances or performance.[477]

Many organisations in both the public and private sector have introduced appraisal systems as part of which an individual's pay is linked to their assessed performance. In legal terms, the effect is to reduce the scope of the contractually-guaranteed wage or salary. In principle, the individual parties are free to agree to a discretionary element in the pay package. Although the contract of employment may then incorporate rules or principles derived from a company handbook or some other document issued by the employer, these normally reserve the final decision on appraisal to management, thereby limiting the degree of wage security enjoyed by the employee.

Profit-related pay seeks to link all or part of an employee's pay not to their individual performance but to the profitability of the company, or a part of it, in which they are employed. Together with share ownership schemes of various kinds which offer employees the chance to buy shares in their companies at discounted or subsidised prices, the practice of linking pay to profits constitutes a form of employee involvement in the enterprise which is referred to as 'financial participation', to distinguish it from more direct forms of participation in management decision-making. Financial participation was actively encouraged from the mid-1980s by a series of tax reliefs and related fiscal measures. Some of these have since been removed. For example, relief on profit-related pay, established by the Finance Act 1987, had been phased out by the start of 2000; too many employers had 'used profit-related pay as a method of cutting wage bills through tax relief'.[478]

Tax reliefs on employee share ownership come in a number of forms, some of which allow the company to give its employees financial assistance for the purchase of shares. In certain cases, tax relief is available when share options are exercised, thereby enabling employees to profit from increases in share values without paying capital gains tax. However, tax legislation provides only limited protection for an employee who loses what may be highly valuable share options as a consequence of termination of employment,[479] thereby leaving open the question of whether, at common law, the employer may be liable in damages for a wrongful dismissal or other act which deprives the employee of valuable options. Employers often attempt to protect themselves from this possibility by including exemption clauses in the scheme rules.

---

[477] Department of Employment, *Employment for the 1990s*, Cm 540, 1988, at pp 23–24.

[478] McLean, 1994: p 8.

[479] The relevant legislation is currently contained in a number of statutes including ICTA 1988 and the Income Tax (Earnings and Pensions) Act 2003. For an account of the relevant principles behind its introduction, see McLean, 1994: ch 3.

In *Thompson v ASDA-MFI Group plc*[480] the claimant was employed by Wades Departmental Stores Ltd which was a wholly-owned subsidiary of the defendant company. Under the rules of an ASDA group employee share option scheme, the claimant was granted a number of options to buy ASDA group shares. ASDA then sold its shares in Wades and wrote to the claimant informing him that the options had automatically lapsed, under the rules of the scheme set up by ASDA, once Wades ceased to be an ASDA subsidiary. Rule 5 of the scheme provided that 'no option shall be exercised at any time when the person seeking to exercise it is excluded from such exercise' by the relevant legislation. Scott J held that at common law, this term validly excluded any contractual rights of the claimant, and he rejected an argument that a term should be implied to the effect that the company would not sell its shares in Wades if the effect was to frustrate the employee's rights.[481]

A similar clause was considered in *Micklefield v SAC Technology Ltd*, a case of wrongful dismissal.[482] The clause was again upheld at common law but on this occasion a challenge was also made to its validity under section 3 of the Unfair Contract Terms Act 1977. Deputy Judge Mowbray held that even if a contract of employment could be held to come within the scope of UCTA section 3, this was a case concerning 'the creation or transfer of securities' to which the Act had no application by virtue of Schedule 1, paragraph 1(e). Since then the Court of Appeal has given a clear indication, in *Commerzbank AG v Keen*,[483] that it does not think that section 3 has any application to terms affecting remuneration for services rendered as an employee.[484]

It would be premature to suggest that financial participation along the lines considered here represents a move towards more complete 'economic democracy' within companies. Forms of direct participation, such as co-determination and statutory information and consultation, enable the employees to present a collective voice to management on issues affecting the organisation of the enterprise. Financial participation, on the other hand, is essentially individual in nature, and in so far as it extends employee ownership it does so by merging employees into the larger mass of shareholders: there is no recognition that the workforce may have interests distinct from those of the managers and owners of the business. A related issue is whether financial participation results in superior employee performance. The evidence here is equivocal: companies which operate profit-related pay and employee share ownership schemes are, on the whole, more productive and profitable than those which do not, but a clear causal link between the success of these companies and the schemes concerned has not been established.[485]

On the other hand, a negative feature of both performance-related and profit-related pay is the degree of wage insecurity which they may induce. Linking all or part of pay to individual performance is nothing new, as the long tradition of piece-work contracting in many industries indicates. Where the measurement of performance is not straightforward, however, the possibility

---

[480] [1988] IRLR 340; H Collins, 1989a; Watson, 1995. Where share options rights have vested prior to dismissal, the termination of the employment will not (all other things being equal) affect their exercise: *Mallone v BPB Industries plc* [2002] IRLR 452.

[481] See also *Tesco Stores Ltd v Pook* [2004] IRLR 618, in which a term was implied to the effect that an employee who had acted in breach of fiduciary duties owed to the employer could not validly exercise certain share options.

[482] [1990] IRLR 218. See also *Levett v Biotrace Ltd* [1999] IRLR 375 and Peninsula Business Services Ltd v Sweeney [2004] IRLR 49, on the construction of such clauses.

[483] [2007] IRLR 132; see also *Brigden v American Express Bank Ltd* [2000] IRLR 94.

[484] Different provisions of UCTA 1977 apply in Scotland which make it less likely that the Act can be disapplied for this reason: *see Chapman v Aberdeen Construction Group plc* [1991] IRLR 505.

[485] See Pendleton, Wilson and Wright, 1998.

of abuse of such payment systems arises. In the past this has been addressed by collective bargaining and through shop-floor custom and practice, as well as by legislation in some exceptional instances. Few of these regulatory constraints now remain in place. As far as profit-related pay and employee share options are concerned, an element of insecurity may be derived to the extent that these variable forms of remuneration displace the previously fixed obligation of the employer to pay for performance rendered by the employee. Share ownership schemes have been termed a modern form of 'truck' or payment in kind,[486] which may turn out to offer illusory gains in so far as the employer retains unilateral powers to limit employee options.

Some of these tensions are reflected in the advisory EU Recommendation concerning the promotion of participation of employed persons in profits and enterprise results (including equity participation) of 1992.[487] The Recommendation noted that financial participation 'may be seen as achieving a wider distribution of the wealth generated by enterprises which the employed persons have helped to produce.'[488] On the other hand, among the points which Member States were invited to consider were the need to frame financial participation schemes so as to ensure that they did not 'stand in the way of normal negotiations dealing with wages and conditions of employment,'[489] a very different emphasis from that of the UK government then and since. The Recommendation also suggested that schemes should recognise that 'apart from the risks of income fluctuation inherent in participation schemes, employed persons may be exposed to additional risk if their participation takes the form of investments that are relatively undiversified; in this context, the possibility of providing for mechanisms to protect against the risk of depreciation in the value of assets merits consideration.'[490]

WORKING TIME

4.75   The regulation of working time is designed to set maximum limits to the 'basic' or 'normal' working day and week. These may be exceeded in return for the employer paying a premium for overtime working; regulation may also set a ceiling to overtime itself, thereby imposing a maximum limit on actual hours worked in a given period. It may also recognise the notion of 'unsocial hours working' by limiting and/or setting premia for nightwork and shift working, and place limits on annual working time by providing for minimum periods of annual paid leave.

The placing of limits on working time is one of the most important objectives of labour law and collective bargaining; it was the goal of the first modern industrial legislation, the British factories legislation of the nineteenth century, and of the first ILO Convention in 1919, which embodied the principle of the 8-hour normal working day. In France, legislation of 1919 established a basic 8-hour day and in 1936 a 40-hour basic working week. In Germany, legislation of 1938 set a basic working day of 8 hours and a basic week of 48 hours. In Britain, however, statutory working time standards of this kind were slow to develop. This was in part a result of the tradition of voluntarism: as with regulation of minimum rates of pay, the state's preference for

---

[486] H Collins, 1989a: p 56.
[487] OJ 1992 L245/92.
[488] OJ 1992 L245/92, Preamble, para 3.
[489] OJ 1992 L245/92, Annex, point 3.
[490] OJ 1992 L245/92, Annex, point 7.

support for collective bargaining over direct legal regulation meant that statutory intervention was confined to sectors of the economy which were characterised by lack of voluntary organisation, or to particular groups of workers (mostly young workers and women in industrial employment). In the 1980s, however, policies of deregulation began which brought about not simply the removal of the limited statutory protections which used to exist in this area, but also a restriction of the coverage of the sector-level collective agreements which were formerly the principal mechanism of regulation of basic hours of work, overtime and shiftwork premia and annual paid holidays. The balance has recently been redressed by recent EC Directives in the areas of working time and the protection of young workers. These impose certain basic standards in respect of the length of the working day and week and annual holidays, subject, however, to numerous and extensive derogations which are reflected in the terms of the Working Time Regulations 1998.

The traditional model: factories legislation and sectoral collective bargaining

4.76   The factories legislation of the nineteenth century was confined to regulating the employment of women, young persons and children in factories and workshops, and failed to develop into a comprehensive code of working time controls as occurred in other European countries. The minority report of the Royal Commission on Labour of 1894 commented that 'for the mass of workers an eight hour day with the effective suppression of overtime can be secured only by further legislative enactment' and rejected the pattern of regulating on a trade by trade basis on the grounds that this 'would not only consume much valuable time, but would, in our judgment, result at best in a lopsided regulation of industry'.[491] The majority, however, rejected the principle of general statutory regulation, and apart from a few exceptional instances of intervention[492] the hours of adult male workers remained outside the scope of legislative controls. The pattern of selective and partial regulation was firmly enough established to lead to British refusal to ratify the first ILO Convention, the Hours of Work Industry Convention of 1919, which embodied a standard 8-hour basic working day and 48-hour basic working week.[493]

Statutory restrictions upon nightwork and Sunday work by women and the limitations upon their weekly hours, together with related controls on breaks, shift work and overtime, were repealed by the Sex Discrimination Act 1986, and the controls on the hours of young persons were repealed by the Employment Act 1989.[494] This left regulations in place only for children under the minimum school leaving age.[495]

The Shops Act 1950, which consolidated a number of earlier statutes, restricted Sunday and evening opening by shops and regulated the working time of retail employees by establishing the right to a weekly half-day holiday for shop assistants, limiting Sunday working hours and specifying minimum breaks for meals. The hours of young workers in shops were also the subject of specific controls. The Act was repealed in 1993;[496] weekday and Saturday opening is now completely

---

[491] *Royal Commission on Labour, Minority Report*, Parliamentary Papers (1894) XXXV.9, at pp 140–141.

[492] These included the Railway Servants (Hours of Labour) Act 1893 and the Coal Mines Regulation Act 1908.

[493] Ewing, 1994a: p 20.

[494] Deakin, 1990a. The repeals of controls specific to women workers were the consequence of EC Directive 76/207.

[495] See generally Deakin, 1990a.

[496] The restrictions on Sunday opening were replaced by those of the Sunday Trading Act 1994, and weekday restrictions were completely repealed by DCOA 1994.

deregulated, while Sunday opening is subject to a more liberal regime than before under which larger shops may open for a maximum of six consecutive hours between 10 am and 6 pm. Under certain circumstances it is automatically unfair to dismiss retail employees for refusing to work on Sundays.[497] Other statutory controls repealed as a consequence of deregulatory policies include those governing the number of hours spent underground by mineworkers[498] and nightwork by bakery workers.[499]

National-level collective agreements for separate industries or sectors were the principal mechanism for the regulation of the basic working week for manual workers from the 1920s, when the 48-hour week was generally established in the engineering industry, to the end of the 1980s, when structures for national-level bargaining began to break up. The national engineering agreement achieved further reductions in the basic working week to 44 hours in 1947, 42 hours in 1960, 40 hours in 1965 and 39 hours in 1979. Reductions in most other sectors of the economy tended to follow on those achieved in the national engineering agreement. Sector-level collective bargaining also achieved gradual improvement to holiday and leave rights. In the early 1970s a basic entitlement to 8 days of paid public holidays and 3 weeks' paid leave per employee was established more or less throughout the economy by this route. A general 4-week entitlement was achieved in the early 1980s, and some sector agreements subsequently achieved a 5-week entitlement. It is largely thanks to collective bargaining that the tradition of respecting 'bank holidays' has been widely followed, since the legislation itself simply prohibits certain financial dealings on the days in question and says nothing about a general right to leave, paid or otherwise.[500]

However, in many respects sector-level bargaining in Britain was less effective than the equivalent forms of statutory control of working time elsewhere in Western Europe. For one thing, British agreements have never sought to impose absolute upper limits on overtime working; nor have they laid down the precise form and limits of shift work. Instead, sector-level agreements have been confined to setting overtime and shift premium payments. In themselves these premia do not provide employers with much of a disincentive to limit overtime working, in particular since they have normally been multiples (such as time-and-a-half or double time) of the national basic wage rate, and not of the higher basic rate which might be set by plant- or company-level agreements. This is one reason why overtime and shift working in Britain has been particularly prevalent for full-time workers, compared to practice on the continent. Actual hours worked in several industries regularly exceed the basic working week of 37–39 hours. [501]

In 1989 national negotiations in the engineering industry for a phased reduction to a basic 37½-hour and then a 35-hour week broke down. Reduced hours were eventually agreed at plant and company level following a series of local strikes, but no new national agreement could be reached and the 1989 dispute marked the effective end, at least for the time being, of national-level bargaining in engineering. Sector-level bargaining, for reasons examined earlier,[502] has undergone a more general decline, with a corresponding loss of effectiveness in working-time regulation. The abolition of the wages councils in 1993 also contributed to this decline. Thanks in large part

---

[497] Sunday Trading Act 1994 and ERA 1996, Part IV and s 101; Deakin, 1994b; see para 5.102 below.
[498] By virtue of the Coal Industry Act 1991.
[499] SDA 1986, s 8, repealing the Banking Industry (Hours of Work) Act 1954.
[500] Banking and Financial Dealings Act 1971, s 1, Sch 1.
[501] See Rubery *et al*, 1994.
[502] See above, para 1.27.

to the tradition of loose regulation, British employment patterns have displayed a wide variety of non-standard working time arrangements.[503]

The new model: regulating the duration and organisation of working time

4.77   The main premise of the Working Time Directive of 1993 was that 'in order to ensure the safety and health of Community workers, the latter must be granted minimum daily, weekly and annual periods of rest and adequate breaks', and that 'it is necessary in this context to place a maximum limit on weekly working hours'.[504] The European Commission argued prior to the adoption of the Directive that reductions in working time were not incompatible with the maintenance of flexibility in operating times, citing evidence that many industrial and service establishments made increasing use of shiftworking and other flexible arrangements to ensure extended daily and weekly continuity of production and services.[505] The legal authority for the Directive was Article 118a of the EC Treaty (now consolidated in Article 153(1)(a) TFEU), which confers powers to adopt instruments, by qualified majority voting, designed to improve the working environment, with regard to health and safety. In *UK v EU Council (Working Time)*[506] the ECJ rejected the United Kingdom's challenge to the validity of the Directive, holding that it could be justified as a health and safety measure, in the process giving a broad definition to Article 118a.[507] Following amendments made in 2000, a consolidated version of the Directive came into force in 2004.[508]

The process of implementing the Working Time Directive only began to take shape following the judgment of the ECJ in the *Working Time* case,[509] which confirmed that the Directive had been validly adopted. Proposals put forward by the Conservative government in 1996 were subjected to further revision following the election of the Labour government in May 1997. In April 1998 the Department of Trade and Industry published a consultation paper and draft regulations[510] for bringing the Working Time Directive and relevant provisions of the Young Workers' Directive (94/33) into force; the Regulations were adopted in 1998[511] and amended in 1999[512] and on a number of subsequent occasions.

---

[503] See Wareing, 1992.

[504] Directive 93/104, Preamble, para 8.

[505] See *Explanatory Memorandum on the Draft Directive concerning Working Time* COM (90) 317. An earlier Regulation (3820/85) governing the hours of lorry drivers had already sets a normal daily limit of nine hours driving which can be extended to ten but with a two-weekly limit of 90 hours and breaks every four and a half hours. See *Prime v Hosking* [1995] IRLR 143; Case C-394/92 *Criminal Proceedings against Michielsen & Geybels Transport Service NV* [1995] IRLR 171; Case C-193/99 *Criminal Proceedings against Hume* [2001] IRLR 103.

[506] Case C-84/94 [1996] ECR I-5755.

[507] See Fitzpatrick, 1997.

[508] See Directives 2000/34/EC and 2003/88/EC respectively.

[509] Case C-84/94 [1996] ECR I-5755.

[510] *Measures to Implement Provisions of the EC Directives on the Organisation of Working Time ('The Working Time Directive') and the Protection of Young People at Work ('The Young Workers' Directive'),* April 1998.

[511] SI 1998/1833 (henceforth WTR 1998); see Barnard, 1999.

[512] SI 1999/3372; see Barnard, 2000.

(i) The Working Time Directive and the Working Time Regulations 1998[513]

4.78   The implementation of the Working Time Directive marked a turning point in the regulation of basic terms and conditions of employment in the UK. For the first time, working time controls were put in place which, in principle, could cover the working population in general, subject only to specific derogations. This reversed the previous approach whereby statutory regulations applied only to certain specified sectors and/or occupations, or to particular groups of workers, leaving the unregulated areas untouched. The Working Time Regulations of 1998 made a second important change in the mode of application of standards. Using the scope for derogations allowed for in the original Directive, the Regulations devolve much of the responsibility for arriving at working time norms to agreement at lower levels, including not just collective agreements but also individual agreements. This form of devolution of law-making authority from statute to collective bargaining (and, beyond that, to individual contract) is unusual in the UK context, although it has a longer history in continental systems.[514]

A central concept under the Regulations is that of a 'relevant agreement'. This is an agreement which is capable of varying or in some cases complementing the statutory standards laid down in the Regulations. A relevant agreement, 'in relation to a worker, means a workforce agreement which applies to him, any provision of a collective agreement which forms part of a contract between him and his employer,[515] or any other agreement in writing which is legally enforceable as between the worker and his employer'.[516] A 'workforce agreement' is, essentially, one made either with specified representatives of the workforce or, in certain circumstances, with a majority of the workers themselves.[517] More precisely, a workforce agreement may not be made in respect of any part of the workforce which is already covered by terms and conditions of employment which derive from a collective agreement between an employer and an independent trade union.[518] It must either cover all members of the employer's workforce whose terms and conditions are not regulated by such a collective agreement, or, alternatively, all such members (known as 'relevant members') who 'belong to a particular group'. A 'particular group' is defined as 'a group of the relevant members of a workforce who undertake a particular function, work at a particular workplace or belong to a particular department or unit within their employer's business'.[519] The agreement must be signed either by representatives of the workforce or, if the agreement only

---

[513] The Regulations should be read together with the regulatory guidance which is contained in Directgov (www.direct.gov.uk) and Businesslink (www.businesslink.gov.uk).

[514] The technique of regulating through a generally-applicable standard from which limited derogations are then carved out is more a feature of continental labour law than it is of British labour law, although there are some British precedents; for example, the health and safety inspectorate had powers to make exemptions from the (now repealed) nightwork provisions of the Factory Acts, but with the right to attach conditions for the protection of the workforce. See Deakin, 1990.

[515] For this purpose, the definition of collective agreement in TULRCA 1992, s 178, is relevant, with the qualification that the agreement must be made by an independent trade union (see the definition of collective agreement in WTR 1998, reg 2(1)), and the common law rules for the incorporation of terms into collective agreements are implicitly adopted (see para 4.27 *et seq* above).

[516] WTR 1998, reg 2(1).

[517] See generally WTR 1998, Sch 1.

[518] WTR 1998, Sch 1, para 2.

[519] WTR 1998, Sch 1, para 2.

covers a 'particular group', by representatives of that group. 'Representatives' here means workers duly elected to represent either the workforce or the group as the case may be.[520] The number of representatives is set by the employer. The candidates must be members of the workforce or group in question. The employer may not unreasonably exclude any member of the workforce who, on this basis, is eligible to stand, from doing so. Arrangements for the election must ensure that the vote is taken in secret, that there is a fair and accurate count, and that the workers are entitled to vote for as many candidates as there are representatives to be elected.[521] The agreement must normally be signed by the relevant representatives who must, for this purpose, be employed by the employer on the date when the agreement is made available for signature;[522] if, on that date, the employer employs 20 or fewer workers, the agreement may be signed by a majority of the workers in employment at that time.[523] Other conditions for the validity of a workplace agreement are that it must be in writing;[524] it must take effect for a specified period not exceeding five years;[525] and, before the agreement is signed, all workers affected by it must be sent a written copy of its contents by the employer and must be given guidance by the employer as to its effect.[526]

In the words of the consultation document which presaged the 1998 Regulations, '[t]he use of workplace agreements may be particularly apt for small and medium size enterprises, perhaps where there are no union members among their workforce. Agreement by signature from the majority of relevant members of the workforce may be appropriate and practical for very small businesses, with election arrangements being confined only to relatively larger ones.'[527] This is an acknowledgement of the need to have a mechanism for achieving flexibility in the application of standards in certain workplaces. However, this aspect of the Regulations raises wider questions concerning the effectiveness and legitimacy of agreements made without the support of an independent union.[528] The Regulations preserve the priority of agreements made through the normal channel of the recognised trade union, but only where arrangements for collective bargaining are in place; otherwise, the employer is free to make a workforce agreement with representatives who may not be 'independent' in the sense used to refer to an independent union. Even more controversial is the third type of relevant agreement, that is, a legally enforceable agreement made between the employer and an individual worker. As we shall see below, by no means all of the standards laid down in the Regulation can be modulated using either workforce agreements or individual agreements. However, among the rights which can be affected in these ways is the core right of workers not to be required to work more than 48 hours on average per week.

---

[520] WTR 1998, Sch 1, para 2.

[521] WTR 1998, Sch 1, para 3.

[522] WTR 1998, Sch 1, para 1(d)(i).

[523] WTR 1998, Sch 1, para 1(d)(ii).

[524] WTR 1998, Sch 1, para 1(a).

[525] WTR 1998, Sch 1, para 1(b).

[526] WTR 1998, Sch 1, para 1(e).

[527] *Measures to Implement Provisions of the EC Directives on the Organisation of Working Time ('The Working Time Directive') and the Protection of Young People at Work ('The Young Workers Directive')*, April 1998, at p 2.

[528] The issue of the legitimacy of workers' representatives is addressed under WTR 1998 Sch 1, para 3, which, as we have just seen, lays down rules governing the process of election; however, this is in principle subject to the test of representativity laid down by the Court of First Instance in Case T-135/96 *UEAPME v Council* [1998] IRLR 602; see Barnard, 1999: p 69.

SCOPE

4.79   The 1993 Directive was stated to apply to all areas of economic activity as defined by the Framework Directive on Health and Safety,[529] but then went on to exclude 'air, rail, road, sea, inland waterway and lake transport, sea fishing, other work at sea and the activities of doctors in training'.[530] These exclusions were subsequently narrowed, or in some cases removed altogether, by the Horizontal Amending Directive of 2000,[531] and additional Directives were put in place for specific sectors.[532] As a result, special rules now apply to mobile workers in sea, road and air transport.[533] With effect from 1 August 2003, non-mobile workers in these sectors, in addition to all workers in rail transport and all workers in other forms of work at sea (such as offshore oil and gas workers), gained the full protection of the 1998 Regulations, and mobile workers in road transport received the benefit of the provisions governing paid annual leave and health assessment for nightwork.[534]

The reference in the 1993 Directive to 'doctors in training' excluded British junior hospital doctors from the scope of protection and left them dependent upon any claim which might have been framed for breach of the employer's common law duty to protect the safety and health of its employees.[535] However, the Horizontal Amending Directive of 2000 improved their position,[536] and from 1 August 2004 the 1998 Regulations were applied to their situation, with two exceptions. Firstly, it was provided that the 48-hour weekly limit for working time would not come into effect in their case until 1 August 2009; a limit of 58 hours would apply from 1 August 2004 to 31 July 2007, and one of 56 hours between 1 August 2007 and 31 July 2009. Secondly, specific rules were put in place for calculating reference periods, based on a normal period of 26 weeks.[537]

Otherwise, the Regulations apply to 'workers',[538] and they also extend to Crown employees, House of Lords and House of Commons staff, the police, and members of the armed forces.[539] However, the Regulations do not apply to situations 'where characteristics peculiar to certain specified services such as the armed forces or the police or to certain specific activities in the civil protection services, inevitably conflict with the provisions of these Regulations'.[540] This exclusion, which is referable to Article 2(2) of the Framework Directive on Health and Safety,[541] 'seems to

---

[529] Directive 89/391, Art 2; see below, para 4.97.

[530] Art 1(3).

[531] Directive 2000/34/EC.

[532] See COM (98) 662 final, laying out a series of proposals for amendments to the 1993 Directive and the adoption of new Directives in relation to mobile workers in the road transport sector, self-employed drivers, and the maritime sector. In May 2000 the Council agreed to amend the 1993 Directive so as to include non-mobile workers in the transport sector, who, it was subsequently confirmed, were outside its scope (Case C-133/00 *Bowden v Tuffnells Parcels Express Ltd* [2001] IRLR 838).

[533] See, respectively, the Seafarers' Directive (1999/63/EC), the Road Transport Directive (2002/15/EC) and the Aviation Directive (2000/79/EC). On the Aviation Directive, see Case C-115/10 *British Airways plc v Williams* [2011] IRLR 948, discussed in para 4.84 below.

[534] This was the effect of changes made to WTR 1998 by a number of amending regulations, principally SI 2003/1684.

[535] *Johnstone v Bloomsbury Health Authority* [1992] QB 333; see above, para 4.8 and below, para 4.95. It is possible that they may be able to invoke Art 4(2) of the ECHR: see *Van der Musselle v Belgium* Judgment of 23 November 1983 (1984) 6 EHRR 163, at para. 37.

[536] Directive 2000/34/EC, Art 1(6), inserting a new para 2.4 in Art 17 of the 1993 Directive; see now Directive 2003/88, Art 17(5).

[537] See WTR 1998, reg 25A.

[538] WTR 1998, reg 2; on the 'worker' concept, see para 3.33, above.

[539] WTR 1998, regs 36–43.

[540] WTR 1998, reg 18(2)(a).

[541] Directive 89/391/EEC, Art 2(2).

envisage a distinction between desk jobs (which are not covered by the exception) and other, frontline jobs'.[542] The Regulations also contain a wide set of exemptions with regard to domestic servants.[543] Finally, the Regulations were held in *Addison v Ashby*[544] to have no application to children below the minimum school age, thereby excluding a paper boy's claim for holiday pay. The EAT held that since the Regulations contain specific provisions governing 'young workers' between the minimum school age and the age of 18[545] and are silent on the position of children below school leaving age, the latter are implicitly excluded.

WORKING TIME LIMITS AND ENTITLEMENTS

THE DEFINITION OF WORKING TIME

4.80   The Directive and Regulations lay down limits on weekly working time, controls on night work and shift work, and minimum daily and weekly rest periods, for the purposes of which it is necessary to define what is meant by 'working time'. The Directive defines 'working time' as 'any period during which the worker is working, at the employer's disposal and carrying out his activity or duties, in accordance with national laws and/or practice', and a rest period is 'any period which is not working time';[546] the Regulations contain a similar provision.[547] In the *SIMAP* case,[548] the ECJ took the view that time spent on call by doctors could be 'working time' if they were required to be present at their place of work during this period, but not otherwise. The Court implicitly viewed the three elements of the 'working time' definition as cumulative rather than alternative, since it took the view that even if the doctors were 'at the disposal of their employer' while away from the workplace, they failed to satisfy the other elements of the definition since in that case they 'may manage their own time with fewer constraints and pursue their own interests'.[549]

WEEKLY LIMITS TO WORKING TIME

4.81   Under the Directive, Member States are required to take 'measures necessary to ensure that, in keeping with the need to protect the health and safety of workers ... the period of weekly working time is limited by means of laws, regulations or administrative provisions or by collective agreements or agreements between the two sides of industry', and to ensure that 'the average working time for each seven-day period, including overtime, does not exceed 48 hours'.[550] The Regulations, likewise, impose a duty upon the employer to 'take all reasonable steps, in keeping

---

[542] Barnard, 1999: 63.

[543] See WTR 1998, reg 19 (the exemptions relate to the rules concerning the weekly limit on working time, night work, and the pattern of work).

[544] [2003] IRLR 211.

[545] See below, para 4.93 for legislation specifically governing the position of children below school leaving age.

[546] Directive 2003/88, Art 2(1), 2(2).

[547] WTR, reg 2(1) (definition of 'working time', which, in the Regulations, is clarified to include 'any period during which ... [a worker] is receiving relevant training').

[548] Case C-303/98 *SIMAP v Conselleria de Sanidad y Consumo de la Generalidad Valenciana* [2000] IRLR 845; to broadly similar effect are Case C-151/02 *Landeshaupstadt Kiel v Jaeger* [2003] IRLR 804 and Case C-14/04 *Dellas v Premier Ministre* [2006] IRLR 225, and, in domestic law, *MacCartney v Oversley House Management* [2006] IRLR 514 and *Hughes v Jones and Jones t/a Graylyns Residential Home*, UK/EAT/0159/08/MAA. See L Rodgers, 2009, and para 4.53 above. The European Commission has proposed a modification of the Directive to provide that on-call time spent at the place of work should not be classed as 'working time': see COM (2004) 607 final.

[549] *SIMAP*, at para 50.

[550] Directive 2003/88, Art 6.

with the need to protect the health and safety of workers', to ensure that the 48-hour limit is 'complied with in the case of each worker employed by him'.[551]

The 48-hour limit is qualified by the concept of the 'reference period' over which actual working hours may be averaged out.[552] The Directive lays down a default reference period of four months in respect of the maximum working week of 48 hours, which in the Regulations is stated as 17 weeks. The starting point of the 17-week period may be set by a 'relevant agreement' but if no such agreement is made, it is any period of 17 weeks of the worker's employment.

The Regulations establish a complex formula for calculating weekly average working time and time spent on night work.[553] The problem addressed here is the one of calculating time spent at work in such a way as to take into account days spent on leave for various reasons, known as 'excluded days'. Essentially, the average figure is arrived at by adding the aggregate hours worked by the worker during the reference period to an additional number of hours in respect of days worked in the *next* reference period which make up for the 'excluded days'. The combined figure is then divided by the number of weeks in the reference period.

NIGHT WORK AND SHIFT WORK

4.82   The Directive and Regulations lay down standards with regard to night work and unsocial hours working.[554] The first of these is a limit to normal average night work of eight hours in any 24-hour period, and an absolute limit of eight hours in any 24 if the work involves special hazards, or heavy physical or mental strain. Nightworkers must be provided with periodic, free health assessments, and those found to be suffering health problems as a result of night work following an assessment by a registered medical practitioner must be transferred, where possible, to suitable day work. The Directive stipulates that in organising working patterns of shifts, employers must also take into account 'the general principle of adapting work to the worker, with a view, in particular, to alleviating monotonous work and work at a predetermined work-rate, depending on the type of activity, and of safety and health requirements, especially as regards breaks during working time'.[555] This provision was based on the principle of the 'humanisation of work' which was borrowed from German labour law.[556]

Nightwork is defined by the Directive as a period of not less than seven hours including at least the period from midnight to 5 am.[557] Under the Regulations, the period between 11 pm and 6 am is used for this purpose, unless a relevant agreement specifies a different seven-hour period between the hours of 10 pm and 7 am. A broad definition of 'nightworker' is used which includes workers who work at night for a least three hours on the majority of days they work or for such number of days as is agreed by a relevant agreement, or, as a residual category, to such extent that they can be said to normally work on a night work basis.[558] In *R v A-G for Northern Ireland, ex p*

---

[551] WTR 1998, reg 4(2).
[552] Directive 2003/88, Art 16.
[553] See regs 4(6) and 6(5).
[554] Directive 2003/88, Arts 8–13; WTR 1998, regs 4, 6–7.
[555] Directive 2003/88, Art 13.
[556] Däubler, 1990: p 321.
[557] Directive 2003/88, Art 2(3).
[558] See WTR 1998, reg 2(1); Barnard, 1999: p 73.

Burns[559] this definition was held to be wide enough to cover a worker who worked between the hours of 9 pm and 7 am in one week in three.

REST PERIODS AND REST BREAKS

4.83 The Directive and Regulations lay down a minimum daily rest period of eleven consecutive hours out of every 24;[560] rest breaks of twenty minutes (unless a different period is set by a collective or workforce agreement) every six hours during the working day;[561] and a period of weekly rest. In Case C-484/04 *Commission v United Kingdom* the ECJ held that the United Kingdom was in breach of the Directive by virtue of a statement in the then DTI guidelines to the effect that 'Employers must make sure that workers can take their rest, but are not required to make sure that they do take their rest'.[562] In the Directive, the weekly rest period is specified to be a period of 35 consecutive hours per week (24 hours plus the eleven hours of minimum daily rest), which may be reduced to 24 hours in total where 'objective, technical or work organisation conditions so justify'.[563] In the Regulations, reference is made to the 24-hour rest period being taken as either two uninterrupted rest periods of 24 hours or one uninterrupted rest period of 48 hours in a 14-day period.[564]

ANNUAL PAID LEAVE

4.84 The Directive makes provision for a minimum paid leave entitlement of four weeks,[565] and the Regulations, in addition to implementing this right,[566] added a provision for 'additional leave', also paid, of 1.6 weeks, with effect from 1 April 2009.[567] The Regulations originally provided for a minimum qualifying period of thirteen weeks continuous employment to apply in respect of the right to annual leave,[568] but this restriction, which is not to be found in the Directive,

[559] [1999] IRLR 315.
[560] Directive 2003/88, Art 3; WTR 1998, reg 10.
[561] Directive 2003/88, Art 4; WTR 1998, reg 12. See *Corps of Commissionaires Management Ltd v Hughes* [2009] IRLR 122, *Hughes v Commissionaires Management Ltd (No 2)* [2011] IRLR 915. A 'rest break' must be fixed in advance of its commencement: see *Gallagher v Alpha Catering Services Ltd* [2005] IRLR 102, at [50] (Peter Gibson LJ).
[562] [2006] IRLR 888.
[563] Directive 2003/88, Art 5.
[564] Directive 2003/88, reg 11.
[565] Directive 2003/88, Art 7.
[566] WTR 1998, reg 13.
[567] WTR 1998, reg 13A (phasing in the additional leave entitlement in stages). See also regs 14 (compensation in respect of leave), 15 (dates of leave), 15A (leave in the first year), 16 (payments in respect of leave). On the requirements for notice by the worker under reg 15, see *Lyons v Mitie Security Ltd* [2010] IRLR 288, and on the employer's right to require that the leave entitlement under the WTR be taken at particular points in the yearly working cycle, see *Russell v Transocean International Resources Ltd.* [2012] IRLR 149.
[568] WTR 1998, reg 13(2).

was successfully challenged before the ECJ[569] and subsequently removed.[570] Article 7(2) of the Directive provides that the right may not be commuted into a payment in lieu, except where the employment is terminated.[571]

According to the Court of Appeal in *Commissioners of Inland Revenue v Ainsworth*,[572] the concept of 'leave' denoted a period in respect of which a worker was freed from an obligation they would otherwise have had to work or to be available to work. On this basis, the Court held that the workers who had been on prolonged leave of absence by virtue of illness and who had exhausted their entitlement to sick pay, some of whom had also been dismissed by the employer by reason of their absence, were not entitled to receive holiday pay under the Regulations. However, the ECJ, on a reference from the House of Lords, then ruled that while it is not incompatible with the Directive for a Member State to restrict the right to take paid annual leave during a period of sick leave, this is conditional upon the worker being able to take the annual leave at a later date. It is not permissible for legislation to provide that the right to take paid leave is extinguished at the end of the year or other relevant period, if the worker does not work by reason of sickness during that year. Similarly, if the employment is terminated, the worker is entitled to receive an allowance in lieu of his or her annual leave rights, by virtue of Article 7(2) of the Directive.[573] When the *Ainsworth* case returned to the House of Lords, the employer conceded that the claimants had been entitled to annual leave in respect of the periods of absence through illness.[574] However the CJEU has recently held that the right to carry over leave is not unlimited; thus, a term to the effect that, if leave could not be taken because of illness, entitlement to it would lapse 15 months after the end of the reference year, was not contrary to the Directive.[575] It was regarded as significant by the Court that the carry-over period in this case exceeded the reference year. In *Dominguez v*

[569] Case C-173/99 *BECTU v Secretary of State for Trade and Industry* [2001] ECR I-4881. In *Gibson v East Riding of Yorkshire Council* [2000] IRLR 598 the Court of Appeal held that the right contained in the Directive was not sufficiently precise to be capable of having direct effect, since, in any given case, the worker's right to leave could only be ascertained once their working time was known; in the Court's view, the Directive itself did not contain a clear or precise enough definition of 'working time' for the nature of the right to leave to be deduced from this source alone. This approach is arguably not reconcilable with that of the ECJ in the *BECTU* case.

[570] SI 2001/3256. In Case C-486/08 *Zentralbetriebsrat der Landeskrankenhäuser Tirols v Land Tirol* [2010] IRLR 631 the ECJ emphasised that 'the right of every worker to paid annual leave must be regarded as a particularly important principle of European Union social law from which there can be no derogations and whose implementation by the competent national authorities must be confined within the limits expressly laid down' by the Directive (at para 28), which 'cannot be interpreted restrictively' (at para 29). See also Case C-155/10 *British Airways plc v Williams* [2011] IRLR 948, referring to the 'fundamental right' to paid leave under Art 31(2) CFREU.

[571] In the event of termination, the employer must make a payment in lieu if worker has used up a lesser proportion of their leave entitlement than that represented by their service for the year in question (WTR 1998, reg 14) but there is no equivalent entitlement to make a deduction from wages due if the worker has taken a higher proportion of their leave entitlement (*Hill v Chapell* [2003] IRLR 19). In Case C-124/05 *Federatie Nederlandse Vakbeweging v Staat der Nederlanden* [2006] IRLR 561 the ECJ held that a provision of Dutch law allowing leave not taken in one year to be carried forward to the next and exchanged for a payment in lieu was contrary to the Directive.

[572] [2005] IRLR 465.

[573] Joined Cases C-520/06 and C-350/06 *Stringer v HMRC and Schultz-Hoff v Deutsche Rentenversicherung Bund* [2009] IRLR 214; see also Case C-227/08 *Pereda v Madrid Movilidad SA* [2009] IRLR 959; *NHS Leeds v Larner* [2011] IRLR 894; cf *Fraser v Southwest London St George's Mental Health Trust* [2010] IRLR 100.

[574] *HMRC v Stringer* [2009] IRLR 677. The House also held that a claim for holiday pay arising under WTR regs 14 and 16 could be pursued as a claim for 'wages' under s 23 ERA 1996, which has a more generous limitation period where there has been a series of deductions (s 23(3)). See above, para 4.73.

[575] Case C-214/10 *KHS AG v Schulte* [2012] IRLR 156. See also Case C-337/10 *Neidel v Stadt Frankfurt am Main* [2012] IRLR 607 (carry-over period shorter than the reference period).

Centre Informatique du Centre Oues Atlantique[576] the CJEU held that Member States may provide that entitlement to paid annual leave in national law may vary according to the reason for the worker's absence on health grounds, provided that the entitlement is always equal to or exceeds the minimum four week period laid down in Article 7 of the Directive.

The ECJ has held that the practice of 'rolled up' holiday pay – whereby a premium is added to wages paid in respect of periods of completed work, to represent holiday pay, and no payment is made in respect of the period of leave itself – is incompatible with Article 7 of the Directive on the grounds 'the point at which the payment for annual leave is made must be fixed in such a way that, during that leave, the worker is, as regards remuneration, put in a position comparable to periods of work', in order to avoid creating a disincentive for the worker to take leave.[577] However, the Court also held that while 'the Member States are required to take the measures appropriate to ensure that practices incompatible with Article 7 of the Directive are not continued',[578] sums paid by way of rolled up holiday pay could be set off against employer's obligations in respect of periods of leave actually taken by workers. The WTR have not been amended in the light of this judgment, and the courts have held that the practice is lawful and set-off possible as long as the arrangements in question meet loosely-framed criteria of transparency and clarity.[579]

A related, although not identical practice, is that of 'consolidated shift pay' which came before the courts in *British Airways plc v Noble*.[580] Here the employer followed a practice of calculating the average weekly shift premium for each worker over a six-month period, and then multiplying that sum by 48 and dividing by 52 to arrive at a consolidated rate of shift pay, which was paid as a supplement to regular weekly earnings both when the worker was working and when the worker took leave. The reduction achieved by multiplying by 48 and dividing by 52 was made on the basis that for the four weeks of annual paid leave, no work was done and so no shift premia would be payable in respect of those weeks. Regulation 16 WTR requires a worker to be paid holiday pay at the 'rate of a week's pay in respect of each week of leave', and a week's pay is determined, for this purpose, by the ERA 1996 which states that when hours differ from week to week or day to day, 'the amount of a week's pay is the amount of remuneration for the average number of weekly normal working hours at the average hourly rate of remuneration'.[581] The Court of Appeal held for the employer, on the grounds that the employer merely had to show under regulation 16 that it paid the same rate for leave periods as for time spent at work. According to Mummery LJ, the gist of the workers' complaints was the manner in which their shift pay was calculated, not the rate at which their holiday pay was worked out, and there was no disincentive to take leave. The lower courts had decided differently on the grounds that the correct rate of holiday pay was the average rate of pay received for the periods when the employees were at work, that is, the basic hourly rate

---

[576] Case C-282/10 [2012] IRLR 321. See also *Neidel* above.

[577] Joined Cases C-131/04 and C-257/04 *Robinson-Steele v RD Retail Services Ltd, Clarke v Frank Staddon Ltd and Caulfield v Hanson Clay Products Ltd* [2006] IRLR 386, at para 59. The issue gave rise to an extensive case law: see *Witley & District Men's Club v Mackay* [2001] IRLR 595; *Blackburn v Gridquest Ltd* [2002] IRLR 604; *MPB Structures v Munro* [2003] IRLR 350; *Bamsey v Albon Engineering and Manufacturing plc* [2004] IRLR 457; *Caulfield v Marshalls Clay Products Ltd* [2004 IRLR 564; *Smith v AJ Morrisroes and Sons Ltd* [2005] IRLR 72.

[578] Joined Cases C-131/04 and C-257/04 *Robinson-Steele v RD Retail Services Ltd, Clarke v Frank Staddon Ltd and Caulfield v Hanson Clay Products Ltd* [2006] IRLR 386, at [67].

[579] *Lyddon v Englefield Brickwork Ltd* [2008] IRLR 198, in which the EAT took a more flexible line than in its earlier decision in *Smith v AJ Morrisroes and Sons Ltd* [2005] IRLR 72.

[580] [2006] IRLR 533.

[581] ERA 1996, s. 222.

supplemented by the average shift pay rate, unaffected by the proportionate reduction for the four weeks of annual leave.

In *British Airways plc v Williams*[582] over 2,000 airline pilots brought claims challenging the basis on which their holiday pay was calculated. Their pay consisted of three parts: basic salary; a 'flying time allowance' set a given hourly rate for time spent in the air; and an allowance paid in respect of periods spent away from their 'base' airport, part of which was treated as a payment in respect of expenses, and part of which was taxable. The employer paid holiday pay by reference only to the first of these, the basic salary. The CJEU ruled that an 'airline pilot is entitled, during his annual leave, not only to the maintenance of his basic salary, but also, first, to all the components intrinsically linked to the performance of the tasks which he is required to carry out under his contract of employment and in respect of which a monetary amount, included in the calculation of his total remuneration, is provided and, second, to all the elements relating to his personal and professional status as an airline pilot.'[583] On the other hand, holiday pay did not need to include those 'components of the worker's total remuneration which are intended exclusively to cover occasional or ancillary costs arising at the time of performance of the tasks which the worker is required to carry out under his contract of employment, such as costs connected with the time that pilots have to spend away from base.'[584] The judgment is notable for its emphasis on the nature of the right to paid annual leave as a fundamental right protected by Article 31(2) CFREU.[585]

WEEKEND WORKING

4.85 The Directive originally provided that the period of weekly rest 'shall in principle include Sunday', but this provision, alone of the terms of the Directive, was struck down by the ECJ in the *Working Time* case.[586] As a result, the issue of weekend working is left untouched by the Directive and Regulations, to the extent that an employer may be able to insist on days of annual leave being taken on a weekend day when the employee either regularly works or has to be available for work on one of those days. Thus in *Sumsion v BBC (Scotland)*[587] it was held that employer could nominate a Saturday as a leave day when the contract gave it the option of requiring the worker to be available for work on that day. In *Copsey v WWB Devon Clays Ltd*.[588] an employee was dismissed for refusing to accept a variation of his contract which would have required him to be available for occasional Sunday work. It was held that he had been dismissed for a potentially fair reason, as the employer had shown a genuine business need for the change, and that the dismissal was reasonable in the circumstances. In *McLean v Rainbow Homeloans Ltd*.[589] the EAT held that where an employee had refused a variation which would have involved additional weekend working and had been dismissed as a result, the dismissal could be automatically unfair

---

[582] Case C-155/10, [2011] IRLR 948. This case was brought under Art 7 of Directive 2000/79/EC, the 'Aviation Directive', implemented in the UK by SI 2004/756, which is the same terms as Art 7 of the Working Time Directive. See also Case C-471/08 *Parviainen v Finnair Oyj* [2011] ICR 99.

[583] Judgment, at para 31.

[584] Judgment, at para 25.

[585] Judgment, at para 18. The Court makes no reference to the UK's 'opt-out' in Protocol 30 of the Lisbon Treaty, on which see para 2.39 above.

[586] [1996] ECR I-5755.

[587] [2007] IRLR 678.

[588] [2005] IRLR 811. The Court of Appeal rejected an argument that Art 9 ECHR was engaged in this case (the claimant had sought to argue that his right to manifest his religious beliefs was being interfered with). See H Collins, 2006.

[589] [2007] IRLR 14.

on the ground that he had refused to accede to a requirement that would have breached the WTR; however, a critical factor here was that he was already working in excess of the statutory upper limit of 48 hours per week.

DEROGATIONS

4.86   Article 17 of the Directive permits Member States to make derogations in five broadly defined areas. These provisions are complex because it is necessary to consider, in some detail, exactly which provisions of the Directive can be derogated from, and the conditions which must be met in order for the derogation to be effective.

WORKERS WITH A SIGNIFICANT DEGREE OF CONTROL OVER THEIR WORKING TIME

4.87   The first category relates to workers with a degree of control over their own working time: 'managing executives or others with autonomous decision-making powers', 'family workers' and those 'officiating at religious ceremonies in churches and religious communities'.[590] This derogation applies to the provisions governing the working week, nightwork, weekly and daily rest, but not to the rights to annual paid leave and to free health assessments. For this group, no required method of derogation is specified; the workers concerned may simply be exempted from the coverage of the relevant national laws. However, the manner in which this exception was implemented in UK law has been problematic. Under WTR regulation 20,[591] the scope of the derogation is referred to in terms of 'unmeasured working time', which means a situation where 'on account of the specific characteristics of the activity in which [the worker] is engaged, the duration of his working time is not measured or predetermined or can be determined by the worker himself'. This vagueness of this formula has created considerable uncertainty in the application of the WTR to professional and managerial workers. In *Sayers v Cambridgeshire County Council*[592] the definition was strictly construed to exclude a senior manager holding 'a high level post', who was nevertheless not 'a managing executive or person with autonomous decision-making powers'.[593]

In an amendment made by the 1999 Regulations,[594] the regulation 20 derogation was amended to cover workers only part of whose work was unmeasured. The limits on working time and night work were then applied only to those parts of the work which were not measured or predetermined,[595] effectively depriving these controls of most of their force. Unsurprisingly, the European Commission began infringement proceedings against the United Kingdom in respect of this amendment, and it was declared to be contrary to the Directive by the ECJ,[596] after the government had already taken steps to restore the original form of regulation 20.[597]

---

[590] Directive 2003/88, Art 17(1); WTR 1998, reg 20.
[591] WTR 1998, reg 20.
[592] [2007] IRLR 29.
[593] [2007] IRLR 29, at [259].
[594] SI 1999/3372, reg 4.
[595] For discussion, see Barnard, 2000: pp 169–171.
[596] Case C-484/04 *Commission v United Kingdom* [2006] IRLR 888.
[597] See SI 2006/99, reg 2.

WORKERS FOR WHOM WORKING TIME CONTROLS ARE DEEMED TO BE INAPPROPRIATE OR IMPRACTICAL

4.88   A second category of derogation relates to a miscellaneous group of workers for whom working time controls may be deemed inappropriate or impractical. These are:[598] those employed at a long distance from their residence; security workers; workers employed in activities requiring continuity of service and production (particularly, health workers, residential care workers, and prison officers; dock or airport workers; media workers; emergency service workers; workers in the utilities sectors; workers employed in continuous process industries ('industries in which work cannot be interrupted on technical grounds');[599] research and development workers; agricultural workers; certain transport workers; workers subject to a 'foreseeable surge in activity' (in particular in agriculture, tourism, and postal services); and those working in emergency or accident situations. Under the Directive, derogations here must take the form of laws, regulations or collective agreements and must involve compensatory rest periods for the workers concerned or, in exceptional circumstances, other appropriate protection;[600] they do not apply to the right to annual paid leave or to the limit upon weekly working time. The Regulations spell out in detail the excluded categories under this heading.[601]

SHIFT WORKERS

4.89   A third set of derogations concerns certain shift workers. Again, these derogations must take the form of laws, regulations or collective agreements (the level of which is not specified in the Directive) and must involve compensatory rest periods for the workers concerned; they apply only to the daily rest and weekly rest provisions.[602]

DEROGATIONS MADE BY COLLECTIVE OR WORKFORCE AGREEMENT

4.90   In a fourth category, the Directive permits derogations to be made without reference to the type of work being carried out, if they are set out in collective agreements at national or regional level, or by lower-level collective agreements made in accordance with the rules laid down by national or regional agreements.[603] Derogating agreements may modify the rules relating to night work, daily and weekly rest periods, and rest breaks. In return they must provide for equivalent rest periods or, in an exceptional case where this is not possible, 'appropriate protection' for the workers concerned, and such agreements may be extended to cover workers outside their express scope. No derogations may be made under this category with respect to annual paid leave, nor to

---

[598] See Directive 2003/88, Art 17(3); see *Hughes v Corps of Commissionaires Management Ltd (No 2)* [2011] IRLR 915.

[599] See *Gallagher v Alpha Catering Services) t/a Alpha Flight Services* [2005] IRLR 102 and Joined Cases C-397/01–C403/01 *Pfeiffer v Deutsches Rotes Kreutz, Kreizverband Waldshut eV* [2005] IRLR 137.

[600] Directive, Art. 17(2), which was narrowly construed in Case 428/09 *Union Syndicale Solidaires Isère v Premier Ministre* [2011] IRLR 84.

[601] WTR 1998, reg 21. As Barnard (1999) points out, these derogations apply to workers employed in activities of a particular kind, and not to all workers in the occupations in question. On compensatory rest, see *Hughes v Corps of Commissionaires Management Ltd (No 2)* [2011] IRLR 915.

[602] See WTR 1998, reg 22 (although note also reg 24(6)).

[603] Directive 2003/88, Art 18.

the length of the maximum working week. However, the default reference period for the calculation of the maximum working week can be extended from four months to up to one year.[604]

This potentially very wide derogating power has been implemented in the Regulations. These allow collective agreements or workforce agreements to make the allowable modifications to the statutory standards which would otherwise apply. These agreements can also extend the reference period for calculating maximum weekly working hours from 17 to 52 weeks where objective or technical reasons, or reasons related to the organisation of work, require this.[605] The Regulations implement the principle that compensatory rest should be provided in return for the derogation.[606]

INDIVIDUAL DEROGATIONS FROM THE 48-HOUR LIMIT TO WEEKLY WORKING TIME

4.91 Finally, Article 22 of the Directive allows Member States to permit individual derogations to be made from the 48-hour limit to weekly working time.[607] This may be done on condition that the power of the employer to require a worker to work more than 48 hours per week may only be exercised where 'he has obtained the worker's agreement' to do so[608] and also on condition that regular records are kept of workers' employed hours over this limit. This derogation was set to operate for a period of seven years after the Directive came into force on 23 November 1996. At the end of 2003 the Commission initiated a review process; since then, a series of further attempts to arrive at a revision of the derogation have failed.[609]

Under the 1998 Regulations, individual derogations from the 48-hour weekly limit were subject to a number of strict conditions; they had to be in writing and allow for termination by the worker by seven days' notice in writing, or such longer period, up to a maximum of three months, as the parties agreed. The 1998 Regulations also imposed upon employers extensive record-keeping requirements, including an obligation to specify those workers agreeing to work in excess of 48 hours, the terms on which they did so, and the hours worked by these workers in each reference period since the agreement came into effect. These provisions were amended in

---

[604] Directive 2003/88, Art 19.

[605] WTR 1998, reg 23.

[606] WTR 1998, reg 24.

[607] A member state must explicitly opt into this derogation to take advantage of it: Case C-243/09 *Fuß v Stadt Halle* [2010] IRLR 1080.

[608] Art 22(1)(a). According to the ECJ in Case C-303/98 *SIMAP* [2000] IRLR 845, this does not include the situation in which a trade union representing the worker makes the agreement on his or her behalf. See Joined Cases C-397/01–C-403/01 *Pfeiffer v Deutsches Rotes Kreutz, Kreizverband Waldshut eV* [2005] IRLR 137 for more general guidance on the conditions that must be met including the need for genuine consent on the part of the worker.

[609] For an account of the background to the Commission's review, together with an overview and assessment of empirical evidence relating to the individual opt-out, see Barnard *et al*, 2004. In the course of 2004 the Commission produced a consultation paper directed to the Member States (COM (2003) 843 final) and initiated a consultation process with the social partners (SEC (2004) 610) before making a proposal to amend the Directive (COM (2004) 607 final). This would have retained the possibility of an individual opt-out from the 48 hour week but only in those workplaces or sectors where there was no applicable collective agreement. It would also have imposed more stringent record-keeping requirements and stricter formalities as conditions of the individual opt-out, and set a new absolute upper limit of 65 hours per week, which could only have been varied by collective agreement. In the event, these proposals were not acceptable to the Member States. The Commission amended its proposals again in 2005 (COM (2005) 246 final), but with no more success than before. After several years of deadlock, the Council reached a common position in June 2008. The text of the revised Directive contained changes to the definition of working time (which would have excluded certain categories of on-call time) and maintained the opt-out from the 48-hour week. In December 2008 the Parliament passed an amendment rejecting these aspects of the revision. At the time of writing, the issue remains deadlocked.

1999. Now there is a simple requirement for the agreement to be in writing and for the employer to record those workers who make an agreement of this kind.[610]

Enforcement

4.92   The Directive permits Member States to comply with its terms either by legislation or by ensuring that the two sides of industry establish the necessary measures by agreement. In the latter case, the Member State is obliged to take any necessary steps to enable them to guarantee at all times that the provisions laid down by this Directive are fulfilled.[611] The Regulations make provision for a range of criminal and civil enforcement methods.[612] The scheme laid down in the Regulations provides that 'working time limits' – the 48-hour weekly limits, and limits on night work – are enforceable through criminal prosecutions and administrative action by the Health and Safety Executive, which would also have responsibility for monitoring record keeping.[613] By contrast, 'working time entitlements' – the rights to rest periods and annual leave – are enforceable by individual workers before employment tribunals.[614] This scheme was upset, however, by the judgment of the High Court in *Barber v RJB Mining Ltd*,[615] in which it was held that the right not to be required to work in excess of 48 hours per week gave rise to a contractual obligation on the part of the employer. On this basis, the 'limits' specified by the Directive and Regulations should be enforceable by individual workers through their contracts. *Barber* has not been followed in subsequent decisions, which have confined enforcement of particular provisions of the Regulation to the remedies explicitly set out for them.[616] However, in *Fuß v Stadt Halle*[617] the ECJ held that the right not to work more than 48 hours per week is sufficiently clear and unconditional to have direct effect in national law. The effect of this judgment is that public sector workers can bring claims directly against their employers for breach of the 48-hour working week, thereby overcoming the restrictions on individual claims to enforce working time limits under WTR.

(ii) The Young Workers Directive and implementing Regulations

4.93   A further EC instrument, the Directive on the Protection of Young Persons at Work,[618] contains provisions regulating the working hours of children and young persons as well as more

---

[610] WTR 1998, reg 4(1), as amended.

[611] Art 18(1).

[612] WTR 1998, regs 28–34.

[613] WTR 1998, regs 28 and 29. Note that local authorities also have an enforcement role in specific circumstances: reg 28(3)–(5).

[614] WTR 1998, reg 30. Rights not to be dismissed or subject to a detriment are provided by reg 31. Note there is no automatic compensation for breach of several of the working time 'entitlements': in *Miles v Linkage Community Trust Ltd* [2008] IRLR 602 the EAT held that an employment tribunal had discretion to award no compensation for breach of the requirement to give compensatory rest periods in lieu of rest periods under WTR reg 24, where the employer acted in good faith and the period of default following the worker's complaint was a relatively brief one.

[615] [1999] IRLR 308; A Edwards, 2000.

[616] See *Sayers v Cambridgeshire County Council* [2007] IRLR 29 (no claim in the tort of breach of statutory duty under WTR reg 4); *Commissioners of Inland Revenue v Ainsworth* [2005] IRLR 465 (a claim for holiday pay cannot be made as a claim for unpaid wages under ERA 1996, s 23 but only under WTR, reg 30, implying a stricter limitation period).

[617] Case C-243/09, [2010] IRLR 1080. See also *Fuß v Stadt Halle* (No 2) [2011] IRLR 176 on EU law governing reparation for a breach of this right.

[618] Directive 94/33.

general measures of a health and safety nature.[619] The employment of children, defined here as persons below the minimum school leaving age or 15 years, whichever is higher, is prohibited. There are exceptions only for work in theatres and films, work experience and/or training, and light work, with strict conditions attached in each case.[620] In particular, children falling within one of these exceptions must not work for more than two hours on any school day or for more than 12 hours a week during term time.[621] Night work by children is prohibited between 8 pm and 6 am.[622] Persons aged between 15 (or the minimum school leaving age) and 18, classified in Britain as 'young persons' for health and safety purposes and termed 'adolescents' in the Directive, are limited to a maximum working day of 8 hours and a maximum working week of 40 hours.[623] Night work by this group is prohibited between the hours of 10 pm and 6 am or 11 pm and 7 am.[624] Minimum daily and weekly rest periods are also laid down for children and adolescents;[625] in addition, there are provisions for derogation from certain of the working-time standards which are similar to those contained in the Working Time Directive.

The UK was granted the benefit of a provision entitling it (but no other Member State) to delay the implementation of most of the Directive for a further four years from the date when the Directive came into force (which was 22 June 1996).[626] Much of the Directive was implemented in the form of regulations adopted in 1997 and 1998.[627] The Working Time Regulations 1998 implement those parts of the Directive which relate to what the 1994 Directive calls 'adolescents' and the Regulations call 'young workers' between the minimum school leaving age and the age of 18.[628]

HEALTH AND SAFETY AND THE WORKING ENVIRONMENT

4.94   The subject of occupational health and safety is a substantial one in its own right. Much of health and safety law operates by imposing regulatory duties upon employers which are enforced through the powers of the health and safety inspectorate and, ultimately, the sanctions of the criminal courts; the detailed provisions of these public-regulatory statutes and their mechanisms of enforcement lie outside the scope of this work.[629] Instead, this section will briefly consider the impact of health and safety standards on the individual employment relationship. In some

[619] On the latter, see footnote 627 below.
[620] Directive 94/33, Arts 4, 5.
[621] Directive 94/33, Art 8(1)(a)–(b).
[622] Directive 94/33, Art 9.
[623] Directive 94/33, Art 8.
[624] Directive 94/33, Art 9.
[625] Directive 94/33, Arts 10–12.
[626] Directive 94/33, Art 17.
[627] The Health and Safety (Young Persons) Regulations, SI 1997/135, implemented Arts 6 and 7 of the Directive which relate to the general obligations of employers with regard to the health and safety of young persons and the prohibition of certain types of employment of young persons. These were then revoked by the Management of Health and Safety at Work Regulations 1999 (SI 1999/3242), reg 19 of which deals with the employment of young persons. The Children (Protection at Work) Regulations, SI 1998/276, implement those parts of the Directive which concern the employment of children (that is, those below the compulsory school leaving age). See generally the Children and Young Persons Act 1933 as amended.
[628] WTR 1998, regs 5A and 6A, as inserted by SI 2002/3128.
[629] See Tolley, 2012; Ford et al, 2010.

cases of a breach of a criminal statute, an individual worker may bring an action for damages *via* the tort of breach of statutory duty; this is an action developed by the courts at common law. In the absence of a specific statute, the employer may be held liable in negligence for its breach of the general common law duty to provide safe working conditions, or may find itself vicariously liable for the tort of an employee. The Health and Safety at Work Act 1974 also imposes a general responsibility on the employer to ensure 'so far as is reasonably practicable' the health, safety and welfare of employees, as well as aiming to incorporate aspects of health and safety observance into managerial practice. Finally, European-level regulation has come to have a major influence in this area, mainly through the 1989 Framework Directive[630] and the 'daughter directives' designed to implement its general objectives in the areas of workplace safety, protection against hazardous substances and specific industries.

Common law duties of the employer

4.95   Employees' actions for damages for personal injury suffered at work were stymied for most of the nineteenth century by the doctrine of common employment. This operated through an implied term in the contract of service, the effect of which was that the employee or servant took the risk of injury or damage caused by a fellow servant's negligence. The employer was thereby absolved of any vicarious liability for a tort committed by one fellow worker against another.[631] If the injury was caused by the employee of another employer, it was highly possible that the victim's claim would be defeated by contributory negligence or *volenti non fit injuria*.[632] The doctrine of common employment was abolished by statute in 1948;[633] around the same time, contributory negligence was made a partial as opposed to a complete defence,[634] and the courts began to take a much more restrictive view than previously of the scope of *volenti*.[635] Even before these changes, developments within the common law had enabled the courts to outflank the broad, pro-employer defences. The defences of *volenti* and common employment were held to be inapplicable to claims based on the civil action for breach of statutory duty, which was widely applied to factories legislation following the decision of the Court of Appeal in *Groves v Lord Wimborne* in 1898.[636] Then in *Wilsons & Clyde Coal Co v English*, decided in 1937,[637] the House of Lords confirmed the existence of an employer's *general* duty of care in tort with regard to the safety of its employees. The duty was affirmative in nature and could not be discharged merely by delegation to an appropriate employee or agent of the employer; the doctrine of common employment, which focused on the negligence of the *employee*, was therefore irrelevant to this claim.

---

[630] Directive 89/391.
[631] *Priestley v Fowler* (1837) 3 M & W 1; *Farwell v Boston and Worcester Railroad Corpn* 4 Metcalf 49 (1842) (Supreme Court of Massachusetts); *Bartonshill Coal Co v Reid* (1858) 3 Macq 266.
[632] See, eg, *Woodley v Metropolitan District Rly Co* (1877) 2 Ex D 384.
[633] Law Reform (Personal Injuries) Act 1948, s 1.
[634] Law Reform (Contributory Negligence) Act 1945.
[635] The restriction of *volenti* began with *Smith v Charles Baker & Sons Ltd* [1891] AC 325, so that by the time contributory negligence had been made a partial defence, volenti had also ceased to be a major obstacle to employees' claims. Since 1945 it has only been applied in somewhat exceptional cases such as *ICI Ltd v Shatwell* [1965] AC 656.
[636] 1898] 2 QB 402. On *volenti* in this context, see *Wheeler v New Merton Board Mills Ltd* [1933] 2 KB 669.
[637] [1938] AC 57.

The *Wilsons* case lays down what is, in effect, a four-fold duty of care. Lord Wright said that the employer's responsibilities related to the provision of competent fellow workers, safe materials and a proper system of work; in addition, there is the category of a safe place of work. The duty to provide safe equipment is now strict, as a result of the Employer's Liability (Defective Equipment) Act 1969. This effectively overruled the decision of the House of Lords in *Davie v New Merton Board Mills Ltd*,[638] according to which an employer cannot be held liable for undiscoverable defects in materials or equipment supplied to it by a third party. The Act imposes liability on the employer if the defect was caused by the fault of the manufacturer or supplier. By contrast, the common law duty to provide a safe place of work and safe working system is still based on fault, and an employer may avoid liability if it can show that, in the circumstances, it took all reasonable steps to ensure the safety of its employees. For example, in determining what is reasonable, the court may take into account the possible costs to the employer of closing down all or part of its operations, if no other means of avoiding the risk of injury was available.[639] Notwithstanding the need to show fault, the scope the employer's duties has been clarified and adjusted over time to reflect changing workplace conditions and societal expectations. One of the more significant recent developments is the emergence of the principle that an employer may be liable for failing to take steps to ensure that an employee is not subjected to harassment and victimisation which results in not just in physical harm but in psychological illness or disease.[640]

The expression of the employer's common law obligations in terms of a duty of care in tort as opposed to an implied contract term is, in many ways, a product of historical accident as much as anything else. As long as the doctrine of common employment operated through an implied contract term, the scope for a contractual solution to the employee's interest in health and safety protection was limited. Moreover, when the *Wilsons* case was decided few aspects of the individual employment relationship were given contractual form; the expression of extensive reciprocal duties through the individual contract of employment is largely a post-1945 development.[641] In *Lister v Romford Ice and Cold Storage Co*,[642] decided in 1955, Lord Radcliffe thought that the employer's implied obligations could be equally well expressed in either contract or tort. In terms of the substance of the obligation it seems that it does not matter whether tort or contract is used, but the distinction is not without significance. In particular, the limitation period for actions in tort begins later than that in contract, namely at the point when the injury or damage is sustained as opposed to the point at which the breach of duty takes place.[643] Moreover, the damages which are recoverable in a tort claim will incorporate an element for loss of earning capacity and loss of

---

[638] [1959] AC 604.

[639] *Latimer v AEC Ltd* [1953] AC 643.

[640] See *Waters v Commissioner of Police of the Metropolis* [2000] IRLR 720. More recently the House of Lords has held that an employer may be vicariously liable for wrongs committed by employees under the Protection from Harassment Act 1997 (*Majrowski v Guy's and St. Thomas's NHS Trust* [2006] IRLR 695) and cases of harassment are now often argued both at common law and under the 1997 Act (see *Green v DB Group Services (UK) Ltd* [2006] IRLR 764) or under the Act alone (see *Rayment v Ministry of Defence* [2010] IRLR 768; *Veakins v Kier Islington Ltd* [2010] IRLR 132 (in which Maurice Kay LJ observed, at [17], that while 'there is nothing in the language of the Act which excludes workplace harassment', stress at work would not 'often' give rise to a claim of this kind, and that 'it is far more likely that, in the great majority of cases, the remedy for high-handed or discriminatory misconduct by or on behalf of an employer will be more fittingly in the employment tribunal'); *Marinello v Edinburgh City Council* [2011] IRLR 669). On the requirements of liability under the 1997 Act, Deakin, Johnston and Markesinis, 2008: pp 473-474.

[641] See above, para 4.4 *et seq.*

[642] [1957] AC 555.

[643] See Deakin, Johnston and Markesinis, 2008: pp 927–938 for an account of the relevant principles.

future earnings which will not normally be recoverable in contract.[644] On the other hand, it may be useful to an employee to be able to show that the employer has acted in breach of contract by disregarding their health and safety; this is the case, for example, where the employee resigns and claims constructive dismissal.[645] In *Waltons & Morse v Dorrington*[646] the applicant, a non-smoker who worked as a secretary for a firm of solicitors, left her employment in protest at her employer's failure to deal adequately with her complaints about being exposed to the cigarette smoke of fellow employees. The EAT, upholding a finding of constructive dismissal, held that 'the correct implied term to deal with the complaint in this case is that the employer will provide and monitor for his employees, so far as is reasonably practicable, a working environment which is reasonably suitable for the performance by them of their contractual duties'.[647] The employment tribunal had been entitled to find, in this case, that it would have been reasonably practicable for the employer to have prohibited employees from smoking inside the building which it occupied.

The employer's common law duty of care extends to an obligation to ensure that the employee is not placed in a position of undue exposure to physical or mental harm through overwork. This is so notwithstanding that the employee may have express contractual commitments to work a certain number of daily or weekly hours or to carry out certain supervisory or managerial tasks. *Johnstone v Bloomsbury Health Authority*[648] is authority for the proposition that where an individual employee foreseeably contracts illness or disease through working excessive hours, the employer cannot avoid liability simply by arguing that the working hours in question were those laid down in the contract. The basis for this ruling is not altogether clear, however, since the majority judges did not offer the same set of reasons.[649] Browne-Wilkinson VC thought that the employer had the right to call on the employee to work hours up to the limit set by the contract (88 per week in total); however, in respect of overtime hours (above 40) this right was qualified by the duty to act in such a way as to maintain the trust and co-operation which was essential to the employment relationship, which in this context meant avoiding placing the employee's health and safety in danger. Stuart-Smith LJ, by contrast, thought that such a contract term was ineffective to oust the common law duty of care. Stuart-Smith LJ's view seems preferable: at the very least, clear words should be needed to override the employer's implied duty with regard to health and safety. It is possible to go further and to suggest that public policy would strike down any contract term purporting to provide for working arrangements which foreseeably endanger an employee's health,[650] but none of the judges in *Johnstone* expressed support for this view.

Johnstone was a case of alleged physical injury; in other cases, employers have been held liable for the negligent infliction of psychiatric harm. In *Walker v Northumberland County Council*[651]

---

[644] On the reasons for the limited extent of damages for breach of contract at common law, see paras 5.21–5.30 below.

[645] On constructive dismissal, see below, paras 5.69–5.72.

[646] [1997] IRLR 488.

[647] [1997] IRLR 488, 490.

[648] [1992] QB 333. The remedies sought in *Johnstone* included a declaration of the parties' rights and an injunction preventing future breaches of contract by the employer. The judgments in that case were pursuant to a striking out application, which was rejected; the case did not subsequently go to trial. In *Barber v RJB Mining Ltd* [1999] IRLR 308 a declaration was granted to support employees' claims that their employer was acting in breach of WTR 1998, reg 4(1), which imposes a statutory obligation requiring employers to observe the 48-hour weekly limit to working time. If this approach were to be widely followed, enforcement of health and safety standards would be significantly strengthened; see A Edwards, 2000: pp 285–287. However, *Barber* has not been followed in later working time cases (see above, para 4.92).

[649] See para 4.8 above.

[650] Weir, 1991. Such a term might also be struck out by virtue of UCTA 1977; see above, para 4.8.

[651] [1995] IRLR 35.

the court held an employer liable for psychiatric illness caused by exposure to a stressful working situation. The employee worked as a senior social services manager. Over a period of years his workload increased considerably, as a large number of child abuse cases were referred to the division which he managed, but without any increase in staff. He complained of overwork but was told that he would have to make do with his existing resources. He suffered a nervous breakdown and, after a short interval, returned to his previous post. Extra staff help was provided for a short period but then withdrawn; he subsequently suffered a second nervous breakdown, following which he was incapable of work and was dismissed on the grounds of ill health. The court held that the *second* nervous breakdown had been foreseeable, and that the employer's response had not been appropriate: the seriousness of the potential risk to the employee, coupled with the high likelihood of further injury following the initial breakdown, made the employer's response unreasonable.

The approach taken in *Walker* was confirmed in a line of cases including several decisions of the higher appellate courts and is now well established.[652] Under this head of liability, employers will not always be liable for the effects of working conditions which induce stress in their employees. The relevant standard is that of the reasonable employer, and as usual in negligence cases, the court will balance the risk of harm and the degree of foreseeability of it occurring against the cost and practicability of preventive measures. In *Walker* itself the employer argued that the allocation of employees between different parts of its organisation was a matter for it to decide, but the court held that while this had to be weighed in the balance against the risk to the employee, it was not decisive on its own. However, it is significant that in *Walker* there were clear warning signs, based not just on the employee's complaints but also on his earlier illness. Employees in positions of managerial responsibility, in particular, may inevitably be exposed to a degree of stress as part of their work, and an employer probably would not be acting unreasonably merely by placing substantial demands upon them.

The question of when an employer is liable for post-traumatic stress disorder suffered by an employee in response to witnessing an accident caused by the employer was discussed by the House of Lords in *White v Chief Constable of South Yorkshire Police*.[653] Here, police officers suffered post-traumatic stress disorder as a result of tending victims of the Hillsborough disaster. The deaths and injuries of the victims were caused by the negligence of a fellow police officer for which their employer was vicariously liable. The House of Lords rejected the claim, on the basis that the claimants were 'secondary victims' who fell outside the normal categories of those who could recover. An employee who is neither a rescuer nor a particularly close relative or possibly friend of the victim is now in no better position than a bystander.[654] However, the post-traumatic stress disorder cases are arguably distinguishable from *Walker* and other cases in which the employee is

---

[652] In *Barber v Somerset County Council* [2004] IRLR 475 the House of Lords affirmed that the overall test is the conduct of the reasonable and prudent employer taking positive thought for the safety of its workers in the light of what it knows or ought to know, a test proposed by Swanwick J in *Stokes v Guest Keen and Nettleford (Bolts and Nuts) Ltd* [1968] 1WLR 1776. See also *Petch v Customs and Excise Comrs* [1993] ICR 789; *Sutherland v Hatton* [2002] IRLR 263; *Marshall Specialist Vehicles Ltd v Osborne* [2003] IRLR 672; *Pratley v Surrey County Council* [2003] IRLR 794; *Bonser v RJB Mining Co (UK) Ltd* [2004] IRLR 164; *Hartman v South Essex Mental Health and Community Care NHS Trust* [2005] IRLR 293; *Dickins v O2 plc* [2009] IRLR 58; *Banks v Ablex Ltd* [2005] IRLR 357; *Intel Corporation (UK) Ltd v Daw* [2007] IRLR 355; *Flood v University of Glasgow* [2010] CSIH 3; Barrett, 1995, 1996, 1999, 2001, 2004.

[653] [1999] IRLR 110.

[654] On this, see *McFarlane v EE Caledonia Ltd* [1994] 2 All ER 1.

more closely analogous to a 'primary' victim of the employer's negligence or breach of contract.[655] This is confirmed by the more recent decision of the House of Lords in *Waters v Commissioner of Police of the Metropolis*,[656] in which it was held that the employer could be liable for exposing the claimant to psychological harm as a result of a failure to treat seriously a claim that she had been sexually assaulted by a fellow officer, and by preventing her from being victimised and harassed by other police officers once she made her initial complaint.

Statutory duties

4.96   The imposition on employers of specific statutory duties to ensure a safe place of work and system of working can be traced back to the earliest Factory Acts of the nineteenth century; as industrialisation developed, successive waves of legislation extended the scope of employers' duties without, however, achieving a general framework of health and safety for all workplaces.[657] Instead, regulation developed in a piecemeal fashion, in response to the needs or demands of particular industries. These measures were eventually collected in a series of separate Acts governing factories, mines and quarries and offices, shops and railway premises.[658] The Factories Act 1961, which consolidated earlier measures, laid down in Part I a series of provisions governing cleanliness, overcrowding, temperature, ventilation, lighting, drainage and sanitation. Part II of the Act was concerned with safety and contained measures relating to, *inter alia*, the construction, fencing and maintenance of machinery; the maintenance of floors, passages, stairs and means of access; the supply of drinking water and washing facilities; and seating facilities. Many of these provisions were regarded, through a process of judicial inference, as giving rise to civil actions for breach of statutory duty.[659]

Unlike the regulation of working time, which was largely confined to women workers and young workers, health and safety legislation was applied also to adult males, although many regulations set differential standards of protection for male and female employees. Women workers were, on the whole, subject to lower limits of exposure to dangerous substances and were excluded from a wide range of jobs which were considered at the time to pose a particular risk to the female physiognomy and reproductive capacity. The scientific basis for most of these distinctions now appears to have been dubious, since many of the substances in question (such as lead and ionising radiation) have been shown to be equally dangerous to men.[660] The vast majority of those regulations which were specific to women were abolished by the Employment Act 1989, as part of the UK's implementation of the EC Directive on Equal Treatment.[661]

---

[655] See Deakin, Johnston and Markesinis, 2008: p 655.

[656] [2000] IRLR 720; see also, on psychiatric harm in the context of the duty of mutual trust and confidence, *Gogay v Hertfordshire County Council* [2000] IRLR 703; *Whiteside v Croydon London Borough Council* [2010] EWHC 320; *Connor v Surrey County Council* [2010] IRLR 521; para 4.105 below. On harassment in the context of statutory health and safety law, see Barrett, 2000; Tolley, 2012: ch H17.

[657] See generally Hutchins and Harrison, 1926.

[658] The Factories Act 1961; the Mines and Quarries Act 1954; and the Offices, Shops and Railway Premises Acts 1963, respectively.

[659] See Deakin, Johnston and Markesinis, 2008: p 377 *et seq*.

[660] See generally Deakin, 1990a

[661] Directive 76/207/EC.

The passage of the Health and Safety at Work Act 1974 marked a change of direction in statutory policy. The Robens report which preceded the Act[662] recommended the enactment of general duties extending to all workplaces and to the self-employed. It also proposed greater encouragement of self-regulation through, amongst other things, the involvement in health and safety issues of workforce representatives. The main achievements of the Act were the imposition of a general statutory duty of care upon all employers; the extension of this duty in some instances to the self-employed; the establishment of a unified inspection and enforcement process, under the Health and Safety Executive; the setting-up of a tripartite Health and Safety Commission (now merged with the HSE) with the responsibility for drafting regulations and Codes of Practice and overseeing the work of the inspectorate; and the making of provision for the election of safety representatives in workplaces with recognised trade unions, with various responsibilities including membership of joint labour-management safety committees.[663]

The aims of the Act include 'securing the health, safety and welfare of persons at work', protecting other persons against risks to health and safety arising from work-related activities, and controlling the use of dangerous substances.[664] The category of 'persons at work' includes employees and the self-employed.[665] The Act imposes a duty on 'every employer to ensure, so far as is reasonably practicable, the health, safety and welfare at work of all his employees'.[666] More specifically, the employer must ensure so far as reasonably practicable that safe plant and systems of work are maintained; arrangements are made for the minimisation of risks from dangerous articles and substances; information, instruction, training and supervision in health and safety matters are made available to employees; the workplace and the means of access to it are kept in a safe condition; and a 'working environment' for employees is provided which is 'safe, without risks to health, and adequate as regards facilities and arrangements for [employees'] welfare at work'.[667] The employer must also prepare a written health and safety policy.[668]

In addition, both employers and the self-employed must ensure so far as reasonably practicable that persons other than employees who may be affected by their activities are not thereby exposed to risks to their health and safety;[669] similar duties with regard to non-employees are also imposed on persons in control of non-domestic premises.[670] Employees themselves must take reasonable care for their own health and safety and, in respect to duties imposed on their employer, must 'co-operate with him so far as is necessary to enable that duty or requirement to be performed or complied with'.[671]

---

[662] *Report of the Committee on Health and Safety at Work*, Cmnd 5034, 1972.

[663] On the 1974 Act in general, see P James and D Lewis, 1986, and on the current provisions relating to safety representatives and safety committees (which were amended in 1996), see paras 9.46–9.47 below.

[664] HSWA 1974, s 1(1).

[665] HSWA 1974, s 51.

[666] HSWA 1974, s 2(1). In Case C-127/05 *Commission v United Kingdom* [2007] IRLR 720 the ECJ held that, in relation to s 2(1), there was no requirement in Art 5 of Directive 89/391 to introduce a strict liability regime into UK health and safety law.

[667] HSWA 1974, s 2(2).

[668] HSWA 1974, s 2(3).

[669] HSWA 1974, s 3; see *R v Associated Octel Co Ltd* [1997] IRLR 123 (discussed by Barrett, 1997); *R v Nelson Group Services (Maintenance) Ltd* [1999] IRLR 646. The Act does not apply to domestic employment, however: HSWA 1974, s 51.

[670] HSWA 1974, s 4. Section 6 imposes duties on manufacturers with regard to articles and substances for use at work.

[671] HSWA 1974, s 7.

The Act provides for enforcement of the duties referred to above by way of powers of inspection (including the use of 'improvement' and 'prohibition' notices) and by criminal sanctions;[672] no civil action by an employee or self-employed person is possible in respect of these general duties.[673] However, the more specific regulations made under the Act are assumed to give rise to a civil action for damages unless the contrary is stated.[674] This provision preserves the civil action for breach of statutory duty in respect of regulations made under the Act which replace earlier provisions made under the Factory Acts and legislation governing mines and non-factory premises.

At the time of its passage it was intended that the 1974 Act would provide a framework for the modernisation and integration of the many industry-specific regulations made under earlier statutes. This process has led to some significant strengthening of regulation, in the area, for example, of the control of dangerous substances.[675]

Protection of the working environment

4.97   While domestic policy was turning towards deregulation in health and safety in the 1980s, a new minimum floor of rights was provided by the EC Framework Directive of 1989 and its 'daughter directives'. The authority for these measures derives from Article 118a of the EC Treaty, which was inserted by the Single European Act of 1986 and is now consolidated in Article 153 TFEU. Prior to this, the Community had adopted only a small number of measures in the field of health and safety: a series of directives concerning safety signs,[676] exposure to certain hazardous agents[677] and exposure to noise at work.[678] Article 118a called on Member States to 'pay particular attention to encouraging improvements, especially in the working environment, as regards the health and safety of workers', and provide for the adoption of directives on the basis of qualified majority voting. The concept of the working environment originated in the Nordic systems of labour law, and as Nielson and Szyszczak explain, refers not simply to health and safety in the traditional sense but more generally to 'the arrangement of the workplace, the physical and socio-psychological conditions under which work is performed, the use of work equipment by workers at work, and the exposure of workers to toxic and other dangerous substances at work'.[679] The notion of the 'working environment' in the TFEU is evidently more extensive than the concept of 'health and safety', to which the Article also refers; however, the precise scope of the Article remains somewhat unclear. It cannot be construed as embracing all aspects of the individual employee's well-being; however, in *United Kingdom v EU Council (Working Time)* the ECJ ruled

---

[672] HSWA 1974, ss 18–42. The criminal sanctions have recently been strengthened by amendments made by the Health and Safety (Offences) Act 2008; see further Barratt, 2009. See also the Corporate Manslaughter and Corporate Homicide Act 2007, discussed by Barratt, 2008.

[673] HSWA 1974, s 47(1).

[674] HSWA 1974, s 47(2).

[675] The principal measure here is the Control of Substances Hazardous to Health Regulations, SI 2002/2677. For a general assessment of the progress made in relation to health and safety practice under the Act of 1974 prior to the implementation of EU law measures on the protection of the working environment, see P James, 1993.

[676] Directive 77/556.

[677] Directives 78/610, 88/1107, 82/605 and 83/477.

[678] Directive 86/188.

[679] Nielsen and Szyszczak, 1997: p 331. See also Hydén, 1992.

that it has a broad scope which, in that case, extended to cover the regulation of working time under Directive 93/104.[680]

The 1989 Framework Directive for the introduction of measures to encourage improvements in the safety and health of workers[681] is intended to provide a generally-applicable set of guidelines and principles for the promotion of health and safety. It does not, however, preclude more specific regulation, being 'without prejudice to more stringent present or future Community provisions',[682] a large number of which have subsequently been adopted. The purposes of the Directive include the economic goal of harmonisation designed to avoid 'competition at the expense of safety and health', but it is also stated that 'the improvement of workers' safety, hygiene and health at work is an objective which should not be "subordinated to purely economic considerations"'.[683] The standards contained in the Directive are minimum levels of protection, upon which Member States may improve.[684]

The Directive applies to 'all sectors of activity, both public and private',[685] and imposes a general duty on employers 'to ensure the safety and health of workers in every aspect related to the work'.[686] The obligations imposed on the employer are effectively six-fold:[687] a duty of awareness, which embraces a duty to be aware of risks, of developments in scientific and technological understanding and an awareness of the capabilities of workers; a duty to ensure safety and health by minimising avoidable risks; a duty to develop a 'coherent overall prevention policy'[688] with regard to risks; a duty to provide health and safety training for the workforce; a duty of information and consultation with regard to health and safety matters;[689] and a duty to maintain the required records and reports to enable national authorities to carry out their responsibilities of monitoring and enforcement. Article 6(2) lists a number of 'general principles of prevention' which employers should observe in implementing health and safety protection: these include the 'principle of substitution',[690] whereby the employer shall '[replace] the dangerous by the non-dangerous or the less dangerous',[691] and the principle of the 'humanisation of work',[692] according to which it must '[adapt] the work to the individual, especially as regards the design of workplaces, the choice of work equipment and the choice of working and production methods, with a view, in particular, to alleviating monotonous work and work at a pre-determined work rate and to reducing their effect on health'.[693] The Directive also imposes a less extensive set of obligations upon workers, who

[680] Case C-84/94 [1996] ECR I-5755; Fitzpatrick, 1997.

[681] Directive 89/391.

[682] Directive 89/391, Preamble, para 15.

[683] Directive 89/391, Preamble, paras 9 and 13 respectively.

[684] Directive 89/391, Preamble, para 2, and Art 1(3); Case C-84/94 *United Kingdom v EU Council (Working Time)* [1996] ECR-I 5755; Case C-2/97 *Società Italiana Petroli SpA v Borsana Srl* [1998] ECR I-8597; Szyszczak, 1999.

[685] Directive 89/391, Art 2(1

[686] Directive 89/391, Art 5(1).

[687] See Neal, 1990.

[688] Directive 89/391, Art 6(2)(g).

[689] Directive 89/391, Art 10. See below, para 9.46.

[690] Nielsen and Szyszczak, 1997: p 340.

[691] Directive 89/391, Art 6(2)(f). For an application of this principle in the context of one of the daughter directives, see Case C-2/97 *Società Italiana Petroli SpA v Borsana Srl* [1998] ECR I-8597, discussed by Szyszczak, 1999.

[692] See above, in the context of working time, at para 4.77.

[693] Directive 89/391, Art 6(2)(d).

must 'take care as far as possible' for their own safety and health in accordance with their training and with the employer's instructions.[694]

The Framework Directive, while similar in its aims to the Health and Safety at Work Act 1974, is at the same time more specific in terms of the detailed obligations it imposes on employers. Accordingly, new regulations were thought necessary in order to transpose the Directive into UK law: these are the Management of Health and Safety at Work Regulations 1999.[695]

The MHSW Regulations, breach of which cannot give rise to a civil cause of action by persons other than the employer and persons in its employment[696] establish a number of additional requirements for employers. In particular, both employers and the self-employed must undertake risk assessments in relation to their employees and to other persons who may be exposed to health and safety risks by their activities. Employers must also put in place health and safety arrangements 'for the effective planning, organisation, control, monitoring and review of the preventive and protective measures' which they must undertake. Further obligations refer to health surveillance, health and safety assistance, procedures for dealing with serious and imminent danger and danger areas within the workplace, the provision of information to employees, and co-operation between employers sharing the same workplace.

The MSHW Regulations also implement certain provisions of one of the daughter directives, namely Directive 91/383 on the safety and health of temporary workers.[697] These impose obligations on employers and self-employed persons to ensure the provision of health and safety information to employees of another employer who are temporarily working in their undertaking, and to their own fixed-term contract employees.[698]

In the period since the adoption of the Framework Directive, numerous 'daughter directives' have been agreed, and in some cases their provisions have already been transposed in UK law by regulations which are gradually replacing the parallel provisions of the Factories Act 1961 and other pre-1974 legislation. These measures fall roughly into three categories: the protection of health and safety in the workplace; protection against exposure to certain substances and agents; and industry-specific regulations. Detailed accounts of their provisions may be found in specialist works on health and safety.[699]

DUTIES OF OBEDIENCE, CO-OPERATION AND CARE

4.98   The employee's obligations of obedience, co-operation and care take the form of terms implied into the contract by the common law. The potential scope of these duties is very wide, but in practice they will tend to be limited by the express terms of the contract and by those implied from custom and practice or collective agreements. The principal role of the common law is therefore to fill in the gaps. This would once have been largely a question of granting

---

[694] Directive 89/391, Art 13.

[695] SI 1999/3242, replacing SI 1992/2051. See P James 1993: p 25 *et seq* for discussion of the 1992 Regulations.

[696] SI 1999/3542, reg 22, as substituted by SI 2006/438.

[697] See above, para 3.51.

[698] Arts 10 and 13 respectively. Oddly, different requirements are imposed for these two groups: for discussion, see P James, 1993: pp 27–29.

[699] See, Tolley, 2012; Ford *et al* 2010.

legal expression to managerial prerogative, but the duty of co-operation, in particular, is now acknowledged to be reciprocal in nature, and to impose certain obligations upon the employer. This development in the law has come to be associated with the concept of the implied term of mutual trust and confidence.

The duty of obedience

4.99   The employee owes an implied obligation to obey lawful and reasonable orders of the employer: this is a 'condition essential to the contract of service'.[700] What is reasonable depends in part upon the substance of the other terms of the contract, and the employee's job title and description, rank and professional status may also be relevant factors. The law has moved on a certain way from *Turner v Mason* (1845),[701] in which the Court of Exchequer Chamber found that a domestic servant had been lawfully dismissed for paying a visit to her mother, who was seriously ill, against her master's wishes. The mother's illness was thought not 'sufficient to justify her in disobedience to his order; there is not any imperative obligation on a daughter to visit her mother under such circumstances, although it may be unkind and uncharitable not to permit her'.[702] The Court considered that only an unlawful order could be deliberately disobeyed.[703] This near-blanket duty of obedience may have been seen as an aspect of the status of a servant, at a time when the law drew a distinction between the categories of 'servant' and 'employee'. In respect of the latter, even nineteenth-century courts recognised contractual limits to the employer's power: as far as an employee hired to buy lace was concerned, 'if he was hired as a buyer, he was not bound to perform services not properly appertaining to that character'.[704] Similarly, isolated acts of disobedience or neglect would not necessarily justify the dismissal of a manager or a journalist.[705]

Today this approach is more generally applied to all employees: 'one act of disobedience can justify dismissal only if it is of a nature which goes to show (in effect) that the servant is repudiating the contract'.[706] But something of old attitudes still remains. In 1978 the EAT decided that an employer was entitled to dismiss an employee who had taken time off work without permission to look after her young son who had just been diagnosed as suffering from diabetes and was having difficulty administering the necessary treatment of insulin.[707]

An employee is always entitled to disobey an unlawful order.[708] In the context of threats to health and safety, the courts have accepted that this would include an order 'to direct a servant to continue where she is in danger of violence to her person, or of infectious disease',[709] but for

---

[700] *Laws v London Chronicle (Indicator Newspapers) Ltd* [1959] 1 WLR 698, 700 (Lord Evershed MR).

[701] 14 M & W 112.

[702] 14 M & W 112, 117 (Parke B).

[703] 14 M & W 112 (Rolfe B).

[704] *Price v Mouat* (1862) 11 CBNS 508 (Erle CJ).

[705] *Cussons v Skinner* (1843) 11 M & W 161 and *Edwards v Levy* (1860) 2 F & F 94, respectively.

[706] *Laws v London Chronicle (Indicator Newspapers) Ltd* [1959] 1 WLR 698, 701 (Lord Evershed MR).

[707] *Warner v Barbers Stores Ltd* [1978] IRLR 109. The employer's power to give orders in this type of situation would now be subject to the statutory right of an employee to take time off for urgent family-related reasons. See below, para 6.121.

[708] *Gregory v Ford* [1951] 1 All ER 121; *Lister v Romford Ice and Cold Storage Co Ltd* [1957] AC 555 (Viscount Simonds); *Morrish v Henlys (Folkestone) Ltd* [1973] ICR 482.

[709] *Turner v Mason* (1845) 14 M & W 112.

this purpose the Privy Council held in a decision now nearly a century old that there must be 'an immediately threatening danger by violence or disease to the person of the servant before an order to remain in the zone of danger can be held to be unlawful'.[710] It is not clear why the danger should be 'immediately threatening', and this decision may no longer be particularly persuasive. In principle, there would seem to be no reason why, if very long working hours could be shown to be likely to induce a stress-related illness, the employee should not be entitled to disobey an order to carry on working beyond the point of danger, even if the impact upon their health was cumulative rather than immediate.[711] In this context, the courts have accepted that statutory health and safety standards may circumscribe the employer's common law right to give orders which may have the effect of endangering the employee. Hence in *Barber v RJB Mining Ltd*[712] the High Court issued a declaration to the effect that employees protected by the statutory right not to work more than 48 hours per week over a specified reference period were entitled to refuse to work excessive hours which would have taken their working time over the threshold. It is also arguable that the duty of obedience is now circumscribed by Convention rights under HRA 1998; hence, if the employer issued an instruction which amounted to breach of such a right, such as the right to respect for private life under ECHR Article 8, special justification might be needed.

While *Barber* suggests that an employee is entitled to refuse to obey an unlawful order, in the sense of an order which would result in the breach of a statutory obligation imposed upon the employer for the protection of the employee, *Macari v Celtic Football and Athletic Co Ltd*[713] rules that this principle does not extend so far as to allow the employee to withhold performance under the contract of employment in circumstances where the employer is acting in breach of the *Malik* term of mutual trust and confidence. Although there are dicta suggesting that an employee might be entitled to refuse to obey a *specific* order made in bad faith by his or her employer[714] – in the sense of an order which would have the effect of harming the employee in a significant way – the Court ruled that an employee who refuses to obey an order which is, in itself, both reasonable and lawful, thereby commits a repudiatory breach of contract, even if the employer is in breach of the duty to maintain trust and confidence in some *other* respect.

The effect of *Macari* is that if the employer commits a generalised breach of the implied duty of co-operation, the employee has the option of terminating the contract and claiming appropriate relief, or of maintaining the contract. If the latter route is chosen, the employee is not entitled to withhold all performance from the employer. The right to withhold performance arises only in respect of those obligations of the employee which correspond to the employer's own breach. Thus it is only if the employer issues a specific order which would result in unlawfulness or would significantly harm the employee that the employee has the right to maintain the employment relationship while also refusing to obey the order in question. However, the reasoning here is not entirely satisfactory, since it turns on regarding the contract in *Macari* as 'not a mutual contract but

---

[710] *Bouzourou v Ottoman Bank* [1930] AC 271, 276; cf *Ottoman Bank v Chakarion* [1930] AC 277.

[711] The issue of long working hours was considered by the Court of Appeal in *Johnstone v Bloomsbury Health Authority* [1992] 1 QB 333. See also the discussion of this issue in the context of ERA 1996, s 100, discussed below at para 5.100.

[712] [1999] IRLR 308; A Edwards, 2000. Note, however, that *Barber* was not followed in *Commissioners of Inland Revenue v Ainsworth* [2005] IRLR 465.

[713] [1999] IRLR 787.

[714] See [1999] IRLR 787, 798 (Lord Caplan); however, this suggestion was not accepted by the Lord President ([1999] IRLR 787, 791–792).

a series of independent obligations.[715] The better approach is to regard a contract of employment as a mutual one under which both parties are obliged to perform their side of the agreement as the condition of being able to enforce the other's performance. If the employer is in breach of the mutual trust term to the extent of having repudiated the contract, it is arguable that it is not entitled to enforce the equally fundamental duty of obedience on the part of the employee.[716]

The implied term of mutual trust and confidence

4.100   The term 'duty of co-operation' is well established in the common law of contracts as referring to an obligation which is implied into a contract to require each party to avoid taking steps to obstruct the other's performance.[717] In the context of the contract of employment, it has been transformed into an affirmative obligation on the part of the employee to use his or her best efforts to ensure the efficient running of the enterprise. More recently, it has become associated with an obligation on the part of both parties not to break the 'mutual trust and confidence' on which the relationship rests.

(i) Obligations of the employee

4.101   The idea of the employee's affirmative duty of co-operation is illustrated by *Secretary of State for Employment v ASLEF (No 2)*.[718] The issue was whether limited industrial action taken by the rail unions involved employees in committing breaches of contract. The unions argued that the employees were performing the contract by sticking to the letter of the work rules book issued by the employer (examples included guards ensuring that a train was safe to leave the station by opening and then closing all its carriage doors, a process which ensured a substantial delay in the train's departure). In the Court of Appeal it was held that breaches of contract had taken place. Lord Denning MR argued that the lack of good faith with which performance was carried out rendered it a breach of contract, and added that '[t]here are many branches of our law when an act which would otherwise be lawful is rendered unlawful by the motive or object with which it is done. So here it is the wilful disruption which is the breach'.[719] Roskill LJ, by contrast, thought that 'questions of intent are usually irrelevant in determining whether or not there has been a breach of contract'. Instead Roskill LJ referred to the presence of an implied term that the employee would not seek so to interpret and act upon the rules as to disrupt the railway system; Buckley LJ spoke of an implied term 'that within the terms of the contract the employee must serve the employer faithfully with a view to promoting those commercial interests for which he is employed'.[720]

---

[715] *Aberdeen City Council v McNeill* [2010] IRLR 374, at [90] (Lady Smith).
[716] Thus in *Aberdeen City Council v McNeill* [2010] IRLR 374 the employee was unable to enforce the duty of mutual trust and confidence against the employer where he had committed an antecedent breach of the same term.
[717] *Shirlaw v Southern Foundries (1926) Ltd* [1939] 2 KB 206.
[718] [1972] 2 QB 455; Napier, 1972.
[719] [1972] 2 QB 455, 492.
[720] [1972] 2 QB 455, 506, 508, 498, respectively.

A crucial step in *ASLEF (No 2)* was, as we have seen,[721] the classification of the rule book: it did not establish contract terms, but simply reflected managerial prerogative. Although this creates a space within which the employer can dispense with contractual consent in setting or altering the form in which performance shall take place, the Court was also at pains to point out that this power is limited by the express contract terms: '[i]t does not mean that the employer could require a man to do anything which lay outside his obligations under the contract, such as to work excess hours of work or to work an unsafe system of work'.[722] In *Fish v Dresdner Kleinwort Ltd*[723] it was held, in similar terms, that a clear contractual right to a bonus payment could not be defeated by reference to the employee's duty to act in the best interests of the employer, while in *Smith v London Metropolitan University* [724] it was held that the implied term of mutual trust and confidence did not entitle the employer to require a university lecturer to teach courses that she was not qualified or contracted to teach.

4.102   Nonetheless, the gap-filling function of the implied terms will grow in importance if the express terms are narrowly construed. In *Sim v Rotherham Metropolitan Borough Council*[725] it was held that schoolteachers who withdrew co-operation in the course of industrial action by refusing to cover for sick and absent colleagues were acting in breach of contract. Their terms and conditions of employment were laid down in a national-level collective agreement whose terms were embodied in the 'Burgundy Book'. However, Scott J held 'these provisions, although in many respects detailed and comprehensive, do not attempt to detail the obligations imposed on teachers by their respective contracts of service'. The contracts were 'silent as to the extent of the teachers' obligations as teachers'; in this case it was appropriate for the court to imply a term on the basis of professional standards 'set both by the profession itself and by public expectation'.[726]

4.103   Similarly, in *Ticehurst v British Telecommunications plc*[727] a managerial employee was held to be subject to the duty of co-operation to exercise 'her judgement and discretion in giving instructions to others and in supervising their work ... faithfully in the interests of the employers'. Her failure to sign an undertaking to work 'normally' was held to amount to a breach of contract: a breach is committed 'when the employee does an act, or omits to do an act, which it would be within her contract and the discretion allowed to her not to do, or to do, as the case may be, and the employee so acts or omits to do the act, not in honest exercise of choice or discretion for the faithful performance of her work but in order to disrupt the employer's business'. The most significant aspect of this case is that the only source of the breach was the employee's refusal to sign the undertaking. The decision effectively adopts Lord Denning's view in *ASLEF (No 2)* that motive can, *in itself,* transform an act from being the lawful exercise of a right into being a breach

---

[721] See paras 4.3 and 4.23 above.
[722] [1972] 2 QB 455, 498 (Buckley LJ). See also *Burgess v Stevedoring Services Ltd* [2002] IRLR 810, discussed para 11.66 below.
[723] [2009] IRLR 1035.
[724] [2011] IRLR 884.
[725] [1987] Ch 216.
[726] [1987] Ch 216, 244–245, 252.
[727] [1992] IRLR 219, 225.

of contract. This is contrary to a 'general principle of English law that the exercise of a right ... will not be rendered unlawful only because of the bad motives of the person exercising that right'.[728]

4.104   A decision which also imposes an extensive affirmative obligation on the employee is *Cresswell v Board of Inland Revenue*,[729] in which Walton J held that employees were acting in breach of contract by refusing to co-operate with the introduction of new, computer-based technology: 'an employee is expected to adapt himself to new methods and techniques introduced in the course of his employment', subject only to an obligation on the part of the employer to offer retraining where 'esoteric skills' were involved which it would not otherwise be reasonable to expect the employee to acquire.[730] If this decision were widely followed, it might be used to justify unilateral alteration of job gradings and other forms of job classification. If the integrity of the contract terms is not to be seriously eroded by this route, Walton J's dictum should perhaps be qualified by the observation that the implied duty of co-operation cannot, in itself, be invoked to override express terms or those derived from collective agreements. In *Bull v Nottinghamshire and City of Nottingham Fire and Rescue Authority*[731] the Court of Appeal distinguished *Cresswell* in holding that firefighters were not contractually obliged to respond to emergency calls from members of the public reporting potentially life-threatening medical conditions where they could respond more promptly than an ambulance crew, a practice known as 'co-responding'. This was not 'a new way of doing firefighting ... it was not firefighting at all as the contract understood it'.[732]

(ii) Obligations of the employer: exploring the implied term of mutual trust and confidence

4.105   The imposition of a general duty of co-operation upon the employer is a comparatively recent development.[733] Its evolution, according to Lord Steyn in *Malik v BCCI SA*,[734] 'is part of the history of the development of employment law in this century. The notion of a "master and servant" relationship became obsolete'. In particular, this shift in the common law was prompted by the development of the unfair dismissal jurisdiction and above all by the statutory concept of 'constructive dismissal', according to which an employee (with the requisite period of qualifying service) has the right to quit and claim unfair dismissal in response to a repudiatory breach of contract by the employer.[735] This statutory jurisdiction greatly increased the frequency with which questions of employer breach of contract came before courts and employment tribunals. An employer who permits an employee to be the victim of persistent verbal abuse[736] or of sexual

---

[728] Hepple, 1981b: p 97, citing Lord Davey in *Allen v Flood* [1898] AC 1, 173.

[729] [1984] IRLR 190.

[730] [1984] IRLR 190, 195.

[731] [2007] ICR 1631.

[732] Above, Buxton LJ at [25].

[733] For overviews of this development, see Brodie, 2001b; Freedland, 2003: pp 154–170.

[734] [1997] IRLR 462, 468.

[735] ERA 1996, s 95(1)(c); *Western Excavating (ECC) Ltd v Sharp* [1978] QB 761, reaffirmed, on this point, in *Bournemouth University Higher Education Corp v Buckland* [2010] IRLR 445. See para 5.69 *et seq* below

[736] *Palmanor Ltd v Cedron* [1978] ICR 1008. For more recent discussion see *Horkulak v Cantor Fitzgerald International* [2003] IRLR 756.

harassment[737] will on the face of it have committed a breach of the duty of mutual trust and confidence; other examples are failing to investigate a legitimate complaint about health and safety,[738] making an unsubstantiated allegation of theft,[739] unjustifiably insisting that the employee should undergo psychiatric examination,[740] providing a 'misleading and potentially destructive reference' to a prospective employer,[741] suspending the employee as an automatic response to unsubstantiated allegations of child abuse,[742] failing to take steps to protect the employee, a schoolteacher, from harassment by parents,[743] undertaking, in a case where the employer and employee had entered into a 'forward contract' in anticipation of the commencement of employment, an illegal and dishonest campaign designed to drive his current employer out of business,[744] and carrying out a restructuring which had the effect of depriving the employee of a chance to earn a contracted-for bonus.[745] The courts have gone so far as to suggest that an employer who 'arbitrarily, capriciously and inequitably' singled out an employee for an inferior pay rise to that granted to her colleagues might thereby have committed a repudiatory breach of contract.[746] At the same time, they have also held that employers have *not* been under implied duties to offer an annual pay rise, or, in general, to treat comparable employees equally for the purpose of pay increases.[747] A further development in this unfolding jurisprudence is the passage of HRA 1998, which raises the possibility (as yet untested) that conduct of the employer which amounts to a breach of a Convention right might be classified as a breach of the duty of co-operation.[748]

The implied term has been described as an obligation that the employer shall not 'without reasonable and proper cause, conduct [itself] in a manner calculated to or likely to destroy or seriously damage the relationship of confidence and trust between employer and employee'.[749] In its most far-reaching form, this development could be said to mark an extension of the duty of co-operation 'from the restricted obligation not to prevent or hinder the occurrence of an express condition upon which performance of the contract depends to a positive obligation to take all

[737] *Wood v Freeloader Ltd* [1977] IRLR 455.

[738] *British Aircraft Corpn v Austin* [1978] IRLR 332.

[739] *Robinson v Crompton Parkinson Ltd* [1978] ICR 401.

[740] *Bliss v South-East Thames Regional Health Authority* [1985] IRLR 308.

[741] *TSB Bank v Harris* [2000] IRLR 157.

[742] *Gogay v Hertfordshire County Council* [2000] IRLR 703.

[743] *Connor v Surrey CC* [2010] IRLR 521.

[744] *Tullett Prebon plc v BGC Brokers LP* [2011] IRLR 420. The effect of the employer's breach was that the employees in question did not commit repudiatory breaches in terminating their contracts and refusing to commence employment with it.

[745] *Takacs v Barclays Services Jersey Ltd* [2006] IRLR 877.

[746] *FC Gardner Ltd v Beresford* [1978] IRLR 63; to similar effect is *Transco v O'Brien* [2002] IRLR 444 in which the Court of Appeal held that the arbitrary refusal to offer the claimant, alone of a group of employees, a new contract of employment with enhanced redundancy terms was a breach of the duty of mutual trust and confidence.

[747] *Bridgen v Lancashire County Council* [1987] IRLR 58; *Murco Petroleum Ltd v Forge* [1987] IRLR 50.

[748] See Hepple, 1998b; see also Brodie, 2008: pp 334-335. Although it would seem highly likely that employer conduct which amounted to an infringement of an employee's Convention right under HRA 1998 would also be a breach of the implied term of mutual trust and confidence and also a repudiatory breach of contract, this is not so with regard to every breach of a statutory provision relating to employment. For example, in *Amnesty International v Ahmed* [2009] IRLR 884, it was held that a finding of unlawful direct discrimination on racial grounds did not give rise to a repudiatory breach of the term of mutual trust.

[749] *Woods v WM Car Services (Peterborough) Ltd* [1981] IRLR 347, 350 (Browne-Wilkinson J), approved in *Lewis v Motorworld Garages Ltd* [1985] IRLR 465; *Imperial Group Pension Trust Ltd v Imperial Tobacco Ltd* [1991] IRLR 66; *Malik v BCCI SA* [1997] IRLR 462, 468 (Lord Steyn); *Brown v Merchant Ferries Ltd* [1998] IRLR 682 (NICA adopting Lord Steyn's test); *Baldwin v Brighton & Hove City Council* [2007] IRLR 232 (clarifying the objective nature of the test).

those steps which are necessary to achieve the purposes of the employment relationship ... this broader, functional view – which rests essentially on a tribunal's view of "good industrial relations practice" – embraces not only the material conditions of employment such as pay and safety, but also those psychological conditions which are essential to the performance by an employee of his part of the bargain'.[750] This seems to be the most appropriate basis for the decision of the EAT in *WA Goold (Pearmak) Ltd v McConnell*,[751] to the effect that a contract of employment contained an implied term requiring the employer to provide a grievance procedure.

4.106   Likewise, in *Malik v BCCI SA*,[752] Lord Steyn gave a broad interpretation to the meaning of the term by holding that in order for there to be a breach, it was necessary neither for the employer's conduct to be directed at the employee as an individual, nor for the employee to have been aware of the breach while it was taking place. This broad interpretation was important in the context of the *Malik* case, which arose out a claim for damages based on the loss of reputation caused by employees' unwitting association with a series of frauds perpetrated by the employer.[753] The post-*Malik* case law has sought to clarify where the limits to the concept may lie.[754] In *BCCI v Ali*[755] and *University of Nottingham v Eyett*[756] the courts substantially qualified the idea that the employer has an affirmative obligation to provide information to the employee which is relevant to the continuing relationship of employment. In *Ali*, this meant that the employer was not in breach of contract for failing to inform its employees about fraudulent activities being undertaken by management; in *Eyett*, the employer was under no obligation to advise and inform employees of the most financially advantageous way in which complex pension rights could be exercised. At one level these decisions seem to be incompatible with the idea of mutual trust and confidence as the core obligation at the heart of the employment relationship. However, they also involve an acknowledgement of the contractual autonomy of the parties. One potentially negative consequence of an over-extensive duty of mutual trust and confidence would be the imposition upon *employees* of a wide-ranging duty to provide information to the employer; the reciprocal nature of the *Malik* term means that decisions in these cases cut both ways.[757]

4.107   It is also the case that the employer's obligations may be limited by the express terms of the contract, just as the employee's are. This makes it difficult to rely on the duty of co-operation as a general guarantor of employee protection: its content is not fixed, but will differ from one case to the next depending on how the express terms are framed. Nevertheless, there is authority to

---

[750] Hepple, 1981b: p 135.

[751] [1995] IRLR 516; see also *Waltons & Morse v Dorrington* [1997] IRLR 488.

[752] [1997] IRLR 462, 468–469; see Brodie, 1996, 1998a, 1998b, 1999a, 1999b, 2001a, 2001b; Lindsay, 2001.

[753] On the admissibility of the damages claim, see para 5.27 below.

[754] In addition to the cases cited in the text, see also *Johnson v Unisys Ltd* [2001] IRLR 279 in which the House of Lords held that the obligation of mutual trust and confidence had limited application in the area of termination of employment by the employer, and its later decision, clarifying *Johnson*, in *Eastwood v Magnox Electric/McCabe v Cornwall County Council* [2004] IRLR 733. These cases are discussed in the context of wrongful dismissal at paras 5.43–5.44 below.

[755] [1999] IRLR 226.

[756] [1999] IRLR 87. See also *Ibekwe v London General Transport Services Ltd* [2003] IRLR 697.

[757] An employee is not obliged at common law to disclose to the employer that he or she has earned sums from third parties from outside employment (*Bell v Lever Bros Ltd* [1932] AC 161; *Nottingham University v Fishel* [2000] IRLR 471, 480–481; *Helmet Integrated Systems Ltd v Tunnard* [2007] IRLR 126) except to the extent that the employee is also a fiduciary (*Neary v Dean of Westminster* [1999] IRLR 288); see below, para 4.112.

suggest that express contractual powers of the employer may be limited by a requirement that these powers be exercised 'in good faith' (again, in parallel with the notion that employees must exercise discretionary contract powers so as not to defeat the interests of the business). In *Imperial Group Pension Trust Ltd v Imperial Tobacco Ltd*[758] the employer had the power, under the rules of an occupational pension scheme, to refuse consent to certain increases in pension benefits proposed by the trustees of the fund. Browne-Wilkinson VC held that the scheme had to be construed against the background of the contract of employment and the implied 'obligation of good faith' which it contained. The employer's powers under the trust deed had to be exercised in accordance with this implied obligation. This did not mean that the employer had to act 'reasonably', but it was required to exercise its rights with regard to the efficient running of the scheme and to consider requests for increases on their merits; it could not give a blanket refusal to consider increases, nor could it refuse them in order to persuade employees to give up their rights under that scheme and transfer to a different one.

But a difficulty here is in knowing when a contractual right or power should be construed so as to be unqualified, and when it is subject to the requirement of good faith. As part of this approach some problematic distinctions have had to be drawn between, for example, an employee's obligation to work basic weekly hours, which was said in *Johnstone v Bloomsbury Health Authority*[759] to be unqualified, and a contractual obligation to work overtime, which was said in the same case to be subject to the implied obligation of the employer not to undermine the relationship by subjecting the employee to excessive hours. In *Hussman Manufacturing Ltd v Weir*[760] the EAT expressed 'very great reservations as to the extent to which [the implied duty of trust and confidence] can bear upon management decisions legitimately taken in terms of agreements between the employer and the employees'.

In principle, it is clear that the *Malik* term, as an implied obligation, can be excluded by an express term which is sufficiently clearly and precisely expressed. The 'default'[761] nature of the *Malik* term, however, does not mean that it has no practical effect. The onus is clearly on the employer to formulate an express term which is capable of overriding the implied obligation. The very imprecision of the *Malik* term works in the employee's favour here; drafting a watertight exclusion may not always be straightforward.

Mutual obligations of care

4.108   The employee impliedly contracts to use the normal degree of skill and care in the performance of his or her work, and will be liable in damages for breach of contract for loss caused to the employer by virtue of his or her negligence. The employer is not obliged by the contract of employment to take out insurance to cover this loss nor to cover the employee against possible liability to third parties. These principles follow from the controversial decision of the House of

---

[758] [1991] IRLR 66. See also *Clark v BET plc* [1997] IRLR 348, discussed below, para 5.22 and *Mallone v BPB Industries Ltd* [2002] IRLR 452.

[759] [1992] QB 333 (Browne-Wilkinson VC). See above, para 4.7.

[760] [1998] IRLR 288, 290; see *Ali v Christian Salveson Food Services Ltd* [1997] IRLR 17; *Hill v General Accident Fire and Life Assurance Corpn plc* [1998] IRLR 641; *Reda v Flag Ltd* [2002] IRLR 747.

[761] See [1997] IRLR 462, 468 (Lord Steyn).

Lords in *Lister v Romford Ice & Cold Storage Co Ltd.*[762] The respondent caused the injury of a fellow worker, who happened to be his father, by his negligent driving, and the employer paid damages to the father on the basis of its vicarious liability for the respondent's negligence. It then sued the respondent for damages for breach of the implied contractual duty to exercise care and skill in the course of employment (the action was brought in the employer's name by its insurers, exercising their rights of subrogation). The action succeeded and appeals to the Court of Appeal and House of Lords were rejected. The House unanimously found that there had been a breach of contract by the employee, but a bare majority held against the implication of a term requiring the employer to indemnify the employee against third party or similar claims. According to Viscount Simonds, such a term could not be formulated with the 'necessary precision'.

Following *Lister*, insurers have observed a practice of not taking up rights of subrogation against employees in this type of situation, but this practice rests upon a 'gentlemen's agreement' and not upon a legally-binding waiver of rights. Aside from its implications from the point of view of insurance,[763] *Lister* is of considerable importance for the employment relationship. An employee may face a claim for a substantial sum either from his or her employer or from a third party. Even if such claims are not often pursued by reason of an employee's limited resources, deductions from wages to reflect employers' losses are common. The relevant duty is not just imposed on highly-skilled employees: 'even in so-called unskilled operations an exercise of care is necessary to the proper performance of duty'.[764]

Since *Lister* was decided, the notion of the employer's duty to maintain the 'trust and confidence' of the employee has been greatly extended,[765] and an argument can be made that, on this basis, an employer is under a responsibility to indemnify the employee against third party claims.[766] Otherwise, an employee who committed an isolated act of negligence could end up facing personal bankruptcy. It is difficult to see how this could be compatible with the employer's obligation to 'take all those steps which are necessary to achieve the purposes of the employment relationship'.[767]

More recent decisions have indeed taken a broader view of the employer's responsibilities for the economic welfare of the employee.[768] In *Scally v Southern Health and Social Services Board*[769] an employer was found to have acted in breach of contract by failing to bring information to employees' attention concerning the exercise of options under their occupational pension scheme, and in *Spring v Guardian Assurance plc*[770] the House of Lords held that an employer owed a duty to

---

[762] [1957] AC 555. For a more recent decision stressing the need to ensure, in the employment context, that the substance of the employer's duty of care in tort and that of the employer's implied obligation to maintain trust and confidence largely coincide, see *Outram v Academy Plastics Ltd* [2000] IRLR 499.

[763] See *Morris v Ford Motor Co Ltd* [1973] QB 792; Deakin, Johnston and Markesinis, 2008: pp 693–695.

[764] *Lister v Romford Ice and Cold Storage Co Ltd* [1957] AC 555, 573 (Viscount Simonds).

[765] See above, paras 4.105-4.107.

[766] It may also be argued that the employer has such a responsibility if it was under a separate statutory duty to take out liability insurance in respect of such claims, on the authority of *Gregory v Ford* [1951] 1 All ER 121; or that if the employer is insured against the relevant loss or liability, it cannot take action against the employee because it suffers no loss (Hepple, 1981b: p 140), although this would not prevent the insurance company bringing an action by way of subrogation.

[767] Hepple, 1981b: p 135. Statute (the Employers' Liability (Compulsory Insurance) Act 1969) imposes a duty on an employer to carry liability insurance to cover claims by third parties against itself, not against its employees.

[768] See Freedland, 2003: pp 140–154 for discussion of this case law.

[769] [1992] 1 AC 294; however, this decision must be read in the light of later decisions limiting the employer's obligation to provide such information (see above, para 4.106).

[770] [1994] 3 All ER 129.

take due care when writing a reference in respect of former or present employees, the duty being owed to the employee both in tort and by way of an implied term in the contract of employment. According to Lord Woolf in *Spring*,[771] the principle in that case and in *Scally* 'recognises that, just as in the earlier authorities the courts were prepared to imply by necessary implication a term imposing a duty on an employer to exercise due care for the physical well being of his employees, so in the appropriate circumstances would the court imply a like duty as to his economic well-being'. In *Scally* the information in question could not easily have been discovered by the employees, whereas the employer could have disclosed it at little cost; in *Spring*, it was recognised that 'it must often be very difficult for an employee to obtain fresh employment without the benefit of a reference from his present or a previous employer ... it is plain that the employee relies on him to exercise due skill and care in the preparation of the reference before making it available to the third party'.[772] The scope of the employer's obligation to provide a reference has been clarified in subsequent case law, the essence of which is that the reference must be 'true, accurate and fair' in the sense of not giving a misleading overall impression through the unfairly selective use of information or the misleading use of information which is in itself accurate; however, there is no obligation upon the employer to report all material aspects of the employee's work record.[773]

Spring and *Scally* might be thought to have opened the way to an extension of the employer's responsibility to have regard for the economic well being of the employee. However, in subsequent judgments the courts have resisted the imposition of a general duty of care in tort with regard to economic interests, and have also narrowly construed the parallel contractual obligation which arises out of the duty of mutual trust and confidence.[774] In particular, the post-*Scally* case law suggests that an employer will only rarely come under an implied duty to bring information about pension scheme arrangements to the attention of the employee.[775] By contrast, an *express* undertaking by an employer to provide information to an employee about pension or other benefits in the context of a transfer of undertaking or similar corporate reorganisation is highly likely to give rise to a duty of care.[776]

Employee mobility

4.109   Contracts of employment frequently contain clauses under which the employer reserves the power to transfer the employee to another place of work or to work of a different kind within the organisation. There is no power at common law to limit or strike down an express mobility or flexibility clause of this kind on the grounds of 'unreasonableness'; instead the court must give priority to the express term over any term which it might have implied in the same

---

[771] [1994] 3 All ER 129, 178.

[772] [1994] 3 All ER 129, 146 (Lord Goff).

[773] See *Bartholomew v London Borough of Hackney* [1999] IRLR 246; *Kidd v Axa Equity & Law Life Assurance Society Ltd* [2000] IRLR 301; *TSB Bank v Harris* [2000] IRLR 157; *Cox v Sun Alliance Ltd* [2001] IRLR 448; *Jackson v Liverpool City Council* [2011] IRLR 1009; Middlemiss, 2004. At the same time, the courts have limited the potential liability in tort of insurers and experts who give advice to employers which has economic consequences for those employers' employees: *Kapfunde v Abbey National plc and Daniel* [1998] IRLR 583; *Briscoe v Lubrizol Ltd* [2000] ICR 694.

[774] See the review of this area by the CA in *Crossley v Faithful and Gould Holdings Ltd* [2004] IRLR 377.

[775] *Outram v Academy Plastics Ltd* [2000] IRLR 499

[776] *Hagen v ICI Chemicals and Polymers Ltd* [2002] IRLR 31; *Lennon v Commissioner of Police of the Metropolis* [2004] IRLR 385.

circumstances.[777] However, the clause, like any other contained in a standard form contract, will be construed *contra proferentem* which in this instance means that any ambiguity will be resolved in favour of the employee. Moreover, the manner in which a mobility clause is invoked can be made subject to the implied duty of co-operation. In particular, an employer is required to give the employee adequate notice of any move.[778] However, it has been held that this is not the same thing as implying a term into the contract to require the employer to 'act reasonably'. In *White v Reflecting Roadstuds Ltd*[779] the EAT held that the obligation is merely to avoid exercising a discretionary power in such a way as to prevent the employee carrying out his or her side of the contract. To insert a general common law obligation to act 'reasonably' into all contracts of employment would not only create uncertainty in the interpretation of contract terms, but could also be seen as an illegitimate judicial usurpation of the statutory jurisdiction of unfair dismissal.[780] But the test formulated in *White's* case is, in its turn, weaker than the version of the duty of co-operation which has been applied in numerous other cases, namely that the employer is under a duty to maintain 'mutual trust and confidence' on which the relationship rests.[781] *White* may be contrasted with *French v Barclays Bank plc*.[782] Here, the defendant bank changed the terms of a bridging loan which it had agreed to make available to the employee in order to assist him in relocating from one office to another. The Court of Appeal held that the employer was not entitled to exercise its discretion in such a way as to impose a significant financial detriment on the employee. By contrast, in *Home Office v Evans*[783] it was held that an employer was entitled to invoke an express mobility clause in order to avoid a situation in which the employee would have been entitled otherwise, by virtue of the change in the place of employment, to claim that there was a redundancy situation.

A term requiring mobility may also be implied into the contract; this can be thought of as an application of the employee's duty of co-operation or, as it has been put more recently, the duty of mutual trust and confidence.[784] However, since the contract will in most cases indicate the employee's normal place of work by way of an express term or one implied from a collective agreement or custom and practice, the scope for implying a duty to move to another place of work must be limited.[785] The scope of any implied mobility clause will also be restricted by the employer's obligations under the implied trust and confidence term. On this basis it could be argued, for example, that any implied right to transfer the employee to another place of work should take account of the latter's family commitments and practical ability to comply with the request, although clear authority on this point is lacking.[786]

---

[777] *Express Lifts Co Ltd v Bowles* [1977] ICR 474.
[778] *United Bank Ltd v Akhtar* [1989] IRLR 507.
[779] [1991] IRLR 331, applying *Rank Xerox (UK) Ltd v Churchill* [1988] IRLR 280; McLean, 1992.
[780] In *White* [1991] IRLR 331 it was said that to imply a general duty to act reasonably would go against the decision of the Court of Appeal in *Western Excavating (ECC) Ltd v Sharp* [1978] ICR 221, on which see below, para 5.69.
[781] *Lewis v Motorworld Garages Ltd* [1985] IRLR 465; *Imperial Group Pension Trust Ltd v Imperial Tobacco Ltd* [1991] IRLR 66.
[782] [1998] IRLR 646.
[783] [2008] IRLR 59.
[784] See paras 4.104-4.106. For a decision implying a mobility clause in the contract of a special needs teacher, see *Luke v Stoke on Trent City Council* [2007] IRLR 305.
[785] See *Aparau v Iceland Frozen Foods plc* [1996] IRLR 119.
[786] See below, para 6.29, for further discussion of this point in the context of indirect sex discrimination; it is also possible that the HRA 1998 will have an impact in this area.

An unusual case of implication was *Courtaulds Northern Spinning Ltd v Sibson*.[787] The employee, who had been a union member, resigned over a dispute concerning the use of union funds; this led the other employees to ostracise him. He refused a request from the employer to transfer to another depot a mile away. It was held in the Court of Appeal that the employer had been entitled to make the request and that the employee should have acceded to it (so there was no constructive dismissal). There was no express term governing mobility; however, partly because the employee was employed as a lorry driver, the Court felt that a term could be implied giving the employer the power to direct him to any place of work which was within reasonable travelling distance of his home. Slade LJ thought it likely that the parties would have agreed this term if asked; but in the absence of an express term an equally plausible interpretation was, arguably, that the employee's normal place of work was the depot at which he had worked for over ten years, and no other.

DUTIES OF FIDELITY, CONFIDENTIALITY AND PRIVACY

4.110   Among the most important obligations of the employee is the duty of fidelity or loyalty which is implied into the contract at common law; there is now growing recognition of corresponding duties of the employer to respect the private life and dignity of the employee.[788] As long as the contract is in force, the employee is bound not to compete with the employer or to work for a competitor without permission. Express terms, so-called 'restrictive covenants', are frequently inserted into contracts for the purposes of clarifying the scope of the employee's duty of fidelity and extending the period during which certain forms of competition are restricted to beyond the life of the contract itself. 'Post-contractual' restraints of the latter kind can only take effect by express agreement; they will not be implied. Post-contractual restraints are also subject to the common law doctrine of public policy, as part of which the courts can strike down terms which are in restraint of trade. However, the court will uphold a particular restraint if the employer shows that it protects a legitimate interest of the business and that its scope is reasonable in the circumstances.[789]

An exceptional feature of the employee's duties of fidelity is that the employer can normally enforce them by way of an injunction; elsewhere, the role of specific relief in the contract of employment is a limited one, damages being the normal remedy for breach of contract.[790] Specific relief may also be available to prevent the use by employees, both during the performance of the contract and for a limited period after it, of confidential information acquired in the course of their employment. There is no general right of the employee to release information which is of a wider public interest, and few protections for 'whistleblowers'; on the contrary, many contracts of employment contain confidentiality clauses designed to prevent employees speaking out about work practices, and these will normally be upheld by the courts. However, the balance has been redressed to some extent by the Public Interest Disclosure Act 1998 (now consolidated in ERA

---

[787] [1988] ICR 451; Holland and Chandler, 1988.
[788] See Hepple, 1999a.
[789] For a detailed analysis of this area see Goulding, 2007.
[790] See paras 5.20 and 5.53 *et seq* below.

1996) and by the enactment of HRA 1998, which makes reference to the Convention right of freedom of expression.[791]

In comparison to the extensive protection granted to employers' interests, there were until recently few controls over the collection, storage and use by an employer of information of a personal nature concerning individual employees. However, the Data Protection Act 1998 (which replaces a less extensive Act of 1984) provides significant protections in relation to the use of information which is collected and held by the employer, and as this body of law comes to be interpreted in the light of the HRA, its influence over employment relations is growing.

The employee's duty of fidelity

(i) The content of the implied duty of fidelity

4.111   An employee is not, in general, prohibited from doing another job during his or her spare time; however, he or she must not work for a rival employer if the effect of this will be seriously to damage the principal employer's business. In *Hivac Ltd v Park Royal Scientific Instruments Ltd*[792] highly skilled employees of the claimant worked for the defendants, who manufactured precisely the same product, in their spare time. This was sufficient for the court to grant an injunction restraining the defendant from taking on the employees, since to do so amounted to inducement to breach their contracts of employment with the claimant. According to Lord Greene MR, 'the obligation of fidelity, which is an implied term of the contract, may extend very much further in the case of one class of employee than it does in others'; the court would be reluctant to impose restraints on manual workers whose obligation of fidelity 'may be one the operation of which will have a comparatively limited scope'.[793] However, 'it would be deplorable if it were laid down that a workman could, consistently with his duty to his employer, knowingly, deliberately and secretly set himself to do in his spare time something which would inflict great harm on his employer's business'.[794]

A critical point about the duty set out in *Hivac* is that it only applies to the period when the contract of employment is in force; if the employer wishes to restrain post-contractual competition by the employee, it must do so by way of a restrictive covenant. If there is no such express term, the employee is allowed, in principle, to take certain steps by way of preparation for setting up in competition with the employer, but must not do so if that involves making use of confidential information.[795] Moreover, the precise scope of what is allowed by allowed by way of advance preparation is far from clear,[796] making this a potentially hazardous step for many employees.

---

[791] ECHR, Art 10.

[792] [1946] Ch 169; *Adamson v B & L Cleaning Services Ltd* [1995] IRLR 193.

[793] [1946] Ch 169, 174.

[794] [1946] 1 Ch 169, 178.

[795] *Helmet Integrated Systems Ltd v Tunnard* [2007] IRLR 126.

[796] For recent decisions on this point, which stress the need for a case by case analysis, see *Helmet Integrated Systems Ltd v Tunnard* [2007] IRLR 126, *Shepherds Investments Ltd v Walters* [2007] IRLR 110 and *Foster Bryant Surveying Ltd v Bryant* [2007] IRLR 425.

(ii) Employees as fiduciaries

4.112   The implied duty of fidelity operates as a term of the contract of employment, which arises as an incident of the employment relationship; it must therefore be distinguished from the separate notion of a fiduciary obligation which may incurred by an employee to his or her employer. Only employees who undertake particular duties and responsibilities, normally associated with a senior position, will become fiduciaries and thereby assume the wide-ranging legal duties which are attached to that status. In particular, fiduciaries come under an open-ended duty of disclosure which is not part of the employee's general duty of fidelity under the contract of employment. Failure to comply with a fiduciary duty of disclosure will generally be grounds for dismissal by the employer, regardless of whether the employee was aware that he or she was under this obligation. The far-reaching effect of such a rule is evident in *Neary v Dean of Westminster*,[797] in which the employee was held to have acted in breach of the duty of mutual trust and confidence in failing to disclose profits which he had made from recording contracts and related arrangements which he entered into by virtue of his position as an organist at Westminster Abbey.

Another relevant feature of fiduciary status for present purposes is that a breach of fiduciary duty may enable the employer to mount a claim for an account of profits or a similar claim in restitution. In a normal breach of contract claim, the employer has to show loss in order to recover damages;[798] the possibility of a claim for breach of fiduciary duty may therefore be highly significant. It was on this basis that a claim for profits made by a university researcher in relation to work undertaken for third parties was mounted in *Nottingham University v Fishel*.[799]

The crucial issue arising from *Neary* and *Fishel* concerns the circumstances in which it is appropriate for a court to imply fiduciary status. A company director necessarily owes fiduciary obligations to the company so that he or she must, among other things, disclose secret profits made in that capacity;[800] but what of employees who are not directors? According to the analysis of Elias J in *Fishel*,[801] while fiduciary obligations may be incurred by a wide range of employees in a variety of circumstances, the employment relationship is not, in itself, a fiduciary relationship. Before fiduciary obligations can be implied, therefore, it is necessary to find specific evidence to support a claim that the employee has undertaken to act for or on behalf of the employer. Moreover, an employee who incurs fiduciary obligations does so only in relation to specific undertakings or commitments of this kind; thus an employee who is entrusted with company property or with confidential information may act as a fiduciary for those purposes, without incurring similar obligations with regard to other aspects of the employment relationship.

Part of the difficulty in determining when the notion of fiduciary responsibility is applicable to employment derives from the similar language used to describe, on the one hand, the position of the fiduciary and, on the other, the status of the employee under the contract of employment.

---

[797] [1999] IRLR 288.

[798] See *A-G v Blake* [1998] Ch 439, [2001] IRLR 36 for discussion of the circumstances in which a claim for restitutionary damages may lie in contract.

[799] [2000] IRLR 471. It should be noted that a breach of fiduciary duty does not, however, entitle the employer to reclaim wages or salary paid to the employee in ignorance of the relevant breach, as the employee is entitled to retain wages or salariy paid in respect of work done under the contract: *Brandeaux Advisers (UK) Ltd v Chadwick* [2011] IRLR 224.

[800] *Regal (Hastings) Ltd v Gulliver* [1967] 2 AC 134n; see *Horcal Ltd v Gatland* [1983] IRLR 459.

[801] [2000] IRLR 471, 482–484; Sims, 2001. Elias J's analysis was approved by the CA in *Helmet Integrated Systems Ltd v Tunnard* [2007] IRLR 126 and applied at first instance in *Crowson Fabrics Ltd v Rider* [2008] IRLR 288 and *Lonmar Global Risks Ltd v West* [2011] IRLR 138.

Hence a leading modern definition of a fiduciary refers to 'someone who has undertaken to act for or on behalf of another in a particular matter in circumstances which give rise to a relationship of trust and confidence. The distinguishing obligation of a fiduciary is the obligation of loyalty'.[802] The main obstacle to the imposition of a fiduciary duty upon employees other than company directors is *Bell v Lever Bros*.[803] However, it has been suggested that 'the development of the specifically fiduciary obligations of directors, on the one hand, and of the obligations of fidelity and loyalty under the contract of employment, on the other, have been congruent with each other, to the point where *Bell v Lever Bros* is quite isolated in so far as it suggests a sharp contrast between the two sets of obligations'.[804] Moreover, the terms 'acting for another', 'duty of loyalty' and 'relationship of trust and confidence' can be read as linked to aspects of the implied obligations of the employee under the 'core' *Malik* term of mutual co-operation.[805] However, it was argued in *Fishel* that 'these concepts are… used in the employment context to describe situations where a party merely has to take into consideration the interests of another, but does not have to act in the interests of that other.'[806] In so far as this may be taken to mean that the employee is not required to subordinate his or her interests to those of the employer except to the extent determined by contract, this is an important reminder of the need for employment law to recognise the contractual autonomy of the parties to the employment relationship.

If this analysis is correct, it would be inappropriate to attach fiduciary duties of a general kind to an employee *solely* on the grounds that he or she owes duties of trust and confidence to the employer.[807] The issue becomes instead one of determining when 'within a particular contractual relationship there are specific contractual obligations which the employee has undertaken which have placed him in a situation where equity imposes [on him] these rigorous [fiduciary] duties'.[808] The introduction of a fiduciary element into the relationship is not dependent on the seniority of the employee concerned, since the most junior of employees can be entrusted with the employer's property in such a way as to give rise to a specific obligation to restore it (together with any secret profits that may have been made through its use).[809] Nevertheless, very senior employees who are in a position of special trust and responsibility with regard to the management of the employer's organisation and assets will almost necessarily incur extensive fiduciary duties to the employer.

Thus in *Sybron Corpn v Rochem Ltd*[810] a group of managers in the claimant company set up the defendant company, along with several others, and then diverted to those companies a series of contracts which had come to them in the course of their work for the claimant. One of the managers, Mr Roques, took early retirement with a pension before the fraud was discovered. The claimant sued for the return of the pension. On the authority of *Bell v Lever Bros Ltd*[811] it was held that Mr Roques could not be held to have acted unlawfully by failing to disclose his own

---

[802] *Bristol and West Building Society v Mothew* [1998] 1 Ch 1, 18 (Millett LJ).
[803] [1932] AC 161.
[804] Freedland, 1984: p 35.
[805] See Brodie, 1998a, 2001; Clarke, 1999; cf Sims, 2001.
[806] [2000] IRLR 471, 483.
[807] In so far as this was the basis for *Neary*, that decision would seem to be irreconcilable with *Fishel*, but *Neary* can be seen as turning on the distinctive position occupied by the employee in an institution of particular national and religious significance.
[808] Elias J in *Fishel*: [2000] IRLR 471, 483.
[809] [2000] IRLR 471, 482.
[810] [1983] ICR 801; Freedland, 1984.
[811] [1932] AC 161.

misconduct, but he could be held in breach of contract for failing to disclose the misconduct of his subordinates. On this basis, he was required to make restitution of the pension on the grounds that the money was paid over under a mistake of fact. An alternative and probably preferable ground for the decision would have been that Mr Roques had committed a breach of fiduciary duty, for which he could have been liable both to make an account of the profits he received and to pay damages to the employer for its losses. In *Fishel*[812] Elias J. held that the defendant was not in a position of being a fiduciary merely by virtue of the research post which he held, since while this was a reasonably senior position, it could not fairly be equated with that of an executive director of a company. He went on to hold that no specific undertaking had been made of the kind which could have given rise to a more limited fiduciary duty. However, the defendant was found to be under a duty to account for income received in respect of work done by other university employees for whom he had been responsible.

The extent of the obligation of a director or employee to disclose their own wrongdoings – in effect, a duty of confession – is an aspect of *Bell* that many courts and commentators have found puzzling. Although in some cases it may make no difference whether the employee has this 'superadded' duty or not,[813] it may have a considerable impact on the adjustment of their respective claims in situations if, as in *Bell* or *Sybron*, the employer can argue that a failure to disclose constitutes grounds for avoiding a severance payment or pension claim. *Bell* may turn on the jury's finding that the appellants did not fraudulently conceal their earlier wrongdoings at the time they entered into the severance agreement which was the subject of the action. The decision is also explicable on the grounds that the appellants were not directors of the respondent company. In *Item Software (UK) Ltd v Fassihi*[814] the Court of Appeal held that a director was under a duty to disclose his own wrongdoing; according to Arden LJ, this could be understood as an integral part of the duty of loyalty which a director owes to the company by virtue of being a fiduciary. Moreover, 'the duties of a director are in general higher than those imposed by law on an employee. This is because a director is not simply a senior manager of the company. He is a fiduciary and with his fellow directors he is responsible for the success of the company's business'.[815] As we have seen, a senior employee may also be a fiduciary under certain circumstances. How far a 'duty of confession' then arises remains unclear.[816] The assimilation of senior employees (a category which is ill-defined) to a fiduciary model developed initially for company directors risks introducing uncertainty into this area of law.

---

[812] [2000] IRLR 471, 484–487.

[813] This was the case in *Fishel*.

[814] [2004] IRLR 928. See also, on the distinction between the director's fiduciary duty of loyalty and the employee's contractual duty of fidelity, the judgments of Deputy Judge Strauss QC at first instance in *Fassihi* ([2003] IRLR 769) *British Midland Tool Ltd v Midland International Tooling Ltd* [2003] EWHC 466, at [77]-[95]; *Crowson Fabrics Ltd v Rider* [2008] IRLR 288, at [77]-[83], *Lonmar Global Risks Ltd v West* [2011] IRLR 138, at [148]-[159] See also *Tesco Stores Ltd v Pook* [2004] IRLR 618; Wynn-Evans, 2005.

[815] [2004] IRLR 928, at [34].

[816] In *Helmet Integrated Systems Ltd v Tunnard* [2007] IRLR 126 it was held that a manager who was not a fiduciary was not under a duty to report to his employer steps taken by way of preparation for setting up in competition with it after he left its employment, under circumstances where this preparation did not amount to a breach of the implied duty of fidelity, and no restrictive covenant was in place.

(iii) Specific enforcement of the duty of fidelity

4.113   If the employee breaks the duty of fidelity, he or she may be dismissed for repudiatory breach of contract if the breach is serious enough.[817] The court may also grant an injunction to prevent an employee from breaking either the implied duty of fidelity or an express agreement not to compete during the period of the contract.[818] This equitable remedy is discretionary, and may be refused if its effect is equivalent to ordering the employee to work for a particular employer. Courts of equity historically would not grant specific performance to enforce the contractual obligation to work, and this practice is now embodied in a statutory rule.[819] However, the granting of a negative injunction preventing the employee from working for a competitor is thought not to infringe the rule against specific performance, as long as the employee is not thereby faced with a choice of 'work or starve' which would drive him or her back to their original employer. 'Work or starve' is not an issue if the individual, finding one line of work closed off by the injunction, is considered to be sufficiently resourceful to find a viable alternative which would enable them to earn a reasonable living.[820] However, it is also open to a court to find that, in a given situation, an alternative career is not a realistic option, in which case an injunction may be refused and the employer limited to a claim in damages and/or restitution.[821]

One means of avoiding the rule against specific performance is for the employer to pay the employee his or her wages or salary for the remainder of the contract period, without requiring them to come into work. During this period of 'garden leave' the employee is financially secure without needing to work for the employer; there is no choice of 'work or starve', and so a court is not prevented from issuing an injunction preventing the employee from working for a competitor. Such clauses are very commonly found in the contracts of professional and managerial employees; employers regard them as essential means of preventing rival businesses from exploiting the specialised knowledge of senior staff. However, garden leave does little to serve the employee's interests: not only is he or she deprived of the chance to get a better paid job, but by being out of employment for a lengthy period their value to any future employer may be greatly reduced.

The possibility of abuse is heightened if the period during which the contract remains formally in force is particularly long. In *Evening Standard Co Ltd v Henderson*[822] a contract of employment contained a clause requiring the employee to give a year's notice of termination, together with an express agreement not to work for a competitor while the contract was in force. He quit to work for a rival firm on only a month's notice. An injunction was granted and was upheld by the Court of Appeal. The employee's action was a repudiatory breach of contract, but the employer had not accepted it and the contract was therefore still in force. Because the employer undertook to pay the employee's normal salary and to allow him to work during his notice period, 'work or starve' was not an issue.

---

[817] Eg, *Boston Deep Sea Fishing Co Ltd v Ansell* (1888) 39 Ch D 339.
[818] An express term may well be necessary to clarify or extend the scope of the implied duty of fidelity: see *Symbian Ltd v Christensen* [2001] IRLR 77.
[819] TULRCA 1992, s 236.
[820] *Warner Bros Pictures Inc v Nelson* [1937] 1 KB 209; cf *Page One Records Ltd v Britton* [1968] 1 WLR 159.
[821] *Warren v Mendy* [1989] 1 WLR 853.
[822] [1987] ICR 588.

A more problematic case is where the employer does not allow the employee to return to work. In *Euro Brokers Ltd v Rabey*[823] it was held that it was not necessary for the employer to offer continuing employment to the employee, a money broker, in order to obtain an injunction against him. In *GFI Group Inc v Eaglestone*[824] an injunction was also issued to prevent a foreign exchange dealer starting work for a competitor before his contractual notice period had expired, although the court exercised its discretion to shorten the period of the restraint from that specified in the notice clause. This was because other employees had been allowed to work for the same competitor after a shorter period of time than the employee's notice clause provided for. By contrast, in *William Hill Organisation Ltd v Tucker*[825] the Court of Appeal declined to grant an injunction to enforce garden leave, on the grounds that the employer was contractually obligated to provide work for the employee during the notice period. In part, this was because of the 'specific and unique post' which the employee held within the organisation.[826] However, Morritt LJ considered that 'as social conditions have changed, the courts have increasingly recognised the importance to the employee of the work, not just the pay';[827] on this basis, there seems to be no reason why the courts not should be willing to imply an obligation to provide work, where it is available, into most contracts of employment.

In a case such as *Henderson* the long notice period could also be attacked on a separate ground, via the doctrine of restraint of trade. This doctrine is normally applied to *post-contractual* restraints but if the contract is for a long, fixed term or contains a provision for a long notice period, there is no reason why it should not apply to restraints which operate during the period when the contract is still subsisting. The doctrine has been applied in this way to recording and agency contracts lasting several years.[828] In *William Hill Organisation Ltd v Tucker*[829] Morritt LJ deprecated the 'trend towards increasing reliance on garden leave provisions in preference to conventional restrictive covenants', and suggested that:

> ... if injunctive relief is sought, then it has to be justified on similar grounds to those necessary to the validity of an employee's covenant in restraint of trade. It seems to me that the court should be careful not to grant [interim] relief to enforce a garden leave clause to any greater extent than would be covered by a justifiable covenant in restraint of trade previously entered into by an employee.

---

[823] [1995] IRLR 206.

[824] [1994] IRLR 119.

[825] [1998] IRLR 313.

[826] [1998] IRLR 313, 317 (Morritt LJ).

[827] [1998] IRLR 313, 317 (Morritt LJ). See also, however, *Standard Life Health Care Ltd v Gorman* [2010] IRLR 233: 'an employee who has a right to work has that right subject to the qualification that he has not as a result of some prior breach of contract or other duty ... rendered it impossible or reasonably impracticable for the employer to provide work': Longmore LJ, at [33].

[828] See eg *A Schroeder Music Publishing Co Ltd v Macaulay* [1974] 1 WLR 1308; *Proactive Sports Management Ltd v Rooney* [2012] IRLR 241.

[829] [1998] IRLR 313, 318. See also *Crédit Suisse Asset Management Ltd v Armstrong* [1996] IRLR 450; *Symbian Ltd v Christensen* [2001] IRLR 77; *SG &R Valuation Service Co LLC v Boudrais* [2008] IRLR 770; *Tullett Prebon plc v BGC Brokers LLP* [2010] IRLR 648, at [219]-[225]. In practice it is common to find garden leave clauses combined with post-contractual restraints. In *TFS Derivatives Ltd v Morgan* [2005] IRLR 246 Cox J declined to hold that the presence of a garden leave clause in a contract made it more likely that a post-contractual constraint would be struck down on the grounds of public policy.

It may also be argued that garden leave clauses should be construed restrictively in the light of the employer's duty to maintain mutual trust and confidence, although the potential of this idea has yet to be fully explored.[830]

Post-contractual restraints on competition and protection of confidential information

4.114   An express agreement not to compete after the contract has come to an end may be highly significant for both parties, since the implied duty of fidelity will not, *in itself*, extend to this period.[831] But as we have just seen, a post-contractual restraint of this sort faces an additional obstacle, namely the doctrine of restraint of trade. This holds that a contract term which purports to restrict competition is *prima facie* void, but can be justified according to a test of 'reasonableness'. As far as employment contracts are concerned, an agreement by the employee not to compete after the contract is over will be struck down unless the employer can point to a more specific 'proprietary interest' which the agreement is designed to protect.[832] This will normally have to be in the form of confidential information or the protection of its existing base of customers, or possibly its employees. Thus in *Herbert Morris Ltd v Saxelby*[833] a term under which the employee agreed not to compete in the relevant trade for a period of seven years after leaving his employer's employment was struck down: according to Lord Parker, there had been no case in which such a restraint against post-contractual competition:

> … has, as such, ever been upheld by the Court. Wherever such covenants have been upheld it has been on the ground, not that the servant or apprentice would, by reason of his employment or training, obtain the skill or knowledge necessary to equip him as a possible competitor in the trade, but that he might obtain such personal knowledge of or influence over the customers of his employer, or such an acquaintance with his employer's trade secrets, as would enable him, if competition were allowed, to take advantage of his employer's trade connection or utilise information confidentially obtained.

Where an employee has acquired specialist knowledge of customers through his or her contacts with them, the employer may legitimately restrain the employee from soliciting them for business after he or she has left the employment.[834] This principle has been applied to solicitors and others working in law offices,[835] and even to a hairdressers' assistant.[836] However, this principle would not justify placing a restraint on an employee who never came into contact with the employer's clients, such as a shop-floor employee, or a restraint which applied to customers with whom the employee had had no dealings.[837] The employer's interest in protecting the client-base it has built

---

[830] It was briefly referred to by Cox J in *TFS Derivatives Ltd v Morgan* [2005] IRLR 246.

[831] *Faccenda Chicken Ltd v Fowler* [1986] IRLR 69; *Wallace Bogan & Co v Cove* [1997] IRLR 453.

[832] See, for example, *Scully (UK) Ltd v Lee* [1998] IRLR 259.

[833] [1916] 1 AC 688, 709.

[834] For an application of this principle see *International Consulting Services (UK) Ltd v Hart* [2000] IRLR 227.

[835] Eg, *Fitch v Dewes* [1921] 2 AC 158; *Fellowes & Son v Fisher* [1976] QB 122.

[836] *Marion White Ltd v Francis* [1972] 1 WLR 1423.

[837] *WRN Ltd v Ayris* [2008] IRLR 889; *Norbrook Laboratories (GB) Ltd v Adair* [2008] IRLR 878; *Landmark Brickwork Ltd v Sutcliffe* [2011] IRLR 976.

up could also arguably extend to its own workforce; an agreement not to recruit former fellow-employees would probably be upheld on this basis.[838]

As far as confidential information is concerned, the courts have traditionally drawn a distinction between specific trade secrets, such as secret designs or recipes, and general know-how: the employer can restrain the use of the former after the employment has ended, but not the latter. It has been suggested that the essence of the distinction is between 'objective knowledge' which is the employer's property and 'subjective knowledge' which relates to the way in which a trade or profession is carried on, and which remains the property of the employee.[839] An express term may help to clarify the categories of information which are sufficiently precise to fall into the category of trade secrets; in addition, the implied duty of fidelity may assist the employer. An employee who copies lists of customers while he or she is still employed and seeks to use them later may be restrained from doing so, whether or not there was an express term not to compete.[840] However, if the information is too vague to be classified as a trade secret, it may be that neither an express nor an implied term will help the employer.

Hence in *Faccenda Chicken Ltd v Fowler*[841] the defendant employee resigned as a sales manager of the claimant and set up in competition against it, taking on many of his former colleagues. His contract did not contain any express terms governing the use of confidential information, nor any express agreement not to compete post-contract. The judge refused to grant an injunction and his view was upheld in the Court of Appeal. The information being used by the defendant was in the nature of general know-how about the nature of the work which he had picked up in the course of his employment and did not rank as a trade secret. Even if there had been an express non-competition clause, it would not have led to the granting of an injunction. According to Neill LJ, 'a restrictive convenant will not be enforced unless the protection sought is reasonably necessary to protect a trade secret or to prevent some personal influence over customers being abused in order to entice them away'.[842]

By contrast, in *Roger Bullivant Ltd v Ellis*[843] an employee, while still employed, acquired a company for the purpose of competing with his employer, and on leaving his employment took with him a card index of customers' names. His contract contained an express term under which he undertook not to enter into similar employment for a period of one year after his employment ended, and this was enforced by an injunction. The information concerning customers was precise in nature and had been illicitly acquired for the purpose of setting up as a competitor.

Most confidential information will not be protected indefinitely. In *Bullivant* the purpose of the injunction was to prevent the ex-employee making unfair use of the information he had acquired, but after a period had elapsed competition would be permitted. This is an application of the 'springboard doctrine': the person entrusted with information while still employed 'should not get a start over others by using the information he received in confidence. At any rate, he should not get a start without paying for it. It may not be a case for an injunction or even an account [of

---

[838] Sales, 1990; *Office Angels Ltd v Rainer-Thomas* [1991] IRLR 214; *Dawnay, Day & Co Ltd v De Braconier d'Alphen* [1997] IRLR 442.

[839] *SBJ Stephenson Ltd v Mandy* [2000] IRLR 233.

[840] *Robb v Green* [1895] 2 QB 315, more recently applied in *British Midland Tool Ltd v Midland International Tooling Ltd* [2003] EWHC 466 and *Crowson Fabrics Ltd v Rider* [2008] IRLR 288.

[841] [1986] IRLR 69; *Lancashire Fires Ltd v SA Lyons & Co Ltd* [1997] IRLR 113.

[842] [1986] IRLR 69, 75.

[843] [1987] ICR 464.

profits], but only for damages, depending on the worth of the confidential information in saving him time and trouble'.[844] But there are also some categories of information whose disclosure will be restrained indefinitely. Secret processes and formulae may fall into this category,[845] and so may details of the personal life of an employer or another, stipulated individual.[846]

The scope of restraints on competition

4.115   The employer will not succeed in enforcing an agreement not to compete merely by showing that it protects a 'proprietary interest'; the restraint must also be shown to be reasonable in its scope. Thus in *Mason v Provident Clothing and Supply Co*[847] the defendant had been employed to canvass business and collect payments from customers in a part of Islington; however, a clause in his contract barred him from entering into similar work within 25 miles of London for a period of three years after his employment came to an end. The clause was struck down as bearing no relation to the protection of the employer's legitimate interest, which was confined to the area in which the employee had previously worked.[848]

In addition to the area of the restraint, its duration will be taken into account. In *Fitch v Dewes*[849] a covenant not to practise as a solicitor's clerk within seven miles of Tamworth Town Hall after leaving the employer's employment was upheld: the clients of the practice tended to stay with it throughout their lives, and so imposing a lifelong restraint on the employee was necessary to protect the practice's business. This was a somewhat unusual case. In *Fellowes & Son v Fisher*[850] Lord Denning thought that a one-year non-solicitation clause would be appropriate for an articled clerk, and in *Bridge v Deacons*[851] the Privy Council upheld a five-year period in the case of a partner in a solicitors' practice. However, more recent decisions have confirmed that an indefinite restraint may be reasonable in certain circumstances as a means of protecting the employer's interests.[852]

What matters here is the balance between the proper interests of the promisee and the interests of the public in the maintenance of healthy competition; the employee's interests appear not to be relevant as such. The courts have, for example, rejected the proposition that the restraint should not be upheld if it confers only a minor benefit on the promisee but a major detriment on the promisor.[853] It is only if the consideration received by the promisor for the restrictive term

---

[844] *Seager v Copydex Ltd* [1967] 1 WLR 923, 931–932 (Lord Denning MR); *Universal Thermosensors Ltd v Hibben* [1992] 1 WLR 840; *UBS Wealth Management (UK) Ltd v Vestra Wealth LLP* [2008] IRLR 965.

[845] *Printers and Finshers Ltd v Holloway* [1965] 1 WLR 1; *Thomas Marshall (Exports) Ltd v Guinle* [1978] ICR 905.

[846] *A-G v Barker* [1990] 3 All ER 257.

[847] [1913] AC 724; on area restraints, see also *Fellowes & Son v Fisher* [1976] QB 122.

[848] This principle also applies to limit the legitimate scope of restraints to those aspects of a business in which the employee concerned was directly employed, and not all aspects of the business of the employer in question: *Turner v Commonwealth & British Minerals Ltd* [2000] IRLR 114. For a decision in which a restraint without specific geographical restriction was held to be reasonable, on the grounds that the employer had a global business, see *WRN Ltd. v Ayris* [2008] IRLR 889.

[849] [1921] 2 AC 158.

[850] [1976] QB 122.

[851] [1984] AC 705.

[852] *Office Angels Ltd v Rainer-Thomas* [1991] IRLR 214; *Dentmaster (UK) Ltd v Kent* [1997] IRLR 636.

[853] *Allied Dunbar (Frank Weisinger) Ltd v Weisinger* [1988] IRLR 60.

is completely inadequate that considerations of injustice to the employee are said to come into play. [854]

A clause which is over-wide in its scope may be saved if the court can 'sever' the offending words, but this may only be done if two conditions are satisfied: the remaining words must make some grammatical sense;[855] and the effect must not be to alter the meaning and nature of the contract.[856] The courts try to resist severance of restraints in contracts of employment, for the reason that to allow it on a regular basis would encourage employers to widen the scope of clauses, safe in the knowledge that they could always fall back on the court-supplied term.[857] In *Attwood v Lamont*[858] the head of the tailoring department in an outfitter's business contracted not to work for a period after leaving the employment in the 'trade or business of a tailor, dressmaker, general draper, milliner, hatter, haberdasher, gentlemen's, ladies', or children's outfitter' within ten miles of the town in which the business was situated. The court rejected an attempt to sever all the parts of the clause not referring to tailoring; it was found that the employer's intention had been to prevent competition across the range of trades mentioned, and not just in respect of the particular work undertaken by the employee; the covenant was held to be void on the grounds that it was wider than necessary for the protection of the employer's interests.

A more recent case which illustrates a questionably liberal attitude to construing restraints is *Littlewoods Organisation Ltd v Harris*,[859] in which the Court of Appeal, by a majority, felt able to construe the broad words of a clause by reference to the protectable interest of the employer: a restriction on the ex-employee working in any similar 'trade or business' was interpreted as referring to any trade or business in which he might use the confidential information he had acquired when working for the company. Browne LJ dissented on the grounds that 'this is re-rewriting the clause, and rewriting it so as to make enforceable what would otherwise be unenforceable ... I think that is something which the court cannot do'.[860]

It was thought, following the judgment of Scott J in *Briggs v Oates*,[861] that covenants which were expressed to apply to any termination of the contract 'howsoever arising' or 'howsoever caused' would necessarily be struck down on the grounds that '[a] restrictive covenant, having effect after the termination of a contract of service or for services, which on its face applies to the employer's benefit even where the termination has been induced by his own breach is necessarily unreasonable'.[862] However, in *Rock Refrigeration Ltd v Jones*[863] the Court of Appeal took a different view. In part, this decision rests on the conceptual point that it is neither necessary nor possible to invoke the restraint of trade doctrine to strike down a restrictive covenant if the employer has

---

[854] *A Schroeder Music Publishing Co Ltd v Macaulay* [1974] 1 WLR 1308. For a more recent example of an 'oppressive' agreement see *Proactive Sports Management Ltd v Rooney* [2012] IRLR 241.

[855] See *T Lucas & Co Ltd v Mitchell* [1974] Ch 129.

[856] See *Goldsoll v Goldman* [1915] 1 Ch 292.

[857] *Mason v Provident Clothing and Supply Co Ltd* [1913] AC 724.

[858] [1920] 3 KB 571.

[859] [1977] 1 WLR 1472; for more recent discussion of the *Littlewoods* test see *Hollis & Co v Stocks* [2000] IRLR 712; *Wincanton Ltd v Cranny and SDM European Transport Ltd* [2000] IRLR 716; *Beckett Investment Management Group Ltd v Hall* [2007] IRLR 793 (in which the Court of Appeal approved the test for severance set out in *Sadler v Imperial life Assurance Co of Canada Ltd* [1988] IRLR 388); *Norbrook Laboratories (GB) Ltd v Adair* [2008] IRLR 878.

[860] [1977] 1 WLR 1472, 1493.

[861] [1990] IRLR 472; see *Living Design (Home Improvements) Ltd v Davidson* [1994] IRLR 69; *PR Consultants Scotland Ltd v Mann* [1996] IRLR 188; *D v M* [1996] IRLR 192.

[862] *D v M* [1996] IRLR 192, 198 (Laws J).

[863] [1996] IRLR 675.

wrongfully repudiated the contract. This is because, under the principle in *General Billposting Co Ltd v Atkinson*,[864] the effect of the employer's repudiation is automatically to release the employee from his contractual obligations, including any restrictive covenants. It follows that there is no justification for holding such a covenant to be invalid in *other* situations, namely where the contract is brought to an end lawfully, or where it is wrongfully terminated by the employee.

The question of whether an employee who is dismissed for refusing to sign an unreasonably wide restraint can bring a claim in unfair dismissal has recently come before the courts. In *Forshaw v Archcraft Ltd*.[865] the EAT held that such a dismissal was necessarily unfair as it would not be for a potentially fair reason, but in *Willow Oak Developments Ltd v Silverwood*[866] the Court of Appeal took a different view, holding that it was open to the employer to establish that such a dismissal was potentially fair under the 'some other substantial reason' category. This approach gives the employer the chance to show that the covenant in question was justified on the basis of its business needs, but it is hard to see how this could be the case if the covenant was unreasonably wide (and hence unenforceable). In the *Willow Oak* case the employer was held to have acted unreasonably in treating the reason given as sufficient for dismissal, so an unfair dismissal finding was arrived at by a different route.

Disclosure of confidential information in the public interest and protection of 'whistleblowers'

4.116   At common law, the disclosure of confidential information by 'whistleblowers' has only very rarely been allowed on the grounds of an overriding public interest. One clear category is the revelation of criminal acts: 'there is no confidence as to the disclosure of iniquity'.[867] In *Initial Services Ltd v Putterill*[868] the Court of Appeal thought that the employee's implied duty of fidelity would not prevent disclosure of documents relating to his employer's attempts to rig the market in laundry services, contrary to the Restrictive Trade Practices Act 1956. The Court discussed, without clearly deciding, the question of whether disclosure in such a case must be made to the relevant authorities, as opposed to the press.

This common-law defence of public interest is limited in scope, and provides little protection for 'whistleblowers' who seek to bring unethical behaviour to the attention of the wider public. Doctors and nurses in the National Health Service, for example, are formally required both by their conditions of service and by the codes of their professional associations to maintain patient confidentiality.[869] This raises the possibility of a conflict between contractual confidentiality and the wider professional obligations of the employee; the courts have not clearly stated, however, that a professional obligation overrides a contract term for the purposes of authorising disclosure of information.[870]

---

[864] [1909] AC 118. This decision is open to question in the light of the House of Lords decision in *Photo Production Ltd v Securicor Transport Ltd* [1980] AC 827 (see [1996] IRLR 675, 678 (Philips LJ)) but it has not been overruled. See Goulding, 2007, paras 5.83–5.143.

[865] [2005] IRLR 600.

[866] [2006] IRLR 607. See further para 5.173.

[867] *Gartside v Outram* (1856) 3 Jur NS 39.

[868] [1968] 1 QB 396.

[869] McHale, 1992, 1993; D Lewis, 1995; Vickers, 1995, 2002.

[870] See generally Cripps, 1995.

If the information is revealed while the employee is still employed, he or she may face the prospect of discipline or dismissal. Prior to the passage of the Public Interest Disclosure Act 1998, there were only isolated statutory provisions allowing for (or in some cases, requiring) disclosure of wrongs committed by the employer.[871] The position of the common law was that whistleblowing would normally be a breach of the employee's obligation of trust and confidence.[872] The employee's duty of fidelity has been a relevant consideration in the application of tests for determining the scope of the public interest in protecting the identity of whistleblowers. In *Camelot Group plc v Centaur Communications Ltd*[873] Camelot, the operators of the national lottery, sought a court order for the return of documents containing the company's draft accounts, which had been leaked to a journalist employed by Centaur. Camelot alleged that the documents had been leaked by a disloyal employee, and that it was necessary for this individual to be identified and dismissed if its operations were not to be disrupted. Centaur invoked section 10 of the Contempt of Court Act, under which '[n]o court may require a person to disclose ... the source of information contained in a publication for which he is responsible, unless it be established to the satisfaction of the court that disclosure is necessary in the interests of justice or national security or for the prevention of disorder or crime'. The judge granted the order requested by Camelot and his ruling was upheld by the Court of Appeal. According to Mummery LJ, 'an employer in the position of Camelot Group has a legitimate and continuing interest in enforcing an obligation of loyalty and confidentiality against an employee who has made unauthorised disclosure and use of documents acquired by him in his employment'. It was also relevant (if rather surprising) that the judges in this case did not consider that any relevant public interest was served by the disclosure of the information in question, which related to the payment of increased salaries to the directors of Camelot. Hence, Mummery LJ thought that '[r]ather than serving a public interest, it appears that the prior and premature disclosure and publication of the draft accounts served a private purpose of the source or a private purpose of Centaur Communications in securing a scoop, ahead of other publications, of information which would have become legitimately available to the public five days later'.[874] Similarly, Schiemann LJ thought that '[t]his is not a case of disclosing iniquity; it is not a whistleblowing case'.[875]

4.117   Specific legal protection of whistleblowers was provided by the Public Interest Disclosure Act 1998, the relevant parts of which have been incorporated into ERA 1996.[876] To be protected, a

---

[871] Under the Pensions Act 1995, s 48, actuaries and auditors of occupational pension schemes came under a *duty* to inform the Occupational Pensions Regulatory Authority of certain breaches of duty by managers and/or trustees of such schemes. Other persons, including trustees or managers of schemes, might make such information available to the Authority. In both cases, the Act specified that no duty to which the person was subject should be regarded as contravened merely because of any information or opinion contained in a report submitted to the Authority. Section 48 was repealed by Pensions Act 2004, s 320, Sch 13 ; see now Pensions Act 2004, ss 69 and 70.

[872] *Thornley v Aircraft Research Association Ltd* (11 May 1977, unreported); Cripps, 1995: pp 315–317.

[873] [1998] IRLR 80. See also the opinions of the House of Lords in *X Ltd v Morgan Grampian (Publishers) Ltd* [1991] 1 AC 1 and *Ashworth Hospital Authority v MGN Ltd* [2002] 1 WLR 2033, and, under Art 10 of the European Convention on Human Rights, that of the European Court of Human Rights in *Goodwin v United Kingdom* (1996) 22 EHRR 123.

[874] [1998] IRLR 80, 85.

[875] [1998] IRLR 80, 84.

[876] See Gobert and Punch, 2000; D Lewis, 1998, 2001; Bowers *et al*, 1999; Cripps, 2000. The provisions of the then Bill (which was introduced as a private members bill with government support) are explained in Consultation Paper on Mr Richard Shepherd's Public Interest Disclosure Bill, Public Concern at Work, 1997.

disclosure must concern subject matter of a certain kind and must be made in a particular way.[877] With regard, first, to subject matter, a 'qualifying disclosure' must be one which, in the reasonable belief of the worker concerned,[878] tends to show that one or more of the following has occurred or is likely to occur: the commission of a criminal offence;[879] the failure of a person to comply with a legal obligation;[880] the occurrence of a miscarriage of justice; the endangering of a person's health and safety; damage to the environment; or the deliberate concealment of information concerning any of the above. However, a disclosure which involves the commission, by the person making it, of a criminal offence,[881] cannot be a 'qualifying disclosure'.[882]

With regard to the mode of disclosure, a 'qualifying disclosure' is most likely to be 'protected' if it is made internally, that is to say, to the worker's employer or a person to whom the employer has authorised this type of disclosure, or, where the worker reasonably believes the failure relates solely or mainly to the conduct of another person, that person.[883] Other potentially protected disclosures are those made to a legal adviser, a Minister of the Crown, or (in essence) a regulatory person or body.[884] 'External' disclosures will only be protected under a very limited range of conditions. These are, first, where the worker can show that he or she reasonably believed that the information disclosed was substantially true;[885] second, that the disclosure was not made for personal gain; third, where the information concerns conduct of 'an exceptionally serious nature'; and fourth, where, in all the circumstances of the case, it is reasonable for the worker to make the disclosure. The worker must also make the disclosure in good faith.[886] Where the conduct is not exceptionally serious, the worker must show, in addition, that he or she believed at the time of the disclosure that they would be subjected to a detriment by the employer if they raised the matter internally; that (in a case where there is no relevant regulatory person or body) the worker reasonably believed that internal disclosure would lead to the concealment of evidence by the employer; that the worker had previously made disclosure of substantially the same information to their employer or to a regulatory person or body; and that in all the circumstances, it was reasonable to make the disclosure. The legislation then goes on to stipulate that 'reasonableness' here depends on factors which include the identity of the person to whom the disclosure is made; the seriousness of the conduct or failure in question; the likelihood of that failure continuing;

---

[877] ERA 1996, ss 43A–43H.

[878] In *Koraski v Abertawe bro Morgannwg University Local Health Board* [2012] IRLR 4 the EAT held that what is reasonable involves 'an objective standard … and its application to the personal circumstances of the discloser': Judge McMullen QC, at [62].

[879] For this purpose, it is sufficient that the claimant reasonably believed that the acts complained of constituted either a criminal offence (or infringed another relevant legal obligation): *Bolton School v Evans* [2006] IRLR 500; *Babula v Waltham Forest College* [2007] IRLR 346 (CA).

[880] The reference to a legal obligation has been widely construed to include a breach by the employer of a contract of employment, including the applicant's own: *Parkins v Sodexho Ltd* [2002] IRLR 109; *Kraus v Penna plc* [2004] IRLR 260. However, it does not cover a case in which an employee simply alleges a repudiatory breach of contract on the part of the employer: *Cavendish Munro Professional Risks Management Ltd v Geduld* [2010] IRLR 38. Wrongdoing by a person other than the employer can come under this provision: *Hibbins v Hesters Way Neighbourhood Project* [2009] IRLR 198.

[881] Particularly relevant here would be offences under the Official Secrets Act 1989. See McColgan, 2000d.

[882] ERA 1996, s 43B.

[883] ERA 1996, s 43C.

[884] ERA 1996, ss 43D–43H; the Public Interest Disclosure (Prescribed Persons) Order 1999, SI 1999/1549, as amended.

[885] The belief must be *reasonable*, not correct: see *Darnton v University of Surrey* [2003] IRLR 133.

[886] See *Street v Derbyshire Unemployed Workers' Centre* [2004] IRLR 687 applied *Koraski v Abertawe bro Morgannwg University Local Health Board* [2012] IRLR 4.

whether the disclosure is made in breach of a duty of confidentiality owed by the employer to another person; action previously taken by the workers' employer or a regulatory person or body in response to the initial disclosure of the information to them; and whether, in making the initial disclosure, the worker had complied with any procedure for disclosure which was laid down by the employer.

The remedies available under the Act include the right of a worker[887] to complain to an employment tribunal that he or she has been subjected to a detriment by reason of having made the disclosure;[888] employees also have the right to complain of unfair dismissal (dismissal in relation to a protected disclosure being categorised as an automatically unfair dismissal under Part X of ERA 1996, for which, unusually, there is no statutory limit on compensation[889]). The Act also renders void any contract term purporting to preclude a worker from making a protected disclosure.[890]

The limited scope of the Act in terms of protecting only disclosures as opposed to a wider range of conduct related to whistleblowing was made clear in *Bolton School v Evans*.[891] Here, a teacher hacked into his school's computer system for the purpose of showing that it was not adequately safeguarding confidential information from general access by pupils. He was given a disciplinary warning for what the employer regarded as an act of misconduct and subsequently resigned after his appeal was dismissed. He claimed that the warning constituted a detriment; that it had been imposed because he had made a public interest disclosure; and that he had been (constructively) unfairly dismissed. The EAT ruled that the claimant had made a protected disclosure at the point when he informed his employer that the system was not secure. However, it held that he had been given a warning not because of the disclosure but because of the act of hacking into the system. Whereas the employment tribunal had treated the disclosure and the claimant's conduct as inseparable, the EAT insisted that the Act provided no protection in relation to acts of the employee aimed at establishing the reasonableness of his belief, as opposed to the disclosure of that belief. The Court of Appeal agreed that the Act did not extend to the employee's conduct leading up to disclosure.[892]

---

[887] ERA 1996, s 47B; on the meaning of the term 'worker', see para 3.33 *et seq* above, and see also s 43K, which contains a particularly wide extension of the term to include a situation in which an individual is introduced or supplied to work for another by a third person under circumstances where the terms on which he works are determined 'not by him but by the person for whom he works or worked, by the third person or by both of them'. In *Douglas v Birmingham City Council*, EAT, 17 March 2003, Appeal No EAT/0518/02 ILB this provision was used to bring within the Act a disclosure made by the applicant to members of the Governing Body of the school for which she worked, when her contract was with the relevant local authority. See also *Croke v Hydro Aluminium Worcester Ltd* [2007] ICR 1303. The claimant must have been a worker at the time of making the disclosure, but need not have been employed at that time by the employer who subjects him or her to the relevant detriment: *BP plc v Elstone* [2010] IRLR 558.

[888] The test is whether 'the protected disclosure is a material factor in the employer's decision to subject the claimant to a detrimental act': *NHS Manchester v Fecitt* [2012] IRLR 64, Elias LJ at [43]. On compensation, see *Virgo Fidelis Senior School v Boyle* [2004] IRLR 268; *Melia v Magna Kansei Ltd* [2006] IRLR 117. The protection continues to apply after the employment has terminated so can cover failure to provide a reference, for example: *Woodward v Abbey National* [2006] IRLR 677. The Court of Appeal has held that, as there is no provision making it unlawful for workers to victimise whistleblowers, there is no scope for vicarious liability for such an act: *NHS Manchester v Fecitt* [2012] IRLR 64, overruling *Cumbria County Council v Carlisle-Morgan* [2007] IRLR 314.

[889] ERA 1996, ss 103A, 124(1A); *Kuzel v Roche Products Ltd* [2008] IRLR 530 (discussing issues of the burden of proof in s 103A claims). On automatically unfair reasons for dismissal in general, see below, para 5.92 *et seq*.

[890] ERA 1996, s 43J.

[891] [2006] IRLR 500. See D Lewis, 2006.

[892] [2007] IRLR 140.

The changes made by the Public Interest Disclosure Act now need to be considered alongside the possible impact of the Human Rights Act 1998, under which domestic legislation must now be interpreted, so far as possible, in such a way as to give effect to Convention rights,[893] and courts and tribunals must have regard to the jurisprudence on those rights developed by the European Court of Human Rights and other specified bodies of the Council of Europe.[894] In addition, the Act creates a new cause of action for breach of Convention rights by public authorities,[895] and opens up the possibility that the common law itself may be open to reinterpretation in the light of the Convention's provisions.[896]

The Human Rights Act came into force in England and Wales in October 2000. If the case law of the European Court of Human Rights is any guide, the impact of the Act on freedom of expression in employment may be limited.[897] This is because of the qualifications placed on the right to freedom of expression in Article 10(2) of the Convention, which legitimises 'such formalities, conditions, restrictions or penalties as are prescribed by law and are necessary in a democratic society, in the interests of national security, territorial integrity or public safety, for the prevention of disorder or crime, for the protection of health or morals, for the protection of the reputation or rights of others, for preventing the disclosure of information received in confidence, or for maintaining the authority and impartiality of the judiciary'. However, in *Heinisch v Germany*[898] the European Court of Human Rights gave Article 10(2) a narrow reading. In this case, a nurse was dismissed for making a complaint to the public prosecutor alleging criminal behaviour by her employer, a state-owned nursing home, in the form of neglect of geriatric patients. The Court ruled that the disclosure of alleged illegal behaviour on the part of a government body by one of its employees was in principle protected by Article 10(1), and that dismissal in the circumstances of this case did not fall within Article 10(2), for the purposes of which the scope of the public interest in disclosure should be widely construed. Relevant factors in judging the appropriateness of an external disclosure under Article 10(2) included the feasibility of any internal disclosure, the authenticity of the information concerned, whether the employee acted in good faith or out of personal grievance towards the employer or a fellow employee, and how far the harm to the employer's reputation was outweighed by the public interest in disclosure.

Protection of employee privacy

(i) The common law

4.118   So far we have considered the remedies available to an employer to restrain an employee's use of confidential information; however, the employer itself may also collect information of a confidential and/or personal kind about its employees. The English common law has traditionally

---

[893] HRA 1998, s 3.
[894] HRA 1998, s 2.
[895] HRA 1998, s 6.
[896] Section 6(3).
[897] For discussion, see McColgan, 2000d: pp 70–72.
[898] [2011] IRLR 922.

been reluctant to recognise a general right to the protection of privacy,[899] with the result that the employer has not to date been prevented from requiring the employee to provide information of a personal kind at the hiring stage.[900] An employee is entitled not to reveal a spent conviction as defined by the Rehabilitation of Offenders Act 1974,[901] but this is the only occasion on which false information may be given without giving rise to the normal legal consequences for misrepresentation.[902] Once the employment has begun, an employer's request for private information could amount to a breach of the duty of mutual trust and confidence.[903] However, the difficulty here lies in knowing how far the courts would balance the employee's interests against what, in an appropriate case, the employer would seek to describe as its business needs.

(ii) Convention rights

4.119   As we have seen, the passage of the Human Rights Act 1998 makes it possible for human rights issues to be presented directly to UK courts which may be called upon to apply the Convention directly and/or as an aid to interpretation.[904] Article 8 of the European Convention on Human Rights states that:

> Everyone has the right to respect for his private and family life, his home and his correspondence.
> There shall be no interference by a public authority with the exercise of this right except such as is in accordance with the law and is necessary in a democratic society in the interests of national security, public safety or the economic well being of the country, for the prevention of disorder or crime, for the protection of health or morals, or for the protection of the rights and freedoms of others.

In *Halford v United Kingdom*[905] the European Court of Human Rights held that Article 8 had been breached where the applicant's employer had intercepted telephone calls which she had made from her place of work, for purposes which allegedly included collecting evidence against her in connection with a claim which she was making for sex discrimination. The Court held that the calls made from her place of work were capable of falling under Article 8, and rejected the United Kingdom government's submission that 'an employer should, in principle, without the prior knowledge of the employee, be able to monitor calls made by the latter on telephones

---

[899] See now, however, *Campbell v MGN Ltd* [2004] 2 AC 457, discussed Moreham, 2005, and *Mosley v News Group Newspapers* [2008] EMLR 20, discussed Hughes, 2009 and *Mosley v UK* Application No 48009/08, noted Hunt, 2011.

[900] For discussion of the implications of HRA 1998 in this area, see G Morris, 2001a and the references in the footnotes above.

[901] See above, para 3.15.

[902] EqA 2010 makes it unlawful for an employer to make enquiries about a job applicant's disability or health before offering work but does not specify the consequences if the applicant gives false information. *Quaere* whether protection against misrepresentation could be inferred.

[903] See paras 4.105–4.107 above.

[904] On privacy and the ECHR in employment, see Ford, 2000; G Morris, 2001a: pp 61–65; Hendrickx, 2001; Ford 2002; H Oliver, 2002; Freedland, 2007

[905] [1997] IRLR 471, 475; see Craig and Oliver, 1998. For an overview of the case law of the ECtHR in relation to Art 8, see Moreham, 2008.

provided by the employer'.[906] The applicant's case was assisted by the fact that she had not been given any prior warning of the interference, that she had been given sole use of a private phone in her office, and that she had been informed in writing that she could use this phone for the purpose of the sex discrimination proceedings. It is unclear whether the employer's conduct would have fallen under Article 8 if these special features of the case had not been present. *Halford* could provide a basis for the use of Article 8 to restrict the use by employers of surveillance and other devices which interfere with employee privacy, although the scope of any such principle is as yet comparatively untested in this context. In *McGowan v Scottish Water*[907] the EAT thought that Article 8 would be engaged in a case of covert surveillance of the employee's home, but that its application was subject to the principle of proportionality; in the instant case, the employer was justified in making videotapes of the employee's comings and goings where these established that he had been falsifying time sheets.

(iii) The interaction of data protection legislation and human rights law

4.120   Highly relevant in this context is the role played by data protection legislation. Once personal information has been collected and stored, its disclosure by the employer to a third party would be subject to the normal rules of breach of confidence, but these rules will not in themselves prevent this information being used by the employer for legitimate purposes internal to the organisation. Certain restrictions are however imposed on the storage and use of employee data by employers under the Data Protection Act 1998, which implements Directive 95/46 and significantly strengthens an earlier Act of 1984.[908]

For the purposes of the 1998 Act, the term 'data' is defined as information which is either 'being processed by means of equipment operating automatically in response to instructions given for that purpose', is recorded with the intention of being processed by such means, or 'is recorded as part of a relevant filing system or with the intention that it should form part of a relevant filing system'.[909] Those, including employers, who process data on individuals within the terms of the Act come under statutory obligations as 'data controllers'. 'Personal data' under the Act means data which relate to a living individual who can be identified from those data or from those data together with other information in the possession of the data controller, including 'any expression of opinion about the individual and any indication of the intentions of the data controller or any other person in respect of the individual'.[910] In *Durant v Financial Services Authority*[911] this definition was clarified by the Court of Appeal. Precisely because the purpose of the Act is to protect the privacy of the individual, 'it is not an automatic key to any information, readily accessible or not, of matters in which he may be named or involved'. In particular, 'mere

---

[906] See [1997] IRLR 471, 475.

[907] [2005] IRLR 167.

[908] See Ford, 1998b; 1999; and on the evolution of EU rules in this area, Simitis, 1998. See Jay, 2007 on UK data protection law and practice.

[909] A 'relevant filing system' must be one which enables 'identification of relevant information with a minimum of time and costs, through clear referencing mechanisms': *Durant v Financial Services Authority* [2004] FSR 28, at [45].

[910] DPA 1998, s 1(1).

[911] [2004] FSR 28. See S Lorber, 2004.

mention of the data subject in a document held by a data controller does not necessarily amount to his personal data'.[912] Auld LJ went on:

> It seems to me that there are two notions that may be of assistance. The first is whether the information is biographical in a significant sense, that is, going beyond the recording of the putative data subject's involvement in a matter or an event that has no personal connotations, a life event in respect of which his privacy could not be said to be compromised. The second is one of focus. The information should have the putative data subject as its focus rather than some other person with whom he may have been involved or some transaction or event in which he may have figured or have had an interest, for example, as in this case, an investigation into some other person's or body's conduct that he may have instigated. In short, it is information that affects his privacy, whether in his personal or family life, business or professional capacity.[913]

It followed that the claimant was unable to obtain disclosure of information relating to the treatment by the Authority of a complaint which he had made against his bank.

The 'processing' of data is widely defined in the Act to refer to 'obtaining, recording or holding the information or data or carrying out any operation or set of operations on the information or data'. Included in this definition are 'adaptation', 'retrieval', 'consultation', 'use', 'disclosure', 'alignment', 'combination', 'blocking', 'erasure' or 'destruction' of data.[914] Personal data can only be processed if the individual concerned has given his or her consent, or if one of a number of other specific conditions has been met.[915] More generally, all processing of data must respect the 'data protection principles'[916] which are derived from the Council of Europe Convention on Data Protection and from Directive 95/46.[917] These require, *inter alia*, that personal data is held only for one or more specified and lawful purposes, that data shall not be disclosed in a manner incompatible with those purposes, and that data shall not be retained for any longer than necessary. The individual is entitled to be informed of the fact that data concerning him or her is held, to have access to that data and to have it corrected or erased in appropriate cases. Failure to comply with the data protection principles does not automatically give rise to criminal liability but it may lead to the Information Commissioner issuing an enforcement notice (with which the data user must comply, on pain of criminal liability).

Particularly stringent controls are imposed on the processing of 'sensitive personal data', a category which includes information relating to the race or ethnic origin of the data subject, his or her political opinions, religious or other beliefs, membership or non-membership of a trade union, physical or mental health or condition, sexual life, and the commission or alleged commission of any offence and any proceedings relating to an offence.[918] At least one of a narrowly-defined set of conditions has to be satisfied: these include the 'explicit consent' of the individual concerned, and processing which is 'necessary for the purposes of exercising or performing any right or obligation

---

[912] [2004] FSR 28, at [27].
[913] [2004] FSR 28, at [28].
[914] DPA 1998, s 1(1).
[915] DPA 1998, s 4, Sch 1 para 1, and Sch 2.
[916] See DPA 1998, Sch 1, Part I.
[917] DPA 1998, s 4 and Sch 1, Part I.
[918] The definition of 'sensitive personal data' is contained in s 2 of the Act; Sch 3 outlines the restrictions which relate to the processing of such data for the purposes of the interpretation of the data protection principles under Sch 1.

which is conferred or imposed by law on the data controller in connection with employment'.[919] These various statutory obligations are complemented by Codes of Practice issued by the Information Commissioner; they may be referred to in enforcement proceedings under the Act. They include an *Employment Practices Code*[920] which makes recommendations on recruitment, employment records, monitoring at work, and information relating to workers' health.

The core individual rights under the Act are the right of access to personal data, the right to know the purposes for which those data will be used, the right to prevent processing which is likely to cause damage or distress, and the right not to be subjected to certain categories of decisions based solely on the automatic processing of personal data. With respect to the latter, the Act provides:

> An individual is entitled at any time, by notice in writing to any data controller, to require the data controller to ensure that no decision taken by or on behalf of the data controller which significantly affects that individual is based solely on the processing by automatic means of personal data in respect of which that individual is the data subject for the purpose of evaluating matters relating to him such as, for example, his performance at work ...[921]

The Act provides a general right to compensation for damage incurred by wrongful processing of data.[922] However, confidential references are not covered by the right of access,[923] nor is a data controller such as an employer obliged to provide information about its stance during negotiations.[924]

Appeals from determinations of the Information Commissioner lie to the Information Tribunal. In addition, specific criminal offences are created in relation to the holding, use, obtaining, disclosure or transfer of personal data which is unauthorised in the sense of going beyond the purposes stated in the entry on the data register. It is also a criminal offence for an employer to require an employee or job applicant to supply it with a 'relevant record' of (among other things) his or her criminal record.[925]

4.121 Additional statutory recognition of the employee's right to control over personal data regardless of whether it is automatically processed is provided by the Access to Medical Records Act 1988. An employer or prospective employer who wishes to gain access to a medical report made on an individual for employment purposes[926] must notify the individual concerned, who is then entitled to see the report before it is supplied to the employer and to request that any errors

---

[919] DPA 1998, Sch 3, paras 1, 2(1). For discussion of the relevance of this provision in one particular context, see Joseph Rowntree Foundation, *Report of Independent Inquiry into Drug Testing at Work* (2004), ch 1.4.

[920] This is regularly updated on the ICO website (www.ico.gov.uk).

[921] DPA 1998, s 12(1).

[922] DPA 1998, s 13.

[923] DPA 1998, s 37 and Sch 7, para 1.

[924] This is the effect of DPA 1998, s 37 and Sch 7, paras 5 and 7.

[925] DPA 1998, s 56.

[926] These are defined as 'the purposes in relation to the individual of any person by whom he is or has been, or is seeking to be, employed (whether under a contract of service or otherwise)': Access to Medical Records Act 1988, s 1(1). Note also that under the Data Protection Act 1998, Sch 3, para 8, processing of health records may only be undertaken by a health professional or by a person who owes a duty of confidentiality equivalent to that which would be owed by a health professional. See also DPA 1998, s 57.

be corrected. The medical practitioner who made the report may refuse to correct the alleged errors, but must then, at the individual's request, attach a statement of the individual's views to his or her report. The court has power to grant a specific order to require compliance with the Act.

4.122   The obligations to respect employee privacy which derive from data protection legislation cut across recent legislation which is designed to enable employers and others to intercept electronic communications for business purposes. The Telecommunications Data Protection Directive,[927] which was implemented in the UK by the Regulation of Investigatory Powers Act 2000, required the confidentiality of electronic communications to be respected, but allowed for certain derogations of which interceptions for business purposes is one. Its successor, the Privacy and Electronic Communication Directive,[928] contains a similar provision. To this end, the Telecommunications (Lawful Business Practice) (Interception of Communications) Regulations 2000[929] legitimise interceptions made for various purposes including establishing compliance with regulatory or self-regulatory practices or procedures, investigating or detecting unauthorised use of telecommunication systems, and monitoring communications to see if they are of a business nature. Such conduct is lawful only if the person making the interception 'has made all reasonable efforts to inform every person who may use the telecommunications system in question that communications transmitted by means thereof may be intercepted'.[930] The Department of Trade and Industry (now BIS) has taken the view that the employer's obligation extends to its own workers and to others making use of the system, but not to those calling, or receiving calls, from outside.[931] Interceptions made with the consent of the persons making and receiving the communications are outside the scope of the primary legislation. The Act and the Regulations, then, permit employers to monitor e-mail communications between employees (and, more generally, between employees and third parties) under a wide range of circumstances. However, any data collected by an employer under this provision would remain subject to the requirements of the Data Protection Act 1998, as outlined above, and of the HRA 1998.[932]

INCOME SECURITY: SICK PAY AND LAY-OFF

4.123   The common law offers some residual protection to employees against loss of income through no fault of their own in the cases of sickness or suspension of employment on account of lack of work ('lay-off'). A common law claim may be brought in the form of wages due as earned, but only if the employee can show that being ready and willing to work is sufficient 'consideration' for payment, and this is normally only the case for salaried employees.[933] If actual performance of work is required for suing in debt, the employee may nevertheless be able to benefit from an implied term that the employer will pay sick pay in the event of illness or, in the case of lay-off,

---

[927] Directive 97/66?EC.

[928] Directive 2002/58/EC.

[929] SI 2000/2699.

[930] SI 2000/2699, reg 3.

[931] See G Morris, 2002a.

[932] In this respect, the Information Commissioner's *Employment Practices Code*, referred to above, provides extensive guidance on various forms of monitoring, including the monitoring of emails.

[933] See above, para 4.62.

ensure that work is available; if the payments are not made, a claim in damages will ensue. However, at common law such claims will only last for a limited period of time. Moreover, if the contract explicitly places the risk of such losses on the employee, or if it is a 'contract at will', containing neither a notice clause nor a term requiring the employer to show good cause for dismissal or suspension, the common law is completely unable to protect the employee's expectations of continuing payment.

These common law rules have been supplemented by collective bargaining and, more recently, by statutory regulation in the form of statutory sick pay and guaranteed pay. These statutory interventions were not principally guided by the aim of ensuring security of income, however. In each case their goal was to shift obligations which had previously been borne by the state social insurance system, in the form of unemployment and sickness benefits, on to individual employers; rather than building on social security entitlements, they replaced them, while in general providing lower levels of payment. The statutory entitlements to which they give rise may also in most cases be set off against the employee's contractual rights.[934]

The right to sick pay at common law

4.124   The question of whether the employee is entitled to receive payments during periods of illness was for a long time treated from the point of view of the construction of the basic wage-work bargain. If the consideration was faithful service as opposed to the completion of work, wages would continue throughout the period of absence, until such time as the employer terminated the contract by giving notice. This principle applied to more senior and salaried employees, such as the production manager employed in a textiles factory in *Orman v Saville Sportswear Ltd*.[935] But in each case, the question was whether the contract of employment was based on an agreement to the effect that the employee would be paid when ready and willing to work, or only for time spent actually working. The employer could resolve the question by posting a notice or otherwise making it clear that wages were not paid during sickness.[936] In the absence of an express term or one implied by custom and practice, most hourly-paid workers and piece workers were regarded as receiving wages only for work done, and so had no inherent right to sick pay. The only clear decision to the contrary, *Marrison v Bell*,[937] was subsequently distinguished in a string of cases,[938] and has had little influence on the subsequent development of the law.

The more modern tendency has been to regard the issue not in terms of the 'consideration' for payment, but to see whether a term can be implied to provide the right to sick pay independently of whether the principle of 'no work, no pay' applies to other situations. In *Howman & Son Ltd v Blyth*[939] a term was implied based on the custom in the *industry* of which the firm was a part, and in *Mears v Safecar Security Ltd*[940] the Court of Appeal was prepared to imply a term as a 'necessary

[934] See generally Szyszczak, 1986.
[935] [1960] 1 WLR 1055.
[936] *Petrie v MacFisheries Ltd* [1940] 1 KB 258.
[937] [1939] 2 KB 187.
[938] *Hancock v BSA Tools Ltd* [1939] 4 All ER 538 (engineering worker); *Petrie v MacFisheries Ltd* [1940] 1 KB 258 (fish packer); *O'Grady v M Saper Ltd* [1940] 2 KB 469 (commissionaire).
[939] [1983] ICR 416.
[940] [1982] ICR 626.

incident' of the employment relationship. This can be done on the basis that the payment of sick pay is necessary to the long-term maintenance of the relationship between the parties. However, there is no presumption either in favour or against such a term and it can easily be excluded by evidence of a contrary intention on the part of the employer, which is what happened in *Mears* itself.

The terms of any express provision made by an employer for sick pay or disability benefits will normally be incorporated into the contracts of employment of individual employees, according to the normal tests. Once incorporation has taken place, the employer is bound to follow the provisions of the scheme, the terms of which fall to be interpreted by the principle that the employer should as far as possible act in good faith and avoid perverse or irrational decisions, thereby aligning the express terms with the implied duty of mutual trust and confidence.[941] Nor can the employer avoid such contractual obligations by purporting to dismiss the employee through the exercise of any general power to terminate the contract by giving notice. This result can be understood by reference to an implied term to the effect that the employer will not give notice under these circumstances. The basis for implying such a term is that neither party could have intended the notice clause to operate in such a case; otherwise, there would have been no point in making provision for sickness benefits in the first place.[942] Alternatively, it is open to the court to decide that, on the true construction of the *express* terms of the contract, the notice clause has been limited by the clause relating to sickness benefits.[943]

Statutory sick pay

4.125   The payment of a short-term benefit in respect of loss of income through illness was for a long period the preserve of social security. A social insurance benefit, sickness benefit, was available to those employees (technically, 'employed earners') with an adequate contribution record;[944] and many employers made payments of occupational sick pay on top of employees' social security entitlements. In 1980 a White Paper[945] proposed to shift the responsibility for the administration of short-term sickness payments from the state to employers, on the grounds that over 80% of employers already had schemes in place for dealing with this problem and could deal with it more effectively than the state could. Accordingly, the Social Security and Housing Benefits Act 1982 introduced statutory sick pay (SSP), which was to be payable by employers for the first eight weeks of illness at one of a number of rates set by the Act. SSP payments were directly set off against employees' contractual entitlements, so ending the 'double compensation' which had operated, *de facto*, under the previous system. The 1982 Act provided for the costs of SSP payments to be recovered in full by employers, in the form of rebates on their own national insurance contributions. Since then the scheme has gradually been amended so that it now covers the first twenty-eight weeks of illness, after which the employee transfers to one of a number of

---

[941] See *Scottish Courage Ltd v Guthrie*, 5 February 2004, Appeal No UKEAT/0788/03/MAA.

[942] *Aspden v Webbs Poultry & Meat Group (Holdings) Ltd* [1996] IRLR 521, 524 (Sedley J); *Villella v MFI Furniture Centres Ltd* [1999] IRLR 468; *Briscoe v Lubrizol Ltd* [2002] IRLR 607; cf. *Hill v General Accident Fire and Life Assurance Corpn plc* [1998] IRLR 641.

[943] *Adin v Sedco Forex International Resources Ltd* [1997] IRLR 280.

[944] On the meaning of the term 'employed earner' and the conditions for making social security contributions, see above, para 3.22.

[945] DHSS, *Income During Sickness: A New Strategy* (1980, Cmnd 7684).

social security benefits.[946] The cost of the scheme to employers was also increased by the withdrawal of the national insurance rebate for all but smaller firms.[947]

The category of employees capable of qualifying for SSP was considered in chapter 3 above:[948] essentially, the individual must be an employed earner with normal weekly wages at or above the lower earnings level for national insurance contributions purposes,

A claim is made in relation to a 'day of incapacity' which is defined as a day 'in relation to a contract of service ... [when] the employee concerned is, or is deemed in accordance with regulations to be, incapable by reason of some specific disease or bodily or mental disablement of doing work which he can reasonably be expected to do under that contract'.[949]

A number of further conditions must then be met for the 'day of incapacity' to count. First, it must fall within a 'period of incapacity' which is a period of at least four consecutive days of incapacity, including days of the week when the employee does not normally work, or holidays.[950] Second, it must fall within a 'period of entitlement'[951] which roughly follows the period of incapacity but which only begins when the employee's contract of employment first takes effect and ends after twenty-eight weeks or when the contract of employment ends, if that is sooner; however, the employer may not terminate the contract for the purposes of avoiding SSP liability.[952] Third, it must fall on a 'qualifying day' which is to be agreed between the employer and employee involved (which could be via a term incorporated from a collective agreement between the employer and a trade union representing the employee). If no such day is agreed, the Statutory Sick Pay (General) Regulations[953] provide that it shall be the normal agreed working days in the week in question or, if there are no such days, the Wednesday of that week. Finally, no SSP is payable for the first three qualifying days in any period of entitlement (the 'waiting days'). However, if there are less than eight weeks between two periods of incapacity then they are treated as one linked period for this purpose, so that the employee does not have to endure three 'waiting days' at the start of the second period.[954]

SSP is paid at a weekly rate which was set at £85.85 from 6 April 2012.[955] SSP payments reduce any contractual entitlement to sick pay by an equivalent amount.[956] The employee's entitlement is exhausted once he or she is paid the equivalent of 28 weeks of sick pay during any one period of entitlement, the maximum length of which is three years.[957] Once SSP entitlement ceases for this reason, the individual's entitlement is transferred to the long-term social security incapacity benefit (now entitled Employment and Support Allowance).[958]

---

[946] Wikeley, 2002: ch 15.

[947] By the SSPA 1994. Another significant reform was the transfer of adjudication of SSP matters from the social security system to the Inland Revenue, by the Social Security Contributions (Transfer of Functions etc) Act 1999. See Wikeley, 2002: p 531.

[948] See para 3.22 above; *Brown v Chief Adjudication Officer* [1997] IRLR 110.

[949] SSCBA 1992, s 151(4); SI 1982/894, reg 2(2).

[950] SSCBA 1992, s 152.

[951] SSCBA 1992, s 153; SI 1982/894, reg 3.

[952] SSCBA 1992, s 153(10); SI 1982/894, reg 4.

[953] SI 1982/894.

[954] SSCBA 1992, s 152(3).

[955] SSCBA 1992, s 157(1), as amended. The daily rate is the weekly rate divided by the number of qualifying days in respect of any claim: SSCBA 1992, s 157(3).

[956] SSCBA 1992, Sch 12, para 2.

[957] SI 1982/894, reg 3(3).

[958] Wikeley, 2002: ch 15.

The employee or somebody acting on his or her behalf must notify the employer of their incapacity for work; the Act and Regulations allow the employer to set the time limit and form in which notification is to take place, as long as it takes reasonable steps to make this known to the employee.[959] The employer is entitled to set a time limit by reference to the first qualifying day. If notification is late, the employer may refuse to pay SSP in respect of that day. The employee must also notify the employer of a day of incapacity even if it is one of the waiting days in respect of which no SSP is payable; if notification is late, the employer is entitled to refuse to pay SSP in respect of the first day when he would otherwise have to do so, but not in respect of any further qualifying days.[960]

Suspension and lay-off at common law

4.126   The employer has no *inherent* or automatic right of lay-off at common law, which starts from the principle that 'there should be either employment or non-employment and that suspension is an uneasy and uncertain limbo'.[961] If work is suspended then the employee is *prima facie* entitled to wages for this period and for any period of notice which the employer would need to have given to terminate the contract lawfully. These basic principles were established in two landmark cases in the development of modern employment law.

In *Devonald v Rosser & Sons Ltd*[962] the employer, which owned a tinplate works, closed the works for lack of business during a depression in the trade, and two weeks later gave notice of one month to terminate the contracts of the manual workforce. During this six-week period the employees, who were piece workers, received no pay. They could not bring a claim in debt, since they were paid for each completed piece of work, and none had been done during the period in question. However, a claim in damages succeeded on the basis of an implied term that the employer would find them work for the period during which they remained in employment. Lord Alverstone CJ said that:

> ... the necessary implication to be drawn from this contract is at least that the master will find a reasonable amount of work up to the expiration of a notice given in accordance with the contract ... it would be no excuse to the master, for non-performance of his implied obligation to provide the workman with work, that he could no longer make his plates at a profit for orders or for stock. It is to be observed that the question of how the works are to be carried on, whether they are to work short or full time, is a matter which rests entirely in the hands of the [employer]...[963]

Gorrell Barnes P also thought that the lack of work 'is not a matter which is not in any sense within the knowledge or control of the workman; it rests entirely with the employer, who can

---

[959] SSCBA 1992, s 156; SI 1982/894, reg 7.
[960] This at least *appears* to be the effect of SSCBA 1992, s 156(2)(b).
[961] McCallum, 1989: p 233.
[962] [1906] 2 KB 728.
[963] [1906] 2 KB 728, 740.

anticipate in respect of such matters ... It seems to me that it is not reasonable to imply that the risk of that was in the contemplation of both sides as being taken by the workman'.[964]

In the second case, *Hanley v Pease & Partners Ltd*[965] the employee was a mineworker who overslept one morning and missed a shift. The employer had a rule that anyone who was more than ten minutes late for a shift would not be allowed to work on that day. On the next day the employee turned up for work on time but he was suspended for that day. He successfully sued for damages for wrongful dismissal. The court held that the contract contained no express right of suspension in respect of the second day, and that no such right could be implied either: 'after declining to dismiss the workman – after electing to treat the contract as a continuing one – the employers took upon themselves to suspend him for one day; in other words to deprive the workman of his wages for one day, thereby assessing their own damages for the servant's misconduct at the sum which would be represented by one day's wages. They have no possible right to do that'.[966]

The effect of these two cases is that in relation to piece workers and others whose right to payment is correlative with their completion of work, the employer is under a certain duty to find work in order to enable the employee to earn his or her wages. If, on the other hand, the employee is salaried, the right to continuing payment arises on the employee simply showing that he or she was ready to work.[967]

The extent of the obligation to find work may be limited, however, if the employer can point to factors beyond its control. In *Minnevitch v Café de Paris (Londres) Ltd*[968] the owner of a cabaret closed his business for six days following the death of King George V. His musicians, who were paid according to performance, received nothing while the club was closed for mourning in this way. The court held that a closure of two days would have been reasonable, but that the employees were entitled to payment for the extra four days. This case could be seen as one of an express contractual right of lay-off, since employment was expressly on the basis of 'no work, no pay'.[969] However, in this respect *Minnevitch* is no different from *Devonald*, in which the employees were expressly to be paid by the piece for work completed; but that did not prevent them from claiming wages for the whole period during which the works was closed. The difference between the two cases is that in *Minnevitch* the employer had an implied right to suspend employment without pay in circumstances where the reason for the suspension was something he could do nothing about, whereas in *Devonald*'s case the lack of work was seen to be the employer's responsibility.

A more problematic case is *Browning v Crumlin Valley Collieries Ltd*.[970] Here, mineworkers were laid off without pay while their mine was closed by reason of flooding. The judge simply applied 'no work, no pay' to decide the case, which is not satisfactory since it does not take into account the possibility of an implied term of the kind found by the court in *Devonald v Rosser & Son Ltd*. As Freedland has argued, to say that the risk was shared between employer and employee in this case is to ignore the point that the responsibility for ensuring that the mine was safe to work

[964] [1906] 2 KB 728, 743.
[965] [1915] 1 KB 698.
[966] [1915] 1 KB 698, 705 (Lush J).
[967] See above, para 4.62.
[968] [1936] 1 All ER 884.
[969] McCallum, 1989: p 215.
[970] [1926] 1 KB 522.

in was, in law and in practice, that of the employer. Courts have declined to follow *Browning* in a number of subsequent decisions,[971] while *Devonald* has been expressly approved.[972]

If the employer wishes to have a right to suspend work without pay, it must contract for it explicitly, and such a term, like any other imposed in a standard form contract, will be construed *contra proferentem*. A contract at will or 'minute contract' under which the employer retains the right to dismiss by giving summary notice effectively achieves the same end: there is no difference here between dismissal and suspension.[973] What might look like suspension is simply dismissal and re-employment; nor will any damages be payable for wrongful dismissal, since the employer is, by definition, entitled to dispense with notice. However, a contract of this kind is now unusual in Britain. This is partly because since the Contracts of Employment Act 1963, statute has implied minimum notice periods into most contracts of employment.[974]

It might be thought, on the authority of *Turner v Sawdon & Co*,[975] that an employer is not obliged to provide work for the employee to do as long as he pays his or her wages for the period of employment. The issue here is whether the employee can quit and claim damages for wrongful and/or unfair dismissal, on the basis that the employer, in failing to provide him or her with work, has committed a repudiatory breach of contract. An employee who needs to work in order to retain the skills necessary to practise his or her chosen trade, or who needs to display their work to a wider audience, could well have a claim of this sort. In *Turner v Sawdon*[976] it was said that 'in the case of an actor who accepts an engagement, it may be an important consideration with him to have an opportunity of displaying his abilities before the public, and it may be that there is an implied obligation on the part of the master to afford such an opportunity'. It is therefore 'necessary to look at the background to the contract to see how it should be construed',[977] and it would be unusual if, given the expansion of the reciprocal duty of co-operation, denying the employee the opportunity to work did not amount to a breach of the obligation of 'mutual trust and confidence' between the two parties.[978]

The implication of a duty to provide work significantly affects the practice of employers insisting on employees taking 'garden leave' before their term of employment may be terminated.[979] If an employee is forced into idleness while waiting to sit out his or her notice, this can be seen as an employer's breach of the obligation to enable a skilled employee to maintain his or her ability to work in his or her chosen trade or livelihood. To avoid a finding of breach by the employer in such a case, it is arguable that 'garden leave' clauses would have to be drafted in such a way as to give the employer an express power to exclude the employee from work for the period of notice.[980] However, this would greatly increase the chances of such clauses being struck down for restraint of trade.[981]

---

[971] *Jones v Harry Sherman Ltd* (1969) 4 ITR 63; Johnson v Cross [1977] ICR 872.

[972] In *Bauman v Hulton Press Ltd* [1952] 2 All ER 1121, 1123; *Bond v CAV Ltd* [1983] IRLR 360, 366; Freedland, 1976b: p 89; McCallum, 1989: pp 216–217.

[973] See *Marshall v English Electric Co Ltd* [1945] 1 All ER 653.

[974] See below, para 5.15.

[975] [1901] 2 KB 653.

[976] [1901] 2 KB 653, 659 (Stirling LJ).

[977] *Breach v Epsylon Industries Ltd* [1976] ICR 316, 321.

[978] On the mutual duty of trust and confidence, see paras 4.105-4.107 above.

[979] *William Hill Organisation Ltd v Tucker* [1998] IRLR 313. See also *SG & R Valuation Service Co LLC v Boudrais* [2008] IRLR 770, approved by the Court of Appeal in *Standard Life Health Care Ltd v Gorman* [2010] IRLR 233.

[980] See the discussion of this point by Morritt LJ in *William Hill Organisation v Tucker* [1998] IRLR 313, 317–318.

[981] See para 4.113 above.

Statutory guaranteed pay

4.127   The statutory right to guaranteed pay was introduced by the EPA 1975 and is now consolidated in Part III of ERA 1996. Prior to 1977 when the relevant provisions were brought into effect, income maintenance for employees who were laid off might come from one of three sources: the individual contract of employment, guaranteed week collective agreements between employers and trade unions, and unemployment benefit. The immediate purpose of the new statutory provision was to provide a 'floor of rights' within the employment relationship, thereby granting a measure of protection to workers who were not covered by a guaranteed week agreement; but at the same time it was also intended to shift the burden of compensation for short-term unemployment away from the state national insurance system onto individual employers.[982]

Employees with continuous employment of at least one month ending with the day before the payment is claimed qualify for protection. The right to the statutory payment arises in relation to each particular day without work, referred to as a 'workless day'.[983] The employee must show that throughout the day in question, he or she was not provided with work by his or her employer by reason of either 'a diminution in the requirements of the employer's business for work of the kind which the employee is employed to do',[984] or 'any other occurrence affecting the normal working of the employer's business'[985] in relation to such work. The employee must also show that the day is one in respect of any part of which 'he would normally be required to work in accordance with his contract of employment'.[986] No claim may be made in any day when the lack of work is caused by a lock-out, strike or other industrial action involving an employee of the employer or an associated employer;[987] and a claim is also excluded if the employee refuses an offer from the employer of alternative work for that day which is 'suitable in all the circumstances, (whether or not it is work which the employee is under his contract employed to perform)'.[988]

The amount of the statutory 'guarantee payment' is calculated by reference to the normal working hours of the employee in question and the minimum 'guaranteed hourly rate'. This is derived by taking the employee's normal weekly pay[989] and dividing it by his or her normal working hours in that week or, if normal working hours differ from week to week, taking a twelve-week average.[990] However, the statutory payment is subject to an upper limit in respect of each day (£23.50 from 1 February 2012), and in any three-month period the employee is restricted to receiving statutory payments for a maximum of five days or the number of days he or she normally works in a week, whichever is less. The statutory payment is claimed by way of complaint to an employment tribunal which must normally be brought within three months of the day in respect

---

[982] See Hepple *et al*, 1977; Szyszczak, 1990: ch 5.

[983] ERA 1996, s 28(1), (3)(a).

[984] The same phrase is used to define 'redundancy' for the purposes of dismissal under ERA 1996, s 139: on its meaning, see below, paras 5.155 *et seq*.

[985] This apparently does not cover a voluntary closure by the employer, for example to observe a Jewish holiday (*North v Pavleigh* [1977] IRLR 461), but it seems highly likely that the employee would have a contractual claim in these circumstances (cf *Minnevitch v Café de Paris (Londres) Ltd* [1936] 1 All ER 884).

[986] ERA 1996, s 28(1).

[987] ERA 1996, s 29(3).

[988] ERA 1996, s 29(4)(a). The employee must also comply with 'reasonable requirements imposed by his employer with a view to ensuring that his services are available' (s 29(5)). On the case law under these provisions, see Szyszczak, 1990: pp 107–111.

[989] This is as defined by ERA 1996, ss 220–224.

[990] ERA 1996, s 30.

of which the claim is made.[991] The statutory payment goes to discharge, by an equivalent amount, any contractual obligation of the employer.[992]

Many of the difficulties associated with these provisions stem from their central premise that normal daily and weekly working hours can be identified in a given case. It is clear that if the employee is not required to work on a particular day, because it falls on a holiday or a weekly break, no claim can be made in respect of *that* day,[993] even if it does arise in respect of other days without work. However, a claim could be defeated completely if the employer can show that the employee had no contractual right to work on *any* particular day. This will be the case if the employee is employed on a casual basis to the degree that there are no normal hours, so that the concept of a 'workless day' becomes meaningless.[994]

Hours may also be varied by agreement, in response, for example, to reduced demand for labour. Where this happens, it is open to an employer to argue that on the days when no work is done, the employee is no longer 'normally ... required to work in accordance with his contract of employment'[995] on those days, and so again they do not count as 'workless days'.[996] This would seem to defeat the purposes of the Act, but the fault appears to lie in the way it was drafted. When calculating the amount of the statutory payment in a case where the contract has been varied for the purposes of short-time working, section 30(5) expressly requires the tribunal to take into account the terms of the original contract before it was varied;[997] but no such provision is made in section 28 which governs the initial determination of the employee's entitlement. It could be argued that section 28 should nevertheless be interpreted by reference to section 30(5), on the grounds that if this were not done, the latter would make no sense.[998]

A further difficulty with the Act is illustrated by the facts of *Trevethan v Sterling Metals Ltd.*[999] The employee was employed as a night-shift worker and worked four ten-hour shifts per week. Employees on the day-shift worked five eight-hour shifts. The factory was closed for a week. The day-shift workers received statutory guarantee payments in respect of five workless days, but the tribunal held that the employee was entitled only to four, since his normal hours were spread over four working days as opposed to five.

A night-shift worker whose working hours span midnight is deemed to be employed on either one of the two days in question, but not both.[1000] However, the wider problem is that the Act measures lack of work in units of days, as opposed to looking simply at the reduction in working hours over the week or month in question. By assuming a normal working week of five days, it indirectly penalises those employees whose normal working week is concentrated into a shorter period.

---

[991] ERA 1996, s 34. On time limits in general, see para 2.17 above.
[992] ERA 1996, s 32.
[993] Cf ERA 1996, s 30(1); *York and Reynolds v Colledge Hosiery Co Ltd* [1978] IRLR 53.
[994] *Mailway (Southern) Ltd v Willsher* [1978] ICR 511; cf *Miller v Harry Thornton (Lollies) Ltd* [1978] IRLR 430; Szyszczak, 1990: p 103.
[995] ERA 1996, s 28(1).
[996] *Clemens v Peter Richards Ltd* [1977] IRLR 332; *Daley v Strathclyde Regional Council* [1977] IRLR 414.
[997] Specifically, under s 30(5) the tribunal must take the last day on which the original contract was in force as the equivalent of the day on which the statutory payment is payable.
[998] See Szyszczak, 1990: p 102.
[999] [1977] IRLR 416.
[1000] ERA 1996, s 28(5).

The upper limit on the amount of statutory payments means that the 'floor of rights' set by the Act is not high in relation to average provision.[1001] The Act also permits the Secretary of State to issue an exemption order, excluding employees already covered by guaranteed week collective agreements from the application of the Act. An agreement does not necessarily have to provide equivalent benefits to those guaranteed by the Act, although it must provide for a dispute-resolution procedure.[1002] A number of orders have been issued from time to time, mainly giving priority to agreements which have been designed with the requirements of particular industries in mind.[1003]

Payment on suspension from work on medical grounds

4.128 ERA 1996 also provides for a right of payment where an employee is suspended from work on medical grounds as a result of a requirement imposed by statute or a recommendation contained in a code of practice issued under the Health and Safety at Work Act 1974, if it is also related to one of a number of matters listed in the Act, which are mainly concerned with exposure to lead, radiation and certain chemical processes.[1004] The employee is entitled to receive a week's pay for each week of suspension, for a period of up to 26 weeks. The qualifying conditions with regard to continuity of employment are basically the same as for statutory guaranteed pay,[1005] and there are similar exclusions for cases in which the employee refuses an offer of suitable alternative work or does not comply with reasonable requirements to ensure that his or her services are available to the employer.[1006] No claim may be made in respect of any period when the employee is incapable of work by reason of disease or disablement.[1007] Statutory payments under these provisions discharge any contractual obligations of the employer by an equivalent amount.[1008]

OCCUPATIONAL PENSION SCHEMES[1009]

4.129 An employee's interest in the receipt of an occupational pension from his or her employer following retirement through age or ill health is likely to be among his or her most valuable financial assets. Employment law plays a surprisingly marginal role in identifying and protecting this interest. In part this is because the state has sought to regulate pension provision through other means, principally through social security law and tax law. However, the goal of providing

---

[1001] See Szyszczak, 1990: p 98.

[1002] ERA 1996, s 35(4).

[1003] For an account of the position up to the late 1980s, see Szyszczak, 1990: pp 112–114.

[1004] ERA 1996, ss 64–65, 69–70.

[1005] ERA 1996, s 65(1)–(2).

[1006] ERA 1996, s 65(4).

[1007] ERA 1996, s 65(3).

[1008] ERA 1996, s 69(3).

[1009] In this section, we focus on those aspects of pensions law which relate closely to the employment relationship; we do not seek to provide a full treatment of the tax and social security aspects of the subject. For fuller detail, specialist works may be consulted. See Wikeley, 2002: ch 17.

comprehensive provision through state social security has been in retreat for some time,[1010] and this is responsible, in part, for refocusing the interest of policy-makers on to employer-based schemes. Another factor has been growing evidence that occupational schemes are vulnerable to predatory employer behaviour. The most dramatic example of this, the fraudulent depletion of the Mirror Group pension funds, is nevertheless atypical. More common and in some ways more problematic from the point of view of legal regulation are practices which, without involving fraud in any way, may enable employers to release pension scheme surpluses to fund merger and takeover activity and other activities of the business, at a potential cost in terms of reduced benefits for future and existing pensioners. The failure of schemes following the employer's insolvency is also becoming more common. The past few years have seen a rise in litigation designed to establish the respective rights of employers, pension fund trustees and beneficiaries in this type of situation and the beginnings of a more systematic approach to statutory pension protection.[1011]

Types of pension scheme

4.130   Pension schemes come in a variety of different forms. It is possible to distinguish between state schemes, employer-based or occupational schemes, and personal or individual schemes.

(i) State pension schemes

4.131   The state retirement pension is a contributory social insurance benefit consisting of two main components. The 'basic pension' is a flat-rate benefit payable to an individual who has reached pensionable age.[1012] There is no longer a retirement condition attached to the receipt of the pension, nor is there any deduction for earnings from employment after reaching pensionable age,[1013] so that the receipt of the pension may be combined with either full- or part-time employment at the option of the individual concerned. Pensionable age under the state scheme was initially set at 65 for men and 60 for women, but measures introduced by the Pensions Act 1995 are giving effect to a gradual equalisation, raising the pensionable age of women to 65 over 10 years starting from April 2010. As a result of changes made by the Pensions Acts 2007 and 2011, the state pensionable age is set to rise to 66 for both sexes by 2020, and to 67 by 2028.

   The right to the basic state pension is based on the individual's national insurance contributions while in employment, or, in some cases, the contributions of his or her spouse. There are also rights to additional payments for dependants and in the case of invalidity, and to a small age-addition for those who have reached the age of 80. The level of the basic pension has undergone a gradual decline since the early 1980s when it began to be uprated with prices,[1014] rather than with whichever of earnings and prices was rising more quickly. The Pensions Act 2007 restored the link with earnings, envisaging its gradual phasing in between 2012 and 2015. However, with effect

---

[1010] On the reasons for this, see Wikeley, 2002: ch 17.
[1011] The principle of equal treatment has also exerted a growing influence. See below, para 6.109.
[1012] See generally Wikeley, 2002: pp 222–240.
[1013] The retirement condition and earnings rule were abolished for most purposes by the SSA 1989, s 7 and Sch 1.
[1014] By virtue of SSA 1980, s 1.

from April 2011 the Coalition government implemented its 'triple lock' policy according to which basic pension must be uprated on an annual basis by 2.5% or by the increase in average earnings or consumer prices over the previous year, if either is higher.

State social security also provides for an additional or 'state second' pension. When introduced in the Social Security Act 1975, the state earnings-related pension scheme (SERPS) was intended to provide a pension equivalent to around one-quarter of the employee's average pre-retirement earnings between the lower and upper earnings limits for national insurance contributions.[1015] The Social Security Act 1986 changed the pension formula with the effect that those reaching pensionable age after April 1999 would receive reduced benefits. Over a ten-year transitional period the rate of accrual was reduced so as to produce a pension based on one-fifth as opposed to one-quarter of average earnings; moreover, these were to be based on an average of earnings in all years of an individual's working life as opposed to the 'best twenty years' as initially provided for.[1016] Further changes were made by the Child Support, Pensions and Social Security Act 2001 and subsequent statutes, culminating in the Pensions Act 2007, which restructured SERPS and renamed it the 'state second pension' (or 'S2P').[1017] In a 'first phase' of these reforms, the S2P focused benefits on to lower earners, replacing the uniform SERPS accrual rate with three separate rates according to earnings levels. In a second phase, the earnings-related element is gradually being withdrawn altogether, to be replaced by a flat-rate pension.

(ii) Occupational pension schemes: final salary or defined-benefit schemes

4.132 Until recently the majority of occupational schemes were 'defined-benefit' or 'salary-related' schemes which guaranteed the employee benefits based on his or her average or final salary and number of years' service with the employer. These types of schemes cover a diminishing number of employees as a result of employers' decisions to close schemes to new entrants or, in some cases, to further contributions from existing members. Tax regulations place implicit limits on the size of the pension payments which schemes of this sort may provide. In the case of schemes which are 'approved' by the Inland Revenue, the fund's investments are free from income tax, and various tax reliefs operate on the employer's and employees' contributions. Pension payments to former employees attract income tax in the normal way but lump sums paid on retirement are not taxed.[1018]

(iii) Occupational pension schemes: money purchase or defined contribution schemes

4.133   Prior to the Social Security Act 1986, only those occupational schemes which offered defined benefits based on the employee's salary could be contracted out of SERPS. Under the 1986 Act it also became possible for employers to contract out by offering employees benefits

---

[1015] On the lower and upper earnings limits, see above, para 3.19.
[1016] See Wikeley, 2002: p 595.
[1017] See generally Wikeley, 2002 pp 620–625.
[1018] See generally Nobles, 1993, for an account of the interaction of tax and social security legislation and trust law in the construction of the legal concepts governing occupational pension schemes.

under a 'money purchase' or 'defined contribution' scheme. Under this arrangement, certain minimum contributions must be paid in but the scheme need not guarantee a pension based on any particular formula. The pension may simply be based, then, on the returns from investments made, and not on the salary and service record of the individual employee. Money purchase schemes do not need to guarantee a certain minimum level of income to the employee in order to qualify for contracting out. In place of a guaranteed income floor, the employee is indirectly protected by regulations governing the form in which the investment may be made. Notwithstanding these protections, the essence of a money-purchase scheme is the transfer of risk from employer to employee. In the past decade, as increasing numbers of defined-benefit schemes have been closed to new members, they have largely been replaced by defined contribution schemes.[1019]

(iv) Personal pension schemes

4.134   The Social Security Act 1986 also introduced a number of measures designed to extend individual choice in relation to pension provision. In particular, it allowed individual employees the option of leaving SERPS (as the state second pension was then known) or their employer's occupational scheme and setting up personal pension schemes of their own, in which the contracted-out portion of their national insurance contributions and those of their employer would then be invested.[1020] These are individual money-purchase schemes which, like their occupational counterparts, do not in themselves guarantee a particular level of final benefit; nor are they required by legislation to match the benefits which the state second pension provides.[1021] As a consequence of the widening of individual choice, an employer may no longer insist on its employees becoming members of an occupational pension scheme;[1022] however, the employer is not obliged to make additional contributions to an employee's individual scheme, beyond its national insurance contribution liability. In practice only a small minority of employers makes such additional contributions.[1023] The tax treatment of individual schemes is in principle more favourable than that governing occupational defined-benefit and money-purchase schemes, but this effect is generally confined to higher earners.[1024]

[1019] See Deakin, 2004; Buchanan and Deakin, 2012. In 2010, there were 5.3 million active members (that is, current employees) of public sector occupational schemes, virtually all of whom were in final salary schemes, and 3 million active members of private sector occupational schemes, a fall from over 6 million in 1991. Of the 3 million or so in private sector occupational schemes in 2010, around 1.8 million were in final salary schemes, 0.8 million were in career average schemes, and just under one million were in defined contribution schemes (ONS, *Occupational Pension Schemes Survey, 2010 Annual Report* (2011)).

[1020] See Wikeley, 2002: p 249.

[1021] See Wikeley, 2002: pp 257–259.

[1022] PSA 1993, s 160.

[1023] In 1991, of full-time male employees with personal pension schemes, fewer than one in five had schemes to which the employer made additional contributions: see Wikeley, 2002: pp 257–258.

[1024] See Dilnot and Disney, 1989.

(v) Stakeholder pensions

4.135   The Welfare Reform and Pensions Act 1999[1025] introduced a requirement that all employers employing more than five employees, and not already providing either an occupational scheme or a personal pension scheme to which the employer makes a specific minimum contribution, had to offer employees with more than three months continuous employment access to a 'stakeholder pension'. This requirement came into effect from 1 April 2001. A stakeholder pension may be (and in practice often will be) provided not by the employer, but by a commercial provider. The employer is not under an obligation to make any contribution; its obligation is to choose a designated scheme, make the necessary deductions of employees' contributions, and arrange for the payment of contributions to the pension provider.

(vi) The National Employment Savings Trust (NEST)

4.136   The Pensions Commission, which issued three reports between 2004 and 2006,[1026] recommended the establishment of a National Pensions Savings Scheme which would offer improved provision to those without access to a workplace based scheme. Broadly in line with the Commission's recommendations, the Labour Government published two White Papers in 2006[1027] which proposed the establishment of a new system of 'personal pension accounts'. More recently rechristened the National Employment Savings Trust or 'NEST' , the system is based on the three principles of automatic enrolment (for those not already in an occupational or stakeholder scheme, and subject to the right to opt out), a low cost administrative structure, and matching worker and employer contributions of at least 3% of wages in each case. The Pensions Act 2008 put in place the statutory architecture for this scheme, which is due to take effect from 2012.

The 'balance of power' in occupational schemes

4.137   Occupational pension schemes are almost invariably constituted in the form of a trust. The immediate reason is that a scheme must be set up in this form if it is to benefit from the tax advantages referred to above. More generally, the great advantage of the trust form from the employer's point of view is its flexibility. The employer can set the 'balance of power'[1028] in its favour at the outset when it drafts the terms of the trust deed laying down the rules of the scheme; because of this, the formal separation of the trust fund from the employer's business assets need not imply a loss of control. Trust deeds may be drafted in such a way as 'to ensure that the employer can use the scheme for its own commercial purposes and keep control of its financial commitments to the scheme'.[1029] However, these powers of the employer are now subject to the

---

[1025] Part I; SI 2000/1403.

[1026] *Pensions: Challenges and Choices* (2004); *A New Pensions Settlement for the Twenty-First Century* (2005); and *Implementing an Integrated Package of Pension Reforms* (2006).

[1027] *Security in Retirement: Towards a New Pensions System*, Cm 6481, and *Personal Accounts: A New Way to Save*, Cm 6975.

[1028] See Nobles, 1993: p 28; Mesher, 1993; Derbyshire *et al*, 2011.

[1029] Mesher, 1993: p 105.

provisions of pensions protection legislation,[1030] as well as to a growing body of case law applying the principles of fiduciary obligation and the contractual notion of good faith.

(i) The fiduciary relationship

4.138   Both the employer and the trustees will necessarily come under certain implied duties by virtue of the general law of contract and trusts respectively, which now interact with the provisions of pensions protection legislation. Two parallel sets of relationships need to be considered here: the *fiduciary* relationship between the trustees on the one hand and the employees and pensioners as future and present beneficiaries on the other; and the *contractual* relationship between the employer and the members of the scheme, both as employee-contributors and benefit recipients.

The trustees owe implied fiduciary duties to the beneficiaries of the trust; this is normally taken to mean that they must not exercise their discretion contrary to the interests of the beneficiaries and, in particular, must not benefit personally from their position.[1031] Within these general constraints, the trustees have a wide discretion to balance the interests of present beneficiaries (pension recipients) against future ones (employees).[1032] Member-nominated trustees owe the same general duties as other trustees.

The same principle may prevent the employer from exercising certain powers in its capacity as trustee for its own benefit. This principle emerges from *Mettoy Pensions Trustees v Evans*[1033] where, following the employer's insolvency, the liquidator sought guidance on how to exercise a power of the employer, under the trust deed, to increase benefits to the members of the pension scheme in the event of a winding up. Warner J held that the liquidator owed a fiduciary duty to the members at the same time as owing a duty to the creditors of the company to advance their interests; since these duties were in irreconcilable conflict, the power had to be exercised by the court. However, there is room for flexibility in the application of this test; courts have on occasion diluted the test of fiduciary duty to the point of simply requiring trustees to act in good faith. In *Icarus (Hertford) Ltd v Driscoll*[1034] this resulted in a finding that a receiver exercising a power originally granted to the employer under the trust deed was entitled, in her discretion, to decline to increase benefits for members on a winding up, so ensuring that the scheme surplus went to discharge the company's debts to its creditors. The receiver's fiduciary obligation to the members was, in this case, no more than a procedural one.[1035]

(ii) The contractual relationship

4.139   In *Mettoy* and *Icarus* the powers concerned had been granted to or were exercised by the employer in its capacity as trustee. However, as we have just noted, the trust deed may grant significant powers to the employer without it being a trustee; in this case, there is no necessary

---

[1030] See below, para 4.141.
[1031] *Regal (Hastings) Ltd v Gulliver* [1967] 2 AC 134n, 137 (Note).
[1032] *Edge v Pensions Ombudsman* [2000] ICR 748.
[1033] [1990] 1 PLR 9.
[1034] [1990] 1 PLR 1.
[1035] See Nobles, 1993: p 88.

presumption that the power in question is a fiduciary one. The employer may nevertheless be subject to the *contractual* duty of good faith, which imposes a lesser, but not insignificant, degree of control than the trust law concept of fiduciary obligation.

In *Imperial Group Pension Trust Ltd v Imperial Tobacco Ltd*[1036] the rules of a trust deed provided that pension benefits were to be increased annually by an amount equivalent to retail price inflation or 5%, whichever was less. The trustees of the fund also had the power to grant a greater increase by altering the rules of the scheme, but this required the consent of the company. Browne-Wilkinson VC held that the power of the company to give its consent was not a fiduciary one; the company was entitled to take its own interests into account, in particular the increased funding burden it would face if higher benefits were to be paid out. However, he went on to hold that the trust deed had to be 'construed against the background of the contract of employment', which meant that 'the pension trust deed and rules themselves are to be taken as being impliedly subject to the limitation that the rights and powers of the company can only be exercised in accordance with the implied obligation of good faith'.[1037] In particular, 'the company's right to give or withhold its consent to an amendment ... is subject to the implied limitation that the right shall not be exercised so as to destroy or seriously damage the relationship of confidence and trust between the company and its employees and former employees'.[1038]

The background to *Imperial Tobacco* was that a hostile takeover bid for the company had been mounted a few years before the action came to trial by Hanson plc. When Hanson's bid was pending, the management of Imperial Tobacco together with the trustees and committee of management of the Imperial Tobacco scheme had amended the trust deed of the scheme, introducing a rule that the scheme would close to new members in the event of the ownership of the company changing hands. The provision for automatic minimum annual increases in pensions of up to 5% was also inserted at that point. The aim had been to make Hanson swallow a 'poison pill' which would make the takeover of Imperial Tobacco less attractive. After the takeover had been concluded, Hanson opened a separate pension scheme for new employees, under which it offered to make provision for annual increases in pension benefits of up to 15%; at the same time it refused to agree to any increase beyond 5% under the Imperial Tobacco scheme. It then invited members of the Imperial Tobacco scheme to transfer over to the new scheme. If all of them had done so, under the arrangements offered by Hanson the surplus in the Imperial Tobacco scheme would have been transferred over to the new scheme, whereupon it would have come under Hanson's control. It is not clear whether this was Hanson's purpose in refusing its consent to the 5% increase suggested by the trustees of the Imperial Tobacco scheme. However, the Vice Chancellor held that 'if the sole purpose of withholding consent to increase benefits out of the fund is to force its present and past employees to give up their accrued rights in an existing fund so as to confer on the company benefits that it cannot enjoy unless the members give up such rights, in my judgment this conflicts with the company's duty to act fairly and in good faith to its employees'.[1039] A similar conclusion on the scope of a power of amendment was reached in

[1036] [1991] IRLR 66; *Engineering Training Authority v Pensions Ombudsman* [1996] OPLR 167; *Hillsdown Holdings plc v Pensions Ombudsman* [1996] OPLR 291; *Wheeler v NBC Pension Trustee Ltd* [1996] OPLR 337; *National Grid Co plc v Laws* [1997] OPLR 247 (Pensions Ombudsman) [1997] PLR 157 (Ch D); *National Grid Co plc v Mayes* [2000] ICR 174 (CA), [2001] IRLR 394 (HL); *Prudential Staff Pensions Ltd v The Prudential Assurance Co Ltd* [2011] EWHC 960 (Ch).
[1037] [1991] IRLR 66, 70.
[1038] [1991] IRLR 66, 71.
[1039] [1991] IRLR 66, 71.

British Coal Corp v British Coal Staff Superannuation Scheme Trustees Ltd.[1040] Here, the employer was prevented from amending the rules so as to enable a scheme surplus to be used to meet its obligations to make additional payments to members who had opted for early retirement.

In general, the principle derived from *Imperial Tobacco* may be regarded as an important and innovative development, which is in line with a general movement in favour of the implication of reciprocal obligations of good faith in the contract of employment.[1041] However, in the context of occupational pension rights, it is not without its problems.[1042] As a matter of construction, because the trustees *must* exercise their discretion in the interests of the beneficiaries, it might be thought that separate powers conferred on the employer do *not* have to be exercised in the same way. In particular, the employer should be able to take into account certain commercial interests of its own. What precisely is permissible here is not clear. This point is a general problem with the use of open-ended implied terms, but it is particularly acute when such terms are applied in the context of tightly-drafted commercial documents such as pension trust deeds. A further difficulty concerns the category of persons whose interests must be taken into account. Is the employer bound to take into consideration the interests of former employees, for example, or those of employees' dependants who may have claims on the fund?

The notion of the implied contractual duty of good faith has also been deployed to assist individual employees in their assertion of rights under pension schemes which form parts of their contracts of employment. At one stage it was thought that the employer was under no contractual duty to individual employees to oversee the effective running of the pension scheme or to ensure the delivery of the intended benefits upon retirement; at most, it was simply required to pay its own, promised pension contributions into the fund.[1043] This view is now no longer tenable. The turning point was *Milhenstedt v Barclays Bank International Ltd*[1044] in which the Court of Appeal held that an employer's power to grant a pension upon an employee's early retirement for ill health implied a contractual obligation to do so if the necessary conditions were satisfied; the employer was contractually bound to consider the employee's claim, take medical advice and form a reasoned opinion of her entitlement. Similarly, in *Scally v Southern Health and Social Services Board*,[1045] the House of Lords held that the employer was under an implied contractual duty to inform employees of their rights to take up certain options under the highly technical terms of a statutory occupational pension scheme.

These decisions make it clear that the establishment of the trust and the appointment of trustees who owe duties of various kinds to the beneficiaries do not exhaust the employer's *contractual* duty to scheme members in their capacity as employees. In particular, the contents

---

[1040] [1994] OPLR 51; see also the ruling of the Pensions Ombudsman in *Laws v National Grid Co plc* [1997] OPLR 73, reversed on appeal to the High Court, *National Grid Co plc v Laws* [1997] PLR 157, reversed in the Court of Appeal, *National Grid plc v Mayes* [2000] ICR 174, and finally reversed again in the House of Lords [2001] IRLR 394; see Nobles, 1998, 2000b.

[1041] Brodie, 1996, 1998, 2001; see paras 4.105–4.107 above.

[1042] See Mesher, 1993: pp 106–108.

[1043] See Moffat and Ward, 1986: p 395.

[1044] [1989] IRLR 522; *Aspden v Webbs Poultry & Meat Group (Holdings) Ltd* [1996] IRLR 521; *Brompton v AOC International Ltd* [1997] IRLR 639; *First West Yorkshire Ltd (t/a First Leeds) v Haigh* [2008] IRLR 182.

[1045] [1991] IRLR 522; but see also later cases qualifying the employer's duty to provide information concerning occupational pension schemes, in particular *Nottingham University v Eyett* [1999] IRLR 87 and *Outram v Academy Plastics Ltd* [2000] IRLR 499.

of the trust deed are capable of being construed so as to impose contractual entitlements on employees which employers must neither deliberately obstruct nor render ineffective.[1046] The judgment in *Milhenstedt* is based on the assumption that certain terms of the pension trust are appropriate for incorporation into individual contracts of employment. In principle there is no reason why those terms which are capable of conferring valuable benefits on employees should not be incorporated.[1047] However, many schemes contain statements indicating that the rules they contain are not intended to have any contractual effect.[1048] The value of a unilateral declaration by the employer of this kind may nevertheless be doubted, in the light of decisions to the effect that it is for the courts to judge, taking into account the available evidence, whether particular arrangements have contractual force, and that they may not treat unilateral statements by one side or the other as conclusive.[1049]

A number of issues remain unclear, however. The trustees have a duty to ensure that pension benefits are paid promptly and in full to the current beneficiaries of the trust, and the employer also has a statutory obligation to make up pension deficits in respect of the accrued rights of both beneficiaries and 'active' members (those who are still contributing).[1050] However, it is not clear whether the employer owes an additional contractual duty to ensure that former employees receive the pension payments which are referable to their past service. In principle, such an obligation could be implied as an aspect of the duty of good faith. It could also survive the ending of the employment relationship by retirement, by analogy with other obligations such as the employee's duty of confidentiality.[1051]

The winding-up of a scheme, or the limitation of restriction of the rights of an individual or of a class of employees, could be seen as a breach of contract by the employer, but the issue is not clear. Even if a scheme contains an express clause allowing the employer to terminate its contributions and wind the scheme up, it is arguable that these powers would be read as subject to the implied duty of good faith, as discussed by Browne-Wilkinson VC in *Imperial Tobacco*.[1052] However, in *Air Jamaica v Charlton*[1053] the Privy Council took the view that the entitlements of the members of an occupational pension scheme derive from trust law, not contract law; although 'pensions are earned by [the members'] services under their contracts of employment as well as by their contributions', and hence 'are often not inappropriately described as deferred pay', this did not mean, according to Lord Millett, that they had 'contractual rights to their pensions'. His Lordship considered that the employer's contractual duties were limited to deducting the employee members' contributions from their salaries and paying them over to the trustees, and paying over its own contributions.

[1046] For discussion, suggesting that the courts are adopting 'circular' reasoning in these cases, see Nobles, 1993: p 58.

[1047] See above, para 4.27.

[1048] See Nobles, 1993: p 54.

[1049] *R v Lord Chancellor's Department, ex p Nangle* [1991] IRLR 343.

[1050] See para 4.141 below.

[1051] See Elias, 1982: p 97.

[1052] It should also be noted that if the power to change the scheme rules is vested in trustees, they will not normally have a free hand but will have to act in compliance with their fiduciary duties to the beneficiaries of the scheme as explained in the text; for some of the implications of this, see *Lloyds Bank Pension Trust Corpn Ltd v Lloyds Bank plc* [1996] OPLR 181.

[1053] [1999] 1 WLR 1399.

Pension benefits as deferred pay

4.140   *Air Jamaica* notwithstanding, decisions to the effect that the rules of occupational schemes might give rise to contractual entitlements offer support for the notion of pension benefits as deferred pay, in other words as an element of the employee's remuneration which is earned by service. Particularly important is the recognition by the courts that pension trusts cannot be analysed in the same way as the standard family trust, in which the beneficiaries are volunteers. This is because the members of a pension trust contribute to their own benefits, either by way of their own periodic contributions or, if the scheme is non-contributory, in the form of their service as employees;[1054] this, in turn, may make it more difficult for both the employer and the trustees to exercise contractual and fiduciary powers, as the case may be, in such a way as to harm the members' interests.

However, the growing judicial acceptance of the notion of deferred pay does not mean that the members' interests will necessarily prevail over those of other parties, such as the employer or its creditors in the event of insolvency. A central issue here is the nature of claims over pension fund surpluses. Many schemes built up surpluses in the 1980s and 1990s when investment returns were high. As a result, it was common for employers to institute 'contribution holidays', reducing or eliminating their own contributions on the grounds that the scheme was already capable of meeting its accrued liabilities. This practice will normally be lawful, according to Vinelott J in *Taylor v Lucas Pensions Trust*:

> The pension fund, to the extent that it is in surplus (that is, that the funds are more than are needed to meet accrued liabilities under the scheme), does not in any intelligent sense belong to anyone. Members and pensioners (present and future) have an interest if and in so far as the fund is capable of being applied in improving benefits or adding new benefits. They also have an interest in ensuring that the fund is retained intact, in that it represents additional security for payment of benefits and may have to be applied for improving benefits for members and pensioners on a winding-up. However, an employer has an interest in so far as a surplus in the fund can be used to relieve him of his obligation to contribute to the fund.[1055]

In practice, decisions on whether to allow a surplus to be returned to the employer tend to turn on the precise construction of the terms of the trust deed, with the general principles of contractual and fiduciary liability playing only a residual role.[1056] In addition, the Pensions Act 1995 provides that any power under the scheme rules to return all or part of the surplus to the employer must be exercised by the trustees, and may only be so exercised if a number of conditions are met.[1057]

[1054] *Mettoy Pension Trustees v Evans* [1990] 1 PLR 9; *Imperial Group Pension Trust Ltd v Imperial Tobacco Lt*d [1991] IRLR 66; *Taylor v Lucas Pensions Trust* [1994] OPLR 29.

[1055] [1994] OPLR 29, 31.

[1056] Compare *British Coal Corpn v British Coal Staff Superannuation Scheme Trustees* [1994] OPLR 51 with the litigation which culminated in *National Grid Co plc v Mayes* [2001] IRLR 394.

[1057] PA 1995, s 37 (as amended by PA 2004, s 250).

Pension scheme protection

4.141 A number of statutory measures for the protection of pension fund assets were introduced following the 1989 report of the Occupational Pensions Board, *Protecting Pensions*,[1058] and again following the report of the Pensions Law Review Committee in 1993. These aimed to protect members' expectations that the real value of benefits would be maintained over time and to limit the use by employers of scheme assets for their own commercial purposes. The principal reform was the introduction by the Pensions Act 1995 of a 'minimum funding requirement' under which the trustees were required to ensure that the value of the scheme's assets exceeded its liabilities. If assets fell below 90% of liabilities, the employer came under a duty to make up the difference. This approach engendered substantial criticism on the grounds that, while stopping short of providing a guarantee that members' rights would be met in full in the event of employer insolvency, it could also distort investment decisions. In September 2000 the Department of Social Security and HM Treasury issued a consultation document laying out a series of options for reform[1059] and after a further consultation process[1060] the requirement was repealed by the Pensions Act 2004. It was replaced by a new 'statutory funding objective' which was intended to provide trustees and employers with greater flexibility to take into account scheme-specific factors, including the scheme's investment policy, the age profile of members, staff turnover and likely future salary increases, when determining the scheme's funding strategy. At the same time, the 2004 Act gave the trustees of a defined-benefit pension scheme (or, failing them, the Pensions Regulator) the power to require that any deficit in a scheme below that set by actuarial accounting standard FRS17 be made up by the employer, resulting in a much stricter regime for such schemes.[1061]

The 2004 Act also introduced new mechanisms for the protection of members against scheme failure. With effect from April 2005 a Pension Protection Fund was set up, funded from levies charged on defined benefit and certain 'hybrid' schemes, with the aim of providing compensation to members of schemes which fail by reason of the insolvency of the employer. The Fund incorporates and extends an earlier scheme of compensation, set up by the 1995 Act, which was, however, confined to cases of misappropriation involving the commission of a criminal offence. In addition, the 2004 Act established a Financial Assistance Scheme to deal with other cases of underfunding involving schemes which have been wound up.[1062]

ASSESSMENT

4.142 This chapter has illustrated the continuing importance of the contract of employment as a means of giving expression to the rights and obligations of the parties to the employment relationship. The basic contractual framework of the relationship remains intact, notwithstanding

---

[1058] 1989, Cm 573.

[1059] See DSS/HM Treasury, *Security for Occupational Pensions. A Consultation Document*, September 2000.

[1060] See DWP, *Simplicity, Security and Choice: Working and Saving for Retirement. Action on Occupational Pensions*, Cm 5835, June 2003. See also the first report of the Pensions Commission, *Pensions: Challenges and Choices* (2004).

[1061] On the wider implications for pension fund governance of this development, see Ashcroft *et al*, 2011; Buchanan and Deakin, 2012.

[1062] See *Action on Occupational Pensions*, Cm 5835, June 2003, for an explanation of the background to these and related changes made by the 2004 Act.

the influence of social legislation and collective bargaining. The body of legislation providing a floor of rights in the employment relationship, while far from negligible, is incomplete in many respects. Fundamental issues concerning the nature of the wage-work bargain, the employee's right to payment and the organisation of working time have until recently been left relatively untouched by statute. The common law is also pre-eminent in relation to the employee's obligations of obedience, co-operation and care, the duty of fidelity, and in the treatment of non-competition clauses. In the areas of income security legislation has had a certain impact, but the main purpose of intervention in the form of statutory guaranteed pay and statutory sick pay was to shift the burden of payments away from social insurance and onto individual employers, rather than seeking to establish a floor of rights for collective bargaining.

The contract of employment has become increasingly important as a device for protecting collectively-agreed terms and conditions of employment against unilateral changes by employers. During the period up to the early 1980s when extension legislation was still in place and provided a basic floor of rights at sector-level, the role of the contract of employment in this regard appears to have been negligible. After the repeal of the Schedule 11 of the Employment Protection Act 1975 and the rescission of the Fair Wages Resolution this constraint was lifted, at the same time as encouragement was given to employers to bargain for more flexible terms and conditions at plant and company level. However, as we have seen the courts, in numerous judgments, affirmed that the abrogation of all or part of a collective agreement, while completely lawful in most cases at the level of management-union relations, did not necessarily entail the abrogation of those terms at the individual level; on the contrary, individual agreement to a variation of contract terms would not lightly be inferred. Another area in which the notion of employees' vested contractual rights has proved to be important is that of occupational pension benefits: an employer may be bound by obligations incurred as part of its funding and payment responsibilities under the pension trust, augmented by statutory protections, and by the common law duty to exercise its powers in good faith.

There are, at the same time, limits to how far the common law can be used to protect employee expectations. In the absence of mandatory regulation, employers can adopt the tactic of describing conditions of employment relating to such matters as occupational benefit schemes as non-contractual. The courts have the final responsibility for determining whether any particular arrangement has legal effect, and disclaimers issued by employers may restrictively construed. However, it is not possible to state as a general rule that conditions of this kind *must* have legal effect, or that such terms are necessarily incorporated into individual contracts of employment: it will be a question of the construction of the contract in each case. With the courts reluctant to bring all the terms of employment contracts within the range of UCTA 1977,[1063] there is no general power to control unconscionable or unreasonable clauses in employment cases as there is in relation to consumer contracts and contracts made on written standard terms of business.

British labour law has never had a comprehensive labour code of the kind found in some civil law systems. Collective bargaining was supplemented by direct statutory regulation in areas where joint regulation had failed to develop. More recently, the policy of deregulation saw the removal of direct statutory regulation of this kind, but without any legal encouragement for voluntary collective bargaining to take its place. However, the passage of the National Minimum Wage Act

---

[1063] *Commerzbank AG v Keen* [2007] IRLR 132.

1998 signified a new turn in the debate over labour standards. The importance of this measure also lies in the justifications given for it: the case for the national minimum wage was put not just in terms of equity, but also by reference to economic criteria such as the need to raise labour productivity and to ensure the adequate operation of work incentives. The primary legislation left open the level at which the wage is set, and the procedure for up-rating it in future years. In these respects, the 1998 Act lacks the comprehensiveness of similar legislation in mainland European systems, in particular the French *SMIC* or minimum growth wage, which is intended to maintain the link between the lowest paid and increases in purchasing power among the working population as a whole.

The cause of basic labour standards was further advanced by the implementation of the Working Time Directive in the Working Time Regulations 1998. The Directive and Regulations together marked a different approach to regulation to that which has traditionally prevailed in relation to working time in Britain. First, these standards have a more or less general application, as opposed to the former practice of industry- or group-specific regulation. Second, the Directive and Regulations make extensive provision for flexibility in implementation, by way of 'bargained derogations', envisaging, from one perspective, a new role for collective agreements as mechanisms for implementing and varying statutory standards, in particular at plant and company level. Bargaining takes place within the broad framework set by legal standards, and is to some extent directed by them;[1064] by contrast, the previous British practice had been to preserve a more formal autonomy of collective bargaining from the state, so that in most sectors pay and working-time issues were dealt with without reference to legally-binding minimum standards of any kind.

It is nevertheless arguable that from the point of view of advancing collective bargaining as a mechanism for the application of labour standards, the Working Time Regulations represent a lost opportunity. By providing for extensive derogations from a wide range of basic standards to be brought about through 'workforce agreeements' which are not concluded by an independent trade union and which offer few, if any, guarantees of equitable treatment for the individuals or groups of workers who sign them, the Regulations deny to independent employee representation the role which was arguably envisaged for it under the Directive. Moreover, in allowing individual derogations to be implemented by employers in a relatively cost-free way, the 1999 amendments open up the possibility for widespread abuse of the opt-out from the 48-hour limit on weekly working time.[1065]

The effectiveness of the basic contractual model of the employment relationship has been extensively debated. The 'primacy' of contractual reasoning is a principal feature of the British system,[1066] in contrast to the civilian systems in which 'contract' is only one aspect of a broader employment 'relationship'. The common law model of contract is, it is suggested, inadequate to the task of expressing the nature of the employment relationship, at least in larger, bureaucratic organisations. Collins has argued that this is because 'the ordinary relations of authority found in employment cannot be reduced to a simple contractual formulation'; the result of attempting to do so is 'a series of artificial and unpersuasive explanations of the content and structure of the employment relation'.[1067] The explanatory force of contract is limited to the hiring process or 'port

---

[1064] Bercusson, 1994a, 1994b, refers to this is an instance of 'bargaining in the shadow of the law'.
[1065] See Barnard *et al*, 2004; Hobbs and Njoya, 2005.
[1066] Honeyball, 1988.
[1067] H Collins, 1986: pp 2–3.

of entry' to the organisation, after which the rules of the workplace, which are better thought of as a private bureaucratic code, govern the relationship. This approach would permit the courts to make greater use of concepts drawn from public law, such as notions of legitimate expectation, whose function is to control the exercise of power.

This analysis has been criticised for placing proceduralism above the protection of substantive rights,[1068] and it arguably also contradicts one of the most important developments of the modern law governing the employment relationship, namely the identification of commitments entered into by employers with regard to pay, hours and working conditions as contractual in nature and hence legally binding upon them. This process, which has involved a considerable limitation of unilateral managerial decision-making, began in regard to the employment of managerial and clerical workers and was extended to the greater body of employees following the passage of the Contracts of Employment Act 1963 and later employment protection legislation. It is still going on today, as we can see from the continuing debate over the extent of the contractual and fiduciary responsibilities of employers with regard to pension fund schemes. Collins suggests that as a matter of 'industrial reality ... the code governing the employment relation, whether or not it is produced by joint regulation, does not create a set of contractual entitlements but provides a set of administrative rules which create expectations which deserve a measure of protection'.[1069] However, this might be thought to do less than justice to the achievements of the doctrine of the incorporation of terms. Not only does this doctrine illustrate the flexibility and adaptability of contract law; given the particular nature of the British system, these contractual entitlements perform, however incompletely, the essential function of providing a floor to employment conditions which in other systems is achieved through statute or collective agreements which have a direct regulatory effect.

In certain other respects it could be argued that Collins's aim of requiring managerial power to be exercised in such a way as to respect the legitimate expectations of the individual employee has been achieved within the framework provided by contractual reasoning. The extension of the implied term of mutual trust and confidence has reached the point where employers have been required to act 'in good faith' and to avoid arbitrary reasoning and collateral purposes. This principle is open to the criticism that its scope is unclear, its practical application is capable of varying from one case to the next and it only offers a residual protection against the employer's superior contractual power. These are, of course, criticisms which can and have been levelled against the public-law model of governance too.[1070] It is not entirely clear what the legitimate expectations of the employees might be under this approach, although it is suggested that they would not be able 'to frustrate changes in tasks performed and work patterns and to inhibit the introduction of new technology by providing a blanket defence of existing styles of work under the guise of the enforcement of terms of the contract'.[1071] The same outcome is achieved under the contract model by way of the employee's open-ended duty of co-operation.[1072]

Despite their superficial similarity, however, the bases of the contractual term of mutual trust and confidence and of the review of powers in public law are not identical. The contractual concept

---

[1068] Fredman and Lee, 1987.
[1069] H Collins, 1986: p 8.
[1070] Fredman and Lee, 1987.
[1071] H Collins, 1986: p 9.
[1072] *Cresswell v Board of Inland Revenue* [1984] IRLR 190.

is based on an extended notion of private bargain, but this does not necessarily detract from the goal of controlling the employer's superior power: on the contrary, it emphasises that mutual respect and reciprocity are essential means of ensuring that both parties realise their expected gains from the relationship.[1073] It represents, in other words, legal recognition of the economic need for co-operation in complex, long-term economic relationships such as employment. The advanced pace of technical change and the increased product-market pressure facing many firms make it more essential than ever to put in place arrangements for eliciting and maintaining workforce co-operation;[1074] from this point of view, the emergence within legal doctrine of the extended duty of contractual co-operation is appropriate and timely. However, it may be questioned how far such developments in the common law, or in the area of basic statutory labour standards, can be made effective in the absence of adequate procedures for ensuring independent and comprehensive collective representation of employees.[1075]

[1073] See Brodie, 1998b, 1999a, 2001b; Freedland, 2003.
[1074] Deakin and Wilkinson, 1996.
[1075] See Ewing, 1998; W Brown et al, 2000.

5

DISCIPLINE AND TERMINATION OF EMPLOYMENT

INTRODUCTION

5.1 The law governing termination of employment occupies a central place in modern labour law. A substantial proportion of litigated disputes arise out of terminations of the employment relationship. In 2010–2011, out of 218,100 claims accepted by employment tribunals, 47,900 concerned unfair dismissal and 16,000 redundancy pay.[1] From a doctrinal point of view, the legislation on unfair dismissal represents a major incursion into the common law, limiting the employer's otherwise open-ended power to bring the contract of employment to an end without the need for substantive justification, and imposing general standards of procedural fairness upon the process of dismissal. Redundancy payments legislation, the other major area of statutory intervention, grants the employee the right to compensation, based loosely on the principle of seniority, for the loss of a job on economic grounds.

At the same time, the law relating to unfair dismissal and redundancy is about much more than the process of termination and its results; it affects the entire structure of the employment relationship. Just as the power of dismissal is 'the fiercest sanction which backs up managerial authority to direct the workforce', so dismissal law has become the 'tail [wagging] the whole dog of the employment relation'.[2] The norms which govern the circumstances in which dismissal is legitimate indirectly set the limits to the employer's power to operate lesser disciplinary sanctions, such as suspension or demotion; accordingly this chapter is also concerned with the law relating to disciplinary procedures and the extent of the employer's power to impose sanctions short of dismissal.[3] Statutory intervention has also qualified the employer's common law rights to insist on unilateral changes to terms and conditions of employment. As long as the employer could terminate the contract of employment at will (or on short notice), it effectively had the right to dismiss and re-employ on those terms which it deemed acceptable. Now that this power of the employer is limited by the principles of unfair dismissal law, dismissal legislation does not simply underpin the accrued contractual rights of the employees; the framework of implied and express terms through which the parties' reciprocal rights and obligations are expressed rests upon the capacity of dismissal law to stabilise the employment relationship (although we shall see below that this

---

[1] HMCTS: *Employment Tribunals and EAT Statistics, 2010-11* Table 1. Claims may cover more than one jurisdiction, eg unfair dismissal and sex discrimination.

[2] H Collins, 1993: pp 1, 270 respectively.

[3] See also the discussion in ch 4 above of the scope of the employee's duties of obedience and care, and the legality of deductions from wages for breaches of discipline.

is far from unqualified). Dismissal protection is also an essential bulwark of those fundamental employment rights which are currently recognised by British legislation: these include rights in relation to trade union membership, health and safety protection, the protection of pregnancy and maternity and, by extension from the equality legislation, rights to equal treatment on the grounds of sex, race, disability, religion or belief, sexual orientation and age.

The structure of this chapter is as follows. The next section considers the aims, forms and impact of dismissal legislation. We then analyse the doctrinal framework of the law governing termination, beginning with an analysis of the common law of wrongful dismissal and the scope and effects of contractual disciplinary procedures and job security clauses. The statutory concept of dismissal is considered next, followed by an analysis of the principles governing fairness of dismissal, with emphasis on the extent of procedural and substantive protections. This is followed by an integrated account of the principles governing economic dismissals, covering the right to redundancy compensation; unfair dismissal in the context of redundancies and reorganisations; the rights of employees in situations of employer insolvency; and dismissals related to business transfers.

DISMISSAL LEGISLATION: FORMS, AIMS AND IMPACT

(i) Forms of dismissal legislation

5.2   Dismissal legislation in Britain takes the form of rights conferred on the individual employee against his or her employer, and administered by the specialised system of labour courts, the employment tribunals, charged with the task of interpreting and enforcing employment protection legislation.[4] In this respect, the UK follows a pattern well established in the systems of mainland Europe.[5] In France and Germany the movement of regulation began in the inter-war period with the imposition of minimum notice periods and of restrictions on the exercise of the right of summary dismissal; in the post-war period, the requirement of good cause as a condition for termination of employment became more widely embodied in legislation.[6] The UK was relatively late to adopt this form of intervention. Notice periods were introduced in the Contracts of Employment Act 1963 and redundancy compensation in the Redundancy Payments Act 1965; unfair dismissal law was introduced as part of the Industrial Relations Act 1971. The relevant provisions of the 1971 Act were re-enacted in 1974, extended in 1975 and currently constitute Parts IX and X of ERA 1996. Part XI of that Act is the successor to the Redundancy Payments Act of 1965. Amendments to these statutory schemes to encourage the use of internal dispute resolution procedures before claims were brought to tribunals were introduced by the Employment Act 2002. However these were repealed by the Employment Act 2008, although provisions allowing more limited adjustments to financial compensation remain.

The regulation of dismissal may take a collective as opposed to an individual form. In the United States regulation exists in the form of arbitration under the umbrella of collective

---

[4] In May 2001 a scheme for the resolution of unfair dismissal disputes by arbitration as an alternative to proceedings in the employment tribunal came into force: see further para 2.20 above.

[5] For an analysis of European provisions on dismissal law, see Hepple, 1997b, Rojot, 2010.

[6] See Vogel-Polskey, 1986; Deakin, 1990b.

bargaining agreements (although these now cover only a small proportion of the total workforce). In the UK, the law accords collective relations an important role in the regulation of economic dismissals, where workforce representatives have the right to be consulted over planned redundancies.[7] Collective arbitration over dismissals also exists, but for the most part alongside and not by way of substitution for unfair dismissal protection.[8] One advantage of arbitration, in addition to the possible reduction of legalism in procedures, is that the arbitrator is closer to the parties concerned than a labour court can be, and may as a result be in a better position to award reinstatement. However, there is disagreement on the question of whether North American arbitration is any more effective than the individual model in protecting employees against the exercise of managerial prerogative;[9] it also suffers from the weakness of providing protection only in those workplaces (a small minority in the USA) where unions are established as representative bargaining agents and have established collective agreements containing job security provisions.

(ii) Aims and influences

5.3   The apparent goal of dismissal legislation, namely the achievement of greater employment security, is neither straightforward in itself, nor the only or even principal objective of statutory intervention. At the outset it is important to clarify the various meanings which might be ascribed to the term 'employment security'.[10] The notion of 'job security', for example, can be taken to imply that a worker is protected in the *particular job* which he or she holds; this in turn presupposes the existence of quite rigid job classifications and, from a regulatory perspective, the placing of limits on the employer's right to change those classifications at will. At the opposite extreme, 'employment security' in its widest sense could be taken to refer to the availability of employment opportunities in a given economy; if this is the goal, economic and regulatory policy should be concerned to maximise the chances of employees finding a job and being able to move between jobs throughout their career, rather than being protected in relation to a given job which they might hold at any one time.[11] Dismissal legislation does not neatly fit either of these definitions. It rarely goes to the lengths of granting a worker absolute protection in relation to a specific job classification; but nor is it concerned simply with individuals' opportunities in the labour market. It focuses instead on employees' positions within employing organisations, and operates on the disciplinary and managerial powers of employers in relation to those who are employees, and not in relation to those who are job seekers or applicants for employment. Moreover, as Büchtemann has pointed out, the term employment security should be distinguished from *de facto* employment stability. The latter describes a situation in which stable, long-term employment relationships are the norm, which may occur even in systems, such as that of the USA, where there

---

[7] TULRCA 1992, ss 188 *et seq*; see para 9.32 *et seq* below. See also ICER 2004, reg 20, discussed at para 9.54 *et seq* below.

[8] ERA 1996, s 110 (as amended by ERDRA 1998, s 12 and EA 2002, s 44) provides a power to exempt employees from the scope of the unfair dismissal provisions of the Act where a collective 'dismissal procedures agreement', designated by order of the Secretary of State, is in place. See para 5.64 below.

[9] For differing views, see H Collins, 1982; Glasbeek, 1984. Arbitration under collective agreements should be distinguished from arbitration systems unilaterally established by employers, on which see Finkin, 2008.

[10] See Büchtemann, 1993.

[11] Lindbeck and Snower, 1989.

are few legal or other controls over managerial prerogative.[12] This situation may persist, thanks to economic circumstances or to shared expectations of the contracting parties, but it cannot be said that the worker in such a situation enjoys security as opposed to the bare expectation that employment will continue. Employment security properly understood, by contrast, refers to the existence of 'explicit or implicit rules and provisions putting a restraint on the ability of firms to dismiss workers "at will",[13] that is to say, without the need to show good cause or to respect certain procedures. In other words, the key to the meaning of employment security is the existence of some form of regulatory intervention designed to protect workers against *arbitrary* managerial decision-making.

5.4   Employment security is sometimes said to confer a form of *job property* or 'ownership of jobs' on workers.[14] The idea should not be taken too literally; an employee is unlikely to be in a position where he or she can sell (or otherwise alienate) their job rights to another, so that any analogy between this form of property and the legally-recognised forms of property rights over tangible and intangible assets is inevitably incomplete. Although legislation or collective agreements may confer on employees the right to be compensated *ex post* for the loss of employment arising from redundancy, it is not clear that anything is gained by describing this as a right to compensation for the expropriation of a property right; a core feature of property is the ability of the right-holder to enjoin, *ex ante*, any interference with his or her enjoyment of it, and not simply to receive compensation after the interference has taken place. Nevertheless the notion of job property could be thought of, less formalistically, as implying a recognition not simply of the dependence of workers on their jobs for economic subsistence but, more broadly, of the need for 'job satisfaction' in the sense of personal self-expression and the fulfilment of career-related and occupational goals. This notion also coincided, for a time, with the practice in large organisations of offering, in effect, lifetime employment to their employees. The expectation was that employment would continue in the absence of good cause justifying dismissal, and that the employee's salary and employment benefits, including occupational pension rights, would be linked to their seniority or length of service with the organisation; job mobility, training and occupational development and career progress would take place largely within the *internal labour market* of the firm itself. While the practice of 'lifetime employment' was most strongly entrenched from a cultural and social point of view in countries such as Japan,[15] it also formed a part of the expectations of many workers in both the private and public sectors in North America and Western Europe. Today, it is widely thought that the idea of the 'job for life' is becoming defunct in western industrialised countries, and it is also under pressure, if not to the same degree, in Japan. But even during the period, roughly from the 1950s to the mid-1970s, when the aim of permanent employment had greater resonance, the expectation of a job for life was rarely translated into a legal guarantee. A few workers, such as civil servants in some European systems, enjoyed *de jure* job security in the sense of being dismissible only for cause.[16] For the most part, however, neither collective bargaining

---

[12] See Addison and Castro, 1987.

[13] See Büchtemann, 1993: p 8.

[14] See Meyers, 1964, and Njoya, 2007 for further discussion.

[15] Dore, 1987.

[16] This was not the case in Britain where, thanks to the long-standing view that civil servants did not have contracts of employment (see para 3.40 above), their legal position was somewhat precarious, even if they enjoyed considerable *de facto* job security.

nor employment protection legislation guaranteed workers against the loss of employment by reason of technical change, changing skills requirements, or shifts in the nature of the demand for labour. It is doubtful if such guarantees can be made legally effective in a market economy: in such an economy, 'employment security can for the vast majority of workers mean security only from ungrounded or arbitrary job terminations'.[17]

5.5   The limitations of the job property model has led to a search for principles which can more legitimately be said to underlie the legal control of managerial power. Collins has suggested in this vein that instead of seeing the individual rights of employees in terms of property rights over jobs, 'the employee's interest in job security is better conceived as a right to dignity combined with the establishment of conditions for autonomy and freedom'.[18] The *right to dignity and autonomy* involves a recognition of the employee's rights to be treated with respect for his or her person and individuality. At the same time, it is to accept the legitimacy of those dismissals which are motivated by rational considerations and which are implemented with regard for due process or procedural fairness. Hence the dismissal of an employee on the grounds that there is no longer any demand for his or her services (redundancy) or that he or she is unable to perform the tasks required of them (incapability) does not involve any infringement of the right of personal dignity, nor are such dismissals 'irrational'; 'where, however, the dismissal is based upon irrelevant considerations, such as conduct wholly unconnected to the employee's performance at work, or the employee's characteristics such as sex or race which the employer views as reasons for treating the employee with less than equal respect, then the dismissal does involve a violation of the right to dignity and so justice requires that it should be prohibited or penalised'.[19] Similarly, the goal of personal autonomy – allowing the individual employee the necessary conditions for self-expression and personal development through his or her work – provides a justification for norms which impose certain procedural obligations upon employers. This requires not just that the employer should put explicit disciplinary rules in place, but also that those rules should be themselves judged by reference to external standards. The set of disciplinary rules should be one which 'satisfies the demands of autonomy … yet which remains compatible with the demands of an efficient and competitive business organisation'.[20]

In this approach there is an explicit borrowing of public law techniques for the regulation of administrative discretion. Here, 'public law properly refers to a function, a kind of activity, and not to an institution'.[21] Hence the norms of public law which require decisions to be based on relevant considerations and which seek to minimise the element of arbitrariness in decision-making may be, up to a point, transmissible to the large private-sector bureaucracies which are found within employing organisations: this involves an acknowledgement that 'the internal management of the firm [is] a form of bureaucratic organisation'.[22]

---

[17] Büchtemann, 1993: p 8.
[18] H Collins, 1993: p 28.
[19] H Collins, 1993: p 17.
[20] H Collins, 1993: p 20.
[21] Selznick, 1980: p 273.
[22] H Collins, 1993: p 23. See also P Davies and M Freedland, 1997, especially pp 323–327. On judicial deference to employers see A Davies, 2009.

5.6   The fundamental notion that managerial power should be exercised so as to be compatible with notions of formal rationality is reflected in ILO Recommendation No 119 of 1963, which was influential in the development of the unfair dismissal laws of many systems including that of the UK.[23] The Recommendation prescribes that '[t]ermination of employment should not take place unless there is a valid reason for such termination connected with the capacity or conduct of the worker or based on the operational requirements of the undertaking, establishment or service'.[24] The idea that certain employee rights should be protected regardless of the costs to the employer or, more widely, to society, of doing so finds its practical application in the creation of a category of reasons for dismissal which 'should not constitute valid reasons for termination of employment': the Recommendation identifies these as reasons related to trade union membership or participation in trade union activities; seeking to become or acting in the capacity of a workers' representative; making, in good faith, a complaint against the employer of alleged violation of laws or regulations; or discriminatory dismissal, defined broadly to include 'race, colour, sex, marital status, religion, political opinion, national extraction or social origin'.[25] As we shall see,[26] the British legislation recognises the principle of 'automatically unfair' reasons, without, however, applying this concept as broadly as the ILO Recommendation suggests.

The ILO Recommendation also lays down procedural guidelines for employers to follow in cases where dismissal is for what, in the language used in our own system, are referred to as 'potentially fair reasons'.[27] In particular, dismissal without notice should not take place except for 'serious misconduct' and where the employer could not 'in good faith be expected to take any other course'. If the employer does not take action within a reasonable time of discovering serious misconduct, it is taken to have waived the right to dismiss on those grounds; and '[b]efore a decision to dismiss a worker for serious misconduct becomes finally effective, the worker should be given an opportunity to state his case promptly, with the assistance where appropriate of a person representing him'.[28] The principle of rational behaviour also extends to economic dismissals. Even though the right of the employer to terminate employment on this ground is recognised, '[p]ositive steps should be taken by all parties concerned to avert or minimise as far as possible reductions of the work force by the adoption of appropriate measures, without prejudice to the efficient operation of the undertaking, establishment or service'.[29] In addition to consultation with the workers' representatives, the employer must observe the principle of rationality in the process of selection for redundancy: this should be done on the basis of precise criteria, notified in advance, and which may take into account the following factors: the 'need for the efficient operation of the undertaking, establishment or service'; the 'ability, experience, skill

---

[23] Note also the later ILO Convention No 158 (1982) concerning termination of employment at the initiative of the employer and the accompanying Recommendation No 166. Convention No 158 defines with greater precision than the 1963 Recommendation certain invalid reasons for dismissal (eg 'family responsibilities'and 'pregnancy'); Recommendation No 166 adds new grounds of invalid dismissal such as age. See further Hepple, 1997b: pp 216–218. To date only a minority of EU Member States have ratified the Convention.
[24] ILO Recommendation No 119, Art 2(1).
[25] ILO Recommendation No 119, Art 2(3).
[26] See paras *5.92 et seq* below.
[27] See paras 5.112-5.114 below.
[28] ILO Recommendation No 119, Art 10(5).
[29] ILO Recommendation No 119, Art 12.

and occupational qualifications of individual workers'; length of service; age; family situation; or 'such other criteria as may be appropriate under national conditions'.[30]

5.7   If the promotion of formal rationality in managerial decision-making can be seen to be the basis for the protection of the fundamental individual right to dignity and autonomy at work, it can also be viewed as the foundation for the enhancement of *managerial efficiency* within the enterprise. This was the view of the Donovan Report of 1968 which supported the adoption of unfair dismissal legislation in the UK, partly by way of implementing ILO Recommendation No 119, which the UK had earlier adopted,[31] but also as part of the wider programme of industrial relations reform put forward by the Royal Commission in its Report. An essential aspect of that programme was the strengthening and formalisation of plant-level procedures. Prior to Donovan, procedures for dealing with disputes over discipline and dismissal operated at sector-level in a number of industries;[32] this resulted in long delays in processing disputes, making their outcome of little relevance for the employees concerned who would have found other work in the meantime, and encouraged resort to unofficial strikes at plant level as the most effective means, for many, of ensuring *de facto* job security. The Royal Commission was concerned both to limit the number and extent of unofficial strikes and to end the division between the two systems of industrial relations, the 'formal system' at the level of the sector and the 'informal system' of plant-level relations. Unfair dismissal legislation, since it took the individual employer and not the multi-employer sector as the focus of regulation, was seen as a means of achieving these goals; even though the introduction of legislation marked a departure from the tradition of voluntarism, it was a central part of Donovan's wider purpose of supporting collective bargaining procedures by deepening and reforming them: 'the central issue for Donovan was how to restore order, peace and efficiency to industrial relations and yet preserve and even extend the voluntarist tradition of collective bargaining'.[33] The result was that the legislation was only partially influenced by considerations of employee rights: the legislation had at the very least a 'dual purpose of ... managerial efficiency and employment protection'.[34]

The legislation was also influenced by a broader efficiency-related theme, that of *labour market flexibility*. Although this aspect came more to the fore in the 1980s, it was implicit in the legislation from the start. The exclusion of protection for part-time workers (removed in 1995[35]) and the potential to exclude protection from workers employed on fixed-term contracts (removed for unfair dismissal in 1999[36] and statutory redundancy payments in 2002[37]) was incorporated into the Redundancy Payments Act 1965 and the first legislation on unfair dismissal in the Industrial Relations Act 1971. More generally, the main aim of the Redundancy Payments Act was not, as it might seem, to recognise a kind of property right in jobs, but to ensure that employees displaced from declining industries were given incentives to abandon resistance to technical change, and

[30] ILO Recommendation No 119, Art 15.
[31] On the relationship between UK law and the various Conventions and Recommendations of the ILO in this field, see Napier, 1983.
[32] See Meyers, 1964.
[33] R Lewis, 1986: p 32.
[34] Anderman, 1986: p 416.
[35] By SI 1995/31; see para 3.55 above.
[36] By ERelA 1999, s 18; see para 5.75 below.
[37] By FTER 2002, Sch 2, para 3(15); see para 5.165 below.

to enhance job mobility by granting displaced workers a form of compensation which would assist them in job search. Since the 1965 Act did not seek to place any restraints on managerial decision-making, it has been suggested that 'to claim that the provisions of the statute amount to an improvement in employment security is akin to arguing that legislating for insurance cover for a proportion of road users would be about road safety'.[38]

5.8   The concern that excessive regulation impairs the responsiveness of firms to changes in the external market environment was a major influence on the reforms of dismissal legislation undertaken by successive Conservative Governments after 1979. The Employment Act 1980 introduced changes to the statutory test of fairness, removing a provision placing the burden of showing fairness on the employer, and allowing for the standard of reasonableness to be modified to take into account the limited size and resources of smaller firms. A more significant change made at around the same time was the lengthening of the qualifying period of service for unfair dismissal from six months to one year in 1979 and eventually to two years for all firms in 1985. From 1989 employees in firms employing fewer than 20 employees ceased to have the right to receive written statements of disciplinary procedures (an exclusion removed in 2004).[39] But in other respects, few substantive changes were made to dismissal law during this period; the bulk of it remained intact. When a Labour Government was returned to office in 1997, it reduced the normal period of qualifying service for unfair dismissal to one year and removed the exemptions from protection for employees employed on fixed-term contracts.[40] In 2002, however, it introduced more radical changes to the structure of unfair dismissal law as part of a wider policy of attempting to reduce the number of cases going to tribunals.[41] These amendments were designed to provide incentives to employers to establish, and both parties to exhaust, workplace dismissal and disciplinary procedures prescribed by statute before a complaint went to a tribunal, although they also had the effect of downgrading the importance of procedural standards beyond the statutory minima. A review of the procedures found that they carried 'an unnecessarily high administrative burden for both employers and employees' and had 'unintended negative consequences' which outweighed their benefits, including the use of formal processes to deal with problems that could have been resolved informally and earlier resort to external advice.[42] They were replaced with effect from 6 April 2009[43] by provisions allowing tribunals to adjust compensatory awards in the event of non-compliance with the ACAS Code of Practice on Disciplinary and Grievance Procedures.[44] In April 2012 the Conservative-Liberal Democrat Coalition Government extended the normal period of qualifying service for unfair dismissal for new employees to two years, citing as reasons improved 'business confidence'; potential benefit to employees undergoing training

---

[38] Fryer, 1973: p 3. For a legal and economic assessment of UK law relating to redundancy compensation, see Deakin and Wilkinson, 1999.

[39] See now ERA 1996, s 3 as amended by EA 2002 and para 4.18 above.

[40] See *Fairness at Work*, 1998, Cm 3968, at paras 3.9–3.13, and paras 5.63 and 5.75 below.

[41] See generally Hepple and Morris, 2002.

[42] *Better Dispute Resolution: A Review of Employment Dispute Resolution in Great Britain* (the 'Gibbons Review'), DTI, March 2007: p 8. See also *Success at Work: Resolving Disputes in the Workplace: a Consultation*, DTI, March 2007 and *Resolving Disputes in the Workplace Consultation: Government Response*, BERR, May 2008.

[43] See SI 2008/3232 for the transitional provisions.

[44] EA 2008, ss 1–3; s 3 inserts TULRCA 1992, s 207A and Sch A2 and amends ERA 1996, s 124A.

whom employers may otherwise dismiss at an earlier stage; and reducing tribunal claims.[45] At the time of writing the Government is seeking evidence on current dismissal processes for businesses employing fewer than ten staff, including whether a system of 'compensated no fault dismissal' should be introduced.[46]

(iii) The effects of the legislation

5.9   The impact of the legislation on personnel practice has been considerable. The Warwick survey of unfair dismissal law and practice, carried out in the mid-1980s, found that the legislation had led to considerable formalisation of plant-level procedures, as well as to changes in their content, and had strengthened the role of central management. Personnel processes had become more highly bureaucratic and there had been a reduction in the discretion accorded to lower levels of management. At the same time, the role of unions in negotiating disciplinary rules was limited, although their participation in the operation of disciplinary procedures was more extensive.[47] A number of studies looked into the issue of recruitment and the question of possible disincentives arising out of regulation.[48] The consensus here has been that the legislation has had an impact in making employers more careful about whom they hire, and in this sense contributed both to greater efficiency in the screening of applicants and to a reduction in the overall rate of dismissals. Nor did employers place much stress on any disincentive effects, at least in larger firms; but this was partly because 'managers in all sized establishments [attributed] little effect to the unfair dismissal provisions in terms of inhibiting dismissal'.[49] The impact of the law on unofficial strikes has been difficult to judge, because of the general decline in strike activity since the late 1960s and even more so since the early 1990s. Throughout the 1980s they remained virtually constant at between 10% and 15% of the total.[50] Recent surveys of strike activity do not break down statistics on this basis.[51]

By promoting developments within plant-level procedures the law contributed to greater security and stability of employment for many workers, but this effect varies according to how far procedures have been formalised and how far trade unions have become involved in them.[52] Formalisation is not necessarily identical with an increase in the level of job security; in respect of individual misconduct and lack of capability, formal procedures may become 'conveyor

---

[45] BIS, *Resolving Workplace Disputes: Government response to the consultation*, November 2011, paras 126-131. The Government acknowledged that there would be a 'degree of disparity of impact' in extending the qualifying period but did not consider that this would be 'considerable' and stated that it was 'a proportionate means of achieving the legitimate aim of improving business confidence to recruit and retain staff': para 130.

[46] BIS, *Dealing with Dismissal and 'Compensated No Fault Dismissal' for Micro Businesses: Call for Evidence*, March 2012.

[47] L Dickens *et al*, 1985.

[48] Daniel and Stilgoe, 1978; W Brown *et al*, 1981; Evans *et al*, 1985.

[49] L Dickens *et al*, 1985: p 257.

[50] See Hepple, 1992: p 87.

[51] In 2009 disputes over 'redundancy' accounted for 60% of days lost in the UK, an unusually high figure,: Hale, 2010, p 54, figs 4 and 5.

[52] See Earnshaw *et al*, 1998; Knight and Latreille, 2000. In 2004, 91% of workplaces with ten or more employees had a formal discipline procedure, although the incidence was lower in workplaces with 10–24 employees (86%) and in certain sectors: Kersley *et al* 2006: pp 213–230.

belts' for dismissal, a more effective means of legitimating managerial decisions.[53] There is, in effect, a dual system in place: employees in workplaces with a trade union presence benefit from joint procedures which are underpinned by the legislation, but they do not need to rely on that legislation directly except in rare instances. By contrast, non-union members or employees in non-unionised workplace have to rely on the tribunals for protection.[54] Since tribunals rarely award reinstatement or re-engagement and the average level of compensation is low (in 2010–2011 the median award was £4,591),[55] the level of job security which these workers enjoy is not greatly increased, although it still represents a substantial advance on the common law. Empirical research suggests that employers who comply with the requirements of procedural fairness very rarely lose in employment tribunals.[56]

5.10   Collective agreements concerning the right of management to make workers redundant have been rare. From time to time, agreements have incorporated a commitment by management of 'no compulsory redundancies', but these are unusual.[57] By far the most common form of collective agreement on redundancies concerns the procedures for their implementation and the levels of compensation above the statutory maximum. The introduction of the Redundancy Payments Act 1965 led to a rapid growth in agreements of this kind,[58] as well as in practices of redundancy management at establishment level. In particular, larger firms were encouraged to make provision for voluntary redundancies, through schemes whose rules were designed to attract older workers to accept generous redundancy terms. Compulsory redundancies were more common in smaller firms and in non-unionised establishments; where redundancies were compulsory, the last-in, first-out principle was widely observed.[59] The Act also encouraged the growth of collective bargaining on redundancy; this was nearly all at establishment or company, rather than at multi-employer level, a practice that accords with the more general trend towards the decentralisation of collective bargaining arrangements in the UK since the late 1960s. In general collective agreements improved on the level set by the Act: survey evidence suggests that in 1984 over 90% did so, with a majority providing for twice the statutory level of payment or better,[60] although patterns varied with the size of firm, with the more generous agreements in larger firms and the manufacturing and public employment sectors.[61] Many schemes were designed to be attractive to older workers and to encourage them to accept voluntary redundancies in the event of business reorganisations. Later, the state followed the same pattern by enacting special statutory schemes to provide additional benefits in government-controlled industries undergoing structural change (in particular coal, steel and shipbuilding).

The effect of these developments was to facilitate the use of *voluntary* redundancy as a mechanism of workforce reduction and to limit the degree to which trade unions could effectively

---

[53] L Dickens *et al*, 1985: p 257.

[54] See Pollert, 2005, 2007.

[55] *HMCTS: Employment Tribunals and EAT Statistics 2010-11*, Table 5.

[56] See Earnshaw *et al*, 1998.

[57] See Deakin and Wilkinson, 1999.

[58] Prior to the Act around 17% of employees were covered by redundancy arrangements derived from collective agreements or unilateral practices of employers: S Parker *et al*, 1971.

[59] Daniel and Stilgoe, 1978; Daniel, 1985 and, for data drawn from the 1990 Workplace Industrial Relations Survey, Millward *et al*, 1992: p 325.

[60] Gordon, 1984: p 27.

[61] Levie *et al*, 1984; Daniel, 1985.

adopt a policy of resisting redundancies as such, which had been the strategy of many unions prior to 1965. Instead their role was largely one of ensuring that where redundancies took place they were voluntary rather than compulsory, and that the resulting payments were as generous as possible: 'whatever their initial feelings might have been, trade unions soon found themselves to be powerless in the face of the growth of voluntary redundancy schemes. If they tried to challenge and oppose the need for redundancies, they were undermined by individual members eager to accept voluntary redundancy terms'.[62] Moreover, the fact that strike action in opposition to redundancies could disqualify the strikers from any entitlement to compensation appears to have limited the willingness of employees to support strategies of opposition. Management also made use of the flexibility provided by their own non-statutory schemes to provide various additional inducements to employees, such as giving them only a short period of time to accept an offer of compensation before it was withdrawn. The combination of widespread provisions for redundancy compensation together with the loose controls on managerial prerogative in the area of dismissal combined in the 1980s to make redundancy the normal mechanism of workforce reduction in circumstances of periodic economic recession and substantial restructuring. Between 1977 and 1983 alone over 3.3 million employees received statutory redundancy payments. The extent of labour shedding during this period has been ascribed to a 'snowball effect' as increasing numbers of employers abandoned practices of labour hoarding: 'there is a threshold level in job loss expectations beyond which employing organisations can shed labour without attracting significant attention to themselves. For some employers there were no better reasons for making labour redundant in 1981 than there had been in 1978 or 1975 or 1972. But because other large employers were announcing job losses, and because of a generally gloomy economic outlook, this has been seized upon as an opportunity to de-man'.[63]

5.11   The collective information and consultation requirements of the 1975 Directive,[64] initially transposed into UK law by the EPA 1975,[65] are more clearly concerned to stabilise and protect the jobs of employees threatened with redundancy. In contrast to the legislation on redundancy payments, however, these provisions have had little influence on the development of management practice. Daniel[66] explains this by the fact that prior to 1975 the practices leading to the acceptance of voluntary redundancy by management, workers and unions alike had already been put in place, under the influence of the earlier 1965 Act. The successful use of dismissal law to prevent employers forcing through unilateral cuts in pay and conditions is rare, largely because it is not conclusively established whether such action amounts to unfair dismissal or whether an injunction can be obtained to restrain breach of the normative terms of collective agreements. Nevertheless, employers who go down this road face potentially high costs in doing so. In 1991 the possibility of legal action is reported to have helped to persuade Rolls Royce to withdraw dismissal notices

---

[62] Daniel, 1985: p 74.

[63] Gordon, 1984: p 72.

[64] Council Directive 75/129 of 17 February 1975 on the approximation of the laws of the Member States relating to collective redundancies; see now Directive 98/59. See also Directive 2002/14/EC on Information and Consultation, implemented in Britain by ICER 2004 on 6 April 2005.

[65] See now TULRCA 1992, s 188. See further para 9.32 *et seq* below.

[66] Daniel, 1985: p 78.

issued to several thousand of its workers as a prelude to the imposition of new contracts, but this also depended on a strong trade union presence within that company.[67]

WRONGFUL DISMISSAL

5.12   We begin our more detailed consideration of the law relating to termination of employment with an analysis of the common law of *wrongful dismissal*. Damages for wrongful dismissal compensate the employee for losses suffered as a result of the wrongful termination of the contract of employment by the employer. In principle, the level of compensation payable by these means could be substantial, but all depends on the terms of the contract (both express and implied) and on the application of the general rules by which contract damages are calculated. In practice, damages for wrongful dismissal are very rarely substantial, essentially for two reasons. The first is that either as a result of express agreement or by way of an implied term, the employer will almost invariably possess the right at common law to terminate the contract simply by giving notice, without needing to have a good reason, or any reason, for doing so (the 'notice rule'). Second, any damages payable to the employee for the employer's failure to give notice will be limited by the principle of mitigation as well as by the principle that the victim of breach of contract may only claim, by way of compensation, damages for those losses which he or she can show derive from a clear contractual entitlement, as opposed to a 'bare' or unprotected expectation. Since, in most cases, the employee is not *entitled* to remain in employment for longer than the minimum period of notice contained in the contract, damages will be limited to a sum representing net salary for the notice period only, and will not normally include an amount for harm done to reputation or for loss of earning capacity.[68] These rules explain why, for most employees, the protection offered by the common law of dismissal is inadequate, and why it was felt necessary for the legislature to intervene by introducing the principle of statutory *unfair dismissal*.

The experience of other legal systems, however, suggests that this restrictive approach to the protection of the employee's interests in job security is not an inevitable feature of the common law. In some states of the USA, courts have implied terms into contracts of employment which require employers to act in good faith or subject to a requirement of reasonableness when taking decisions relating to discipline or dismissal.[69] In Australia the focus has been on the terms of disciplinary procedures incorporated into individual contracts from collective arbitration awards; the courts have required employers to observe these procedures and have made substantial awards of damages where they have failed to do so.[70] The award of substantial damages is far from being automatic in these jurisdictions, however, and in the United States many states continue to apply a version of the traditional American rule of 'employment at will', which allows either party to

---

[67] Jeremy McMullen and Philippa Kaufman, 1991.

[68] For further discussion of this point see *Malik v BCCI SA* [1997] IRLR 462, *Johnson v Unisys Ltd* [2001] IRLR 279, *Eastwood v Magnox Electric plc* [2004] IRLR 733, and paras 5.26 and 5.27 below.

[69] See Pitt, 1989; Stone, 2007.

[70] *Gregory v Philip Morris Ltd* (1988) 80 ALR 455; see Ewing, 1989. However in *Byrne and Frew v Australian Airlines Ltd* (1995) 131 ALR 422 the High Court of Australia held that this principle was limited to cases where there was an express agreement between employer and employee to incorporate the terms of the award into the employment contract: see further John McMullen, 1996.

terminate the contract at short notice or without any notice at all.[71] Nevertheless, the diversity of approaches to be found elsewhere in the common law world suggests that the English-law rule of minimal compensation for wrongful dismissal is not immutable.

At one stage the English common law itself was developing in ways which suggested that the traditional rule required reassessment. The first development was the preparedness of the courts to grant more extensive damages in cases where employers had failed to observe contractual disciplinary procedures;[72] the second, their willigness to grant specific relief in equity in order to restrain certain breaches of contract by the employer.[73] In both instances, the normal 'notice rule' is effectively undermined: as a result of the court's intervention, the employer can no longer rely on the power of the notice term to dispense with the need for procedural fairness or for adequate substantive grounds for an act of discipline or dismissal. However the first of these developments must now be considered in the light of the 2011 Supreme Court decision in the co-joined appeals in *Edwards v Chesterfield Royal Hospitals NHS Foundation Trust* and *Botham v Ministry of Defence*,[74] which we discuss in para 5.45 below. The potential for equitable relief to restrain a breach of a contractual disciplinary procedure was affirmed in *Edwards* but as we discuss in para 5.54 *et seq*, below, such relief is discretionary, and to date has been granted only exceptionally and generally only in relation to public sector workers. Whether the courts would be prepared to grant applications in a wider range of circumstances is currently unclear.

Notice and duration

5.13   Where a contract of employment is silent on the question of termination it will normally be construed as being of an indeterminate duration. If so, a term will normally be implied at common law to make provision for notice. The principal function of this 'notice rule' is to give both sides the option of escaping from the arrangement at low cost. However, the length of notice may be set so as to grant one or both of the parties some degree of warning of, and monetary compensation for, the ending of the relationship.

(i) The development of the common law notice rule

5.14   The development of the notice rule at common law is linked, historically, to changes in the typical duration of contracts of employment. When it became normal for contracts to have an *indefinite or indeterminate* duration – as opposed to a duration for a *fixed term* – it became necessary for the parties, or for the courts through the technique of implied terms, to make provision for termination by notice. During the industrial revolution there was a legal presumption that servants in agriculture were hired for a fixed term of a year. This rule was originally based on

---

[71] See Estlund, 2002: pp 205–209.

[72] *Gunton v Richmond-upon-Thames London Borough Council* [1981] Ch 448; *Dietman v Brent London Borough Council* [1987] ICR 737; *Boyo v Lambeth London Borough Council* [1995] IRLR 50.

[73] See, in particular, *Powell v Brent London Borough Council* [1987] IRLR 466; *Jones v Gwent County Council* [1992] IRLR 521; see further para 5.54 *et seq* below.

[74] [2012] IRLR 129.

the Statute of Artificers of 1562 and on the poor laws of the seventeenth century which conferred a parish settlement (or right to relief) on servants with a yearly hiring, but survived the abolition of this legislation to become a presumption of the common law.[75] It was formally removed from the law by the Court of Appeal in 1969,[76] but had fallen into disuse long before then. By the middle of the nineteenth century indefinite hirings were becoming common, and the modern notice rule began to emerge: either party could terminate the contract by giving the other reasonable notice.[77] In the absence of an express clause, what was 'reasonable' tended to be determined by one of two rival criteria, namely the period by which the wage or salary was calculated, and the custom in the relevant trade. An employee whose wage was calculated by the week might, for that reason, be entitled to receive at least a week's notice of termination;[78] otherwise, 'general usages are tacitly annexed to all contracts relating to the business with reference to which they are made, unless the terms of such contracts expressly or impliedly exclude them'.[79] For domestic servants, a month's notice was customary; for professional or managerial employees, periods of minimum notice ranged from a month to a quarter or, less usually, a year.[80] In other cases, employers made use of express notice clauses to prevent workers quitting on short notice; the contracts of many industrial workers contained long notice clauses which bound them to their employer for a certain period and also had the effect of triggering the application of the Master and Servant Acts, which imposed criminal sanctions for certain breaches of contract.[81]

The English judges of the nineteenth century did not develop a legal presumption that employment contracts were terminable 'at will', or on summary notice, as the American courts did during the last quarter of the nineteenth century.[82] However, the use of contractual presumptions in the English common law could often produce a similar result: in England, so-called 'minute contracts' were common during this period in industries such as the docks, construction and engineering where short-term engagements and sub-contracting were widespread. The contracts of employment of the workers in *Allen v Flood*,[83] for example, the leading case on the law of tortious interference with trade and livelihood, were all terminable at short notice by either side, which was one reason why the organiser of strike activity in that case incurred no liability in tort. In later cases, too, the courts construed the contracts of hourly-paid industrial workers (that is to say, workers who were paid on the basis of an hourly rate for work done) as terminable by an hour's notice on either side. One effect of this was to reduce the contractual security of the

[75] Settlement by hiring was abolished by the Poor Law Amendment Act 1834, s 64, and the provisions of the Statute of Artificers 1563 requiring yearly hirings in agriculture were repealed in 1875. On the survival of the presumption into the middle of the nineteenth century, see Jacoby, 1982.

[76] *Richardson v Koefod* [1969] 1 WLR 1812.

[77] See *Baxter v Nurse* (1844) 6 Man & G 935; and for modern restatements of the rule, Lord Oaksey in *McClelland v Northern Ireland General Health Service Board* [1957] 1 WLR 594, 599 and Lord Millett in *Reda v Flag Ltd* [2002] IRLR 747, [57] (emphasising that the rule is confined to contracts that contain no provision for determination and does not apply to fixed term contracts).

[78] *Baxter v Nurse* (1844) 6 Man & G 935 (Coltman J).

[79] *Metzner v Bolton* (1854) 9 Exch 518, 521 (Parke B).

[80] See Jacoby, 1982.

[81] Industrial workers came under the master and servant regime if they had an agreement for 'exclusive service' with an employer for a certain period; long notice clauses were regarded as important evidence of this. See, eg, *Whittle v Frankland* (1862) 2 B & S 49.

[82] *Payne v Western & Atlantic Railroad* 81 Tenn 507 (1884); see Jacoby, 1982, for discussion of the reasons for the divergence between the English and American systems.

[83] [1898] AC 1. See para 11.10 below.

hourly-paid worker practically to nothing. In *Marshall v English Electric Co Ltd*[84] the Court of Appeal considered whether the employer had the implied right under such a contract to impose a disciplinary suspension on the employee. They concluded that it had, on the basis that 'what is called suspension is in truth dismissal with an intimation that at the end of so many days, or it may be hours, the man will be re-employed if he chooses to apply for reinstatement'.[85] Because the minimum period of notice was so short, the employer's power to terminate the contract effectively embraced an unconditional power of suspension too. This approach was not followed for all employees: as a matter of construction, salaried employees, who were paid by the month or longer period, enjoyed superior rights to minimum notice. In *Nokes v Doncaster Amalgamated Collieries Ltd*[86] Lord Atkin contrasted the position of manual workers, at best 'confined to weekly or fortnightly contracts', with 'the longer-term contracts of accountants, managers, salesmen, doctors, and … managing directors employed for a term of years'. The EAT has indicated that, although where there is no express term the court must imply an appropriate term from all the circumstances, 'an extremely significant circumstance will be the parties' own assessment of the appropriate period'.[87] This is very likely, however, to be a matter of dispute.

(ii) Statutory minimum notice periods

5.15   Minimum periods of notice are now inserted into the contracts of employment of all employees with continuity of employment of at least one month. The relevant legislation, which was first enacted as part of the Contracts of Employment Act 1963, is now contained in section 86 *et seq* of ERA 1996. The employee is entitled, after one month's continuous employment, to receive a minimum of one week's notice of dismissal; after two years this rises to two weeks, and goes on rising by one week for each additional year of continuous employment up to a limit of twelve weeks' minimum notice.[88] In the event of breach by the employer, the employee has available the common law action for damages for breach of contract. For this purpose the Act provides that its provisions prevail over any shorter period of notice in the contract[89] and that the employer's failure to comply with these provisions is to be taken into account in assessing its liability for breach of contract.[90] The effect is that damages will be based, at least, on the minimum notice period provided for by statute. The courts have also inferred that in claiming damages for breach of the statutory provisions, the employee must mitigate his or her loss according to normal contract law principles.[91] Conversely, after one month of continuous employment the employee

---

[84] [1945] 1 All ER 653.

[85] [1945] 1 All ER 653, 655.

[86] [1940] AC 1014, 1028.

[87] *Clark v Clark Construction Initiatives Ltd* [2008] IRLR 364, [109] (Elias P).

[88] Where an employee has been continuously employed for three months or more under a 'contract for a term certain of one month or less' the contract has effect as if it were for an indefinite period and the statutory minimum periods of notice of termination apply: ERA 1996, s 86(4); for the application of this provision in relation to entitlement to statutory sick pay see *Brown v Chief Adjudication Officer* [1997] IRLR 110. See also s 86(5).

[89] ERA 1996, s 86(3). Note, however, that they do not affect the right of either party to terminate the contract without notice by reason of the conduct of the other: s 86(6).

[90] ERA 1996, s 91(5).

[91] *Secretary of State for Employment v Wilson* [1978] ICR 200, 203–204 (Phillips J); *Westwood v Secretary of State for Employment* [1985] ICR 209, 218–219 (Lord Bridge).

is obliged to give the employer at least one week's notice of termination of the contract.[92] The Act is silent on the question of the employee's liability for breach of contract for failure to give the minimum statutory notice. The Act does not rule out the parties themselves agreeing to longer minimum periods on either side,[93] nor does it prevent either party from waiving their right to notice on any occasion or from accepting a payment in lieu of notice.[94]

Once either party gives notice, sections 87–91 of the Act govern the rights and liabilities of the parties during the period of notice.[95] In particular, the employee is entitled to receive wages based on his or her normal working hours even if no work is done by reason of lay-off, incapability through sickness or injury, absence by virtue of pregnancy, childbirth, adoption, parental or paternity leave, or absence on holiday; however, if the employee receives any other contractual or statutory payments from the employer in respect of his or her absence, such as statutory sick pay or contractual holiday pay, these will go to discharge this liability.[96]

(iii) The implications of the notice rule

5.16   Notwithstanding the minimum periods imposed by the Act, the reciprocal right to give notice to terminate the contract means that the employer has only a limited right to the future services of the employee. The employee normally has an unfettered right to resign by giving the notice required by the contract. In giving notice, the employee is exercising a contractual power to bring the contract to an end; it follows that the employee cannot unilaterally revoke the notice once it is given.[97]

The converse to this is, however, that the employee has only a limited right to job security, at least at common law. The employee 'has no right to any particular employment if it depends on the will of another'.[98] The Privy Council has held that where a contract expressly gives the employer the power to dismiss the employee without cause this power cannot be made subject to any implied qualification, such as the implied term of trust and confidence.[99] However, there are cases where the contract itself expressly or impliedly places restrictions on the employer's right to give notice, such as those which may be inferred from the existence of disciplinary procedures. We return to this issue in the context of our discussion of contractual job security clauses below.[100]

---

[92] ERA 1996, s 86(2).

[93] At common law, where a notice term was implied it normally provided for the same length of minimum notice to be given by both sides: *Creen v Wright* (1876) 1 CPD 591. The Act departs from this principle of strict reciprocity by providing for longer minimum periods in the case where notice is given by the employer.

[94] ERA 1996, s 86(3).

[95] Note that these provisions do not apply if the contractual notice to be given by the employer to terminate the contract is at least one week more than the statutory minimum: ERA 1996 s 87(4) as interpreted in *Scotts Company (UK) Ltd v Budd* [2003] IRLR 145 where the EAT accepted that this was a 'curious result'; *Langley v Burlo* [2006] IRLR 460.

[96] ERA 1996, s 88. Section 89 deals with the situation in which the employee has no normal working hours.

[97] *Riordan v War Office* [1959] 1 WLR 1046; *a fortiori* if the employee resigns in breach of contract, whereupon the employer has the right to accept the repudiation and will not easily be taken to have waived the right to do so. The employee may be liable for damages for breach of contract in this situation, assuming that the employer can show loss, which may be difficult.

[98] *Allen v Flood* [1898] AC 1, 172 (Lord Davey).

[99] *Reda v Flag Ltd* [2002] IRLR 747.

[100] See para 5.31 *et seq.*

(iv) The implications of no provision for notice

5.17   Contracts containing neither an express nor an implied notice term are, by their nature, rare. In a contract of fixed-term duration, the absence of an express notice clause might not be surprising: both parties might expect the contract to be worked out for the period agreed.[101] Where, on the other hand, the contract is 'permanent' or for an indeterminate duration, there is a presumption that a notice clause will be implied according to the normal common law tests,[102] with the Act now prescribing its minimum length. It would be normal to imply a notice term for the benefit of the employee, who would otherwise be bound to serve a particular employer indefinitely. However, there may be certain cases in which the implication of a clause granting the *employer* the right to give notice is not appropriate. This occurred in *McClelland v Northern Ireland General Health Services Board*,[103] where the House of Lords concluded that the omission of such a clause from the contract of a senior health service employee in the public sector was deliberate, since it reflected the high level of job security which was part of the contractual package agreed by the parties. The employee's contract incorporated an extensive procedure, known as the 'September Conditions', governing dismissal for misconduct, inefficiency and unfitness; no mention was made of any express right to dismiss for redundancy. The effect of this was that the employee had a contractual right to remain in the employment until she reached the retirement age, subject only to the possibility of dismissal for good cause which on the facts was not made out (she was dismissed for having married). She was granted a declaration to the effect that her contract of employment was still subsisting, in effect nullifying the purported dismissal.[104]

It must be said that while the principle behind *McClelland* is clear, not many employees are in a position to benefit from it. It was always unlikely that a court would assume that the parties intended to create such a stable employment environment in anything other than the public sector, and it is difficult to think of any major group of workers that would now fall within this protected category.[105]

Summary dismissal

5.18   The employer is entitled to dispense with contractual notice, or with the minimum notice prescribed by statute,[106] and summarily dismiss an employee who has committed a repudiatory breach of contract. This is an application of the general rule of contract law that following repudiatory breach, the innocent party has the option to terminate or to affirm the contract.[107] The nature of the conduct which is considered to constitute repudiation by the employee has to

---

[101] The presence of a notice clause will not, on the other hand, prevent a fixed-term contract being defined as such for the purposes of ERA 1996, s 235(2B)(a) or FTER 2002: see paras 3.52 and 5.75.
[102] See para 4.4 *et seq.*
[103] [1957] 1 WLR 594.
[104] See further para 5.40 *et seq* below.
[105] *McClelland* has never been available to civil servants, who are regarded as dismissible at will: see para 3.40. On the position of university teachers, see Farrington and Palfreyman, 2006.
[106] Cf ERA 1996, s 86(6).
[107] *White and Carter (Councils) Ltd v McGregor* [1962] AC 413.

some degree changed over time, to reflect changing social values.[108] It is no longer sufficient for the employee to have committed an isolated and minor act of disobedience or negligence. For an isolated breach to suffice it must be such 'as to show the servant to have disregarded the essential conditions of the contract of service',[109] or to be 'inconsistent with the continuance of confidence' between employer and employee.[110] The wilful disobedience of a reasonable and lawful order, or the unauthorised taking of the employer's property, will almost certainly justify summary dismissal at common law.[111] If, however, it is the employer who provokes, by its own conduct, the breakdown of relations of trust and confidence, summary dismissal will not be justified, and the employer itself will be liable for wrongful dismissal.[112] In these circumstances the employee will need to ensure that he or she terminates the relationship first; the employer, even if in breach of the trust and confidence term, will not itself be barred from dismissing the employee summarily for good cause if the relationship is still continuing.[113]

5.19   At common law the right to summary dismissal applies even though, at the time of the dismissal, the employer was not aware of the breach in question or of its seriousness. In *Boston Deep Sea Fishing and Ice Co v Ansell*[114] the claimant, the manager of the defendant's business, was dismissed for reasons which Kekewich J found to be groundless. However, after the dismissal had taken place the defendant discovered that the claimant had, several years earlier, accepted a secret commission which should have been directed to the business. This misconduct would have justified summary dismissal, had the employer been aware of it. The Court of Appeal found that the dismissal had not been wrongful, 'even though [the employer] did not discover the fraud until after [it] had actually pronounced the sentence of dismissal'.[115]

In effect, this is saying that the employee did not lose anything of value by virtue of his dismissal: by virtue of his earlier fraud, he had no right to continuing employment.[116] A different outcome will occur if the employer, knowing of the breach, expressly waives the right to terminate the contract in response to it. If, alternatively, it takes no action, then after a reasonable period has elapsed it will again be taken to have waived the right of dismissal;[117] delay or inaction may lead a

---

[108] See the discussion of Edmund Davies LJ in *Wilson v Racher* [1974] ICR 428.
[109] *Laws v London Chronicle (Indicator Newspapers) Ltd* [1959] 1 WLR 698, 700 (Lord Evershed MR).
[110] *Sinclair v Neighbour* [1967] 2 QB 279, 289 (Sachs LJ).
[111] See the cases cited in the two notes above and for more recent examples *Macari v Celtic Football and Athletic Club* [1999] IRLR 787 (discussed at para 4.99); *Briscoe v Lubrizol Ltd* [2002] IRLR 607; *Dunn v AAH Ltd* [2010] IRLR 709 and *A v B* [2010] IRLR 844. On the scope of the duty of obedience see para 4.99 *et seq* above, and on aspects of the duty of fidelity which are relevant in this context, see para 4.111 *et seq.*
[112] *Wilson v Racher* [1974] ICR 428.
[113] *Brandeaux Advisers (UK) Ltd v Chadwick* [2011] IRLR 224, QBD at [32].
[114] (1888) 39 Ch D 339.
[115] Bowen LJ at 364. Cf *Welsh v Cowdenbeath Football Club Ltd* [2009] IRLR 362, where in contrast to the secret commission in *Boston Deep Sea Fishing*, the conduct complained of 'could hardly have been more public' (Lord Malcolm at [14]).
[116] *Quaere* whether the same principle would apply if the employee committed a repudiatory breach *after* the employer's breach; cf *Ridgway v Hungerford Market Co* (1835) 3 Ad & El 171, discussed by Hepple, 1981a: pp 253–254. In *Lakshmi v Mid Cheshire Hospitals NHS Trust* [2008] IRLR 956, QBD, [32] it was suggested that the principle in *Boston Deep Sea Fishing* applied only where there was no disciplinary process in existence although it remained relevant to the remedy to be sought. This may be a desirable result but it is not clear that it is compatible with *Boston*.
[117] Cf, in a different context, *Peyman v Lanjani* [1985] Ch 457.

court to conclude either that the contract has been affirmed or that there is no genuine causal link between the misconduct and dismissal.[118]

These aspects of the common law of summary dismissal must now be read subject to the requirements imposed by unfair dismissal law in cases which fall within the scope of ERA 1996. Importantly, in contrast to the common law, the statutory regime does not permit an employer to advance as a reason for dismissal one which it did not actually rely upon at the time.[119]

Damages for wrongful dismissal

5.20   An employer's failure to give notice as due under the contract of employment gives rise to a distinctive type of damages claim which has come to be known as an action for 'wrongful dismissal'.[120] As a basis for an action for wages or salary, claims for damages are clearly inferior to claims in debt: in debt, the employee has no general duty to mitigate loss and can claim the liquidated sum set by the contract itself, as opposed to the unliquidated damages which are ascertained by the court and subject to deductions of various kinds.[121] However, as we shall see, the employee is only able in exceptional circumstances to maintain the contract in force after a summary dismissal has taken place, and even then any claim in debt for wages due will only operate for a limited period.[122] In the vast majority of cases, the ending of the employment relationship by the employer, even where it is a wrongful act, has the effect of confining the employee to a claim in damages.

(i) The measure of damages: general principles

5.21   Consistently with general principles of contract law:

> … where a servant is wrongfully dismissed, he is entitled, subject to mitigation, to damages equivalent to the wages he would have earned under the contract from the date of dismissal to the end of the contract. The date when the contract would have come to an end, however,

---

[118] *McCormack v Hamilton Academical Football Club Ltd* [2012] IRLR 108, Court of Session, [8].

[119] See para 5.86 below.

[120] For discussion of the circumstances in which other kinds of claim may lie in respect of wrongful termination, see paras 5.31 *et seq* below.

[121] Note that even where an employee has been dismissed without notice, if the contract provides for payment in these circumstances the claim may be brought in debt. See *Abrahams v Performing Rights Society* [1995] IRLR 486 where the employer had the right to terminate the employee's contract by giving two years' notice or an equivalent payment in lieu; the Court of Appeal held that the effect of this agreement was that the claimant was entitled to payment in lieu as a contractual debt when his contract was terminated without notice. The agreement in that case was distinguished by the Court of Appeal in *Gregory v Wallace* [1998] IRLR 387 where the employee's contract was not terminated in accordance with the procedure specified in that contract and the claim was held to lie in damages. However, because the employee's contract specifically permitted him to take other employment during the notice period, he was entitled to damages undiminished by earnings in his new employment, this being the appropriate measure of his loss. See also *Cerberus Software Ltd v Rowley* [1999] IRLR 690, [2001] IRLR 160, and Fodder and Freer, 2001. Failure to give the period of notice prescribed by ERA 1996, s 86 gives rise to a claim in damages, not debt: *Hardy v Polk (Leeds) Ltd* [2004] IRLR 420. For guidance as to when a liquidated damages clause may be regarded as a penalty, see *Murray v Leisureplay plc* [2005] IRLR 946.

[122] See paras 5.36 *et seq* and 5.54 *et seq* below.

must be ascertained on the assumption that the employer would have exercised any power he may have had to bring the contract to an end in the way most beneficial to himself; that is to say, that he would have determined the contract at the earliest date at which he could properly do so.[123]

It follows from this and from the notice rule that in the case of an indefinite hiring, damages for wrongful dismissal will normally be restricted to net salary for the notice period. An employee who is employed under a fixed-term contract which does *not* contain a notice clause is on the face of it entitled to receive net salary for the unexpired period of the contract. 'Net salary' here means the employee's normal weekly or monthly wage or salary, after making deductions for the normal incidence of income tax.[124] The impact of income tax on the earnings which the employee would have had in the notice period is 'something which the law does not regard as too remote';[125] if, conversely, the employee has to pay income tax on the damages which the court then awards, the damages will be grossed up to ensure that he or she is fully compensated for his or her loss.[126] This will occur where the damages exceed £30,000.[127] It is also common for deductions to be made in respect of the employee's national insurance contributions and contributions, if any, to an occupational pension or similar employee benefit scheme,[128] but there is some authority to suggest that these deductions should not be made unless the employee also receives some compensation for loss of the insurance-related benefits to which his or her previous contributions were directed.[129]

(ii) Claims for lost opportunities to earn financial benefits

5.22   Whether the employee can recover for the loss of benefits other than salary depends on whether these benefits are ones to which the employee is entitled under the terms of the contract. In *Lavarack v Woods of Colchester Ltd*[130] the dismissed employee was unable to claim damages for the lost opportunity to earn bonuses which had been made available by the directors at their discretion in the past, but which the company was under no contractual obligation to maintain. This decision may be contrasted with those in which the employer was under a contractual

---

[123] *Gunton v Richmond-upon-Thames London Borough Council* [1980] ICR 755, 772 (Buckley LJ). See also *Abrahams v Herbert Reiach Ltd* [1922] 1 KB 477, 482 (Scrutton LJ); *Lavarack v Woods of Colchester Ltd* [1967] 1 QB 278, 294 (Diplock LJ); *Janciuk v Winerite Ltd* [1998] IRLR 63, 64; *Morran v Glasgow Council of Tenants' Associations* [1998] IRLR 67.

[124] This may involve consideration of whether the employee would have received an increase during the unexpired period of the contract. In *Clark v BET plc* [1997] IRLR 348, the employee's service agreement provided for a basic salary 'which shall be reviewed annually and be increased by such amount if any as the board shall in its absolute discretion decide'. The Court held that it would have been a breach of contract for the board to have exercised its discretion capriciously or in bad faith to award a nil increase, and on the basis of the evidence the claimant would have been entitled to an annual increase of 10%. See also *Clark v Nomura International plc* [2000] IRLR 766; *Horkulak v Cantor Fitzgerald International* [2004] IRLR 942.

[125] *Shove v Downs Surgical plc* [1984] ICR 532, 537 (Sheen J).

[126] [1984] ICR 532, 537.

[127] ITEAP 2003, ss 401–404. For criticism of the court's approach to taxation in the measurement of damages, see Bishop and Kay, 1987.

[128] See *Shove v Downs Surgical plc* [1984] ICR 532, 538–539.

[129] *Gothard v Mirror Group Newspapers Ltd* [1988] ICR 729, 734 (Lord Donaldson MR).

[130] [1967] 1 QB 278.

obligation to pay commission in return for performance, and where damages for wrongful dismissal included an amount for the normal commission or bonus which the employee could have expected to earn in the notice period (or the unexpired period of the contract term).[131] In the light of recent case law, recovery may be possible even if a benefit is expressed to be discretionary. In *Horkulak v Cantor Fitzgerald International* the Court of Appeal held that *Laverack* had no application to cases where there was a contractual entitlement to a bona fide and rational exercise by the employer of its discretion as to whether the employee should receive a bonus and, if so, how much.[132] In such circumstances the court should put itself in the shoes of those making the decision and decide what figure would have been arrived at had the discretion been exercised in accordance with these principles.[133] It may also be necessary to consider whether entitlement to benefits is dependent upon the maintenance of the employment relationship. In *Micklefield v SAC Technology Ltd*,[134] for example, the effect of the employee's dismissal was that certain share options which would otherwise have been available to him automatically lapsed under the rules of the company scheme in question. As a result he was not entitled to any compensation in respect of this head of loss. In *Commerzbank AG v Keen*[135] the employee's contract stated that no bonus would be paid to him if on the date of payment he was not employed by the bank. The Court of Appeal held that the employee's argument that the bank had acted irrationally or perversely in not awarding him a bonus in respect of the period of the year for which he had worked, even though his employment had been terminated by the date of payment, stood no real prospect of success.

Ultimately, in any given case the outcome depends on whether the benefit can be construed as one to which the employee is contractually or otherwise legally entitled. For example in *Shove v Downs Surgical plc*[136] damages included amounts in respect of the employee's exclusion from the employer's life insurance scheme, the loss of his subscription to a private health care scheme and his loss of the use of a company car. An employee will also normally recover damages for loss of accrued holiday pay: in other words, he or she will receive a sum in respect of days of paid leave to which he or she was entitled on the basis of past service, but had not yet taken at the time of the dismissal.[137] The Court of Appeal has held that an employee who is wrongfully dismissed before he or she has acquired the necessary period of service to bring an unfair dismissal claim cannot claim damages for the loss of opportunity to bring such a claim; to permit this would subvert the statutory provision that in effect extends the period of employment of a summarily dismissed employee for this purpose by the *statutory minimum*, not the contractual, period of notice to which the employee is entitled.[138]

---

[131] *Turner v Goldsmith* [1891] 1 QB 544; *Addis v Gramophone Co Ltd* [1909] AC 488; *Clark v BET plc* [1997] IRLR 348; *Clark v Nomura International plc* [2000] IRLR 766, *Horkulak v Cantor Fitzgerald International* [2004] IRLR 942. The same principle would apply to a contract under which the employee was paid according to a piece rate for work completed.

[132] [2004] IRLR 942, [46] (Potter LJ).

[133] Above, [72].

[134] [1990] IRLR 218. See also *Thompson v ASDA-MFI Group plc* [1988] IRLR 340, but cf *Mallone v BPB Industries plc* [2002] IRLR 452.

[135] [2007] IRLR 132. The Court of Appeal rejected the argument that this was an unfair contract term under UCTA 1977; see further para 4.34.

[136] [1984] ICR 532.

[137] See, eg, *Shove v Downs Surgical plc* [1984] ICR 532, 542.

[138] *Harper v Virgin Net Ltd* [2004] IRLR 390, applying the reasoning in *Johnson v Unisys Ltd* [2001] IRLR 279, discussed in paras 5.43 and 5.44 below, applied *Wise Group v Mitchell* [2005] 1 ICR 896. For discussion of the relevant statutory provision – ERA 1996, s 97(2) – see para 5.81 below.

(iii) The duty to mitigate loss

5.23   The employee's duty to mitigate his or her loss normally requires him or her to claim the jobseeker's allowance[139] and to look for alternative work; failure to do so will reduce his or her damages. For this purpose the employee is not normally required to accept a job entailing a lower rate of pay or an inferior position to the one he or she previously occupied;[140] nor is it normally unreasonable to refuse an offer of re-employment from the employer who has just committed a wrongful dismissal.[141] If the employee is successful in mitigation and earns salary or fees from work found after the dismissal, these sums will go to reduce the employer's obligation to pay damages.[142]

(iv) Other deductions

5.24   Where the employee receives the jobseeker's allowance following dismissal, this will be deducted from damages on the grounds that it is a direct replacement for the claimant's lost earnings.[143] However, in certain circumstances it is possible that the full amount received will not be subject to deduction. The jobseeker's allowance is composed of a contribution-based allowance, available for six months, and an income-based allowance, which is subject to a household means test. The failure to allow the employee to work out his or her notice may deprive him or her of time during which he or she could have found alternative work and postponed a claim for the jobseeker's allowance; if, as a result, his or her entitlement to the contribution-based allowance runs out sooner than it would otherwise have done he or she has suffered a loss attributable to the employer's breach of contract. In *Westwood v Secretary of State for Employment*[144] the House of Lords, dealing with a situation where an employee's entitlement to unemployment benefit expired and he qualified only for the lower 'supplementary benefit' then available, dealt with the loss constituted by the 'premature expiry of the unemployment benefit'[145] by deducting from the sum based on the employee's net wages for the notice period not the actual (unemployment) benefit he had received during that period but the lesser sum received as supplementary benefit after the unemployment benefit had prematurely expired. This sum properly represented the net gain for which he was bound to give account by way of mitigation. It seems likely that the same approach would be followed, *mutatis mutandis*, in relation to the respective elements of the jobseeker's allowance.

5.25   What other deductions may be made from a wrongfully dismissed employee's award of damages? The compensatory award for unfair dismissal, as its name implies, is designed to

---

[139] See para 3.16 above.

[140] *Yetton v Eastwoods Froy Ltd* [1967] 1 WLR 104. To this extent, the common law is considerably less disciplinary in its effects on the unemployed worker than the law of social security: see para 3.16 above.

[141] *Shindler v Northern Raincoat Co Ltd* [1960] 1 WLR 1038.

[142] For example *Shove v Downs Surgical plc* [1984] ICR 532, 542–543.

[143] *Parsons v BNM Laboratories Ltd* [1964] 1 QB 95. Unemployment benefit, at issue in this case, was the precursor of the jobseeker's allowance.

[144] [1985] ICR 209.

[145] [1985] ICR 209, 221 (Lord Bridge).

replace earnings lost after the dismissal.[146] Where an employee has been awarded unfair dismissal compensation, the 'best view is that those elements of the compensatory award which are capable of being allocated to any of the heads of damages for wrongful dismissal should be deducted from the award of damages, but only to the extent that they are capable of being so allocated'.[147] By contrast, statutory redundancy payments are not normally set off against damages in this way. This is said to be because they represent 'compensation for loss of an established job, not for loss of future earnings'.[148] The basis of calculation is the past service of the employee not the effect of dismissal on his or her future earning capacity, as a result of which the statutory payment is 'payable even though the dismissed employee at once finds work elsewhere at higher wages'.[149] On the face of it, then, the employee is entitled to be given notice of dismissal for redundancy and then to receive the statutory payment in addition.[150] Similarly, common law damages will not be affected either by the receipt of the basic award for unfair dismissal,[151] since it is not regarded as compensatory in nature; nor is any deduction made in respect of the receipt of long-term occupational sickness or pension benefits paid under contributory schemes.[152] The total award of damages will suffer a further reduction to reflect the fact that the payment is an accelerated single receipt of entitlements covering the whole unexpired term, and the fact that the 'vicissitudes of life' might shorten the period of salary entitlement.[153]

(v) Damages for lost reputation or lost earning capacity?

5.26   A controversial issue in this area has been whether an employee should be able to claim damages for lost reputation or for lost earning capacity arising from a wrongful dismissal. For many years the leading authority on this point was the decision of the House of Lords in *Addis v Gramophone Co Ltd*.[154] The employee, who managed the employer's business in Calcutta, was employed under a contract which entitled him to receive six months' notice of dismissal. He was summarily dismissed and prevented from working out his notice; in compensation he received six months' salary from his employer. A jury awarded him a substantial sum for lost salary extending beyond the period of notice, as well as a sum representing lost commission for the period when he was not allowed to work. In the House of Lords his damages were confined to salary and commission for the notice period only. According to Lord Loreburn LC, damages for wrongful dismissal 'cannot include compensation either for the injured feelings of the servant, or for the

---

[146] See further paras 5.145 *et seq* below.
[147] Upex, 2001: para 10.68. Cf *O'Laoire v Jackel International Ltd (No 2)* [1991] IRLR 170 at 175–176, where the defendants could not show that the claimant would be obtaining compensation under two heads for the same loss.
[148] *Wilson v National Coal Board* [1981] SLT 67, 72 (Lord Keith of Kinkel).
[149] [1981] SLT 67, 72.
[150] There are exceptions to this in personal injury cases where it can be shown that the employee would not have been made redundant but for the injury: *Wilson v National Coal Board* [1981] SLT 67; *Colledge v Bass Mitchells & Butlers Ltd* [1988] ICR 125; or, in a case of wrongful dismissal, where the right to the statutory redundancy payment only arose because the employee was summarily dismissed, thereby ensuring that he was made redundant before a special scheme offering favourable terms expired: *Baldwin v British Coal Corpn* [1995] IRLR 139.
[151] *Shove v Downs Surgical plc* [1984] ICR 532, 543. On the basic award, see para 5.144, below.
[152] *Hopkins v Norcross plc* [1994] ICR 11, applying *Parry v Cleaver* [1970] AC 1; see Deakin *et al*, 2008: pp 956–960.
[153] See Upex, 2001: para 10.74.
[154] [1909] AC 488.

loss he may sustain from the fact that his having been dismissed of itself makes it more difficult for him to obtain fresh employment'.[155]

5.27   Until relatively recently both aspects of this rule were applied in an unquestioning way[156] and, indeed, the first limb reflects the limited nature of this head of recovery in the common law in general for injury to feelings.[157] However, in *Malik v BCCI SA*[158] the House of Lords held, in relation to the second limb, that an employee might be able to recover damages where a breach by the employer of the implied term of trust and confidence harmed his or her reputation in such a way as to limit opportunities for alternative employment. In this case the claimants lost their jobs with the defendant bank when it collapsed. The claimants argued that, because the bank had operated its business dishonestly and corruptly, they, although personally innocent, were stigmatised by reason of their employment by it, and consequently disadvantaged in the labour market. The House of Lords held that on the assumption that the conduct of the bank had been as pleaded, the bank had breached the trust and confidence owed to its employees and the claimants were not barred from recovering loss flowing from that breach by reason of discovering the conduct only after termination of their employment. The court distinguished *Addis* on the basis that it had been decided before the implied term of mutual trust and confidence had been developed.[159] However, in the later decision of *Johnson v Unisys Ltd*[160] the majority of the House of Lords held that *Malik* could not be invoked to support a cause of action for lost reputation as a result of a wrongful dismissal. *Addis* itself was not regarded as an insuperable obstacle to reliance on *Malik*[161] in these circumstances; rather, the difficulty lay, in the view of the majority, in the argument that implying a duty to act fairly (the term preferred in this context to trust and confidence)[162] in relation to the employer's power of dismissal would go contrary to the will of Parliament in establishing a statutory unfair dismissal scheme which was limited in its application.[163] In *Edwards v Chesterfield Royal Hospitals NHS Foundation Trust; Botham v Ministry of Defence*[164] the majority of the Supreme Court used the same justification to deny a remedy in damages for loss resulting from an employer's breach of an express disciplinary procedure.

In essence, two issues arise here: a narrow issue, of the damages properly awardable for an employer's failure to give notice under the contract; and a wider issue of the relationship between express notice clauses and the implied term of mutual trust and confidence. The opinions in

---

[155] [1909] AC 488, 491.

[156] *Cox v Philips Industries Ltd* [1976] 1 WLR 638; *Shove v Downs Surgical plc* [1984] ICR 532; *Bliss v South East Thames Regional Health Authority* [1985] IRLR 308; *Malik v BCCI SA (in compulsory liquidation)* [1995] IRLR 375.

[157] For the argument that the implied duty of trust and confidence is relevant to recovery of damages for distress see John McMullen, 1997.

[158] [1997] IRLR 462; see Brodie, 1998b; para 4.105 *et seq* above.

[159] [1997] IRLR 462, 465–466 (Lord Nicholls, with whom Lord Goff and Lord MacKay concurred). Lord Steyn (referring to Enonchong, 1996: p 596) held that *Addis* was irrelevant because it merely decided that the loss of reputation there was not caused by a breach of contract: 470. The claimants in *Malik* failed at trial on the issue of causation: *BCCI SA v Ali (No 3)* [2002] IRLR 460.

[160] [2001] IRLR 279.

[161] See Lord Hoffmann at [44], Lord Millett at [77]. Lord Bingham agreed with both these opinions.

[162] For the view that this term should be preferred in relation to the power of dismissal: see Lord Hoffmann at [46], Lord Millett at [78]-[79].

[163] See also *Eastwood v Magnox Electric plc, McCabe v Cornwall County Council* [2004] IRLR 733, discussed in para 5.44 below.

[164] [2012] IRLR 129.

Johnson address the second, wider issue and we will return to this below, followed by an analysis of the broader implications of *Edwards* and *Botham*.[165] The narrower issue turns on whether the employee can show that the employer's failure to give notice, assuming this is a breach of contract, caused him or her loss over and above net wages or salary for the notice period. At one level, the question can simply be approached as one of causation. If this is done, it is far from obvious that an employer should escape liability for causing unwarranted harm to an employee's reputation by the manner of dismissal. If notice is dispensed with, the implication is that the employer has grounds for doing so. If there are no such grounds, the employee can argue that the stigma which attaches to him or her as a result is the direct consequence of the employer's breach of contract. The failure to allow the employee to serve out the notice period may also make it more difficult than it would otherwise have been to find alternative work; in general it is more costly and time consuming for an unemployed person to find suitable work than it is for an employed person to find a similar job with a different employer. It may be that an employee faces a high evidentiary burden in demonstrating losses of this kind, and that as a result claims of this kind will rarely succeed,[166] but this is not the same thing as saying that the cause of action, as a matter of law, cannot be sustained.

In *Johnson*, the point discussed above was only indirectly addressed; the case was pleaded in terms of the employer's breach of the implied duty of mutual trust and confidence,[167] and it was in this context that the majority of the House (Lord Steyn dissenting on this point) ruled that the employee's claim should be struck out as disclosing no cause of action. In *Johnson*, Lord Steyn argued that the aspect of Lord Loreburn's judgment in *Addis* which dealt with reputational losses did not clearly command the consent of a majority of the judges in that case, and that, in any event, it was contrary to basic principles of contract law which allow recovery of financial losses flowing from breach as long as a causal link can be established. In his opinion, Lord Hoffmann (with whom Lords Bingham and Millett agreed) concluded that in the light of the express terms of the contract in *Johnson*, '[t]he action for wrongful dismissal could ... yield no more than the salary which should have been paid during the contractual period of notice'.[168] However, this conclusion rested not simply on the express notice clause in Mr Johnson's contract, but also on a provision under which the company reserved the right to make a payment in lieu of notice (or 'PILON') in the event of dismissal, a right which it exercised. On this basis, Mr Johnson's contract contained a PILON clause which Lord Hoffmann appears to have construed as permitting the company to dismiss him summarily without thereby committing any breach, as long as it paid a sum equivalent to net wages for the notice period.[169] On the basis of this interpretation of *Johnson*, it remained open to courts in future cases not involving a similar PILON clause to reconsider the issue of precisely what was decided in *Addis* and whether that decision was consistent with basic principles governing the award of damages for breach of contract. To date there has been no such reconsideration of *Addis* on this or any other ground. In *Edwards v Chesterfield Royal*

---

[165] See para 5.45.
[166] This was the basis on which Lord Steyn ruled that the claim in *Johnson* should be struck out ([2001] IRLR 279, at [29]).
[167] This was also the case in *Eastwood v Magnox Electric plc* and *McCabe v Cornwall County Council* [2004] IRLR 733.
[168] [2001] IRLR 279, [41].
[169] See para 5.28 below for further discussion of PILON clauses. It is not entirely clear that Mr Johnson's contract contained a true PILON clause; if it did, he would not have had a wrongful dismissal claim for net wages, as Lord Hoffmann appears to imply, but, for reasons we explain below, no action for wrongful dismissal at all.

Hospitals NHS Foundation Trust and *Botham v Ministry of Defence* reputational loss was alleged to have resulted from the respective employers' failures to carry out a contractual disciplinary procedure prior to dismissal.[170] The majority of the Supreme Court regarded *Addis* and *Johnson* as a barrier to these claims. It had been argued for the claimants that Parliament, in enacting protection against unfair dismissal, could not be taken to have intended to remove an employee's common law rights. Lord Dyson (with whom Lord Walker agreed) acknowledged that there was debate about what *Addis* had decided but held that it was unnecessary to enter into this debate as the Donovan report which inspired the introduction of unfair dismissal protection in IRA 1971 assumed that the law was as summarised in the headnote, which stated that the damages available to a wrongfully dismissed employee could not include compensation for the manner of dismissal. In the absence of cases prior to IRA 1971 where an employee had been awarded damages for the unfair manner of dismissal, Lord Dyson held that it could not be said that the reasoning in *Johnson* should be rejected on the basis that IRA took away an employee's existing rights.[171] Lord Mance also supported an approach which did not outflank *Addis* and *Johnson*,[172] as did Lord Phillips, although the latter acknowledged that this was an area of law which might merit 'fundamental review'.[173] Whether *Addis* was correct in principle did not seem to have been challenged in the Supreme Court by the claimants[174] and those judges who dissented in *Edwards* did so without reversing it. Lady Hale, who considered that loss that flowed from breach of contractually agreed procedures should be recoverable, distinguished *Addis* on the basis that there was no contractually agreed process in that case.[175] Lord Kerr (with whom Lord Wilson agreed) did not consider *Addis* to be a barrier where the claim was based on a breach of disciplinary procedure separate from that of wrongful dismissal.[176] As we discuss in para 5.44 below, the idea that statute has 'occupied the field' in relation to dismissal procedure is highly contentious, but the approach of the majority in *Edwards* may make it more difficult to persuade a court to undertake the type of re-examination of *Addis* which *Johnson* alone might have permitted.

(vi) The effect of the payment of wages in lieu of notice

5.28   It is often the case in practice that an employer will summarily dismiss an employee and, at the same time, pay him or her the net wages which he or she would have received during the period of minimum notice to which he or she was entitled (a 'payment of wages in lieu of notice' or 'PILON').[177] This may or may not be a wrongful dismissal, depending on the circumstances. An employee is entitled to waive the right to receive notice, just as with any other contractual right,

---

[170] Further details of the claim, and of that in *Botham v Ministry of Defence*, are given in para 5.45 below.
[171] [2012] IRLR 129 at [43].
[172] Above at [102].
[173] At [87]-[88].
[174] Lord Phillips at [85].
[175] At [116].
[176] At [146]-[147]. Lords Kerr and Wilson considered that Mr Edwards' claim should be allowed to proceed but not that of Mr Botham: see further para 5.45 below.
[177] In *Locke v Candy and Candy Ltd* [2011] IRLR 163 the Court of Appeal emphasised that the amount to be paid under a PILON would depend on the construction of the contract; there was no presumption that the former employee would receive what he would have received had he remained employed during the notice period (in this case, a bonus).

whereupon the dismissal will not be wrongful.[178] However, for a waiver of contractual rights to be effective it must be given in return for consideration of some kind, or be subject to an estoppel. If an employee voluntarily accepts a payment of wages in lieu of notice, this would normally be seen as discharging his or her contractual rights against the employer. It is also possible for an employee to give up the rights both to notice and to receive wages in lieu, in return for receiving some other benefit. In *Baldwin v British Coal Corpn*[179] the employee's contract was terminated without him receiving the twelve weeks' notice to which he was entitled. This was done in order to enable him to receive a redundancy payment of £5,000 under a statutory scheme, the terms of which would have been inapplicable had he been dismissed at a later date. It was held that he had thereby waived any right to receive, in addition, net salary for the contractual notice period.

Conversely, where the employment relationship is ended consensually on the basis that the employee will receive wages in lieu of notice, this arrangement could be construed as involving a promise by the employer to pay a sum equivalent to *gross* salary for the period in question. Because the contract is discharged by agreement there is no question of there being a wrongful dismissal, and no presumption that the sum payable by the employer in return for ending the relationship should be the same as the sum normally awarded by a court by way of damages for failure to give notice. Thus in *Gothard v Mirror Group Newspapers Ltd*[180] the Court of Appeal thought that the most natural construction of an agreement for voluntary early retirement was that the payment of wages in lieu of notice would be made gross. The same principle may apply to a PILON clause, that is to say, a clause in the contract which provides that the employer has a choice of either giving notice or making a payment in lieu. If the employer fails to give notice, the payment in lieu may be characterised as a contractual debt rather than as a payment of damages. Where the payment in lieu can be characterised in this way (an issue which turns on the construction of the contract terms) the effect (among other things) is that the employee has no duty of mitigation, and no deduction may be made to take account of the accelerated receipt of wages or salary.[181]

(vii) A 'right to work'?

5.29 What happens where the employee does not agree to waive the right to notice? Under these circumstances, it is far from clear that he or she has any enforceable right to work out the period of notice. A payment of wages in lieu of notice will normally be seen as discharging in full the employer's liability to pay damages for breach of contract. This follows from *Addis v Gramophone*

---

[178] *Trotter v Forth Ports Authority* [1991] IRLR 419; *Baldwin v British Coal Corpn* [1995] IRLR 139. This rule is preserved in the context of the statutory minimum notice periods by ERA 1996, s 86(3). In *Société Générale v Geys* [2011] IRLR 482 the Court of Appeal held that there was no requirement for the employee to be given notice of the exercise of the PILON clause where the contract did not provide for this and distinguished termination at common law from the statutory 'effective date of termination' (see para 5.80 below).

[179] [1995] IRLR 139.

[180] [1988] ICR 729.

[181] See *Cerberus Software Ltd v Rowley* [1999] IRLR 690, which was overturned on the basis of a different construction of the contract by the Court of Appeal [2001] IRLR 160; see also *EMI Group Electronics Ltd v Coldicott (Inspector of Taxes)* [1999] IRLR 630 (where the contract makes provision for a payment in lieu of notice, the amount is taxable as an emolument from employment, which will not be the case if the payment is made as damages for breach of contract). In *Cavenagh v William Evans Ltd* [2012] EWCA Civ 697 the Court of Appeal held that once the employer had terminated the employee's contract using a PILON a debt was accrued and the employer could not then rely on the *Boston Deep Fishing and Ice Co v Ansell* principle (see para 5.19 above).

Co Ltd.[182] It is only in exceptional cases that an employer may be liable for an additional breach of contract in refusing to allow the employee to work. In cases involving actors and others whose work is displayed to the public at large, the employer's failure to permit the employee to perform as contractually agreed has been held to give rise to claims for harm to reputation, which the courts have been prepared to quantify.[183] However, in other contexts quantification may be more difficult. The courts are unlikely to grant an order for specific performance of a contract of employment[184] and, in practice, the issue is likely to arise most frequently in relation to situations where the employer wishes the employee to remain on 'garden leave', but employees, to preserve their skills, wish to start working for another employer.[185]

The position with regard to the protection of skills and earning capacity is more clearly defined in the case of a contract of apprenticeship, which will normally be for a fixed term without provision for the employer to terminate the contract by giving notice. The apprentice is entitled not simply to be employed, but also to receive training and instruction. The employer has no general power to dismiss without giving a reason, and the range of conduct for which the apprentice may be summarily dismissed is highly restricted: in *Dunk v George Waller & Son Ltd*[186] it was not enough that the apprentice had failed certain examinations. If the apprentice is wrongfully dismissed, he or she is entitled to damages not just for lost wages but also for the loss of training opportunities and the consequent harm done to his or her chances of eventually obtaining a good job.

The right to training is an integral part of the contract of apprenticeship. It is not necessarily a part, integral or otherwise, of the contract of employment. However, a contract of employment may contain a term providing a right to training or to retraining, either by way of incorporation from a collective agreement or other external source, or by way of an implied term.[187] Under these circumstances, there seems to be no reason why an employee who is wrongfully dismissed should not receive an award of damages to reflect the loss of these rights, by way of analogy with the apprenticeship cases.

(viii) Clauses providing for dismissal 'with immediate effect'

5.30   Contracts of employment sometimes contain clauses specifying that the employer shall have the right to bring the employment to an end 'with immediate effect' in the event of a breach of contract of a certain kind by the employee. In *T & K Home Improvements Ltd v Skilton*[188] the

---

[182] [1909] AC 488. See also *Dixon v Stenor* [1973] ICR 157, 158 (Sir John Donaldson P); *Gothard v Mirror Group Newspapers Ltd* [1988] ICR 729, 733 (Lord Donaldson MR).

[183] See *Herbert Clayton and Jack Waller Ltd v Oliver* [1930] AC 209; para 4.126 above.

[184] See Brodie, 1998. On injunctions and declarations to maintain the contract of employment, see para 5.54 *et seq* below.

[185] See *William Hill Organisation Ltd v Tucker* [1998] IRLR 313 in which the Court of Appeal held, somewhat unusually, that the employer was under a contractual obligation to supply the employee with work and, as it was in breach of this term during the notice period, was not entitled to an injunction restraining him from working for a competitor during the notice period.

[186] [1970] 2 QB 163. See also *Wallace v CA Roofing Services Ltd* [1996] IRLR 435; *Whitely v Marton Electrical Ltd* [2003] IRLR 197 (employment under a 'modern apprenticeship pact'); *Flett v Matheson* [2006] IRLR 277 (tripartite 'individual learning plan').

[187] See *Cresswell v Board of Inland Revenue* [1984] IRLR 190; para 4.104 above.

[188] [2000] IRLR 595.

Court of Appeal held that such a clause was effective in allowing the employer to end the contract without notice, and that the employee was not entitled to work or to be on the employer's premises after that point. However, the Court found that, on the construction of the particular contract before it, the 'immediate effect' clause did not override another clause in the contract under which the employee was entitled to receive three month's written notice of termination.[189] The employee was therefore entitled to receive a payment of wages in lieu of notice for this period. In other words, the Court construed the 'immediate effect' clause as qualifying the employee's right to work during the notice period, but not his right to receive a payment in lieu.

Contractual job security

5.31   Contracts of employment may contain express terms, or terms incorporated from external sources, which purport to provide guarantees of job security going beyond that provided by the right to minimum notice. It is possible, for example, for a contract to incorporate a guarantee that the employer will not make the employee compulsorily redundant, although such terms are rare and may even, in respect of some public-sector employments, be open to legal challenge as illegitimately fettering the employer's discretion.[190] It is more common, but still rare, for a contract to omit the normal provision allowing the employer to terminate the contract by simply giving notice: this may have the same effect as preventing compulsory redundancy.[191] Alternatively, a contract could incorporate a term making compulsory redundancy conditional upon a particular selection procedure being followed.[192] Contracts may also incorporate the terms relating to the exercise by the employer of powers of discipline and dismissal. These may provide superior protection to that which is available under unfair dismissal legislation, in terms of such procedural issues as the employee's rights to be represented (rather than merely accompanied)[193] at a hearing of the issues and more specific rights in relation to the conduct of a hearing.[194] Terms of this kind normally require the employer to follow a particular procedure as a pre-condition of exercising the power, under the contract, to discipline or dismiss an employee who has been found guilty of misconduct. They can be read, then, as doing one or both of two things: they impose a procedure which the employer must observe when exercising a disciplinary power; and they impliedly restrict the right of the employer to circumvent this procedure by dismissing an employee for no reason at all by simply invoking the right to give notice under the contract. In other words, the

---

[189] Here, the notice term was express, but it is also possible that similar notice clauses (of varying lengths) could take effect in contracts by virtue of ERA 1996, ss 86 *et seq* (see para 5.15 above). It would arguably be contrary to principle (and, more specifically, contrary to ERA 1996, s 203) to allow the employer to contract out of the obligation to give notice which arises by virtue of this legislation.

[190] See Ewing, 1989: p 217.

[191] On notice clauses, see *McClelland v Northern Ireland General Health Services Board* [1957] 1 WLR 594 and the discussion in para 5.17 above. Cf *Kaur v MG Rover Group Ltd* [2005] IRLR 40.

[192] *Anderson v Pringle of Scotland* [1998] IRLR 64; *Peace v City of Edinburgh Council* [1999] IRLR 417; cf *Alexander v Standard Telephones and Cables (No 2)* [1991] IRLR 286. A further possibility is that the contract incorporates an equal opportunities policy which qualifies the employer's powers of dismissal: see *Taylor v Secretary of State for Scotland* [2000] IRLR 502.

[193] ERA 1999, ss 10–15 gives a right to be accompanied; see further para 5.121 *et seq.*

[194] See para 5.129 below for the provisions of the ACAS Code of Practice on Disciplinary and Grievance Procedures 2009 in relation to the conduct of disciplinary meetings.

effect of these clauses could be both procedural and substantive: if the protection against arbitrary discipline is to mean anything, the employer must have impliedly given up the right, which the notice rule otherwise confers, to end the contract without needing to have a reason for doing so.[195]

5.32   In addition to the higher standards which they frequently embody, contractual job security clauses have other advantages over statutory protection against unfair dismissal. As we shall see,[196] an employee may under certain circumstances be able to enforce his or her contractual rights by way of an injunction or declaration. This remedy – effectively enabling a dismissal to be nullified and the employment relationship maintained – is not normally available under unfair dismissal legislation. This legislation is only triggered once dismissal has already taken place,[197] and although re-employment is in principle the primary remedy for unfair dismissal,[198] it is very rarely awarded in practice.[199]

Nor does unfair dismissal law provide fully adequate protection to an employee who suffers disciplinary action short of dismissal. Unless the action in question falls into one of a number of specific cases in which a worker or employee can bring a claim based on being subjected to a detriment without necessarily being dismissed,[200] the employee's only option under the Act is to accept that the contract has come to an end and claim unfair dismissal. This need not always lead to the employee resigning; in some cases the courts have accepted that the employee can bring a claim for unfair dismissal while continuing to work for the employer under a new contract.[201] But even if a tribunal finds that there was an unfair dismissal in these circumstances, the employee is unlikely to get the previous contract terms reinstated: financial compensation is the much more likely outcome.[202] Where it would be preferable from the employee's point of view to have the wrongful disciplinary action *nullified* as opposed to being compensated for its effects, this can only be effectively achieved by way of an injunction or declaration under the common law.

Finally, in a case where a specific order of injunction or declaration is not available, the employee may nevertheless be able to obtain substantial damages for breach of a contractual job security clause. This will be important in cases where unfair dismissal compensation falls short of meeting the employee's losses in full, thanks to the upper limits on compensation which apply to claims under the Act.[203] Whether damages will be available must now be considered in the light of

---

[195] See further para 5.40–5.42 below.

[196] See para 5.54 *et seq* below.

[197] Note, however, the provisions of the ACAS Code of Practice on Disciplinary and Grievance Procedures on procedures to be followed prior to dismissal and the discretion of employment tribunals to adjust awards in the event of non-compliance with the Code: see further para 5.125 *et seq* below.

[198] ERA 1996, ss 112 and 113.

[199] See para 5.142 below.

[200] These include the situations listed in TULRCA 1992, s 146 and Sch A1, para 156; ERA 1996, ss 43M–47E; NMWA 1998 s 23; ERelA 1999, s 12; TICER 1999, reg 31; PTWR 2000, reg 7; FTER 2002, reg 6; FWPR 2002, reg 16; ICER 2004, reg 32; ECSIER 2006, reg 33; CCBMR 2007, regs 49–51; EPLLCEIR 2009, reg 31; ERABR 2010, reg 9; and AWR 2010, reg 17.

[201] *Hogg v Dover College* [1990] ICR 39; *Joseph v British Railways Board* (2 September 1993, IT, unreported) noted by Curran, 1994; *Alcan Extrusions v Yates* [1996] IRLR 327.

[202] See para 5.142 below.

[203] See para 5.145 *et seq* below. A contract clause which requires the employer to observe the substance of unfair dismissal protection might be one means of seeking to combine the strengths of unfair dismissal with those of the common law, while seeking to avoid their respective weaknesses. See Ewing, 1989.

the co-joined appeals in *Edwards v Chesterfield Royal Hospitals NHS Foundation Trust* and *Botham v Ministry of Defence*,[204] which we discuss in para 5.45 below.

A further possibility is that a degree of contractual job security may be provided by implied terms, and, in particular, by the implied duty of mutual trust and confidence.[205] Where this is the case, it may be open to an employee to argue that substantial damages should be awarded, going beyond the net wages and salary for the notice period which is the usual measure of damages for a 'direct' wrongful dismissal claim. However, the application of the implied obligation of trust and confidence in relation to termination of employment raises complex and difficult questions, which we discuss in paras 5.43 and 5.44 below.

(i) The legal effect of express job security clauses

5.33 We begin our analysis with a closer examination of the legal status of express job security clauses. The first question that arises is whether the clause has been incorporated into the individual contract of employment; if so, it is then necessary to consider whether the clause can survive a wrongful summary dismissal.

IS THE TERM INCORPORATED INTO THE CONTRACT?

5.34 In the first place, it may be that the clause is not effectively incorporated into the individual contract of employment. There should be no difficulty, in principle, on the grounds of the term's *appropriateness* for incorporation:[206] such clauses can be seen as intended to regulate the individual relationship, and are not normally a matter for collective relations only. In *Alexander v Standard Telephone and Cables Ltd (No 2)*[207] Hobhouse J held that a clause in a collective agreement laying down a 'last-in, first-out' procedure for redundancy selection was not intended to give rise to individual rights and was not incorporated at the level of the individual contract. However, this was a somewhat exceptional outcome[208] and goes against the tide of numerous other decisions in which contractual job security clauses have been regarded as incorporated into individual contracts, almost as a matter of course.[209]

It may nevertheless be open to an employer to deny normative force to the clause by stating that it is not intended to have legal effect. Against this, the courts have insisted that they, and not the parties, are the final arbiters of whether an agreement is a legally-binding contract or not.[210] If, in all other respects, a clause of this kind possesses the necessary attributes of a binding contract

---

[204] [2012] IRLR 129, SC.

[205] On the implied term of mutual trust and confidence, see para 4.105 *et seq* above.

[206] See para 4.30 above.

[207] [1991] IRLR 286; see para 4.30 above.

[208] Cf, in the context of redundancy, the Court of Session decision in *Anderson v Pringle of Scotland* [1998] IRLR 64, discussed further in para 5.61. In *Kaur v MG Rover Group Ltd* [2005] IRLR 40, however, a clause in a collective agreement stating '[t]here will be no compulsory redundancy' was found in the circumstances not to be apt for incorporation.

[209] This is so in virtually all the cases discussed in this and the following paragraph. Cf *Lakshmi v Mid Cheshire Hospitals NHS Trust* [2008] IRLR 956, QBD, [24]–[29], where it was held that the employer's disciplinary policy constituted policy guidelines rather than being expressly incorporated into the employee's contract, but that it was an implied term that the employer would comply with the policy unless it could establish good reason not to do so.

[210] *R v Lord Chancellor's Department, ex p Nangle* [1991] IRLR 343.

term, the courts should arguably be reluctant to rubber-stamp a bare statement by the employer to the effect that the clause is binding in honour only.

5.35   At one time the opinion of Lord Hoffmann in *Johnson v Unisys Ltd* [211] seemed to raise a further difficulty, although this must now be considered in the light of *Edwards v Chesterfield Royal Hospitals NHS Foundation Trust* and *Botham v Ministry of Defence*,[212] discussed below. In *Johnson*, Mr Johnson sought unsuccessfully to maintain that he had a cause of action based on the employer's breach of the implied duty of trust and confidence in respect of the psychological illness which he alleged had been caused by his summary dismissal without a fair hearing and in breach of the company's disciplinary procedure. He did not argue that the provisions of the disciplinary procedure constituted express terms of his contract of employment. Lord Hoffmann, with whose opinion Lords Bingham and Millett agreed, nevertheless decided that it would be useful to 'examine the matter in a little more detail'.[213] In lengthy *obiter* remarks, he stated that the employee handbook 'has to be construed against the relevant background and the background which fairly looms over the disciplinary procedure is Part X of the [Employment Rights Act]', that is, the legislation conferring on employees the right to claim compensation and/or re-employment for unfair dismissal.[214] From this perspective, in Lord Hoffmann's view, the main purpose of the disciplinary procedure was to ensure that an employee was not unfairly dismissed. Procedures of this kind were, he argued, included in employee handbooks out of concern for the provisions of ERA 1996, Part X and the Code of Practice on Disciplinary and Grievance Procedures (as it now is) issued by ACAS, and in order to comply with the obligation in section 3 of ERA 1996 to notify employees in writing of disciplinary procedures governing their employment. Lord Hoffmann then went on to say:

> ... given this background to the disciplinary procedures, I find it impossible to believe that Parliament, when it provided in section 3(1) of the 1996 Act that the statement of particulars of employment was to contain a note of any applicable disciplinary rules, or the parties themselves, intended that the inclusion of those rules should give rise to a common law action in damages which would create the means of circumventing the restrictions and limits which Parliament had imposed on compensation for unfair dismissal ... It is, I suppose, possible that they may have contractual effect in determining whether the employer can dismiss summarily in the sense of not having to give four weeks' notice or payment in lieu. But I do not think they can have been intended to qualify the employer's common law power to dismiss without cause on giving such notice, or to create contractual duties which are independently actionable.[215]

---

[211] [2001] IRLR 279.
[212] [2012] IRLR 129, SC.
[213] [2001] IRLR 279, [60]
[214] [2001] IRLR 279, [63].
[215] [2001] UKHL 13, [2001] IRLR 279, [66]. Lord Hoffmann's reference to the role of the written statement of disciplinary procedures in this context is difficult to understand. As we have seen (para 4.23), the courts have held that the employer is only obliged to record in the statement those terms and conditions (including disciplinary procedures) which have contractual effect. A disciplinary procedure which, applying Lord Hoffmann's reasoning in *Johnson*, had no contractual effect, would not need to be referred to in a written statement. On this basis, it is arguable that the enactment of ERA 1996, s 3 is evidence that Parliament intended disciplinary procedures to have contractual effect unless there was clear intention to the contrary.

This statement is capable of being read in a number of ways. It could be construed as meaning that the existence of Part X of the 1996 Act must be interpreted as preventing courts giving effect to contractual disciplinary procedures which provide rights over and above those supplied by statute. An alternative reading is that there is merely a strong presumption against giving contractual effect to disciplinary procedures adopted by employers in order to comply with their statutory obligations. In either case, this would be a highly novel approach to the interpretation of protective employment legislation and of its relationship to contract. It is normal for such legislation to limit the degree to which the parties to the employment relationship can contract out of provisions designed for the protection of the employee.[216] However, far from preventing the parties from contracting for superior or complementary protections, one of the aims of such legislation is precisely to induce improvements at this kind, hence its characterisation as a *'floor* of rights'.[217] If Lord Hoffmann's analysis were to be widely followed, statutory standards of this kind would in future act as a 'ceiling' rather than as a 'floor' for contractual rights and obligations. This would create the anomalous situation that employees may be better protected in areas in which Parliament has failed or chosen not to legislate than those in which it has.

Obiter dicta in the seven-judge Supreme Court decision in *Edwards* and *Botham*[218] give some support to the view that disciplinary procedures should be treated as contractual although, in the light of the decision as a whole, this may be little comfort to a claimant. Lord Dyson concluded that the effect of ERA 1996, ss 1 and 3(1) was that Parliament had decided 'at least in most cases, that contractual force should be given to applicable rules and procedures'.[219] He reached this view on the basis that the written statement of employment terms may be regarded in practice by one or both of the parties as equivalent to contract and that it represented strong prima facie evidence of the contract when it favoured an employee.[220] However, he noted that Lord Hoffmann in *Johnson* had stated that the disciplinary procedures were 'intended to operate within the scope of the law of unfair dismissal'. Lord Dyson agreed, citing the provisions in TULRCA 1992, EA 2002 and EA 2008 which Parliament had adopted 'linking a failure to comply with disciplinary or dismissal procedures with the outcome of unfair dismissal proceedings'.[221] This meant that 'if provisions about disciplinary procedure are incorporated as express terms into an employment contract, they are not ordinary contractual terms agreed by parties to a contract in the usual way'.[222] Parliament, having specified the consequences of a failure to comply with such provisions in unfair dismissal proceedings:

> ... could not have intended that the inclusion of these provisions in a contract would also give rise to a common law claim for damages ... It is necessarily to be inferred from this statutory

---

[216] See, eg, ERA 1996, s 203; and see our discussion of the relationship between statutory standards and the contract of employment at para 4.11 above.

[217] See our discussion at para 4.11 above, and, for an empirical analysis of this effect in practice, see W Brown *et al*, 2000, cited by Lord Steyn in his dissenting judgment in *Johnson* [2001] IRLR 279, [23].

[218] [2012] IRLR 129, SC.

[219] At [28].

[220] See para 4.25 above, cited by Lord Dyson. As we indicate in para 4.25, contract and statement are conceptually discrete and we do not agree that the fact that a party regards it as being 'equivalent to a contract' is sufficient to give a statement contractual effect. However, for the reasons we give in note 215 above, it is possible to maintain that, in enacting ERA 1996, s 3, Parliament intended to accord disciplinary procedures contractual effect unless the contrary is indicated.

[221] At [37]. See paras 2.20 above and 5.125 below.

[222] At [38].

background that, unless they otherwise expressly agree, the parties to an employment contract do not intend that a failure to comply with contractually binding disciplinary procedures will give rise to a common law claim for damages. In these circumstances, I agree entirely with para 66 of Lord Hoffmann's speech [quoted above].... That is not to say that an employer who starts a disciplinary process in breach of the express terms of the contract of employment is not acting in breach of contract. He plainly is. If that happens, it is open to the employee to seek an injunction to stop the process and/or to seek an appropriate declaration ... [A]n injunction to prevent a threatened unfair dismissal does not cut across the statutory scheme for compensation for unfair dismissal.[223]

Lord Walker agreed with the entirety of Lord Dyson's judgment, and Lord Mance, too, appeared to assume that disciplinary procedures would have the effect Lord Dyson indicated.[224] Lord Phillips thought it 'artificial' to impute to every party to a contract of employment the same intention that Lords Hoffmann and Dyson had ascribed to Parliament in relation to disciplinary procedures, but conceded that it 'may be a legitimate approach to making sense of this area of the law'.[225] Lord Kerr (with whom Lord Wilson agreed) and Baroness Hale did not comment on the general principle of whether disciplinary procedures should or should not be regarded as contractual but considered that if they were incorporated in the contract, by statute or agreement, they should be enforceable in the normal way.[226] We discuss the implications of these judgments for the remedies available for breach of disciplinary procedures in greater detail in para 5.45 below.

It was accepted by the parties in *Edwards* and *Botham* that the disciplinary procedures in question were contractually binding and, assumed for the purposes of the appeal, that they had been breached; arguments centred on the damages potentially available for breach. The statements as to the contractual status of disciplinary procedures in general are, therefore, as in *Johnson*, *obiter*, but significant weight is likely to be accorded to them. The conclusions of Lords Dyson and Mance are open to the same objections which we set out above in relation to the opinion of Lord Hoffmann: it is contrary to the generally accepted approach to the interpretation of protective employment legislation to treat statutory rights as a ceiling rather than as a floor of rights. We agree with the views of Lord Kerr and Baroness Hale in *Edwards* and *Botham* that there is no justification for the proposition that the parties would need expressly to state that they intend a contractually binding procedure to give rise to a claim for damages, if breached, for damages to be available.[227] As Lord Kerr explained, this 'seems a curious result' which can be reached only 'for some unstated policy reason. And if it is the case that the proposition is underpinned by a public policy consideration, it seems highly curious that it can be displaced by the express agreement of the parties'.[228] Finally, there is considerable force in the view expressed by Lord Phillips that the legal effect of specific procedures should be ascertained by examining the parties' individual agreement unless statute clearly specifies otherwise.

---

[223] At [39] and [44].

[224] At [94].

[225] At [79].

[226] At [153] and [116] respectively. However Lord Kerr, unlike Baroness Hale, excluded damages claims 'inextricably linked to the fact of .... dismissal' (at [156]).

[227] At [154] and [122] respectively

[228] At [154].

THE 'ELECTIVE' AND 'AUTOMATIC' THEORIES OF CONTRACT TERMINATION

5.36   If a job security clause has been incorporated into a contract. it may then be necessary to consider the effect of a wrongful summary dismissal on the future contractual obligations of the parties. According to the 'automatic' or 'unilateral' theory of contract termination, the act of summary dismissal of itself brings the contract to an end, as would the employee's abrupt walk-out or resignation; the employer's obligations under the job security clause are discharged along with the rest of the contract. This theory seeks to draw distinctions between different kinds of repudiatory breach. A repudiatory breach which is not aimed at bringing the relationship to an end, such as an employer's failure to pay wages or salary as agreed, does not, it is said, terminate the contract.[229] However, it is also said that the *contract* cannot be maintained in force once the *relationship* of employment has come to an end by virtue of the deliberate act of either party.[230] The result would be that following summary dismissal, the employee could not rely on a contractual job security clause to protect his or her expectations of continuing employment. This argument has, however, been discredited in the context of the law of contract more generally, where an unaccepted repudiation is regarded as 'a thing writ in water':[231] the contract is only brought to an end if the innocent party chooses to terminate it in response to the repudiatory breach.[232] This 'bilateral' or 'elective' theory of termination is also supported by decisions specific to the contract of employment. The elective theory explains, for example, why an employer may be able to obtain an injunction against a former employee, restraining him or her from making use of confidential information or for working for a competitor for a certain period.[233] For this purpose, the contract term in question must have survived the employee's wrongful repudiation of the contract. If this principle works in favour of the employer, contractual reciprocity requires that it should work in favour of the employee too.[234]

5.37   It is nevertheless maintained by some that the application of the bilateral theory to the ending of the contract of employment is impractical, and that these practical considerations should outweigh more abstract arguments in favour of aligning contracts of employment with the rule which applies to other contracts.[235] For example, it has been suggested that the effect of the elective theory is to allow the employee, following a refusal to accept that the contract has been brought to an end by the summary dismissal, to 'sit in the sun' and claim his or her wages indefinitely, without needing to do any work for them. This is because no duty to mitigate loss arises in the context of a debt claim, to which the employee might, under these circumstances, be

---

[229] *Rigby v Ferodo Ltd* [1988] ICR 29; *Boyo v Lambeth London Borough Council* [1995] IRLR 50, 59 (Ralph Gibson LJ).
[230] *Sanders v Ernest A Neale Ltd* [1974] IRLR 236 (Sir John Donaldson P); *Gunton v Richmond-upon-Thames London Borough Council* [1980] ICR 755, 762 (Shaw LJ, dissenting); *London Transport Executive v Clarke* [1981] ICR 355 (Lord Denning MR, dissenting); *R v East Berkshire Area Health Authority, ex p Walsh* [1984] ICR 743, 756 (May LJ); *Boyo v Lambeth London Borough Council* [1995] IRLR 50, 57 (Ralph Gibson LJ), 49 (Staughton LJ), 60 (Sir Francis Purchas).
[231] *Howard v Pickford Tool Co Ltd* [1951] 1 KB 417, 421 (Asquith LJ), itself an employment case.
[232] *White and Carter (Councils) Ltd v McGregor* [1962] AC 413.
[233] *Thomas Marshall (Exports) Ltd v Guinle* [1979] Ch 227; *Evening Standard Co Ltd v Henderson* [1987] ICR 588.
[234] It accordingly seems beside the point that the employer cannot obtain an order of *specific performance* against the employee (cf *Boyo v Lambeth London Borough Council* [1995] IRLR 50, 60, per Sir Francis Purchas). If the employer can obtain prohibitory injunctions against the employee after the relationship of employment has come to an end, why should not the employee have the reciprocal right? There is a distinction here between specific performance, which is generally not available to either party, and a prohibitory injunction, which may be. See further para 5.54 below.
[235] For discussion, see John McMullen, 1982 and 1995.

entitled.[236] However, this would only be the case if the employee were entitled to wages for being ready and available for work, as opposed to receiving wages for work actually done.[237]

Even then, it is an established principle of contract law that the innocent party is not entitled to uphold the contract in all circumstances. He or she only has the right to do so if they have a 'legitimate interest' in maintaining that contract in force as opposed to any other. The unavailability of alternative work might be such an interest.[238] Where the innocent party has no 'legitimate interest', however, he or she may be taken to have accepted the other's repudiatory breach, and is then left only with a claim for damages. This would seem to deal fully with the point at issue here. In the context of employment, an employee would have a legitimate interest in maintaining the contract if he or she were genuinely seeking to keep the relationship intact by asserting their rights to a fair hearing under the contract, but in few other cases.[239] Moreover, acceptance is easily implied by, for example, the act of seeking alternative employment.[240] The danger of an employee 'sitting in the sun' and claiming wages indefinitely is also simply enough avoided, in these circumstances, by the employer agreeing to operate the procedure as required by the contract.

5.38   A related objection is that the elective theory does not work very well in the context of unfair dismissal, which adopts the common law notion of dismissal for a number of purposes.[241] Without a dismissal, the employment tribunal has no jurisdiction to hear the employee's complaint. Section 95(1) of ERA 1996 defines dismissal as including the case where the contract is 'terminated by the employer (whether with or without notice)'. If the elective theory were correct, this section would have no application to the case of a wrongful summary dismissal in which the contract was brought to an end not by the employer's breach, but by the employee's acceptance of that breach. This point is easily enough dealt with, however, by the provision made for constructive dismissal in section 95(1)(c), which states that there is a dismissal for the purposes of the Act where the 'employee terminates the contract under which he is employed (with or without notice) in circumstances in which he is entitled to terminate it without notice by reason of the employer's conduct'. This provision extends the jurisdiction of the tribunal to cover the case where the employee accepts the repudiatory breach of the employer.

However, where the contract is terminated by the employee's acceptance in this way, it may be difficult to establish precisely when the contract was brought to an end, in particular in a case where the employee is *taken* to have waived the right to affirm the contract by virtue

---

[236] *White and Carter (Councils) Ltd v McGregor* [1962] AC 413; *Sanders v Ernest A Neale Ltd* [1974] IRLR 236; *Boyo v Lambeth London Borough Council* [1995] IRLR 50, 57, 59.

[237] On this, see para 4.62 above.

[238] *White and Carter (Councils) Ltd v McGregor* [1962] AC 413, *per* Lord Reid.

[239] Another possibility might be an interest in keeping the contract on foot in order to acquire the necessary continuity of employment to claim unfair dismissal. This is discussed further at para 5.80 *et seq* below. The result of *Edwards v Chesterfield Royal Hospitals NHS Foundation Trust and Botham v Ministry of Defence* [2012] IRLR 129, discussed in para 5.45 below, may be to encourage employees to seek to uphold the contract in a wider range of circumstances.

[240] *Dietman v Brent London Borough Council* [1987] ICR 737. The judgments of the Court of Appeal in *Boyo v Lambeth London Borough Council* [1995] IRLR 50 express doubt on this point (see eg [1995] IRLR 50, 59, *per* Ralph Gibson LJ) but it seems well enough established by authority and by principle. In *Soares v Beazer Investments Ltd* [2004] EWCA Civ 482, however, the Court of Appeal held that if there is an evidential lacuna about acceptance it should benefit the employee not the employer ([26], Maurice Kay LJ).

[241] See *London Transport Executive v Clarke* [1981] ICR 355, discussed at para 5.73 below.

of having no legitimate interest in keeping it alive. In *Robert Cort & Son Ltd v Charman*[242] the EAT concluded that in a case of summary dismissal, the 'effective date of termination' ('EDT') for statutory purposes should be set by reference to the date of that summary dismissal, even if the elective view was correct and the contract would be determined only where the employee accepted the repudiation.[243] In *Société Générale v Geys*[244] the Court of Appeal endorsed this view, and emphasised that the EDT and the date when the contract terminated for contractual purposes were different questions.[245] Thus, even if the unilateral theory has to be adopted for reasons of certainty in relation to the EDT, this is no reason for applying the same rule in the common law, where its effect would be to deny all normative force to contractual job security clauses: that would surely be a case of the tail wagging the dog.

5.39 In terms of contract principle, there would seem to be no good reason to depart from the general rule in favour of giving the innocent party the option to keep the contract on foot for the pursuit of a 'legitimate interest'. The alternative can be seen as unjust, in the sense that it would allow the party in breach to profit from its own wrong.[246] A number of judges have also questioned the idea that the subjective intention of the guilty party to end the relationship should determine the extent of the other's contractual rights.[247] The application of the elective theory to the contract of employment is, in effect, one further aspect of the courts' recognition that terms incorporated from collective agreements and other external sources have normative force at the level of the individual relationship. To deny the application of the elective theory would be to deny the fundamentally reciprocal nature of the parties' obligations under the individual contract of employment, and to return to a more hierarchical, master-servant model of the employment relationship.

There is also support for the elective theory from the point of view of authority. It was accepted by a majority of the Court of Appeal in *Gunton v Richmond-upon-Thames London Borough Council*[248] and was approved after extensive analyses at first instance in *Thomas Marshall (Exports) Ltd v Guinle*[249] and *Dietman v Brent London Borough Council*.[250] Numerous decisions in which employees have been granted declarations or injunctions to prevent employers acting in breach of disciplinary procedures also depend on the application of the elective theory, including the decision of the House of Lords in *McClelland v Northern Ireland General Health Services Board*;[251] it is not clear if or how far these decisions constitute some kind of exceptional category.[252] In *Rigby*

---

[242] [1981] IRLR 437. See also *Octavius Atkinson and Sons Ltd v Morris* [1989] ICR 431. See Freedland, 2003: pp 382–384 for a critique of these decisions, which allow the employing entity 'to take advantage of its own breach of contract' (p 383).

[243] See para 5.80 *et seq* below for discussion of the EDT. The decision in *Charman* should be considered in the light of *Gisda Cyf v Barratt* [2010] IRLR 1073, where the Supreme Court held that an employee should be entitled to be informed of, or at least have a reasonable chance of finding out about, his or her dismissal before time began to run.

[244] [2011] IRLR 482.

[245] Rimer LJ at [19].

[246] *Thomas Marshall (Exports) Ltd v Guinle* [1979] Ch 227, 240 (Sir Robert Megarry, VC).

[247] [1979] Ch 227. See also *Rigby v Ferodo Ltd* [1988] ICR 29, 35 (Lord Oliver).

[248] Shaw LJ dissented.

[249] By Sir Robert Megarry VC.

[250] By Hodgson J.

[251] [1957] 1 WLR 594. See also *Vine v National Dock Labour Board* [1957] AC 488; *Hill v CA Parsons & Co Ltd* [1972] Ch 305.

[252] See para 5.54 *et seq* below.

v Ferodo Ltd[253] the House of Lords declined to decide the matter, in a case not directly concerned with dismissal but with a cut in wages imposed, in breach of contract, by the employer. However, Lord Oliver said:

> I entirely fail to see how the continuance of the primary contractual obligation can be made to depend on the subjective desire of the contract-breaker and I do not understand what is meant by the injured party having no alternative but to accept the breach … I can see no reason in law or in logic why, leaving aside for the moment the extreme case of outright dismissal or walk-out, a contract of employment should be on any different footing from any other contract ….[254]

Despite this the application of the elective theory continues to be controversial, and it is unfortunate that the House of Lords did not choose to clarify the law when it could arguably have done so in *Rigby v Ferodo Ltd*.[255] More recently, in *Boyo v Lambeth London Borough Council*[256] a unanimous Court of Appeal took the opportunity to cast fresh doubt on the elective theory, while at the same time feeling bound to apply the majority ruling in an earlier judgment of the Court of Appeal, *Gunton v Richmond-upon-Thames London Borough Council*.[257] *Gunton*, according to the Court in *Boyo*, had produced law 'distinctly lacking in rhyme and reason',[258] and was not to be preferred, in principle, to the judgment of Sir John Donaldson P in *Sanders v Ernest A Neale Ltd* laying out the case for the automatic theory.[259] Although, at present, the elective theory has prevailed,[260] in the light of powerful *dicta* casting doubt on it, its future can hardly be regarded as assured.[261]

(ii) The relationship between contractual job security clauses and the notice rule

5.40   Even if the application of the elective theory would remove an important obstacle to the effectiveness of contractual job security clauses, it would not settle the question of the legal meaning of such clauses. This is because their relationship to the notice rule has not been properly resolved. Arguably, job security clauses of this kind can only be truly effective if they limit the notice rule. One possible construction of contracts containing these clauses is that they limit the employer's normal right to dismiss by giving notice: in the absence of an express clause empowering the employer to dismiss for redundancy, for example, it may only terminate the contract for good cause as laid down in the contractual procedure. If this is seen as a far-reaching and possibly unintended restriction upon the employer's powers, a second possibility is that where the employer seeks to dismiss for misconduct or breach of discipline, it may only do so after adhering to the contractual

---

[253] [1988] ICR 29.
[254] [1988] ICR 29, 35.
[255] [1988] ICR 29, 35.
[256] [1995] IRLR 50.
[257] [1980] ICR 755.
[258] [1995] IRLR 50, 50 (Staughton LJ).
[259] [1995] IRLR 50, 57 (Ralph Gibson LJ), 60 (Sir Francis Purchas).
[260] *Soares v Beazer Investments Ltd* [2004] EWCA Civ 482, [17] (Maurice Kay LJ); *Société Générale v Geys* [2011] IRLR 482, CA. See para 5.45 below for dicta on *Gunton* in *Edwards v Chesterfield Royal Hospital NHS Foundation Trust* and *Botham v Ministry of Defence* [2012] IRLR 129, SC.
[261] See also the discussion of this point by Sedley LJ in *Cerberus Software Ltd v Rowley* [2001] IRLR 160, 164–165.

procedures laid down for *these* situations; but that otherwise, it remains free to dismiss for no reason at all, simply by giving notice.[262] If this were the case, however, the employer could easily evade the job security clause by relying on its general power of dismissal. The employee would be back at square one. As Shaw LJ put it in his judgment in *Gunton* (which, on this point, departed from the majority view):

> How is the [procedural] code as to dismissal for breaches of discipline to be reconciled with the express provision for the termination of the [claimant's] contract of service by one month's notice on either side? A possible solution is that the code extends or varies that express provision where the council purports to dismiss on disciplinary grounds, but that in any other circumstances the contract of service may be determined by reference to the express provision. This, however, would produce a grotesque result, for it would mean that the council could, without assigning any reason, terminate the [claimant's] employment by a month's notice, but could not, if they complained of misconduct on his part, determine that employment save by what might prove a long protracted process.[263]

5.41 In *Gunton* the employee was dismissed for misconduct without the benefit of a hearing to which he was contractually entitled. The majority of the Court concluded that the contractual procedure was binding on the employer, and awarded the employee damages representing net salary for the period during which the procedure should have been operated, plus damages for the notice period laid down under his contract.[264] The majority appears to have assumed that the employer was under an obligation to operate the procedure, but was not bound to reach a particular result; and, moreover, that after the hearing, it could have exercised its right to dismiss the employee without needing to offer a reason, by giving the minimum period of contractual notice to terminate the contract. In that case, however, why could not the employer have given notice at the outset?

The notion of extended damages representing salary for the period of the disciplinary period was also applied, but with evident reluctance, in the later Court of Appeal judgment in *Boyo v Lambeth London Borough Council*.[265] In this case the claimant was suspended from work on full pay after he was charged with an alleged fraud against the council. Later he was prevented, as a condition of his bail, from having contact with certain of his colleagues. At that stage the council attempted to argue that the contract had been frustrated, and that Mr Boyo's employment was at an end. It was later accepted that the council's conduct amounted to a repudiation of Mr Boyo's contract, which had not been frustrated. Mr Boyo was acquitted of fraud and brought an action for his salary on the basis that his contract of employment was still in force. The trial judge held that once Mr Boyo agreed to go ahead with a contested hearing of this action, his employment was at an end, but that he was entitled to damages representing net salary for the period of his contractual notice plus five months, which was deemed a reasonable length of time

---

[262] This analysis was suggested by the Court of Appeal in *Kaur v MG Rover Ltd* [2005] IRLR 40, [27] (in that context, on the hypothesis that a 'no compulsory redundancy' provision in a collective agreement had been incorporated into an employee's contract of employment).

[263] [1980] ICR 755, 760.

[264] See also *Dietman v Brent London Borough Council* [1987] ICR 737, for a similar decision on the measure of damages to be awarded in such a case.

[265] [1995] IRLR 50.

for the carrying out of disciplinary proceedings against him. The Court of Appeal, regarding itself as bound by *Gunton*, upheld the order of the judge, in the process rejecting a claim for damages based on the assumption that the claimant would have stayed with the council for most of the rest of his working life – 'a claim of this magnitude offends against common sense and reason, when it is to be remembered that the whole engagement could be brought to a conclusion by one month's notice on either side'.[266]

5.42   Although the solution arrived at in *Gunton* and *Boyo* has a certain practical value – the employee is given something by way of damages to represent the loss of his or her procedural rights – it does not otherwise have much to commend it. It would have been more consistent, on the one hand, to have confined the employee to net salary for the notice period (the traditional rule), on the basis that the notice rule was effective in limiting the employee's right to continuing employment, or, on the other, to have awarded him more substantial damages for the loss of his employment, on the basis that the job security clause placed a substantive restriction on the employer's right to terminate the contract by giving notice.[267]

The first of these alternatives was, in essence, the conclusion reached by Hobhouse J in *Alexander v Standard Telephones and Cables (No 2)*:[268] where the contract contains a notice clause, he considered that:

> ... it is always open to an employer, as a matter of contract, to say to his employee that after the expiry of the contractual notice period the employer will only continue the contract of employment on different terms ... The employer's right to vary the contract is effectively equivalent to his right to terminate the contract.

The second alternative, the award of extended damages on the basis that contractual job security clauses can place substantive limits on the notice rule, has some authority to support it,[269] although the impression given by the decisions of the Court of Appeal and House of Lords in *R v Lord President of the Privy Council, ex p Page*[270] was that the courts are unwilling to construe contracts of employment in such a way as to achieve this end. Mr Page was employed as a university lecturer from October 1966, under terms in his letter of appointment which provided for his employment to be terminated 'by either party on giving three months' notice in writing expiring at the end of a term or of the long vacation'. No fixed term was set for the contract's duration, but

---

[266] [1995] IRLR 50, 59 (Sir Francis Purchas).

[267] A further possible solution is the idea of damages for loss of a chance (cf *Chaplin v Hicks* [1911] 2 KB 786) although this was rejected by the EAT in *Janciuk v Winerite Ltd* [1998] IRLR 63. For discussion see Ford, 1998a. On contractual job security clauses and the '*Johnson* exclusion zone' see the Supreme Court decision in the co-joined appeals *Edwards v Chesterfield Royal Hospital NHS Foundation Trust* and *Botham v Ministry of Defence* [2012] IRLR 129, discsussed at para 5.45 below.

[268] [1991] IRLR 286, 296.

[269] *Aspden v Webbs Poultry and Meat Group (Holdings) Ltd* [1996] IRLR 521 (employer's contractual power to give notice to terminate the contract should not be exercised to frustrate the employee's entitlement to benefit under the permanent health insurance scheme); *Adin v Sedco Forex International Resources Ltd* [1997] IRLR 280 (employee's contractual rights under a disability benefit scheme could not be defeated by the employer's decision to dismiss him under a notice provision in the contract). See Ford, 1998a. See also *Jenvey v Australian Broadcasting Corporation* [2002] IRLR 520; *Briscoe v Lubrizol Ltd* [2002] IRLR 607; *Kaur v MG Rover Ltd* [2005] IRLR 40, [27] (*obiter*); and *Takacs v Barclays Services Jersey Ltd* [2006] IRLR 877.

[270] [1993] ICR 114, HL, in the Court of Appeal *sub nom R v Hull University Visitor, ex p Page* [1992] ICR 67.

the contract incorporated a term from the University's statutes stating that the employee would retire not later than the September following his 67th birthday. The contract also incorporated from the University statutes a term whereby employees 'holding their appointments until the age of retirement may be removed by the Council for good cause', as well an extensive disciplinary procedure to be operated in a case where good cause was alleged. In 1988 Mr Page was given three months' notice of dismissal on the grounds of redundancy. He complained to the Visitor that the University was not entitled to dismiss him except for good cause. The Visitor (the Lord President) rejected his petition and proceedings for judicial review followed.

The Divisional Court found that the Visitor had made an error of law and quashed his decision. This ruling was overturned by the Court of Appeal on the merits, but in the House of Lords the Visitor succeeded in showing that his decision, even if it were based on an error of law, was outside the scope of judicial review.[271] Lords Slynn and Mustill dissented from this part of the ruling, and Lord Slynn (with whom Lord Mustill agreed) went on to find that, on the merits, no error of law had been committed. Lord Browne-Wilkinson, who gave the principal judgment of the majority, found it 'unnecessary to express any view on the proper construction of the charter and statutes beyond saying that I have heard nothing which persuades me that the views of [the Visitor] and the Court of Appeal were wrong'.[272]

The views on the merits of the majority were *obiter* since they were unnecessary for the decision in *Page*, which was that judicial review would not lie against the Visitor; nor is the minority view of Lords Slynn and Mustill strictly binding on lower courts. However, these statements are evidently an important indication of judicial thinking in this area. According to Lord Slynn, the provision in Mr Page's contract for compulsory retirement at the age of 67 did not mean that he was entitled to stay in post until he reached that age:

> ... whether members of staff can so continue depends on the other terms and conditions of the employment. Those terms in this case include provision for termination for good cause ... and on three months' notice as one of the terms of the appointment ... This result could have been spelled out more clearly in the statutes but it seems to me to follow from the provisions of the statutes as they stand and, contrary to the argument of Mr Page, no more curious than the alternative for which he contends.[273]

The judgments on the merits of the Court of Appeal were not *obiter*, and can be seen as direct authority for the view that the notice rule will prevail unless it is explicitly limited by the contract itself, notwithstanding the presence of a procedural clause dealing with the case of good-cause dismissal. However, their weight is somewhat weakened by their failure to mention *Gunton* or, apparently, to appreciate the significance of that case for the issue of construction addressed in *Page*. In *Kaur v MG Rover Ltd* the Court of Appeal expressed the view that *Page* did not establish a general principle of law to the effect that notice clauses are to prevail over other express terms concerned with termination; rather '[i]t will in all cases be a matter of construing the individual contract of employment'.[274]

---

[271] A fuller consideration of this question lies outside the scope of this book. See H Wade, 1993.
[272] [1993] ICR 114, 129.
[273] [1993] ICR 114, 137.
[274] [2004] EWCA Civ 1507, [2005] IRLR 40, [26] (*obiter*).

In *Page* the courts were faced with a situation which was also essentially the situation which arose in *Gunton* and *Boyo*, namely that of a contract of employment containing two clauses, one dealing with a power to dismiss with notice and the other with dismissal via a complex disciplinary procedure, whose legal effects were apparently irreconcilable. The outcome arrived at by the courts in *Page*, while apparently containing 'nothing improbable',[275] nevertheless suffers from the major weakness that it deprives the procedure clause of virtually all legal force.[276] At no point in the judgments in *Page* did the courts explain why the procedure clause, as opposed to the notice clause, should be the one to be denied legal force in this way. One possible construction which would have reconciled the two would have been to regard the procedure clause as limiting the employer's general power to dismiss, and the notice clause as applying in the event of good cause being established; in other words, the employee could only be dismissed for good cause, as defined by the statutes, *and* with the minimum notice required by Mr Page's conditions of appointment. But this construction was explicitly rejected by the Court of Appeal and by Lord Slynn. Despite more recent indications that the courts may be prepared to constrain an employer's reliance on a notice clause in specific circumstances,[277] the point has yet to be established by higher appellate authority in England.[278]

(iii) The role of the implied duty of mutual trust and confidence

5.43   Many of the same issues of conflicts between notice clauses and other terms of the contract of employment arise in the context of discussion of the effect upon termination of the implied duty of mutual trust and confidence. As we have seen, the centrality of the term to the modern analysis of the contract of employment was affirmed by the House of Lords in *Malik v BCCI SA*.[279] In *Johnson v Unisys Ltd*,[280] however, the House of Lords concluded that the implied term could not have the effect of restricting the employer's common law power to end the contract without the need to show good cause. The judgments in *Malik* confirmed that the implied duty operates as a default term, which can be ousted by a clear, express term to the contrary.[281] However, this was not the central issue on which the decision in *Johnson* turned. Lord Hoffmann, while noting that, in the light of the express term governing dismissal with notice (or by way of a payment of wages in lieu of notice), it was 'very difficult to imply a term that the company should not do so except for some good cause and after giving [Mr Johnson] a reasonable opportunity to demonstrate that

---

[275] [1992] ICR 67, 81 (Staughton LJ).

[276] *Quaere*, moreover, whether it could be argued that it would be an abuse of power under public law for the University to rely upon the notice clause in circumstances falling within the definition of 'good cause'. See also Ford, 1998a.

[277] See the cases referred to in note 269 above.

[278] *Adin v Sedko Forex International Resources Ltd* [1997] IRLR 280 was a decision of the Court of Session; in *Briscoe v Lubrizol Ltd* [2002] EWCA Civ 508, [2002] IRLR 607 it was not disputed that the employer could not terminate employment save for a cause other than ill health as a means of removing an employee's entitlement to benefit under a long-term disability scheme (see [21]). On contractual job security clauses and the '*Johnson* exclusion zone' see the Supreme Court decision in the co-joined appeals *Edwards v Chesterfield Royal Hospital NHS Foundation Trust* and *Botham v Ministry of Defence* [2012] IRLR 129, discsussed at para 5.45 below.

[279] [1997] IRLR 462.

[280] [2001] IRLR 279; see paras 5.27 and 5.35 above for other aspects of the case. See H Collins, 2001c; Brodie, 2001b; Freedland, 2003: pp 162–167, 303–305, 342–345; Barmes, 2004.

[281] See generally para 4.105 *et seq* above, and see also *Reda v Flag Ltd* [2002] IRLR 747, [45].

no such cause existed',[282] was nevertheless prepared to accept the existence within the contract of 'a separate term that the power of dismissal will be exercised fairly and in good faith'.[283] Such a term, he felt, would not have contradicted the express term that the employer had the power to dismiss without cause. Lord Millett, likewise, was prepared to countenance a common law term imposing upon the employer a 'general obligation … to treat his employee fairly even in the manner of his dismissal'.[284]

What, instead, proved decisive in turning the outcome in *Johnson* against the application of the implied term was concern that to develop the common law in this way would frustrate the intention of Parliament in enacting unfair dismissal legislation. As Lord Hoffmann put it, '[f]or the judiciary to construct a general common law remedy for unfair circumstances attending dismissal would be to go contrary to the evident intention of Parliament that there should be such a remedy but that it should be limited in application and extent'.[285] The statutory limits to which Lord Hoffmann referred here include the necessity for a minimum qualifying period of service prior to dismissal and the upper limit on compensation for unfair dismissal.[286] Lord Millett adverted to the possibility of overlapping systems of statutory and common law jurisdiction as a 'recipe for chaos'.[287] More specifically, it was suggested that Parliament adopted the unfair dismissal legislation on the assumption that the House of Lords decision in *Addis v Gramophone Co Ltd*,[288] apparently limiting a claim for damages for wrongful dismissal to net wages for the notice period, was correctly decided.[289]

5.44   The argument that Parliament had intended to exclude the development of the common law by creating a statutory remedy for unfair dismissal was a highly contentious one; the absence of any reference to the common law in the legislation may have occurred because Parliament was content to let the courts develop it in the usual way.[290] Indeed, it would be open to the courts to reason by analogy that a requirement for employers to follow a fair procedure is not regarded by Parliament as unduly onerous.[291] Moreover the majority's reasoning created the anomalous position that, although the courts had accepted that lesser powers, including the power to suspend

---

[282] [2001] IRLR 279, [42].

[283] [2001] IRLR 279, [46].

[284] [2001] IRLR 279, [79]. See also Lord Nicholls, [2001] IRLR 279, [2], and the judgment of McLachlin J in *Wallace v United Grain Growers Ltd* (1997) 152 DLR (4th) 1, discussed by Lord Hoffmann in *Johnson*. See Fudge, 2007.

[285] *Johnson*, above, [58].

[286] See generally paras 5.63 and 5.145 *et seq* below.

[287] *Johnson* [2001] IRLR 279, [80]; see also Lord Nicholls, at [2].

[288] See paras 5.26–5.27 above.

[289] Cf the dissenting opinion of Lord Steyn on this point, who argued that '[I]t cannot be said that the unfair dismissal legislation would be unworkable if the House departs from *Addis's* case' (*Johnson*, at [22]) and suggested that '[I]f Parliament is deemed to have been aware of the *Addis* decision, one must also deem Parliament to have been aware that the system it was creating was only capable of dealing effectively and justly with less serious cases where the threshold of a breach of contract was not necessarily established' (at [23]).

[290] H Collins, 2001c: p 306. See also Freedland, 2003: p 304: 'As an account of the intention of Parliament … that was more than slightly artificial. It was really an assertion of their Lordships' 'own underlying view' that the law concerning the termination of personal work or employment contracts now had two distinct context-specific aspects … and that developments in one sphere should not necessarily be replicated in the other sphere.'

[291] Cf J Beatson, 1997: p 310.

an employee,[292] must be exercised with due regard to trust and confidence, the 'more drastic power of dismissal was free from any equivalent constraint'.[293] In *Eastwood v Magnox Electric plc, McCabe v Cornwall County Council*,[294] however, the majority of the House of Lords reaffirmed the '*Johnson* exclusion area', whereby claims for loss resulting from dismissal fell within that area whereas a cause of action acquired prior to dismissal, which by definition existed independently of the dismissal, did not.[295] Their Lordships recognised that this 'boundary line' produced 'strange results', such as rendering it potentially cheaper for an employer to dismiss an employee than to suspend him or her.[296] They also acknowledged that the boundary line could be difficult to apply, particularly in cases concerning financial loss flowing from psychiatric illnesses. In some cases a continuing course of conduct, typically a disciplinary process followed by dismissal, 'may have to be chopped artificially into separate pieces',[297] and the division of remedial jurisdiction between courts and tribunals would lead to a duplication of proceedings. Moreover,

> In cases of constructive dismissal a distinction will have to be drawn between loss flowing from antecedent breaches of the trust and confidence term and loss flowing from the employee's acceptance of these breaches as a repudiation of the contract.[298] The loss flowing from the impugned conduct taking place before actual or constructive dismissal lies outside the *Johnson* exclusion area, the loss flowing from the dismissal itself is within that area. In some cases this legalistic distinction may give rise to difficult questions of causation in cases such as those now before the House, where financial loss is claimed as the consequence of psychiatric illness said to have been brought on by the employer's conduct before the employee was dismissed.[299] Judges and tribunals, faced perhaps with conflicting medical evidence, may have to decide whether the fact of dismissal was really the last straw which proved too much for the employee, or whether the onset of the illness occurred even before he was dismissed.[300]

The majority did not, however, conclude that 'an inter-relation between the common law and statute having these awkward and unfortunate consequences' should lead to *Johnson* being

---

[292] *Gogay v Hertfordshire County Council* [2000] IRLR 703. See also *King v University Court of the University of St Andrews* [2002] IRLR 252, discussed by Brodie, 2002; *Mezey v South West London and St George's Mental Health NHS Trust* [2007] IRLR 237, QBD and 244, CA.

[293] Hepple and Morris, 2002: p 254.

[294] [2004] IRLR 733. See Barratt, 2004; Brodie, 2004.

[295] [2004] IRLR 733, [27] (Lord Nicholls, with whom Lords Hoffmann, Rodger and Brown agreed).

[296] [2004] IRLR 733, [32].

[297] [2004] IRLR 733, [30] and [31]. See *Lakshmi v Mid Cheshire Hospitals NHS Trust* [2008] IRLR 956, [38]-[43].

[298] See para 5.69 *et seq* below. There was room for doubt as to whether *Johnson* applied to constructive dismissal: see Freedland, 2001. *Eastwood* assumes that it does. This means that an employee who affirms the contract and continues working may be in a better position than one who purports to accept the repudiation: see Barmes, 2004. Moreover, '[t]he more outrageous the breach the less likely it is that the employee can affirm the contract': *Eastwood*, above, at [40] (Lord Steyn). In *GAB Robins (UK) Ltd v Triggs* [2008] IRLR 317 the Court of Appeal held that the claimant's reduced earning capacity due to an illness caused by breaches by her former employer of the implied duty of trust and confidence which occurred prior to her election to treat this as constructive dismissal could not be regarded as a loss suffered 'in consequence of the dismissal' under ERA 1996, s 123 as the right to sue in respect of that loss had accrued before the dismissal.

[299] In *Eastwood* the claimants alleged that they had suffered psychiatric illnesses caused by a deliberate course of conduct by certain individuals using the machinery of the disciplinary process; in *McCabe* the claimant alleged that he had sustained psychiatric illness as a result of his suspension and the employer's failure properly to investigate allegations against him or to inform him of those allegations.

[300] *Eastwood*, at [31] (Lord Nicholls).

reconsidered;[301] rather, it attributed the difficulties to the statutory cap on the compensatory award for unfair dismissal, which precluded tribunals from awarding full compensation for a dismissed employee's financial loss, so leading employees to attempt to construct a claim at common law. This situation 'merit[ed] urgent attention by the government and the legislature'.[302]

The majority in *Eastwood* reiterated the argument in *Johnson* that Parliament had 'occupied the field' relating to unfair dismissal and that it would be wrong for the courts 'to expand a common law principle into the same field and produce an inconsistent outcome'.[303] As we noted at the beginning of this paragraph, however, this is not the only sustainable analysis of the position. Moreover this argument, would, if more generally applied, have already prevented the application of the implied term of mutual trust and confidence to many other aspects of the employment relationship.[304] It may be argued that just as employment legislation normally acts as a 'floor of rights' in relation to the contract of employment, implicitly encouraging the parties to improve on the basic standards supplied by statute, so the courts should be willing, in appropriate cases, to use the enactment of protective legislation as a basis for extending, rather than limiting, recognition of the legitimate common law interests of the employee.[305]

(iv) Contractual job security clauses and the Johnson exclusion zone: the decision in Edwards v Chesterfield Royal Hospital NHS Foundation Trust and Botham v Ministry of Defence

5.45 We referred in para 5.44 above to the difficulties and anomalies caused by the *Johnson* exclusion area in relation to the application of the implied term of trust and confidence in the context of dismissal. In the co-joined appeals in *Edwards v Chesterfield Royal Hospital NHS Foundation Trust* and *Botham v Ministry of Defence*[306] a seven-judge Supreme Court had the opportunity to consider whether the reasons used to justify the exclusion area in *Johnson* and *Eastwood* also applied to an employer's breach of an express disciplinary procedure.

Edwards concerned the dismissal of a consultant surgeon. He brought two separate damages claims for breach of contract: (i) a claim for wrongful dismissal, based on termination of his contract without notice; and (ii) a claim that his employer had failed to carry out the proper contractual disciplinary procedure, resulting in a finding of misconduct which damaged his

---

[301] [2004] IRLR 733, [33]. Cf Lord Steyn, who acknowledged that oral argument had not been heard from counsel on the correctness of *Johnson* but sought to provide 'some focus for a future re-examination of the position' (at [36]) in the light, *inter alia*, of critical academic commentary of the majority opinions.

[302] [2004] IRLR 733, [33].

[303] *Eastwood*, at [14] (Lord Nicholls).

[304] Thus there has been extensive statutory intervention in the areas of health and safety at work, grievance procedures, and the exercise of employer discretion in relation to occupational pension schemes, all of which have been the subject of judicial innovation in respect of the duty of mutual trust and confidence and which were accepted as legitimate in both *Malik* and *Johnson*. See generally para 4.105 *et seq* above.

[305] This is arguably what happened prior to *Johnson*; the enactment of unfair dismissal legislation in the early 1970s was a catalyst for the development of the implied term of trust and confidence, so making the protection offered by that legislation more effective. See Hepple, 1981: pp 134–135; Deakin, 1997; Brodie, 2001; and Lord Steyn in *Johnson* [2001] UKHL 13, [2001] IRLR 279, [18] and [21]. For a wider discussion see the third of Professor Sir Bob Hepple's 2004 Hamlyn Lectures (Hepple, 2005a).

[306] [2012] IRLR 129.

reputation, leading to loss of earnings in excess of £3.8 million.[307] The Trust applied for an order to strike out Mr Edwards' claim for damages in respect of any period exceeding his three months' contractual notice period. The District Judge acceded to the application; on appeal, Nicol J allowed the appeal but only to the extent of adding compensation for the additional period that it would have taken to conduct the disciplinary procedure if it were conducted and completed with reasonable expedition (the 'Gunton extension', discussed in paras 5.40-5.41 above). The Court of Appeal held that Mr Edwards' second claim did not fall within the Johnson exclusion area and that he was in principle entitled to recover whatever damages he could prove he had suffered as a result of the employer's failure to carry out the proper procedure. The Trust appealed to the Supreme Court. For the purpose of these proceedings it was accepted by the Trust that the court should proceed on the assumption that Mr Edwards would succeed in establishing the allegations made.

Botham concerned the dismissal of a youth community worker who had been employed by the Ministry of Defence ('MoD'). He was suspended from work and later charged with gross misconduct; following disciplinary proceedings he was summarily dismissed and because his dismissal was for gross misconduct in relation to young people, he was placed on a list of persons deemed unsuitable to work with children (the 'POCA register'). He claimed unfair dismissal and wrongful dismissal, both of which claims were upheld by an employment tribunal, which found that the MoD had breached express terms of the Discipline Code. The MoD's appeal against liability to the EAT was dismissed. Mr Botham then issued High Court proceedings seeking damages for breach of contract, including loss of future earnings, relying on findings by the tribunal that in conducting the disciplinary process the MoD had failed to comply with the Discipline Code. He argued that as a result of the various breaches he was dismissed; suffered a loss of reputation; was placed on the POCA register; and was precluded from further employment in his chosen field. His claim was dismissed in the High Court as falling within the Johnson exclusion area; in view of the Court of Appeal decision in Edwards his appeal was allowed by consent in the Court of Appeal and the MoD given permission to appeal to the Supreme Court. [308]

Both claims were dismissed by the Supreme Court; Edwards by a majority of 4/3; Botham by 6/1. However, even among judges who were agreed on the outcome, different lines of reasoning were employed.

As we discussed in para 5.35 above, Lord Dyson (with whom Lord Walker agreed) considered that Parliament had intended that compliance with contractual disciplinary procedures should be relevant only to whether a dismissal was unfair. It was 'necessarily to be inferred from ... [the] ... statutory background that, unless they otherwise expressly agree, the parties to an employment contract do not intend that a failure to comply with contractually binding disciplinary procedures will give rise to a common law claim for damages'.[309] The unfair dismissal legislation, with its 'carefully crafted' limitations, precluded a claim for damages for breach of contract in relation to the manner of dismissal regardless of whether it was formulated as a breach of an express or an implied term.[310] If an employer started a disciplinary process in breach of the express terms of the contract, the employee could seek an injunction to stop the process and/or seek an appropriate

---

[307] The second claim was not pleaded in the original particulars of claim but was advanced in the Court of Appeal and the pleading point was not taken there: Lord Dyson at [12].

[308] These summaries of Edwards and Botham are taken from the judgment of Lord Dyson at [3] -[18].

[309] At [39].

[310] At [40].

declaration; this would not 'cut across' the statutory scheme for unfair dismissal compensation and so 'jeopardise the coherence of our employment laws'.[311] Lord Dyson agreed with Lord Nicholls in *Eastwood* that drawing the boundary line in this way led to 'unsatisfactory and anomalous results', so that an employer may be better off dismissing than suspending an employee, but this was 'the inevitable consequence of the interrelation between the common law and statute. The unfair dismissal legislation occupies the unfair dismissal territory to the exclusion of the common law, but it does not impinge on any cause of action which is independent of a dismissal'.[312] In Lord Dyson's view, the claims by Edwards and Botham could not be divorced from their dismissal. Lord Mance agreed with Lord Dyson's reasoning and conclusions; 'in the absence of express contrary agreement, the *Johnson* exclusion area must be taken to cover both loss arising from dismissal and … loss arising from failures in the steps leading to such dismissal'.[313] Lord Phillips, too, agreed with Lord Dyson that each claim arose out of the manner of dismissal although he preferred to analyse the issue as one of remoteness of damage rather than the imputed intention of the contracting parties. Until *Addis v Gramophone Co Ltd*[314] - which Lord Phillips regarded as being a case on remoteness - was reversed, damages for reputational loss ('stigma damages') could not be awarded for wrongful dismissal nor, following *Johnson* and *Eastwood*, could they be awarded for failure to comply with a disciplinary code leading to dismissal, where the chain of causation was 'more tenuous'.[315] More generally, to permit a claim based on failure to comply with a disciplinary code would subvert the reasoning in *Johnson* and *Eastwood*. These four judges all agreed, therefore, that the claims of both Mr Edwards and Mr Botham should be dismissed.

Of the remainder, Lord Kerr (with whom Lord Wilson agreed) did not accept that there was evidence of any intention on the part of Parliament to subsume reputational damage into an unfair dismissal claim or otherwise to restrict an employee's contractual rights. In addition, to accept there would be a claim in damages for breach of a disciplinary procedure if there was no termination of employment but not if there were would be 'an impossibly anomalous situation', which would not be rectified by the availability of injunctive relief: ' an injunction is available on the basis that a legal wrong is anticipated … [i]f … [it] materialises, why should it not be actionable? [316] Lord Kerr noted in relation to Mr Edwards that the Trust had conceded that he could have applied for an injunction to stop the disciplinary tribunal from considering his case, which itself assumed that Mr Edwards already had a cause of action at that stage. On that basis, following *Eastwood*, Mr Edwards' cause of action should remain unimpaired by his subsequent dismissal. By contrast, in Mr Botham's case the reputational damage was directly linked to his dismissal rather than any defects in the procedure leading up to it and his claim should be dismissed.

Baroness Hale alone held that the losses in both *Edwards* and *Botham* should be recoverable according to ordinary contractual principles.[317] She did not consider that there was any reason to think that Parliament intended to reduce the remedies available to employees whose employers acted in breach of contract and thought that *Johnson* should be confined to dismissals in breach of

---

[311] At [44].
[312] At [52].
[313] At [94].
[314] [1909] AC 488; see further para 5.26 above.
[315] At [87].
[316] At [134] and [135]..
[317] As we indicated in para 5.27 above, Baroness Hale distinguished *Addis* on the basis that there was no contractually-agreed process in that case.

an implied term. Like Lord Kerr, she was 'puzzled' as to how there could be a right to an injunction but not damages.[318]

Technically *Edwards* leaves open the possibility of a claim for damages for breach of a contractual disciplinary procedure even if the parties have not expressly agreed to this. Lady Hale and Lords Kerr and Wilson explicitly supported this. Lord Phillips, who sided with Lords Dyson, Walker and Mance in deciding that Mr Edwards' claim should be struck out, did so on the basis that, on the authority of *Addis*, reputational loss was too remote. He thus left open the potential for claiming other losses for breach of a contractual procedure, although in practice reputational damage is likely to be the most substantial head of loss. Moreover, the view of Lords Kerr and Wilson in support of a damages claim depend upon the cause of action having arisen prior to the dismissal. Where financial loss is consequent upon dismissal itself, compensation for damage to reputation may be sought only as part of a claim for unfair dismissal. This, effectively, applies the *Johnson* exclusion area in a different place, although it is not clear why the separate contractual right to damages arising from breach of the disciplinary procedure should be extinguished at this stage.

The judgments in *Edwards* leave open two further areas of uncertainty. The first is the status of *Gunton*. As we indicate above, Nicol J had awarded Mr Edwards damages based on the '*Gunton* extension' and the Trust did not appeal against this. Nevertheless it was relevant to the argument as to whether any damages for breach of a disciplinary process leading to dismissal could be claimed. Lords Dyson and Phillips distinguished *Gunton* as not undermining *Johnson* but, like Lord Mance, left open whether it had been correctly decided.[319] On one view, if Parliament is indeed to be treated as having 'occupied the field' in relation to the manner of dismissal, it is hard to see why any damages for failure to carry out a disciplinary procedure correctly should be awarded. If, however, the time needed to carry out the procedure is effectively regarded as part of the employee's notice period it may survive. The second area of uncertainty relates to clauses which state that dismissal can only be for specified reasons: 'good cause' dismissals. Lord Mance distinguished 'good cause' clauses from procedural clauses,[320] and Baroness Hale's dissenting judgment supports damages being available in the event that they are breached. The remaining judgments are silent on the issue. Damages for breach of such clauses may still be claimable but this cannot be regarded as clear-cut. [321]

(iv) Contractual job security: the way ahead?

5.46   Many of the fears expressed at the possible extension of the wrongful dismissal action to include financial losses going above and beyond net wages for the notice period are arguably misplaced. There seems no reason in principle why substantial, extended damages for lost earnings capacity should not be awarded in a case where a job security clause can be shown to be effective in limiting the notice rule. This has been done not simply in a number of US and Australian

---

[318] At [122].

[319] See [48], [61], [87] and [107]-[108].

[320] At [96].

[321] Baroness Hale stated in *Edwards* at [122] that she was uncertain how the majority would regard the case of an employee with the contractual right only to be dismissed for cause.

cases,[322] but also, in a slightly different British context, in cases involving dismissals in breach of equality law.[323] The result need not and should not involve the employee receiving salary for the rest of his or her working life. As explained above, a debt claim is ruled out here; the claim can only be in damages, and while these can extend to a period going beyond both the notice period and the period envisaged for any procedure, the relevant period would not be that from dismissal to retirement: the relevant period would be the expected time out of employment, which would have to be calculated in such a way as to take into account the possibility of the employee finding alternative work. The court would also reduce the period in respect of which damages were payable by the chance that the employee's working life would be shortened by injury or illness, as is routinely done in cases involving compensation for work-related injuries.[324] If it still remains to be seen precisely how the general principles of the law of damages could be adapted to the extended action for wrongful dismissal, there seems to be less doubt that they *could* be effectively applied in some way or other, if the law in this area were to continue to evolve in the direction of stronger employment protection.

As we have just seen, the main obstacle to the further development of the common law in this area is the concern that the unfair dismissal jurisdiction would thereby be undermined. However, as Lord Steyn opined in *Eastwood*, if the statutory cap on unfair dismissal awards 'is allowed to constrain the development of the common law it may come at too high a price in the failure of corrective justice'.[325] The coherence of employment law in this area is also greatly diminished by the failure in *Johnson*, as confirmed in *Eastwood*, to apply the implied term of mutual trust and confidence to issues of termination, when its application to most other aspects of the employment relationship (including the disciplinary process prior to, and short of, dismissal)[326] has been generally accepted.[327]

Specific remedies in public law

5.47 The most effective remedy for an employee who seeks to resist dismissal is an order of the court which prevents the dismissal taking effect. Public employees may be able to bring proceedings for judicial review against their employer, challenging the decision on the grounds of illegality, '*Wednesbury* unreasonableness' or procedural impropriety.[328] If successful this can lead to the decision being quashed.[329] In the case of dismissal it is thus akin to the statutory

---

[322] See para 5.12 above; Pitt, 1989; Ewing, 1989, 1993, discussing *Gregory v Philip Morris Ltd* (1988) 80 ALR 455; although cf *Byrne and Frew v Australian Airlines Ltd* (1995) 131 ALR 422 (High Court of Australia), discussed by John McMullen, 1996.

[323] See para 6.66 below.

[324] See Deakin *et al*, 2008: pp 990–992.

[325] *Eastwood v Magnox Electric plc, McCabe v Cornwall County Council* [2004] IRLR 733, [51].

[326] This was expressly recognised in *Eastwood*: see above, [15] and [32] (Lord Nicholls).

[327] See paras 4.4 *et seq* and 4.105 *et seq* above.

[328] This is the classification adopted by Lord Diplock in *Council of Civil Service Unions v Minister for the Civil Service* [1985] AC 374. It continues to survive, although *Wednesbury* unreasonableness has become a concept of 'variable intensity' depending on the context: see Le Sueur, 2005; *Doherty v Birmingham City Council* [2008] 3 WLR 636.

[329] This is done by way of the public law remedy of a quashing order (formerly known as *certiorari*). An order to require the employer to perform a duty may also be sought by means of the remedy of a mandatory order (formerly known as *mandamus*). For a detailed account of the remedies available in public law see H Wade and C Forsyth, 2009: Part VII; C Lewis, 2008; Woolf *et al*, 2009, Part III.

remedy of reinstatement following unfair dismissal, with the difference that the dismissal is deemed never to have taken place. Thus the individual 'remains in office, entitled to the remuneration attaching to such office, so long as he remains ready, willing and able to render the service required of him, until his tenure of office is lawfully brought to an end by resignation or lawful dismissal'.[330] Moreover, judicial review does not depend upon the applicant having met the general requirements of a minimum period of continuous employment or, indeed, being an 'employee'. Judicial review may also afford a remedy in cases of disciplinary action short of dismissal which in private law could, until recently, only be remedied by an action for damages for breach of contract, for which quantifiable loss would have to be shown.[331] This is now subject to the possibility, analysed below,[332] that a court may grant an injunction or declaration in equity to prevent dismissal or disciplinary action by the employer in breach of contract; but this private law remedy is by no means generally available and, as we have seen, it suffers from the difficulty that the legal status of contractual job security clauses is not altogether clear. Alternatively, an employee who is subject to disciplinary action which breaches the contract may seek to show that this amounts to constructive dismissal, and then bring a statutory claim for unfair dismissal; but, once again, this requires the necessary conditions to be met. As we saw in para 5.45 above, the Supreme Court decision in the co-joined appeals in *Edwards v Chesterfield Royal Hospital NHS Foundation Trust* and *Botham v Ministry of Defence*[333] restricts what may be claimed in damages for dismissal in breach of contractual procedures. Judicial review has other potential advantages over private law routes to employee protection. In particular, judicial review may be used to overturn a decision relating to a group of employees; although an action in private law may, in practice, be treated as a 'test case', in strict terms it only binds the parties to the particular action.[334]

(i) When is judicial review available?

5.48   For all the reasons indicated above judicial review has proved a popular route for public employees who have been subject to dismissal or to other disciplinary action short of dismissal.[335] However, it is not available as of right to public employees, merely because their employer is a

---

[330] *McLaughlin v The Governor of the Cayman Islands* [2007] UKPC 50, [14] (Lord Bingham). This statement applies where the order renders the dismissal null, void and without legal effect; as the Privy Council noted, the discretionary nature of public law remedies means that a claimant may not always obtain the full relief sought: [16].The Privy Council distinguished the case from one of wrongful dismissal, 'where a dismissal may be unlawful but nonetheless effective': [17].

[331] However, see the limitation in *R (on the application of Tucker) v Director General of the National Crime Squad* [2003] IRLR 439, discussed in para 5.50 below.

[332] See para 5.54 *et seq*.

[333] [2012] IRLR 129.

[334] See, for example, *R v Liverpool City Council, ex p Ferguson* (1985) Times, 20 November (noted by G Morris, 1986), where the court found that dismissal notices issued by the council to its employees terminating their employment from a specified date on the ground that the Council would thereafter be unable to pay their wages, and offering them re-employment one month later, were *ultra vires* and void because the decision to dismiss arose out of the setting of an illegal rate, and a consequent failure by the Council to balance its budget. Here, a remedy was granted even though there was no breach of contract on the part of the employer.

[335] See para 5.69 *et seq* below, on constructive dismissal.

public body; rather, it requires showing that the claim falls on the 'public side' of the procedural divide erected between public and private law.[336]

In deciding whether judicial review should be available in the employment context, the courts have formulated a series of (sometimes conflicting) tests. In broad terms these relate to the existence of a contract between the parties; the subject-matter of the claim; and the availability of alternative remedies. We consider here the application of each of these criteria as they relate specifically to dismissal and other disciplinary action.[337]

5.49   The use of contract as a line of demarcation stems from the decision of the Court of Appeal in *R v East Berkshire Area Health Authority, ex p Walsh*.[338] Mr Walsh, a senior nursing officer in the National Health Service, was dismissed for misconduct. He sought to have the decision quashed by way of proceedings for judicial review, on the grounds that the decision had been taken in breach of natural justice and contrary to the disciplinary procedure which formed part of his conditions of service under the relevant Whitley Council collective agreement. The Court of Appeal, overruling Hodgson J, held that an application for judicial review was inappropriate, since the issue raised by the applicant was one of 'private law' only. Sir John Donaldson MR affirmed that 'employment by a public authority does not *per se* inject any element of public law. Nor does the fact that the employee is in a "higher grade" or is an "officer"'.[339] The applicant's employment was founded on a contract of employment, and was no less contractual simply because the terms of the Whitley Council collective agreement were incorporated into it by a statutory instrument.[340] Similarly, Purchas LJ held that:

> … the rules of natural justice may well be imported into a private contractual relationship …
> but in such circumstances they would go solely to the question of rights and duties involved
> in the performance of the contract of employment itself. The manner in which the authority
> terminated, or purported to terminate, the applicant's contract of employment related to
> their conduct as employers in a pure master and servant context and not the performance
> of their duties, or exercise of their powers as an authority providing a health service for the
> public at large.[341]

On the basis of *Walsh* the only circumstances in which an individual could invoke judicial review to challenge a decision of his or her employer would be where the employment relationship is not expressed in contractual terms (as in the case of the police) or where, despite the existence of a contract, the matter in dispute does not concern the exercise of contractual rights. On the latter point it was accepted in *Walsh* that had the relevant terms of the Whitley Council collective agreement not been incorporated into the applicant's contract of employment as required by

---

[336] See para 2.5 above.

[337] For a general critique of these tests, see Fredman and Morris, 1991a, 1994; see also T Poole, 2000 and SH Bailey, 2007.

[338] [1984] ICR 743.

[339] [1984] ICR 743, 751. Cf *R (on the application of Shoesmith) v OFSTED* [2011] IRLR 679, discussed below, where the Court of Appeal referred to protections that have 'long been accorded to responsible and accountable office-holders' (Maurice Kay LJ at [65])

[340] SI 1974/296; see [1984] ICR 743, 752.

[341] [1984] ICR 743, 768.

statute, that would have provided a basis for judicial review to order the employer to comply with its duty to include it.[342] As an illustration of the former category of cases, in *R v Secretary of State for the Home Department, ex p Benwell*[343] Hodgson J was able to allow an application for judicial review to proceed in a case concerning disciplinary action against a prison officer, notwithstanding *Walsh*. The critical factors here were the absence of a contractual nexus between the parties[344] and the fact that the power of the employer to take disciplinary action had a specific statutory source. Also material was the fact that, at this stage, prison officers were excluded from the scope of unfair dismissal legislation (they are now included).[345]

5.50   In *Benwell* the court was clearly influenced by the fact that to have denied the applicant access to judicial review would have left him without any legal means of redress.[346] The converse view has also been applied; the courts have consistently regarded the possibility of a remedy in private law as a justification for denying judicial review. Thus in *Walsh*[347] May LJ thought that in 'the great majority of cases involving disputes about the dismissal of an employee by his employer, the most appropriate forum for their resolution is an [employment] tribunal', and in *R v Civil Service Appeal Board, ex p Bruce*[348] the Court of Appeal rejected a civil servant's application for judicial review of the board's decision largely on these grounds. Since then, civil servants have lost further ground as a result of the Divisional Court's decision in *R v Civil Service Appeal Board, ex p Nangle*,[349] to the effect that their relationship with the Crown is based on contract and not on a distinctive public law status.[350] Since *Benwell* the status of prison officers has been altered by legislation in such a way as to bring them within the scope of ERA 1996.[351] This could mean that the courts will henceforth exercise their discretion to exclude them from judicial review in relation to dismissal on the ground that an alternative remedy exists. However, in their case it is possible that statutory underpinning in the form of the Code of Discipline governing the service[352] may, for reasons we consider below, persuade the courts to continue to allow judicial review to lie.

The idea that by comparison with judicial review an unfair dismissal claim is adequate protection for the employee is, to say the least, debatable, since the statutory jurisdiction contains no mechanism for nullifying an abuse of power by the employer, as opposed to granting the

---

[342] [1984] ICR 743, 752 (Sir John Donaldson MR).

[343] [1985] IRLR 6; cf *McClaren v Home Office* [1990] IRLR 338, in which a prison officer's action which had been begun by writ was allowed by the Court of Appeal to proceed. See Fredman and Morris, 1991b: p 307.

[344] This decision preceded *R v Lord Chancellor's Department, ex p Nangle* [1991] IRLR 343.

[345] See para 3.44 above.

[346] Although Dillon LJ in *R v Derbyshire County Council, ex p Noble* [1990] IRLR 332, 337 refused to regard the non-availability of an alternative remedy as a reason for granting judicial review; see also Stuart-Smith LJ in *Nangle* [1991] IRLR 343, 348.

[347] [1984] ICR 743, 757.

[348] [1989] ICR 171. For an example of circumstances where judicial review was permitted despite the availability of an alternative, internal remedy, see *R v Chief Constable of the Merseyside Police, ex p Calveley* [1986] 1 All ER 257.

[349] [1991] IRLR 343; see para 3.40 above.

[350] Fredman and Morris, 1991b. Note that some aspects of civil servants' employment remain susceptible to review, however: see, for example, *Council of Civil Service Unions v Minister for the Civil Service* [1985] AC 374; *R v Civil Service Appeal Board, ex p Cunningham* [1991] IRLR 297 (although note also *R v Secretary of State for the Home Department, ex p Moore* [1994] COD 67).

[351] See para 3.44 above.

[352] The Code is made under the Prison Rules (SI 1999/728), which are made under the Prison Act 1952, s 47.

employee redress after the event, and re-instatement is rarely granted.[353] Nor, in relation to the protection of contractual rights, is an equivalent remedy commonly granted. From a wider perspective, to deny judicial review on the grounds of the availability of an alternative remedy for the individual is to ignore the fact that the remedy of judicial review is concerned with the exercise of public power, scrutiny of which should not be obstructed by a co-existent remedy concerned only with private rights. The two jurisdictions could more usefully be seen as complementary and not as alternatives. This approach was adopted by the Court of Appeal in the recent case of *R (on the application of Shoesmith) v OFSTED* where the court referred to judicial review being available where the case 'raises significant issues falling outwith the inquiry which could take place in the employment tribunal', as well being one where the inadequacy of the financial compensation made the alternative remedy in the employment tribunal 'inappropriate or less appropriate'.[354] It remains to be seen whether this marks the beginning of a more expansive approach to jurisdiction. On the basis of the previous case law, only members of a public sector group which has no possibility of an action in private law for individual claims arising out of disciplinary action, most notably the police,[355] could feel moderately confident of a potential remedy in judicial review. Even then, however, a claimant may now have to surmount an additional obstacle that asks not only whether the function performed by the public body is public or private in nature but further whether 'the defendant was performing a public duty owed to the claimant in the particular circumstances under consideration'.[356] On this basis the Court of Appeal concluded that the decision to send a detective inspector of police seconded to the National Crime Squad back to his local force because of perceived deficiencies in his skills and conduct was a 'decision tailor-made' to him and of an 'operational nature' and for these reasons did not involve the performance of a public duty,[357] even though it is likely to have had repercussions for his reputation and career prospects.[358]

5.51 The *Walsh* principle had the potential to exclude large areas of public employment from the purview of judicial review, regardless of the context, scope, and nature of the employer's conduct. In the event the courts shied away from a consistently rigorous application of *Walsh* by indicating that the availability of judicial review may also be influenced by the subject-matter of the claim. The emphasis on subject-matter was developed by Lord Woolf in a series of judgments

[353] See para 5.142 below. See also *R (on the application of Dunbar) v Hampshire Fire and Rescue Service* [2003] EHWC 431 (Admin), [2004] ACD 148.

[354] [2011] IRLR 679, Maurice Kay LJ at [87]. See Buxton, 2011, for a critique of this decision.

[355] The capacity to seek judicial review seems to be well established for officers of all ranks, including probationary officers. See *Chief Constable of the North Wales Police v Evans* [1982] 1 WLR 1155; and on the nature of the employment relationship in the context of the police, see para 3.43 above.

[356] *R (on the application of Tucker) v Director General of the National Crime Squad* [2003] IRLR 439, [24] (Scott Baker LJ).

[357] [2003] IRLR 439, [25]. The line between the operation of formal disciplinary proceedings, which the court acknowledged remained amenable to review, and 'operational and management decisions, where the police are entitled to run their own affairs without the interference of the courts' [35] may not be as clear cut as this judgment suggests. Cf *R (on the application of Hodgson) v South Wales Police Authority* [2008] EWHC 1183 (Admin), where the decision to require the applicant, who had been retained in the force under the '30-plus' scheme, to retire on the grounds that his retention would not be in the general interests of efficiency, was susceptible to judicial review.

358 See also *R (On the Application of Morgan) v Chief Constable of South Wales* [2001] EWHC Admin 262, [19], where Scott Baker LJ opined that the courts should only in the most exceptional circumstances, if ever, interfere with a decision to remove the claimant from a pool awaiting promotion due to an operational incident that resulted in admonishment.

and extra-judicial writings.[359] Lord Woolf took as his starting point the proposition that the employment relationship is an essentially private one, enforceable by ordinary action and not appropriate for judicial review.[360] This demarcation is based upon the fact that it is the 'public as a whole ... who are the beneficiaries of what is protected by public law and it is the individuals or the bodies entitled to the rights who are the beneficiaries of the protection provided by private law'.[361] However, he also accepted that there may be situations in which judicial review may be appropriate. The first is where the employee 'contends that he is adversely affected by a decision of general application by his employer' which is argued to be flawed on the grounds of *Wednesbury* unreasonableness.[362] In *R v Derbyshire County Council, ex p Noble*[363] this question was reduced to a numerical measure – if the decision affected only one individual it was a private law issue, whereas if it affected many it could become one of public law. Lord Woolf viewed the availability of a remedy in the case of the ban on membership of national civil service trade unions at GCHQ as an example of this exception.[364] This was a welcome recognition of the public dimension to employers' decisions in this context; however, it is difficult to see why a decision affecting a single individual, rather than a group, is, from this point of view, any less worthy of supervision by the courts.

Another situation in which judicial review may lie on the basis of the subject-matter of a dispute concerns the exercise of a statutory discretion in such a way as to interfere with an individual's exercise of his or her trade or livelihood. In *R v Broxtowe Borough Council, ex p Bradford*,[365] the Court of Appeal granted judicial review of the Council's decision to exclude the applicant from coaching young children on its tennis courts on the grounds that allegations of child abuse had been made against him in respect of previous employments, without giving him the right to respond to these allegations. According to Lord Woolf, the council 'have a responsibility not to use their position as a local authority to interfere with an individual's right to earn his living without proper cause and without extending to the individual concerned the basic requirements of fairness'.[366] This was not a case in which the council was the applicant's employer; rather, he was applying for employment with the council, and the effect of its decision would also be to restrict his existing employment with a tennis club which used the council's courts. Thus it is not clear how far this decision can be read as providing protection to employees. However, it is arguable that the principle enunciated by Lord Woolf in this case could equally well apply to decisions taken by statutory authorities with regard to their employees, as it did to the applicant in this case. The Supreme Court has recently held that where the outcome of disciplinary proceedings against a worker by a 'public authority' 'will have a substantial influence or effect' on the individual's right to practise his or her profession he or she may (not necessarily will) by force of Article 6 of the

---

[359] Lord Woolf more recently acknowledged that his attempts to find 'indicators that would penetrate the gloom' in clarifying a distinction between public and private in the realm of public employment were not wholly successful: Woolf, 1995: p 64.

[360] Woolf, 1986: p 223; and see also Woolf J in *R v BBC, ex p Lavelle* [1983] ICR 99.

[361] Woolf, 1986: p 222.

[362] *McClaren v Home Office* [1990] IRLR 338, 342. See *R v Sunderland City Council, ex p Baumber* [1996] COD 211.

[363] [1990] IRLR 332.

[364] *Council of Civil Service Unions v Minister for the Civil Service* [1985] AC 374.

[365] [2000] IRLR 329. See also *R (on the application of Montgomery) v Hertfordshire County Council* [2006] IRLR 787.

[366] [2000] IRLR 329, 330.

ECHR enjoy appropriate procedural rights.[367] Thus, where the consequences of the employer's decision are that another body will consider barring the individual from practising his or her profession, there must be a sufficient nexus between the two sets of proceedings.

The second major situation where Lord Woolf took the view that judicial review may be appropriate is 'where there exists some disciplinary or other body established under the prerogative or by statute [which has] a sufficient public law element, which it almost invariably will have if the employer is the Crown, and it is not domestic or wholly informal'.[368] The public law element arises from a statutory or similar underpinning which must relate to the procedure for dismissal.[369] This is one of the bases on which *Benwell* was decided, and it may mean that the courts continue to grant judicial review to prison officers despite their now having access to unfair dismissal protection. It has also been invoked to explain pre-*O'Reilly v Mackman*[370] decisions such as those in *Ridge v Baldwin*[371] and *Malloch v Aberdeen Corpn*,[372] to which we refer below. But even in this category of case, it may be that other factors weigh against judicial review in a purely individual case, as the decisions of the Court of Appeal in *Bruce* and *Nangle* demonstrate. In *R (on the application of Shoesmith) v OFSTED* the Court of Appeal held that in a case where the position was 'created, required and defined by and under statute' there was no requirement for the dismissal itself to be circumscribed by statutory provision in order for judicial review to lie.[373] It remains to be seen whether this is a decision which is confined to the relatively unusual category of post (that of Director of Children's Services) at issue in this case.

5.52   The circumstances in which the courts will grant employees access to judicial review remain unpredictable,[374] and the courts generally have shown a willingness to construct new obstacles to such access.[375] Whether the procedural divide between public law and private law should be maintained is a larger issue upon which opinions sharply differ.[376] In the area of public employment one of the most undesirable consequences of its existence in the past was the opportunistic litigation which it encouraged; employees and their advisers were unable to predict with confidence whether a particular dispute should be litigated under the 'public' procedure or

[367] *R (on the application of G) v Governors of X School and Y City Council* [2011] IRLR 756, Lord Dyson at [69], approving the test by Laws LJ at [2010] IRLR 222, [37]. Unlike the Court of Appeal, the Supreme Court did not consider that there was a sufficient connection between the two sets of proceedings on the facts. See also *R (Wright) v Secretary of State for Health* [2009] 1 AC 739, ; *Kulkarni v Milton Keynes Hospital NHS Trust* [2009] IRLR 829; *R (on the application of Puri) v Bradford Teaching Hospital NHS Trust* [2011] IRLR 582; *Mattu v The University Hosptials of Coventry and Warwickshire NHS Trust* [2012] EWCA Civ 641.
[368] [1990] IRLR 338, 342.
[369] *R v Derbyshire County Council, ex p Noble* [1990] IRLR 332.
[370] [1983] 2 AC 237; see para 2.5 above, n 35.
[371] [1964] AC 40.
[372] [1971] 1 WLR 1578.
[373] [2011] IRLR 679, Maurice Kay LJ at [91].
[374] In *R v CPS, ex p Hogg* [1994] 6 Admin LR 778 the Court of Appeal suggested that if a case arose where the independence of a Crown Prosecutor was at stake, the necessary public law element for judicial review might be present. It is also possible to argue that an infringement of an individual's 'Convention right' under HRA 1998 may afford the requisite 'public element': see G Morris, 1998c: pp 299–303.
[375] *R (on the application of Tucker) v Director General of the National Crime Squad* [2003] IRLR 439, discussed in para 5.50 above. *R (on the application of Shoesmith) v OFSTED* [2011] IRLR 679 is an exception to this general trend.
[376] In 1994 the Law Commission recommended maintaining it, although with greater flexibility for cases to transfer between the public law route and the claim form procedure: *Administrative Law: Judicial Review and Statutory Appeals*, Law Com No 226, HC 669, 1994, Part III.

by way of an action begun in private law, while employers did not lose the chance to argue that judicial review was inappropriate and that, whichever forum was chosen, it was the wrong one. Thus in *Benwell* the Home Department attempted to argue that judicial review was inappropriate and that the application should have been begun by writ, only to argue the opposite in *McClaren v Home Office* even though that case also concerned the employment of a prison officer. The Civil Procedure Rules now encourage greater procedural flexibility and afford the possibility of the court ordering the consolidation of claims for judicial review and ordinary civil claims or the transfer of a judicial review claim as if it had not been commenced under CPR Part 54.[377] However, the courts are still required to decide if a matter is properly amenable to judicial review, a particularly important issue where the remedy sought has no equivalent in private law. The dividing line formulated in *Walsh* is based on the assumption that the private can easily be disentangled from the public. As the discussion above makes clear, this is not the case.

(ii) Public law standards in private law claims

5.53   A further method of dealing with the dual dimension, which also has much wider implications, is to introduce public law standards into the employment relationship as implied terms in the contract of employment. In *Ridge v Baldwin*,[378] an action begun by writ, the House of Lords indicated that there could be an implied right to a hearing in special cases, such as those of 'office holders', although not in relation to the 'pure master and servant relationship' or in the case of those employed 'at the pleasure' of their employer and hence subject to an open-ended power of dismissal by the giving of notice. A classic office-holder was an individual, such as the Chief Constable in *Ridge*, who not only held a high-status position but who also had the express protection of certain procedural guarantees in the event of being subjected to suspension or exclusion from the office in question.

In *Malloch v Aberdeen Corpn*[379] this notion was extended to cover a school-teacher who, under the relevant Scottish legislation, was stated to 'hold office' under statutorily-constituted local school boards and to be dismissible only after 'due deliberation', in particular after three weeks' notice had been given of any motion for dismissal. The intervention of the court rested, here, partly upon the public nature of the employment and partly upon the existence of statutory rules underpinning both the employment in general and the power to dismiss in particular. According to Lord Reid:

> An elected public body [such as the school board] is in a very different position from a private employer. Many of its servants in the lower grades are in the same position as servants of a private employer. But many in the higher grades or 'offices' are given special statutory status or protection. The right of a man to be heard in his own defence is the most elementary protection of all and, where a statutory form of protection would be less effective if it did not carry with it a right to be heard, I would not find it difficult to imply this right.[380]

---

[377] Woolf *et al* 2007: paras 3-103–3-104.

[378] [1964] AC 40, 65. See also *R (on the application of Shoesmith) v OFSTED* [2011] IRLR 679, Maurice Kay LJ at [91] where the Court of Appeal drew an analogy between the role of Director of Children's Services and that of the Chief Constable in *Ridge v Baldwin*.

[379] [1971] 1 WLR 1578.

[380] [1971] 1 WLR 1578, 1586.

Similarly, Lord Wilberforce defined the scope of the principle in these terms:

> One may accept that if there are relationships in which all requirements of the observance of rules of natural justice are excluded (and I do not wish to assume that this is inevitably so), these must be confined to what have been called 'pure master and servant cases', which I take to mean cases in which there is no element of public employment or service, no support by statute, nothing in the nature of an office or a status which is capable of protection. If any of these elements exist then, in my opinion, whatever the terminology used, and even though in some inter partes aspects the relationship may be called that of master and servant, there may be essential procedural requirements to be observed, and failure to observe them may result in dismissal being declared to be void.[381]

The principle was extended still further in *Stevenson v United Road Transport Union*,[382] a decision concerning a trade union official who, as an employee of the union, was neither in public employment nor in an office underpinned by statutory rules. The Court of Appeal nevertheless granted the employee a declaration to the effect that a decision to dismiss him made by the union's executive committee was void on the grounds of *ultra vires* and Buckley LJ formulated the following broad test:

> Where one party has a discretionary power to terminate the tenure or enjoyment by another of an employment ..., is that power conditional upon the party invested with the power being first satisfied upon a particular point which involves investigating some matter upon which the other party ought in fairness to be heard or to be allowed to give his explanation or put his case? If the answer to the question is 'Yes', then unless, before the power purports to have been exercised, the condition has been satisfied after the other party has been given a fair opportunity of being heard or of giving his explanation or putting his case, the power will not have been well exercised.[383]

If the notion of office-holder is defined so widely as to cover any employee who has a legal right to protection against arbitrary dismissal, then it could be argued that it should extend at least to all employees with the benefit of a contractual disciplinary procedure, and possibly even further to all those qualifying for statutory unfair dismissal protection.[384] Indeed, it has been suggested that the time has come to consider the implication of public law doctrines of procedural fairness, at the very least, into all contracts of employment.[385] At present, however, the law is some way off recognising the existence of such a generally-applicable implied term, and, indeed, the House of Lords decision in *Johnson v Unisys Ltd*[386] constitutes a formidable obstacle to a development of this nature in the context of dismissal.

---

[381] [1971] 1 WLR 1578, 1595–1596.

[382] [1971] 1 WLR 1578, 1595–1596.

[383] [1977] ICR 893, 902.

[384] This extension of the notion of office-holder was considered by Woolf J in *R v BBC, ex p Lavelle* [1983] ICR 99, although he refused to allow an application for judicial review in that case on the grounds that only contractual rights were at stake: see Ewing and Grubb, 1987: pp 146, 156–157.

[385] *R v Derbyshire County Council, ex p Noble* [1990] IRLR 332, 337; Sedley, 1994; Laws, 1997.

[386] [2001] IRLR 279; see further paras 5.43 and 5.44 above.

Specific remedies and contractual rights

5.54   The failure of public law to develop a fully-fledged system of employment protection has proved to be less significant than it might have seemed, thanks to 'breathtaking developments' in the remedies available under the common law of contract: 'in appropriate cases injunctive relief may be available to restrain not only an attempt by an employer unilaterally to vary the contract, but also dismissal of an employee in breach of its terms'.[387] The basis for the court's intervention here is its equitable jurisdiction to grant injunctions or declarations in support of the parties' private rights, in this case their rights under the contract of employment. Only a short time ago, it seemed unlikely that specific relief would be available in these situations, thanks to the rule against specific performance of contracts of employment. This long-standing rule is based on a number of considerations: the assumed adequacy of damages in most cases; the difficulty facing the court in supervising the performance of either party;[388] the potential oppression of either party, but in particular the employee, in being required to maintain a contract involving the supply of personal services;[389] and the need for the parties to maintain 'mutual trust and confidence' in one another for the order to have any purpose.[390] Nonetheless, the courts have always accepted some exceptions to the rule: in *CH Giles & Co Ltd v Morris*[391] Sir Robert Megarry VC did 'not think that it should be assumed that as soon as any element of personal service or continuous services can be discerned in a contract the court will, without more, refuse specific performance'. Legislation prohibits orders for specific performance against employees on one of the grounds also recognised by the common law, namely the need to protect the individual against direct legal compulsion to work.[392] Reciprocity between employer and employee would seem to demand that the employer should be equally free from specific enforcement, but the matter is not so straightforward. Employers are able to obtain negative injunctions against employees preventing them from working for competitors in breach of contract, as long as the circumstances do not constitute the equivalent of requiring the employee to work for the employer against their will. An injunction will normally be issued in a case where the employee is not faced with a direct choice of 'work or starve', which is tantamount to making him or her perform the contract.[393] By extension, it should be and is possible for negative injunctions to be issued in certain circumstances against the employer, to prevent a disciplinary action or the dismissal of the employee being carried out in breach of contract. Again, the courts must respect the principle that no injunction should be granted in an employment case if its effects are equivalent to specific performance. But recent decisions have shown the traditional objections to specific orders to have lost much of their force.

The principal situation to be considered is that in which an employer purports to dismiss the employee without granting him or her the benefit of a contractual procedure, or without having established a good substantive reason when required to do so by the contract. The employee may

---

[387] Ewing, 1993b: p 406. See also John Hendy and Jeremy McMullen, 1987; John McMullen, 1995.

[388] *Ryan v Mutual Tontine Westminster Chambers Association* [1893] 1 Ch 116.

[389] *De Francesco v Barnum* (1890) 45 Ch D 430, 438.

[390] For a summary of the traditional reasons for denying specific performance, see *Chappell v Times Newspapers Ltd* [1975] 1 WLR 482. For a critique of the traditional view, see Brodie, 1998a.

[391] [1972] 1 WLR 307, 324.

[392] TULRCA 1992, s 236.

[393] *Warner Bros Pictures Inc v Nelson* [1937] 1 KB 209; see para 4.113 above.

then refuse to accept that the employer's repudiatory breach has brought the contract to an end,[394] and seek an injunction or declaration to restrain the employer from treating the employee as dismissed until the correct procedure is operated and/or a good reason established.[395] A specific order may also be sought to prevent a unilateral variation of the contract terms,[396] unauthorised disciplinary action short of dismissal,[397] or suspension in breach of contract.[398] These actions are begun by claim form in the High Court, separately from the special procedure for judicial review under CPR Part 54. Any injunction will normally be interim, pending a full trial or the completion of the agreed procedure, but it may alternatively be permanent in form.[399] The effect of an injunction is to require the employer to refrain from undertaking the action enjoined, on pain of being found to be in contempt of court. A declaration may also be issued, normally if the court is satisfied that the parties will act on this statement of their rights and obligations without the need to invoke the threat of contempt of court proceedings.

(i) The need to retain mutual trust and confidence

5.55   A key issue is whether the employer can be said to retain trust and confidence in the capacity of the employee to carry out his or her work. In *Hill v CA Parsons & Co Ltd*[400] an injunction was granted in rather unusual circumstances: the employee, who had refused to join a trade union which operated a closed shop in the establishment where he worked, had been dismissed as a result of pressure from the union. The aim of the injunction was to prevent the dismissal from taking effect until after the expiry of the period of notice to which the employee was entitled, by which time the Industrial Relations Act 1971 would have come into force and rendered the employee's dismissal on grounds related to his non-membership of the union unlawful. In this case, because the only reason for dismissal was the pressure exercised by a third party and there was no loss of mutual confidence between the two parties to the contract, an injunction was deemed appropriate.

Although the facts of *Hill* were exceptional and unlikely to be repeated, the principle it enunciated was not exceptional: in an appropriate case, an injunction could be issued to maintain the employment relationship if there was still mutual trust and confidence between the parties. The application of this principle to a broader category of cases of discipline and dismissal was achieved,

---

[394] See paras 5.36–5.39 above, for discussion of the competing 'elective' and 'automatic' theories of contract termination.

[395] *Jones v Lee* [1980] ICR 310; *Irani v Southampton and South West Hampshire Health Authority* [1985] IRLR 203; *Robb v Hammersmith and Fulham London Borough Council* [1991] IRLR 72; *Ali v Southwark London Borough Council* [1988] ICR 567; *Jones v Gwent County Council* [1992] IRLR 521; *Gryf-Lowczowski v Hinchingbrooke Healthcare NHS Trust* [2006] IRLR 100; see also *Edwards v Chesterfield Royal Hospital NHS Foundation Trust* and *Botham v Ministry of Defence* [2012] IRLR 129, discussed at para 5.45 above.

[396] *Burdett-Coutts v Hertfordshire County Council* [1984] IRLR 91; *Keir and Williams v County Council of Hereford and Worcester* [1985] IRLR 505; *Hughes v Southwark London Borough Council* [1988] IRLR 55; *Rigby v Ferodo Ltd* [1988] ICR 29; *Powell v Brent London Borough Council* [1988] ICR 176; *McLaren v Home Office* [1990] IRLR 338.

[397] *Honeyford v Bradford Metropolitan City Council* [1986] IRLR 32.

[398] *Mezey v South West London and St George's Mental Health NHS Trust* [2007] IRLR 237, QBD and 244, CA.

[399] As in *Jones v Gwent County Council* [1992] IRLR 521; see also *Mezey v South West London and St George's Mental Health NHS Trust* [2010] IRLR 512, CA.

[400] [1972] Ch 305.

to striking effect, in *Irani v Southampton and South West Hampshire Health Authority*.[401] In this case the employee, an ophthalmologist, was dismissed after he fell out with a senior consultant at the hospital where he worked. The health authority made no complaint about the employee's own work. His dismissal had taken place in breach of procedures incorporated into his contract of employment from the 'blue book' of NHS terms and conditions. Warner J granted a declaration that the purported dismissal had been in breach of contract and issued an interim injunction to prevent the employer acting on the dismissal until it had operated the contractual disciplinary procedure, 'the effect of which [was] to compel the defendant authority to continue to employ Mr Irani until the trial or at all events until it had in the meantime completed the procedure'.[402] In the judge's view, 'it remains the fact that the defendant authority has perfect faith in the honesty, integrity and loyalty of Mr Irani';[403] as in *Hill*, an injunction could be issued where the dismissal was not caused by any lack of confidence in the employee.

5.56   More problematic are cases where an employer insists before the court that the reinstatement of the employee would be impractical, notwithstanding the absence of fault on the employee's part, because of irreconcilable personal differences between that individual and other members of the organisation, in particular close colleagues or immediate superiors in the managerial hierarchy. Case law nevertheless suggests that this is not an insuperable obstacle to the issue of a specific order. In *Powell v Brent London Borough Council*[404] the Council attempted to revoke Mrs Powell's promotion to a more senior post within the organisation, for reasons relating to an alleged procedural impropriety concerning her appointment (these were found by the court to be groundless). No complaint was made concerning Mrs Powell's ability to do the job to which she had been appointed, and which she was carrying out at the time of the legal proceedings. Mrs Powell sought an interim injunction to prevent the Council re-advertising the post and to require them to treat her as employed in that capacity. Knox J refused to grant the order on the grounds that mutual trust and confidence were lacking, but the Court of Appeal allowed an appeal. The relevant test of confidence was, in the view of Ralph Gibson LJ, to 'be judged by reference to the circumstances of the case, including the nature of the work, the people with whom the work must be done and the likely effect upon the employer and the employer's operations if the employer is required by injunction to suffer the [claimant] to continue in the work'.[405] In this case, it was relevant that 'Brent Council is a large organisation employing many people in different departments';[406] in an organisation of such size, the clearest evidence of a breakdown of personal relations would be required, particularly where there was no rational reason for the claimant's competence to be questioned.

---

[401] [1985] IRLR 203. *Irani* is not quite the first case of this kind; there is a long line of case law concerning the grant of injunctions or declarations to protect the position of schoolteachers which do not appear to rest on any principle of public law (see *Young v Cuthbert* [1906] 1 Ch 451; *Crisp v Holden* (1910) 54 Sol Jo 784; *Smith v McNally* [1912] 1 Ch 816; *Jones v Lee* [1980] ICR 310). See John Hendy and Jeremy McMullen, 1988: p 28.
[402] [1985] IRLR 203, 206.
[403] [1985] IRLR 203, 209.
[404] [1987] IRLR 466; see Ewing and Grubb, 1987.
[405] [1987] IRLR 466, 473.
[406] [1987] IRLR 466, 473.

5.57   *Jones v Gwent County Council*[407] is an even stronger case. Mrs Jones, who was employed by the Council as a lecturer, was accused of misconduct on a number of grounds and her case was considered twice by an internal disciplinary committee of the college at which she worked, in accordance with her contractual disciplinary procedure. She was cleared on each occasion, but the governors of the college nevertheless decided to continue to suspend her from work on full pay and then to dismiss her since they believed that 'your return to the college would cause an irrevocable breakdown in the relationships between staff and between management and staff based on your past behaviour'. The judge assumed this view to be 'sincerely held' but based on a perception of the claimant's past conduct which had not been substantiated. He issued a declaration under Rules of the Supreme Court, Order 14A, rule 1, to the effect that the continuing suspension of the claimant was in breach of contract; an interim injunction preventing the claimant from being dismissed in breach of the procedure laid down in her contract; and a permanent injunction preventing the Council acting on the governors' previous decision to dismiss her.

CPR Part 24 permits the court to give summary judgment against a claimant or defendant if (a) it considers that the claimant has no real prospect of succeeding on the claim or issue, or the defendant has no real prospect of successfully defending the claim or issue and (b) there is no other compelling reason why the case or issue should be disposed of at a trial. CPR Part 24 permits summary disposal in three types of cases which were previously dealt with by separate provisions, one of which – RSC Order 14A – allowed summary disposal of a case on a point of law or construction of a document.[408] In *Jones v Gwent County Council*, Chadwick J thought that so far as Order 14A was concerned, the issue of mutual trust and confidence between the parties was not relevant: to argue otherwise was 'to misunderstand the nature of the power conferred by that Order', which was to determine issues of construction which do not depend on trust and confidence. His judgment can be seen as having 'elided completely the requirement of continuing confidence as a condition of injunctive relief'.[409] A court acting under CPR Part 24 may take a more restrictive view. However, *Jones v Gwent County Council* remains significant in suggesting that mutual confidence cannot be denied simply by the subjective assertion of the contract-breaker, where, on objective grounds, there is no good reason to believe that the employee cannot carry out his or her work effectively.

On the same grounds, it can be argued more generally that where an employee is seeking to enforce the terms of a disciplinary procedure, mutual confidence should hardly ever be an issue, for the reason that until the procedure is properly carried out the employer is not justified in regarding the employee as unfit to continue in employment.[410] To regard it as a relevant consideration can be said to be allowing the employer to take advantage of its own wrong. Nor should it be an issue in cases where the employee is attempting to resist a unilateral change in terms and conditions of

---

[407] [1992] IRLR 521.

[408] Of the other provisions, RSC Order 14 dealt with summary judgment; RSC Order 18, r 19 with striking out proceedings. See now Practice Direction – the Summary Disposal of Claims, para 1.3.

[409] Ewing, 1993b: p 435. Order 14A was used more generally as a means of acquiring a declaration of rights in cases concerning, for example, transfers of employment: *Kenny v South Manchester College* [1993] IRLR 265.

[410] Ewing, 1989; *Robb v Hammersmith and Fulham London Borough Council* [1991] IRLR 72; *Barros D'Sa v University Hospital Coventry and Warwickshire NHS Trust* [2001] EWCA Civ 983, [2001] IRLR 691; *Gryf-Lowczowski v Hinchingbrooke Healthcare NHS Trust* [2006] IRLR 100, although cf the decisions apparently to the contrary in *Ali v Southwark London Borough Council* [1988] IRLR 100 and *Lakshmi v Mid Cheshire Hospitals NHS Trust* [2008] IRLR 956.

employment which is unrelated to any question of his or her personal misconduct. Thus in *Keir and Williams v County Council of Hereford and Worcester*[411] an injunction was granted to prevent an employer removing car expense allowances in breach of terms incorporated into contracts from national and local-level collective agreements, while in *Hughes v Southwark London Borough Council*[412] an injunction was granted to prevent an employer implementing an order, made in breach of contract, purporting to change the claimant social worker's place of work and to alter her job description.[413]

(ii) The balance of convenience

5.58   Under the general principles laid down by the House of Lords in *American Cyanamid Co v Ethicon Ltd*[414] the claimant seeking an interim injunction or declaration is not necessarily required to show a *prima facie* case that they will succeed at full trial, but rather that there is a serious issue to be tried and that damages would not be adequate, whereupon the court will decide whether to issue the order by weighing up the 'balance of convenience' between the parties. This test, because it favours the status quo, inherently favours the employee who is seeking to defend the position he or she occupied prior to the allegedly unlawful act of the employer. Damages rarely will be adequate, since the employee is unlikely to be entitled to receive substantial compensation for wrongful dismissal or for breach of a disciplinary procedure leading to dismissal at common law[415] nor will unfair dismissal normally be a viable alternative, since, for reasons examined below,[416] it is unlikely to lead to reinstatement. It nevertheless remains open to the court, in its discretion, to refuse to grant an equitable order on the grounds that damages would be sufficient in the circumstances,[417] or to refuse to do so because it finds that the claimant's own conduct has not been above reproach.[418] The right to seek equitable relief may also be lost if the employee has, at some stage, accepted the employer's repudiatory breach of contract, for example by looking for or taking work elsewhere;[419] he or she will then be limited to a claim for damages, or to a claim for unfair dismissal.

---

[411] [1985] IRLR 505.

[412] [1988] IRLR 55.

[413] Declarations have also been granted in cases concerning attempts by employers to implement unilateral wage cuts: *Burdett-Coutts v Hertfordshire County Council* [1984] IRLR 91; *Miller v Hamworthy Engineering Ltd* [1986] ICR 846; *Rigby v Ferodo Ltd* [1988] ICR 29.

[414] [1975] AC 396; see further para 11.49.

[415] *Powell v Brent London Borough Council* [1987] IRLR 466, 474; *Hughes v Southwark London Borough Council* [1988] IRLR 55; *Gryf-Lowczowski v Hinchingbrooke Healthcare NHS Trust* [2006] IRLR 100, although cf *Marsh v National Autistic Society* [1993] ICR 453; *Edwards v Chesterfield Royal Hospital NHS Foundation Trust* and *Botham v Ministry of Defence* [2012] IRLR 129, discussed at para 5.45 above.

[416] See para 5.138 *et seq* below, and *Robb v Hammersmith and Fulham London Borough Council* [1991] IRLR 72; *Gryf-Lowczowski v Hinchingbrooke Healthcare NHS Trust* [2006] IRLR 100.

[417] *Marsh v National Autistic Society* [1993] ICR 453.

[418] *Wadcock v Brent London Borough Council* [1990] IRLR 223.

[419] *Dietman v Brent London Borough Council* [1987] ICR 737.

(iii) The effect of an injunction or declaration

5.59   The practical effect of an injunction or declaration is to reinstate the employee into his or her employment, or to re-establish the agreed terms of the contract of employment; but this may depend both on the nature of the contract terms which the employee is seeking to uphold and on the way in which the court chooses to exercise its equitable discretion. In a situation where the employment relationship is continuing and the employer is not seeking to dismiss the employee, equitable relief would normally have the desired effect of realigning the relationship with the agreed contract terms, as well as confirming the employee's right to bring an action in debt or damages for the preceding breach of contract and for any continuing breach.[420] What happens where, following the issue of an injunction, the employer then seeks to dismiss the employee by properly operating the disciplinary procedure in question? One effect of the court's intervention may be to ensure that the employee receives his or her normal salary while the procedure is continuing,[421] but the wider question is whether it will result in the employee keeping their job once the process is exhausted. We suggested above[422] that contractual job security clauses of the kind which are now frequently found in practice have an effect which is both procedural and substantive: they do not simply require a certain procedure to be observed, they also limit the employer's power of arbitrary dismissal. It should follow from this that the employer does not meet its contractual obligations by simply going through the motions of a given procedure; there must also be good objective grounds, at the end of the procedure, for arriving at a decision to discipline or dismiss the employee. Accordingly, there is no reason why an injunction should not be granted to restrain a *substantive* breach of contract in an appropriate case. For example, in *Jones v Gwent County Council*[423] the interim injunction granted by Chadwick J restrained the defendant from 'dismissing [the claimant] unless proper grounds exist and until after a proper procedure has been carried out, both in accordance with the [claimant's] contract of employment'. Since the intervention of the court derives from its equitable jurisdiction and is designed to protect the private rights of the parties, it would seem appropriate for it to have the power to protect the *substance* of those rights and not simply the procedural aspects of the contract. Judicial review is more clearly limited to providing procedural protection for the party whose legitimate expectations are affected by the relevant determination; but there would seem to be no reason, in principle, for extending the public law distinction between substance and procedure to actions begun by claim form.

(iv) The significance of the notice rule

5.60   One remaining barrier to this result could be the notice rule which, as we saw earlier,[424] may provide the employer with a residual right to bring the contract to an end without needing to invoke any given procedure or to offer a reason for doing so. Implicitly, the cases which we have

---

[420] See, eg, *Rigby v Ferodo Ltd* [1987] ICR 457; affd [1988] ICR 29.
[421] *Robb v Hammersmith and Fulham London Borough Council* [1991] IRLR 72.
[422] See para 5.31 *et seq.*
[423] [1992] IRLR 521, 527.
[424] See paras 5.40–5.42 above.

just been considering make little or no sense unless they are seen as limiting the notice rule: what is the point of the court intervening to uphold a given procedure if the employer can outflank it by simply giving notice of termination to the employee? Here, as in relation to the question of damages,[425] the issue remains unclear. It was briefly considered in *Powell v Brent London Borough Council* where Ralph Gibson LJ said:

> The length of the security of tenure in the post which the [claimant] might enjoy is very short. The defendants say three weeks. The [claimant] says 10, because of continuing service with other local authorities. The period of notice does not seem to me to delimit the legitimate interests of the [claimant] in retaining her alleged right to the post … It is not probable that the Borough of Brent will treat the [claimant] unfairly or contrary to their normal policy. If the [claimant] can prove her right to the post, even if it causes disappointment to the legal department, she will probably keep it until she secures further promotion or, if things go ill, she is removed under the disciplinary procedures or however else Brent Council may lawfully proceed.[426]

This does not quite answer the point: could the Council 'lawfully proceed' to dismiss Mrs Powell by giving notice, or would they be obliged to operate the disciplinary procedure and find good cause for dismissal? It is one thing to talk of the *expectation* that Mrs Powell would keep her job, another to consider whether she had the *right* to do so indefinitely. Where the contract contains no notice clause (either express or implied), *McClelland v Northern Ireland General Health Services Board*[427] indicates that a declaration may be issued to prevent the employer treating the employee as dismissed. It seems from the dissenting opinion of Lord Keith of Avonholm that the purpose of the declaration in this case was to establish the claimant's right to substantial damages for breach of contract, although the point does not emerge clearly from the report.[428] If a declaration could be granted for this purpose, it is only a short step to granting an injunction, which would be as good as reinstatement as the employer would then be threatened with contempt of court proceedings for non-compliance. The same result could follow even in cases where the contract contains an express notice clause, if the court is able to construe a contractual job security clause as impliedly limiting the employer's right to give notice. This point does not seem to have been expressly considered in *Jones v Gwent County Council*,[429] but Chadwick J nevertheless granted the injunction sought 'expressly on the basis that the seriousness of being in breach of a court order, if the council continues on the course that it has so far adopted, may perhaps concentrate the minds of those responsible for its affairs'.[430]

---

[425] See para 5.20 *et seq.*

[426] [1987] IRLR 466, 475.

[427] [1957] 1 WLR 594.

[428] See Ewing, 1993b: pp 425–426.

[429] The claimant's contract provided for her to be dismissed on notice of not less than two months, but to have the right even then to make representations to the effect that the dismissal was not for good cause. See [1992] IRLR 521, 525. This could be read as qualifying the employer's residual power of arbitrary dismissal.

[430] [1992] IRLR 521, 527.

(v) The employment relationships covered by the principle

5.61   There remains, as a final question, the issue of how far the principle enunciated in these decisions extends to different varieties of employment relationship. There is no reason why the equitable intervention of the courts should be limited to public sector employment relationships, nor to employees of a particular status, although employees in insecure employment are unlikely to have the kind of express job security clauses which the courts have to date intervened to protect. The courts have not taken any further the suggestion of Woolf J in *Lavelle*,[431] that office-holder status be extended to all employees benefiting from the protection of unfair dismissal legislation,[432] and, indeed, *Johnson v Unisys Ltd*[433] constitutes a formidable obstacle to this. As we discussed in para 5.35 above, *obiter dicta* in the Supreme Court decision in *Edwards v Chesterfield Royal Hospital NHS Foundation Trust* and *Botham v Ministry of Defence*[434] give some support to the view that all disciplinary procedures should be treated as contractual. The decision of the majority that damages for breach of such clauses should not cover the manner of dismissal may strengthen the case for an injunction and/or declaration to halt the disciplinary process and, indeed, Lord Dyson expressly envisages employees seeking such remedies.[435] In practice, however, many employees are unlikely to have access to the expertise and resources required to apply for these orders and experience to date suggests that the courts are unlikely to be sympathetic to applications from employees in general. To date, virtually all the cases in which injunctions or declarations have been issued to prevent dismissal have concerned employees in secure jobs in the public sector. The case law appears not to have shaken off entirely the traditional notion of an office holder as one occupying a post which has 'a subsisting, permanent, substantive position',[436] a description which can only with difficulty be applied to any private-sector employment, no matter how elevated. Where private-sector employees have sought specific relief to retain their jobs they have, until recently, failed to do so, although the reasons given by the courts do not formally discriminate between employment in the public and private sectors.

Thus in *Marsh v National Autistic Society*[437] an injunction was refused on the grounds that damages would be an adequate remedy. An injunction was also refused in *Alexander v Standard Telephones and Cables Ltd*[438] where it was sought to enforce the terms of a 'last-in, first-out' redundancy selection procedure by nullifying the dismissals of employees who had been dismissed when fellow workers with less seniority had been kept on. According to Aldous J, 'it cannot be said that the defendant has complete confidence in the [claimants], as it has less confidence that they can do the work than the other members of the workforce that have been retained. The relationship of employer and employee has in fact broken down'.[439] In *Anderson v Pringle of Scotland Ltd*,[440]

---

[431] [1983] ICR 99. See para 5.53 above.

[432] The substantial costs of High Court litigation will also be a practical bar to most employees who are not supported financially by their trade unions and even, perhaps, to many who are: Ewing, 1993b: p 436.

[433] [2001] IRLR 279; see paras 5.43 and 5.44 above.

[434] [2012] IRLR 129.

[435] At [44].

[436] *Great Western Rly Co v Bater* [1920] 3 KB 266, 273–274. On the notion of 'office holder', see para 3.46 above.

[437] [1993] ICR 453.

[438] [1990] IRLR 55.

[439] [1990] IRLR 55, 61.

[440] [1998] IRLR 64. Anderson was applied in a public-sector context in *Peace v City of Edinburgh Council* [1999] IRLR 417.

however, where the facts were in material respects identical to those of *Alexander,* the Court of Session, Outer House dismissed such an argument. Lord Prosser was 'not persuaded' that there was 'any true analogy between the respondents' preference for other employees and the need for confidence which is inherent in the employer/employee relationship'.[441] Moreover, while it may be 'very inconvenient or difficult for the respondents to abide by the priorities' they had agreed to, 'they can hardly call it unfair to be held to their own bargain'.[442] The court therefore granted interim relief to prevent the employer selecting employees for redundancy on any basis other than the agreed procedure.

We would suggest that *Anderson* shows a much more appropriate approach to the enforcement of redundancy selection procedures than *Alexander.* It also demonstrates that there is no reason why a court should not grant an injunction or declaration to a private-sector employee in an appropriate case. It remains to be seen whether it will mark the beginning of a trend towards the more extensive protection of the contractual rights of private, as well as public, sector employees.

THE STATUTORY CONCEPT OF DISMISSAL

5.62   We now turn to the legislation governing the employer's liability for unfair dismissal. For the unfair dismissal jurisdiction to be invoked the employee must first satisfy a number of qualifying conditions, the most important of which, for present purposes, is that he or she has been *dismissed.*[443] This is also a pre-requisite for a claim to statutory redundancy compensation.[444] The statutory concept of dismissal builds on the common law of the contract of employment.[445] Under section 95(1) of ERA 1996:

> … an employee is treated as dismissed by his employer if (and … only if)-
> (a)   the contract under which he is employed is terminated by the employer, (whether with or without notice),
> (b)   he is employed under a limited-term contract and that contract terminates by virtue of the limiting event without being renewed under the same contract,[446] or
> (c)   the employee terminates the contract under which he is employed (with or without notice) in circumstances in which he is entitled to terminate it without notice by reason of the employer's conduct.[447]

---

[441] [1998] IRLR 64, 67.

[442] [1998] IRLR 64. The court in *Anderson* considered that, for the purposes of the interim application before it, there was sufficient evidence that the terms of the collective agreement had been incorporated into individual contracts. It is notable that the question as to whether the terms were appropriate for incorporation did not arise: cf *Alexander v Standard Telephones and Cables Ltd (No 2)* [1991] IRLR 286 and *Kaur v MG Rover Group Ltd* [2005] IRLR 40; see further para 4.30above.

[443] Elias, 1978.

[444] On this, see para 5.155 *et seq* below.

[445] *Western Excavating (ECC) Ltd v Sharp* [1978] QB 761.

[446] As amended by FTER 2002, Sch 2, Part 1. See ERA 1996, s 235(2A), (2B) for the definition of 'limited-term contract' and 'limiting event'.

[447] This is subject to s 95(2) (employee who has been given notice of termination who then himself or herself gives notice to expire at an earlier date still treated as dismissed). Section 95(1) and s 136(1) (redundancy) are in substantially similar terms. Those respects in which the definition of dismissal for the purposes of redundancy compensation differs from that for unfair dismissal are considered at para 5.163 below.

Partly through its reliance on the common law of contract and partly as a consequence of derogations contained elsewhere in the Act, this statutory concept is not completely comprehensive, and certain important cases of non-consensual termination of employment fall outside its scope. The principal statutory derogation involves the expiry of certain fixed-term contracts[448] in a case where the employee has signed a valid waiver prior to 25 October 1999; employees protected by a collective agreement establishing dismissal procedures may also be excluded.[449] To these the courts have added a number of situations which, in their view, fall outside the scope of section 95(1): these include the discharge of the contract by way of frustration.[450] All of these derogations or exclusions go to the employment tribunal's jurisdiction, so that where they apply the tribunal is unable to decide the applicant's claim on the merits.[451] Where an employee is claiming to have been constructively dismissed (ie a dismissal as defined in section 95(1)(c) above) he or she will risk the employment tribunal reducing any eventual compensatory award by up to 25% if he or she has failed to comply with the ACAS Code of Practice on Disciplinary and Grievance Procedures and that failure was unreasonable.[452] If an employer has failed to comply with the Code and that failure was unreasonable the tribunal may increase an award by up to 25% if the dismissal takes the form of termination of the employee's contract by the employer.[453] The Code itself excludes dismissals due to redundancy and non-renewal of fixed-term contracts on their expiry from its scope.[454]

Initial qualifying conditions

5.63   The applicant must have been employed as an employee[455] and (for employees employed from 6 April 2012) must normally have had continuity of employment of not less than two years[456] at the time of the dismissal, the 'effective date of termination'.[457] Continuity of employment is only unnecessary in respect of a limited category of dismissals for automatically unfair reasons, which are considered in more detail below.[458] The employment must also have fallen within the territorial scope of UK labour legislation.[459]

---

[448] ERA 1996, s 197, now repealed; see para 5.75 below.

[449] ERA 1996, s 110; see para 5.64 below.

[450] See para 5.77 *et seq* below.

[451] The exclusion of retirement dismissals which fell within ERA 1996, 109(1) was repealed as from 1 October 2006 by EE(A)R 2006; the relevant provisions of EE(A)R 2006 were in turn revoked by SI 2011/1069.

[452] TULRCA 1992, s 207A, inserted by EA 2008, s 3; ERA 1996, s 124A, as amended by EA 2008, s 3(4); see further paras 2.21 above and 5.125 *et seq* below.

[453] TULRCA 1992, s 207A, inserted by EA 2008, s 3; see further para 5.151 below.

[454] Acas Code of Practice on Disciplinary and Grievance Procedures 2009, introduction (which refers to 'fixed-term contracts' rather than using the broader term 'limited-term contract', discussed in para 5.75 below). The legislation itself does not exclude such dismissals so it is conceivable that a subsequent Code could cover them.

[455] ERA 1996, ss 95(1), 230(1); see para 3.19 *et seq* above. On the position of civil servants and members of the armed forces, see above, paras 3.40 and 3.41.

[456] ERA 1996, s 108(1), as amended by SI 2012/989. Where the employee's period of continuous employment began before 6 April 2012 the period is one year. On changes to the qualifying period for unfair dismissal since the inception of this legislation in 1971, see para 5.8 above.

[457] On this, see para 5.80 *et seq* below.

[458] See para 5.92 *et seq* below.

[459] See *Lawson v Serco Ltd* [2006] IRLR 289, discussed at para 2.46 above.

Derogation for collective dismissal procedures

5.64   A special derogation for certain collective agreements establishing dismissal procedures is allowed for under the Act.[460] This provision, a concession to the wish of collective parties to disputes procedures to avoid recourse to law, has to date only been exercised in one case, concerning the Joint Industry Board for the Electrical Contracting Industry, although the order granting exemption was revoked on 1 June 2001 on the ground that the agreement no longer satisfied the relevant statutory conditions.[461] The Secretary of State may by order exempt from the scope of the legislation those employees covered by a collective 'dismissal procedure agreement'. The agreement then displaces the legislation, excluding the right of the employees concerned to bring complaints of unfair dismissal before employment tribunals.[462] To be valid, the agreement must be agreed by or on behalf of one or more independent trade unions and one or more employers or employers' associations,[463] and must also meet certain conditions to the satisfaction of the Secretary of State. These are, among other things, that the agreement lays down procedures which apply to all employees within the scope of the agreement without discrimination; that the agreement either makes general provision for arbitration or, alternatively, allows arbitration where an initial decision cannot be reached and on a point of law; and that 'the remedies provided … in respect of unfair dismissal are on the whole as beneficial as (but not necessarily identical with) those provided in respect of unfair dismissal' by the Act.[464] The legislation itself provides that an award made under a 'designated dismissal procedure agreement' (that is to say, one approved by the Secretary of State) may be enforceable in the same way as a judgment of the County Court.[465]

Dismissal by the employer

5.65   The first of the three categories of dismissal listed in section 95(1)(a) of ERA 1996 consists of the termination of contract under which the employee is employed, either with or without notice. For this, no formalities are required: the act of dismissal may be carried out in writing or by words or conduct. Whether words and/or conduct amount to a dismissal in a given case depends in part upon the intentions of the employer and in part upon the reasonable understanding of the employee:

> … the test which has to be applied in cases of this kind is along these lines. Were the words spoken those of dismissal, that is to say, were they intended to bring the contract of employment to an end? What was the employer's intention? In answering that a relevant,

---

[460] ERA 1996, s 110.

[461] SI 2001/1752.

[462] Prior to 1 August 1998, s 110(2) excluded dismissals relating to pregnancy or maternity or the assertion of a statutory right. ERDRA 1998, s 12 amended the section to exclude only those descriptions of dismissal excluded by the agreement itself, with the aim of making dismissal procedure agreements more flexible.

[463] ERA 1996, s 235(1).

[464] ERA 1996, s 110(3).

[465] ERA 1996, s 110(6), as inserted by ERDRA 1998, s 12.

and perhaps the most important, question is how would a reasonable employee, in all the circumstances, have understood what the employer intended by what he said and did?[466]

This test is equally applicable to words and conduct of the employee which might be taken as indicating an intention to resign. Again, no formalities are required by law for an employee to resign his or her employment. Unless it can be construed as a 'constructive dismissal', which, as we shall see, requires the employee to resign in response to a repudiatory breach of contract by the employer,[467] resignation is outside the scope of section 95(1). Leaving the case of constructive dismissal to one side for the moment,[468] the question becomes whether the employer or the employee was the one to bring the contract to an end. Some basic principles of contract law for ascertaining the intentions of the parties are relevant here: one party cannot rely on an undisclosed intention which the other party could not reasonably have ascertained; but if both parties subjectively understand the contract to have been terminated, the reasonableness of their views is irrelevant.[469] The court may also construe the words used by reference to their accepted or customary meaning in the trade in question.[470]

Where words are uttered in the heat of the moment, the tribunal 'ought to be careful to ensure that what has taken place really is a dismissal' or, conversely, a resignation, 'and not merely some words uttered for particular reasons which everybody quite understood were little more than abuse or something of that sort'.[471] However, some words are sufficiently unambiguous as to leave nobody in any doubt as to their meaning, even when they are spoken in anger. If the employee says 'I am resigning', these words are not ambiguous, according to the Court of Appeal: they signify a present intention to resign, with immediate effect, and if the employer understands them in this way that is the end of the matter. Otherwise it would be difficult for mere words ever to effect a valid resignation.[472] Where there is ambiguity, however, 'if one is concerned with an immature employee, or decisions taken in the heat of the moment, then what might otherwise appear to be a clear resignation, should not be so construed'.[473] In these 'special circumstances', although it would be going too far to say that the employer is necessarily under a responsibility to take steps to ascertain the true intention of the employee, nevertheless 'a reasonable period of time should be allowed to lapse and if circumstances arise during that period which put the employer on notice that further inquiry is desirable to see whether the resignation was really intended and can properly be assumed, then such inquiry is ignored at the employer's risk'.[474] The Court of Appeal has recently emphasised that the 'special circumstances' exception is not an exception to the rule that notice, once given, cannot be withdrawn except by consent; rather, it is a situation

---

[466] *Tanner v DT Kean Ltd* [1978] IRLR 110, 111.
[467] ERA 1996, s 95(1)(c).
[468] It is discussed in para 5.69 *et seq* below.
[469] *Sothern v Frank Charlesly & Co* [1981] IRLR 278.
[470] *Futty v D and D Brekkes Ltd* [1974] IRLR 130.
[471] *Chesham Shipping Ltd v Rowe* [1977] IRLR 391, 392.
[472] *Sothern v Franks Charlesly & Co* [1981] IRLR 278; *BG Gale Ltd v Gilbert* [1978] ICR 1149 ('I am leaving, I want my cards').
[473] *Sovereign House Security Services Ltd v Savage* [1989] IRLR 115, 116 (the employee said he was 'jacking the job in': held, no resignation); *Barclay v City of Glasgow District Council* [1983] IRLR 313 ('mentally defective employee'); *Futty v D and D Brekkes Ltd* [1974] IRLR 130 (no dismissal intended when manager and employee had an altercation).
[474] *Kwik-Fit (GB) Ltd v Lineham* [1992] ICR 183, 191.

in which 'the giver of the notice is afforded the opportunity to satisfy the recipient that he never intended to give it in the first place'.[475]

5.66   The employer will be deemed to have dismissed the employee if it prompts or induces the latter to resign by way of a threat of dismissal: 'if an employee is told that she is no longer required in her employment and is expressly invited to resign, a court of law is entitled to come to the conclusion that, as a matter of common sense, the employee was dismissed'.[476] The question is seen as one of causation. If it can be shown that the employee agreed to go because, for example, of the severance terms which he or she is offered, a tribunal may find that the generosity of the severance terms and not the initial threat of dismissal was the operative cause of the contract coming to an end, in which case there will have been no dismissal.[477] This doctrine can place employees in a dilemma where they are offered incentives for voluntary redundancy or early retirement. In *Birch v University of Liverpool*[478] the University, faced with the need to make cuts in staff, introduced a scheme under which employees taking early retirement would receive a pension and lump sum from the University's pension fund. Mr Birch made an application under the scheme which the University accepted; he later lodged a separate claim for a statutory redundancy payment. The University claimed that he had not been dismissed, and this contention was upheld. There had been no threat of compulsory early retirement and no other pressure on Mr Birch to resign, and the contract had therefore been terminated by mutual consent.[479] By contrast, in *Scotch Premier Meat Ltd v Burns*[480] the EAT took the robust view that 'where the whole background to the departure was determination by the employer to close a factory and make the employees inevitably redundant, the fact that some employees accepted a package as the means of effecting that decision does not in our opinion preclude a finding that there was a dismissal'.[481] This decision turned on the meaning of the term 'dismissal' in the context of an employee's entitlement to remuneration under a protective award granted in respect of the employer's failure to consult and inform employee representatives of proposed redundancies,[482] but it would be just as appropriate for it to be applied to individual applications in relation to unfair dismissal and/or redundancy compensation. In *Sandhu v Jan de Rijk Transport Ltd* Wall LJ reviewed the authorities and concluded that:

> ... in none of the cases in which the employee has been held to resign has the resignation occurred during the same interview/discussion in which the question of dismissal has been raised, and in no case in which the termination of the employee's employment has occurred in a single interview has a resignation been found to have taken place. The reason for this

[475] *Willoughby v CF Capital Plc* [2011] IRLR 985, Rimer LJ at [37]-[38].
[476] *East Sussex County Council v Walker* (1972) 7 ITR 280, 281 (Sir John Brightman).
[477] *Sheffield v Oxford Controls Co Ltd* [1979] ICR 396; see also *Catherall v Michelin Tyre plc* [2003] IRLR 61 (case remitted to tribunal to determine whether, where an employee was given the choice between redundancy and retirement through ill health, the absence of choice was the cause of the termination or whether the situation provided the opportunity for satisfactory terms to be negotiated for the termination of employment).
[478] [1985] ICR 470. See also *Optare Group Ltd v TGWU* [2007] IRLR 931.
[479] See also, in the context of provisions of a pension scheme, *AGCO Ltd v Massey Ferguson Works Pension Trust Ltd* [2003] IRLR 793 (voluntary redundancy was 'retirement at the request of the employer' and in reality 'consensual dismissal' (sic); compulsory redundancy was not).
[480] [2000] IRLR 639.
[481] [2000] IRLR 639, 642.
[482] See generally para 9.33 below.

... is not far to seek. Resignation ... implies some form of negotiation and discussion; it predicates a result which is a genuine choice on the part of the employee. Plainly, if the employee has had the opportunity to take independent advice and then offers to resign, that fact would be powerful evidence pointing towards resignation rather than dismissal.[483]

In this case the claimant had been summoned to a meeting with senior managers without being warned of the purpose of the meeting in advance. The meeting had begun with the claimant being told that his contract was going to end. The claimant then negotiated his leaving date and retention of his company car and mobile phone. The Court of Appeal held that the claimant was "doing his best on his own to salvage what he could from the inevitable fact that he was going to be dismissed". This was "the very antithesis of free, unpressurised negotiation"[484] and the tribunal's conclusion that he had resigned was set aside as perverse.

Employees need to avoid resigning prematurely, before a threat of dismissal becomes operative. In *Logan Salton v Durham County Council*[485] the employee was the subject of disciplinary proceedings which reached the stage of the Council recommending that he be summarily dismissed. Before this recommendation could be considered by the internal committee convened to deal with the matter, the employee decided to resign and agreed severance terms with the Council. It was held that his employment had been terminated by agreement. In *Roberts v West Coast Trains Ltd*[486] a further potential trap for employees was exposed. The applicant was dismissed following a disciplinary hearing. He launched an internal appeal against that decision but before the outcome of that appeal was known he started proceedings in the employment tribunal claiming unfair dismissal. Following the internal appeal he was informed that his punishment had been reduced from dismissal to demotion. The sanctions of demotion and suspension without pay were specified in the contractual disciplinary procedure. When the applicant pursued his unfair dismissal claim the Court of Appeal affirmed the decisions of the tribunal and EAT that he had not been dismissed. The terms of the employment contract permitted the employer to demote the employee in place of the earlier decision to dismiss, so that they could retrospectively achieve a position where he was not dismissed for the purposes of bringing an unfair dismissal claim. In this case the court emphasised that the initial dismissal would have stood if the applicant had never instituted an appeal and/or if he had withdrawn his appeal before a decision was made. A dismissed employee who failed to appeal against dismissal would now risk a reduction of up to 25% in any eventual award of compensation.[487] The issue of whether an employee who is initially dismissed but subject to a lesser sanction on appeal should be treated as a dismissed employee who has been offered re-instatement or re-engagement, or not dismissed at all, may become increasingly important in future litigation.[488]

5.67   Where the employer has given notice to the employee to terminate the contract, the courts are reluctant to conclude that any subsequent agreement to end the employment before the notice

---

[483] [2007] IRLR 519, [37]. The other members of the Court agreed with Wall LJ's judgment.
[484] Above, [51].
[485] [1989] IRLR 99.
[486] [2004] IRLR 788.
[487] See para 5.131 and 5.151.
[488] An employee who is subject to a disciplinary sanction which he or she considers to be a repudiatory breach of contract could claim to have been constructively dismissed. Constructive dismissal was not argued in *Roberts*.

expires amounts to termination by consent. The initial decision to dismiss will be regarded as the operative one, particularly if there is any evidence of the employee being pressurised into leaving.[489] If, having been given notice by the employer, the employee then gives notice of his or her resignation to take effect before the employer's notice has expired, section 95(2) provides that the employee is nevertheless to be taken to have been dismissed by the employer, for the reasons which the employer had at the time the initial notice was given. There is no specified minimum period of notice which the employee must comply with in order for this provision to apply.[490] However, if the employee fails to give the minimum notice required by the contract, it is possible that the employer will thereby acquire a claim against him or her for damages for breach of contract, which is not precluded in any way by section 95(2). Where the employee gives notice of his or her intention to resign and subsequently receives shorter notice of termination from the employer, the employer will be taken to have terminated the contract and there is a dismissal.[491] Depending on the reason for dismissal, an employer in that situation may need to have regard to the ACAS Code of Practice on Disciplinary and Grievance Procedures.[492]

5.68 Dismissal under section 95(1)(a) normally involves the ending of the employment relationship, but this is not inevitable as *Hogg v Dover College*[493] shows. Mr Hogg was employed full-time as a teacher and head of department at the College. Then, following an illness, he received a letter from the headmaster of the College offering him teaching on a part-time basis with a reduced salary. In response he lodged a claim for unfair dismissal while continuing to work under the new arrangement, making it clear that this was done under protest. The employment tribunal found that the headmaster's letter did not amount to a dismissal under section 95(1)(a), and that Mr Hogg could not claim constructive dismissal either under section 95(1)(c) as he had waived the employer's repudiatory breach of contract. The EAT overturned this ruling in both respects. The headmaster's letter amounted to a termination of Mr Hogg's *contract*, as required by section 95(1)(a), regardless of whether he carried on in employment: 'he was being told that his former contract was from that moment gone'.[494] Alternatively there was a constructive dismissal since his employment continued under a *new* contract, Mr Hogg having terminated the old one by accepting the employer's repudiation.

The application of the principle in *Hogg* was upheld in *Alcan Extrusions v Yates*.[495] Here the employers had imposed a continuous rolling shift system, which had knock-on effects for pay and holidays, in place of the shift system prescribed in their employees' contracts of employment. The EAT affirmed that in this case the departure from the terms of the existing contract was sufficiently substantial to constitute withdrawal of the contract.

Hogg and *Alcan* are potentially far-reaching decisions which make it possible for employees to use unfair dismissal legislation to challenge unilateral variations or impositions of contract terms,

[489] *Lees v Arthur Greaves (Lees) Ltd* [1974] ICR 501.
[490] *Cardinal Vaughan Memorial School Governors v Alie* [1987] ICR 406.
[491] *British Midland Airways Ltd v Lewis* [1978] ICR 782.
[492] See para 5.125 *et seq*
[493] [1990] ICR 39.
[494] [1990] ICR 39, 42.
[495] [1996] IRLR 327.

and disciplinary action short of dismissal,[496] without the need to resign from their employment and find another job.[497] The possible weak link in the reasoning of the EAT in these cases is the argument that there were two different contracts of employment here, one before and one after the change in working hours took place. While it is true that for there to be a dismissal under section 95(1) it is enough for the *contract* and not the *relationship* of employment to be brought to an end, it may be a matter of fine judgement whether, in a given case, a unilateral change in working conditions leads to a new contract being created or simply amounts to a purported variation of the old one. There is authority to suggest that where the employer seeks to change an important element of a contractual package, 'if an employee goes on working, having made his protest about the exclusion of the important element, the true position in law is that he has been dismissed but re-engaged on a fresh contract'.[498] However the the EAT's suggestion in *Alcan* that whether the departure from the original contract is sufficiently radical to amount to the termination of that contract and its replacement by a different one is a question of fact for the employment tribunal to decide[499] can only be a recipe for uncertainty in the law in this area.[500]

Constructive dismissal

5.69   There is a dismissal where the employee terminates the contract, either with or without notice, 'in circumstances in which he is entitled to terminate it without notice by reason of the employer's conduct'.[501] On general principles, it is not necessary for the employee to inform the employer, at the time of the termination, of his or her reason for leaving the employment; the test is simply one of causation, that is to say, was the employee's departure caused by the employer's conduct?[502] However employees who leave without previously raising their grievance and otherwise complying with the ACAS Code of Practice on Disciplinary and Grievance Procedures risk having any eventual compensatory award reduced by up to 25% if this failure

---

[496] *Joseph v British Railways Board*, IT (2 September 1993, unreported) noted by Curran, 1994; cf *Hunt v British Railways Board* [1979] IRLR 379.

[497] Curran, 1994; R White, 1997. *Waite v Government Communications Headquarters* [1983] ICR 653 is another case in which the employee brought a claim for unfair dismissal while still working for the employer; at no point does it seem to have been argued that the claimant had not been dismissed.

[498] *Land v West Yorkshire Metropolitan County Council* [1979] ICR 452 (Kilner Brown J); cf *Marriott v Oxford and District Co-operative Society Ltd (No 2)* [1970] 1 QB 186.

[499] [1996] IRLR 327, 329. See R White, 1997 for a critique of this decision.

[500] See *Robinson v Tescom Corp* [2008] IRLR 408 (discussed at para 4.42 above) for a case in which it was found that a purported variation by the employer was not sufficiently serious to amount to a dismissal under *Hogg v Dover College*.

[501] ERA 1996, s 95(1)(c).

[502] *Weathersfield Ltd (t/a Van & Truck Rentals) v Sargent* [1999] IRLR 94, CA, overruling *Holland v Glendale Industries Ltd* [1998] ICR 493, EAT. The employee must communicate to the employer the intention to terminate the employment: *Edwards v Surrey Police* [1999] IRLR 456. In *Rai v Somerfield Stores Ltd* [2004] IRLR 124 the EAT held that presentation of an originating application to the tribunal did not constitute the requisite communication. In *RDF Media Group plc v Clements* [2008] IRLR 221 it was suggested that causation could also be relevant to whether there had been a repudiatory breach by the employer on which the employee could rely to support constructive dismissal; if the employee had himself committed an anterior breach by his misconduct, that anterior breach, and not that of the employer, had destroyed the relationship between them: see [141]; see also *Aberdeen City Council v McNeill* [2010] IRLR 374, but cf *Tullett Prebon plc v BGC Brokers LP* [2010] IRLR 648, Jack J at [83]-[85].

was unreasonable.[503] The test of employer misconduct in the context of constructive dismissal implicitly incorporates the common law of contract relating to the employee's right to resign in the face of a repudiatory breach of contract by the employer.[504] For a time, tribunals applied a more general test of whether the employer had acted 'unreasonably' in prompting the employee to quit the employment.[505] However, in *Western Excavating (ECC) Ltd v Sharp*[506] the Court of Appeal, in a judgment subsequently regarded as authoritative,[507] imposed a contract test. This was done in large part in order to avoid duplicating within the concept of dismissal the test of reasonableness provided for separately by what is now section 98(4) of ERA 1996.[508] Although the effect of this ruling might have been to limit the scope of the Act by reference to the highly technical law of repudiatory breach of contract, this has not happened largely because of the expansion of the implied duty of co-operation within the contract of employment. In this way, the law of unfair dismissal has been indirectly responsible for one of the most important recent developments within the common law of employment.[509]

5.70   In *Western Excavating*[510] Lawton LJ found it neither 'necessary [nor] advisable to express any opinion as to what principles of law operate to bring a contract of employment to an end by reason of an employer's conduct' and suggested that it would be a 'waste of legal learning' for tribunals to expend much time and effort examining the law of repudiatory breach. The voluminous case law which has developed around section 95(1)(c) simply indicates that the circumstances giving rise to a constructive dismissal are as varied as those of employment itself. A breach by the employer of the duty to maintain mutual trust and confidence, which is part of the reciprocal duty of co-operation, will be regarded as sufficient.[511] Conduct falling into this category has included subjecting the employee to abusive and insulting language;[512] refusing

---

[503] TULRCA 1992, s 207A, inserted by EA 2008, s 3; see further para 2.21. Under the general law, an alleged failure by an employee to follow a grievance procedure is irrelevant: *Tolson v Governing Body of Mixenden Community School* [2003] IRLR 842.

[504] The employee must leave because of the breach (*Walker v Josiah Wedgwood & Sons Ltd* [1978] IRLR 105). In *Jones v F Sirl & Son (Furnishers) Ltd* [1997] IRLR 493, 495 the EAT held that the breach need not be the sole cause as long as it is the 'effective cause' but in *Nottinghamshire County Council v Meikle* [2004] IRLR 703 the Court of Appeal warned against getting drawn too far into questions about the employee's motives (Keene LJ at [33]). The fact that an employee has another job to go to may not prevent a finding of constructive dismissal if the employer's breach was the main operative cause of his or her resignation: [1978] IRLR 105.

[505] *Gilbert v Goldstone Ltd* [1977] ICR 36; *Turner v London Transport Executive* [1977] ICR 952.

[506] [1978] QB 761.

[507] For an argument that the courts might have chosen to follow the prior Court of Appeal judgment in *Turner v London Transport Executive* [1977] ICR 952, see Elias *et al*, 1980: p 563.

[508] [1978] QB 761, 770 (Lord Denning MR); on s 98(4), see para 5.115 *et seq* below.

[509] See para 4.105 *et seq* above.

[510] [1978] QB 761, 772.

[511] In *Morrow v Safeway Stores plc* [2002] IRLR 9 the EAT held that a breach of the implied term of trust and confidence would always be repudiatory; there is no room for assessing the seriousness of the breach. See also *London Borough of Waltham Forest v Omilaju* [2005] IRLR 35, [14] (Dyson LJ). In *Buckland v Bournemouth University* [2010] IRLR 445, the Court of Appeal rejected the argument that the 'range of reasonable responses' test was relevant in determining whether the employer had breached the trust and confidence term; see also *Burton, McEvoy and Webb v Curry* UKEAT/0174/09, 21 April 2010 and see Cabrelli, 2011; Bogg, 2010b.

[512] *Palmanor Ltd v Cedron* [1978] ICR 1008.

to investigate a justified complaint relating to health and safety;[513] making an unsubstantiated allegation of theft against the employee;[514] issuing a final written warning in respect of a relatively minor incident;[515] insisting without good cause that the employee should undergo a psychiatric examination;[516] 'arbitrarily, capriciously and inequitably' singling out an employee for an inferior pay rise to that received by other employees;[517] unjustifiably demoting the employee for a minor disciplinary offence;[518] denying the employee access to the company's premises by changing the locks, and telling customers that the employee no longer worked for the company;[519] failing to support the employee, who was a supervisor, in his relations with shop-floor workers;[520] failing reasonably and promptly to afford a reasonable opportunity to obtain redress of grievances;[521] apparent bias in an internal grievance appeal panel;[522] instructing the employee to change her place of work in the absence of a term authorising this;[523] allowing an employee to be subjected to sexual harassment;[524] giving the employee an instruction which amounted to discrimination on racial grounds;[525] writing a misleading reference for a prospective employer;[526] failing to inform an employee on maternity leave about a vacancy for which she would have applied had she known about it;[527] rejection of a request for flexible, including part-time, working;[528] a serious breach of the obligation under the equality legislation relating to disability to make reasonable adjustments;[529] and suspending the employee in response to unsubstantiated allegations of child abuse.[530] However, the notion of reciprocal co-operation has so far stopped short of imposing an obligation on an employer to offer an annual pay rise or an offer of regrading.[531] On the other hand, an attempt by the employer unilaterally to vary the express contract terms, by, for example, cutting pay,[532] reducing hours,[533] or requiring the employee to relinquish his principal job in

---

[513] *British Aircraft Corpn v Austin* [1978] IRLR 332. Note, however, *Marshall Specialist Vehicles Ltd v Osborne* [2003] IRLR 672 (need to apply approach in *Sutherland v Hatton* [2002] IRLR 263 in examining whether breach of implied term to take reasonable care for the safety of employees in context of alleged overwork).

[514] *Robinson v Crompton Parkinson Ltd* [1978] ICR 401.

[515] *Stanley Cole (Wainfleet) Ltd v Sheridan* [2003] IRLR 52.

[516] *Bliss v South East Thames Regional Health Authority* [1985] IRLR 308.

[517] *FC Gardner Ltd v Beresford* [1978] IRLR 63.

[518] *BBC v Beckett* [1983] IRLR 43.

[519] *Brown v JBD Engineering Ltd* [1993] IRLR 568.

[520] *Industrial Rubber Products v Gillon* [1977] IRLR 389.

[521] *WA Goold (Pearmak) Ltd v McConnell* [1995] IRLR 516.

[522] *Watson v University of Strathclyde* [2011] IRLR 458.

[523] *Aparau v Iceland Frozen Foods plc* [1996] IRLR 119.

[524] *Wood v Freeloader Ltd* [1977] IRLR 455; *Western Excavating (ECC) Ltd v Sharp* [1978] QB 761, 772 (Lawton LJ).

[525] *Weathersfield Ltd (t/a Van & Truck Rental) v Sargent* [1999] IRLR 94. In *Amnesty International v Ahmed* [2009] IRLR 884 the EAT held that in the 'peculiar circumstances' of the case unlawful discrimination did not support a finding of constructive dismissal: Underhill P at [72].

[526] *TSB Bank plc v Harris* [2000] IRLR 157.

[527] *Visa International Service Association v Paul* [2004] IRLR 42.

[528] *Shaw v CCL Ltd* [2008] IRLR 284.

[529] *Greenhof v Barnsley Metropolitan Borough Council* [2006] IRLR 98.

[530] *Gogay v Hertfordshire County Council* [2000] IRLR 703. See also observations of the Court of Appeal in *Crawford v Suffolk Mental Health Partnership NHS Trust* [2012] IRLR 402.

[531] *Murco Petroleum Ltd v Forge* [1987] IRLR 50 and *Bridgen v Lancashire County Council* [1987] IRLR 58 respectively. On whether HRA 1998 may lead to a widening of the employer's duties of co-operation and good faith, see Hepple, 1998b; 2001a.

[532] *Industrial Rubber Products v Gillon* [1977] IRLR 389; *Cantor Fitzgerald International v Callaghan* [1999] IRLR 234.

[533] *Hogg v Dover College* [1990] ICR 39.

favour of another role,[534] will almost certainly be regarded as a repudiation.[535] The obligation to maintain trust and confidence can arise before the actual commencement of employment, so entitling the prospective employee to terminate the employment if it is breached.[536]

A series of separate acts, taken together, may amount to good grounds for repudiation.[537] It is not necessary for the 'final straw' itself to be a breach of contract to result in a breach of the implied term of trust and confidence, but:

> ... the quality that the final straw must have is that it should be an act in a series whose cumulative effect is to amount to a breach of the implied term ... The act does not have to be of the same character as the earlier acts. Its essential quality is that, when taken in conjunction with the earlier acts on which the employee relies, it amounts to a breach of the implied term of trust and confidence. It must contribute something to that breach, although what it adds may be relatively insignificant.[538]

The tribunal may need to investigate closely whether the conduct of the employee is such as to disentitle him or her to rely upon acts that may have preceded the 'final straw' by some time.[539]

5.71   The concept of constructive dismissal has not entirely escaped the more specific, technical aspects of the law of repudiatory breach. The test is whether 'looking at all the circumstances objectively, that is from the perspective of a reasonable person in the position of the innocent party, the contract breaker has clearly shown an intention to abandon and altogether refuse to perform the contract'.[540] There must be an immediate threat to the express contract terms for the employer to have committed a repudiation; it may not be enough for the employer merely to voice a difference of opinion about the contract terms, even if it should subsequently turn out that the employee was right. This is an application of the principle, enunciated by the House of Lords in *Woodar Investment Development Ltd v Wimpey Construction UK Ltd*,[541] that an assertion of a contractual right, unless it is made in bad faith, does not amount to a repudiation merely because it 'has proved to be wrong in law'. For the assertion to amount to a repudiation, the guilty party must '[evince] an intention not to be bound by the contract'.[542] Similarly, '[t]he mere fact that an employer is of the opinion, albeit mistakenly, that there is something to be discussed with his

---

[534] *Hilton v Shiner Ltd – Builders Merchants* [2001] IRLR 727. In *Land Securities Trillium Ltd v Thornley* [2005] IRLR 765 the EAT held that it was permissible for the employment tribunal to analyse both the claimant's job description and how her duties operated in practice and also to conclude that the extent and nature of the changes to her duties did not fall within the scope of the contract. See also *McBride v Falkirk Football and Athletic Club* [2012] IRLR 22: imposition of a change of role without prior notice, consultation or discussion.
[535] A wholly exceptional case is *Adams v Charles Zub Associates Ltd* [1978] IRLR 551, where an employer's failure to pay on time was excused on the grounds of unanticipated cash-flow difficulties.
[536] *Tullett Prebon plc v BGC Brokers LP* [2011] IRLR 420.
[537] *Lewis v Motorworld Garages Ltd* [1985] IRLR 465.
[538] *London Borough of Waltham Forest v Omilaju* [2005] IRLR 35, [19] (Dyson LJ); see also *GAB Robins (UK) Ltd v Triggs* [2007] IRLR 857.
[539] *Logan v Commissioners of Customs and Excise* [2004] IRLR 63, [30]–[33] (Ward LJ); *Royle v Greater Manchester Police Authority* [2007] ICR 281.
[540] *Eminence Property Developments Ltd v Heaney* [2010] EWCA Civ 1168, Etherton LJ at [61], approved in *Tullett Prebon plc v BGC Brokers LP* [2011] IRLR 420, Maurice Kay LJ at [20].
[541] [1980] 1 WLR 277, 280 (Lord Wilberforce).
[542] [1980] 1 WLR 277, 299 (Lord Scarman).

employee about the contract is a very long way from the employer taking up the attitude that he is not under any circumstances at all going to be bound by it'.[543]

This doctrine could place an employee in a difficult position where the employer fails to respect contractual rights to which the employee believes, with reason, he or she is entitled. However, it should not be taken as exempting employers from the consequences of actual, as opposed to anticipatory, breaches of the express contract terms relating to pay and hours; nor does it prevent the operation of the implied obligation to maintain trust and confidence in an appropriate situation. The best view would seem to be that the assertion of a genuine but mistaken view of the contract *might* give rise to a repudiation in a given case, where other factors also point in that direction; at least as far as employment contracts are concerned, there is no rule to the effect that the good faith nature of an erroneous assertion of rights, by itself, prevents there being a repudiation.[544] In *BBC v Beckett*[545] the employee was at first dismissed for committing an act of negligence which led to the injury of a fellow worker and then, on appeal, offered a job at a lower grade and in a different department. He refused to accept this and resigned. The employment tribunal found that the punishment inflicted on the employee was out of proportion to his offence, and that the employer's conduct amounted to a repudiation. On appeal it was argued that the employer had purported to exercise an express power in good faith and therefore could not be said to have committed a repudiatory breach, but the EAT held that the principle in *Woodar v Wimpey*[546] did not 'derogate from the general proposition that a party to a contract may so act that his conduct viewed objectively amounts to a fundamental breach of his contractual obligations':[547] accordingly, there had been a constructive dismissal.

As we have seen, the decisions of the EAT in *Hogg v Dover College*[548] and *Alcan Extrusions v Yates*[549] indicate that an employee faced with a repudiatory breach short of dismissal may not necessarily have to resign in order to force the issue of constructive dismissal; he or she may have the right to accept the repudiation and bring the original contract to an end, while then remaining in employment under a new contract.[550] This is because '[t]he question is not whether the relationship between the parties has ceased; the question is not whether there was any contract between the parties; the question is whether the particular contract under which the employee was employed by the employer at the relevant time was terminated by the employer'.[551] If the employee makes it clear that he or she is working under protest, they are not taken to have waived the right to terminate the original contract.[552] If this doctrine is correct it would mean, for example, that Mr Beckett could have accepted the inferior post offered to him by the BBC and

---

[543] *Financial Techniques (Planning Services) Ltd v Hughes* [1981] IRLR 32, 35 (Lawton LJ); see also *Frank Wright & Co (Holdings) Ltd v Punch* [1980] IRLR 217.

[544] *Financial Techniques (Planning Services) Ltd v Hughes* [1981] IRLR 32, 36–37 (Templeman LJ); see also *Brown v JBD Engineering Ltd* [1993] IRLR 568. See also Reynold and Palmer, 2005.

[545] [1983] IRLR 43.

[546] [1980] 1 WLR 277.

[547] [1983] IRLR 43, 46 (Neill J).

[548] [1990] ICR 39.

[549] [1996] IRLR 327.

[550] It should however be noted that not every purported variation by the employer will be classified as repudiatory: see *Robinson v Tescom Corp* [2008] IRLR 408, discussed at para 4.42 above.

[551] [1990] ICR 39, 43.

[552] Cf [1990] ICR 39, 44: 'the applicant accepted the employer's conduct as repudiatory and cannot, by his subsequent conduct, be said to have affirmed the original contract or any original contract as varied' (Garland J). See also *WE Cox Toner (International) Ltd v Crook* [1981] IRLR 443, *Henry v London General Transport Services* [2002] IRLR 472.

then brought an action for unfair dismissal, without needing to quit; the employment tribunal, on finding that he was unfairly dismissed, would then have had the power to order his reinstatement into the job which he previously occupied.[553] Reinstatement is very rarely awarded, and financial compensation is a much more likely outcome;[554] nonetheless, *Hogg* and *Alcan* place the employee in a far better position than decisions which suggest that the employee has no choice but to resign if he or she wishes to claim unfair dismissal in response to unjustified disciplinary action or a unilateral change in terms and conditions.[555]

More generally, there will be no ready assumption of waiver or estoppel in a case where the employee's hesitation is due to ignorance of his or her rights;[556] where the employer's breach of contract also amounts to a statutory wrong which the employee has no power to waive;[557] or where the breach is regarded as a continuing one involving the making of unlawful pay deductions month to month.[558] The Court of Appeal has confirmed that once a fundamental breach has occurred the option of acceptance or affirmation lies with the innocent party[559] although differing views were expressed on how ready tribunals should be to find affirmation in an employment context.[560]

5.72   Although a constructive dismissal necessarily entails a repudiatory breach of contract by an employer, this does not mean that the dismissal is automatically unfair. The tribunal may find that the dismissal was for a potentially fair reason and that the employer acted reasonably in the circumstances; a unilateral cut in pay could, for example, be justified by external cuts in the funding received by the employer.[561] This means that while unfair dismissal law goes part of the way to entrenching the existing contract terms against unilateral variation, it also grants overriding priority to certain interests of the employer, in particular its claims to have the right to reorganise production processes in the interests of efficiency.[562]

'Self-dismissal' and resignation

5.73   Where the employee commits a repudiatory breach of contract, the elective theory holds that the contract is only terminated once the employer, as the innocent party, has accepted the breach. Since the contract is ended by the employer, there is a dismissal for the purposes of section 95(1)(a). Because, *ex hypothesi*, the employee has committed a serious contractual breach, the employer may not find it difficult to establish that there was a potentially fair reason for the dismissal and that it acted reasonably in the circumstances, but this does not inevitably follow. A more effective way of protecting the employer in these circumstances is the idea of 'self-

---

[553] ERA 1996, ss 113–114.
[554] See para 5.142 below.
[555] *Hunt v British Railways Board* [1979] IRLR 379, distinguished in *Hogg* [1990] ICR 39, 44.
[556] *Peyman v Lanjani* [1985] Ch 457.
[557] *Reid v Camphill Engravers Ltd* [1990] IRLR 268.
[558] *New Southern Railway Ltd v Quinn* [2006] IRLR 266.
[559] *Buckland v Bournemouth University* [2010] IRLR 445.
[560] See Sedley LJ at [44], where he stated that tribunals 'can take a reasonably robust approach to affirmation'; cf. Jacob LJ at [54]-[56]: it takes 'rather a lot to find affirmation on the facts in an employment contract' given the difficulties that employees may face.
[561] Eg *Kent County Council v Gilham* [1985] ICR 227. See paras 5.114 and 5.173 *et seq* below.
[562] See para 5.173 *et seq* below.

dismissal', but this doctrine is of doubtful validity. In *Gannon v JC Firth Ltd*[563] it was suggested that employees who walked out of their employment in the course of a wildcat strike had thereby 'dismissed themselves', and in *London Transport Executive v Clarke*[564] Lord Denning MR argued that the same reasoning should apply in a case where the employee took seven weeks' leave of absence without permission. The majority of the Court of Appeal found, however, that there had been a dismissal in this case, and applied the elective theory to section 95(1). According to Templeman LJ, 'the acceptance by an employer of repudiation by a worker who wishes to continue his employment notwithstanding his repudiatory conduct constitutes the determination of the contract of employment by the employer ...'[565] However, his Lordship distinguished the situation where the employee walked out *without* wishing to continue the relationship of employment; here, the employer accepted the repudiation by taking no action to affirm the contract and the unfair dismissal legislation could apply only if there was a constructive dismissal, in the sense that the employee was responding to a repudiatory breach by the employer.[566] The latter part of this dictum amounts to saying that in such a situation the elective theory will not, in fact, apply.

It is already the case that the application of the elective theory to section 95 causes a certain blurring of the categories of termination by the employer, on the one hand, and constructive dismissal, on the other.[567] Leaving aside the questions of the employee's common law rights[568] and the effective date of termination[569] it should make little or no difference to the outcome of an unfair dismissal claim whether the dismissal falls into one category or the other. There is no particular advantage a finding that the dismissal is constructive since it is possible for the tribunal to hold that a constructive dismissal is fair in the circumstances[570] just as much as in the case of dismissal by the employer. Although tribunals have a discretion to increase or reduce compensatory awards if there is a failure to comply with applicable provisions of the ACAS Code of Practice on Disciplinary and Grievance Procedures they can do so only where this failure is 'unreasonable';[571] it is to be hoped that a failure properly to identify whether a dismissal is 'direct' or 'constructive' and to act accordingly would not be held to constitute unreasonable failure. However, if the elective theory is strictly applied to the case of the employee who quits employment without good reason, what looks at first sight like resignation could turn out to be dismissal by the employer: if the employee's departure is analysed as a repudiatory breach, the contract is only brought to an end by the employer's acceptance, which would bring the situation within section 95(1)(a). This

[563] [1976] IRLR 415; not followed in *Rasool v Hepworth Pipe Co Ltd* [1980] IRLR 88.
[564] [1981] ICR 355.
[565] [1981] ICR 355, 368.
[566] [1981] ICR 355, 368.
[567] See, eg, *Hogg v Dover College* [1990] ICR 39, where the employer's repudiation was analysed alternately as a dismissal under s 95(1)(a) and as a constructive dismissal under s 95(1)(c), and *Shook v Ealing London Borough Council* [1986] ICR 314 where it was suggested that in a case where the employer gave notice in breach of contract, this was best analysed as a constructive dismissal. Curran, 1994, argues that employer repudiation is best analysed as a dismissal under paragraph (a); cf R White, 1997.
[568] For employees to gain a specific remedy to prevent the employer acting on a wrongful dismissal, they must show that they have refused to accept the employer's repudiatory breach and are seeking to keep the contract on foot (see para 5.54 *et seq* above). If this common law action fails, an action for unfair dismissal may subsequently be brought on the basis that the dismissal was constructive; for these purposes, a provisional claim may be lodged with the employment tribunal: *R v East Berkshire Health Authority, ex p Walsh* [1984] ICR 743, 749 (Sir John Donaldson MR); *Shook v Ealing London Borough Council* [1986] ICR 314, 325.
[569] See para 5.80 *et seq* below.
[570] *Kent County Council v Gilham* [1985] ICR 227.
[571] TULRCA 1992, s 207A, inserted by EA 2008, s 3; see further paras 2.21 and 5.151.

would leave very little room for an effective concept of employee resignation, and may explain why in *Clarke* Templeman LJ was reluctant to apply the elective theory to this kind of case.

As the law currently stands, then, the notion of self-dismissal is not completely discredited: conduct of the employee which evinces an intention not to carry on with the relationship of employment may be regarded as terminating the contract of employment, according to the automatic theory. Such conduct may be regarded, in effect, as a form of resignation; but the conditions for drawing such an inference are strict. In principle it should not be appropriate to do so, for example, in the context of industrial action, since it is very rarely the intention of striking employees to give up the employment in question and seek another; by definition, they are normally seeking improvement to the terms and conditions contained in their *existing* contracts of employment. This is not to say that conduct of this sort is not *repudiatory*, simply that it is not, in itself, the equivalent of resignation.

5.74   An agreement by the employee that he or she will be taken to have resigned in the event of committing a particular breach of discipline or some other act is likely to be struck down for statutory purposes by section 203(1) of ERA 1996, which, subject to some stated exceptions, renders void any contract or contract term purporting to exclude the operation of the Act. In *Igbo v Johnson Matthey Chemicals Ltd*[572] the employee was granted extended holiday leave, as a condition of which she signed a document stating that if she failed to return to work on an agreed date, 'your contract of employment will automatically terminate on that date'. When she came back from her holiday she was ill, sent her employer a medical certificate and reported for work after the date agreed for her return. She was told that her employment had come to an end. In the Court of Appeal it was held that Mrs Igbo had been dismissed, the agreement for self-dismissal being void under section 203(1) (previously section 140 of EPCA 1978): otherwise 'the whole object of the Act can be easily defeated by the inclusion of a term in a contract of employment that if the employee is late for work on the first Monday in any month, or indeed on any day, no matter for what reason, the contract shall automatically terminate'.[573]

On the other hand, section 203(1) will not be read as invalidating a genuinely consensual termination of employment. Where it can be shown that the employee agreed to resign by virtue of the severance terms offered by the employer, the resignation will probably not, as we have seen, constitute a dismissal;[574] nor will the severance agreement necessarily be struck down under section 203. This is because 'in the resolution of industrial disputes it is in the best interests of all concerned that a contract made without duress, for good consideration, preferably after proper and sufficient advice, and which has the effect of terminating a contract of employment by mutual agreement (whether at once or on some future date) should be effective between the contracting parties'.[575]

---

[572] [1986] IRLR 215, overruling *British Leyland (UK) Ltd v Ashraf* [1978] IRLR 330; see also *Midland Electric Manufacturing Co Ltd v Kanji* [1980] IRLR 185; *Tracey v Zest Equipment Co Ltd* [1982] IRLR 268. See the useful discussion of this decision in Freedland, 2003: pp 432–439.
[573] [1986] IRLR 215, 217 (Parker LJ).
[574] *Logan Salton v Durham County Council* [1989] IRLR 99.
[575] [1989] IRLR 99, 103.

Expiry of limited-term contract

5.75 Section 95(1)(b) provides that there is a dismissal for the purposes of the Act where an employee is employed under a limited-term contract and that contract terminates by virtue of the limiting event without being renewed under the same contract.[576] A 'limited-term contract' is one where '(a) the employment under the contract is not intended to be permanent, and (b) provision is accordingly made in the contract for it to terminate by virtue of a limiting event'.[577] A 'limiting event means:

(a) in the case of a contract for a fixed-term,[578] the expiry of the term,
(b) in the case of a contract made in contemplation of the performance of a specific task, the performance of that task, and
(c) in the case of a contract which provides for its termination on the occurrence of an event (or the failure of an event to occur), the occurrence of the event (or the failure of the event to occur).[579]

Prior to 1 October 2002 the legislation was confined to expiry of a fixed-term contract without renewal, a provision which excluded 'task contracts' to carry out a particular job unless they contained a set date when they were due to terminate.[580] In addition the legislation did not restrict the use of fixed-term contracts, unlike many continental systems which provided that if there was no good reason for the use of a fixed-term contract, or if a contract was renewed more that the minimum number of times allowed for by legislation, the employee was treated as if he or she was employed on a contract of indefinite duration, with the full protection of dismissal law.[581] Since 1 October 2002 protection against non-renewal of the more widely-defined 'limited-term contract' has applied, and restrictions have been introduced on the use of successive fixed-term contracts by FTER 2002 in order to comply with Directive 99/70/EC.[582] A provision that restricts the duration of a contract, where that contract (referred to here as the 'subsequent contract') has previously

---

[576] This provision was substituted by FTER 2002, reg 11, Sch 2, para 3(1), (7). Prior to 25 October 1999, s 197(1) of ERA 1996 provided that, if the employment was in the form of a fixed term of at least one year and the dismissal took the form of the non-renewal of the contract under s 95(1)(b), the employee lost the right to claim unfair dismissal if he or she agreed in writing, before the expiry of the term, to exclude this right. This provision was repealed by ERelA 1999 and only valid waivers agreed before 25 October 1999 remain effective.

[577] ERA 1996, s 235(2A).

[578] A provision for earlier termination by notice does not prevent a contract being for a 'fixed term': *Allen v National Australia Group Europe Ltd* [2004] IRLR 847.

[579] ERA 1996, s 235(2B).

[580] *Wiltshire County Council v NATFHE* [1980] ICR 455. Curiously the Acas Code of Practice on Disciplinary and Grievance Procedures 2009 excludes only the non-renewal of fixed-term contracts and not limited-term contracts from its scope.

[581] On Spain, see Auvergnon and Gil y Gil, 1994; on Germany, Daübler and Le Friant, 1985; on France, Pélissier, Supiot and Jeammaud, 2008: pp 421–442.

[582] See further para 3.52. Clause 5.1 of the Framework Agreement required Member States to introduce one or more of the following measures: (a) objective reasons justifying the renewal of such contracts or relationships; (b) the maximum total duration of successive fixed-term contracts; and (c) the number of renewals of such contracts or relationships. Clause 5.2 required Member States to determine under what conditions fixed-term employment contracts or relationships are to be regarded as 'successive' and deemed to be contracts or relationships of indefinite duration. In Case C-268/06 *Impact v Minister for Agriculture and Food* [2008] IRLR 552 the ECJ held that clause 5(1) did not have direct effect as it did not contain any unconditional and sufficiently precise obligation capable of being relied on by an individual before a national court.

been renewed[583] or the employee has previously been employed on a fixed-term contract, will be of no effect and the employee will be deemed to be a permanent employee, provided that:

(a) the employee has been continuously employed under the subsequent contract, or under that contract taken with a previous fixed-term contract, for a period of four years or more (disregarding any period of employment before 10 July 2002)[584] and
(b) the employment of the employee under a fixed-term contract was not justified on objective grounds –
　(i)　where the subsequent contract has been renewed, at the time when it was last renewed;
　(ii)　where the subsequent contract has not been renewed, at the time when it was entered into.[585]

The employee is deemed to be permanently employed as from the date on which he or she acquired four years' continuous employment or the date on which the subsequent contract was last entered into or renewed, whichever is the later. The application of these measures may be modified in relation to a particular employee or description of employees by means of a 'collective agreement'[586] or 'workforce agreement'. [587]

　The 'objective grounds' that may justify continued employment under a fixed-term contract are not defined in the Regulations or the Directive. However in *Adeneler v Ellinikos Organismos Galaktos* the ECJ held that the concept of 'objective reasons', which was designed to prevent abuse:

> ... must be understood as referring to precise and concrete circumstances characterising a given activity, which are therefore capable in that particular context of justifying the use of successive fixed-term employment contracts. Those circumstances may result, in particular, from the specific nature of the tasks for the performance of which such contracts have been concluded and from the inherent characteristics of those tasks or, as the case may be, from pursuit of a legitimate social-policy objective of a Member State.[588]

On this basis a national rule that there was an objective reason if the conclusion of a fixed-term contract was required by legislation did not suffice as if did not "permit objective and transparent criteria to be identified in order to verify whether the renewal of such contracts actually responds to a genuine need, is appropriate for achieving the objective pursued and is necessary for that purpose".[589]

---

[583] Renewal includes extension: FTER 2002, reg 1(2).

[584] The date by which the Directive should have been transposed. The UK Government took the view that giving any retrospective effect to the restrictions on renewal would place unnecessary burdens on business: *Government Response to the Final Consultation on the Draft Fixed Term Employees (Prevention of Less Favourable Treatment) Regulations 2002*, DTI, 2002.

[585] Reg 8. See Case C-251/11 *Huet v Université de Bretagne occidentale* for the requirements of the Directive in relation to the permanent contract.

[586] See para 2.8 above.

[587] See para 2.11 above.

[588] Case C-212/04, [2006] IRLR 716, paras 69, 70. See generally Zappala, 2006.

[589] Above, para 74. See also *Deutsche Lufthansa v Kumpan* [2011] ICR 1278; *Duncombe v Secretary of State for Children, Schools and Families* [2011] IRLR 498, discussed at para 3.52 above.

5.76   The requirement in the British Regulations for employment to be 'continuous' in order for the measures against abuse to apply could constitute a considerable restriction on their effectiveness, given the ease with which continuity can be broken by employers;[590] applying general principles would allow employees to be employed on successive fixed-term contracts of less than four years' duration indefinitely, provided that the employer ensured that there was a two-week gap between them to break continuity. In *Adeneler v Ellinikos Organismos*[591] the ECJ held that a national rule which provided that fixed-term contracts were not regarded as 'successive' if they were separated by more than 20 working days was precluded by the Directive. On this basis the British courts should attempt to construe the continuity rules differently in this context to prevent the purpose of the Directive being circumvented.

The Labour Government declined to make it automatically unfair under FTER 2002 to dismiss an employee to prevent him or her acquiring permanent status,[592] concluding that it was unnecessary to do so because it is unlawful to dismiss a fixed-term employee for enforcing or seeking to enforce their rights.[593] However it is far from clear that it was unnecessary. An employee who is dismissed prior to acquiring permanent status never acquires a right to permanence and it is difficult, under these circumstances, to identify any other right that has been infringed.[594] If this view is correct, such a dismissal would need to be judged on ordinary unfair dismissal principles.

Frustration

5.77   At common law a contract discharged by frustration is terminated automatically, regardless of the 'opinions, or even knowledge' of the parties concerned;[595] accordingly, a contract of employment discharged in this way cannot be said to have been terminated by a dismissal within the meaning of section 95(1)(a) or (c), each of which relies on one of the parties taking steps to bring the contract to an end. There is no doubt that the doctrine of frustration can apply to a contract of employment, as to most other kinds of contract. Supervening events which could, potentially, give rise to frustration include the death of either party[596] (although, for the purposes of redundancy compensation only, the death of the employer is deemed by the Act to be a dismissal[597]); an illness or injury of the employee which is either immediately disabling or, over

[590] *Booth v United States of America* [1999] IRLR 16; see generally para 3.59 *et seq*.
[591] Above note 588.
[592] *Government Response to the Final Consultation on the Draft Fixed Term Employees' (Prevention of Less Favourable Treatment) Regulations 2002*, DTI, 2002, regulation 6. Cf the proposal by the TUC: *The Fixed-Term Employees (Prevention of Less Favourable Treatment) Regulations 2002*, TUC.
[593] FTER 2002, reg 6.
[594] Unless the employee has refused or proposed to refuse to forego the right to acquire permanent status, so bringing him or her within Regulation 6(3)(a)(vi). In *Department for Work and Pensions v Webley* [2005] IRLR 288 the Court of Appeal held that the termination of a fixed-term contract by effluxion of time could not, of itself, constitute less favourable treatment by comparison with a permanent employee nor could it represent a 'detriment'.
[595] *Hirji Mulji v Cheong Yue SS Co Ltd* [1926] AC 497, 509; *GF Sharp & Co Ltd v McMillan* [1998] IRLR 632.
[596] Eg, *Cutter v Powell* (1795) 6 Term Rep 320, which would now be classified as a case of frustration.
[597] ERA 1996, s 136(5). Other events which in accordance with any statute or rule of law operate to terminate the contract are also treated as dismissal by the employer for the purposes of statutory redundancy payments: s 136(5).

a longer term, leads to prolonged absences;[598] and the imprisonment of the employee.[599] However, it is also an established principle that a contract will not be frustrated merely by a supervening event or *force majeure* if the parties have made provision for that event in their contract, and have expressly allocated the risk of its occurring; nor if the frustrating event is brought about by the fault of one of the parties. The application of these principles to the contract of employment has been far from straightforward.

5.78   There is much to be said for the view that in the normal contract of employment which is terminable by either party on short notice, the risk of a supervening event is already dealt with in the contract; if, for example, the employee is incapable of working by virtue of injury or illness, the employer has the option of terminating the contract by giving notice. Similarly, if the employee is imprisoned as a consequence of committing a criminal offence, it might be thought that he or she has thereby committed a repudiatory breach of contract, for which the employer may summarily dismiss him or her. In these cases, the doctrine of frustration is simply not needed to protect the employer's position at common law. The doctrine is invoked only because the employer wishes to avoid dismissing the employee under section 95(1)(a) and thereby triggering the unfair dismissal jurisdiction.

In *Harman v Flexible Lamps Ltd*[600] this prompted Bristow J to observe that 'in the field of employment the concept of discharge by operation of law, that is frustration, is normally only in play where the contract of employment is for a long term which cannot be determined by notice. Where the contract is terminable by notice, there is really no need to consider the question of frustration'. This sensible approach was, nevertheless, disapproved by the Court of Appeal in *Notcutt v Universal Equipment Co (London) Ltd*.[601] Dillon LJ gave two reasons for his view that frustration could apply to a contract terminable by short notice: such a contract 'may none the less be intended in many cases by both parties to last for many years'; and 'the power of the employer to terminate the contract by notice is subject to the provisions for the protection of employees against unfair dismissal'. Neither reason is very convincing. The bare expectation of the parties that the contract will continue indefinitely in no way detracts from the employer's right, at common law, to terminate it by giving notice;[602] while Dillon LJ's second observation is the very reason normally given for limiting the doctrine of frustration, namely that it could defeat the aim of the Act in providing a degree of job security for the employee. In the case of long-term illness, for example, unfair dismissal law normally imposes certain minimum procedural requirements on the employer, in relation to the need to establish the nature of the illness, investigate the possibility of the employee being found alternative work and consider the feasibility of hiring a temporary replacement.[603] These procedural obligations are avoided at a stroke if the illness is regarded as frustrating the contract, thereby bringing it to an end without any dismissal.

Nor does a finding of dismissal necessarily decide the issue of fairness in the employee's favour; on the contrary, the tribunal may go on to find that the employer acted reasonably in

---

[598] *Egg Stores (Stamford Hill) Ltd v Leibovici* [1977] ICR 260; *GF Sharp & Co Ltd v McMillan* [1998] IRLR 632.

[599] *FC Shepherd & Co Ltd v Jerrom* [1986] IRLR 358.

[600] [1980] IRLR 418, 419.

[601] [1986] IRLR 218, 220–221.

[602] See para 5.12 *et seq* above; there may be an exception if the contract contains a job security clause, see para 5.31 *et seq*.

[603] *Lynock v Cereal Packaging Ltd* [1988] IRLR 510; see para 5.135 below.

the circumstances under section 98(4) of the Act. It would be difficult to envisage the tribunal reaching any other conclusion in a case, for example, where the employee's criminal conduct, whether in or out of work, had resulted in his imprisonment for a substantial period of time. The event which is alleged to give rise to frustration will normally constitute a potentially fair reason for dismissal,[604] but there is a difference between using the notion of a supervening event to find that dismissal was fair, and invoking the doctrine of frustration to decide that no dismissal even took place: the former route allows the tribunal to consider the merits of the case, the latter does not. The effects of frustration, in terms of wiping out statutory entitlements, may be far reaching. An employee whose contract is frustrated cannot qualify for a statutory redundancy payment, nor for the statutory right to receive notice prior to the termination of employment, since both these sets of rights depend on upon there being a dismissal.[605] Moreover, where the contract is discharged by frustration, the parties may have great difficulty in determining precisely when the contract came to an end.

Notwithstanding *Notcutt*, the EAT stressed in *Williams v Watsons Luxury Coaches Ltd*[606] that cases of frustration of employment contracts will be 'rare occurrences' and that 'the court must guard against too easy an application of the doctrine'; the lay members in this case also thought that 'the doctrine of frustration when applied to employment contracts is one which, unless severely limited in its scope, can do harm to good industrial relations as it provides an easy escape from the obligations of investigation which should be carried out by a conscientious employer',[607] but this is not a view which had the support of Wood J.

5.79   In deciding whether a particular contract of employment is frustrated, the essential question is whether it can be said that the future performance of the employee had become impossible at the time in question. For this purpose a distinction should be drawn between, on the one hand, 'an event (eg a crippling accident) so dramatic and shattering that everyone concerned will realise immediately that to all intents and purposes the contract must be regarded as at an end' and, on the other, 'an event, such as illness or accident, the course and outcome of which is uncertain'.[608] For example, in the case of illness the court will look both at the nature of the disabling event (the length of the illness, its likely future duration, its effect on the employee's ability to work) and at the contract terms to see whether the provision made for termination and for payment of wages or sick pay in the event of illness impliedly exclude the doctrine. In *Egg Stores (Stamford Hill) Ltd v Leibovici*[609] the EAT listed a number of other factors to be considered, including the length of the employee's previous employment, the parties' expectations of continuing employment, the availability of a replacement, the risk to the employer of incurring statutory or other obligations by retaining the employee in employment, and 'whether in all the circumstances a reasonable employer could be expected to wait any longer'. This type of inquiry is very wide-ranging, and seems to be inviting the tribunal to consider issues which should, more properly, be considered under the heading of the test of fairness under section 98(4). In *Notcutt v Universal Equipment Co*

---

[604] See para 5.112 below.
[605] See generally *GF Sharp & Co Ltd v McMillan* [1998] IRLR 632.
[606] [1990] IRLR 164, 166.
[607] [1990] IRLR 164, 167.
[608] *Egg Stores (Stamford Hill) Ltd v Leibovici* [1977] ICR 260, 265.
[609] [1977] ICR 260, 265. See also *Marshall v Harland and Wolff Ltd* [1972] IRLR 90.

(London) Ltd[610] the Court of Appeal took a somewhat simpler approach in concluding that once the employee's doctor had told him that he would probably never work again following a heart attack, the contract was frustrated.

The Court of Appeal has also held that the imprisonment of the employee may give rise to frustration on the grounds of his or her resulting inability to perform the contract, notwithstanding that, at common law, 'self-induced frustration' of this kind would not normally suffice to discharge the primary obligations of the party at fault.[611] This seems nothing more than an opportunistic use of the doctrine to avoid the application of the Act,[612] and although the result may well have been the right one, the same end could have been achieved more consistently with principle by a finding that the dismissal was fair in the circumstances. The same objection can be made to the application of the doctrine to incapability of performance arising out of the need for an employee to be suspended pending a period of re-skilling.[613]

Effective date of termination

5.80   The date of dismissal, known as the 'effective date of termination' (or EDT), is important for a number of purposes under the Act and can affect the employee's claim for unfair dismissal in two particularly significant ways. The first concerns the length of the employee's continuous employment: leaving aside the few cases where no qualifying service is needed, the employee must have been continuously employed for a period of two years 'ending with the effective date of termination' if employed on or after 6 April 2012 (or for a period of one year if the period of continuous employment began before that date).[614] The second relates to what is, in effect, the limitation period for unfair dismissal claims: the employment tribunal shall not consider the applicant's complaint unless it is presented before the end of a period of three months beginning with the EDT, subject to a limited power of the tribunal to extend this period where the employee can show that it was not reasonably practicable to present the complaint within the time limit.[615] The EDT is a 'statutory construct which depends on what has happened between the parties over

---

[610] [1986] IRLR 218.

[611] *FC Shepherd & Co Ltd v Jerrom* [1986] IRLR 358; cf *Hare v Murphy Bros Ltd* [1974] IRLR 342; *Four Seasons Healthcare Ltd v Maughan* [2005] IRLR 324.

[612] The Court of Appeal in *Shepherd* was influenced by the argument that it was the *applicant* who was attempting to rely on his own fault to exclude frustration in what was regarded as a mirror image of the usual context in which frustration is pleaded: Lawton LJ at 362, Mustill LJ at 364; see also *Ananwu v London South Bank Students Union* ULEAT 0280/03, EAT 20 November 2003. However this is not an answer to the wider policy objections to the operation of the doctrine in this context.

[613] In *Gryf-Lowczowski v Hinchingbrooke Healthcare NHS Trust* [2006] IRLR 100 Gray J held that the contract of the claimant, a specialist consultant surgeon, had not been frustrated as there was a realistic possibility of another NHS Trust agreeing to re-skill him to enable him to resume his duties but did not regard the situation as one where the doctrine should not apply.

[614] ERA 1996, s 108(1) as amended by SI 2012/989. On continuity of employment, see para 3.59 *et seq* above.

[615] ERA 1996, s 111(2). Where a dismissal is with notice, the tribunal can consider a complaint after the notice is given but before the EDT: s 111(3). In *Rai v Somerfield Stores Ltd* [2004] IRLR 124 the EAT held that a notice which enables the employer to terminate the contract of employment only if the employee does or does not perform a particular act specified in the notice, which only the employee can choose whether or not to perform, is not a 'notice' for the purpose of s 111(3).

time and not on what they may agree to treat as having happened'.[616] It cannot, therefore, be fixed by agreement between the parties.[617]

5.81   Under section 97(1) of the Act, the 'effective date of termination':

(a) in relation to an employee whose contract of employment is terminated by notice, whether given by his employer or by the employee, means the date on which the notice expires;

(b) in relation to an employee whose contract of employment is terminated without notice, means the date on which the termination takes effect; and

(c) in relation to an employee who is employed under a limited-term contract which terminates by virtue of the limiting event without being renewed under the same contract, means the date on which the termination takes effect.[618]

The principal issue which this provision leaves open is the effect on the EDT of a breach of contract by the employer. If, for example, the employer fails to give sufficient notice of termination, is the EDT the date on which the notice expires, or the date when it should have expired? The courts have opted for the first of these possibilities,[619] which is apparently in line with the reference to 'the notice', read as the notice actually given, in section 97(1)(a). However, the Supreme Court has held that the EDT cannot be earlier than the date on which the employee 'knows - or, at least, has a reasonable chance to find out - that he or she has been dismissed'.[620] The Court held that the doctrine of constructive knowledge had no place in this context and that the tribunal could consider the employee's behaviour in assessing whether she had had a reasonable opportunity to find out what the letter dismissing her contained; there was a need 'to be mindful of the human dimension' in deciding what was reasonable. [621]More generally the Court did not consider that:

> ... what has been described as 'the general law of contract' should provide a preliminary guide to the proper interpretation of s 97 of the 1996 Act, much less that it should be determinative of that issue... Section 97 should be interpreted in its setting. It is part of a charter protecting employees' rights. An interpretation that promotes those rights, as opposed to one which is consonant with traditional contract law principles, if to be preferred.[622]

---

[616] *Fitzgerald v University of Kent at Canterbury* [2004] IRLR 300, [20] (Sedley LJ). In *Wang v University of Keele* [2011] IRLR 542 the EAT held that in the case of both oral dismissal and dismissal by written notice, unless the contract provides otherwise, a notice given during the working day cannot take effect until the following day.

[617] In addition, any such agreement would be void under ERA 1996, s 203: *Fitzgerald*, above, [22] (Sedley LJ).

[618] Substantially the same provision applies in the context of redundancy compensation (the 'relevant date': ERA 1996, s 145) but with some further qualifications: see para 5.163 below. On the meaning of 'limited-term contract' and 'limiting event' see para 5.75 above.

[619] *TBA Industrial Products Ltd v Morland* [1982] IRLR 331. On the difficult questions of construction which may arise in this context, see *Dedman v British Building and Engineering Appliances Ltd* [1974] ICR 53; *Chapman v Letherby and Christopher Ltd* [1981] IRLR 440. In a case of constructive dismissal the EDT will normally be the date on which the employee communicates to the employer his or her decision to leave the employment: *Edwards v Surrey Police* [1999] IRLR 456.

[620] *Gisda Cyf v Barratt* [2010] IRLR 1073, Lord Kerr at [34]

[621] Lord Kerr at [30].

[622] Lord Kerr at [37]. The Court considered that the very short time limit for applying for interim relief, discussed in para 5.153 below, put the matter 'beyond plausible debate': Lord Kerr at [44].

The Court rejected arguments that this would provoke uncertainty, and:

> ... [i]n any event, certainty, although desirable, is by no means the only factor to be considered in determining the proper interpretation to be given to s 97. What will most strongly influence that decision is the question of which construction most conduces to the fulfilment of the legislative purpose. And, of course, an employer who wishes to be certain that his employee is aware of the dismissal can resort to the prosaic expedient of informing the employee in a face-to-face interview that he or she has been dismissed.[623]

Section 97(2) provides that where the employee does not receive the minimum *statutory* notice to which he or she was entitled, the EDT shall be extended for certain purposes[624] to the date on which the statutory notice, had it been given, would have expired; the existence of this provision can be read as impliedly supporting the proposition that *contractual* notice cannot be taken into account under section 97(1)(a), if it is not actually given. If, having received notice from the employer, the employee exercises the statutory right to give a shorter counter-notice under section 95(2), the EDT will be the date on which the counter-notice expires.[625] Where the employer's notice is deemed still to be the operative cause of the termination of employment but the employee accepts the employer's invitation to leave early, the position is more complex; for clarity's sake employers would be best advised to withdraw the original notice and substitute a second notice which contains the earlier date. [626]

5.82   A second situation to consider is that in which the employer summarily dismisses the employee without good cause: is the contract terminated forthwith, or at some later date when the employee has accepted the employer's repudiatory breach? The elective theory would give the employee the right to delay acceptance where he or she has a 'legitimate interest' in doing so, and it would not perhaps be stretching the notion of 'legitimate interest' too far to include a case where the employee sought to delay the EDT in order to ensure that he or she acquires the necessary continuity of employment. This argument could be applied for example, to the situation in which the employer dismisses the employee a few days or weeks short of the completion of the qualifying period, for the sole purpose of ensuring that the employee does not acquire the protection of the Act. However, in general the attitude of the courts has been that in the interests of certainty, the automatic theory should determine the EDT under section 97(1)(b), so that the termination

---

[623] Lord Kerr at [43].

[624] These include the establishment of the period of continuity of employment for the purposes of s 108(1) and the calculation of the basic award for unfair dismissal (s 119(1)) but not the period of three months for the claim in time under s 111(2). See *Fox Maintenance Ltd v Jackson* [1977] IRLR 306. In *Harper v Virgin Net Ltd* [2004] IRLR 390, s 97(2)(b) was invoked to preclude a claim for damages for loss of a chance of recovering compensation for unfair dismissal in circumstances where the employee had not been given the three months' notice to which she was entitled under her contract; see further para 5.22 above.

[625] *Thompson v GEC Avionics Ltd* [1991] IRLR 488. The effect of s 95(2) is that the employee is still regarded as having been dismissed in this situation.

[626] *TBA Industrial Products Ltd v Morland* [1982] IRLR 331. In *Palfrey v Transco plc* [2004] IRLR 916 the EAT found on the facts that the employers had done this, but also opined that there should be scope for variation even if they had not and that *TBA Industrial Products Ltd* was *per incuriam*.

'takes effect' when the act of summary dismissal takes place.[627] In *Stapp v Shaftesbury Society*[628] the Court of Appeal expressly ruled out the possibility of using the elective theory to extend the period of continuous employment by holding that 'the effect of ... summary dismissal in fixing the effective date of termination' cannot be questioned, although this was not a case where the employer was found to have ended the contract for the sole purpose of avoiding the application of the Act. It is possible that the approach of the Supreme Court to this area, described above in para 5.81, may persuade the courts to take a different view in future.

5.83   A third situation is that in which the employer, this time in accordance with the contract, operates a disciplinary procedure which results in the confirmation of an earlier decision to summarily dismiss the employee: is the EDT the date upon which an initial decision to dismiss is taken, or is the employee dismissed only once his or her internal rights of appeal are exhausted? The courts have taken the view that the EDT is normally the earlier of these two dates, unless the contract itself provides for the employee to be suspended from employment, but continuing to receive wages or salary, during the period of any appeal (as opposed to being dismissed with the possibility of reinstatement), in which case the EDT is the date on which the employer informs the employee of the outcome of the appeal.[629]

Employees who fail to comply with the three-month time limit for presenting an unfair dismissal complaint because they are awaiting the outcome of an internal appeal may seek to rely on section 111(2) of ERA 1996, whereby the period for presenting a complaint may be extended where the tribunal 'is satisfied that it was not reasonably practicable for the complaint to be presented before the end' of this period. Whether or not an extension is granted is a matter for the discretion of the individual tribunal.[630] Section 111(3)–(4) of ERA 1996 makes explicit provision for a complaint to be made after notice of dismissal has been given but while the employee is still in employment, and in a case where the employee seeks to keep the contract on foot by applying to the High Court for a declaration or injunction it has been normal for him or her to make an application to an employment tribunal at the same time, pending the outcome of the other action.[631] Employees now need to be mindful of the provisions of the Acas Code of Practice on

---

[627] The leading judgment is that of Browne-Wilkinson J in *Robert Cort & Son Ltd v Charman* [1981] IRLR 437; see also *Dedman v British Building and Engineering Appliances Ltd* [1973] IRLR 379; *Stapp v Shaftesbury Society* [1982] IRLR 326; *Batchelor v British Railways Board* [1987] IRLR 136; *BMK Ltd v Logue* [1993] IRLR 477; *Kirklees Metropolitan Council v Radecki* [2009] IRLR 555 (EDT when employee ceased to pay salary, the last vestige of any performance of the contract, which it had indicated it would cease to do and employee knew it had done); although cf *Shook v Ealing London Borough Council* [1986] ICR 314.

[628] [1982] IRLR 326, 330.

[629] *Drage v Governors of Greenford High School* [2000] IRLR 314, CA, reviewing earlier case law including *Savage v J Sainsbury Ltd* [1981] ICR 1. See also *McMaster v Antrim Borough Council* [2011] IRLR 235, NICA, where the employer refused to reinstate the employee following a successful appeal. On the use of the time limit provisions in ERA 1996 s 111 to overcome restrictive readings of the EDT, see para 2.17 above.

[630] *Bodha v Hampshire Area Health Authority* [1982] ICR 200, not following *Crown Agents for Overseas Governments and Administration v Lawal* [1979] ICR 103, where it was suggested that an extension would regularly be granted where an application was delayed by reason of an internal procedure; see further para 2.17. In *Marley (UK) Ltd v Anderson* [1996] IRLR 163 the Court of Appeal held that although an employee's complaint on the initial ground put forward was time-barred, the tribunal did have jurisdiction to consider the complaint on a different ground which had subsequently come to light and which the employee had raised, by amendment to his existing claim, within a reasonable period after acquiring the relevant knowledge. See also *Cambridge and Peterborough Foundation NHS Trust v Crouchman* UKEAT/0108/09, CEA, 8 May 2009.

[631] This course was recommended in *R v East Berkshire Health Authority, ex p Walsh* [1984] ICR 743, 753 and *Shook v Ealing London Borough Council* [1986] ICR 314, 325.

Disciplinary and Grievance Procedures, particularly the requirement to appeal against the initial decision to dismiss.[632]

5.84   The three-month period for bringing claims is extremely short in comparison to the normal six-year limitation period for actions in breach of contract,[633] but the justification for this is the less formal procedure which operates in employment tribunals.[634] Under the early unfair dismissal legislation a 28-day period applied; when this was extended to the current three months, Lord Denning thought that as a result there was even 'less reason for granting an indulgence to the complainant'.[635] The circumstances when it will be regarded as not 'reasonably practicable' to make a claim in time are limited.[636] It is not normally acceptable to delay a claim pending the outcome of other legal proceedings, such as criminal proceedings relating to an alleged offence or a claim for the jobseeker's allowance,[637] although it will normally be relevant that the employee was hoping to avoid litigation by seeking alternative remedies.[638]

FAIRNESS OF DISMISSAL

5.85   Section 98 of ERA 1996 sets up a two-stage test of fairness which separates the *reasons for dismissal* from the *reasonableness of the employer's conduct*. At the first stage the employer is required to show that the dismissal took place for reasons which were 'potentially fair', that is to say capable of providing a legitimate basis for the termination of employment. Although the burden of proof is placed on the employer at this stage, the statutory categories of potentially fair reasons are very broadly defined, and only a completely unreasoned or arbitrary dismissal (or one where the tribunal is not satisfied that the potentially fair reason was the real reason) is likely to fall outside their scope. However, the employee may nevertheless win the case at this point if the tribunal finds that the dismissal took place for one of a strictly-defined set of automatically unfair reasons which are deemed to be illegitimate *per se*. Conversely, the employer may be able to show that the dismissal took place in circumstances where it enjoys an immunity (these are also narrowly defined). Otherwise, the tribunal proceeds to the second stage, at which it assesses whether the employer 'acted reasonably or unreasonably' in treating the reason relied upon as a sufficient reason, in the circumstances, for dismissing the employee. The Act's explicit reference to the employer's conduct stresses that the standard here is more procedural than substantive, that is to say, concerned less with the fairness of the outcome than with the fairness of the process by which it was arrived at. The standard is also variable, in the sense that the tribunal must take into account the 'size and administrative resources of the employer's undertaking', and embodies a strong element of discretion: the tribunal must decide whether the employer acted reasonably 'in accordance with equity and the substantial merits of the case' in question.

---

[632] See further paras 5.125 *et seq.*

[633] Limitation Act 1980, s 5.

[634] This point was discussed by the Donovan Commission, which recommended a maximum period of five working days from the dismissal: Cmnd 3623, 1968: p 147.

[635] *Wall's Meat Co Ltd v Khan* [1979] ICR 52, 59.

[636] See para 2.17 above.

[637] *Wall's Meat Co Ltd v Khan* [1979] ICR 52.

[638] See *Schultz v Esso Petroleum Ltd* [1999] IRLR 488.

Discretion also affects the question of remedies. The grant of the remedies of reinstatement and re-engagement is discretionary, and an employer may be able to resist one or the other on the grounds of its impracticability. Even if an order involving re-employment is made, it cannot be specifically enforced; at best the employee will obtain additional compensation. Compensation may be awarded under a wider range of heads of loss than allowed at common law, but the tribunal may reduce the compensatory award for, among other things, the employee's non-compliance with the ACAS Code of Practice on Disciplinary and Grievance Procedures or contributory fault.

Relevant reasons

5.86 Under section 98(1) of ERA 1996, the employer is required to show 'the reason (or, if more than one, the principal reason) for the dismissal' and to show that it comes within one or other of the 'gateways' of potentially fair reasons.[639] The Court of Appeal has recently set out the correct approach to the burden of proof where the employee contests the reasons put forward by the employer.[640] There is no burden on the employee to disprove those reasons, let alone positively to prove a different reason even where he or she alleges that there was an automatically unfair reason for dismissal, although some evidence to support that allegation will need to be provided. 'It is sufficient for the employee to challenge the evidence produced by the employer to show the reason advanced by him for the dismissal and to produce some evidence of a different reason'.[641] It is then for the tribunal to consider the evidence as a whole and make findings of primary fact on the basis of direct evidence or by reasonable inferences from primary facts established by the evidence. If the tribunal is not satisfied that the principal reason was that asserted by the employer, it may – but need not – find the reason to be that asserted by the employee; the employer may fail in establishing a potentially fair reason but may not fail in disputing the case advanced by the employee.[642]

The only relevant 'reason' or 'principal reason' for the purpose of section 98(1) is one which the employer had at the time of the dismissal;[643] and it is in relation to *this* reason that the employer's conduct is to be judged. Under section 98(4), whether a dismissal is fair depends on whether 'the employer acted reasonably or unreasonably in treating *it* as a sufficient reason' (emphasis added); the 'it' is the reason actually relied on.[644] As a result 'what must be shown to be reasonable and sufficient is the employer's action in treating the reason shown by him (the employer) as the reason for dismissing the employee'.[645] The distinction between the two stages of inquiry – the first, at which the reason or reasons for dismissal are established and classified as potentially fair or otherwise, and the second, at which the reasonableness of the employer's conduct is assessed – is fundamental to the approach of the Act to evaluating fairness in dismissal.[646] On the face

---

[639] ERA 1996, s 98(1).

[640] *Kuzel v Roche Products Ltd* [2008] IRLR 530.

[641] Mummery LJ (who gave the only reasoned judgment), above, at [57].

[642] Above, [58]–[60].

[643] See the discussion below for what constitutes the time of dismissal in this context.

[644] *W Devis & Sons Ltd v Atkins* [1977] IRLR 314, 338 (Viscount Dilhorne).

[645] *W Devis & Sons Ltd v Atkins* [1977] IRLR 314, 320 (Lord Simon of Glaisdale).

[646] *Beedell v West Ferry Printers Ltd* [2000] IRLR 650, 655; *Post Office v Foley; HSBC Bank plc v Madden* [2000] IRLR 827; cf *Midland Bank plc v Madden* [2000] IRLR 288, 291–292, which undermined this distinction.

of it, the first stage begins with a purely factual inquiry – what was the reason actually relied on by the employer? – while the question of whether that reason was objectively justifiable in the circumstances is one for the second stage.

5.87   The main issue facing the tribunal under section 98(1), properly understood, is the identification of the reason which motivated the dismissal. Some leeway is allowed to the employer by the principle that in an appropriate case the tribunal may infer, from the evidence offered, that the employer was motivated by a reason which was not clearly expressed as such at the relevant time. In *Abernethy v Mott, Hay and Anderson*[647] Cairns LJ said:

> A reason for the dismissal of an employee is a set of facts known to the employer, or it may be of beliefs held by him, which cause him to dismiss the employee. If at the time of his dismissal the employer gives a reason for it, that is no doubt evidence, at any rate as against him, as to the real reason, but it does not necessarily constitute the real reason.

Cairns LJ gave three examples of situations in which the given reason might not be the 'real reason': where a false reason is given out of kindness; where the employer 'might have difficulty in proving the facts that actually led him to dismiss'; and where he 'may describe his reason wrongly through some mistake of language or of law'. In the first case, where a false reason is deliberately given, the burden on the employer of showing that he had a different reason to that given at the time may be particularly heavy, but is not insurmountable. In the second case, where the employer did not have good grounds at the time for taking the decision to dismiss, the reason may well be potentially fair but it is doubtful that the employer will be held to have acted reasonably under section 98(4). For the tribunal 'to accept as a reasonably sufficient reason for dismissal a reason which, at least, in respect of an important part was neither established in fact nor believed to be true on reasonable grounds is ... an error of law'.[648] This is because, as we shall see, the requirements of procedural fairness normally impose an obligation upon the employer at the very least to formulate the charges against an employee; if the employer is not even clear, at the time of dismissal, what the reason for it was, a breach of procedural fairness is likely to be made out. By extension, if the tribunal finds that the employer could have dismissed the employee fairly for one reason which was backed up by evidence, but that the employer was in fact motivated by a different reason for which there was no adequate evidence, the dismissal will most likely be held to be unfair on procedural grounds: the tribunal cannot impute to the employer a reason which it did not have at the time.[649] If the tribunal is not satisfied that the reason given by the employer, albeit potentially fair, was the real or principal reason it is under no obligation to determine what the real reason was; the dismissal will be unfair regardless of whether there are additional procedural defects.[650]

Cairns LJ's third category, that of misdescription, is the one most likely to assist the employer. The employer does not necessarily have to have used the same words as those used in the statutory definition of the potentially fair reasons, such as 'misconduct' or 'incapability', when dismissing the employee. The *Abernethy* principle can even extend to a case of constructive dismissal, where

[647] [1974] IRLR 213, 215.
[648] *Smith v Glasgow City District Council* [1987] ICR 796, 804.
[649] *Smith v Glasgow City District Council* [1987] ICR 796, 804.
[650] *ASLEF v Brady* [2006] IRLR 576, [72]-[84].

the employer may not realise at the time that a dismissal is taking place. In *Ely v YKK Fasteners (UK) Ltd*[651] Waite LJ said that 'if resort can be had to a state of facts known to and relied on by the employer at the time, for the purpose of substituting a valid reason for any invalid or misdescribed reason given by the employer through misapprehension or mistake, there seems to me to be every justification for extending that principle to enable resort to be had to a state of facts known to and relied on by the employer, for the purposes of supplying him with a reason for dismissal which, as a consequence of his misapprehension of the true nature of the circumstances, he was disabled as treating as such at the time'.

In this case, the employee led his employer to believe that he was about to resign, but changed his mind before a formal resignation was submitted. The employer treated the employment at an end; this was found to be a constructive dismissal. It was held that the employer was entitled to argue that the dismissal was for 'some other substantial reason' under section 98(1)(b) of the Act. In effect, the employer can treat as the reason for dismissal the reason it had for the *conduct which gave rise to the dismissal*, in other words the conduct which amounted to a repudiatory breach; or, as Lord Browne-Wilkinson has put it, 'the only way in which the statutory requirements of the Act of ... [1996] ... can be made to fit a case of constructive dismissal is to read section ... [98(1)] as requiring the employers to show the reasons for their conduct which entitled the employee to terminate the contract thereby giving rise to a deemed dismissal'.[652] This might seem to be a considerable enlargement of the *Abernethy* principle, but it needs to be remembered that a constructive dismissal is not automatically unfair.[653] It therefore seems unavoidable that an employer can seek to show that its reasons for acting as it did are also the reasons for the dismissal for statutory purposes; otherwise it would be impossible to find that a constructive dismissal was ever fair. *Ely* does not formally seek to disturb the principle that the tribunal cannot substitute for the reason given a reason which the employer did not actually rely on.

5.88 The ACAS Code of Practice on Disciplinary and Grievance Procedures states that an employee should be informed of the reasons for dismissal.[654] In addition the employer is under a separate statutory obligation, contained in section 92 of ERA 1996, to give a written statement of the reasons for dismissal within 14 days of the employee requesting such a statement,[655] except where the dismissal was constructive.[656] The statement is admissible in any proceedings, and it seems that the main justification for the right to such a statement is to assist the employee in relation to legal claims arising out of the dismissal.[657] However, in general[658] the right vests only in employees with at least two years' continuity of employment at the time of dismissal for those employed on or after 6 April 2012 (or one year's continuity of employment for those whose period

---

[651] [1993] IRLR 500, 503.

[652] *Berriman v Delabole Slate Ltd* [1985] ICR 546, 555–556.

[653] See para 5.72 above.

[654] Code of Practice, para 21; see further para 5.125 *et seq*.

[655] ERA 1996, s 92(2). An employee who is dismissed while pregnant or during a period of ordinary or additional maternity or adoption leave is entitled to a statement without having to request one: ERA 1996, 92(4), (4A).

[656] ERA 1996, s 92(1).

[657] ERA 1996, s 92(5).

[658] No minimum period of employment is required if an employee is dismissed while pregnant or during a period of ordinary or additional maternity or adoption leave: ERA 1996, s 92(4), (4A).

of continuous employment began before that date).[659] The requirement for a lengthy period of continuous employment to enjoy the right was introduced by the Employment Act 1989, which set a period of two years;[660] before that only six months' continuity was needed. At the time it was argued that the qualifying period for this purpose should be the same as that applying to unfair dismissal generally,[661] and this remains the case. This is not a very convincing reason since numerous legal rights arising out of dismissal are not dependent on continuity in this sense. These include claims for the jobseeker's allowance, for the purposes of which it may be important to establish that the claimant was not dismissed for good cause, in which case he or she faces disqualification for being 'voluntarily unemployed'. The employee may also wish to show that dismissal took place for an automatically unfair reason, for which in most cases no period of continuity is needed, or to bring a claim for damages for wrongful dismissal.

The employer is required to provide a statement as a distinct document which must 'be of such a kind that the employee, or anyone to whom he may wish to show it, can know from reading the document itself why the employee has been dismissed'; the document may refer to other materials but must in itself 'contain a simple statement of the essential reasons for the dismissal'.[662] If the employer unreasonably fails to provide a written statement, or provides one whose particulars are inadequate or untrue, the employee may complain to an employment tribunal, which has the power to declare what it considers to have been the real reasons for dismissal and to award the employee a sum equal to two weeks' pay.[663]

It does not follow, however, that the reasons given by the employer in this written statement will necessarily be those found to be the relevant ones for the purposes of an unfair dismissal claim. Under the *Abernethy* principle, the employer may apparently still seek to show that the reasons given at the time were misdescribed, and that the real reasons were otherwise. But the result is unfortunate, since the penalty against the employer for misleading the employee in this way is the relatively insignificant award of two weeks' pay. It is arguable that the courts should invoke in this context the principle of estoppel, to restrict the right of the employer to seek to go back on its statement to the employee.

5.89   The principle that the employer cannot rely on a reason which it did not have at the time of dismissal but only *might* have had means that facts emerging after the dismissal cannot be taken into account in the employer's favour in establishing what the relevant reason was or in showing that it acted reasonably in treating as sufficient.[664] It follows that the time of dismissal needs to be pinpointed with some degree of precision for this rule to operate. On one view of the statute the date of 'dismissal' is defined by reference to the 'effective date of termination'. In other words, when the termination is by notice, this is the date upon which that notice expires.[665] However, this creates the risk of undermining procedural fairness in potentially allowing the employer

---

[659] ERA 1996, s 92(3), as amended by SI 2012/989.
[660] EA 1989, ss 15(1) and 29(6) and Sch 9, amending EPCA 1978, s 53(2), now ERA 1996, s 92(3).
[661] Mr Patrick Nicholls, HC Official Report, Standing Committee A, col 374, 28 February 1989.
[662] *Horsley Smith and Sherry Ltd v Dutton* [1977] ICR 594, 597.
[663] ERA 1996, s 93. The complaint must be presented within the same time limits as a claim for unfair dismissal in respect of that dismissal: s 93(3). The provision for adjusting an award for non-compliance with the Acas Code of Practice on Disciplinary and Grievance Procedures, described in para 2.21 above, does not apply to such complaints.
[664] *W Devis & Sons Ltd v Atkins* [1977] IRLR 314.
[665] ERA 1996, s 97(1).

to find a reason, or justification, for dismissal subsequent to having given the employee notice (although equally it means that a change in circumstances after notice but before the EDT may make an otherwise fair dismissal unfair[666]). In *Parkinson v March Consulting Ltd*[667] the Court of Appeal held that where the employment was terminated by notice, the employer's reason should be determined both by reference to the reason for giving the prior notice to terminate and the reason at the time the dismissal occurred. This decision was applied in the later Court of Appeal decision in *Alboni v Ind Coope Retail Ltd.*[668] The approach in these cases has been criticised as confusing the point at which a dismissal takes place with the reason for dismissal, which should be identified by reference to the date when 'the reason has crystallised by the employer giving notice of dismissal to the employee'.[669] There is considerable substance in this criticism. However, in terms of the language, if not the purpose, of the statute it is defensible to say that 'dismissal' means the termination of the employee's actual employment.[670]

5.90   A further problem has been created by the insistence of the courts that where there are internal disciplinary proceedings which result in summary dismissal, the EDT is the date of any initial decision to dismiss and not the later date upon which the dismissal is confirmed by a higher tribunal or authority within the internal process.[671] This principle has been only partially qualified by the more recent view that the EDT can be extended to the end of the appeal in a case where the employee was suspended pending the hearing of the appeal.[672] While this qualification is helpful, it does not address the situation of an employee who is excluded from employment altogether during the hearing of the appeal and therefore only has the hope of 'reinstatement' if the appeal goes in his or her favour. In such cases, employees who wish to preserve their statutory rights may be forced to present what may be an otiose complaint of unfair dismissal in order to avoid being out of time.[673] Moreover, if the rule against taking into account irrelevant reasons is taken literally, reasons which emerge *after* the initial decision is made cannot help the employer; nor can conduct based on those reasons. In *West Midlands Co-operative Society Ltd v Tipton*[674] the House of Lords modified the effect of the rule just stated by deciding that the appeal process should be taken as one with the rest of the internal procedure for the purposes of assessing whether the employer acted reasonably. However, the House of Lords held in the same decision that evidence emerging during the appeal could only be used to support the original reason given, and not a separate and better reason which had not been relied on at the time. An employer faced with a newly-emerging reason would, it seems, have to rescind the dismissal and start the internal process all over again, whether or not this was objectively necessary to safeguard the employee's right to procedural fairness.

---

[666] See *Stacey v Babcock Power Ltd* [1986] ICR 221 (failure to offer employee given notice of redundancy fresh employment when it became available before his notice expired); *White v South London Transport Ltd* [1998] ICR 293.

[667] [1997] IRLR 308, 312 (Evans LJ).

[668] [1998] IRLR 131.

[669] [1998] IRLR 107: editorial commentary on *Alboni*.

[670] *Parkinson v March Consulting Ltd* [1997] IRLR 308, 312 (Evans LJ).

[671] *J Sainsbury Ltd v Savage* [1981] ICR 1.

[672] *Drage v Governors of Greenford High School* [2000] IRLR 314.

[673] See para 5.83 above.

[674] [1986] AC 536.

Employer's immunity

5.91   The employer is effectively immune from unfair dismissal liability in two situations. The first situation of immunity is in relation to complaints where 'it is shown that the action complained of was taken for the purpose of safeguarding national security'; thereupon, 'the tribunal shall dismiss the complaint'.[675] The second situation arises where, at the time of dismissal, the employee was taking part in a strike or other industrial action in the circumstances defined by sections 237 and 238 of TULRCA 1992. Section 237 covers situations where there is an unofficial strike or industrial action. Section 238 refers to situations of 'non-unofficial' strikes or industrial action where all those taking part at the relevant time at the applicant's establishment are dismissed and none of them is re-employed by the same employer or an associated employer for a period of three months. The immunity provided to the employer by section 238, however, has no application where the employee is dismissed for taking 'protected industrial action' within the meaning of the Act.[676] Neither do the immunities provided by either section apply where the employee is dismissed, or selected for redundancy,[677] for one of a number of specified reasons, as defined in the Act.[678] The reasons specified relate to leave for family reasons; health and safety; acting as a representative of the workforce for the purpose of the Working Time Regulations or as a candidate for such a position; acting as an employee representative or as a candidate for such a position; the taking of time off for dependants; flexible working; jury service; and (in the case of section 237 only) making a protected disclosure. The rationale for this list is not immediately clear. The first five categories arise out of the requirements of EC Directives on the matters concerned, but this is not true of the others. If compliance with EU law is not the issue here, there seems no reason for not extending the same approach to all cases of automatically unfair dismissal.[679] Nor is it at all clear (unless it is simply the result of a drafting mistake) why the immunity should be lifted in the case of a protected disclosure for cases of unofficial industrial action under section 237, but not under section 238. It should also be noted in this context that neither section 237 nor section 238 prevents an employee who was the victim of unlawful discrimination in dismissal from bringing a claim to an employment tribunal under EqA 2010[680]

Automatically unfair reasons

5.92   The following reasons for dismissal, or for selection on grounds of redundancy,[681] are automatically unfair:[682] reasons related to the employee's membership or non-membership of an

---

[675] ETA 1996, s 10(1). Cf *B v BAA plc* [2005] IRLR 927, where the EAT held that the HRA 1998 required that the impact of ERA 1996, s 98(4) should not be excluded from such cases. It is difficult to reconcile this decision with the statutory language.

[676] TULRCA 1992, s 238A. See para 11.79 *et seq* below.

[677] Within the meaning of ERA 1996, s 105(1), (9).

[678] TULRCA 1992, ss 237(1A), 238(2A).

[679] On the automatically unfair reasons, see para 5.92 below.

[680] See further ch 6.

[681] In these cases it must be shown that the circumstances constituting the redundancy applied equally to one or more other employees in the same undertaking who held positions similar to that held by the employee and who have not been dismissed: ERA 1996, s 105(1)(b).

[682] The term 'automatically unfair' is not used in the Acts, but has entered general usage.

independent trade union, participation in the activities, or use of services, of such a union at the appropriate time, or failure to accept an employer's offer that is designed to move workers away from collectively-agreed terms of employment;[683] reasons relating to a 'prohibited list' under the blacklisting regulations;[684] reasons related to leave for family reasons or flexible working;[685] the employee's assertion of certain statutory rights against the employer;[686] the exercise of rights relating to the protection of part-time workers, employees on fixed-term contracts and agency workers;[687] reasons relating to statutory working time standards,[688] the enforcement of the national minimum wage,[689] and claims for employment-related tax credits;[690] certain reasons concerned with health and safety at work;[691] in the case of certain retail employees, the employee's refusal to work on Sundays;[692] the making by an employee of a 'protected disclosure';[693] jury service;[694] exercising rights in relation to study and training;[695] taking part in specified circumstances in protected industrial action;[696] performing the functions of an employee representative or candidate for such position;[697] fulfilling specified representative roles, or being a candidate for such positions, in relation to the establishment or operation of a European Works Council or information or consultation procedure;[698] fulfilling specified representative roles, or being a candidate for such positions, or engaging in specified activities in relation to information and consultation at national level[699] or in relation to a European Public Limited-Liability Company or European Cooperative Society;[700] performing the functions of a trustee of an occupational pension scheme;[701] and specified acts relating to the statutory recognition and derecognition procedures.[702] It is also automatically unfair to dismiss an employee[703] for the exercise of the right to be accompanied, or to accompany, at a grievance or disciplinary hearing or hearing relating to flexible working[704] or for the transfer of an undertaking or a reason connected with the transfer that is not an 'economic, technical or organisational reason entailing changes in the workforce'.[705]

[683] TULRCA 1992, ss 152(1), 153. See further para 8.5 below.
[684] ERA 1996, ss 104F, 105(7M); ERABR 2010, reg 12.
[685] ERA 1996, ss 99, MPLR 1999, reg 20; ERA 1996, ss 104C, 105(1).
[686] ERA 1996, ss 104, 105(1), (7).
[687] PTWR 2000, reg 7; FTER 2002, reg 6; AWR 2010, reg 17; ERA 1996, s 105(1), (7E), (7F), (7N).
[688] ERA 1996, ss 101A, 105(1), (4A).
[689] ERA 1996, ss 104A, 105(1), (7A).
[690] ERA 1996, ss 104B, 105(1), (7B).
[691] ERA 1996, ss 100, 105(1), (3).
[692] ERA 1996, ss 101, 105(1), (4).
[693] ERA 1996, ss 103A, 105(1), (6A).
[694] ERA 1996, ss 98B, 105(1), (2A).
[695] ERA 1996, ss 104E, s105(7BB).
[696] TULRCA 1992, s 238A; ERA 1996, s 105(1), (7C).
[697] ERA 1996, ss 103, 105(1), (6).
[698] TICER 1999, reg 28; ERA 1996, s 105(1), (7D).
[699] ICER 2004, reg 30; OPPSCER 2006, reg 17, Sch, para 5; ERA 1996, s 105(1), (7H), (7I);
[700] ECSIER 2006, reg 31; EPLLCEIR 2009, reg 29; see also CCBMR 2007, regs 46, 47; ERA 1996, s 105(1), (7G), (7J), (7K).
[701] ERA 1996, ss 102, 105(1), (5).
[702] TULRCA 1992, Sch A1, paras 161, 162. There is also provision to make it automatically unfair to dismiss or select for redundancy on grounds relating to participation in education or training (ERA 1996, ss 101B, 105(4B)) and pension enrolment (ERA 1996, ss 104D, 105(7JA)) but at the time of writing these provisions have not been brought into force.
[703] But not to select an employee for redundancy in relation to the right to accompany or to be accompanied at disciplinary or grievance hearings or hearings relating to flexible working; the reasons for this omission are unknown.
[704] ERelA 1999, s 12; FWPR, reg 16.
[705] TUPE 2006, reg 7(1).

In addition a 'spent conviction' under the Rehabilitation of Offenders Act 1974 is not a proper ground for dismissal.[706]

5.93   The principal advantage of these provisions is that where they apply, they close off any possibility of the conduct being shown to be reasonable under section 98(4): the second stage of inquiry is short-circuited and the tribunal makes an immediate finding of unfair dismissal. This prevents the employer from seeking to justify the dismissal by showing that the needs of the business or some other instrumental consideration made it reasonable to dismiss the employee; nor is it a defence that the employer acted reasonably in the sense of following a course of action which a reasonable employer, in the same circumstances, might have followed; nor is it enough for the dismissal to have complied with the requirements of procedural fairness. The categories of automatically unfair reasons therefore represent substantive rights of employees which may not, on the whole, be weighed in the balance against the managerial or business-related interests of the employer. In addition, no qualifying period of employment is needed to assert these rights (with the exceptions of dismissal in connection with a transfer of the undertaking[707] and a remedy for dismissal for a 'spent conviction'[708]).

Where the employee has the requisite continuity of employment to bring a complaint of unfair dismissal to an employment tribunal section 98(1) places the burden of identifying the reason on the employer, whether or not the employee is seeking to argue that the reason is automatically unfair.[709] Where the employee lacks continuity it had for many years been assumed that the burden of proof in establishing an automatically unfair reason rested with the employee because, without continuity, the categorisation of the reason as automatically unfair is a point which goes to the jurisdiction of the tribunal, and, as such, must be established by the complainant (the employee) on the balance of probabilities. This was the ruling of the Court of Appeal (Lord Denning MR dissenting) in the trade union membership case of *Smith v Hayle Town Council*.[710] Eveleigh LJ considered that the statutory provision for automatically unfair dismissal had to be construed narrowly as an exception to the general rule requiring an employee to show continuity of employment:

> ... when one considers that [TULRCA 1992, section 152] is in fact introducing an exception, one bears in mind the principle that it is for the person relying upon the exception to bring himself within it. Once the employer has established ... that the employee has not been employed for ... [the requisite period], the employer has, as it were, put up an obstacle to the employee obtaining advantage under ... [ERA 1996, s 98]. So [TULRCA 1992, s 152], in my

---

[706] Section 4(3)(b).

[707] TUPE 2006, reg 7(6).

[708] The Rehabilitation of Offenders Act 1974 does not provide a remedy for breach of s 4(3)(b); employees need to rely on the general unfair dismissal law: see *Property Guards Ltd v Taylor* [1982] IRLR 175.

[709] *Maund v Penwith District Council* [1984] ICR 143; *Kuzel v Roche Products Ltd* [2008] IRLR 530. Dismissal for taking part in 'protected industrial action' is an exception to this principle since, in that case, the employee must establish that this is the reason for dismissal in order for the tribunal to have jurisdiction. See para 11.79 below.

[710] [1978] ICR 996.

view, is worded to the intent that, and by the nature of its being an exceptions paragraph, the burden of proof must be upon the employee.[711]

This approach negated much of the benefit the employee derived from not needing to show continuity as it will inevitably be difficult to contradict the employer's own assertion of the reason which motivated it. In *Kuzel v Roche Products*,[712] discussed in para 5.86 above, the Court of Appeal, in setting out the general principles applicable to the burden of proving the reason for dismissal, which it saw as lying on the employer for all unfair dismissal cases governed by the 1996 Act, did not distinguish between cases where continuity was established and those where it was not.[713] Nor, however, did it expressly cast doubt on *Smith* which was rather puzzlingly described as ' a case on the issue of sufficiency of qualifying service for bringing an ordinary case of unfair dismissal rather than on the reason for dismissal'.[714] It seems, therefore, as if the burden of proof in cases where continuity has not been established may still remain with the employee although the matter is not free from doubt. Even if it does not so remain, where employers produce sufficient evidence to show that the reason was one other than the automatically unfair reason alleged by the employee this may suffice to defeat the claim. *Kuzel* itself (where the complainant had more than the year's continuous employment then required to claim) illustrates the point. Here, the employer failed to establish a potentially fair reason for dismissal but the complainant's allegation that she had been dismissed for making protected disclosures was also not 'made out'; rather, the reason for the complainant's dismissal was the 'catastrophic loss of temper' and failure to follow advice of his human resources director on the part of her line manager.

5.94 The content of the present categories of automatically unfair reasons owes as much to historical accident and *ad hoc* concerns of the legislature as anything else; it can hardly be regarded as an attempt to make a comprehensive statement of employees' civil or personal rights at work.[715]

(i) Reasons related to trade union membership and non-membership and blacklisting

5.95 The category of dismissals related to trade union membership and non-membership and trade union activities is largely a legacy of the legislation of the 1970s concerning freedom of association and the closed shop. Here, it seems that unfair dismissal law has simply been the mechanism through which policy towards the exercise of collective power has been implemented; if Parliament had intended to protect employees' expressions of opinion as such, it is odd that it

---

[711] [1978] ICR 996, 1002. Sir David Cairns at 1003 based his judgment more specifically on the wording of TULRA 1974, Sch 1, para 11(1) (now repealed) which required it to be 'shown' that the principal reason for dismissal was 'inadmissible' (the statutory language previously used to denote an automatically unfair reason for dismissal) in order for the requirement for a specified period of continuous employment to be disapplied.

[712] [2008] IRLR 530.

[713] TULRCA 1992, s 152 states that a dismissal shall be regarded as unfair for the purposes of Part X of ERA 1996 if it is for one of the reasons specified in s 152; s 154 disapplies the qualifying period.

[714] Mummery LJ (who gave the only reasoned judgment) at [41]. In the EAT *Smith* was assumed to govern cases where the complainant lacked continuity: [2007] IRLR 309 at [27].

[715] Deakin, 1996.

should have done so only in relation to trade union membership and not more broadly, extending to the expression of political opinions, for example. ERelA 2004 added protection against dismissal for failing to accept an offer by an employer that is designed to move workers away from terms of employment that are collectively agreed. ERABR 2010, in turn, added protection against dismissal in the context of blacklisting. The details of these statutory provisions are considered at greater length in our discussion of freedom of association and collective rights in chapter 8 below.

(ii) Reasons related to leave for family reasons or flexible working

5.96   Although pregnancy was established as an automatically unfair reason for dismissal with the introduction of this category in the EPA 1975, it was only in 1993 that the two-year qualifying period was removed, together with certain defences which had been available to employers.[716] Further changes were introduced partly as a consequence of decisions of the ECJ interpreting Directive 76/307 on Equal Treatment, and partly by virtue of Directive 92/85 on the Protection of Pregnant Workers. With the enactment of the Employment Relations Act 1999, further provision was made for protection in relation to maternity leave and, more generally, parental leave (following the adoption of EC Directive 96/34 on Parental Leave), and for protection with respect to time off for dependants.[717] The Employment Act 2002 introduced specific rights to paternity and adoption leave, and a right to request flexible working, with protection against dismissal in relation to the exercise of these rights.[718] The protection given to employees in relation both to pregnancy and to these other aspects of leave for family reasons is considered in chapter 6, below.

(iii) Assertion of a statutory right

5.97   Section 104 of the Act protects the employee against dismissal for the assertion of a 'relevant statutory right', either by initiating proceedings against the employer or by alleging an infringement of that right. This right, introduced initially by TURERA 1993, closed what had previously been an obvious gap in the law. Although it is immaterial whether the employee actually had the right, or whether it had been infringed, he or she must have made the claim in question 'in good faith',[719] and it is sufficient that he or she made it 'reasonably clear' to the employer what the right was, without specifying it exactly.[720] The provision applies to any right contained in ERA 1996 which is enforced by way of a complaint to an employment tribunal; the statutory right to minimum notice of termination of employment;[721] rights conferred by WTR 1998;[722] and certain of the rights contained in TULRCA 1992, namely the right not to have union dues deducted from pay

---

[716] TURERA 1993, s 24(1).

[717] See ERelA 1999, ss 7–8 and Sch 4. The relevant law is now contained in ERA 1996, ss 57A–57B, Part VIII and s 99, and in SI 1999/3312.

[718] See EA 2002, ss 1, 3, 47 and SI 2002/2788, SI 2002/3207 and SI 2002/3236.

[719] ERA 1996, s 104(2).

[720] ERA 1996, s 104(3).

[721] ERA 1996, s 86.

[722] Together with legislation applicable to merchant shipping and fishing vessels. See *McLean v Rainbow Homeloans Ltd* [2007] IRLR 14 and para 4.85 above.

without consent, the right not to be subjected to a detriment on specified trade union or collective bargaining grounds, and the right to time off for carrying out trade union duties or activities of a learning representative.[723] It does not, however, apply to infringements of contractual rights.[724]

(iv) The exercise of rights relating to study and training

5.98 It is automatically unfair to dismiss an employee for making a request in relation to study or training under the statutory provisions governing such requests or proposing to do so; bringing proceedings in relation to that right or alleging the existence of a circumstance which would constitute a ground for bringing such proceedings.[725] At the time of writing 'small employers' (those with fewer than 250 employees) are excluded from the rights relating to study and training.[726]

(v) The exercise of rights relating to the protection of part-time workers; employees on fixed-term contracts; and agency workers

5.99 The right of a part-time worker to be treated no less favourably than a comparable full-time worker unless that treatment can be justified objectively came into force in 2000;[727] that of a fixed-term employee to be treated no less favourably than a comparable permanent employee in 2002;[728] and that of an agency worker to the same basic working and employment conditions and other specified rights as non-agency workers recruited by the hirer in 2011.[729] All these rights were introduced as a result of EC Directives (Directive 98/23; Directive 99/70 and Directive 2008/104 respectively). There is protection against dismissal for a wide range of activities: bringing proceedings against the employer;[730] giving evidence or information in connection with proceedings brought by another worker or otherwise doing anything under the respective Regulations in relation to the employer or any other worker; alleging that the employer had infringed the Regulations (unless the allegation is false and not made in good faith); requesting a written statement of reasons for less favourable treatment (or, in the case of the Regulations relating to fixed-term employees, a statement of variation); or refusing or proposing to forego a

---

[723] TULRCA 1992, ss 68, 86, 145A, 145B, 146, 168, 168A, 169 and 170 respectively.

[724] In *Mennell v Newell & Wright (Transport Contractors) Ltd* [1997] IRLR 519 the applicant argued unsuccessfully that he was asserting a right relating to deductions from his wages under ERA 1996, ss 13–27 when he refused to sign a new contract, one term of which related to deduction of training costs from final salary; he could not show that he had ever alleged that the employer was in breach of a statutory right as required by s 104. A complaint about alleged unlawful deductions from wages and for threatening to commence tribunal proceedings is capable of amounting to asserting a statutory right: *Pearce v Dyer* UKEAT/0465/04/LA, 20 October 2004. In *Elizabeth Claire Care Management Ltd v Francis* [2005] IRLR 858 the EAT confirmed that failure to pay any of the claimant's salary constituted a breach of a relevant statutory right.

[725] ERA 1996, s 104E.

[726] SI 2010/303.

[727] ERelA 1999, s 19; SI 2000/1551.

[728] EA 2002, ss 45, 51(1); SI 2002/2034.

[729] SI 2010/93.

[730] For agency workers, the protections apply in relation to proceedings brought against the temporary work agency or hirer or other specified activities carried out in relation to them: AWR 2010, reg 17.

right conferred by the Regulations.[731] In the case of the Regulations covering fixed-term employees there is also protection against dismissal for refusal to sign a workforce agreement which can modify the statutory standards designed to prevent abuse of successive fixed-term contracts (the maximum total period for which employees may be employed on a fixed-term contract, the maximum number of successive fixed term contracts, and the objective grounds justifying the renewal of fixed-term contracts or engagement under successive fixed-term contracts) and for performing the functions or activities of a workforce representative or candidate for such a position.[732] However there is no express provision making it automatically unfair to dismiss a fixed-term employee to prevent him or her acquiring permanent status and it is open to doubt whether this is covered by the protection for enforcing or seeking to enforce a right under the Regulations.[733]

(vi) Enforcement of statutory rights in relation to working time, the national minimum wage and tax credits

5.100   In addition to the general right contained in section 104, specific provisions make it automatically unfair for the employer to dismiss the employee for reasons related to statutory standards in relation to working time, the national minimum wage, and employment-related tax credits (the working family tax credit and associated benefits). Dismissal of an employee for asserting rights under WTR 1998 is already covered by section 104.[734] In addition, it is automatically unfair to dismiss an employee for refusing, or proposing to refuse, to comply with a requirement imposed by the employer in contravention of a requirement contained in WTR 1998;[735] for refusing, or proposing to refuse, to forego a right conferred by those Regulations; and for failing to sign a workforce agreement or refusing to enter into, or to agree to vary or extend, any other agreement with the employer which may vary working time standards under those Regulations. Specific protection is also accorded against dismissal for performing the functions or activities of a workforce representative or candidate for such a position.[736] The provisions relating to the national minimum wage and tax credits also closely follow the model of section 104. Hence dismissal in respect of any action taken or proposed to be taken by or on behalf of the employee with a view to enforcing or otherwise securing the benefit of these rights, or in respect of action leading to the prosecution of the employer under the relevant legislation, is automatically unfair,[737] as is any dismissal taken for the reason that the employee either qualifies, or will or might qualify, for these rights. In relation to dismissals in relation to actions taken by

---

[731] SI 2000/1551, reg 7; SI 2002/2034, reg 6; SI 2010/93, reg 17. Employees are also protected against dismissal on the ground that the employer (or hirer or temporary work agency, as appropriate) believes or suspects that the employee has done or intends to do any of these things.

[732] See further paras 2.11 and 3.52 for the role of such agreements and representatives.

[733] This point is discussed further in para 5.76 above.

[734] ERA 1996, s 104(4)(d).

[735] In *McLean v Rainbow Homeloans Ltd* [2007] IRLR 14 the EAT held that the dismissal need not have occurred because the employee had positively asserted a right under WTR 1998; it was sufficient that the employee had refused to accede to a requirement that would have breached WTR and that the dismissal was because of that refusal.

[736] ERA 1996, s 101A.

[737] See ERA 1996, ss 104A(1) (minimum wage) and 104B (tax credit). The precise rights under NMWA 1998 and TCA 2002 in respect of which these provisions apply are spelled out in ss 104A(3) and 104B(1).

or on behalf of the employee, it is not necessary that the employee should actually have had the right in question or that it should have been infringed by the employer, as long as the claim to that effect is made in good faith.[738]

(vii) Health and safety

5.101   Section 100 of the 1996 Act, which governs dismissals on grounds related to health and safety, derives from European Union law, in this case Framework Directive 89/391 on Health and Safety.[739] Dismissal is deemed to be unfair if the reason or principal reason is that the employee was carrying out activities relating to his or her duties as a health and safety representative, or in connection with their membership of a health and safety committee, either in accordance with arrangements established pursuant to legislation or having been acknowledged as such a representative or member by the employer. Provision is also made for protection for employees who are designated by the employer to carry out activities in connection with the prevention or reduction of health and safety risks at work.[740]

Section 100 also provides that in a workplace where there is neither a health and safety committee nor health and safety representatives,[741] an employee who brings 'to his employer's attention, by reasonable means, circumstances connected with his work which he reasonably believed were harmful or potentially harmful to health and safety', may not be dismissed for doing so.[742] Employees are also protected against dismissal for taking part in consultations with their employer pursuant to the Health and Safety (Consultation) Regulations 1996[743] or in the election of representatives of employee safety.[744] Finally, in all workplaces, where an employee reasonably apprehends a 'serious and imminent' danger which he could not reasonably be expected to avert, he or she may not be dismissed for leaving the place of work or the dangerous part of it or, while the danger persists, refusing to return to it;[745] and in the same circumstances, an employee may not be dismissed for taking 'appropriate steps to protect himself or other persons from the danger',[746] these steps to be assessed by reference to circumstances including the employee's own knowledge

---

[738] ERA 1996, ss 104A(2), 104B(2).

[739] See para 4.95 above. See also ERA 1996, s 44, which provides protection against detrimental action short of dismissal in cases involving health and safety representatives.

[740] ERA 1996, s 100(1)(a), (b). In *Goodwin v Cabletel UK Ltd* [1997] IRLR 665, the EAT held that the way in which a designated employee carries out health and safety activities, as well as the actual doing of them, can fall within the protection.

[741] Or if there is such a representative or committee but it was not reasonably practicable for the employee to raise the matter by those means.

[742] ERA 1996, s 100(1)(c). See *Balfour Kilpatrick Ltd v Acheson* [2003] IRLR 683. This provision is not limited to harm at the employee's place of work or to employees: *Von Goetz v St George's Healthcare NHS Trust* EAT 1395/97.

[743] SI 1996/1513.

[744] ERA 1996, s 100(1)(ba); see further para 9.46.

[745] The source of the danger may be the behaviour of a fellow employee: *Harvest Press Ltd v McCaffrey* [1999] IRLR 778.

[746] The category of 'other persons' extends to protection of members of the public and is not confined to fellow employees of the applicant: *Masiak v City Restaurants (UK) Ltd* [1999] IRLR 780; *Von Goetz v St George's Healthcare NHS Trust* EAT 1395/97. In *Balfour Kilpatrick Ltd v Acheson* [2003] IRLR 683 the EAT suggested that the words 'or to communicate these circumstances by any appropriate means to the employer' be added to give effect to Art 13 of the Directive.

and the facilities and advice available to him at the time.[747] In this last case only, the dismissal will not be automatically unfair if the employer can show that the steps taken were so negligent that a reasonable employer would have dismissed the employee.[748]

A number of points arise for discussion here. First, it should be noted that section 100 confers greater protection on individual employees to make complaints in workplaces where there is no statutory or other representation,[749] out of recognition of the necessarily greater role played by the individual in these circumstances. Second, the protection conferred on employees who take steps to avert a danger to themselves or to 'other persons' complements the protection otherwise provided for 'whistleblowers' who alert third parties to dangers arising at the workplace.[750] However, the legislation contains the important qualification allowing the employer a defence where the 'reasonable employer' would have dismissed the employee for negligence. The notion of the 'reasonable employer' is derived from the extensive case law applying the test of reasonableness under section 98(4); its appearance here reintroduces into section 100 the kind of balancing act between employee rights, on the one hand, and the business needs of the employer, on the other, which is more characteristic of the general test of fairness in dismissal than it is of cases of automatically unfair dismissal. Finally the EAT has held that industrial action does not constitute 'reasonable means' of bringing an employer's attention to health and safety concerns, although an employee who leaves a workplace where he or she reasonably apprehends a 'serious and imminent' danger he or she cannot reasonably be expected to avert, and refuses to return to it while the danger persists, may not be dismissed.[751] Employees who leave the workplace when the terms of protection are not met may risk dismissal without redress if they are regarded as taking unofficial industrial action.[752] The line between the two may not be an easy one to draw.

(viii) Sunday work

5.102   The explicit right to protection against dismissal in relation to Sunday work only applies to retail workers.[753] The reason for their particular treatment is that until relatively recently, legislation prevented most shops from opening on Sunday, thereby indirectly protecting retail workers from being required to work on that day of the week.[754] When it was proposed that the legislation governing opening hours was liberalised, it was accepted by a number of employers'

---

[747] ERA 1996, ss 100(1)(d), (e), 100(2). In *Kerr v Nathan's Wastesavers Ltd* EAT 91/95, discussed IRLB 564, March 1997: p 9 the EAT warned against placing 'an onerous duty of enquiry' on an employee in a case such as this. The fact that the employer disagreed with the employee as to whether, for example, there were 'circumstances of danger' is irrelevant: *Oudahar v Esporta Group Ltd* [2011] IRLR 730.

[748] ERA 1996, s 100(3).

[749] Section 100(1)(c).

[750] On the wide scope of the phrase 'other persons' in this context see *Masiak v City Restaurants (UK) Ltd* [1999] IRLR 780 and *Von Goetz v St George's Healthcare NHS Trust* EAT 1395/97, and on protection for whistleblowers who make 'protected disclosures' see para 4.117 above.

[751] *Balfour Kilpatrick Ltd v Acheson* [2003] IRLR 683.

[752] See para 11.85 below.

[753] For discussion of discrimination on grounds of religion see para 6.46. See also *Copsey v WWB Devon Clays Ltd* [2005] IRLR 811, where the dismissal of a non-retail worker who refused, because of his religious beliefs, to agree to a contractual variation in his working hours which meant that he could be required to work on Sundays was found in the circumstances not to be unfair.

[754] See para 4.76 above.

groups and by the government that this should be done on condition that new protections were introduced for employees in these sectors.[755] This compromise was subsequently embodied in the Sunday Trading Act 1994 and is now consolidated in ERA 1996.

There are two broad categories of shop workers who potentially fall within the scope of protection. The first consists of 'protected shop workers', those employed as shop workers at the commencement of the 1994 Act (but not to work only on Sunday) and subsequently continuously employed in that capacity, and those who work under contracts such that they may not be required to work on Sunday even if the provisions of ERA 1996 were disregarded.[756] It is automatically unfair for an employer to dismiss a protected shop worker for refusing or proposing to refuse to do shop work on Sundays in general or on a particular Sunday.[757] However, a protected shop worker may lose this protected status at any time on or after the commencement date by agreeing to carry out Sunday work *and* giving the employer an 'opting-in notice' in the prescribed form: the notice must be in writing, must be dated and signed by the employee and must state that he or she wishes to work on Sunday and has no objection to working on Sunday.[758] The employer is also required to issue a written explanatory statement detailing these statutory rights.[759]

The second protected status created by the Act is that of 'opted-out shop worker'. This refers to workers who are not 'protected' and may therefore be required to work on Sundays, either because they were not employed as a shop worker by their current employer when the Act came into force or because, having been protected, they gave the employer an opting-in notice. Such a worker may give the employer an opting-out notice to the effect that he or she objects to Sunday working (and which must also be in writing, signed and dated). There is then a three-month gap before automatic unfair dismissal protection is acquired, but during which the employee may not be dismissed for having given the opting-out notice.[760] Two groups are not protected by ERA 1996 at all: these are shop workers who are 'opted-in'; and those employed to work only on Sundays.[761] These groups must rely on any protection they might have under general unfair dismissal law.

(ix) Protected disclosures

5.103 An employee who is dismissed for making a 'protected disclosure'[762] is regarded as automatically unfairly dismissed for the purposes of ERA Part X.[763] The law relating to protected disclosures is analysed in more detail in our discussion of protection of 'whistleblowers'.[764]

---

[755] For the background to the campaign to reform the Sunday trading laws, see Diamond, 1991, and on the controls over opening introduced in 1994, see Deakin, 1994b.

[756] ERA 1996, s 36.

[757] ERA 1996, s 101. Such workers are also protected against being subjected to any detriment for this reason: s 45.

[758] ERA 1996, s 36(5), (6).

[759] ERA 1996, s 42.

[760] ERA 1996, ss 40–42, 101(2), (3). Parallel provisions apply to detrimental action short of dismissal: s 45.

[761] ERA 1996, s 40(3)(b).

[762] 'Protected disclosures' are defined in detail in ERA 1996, ss 43A–43L. All the requirements of these provisions must be satisfied on the evidence: *Alm Medical Services Ltd v Bladon* [2002] IRLR 807.

[763] ERA 1996, s 103A.

[764] See para 4.117

(x) Jury service

5.104   It is automatically unfair to dismiss an employee for having been summoned for jury service, or for having been absent from work because he or she attended for jury service.[765] However this will not be the case if the employer can show that the circumstances were such that the employee's absence in pursuance of being so summoned was likely to cause substantial injury to the employer's undertaking; that the employer brought those circumstances to the attention of the employee; that the employee refused or failed to apply to the appropriate officer for excusal from or a deferral of the obligation to attend in pursuance of being so summoned; and that the refusal or failure was not reasonable.[766]

(xi) Participation in protected industrial action

5.105   It is automatically unfair to dismiss an employee for taking part in protected industrial action, that is to say, action which is not actionable in tort by virtue of the statutory immunities contained in TULRCA 1992, section 219, during the first twelve weeks of the employee's participation in that action. (If the employee is locked-out by the employer at any time during this twelve week period the period of protection is extended by the number of days for which this occurs.) After the twelve-week period (extended if appropriate for lock-out days), dismissal for this reason is automatically unfair only if the employee had stopped taking protected industrial action before the end of that period or if the employer had not taken all reasonable procedural steps to resolve the dispute.[767] We consider these provisions, and their relationship to other provisions bearing upon industrial action and dismissal, in our discussion of industrial action, below.[768]

(xii) Activities of employee representatives and other representative roles

5.106   There is an automatically unfair dismissal if the employee was an employee representative for the purposes of information and consultation relating to collective redundancies, transfers of undertakings, or occupational pension schemes, or was a candidate for election to such a position, and was dismissed for performing or proposing to perform the activities of such a representative.[769] In addition, it is automatically unfair to dismiss an employee for taking part in the election of employee representatives under these provisions.[770] There are analogous protections for those acting, or standing as candidates for, representative positions in relation to the establishment or operation of a European Works Council or information or consultation procedure; information and consultation at national level; and in relation to a European Public Limited-Liability Company or European Cooperative Society, and for employees exercising specified rights in

---

[765] ERA 1996, s 98B(1). Parallel provisions apply to detrimental action short of dismissal: s 43M.
[766] ERA 1996, s 98B(2). 'Appropriate officer' is defined in s 98B(3).
[767] TULRCA 1992, s 238A, as inserted by ERelA 1999, s 16 and Sch 5 and amended by ERelA 2004, ss 26-28.
[768] See para 11.79 *et seq.*
[769] ERA 1996, s 103(1); OPPSCER 2006, reg 17, Sch, reg 5.
[770] ERA 1996, s 103(2); OPPSCER 2006, reg 17, Sch, reg 5 (which also extends protection to a range of other activities).

relation to these procedures.[771] We examine the status and functions of employee representatives and the rights of employees in relation to these various provisions in our discussion of employee representation.[772]

(xiii) Functions of pension fund trustees

5.107   It is automatically unfair to dismiss an employee for carrying out the functions of the trustee of a relevant occupational pensions scheme.[773]

(xiv) Protection of workers for acts relating to the statutory recognition and derecognition procedures

5.108   It is automatically unfair for an employer to dismiss a worker (not just an employee) if the reason or main reason is one of a number of specified acts relating to the statutory procedures for the recognition and derecognition of a trade union, under Schedule A1 of TULRCA 1992.[774] These provisions are considered in chapter 9, below.

(xv) The right to be accompanied, and to accompany, for the purposes of a grievance or disciplinary hearing or a hearing relating to a request for flexible working [775]

5.109   Under ERelA 1999, section 10, as amended by ERelA 2004, a worker has the right to be accompanied at a grievance or disciplinary hearing by another person of his choice who may either be an official employed by a union, any other union official whom the union has reasonably certified in writing as having experience of, or having received training in, accompanying workers at disciplinary or grievance hearings, or any other worker of the employer in question. A worker who is unfairly dismissed for exercising the right to be accompanied, or for seeking to accompany another worker (not necessarily employed by the same employer) for this purpose, will be regarded as automatically unfairly dismissed.[776] The right to be accompanied is examined in more detail below, in our discussion of the law relating to disciplinary procedures.[777] The same protections are accorded to employees in relation to the right to be accompanied at meetings to request flexible

---

[771] TICER 1999, reg 28; ICER 2004, reg 30; ECSIER 2006, reg 31; EPLLCEIR 2009, reg 29; see also CCBMR 2007, regs 46, 47.

[772] See ch 9 below.

[773] ERA 1996, s 102. On pension fund trustees, see para 4.137 et seq above.

[774] TULRCA 1992, Sch A1, para 161.

[775] For categories (i)–(xiv) above, selection for redundancy on the specified ground is automatically unfair. This is not the case for category (xv) nor for categories (xvi) and (xvii).

[776] ERelA 1999, s 12. This provision refers to the dismissal of a 'worker' which, as defined in s 13, includes not just 'workers' in the sense of ERA 1996, s 230(3), but also 'agency workers' and 'home workers' along the same lines as NMWA 1998 (see para 4.47 above). The unfair dismissal provisions of ERA 1996 are deemed to apply to 'workers' as so defined, and not just employees, for this purpose: see ERelA 1999, s 12(6). Parallel provisions apply to detrimental action short of dismissal: s 12(1), (2).

[777] See para 5.121 et seq.

working or to appeal against an employer's decision to refuse an employee's application.[778] They are also extended to workers who accompany or seek to accompany an employee for any such purposes.[779]

(xvi) Transfer of the undertaking

5.110   Dismissal for the transfer of an undertaking falling within the scope of TUPE 2006 or a reason connected with the transfer is automatically unfair, unless it is for an 'economic, technical or organisational reason entailing changes in the workforce' in which case it is potentially fair. These provisions are analysed in our discussion of redundancies and business reorganisations.[780]

(xvii) Spent convictions

5.111   A further category of automatically unfair reasons is that of dismissal for a spent conviction. Under the Rehabilitation of Offenders Act 1974, the possession of a spent conviction or the failure to disclose it 'shall not be a proper ground for dismissing or excluding a person from any office, profession, occupation or employment, or for prejudicing him in any way in any occupation or employment'.[781] This is broadly equivalent to categorising such action as an automatically unfair reason for dismissal. A conviction cannot become spent if, *inter alia*, it results in a sentence of imprisonment exceeding thirty months.[782] Otherwise, various rehabilitation periods apply, ranging from three to ten years, in order for the conviction to become spent. There are numerous exemptions in relation to public employment, the professions and occupations involving trust and confidence, such as those in the medical and financial service sectors.[783] Dismissal for a conviction which, for one reason or another, is not spent in the sense laid out in the Act, will almost certainly be for a potentially fair reason.[784]

Potentially fair reasons

5.112   The Act lists five categories of potentially fair reasons: reasons related to the individual's capability or qualifications for performing work of the kind he or she was employed to do; reasons related to the employee's conduct; redundancy; a statutory prohibition upon the employee continuing to work in the position he or she holds; and 'some other substantial reason of a kind such as to justify the dismissal of an employee holding the position which the employee held'.[785]

---

[778] FWPR 2002, reg 16.

[779] Above

[780] See para 5.182 *et seq* below.

[781] Rehabilitation of Offenders Act 1974, s 4(3)(b); *Property Guards Ltd v Taylor* [1982] IRLR 175.

[782] Rehabilitation of Offenders Act 1974, s 5(1)(b).

[783] SI 1975/1023 as amended. On the interpretation of the exception in the case of the provision of social services to persons over 65 see *Wood v Coverage Care Ltd* [1996] IRLR 264.

[784] Cf *Torr v British Railways Board* [1977] IRLR 184.

[785] ERA 1996, s 98(1)–(2).

Capability and qualifications are defined to mean, respectively, 'capability assessed by reference to skill, aptitude, health or any other physical or mental quality', and 'any degree, diploma or other academic, technical or professional qualification relevant to the position' which the employee held.[786] Redundancy bears the same meaning here as in the context of the right to statutory redundancy compensation, namely a situation in which the business where the employee works ceases, or in which there is a diminution in the business' requirements for employees to do work of a particular kind.[787]

These potentially fair reasons are simply the 'gateways' through which the employer has to pass if it is to demonstrate that the dismissal was fair. The employer only has to show, at this stage, that the dismissal was motivated by reasons which fall within one of these gateways; it does not have to show that the facts justify the dismissal in question.[788] A potentially fair reason is 'one which can justify the dismissal, not which *does* justify the dismissal'.[789] Even when it comes to the second stage, the Act does not lay down in detail the circumstances under which, for example, a dismissal by reason of misconduct or lack of capability is deemed to be fair or unfair. The test of fairness under section 98(4) is essentially procedural and, as we shall see, an employer may escape liability if it can show that the procedure it adopted was fair in the circumstances, even if the substantive outcome was one with which the tribunal might have disagreed.[790]

It has not greatly mattered in the past, in most cases, which of the potentially fair reasons under section 98(1)–(2) was being relied on by the employer. Case law has given rise to specific guidelines to be followed in relation to dismissals of different types,[791] but the norms thereby established are no more than applications of the general test of reasonableness in dismissal, and that there is considerable overlap in the guidelines which apply to dismissals of different types.[792] The reason relied upon may be more significant where there is scope for argument as to whether the ACAS Code of Practice on Disciplinary and Grievance Procedures 2009 governs the dismissal. Where the Code applies to the dismissal and there was a failure by one or other party to comply with the Code which is found to have been unreasonable the tribunal has the discretion to increase or reduce an award to an employee whose complaint has been upheld by up to 25%.[793] The Code applies to misconduct and/or poor performance and specifically excludes redundancy dismissals.[794] Thus where an employee with a written warning for misconduct or poor performance is selected for redundancy, for example, the designation of the principal reason for dismissal may prove to be important if the employer has failed to complete the procedure in the Code prior to dismissing the employee.

---

[786] ERA 1996, s 98(3).
[787] ERA 1996, s 139(1), (2).
[788] See para 5.89 above.
[789] *Mercia Rubber Mouldings Ltd v Lingwood* [1974] ICR 256, 257 (Sir John Donaldson P).
[790] See para 5.125 *et seq* below. Note, however, the possible implications of HRA 1998 in this context.
[791] For examples of cases where this made a difference see *Wilson v Post Office* [2000] IRLR 834, where the employer successfully sought to argue that the case was one of misconduct, not incapability, and *Ezsias v North Glamorgan NHS Trust* [2011] IRLR 550, where the tribunal found that the breakdown of relationships, rather than the employee's conduct, was the reason for dismissal.
[792] See, for example, *Perkin v St George's Healthcare NHS Trust* [2005] IRLR 934, Wall LJ at [65].
[793] TULRCA 1992, s 207A.
[794] Code of Practice, para 1. See para 5.125 *et seq* for more detailed discussion of the Code.

5.113   The four specific categories contained in section 98(2) are, in themselves, broadly defined. The reason must in each case be 'substantial',[795] so that if the reason relied on by the employer was completely trivial, the dismissal is not capable of being justified. On the other hand, the reference to a reason which 'relates to' capability, qualifications and misconduct means that these categories are even wider than they might otherwise be;[796] the Act does not say that the reason must relate 'wholly or mainly to' the category in question, for example (although, in terms of the second-stage test of fairness, the reason will have to be a 'sufficient' one in the circumstances for dismissal to be actually fair). The category of misconduct has broadly been defined to include, for example, a refusal to obey an order to carry out extra-contractual duties. In *Redbridge London Borough Council v Fishman*[797] a dismissal was held to be potentially fair on these grounds where the employee, who had been employed at a school in an essentially managerial capacity, was asked to undertake some teaching. She refused and was dismissed. The tribunal made a finding of unfair dismissal which was upheld, in part, on the grounds that the order was one she was not contractually obliged to obey. However, the point for present purposes is that the dismissal was for a reason which could have been justified in slightly different circumstances; elsewhere, tribunals and courts have made findings of fair dismissal in cases where employees were dismissed for resisting unilateral changes to their existing terms and conditions of employment.[798] In a similarly broad interpretation, it has been held that the potentially fair reason of lack of capability does not have to be established in relation to each and every aspect of an employee's contractual duties.[799]

Dismissal by reason of a statutory contravention under section 98(2)(d) applies where the employee could not continue to work 'in the position which he held' without contravening, or causing the employer to contravene, a 'duty or restriction' imposed by legislation. This is only a potentially fair reason. The employer may be found to have acted unreasonably in failing to allow an employee time to acquire a necessary licence or permit,[800] or in failing to look into the possibility of suitable alternative employment.[801]

The definition of redundancy is particularly important since in addition to opening the gateway to a fair dismissal, it also grants the employee an entitlement to receive a statutory redundancy payment, if he or she is otherwise qualified to do so.[802] A dismissal for economic reasons which falls outside the scope of redundancy may be potentially fair on the separate grounds that it falls within the category of 'some other substantial reason' in section 98(1)(b); the employee will not then receive statutory redundancy compensation. The extensive case law in this area is examined later in this chapter in the discussion of redundancies and business reorganisations.[803]

---

[795] This follows from the reference to 'some other substantial reason' in ERA 1996, s 98(1)(b).

[796] *Shook v Ealing London Borough Council* [1986] ICR 314, 326.

[797] [1978] ICR 569.

[798] Eg, *Industrial Rubber Products v Gillon* [1977] IRLR 389; and see generally *Gilham v Kent County Council (No 3)* [1986] IRLR 56. In *Farrant v Woodroffe School* [1998] IRLR 176, the EAT upheld a finding that the employers had acted reasonably in dismissing the employee because of their genuine, if mistaken, view that they were contractually entitled to require him to work to a new job description and that he was guilty of gross misconduct in refusing to do so.

[799] *Shook v Ealing London Borough Council* [1986] ICR 314.

[800] *Sutcliffe and Eaton Ltd v Pinney* [1977] IRLR 349, discussed *Kelly v University of Southampton* [2008] ICR 357.

[801] *Appleyard v FM Smith (Hull) Ltd* [1972] IRLR 19.

[802] Note that in the context of an unfair dismissal complaint it will be for the employer to show redundancy as a 'fair' reason (s 98(1)) whereas for the purposes of a statutory redundancy payment a dismissal is presumed to be for redundancy unless otherwise shown: ERA 1996, s 163(2).

[803] See para 5.173 *et seq.*

5.114   If a dismissal does not come under any of the four specific gateways in section 98(2), it is more than likely that it will qualify under the heading of the residual category of 'some other substantial reason of a kind such as to justify the dismissal of an employee holding the position which the employee held' (or SOSR).[804] In addition to greatly expanding the scope of legitimate economic reasons for dismissal, as we have just noted, the concept of SOSR also blurs the edges of the other specific reasons listed by the Act. If an employer dismisses an employee whom he mistakenly thinks lacks the necessary work permit, when in fact the employee had the permission needed, the dismissal may fail to be justifiable by reference to a statutory prohibition within the meaning of section 98(2)(d), but may, instead, qualify as an SOSR.[805] Dismissals for reasons which could only with difficulty be classified as related to conduct or incapability have also come under the SOSR category. Such cases include the dismissal of an employee for failure to reveal a history of mental illness when asked about this at the job interview,[806] a dismissal brought about by pressure from a major customer or client of the employer,[807] dismissal of a senior employee who could not or would not work harmoniously with others;[808] and dismissal following the receipt of information under an official disclosure regime that the employee poses a risk to children.[809]

The scope of SOSR is not, however, limited to reasons similar to those cited in section 98(2). This has been the view of the courts since the early decision of Brightman J in *RS Components Ltd v Irwin*.[810] The employment tribunal had proceeded on the basis that 'a reason for dismissal is not capable of being "some other substantial reason" unless it is a reason *ejusdem generis* with the reasons specified in subsection (2)'. This was rejected on appeal, on the basis that:

> ... there are not only legal, but also practical objections to a narrow construction of 'some other substantial reason'. Parliament may well have intended to set out in section [98(2)] the common reasons for a dismissal, but can hardly have hoped to produce an exhaustive catalogue of all the circumstances in which an employer would be justified in terminating the services of an employee.[811]

This assertion, for which no grounds were offered, is in any case beside the point; Parliament might well have intended to give employers some flexibility via the notion of SOSR, while still

---

[804] See Bowers and Clarke, 1981. The requirement that the reason justifies the dismissal of an employee 'holding the position which the employee held' may, on occasion, be significant: see *Cobley v Forward Technology Industries plc* [2003] IRLR 706, para 21 (in deciding whether there was a substantial reason to dismiss a chief executive after a hostile takeover, different considerations would apply to him than to a case of a secretary or storeman: *per* Mummery LJ). Dismissal of an employee engaged to replace an employee who is absent because of maternity, adoption, or paternity leave is deemed to be for SOSR provided that specified conditions are met: see *Victoria and Albert Museum v Durrant* [2011] IRLR 290.

[805] *Bouchaala v Trusthouse Forte Hotels Ltd* [1980] ICR 721. See also *Hounslow London Borough Council v Klusova* [2008] ICR 396 (immigrant in UK with limited right to remain who had made a relevant in-time application to extend leave to remain entitled to continue in employment pending determination of the application).

[806] *O'Brien v Prudential Assurance Co Ltd* [1979] IRLR 140. Note now EqA 2010, s 60, discussed in para 6.129.

[807] *Scott Packaging and Warehousing Ltd v Patterson* [1978] IRLR 166; *Henderson v Connect (South Tyneside) Ltd* [2010] IRLR 466.

[808] *Perkin v St George's Healthcare NHS Trust* [2005] IRLR 934, Wall LJ (giving the only reasoned judgment) at [62]–[63]; see also *Ezsias v North Glamorgan NHS Trust* [2011] IRLR 550.

[809] *A v B* [2010] IRLR 844.

[810] [1973] ICR 535.

[811] [1973] ICR 535, 540. See, more recently, *Cobley v Forward Technology Industries plc* [2003] IRLR 706, [22] (Mummery LJ).

linking that concept to the specific categories listed in section 98(2), so that it should be construed *ejusdem generis* with them. The residual category would then have operated as a safety valve, allowing a potentially fair dismissal in situations closely analogous to those listed. If, by contrast, the category of SOSR is capable of extending to *any* substantial reason, what was the point of enacting section 98(2)? The principal concern of the NIRC in *RS Components* was apparently to preserve free of legal control the power of the employer to initiate changes beneficial to the 'development of industry',[812] without incurring the costs of unfair dismissal or of redundancy compensation. This has led to an important narrowing of the concept of redundancy. It has also had a more general effect, practically removing the check on employers apparently imposed by section 98(1)–(2): 'in very few reported cases have employers not reached the threshold of "substantiality"'.[813] To date this approach to the concept of 'substantiality' has yet to be affected by the enactment of the Human Rights Act 1998.

Reasonableness: issues of fact and law

5.115   Under section 98(4), 'the determination of the question whether the dismissal is fair or unfair (having regard to the reason shown by the employer) – (a) depends on whether in the circumstances (including the size and administrative resources of the employer's undertaking) the employer acted reasonably or unreasonably in treating it as a sufficient reason for dismissing the employee and (b) shall be determined in accordance with equity and the substantial merits of the case'. The Employment Act 1980[814] inserted the reference to the size and resources of the employer's undertaking and removed a provision which had previously placed the burden of proof on the employer under this subsection; the burden of proof is now neutral as between the two parties.

The appellate courts have, through various self-denying ordinances, consistently preserved a broad area of autonomy for individual tribunals in determining the question set out in section 98(4). The statute signals the discretionary nature of the tribunal's task by its reference to 'equity and the substantial merits of the case'. 'Equity' here means 'common fairness': the result is that the tribunal 'has to look at the question in the round and without regard to lawyers' technicalities. It has to look at it in an industrial relations context'.[815] EA 2008 introduced a discretion for tribunals to increase or decrease the compensatory award to an employee whose complaint is upheld where the ACAS Code of Practice applies to the dismissal and there was a failure by the relevant party to comply with the Code but the tribunal must find that the failure was 'unreasonable'[816] and the Code itself makes clear that it may not be practicable for all employers to take all the steps set out in it.[817]

An appeal only lies to the EAT (and further to the Court of Appeal and Supreme Court) on a point of law,[818] and a tribunal will only commit an error of law if it either misdirected itself on

---

[812] [1973] ICR 535.
[813] Bowers and Clarke, 1981: p 35.
[814] Section 6.
[815] *Union of Construction Allied Trades and Technicians v Brain* [1981] ICR 542, 550 (Donaldson LJ).
[816] EA 2008, ss 1–3, inserting TULRCA 1992, s 207A and Sch A2 and amending ERA 1996, s 124A.
[817] Code of Practice, para 3.
[818] ETA 1996, s 21.

the relevant legal test or misunderstood or misapplied the law; made a finding of fact for which there was no evidence; or the decision was 'perverse' in that it was one which no reasonable tribunal, directing itself properly on the law, could have reached or, alternatively, was one which was obviously wrong.[819] In practice it will be very difficult to classify as 'perverse' a decision which did not fall within one of these categories.

In the context of unfair dismissal it has been held that decisions applying the fairness test in section 98(4) to particular situations do not create precedents which are strictly binding on future tribunals or courts.[820] Nor are tribunals required rigidly to follow guidelines for the interpretation of section 98(4) which are laid down by the EAT.[821] So although the EAT has given guidance of a general kind in relation, for example, to the procedures to be followed in cases of dismissal for misconduct,[822] incapability[823] and redundancy,[824] it is not necessarily an error of law for a tribunal to decline to follow these guidelines (which should in any event be read in the light of the ACAS Code of Practice on Disciplinary and Grievance Procedures 2009, discussed below). In general, 'it should ... be very rare for any decision of an ... [employment] ... tribunal under this section to give rise to any question of law'.[825]

Although the intention here was to limit the number of legal citations made before tribunals, to respect the comparative informality of tribunal proceedings and preserve their autonomy of decision-making, the effect has also been to deny a degree of certainty and consistency in the application of the law. It is quite possible that different tribunals may reach different decisions on essentially similar facts, as occurred in *Kent County Council v Gilham*.[826] The Court of Appeal considered a number of appeals from determinations of tribunals (and of the EAT) in cases where dinner ladies employed by various local government authorities had been dismissed for refusing to accept a cut in pay. In each case the employers argued that cuts in their budgets, imposed by central government, had forced them to make savings on wage costs. Most tribunals accepted that this constituted a potentially fair reason for dismissal; some tribunals, the majority, then went on to find the dismissals to be fair in the circumstances, others that the dismissals had been unfair. The Court of Appeal held that it was permissible for the tribunals concerned to disagree, and that the decisions made by one tribunal did not bind the others.

[819] *British Telecommunications plc v Sheridan* [1990] IRLR 27, 30 (Lord Donaldson MR); *Neale v Hereford and Worcester County Council* [1986] ICR 471, 483 (May LJ); *Piggott Bros & Co Ltd v Jackson* [1991] IRLR 309, 312 (Lord Donaldson MR); *Watling v William Bird & Son (Contractor) Ltd* (1976) 11 ITR 70, 71. See also *Fuller v London Borough of Brent* [2011] IRLR 414; *Bowater v Northwest London Hospitals NHS Trust* [2011] IRLR 331.
[820] *Jowett v Earl of Bradford (No 2)* [1978] ICR 431.
[821] *Bailey v BP Oil (Kent Refinery) Ltd* [1980] ICR 642; *Union of Construction Allied Trades and Technicians v Brain* [1981] ICR 542.
[822] *ILEA v Gravett* [1988] IRLR 497.
[823] *Lynock v Cereal Packaging Ltd* [1988] IRLR 510.
[824] *Williams v Compair Maxam Ltd* [1982] IRLR 83.
[825] *Union of Construction Allied Trades and Technicians v Brain* [1981] ICR 542, 550 (Donaldson LJ). Note, however, that it is highly likely that a tribunal that found that an employer who had violated an employee's Convention rights in dismissing him or her had acted 'reasonably' would be regarded as having misapplied the law: see *Pay v Lancashire Probation Service* [2004] IRLR 129, [32], [33]; *X v Y* [2004] IRLR 625, CA.
[826] [1985] ICR 227.

Reasonableness test: the band of reasonable responses

5.116   The tribunal must determine whether the employer 'acted reasonably' in treating as sufficient the reason which was the basis for the dismissal. This emphasis on the employer's conduct means that the substantive justice of the dispute is, by and large, a secondary consideration. As Viscount Dilhorne said in *W Devis & Sons Ltd v Atkins*,[827] section 98(4) directs the tribunal 'to focus on the conduct of the employer and not on whether the employee in fact suffered any injustice'. Moreover, (infringement of Convention rights apart) the employer's conduct is judged not by reference to the nature of the right of the employee which might have been infringed, but by reference to the standard set by a notional 'reasonable employer'. The relevant principles were summarised by Browne-Wilkinson J on behalf of the EAT in *Iceland Frozen Foods Ltd v Jones*:[828]

> ... in judging the reasonableness of the employer's conduct an ... [employment] ... tribunal must not substitute its decision as to what was the right course to adopt for that of the employer – in many, though not all, cases there is a band of reasonable responses to the employee's conduct within which one employer might reasonably take one view, another may quite reasonably take another; ... the function of the ... [employment] ... tribunal, as an industrial jury, is to determine whether in the particular circumstances of each case the decision to dismiss the employee fell within the band of reasonable responses which a reasonable employer might have adopted.

5.117   The fundamental difficulty with this test, as Collins has written, is that 'the idea of a range of reasonable conduct broadens the scope for legitimate disciplinary action by denying implicitly that a fixed standard of reasonableness should be applied'.[829] In *Haddon v Van den Bergh Foods*[830] the EAT, under the presidency of Morison J, took the view that the band of reasonable responses test was an unjustifiable gloss on the statute and that the basic test of fairness in section 98(4) should be applied 'without embellishment'.[831] The reasonable responses test was illegitimate because it 'led tribunals to adopt a perversity test of reasonableness',[832] that is to say, one in which an employer's decision could not be disturbed unless it was one which no reasonable employer could have arrived at. However, decisions coming after *Haddon* saw a reversion to the traditional approach. In *Midland Bank plc v Madden*[833] and *Beedell v West Ferry Printers Ltd*[834] the EAT accepted that the reasonable responses test, having been approved by the Court of Appeal, could not be overturned by a decision of the Appeal Tribunal. At the same time, while it was agreed that a 'perversity test' was not compatible with the language of section 98(4), it was also asserted in *Madden* that 'the band test has always been intended not to lead to one of perversity'.[835] In *Beedell* the EAT went further in stressing that the tribunal was not entitled to substitute its judgment for

---

[827] [1977] IRLR 314, 317.
[828] [1983] ICR 17, 24–25. See also Lord Denning in *British Leyland (UK) Ltd v Swift* [1981] IRLR 91, referring to a 'band of reasonableness'.
[829] H Collins, 1993: p 38. See also H Collins, 2004: ch 5 for a more recent critique of this test.
[830] [1999] IRLR 672; see also *Wilson v Ethicon Ltd* [2000] IRLR 4; H Collins, 2000c; Freedland, 2000.
[831] [1999] IRLR 672, 676.
[832] [1999] IRLR 672, 676.
[833] [2000] IRLR 288.
[834] [2000] IRLR 650.
[835] [2000] IRLR 288, 295. See also *Beedell v West Ferry Printers* [2000] IRLR 650, 656.

that of the employer at any point in the application of section 98(4): 'the employment tribunal should not put themselves in the place of management to decide whether they, the employment tribunal members, would have dismissed the applicant or not'; equally, 'it is not for the employment tribunal to re-try the factual issues before the employer at the dismissal (including appeal) stage'.[836] In *Post Office v Foley; HSBC Bank v Madden*[837] the Court of Appeal did its utmost to restore the pre-*Haddon* position, by asserting that the EAT in that case had made 'an unwarranted departure from binding authority'.[838] The Court took the view that an authority which had 'been followed almost every day in almost every employment tribunal and on appeals for nearly 20 years [should] remain binding' until such time as Parliament chose to change the basic statutory text underpinning the test.[839] In 2002, even more controversially, the Court of Appeal held that the third element of this test – whether investigation into suspected misconduct was reasonable in the circumstances – was subject to the 'band of reasonable responses' test.[840] We discuss the implications of this further in para 5.134 below.

5.118 The courts may be thought of as having adapted to the employment context an approach of the common law of tort and contract to the assessment of the standard of care expected of professionals in negligence cases: the same notion of a range of legitimate responses is used there to create a space for professional discretion and judgment.[841] Adopting this suggestion in *Beedell*, the EAT commented: '[j]ust as the question of a doctor's negligence will depend upon whether a reasonable body of medical practitioners would have accepted the practice which he followed, even if another body of equally reasonable practitioners would have acted differently (a band of reasonable responses), so it may be said that the question of whether an employer has acted reasonably in dismissing his employee will depend upon the range of responses of reasonable employers'.[842]

However, this is not the only conceivable approach to the setting of the relevant standards in the common law, and if the courts wish to draw inspiration from the analogy with *Bolam* they should also look to decisions which have qualified the traditional test by making reference to the *reasonable expectations of treatment of the claimant* (or, here, the employee).[843] It remains the case that there is nothing in section 98 to indicate that Parliament intended a 'band of reasonableness' test to be applied by employment tribunals, in contrast to the clear authority in the statutory scheme for the separation of reasons and reasonableness, which the Court of Appeal also (and correctly) reasserted in *Madden*.[844] In the final analysis, there remains a strong case for reviewing the band of reasonableness test given that it is essentially a judicial addition to the statutory formula, and, arguably, one which has done much to limit the effectiveness of the statutory protection provided to employees, no matter how hallowed it has become with the passage of time.

[836] [2000] IRLR 650, 656.
[837] [2000] IRLR 827.
[838] [2000] IRLR 827, 829 (Mummery LJ).
[839] [2000] IRLR 827, 830 (Mummery LJ). Cf Anderman, 2004: p 127, who states that '[t]he inability of judges to see that the current interpretation of section 98(4) *is* a form of judicial legislation is evidence of their underlying assumptions about exclusive employer property rights in the contract of employment'.
[840] *Sainsbury's Supermarkets Ltd v Hitt* [2003] IRLR 23.
[841] *Bolam v Friern Hospital Management Committee* [1957] 1 WLR 582.
[842] [2000] IRLR 650, 656.
[843] See, in particular, the opinion of Lord Scarman in *Sidaway v Bethlem Royal Hospital* [1985] AC 871.
[844] See para 5.117 above.

Procedural fairness

(i) An overview

5.119   As we discussed above, the statute directs attention to the employer's conduct rather than to the overall fairness of the outcome. In assessing whether an employer has acted reasonably a crucial source of the employer's obligations has been the ACAS Code of Practice on Disciplinary and Grievance Procedures, originally issued in 1977 and revised in 1997, 2000, 2004, and, most recently, in 2009. Like other Codes issued by virtue of powers now contained in TULRCA 1992, the Disciplinary Code must be taken into account by employment tribunals where it appears to be relevant to any matter arising in the course of the proceedings,[845] and more than 20 years ago the House of Lords confirmed that it should be regularly consulted in cases of disciplinary dismissal.[846] Despite the status of the Code, however, the importance accorded by courts and tribunals to procedural fairness has oscillated since the unfair dismissal protection came into being.[847] Initially the courts 'demanded scrupulous attention to detailed procedural guidelines' and maintained that an unfair procedure alone could render a dismissal unfair.[848] This was replaced by an approach that allowed substantive standards to prevail. According to the test expressed in *British Labour Pump v Byrne*[849] a dismissal which had not been preceded by the appropriate procedural steps could nevertheless be fair if an employment tribunal was satisfied, on the balance of probabilities, that the result would have been the same had the proper procedure been followed and the employer could show that, in the light of the information it would thereby have acquired, it would have been behaving reasonably in deciding to dismiss. In 1987, in *Polkey v AE Dayton Services Ltd*,[850] this approach, which had been subject to considerable criticism, was overruled by the House of Lords as inconsistent with the statutory language. Lord Mackay said:

> Where there is no [automatically unfair dismissal] the subject matter for the tribunal's consideration is the employer's action in treating the reason as a sufficient reason for dismissing the employee. It is that action and that action only that the tribunal is required to characterise as reasonable or unreasonable. That leaves no scope for the tribunal considering whether, if the employer had acted differently, he might have dismissed the employee. It is what the employer did that is to be judged, not what he might have done. On the other hand, in judging whether what the employer did was reasonable it is right to consider what a reasonable employer would have had in mind at the time he decided to dismiss as the consequence of not consulting or not warning.[851]

The result of *Polkey* was to reaffirm the significance of adherence to procedures, although it did not mark a return to the initial strict approach. Under this test an employer could dispense with procedure in a case where a reasonable employer would have decided to dismiss the employee

---

[845] TULRCA 1992, s 207; see *Lock v Cardiff Rly Co Ltd* [1998] IRLR 358.
[846] *West Midlands Co-operative Society Ltd v Tipton* [1986] AC 536.
[847] See H Collins, 1992: pp 111–120.
[848] H Collins, 1992: p 112.
[849] [1979] IRLR 94, affirmed by the Court of Appeal in *W and J Wass Ltd v Binns* [1982] IRLR 283.
[850] [1987] IRLR 503.
[851] [1988] ICR 142, 153.

summarily: 'there may be cases where the offence is so heinous and the facts so manifestly clear that a reasonable employer could take the view that whatever explanation the employee advanced it would make no difference'.[852] Similarly, an employer might legitimately dispense with a disciplinary procedure 'where, on the undisputed facts, dismissal was inevitable, as for example where a trusted employee, before dismissal, was charged with, and pleaded guilty to, a serious offence of dishonesty committed in the course of his employment'.[853] As Collins explained, this allowed an element of flexibility in exceptional cases albeit at the expense of the principle of respect for the dignity of the individual worker that a stricter adherence to procedural fairness embodies.[854]

5.120 The principles laid down in *Polkey* governed the position prior to the entry into force on 1 October 2004 of fundamental and controversial changes to unfair dismissal law introduced by EA 2002.[855] The 2002 Act eroded the *Polkey* principle from two directions. First, it introduced rudimentary statutory dismissal and disciplinary procedures which, other than in limited circumstances, all employers were required to follow.[856] A dismissal was automatically unfair if the relevant statutory procedure had not been completed and non-completion was 'wholly or mainly attributable to failure by the employer to comply with its requirements'. The dismissed employee was entitled to a minimum of four week's pay (unless the tribunal considered that it would result in 'injustice' to the employer) and the compensatory award could be increased by 10% (unless there were exceptional circumstances which would make such an increase 'unjust or inequitable') and could be increased by up to 50%. An employee's failure to complete the applicable procedure also had legal consequences; tribunals were required (exceptional circumstances apart) to reduce the compensatory award for unfair dismissal by 10%, and had a discretion to reduce it by up to 50%. Secondly, EA 2002 provided that, subject to the requirement, where applicable, to follow the statutory minimum, 'failure by an employer to follow a procedure in relation to the dismissal of an employee shall not be regarded ... as by itself making the employer's action unreasonable if he shows that he would have decided to dismiss the employee if he had followed the procedure'. This provision, in effect, reinstated the 'no difference' rule removed by *Polkey* for procedures beyond the statutory minima, including those that were enshrined in the ACAS Code.[857]

A review of the statutory procedures found that they carried 'an unnecessarily high administrative burden for both employers and employees' and had 'unintended negative consequences' which outweighed their benefits, including the use of formal processes to deal with problems that could have been resolved informally and earlier resort to external advice.[858] Following the consultation exercise which we outlined in para 2.20 above, they

---

[852] *Sillifant v Powell Duffryn Timber Ltd* [1983] IRLR 91, 97 (Browne-Wilkinson J), an analysis approved by Lord MacKay in *Polkey* [1988] ICR 142, 157.
[853] *West Midlands Co-operative Society Ltd v Tipton* [1986] AC 536, 548 (Lord Bridge of Harwich).
[854] H Collins, 1992: pp 118–126.
[855] See Hepple and Morris, 2002; G Morris, 2005.
[856] EA 2002, s 98A; Sch 2, Part 1. These procedures, and the circumstances in which they applied, were discussed in detail in our fourth edition.
[857] Hepple and Morris, 2002: p 264.
[858] *Better Dispute Resolution: A Review of Employment Dispute Resolution in Great Britain* (the 'Gibbons Review'), DTI, March 2007: p 8. See also *Success at Work: Resolving Disputes in the Workplace: a Consultation*, DTI, March 2007 and *Resolving Disputes in the Workplace Consultation: Government Response*, BERR, May 2008 and Sanders, 2009.

were replaced with effect from 6 April 2009[859] by provisions allowing tribunals to adjust compensatory awards in the event of non-compliance with the ACAS Code of Practice on Disciplinary and Grievance Procedures.[860] The decision to repeal the statutory procedures also necessitated a review of the 'no difference' rule contained in the 2002 Act. The Labour Government consulted on three options: to reinstate *Polkey*; reverse *Polkey* and revert to the 'no difference' rule in *British Labour Pump*; or to distinguish between dismissals which were unfair on procedural and substantive grounds, with those unfair on procedural grounds alone having a lower limit of compensation.[861] Although initially attracted to the last of these options, the Government was persuaded following consultation to reinstate *Polkey* which was regarded as a well-understood position which achieved a fair balance between the interests of employers and employees.[862]

We discussed the grievance procedures in the ACAS Code of Practice and the consequences of failure to follow them in para 2.21 above. These procedures will be relevant to unfair dismissal complaints based on constructive dismissal. For those based on termination by the employer (other than non-renewal of fixed-term contracts on expiry)[863] both employer and employee will need to comply with the provisions of the Code that relate to disciplinary procedures if they are not to risk any eventual compensatory awards being increased or decreased by up to 25%. This will require tribunals to distinguish between elements of procedural fairness that are contained in the Code and those that are not. We discussed in para 2.21 the areas which may give rise to litigation in relation to grievances under the new regime and many of the points which we made there apply equally in this context. We discuss those relating specifically to discipline in our discussion of the substantive provisions of the Code and the framework within which adjustments may be made.

In the following discussion of procedural fairness we first outline the free-standing statutory right to be accompanied at disciplinary and grievance hearings (the latter being relevant to complaints of unfair constructive dismissal). We then examine the standards of procedural fairness that are laid down in the ACAS Code together with those that have been developed by courts and tribunals. It is important to emphasise that, although there is considerable overlap between the Code and the principles developed by the courts, the two are not wholly co-extensive. Thus, the courts have in the past found a dismissal to be fair if there has been a clear breach of acceptable behaviour by the employee even if the employer lacks the formalised rules and procedures the Code requires. Moreover, application of the *Polkey* principle may mean that there is no compensation which can be made the subject of an adjustment. It remains to be seen whether the new statutory regime may make courts and tribunals more reluctant, even in extreme cases, to dispense with the requirement to adhere to the basic procedural standards which the current Code contains.

---

[859] See SI 2008/3232 for the transitional provisions.

[860] EA 2008, ss 1–3; s 3 inserts TULRCA 1992, s 207A and Sch A2.

[861] *Supplementary review of options for the law relating to procedural fairness in unfair dismissal* DTI, 2007.

[862] *Resolving Disputes in the Workplace Consultation: Government Response*, BERR, May 2008, paras 2.13–2.23; EA 2008, s 2.

[863] Code of Practice, para 1.

(ii) The right to be accompanied

5.121   The right to be accompanied at disciplinary and grievance hearings was introduced by ERelA 1999.[864] Provisions relating to the right are also included in the ACAS Code of Practice on Disciplinary and Grievance Procedures 2009. ACAS was aware that including the right to be accompanied in the Code could leave employers open to a 'double penalty for the same offence' in the form of a 25% increase in compensation where the employee's complaint for unfair dismissal was upheld in addition to the specific penalty for breach of the right laid down in ERelA 1999 itself, discussed below. ACAS decided in favour of inclusion on the basis that employment tribunals were sufficiently experienced in such matters to take a 'commonsense approach' and avoid this being an issue in practice.[865] As we indicate in para 5.122 below, the right to be accompanied applies to 'workers' whereas the Code of Practice in some places refers only to 'employees'.[866] The latter reflects the general scope of the unfair dismissal legislation but could have the potential to mislead those seeking guidance only on the right to be accompanied. In the discussion which follows we refer to 'employees' where this reflects the language of the Code.

ERelA 1999 provides that where a worker is 'required or invited by his employer to attend a disciplinary or grievance hearing' and 'reasonably requests to be accompanied' at that hearing, the employer must allow him or her to be accompanied by any one of the following: a trade union official employed by the union itself; any official of a trade union (including a lay official or shop steward) whom the union has reasonably certified as either having experience of, or having received training in, acting as a worker's companion for these purposes; or any other worker of the employer.[867] The ACAS Code states that employers should advise employees who are notified of a disciplinary meeting of their right to be accompanied at disciplinary meetings[868] but this is not a statutory obligation.

It is not clear on what if any grounds the courts could decide that a request to be accompanied was not 'reasonable'; since section 98(4) is not in point here, there would seem to be no adequate basis for invoking the 'band of reasonableness' test, described in para 5.116, in this context. The ACAS Code states that it would not normally be reasonable for workers to insist on being accompanied by a companion whose presence would prejudice the hearing nor would it be reasonable for a worker to ask to be accompanied by a companion from a remote geographical location if someone suitable and willing was available on site.[869] It is not clear that this accords with the statutory language, however; the statute refers to the reasonableness of the request *to be accompanied* not to the choice of companion, which appears to be for the worker himself or herself to decide. If a union official is chosen, he or she can be an official of any union; the worker does not have to be a member of that union, nor need that union be recognised by the employer for the purposes of collective bargaining. There is no requirement that the union is independent.[870] The

---

[864] ERelA 1999, ss 10–15. See generally Clancy and Seifert, 2000, and on the impact of the right in practice see Antcliff and Saundry, 2009, and Saundry *et al*, 2011.

[865] *Discipline and Grievance Code of Practice – Consultation Outcome*, ACAS, October 2008, para 22.

[866] See, for example, para 10 and the heading to paras 13-16.

[867] ERelA 1999, s 10 as amended by ERelA 2004, s 37.

[868] Code of Practice, para 10. In contrast to ERelA 1999, which refers to 'hearings' throughout, the Code refers in some places to disciplinary and grievance 'meetings', although consistently to appeal 'hearings'.

[869] Code of Practice, paras 15, 36.

[870] See para 7.23 for the meaning of this term.

Act imposes no *duty* upon the chosen companion to act if he or she does not wish to do so. Where a group of workers is invited to a disciplinary or grievance hearing each may choose a different companion or they may select a single companion to support them all.[871]

If the chosen companion is not available at the time set by the employer for the hearing, the employer must agree to a postponement of the hearing to an alternative time proposed by the worker which must be 'reasonable' and within five working days beginning with the first working day after the day proposed by the employer.[872]

5.122   The right to be accompanied is a free-standing statutory right which is separate from the right to claim unfair dismissal, although denial of the right may, depending on the circumstances, render a dismissal unfair on general principles under the reasonableness test.[873] It may be claimed by a 'worker', a term which, in particular in this context, is considerably wider than the category of 'employee' which is relevant for the purposes of unfair dismissal law. Not only does it cover, for example, home workers and agency workers, but in relation to agency workers it is specified that the employer can be either the user (or 'principal') or the agency, in an appropriate case.[874] Breach by the employer can give rise to a claim for up to two weeks' pay (subject to the normal upper limits on compensation) by the worker, in addition to any compensation that may be awarded in relation to any other complaint that may be brought at the same time, such as unfair dismissal.[875] A worker and/or his or her companion who is subjected to a detriment or dismissal in connection with the exercise of rights under this provision may also bring a complaint to an employment tribunal.[876] The companion has a statutory right to paid time off during working hours to fulfil his or her responsibilities, but only if employed by the same employer as the worker.[877]

5.123   A key issue is when the right to be accompanied arises. The Act defines a disciplinary hearing as one which could result in either the administration by the employer of a formal warning; the taking of some other action by the employer with regard to the worker (such as dismissal or some lesser penalty); or the confirmation of a previously issued warning or of some other action taken by the employer.[878] Whether there has been a 'hearing' for the purposes of the right may not be self-evident; the courts have declined to specify criteria and held that this is a matter for the tribunal to decide on the facts.[879] Moreover, whether a warning is 'formal' may also involve looking beyond the terminology used by the employer; thus a hearing that results in what is described as a 'informal oral warning' may, in practice, attract the right to be accompanied if that

---

[871] This interpretation was confirmed by Lord Triesman, HL Debs col GC 163, 15 June 2004.

[872] ERelA 1999, s 10(4),(5).

[873] See further paras 5.125 *et seq.*

[874] See ERelA 1999, s 13(2).

[875] ERelA 1999, s 11.

[876] ERelA 1999, s 12.

[877] This is the effect of ERelA 1999, s 10(6)–(7).

[878] ERelA 1999, s 13(4). In *London Underground Ltd v Ferenc-Batchelor* [2003] IRLR 252 the EAT held that 'some action' in this context meant some form of disciplinary sanction and would not, therefore, normally cover imposed training, coaching or counselling. See also *Skiggs v South West Trains Ltd* [2005] IRLR 459. In *Heathmill Multimedia ASP Ltd v Jones* [2003] IRLR 856 the EAT held that a meeting at which the applicants were dismissed on grounds of redundancy was not a 'disciplinary hearing'.

[879] *London Underground Ltd v Ferenc-Batchelor* [2003] IRLR 252.

warning has a degree of formality attached to it and becomes part of the employee's disciplinary record.[880]

Grievance procedures are defined by the Act as hearings which concern 'the performance of a duty by an employer in relation to a worker'.[881] The ACAS Code states that this would cover complaints that the employer is not honouring the worker's contract, for example, or is in breach of legislation.[882] Thus whether an individual's request for a pay rise is covered may depend upon whether there is a contractual right to such an increase or an issue about equal pay is raised.[883]

5.124   A further crucial issue is the role of the companion at the relevant hearing. The activities the companion may undertake were spelt out in more detail in ERelA 2004 in an attempt to deal with uncertainties arising from the original definition. It is now made clear that the companion must be permitted by the employer to address the hearing to put the worker's case, sum up that case, and respond on the worker's behalf to any view expressed at the hearing. The companion may also confer with the worker during the hearing.[884] However, importantly, the employer is not required to permit the companion to answer questions on behalf of the worker;[885] the Labour Government rejected calls from unions to change the right to be accompanied to a right to be represented.[886] Nor need the companion be permitted by the employer to use the statutory powers in a way that prevents the employer from explaining its case or any other person at the hearing from contributing to it, nor to address the hearing if the worker indicates at it that he or she does not wish the companion so to do.[887] This latter provision is designed to ensure that the worker remains in control of how the proceedings are conducted on his or her behalf.

(iii) General standards of procedural fairness

5.125   The right to be accompanied, described above, is important in the context of dismissal and other disciplinary action, although, as we have indicated, it extends to many situations beyond those. We now consider the broader principles that apply in considering the fairness of a dismissal. As we indicated in para 5.115 above, the ACAS Code of Practice on Disciplinary and Grievance Procedures is a crucial source of the obligations of both parties, and failure to comply with the Code gives tribunals the discretion to increase or decrease any eventual compensatory award by up to 25% in the event that the employment tribunal considers the failure to have been 'unreasonable'.[888] We examine the contents of that Code, and the principles developed by courts and tribunals, in the paragraphs that follow. As we discussed in para 5.120, while there is

---

[880] [2003] IRLR 252.

[881] ERelA 1999, s 13(5).

[882] Code of Practice, para 34. The Code adopts a wider definition of 'grievances' as 'concerns, problems or complaints that employees raise with their employers': para 1.

[883] Code of Practice, paras 101–102.

[884] ERelA 1999, s 10(2B).

[885] ERelA 1999, s 10(2C)(a).

[886] *Review of the Employment Relations Act 1999: Government Response to the Public Consultation*, DTI, December 2003, para 3.47. The Government disputed the argument that a right to be represented was required by the ECtHR: *Wilson and Palmer v UK* [2002] IRLR 568; see further para 7.9 below.

[887] ERelA 1999, s 10(2), (2C)(b), (c).

[888] TULRCA 1992, s 207A, inserted by EA 2008, s 3.

considerable overlap between the Code and judicially-developed principles, they are not wholly co-extensive and in some instances in the past the courts have found dismissals to be fair even though the provisions of the predecessor Code were not followed.

The 2009 version of the Code is less detailed than its predecessor and ACAS has also produced detailed good practice advice for employers dealing with discipline and grievances at work.[889] Unlike the Code, tribunals are not required to have regard to this advice in making their decisions and space does not permit us to discuss it here. The Code states that '[d]isciplinary situations include misconduct and poor performance'. It indicates that employers who have a separate capability procedure may prefer to address performance issues under that procedure but makes clear that the basic principles of fairness set out in the Code should still be followed, albeit that they may need to be adapted.[890] The Code states that it does not apply to non-renewal of fixed-term contracts on their expiry and redundancy dismissals but does not specifically exclude dismissals for other reasons, such as sickness absence or reorganisation. However these would seem to be excluded by implication.

It should be remembered at this stage that tribunals are required to have regard to the size and administrative resources of an employer's undertaking in deciding whether it has acted reasonably,[891] and the Code makes clear that it may sometimes not be practicable for all employers to take all the steps set out in the Code.[892] Having said that the Code identifies a number of basic elements to fairness which all employers should apply whenever a disciplinary process is being followed. These are to raise and deal with issues promptly; act consistently; carry out any necessary investigations to establish the facts of the case; inform employees of the basis of the problem and give them an opportunity to put their case in response prior to making a decision; allow employees to be accompanied at any formal meeting; and to allow employees to appeal against any formal decision made.[893]

FORMALISATION OF RULES AND PROCEDURES

5.126   The Code emphasises that '[f]airness and transparency are promoted by developing and using rules and procedures for handling disciplinary ... situations'. These should be set down in writing, be specific and clear. Employees and, where appropriate, their representatives should be involved in the development of rules and procedures. It is also important to help employees and managers understand what the rules and procedures are, where they can be found and how they are to be used.[894] The Code states that disciplinary rules should give examples of acts which the employer regards as acts of gross misconduct.[895] It also states that a decision to dismiss should only be taken by a manager who has the authority to do so,[896] a stipulation which may encourage employers who have not already done so to formalise the granting of authority.

---

[889] *Discipline and grievances at work : The Acas Guide*, ACAS, 2009
[890] Code of Practice, para 1.
[891] ERA 1996, s 98(4).
[892] Code of Practice, para 3
[893] Code of Practice, para 4.
[894] See para 4.18 above for the information required to be included in the written statement of employment terms issued to employees. Note that there is no requirement for an employer to distinguish between what is and what is not required by the Code of Practice, nor to notify employees of the consequences of failing to comply with the Code.
[895] Code of Practice, para 23.
[896] Code of Practice, para 21.

As we indicated in para 5.120 above, the provision for adjustment of awards due to non-compliance with the Code has the potential to generate litigation concerning the Code itself. May it be a ground for adjustment that employees or their representatives were not involved in the development of rules and procedures? How extensive should any such involvement be? Although ACAS took the view that having to obtain the agreement of employees or their representatives was too stringent a requirement,[897] what of rules and procedures which employees consider to be manifestly unfair? Although dismissal pursuant to such procedures may result in a finding of unfair dismissal, should it also support an adjustment of the compensatory award? These are examples of the kind of issues with which tribunals may be required to deal.

5.127 Courts and tribunals have held that the non-existence of formalised rules, or the failure to communicate them to employees, does not necessarily prevent the employer from taking disciplinary action in a case of a clear breach of acceptable behaviour, such as theft or fighting at work,[898] or even a serious criminal offence committed outside work.[899] Nor does the mere existence of a rule make a dismissal automatically fair, since a tribunal may conclude that either the rule itself or its application in this case was arbitrary or otherwise unfair.[900] If the rules are incorporated into the employee's contract of employment this may be a factor weighing in the employer's favour,[901] but it is still open to the tribunal to find that while a dismissal was contractually justified, it was unfair under the Act, or vice versa. The contract terms are not in themselves decisive, for example, in determining whether dismissal for a refusal to obey orders was justified. Although it would not be normal for dismissal to be fair where the employee insists on doing only what he or she is required to do by the contract,[902] in exceptional circumstances the employer may be able to argue that the order was reasonable in the light of the need for flexibility.[903] In so far as the employee's implied duty of obedience is concerned, there may well be a high degree of overlap between reasonableness at common law and under the Act, since in each case the tribunal or court will take into account the nature of the work the employee is employed to do as well as the wider needs of the business. Dismissal for refusal to obey an unlawful order is very unlikely to be fair.[904]

INVESTIGATIONS AND SUSPENSION PRIOR TO A DISCIPLINARY HEARING

5.128 The Code states that it is important to carry out necessary investigations of potential disciplinary matters without unreasonable delay to establish the facts of the case. In some cases

---

[897] *Discipline and Grievance Code of Practice – Consultation Outcome*, ACAS, October 2008, para 14.

[898] *Pringle (RA) v Lucas Industrial Equipment Ltd* [1975] IRLR 266.

[899] *Mathewson v RB Wilson Dental Laboratory Ltd* [1988] IRLR 512: an employee arrested and, later, convicted for possession of cannabis, had committed a serious offence since the crime was deliberate and he was in a position of trust.

[900] *Greenslade v Hoveringham Gravels Ltd* [1975] IRLR 114; *Taylor v Parsons Peebles Nei Bruce Peebles Ltd* [1981] IRLR 119; *Ladbroke Racing Ltd v Arnott* [1983] IRLR 154.

[901] Note that the classification of the conduct may be material where the contract provides for differing procedures to deal with different forms of misconduct: *Skidmore v Dartford and Gravesham NHS Trust* [2003] IRLR 445 (although note that the procedure in question has now been withdrawn and replaced by 'maintaining high professional standards in the modern NHS').

[902] As in *Redbridge London Borough Council v Fishman* [1978] ICR 569 but cf *Farrant v Woodroffe School* [1998] IRLR 176.

[903] For example, *Simmonds v Dowty Seals Ltd* [1978] IRLR 211.

[904] *Morrish v Henlys (Folkestone) Ltd* [1973] ICR 482.

this will require the holding of an investigatory meeting with the employee before proceeding to any disciplinary hearing. In others, the investigatory stage will be the collation of evidence by the employer for use at any disciplinary hearing. In misconduct cases, where practicable, different people should carry out the investigation and disciplinary hearing. The Code emphasises that if there is to be an investigatory meeting, this should not by itself result in any disciplinary action. Although there is no statutory right for an employee to be accompanied at an investigatory meeting, the Code states that employers may make provision for this under their own procedure. If a period of suspension with pay is considered necessary, this period should be as brief as possible and should be kept under review and it should be made clear that suspension is not considered a disciplinary action.[905]

DISCIPLINARY HEARINGS

5.129   If it is decided that there is a disciplinary case to answer the Code states that the employee should be notified of this in writing, with sufficient information about the alleged misconduct or poor performance and its possible consequences to enable the employee to prepare the case to answer at a disciplinary meeting. It would normally be appropriate to provide copies of any written evidence, which may include any witness statements, with the notification. The notification should also give details of the time and venue for the disciplinary meeting and advise the employee of his or her right to be accompanied at the meeting. The meeting should be held without unreasonable delay, whilst allowing the employee reasonable time to prepare his or her case, and employers, employees and their companions should make every effort to attend.[906] Rather surprisingly, the Code does not refer to the statutory right to have the meeting postponed in the event that the companion is not available at the stipulated time which we discussed in para 5.121 above. Where an employee is persistently unable or unwilling to attend a disciplinary meeting without good cause, the Code provides that the employer should make a decision on the evidence available.[907]

At the meeting the employer should explain the complaint against the employee and go through the evidence that has been gathered. The employee should be allowed to set out his or her case; to answer any allegations made; and should be given a reasonable opportunity to ask questions, present evidence, call witnesses and be given an opportunity to raise points about any information provided by witnesses. Where an employer or employee intends to call relevant witnesses they should give advance notice that they intend to do this.[908]

Beyond the basic principles of the Code, only a general standard of fairness applies to the conduct of hearings. Thus in *Hussain v Elonex plc*[909] the Court of Appeal rejected a plea by the applicant that his employer's failure to disclose the existence of witness statements to him during the hearing invalidated the procedure. According to Mummery LJ, '[i]t is a matter of what is fair and reasonable in each case', so that, in the absence of a contractual disciplinary procedure, 'there are no hard and fast rigid rules' beyond the basic requirement that the employee should be

---

[905] Code of Practice, paras 5–8. See the observations of the Court of Appeal in *Crawford v Suffolk Mental Health Partnership NHS Trust* [2012] IRLR 402 on the use of suspension.

[906] Code of Practice, paras 9–12.

[907] Code of Practice, para 24.

[908] Code of Practice, para 12.

[909] [1999] IRLR 420. See also *Spence v Department of Agriculture and Rural Development* [2011] IRLR 806, NICA.

informed of the case against him or her and given a chance to respond to it.[910] However it 'is a basic proposition ... that the charge against ... the employee facing dismissal should be precisely framed, and that evidence should be confined to the particulars given in the charge'.[911] The 'circumstances in which it is permissible to go beyond that charge in a decision to take disciplinary action are very limited'.[912] There is no rule of law requiring an employer to give an employee the opportunity to cross-examine a person making a complaint; this will depend upon the circumstances.[913] It may be even be reasonable in certain situations to dismiss an employee on the basis of written statements from fellow employees whose identities remained anonymous to the investigating and the dismissing officer, as well as to the dismissed employee, on the ground that, in a close-knit community, they feared retaliation in the event that their identities were disclosed.[914]

DISCIPLINARY ACTION

5.130 The Code provides that following a disciplinary meeting the employer should decide whether any disciplinary action is justified and inform the employee accordingly in writing. Where misconduct is confirmed or the employee is found to be performing unsatisfactorily the Code states that it is usual to give the employee a written warning; a further act of misconduct or failure to improve performance within a set period would normally result in a final written warning. However, if an employee's first misconduct or unsatisfactory performance is sufficiently serious – where his or her actions are liable to have a serious or harmful impact on the organisation, for example – it may be appropriate to move directly to a final written warning.[915]

The Code states that a written warning should set out the nature of the misconduct or poor performance and the change in behaviour or improvement in performance required, with timescale. The employee should be told how long the warning will remain current and informed of the consequences of further misconduct or failure to improve performance within the set period following a final warning. If a decision to dismiss is taken, the employee should be informed as soon as possible of the reasons for the dismissal, the date on which the employment contract will end, the appropriate period of notice, and the right of appeal.[916] The Code acknowledges that some acts are so serious in themselves or have such serious consequences that they may call for dismissal without notice (ie. summary dismissal) for a first offence[917] but emphasises that a fair disciplinary process should always be followed.[918] The statement in the Code that disciplinary rules should give *examples* of acts which the employer regards as acts of gross misconduct means

---

[910] [1999] IRLR 420, 423. Cf *A v B* [2004] IRLR 405. In *Rhondda Cynon Taf County Borough Council v Close* [2008] IRLR 868 the EAT held that in circumstances where a disciplinary hearing was delayed for two-and-a-half years after the employee's suspension pending a police investigation it was not unreasonable for the employer to put before the hearing references to the charges from the witnesses statements obtained in the police investigation.

[911] *Strouthos v London Underground Ltd* [2004] IRLR 636, [12] (Pill LJ).

[912] *Strouthos v London Underground Ltd* [2004] IRLR 636, [41].

[913] *Santamera v Express Cargo Forwarding t/a IEC Ltd* [2003] IRLR 273.

[914] *Ramsey v Walkers Snack Foods Ltd* [2004] IRLR 754.

[915] Code of Practice, paras 17–19.

[916] Code of Practice, paras 20, 21.

[917] See para 5.18 above for acts that may justify summary dismissal at common law.

[918] Code of Practice, para 22; see also *Retarded Children's Aid Society Ltd v Day* [1978] IRLR 128; *Mathewson v RB Wilson Dental Laboratory Ltd* [1988] IRLR 512. In *Sarkar v West London Mental Health NHS Trust* [2010] IRLR 508 it was unfair to dismiss an employee for gross misconduct when the employer had agreed to use the 'Fair Blame Policy', under which the maximum sanction was a final written warning , for the same matters.

that the fact that a particular act is not specified will not of itself be fatal to the employer's case. The courts have held that, in general, the penalty should be proportionate to the nature of the offence; the position and seniority of the employee; and the degree of wilfulness with which it was committed.[919] It should also be reasonably consistent with the employer's previous practice in similar cases [920] although tribunals have been urged to scrutinise arguments based on disparity with particular care and to bear in mind that ultimately the question is whether in the particular case dismissal is a reasonable response to the misconduct in question.[921]

The previous Code of Practice stated that warnings should be disregarded for disciplinary purposes after a specified period: six months was suggested for a first formal warning, twelve for a final written warning.[922] The current Code is less prescriptive in order to take account of the Court of Appeal decision in *Airbus UK v Webb*.[923] In this case the court was required to consider whether a dismissal was necessarily unfair if the employee would not have been dismissed but for the employer taking into account an expired disciplinary warning. The court regarded the arguments as 'finely balanced' but concluded that there was nothing in the wording of s 98(4) prescribing that the circumstance of the employee's previous misconduct must be ignored by the employer. In reaching this conclusion the court distinguished between the warning itself and the misconduct.[924] According to Mummery LJ:

> ... [a]lthough the warning penalty and the record of it on the file was time limited, the misconduct in respect of which it was given was not .... The language of s 98(4) is wide enough to cover the employee's earlier misconduct as a relevant circumstance of the employer's later decision to dismiss the employee, whose later misconduct is shown by the employer to the ET to be the reason or principal reason for the dismissal. The expired warning does not make the earlier misconduct an irrelevant circumstance under the subsection.[925]

In *Diosynth v Thomson* the Court of Session had held that it was unreasonable for an employer to treat an expired warning as 'tipping the balance in favour of dismissal'.[926] This decision was regarded as distinguishable on the basis that in *Webb* the subsequent misconduct on its own was shown to have been the principal reason for dismissal; the previous misconduct and the expired warning were relevant only to the reasonableness of the employer's response.

Although agreeing that the appeal should be allowed, David Richards J warned that the decision in *Webb* should not encourage reliance on an expired warnings as a matter of course. He also did not consider that there was any 'real distinction' between a warning and the misconduct that gave rise to it.[927] We share this view. As Elias P stated in the EAT it is always open to employers to tailor warnings to the particular circumstances and to make provision for a longer or extended

---

[919] *Ladbroke Racing Ltd v Arnott* [1983] IRLR 154.
[920] *Cain v Leeds Western Health Authority* [1990] IRLR 168.
[921] *Hadjioannou v Coral Casinos* [1981] IRLR 352; *Paul v East Surrey District Health Authority* [1995] IRLR 305.
[922] Code of Practice 2004, paras 20, 22, 24.
[923] [2008] IRLR 309. Greater detail is given in the non-statutory *Discipline and grievances at work: the Acas guide*, 2009, paras 95–97.
[924] Mummery LJ at [44]. Thomas LJ agreed with Mummery LJ's judgment.
[925] Above, note 923, at [55], [56].
[926] [2006] IRLR 284, Lord Philip at [22], [27].
[927] Above note 923 at [86].

time limit if the conduct so warrants.[928] This would be preferable to the convoluted approach in *Webb* which creates further confusion in a context where clarity is crucial.

THE RIGHT TO APPEAL

5.131 The Code states that where an employee feels that the disciplinary action against him or her is wrong or unjust he or she should appeal against the decision, putting the grounds for appeal in writing. Appeals should be heard without unreasonable delay and ideally at an agreed time and place. The appeal should be dealt with impartially and, wherever possible, by a manager who has not previously been involved in the case. Employees should be informed in writing of the results of the appeal as soon as possible.[929]

The courts have held that failure to allow an appeal may result in a finding of unfairness, particularly where the right to appeal forms part of a contractual disciplinary procedure,[930] and a failure to apply the appeal process fairly and fully may do likewise.[931] The Court of Appeal has held that where the initial hearing was unfair or defective in some way tribunals should examine any subsequent proceeding with particular care. However it considered previous dicta requiring the appeal to be 'in essence a rehearing and not a mere review'[932] risked leading tribunals to undertake 'inappropriate' categorisation. The purpose of a tribunal's examination was, rather, 'to determine whether, due to the fairness or unfairness of the procedures adopted, the thoroughness or lack of it of the process and the open-mindedness (or not) of the decision-maker, the overall process was fair, notwithstanding any deficiencies at the early stage'.[933]

SPECIAL CASES

5.132 The Code makes particular provision for two categories of special case.[934]

The first concerns trade union representatives. The Code states that where disciplinary action is being considered against an employee who is a trade union representative the normal disciplinary procedure should be followed. Depending on the circumstances, however, it is advisable to discuss the matter at an early stage with an official employed by the union, after obtaining the employee's agreement.

The second concerns employees who are charged with or convicted of a criminal offence. The Code emphasises that this is not normally in itself reason for disciplinary action. Consideration needs to be given to what effect this has on the employee's suitability to do the job and the relationship with the employer, work colleagues and customers.[935] However the courts have found that where an employee admits to having committed an offence outside work, summary dismissal may be

---

[928] Cited above note 923 at [12].
[929] Code of Practice, paras 25–28.
[930] *West Midlands Co-operative Society Ltd v Tipton* [1986] AC 536, although failure to observe the contractual procedure in every respect does not inevitably make the dismissal unfair: *Westminster City Council v Cabaj* [1996] IRLR 399 (appeal panel composed of two members instead of three).
[931] *Tarbuck v Sainsbury's Supermarkets Ltd* [2006] IRLR 664, Elias P at [80].
[932] *Whitbread & Co plc v Mills* [1988] IRLR 501, 509; *Whitbread plc (t/a Whitbread Medway Inns) v Hall* [2001] IRLR 275.
[933] *Taylor v OCS Group Ltd* [2006] IRLR 613, Smith LJ at [46],[47].
[934] Code of Practice, paras 29, 30.
[935] Code of Practice, para 43. See, for example, *X v Y* [2004] IRLR 625.

justified depending on the circumstances. In *Mathewson v RB Wilson Dental Laboratory Ltd*[936] a skilled and senior employee who was arrested for possession of cannabis during his lunch break was summarily dismissed on returning to work an hour late and explaining the circumstances to his employer. The dismissal was found to be fair, taking into account 'involvement in the use of prohibited drugs; the intervention of the police; the admission by the appellant ...; the possible influence on other members of staff; and the suitability of continuing to employ the appellant in the job for which he was employed'. In respect of allegations of criminal behaviour which are work related, the EAT has suggested that the employer should initiate an investigation if it has not already done so, although being careful 'not to trap the employee into making any sort of admission against his interests'.[937] It would only be in an exceptional case in which 'the circumstances may be so blatant, and the circumstances sufficiently brought to the attention of the employer to warrant a reasonable belief as to guilt', that further investigation may be dispensed with. In *A v B*[938] the EAT emphasised that an investigator should 'focus no less on any potential evidence that may exculpate or at least point towards the innocence of the employee as he should on the evidence directed towards proving the charges against him' particularly where the employee in question is suspended and denied the opportunity of contacting potentially relevant witnesses. These dicta must now be considered in the light of the decision of the Court of Appeal to the effect that the issue of whether investigation into suspected misconduct was reasonable in the circumstances is subject to the 'band of reasonable responses' test.[939] We discuss the implications of this further in para 5.134 below.

(iv) The effect of a failure to comply with procedural requirements

5.133   As we saw in para 5.120, failure to comply with the minimum procedural requirements described above will generally, although not inevitably, result in a finding of unfair dismissal. It is not open to the employer to argue that, notwithstanding a breach of procedure, the dismissal was fair on substantive grounds, either because of facts which emerged later[940] or because, viewed objectively, the failure to operate the procedure would have made no difference to the outcome[941] (although should facts have emerged later that showed that a disciplinary dismissal could have been justified, or that a failure to consult over redundancy would have made no difference, the compensation payable to the employee may be reduced, possibly to nothing[942]). Where the complaint of unfair dismissal is upheld and compensation is awarded, if the tribunal finds that the employer has failed to comply with the ACAS Code of Practice on Disciplinary and Grievance Procedures and that failure was 'unreasonable' the tribunal may, if it considers it just and equitable in all the circumstances to do so, increase any compensatory award it makes to the employee by no more than 25%.[943] There are equivalent provisions permitting the reduction of an award if the

---

[936] [1988] IRLR 512, 513–514.
[937] *Lovie Ltd v Anderson* [1999] IRLR 164, 165.
[938] [2003] IRLR 405, 409.
[939] *Sainsbury's Supermarkets Ltd v Hitt* [2003] IRLR 23.
[940] *W Devis & Sons Ltd v Atkins* [1977] IRLR 314.
[941] *Polkey v AE Dayton Services Ltd* [1987] IRLR 503.
[942] *Sillifant v Powell Duffryn Timber Ltd* [1983] IRLR 91, 97 (Browne-Wilkinson J).
[943] TULRCA 1992, s 207A and Sch A2, inserted by EA 2008; ERA 1996, s 124A, amended by EA 2008, s 3(4).

employee unreasonably fails to comply with the Code, for example by failing to appeal against a disciplinary decision. We discussed the factual disputes that may arise in relation to compliance with the Code, such as whether steps have been taken 'without unreasonable delay', in para 2.21 above and the same points arise in this context. Equally the same points are relevant to the scope for appeal against decisions to adjust awards. It remains to be seen whether the new provisions are more successful than their predecessor in encouraging disputes to be resolved at workplace level and whether they, too, generate additional litigation.

It should be noted that dismissals effected by employers who have complied with the requirements of the Code of Practice and the general principles of procedural fairness established by the courts are likely to be fair, even if it later appears that the employee was innocent of the disciplinary charges brought against him or her, or if a more thorough investigation would have revealed this to be the case. This is because the procedural obligation imposed on the employer is far from absolute; the employer's internal procedures do not have to resemble those of a court or tribunal, nor do they have to comply with the strict requirements of natural justice – such as the rule against personal bias or the employer being judge in his own cause – in so far as they go further than the Code.[944] Moreover the requirement for tribunals to consider the size and administrative resources of the undertaking in deciding reasonableness[945] means that less stringent standards may be demanded where the business is relatively small.

(v) Misconduct: particular features

5.134   In a case of dismissal for a serious disciplinary offence, such as theft or fighting, the courts applied for many years a three-fold test, requiring an employer to show first, that it honestly believed that the employee had committed the offence in question; second, that it had reasonable grounds upon which to sustain that belief; and third, that the employer had at the stage at which the belief was formed carried out as much investigation into the matter as was reasonable in the circumstances of the case.[946] On this the EAT suggested that there was, in effect, a sliding scale of responsibility:

> ... at one extreme there will be cases where the employee is virtually caught in the act and at the other there will be situations where the issue is one of pure inference. As the scale moves towards the latter end, so the amount of inquiry and investigation, including questioning of the employee, which may be required is likely to increase. The sufficiency of

---

[944] *Slater v Leicestershire Health Authority* [1989] IRLR 16.

[945] ERA 1996, s 98(4)(a).

[946] *British Home Stores Ltd v Burchell* [1978] IRLR 379; *W Weddell & Co Ltd v Tepper* [1980] ICR 286. In *Boys and Girls Welfare Society v McDonald* [1996] IRLR 129 the EAT held that a 'simplistic application' (at 132) of the *Burchell* test, promulgated when the onus lay on employers to show that they had acted reasonably, could lead tribunals into error. In practice, however, it is difficult to see how an employer who did not act in accordance with its terms could nevertheless have acted reasonably, a view affirmed by the Court of Session in *Scottish Daily Record and Sunday Mail (1986) Ltd v Laird* [1996] IRLR 665. In *Perkin v St George's Healthcare NHS Trust* [2005] IRLR 934 the Court of Appeal held that there was no reason why the *Burchell* principles should be limited to conduct cases: Wall LJ at [65]. In *Orr v Milton Keynes Council* [2011] IRLR 317, the Court of Appeal held that in a large organisation the person deputed to carry out the employer's functions under s 98 was the person whose state of mind was intended to count as that of 'the employer', and that knowledge should not be imputed to that person which he or she did not have and could not reasonably have obtained.

the relevant evidence and the reasonableness of the conclusion seem to us to be inextricably intertwined.[947]

In 2002, however, the Court of Appeal held that the third element of this test – whether investigation into suspected misconduct was reasonable in the circumstances – was subject to the 'band of reasonable responses' test discussed in para 5.116 *et seq*.[948] Thus, tribunals should not substitute their own view as to what was a reasonable and adequate investigation; rather they should apply 'the objective standard of the reasonable employer as to what was a reasonable investigation'.[949] The general criticisms that we made of the 'band of reasonable responses' test in our discussion above apply with even greater strength in this context; the idea that a very basic principle of procedural justice should itself be subject to the broad and highly speculative test of whether a reasonable employer might have considered what was done to be reasonable is particularly troubling in the light of the severe consequences for an employee's reputation of dismissal for theft or other acts of serious misconduct.[950]

A further issue that may arise in the context of misconduct dismissals is whether it is fair to dismiss more than one employee if it is not possible to identify which of them was responsible for offences being committed. Since the employer is normally required to take into account not simply the circumstances surrounding the alleged offence but also the seniority and past record of the individual employee concerned, it would be difficult to justify a group dismissal which takes no account of such individual circumstances. Nonetheless, in an exceptional case a group dismissal may be possible, where, for example, an employer reasonably concludes, following an investigation, that a number of employees could have committed the act in question, that each member of the group in question was capable of having done so and that 'as between members of the group the employer could not reasonably identify the individual perpetrator; then, provided that the beliefs were held on solid and sensible grounds at the date of dismissal, an employer is entitled to dismiss each member of the group'.[951]

(vi) Capability: particular features

5.135   Broadly the same principles concerning procedural fairness apply by extension to cases of dismissal for incapability on the grounds of lack of competence or illness.[952] According to the EAT, where illness causes intermittent absences from work, 'it is important to realise that these cases are not cases of disciplinary situations; what is important is that the employers should treat each case individually where there is genuine illness and with sympathy, understanding and compassion'.

---

[947] *ILEA v Gravett* [1988] IRLR 497, 499.

[948] *Sainsbury's Supermarkets Ltd v Hitt* [2003] IRLR 23.

[949] *Sainsbury's Supermarkets Ltd v Hitt* [2003] IRLR 23, [28] (Mummery LJ).

[950] Cf *A v B* [2003] IRLR 405, [58] *et seq* and *Salford Royal NHS Foundation Trust v Roldan* [2010] IRLR 721, where Elias LJ emphasised at [13] that it was particularly important that employers took seriously their responsibilities to conduct a fair investigation where the employee's reputation or ability to work in his or her chosen field of employment was potentially apposite.

[951] *Parr v Whitbread and Co plc* [1990] ICR 427, 432 (Wood J); *Monie v Coral Racing Ltd* [1981] ICR 109.

[952] For the suggestion that employers may, in certain circumstances, have a duty to dismiss employees on health grounds for their own good, see *Coxall v Goodyear Great Britain Ltd* [2002] IRLR 742, [29] (Simon Brown LJ), discussed by Elvin, 2003.

The purpose of a warning in this context is not to get the individual to change his or her behaviour, but 'to give a caution that the stage has been reached where with the best will in the world, it becomes impossible to continue with the employment'.[953] The employee need not necessarily be absent from work at the time of dismissal, nor need the employer require firm medical evidence that the absences will continue, if there has been a regular pattern in the past; factors to be taken into account in considering whether to dismiss include the nature of the illness; the likelihood of its recurring; the length of the absences in relation to the periods of good health; the employer's dependence on the work done by the employee; the effect of their absence on fellow workers; the ease with which the employee's work could be redeployed during their absence; and 'the extent to which the difficulty of the situation and the position of the employer has [sic] been made clear to the employee so that the employee realises that the point of no return, the moment when the decision was ultimately being made may be approaching'.[954] In the case of long-term sickness proper consideration should be given to al ill-health retirement scheme before dismissal.[955] The Court of Appeal has confirmed that the fact that an employer has caused the incapacity in question, however culpably, cannot preclude it from effecting a fair dismissal, although it may be relevant to whether and, if so, when it is reasonable to dismiss the employee for that incapacity; thus, it may be necessary to 'go the extra mile' in finding alternative employment for such an employee or to allow a longer period of sickness absence than would otherwise be reasonable. However tribunals should not substitute an unfair dismissal award for the compensation for injury to which an employee may be entitled in the ordinary courts.[956]

Substantive fairness

5.136   To what extent, if at all, does section 98 of the Act embody a notion of substantive fairness in dismissal, which can be related to the result and not simply to the process or procedure leading up to it? Whether the individual's interest in job security is viewed as akin to a 'property right' in the job[957] or, more justifiably, as a right to the recognition of their personal dignity and autonomy,[958] the protection accorded by section 98 is highly qualified. To date, limitations placed on the free speech or self-expression of employees have generally been permitted if the employer could show that they were loosely justified on business-related grounds. What the tribunal aims for 'is the striking of a balance between the need of the employer to control the business for which he is responsible, in the interests of the business itself – and after all, it is upon its continued prosperity that everybody's interests depend – a balance between that need, on the one hand,

---

[953] *Lynock v Cereal Packaging Ltd* [1988] IRLR 510, 511.

[954] [1988] IRLR 510, 512. See also the earlier case of *Spencer v Paragon Wallpapers Ltd* [1977] ICR 301, and on warnings in the context of incompetence, *James v Waltham Holy Cross UDC* [1973] ICR 398. There is no rule that an employer, in operating a sickness absence procedure, must leave out of account disability-related absences: *Royal Liverpool Children's NHS Trust v Dunsby* [2006] IRLR 351. In Case C-13/05 *Chacon Navas v Eurest Colectividades SA* [2006] IRLR 706 the ECJ held that a person who has been dismissed solely on account of sickness is not protected by the prohibition against discrimination on grounds of disability in Framework Directive 2000/78.

[955] *First West Yorkshire Ltd t/a First Leeds v Haigh* [2008] IRLR 182.

[956] *McAdie v Royal Bank of Scotland plc* [2007] IRLR 895.

[957] Cf Meyers, 1964.

[958] H Collins, 1993: p 28; see para 5.5 above.

and the reasonable freedom of the employee, on the other'.[959] The employer has accordingly been accorded a wide discretion to impose rules relating, for example, to dress codes, or guidelines governing the personal appearance of employees;[960] conversely, the employer has been given a discretion 'to instruct an employee not to wear some sign or symbol that could be offensive to fellow-employees and customers'.[961] Moreover the 'band of reasonable responses' test discussed in para 5.116 *et seq*, in embodying a reactive standard that incorporates not the best employer practice but an ill-defined 'middle ground', also diminishes standards of substantive fairness.[962]

These decisions may now require reconsideration in the light of the Human Rights Act 1998; more generally, it is strongly arguable that the 'band of reasonable responses' test should not be applied in its existing form where an employee's Convention rights have been violated, although to date judicial comments to this effect have been *obiter*.[963] To date, however, the HRA has not led to the application of the more rigorous test of proportionality in the context of the reasonableness test for unfair dismissal that some had argued for when an employee's Convention rights are at issue.[964]

The courts have attempted to give some general guidance on how tribunals should consider HRA points in the context of unfair dismissal cases. The Court of Appeal has confirmed that section 3 of the HRA requires tribunals to read and give effect to the unfair dismissal legislation in a way that is compatible with Convention rights so far as it is possible to do so regardless of the legal identity of the employer.[965] However according to Mummery LJ, in general section 3 can be ignored; 'the reasonable expectation is that a decision that a dismissal was fair under s 98 would not be incompatible with Article 8 or Article 14 of the Convention'[966] (an assertion for which, unfortunately, no clear authority or justification was provided). He proposed that in cases between private litigants, tribunals should ask first whether the circumstances of the dismissal fall within the ambit of a Convention right; second, if so, whether the state has a positive obligation to secure enjoyment of that right between private persons (since, if not, the right is unlikely to affect the outcome of the claim);[967] and third, if the state does have such an obligation, whether the interference with the right in question is justified. If the interference is not justified, the tribunal should then ask whether there is a permissible reason for the dismissal which does not involve unjustified interference with a Convention right: if not the dismissal would be unfair. If there

---

[959] *Boychuk v HJ Symons Holdings Ltd* [1977] IRLR 395, 396. See Mantouvalou, 2008 for a critique of decisions relating to dismissal for activities outside the workplace and outside working hours.

[960] *Schmidt v Austicks Bookshops Ltd* [1978] ICR 85; *Department for Work and Pensions v Thompson* [2004] IRLR 348.

[961] *Boychuk v HJ Symons Holdings Ltd* [1977] IRLR 395, 396.

[962] Its most controversial application was the decision of the EAT in *Saunders v Scottish National Camps Association* [1980] IRLR 174, where the dismissal of an attendant in a boys' camp on the grounds solely of his homosexuality was found to be fair, even though he regarded his sexuality as an entirely private matter and there was no evidence of it affecting the way he performed his job. This would now be contrary to EqA 2010, but the court's approach to the band of reasonable responses in this case may still apply in other contexts.

[963] *Pay v Lancashire Probation Service* [2004] IRLR 129, [33]–[34]. In *Pay v UK* [2009] IRLR 139 the ECtHR declared inadmissible the complaint that the probation officer's dismissal for his bondage, domination and sado-masochist performances violated Art 8 of the ECHR; even if Art 8 was applicable (which was not decided), dismissal was not a disproportionate response in the circumstances. The interference with his freedom of expression under Art 10 was also held to be justified, and there was a reasonable and objective justification under Art 14. See further Mantouvalou and Collins, 2009.

[964] *Copsey v WWB Devon Clays Ltd* [2005] IRLR 811; H Collins, 2006; Mantouvalou, 2008

[965] *X v Y* [2004] IRLR 625.

[966] *X v Y* [2004] IRLR 625, [58(5)]. Arts 8 and 14 were the Convention rights at issue in that case.

[967] In practice, this is highly likely to be the case.

is justification for the interference, the tribunal should then ask whether the dismissal was fair, reading and giving effect to section 98 of ERA 1996 under section 3 of the HRA so as to be compatible with the Convention right.[968]

5.137 It should be noted that, equality law aside, the employer can make the out-of-work activities of the employee a relevant matter from the point of view of employment by raising them prior to the formation of the contract of employment. The lack of effective controls over the hiring stage is also significant here.[969] An employee who conceals his past or his out-of-work activities is open to dismissal on the ground of misrepresentation, however irrelevant the matter might be to the subsequent performance of his or her job, although this is now subject to restrictions on pre-employment health questions which we discuss in chapter 6.[970]

The Rehabilitation of Offenders Act 1974 establishes a special category of cases in this area: an employee is entitled to mislead a prospective employer at the point of hiring by not revealing the existence of a spent conviction, and grounds related to the conviction cannot constitute a proper ground for dismissal thus rendering a dismissal for this reason, in effect, automatically unfair. More generally, the categories of automatically unfair reasons creates a space in which the 'balancing act' between substantive rights and the employer's business interests is, by and large, avoided; however, these categories are, as we have seen, an essentially arbitrary grouping.

REMEDIES FOR UNFAIR DISMISSAL

Re-employment

5.138 ERA 1996 provides[971] that if, on a finding of unfair dismissal, the employee indicates a wish to be re-employed, the tribunal may make an order of either reinstatement or re-engagement under sections 114 and 115; if no order is made under this section, it must make an award of compensation calculated in accordance with sections 118 to 126. Accordingly, 'the preferred remedies for unfair dismissal are reinstatement, re-engagement and monetary compensation in that order'.[972] The term 're-employment', while not appearing in the Act, is used here as a genus term covering both reinstatement and re-engagement.

5.139 An order for reinstatement requires the employer to 'treat the complainant in all respects as if he had not been dismissed', and must specify any amount payable by the employer in respect of the period during which the employee should have been, but was not, in employment, including back pay, and also any rights and privileges, including seniority and pension rights,

---

[968] [2004] IRLR 625, [63].

[969] See paras 3.14 and 3.15 above.

[970] See EqA 2010, s 60, discussed in para 6.129 below. See *O'Brien v Prudential Assurance Co Ltd* [1979] IRLR 140 for an example of an employee whose dismissal was for SOSR and fair when he had failed to disclose on his application form a history of mental illness.

[971] Section 116(1), (2).

[972] *O'Laoire v Jackel International Ltd* [1990] ICR 197, 200 (Lord Donaldson MR).

which should be restored to the employee.[973] In effect, then, the employee is put back into the job which he or she occupied, restored to the benefits he or she enjoyed and compensated for those lost in the interim. Re-engagement, by contrast, involves re-employment by the employer or an associated employer in employment 'comparable to that from which he was dismissed or other suitable employment'.[974] The order for re-engagement must specify the identity of the employer, the nature of the employment, the remuneration to be paid, an amount payable for lost benefit in the period following dismissal, and rights and benefits to be restored to the employee.[975] Orders for reinstatement and re-engagement must also indicate the date by which they must be complied with.

In each case the award is discretionary. In deciding upon reinstatement, the tribunal must consider not simply whether the complainant wishes to be reinstated, but also 'whether it is practicable for the employer to comply with an order for reinstatement' and, in a case where the employee contributed to the dismissal, whether reinstatement would be 'just'.[976] If reinstatement is not deemed appropriate the tribunal will go on to consider re-engagement, whereupon it will take the same factors into account.[977] Except in a case where the employee contributed to his or her own dismissal, an order for re-engagement must be on terms 'which are, so far as reasonably practicable, as favourable as an order for reinstatement'.[978] In exercising its discretion to make either order, the tribunal may not take into account the fact that the employer has hired a permanent replacement for the complainant unless the employer can show that it was not practicable to do otherwise or that it engaged the replacement after a reasonable period had elapsed without the complainant indicating that he or she wished to be re-employed.[979]

5.140   The statutory order for re-employment is unlike an equitable order restraining dismissal by way of an injunction or declaration in two important respects. First, the statutory order necessarily assumes that there has been a dismissal and, as a result, that not just the employment but also the contractual nexus itself has been broken. This is one reason why reinstatement, although the 'primary' remedy for unfair dismissal, is 'something of a rarity... [It] may be that by the time that the complaint reaches the ... [employment] ... tribunal, relations between the complainant and his employer have usually reached a stage at which reinstatement has ceased to be a realistic option'.[980] It seems that it is formally or perhaps psychologically more difficult to put the employee back into a job which he or she has 'lost' than it is to enable them to retain it; for the employment tribunal, the status quo is the dismissal which the statutory order must reverse, whereas for the

---

[973] ERA 1996, s 114(1), (2). If the employee would have benefited from a further improvement in terms and conditions during the period in question, that must also be taken into account from the date when such improvement would have come into effect: s 114(3). Note also the provision for adjustment of the amount payable to the employee where he or she has been in receipt of certain payments: s 114(4).

[974] ERA 1996, s 115(1).

[975] ERA 1996, s 115(2).

[976] ERA 1996, s 116(1).

[977] ERA 1996, s 116(2). In *King v Royal Bank of Canada Europe Ltd* [2012] IRLR 280, the EAT held that the relevant time to consider the question of re-engagement in alternative employment was the time of the hearing.

[978] ERA 1996, s 116(4). In *Rank Xerox (UK) Ltd v Stryczek* [1995] IRLR 568 the EAT held that re-engagement could not be on *more* favourable terms than reinstatement.

[979] ERA 1996, s 116(5), (6).

[980] *O'Laoire v Jackel International Ltd* [1990] ICR 197, 201 (Lord Donaldson MR).

High Court the status quo is the position prior to the employer's alleged breach of contract, so that in the latter case the 'balance of convenience' inherently favours the employee.[981]

The second major difference is that the employer will not incur contempt of court proceedings for refusing to implement a statutory order for re-employment. The statutory order does not have the power to 'concentrate the mind'[982] in the way that the equitable order can. Under section 117 of the Act, in a case where an order for reinstatement or re-engagement is not fully complied with, the only option is for the tribunal to make one or more of a number of compensatory awards to the employee. Two situations need to be considered. The first is where the employee is taken back into employment, but the terms of the order are not fully complied with. Here the tribunal can make an award of compensation of such amount as it thinks fit, having regard to the employee's loss. This sum is calculated according to the principles laid down for the computation of the compensatory award in section 124 of the Act, except that the statutory maximum for such an award (as of 1 February 2012 and at the time of writing £72,300)[983] may be exceeded to the extent necessary to enable the award fully to reflect the amount specified in the reinstatement or re-engagement order as payable for the period between termination of employment and the date of re-employment.[984] A more highly-paid employee might therefore receive substantial compensation under this head.

The second situation is where the employee is not reinstated or, in an appropriate case, re-engaged. Here the tribunal makes a basic award, a compensatory award and a further 'additional award' to reflect the employer's failure to comply with that order.[985] The additional award is an amount equivalent to between 26 and 52 weeks' pay.[986] Once again the statute allows the limits on the compensatory award to be exceeded, in this context to enable the aggregate of the compensatory and additional awards to reflect the amount specified as payable in the re-instatement and re-engagement order.[987] However the courts have held that the arrears of pay that would have been payable had reinstatement or re-engagement taken place are subsumed in the compensatory award, so where those arrears do not themselves exceed the statutory limit on the compensatory award, the total award is subject to the statutory cap.[988]

5.141   The employer may avoid the additional award by showing that it was not practicable to comply with the order.[989] This means that the employer gets two chances to argue for the impracticability of re-employment. According to the EAT, 'one process looks forward, the other looks back and although it may be that a cherry that is rejected at the first bite will be likely to be regarded as indigestible at the second, there is in our view no doubt at all that two bites are allowed'.[990] The determination of practicability at the first stage does not raise an estoppel against

---

[981] See para 5.58 above.

[982] *Jones v Gwent County Council* [1992] IRLR 521, 527. Cf also the provisions of the Reserve Forces (Safeguard of Employment) Act 1985, as amended.

[983] ERA 1996, s 124(1), as amended; see para 5.145 below.

[984] ERA 1996, s 124(3). Any award under s 112(5) is deducted from this award.

[985] ERA 1996, s 117(3).

[986] ERA 1996, s 117(3). Again this is subject to the statutory maximum limit, which stands £430 at 1 February 2012 and at the time of writing: ERA 1996, s 227(1).

[987] Section 124(4).

[988] *Parry v National Westminster Bank plc* [2005] IRLR 193; see also *Selfridges Ltd v Malik* [1997] IRLR 577.

[989] ERA 1996, s 117(4)(a).

[990] *Mabrizi v National Hospital for Nervous Diseases* [1990] IRLR 133, 135 (Knox J).

the employer putting a different point of view at the second stage.[991] At the first stage, the tribunal is simply required to 'take into account' the question of practicability, but must nevertheless make a determination that the remedy would be practicable and so must give due consideration to arguments that it is not.[992] At the second stage, the burden is clearly placed on the employer to satisfy the tribunal that re-employment was not practicable.[993]

At both stages, the courts have made it clear that what is practicable should not be equated with what is possible. The tribunal should not award re-engagement, it has been said, where 'the evidence points overwhelmingly to the conclusion that the consequence of any attempt to re-engage the employee will result in serious industrial strife'.[994] Nor would it be appropriate where the parties had been in a 'close personal relationship' which has irretrievably broken down,[995] or where the employer, no matter how unreasonably, remains convinced of the employee's wrongdoing.[996] To this extent, the exercise of the tribunal's statutory discretion follows the approach of the courts at common law: factors of the kind to be taken into account are 'the fact that the atmosphere in the factory is poisoned ... the fact that the employee has displayed her distrust and lack of confidence in her employers and would not be a satisfactory employee on reinstatement ... insufficient employment for the employee'.[997]

The Court of Appeal has also said that the tribunal must avoid substituting its commercial judgment for that of the employer. In *Port of London Authority v Payne*[998] a decision that re-engagement was not impracticable on the grounds that the employer could have considered offering voluntary redundancy to existing staff in order to make way for the applicant was held to have been incorrect. The tribunal:

> ... should give due weight to the commercial judgment of the management unless of course the witnesses are disbelieved. The standard must not be set too high. The employer cannot be expected to explore every possible avenue which ingenuity might suggest. The employer does not have to show that reinstatement or re-engagement was *impossible*. It is a matter of what is practicable in the circumstances of the employer's business at the relevant time.

One difficulty with this approach is that it creates a further stage at which the employee's rights can be defeated by the invocation of business-related factors which, by their nature, are exceptionally difficult for a tribunal to challenge or to second-guess; the 'band of reasonableness' test is carried over to the stage of remedies.

5.142   Orders of re-engagement and reinstatement have amounted on average to around only 5% of successful unfair dismissal claims and 1% of all claims proceeding to a hearing since the

---

[991] *Timex Corpn v Thomson* [1981] IRLR 522; *Port of London Authority v Payne* [1994] IRLR 9.

[992] *Port of London Authority v Payne* [1994] IRLR 9, 14; Bennett, 1994.

[993] ERA 1996, s 117(4)(a); see also *Port of London Authority v Payne* above.

[994] *Bateman v British Leyland UK Ltd* [1974] ICR 403, 406; *Coleman and Stephenson v Magnet Joinery Ltd* [1975] ICR 46.

[995] *Enessy Co SA (t/a Tulchan Estate) v Minoprio* [1978] IRLR 489.

[996] *Wood Group Heavy Industrial Turbines Ltd v Crossan* [1998] IRLR 680; D Lewis,1999.

[997] *Rao v Civil Aviation Authority* [1992] IRLR 203, 207.

[998] [1994] IRLR 9, 16. This was a case concerning entitlement to enhanced compensation as part of the special award for trade-union related dismissals under what is now TULRCA 1992, s 158, where the same test of practicability applies. See also *Cold Drawn Tubes Ltd v Middleton* [1992] IRLR 160; and see further, para 8.5 below.

introduction of the present remedy in 1975. The Warwick survey of the employment tribunal system which was carried out by the Industrial Relations Research Unit in the early 1980s reported a figure of 7.6% of cases in a survey sample resulting in re-employment, and there is some evidence that the Department of Employment figures might underestimate the true extent of re-employment by not counting cases in which it is brought about by agreement between the parties rather than being ordered by the tribunal.[999] In 2010/11 only 8 cases out of 4,200 unfair dismissal claims upheld by a tribunal resulted in orders of reinstatement or re-engagement.[1000]

Research in this area has shown several reasons for the low rate of re-employment. One is that applicants may not ask to be reinstated; this is especially likely to be the case in smaller firms, where employees in this position are unlikely to benefit from a protective union environment and where they will come into personal contact with the manager or owner who was responsible for their dismissal.[1001] But another factor is the reluctance of tribunals to make this order in all but the most exceptional cases. The Warwick survey concluded that:

> ... the [employment] tribunals pay a lot of attention to the employers' views regarding the acceptability and practicability of re-employment and rarely award the remedy in the face of employer opposition. This is partly because of a view that re-employment which has to be imposed will not work.[1002]

This perception may not be justified; research published in 1981 found that re-employment rarely produces disruption to relations within the undertaking concerned and that most reinstated or re-engaged employees stay with the employer for a reasonable length of time after the order is made.[1003]

Compensation

5.143   In a case where no order of re-employment is made, the Act envisages an award of compensation which comes in two parts, a basic and a compensatory award.[1004]

(i) The basic award

5.144   The basic award is meant to reflect the loss of accrued continuity of employment following the dismissal: on finding new employment, the employee will have to begin again to acquire the continuity needed for the purposes of entitlement to a statutory redundancy payment. Under the original unfair dismissal jurisdiction conferred by the Industrial Relations Act 1971, the courts would include within damages a sum representing the discounted value of lost unfair dismissal

---

[999] L Dickens *et al*, 1985: p 110; and see the discussion in para 2.16 *et seq* above.
[1000] HMCTS *Employment Tribunals and EAT Statistics, 2010-11*, Table 3.
[1001] L Dickens *et al*, 1985: pp 114–119; K Williams, 1983.
[1002] L Dickens *et al*, 1985: p 138.
[1003] K Williams and D Lewis, 1981. To date only a small number of cases have been determined under the ACAS arbitration scheme, discussed in para 2.20.
[1004] ERA 1996, s 118.

and redundancy rights;[1005] the present basic award was introduced by the EPA 1975 in order to put this practice on a firmer statutory basis as far as redundancy is concerned. Accordingly, the basic award is calculated in precisely the same way as a statutory redundancy payment, so that it is a function of the employee's age, length of service and normal weekly pay at the time of dismissal;[1006] it is also reduced by the amount of any statutory redundancy payment actually received by the employee in respect of the dismissal.[1007] From 1 February 2012 and at the time of writing, the maximum amount which may be awarded under this head is £12,900 as a result of the present upper limit of £430 applicable to an employee's normal weekly pay for these purposes.[1008] If, however, the employee is made redundant in circumstances such that he or she is unfairly dismissed but does not qualify for a redundancy payment, either because they refuse to accept a suitable offer of re-employment[1009] or because their contract is renewed or they are re-engaged within four weeks of the dismissal,[1010] the Act provides that they should receive a basic award equivalent to two weeks' pay.[1011] Because the basic award covers only redundancy compensation and not unfair dismissal rights, a sum representing the loss of the latter may be included in the compensatory award; it is common to award an amount of around a few hundred pounds under this head.

A minimum basic award of £5,300 is payable if the employee was dismissed or selected for redundancy on grounds related to trade-union membership or activities, blacklisting, or on grounds of activities as a health and safety representative, employee representative (including representation for the purposes of working time), or trustee of an occupational pension scheme.[1012] In general, reductions in the basic award may be made for the employee's contributory fault[1013] and for the employee's refusal to accept an offer of reinstatement; both of these may also go to reduce the minimum amount payable in the special cases stated above.[1014] A reduction may also be made in respect of the employee's misconduct prior to the dismissal,[1015] and for any redundancy payment awarded in respect of the same dismissal or other payment by the employer on the ground that the dismissal was by reason of redundancy.[1016]

[1005] *Norton Tool Co Ltd v Tewson* [1972] ICR 501 (Sir John Donaldson P).

[1006] ERA 1996, s 119, as amended; on the calculation of the statutory redundancy payments, see para 5.164 below. *Quaere* whether the age -related structure of the award is compatible with EU law in the light of Case C-555/07 *Kücükdevici v Swedex GMBH and Co KG* [2010] IRLR 346.

[1007] ERA 1996, s 122(4). However, this applies only where the dismissal was, in fact, by reason of redundancy; thus, no deduction should be made under s 122(4) for the element of an *ex gratia* payment expressed as incorporating the employee's statutory redundancy entitlement: *Boorman v Allmakers Ltd* [1995] IRLR 553.

[1008] ERA 1996, s 227. The calculation of a week's pay in this context (and the loss of earnings for the compensatory award) is subject to the national minimum wage: *Paggetti v Cobb* [2002] IRLR 861.

[1009] ERA 1996, s 141(2)–(4).

[1010] ERA 1996, s 138(1).

[1011] ERA 1996, s 121.

[1012] TULRCA 1992, s 156(1); ERA 1996, s 120(1).

[1013] This does not apply in a redundancy case unless the reason for selecting the employee for dismissal was one of those in respect of which a minimum award is payable under section 120(1); in that case s 122(2) applies only to so much of the basic award as is payable because of s 120(1): s 122(3).

[1014] ERA 1996, s 122(1)–(3); the parallel provision in trade union cases is TULRCA 1992, s 156.

[1015] ERA 1996, s 122(2)–(3); see below.

[1016] ERA 1996, s 122(4). See also s 122(3A) in respect of awards under a designated dismissal procedures agreement.

(ii) The compensatory award

5.145 The compensatory award payable under section 123 is 'such amount as the tribunal considers just and equitable in all the circumstances having regard to the loss sustained by the complainant in consequence of the dismissal in so far as that loss is attributable to action taken by the employer'.[1017] Awards under this head are currently subject to an upper limit which since 1 February 2012 and at the time of writing stands at £72,300.[1018] The Labour Government's *Fairness at Work* White Paper proposed the abolition of the maximum limit to the compensatory award, on the grounds that this would both enable individuals to be fully compensated for their losses and encourage employers to establish more effective voluntary systems.[1019] This proposal followed a decades-long decline in the value of the upper limit relative to average earnings since it was first set in the Industrial Relations Act 1971. The Secretary of State had power to raise this sum by order[1020] but, in contrast with the regulations governing the up-rating of most social security benefits, he or she had no obligation to make an annual increase, nor need any increase be linked to inflation. ERelA 1999 substituted a new requirement on the Secretary of State to adjust (upwards or downwards) the upper limit once a year in line with any changes in the retail prices index 'as soon as practicable' following the publication of the September year-on-year figures.[1021] The upper limit does not apply to dismissal (or, subject to specified conditions, selection for redundancy) on health and safety grounds, nor to dismissal for making a 'protected disclosure'.[1022] More generally, no upper compensation limits applies to compensation under EqA 2010. The upper limit was removed for cases involving sex discrimination on the grounds of its incompatibility with Directive 76/307,[1023] and a parallel change was later made in relation to cases of racial discrimination[1024] and applied to disability discrimination and discrimination on grounds of religion or belief, sexual orientation, and age.[1025] The cap on the compensatory award, which may preclude tribunals from awarding full compensation for a dismissed employee's financial loss, was blamed by the House of Lords as the principal cause of the 'awkward and unfortunate consequences' flowing from the unsatisfactory inter-relation between the common law and statute in the context of dismissal,[1026] discussed in para 5.44 above.

[1017] ERA 1996, s 123(1). The loss must be *in consequence of* the dismissal rather than antecedent breaches of the implied term of trust and confidence; on the implications of this in the context of unfair constructive dismissal see *GAB Robins (UK) Ltd v Triggs* [2008] IRLR 317.

[1018] ERA 1996, s 124(1) (as amended by SI 2008/3055). The Enterprise and Regulatory Reform Bill contains provisions allowing the Secretary of State to specify different awards for 'different descriptions' of employers.

[1019] *Fairness at Work*, Cm 3968, 1968, para 3.5.

[1020] ERA 1996, ss 124(2), 236(3), now repealed.

[1021] ERelA 1999, s 34. The Coalition Government decided to retain this formula, with the amendment that rounding should be to the nearest pound: *Resolving Workplace Disputes: Government response to the consultation*, paras 147–153.

[1022] ERA 1996, s 124(1A).

[1023] *Marshall v Southampton and South West Hampshire Area Health Authority (No 2)* Case C-271/91 [1993] IRLR 445; SI 1993/2798; see para 6.66 below.

[1024] Race Relations (Remedies) Act 1994.

[1025] See now EqA 2010, s 124(2)(b), discussed para 6.66 below. The CA has held that where an employee has been subject to discrimination, unfair dismissal does not break the chain of causation for the purposes of assessing loss: *HM Prison Service v Beart (No 2)* [2005] IRLR 568.

[1026] *Eastwood v Magnox Electric plc* [2004] IRLR 733, para 33 (Lord Nicholls).

5.146   The object of the compensatory award 'is to compensate, and to compensate fully, but not to award a bonus'.[1027] At the same time, the common law categories of loss are not directly relevant: the statutory claim is 'an entirely new cause of action'.[1028] The limited common law right of the employee to continued employment – the consequence of the notice rule[1029] – no longer poses an automatic barrier to substantial compensation claims. In a creative gloss on the statute the NIRC suggested that 'in the context of unfair dismissal … it is appropriate and in accordance with the intentions of Parliament that we should treat an employee as having suffered a loss in so far as he receives less than he would have received in accordance with good industrial practice'.[1030] The principal application of this idea was in a series of cases ruling that an employee should be entitled to receive compensation representing wages in lieu of notice, regardless of actual earnings he or she may have had from alternative employment during the notice period. At common law, such earnings would automatically reduce the damages payable by the employer, but under the Act the NIRC considered that it was 'good industrial practice' for an employer to pay wages in lieu as a matter of course, and that there should accordingly be no deduction from this payment in respect of the employee's earnings.[1031] This was a surprising interpretation in the light of an express statutory instruction to the effect that 'the tribunal shall apply the same rule concerning the duty of a person to mitigate his loss as applies to damages recoverable under the common law',[1032] and produced the anomalous result that a failure to mitigate by looking for work counted against the employee when actual mitigation did not. In *Burlo v Langley*[1033] the Court of Appeal confirmed that the 'narrow principle' established in *Norton Tool* that there should be no requirement to give credit for sums earned from other employers during the notice period should continue to be applied until the House of Lords decided otherwise. However the Court held that *Norton Tool* should not be extended to allow principles of good employment practice to be relied upon in other areas where this would result in an award greater than the loss caused to the employee in consequence of the dismissal. Thus, where the employee was sick during the notice period and was entitled under her contract to SSP only, she could not claim loss of pay in lieu of notice at her normal rate of pay even if it would have been good industrial relations practice to pay this. In *Stuart Peters Ltd v Bell* the Court of Appeal held that the *Norton Tool* principle did not apply to constructive dismissal on the ground that what may be good industrial relations practice when termination was triggered deliberately by an employer was different to what occurs when it is triggered by an employee.[1034]

[1027] *Norton Tool Co Ltd v Tewson* [1972] ICR 501, 504 (Sir John Donaldson P).
[1028] [1972] ICR 501.
[1029] See para 5.13 *et seq.*
[1030] *Norton Tool Co Ltd v Tewson* [1972] IRLR 86, 88 (Sir John Donaldson P).
[1031] [1972] IRLR 86. This was followed by the EAT in *TBA Industrial Products Ltd v Locke* [1984] IRLR 48 and approved in *Babcock Fata Ltd v Addison* [1987] IRLR 173, although cf an earlier EAT judgment, *Tradewinds Airways Ltd v Fletcher* [1981] IRLR 272.
[1032] ERA 1996, s 123(4). For this purpose, no account is taken of job offers received before the dismissal took place: *Savoia v Chiltern Herb Farms Ltd* [1981] IRLR 65; *McAndrew v Prestwick Circuits Ltd* [1988] IRLR 514. On the principles to be applied in determining whether a dismissed employee who has refused an offer of re-employment has failed in his duty to mitigate his loss, see *Wilding v British Telecommunications plc* [2002] IRLR 524. On the principles to be applied where a dismissed employee has set up his or her own business, see *Aon Training Ltd (formerly Totalamber plc) v Dore* [2005] IRLR 891.
[1033] [2007] IRLR 145.
[1034] [2009] IRLR 941, Elias LJ at [13].

The emphasis on the compensatory function of the compensatory award is also reflected in the principle, established by the Court of Appeal in 1987, that where the employer has made a payment in lieu of notice this will be deducted from the employee's compensation for lost earnings even if the employee fails to get another job during the notice period.[1035] The argument that entitlement to wages in lieu of notice was an 'independent right' of the employee, for which he should be compensated *in addition to* lost wages for the period spent out of, or in less well paid, employment was rejected. In Ralph Gibson LJ's words, 'if the employer has paid the wages due in lieu of notice at the time of dismissal, the employer has complied with good industrial practice. If the employee does not get employment during the period of notice, no principle of good industrial practice can secure to the employee any further payment by way of lost wages in respect of the period of notice; he has received the wages for that period and if he is to recover the same amount again it must be by reference to some rule of law outside the provisions of the ... [1996 Act] ... and in my view no such rule exists'.[1036]

A sum paid *ex gratia* by the employer to the employee will also normally be taken into account in reducing the employer's liability,[1037] and if the employer makes a statutory or contractual redundancy payment to the employee which is in excess of the basic award, the difference will also go to reduce the amount of any compensatory award for unfair dismissal.[1038]

5.147 Jobseeker's allowance or income support received by the applicant while unemployed, which at common law would be deducted from damages representing lost earnings, is dealt with by special recoupment regulations as far as the statutory claim is concerned.[1039] In respect of lost earnings up to the tribunal hearing, the tribunal must make an award of compensation in full against the employer, taking no account of any receipt of jobseeker's allowance or income support by the applicant up to that point. The Secretary of State may then serve a recoupment notice on the employer, claiming back an amount equivalent to the benefit paid out to the applicant for the period in question. As a result, the employee only *receives* compensation based on his or her *net* loss, but the employer must pay out in full, the difference going to the state. In effect the state is subrogated to the employee's claim against the employer, to the extent needed to reimburse it for the costs of paying out the benefit. The recoupment regulations do not apply to payments of unfair dismissal compensation made by way of a settlement between the parties; this is a strong incentive, then, to settle out of the tribunal.

Different rules apply to the period after the tribunal hearing, that is to say for *future* lost earnings. The tribunal may award compensation under this head without making any deduction for any jobseeker's allowance which might be received; however, this amount is then treated as earnings for the purposes of calculating entitlement to jobseeker's allowance.[1040] The recoupment

---

[1035] *Babcock FATA Ltd v Addison* [1987] IRLR 173.

[1036] [1987] IRLR 173, 178. Cf the different approach taken by the Scottish Division of the EAT in *Finnie v Top Hat Frozen Foods* [1985] ICR 433.

[1037] *Finnie v Top Hat Frozen Foods Ltd* [1985] ICR 433; *Horizon Holidays Ltd v Grassi* [1987] IRLR 371.

[1038] ERA 1996, s 123(7). In *Digital Equipment Co Ltd v Clements (No 2)* [1998] IRLR 134 the Court of Appeal held that the full amount of any payment should be deducted from the compensatory award after it had been subject to a percentage reduction to reflect the chance of the employee remaining in employment if the dismissal had not been procedurally unfair.

[1039] Employment Protection (Recoupment of Jobseeker's Allowance and Income Support) Regulations, 1996, SI 1996/2349.

[1040] Jobseeker's Act 1995, ss 2–4; Jobseeker's Allowance Regulations 1996, SI 1996/207, reg 98.

regulations do not apply to other social security benefits. Receipt of incapacity benefits does not preclude an employee from claiming compensation for loss of earnings, although credit should be given for the sums received. [1041]

In calculating lost earnings, the court will have regard to evidence of actual loss up to the hearing or, if the employee has found a permanent better-paid job, up to the point where he or she ceased to be unemployed[1042] or, in an exceptional case, beyond that point, if the employee is dismissed by the new employer under circumstances where a causal link with the original dismissal can be established.[1043] If the applicant is unemployed at the time of the hearing the tribunal may also allow a claim for losses in the future, depending on the circumstances. The employee is most unlikely to recover a sum approaching net salary for the rest of his or her working life. This is not just because of the statutory upper limit; even if that were removed, future earnings would be discounted to take into account the chance that illness or redundancy would have brought an end to the employment lawfully, or that the employee would in any case have moved on from that job to another, as well as the chances of the employee finding work following the dismissal.[1044] Nor have the courts taken the chance to escape completely certain other limitations of the common law. No sum is recoverable, for example, for any form of non-economic loss, such as hurt feelings or distress arising from the manner of the dismissal,[1045] or for lost job satisfaction.[1046] A claim for damages for lost reputation arising from an unjustified summary dismissal may only be made 'if there is cogent evidence that the manner of the dismissal caused financial loss, as, for example, by making it more difficult to find future employment';[1047] nor were damages awarded in a case where a failure to provide a written reference in good time was alleged to have affected the employee's chances of getting alternative work.[1048] Nevertheless, some courts remain true to the flexibility shown by the NIRC in the Norton case. In *Leonard v Strathclyde Buses Ltd*[1049] the Court of Session stressed that an employment tribunal was required 'to apply the statutory test as a whole and assess what is just and equitable having regard to the loss so far as attributable to

---

[1041] *Sheffield Forgemasters International Ltd v Fox* [2009] IRLR 192. In *Savage v Saxena* [1998] IRLR 182 the EAT held that no deduction should be made in respect of housing benefit.

[1042] *Fentiman v Fluid Engineering Products Ltd* [1991] IRLR 150; *Whelan (t/a Cheers Off Licence) v Richardson* [1998] IRLR 114. The former employer cannot rely on the employee's increased earnings to reduce the loss sustained prior to the new employment being taken up.

[1043] *Dench v Flynn & Partners* [1998] IRLR 653; *Aegon UK Corp Services Ltd v Roberts* [2009] IRLR 1042.

[1044] In *Kingston upon Hull City Council v Dunnachie (No 3)* [2003] IRLR 843 the EAT held that tribunals should consider the use of the 'Ogdon tables' ('actuarial tables with explanatory notes for use in personal injury and fatal accident tables') in calculating compensation for future loss of earnings only where it is established that there is a prima facie career-long loss. In *Scope v Thornett* [2007] IRLR 155 the Court of Appeal confirmed that where there is evidence that the employment would not have continued indefinitely the tribunal needs to make a prediction as to how long it would have lasted.

[1045] *Dunnachie v Kingston upon Hull City Council* [2004] IRLR 727, affirming *Norton Tool Co Ltd v Tewson* [1972] ICR 501. See Brodie, 2004: pp 352–354. For the difficulties of distinguishing between acts constituting detriment short of dismissal, for which non-economic loss is recoverable, and dismissal, see Bowers and Lewis, 2005: pp 87–89.

[1046] *Robert Normansell (Birmingham) Ltd v Barfield* (1973) 8 ITR 171.

[1047] *Vaughan v Weighpack Ltd* [1974] ICR 261, 265–266; cf *Chagger v Abbey National plc* [2010] IRLR 47, CA, in relation to compensation for stigma resulting from having brought discrimination proceedings. On the common law position see now *Malik v BCCI SA* [1997] IRLR 462 ; *Johnson v Unisys Ltd* [2001] IRLR 279; and *Edwards v Chesterfield Royal Hospital NHS Foundation Trust* and *Botham v Ministry of Defence* [2012] IRLR 129 discussed at paras 4.105 *et seq* and 5.43–5.45 above.

[1048] *Lewis Shops Group v Wiggins* [1973] ICR 335.

[1049] [1998] IRLR 693, 696. In this case, the flexible approach adopted by the court to the calculation of damages for loss of share options may be contrasted with the more rigid approach adopted at common law in *Micklefield v SAC Technology Ltd* [1990] IRLR 218; see para 4.74 above.

the employer'; this meant that it was inappropriate 'to introduce principles of foreseeability or remoteness in the technical sense in which those concepts apply in other legal contexts'. Such flexibility was demonstrated in *Ignarski v BBC*, in which the EAT indicated that, in principle, compensation might be awarded for the additional child care costs of an applicant who had been unfairly dismissed from a night-work job which she had taken so that she and her husband, who worked a day-shift, could share child care responsibilities, if it could be shown that she could not find an alternative night-work employment.[1050]

5.148 Where an employee has suffered no loss as a result of the dismissal the compensatory award may be nil. If, for example, the employer can show that a failure to consult would have made no difference since no work could have been found even if the correct procedure had been followed, this will be reflected in reduced compensation payable to the employee, even though the decision of the House of Lords in *Polkey v AE Dayton Services Ltd*[1051] makes it clear that the dismissal itself is unfair.[1052]

5.149 By virtue of section 123(2), the compensatory award may include amounts in respect of expenses reasonably incurred by the employee as a consequence of the dismissal and 'loss of any benefit which he might reasonably be expected to have had but for the dismissal'. The first of these rules essentially follows the common law; expenses incurred in search of alternative employment would normally be taken into account in relation to mitigation, for example. The second category would seem to be broad enough to capture some benefits which the employee would have normally expected to receive, even though they contain a discretionary element and so may not be recoverable at common law. The point has not been clearly settled. Employees have recovered sums in respect of such perks as a company car and share options,[1053] although there seems to be no hard and fast rule that such losses will be recoverable in every case.

Often the most important prospective benefit is the retirement pension which the employee would have expected to receive under an occupational pension scheme; but the difficulties in calculating this loss are considerable. The government has issued guidelines, *Compensation for Loss of Pension Rights: Employment Tribunals*, which are not strictly binding on tribunals but which may be taken into account,[1054] and regularly are in practice. The calculation depends upon what type of occupational scheme is being considered.[1055] If it is a money-purchase scheme, the employee's loss will normally be the value of the employer's future contributions to the pension.

[1050] Unreported, discussed by L Blake, 1991; see further our discussion of work-life balance issues in ch 6 below, at para 6.119 *et seq*.

[1051] [1987] IRLR 503.

[1052] *British United Shoe Machinery Co Ltd v Clarke* [1978] ICR 70. Reductions of between 50% and 75% of compensation are known: *Hough v Leyland DAF Ltd* [1991] IRLR 194; *Campbell v Dunoon and Cowal Housing Association Ltd* [1992] IRLR 528. 100% deductions are possible in the case of misconduct dismissals: *Fisher v California Cake & Cookie Ltd* [1997] IRLR 212. In *Perkin v St George's Healthcare NHS Trust* [2005] IRLR 934 the Court of Appeal upheld a 100% deduction although also holding that the reason for dismissal could have been 'some other substantial reason' rather than conduct.

[1053] *Crampton v Dacorum Motors Ltd* [1975] IRLR 168; *Bradshaw v Rugby Portland Cement Ltd* [1972] IRLR 46.

[1054] *Bingham v Hobourn Engineering Ltd* [1992] IRLR 298. However, in *Port of Tilbury (London) Ltd v Birch* [2005] IRLR 92, the EAT emphasised that there is no duty on tribunals to follow these guidelines and it is an error of law for a tribunal to reject a party's submissions on the basis that they do not reflect an assessment suggested in them.

[1055] On the distinctions between money purchase and defined benefit or salary-related schemes, see paras 4.132 and 4.133 above.

In a defined-benefit scheme, it will be the difference between the deferred pension which the employee is entitled to receive, upon retirement, on the basis of service prior to the dismissal,[1056] and the pension which he or she would have received had they stayed in the employment in question. This means taking the value of the deferred pension and applying to it a multiplier which is a function of the service thought to be necessary to earn the full pension. The tribunal must also take into account the likelihood that the employee might have withdrawn from the scheme in any event, by virtue of ill health or resignation, or that he or she might have been fairly dismissed.[1057] These factors may lead to very considerable reductions in the amount awarded under this head.

5.150   Under section 123(6), 'where the tribunal finds that the dismissal was to any extent caused or contributed to by any action of the complainant, it shall reduce the amount of the compensatory award by such proportion as it considers just and equitable having regard to that finding'.[1058] Misconduct may qualify as contributory fault if it is found to have prompted the employer's action, and where section 123(6) may be invoked the courts have held that a 100% deduction, while unlikely, is not ruled out by the Act.[1059] Mere incompetence of the employee, on the other hand, is unlikely to be enough.[1060] Participation in trade union activities, or the employee's being or not being a member of an independent trade union, may not constitute contributory fault;[1061] nor, the House of Lords has held, may taking part in industrial action in the absence of individually blameworthy conduct additional to or separate from the mere act of participation.[1062] A similar but not quite identical provision applies in the case of the basic award; here, the tribunal may make a deduction by reason of 'any conduct of the complainant before the dismissal'.[1063] The difference is that with the basic award, there need not be any causal link between the dismissal and the conduct of the employee.

5.151   As we discussed in para 5.120 above, TULRCA 1992, s 207A provides that if it appears to an employment tribunal that the employee's claim concerns a matter to which the ACAS Code of Practice on Disciplinary and Grievance Procedures applies; that the employer has failed to comply with the Code in relation to that matter; and that failure was unreasonable, the tribunal *may*, if it considers it just and equitable in all the circumstances to do so, increase any award it makes to the employee by a maximum of 25%. There are equivalent provisions permitting the reduction of an award by a maximum of 25% if the employee unreasonably fails to comply with the Code.[1064]

[1056] An 'early leaver' has certain rights to have the deferred pension preserved and revalued in line with price inflation.

[1057] *TBA Industrial Products Ltd v Locke* [1984] ICR 228.

[1058] The deduction can only be made in respect of the award made by the tribunal and not in respect of any payment of wages in lieu of notice which the employer may make to the employee: *Heggie v Uniroyal Englebert Tyres Ltd* [1999] IRLR 802.

[1059] *W Devis & Sons Ltd v Atkins* [1977] IRLR 314. For a more recent example see *Perkin v St George's Healthcare NHS Trust* [2005] IRLR 934.

[1060] *Kraft Foods Ltd v Fox* [1977] IRLR 431.

[1061] TULRCA 1992, s 155.

[1062] *Crosville Wales Ltd v Tracey (No 2)* [1997] IRLR 691.

[1063] ERA 1996, s 122(2). Note also s 122(3).

[1064] TULRCA 1992, s 207A(1)–(4), inserted by EA 2008, s 3.

The Code itself excludes dismissals due to redundancy and non-renewal of fixed-term contracts on their expiry from its scope.[1065]

As we discussed in para 2.21, in the case of the repealed procedures the EAT in England and Wales took the view that the size of the award itself should not be subject to appeal provided that there were sufficient reasons why a reasonable tribunal might have chosen the percentage which it did.[1066] This case law is of continuing relevance. The EAT held that it was 'good practice' for the tribunal to specify the factors influencing its decision.[1067] It also held that although in 'routine cases' the tribunal would arrive at the percentage by which an award should be adjusted without regard to the initial size of the award, this did not preclude the tribunal taking size into account where the tribunal considered it just and equitable provided that it explained that it was so doing.[1068] In applying the uplift, there is no requirement to have regard to an employee's loss, which will in any event have been taken into account under section 123(1). By analogy with the remedies for detriment short of dismissal,[1069] there seems no reason to exclude injury to feelings due, for example, to the suddenness of a decision to dismiss or a failure to allow an employee to explain his or her case. Tribunals may then be faced with the difficult task of separating injury resulting from breach of the procedure, which may be compensated, from injury resulting from the dismissal itself, which is not.[1070]

If, in addition to a finding of unfair dismissal, the employer is found to have breached its duty to give the employee a written statement of initial employment particulars or to notify the employee of changes in those particulars,[1071] EA 2002, s 38 requires the tribunal (exceptional circumstances apart) to award the employee a minimum of two weeks' pay and it may award four weeks' pay if it considers this 'just and equitable in all the circumstances'.[1072] Any adjustment under TULRCA 1992, s 207A is to be made before any adjustment under EA 2002, s 38.[1073]

(iii) The level of awards

5.152 In practice, the average award of compensation in unfair dismissal cases is much less than the various statutory maxima allow. In 2010/11 the median award was £4,591; in 1990/91 it was £1,773 and in 1986/87 it was £1,676.[1074] The rate of awards is low, in part, because many of the applicants for unfair dismissal protection are comparatively low earners with short service, but also because of the manner in which the employee's loss is calculated by the tribunal and

---

[1065] Code of Practice, para 1.

[1066] *CEX Ltd v Mark Lewis* UKEAT/0013/07/DA, para 49; *Home Office v Khan and King* UKEAT/0257/07/CEA, para 39; cf the decisions of the EAT in Scotland in *Aptuit (Edinburgh) Ltd v Kennedy* UKEATS/0057/06 and *McKindless Group v McLaughlin* UKEATS/0010/08.

[1067] *Home Office v Khan and King*, above, [40].

[1068] *Abbey National v Chagger* [2009] IRLR 86, [135].

[1069] See, for example, para 8.16.

[1070] See generally Bowers and Lewis, 2005: pp 92–95.

[1071] ERA 1996, ss 1, 4. See para 4.14 *et seq.*

[1072] EA 2002, s 38. A 'week's pay' is subject to the statutory maximum, which at 1 February 2012 and at the time of writing stands at £430.

[1073] TULRCA 1992, s 207A, inserted by EA 2008, s 3.

[1074] HMCTS, *Employment Tribunals and EAT Statistics, 2010-11*, Table 5; *Labour Market Trends*, September 1999, 494; HC Debs col 542, 30 June 1992 (written answers).

the possibility of deductions for contributory fault and failure to mitigate. According to research published by Dickens and her colleagues in 1985:

> ... the explanation [lies] in the statutory principles underlying the calculation of compensation and in the way in which tribunals exercise the discretion granted to them by statute in determining what would be just and equitable. Only certain kinds of loss are compensatable. There is no intention that the employer should be penalised for dismissing unfairly. A deterrent-regulatory view of money awards is not taken and to adopt anything other than *restitutio in integrum* (that is, putting the applicant in the position in which he or she would have been if the wrong had not been sustained) would be seen by the courts to represent 'punishment' of the employer ... Taken together, the limited use of the re-employment remedy and the way in which compensation is assessed serve typically to set a low price on the unfair deprivation of a job and can have little deterrent value for most employers.[1075]

Interim relief

5.153   Exceptionally, the employment tribunal has the power to maintain the applicant in his or her employment pending the hearing of an unfair dismissal claim, if the applicant is claiming that the principal reason for the dismissal is one which relates to trade union membership or activities; their position as a health and safety or employee representative (including representatives for working time purposes); their position as a trustee of an occupational pension scheme; the making of a protected disclosure; the exercise of rights relating to trade union recognition and derecognition procedures; and the exercise of the right to be accompanied (or the accompaniment of another worker) at a grievance or disciplinary hearing.[1076] The claim must be lodged within seven days of the EDT.[1077] The tribunal must be satisfied that at the full hearing it is likely to accept the employee's claim of automatically unfair dismissal under one or other of the above heads.[1078] The tribunal may then make an interim order of either reinstatement or, in an appropriate case, re-engagement, but only if the employer states that it is willing to accept re-employment.[1079] If the employer either does not attend the hearing or refuses to re-employ the employee, the tribunal must make an order for the interim continuation of the contract of employment: this is an order to the effect that the contract of employment is still in force for the purposes of the employee's pay and benefits under the contract, and for the purposes of the computation of statutory continuity of employment.[1080] An order for the continuation of the contract may also be made, along with

---

[1075] L Dickens *et al*, 1985: pp 138–139.

[1076] ERA 1996, ss 128–132; TULRCA 1992, ss 161–166; ERelA 1999, s 12(5); see also para 8.5 below. Selection for redundancy on one of these grounds is not included. In *McConnell v Bombardier Aerospace/Short Brothers plc* [2009] IRLR 201 the NICA confirmed that if it was likely that dismissals were for the principal reason of redundancy, even if the complainants were likely to succeed in establishing that they had been unfairly selected for their union activities, a claim for interim relief could not succeed.

[1077] ERA 1996, s 128(1), (2).

[1078] ERA 1996, s 129. On the approach to whether the employee is 'likely' to win at the full hearing, see *Taplin v C Shippam Ltd* 1978] ICR 1068; *Ministry of Justice v Sarfraz* [2011] IRLR 562 (where the approach in the context of a 'protected disclosure' was also discussed).

[1079] ERA 1996, s 129.

[1080] ERA 1996, s 129(9), 130.

an order of compensation, if the employer fails to comply with an order of interim reinstatement or re-engagement.[1081]

This power, remarkable as it is, is confined to the instances cited above, where protection against victimisation of employee representatives and those making protected disclosures was thought particularly important. Were interim relief available more widely, the effectiveness of the unfair dismissal jurisdiction in preserving employment could be much greater than it currently is, and tribunals might be more willing to order reinstatement as the primary remedy for unfair dismissal. The extension of interim relief to support the right to be accompanied at a grievance or disciplinary hearing is a significant step in this regard.

ECONOMIC DISMISSALS

5.154   Economic dismissals – dismissals involving redundancy, reorganisation and business transfers – form a distinct category within the law governing termination of employment. They touch on the key area of managerial prerogatives in the organisation of work and raise countervailing claims of job ownership by employees. Distributional conflicts of interest are particularly sharp: 'economic dismissals pose the question of how should the social costs resulting from economic dislocation be distributed between the workers and their employer'.[1082] Where termination arises out of the failure or economic difficulty of the business concerned, third parties are directly affected by decisions on the extent of the employer's liability; these include potential purchasers of the business, who may inherit these liabilities as a result of a transfer of employment, and creditors of the insolvent company, who may find their claims ranked behind those of the employees. The state also has an interest, since it retains a residual responsibility to meet certain liabilities of insolvent or bankrupt employers.

We begin our analysis by examining the concept of redundancy. Where a dismissal is for redundancy, a statutory redundancy payment is available to employees who have met the qualifying conditions, and a complaint for unfair dismissal is also possible.[1083] Where, on the other hand, dismissal falls into the SOSR category, no statutory redundancy payment is due, and the dismissal may well be fair, leaving the employee with nothing. We then consider employees' claims in insolvency against their former employer and against the state. Finally, we examine the extent to which the TUPE Regulations 2006 apply to sales and transfers of businesses, and their impact on the rights of the parties involved in these transactions.

[1081] ERA 1996, s 132.

[1082] H Collins, 1993: p 65.

[1083] Note that the ACAS Code of Practice on Disciplinary and Grievance Procedures 2009 (non-compliance with which can lead to the adjustment of awards under TULRCA 1992, s 207A) does not apply to redundancy dismissals: Code of Practice, para 1.

The scope of redundancy

5.155   A finding of redundancy means that a dismissal is potentially fair,[1084] but it also makes the employer liable to pay a redundancy payment to the employee, calculated by reference to the employee's seniority, normal weekly pay and age.[1085] This dual purpose of the definition has led to some difficulty in its interpretation by the courts.

A curious result follows from the rule that, for a redundancy payment, a dismissal is presumed to be by reason of redundancy,[1086] whereas for the purposes of defending an unfair dismissal claim the employer must demonstrate what the reason was.[1087] In finely-balanced circumstances this means that a dismissal can be found to be for redundancy for the former purpose but not the latter.[1088]

Under section 139(1) of ERA 1996, a dismissal of an employee is taken to be by reason of redundancy if it is attributable wholly or mainly to one of two circumstances:

> (a) the fact that his employer has ceased, or intends to cease –
>> (i)   to carry on the business for the purposes of which the employee was employed by him, or
>> (ii) to carry on that business in the place where the employee was so employed, or
>
> (b) the fact that the requirements of that business –
>> (i)   for employees to carry out work of a particular kind, or
>> (ii) for employees to carry out work of a particular kind in the place where the employee was employed by the employer,
>
> have ceased or diminished or are expected to cease or diminish.

These two criteria are referred to respectively as 'cessation of business' and 'diminishing requirements'. 'Cease' and 'diminish' mean 'cease and diminish either permanently or temporarily and for whatever reason'.[1089]

(i) The relevance of the employer's motives

5.156   In their interpretation of section 139(1) the courts have, on the whole, respected the employer's right to decide matters concerning the size, scope and direction of the enterprise. In particular, the test of whether there is a 'cessation of business' is not concerned with the wider purposes of the employer in making decisions of this kind. In *Moon v Homeworthy Furniture (Northern) Ltd*[1090] the EAT held that it was not the tribunal's task to inquire into management's motives for the closure of a factory (it had been alleged that the factory was closed out of retaliation for union activism). The mere fact of closure was sufficient for there to be a redundancy in law.

[1084] ERA 1996, s 98(2)(c).
[1085] ERA 1996, s 162.
[1086] ERA 1996, s 163(2).
[1087] ERA 1996, s 98(1), (2).
[1088] *Midland Foot Comfort Centre Ltd v Moppett* [1973] ICR 219.
[1089] ERA 1996, s 139(6).
[1090] [1977] ICR 117, 121.

According to Kilner Brown J there 'cannot be any investigation into the rights and wrongs of the declared redundancy'.

This case indicates that it is essentially for the employer to decide if and when to close down a business, and that the law regards a clear cessation of business as a redundancy situation. However, it is also important to be clear what *Moon* does not decide. It does not decide that the subjective opinion of the employer is decisive in classifying the dismissal as potentially fair or otherwise. The employer must show evidence that it had the relevant motive at the time of the dismissal.[1091] In *Moon* the tribunal found that there were good objective grounds for a finding of redundancy, and when the EAT agreed with this finding only one outcome was possible. It seems unlikely that a decision to shut down a whole business could ever be anything but redundancy, but this begs the question of whether the business has indeed ceased to be carried on at the place of work in question, and in a case of a sham closure there is no reason, in principle, why a tribunal should not find that no redundancy has occurred, or that the dismissals, although potentially fair, were not fair in the circumstances under section 98(4) of the Act.

(ii) 'Place where the employee was so employed'

5.157   The reference in section 139(1) to the 'place where the employee was so employed' has given rise to a considerable body of case law concerning contractual mobility clauses. Where part of a business is shut down, the contents of the employee's contract may determine if there is a redundancy or not. If the contract of employment contains an express or implied mobility clause, the employee may be required by the contract to move to a new location, which may prevent there being a redundancy under section 139(1)(a).[1092] If there is an express clause the court cannot formally limit its scope by reference to the concepts of good faith or reasonableness,[1093] but it can invoke the principle of construction *contra proferentem* or require the employer to give the employee a reasonable period of notice of the move.[1094] A mobility clause favouring the employer may also be implied into the contract.[1095] However, an implied term will not normally require the employee to move beyond a reasonable travelling distance from home.[1096]

In recent years the courts have taken the view that the contract should not be the exclusive test of the employee's place of work for the purpose of determining whether the employee is redundant, in particular where the employer has inserted a mobility or flexibility clause which is particularly broad or which has not, in practice, been invoked. In *High Table Ltd v Horst*[1097] the applicants were employed as silver-service waitresses by a company which provided catering services for companies in the City of London and elsewhere. The employer's staff handbook, which formed part of their terms of employment, provided that '[y]our place of work is as stated in your

---

[1091] See also *Hindle v Percival Boats Ltd* [1969] 1 WLR 174; *Baxter v Limb Group of Companies* [1994] IRLR 572.

[1092] *Sutcliffe v Hawker Siddley Aviation Ltd* [1973] ICR 560; *United Kingdom Atomic Energy Authority v Claydon* [1974] ICR 128; *Home Office v Evans* [2008] IRLR 59 (claim for unfair dismissal by immigration officers: no requirement for the Home Office to follow its redundancy procedure where a mobility clause was invoked).

[1093] *Express Lifts Co Ltd v Bowles* [1977] ICR 474.

[1094] *United Bank Ltd v Akhtar* [1989] IRLR 507.

[1095] See para 4.109 above.

[1096] *O'Brien v Associated Fire Alarms Ltd* [1969] 1 All ER 93.

[1097] [1997] IRLR 513. See also *Bass Leisure Ltd v Thomas* [1994] IRLR 104.

letter of appointment which acts as part of your terms and conditions. However, given the nature of our business, it is sometimes necessary to transfer staff on a temporary or permanent basis to another location. Whenever possible, this will be within reasonable daily travelling distance of your existing place of work'. In practice the applicants had all worked for one particular client, Hill Samuel, from 10am to 4pm on weekdays for a number of years. In 1993 cuts in Hill Samuel's catering budget necessitated a reorganisation of the services provided by the employers which resulted in a need for fewer waitresses working longer hours, and the applicants were dismissed. The Court of Appeal upheld the employer's claim (in defence of a complaint of unfair dismissal) that the applicants were redundant, rejecting the argument that 'the place where the employee was so employed' extended to every place where the employee could be required to work. Peter Gibson LJ, giving the judgment of the court, stated that the question of where the employee was employed:

> ... is one to be answered primarily by a consideration of the factual circumstances which obtained until the dismissal. If an employee has worked in only one location under his contract of employment for the purposes of the employer's business, it defies common sense to widen the extent of the place where he was so employed, merely because of the existence of a mobility clause. Of course, the refusal by the employee to obey a lawful requirement under the contract of employment for the employee to move may constitute a valid reason for dismissal, but the issues of dismissal, redundancy and reasonableness in the actions of an employer should be kept distinct. It would be unfortunate if the law were to encourage the inclusion of mobility clauses in contracts of employment to defeat genuine redundancy claims ... If the work of the employee for his employer has involved a change of location ... then the contract of employment may be helpful to determine the extent of the place where the employee was employed. But it cannot be right to let the contract be the sole determinant, regardless of where the employee actually worked for the employer.[1098]

(iii) Diminished requirements for 'work of a particular kind'

5.158   On the face of it, the test of 'diminishing requirements' under section 139(1)(b) of the Act is sufficiently wide to cover both the situation in which reduced demand for labour is the result of business difficulties, and the situation in which it is the result of technological change or workforce reorganisation. However, its application to the second situation is unclear. This is not simply the fault of the courts. The definition contained in ERA 1996, section 139(1) is significantly narrower, for example, than the definition of redundancy used for the purposes of defining the collective consultation and information rights of trade union representatives, 'dismissal for a reason not related to the individual concerned'.[1099] This wider definition was introduced to comply with Directive 75/129; no plans have been announced to extend it to section 139(1) of the 1996 Act.

5.159   In interpreting the concept of 'work of a particular kind' in section 139(1)(b) the courts have traditionally drawn a distinction between the employer's 'requirement' for employees to

---

[1098] [1997] IRLR 513, 518.
[1099] TULRCA 1992, s 195, as amended by TURERA 1993, s 34. See para 9.32 below.

perform a particular quantum of work and its needs for that quantum of work to be performed in a particular way or on specific terms and conditions. The demand for employees to perform the quantum may remain the same even though the interests of the business demand that the work should in future be performed according to a different working schedule, or even through the use of different technology. In *Chapman v Goonvean and Rastowrack China Clay Co Ltd*[1100] the employer withdrew free transport from a group of employees on the grounds of cost and employed local workers in their stead. It was found that there had been no redundancy. According to Lord Denning MR, 'it is very desirable, in the interests of efficiency, that employers should be able to propose changes in the terms of a man's employment for such reasons as these: so as to get rid of restrictive practices: or to induce higher output by piece work or to cease to provide free transport at an excessive cost'.[1101] Buckley LJ thought that while 'the employer must ... justify his expectation by reference to objective circumstances relating to the commercial situation of his business and those commercial and economic conditions which exist generally, at the relevant time or which could then reasonably be anticipated in the future', there was 'nothing in the language of the section to suggest that the employer should be treated as bound or likely to carry on his business in all, or indeed in any, respects in precisely the way in which he was carrying it on at the time when the facts have to be considered'.[1102]

For similar reasons, it seems that a redundancy will not normally arise in cases where the employer rearranges working-time schedules in the interests of greater efficiency, such as might be involved in adopting a different pattern of shift work.[1103] The courts have been explicit in the reasoning behind these decisions, namely to cut the potential costs to the employer of business reorganisation: 'an employer is entitled to reorganise his business in order to improve its efficiency and in doing so to propose to his staff a change in the terms and conditions of employment; and to dispense with their services if they do not agree';[1104] similarly, it is said that 'nothing should be done to impair the ability of employers to reorganise their workforce and their terms and conditions of work so as to improve efficiency'.[1105]

Other decisions have denied employees the right to redundancy compensation where they were unable to adapt to changing methods of working, on the grounds that the change in the nature of their work was not sufficient. In *North Riding Garages Ltd v Butterwick*[1106] the employee, who was manager of a garage, was dismissed following the introduction by new owners of different methods of working, which involved him in more paperwork and less engineering work than previously. He claimed redundancy compensation but this was rejected. Widgery J held that for these purposes, 'an employee who remains in the same kind of work is expected to adapt himself to new methods and techniques and cannot complain if his employer insists on higher standards of efficiency than those previously required; but if new methods alter the nature of the

[1100] [1973] ICR 310.
[1101] [1973] ICR 310, 315.
[1102] [1973] ICR 310, 318.
[1103] In *MacFisheries Ltd v Findley* [1985] ICR 160, however, the EAT upheld the finding of the employment tribunal that on the facts night work (as compared to day work) was 'work of a particular kind'.
[1104] *Johnson v Nottinghamshire Combined Police Authority* [1974] ICR 170, 184. However, an employer cannot escape a finding of redundancy by arguing that it still has a need for certain work to be done, but because of funding cuts can no longer afford to pay for the work done by the employee: *Association of University Teachers v University of Newcastle-upon-Tyne* [1988] IRLR 10.
[1105] *Lesney Products & Co Ltd v Nolan* [1977] ICR 235, 238.
[1106] [1967] 2 QB 56, 63; cf *Robinson v British Island Airways Ltd* [1977] IRLR 477.

work required to be done it may follow that no requirement remains for employees to do work of the particular kind which has been superseded and that they are truly redundant'. In this case, the work for which the employee was employed remained essentially the same, since the vehicle workshop remained, as did the requirement for a workshop manager.[1107]

5.160   These decisions, dating from the early 1970s and never formally overruled, nevertheless run counter to one of the principal aims of the redundancy compensation scheme at its inception in 1965. By ensuring that employees who were displaced from employment by technological change would receive compensation, it was hoped to encourage firms to embark on necessary economic restructuring and at the same time to provide displaced workers with financial assistance for mobility and job-search in the labour market.[1108] Moreover, for the early part of its life (including the period during which this case law developed) the redundancy payments scheme subsidised the costs of these payments to individual employers, by refunding varying proportions of redundancy payments through the rebate system (this was repealed in 1989).[1109] Since all employers contributed to the Redundancy Payments Fund through a supplementary levy to their national insurance (social security) contributions, the costs of redundancy were spread beyond the individual business. Even during the period the rebate scheme was in force the 'cost-spreading' aspect was ignored by the courts, who seem to have thought that managerial prerogatives were somehow under threat when redundancies were alleged to exist.

5.161   The test put forward in this line of case law has been described as the 'job function' test since, as we have just seen, it attempts to identify a redundancy in terms of the economic requirement for employees to perform a particular quantum of work. A rival approach, the 'contract test', suggests on the contrary that in order to determine whether there is a redundancy it is necessary to ascertain whether there is a diminished requirement by reference to the whole range of contractual duties which the employee could be required to perform, not merely those which he had been performing. This latter test is exemplified by *Cowen v Haden Ltd*,[1110] where the EAT felt itself bound by the earlier decision of the Court of Appeal in *Nelson v BBC*[1111] to hold that 'it is not sufficient in order to establish redundancy to show merely that the requirements of the employers for employees to carry out work of the kind on which the employee was actually engaged had ceased or diminished; it is necessary to show that such diminution or cessation

---

[1107] See also *Cresswell v Board of Inland Revenue* [1984] IRLR 190, discussed in para 4.104 above. However, some changes will be so complete as to amount to a redundancy, as in a case where the introduction of new heating equipment meant that the employer needed a heating engineer rather than a plumber with the result that the applicant was made redundant: *Murphy v Epsom College* [1985] ICR 80.

[1108] See para 5.7 above.

[1109] EA 1989, s 17. Under the initial scheme the rebate represented between 66% and 78% of compensation, with the higher rebate paid in respect of older employees. In 1969 a general rebate of 50% was introduced and in 1977 this became 41%. In 1986 it was confined to firms employing fewer than ten employees and reduced to 35% before being abolished completely in 1989. At the same time the redundancy contribution was abolished and in 1990 the Redundancy Fund was merged into the National Insurance Fund: EA 1990, s 16.

[1110] [1983] ICR 1.

[1111] [1977] ICR 649; *Nelson v BBC (No 2)* [1980] ICR 110: the employee was employed as a managerial producer and editor grade 3 who could be required to work in any country or capacity which the BBC decided. When the Caribbean Service, in which he worked, closed down he was held not to be redundant because there was no diminution in the work of producers and editors grade 3.

was in relation to any work that he could have been asked to do'.[1112] In this case the contract of employment contained a broad flexibility clause, under which the employee could have been called on to perform 'any and all duties which reasonably fall within the scope of his capabilities'; he attempted to argue (for the purposes of an unfair dismissal claim) that he had not been made redundant, since his contractual duties were sufficiently extensive for him to have been redeployed to do new work without entering into a new contract. The Court of Appeal reversed the EAT's finding of no redundancy on the facts, holding that the employee had been employed to carry out the particular kind of work of a divisional contracts surveyor, but did not disturb the wider legal principle relied upon.

In *Nelson* and *Cowen* the contract test was invoked by employees in order to show that their employers, by failing to redeploy them on other duties which they could be contractually required to perform, would be unable to show redundancy as a potentially fair reason for dismissal.[1113] In other cases, the principle in *Nelson* was deployed by employers to avoid a finding of unfair dismissal by extending the notion of redundancy to embrace a wider range of functions than those actually performed by the employee and thus create a test which, in certain situations, may be easier to satisfy.[1114] The confusion between the 'job function' and 'contract' tests arose, then, largely because the statutory definition of redundancy serves the two different purposes referred to earlier; it is the gateway to automatic statutory compensation, but also to a potentially fair dismissal.

5.162   In the second half of the 1990s the EAT showed impatience with both the 'function' and the 'contract' tests, regarding both as distorting the statutory language. In *Safeway Stores v Burrell* the court considered that in examining whether the requirements of the business for employees to carry out work of a particular kind have diminished, employees' contractual terms are irrelevant; they become relevant only when asking whether the dismissal was attributable to redundancy, as compared, for example, to a refusal to transfer to another job where the employee's contract requires this.[1115] In *Church v West Lancashire NHS Trust*[1116] a differently-constituted EAT affirmed that 'the proper test is neither contractual nor functional but a sensible blend of the two', as exemplified by the approach in *High Table Ltd v Horst*,[1117] discussed in para 5.157 above. This more flexible approach subsequently received the support of the House of Lords. In *Murray v Foyle Meats Ltd*[1118] Lord Irvine LC commented that 'both the contract test and the function test miss the point. The key work in the statute is "attributable" and there is no reason in law why the dismissal of an employee should not be attributable to a diminution in the employer's need for employees irrespective of the terms of his contract or the function which he performed'.[1119] The suggestion, then, is that a test of factual causation should be applied; the correct approach is to

---

[1112] [1983] ICR 1, 7.
[1113] For a further example see *Johnson v Peabody Trust* [1996] IRLR 387.
[1114] *Pink v White* [1985] IRLR 489: the employee under his contract was a making and finishing room operative, although his actual work was sole layer/pre-sole fitter; as there was a diminished requirement for the former (although not the latter) the employee was redundant.
[1115] *Safeway Stores plc v Burrell* [1997] IRLR 200, 206–207 (Judge Peter Clark).
[1116] [1998] IRLR 4, 9 (Morison J).
[1117] [1997] IRLR 513.
[1118] [1999] IRLR 562.
[1119] [1999] IRLR 562, 564.

treat the question as 'a factual inquiry, without any artificial subtlety'.[1120] Stated in this way, the test has the merit of potentially bringing within the scope of redundancy so-called 'bumping' cases in which an employee is dismissed to make way for another employee who would otherwise have been made redundant. To treat this part of the definition of redundancy as turning on a predominantly factual inquiry, however, is to invite inconsistency in the application of the law by tribunals.

Redundancy compensation

5.163   In order to claim a redundancy payment, the employee must have been dismissed; for this purpose, the same basic definition of dismissal applies as for unfair dismissal.[1121] There are some slight differences which are specific to the issue of redundancy compensation. First, under certain circumstances, there will be no dismissal if the employer offers the employee suitable alternative employment.[1122] This is explored in more detail below. Second, if the employee, having received notice of dismissal, then gives a counter-notice to terminate the contract at an earlier date, the employer may require the employee to withdraw the counter-notice on pain of losing any right to a redundancy payment. However, the employee may still receive some payment if an employment tribunal concludes that 'having regard to – (a) the reasons for which the employee seeks to leave the employment, and (b) the reasons for which the employer requires him to continue in it' it is 'just and equitable' that he or she should receive the whole or a part of the redundancy payment to which he or she would otherwise have been entitled.[1123] Third, the definition of dismissal is given a special extension, for the purposes of redundancy compensation only, to cover cases of 'implied or constructive termination of contract'. This means that there is a dismissal where '(a) an act on the part of an employer, or (b) any event affecting an employer (including, in the case of an individual, his death) operates to terminate' the contract of employment.[1124] The dismissal, so defined, will be deemed to be for redundancy if the employee is not then re-employed for a reason which falls under section 139(1).[1125]

To be eligible for a statutory redundancy payment, the employee must have had two years' continuity of employment up to the 'relevant date'.[1126]

[1120] [1999] IRLR 562, 565 (Lord Clyde). See also *Shawkat v Nottingham City Hospital NHS Trust* [2001] IRLR 555.

[1121] ERA 1996, s 136(1). Many of the same problems arise, particularly with reference to resignation. See *Morton Sundour Fabrics Ltd v Shaw* (1966) 2 ITR 84; *Maher v Fram Gerrard Ltd* [1974] ICR 31; *Birch v University of Liverpool* [1985] ICR 470.

[1122] ERA 1996, s 138; see para 5.167 *et seq* below.

[1123] ERA 1996, s 142.

[1124] ERA 1996, s 136(5). See *Rose v Dodd* [2005] IRLR 977 for the effect of an intervention by the Law Society on the contracts of employment of those employed by solicitors.

[1125] ERA 1996, s 139(4).

[1126] ERA 1996, s 155. The notion of the 'relevant date' under ERA 1996, s 145, broadly corresponds to that of the EDT under s 97(1), adapted to the particular variations on the concept of dismissal which are discussed in the text. A tribunal only has jurisdiction where an employee has been dismissed with notice after expiry of the notice period: ERA 1996, ss 135(1)(a), 145: *Watts v Rubert Owen Conveyancer Ltd* [1977] IRLR 112; *Foster v Bon Groundwork Ltd* [2011] IRLR 645 (cf ERA 1996, s 111(3) in relation to unfair dismissal claims).

5.164 The statutory redundancy payment is calculated as a function of the age, weekly pay and seniority of the employee.[1127] The employee receives one-and-a-half week's gross pay for each year of employment in which he or she was not below the age of 41; one week's pay for each year he or she was 22 and over (but below 41); and half a week's pay for each year he or she was below 22. A maximum of 20 years' employment can be taken into account.[1128] There is a statutory ceiling on the gross weekly wage which can be used in this calculation, which as of 1 February 2012 and at the time of writing stands at £430,[1129] making the maximum sum which may currently be awarded £12,900. The redundancy payment therefore incorporates some elements of a reward for seniority, but in other respects it does not resemble a seniority payment. It is not available as of right in return for service in the manner of a retirement pension, but only in the event of a redundancy dismissal. The policy of promoting job search is reflected in the enactment of a statutory right of employees under notice of redundancy to take time off to look for alternative work.[1130]

Either party may refer to an employment tribunal the issue of entitlement to a redundancy payment or the appropriate quantum.[1131] Where the tribunal determines that the employee has the right to a redundancy payment it may order the employer to pay him or her such amount as the tribunal considers appropriate in all the circumstances to compensate him or her for any financial loss sustained which is attributable to the non-payment.[1132]

5.165 The employee's statutory rights may be waived collectively if there is an exemption order in force, granting effect to a collective agreement. An order shall not be made under this provision unless the Secretary of State is satisfied that the parties are willing to submit questions of an individual's entitlement to an employment tribunal.[1133] Prior to 1 October 2002, an employee employed under a contract of employment for a fixed term of two years or more could agree in writing to exclude any right to a redundancy payment in the event of the expiry of that term without renewal.[1134] This provision was repealed in order to comply with Directive 99/70/EC on Fixed-Term Work.

5.166 The employer may avoid the obligation to make a redundancy payment in one of a number of situations.

[1127] ERA 1996, s 162. Normal weekly pay is in accordance with ss 221–227. *Quaere* whether the age -related structure of the award is compatible with EU law in the light of Case C-555/07 *Kücükdevici v Swedex GMBH and Co KG* [2010] IRLR 346.

[1128] ERA 1996, s 162(3).

[1129] ERA 1996, s 227(1); SI 2008/3055. The concept of a week's pay is based on the employee's 'normal working hours', a phrase which normally excludes consideration of overtime hours: *Tarmac Roadstone Holdings Ltd v Peacock* [1973] ICR 273. On bonuses, see *British Coal Corpn v Cheesebrough* [1990] ICR 317.

[1130] ERA 1996, ss 52–54.

[1131] ERA 1996, s 163(1). See s 164 for time limits in relation to this matter.

[1132] ERA 1996, s 163(5), inserted by EA 2008, s 7(2).

[1133] ERA 1996, s 157; Redundancy Payments (Exemption) Order 1980, SI 1980/1052 (covering certain employees of Lancashire County Council).

[1134] ERA 1996, s 197, repealed by FTER 2002, SI 2002/2034, Sch 2, Part 1, para 3: see *Wiltshire County Council v NATFHE* [1980] ICR 455; *Housing Services Agency v Cragg* [1997] IRLR 380; *BBC v Kelly-Phillips* [1998] IRLR 294. Agreements entered into and taking effect before 1 October 2002 that comply with the conditions of the repealed s 197 remain effective only where the contract was entered into before 1 October 2002 or, where there have been one or more renewals, the only or most recent renewal was agreed before that date: SI 2002/2034, Sch 2, Part 2, para 5.

(i) An offer of renewed or alternative employment

5.167   An offer of renewed or alternative employment by the employer, or an associated employer,[1135] may prevent an employee being entitled to a redundancy payment.[1136] The provisions governing this situation are complex and operate in two separate ways: either they result in the employee not being treated as having been dismissed for the purposes of claiming a redundancy payment,[1137] or they disentitle an employee who is treated as dismissed from receiving a redundancy payment which would otherwise be payable.

5.168   Section 138(1) provides that employees who have been given notice of dismissal for redundancy (or have been constructively dismissed) *will not be regarded as dismissed* if (a) their contract of employment is renewed, or they are re-engaged under a new contract in pursuance of an offer made before the end of the employment under the previous contract[1138] and (b) the renewal or re-engagement takes effect either immediately on, or after an interval of not more than four weeks after, the end of that employment. Where the provisions of the contract as renewed, or the new contract, differ from those of the previous contract a four-week 'trial period' operates.[1139] If the employee leaves or is dismissed during the trial period (for a reason connected with or arising out of any difference between the renewed or new contract and the previous one), he or she is treated as having been dismissed on the date on which his or her employment under the previous contract ended, for the reason for which he or she would have been dismissed had the offer of re-employment not been made.[1140] Once the employee is treated as dismissed, he or she may still be disentitled from receiving a redundancy payment for the reasons provided in section 141, discussed below.

The timing of the four-week trial period has been considered in the context of the employee's broader rights to refuse to accept a repudiatory breach of contract by the employer which amounts to a dismissal. Where the employer commits such a breach, the employee is entitled at common law to carry on working under protest without being taken to have waived the rights under the original terms and conditions, at least for a certain period. The courts have held that for the purposes of redundancy compensation, the employee may resign and claim constructive dismissal even after the end of the four-week trial period envisaged by section 138: this provision does not take away the more general rights of the employee. Thus, the employee who is dismissed by the employer and then offered a new contract is subject to the four-week trial period, and will be taken not to have been dismissed if he or she stays in the new job after the end of that

---

[1135] ERA 1996, s 146(1). See para 3.65 for the definition of 'associated employer'.

[1136] ERA 1996, ss 138, 141.

[1137] Note that these provisions apply only for the purposes of Part XI of the Act: see *Jones v Governing Body of Burdett Coutts School* [1997] ICR 390.

[1138] 'Renewal' includes 'extension': ERA 1996, s 235(1). In *SI (Systems and Instrumentation) Ltd v Grist* [1983] ICR 788 the EAT opined that it is only in cases of re-engagement that the offer needs to be made before termination of the contract of employment, but cf the terms of s 141(1) where it is clear that this condition applies to both.

[1139] Section 138(2), (3). The period begins at the end of the employee's employment under the previous contract and ends with the period of four weeks beginning with the date on which the employee starts work under the renewed or new contract. The parties may agree a longer trial period but only where this is for the purpose of retraining: see s 138(3)(b)(ii), (6).

[1140] ERA 1996, s 138(2)(b), (4).

period.[1141] If, on the other hand, the employer simply announces that the old employment is at an end and offers new terms, the effect is that of a repudiation, and the employee may well have the benefit of a common law trial period extending well beyond the four weeks provided for by the Act.[1142] In *Turvey v CW Cheney & Son Ltd*[1143] it was held that the two could be combined, so that the statutory four-week trial period may begin only after the common law period had come to an end. This seemed a particularly anomalous outcome and it was rejected in *Optical Express Ltd v Williams* where the EAT clarified the position in the following terms:

> ... if there was a constructive dismissal, with no accompaniment of an offer, then accepted, of alternative employment, the employee would have the common law opportunity to accept or reject; and the fact that the employee went on working, either on the same or on different terms, would not, absent evidence of waiver, prevent acceptance of repudiation and hence a constructive dismissal after a common law trial period. But where ... there is an express offer and an express acceptance of a s138 contract of re-engagement for a trial period, ... it is impossible to suggest that the common law period runs alongside.[1144]

On this basis, once the statutory trial period had expired the employee could no longer claim to have been dismissed.

5.169 Section 141 deals with the position of the employee *who is treated as dismissed for redundancy but disentitled from receiving a redundancy payment*. This occurs if the employee unreasonably refuses an offer of alternative employment under a renewed contract or a new contract.[1145] Where the provisions of the renewed or new contract differ from the corresponding provisions of the previous contract, the right to a payment will be lost only if the employment also satisfies the condition of being 'suitable'. (This question does not arise if the provisions of the new contract do not differ from those of the old.) If the employee embarks upon a trial period pursuant to section 138 and then leaves during it, entitlement to a payment will be lost if the new employment was suitable and the termination of the employment during the trial period was unreasonable.[1146]

The essential questions under these provisions, then, are whether an alternative job offer is suitable and whether an employee's refusal to accept the new job is unreasonable. In *Taylor v Kent County Council*[1147] Lord Parker CJ thought that suitability should be assessed by reference to the individual concerned, and that 'suitability means something substantially equivalent to the employment which has ceased'. A significant change in salary or status – such as, in *Taylor*, the demotion of a headmaster to a position which was effectively that of a supply teacher – would be

---

[1141] Eg *Meek v J Allen Rubber Co Ltd* [1980] IRLR 21.

[1142] *Shields Furniture Ltd v Goff* [1973] ICR 187; *Sheet Metal Components Ltd v Plumridge* [1974] ICR 373; *Air Canada v Lee* [1978] ICR 1202.

[1143] [1979] ICR 341. See also *East Suffolk Local Health Services NHS Trust v Palmer* [1997] ICR 425.

[1144] [2007] IRLR 936, Burton P at [29].

[1145] ERA 1996, s 141(1). The offer must have been made before the end of the employment, with renewal or re-engagement to take effect either immediately on, or after an interval of not more than four weeks after, the end of the employment.

[1146] ERA 1996, s 141(4).

[1147] [1969] 2 QB 560; for a more recent illustration, see *Cambridge & District Co-operative Society Ltd v Ruse* [1993] IRLR 156.

likely to render the alternative job unsuitable. In *Thomas Wragg & Sons Ltd v Wood*[1148] factors which the EAT held could be taken into account included the fact that the offer was made very late in the day; the employee's acceptance, by that date, of other work; and his fear of continuing to work in a declining industry.

(ii) Misconduct

5.170   Where the employee has committed a repudiatory breach of contract which would entitle the employer to dismiss him or her summarily, the employer may avoid any liability for redundancy which it would otherwise have had by either dismissing the employee without notice; dismissing him or her by giving shorter notice than, but for the employee's breach, would have been required; or by giving the employee the normal contractual or statutory notice to which he or she was entitled, but including with that a written statement to the effect that the employer would have been entitled to dismiss the employee without notice.[1149] At first sight it is not easy to see the point of this provision since if dismissal was for misconduct, there would be no redundancy in the first place; however, section 140(1) pre-dates the introduction of unfair dismissal legislation, which may account for its existence and rather convoluted form. As it is, the provision could apply in a situation where the employee was first dismissed for redundancy, but then, in the period of notice, committed an act which justified summary dismissal.[1150] Even where section 140(1) applies, if the employee is dismissed during the 'obligatory period of notice', which means the minimum period of notice to which the employee is entitled, the tribunal has the power to award the employee all or part of the redundancy payment to which, in the absence of section 140(1), he or she would have been entitled.[1151]

(iii) Participation in a strike

5.171   In some circumstances the employee may not lose his or her entitlement by virtue of taking part in a strike. This provision forms an exception to the general disqualification for misconduct,[1152] which would otherwise apply since the act of going on strike is a repudiatory breach of contract by the employee which entitles the employer to terminate the contract without notice.[1153] Section 140(2) provides that the misconduct disqualification has no application in a case where the employee has been given notice of dismissal by the employer and who then takes part in a strike during the 'obligatory period of notice' and is dismissed for so doing. This exception was designed to give employees some protection in the case of a strike called to protest against redundancy. However, the protection is not very effective since it does not apply to the interval

---

[1148] [1976] ICR 313.
[1149] ERA 1996, s 140(1).
[1150] Elias *et al*, 1980: p 698. In *Simmons v Hoover Ltd* [1977] ICR 61 the EAT affirmed that s 140(1) applies both where there is a 'single' dismissal (ie, a dismissal for redundancy and not explicitly for misconduct) as well as a 'double' dismissal (ie, a dismissal for redundancy followed by a dismissal for misconduct).
[1151] ERA 1996, ss 140(3)–(5), 136(4).
[1152] Cf s 140(1).
[1153] *Simmons v Hoover Ltd* [1977] ICR 61.

between an employer's announcement of impending redundancies and the issue of notices to individual workers. If a strike starts during this interval, the employees concerned will forfeit any rights to redundancy compensation.[1154] Even where the strike begins after notices have been sent out, the employer may still require the employee to work the extra period of days lost by virtue of the strike in order to receive the redundancy payment.[1155] Industrial action short of a strike which constitutes a repudiatory breach of contract will be dealt with under section 140(1); see further para 11.86 below.

(iv) Lay-off or short-time working

5.172 A fourth exclusion relates to a situation of temporary lay-off or short-time working. The Act attempts, in an exceptionally complicated fashion, to deal with the overlap between the right to redundancy compensation and the guaranteed pay provisions of the ERA 1996.[1156] Where an employee is 'laid off or kept on short time' there may be no right to a redundancy payment, even if there would otherwise have been a redundancy. For these purposes, lay-off describes a situation in which the employee does not receive work under the contract of employment and, as a result, receives no pay;[1157] short-time is a situation in which, by reason of a diminution in the employee's work, the remuneration received is less than half a week's pay.[1158] Under these circumstances, there is only a redundancy if the employee has been laid off or kept on short time for four or more consecutive weeks, or has been laid off or kept on short time for six or more weeks (of which not more than three were consecutive) in any period of thirteen weeks.[1159] To be entitled to claim redundancy compensation, the employee must then give the employer a notice of intention to claim a redundancy payment, which must be issued within four weeks of the last of the four or six weeks of lay-off and/or short-time, as just described.[1160] This notice will be of no effect if, on the date it was served, it was reasonably expected that within four further weeks the employee's employment would return to normal and that he or she would then enter into a period of uninterrupted employment lasting at least thirteen weeks,[1161] and the employer also gives the employee a counter-notice that it will contest liability for redundancy compensation.[1162] Assuming the notice of claim is effective, the employee must finally give the employer a further notice of termination of the contract of employment, which must be notice of at least a week, and must be more if the terms of the employee's contract of employment provide for that; and this

---

[1154] *Simmons v Hoover Ltd* [1977] ICR 61. Note also s 136(2) which provides that if an employee terminates his or her contract of employment without notice in response to a lock-out which constitutes a repudiatory breach of contract, this is excluded from the definition of 'constructive dismissal', so denying the employee any form of statutory redundancy payment.

[1155] ERA 1996, s 143. See further para 11.86.

[1156] ERA 1996, ss 147–152; on guaranteed pay see ERA 1996, ss 28–35; see para 4.127 above.

[1157] ERA 1996, s 147(1).

[1158] ERA 1996, s 147(2).

[1159] ERA 1996, s 148(2).

[1160] ERA 1996, s 148(1), (2).

[1161] This means uninterrupted in the sense of there being neither lay-off nor short-time for any week in this period: ERA 1996, s 152(1). However, this exception in the employer's favour does not apply if, in the four weeks after the employee issues the notice of claim, he or she is laid off or kept on short time for each of those four weeks: ERA 1996, s 152(2), 154.

[1162] ERA 1996, ss 149, 152(1)(b).

notice of termination must be given within a period which, for most purposes, is four weeks from the date upon which the initial notice of claim was given.[1163]

Unfair dismissal in cases of redundancy and reorganisation

5.173   Both redundancy and some other substantial reason (SOSR) are potentially fair reasons for an economic dismissal. Whereas the statutory definition of a 'redundancy' has been narrowly confined by case law, the residual SOSR category has been greatly expanded to cover most economic dismissals which do not fall into the category of redundancy. The effect is that an economic dismissal will not be unfair just because it cannot be classified as a redundancy; it will most likely fall into the SOSR category and so be potentially fair. On the other hand, if a dismissal is categorised as falling into the SOSR category, there is no automatic compensation for loss of employment as there is in the case of redundancy.

The category of SOSR has been held to cover, for example, cases in which employees have been dismissed for refusing to accept changes in working hours and shift arrangements made in the business interests of the employer.[1164] This is so even where the employer attempts to make unilateral changes to contract terms and conditions, and the employee resigns in response to the employer's repudiatory breach of contract.[1165] SOSR has also applied where temporary workers employed on a succession of fixed-term contracts were dismissed upon the expiry of the final agreement.[1166] The type of reason which the employer needs to put forward has been described simply as a 'sound, good business reason'.[1167] The burden of proof on the employer is easily met: 'it is not an onus which it is at all difficult to discharge'.[1168] Although the tribunal has the right to disregard the reason put forward by the employer and conclude that, objectively speaking, no good business reason existed,[1169] it may not substitute its judgment of what is in the commercial interests of the business for that of the employer. Nor may the tribunal find that there is no SOSR because it considers that the new covenants the employer proposes for the protection of its legitimate interests are so unreasonable that the employee could not be expected to sign them: the question at this stage is merely whether the reason falls within a *category* that is not excluded by the law as a ground for dismissal.[1170] Although a finding of SOSR does not necessarily lead to a finding that the dismissal was fair in the circumstances – SOSR is only a potentially fair reason,

---

[1163] See ERA 1996, s 150(3), (4) for further details dealing with the various situations which may exist with regard to the employer's counter-notice.

[1164] *Ellis v Brighton Co-operative Society* [1976] IRLR 419. See also *Copsey v WWB Devon Clays Ltd* [2005] IRLR 811 where the Court of Appeal held that the employment tribunal had been entitled to find that the dismissal of an employee who refused to agree, because of his religious beliefs, to a contractual variation which meant that he could be required to work on Sundays was fair in the circumstances, discussed H Collins, 2006.

[1165] *Knighton (RG) v Henry Rhodes Ltd* [1974] IRLR 71; *Bumpus (JF) v Standard Life Assurance Ltd* [1974] IRLR 232; Bowers and Clarke, 1981: p 40.

[1166] *North Yorkshire County Council v Fay* [1985] IRLR 247; *Terry v East Sussex County Council* [1976] ICR 536. Note now the limitation on successive fixed-term contracts in FTER 2002, SI 2002/2034, reg 8, discussed at paras 5.75–5.76.

[1167] *Hollister v National Farmers' Union* [1979] ICR 542, 551 (Lord Denning MR).

[1168] *Banerjee v City and East London Area Health Authority* [1979] IRLR 147, 150 (Arnold J).

[1169] *Orr v Vaughan* [1981] IRLR 63; *Ladbroke Courage Holidays Ltd v Asten* [1981] IRLR 59.

[1170] *Willow Oak Developments Ltd (t/a Windsor Recruitment) v Silverwood* [2006] IRLR 607.

and the employer must not make demands on the employee which are wholly excessive – it has to date tended to do so in all but the most exceptional of cases.[1171]

5.174 It remains axiomatic that under section 98(4) there is an area of economic decision-making which is beyond the legitimate scope of tribunal review: in one redundancy case the Court of Appeal reiterated the view that 'it was not open to the court to investigate the commercial and economic reasons which prompted the closure. It may be that the court should have this power, but it does not have [it] at present'.[1172] This does not mean that either redundancy or SOSR is an *automatically* fair reason for dismissal. There is a world of difference between saying that a dismissal is for a potentially fair reason, and concluding that the employer acted reasonably as treating that reason as sufficient in the particular circumstances of the case. Thus even if the decision is motivated by economic considerations, the employer must still show that there were grounds upon which a reasonable employer could conclude that there was a need for changes leading to redundancy or re-organisation.[1173] If the employer fails to offer any convincing evidence of business pressures leading to change, the tribunal may legitimately find the dismissal to have been unfair.[1174]

Nonetheless, in SOSR cases courts have found that an employer may be acting reasonably in forcing through changes which amount to a unilateral abrogation of existing collective agreements and, by extension, of terms incorporated from those agreements into individual contracts of employment. There is nothing in the Act to say that either a constructive dismissal or any other dismissal in which the employer acts in repudiatory breach of contract must be unfair; and it is also important to bear in mind that the contract terms have no greater stability, for much of the time, under the common law than they do under statute, since the common law normally allows the employer to end the contract by giving notice. However, there is a good case for saying that 'since the statute was arguably enacted to enhance employee rights, it would have been perfectly proper to treat the contract and collective agreement as establishing minimum rights for employees to be improved upon by the statute'.[1175] Instead, redundancy or reorganisation in breach of contract is a potentially fair reason, which the employer can show was fair in the circumstances by producing evidence of business necessity in some form or other.

Even if the employer can produce evidence of cost savings or enhanced efficiency, however, dismissal may be unfair if the new demands being placed on the employee are excessive. In *Evans v Elemeta Holdings Ltd*[1176] the employee was offered new terms, as part of a reorganisation, which would have required him to work overtime, unpaid, up to an unspecified number of hours per week. He resigned and claimed constructive dismissal. The EAT, reversing the tribunal, found that the unreasonableness of the terms offered made the dismissal unfair. However, the unreasonableness of the terms offered may not, in itself, be enough to justify such a finding. In *St*

[1171] See below.
[1172] *James W Cook & Co (Wivenhoe) Ltd v Tipper* [1990] IRLR 386.
[1173] *Orr v Vaughan* [1981] IRLR 63. On the band of reasonableness test in this context, see *Richmond Precision Engineering Ltd v Pearce* [1985] IRLR 179, *Cobley v Forward Technology Industries plc* [2003] IRLR 706.
[1174] *Ladbroke Courage Holidays Ltd v Asten* [1981] IRLR 59.
[1175] Anderman, 1986: p 428.
[1176] [1982] IRLR 143.

John of God (Care Services) Ltd v Brooks[1177] a hospital funded by the NHS, faced with substantial cuts in its funding, offered its employees new contracts involving lower rates of pay, the abolition of holiday entitlements and the abolition of overtime premia for weekend and holiday work. The tribunal found that the resulting dismissals were unfair because no reasonable employer could have expected the employees to agree to such terms. By a majority the EAT overruled this decision, holding that the tribunal had applied the wrong test: it was wrong to focus on the offer, to the exclusion of other factors; and the tribunal's approach 'tends to lead to giving undue importance to the factor that the employee is acting reasonably in refusing the offer'.[1178]

5.175   If the law of unfair dismissal places few restraints on the employer's right to direct the business and organise the workforce as it sees fit, it places more effective restraints on the manner in which the employer conducts the process of redundancy and in particular its selection of the employees to be dismissed. It used to be the case that two forms of redundancy selection were automatically unfair: selection for reasons related to trade union activities and membership or non-membership, and selection contrary to an agreed or customary procedure. The latter provision, which applied to procedures such as 'last-in, first-out' (LIFO), was repealed in 1994.[1179] The former is still retained and the model it embodies has been extended to cover a number of other automatically unfair reasons.[1180] The normal qualifying period of service does not apply in these cases.[1181]

Although selection contrary to an agreed or customary procedure is no longer automatically unfair, the process of selecting an employee must still comply with section 98(4) of ERA 1996. As Millett LJ explained:

> Criticism of the fairness of the process of selection for redundancy may take either or both of two forms. It may take the form of a challenge to the fairness of the system of selection which the employer adopted, including the criteria for redundancy, safeguards against bias and extent of consultation; or it may take the form of a challenge to the fairness of the manner in which the system was applied in practice.[1182]

5.176   In order successfully to challenge the operation of selection criteria it will often be important to know the points awarded or assessments given to those who were not selected for redundancy. In *British Aerospace plc v Green*[1183] the Court of Appeal took a restrictive approach to this question, holding that the 530 employees selected for redundancy out of a workforce of 7,000 were not entitled to discovery of the assessment forms of those who had not been selected. Millett LJ indicated that an applicant who sought an order for discovery 'must specify the respect in which he claims that the process was unfairly applied with sufficient particularity to demonstrate

---

[1177] [1992] ICR 715. See also *Catamaran Cruisers Ltd v Williams* [1994] IRLR 386, discussed at para 4.41 above; *Garside and Laycock Ltd v Booth* [2011] IRLR 735.

[1178] [1992] ICR 715, 722.

[1179] DCOA 1994, s 36(1).

[1180] See para 5.92 above.

[1181] ERA 1996, s 108(3).

[1182] *British Aerospace plc v Green* [1995] IRLR 433, 437. See, for example, *Watkins v Crouch (t/a Temple Bird Solicitors)* [2011] IRLR 382.

[1183] [1995] IRLR 433.

the relevance of the material the discovery of which is sought'.[1184] In many cases, however, this will place an impossible burden on an employee. This point was recognised by the EAT in a decision reached shortly after *British Aerospace* where the employee was selected for redundancy from a group of eight, despite the fact that length of service was one of the criteria for selection; he had longer service than one of those retained; and there had never been any complaints about his performance. The EAT dismissed the employer's appeal against an order for discovery; only by knowing the applicant's markings and how they compared with those of the other seven employees was it possible to know whether the selection criteria had been applied fairly and reasonably to him.[1185] In *John Brown Engineering Ltd v Brown* the EAT went further in holding that 'a policy decision to withhold all markings in a particular selection process may result in individual unfairness if no opportunity is thereafter given to the individual to know how he has been assessed. We recognise it may be invidious to publish the whole identified "league tables", but in choosing not to do so the employer must run the risk that he is not acting fairly in respect of individual employees'.[1186] Adoption of a more transparent approach of this nature also avoids protracted litigation over the boundaries of appropriate discovery orders in this context.

5.177   The process of redundancy may also be unfair by reason of a general breach of procedural fairness under section 98(4) of ERA 1996. The employer may come under an obligation, depending on the circumstances, to give prior warnings to the employees; to enter into consultations with their trade union; to investigate the possibility of alternative employment; to consider the timing of the redundancies and their financial implications; and to allow for an appeal.[1187] A lower standard of procedural propriety is set in the case of smaller firms,[1188] consonant with the reference in the subsection to the need to take into account the 'size and administrative resources of the employer's undertaking'. Generally, however, these provisions require the employer to produce some objective justification of the process adopted.[1189] The obligations imposed by section 98(4) do not replicate precisely the obligations placed upon the employer to consult at a collective level with employee or union representatives.[1190] However in *Rowell v Hubbard Group Services Ltd*[1191] the EAT thought that it would be normal for a tribunal to follow the approach suggested for collective consultation by Glidewell LJ in *R v British Coal Corpn and Secretary of State for Trade*

[1184] [1995] IRLR 433, 438.

[1185] *FDR Ltd v Holloway* [1995] IRLR 400, 402. Although it could be argued that the applicant in this case met the test set out by Millett LJ in *British Aerospace*, the decision in *FDR* was regarded by the Court of Session in *King v Eaton Ltd* [1996] IRLR 199, 201 as 'irreconcilable' with *British Aerospace*, which was affirmed to be correct.

[1186] [1997] IRLR 90, 91 (Lord Johnston).

[1187] See generally the judgment of the EAT in *Williams v Compair Maxam Ltd* [1982] IRLR 83; see also *Langston v Cranfield University* [1998] IRLR 172; *Lloyd v Taylor Woodrow Construction* [1999] IRLR 782. In *Morgan v Welsh Rugby Union* [2011] IRLR 376 the EAT held that *Compair Maxam* did not apply to the filling of new, different roles where redundancy arose in the course of a reorganisation; appointment to a new role was likely to involve something more like an interview process and a substantial element of judgement by the employer.

[1188] *Gray v Shetland Norse Preserving Co* [1985] IRLR 53.

[1189] *Williams v Compair Maxam Ltd* [1982] IRLR 83; *NC Watling & Co Ltd v Richardson* [1978] ICR 1049; *Thomas and Betts Manufacturing v Harding* [1978] IRLR 213.

[1190] TULRCA 1992, ss 188 *et seq*; see para 9.32 *et seq* below. Nor does consultation with the union over selection criteria release the employer from consulting with the individual employee: see *Mugford v Midland Bank plc* [1997] IRLR 208. On fair consultation with an individual during a redundancy selection process, see *Pinewood Repro Ltd (t/a County Print) v Page* [2011] ICR 508.

[1191] [1995] IRLR 195, 197.

and Industry, ex p Price:[1192] in particular, there should be consultation at an early stage of the formulation of the proposals; there should be adequate provision of information to the employees or, where appropriate, their representatives; they should be given adequate time to respond; and their response should be conscientiously considered by the employer.

5.178   Finally, selection must comply with the general requirements of the equality legislation, which outlaws discrimination on the grounds of race, sex, disability, religion or belief, sexual orientation and age.[1193] In *Clarke v Eley (IMI) Kynoch Ltd*[1194] the EAT held that a practice of dismissing all the part-time workers at the establishment, before any full-time workers were dismissed, amounted to indirect sex discrimination since the large majority of the part-time staff were female. The prior selection of the part-time staff amounted to the imposition of a requirement which the women in the establishment were proportionally less able to meet than the men. The employer failed in a defence of justification. The EAT also discussed the possibility that LIFO itself might be discriminatory on the grounds that women were, as a consequence of breaks in service for childcare and other purposes, less likely to have long service than men. The question was left open; it is possible that an employer might successfully invoke the justification defence to support LIFO. In *Eversheds Legal Services v De Belin*[1195] the selection of the claimant solicitor for redundancy was found to be both unfair and to constitute sex discrimination when a colleague absent on maternity leave was given the maximum score under the criterion of 'lock-up' (which measures the length of time between undertaking a piece of work for a client and receipt of payment for it) and he was given his actual score in circumstances where, had this approach not been adopted, he would not have been selected.

   In *Rolls Royce plc v Unite the Union*[1196] the High Court was asked to determine whether the retention of length of service as a criterion within a selection matrix for redundancy, as contained within the collective agreements applicable to two of the employers' sites, was lawful under EE(A)R 2006. The court concluded that it was. First, the service-related selection criterion constituted a 'benefit' under reg 32(1) of EE(A)R (now EqA 2010, Sch 9, para 10) and '[w]here there is an agreed redundancy scheme, negotiated with a recognised trade union, which uses a length of service requirement as part of a wider scheme of measured performance, it is probable … that such would be regarded as reasonably fulfilling a business need'.[1197] Second, even without reg 32, the parties had adopted a scheme which enabled the employer to succeed in a defence to an age discrimination claim under reg 3 (now EqA 2010, s 13(2)): 'the legitimate aim is the

---

[1192] [1994] IRLR 72. See also *King v Eaton Ltd* [1996] IRLR 199.

[1193] See ch 6.

[1194] [1983] ICR 165. See generally paras 3.49 *et seq* above. The application of the Part-Time Workers (Prevention of Less Favourable Treatment) Regulations 2000, SI 2000/1551 would now need to be considered: see para 3.58

[1195] [2011] IRLR 448,

[1196] [2009] IRLR 49. Sir Thomas Morison, sitting as judge of the High Court, said at [2] that he acceded to the request of both parties to determine the specified questions with 'considerable misgivings' given that he was sitting without the 'benefit of the advice and wisdom' which lay members of employment tribunals and the EAT brought to such questions. The Court of Appeal was also 'anxious' (Wall LJ at [59]) about addressing the issues raised in these circumstances and Wall LJ emphasised at [60] that nothing in the judgment should be read as inhibiting potential ET claimants from arguing that the redundancy process was unfair: [2009] IRLR 576.

[1197] Above at [16], [17]. As the editorial to the IRLR report notes, this expansive interpretation of the meaning of 'benefit' 'would have the effect of virtually immunising service-based criteria from the scope of the age discrimination prohibition', so conflicting with the principle that exceptions to the legislation should be strictly construed. See also Wynn-Evans, 2009.

advancement of an employment policy which achieves a peaceable process of selection agreed with the recognised union. The criterion of length of service respects the loyalty and experience of the older workforce and protects the older employees from being put onto the labour market at a time when they are particularly likely to find alternative employment hard to find'.[1198] The Court of Appeal upheld the conclusions reached by the High Court although Wall LJ criticised the failure to address explicitly whether the criterion was a proportionate means of achieving a legitimate aim.[1199]

Employer insolvency

5.179 Legislation provides certain guarantees to employees in the event of their employer's insolvency.[1200] It may be possible for the employees to claim, first of all, against the insolvent employer in their capacity as preferred creditors. Accrued wages for four months up to a limit of £800, together with accrued holiday pay and certain other payments, are protected in this way.[1201] In practice, even the employees' preferred claims against the estate of the insolvent employer will be defeated in most cases by the prior claims of any creditor holding a fixed charge over the company's assets, and will in any event only be ranked *pari passu* with those of other preferred creditors. Where wages in excess of £800 are owed, employees rank *pari passu* with other unsecured creditors.

More useful in practice is the second possibility, which is that the employees can make a claim for certain payments against the National Insurance Fund.[1202] The Fund is then statutorily subrogated to the employees' claims, in respect of these sums, against the insolvent employer. The claims met by the Fund include certain arrears of wages for up to eight weeks (and subject to a ceiling which from 1 February 2012 and at the time of writing stands at £430 per week);[1203] statutory guaranteed pay; the protective award; holiday pay; wages for the statutory notice period; any basic award of unfair dismissal compensation (but not the compensatory award or any further

[1198] Above at [15].
[1199] [2009] IRLR 576, [98]-[99]. Cf Arden LJ at [162] on this point.
[1200] For a more detailed examination of the complex area of corporate rescue and insolvency see Belcher, 1997.
[1201] IA 1986, ss 386–387 and Sch 6, para 9; SI 1986/1996.
[1202] ERA 1996, ss 166–170 and 182–190, which implement the UK's commitments under EC Council Directive 80/987/EC as amended by Directive 2002/74/EC. On the definition of insolvency for this purpose see ERA 1996, s 183, which was amended by the Enterprise Act 2002 to include a reference to companies in administration (see s 183(3)(aa); *Mann v Secretary of State for Employment* [1999] IRLR 566; *Secretary of State for Trade and Industry v Walden* [2000] IRLR 168.
[1203] ERA 1996, s 186. In *Potter v Secretary of State for Employment* [1997] IRLR 21 the Court of Appeal left open the question whether the statutory ceiling on the total amount payable by the Secretary of State was in accordance with the social policy objective of the Insolvency Directive. A reference to the ECJ on this point was held not to be necessary to dispose of the case. The EAT has held that the statutory ceiling should be applied before making any deductions for national insurance contributions and any relevant benefits to be recouped: *Titchener v Secretary of State for Trade and Industry* [2002] IRLR 195. Art 4(3) of the amended Directive states that ceilings set 'must not fall below a level which is socially compatible with the social objectives' of the Directive. In *Mann v Secretary of State for Employment* [1999] IRLR 566 Lord Hoffmann suggested that employees can choose the eight weeks they regard as most favourable to them for the purposes of the claim against the Secretary of State.

additional award); and any statutory redundancy payment.[1204] Where the Secretary of State fails to make a payment, or pays too little, the employee may complain to an employment tribunal, which may declare the amount of payment due.[1205]

The statutory scheme therefore provides only limited protection for employees in a direct claim against the remaining assets of the insolvent employer, and envisages that in most cases the state will have to meet the employer's residual liabilities. However, this compromise is capable of being upset in situations where administrators are appointed to run insolvent companies with a view to saving the businesses concerned, as opposed to simply realising their assets as quickly as possible.[1206] Before examining the reasons for this, it is necessary briefly to consider the types of insolvency which may arise and their impact on the employees of the company.

5.180   Traditionally, a receiver (referred to as an 'administrative receiver' by modern insolvency legislation) was appointed by a secured creditor, typically a debenture-holder with a fixed and/or floating charge over the company's assets, in order to realise that creditor's security interest in the event of default.[1207] The Insolvency Act 1986 then made provision for an administrator to be appointed by order of the court, on a petition from one of the company's creditors, to run a company which could not meet its debts as they fell due, with the purpose of effecting a rescue. In the interests of further promoting the 'rescue culture', the Enterprise Act 2002 substantially limited the right of a floating charge holder to appoint a receiver; this possibility is now restricted to cases where the charge was created before the 2002 Act came into force, and various special cases (including certain complex capital market transactions and public-private partnerships). Thus the case of receivership is now of diminishing relevance. The 2002 Act also made it possible for an administrator to be appointed by the company itself, its directors or a floating-charge holder, without a court order. A further possibility is that a liquidator is appointed by the creditors following a voluntary liquidation; rather than aiming to save the company, the liquidator's principal role is to sell its assets, with a view to maximising returns to the creditors. The court can also order a compulsory winding up, again with a view to selling the remaining assets and returning the proceeds to the creditors.

An administrator is deemed to act as the agent of the company and is thereby empowered to make contracts on its behalf.[1208] Case law from before the passage of the 1986 and 2002 Acts indicates that where an administrator (or liquidator) acts as the company's agent, his or her appointment does not, of itself, terminate the contracts of employment of the company's

---

[1204] ERA 1996, s 184. The EAT has held that the list of payments in s 184 is exhaustive and that payments under contractual guaranteed pay provisions in respect of lay-offs that exceed the statutory entitlement, or payments in respect of absence through sickness or maternity due under the contract, are not recoverable: *Benson v Secretary of State for Trade and Industry* [2003] IRLR 748.

[1205] ERA 1996, ss 182–188. The ECJ has held that if the employer discharges part of the debt owed to an employee, this goes to reduce the employer's liability *outside* the three-month protected 'reference' period under the Directive, leaving the residual liability of the 'guarantee institution' (in the UK, the National Insurance Fund) within the reference period unaffected: Case C-125/97 *Regeling v Bestuur van de Bedrijfsvereniging Voor de Metaalnijverheid* [1999] IRLR 379.

[1206] P Davies, 1994a.

[1207] On receivership, see Armour and Frisby, 2001.

[1208] IA 1986, Sch B1, para 69, as inserted by the Enterprise Act 2002.

employees.[1209] This case law also suggests that if an administrator enters into new contracts with the employees (or some of them) after being appointed, he or she might then become personally liable to those employees for debts arising out of their employment or for any claims in damages for wrongful dismissal which might arise.[1210] Under insolvency legislation, the administrator has a right to be indemnified out of the company's assets in respect of any such personal liabilities, and expenses and debts incurred in this way are a first charge on the assets of the company.[1211] Thus if the employees can establish a personal claim against the administrator, the effect is to gain a 'super-priority' placing them above all other creditors, since their claims would reduce the sums available to meet the company's other debts.[1212] Perhaps this does not greatly matter, since giving the employees a first charge on the company's assets could be thought to be protecting those who are most sharply affected by the company's collapse. But even if the point about the vulnerability of the employees is right, there is a problem in short-circuiting the intended statutory ranking of creditors in this way; and, from a more practical point of view, it could give administrators a strong disincentive to keep the employees in employment while attempting to salvage the fortunes of the business. Faced with the prospect of open-ended liability to the employees, they might be more likely to seek a quick sale of assets in order to meet the claims of the charge-holder and other commercial creditors.

5.181 The Insolvency Act 1986 attempted to strike a balance between these conflicting considerations by providing that administrators were to be personally liable on contracts entered into in the course of carrying out their functions, as well as any contracts of employment adopted by them; but that, on the other hand, they should not be taken to have adopted a contract of employment in respect of anything done within 14 days of their appointment.[1213] Subsequently, in *Re Specialised Mouldings*[1214] Harman J held that an insolvency practitioner could avoid liability under these provisions even if he or she continued with the contracts of employees beyond 14 days, merely by writing to the employees concerned informing them that he or she would not be adopting their contracts and would not be personally liable on them. There was nothing in the Act to justify such an exclusion , and the decision in *Re Specialised Mouldings* also appeared to elide the distinction between adopting and continuing a contract of employment in such a way to undermine the apparent aim of the 1986 amendments. Nevertheless, the judgment was widely relied on as providing insolvency practitioners with a means of keeping on the core employees of the business without incurring extensive liability to them. However, in *Re Paramount Airways (No 3), Powdrill v Watson*[1215] Harman J's interpretation of the Act was rejected as unfounded, first in the Court of Appeal and then in the House of Lords.

[1209] *Reigate v Union Manufacturing Co (Ramsbottom) Ltd* [1918] 1 KB 592 (liquidator). By contrast, an appointment made by the court was thought to terminate contracts of employment, on the grounds that an agency relationship was lacking in that case: *Reid v Explosives Co Ltd* (1887) 19 QBD 264. This would no longer be so in the case of an administrator appointed by the court, due to the statutory deeming provision in IA 1986, referred to above.

[1210] *Re Mack Trucks (Britain) Ltd* [1967] 1 All ER 977; cf *Nicoll v Cutts* [1985] BCLC 322, where the Court of Appeal drew a distinction between continuing and adopting contracts of employment. The matter is now dealt with by IA 1994 and consequent amendments to IA 1986: see para 5.181 below.

[1211] IA 1986, Sch B1, para 99(3).

[1212] P Davies, 1994a.

[1213] IA 1986, s 19(5) (now repealed).

[1214] 13 February 1987, unreported.

[1215] [1994] IRLR 295; affd [1995] 2 AC 394.

Following the Court of Appeal's ruling, Parliament enacted the Insolvency Act 1994 which amended the 1986 Act in such a way as to restrict the impact of the *Paramount Airways* judgment. The administrator is now only liable for 'qualifying liabilities', that is to say wages and salary (including contractual holiday and sickness payments) and occupational pension contributions arising in respect of service after the point at which the contract was adopted. This formula was retained in the changes made by the Enterprise Act 2002.[1216] Thus amounts payable in respect of wrongful dismissal, as well as any claims for wages in respect of previous service, simply rank as unsecured debts and are subject to the general rules concerning the priority of such debts. Nor is the administrator liable under these provisions for sums payable to the employees by way of a protective award, which has been held not to give rise to a 'liability arising under a contract of employment' within the meaning of the Insolvency Act.[1217]

Dismissal and transfers of employment

5.182   At common law, the transfer of a business from one employer (the 'transferor') to another (the 'transferee') often precipitates the dismissal of the employees who work in that business. They may be dismissed by the transferor, for redundancy or for some other business-related reason, at some point before the transfer takes place; alternatively, if they are still employed when the business is sold, the sale constitutes a repudiatory breach of contract by the employer which, at common law, the employees are entitled to treat as a wrongful dismissal.[1218] If the business is insolvent, the appointment of an administrator or liquidator does not normally, as we have seen, automatically terminate the employee's contracts;[1219] if the business is subsequently sold, however, there is normally a dismissal at that point.

The concept of a 'relevant transfer' of an 'undertaking' under the Transfer of Undertakings (Protection of Employment) Regulations 2006 and the effect of the Regulations on the contract of employment and the rights and liabilities of the parties were considered in chapter 3 above.[1220] By virtue of regulation 7(1) of TUPE (formerly regulation 8(1) of the 1981 Regulations), it is automatically unfair to dismiss an employee of either the transferor or the transferee where the reason or principal reason for the dismissal is 'the transfer itself' or 'a reason connected with the transfer' that is not an ETOR (on which see below).[1221] This is so whether the dismissal takes effect

---

[1216] See now IA 1986, Sch B1, para 99(4)–(6).

[1217] *Krasner (administrator of Huddersfield Fine Worsteds Ltd. and Globe Worsted Co. Ltd.) v McMath* [2005] IRLR 995. The logic of this decision extends, on the face of it, to liabilities under other statutory employment protection provisions.

[1218] See *Nokes v Doncaster Amalgamated Collieries Ltd* [1940] AC 1014, 1019 (Viscount Simon); *Litster v Forth Dry Dock and Engineering Co Ltd* [1989] IRLR 161, 169 (Lord Oliver). It is doubtful that the employees have a sufficient 'legitimate interest' at common law to keep the contract alive against the transferor, if it no longer owns the business, nor can the common law (as opposed to TUPE) grant the employees automatic rights of continuing employment against the transferee.

[1219] See para 5.180 above. The same reasoning may not apply, however, if the liquidator or administrator is appointed by the court.

[1220] SI 2006/246; see para 3.66 *et seq* above.

[1221] See para 5.183.

before or after the transfer. The employee is required to satisfy the normal qualifying period to claim unfair dismissal,[1222] as well as any other relevant qualifying conditions.[1223]

5.183   Regulation 7 qualifies the principle of automatically unfair dismissal by providing that a dismissal shall be for a potentially fair reason[1224] where it is for 'an economic, technical or organisational reason entailing changes in the workforce of either the transferor or the transferee before or after a relevant transfer'.[1225] The scope of this 'ETOR' exception is therefore central to the question of determining the effect of regulation 7 as a whole. The concept of ETOR has been interpreted as being in some ways wider and in some ways narrower than the notion of SOSR which is its rough counterpart under ERA 1996. It is wider in the sense that ETOR embraces a dismissal by reason of redundancy;[1226] otherwise, redundancy, although generally a potentially fair reason for dismissal, would cease to be so for the purposes of business transfers, which can hardly have been the intention here. However, it is also significantly narrower in that it does not cover a range of economic dismissals which would, under the Act of 1996, fall into the SOSR category and hence be potentially fair; in the context of a transfer these dismissals are automatically unfair under regulation 7(1). This occurs largely because the concept of an ETOR as set out in regulation 7(2) (formerly 8(2)) covers only economic reasons 'entailing changes in the workforce' of either employer; as a result, dismissals which would almost certainly have been classed as SOSR reorganisations, because of their aim of job flexibility or cost-cutting, fail to qualify here as potentially fair.[1227]

5.184   In evaluating the impact of regulation 7 on transfer situations, it must be considered together with regulation 4 (formerly regulation 5), which provides for automatic novation of the contracts of employment of the transferor which would otherwise have been terminated by the transfer, unless the individual employees concerned object,[1228] and for the transmission to the transferee of all rights and liabilities arising in or under these contracts. Where the transferor is insolvent or approaching insolvency, the price paid for a business by the transferee may well be affected by whether or not it inherits the pre-existing liabilities of the transferor to its employees; these might take the form of common law obligations to pay accrued wages or damages for wrongful dismissal, or statutory obligations with regard to unfair dismissal, redundancy and other employment rights. Equally, the price might be higher if the transferee has a free hand, after the transfer, to employ whom it wishes, or to offer whatever terms it thinks fit. The prospective imposition of these various obligations may mean that the sale does not go ahead. Where that is so, the employees of the transferor will lose their chance of continuing employment; this raises

---

[1222] One year for employees whose period of continuous employment began before 6 April 2012; two years for those employed on or after that date: ERA 1996, s 108, as amended by SI 2012/989.

[1223] See TUPE 2006, reg 7(6). TUPE 1981, reg 8(5)(b), its predecessor, was inserted by the Collective Redundancies and Transfer of Undertakings (Protection of Employment)(Amendment) Regulations 1995, SI 1995/2587, overruling *Milligan v Securicor Cleaning Ltd* [1995] IRLR 288. Note, however, that ERA 1996, s 218 applies regardless of whether there is a TUPE transfer: *Oakland v Wellswood (Yorkshire) Ltd* [2010] IRLR 82.

[1224] This is the combined effect of reg 7(1)(b), (2) and (3)(a).

[1225] TUPE 2006, reg 7(2).

[1226] This is the effect of TUPE 2006, reg 7(3)(b). Previously the matter had been unclear. See DTI, *TUPE Draft Revised Regulations Public Consultation Document*, March 2005, at para 52.

[1227] *Berriman v Delabole Slate Ltd* [1985] ICR 546; *Crawford v Swinton Insurance Brokers Ltd* [1990] ICR 85.

[1228] See para 3.75 above.

the possibility that the level of protection conferred by the TUPE Regulations might be counter-productive from the point of view ensuring *de facto* security of employment.[1229] Whether, from a legal point of view, the Regulations strictly apply in all situations of restructuring which accompany a transfer is unclear. Four issues need to be considered: the application of the Regulations to pre-transfer dismissals; the significance, if any, of the transferor's insolvency; the effect of post-transfer dismissals; and the issue of the joint liability of transferor and transferee.[1230]

(i) Pre-transfer dismissals

5.185   The decision of the House of Lords in *Litster v Forth Dry Dock and Engineering Co Ltd*[1231] made it difficult for the Regulations to be avoided by collusion between the two employers designed to ensure that, at the point of transfer, the employees of the transferor had already been dismissed. This had seemed a possibility for a while when the Court of Appeal, in *Secretary of State for Employment v Spence*,[1232] overruled a number of earlier decisions[1233] to hold that the completion of a transfer takes place at a single point in time, and cannot be deemed to be spread over a number of hours or days. In *Spence* this meant that employees dismissed by the transferor for redundancy at 11.00am, some three hours before an agreement was completed for the sale of the business, did not thereby become employees of the transferee: the time of the transfer was 2.00pm, and not the day as a whole. Because it was only the contracts of those employees who were employed 'immediately before the transfer' which were subject to regulation 5 (as it then was), this meant that, as the EAT had noted in an earlier decision, 'it would be very easy for a transferor without funds to agree with a transferee, for reasons convenient to them both, that employees should be dismissed a short time before transfer, thus leaving them with a worthless remedy and so defeating the protection afforded by the Regulations'.[1234]

In *Litster* this scenario was realised. The transferor (Forth Dry Dock), which was in receivership, dismissed its workforce one hour before the completion of a transfer of business assets to the transferee (Forth Estuary), which also took a lease of the business premises concerned (together these were found to constitute a relevant transfer). Forth Estuary declined to take on any of the workforce of the insolvent company, since it had hired employees who were willing to work for lower pay. Forth Dry Dock's receivers were unable to meet its liabilities to its employees by way of holiday pay and damages for wrongful and unfair dismissal, since there were no assets left after the debenture holder had realised its security. The employees made claims for compensation instead against Forth Estuary, which was solvent. The Court of Session, applying *Spence*, ruled that none of the employees had been employed by Forth Dry Dock immediately before the transfer, and so had no claim against Forth Estuary. The House of Lords allowed an appeal.

[1229] On this, see Frisby, 2000; Armour and Deakin, 2000, 2003.

[1230] Issues of dismissal law may also arise in the context of an employee's refusal to enter the employment of the transferee; these are discussed at para 3.75 above.

[1231] [1989] IRLR 161.

[1232] [1986] IRLR 248.

[1233] *Apex Leisure Hire v Barratt* [1984] ICR 452; *Secretary of State for Employment v Anchor Hotel (Kippford) Ltd* [1985] IRLR 452.

[1234] *Apex Leisure Hire v Barratt* [1984] ICR 452, 457 (Tudor Evans J).

Lord Oliver thought that under the Directive, as construed by the European Court of Justice, a dismissal effected before the transfer and solely because of the transfer of the business was, in effect, prohibited and so was, for the purpose of considering the application of the Directive to UK law, required to be treated as ineffective.[1235] This interpretation should, in his Lordship's view, legitimately be extended to regulation 5 of TUPE 1981, as it then was, notwithstanding the substantial difference between its wording and that of the Directive, on the grounds that the aim of both the Directive and the Regulations was to safeguard the rights of the employees on a transfer and to provide effective remedies to this end. The remedies provided 'in the case of an insolvent transferor are largely illusory unless they can be exerted against the transferee'.[1236] Accordingly, the Directive had to be read as applying both to an employee actually employed immediately before the transfer and to one who 'would have been so employed if he had not been unfairly dismissed in the circumstances described in regulation 8(1)' (as it then was).

It followed that *Spence* had been correct on the question of the timing of the transfer, a decision subsequently confirmed by the ECJ.[1237] *Spence* was also correctly decided on its facts, since the dismissals in that case were genuinely for redundancy and were not connected to the transfer.[1238] Where, however, a dismissal which took place prior to the transfer was automatically unfair under the then regulation 8(1), *Litster* decided that the transferee would inherit the pre-existing liabilities of the transferor towards its employees. The employees were thereby able to bring outstanding claims for compensation against the transferee. However, where a dismissal fell under regulation 8(2) (as it then was), the transfer, although the reason for the dismissal,[1239] was not the reason for that dismissal being *unfair*, in contrast to the position under regulation 8(1). As a result, only automatically unfair dismissals under regulation 8(1) triggered the principle enunciated in *Litster*.[1240] This point has now been clarified in the new version of TUPE enacted in 2006.[1241]

5.186   A broad reading has been given to regulation 7(1) (previously regulation 8(1)). In *Spaceright Europe Ltd v Baillavoine*[1242] some employees, including the claimant, were dismissed by the administrators of the transferor prior to a TUPE transfer. The Court of Appeal held that the 'natural and ordinary meaning of the language of regulation 7(1) does not require a particular transfer or transferee to be in existence or in contemplation at the time of dismissal... [Thus] ... a dismissal prior to the transfer could have been for a reason "connected with the transfer" even

---

[1235] [1989] IRLR 161, 172. The judgments of the ECJ which Lord Oliver relied on directly were Case 19/83 *Wendelboe v LJ Music ApS* [1985] ECR457; Case 324/86 *Foreningen af Arbejdsledere i Danmark v Daddy's Dance Hall* [1988] IRLR 315; and Case 101/87 *P Bork International A/S v Foreningen af Arbejdsledere i Danmark* [1989] IRLR 41.

[1236] [1989] IRLR 161, 172.

[1237] Case C-478/03 *Celtec Ltd v Astley* [2005] IRLR 647.

[1238] See Lord Oliver in *Litster* [1989] IRLR 161, 171; *Porter and Nanyakkara v Queen's Medical Centre (Nottingham University Hospital)* [1993] IRLR 486; and *Dynamex Friction Ltd v Amicus* [2008] IRLR 515 where the tribunal held that a claim of collusion was not made out on the facts.

[1239] *Warner v Adnet Ltd* [1998] IRLR 393, cf *Whitehouse v Charles A Blatchford & Sons Ltd* [1999] IRLR 492.

[1240] See *Kerry Food Ltd v Creber* [2000] IRLR 10, 12; *Thompson v SCS Consulting Ltd* [2001] IRLR 801; *Dynamex Friction Ltd v Amicus* [2008] IRLR 515. See also *BSG Property Services v Tuck* [1996] IRLR 134, where the EAT held that where notice was given by the transferor which expired after the date of transfer, it was the transferor's reason for dismissing which was material, even though liability in connection with the dismissal was transferred to the transferee.

[1241] TUPE 2006, reg 4(3); see DTI, *TUPE Draft Revised Regulations Public Consultation Document*, March 2005, para 43.

[1242] [2012] IRLR 111. See paras 5.188 and 5.190 for the application of TUPE to situations of insolvency.

though that particular transfer or transferee was not known, identified or contemplated at the date of dismissal'.[1243]

Conversely, a narrow reading has been given to what is now regulation 7(2) (previously regulation 8(2)) Where a prospective purchaser puts pressure on the vendor to make a number of dismissals as a precondition of the sale going ahead, or as a precondition of a higher price, it could be argued that the dismissals fall into the ETOR category; but in *Wheeler v Patel*[1244] the EAT ruled that in these circumstances, where the dismissals were motivated by purely financial considerations, the dismissals were not 'economic' within the meaning of regulation 8(2). The term 'economic' is, for this purpose, to be construed *ejusdem generis* with 'technical and organisational', so as to require there to be good business-related reasons for re-structuring the workforce.[1245] Reasons for dismissal by the transferor must relate to the future conduct of its own business, not that of the transferee.[1246] In *Spaceright Europe Ltd v Baillavoine*[1247] the Court of Appeal held that, for an ETOR to be available, there must be an intention to change the workforce and to continue to conduct the business, as distinct from the purpose of selling it. 'It is not available in the case of dismissing an employee to enable the adminstrators to make the business of the company a more attractive proposition to prospective transferees of a going concern'.[1248]

5.187   It was unclear following *Litster* whether the judgment in that case had an application beyond the issue of whether employees could claim compensation for unfair dismissal from the transferee. In *P Bork International A/S v Foreningen af Arbejdsledere i Danmark* the ECJ said that 'workers employed by the undertaking whose contract of employment or employment relationship has been terminated on a date before that of the transfer, in breach of Article 4(1) of the Directive, must be considered as still employed in the undertaking on the date of the transfer with the consequence, in particular, that the obligations of an employer towards them are fully transferred from the transferor to the transferee, in accordance with Article 3(1)'.[1249] This could be read as meaning that the dismissals in question were to be regarded as a nullity. In *Litster* Lord Oliver spoke of such a dismissal being 'prohibited' and, for the purposes of applying the Directive, 'required to be treated as ineffective'; as a result the employment was 'statutorily continued'.[1250] The notion of a dismissal being nullified in this way is not, however, one which is generally present in the law of unfair dismissal, and there was authority to suggest that the English and Scottish courts would not be obliged to adopt a remedy which did not already have a place in national law: in *Wendelboe v LJ Music ApS*[1251] Advocate-General Slynn thought that 'whether the remedy for such unlawful dismissal consists in a court order declaring that dismissal to be a nullity or the award of damages or some other effective remedy is for member states to determine'.

[1243] Above, Mummery LJ at [43], [45].
[1244] [1987] IRLR 211; see also *Whitehouse v Charles A Blatchford & Sons Ltd* [1999] IRLR 492; *Thompson v SCS Consulting Ltd* [2001] IRLR 801; *Hynd v Armstrong* [2007] IRLR 338.
[1245] In *Meter U Ltd v Ackroyd* [2012] IRLR 367, the EAT held that 'workforce' did not include corporate franchisees.
[1246] See, on this point, *Hynd v Armstrong* [2007] IRLR 338.
[1247] Above note 1242.
[1248] Mummery LJ at [47].
[1249] [1989] IRLR 41, 44.
[1250] [1989] IRLR 161, 172.
[1251] [1985] ECR 457, 460.

In *Wilson v St Helens Borough Council/British Fuels Ltd v Baxendale and Meade*,[1252] Lord Slynn repeated this view: 'the overriding emphasis in the European Court's judgment is that the existing rights of employees are to be safeguarded if there is a transfer ... But neither the Regulations nor the Directive nor the jurisprudence of the Court create a Community law right to continue in employment which does not exist under national law'. Because UK labour law has no general concept of the nullity of a dismissal, then, *Litster* was confined to providing dismissed employees with a right to compensation from the transferee.

TUPE 2006 codifies the *Litster* ruling by extending the coverage of the Regulations to the transfer of any person 'employed immediately before the transfer, or who would have been so employed if he had not been dismissed in the circumstances described in regulation 7(1)'.[1253] There is no reference here to the dismissal being a 'nullity'. The Consultation Document on TUPE issued by the DTI in 2005 also refers to a regulation 7(1) dismissal being *unfair*, not *void*.[1254] But this attempt at clarification may not be the last word on the matter. As we have just seen, the crucial step in Lord Slynn's judgment in *Wilson* was the argument that the concept of nullity has no place in UK labour law. The amendments made in 2006 introduce the notion of nullity in the context of variations by reason of the transfer or a reason connected with the transfer which is not an ETOR by expressly stating that any purported variation shall be void.[1255] If the concept of nullity can be applied to variations, its application to dismissals, as intended by the ECJ in the *Bork* case, may have been facilitated.

(ii) The application of the Regulations to a situation of insolvency

5.188 The original draft of the Directive only applied to certain situations of insolvency. As a result of the jurisprudence of the ECJ, it was understood to apply to insolvency proceedings whose object was, broadly speaking, to effect a corporate rescue with a view to keeping the business intact where possible, but not to insolvency proceedings whose purpose was to liquidate the assets of the transferor. Member States were free to apply the provisions of the Directive in the second set of situations,[1256] but were not obliged to do so. The basis of this distinction was Article 1(1) of the Directive, which limited its scope to transfers made 'as a result of a legal transfer or merger'; this expression was held not to cover certain insolvency proceedings in the national legal systems of Member States. In *Abels v Bedrijfsvereniging Voor de Metaalindustrie en de Electrotechnische Industrie*[1257] the ECJ held that there was no 'legal transfer' within the meaning of the Directive in a case where a transfer took place 'in the context of insolvency proceedings instituted with a view to the liquidation of the assets of the transferor under the supervision of the competent judicial authority'.

[1252] [1998] IRLR 706, 713–714, overturning the judgment of the Court of Appeal ([1997] IRLR 505). See also the similar emphasis of the ECJ on the relationship between national law and the Directive in Case C-343/98 *Collino and Chiappero v Telecom Italia Spa* [2000] IRLR 788, and see para 3.76 above for discussion of the implications of the *British Fuels* decision for post-transfer variation of contract terms.
[1253] TUPE 2006, reg 4(3).
[1254] DTI, *TUPE Draft Revised Regulations Public Consultation Document*, March 2005, paras 50–51.
[1255] TUPE 2006, reg 4(4): see DTI, *TUPE Draft Revised Regulations Public Consultation Document*, March 2005, paras 44–45, and para 3.76 above.
[1256] Directive 77/187, Art 7.
[1257] Case 135/83 [1985] ECR 469.

Two reasons were given for the ruling in *Abels*. The principal reason relied on was the fear that the application of the Directive in this situation would be counter-productive; the employees' interests in job security would best be met by enabling the sale of assets to go ahead as quickly as possible, without being restricted by the imposition of the insolvent company's liabilities on any prospective purchaser.

The second reason was the 'specificity of insolvency law', or the principle that the ranking of creditors in insolvency law should not easily be upset by contrary principles of employment law. As Advocate General Van Gerven put it in the later case of *d'Urso v Ercole Marelli Elettromeccanica Generale SpA*,[1258] 'insolvency law is characterised by special procedures intended to weigh up the various interests involved, in particular those of the various classes of creditors, which implies that in all the Member States there are specific rules which may derogate, at least partially, from other provisions, of a general nature, including provisions of social law'. This is the problem of the employees' 'super-priority' which we also encountered in the context of the personal liability of administrators.[1259] Where, under *Litster*, the transferee inherited the pre-existing employment law liabilities of the transferor, the employees alone of all the creditors had the benefit of a direct claim for their loss against the solvent transferee; all the other creditors had was a claim against the assets of the insolvent transferor. Because the price paid by the transferee was likely (other things being equal) to be reduced to the extent that it had to meet in full the claims of the workforce, the employees' gain was the other creditors' loss. The problem of 'super-priority' was therefore two-fold: not only were the employees ranked above all other creditors, but their claims were met in full when those of the others (with the possible exception of the debenture holder) would almost certainly have been met only in part.[1260] Since, in the British context, legislation guarantees that part (although not all) of the employee's claims against an insolvent transferor will be met by the National Insurance Fund in any event,[1261] it could be argued that there was less reason to give the employees claims in full against the solvent transferee.

5.189   The 1981 Regulations attempted, in an indirect way, to exclude certain insolvency situations from their scope, by virtue of regulation 4 which purported to permit the practice of 'hiving down'. This was a process whereby an administrator or other insolvency practitioner transferred the business of an insolvent company to a specially-created subsidiary, while retaining the employees in the employment of the insolvent parent. The parent then lent the use of the employees' labour to the subsidiary. The subsidiary was sold to a third party which took the business without being required to take the employees as well. Regulation 4 deemed the transfer of the parent's undertaking to the subsidiary to take place no sooner than the moment immediately before the subsidiary's business was sold to the transferee, or the transferee took a controlling shareholding in the subsidiary. As a result the administrator could dismiss the employees, who remained employed by the parent, before the point at which the Regulations bit, so that they never entered the subsidiary's employment and so could not be transferred to the ultimate purchaser of the business. After *Litster*, however, the validity of regulation 4 was plainly in doubt, since it

---

[1258] Case C-362/89 [1992] IRLR 136, 142. See also Case C-319/94 *Jules Dethier Equipement SA v Dassy and Sovram SPRL* [1998] IRLR 266. *Abels* was applied in the UK context in *Perth and Kinross Council v Donaldson* [2004] IRLR 121.
[1259] See para 5.180 above, and see Pollard, 1996.
[1260] See H Collins, 1989b; P Davies, 1989; Schumacher, 1994.
[1261] See para 5.179 above.

could be argued that at the point when the administrator, at the purchaser's behest, dismissed the employees, the dismissal had to be disregarded and their employment 'statutorily continued', first with the subsidiary and then with the transferee, at the point when it either bought the subsidiary's business or took a controlling interest in its shares.[1262] Accordingly, the hiving down provisions were removed from the Regulations when they were revised in 2006.

The 2006 version of the Regulations now contain a provision, regulation 8(7), to the effect that regulation 4 (novation of the contract of employment) and regulation 7 (unfair dismissal) have no application in case where 'the transferor is the subject of bankruptcy proceedings or any analogous insolvency proceedings which have been instituted with a view to the liquidation of the assets of the transferor and are under the supervision of an insolvency practitioner'.[1263] This provision more or less copies out Article 5(1) of the 2001 version of the Directive, which codified *Abels*. As such, it should be confined to insolvency proceedings such as creditors' voluntary liquidations and windings up in which the object is to liquidate the company's assets; it should not, in principle, be extended to situations, such as administration, in which the main purpose of the proceedings is to rescue the underlying business.[1264] However, the 2006 Regulations do not precisely specify which insolvency situations (as defined by British insolvency law) fall under regulation 8(7), and there were conflicting EAT decisions on whether administrations could be covered.[1265] In *Key2Law (Surrey) LLP v De'Antiquis*[1266] the Court of Appeal confirmed that administrations were not within regulation 8(7) regardless of the surrounding circumstances. The Court of Appeal noted that regulation 8(7) adopted Article 5(1) 'almost verbatim'.[1267] The focus of that article, as interpreted in the case law of the Court of Justice, was 'the purpose of the procedure in question and not on the reasons for which the procedure is invoked or the result which it is anticipated will be reached'.[1268] Given that an adminstrator's prime objective was to rescue the company it could not be concluded that these were proceedings which had been 'instituted with a view to the liquidation of the assets of the transferor' even if that was the eventual outcome in some cases. Moreover, an 'absolute' rather than 'fact-based' approach had the advantage of 'legal certainty.[1269]

5.190   The 1977 Directive was amended in 1998 in such a way as to encourage greater flexibility in its application to insolvency. Article 5(2) of the 2001 Directive now provides for two derogations which may be applied to 'insolvency proceedings which have been opened in relation to a transferor

---

[1262] See *In the matter of Maxwell Fleet and Facilities Management Ltd (No 2)* [2000] IRLR 368.

[1263] TUPE 2006, reg 8(7). See *Secretary of State for Trade and Industry v Slater* [2007] IRLR 928 on when insolvency proceedings have been 'instituted' for the purpose of regulation 8(7).

[1264] According to guidance issued by BERR at the time of the implementation of the 2006 Regulations, reg 8(7) excludes from the scope of TUPE bankruptcies, compulsory liquidations and creditors' voluntary liquidations, but not members' voluntary liquidations (because these apply only to solvent companies), administration (as the purpose of administration is not to realise the remaining assets of the debtor), voluntary arrangements (as these leave the assets in the control of the debtor), and administrative and other receiverships (as these are not analogous to bankruptcy proceedings). See BERR, *The Transfer of Undertakings (Protection of Employment) Regulations 2006 (TUPE): redundancy and insolvency payments guidance* (2006), URN 06/1368. See also John McMullen, 2006: p 132,

[1265] *Oakland v Wellswood (Yorkshire) Ltd* [2009] IRLR 250 (the Court of Appeal found for the claimant on a different point: see [2010] IRLR 82 and note 1223 above); *OTG v Barke* [2011] IRLR 272.

[1266] [2012] IRLR 212.

[1267] Above, Rimer LJ at [83].

[1268] Warren LJ at [106]; see also Rimer LJ at [101].

[1269] Rimer LJ at [103].

(whether or not those proceedings have been instituted with a view to the liquidation of the assets of the transferor) and provided that such proceedings are under the supervision of a competent public authority (which may be an insolvency practitioner determined by national law)'.[1270] The first derogation[1271] allows the Member State to specify that debts of the transferor which arise from contracts of employment or employment relationships are not transferred to the transferee, as long the employees have protection (in respect of their claims against the transferor) equivalent to that laid down in the Insolvency Directive.[1272] The second derogation permits a Member State to make a provision according to which 'the transferee, transferor, or person or persons exercising the transferor's functions, on the one hand, and the representatives of the employees on the other hand may agree alterations, insofar as current law or practice permits, to the employees' terms and conditions of employment designed to safeguard employment opportunities by ensuring the survival of the undertaking, business or part of the undertaking or business'.[1273]

In 2001 the Government indicated an intention to take advantage of these derogations in revising TUPE,[1274] and they are now contained in the 2006 version of the Regulations.[1275] They apply to 'relevant insolvency proceedings', which are defined in regulation 8(6) as 'insolvency proceedings which have been opened in relation to the transferor not with a view to the liquidation of the assets of the transferor and which are under the supervision of an insolvency practitioner'. Thus they are intended to apply to those insolvency situations, such as administrative receivership, in which the purpose of the procedure is, broadly speaking, to maintain the business as a going concern as opposed to liquidating its remaining assets and returning them to the creditors. As we saw in para 5.189 above, the Court of Appeal has now confirmed that administrations are not proceedings which have been opened with a view to liquidation of the assets of the transferor.[1276] One remaining difficulty in ascertaining the scope of regulation 8(6), however, is that it only applies where insolvency proceedings have been opened and are already under the supervision of an insolvency practitioner. Thus the timing of the transfer in relation to the opening of insolvency proceedings may well determine the application of the derogations.[1277]

The first derogation refers to the liabilities relating to employees who have passed from the transferor to the transferee by virtue of a relevant transfer, or would have done but for a *Litster*-type dismissal. Liabilities falling under the statutory insolvency payments provisions,[1278] together

---

[1270] Directive 2001/23, Art 5(2).

[1271] Directive 2001/23, Art 5(2)(a).

[1272] Directive 80/987; see para 5.179 above.

[1273] Directive 2001/23, Art 5(2)(b). It is also specified that a Member State may take advantage of this particular derogation in the case of 'any transfers where the transferor is in a situation of serious economic crisis, as defined by national law, provided that the situation is declared by a competent national authority and open to judicial supervision, on condition that such provisions already existed in national law by 17 July 1998' (Art 5(3)); this would seem to have no application to the UK, and has not been relied on by the UK Government in reforming TUPE (see below).

[1274] See generally *Transfer of Undertakings (Protection of Employment) Regulations 1981: Government Proposals for reform*, DTI, September 2001, paras 84–97. A DTI Press Release of 14 February 2003 then stated that the Government intended to 'introduce new flexibility into the Regulations' application in relation to the transfer of insolvent businesses, giving a significant boost to our promotion of the "rescue culture"'. For discussion of the potential implications of the derogations for the UK see P Davies, 1998; Frisby, 2000; Armour and Deakin, 2000, 2003.

[1275] TUPE 2006, regs 8(1)-(6) and 9; DTI, *TUPE Draft Revised Regulations Public Consultation Document*, March 2005, paras 54–72; John McMullen, 2006: 132–134.

[1276] *Key2Law (Surrey) LLP v De'Antiquis* [2012] IRLR 212.

[1277] See *Secretary of State for Trade and Industry v Slater* [2007] IRLR 928.

[1278] See para 5.179 above.

with statutory redundancy payments,[1279] do not now transfer to the transferee, but may be claimed against the Secretary of State under the insolvency scheme.[1280] In *Pressure Coolers Ltd v Molloy*[1281] the EAT held that the relevant debts needed to arise before the transfer in order for a claim to lie against the Secretary of State. As well as basing its decision on the wording of the legislation, the court considered that this interpretation was consistent with its underlying rationale: to minimise the burden on acquiring employers of transferring employees, an objective which did not apply post-transfer. The second derogation creates a category of 'permitted variations' to terms and conditions of employment, which may be negotiated by 'appropriate representatives' of the employees assigned to the organised grouping involved in the relevant transfer.[1282] 'Permitted variations' are those designed to 'safeguard employment opportunities by ensuring the survival' of the undertaking or business, of the part of it, that is involved in the transfer. The 'appropriate representatives' are defined in essentially the same way as they are for the purposes of information and consultation requirements arising under TUPE 2006.[1283]

(iii) Post-transfer dismissals

5.191   If, following the transfer, the transferee takes into its employment the employees of the business concerned, it may not immediately seek unilaterally to change their terms and conditions of employment. Any such change would be not simply a constructive dismissal, but could be automatically unfair by virtue of regulation 7(1): the employee concerned could argue that the dismissal arose in connection with the transfer and was not potentially fair under the ETOR exception. This is because, as noted earlier, the concept of ETOR is significantly narrower than that of SOSR under section 98(1) of the Act of 1996. In *Berriman v Delabole Slate Ltd*[1284] the transferee attempted, after the transfer had taken place, to harmonise the terms and conditions of employment of staff previously employed by the transferor, by cutting their entitlement to a guaranteed basic wage. Mr Berriman resigned and claimed constructive dismissal. The tribunal found that he had been constructively dismissed and that the reason was an ETOR. The EAT and Court of Appeal both took a different view, namely that the reason for the dismissal was the employer's wish to alter the terms and conditions of the transferred staff. Here, 'the reason itself (ie to produce standardisation of pay) does not involve any change either in the number or the functions of the workforce. The most that can be said is that such organisational reasons *may* (not must) lead to the dismissal of those employees who do not fall into line'.

However, there does not necessarily need to be a net drop in the number of employees employed by the transferee for there to be an ETOR. In *Crawford v Swinton Insurance Brokers Ltd*[1285] a transferred employee, who had been employed as a clerk, was offered different work as

---

[1279] See paras 5.163 *et seq* above.
[1280] TUPE 2006, reg 8(3)–(5); see DTI, *TUPE Draft Revised Regulations Public Consultation Document*, March 2005, paras 57–65.
[1281] [2011] IRLR 630.
[1282] TUPE 2006, reg 9; see DTI, *TUPE Draft Revised Regulations Public Consultation Document*, March 2005, paras 66–72.
[1283] See para 9.43 below.
[1284] [1985] ICR 546, 551.
[1285] [1990] ICR 85.

an insurance salesman, which he refused. It was held that his resulting dismissal was for an ETOR since the aim was to bring about a 'change in the workforce', substituting a worker doing one job for one doing another. In *Nationwide Building Society v Benn*[1286] the EAT held that there was no requirement for an organisational reason to affect the entirety of the workforce.

The effect of *Berriman* is that a transferred employee is, for a while, in a better position than those who have worked for the transferee throughout, who cannot protect their terms and conditions of employment against a re-organisation on efficiency grounds which constitutes an SOSR. The question is how long this period of protection lasts in the case of the transferred employees: at what point would their dismissal for refusing new terms cease to be for a reason connected with the transfer?[1287] The Regulations provide no answer. Interestingly, the Directive provides that following the transfer, the transferee should observe the terms of any applicable collective agreement of the transferor for a period which Member States may limit to one year.[1288] This provision does not fit easily into the context of British labour law, where the collective agreement is not in any case normally binding between employer and trade union, and was not transposed into the Regulations. Nor is the issue of post-transfer dismissals confined to the effect of collective agreements. However, the clear implication of this provision is that after one year the transferee is entitled to insist on harmonising the terms and conditions of the transferred employees with those of its own staff; whether it could be relied on by employment tribunals applying the Regulations is an open question. Further issues have been raised by the recent decision of the ECJ in *Scattolon v Ministero dell'Istruzione, dell'Universita e della Ricerca*[1289] that it is lawful for the transferee to apply, from the date of the transfer, the working conditions laid down by the collective agreement in force with it provided that this does not have the aim or effect of imposing on those workers conditions which are, overall, less favourable than those applicable before the transfer. We discuss this decision further in para 9.27 below.

In *Berriman*, the court found that the attempt by the transferee to impose new terms and conditions of employment amounted to a constructive dismissal; however, this will not always be the case. In *Rossiter v Pendragon plc*[1290] a dispute over commission payments was held not to give rise to a breach of contract by the employer. In the alternative, the employee was held to have affirmed any such breach. In *Air Foyle Ltd v Crosby-Clarke*[1291] the transferee's decision to alter the employee's working hours was held to be contractually justified, since it was done to comply with mandatory legislation setting limits to the working time of pilots. The Court of Appeal held that, in each case, there had been no constructive dismissal, rejecting an argument that under regulation 5(5) of TUPE, as it then was, a substantial change in working conditions was enough to trigger the protection of the Regulations, whether or not it amounted to a repudiatory breach by the employer. Regulation 4(9) of TUPE 2006 now provides that 'where a relevant transfer involved or would involve a substantial change in working conditions to the material detriment of a person whose contract of employment is or would be transferred ... such an employee may treat the contract of employment as having been terminated, and the employee shall be treated

---

[1286] [2010] IRLR 922. In *Meter U Ltd v Ackroyd* [2012] IRLR 367 the EAT held that 'workforce' does not include corporate franchisees.

[1287] See also discussion of this issue in relation to consensual variations in para 3.76 above.

[1288] Directive 2001/23, Art 3(3).

[1289] Case C-108/10 [2011] IRLR 1020.

[1290] [2002] IRLR 483.

[1291] [2002] IRLR 483.

for any purpose as having been dismissed by the employer'.[1292] The EAT has held that, in deciding whether there is 'material detriment' it is necessary to consider the proposed change from the employee's point of view and whether, if the employee finds it detrimental, this is a reasonable position for him or her to adopt.[1293] The EAT has also held that the term 'working conditions' is wider than 'contractual conditions'; '[w]orking conditions are not contractual conditions, though they may be affected by them, and they may take those contractual terms into account'. [1294]

(iv) Joint liability

5.192 A final question to consider here is whether the transfer of employment from one employer to another puts an end to all liabilities of the transferor. In the context of insolvency this question is often irrelevant, but it has considerable importance where work is contracted out from one employer to another, and both remain solvent. The Directive permits, but does not require, Member States to maintain the liability of the transferor after the transfer.[1295] After some hesitation the British courts held that clear provision would be required in order for the transferor's liability to be maintained, and that not only was there no such provision in TUPE, but that regulation 5 of TUPE 1981, which provided for all the transferor's liabilities to be transferred to the transferee, prevented any such interpretation.[1296] The 2006 Regulations preserve this basic position but now specify two situations in which there will be joint liability. The first is where liability arises for the failure of the transferor to inform and consult appropriate employee representatives or in respect of failure to pay compensation which either the transferor or transferee has previously been ordered to pay.[1297] The second is where the transferor is not obliged to carry statutory employer's liability insurance. This is the case for certain public sector employers. Under these circumstances, both the transferor and the transferee are liable in respect of personal injury claims arising against the transferor.[1298]

ASSESSMENT

5.193 As this chapter has shown, the law governing termination of employment is of pivotal importance in contemporary labour law. It has also exhibited a degree of stability which was surprising at a time when deregulation became the predominant tendency in other areas. Unfair dismissal law was not left untouched by the reforms of the 1980s and 1990s, not least of which was the extension of the qualifying period from six months in 1979 to two years (subsequently reduced

[1292] See DTI, *TUPE Draft Revised Regulations Public Consultation Document*, March 2005, para 46, for discussion of this change
[1293] *Tapere v South London and Maudsley NHS Trust* [2009] IRLR 972.
[1294] *Abellio London Ltd (formerly Travel London Ltd) v Musse and Centrewest London Buses Ltd* [2012] IRLR 360, Langstaff P at [22].
[1295] Directive 2001/23, Art 3(1).
[1296] *Stirling District Council v Allan* [1995] IRLR 301; see also *Thompson v Walon Car Delivery and BRS Automotive Ltd* [1997] IRLR 343.
[1297] TUPE 2006, reg 15(9). See further para 9.45 below.
[1298] TUPE 2006, reg 17(2).

to one by the Labour Government, and increased again to two for those employed on or after 6 April 2012 by the Conservative-Liberal Democrat Coalition). Recent amendments have sought to encourage recourse to basic workplace dismissal procedures. Nonetheless, the preservation of the basic structure of unfair dismissal protection much as it was when it was enacted in the 1970s is, perhaps, testimony to a general acceptance of the principle that there should continue to be legal regulation of employment terminations. In this respect, Hepple has suggested that unfair dismissal law has survived thanks to its 'chameleon-like qualities both of protecting individuals against arbitrary management, and simultaneously of strengthening managerial legitimacy and control'.[1299] Three aspects of dismissal law will be considered in the light of this statement: the extent to which the law has led to greater control of managerial prerogative; the impact of legal procedures and processes on the resolution of individual disputes; and the wider social and economic implications of job security.

(i) Controlling managerial prerogative

5.194   A key issue here is how far the present body of law is effective in imposing controls on management decision-making. Collins has argued that dismissal legislation sees the employment relationship not as an individualised transaction (the model he associates with contract), but instead as embedded in the structure of bureaucratic rules which characterise the business enterprise. If the enterprise is viewed as a bureaucratic organisation, it can be said that managerial decisions are most effective where they comply with notions of formal rationality which are similar to those which are found in the public law model of control of discretionary powers. 'Rationality' here means that employers should exercise disciplinary powers for a rational purpose, which means 'one which avoids substantial harm to the business', and in a rational manner, or in 'a way which is conducive to efficient decisions'.[1300] It also means respecting certain fundamental rights of employees. The law is entitled to intervene to require this of employers because managerial prerogative, in common with other examples of discretionary power, 'can only be legitimate if exercised for rational business purposes and without infringement of individual rights'.[1301] Legal regulation is necessary, then, both to protect individuals from potential injustice, but also to underpin good practice by employers which, in the long run, is conducive to the more efficient operation of organisations.

Collins's formulation of the aims of dismissal protection is valuable not least because it helps to explain why dismissal legislation in Britain falls a long way short of providing absolute protection against loss of a job, or a 'job property' right on the part of the employee. Except in the relatively few cases of automatically unfair dismissals (and subject to the potential impact of the HRA 1998), the essence of the obligation imposed by the law on the employer is procedural. Fundamental principles applied by the courts under section 98(4), such as the principle that the tribunal must not substitute its judgment for that of the employer and that it must apply a 'band of reasonableness' test when judging the employer's conduct, testify to the peripheral place occupied by notions of substantive fairness in this area of the law; the focus is above all on the process of

---

[1299] Hepple, 1993: p 95.
[1300] H Collins, 1993: p 272.
[1301] H Collins, 1993: p 273.

dismissal or discipline, and only second on the outcome.[1302] But this does not mean that the law is necessarily failing in the task which it was set. It should be borne in mind that the Donovan Commission placed little emphasis on the goal of substantive justice for individual employees when making the case for what became unfair dismissal legislation. The Commission regarded dismissal legislation as a means of streamlining and formalising plant-level procedures, with a view to strengthening managerial decision-making at this level; the subsequent experience of the legislation could be seen as largely fulfilling this aim.

Whether the law goes far enough in imposing procedural requirements over the exercise of disciplinary powers is much more open to debate. It still remains to be seen whether the provisions introduced by EA 2008 to encourage adherence to the ACAS Code of Practice on Disciplinary and Grievance Procedures 2009 will lead to more disputes being settled at workplace level and whether, if they do, the benefits will outweigh any greater scope for litigation that the provisions for adjustment of compensatory awards may create. It is clear, however, that a major weakness of the current law is that the protection of employees against unfair disciplinary action short of dismissal is limited. In most cases, an employee who is subjected to such action has the option to resign and claim constructive dismissal, but making a complaint while still remaining in employment is much more difficult to do.[1303] More generally, remedies associated with unfair dismissal are widely regarded as being too weak. Although the statutory ceiling on the compensatory award has been raised substantially, the ease with which the employer can resist re-employment continues to pose a major obstacle to effective employment protection.

The limited nature of statutory protection in the case of individual dismissals for misconduct or lack of capability is one reason for the growth of interest in alternative routes to protection which utilise either public law or the common law of contract. Both judicial review and the equitable remedies of injunction and declaration can, in principle, be deployed to counter disciplinary action short of dismissal, and can also have an effect which is essentially that of nullifying a purported dismissal, a power denied to the employment tribunals in their statutory jurisdiction. The use of the common law to uphold contractual job security clauses also illustrates how the law can confer protection which is substantive and not simply procedural in nature, although the Supreme Court has now cast doubt on their effectiveness where equitable relief is not available, at least as far as disciplinary procedures are concerned.[1304] Moreover, the difficulty here continues to be that only a small group of employees, mainly in the public sector, has succeeded in deploying these legal mechanisms, while the courts retain a wide discretion in granting injunctions and declarations. Continuing doubt over the correctness of the 'bilateral' theory of contract termination also qualifies the advantages offered by these routes to protection. Finally, the refusal of the courts to subject the contractual power of dismissal to a duty to act fairly on the ground that such a term would subvert the statutory unfair dismissal scheme has left the law in a regrettably incoherent and unsatisfactory state.

In the area of economic dismissals, the extent of the employer's duty is, in most cases, to act with regard to the rational business needs of the enterprise; there may be procedural restrictions,

---

[1302] For the argument that the interpretation of the unfair dismissal legislation has been distorted by judicial defence of employers' property rights see Anderman, 2004.

[1303] See, however, *Hogg v Dover College* [1990] ICR 39 and *Alcan Extrusions v Yates* [1996] IRLR 327, discussed at paras 5.68 and 5.71.

[1304] See *Edwards v Chesterfield Royal Hospital NHS Foundation Trust* and *Botham v Ministry of Defence* [2012] IRLR 129, discussed at para 5.45 above.

in the form of a duty to inform and consult at collective level, but requirements at the individual level are limited. Compensation for loss of employment may then be left up to the system of social security, on the grounds that the costs of displacing employees from their jobs are best met collectively through national insurance and the taxation system. In practice, this is what the redundancy payment scheme did for much of its life, via the system of redundancy rebates which operated until 1990. As the value of redundancy rebates was reduced prior to their complete abolition, the potential costs of restructuring to individual employers were increased, whilst amendments made to comply with EU obligations significantly added to the content of the employer's collective obligations of consultation and information.[1305] In these ways, the law now imposes firmer procedural obstacles to the implementation of redundancies than it has at any point since the introduction of redundancy compensation in 1965, but their value for workers might have been greater during the period of large-scale job losses in industry in the 1980s. In general, as we saw in our earlier discussion,[1306] there can be little doubt that the overall effect of legal intervention in this area since 1965 has been to facilitate job restructuring through redundancy or reorganisation, sometimes at the expense of agreed contract terms, and not to support job security as such.

The law has also been weak in the area of civil liberties or 'public rights' dismissals. While the goal of protecting individual dignity and autonomy at work is recognised to be an important objective of dismissal law[1307] (and, indeed, of labour law more generally),[1308] it is a different matter to argue that this objective is even close to being fulfilled in the current law. The technique of making certain reasons for dismissal automatically unfair provides a potentially useful model for entrenching certain rights against instrumental arguments based on considerations of efficiency or business rationality. However, as Pitt suggests with regard to the existing categories of automatically unfair dismissal, 'no coherent philosophy such as protection for public rights or civil liberties underpins their special status; rather, there are separate reasons for each category'.[1309] This is so notwithstanding the continuing growth of new categories of automatically unfair reasons. There is no good reason, it would seem, for the inclusion within the legislation of discrimination on grounds related to trade union membership or activities, on the one hand, and the absence, on the other, of any reference to political opinions, to give but one example. For the most part, the merits of 'public rights dismissals', just like any others, fall to be determined under section 98(4). Here, considerations of 'efficiency' or business rationality, very loosely defined, regularly prevail over employees' claims to rights-based protection.[1310] There is an instructive contrast here with the approach under the equality legislation, where the test of proportionality in indirect discrimination requires arguments about efficiency to be much more precisely formulated than is possible under the 'band of reasonableness' test, and where the weighing exercise must be undertaken with a view to limiting, as far as possible, any infringement of the fundamental right

---

[1305] See para 9.30 *et seq* below.
[1306] See in particular paras 5.10, 5.154 and 5.173 above.
[1307] See H Collins, 1993: pp 16–21.
[1308] See Hepple, 1995
[1309] Pitt, 1993: p 264.
[1310] See para 5.173 *et seq* above.

whose application is at stake.[1311] At the time of writing this approach has yet to be adopted in cases where the HRA 1998 has been at issue.[1312]

In short, as a result of unfair dismissal legislation, the law no longer permits the employer to act wholly arbitrarily in the area of discipline and dismissal, and an element of the rule of law has been injected into relations within the firm. However, the relevant statutory standards are set at too low a level, and the remedies established by statute, in their existing form, arguably do little to persuade employers who are bent on dismissal to take a contrary course of action. Nor has the common law evolved to the point of providing a satisfactory alternative. The common law has stopped well short of implying into all contracts of employment an obligation upon the employer to observe natural justice, or, less specifically, to act fairly, when exercising a contractual power to discipline or dismiss; nor have doubts about the availability of specific remedies in equity, or by way of judicial review, been satisfactorily resolved. Under these circumstances, it may be premature to speak of a 'new paradigm' of the employment relationship based around the control of bureaucratic power; at the very least, as Collins accepts, this paradigm is still 'struggling to the surface of popular and legal consciousness'.[1313]

(ii) The role of the law and 'legalism' in dispute resolution

5.195   Dismissal legislation is one of the clearest examples of the process of the 'juridification' of employment relations. Juridification does not simply signify an increase in legal regulation; more specifically it involves the displacement of contractual autonomy of the parties by legislative rules which are designed to bring about certain goals of public policy.[1314] A potentially negative feature of juridification is the possibility of 'regulatory failure', which may be the result of regulation which fails to take into account the role of autonomous social and economic processes governing the object of regulation. As we have seen,[1315] there is some uncertainty as to whether this has been true of the impact of dismissal legislation in Britain. Although it has fallen short of providing strong guarantees of job protection, it is arguable that this was never a clear aim of the legislation. Moreover, in stimulating the growth of more formal procedures at plant level, the legislation may be said to have a considerable indirect impact which is consonant with the goals set out by the Donovan Commission. At any rate, the apparent inability of the legislation to provide an effective right against being unfairly dismissed does not necessarily mean that, in this case, the process of intervention can be said to have been subject to 'regulatory failure' in the sense referred to above.

There has been a substantial debate since the inception of unfair dismissal legislation concerning the desirability of introducing formal legal processes into individual employment disputes, and in particular into the role played by the employment tribunal system. Although employment tribunals were meant to provide an informal setting for the resolution of disputes and to avoid recourse to over-extensive legal argument, this has proved difficult to achieve. Proceedings before employment tribunals are inevitably adversarial, with cross-examination

---

[1311] See Deakin, 1996; para 6.30 below.
[1312] H Collins, 2006; Mantouvalou, 2008.
[1313] H Collins, 1993: p 273.
[1314] Simitis, 1987.
[1315] See para 5.9 *et seq* above.

of witnesses and opposing arguments being presented by the two sides, and frequently involve discussion of highly technical points of law (such as the definition of the terms 'employee' or 'dismissal'). The formality, cost and 'excessive legalism' of tribunal proceedings have been unfavourably compared with voluntary arbitration; the latter is said to be 'cheaper, speedier, more informal, and more accessible, it avoids the legalism and publicity associated with the tribunals, and offers the possibility of a more flexible range of remedies, including a greater likelihood of reinstatement and re-engagement'.[1316]

Two points may be made in the context of this long-running debate. The first is that it was probably unavoidable that the employment tribunals would come to operate in a judicial fashion, given that their jurisdiction involves adjudication on questions of legal rights which have a wider significance than the particular disputes which come before them.[1317] The second is that while 'legalism' may have certain unattractive features, it is a necessary part of the process by which certain clear legal limits are set to managerial prerogative. If, for example, dismissal law is to play a more extensive role in future in protecting employees in the context of public-rights dismissals,[1318] a clearer statutory articulation of those rights will have to be made, and their enforcement entrusted to adjudicatory bodies to which the employee has access whether or not the employer agrees. This is not to deny that alternative dispute resolution does not have a valuable role to play in processing individual disputes, merely to point out that this is unlikely to be at the expense of a continuing role for more formal mechanisms of legal enforcement. To date little use has been made of the scheme by ACAS for the resolution of unfair dismissal disputes by arbitration, discussed in para 2.20 above.[1319] It remains to be seen whether the regime for encouraging resolution of disputes before they reach tribunals introduced by EA 2008 will be more successful than its predecessor in EA 2002. At the time of writing the Enterprise and Regulatory Reform Bill contains further reforms, requiring details of potential claims to be submitted to ACAS so that early conciliation can be offered.

(iii) The social and economic implications of job security

5.196   An assessment of dismissal legislation must also take into account the degree to which developments in the forms of employment and in the labour market more generally have undermined the goal of job security, or have confined its achievement to a minority of workers in the 'core'. Legislation has encouraged this development, in the United Kingdom and elsewhere in western Europe, by exempting certain categories of temporary employment from dismissal protection; there has also been a rise in forms of casual employment which involve only minimal guarantees, on the part of the employer, of work and payment.[1320] In addition there has been a direct challenge to the legitimacy of dismissal protection from accounts which argue that the model of the contract at will is, after all, an efficient basis for constituting the employment relationship.

[1316] R Lewis and J Clark, 1993: p 33; see also L Dickens, 1988, and our discussion at para 2.20 above.
[1317] See Munday, 1981.
[1318] Cf Pitt, 1993.
[1319] Between May 2001, when the scheme came into force, and the end of March 2008 a total of 60 cases (including those relating to requests to work flexibly) have been accepted for resolution by this means. ACAS Annual Reports no longer include this information.
[1320] See paras 3.47 *et seq* and 3.29 *et seq* above.

It is said that the advantage of the contract at will is that both parties can exercise at low cost the option of quitting the relationship and re-entering the market in search of another contract. An employer who acts arbitrarily in its treatment of an employee will be punished not by the law but by the market; the employee will leave to get better employment and the employer will pay a price for its behaviour in terms of its diminished reputation for fair treatment, which will make it more difficult to attract and retain high-quality employees.[1321] This argument correctly points to the existence of non-legal sanctions for breach of contract, which its proponents claim also explains why the common law traditionally provided so little in the way of formal employment protection; however, its weakness is its failure to deal with the point that market failures of various kinds will frequently make it impossible for these non-legal sanctions to be effectively deployed.[1322] Nor does it answer the objection that the market cannot provide a remedy, after the event, for injustices which may have been suffered by individual employees; the employer who acts arbitrarily may suffer from a diminished reputation, without the employee necessarily receiving adequate compensation for the psychic and financial costs arising from job loss.

As we have seen, security of employment is not necessarily the same thing as the right not to be dismissed from a particular job;[1323] it may be that the interests of society as a whole and of individual employees would be better served by a system which ensured that all individuals had a wide choice of jobs in the labour market, rather than allowing a minority the privilege of absolute job protection at the cost, perhaps, of limiting opportunities for the rest. To the extent that dismissal legislation has this effect (which is not consistently borne out by empirical studies),[1324] the answer may lie not so much in deregulation as in the development of mechanisms which might secure individual economic security at the level of the labour market as a whole, rather than at the level of the individual business enterprise.[1325] Nor should it be assumed from this that the goal of job security is necessarily outmoded. Although 'atypical' or 'non-standard' jobs take up a significant number of new hirings, the majority of employees in the United Kingdom continue to work in jobs which take the form of contracts for an indefinite duration,[1326] and a secure job is still an essential aspect, for most individuals, of their long-term economic security. This suggests that dismissal protection will remain an important aspect of labour market regulation, even if other forms of intervention based on active labour market policy and social security transfers may come to play a more important role in future than they have in the past.

[1321] Epstein, 1984.

[1322] Mückenberger and Deakin, 1989: p 187 *et seq.*

[1323] See our discussion in para 5.3 above.

[1324] See Büchtemann, 1993.

[1325] See Deakin and Wilkinson, 1991, for a discussion of the form which might be taken by labour-market rights in this context.

[1326] Coutts and Rowthorn, 1995; Burchell *et al*, 1999; findings from the Working in Britain in 2000 survey, discussed Taylor, (no date given); see above, paras 3.33–3.35 and 3.49 for more recent figures on the numbers employed in non-standard forms of employment.

6

EQUALITY IN EMPLOYMENT

INTRODUCTION

6.1   The law recognises the right of an individual not to be discriminated against because of one or more of a number of 'protected characteristics' which include sex, gender reassignment, sexual orientation, race, religion or belief, disability, and age. By these means, employers' decisions in all aspects of the employment relationship, from hiring through to termination, are subjected to a distinct form of legal scrutiny which operates on two levels. At the first level, the law requires that 'like must be treated alike' in the sense that access to benefits (or, conversely, the imposition of detriments) must not be determined by reference to a protected characteristic. This is the prohibition of 'direct discrimination'. At the second level, the law entails a legal examination of the effects of policies, practices and requirements which, while apparently neutral, may result in disadvantage to the members of a group which is defined by reference to one of the protected characteristics. This is the prohibition of 'indirect discrimination'. Together these concepts form the basis of equality law as it relates to the employment relationship.

The common law, with its emphasis on freedom of contract, sees nothing inherently wrong with discrimination in the sense just described, as long as no pre-existing contractual or property right is infringed. Statutory intervention in this area therefore represents an erosion of contractual autonomy.[1] Three potential justifications, which are not necessarily complementary, may be offered for this. One stresses the role of labour law in protecting the dignity of the individual worker in a situation where he or she is in a relationship of economic subordination; the second emphasises the role of the law in correcting for systematic disadvantage suffered by particular groups; and the third sees equality law as a means of overcoming certain market failures, in particular barriers to market access on the part of excluded groups, in such a way as to make the labour market more transparent. As we shall see, each of these elements may be found within the present body of law, and the tensions between them help to account for the dynamic nature of this area of doctrine.

The first race relations legislation dates from 1965, legislation governing equal pay for equal work from 1970, and more general anti-discrimination legislation in respect of both sex and race from 1975 and 1976 respectively. The Equal Pay Act 1970 and the Sex Discrimination Act 1975 were much amended in the years following their enactment, largely as a consequence of the influence of European Union law. The Race Relations Act 1976 saw fewer changes, in part because the European Union was less of a direct influence until the passage in 2000 of an EC Directive prohibiting racial discrimination. Legislation concerning disability discrimination, the Disability Discrimination Act, was introduced in the UK in 1995. In 2000 the European Community adopted

---

[1]   See Epstein, 2002, discussed by Deakin, 2002.

a Framework Directive prohibiting discrimination in employment on grounds including age, religion or belief, or sexual orientation. The parts of the Directive relating to sexual orientation and to religion and belief were implemented in the UK 2003; amendments to disability discrimination legislation required to comply with the Directive came into force in 2004; and provisions relating to age discrimination were implemented in 2006. The Equality Act 2010 brought together the different strands of anti-discrimination legislation and provided a unified conceptual framework for this body of law which extends beyond employment to cover discrimination in relation to the provision of certain services.[2] The 2010 Act made few changes of major substance to the law on discrimination in relation to employment, but some, particularly those relating to discrimination on the grounds of disability and age, and to the scope for positive action to address persistent inequalities, are potentially significant for law and practice.

This chapter continues with an account of the origins, rationales and impact of equality law in the area of employment. This is followed by an account of the legal concept of discrimination and related forms of prohibited conduct (harassment and victimisation), an examination of the definitions of the protected characteristics, an analysis of the scope of the protection against discrimination in the employment context, and an examination of the scope allowed for positive action. This is followed by an examination of three areas requiring specific analysis, namely equal pay between women and men, work and family rights, and disability discrimination.

THE ORIGINS, RATIONALES AND IMPACT OF EQUALITY LAW

Historical development and influences

6.2   The present legislation on equality in employment has been influenced by diverse social and political forces; these include the pressure exercised by campaigning groups and also, to a degree not matched elsewhere in labour law, the models established in other jurisdictions and also given expression in transnational labour standards, in particular those contained in European Union law. The statutory form taken by the principle of equal treatment in this country is heavily reliant on the model first established by the US Civil Rights Act of 1964, while European Union law, which had a marginal effect initially, has become increasingly important in shaping the form and substance of the law of equal pay and sex discrimination and has thereby indirectly also influenced race relations law. In recent years it has been crucial to the introduction of legislation prohibiting discrimination on grounds of sexual orientation, religion or belief and age.

(i) Early campaigns for sexual and racial equality

6.3   The campaign for equal pay and equal access of men and women to employment goes back well into the nineteenth century, when it was linked to the causes of factory reform and the extension of the right to vote in public elections. The first government inquiry was undertaken at the end of the

---

[2] The law governing discrimination in relation to services is beyond the scope of this book. See Hepple, 2011a: ch 5, for an overview.

1914–1918 war,[3] and in the following year Parliament passed the Sex Disqualification (Removal) Act 1919 which abolished formal restrictions on women entering certain professions (including the solicitors' profession), the civil service and the universities. Section 1 provided that 'a person shall not be disqualified by sex or marriage from the exercise of any public function, or from being appointed to or holding any judicial office or post or from entering or assuming or carrying on any profession or vocation'. Many trade union campaigns for equal pay had at this time a dual rationale of advancing women's rights while also maintaining the model of the male worker's 'breadwinner wage'; 'support among trade unionists for equal pay was, in effect, a demand for protection of male employment',[4] since it was expected that increases in women's pay would neutralise their value to employers as a source of 'cheap labour'. There was also a strong lobby among trade unionists at the time of the Trade Boards Act 1909 which 'wanted more protective legislation to restrict the extent of female labour' on the grounds that 'women should not have to engage in waged work'.[5] Both world wars saw a great influx of female labour into industrial occupations where they carried out jobs which had previously been restricted to men. The response of the industrial unions during the second world war was to support the campaign for the phased introduction of equal pay, which began in the public sector, and to couple this with demands for nurseries and a right to maternity pay. After the war the TUC echoed the call for the introduction of equal pay in public-sector employment, but it was not until 1961 that it called on the government to take measures to implement ILO Convention No 100 of 1951 on Remuneration for Men and Women Workers, and only in 1963 did it make its first clear recommendation for legislation.[6]

A number of local authorities introduced the principle of equal pay for equal work for men and women in their employment in the 1920s. However, in *Roberts v Hopwood*[7] this practice was successfully challenged as being *ultra vires*, with Lord Atkinson describing as unlawful payment systems which were motivated by 'eccentric principles of socialistic philanthropy, or by a feminist ambition to secure the equality of the sexes'.[8] The inter-war period also saw judicial confirmation of the marriage bar, or the practice of dismissing women upon marriage which was common in the case of schoolteachers employed by local authorities, notwithstanding the apparently clear words of the Sex Disqualification (Removal) Act 1919.[9] Further progress in this area had to wait until after 1945. In 1955 the government accepted the principle of equal pay in the civil service and, shortly afterwards, in other areas of public-sector employment including education and local government.[10] When a Labour government was elected in 1964 there was at first a reluctance to legislate, but a series of strikes over equal pay helped force the government's hand and a commitment to introduce statutory mechanisms was made in 1968 by the Secretary of State for Employment and Productivity, Barbara Castle.[11] The result was the Equal Pay Act 1970, which embodied a limited version of equal

---

[3] *Report on the War Cabinet Committee on Women in Industry*, Cmd 135, 1918.

[4] Meehan, 1985: p 37.

[5] J Morris, 1986: p 221. Nor was it impossible for this attitude to be expressed in public relatively recently: Meehan, 1985: p 41, reports that in 1973 a trade union official 'told the Select Committee on Expenditure that he did not believe in women working'.

[6] Meehan, 1985: pp 37–38.

[7] [1925] AC 578.

[8] [1925] AC 578, 594.

[9] *Price v Rhondda Urban District Council* [1923] 2 Ch 372; *Short v Poole Corp* [1926] Ch 66. A major weakness of the Act was its failure to provide an aggrieved individual with a remedy for its breach.

[10] Meehan, 1985: p 43. See Fredman and Morris, 1989: ch 9.

[11] Meehan, 1985: p 38.

pay for equal work: the right to equality was confined to situations where a female worker could point to a male worker in the same employment who was employed on 'like work' or 'work rated as equivalent' by a job evaluation scheme instituted by the employer. Since there was no means of requiring an employer to adopt job evaluation or of challenging the results of a particular job evaluation scheme, this was something less than the principle of 'equal pay for work of equal value' contained in ILO Recommendation No 90.[12] This stipulated that:

> ... where appropriate for the purpose of facilitating the determination of rates or remuneration in accordance with the principle of equal remuneration for men and women workers for work of equal value, each Member should, in agreement with the employers' and workers' organisations concerned, establish or encourage the establishment of methods for objective appraisal of the work to be performed, whether by job analysis or by other procedures, with a view to providing a classification of jobs without regard to sex ...[13]

Moreover, the implementation of the 1970 Act was to be delayed for five years, in order to give employers time to adjust, as well as encouraging voluntary compliance through collective bargaining. When the Act was finally brought into force, Parliament enacted, at the same time, the Sex Discrimination Act 1975 which embodied a more general principle of equal treatment in employment, proscribing discrimination against applicants, employees and other employed persons on the grounds of sex.[14]

The common law took the view that race discrimination, like sex discrimination, was a legitimate exercise of the employer's right to freedom of contract.[15] In the absence of any equivalent to the Sex Disqualification (Removal) Act 1919 for acts of racial discrimination,[16] no legal means were available to prise open access to particular occupations and employments until the 1960s. The catalyst for reform was provided by the large-scale entry into the United Kingdom of immigrants from the 'new commonwealth' during the post-war boom. The Race Relations Acts of 1965 and 1968 were part of a cross-party consensus 'that there was a need to control the numbers of immigrants and a requirement to eradicate the discrimination that was increasingly being directed at those already settled in Britain. Thus a twin strategy – inherently contradictory – was adopted',[17] which saw the enactment of anti-discrimination legislation on the one hand and the introduction of curbs over entry into the United Kingdom by immigration legislation on the other. The Race Relations Act 1965 prohibited racial segregation and discrimination in public places such as hotels, restaurants, dance halls and sports grounds; it did not touch on employment, or on the question of access to housing. Awareness of the legal issues surrounding racial discrimination in employment was raised by the Street Report which was published in 1967

---

[12] The Recommendation is more precise, in this respect, than ILO Convention No 100, which was adopted in the same year (1951).

[13] Art 5. See also Convention No 100, Art 2.

[14] Sex discrimination in employment, including discrimination leading to unequal pay between women and men, now falls under the Equality Act 2010.

[15] This was expressed in Lord Davey's often-cited dictum in *Allen v Flood* [1898] AC 1, 172, that an 'employer may refuse to employ [an individual] for the most mistaken, capricious, malicious or morally reprehensible motives that can be conceived, but the workman has no right of action against him'. See also *Nagle v Feilden* [1966] 2 QB 633.

[16] See *Weinberger v Inglis (No 2)* [1919] AC 606.

[17] Mirza, 1995: p 1; see Hepple, 1968; Sooben, 1990.

by Political and Economic Planning (the forerunner of the Policy Studies Institute);[18] however, the Race Relations Act 1968 stopped short of establishing a fully effective set of measures for combating discrimination. This was in part because of 'concerted action by the TUC and the CBI who both argued against legal intervention, preferring to maintain the tradition of voluntarism'.[19] Although the Act introduced the right to equal treatment on the grounds of race for both applicants and individuals in employment, it contained a complex dispute resolution procedure, as part of which individuals had to complain to the Secretary of State who could then refer the matter to voluntary arbitration or to the Race Relations Board.

(ii) The influence of US civil rights legislation

6.4   The strengthening of anti-discrimination legislation which took place in the 1970s borrowed directly from the model established in Title VII of the US Civil Rights Act 1964. The Civil Rights Act was the federal legislature's response to the civil rights movement and its campaign for equality of access to facilities and jobs and for equal treatment within employment. The main target of the Act was discrimination based on race and colour; a prohibition on sex discrimination was added at a late stage, initially by opponents of the measure who thought it might discredit it. In other respects, though, the addition of sex discrimination was a natural extension of an earlier measure, the federal Equal Pay Act of 1963, and of a number of equal treatment statutes at state level.[20] In addition to prohibiting 'disparate treatment' based on an individual's race or sex, the 1964 Act was interpreted as applying also to 'disparate impact' or measures which, while facially neutral, disproportionately affected one racial group, or the members of one sex, as opposed to the other. A classic example of this was the use of aptitude tests which tended to exclude members of racial minorities from access to particular grades or occupations. The concept of disparate impact, arrived at by the Supreme Court in *Griggs v Duke Power Co*,[21] greatly extended the reach of the law. The Sex Discrimination Act 1975 incorporated a version of disparate impact which, in the British context, has come to be termed 'indirect discrimination' to distinguish it from 'direct discrimination' or disparate treatment.[22] The Act of 1975, like the Equal Pay Act 1970, provided for an individual right of recourse to an employment tribunal; this right was extended to cases of racial discrimination in the Race Relations Act 1976, which also embodied the concept of indirect discrimination. A further important feature of this legislation was the establishment of bodies, outside the departmental structure of central government, charged with the task of monitoring the new law, supporting litigation financially and with advice, and themselves having powers to enforce certain of its provisions: these bodies were the Equal Opportunities Commission ('EOC')

---

[18] Street *et al*, 1967.
[19] Mirza, 1995: p 3.
[20] See generally Meehan, 1985: ch 2.
[21] 401 US 424 (1971).
[22] See below, para 6.12 *et seq*.

and the Commission for Racial Equality ('CRE').[23] The model thereby established was later adopted in the case of disability discrimination, with the establishment of the Disability Rights Commission ('DRC'),[24] and later extended to cover anti-discrimination law in general with the setting up of the Equality and Human Rights Commission ('EHRC').[25]

American influence was also important in the adoption of the Disability Discrimination Act 1995.[26] Two federal US statutes, the Rehabilitation Act 1973 and the Americans with Disabilities Act 1990, provided a conceptual basis for legislation aimed at combating disability discrimination, in particular through the notion of the employer's duty to make reasonable accommodation to the known physical or mental incapacities of an otherwise qualified applicant or employee. Legislation embodying the US approach was adopted in Canada, Australia and New Zealand in the 1970s and 1980s. Private members' bills were unsuccessfully introduced in the UK Parliament every year from 1982 and a number of extra-Parliamentary organisations maintained a campaign for reform under the umbrella group Voluntary Organisations for Anti-Discrimination Legislation (later renamed the Right Now Campaign). The then Conservative government brought forward the 1995 Act apparently in order to forestall a more far-reaching private members' bill, the Civil Rights (Disabled Persons) Bill. The 1995 Act reflected this rather lukewarm support of the government of the day, since it was by far the weakest of the principal anti-discrimination statutes, although it has since been strengthened considerably by a number of amendments, many of them introduced to comply with European Union law.

(iii) The influence of European Union law

6.5   The United Kingdom's membership of the European Union appears to have had little or no influence on the form and substance of the Sex Discrimination Act 1975. Lord Lester, who in the mid-1970s was a special adviser on discrimination law to the Home Secretary, has explained that the Act was drafted without regard to the Equal Treatment Directive, which was being prepared at around the same time and which was adopted in 1976.[27] The full significance of European Union law as a source of UK law in this area only began to become clear following the ruling of the ECJ in the second *Defrenne* case,[28] to the effect that the principle of equal pay for equal work in Article 119 of the Treaty of Rome (subsequently Article 141 TEC and now Article 157 TFEU) had direct effect in national law.

Article 119 owed its presence in the Treaty of Rome to a compromise on the issue of social policy harmonisation which was made at the time of the Treaty's adoption. Article 119, together with Article 120 concerning annual paid leave, represented limited concessions to the possibility

---

[23]   Further significant amendments were made to RRA 1976 by the Race Relations (Amendment) Act 2000, which (among other things) imposed a general duty on specified public authorities, when carrying out their functions, to have regard to the need to 'eliminate unlawful racial discrimination' and 'to promote equality of opportunity and good relations between persons of different racial groups' (RRA 1976, s 71 as amended by RR(A)A 2000, s 2). See O'Cinneide, 2001. Racial discrimination in employment is now governed by the Equality Act 2010.

[24]   By the Disability Rights Commission Act 1999.

[25]   Under the Equality Act 2006. The EHRC assumed the previous powers of the EOC, CRE and DRC. See below para 6.69.

[26]   See Doyle, 1995, 1996; Gooding, 1996; Stacey and Short, 2000.

[27]   See Lester, 1994.

[28]   Case 43/75 *Defrenne v SA Belge de Navigation Aérienne* [1976] ECR 455.

that economic integration could be impeded by distortions of competition arising from social policy differences between Member States. The Community essentially adopted the position taken by a group of experts chaired by the Swedish economist Bertil Ohlin, whose 1956 Report for the ILO looked into the question of labour costs and economic integration. Ohlin rejected pleas for general harmonisation of social policy, on the grounds that differences in costs *between* Member States were a reflection, by and large, of differences in the productivity of labour. However, Ohlin also accepted that in some instances, transnational harmonisation of social policy was needed to eliminate 'such discrepancies within each country as would substantially distort international trade'. The problem arose not because the general level of wages in a given country might be low in comparison to that in another, but because, instead, an industry might enjoy an advantage in terms of wage levels and/or social charges which were exceptionally low in relation to the general level of costs in *that country*. If this advantage were unrelated to productivity, 'the whole situation … [would be] … economically unsound' and workers and employers in other countries could justifiably complain about 'unfair competition'. The low-cost producer would obtain the benefit of what was in effect a subsidy, since differences in national exchange rates, which reflect general prices and productivity within states, would not cancel out the advantage enjoyed by just one industry. Thus:

> … a certain distortion of international competition arises from differences in the extent to which the principle of equal pay for men and women applies in different countries. Countries in which there are large wage differentials by sex will pay relatively low wages in industries employing a large proportion of female labour and these industries will enjoy what might be considered a special advantage over their competitors abroad where differentials according to sex are smaller or non-existent.[29]

In *Defrenne v SA Belge de Navigation Aérienne* the ECJ affirmed the economic origins of Article 119 by stating that it had a 'double aim, which is at once economic and social'.[30] Its economic purpose was to 'avoid a situation in which undertakings established in States which have actually implemented the principle of equal pay suffer a competitive disadvantage in intra-Community competition as compared with undertakings established in States which have not yet eliminated discrimination against women workers as regards pay'.[31] But at the same time, Article 119 was 'part of the social objectives of the Community, which is not merely an economic union, but is at the same time intended, by common action, to ensure social progress and to seek the constant improvement of the living and working conditions of their peoples'.[32] As we shall examine further below,[33] the Court has since given Article 157 TFEU (as it has become) a broad interpretation at the same time as ensuring that its direct effect, which here is both horizontal and vertical, means that individuals have the benefit of its protection, regardless of the position adopted in national legislation.

---

[29] ILO, 1956: p 107.
[30] Case 43/75 [1976] ECR 455, at para 12.
[31] Case 43/75 [1976] ECR 455, at para 9.
[32] Case 43/75 [1976] ECR 455, at para 10.
[33] See para 6.79 below.

The Equal Pay Directive of 1975[34] and the Equal Treatment Directive of 1976[35] also had a substantial impact on domestic law. The 1975 Directive led to the amendment in 1983 of the Equal Pay Act 1970, introducing the principle of equal pay for work of equal value, after the ECJ had held in favour of the Commission in infringement proceedings brought against the UK.[36] The impact of the Equal Treatment Directive was felt in a number of areas including the removal of protective legislation limiting women's working hours and access to particular kinds of employment,[37] the imposition of equal retirement ages for men and women[38] and the extension of the rights of pregnant workers.[39] The ECJ's broad interpretation of Article 119 caused upheaval in the law of occupational pensions following its decision in 1990 in *Barber v Guardian Royal Exchange Assurance Group*,[40] and also contributed to the removal in 1995 of legislation discriminating against part-time workers by excluding those working for fewer than 8 or, in some cases, 16 hours, from employment protection rights. In *R v Secretary of State for Employment, ex p EOC*[41] the House of Lords, applying principles of European Community law which had been fashioned by the ECJ, decided that these qualifying thresholds amounted to indirect sex discrimination on the grounds that they significantly affected women more than men and could not be justified by reference to wider considerations of social and economic policy. During this period the case law of the ECJ had an indirect impact on the law of racial discrimination, as it proved politically impossible to introduce certain improvements to sex discrimination law without also extending them to the Race Relations Act: thus when the statutory upper limit on compensation for acts of sex discrimination was removed following the ruling of the ECJ in *Marshall v Southampton and South West Hampshire Health Authority (No 2)*,[42] it was felt both desirable and necessary to take the same step under the Race Relations Act.[43]

European Union law set the context for attempts to extend the principle of equal treatment into new areas. The open-ended quality of Article 119 of the Treaty of Rome and the various directives relating to equal treatment provided opportunities for innovative interpretations which were not available under the more rigidly-confined terms of domestic legislation. In *P v S and Cornwall County Council*[44] the ECJ accepted that discrimination against a transsexual was an infringement of the Equal Treatment Directive; however, in *Grant v South West Trains Ltd*[45] it

---

[34] Directive 75/117.

[35] Directive 76/207.

[36] Case 61/81 *EC Commission v United Kingdom of Great Britain and Northern Ireland* [1982] ICR 578.

[37] In the SDA 1986 and the EA 1989. See Deakin, 1990a; below, para 6.56.

[38] SDA 1986, introduced following the decision of the ECJ in Case 152/84 *Marshall v Southampton and South West Hampshire Health Authority* [1986] IRLR 140.

[39] See generally para 6.111 below.

[40] Case C-262/88 [1990] IRLR 240; see below, para 6.109.

[41] [1994] IRLR 176; see below, para 6.31. The EOC's case was argued under Art 119 and the Equal Treatment Directive. Although the House of Lords was content to decide the case solely by reference to the Directive, other courts subsequently decided that Art 119 was also applicable in this context, so as to give the equal pay principle both horizontal and vertical direct effect.

[42] Case C-271/91 [1993] IRLR 445; SI 1993/2798.

[43] Race Relations (Remedies) Act 1994.

[44] Case C-13/94 [1996] IRLR 347. Following this judgment, the relevant UK law was amended by the Sex Discrimination (Gender Reassignment) Regulations 1999, SI 1999/1102. On discrimination against transsexual persons, see para 6.38 below.

[45] Case C-249/96 [1998] IRLR 206. The conceptual approach of the ECJ in *Grant* was broadly followed by the House of Lords in *MacDonald v Advocate General for Scotland, Pearce v Governing Body of Mayfield School* [2003] IRLR 512. On discrimination on the grounds of sexual orientation, see below, para 6.40.

held that discrimination on the grounds of an individual's sexual orientation did not contravene Article 141 TEC (as it then was), using reasoning which appeared to cast doubt on the broad application of the equality principle which it had made in *P v S*. The Court also gave an important but qualified recognition to the possibility of affirmative action under EC law.[46]

The continuing importance of European Union law in the legislative field was confirmed by the adoption through the Treaty of Amsterdam in 1997 of what became Article 13 TEC and is now Article 19 TFEU. This provided a new power to the Community to legislate across the whole range of discrimination issues including sex, sexual orientation, racial or ethnic origin, religion or belief, disability, and age. Two Directives were adopted in 2000 under this provision. The Race Directive[47] prohibits discrimination on the grounds of race and ethnic or national origin in respect of a range of matters relating to employment, social protection, social advantages, and access to goods and services. Implementation took place in 2003.[48] The Framework Directive[49] prohibits discrimination in relation to employment and occupation on the grounds of religion or belief, disability, age, and sexual orientation. The provisions on religion, belief and sexual orientation were implemented in 2003; those relating to disability in 2004;[50] and those relating to age in 2006.[51] Other important changes were made by the Burden of Proof Directive of 1997,[52] which altered the meaning of the concept of discrimination in the context of sex discrimination law,[53] and a Directive of 2002[54] which amended the 1976 Directive on equal treatment for men and women in employment.[55]

Conceptions of equality

6.6   As a consequence of these developments, the legal principle of equality in employment is now firmly established. However, the rapid pace of legal change has tended to obscure some underlying uncertainties concerning the nature and rationale of this body of legislation. Within the law as it currently stands there are several different, competing conceptions of the equality principle.

---

[46] Case C-409/95 *Marschall v Land Nordrhein-Westfalen* [1998] IRLR 39; cf Case C-450/93 *Kalanke v Freie Hansestadt Bremen* [1995] IRLR 660; see below, para 6.72.

[47] Directive 2000/43/EC. See further para 6.45 below.

[48] By virtue of the Race Relations Act 1976 (Amendment) Regulations 2003, SI 2003/1626.

[49] Directive 2000/78/EC.

[50] By virtue of the Employment Equality (Sexual Orientation) Regulations, SI 2003/1661 (henceforth referred to as EE(SO)R); the Employment Equality (Religion or Belief) Regulations, SI 2003/1660 (henceforth referred to as EE(RB)R); and the Disability Discrimination Act 1995 (Amendment) Regulations 2003, SI 2003/1673. The provisions relating to disability were not required to be implemented until 2 December 2006. These provisions, as amended, are now incorporated into the Equality Act 2010.

[51] Through the Employment Equality (Age) Regulations, SI 2006/1031 (henceforth referred to as EE(A)R), now incorporated, as amended, in the Equality Act 2010.

[52] Directive 97/80/EC.

[53] See in particular para 6.23 below.

[54] Directive 2002/73/EC.

[55] It should also be noted that the European Convention on Human Rights, in Art 14, contains a prohibition of discrimination on grounds of 'sex, race, colour, language, religion, political or other opinion, national or social origin, association with a national minority, property, birth or other status', but this only covers discriminatory treatment in relation to the 'enjoyment of the rights and freedoms set forth in this Convention'. It is therefore necessary to find that the discriminatory treatment falls within the ambit of one of the other Convention rights. On the overlap between Art 14 ECHR and EU law, see Bamforth, 2006.

(i) Protection of the dignity and autonomy of the individual

6.7   The principal conception is that of equal treatment as part of the individual worker's right to respect for their *personal dignity*: each person has the right to be treated on the basis of their *individual* characteristics, merits and achievements, and not on the basis of stereotypical assumptions about them which are based on their sex, race or other relevant *group-based* characteristic. This was clearly recognised, for example, in the White Paper, *Equality for Women*, which preceded the Sex Discrimination Act 1975: 'the variations of character and ability within each sex are greater and more significant than the differences between the sexes'.[56] Feminist social and legal theory has shown that many of the assumed differences between men and women in terms of their capacity for particular kinds of tasks are not the product of differences between the biological sexes, but are based on assumptions originating in social practices which are nationally and historically contingent and, in many cases, backed up by legal rules either requiring or condoning segregation and discrimination.[57]

(ii) Addressing group disadvantage

6.8   The notion of the right to equality as the individual's right to personal dignity is most clearly reflected in the concept of direct discrimination, which is the legal form of the principle that 'like should be treated alike'.[58] The law also recognises a second conception of the equality principle, which sees its rationale as remedying the social and economic disadvantage suffered by particular *groups*.[59] From the point of view of direct discrimination, the adverse treatment of men on the grounds of their sex or of white individuals on the basis of their colour is inherently wrong, and a breach of the personal rights of the individuals concerned, as the adverse treatment of women and of members of ethnic minorities is for the same reasons; if, however, remedying collective disadvantage is the aim of anti-discrimination legislation, space should be created for measures designed to enhance the standing and opportunities of those groups who were previously the victims of unequal treatment, if necessary through affirmative action which may involve an element of 'reverse discrimination'. Title VII of the US Civil Rights Act incorporated a compromise between these two ideas: the prohibition on disparate treatment was broadly worded and came to be interpreted in such a way as to permit certain limited forms of affirmative action on the basis of past disadvantages suffered by particular groups.[60] This interpretation was coupled with the enactment of Federal Executive Order 11246 which instituted a wide-ranging programme of contract compliance, aimed at requiring government contractors to promote affirmative action in

---

[56]   Cmnd 5724, 1974, at para 16.

[57]   See Pannick, 1985: pp 14 *et seq*; Fredman, 1997c: ch 1. There is a potentially important analytical distinction here between practices which are based on *gender*, that is to say on the *assumed or attributed characteristics* of men and women, and those based on the biological differences between the sexes (see Oakley, 1972); the vast majority of acts of 'sex discrimination', as the law describes it, fall into the former category. The term 'sex discrimination' is the term given by the law to what may more accurately be referred to as 'gender discrimination'; in this book we use the phrase 'sex discrimination' because of the legal meaning which it has come to acquire, but this is not to assume that the practices which constitute sex discrimination in the eyes of the law are based on biological factors.

[58]   See below, paras 6.14-6.21.

[59]   Lacey, 1992; and on the relationship between discrimination law and social inclusion, see H Collins, 2003.

[60]   *United Steelworkers of America v Weber* 443 US 193 (1979); see below, para 6.71.

their own personnel policies. Affirmative action continues to have a major role to play in US anti-discrimination law, notwithstanding a continuing, heated debate over its legitimate scope.

In Britain, the issue of affirmative action was dealt with differently from the start. The definition of direct discrimination in the Acts of 1975 and 1976 was more precisely formulated than its counterpart in the Civil Rights Act 1964, in such a way as clearly to rule out reverse or 'positive' discrimination; this was a conscious policy choice to which only one formal concession was made, in the case of training designed to benefit members of a particular sexual or racial group which was under-represented in an area of employment or in a particular organisation.[61] The Equality Act 2010 has extended the scope of these positive action provisions and has also loosened the rules on positive discrimination in recruitment and promotion to allow employers to take under-representation into account when choosing from two equally well-qualified persons, in line with EU law.[62]

There is a more general difficulty in attempting to use the legislative model established in the Civil Rights Act and in EqA 2010 to promote greater sexual and racial equality. The notion that 'like should be treated alike' requires comparisons to be made on the basis of a 'white male norm' which may be inappropriate: 'the doctrine inherently assumed that the goal is assimilation to an existing standard without questioning the desirability of that standard'.[63] A strict comparison of 'like with like' is capable of being counter-productive where the rights of (female) part-time workers are compared to those of (male) full-timers,[64] or where the position of pregnant women is compared to that of men who are absent from work on account of illness.[65] In both these cases, notwithstanding the use of the equality principle to bring about far-reaching improvements, there is a case for saying that improvements in the position of the disadvantaged group would best be brought about by regulation which deals with the specific situation in question, such as legislation outlawing the adverse treatment of part-timers and pregnant workers as such, and not by always attempting to fit these cases into the framework provided by equality legislation.[66]

(iii) Equality and the market

6.9 A third conception of equality sees its role in terms of the promotion of *equality within a market order*:[67] here the principal aim is to do what is necessary to ensure free and equal competition in the labour market, and to regulate outcomes in terms of the distribution of economic and social resources as little as possible. The view of equality legislation which sees it in terms of opening access and extending competition is hostile to equal value legislation, on the grounds that this is an unwarranted interference with the outcomes of private bargaining; on the other hand, it might be favourably disposed to certain affirmative action policies designed to break down

---

[61] SDA 1975, ss 47–48; RRA 1976, ss 37–38.

[62] EqA 2010, ss 158-159. See Government Equalities Office, *Framework for a Fairer Future – the Equality Bill*, Cm 7431, June 2008, ch. 4 (henceforth '*Framework for a Fairer Future*'), presaging this change in the law, discussed further at para 6.73 below.

[63] Finley, 1986: p 1143; see also Fredman, 1992b, 1997c: ch 1.

[64] Case C-399/92 *Stadt Lengerich v Helmig* [1995] IRLR 216, discussed below at para 6.98.

[65] *Webb v EMO Air Cargo Ltd* [1993] IRLR 27, HL; refd [1994] IRLR 482, ECJ; *(No 2)* [1995] IRLR 645, HL; see below, at para 6.111.

[66] See Finley, 1986; Hepple, 1990a; Fredman, 1994b.

[67] See Deakin, 1990a; Fredman, 1992b, 1997c: ch 9, part III; McColgan, 1997.

women's entry into previously closed occupations and professions.[68] However, many neoliberal accounts are simply against equality legislation in principle, on the grounds that the free market is capable of arriving at the necessary economic equilibrium unaided, and that the interference with freedom of contract which all such legislation entails is illegitimate. According to Becker's influential economic theory of discrimination, discrimination on grounds of sex or race arises from employers' subjective preferences or 'tastes'; if certain employers behave irrationally, for example hiring men when women would work more productively, the market will require them to pay a price in the form of competition from employers who have no such predelictions.[69] Where there is job segregation, it is often explicable, according to Becker, on the basis of individual choice: women, by preferring domestic responsibilities over continuous participation in the labour market, thereby 'choose' to diminish their own human capital, and to reduce their value to employers.[70] This point of view has been challenged by labour market segmentation theory, which stresses the institutional forces shaping labour supply decisions and the role of customary assumptions about relative worth which tend to undervalue the labour of particular groups. From this point of view, the 'unregulated' labour market is one in which social norms serve to reinforce racial and sexual stereotypes, thereby opening up the possibility of institutionalised discrimination and providing an economic basis for more extensive legal intervention.[71]

There are elements in the law of equal treatment which support both of these approaches. Equal value legislation, for example, openly challenges the assumption that rankings arrived at by job evaluation systems are necessarily objective. On the other hand, there is a sense in which anti-discrimination legislation can also be used to justify the removal, as part of a policy of deregulation, of practices whose aim is principally protective. One of the results of the Equal Treatment Directive, for example, has been the removal from domestic law of protective legislation regulating nightwork by women and limiting their exposure to certain dangerous substances; when the relevant legislation was repealed by the Sex Discrimination Act 1986 and the Employment Act 1989, nothing was put in its place, although the alternative would have been to enact a general measure providing protection for *all* workers.[72] The point is that there is nothing in Article 157 TFEU or in the Equality Directives which specifically requires what may be called 'levelling up' of the disadvantaged group to the level of the advantaged group.[73] An example of the problems this creates is provided by the occupational pension case, *Smith v Avdel Systems Ltd*,[74] in which the ECJ condoned employers' practice of raising the pensionable age of women from 60 to 65, in order to achieve formal equality with male employees. In short, in certain of its guises the equality principle is only capable of dealing with the issue of 'horizontal equality' between comparable individuals or groups; it may have nothing to say about 'vertical equality', or the redistribution of social and economic resources between groups in the labour market hierarchy. In so far as equality legislation achieves such a redistribution, it only does so in conjunction with other forms of social protection, including collective bargaining and regulatory legislation, which set a floor

---

[68]   Fischel and Lazear, 1986.

[69]   Becker, 1971.

[70]   Becker, 1975. See Mayhew and Addison, 1983.

[71]   See Rubery, 1988; Rubery, *et al*, 1989; Deakin and Wilkinson, 1992; Humphries and Rubery, 1995.

[72]   See Deakin, 1990a. A similar debate took place in France in regard to Art L 213-1 *et seq* of the French *Code du Travail*, which were declared incompatible with Directive 76/307 by the ECJ (Case C-345/89 *Re Stoeckel* [1991] ECR I-4047).

[73]   Deakin, 1995a.

[74]   Case C-408/92 [1994] IRLR 602.

of minimum standards upon which any 'equalisation' of rights must build, and alongside more results-orientated forms of affirmative action in support of disadvantaged groups.

The economic and social impact of equality legislation

6.10   This last point highlights some of the reasons for the limited impact, in certain respects, of equal treatment legislation in Britain: British legislation tends to be characterised by an emphasis on horizontal as opposed to vertical equality and accepts only a marginal role for affirmative action, and is heavily dependent on other regulatory instruments, in particular collective bargaining, for its effective implementation. Following the passage of the Equal Pay Act in 1970 there was a substantial narrowing of the pay gap between men and women. Average hourly wages for women, which had been below 60% of men's in 1970, rose to over 70% by 1980. Although incomes policies, which at that time embodied a strong tendency to favour the lower paid, may also have contributed to the narrowing of the pay gap, it has been argued that neither incomes policies nor changes in the industrial structure would have been decisive on their own; instead, the Act itself was chiefly responsible for the change, in combination with the use of centralised pay bargaining to achieve equalisation.[75] Thus the improvement began in the early 1970s, before the Act came into force, as sector-level collective agreements were voluntarily amended in anticipation of the law becoming formally operative.[76] As originally enacted, the Act contained a mechanism by which payment structures of this kind could be amended by an award of the Central Arbitration Committee,[77] and the threat of this legal sanction appears to have directly influenced collective bargaining behaviour. What this finding suggests is that the Act was successful because it was combined with an effective collective procedure for enhancing pay and conditions. There is ample evidence, by contrast, that individual actions for pay equality are extremely costly and difficult to mount, are diffuse in their effects and often unsatisfactory for the workers concerned, who may face subsequent victimisation.[78] Since 1986, however, when the CAC's jurisdiction over equal pay issues was repealed,[79] the individual route is effectively all that remains. It is not clear whether the introduction of equal value legislation in 1983 has been responsible for the small but steady improvement in the relative position of women's pay since then: for example, the proportion of female to male full-time hourly earnings rose from 75% in 1988 to 79% in 1992, 82% in 2000 and 91% by 2011.[80] One possible cause of the improvement in the 1990s was the combination of a decline in the degree of occupational segregation and a rise in women's full-time working.[81] More generally, the decline of sector-level collective bargaining in Britain poses a major problem for the full implementation of the principle of equal pay for work of equal value: a comparative study of gender inequality in OECD countries concluded that 'a centralised industrial relations

---

[75] Zabalza and Tsannatos, 1985.

[76] Zabalza and Tsannatos, 1985.

[77] EqPA 1970, s 3, repealed by the SDA 1986; see below, para 6.106. Prior to 1975 the relevant body was the Industrial Arbitration Board.

[78] See Leonard, 1987; Fredman 1997c: p 251 *et seq.*

[79] See below, para 6.106.

[80] For recent figures, see GEO, *Framework for a Fairer Future*, at p 4, and ONS figures for 2011, available at www.ons. gov.uk.

[81] Hakim, 1993: p 107.

system, high levels of public employment relative to total employment and sustained expenditure on active labour market programmes are most likely to deliver relatively high earnings for women', and that as a result 'the emancipatory potential of legislative moves will be best enhanced within a "collective" framework'.[82]

For similar reasons, the failure of the Race Relations Act 1976 to counter increasing levels of relative poverty and unemployment among ethnic minority groups needs to be put in the context not simply of the limits to the role of the law in economic and social regulation, but also of the clear shortcomings of that particular legislation.[83] Unemployment rates for ethnic minority groups are substantially higher than those for white people, although it should be noted that there are significant variations in the activity rates of different ethnic groups.[84] There is evidence of institutionalised racial discrimination both in recruitment and in the selection of workers for redundancy. Weaknesses in the Act of 1976 included difficulties inherent in the burden of proof in discrimination cases; the lack of a class action procedure; the complexity of the statutory definition of indirect discrimination; the large range of exemptions contained in the Act; and the failure to entrench the Act against other legislative measures which may contradict its aims. Research in the mid-1990s showed that success rates in race discrimination cases before employment tribunals were about 20%, which was about half the rate for sex discrimination and unfair dismissal cases, and that race discrimination cases were the most likely to be withdrawn and the least likely to be settled without a hearing.[85] These and other difficulties were raised by the CRE in two reviews of the legislation in the 1980s and 1990s[86] as well as by independent research.[87] Following these reviews the 1976 Act was amended and some of its structural weaknesses addressed, although how far these changes were successful in their aim of removing barriers to racial equality in employment is an open question.[88]

The Equality Act 2010

6.11   In part as a consequence of the multiplication of new grounds for discrimination claims, discrimination law became exceedingly complex. By the middle of the last decade there were 'nine major pieces of discrimination legislation, around 100 statutory instruments setting out connected rules and regulations and more than 2,500 pages of guidance and statutory codes of practice'.[89] In 2005 the government launched a Discrimination Law Review to consider, among other things, proposals for a 'clearer and more streamlined equality legislation framework... reflecting better

---

[82] Whitehouse, 1992: p 63; see also McColgan, 1997.

[83] See Hepple, 1991, and D Bell, 1992 for an assessment of the limited impact, in this respect, of civil rights legislation in the USA.

[84] For data from the 1980s and 1990s, see R Jenkins, 1988: pp 314–315 and McCrudden *et al*, 1991. According to more recent government figures, members of ethnic minorities have a substantially lower likelihood of finding work than white people, with the gap narrowing only slightly since the late 1990s (GEO, *Framework for a Fairer Future*, at p 4.).

[85] Mirza, 1995: p 14.

[86] *Review of the Race Relations Act 1976: Proposals for Change*, CRE 1985; *Second Review of the Race Relations Act 1976*, CRE 1992.

[87] McCrudden *et al*, 1991; Hepple *et al*, 2000.

[88] See the evidence referred to in GEO, *Framework for a Fairer Future*, at p 4.

[89] GEO, *Framework for a Fairer Future*, at p 6.

regulation principles'.[90] A consultation paper published in June 2007, in addition to making the case for a single Equality Act on the grounds of simplification and rationalisation of the law, advocated a mix of statutory modifications, self-regulation and market-based incentives as a basis for addressing inequalities which had proved resistant to legal intervention.[91] The apparent downplaying of the role of statutory regulation came in for substantial criticism.[92] In 2008 the Government Equalities Office ('GEO') published a short White Paper, *Framework for a Fairer Future – the Equality Bill*,[93] and a more detailed set of responses to the earlier consultation.[94] These two documents placed less stress on the 'better regulation' agenda and proposed a series of substantive and potentially far reaching legal changes.[95] The proposals included putting in place a single equality duty for public authorities; streamlining existing duties in respect of the different heads of discrimination law; requiring public authorities to make annual reports on compliance with the equality duty; changing the law on discrimination on the grounds of gender reassignment, to make provision for associative discrimination and indirect discrimination; prohibiting 'secrecy clauses' which prevent workers revealing their pay for the purposes of equal pay claims; extending the scope for positive discrimination by employers; and granting new powers to employment tribunals to make workforce-wide recommendations following a finding of discrimination against an employer. In relation to simplification, the proposed changes included measures harmonising the different tests of indirect discrimination; bringing equal pay into the single Equality Act with some streamlining and codification on the issue of the burden of proof and employer defences, while retaining distinct approaches for dealing with contractual and non-contractual pay matters; and removing the need for a comparator in victimisation cases, in favour of a looser 'detriment' test.

A Bill incorporating these proposals was laid before Parliament in April 2009 and enacted as the Equality Act 2010 (henceforth 'EqA 2010').[96] The Act was passed shortly before the General Election of 2010 which led to the removal of the then Labour government from office. The Conservative-Liberal Democrat Coalition government which took office in May of that year proceeded to bring most of the Act into force with effect from October 2010. The Act's provisions on positive action in recruitment and promotion and the public sector equality duty were brought into force from April 2011, with more specific aspects of the public sector equality duty being introduced by regulation with effect from September 2011.[97] In the March 2011 Budget Statement, the Chancellor of the Exchequer announced that the government would not be bringing into force

[90] See *The Equality Bill – Government Response to the Consultation*, Cm 7454 (henceforth *Government Response to the Consultation*), July 2008, at p 13.

[91] Department for Communities and Local Government, *A Framework for Fairness: Proposals for a Single Equality Bill for Great Britain*, June 2007.

[92] McCrudden, 2007c.

[93] Cm 7431.

[94] *Government Response to the Consultation*, Cm 7454. See also GEO, *A Fairer Future. The Equality Bill and other action to make equality a reality*, April 2008.

[95] The most important of these are outlined in the text below. We refer to specific proposals in more detail in the relevant sections of this chapter.

[96] The *Explanatory Notes to the Act* (henceforth '*Explanatory Notes*'), available online on the OPSI website (www.opsi. gov.uk/legislation), and the EHRC *Employment Statutory Code of Practice* (2011) (henceforth '*EHRC Employment Code of Practice*') provide important sources of guidance on its provisions. For academic commentary on the Act, see Hepple, 2011a, 2011b; Fredman, 2011; Lawson, 2011; Pitt, 2011; Solanke, 2011.

[97] SI 2011/2260.

the Act's provisions on combined or dual discrimination,[98] and that there would be consultation on the possible repeal of measures relating to employers' liability for third-party harassment.[99] The Coalition government has also decided against bringing into force those parts of the Act dealing with socio-economic inequalities[100] and employers' reporting of gender-related pay differences,[101] although without formally repealing them.

DISCRIMINATION AND PROHIBITED CONDUCT

The forms of prohibited conduct

6.12   The 2010 Act sets out a number of types of 'prohibited conduct' which are, in effect, statutory wrongs producing a form of civil liability which is closely analogous to that which arises in the common law of tort. The principal forms of prohibited conduct are the 'statutory torts' of direct and indirect discrimination.[102] Separate provision is made for wrongs of harassment[103] and victimisation,[104] and for a number of forms of secondary civil liability based on instructing, causing, inducing or aiding contraventions of the Act.[105]

The distinction between direct and indirect discrimination

6.13   The distinction between direct and indirect discrimination is at the conceptual core of equality law. *Direct discrimination* denotes unequal treatment of an individual on the basis of a given protected characteristic, while *indirect discrimination* describes inequality resulting from the application of a provision, criterion or practice which is apparently neutral, but which has a disadvantageous effect upon persons sharing a given protected characteristic. In principle, the two categories are mutually exclusive, and so operate in the alternative. The distinction between them is important because in the case of indirect discrimination only, the legislation grants the employer (or other respondent) the benefit of an open-ended defence of justification. It is not true to say that adverse treatment of the kind involved in direct discrimination can never be justified; such justification is, in effect, the function of the statutory genuine occupational requirement (GOR) defence[106] and of certain exceptions to the equality principle which are expressly laid down in the legislation itself.[107] The GOR defences, however, are more narrowly framed than the

---

[98]   See para 6.22.

[99]   See para 6.33.

[100]   See para 6.76.

[101]   See para 6.108.

[102]   EqA 2010, ss 13 (direct discrimination), 19 (indirect discrimination). On the tort-like nature of liability for contraventions of the 2010 Act, see below, para 6.66.

[103]   EqA 2010, s 26 . See para 6.33 below.

[104]   EqA 2010, s 27. See para 6.34 below.

[105]   EqA 2010, ss 111, 112. See para 6.54. below.

[106]   EqA 2010, Sch 9; see para 6.55 below.

[107]   See, in particular, EqA 2010, ss 192-195; paras 6.56-6.61 below.

justification defence for indirect discrimination, although they are not a closed set, as the pre-2010 GOQ defences were.[108]

If the distinction between the two forms of discrimination nevertheless is a critical issue, its precise basis is elusive.[109] Both the UK courts and the ECJ, in interpreting the relevant provisions of European Union law, have rejected the proposition that direct discrimination is based on the intention or motive of the employer. Under UK law, the court will only look to evidence of the alleged discriminator's intention in a case where the basis of a decision is not clear.[110] For the most part emphasis is placed, instead, on the existence of a causal link between the unfavourable treatment suffered by the victim and the relevant protected characteristic. To see the gist of discrimination in terms of the impact on the victim is an important aspect of the equality principle; as Ellis stresses, 'it is at the very heart of the notion of discrimination that it is the *effect* on its victims with which the law is truly concerned, not the precise nature of the conduct of its perpetrators'.[111] At the same time, by marginalising the role of intention, the courts have, perhaps unavoidably, blurred the boundary between direct and indirect discrimination, leading to suggestions, so far rejected by the ECJ, that, at the level of European Union law, the open-ended justification defence should be extended to cases of direct discrimination.[112]

The division between direct and indirect discrimination is also relevant in the context of equal pay claims. The Equal Pay Act 1970 made no explicit reference to the distinction between direct and indirect discrimination and, although it allowed for defences of material difference and 'material factor' which operated in a manner akin to the defence of justification in indirect discrimination, it did not clearly state that a finding of adverse impact had to be made before the employer was required to justify the difference in pay. In *Strathclyde Regional Council v Wallace*[113] Lord Browne-Wilkinson argued that the 1970 Act nevertheless had to be considered in the light of the jurisprudence of the ECJ, which, in relation to Article 157 TFEU (as it now is), had accepted the existence of the distinction between direct and indirect discrimination.[114] This meant that in the context of claims for equal pay, 'the only circumstances in which questions of "justification" can arise are those in which the employer is relying on a factor which is sexually discriminatory. There is no question of the employer having to "justify"... all disparities of pay'. However, the attempt, which began with the *Strathclyde* case, to align the 1970 Act with the general conceptual framework of the principle of equal treatment, led to considerable uncertainty in the context of already complex litigation.[115] EqA 2010[116] attempts a resolution of this issue by specifying that a defence of material factor can only be made out where the discrimination in question is indirect as opposed to direct, and by setting out a definition of the material factor defence which aligns

---

[108] In the context of age discrimination, a justification defence is available for both direct and indirect discrimination (EqA 2010, s 13(2)) and, somewhat superfluously in the case of direct age discrimination, a GOR defence is also available (Sch 9, para 1). See further para 6.42 below. On the thinking behind replacing the GOQs with GORs, see *Government Response to the Consultation*, at paras 8.5–8.13

[109] Case C-132/92 *Birds Eye Walls Ltd v Roberts* [1994] IRLR 29, 35 (Advocate General Van Gerven).

[110] R *(on the application of E) v JFS* [2010] IRLR 136; see below, para 6.19.

[111] Ellis, 1994: pp 564–565; for discussion, see Watt, 1998.

[112] Most notably from Advocate General Van Gerven in his opinions in Case C-152/91 *Neath v Hugh Steeper Ltd* [1994] IRLR 91, Case C-132/92 *Birds Eye Walls Ltd v Roberts* [1994] IRLR 29 and Case C-32/93 *Webb v EMO Air Cargo Ltd* [1994] IRLR 482. See also Bowers and Moran, 2002; Gill and Monaghan, 2003; Bowers, Moran and Honeyball, 2003.

[113] [1998] 1 WLR 259, 265.

[114] In particular, in Case 170/84 *Bilka-Kaufhaus GmbH v Weber von Hartz* [1986] IRLR 317.

[115] See our discussion below, at para 6.80.

[116] EqA 2010, ss 69(1), (2); see below, para 6.96.

it with the concept of justification by reference to proportionate means of achieving a legitimate aim, of the kind which applies in other areas of equality law.

The statutory definitions of direct and indirect discrimination have evolved considerably since they were first introduced. The definition of discrimination contained in the SDA 1975 was first amended in order to comply with a wider test set out in the Burden of Proof Directive of 1997.[117] The Framework Directive and Race Directive of 2000 contained a further definition of discrimination which was wider than that set out in British law as it then stood, in particular as it related to indirect discrimination.[118] This widened definition of indirect discrimination was incorporated into the SDA 1975[119] and RRA 1976,[120] but only to the extent necessary to comply with EU law. The result, in the context of the 1976 Act, was that the concept of indirect discrimination had a wider meaning when it was applied to the grounds of race or national or ethnic origins, which are covered by the Race Directive, than it did when applied to the grounds of colour or nationality, which are outside that Directive. This wider definition was applied to discrimination on the grounds of sexual orientation, religion or belief, and age,[121] under the provisions of legislation implementing the relevant parts of the Framework Directive. Thus the meaning of the concept of indirect discrimination shifted according to the precise context being considered. Under EqA 2010, a single, revised set of definitions for direct and indirect discrimination is now applied to each of the protected characteristics.[122]

The Disability Discrimination Act 1995, in its turn, adopted a yet further, distinctive concept of discrimination.[123] EqA 2010 extends the concept of indirect discrimination to cases of disability but also retains aspects of the previous test for disability discrimination which continue to make it to some degree *sui generis*.[124]

Direct discrimination

6.14   Under section 13 EqA 2010, 'a person (A) discriminates against another (B) if, because of a protected characteristic, A treats B less favourably than A treats or would treat others'. This is the right of an individual to be treated on the basis of their own qualities rather than by reference to those associated with membership of a particular group.[125] In general, it is not necessary for the complainant to be a member of that group. On this last point, EqA 2010 marks a change in the law. Under section 1(2)(a) of SDA 1975, a person was taken to discriminate against a woman if 'on the ground of *her sex* he treats her less favourably than he treats or would treat a man' (emphasis

---

[117] See SI 2001/2660.

[118] In each case, this definition is contained in Art 2(2)(b) of the Directive.

[119] SDA 1975, s 1(2)(b), as substituted by SI 2005/2467. This change was required by virtue of the revisions made to the Equal Treatment Directive by Directive 2002/73/EC: see now the recast Equal Treatment Directive, Directive 2006/54/EC, Art 2(1)(b).

[120] RRA 1976, s 1A, as inserted by SI 2003/1626.

[121] EE(SO)R 2003, reg 3, EE(RB)R 2003, reg 3 and EE(A)R 2006, reg 3, respectively.

[122] EqA 2010, ss 13, 19. See *Government Response to the Consultation*, at paras 7.17–7.26.

[123] See below, para 6.124.

[124] EqA 2010, ss 13 (direct discrimination), 15 ('disability-related discrimination'), 20 ('duty to make adjustments'), and 19 (indirect discrimination); on the background to this aspect of the 2010 Act, see *Government Response to the Consultation*, at paras 11.12–11.28.

[125] See Pannick, 1985; p 37.

added). Under the new definition of direct discrimination, it is enough if the respondent treats the complainant differently on the grounds of a protected characteristic of another with whom the complainant has an association ('associative discrimination'), or on the basis of a belief or perception that the complainant has the characteristic in question ('perceptual discrimination'). An exception to this rule is made in the case of discrimination on the grounds of marital status; here, the complainant must actually be married or a civil partner.[126] In addition, protection against pregnancy-related discrimination operates only in relation to the complainant's own pregnancy or maternity.[127]

Section 13 makes a number of further modifications of the basic direct discrimination test for particular protected characteristics. In general, the test of direct discrimination is symmetrical: the prohibition of sex discrimination protects men and women equally. In the case of disability discrimination, however, the protection only operates in favour of disabled persons,[128] and the Act's provisions on discrimination on the grounds of gender reassignment only protect transgender people.[129] Section 13 also indicates that special treatment accorded to a woman 'in connection with pregnancy or childbirth' is not to constitute sex discrimination against men.[130] In the case of marriage and civil partnership, Part 5 of the Act (covering work) applies only if the complainant is married or a civil partner, so does not cover discrimination against unmarried persons.[131] Conversely, in two instances section 13 is explicit on what does constitute discrimination: these are, in the context of racial discrimination, 'segregating [the complainant] from others'[132] and, in the context of sex discrimination against women, 'less favourable treatment of [the complainant] ... because she is breast-feeding'.[133] Finally, while, in general, direct discrimination cannot be justified, section 13 provides that this is possible in the case of discrimination on the grounds of age 'if A can show A's treatment of B to be a proportionate means of achieving a legitimate aim'.[134]

(i) Associative discrimination

6.15 Prior to the coming into force of EqA 2010, there were different approaches to the issue of associative discrimination in respect of the different prohibited grounds. As we have seen, under the SDA 1975, it was necessary for the differential treatment to be on the grounds of the complainant's own sex. By contrast, associative claims were possible in respect of discrimination

---

[126] EqA 2010, s 13(4).
[127] EqA 2010, s 18(2) ('a pregnancy of hers').
[128] EqA 2010, s 13(3).
[129] This is the effect of EqA 2010, s 7(2), referring to 'transsexual persons'. See below, para 6.38.
[130] EqA 2010, s 13(6)(b).
[131] EqA 2010, s 13(4).
[132] EqA 2010, s 13(5).
[133] EqA 2010, s 13(6)(a).
[134] EqA 2010, s 13(2).

on the grounds of race,[135] religion or belief, [136] and sexual orientation.[137] Under the DDA 1995, the relevant disability had to be that of the complainant.[138] However, in *Coleman v Attridge Law*[139] the ECJ held that the prohibition on disability discrimination in the Framework Directive could extend to the case of the adverse treatment of the primary carer of a disabled child. The Framework Directive defines direct discrimination as a situation where 'where one person is treated less favourably than another is, has been or would be treated in a comparable situation, on any of the grounds referred to in Article 1', grounds which include disability.[140] According to the Court, in the light of the purposes of the Directive which include combating 'all forms of discrimination on the grounds of disability', the principle of equal treatment set out in the Directive 'applies not a particular category of person but by reference to the grounds mentioned in Article 1'.[141] The existence of certain provisions of the Directive which could only be read as applying to disabled persons exclusively did not mean that the personal scope of the Directive as a whole was similarly confined.[142] The Court also explicitly held that the concept of harassment contained in the Directive was capable of covering associative discrimination.[143] Although *Coleman* was a decision on disability discrimination, there was nothing in the ECJ's judgment to suggest that its reasoning could not extend to the other grounds of discrimination, and the new formula in section 13 was adopted in order to bring UK law into line with this interpretation of the Directive.[144]

(ii) Perceptual discrimination

6.16   The definition of direct discrimination in the context of race, religion and belief and sexual orientation cases prior to the implementation of EqA 2010 extended to cases in which the respondent acted on a mistaken belief that the complainant or (where relevant) another person had the characteristic in question ('perceptual discrimination'),[145] and the same result was achieved in the case of age discrimination by virtue of an explicit statutory provision to the effect that 'age' included the 'apparent age' of the complainant.[146] With the coming into force of

---

[135]   RRA 1976, s 1(1)(a), on which see *Showboat Entertainment Centre Ltd v Owens* [1984] IRLR 7; *Weathersfield Ltd v Sargent* [1998] IRLR 14, [1999] IRLR 94; *MacDonald v A-G for Scotland, Pearce v Governing Body of Mayfield School* [2003] IRLR 512 at [80]–[82] (Lord Hope); *Redfearn v Serco Ltd* [2006] IRLR 623.

[136]   EE(RB)R 2003, reg 3(1)(a); *Saini v All Saints Haque Centre* [2009] IRLR 74 (a decision on the harassment provisions in EE(RB)R 2003, reg 5 which also covered associative claims).

[137]   EE(SO)R 2003, reg 3(1)(a).

[138]   DDA 1995, s 3A.

[139]   Case C-303/06 *Coleman v Attridge Law* [2008] IRLR 722.

[140]   Directive 2000/78/EC, Art 2(1)(a).

[141]   *Coleman v Attridge Law*, at para 38.

[142]   *Coleman v Attridge Law*, at paras 42–43.

[143]   *Coleman v Attridge Law*, at para 63. See Pilgerstorfer and Forshaw, 2008 (discussing the wider concept of 'transferred discrimination').

[144]   See *Government Response to the Consultation*, at paras 9.3–9.11. It is possible that the changes made to the definition of discrimination by EqA 2010 will not catch all cases of unfavourable treatment of carers of disabled or other (eg elderly) persons: see Hepple, 2011a: pp 60-61.

[145]   See DTI, *Explanatory Notes for the Employment Equality (Sexual Orientation) Regulations 2003 and the Employment Equality (Religion or Belief) Regulations 2003* (2003), at para 25.

[146]   EE(A)R 2006, reg 3(3)(b).

the 2010 Act, perceptual discrimination claims can be brought in respect of each of the protected characteristics with the exception of marital status.[147]

In the pre-2010 Act case of *English v Thomas Sanderson Blinds Ltd*[148] the complainant was subjected to a course of harassment by fellow workers *as if he had been* gay. The employment tribunal and the EAT rejected his claim on the basis that he was neither gay, nor was perceived to be by his colleagues. The Court of Appeal reversed on the basis that, as Sedley LJ put it, there is no real difference between harassing a man who is wrongly assumed to be gay, and harassing a man as if he is gay when he is not:

> If, as is common ground, tormenting a man who is believed to be gay but is not amounts to unlawful harassment, the distance from there to tormenting a man who is being treated as if he were gay when he is not is barely perceptible. In both cases the man's sexual orientation, in both cases imaginary, is the basis – that is to say, the ground – of the harassment. There is no Pandora's box here: simply a consistent application of the principle that, while you cannot legislate against prejudice, you can set out in specified circumstances to stop people's lives being made a misery by it.[149]

This decision suggests that the idea of perceptual discrimination will be flexibly applied by the courts.

(iii) The need for a comparator

6.17   Direct discrimination derives from the concept originally developed in US law and known as 'disparate treatment': this involves comparing the treatment received by the complainant with the treatment which either is or would have been received by a person lacking the relevant protected characteristic but in all other material respects comparable to the complainant. Adapting this notion, EqA 2010 provides that '[o]n a comparison of cases for the purposes of section 13... there must be no material difference between the circumstances relating to each case'.[150] The Discrimination Law Review which preceded EqA 2010 considered the question of whether a comparator was needed in all cases. In its response to the consultation, the government concluded that a comparator requirement should in general be retained on the grounds that 'discrimination is principally about equal rather than fair treatment'[151] and, more specifically, that 'organisations would find it more difficult to address actual rather than hypothesized discrimination in the absence of a comparator'.[152] The Act makes an exception to this in the case of discrimination on the

---

[147] By virtue of EqA 2010, s 13(4).
[148] [2008] IRLR 342; [2009] IRLR 206.
[149] [2009] IRLR 206, at [38].
[150] EqA 2010, s 23(1).
[151] On this point, see the pre-2010 Act cases of *Zafar v Glasgow City Council* [1998] IRLR 36 (noted by Watt, 1998); *Martins v Marks & Spencer plc* [1998] IRLR 326; *Chief Constable of West Yorkshire v Vento* [2001] IRLR 124; *Shamoon v Chief Constable of the Royal Ulster Constabulary* [2003] IRLR 285; *Bahl v Law Society* [2004] IRLR 799.
[152] *Government Response to the Consultation*, at para 7.10.

grounds of pregnancy or maternity,[153] where a series of ECJ decisions had earlier established that a comparison between the position of a pregnant female worker and a male worker who was absent from work on account of illness was inappropriate when determining whether discrimination had occurred.[154] It also specifies that where the protected characteristic is sexual orientation, the fact that one person is a civil partner while another is married is not to be treated as a material difference for the purposes of the comparator test.[155]

In cases other than pregnancy, the critical issue for the court is to identify whether the position of the complainant is materially different from that of the comparator. This is to some degree an impressionistic test. In *P v S*[156] the ECJ held that the appropriate comparator in the case of a transsexual person is a person 'of the sex to which [the complainant] was deemed to belong before undergoing gender reassignment'; on this basis, discrimination against an individual on the grounds of their decision to undergo gender reassignment was categorised as sex discrimination. The Court might have ruled that the comparator was a person of the opposite original sex to the complainant, who was also undergoing gender reassignment, in which case there would have been no discrimination. The flexible approach in *P v S* stands in contrast to that in *Grant v South West Trains Ltd*.[157] in which the ECJ ruled that the appropriate comparator in a claim of sex discrimination brought by a complainant alleging discrimination on the grounds that they had a same-sex partner was a homosexual person of the opposite sex. To some degree, the problem of identifying the comparator in these so-called 'sex plus' claims[158] has been overcome by the introduction of gender reassignment and sexual orientation as protected characteristics in their own right.[159]

(iv) Less favourable treatment

6.18   In the first case under SDA 1975 to reach the higher courts, *Peake v Automotive Products Ltd*,[160] Mr Peake challenged his employer's practice of allowing female shop floor workers to leave five minutes earlier than their male colleagues at the end of a shift. Lord Denning MR thought

---

[153]   Under EqA 2010 s 18(2), a person discriminates against a person on the grounds of her pregnancy if he 'treats her unfavourably' because of the pregnancy or a pregnancy-related illness, a formula which implies that the comparator requirement does not operate in this case.

[154]   Case 177/88 *Dekker v VJV Centrum* [1991] IRLR 27; Case C-32/93 *Webb v EMO Air Cargo Ltd* [1994] IRLR 482. See also *Webb v EMO (Air Cargo) Ltd (No 2)* [1995] IRLR 645 (HL); *EOC v Secretary of State for Trade and Industry* [2007] IRLR 327.

[155]   EqA 2010, s 23(3).

[156]   Case C-13/94 [1996] IRLR 347, 354; see also Case C-117/01 *KB v National Health Service Pensions Agency* [2004] IRLR 240 and our analysis in para 6.38 below.

[157]   Case C-249/96 *Grant v South West Trains Ltd* [1998] IRLR 206; see para 6.40 below. See also the judgment of the House of Lords in *MacDonald v A-G for Scotland, Pearce v Governing Body of Mayfield School* [2003] IRLR 512.

[158]   That is to say, claims in which the basis of the claim was the sex of the claimant 'plus' another factor such as gender reassignment or sexual orientation.

[159]   Thus it is sufficient now to compare the position of a transsexual person to one not who is not transsexual, and the position of a claimant in a sexual orientation claim to a person of a different sexual orientation (EqA 2010 s 13, read with ss 7 and 12). Note, however, that in the case of absence from work because of gender reassignment, the claimant's treatment must be compared to that which he or she would have received if their absence had been caused by 'sickness or injury' or for some other reason and it is not reasonable for the claimant to be treated less favourably (EqA 2010, s 16; see para 6.38 below).

[160]   [1977] QB 780; revsd [1978] QB 233.

that 'it is not discrimination for mankind to treat womankind with the courtesy and chivalry which we have been taught to believe is right conduct in our society', while Shaw LJ considered that unequal treatment 'involves an element of something which is inherently adverse or hostile to the interests of the persons of the sex which is said to be discriminated against'.[161] However, in *Ministry of Defence v Jeremiah*,[162] Lord Denning repudiated his earlier comments about chivalry, and attempted to justify the outcome in *Peake* on *de minimis* grounds. This is not a convincing argument, since the five minutes extra working time per day which the men had to complete takes on a different aspect when it is translated into an extra half-hour or so of work each week. Subsequent decisions have made it clear that if there is a *de minimis* principle in this area of law, it has very little scope of application, and that, in general, deprivation of choice can amount to adverse treatment.[163] However, it is still necessary to show that the complainant has been put at a disadvantage by the treatment he or she received. Thus in decisions on the application of the principle of non-discrimination to the imposition of gender-specific dress codes, the courts have found a gateway to legality for employers by ruling, somewhat controversially, that it is not unfavourable treatment to require an employee to abide by conventional rules on dress and appearance for persons or his or her sex.[164]

(iv) Irrelevance of motive or intention: the 'but-for' test of causation

6.19   The irrelevance of motive to direct discrimination was established in two decisions of the House of Lords, *R v Birmingham County Council, ex p EOC*[165] and *James v Eastleigh Borough Council*.[166] In the former, the Council operated a number of single-sex grammar schools to which entry was by competitive examination; as there were fewer schools for girls than for boys, the pass mark for girls was set at a higher level. This practice was ruled unlawful. According to Lord Goff:

> There is discrimination under the statute if there is less favourable treatment on the ground of sex, in other words if the relevant girl or girls would have received the same treatment as the boys but for their sex. The intention or motive of the defendant to discriminate ... is not a necessary condition to liability; it is perfectly possible to envisage cases where the defendant had no such motive, and yet did in fact discriminate on the ground of sex.[167]

In *James* the issue was whether the Council was entitled to offer free entry to its swimming pool to individuals who had reached the state pensionable age of 65 for men and 60 for women. Mr James, who was 61, complained that he had to pay to gain admission when his wife, who was the same age, did not. The Court of Appeal concluded that this was not a case of direct discrimination, since

---

[161] [1978] QB 233, 238, 240 respectively.
[162] [1980] ICR 13.
[163] *Greig v Community Industry* [1979] ICR 356; *Gill v El Vino Co Ltd* [1983] QB 425.
[164] *Schmidt v Austick Bookshops Ltd* [1977] IRLR 360; *Burrett v West Birmingham Health Authority* [1994] IRLR 7, EAT, 3 March 1994, unreported, CA; Cunningham, 1995; see para 6.51 below.
[165] [1989] IRLR 173.
[166] [1990] IRLR 288; see also *Chief Constable of Greater Manchester Police v Hope* [1999] ICR 338.
[167] [1989] IRLR 173, 175.

'one is looking not to the causative link between the defendant's behaviour and the detriment to the plaintiff but to the reason why the defendant treated the plaintiff less favourably'.[168] The House of Lords reversed this ruling by a bare majority. According to Lord Bridge, the criterion of pensionable age was 'no more than a convenient shorthand expression which refers to the age of 60 in a woman and to the age of 65 in a man'; in this context, 'it cannot possibly make any difference whether the alleged discriminator uses the shorthand expression or spells out its full meaning'.[169] Although the Council had no intention to discriminate in favour of women and had acted from the laudable motive of providing a concession to those it assumed were retired and no longer in receipt of income from full-time employment, in adopting the criterion of state pensionable age it relied on a ground which was objectively based on a prohibited ground or, now, protected characteristic, and so contravened the Act.

It is arguable that the Council could have acted lawfully by making the offer of free admission to those who were *actually* retired from full-time employment, since this group would not necessarily have been coterminous with those who had reached state pensionable age; thanks mainly to early retirements, such a classification would arguably not have been one which was formally based on sex.[170] Had this been the case, the Council's actions could have given rise to a prima facie finding of indirect discrimination, but its reasons for acting would have been relevant to the justification defence. As it was, arguments in favour of the Council's practice could not be weighed in the balance as potentially justifying factors once it had been decided that the discrimination was direct as opposed to indirect.

The effect of *James* is that neither the lack of an intention to discriminate, nor (which is a different thing) a superior motive, will deprive treatment which is causally connected to a protected characteristic of its character as direct discrimination. In principle, the applicant must still show that the respondent *treated* him or her less favourably, and in so far as this entails deliberate conduct of some kind it could be said to necessitate the intentional commission of an act constituting the unequal treatment. It has not so far been suggested, in this context, that the equality legislation does not prohibit a mere *omission* to extend to one individual a benefit extended to another. The act-omission distinction is without merit here, since treating one person differently from another is both an act and an omission.[171]

The *James* test was reconsidered and, in its essential aspects, reaffirmed by the Supreme Court in its ruling in *R (on the application of E) v Governing Body of JFS and the Admissions Appeal Panel of JFS*.[172] The complainant was refused admission to the JFS (previously the 'Jewish Free School'), a state maintained 'faith school' with an Orthodox Jewish character, on the grounds that he did not have the requisite religious status under guidance drawn up by the Office of the Chief Rabbi of the United Hebrew Congregation of the Commonwealth (the 'OCR'). This guidance indicated that an applicant for a place at the school would be considered if he or she was the child of a mother who was 'Jewish by birth' or had converted to Judaism under Orthodox 'auspices'.[173] These admissions criteria were based on the view that '[either] matrilineal descent or conversion

[168] [1989] IRLR 318, 321 (Browne-Wilkinson VC).
[169] [1990] IRLR 288, 291.
[170] See G Mead, 1990.
[171] It should also be noted that EqA 2010, s 212(2) specifies that 'act' includes 'omission'.
[172] [2010] IRLR 136; Connolly, 2010.
[173] See the judgment of Lord Hope, at [181].

is the requirement for membership of the Jewish faith according to the law of that faith'.[174] The complainant's application for admission failed because his mother, who was of Italian origin and had been a Roman Catholic prior to her conversion to Judaism, had undergone that conversion in a non-Orthodix synagogue, and so was not considered to be Jewish under the criteria operated by the OCR, which required an Orthodox conversion. The complainant argued that his exclusion amounted to discrimination on racial grounds under RRA 1976, and, specifically, to unfavourable treatment on the basis of his 'ethnic origins'.

The issue in the *JFS* case was whether the criteria adopted by the OCR and applied by the school were ethnic in nature. There was no doubt that discrimination on the grounds of religion had occurred, but this was permitted under legislation governing admissions to faith schools. The legislation in question provided no defence, on the other hand, to a claim of racial discrimination.[175]

For reasons we will explore in more detail later when we consider the meaning of the protected characteristic of race,[176] the majority in the *JFS* case ruled that there had been direct discrimination on racial grounds. Because one of the defining features of the religious test applied by the school had been qualification by descent through the matrilineal line, the criteria applied were, in the view of the majority, inherently or objectively based on ethnic grounds. Had the complainant's mother been Jewish by birth, he would have qualified for a place in the school. Thus, as Baroness Hale put it, 'it was because his mother was not descended in the matrilineal line from the original Jewish people that he was rejected'.[177]

It was agreed by all those represented in the *JFS* case that the Chief Rabbi, in adopting the OCR criteria, had not intended to act on racial grounds. According to the minority judgments, this was relevant to the disposal of the key issue in the case: the state of mind of the alleged discriminator should be taken into account in cases where the reason for the action giving rise to the treatment in question is unclear. This is not, Lord Hope said, the same thing as considering motive: 'the statutory ground of discrimination, once it has been established, is unaffected by the underlying motive for it'. However, 'where the complaint is that a black or female employee has not been selected for promotion, or has been taken off some particular duty, there will usually be a disputed issue as to the reason. This will require the tribunal to inquire more closely into the mind of the alleged discriminator'.[178] This view, while having some authority in its favour on the basis of dicta in earlier House of Lords decisions,[179] was rejected by the majority in the *JFS* case as being contrary to the objective, causal test of direct discrimination that was set out in *James*.[180] The majority position is consistent with the view that the law in this area is concerned with the effects of the employer's conduct on the complainant, not with identifying fault on the part of the

---

[174] Lord Phillips, at [50].

[175] On the statutory context of the *JFS* case, see the judgment of Lord Hope at [173]-[180]. See now EqA 2010, s 85, Sch 3, paras 6 and 7, and Sch 11, para 5; Hepple, 2011a: pp 119-121. Consideration of this legislation, which gives rise to issues of education law, is outside the scope of this book.

[176] See below, para 6.45.

[177] *R (on the application of E) v Governing Body of JFS* [2010] IRLR 136, at [66].

[178] At [196].

[179] *Nagarajan v London Regional Transport* [1999] IRLR 572, 575 (Lord Nicholls); *Chief Constable of West Yorkshire Police v Khan* [2001] IRLR 830 at [29] (Lord Nicholls).

[180] See, in particular, the judgment of Lord Clarke at [137]-[145].

employer.[181] It is only in a case where the prohibited conduct can *only* be established by reference to the employer's intention or motive that an inquiry into mental states should be conducted.[182]

Although a test based identifying the objective or factual basis for the employer's decision may be preferable, from a policy perspective, to one based on the court's assessment of mental states, the court is still left, under the but-for test, with the task of identifying a *sufficient* causal link between the treatment received by the complainant and the relevant protected characteristic.[183] This can be far from straightforward. In *Dhatt v McDonald's Hamburgers Ltd*[184] the complainant, who was Indian by birth and nationality but who had acquired the right to live and work in the UK, was asked on an application form to provide evidence of his right to do so. The employer would not have made the same request of a British citizen or other EC national. The complainant produced his passport, which was stamped 'Given leave to enter the United Kingdom for an indefinite period' and hence, properly understood, gave him the right to work; however, the employer did not accept this as adequate evidence and he was dismissed. The Court of Appeal held that there had been no infringement of the RRA 1976. According to Neill LJ, the treatment accorded to Mr Dhatt was not based on his nationality as such, but on the statutory rules, deriving from immigration legislation, that required non-UK and non-EC nationals to have the necessary authority in order to enter into employment. Stocker LJ thought that the 'vital distinction' between this case and *James* was that whereas the Council in *James* adopted the criterion of state pensionable age out of convenience, in *Dhatt* the employer 'had no alternative but to enquire whether or not an applicant was lawfully entitled to accept employment'.[185]

(v) Stereotyping

6.20   The anti-discrimination principle catches disparate treatment caused by stereotypical assumptions about the members of one group, as opposed to a belief which is specific to a particular individual. In *Horsey v Dyfed County Council*[186] Browne-Wilkinson J thought that the words 'on the grounds of' in the definition of direct discrimination in the SDA 1975 were wide enough to cover 'cases where the alleged discriminator acts on generalised assumptions as to the characteristics of women or married or coloured persons' and not just those cases where 'the sole factor influencing the decision of the alleged discriminator is the sex, marital status or race of the complainant'. In this case, Mrs Horsey lived in Aberystwyth; her husband got a job

---

[181]   Ellis, 1994: pp 564–565; para 6.12 above. The change of wording from 'on the grounds of' to 'because of' in the definition of direct discrimination in EqA 2010, s 13, was not intended by the government to effect any change in the law, and it is unlikely that such a major change in the law could have been effected in this way (see Hepple, 2011a: p 59).

[182]   *R (on the application of E) v Governing Body of JFS* [2010] IRLR 136, at [137] (Lord Clarke). For a different view, suggesting that the *JFS* case implies the 'demise' of the but-for test, see Connolly, 2010, discussing also the judgment of Underhill J in the pre-*JFS* case of *Amnesty International v Ahmed* [2009] IRLR 884, and dicta of Lord Phillips in *JFS* at [16], expressing some scepticism towards the but-for test.

[183]   In addition to the examples from racial discrimination cases discussed in this para, see the discussion of issues of causation in the context of pregnancy discrimination by Ellis, 1994: p 567. As pregnancy is now a protected characteristic in its own right, as opposed to being seen as a subset of sex discrimination, some of these difficulties have now been mitigated, although a necessary causal link must still be shown. See our discussion at paras 6.111-6.113 below.

[184]   [1991] IRLR 130; see para 3.13 above for discussion of the importance of this case in the context of access to the labour market. See also *Bullock v Alice Ottley School* [1992] IRLR 564; *Barclays Bank plc v Kapur (No 2)* [1995] IRLR 87.

[185]   [1991] IRLR 130, 134.

[186]   [1982] IRLR 395, 397. See also *Hurley v Mustoe* [1981] IRLR 208.

in London and she applied for secondment to a social service course in Maidstone so that she could live with him near his place of work. This was denied on the basis that she was unlikely to return; this view, in turn, was found to be based on a 'generalised assumption that married women follow their husband's jobs'. The EAT found that Mrs Horsey had been the victim of discrimination on the ground of her sex: she would have been treated differently had she been a comparable man.[187]

In *R (on the application of European Roma Rights Centre) v Immigration Officer at Prague Airport*[188] it was found that UK immigration officers in Prague who were operating a pre-clearance scheme for asylum seekers were subjecting Czech Roma to longer and more intrusive questioning than was the case with non-Roma. This was because 'Roma alone as a group suffer discrimination (whether or not amounting to persecution) in the Czech Republic and so in general have a much greater incentive than others to seek asylum and therefore, when being questioned at Prague airport, to lie about their intentions in visiting the United Kingdom'; as a result, the immigration officers 'are inevitably more sceptical of a Roma applicant's true intentions than those of a non-Roma, and are less easily persuaded that the Roma is genuinely intending to come only for a limited purpose'.[189] The majority of the Court of Appeal considered that this practice was not discriminatory on the grounds of race; the immigration officers had not departed from the principle that each case had to be treated on its individual merits. According to Simon Brown LJ, an employer would be entitled to take sex or race into account to the extent of questioning individual applicants for employment more intensively if this was relevant to the job in question: an employer 'interviewing for a job involving heavy lifting' was entitled 'to question a female applicant for the job more sceptically and rigorously than her male counterpart'.[190] By contrast, in his dissent (on this point), Laws LJ regarded the practice of the immigration officers as an 'inescapable' case of stereotyping.[191] On appeal to the House of Lords this view of the facts of the case was accepted, and the majority decision of the Court of Appeal overturned. As Baroness Hale put it, 'the object of the legislation is to ensure that each person is treated as an individual and not assumed to be like other members of the group'.[192]

(vi) Shared characteristics

6.21 It is not a defence to claim of direct discrimination that the employer or other respondent shares the protected characteristic which forms the basis for the claim. This was previously spelled out in the case of discrimination on the grounds of religion or belief, but now applies to each of the relevant protected characteristics.[193]

[187] See also *Skyrail Oceanic Ltd v Coleman* [1980] IRLR 226.
[188] [2003] IRLR 577 (CA), [2005] IRLR 115, HL.
[189] [2003] IRLR 577, at [67].
[190] [2003] IRLR 577, at [81].
[191] [2003] IRLR 577, at [109].
[192] [2005] IRLR 115, at [82].
[193] EqA 2010, s 24(1).

Combined or dual discrimination

6.22   Under section 14 of the 2010 Act, '[a] person (A) discriminates against another (B) if, because of a combination of two relevant protected characteristics, A treats B less favourably than A treats or would treat a person who does not share either of those characteristics'.[194] The protected characteristics to which this provision applies are age, disability, gender reassignment, race, religion or belief, sex and sexual orientation.[195] The employer has a defence under this section if it would have had the benefit of a defence or exception, such as the defence of occupational requirement, in relation to one of the relevant protected characteristics.[196] The aim of section 14 is to provide for a claim in circumstances where 'those who have experienced less favourable treatment because of a combination of two relevant characteristics' would fail under the 'single strand' approach which generally applies under the Act.

The Coalition government has decided not to bring section 14 into force, describing the provision as 'costly' to employers.[197] It is not clear, however, that the provision was necessary, or, conversely, that its non-implementation will make any difference to the operation of the law. The issue is one of identifying the correct comparator for the purposes of the various 'single strand' claims. The *Explanatory Notes*[198] give the following example (among others):

> A black woman has been passed over for promotion to work on reception because her employer thinks black women do not perform well in customer service roles. Because the employer can point to a white woman of equivalent qualifications and experience who has been appointed to the role in question, as well as a black man of equivalent qualifications and experience in a similar role, the woman may need to be able to compare her treatment because of race and sex combined to demonstrate that she has been subjected to less favourable treatment because of her employer's prejudice against black women.

It is arguable that, in a case such as this, the complainant would be able to succeed on both counts. If the case were brought as a sex discrimination claim, the appropriate comparator would be a black man; if it were brought as a race discrimination claim, the comparator would be a white woman. Since, in both cases, the complainant could show that 'but for' the protected characteristic she would not have been treated less favourably, a claim should lie. There is nothing in principle to prevent more than one type of discrimination being made out on the same facts. Thus whether, in practice, the failure to bring section 14 into force has a chilling effect on claims of 'stereotyping' based on multiple characteristics, depends on how flexibly the courts apply the comparator test. It is also arguable that the non-implementation of section 14 will diminish the exemplary effect that its enactment was intended to have, in highlighting the cumulative disadvantages suffered by particular groups.[199]

---

[194] EqA 2010, s 14(1).
[195] EqA 2010, s 14(2).
[196] EqA 2010, s 14(4).
[197] Chancellor of the Exchequer, George Osborne MP, Budget Statement, March 2011.
[198] At para 68.
[199] See Solanke, 2011, and Hepple, 2011a: pp 61-62, discussing the concepts of 'multiple' and 'intersectional' discrimination.

Indirect discrimination

6.23   The concept of indirect discrimination originates in the case law of the US Supreme Court in interpreting Title VII of the Civil Rights Act 1964.[200] Section 703(a) of that measure provides that:

> It shall be an unlawful employment practice for an employer -
> (1) to fail or refuse to hire or to discharge any individual, or otherwise to discriminate against any individual with respect to his compensation, terms, conditions, or privileges of employment, because of such individual's race, color, religion, sex, or national origin ...[201]

At first sight, this provision might appear to stretch no further than the notion of direct discrimination in UK law. However, in *Griggs v Duke Power Co*[202] the Supreme Court held that it also applied to a situation of institutional or structural discrimination arising from the common application of a rule or practice which was, *in itself*, free of racial bias. Prior to the coming into force of the Civil Rights Act, the employer in this case had discriminated against black employees by offering jobs in grades with a higher level of pay and conditions only to whites. After the Act came into effect, this practice was ended, but the employer made it a condition of transfer to the jobs in the higher grades that an employee should pass a standardised educational test. It was found that the employer had not introduced this test with any intention of perpetuating its discrimination against blacks, but, in addition, that the test was unrelated to the requirements of the jobs in question and, at the same time, tended to disqualify black applicants at a significantly higher rate than white applicants. The Court held that the use of such a test by the employer was prohibited. According to Burger CJ, 'the Act proscribes not only overt discrimination but also practices that are fair in form, but discriminatory in operation. The touchstone is business necessity. If an employment practice which operates to exclude [members of one racial group] cannot be shown to be related to job performance, the practice is prohibited'.[203]

The concept of indirect discrimination which was originally enacted in the SDA 1975 and the RRA 1976 was based on *Griggs*.[204] That definition provided that sex discrimination (for example) occurred where a person:

> ... applies to [a woman] a requirement or condition which he applies or would apply equally to a man but –
> (i)   which is such that the proportion of women who can comply with it is considerably smaller than the proportion of men who can comply with it, and
> (ii) which he cannot show to be justified irrespective of the sex of the person to whom it is applied, and
> (iii) which is to her detriment because she cannot comply with it.[205]

---

[200] See McCrudden, 1985.

[201] 42 USC s 2000e-2(a).

[202] 401 US 424 (1971).

[203] 401 US 424, 431.

[204] See Lester, 1994: p 227; *Steel v Union of Post Office Workers* [1978] ICR 181, 188; *Clarke v Eley (IMI) Kynoch Ltd* [1983] ICR 165, 171. It should be noted that later US case law on the meaning of disparate impact has qualified *Griggs* (see *Wards Cove Packing Co v Atonio* 460 US 642 (1989)) and that a number of amendments have been made to the definition of discrimination under Title VII of the Civil Rights Act 1964.

[205] SDA 1975, s 3(1)(b); RRA 1976, s 1(1)(b).

This definition was referred to by leading authorities on discrimination law as 'technical and crabbed'[206] and 'so vague ... that the effective use of the concept still depends on sympathetic judicial interpretation'.[207] In relation to discrimination on the grounds of sex, a series of changes were made with effect from October 2001, as part of the process of implementing the Burden of Proof Directive.[208] The words 'requirement or condition' were replaced by the expression 'provision, criterion or practice', sub-paragraph (i) was modified to refer to an adverse impact which was 'to the detriment of a considerably larger proportion of women than of men', the term 'justifiable' replaced 'justified' in sub-paragraph (ii), and the words 'because she cannot comply with it' in sub-paragraph (iii) were removed.

Then, under the Framework Directive on Discrimination of 2000, a completely different definition was provided. This referred to a situation where:

> ... an apparently neutral provision, criterion or practice would put persons having a particular religion or belief, a particular disability, a particular age, or a particular sexual orientation at a particular disadvantage compared with other persons, unless (i) that provision, criterion or practice is objectively justified by a legitimate aim and the means of achieving that aim are appropriate and necessary...[209]

This test, a version of which was also adopted in the context of the Race Directive[210] and later in the amended version of the Equal Treatment Directive,[211] was significantly wider than both the original test and the modified version which has been introduced for sex discrimination in 2001. It was incorporated into UK law for the purposes of employment discrimination under the SDA 1975, for those parts of the RRA 1976 which covered discrimination on the grounds of race and national or ethnic origin, and in respect of the new heads of discrimination on the grounds of sexual orientation, religion or belief, and age. Racial discrimination on the grounds of nationality or colour, which fell outside the scope of the Race Directive, was still governed by the original definition.[212] However, under the 2010 Act,[213] the new definition applies to each of the relevant protected characteristics,[214] without reference to their particular origins under UK or EU law. Section 19 EqA 2010 now provides:

> (1) A person (A) discriminates against another (B) if A applies to B a provision, criterion or practice which is discriminatory in relation to a relevant protected characteristic of B's.

---

[206] Lester, 1994: p 227.

[207] Pannick, 1985: p 40.

[208] This change took effect by virtue of the insertion of a new s 1(2) into the Act and by amending s 3 in relation to discrimination against married persons (see SI 2001/2660, reg 3).

[209] Directive 2000/78/EC, Art 2(2)(b). Sub-paragraph (ii) of Art 2(2)(b) refers to aspects of the definition which are specific to disability discrimination, on which, see paras 6.123 *et seq.*

[210] Directive 2000/43/EC, Art 2(2)(b).

[211] Directive 76/207/EEC, Art 2(2), as amended by Directive 2002/73/EC. See also Directive 2006/54/EC, Art 2(1)(b) (replacing Directive 76/207 with effect from 15 August 2009).

[212] For an illustration of the potential problems caused by this bifurcation of the legal tests for determining discrimination in race-related cases, see *Abbey National plc v Chagger* [2009] IRLR 86, [2010] IRLR 47.

[213] EqA 2010, s 19.

[214] The protected characteristic of pregnancy or maternity is not covered, with the result that indirect discrimination claims relating to this characteristic must be brought as indirect sex discrimination claims. See para 6.112 below.

(2) For the purposes of subsection (1), a provision, criterion or practice is discriminatory in relation to a relevant protected characteristic of B's if –

(a) A applies, or would apply, it to persons with whom B does not share the characteristic,

(b) it puts, or would put, persons with whom B shares the characteristic at a particular disadvantage when compared with persons with whom B does not share it,

(c) it puts, or would put, B at that disadvantage, and

(d) A cannot show it to be a proportionate means of achieving a legitimate aim.[215]

(i) From 'requirement or condition' to 'provision, criterion or practice'

6.24 A key aspect of the original 'requirement or condition' test was that the complainant should be able to point to a specific requirement which imposed an 'absolute bar' upon compliance. In *Perera v Civil Service Commission (No 2)*[216] Mr Perera, a Sri Lankan by birth who had lived in Britain for several years, claimed that he had been denied the post of legal assistant in the civil service, for which he had the necessary professional qualifications, on racially motivated grounds. He argued that other criteria taken into account by the selection board, including the candidate's age, his or her command of the English language, their experience in the UK and whether they were, or had applied to become, British citizens, had an adverse impact on him on the grounds of his race. His claim failed on the grounds that 'none of those factors could possibly be regarded as a requirement or a condition in the sense that the lack of it, whether of British nationality or even of the ability to communicate well in English, would be an absolute bar. The whole of the evidence suggests that a brilliant man whose personal qualities made him suitable as a legal assistant might well have been sent forward on a short list by the interview board in spite of being, perhaps below standard on his knowledge of English and his ability to communicate in that language'.[217]

This test set an exceptionally high hurdle for claims. By contrast, the test formulated by the US Supreme Court in *Griggs v Duke Power Co*[218] focused on 'employment practices', and this was relied on by the EAT to give a broad interpretation to the notion of 'requirement or condition' in a number of decisions which preceded *Perera*.[219] In its later decision in *Wards Cove*[220] the Supreme Court held that the plaintiff had to point to a specific employment practice as the source of adverse treatment and could not simply rely on statistical evidence of a racial or sexual imbalance between different employment categories; however, the Court did not go as far as the Court of Appeal in *Perera* in insisting on an *absolute* barrier to employment, promotion or some other benefit. The US Civil Rights Act 1991, which partially reversed *Wards Cove*, also retained the expression 'employment practice', and enabled a number of separate practices to be taken as one for the

---

[215] Section 19 largely re-enacts the previous law, but with some slight modifications to the statutory formula which amount to clarifying its application to those deterred by the potential effects of a provision, criteria or practice. See the *Explanatory Notes* at paras 77-81.

[216] [1983] ICR 428; see also *Meer v Tower Hamlets London Borough Council* [1988] IRLR 399.

[217] [1983] ICR 428, 437–438 (Stephenson LJ).

[218] 401 US 424 (1971).

[219] *Price v Civil Service Commission* [1978] ICR 27; *Clarke v Eley (IMI) Kynoch Ltd* [1983] ICR 165; *Watches of Switzerland Ltd v Savell* [1983] IRLR 141; see Pannick, 1985: p 42.

[220] 460 US 642 (1989).

purposes of defining their adverse impact if the 'decision-making process' was not sufficiently clear for them to be analysed individually.

Even prior to the 2000 Framework Directive, European Union law took a more flexible line on the definition of indirect discrimination. In *Enderby v Frenchay Health Authority*[221] it was held that a prima facie case of discrimination arose where there was an 'appreciable difference in pay between two jobs of equal value, one of which is carried out almost exclusively by women and the other predominantly by men'.[222] Hence statistical evidence of a significant disparity was sufficient to shift the burden of proof on to the employer by requiring it to justify the differential in pay, even though no precise 'requirement' or 'condition' could be established. According to Advocate General Van Gerven, 'attention should be directed less to the existence of a requirement or a hurdle by means of which women suffer a disadvantage, and more to the discriminatory result'.[223] By adopting this test, the ECJ went significantly further than the Supreme Court, which in *Wards Cove* rejected precisely this proposition: the majority in that case held that 'racial imbalance in one segment of an employer's work force does not, without more, establish a *prima facie* case of disparate impact with respect to the selection of workers'.[224] Even the US Civil Rights Act 1991 did not go as far as *Enderby* since it retained the need to show that adverse impact arose from a specific employment practice. The liberal line taken in *Enderby* was repeated in the Framework, Race and Equal Treatment Directives, each of which, as we have seen, refers to a 'provision, criterion or practice' in its definition of indirect discrimination. The incorporation of this formulation into UK law should clearly be interpreted as qualifying the rigid *Perera* test. Courts were already leaning in that direction. In *Bhudi v IMI Refiners Ltd*[225] the EAT held that an employment tribunal had erred in deciding that the employer had not imposed a requirement under section 1(1)(b) of the SDA 1975, in a case where it dismissed part-time workers for redundancy ahead of full-timers. This is consistent with a number of earlier decisions in which tribunals and courts have taken the view that such practices constitute an implicit requirement that employees should be employed on a full-time basis or its equivalent in order to retain their employment or to gain access to a particular employment-related benefit.[226] In *Falkirk Council v Whyte*[227] the EAT refused to follow *Perera*, holding that the term 'requirement' in the Act of 1975 should be given a 'liberal' interpretation with the result that it applied to a statement by the prospective employer that a certain level of training and supervisory experience was 'desirable'.[228]

---

[221] [1991] IRLR 44; on appeal [1992] IRLR 15; refd Case C-127/92 [1993] IRLR 591.

[222] [1993] IRLR 591, 595.

[223] [1993] IRLR 591, 601.

[224] 490 US 642, 653 (1989).

[225] [1994] IRLR 204.

[226] See *Clarke v Eley (IMI) Kynoch Ltd* [1983] ICR 165 and *Allonby v Accrington and Rossendale College* [2001] IRLR 364 (stressing that for this purpose, it is of no relevance that the employer might be able to point to an alternative, unobjectionable requirement); cf *Kidd v DRG (UK) Ltd* [1985] ICR 405; *Clymo v Wandsworth London Borough Council* [1989] ICR 250.

[227] [1997] IRLR 560.

[228] The reasons given by the EAT in the *Whyte* case included the existence of allegedly conflicting authority in the Court of Appeal (*Meer v Tower Hamlets London Borough Council* [1988] IRLR 399) and the need to construe the SDA 1975 in the light of Directive 76/207 (which had not then been amended). See the discussion of Connolly, 1998.

(ii) From 'adverse impact' to 'particular disadvantage'

6.25   The second element of the concept of indirect discrimination is that the provision, criterion or practice, although on the face of it applied in the same way to members of two identifiable groups or categories, should result in the members of one of those groups being disadvantaged. In determining whether 'adverse' or 'disparate impact' or, as it is now put under the current definition, 'particular disadvantage',[229] has occurred, two sets of issues arise. The first is concerned with the definition of the relevant groups or categories or, as it is sometimes put, the 'pool' which serves as the basis for comparison. The second set of issues relates to the question of whether the treatment of the two groups is materially different, in the sense of giving rise to a relevant disadvantage.

BASIS FOR COMPARISON: THE 'POOL'

6.26   In deciding whether there is disparate impact or disadvantage, it is necessary to identify a 'pool' or population within which a meaningful comparison between the advantaged and disadvantaged groups can be made. According to Sedley LJ in *Grundy v British Airways plc*,[230] the pool must be one which 'suitably tests the particular discrimination complained of'; later in his judgment he referred to the need to 'identify a cohort within which the [justification] defence can be objectively tested'.[231] Within this broadly framed approach, the identification of the pool is a question of fact for the employment tribunal; thus 'the tribunal cannot be said to have erred in law even if a different pool, with a different outcome, could equally legitimately have been chosen'.[232]

It is possible to be slightly more precise about what the notion of the pool entails. The pool, first, must contain some members of both the advantaged and disadvantaged groups. Otherwise, no comparison is possible. Thus 'it is usual to regard the pool as consisting of the aggregate of the advantaged and the disadvantaged'.[233] Second, the boundary between these two groups must have something to do with the protected characteristic which, according to the complainant, forms the basis of the disadvantage in question (that is, their sex, race, and so on). Third, the pool should consist *only* of those persons to whom the relevant provision, criterion or practice has been or could be applied: 'one should not be bringing into the comparison people who have no interest in the advantage in question'.[234] Finally, those in the pool should, aside from the characteristic in question, be in a comparable position to the complainant. This follows from the 'comparator requirement' which applies to indirect discrimination cases just as it does to direct discrimination ones.[235]

Some of the conceptual difficulties at issue here are illustrated by *Lord Chancellor v Coker*.[236] The complainants alleged, respectively, sex and race discrimination arising from the

---

[229] On the significance of the transition to the broader definition under the pre-2010 law, see the judgment of Elias P in *Eweida v British Airways plc* [2009] IRLR 78.

[230] *Grundy v British Airways plc* [2008] IRLR 74, at [27]. See also *BMA v Chaudhary* [2007] IRLR 800.

[231] *Grundy v British Airways plc* [2008] IRLR 74, at [27] and [35] respectively.

[232] *Grundy v British Airways plc* [2008] IRLR 74, at [31].

[233] *Rutherford v Secretary of State for Trade and Industry (No 2)* [2006] IRLR 551, at [60] (Lord Walker of Gestingthorpe).

[234] *Rutherford v Secretary of State for Trade and Industry (No 2)* [2006] IRLR 551, at [77] (Baroness Hale); see also *Jones v University of Manchester* [1993] IRLR 218, 226 (Ralph Gibson LJ).

[235] EqA 2010, s 23. See para 6.17 above.

[236] [1999] IRLR 396, ET; [2001] IRLR 116 EAT, [2002] IRLR 80, CA.

Lord Chancellor's decision to appoint a close acquaintance, who happened to be male, to be his special adviser, without advertising the post. The employment tribunal and the EAT accepted that a 'requirement' had been imposed as result of this method of recruitment, namely that the successful candidate had to be personally known to the Lord Chancellor. The employment tribunal went to hold, in a rather impressionistic way, that the proportion of women who could comply with this requirement was substantially smaller than the proportion of men, and that the same was true with regard to members of ethnic minority groups by comparison to whites. The EAT, in a majority judgment, reversed on the grounds that 'the Lord Chancellor determined upon only one person and thus can be said to discriminate against *everybody else* … be they men or women, and accordingly there is no relevant pool'.[237] The point was put slightly differently and, arguably, more accurately in the Court of Appeal: there was a pool of potential applicants, but because nearly everyone in it was disqualified, there could not be said to have been adverse impact. As a result, 'making an appointment from within a circle of family, friends and personal acquaintances is seldom likely to constitute indirect discrimination. Those known to the employer are likely to represent a minute proportion of those who would otherwise be qualified to fill the post'.[238]

In practice, the critical issue in determining the pool tends to be whether it is broadly or narrowly defined. In *R v Secretary of State, ex p EOC*,[239] in which the EOC successfully invoked the Equal Treatment Directive to challenge the 8- and 16-hour qualifying thresholds for employment protection rights contained in the ERA 1996, the relevant pool was taken to be the working population as a whole, and it was accepted on both sides that a prima facie case of adverse impact was made out: it was 'common ground that a very large majority of part-time employees are women and a majority of full-time employees are men, and it is common ground also that the main reason why women seek part-time employment is their responsibility as carers for children or elderly relatives'.[240] In the House of Lords decision of *Rutherford v Secretary of State for Trade and Industry (No 2)*,[241] a wide pool was used to determine whether legislation excluding employees over the age of 65 from entitlement to a redundancy payment gave rise to indirect sex discrimination. According to the Court of Appeal, it was necessary to focus on the adult workforce of Great Britain as a whole when addressing this question. An alternative approach would have been to focus on a subset of older employees, such as those employees who were approaching the age of 65 (those over 50 years old, for example) or who had passed it. A 'narrow' pool of this kind, consisting of those who were arguably most affected by the exclusionary rule, was one in which there were significantly more men than women. By contrast, in the 'wide' pool chosen by the Court of Appeal, the proportions of men and women were almost identical. In the House of Lords, Lords Nicholls and Walker followed the Court of Appeal's approach and reached the same conclusion, namely that the gap in treatment between the two groups was not sufficiently large to merit a finding of adverse impact. The majority, consisting of Lords Scott and Rodger and Baroness Hale, decided the case on other grounds. In so far as *Rutherford (No 2)* can be read as

[237] [2001] IRLR 116, 121.
[238] [2002] IRLR 80, at [39].
[239] [1991] IRLR 493; affd [1993] IRLR 10; on appeal [1994] IRLR 176; see para 3.55 above. See also, on this point, Case C-167/97 *R v Secretary of State for Employment, ex p Seymour-Smith* [1999] IRLR 253.
[240] [1993] IRLR 10, 13 (Dillon LJ); cf the sceptical comments of Nolan LJ in the Divisional Court [1991] IRLR 493, 500.
[241] [2006] IRLR 551.

providing guidance on the correct definition of the pool,[242] the approach of Lords Nicholls and Walker implies that when considering the legality of legislation which is national in its scope, the starting point is to consider its impact on the workforce as a whole, and only to narrow the focus on to a subset of it if to do so can be justified by reference to an objective factor of some kind. In this case, all workers in Great Britain were potentially affected by the exclusionary rule, and it was not possible to identify a narrower category by reference to age, in the way argued by the complainants, without drawing arbitrary boundaries within this wider group.

A further decision in which widening the pool operated to the complainant's disadvantage is *Jones v University of Manchester*.[243] Here the respondent advertised for a career officer who had to be 'a graduate, preferably aged 27–35 years with a record of successful experience in an industrial, commercial or public service setting'. Miss Jones, who was aged 46 when she applied for the post but was otherwise well qualified for it, was not shortlisted, apparently on the grounds of her age. She had attended university as a mature student and had obtained her degree when aged 38. The employment tribunal found that she had been the victim of unlawful sex discrimination. For this purpose, the relevant pool was taken to consist of all mature students graduating after the age of 25. Of this group, the proportion of women who took their degrees after the age of 30 was considerably larger than the proportion of men; on this basis, the tribunal concluded that the proportion of women able to comply with the age condition in the advertisement was considerably smaller than the proportion of men. The EAT reversed this aspect of the tribunal's decision on the grounds that the wrong pool had been used, and their view was upheld on appeal. The Court of Appeal held that the correct total in this case was *all graduates*, and not just those who graduated as mature students. This was because the job was open to all those with a degree and not just those who had been mature students. As a result, the proportion of women capable of meeting the requirement was greater than it would otherwise have been and considerably closer to the relevant proportion of men.

The pool may also be confined to a subset of the members of a particular organisation. In *Staffordshire County Council v Black*[244] an employer decided, under the terms of its pension scheme, to credit full-time workers with additional contributions on the basis of past service, but to credit additional contributions to part-time workers only in respect of their past service under their regular contracts of employment, without regard for additional duties carried out under supply contracts and temporary contracts of employment. The tribunal took as the relevant pool those employees of the council who were aged 50 or more at the time Mrs Black was made redundant, on the grounds that only this group had been eligible for the additional contributions in question. It found that of this group, 89.5% of women worked full-time (and so qualified for the higher rate of additional contribution), compared to 97% of men. On this basis it concluded that the

---

[242] It is hard to identify a clear *ratio decidendi* from the majority opinions. One possible ratio is that there was no true exclusionary rule, or as it would now be put, no relevant provision, criterion or practice, in this case. As Lord Scott put it (at [16]), 'everyone who survives and for whom employment is available can decide, by not entering or continuing in employment, to be a person unaffected by the disadvantage'. This view is surprising, since the rule being considered in *Rutherford (No2)* was arguably no different, in this respect, to the qualifying conditions under employment protection legislation which had previously been treated as potentially giving rise to adverse impact (as in the *Ex p EOC* case [1994] IRLR 176). The loosening of the definition of indirect discrimination which has occurred since the facts of the *Rutherford* litigation arose makes it unlikely that this aspect of the case will be followed in future.

[243] [1993] IRLR 218, 226.

[244] [1995] IRLR 234.

proportion of women capable of complying with the full-time requirement was not considerably smaller than the proportion of men, and the EAT agreed that this difference was 'very small'.[245]

In *Black*, the choice of a pool which was confined to a particular category of employees in a particular organisation limited the complainant's chances of success, because she happened to work in a profession and for an organisation where an unusually large proportion of women worked full-time. In *Ex p EOC* and *Rutherford (No 2)* the courts were considering the impact of legislation affecting all employees working in Great Britain: this made the broad scale of the comparison appropriate. But more generally, it is arguable that to narrow the size of the relevant pool, as occurred in *Black*, is to undermine the purpose of indirect discrimination: Pannick, for example, suggests that 'section 1(1)(b) and the principle of disparate impact do not intend to make one's rights dependent on the arbitrary factors of where one works, and the number of men and women who do particular jobs there'.[246] Similarly, in *R v Secretary of State for Education, ex p Schaffter*[247] Schiemann J commented that with the choice of a very small pool, there is a 'real risk that you have incorporated an act of discrimination into your definition'.

By contrast, a narrow pool can sometimes assist a claim. In *Somerset County Council v Pike*[248] the complainant was a schoolteacher who took early retirement on the grounds of ill health and subsequently returned to work on a part-time basis. She challenged a rule of her pension scheme under which part-time employment after retirement was not pensionable, but full-time employment was. She argued that the relevant pool consisted only of those teaching after retirement, on the basis of which she was able to show that women teachers were significantly more adversely affected than men. The employer argued for a wider pool, consisting of all teachers, pre- and post-retirement, in which case the evidence of adverse impact was much less clear. The Court of Appeal ruled that the narrower pool was appropriate in this case since, applying the *Rutherford* test, pre-retirement teachers had no interest in the application of the rule.

These cases suggest that it is difficult to generalise from individual decisions on the question of whether a 'wide' or 'narrow' pool is appropriate. There is much to be said for an approach in which the decision on the size of the pool is established by the tribunal after comparing the alternatives available to it in the light of the particular claim it is considering.[249]

Degree of impact

6.27   The original statutory formula required the complainant to show that a 'considerably smaller proportion' of the allegedly disadvantaged group could comply with the requirement or condition. The current test requires the complainant to show that the members of one group suffered a 'particular disadvantage' as opposed to the other. In *R v Secretary of State for Employment, ex p Seymour-Smith*,[250] it was found that the proportion of women meeting the then two-year

---

[245] [1995] IRLR 234, 238.

[246] Pannick, 1985: p 47.

[247] [1987] IRLR 53, 56.

[248] [2009] IRLR 870.

[249] See *Ministry of Defence v DeBique* [2010] IRLR 471, in which the tribunal's carefully reasoned choice of a narrow pool was upheld by the EAT. See also the judgment of Sedley LJ in *Eweida v British Airways plc* [2010] IRLR 322 at [14], expressing scepticism on attempts to produce a workable general definition of the 'pool'.

[250] [1994] IRLR 448, DC; varied [1995] IRLR 464, CA; refd [1997] IRLR 315, HL; Case C-167/97 [1999] IRLR 253, ECJ; [2000] IRLR 263, HL; Freedland, 1994; Barnard and Hepple, 1999, 2000; Townshend-Smith, 2000. See also para 3.50 above.

qualifying period for unfair dismissal protection was approximately 90% of the proportion of men who met this requirement; put differently, about 77% of all male employees in the United Kingdom at the relevant time were capable of qualifying under this rule, compared to 69% of all female employees. The House of Lords, applying a ruling of the ECJ, held that although this was not in itself a sufficiently large gap, a finding of adverse impact was justified because the disparity persisted at a more or less constant level over many years.[251]

In *London Underground Ltd v Edwards (No 2)*[252] the Court of Appeal held that in a case where 100% of male employees could comply with a requirement for flexible hours working, but only 95% of women could comply, there was again a sufficient difference in treatment for a finding of adverse impact. This case suggests that there is more to the test than a purely mechanical application of statistical differences. In *Edwards*, the complainant (who was a single parent) was the only woman out of 21 female train drivers who was unable to comply with the requirement; but there were over 2,000 male train drivers, all of whom could comply with it. The Court held that it was not appropriate to apply any rule of thumb defining the threshold level below which a difference in the impact of the requirement could not be regarded as sufficient, and that, in this case, the tribunal had been entitled to have regard to the very large disparity between the number of male and female train drivers employed by the respondent. It was also relevant in this case that, among the working population as a whole, women were much more likely than men to be single parents and hence unable to comply with an employer's requirement for flexible working.

Under US anti-discrimination law some courts have applied a presumption that the success rate of those in the disadvantaged group should not be more than 80% of the success rate for the other group.[253] This standard was derived from the Uniform Guidelines of the US Equal Employment Opportunities Commission, but it is not strictly binding and many courts apply instead a more open-ended test of what amounts to 'substantial' or 'significant' impact.[254] More generally, there is a good argument that in principle it should be 'inappropriate to deny the character of [indirect] discrimination to any disparity which is more than *de minimis*',[255] although the courts are currently a long way from accepting this.[256]

A plausible reading of the current definition of indirect discrimination is that the court or tribunal is no longer required to identify a particular level of statistical discrepancy in the treatment of the two groups. The Labour Government's proposals for a single Equality Bill envisaged that what is now section 19 would open up 'the possibility of expert evidence or witness evidence being used rather than detailed statistical analysis to show particular disadvantage', an important change 'for strands such as sexual orientation and religion or belief, where reliable

---

[251] See also Lord Walker's opinion in *Rutherford (No 2)* at [59]–[60] for an assessment of the degree of disparity in that case (discussed above, at para 6.26). See para 5.8 above for changes to the qualifying period for unfair dismissal and the current position.

[252] [1998] IRLR 364. See also, on the issue of the degree of adverse impact, *Whiffen v Milham Ford Girls' School* [2001] IRLR 468; *Chief Constable of Bedfordshire Constabulary v Graham* [2002] IRLR 239.

[253] See, eg, *United States v City of Chicago* 648 F 2d 531 (1982); and see *McCausland v Dungannon District Council* [1993] IRLR 583, a case under the Fair Employment (Northern Ireland) Act 1989, in which 1.5% of all Catholics and 2.1% of all Protestants were able to meet a qualifying condition for a post. As the one figure was calculated as 71% of the other, the Northern Ireland Court of Appeal held that a 'considerably smaller proportion' of Catholics could comply.

[254] See *Moore v South Western Bell Telephone Co* 593 F 2d 607 (1982).

[255] Freedland, 1994: p 340.

[256] See, eg, *Nelson v Carillion Services Ltd* [2003] IRLR 428, in which the Court of Appeal held that it was possible to ignore a statistical disparity based on a small pool which the court considered to be 'fortuitous' rather than 'significant'.

statistics are not available, and where there are issues of privacy involved in gathering data which might provide statistics'.[257]

6.28   The approach to adverse impact contained in the 'old' definition required a comparison of relative success rates, and appeared to rule out alternative bases of comparison, such as a focus on relative failure rates. If failure rates had been considered in *Black*, for example, the result there could have been expressed as a finding that the proportion of women failing to meet the requirement was three times as great as it was for men (10% as opposed to 3%). In *R v Secretary of State for Employment, ex p Seymour-Smith*[258] it was suggested by the Divisional Court, at an early stage of the litigation, that the use of comparative failure rates would only be appropriate if success rates in each case were very low; the House of Lords left the matter open when applying the ruling of the ECJ on this issue.[259] In *Rutherford v Secretary of State for Trade and Industry (No 2)* the Court of Appeal held that a focus on the disadvantaged group was not required by the Burden of Proof Directive: that Directive did not prescribe a particular methodology for assessing the statistical evidence, thereby leaving it up to national courts to 'work out from case to case a satisfactory method … applying considerations of logic, relevance and common sense'.[260] Section 1(2) SDA 1975, as it then was, as amended in the light of the Directive, directed attention to a provision, criterion or practice 'which is such that it would be to the detriment of a considerably larger proportion of women than of men'; by contrast, the original formula under section 1(1)(b) of the Act referred to a requirement 'which is such that the proportion of women who can comply with it is considerably smaller than the proportion of men who can comply with it'. The implication of the Court of Appeal judgment in *Rutherford* is that this change made no difference to the law, but if this is so, given the change in the relevant wording, it is surprising. When *Rutherford (No 2)* reached the House of Lords, Lord Walker, while not ruling out the use of the disadvantage-based approach, referred to the difficulty in taking a disadvantage-based approach 'with any intellectual consistency' in a case where the advantaged formed the vast majority of the pool.[261] As we have seen, the majority of the House decided the case on other grounds.

A more radical alternative approach to the assessment of adverse impact is not to compare the relative success rates of the two groups (for example, women and men) but to compare instead the sexual or racial composition of the group of those who are able to comply with the composition of the group consisting of those who cannot. For example, it may be that in a given case, women and men make up roughly 50% each of the relevant pool. We would then expect roughly the same proportion of women and men to be found in the two groups of those able and those not able to comply with the requirement. Where there is a significant disparity, there may be the basis for a finding of adverse impact. What is being compared here is not the relative success rate of women and men, but the sexual composition of the failed group and the successful group; and the picture presented may be completely different as a result.

---

[257] *Government Response to the Consultation*, at para 7.25.
[258] [1994] IRLR 448; Freedland, 1994.
[259] See Case C-167/97, [1999] IRLR 253, ECJ; [2000] IRLR 263, HL.
[260] [2004] IRLR 892, at [35] (Mummery LJ).
[261] [2006] IRLR 551, at [67].

Hence in *Staffordshire County Council v Black*[262] the pool consisted of 1,772 teachers who were over the age of 50. Of these, 1,141 were women (64% of the total) and 631 were men (36%). One hundred and thirty-nine persons out of the group as a whole could not comply with the full-time requirement imposed by the employer; of these, 120 were women (86%) and 19 were men (14%). So whereas women made up 86% of the failed group, they represented only 64% of the pool as a whole, arguably a substantial difference, and certainly a more substantial adverse impact than appears from the measurement of comparative success rates.

This 'compositional' approach is not necessarily a better way of assessing adverse impact than the comparison of success rates; but it is not clear that it is any worse, in principle. In particular, it may be appropriate to use the compositional approach in situations where, as in the example just given, numbers in the disadvantaged group are small in relation to the pool as a whole. This is because '[t]he smaller the disadvantaged group in proportionate terms, the narrower will be the differential' in terms of comparative success rates.[263] As far as cases brought under the British anti-discrimination Acts were concerned, the original definition of indirect discrimination in section 1(1)(b) of SDA 1975 and RRA 1976, because it expressly directed the attention of the tribunal to relative success rates, could be read as ruling out the 'compositional' approach. However, under European Union sex discrimination law it would seem to be a viable option. Such a test seems implicit, for example, in the concept of indirect discrimination adopted by ECJ in *Enderby v Frenchay Health Authority*: 'if the pay of speech therapists is significantly lower than that of pharmacists and if the former are almost exclusively women while the latter are predominantly men, there is a prima facie case of sex discrimination, at least where the two jobs are of equal value'.[264] This would benefit complainants who were in a position to invoke the doctrine of direct effect to claim rights under Article 157 TFEU and the Equal Treatment Directive. There should also be more scope to apply the compositional approach in the light of the progressive loosening of the test of indirect discriminaton, under the influence of EU law standards, which has resulted in its current formulation in section 19 of the 2010 Act. Thus in *Rutherford (No 2)* Lord Walker, after exploring both the relevant EU law jurisprudence and the domestic cases, discussed a hypothetical case in which 'the advantaged 95% were split equally between women and men, but the disadvantaged 5% were all women'; in such a case, 'the very strong disparity of disadvantage would, I think, make it a special case, and the fact that the percentages of the advantaged were not greatly different... would not be decisive'.[265]

To similar effect is the decision of the Court of Appeal in *Grundy v British Airways plc*.[266] Here the complainant was part of a group employed on flexible working arrangements who claimed to be disadvantaged by a scheme under which they did not qualify for increments as

---

[262] [1995] IRLR 234.

[263] *Barry v Midland Bank plc* [1999] IRLR 581, 586 (Lord Nicholls of Birkenhead). Although Lord Nicholls concurred in the result in this case, the reasoning he offered on the point of adverse impact was not that of the majority, so the validity of his approach remains open to further argument. See Thomas, 2000.

[264] Case C-127/92, [1993] IRLR 591, 595; the same approach was recommended by the ECJ in Case C-236/98 *Jämställdhetsombudsmannen v Örebro Läns Landsting* [2000] IRLR 421. It was also adopted by Mustill LJ in *Jones v Chief Adjudication Officer* [1990] IRLR 533, a decision on the meaning of Directive 79/7 on equality in state social security, and approved by Ralph Gibson LJ and Evans LJ in *Jones v University of Manchester* [1993] IRLR 218, although neither judge in that case seems to have considered the argument that this might not be compatible with the formula in SDA 1975, s 1(1)(b), which was being applied in that case.

[265] [2006] IRLR 551, at [67].

[266] [2008] IRLR 74.

full-time, regular staff did. The employment tribunal held that there was adverse impact as the disadvantaged group was predominantly female (by a ratio of around 20 to 1). The EAT reversed on the grounds that that the tribunal should have focused on the advantaged group which was also female-dominated (by a ratio of around 2 to 1). Of the total pool, over 90% were in the advantaged group. The Court of Appeal restored the tribunal's ruling, holding that it had not erred in its choice of pool. As we have seen,[267] it held that the correct test was whether there was a causative link involving discrimination between the treatment of the applicant and the inequality of pay. Assessing adverse impact was a question of fact for the tribunal and it had discretion to determine how to define the pool, as long as it was done in such a way as to identify a cohort within which the material factor defence could be objectively tested.

COMPLIANCE AND DISADVANTAGE

6.29   Under the 'old' test, the complainant had to show that the members of one group were proportionately *less able to comply* with the relevant condition of requirement. The phrase 'can comply' was, on the whole, flexibly interpreted. In *Mandla v Dowell Lee*[268] a school refused to allow Sikh students to wear turbans, on the grounds that this was not an acceptable part of the school uniform. The House of Lords held that this amounted to indirect discrimination. According to Lord Fraser, the phrase 'can comply', in the context of the concept of indirect discrimination, should be read 'not as meaning "can physically"', so as to indicate a theoretical possibility, but as meaning "can in practice" or "can consistently with the customs and cultural traditions of the racial group"'.

Similarly, in *Price v Civil Service Commission*[269] the EAT thought that it 'should not be said that a person "can" do something merely because it is theoretically possible for him to do so; it is necessary to see whether he can do so in practice'. This case concerned a maximum age bar for a particular employment which Mrs Price claimed was indirectly discriminatory on the grounds of sex. The EAT held that 'it is relevant in determining whether women can comply with the condition to take into account the current usual behaviour of women in this respect, as observed in practice, putting on one side behaviour and responses which are unusual or extreme'. In this respect, 'knowledge and experience suggest that a considerable number of women between the mid-twenties and the mid-thirties are engaged in bearing children and in minding children, and that while many find it possible to take up employment many others, while desiring to do so, find it impossible, and that many of the latter as their children get older find that they can follow their wish and seek employment'. This flexible approach is one which the courts followed in numerous other decisions on the application of the 'old' test, with the result that working practices involving full-time working for a standard or regular working week were found, on the whole, to disadvantage female employees as a group.[270]

---

[267] See para 6.26 above.
[268] [1983] ICR 385, 394; *JH Walker Ltd v Hussain* [1996] IRLR 11.
[269] [1978] ICR 27, 31.
[270] See *Meeks v NUAAW* [1976] IRLR 198; *Home Office v Holmes* [1984] ICR 678; *Clarke v Eley (IMI) Kynoch Ltd* [1983] ICR 165; *Bhudi v IMI Refiners Ltd* [1994] IRLR 204; *Meade-Hill v British Council* [1995] IRLR 478 ; *Shaw v CCL Ltd* [2008] IRLR 284; although there were cases in which this argument failed (see *Clymo v Wandsworth London Borough Council* [1989] ICR 250; *Kidd v DRG (UK) Ltd* [1985] IRLR 405).

Under the current test, there is no need to show that members of the disadvantaged group suffered a disadvantage because they were unable to comply with the relevant provision, criterion or practice. Their disadvantage might, indeed, have arisen precisely by virtue of their ability to comply with it. In that sense, the new test would seem to be more flexible than the old one.[271] However, the new test may present fresh conceptual difficulties of its own, in the sense of blurring the boundaries between the advantaged and disadvantaged groups. In *Eweida v British Airways plc*[272] the complainant, a devout practising Christian, was disciplined for insisting on wearing a plain silver cross while working as a member of the respondent airline's check-in staff. The employer allowed religious items to be worn in a visible way only if they were 'mandatory' religious requirements, could not be concealed beneath the wearer's uniform, and had specific management approval. The complainant did not argue that wearing a cross while at work was a 'mandatory' requirement of her religion, but she did claim that to do so was an expression of her religious beliefs. Her claim was rejected, the EAT ruling that the tribunal had been correct to find that there had been no indirect discrimination on the grounds of religion or belief. It was necessary, the EAT held, for the complainant to show that Christians generally, including those who were willing to comply with the restriction imposed by the employer, would have regarded themselves as disadvantaged by it. The EAT's ruling was upheld by the Court of Appeal, which held that in the context of an indirect discrimination claim, it was insufficient to show that the individual claimant had suffered disadvantage; there had to be adverse impact on an identifiable group, of which she could show she was a member. According to the Court of Appeal, whether the disadvantaged group was defined more or less expansively in *Eweida*, the claim failed. *Eweida* can be seen as a decision in which, in the comparatively new field of discrimination based on religion or belief, the courts did not feel able to make the type of broad assumptions about social norms and practices that have become widely accepted in sex and race discrimination cases,[273] but it also indicates the potential for high evidential burdens of a novel kind to be raised in the context of the new indirect discrimination test.

The original indirect discrimination test stipulated that the requirement or condition had to be to the 'detriment' of the complainant because he or she 'cannot comply with it'.[274] This provision was meant to make it clear that the individual complainant must have been disadvantaged by the requirement in question, but it was not clear that it succeeded in this.[275] The current definition of indirect discrimination refers to a provision, criterion or practice which, in addition to putting members of the group at a particular disadvantage compared to others, also 'puts [the complainant] at that disadvantage',[276] thereby capturing essentially the same idea. The old case law established that individual detriment had to be assessed at the time at which the condition or requirement was to be fulfilled, and not at some future hypothetical time;[277] the same principle would seem to apply under the current test. We examine the meaning of 'detriment' and individual 'disadvantage', in greater detail in our discussion of the substantive scope of the employment discrimination legislation.[278]

---

[271] See *Eweida v British Airways* [2009] IRLR 78, at [44] (Elias P).
[272] [2009] IRLR 78.
[273] See the judgment of Elias P at in the EAT, [2009] 78, at [51]–[54], and that of Sedley LJ in the CA, [2010] IRLR 322, at [40].
[274] SDA 1975, s 1(1)(b)(iii); RRA 1976, s 1(1)(b)(iii).
[275] See Pannick, 1985: pp 54–55, for an account of the legislative history of this provision in the SDA 1975.
[276] EqA 2010, s 19(2)(c).
[277] *Steel v Union of Post Office Workers* [1978] ICR 181, 186.
[278] See para 6.51 below.

(iii) Justification

THE TEST OF PROPORTIONALITY

6.30   The respondent could escape liability under the 'old' definition contained in the SDA 1975 if it could show the requirement or condition to be justifiable 'irrespective of the sex of the person to whom it is applied' or, in the case of the original formula of the RRA 1976, to be justifiable irrespective of their 'colour, race, nationality or ethnic or national origins'.[279] The current definition allows a defence where the respondent cannot show the provision, criterion or practice 'to be a proportionate means of achieving a legitimate aim'.[280] It is likely that the new test will not be significantly different from the old one in this respect, since the concepts of proportionality and legitimacy had already been read into the statutory formula by virtue of the influence of EU law, in particular the relevant case law of the ECJ.[281] The low point in the evolution of the test was *Ojutiku v Manpower Services Commission*[282] in which the Court of Appeal thought that 'if a person produces reasons for doing something, which would be acceptable to right-thinking people as sound and tolerable reasons for so doing, then he has justified his conduct'.[283] Moreover, this implied 'a lower standard than the word "necessary"'.[284] By contrast, the proportionality test developed by the ECJ requires,[285] first of all, that the practice be capable of justification by reference to an objective which is, in itself, legitimate; second, that it employs means which are appropriate and necessary to the achievement of that end; and third that, on balance, the means chosen do not unduly interfere with the principle of equality. This is a much stricter test since it enables the tribunal not just to judge the value of the objective being put forward by the alleged perpetrator, but also the legitimacy of the means chosen to implement it and their relationship to the end in question. In particular, it strikes at discriminatory practices in cases where alternative means were available which could have achieved the objective sought without interfering to the same extent with the principle of equality.[286]

In *R v Secretary of State for Employment, ex p EOC*[287] the House of Lords, applying the proportionality test, struck down the 8- and 16-hour qualifying thresholds which were at that time contained in Schedule 13 of the EPCA 1978, on the grounds that they were incompatible with the Equal Treatment Directive. The *EOC* case indicates, firstly, that the burden of demonstrating justification is on the respondent once a prima facie finding of adverse impact is made, and, secondly, that a strict standard of proof will be applied to claims of the effectiveness of the means chosen to meet the end being aimed at. The defence offered by the Secretary of State was that the hours thresholds, by excluding certain part-time workers from statutory employment protection

---

[279] SDA 1975, s 1(1)(b)(ii); RRA 1976, s 1(1)(b)(ii). The original RRA definition still applies to colour and nationality. See para 6.46 below.

[280] EqA 2010, s 19(2)(d).

[281] See Baker, 2008.

[282] [1982] ICR 661.

[283] [1982] ICR 661, 668 (Eveleigh LJ).

[284] [1982] ICR 661, 670 (Kerr LJ).

[285] See in particular Case 170/84 *Bilka-Kaufhaus GmbH v Weber von Hartz* [1986] IRLR 317; Case 171/88 *Rinner-Kühn v FWW Spezial-Gebäudereinigung Gmbh* [1989] IRLR 493; Case C-1/95 *Gerster v Freistaat Bayern* [1997] IRLR 699; Case C-100/95 *Kording v Senator für Finanzen* [1997] IRLR 710.

[286] A similar approach has been adopted by some US courts under Title VII: see eg *Robinson v Lorillard Corpn* 444 F 2d 791 (1971).

[287] [1994] IRLR 176.

rights, encouraged employers to hire more workers than they would otherwise have done to work on a part-time basis. Although the promotion of jobs was accepted to be a legitimate goal of social policy, the House of Lords held that the Secretary of State had failed to show that the means chosen were appropriate to this end. There was, said Lord Keith, no 'factual evidence'[288] to support the argument being offered.

This strict test was however put in doubt as a result of the litigation which took place over the lawfulness of the two-year qualifying period for unfair dismissal in *R v Secretary of State for Employment, ex p Seymour-Smith*.[289] In contrast to the rather brief discussion in *ex p EOC*, on this occasion there was an extended analysis by the courts of the statistical and other evidence offered by the government. The Divisional Court and Court of Appeal considered the evidence to be inadequate, with some critical comments being passed on the value of the surveys which the Department of Employment had carried out in the mid-1980s in support of the policy of labour market deregulation.[290] When, however, the case reached the ECJ on a preliminary reference from the House of Lords, the Court enunciated a more flexible test which, when applied by the House, resulted in a finding in favour of the government. A plausible reading of *Seymour-Smith* is that it liberalised the basic test for cases of legislative policy only,[291] with the result that it is necessary to consider this category separately from other cases.

In the *JFS* case it was not necessary for the majority to consider the issue of indirect discrimination, as they held that direct discrimination on racial grounds was made out on the facts, but the nature of the test for indirect discrimination received extensive argument before the Supreme Court and was considered by all the Justices except Lord Phillips. It was generally accepted that there had been adverse impact in this case as the school's admissions criteria disadvantaged applicants who were not Jewish by reference to the criterion of descent through the matrilineal line. The judgments of both the majority and minority Justices contain important guidance on the approach to be taken when applying the proportionality test. Lord Mance, with whose judgment three other majority Justices agreed on this point,[292] held that the correct test to apply was the 'exacting EC test of proportionality'[293] set out by Mummery LJ in *R (Elias) v Secretary of State for Defence*.[294] Mummery LJ's judgment in *Elias* makes it clear that the burden of proving justification is on the alleged discriminator, which must show that it addressed the issue of adverse impact when formulating the provision, criterion or practice in question, at least where it is a public body. In the employment context, applying *Elias* by extension, the provision must correspond to a real need of the employer and it must be shown that the means used were appropriate and necessary to that aim, with the seriousness of the detriment to the disadvantaged group being weighed against the employer's needs. Where this strict test is applied, the effect is that an employer may be unable to demonstrate justification if an alternative means of meeting

[288] [1994] IRLR 176, 182; see also para 3.55 above, and Deakin, 1994a.

[289] [1994] IRLR 448, DC; varied [1995] IRLR 464, CA; refd [1997] IRLR 315, HL; Case C-167/97 [1999] IRLR 253, ECJ; [2000] IRLR 263, HL.

[290] For discussion of this point see Freedland, 1994: p 341.

[291] Although see the judgment of the EAT in *Lord Chancellor v Coker* [2001] IRLR 116, 122, assuming the opposite point of view; but the specific context of the *Seymour-Smith* decision was apparently not considered in that case.

[292] Baroness Hale and Lords Kerr and Clarke.

[293] *JFS*, [2010] IRLR 136, at [97].

[294] [2006] IRLR 934, at [151]. *Elias*, like *JFS*, was not an employment case (it concerned claims for compensation under a government scheme set up to provide assistance to former prisoners of war), but the principles it lays down on the issue of the definition of indirect discrimination are of general application.

its needs could have been used, which would have involved less disadvantage to the interests of the affected group. In the *JFS* case the four majority Justices who considered the matter thought that the school's policy failed the justification test because it could not be shown that it promoted the aim of maintaining the school's religious ethos.[295] Two of the minority Justices, Lords Hope and Walker, also held against the school on the slightly different ground that the school had not done enough to show that alternative means of achieving its goal, which would have avoided adverse impact on racial grounds, were considered.[296] Lords Brown and Rodger, on the other hand, thought that the school had done enough to satisfy the proportionality test, and pointed to the dangers of the courts interfering in the school's admissions policy or in the criteria for entry drawn up by the Office of the Chief Rabbi.[297] On the whole, the *JFS* judgments show that a strict approach to the test of proportionality can result in a high level of external scrutiny of decisions which result in group disadvantage.

LEGITIMATE JUSTIFICATIONS: STATE POLICY

6.31   The range of potentially legitimate justifying factors is extensive at the level of state policy. It not only covers the goals of increasing labour market participation and job creation which were defended in *ex p EOC* and *ex p Seymour-Smith*, but also measures taken to promote the growth of smaller firms. Thus in *Kirshammer-Hack v Sidal*[298] the ECJ considered, from this point of view, the validity of a German law which excluded from dismissal protection undertakings employing five or fewer employees, and for this purpose did not count employees working less than ten hours per week or 45 hours per month. The German government argued that this legislation was 'intended to alleviate the constraints on small businesses, which play an essential role in economic development and job-creation within the Community'. The Court held that even if there was a prima facie case of indirect discrimination in this instance (which it doubted), the grounds put forward in defence of the legislation were potentially legitimate: Article 118a of the EC Treaty (now Article 153 TFEU), which qualified the power to adopt directives in the area of health and safety by reference to the need to avoid 'imposing administrative, financial and legal constraints in a way which would hold back the creation and development of small and medium-sized undertakings', meant that under Community law 'these undertakings can be the object of special economic measures'.[299]

In other decisions under EU sex discrimination law, the ECJ has held that Member States have a wide 'margin of discretion' in determining the range of relevant factors which may be weighed in the balance against the principle of equal treatment.[300] In *Seymour-Smith* it stated that the relevant test was whether 'the … rule reflects a legitimate aim of [the government's] social policy, that that aim is unrelated to any discrimination based on sex, and that … [the government]

---

[295]   *JFS*, at [100] (Lord Mance).

[296]   *JFS*, at [211]-[214] (Lord Hope) and [235] (Lord Walker).

[297]   *JFS*, at [255]-[256] (Lord Brown), and [233] (Lord Rodger).

[298]   Case C-189/91 [1994] IRLR 185.

[299]   [1994] IRLR 185, 188.

[300]   Case C-317/93 *Nolte v Landesversicherungsanstalt Hannover* [1996] IRLR 225; Case C-444/93 *Megner and Scheffel v Innungskrankenkasse Vorderpfalz* [1996] IRLR 236; but see also the limits to the margin of discretion laid down in Case C-226/98 *Jorgensen v Foreningen Af Speciallæger and Synesikringens Forhandlingsudvalg* [2000] IRLR 726.

… could reasonably consider that the means chosen were suitable for attaining that aim'.[301] It was in applying this test that the House of Lords ruled in favour of the UK Government.[302]

EMPLOYERS' JUSTIFICATIONS

6.32   At the level of practices undertaken by individual employers, numerous justifying factors are also available. On the whole, even though, under the test enunciated by the House of Lords in *Rainey*,[303] objective grounds of an economic, technical or administrative nature must be advanced, this category has been widely defined. In *Clymo v Wandsworth London Borough Council*[304] the employer was found to be justified in refusing to allow a job-sharing arrangement for what it claimed were reasons of managerial efficiency. In *Mandla v Dowell Lee*[305] the House of Lords could find no objective justification in a rule that forbade pupils from wearing a turban at a school, but in *Board of Governors of St Matthias Church of England School v Crizzle*[306] a school was held to be justified in requiring that its headteacher should be a communicant Christian (thereby causing a situation of adverse impact on racial grounds against the complainant, who was an Asian), since this was thought necessary to sustain the particular religious nature of the school as defined by its governors.[307] In *Eweida v British Airways plc*[308] the employment tribunal found that the employer had failed to justify a rule that check-in staff could not wear visible religious items (in this case, a plain silver cross) except under strict conditions; the EAT reversed on other grounds but dismissed an appeal on this point.[309] By contrast, in *Azmi v Kirklees Metropolitan Borough Council*[310] the EAT held that the employment tribunal had been entitled to find that a requirement that a Muslim schoolteacher should not wear a veil while teaching children was a proportionate means of meeting a legitimate aim, namely that of ensuring that the children could learn effectively, while in *Ladele v London Borough of Islington*[311] the Court of Appeal held that the employer's policy of instructing the complainant to conduct civil partnership registrations, to which she has objected on religious grounds, was a proportionate means of implementing its anti-discrimination policy.[312] In contrast to the specific grounds of justification relied on in these cases, employers have not generally succeeded in arguing that simple cost avoidance, in and of itself, is a legitimate goal, although on the rather unusual facts of *Woodcock v Cumbria*

---

[301]   Case C-167/97 [1999] IRLR 253, Judgment, at para 77.

[302]   [2000] IRLR 263. Cf *Hockenjos v Secretary of State for Social Security* [2005] IRLR,471. In *Rutherford v Secretary of State for Trade and Industry (No 2)* [2004] IRLR 892, [2006] IRLR 551 a number of policy-related grounds were put forward for justifying the denial of redundancy compensation to employees over the age of 65; in the event, the case was decided on other grounds. See below, para 6.44, for a discussion of possible justifications for age discrimination of this kind.

[303]   [1987] IRLR 26.

[304]   [1989] ICR 250.

[305]   [1983] IRLR 209.

[306]   [1993] IRLR 472.

[307]   *Crizzle* would now be seen as a case of direct discrimination on religious grounds, and would thereby trigger consideration of the scope of the GOR defences for religious employers under EqA 2010, Sch 9. See below, para 6.55.

[308]   [2009] IRLR 78.

[309]   The point was not considered by the Court of Appeal, which also ruled in favour of the employer ([2010] IRLR 322).

[310]   [2007] IRLR 484.

[311]   [2010] IRLR 211.

[312]   See below, para 6.46 for further discussion of these and other recent cases on the application of the indirect discrimination concept to cases involving religion and belief.

Primary Care Trust[313] the EAT was prepared to find that age discrimination was justified to avoid incurring 'disproportionately high' redundancy costs. The Court of Appeal dismissed an appeal, although emphasising that saving or avoiding costs could not, without more, amount to achieving a legitimate aim.[313a]

Much of the relevant case law in this area has arisen in the context of the equal pay defences, and is considered later in this chapter.[314] The decision of the ECJ in *Enderby v Frenchay Health Authority*[315] establishes that factors such as individual seniority[316] and scarcity of particular categories of labour can be relied upon to justify differences in pay for work of equal value under Article 157 TFEU and the Equal Pay Directive, but that the mere existence of separate collective bargaining arrangements for different groups is unlikely to be enough.[317] Nor is *Enderby* properly to be regarded as authority for the proposition that market forces *in themselves* – or the willingness of individuals to work for low pay – can justify unequal pay for equal work.[318] In relation to the differential treatment of part-time work, an employer may be able to justify lower rates of pay and benefits by arguing that these are intended to *discourage* part-time employment, on the grounds of the higher proportionate overhead costs which it involves.[319] However, since employers more usually often hire part-timers in preference to full-timers and see advantages in their employment in terms of flexibility and high productivity for those working shorter periods of time, it would seem that such arguments should not often be valid. On the other hand, the practice of not paying overtime premia to part-time workers until their hours exceed the normal weekly limit for a full-time worker, as opposed to their own normal weekly limit, was held to be justified by reference to 'the additional physical effort and the restriction on the use of free time entailed in working overtime' in the case of full-timers.[320] In this context, the range of justifying factors in employers' cases is wide, although narrower than the margin of discretion granted to states.[321]

---

[313] [2011] IRLR 119.

[313a] *Woodcock v Cumbria Primary Care Trust* [2012] IRLR 491.

[314] See paras 6.92–6.101 below.

[315] Case 127/92 [1993] IRLR 591.

[316] On seniority, see also Case C-17/05 *Cadman v HSE* [2006] IRLR 969; *Wilson v HSE* [2010] IRLR 59; Rowbottom, 2010.

[317] In *Redcar & Cleveland Borough Council v Bainbridge (No 1), Surtees v Middlesborough Borough Council and Equality and Human Rights Commission (Intervener), Redcar & Cleveland Borough Council v Bainbridge and Equality and Human Rights Commission (No 2)* [2008] IRLR 776 the Court of Appeal held that separate collective bargaining arrangements can provide grounds for a 'genuine material factor' defence and therefore a complete answer to an equal pay claim, but not where those collective agreements are tainted by discrimination. In *Allen v GMB* [2008] IRLR 690 a trade union had a policy, as part of collective bargaining following implementation of a single status agreement, of prioritising the 'pay protection' of mainly male members over past equal pay claims of mainly female members. It was held that there was disparate impact and that the actions taken were not proportionate. See generally para 6.100 below

318 See the discussion in para 6.99 below, and on the approach that should be taken to employers' arguments based on the need to cut costs or impose tighter budgetary controls, see the judgment of Sedley LJ in *Allonby v Accrington and Rossendale College* [2001] IRLR 364.

[319] See Case 170/84 *Bilka-Kaufhaus v Weber von Hartz* [1986] IRLR 317.

[320] Case C-399/92 *Stadt Lengerich v Helmig* [1995] IRLR 216, 219 (Advocate General Van Gerven). In that case, the ECJ held that the practice referred to did not even raise a prima facie finding of adverse impact, but it reached a different outcome on the adverse impact point in Case C-285/02 *Elsner-Lakeberg v Land Nordrhein-Westfalen* [2005] IRLR 290.

[321] On this, see Case C-281/97 *Krüger v Kreiskrankenhaus Ebersberg* [1999] IRLR 808.

Harassment

6.33 Under section 26 EqA 2010, harassment is a free-standing wrong and distinct form of prohibited conduct, separate from the concepts of direct and indirect discrimination. Under the core definition of harassment, a person (A) harasses another (B) where '(a) A engages in unwanted conduct related to a relevant protected characteristic, and (b) the conduct has the purpose or effect of (i) violating B's dignity, or (ii) creating an intimidating, hostile, degrading, humiliating or offensive environment for B'. This definition is clarified in two cases relating to harassment of a sexual nature. Harassment occurs where 'A engages in unwanted conduct of a sexual nature' which has the purpose or effect referred to in (b)(ii) above,[322] and where 'A or another person engages in unwanted conduct of a sexual nature or that is related to gender reassignment or sex', the conduct has the purpose or effect referred to above, and 'because of B's rejection of or submission to the conduct, A treats B less favourably than A would treat B if B had not rejected or submitted to the conduct'.[323] In determining whether harassment has the 'effect' of 'creating an intimidating, hostile, degrading, humiliating or offensive environment for B' the tribunal or court must take into account 'the perception of B', 'the other circumstances of the case' and 'whether it is reasonable for the conduct to have that effect'.[324] Section 26 covers all the protected characteristics except pregnancy and maternity and marriage and civil partnership.[325] The exclusion of pregnancy and maternity was defended by the Labour Government on the ground that the prohibition of sex discrimination adequately met this point, and that of marriage and civil partnership on the ground that there was no evidence that this was a serious problem in practice.[326]

The 2010 Act also contains a further provision, designed to specify the nature and extent of the employer's liability for act of harassment committed by third parties. Where an employee commits harassment against a fellow employee under section 26, the employer will generally be vicariously liable for this wrong.[327] Under section 40 of the Act, an employer (A) will in addition be liable for harassment of an employee (B) where a third party, that is a non-employee,[328] harasses B 'in the course of B's employment' and 'A failed to take such steps as would have been reasonably practicable to prevent the third party from doing so'.[329] This will not be the case unless 'A knows that B has been harassed in the course of B's employment on at least two other occasions by a third party', for the purposes of which 'it does not matter whether the third party is the same or a different person on each occasion'.[330]

The background to the enactment of sections 26 and 40 was the gradual but incomplete acceptance by the courts of the possibility that harassment on the grounds of what would now be known as a protected characteristic could constitute direct or indirect discrimination. The problem in framing a harassment claim as one based on direct or indirect discrimination was, firstly, that the courts were not consistently prepared to see cases of distress caused by sexually

---

[322] EqA 2010, s 26(2).
[323] EqA 2010, s 26(3).
[324] EqA 2010, s 26(4).
[325] EqA 2010, s 26(5).
[326] For discussion of these exclusions, see Hepple, 2011a: 79-80.
[327] On vicarious liability under EqA 2010, see below, para 6.54.
[328] EqA 2010, s 40(4). For this purpose, the term 'employee' has the broad meaning, akin to the term 'worker', that is generally accorded to it in equality legislation. See below, para 6.47.
[329] EqA 2010, s 40(2).
[330] EqA 2010, s 40(3).

or racially abusive remarks as amounting to a 'detriment' or disadvantage to the complainant,[331] and, secondly, that the comparator requirement led to claims being ruled out on the basis that the treatment suffered by the claimant was not sufficiently related to their sex, race, or other relevant characteristic. On the last point, the early decision in *Porcelli v Strathclyde Regional Council*[332] had found that sex discrimination was established where sexual insults and physical intimidation of a female employee by two male colleagues amounted to 'a particular kind of weapon, based upon the sex of the victim, which… would not have been used against an equally disliked man'.[333] However, later decisions, culminating in the decision of the House of Lords in *Pearce v Governing Body of Mayfield School*,[334] took a more restrictive approach. In that case, a claim for sex discrimination failed on the basis that the harassment suffered by the claimant because she was a lesbian could equally well have been experienced by a gay male employee.[335]

Section 26 EqA 2010 is based on the definition of harassment in the amended Equal Treatment Directive, the Framework Directive and Race Directive, each of which define harassment as a form of discrimination which occurs when 'unwanted conduct related to [a prohibited ground] takes place with the purpose or effect of violating the dignity of a person and of creating an intimidating, hostile, degrading, humiliating or offensive environment'.[336] This more open-ended formula was initially incorporated into those parts of British law which are derived from the amended Equal Treatment Directive and the Framework and Race Directives, and now has more general application. The British test is more flexible in that it refers to harassment being established if there is either unwanted conduct *or* an intimidating environment, whereas the EU law requires both. The Labour Government felt that it would be inappropriate to use the passage of the 2010 Act as an occasion to reduce the level of protection for victims of harassment, partly on the grounds that to do would contravene the non-regression clauses in the Directives which prevent their use to level-down more favourable provisions of national law.[337]

The Framework Directive's definition of harassment indicates that it is to be understood as a 'form of discrimination' and hence refers back to the definitions of direct and indirect discrimination set out in the Directive.[338] The definition of direct discrimination refers, in turn, to the treatment

[331] See, for varying approaches and outcomes, *Insitu Cleaning v Heads* [1995] IRLR 4; *De Souza v Automobile Association* [1986] IRLR 103; *Bracebridge Engineering Ltd v Darby* [1990] IRLR 3; *Mecca Leisure Group plc v Chatprachong* [1993] IRLR 531; *Driskel v Peninsula Business Services* [2000] IRLR 151; *Thomas v Robinson* [2003] IRLR 7.

[332] [1986] IRLR 134.

[333] [1986] IRLR 134, 137; see also, on this point, *Pearce v Governing Body of Mayfield School* [2003] IRLR 512, at [90]–[94] (Lord Hope).

[334] [2003] IRLR 512, at para 30 (Lord Nicholls). See also *Stewart v Cleveland Guest (Engineering) Ltd.* [1994] IRLR 440; *Brumfit v Ministry of Defence* [2005] IRLR 4. More flexible approaches were adopted in *Scott v Commissioners of Inland Revenue* [2004] IRLR 713 and *Moonsar v Fiveways Express Transport Ltd.* [2005] IRLR 9.

335 Pearce would now be decided as a claim of sexual orientation discrimination, in the context of which the argument about the treatment of a gay man would be irrelevant. More generally, it should be noted that claims for harassment in the context of employment may be brought without reference to EqA 2010. For an argument that harassment is best regarded as an employment-related wrong in itself, without reference to the element of discrimination, see Dine and Watt, 1995, discussing the seminal work of McKinnon, 1979; on this question, see also Conaghan, 1996; Hepple, 2000: p 180. In this context it is noteworthy that the Protection from Harassment Act 1997 creates both criminal and civil liability where a person pursues a course of conduct which he or she knows or ought to know amounts to the harassment of another; in *Majrowski v Guy's and St Thomas's NHS Trust* [2006] IRLR 695 the House of Lords held that an employer could be vicariously liable for an employee's breach of the Act, committed in the course of employment. See also *Sunderland City Council v Conn* [2008] IRLR 324.

[336] Directive 76/207, Art 2(2); Directive 2000/78, Art 2(3); Directive 2000/42, Art 2(3).

[337] See Hepple, 2011a: 78,

[338] See Directive 2000/78, Art 2(2)(a).

of another in a 'comparable situation', while the definition of indirect discrimination refers to the disadvantage suffered by the complainant 'compared with other persons'. Sections 26 makes no such references back to the concepts of direct and indirect discrimination, indicating the free-standing nature of the harassment wrong. However, it must still be shown that the harassment was 'related to'[339] the relevant protected characteristic. Thus the element of comparison is not completely absent; rather it is open to the courts to approach the process of comparison more flexibly in future. In particular, the requirement that there should be a hypothetical comparator whose position was in all material respects similar to that of the complainant is no longer relevant in this context.

Section 40 addresses the issue which arose in *Burton v De Vere Hotels*.[340] Here, two black women who were employed as waitresses succeeded in an action for racial discrimination against their employer when they were subjected to racial harassment by a comedian, who was not an employee of the hotel, giving an after-dinner speech. In *Pearce v Governing Body of Mayfield School*[341] the House of Lords held that *Burton* was wrongly decided, since white waitresses might have been just as insulted as the complainants were, and also cast doubt on the idea that an employer could be liable for the act of a third party. Section 40 only goes part of the way towards providing a remedy in this type of situation, as it requires at least two previous occasions of harassment of a particular employee to have occurred, and for the employer to have been aware of this. In principle, a claim for direct or indirect discrimination could be brought if the section 40 claim failed, but would face the problem of the comparator test which led to the rejection of the claim in *Pearce*. Although Section 40 has been brought into force, it is currently under review by the Coalition Government.[342]

Victimisation

6.34 EqA 2010 provides for a free-standing wrong of victimisation. Under earlier legislation, victimisation arose where the 'discriminator' treated the 'person victimised' less favourably than it treats or would treat other persons by reason of one of the a number of 'protected acts'. The leading case on the pre-EqA 2010 law was *Chief Constable of West Yorkshire Police v Khan*.[343] Mr Khan made a complaint of racial discrimination against the Chief Constable in respect of his failure to gain promotion. He then applied for a post in another police force, and asked the Chief Constable to write a reference on his behalf. The Chief Constable refused on the grounds that to comment on Mr Khan's application would prejudice the Chief Constable's case in the proceedings brought by Mr Khan against him. This refusal formed the basis of Mr Khan's claim for victimisation. According to Lord Nicholls, who gave the leading opinion in the House of Lords, Mr Khan had suffered less favourable treatment within the meaning of the Act: the relevant comparator group in this context was, simply, 'other employees who have not done the protected act',[344] which in this

---

[339] EqA 2010, s 26(1)(a).
[340] [1996] IRLR 596.
[341] [2003] IRLR 512.
[342] This review was announced in the Chancellor of the Exchequer's March 2011 Budget Statement.
[343] [2001] IRLR 830.
[344] [2001] IRLR 830, at para 27. For earlier, varying approaches to this issue, see *Kirby v Manpower Services Commission* [1980] IRLR 229; *Aziz v Trinity Street Taxis Ltd.* [1988] IRLR 204; *Nagarajan v London Regional Transport* [1998] IRLR 73; *St. Helens MBC v Derbyshire* [2007] IRLR 540; and see Connolly, 2000.

case was the act of making the initial complaint of racial discrimination. However, Lord Nicholls went on to hold that the Chief Constable's refusal to give Mr Khan a reference was not 'by reason that' Mr Khan had made the first complaint of discrimination: as long as he was acting 'honestly and reasonably' he was entitled to protect his position in respect of the pending proceedings.

Section 27 EqA 2010 addresses the shortcomings in the previous definition of victimisation. It establishes that victimisation occurs where A subjects B to a detriment because - (a) B does a protected act, or (b) A believes that B has done, or may do, a protected act.[345] This avoids the need to show that a comparator would have been treated differently. As before, there is no need to demonstrate a conscious decision to victimise or discriminate. The protected acts are defined as bringing proceedings under the Act, giving evidence or information in connection with proceedings under the Act, doing any other thing for the purposes of or in connection with the Act, and making an allegation of a contravention of the Act.[346] Giving false evidence or information or making a false allegation are not protected if done 'in bad faith'.[347] Only an individual, and not a corporate or other similar legal entity, may bring a claim under this provision.[348]

PROTECTED CHARACTERISTICS

6.35   We now turn to an analysis of the definitions of each of the protected characteristics under the 2010 Act. Sex, pregnancy and maternity, marriage and civil partnership,[349] gender reassignment, sexual orientation, race (broadly defined), religion or belief, age and disability are the grounds upon which employment discrimination is explicitly prohibited under the law of Great Britain.[350] By contrast, ILO Convention No 111 of 1958 on Discrimination in respect of Employment and Occupation refers to 'any distinction, exclusion or preference made on the basis of race, colour, sex, religion, political opinion, national extraction or social origin'[351] (although omitting disability, age, and sexual orientation). Article 19 TFEU, which was originally inserted as Article 13 TEC by the Treaty of Amsterdam, provided the Community (now the Union) with the power to legislate across a range of matters relating to discrimination on grounds of sex, racial or ethnic origin, religion or belief, disability, age or sexual orientation.[352] This paved the way for the Framework Directive on Discrimination which was adopted in November 2000.[353] Under its terms, Member States had to implement prohibitions on discrimination on the grounds of religion or belief and sexual orientation by 2 December 2003, and prohibitions on discrimination on the grounds of age and disability by 2 December 2006. The relevant implementing provisions are now incorporated into EqA 2010.

---

[345] EqA 2010, s 27(1).

[346] EqA 2010, s 27(2).

[347] EqA 2010, s 27(3).

[348] EqA 2010, s 27(4).

[349] The status of civil partnership was created by the Civil Partnership Act 2004. See para 6.40 below.

[350] EqA 2010, s 4. Other grounds which are the subject of partial prohibitions are an individual's trade union membership or non-membership (see ch 8 below), and his or her having a criminal conviction which is now spent under the Rehabilitation of Offenders Act 1974 (see paras 3.15 and 5.111 above). In addition, other kinds of discrimination may violate specific Convention rights contrary to HRA 1998.

[351] Art 1(1)(a).

[352] See L Waddington, 1999, 2000; M Bell, 2000.

[353] Directive 2000/78/EC.

Sex

6.36   The term 'sex' was not defined in the SDA 1975. In the absence of any specific statutory guidance in this context, the UK courts first took the view that the criteria for determining the sex of an individual were biological as opposed to being psychological or social. This was the approach taken by the courts in other contexts at this time,[354] and it was followed at tribunal level under the SDA 1975,[355] with the result that transsexuals and other transgender persons were regarded for these purposes as retaining the sex with which they were born; the effect was to exclude discrimination by employers against transsexuals from the scope of the Act. However, the ECJ in *P v S and Cornwall County Council*[356] reversed this line of reasoning, holding that discrimination against an individual on the grounds that they were proposing to undergo or have undergone gender reassignment was contrary to the Equal Treatment Directive. The Court's ruling was based on the argument that such discrimination 'is based, essentially if not exclusively, on the sex of the person concerned. Where a person is dismissed on the ground that he or she intends to undergo, or has undergone, gender reassignment, he or she is treated unfavourably by comparison with persons of the sex to which he or she was deemed to belong before undergoing gender reassignment.'[357] Thus the Court assumed that the effect of gender reassignment was to alter the sex of the individual concerned for the purposes of the principle of equal treatment. It also made a crucial choice of hypothetical comparator, namely, a person of the sex to which the individual belonged prior to the reassignment. Underlying the Court's approach was a broad view of the Equal Treatment Directive as protecting 'the dignity and freedom to which [an individual] is entitled',[358] for the purposes of which it was necessary to assert, in the words of Advocate General Tesauro, 'the irrelevance of a person's sex with regard to the rules regulating relations in society'.[359]

Gender reassignment is now a protected characteristic in its own right,[360] and EqA 2010 continues the line taken by the 1975 Act of not offering a definition of 'sex', other than to say that a reference to a person who has the protected characteristic of sex is 'a reference to a man or to a woman', and that a reference to persons who share this protected characteristic is 'a reference to persons of the same sex'.[361]

Pregnancy and maternity

6.37   Following judgments of the ECJ which established that discrimination against a person on the grounds of her pregnancy or maternity would generally amount to direct discrimination,[362]

---

[354]   Eg *Corbett v Corbett* [1970] 2 All ER 33 (marriage); *R(P) 1/75, R(P) 1/80* (social security). See Earnshaw and Pace, 1991: p 243.

[355]   *Calvin v Standard Telephone and Cables plc* London (North) Employment tribunal 16.1.86, COIT 1835/37; *White v British Sugar Corpn Ltd* [1977] IRLR 121, both discussed by Earnshaw and Pace, 1991: p 249. See also the same approach under Title VII of the US Civil Rights Act in *Holloway v Arthur Anderson & Co* 566 F 2d 659 (1977).

[356]   Case C-13/94 [1996] IRLR 347.

[357]   [1996] IRLR 347, 354.

[358]   [1996] IRLR 347, 354.

[359]   [1996] IRLR 347, 352.

[360]   See para 6.38 below.

[361]   EqA 2010, s 11.

[362]   See below, para 6.112.

the amended Equal Treatment Directive introduced a specific provision to the effect that discrimination on the grounds of sex included 'any less favourable treatment of a woman related to pregnancy or maternity leave'[363] and this led to a series of changes to the SDA 1975.[364] EqA 2010 now provides that pregnancy and maternity is a protected characteristic in its own right.[365] Section 18 prohibits direct discrimination on the grounds of pregnancy which it defines as occurring where a person treats a woman unfavourably because of a pregnancy of hers or because of an illness suffered by her as a result of it, in both cases only during the 'protected period' in relation to that pregnancy.[366] The 'protected period' means the period beginning with the pregnancy and ending, if the claimant is entitled to ordinary and additional maternity leave, at the end of the additional period or at the point, if earlier, when she returns to work after the pregnancy, or, any other case, the period of two weeks from the end of the pregnancy.[367] Section 18 also provides that there is direct discrimination on the grounds of pregnancy where a person treats a woman unfavourably because she is on compulsory maternity leave or is exercising or seeking to exercise, or has exercised or sought to exercise, the right to ordinary or additional maternity leave.[368] Section 18 does not extend to cases of indirect discrimination on the grounds of pregnancy, and the Act's provisions on harassment do not apply here either.[369] In these cases, a claim may be framed in terms of sex discrimination. Direct discrimination on the ground of pregnancy or maternity outside the protected period or outside the scope of protection in relation to the taking of compulsory, ordinary or additional maternity leave may give rise to a sex discrimination claim under section 13 of the Act.[370]

We consider the law's treatment of pregnancy and maternity in relation to employment on a more general basis later in this chapter.[371]

Gender reassignment

6.38   Following the ruling in *P v S*,[372] the Sex Discrimination Act was amended[373] to prohibit direct discrimination on grounds related to gender reassignment. The 2010 Act goes further, applying direct and indirect discrimination[374] as well as the harassment wrong[375] to the protected characteristic of gender reassignment. Retaining a provision from earlier legislation, the Act also states that it is unlawful for the employer to apply rules concerning absence which are less favourable than those which would apply either to a worker absent on the grounds of sickness or

---

[363] This is now Directive 2006/54/EC, Art 2(2)(c).
[364] See below, para 6.111.
[365] EqA 2010, ss 18, 25(5).
[366] EqA 2010, s 18(2).
[367] EqA 2010, s 18(6).
[368] EqA 2010, ss 18(3), (4).
[369] See EqA 2010, s 26(5).
[370] On the relationship between ss 13 and 18, see s 18(7).
[371] See below, paras 6.111-118.
[372] Case C-13/94 [1996] IRLR 347; see para 6.36 above.
[373] By SI 1999/1102. See also *Consultation Paper: Legislation Regarding Discrimination on Grounds of Transsexualism* (DfEE, 1998).
[374] EqA 2010, s 25(3).
[375] EqA 2010, s 26(5).

injury, or which are less favourable than those which would apply if the absence was 'for some other reason and it is not reasonable for '[the complainant] to be treated less favourably'.[376] A person has the protected characteristic of 'gender reassignment' where that person 'is proposing to undergo, is undergoing or has undergone a process (or part of a process) for the purpose of reassigning the person's sex by changing physiological or other attributes of sex'. This definition is wider than its predecessor which referred to 'a process which is undertaken under medical supervision for the purpose of reassigning a person's sex by changing physiological or other characteristics of sex'.[377] The effect of the change is that a person who 'passes' as a person of the chosen gender without having sought medical advice will have the protected characteristic of gender reassignment.[378] Although a general GOR defence applies to this protected characteristic as it does to others,[379] a number of specific GOQs which were formally applied to persons undergoing gender reassignment no longer apply.[380]

Marriage and civil partnership

6.39   The prohibition on discrimination against married persons on the grounds of their marital status in the SDA 1975 was principally introduced to outlaw the 'marriage bar' which operated in a highly public way in a number of occupations, including public sector employment, as late as the 1950s. Because the marriage bar only operated, in practice, against married *women*, its application would probably have amounted to unlawful sex discrimination even without the reference to marital status in section 3 of the SDA 1975.[381] As it was, section 3 put the matter beyond doubt.[382] It was later extended to cover cases of civil partnership,[383] but not to cases of those intending to get married,[384] those in cohabiting relationships or partnerships not recognised by the law. EqA 2010 continues this approach,[385] and also provides no protection, on this ground, to those who are single, widowed or divorced.[386] It may be possible to argue that unfavourable treatment in some of these circumstances violates the Convention right to respect for private life.[387]

---

[376] EqA 2010, s 16(2), replacing SDA 1975, s 2A(3).

[377] SDA 1975, s 82(1).

[378] *Explanatory Notes*, at para 43. The Gender Recognition Act 2004 provides for a transgender person to obtain a gender recognition certificate, for which it is not necessary to have completed a medical procedure. The Act was adopted in response to the decision of the ECtHR in *Goodwin v UK* (2002) 35 EHRR 447.

[379] EqA 2010, Sch 9; see below, para 6.55.

[380] See the 5th edition of this book, at para 6.38.

[381] *McLean v Paris Travel Service Ltd* [1976] IRLR 202, IT.

[382] See *Skyrail Oceanic Ltd v Coleman* [1981] ICR 864.

[383] By virtue of the Civil Partnership Act 2004, s 251.

[384] *Bick v Royal West of England Residential School for the Deaf* [1976] IRLR 326.

[385] EqA 2010, s 8.

[386] For discussion of the shortcomings of the Act in this regard, see Hepple, 2011: p 49. There is no protection against harassment related to marriage or civil partnership.

[387] Under Art 8, ECHR. There is discussion of the continuing relevance of this head of sex discrimination in the consultation document on the Equality Bill: see *Government Response to the Consultation*, paras 15.35–15.41 (the Labour Government's position was that the provision should be retained in its current form).

Sexual orientation

6.40   Although discrimination on the grounds of a person's sexual orientation was not expressly prohibited by the SDA 1975, attempts were made to bring it within the scope of the Act. One such argument was based on the application of what in US law was known as 'sex plus' discrimination, in other words discrimination based on the victim's sex plus some other characteristic which was related to it. This idea was also recognised in the UK case law: an example is *Hurley v Mustoe*,[388] in which the complainant was dismissed on the grounds that she was a mother with a young family, which her employer considered made her unreliable as a worker. The difficulty with using this idea to counter discrimination on the grounds of an individual's sexual orientation, however, is that the complainant had to show that a comparable individual of the opposite sex would have been treated less favourably.[389] It was open to a tribunal to conclude that an individual's sexuality was not a relevant circumstance for this purposes of the comparator test, with the result that the adverse treatment of a homosexual male could have been compared, for this purpose, to the treatment which would have been accorded to persons generally of the opposite sex.[390] This argument was rejected, however, both by the domestic courts and by the ECJ, applying Article 141 as it then was (now Article 157 TFEU), and the Equal Treatment Directive. In *Grant v South West Trains*[391] the ECJ, considering a case in which only employees who were married or who had a partners of the opposite sex could qualify for cheap rail fares for their spouse or partner, ruled that '[t]hat condition, the effect of which is that the worker must live in a stable relationship with a person of the opposite sex in order to benefit from the travel concessions, is, like the other alternative conditions prescribed in the [employer's] regulations, applied regardless of the sex of the worker concerned. Thus travel concessions are refused to a male worker if he is living with a person of the same sex, just as they are to a female worker if she is living with a person of the same sex'. However, at no point did either the Divisional Court or the ECJ explain its choice of comparator. There was a striking contrast with *P v S*, in which the ECJ compared the position of a male to female transsexual not with that of a female to male transsexual, but with the position of a male employee who was not undergoing gender reassignment.

In *Smith and Grady v United Kingdom*[392] the European Court of Human Rights held that the policy of conducting investigations into the alleged homosexuality of members of the armed forces and discharging from service those found to be of homosexual orientation contravened the right to respect for private life in Article 8 of the Convention. The Court ruled that the UK government had not offered sufficient justification for these practices. In particular, no evidence had been presented to support the government's argument that the morale and effectiveness of the armed forces would otherwise be undermined, except for indications of 'a predisposed bias on the part of a heterosexual majority against a homosexual minority'.[393] The Court noted that 'these negative attitudes cannot, of themselves, be considered by the Court to amount to sufficient justification for the interferences with the applicants' rights [under Article 8] any more than similar negative

---

[388] [1981] ICR 490.

[389] SDA 1975, s 5(3).

[390] Earnshaw and Pace, 1991: p 248. See also Bamforth, 1994, 1998 and Wintemute, 1997a, 1997b, for general analyses of discrimination law relating to sexual orientation.

[391] Case C-249/96 [1998] IRLR 206, 218; Barnard, 1998; Bamforth, 2000.

[392] [1999] IRLR 734.

[393] [1999] IRLR 734, 748.

attitudes towards those of a different race, origin or colour'.[394] Together with the Human Rights Act, *Smith* made it possible to argue that the SDA 1975 should be interpreted in such a way as to bring discrimination on the grounds of sexual orientation within the scope of the equality principle. However, this argument was rejected by the House of Lords in two cases heard together, *MacDonald v A-G for Scotland* and *Pearce v Governing Body of Mayfield Secondary School*,[395] essentially on the grounds, as in *Grant v South West Trains*,[396] that the sexual orientation of the applicant constituted 'relevant circumstances' for the purposes of then version of the comparator test in the SDA 1975.

The reform of UK law had to await the implementation of the Framework Directive on Discrimination, which prohibits both direct and indirect discrimination on the grounds of sexual orientation.[397] This part of the Directive was brought into effect from 1 December 2003 by the Employment Equality (Sexual Orientation) Regulations 2003.[398] Section 12 of EqA 2010 now defines the protected characteristic of sexual orientation in terms of 'a person's sexual orientation towards (a) persons of the same sex, (b) persons of the opposite sex, and (c) persons of either sex'.[399] Each of the relevant grounds of prohibited conduct (direct and indirect discrimination, and harassment) applies to this characteristic,[400] which is subject to a general GOR defence.[401] In addition, certain religious employers may invoke a specific GOR to justify discrimination on the grounds of sexual orientation.[402]

Age

(i) The European Context

6.41   Article 19 TFEU, formerly Article 13 TEC, empowers the Council to take appropriate action to combat discrimination based on age, among other things, and the Framework Directive[403] contains a specific prohibition on age discrimination. The 25th recital to the Directive states that while the prohibition of age discrimination should be 'an essential part' of the European employment strategy and a basis for diversity in the workforce, differences in treatment on the grounds of age may nevertheless be justified. Article 6(1) of the Directive accordingly states that Member States may provide that 'differences of treatment on grounds of age shall not constitute discrimination, if, within the context of national law, they are objectively and reasonably justified by a legitimate

---

[394] [1999] IRLR 734, 748. The Court also found a breach of Art 13 of the Convention (lack of access to a legal remedy) but rejected claims under Art 3 (degrading treatment) and did not consider a claim under Art 10 (freedom of expression).
[395] [2003] IRLR 512.
[396] Case C-249/96 [1998] IRLR 206.
[397] For the background to this aspect of the Framework Directive, see *Proposal for a Council Directive Establishing a General Framework for Equal Treatment in Employment and Occupation*, COM (1999) 565 final, which notes that 'employment is an area in which people may hide their sexual orientation for fear of discrimination and harassment' (p 4). The scope of the Directive is discussed by the ECJ in Case C-267/06 *Maruko v Versorgungsanstalt der Deutschen Bühnen* [2008] IRLR 450.
[398] SI 2003/1661.
[399] EqA 2010, s 12(1).
[400] EqA 2010, ss 25(9), 26(5), 27.
[401] EqA 2010, Sch 9, para 1. See below, para 6.55.
[402] EqA 2010, Sch 9, para 2. See below, para 6.55.
[403] Directive 2000/78/EC.

aim, including legitimate employment policy, labour market and vocational training objectives, and if the means of achieving that aim are appropriate and necessary'. This derogation is applies to both direct and indirect forms of discrimination.[404] Article 6(1) goes on to state that such legitimate differences of treatment may include the setting of age-related conditions on access to employment and vocational training which are designed to promote vocational integration or to protect the workers concerned; the fixing of minimum conditions of age, professional experience or seniority for access to employment or employment-related benefits; and the fixing of maximum ages for recruitment where this is based on training requirements or on the need for a 'reasonable period of employment before retirement'.[405]

In *Mangold v Helm*[406] the ECJ considered a German law removing restrictions on the duration or number of fixed-term contracts of employment which could be entered into in the course of a single employment relationship where the worker was above a certain age (originally 60, then 58 from 2001, then 52 from 2003 until 2006). The Court held that this was contrary to the prohibition of age discrimination in EU law. Although the measure was aiming to fulfil a legitimate goal, namely the promotion of the employment opportunities of older workers, it did not pass the proportionality test because of the blanket nature of the exemption for older workers: 'it has not been shown that fixing an age threshold , as such, regardless of any other consideration linked to the structure of the labour market in question or the personal situation of the person concerned, is objectively necessary to the attainment of the objective which is the vocational integration of unemployed older workers'.[407]

Mangold was a controversial decision because the original dispute in that case arose before the point which the age discrimination provisions of the Framework Directive were due to be implemented by the Member States. In *Bartsch v Bosch und Siemens Hausgeräte (BSH) Altersfürsorge GmbH*[408] the ECJ interpreted Mangold not as a decision under the Framework Directive at all, but as a decision applying the general principle of equality in European Union law in the context of an interpretation of the Directive relating to the Framework Agreement on Fixed-Term Employment.[409] *Bartsch* concerned an allegedly age-discriminatory provision governing survivors' benefits under an occupational pension scheme, with the events again relating to a time before Directive 2000/78 came into force. The Court ruled that there was no EU law measure, equivalent to the Framework Agreement on Fixed-Term Work, on which the principle of equal treatment could bite.[410] The importance of the prohibition on age discrimination as a general principle of EU law was nevertheless reasserted by the Court of Justice in its ruling in the *Kücükdevici* case,[411] in which it held that German legislation which discounted periods of employment before the age of 25 when calculating notice period rights was directly discriminatory on the grounds of age.

---

[404] This appears to be the significance of the cross-reference to Art 2(2) in Art 6(1); see also COM (1999) 565 final, at pp 10–11. These derogations are additional to the genuine occupational requirements referred to in Art 4.

[405] See also Art 6(2) which allows Member States to provide for differential pensionable ages in occupational (employer-run) social security schemes; state-run social security schemes and employment subsidies are stated to be outside the scope of the Directive (see Art 3(3)). Member States may also provide that the armed forces are exempt from the age discrimination requirements of the Directive (Art 3(4)).

[406] Case C-144/04 *Mangold v Helm* [2006] IRLR 143; Schiek, 2006

[407] Case C-144/04 *Mangold v Helm* [2006] IRLR 143, at para 64.

[408] Case C-427/06 *Bartsch v Bosch und Siemens Hausgeräte (BSH) Altersfürsorge GmbH*, opinion of 22 May 2008, judgment of 23 September 2008.

[409] Directive 99/70/EC.

[410] See the opinion of Sharpston AG on this point, at para 88.

[411] Case C-555/07 *Kücükdevici v Swedex GmbH & Co KG* [2010] ECR I-365.

(ii) Age discrimination under the Equality Act 2010

6.42   Following a consultation process which began in 2003,[412] Regulations implementing the age discrimination provisions of the Framework Directive were adopted in 2006 and came into force in October of that year. These provisions, the Employment Equality (Age) Regulations, have now been incorporated, with some significant amendments, into EqA 2010.[413]

The Act defines the protected characteristic of age in terms of membership of a particular age group. Thus a reference to a person who has the protected characteristic is 'a reference to a person of a particular age group' and a reference to persons who share that characteristic is a reference to persons 'of the same age group'.[414] A reference to an age group can include a reference 'to a particular age or to a range of ages'.[415]

Both direct and indirect discrimination on the grounds of age are prohibited, as is harassment relating to age,[416] but, in a departure from the approach taken for other protected characteristics, direct discrimination, and not just indirect discrimination, may be justified if the employer shows that the measure in question is a proportionate means of achieving a legitimate aim.[417] There is also a general GOR for age[418] and a number of specific exemptions concerning minimum wages and childcare provision.[419]

The meaning of indirect discrimination in the context of age was considered in *Chief Constable of West Yorkshire Police v Homer*.[420] The complainant was denied access to a higher pay grade on the grounds that he did not have one of the requirements for that grade, namely a law degree. He had previously been offered the opportunity to undertake a law degree but had declined on the grounds that he would not have completed it until after his retirement at the age of 65. He argued that the denial of the higher pay grade was indirectly discriminatory on the grounds of his age. The employment tribunal found that the complainant had been put at a particular disadvantage by virtue of his age and that the employer's conduct could not be justified. The EAT reversed on the grounds that there was 'no basis for concluding that there was

---

[412]   See DTI, *Equality and Diversity: Age Matters. Age Consultation 2003* (2003). A number of extra-legal initiatives had previously been adopted, including a non-statutory Code of Practice drawn up by the DfEE in 1999. See generally Sargeant, 1999; Desmond, 2000, 2003; Fredman and Spencer (eds), 2003.

[413]   Prior to the coming into force of the 2006 Regulations, a number of challenges to age discriminatory practices were mounted using arguments based on sex discrimination. See *Jones v University of Manchester* [1993] IRLR 218; *Nash v Mash/Roe Group Ltd* [1998] IRLR 168; *Rutherford v Secretary of State for Employment (No 2)* [2004] IRLR 892; [2006] IRLR 551. With the advent of age discrimination legislation these decisions are of limited interest although they remain relevant in relation to the approach to the definition of indirect discrimination, on which see above, para 6.23 *et seq*.

[414]   EqA 2010, s 5(1).

[415]   EqA 2010, s 5(2).

[416]   EqA 2010, ss 25(8), 26(5).

[417]   EqA 2010, s 13(2). In *Woodcock v Cumbria Primary Care Trust* [2011] IRLR 119 the EAT ruled that there was no basis for giving the justification test an unduly narrow reading under what is now s 13(2), merely because the context in which the test was being applied was one in which the discrimination was direct. This decision is also notable for the flexible reading given to the notion of the employer's costs as a possible basis for a justification defence but note the more restrictive approach of the Court of Appeal in that case: *Woodcock v Cumbria Primary Care Trust* [2012] IRLR 491. See also the discussion of justification for age discrimination in the context of a 'pay protection scheme' in *Pulham v London Borough of Barking and Dagenham* [2010] IRLR 184.

[418]   EqA 2010, Sch 9, para 1. For an application of the GOR defence under Art 4(1) of the Directive to case of a maximum age for recruitment to the fire service, see Joined Cases C-229/08 and C-341/08 *Wolf v Stadt Frankfurt am Main* [2010] IRLR 244.

[419]   See EqA 2010, Sch 9, paras 11-12 (national minimum wage rates), and para 15 (provision of childcare).

[420]   [2009] IRLR 262.

any particular disadvantage which affected persons falling within the age bracket of 60–65'.[421] It was not intrinsically more difficult for persons in that age group to obtain a degree. While it was the case that a degree would be less valuable to persons over the age of 60 than it would to their younger colleagues because they would have less time to benefit from the higher pay that went with it, the EAT held that 'the financial disadvantage – if it can properly be so described – resulting from the operation of this criterion is the inevitable consequence of age; it is not a consequence of age discrimination'.[422] The Court of Appeal upheld this decision on the grounds that 'the particular disadvantageous impact of the apparently neutral law degree provision results from the appellant's impending retirement, and not from his age'.[423] If this is correct, *Homer* might be better understood as a case turning on the scope of the derogation from the principle of age discrimination for cases involving the application of employers' provisions on retirement,[424] but if that is so it is hard to avoid the conclusion that the provision in question was one which the employer should have had to justify.[425] At the time of writing *Homer* is being considered by the Supreme Court.

Length of service

6.43   In addition to the defences mentioned above, an employer has a defence to an age discrimination claim if unfavourable treatment on the grounds of age is based on differences in length of service.[426] This provision takes advantage of Article 6(1) of the Directive, which allows a derogation for 'seniority in service' provided that this can be justified. In a case where the disadvantaged worker has more than five years' service, the employer has to cross an additional hurdle by showing that it reasonably believed that the use of the seniority criterion 'fulfils a business need'.[427] In addition, employers are allowed to make 'enhanced redundancy payments' based on seniority.[428] This provision is meant to allow employers to make redundancy payments which are more generous than the statutory redundancy payments scheme in Part XI of ERA 1996 without committing age discrimination provided that specified criteria are met.[429]

In *Rolls Royce plc v Unite*[430] the employer challenged before the High Court a redundancy scheme which it had itself agreed with the respondent trade union. The scheme provided for length of service to be taken into account in redundancy selection, although it was not a pure 'last in, first out' scheme. The court held that the scheme was acceptable under both the general justification

---

[421] [2009] IRLR 262, at [35].

[422] [2009] IRLR 262, at [39].

[423] [2010] IRLR 619, at [49] (Mummery LJ).

[424] See below, para 6.44.

[425] The default retirement age derogation in force when *Homer* was decided, and since repealed, gave the employer a blanket immunity only if the employee was dismissed for retirement under the procedure then set out in the relevant legislation. In other cases, as now more generally, the employer would only have had a defence to discriminatory treatment related to the application of an age-based retirement provision if it could show that the application of the provision was a proportionate means of achieving a legitimate aim: see below, para 6.44.

[426] EqA 2010, Sch 9, para 10.

[427] EqA 2010, Sch 9, para 10(2).

[428] EqA 2010, Sch 9, para 13.

[429] See DTI, *Employment Equality (Age) Regulations 2006. Notes on Regulations*, paras 127–135.

[430] [2009] IRLR 49; see further para 5.178 above. See also *MacCulloch v Imperial Chemical Industries plc* [2008] IRLR 846; *Loxley v BAE Systems (Munitions & Ordnance) Ltd.* [2008] IRLR 853.

defence for age discrimination, and under the specific length of service derogation. Both sides had a legitimate business interest under the general defence, in the form of 'the advancement of an employment policy which achieves a peaceable process of selection agreed with the recognised union'.[431] It was accepted that the process of collective bargaining involves a compromise:

> If employers were unconstrained by concepts of fairness to their staff, they would choose to retain those members of staff whom they considered to be best for the business… [T]he union is in principle opposed to compulsory redundancy. That is because the union sees its role as the protector of the staff from the unconstrained power of the employer to run his business as he will…The collective agreements represent a compromise between them.[432]

In addition, the length of service derogation was relevant, as the 'business need' test was met: '[w]here there is an agreed redundancy scheme, negotiated with a recognised trade union, which uses a length of service requirement as part of a wider scheme of measured performance, it is probable… that such would be regarded as reasonably fulfilling a business need'.[433] The Court of Appeal upheld the conclusions reached by the High Court, although Wall LJ criticised the failure explicitly to address whether the criterion of length of service was a proportionate means of achieving a legitimate aim.[434]

RETIREMENT

6.44 The Employment Equality (Age) Regulations 2003 contained a highly complex and controversial derogation for retirement in situations where an employer operated a so-called 'default retirement age' (DRA) of 65 or above. The employer was able to show that dismissal on the grounds of retirement was fair and that no claim of unlawful discrimination arose under the Regulations if it followed a procedure, set out in the legislation, for considering requests by employees to carry on working beyond the retirement age.[435]

The DRA was challenged in an action brought by Age Concern (England) (since renamed Age UK) in the High Court. The High Court referred a number of issues to the ECJ for a preliminary ruling, although it stopped short of asking the ECJ to rule on the substance of the retirement scheme. The ECJ ruled that the retirement scheme was subject to the Framework Directive, but that the United Kingdom was not in breach of the Directive by failing to set out in the Regulations a specific list of differences in treatment which could be regarded as meeting legitimate aims under the Directive. The Court held that the legitimate aims referred to in Article 6 were illustrative, not exhaustive.[436] It went on to hold that Article 6 did not impose a more restrictive test of justification for age than the general test set out in Article 2 of the Directive, notwithstanding some difference

---

[431] [2009] IRLR 49, at [15].

[432] [2009] IRLR 49, at [14]-[15].

[433] [2009] IRLR 49, at [17].

[434] [2009] IRLR 576. Note also Wall LJ at [59] and [60]. See above, para 5.178.

435 On the working of the DRA, see *Compass Group plc v Ayodele* [2011] IRLR 802 and the 5th edition of this work at paras 5.138–5.145.

[436] Case C-388/07 *R on the application of The Incorporated Trustees of the National Council on Ageing (Age Concern England) v Secretary of State for Business, Enterprise and Regulatory Reform*, judgment of 5 March 2009, [2009] IRLR 373.

of wording.[437] The crux of its decision was its guidance on the approach the national court should take in assessing the social policy justifications put forward by the government. According to the ECJ:

> ... in choosing the means capable of achieving their social policy objectives, the Member States enjoy broad discretion... However, that discretion cannot have the effect of frustrating the implementation of the principle of non-discrimination on grounds of age. Mere generalisations concerning the capacity of a specific measure to contribute to employment policy, labour market or vocational training objectives are not enough to show that the aim of the measure is capable of justifying derogation from that principle and do not constitute evidence on the basis of which it could reasonably be considered that the means chosen are suitable for achieving that aim.[438]

When the case was remitted to the High Court, Blake J ruled that the DRA scheme was compatible with the Directive, on the grounds that it was a proportionate means of achieving a number of national-level social policy goals, which he summed up in the idea of 'maintaining confidence in the labour market'.[439] He suggested, however, that setting the normal DRA at 65, while proportionate at the point when the 2006 Regulations had been introduced, was no longer so, in the light of changes to state policy which included the gradual raising of the state retirement age to 68. Following this judgment, the government announced a review of the DRA. Although EqA 2010, as initially enacted, continued the default retirement age derogation in force, it was repealed with effect from 1 October 2011, with transitional arrangements taking effect from 1 April of that year.[440]

The effect of these repeals is to throw into doubt the legality of the practice of compulsory retirement. Although the government, in its consultation on the proposed abolition of the DRA,[441] suggested that it would remain open to employers to adopt a so-called 'employer justified retirement age' (EJRA) by reference to the justification defence to direct age discrimination set out in section 13(2) of the Act, the circumstances under which an EJRA would be lawful are unclear until the matter is tested in the courts. For the time being, the only guidance is that of the Court of Justice, which has indicated, in a series of rulings from other member states, that there is a wide margin of appreciation under the terms of the derogations set out in the Framework Directive, but that the discretion given to member states is not boundless. In *Palacios de la Villa v Cortefiel Servicios SA*[442] the Court considered a case arising from a Spanish collective agreement which provided for compulsory retirement where the worker concerned had reached the normal state retirement age and had satisfied the conditions for entitlement to a contributory retirement pension. The Court held that

---

[437] The Court noted, at para 65, that Art 6 gives Member States the option of providing that certain forms of treatment do not constitute discrimination within the meaning of the Directive if they are 'objectively and reasonably' justified, but ruled that there was no significance to the inclusion of the word 'reasonably' in Art 6 when it did not appear in Art 2; a measure which was justified by reference to a legitimate aim and achieved by appropriate and necessary means could not be other than 'reasonable'. See also discussion of the meaning of Art 6(1) in *R (on the application of Unison) v First Secretary of State* [2006] IRLR 926.

[438] Case C-388/07 *R on the application of The Incorporated Trustees of the National Council on Ageing (Age Concern England) v Secretary of State for Business, Enterprise and Regulatory Reform* [2009] IRLR 173, at para 51.

[439] *R (on the application of Age UK) v Secretary of State for Business, Enterprise and Regulatory Reform* [2009] IRLR 1017, at [103].

[440] SI 2011/1069, repealing EqA 2010, Sch 9, paras 8-9, and ERA 1996, ss 98ZA-98ZH.

[441] BIS, *Phasing Out the Default Retirement Age. Consultation Document* (2010), paras 7.2.7-7.2.8.

[442] Case C-411/05 [2007] IRLR 989.

the measure fell under Article 6: it was aiming at a legitimate goal, promoting employment, which was specifically referred to in the collective agreement in question, and it was not unreasonable for the authorities to conclude that it was 'appropriate and necessary' to achieve that goal. The national legislation, by delegating the decision on compulsory retirement to the collective bargaining process, had put in place a mechanism which allowed for flexibility. In particular, it was possible for collective agreements to take into account the overall labour market situation and the nature of the jobs affected when providing for compulsory retirement. In a series of further decisions, the Court has stressed the need for national courts to allow for flexibility in the application of the derogations contained in the Directive. Compulsory retirement may be a proportionate means of achieving certain legitimate social policy goals, including ensuring access to the labour market on the part of younger workers, if it is combined with availability of a sustainable level of pension provision and with flexibility in dealing with requests to continue working after retirement. Another factor present tending towards the proportionality of retirement provisions is the involvement of the social partners, through collective bargaining, in the negotiation of such schemes.[443]

The DRA applied only to employees. In *Seldon v Clarkson, Wright and Jakes*[444] a challenge was mounted to the practice of a firm of solicitors which required its partners to retire at 65. The EAT upheld a ruling of the employment tribunal to the effect that the practice of having a compulsory retirement age was justified, on grounds which included providing associates with opportunities for promotion and maintaining collegiality between partners (which would be undermined, it was suggested, by a practice of subjecting partners to regular performance management reviews). However, the EAT reversed the tribunal on the issue of whether the particular age of 65 chosen in this case could be justified, on the grounds that there was no evidence that there was a significant deterioration in performance around that age. In the Court of Appeal, the EAT's ruling on the legality of the compulsory retirement age in principle was upheld and the Court also restored the tribunal's decision on the choice of 65 as the particular age in this case. According to Sir Mark Waller, some age had to be chosen and while 65 involved a greater degree of discrimination than a higher age, '[t]he Directive (recital 14) seems to contemplate the legitimacy of a retirement age and it cannot thus have envisaged that it would be impossible to justify one age because a different age would be less discriminatory to persons of the age chosen'.[445] At the time of writing *Seldon* is being considered by the Supreme Court.

Race, nationality, ethnic and national origin, and colour

6.45   EqA 2010 defines the protected characteristic of 'race' as including 'colour', 'nationality' and 'ethnic or national origins'.[446] Prior to the coming into force of the 2010 Act, the extended

---

[443]   See Case C-341/08 *Petersen v Berufungsausschuss für Zahnärzte für Bezirk Westfalen-Lippe* [2010] IRLR 254; Case C-45/09 *Rosenbladt v Ollerking Gebaüdereinigungs GmbH* [2011] IRLR 51; Case C-250/09 and Case C-268/09 *Georgiev v Technicheski universitet – Sofia, filial Plovdiv* [2011] 2 CMLR 179; Case C-159/10 *Fuchs v Land Hessen* [2011] IRLR 1043; Case C-447/09 *Prigge v Deutsche Lufthansa AG* [2011] IRLR 1052. Kilpatrick, 2011, argues that the approach to proportionality taken by the Court of Justice in its case law on age discrimination is looser than that adopted in other areas of discrimination law and in EU law more generally.
[444]   [2009] IRLR 267, [2010] IRLR 865.
[445]   [2010] IRLR 865, at [38].
[446]   EqA 2010, s 9(1).

definition of indirect discrimination in the amended RRA 1976 did not extend to discrimination on the grounds of nationality or colour, which are outside the scope of the Race Directive.[447] Under the 2010 Act, the various forms of prohibited conduct apply equally to each of the different aspects of the protected characteristic of race.[448]

The leading case on the definition of the protected characteristic of race is a decision under the 1976 Act, *Mandla v Dowell Lee*,[449] in which the House of Lords held that Sikhs constituted an identifiable ethnic group. Lord Fraser said:

> For a group to constitute an ethnic group in the sense of the Act of 1976, it must, in my opinion, regard itself, and be regarded by others, as a distinct community by virtue of certain characteristics. Some of these characteristics are essential: others are not essential but one or more of them will commonly be found and will help to distinguish the group from the surrounding community. The conditions which appear to me to be essential are these: (1) a long shared history, of which the group is conscious as distinguishing it from other groups, and the memory of which it keeps alive; (2) a cultural tradition of its own, including family and social customs and manners, often but not necessarily associated with religious observance. In addition, to those two essential characteristics the following characteristics are, in my opinion, relevant: (3) either a common geographical origin, or descent from a small number of common ancestors; (4) a common language, not necessarily peculiar to the group; (5) a common literature peculiar to the group; (6) a common religion different from that of neighbouring groups or from the general community surrounding it; (7) being a minority or being an oppressed or a dominant group within a larger community ...[450]

On this basis, although Sikhs are not (as the courts decided in this case) distinguishable in a biological sense from other inhabitants of the Punjab, their distinctive history and tradition and their own religion and written language mean that they are protected by the protected characteristic of race. The Act has also been held to extend to discrimination against Jews[451] and gypsies.[452] However, in *Dawkins v Department of the Environment*[453] it was held that Rastafarians were not an ethnic group, in part on the grounds that they had only been an identifiable group, separate from other Jamaicans, for around sixty years.

In the *JFS* case,[454] the issue before the Supreme Court was whether a faith school's policy of excluding pupils who were not classified as Jewish according to criteria set out by the Office of the Chief Rabbi of the Commonwealth (OCR) was racially discriminatory. The OCR criteria defined as Jewish any person who was the child of an ethnically Jewish mother (the 'matrilineal line' criterion) and any person whose mother had converted to Judaism under Orthodox auspices. The complainant was excluded because his mother, who was of Italian origin and had been a

---

[447] On the changes the 2010 Act was intended to make on this point, see *Government Response to the Consultation*, ch 7, and Hepple, 2011a: 36-37.

[448] EqA 2010, ss 25(6), 26(5).

[449] [1983] IRLR 209.

[450] [1983] IRLR 209, 211.

[451] *Seide v Gillette Industries Ltd* [1980] IRLR 427.

[452] *Commission for Racial Equality v Dutton* [1989] IRLR 8.

[453] [1993] IRLR 284. In *Northern Joint Police Board v Evans* [1997] IRLR 610 the EAT held that the Scots and the English were separate racial groups defined by reference to 'national origins', although they did not have separate 'ethnic origins'; see also *BBC Scotland v Souster* [2001] IRLR 150.

[454] [2010] IRLR 136.

Roman Catholic prior to converting to Judaism on her marriage to the complainant's father, had converted under non-Orthodox auspices. The Supreme Court held by a majority that the complainant's exclusion was on racial grounds.

The difficulty in this decision derives from the possibility of entry into the Jewish faith via conversion. On the one hand, the complainant was treated less favourably than he would have been had his mother been born a Jew. This looks at first sight like an ethnic criterion, which would undoubtedly be within the definition of racial discrimination.[455] On the other hand, the possibility of entry into the faith by conversion implies that descent by the matrilineal line need not necessarily imply ethnic origin. Had the complainant's mother been born the child of a mother who had herself converted to Judaism via the Orthodox route, he would have qualified for entry into the school, regardless of the ethnic origins of his mother and grandmother. On one view, conversion into the Jewish faith implies assimilation to the Jewish ethnic group: '[t]o the Jew, the matrilineal descendant is a member of the Jewish family and a member of the Jewish religion. The two are inextricably intertwined'.[456] But this perspective perhaps does less than full justice to the argument that the criteria applied by the Chief Rabbi were fundamentally religious in nature, rather than ethnic, since '[a]n approach to this case which assumes that Jews are being divided into separate subgroups on the grounds of ethnicity is an artificial construct which Jewish law, whether Orthodox or otherwise, does not recognise'.[457] The obstacles to a clear resolution of the *JFS* case arguably lay in the *Mandla* judgment, which in linking the definition of an ethnic group at least in part to religious observance, risks conflating ethnic and religious identity.

It is apparent from the *JFS* case that the definition of a racial group is to some degree context-dependent, that is to say, it depends in part on the nature of the claim being made and the comparison on which it is based. The complainant in that case was, it was agreed, part of the wider Jewish community that formed an ethnic group under the *Mandla* test. He was also, according to the majority of the Supreme Court, part of a sub-group within that group, which, because it was in part defined by ethnic origin, was a separate racial group for the purposes of the Act. The 2010 Act explicitly provides that 'the fact that a racial group comprises two or more distinct racial groups does not prevent it from constituting a particular racial group'.[458]

Religion or belief

6.46 The RRA 1976 did not protect individuals against discrimination on the grounds of their religion, except in so far as that formed one aspect of discrimination on racial grounds as that was defined in the Act: as we have just seen, an ethnic group may be defined by its religion, amongst other factors. Religious discrimination may constitute indirect discrimination on racial grounds where, for example, employers' practices of denying Muslim employees time off to attend the mosque can be seen as imposing a condition which black individuals are less able to comply

---

[455] See Hepple, 2011a: p 39.
[456] *JFS*, [2010] IRLR 136, at [43] (Lord Phillips).
[457] *JFS*, [2010] IRLR 136, at [184] (Lord Hope).
[458] EqA 2010, s 9(4).

with than white individuals.[459] The Framework Directive on Discrimination introduced a general prohibition on discrimination on the grounds of 'religion or belief' which was implemented in the Employment Equality (Religion or Belief) Regulations 2003. Section 10 EqA 2010 now provides that '[r]eligion means any religion and a reference to religion includes a reference to a lack of religion', while '[b]elief means any religious or philosophical belief and a reference to belief includes a reference to a lack of belief'.[460] This definition, in providing symmetrical protection to those who do and those who do not profess a particular belief, follows the ECtHR's case law, which indicates that discrimination on the grounds of a belief structure which involves the absence of certain beliefs should be protected: 'if a Christian employer refuses an individual a job, because he is not Christian, regardless of whether he is Muslim, Hindu, atheist (etc.), that would be direct discrimination on the grounds of that individual's religious belief, which can be described as "non-Christian"'.[461]

The DTI's *Explanatory Notes* on the 2003 Regulations suggested that the term 'religion', if it was to be construed in line with the case law of the European Court of Human Rights interpreting Article 9 of the Convention, would cover all religions widely recognised in the UK, as well as sects within religions, such as the Catholic and Protestant branches of the Christian Church.[462] The Convention jurisprudence, which requires a religion to have a clear structure and belief system,[463] thereby incorporates such belief systems as those of Druidism and the Church of Scientology in the definition of a religion. The term 'religious belief', the 2003 *Notes* indicated, would also include 'beliefs founded in a religion, if they attain a certain level of cogency, seriousness, cohesion and importance, provided the beliefs are worthy of respect in a democratic society and are not incompatible with human dignity'.[464] The third category, 'philosophical belief', was intended to cover those philosophical and political beliefs which are similar to religious beliefs, as just defined. The *Notes* suggested that 'the belief should occupy a place in the person's life parallel to that filled by the God/Gods of those holding a particular religious belief'.[465] The Explanatory Notes to the 2010 Act indicate that the 'criteria for determining what is a "philosophical belief" are that it must be genuinely held; be a belief and not an opinion or viewpoint based on the present state of information available; be a belief as to a weighty and substantial aspect of human life and behaviour; attain a certain level of cogency, seriousness, cohesion and importance; and be worthy of respect in a democratic society, compatible with human dignity and not conflict with the fundamental rights of others'.[466] In applying this approach the courts and tribunals have held that belief in climate change was capable of amounting to a philosophical belief[467] as were belief in the higher purpose of public service broadcasting,[468] and belief in the sanctity of all life, entailing

---

[459] *Yassin v North-West Homecare Ltd* (1994) 19 *EOR Case Law Digest*; see Mirza, 1995: p 20; *JH Walker Ltd v Hussain* [1996] IRLR 11.

[460] EqA 2010, s 10(1),(2).

[461] DTI, *Explanatory Notes for the Employment Equality (Sexual Orientation) Regulations 2003 and the Employment Equality (Religion or Belief) Regulations 2003* (2003), at para 14, referring to *Kokkanikis v Greece* (1994) 17 EHRR 397.

[462] *Explanatory Notes* (2003), at para 11.

[463] *X v UK* (1977) 11 DR 55.

[464] *Explanatory Notes* (2003), at para 12, referring to *Campbell and Cousans v UK* (1982) 4 EHRR 293.

[465] *Explanatory Notes* (2003), at para 13. See *McClintock v Department of Constitutional Affairs* [2008] IRLR 29.

[466] *Explanatory Notes* (2011), at para 52. For discussion, see Pitt, 2011.

[467] *Grainger v Nicholson* [2010] IRLR 4.

[468] *Maistry v BBC* ET/1313142/10.

opposition to fox-hunting and hare-coursing,[469] but that membership of a political party,[470] belief in spiritualism[471], belief in the idea that 9/11 and 7/7 were 'false flag' operations organised as part of a government-led conspiracy,[472] and belief in the importance of wearing a Remembrance day poppy,[473] were not.

The 2003 *Notes* suggested that a distinction should be drawn, for the purposes of determining whether direct or indirect discrimination had occurred, between a 'manifestation' of religious belief, for example in the form of clothing or the expression of certain views, and the belief itself.[474] The effect of taking this view is that unfavourable treatment or disadvantage associated with manifestations of belief will be, at best, indirect discrimination, and so allow the employer a justification defence. Thus in *Azmi v Kirklees Metropolitan Borough Council*[475] the employment tribunal ruled that a requirement that a Muslim teaching assistant should not wear the niqab (the full-face veil) in class, did not constitute direct discrimination on the grounds of religion, but consisted instead of the application of a formally neutral provision, criterion or practice, which was justifiable in the circumstances as it was necessary for the pupils to see her face when she was carrying out her duties. The EAT upheld this ruling, while suggesting that there was no bar, in principle, to disadvantage associated with a manifestation of belief amounting to direct discrimination; each case would turn on its own facts.[476] In *Eweida v British Airways*[477] the complainant, who had been disciplined for wearing a plain silver cross in breach of the employer's rules on dress and appearance, which ruled out the wearing of religious items unless they could be shown to be 'mandatory' requirements of the religion in question, failed even to establish that there had been adverse impact related to her religious beliefs.

The courts have generally taken a broad view of the justification defence which is available to employers in cases of indirect discrimination on the grounds of religion and belief. In *Ladele v London Borough of Islington*[478] the complainant, a registrar of births and marriages, was disciplined for refusing to conduct civil partnership registrations (which under the Civil Partnership Act 2004 are available only to same-sex partners) on grounds related to her Christian beliefs. The Court of Appeal accepted the employer's argument that to allow the complainant to be exempted from the duty to perform civil partnership registrations would contravene its 'dignity for all' policy, the aim of which was to avoid discrimination within employment and also in the provision of services by the Council to the community it served. A relevant factor in this case was that the Council had offered the complainant a compromise under which she would not have been required to officiate at civil partnership ceremonies which went beyond the simply signing process, which she had rejected.

---

[469] *Hashman v Milton Park (Dorset) Ltd t/a Orchard Park* ET/3105555/2009.

[470] *Baggs v Fudge* ET/1400114/05 (membership of the British National Party). In *Kelly v Unison* ET/2203854/08 an employment tribunal found that Trotskyist views did not constitute a philosophical belief, but it would seem that belief in an organised political philosophy or doctrine should in principle come under the protection of the Act (see *Maistry v BBC* ET/1313142/10).

[471] *Greater Manchester Police Authority v Power* UKEAT/04334/09.

[472] *Farrell v South Yorkshire Police Authority* ET/2803805/10.

[473] *Lisk v Shield Guardian Co Ltd.* ET/3300873/11.

[474] *Explanatory Notes* (2003), at para 15.

[475] [2007] IRLR 484.

[476] [2010] IRLR 322, at [75]-[77].

[477] [2009] IRLR 78 (EAT), [2010] IRLR 322 (CA).

[478] [2010] IRLR 211. See also *Macfarlane v Relate Avon* [2010] IRLR 872.

THE SCOPE OF PROTECTION AGAINST DISCRIMINATION IN EMPLOYMENT

Personal scope

6.47   We now analyse some issues relating to the scope of the prohibition of discrimination relating to employment.[479] Equality legislation applies to all aspects of the employment relationship, from hiring through to (and in some cases beyond) termination. A first point to note is that the legislation applies both to 'employees' as they are normally defined, referring to persons employed under a contract of employment or apprenticeship, and to those who are employed under contracts for services, where these give rise to an obligation 'personally to do work'.[480] Somewhat confusingly, given its normal meaning,[481] the 2010 Act applies the term 'employee' to each of these groups.[482] Agency workers have the benefit of the protection of the legislation in their relationships both with the agency or 'employment service-provider',[483] and with the user or 'principal'.[484] These are useful extensions to the coverage of the law. However, they by no means solve all the problems of classification which may arise. For example, the courts asserted that, under the test for identifying employment under the RRA 1976, not only was mutuality of obligation required for there to be a contract for services,[485] but that a clear personal commitment to provide work or labour, on the part of the complainant, was essential,[486] while more recently they have held, highly questionably, that the test for identifying employment in cases of religion or belief discrimination excludes work relationships lacking the feature of 'subordination'.[487] The requirement that there be a contract for the exchange of personal service or services for remuneration has also been invoked to explain the exclusion of a claim for disability discrimination brought by a volunteer worker in a citizens advice bureau.[488]

In relation to agency work, the fragmentation of the normal responsibilities of the employer between two distinct entities – the agency and the user or 'principal' – gives rise to problems which are not fully addressed by the present law. Although the issue is not free from doubt, the legislation can be read as imposing upon the user or principal an obligation to treat agency workers equally with comparable 'permanent' workers in relation, for example, to the general working

---

[479] For discussion of the territorial scope of the 2010 Act, see para 2.47 above. The Act is mostly silent on the issue of territorial effect so that the relevant general principles of law apply, but allows for Ministers to determine the application of the Act to employment on board ships and hovercrafts and on offshore installations by order: see EqA 2010, ss 81, 82; SI 2011/1771; SI 2010/1835.

[480] EqA 2010, s 83(2). See our discussion in ch 3 above, at para 3.33.

[481] See ch 3 above, at para 3.19.

[482] EqA 2010, s 83(4).

[483] EqA 2010, ss 55-56.

[484] EqA 2010, s 41, which amends earlier provisions to make it clear that there does not need to be a direct contractual relationship between the agency and the user or principal (see Hepple, 2011a: p 87). See above, para 3.35. Note that office-holders who do not otherwise fall under the relevant definitions are also covered, with certain specified exceptions: EqA 2010, ss 49-52.

[485] *Mingeley v Pennock* [2004] IRLR 373.

[486] See, for various applications of this test, *Loughran and Kelly v Northern Ireland Housing Executive* [1998] IRLR 593; *Perceval-Price v Department of Economic Development* [2000] IRLR 380; *Patterson v Legal Services Commission* [2004] IRLR 153.

[487] *Jivraj v Hashwani* [2011] IRLR 827. See our analysis in ch 3 above, at para 3.33; McCrudden, 2012; Freedland and Kountouris, 2012.

[488] *X v Mid-Sussex CAB* [2011] IRLR 335.

environment in the employment in question. But in so far as the user is not directly responsible for setting terms and conditions of employment, which are normally determined by the agency, it is arguable that, for this purpose, there can be no comparison of, for example, the pay and hours of agency staff and those of the 'permanent' workers in the same employment under EqA 2010.[489]

Discrimination against partners and applicants for partnerships falls under the Equal Treatment, Framework and Race Directives and now under the 2010 Act.[490] Trade unions, employers' associations and trade associations fall under the 2010 Act in respect of their treatment of applicants and members,[491] and 'qualifying' or 'qualification' bodies which are responsible for conferring authorisations or qualifications for professional purposes are also covered,[492] as are providers of vocational training.[493] EqA 2010 applies to Crown employment and to Parliamentary staff,[494] to the police,[495] and to the armed forces.[496]

Hiring

6.48   It is unlawful for an employer (A) to discriminate against a person (B) '(a) in the arrangements A makes for deciding to whom to offer employment; (b) as to the terms on which A offers B employment; [or] (c) by not offering B employment',[497] with parallel provisions applying to victimisation.[498]   Case law under earlier versions of this provision suggests that in addition to being able to show that the employer contravened the equality principle by refusing or omitting to hire him or her on grounds which were discriminatory, the complainant may also challenge the arrangements made by the employer for determining who is appointed, including the composition of the shortlist and the form of the interview,[499] as well as the terms on which the job is offered. Although difficulties of proof are substantial here, they may be eased by the use of the statutory questionnaires to elicit from the respondent the reasons for its decision,[500] as well as by the willingness of the courts, following *West Midlands Passenger Transport Executive v Singh*,[501]

---

[489]   See the judgment of the Court of Appeal in *Allonby v Accrington and Rossendale College* [2001] IRLR 364, at [34]– [36] (Sedley LJ). In this case the Court of Appeal referred questions relating to the scope of comparison under the EqPA 1970 to the ECJ, which decided on a narrow reading of Art 141 TEC (now Art 157 TFEU), under which comparisons across undertakings are generally not possible (Case C-256/01 *Allonby v Accrington and Rossendale College* [2004] IRLR 224). See further our analysis at para 6.82 below. Agency workers may now make a claim for equal treatment with permanent workers of the user or 'hirer' under AWR 2010: see para 3.53 above.

[490]   EqA 2010, ss 44-46. On discrimination against barristers and advocates, see EqA 2010, ss 47-48.

[491]   EqA 2010, s 57 (for an application of one of the the predecessor provisions, s 12 SDA 1975, in action against a trade union, see *Allen v GMB* [2008] IRLR 690).

[492]   EqA 2010, ss 53, 96-97.

[493]   This is the effect of EqA 2010, s 56, extending the scope of s 55 on employment service-providers.

[494]   EqA 2010, s 83(2)(b), (c), (d).

[495]   EqA 2010, ss 42-43.

[496]   EqA 2010, s 83(3). The armed forces nevertheless benefit from a 'combat readiness' exception (see below, para 6.60). Note also EqA 2010, s 121 requiring a 'service complaint' to be made prior to applying to an employment tribunal.

[497]   EqA 2010, s 39(1).

[498]   EqA 2010, s 39(3).

[499]   See *Roadburg v Lothian Regional Council* [1976] IRLR 283; *Saunders v Richmond-upon-Thames London Borough Council* [1978] ICR 75.

[500]   EqA 2010, s 138; SI 2010/2194. See *King v Great Britain-China Centre* [1991] IRLR 513, discussed in para 6.64 below.

[501]   [1988] ICR 614.

to countenance the use of statistical evidence concerning the composition of the workforce and patterns of previous hirings as evidence of discriminatory practices. The changes made to the definition of discrimination as a result of the implementation of the Burden of Proof Directive, together with similar provisions in the Framework and Race Directives, have also helped in this regard.[502] The remedies available to a disappointed applicant may also be significant; because damages for injury to feelings may be awarded[503] and because there is no upper limit on compensation,[504] damages may well be more than nominal, and there is also the possibility (albeit not a very strong one) that the tribunal could make a recommendation that the complainant be hired on the next occasion of a vacancy arising.[505]

Terms of employment, access to promotion, transfer and training, and detrimental treatment in employment

6.49   An employer (A) must not discriminate against an employee in its employment (B) '(a) as to B's terms of employment; (b) in the way A affords B access, or by not affording B access, to opportunities for promotion, transfer or training or for receiving any other benefit, facility or service; (c) by dismissing B; or (d) by subjecting B to any other detriment'.[506] Parallel provisions apply to victimisation of an employee by their employer.[507]

(i) Sex equality clause exclusion

6.50   The scope of the prohibition of sex discrimination in employment is artificially restricted in order to ensure that it does not trespass on the ground covered by the provisions of the Act on equal pay between women and men. The latter, which are inherited (with some amendments) from the Equal Pay Act 1970, are limited in significant respects; unlike the general prohibition on discrimination, which enables a comparison to be made between the complainant and a hypothetical comparator, the equal pay provisions of the Act require an actual comparator who also falls into one of the three situations specified in the legislation, namely like work, work rated as equivalent and work of equal value with that of the applicant.[508] Notwithstanding these limits, the general prohibition has no effect in relation to terms of the contract that would be modified by, or included by virtue of, the sex equality clause which gives effect to the equal pay provision (or would be so modified or included but for the operation of a defence of material factor),[509] unless the case is one of direct sex discrimination in relation to contractual pay.[510] The effect of this is

---

[502] See para 6.63 below.
[503] EqA 2010, s 119(4), read with s 124(6).
[504] See below, para 6.66.
[505] See *North West Thames Regional Health Authority v Noone* [1988] ICR 813.
[506] EqA 2010, s 39(2).
[507] EqA 2010, s 39(4).
[508] See below, paras 6.88-6.91.
[509] EqA 2010, s 70 (referring also to the sex equality rule that operates in the context of occupational pension schemes); see also s 39(6) on discriminatory hiring. For decisions under the pre-2010 law, see *Meeks v NUAAW* [1976] IRLR 198; *Hosso v European Credit Management Ltd.* [2012] IRLR 235.
[510] EqA 2010, s 70. Such cases will, by their nature, be rare. See below, para 6.80.

that once the employment has begun, other than in cases of direct sex discrimination in relation to contractual pay, differences in contractual terms and conditions falling under the equal pay principle must be judged under the more narrow provisions of the sex equality clause.[511]

(ii) Detriment

6.51   The term 'detriment' has been broadly defined since the introduction of employment discrimination legislation. The approach in *Peake v Automotive Products Ltd*[512] in which the Court of Appeal held that the employer's practice of allowing women workers to leave the factory floor five minutes earlier than their male colleague was held to be, in Lord Denning's words, 'perfectly harmless',[513] has not been followed. In *Ministry of Defence v Jeremiah*[514] the requirement that men, but not women, should agree to undertake dirty and unpleasant work in order to be eligible for overtime, was held to be a detriment. In this case there was a 'deprivation of choice', and it was irrelevant that the complainant received financial compensation for doing the work in question. In *Kirby v Manpower Services Commission*[515] the transfer of the employee to a less interesting job was held to be a 'detriment' for this purpose. In *Shamoon v Chief Constable of the Royal Ulster Constabulary*[516] the House of Lords stressed that it is not necessary for an applicant to demonstrate some physical or economic consequence, but the tribunal must find that by reason of the act complained of a reasonable worker might take the view that he or she had thereby been disadvantaged in the circumstances in which they had thereafter to work. A detriment can arise from psychological illness or stress but transient hurt feelings may not suffice.[517] In *Moyhing v Barts and London NHS Trust*[518] a male nurse was subjected to a detriment by virtue of a requirement that he should be 'chaperoned' when he carried out certain procedures on female patients, when the same rule did not apply to female nurses treating male patients.

A persistently controversial issue has been the application of the notion of detriment in the context of sex-specific dress codes. At the level of the contract of employment, it is clear that the employer has an inherent power to lay down rules governing dress and appearance at work ('dress codes'). Such rules are unlikely, in themselves, to be terms of the contract; it is more likely that they are akin to the rule book issued in *ASLEF (No 2)*,[519] which was no more than an emanation of the employer's managerial prerogative. Like other rules of this kind, dress codes are subject to the

---

[511]   See Hepple, 2011: pp 98-99. It is not clear whether Art 157 TFEU and the Equal Treatment Directive are mutually exclusive in the same way. For a view that the Equal Treatment Directive, prior to its amendment, was applicable to certain issues of contractual terms and conditions and employment-related benefits which might also fall under Art 157, see the Opinion of Advocate General Van Gerven in Case C-262/88 *Barber v Guardian Royal Exchange Assurance Group* [1990] IRLR 240 (and see Ellis, 1991: p 136); for a decision suggesting the opposite, see the Judgment of the ECJ in Case C-77/02 *Steinicke v Bundesanstalt für Arbeit* [2003] IRLR 892.

[512]   [1978] QB 233.

[513]   [1978] QB 233, 239.

[514]   [1980] ICR 13.

[515]   [1980] IRLR 229. See also *Gloucester Working Men's Club & Institute v James* [1986] ICR 603, 606 (threatening a person with dismissal may be a 'detriment' even though that threat is not carried out).

[516]   [2003] IRLR 285.

[517]   *Jiad v Byford* [2003] IRLR 232.

[518]   [2006] IRLR 860.

[519]   *Secretary of State for Employment v ASLEF (No 2)* [1972] 2 QB 455.

common law notion of the reciprocal duty of co-operation; if an employer were to impose rules which were clearly oppressive to individuals in the sense of undermining their personal dignity,[520] or which not were reasonably related to the jobs which they carried out, it is arguable that *to that extent* the rules could not be enforced, in the sense that to do so would be a breach of contract by the employer. However, this common law constraint on the employer's power is residual, at best, and unlikely to provide a firm foundation for a challenge mounted by an employee. More concrete support may be provided by HRA 1998; dress codes may constitute an interference with respect for private life or freedom of expression unless they can be justified, although they are likely to be easier to justify if confined to the workplace than if they also intrude on conduct outside work.[521]

However, the contractual position on dress codes is necessarily subject to the principle of equal treatment. In practice the greatest difficulty here is caused by rules which formally differentiate between the sexes.[522] If such rules amount to direct discrimination there is no possibility of the open-ended justification defence being invoked, so that managerial prerogative in an important area would then be significantly qualified. Whatever the business justifications for dress codes, there is an argument to the effect that dress codes, at least in certain forms, reinforce sex-based stereotypes which the Act is intended to address.[523] The courts have struggled to find a clear line which might successfully reconcile these two positions.

In *Schmidt v Austick Bookshops Ltd*[524] the EAT was faced with a complaint about a rule that female employees were not allowed to wear trousers at work. A variety of grounds were offered for concluding that no sex discrimination had taken place. One was that male and female employees were not being treated unequally: 'there were in force rules restricting wearing apparel and governing appearance which applied to men and also applied to women, although obviously, women and men being different, the rules in the two cases were not the same'.[525] In *Smith v Safeway plc*[526] the EAT interpreted *Schmidt* as establishing the principle that 'the law permits different rules to be applied to men and women provided they enforce a common principle of smartness if read as a whole'. The difficulty with this view, plausible as it might seem, is that it strikes at the core of the concept of direct discrimination: as Cunningham points out, 'the whole purpose of the Act is to limit the extent to which women and men, different as they are, can be differently treated'. To say that the undeniable difference between men and women is a sufficient reason for applying different rules to women than to men is 'to demolish it in its entirety'.[527] This aspect of *Schmidt* is even more difficult to defend in the light of the 'but-for' test applied by the

---

[520] An example of this might be a rule requiring an employee to wear a uniform which was sexually provocative and which exposed him or her to sexual harassment: see, eg, the US case of *EEOC v Sage Realty Corpn* 507 F Supp 599 (1981), in which a rule of this kind was found to violate Title VII of the Civil Rights Act.

[521] *Kara v UK*, Application No 36528/97; see G Morris, 2001a.

[522] On dress and appearance in the context of manifestations of religious belief, see para 6.46 above.

[523] See generally Flynn, 1995, and for a review of the issue of legal regulation of dress and appearance, Skidmore, 1999. In the context of discrimination on the grounds of religion or belief, dress code issues tend to give rise to claims of indirect rather than direct discrimination, and so may be justified, or may not give rise to any discrimination at all: see above, para 6.46.

[524] [1977] IRLR 360.

[525] [1977] IRLR 360, 361.

[526] [1995] IRLR 132, 133.

[527] Cunningham, 1995: p 178.

House of Lords in the *Birmingham County Council*[528] and *James*[529] cases: clearly, the complainant would not have been treated in the same way had she been a man.[530]

A more coherent (if, nonetheless, still debatable) ground offered in *Schmidt* was that the complainant in that case suffered no 'detriment' by being required to wear a skirt or dress when at work. Similarly, in *Burrett v West Birmingham Health Authority*[531] the EAT and Court of Appeal decided that a female nurse who was required to wear a cap as part of her uniform, when male nurses were not required to do so as part of theirs, had not thereby been sufficiently disadvantaged for a detriment to arise, despite the complainant arguing that it was demeaning. The Court of Appeal went on to hold that while the complainant had later suffered a detriment when she was disciplined for refusing to wear the cap, this was not an act of sex discrimination since a man in the same position, who had refused to wear part of his uniform, would also have been subjected to a disciplinary sanction.

In *Smith v Safeway plc*[532] the Court of Appeal, overturning a ruling of the EAT, held that a male shop assistant in a supermarket delicatessen who was dismissed for having a pony-tail had not thereby been discriminated against on the grounds of his sex. Safeway operated two different rules, one for men and one for women. Men were required to have 'tidy hair not below shirt collar length', for women, 'shoulder-length hair must be clipped back'. The majority of the EAT (Pill J dissented) distinguished *Schmidt* on the grounds that that case was concerned with the issue of dress and appearance while at work; *Smith*, on the other hand, addressed 'the issues of appearance which extend beyond working hours and thereby affect individual choice detrimentally at all times'. The majority also thought that it was unnecessary for the employer to have imposed differential rules on hair-length for men and women: 'the need to present a conventional appearance at work is already met by the standards laid down as to hairstyle which, in the case of a pony-tail, is specifically capable of being treated the same for both men and women'.[533] In the Court of Appeal, by contrast, Peter Gibson LJ considered that an employer would not be acting unlawfully by adopting a 'code which applies conventional standards' to both sexes.[534]

The concept of detriment arguably needs to be given a broad meaning if the legislation is not to be stymied, and should be concerned solely with the question of whether the complainant has suffered a tangible disadvantage and not with the quite separate issue of whether the disadvantage was *justifiable*, since that would be to undermine the distinction between direct and indirect discrimination.[535] Of the cases just considered, *Burrett* suggests that the courts could limit the scope of the equality principle by defining 'detriment' narrowly and by drawing a distinction between the effect of the rule itself, which may be discriminatory but not a detriment, and the effect of the disciplinary action designed to enforce the rule, which may be a detriment but not discriminatory. But perhaps it is the case that 'a reading of the Act which has the result that

---

[528] [1989] IRLR 173.
[529] [1990] IRLR 288.
[530] On the but-for test in this context, see above, para 6.19.
[531] [1994] IRLR 7, EAT; (3 March 1994, unreported), CA, discussed by Cunningham, 1995.
[532] [1996] IRLR 456.
[533] [1995] IRLR 132, 134.
[534] [1996] IRLR 456, 459. To similar effect is the decision of the EAT in *Department for Work and Pensions v Thompson* [2004] IRLR 348.
[535] Cunningham, 1995.

employers may not in general enforce different dress codes on their male and female employees suggests a more radical contempt for social *mores* than can have been intended when the Act was drafted'.[536]

(iii) Dismissal

6.52   Dismissal is one of the specific employment-related wrongs covered by EqA 2010. Dismissal is defined as including the termination of a limited-term contract ('the termination of … [a person's] employment… by the expiry of a period (including a period expiring by reference to an event or circumstance', unless 'immediately after the termination, the employment is renewed on the same terms') and a constructive dismissal (the termination of employment by an act of that person (including giving notice) such that he or she 'is entitled, because of [their employer's] conduct, to terminate the employment without notice').[537]

Discriminatory dismissal is almost bound to be unfair under ERA 1996, although it is not automatically unfair in the sense that certain other categories of reasons are.[538] In practice, where the complainant can choose between these statutory claims, resort to the 2010 Act is more likely. In contrast to most unfair dismissal claims, no qualifying period is required under equality legislation. Nor are there any statutory upper limits on compensation. The changes made to the law governing the burden of proof[539] have made a discrimination-based claim more attractive, by comparison to an unfair dismissal claim, than used to be the case. In addition, the right to claim unfair dismissal under ERA 1996 is confined to employees, whereas the anti-discrimination legislation extends to a wider category of employed persons.[540]

Post-contractual and post-relationship discrimination

6.53   In *Rhys-Harper v Relaxion Group plc*[541] the House of Lords held that certain discriminatory acts occurring after the termination of the complainant's contract of employment were within the coverage of the pre-2010 legislation. This issue initially arose in the context of employees who, following an initial decision to dismiss, lodged an appeal under the employer's internal disciplinary procedures. According to the Court of Appeal in *Post Office v Adekeye (No 2)*,[542] any discrimination occurring at this later stage applied to a period when the complainant was no longer 'employed'. In *Coote v Granada Hospitality Ltd*.[543] the ECJ held that, under the Equal Treatment Directive (prior to its amendment[544]), a remedy had to be provided for ex-employees

---

[536] Cunningham, 1995: p 179.

[537] EqA 2010, s 39(7).

[538] See para 5.92 *et seq* above.

[539] See below, para 6.63.

[540] See para 6.47 above.

[541] *Rhys-Harper v Relaxion Group plc, D'Souza v London Borough of Lambeth, Jones v 3M Healthcare Ltd, Kirker v British Sugar plc, Angel v New Possibilities NHS Trust, Bond v Hackney Citizens Advice Bureau* [2003] IRLR 484.

[542] [1997] IRLR 105. See also *Nagarajan v Agnew* [1994] IRLR 61.

[543] Case C-185/97 *Coote v Granada Hospitality Ltd* [1998] IRLR 656, applied in *Coote v Granada Hospitality Ltd (No 2)* [1999] IRLR 452.

[544] By Directive 2002/73.

who were the subject of victimisation by their employer. The EAT and Court of Appeal in *Rhys-Harper* held that this decision had no application beyond victimisation cases.[545] When the case reached the House of Lords, the majority concluded that the reference to an 'employed' person was, after all, sufficiently wide to cover ex-employees as long as certain elements of the employment relationship remained in place notwithstanding the termination of the complainant's contract. In Lord Nicholls' view:

> ... the natural and proper interpretation of s 6(2) of the Sex Discrimination Act and the corresponding provisions of the [Race Relations Act and Disability Discrimination Act] in this context is that once two persons enter into the relationship of employer and employee, the employee is intended to be protected against discrimination by the employer in respect of all the benefits arising from that relationship ... This being the purpose, it would make no sense to draw an arbitrary line at the precise moment when the contract of employment ends, protecting the employee against discrimination in respect of all benefits up to that point but in respect of none thereafter.[546]

According to Lord Rodger, the Acts applied where 'there is a substantive connection between the discriminatory conduct and the employment relationship',[547] while Lord Hobhouse pointed to the need to show that a given dispute fell within the 'employment field'[548] in order for an employment tribunal to have jurisdiction. Lord Hope, drawing more explicitly on the ECJ judgment in *Coote*, argued that 'the relationship between the employer and the employee does not necessarily come to an end at the precise moment when their contract terminates'. Under section 6(2) of the SDA as interpreted by reference to the Directive, a former employee was protected as 'long as the transactions that remain to be completed are attributable to a continuation of [the] relationship of employer and employee', and there was, in his view, no reason not to extend this meaning to the similar expressions used in the RRA and DDA.[549] Lord Scott took a more restricted view of the reach both of the Acts and of the Directive and confined his opinion to ruling that, on its proper interpretation, the legislation could apply to cases of internal appeal procedures, but not to other instances of post-employment discrimination beyond a limited range of scenarios.[550]

The effect of the ruling in *Rhys-Harper* and a series of other cases decided at the same time was that a failure of the employer to apply an internal disciplinary procedure, to respond to a reasonable request for a reference or to return property to the employee, in so far as they involved a breach of the equal treatment principle, were all capable of coming under the anti-discrimination statutes. Although an employer's refusal to comply with a reinstatement or re-engagement order issued by an employment tribunal was held not to be covered by this principle,[551] a failure to honour a tribunal award of compensation for unfair dismissal and discrimination was.[552]

---

[545] [2000] IRLR 810; [2001] IRLR 460.
[546] [2003] IRLR 484, at [37].
[547] [2003] IRLR 484, at [215].
[548] [2003] IRLR 484, at [150,] referring to SDA 1975, s 63(1), RRA 1976, s 54(1) and DDA 1995, s 8(1).
[549] [2003] IRLR 484, at [114–115].
[550] [2003] IRLR 484, at [200].
[551] This was the effect of the ruling in *D'Souza v London Borough of Lambeth* [2003] IRLR 484.
[552] *Rank Nemo (DMS) Ltd v Lance Coutinho* [2009] EWCA Civ 454, 20 May 2009.

The issue of post-contractual discrimination has also received the attention of the legislature. By virtue of amendments made while the *Rhys-Harper* case was still being decided and now contained, in an amended form, in EqA 2010, a person (A) must not discriminate against another (B) where 'the discrimination arises out of and is closely connected to a relationship which used to exist between them', and 'conduct of a description constituting the discrimination would, if it occurred during the relationship', amount to a contravention of the Act.[553] This provision does more than clarify the meaning of *Rhys-Harper*. The opinions of the House of Lords refer to discrimination which is post-contractual but within the period when the 'relationship' of employment is still subsisting. By referring to a 'post-relationship' period, the Act furthers extends the reach of the equality principle.

Personal and vicarious liability

6.54   Employers may be liable under EqA 2010 either personally or vicariously, and employees may also incur liability in circumstances where their conduct triggers the vicarious liability of their employer. The employer's vicarious liability is provided for by section 109 EqA 2010, under which '[a]nything done by a person (A) in the course of A's employment must be treated as also done by the employer',[554] whether or not it is done with the employer's knowledge or approval.[555] The employer has a defence if it can show that it took 'all reasonable steps' to prevent the employee from doing the thing which gave rise to liability or 'anything of that description'.[556] In *Jones v Tower Boot Co Ltd*[557] the complainant was subjected to racial taunts and acts of violence by his fellow employees, of a kind which were sufficiently extreme to fall outside the course of those employees' course of employment as defined by the common law. The Court ruled that, for this purpose, the phrase 'course of employment' in the context of the RRA 1976 had to be given a purposive interpretation, precisely in order to avoid the conclusion that 'the more heinous the act of discrimination, the less likely it will be that the employer would be liable'. To apply the traditional common law test would, thought Waite LJ, 'seriously undermine the statutory scheme of the Discrimination Acts and flout the purposes which they were passed to achieve'.[558]

The personal liability of the employee is established in circumstances where he or she does something which gives rise to vicarious liability on the part of the employer, as just defined.[559] For this purpose, it is no bar to the claim that the employer has the benefit of the defence that

---

[553] EqA 2010, s 108(1).
[554] EqA 2010, s 109(1).
[555] EqA 2010, s 109(3).
[556] EqA 2010, s 109(4).
[557] [1997] IRLR 168, reversing the EAT ([1995] IRLR 529).
[558] [1997] IRLR 168, 172; a similarly broad construction was given to the term 'course of employment' in a different context in *Chief Constable of the Lincolnshire Police v Stubbs* [1999] IRLR 81. Although the courts accept the need to go beyond the common law test when deciding discrimination claims, they have continued to recognise limits to the employer's responsibility for incidents, such as assaults, occurring away from the place of employment: see *Sidhu v Aerospace Composite Technology Ltd.* [2000] IRLR 602. On the development of the common law test, which over time has moved closer to the statutory version of the test applied in *Jones*, see *Lister v Hesley Hall Ltd* [2001] IRLR 472; *Maga v Archbishop of Birmingham* [2010] 1 WLR 1441; *Various Claimants v Institute of the Brothers of the Christian Schools* [2010] EWCA Civ 1106; *JGE v English Province of Our Lady of Charity* [2012] IRLR 301; *Weddall v Barchester Healthcare Ltd; Wallbank v Wallbank Fox Designs Ltd* [2012] IRLR 307.
[559] EqA 2010, s 110(1).

it took all reasonable steps to prevent the relevant conduct of the employee.[560] It is, however, a defence for an employee to show that he or she reasonably relied on a statement by their employer 'that doing that thing is not a contravention of this Act'.[561] The legislation also makes provision for liability where one person knowingly helps another to contravene the Act,[562] and for liability for instructing, causing or inducing another to do anything in relation to a third party which contravenes the Act.[563]

It can be argued that an employer which fails to put in place a policy of discouraging harassment in relation to one or more of the protected characteristics, which may be inferred if it lacks a procedure for dealing with complaints, may for that reason be *personally* liable under EqA 2010 for subjecting employees for example, to a working environment in which sexual or racial harassment is possible. This is consistent with the European Commission's Recommendation of 27 November 1991 on the protection of the dignity of women and men at work.[564] The Recommendation calls on Member States to take action to promote awareness that sexual harassment, or 'conduct of a sexual nature, or other conduct based on sex affecting the dignity of women and men at work' is unacceptable, which will be the case where it is 'unwanted, unreasonable and offensive to the recipient'; leads to the victim being adversely treated in his or her employment; and/or 'creates an intimidating, hostile or humiliating work environment'.[565] The Commission's Code of Practice, which is appended to the Recommendation, lays out a number of suggestions to be followed by employers and by trade unions. It notes that 'as sexual harassment is often a function of women's status in the employment hierarchy, policies to deal with sexual harassment are likely to be most effective where they are linked to a broader policy to promote equal opportunities and improve the position of women'.[566] It is suggested that employers should have a clear policy stating that sexual harassment at work will not be permitted and should put in place procedures for dealing with complaints, including provision for investigations and disciplinary offences.

A robust approach to the issue of harassment was taken in the racial discrimination case of *Burton v De Vere Hotels*.[567] Here, two black women who were employed as waitresses alleged that they had suffered racial harassment as a result of racial remarks made by a stand-up comedian and by customers during a dinner at which they were serving. The employment tribunal found that they had been subjected to a detriment, but that the employer was not responsible for it. The EAT reversed on the basis that the employer had itself 'subjected' the complainants to a 'detriment' under section 4(2)(c) of the RRA 1976, by failing to take steps to prevent the harassment occurring when it could have done so. According to Smith J, '... an employer subjects an employee to the detriment of racial harassment if he causes or permits the racial harassment to occur in circumstances in which he can control whether it happens or not'.[568] However, in *Pearce v Governing Body of Mayfield School*[569] the House of Lords held that *Burton* had been wrongly decided: the harassment

---

[560] EqA 2010, s 110(2).
[561] EqA 2010, s 110(3).
[562] EqA 2010, s 112.
[563] EqA 2010, s 111.
[564] The Recommendation built on an expert report carried out by Rubinstein, 1988.
[565] Art 1.
[566] Code of Practice, para 3.
[567] [1996] IRLR 596.
[568] [1996] IRLR 596, 600.
[569] [2003] IRLR 512.

in question was carried out by a third party for whose conduct the employer could not have been vicariously liable. The 'control' test suggested in *Burton* was explicitly rejected.[570]

The coming into force of a free-standing statutory wrong of harassment[571] does not completely overcome the limitations inherent in *Pearce*: it is still necessary to establish that the employer is either personally or vicariously liable for the conduct which amounts to the harassment. The addition of liability for third party harassment, in circumstances where the employer knows that the employee has been harassed by a third party on at least two prior occasions and has failed to take such steps as were reasonably practicable to prevent the harassment,[572] may help overcome the limitations of *Pearce*. However, at the time of writing, this provision is under review by the Coalition Government.[573]

Genuine occupational requirements

6.55   The concept of a 'genuine occupational qualification' or 'genuine occupational requirement' refers to a feature of a particular job or position which potentially justifies the exclusion of an individual from that employment on grounds which would otherwise be prohibited. These concepts draw on the notion of 'bona fide occupational qualifications' (or BFOQs) in the US Civil Rights Act 1964. Under that legislation, a BFOQ arises where 'religion, sex, or national origin is a bona fide occupational qualification reasonably necessary to the normal operation of that particular business or enterprise'.[574] Guidelines issued by the US Equal Employment Opportunity Commission provide more specific indications of what is permitted and what is not, in particular by prohibiting refusals to hire based on:

> ... stereotyped characterisations of the sexes. Such stereotypes include, for example, that men are less capable of assembling intricate equipment; that women are less capable of aggressive salesmanship [sic]. The principle of non-discrimination requires that individuals be considered on the basis of individual capacities and not on the basis of any characteristics generally attributed to the group.[575]

The SDA 1975 and the RRA 1976, as initially drafted, made reference to a number of specific genuine occupational qualifications (or 'GOQ's). The list was exhaustive: a GOQ could only arise where the case fell under one of the situations outlined in section 7 of the SDA 1975 or section 5 of the RRA 1976. The concept of the genuine occupational requirement (or 'GOR') was introduced with reference to UK law by the Framework and Race Directives of 2000:[576]

---

[570] [2003] IRLR 512, at paras 31–35 (Lord Nicholls), 100 (Lord Hope), 204 (Lord Rodger).
[571] See para 6.33 above.
[572] EqA 2010, s 40. See para 6.33 above.
[573] See para 6.33 above.
[574] Civil Rights Act 1964, s 703(e); 42 USC 2000e-2(e).
[575] EEOC Guidelines on Discrimination Because of Sex, s 1604.2(a)(1)(ii); 29 CFR s 1604.2(a)(1)(ii).
[576] Art. 4(1) of the Framework Directive (2000/78) and Art 4 of the Race Directive (2000/43).

> Member States may provide that a difference of treatment which is based on a characteristic related to [one or more of the prohibited] grounds … shall not constitute discrimination where, by reason of the nature of the particular occupational activities concerned or of the context in which they are carried out, such a characteristic constitutes a genuine and determining occupational requirement, provided that the objective is legitimate and the requirement is proportionate.

This provision, with some modifications, now operates as a general GOR defence under EqA 2010, applying to each of the protected characteristics.[577] The effect is to introduce an open-ended defence based on occupational requirements, akin to the US concept of the BFOQ. The more specific GOQs set out under the SDA 1975 and RRA 1976 have been repealed.

The general GOR defence applies where an employer applies in relation to work a requirement to have a particular protected characteristic where it can show, 'having regard to the nature or context of the work', that the requirement is an occupational one, that its application is a proportionate means of achieving a legitimate aim, and either that the person to whom the requirement is applied does not meet it or that the employer has reasonable grounds for not being satisfied that he or she does meet it.[578] The condition in question must be a 'requirement', which the *Explanatory Notes* on the 2010 Act explain means that it 'must be crucial to the post, and not merely one of several important factors. It also must not be a sham or pretext'.[579]

That there is a GOR not simply where the complainant objectively speaking, does not satisfy the relevant requirement but also where the employer reasonably thinks that they do not was unsuccessfully challenged in relation to EqA 2010's predecessor legislation as being contrary to the Framework Directive in *R (on the application of Amicus – MSF Section) v Secretary of State for Trade and Industry*.[580] According to Richards J, the formula used in the Regulations fell within the scope of the phrase 'based on a characteristic related to' sexual orientation in the Directive,[581] and, moreover, met the need to protect employers in cases where they would otherwise be required to take at face value an assertion by the complainant that they met the requirement in question.

Two further definitions of the GOR concept apply in cases involving religious employment. In the first,[582] an employer may apply one of a number of requirements if it can show that the employment is for the purposes of an organised religion, that the application of the requirement engages the 'compliance' principle or the 'non-conflict' principle, and that either the person to whom the requirement is applied does not meet it or the employer has reasonable grounds for not being satisfied that they do.[583] The 'compliance' principle is triggered where 'the requirement is applied so as to comply with the doctrines of the religion',[584] and the 'non-conflict' principle is

---

[577] EqA 2010, Sch 9, para 1.
[578] EqA 2010, Sch 9, para 1(1). Note that in the case of the protected characteristic of marriage and civil partnership and of that of gender reassignment, the defence works asymmetrically: it can be a defence to make it a requirement that a person *not* be married or a civil partner, and in the same way it can be a defence to require that a person *not* be a transsexual person (para 1(3)), but not, in either case, vice versa. This is because, in these two cases, no discrimination is committed if the employer imposes a requirement that the person should have the relevant protected characteristic. See above, paras 6.38, 6.39.
[579] *Explanatory Notes* (2010), at para 787.
[580] [2004] IRLR 430.
[581] Directive 2000/78, Art 4.
[582] EqA 2010, Sch 9, para 2.
[583] EqA 2010, Sch 9, para 2(1).
[584] EqA 2010, Sch 9, para 2(5).

triggered where 'because of the nature or context of the employment, the requirement is applied so as to avoid conflicting with the strongly held religious convictions of a significant number of the religion's followers'.[585] The requirements that the employer can apply under this provision are: a requirement that a person should be of a particular sex; a requirement that a person should not be a transsexual person; a requirement that a person should not be married or a civil partner; a requirement that a person should 'not be married to, or the civil partner of, a person who has a living former spouse or civil partner'; a requirement 'relating to the circumstances in which a marriage or civil partnership came to an end'; and 'a requirement related to sexual orientation'.[586] According to the 2010 *Explanatory Notes*, this provision is intended to 'cover a very narrow range of employment: ministers of religion and a small number of lay posts, including those that exist to promote and represent religion'.[587] As with the general GOR, the Notes suggest that the requirement must be 'crucial'.[588] The defence is apparently intended to apply 'to a requirement that a Catholic priest be a man and unmarried' but not to 'a requirement that a church youth worker who primarily organises sporting activities is celibate if he is gay, but it may apply if the youth worker mainly teaches Bible classes'.[589]

In the case of the second additional GOR, a defence is made out if the employer shows that it has a particular 'ethos based on religion or belief', and that 'having regard to that ethos and to the nature and context of the work', the employer applies an occupational requirement which is a proportionate means of achieving a legitimate aim, and either that the person to whom the requirement is applied does not meet it or the employer has reasonable grounds for not being satisfied that they do.[590] This provision is meant to apply to a case where, for example, 'a religious organisation … [wishes] to restrict applicants for the post of head of its organisation to those people that adhere to that faith' since 'to represent the views of that organisation accurately it is felt that the person in charge of that organisation must have an in-depth understanding of the religion's doctrines', but 'other posts that do not require that sort of in-depth understanding, such as administrative posts, should be open to all people regardless of their religion or belief'.[591]

Other exceptions

(i) Health and safety

6.56   The original section 51 of the SDA 1975 provided an exemption in respect of acts done under the authority of statutory requirements pre-dating the Act of 1975. The main purpose of this was to enable access to certain jobs by women to be restricted on the grounds of health and

---

[585] EqA 2010, Sch 9, para 2(6).
[586] EqA 2010, Sch 9, para 2(4).
[587] At para 790.
[588] At para 791.
[589] At para 793.
[590] EqA 2010, Sch 9, para 3.
[591] *Explanatory Notes* (2010), para 796. In *Jivraj v Hashwani* [2011] IRLR 827 the Supreme Court held that the requirement that an arbitrator in a commercial dispute between two members of Ismaili community should be a member of that religious group would have fallen under the 'religious ethos' GOR had it been necessary to decide this point (the claim of discrimination failed on the separate ground that the role of arbitrator was not an employment within the meaning of the Religion or Belief Regulations 2003; see above, para 6.47).

safety, and the point was reinforced by section 7(2)(f) which made it a GOQ to discriminate against a woman on the grounds that 'the job needs to be held by a man because of restrictions imposed by the laws regulating the employment of women'. By contrast, Title VII of the US Civil Rights Act 1964 provided that the principle of equal treatment should prevail over contrary state law which 'purports to require or permit' the doing of acts contrary to Title VII.[592] Similarly, the Equal Treatment Directive, in its original form, called on Member States to revise discriminatory protective statutes 'when the concern for protection which originally inspired them is no longer well founded',[593] with the exception of regulations concerning pregnancy and maternity;[594] a four-year timetable for review of such regulations by the individual Member States was laid down.[595] The derogation for regulations concerning pregnancy and maternity was given a narrow interpretation by the ECJ in its 1986 decision in *Johnston v Chief Constable of the Royal Ulster Constabulary*,[596] and in 1987 the European Commission issued a communication to Member States suggesting that they should implement the Equal Treatment Directive by a combination of measures removing restrictions on women's access to certain employments and 'levelling up' where appropriate by extending similar rights to men. The Commission also suggested that sex-specific regulations should only be retained where they could be justified by the 'separate biological condition' of one sex.[597]

The United Kingdom chose to implement this aspect of the Equal Treatment Directive in a series of steps. First, certain protective legislation affecting women was repealed entirely. The SDA 1986 removed controls on nightworking by women and the EA 1989 repealed restrictions on women working underground in mines and quarries, as well as certain restrictions on employment in textiles and in jute, pottery and cement manufacture.[598] Second, the EA 1989 provided that any remaining statutes which required sex discrimination contrary to the SDA 1975 were to that extent overriden,[599] and as a sweeping-up measure the Secretary of State for Employment was given the power to repeal such legislation by order.[600] Third, the EA 1989 amended section 51 of the SDA 1975 to provide for a more limited defence than previously: this was confined to cases where action in relation to a woman was necessary in order to comply with a statute concerning the protection of women with regard to '(i) pregnancy or maternity, or (ii) other circumstances giving rise to risks specifically affecting women', or necessary to comply with general health and safety legislation.[601] Fourth, for the avoidance of doubt, certain legislation restricting access to employment on grounds of a woman's pregnancy was specifically preserved.[602] Under EqA 2010, these exemptions are continued in force.[603]

---

[592] Civil Rights Act 1964, s 708; *Rosenfeld v Southern Pacific Co* 444 F 2d 1219 (1971).

[593] Directive 76/207, Arts 3(2)(c), 5(2)(c).

[594] Directive 76/207, Art 2(3).

[595] Directive 76/207, Art 9(1).

[596] Case 222/84 [1986] IRLR 263.

[597] *Protective Legislation for Women in the Member States of the European Community*, Communication of 20 March 1987, COM (87) 105 final.

[598] See generally Deakin, 1990a.

[599] EA 1989, s 1.

[600] EA 1989, s 2. He or she also has the power to disapply the override: EA 1989, s 6. On the statutory override generally, see Deakin, 1990a: pp 8–9.

[601] In particular, s 2(1) of the HSWA 1974: see *Page v Freight Hire (Tank Haulage) Ltd* [1981] IRLR 13.

[602] EA 1989, s 5.

[603] EqA 2010, Sch 22, para 2.

(ii) Statutory authority

6.57   Unlike the SDA 1975, other anti-discrimination statutes contained certain generally-phrased exclusions with regard to acts of discrimination done in pursuance of statutory authority, and these are also continued in force under EqA 2010.[604]

(iii) National security

6.58   Acts done for the purpose of safeguarding national security do not contravene the 2010 Act if they are 'proportionate ... for that purpose'.[605]

(iv) Charities and educational bodies

6.59   Charitable instruments may lawfully restrict the provision of benefits to persons who share a protected characteristic where to do so is a proportionate means of achieving a legitimate aim or is for the purpose of preventing or compensating for a disadvantage linked to the protected characteristic.[606] Certain specified educational appointments may also be restricted to persons of a certain sex or to members of certain religious orders.[607]

(v) The armed forces

6.60   Discrimination against women and transsexual persons in relation to recruitment, access to training, promotion and transfer opportunities, and any other benefit, facility or service, is permitted where it can be shown to be a proportionate means of ensuring 'the combat effectiveness of the armed forces', and the armed forces also have a general exemption from the prohibitions on age and disability discrimination in employment.[608]

(vi) Sport

6.61   EqA 2010 permits the separate organisation of sporting events for men and women by virtue of a provision which applies to 'gender-affected activities', which are defined as 'any sport, game or other activity of a competitive nature in circumstances in which the physical strength, stamina or physique of average persons of one sex would put them at a disadvantage compared to average persons of the other sex as competitors in events involving the activity',[609] and declares

---

[604] See EqA 2010, Sch 22 para 1 and Sch 23, para 1.
[605] EqA 2010, s 192.
[606] EqA 2010, s 193.
[607] EqA 2010, Sch 22, para 3.
[608] EqA 2010, Sch 9, para 4(1)-(3). See Hepple, 2011a: pp 110-111. On the position of the armed forces exclusion under EU law, see Case C-273/97 *Sirdar v Army Board and Secretary of State for Defence* [2000] IRLR 47.
[609] EqA 2010, s 195(3).

lawful for this purpose the doing of 'anything in relation to the participation of another as a competitor' in such an activity.[610] In addition, the doing of 'anything in relation to the participation of a transsexual person as a competitor in a gender-affected activity' is permitted if it is necessary in order to secure either 'fair competition' or 'the safety of competitors'.[611]

ENFORCEMENT

6.62   We now turn to issues of enforcement. We firstly consider some specific issues relating to individual claims, concerning the burden of proof, and the obtaining of evidence relating to discrimination. Then we look at the remedies available in individual claims, before examining administrative enforcement through the EHRC.

The burden of proof in discrimination, harassment and victimisation cases

6.63   It has been accepted since the early days of the legislation that a finding of discrimination depends on the court or tribunal drawing an inference from the primary facts. In *Chattopadhyay v Headmaster of Holloway School*[612] Browne-Wilkinson J went so far as to say that 'if an applicant shows that he has been treated less favourably than others in circumstances which are consistent with that treatment being based on racial grounds, the employment tribunal should draw an inference that such treatment was on racial grounds, unless the respondent can satisfy the employment tribunal that there is an innocent explanation'. According to Neill LJ in *King v Great Britain-China Centre*, given that it is 'unusual to find direct evidence of racial discrimination', the tribunal was entitled to draw an inference from the primary facts and to reach a conclusion 'bearing in mind both the difficulties which face a person who complains of unlawful discrimination and the fact that it is for the complainant to prove his or her case'.[613] When these cases were decided, a court or tribunal was not *bound* to draw an inference of discrimination merely because no clear explanation was offered by the employer. However, the position was altered over time to bring UK law into line with EU requirements. The model here was section 63A of the SDA 1975, inserted by way of compliance with the Burden of Proof Directive of 1997. This provided that where the complainant 'proves facts from which the tribunal could ... conclude in the absence of an adequate explanation that the respondent ... has committed an act of discrimination ... the tribunal shall uphold the complaint unless the respondent proves that he did not commit ... that act'. Section 136 EqA 2010 now provides that '[i]f there are facts from which the court could decide, in the absence of any other explanation, that a person (A) contravened the provision concerned, the court must hold that the contravention occurred',[614] unless 'A shows that A did not

---

[610]   EqA 2010, s 195(1).

[611]   EqA 2010, s 195(2).

[612]   [1981] IRLR 487, 490. See also *Khanna v Ministry of Defence* [1981] IRLR 331; *North West Thames Regional Health Authority v Noone.* [1988] ICR 813, 822 (May LJ); *King v Great Britain-China Centre* [1991] IRLR 513.

[613]   [1991] IRLR 513, 518. This test was approved by the House of Lords in *Zafar v Glasgow City Council* [1998] IRLR 36, 38.

[614]   EqA 2010, s 136(2). References to a court include an employment tribunal: s 136(6).

contravene the provision'.[615] This provision applies to any proceedings relating to a contravention of the Act,[616] and hence not just in respect those protected characteristics covered by EU law as was the case prior to 2010.

Case law decided under the pre-EqA 2010 legislation established that the complainant had to show, on the balance of probabilities, that there were facts from which an inference of discrimination could be drawn; only then would the burden shift.[617] The 2010 Act no longer refers to the need for the complainant to 'prove facts' on which an inference of discrimination can be based, and so would appear to have made the so-called first stage of the reverse-burden test somewhat more flexible, although it will presumably still be for the complainant to adduce facts from which an inference can be drawn.[618] Once the burden shifts, pre-2010 case law suggests that the tribunal should require 'cogent evidence' of non-discrimination from the employer.[619] However, the tribunal should not draw an inference of discrimination merely because it considers that the complainant has been treated unreasonably or unfairly.[620]

Evidence of discrimination

6.64   The burden on the complainant is also eased by the provision made for the tribunal to admit in evidence the respondent's response to a questionnaire which the complainant is entitled to send it, requiring the respondent to explain its conduct.[621] The form of the questionnaire is laid down by statutory instrument.[622] The respondent is called on to explain, among other things,

---

[615]   EqA 2010, s 136(3).

[616]   EqA 2010, s 136(1).

[617]   *Barton v Investec Henderson Crosthwaite Securities Ltd* [2003] IRLR 332, at [25], approved, in amended form, by the Court of Appeal in *Igen Ltd (formerly Leeds Careers Guidance) v Wong* [2005] IRLR 258, at [76]; see also *Madarassy v Nomura International Ltd* [2007] IRLR 246. Evidence of bias on the part of a selection panel was held to give rise to a finding of discrimination even in a case where it was only one factor in the employer's decision: *O'Donoghue v Redcar and Cleveland Borough Council* [2001] IRLR 615.

[618]   See Hepple, 2011a: p 166-7.

[619]   *Barton v Investec Henderson Crosthwaite Securities Ltd.* [2003] IRLR 332, at [25]; *Igen Ltd (formerly Leeds Careers Guidance) v Wong* [2005] IRLR 258, at [76]; *Laing v Manchester City Council* [2006] IRLR 748; *Brown v Croydon LBC* [2007] IRLR 259; *Appiah v Governing Body of Bishop Douglass Roman Catholic High School* [2007] IRLR 264.

[620]   *Zafar v Glasgow City Council* [1997] IRLR 229, Ct of Sess; affd [1998] IRLR 36, HL; *Martins v Marks & Spencer plc* [1998] IRLR 326; *Madden v Preferred Technical Group Cha Ltd* [2005] IRLR 46. The employer is *not* required to prove on the balance of probabilities, in the event of unreasonable treatment of the complainant, that a similarly situated comparator of the complainant would have been treated just as unreasonably (see *Anya v University of Oxford* [2001] IRLR 377, at [14], discussed in *Bahl v Law Society* [2003] IRLR 640, at [97], [2004] IRLR 799, at [101]). Thus the respondent does not as such have the burden of disproving a discrimination claim (*Parliamentary Commissioner for Administration v Fernandez* [2004] IRLR 22) and an employment tribunal must set out the facts from which it has drawn an inference of discrimination in looking to the respondent to explain the conduct in question (*Sinclair, Roche and Temperley v Heard* [2004] IRLR 763). On the circumstances under which the burden of proof can shift in particular kinds of cases, see *Dresdner Kleinwort Wasserstein v Adebayo* [2005] IRLR 514; *Network Rail Infrastructure v Griffiths-Henry* [2007] IRLR 865; *EB v BA* [2006] IRLR 471; *Nelson v Newry and Mourne DC* [2009] IRLR 548; *B v A* [2010] IRLR 400; *Pothecary Witham Weld v Bullimore* [2010] IRLR 572.

[621]   EqA 2010, s 138, replacing SDA 1975, s 74 and parallel provisions under the other anti-discrimination statutes. These provisions were interpreted as allowing an inference of discrimination to be drawn from incorrect information provided by the employer in a form other than that prescribed for the statutory questionnaires: *Dattani v Chief Constable of West Mercia Police* [2005] IRLR 327. See now EqA 2010, s 138(3).

[622]   SI 2010/2194, Sch 1, governing claims relating to prohibited conduct under the 2010 Act. Part 2 deals with equal pay claims (see below, para 6.94).

why it disputes the claim of unlawful discrimination; why the complainant received the treatment accorded to him or her; and how far the relevant protected characteristic affected the treatment they received. The court or tribunal may 'draw an inference' from the respondent's failure to reply to the questionnaire within an eight week period, or from an 'evasive or equivocal' answer,[623] unless the respondent invokes one of a number of exemptions, including the risk of prejudicing criminal proceedings.[624]

In *King v Great Britain-China Centre*[625] the complainant was Chinese by origin and had lived most of her life in the UK. She made an application for the post of deputy director of the Centre but was not shortlisted for interview despite being very well qualified on paper. The majority of the employment tribunal held that she had been treated less favourably than certain other candidates who, while in a similar position, had been interviewed; they also considered that the employer, who had been sent a statutory questionnaire, had failed to give an adequate explanation of its conduct. A finding of racial discrimination was accordingly made, and was upheld on appeal.

Statistical evidence of a racial or sexual imbalance between different job grades or groups within the employer's workforce may also be used to draw an inference of direct discrimination. This was accepted by the Court of Appeal in *West Midlands Passenger Transport Executive v Singh*.[626] According to Balcombe LJ:

> Statistics obtained through monitoring are not conclusive in themselves, but if they show racial or ethnic imbalance or disparities, then they may indicate areas of racial discrimination. If a practice is being operated against a group then, in the absence of a satisfactory explanation in a particular case, it is reasonable to infer that the complainant, as a member of the group, has himself been treated less favourably on grounds of race. Indeed, evidence of discriminatory conduct against the group in relation to promotion may be more persuasive of discrimination in the particular case than previous treatment of the applicant, which may be indicative of personal factors peculiar to the applicant and not necessarily racially motivated.

In particular, statistical evidence may assist an applicant first in showing that racial or sexual discrimination was an effective cause of the treatment he or she received, and second, in rebutting an employer's argument that it was operating an effective equal opportunities policy.[627]

The employment tribunal has the power to order disclosure of documents by the respondent on the application of the complainant or of its own motion,[628] and this may help him or her to overcome the burden of proof. In exercising this power, however, the tribunal must balance the importance of the documents or information in question for the conduct of the proceedings with the need to preserve confidentiality.[629] Confidentiality is very likely to be an issue where the complainant seeks disclosure of documents relating to an employment or promotion which he or

---

[623] EqA 2010, s 138(4). For the view, under the pre-2010 law, that giving an answer to a question in a discrimination questionnaire does not automatically give rise to a presumption of discrimination where there was a good reason for the failure, such as the excessive cost of gathering the requested information, see *D'Silva v NATFHE* [2008] IRLR 412.

[624] EqA 2010, s 138(5). See also SI 2010/2194 (referring to national security).

[625] [1991] IRLR 513.

[626] [1988] ICR 614, 619, effectively overruling, on this point, *Jalota v Imperial Metal Industry (Kynoch) Ltd* [1979] IRLR 313.

[627] [1988] ICR 614, 621; *Home Office v Coyne* [2000] IRLR 838.

[628] See SI 2004/1861, Sch 1, para 10.

[629] *Science Research Council v Nassé* [1978] ICR 1124; affd [1979] ICR 921.

she failed to secure. Another possibility is that the complainant will seek disclosure of statistical evidence concerning the composition of parts of the employer's workforce, for example; as we have just seen, although the Court of Appeal accepted in *West Midlands Passenger Transport Executive v Singh*[630] that this could in principle form evidence of a discriminatory practice which operated to the detriment of a particular individual, it also warned against 'oppressive disclosure', which would include the provision of information which is only available at great expense or which would add unreasonably to the cost and length of the hearing.

Remedies

(i) Complaint to an employment tribunal

6.65   The three remedies which are potentially available to employment tribunals in respect of discrimination are a declaration of rights, an award of compensation and a recommendation.[631] The complainant must make their application to an employment tribunal within three months of the occurrence of the 'act to which the complaint relates',[632] although the tribunal also has the power to hear a complaint which is out of time if it considers that it is just and equitable to do so.[633] These provisions have on the whole been flexibly applied, in contrast to the rather more restrictive approach taken under the claim-in-time provisions of ERA 1996.[634] Complainants may also be helped in this regard by the notion of 'continuing discrimination'. The legislation provides that 'conduct extending over a period' can be brought within three months of the end of that period'.[635] This provision was applied by the House of Lords in *Barclays Bank plc v Kapur*[636] to hold that a failure by the employer to count a period of previous service towards an employee's pension rights continued up to the point at which the complaint was lodged.

(ii) Compensation

6.66   Compensation is payable according to the principles which would apply to a civil claim in tort,[637] and for this purpose it is declared for 'the avoidance of doubt' that 'damages may include

---

[630] [1988] ICR 614.

[631] EqA 2010, s 124(2).

[632] EqA 2010, s 123(1).

[633] EqA 2010, s 123(1)(b).

[634] See *Hutchinson v Westward Television Ltd* [1977] IRLR 69; *Lupetti v Wrens Old House Ltd* [1984] ICR 348; and on claim in time under ERA 1996, see para 2.17 above.

[635] EqA 2010, s 123(3).

[636] [1991] IRLR 136; see also *Sougrin v Haringey Health Authority* [1992] IRLR 416; *Owusu v London Fire and Civil Defence Authority* [1995] IRLR 574; *Rovenska v General Medical Council* [1997] IRLR 367; *Cast v Croydon College* [1998] IRLR 318; *Tyagi v BBC World Service* [2001] IRLR 465; *Hendricks v Commissioner of Police of the Metropolis* [2003] IRLR 96.

[637] EqA 2010, s 119(2)(a) (applied to employment tribunals by virtue of s 124(6)). On the tort-based nature of damages, see *Ministry of Defence v Cannock* [1994] IRLR 509; *Sheriff v Klyne Tugs (Lowestoft) Ltd* [1999] IRLR 481 *ICTS (UK) Ltd v Tchoula* [2000] IRLR 643; *Essa v Laing Ltd* [2004] IRLR 313 (holding that losses could be recovered if they flowed naturally and directly from the wrong, thereby rejecting a test based on foreseeability).

compensation for injured feelings'.[638] This marks an important distinction between awards under EqA 2010 and those under ERA 1996 for unfair dismissal;[639] another difference is that EqA 2010 makes no provision for a reduction in damages for the complainant's contributory fault. Although an award for injury to feelings is not automatic, substantial damages may be awarded under this head. In *Deane v Ealing London Borough Council*,[640] where there was detailed evidence of the complainant's hurt feelings on being denied promotion on grounds of his race, an award of £1,000 was made, and in *Noone v North West Thames Regional Health Authority*[641] the Court of Appeal ordered £3,000 damages under this head for 'the affront and distress caused to Dr Noone by having her legitimate and honourable ambition to become a consultant microbiologist thwarted'. In *Doshoki v Draeger Ltd*[642] £4,000 was awarded by the EAT in respect of persistent racial taunts and insults, overturning an award of £750 by the employment tribunal. In *Armitage v Johnson*[643] the complainant was awarded £21,000 under this head for the effects of a systematic campaign of racial harassment, although in *Vento v Chief Constable of West Yorkshire Police (No 2)*[644] the tribunal's award of £50,000 for injury to feelings was reduced to £18,000. In *Vento* the Court of Appeal identified three broad bands of compensation, which, as later updated in *Da'Bell v NSPCC*,[645] are: £18,000–£30,000 for 'the most serious cases'; £6,000–£18,000 for 'serious cases'; and £500-£6,000 for 'less serious cases, such as where the act of discrimination is an isolated or one-off occurrence'. In general, awards of less than £500 should be avoided 'as they risk being regarded as so low as not to be a proper recognition of injury to feelings'. [646]

The courts have held in the past that exemplary or punitive damages, which are not compensatory in nature but are designed purely as a deterrent, may not normally be awarded in discrimination cases,[647] on the basis of what was understood at one time to be the general position in tort law.[648] However, in *Sivanandan v London Borough of Hackney*[649] the EAT reconsidered the issue and decided that, in line with developments in tort law, exemplary damages could be awarded for oppressive, arbitrary or unconstitutional action, although it declined to make such an award in this case. Aggravated damages, understood as damages payable in respect of intentional or malicious damage inflicted on the complainant, are properly regarded as compensatory in nature, and so may be awarded in an appropriate discrimination case. In *Armitage v Johnson*[650] the EAT made an award of aggravated damages on top of damages to injury to feelings, an approach

---

[638] EqA 2010, s 119(4).
[639] See para 5.147 above.
[640] [1993] IRLR 209; cf *Alexander v Home Office* [1988] IRLR 190; *Owusu v London Fire and Civil Defence Authority* [1995] IRLR 574.
[641] [1988] IRLR 195, 204.
[642] [2002] IRLR 340.
[643] [1997] IRLR 163; *ICTS (UK) Ltd v Tchoula* [2000] IRLR 643; *British Telecommuncations plc v Reid* [2004] IRLR 327.
[644] [2003] IRLR 102.
[645] [2010] IRLR 19.
[646] Mummery LJ at [65]. See *Al Jumard v Clwyd Leisure Ltd* [2008] IRLR 354 for the approach to be taken in relation to different forms of discrimination.
[647] *Deane v Ealing London Borough Council* [1993] IRLR 209; *Ministry of Defence v Cannock* [1994] IRLR 509.
[648] *AB v South West Water Services Ltd* [1993] 1 All ER 609. This decision has since been overruled by *Kuddus v Chief Constable of Leicestershire Constabulary* [2002] 2 AC 122.
[649] [2011] IRLR 740. This judgment is also notable for the EAT's carefully reasoned application of tort law rules on apportionment and contribution to the discrimination law context. See also *Ministry of Defence v Fletcher* [2010] IRLR 25.
[650] [1997] IRLR 163; *Minstry of Defence v Fletcher* [2010] IRLR 25.

followed in later case law.[651] The Law Commission has suggested that exemplary or punitive damages should be available on a more general basis in anti-discrimination cases.[652]

Until 1993 the legislation applied an upper limit to the amount of compensation which an employment tribunal could award, which was equivalent to the limit to the compensatory award for unfair dismissal.[653] However, the application of an upper limit in sex discrimination cases was successfully challenged before the ECJ on the grounds of its incompatability with the Equal Treatment Directive, in *Marshall v Southampton and South West Hampshire Area Health Authority (No 2)*.[654] The Court ruled that 'the fixing of an upper limit of the kind at issue ... cannot, by definition, constitute proper implementation of Article 6 of the Directive, since it limits the amount of compensation *a priori* to a level which is not necessarily consistent with the requirement of ensuring real equality of opportunity through adequate reparation for the loss and damage sustained as a result of discriminatory dismissal'.[655] The Court also held that Article 6 required that an award of interest be made on compensation, and that in both these respects the Article had vertical direct effect in national law, so conferring immediate rights on employees in claims against organs of the state. Following *Marshall (No 2)*, the upper limits under both the SDA 1975 and the RRA 1976 were abolished and employment tribunals were granted the right to award interest on compensatory awards.[656]

The correct approach to the awards of compensation under the amended provisions can be seen from *Ministry of Defence v Cannock*,[657] a set of test cases arising from dismissals of members of the armed forces on the grounds of pregnancy. In relation to the extent of compensation, the EAT held that the relevant principles of tort law should apply to claims under the Directive, as they would to claims under the SDA 1975. This meant that the award of compensation should be designed so as to put the complainants in the position which they would have occupied had the Ministry of Defence not dismissed them unlawfully on the grounds of pregnancy. In this respect, the EAT held that there was an important difference between a situation of unlawful dismissal such as the present one, where the career prospects of the complainant would be harmed but without her necessarily being thereby disabled from finding another employment at some point, and a situation of personal injury of the kind more normally litigated through a claim in tort, where a complainant's claim for loss of earning capacity might well be much more extensive: 'to this extent, [the complainants'] compensation for loss of earnings is not likely to be different from the thousands of cases of unfair dismissal with which the Employment tribunals are having to deal each year, albeit that there is no cap on the award'.[658] Later case law has established that while it is unlikely that, following discriminatory dismissal, a complainant will be awarded compensation for loss of earnings for the whole period from dismissal up to their likely date of retirement,

---

[651] See *Vento v Chief Constable of West Yorkshire Police (No 2)* [2003] IRLR 102; *Scott v Commissioners of Inland Revenue* [2004] IRLR 713; *Commissioner of Police of the Metropolis v Shaw* [2012] IRLR 291 (applying the same principles in the context of a protected disclosure case under ERA 1996, Part IVA (on which, see para 4.117 above)).

[652] Law Commission Report No 247, *Aggravated, Exemplary and Restitutionary Damages* (1997).

[653] See para 5.145 above.

[654] Case C-271/91 [1993] IRLR 445.

[655] [1993] IRLR 445, 449.

[656] SI 1993/2798; Race Relations (Remedies) Act 1994.

[657] [1994] IRLR 509; *Ministry of Defence v Meredith* [1995] IRLR 539; *Ministry of Defence v Hunt* [1996] IRLR 139; see also *Ministry of Defence v Wheeler* [1998] IRLR 23 (on the correct approach to percentage deductions for loss of a chance).

[658] [1994] IRLR 509, 525.

substantial compensation for lost future earnings may nevertheless be awarded to reflect the true loss of the complainant,[659] including 'stigma' damages in respect of the greater difficulty they are likely to face in finding future work as a result of bringing a discrimination claim.[660]

Prior to the implementation of the 2010 Act, a tribunal had no power generally (with some exceptions) to award compensation in a case of indirect discrimination if it was satisfied that the employer had not intended to discriminate against the complainant. This restriction has now been removed, and the tribunal may now award compensation in an indirect discrimination case, although only after first considering whether to grant a declaration of rights or make a recommendation.[661]

(iii) Recommendation

6.67   The remedy of a recommendation enables the tribunal to recommend that 'within a specified period the respondent takes steps for the purpose of obviating or reducing the adverse effect of any matter to which the proceedings relate... (a) on the complainant; [and] (b) on any other person'.[662] Prior to the coming into force of the 2010 Act, the tribunal could only consider the effect on the complainant. If the respondent fails to comply with the recommendation 'without reasonable excuse', the tribunal may order compensation to be paid or increase the amount of compensation it has already ordered to be paid.[663]

In pre-EqA 2010 cases the courts gave the remedy of recommendation a highly restrictive application. In *Noone v North West Thames Regional Health Authority (No 2)*,[664] where the complainant was not appointed as a consultant microbiologist on grounds which were found to be racially motivated, the Court of Appeal declined to approve a recommendation that the next time a vacancy came up within the organisation for the post in question, it should not be advertised, the aim being to ensure that the complainant would be appointed. This was because the failure to advertise the post would have set at nought the statutory procedure for making the appointment. In *British Gas plc v Sharma*[665] the EAT overruled a tribunal recommendation to the effect that the complainant be promoted to the post from which she had been wrongfully excluded the next time a suitable vacancy arose, on the grounds that a recommendation had to indicate the action to be taken 'within a specified period'; since it was not known when a vacancy might arise in the future, the recommendation made by the tribunal was invalid. The need for the recommendation to be acted on within a specified period remains in force under the 2010 Act.[666]

The introduction of a power to make recommendations in respect of other persons nevertheless makes it possible for the recommendation remedy to be used more proactively in future. The *Explanatory Notes* to the 2010 Act suggest that it could be used, *inter alia*, to recommend the introduction of an equal opportunities policy, the more effective implementation of a harassment

---

[659]   *Vento v Chief Constable of West Yorkshire Police (No 2)* [2003] IRLR 102; *Orthet Ltd. v Vince-Cain* [2004] IRLR 857; *Chagger v Abbey National plc* [2010] IRLR 47; *Crédit Agricole Corporate and Investment Bank v Wardle* [2011] ICR 1290.

[660]   *Chagger v Abbey National plc* [2010] IRLR 47.

[661]   EqA 2010, s 124(4)-(5).

[662]   EqA 2010, s 124(3).

[663]   EqA 2010, s 124(7).

[664]   [1988] IRLR 530.

[665]   [1991] IRLR 101. See also *Irvine v Prestcold Ltd* [1981] IRLR 281.

[666]   EqA 2010, s124(3).

policy, the setting up of a review panel to deal with equal opportunities-related grievances, staff retraining, and making public the criteria used for the transfer or promotion of staff.[667]

(iv) Removal or modification of contract terms

6.68   A term of a contract is unenforceable against a person in so far as it constitutes, promotes or provides for treatment of that or another person which is prohibited by the Act [668] and a person with 'an interest' in the contract in question may apply to the county court for an order to have the term removed or modified.[669] For disability alone this also applies to non-contractual terms relating to the provision of employment services or group insurance arrangements for employees ('relevant non-contractual terms').[670] A contract term or relevant non-contractual term which purports to exclude or limit the application of the Act is unenforceable by the person in whose favour it would operate.[671] In addition, any term of a collective agreement is void in so far it constitutes, promotes or provides for treatment of a description prohibited by the Act, and any rule of an undertaking which similarly contravenes the Act is unenforceable.[672] Provision is made in each case for an application to be made to an employment tribunal for a declaration of nullity.[673]

Administrative enforcement and the role of the EHRC

6.69   The responsibility for enforcing certain provisions of EqA 2010 is devolved to the Equality and Human Rights Commission,[674] which inherited the powers of the EOC, CRE and DRC.[675] The Commission has powers to undertake inquiries[676] and investigations[677] and issue unlawful act notices[678] which can lead, among other things, to a requirement to adopt an action plan to avoid repetition of the unlawful acts in question.[679] It can also enter into binding agreements

---

[667] *Explanatory Notes* (2010), at para 406.

[668] EqA 2010, s 142(1). On the meaning of a relevant non-contractual term, see s 141(3).

[669] EqA 2010, s 143.

[670] EqA 2010, ss 142(2),(3); 143.

[671] EqA 2010, s 144.

[672] EqA 2010, s 145. 'Collective agreement' has the meaning given in TULRCA 1992, s 178: EqA 2010, s 148; see further para 9.26 below.

[673] EqA 2010, s 146. The section specifies those persons who may apply to an employment tribunal under this procedure.

[674] A full account of the Commission's operations and functions lies outside the scope of this book. See Hepple, 2011a: pp 145-154; Hepple, 2011b; 2012.

[675] With the establishment of the additional prohibited grounds of discrimination, relating to sexual orientation, religion or belief, and age, the case for the integration of the different bodies with responsibilities for enforcing and overseeing anti-discrimination law was raised. In October 2003 the government announced that it was in favour of an integrated body, and in May 2004 published a White Paper, *Fairness for All: A New Commission for Equality and Human Rights: White Paper* Cm 6185, 2004, setting out its proposals, which were subsequently enacted in the Equality Act 2006. See para 2.34 above; O'Cinneide, 2007.

[676] EqA 2006, s 16.

[677] EqA 2006, s 20.

[678] EqA 2006, s 21.

[679] EqA 2006, s 22.

with employers and others[680] and issue a compliance notice in the case of non-compliance with a public authority's duty to promote equality.[681] The Commission has the power to seek a court order requiring compliance with one of its notices.[682]

In addition, under provisions inserted by EqA 2010, the Commission can use any of its general investigatory and compliance powers in relation to acts of direct or indirect discrimination in employment (as well as in other contexts relevant to the 2010 Act),[683] and can also intervene where an employer makes prohibited inquiries about job applicants' disabilities or health.[684] These provisions replace earlier ones relating to discriminatory advertisements and related discriminatory practices.

POSITIVE ACTION

6.70 We now analyse the legality of positive action to address discrimination. The 2010 Act has made a number of significant changes to the law on this issue, firstly by allowing employers generally to take steps to address situations in which the numbers of persons with a given protected characteristic is disproportionately low and to take positive action, within strictly defined limits, in recruitment and promotion, and secondly by extending the duty of public authorities to have due regard to the need to eliminate discrimination, advance equality of opportunity and foster relations between groups, in such a way as to enhance the scope for positive action.

Positive action by employers

(i) The pre-2010 Act law

6.71 In the USA, private-sector voluntary affirmative action programmes designed to remedy conspicuous racial imbalances in an employer's workforce, designed to be temporary in nature and striking a balance between the interests of different groups of employees (particularly in relation to accrued seniority rights), were declared lawful under Title VII by the Supreme Court in *United Steelworkers of America v Weber*.[685] In addition to this permissive interpretation of the Civil Rights Act, Executive Order 11246, adopted in 1965, required federal government contractors to take 'affirmative action' to recruit, hire and promote women and racial minorities where they had previously been 'under-utilised' in the employer's workforce. The legality of this type of practice

---

[680] EqA 2006, s 23.
[681] EqA 2006, s 32; see below, para 6.75.
[682] EqA 2006, s 22(6), 32(8). Under the law governing the investigatory functions of the EOC and CRE, the courts took a limited view of the Commissions' powers: see the fourth edition of this book (2005), at para 6.70. For an assessment of the changes made by EqA 2006, see O'Cinneide, 2007.
[683] EqA 2006, s 24A. The exercise by the Commission of these powers does not rule out an individual claim arising from a breach of the Act: s 24A(4).
[684] EqA 2010, s 60.
[685] 443 US 193 (1979).

has however been called into question, both in the employment field and more widely, both under Title VII and under the Fourteenth Amendment to the US Constitution.[686]

By contrast, in the UK context, 'positive' or 'reverse' discrimination, in so far as that is understood to mean preferential treatment of an individual on the grounds of his or her sex, or racial group, was until recently ruled out by the strict nature of the direct discrimination test.[687] The House of Lords' decision in *James v Eastleigh Borough Council*,[688] which determined that motive is irrelevant in the context of direct discrimination, reinforced this position. The principal anti-discrimination Acts contained a derogation which was designed to permit preferential treatment relating to arrangements for training and the encouragement of employment opportunities. Under section 47 of the SDA 1975, access to training facilities could be made available to women only or to men only, or the employer could encourage women only or men only to take up opportunities for doing certain work, where it reasonably appeared to the provider that in the preceding twelve months there were no persons of that sex doing work of that kind in Great Britain, or that the number of such persons was comparatively small. Similarly, an employer was entitled by section 48 of the SDA 1975 to make similar access available to training in relation to work in its employment, again where there were either no members of that sex doing such work or a comparatively small number within the preceding twelve months. The same approach was taken to the provisions of training facilities for particular racial groups under sections 37 and 38 of the RRA 1976.

The Framework Directive on Discrimination[689] and the Race Directive[690] contain provisions according to which '[w]ith a view to ensuring full equality in practice, the principle of equal treatment shall not prevent any Member State from maintaining or adopting specific measures to prevent or compensate for disadvantages linked to' the ground of discrimination in question. In line with this provision, British legislation enacting the provisions of the Directive in the early 2000s permitted positive action to be taken to afford persons of a particular religion or belief, sexual orientation or age, access to facilities for training that would help fit them for particular work, or to encourage such persons to take advantage of opportunities for doing particular work, to compensate them for disadvantages linked to their religion or belief, sexual orientation or age.[691]

(ii) Positive action and sex discrimination under EU law

6.72   The legality of positive action under EU law was first considered in *Kalanke v Freie Hansestadt Bremen*.[692] In this case the rule in question 'automatically gave priority to women in sectors where they are underrepresented, underrepresentation being deemed to exist when women do not make up at least half of the staff in the individual pay brackets in the relevant

---

[686] See *Johnson v Santa Clara County* 480 US 616 (1987); *Richmond v JA Croson* 488 US 469 (1989); *Podbersky v Kirwan* 38 F 3d 147 (1994); *Gratz v Bollinger* 539 US 244 (2003).

[687] See Barmes, 2003.

[688] [1990] IRLR 288.

[689] Directive 2000/78/EC, Art 7.

[690] Directive 2000/42/EC, Art 5.

[691] EE(SO)R 2003, reg 26; EE(RB)R 2003, reg 25; EE(A)R 2006, reg 29.

[692] Case C-450/93 [1995] IRLR 660. See Schiek, 1996, 2000; Prechal, 1996; Fredman, 1997a; Barnard, 1998; Betten and Shrubshall, 1998; Barnard and Hepple, 2000.

personnel group'.[693] The Court considered that a rule which meant that 'where women and men who are candidates for the same promotion are equally qualified, women are automatically to be given priority in sectors where they are underrepresented, involves discrimination on grounds of sex'[694] and so was contrary to the Equal Treatment Directive. It also refused to bring this type of practice within the derogation provided by Article 2(4) of the Directive, which, at that point, permitted 'measures to promote equal opportunity for men and women, in particular by removing existing inequalities which affect women's opportunities',[695] ruling that the derogation had to be narrowly construed. By contrast, in *Marschall v Land Nordrhein Westfalen*[696] the Court held that a form of affirmative action under which, in a situation of underrepresentation of female employees, an equally well qualified female applicant would be given preference over a male, did not contravene the Equal Treatment Directive, as long as the following conditions were met: first, the employer made provision for a 'saving clause' under which it could take into account objective factors which were specific to an individual male; and, second, the criteria involved in such a process were not such as to discriminate against the female candidates. The basis for the ruling was that the derogation in Article 2(4) could be triggered, subject to the need for the saving clause, where affirmative action was aimed at counteracting 'the prejudicial effects on female candidates' of stereotypical attitudes and behaviour relating to the roles and capacities of women in working life.[697] A substantial case law has built up applying this test, the effect of which is that measures to promote the underrepresented sex are in principle permitted, but will be strictly scrutinised to see if they pass the test of proportionality under Article 2(4). Thus hiring rules which did not permit sufficient flexibility in their application, to take into account the objective merits of the candidates, have been struck down as going beyond the scope of Article 2(4),[698] as have rules which indiscriminately favour all widows over all widowers, regardless of individual circumstances,[699] whereas the restriction of child care places to female employees was held to be permissible as long as their benefit was also extended to male employees with child-care responsibilities.[700]

The legality of affirmative action was confirmed by the amendments to the EC Treaty which were agreed in the Treaty of Amsterdam. In relation to equal treatment between men and women, Article 157(4) TFEU, as it now is, contains a wide derogation intended to permit Member States to maintain or adopt 'measures providing for specific advantages in order to make it easier for the under-represented sex to pursue a vocational activity or to prevent or compensate for disadvantages in professional careers', with the aim of 'ensuring full equality in practice between men and women in working life',[701] a phrase which could be interpreted as going beyond the restricted notion of equality of opportunity which the ECJ relied on in *Kalanke*.

---

[693] [1995] IRLR 660, 667.

[694] [1995] IRLR 660, 667.

[695] Art 2(4) has now been superseded by Art 3 of the recast Equal Treatment Directive, which provides that 'Member States may maintain or adopt measures within the meaning of Article [157 TFEU] with a view to ensuring full equality in practice between men and women in working life'.

[696] Case C-409/95 [1998] IRLR 39. See, to similar effect, Case C-158/97 *Application by Badeck and others* [2000] IRLR 432.

[697] [1998] IRLR 39, 48.

[698] Case C-407/98 *Abrahamsson and Anderson v Fogelqvist* [2000] IRLR 732; Case E-1/02 *EFTA Surveillance Authority v Kingdom of Norway* [2003] IRLR 318.

[699] Case C-319/03 *Brihèche v Ministre de l'Intérieure* [2005] 1 CMLR 4.

[700] Case C-476/99 *Lommars v Minster van Landbouw, Natuurbeheer en Visserij* [2002] ECR-I 2891; see also Case C-366/00 *Griesmar v Ministre de l'Économie, des Finances et de l'Industrie* [2001] ECR-I 9383.

[701] As noted above (this para), Directive 2006/54/EC, Art 3, is in similar terms and cross-refers to Art 157(4).

(iii) Positive action under the Equality Act 2010

6.73   Two provisions of the 2010 Act widen the scope for positive action in employment, in line with the evolution of EU law. Section 158 applies where a person reasonably thinks that persons sharing a protected characteristic suffer a disadvantage connected to that characteristic or have needs different from the needs of the persons who do not share it, or where that person reasonably thinks that participation in an activity by persons sharing a protected characteristic is 'disproportionately low'. Under these circumstances, section 158 provides that the Act will not prevent a person taking action which is a proportionate means of achieving the following aims: enabling or encouraging persons with the shared protected characteristic to overcome or minimise that disadvantage; meeting the needs connected to the characteristic; and enabling persons with the characteristic to take part in the relevant activity. This provision supersedes the limited positive action provisions of the SDA 1975 and RRA 1976 and effectively extends to each of the protected characteristics the model introduced at an earlier point for age, sexual orientation and religion or belief discrimination.

   Section 159 of the Act gives effect to the aim, identified by the government in the period of consultation prior to the adoption of the 2010 Act, of enabling 'employers, where they feel it is appropriate, and where there is a choice between two equally qualified candidates, to take under-representation into account when making recruitment or promotion decisions, providing there is not an automatic rule favouring those with any particular protected characteristic'.[702] Where a person reasonably thinks that persons with a given protected characteristic suffer a disadvantage connected with it, or have disproportionately low rate of participation in a given activity, that person may take action to encourage persons with the characteristic to overcome or minimise that disadvantage or to participate in the activity.[703] The action must take the form of 'treating a person... more favourably in connection with recruitment or promotion than another person' because the former has the protected characteristic and the latter does not.[704] This can only be done where the two persons are 'as qualified' as each other to be recruited or promoted and where the action is a proportionate means of achieving the aim referred to.[705] In addition, the person taking action in this way must 'not have a policy of treating persons who share the protected characteristic more favourably in connection with recruitment or promotion than persons who do not share it'.[706]

   The effect of requiring the two candidates to be 'as qualified' as each other is to give the employer some leeway in applying section 159. The *Explanatory Notes* to the Act suggest that the provision is 'intended to allow the maximum extent of flexibility' which is consistent with European law,[707] and that 'the question of whether one person is as qualified as another is not a matter only of academic qualification, but rather a judgement based on the criteria the employer uses to establish who is best for the job which could include matters such as suitability, competence and professional performance'.[708] The reference to the impermissibility of a 'policy' is perhaps not

---

[702] *Government Response to the Consultation*, at para 5.20.
[703] EqA 2010, s 159(1)-(2).
[704] EqA 2010, s 159(3).
[705] EqA 2010, s 159(4)(a), (c).
[706] EqA 2010, s 159(4)(b).
[707] At para 519.
[708] At para 518.

as clearly drafted as it might have been, but need not be taken to imply that an employer cannot invoke section 159 in any case where two candidates are found to be of 'substantially equivalent merits'.[709]

(iv) Positive action and the GOR defence

6.74 Employers engaging in positive action may seek to invoke one of the defences to direct discrimination. The GOQ defences under the SDA 1975 and the RRA 1976 were restrictively defined in this context. Section 5(2)(d) of the RRA 1976 allowed a GOQ on grounds of race where 'the holder of the job provides persons of that racial group with personal services promoting their welfare, and those services can most effectively be provided by a person of that racial group'. This provision was given a narrow construction in *Lambeth London Borough Council v Commission for Racial Equality*,[710] where the Council attempted to restrict two housing managers' posts to Afro-Caribbean and Asian applicants on the grounds that they wished to make the delivery of their housing services more sensitive to the needs of these racial groups. The employment tribunal held that the jobs in question did not involve personal services, a ruling which is highly debatable but which was not upset on appeal. Balcombe LJ was 'wholly unpersuaded that one of the two main purposes of the Act is to promote positive action to benefit racial groups'.[711] However, with the adoption of more general GOR defences to each of the main heads of discrimination legislation, an open-ended defence is now available to direct discrimination claims,[712] and it is possible that employers will, as a result, have greater flexibility in future to engage in positive action. Because, in addition, a justification defence to a direct discrimination claim is possible in the context of age discrimination,[713] there may also be further scope for positive action in this context.

The public sector equality duty

6.75 Under section 149 EqA 2010, if the employer is a public authority it has a duty in carrying out its functions to have due regard to the need to eliminate discrimination, harassment, victimisation and any other conduct prohibited by the Act; advance equality of opportunity between persons who share a relevant protected characteristic and those who do not; and foster good relations between persons who share a protected characteristic and those who do not.[714] An employer that is not a public authority but exercises public functions has the same duties with regard to the exercise of those functions.[715] This single 'public sector equality duty' replaces separate duties previously in force in relation to sex, race and disability discrimination.[716] The Act specifies that

---

[709] Hepple, 2011a: p 131.
[710] [1990] ICR 768.
[711] [1990] ICR 768, 774. See Pitt 1992.
[712] EqA 2010, Sch 9. See above, para 6.55.
[713] EqA 2010, s 13(2).
[714] EqA 2010, s 149(1).
[715] EqA 2010, s 149(2).
[716] On the race equality duty, the first to be adopted, see O'Cinneide, 2001.

advancing equality of opportunity means having due regard in particular to the need to remove or minimise relevant disadvantages suffered by people sharing a given protected characteristic, taking steps to meet the needs of such persons, and encouraging them to 'participate in public life or in any other activity in which participation by such persons is disproportionately low'[717]. In the case of disability, steps taken with regard to meeting the needs of persons who are disabled must take account, in particular, of their disabilities.[718] Fostering good relations means having due regard in particular to the need to 'tackle prejudice' and 'promote understanding'.[719] The Act makes it clear that these duties may imply a form of positive action ('treating some persons more favourably than others'), and that where this is so, the action will be protected, as long as it is not otherwise prohibited by or under the Act.[720] The duty to have regard to the elimination of discrimination applies to all the protected characteristics; the duties to have regard to the need to advance equality of opportunity and foster good relations apply to them all except marriage and civil partnership.[721]

The *Explanatory Notes* on the 2010 Act spell out the possibility of positive action and give a number of examples of how, more generally, public authorities and bodies exercising public functions could approach the implementation of the equality duty.[722] These include a police authority reviewing its recruitment procedures to ensure that they do not unintentionally deter ethnic minority applicants, targeting training and mentoring schemes, and a government department providing its staff with training and guidance with the aim of fostering good relations between transgender staff and others.[723]

The Act confers a general power on Ministers to impose more specific duties by order.[724] The Labour Government envisaged, during the passage of the Act, that these would include reporting duties for public bodies employing over 150 employees, in respect of the gender pay gap, the ethnic minority employment rate, and the disability employment rate.[725] However, regulations introduced by the Coalition Government impose a much looser obligation upon a public authority or body exercising public functions to 'prepare and publish one or more objectives it thinks it should achieve to do any of the things' listed in section 149(1) of the Act.[726]

The public authorities covered by the duty are listed in Sch 19 to the Act. They include central and local government bodies, the armed forces, the police, the National Health Service, and state-maintained schools, further education colleges and higher education institutions. These bodies are subject to the equality duty in respect of all their public functions unless, as in some cases, they are only listed with regard to certain of them. A 'public function' is a 'function of a public nature' as defined under the Human Rights Act 1998.[727] Failure to perform an aspect of the duty does not

---

[717] EqA 2010, s 149(3).
[718] EqA 2010, s 149(4).
[719] EqA 2010, s 149(5).
[720] EqA 2010, s 149(6).
[721] This is the effect of EqA 2010, s 149(7).
[722] At para 482.
[723] At para 484. On the interaction between the public sector equality duty and public procurement, see para 2.6 above.
[724] EqA 2010, s 153.
[725] Harriet Harman MP, Minister for Women and Equality, Hansard, HC Vol 492, col 556 (11 May 2009).
[726] SI 2011/2260.
[727] EqA 2010, s 150(5).

give rise to a private cause of action,[728] but may be the basis for an action in judicial review.[729] In addition, the EHRC may issue an enforcement notice for a failure to comply with the duty.[730]

The socio-economic duty

6.76   Section 1 of the 2010 Act sets out a duty on the part of certain public authorities, when making 'decisions of a strategic nature' concerning the exercise of their functions, to 'have due regard to the desirability of exercising them in a way that is designed to reduce the inequalities of outcome which result from socio-economic disadvantage'. As in the case of the public sector equality duty, the socio-economic duty cannot be enforced through a private civil law claim,[731] but judicial review may lie in respect of a breach of the duty. The socio-economic duty was intended by the Labour government that was responsible for the drafting of the 2010 Act to encourage public bodies with strategic functions, a group which includes central government departments, local government and the National Health Service, to consider the impact of their decisions on 'inequalities in education, health, housing, crime rates, or other matters associated with socio-economic disadvantage'. The Coalition government has decided not to bring section 1 into force, thereby depriving equality law of a mechanism would usefully supplement the wider public sector equality duty.[732]

EQUAL PAY

6.77   The principle of equal treatment takes a distinctive form in the context of sex discrimination in the area of pay. The SDA 1975 had no application to issues of pay which were governed by the complainant's contract of employment or other relevant contract; instead these were resolved under the EqPA 1970, an earlier Act with a different conceptual structure from the other anti-discrimination statutes. At European Union level, the issue of equal pay has particular prominence as a result of the presence in the Treaty of Rome of Article 119, now Article 157 TFEU, and of the case law of the ECJ, which not only gave Article 119 a broad interpretation but has ensured that it conferred rights directly on individuals in national law, through the doctrine of direct effect. The influence of the Equal Pay Directive of 1975[733] was felt, not least in bringing about the amendment of the EqPA 1970 in 1983 with the introduction of the principle of equal pay for work of equal value.

Chapter 3 of Part 5 of EqA 2010 has continued the distinctive treatment of equal pay in employment, separating it from the provisions of the Act defining the forms of prohibited conduct

---

[728]   EqA 2010, s 156.
[729]   On the judicial review case law on the 'due regard' test, which has so far not touched on employment issues, see Fredman, 2011. Hepple, 2011a: pp 134-40 and Fredman, 2012, discuss the implications of the public sector equality duty as a mechanism for promoting equality.
[730]   EqA 2006, ss 31, 32.
[731]   EqA 2010, s 3.
[732]   Fredman, 2011: 427. See also Hepple, 2011a: pp 141-143.
[733]   Directive 75/117.

and the scope of discrimination in employment.[734] Although the 2010 Act has brought about some improvements to the drafting of the relevant legislation and has made substantive changes in a few places,[735] the legislation 'remains unnecessarily complex and to some extent unintelligible'.[736] While this is unfortunate, it is even more regrettable that limitations on the capacity of the law to address pay inequality, which are the result of the failure to integrate equal pay law into the mainstream of equality law, remain in place under the 2010 Act.[737]

We begin our analysis of equal pay by outlining the framework of British and European law on this area before examining in greater detail the substance of the law in terms of the scope and bases of comparison of pay and conditions; the defences available to employers; and the mode of implementation of awards. Our analysis will conclude with a study of the application of the principle of equal treatment to occupational pension schemes and to collective agreements.

The relationship between equal pay and the principle of non-discrimination

6.78   As we have seen,[738] cases of direct sex discrimination relating to contractual pay aside,[739] the 2010 Act's prohibition of sex discrimination in employment has no application to any term of the complainant's contract that 'is modified by, or included by virtue of, a sex equality clause' or to a term which is less favourable than it should be given the effect of the sex equality clause.[740] The sex equality clause is the statutorily implied term which has the effect of modifying the terms of the complainant's contract so as to ensure that they are no less favourable than those of a comparable person of the opposite sex in the same employment (the 'comparator').[741] The sex equality clause affects *all* contract terms and not simply those governing pay;[742] in this sense, the scope of the equal pay principle is wider than it strictly needs to be to fill the gap left by the exclusion of the issue of pay from the general prohibition on sex discrimination in employment. However, for the purpose of identifying a comparator, only certain individuals may be chosen:[743] a female worker (for example) is only permitted to compare her pay and conditions with those of a man who is employed on either 'like work', on work 'rated as equivalent' under a job evaluation scheme, or on work of 'equal value' to hers. The result of this is that the basis of comparison

---

[734] Note that Chapter 3 of Part 5 of the 2010 Act also enacts a right to maternity pay via a maternity equality clause, the effect of which is to align maternity pay during the 'protected period' of maternity leave with certain increases to which the complainant would have been entitled had she not been on leave. See further para 6.118 below.

[735] Where there has been a substantive change, this is noted in our analysis in the following paragraphs. For the most part, despite drafting changes aimed at improving the clarity of the legislation, its substance remains unchanged, so the pre-2010 Act case law continues to be relevant.

[736] Hepple, 2011a: p 98.

[737] See Hepple, 2011a: pp 94-98.

[738] See para 6.50 above.

[739] EqA 2010, s 71.

[740] EqA 2010, s 70(1), (2). For a decision on the predecessor statute, SDA 1975, s 6(6), see *Hoyland v Asda Stores Ltd* [2006] IRLR 468.

[741] EqA 2010, s 66. See below, paras 6.102.

[742] This is the effect of EqA 2010, s 66(2).

[743] See para 6.88 below.

under the equal pay provisions of the 2010 Act is much more restricted than under the general provisions of the Act.[744]

The interaction of domestic legislation and European Union law

6.79   Article 157 TFEU, continuing in force Article 119 of the Treaty of Rome, requires Member States to 'ensure that the principle of equal pay for male and female workers for equal work or work of equal value is applied';[745] for this purpose it defines pay as 'the ordinary basic or minimum wage or salary and any other consideration, whether in cash or in kind, which the worker receives directly or indirectly, in respect of his employment, from his employer.'[746] Article 1 of the Equal Pay Directive 1975[747] specified that:

> The principle of equal pay for men and women outlined in Article 119 of the Treaty ... means, for the same work or for work to which equal value is attributed, the elimination of all discrimination on grounds of sex with regard to all aspects and conditions of remuneration.
> In particular, where a job classification system is used for determining pay it must be based on the same criteria for both men and women and so drawn up as to exclude any discrimination on grounds of sex.

The ECJ held that Article 1 of the 1975 Directive was 'principally designed to facilitate the practical application of the principle of equal pay outlined in Article [157] of the Treaty', and 'in no way alters the content or scope of that principle as defined in the Treaty'.[748] As Ellis comments, 'if the Directive therefore merely spells out the detail of Article 119, without in any way undermining its scope, it follows that its chief practical effect today is to shed light on the more obscure objects of Article 119'.[749] This was highly significant at a time when Article 119, as it then was, made no reference to the principle of equal value; that reference was inserted through the revisions to the EC Treaty following the Treaty of Amsterdam in 1997. The ECJ had already held, on a number of occasions, that Article 119 incorporated the principle of equal value.[750] As it is, there has for some time been no doubt that the principle of equal value has horizontal, and not simply vertical, direct effect in UK law. In addition, because the Equal Pay Directive 1975 is the immediate source of the 1983 amendments to the EqPA 1970 which introduced the principle of equal pay for work of equal value into the Act, its successor, Chapter 3 of the 2010 Act is to be purposively interpreted

---

[744] For an example of a claim which might have succeeded had it fallen under the SDA 1975 but failed under the EqPA 1970, see *Meeks v National Union of Agricultural and Allied Workers* [1976] IRLR 198.

[745] Art 157(1).

[746] Art 157(2). See para 6.5 above for an account of the origins of Art 157. For an account of the general development of EC equality law which examines in detail the case law under Art 157's predecessors, Art 119 of the Treaty of Rome and Art 141 TEC, see Hepple, 1997.

[747] This Directive was replaced by Directive 2006/54/EC, which consolidated several equal treatment directives, with effect from 15 August 2009.

[748] Case 96/80 *Jenkins v Kingsgate (Clothing Productions) Ltd* [1981] IRLR 228, 234.

[749] Ellis, 1991: p 97.

[750] Case 69/80 *Worringham v Lloyd's Bank Ltd* [1981] IRLR 178; Case 96/80 *Jenkins v Kingsgate (Clothing Productions) Ltd* [1981] IRLR 228; Case 157/86 *Murphy v Bord Telecom Eireann* [1988] ECR 673.

by reference to the Directive and its objectives.[751] Article 1 of the 1975 Directive has now been superseded by Article 4 of the recast Equal Treatment Directive,[752] which is in a similar form but no longer refers back to Article 157 (as it now is) of the Treaty.

Although it is neither necessary nor permissible for a domestic court to consider Article 157 if the 2010 Act provides a fully adequate remedy,[753] in cases where European Union law provides rights over and above domestic legislation the courts have held that employment tribunals should apply Article 157 directly.[754] The ECJ has given a broad interpretation both to the substance of Article 157 and to the circumstances in which it has direct effect in national law. After some initial uncertainty, the Court confirmed that Article 157's predecessor, Article 119 of the Treaty of Rome, had direct effect in situations of indirect as well as direct discrimination, and regardless of whether the discrimination is intentional.[755] Of particular importance is the wide definition which the Court has consistently given to the concept of 'pay' in this context. In *Barber v Guardian Royal Exchange Assurance Group*[756] it held that the definition contained in Article 119 was sufficiently broad to extend to payments made by an employer under an occupational pension scheme, even though this was a contracted-out scheme which, under domestic UK law, operated in partial substitution for benefits under the state social security system.[757] The most important division is now between employer-based payments, which in principle fall under Article 157 TFEU and the Equal Treatment Directive, and social security payments which fall under the Directive on Equality in State Social Security.[758] Unemployment benefits, for example, and payments made through the basic state pension and state earnings-related pension schemes are governed by the latter; but this leaves a large category of payments within Article 157, including occupational sick pay and maternity pay;[759] rules governing access to pay increments based on seniority;[760] ex gratia payments made to employees on termination of employment;[761] redundancy compensation;[762] unfair dismissal compensation[763] and payments made in respect of time off to take part in training courses for the purposes of employee representation.[764] It is irrelevant for this purpose that the

---

[751] *Pickstone v Freemans plc* [1988] IRLR 357. In *Webb v EMO Air Cargo Ltd* [1993] IRLR 27, 32, Lord Keith accepted the principle of the 'indirect effect' of directives regardless of whether the domestic legislation in question was enacted before or after the adoption of the Community measure.

[752] Directive 2006/54/EC, Art 4.

[753] *Blaik v Post Office* [1994] IRLR 280.

[754] *McKechnie v UBM Building Supplies (Southern) Ltd* [1991] IRLR 283.

[755] Case 170/84 *Bilka-Kaufhaus GmbH v Weber von Hartz* [1986] IRLR 317.

[756] Case 262/88 [1990] IRLR 240; see also Case C-243/95 *Hill and Stapleton v Revenue Commissioners* [1998] IRLR 466.

[757] To a large extent the benefit of this ruling was limited by the Court's ruling that it should only apply to benefits vesting on or after the date of its ruling, 17 May 1990: see below, para 6.109. In Case C-267/06 *Maruko v Versorgunsanstalt der Duetschen Bühnen* [2008] IRLR 450 a survivor's pension under an occupational pension scheme was held to constitute 'pay'.

[758] Directive 79/7/EEC.

[759] Case 171/88 *Rinner-Kühn v FWW Spezial Gebäudereinigung GmbH* [1989] IRLR 493; C-342/93 *Gillespie v Northern Health and Social Services Board* [1996] IRLR 214; Case C-147/02 *Alabaster v Woolwich plc* [2004] IRLR 486; Case C-191/03 *North Western Health Board v McKenna* [2005] IRLR 895.

[760] Case C-184/89 *Nimz v Freie und Hansestadt Hamburg* [1991] IRLR 222.

[761] Case 262/88 *Barber v Guardian Royal Exchange Assurance Group* [1990] IRLR 240.

[762] Case 262/88 *Barber v Guardian Royal Exchange Assurance Group* [1990] IRLR 240.

[763] Case C-167/97 *R v Secretary of State for Employment, ex p Seymour-Smith and Perez* [1999] IRLR 253.

[764] Case C-457/93 *Kuratorium für Dialyse und Nierentransplantation e V v Lewark* [1996] IRLR 637; *Davies v Neath Port Talbot County Borough Council* [1999] IRLR 769, holding that *Manor Bakeries Ltd v Nazir* [1996] IRLR 604 was incorrectly decided on this point.

making of the particular payment is mandated by legislation (as it would be in the case of unfair dismissal and redundancy compensation). This extension of the concept of 'pay' proved to be highly significant as a means of calling into question derogations from the principle of equal treatment under domestic law which had previously seemed safe from review. *Barber* itself prompted the equalisation of pensionable ages in occupational pension schemes, thereby rendering ineffective a derogation inserted into the EqPA 1970;[765] it also prompted litigation which eventually led to the removal of the 8- and 16-hour weekly qualifying thresholds from the law of redundancy and unfair dismissal.[766] On the other hand, the Court held that the concept of pay did not extend to the contributions made by an employer into an occupational pension scheme, thereby allowing differential payments to be made in respect of male and female employees according to sex-based actuarial calculations.[767]

At points in the evolution of equal pay law, EU law has allowed claims that were beyond the scope of British legislation. Under Art 157, a comparison may be made between the pay of a female complainant and a male predecessor[768] or successor[769] in the employment in question. These types of claim were ruled out under the EqPA 1970, which required the employment of the complainant and her comparator to be contemporaneous, but are allowed under the 2010 Act.[770] EU law may also allow a claim between a female complainant and a male worker earning the same wage but employed on work of less than equal value with hers,[771] a claim which is not possible under EqA 2010.

The role of the concept of discrimination in equal pay claims

6.80 The regime set up by the EqPA 1970 appeared, at first sight, to be more flexible than that operating for other sex discrimination claims in one significant respect. In particular, it was arguable that once the claimant had identified a relevant comparator who was paid more than she was, sex discrimination was presumed, allowing the court to proceed directly to a consideration of the material factor defence, which in this context operated as a variant of the justification defence.[772] In *Glasgow City Council v Marshall* Lord Nicholls said of the 1970 Act:[773]

> The scheme of the Act is that a rebuttable presumption of sex discrimination arises once the gender-based comparison shows that a woman, doing like work or work rated as equivalent

---

[765] EqPA 1970, s 6(1A)(b).

[766] *R v Secretary of State for Employment, ex p EOC* [1994] IRLR 176; see above, para 3.54.

[767] C-152/91 *Neath v Hugh Steeper Ltd* [1994] IRLR 91; Case C-200/91 *Coloroll Pension Trustees Ltd v Russell* [1994] IRLR 586; see below, para 6.109. The legality of such sex-based criteria must now be read in the light of the judgment of the Court of Justice in Case C-236/09 *Association Belge des Consommateurs Tests-Achats v Conseil des Ministres* [2011] 2 CMLR 38, ruling that a derogation allowing sex-based actuarial factors to be used in private insurance contracts (contained in Directive 2004/113/EC, Art 5) was invalid, in part because of the application of Arts 21 and 23 CFREU.

[768] Case 129/79 *Macarthys Ltd v Smith* [1980] IRLR 210; *Walton Centre for Neurology and Neurosurgery NHS Trust v Bewley* [2008] IRLR 588.

[769] *Diocese of Hallam Trustee v Connaughton* [1996] IRLR 505.

[770] By virtue of EqA 2010, s 64(2). See below, para 6.86.

[771] Case 157/86 *Murphy v Board Telecom Eirrean* [1988] ECR 673.

[772] *Home Office v Bailey* [2005] IRLR 369, at [34] (Waller LJ). *Grundy v British Airways* [2008] IRLR 74, at [25] (Sedley, LJ).

[773] [2000] IRLR 272, at [18]–[19].

or work of equal value to that of a man, is being paid or treated less favourably than the man. The variation between her contract and the man's contract is presumed to be due to the difference of sex. The burden passes to the employer to show that the explanation for the variation is not tainted with sex. In order to discharge this burden, the employer must satisfy the tribunal on several matters. First, that the proffered explanation, or reason, is genuine, and not a sham or pretence. Second, that the less favourable treatment is due to this reason ... Third, that the reason is not the 'difference of sex'. This phrase is apt to embrace any form of sex discrimination, whether direct or indirect. Fourth, that the factor relied upon is or, in a case within section 1(2)(c), may be a 'material' difference, that is, a significant and relevant difference, between the woman's case and the man's case.

A plausible reading of Lord Nicholls' judgment is that the discrimination concept was embedded in section 1 of the 1970 Act. Once a valid comparison was made and inequality of pay was revealed, the employer could refute the claim by showing that there was neither adverse treatment nor adverse impact (stages 1–3 in Lord Nicholls' analysis), or that the difference was justified under the genuine material factor defence (stage 4). The burden was not on the claimant of demonstrating either adverse treatment or adverse impact. This point did not arise clearly in *Marshall* since the complainants conceded that there was no adverse impact. For this reason, *Marshall* is not a strong authority for the suggestion, later made in *Nelson v Carillion Services Ltd*.[774] that the complainant should in all cases have the burden of showing adverse impact.[775] However, in *Armstrong v Newcastle upon Tyne NHS Hospital Trust*[776] Buxton LJ, with whose judgment Latham LJ agreed, argued that the claimant did have the burden of showing disparate impact, after which the burden shifted to the employer, which had to establish a genuine material factor defence. The matter was considered by the Court of Appeal again in *Redcar & Cleveland Borough Coumcil v Bainbridge (No 1), Surtees v Middlesborough Borough Council and Equality and Human Rights Commission (Intervener), Redcar & Cleveland Borough Council v Bainbridge and Equality and Human Rights Commission (No 2)*.[777] Mummery LJ, giving the judgment of the Court, offered yet a further interpretation: he said that *Armstrong* was authority for the proposition that 'merely because it has been shown that the pay arrangements have a disparate, adverse impact on women, it does not necessarily follow that the employer will have to show objective justification'; it could avoid this if, under the genuine material factor defence, it could show that 'the pay differential was not due to the difference in sex, directly or indirectly, or was not tainted by sex'.[778] On this reading, the employer had the opportunity to avoid going down the objective justification route by establishing that a genuine material factor, which was not based on sex, was the reason for the pay differential. It was argued by counsel in *Redcar* that this was 'to insert into the process of decision-making an additional stage, which ought not to be inserted, which made the process more complicated and gave the employer a further opportunity to avoid liability'.[779] However,

---

[774] *Nelson v Carrillion Services Ltd* [2003] IRLR 428, at [39] (Simon Brown LJ). It should nevertheless be noted that *Marshall* was not the only HL authority relied on *Nelson*; the Court of Appeal also referred to *Barry v Midland Bank plc* [1999] IRLR 581 in which the House of Lords adopted a strict test of indirect discrimination (see the discussion of Thomas, 2000).

[775] See *Home Office v Bailey* [2005] IRLR 369, at [37] (Waller LJ).

[776] [2006] IRLR 124, at [103].

[777] [2008] IRLR 776.

[778] [2008] IRLR 776, at [57]. See also *Villalba v Merrill Lynch & Co Inc* [2006] IRLR 437.

[779] [2008] IRLR 776, at [58] (Mummery LJ paraphrasing the submissions of Robin Allen QC and Lord Lester QC).

the Court declined to accept this invitation to clarify or, alternatively, overrule *Armstrong*, on the grounds that it was not necessary for it to do so on the facts of the *Redcar* case.[780]

As a consequence of this line of cases, the pre-2010 Act law was left in a highly uncertain state. The most straightforward solution would have been to apply to equal pay cases the normal test of indirect discrimination, involving the two elements of adverse impact and justification based on the concept of proportionate steps to meet a legitimate goal, as required by EU law.[781] This would mean, on the one hand, requiring the claimant to show either direct or indirect discrimination in each case and, in a case of indirect discrimination, requiring the employer to justify the adverse impact of its policies or practices. The changes made by EqA 2010 have arguably achieved this much needed clarification. Under section 69, the employer can rebut a claim for equal pay using the material factor defence if it can show, firstly, that it relied on a factor which does not involve treating A, the complainant, 'less favourably because of A's sex than [the employer] treats' B, the comparator.[782] This effectively incorporates the definition of direct discrimination into equal pay claims. In addition, the employer must show that the material factor is a proportionate means of achieving a legitimate aim,[783] in any case where, 'as a result of the factor, A and persons of the same sex doing work equal to A's are put at a particular disadvantage when compared with persons of the opposite sex doing work equal to A's'.[784] This requirement embeds the indirect discrimination concept in equal pay claims. Although simpler means might have been found for realigning the definition of equal pay with the mainstream definition of discrimination than using the material factor defence to this end, the new provision should finally have resolved a matter which, in the course of litigation over the preceding decade, had only become more complex.

The scope of comparison: same employment

6.81 The complainant may not compare her treatment to that which a comparable person of the opposite sex would *hypothetically* have received, as is possible under a general claim of sex discrimination.[785] Instead, an equal pay claim may only be brought under Chapter 3 of Part 5 of the 2010 Act where the complainant (A) can show that she is employed on equal work with that of a comparator (B) who is 'employed by A's employer or by an associate of A's employer' and works 'at the same establishment' as A,[786] or at another establishment where 'common terms' apply, with parallel provisions applying to office holders.[787]

---

[780] [2008] IRLR 776, at [60]. Counsel had argued that the Court should formally overrule *Armstrong* on the basis that it was *per incuriam*, by reason of omitting to consider the ECJ's judgment in Case C-127/92 *Enderby v Frenchay Health Authority* [1993] IRLR 591. In *Gibson v Sheffield City Council* [2010] IRLR 311 the Court of Appeal held that *Armstrong* had not been decided *per incuriam*, on which point see also the judgment of the EAT in *Bury Metropolitan Borough Council v Hamilton* [2011] IRLR 358. See further our discussion of the revised material factor defence below, paras 6.96-6.101.

[781] See Case C-127/92 *Enderby v Frenchay Health Authority* [1993] IRLR 591 and Case C-381/99 *Brunnhofer v Bank der Österreichischen Postsparkasse AG* [2001] IRLR 571, discussed below at para 6.99; *Coventry City Council v Nicholls* [2009] IRLR 345, at [10] (Elias LJ).

[782] EqA 2010, s 69(1)(a).

[783] EqA 2010, s 69(1)(b).

[784] EqA 2010, s 69(2).

[785] See above, para 6.17.

[786] EqA 2010, s 79(3).

[787] EqA 2010, s 79(4). On private and public offices within the Act, see EqA 2010, ss 49-52.

(i) Identifying the employer in equal pay claims

6.82   Associated employers, here as elsewhere in labour legislation, are defined according to a test of control borrowed from company law: 'employers are associated... if one is a company of which the other (directly or indirectly) has control, or both are companies of which a third person (directly or indirectly) has control'.[788] In *Scullard v Knowles*[789] the EAT gave an almost identically worded provision under EqPA 1970 a narrow reading, but applied Art 119 (now 157 TFEU) directly to hold that a comparison could be made between the complainant's pay and those of male comparators employed by different entities controlled by the same charitable employer.

In *Lawrence v Regent Office Care Ltd*[790] the ECJ ruled that under EU law, dinner ladies whose employment had been transferred from a local authority to private contractors could not claim equal pay with employees of the council for which they used to work, and whose work had been rated of equal value to their own prior to the transfer. The basis for this ruling was that Article 157 required the identification of a 'single source' which was responsible for the discrimination and could put it right. Thus the Article:

> ... is addressed to those who may be held responsible for the unauthorised difference in terms and conditions of employment ... these are the legislature, the parties to a collective works agreement and the management of a corporate group. They may be held accountable in this regard. On the other hand, if differences in pay arise as between undertakings or establishments in which the respective employers are separately responsible for the terms and conditions of employment within their own undertaking or establishment, they cannot possibly be held individually accountable for any differences in the terms and conditions of employment between those undertakings.[791]

The ECJ proved equally unreceptive to arguments for allowing a broad scope of comparison in *Allonby v Accrington and Rossendale College*.[792] The claimant, a part-time lecturer in a further education college, was dismissed and re-employed, to carry out the same work on a lower rate of pay, via an employment agency. She claimed equal pay with a comparator who was a full-time, directly employed employee of the college. Her claim failed under UK law on the grounds that the agency and the college were not associated employers under section 1(6) of the 1970 Act. The ECJ ruled that 'the fact that the level of pay received by Ms Allonby is influenced by the amount which the College pays the [agency] is not a sufficient basis for concluding that the College and [the agency] constitute a single source to which can be attributed the differences identified in Ms. Allonby's conditions of pay and those of the male worker paid by the College'.[793]

Ellis had earlier argued[794] that since job content, measured objectively, was taken to be the principal criterion of equal work under the Equal Pay Directive of 1975 and hence, by extension,

[788] EqA 2010, s 79(9). For discussion of the phrase 'associated employer', see above, para 3.65.
[789] [1996] IRLR 344. See also, under the pre-2010 case law, *Halsey v Fair Employment Agency* [1989] IRLR 106; *South Ayrshire Council v Morton* [2001] IRLR 28, [2002] IRLR 256.
[790] Case C-320/00, [2002] IRLR 822.
[791] Case C-320/00 *Lawrence v Regent Office Care* [2002] IRLR 822, Opinion of Advocate General Geelhoed, at para 52. See also the Judgment of the Court, at para 18.
[792] Case 256/01, [2004] IRLR 224. See Fredman, 2004c.
[793] Case 256/01 *Allonby v Accrington and Rossendale College* [2004] IRLR 224, at [48].
[794] Ellis, 1991: p 62.

under Article 157, comparisons should be confined neither to individual establishments nor even to individual employers. Some authority for her argument was to be found in the early case of *Defrenne v Sabena*[795] in which the ECJ referred to the principle of equal pay for equal work as applying broadly to men and women 'in the same establishment or service', and to a later suggestion from Advocate General Van Themaat that the comparison should not be confined to individual establishments.[796] However, if the employment unit is not to set the limits to comparison, another acceptable basis must be found. It is not clear that job evaluation techniques, without more, are capable of providing objective guidance on such a scale.[797] Where, on the other hand, a number of employers come under the scope of a common institutional framework for regulating pay and conditions, such as a sector-level collective agreement or a single job evaluation exercise, this objection would have less force. In *Lawrence* itself the ECJ agreed that there was 'nothing in the wording of Article [157 TFEU] to suggest that the applicability of that provision is limited to situations in which men and women work for the same employer' and accepted that its earlier case law had established that the principle could be invoked 'in cases of discrimination arising directly from legislative provisions or collective labour agreements'.[798]

There are several problematic aspects to the *Lawrence* and *Allonby* decisions. Article 157 makes no reference to the employment unit as the sole basis for comparison. Although it was claimed, in both cases, that there would be practical difficulties in allowing comparisons across employment boundaries, these did not arise in the cases before the Court: as we have seen, *Lawrence* was a case of a unified job evaluation exercise and *Allonby* involved work in a single establishment, while in both cases comparisons were being made with former co-employees. It is also a matter of concern that the supposedly fundamental right contained in Article 157 can so easily be evaded by employer action of the kinds seen in these cases.

Nothwithstanding these difficulties, the concept of the 'single source' was held by the Court of Appeal in *Robertson v DEFRA*[799] to be of relevance to comparisons made *within* employment units. Here, civil servants employed by one government department tried to compare their pay to more highly-paid civil servants in another. They were not employed at the same establishment and their employment was not governed by common terms and conditions, as a result of the delegation of the power to set the terms and conditions of employment of civil servants to individual departments which occurred in the early 1990s.[800] Thus they could not bring their case under the 1970 Act.[801] The Court of Appeal held that, under Article 157, the Crown was not a 'single source' by virtue of its retaining a residual power to determine civil servants' pay, and that neither the Treasury nor the Minister for the Civil Service could be said to exercise sufficient de facto control to qualify. Accordingly, the claim failed. However, in *North Cumbria Acute Hospitals NHS Trust v Potter*[802] the EAT held that a single employer such as an NHS trust could be regarded as a single source and held, moreover, that the EU law test could not have the effect of narrowing

---

[795] Case 43/75 [1976] ECR 455, at para 22.

[796] Case 143/83 *EC Commission v Denmark* [1985] ECR 427.

[797] On job evaluation, see below, paras 6.90 and 6.93.

[798] Case C-320/00 *Lawrence v Regent Office Care* [2002] IRLR 822, at para 17.

[799] [2005] IRLR 363; Steele, 2005. *Robertson* was applied in *Armstrong v Newcastle upon Tyne NHS Trust* [2006] IRLR 124. In *North Cumbria Acute Hospitals NHS Trust v Potter* [2009] IRLR 176 the EAT upheld an argument that the 'single source' concept was not incorporated into EqPA 1970, s 1(6).

[800] See [2005] IRLR 363, [35].

[801] See above, this paragraph.

[802] [2009] IRLR 176.

down the scope of comparison permitted by domestic law, which could, in principle, be more protective than the European standard.

(ii) Establishment

6.83   The complainant and her comparator must be employed or have been employed at the same 'establishment' or at different establishments to which 'common terms apply' either generally or as between the two of them.[803] For this purpose, 'establishment' is left undefined. Although the concept has received extensive discussion in other labour law contexts,[804] it has not been much analysed in equal pay cases. An exception is the recent decision of the EAT in *City of Edinburgh v Wilkinson*.[805] The EAT held that 'establishment' did not necessarily mean a geographical work location, and that in order to give the concept of equal pay an appropriately broad reading under Article 157, an undertaking such as a local government unit should be presumed to be a single establishment unless it could be shown that it consisted of discrete administrative or organisational sub-units. The Court of Session reversed on this point, ruling that there was no presumption that an undertaking was a single establishment, and suggesting that the statutory reference to employment 'at' an establishment 'conveys an association with a locality'.[806]

(iii) Common terms

6.84   Under the 2010 Act, comparison across establishments is possible if 'common terms apply at the establishments (either generally or as between A and B)',[807] and terms of a person's work are defined for this purpose as 'the terms of the person's employment that are in the person's contract of employment'.[808] In *Leverton v Clwyd County Council*[809] Lord Bridge said that 'the concept of common terms and conditions of employment observed generally at different establishments necessarily contemplates terms and conditions applicable to a wide range of employees whose individual terms will vary greatly *inter se*. Terms and conditions of employment governed by the same collective agreement seem to me to represent the paradigm, though not necessarily the only example, of the common terms and conditions of employment contemplated' by the Act. The application of the Act is, to that extent, dependent on the types of arrangement which happen to be in place for a particular employment; in so far as bargaining is decentralised as part of company strategies to that effect, and as sector-level collective bargaining is further weakened,[810] the range of opportunities for comparison under the Act is necessarily reduced.

---

[803] EqA 2010, s 79(4)(b), (c).

[804] See para 3.62 above and para 9.32 below.

[805] [2010] IRLR 756, [2012] IRLR 202.

[806] [2012] IRLR 202, at [20] (Lord Eassie).

[807] EqA 2010, s 79(4)(c). According to the *Explanatory Notes* to the Act (para 282), no change to the law was intended at this point, and in line with this indication of legislative intent it would seem that the addition of the words 'either generally or as between A and B' was clarificatory only and, given the disjunctive sense of the new formula, should accommodate a flexible reading of this concept.

[808] EqA 2010, s 80(2)(a).

[809] [1989] IRLR 28, 31.

[810] On this, see paras 1.27–1.28 above.

In *Leverton*, a single collective agreement which formed the basis for the 'Purple Book' of terms and conditions governed the pay of the complainant and her chosen comparator. In contrast, in *British Coal Corpn v Smith*[811] three separate sets of agreements governed the terms and conditions of, respectively, canteen workers, clerical workers and surface mineworkers employed by British Coal. However, at the relevant time all of the employees had their pay and conditions set through centralised, industry-level agreements; and although the surface mineworkers enjoyed production bonuses which were calculated at local level, the tribunal considered that these could be seen in each case as 'a locally varied fulfilment of the same universally accepted central terms'. This decision was overturned in the Court of Appeal, which applied the following test:

> ... section 1(6) ... requires and permits the choice of a male comparator from a separate establishment, if he has the same employer or an associated employer, and if the terms and conditions of employment for men of the relevant class at his establishment are common with, meaning the same as, those of men of the relevant class employed at the woman's establishment, or which would be available for male employees for that work at her establishment. It is necessary that the selected male comparator should be representative of the class, or group, of male employees from whom he is selected, as regards the relevant terms etc of his contract of employment.[812]

The ruling that the relevant terms and conditions should be *the same as* those applying in the comparator's establishment seems a restrictive reading of the concept of '*common* terms and conditions'; in addition, the requirement that the male comparator be 'representative' of a group of men sharing the same terms as men employed at the complainant's establishment is arguably an unjustifiable gloss on the statute. The House of Lords allowed an appeal in *Smith*; according to Lord Slynn, 'the terms and conditions do not have to be identical'; it was enough if they were 'substantially comparable'.[813] However, the courts have continued to apply the highly artificial idea that the complainant has to show that the comparator was employed on terms similar to those which applied to similar male workers in her own establishment, or would have applied if there were any such workers.[814] This is at best a gloss on the statute for which the Act provides no obvious justification. More generally, the confinement of claims to workers employed in the same establishment or those employed in different establishments on narrowly defined 'common terms' would appear on the face of it to be contrary to the 'single source' test in EU law, which at no point requires that comparison across sub-units of the same employment unit should be limited in this way.

Comparison within the scope of discrimination

6.85 On the face of it, the Act leaves the claimant a free choice of comparator, as long as the 'same employment' hurdle is passed.[815] However, the comparator's choice may be circumscribed

---

[811] [1994] IRLR 342; revsd [1996] IRLR 404; applied in *South Tyneside Metropolitan Borough Council v Anderson* [2007] IRLR 715.
[812] [1994] IRLR 342, 358 (Balcombe LJ).
[813] [1996] IRLR 404, 410.
[814] *North v Dumfries and Galloway Council* [2011] IRLR 239; *City of Edinburgh Council v Wilkinson* [2012] IRLR 202.
[815] Within the meaning of the Act: see paras 6.81–6.84 above.

in practice by the need for the claimant to show that discrimination has occurred. In *Cheshire & Wirral NHS Trust v Abbott*[816] the Court of Appeal held that the comparison must be meaningful under the disparate impact test of European Union law. In the context of equal pay, this requires the tribunal to make a comparison between the advantaged and disadvantaged groups, using as large a pool as possible in order to generate a meaningful statistical comparison,[817] although the numbers required will depend on the size of employer and the nature of the element of pay at issue.[818]

Predecessor and successor comparators

6.86   Under the EqPA 1970 the male comparator had to be employed, or have been employed, at the same time as the complainant.[819] In *Macarthys Ltd v Smith* the female complainant was taken on as a factory manager at a wage of £50 per week; the previous holder of the job, a man, had earned £60 per week. The ECJ held on a preliminary reference that the scope of the concept of equal work, 'which is entirely qualitative in character in that it is exclusively concerned with the nature of the services in question, may not be restricted by the introduction of a requirement of contemporaneity'.[820] The Court nevertheless declined to interpret Article 119 (now 157 TFEU) as extending to cases of hypothetical comparisons.[821] EqA 2010 has brought British legislation into line with the *Macarthys* case by providing that the work of the complainant and her comparator need not be 'done contemporaneously'.[822]

'Piggyback' claims

6.87   If a female complainant succeeds in a claim for equal pay with a male comparator, other male workers may then be able to bring a claim for equality with her, and in this way 'piggy back' on her claim. This was confirmed by the EAT in *Hartlepool Borough Council v Llewellyn*.[823] The equal pay legislation draws no distinction between a comparator whose pay has been raised by virtue of successful litigation, as here, and any other case. Thus, according to the EAT judgment in *Llewellyn*, not to extend the increase in pay enjoyed by the female complainant in the original action to similarly placed male workers would amount to direct sex discrimination. Nor would the employer be able to resist the claims of the male workers on the basis of the defence of material factor.

---

[816]   [2006] IRLR 546; see also *Grundy v British Airways plc* [2008] IRLR 74.

[817]   On the definition of the 'pool' in indirect discrimination cases, see above, para 6.26.

[818]   See [2006] IRLR 546, Keene LJ at [22], who emphasised that employees in small firms should not be debarred from establishing disparate impact.

[819]   *Walton Centre for Neurology and Neurosurgery NHS Trust v Bewley* [2008] IRLR 588.

[820]   Case 129/79 [1980] ECR 1275, at para 11.

[821]   Case 129/79, at paras 14–15. In *Walton Centre for Neurology and Neorosurgery NHS Trust v Bewley* [2008] IRLR 588 the EAT held that comparison with a successor, unlike that of comparison with a predecessor, was not required by Art 141 TEC and that *Diocese of Hallam Trustee v Connaughton* [1996] IRLR 505 to the contrary was *per incuriam*.

[822]   EqA 2010, s 64(2).

[823]   [2009] IRLR 796.

Scope of comparison: nature of work

6.88 As we have just seen, the complainant (A) and the comparator (B) must be employed on 'equal work'. A's work is 'equal' to B's where it is 'like B's work', 'rated as equivalent to B's work' or of 'equal value' to it.[824]

(i) Like work

6.89 There is like work under the Act if 'A's work and B's work are the same or broadly similar' and 'such differences as there are between their work are not of practical importance in relation to the terms of their work'.[825] For this purpose the Act requires the tribunal to take into account 'the frequency with which differences between their work occur in practice' and 'the nature and extent of the differences'.[826] In the first case decided under the 1970 Act, *Capper Pass Ltd v Lawton*,[827] the EAT held that 'the work need not be of the *same* nature in order to be like work. It is enough if it is of similar nature. Indeed, it need only be broadly similar'; and 'trivial differences, or differences not likely in the real world to be reflected in the terms and conditions of employment, ought to be disregarded'.

The test has been applied in a fairly broad brush manner since then. One particular area of contention has been working-time arrangements, but courts and tribunals have been reluctant to classify otherwise identical jobs as dissimilar simply on the basis that one was part-time and the other full-time, or that one involves shift-working. In *Dugdale v Kraft Foods Ltd*[828] female quality control inspectors who were employed on day shifts compared their pay to those of men doing the same job on a regular night shift. The men received a higher basic rate of pay. All employees received shift premia of some kind, but the women were restricted from working at night by legislation which was in force at that time. The EAT held that 'the mere time at which the work is performed should be disregarded when considering the differences between the things which the woman does and the things which the man does'. Nor was this unjust, since 'where the work done is the same, and the only difference is the time at which it is done, the men will be compensated for the extra burden of working at night or on Sundays by the shift payment or premium. There seems no reason why the women should not have equality of treatment in respect of the basic wage'.[829]

Where one employee has extra responsibilities or extra duties, it is a question of fact in each case whether these are so substantial as to merit a finding that the jobs are dissimilar;[830] and even if the tribunal rules in favour of the complainant at this point, it remains open to the employer to argue that the difference is a 'material factor' and hence justifiable on those

---

[824] EqA 2010, s 65(1).

[825] Eq A 2010, s 65(2).

[826] EqA 2010, s 65(3).

[827] [1976] IRLR 366, 367–368.

[828] [1976] IRLR 368, 370, 371; see also *Electrolux Ltd v Hutchinson* [1976] IRLR 410; *Thomas v National Coal Board* [1987] IRLR 451.

[829] By contrast, there is EU law authority to suggest that employees with different professional qualifications and career structures may have difficulty demonstrating like work: see Case C-309/97 *Angestelltenbetriebsrat der Wiener Gebietskrankenkasse v Wiener Gebietskrankenkasse* [1999] IRLR 804.

[830] See *Waddington v Leicester Council for Voluntary Services* [1977] IRLR 32; *Eaton Ltd v Nuttall* [1977] IRLR 71.

grounds.[831] In *Shields v E Coomes Holdings Ltd*[832] the employer, which ran a chain of betting shops, paid a higher hourly rate to male counterhands than to female counterhands, on the basis that men were employed in shops where there was a risk of trouble from customers. Lord Denning, deciding that the jobs were similar, held that the time rate paid should be the same and that any extra duties undertaken by the men should be reflected in additional payments which would have to be justified under what is now the material factor defence.

(ii) Work rated as equivalent

6.90   The complainant (A) and her comparator (B) will be employed on 'work rated as equivalent' if a job evaluation study 'gives an equal value to A's job and B's job in terms of the demands made on a worker' or 'would give an equal value to A's job and B's job in those terms were the evaluation not made on a sex-specific system.'[833] A job evaluation study is 'a study undertaken with a view to evaluating, in terms of the demands made on a person by reference to factors such as effort, skill and decision making, the jobs to be done... by some or all of the workers in an undertaking or group of undertakings.'[834] A system is 'sex-specific' if 'for the purpose of one or more of the demands made on a worker, it sets values for men different from those it sets for women.'[835]

The assumption underlying this provision is that the employer has carried out a voluntary job evaluation which has either resulted in an equal ranking for the two jobs, or would have done but for sex discrimination in the way the scheme was set up. The Act does not require the employer to undertake a job evaluation scheme if it does not wish to. Moreover, the grounds on which an existing classification may be relied on are extremely difficult to meet. First, the employee has no basis for a claim if the scheme is not 'analytical'. The employee may, ironically, lose out at this point on the grounds of the study's inadequacy. An 'analytical' study is one which is 'thorough in analysis and capable of impartial application'; this will not be the case if the study 'requires the management to make a subjective judgment concerning the nature of the work before the employee can be fitted into the appropriate place in the appropriate salary grade.'[836] The study must also have been accepted as legitimate by the parties who commissioned it (usually the employer and possibly also any relevant trade union); it is not enough for consultants to have completed an analysis which is then rejected as inadequate by the employer, since it is no part of the purpose of the Act to force job evaluation schemes on those who do not want them.[837]

The second substantial hurdle which the complainant has to cross is the need to show, in a case where the study has ranked the jobs unequally, that the study was based on clear discrimination in

---

[831] On the material factor defence, see below, paras 6.96-6.101.

[832] [1978] IRLR 263.

[833] EqA 2010, s 65(4).

[834] EqA 2010, s 80(5) (which also extends to job evaluation studies carried out in the context of the armed forces).

[835] EqA 2010, s 65(4), (5). In *Redcar and Cleveland Borough Council v Bainbridge (No 1)* [2007] IRLR 984, the Court of Appeal held that the words 'or her job had been given a higher value' and 'her job would have been given a higher value' should be read into s 1(5) EqPA 1970, the predecessor statute to EqA 2010 s 65(4)-(5), in order to allow a claim against a comparator who had been placed in a lower band but received more pay. See also *Home Office v Bailey* [2005] IRLR 757, EAT (employment tribunal erred in finding that jobs of the complainants and their comparators had been given an equal value when the complainants scored lower than their comparators).

[836] *Eaton Ltd v Nuttall* [1977] IRLR 71, 74.

[837] *Arnold v Beecham Group Ltd* [1982] IRLR 307; cf *O'Brien v Sim-Chem Ltd* [1980] IRLR 373.

the values set for the work of men and women respectively. This involves something akin to 'a plain error on the face of the record'.[838] In essence the contention is that the study would have resulted in a finding of equality if 'purged of some discriminatory element'; but what the complainant is unable to do 'is to base his claim on the footing that if the evaluation study had been carried out differently from the way in which it has in fact been carried out he would be entitled to the relief claimed. The claimant must take the study as it is'.[839] As a result, the chances of a successful claim being made under this head are remote.

A claim for equal pay based on a job evaluation study that has ranked the work of the complainant and the comparator equally may only be made with effect from the point at which the study in question became effective. The consequence of this rule is that a claim for arrears of pay going back to before that point must be brought as an equal value claim, in the context of which the job evaluation study, while of probative value, will not be decisive.[840]

(iii) Work of equal value

6.91   Under EqA 2010, the work of the complainant (A) is of equal value to that of the comparator (B) if A's work is 'equal to B's work in terms of the demands made on A by reference to factors such as effort, skill and decision-making'.[841] The concept of work of equal value was introduced into UK law in 1983 following the ruling of the ECJ in *EC Commission v United Kingdom*[842] to the effect that the 1970 Act, which as it then stood only contained the two bases of comparison referred to above, failed to comply with the standards set by the Equal Pay Directive. The Court noted that 'British legislation does not permit the introduction of a job classification system without the employer's consent. Workers in the United Kingdom are therefore unable to have their work rated as being of equal value with comparable work if their employer refuses to introduce a classification system'.[843] The Court did not hold that the Directive required the general introduction of job evaluation techniques into employing organisations, but rather that it required Member States to put in place the means by which equal value could be attributed to particular work 'notwithstanding the employer's wishes, if necessary in the context of adversarial proceedings';[844] the United Kingdom's argument that 'the criterion of work of equal value is too abstract to be applied by the courts' was brushed aside.[845]

The 1983 Equal Pay (Amendment) Regulations[846] established a complex procedure for the adjudication of equal value claims, which has been amended over time and is now set out in the Employment Tribunals (Constitution and Rules of Procedure) Regulations 2004.[847]

---

[838] *Green v Broxtowe District Council* [1977] ICR 241, 243.

[839] *England v Bromley London Borough Council* [1978] ICR 1, 5.

[840] *Redcar and Cleveland Borough Council v Bainbridge (No 2)* [2008] IRLR 776; *Hovell v Ashford and St. Peter's Hospital NHS Trust* [2009] IRLR 734. Arrears may be claimed for up to six years from the date of the claim: see below, para 6.105.

[841] EqA 2010, s 65(6)(b).

[842] Case 61/81 [1982] ICR 578.

[843] Case 61/81 [1982] ICR 578, para 5.

[844] Case 61/81 [1982] ICR 578, para 13.

[845] Case 61/81 [1982] ICR 578, para 12.

[846] SI 1983/1794.

[847] SI 2004/1861, as amended.

THE 'TOKEN MAN' DEFENCE

6.92   An artificial obstacle faced by early complainants arose from the peculiar drafting of the amending Regulations, which were introduced under the European Communities Act 1972 and so were not subject to any amendment in the course of their parliamentary passage. In order for work to be of equal value under section 1(2)(c) of the Act, it has to be 'work in relation to which paragraph (a) or (b) above applies', paragraphs (a) and (b) referring to the 'like work' and 'work rated as equivalent' provisions of the Act. The intention here was to require complainants first of all to exhaust any rights they might have under paragraphs (a) and (b) before mounting an equal value claim. But this is not quite what paragraph (c) said: it appeared to rule out a claim for equal value where, for example, there was male worker doing the same job as the complainant ('like work'). The House of Lords held in *Pickstone v Freemans plc*[848] that the Regulations should be given a purposive interpretation which was consonant with the Directive which they were intended to implement and with Parliament's intentions, namely that 'paragraph (c) will only apply if paragraphs (a) and (b) are first held by the Tribunal not to apply in respect of the work of the woman and the work of the man with whom she seeks parity of pay'.[849] EqA 2010 now provides that an equal value claim only lies if the complainant's work is neither like that of the comparator nor rated as equivalent to it.[850]

PRE-EXISTING JOB EVALUATION SCHEME

6.93   Before proceeding to determine whether the work of the complainant and her comparator are of equal value, the tribunal must consider whether there is evidence to the effect that a job evaluation scheme has already ranked the jobs unequally.[851] For this purpose, a 'stage 1 equal value hearing' must be conducted.[852] For the defence to apply, the work of the complainant and her comparator must 'have been given different values' by a job evaluation study within the meaning of the Act.[853] The tribunal must reject the claim unless it has 'reasonable grounds for suspecting that the evaluation contained in the study … was based on a system which discriminates because of sex' or is 'otherwise unreliable'.[854] For this purpose there is sex discrimination where 'a difference, (or coincidence) between values that the system sets on different demands is not justifiable regardless of the sex of the person on whom the demands are made'.[855]

There are three requirements of this defence: the two jobs in question must have been ranked unequally; the study carried out must be an 'analytical' one within the meaning of the case law interpreting section 1(5) of the 1980 Act (now section 80(5) of the 2010 Act); and it must not be tainted by sex discrimination or be otherwise unsuitable. The first requirement is self-explanatory. The second necessitates some consideration of the kinds of job evaluation techniques which are acceptable for this purpose and of the extent to which the courts are prepared to scrutinise the

---

[848]   [1988] IRLR 357.
[849]   [1988] IRLR 357, 363. This case was an early example of the use of Hansard to clarify the meaning of a statute derived from an EU law source.
[850]   EqA 2010, s 65(6).
[851]   EqA 2010, s 131(5), (6).
[852]   SI 2004/1861, Sch 6, para 4.
[853]   That is to say, as defined by EqA 2010, s 80(5). See above, para 6.90.
[854]   EqA 2010, s 131(6).
[855]   EqA 2010, s 131(7).

findings of studies which have been carried out. ACAS Guide No 1 on job evaluation, which was judicially noted by the EAT in *Eaton Ltd v Nuttall*[856] identified five possible techniques: *job ranking*, where the jobs are individually assessed, then ranked in order and finally grouped into grades which form the basis of pay rates; *paired comparison*, which involves the comparison of particular pairs of jobs in turn, leading again to a ranking order; *job classification*, where 'benchmark' or typical jobs are assigned places in a pre-set grading structure and other jobs slotted in around them; *points assessment*, whereby jobs are broken down into a number of factors such as skill, responsibility, working conditions and physical and mental requirements to which points are awarded according to a predetermined scale, on the basis of which each job is given a points total which determines its place in the ranking; and *factor comparison*, whereby, for a number of 'key' jobs which serve as benchmarks, the proportion of pay which is determined by particular factors is identified, thereby producing a rate for these factors from which a composite wage can be deduced for each job. As we saw above,[857] the EAT in *Eaton* held that section 1(5) is only satisfied by a study, of whatever sort, which is capable of impartial application and does not require management to make a subjective judgment.

The degree of precision and of 'objectivity' needed was considered further by the Court of Appeal in *Bromley v H & J Quick Ltd*.[858] The employer had adopted a job evaluation study as part of which benchmark jobs were ranked on the basis of paired comparison, separate factors identified and their contribution weighted using multiple regression analysis, and grade boundaries established around the jobs. The resulting rankings were then discussed by a joint panel of management and employees on a 'felt fair' basis. Once the rankings were agreed, other jobs, for which there was no written job descriptions, were slotted into the structure on the basis of a general assessment of their worth by management, without a more specific factor-based analysis. The Court of Appeal held that this last stage of the process did not meet the requirements of section 1(5). According to Dillon LJ, the scheme must be analytical in the sense that 'the jobs of each worker covered by the study must have been valued in terms of the demands made on the worker under various headings',[859] and this was not the case here.

Quick suggests that it is expecting too much of schemes to avoid subjective judgments entirely, but that if the scheme is to be valid under section 1(5) these judgments must be placed within the framework of a 'transparent' or objectively justifiable *process* of evaluation. Dillon LJ accepted that 'there are no universally accepted external criteria for measuring how much of a factor or quality is involved in a particular job or for measuring what relative weights ought to be attached to different factors or qualities involved, to differing extents, in various jobs'. Hence, there could be 'subjective elements' but only 'in an objective process', and 'where there are such subjective elements, care has to be taken to see that discrimination is not, inadvertently, let in'.[860]

The third element in the defence, the test of discrimination, involves an examination of the criteria or weightings used in the process of evaluation to see whether they give rise to either direct or indirect discrimination and, if the latter, whether they are justifiable. The Act must be

---

[856] [1977] IRLR 71, 74.
[857] See above, this paragraph.
[858] [1988] IRLR 249.
[859] [1988] IRLR 249, 253–254.
[860] [1988] IRLR 249, 253–254.

interpreted here by reference to the standards applicable under Article 157 TFEU (previously Article 141 EC) and the Equal Pay Directive.[861]

In *Rummler v Dato-Druck GmbH*[862] the ECJ was called on to consider the position, under the Directive, of a job evaluation process under which high weightings were attached to the factor of muscular effort involved in particular jobs. The Court ruled that under the Directive a job evaluation process has to operate 'objectively' and 'must not be organised, as a whole, in such a manner that it has the practical effect of discriminating generally against workers of one sex'.[863] It held that the use of a criterion, such as muscular effort, which tended to favour men was not ruled out as such but that any discriminatory effect should be measured by reference to the job classification system as a whole, and that in comparing jobs the classification system should take into account 'other criteria in relation to which women workers may have a particular aptitude'.[864] The use of a criterion favouring one sex was also justifiable by reference to 'the nature of the job when such a difference is necessary in order to ensure a level of pay appropriate to the effort required by the work and thus corresponds to a real need on the part of the undertaking'.[865]

Rummler, together with the similar decision of the ECJ in *Danfoss*,[866] which concerned the criteria established by a collective agreement for determining pay increments, lay down a requirement of 'transparency' in pay classification systems, which means in this context that the burden is on the employer under the Act to account for the process used and to rebut suggestions of discriminatory bias: 'it is for the employer to explain how any job evaluation study worked and what was taken into account at each stage',[867] and to show that any subjective adjustments to the placings of jobs in a ranking scheme were not the result of ingrained attitudes of discrimination.

ESTABLISHING EQUAL VALUE: THE ROLE OF THE TRIBUNAL AND OF THE INDEPENDENT EXPERT

6.94   If the tribunal does not reject the claim on the basis of the pre-existing job evaluation scheme defence, it must make a number of orders at the stage 1 hearing, the purpose of which is to put in place a procedure for establishing the relevant facts of the case.[868] By these means, the claimant can be required to disclose to the employer the name of the chosen comparator or such information as will enable the comparator to be identified. If it has been supplied with sufficient detail to do so, the employer must respond by providing the claimant with the comparator's name. The parties then have to provide written job descriptions for the claimant and comparator, and identify to each other the facts which they consider relevant to the question of equal value.

The tribunal must also decide at the stage 1 hearing whether to require a report to be prepared by a member of the panel of independent experts which is constituted for this purpose by ACAS.[869] In deciding whether or not to require a report, it may, on the application of a party, take into

---

[861] *Bromley v H & J Quick Ltd* [1988] IRLR 249.

[862] Case 237/85 [1986] ECR 2101.

[863] Case 237/85 [1986] ECR 2101, at para 13.

[864] Case 237/85 [1986] ECR 2101, at para 15.

[865] Case 237/85 [1986] ECR 2101, at para 24.

[866] Case 109/88 *Handels-og Kontorfunktionaerernes Forbund i Danmark v Dansk Arbejdsgiver-forening (acting for Danfoss)* [1989] IRLR 532; Case C-400/93 *Royal Copenhagen* [1995] IRLR 648 (applying the principle to piecework payment systems).

[867] *Bromley v H & J Quick Ltd* [1988] IRLR 249, 254 (Dillon LJ).

[868] SI 2004/1861, Sch 6, para 5.

[869] EqA 2010, s 131(2); SI 2004/1861, Sch 6, para 4(3)(b).

account representations of both of the parties on the availability to the employer of the defence of genuine material factor.[870] If no independent expert is appointed, the tribunal must set a date for the main hearing according to an indicative timetable set out in the Regulations, at which it must resolve the issue of equal value. If, on the other hand, an independent expert is appointed, the tribunal must first conduct a 'stage 2 equal value hearing' at which it determines the facts on which the independent expert must, exclusively, base the report. The role of determining the relevant facts, in so far as they are not agreed by the parties themselves, rests with the tribunal and not the independent expert,[871] but the tribunal may call on the independent expert to assist it in fact finding under certain specified circumstances.[872] The independent expert may apply for some or all of the facts, as determined by the tribunal, to be amended, supplemented or omitted.[873]

Once appointed, the independent expert has a number of duties, the most important one of which is to prepare a report and send it to the tribunal and the parties.[874] The tribunal has powers to manage proceedings during this process, including the power to order the parties to provide relevant information and documents to the independent expert.[875] The employer may be required to grant access to its premises and to allow the independent expert to carry out interviews with relevant persons.[876]

The tribunal may withdraw the requirement to prepare the report and order the independent expert to provide it with documentation and to accede to any other request related to the withdrawal of the requirement.[877] If it does not withdraw the requirement, the tribunal must not determine the issue of equal value without receiving the report[878] and admitting it at the final hearing.[879] The scope for argument at the full hearing is tightly circumscribed: the tribunal may refuse to hear evidence or argument on issues which were not properly disclosed in advance under the rules set out above, unless it was not reasonably practicable for the party concerned to have done so.[880] However, the purpose of the hearing is not simply to rubber-stamp the report. If the tribunal decides that the report is not based on the relevant facts, it may decide the issue of equal value without reference to the report, or commission another one.[881] This last provision could be read as implying that the tribunal must, in all other cases, accept the independent expert's conclusions. However, the Regulations also provide that the parties may, with the tribunal's permission, submit an expert report of their own and/or call such an expert to give evidence at the hearing.[882] In addition, they may challenge the report of the independent expert, or that of a rival expert, by putting questions to them in writing prior to the hearing.[883] Because the independent expert's report can be challenged in this way, case law under pre-2004 Regulations which suggested that

---

[870] SI 2004/1861, Sch 6, reg 4(5). On the material factor defence, see paras 6.96–6.101 below.
[871] This is the effect of SI 2004/1861, Sch 6, paras 7(3) and 8(1)(b).
[872] SI 2004/1861, Sch 6, para 6.
[873] SI 2004/1861, Sch 6, para 7(6).
[874] SI 2004/1861, Sch 6, para 10(2)(f).
[875] SI 2004/1861, Sch 6, para 3(1)(d).
[876] SI 2004/1861, Sch 6, para 5(1)(c).
[877] EqA 2010, s 131(2); *Hovell v Ashford and St. Peter's Hospital NHS Trust* [2009] IRLR 734.
[878] EqA 2010, s 131(4).
[879] SI 2004/1861, Sch 6, para 9(1).
[880] SI 2004/1861, Sch 6, para 9(3).
[881] SI 2004/1861, Sch 6, para 9(2).
[882] SI 2004/1861, Sch 6, para 11. See *Middlesborough Borough Council v Surtees (No 2)* [2007] IRLR 981.
[883] SI 2004/1861, Sch 6, para 12.

it was open to the tribunal, having admitted the report, to disagree with its conclusions, without needing to commission a new one,[884] is probably still valid.

Proportionate pay claims

6.95   The Act provides a right to equal treatment only where the work of the complainant and her comparator are 'equal'; it does not provide a right to 'proportionate' pay in a case where, for example, it is shown by job evaluation or by some other means that the complainant's work is worth 95% of the comparator's but she receives only 70%.[885] Nor does it apparently provide a right to equal pay in a case where the work done by the complainant is *more valuable* than the comparator's.[886] In the former situation, Article 157 and the Equal Treatment Directive may provide a solution but only if they are clearly seen to extend to the situation of the 'hypothetical' male comparator, in other words to the situation which the complainant would have been in had she been male.[887] The latter situation is clearly covered by Article 157 as a consequence of the ECJ's ruling on a preliminary reference in *Murphy v Bord Telecom Eireann*:[888] 'a contrary interpretation would be tantamount to rendering the principle of equal pay ineffective and nugatory'.[889] *Murphy* was applied by the Court of Appeal to a claim based on a rating under a job evaluation scheme in *Redcar v Cleveland Borough Council v Bainbridge (No 1)*.[890]

Material factor defence

6.96   Under section 1(3) of the EqPA 1970, the equality clause had no application in relation to a variation in terms and conditions between the complainant and her comparator where 'the variation is genuinely due to a material factor which is not the difference of sex'. In the case of claims in respect of like work and work rated as equivalent, this factor also had to be a 'material difference'.[891] Now, section 69 EqA 2010 applies the material factor defence where the employer can show that a difference in pay arises 'because of a material factor reliance on which... does not involve treating [the complainant] less favourably because of [her] sex' than the comparator is treated, and, in a case where there is adverse impact,[892] the factor is 'a proportionate means of achieving a legitimate aim'.[893] The concept of 'material factor' thereby embodies both the definition of direct discrimination, for the purposes of which justification is no defence, and the concept of

---

[884] *Tennants Textile Colours Ltd v Todd* [1989] IRLR 3; *Aldridge v British Telecommunications plc* [1990] IRLR 10.
[885] As in the US case, *County of Washington v Gunther* 452 US 161 (1981); McCrudden, 1983: p 209.
[886] At least, this may be inferred from the like work case of *Waddington v Leicester Council for Voluntary Services* [1977] IRLR 32, where it was concluded in such circumstances that s 1(1)(a) of the Act was not satisfied.
[887] See Szyszczak, 1985: p 151.
[888] Case 157/86 [1988] IRLR 267.
[889] [1988] IRLR 267, 269.
[890] [2008] IRLR 876.
[891] EqPA 1970, s 1(3)(a).
[892] That is, a case in which, as a result of a material factor, A, the complainant, 'and persons of the same sex doing equal work to A's are put at a particular disadvantage when compared with persons of the opposite sex doing equal work to A's': EqA 2010, s 69(2).
[893] EqA 2010, s 69(1).

indirect discrimination, for which it is. Here, as elsewhere in equality law, the two categories of direct and indirect discrimination should be treated as mutually exclusive:[894] thus it should not be a defence to a claim based on *indirect* discrimination that the employer did not commit *direct* discrimination in the sense of treating the complainant less favourably on the ground of her sex.[895] Contrary to the pre-2010 Act case law on this point,[896] the employer should only have a material factor defence in a case of adverse impact if it can show that the factor relied on was a proportionate means of achieving a legitimate aim. Conversely, the complainant should fail if she cannot establish either less favourable treatment because of her sex (direct discrimination) or adverse impact on the members of her sex (indirect sex discrimination).[897] This interpretation would realign UK law with EU law as set out in the *Danfoss* and *Enderby* cases.[898]

If this approach is correct, analysis of the material factor defence will turn on the existence, in indirect discrimination cases, of a legitimate aim and on the proportionality of the means taken to achieve it. We will consider four types of aim, consisting respectively of personal, organisational, labour-market related and collective-bargaining related factors, before analysing the application of the proportionality test in this context.

(i) Personal factors

6.97 The early case law of the domestic courts confined the defence of material factor and/or material difference to factors specific to the individual complainant and her comparator. In *Clay Cross (Quarry Services) Ltd v Fletcher*[899] the Court of Appeal held that in applying section 1(3), the tribunal 'is to have regard to... the personal equation of the woman as compared to that of the man B irrespective of any extrinsic forces which led to the variation in pay'.[900] The kind of factors permissible here include the greater seniority of a given individual; his or her superior qualifications for the job; their greater productivity; or the difference between permanently-established workers and secondees.[901] Also covered are cases of so-called 'red circling'. This occurs where it is 'necessary to protect the wages of an employee, or a group of employees, moved from a better paid type of work to a worse paid type of work, perhaps because the first is no longer being undertaken'.[902] In judging whether the red circling is legitimate in a given case, the tribunal should take into account such factors as whether the differential treatment was intended to be temporary or permanent; whether the class of those protected in this way was open or closed;

---

[894] See above, para 6.13.
[895] See Hepple, 2011a: pp 103-104.
[896] In particular *Armstrong v Newcastle-upon-Tyne NHS Trust* [2006] IRLR 124; *Gibson v Sheffield City Council* [2010] IRLR 311.
[897] It may be noted that if the complainant can establish direct sex discrimination relating to contractual pay, she can most straightforwardly bring a claim of direct sex discrimination under ss 13 and 26(8)(a) EqA 2010, to which the sex equality clause exclusion has no application: EqA 2010, s 71; see above, paras 6.50, 6.78.
[898] Case 109/88 *Handels-og Kontorfunktionaerernes Forbund i Danmark v Dansk Arbejdsgiver-forening (acting for Danfoss)* [1989] IRLR 532; Case C-127/92 *Enderby v Frenchay Health Authority* [1993] IRLR 591. See also, for a restatement of the need for objective justification and for the application of a proportionality test, Case C-381/99 *Brunnhofer v Bank der Österreichischen Postsparkasse AG* [2001] IRLR 571.
[899] [1978] IRLR 361.
[900] [1978] IRLR 361, 363 (Lord Denning MR).
[901] On this last point see *Wakeman v Quick Corporation* [1999] IRLR 424, a race discrimination claim.
[902] *Snoxell v Vauxhall Motors Ltd* [1977] IRLR 123, 125 (Phillips J).

whether it had been the subject of collective negotiation; whether it originated in an act of sex discrimination; and whether movement between the grades in question was equally possible for men and women.[903]

In *Snoxell v Vauxhall Motors Ltd* the employers red circled a group of male inspectors who, before 1970, had been in a high grade for male inspectors only; there were two other grades, a lower grade for male inspectors and a grade exclusively for women inspectors. When the Act was passed all the male and female grades were merged but those employees who had been in the higher male grade kept their higher rate of pay. The EAT held that the employer had failed to make out a section 1(3) defence since 'past sex discrimination has contributed to the variation'.[904] *Snoxell* was applied in *Redcar and Cleveland Borough Council v Bainbridge*,[905] where the Court of Appeal held that the employer could not rely on a pay protection scheme as a valid material factor defence given that the claimant women had been entitled in the past to the same pay as the men who had previously received bonuses and who were in receipt of pay protection due to losing those bonuses: '[T]he reason for the new pay differential was causally related to the historic unlawful sex discrimination'. [906]

An arguably illegitimate extension of the category of 'personal factors' is the acceptance by some courts of an employer 'error' as the basis for a material factor defence.[907] Where, for example, an employee is placed in the wrong job category by mistake and thereafter retains his or her advantage through red circling, there seems a strong case for concluding that this should not be treated as a 'material' factor.[908]

(ii) Organisational factors

6.98   In *Rainey v Greater Glasgow Health Board*[909] the House of Lords held that the scope of the defence of material factor cannot be confined to the 'personal equation' as suggested in *Clay Cross*;[910] at least in a case where there was no intention to discriminate, 'a difference which is connected with economic factors affecting the efficient carrying on of the employer's business or other activity may well be relevant'.[911] The ECJ referred, in *Bilka-Kaufhaus*, to measures which 'correspond to a real need on the part of the undertaking, are appropriate with a view to achieving the objectives pursued and are necessary to that end'.[912] This is a precise test, in which the Court broadly accepted the argument put forward by the European Commission in that case, namely that 'it is not sufficient to show that in adopting a pay practice which discriminates against women

[903] [1977] IRLR 123, 126. A red circling defence may have to be periodically reviewed to see if it is still valid: *Home Office v Bailey* [2005] IRLR 757; *Fearnon v Smurfit Corrugated Cases (Lurgan) Ltd* [2009] IRLR 132.
[904] [1977] IRLR 123, 128; see also *United Biscuits Ltd v Young* [1978] IRLR 15; *Outlook Supplies Ltd v Parry* [1978] ICR 388.
[905] [2008] IRLR 776.
[906] Mummery LJ, giving the judgment of the court, at [106].
[907] *Yorkshire Blood Transfusion Service v Plaskitt* [1994] ICR 74; cf the decision of the NICA in *McPherson v Rathgael Centre for Children and Young People* [1991] IRLR 206.
[908] Kilpatrick, 1994: p 325.
[909] [1987] IRLR 26.
[910] [1978] IRLR 361.
[911] [1987] IRLR 26, 29.
[912] Case 170/84 *Bilka-Kaufhaus v Weber von Hartz* [1986] IRLR 317, 320.

workers the employers sought to achieve objectives other than discrimination against women ... It is also necessary to ascertain whether the pay practice in question is necessary and in proportion to the objectives pursued by the employer.[913]

The Court held in the *Danfoss*[914] case that once a *prima facie* finding of adverse impact has been made, the burden of proof lies on the employer. Here, the effect of a pay classification system operated by the employer under a collective agreement was that in each grade the pay of women was around 7% lower than that of men. The Court ruled that 'where an undertaking applies a system of pay which is characterised by a total lack of transparency, the burden of proof is on the employer to show that his pay practice is not discriminatory, where a female worker establishes, by comparison with a relatively large number of employees, that the average pay of female workers is lower than that of male workers.'[915] The Court also held that pay differentials arising from the operation of seniority systems were, in principle, capable of providing an adequate justification, as long as the criteria being applied were not themselves tainted by sex.[916]

The issue in many of the cases which have arisen in this area concerns how far institutional rules or practices governing working time arrangements, seniority, labour flexibility and access to benefits can be justified. In *Bilka- Kaufhaus*[917] the Court accepted that the differential treatment of part-time workers (in this case, exclusion from an occupational pension scheme) could in principle be justified by reference to the needs of the business if it was the aim of the employer to *reduce* the numbers of part-timers employed, for example because of high overhead and training costs. However, in *Steinicke*[918] the Court held that, in such a case, it was insufficient for an employer to make generalised observations concerning the need to encourage the recruitment of full-time workers, in the absence of evidence which could enable a court to judge whether the means chosen were proportionate to that aim. Moreover, it was not open to an employer to justify an otherwise discriminatory practice simply on the grounds that it reduced its costs.[919]

Payment systems favouring 'labour flexibility', in the sense of the 'adaptability of the worker to variable work schedules and places of work', which could disadvantage female workers on account of their greater household and family duties, have to be justified by reference to 'the performance of the specific duties entrusted to the worker concerned', as do requirements of vocational training which may also have an adverse impact.[920] Rules incorporating the principle that benefits accrue with seniority do not, on the other hand, need to be justified by reference to *specific duties* in this way, since 'seniority goes hand in hand with experience which generally places a worker in a better position to carry out his [sic] duties.'[921] However, this does not mean that seniority rules which have

---

[913] Case 170/84 *Bilka-Kaufhaus v Weber von Hartz* [1986] IRLR 317, 320; for a more recent reassertion of this principle, see Case C-243/95 *Hill and Stapleton v Revenue Commissioners* [1998] IRLR 466.

[914] Case 109/88 [1989] IRLR 532.

[915] [1989] IRLR 532, 537.

[916] See also, on seniority, Case C-17/05 *Cadman v HSE* [2006] IRLR 969; *Wilson v HSE* [2010] IRLR 59; Rowbottom, 2010.

[917] Case 170/84 *Bilka-Kaufhaus v Weber von Hartz* [1986] IRLR 317, 320; see also Case C-33/89 *Kowalska v Freie und Hansestadt Hamburg* [1990] IRLR 447.

[918] Case C-77/02 *Steinicke v Bundesanstalt für Arbeit* [2003] IRLR 892.

[919] To similar effect, on this last point, are the judgment of the Court of Appeal in *Allonby v Accrington and Rossendale College* [2001] IRLR 364 and the ECJ's judgments in Case C-187/00 *Kütz-Bauer v Freie und Hansestadt Hamburg* [2003] IRLR 368 and Joined Cases C-4/02 and C-5/02 *Schönheit v Staft Frankfurt am Main, Becker v Land Hessen* [2004] IRLR 983.

[920] Case 109/88 *Danfoss* [1989] IRLR 532, 536–537.

[921] Case 109/88 *Danfoss* [1989] IRLR 532, 536–537.

an adverse impact do not need to be justified *at all*, as, for example, in a context where only a limited proportion of part-timers' accrued service was recognised for seniority purposes.[922] In *Cadman v HSE*[923] the Court of Appeal made a reference to the ECJ in an attempt to clarify the relationship between the *Danfoss* and *Nimz* judgments. The ECJ reiterated that an employer could reward length of service without needing to relate its importance to the performance of specific tasks but went on to state that there 'may be situations in which recourse to the criterion of length of service must be justified by the employer in detail'. This would be the case, in particular, where the worker 'provides evidence capable of giving rise to serious doubts as to whether recourse to the criterion of length of service is … appropriate to attain' the objective of performing his duties better.[924]

Although the extensive case law at both domestic and European Union level concerning the impact of the principle of equal treatment on working-time arrangements has established that it is not, in general, permissible to differentiate between part-time and full-time workers in terms of the basic rate of their wage or salary, a much more contentious area is that of fringe benefits including overtime and premium payments for shifts. In *Stadt Lengerich v Helmig* Advocate General Van Gerven considered that where overtime premia were restricted to employees who worked more than the normal *full-time* working week, 'the additional physical effort and the restriction on the use of free time entailed in working overtime constitute objective reasons to be appraised by the national courts, which may justify a difference in treatment as between part-time and full-time employees'.[925] Similarly, in *Calder v Rowntree Mackintosh Confectionery Ltd*[926] the Court of Appeal refused to upset a finding of an employment tribunal to the effect that a defence of justification was made out where the employer paid shift premia to full-time employees (mainly men) working on rotating daytime and night-time shifts which was not available to part-time employees (mainly women) who worked a regular twilight shift, partly because of the 'inconvenience of rotation, which we understand can cause physical problems, eg disturbance of sleeping patterns [and] is disruptive of family life'.[927] However, in *Krüger v Kreiskrankenhaus Ebersberg*[928] a collective agreement which excluded part-time workers from eligibility from a Christmas bonus simply on the grounds that to do so mirrored a rule in the state social security system was held not be justified.

(iii) Labour market factors

6.99   In *Fletcher v Clay Cross (Quarry Services Ltd).*[929] the Court of Appeal held that the defence of material difference did not cover a case where, thanks to external market forces, the employer

---

[922] Case C-184/89 *Nimz v Freie und Hansestadt Hamburg* [1991] IRLR 222.

[923] [2004] IRLR 971; see also *Wilson v HSE* [2010] IRLR 59; Rowbottom, 2010.

[924] Case C-17/05 *Cadman v HSE* [2006] IRLR 969, paras 33–40; Rowbottom, 2010

[925] Case C-399/92 [1995] IRLR 216, 219. The Court reached the same conclusion in this case but on a different ground: see para 6.99 below. In Case C-285/02 *Elsner-Lakeberg v Land Nordrhein Westfalen* [2005] IRLR 209 the ECJ ruled that the application to part-time and full-time workers of different rules for calculating overtime work required justification, but did not consider the precise grounds for such justification.

[926] [1993] IRLR 212.

[927] [1993] IRLR 212, 217.

[928] Case C-281/97 [1999] IRLR 808. It is surprising that a similar argument should have succeeded in the context of pension benefits in *Trustees of Uppingham School Retirement Benefits Scheme for Non-Teaching Staff v Shillcock* [2002] IRLR 702.

[929] [1978] IRLR 361, 363.

found it necessary to hire an individual at a higher rate than those already employed. Under these circumstances, the employer came under a duty to raise the pay of the latter group:

> … the Tribunal is not to have regard to any extrinsic forces which have led to the man being paid more. An employer cannot avoid his obligations under the Act by saying: 'I paid him more because he asked for more', or 'I paid her less because she was willing to work for less'. If any such excuse were permitted, the Act would be a dead letter. Those are the very reasons why there was unequal pay before the Statute. They are the very circumstances in which the Statute was intended to operate.

This statement is not necessarily an inaccurate one in the context of the circumstances which the Court had to deal with in *Clay Cross*, despite the later overruling of the Court's decision that comparisons could never extend to 'extrinsic factors'. Although *Rainey v Greater Glasgow Health Board*[930] opened up the possibility of external market forces constituting a defence, the House of Lords did not, in that case, accept that *any* form of this argument would succeed.

In *Rainey* a disparity in pay arose between a group of medical professionals, prosthetists, who were hired to join the NHS from the private sector when a prosthetic service was set up for the first time in Scotland, and their colleagues who were either hired from other regions within the NHS or joined after the service was established. The former group had been paid at a higher rate which matched their private-sector salaries because of the difficulties experienced in recruiting entirely from within the NHS. The House of Lords held that the difference in pay was justified under section 1(3).

Rainey can be explained on the basis that the higher paid group were 'red circled'; moreover, there was specific evidence of a labour shortage causing the difficulty in recruitment. Arguably it would not affect the outcome in *Clay Cross*, where the employer was basically doing little more than asserting that because Mrs Fletcher had been prepared to work for less than her male comparator, the difference between their pay was caused by 'market forces' in the sense of supply and demand.

The view that differential pay rates are legitimate *solely* because they are the outcome of an agreement between the parties which may be assumed to have been influenced to some degree by supply and demand, although apparently acceptable to some US courts in the context of the Equal Pay Act 1963 and Civil Rights Act 1964,[931] has not been accepted at any point either by the domestic UK courts or by the ECJ: on the contrary, they have insisted on specific evidence of labour scarcity or geographical factors causing differential pay rates. In the leading case under Article 157, *Enderby v Frenchay Health Authority*,[932] the ECJ held that 'the state of the employment market, which may lead an employer to increase the pay of a particular job in order to attract candidates, may constitute an objectively justified economic ground'; but it was also necessary 'for the national court to determine, if necessary by applying the principle of proportionality, whether and to what extent the shortage of candidates for a job and the need to attract them by higher pay constitutes an objectively justified economic ground for the difference in pay between the jobs in question'.[933] This suggests that the

---

[930] [1987] IRLR 26.
[931] *Christiansen v Iowa* 563 F 2d 706 (1980); *American Nurses Association v State of Illinois* 783 F 2d 716 (1986).
[932] Case C-127/92 [1993] IRLR 591; Fredman, 1994a.
[933] [1993] IRLR 591, 595.

employer must do considerably more than merely assert that a given pay differential is the outcome of 'supply and demand'. In particular, objective evidence must be provided of the basis for retention bonuses and other incentive payments which are offered to individuals on a selective basis.[934] The ECJ in *Enderby* also rejected an argument that the mere existence of separate collective bargaining processes for given grades of workers can amount to justification.[935]

A further decision which limits the 'market forces' defence is *Ratcliffe v North Yorkshire County Council*.[936] Here the Council's direct service organisation cut the pay of a group of employees in order to enable it to place a low bid to carry out work which was being put out to competitive tender under the Local Government Act 1988. The Court of Appeal accepted a view that 'the "material factor" which led to the lower rates of pay ... was the operation of market forces resulting from the statutory requirement in the 1988 Act that [the employer's] tender could not succeed unless it took full account of those forces'.[937] However, the House of Lords took a different view. According to Lord Slynn the employer was not entitled to make cuts in pay simply in order to compete with an external contractor, which was apparently able to set wages at rates below those set by national collective bargaining by employing only women to do the work in question: 'though conscious of the difficult problem facing the employers in seeking to compete with a rival tenderer,' to reduce the women's wages below those of their male comparators was 'the very kind of discrimination in relation to pay which the [1970] Act sought to remove'.[938]

A contrasting decision is *Armstrong v Newcastle upon Tyne NHS Trust*.[939] Here, the claimants were female domestic ancillary workers who were comparing their pay to male porters. The ancillary work had been contracted out in the 1980s and an in-house bid had been successful, as part of which bonus payments for the ancillary workers were withdrawn while the porters retained theirs. At a later point the two groups were again employed by the same employer. The tribunal held that the initial decision to put the ancillary work out to tender, but not the portering work, had been tainted by discriminatory assumptions on the part of the employer concerning the state of the local labour market and the willingness of the predominantly male employees to accept the loss of bonuses. The EAT upheld this decision but the Court of Appeal reversed, holding that the tribunal's decision was not based on an objective reading of the facts, and depended too much on unsubstantiated inferences. The case was remitted to the employment tribunal.

(iv) Collective bargaining

6.100   One of the issues considered in *Enderby*[940] was whether collective bargaining arrangements could provide the basis for a justification defence. In that case the ECJ ruled that the existence of separate collective bargaining arrangements for the two groups of employees being considered

---

[934] *Barton v Investec Henderson Crosthwaite Securities Ltd.* [2003] IRLR 332.
[935] Case C-127/92 [1993] IRLR 591; on collective bargaining, see further para 6.100 below. In Case C-243/95 *Hill and Stapleton v Revenue Comrs and Department of Finance* [1998] IRLR 466 the ECJ affirmed that an employer could not justify discrimination arising from a jobsharing scheme solely on the ground that avoidance of such discrimination would involve increased costs.
[936] [1994] IRLR 342; revsd [1995] IRLR 439; H Collins, 1994.
[937] [1994] IRLR 342, 363.
[938] [1995] IRLR 439, 443.
[939] [2006] IRLR 124.
[940] Case C-127/92 *Enderby v Frenchay Health Authority* [1993] IRLR 591.

did not, without more, provide an adequate justification for unequal pay. The issue came to the fore again in a number of cases decided under the 1970 Act. Many of these arose from the practice of 'pay protection', that is to say, preserving the higher pay of a previously advantaged group at the point when payment structures which are tainted by sex or in some way discriminatory are reorganised. Such reorganisations became widespread in local government and other parts of the public sector as part of moves to harmonise the terms and conditions of manual and non-manual staff. The leading decision is the 2008 judgment of the Court of Appeal in the *Redcar* and *Middlesborough* cases.[941] This complex litigation arose from the phasing out of local government collective agreements (the 'White Book', for manual workers, and the 'Purple Book', for non-manual workers) which contained discriminatory elements, and their replacement by the single status 'Green Book'. The principal issues were: could a pay protection scheme for staff whose pay was reduced upon the elimination of discriminatory pay structures provide the basis for a material factor defence or, alternatively, objective justification for indirect discrimination; could the existence of separate collective agreements for some of the relevant jobs constitute a material factor; and could the complainants rely on the Green Book job evaluation study to found a claim for equal pay for work rated as equivalent in periods prior to its implementation? The Court of Appeal found for the claimants on the first two points and for the employer on the third one.[942] The essence of the judgment on the pay protection point is that the schemes in question could not provide a genuine material factor defence because they were themselves tainted by sex. The employees covered by the pay protection scheme were predominantly male workers who had benefited from unlawful discrimination against female colleagues in the past. This left open the question of whether the employer could justify its practices under the indirect discrimination test. The answer, according to the Court, depended on the employer's state of knowledge. Where the employer was aware of the sex-tainted nature of the practices it was now abandoning, and did not consider whether it should exclude the discrimination after the changeover was made, it could not rely on the justification defence (*Redcar*). In the *Middlesborough* case, the Court of Appeal held for the claimants on other grounds: the EAT had been wrong to interfere with the employment tribunal's decision for the claimants on justification (suggesting that justification was essentially an issue for the tribunal as an 'industrial jury'), and it had also been wrong to suggest that instituting a pay protection scheme with the motive of mitigating the effects of a pay reduction would necessarily be justified, without more. More generally, the Court held that the existence of separate collective agreements could be a material factor and therefore a complete answer to an equal pay claim, but not where the collective agreements were tainted by discrimination. Finally, it ruled that the Green Book job evaluation scheme could did not have retroactive effect for the purposes of a work rated as equivalent claim.

---

[941]   *Redcar & Cleveland Borough Council v Bainbridge (No 1), Surtees v Middlesborough Borough Council and Equality and Human Rights Commission (Intervener), Redcar & Cleveland Borough Council v Bainbridge and Equality and Human Rights Commission (No 2)* [2008] IRLR 776. See also *Newcastle-upon-Tyne City Council v Allan, Degnan v Redcar and Cleveland Borough Council* [2005] IRLR 504; *Degnan v Redcar and Cleveland Borough Council* [2005] IRLR 615; *South Tyneside Metropolitan Borough Council v Anderson* [2007] IRLR 715; *Cumbria County Council v Dow (No 1)* [2008] IRLR 91; *Coventry City Council v Nicholls* [2009] IRLR 345; *Bury Metropolitan Borough Council v Hamilton* [2011] IRLR 358.
[942]   On this last point, see also *Hovell v Ashford and St. Peter's Hospital NHS Trust* [2009] IRLR 734; para 6.90 above.

Allen v GMB,[943] although not an equal pay claim but a claim brought against a trade union for sex discrimination,[944] raises similar issues concerning the scope of the justification defence in the context of collective bargaining over the introduction of single status arrangements. It was found that the union had a policy of prioritizing pay protection for mainly male members and achieving equality for the future, over past equal pay claims of mainly female members. The employment tribunal found that the policy was indirectly discriminatory, and that while the goals sought were legitimate in the light of the limited resources at the union's disposal and the need for it to balance the competing claims of different groups of members, the actions it took were not proportionate as (among other things) excess pressure was placed on female members to settle claims. The EAT held that while the union's actions might have been questionable in certain respects and could, possibly, have given rise to a claim for breach of an implied duty of fair representation, or action in misrepresentation, they could nevertheless be regarded as a proportionate means of attaining a legitimate end. The Court of Appeal restored the tribunal's finding on justification.

(v) The proportionality test

6.101   The width of the justifications which may in principle be put forward in defence of pay inequality is balanced by the precision required of respondents by the proportionality test. Under European Union law, this requires both that the aim being pursued by the employer is legitimate in itself and that the means chosen are necessary to achieve it, while also interfering with the principle of equal treatment as little as possible.[945] One aspect of the ECJ's decision in *Enderby*[946] is that although a discriminatory practice may *to some extent* justify a differential in pay, it may not be capable of explaining all of it: where 'the national court has been able to determine precisely what proportion of the increase in pay is attributable to market forces, it must necessarily accept that the pay differential is objectively justified to the extent of that proportion'.[947] Thus the defence of material factor under section 69 of the 2010 Act is arguably not made out where *all* of the variation in pay cannot be justified by the factor in question.[948]

Effect of the sex equality clause

6.102   The effect of the sex equality clause on the contract of the complainant (A) by reference to that of the comparator (B) is that 'if a term of A's is less favourable to A than a corresponding term of

---

[943] [2008] IRLR 690.

[944] Under SDA 1975, s 12.

[945] See paras 6.30–6.32 above. The pre-2010 Act case law suggests that bonus schemes may, in principle, be an appropriate means of achieving the legitimate goal of enhancing productivity, but that an employer has to do more than simply assert that they reach this objective: see *Hartlepool Borough Council v Dolphin* [2009] IRLR 168; *Coventry City Council v Nicholls* [2009] IRLR 345; *Gibson v Sheffield CC* [2010] IRLR 311; *Bury Metropolitan Borough Council v Hamilton* [2011] IRLR 358.

[946] Case C-127/92 [1993] IRLR 591; Fredman, 1994a.

[947] Case C-127/92 [1993] IRLR 591, para 27.

[948] See Kilpatrick, 1994, on the pre-2010 Act case law, discussing the divergent approaches of the domestic courts on this point in *National Coal Board v Sherwin* [1978] IRLR 122 and *Calder v Rowntree Mackintosh Confectionery Ltd* [1993] IRLR 212.

B's is to B, A's term is modified so as not to be less favourable', while 'if A does not have a term which corresponds to a term of B's that benefits B, A's terms are modified so as to include such a term'.[949] It was established in pre-2010 Act case law that the process of implementing the sex equality clause involves identifying the precise source of the inequality of treatment, and remedying it accordingly. Following the decisions of the House of Lords in *Hayward v Cammell Laird Shipbuilders Ltd*[950] and of the ECJ in *Barber v Guardian Royal Exchange Assurance Group*[951] it was established that the correct approach is to take each significant term of the contract separately; the employer is not entitled to argue that inequality with regard to one term is outweighed by an advantage elsewhere in the terms and conditions of the complainant and his or her comparator. It may not be argued, for example, that differences in the basic rate of pay should be offset by differences in working hours or in fringe benefits such as free meals;[952] this, according to the ECJ, is because 'if the national courts were under an obligation to make an assessment and a comparison of all the various types of consideration granted, according to the circumstances to men and women, judicial review would be difficult and the effectiveness of Article [157] diminished as a result'.[953] The employer is not, in any case, prevented from raising any relevant differences between the two cases in the separate context of the material factor defence.[954]

It may nevertheless be the case that at the level of an individual 'element' of the pay package, no inequality is found to exist. This may be a far from straightforward issue, as the judgment of the ECJ in *Stadt Lengerich v Helmig*[955] illustrates. The Court ruled that the employer's failure to pay overtime premia to part-time employees when they exceeded their normal *part-time* working week, on the grounds that premia were only payable to employees working in excess of the normal *full-time* week, did not give rise to unequal treatment:

> There is unequal treatment wherever the overall pay of full-time employees is higher than that of part-time employees for the same number of hours worked on the basis of an employment relationship. In the circumstances considered in these proceedings, part-time employees do receive the same overall pay as full-time employees for the same number of hours worked. A part-time employee whose contractual working hours are 18 receives, if he works 19 hours, the same overall pay as a full-time employee who works 19 hours.[956]

It is arguable, however, that the treatment received here was differential, in that part-time employees would have had to work greatly in excess of *their* normal working hours in order to qualify for the premium; while such a difference could, perhaps, have been justified, the burden of

---

[949] EqA 2010, s 66(2).

[950] [1988] ICR 464.

[951] Case C-262/88 [1990] IRLR 240; but cf the race discrimination case of *Wakeman v Quick Corporation* [1999] IRLR 425, adopting a more impressionistic approach, and *Redcar and Cleveland Borough Council v Degnan* [2005] IRLR 179, in which the EAT in effect amalgamated, for this purpose, a number of different bonus schemes into a single significant contract term. This approach was upheld by the CA: *Degnan v Redcar and Cleveland BC* [2005] IRLR 615 (CA) but in *Brownbill v St. Helens and Knowsley Hospital NHS Trust* [2011] IRLR 128, [2011] IRLR 815 the EAT and CA adopted a more fine-grained approach to the identification of separate terms on pay and bonuses, distinguishing *Degnan*.

[952] As in *Hayward* [1988] ICR 464.

[953] Case C-262–88 *Barber*, at para 34.

[954] See above, para 6.96.

[955] Case C-399/92 [1995] IRLR 216.

[956] [1995] IRLR 216, 223.

doing so should have rested on the employer. This was the view subsequently taken in by the ECJ in *Elsner-Lakeberg v Land Nordrhein Westfalen*.[957]

Limitation periods and claims for arrears

6.103   A claim for equal pay must be brought within six months of the end of the complainant's employment, which is flexibly defined for this purpose, and, if the claim is successful, an award, in addition to its prospective effect, may allow for arrears of pay for a period of up to six years before the relevant legal proceedings were instituted.[958] These rules, which are now to be found, respectively, in sections 129 and 132 of the 2010 Act, were inserted into the predecessor statute, the EqPA 1970, with effect from July 2003, as a result of amendments made to bring the law into line with a number of rulings of the ECJ and UK courts applying Article 141 TEC (as it then was).[959] The trigger for change was the ECJ's decision in *Barber v Guardian Royal Exchange Assurance Group*[960] to the effect that benefits paid under occupational pension schemes fell under the equal pay principle, coupled with its ruling that Article 141 prohibited indirect discrimination in the terms of access to occupational pension schemes.[961] This seemed to open the way for compensation to be claimed by part-time workers excluded from schemes all the way back to 1976, the point at which the ECJ decided the issue of the direct effect of Article 141 in *Defrenne v Sabena*.[962] Over 60,000 such claims were made before employment tribunals in the mid-1990s. However, in the case of domestic legislation applying the principle of equal treatment to occupational pension schemes which was introduced in 1995 in the aftermath of *Barber*, there was in force at this point a two-year limit on any claim to backdated membership.[963] Employers also resisted claims brought directly under Article 141 TEC on the grounds that claims under the 1970 Act were then subject to a two-year limit on arrears, while proceedings to be instituted within six months of the end of employment with no room for flexibility on the application of this time limit.

In *Magorrian and Cunningham v Eastern Health and Social Services Board*[964] a claim made under Northern Ireland legislation, the ECJ ruled on a preliminary reference that the two-year limit on arrears was contrary to Article 141 TEC, on the grounds that the limitation struck 'at the very essence of the rights conferred by the Community legal order' and was 'such as to render

---

[957]   Case C-285/02 [2005] IRLR 209.

[958]   Note also that the employment tribunal may make a declaration of right in relation to an equal pay claim: EqA 2010, s 132(2)(a).

[959]   EqPA 1970 as originally enacted imposed a two-year limitation period, but in Case C-326/96 *Levez v TH Jennings (Harlow Pools) Ltd* [1999] IRLR 36 the ECJ held that this was contrary to Art 141 TEC (now Art 157 TFEU) and to the Equal Treatment Directive; when the case returned to the EAT, the six-year limitation period was applied (*Levez v TH Jennings (Harlow Pools) Ltd (No 2)* [1999] IRLR 764). See also *National Power plc v Young* [2001] IRLR 32.

[960]   Case C-262/88 [1990] IRLR 240.

[961]   Case C-262/88 [1990] IRLR 240. See Tether, 1995.

[962]   Case 43/75 [1976] ECR 445.

[963]   At this point PA 1995, ss 62–65 deemed an occupational pension scheme to contain an 'equal treatment rule' which operated in a manner akin to the equality clause under EqPA 1970, and SI 1995/3183 provided for remedies in relation to sex discrimination in occupational schemes which included the power of a court or tribunal to declare a right of admission to a scheme and to require the employer to provide additional resources to the scheme in connection with the right of access only in respect of a period of two years preceding the institution of the claim. On equality in occupational pension schemes, see below, para 6.109.

[964]   Case C-246/96 [1998] IRLR 86.

any action by individuals relying on Community law impossible in practice'.[965] In *Preston v Wolverhampton Healthcare NHS Trust*[966] the House of Lords ruled that *Magorrian* had not settled a number of complex issues which arose in the context of the English litigation, and referred several questions to the ECJ for further consideration; the ECJ, however, basically affirmed its earlier rulings in holding that the two-year limitation period in under the EqPA 1970 was contrary to Article 141 TEC.

The ECJ also held in the *Preston* case that the six-month time limit for bringing claims under the 1970 Act was potentially compatible with Article 141 TEC in so far as it satisfied the principle of equivalence between remedies. However, when the case returned to the House of Lords in *Preston (No 2)*[967] it was held that, where an employee was employed on a series of short-term contracts, it was contrary to the principle of the effectiveness of remedies to require the complainant to lodge a claim within six months of the end of *each* contract, so long as there was evidence of a 'stable employment relationship' spanning different contracts. This, along with related rulings of the ECJ and the House of Lords on time limits, led to further changes to the 1970 Act, which have been carried over in substantially the same form into the 2010 Act.

However, even these time limits may now be subject to the possibility of a complainant bringing a claim for equal pay arrears in the form of a claim for breach of contract, for which the six year limitation period applies. In *Abdulla v Birmingham City Council*[968] a breach of contract claim was brought on the basis that the effect of the equality clause was to align the complainant's contract terms with those of the comparator as a matter of contract law. The employer sought to have the claim struck out under section 2(3) of the 1970 Act, now section 128 of the 2010 Act, which applies where a court considers that a claim can 'more conveniently be determined by an employment tribunal'. The Court of Appeal, overruling an earlier High Court decision on this point,[969] held that it was not appropriate to strike out a contract claim simply because the statutory claim was out of time. The Court of Appeal considered that striking out would not normally be appropriate in a case where the exercise of the tribunal's specialist jurisdiction, for example to resolve whether work was of equal value of if a material factor defence applied, was not required.

(i) Time limits

6.104 Proceedings under the 2010 Act must be instituted before the end of the 'qualifying period', which is defined in section 129. In a so-called 'standard case', the qualifying period is

---

[965] [1998] IRLR 86, 100; here the Court in effect distinguished its earlier judgments on time limits in Case C-410/92 *Johnson v Chief Adjudication Officer (No 2)* [1995] IRLR 157 and Case C-338/91 *Steenhorst-Neerings v Bestuur van de Bedrijfsvereniging voor Detailhandel, Ambachten en Huisvroouwen* [1994] IRLR 244.

[966] [1998] IRLR 197. In addition to the basic issue of the time limits in domestic law which *Magorrian* seemed to have settled (since the limits in *Preston* and *Magorrian* were, in essence, identical), the House of Lords also referred a number of questions concerning the relevance of the timing of the UK's accession to the EC (in 1972, after the passage of EqPA 1970) and the treatment of fixed-term contract employees.

[967] *Preston v Wolverhampton Healthcare NHS Trust (No 2)* [2001] IRLR 237. See *Powerhouse Retail Ltd v Burroughs* [2006] IRLR 381 and *Gutridge v Sodexo* [2009] IRLR 721 for applications of the *Preston* case in the context of transfers of undertakings.

[968] [2012] IRLR 116.

[969] *Ashby v Birmingham City Council* [2011] IRLR 473.

the period of six months beginning with the last day of the employment (or, in the case of an office, appointment).[970] A 'standard case' is any case which is not one of four other cases set out in section 129.[971] The first of these is a 'stable work case'. This refers to the situation which was the focus of the House of Lords decision in *Preston (No 2)*, and which is defined here as a case where the 'proceedings relate to a period during which there was a stable working relationship between the worker' and the employer, including 'any time after the terms of work had expired'.[972] The qualifying period is six months beginning with the day on which the stable employment relationship ended.[973] This has the effect of enabling a complainant to ignore gaps between contracts, and to choose the end of the last contract as the point from which time begins to run. It may also be possible to invoke it after that point if some elements of the employment relationship remain. This is therefore a provision which could potentially be applied to cover situations of extra-contractual family or educational leave, although whether this turns out to be the case remains to be seen.[974]

A 'concealment' case is a situation in which the employer deliberately concealed from the claimant a 'qualifying fact' which was relevant to the complaint and without knowledge of which the complainant could not reasonably have been expected to institute proceedings.[975] In this case the qualifying period is the period of six months beginning with the day on which the worker discovered or could with reasonable diligence have discovered the qualifying fact.[976] An 'incapacity case' occurs where the claimant had an incapacity at any time during the six months after the 'relevant day', which means the end of the employment or stable employment relationship, as the case may be;[977] here time begins to run six months from the date on which the complainant ceased to have the incapacity.[978] If the case is one of both concealment and incapacity, the qualifying period begins on whichever of the two relevant dates is later.[979]

---

[970] In the case of the armed forces, the qualifying period is nine months, and this period applies, *mutatis mutandis*, to each of the other time limit cases set out in ss 129 and 130 (see s 129(4)).

[971] This is the effect of s 130(2). In *Potter v North Cumbria Acute Hospitals NHS Trust (No 2)* [2009] IRLR 900 the EAT rejected an argument by the employer that the introduction of new terms and conditions of employment via the NHS 'Agenda for Change' programme had brought about a termination of existing contracts of employment and their replacement by new ones, ruling that there had been a variation of existing contracts, with the result that the claims in this case were not out of time.

[972] EqA 2010, s 130(3).

[973] EqA 2010, s 129(3).

[974] The general approach to be taken in applying these provisions was set out by the EAT in *Secretary of State for Health v Rance* [2007] IRLR 665. See also *Cumbria County Council v Dow (No 2)* [2008] IRLR 109, EAT, and the appeal in that case sub nom *Slack v Cumbria County Council and EHRC* [2009] IRLR 463, CA, and *North Cumbria University Hospitals NHS Trust v Fox* [2010] IRLR 804, applying the principle of a 'stable employment relationship' to an uninterrupted succession of contracts.

[975] EqA 2010, s 130(4).

[976] EqA 2010, s 129(3).

[977] EqA 2010, s 130(7), (10). In addition, an 'incapacity case' includes one in which the complainant was under an incapacity at any time during the period of six months beginning with the day on which she either discovered or could with reasonable diligence have discovered the 'qualifying fact' deliberately concealed from her by the employer, if later: s 130(7)(b).

[978] EqA 2010, s 129(3).

[979] EqA 2010, s 129(3).

(ii) Arrears

6.105   Section 132 of the 2010 Act provides that the normal period for which arrears may be awarded, in a 'standard case', is set by reference to an 'arrears day' which is the day falling six years before the day on which proceedings were instituted.[980] The arrears day is altered in a 'concealment' or 'incapacity' case. For this purpose, a 'concealment' case is defined as one in which the employer deliberately concealed a 'qualifying fact'[981] and the complainant commenced the proceedings before the end of the period of six years beginning with the day on which she either discovered or could have with reasonable diligence have discovered that fact[982] and an 'incapacity case' is one in which she had an incapacity when the breach first occurred and commenced the proceedings before the end of the period of six years beginning with the day on which she ceased to have the incapacity.[983] Under these circumstances, the arrears date is, simply, the date on which the breach first occurred.[984]

Amendment of collective agreements

6.106   Prior to 1986 it was possible to obtain a remedy which would lead to the amendment of an entire payment structure, such as a collective agreement or wages order, to comply with the principle of equal treatment in matters of pay; this took the form of unilateral arbitration before the Central Arbitration Committee.[985] However, the effectiveness of this route for the ending of discrimination based on segregation was restricted by the Court of Appeal's decision in *R v Central Arbitration Committee, ex p Hy-Mac Ltd*,[986] limiting the jurisdiction of the Committee under the Act to situations of *direct discrimination*. This meant that only those provisions of a collective agreement which set differential rates for men and women as such could be challenged using this route.

   Rather than extending the jurisdiction of the Central Arbitration Committee to cover indirect discrimination, the Sex Discrimination Act 1986 abolished it completely and replaced it with a provision which rendered 'void' any term of a collective agreement which had the effect of providing for the inclusion, within a contract, of a term which would render necessary the application of the equality clause. The county court had the power to make an order 'removing or modifying any term made unenforceable' by this provision.[987] The successor to this provision is the power of an employment tribunal to rule that a term in a collective agreement is void if it 'constitutes, promotes or provides for treatment of a description prohibited by this Act'.[988]

   This provision is considerably less helpful than the remedy up to the late 1970s of unilateral arbitration before the Central Arbitration Committee. The latter enabled the Committee to

---

[980] EqA 2010, s 132(4).
[981] On which, see para 6.104 above.
[982] EqA 2010, s 135(3).
[983] EqA 2010, s 135(5).
[984] EqA 2010, s 132(4).
[985] EqPA 1970, s 3, as amended by the EPA 1975.
[986] [1979] IRLR 461.
[987] SDA 1975, s 77(5).
[988] EqA 2010, s 145(1), to be read with s 146. See above para 6.68.

make a positive amendment to the terms of collective agreements which could, if necessary, be inserted into the individual contracts of the employees and others whose contracts were governed by it, thereby ensuring the levelling-up of the disadvantaged group. The current provision merely enables a discriminatory term to be removed from the collective agreement, without specifying a means by which this might lead to the improvement of individual terms and conditions of employment.[989]

The amendment originally made by the 1986 Act was the product of a decision of the ECJ in infringement proceedings brought against the United Kingdom, to the effect that the EqPA 1970 did not comply with Article 4(b) of the Equal Treatment Directive.[990] Since Article 4(b) provides that 'any provisions contrary to the principle of equal treatment which are included in collective agreements ... shall be, or may be declared, null and void *or may be amended*' (emphasis added),[991] it is not at all obvious that the abolition of the Central Arbitration Committee's jurisdiction was compatible with the Directive. Nor would British domestic law appear to have an effective means, in this context, of complying with Article 157 TFEU, which according to the ECJ has the effect that 'where there is indirect discrimination in a provision of a collective agreement, the members of the group which is disadvantaged because of that discrimination must be treated in the same way and have the same system applied to them as the other workers, in proportion to their hours of work'.[992]

Pay disclosures

6.107   EqA 2010 introduces a new provision under which a term in a contract is unenforceable to the extent that it purports to prevent or restrict a person from making a 'relevant pay disclosure' about the terms of their work, or from seeking such a disclosure from a colleague or former colleague.[993] Seeking a relevant pay disclosure, making or seeking to make one, or receiving information disclosed in one, are all 'protected acts' for the purpose of a victimisation claim.[994] A 'relevant pay disclosure' is one about the terms of work which is 'made for the purpose of enabling the person who makes it, or the person to whom it is made, to find out whether or to what extent there is, in relation to the work in question, a connection between pay and having (or not having) a particular protected characteristic'.[995] Thus this provision only operates in so far as the disclosure relates to unlawful pay discrimination under the Act; it does not protect more general disclosures of pay.

---

[989]   The issue of incorporation is particularly important since the collective agreement is most unlikely to be binding between the parties to it, by virtue of TULRCA 1992, s 179: see further para 9.26 below.

[990]   Case 165/82 *EC Commission v United Kingdom* [1984] IRLR 29.

[991]   Directive 76/207/EC, Art 4(b). 75/117/EC, Art 4 was in substantially the same terms. See now Directive 2006/54/EC, Art 23(b).

[992]   Case 33/89 *Kowalska v Freie und Hansestadt Hamburg* [1990] IRLR 447, at para 20.

[993]   EqA 2010, s 77(1), (2).

[994]   EqA 2010, s 77(4).

[995]   EqA 2010, s 77(3).

Gender pay gap information

6.108   Section 78 of the 2010 Act creates a power to make regulations requiring larger employers (those employing 250 workers or more) to publish information for the purpose of showing whether there is a gender 'pay gap', that is, on 'differences in the pay of male and female employees'.[996] The sanction envisaged for breach of this provision is a fine not exceeding level 5 on the standard scale.[997] The costs and benefits of a pay disclosure rule of this kind have been extensively debated for over a decade, with a number of official inquiries and reports seeing it as a potentially valuable device for encouraging employers to address persistent pay inequalities, and public sector employers have been subject for some time to *de facto* obligations to publish pay gap data as a result of initiatives including the local authority National Joint Council pay agreement, the Agenda for Change programme in the NHS, and the Civil Service Reward Principles.[998] The Labour Government which introduced the Equality Act 2010 envisaged making the publication of pay gap data by employers employing 150 workers or more one of the specific duties under the public sector equality duty, but the regulations introduced by the Coalition stop short of imposing a specific reporting duty of this kind, simply requiring public authorities and other bodies exercising public functions to comply with a more broadly framed duty to report on progress in addressing inequalities.[999] Section 78 was to have extended pay gap reporting to the private sector. However, the Conservative-Liberal Democrat Coalition Government has announced that it will not be taking this provision forward.[1000]

Occupational pensions

6.109   When the ECJ decided, in *Barber v Guardian Royal Exchange Assurance Group*,[1001] that benefits under occupational pension schemes fell under Article 119 of the Treaty of Rome (now Article 157 TFEU),[1002] the effect was to override a number of derogations contained in the Directive on Equality in Occupational Social Security[1003] which would have permitted, among other things, the maintenance of unequal pensionable ages and the use of actuarial factors to set different benefit and contribution rates for male and female employees. For this reason, the Court limited the effect of *Barber* to claims already instituted[1004] and, in other cases, to 'acquisition of

---

[996] EqA 2010, s 78(1).

[997] EqA 2010, s 78(5). At the time of writing this is a maximum of £5,000.

[998] See Hepple, 2011: pp 107; Deakin, Chai and McLaughlin, 2012.

[999] See para 6.75 above.

[1000] See http://www.homeoffice.gov.uk/equalities/equality-act/commencement/ (last accessed 26 March 2012). The BIS consultation on modern workplaces, initiated in May 2011, invited discussion on a proposal to require employers to conduct a pay audit if they were found to have breached equal pay law: see BIS, *Consultation on Modern Workplaces* (May 2011), ch 6.

[1001] Case C-262/88 [1990] IRLR 240.

[1002] The following fall within Art 157 TFEU: survivors' pensions (both widows' and widowers'); and benefits under occupational pension schemes which are 'supplementary' or additional to state retirement pensions (as well as benefits under those which are 'contracted-out', that is, operate in partial substitution for the state pension, as in *Barber* itself). See Case C-109/91 *Ten Oever v Stichting Bedrijfspensioenfonds voor het Glazenwassers-en Schoonmaakbedrijf* [1993] IRLR 601; Case C-110/91 *Moroni v Firma Collo GmbH* [1994] IRLR 130; Case C-152/91 *Neath v Hugh Steeper Ltd* [1994] IRLR 91.

[1003] Directive 86/378.

[1004] For an application of this aspect of the *Barber* ruling, see *Howard v Ministry of Defence* [1995] IRLR 570.

entitlement to a pension as from the date of this judgment' (17 May 1990). This was because the Member States, in common with many employers, had assumed, by virtue of the Directive on Occupational Social Security, that Article 157 TFEU (as it now is) was irrelevant to the question of pensions equality; under these circumstances 'overriding considerations of legal certainty preclude legal situations which have exhausted all their effects in the past from being called in question where that might upset retroactively the financial balance' of schemes constructed on this assumption.[1005] The implementation of *Barber* was, in effect, suspended while a number of further references were made to the Court to establish precisely what was meant by its ruling on non-retroactivity.

In *Ten Oever v Stichting Bedrijfspensioenfonds voor het Glazenwassers-en Schoonmaakbedrijf*[1006] the Court decided that the predecessor of Article 157 TFEU only applied to occupational pension benefits which were payable in respect of periods of service after the date of the *Barber* judgment, thereby fortuitously finding common cause with Protocol No 2 to the Maastricht Treaty which provided that '[f]or the purposes of [Article 157 TFEU] benefits under occupational social security schemes shall not be considered as remuneration if and so far as they as they are attributable to periods of employment prior to 17 May 1990'. According to Advocate General Van Gerven, in the case of a defined-benefit pension scheme there is 'a distinction between the coming into being of pension rights, namely as a result of the *accrual* of the pension on the basis of completed periods of service, and those rights becoming exercisable, namely when the pension *falls to be paid for the first time*'.[1007] This meant that a male employee in a scheme setting a lower pensionable age for women (say, 60) could become entitled to a part of his pension at that age, the part-pension being referable to his service after 17 May 1990.[1008]

The effects of *Barber* were also limited by two further preliminary rulings of the ECJ. First, in *Neath v Hugh Steeper Ltd*[1009] the Court held that the predecessor of Article 157 did not prohibit sex-based inequalities in employers' contributions in defined-benefit or final-salary schemes where these are justified by actuarial factors. Although employees' contributions were 'pay', at least where they were deducted from salary or wages,[1010] the Court concluded that Article 157 'does not necessarily have to do with the funding arrangements chosen to secure the periodic payment of the pension, which thus remain outside the scope of application of Article [157]'.[1011]

Second, the ECJ ruled in *Smith v Avdel Systems Ltd*[1012] that the predecessor of Article 157 'does not preclude measures which achieve equal treatment by reducing the advantages of the persons previously favoured'. The Court drew what was arguably an artificial distinction between

---

[1005] *Barber*, Case C-262/88, at para 44.

[1006] Case C-109/91 [1993] IRLR 601; Fitzpatrick, 1994.

[1007] Case C-109/91 *Ten Oever*, Opinion of Advocate General Van Gerven, at para 17.

[1008] On the Barber Protocol, see *Quirk v Burton Hospitals NHS Trust* [2001] IRLR 198, [2002] IRLR 353; Joined Cases C-4/02 and C-5/02 *Schönheit v Staft Frankfurt am Main, Becker v Land Hessen* [2004] IRLR 983.

[1009] Case C-152/91 [1994] IRLR 91.

[1010] Case 69/80 *Worringham v Lloyds Bank Ltd* [1981] ECR 767.

[1011] Case C-152/91 *Neath*, at para 30. However, the use of sex-based criteria to set contribution rates is almost certainly unlawful as a result of the later judgment of the Court of Justice in Case C-236/09 *Association Belge des Consommateurs Tests-Achats v Conseil des Ministres* [2011] 2 CMLR 38, ruling that a derogation allowing sex-based actuarial factors to be used in private insurance contracts (contained in Directive 2004/113/EC, Art 5) was invalid, in part because of the application of Arts 21 and 23 CFREU.

[1012] Case C-408/92 [1994] IRLR 602, at para 21; see also Case C-28/93 *Van den Akker v Stichting Shell Pensioenfonds* [1994] IRLR 616, at para 19; Case C-200/91 *Coloroll Pension Trustees Ltd v Russell* [1994] IRLR 586, at para 33; Deakin, 1995a; Tether, 1995.

the immediate period following a court's ruling that a particular practice contravenes the Article, during which time there had to be levelling-up, and the period after which the employer (or the Member State, as the case may be) took formal steps to purge the discriminatory practice and establish equality. With regard to the first of these two periods, the Court reasoned that levelling-up was obligatory since at this time, the 'only valid point of reference' was the level of advantage enjoyed 'by the persons in the favoured class'.[1013] However, once the discrimination was purged, the Court held, there was nothing in Article 157 (as it now is) to prevent levelling-down from then on. An employer might therefore implement the requirement of equality of pensionable ages in occupational schemes by raising the relevant age for women employees from 60 to 65, rather than by lowering the age for men from 65 to 60.

The outcome was complicated by *Barber*'s non-retroactive effect as interpreted in *Ten Oever*. The result in a case such as *Avdel Systems* was, first, that no rights accruing prior to 17 May 1990 were affected by *Barber*, so that women retained a right to a pension at 60 in respect of service up to that point; second, that men and women alike could claim a pension at the age of 60 in respect of service from 17 May 1990 to the point at which the common pensionable age of 65 was introduced, which in *Advel Systems* itself was 1 July 1991; but, finally, that service from that date would only earn a pension at 65 for men and women alike.

Domestic British legislation prevents levelling-down of the kind approved by the Court in *Avdel Systems*. Under the EqPA 1970, the equality clause required levelling-up: the contract of the complainant was to be 'treated as so modified as not to be less favourable' than that of the comparator, and this approach is maintained under the 2010 Act.[1014] Specific provisions now govern the operation in the context of occupational pension schemes of the 'sex equality rule' which operates in the same way, *mutatis mutandis*, as the sex equality clause in contracts of employment and other relevant contracts for work.[1015]

PROTECTION OF PREGNANCY, MATERNITY AND FAMILY TIME

6.110   Legislation protecting employees from dismissal on the grounds of pregnancy and/or maternity and providing a right to maternity leave was first introduced in the EPA 1975, together with a statutory right to receive maternity pay from the employer. In each case there were extensive qualifying requirements and restrictions on the scope of substantive rights. The impetus for the removal of most of these restrictions came initially from Directive 92/85 on measures to encourage improvements in the safety and health of pregnant workers and workers who have recently given birth (the 'Pregnant Workers Directive'). This Directive was derived not from the principle of equal treatment as expressed in Article 157 TFEU (as it now is) or in the Directives on Equal Pay and Equal Treatment, but instead from Article 118a of the EC Treaty (now part of Article 153 TFEU) which was concerned with the promotion of improvements in the working environment. The Employment Relations Act 1999 marked another important turning point. In addition to a further streamlining of maternity protection, this legislation introduced rights to parental leave

---

[1013] Case C-408/92 *Avdel Systems*, at paras 16–17.
[1014] EqA 2010, s 66(1)(a).
[1015] EqA 2010, ss 67-68, replacing PA 1995, ss 62–66.

and to take time off work to look after dependants as part of the 'family friendly' policies being pursued by the Labour Government elected in 1997. The Employment Act 2002 took this process several steps further by enacting rights to statutory paternity pay and leave and adoption pay and leave, as well as a right to request flexible working. These rights were extended further by the Work and Families Act 2006.[1016] We begin our analysis by examining the relationship between pregnancy and the principle of equal treatment before turning to the substance of the various statutory provisions which now operate in this area.

Pregnancy and the principle of equality

6.111   As we have seen in earlier sections of this chapter, the protection of pregnancy and maternity has not consistently been seen as assimilable to the principle of equal treatment. The EqPA 1970, the SDA 1975 and the Equal Treatment Directive all contained derogations designed to ensure that protective provisions in respect of maternity and pregnancy did not constitute sex discrimination against men.[1017] A similar debate took place in US discrimination law: courts initially held that employers' practices excluding pregnancy from disability protection schemes did not contravene Title VII of the Civil Rights Act 1964,[1018] before the federal Congress passed the Pregnancy Discrimination Act in 1978. This amended Title VII to provide that discrimination on the grounds of sex included discrimination on the grounds of pregnancy, and specifically stated that 'women affected by pregnancy, childbirth, or related medical conditions shall be treated the same for all employment-related purposes, including receipt of benefits under fringe benefit programs, as other persons not so affected but similar in their ability or inability to work.'[1019] In addition, the Supreme Court held that state-level laws providing for minimum maternity leave do not thereby contravene the principle of equal treatment in Title VII.[1020]

Thus the principle of non-discrimination does not, on the whole, *prohibit* legislation protecting pregnancy and maternity. Turning the question around, does the equal treatment principle *require* a certain degree of protection for pregnant workers? The decisions of the ECJ in *Dekker v VJV-Centrum*[1021] and *Webb v EMO Air Cargo Ltd*[1022] established that, in principle, the adverse treatment of an employee on pregnancy-related grounds amounted to *direct* sex discrimination contrary to the Equal Treatment Directive, and could not be justified.[1023] There was some doubt as to how far the principle first enunciated in *Dekker* extended: as a consequence

---

[1016] See G James, 2006.

[1017] EqPA 1970, s 6(1)(b); SDA 1975, s 2(2); Directive 76/207, Art 2(7) (as later amended by Directive 2002/73).

[1018] *Geduldig v Aiello* 417 US 484 (1974); *General Electric Co v Gilbert* 429 US 125 (1976).

[1019] Civil Rights Act 1964, Title VII, s 701(k); 42 USC s 2000e-2(k).

[1020] *California Savings & Loan Association v Guerra* 479 US 272 (1987); see Deakin, 1990a: p 11.

[1021] Case C-177/88 [1991] IRLR 27; see also Case C-207/98 *Mahlburg v Land Mecklenburg-Vorpommern* [2000] IRLR 277.

[1022] Case C-32/93 [1994] IRLR 482.

[1023] See also Case C-506/06 *Mayr v Bäckerei und Konditorei Gerhard Flöckner OHG* [2008] IRLR 387 in which the ECJ held that dismissal of a female worker on the grounds that she was undergoing in vitro fertilisation was direct sex discrimination contrary to Art 2(1) of Directive 76/207 because that treatment 'directly affects only women' (at para 50). However, dismissal before the point where the fertilised ova were transferred to the uterus was not dismissal during pregnancy, and so was not contrary to Art 10 of Directive 92/85.

of the Court's ruling in *Hertz*,[1024] it appeared not to cover a case of dismissal on the grounds of a pregnancy-related illness after the period of maternity leave came to an end, although it is hard to see why this should be so since the employee in such a case could argue that the substantial cause of her dismissal was her pregnancy. In *Brown v Rentokil Ltd*[1025] the ECJ affirmed that dismissal on the grounds of a pregnancy-related illness during pregnancy, as well as during maternity leave, constituted direct sex discrimination.[1026]

The ECJ's judgment in *Brown* was consistent with its earlier decision in *Habermann-Beltermann*[1027] where the Court held that it was a breach of the Directive for an employer to dismiss a pregnant worker who was employed as a night attendant in a residential home, solely on the grounds of a statutory prohibition upon employees working at night while pregnant. The Court concluded that 'the termination of a contract without a fixed term on account of the woman's pregnancy, whether by annulment or avoidance, cannot be justified on the ground that a statutory prohibition, imposed because of pregnancy, temporarily prevents the employee from performing night-time work'.[1028] An important aspect of this decision was the use made of the pregnancy derogation in Article 2(3) of the Directive (as it then was), which provided that the Directive 'shall be without prejudice to provisions concerning the protection of women, particularly as regards pregnancy and maternity'. According to the Court, Article 2(3) 'recognises the legitimacy, in terms of the principle of equal treatment, of protecting, first, a woman's biological condition during and after pregnancy, and secondly, the special relationship between a woman and her child over the period which follows pregnancy and childbirth'. In other words, Article 2(3) was not a denial of the principle of equal treatment but marked an extension of it to take into account the *particular* position of women with regard to pregnancy and maternity and the potential discrimination which may result from that, in particular 'the disadvantages which women, by comparison with men, suffer with regard to the retention of employment'.[1029]

The position under the SDA 1975, as it then was, was determined by the House of Lords when it reconsidered *Webb* in the light of the ECJ's ruling in that case. In *Webb (No 2)*[1030] their Lordships ruled that in a case where a female employee was employed under a contract for an indeterminate period, her dismissal for a pregnancy-related reason was for a reason relating to her sex. However, the same reasoning would not necessarily apply to a case where the employment was for a limited term which would have expired by the time the employee was ready to return to work after her period of maternity leave.[1031] The basis for this view is obscure. Lord Keith, giving the principal judgment in *Webb*, seems to have regarded himself as bound to accept the ruling of the ECJ in that case, and conclude that, at least in the case of an open-ended contract of employment, dismissal for pregnancy amounted to *direct* sex discrimination. In *Jiménez-Melgar v Ayuntamiento*

[1024] Case C-179/88 *Hertz v Aldi Marked K/S* [1991] IRLR 31.

[1025] Case C-394/96 [1998] IRLR 445; *Abbey National plc v Formoso* [1999] IRLR 222. See Wynn, 1999.

[1026] In so deciding, the ECJ did not follow its earlier decision in Case C-400/95 *Handels-OG Kontorfunktionaerernesforbund, acting on behalf of Larsson v Dansk Handel & Service, acting on behalf of Føxted Supermarked A/S* [1997] IRLR 643.

[1027] Case C-421/92 *Habermann-Beltermann v Arbeiterwohlfahrt, Bezirksverband Ndb/pf eV* [1994] IRLR 364.

[1028] [1994] IRLR 364, 367.

[1029] [1994] IRLR 364, 367.

[1030] [1995] IRLR 645. This decision has since been applied in *British Telecommunications v Roberts* [1996] IRLR 601 and in *Iske v P & O European Ferries (Dover) Ltd* [1997] IRLR 401 (on which, see the Suspension from Work on Maternity Grounds (Merchant Shipping and Fishing Vessels) Order 1998, SI 1998/587).

[1031] In *Caruana v Manchester Airport plc* [1996] IRLR 378 the EAT held that any special rule for fixed-term contracts was limited to cases where the employee would not be available for any part of the term.

de los Barrios the ECJ took a similar view, holding that the non-renewal of a pregnant worker's fixed-term contract (which the Court treated as a refusal of employment) on the grounds of her pregnancy was directly discriminatory under the Equal Treatment Directive.[1032] An alternative solution would have been to hold that the adverse treatment of a worker on pregnancy-related grounds was a form of *indirect* sex discrimination which might therefore be justified by business necessity or some similar criterion.[1033]

Later decisions of the ECJ have focused on issues surrounding the provision of maternity pay and related benefits both before and during the period of maternity leave, and on the relationship between the equal treatment principle and the Pregnant Workers Directive. The Court has sought to draw a line between the adverse treatment of pregnant workers prior to and following maternity leave – which can in principle amount to sex discrimination – and the position during maternity leave itself. The basis for this distinction is the view of the Court that it is inappropriate to compare the position of a pregnant worker with that of a male employee who is absent from work on the grounds of sickness.[1034] The Court has taken the view that the Pregnant Workers Directive, rather than the Equal Treatment and Equal Pay Directives, should be the focus of rights to maternity leave and maternity pay. This is not to say that certain pregnancy-related rights *outside* the leave period cannot be read in a way which incorporates and builds on the non-discrimination principle.[1035] The Court's jurisprudence has been criticised for its assumption of 'a stereotyped idea of motherhood', according to which care of newly-born children is undertaken mainly by the mother rather than being shared by both parents.[1036]

Pregnancy as a protected characteristic

6.112   The ECJ's pregnancy jurisprudence, with its emphasis on pregnancy protection as a distinct variant of the wider concept of sex discrimination, came to be reflected in the terms of the revised Equal Treatment Directive, which currently provides that '[l]ess favourable treatment of a woman related to pregnancy or maternity leave… shall constitute discrimination' related to sex. In addition, the Directive provides that '[a] woman on maternity leave shall be entitled, after the end of her period of maternity leave, to return to her job or to an equivalent post on

---

[1032] Case C-438/99, [2001] IRLR 848. See also Case C-294/04 *Sarkatzis Herrero v Instituto Mardrileno de la Salud* [2006] IRLR 296.

[1033] See generally Wintemute, 1998; cf the discussion of Honeyball, 2000.

[1034] See, in particular, Case C-411/96 *Boyle v Equal Opportunities Commission* [1998] IRLR 717; Case C-66/96 *Handels-og Kontorfunktionærernes Forbund i Danmark (acting for Hój Pedersen) v Fællesforeningen For Danmarks Brugsforeninger* [1999] IRLR 55; Case C-218/98 *Abdoulaye v Régie Nationale des Usines Renault* [1999] IRLR 811; Case C-147/02 *Alabaster v Woolwich plc and Secretary of State for Social Security* [2004] IRLR 486. See the discussion of this line of case law in *Eversheds Legal Services v De Belin* [2011] IRLR 448, discussed below, para 6.113.

[1035] See, in addition to the cases cited above, Case C-320/01 *Busch v Klinikum Neustadt GmbH & Co Betriebs-KG* [2003] IRLR 625 (refusal to allow a worker to return to work before the end of her parental leave, on the grounds of her pregnancy, was contrary to the Equal Treatment Directive and the Pregnant Workers' Directive), and Case C-342/02 *Merino Gómez v Continental Industries del Caucho SA* [2004] IRLR 407 (a pregnant worker had the right to take her annual leave entitlement in addition to her maternity leave). The UK courts also took the view that the SDA 1975 should be read in the light of the Pregnant Workers Directive: see *Hardman v Mallon* [2002] IRLR 516, in which a failure to provide a health and safety risk assessment to a pregnant worker was held to be sex discrimination, although this will not always be the case: *O'Neill v Buckinghamshire CC* [2010] IRLR 284.

[1036] See generally Caraciollo di Torella, 1999.

terms and conditions which are no less favourable to her and to benefit from any improvement in working conditions to which she would be entitled during her absence.[1037] These provisions are now implemented in UK law in the form of the prohibition of discrimination on the grounds of the protected characteristic of pregnancy and maternity, under section 18 of the 2010 Act.[1038] A person (A) discriminates against a woman if 'in the protected period in relation to a pregnancy of hers' A treats her unfavourably 'because of the pregnancy' or 'because of illness suffered by her as a result of it.[1039] Pregnancy discrimination also occurs where a person treats a woman unfavourably because she is on compulsory maternity leave, or is exercising or seeking to exercise, or has exercised or sought to exercise, rights to ordinary or additional maternity leave.[1040] The protected period is the period which begins when the pregnancy begins and ends, if she is entitled to ordinary and additional maternity leave, at the end of the period of additional maternity leave, or when she returns to work if that is earlier. If she is not entitled to ordinary and additional maternity leave, it is the end of the period of two weeks from the end of the pregnancy.[1041]

The protection provided by section 18 only applies in favour of workers with the protected characteristic of pregnancy or maternity, which is not defined in the Act, and is based on the notion of 'unfavourable treatment' which does not depend on comparing the position of the complainant with that of a hypothetical or real comparator. Only direct discrimination is covered by this provision. Indirect discrimination on pregnancy-related grounds, or discrimination on pregnancy-related grounds outside the protected period, may give rise to claim of sex discrimination under the Act.[1042]

Pregnancy protection and sex discrimination

6.113   In addition, the 2010 Act continues in force the derogation from the principle of equality between women and men for measures taken to protect women in relation to pregnancy and maternity. Thus where the complainant 'is a man, no account is to be taken of special treatment afforded to a women in connection with pregnancy or childbirth.[1043] In *Eversheds Legal Services v De Belin*[1044] the EAT held, in a case concerning dismissal for redundancy, that the predecessor

---

[1037] Directive 2006/54/EC, Art 15.

[1038] This provision was first introduced as SDA 1975, ss 3A and 6A, as inserted by SI 2005/2467. In *EOC v Secretary of State for Trade and Industry* [2007] IRLR 327 the High Court ruled that the reference to a non-pregnant female comparator in the test of discrimination on pregnancy grounds in s 3A(1) was an incorrect implementation of Directive 2002/73, and an amendment was then made by SI 2008/656, which also inserted a new version of s 6A; cf. *Madarassy v Nomura International plc* [2007] IRLR 246, in which the Court of Appeal held that it was relevant to consider how a hypothetical male comparator would have been treated in a claim of sex discrimination related to pregnancy, a decision which would not now be followed. In general, it is irrelevant that a male comparator who was absent through illness would have been treated in the same way as the claimant, but if it can be shown that a male employee absent on the grounds of illness would have been *better* treated than the claimant, a claim may arise on those grounds: see *Fletcher v Blackpool Fylde and Wyre Hospitals NHS Trust* [2005] IRLR 689.

[1039] EqA 2010, s 18(1), (2).

[1040] EqA 2010, s 18(3), (4).

[1041] EqA 2010, s 18(6). On maternity leave, see para 6.115 below.

[1042] See EqA 2010, s 18(7), excluding the application of s 13, in so far as it relates to sex discrimination, to claims under s 18(2)-(4), and the *Explanatory Notes* on the Act, para 75.

[1043] EqA 2010, s 13(6)(b).

[1044] [2011] IRLR 448.

of this provision[1045] could only be relied on by an employer if it could show that the action taken was a proportionate means of achieving a legitimate aim, in this case ensuring that employees who were absent from work because of maternity were not unduly disadvantaged when their position was being compared, for the purposes of redundancy selection, with other employees. In the context of the 2010 Act, which makes extensive references elsewhere to the test of proportionality as a basis for defences of justification and positive action but does not do so here, the decision is questionable.

Dismissal on the grounds of pregnancy and maternity

6.114   Under ERA 1996, section 99, it is automatically unfair to dismiss an employee for taking 'leave for family reasons' which includes a reason relating to pregnancy, childbirth or maternity, or to 'ordinary, compulsory or additional maternity leave'.[1046] For this purpose, 'ordinary' leave refers to the basic statutory right to leave of 26 weeks; 'compulsory leave' is the period of two weeks' absence following childbirth which is mandated by law; and 'additional leave' is the extra period of leave of twenty-six weeks following ordinary leave.[1047] When the forerunner of section 99 was introduced in the EPA 1975, the rights it contained were so hedged about with restrictions as to put its effectiveness in doubt.[1048] The provision which, following consolidation, is now ERA 1996, section 99, was first introduced by TURERA 1993 in order to comply with the requirements of the Pregnant Workers Directive, and was amended further by the Employment Relations Act 1999. The substance of this legislation is no longer to be found in the body of the Act itself, but instead in the Maternity and Parental Leave etc. Regulations 1999 ('MPLR').[1049] No qualifying period of service is now required. The claimant can complain of dismissal on the grounds of maternity in a number of cases. These include situations in which dismissal occurs by reason of the 'pregnancy of the employee';[1050] where the employee gives birth, with dismissal ending the period of ordinary or additional maternity leave; where the employee is dismissed because she is suspended from work on maternity grounds for reasons relating to health and safety;[1051] and where the employee takes or seeks to take ordinary or additional maternity leave.[1052] It is also automatically unfair to select an employee for redundancy on one of the above grounds (where others in the same position were not dismissed),[1053] and unlawful for the employer to subject the employee to a detriment for one of these reasons.[1054]

These provisions fall to be interpreted in the light of the Pregnant Workers Directive, Article 10 of which states that Member States must take steps to 'prohibit the dismissal of workers ... during the period from the beginning of their pregnancy to the end of the maternity leave [period]

[1045] SDA 1975, s 2(2).
[1046] ERA 1996, s 99(1), (3). Other aspects of 'family leave' under s 99(3) are considered in paras 6.119-120 below.
[1047] See generally para 6.115 below.
[1048] See Bailey, 1989.
[1049] SI 1999/3312.
[1050] On the meaning of this phrase, see *Brown v Stockton-on-Tees Borough Council* [1989] AC 20.
[1051] On suspension from work on maternity grounds, see para 6.116 below.
[1052] MPLR 1999, reg 20(3).
[1053] MPLR 1999, reg 20(2).
[1054] MPLR 1999, reg 19; ERA 1996, ss 47C, 48–49, providing for a right to bring a complaint to an employment tribunal; *New Southern Railway v Quinn* [2006] IRLR 266. See also *Eversheds Legal Services Ltd v De Belin* [2011] IRLR 448.

save in exceptional cases not connected with their condition which are permitted under national legislation and/or practice.'[1055] In *Caledonia Bureau Investment & Property Ltd v Caffrey*[1056] the EAT held that the forerunner of the general right not to be dismissed on the grounds of pregnancy extended to a situation in which the employee was dismissed after her period of maternity leave had come to an end; dismissal for a pregnancy-related illness, in this case post-natal depression, was for a reason connected with pregnancy. The EAT also held that the dismissal in this case amounted to unlawful sex discrimination.

The right to claim automatically unfair dismissal is qualified where it is not reasonably practicable for the employer to allow the employee to return to work for a reason other than redundancy; an associated employer makes an offer of alternative employment which is appropriate and suitable; and the employee either unreasonably refuses or accepts that offer.[1057]

Maternity leave

6.115   The right not to be dismissed for pregnancy-related reasons would be of limited use were no provision also made for a minimum period of maternity leave and for the maintenance of employment-related benefits during that period. Accordingly the Pregnant Workers Directive provides for a continuous minimum period of maternity leave of 14 weeks.[1058] ERA 1996 and MPLR 1999 now provide for a period of 26 weeks' leave (increased from 18 weeks in 2003), known as 'ordinary maternity leave'. There is no minimum qualifying period of service. The leave begins on the date indicated by the employee, which may not be earlier than the eleventh week before the expected week of childbirth,[1059] or, alternatively, the first day after the beginning of the fourth week before the expected week of childbirth on which she is absent from work wholly or partly because of pregnancy, whichever of these two dates is the earlier.[1060] The latest day on which the leave can begin is the day following that on which the birth occurs.[1061] During this period of leave, the employee is entitled to all the normal terms and conditions of her employment and to benefits which would have applied if she had not been absent, with the exception of any right to remuneration, and is bound by any obligations arising under those terms and conditions, with the exception of any obligation to be present at work.[1062] In the absence of a contractual right to remuneration, minimum income maintenance during pregnancy takes the form, as we shall see,[1063] of the right to statutory maternity pay. However, the latter is unavailable to employees with

---

[1055] Directive 92/85, Art 10(1). Where dismissal takes place within the scope of the exception allowed by Art 10(1), Art 10(2) requires the employer to cite 'duly substantiated grounds' for this. Art 10 is sufficiently clear, precise and unconditional to have direct effect in national law: Case C-438/99 *Jiménez Melgar v Ayuntamiento de los Barrios* [2001] IRLR 848, and applies in a case where the worker was employed on a fixed-term contract and did not tell her employer prior to the hiring that she was pregnant, even though she was aware of this: Case C-109/00 *Tele Danmark A/S v Handels-Og Kontorfunktionaerernes Forbund I Danmark (HK), acting on behalf of Brandt-Nielsen* [2001] IRLR 853.

[1056] [1998] IRLR 110.

[1057] MPLR 1999, reg 20(7).

[1058] Directive 92/85/EC, Art 8.

[1059] This is the effect of the written notification requirement contained in MPLR 1999, reg 4(2).

[1060] MPLR 1999, reg 6(1).

[1061] MPLR 1999, reg 6(2).

[1062] ERA 1996, s 71(4)–(5); MPLR 1999, reg 9 (on which, see *Hoyland v Asda Stores Ltd.* [2005] IRLR 438).

[1063] See below, para 6.118.

less than 26 weeks' continuous employment; there is therefore a category of employees who have the right to ordinary maternity leave, but not the right to income maintenance to go with it.

The right to ordinary maternity leave is conditional upon the employee meeting certain notification requirements which are laid down in the Act. She must inform the employer (in writing if the employer so requests) that she is pregnant no later than the end of the fifteenth week before her expected week of childbirth or, if that is not reasonably practicable, as soon as it is reasonably practicable. She must at the same time indicate to the employer the expected week of childbirth and the date on which she intends her ordinary maternity leave to start. She must also, if requested by the employer to do so, provide it with a certificate from a registered doctor or midwife stating the expected week of childbirth.[1064] She may vary the commencement of the maternity leave by doing so at least 28 days before either the varied date or the new date, whichever is the earlier, or, if that is not reasonably practicable, as soon as is reasonably practicable.[1065]

At the end of the ordinary maternity leave period, the employee has the right to return to work to the job in which she was employed before her absence.[1066] Her seniority, pension rights and similar rights must be the same as they would have been if she had not been absent, and that the terms and conditions on which she returns must be not less favourable.[1067] If, however, during the leave period it becomes no longer practicable to continue to employ the employee by reason of redundancy, she is entitled to be offered suitable alternative employment.[1068] If an employee has a contractual right to leave in addition to the statutory right, she may not accumulate the two rights, but she may exercise a 'composite' right which means that she can rely on whichever of the two rights is more favourable in relation to a particular aspect of her leave entitlements.[1069]

In addition, legislation provides for 'compulsory' maternity leave of two weeks commencing on the day of childbirth. The employer must not permit the employee to work during this period, subject to the possibility of criminal conviction and a fine not exceeding level 2 on the standard scale.[1070]

Legislation also provides for the right to take 'additional maternity leave'.[1071] The equivalent of this right originated in the Employment Protection Act 1975; the relevant provisions have since been much amended, in particular by the Trade Union Reform and Employment Rights Act 1993, the Employment Relations Act 1999, the Employment Act 2002 and the Work and Families Act 2006, along with relevant regulations. The principle of a full year's leave, taking the 'ordinary' and 'additional' periods together, came in by virtue of the 2002 changes. Initially, 26 weeks of qualifying service were required to trigger this right. This qualifying period was removed by the amendments made in 2006, and the qualifying conditions for additional leave are now the same as those for ordinary maternity leave.[1072] The employee has the right to leave of 26 weeks beginning from the day after her ordinary maternity leave comes to an end.[1073] If she wishes to return to

---

[1064] MPLR 1999, reg 4(1).

[1065] MPLR 1999, reg 4(1A).

[1066] MPLR 1999, reg 18(1); *Blundell v Governing Body of St Andrew's Roman Catholic Primary School* [2007] IRLR 652.

[1067] ERA 1996, S 71(4)(c), (7); MPLR 1999, reg 18A.

[1068] ERA 1996, s 74; MPLR 1999, reg 10.

[1069] MPLR 1999, reg 21.

[1070] See ERA 1996, s 72 and MPLR 1999, reg 8.

[1071] ERA 1999, s 73.

[1072] See MPLR 1999, reg 4.

[1073] See MPLR 1999, regs 6, 7.

work before the end of the additional maternity leave period, she must give eight weeks' notice of her intention to do so: otherwise the employer is entitled to postpone her return to work for such time until the eight weeks' notice is given (although not beyond the end of the additional maternity leave period), and is under no obligation to pay her if she returns to work before the postponed date.[1074] During the additional leave period, the employee is not entitled to the benefit of the normal terms and conditions of employment as in the case of ordinary maternity leave, but instead only receives the benefit of the employer's implied obligation of trust and confidence and any terms and conditions of employment relating to notice of termination, compensation in the event of redundancy, and disciplinary or grievance procedures. The Regulations also state that during the additional leave period, the employee is bound by her implied obligation to her employer of good faith and any terms governing notice of termination, the disclosure of confidential information, the acceptance of gifts or other benefits, or the employee's participation in any other business.[1075] At the end of the additional leave period, the employee is entitled to return to her own job or, if that is not reasonably practicable, to another job 'which is both suitable for her and appropriate for her to do in the circumstances'.[1076]

As a result of a change made in 2006, an employee may do up to 10 days' work for the employer during the period of maternity leave (except during the two week period of compulsory leave) without this counting as a return to work or otherwise bringing the period of maternity leave to an end. Nor does any such work have the effect of extending the period of leave. This is designed to enable the employee to keep in touch with the workplace. The Regulations also state that reasonable contact between employer and employee during maternity leave, for example to discuss the employee's return to work, does not end the period of maternity leave.[1077]

Until December 1999, legislation provided that an employer who did not allow the employee to return to work after she had exercised her right to do so in the manner prescribed by the Act was to be treated as having dismissed her.[1078] This provision was extremely complex, and, arguably, was not even necessary, on the ground that the contract continued in force during the period of the employee's absence; if the employer refused to take the employee back, it would be committing a repudiatory breach of contract which would amount to a constructive dismissal. As we have just seen, the legislation now specifies the terms and conditions of employment which are to remain in force during periods of ordinary and additional maternity leave. A plausible reading of these provisions is that the contract of employment remains in force for a number of purposes during the period of leave; this can also be inferred from Articles 8 (concerning leave) and 10 (concerning dismissal) of the Pregnant Workers Directive. What happens to the contract of employment if the employee does not exercise the right to take leave or does not notify her employer of her wish to return to work within the terms set out by legislation is less clear. Under the now-repealed legislation, the courts failed to reach a consensus on this question, but there seems no reason in principle why it should not be open to them to find that an employer who

---

[1074] MPLR 1999, reg 11.
[1075] MPLR 1999, reg 17.
[1076] MPLR 1999, reg 18(2).
[1077] See MPLR, reg 10.
[1078] ERA 1996, s 96, now repealed. See *Halfpenny v IGE Medical Services Ltd* [2001] IRLR 96 for a decision under the old law which illustrates its extreme complexity.

excludes an employee from employment when she wishes to return thereby dismisses her, even if the statutory requirements for notification were not complied with.[1079]

The amendments made in 2006 included a power for the Secretary of State to make regulations providing for the mother to return to work before the end of a period of ordinary or additional maternity leave, in return for the father becoming eligible for additional paternity leave of up to twenty-six weeks,[1080] and measures to this effect were implemented with effect from 6 April 2010.[1081] The effect of these provisions is that the right to additional paternity leave is triggered where the mother is entitled to ordinary or maternity leave, but returns to work before the leave period comes to an end.[1082] As part of the procedure for a father taking additional paternity leave, the mother must sign a 'mother declaration' indicating her intention to return to work.[1083]

Suspension from work on grounds of maternity

6.116   As a result of an amendment made in 1993, where the employee is suspended from work on maternity grounds by virtue of a statutory prohibition or of a recommendation contained in a code of practice issued under the HSWA 1974, she is entitled to be offered any available suitable alternative work or, failing that, to be paid during her period of suspension. If she is suspended without an offer of suitable alternative work when that was available, she has the right to complain to an employment tribunal which may make an award of compensation.[1084] No qualifying period applies here.

Right to paid time off for ante-natal care

6.117   The employee has the right to paid time off during working hours in order to keep an appointment for the purpose of receiving ante-natal care. There is no qualifying period, and the remedy is by way of a complaint to an employment tribunal.[1085]

[1079] See *Lewis Woolf Griptight Ltd v Corfield* [1997] IRLR 432; *Caledonia Bureau Investment & Property v Caffrey* [1998] IRLR 110. In *Curr v Marks and Spencer plc* [2003] IRLR 74 the Court of Appeal held that the contract of employment was not in force during a period of extended childcare leave (which is not the same as a period of statutory maternity leave).

[1080] See now ERA 1996, s 88AA.

[1081] The Additional Paternity Leave Regulations ('APLR'), SI 2010/1055. The Coalition government's consultation on modern workplaces, initiated in May 2011, sets out further proposals for leave-sharing between parents (BIS, *Consultation on Modern Workplaces*, May 2011). The government is due to report on responses to the consultation in the spring of 2012.

[1082] APLR, regs 4, 35.

[1083] APLR, reg 6. See further below, para 6.120 below.

[1084] ERA 1996, ss 66–70. On what counts as suspension under these provisions, see *New Southern Railway v Quinn* [2009] IRLR 266.

[1085] ERA 1996, ss 55–57.

Statutory maternity pay

6.118   Although the statutory right to maternity pay was introduced in the EPA 1975, the present form of SMP derives from the SSA 1986, which modelled the right on the form taken by statutory sick pay: the employer is primarily responsible for making the relevant payments, but recovers the cost of doing so by way of a rebate on national insurance contributions, the extent of which varies according to the size of the employer.[1086]

The 1992 Directive requires the 'maintenance of a payment to, and/or entitlement to an adequate allowance' for the pregnant worker during the period of maternity leave;[1087] it also stipulates that this payment must be 'at least equivalent to that which the worker concerned would receive in the event of a break in her activities on grounds connected with her state of health, subject to any ceiling laid down under national legislation'.[1088] In response to the Directive, the Department of Social Security proposed aligning the level of SMP with the standard rate for SSP, and at one stage also considered abolishing entirely the qualifying period for SMP,[1089] a move which would have integrated income maintenance under this head with the introduction of the right to 14 weeks' maternity leave at this time. However, in the event the amending legislation for SMP retained a 26-week qualifying period, and it was only from December 1999 that the basic period of 'ordinary maternity leave' was harmonised with the then 18 weeks of SMP entitlement. By virtue of changes made by the Employment Act 2002, the leave period was extended to 26 weeks for both pay and leave purposes. The maternity pay period was later extended to 39 weeks and currently stands at 52 weeks.[1090]

SMP is available to an employee who has been continuously employed in employed earner's employment[1091] for 26 weeks up to the fifteenth week before the expected week of confinement, and whose average weekly earnings in the eight weeks up to the qualifying week are at least equal to the lower earnings limit for national insurance contributions.[1092] Self-employed workers, and others unable to meet this qualifying condition, may nevertheless qualify for the state maternity allowance on the basis of having paid Class 1 or Class 2 national insurance contributions in any 26 weeks in the 66 weeks ending with the qualifying week.[1093] In order to receive SMP, the employee must still be pregnant at the eleventh week before the expected week of confinement or have been confined by that time.[1094] She must also have ceased to work. A set of notification requirements must again be complied with. The employee must give the employer at least 28 days' notice of her intended absence for reasons of pregnancy or confinement, unless it is not reasonably practicable to do so; if the employer insists, this notice must be in writing.[1095]

[1086] See SSCBA 1992, s 167.
[1087] Directive 92/85, Art 11(1); Case C-471/08 *Parviainen v Finnair Oyj* [2011] ICR 99.
[1088] Directive 92/85, Art 11(3).
[1089] Department of Social Security, *Changes in Maternity Pay: Proposals for Implementing the EC Pregnant Workers Directive* (1993).
[1090] SSCBA 1992, s 165(1).
[1091] This expression, used in social security law, effectively reproduces the requirement that an individual be employed as an employee. See ch 3 above, at para 3.19.
[1092] SSCBA 1992, s 164(2)(a), (b). A claim by a part-time worker that her exclusion from statutory maternity pay on the grounds that she earned less than the lower earnings limit contravened Art 119 (now Art 157 TFEU) failed in *Banks v Tesco Stores and (2) Secretary of State for Employment* (3 June 1997, unreported), case no 18985/95/C.
[1093] See SSCBA 1992, s 35.
[1094] SSCBA 1992, s 164(2)(c).
[1095] SSCBA 1992, s 164(4), (5); SMPR 1986, reg 23.

The employee receives SMP for the duration of the maternity pay period of 52 consecutive weeks. SMP is payable at 90% of the employee's normal average weekly earnings for a period of six weeks (the 'earnings-related rate') and at a rate set by statute for the remainder of the maternity pay period.[1096] The payment period will normally begin in the week when the employee has either ceased to work in conformity with the notice given by her to the employer, which may not be earlier than the start of the eleventh week before the expected week of confinement, or she is confined.[1097]

When an employer is in default, a claim may be made by the employee against the Commissioners for Her Majesty's Revenue and Customs.[1098] Alternatively, an employee may argue that a failure to pay statutory maternity pay amounts to an unlawful deduction from wages due under Part II of the ERA 1996.[1099]

Laws and practices relating to maternity pay and leave have been analysed by the ECJ in a series of cases. In *Gillespie v Northern Health and Social Services Board*[1100] the Court held that although statutory maternity pay fell within the definition of 'pay' in Article 119 of the Treaty of Rome (now 157 TFEU), it was not a breach of Article 119 for the amount of SMP to be set at a level below the earnings which an individual was receiving while she was in employment, since this did not give rise to a case of unequal treatment on the grounds of sex, but that it would be a breach if pay rises awarded during the period of leave were not taken into account in the calculation of maternity pay. In further litigation, the Northern Ireland Court of Appeal held that statutory maternity pay which was set at a higher level than statutory sick pay under the relevant legislation could not be categorised as 'inadequate' under Article 11(3) of the Pregnant Workers Directive.[1101]

The principle in *Gillespie* has since been interpreted as turning on a distinction between the period of maternity leave, on the one hand, and the period of employment prior to and after the leave, on the other. During the leave period, according to the Court, it is illegitimate to compare the position of a pregnant woman with either that of a sick man or with that of a woman in regular employment. In effect, the equal treatment principle is suspended while the leave period is in effect, and the Pregnant Workers Directive is the sole source of protection. This principle has been interpreted as meaning that it is not unlawful for an employer to operate a rule requiring pregnant employees who do not return to work after their leave has ended to repay the difference between their contractual maternity pay and their basic SMP entitlement, even though such a rule would not be applied to employees who were in receipt of sick pay or some other contractual payment while absent from work.[1102] Nor, for the same reason, is it a breach of the equal treatment principle for an employer to pay a maternity bonus to women on maternity leave, thereby engaging in what might otherwise have been a form of positive discrimination in

[1096] SSCBA 1992, s 166. The rate was set at £135.45 with effect from 6 April 2012; SMPR 1986, reg 6.
[1097] SSCBA 1992, s 165; SMPR 1986, regs 2 and 8–9 as amended; *Wade v North Yorkshire Police Authority* [2011] IRLR 393.
[1098] SMPR 1986, regs 7 and 30.
[1099] This is the combined effect of ERA 1996, ss 13(3), 23 and 27(1)(c); see *Alabaster v Woolwich plc* [2000] IRLR 754.
[1100] Case C-342/93 [1996] IRLR 214.
[1101] *Gillespie v Northern Health and Social Services Board (No 2)* [1997] IRLR 410. The same principle was applied in *Edwards v Derby City Council* [1999] ICR 115 and *British Airways (European Operations at Gatwick) v Moore and Botterill* [2000] IRLR 296, although cf *P & O European Ferries (Dover) Ltd v Iverson* [1999] ICR 1088. See also Case C191/03 *North Western Health Board v McKenna* [2005] IRLR 895.
[1102] Case C-411/96 *Boyle v Equal Opportunities Commission* [1998] IRLR 717.

favour of women.[1103] By contrast, it is unlawful for an employer to make a deduction from the pay of a pregnant worker who is absent from work on the grounds of illness *before* the start of her maternity leave, if the same deduction would not be made from the pay of a sick man;[1104] and it is unlawful to deny to a worker a performance appraisal which could result in her later promotion simply because, at the relevant time, she was absent from work, since this affects her employment after the leave period comes to an end.[1105] It is far from obvious that the distinction drawn by the Court in this context between the leave period and other periods is justifiable, in particular given the assumption contained in the Pregnant Workers Directive[1106] (and, as we have seen, now translated into UK law) that the employment relationship continues during maternity leave.[1107] In *Alabaster v Woolwich plc and Secretary of State for Social Security*,[1108] the ECJ held that under Art 157 (as it now is), maternity pay paid during the period of maternity leave had to take into account a relevant pay rise occurring after the leave began, rejecting the advice of the Advocate General that, to be consistent with the post-*Gillespie* case law, this issue fell to be decided by reference to the Directive and not Art 157.

The relationship between maternity pay and the pay normally received by the pregnant worker prior to taking maternity leave is now regulated by Chapter 3 of Part 5 of EqA 2010. This inserts a 'maternity equality clause' into the worker's contract, the effect of which is to align her pay with any increases that she would have received had she not been on maternity leave,[1109] consistently with the ECJ's decision in *Alabaster*.[1110]

Parental leave

6.119   Parents have the right to take unpaid parental leave for the purposes of caring for a child under legislation introduced as part of the Employment Relations Act 1999. The legislation implements the EU Parental Leave of Directive 1996 which, in its turn, refers to a Framework Agreement made by the social partners under the process of European social dialogue.[1111] The

---

[1103] Case C-218/98 *Abdoulaye v Régie Nationale des Usines Renault* [1999] IRLR 811.

[1104] Case C-66/96 *Handesl-Og Kontorfunktionærernes Forbund i Danmark, acting on behalf of Hoj Pedersen v Fællesforeningen for Danmarks Brugsforeninger, acting on behalf of Kvickly Skive* [1999] IRLR 55.

[1105] Case C-136/95 *Thibault v Caisse Nationale D'Assuarance Vieillesse des Travailleurs Salariés* [1999] ICR 160; applied in *Gus Home Shopping Ltd v Green* [2001] IRLR 74. In *Halfpenny v IGE Medical Systems Ltd* [2001] IRLR 96 the HL rejected a claim of sex discrimination on the grounds that the applicant, when attempting to return to work following maternity leave, was not at that point in employment within the meaning of SDA 1975. This decision, which was questionable as a matter of contractual construction, also looks suspect in the light of *Thibault*.

[1106] In particular, Arts 8 (maternity leave) and 10 (dismissal).

[1107] See *Gus Home Shopping Ltd v Green* [2001] IRLR 74; cf the decision of the Court in Case C-333/97 *Lewen v Denda* [2000] IRLR 67, applying Art 119 (now 157 TFEU) to a situation in which a pregnant worker absent from work during *parental* leave (as opposed to maternity leave) was denied a pay-related benefit (a Christmas bonus) in a discriminatory fashion. It is far from clear on what basis the equal treatment principle should be applicable to a period of parental leave but not to a period of maternity leave. For discussion of the inconsistencies of the ECJ's approach in these cases, see P Lewis, 2000.

[1108] Case C-147/02, [2004] IRLR 486. See also *Alabaster v Barclays Bank plc and Secretary of State for Soacial Security (No 2)* [2005] IRLR 576.

[1109] EqA 2010, ss 73-74.

[1110] Case C-147/02, [2004] IRLR 486.

[1111] Directive 96/34/EC on the framework agreement on parental leave concluded by UNICE, CEEP and the ETUC, extended to the UK by Directive 97/75/EC.

1996 Directive was repealed and replaced by a new Directive, incorporating the provisions of a new Framework Agreement, with effect from 8 March 2012.[1112] The recast Parental Leave Directive extends the minimum period of parental leave from three months to four, raises the maximum age of the child in respect of whom the leave may be taken from five to eight, and makes provision for at least one of the four months of leave to be non-transferable as between the parents of the child, in order to 'encourage a more equal take-up of leave by both parents'.[1113] The recast Directive allows a Member State to delay implementation for up to a year after the coming into force of its provisions, and the UK government has taken advantage of this derogation,[1114] with a view to bringing revisions to the relevant UK legislation into force by March 2013.

The implementing legislation for the Parental Leave Directive is distinctive, in the British context, in leaving much of the application of the law to workplace- or enterprise-level agreements between employers and employees (or their representatives), subject only to a 'default' or 'fallback' scheme if the parties fail to agree. The statutory framework is provided by ERA 1996, sections 76-80, and the details of the right are contained in MPLR 1999.[1115] The Regulations provide for an employee with continuous employment of not less than one year to take parental leave of up to thirteen weeks in respect of any individual child for whom he or she has responsibility.[1116] The thirteen weeks' leave may be taken at various points up to the child's fifth birthday or, if the child is disabled and entitled to disability living allowance, his or her eighteenth birthday. In the case of an adopted child, the leave may be taken up to the fifth anniversary of the date on which the placement of the child began, or his or her eighteenth birthday, whichever is the earlier. The meaning of a 'week' of leave for this purpose is calculated by reference to the normal working time of the employee; if his or her weekly working time varies, an annualised average is used.[1117]

An employee has the right not to be subjected to any detriment[1118] and not to be dismissed for taking parental leave.[1119] During the period of leave, certain terms and conditions of employment

---

[1112] Directive 2010/18/EU implementing the Framework Agreement on parental leave concluded by BUSINESSEUROPE, UEAPME, CEEP and ETUC and repealing Directive 96/34/EC.

[1113] Framework Agreement, cl 2(2).

[1114] Directive 2010/18/EU, Art 3(2). The derogation applies where a member state can show that delay is necessary 'to take account of particular difficulties or implementation by collective agreement'. The UK government has justified the delay in the implementation of the Directive by reference to its consultation on modern workplaces which was initiated in 2011, and on which it is due to respond in the spring of 2012. See BIS, *Consultation on Modern Workplaces*, May 2011.

[1115] MPLR 1999, regs 13–16.

[1116] As originally drafted, the right to parental leave was confined to parents of children born after 15 December 1999. In *R v Secretary of State for Trade and Industry, ex p TUC* [2000] IRLR 565 the TUC argued that, under the Directive, the right to leave should have been provided in respect of all children under the age of five at the date the Regulations came into force, and not those born on or after that date. The Divisional Court referred the question to the ECJ and declined to grant an interim order for the protection of parents affected by the alleged failure to transpose the Directive correctly, even though it considered the TUC's argument likely to prevail before the ECJ. The Regulations were subsequently amended (by SI 2001/4010) to provide that parents of children born between 15 December 1994 and 15 December 1999 had until 31 March 2005 to exercise the right to leave, and might include service with a previous employer for the purposes of computing their continuity of employment, provided that this was notified to the current employer. See now MPLR 1999, regs 13(1A), 15(2) and Sch 2, para 2A.

[1117] MPLR 1999, reg 14.

[1118] ERA 1996, s 47C(2)(c). A 'detriment' includes subjecting the employee to a disciplinary hearing and a warning in respect of an otherwise unauthorised period of absence; however, a successful claim can be made under the Act only if the employee can show that they were entitled to the statutory right: *South Central Trains Ltd v Rodway* [2004] IRLR 777, [2005] IRLR 583.

[1119] ERA 1996, s 99(3)(c).

are deemed to remain in place.[1120] If the period of leave is four weeks or less, the employee has the right to return to the same job as before; if the leave is longer than four weeks, the employer may offer alternative employment if it is not reasonably practicable to reinstate the employee in the old job. The new employment must, however, be suitable and appropriate for the employee, and must offer terms and conditions which are not less favourable than those which applied before.[1121] Seniority rights must be preserved during the period of leave according to the same principle that applies for maternity rights.[1122] An employee whose employer unreasonably postpones a requested period of parental leave or who prevents or attempts to prevent the employee from taking parental leave may make a claim to an employment tribunal which has the power to award compensation as well as issuing a declaration.[1123]

The Regulations provide for the detail of the operation of parental leave schemes to be worked out by agreement between employers and employees. If no agreement is made, a default scheme operates.[1124] This scheme appears to provide for leave to be taken in blocks or multiples of a week.[1125] In *South Central Trains Ltd v Rodway*[1126] it was held that, as a result, there was no right to take leave for a period of less than a week, rejecting an argument that such an absence was to be treated as exhausting a week's entitlement. The default scheme also sets an upper limit of four weeks' leave in any one year. The employee must give notice of 21 days before taking leave. The employer has the right to postpone the taking of leave for up to six months if it 'considers that the operation of his business would be unduly disrupted if the employee took leave during the period identified in [his or her] notice'; the employer must agree alternative dates on which the leave is to be taken within the six-month period.[1127]

In order to displace the provisions of the default scheme, the employer must make either a collective agreement or a workforce agreement governing the operation of parental leave, and ensure that the relevant terms of the agreement are incorporated into the contracts of employment of the employees.[1128] A 'collective agreement', for this purpose, must be one which is made with an independent trade union.[1129] A workforce agreement[1130] may only be made if there is no collective agreement (in the sense just defined) governing the terms and conditions of the employees in

[1120] MPLR 1999, reg 17. Parental leave is assimilated, for this purpose, to the statutory regime for additional maternity leave (see para 6.115 above).

[1121] MPLR 1999, reg 18.

[1122] MPLR 1999, reg 18A.

[1123] ERA 1996, s 80.

[1124] MPLR 1999, reg 16 and Sch 2. In this context, it should be noted that an employee who makes an individual agreement with his or her employer on the matter of parental leave is able to exercise a 'composite right' along the same lines as that which applies to cases of maternity leave, enabling them to claim the advantage of whichever scheme (the contractual scheme or the statutory 'default' scheme) provides superior benefits with regard to a particular aspect of the leave (MPLR 1999, reg 21).

[1125] Sch 2, para 7, except in the case of a parent of a child in receipt of disability living allowance. In *South Central Trains v Rodway* [2004] IRLR 777 the EAT held that reg 14(4), which appears to envisage periods of leave for less than one week, only applies to the disability living allowance case. However, the DTI Guidance of the time assumed that reg 14(4) applies more generally: *Parental Leave (PL 509 rev 1): A Guide for Employers and Employees* (2004), at para 2.3. The EAT's interpretation of reg 14(4) was doubted by the CA: see [2005] IRLR 583, [24] (Keane LJ).

[1126] [2004] IRLR 777, [2005] IRLR 583.

[1127] MPLR 1999, Sch 2, para 6.

[1128] MPLR 1999, reg 16 (under which it is also sufficient if the contract of employment otherwise 'operates by reference to' the collective or workforce agreement).

[1129] MPLR 1999, reg 2(1).

[1130] See generally MPLR 1999, Sch 1.

question. A workforce agreement must be made in writing, have effect for a specified period not exceeding five years, and be concluded with representatives of the workforce in question[1131] or the relevant part of it; if, however, the employer employs fewer than 21 employees on the date the agreement was first made available for signature, the agreement may be made with the workforce representatives or with a majority of the employer's employees. In addition, prior to making the agreement available for signature, the employer must send written copies of it, together with appropriate guidance, to the employees whom it will affect.

Rights arising in connection with paternity and adoption

6.120   Rights to statutory paternity leave and pay and to statutory adoption leave and pay were introduced with effect from April 2003 by virtue of the Employment Act 2002,[1132] as amended by the Work and Families Act 2006, and associated regulations.[1133] With effect from April 2010, rights to additional paternity leave and pay came into force.[1134]

To qualify for ordinary paternity leave, an individual must be an employee with 26 weeks' continuous employment up to the fifteenth week before the expected week of the child's birth, and must be either the father of the child or, if not the father, married to or the partner of the child's mother.[1135] A 'partner' is 'a person (whether of a different sex or the same sex) who lives with the mother … and the child in an enduring family relationship but is not a relative of the mother'.[1136] Thus despite its name, 'paternity' leave is confined neither to fathers, nor to male partners. In addition, the claimant must have or expect to have, if he is the father, 'responsibility for the upbringing of the child', and, in any other case, 'the main responsibility (apart from any responsibility of the mother) for the upbringing of the child'.[1137] The leave must be taken for the purpose of 'caring for a child or supporting the child's mother'.[1138] The entitlement consists of two weeks' leave which either be taken as a single block, or in two blocks of a week each, and it must be taken within 56 days of the birth or, if earlier, the expected week of childbirth.[1139] The leave entitlement is not increased if more than one child is born from the relevant pregnancy.[1140] The employee must give notice to the employer specifying the expected week of childbirth, the intended period of leave and the date on which he or she has chosen

---

[1131] Rules governing the election or appointment of workforce representatives are laid down in MPLR 1999, Sch 2, para 3.

[1132] The relevant parts of the 2002 Act (ss 1–16) took effect through amendments to other legislation. For statutory paternity and adoption leave, see ERA 1996, ss 80A–80E and 75A–75D respectively, and for statutory paternity and adoption pay, SSCBA 1992, ss 171ZA–171ZK and 171ZL–171ZT, respectively. These statutory provisions set out the framework for the relevant rights; the substantive details are contained in regulations (see next footnote).

[1133] The most important of these are the Paternity and Adoption Leave Regulations ('PALR'), SI 2002/2788, and the Statutory Paternity Pay and Statutory Adoption Pay (General) Regulations ('SPPR'), SI 2002/2822.

[1134] The Additional Paternity Leave Regulations ('APLR'), SI 2010/1055, and the Additional Statutory Paternity Pay (General) Regulations ('ASPPR'), SI 2010/1056.

[1135] PALR 2002, reg 4(2)(a)–(b). On continuity if the child is born before the expected week of childbirth, see reg 4(3).

[1136] PALR 2002, reg 1(1).

[1137] PALR 2002, reg 4(2)(c).

[1138] PALR 2002, reg 4(1).

[1139] PALR 2002, reg 5.

[1140] PALR 2002, reg 4(6).

to start the leave. The notice must be given in or before the fifteenth week before the expected week of childbirth or, if that is not possible, as soon as reasonably practicable; if the employer requires, the employee must provide a written declaration that he or she is taking leave for the relevant purpose, and that they have met the conditions of entitlement.[1141] The continuation of certain terms and conditions of employment during the paternity leave, and the provisions governing the employee's right to return to work after the completion of leave, mirror those for ordinary maternity leave.[1142]

To qualify for ordinary statutory paternity pay, the employee must meet the conditions for paternity leave which have just been outlined, and must, in addition, be in employed earner's employment for 26 weeks ending with the fifteenth week before the expected week of childbirth, and have had earnings at or above the lower earnings limit for national insurance contributions for the last eight weeks of that period.[1143] A number of notification requirements have to be met which, essentially, are the same as those which apply to paternity leave. The amount of ordinary paternity pay is 90% of the employee's average weekly earnings, up to a ceiling set by statute,[1144] and it is payable for a period of up to two weeks within the 'qualifying period' of 56 days from the child's birth.[1145]

The Work and Families Act 2006 created powers to make regulations providing for a right to additional paternity leave of up to 26 weeks in the year following birth or adoption.[1146] The aim was to establish a right to additional leave which could be taken during a period when the mother is entitled to take either ordinary or additional maternity leave, but returned to work before the end of the leave period. The relevant regulations were brought into force with effect from 6 April 2010.[1147] The basic qualifying conditions are the same as for paternity leave.[1148] In addition, the mother must have qualified for one or more of statutory maternity leave, SMP or maternity allowance, and must have returned to work before the end of the leave period.[1149] In addition, the mother must sign a 'mother declaration' indicating her intention to return to work.[1150] The leave must be taken in the form of a continuous period consisting of multiples of complete weeks, between the period of twenty weeks and one year from the child's birth, and may last from two to 26 weeks.[1151] Separate regulations[1152] provide for the payment of additional statutory paternity pay, payable at the same rate as statutory paternity pay, during the period of additional paternity leave. The basic qualifying conditions, in terms of length of service and requisite minimum

---

[1141] PALR 2002, reg 6, which also provides for the date on which leave commences to be varied by notice of 28 days prior to the relevant date.

[1142] PALR 2002, regs 12–14.

[1143] SSCBA 1992, s 171ZA(2)(b)–(d).

[1144] SI 2002/2818, reg 2. The ceiling was set at £135.45 with effect from 1 April 2012.

[1145] See generally SSCBA 1992, s 171ZE; SI 2002/2822, reg 8.

[1146] ERA 1996, ss 80AA and 80BB (the latter governing additional adoption leave), as inserted by WFA 2006.

[1147] APLR 2010 (SI 2010/1055). On the Coalition government's proposals to extend leave-sharing between parents, see BIS, *Consultation on Modern Workplaces* (2011), ch 3. The government is due to respond to the consultative process on this document in the spring of 2012.

[1148] APLR 2010, reg 4.

[1149] On the meaning of 'return to work', see APLR, reg 25.

[1150] APLR 2010, reg 6.

[1151] APLR 2010, reg 5.

[1152] ASPRR 2010 (SI 2010/1056).

earnings, are the same as those for ordinary statutory paternity pay.[1153] In addition, the applicant must intend to care for the child during the additional paternity pay period.[1154]

The right to statutory adoption leave vests in an employee with 26 weeks' continuous employment ending with the week in which he or she is notified by a UK adoption agency that he or she has been matched with a child for the purposes of adoption.[1155] The employee must inform the employer of their intention to take adoption leave within seven days of receiving the notice of matching from the adoption agency.[1156] The leave may begin either on the date on which the child is placed with the employee for adoption or up to 14 days before the expected date of placement.[1157] The employee is then entitled to take 'ordinary' adoption leave of 26 weeks[1158] and 'additional' leave of a further 26 weeks,[1159] unless the ordinary leave is disrupted (by, for example, the death of the child or the return of the child to the adoption agency) or the employee is dismissed prior to its completion.[1160] During ordinary leave, the normal terms and conditions of employment apply, with the exception of the employee's obligation to be present at work;[1161] during additional leave a more limited subset of the normal terms and conditions are continued in force.[1162] At the end of the leave the employee is entitled to return to their previous employment, if they took ordinary leave; if they took additional leave as well, they are entitled either to return to their previous employment or, if that is not reasonably practicable, to one which is 'both suitable for him and appropriate for him to do in the circumstances'.[1163]

To qualify for statutory adoption pay, an employee must show that, in addition to meeting the qualifying conditions for leave, he or she was in employed earner's employment for 26 weeks up to the week in which they were notified that they had been matched with the child, and had earnings at or above the lower earnings limit for national insurance contributions for the last eight weeks of that period.[1164] Adoption pay is payable at 90% of the employee's average weekly earnings up to a ceiling set by statute,[1165] for a period of 39 weeks.[1166]

A child may be adopted by one member of a couple, or by both of them. Until the coming into force in 2004 of the Adoption and Children Act 2002, joint adoption was only possible if the coupled were married, but this possibility now also extends to unmarried couples who are partners living in an enduring family relationship, and to members of a civil partnership, which is the quasi-marital status created for members of same-sex relationships.[1167] Where joint adoption occurs, only one member of the couple may opt to take the relevant statutory adoption leave

[1153] See SSCBA 1992, s 171ZEA; ASPRR 2010, reg 4.
[1154] See SSCBA 1992, s 171ZEA(2)(h); ASPPR 2010, reg 4(1)(c).
[1155] PALR 2002, reg 15.
[1156] PALR 2002, reg 17(2).
[1157] PALR 2002, reg 16.
[1158] PALR 2002, reg 18.
[1159] PALR 2002, reg 20.
[1160] PALR 2002, regs 22, 24.
[1161] PALR 2002, reg 19.
[1162] PALR 2002, reg 20.
[1163] PALR 2002, reg 26.
[1164] SSCBA 1992, s 171ZL(2)(b)–(d).
[1165] SI 2002/2818, reg 3. The ceiling was set at £135.45 with effect from 1 April 2012.
[1166] SPPR 2002, reg 21(5).
[1167] For this purpose the definition of 'couple' is that contained in the Adoption and Children Act 2002, s 144(4), as amended by the Civil Partnership Act 2004, s 79.

and/or pay.[1168] The other member of the couple – whether or not they jointly adopted the child – may then be entitled to statutory paternity leave of two weeks for the purposes of supporting the adopter or caring for the newly adopted child, and to statutory paternity pay for the same period, if in all other respects they meet the relevant qualifying conditions. They also qualify for statutory additional paternity pay and leave. The provisions governing statutory paternity pay in relation to birth apply, *mutatis mutandis*, to these rights in relation to adoption,[1169] as do those relating to statutory additional paternity leave and pay.[1170]

An employee may not be subjected to a detriment or be dismissed for taking or seeking to take paternity or adoption leave.[1171] An employer's failure to make a payment of statutory paternity or adoption pay may be referred to the Commissioners of Revenue and Customs for adjudication,[1172] or the employee may make an application for the payment of wages due under Part II of ERA 1996.[1173]

The right to time off to provide urgent assistance to dependants

6.121 By way of implementation of the original Parental Leave Directive,[1174] the Employment Relations Act 1999[1175] established a new right for employees[1176] to take a reasonable amount of time off during working hours to provide urgent assistance to dependants. The right is principally set out in section 57A of ERA 1996. There is no qualifying period of continuous employment for this right. Specifically, an employee has the right to time off to provide assistance if a dependant falls ill, gives birth, or is injured or assaulted; to make arrangements for the care of a dependant who is ill or injured; in consequence of the death of a dependant; because of unexpected disruption or termination of arrangements for care of a dependant; or to deal with an incident involving the employee's child during a time when an educational establishment would normally be responsible for that child.[1177] The employee must notify the employer as soon as reasonably practicable of his or her intention to take time off, and how long he or she expects to be absent (unless it was not possible to tell the employer in advance).[1178] The category of dependants includes not just a spouse, child or parent, but also a person living in the same household (other than a tenant, lodger

[1168] See PALR 2002, reg 2(1) (defining 'adopter') and SSCBA 1992, ss 171ZB(2)(e) and 171ZL(2)(e) (governing election to receive statutory paternity pay and statutory adoption pay respectively).
[1169] See ERA 1996, s 80B; PALR 2002, regs 8–14; SSCBA 1992, Part XIIZA; ASPPR 2002, regs 11–16.
[1170] APLR 2010, regs 14–23; ASPPR 2010, regs 12–18.
[1171] See ERA 1996, s 47 (detriment) and 99 (dismissal), and PALR 2002, regs 28 (detriment) and 29 (dismissal). There are parallel provisions in relation to additional leave under APLR 2010.
[1172] SI 2002/2820, reg 12. If the employer does not pay, the Commissioners of Revenue and Customs may become responsible under certain circumstances for making the payment to the employee: see SPPR 2002, reg 43; ASPRR, reg 35.
[1173] Statutory paternity pay and statutory adoption pay (and additional pay) fall under the definition of 'wages' for this purpose: ERA 1996, s 27(1)(ca), (cb).
[1174] Directive 96/34, Framework Agreement, cl 3, referring to 'time off from work on grounds of force majeure … for urgent family reasons in cases of sickness or accident making the immediate presence of the worker indispensable'.
[1175] ERelA 1999, s 8 and Sch 4, Part II, inserting ERA 1996, ss 57, 57A.
[1176] The police and members of the armed forces may also qualify for statutory paternity pay and adoption pay, but not for paternity leave and adoption leave. See above at paras 3.33 and 3.41, respectively.
[1177] ERA 1996, s 57A(1).
[1178] ERA 1996, s 57A(2). However, this does not give rise to an obligation to keep the employer informed of the situation on a daily basis: *Qua v John Ford Morrison Solicitors* [2003] IRLR 184, at [28].

or boarder) and, for relevant purposes, any person who reasonably relies on the employee for assistance when that person falls ill or is injured or assaulted, or for the making of arrangements for care.[1179] An employee who is unreasonably refused time off may make a complaint to an employment tribunal which has the power to issue a declaration and to order compensation in an appropriate case,[1180] and dismissal of the employee for seeking to exercise this right is automatically unfair.[1181]

The right is one 'to be permitted to take a reasonable amount of time off work during working hours in order to deal with a variety of unexpected or sudden events affecting their dependants, as defined, and in order to make any necessary longer-term arrangements for their care'.[1182] It follows that it does not cover leave of an extended duration to care for a sick dependant. Even if the employee gives notice to the employer and takes only a reasonable amount of time off on each occasion, although time off may be taken for the purposes of organising long-term care, any right to further leave on the part of employee himself or herself must be brought under the parental leave provisions of the Act and Regulations.[1183] Nor does section 57A provide a right to compassionate leave following a bereavement, although it may well cover 'many other matters' consequent upon the death of a dependant, such as registering the death and dealing with the administration of the deceased's estate.[1184] However, 'what is reasonable time off in the particular situation which has arisen will depend on what has occurred and the individual employee's own circumstances'; in this context, 'the operational needs of the employer cannot be relevant to a consideration of the amount of time an employee reasonably needs to deal with emergency circumstances of the kind specified'.[1185]

The right to request flexible working in relation to family responsibilities

6.122   Since April 2003,[1186] an employee[1187] has had the right to apply to his or her employer for a change in his or her terms and conditions of employment for the purposes of enabling him or her to carry out childcare responsibilities. In April 2007 this right was extended to caring for certain adults in need of care.[1188] Specifically, the change must relate to the hours which the employee is required to work, the times at which he or she is required to work, and 'where, as between his home and a place of business of his employer, he is required to work'.[1189] The employee must have had 26 weeks of continuous employment with the employer at the time of making

---

[1179]   ERA 1996, s 57A(3)–(5).

[1180]   ERA 1996, s 57B.

[1181]   ERA 1996, s 99(3)(d); see *Qua v John Ford Morrison Solicitors* [2003] IRLR 184.

[1182]   [2003] IRLR 184, at [15]. On what constitutes an 'unexpected' event, see *Royal Bank of Scotland v Harrison* [2009] IRLR 28.

[1183]   [2003] IRLR 184, at [21].

[1184]   *Forster v Cartwright Black* [2004] IRLR 781, at [17] (EAT).

[1185]   *Qua v John Ford Morrison Solicitors* [2003] IRLR 184, at [22].

[1186]   The right was introduced by the Employment Act 2002, s 47, and is now to be found in ERA 1996, ss 80F–80I, the Flexible Working (Procedural Requirements) Regulations (henceforth 'FWPR'), SI 2002/3207, and the Flexible Working (Eligibility, Complaints and Remedies) (henceforth 'FWER'), SI 2002/3236, as amended.

[1187]   This right does not apply to members of the armed forces. See para 3.41 above.

[1188]   The BIS consultation on modern workplaces has set out proposals to extend the right to request flexible working to all employees. See BIS, *Consultation on Modern Workplaces* (2011), ch 4.

[1189]   ERA 1996, s 80F(1)(a).

the request.[1190] The request must be made before the day on which the child concerned reaches the age of seventeen or, if disabled,, eighteen,[1191] or in relation to an adult person for whom the employee cares or expects to care.[1192] In the case of caring for a child, the employee must be either the mother, father, adopter, guardian or foster parent of the child, or a person in whose favour there is a residence order for the child, or married to or the partner of one of the above.[1193] For the purpose of the Regulations 'partner' is defined as 'the other member of a couple' consisting of a man and a woman living together as if they were husband and wife or as if they were civil partners.[1194] The employee must also have or expect to have 'responsibility for the upbringing of the child'.[1195] In the case of caring for an adult, the adult person must be either married to the employee or their partner; a relative of the employee; or a person living at the same address as the employee. The application must be made in writing to the employer[1196] and must state, among other things, the change being requested and 'what effect, if any, the employee thinks making the change applied for would have on his or her employer and how, in his or her opinion, any such effect might be dealt with'.[1197] If a previous application was made, the employee must wait twelve months before making another one.[1198]

The employer is under no obligation to accede to the request, no matter how reasonable it might be. However, the employer may only refuse an application on one of a number of specified grounds. These are listed as: a 'burden of additional costs'; a 'detrimental effect' on the employer's 'ability to meet customer demand'; its 'inability to re-organise work among existing staff' or to 'recruit additional staff', a 'detrimental impact on quality' or 'on performance'; 'insufficiency of work during the periods the employee proposes to work'; and 'planned structural changes'.[1199] The Secretary of State is empowered to add to this list by regulation.[1200] Regulations set out the procedure which should be followed when an application is made; among other things, these provide for the employee to have the right to be accompanied at relevant meetings.[1201] An employee may not be subjected to a detriment or dismissed in connection with the rights created by these provisions,[1202] and may make a complaint to an employment tribunal if the employer fails to comply with the requirement to deal with the request according to the Act or makes a decision on the basis of incorrect facts.[1203] The tribunal has power to order the application to be reconsidered, and/or to award such sum of compensation as it considers just and equitable in the circumstances,[1204] up to a maximum of two weeks' pay.[1205]

[1190] FWER 2002, reg 3(1)(a).
[1191] ERA 1996, s 80F(1)(b)(i); FWER 2002, reg 3A.
[1192] ERA 1996, s 80F(1)(b)(ii); FWER 2002, reg 3B.
[1193] FWER 2002, reg 3(1)(b).
[1194] FWER 2002, reg 2(1).
[1195] FWER 2002, reg 3(1)(c).
[1196] FWER 2002, reg 4.
[1197] ERA 1996, s 80F(2).
[1198] FWER 2002, reg 80F(4).
[1199] ERA 1996, s 80G(1)(b).
[1200] ERA 1996, s 80G(1)(b)(ix).
[1201] See FWPR 2002, in particular reg 14.
[1202] FWPR 2002, reg 16.
[1203] ERA 1996, s 80H(1); FWER 2002, reg 6.
[1204] FWER 2002, reg 80I.
[1205] SI 2002/3207, reg 15. This is subject to the statutory maximum in ERA 1996, s 227(1), which at 1 February 2012 and at the time of writing stands at £430 per week.

In *Commotion Ltd v Rutty*[1206] the claimant asked to move from a full-time working week to a three day week upon becoming responsible for the care of her grandchild. Her request was refused on the grounds that the employer wanted to 'promote team spirit' as part of which all employees were expected to work full time. The EAT upheld a finding in favour of the claimant, noting that while the tribunal was not able to make a judgment of whether the employer's refusal was reasonable, it was able to judge whether the refusal had been on one of the grounds set out in the Act.

DISABILITY DISCRIMINATION

North American and European antecedents

6.123   The issue of disability discrimination was the subject of repeated attempts at legislative reform from the early 1980s onwards. The Disabled Persons (Employment) Act 1944 established a quota scheme for the employment of disabled persons which was widely considered to have been ineffective.[1207] In the United States, the civil rights model of anti-discrimination law was extended to cover disability discrimination as a result of two federal statutes, the Federal Rehabilitation Act 1973 and the Americans with Disabilities Act 1990. Title V of the 1973 Act imposed an obligation upon the federal government in its capacity as employer to adopt affirmative action programmes for the hiring, promotion and advancement of disabled persons, and put in place a federal contract compliance programme covering the employment practices of government contractors. The 1990 Act prohibited discrimination on the grounds of disability in both the private and public sectors, and covered not just employment but also housing, education, recreation and health services, as well as a number of other areas.

In 1986 a European Community Recommendation on the Employment of Disabled People was adopted which called upon Member States to eliminate discrimination by, amongst other things, 'limiting exceptions to the principle of equal treatment in access to training or employment to the cases justified on the ground of a specific incompatibility between a particular activity forming part of a job or course of training and a particular disability; if necessary, it should be possible to have this incompatibility confirmed by a medical certificate'.[1208] The Recommendation also contained a guideline framework for positive action to be taken by employers, workers' organisations and the state.

In 1990 the British Conservative Government responded to the growing pressure for reform of domestic legislation by issuing a consultative document which rejected the extension of anti-discrimination legislation to disability, on grounds which included the observation that 'a major difficulty is that disability, unlike sex or race, can be relevant to job performance and what might seem like discrimination may in reality be recruitment based on legitimate preferences and likely performance'.[1209] As Doyle commented, this argument 'does not withstand close scrutiny ... If a

---

[1206] [2006] IRLR 171; see also *Shaw v CCL Ltd* [2008] IRLR 284.

[1207] See Doyle, 1995: ch 2.

[1208] Recommendation 86/379, Art 2(a)(iii).

[1209] Department of Employment, *Employment and Training for People with Disabilities: Consultative Document*, 1990, at para 5.14.

disabled person is refused an employment opportunity because he or she cannot perform the work or is ill-suited to the job, that is not unlawful discrimination and it is not proposed that it should be so'.[1210] By January 1995 there had been a change in the official line, and a White Paper was published accepting the principle of legislative intervention.[1211] A government measure, the Disability Discrimination Bill, was published early in 1995; a more far-reaching private members' bill, the Civil Rights (Disabled Persons) Bill was introduced at about the same time but was pre-empted by the government's intervention.

The DDA 1995 repealed the quota system which operated under the Disabled Persons (Employment) Act 1944,[1212] and introduced a new framework of rights which was based on the then anti-discrimination model but only partially assimilated to it. The 1995 Act contained a distinctive definition of discrimination which was a 'hybrid, incorporating elements of direct and elements of indirect discrimination',[1213] but was not entirely like either of them. The Act only conferred rights on disabled people, not on the non-disabled; thus it left scope for positive action in favour of the disabled. It also introduced the concept of the employer's duty to make reasonable adjustments to the arrangements on the basis of which employment was offered, and to 'any physical feature of premises' which placed a disabled person 'at a substantial disadvantage in comparison with persons who are not disabled'.[1214]

The 1995 Act provided inspiration for the incorporation of a prohibition on disability discrimination into the EC Framework Directive on Discrimination in Employment which was adopted in December 2000,[1215] and this led, in its turn, to further amendments to the British legislation, strengthening and clarifying it.[1216] EqA 2010 made a number of further amendments to disability discrimination law in the context of employment, as well as more generally.[1217] The major change was to align disability discrimination for the first time with the core definitions of direct and indirect discrimination as set out, respectively, in sections 13 and 19 of the 2010 Act Some specific features of disability discrimination remained in place. The pre-2010 Act concept of 'disability-related discrimination' was retained in a strengthened form as 'discrimination arising from disability', on the basis that the extension of the concept of indirect discrimination to disability might not be sufficient to deal with all the situations that came within the scope of the earlier legislation.[1218] The duty of reasonable adjustment also remained, again in a strengthened form. The statutory definition of disability was little changed in substance from what went before. The UK's ratification in 2009 of the UN Convention on the Rights of Persons with Disabilities

[1210] Doyle, 1995: p 47.

[1211] *Ending Discrimination against Disabled People*, Cm 2729, 1995.

[1212] The 1995 Act retained the system of 'supported employment' in organisations providing work specifically designed for disabled persons, mostly in manufacturing. At that point, 13,000 persons worked in such employment: see Gooding, 1996: p 29. By 2011, the figure had fallen to below 3,000, and following the 'Sayce Review' of that year (Department for Work and Pensions, *Getting In, Staying In and Getting On: Disability Employment Support Fit for the Future*, Cm 8081, June 2011) the Coalition Government decided to withdraw funding for supported employment, the likely result of which is that the factories providing it will close ('Sayce Review response', DWP website, 7 March 2012 (www.dwp.gov.uk)).

[1213] *O'Neill v Symm & Co Ltd* [1998] IRLR 233, 235.

[1214] DDA 1995, s 6(1), as originally enacted.

[1215] Directive 2000/78/EC; see above, para 6.5.

[1216] In particular SI 2003/1673 and DDA 2005.

[1217] The changes made to the operation of the law in the employment sphere were, in general, less extensive than those affecting services and premises. See Hepple, 2011a: 32-34, 72-77; Lawson, 2011.

[1218] See Hepple, 2011a: 73-75; Lawson, 2011: pp 364-367.

appears to have had little impact on the drafting of the 2010 Act,[1219] a point to which we return in our analysis below.[1220]

The concept of discrimination in the context of disability

6.124   Under the 2010 Act, there are four variants of the statutory wrong of discrimination in relation to disability: direct disability discrimination, for which, as is normal under the Act, justification is no defence;[1221] the duty to make reasonable adjustments to avoid substantial disadvantage to a disabled person, a form of discrimination which is *sui generis* to disability;[1222] discrimination arising from disability, another statutory wrong that is distinctive to disability, and which extends the scope of the law's protection to a number of cases not covered by the core conceptions of discrimination, and which is subject to a justification defence;[1223] and finally indirect disability discrimination,[1224] which, as elsewhere under the Act, requires the employer to justify practices which result in group disadvantage, by reference to a test of proportional means to achieve a legitimate aim.

(i) Direct discrimination

6.125   The 2010 Act applies the statutory tort of direct discrimination to cases of disability,[1225] in this respect re-enacting the substance of the pre-2010 law. This, then, is the requirement that disability should not, as such, form the basis for decisions taken in the context of employment.[1226] There is no defence of justification to a direct disability discrimination claim.[1227]

As more generally in cases of direct discrimination, the critical issue concerns the identification of the relevant features of the comparator. Under the pre-2010 law, direct disability discrimination was defined as discrimination against a disabled person where 'on the ground of the person's disability, [the respondent] treats the disabled person less favourably than he treats or would treat a person not having that particular disability whose relevant circumstances, including his abilities, are the same as, or not materially different from, those of the disabled person.'[1228] The essence of this test is retained under the 2010 Act, which provides that, in general, 'there must be no material difference between the circumstances relating to' the case of the complainant and

---

[1219] The CRPD was adopted in 2006. For discussions of the CRPD which reach different conclusions on its meaning and significance for UK law but which nevertheless both see the 2010 Act as a limited response, at best, to the challenges posed by the Convention, see Lawson, 2011; Fraser Butlin, 2011.

[1220] See below, para 6.135.

[1221] See below, para 6.125.

[1222] See below, para 6.126.

[1223] See below, para 6.127.

[1224] See below, para 6.128.

[1225] EqA 2010, ss 13(1), 25(2)(a). On the definition of direct discrimination, see paras 6.14-6.21 above.

[1226] See *J.P. Morgan (Europe) Ltd v Chweidan* [2011] IRLR 673, at [5] (Elias LJ).

[1227] A defence of justification did apply to cases of direct disability discrimination under the original DDA 1995, but this defence was removed in the early 2000s when the provisions of the EC Framework Directive were implemented in UK law. See Lawson, 2011: p 371.

[1228] DDA 1995, s 3A(5).

the comparator,[1229] and that these circumstances 'include a person's abilities' in a case where the protected characteristic is disability.[1230]

Thus the application of the direct discrimination concept involves a comparison of the treatment of the complainant with that accorded to a person whose circumstances were in all relevant respects similar to that of the complainant, with the exception that they did not have the particular disability in question. The comparator can be either hypothetical or real. The EHRC *Employment Code of Practice* provides the following illustration of the operation of direct disability discrimination:

> A disabled man with arthritis who can type at 30 words per minute applies for an administrative job which includes typing, but is rejected on the grounds that his typing is too slow. The correct comparator in a claim for direct discrimination would be a person without arthritis who has the same typing speed with the same accuracy rate.[1231]

But applying the concept of direct discrimination in the context of disability will not always be straightforward. In *High Quality Lifestyles Ltd v Watts*[1232] the claimant was a support worker for an employer providing specialist services to people with learning difficulties. The employee was frequently scratched and cut as part of his work. He had been diagnosed as HIV positive prior to his application and revealed his condition to the employer, but only after several instances of cutting and scratching had occurred. The employer dismissed him after carrying out a risk assessment which found that injuries caused by cutting were commonplace. The grounds of dismissal were his alleged dishonesty in not reporting his condition earlier and the risk to patients of contracting HIV (although the employee's consultant had said the risk of HIV being transmitted was very small). The EAT held that the appropriate comparator was someone with an 'attribute, whether caused by a medical condition or otherwise, which is not HIV positive'. This attribute had to 'carry the same risk of causing to others illness or injury of the same gravity, here serious and possibly fatal'. [1233] As such a person would also have been dismissed in similar circumstances, there was no adverse treatment.

By contrast, the Court of Appeal judgment in *Aylott v Stockton-on-Tees Borough Council*[1234] demonstrates the scope for a more flexible approach. Here, the complainant, who was suffering from bipolar affective disorder, was dismissed for performance-related reasons, including inability to work to deadlines and confrontations with colleagues. The employment tribunal held that an appropriate comparator was an employee whose performance had been affected by a non-disability related reason such as a surgical procedure. On this basis, the tribunal ruled that there had been direct discrimination against the complainant on the grounds of his disability. The EAT reversed this ruling on the grounds that the appropriate comparator was an employee whose work record had caused similar concerns to those raised in the case of the complainant, as these were 'relevant circumstances' which the tribunal should have taken into account. The Court of Appeal restored the tribunal's ruling. According to Mummery LJ, the tribunal's choice of comparator was

---

[1229] EqA 2010, s 23(1).
[1230] EqA 2010, s 23(2)(a).
[1231] EHRC *Employment Code of Practice*, para 3.30.
[1232] [2006] IRLR 850.
[1233] [2006] IRLR 850, at [48].
[1234] [2010] IRLR 994.

one that was 'reasonably open' to it.[1235] He also warned against too literal a reading of the 'relevant circumstances' test, particularly in cases where, as here, there was evidence of stereotyped attitudes influencing the employer. *Aylott* was however distinguished in the subsequent Court of Appeal decision of *Aitken v Commissioner of Police of the Metropolis*,[1236] in a case where the employer's approach was said to be based not on stereotyping but on objectively verifiable observations of an employee's behaviour.

In principle, the 2010 Act allows claims for associative and perceptual discrimination on the grounds of disability. An associative claim of the kind raised in *Coleman v Attridge Law*,[1237] where the carer of a disabled person argued that her employer had treated her less favourably on grounds related to her son's disability, may now succeed without the need to invoke the Framework Directive as an aid to the interpretation of domestic legislation, as was necessary under the pre-2010 law.[1238] Direct discrimination may also arise on the basis of a perceived disability, but a practical problem here is that it may not be straightforward to establish that the employer thought that the complainant's condition was sufficiently serious to amount to a 'disability' in the specific sense required by the Act.[1239]

As under the pre-2010 law, EqA 2010 only confers rights on disabled people, not, by way of symmetry, on the non-disabled.[1240] Thus there is greater scope, in this context, for reconciling positive action for disadvantaged groups with the prohibition on direct discrimination.[1241]

(ii) The duty to make reasonable adjustments

6.126   A second form of disability discrimination occurs where an employer fails to make reasonable adjustments to avoid a substantial disadvantage to a disabled person.[1242] This statutory wrong dates back to the 1995 Act and so predates the EU Framework Directive, whose content it influenced.[1243] In contrast to the requirement, implicit in the idea of direct discrimination, that like should be treated alike, the logic of reasonable adjustment 'necessarily entails an element of more favourable treatment' for disabled persons.[1244]

Under section 20 EqA 2010, the duty comprises three requirements: firstly, a requirement 'where a provision, criterion or practice of [the employer's] puts a disabled person at a substantial

---

[1235] [2010] IRLR 994, at [44].

[1236] [2011] EWCA Civ 582, discussed by Lawson, 2011: pp 372-3.

[1237] Case C-303/06 *Coleman v Attridge Law* [2008] IRLR 722.

[1238] See *EBR Attridge Law v Coleman (No 2)* [2010] IRLR 10. It should be noted that, notwithstanding the changes made by EqA 2010 to the definition of direct discrimination, carers of disabled persons remain unprotected in certain significant respects, for example in relation to the duty of reasonable adjustment (see Lawson, 2011: p 373; Hepple, 2011a: pp 60-61).

[1239] See Lawson, 2011: pp 373-75, discussing *J v DLA Piper UK LLP* [2010] IRLR 936 and *Aitken v Commissioner of Police of the Metropolis* [2011] EWCA Civ 582, both arising under the pre-2010 law.

[1240] EqA 2010, s 13(3).

[1241] See our discussion of this point in the wider context of the concept of direct discrimination at paras 6.14–6.21 above. It should also be noted that although the Act thereby permits positive action in favour of disabled persons, it does not require it, although this may be the effect of the duty to make reasonable adjustments (see below, para 6.126).

[1242] EqA 2010 s 21(2) provides that 'A discriminates against a disabled person if A fails to comply with' the duty to make reasonable adjustments 'in relation to that person'.

[1243] See Lawson, 2011: p 367.

[1244] *Archibald v Fife Council* [2004] IRLR 651, at [47] (Baroness Hale).

disadvantage in relation to a relevant matter in comparison with persons who are not disabled, to take such steps as it is reasonable to have to take to avoid the disadvantage';[1245] secondly, a requirement again to take such steps where 'a physical feature puts a disabled person at a substantial disadvantage in relation to a relevant matter in comparison with persons who are not disabled';[1246] and thirdly, a requirement 'where a disabled person would, but for the provision of an auxiliary aid, be put at a substantial disadvantage in relation to a relevant matter in comparison with persons who are not disabled, to take such steps as it is reasonable to have to take to provide the auxiliary aid'.[1247] The application of the third of these requirements to the employment sphere is new to the 2010 Act. Section 20 specifies that where, in relation to the first and third requirements, the employer's duty involves the provision of information, the steps to be taken 'include steps for ensuring that in the circumstances concerned the information is provided in an accessible format'.[1248] It also provides that a person subject to the duty of reasonable adjustment may not require a disabled person to pay 'to any extent' the costs of complying with that duty.[1249] In the context of section 20, as elsewhere under the Act, a 'substantial' disadvantage is one which is 'more than minor or trivial'.[1250]

Schedule 8 of the Act specifies the scope of the duty in relation to employment, largely re-enacting the prior law. Thus the 'relevant matter' in respect of which a substantial disadvantage must be avoided is the decision to whom to offer employment, in the case of applicants for that employment, and employment by the employer, in the case of both applicants and employees.[1251] Similar provisions apply, *mutatis mutandis*, to define the scope of the duty of employers and principals of contract workers, partnerships and LLPs, barristers and advocates and their respective clerks, persons making appointments to offices, qualifications bodies, employment service-providers, trade unions and employers' associations ('trade organisations'), and local authorities.[1252]

Although the parts of the 2010 Act governing the duty of reasonable adjustment in the context of services and premises impose certain 'anticipatory' duties, those operating in the employment sphere are entirely 'reactive' in the sense of being triggered only if the employer has knowledge, or reasonably should have had knowledge, of the circumstances of the complainant. Thus in the case of applicants for employment, the duty only applies to arrangements for determining to whom employment is offered if the disabled person has notified the employer that he or she is an applicant for the employment in question.[1253] More generally, the employer is under no duty if it 'does not know, or could not reasonably be expected to know', that the disabled person is or may be an applicant for the work in question or, if already employed, 'has a disability and is likely to be placed' at a substantial disadvantage.[1254]

[1245] EqA 2010, s 20(3).
[1246] EqA 2010, s 20(4).
[1247] EqA 2010, s 20(5).
[1248] EqA 2010, s 20(6).
[1249] EqA 2010, s 20(7).
[1250] EqA 2010, s 212(1).
[1251] EqA 2010 , Sch 8, para 5(1).
[1252] See generally EqA 2010, Sch 8, Part 2.
[1253] EqA 2010, Sch 8, para 5(1).
[1254] EqA 2010, Sch 8, para 20. For pre-2010 Act case law on this point, see *O'Neill v Symm & Co Ltd* [1998] IRLR 233; *Ridout v TC Group* [1998] IRLR 628; *Fu v London Borough of Camden* [2001] IRLR 186; *Eastern and Coastal Kent Primary Care Trust v Grey* [2009] IRLR 429; *Secretary of State for Work and Pensions v Alam* [2010] IRLR 283.

The leading case on the meaning of the duty of reasonable adjustment under the pre-2010 law is the decision of the House of Lords in *Archibald v Fife Council*.[1255] The complainant, who was employed in a manual occupation, had a spinal anaesthetic for a minor operation, after which she was unable to walk without considerable pain. She received retraining for other jobs including non-manual work, but was unable to obtain a new position with the Council despite applying for over 100 posts. About two years after the operation, she was dismissed on the grounds that all efforts to redeploy her had failed. She claimed that, rather than being required to apply for a new post on the basis of competitive interviews, she should have been reallocated to a suitable alternative post once it became available. The employment tribunal held that the employers had not failed to comply with the duty to make reasonable adjustments. The House of Lords, remitting the case for a new hearing, held that the tribunal in this case had erred in rejecting the claimant's contention that it would have been a reasonable adjustment not to require her to go through competitive interviews if she could show that she was qualified and suitable for an existing vacancy. *Archibald* clearly shows that the duty to make adjustments may require the employer to treat a disabled person more favourably than persons without the disability in question, in order to remove the disadvantage that is attributable to the disability.

The statutory formula defining the duty of reasonable adjustment requires the tribunal to determine whether the complainant was put at a substantial disadvantage 'in comparison with persons who are not disabled'. In *Fareham College Corp v Walters*[1256] the EAT ruled that this formula does not require the tribunal to determine whether a non-disabled comparator would have been treated differently from the complainant; in this context, a 'like-for-like comparison' is not required.[1257] Rather, the tribunal must simply decide whether the disadvantage suffered by the complainant was related to the disability, for the purposes of which it may not be necessary to identify a precise class of comparators.[1258]

(iii) Discrimination arising from disability

6.127   A third form of disability discrimination arises under the 2010 Act where 'A treats B unfavourably because of something arising in consequence of B's disability',[1259] and A cannot show that the treatment is a proportionate means of achieving a legitimate aim.[1260] A must

---

[1255] [2004] IRLR 651. A substantial, if somewhat fact-specific, case law developed on the duty of reasonable adjustment following *Archibald*. See *Williams v J Walter Thompson Group Ltd* [2005] IRLR 376 (employer failed to provide promised equipment to enable a blind software operator to do her job); *Southampton City College v Randall* [2006] IRLR 18 (the employer did not do enough to provide assistance to a lecturer suffering from voice strain, such as providing voice enhancement equipment); *Rothwell v Pelikan Hardcopy Scotland Ltd* [2006] IRLR 24 (employer did not do enough to consult the employee, who had Parkinson's disease, about options with regard to his continuing employment); *O'Hanlon v Revenue and Customs Commissioners* [2007] IRLR 404, CA (the employer was not required to carry on paying an employee, absent through sickness, at her normal rate of remuneration); *Chief Constable of South Yorkshire Police v Jelic* [2010] IRLR 744 (tribunal entitled to find that the employer should have arranged a job-swap between the complainant and a fellow police officer). See also ch. 6 of the EHRC *Employment Code of Practice* (2011), and paras 82-88 of the *Explanatory Notes* on the 2010 Act.

[1256] [2009] IRLR 991, clarifying *Environment Agency v Rowan* [2008] IRLR 20.

[1257] [2009] IRLR 991, at [58].

[1258] See further the EHRC *Employment Code of Practice*, para 6.16.

[1259] EqA 2010, s 15(1)(a).

[1260] EqA 2010, s 15(1)(b).

know, or could reasonably have been expected to know, that B had the disability.[1261] Under the pre-2010 law, the equivalent provision to this required the complainant to show that 'for a reason which relates to the disabled person's disability, [the respondent] treats him less favourably than he treats or would treat others to whom that reason does not or would not apply' and 'he cannot show that the treatment in question is justified.'[1262] The comparator requirement embedded in this provision was flexibly interpreted by the Court of Appeal in *Clark v Novacold*[1263] to mean that the correct comparison was with a person to whom the reason for the less favourable treatment did not apply. The effect was that once a sufficient causal link between the complainant's disability and the less favourable treatment had been established, the focus shifted to the issue of justification. However, in *Lewisham London Borough Council v Malcolm*[1264] the House of Lords, in a housing case, ruled that *Clark v Novacold* had been wrongly decided. The claimant was a council tenant who had been given notice to quit for sub-letting. The tenant was suffering from schizophrenia and had stopped taking his medicine at the relevant time. The issue was whether the comparator was a tenant who had not sub-let, or one who had. The majority in *Malcolm* held that the correct comparator was a person who had sub-let and who did not have a mental disability. Baroness Hale's dissenting opinion, by contrast, drew on the legislative history of the DDA 1995 as well argument from its structure and intent to defend the decision in the *Novacold* case.

The new definition of 'discrimination arising from disability' in effect reverses *Malcolm* by removing the comparator requirement completely and by simplifying the statutory formula in a way that is designed to restore a test of causal connection between the complainant's disability and their unfavourable treatment.[1265] In addition, the new formulation of the proportionality test in the 2010 Act helpfully aligns the justification defence for this type of disability discrimination with similar definitions elsewhere in the Act.[1266]

The Labour government which drafted the 2010 Act was initially against the retention of this head of disability discrimination, arguing that the extension of the concept of indirect discrimination to cases of disability would be sufficient to deal with cases of unfavourable treatment arising from the application of a facially neutral provision, criterion or practice. It was finally persuaded to accept an argument to the effect that the concept of indirect discrimination, because of its emphasis on the need to show adverse impact arising from group disadvantage, might not capture all cases covered by the pre-2010 law (at least as it was interpreted prior to the decision of the House of Lords in the *Malcolm* case).[1267]

[1261] EqA 2010, s 15(2). For discussion of the background to the insertion of this knowledge requirement, see Hepple, 2011a: p 74.

[1262] DDA 1995, s 3A(1).

[1263] [1999] IRLR 318.

[1264] [2008] IRLR 700; see Horton, 2008.

[1265] See the *Explanatory Notes* on the 2010 Act , paras 69-70; Hepple, 2011a: p. 74; Lawson, 2011: pp 364-65.

[1266] See Lawson, 2011: p 365. The pre-2010 case law had applied, in this context, a test similar to the 'band of reasonable responses' test in unfair dismissal law (on which, see above, para 5.136); see *Jones v Post Office* [2001] IRLR 384; *Surrey Police v Marshall* [2002] IRLR 843; *Murray v Newham Citizens Advice Bureau Ltd* [2003] IRLR 340; *Mid-Staffordshire General Hospitals NHS Trust v Cambridge* [2003] IRLR 566; *Paul v National Probation Service* [2004] IRLR 190; *Williams v J Walter Thompson Group Ltd* [2005] IRLR 376.

[1267] See Lawson, 2011: p 366.

Indirect discrimination

6.128   The 2010 Act applies the statutory tort of indirect discrimination to disability for the first time.[1268] This is a significant step in particular because of the limitation of the duty of reasonable adjustment, in the employment context, to 'reactive' as opposed to 'anticipatory' measures.[1269] A convincing argument may be made to the effect that the case law on the extent of the 'anticipatory' duty of adjustment in the context of services could be called in aid in the interpretation, in future, of the concept of indirect disability discrimination.[1270] If this argument is correct, the flexible meaning given to the notion of group disadvantage in services cases[1271] could turn out to be of relevance in the employment context.

Pre-employment health enquiries

6.129   A new provision inserted by the 2010 Act makes it unlawful for a person (A) to 'whom an application for work is made' to 'ask about the health of the applicant (B)' either 'before offering the work to B' or, where A is not in a position to offer the work, 'before including B in a pool of applicants from whom A intends (when in a position to do so) to select a person to whom to offer work'.[1272] A breach of the provision may be relied on by an individual complainant in a claim of disability discrimination before an employment tribunal,[1273] and can also form the basis for enforcement by the EHRC.[1274] There are, however, a number of exceptions on which employers may seek to rely as justification for maintaining the practice of pre-employment health checks 'which frequently operates disproportionately to the disadvantage of people with one of the protected characteristics', including disability.[1275] The exceptions apply where the purpose of the question is to establish whether 'B will be able to comply with a requirement to undergo an assessment' or in establishing whether a duty to make reasonable adjustments will be imposed on A with respect to B in connection with such a requirement; in establishing whether 'B will be able to carry out a function that is intrinsic to the work concerned';[1276] in monitoring diversity in the range of persons applying to A for work; in taking positive action in recruitment or promotion under section 158 of the Act; and in determining whether B has a particular disability, which is an occupational requirement for the post in question.[1277]

[1268] EqA 2010, ss 19(3), 25(2)(c); on the elements of indirect discrimination, see paras 6.23-6.32 above. As Lawson (2011: p 375) explains, the government previously sought to rely on the derogation contained in Art 2(2)(b)(ii) of the Framework Directive to justify the non-application of indirect discrimination in the disability context, but this interpretation of the derogation was questionable.

[1269] See above, para 6.126.

[1270] Lawson 2011: pp 375-379; see also Hepple, 2011a: 77.

[1271] See, in particular, the judgment of Sedley LJ in *Roads v Central Trains* [2004] EWCA Civ 1540.

[1272] EqA 2010, s 60(1).

[1273] EqA 2010, s 60(3)-(5).

[1274] EqA 2010, s 60(2).

[1275] Lawson, 2011: p 371.

[1276] For discussion of this exception, see Lawson, 2011: pp 370-371.

[1277] EqA 2010, s 60(6).

Disability as a protected characteristic

6.130 For the purpose of EqA 2010, a 'disabled person' is a person 'who has a disability'[1278] or has had one.[1279] A person (P) has a disability if 'P has a physical or mental impairment' and 'the impairment has a substantial and long-term adverse effect on P's ability to carry out normal day-to-day activities'.[1280] A reference to a person with the protected characteristic of disability is a reference to a person 'who has a particular disability' and references to persons who share that characteristic is a reference to persons 'who have the same disability'.[1281]

The definition of disability is essentially unchanged from the pre-2010 Act law. The government has issued guidance on the meaning of disability in this context (henceforth '*Disability Guidance*').[1282] This breaks down the elements of the statutory definition into the linked components of 'impairment', 'substantial and adverse effect', 'long-term effect', and 'effect on normal day-to-day activities'. We shall consider each of these in turn.

(i) Impairment

6.131 The term 'impairment' is not defined in the Act. According to the *Disability Guidance*, the term 'should be given its ordinary meaning'.[1283] The Guidance states that an impairment need not arise from an illness, and that its precise cause does not have to be established.[1284] It also indicates that while an exhaustive list of conditions that qualify as impairments cannot be provided, and would in any event be subject to advances in medical knowledge, a disability can arise from 'a wide range of impairments'. These are set out[1285] in a non-exhaustive list which, building in part on case law, includes: sensory impairments affecting sight or hearing; impairments with fluctuating or recurring effects such as rheumatoid arthritis, myalgic encephalitis, chronic fatigue syndrome,[1286] fibromyalgia, and epilepsy; progressive conditions, such as motor neurone disease, muscular dystrophy, and forms of dementia; auto-immune conditions such as systemic lupus erythematosis; organ-specific and respiratory conditions,[1287] such as asthma, and cardiovascular diseases, including thrombosis, stroke and heart disease; developmental conditions, such as autistic spectrum disorders,[1288] dyslexia[1289] and dyspraxia; learning disabilities; mental health conditions with symptoms such as anxiety, low mood, panic attacks, phobias or unshared perceptions, eating disorders, bipolar affective disorders, post traumatic stress disorder and some self-harming behaviour; mental illnesses, such as

---

[1278] EqA 2010, s 6(2).
[1279] EqA 2010, s 6(4).
[1280] EqA 2010, s 6(1))
[1281] EqA 2010, s 6(3).
[1282] *Guidance on matters to be taken into account in determining questions relating to the definition of disability* (2011). The Guidance must be taken into account by a tribunal or other adjudicating body in any case where it appears to be relevant (EqA 2010, s 6(5); Sch 1, para 12
[1283] *Disability Guidance*, para A3.
[1284] Disability Guidance, para A3.
[1285] *Disability Guidance*, para A5.
[1286] *O'Neill v Symm & Co Ltd* [1998] IRLR 233.
[1287] *Ministry of Defence v Hay* [2008] IRLR 928 (tuberculosis).
[1288] *Hewett v Motorola Ltd* [2004] IRLR 545.
[1289] *Paterson v Commissioner of Police of the Metropolis* [2007] IRLR 763.

depression[1290] and schizophrenia;[1291] and conditions produced by injury to the body, including to the brain.

Under the pre-2010 law, an impairment affected a person's ability to carry out 'normal day-to-day activities' only if it affected one of the following: mobility; manual dexterity; physical co-ordination; continence; ability to lift, carry or otherwise move everyday objects; speech, hearing or eyesight; memory or ability to concentrate, learn or understand; and perception of the risk of physical danger. This 'checklist' has now been repealed.[1292] Regulations currently exclude a number of conditions from the definition of impairment: these are addictions to alcohol, nicotine or any other substance; pyromania, kleptomania, a tendency to physical or sexual abuse; exhibitionism and voyeurism; and seasonal allergic rhinitis (or hay fever).[1293] Conversely, cancer, HIV and multiple sclerosis are automatically characterised as disabilities,[1294] while persons who are certified as blind, severely sight impaired, sight impaired or partially sighted by a consultant ophthalmologist are deemed to be disabled for the purposes of the Act.[1295]

(ii) Substantial adverse effect

6.132   A 'substantial' effect is defined by the Act as one which is 'more than minor or trivial'[1296] and the *Disability Guidance* amplifies this by stating that 'the requirement that an adverse effect on normal day-to-day activities should be a substantial one reflects the general understanding of disability as a limitation going beyond the normal differences in ability which may exist among people'.[1297] This approach reflects the pre-2010 Act case law. In *Goodwin v Patent Office*[1298] the EAT suggested that '[w]hat the Act is concerned with is an impairment on the person's *ability* to carry out activities. The fact that a person can carry out such activities does not mean that his ability to carry them out has not been impaired'. *Goodwin* also established that the effect of a disability might be cumulative in the sense of impairing more than one capacity. The *Disability Guidance*[1299] sets out a number of factors which may have a bearing on whether an effect is 'substantial': these include the time taken to carry out an activity, the way in which an activity is carried out, the cumulative effects of an impairment, the modification by the person of his or her behaviour, and the effects of the working environment.

[1290] *Kapadia v London Borough of Lambeth* [2000] IRLR 699; *Greenwood v British Airways plc* [1999] IRLR 600; *Tarbuck v Sainsbury's Supermarkets Ltd* [2006] IRLR 664.

[1291] *Goodwin v Patent Office* [1999] IRLR 4.

[1292] See Hepple, 2011a: pp 34–35.

[1293] Equality Act (Disability) Regulations 2010, SI 2010/2128 (henceforth 'EADR 2010'), regs 3–5. A recognised condition, such as depression, is not outside the Act merely because it is induced in part by one of the listed exceptions: *Power v Panasonic UK Ltd* [2003] IRLR 151.

[1294] EqA 2010, Sch 1, para 7.

[1295] EADR 2010, reg 7.

[1296] EqA 2010, s 212(1).

[1297] *Disability Guidance*, para B1.

[1298] *Goodwin v Patent Office* [1999] IRLR 4, 7. See also *Leonard v Southern Derbyshire Chamber of Commerce* [2001] IRLR 19, suggesting that employment tribunals should focus on what applicants cannot do, or cannot do easily, rather than on what they can do, in determining whether the substantial adverse effect condition is satisfied. In *Paterson v Commissioner of Police of the Metropolis* [2007] IRLR 763 (applying the judgment of the ECJ in Case C-13/05 *Chacún Navas v Eurest Colectividades SA* [2006] IRLR 706) dyslexia was found to have had a substantial and long-term adverse effect on the claimant's ability to carry out his duties as a senior police officer.

[1299] Paras B2–B11.

In a number of cases the Act spells out what more precisely is meant by a 'substantial and adverse effect'. The first of these relates to the effect of medical treatment.[1300] An impairment is taken to have a substantial and adverse effect if 'measures are being taken to treat or correct it' and but for those measures the impairment 'would be likely to have that effect'. In *SCA Packaging v Boyle*[1301] the House of Lords gave this formula a broad meaning, ruling that it did not require the complainant to show that the effect was more probable than not, but that it 'could well happen'. In this context, relevant medical measures include 'medical treatment and the use of a prosthesis or other aid'. On the other hand, a sight impairment that is correctable by spectacles or contact lenses, or by similar means, does not fall within this provision. The *Guidance* suggests that a distinction needs to be drawn between a case in which the effect of medical treatment is to create a permanent improvement as opposed to a merely temporary one; in the former case, once the impairment is cured, no substantial adverse effects will remain. However, a person who is cured of a disability in this way may have a claim on the basis that he or she had a disability in the past.[1302]

A second situation that receives a more specific treatment in the Act is that of progressive conditions which 'increase in severity over time',[1303] such as motor neurone disease, muscular dystrophy, and forms of dementia. If a person (P) has a progressive condition which has an effect on his or her ability to carry out day-to-day activities, but that effect is not a substantial adverse one, 'P is to be taken to have an impairment which has a substantial adverse effect if the condition is likely to result in P having such an impairment'.[1304] As we have seen, the Act separately provides that the conditions of cancer, HIV and multiple sclerosis necessarily give rise to a disability,[1305] whether or not they meet this test.

A third case dealt with specifically by the legislation is that of severe disfigurements. These are treated as meeting the substantial adverse effect condition,[1306] unless they one of a number of deliberately acquired disfigurements set out in regulations.[1307]

(iii) Long-term effect

6.133 A 'long-term' effect is defined in the Act as one which has either 'lasted for at least 12 months', is 'likely to last for at least 12 months' or 'is likely to last for the rest of the life of the person affected' at the time the discrimination occurs.[1308] If the impairment ceases to have a substantial adverse effect, it is to be treated as continuing to have it 'if that effect is likely to recur'.[1309]

[1300] EqA 2010, Sch 1, para 5. See *Abadeh v British Telecommunications* plc [2001] IRLR 23; *Woodrup v London Borough of Southwark* [2003] IRLR 111; *Carden v Pickerings Europe Ltd.* [2005] IRLR 720.

[1301] [2009] IRLR 746.

[1302] *Disability Guidance*, para B17. On past disabilities, see para 6.130 above.

[1303] *Disability Guidance*, para B18.

[1304] EqA 2001, Sch 1, para 8.

[1305] EqA 2010, Sch 1, para 6.

[1306] EqA 2010, Sch 1, para 3. For examples of such disfigurement, see the *Disability Guidance*, para B25.

[1307] EADR 2010, reg 5 (tattoos and body piercings).

[1308] EqA 2010, Sch 1, para 2(1). The House of Lords' flexible ruling on the meaning of the term 'likely', taking it to refer to something would 'could well happen', applies here too (*SCA Packaging Ltd. v Boyle* [2009] IRLR 746.

[1309] EqA 2010, Sch 1, para 2(2); see *Greenwood v British Airways* plc [1999] IRLR 600; *Swift v Chief Constable of Wiltshire Constabulary* [2004] IRLR 540; *SCA Packaging Ltd v Boyle* [2009] IRLR 54.

The *Guidance* provides a number of indications of how these provisions are intended to operate. Firstly, the cumulative effect of a number of linked impairments should be taken into account. Thus 'the substantial adverse effect of an impairment which has developed from, or is likely to develop from, another impairment should be taken into account when determining whether the effect has lasted, or is likely to last at least 12 months, or for the rest of the life of the person affected'.[1310] Case law under the essentially equivalent pre-2010 legislation establishes that wholly unconnected impairments cannot be aggregated in this way, but that 'fine distinctions between one medical condition and its development into another are to be avoided'.[1311]

Secondly, the *Guidance* considers the issue of recurring and fluctuating effects. It suggests that examples of conditions which are likely to have recurring or fluctuating effects beyond 12 months are Menières disease, epilepsy, schizophrenia, bipolar affective disorder and certain types of depression.[1312] The *Guidance* notes that 'it is not necessary for the effect to be the same throughout the period which is being considered' and that an effect may disappear temporarily without ceasing to be 'long-term'.[1313] In relation to the issue of likelihood of recurrence, it suggests that while account should be taken of steps that a person can reasonably be expected to take to prevent the impairment from having a substantial and adverse long-term effect, difficulties in control or avoidance routines should also be considered.[1314]

Thirdly, the *Guidance* seeks to clarify the application of the Act to cases of past disability. Consistently with the inclusion of past disabilities within the scope of the legislation,[1315] it suggests that 'in deciding whether a past condition was a disability, its effects count as long-term if they lasted 12 months or more from the first occurrence, or if a recurrence happened or continued until more than 12 months after the first occurrence'.[1316]

(iv) Effect on normal day-to-day activities

6.134   The term 'normal day-to-day activities' is not defined in the legislation. The *Guidance* suggests that it does not cover 'activities which are normal only for a particular person, or a small group of people',[1317] although it indicates that the term can include activities which are not carried out 'by the majority of people' such as activities carried out predominantly by persons of a particular gender, giving breast-feeding as an example.[1318] In determining whether an activity is a 'day-to-day' one, it is suggested that account should be taken of 'how far it is carried out by people on a daily or frequent basis'.[1319] For this purpose, day-to-day activities can include both

---

[1310] *Disability Guidance*, para C2.
[1311] *Patel v Oldham Metropolitan Borough Council* [2010] IRLR 280, at [15] (Slade J). See also *College of Ripon and York St. John v Hobbs* [2002] IRLR 185; *McNicol v Balfour Beatty Rent Maintenance Ltd.* [2002] IRLR 711; *Ministry of Defence v Hay* [2008] IRLR 928.
[1312] *Disability Guidance*, para C6.
[1313] *Disability Guidance*, para C7.
[1314] *Disability Guidance*, para C10.
[1315] EqA 2010, s 6(4). See above, para 6.130.
[1316] *Disability Guidance*, para C12.
[1317] *Disability Guidance*, para D4.
[1318] *Disability Guidance*, para D5.
[1319] *Disability Guidance*, para D4.

work-related activities and those related to daily life outside work.[1320] Certain highly 'specialised' activities, such as working with specialised tools or playing a musical instrument to a high standard of achievement, will not, the *Guidance* suggests, be 'normal day-to-day' activities.[1321] The role of environmental factors and the possibility of indirect effects on activities are also clarified by the *Guidance*.[1322]

The adverse effect on normal day-to-day activities which arises from an impairment must be distinguished from the less favourable or unfavourable treatment which constitutes the gist of the statutory tort of discrimination (in whichever form is relevant in a particular case). In *Chief Constable of Lothian and Borders Police v Cumming*[1323] the complainant's application to join the respondent police force was rejected on the grounds that she did not meet the relevant eyesight standards for the post. The complainant suffered from a minor sight impairment in her left eye. She did not argue that this impairment, in itself, prevented her from carrying out the relevant work; on the contrary, she claimed that she could perfectly well perform the tasks that would have been required of her, having performed them already as a special constable. She claimed instead that the refusal of the respondent to offer her employment in itself amounted to an 'adverse effect' on her participation in professional life which amounted to disability discrimination. This claim was rejected, with the EAT ruling that 'the potential employer's refusal to progress the application is not a physical effect. If it was then a person who themselves suffered no adverse effects from a subsisting physical impairment would be rendered disabled if a potential employer rejected their application on the ground of that impairment'.[1324] The core of the decision is the EAT's insistence that 'the status of disability for the purposes of the DDA cannot be dependent on the decision of the employer as to how to react to the employee's impairment'.[1325] With the enactment of EqA 2010 and the extension of the concept of direct disability discrimination to cover perceived discrimination, a different outcome might now be possible in a case such as this, although some of the difficulties inherent in the concept of perceptual discrimination in this context need to be borne in mind.[1326]

Extending the concept of disability: 'medical' and 'social' models of disability

6.135 The UN Convention on the Rights of Persons with Disabilities ('CRPD') defines persons with disabilities as 'those who have long-term physical, mental, intellectual or sensory impairments which in interaction with various barriers may hinder their full and effective participation in society on an equal basis with others',[1327] and in its preamble refers to disability arising from 'interactions between persons with impairments and attitudinal and environmental factors'.[1328]

[1320] *Disability Guidance*, para D3.
[1321] *Disability Guidance*, paras D8-D10. See *Chief Constable of Dumfries and Galloway v Adams* [2009] IRLR 612 (working night shifts was a 'normal day-to-day activity' for a police officer).
[1322] *Disability Guidance*, paras D20-D22.
[1323] [2010] IRLR 109. See also *Paterson v Chief of Police of the Metropolis* [2007] IRLR 763.
[1324] [2010] IRLR 109, at [36] (Lady Smith).
[1325] [2010] IRLR 109, at [36] (Lady Smith).
[1326] See the discussion of this point by Underhill P in *J v DLA Piper UK LLP* [2010] IRLR 936, on the pre-2010 law, and our discussion at para 6.125 above.
[1327] CRPD 2006, Art 1.
[1328] CRPD, 2006, Preamble, para e.

This Convention thereby 'evinces a predominantly social model of disability, only partially circumscribed by a medical perspective'.[1329] A social model of disability is one which focuses on the institutional and organisational barriers to full participation in employment and society more generally on the part of disabled people, rather than on the medical conditions which are associated with the concept of 'impairment'.[1330] The CRPD, in addition to being ratified by the UK in 2009, was also ratified by the EU in the same year, and has been designated a 'Community treaty' within the meaning of section 1(2) of the European Communities Act 1972.[1331] This means that UK courts must give effect to its provisions.[1332] In practice this entails interpreting the EU Framework Directive and the domestic law of disability discrimination in line with the CRPD, in so far as that is possible. At present, the definition of disability under EqA 2010 more closely follows the medical model than the social one,[1333] and the same is arguably true of the conception of disability favoured by the ECJ.[1334] Even with the changes made by the 2010 Act, in particular the legislative recognition of the possibility of perceptual discrimination relating to disability, there may be limited scope for a move away from the medical model through judicial interpretation alone. The ratification of the CRPD may therefore prompt legislative reconsideration of the definition of disability. The current 'medical' model is arguably deficient in requiring 'gruelling and personally invasive' examination of the medical conditions of applicants, at the same time as 'distracting judicial and other attention from the behaviour of the alleged discriminator'.[1335]

ASSESSMENT

6.136   In numerous respects, equality law, as applied in the employment sphere, marks a radical departure from more traditional forms of labour law regulation. It provides a model for a type of labour legislation which extends beyond a narrow focus on the relationship of employer and employee. By regulating the hiring stage as well as aspects of the continuing employment relationship and by protecting certain economically dependent workers who are not 'employees' in the sense required by most of employment protection and social security legislation, it expresses the growing importance of rights operating at the level of the labour market and not simply at the level of the individual business enterprise. Equality legislation also explicitly recognises the individual's right to occupational training and development, by requiring equal access to professional and other associations and by supporting positive action in favour of minorities with regard to training and promotion and employment opportunities within employment.

In other ways, it is clear that the substantive scope of the legislation has until recently been restricted. If the goal of equal treatment legislation was a deeper recognition of the values of individual dignity and autonomy at work, it made no sense to limit the intervention of the law

---

[1329]   Fraser Butlin, 2011: p 432.

[1330]   Oliver, 1996; Lawson, 2011: p 361; Fraser Butlin, 2011: p 432.

[1331]   By SI 2009/1181.

[1332]   ECA 1972, s 2(1). In addition, there is the option of a complaint to the UN Committee on the Rights of Persons with Disabilities, under the Optional Protocol to the CRPD, which the UK has also ratified. See Fraser Butlin, 2011: p 429.

[1333]   In particular, through its stress on the need to show an 'impairment'. See above, paras 6.130–6.131.

[1334]   This is broadly the effect of the Court's judgment in Case C-13/05 *Chacún Navas v Eurest Colectividades SA* [2006] IRLR 706.

[1335]   Lawson, 2011: pp 361-62.

to discrimination on the grounds of sex, race and disability. Tangible progress had to await the adoption of Article 19 TFEU (as it now is) in the Treaty of Amsterdam in 1997, followed by agreement on the Race and Framework Directives of November 2000, and the subsequent revisions to the Equal Treatment Directive. These developments set in train the extension of domestic equality law to cover sexual orientation, gender assignment, religion or belief, and age. The EU measures also made significant changes to the core definitions of direct and indirect discrimination, by clarifying, in the case of the former, the concepts of associative and perceptual discrimination, and, in the case of the latter, by replacing the rigid language of the original anti-discrimination Acts with more flexible formulae.

Notwithstanding these changes, questions remain concerning the two-pronged approach to defining discrimination. The principle that like should be treated alike, which is enshrined in the concept of direct discrimination, is arguably at the core of the principle of equality. However, there are limits to the usefulness of this concept for remedying group disadvantage. In this respect, British legislation has historically made very few concessions to the goals of affirmative or positive action, and certainly far fewer than the US Civil Rights Act 1964. This is not just a question of sanctioning preferential treatment or reverse discrimination. That may be an important aspect of positive action programmes, but it is far from being the only one, and a strong argument can be made that what affirmative action is concerned with is not reverse discrimination as such but rather a notion of equality which fully recognises the role played by institutional forces and by stereotyped assumptions in reproducing the conditions for social disadvantage and injustice. In US practice, for example, affirmative action programmes were permitted by the Supreme Court precisely because in many cases they were put in place to overcome the historical legacy of institutionalised discrimination; this was not a denial of the principle of equal treatment but rather a means of strengthening it. The Supreme Court was able to sanction positive action in decisions taken in the years following the enactment of Title VII of the Civil Rights Act 1964 in part because the definition of adverse treatment in Title VII was relatively loose. By contrast, the definition of direct discrimination set out in section 1 of the SDA 1975 and of the RRA 1976 provided little scope for even the temporary and limited kind of affirmative action programme which the Supreme Court upheld in *United Steelworkers of America v Weber*.[1336] The changes made to EU law in the Treaty of Amsterdam, in particular the amendment of Article 157 TFEU (as it now is) to accommodate a wider notion of positive action, paved the way for the changes which were eventually enacted in section 159 of the Equality Act 2010, extending the scope for positive action in recruitment and employment.

The lack of a clear commitment in the legislation to a concept of equality more clearly focused on remedying collective disadvantage is also evident in the structure of enforcement mechanisms which is provided for. Over time the role of collective enforcement under the British legislation has diminished, thanks to the abolition of collective arbitration of equal pay claims before the Central Arbitration Committee. The courts' restrictive interpretations of the administrative enforcement powers of the EOC and CRE during the 1970s and 1980s demonstrated a similar reluctance to countenance the use of the Acts to tackle institutional disadvantage, although the powers granted to the Equality and Human Rights Commission by the Equality Act 2006 are more extensive than those of its predecessors. The risks and costs of individual litigation have been exacerbated by the

---

[1336] 443 US 193 (1979).

enormous complexity, in particular, of the procedures put in place for the adjudication of equal pay claims.[1337]

The scope of the defences to discrimination claims has also proved to be a critical issue. Much of the case law of the ECJ and of the domestic courts has been concerned with issues arising from the tension between the economic, efficiency-related goals of the legislation and the aim of eradicating institutional discrimination. The 'economic goal' of regulating labour market competition was one of the twin bases of Article 157 TFEU and of its development by the Court of Justice.[1338] As the technique of identifying adverse impact in apparently sex-neutral practices advanced, so did the range of arguments placed against it by way of justification; whereas these were at one time confined, in the context of equal pay, to the 'personal equation' of the applicant and his or her comparator, they have now broken the bounds set by the organisational limits of the business enterprise to embrace a variety of factors operating at the level of the labour market, including labour scarcity or simply, and more crudely, 'market forces'. A vital issue here is how far the courts will be prepared to take arguments concerning efficiency at their face value. In its landmark judgment in *R v Secretary of State for Employment, ex p EOC*[1339] the House of Lords was sceptical of such arguments, insisting that the respondent had not met the high burden of proof imposed on the respondent in adverse impact cases, and over time the courts have taken a stricter approach to the analysis of the justification defence, encouraged in this direction by the statutory tightening of the test of proportionality, again influenced by EU law.

The Equality Act 2010 has been described as 'a major landmark in the long struggle for equal rights',[1340] and it can be justifiably be seen as having achieved a number of the objectives set out by the Labour Government at the outset of the process of deliberation and consultation which led to its drafting and enactment. The Act harmonised and simplified the core concepts of equality law and made significant substantive changes in the form of the greater encouragement given to positive action. In other respects, however, the Act was a less than radical measure. It retained the approach of legislating for each of the different protected characteristics separately, neglecting arguments for more 'synergistic' approaches to addressing the causes of social disadvantage.[1341] In harmonising the treatment of the different protected characteristics, the Act risked extending the non-discrimination model into areas, in particular those relating to expressions of religious and other beliefs in the workplace, in which its operation not just highly contentious but also potentially counter-productive when set in the context of the wider goals of equality law.[1342] It missed the opportunity provided by the UK's ratification of the UN Convention on the Rights of Persons with Disabilities to move disability discrimination law away from a 'medical' model of disability. The Act did little to minimise the high costs of the predominant litigation-based approach to remedying inequality, notably failing to address the complexities of the procedures for determining equal pay claims.[1343] The unwillingness of the Coalition Government which came into office in 2010 to bring into force certain of the Act's provisions, such as those relating to the disclosure of information on the gender pay gap, and its watering down of others which had been

[1337] Gilbert, 2012.
[1338] Case 43/75 *Defrenne v Sabena* [1976] ECR 455.
[1339] [1994] IRLR 176.
[1340] Hepple, 2011a: p 1.
[1341] Solanke, 2011; Hepple, 2011a: p 185.
[1342] Pitt, 2011.
[1343] See Gilbert, 2012; Deakin, Chai and McLoughlin, 2012.

designed to encourage a proactive approach to inequality issues, most notably in the case of the public sector equality duty,[1344] have further limited the Act's effectiveness, at least for the time being. The 2010 Act marks not so much the culmination of equality law as a 'new beginning',[1345] and debates over its aims and effectiveness are likely to continue for some time.

[1344] See Hepple, 2011b; Fredman, 2011.
[1345] Hepple, 2011a: 186.

7

COLLECTIVE ORGANISATION: TRADE UNIONS AND EMPLOYERS' ASSOCIATIONS

INTRODUCTION

7.1   We have described in earlier chapters the central role which collective bargaining has played as a source of norms in labour law in Britain. In this chapter we examine from a broader perspective the nature and functions of collective organisations in the employment context and the relationship between such organisations and the law. In doing so we provide a framework for the more detailed analysis of the substantive law which follows in chapters 8 to 10. We discuss the development of the law relating to industrial action in chapter 11.

   This chapter begins by outlining the rationale for, and role of, collective organisation on the part of workers and employers respectively. We do not attempt to describe exhaustively here how these organisations have developed, the variety of structures which they may assume and the disparate range of functions which they may perform; these are areas upon which many library shelves can be filled. Our focus is to explain in basic terms the factors which stimulate the formation of such organisations and the ways in which they may attempt to influence decisions both in the workplace and beyond. We then discuss the various international standards relevant to this area. There follows an overview of the history of legal policy in this country towards collective organisation, with particular reference to the ideology which has shaped the current law. We then analyse some basic legal concepts in this area: the definition of a 'trade union', of an 'employers' association', and of trade union 'independence' and 'recognition', terms which are crucial in discussing the application of a series of statutory provisions dealt with in later chapters and which also embody some important assumptions about the legitimate functions of such organisations. We conclude the chapter by commenting briefly upon the influence which trade unions now exercise in contemporary employment relations and the challenges which they face in a changing labour market.

THE RATIONALE AND ROLE OF COLLECTIVE ORGANISATION

7.2   On the workers' side there are compelling reasons for collective action. In advanced industrial societies the employer almost always has greater economic and social power than any individual worker. Occasionally a worker may be in a stronger bargaining position if he or she possesses skills or experience which are much in demand although even then entry into a contract of employment may, as we explain in chapter 3, entail subordination to the commands of the employer. However, for workers in general to have any effective power in the employment relationship they must join together to further their demands on a collective basis; only then can they stand any chance of counterbalancing the power of the employer.[1]

The means by which workers' organisations have sought to exercise this function has varied over time and between countries. In analysing the development of British unions Turner's distinction between 'open' and 'closed' unions is a helpful one.[2] 'Closed' unions were those whose primary interest consisted of regulating the supply of labour to particular occupations and which maintained an exclusive claim to employment within those occupations. As a result these organisations had little interest in increasing their numerical strength; indeed their interest lay rather in the opposite direction. By contrast the larger 'open' unions were 'content to recruit all workers in those occupations whom the employers themselves engage[d]'. Being usually unable to bring pressure on employers through controlling labour supply they relied instead upon strength of numbers for their bargaining power.

7.3   Since the nineteenth century British trade unions have, in general, perceived their primary role as the improvement of their members' terms and conditions of employment through the mechanism of collective bargaining. As we have seen already this is not merely the functional equivalent of individual bargaining on a collective scale; rather it is more accurately described as a process of joint regulation which prescribes not only the terms upon which individual contracts should draw but may also extend to broader aspects of job regulation and the working environment, such as disciplinary and grievance procedures and training.[3] As such it is capable of serving as a conduit for wider democratic participation on the part of workers in the operation of the enterprise although clearly the extent to which it performs this function will depend upon a variety of different factors.

A further benefit of effective collective organisation is that it may assist workers to enforce their legal rights. The provision of statutory rights is sometimes seen as antipathetic to collective organisation which, it is argued, can be rendered otiose if workers can enforce their rights directly through the legal system or by complaint to an administrative agency. Kahn-Freund, for one, would have given short shrift to such an argument. Evidence relating to compliance with nineteenth-century legislation regulating deductions from workers' wages led him to conclude that:

> Where labour is weak ... Acts of Parliament, however well intentioned and well designed, can do something, but cannot do much to modify the power relation between labour and management. The law has important functions in labour relations but they are secondary if compared with the impact of the labour market ... and ... with the spontaneous creation of a social power on the workers' side to balance that of management. Even the most efficient inspectors can do but little if the workers dare not complain to them about infringements of the legislation they are seeking to enforce ...[4]

---

[1] See P Davies and M Freedland, 1983: ch 1.
[2] See H Turner, 1962: pp 241–242.
[3] See generally Flanders, 1970.
[4] P Davies and M Freedland, 1983: p 19

Although there is now statutory protection in some areas for workers who are discriminated against for attempting to enforce certain statutory rights[5] the protection which the law can provide in this respect is ultimately limited and it seems likely that Kahn-Freund's argument is no less applicable today. Polls have shown that many workers join unions because of the access which this gives to legal representation.[6] Representation by an organisation which has the knowledge to recognise the potential of test cases is additionally beneficial in putting pressure on employers to comply with their legal obligations. It can also mean that cases are more likely to be brought which clarify the law in workers' interests; where, for example, it is necessary to test compliance with European Union obligations. Nevertheless, although the provision of this and other benefits to members, such as welfare and financial benefits, has been a traditional part of union activity it has generally been regarded as secondary to collective bargaining. This focus is, indeed, reflected in the statutory definition of a 'trade union' which requires such an organisation to have as among its principal purposes the regulation of relations between workers and employers.[7] This definition, which we explore in greater detail in para 7.20, has been interpreted to mean that the organisation must at least have sought recognition from an employer for the purposes of collective bargaining to constitute a 'trade union'.[8] Although other forms of representation, such as assistance in disciplinary and grievance proceedings,[9] are also important, collective bargaining remains fundamental to trade union purposes.

7.4 The commitment to collective bargaining has also been important in shaping unions' activities beyond the workplace. As we discussed in chapter 1, unions in this country, unlike some of their European counterparts, achieved industrial power before they achieved political power through the extension of the franchise, and reliance upon collective bargaining rather than legislation as the preferred method of securing the best possible terms and conditions of employment remained even after they obtained greater access to political influence. This is not to say that the union movement stayed wholly aloof from the political process; for any interest group it is essential to ensure that the legal and economic environment is hospitable to its goals and operation and that the views of its members are adequately represented in the political process by lobbying and other means. Indeed the TUC – the first permanent federation on a multi-union basis – was formed in 1868 as an annual meeting of unions to discuss matters of common interest, with a 'parliamentary committee' which directed union campaigns between such meetings to influence the political parties to support pro-union legislation. Moreover, the Labour Party in its inception was a product of the trade union movement; a number of TUC-affiliates combined with the Marxist Social-Democratic Federation, the Independent Labour Party and the Fabian Society to establish a Labour Representation Committee from which emerged the modern Labour Party. It is notable, however, that it was the landmark case of *Taff Vale Rly Co v ASRS*,[10] where the House of Lords decided that trade unions, although not corporate bodies, could be sued for the torts of

---

[5] ERA 1996, s 104; see para 5.98 above. For the protection afforded by the equality legislation see ch 6.
[6] Mr John Monks, General Secretary TUC, Evidence to the House of Commons Employment Committee, Session 1993–1994, Third Report, The Future of Trade Unions, Volume II, p 20, Q 31.
[7] TULRCA 1992, s 1(a).
[8] See *Midland Cold Storage Ltd v Turner* [1972] ICR 230, NIRC, discussed at para 7.20 below.
[9] See ERelA 1999, ss 10–15 for the statutory right to be accompanied; see further para 5.121 *et seq*.
[10] [1901] AC 426.

their officials,[11] which inspired the TUC to participate in this project; once unions had obtained as much as they thought possible in the Trade Disputes Act 1906 they returned to industrial activity.[12] The law has explicitly recognised the legitimacy of trade unions pursuing political objects since the Trade Union Act 1913 although subject to approval of the establishment of a separate political fund for expenditure on such objects from which members must be able to claim exemption from contributing.[13] This provision thus assumes and incorporates a distinction between the industrial and the political realms. Although it may be argued that this is an impossible line to draw, particularly at times when legislation in the labour field is central to the programmes of the major political parties, it nevertheless remained undisturbed even during periods when the Labour Party was in power and has continued to this day.

7.5   As well as being affiliated to a political party or acting as a pressure group trade unions may also be more closely integrated into the political process. Again the extent to which this occurs varies widely between countries and within individual countries at particular times. In France, Belgium, the Netherlands, Portugal and Luxembourg, for example, there has been an obligation to consult national tripartite or bipartite bodies before new labour legislation is introduced.[14] In a number of European countries the concept of unions and employers' organisations as 'social partners' is much more developed than in Britain, a concept which, as we saw in chapter 2, has been reflected in European Union law. In some states tripartite agreements between unions, employers and government have been concluded to attempt to reconcile collective bargaining with the government's economic objectives, agreements which may also embrace aims such as increasing employment, combating price rises and helping the low-paid.[15] In addition, tripartite bargaining may be used as a basis for introducing labour market reforms.[16] In this country the role of unions has been subject to considerable variation. During the two World Wars trade union leaders were appointed to ministerial office in order to ensure co-operation of the labour movement in promoting the war effort. During the 1945–1951, 1964–1970 and 1974–1979 Labour Governments unions were brought into the political process through attempts to constitute arrangements whereby they would exercise restraint in pursuing pay demands in return for legislative and administrative policies which were perceived to further the interests of union members. The legislation of the 'Social Contract' period of the 1974–1979 Labour Government was a striking illustration of this process. Even under Conservative governments before 1979 trade unions exercised a measure of influence, such as participation in the National Economic Development Council, a (tripartite) body established in 1962 with policy functions in relation to economic planning and in the organisation of industrial training.[17] The NEDC was abolished in 1992 and, indeed, from 1979 until 1997 unions were progressively marginalised in relation to the political process, an element in the broader strategy of undermining their role as socially legitimate organisations. The election of a Labour Government

---

[11] Between 1906 and 1982 trade unions could not, with specified exceptions, be sued in tort. The Employment Act 1982 removed this immunity.

[12] Hepple, 1986a: p 25.

[13] See further para 10.18 *et seq.*

[14] Deakin *et al*, 1992: p 21.

[15] Bamber *et al*, 2010.

[16] Deakin *et al*, 1992: p 21.

[17] See P Davies and M Freedland, 1993: pp 333–345 for the activities of the Heath Conservative Government in this area and see paras 1.20 and 1.21 above.

in 1997 produced a more hospitable environment, with a greater emphasis on 'social partnership' and enhanced institutionalised participation in specific areas, such as training.[18] However, the government was keen from the outset to avoid the appearance that the union movement would enjoy any favoured status; indeed, one commentator observed that '[t]rade unions were from the start treated as an embarrassing relic, as welcome as elderly working class relatives at an Islington party',[19] another that Prime Minister Blair 'appeared to give more of his time to wooing big business tycoons like Rupert Murdoch of News International' than to union leaders.[20] The entry into office of a Coalition Government in 2010 has not, at the time of writing, led to a substantial shift in policy towards trade unions.

In addition to their marginalisation by government during the 1979–1997 Conservative administration, the collective bargaining role of unions was also subject to severe challenge and trade unions were left fighting a difficult struggle to maintain their role as bargaining partners and to retain their membership. We shall see in para 7.30 and later chapters the variety of attempts which they made to counteract these trends by, *inter alia*, becoming publicly more open to other forms of representative structures, such as consultative bodies, and broadening the range of services which they offer their members. There have been signs of a reduction in the rate of decline in union membership in recent years,[21] and factors such as complex employment protection legislation and the right for individuals to be accompanied by a union representative during disciplinary and grievance hearings, as well as the statutory recognition and information and consultation procedures, may encourage workers to join.[22] The range of roles that unions may play in the rapidly changing political and economic environment should not disguise the quintessential rationale for the existence of trade unions, however: in Kahn-Freund's ringing phrase, on the side of labour the (only) power is collective power.[23]

7.6   On the employers' side the rationale for collective organisation is different from that of workers. Although employers do form associations both at sectoral and national multi-industry level these are not the functional equivalent of trade unions in that the individual employer is already a 'collective power' in being a holder of capital. In Europe the reasons historically which led to associations being formed vary from the desire to oppose the labour movement (Denmark and Germany) to exerting an influence upon legislators (the Netherlands and Italy).[24] In Britain 'it was the realisation by employers in industries such as building, engineering and printing that they could be defeated one by one by the craft unions that led them to associate, as in the Engineering Employers' Federation (1897)'.[25] After the First World War employers' associations became more significant negotiators in collective bargaining. In industries where firms were small

---

[18] See W Brown, 2000, who notes the importance for the legitimacy of recommendations made by the Low Pay Commission that three of its members were, in practice, from union backgrounds: see further para 4.46.

[19] W Brown, 2008: p 188.

[20] Taylor, 2000: p 265. See also, on 'New Labour' and the trade unions, J Waddington, 2003a; P Smith and Morton, 2006; P Davies and M Freedland, 2007: pp 236-40; McIlroy and Daniels, 2009; McIlroy, 2009.

[21] See Achur, 2011: p 3; and para 7.30 below. Note, however, that budget cuts in public services, where union density is greatest, may accelerate the decline in membership.

[22] Aggressive anti-union tactics by employers may also be significant, however, together with a range of other variables: see generally Charlwood 2003, 2004a; Freeman and Diamond, 2003; Simms and Charlwood, 2010.

[23] P Davies and M Freedland, 1983: p 17.

[24] A Jacobs, 1986: pp 222–223.

[25] A Jacobs, 1986: p 223.

the knowledge and experience of the association could be particularly advantageous. Since the Second World War the significance of employers' associations in that area has declined in tandem with the decline in sectoral bargaining, a trend which accelerated further during the 1980s.[26] Their other major traditional role, as a source of information and advice to employers, has also diminished,[27] although this varies between sectors.[28] The main national employers' organisation, the Confederation of British Industry, was formed in 1965 by the merger of three earlier bodies; its membership is largely drawn from the manufacturing sector. As in the case of unions the 'social dialogue' has afforded the CBI the opportunity of a wider role.

INTERNATIONAL STANDARDS RELATING TO COLLECTIVE ORGANISATION

Overview

7.7   Freedom of association is regarded as a fundamental right under international human rights conventions. An important element of this right is the freedom of workers to associate in order to further and defend their interests.[29] The fundamental importance of freedom of association in this context is emphasised by its presence in treaties dealing both with civil and political rights, on the one hand, and economic, social and cultural rights on the other. The Universal Declaration of Human Rights, adopted by the United Nations General Assembly in 1948, proclaims that '[e]veryone has the right to form and to join trade unions for the protection of his interests', a right which was given effect in international law by the International Covenant on Economic, Social and Cultural Rights (ICESCR) and the International Covenant on Civil and Political Rights (ICCPR) of 1966.[30] Freedom of association has been a fundamental principle of the ILO since its inception in 1919; the ingredients of the freedom are spelt out in a number of instruments, the most important being the Freedom of Association and the Right to Organise Convention 1948 (No 87) and the Right to Organise and Collective Bargaining Convention 1949 (No 98).[31]

---

[26] Roderick Martin, 1992: p 83. In contrast to the demise of multi-employer bargaining over pay in Britain, this structure continues to prevail in many other Western European countries although an element of decentralisation is becoming more common: Carley, 2008. As of 31 March 2011 there were 106 known employers' associations: The *Annual Report of the Certification Officer for 2010–2011* paras 1.7, 1.13. However, in many sectors membership fails to reach 50% of the eligible companies: P Edwards *et al*, 1998: p 19; see also Millward *et al*, 2000: p 75. As of 31 March 2008 there were 146 employers' associations so the number has declined sharply within a three-year period: The *Annual Report of the Certification Officer for 2007–2008* para 1.13. Cockburn states that an increasing number of employers' associations are reorganising themselves as trade associations, removed from any involvement in industrial relations: Cockburn, 2006: p 96.

[27] Millward *et al*, 2000: pp 73, 75; Kersley *et al*, 2006; p 53.

[28] See the role of the Engineering Employers' Federation, for example, which claims to have around a quarter of the UK's manufacturing businesses as members: see www.eef.org.uk.

[29] The freedom of employers to associate is also affirmed in ILO Conventions and the European Social Charter and is implicit in general guarantees.

[30] On the background to the right in the ICESCR, see Craven, 1998.

[31] Other ILO Conventions which seek to ensure respect for the principles of freedom of association are: Right of Association (Agriculture) 1921 (No 11); Right of Association (Non-Metropolitan Territories) 1947 (No 84); Workers' Representatives, 1971 (No 135); Rural Workers' Organisations 1975 (No 141); Labour Relations (Public Service) 1978 (No 151); Collective Bargaining 1981 (No 154); and Private Employment Agencies 1997 (No 181). On ILO standards in this area see generally Creighton, 2010.

However, it is assumed that the very fact of membership of the ILO carries with it a constitutional obligation to respect these principles.[32] The right is also expressed in treaties agreed at a regional level including the European Convention on Human Rights (ECHR) and the European Social Charter (ESC), and, most recently, the Charter of Fundamental Rights of the European Union.[33] In addition, as we discuss in para 7.11, there is authority for its recognition as a 'fundamental right' within the EU legal order, albeit that it is excluded from the Social Policy provisions of TFEU.[34]

There is, therefore, wide agreement upon the importance of the right of workers to associate both as the hallmark of a democratic society and more specifically in their role as economic actors. There is less consensus, however, about the scope of this right in practice, beyond the basic right to form and to join trade unions.[35] Does it, for example, include the right to form or join a union of one's choice regardless of the impact upon industrial relations? Does it include the right not to join a union?[36] Does it include a right to organise? Does it include a right for trade unions to engage in collective bargaining? Does it imply a right to strike? What level of interference, if any, by the state in the affairs of unions should be permitted? In this section we discuss, in broad terms, the approach to the scope of freedom of association adopted by various international bodies; the implications of their conclusions for British law is analysed in greater detail at appropriate points in the chapters which follow.

7.8 The most detailed elaboration of the right to freedom of association is contained in the relevant ILO Conventions, supplemented by the jurisprudence of the Governing Body's Committee on Freedom of Association[37] and reports of the Committee of Experts on the Application of Conventions and Recommendations.[38] Convention No 87 provides that all workers 'without distinction whatsoever, shall have the right to establish and, subject to the rules of the organisation concerned, to join organisations of their own choosing without previous authorisation'.[39] Such organisations also have the right to establish and join federations and confederations and to affiliate with international organisations of workers.[40] In addition there are guarantees relating to the free functioning of organisations.[41] Member States undertake to take 'all necessary and appropriate measures' to ensure that workers may exercise freely the right to organise, and the law of the land shall not impair guarantees in the Convention.[42] Convention No 98 provides that workers should enjoy adequate protection against acts of anti-union discrimination in respect of their employment and their organisations should enjoy adequate protection against interference by other organisations and by employers in their establishment, functioning and

---

[32] See now the *ILO Declaration on Fundamental Principles and Rights at Work and its Follow-Up*, ILO, 1998, reaffirmed in *ILO Declaration on Social Justice for a Fair Globalization*, 2008, and on the special machinery to deal with alleged failures of compliance in this area see para 2.41 above.

[33] See further para 2.39 for the status of the Charter. For further regional instruments in other areas of the world see Creighton, 2010.

[34] Art 153(5).

[35] See generally Wedderburn 1987b; Christian and Ewing, 1988; Leader, 1992; Betten, 1993; G Morris, 1994a; Bercusson 2000: pp 416–420; Novitz, 2003.

[36] We discuss the scope of the right not to join in para 8.28 *et seq* below.

[37] The key features of this jurisprudence are digested in ILO, 2006

[38] For a general survey of reports to the date of publication, see ILO, 1994.

[39] Art 2.

[40] Art 5.

[41] Art 3.

[42] Arts 11 and 8(2). See generally Gernigon *et al*, 2000.

administration.[43] The Convention also states that measures appropriate to national conditions should be taken, where necessary, to encourage and promote collective bargaining machinery.[44] However ILO supervisory bodies have said that this does not require governments to enforce collective bargaining by compulsory means with a given organisation as such an intervention would alter the voluntary nature of collective bargaining, although 'this does not mean that governments should abstain from any measure whatsoever aiming to establish a collective bargaining mechanism'.[45] There is no express reference in either of these Conventions to the right to strike. However, ILO supervisory bodies have derived this right from them on the basis that it is one of the essential and legitimate means by which workers and their organisations may promote and defend their economic and social interests and is therefore integral to the free exercise of the rights they guarantee (with the proviso that in the case of public officials recognition of the freedom to associate does not necessarily imply the right to strike).[46] Although less detailed than the ILO Conventions the ICESCR also obliges signatory states to ensure the right of everyone to join the union of their choice, subject to the union's rules; the right of unions to join federations, confederations and international union organisations; and the right of unions to function freely.[47] In addition it explicitly guarantees the right to strike, although subject to the proviso that 'it is exercised in conformity with the laws of the particular country'.[48] The ESC, the economic and social counterpart to the ECHR, also expressly includes, in Article 6, obligations to promote joint consultation between workers and employers and, where necessary and appropriate, collective bargaining machinery and the right to strike.[49]

7.9   The ICCPR and ECHR both articulate trade union freedom as a manifestation of a broader freedom to associate. Article 11 of the ECHR provides that 'Everyone ... has the right to freedom of association with others, including the right to form and to join trade unions for the protection of his interests'. Until recently the European Court of Human Rights (ECtHR) adopted a narrow interpretation of this right which failed to take account of its function in the employment context.[50] In 1975 it held that the Article did not give union members a right that their union should be able

---

[43] Art 1 and 2. Again there is an obligation to establish 'machinery appropriate to national conditions', where necessary, to ensure respect for the right to organise: Art 3.

[44] Art 4. See also Convention 154 Concerning the Promotion of Collective Bargaining (1981) (not ratified by the UK) and Recommendations 92 on Voluntary Conciliation and Arbitration (1951), 130 on Examination of Grievances (1967) and 163 on Collective Bargaining (1981).

[45] ILO 2006: para 929.

[46] ILO, 2006: paras 520 *et seq*. See also Hodges-Aeberhard and Odero de Dios, 1987; Ben-Israel, 1988; Gernigon *et al*, 1998; Novitz, 2003: ch 8. For discussion of the permissible restrictions on this right, and of the scope of the right to strike under other international treaties, see paras 11.3 and 11.4 below.

[47] Art 8. See Craven 1998: ch 7; Joseph, 2010.

[48] Art 8(1)(d).

[49] A revised ESC, which accords additional rights in the field of employment, was open for signature in May 1996: see para 2.43. The UK signed the revised Charter in November 1997, but at the time of writing has not ratified it. Arts 5 and 6, and the terms of Art 31, remain the same in both versions of the Charter; Art 31 is Art G in the new Charter.

[50] For an overview to the date of publication, see Novitz, 2003: pp 224 *et seq*. See also *Collymore v A-G of Trinidad and Tobago* [1970] AC 538, where the Privy Council held that constitutional protection of freedom of association does not extend to collective bargaining and the right to strike. Cf Hendy and Walton, 1997. In *Health Services and Support-Facilities Subsector Bargaining Association v British Columbia* 2007 SCC 27 the Supreme Court of Canada overruled its previous jurisprudence in holding that freedom of association in the Canadian Charter of Rights and Freedoms 1982 extended to collective bargaining: see further Fudge, 2008, although see also *AG of Ontario v Fraser* 2011 SCC 20, discussed Fudge, 2012.

to engage in collective bargaining nor even that it should be consulted by their employer. The Court denied that this rendered otiose the words 'for the protection of his interests' in Article 11. The words showed that:

> ... the Convention safeguards freedom to protect the occupational interests of trade union members by trade union action, the conduct and development of which the Contracting States must both permit and make possible ... It follows that the members of a trade union have a right, in order to protect their interests, that the trade union should be heard. [However the article] leaves each State a free choice of the means to be used towards this end. While consultation is one of these means, there are others. What the Convention requires is that under national law trade unions should be enabled, in conditions not at variance with Article 11, to strive for the protection of their members' interests.[51]

The Court also stated that:

> In view of the sensitive character of the social and political issues involved in achieving a proper balance between the competing interests and, in particular, in assessing the appropriateness of State intervention to restrict union action aimed at extending a system of collective bargaining, and the wide degree of divergence between the domestic systems in the particular area under consideration, the Contracting States should enjoy a wide margin of appreciation in the choice of the means to be employed.[52]

In its 2002 decision in *Wilson and NUJ v UK; Palmer, Wyeth and RMT v UK* and *Doolan v UK*,[53] however, the Court showed greater appreciation of the rationale of freedom of association in the context of employment. In these cases the employers had each refused a pay rise to employees who refused to transfer to personal contracts in place of collectively agreed terms and conditions of employment. These contracts also required those who signed them to forgo the entitlement to be represented by a union in some or all of their dealings with the employer. While continuing to state that collective bargaining was 'not indispensable for the effective enjoyment of trade union freedom' the Court affirmed that '[t]he union and its members must, however, be free, in one way or another, to seek to persuade the employer to listen to what it has to say on behalf of its members'.[54] Moreover, it was 'of the essence of the right to join a trade union for the protection of their interests that employees should be free to instruct or permit the union to make representations to their employer or to take action in support of their interests on their behalf.[55] Here, UK law had permitted employers to treat less favourably employees who were not prepared to renounce a freedom that was an essential feature of union membership, so allowing an employer 'effectively to undermine or frustrate a trade union's ability to strive for the protection of its members'

---

[51] *National Union of Belgian Police v Belgium* judgment of 27 October 1975, (1979–80) 1 EHRR 578 at para 39; *Swedish Engine Drivers Union v Sweden* judgment of 6 February 1976, (1979–80) 1 EHRR 617, para 40.

[52] *Gustafsson v Sweden* judgment of 28 March 1996, (1996) 22 EHRR 409, para 45. In this case (noted Novitz, 1997) the Court affirmed that the Convention did not guarantee a right not to enter a collective agreement.

[53] Judgment of 2 July 2002, [2002] IRLR 568. For differing opinions on the implications of this decision, see Ewing, 2003; cf *Review of the Employment Relations Act 1999: Government Response*, DTI, 2003, ch 3. See also paras 8.17 *et seq* below.

[54] Para 44.

[55] Para 46.

interests'.[56] By permitting employers to use financial incentives to induce employees to surrender important union rights, the State had failed in its positive obligation to secure the enjoyment of the rights under Article 11 of the Convention, a violation as regards both the applicant unions and the individual applicants.[57]

This decision was seen as representing 'a significant break with the past'[58] but it did not, as 'yet',[59] accord a specific right to recognition or consultation.[60] Finally, in the landmark case of *Demir and Baykara v Turkey*, the ECtHR unanimously decided that its previous jurisprudence should be 'reconsidered, so as to take account of the perceptible evolution in such matters, in both international law and domestic legal systems'.[61] Having reviewed the terms of ILO Conventions, the ESC (as interpreted by the ECSR), the EU Charter of Fundamental Rights,[62] and the practice of European States, including Turkey, the Court concluded that:

> ... the right to bargain collectively with the employer has, in principle, become one of the essential elements of the 'right to form and to join trade unions for the protection of [one's] interests' set forth in Article 11 of the Convention, it being understood that States remain free to organise their system so as, if appropriate, to grant special status to representative trade unions. [63]

Accordingly, any interference with this right must comply with the requirements of Article 11(2), which states that no restrictions shall be placed on the exercise of the rights in Article 11(1) other than such as are 'prescribed by law and are necessary in a democratic society in the interests of national security or public safety, for the prevention of disorder or crime, for the protection of health or morals or for the protection of the rights and freedoms of others'. The Court affirmed that, in determining whether any interference with the exercise of trade union rights was justified, or the State had failed in its positive duty to take reasonable and appropriate measures to secure an applicant's rights, the State had only a 'limited margin of appreciation'.[64]

Demir and Baykara concerned the annulment by the Turkish courts of an existing collective agreement between a union representing municipal civil servants and a Municipal Council, which was found by the ECtHR to constitute a violation of Article 11. This decision did not require the ECtHR to consider the broader scope of the right to bargain collectively under that article. Does it exceed the right not to be subject to State interference in relation to collective bargaining? If so,

---

[56] Para 48.

[57] Para 48.

[58] Ewing, 2003: p 5.

[59] The term interestingly, used by the ECtHR in *Wilson* and *Palmer* above, note 53, at para 44.

[60] On Arts 11 and 14 together see *Swedish Engine Drivers Union v Sweden* judgment of 6 February 1976, (1979–80) 1 EHRR 617, paras 44–48. See also *National Union of Belgian Police v Belgium* judgment of 27 October 1975, (1979–80) 1 EHRR 578, paras 43–49 and *Schettini v Italy* admissibility decision of 9 November 2000.

[61] Judgment of 12 November 2008, [2009] IRLR 766, para 153. This was a decision of the Grand Chamber of 17 judges.

[62] Art 28 provides that workers and employers, or their respective organisations, have, in accordance with Community law and national laws and practices, the right to negotiate and conclude collective agreements at the appropriate levels. See para 2.39 for the status of the Charter.

[63] Above, note 61, para 154.

[64] Above, note 61, para 119.

what is the nature of any positive obligation on the state?[65] Does it require the state as employer to bargain in good faith and the state as legislator to require private employers so to do? If so, does it require bargaining to take place with representative unions or is the employer free to choose its bargaining partner, however unrepresentative it may be? Does it require an obligation to conclude collective agreements and to apply the terms and conditions they contain? What does it require in the event that parties fail to reach an agreement?[66] These are questions which are likely to come before the Court in future cases. An important feature of *Demir and Baykara* is the willingness of the Court to have regard to other international norms regardless of whether they had been accepted by Turkey. Although the Court said that in 'searching for common ground among the norms of international law' it had never distinguished between sources according to whether or not they had been signed or ratified by the respondent State,[67] in the past the fact that the ESC allows contracting states some discretion as to the articles they accept was relied upon by the ECtHR to bolster a narrow interpretation of Article 11. Thus the Court took the view that, given that a state may not have accepted Article 6 of the ESC, to conclude that a right to joint consultation derived directly from Article 11 would 'amount to admitting that the 1961 Charter took a retrograde step in this direction'.[68] *Demir and Baykara* suggests that this line of reasoning has now been abandoned.

Demir and Baykara is important in Britain for three reasons. First, as we explain in para 9.7, it may expose British law to challenge. In this regard, the significance accorded by the ECtHR to other jurisprudence, including that of the ILO, may make domestic courts more receptive to arguments based on that jurisprudence when considering what is required by the HRA 1998.[69] Second, the UK Government has consistently failed to comply with the conclusions of ILO bodies and the ECSR in the area of collective labour law whereas decisions of the ECtHR have carried much greater weight. Third, recognition by the ECtHR that Article 11 supports a right to bargain collectively makes it likely that the ECJ will also hold that this right can be derived from the right to freedom of association which, as we discuss in para 7.11 below, has been recognised as a fundamental right in EU law.

The application in *Demir and Baykara* did not require the ECtHR to consider whether Article 11 gave a right to strike in the event that collective bargaining proved unsuccessful.[70] Unlike the supervisory organs of the ILO, the ECtHR had not, until very recently, been prepared to derive the right to strike from the general principle of freedom of association, traditionally taking the view that while it is 'one of the most important' of the means by which the occupational interests of trade union members may be protected by trade union action, 'there are others'.[71] This approach was modified somewhat in 2002 in *UNISON v UK*, where it was argued that the right to strike, and thereby freedom of association, was unjustifiably restricted under UK law. Here,

---

[65] The ECtHR reiterated the principle established in previous case law that Art 11 may impose positive obligations on the state to secure the effective enjoyment of the rights protected: above, note 61, para 110.

[66] For the principles applied by the ILO, see ILO, 2006, ch 15 and Creighton, 2010. On the narrow scope accorded to the right by the Canadian Supreme Court, see Fudge, 2008, 2012.

[67] Above, note 61, para 78.

[68] *Belgian Police v Belgium*, above, note 60, para 38.

[69] See further para 11.9 below.

[70] Above, note 61, para 158.

[71] *Schmidt and Dahlstrom v Sweden* judgment of 6 February 1976, (1979–80) 1 EHRR 632 at para 36. See also *X v Germany* Application No 10365/83,(1985) 7 EHRR 461. Ben-Israel, 1988: pp 28–29, however, considers that the Court provided 'powerful support' for the argument that freedom to strike is essential to freedom of association.

the Court was prepared to acknowledge that the strike in question concerned 'the occupational interests of the applicant's members' and therefore fell within the scope of Article 11, although it concluded that the prohibition on the strike could be justified under Article 11(2) on the ground that it protected the rights of the employer, including its ability to contract with other bodies.[72] As Ewing remarks, this decision accorded the right to strike 'a curious twilight status'; although not formally protected, the Court regarded restrictions on the right as falling within Article 11(1).[73] In *Enerji Yapi-Yol Sen v Turkey*[74] the ECtHR held that a ban preventing public sector employees from taking part in a one-day national strike in support of the right to a collective-bargaining agreement violated Article 11. This decision, together with other case law of the ECtHR, has been widely interpreted (including judicially) as supporting the conclusion that the right to strike is conferred by Article 11(1),[75] leaving the extent of permissible restrictions to be governed by Article 11(2).

The ECtHR has also taken into account ILO Convention No 87 and the ESC (and conclusions of the ECSR) when considering the freedom of unions to choose their members.[76] In *ASLEF v UK* the Court confirmed that:

> The right to form trade unions involves ... the right of trade unions to draw up their own rules and to administer their own affairs. Such trade union rights are explicitly recognised in Articles 3 and 5 of ILO Convention No. 87 ... .
>
> Article 11 cannot be interpreted as imposing an obligation on associations or organisations to admit whosoever wishes to join. Where associations are formed by people who, espousing particular values or ideals, intend to pursue common goals, it would run counter to the very effectiveness of the freedom at stake if they had no control over their membership. By way of example, it is uncontroversial that religious bodies and political parties can generally regulate their membership to include only those who share their beliefs and ideals. Similarly, the right to join a union 'for the protection of his interests' cannot be interpreted as conferring a general right to join the union of one's choice irrespective of the rules of the union: in the exercise of their rights under Article 11(1) unions must remain free to decide, in accordance with union rules, questions concerning admission to and expulsion from the union ... .[77]

In assessing whether an intervention in internal trade union matters could be justified under Article 11(2), the Court reiterated its long-standing view that pluralism, tolerance and broadmindedness are hallmarks of a 'democratic society' and stated that:

> ... democracy does not simply mean that the views of a majority must always prevail: a balance must be achieved which ensures the fair and proper treatment of minorities and avoids any

---

[72] Admissibility decision of 10 January 2002, [2002] IRLR 497. See further para 11.26 for discussion of this case.
[73] Ewing, 2003: p 18.
[74] Judgment of 21 April 2009.
[75] *RMT v Serco Docklands*; *ASLEF v London Midland* [2011] IRLR 399, CA, Elias LJ at [8]; see also Ewing and Hendy 2010, 2011. Countouris and Freedland, 2010.
[76] *ASLEF v UK* judgment of 27 February 2007, [2007] IRLR 361, paras 22-25, 38, 39; see also the decision of the European Commission on Human Rights in *Cheall v UK* Application No 10550/83, (1986) EHRR 74. For discussion of the implications of this decision see paras 10.3, 10.10 and 10.21 below.
[77] Above, paras 38 and 39.

abuse of a dominant position. For the individual right to join a union to be effective, the State must nonetheless protect the individual against any abuse of a dominant position by trade unions ... Such abuse might occur, for example, where exclusion or expulsion from a trade union was not in accordance with union rules or where the rules were wholly unreasonable or arbitrary or where the consequences of exclusion or expulsion resulted in exceptional hardship.[78]

The Court affirmed that, since this was 'not an area of general policy, on which opinions within a democratic society may reasonably differ widely' the margin of appreciation available to the domestic policy-maker would 'play only a limited role'.[79]

7.10   The discussion above indicates a much greater willingness by the ECtHR to take account of other international treaties in interpreting the scope of the right to freedom of association.[80] In *Demir and Baykara* the ECtHR also adopted this approach in relation to the permissible exceptions to the freedom to associate. All the treaties which guarantee the right exempt specific groups from its application, leaving their position to be regulated entirely by national law; some also allow restrictions to meet specified objectives.[81] For most treaties the armed forces and the police are the only categories specifically exempted; however, the ECHR and the ICESCR also allow 'lawful restrictions' on the exercise of this right by 'members ... of the administration of the state'. The dangers of these disparities were demonstrated when, in 1984, the UK Conservative Government peremptorily banned membership of national civil service unions by workers at Government Communications Headquarters (GCHQ), which safeguards the security of the UK's military and official communications and provides signals intelligence for the government.[82] This ban was found to breach ILO principles of freedom of association.[83] However a complaint that it infringed Article 11 of the ECHR was ruled inadmissible by the (now defunct) European Commission on Human Rights on the ground that workers at GCHQ were 'members ... of the administration of the state',[84] a finding invoked by the Government to add weight to its refusal to accept the finding by the ILO.[85] In later cases the ECtHR held that the concept of 'members ... of the administration of the state' should be ' interpreted 'narrowly, in the light of the post held by

---

[78] Above, para 43.

[79] Above, para 46.

[80] For a more recent example see *Paloma Sanchez v Spain* judgment of 12 September 2011, [2011] IRLR 934.

[81] For a detailed examination of the scope of these exemptions, see G Morris, 1994a.

[82] See G Morris, 1985b for the background to this ban.

[83] Freedom of Association Committee, Case 1261, whose recommendation was adopted by the Governing Body of the ILO in June 1984. The ILO regularly and repeatedly exhorted the UK government to reach an agreement with the unions which would reconcile the government's wish for continuity of operations with the application of freedom of association principles and welcomed the decision by the Labour Government to do this: see the Provisional Record of the International Labour Conference, Eighty-Fifth Session, Geneva, 1997, Report of the Committee on the Application of Standards, 19/100–19/101.

[84] *CCSU v UK* Application No 11603/85 (1987) 10 EHRR 269. The Commission also rejected the applicants' argument that 'restrictions' in Art 11(2) did not extend to a complete ban. See further Fredman and Morris, 1988.

[85] See Report of the ILO Committee of Experts on the Application of Conventions and Recommendations, Report III (Part 4A), 1992: pp 242–243 and see generally Creighton, 1994; G Morris, 1994a; Ewing, 1994a and Mills, 1997. The ban on union membership at GCHQ was also found not to infringe the ESC (see ESC Committee of Independent Experts Conclusions X-1 (1989), 80) although the reasons for this were not spelled out.

the official concerned'[86] and in *Demir and Baykara* the Court affirmed that restrictions imposed on any of the three groups specified 'must not impair the very essence of the right to organise' and the State must show the legitimacy of any such restrictions.[87] This goes some way to reducing the difficulties caused by the broader terms of Article 11 although ideally the standards set by the tripartite ILO have the greatest claim to legitimacy in this area.

Freedom of Association in EU Law and EU Competition Law

7.11   As we indicated in para 7.7 above, the Social Policy provisions of the TFEU (like its predecessor) expressly exclude the right of association and the right to strike.[88] However, despite this barrier to future legislation on these matters, the ECJ has recognised them as 'fundamental rights' within EU law. As we saw in para 2.39, the Treaty on European Union explicitly bound the EU to respect as general principles of Community law fundamental rights as guaranteed by the ECHR, and as they result from the constitutional traditions common to the Member States,[89] and this is reflected in the current treaty.[90] However, even before this provision was introduced, the ECJ had held that fundamental rights were integral to Community law,[91] so obliging both Community institutions and Member States when acting in the field of Community law to respect them. The status of freedom of association as a fundamental right was affirmed by the ECJ in *Bosman*.[92] Furthermore, the ECJ had held, in the context of considering the ambit of the right to union membership enshrined in EU Staff Regulations, that this right entailed that staff associations are 'free to do anything lawful to protect the interests of their members as employees',[93] and that Community institutions may not penalise their staff from participating in union activities.[94] In *Albany* Advocate General Jacobs considered, on the basis of these authorities, that the collective right of workers to take action, in addition to the right to form and join a union, had thereby been confirmed as a fundamental right in EU law.[95] In 2007, in *ITWF v Viking Line*, the ECJ, referring to various international instruments including the EU Charter of Fundamental Rights,[96] agreed that 'the right to take collective action, including the right to strike, must ... be recognised as a

[86] *Vogt v Germany* judgment of 26 September 1995, (1996) 21 EHRR 205, para 67; *Grande Oriente D'Italia di Palazzo Giustiniani v Italy* judgment of 2 August 2001, para 31.
[87] Above, note 61, para 97. The ECtHR did 'not share the view of the Commission' in *CCSU v UK*, above, note 84, that 'lawful' in Art 11(2) required no more than that the restriction in question should have a basis in national law and not be arbitrary.
[88] Art 153(5).
[89] Art 6(2) EU.
[90] Art 6(3) TFEU.
[91] Case 11/70 *Internationale Handelsgesellschaft mbH v Einfuhr und Vorratsstelle fur Getreide und Futtermitte* [1970] ECR 1125, 1134; Case 4/73 *Nold v Commission* [1974] ECR 491, para 13.
[92] Case C-415/93 *Union Royale Belge des Societes de Football Association ASBL v Jean-Marc Bosman* [1995] ECR I-4921, paras 79 and 80. See also Case C-499/04 *Werhof v Freeway Traffic Systems Gmbh and Co KG* [2006] IRLR 400, para 33, where the ECJ relied on ECtHR jurisprudence to hold that this included the right not to join an association or union.
[93] Case 175/73 *Union Syndicale, Massa and Kortner v Commission* [1974] ECR 917, para 14.
[94] Joined Cases C-193/87 and C-194/87 *Maurissen and European Public Service Union v Court of Auditors of the European Communities* [1990] ECR I-95, paras 11–16 and 21.
[95] Case C-67/96 *Albany International BV v Stichting Bedrijfspensioenfonds Textielindustrie* Opinion of 28 January 1999, [1999] ECR I-5751, para 139. See also Council Regulation 2679/98, art 2.
[96] Art 28.

fundamental right which forms an integral part of the general principles of Community law'.[97] However, as we discuss in para 11.52 below, it did so in a context where this right operated as a defence to employers' claims that their free movement rights under the EC Treaty had been infringed by trade unions and, as such, the Court required individual instances of collective action to be subject to forms of scrutiny which may severely limit the scope of the right in practice. As the right recognised by the ECJ is also subject to provisions of national law the Court's decision has the effect of adding new restrictions to those already present in relation to disputes with a cross-border dimension.

In *Albany*, Advocate General Jacobs considered whether collective bargaining could be considered a fundamental right.[98] He concluded that it could not, despite the emphasis placed upon the concept of 'social dialogue' and collective agreements within the EU legal order. In his view, national legal systems and international instruments did not sufficiently converge in recognising such a right: the guarantee of the right to bargain collectively in Article 6 of the ESC did not accord it fundamental status, given that acceptance of Article 6 was optional on the part of signatory states;[99] ILO Convention 98 merely imposed an obligation to 'encourage and promote' collective bargaining, and no such right could be derived from Article 11 of the ECHR. He also opined that the collective bargaining process, like any other negotiation between economic actors, was sufficiently protected by the general principle of freedom of contract, so obviating the need for more specific protection.[100] In so reasoning, Advocate General Jacobs overlooked the fact that, as we have emphasised in earlier chapters, collective bargaining is not merely the functional equivalent of individual negotiation.

Since *Albany*, there have been two important developments which cast further doubt on Advocate General Jacobs' conclusion that collective bargaining is not a fundamental right in EU law. First, the EU Charter of Fundamental Rights provides that '[w]orkers and employers, or their respective organisations, have, in accordance with Community law and national laws and practices, the right to negotiate and conclude collective agreements at the appropriate levels'.[101] Although not legally binding, as we discuss in para 2.39 the Charter has been used by the ECJ as a source of general principles of EU law. Second, as we saw in para 7.9 above, the ECtHR has now 'reconsidered' its previous case law, which influenced Advocate General Jacobs, and held that the right to bargain collectively is inherent in Article 11 of the ECHR.

The issue of the status of collective bargaining arose in *Albany* because the ECJ was required to consider for the first time the crucial question of the relationship between collective agreements and social policy measures, on the one hand, and EU competition law on the other. Article 101 TFEU (formerly Article 81 EC) prohibits agreements between undertakings, decisions by associations of undertakings and concerted practices which may affect trade between Member States and which have as their object or effect the prevention, restriction or distortion of competition within the common market, and renders such agreements void. In *Albany*, the Court

---

[97] Case C-438/05, para 44, [2008] IRLR 143. See also Case c-341/05 *Laval Un Partneri Ltd v Svenska Byggnadsarbetareforbundet* [2008] IRLR 160, para 91.

[98] For discussion of *Albany*, see Barnard and Deakin, 2000; Vousden, 2000; Evju, 2001b. For a comparison between the *Albany* test and 'EFTA Guidelines', see Johansen, 2004.

[99] Advocate General Jacobs also, controversially, classified the rights in the ESC as mere 'policy goals', given that they were not 'enforceable rights': Opinion, para 146.

[100] Opinion, paras 131–161.

[101] Art 28.

had to decide whether a sector-level collective agreement establishing a pension fund, which had been given compulsory legal effect, was contrary to Article 101. Advocate General Jacobs rejected the argument of the pension funds that social policy was outside the ambit of the competition rules altogether; there was no provision authorising such exemption in the Treaty.[102] He also rejected the Commission's view that collective agreements should be excluded; even if, contrary to his view, collective bargaining was a fundamental right, this would not suffice to shield it from competition law.[103] However, he recognised that there were provisions of the Treaty and the then Agreement on Social Policy (now incorporated in the Social Policy provisions of the Treaty) that encouraged collective bargaining, and which thereby assumed that collective agreements were in principle lawful. On this basis, he proposed that a collective agreement should have immunity from review under competition rules if it complied with three conditions: first, it had been made 'within the formal framework of collective bargaining between both sides of industry'; second, it was made 'in good faith', and third, it dealt with 'core subjects of collective bargaining such as wages and working conditions which do not directly affect third markets and third parties'.[104] The third of these conditions was particularly restrictive, and would have opened up many multi-employer agreements to the review of competition policy authorities.[105] By contrast, the Court, which emphasised the general social policy objectives of the Treaty in addition to the provisions encouraging social dialogue, adopted a much broader view of the exemption. It affirmed that it was:

> ....[b]eyond question that certain restrictions of competition are inherent in collective agreements between organisations representing employers and workers. However, the social policy objectives pursued by such agreements would be seriously undermined if management and labour were subject to ... [Article 101 TFEU] ... when seeking jointly to adopt measures to improve conditions of work and employment. It therefore follows from an interpretation of the provisions of the Treaty as a whole which is both effective and consistent that agreements concluded in the context of collective negotiations between management and labour in pursuit of such objectives must, by virtue of their nature and purpose, be regarded as falling outside the scope of ... [Article 101][106]

This test, which focuses upon the aims the social partners are pursuing in negotiations, accords much greater respect to the autonomy of the social partners than the criteria propounded by the Advocate General.[107] Nevertheless it is not free from difficulty. Collective bargaining may take place on a range of matters whose relationship with the improvement of conditions of work and employment may be tangential, such as those relating to family life, for example.[108] It remains to be seen whether *Albany* will mark the beginning of a tide of litigation relating to the application of

---

[102] Opinion, paras 120–130. Art 101(3) allows the provisions of Art 101(1) to be declared inapplicable in specified circumstances, but none relates to social policy objectives.

[103] Opinion, para 163.

[104] Opinion, paras 165–194.

[105] Barnard and Deakin, 2000: p 335.

[106] [1999] ECR I-5751, paras 59 and 60.

[107] See also Case C-222/98 *Van der Woude v Stichting Breatrixoord* [2000] ECR I-7111, where the Advocate General considered that the scope of the exception from Art 101 is not 'limited to matters that the parties to the agreement are capable of carrying out themselves'. The Court did not expound on this view. See generally Evju, 2001b.

[108] See further Vousden, 2000.

the boundary it establishes,[109] but there seems much to be said in favour of amending the Treaty specifically to exclude social policy measures from the application of competition rules.[110]

LEGAL POLICY RELATING TO COLLECTIVE ORGANISATION[111]

7.12   Legal policy relating to collective organisation in this country has passed through a series of radical changes. In common with the rest of Western Europe, the initial response to the growth of trade unionism was to attempt to suppress it by means of the criminal law.[112] As we saw in chapter 1, during the eighteenth century a number of Acts of Parliament forbade combinations in specific trades and places (clothing and London respectively in particular)[113] and combining workers could also be prosecuted for conspiracy at common law. At the turn of the century a new and more comprehensive statutory offence was created by the famous Combination Acts of 1799 and 1800 which made all combinations of workmen unlawful.[114] These Acts applied also to employers who combined for specified purposes but there appears to be no record of employers being convicted under them, possibly because 'the justices [who heard proceedings] were from the employers' class and would likely be their close neighbours or personal acquaintances'.[115] In practice the Acts were enforced only infrequently even against unions, perhaps because there was no shortage of other legal weapons available, including the Master and Servant Acts which made it a criminal offence to break a contract of employment.

In 1824/25 Britain became the first country in Western Europe to remove criminal sanctions from trade unions when the Combination Acts and other legislation forbidding combinations were repealed. Interestingly the leading campaigner for their repeal, Francis Place, was not a champion of trade union organisation; rather he believed that recruits were attracted to joining associations because of their illegal status and that once the prohibitions were repealed they would wither away. This did not happen; indeed, the newly-legalised organisations[116] demanded higher wages, and furthered these demands by strikes. This led to amending legislation in 1825 which modified the 1824 Act in two important ways. First, whilst confirming the repeal of the previous statutory restrictions, it excluded the application of common law conspiracy only for combinations (both of workmen and, *mutatis mutandis*, of employers) concerned with wages, prices and hours of work. Secondly, it severely restricted the freedom to strike by creating criminal offences involving

---

[109] See also Case C-271/08 *Commission v Germany* [2011] All ER (EC) 912, discussed Syrpis, 2011.

[110] For further discussion of this point in relation to the impact on industrial action of EU law on freedom of movement, see para 11.52 below.

[111] The account which follows is intended merely to highlight in broad terms the strategies which have lain behind the development of the law and to provide a backcloth for the more detailed analysis of the contemporary law which follows in subsequent chapters. For recent histories of this area see Orth, 1991; P Davies and M Freedland, 1993; Rubin, 2000; P Davies and M Freedland, 2007.

[112] See A Jacobs, 1986.

[113] See Orth, 1991: ch 2.

[114] The Acts appear to have been inspired partly by fears of the potentially revolutionary nature of trade unionism and partly because industrial action was obstructing trade: Elias and Ewing, 1987: p 1.

[115] Elias and Ewing, 1987: p 1.

[116] Sidney and Beatrice Webb found no instance of the use of the term 'trade union' in the first third of the nineteenth century: Webb and Webb, 1920: p 113.

vague and indeterminate terms such as violence to the person or property, intimidation and molestation.

The repeal of the statutory prohibitions on combinations, whilst removing the fear of prosecution, did not accord any specific legal status to workers' organisations and their position was, in fact, problematic. As unincorporated associations they were prey to officials embezzling their funds who, because the property was owned jointly by all the members, were merely taking their own property in so doing. The Friendly Societies Act 1855 enabled the officials of societies with benefit functions to be prosecuted in case of fraud and it was assumed that the Act applied to trade unions provided they complied with specified formalities. However, in *Hornby v Close*[117] the court declared that because the purposes of trade unions were in restraint of trade they were 'illegal' and thereby fell outside the scope of this Act. In 1867 a Royal Commission was established to investigate the whole question of trade unionism. This produced a majority report which proposed that unions should be governed by a highly restrictive regime, and a minority report, drafted by union sympathisers, which recommended that unions be accorded the legal protections which they required in order to function but otherwise should be free from legal supervision. The minority approach prevailed with the Liberal government which accepted the principle of non-intervention in union affairs. This led to the Trade Union Act 1871 which provided that the purposes of trade unions should not, by reason of being in restraint of trade, be deemed unlawful so as to render any member liable to criminal prosecution (section 2) and stipulated that the restraint of trade doctrine should not render trade union agreements or trusts void or voidable (section 3). A further provision (section 4) which precluded any of their agreements from being directly enforceable or subject to damages for breach was designed to exclude union rules from the purview of the courts although, due to tortuous drafting, it achieved only partial success in this endeavour.[118] The Act also introduced a system of voluntary registration, carrying some small advantages, and most unions did, indeed, register under it.[119]

7.13   The Trade Union Act 1871 provided the legal basis for trade union freedom for about a century. It also initiated a strategy which was to be replicated in the area of industrial action; that of according statutory immunity against common law liability but without bestowing any positive rights. As we described in chapter 2 this approach left unions vulnerable to the resurgence of common law doctrines; thus in *Edwards v SOGAT*,[120] for example, it was suggested that a rule which enabled unions to act in a 'capricious and despotic' manner was not proper to the purposes of a union and therefore unprotected by section 3.[121] It also meant that, although individuals were free to join unions in so far as this was not specifically forbidden,[122] workers have been left unprotected against any curtailment of this freedom by the state. In 1919 the police were

---

[117] (1867) LR 2 QB 153. See also *Hilton v Eckersley* (1855) 6 E & B 47, where an agreement between a group of employers to adopt a common policy on matters such as wages and hours was held to be unenforceable as being in restraint of trade.

[118] See Elias and Ewing, 1987: pp 6–12.

[119] TUA 1871, s 6.

[120] [1971] Ch 354.

[121] Per Sachs LJ at 382. Protection against the restraint of trade doctrine was extended to trade union rules in TULRA 1974 and this has continued ever since: see now TULRCA 1992, s 11.

[122] Thus members of the armed forces, for example, may join trade unions, given that there is no legislation to the contrary, provided that this does not involve them in activities which would conflict with their military duties.

forbidden by statute from joining trade unions on the ground that this was incompatible with their law enforcement role and since that time they have been restricted to membership of bodies confined to the service. The lower ranks are automatically members of the Police Federation whose constitution and activities are tightly defined by statute.[123] In 1984, as we discussed in para 7.10, a ban on membership of national civil service unions at GCHQ was imposed (and remained in force until the advent of a Labour Government in 1997). Here the decision was the subject of an application for judicial review in which the House of Lords accepted the unions' argument that they had a public law right to be consulted before their members' terms and conditions were varied although in the circumstances this right was outweighed by the interests of the state in national security.[124] However, this right of consultation was not specifically related to the nature of the freedom being curtailed. Finally, the lack of any independent right to freedom of association has meant that workers may be discriminated against with impunity by employers on the grounds of their union membership and activities unless they fall within the relatively limited statutory protection against such action which has been in force in various forms since the Industrial Relations Act 1971. This 'negative' approach stands in marked contrast to systems where freedom of association is a fundamental, sometimes even a constitutional, right. Whether such a right serves as an adequate guarantee of collective organisation depends upon the way in which it is drafted and interpreted and any qualifications to which it is made subject; it is not, of itself, a panacea. Nevertheless it is undoubtedly the case that, in legal terms, reliance purely upon a system of immunities left trade unions and their members in a fragile situation. The Human Rights Act 1998, in giving 'further effect' in UK law to rights and freedoms guaranteed under the ECHR, grants for the first time a positive right to join trade unions. This is particularly significant because the right applies to '[e]veryone', not only 'workers' who alone at present are covered by the statutory protections against detriment on grounds of union membership and activities. However, there is a free-standing right of action only against public authorities (or, possibly, 'pure' public authorities); those who are discriminated against by other employers will have to invoke an existing common law right of action or defence, or a statutory right, in order to rely upon the general principle of freedom of association in proceedings. Moreover, as we noted in para 7.9, there are specified groups, including the police, whose exercise of the right may be restricted. Nevertheless there are areas in which the HRA 1998 may extend greater protection to unions and their members than has been accorded to them to date. The extent to which the Act has the potential to influence the interpretation of existing legislation, or the development of the common law, is discussed in greater detail in specific contexts.

7.14   The 'negative' legal strategy adopted towards collective organisation by the 1871 Act did not mean that governments remained wholly indifferent to trade unions. In parallel to their attitude towards collective bargaining, which we describe below, government policy shifted from one of tolerance towards more positive encouragement. However, this was expressed not through legislation but by the government's own conduct as an employer by which it hoped to set an example to be followed by the private sector.[125] Initially union activity in the civil service, which

---

[123] Police Act 1996, s 59; Police Federation Regulations 1969, SI 1969/1789, as amended; Fredman and Morris, 1989: pp 95–98.
[124] For a critique of this decision see Fredman, 1985. See also Blom-Cooper and Drabble, 2010.
[125] See generally Fredman and Morris, 1989: ch 4, from which the material which follows is taken.

began on a regular basis in the 1880s and 1890s, was met by considerable opposition. In 1898, however, the Secretary of the Treasury confirmed that Post Office workers were free to enter combinations[126] and in 1906 the Postmaster-General in the new Liberal Government affirmed the value of their doing so.[127] The final seal of approval on public service trade unionism came in 1919 when the government adopted collective bargaining in the civil service.[128] It then became official practice to encourage civil servants to join an appropriate trade union on the grounds that fully representative organisations promoted good staff relations and contributed to greater efficiency, as well as benefiting the individual,[129] a policy reflected in later years in local government and the National Health Service. The impact of this policy was amply demonstrated by the high level of trade union membership in the public as compared with the private sector: in 1948, when overall union density was 45.2%, density in central government was 52.9%, in local government and education 69.4% and in posts and telecommunications (then a government department) 87.3%.[130] By 1974 the disparity was even greater; trade union density in the public sector as a whole was estimated at 83% as compared with 38.6% in the private sector.[131] This pattern has continued; in 2010 union density in the UK public sector stood at 56.3% as compared with 14.2% in the private sector.[132]

The first step towards more direct encouragement of union membership in the private sector came in 1946 when the House of Commons Fair Wages Resolution of that year, unlike its predecessors, included a clause that government contracts with private employers should require contractors to recognise the freedom of their workers to be members of trade unions.[133] Although not covered by the Resolution, many local authorities followed this example and inserted such clauses in their contracts for works, supplies and services.[134] Due to inadequate monitoring and enforcement the efficacy of the Fair Wages Resolution in upholding freedom of association in practice has been doubted.[135] Nevertheless it constituted important symbolic support for the principle of trade unionism although, as we discuss further in para 8.2, not all employers were persuaded to follow the example set.

7.15   The approach of the government towards trade union organisation needs to be viewed in tandem with its attitude towards collective bargaining. From the last years of the nineteenth century and more actively from the end of the First World War it became government policy to support collective bargaining as the preferred method of determining terms and conditions of employment. Again this was furthered in the main by example rather than by statute. The government resolved actively to promote collective bargaining in the wake of a landmark report by the Whitley Committee, established in 1916, a time of considerable industrial unrest, to make

---

[126] Hans (4th Ser) vol LIII col 1136 (18 February 1898).

[127] Hans (4th Ser) vol CLIX col 396 (21 June 1906).

[128] See below.

[129] Civil servants' freedom of association was temporarily restricted by the Trade Disputes and Trade Unions Act 1927. Passed in the wake of the General Strike, the Act prohibited established civil servants from joining unions which, *inter alia*, were not confined to Crown servants. The Act was repealed by the Labour Government in 1946.

[130] Bain and Price, 1983: tables 1.1 and 1.5.

[131] Price and Bain, 1976: table 2, p 342.

[132] Achur, 2011: p 4.

[133] See para 2.6 for the status of the Resolution and the sanction for non-compliance with its terms.

[134] Hepple and O'Higgins, 1971: p 60.

[135] Bercusson, 1978: ch 17.

recommendations 'for securing a permanent improvement in the relations between employers and workmen'.[136] The Committee recommended that henceforth rates of pay and major terms of employment should be jointly determined by management and labour through a system of joint (national) industrial councils, district councils and works committees. The Ministry of Labour endorsed these proposals and drew up a model Joint Industrial Council constitution for industry to follow. It also encouraged the formation of employers' associations. The government demonstrated its own commitment to collective bargaining by establishing a system of 'Whitley Councils' for the civil service, despite reservations as to the appropriateness of this model in this context.[137] By 1921, 74 Joint Industrial Councils had been established in the private sector. Although the active promotion of collective bargaining ceased during that year with the advent of the post-war depression, the Whitley model was sufficiently well established to survive in many industries until national-level bargaining itself went into decline in the 1960s.

Although the prevailing theme in relation to collective bargaining was one of state abstentionism, there were a number of measures which lent it auxiliary support.[138] First, in a scheme dating back originally to 1909, provision was made for trade boards (later called wages councils) to be established in any industry in which there was no effective collective bargaining machinery.[139] These bodies, composed of union and employer representatives and independent members, were empowered to determine binding terms and conditions of employment for individual sectors. Once embodied in a ministerial order, these terms took automatic effect in the contracts of employment of those working in the industry and could be enforced in the same way as any other contractual terms.[140] It was also a criminal offence for an employer to breach an order. By the end of 1921 there were 63 trade boards in existence; by the early 1950s, 12% of the workforce was covered by them. Their success in extending voluntary collective bargaining has been doubted (although it seems that the threat of establishing a board was a useful lever in persuading employers to establish joint industrial councils in the period after the First World War).[141] However, in formal terms at least, they endorsed the view that vulnerable groups of workers should be protected against exploitation.

The next layer of support was constituted by the House of Commons Fair Wages Resolutions. The first Resolution, passed in 1891, required the government, in concluding contracts, to 'make every effort to secure the payment of the rate of wages generally accepted as current for a competent workman in his trade'. This was designed to combat sweated labour by removing government support for employers who paid low wages and in 1909 was extended to hours of work. The further Resolution passed in 1946 made explicit reference to collective agreements as a yardstick for determining appropriate conditions, thus enshrining a commitment to secure

[136] For a summary of the Committee's recommendations, and references to interim reports, see Ministry of Reconstruction: Committee on Relations between Employers and Employed: *Final Report*, Cd 9153 (1918).

[137] The ultimate power of government and Parliament to decide upon terms and conditions of employment was constantly affirmed. For an analysis of collective bargaining, and other methods of determining terms and conditions of employment in the public services, such as the role of 'Review Bodies', see Fredman and Morris, 1989: ch 5.

[138] See P Davies and M Freedland, 1993: ch 1, for the argument that these measures taken collectively made considerable inroads into the doctrine of collective laissez-faire, and that had they had greater impact the collective bargaining system may have been much more dependent upon statutory support than the traditional view suggests.

[139] See Deakin and Green, 2009; Blackburn, 2009.

[140] See para 4.44 above.

[141] See P Davies and M Freedland 1993: 29–30, 40. On the wages councils in general see Bayliss, 1962; Deakin and Wilkinson, 2005: 226–243.

observance of collectively-agreed terms in sectors where it could be applied. Express support was also accorded in the post-war statutes which nationalised a number of important industries and services (denationalised during the 1980s), such as coal, iron and steel, electricity and transport; these placed a legal obligation on the new public corporations to seek or enter into consultation with appropriate organisations with a view to establishing joint bargaining and consultative machinery. Last, a procedure introduced during the Second World War for enforcing recognised terms and conditions of employment determined in collective bargaining as the *quid pro quo* for a prohibition on strikes,[142] was continued after the war (although the ban on strikes was removed in 1951[143]) and then re-enacted in 1959.[144] Although used only infrequently it again provided an important demonstration of commitment to the collective bargaining process. Moreover, as one of us has commented elsewhere, its existence, together with that of the Fair Wages Resolution, may have served as an disincentive to denying collective bargaining rights: '[a]s long as a sector-level agreement could be made legally binding, through arbitration, on all employers in a certain trade, any cost advantages which might accrue to employers from non-recognition or the withdrawal of collective bargaining rights were limited'.[145]

7.16   This structure remained in place until the Conservative Government led by Edward Heath introduced the Industrial Relations Act 1971. As we indicated in chapter 1, this Act was a bold but ultimately unsuccessful attempt to bring British industrial relations within a framework of legal regulation at one stroke. The causes of its failure have been analysed in detail elsewhere.[146] In this context, and from our present day perspective, it is important merely to note that, whilst the Act sought to transform the legal culture within which collective bargaining was conducted, unlike later Conservative legislation it was clearly grounded in a continuing belief in the value of collective organisation and collective bargaining, albeit coupled with a greater degree of intervention in internal union affairs. Thus, for the first time, a statutory right to join a trade union, and participate in its activities, was created (although a right not to join a union was also introduced). Moreover, a trade union (or group of unions) which had been denied recognition could seek, through a statutory procedure, designation as the sole bargaining agent for a specified bargaining unit, whereupon the employer would be legally obliged to bargain with it. An employer could be required to disclose to union representatives information required for collective bargaining purposes.[147]

In the event these rights had very little practical impact because they could be invoked only by unions, and members of such unions, which were registered under the Act, and TUC policy opposed such registration. However, they heralded what turned out to be a lasting departure from the abstentionist tradition in the area of collective labour law.[148] Although the Act itself was repealed by the Trade Union and Labour Relations Act 1974 when the Labour Party was returned to power, what has come to be known as the 'Social Contract' legislation incorporated statutory

---

[142] SR&O 1940, No 1305; see further para 4.27 above.

[143] Industrial Disputes Order, SI 1951/1376.

[144] Terms and Conditions of Employment Act 1959, s 8.

[145] Deakin *et al*, 1992: p 12.

[146] Weekes *et al*, 1975. For a more recent analysis of its provisions see P Davies and M Freedland, 1993: ch 7.

[147] This provision was never brought into force.

[148] As we point out in ch 1, incomes policies and some employment protection legislation had also modified the tradition of state abstentionism.

rights which promoted a much more extensive and coherent role for the law than heretofore in supporting trade unions and collective bargaining. Thus employees were accorded a statutory right not to be dismissed or otherwise discriminated against for joining or participating in the activities of an independent trade union. Moreover, although closed shop agreements remained voluntary on the part both of unions and employers, where they had been agreed it was, as from 1976, (with a very limited exception) automatically fair to dismiss an employee who refused to join a specified union or unions. The terms of reference of the newly-constituted ACAS explicitly referred to encouraging the extension of collective bargaining and independent unions could apply, under a statutory procedure, for recognition or extended recognition from employers. Where recognised, such unions had rights to information from employers for collective bargaining purposes and the results of collective bargaining could be extended by law to other employers who did not pay the going rate.[149] Recognised unions also had rights to be consulted by employers in the areas of health and safety, dismissals for redundancy and occupational pensions, and their officials had the right to time off with pay during working hours for the performance of duties connected with the conduct of industrial relations, with members having a similar right (unpaid) for union activities. As Davies and Freedland have emphasised, this programme, although superficially ambitious, was characterised by a considerable degree of tentativeness about harnessing the law to promote collective bargaining, as manifested, for example, in the weakness of the sanctions for breach of these provisions.[150] Thus in relation to the recognition procedure, the 'linchpin' of the system, an employer could not legally be forced to give the requisite information to ascertain the views of the workforce on a recognition claim, nor could it be required ultimately to bargain with a union if such a claim were successful; refusal met only with compulsory unilateral arbitration of the terms and conditions of employment of employees covered by the recommendation. This approach was echoed in the provisions relating to disclosure of information. Despite these limitations, however, the legislation was significant in marking another step away from the abstentionist tradition.

7.17   The advent of a Conservative Government in 1979 under Mrs Thatcher, elected in the wake of a period of strikes dubbed the 'winter of discontent', quickly brought a reversal of this strategy. Her government viewed the free market as the most efficient economic principle. The reform of collective labour law was seen as integral to the government's broader economic agenda and, in particular, to the restructuring of the labour market.[151] Trade unions were characterised as legally-overprivileged bodies which, by their very nature obstructed the operation of market forces and threatened individual freedoms. Collective bargaining was also seen as an undesirable constraint upon a market which required the individualisation of the employment relationship in order to function properly. The 'unique' character of trade unions was said to justify an unprecedented degree of statutory intervention in their internal affairs and individuals were accorded rights against them ostensibly to secure union democracy and prevent the abuse of union power but with the effect in practice of prejudicing their ability to function as effective organisations. It is immediately apparent therefore that the policies of this Government marked a reversal not only of those of its immediate Labour predecessor but also of the approach to industrial relations which had prevailed for most of the century. They were further marked by a series of measures which

---

[149] See Bercusson, 1976.
[150] P Davies and M Freedland, 1993: p 385 *et seq*; see also L Dickens and G Bain, 1986.
[151] See P Davies and M Freedland, 1993: ch 9 *et seq*; W Brown *et al*, 1997; and para 1.25 *et seq* above.

imposed increasingly complex and restrictive requirements upon the organisation of industrial action and reduced the already limited protections available to those participating in it.

On this occasion, unlike 1971, the Conservative Government did not attempt to achieve its goals (which in any case evolved rather than being precisely formulated at the outset) in a single piece of legislation; rather they introduced reforms on an incremental basis. They began by dismantling major supports to collective bargaining; the (admittedly defective) recognition procedure and the extension procedure were repealed without replacement by the Employment Act 1980. This Act also made inroads into the closed shop by extending the categories of employee exempted from non-membership and requiring a high majority of the workforce to be in favour before new closed shops could be established. The 1982 Employment Act extended further these exempted categories and also required a ballot for a closed shop to continue with protection from the law. This Act also brought a more direct attack upon collective organisation by making it unlawful for persons awarding contracts for the supply of goods or services to make decisions by reference to whether the contractor used union (or non-union) labour or recognised a union (and made void any contractual specification of these matters). A major focus of the 1984 Trade Union Act was the regulation of trade unions' internal affairs; its provisions included a novel requirement for members of the principal executive committee to undergo periodic elections, the extension of the 'political objects' for which a separate political fund was needed and an obligation to approve the continued existence of such a fund in a ballot held at least once every ten years. This process was continued by the Employment Act 1988 which imposed further restrictions upon trade unions in relation to elections and gave a broad range of additional rights to union members, including the right not to be 'unjustifiably disciplined' by their union, the right to inspect union accounting records and the right to prevent the unlawful use of union property. Another radical development was the creation of a Commissioner for the Rights of Trade Union Members, with power to grant assistance, including financial assistance, to individuals contemplating High Court proceedings against their union. In the light of the unavailability of legal aid for proceedings in employment tribunals this move sent another clear message as to where government priorities lay. This Act also removed the remaining legal protection from employers who dismissed or otherwise discriminated against employees for non-membership of a union, thus preventing altogether the enforcement of closed shops. This was followed in 1990 by legislation which, for the first time since the Industrial Relations Act, extended protection to those refused employment for non-membership (or membership) of a trade union. The final major statute in this area, the Trade Union Reform and Employment Rights Act 1993, made further major inroads into trade union autonomy by providing that unions could only lawfully exclude or expel individuals from membership on grounds specified in the legislation. It also required them to comply with more onerous reporting requirements and gave the Certification Officer extensive powers to investigate their affairs. The pursuit of individualism was further facilitated by a provision intended to remove any obstacle to employers offering employees inducements to move from collectively-agreed terms and conditions of employment to personal contracts. Finally, and significantly from a symbolic point of view, the goal of encouraging the extension of collective bargaining was removed from the terms of reference of ACAS.

Hostility to collective organisation was also manifested in the Conservative Government's role as contractor and as employer.[152] In 1982 it gave notice of its intention to rescind the Fair Wages

---

[152] See generally Fredman and Morris, 1989.

Resolution, a step which necessitated denouncing an ILO Convention in whose formulation British practice had been highly influential. Despite having been in force in various forms since 1891 it was perceived by the government as a damaging anachronism which impeded competitiveness, destroyed jobs and undermined established pay structures. The ban on national civil service unions at GCHQ, discussed in para 7.10, was a particularly dramatic demonstration of its new role as employer; other less direct attacks included threats to trade unionists' freedom of expression and withdrawal of check-off facilities for union subscriptions during official industrial action. This hostility to collective organisation was mirrored in the treatment of collective bargaining in public services where government sought to undermine national bargaining structures by encouraging more local bargaining, and the introduction of individualised reward structures, most notably performance-related pay. Collective bargaining machinery was withdrawn altogether for schoolteachers, to be replaced by unilateral determination of terms and conditions, after following only limited advisory and consultation procedures, by the Secretary of State.[153] Union influence was further reduced by programmes of compulsory competitive tendering in local government and the National Health Service reinforced, in the case of local government, by restrictions in the Local Government Act 1988 which made it unlawful for local authorities and other specified public bodies to have regard to 'non-commercial matters', including, *inter alia*, the payment of fair wages, when awarding and operating contracts.[154]

As even this short summary makes clear, at the time the Conservative administration left office in 1997, the law relating to collective organisation was extremely complex and, in general, restrictive. This is not to say that some remnants of earlier strategies did not remain; it was still unlawful for employers to discriminate against trade union members, for example, although the scope of this protection was radically reduced, and obligations under EU law necessitated the provision of some specific collective rights of information and consultation. However, the predominant aim was to undermine the capacity of trade unions to act as effective organisations. In this respect legal policy in Britain towards collective organisation came almost full circle; from state abstentionism to positive support returning to hostility, although this was manifested in a rather more sophisticated form than at the beginning of the nineteenth century. It was notable that a number of those changes brought the UK into conflict with international standards, particularly those formulated by the ILO,[155] a development which was particularly poignant given the leading role which the UK took initially in their formulation.[156] We consider these conflicts in greater detail when we discuss individual provisions.

7.18   The election of a Labour Government in May 1997 heralded a less hostile environment for trade unions, with emphasis upon a culture of 'partnership' in the conduct of industrial relations.[157] There were two immediate changes of considerable symbolic significance to collective labour law: the restoration of the freedom of workers at GCHQ to join national civil service unions, and at EU level, a commitment to adopt the Agreement on Social Policy (which became the new Social

---

[153] Teachers' Pay and Conditions Act 1987, itself replaced by the School Teachers' Pay and Conditions Act 1991, discussed Fredman and Morris, 1992; see now Education Act 2002, Part 8 and Sch 11.

[154] LGA 1988, s 17.

[155] See Creighton, 1994; Ewing, 1994a; Mills, 1997.

[156] Creighton, 1994.

[157] See *Fairness at Work*, Cm 2968, 1998, and generally W Brown, 2000.

Chapter of the revised EC Treaty) and the European Works Council Directive adopted under it. The most comprehensive development at a collective level was the enactment of the Employment Relations Act 1999, the 'industrial relations settlement' for the duration of the government's first term of office.[158] The Act significantly extended the protection for union members against discrimination by employers. However, its most controversial aspect was the re-introduction of a procedure for the mandatory recognition of trade unions by employers. This procedure showed that lessons had been learnt from its 1975 predecessor in that it specified the criteria for designating a bargaining unit and imposed a duty on employers to co-operate with the balloting process.[159] However, in some ways it is less far-reaching: the scope of mandatory recognition is confined to 'pay, hours and holidays'; if the employer fails to comply with the collective bargaining method imposed by the Central Arbitration Committee (CAC) which is charged with operating the procedure, the sanction is confined to specific performance of that method; and those employing fewer than 21 workers[160] are excluded. Employers can also avoid the procedure altogether if they voluntarily recognise any other union, regardless of its level of support among the workforce and (usually) even if it lacks a certificate of independence. Moreover, even where there is recognition (voluntarily or otherwise) the capacity of individual employers and workers to negotiate terms and conditions of employment which differ from those collectively agreed has been explicitly affirmed, although, following the ECtHR decision in *Wilson* and *Palmer*, discussed in para 7.9, ERelA 2004 introduced a right not to be induced to abjure collective standards.

There were other indications that, while there was greater acknowledgement of the legitimacy of collective bargaining than under the Conservatives, its promotion was very far from being a central plank of the Labour Government's labour market policy. The statutory recognition procedure was paralleled by a mechanism for compulsory derecognition of unions which had been recognised under the statutory procedure, and the CAC is required to assist the parties to agree, *inter alia*, to end the bargaining arrangements in the same way as it assists a recognition application. The pre-1993 statutory duty upon ACAS to extend collective bargaining was not reinstated (although arguably its general duty 'to promote the improvement of industrial relations' can accommodate this).[161] Finally, the prohibition against requiring contractors to recognise trade unions (but not against requiring them not to do so), introduced by the Conservative Government, remained intact, although there was greater emphasis on consultation with trade unions in areas of the public sector, and the list of prohibited 'non-commercial matters' to which local authorities and other public bodies may not have regard when awarding and operating contracts was shortened.[162]

Other important aspects of the Conservative legacy remained substantially untouched. The reform of the law relating to the internal affairs of trade unions stayed in place in its essentials, although the symbolically significant (but under-used) office of the Commissioner for the Rights

---

[158] See generally Ewing, 1999a; Wedderburn, 2000; G Morris and T Archer, 2000; Novitz and Skidmore, 2001; L Dickens and M Hall, 2003; Fredman, 2004a; P Davies and M. Freedland, 2007.

[159] For an assessment of the new procedure and comparison, variously, with its predecessors and with US and Canadian procedures, see S Wood and J Godard, 1999; McCarthy, 1999; Towers, 1999; Adams, 1999; Hepple 2000a; Dubinsky, 2000; S Wood *et al*, 2002, 2003; Dukes, 2008b; Bogg, 2009a. For lessons that the British procedure may hold for the US, see Brudney, 2007; Peters, 2004. For discussion of various other strategies for structuring a recognition procedure, see Simpson, 1991; Townley, 1987; Ewing, 1990a and Ewing, 1996: ch 7; Bercusson *et al*, 1998.

[160] Including those employed by any associated employer (see para 3.65).

[161] Hepple, 2000a: p 153.

[162] See generally G Morris, 2004a: pp 170–172.

of Trade Union Members was abolished and greater powers granted to the Certification Officer. This meant that the UK continued to violate ILO standards in a number of important areas.[163] However some changes were forced on the government by external pressures. In 2001 the government reluctantly accepted the Information and Consultation Directive, having secured a longer transposition period for its full implementation, after other EU Member States which had previously also opposed the mandatory national-level information and consultation it requires indicated their willingness to compromise. In addition, the Employment Relations Act 2004 extended the scope of protection against anti-union discrimination in the light of the *Wilson* and *Palmer* judgment, although there remained questions as to whether the law, even after these amendments, was fully in compliance with international standards. Finally, in the wake of *ASLEF v UK* the Employment Act 2008 granted unions greater discretion to exclude or expel individuals on the grounds of their party political membership but the government declined to conduct a broader review of the constraints on union autonomy despite the exhortations of international supervisory bodies. In summary, therefore, the advent of a Labour Government undoubtedly brought a more hospitable approach to collective organisation than its predecessor, but there were evident limits to that hospitality.

The entry into office of the (Conservative and Liberal Democrat) Coalition Government has not, at the time of writing, brought major statutory reforms to collective labour law, although changes to the requirements for consultation on collective redundancies are being considered and the CBI is pressing for greater restrictions in the area of industrial action. In general, however, the most significant changes implemented or announced by the Coalition Government to date relate to the enforcement of individual employment rights which we discuss in earlier chapters of this work.[164]

BASIC DEFINITIONS AND CONCEPTS

7.19 In this section we examine the various legal categories into which collective organisations are divided and summarise the legal implications of such categorisation. We begin by analysing the legal definition of a 'trade union'. In Britain important legal consequences follow if an organisation falls within this definition. Some are beneficial, others onerous. On the one hand trade unions are protected against the application of some common law doctrines; their rules and purposes are protected against the doctrine of restraint of trade and their liability for damages in tort (with some exceptions) is subject to statutory limits. On the other, only trade unions are subject to the intricate statutory requirements regulating the selection of their executive committees; restrictions upon those whom they admit to, and expel from, membership; and the grounds upon which they discipline their members. We also outline here the definition of an 'employers' association'. Such bodies share some of the legal attributes of trade unions and a few, but by no means all, of their burdens.

---

[163] See Novitz, 2000; G Morris, 2001b.
[164] See our discussion of employment tribunals in para 2.15 *et seq* and the increased qualifying period generally required to claim unfair dismissal, discussed in para 5.63 above.

Trade unions themselves are sub-divided into categories which also have significant implications. First, they may be listed or unlisted. 'Listed' unions are those that appear on the Certification Officer's list of unions; while not compulsory, listing brings significant advantages. Second, they may be independent or non-independent. One important consequence of a union being independent is that its 'worker' members have the right not to be discriminated against on the grounds of their union membership or activities. Another is that only independent unions may invoke the statutory recognition procedure. Third, unions may be recognised or unrecognised. Unlike independence or, indeed, trade union status itself, 'recognition' is relevant only to the status of the union in relation to a particular employer; a union may be recognised by one employer but not by another. Being recognised entitles unions to a variety of statutory rights. We examine each of these concepts in turn. We then summarise the legal status and attributes of 'trade unions' and of 'employers' associations'.

The definition of a 'trade union' and an 'employers' association' and the concept of 'listing'

7.20   A 'trade union' means an organisation (whether temporary or permanent) which consists wholly or mainly of workers of one or more descriptions and whose principal purposes include the regulation of relations between workers of that description or those descriptions and employers or employers' associations.[165] As we saw in para 3.33 *et seq* the definition of 'worker' goes beyond those who work under a contract of employment to include any other contract whereby a person 'undertakes to do or perform personally any work or services for another party to the contract who is not a professional client of his'.[166] It also covers those who seek to work under such arrangements; thus an organisation composed solely of the unemployed could, in theory, constitute a trade union although it may have difficulty satisfying other elements of the definition. The exclusion of those who work for 'professional clients' means that the Law Society is not a trade union,[167] although it is not clear whether an organisation of *employed* solicitors could be.[168] The requirement for 'an organisation' may mean that a body that is no more than a part of the employer's consultative procedures does not satisfy the test.[169] 'Similarly, a body may not "consist" wholly or mainly of workers within the definition if it merely deems all employees of a particular employer to be its members, without individual employees having indicated any wish to join'.[170]

The need to engage in the 'regulation of relations' probably requires the organisation directly to regulate relations between employers and workers rather than simply engaging in political activities which may influence industrial relations or eschewing collective bargaining in favour of statutory regulation of terms and conditions. It has been suggested that the organisation must at

---

[165] TULRCA 1992, s 1(a).

[166] TULRCA 1992, s 296(1). The police and armed forces are specifically excluded from the definition: ss 280, 274. Otherwise, with limited exceptions, TULRCA 1992 has effect in relation to persons in Crown employment as in relation to other workers: s 273.

[167] *Carter v Law Society* [1973] ICR 113. See generally *R (on the application of the BBC) v CAC* [2003] IRLR 460.

[168] Specified health service practitioners are specifically included within the definition: s 279.

[169] *Frost v Clark and Smith* [1973] IRLR 216: a works committee is unlikely to satisfy the definition of a 'trade union' because it will probably lack the attributes of an 'organisation'.

[170] *Annual Report of the Certification Officer 2003–2004*, p 2.

least have sought recognition from employers. In *Midland Cold Storage Ltd v Turner*[171] the issue arose as to the status of a shop stewards' committee whose apparent activity was to recommend the taking or abandonment of industrial action in the London docks and organising any action which might be decided upon. There was no evidence that it sought recognition from the employers; rather, it left the conduct of negotiations to the established union machinery. The court held that no body whose principal purposes included the regulation of relations between workers and employers could fail at least to seek recognition from employers.

The organisation need not be of a minimum size or demonstrate any particular effectiveness or frequency of intervention in regulating relations, however; the crucial point is that its principal purpose includes such regulation.[172] This purpose need not be stated expressly in its constitution provided that it can be inferred from all the circumstances. Thus the British Association of Advisers and Lecturers in Physical Education was found to be a 'trade union' despite the fact that its constitution merely stated that it should be 'concerned with the professional interests of its members' since in practice it concerned itself with the pay and working conditions of its employed members through national negotiating machinery.[173] However there are strong grounds for concluding that, regardless of its constitution, an organisation cannot regulate the relations of a group of workers if it has no such workers in membership.[174] On the basis of existing authorities an organisation of workers which sought only to be consulted by employers would not qualify as a trade union; to extend the definition to such organisations would require taking a much broader view of the concept of 'regulation' than heretofore. In the light of the current emphasis upon consultation, it is arguable that such an extension should be considered, subject to the other elements of the definition of being satisfied. Although the existing definition focuses upon the traditional role of unions in engaging and seeking to engage in collective bargaining, there is nothing to prevent a union having other lawful objects, including political objects;[175] indeed in 2005 Ewing stated that the 'trade union regulatory function has [now] become political as much as industrial with regulatory ambitions to be secured by political campaigning and by legislation rather than by collective bargaining'.[176] However, as we describe in chapter 10, where a union wishes to spend money on 'political objects' as statutorily defined it must establish a separate 'political fund' in accordance with a specified procedure.

Organisations which themselves consist wholly or mainly of trade unions or representatives of trade unions, and whose principal purposes include the regulation of relations between workers and employers or employers' associations, or the regulation of relations between their constituent or affiliated organisations, are also regarded as 'trade unions'.[177] Thus the TUC, for example, is a

---

[171] [1972] ICR 230. See also *Midland Cold Storage v Steer* [1972] ICR 435, on the same set of facts.

[172] *BAALPE v NUT* [1986] IRLR 497. In his report for 2010-2011 the Certification Officer stated that an increasing number of bodies were wishing to be listed seemingly to exercise the right to accompany workers at disciplinary and grievance hearings under ERelA 1999, s 10 (see para 5.121 *et seq*), frequently for a fee. He considered carefully if such bodies satisfied the statutory definition or were commercial bodies seeking to take advantage of the s 10 right: *Annual Report of the Certification Officer for 2010-2011*, p 2.

[173] *BAALPE v NUT* [1986] IRLR 497.

[174] See the CAC decision in *BECTU v City Screen Ltd* TURI/309/2003, 10 December 2003, para 32.

[175] This has been the case since the TUA 1913; before that the objects of a union were stated exhaustively and in *ASRS v Osborne* [1910] AC 87 the House of Lords held that funding the candidature of prospective Labour MPs was not within the statutory object of the regulation of relations between workers and employers.

[176] Ewing, 2005: p 15.

[177] TULRCA 1992, s 1(b). Note that some provisions which apply to trade unions as defined in s 1(a) do not apply to these organisations or apply with modifications: see s 118.

'trade union'.[178] From the opposite end of the scale the courts have held that a branch or division of a trade union can itself constitute a 'trade union' where it satisfies the statutory criteria, despite the fact that members of the branch are also members of the main trade union.[179] This may be significant in relation to the statutory limits on damages payable by a trade union in tort, for example.[180]

7.21   Unlike in some systems, there is no requirement for trade unions to be registered in order legally to exist. However, the Certification Officer maintains a list of trade unions and any union which complies with specified formalities is entitled to have its name entered on the list.[181] Being listed has a number of advantages for a union. It is evidence (although not conclusive evidence)[182] that the organisation is, indeed, a trade union;[183] it entitles the union to tax relief on income tax, corporation tax and chargeable gains applied for the purpose of 'provident benefits' provided certain conditions are met;[184] and there is a simplified procedure for vesting union property in newly appointed trustees.[185] Moreover, inclusion on the list is an essential preliminary to an application for a certificate of independence, described below. Thus, although listing is theoretically voluntary, a union is highly likely to seek entry to the list. It is irrelevant to a union's application that there may be other organisations which already recruit members in the same area of work, although if the organisation's name is the same as that of a listed union, or so closely resembles it as to be likely to deceive the public, listing will be refused.[186] The Certification Officer may remove a union from the list if he or she considers that it is not a union (after allowing the organisation to make representations) or if the organisation requests removal, or he is she is satisfied that it has ceased to exist (for example, as a result of merger with another union).[187] There is a right of appeal to the EAT on a question of law against the Certification Officer's decision not to list a union, or to remove it from the list.[188] At the end of March 2011 there were 162 listed trade unions and a further 15 which had not sought to be listed.[189]

The Certification Officer also maintains a list of employers' associations, and at the end of March 2011 there were 62 on this list.[190] Again listing is not mandatory (and a further 44 were

---

[178] Another example is the Iron and Steel Trades Confederation.

[179] *BAALPE v NUT* [1986] IRLR 497; *News Group Newspapers Ltd v SOGAT '82 (No 2)* [1986] IRLR 337.

[180] See para 11.47 below.

[181] TULRCA 1992, ss 2, 3. Unions listed under the Trade Union and Labour Relations Act 1974 (now repealed) were automatically entered on the list; this statute, in turn, automatically listed organisations registered under the provisions of the TUA 1871 (or organisations formed by an amalgamation of such organisations) and those affiliated to the TUC.

[182] This may be important in the context of the recognition procedure, for example: see the CAC decision in *BECTU v City Screen Ltd* TURI/309/2003, 10 December 2003.

[183] TULRCA 1992, s 2(4).

[184] Corporation Tax Act 2010, s 981; see s 982 for the meaning of 'provident benefits'.

[185] TULRCA 1992, ss 13, 14.

[186] TULRCA 1992, s 3(4). The protection of its name is, therefore, another advantage for a union of being listed.

[187] TULRCA 1992, s 4.

[188] TULRCA 1992, s 9, as amended by ERelA 2004, s 51, which removed the right of appeal on questions of fact.

[189] *Annual Report of the Certification Officer for 2010–2011*, paras 1.7, 1.13 and 1.14. Being unlisted does not limit an organisation's statutory responsibilities, including the requirement to submit annual returns to the Certification Officer (although 'federated' trade unions, whether listed or unlisted, are exempted from several statutory obligations).

[190] *Annual Report of the Certification Officer for 2010–2011*, paras 1.13 and 1.14.

not listed),[191] but it constitutes evidence that the organisation falls within the legal definition.[192] An 'employers' association' means an organisation (whether temporary or permanent) which consists wholly or mainly of employers or individual owners of undertakings of one or more descriptions whose principal purposes include the regulation of relations between employers of that description or those descriptions and workers or trade unions.[193] There is no case law directly on the interpretation of this definition[194] but one would expect the same approach to be applied to phrases such as the 'regulation of relations' as apply in the context of trade unions. Organisations consisting wholly or mainly of constituent or affiliated organisations which themselves fulfil the definition of an employers' association or representatives of such organisations are also included provided, again, that their principal purposes include regulating relations with workers or trade unions or between their constituent or affiliated organisations.[195]

The concept and implications of trade union 'independence'

7.22   Once a union has been entered on the Certification Officer's list it is eligible to apply to him or her for a certificate of independence. Satisfying the test of 'independence' (which refers to independence from employers rather than the state) is essential for access to a number of statutory rights: only ('worker') members of independent unions are protected against subjection to a detriment by their employers on grounds of their union activities; only independent unions may invoke the statutory recognition procedure; and only independent recognised unions have certain rights to information and consultation and their members the right to claim time off to participate in union activities.[196] In broad terms the concept is intended to preclude access to these rights by employer-dominated 'house unions' or 'staff associations'. This was particularly significant when, in the past, employees could be fairly dismissed for refusing to join a union with which the employer had agreed a 'closed shop'. A certificate is not a prerequisite of independent status but it constitutes conclusive proof of such and if the question of the independence of a non-certificated union arises in any proceedings they must be stayed pending a decision by the Certification Officer on the matter.[197]

On receiving an application for a certificate, which is entered on a record open to public inspection for at least a month, the Certification Officer must make such inquiries as he or she thinks fit and take into account any relevant information submitted by any person.[198] If a certificate

[191] As above, paras 1.7, 1.13 and 1.14.
[192] TULRCA 1992, s 123. The procedure required to gain entry to the list, and provision for appeal against refusal, is set out in ss 123–126 and is the same, *mutatis mutandis*, as that applicable to trade unions. In 1983 there were 502 unions and 375 employers' associations: *Annual Report of the Certification Officer for 2010-2011*: p 2.
[193] TULRCA 1992, s 122.
[194] Although see *National Federation of Self-Employed and Small Businesses v Philpott* [1997] IRLR 340, where the Federation was held to be an 'organisation of employers' for the purposes of the SDA 1975, s 12, notwithstanding that not all its members employed labour, given that the majority did.
[195] TULRCA 1992, s 122.
[196] See chs 8 and 9.
[197] TULRCA 1992, ss 6(1), 8. On 31 March 2011 there were 110 unions with a certificate of independence: *Annual Report of the Certification Officer for 2010-2011*, p 15.
[198] TULRCA 1992, s 6. See *Independence: a guide for trade unions wishing to apply for a certificate of independence*, Certification Office, 2011, for further details about the procedure which is followed.

is refused the Certification Officer must give reasons for this decision; he or she may also withdraw a certificate after following a procedure similar to that laid down for applications.[199] An appeal lies to the EAT on a question of law against the Certification Officer's decision to refuse, or withdraw, a certificate of independence.[200] A union which has been refused a certificate may reapply at a later stage, although it would be advised to scrutinise carefully its constitution, finances and conduct before doing this. There is no right of appeal for a third party which wishes to contest the granting of a certificate (which it may wish to do now, perhaps, for purposes relating to the statutory recognition procedure).[201] The only way in which such an third party could proceed would be to attempt to obtain an order for judicial review to overturn the Certification Officer's decision, but as this would require showing that the decision was vitiated by a procedural irregularity, illegality, or 'irrationality' it would probably be a difficult task.

7.23   A trade union is 'independent' if it is not under the domination or control of an employer or group of employers or one or more employers' associations and is not liable to interference by an employer or any such group or association (arising out of the provision of financial or material support or by any other means whatsoever) tending towards such control.[202] This test directs attention therefore both to whether the employer in fact exercises domination or control over the union and whether it is exposed to the risk of interference tending towards such control. 'Liability to interference' has been interpreted by the courts as 'vulnerable to interference'; thus there is no need to show that such interference is likely in the circumstances.[203]

Beyond this general test the statute does not specify the criteria relevant to independence, although further guidance is available from the decisions of the Certification Officer and the courts. Among the factors which the Certification Officer considers relevant are the union's history (if it began with employer support in the recent past, this would be a powerful argument against granting a certificate); the scope of its membership base; its organisation and structure, both as set out in the rule book and in practice (which should exclude any form of employer involvement or influence in its internal affairs); the strength and sources of the union's finances; and its negotiating record.[204] An earlier iteration of these criteria was referred to with approval in the judgment of the EAT in *Blue Circle Staff Association v Certification Officer*,[205] a case where the decision of the Certification Officer to refuse a certificate of independence was confirmed. The background to this case demonstrates the need for vigilance in this area. In 1971 the employer realised that its salaried staff (some 4,000 in number) wanted some form of collective voice. The employer was

---

[199] TULRCA 1992, ss 6, 7.
[200] TULRCA 1992, s 9. as amended by ERelA 2004, s 51, which removed the right of appeal on questions of fact.
[201] *GMWU v Certification Officer* [1977] ICR 183.
[202] TULRCA 1992, s 5.
[203] *Squibb UK Staff Association v Certification Officer* [1979] IRLR 75. After the ban on membership of national civil service unions, described in para 7.10, it became a condition of service for staff at GCHQ that they could only belong to a departmental staff association approved by the director of GCHQ, and industrial action could lead to disciplinary action. The EAT confirmed the decision of the Certification Officer that the association in question was 'vulnerable to interference': see *Government Communications Staff Federation v Certification Officer* [1993] IRLR 260. For the grounds of refusal of a subsequent application by the Federation to the Certification Officer, see *Annual Report of the Certification Officer for 1996*, para 2.9. In May 2001 the Certification Officer refused an application from NISA (the News International Staff Association) on the grounds that it was liable to interference from the employer.
[204] Guide, note 198 above, para 17 *et seq.*
[205] [1977] IRLR 20.

eager that any emerging body should represent only its own employees and, following a ballot, an organisation called a 'staff consultative organisation', dominated by the employer, was formed. The organisation had a central committee on which the employers had five representatives; the chairman of the committee was nominated by the employers, and there were area committees on which management had a right of representation. Members with less than three years' service with the employer were not eligible for election as representatives. The employer provided facilities and paid virtually all the expenses, although members had to pay a nominal subscription. Initially the organisation was empowered only to make recommendations to the employer but in 1974 it was given negotiating rights. Between 1975 and February 1976 further changes were made to its structure, including renaming it a staff association, in order to strengthen its independence.

The Certification Officer took the view that, given the degree of dependence to which the organisation had been subject in the first five years of its life, that history imposed a duty to look scrupulously at all the facts to see that it had changed its character. In this case, although the association had taken steps towards independence it had not gone far enough along this road and he thought that it should establish some record for itself which he expected to take some time.

The EAT, looking at the issue afresh,[206] agreed with the Certification Officer's decision. The rules still showed traces of the old dependence – for example, it was for the employer to appoint the chairman of the Joint Central Committee, those with less than three years' service were still excluded from office, irrespective of their negotiating experience, and the employer had the right to withdraw recognition of a representative regardless of the views of the association's central council. Moreover, the association was dependent on the goodwill of the employer for the bulk of its communications with its members and its very slender financial base gave rise to doubt as to its viability. The court found that it was 'difficult to identify any real sign that anything has changed in this Association except the formal documents that came into existence ... when the management was helping the Staff Consultative Organisation to find new clothes to make it respectable for its introduction to the Certification Officer'. It was:

> ... unlikely that the employer's dominant role would have been modified at all had it not been the view of the employer that it was in its interest to concert with the Association a constitution and negotiating machinery consistent with the end of the existing company control ... When the matrix of the new constitution is regarded, it is found to be an organisation whereby the association of the salaried staff members was penetrated at every point by the interference and control of the management. There must be a heavy onus on such a body to show that it has shaken off the paternal control which brought it into existence and fostered its growth, and which finally joined in drafting the very rules by which the control appears to be relaxed.[207]

The court concluded by warning the association that, although it was open to it at any time to make a fresh application for a certificate, 'they must recognise that the process of asserting genuine and effective independence after some years of such domination by management ... is likely to be protracted'.[208]

---

[206] Prior to 6 April 2005, appeals could be made to the EAT on questions of fact as well as questions of law.
[207] *Blue Circle Staff Association v Certification Officer* [1977] IRLR 20, 24.
[208] *Blue Circle Staff Association v Certification Officer* [1977] IRLR 20, 24.

7.24   It is important to emphasise that the criteria listed by the Certification Officer are only guidelines whose relevance and weight may vary depending on the circumstances; thus, whilst single company unions, for example, are scrutinised more carefully because their membership base makes them more vulnerable to employer interference, they are not precluded altogether and this is less likely to be a critical factor for a well-established union backed up by strong resources.[209] Similarly, the provision of facilities by an employer is not of itself a bar to independence and, indeed, the ACAS Code of Practice on Time Off for Trade Union Duties and Activities (Including Guidance on Time Off for Union Learning Representatives) 2010 states that they should be provided.[210] In an analysis of the management of unions' financial resources during the period 1980–89, Willman *et al* indicated the difficult passage which unions may need to steer in this respect, pointing out that:

> ... [d]ependence is ... to some extent, an indication of negotiating success, given the structure of British unions. Lay involvement, the key to cost control and perhaps to a wider range of union objectives, depends on employer support. But too much employer support may threaten independence and in fact usurp the union's role unless the employer is simultaneously dependent on the union. The issue, then, is one of managing this dependence, of making such dependence mutual.[211]

The crucial question would seem to be whether the union could survive if its facilities were suddenly withdrawn. As the Certification Officer's guide explains:

> A distinction can properly be drawn between a broadly-based union which could continue to function even if an employer withdrew facilities from one or more of its branches and a single company union which might well find it difficult or even impossible to carry on at all if such action were taken by the company which employs its entire membership.[212]

A strong negotiating record is regarded as indicative of independence although, again, this varies with the circumstances; in the case of a 'good, tactful and sensitive employer' these could be difficult to demonstrate.[213] Willingness to take industrial action is not a statutory criterion of independence and organisations whose rules forbid this have been granted certificates. In view of this it is interesting to note that legislation clarifying the position of prison officers, which also removed their freedom to take industrial action, provided that the Certification Officer should disregard their inability lawfully to take industrial action in determining whether their unions are independent.[214]

---

[209] For example, the National Union of Railwaymen (now the National Union of Rail, Maritime and Transport Workers) and the National Union of Mineworkers were not refused certificates during periods when virtually all their members were employed by single employers in the form of nationalised state corporations.

[210] Para 46; see further para 8.46.

[211] Willman *et al*, 1993: p 207.

[212] Above note 198, para 23. See also the *Annual Report of the Certification Officer for 1996*, para 2.9, regarding GCHQ, referred to in note 203 above.

[213] *Blue Circle Staff Association v Certification Officer* [1977] IRLR 20, 23.

[214] CJPOA 1994, s 127(7). See further G Morris, 1994b and 1994c.

7.25   The concept of independence is a crucial one in the context of freedom of association. ILO Convention No 98 emphasises the need for workers' (and employers') organisations to enjoy 'adequate protection against any acts of interference by each other or each other's agents or members in their establishment, functioning and administration'. In particular acts 'designed to promote the establishment of workers' organisations under the domination of employers or employers' organisations, or to support workers' organisations by financial or other means, with the object of placing ... [them] under the control of employers or employers' organisations' are deemed to constitute acts of interference.[215] The Freedom of Association Committee of the ILO Governing Body considers that legislation should make express provision for appeals and establish sufficiently dissuasive sanctions against acts of interference by employers.[216] In the United States, for example, it is an unfair labour practice for an employer to provide financial assistance to a labour organisation and it can be ordered to desist from doing so.[217] It is notable that under English law there is nothing to prevent an employer establishing and supporting a non-independent union. It is strongly arguable that the law should be changed in this respect; even though an employer cannot lawfully dismiss or otherwise discriminate against a worker, or deny employment to someone, because they refuse to join a non-independent union, nevertheless the social pressures to join may be strong and the very existence of such an organisation may discourage workers from joining independent unions. Moreover, the Employment Relations Act 1999 has given a further incentive to employers to establish non-independent unions; recognition of a non-independent union will (usually) bar a claim for recognition by an independent union under the statutory recognition procedure, a position which it can be argued violates ILO Convention 98.[218] Finally, it is inappropriate that an employer which does not recognise an independent union can fulfil its statutory obligations to inform and consult in a number of important areas, such as collective redundancies and matters covered by the Information and Consultation Regulations,[219] by informing and consulting worker representatives whose position may not comply in a number of respects with the criteria of independence outlined above, not least because it is a condition that they are employed by the employer at the time of their selection as such representatives.[220] This is another area in which the law is in urgent need of reform. Indeed, it may be thought desirable to consider extending the application of the concept of independence to enterprise worker representative bodies in general, even though they may be single employer organisations and may not seek to engage in collective bargaining, only consultation, and may not therefore fall within the current definition of a 'trade union'.

The concept and implications of union 'recognition'

7.26   An employer may elect to 'recognise' a trade union; it may also (if 21 or more workers are employed) be compelled to recognise an independent union in relation to pay, hours and holidays

---

[215] Art 2.
[216] ILO 1996, para 764.
[217] 29 USC para 158(a)(2), 160(c) (1976).
[218] See further para 9.7 and Ewing, 2000a.
[219] SI 2004/3426.
[220] See further ch 9.

pursuant to a statutory procedure. Recognition of an independent trade union, voluntary or otherwise, has a number of important legal consequences. Recognition entitles the union to claim disclosure of information for collective bargaining purposes (see para 9.22); union representatives and members are entitled to time off work for specified activities (see para 8.40 *et seq*); and a variety of statutory consultation rights, which we describe in para 9.29 *et seq* apply. Recognised unions therefore have significant rights which are not available to those which are unrecognised. Furthermore, recognition has significant implications for the operation of the statutory recognition procedure: where an employer recognises an independent union for a particular group of workers, an application by another union in respect of a bargaining unit which overlaps to any extent with that group will not be accepted by the CAC; perhaps surprisingly, the same principle generally applies even where a non-independent union is recognised (see para 9.7). Finally, an employer must consult a recognised independent union on training matters where that union is recognised in accordance with the statutory procedure and a method for the conduct of collective bargaining has been specified by the CAC (see para 9.49).

7.27   'Recognition' in relation to a trade union means 'the recognition of the union by an employer, or two or more associated employers, to any extent, for the purposes of collective bargaining'.[221] 'Collective bargaining' means 'negotiations relating to or connected with' one or more of the matters specified in the Trade Union and Labour Relations (Consolidation) Act 1992, section 178(2).[222] These matters are:

(a)   the terms and conditions of employment, or the physical conditions in which any workers[223] are required to work;

(b)   engagement or non-engagement, or termination or suspension of employment or the duties of employment, of one or more workers;

(c)   allocation of work or the duties of employment as between workers or groups of workers;

(d)   matters of discipline;

(e)   a worker's membership or non-membership of a trade union;

(f)   facilities for officials of trade unions; and

(g)   machinery for negotiation or consultation, and other procedures, relating to any of the above matters, including the recognition by employers or employers' associations of the right of a trade union to represent workers in such negotiation or consultation or in the carrying out of such procedures.

The phrase 'to any extent' in the definition of 'recognition' means that it is sufficient that the employer negotiates with a union on any one of these matters for the union to be recognised within the meaning of the statute, although the precise extent of recognition is relevant to the scope of the rights to disclosure of information and time off. Recognition may be the product of an express agreement between the parties or implied from their conduct, probably only over a period of time.[224] We discuss in para 9.3 the considerations which are relevant in determining whether recognition can be implied. Even where express, voluntary recognition, granted wholly outside

---

[221] TULRCA 1992, s 178(3).
[222] TULRCA 1992, s 178(1).
[223] Defined TULRCA, s 296; see para 3.33 *et seq* above.
[224] *NUGSAT v Albury Bros Ltd* [1978] IRLR 504.

the statutory procedure, may be varied or withdrawn unilaterally by the employer although, as we outline in 9.4, derecognition may have legal implications which employers need to take into account. By contrast, as we explain in para 9.20, where a union has been recognised pursuant to a request under the statutory procedure, it may not normally be derecognised within three years, and if recognition was granted pursuant to a finding that a majority of workers were members of the applicant union or consequent upon a ballot, the employer may derecognise only if the requisite support for this course of action has been demonstrated in a ballot.

Although the legislation does not prevent employers and unions negotiating on matters outside the definition of 'collective bargaining', the list of matters specified in section 178(2) reflects a perception of the matters which are likely to be viewed as appropriate for joint regulation. Thus it does not extend to future investment strategy or product development, for example.[225] These matters are identical to those which constitute the subject-matter of a 'trade dispute' for the purpose of the statutory immunities relating to industrial action; the scope of 'legitimate' industrial action and that of 'collective bargaining' are therefore co-extensive. The case law relating to the interpretation of these matters (holding, for example, that in (a) 'terms of employment' extends beyond contractual terms and (b) can cover fear of future redundancies) has, in fact, issued from the industrial action context and we discuss it therefore in para 11.27.

The legal status and attributes of trade unions and of 'employers' associations'

7.28   At common law the legal nature of trade unions is based on an association of individuals bound together by a contract of membership which regulates the relationship between those members. Although this remains their legal basis, in reality they are subject to a complex overlay of statutory provisions which modify the common law position in most important areas.[226] Thus, for example, all property belonging to the union must be vested in trust for the union (not, notably, for its members)[227] and unions can only exclude individuals from membership on grounds specified by statute.[228] In this section we outline those provisions which relate to the legal status of unions and indicate in broad terms the scope of public accountability.[229] We analyse in greater detail in chapter 10 the extensive statutory constraints upon the conduct of internal trade union affairs, enforceable by union members. Their intricacy and complexity casts doubt on whether unions can in any sense now be regarded as voluntary autonomous bodies.

---

[225] Cf the wider range of matters on which employers must inform and consult information and consultation representatives under the standard provisions in ICER 2004, reg 20: see further para 9.54.

[226] We refer here only to the modern law. For further detail on the history of the law in this area see Elias and Ewing, 1987, and references therein.

[227] TULRCA 1992, s 12 and see *Hughes v TGWU* [1985] IRLR 382 (individual members have no interest severable or in common in union property); cf the puzzling wording of s 23(2)(b) which refers to 'property belonging to any member of the union otherwise than jointly or in common with the other members'.

[228] See para 10.9 below.

[229] For a more detailed consideration of these matters see G Morris and T Archer, 2000: paras 2.8–2.11.

The significant features of the legal status of trade unions fall into three broad categories. First, although they cannot be incorporated,[230] they have been accorded by statute many of the attributes of incorporated bodies. Thus, they are capable of making contracts; they can sue[231] and be sued, and are amenable to criminal prosecution, in their own name; and judgments, awards and orders may be enforced against any property held in trust for the union (although certain property is protected against the enforcement of any award of damages, costs or expenses).[232] Second, they have statutory protection against the common law doctrine of restraint of trade, without which it would be impossible for most unions to function lawfully;[233] the purposes of a trade union are not, by reason only that they are in restraint of trade, unlawful so as to make any members liable to criminal proceedings or so as to make any agreement or trust void or voidable, nor is any union rule unlawful or unenforceable on that ground.[234] Finally, although trade unions have been potentially liable in tort since the Employment Act 1982, there are statutory limits on the amount of damages which may be awarded against a union in any proceedings in tort (with specified exceptions).[235] We discuss further in para 11.47 the nature and importance of these limits in relation to liability for organising industrial action which is the context in which, in practice, they are likely to be most relevant.

Unlike trade unions, employers' associations may be either incorporated or unincorporated.[236] Where unincorporated, they have the same attributes of incorporated bodies as do trade unions.[237] Again, all the property must be vested in trust for the association.[238]

7.29   Both trade unions and employers' associations[239] (regardless of whether they are listed) are subject to detailed obligations in respect of their accounting practices.[240] They must also submit an annual return to the Certification Officer which includes audited revenue accounts and such other audited accounts as he or she requires, together with a balance sheet and a

---

[230] TULRCA 1992, s 10(1), (2) (cf the Industrial Relations Act 1971, s 74, which accorded registered trade unions corporate status). There is an exception in the case of the 13 (as at the end of March 2011) 'special register bodies' which are companies registered under the Companies Act 1985 or incorporated by charter or letters patent whose names appeared on a special register maintained under the Industrial Relations Act 1971, s 84: TULRCA 1992, s 117. These organisations are bodies whose principal purposes are to maintain professional standards or training but which also became involved in negotiating terms and conditions of employment for their members. Most are in the public services; they include the Royal College of Nursing of the United Kingdom and the British Medical Association. Special register bodies whose principal purposes do not include employer-worker relations cannot be listed or seek a certificate of independence. There are various exceptions and modifications to the legislation governing trade unions which apply to these bodies: TULRCA 1992, s 117(3), (4).
[231] There has been some doubt as to whether unions can sue in defamation: in *EETPU v Times Newspapers Ltd* [1980] 1 All ER 1097, it was held they could not, but cf *NUGMW v Gillian* [1946] KB 81, cited without adverse comment by the House of Lords in *Derbyshire County Council v Times Newspapers Ltd* [1993] 1 All ER 1011.
[232] TULRCA 1992, s 12(2). See s 23 for the definition of protected property.
[233] In *Hornby v Close* (1867) LR 2 QB 153 it was held that the purposes of a union whose rules enabled a majority to control the terms on which all members disposed of their labour were unlawful. The TUA 1871 granted protection as far as trade union purposes were concerned; this was extended to trade union rules by TULRA 1974 following the suggestion in *Edwards v SOGAT* [1971] Ch 354 that the 1871 Act did not protect rules in restraint of trade.
[234] TULRCA 1992, s 11.
[235] TULRCA 1992, s 22.
[236] TULRCA 1992, s 127.
[237] TULRCA 1992, s 127.
[238] TULRCA 1992, s 129.
[239] Except those which consist wholly or mainly of representatives of constituent or affiliated organisations.
[240] TULRCA 1992, ss 28 and 131.

copy of the organisation's rules.[241] In relation to trade unions, details of the salary paid to, and other benefits provided to or in respect of, the president, general secretary and each member of the executive during that period must also be included.[242] Unions and employers' associations must supply any person on request with a copy of their most recent annual return and of their rules (either free or on payment of a reasonable charge) and the Certification Officer must keep copies of all returns available for public inspection.[243] In addition, union members must be supplied with a statement containing specified information, including the total income and expenditure for the period to which the return relates; how much income consisted of payments in respect of membership; the income and expenditure of the political fund, if relevant; and information as to the salary and benefits referred to above.[244] It should also include the auditor's report together with a prescribed statement which advises members of the action they may take should they consider that some irregularity may be occurring, or has occurred, in the conduct of the union's financial affairs.[245] It is a criminal offence for a union or employers' association to refuse or wilfully neglect to perform any of these duties, punishable by a fine of up to level 5 on the standard scale.[246] Where the organisation is guilty of such an offence it is deemed also to have been committed by any officer bound by the rules to discharge the relevant duty or, if none, every member of the general committee of management.[247] It is also an offence, punishable with up to six months' imprisonment as well as a fine, wilfully to alter a document required for the statutory purposes, to falsify it or to enable the organisation to evade any statutory requirements.[248] Unions have a duty to ensure that no person convicted of any of these offences holds any office in the union covered by the mandatory election requirements described in para 10.14.[249] The Certification Officer is responsible for enforcing the statutory requirements[250] and since 1993 has been granted extensive powers of investigation in relation to the financial affairs both of unions and employers' associations including the power, in specified circumstances, to appoint an inspector to conduct an investigation.[251]

---

[241] TULRCA 1992, ss 32 and 131.

[242] TULRCA 1992, s 32(3)(aa). See para 10.14 below for the definition of these posts.

[243] TULRCA 1992, ss 27, 32, 131.

[244] TULRCA 1992, s 32A(3).

[245] TULRCA 1992, s 32A(5), (6).

[246] TULRCA 1992, ss 45, 45A, 131. At the time of writing £5,000 is level 5 on the standard scale established by the Criminal Justice Act 1982, s 37(2), as amended.

[247] TULRCA 1992, ss 45, 131.

[248] TULRCA 1992, ss 45, 131.

[249] TULRCA 1992, s 45B.

[250] Note, however, that the Certification Officer does not generally undertake prosecutions for offences such as theft or fraud which would normally be dealt with by other prosecuting authorities: *Annual Report of the Certification Officer for 2007–2008*, para 3.11.

[251] TULRCA 1992, s 37A–37E; s 131. Up to 31 March 2011 the Certification Officer had used his powers to appoint an inspector on four occasions. Where the Certification Officer looks into a possible financial irregularity which has been raised by a union member and decides not to appoint an inspector he must notify that member of his decision and, if he thinks fit, give his reasons: *Annual Report of the Certification Officer for 2010-2011*, para 3.25.

THE ROLE OF TRADE UNIONS IN CONTEMPORARY INDUSTRIAL RELATIONS

7.30   Trade unions currently face an uncertain future.[252] First, and most fundamentally, the number of workers who are union members has fallen substantially, from a post-war peak of 13.2 million in 1979 to just over 7.3 million in 2009/10,[253] although the decline in recent years has been relatively modest (in 1998 there were 7.8 million union members) and for a short period there were slight increases. [254] As well as being a decline in absolute numbers since 1979, the statistics show a large fall in the proportion of the active labour force in the UK who are unionised; over half in 1979, 26.6% in 2010.[255] It is also notable that membership is concentrated in the public services; in 2010 union density in the public sector was 56.3% as compared with 14.2% in the private sector.[256] A particularly worrying feature for the unions is the low proportion of young workers in trade unions.[257]

Several reasons have been identified for the decline in union membership since 1979 although the weight of their respective contributions is more difficult to assess.[258] The evidence suggests that in the first half of the 1980s the demise of large, highly-unionised manufacturing plants was an important factor.[259] Moreover, employment growth has been concentrated in areas in which unions have traditionally not been well represented – smaller enterprises and private sector services, where work is often offered on a part-time, casualised or self-employed basis; indeed, the failure to organise in establishments and firms set up since 1980 has been claimed to be the critical factor in union decline.[260] However, this alone does not provide a sufficient explanation, given that the decline in membership and density is a feature of all categories of employment.[261] More difficult to measure, but also influential, was the anti-union culture which, as we saw in para 7.17, it was the policy of the 1979–1997 Conservative Government to promote; in the words of Professor Brian Towers 'a climate in which employers ... increasingly adopted anti-union or union

---

[252] For surveys of the issues see the Report of the House of Commons Employment Committee, Session 1993–94, *The Future of the Trade Unions*, HC 676-I; Taylor, 1994; Fairbrother, 2000; Machin, 2000; J Waddington, 2003b; Gospel and Wood, 2003; Heery *et al*, 2003; Charlwood, 2004b; Metcalf, 2004; Ewing, 2005; Simms and Charlwood, 2010. Note that the challenges facing unions are not confined to the UK (see Hyman, 1994; W Brown *et al*, 1997: p 74; Crouch, 2000; Raday, 2002; Kochan, 2003; Blanchflower, 2007), although the nature of these challenges may vary between countries.

[253] *Annual Report of the Certification Officer for 2010-2011*, para 4.3 *et seq*; App 4. This figure is based on returns from unions and includes all members (eg retired and unemployed members), not only those paying contributions; the total number of contributing members was around 8.5% less than the figure for total membership: para 4.8. Estimates derived from the Labour Force Survey show a lower figure for 2010 but the two sources are not directly comparable: see Achur, 2011: p 42.

[254] *Annual Report of the Certification Officer for 2009–2010*, p 2.

[255] Achur, 2011 : p 1. Achur, 2011 contains a detailed breakdown of union membership by occupational group, gender, age etc. and of trends over time.

[256] Achur, 2011 : p 4.

[257] In 2010 UK employees aged 16-24 accounted for 4.8% of union members Achur, 2011: p 18; see also Table 3.5. This phenomenon is not confined to Britain: see Blanchflower, 2007.

[258] See the Memorandum from Professor Brian Towers to the Employment Committee, Volume III, Appendices to the Minutes of Evidence, HC 676-III; Kessler and Bayliss, 1995; J Waddington and C Whitson, 1995; W Brown *et al*, 1997: p 74; Millward *et al*, 2000: pp 230–234; Crouch, 2000; Machin, 2000, 2003; Bryson and Gomez, 2005; Simms and Charlwood, 2010.

[259] Millward *et al*, 1992: pp 101–102.

[260] Cully *et al*, 1999: pp 234–238; Machin, 2000

[261] Cully and Woodland, 1997: p 232; see also Millward *et al*, 2000: pp 84–95. There is a rising number of employees who have never been union members: Bryson and Gomez, 2005.

avoidance policies and public policy and legislation ... sought to weaken trade union authority and influence at the place of work and in political and economic institutions affecting policy.'[262] A further contributory factor in the decline of union influence was the reduction in the proportion of employers recognising trade unions and the consequent reduction in the coverage of collective bargaining. As we indicate in chapter 9, employers found alternative methods of communicating with their workers which may leave little room for trade union involvement.

Unions have responded in a number of different ways to these various pressures. First, there has been a growing movement for individual unions to seek partners for mergers.[263] In 1962 there were 182 unions affiliated to the TUC;[264] in March 1998, 73; and by December 2011, 58.[265] A prominent example of this process was the amalgamation between the National and Local Government Officers Association, the National Union of Public Employees and the Confederation of Health Service Employees to form UNISON – The Public Service Union in 1993 which, with over 1.5 million members at the time of merger, became at the time the largest union in the country (although its membership has since decreased[266]). Another was the amalgamation of the Manufacturing Science and Finance Union with the Amalgamated Engineering and Electrical Union in 2002 to form Amicus, with more than a million members.[267] In 2007, Amicus itself merged with the Transport and General Workers' Union to form Unite the Union, with an estimated 1,938,000 members.[268] Unions embarking upon mergers claim that the resulting economies of scale allow them to provide better services more effectively. It is also a development which some employers seem to favour because of its effect in simplifying bargaining structures. It carries the danger, however, that such unions can become monolithic and remote from their members.[269] Moreover, far from simplifying the trade union structure, mergers have merely added to its complexity; because mergers have taken place across industrial and occupational boundaries, unions have created complex forms of internal representation which have thus 'transformed traditional issues of inter-union relations into intra-union relations, with no obvious benefits in terms of strategic advantage.'[270]

Second, unions adopted a 'managerial servicing relationship' in which they sought 'to research members' needs and design and promote attractive servicing packages in response,'[271] placing greater emphasis on benefits beyond collective bargaining, such as legal services, professional advice, cash benefits covering accident insurance and convalescence, representation at work or in employment tribunals, and advantageous deals on mortgages and loans, life assurance, credit cards, home and motor insurance and travel. Unions recognised that 'consumerist' benefits would not

---

[262] Note 258 above.

[263] This is not only a British phenomenon: see J Waddington, 2006.

[264] Evidence of the TUC to the Employment Committee, Vol II, p 40.

[265] See www.tuc.org.uk. In 2010/11 the 14 unions with over 100,000 members accounted for 85.7% of total union (TUC and non-TUC affiliated) membership: *Annual Report of the Certification Officer for 2010–2011*, para 4.5.

[266] In 2009/10 it stood at 1,374,500: *Annual Report of the Certification Officer for 2007–2008*, App 4.

[267] *Annual Report of the Certification Officer for 2003–2004*, App 4.

[268] *Annual Report of the Certification Officer for 2007–2008*, para 6.12. The two unions merged in 2007 and changed the name of the new union to Unite the Union in 2008. In 2009/10 the total membership of Unite the Union was 1,572,995: *Annual Report of the Certification Officer for 2010-2011* App 4.

[269] House of Commons Employment Committee, above, note 252, paras 90–101.

[270] Heery *et al*, 2003: p 84; see also J Waddington, 2003: pp 222–224 and J Waddington, 2006, where it is argued that the intended objectives are rarely achieved in the merger process and energies are diverted from union renewal.

[271] Heery, 1996: p 187; see also Ewing, 2005, for discussion of these developments.

of themselves suffice to attract members,[272] and recent developments have the potential to bring more work-related services to the fore again, such as helplines on individual rights, representation at disciplinary and grievance hearings (now a statutory right),[273] and collective consultation and collective bargaining.[274] The advent of the Labour Government brought unions a greater role in workplace training, with £81 million of public money having been given to unions from a 'Union Learning Fund' by 2006[275] and, since 2003, 'union learning representatives' having a right to paid time off from work.[276] In addition the TUC established an 'Organising Academy' to which unions can send representatives to train as specialist membership recruiters.[277] The ERelA 2004 gave the Secretary of State authority to provide financial assistance to independent trade unions for, *inter alia*, improving the way they carry out their functions and increasing the range of services they offer to their members.[278] In total £5-10 million was allocated to the 'Union Modernisation Fund', with funding spread over several years, with the aim of supporting innovative projects which would speed unions' adaptation to changing labour market trends and new ways of working, and provide examples of best practice for other unions to follow.[279]

In relation to employers, unions have sought to emphasise their ability to co-operate as partners, rather than as adversaries, in introducing greater flexibility and change whilst at the same time protecting the interests of employees.[280] 'Partnership' is a difficult concept to define,[281] but in 1999 the TUC identified what it regarded as the principles underlying it: shared commitment to the organisation's business goals; recognition that the partners may have legitimate differences which needed to be heard; recognition that flexibility of employment should not be at the expense of employees' security, which should be protected by measures such as ensuring transferable skills and qualifications; the need to improve the personal development of employees; open and well informed consultation, involving genuine dialogue; and 'adding value' by raising employee motivation.[282] In 2001 the TUC launched a Partnership Institute to help organisations improve industrial relations and develop partnerships between unions and employers.[283] The CBI also associated itself with this initiative, and partnership deals have been signed at a wide variety of workplaces, although their content varies significantly,[284] ranging from 'some that do indeed seek to nurture trade unions as genuinely representative and independent, albeit on a cooperative basis, through to some that are thinly veiled devices to limit and constrain union influence.'[285] Research suggests, however, that 'any "partnership movement", if it ever got going, has run out

---

[272]   Heery, 1996: p 190.

[273]   ERelA 1999, ss 10–15; see para 5.121 *et seq*.

[274]   On unions and the enforcement of individual statutory rights, see Colling, 2006.

[275]   McIlroy, 2008, p 296; see pp 295–298 for the history and operation of the fund. See Hayes and Rainbird, 2011 for an analysis of the Fund's use by UNISON and Findlay and Warhurst, 2011 for an evaluation of the Scottish Union Learning Fund.

[276]   TULRCA 1992, s 168A. See further para 8.44.

[277]   Heery *et al*, 2003; Heery and Simms, 2008; Gall, 2010b.

[278]   TULRCA 1992, s 116A, inserted by ERelA 2004, s 55. There is a specific prohibition on funds being added to a union's political fund: s116A(4)–(7).

[279]   For an evaluation of two out of the three funding rounds, see Stuart *et al*, 2009, 2010.

[280]   See Taylor, 1994: ch 5; Taylor, 2000: ch 8.

[281]   See Guest *et al* 2008.

[282]   *Partners for Progress: New Unionism at the Workplace*; see W Brown 2000: pp 305–306.

[283]   W Brown and S Oxenbridge, 2004: p 73.

[284]   W Brown 2000: p 306; Bacon and Storey, 2000; Guest and Peccei, 2001; Heery, 2002; Oxenbridge and Brown, 2004; Taylor, 2004; Stuart and Martinez-Lucio, 2005.

[285]   W Brown and S Oxenbridge, 2004: p 73.

of steam'.[286] Other signs of revival in collective representation may also have stalled. The period 1998-2004 showed an increase in the incidence of voluntary recognition agreements, reached in the shadow of the statutory recognition procedure[287] but as we discuss in para 9.2 this has not resulted in an extension of collective bargaining coverage. The legislation on information and consultation, which came into force in April 2005,[288] has the potential to encourage the establishment of consultative bodies on a voluntary basis, but these are not confined to union representatives and, perhaps surprisingly, to date unions have made limited use of ICER 2004.[289] Finally, the role of unions (and employers) as social partners has been enhanced at European Union level, within the framework of the 'social dialogue', although there are unresolved issues of 'representativity' in this area, given that the TUC does not represent all workers nor even all trade unionists, nor does the CBI represent all employers. To some extent the practice of social dialogue was reflected in discussions involving the TUC and CBI which preceded the enactment of the statutory recognition procedure under ERel 1999, the information and consultation provisions in ICER 2004 and the AWR 2011. Although this process has no formal status in British law, the legislative passage of measure based on agreements between the social partners is likely to be eased and the risk reduced that they will be subjected to legal challenge in domestic courts where they are introduced to implement EU obligations. For example, as we explain in para 9.58 below, the fact that the requirement for a minimum level of employee support before employers are required to establish an information and consultation procedure under ICER 2004 was the product of TUC and CBI agreement made it less likely their compatibility with Directive 2004/14 would be challenged in judicial review proceedings.

During the period of the 1979–1997 Conservative Government trade unions became increasingly excluded from the political process, collective bargaining coverage contracted, and the decline in membership seemed irreversible. The picture now is more mixed. At the time of writing the future of trade unions continues to be unpredictable. The Labour Government of 1997-2010 produced a more (if not wholly) hospitable political environment, as reflected in changes to the law relating to recognition, consultation and representation of workers, and the Coalition Government has not, at the time of writing, sought materially to amend these provisions. However, given the significant disparity in levels of union membership in the public and private sectors, the budget cuts to public services and consequent reductions in staffing levels pose the biggest single challenge for trade unions in the immediate future.

---

[286] Guest *et al*, 2008: p 149.
[287] Gall and McKay, 1999; Gall, 2004; S Wood *et al*, 2002; Moore *et al*, 2004, 2005.
[288] See para 9.50.
[289] See further para 9.29.

8

FREEDOM OF ASSOCIATION AND THE RIGHT TO ORGANISE

INTRODUCTION

8.1   As we saw in chapter 7, workers' freedom to associate and organise may potentially be subject to restriction by the state, by employers, or, arguably, by trade unions exercising power to admit, or expel from, membership. There we examined the history and current scope of restrictions on freedom of association imposed by the state. In this chapter we analyse workers' rights in relation to trade union membership and activities as regards employers. The rights which the law gives individuals in relation to trade unions are discussed in chapter 10.

   The chapter begins by analysing the legal position of workers who are denied employment, or dismissed or otherwise disadvantaged, because of their trade union membership or activities. This includes consideration of the right not to be induced to move from terms of employment that have been collectively agreed. We also examine the remedies of those who are subject to disadvantageous treatment because they *refuse* to join a union, although whether the right not to join should be regarded as intrinsic to freedom of association in the employment context, and of equal status to the right to join, is a contentious issue which we address later in the chapter. We discuss this question within this framework because the development of the legislation which upholds the right to join cannot be properly understood in isolation from it. We also, in this connection, outline restrictions upon the operation of contract compliance policies relating to union membership or non-membership. We then consider the extent to which the law provides more positive support for union organisation by requiring employers to allow time off during working hours for union representatives and other union members. Unlike the provisions relating to anti-union discrimination, these rights are confined to members of unions which are recognised. Finally, we examine the legal restrictions which surround the practice of the 'check-off' whereby employers deduct union subscriptions from workers' pay and pass them directly to the union. As this summary demonstrates the chapter involves a heterogenous collection of rights whose fragmented nature can be properly understood only in the light of their legislative history.

PROTECTION OF TRADE UNION MEMBERSHIP AND ACTIVITIES IN RELATION TO EMPLOYERS

8.2   All workers other than the police[1] are now free to form and join trade unions.[2] However, this negative freedom from restraint means little if its exercise can be thwarted by employers refusing to employ, or dismissing or otherwise discriminating against, trade union members. This point is emphasised by ILO Convention No 98 which states that '[w]orkers shall enjoy adequate protection against acts of anti-union discrimination in respect of their employment', more particularly in relation to acts 'calculated to (a) Make the employment of a worker subject to the condition that he shall not join a union or shall relinquish trade union membership; (b) Cause the dismissal or otherwise prejudice a worker by reason of union activities or because of participation in union activities outside working hours or, with the consent of the employer, within working hours'.[3]

As we saw in chapter 7, legal intervention in Britain in this area came late. Official encouragement of trade union membership and participation following the reports of the Whitley Committee[4] was manifested by the Government seeking to set an example to the private sector by its own employment practices rather than by introducing legislation upholding the right to organise.[5] However, exhorting public servants to join trade unions was not universally successful in persuading other employers, particularly in the white-collar sectors, to follow suit.[6] Employer strategies to discourage union organisation ranged from making it a term of the contract of employment that employees should not join trade unions, denying union members promotion and pay rises, and continuously transferring active unionists between departments, on the one hand, to establishing 'company unions' to ward off external organisations and offering rewards to 'loyal' employees on the other.[7] The 1946 version of the House of Commons Fair Wages Resolution (now rescinded) specified that government contracts with private employers should require contractors to recognise the freedom of their workers to be members of trade unions. However, although symbolically significant, the Resolution appears to

---

[1] Police Act 1996, s 64. See further para 7.13 above.

[2] Members of the armed forces (as well as the police) are specifically excluded from the anti-union discrimination provisions: TULRCA 1992, ss 274, 280. Note also s 275 which permits particular groups of persons, or particular individuals, in Crown employment to be exempted from the application of the Act, and thus from the statutory protections against anti-union discrimination, for the purpose of safeguarding national security; this enables it to be made a valid term of employment for members of the security and intelligence agencies that they will not join a trade union. See para 7.10 above on the withdrawal of the freedom of workers at Government Communications Headquarters to join national civil service trade unions (now reinstated). In addition, if on a complaint of unfair dismissal, or a complaint relating to an inducement or detriment under TULRCA 1992, ss 145A, 145B or 146, it is shown that the action complained of was taken for the purpose of safeguarding national security, the employment tribunal must dismiss the complaint: ETA 1996, s 10(1), as substituted by ERelA 1999 and amended by ERelA 2004.

[3] Convention Concerning the Application of the Principles of the Right to Organise and to Bargain Collectively, 1949, Art 1.

[4] For a summary of the Committee's recommendations, and references to interim reports, see Ministry of Reconstruction: Committee on Relations between Employers and Employed: *Final Report*, Cd 9153 (1918).

[5] See generally Fredman and Morris, 1989: ch 4.

[6] See the *Report of the Royal Commission on Trade Unions and Employers' Associations 1965–1968* (the Donovan Commission), Cmnd 3623, 1968, paras 213–224.

[7] See Bain, 1970: pp 131–135, who divides such strategies into those of 'forceful opposition' and 'peaceful competition'.

have been of little practical effect in influencing employment practices due to inadequate monitoring and enforcement.[8]

8.3   The United Kingdom was the first country to ratify ILO Conventions 87 and 98 (in 1949 and 1950 respectively). However, the first statutory intervention to uphold freedom of association came only in 1971,[9] when the Industrial Relations Act extended protection to workers against discrimination by employers on grounds of trade union membership and participation in union activities (as well as bestowing correlative rights not to join). As these rights applied only to membership of unions which 'registered' under the Act, and it was TUC policy not to do this, they had little practical effect. They were maintained in an amended form in the 1974–1979 Labour Government's 'Social Contract' legislation and have continued in force, with important modifications, ever since. Their survival – and indeed, extension[10] – in a climate hostile to trade unions during the period of the 1979–1997 Conservative Government can be understood only by appreciating that the real target of that government's policy was the protection of the right not to join a union, a right to which these provisions were perceived as the corollary. Initially the Labour Government which succeeded it maintained the basic framework intact in its essentials. However ERelA 2004 significantly extended the scope of protection to give effect to the decision of the European Court of Human Rights in *Wilson and NUJ v UK, Palmer, Wyeth and RMT v UK* and *Doolan and others v UK*,[11] discussed in para 7.9 above. In these cases the employers had each refused a pay rise to employees who refused to transfer to personal contracts in place of collectively agreed terms and conditions of employment. These contracts also required those who signed them to forego the entitlement to be represented by a union in some or all of their dealings with the employer. The ECtHR held that the UK had failed in its positive obligation to secure the enjoyment of rights guaranteed by Article 11 of the ECHR by permitting employers to use financial incentives to induce employees to surrender important union rights. 'This failure amounted to a violation of Article 11, as regards both the applicant unions and the individual applicants.'[12] In response to the judgment, the government introduced a new right for a worker not to have an offer made to him or her by an employer where the employer's sole or main purpose is that workers' terms of employment, or any such term, will not be determined by collective agreement.[13] It is also now unlawful to offer a worker an inducement not to join an independent union, or to participate in its activities or use its services, or to join a union.[14] These provisions are in addition to the more long-standing remedies against discrimination by employers on trade union grounds. The Labour Government also introduced amendments to the pre-existing law to

---

[8] See Bercusson, 1978: ch 17. The Local Government Act 1988 made it unlawful for local authorities and certain other bodies to stipulate such requirements; see now the Local Government Act 1999, s 19 and SI 2001/909, discussed at para 2.6; see also TULRCA, 1992, ss 144 and 145, discussed in para 8.38 below.

[9] The Donovan Commission (above, note 6) pointed out (para 243) that these Conventions were not drafted in terms which required legislation; 'successive British Governments' had taken the view that the trade union movement was sufficiently strong to make legislation unnecessary and the TUC had not pressed for it.

[10] For example the introduction of enhanced compensation levels and protection against discriminatory hiring.

[11] Judgment of 2 July 2002, [2002] IRLR 568. See Ewing, 2003.

[12] Above, para 48.

[13] TULRCA 1992, s 145B–145F, inserted by ERelA 2004, s 29.

[14] TULRCA 1992, s 145A, 145C–145F, inserted by ERelA 2004, s 29.

deal with matters it considered would have been regarded by the Court as contrary to Article 11 had they been at issue.[15]

In broad terms the legislation now provides access to remedies (which cannot be excluded by contract) in relation to three major forms of discrimination by employers,[16] although, as the more detailed analysis below reveals, their application is hedged around with restrictions. First, employees have the right not to be dismissed (or selected for redundancy[17]) on account of their membership of an independent trade union or participation in the activities of, or making use of the services of, such a union at an appropriate time.[18] Protection also extends to dismissal (or selection for redundancy) for failing to accept an inducement not to be a union member or engage in such activities or to move from terms of employment that have been collectively agreed. Second, workers (not only 'employees') have the right not to be subjected to any detriment by any act, or deliberate failure to act, to penalise or deter such membership or activities or because of the worker's failure to accept an inducement.[19] The detriment in question may amount to dismissal, but only for workers who are not 'employees'; those who are employees must rely upon the protection described above.[20] Last, it is unlawful to refuse a person employment because he or she is a member of a union.[21] Significantly, however, it is not unlawful to refuse employment because of participation in union activities unless such a refusal relates to a 'prohibited list' (colloquially known as a 'blacklist').[22]

8.4   We examine the scope of each of these rights in turn before assessing, from a broader perspective, their effectiveness in protecting the freedom to associate and organise. It should be noted that despite the changes introduced by ERelA 2004 there are still respects in which the legislation, and case law interpreting that legislation, does not fully comply with international

---

[15] Memorandum from the DTI in response to concerns raised by the Committee in its Third and Fourth Progress Report of Session 2003–2004, Joint Committee on Human Rights, Thirteenth Report, Session 2003–2004. Appendix 2a, para 44. Examples given of such additional matters include new TULRCA 1992, s 145A and the application of ss 145A, 145B, and 146 to 'workers' rather than 'employees'. ERelA 2004 also repealed the notorious 'Ullswater Amendment' contained in s 148(3)–(5) and ERelA 1999, s 17 (the latter was never brought into force). See G Morris and T Archer, 2000: paras 3.12 and 4.72 for an analysis of these repealed provisions.

[16] Certain categories of worker are excluded from these rights: see note 2 above. For the protections against prejudicial action for those involved in health and safety activities see para 5.104 above.

[17] Here it must be shown that the circumstances constituting the redundancy (the principal reason for dismissal) applied equally to one or more other employees in the same undertaking who held positions similar to that held by the applicant and who have not been dismissed by the employer, and the reason or principal reason for selection was one of those specified in TULRCA 1992, s 152(1): TULRCA 1992, s 153. There is no requirement to find that employers were motivated by malice or the deliberate desire to be rid of a union activist: *Dundon v GPT Ltd* [1995] IRLR 403, EAT. In determining whether the dismissed employee and his or her comparator hold similar 'positions', regard should be paid only to their relative positions as employees; no account should be paid to what any of them did, or had a contractual right to do, in other capacities, such as a union official: *O'Dea v ISC Chemicals Ltd (t/a Rhône-Poulenc Chemicals)* [1995] IRLR 599, CA. Moreover, the way in which employees carry out their duties as union officials should not count either in their favour or against them: *Smiths Industries Aerospace and Defence Systems v Rawlings* [1996] IRLR 656 (a case concerning a health and safety representative).

[18] TULRCA 1992, s 152, as amended by ERelA 2004, s 32. In *Driver v Cleveland Structural Engineering Co Ltd* [1994] IRLR 636 the EAT held that this section could also cover the situation where a redundant employee was not offered alternative employment within the organisation; if this was on grounds of trade union membership or activities it would be automatically unfair.

[19] TULRCA 1992 s 146, as amended by ERelA 2004, ss 30, 31.

[20] TULRCA 1992, s 146(5A), inserted by ERelA 2004, s 30(6).

[21] TULRCA 1992, s 137.

[22] Employment Relations Act 1999 (Blacklists) Regulations 2010, SI 2010/493.

standards. The HRA 1998 may be invoked to persuade courts and tribunals towards a more expansive interpretation of some of these provisions, and may afford a free-standing right to individuals and unions discriminated against by public authorities (or, at least, 'pure' public authorities) who lie outside the ambit of the specific protections or whose particular activities are not protected;[23] Article 11 of the ECHR, which guarantees the right to join to trade unions, applies to '[e]veryone', as does Article 10, which guarantees the right to freedom of expression.[24] In addition, as we saw in para 7.11, there is authority in EU law to support the recognition of freedom of association as a fundamental right,[25] and the ECJ has derived from the right to join trade unions a right to participate in their activities. However, the scope of these rights awaits clarification. From another perspective it should also be noted that legislation to implement EU law obligations, in particular rights to information and consultation, which we discuss in chapter 9, may encourage the fragmentation of worker representation away from the single channel of trade unions, the traditional repository of this role in Britain, to a dual channel system which also incorporates the establishment of representative bodies existing separately from unions, although union members and officials may be elected to them. Those who serve on these representative bodies are protected against dismissal or other detriment for exercising their functions, as are employees who participate in activities related to their establishment, but there is no broader protection against discrimination of the kind that applies in relation to trade unions and their activities. The more frequent establishment of bodies of this nature prompts the question as to whether the scope of protection for freedom of association and the right to organise should expand commensurately to cover collective organisation and activity beyond the ambit of traditional trade unionism.

Protection for employees against dismissal: procedure and remedies

8.5   Protection for employees against dismissal for trade union membership and activities is secured through the unfair dismissal procedure described in chapter 5.[26] It is thus confined at the time of writing to 'employees'.[27] However, since 1 October 2004, protection against subjection to a detriment has applied to the broader category of 'workers', and 'workers' who are not 'employees' may rely upon that protection, discussed in para 8.13 *et seq* below, in the event of dismissal.[28] However, as we discuss in para 3.33 *et seq*, this may still leave some categories of dependent labour, such as casual workers, unprotected unless courts and tribunals can be persuaded, in accordance

---

[23] Sections 6, 7.

[24] See *Paloma Sanchez v Spain* judgment of 12 September 2011, [2011] IRLR 934, ECtHR, which also emphasises the positive obligation of the state in this area.

[25] Note also Art 12 of the Charter of Fundamental Rights of the European Union, which affirms the right to form and join trade unions in similar terms to Art 11 of the ECHR. See para 2.39 for the status of the Charter.

[26] In addition to the protections described in this section, there is additional protection against dismissal relating to a blacklist. As the latter differs in some important respects from the protections we describe here we analyse it separately in para 8.27 *et seq* below.

[27] See para 3.19 *et seq*. As with the general provisions Crown employment (other than the armed forces and those excluded under TULRCA 1992, s 275) is included.

[28] TULRCA 1992, s 146, as amended by ERelA 2004, s 30. 'Employees' are excluded from that protection in relation to dismissal by s 146(5A). See s 151(1B) for the definition of 'worker' for the purposes of ss 146–150.

with the HRA 1998,[29] to construe the term more broadly than in other contexts in order to give effect to the protection afforded by Articles 10 and 11 of the ECHR to '[e]veryone'.[30] As we discuss in para 8.13 below, requiring 'employees' to rely upon the 'unfair dismissal' protection rather than the general protection against 'detriment' in this context can, in some respects, put them at a disadvantage, and may produce the unusual situation of individuals arguing that they are 'workers' other than 'employees'.

Subject to the constraint on its personal scope, the legislation accords some specific recognition of the position of trade unions in that dismissal,[31] and (with one exception[32]) selection for redundancy, on grounds of union membership and activities are subject to some special provisions (which also apply to dismissals on certain other grounds[33]).

First, once such a reason is found by the employment tribunal, the dismissal is automatically unfair; an employer cannot argue that it was reasonable in the circumstances.

Second, no minimum period of employment is required.[34] As we discussed in para 5.94, it had for many years been assumed, following the Court of Appeal decision in *Smith v Hayle Town Council*,[35] that where employees are claiming in circumstances where they would not otherwise qualify to claim, it is for them to prove the reason, or principal reason, for dismissal given that they are invoking a jurisdiction which the tribunal would otherwise not have.[36] Doubt has recently been cast on this position by *Kuzel v Roche Products Ltd*[37] where, in setting out the general principles applicable to the burden of proving the reason for dismissal, the Court of Appeal saw the burden as lying on the employer in all cases governed by the 1996 Act,[38] without distinguishing between those where continuity was established and those where it was not. However, it did not expressly cast doubt on *Smith*.[39] It seems, therefore, as if the burden of proof where continuity has not been established may continue to remain with the employee. This may be a difficult burden to satisfy, particularly as employers will generally take care to ensure that other reasons, such as poor work or a disciplinary offence, are attributed to such dismissals,[40] although the need to comply with the Code of Practice on Disciplinary and Grievance Procedures prior to dismissal may make it easier for an employee to refute a

---

[29] Section 3.

[30] See para 7.10 above for the exceptions to these guarantees. In cases where it is not possible for an individual to be deemed to be a 'worker', they will probably be denied a remedy unless they are employed by a 'public authority' against whom proceedings may be brought directly: HRA 1998, ss 6, 7.

[31] See para 5.65 *et seq* for the definition of 'dismissal'. In this context, as in relation to complaints of unfair dismissal on other grounds, 'constructive dismissal' is included.

[32] The remedy of 'interim relief' described below.

[33] See para 5.92 *et seq* above.

[34] TULRCA 1992, s 154, as substituted by ERelA 2004, s 35. The EAT has held that an employee can claim for unfair dismissal if her contract of employment is terminated for an 'anti-union' reason before she has taken up her duties: *Sarker v South Tees Acute Hospitals NHS Trust* [1997] IRLR 328.

[35] [1978] ICR 996.

[36] See also *Marley Tile Co Ltd v Shaw* [1980] ICR 72. Where an employee would otherwise qualify to claim, the employer must show that the reason for dismissal was one of those specified in ERA 1996, s 98(1), (2) in the usual way in order to defend the claim: *Maund v Penwith District Council* [1984] IRLR 24; *Kuzel v Roche Products Ltd* [2008] IRLR 530.

[37] [2008] IRLR 530.

[38] TULRCA 1992 s 152(1) states that *for the purposes of Part X of ERA 1996* the dismissal of an employee shall be regarded as unfair if it is for a reason specified in s 152.

[39] See Mummery LJ (who gave the only reasoned judgment) at [41]. In the EAT *Smith* was assumed to govern cases where the complainant lacked continuity: [2007] IRLR 309 at [27].

[40] Evans and Lewis, 1987: p 95. Cf the position under the 'blacklisting' provisions, discussed in para 8.27 *et seq* below.

specious reason.[41] The treatment of employees who have not been dismissed is usually irrelevant to whether the dismissal of the applicant is unfair. In this context, however, it may be important for the employee to show that non-unionists in a similar position have not been dismissed in order to undermine the credibility of the employer's evidence.[42] The difficulty of the employee's task in discharging the burden of proof may be exacerbated if the decision was taken by a group of persons, as the facts of *Smith v Hayle Town Council* exemplify. The applicant was a town clerk who applied to join a union. He told two councillors that he had done this. Shortly afterwards he was dismissed at a council meeting by a vote of six to five. The evidence showed that at least one member of the council had voted for dismissal because of his application to join a union but there was no evidence to show why the remaining five had voted as they did. The Court of Appeal concluded that, although there was an 'element of [anti-union] prejudice', that had not been shown to be the principal reason behind the thinking of the 'corporate mind'.[43]

The final departure from the norm in relation to dismissals for 'anti-union' reasons lies in the area of remedies. Here there are two distinctive features. First, the dismissed employee may apply for 'interim relief' pending the outcome of the tribunal hearing, provided that the application is presented within seven days of the effective date of termination[44] and is supported by a certificate signed by an official[45] of the union authorised to act for this purpose.[46] If the tribunal finds that the employee's claim is 'likely'[47] to succeed at the full hearing it may order his or her reinstatement or re-engagement pending the determination or settlement of the complaint or, if the employer refuses this, order the continuation of the contract, thus continuing the other benefits of employment until that time.[48] This provision reduces the need for the employee to seek other employment pending the tribunal hearing. Second, if the unfair dismissal complaint succeeds a minimum basic award of £5,300 is payable.[49] Prior to ERelA 1999 a complainant who sought reinstatement or re-engagement[50] was also entitled to a special award in addition to the

---

[41] See further para 5.125 *et seq*. Note para 29 of the Code in relation to disciplinary action against union representatives.

[42] Employment Tribunals (Constitution and Rules of Procedure) Regulations 2004, SI 2004/1861, Sch 1, para 10. Note that there is no equivalent under TULRCA 1992 to the Sex Discrimination (Questions and Replies) Order 1975, SI 1975/2048 or other similar provisions in the areas of race, disability, religion or belief, age or sexual orientation discrimination.

[43] [1978] ICR 996, 1003 (Eveleigh LJ).

[44] See para 5.80 *et seq* above.

[45] Defined in TULRCA 1992, s 119. Note that this is wide enough to cover shop stewards. On authorisation see *Sulemany v Habib Bank Ltd* [1983] ICR 60, EAT. For the required content of the certificate see s 161(3) and *Barley v Amey Roadstone Corpn Ltd* [1977] IRLR 299, EAT; *Stone v Charrington and Co Ltd* [1977] ICR 248, EAT; *Bradley v Edward Ryde and Sons* [1979] ICR 488, EAT; *Sulemany v Habib Bank*, above; *London Borough of Camden v Maharaj* EAT/1323/00, 9 November 2000.

[46] See generally TULRCA 1992, ss 161–166. Note that this remedy is also available where the applicant alleges that the dismissal is unfair on certain other grounds: see para 5.153 above. It does not apply to selection for redundancy on union grounds.

[47] This has been interpreted as 'pretty good': *Taplin v C Shippam Ltd* [1978] ICR 1068.

[48] *Quaere* whether, if a shop steward had a contractual right to be on the premises to exercise his or her functions (see *City and Hackney Health Authority v NUPE* [1985] IRLR 252, CA) this would be covered by TULRCA 1992, s 164(1), which includes 'any ... benefit derived from the employment ...' In practice such circumstances are likely to be rare. In *Dowling v ME Ilec Haulage and Berkeley Logistics Ltd* UKEAT/0836 it was held that liability under a continuation order did not transfer under TUPE.

[49] TULRCA 1992, s 156; rate as of 1 February 2012 and at the time of writing. This also applies if an employee has been selected for redundancy on trade union grounds under TULRCA 1992, s 153. However, the award may be reduced on the same grounds as in other cases subject to s 156(2) in cases of unfair selection for redundancy.

[50] See para 5.138 *et seq* above for the meaning of these terms and criteria for granting orders.

basic and compensatory awards.[51] This has now been abolished, and, as in other cases where employers fail to comply with an order to reinstate or re-engage an unfairly dismissed employee, an additional award which is limited to 26–52 weeks' pay may be made unless the employer shows that it was not reasonably practicable to comply with the order. As we indicated in para 5.141, the Court of Appeal has adopted a broad view of the concept of practicability in this context.[52] The restricted level of compensation for dismissal for trade union reasons stands in marked contrast to dismissal for 'whistleblowing' and reasons relating to health and safety, where there is no limit on the compensatory award.[53] We discuss the adequacy of the remedies in general further in para 8.26.

The scope of protection

8.6   The provisions outlined above apply where the principal reason for dismissal falls into one of four categories:[54] first, if the employee was, or proposed to become, a member of an independent trade union;[55] second, if the employee had taken part, or proposed to take part, in the activities of an independent trade union at an appropriate time;[56] third, if the employee had made use, or proposed to make use, of trade union services at an appropriate time;[57] and fourth, if an employee had failed to accept an offer made for a specified unlawful purpose.[58]

(i) Membership of an independent trade union

8.7   Dismissal for membership of an independent trade union has been held to cover membership of a particular union as well as unions in general so employees are protected if they are dismissed for joining union X instead of union Y.[59] This prevents employers from inhibiting employees' freedom to join the union of their choice. However, as a result of restrictive judicial interpretation of this provision, the extent to which the concept of union membership goes beyond a bare right

---

[51]   At the time of abolition, this stood at a minimum of £14,500 and a maximum of £29,000 if reinstatement or re-engagement was not ordered, and a minimum of £21,800 and a maximum of 156 weeks' pay if an order was made and not complied with.

[52]   See *Port of London Authority v Payne* [1994] IRLR 9.

[53]   ERA 1996, s 124(1A).

[54]   Note that where the terms of TULRCA 1992, s 152 (or s 153) are not satisfied an anti-union dismissal may still be unfair under the ordinary unfair dismissal provisions.

[55]   TULRCA 1992, s 152(1)(a). See para 7.23 above for the definition of an 'independent' trade union. The restriction means that members of 'embryonic' unions may be excluded: Todd, 2000: p 579. The employee need not have decided which particular union he or she wishes to join: *Cotter v Lynch Bros* [1972] IRLR 20. Membership of a union includes membership of a particular branch or section of that union or one of a number of such branches or sections, and references to taking part in the activities of a union and to services made available by a union are to be similarly construed: s 152(4), (5).

[56]   TULRCA 1992, s 152(1)(b). Where the employee is dismissed for proposing to take part in union activities there is no requirement to identify the precise activities: see *Fitzpatrick v British Railways Board* [1991] IRLR 376.

[57]   TULRCA 1992, s 152(1)(ba).

[58]   TULRCA 1992, S 152(1)(bb). See further para 8.17 *et seq* below.

[59]   *Ridgway and Fairbrother v National Coal Board* [1987] IRLR 80, CA. Although *Ridgway* was overruled in *Associated Newspapers Ltd v Wilson; Associated British Ports v Palmer* [1995] IRLR 258, this element of the reasoning in that case would appear to remain valid.

to hold a union card, and in particular whether it covers making use of union services, became unclear.[60] Prior to the introduction of extended protection against dismissal by ERelA 2004, this constituted a serious limitation, given that employers are likely to object not to the mere act of joining a union but to its practical implications. The specific protection now accorded against dismissal for making use of trade union services has removed much of the practical significance of this debate, although the issue may still arise if the individual's act (clarifying terms of employment, for example) is not at an 'appropriate time'; there is no such limitation in relation to union membership.

(ii) Participation in the activities of an independent trade union at an appropriate time

8.8   Crucial to the second reason are the concepts of '*activities of an independent trade union*' and '*appropriate time*'. '*Activities*' are not defined in the legislation; they clearly include activities connected with internal union organisation and industrial relations and should, in theory, extend to any activities which a union may lawfully undertake (although, in applying this term within the time off provisions, certain political activities have been excluded).[61] The courts have held that, because it is dealt with elsewhere in the legislation,[62] participation in industrial action (as opposed to preparation for it)[63] is not within the scope of protected activities[64] although, as others have argued,[65] this conclusion does not necessarily follow from the structure of the legislation: this separate provision relates only to whether the tribunal has jurisdiction to hear a claim; where it does have such jurisdiction there seems no reason why industrial action should not be a union activity. Ultimately this debate is of little practical significance as, to be effective, industrial action is unlikely to be at an 'appropriate time' (see below).

8.9   More problematic is the decision as to when activities are those '*of the union*'. The courts have emphasised that it is not sufficient that a union member is taking part in the type of activities which his or her union pursues ('trade union' is not 'adjectival');[66] rather, it seems that the union must in some sense have 'authorised' the individual to act on its behalf. Such authorisation will usually derive from custom and practice rather than being direct and specific. Thus, union members will generally be protected while participating in internal union affairs, such as recruitment and

---

[60] See *Discount Tobacco and Confectionery Ltd v Armitage* [1990] IRLR 15, EAT (membership extended to using the 'essential services' of the union); *Associated Newspapers Ltd v Wilson; Associated British Ports v Palmer* [1995] IRLR 258, HL (membership of a union and making use of its services could not be equated); *Speciality Care plc v Pachela* [1996] IRLR 248, EAT (observations in *Wilson* were *obiter*).

[61] See *Luce v London Borough of Bexley* [1990] IRLR 422, EAT, discussed in para 8.45 below. *Paloma Sanchez v Spain* judgment of 12 September 2011, [2011] IRLR 934, ECtHR may support a wider interpretation in this context.

[62] See para 11.73 *et seq*.

[63] *Britool Ltd v Roberts* [1993] IRLR 481, EAT.

[64] *Drew v St Edmundsbury Borough Council* [1980] IRLR 459, EAT.

[65] See, for example, P Davies and M Freedland, 1984: p 191; Harvey, 1972, as updated: Division NI, para 517 *et seq*. The strength of this argument may be reduced by the creation of protection against dismissal for taking 'protected industrial action' (see para 11.79), which could be seen as demonstrating the intention of the legislature that protection against dismissal should be confined to participation only in a restricted form of industrial action.

[66] *Dixon and Shaw v West Ella Developments Ltd* [1978] IRLR 151, 153 (Phillips J).

other organisational activities,[67] attending union meetings,[68] and discussing union matters.[69] Contacting a union official for advice in certain circumstances has also been included,[70] although since 1 October 2004 it would be preferable to rely on the specific protection for use of trade union services, discussed in para 8.11 below. On the basis of the case law, individual union members probably have little or no authority to act on behalf of the union in any dealings with the employer. In *Chant v Aquaboats Ltd*[71] a union member who organised a petition complaining about safety standards in the workplace was found not to have been taking part in the activities 'of the union' in presenting the petition to the employer, despite the fact that a union official had approved the petition before it was presented; this did not make it a communication of the union given that Mr Chant was not a shop steward and the petition had been signed by a majority of workers who were not union members. By contrast, union representatives, such as shop stewards,[72] would seem to be 'authorised' to perform a wider range of activities, such as taking up members' grievances with management, calling meetings of the workforce (regardless of whether they are critical of more senior officials),[73] and any other activities normally associated with officials of their grade, provided that they act in accordance with union practice.[74]

As well as differentiating between activities of individual trade unionists and those 'of the union' the courts have also, from the opposite perspective, distinguished between an employer's reactions to an individual employee's activities in a union context and activities of the union. In *Therm A Stor Ltd v Atkins and Carrington*[75] between 60 and 65 of the company's 70 employees had joined the Transport and General Workers Union, and representatives of those employees asked the union's district secretary to apply to the company for recognition. The company then instructed its chargehands to select 20 employees for dismissal. The employment tribunal found that, although the employers were strongly anti-union and the dismissals were in reaction to the union's letter seeking recognition, the chargehands had not taken account of the actual or proposed union membership of, or participation in union activities by, the employees concerned and therefore those employees could not show that this was the reason for their dismissal. The EAT allowed the appeal and said that failure to construe the legislation to cover dismissal of individuals by

---

[67] *Lyon v St James Press Ltd* [1976] IRLR 215. It is irrelevant that these activities are not disclosed to the management.. It was suggested in this case that 'wholly unreasonable, extraneous or malicious acts' done in support of union activities may not be protected. See also *Bass Taverns Ltd v Burgess* [1995] IRLR 596, where Pill LJ opined at 599 that malicious, untruthful or irrelevant statements at a union recruitment meeting may not fall within the scope of trade union activities and *Paloma Sanchez v Spain* judgment of 12 September 2011, [2011] IRLR 934, ECtHR (dismissal for use of offensive cartoons not a violation of Art 11 ECHR).

[68] *Rasool v Hepworth Pipe Co Ltd (No 2)* [1980] IRLR 137; *British Airways Engine Overhaul Ltd v Francis* [1981] IRLR 9.

[69] *Zucker v Astrid Jewels Ltd* [1978] IRLR 385.

[70] *Brennan and Ging v Ellward (Lancs) Ltd* [1976] IRLR 378, EAT; *Dixon and Shaw v West Ella Developments Ltd* [1978] IRLR 151 (but note the limitation suggested there – of questionable authority – that the union should take some action in response to this approach for the employee to be protected. There is no such limitation in TULRCA 1992, s 152(1)(ba)).

[71] [1978] ICR 643.

[72] Union representatives are often referred to as 'shop stewards', especially among blue-collar workers, but sometimes have other titles (eg convenor, or Father or Mother of the Chapel): Cully *et al*, 1999: p 214, n 1. In this chapter we use the term 'union representative' to cover all lay union representatives.

[73] *British Airways Engine Overhaul Ltd v Francis* [1981] IRLR 9.

[74] See, for example, *British Airways Engine Overhaul Ltd v Francis* [1981] IRLR 9; *Marley Tile Co Ltd v Shaw* [1980] IRLR 25.

[75] [1983] IRLR 78.

way of reprisal for the involvement of the union would render the legislation 'wholly inoperative' in many instances where it must have been intended to apply. The Court of Appeal, however, restored the decision of the employment tribunal, holding that the reason for dismissal was not related to anything which the employees personally had done. The Court rejected the argument of the applicants' counsel – that union activities were essentially collective and that where reasons for dismissal were the activities of the group (ie, the union) they were, therefore, those of individuals – as a 'valiant attempt at purposive construction' which went beyond permissible limits'.[76]

It is strongly arguable that this very narrow interpretation of the legislation does not take adequate account of the fact that the union was acting on behalf, and at the request, of individual members. It is also arguable that, as a result of the decision in *Therm A Stor*, UK law on this point violates Article 11 of the ECHR.[77] More broadly, it highlights the limitations of locating the protection of collective activity wholly within a framework of individual rights, a theme to which we return in para 8.24. In relation to the decision itself the burden of proof may have been a crucial factor. The applicants in the case lacked the period of continuous employment needed to bring a general unfair dismissal claim and thus were required to prove that their dismissal was for union activities. Had they been qualified to bring such a claim it is difficult to see that the employers would have been able to demonstrate a potentially fair reason for dismissal.[78] The *Therm A Stor* decision now stands in marked contrast to the situation where a union has sought recognition pursuant to the statutory procedure, discussed in chapter 9; in that context workers have protection against dismissal or selection for redundancy (or subjection to other detriment) for specified acts relating to the recognition procedures, including acting with a view to obtaining, or indicating support for, recognition.[79] Given that it is official policy to encourage unions and employers to reach voluntary recognition agreements outside the statutory procedure, it is most unfortunate that these protections were not extended to situations where no request for recognition has been made pursuant to the statute.[80] As we explain in para 8.11 below, the applicants in *Therm A Stor* would not be regarded as making use of 'trade union services' under the provisions introduced by ERelA 2004.

8.10   An '*appropriate time*' in relation to union activities means a time outside the employee's working hours, or a time within his or her working hours at which, in accordance with arrangements

---

[76] Per Sir John Donaldson at 80.

[77] See *Palomo Sanchez v Spain* judgment of 12 September 2011, [2011] IRLR 934, ECtHR; *Demir and Baykara v Turkey* judgment of 12 November 2008, [2009] IRLR 766, ECtHR, discussed para 7.9 above; *Wilson and NUJ v UK, Palmer, Wyeth and RMT v UK* and *Doolan v UK* judgment of 2 July 2002, [2002] IRLR 568, para 46: 'The Court agrees with the Government that the essence of a voluntary system of collective bargaining is that it must be possible for a trade union which it not recognised by an employer to take steps including, if necessary, organising industrial action, with a view to persuading the employer to enter into collective bargaining with it on those issues which the union believes are important for its members' interests. Furthermore, it is of the essence of the right to join a trade union for the protection of their interests that employees should be free to instruct or permit the union to make representations to their employer or to take action in support of their interests on their behalf'. This argument may be more successfully located in the context of dismissal on the grounds of union membership rather than union activity, given that it starts from the perspective of the individual rather than the union.

[78] See further para 5.112 *et seq* above. As we discuss in para 8.5 above, whether the burden of proof, since *Kuzel v Roche Products Ltd* [2008] IRLR 530, rests with the employee where he or she lacks the requisite continuity to bring a general claim is unclear.

[79] TULRCA 1992, Sch A1, paras 156–165.

[80] See also CEACR, Individual Observation concerning Right to Organise and Collective Bargaining Convention 1949 (No 98) UK, 2007. *Quaere* whether an employee who voiced support for voluntary recognition where it was official policy to seek it could be regarded as 'authorised' by the union.

agreed with or consent given by the employer, participation in the activities of a union is permissible.[81] 'Working hours', in relation to an employee, means any time when, in accordance with his or her contract of employment, he or she is required to be 'at work'[82] and 'at work' has been held to mean when actually working.[83] This means that no permission is required for union activities during recognised breaks or before or after the working day, even if the employee is paid during these times. The House of Lords has inferred from this an entitlement for employees to take part in union activities on the employer's premises, using facilities normally available to the employer's workers, provided that this does not require the employer to incur expense or cause substantial inconvenience either to it or to fellow workers who are not union members.[84] In this respect employers 'must tolerate minor infringements of their strict legal rights which do them no real harm.'[85] Whether activities do cause 'substantial inconvenience' will be a question of fact; thus, a union meeting in the staff canteen at lunchtime may be permissible if all, or a significant majority, of staff are union members but not if only a minority are.[86]

Consent to union activities during working hours may be express (an agreement to hold union meetings during working hours, for example[87]) or implied from the circumstances, although consent cannot be implied purely from an employer's silence when the intention to conduct the activity is announced.[88] The principle of implied consent was invoked to mean that employees who were permitted to converse with fellow employees while working could discuss union, as well as other, matters.[89] In relation to union representatives, once an employer has accepted the appointment of an employee as such, or if it is custom and practice for a union to nominate a representative for a particular workgroup, the employer's consent to the employee carrying out the duties of a representative during working hours will probably be implied[90] unless there is an express agreement which limits this.[91]

The definition of 'appropriate time' might appear to conflict with the extension of protection to those who 'propose' to take part in union activities. However the courts have avoided this result by adopting a purposive interpretation to the legislation in this context in holding that the precise

---

[81]   TULRCA 1992, s 152(2).

[82]   TULRCA 1992, s 152(2).

[83]   *Post Office v Union of Post Office Workers* [1974] ICR 378 (decided under the equivalent provisions of the Industrial Relations Act 1971).

[84]   *Post Office v Union of Post Office Workers* [1974] ICR 378, applied in *Zucker v Astrid Jewels Ltd* [1978] ICR 1088. It may be possible to apply this reasoning to the use of e-mail and the internet for union activities: see generally G Morris, 2002a.

[85]   *Post Office v Union of Post Office Workers* [1974] ICR 378, 400 (Lord Reid). It is unlikely that this principle is open to challenge under the HRA 1998 as interfering with the peaceful enjoyment of possessions under Art 1 of Protocol 1 of the ECHR: see further para 9.16.

[86]   Cf, for example, the employment tribunal decision in *Carter v Wiltshire County Council* [1979] IRLR 331 (meeting in a social club where all but one employee a union member).

[87]   In *Bass Taverns Ltd v Burgess* [1995] IRLR 596 the Court of Appeal rejected the suggestion that the employer's consent to the applicant addressing trainee managers to recruit them to the union was subject to an implied limitation that he would not use the occasion to criticise the company. Pill LJ emphasised (at 598) that a consent to recruit 'must include a consent to underline the services which the union can provide. That may reasonably involve a submission to prospective members that in some respects the union will provide a service which the company does not'.

[88]   *Marley Tile Co Ltd v Shaw* [1980] IRLR 25.

[89]   *Zucker v Astrid Jewels Ltd* [1978] ICR 1088. Similar reasoning could be invoked in relation to access to notice boards or e-mail or the internet for matters not pertaining directly to the employment.

[90]   See *Marley Tile Co Ltd v Shaw* [1980] IRLR 25.

[91]   Cf *Robb v Leon Motor Services Ltd* [1978] ICR 506.

activities need not be identified.[92] Moreover, although the 'activities' referred to are those in the employment from which the employee has been dismissed, this does not necessarily mean that past activities are irrelevant if a sufficient link with the current employment can be shown. In *Fitzpatrick v British Railways Board*[93] the applicant, when she obtained her job, deliberately failed to give full details of her previous employment or to disclose her former participation in union activities. She joined the National Union of Railwaymen and engaged in some union activity and intended to seek an official position in the union. In the meantime another British Railways employee read a newspaper article in which the applicant was referred to as a union activist with links with some ultra-left Trotskyite groups. When the employers learned of this they decided to dismiss her. The employment tribunal concluded that the principal reason for her dismissal was her previous union activities, which gave her a reputation for being a disruptive force and that she did not, therefore, fall within the legislation. The EAT dismissed her appeal. The Court of Appeal, however, held that the tribunal had failed to ask the critical question: *why* had the employers dismissed the employee because of her previous activities? The Court recognised that where an employer, having learnt of an employee's previous trade union activities, decides that it wishes to dismiss that employee, 'that is likely to be a situation where almost inevitably the employer is dismissing ... because ... [it] ... feels that the employee will indulge in industrial activities of a trade union nature in his [or her] current employment'. When the only 'rational explanation' for dismissal is the employer's fear that the employee will 'repeat those ... activities in [his or] her employment with them' the dismissal will be unfair.[94] However, if an employee obtains employment by deceit and such deceit was the principal reason for dismissal, then even though the deceit relates to previous union activities he or she will then be outside the scope of the statutory protection.[95] This approach invites employers to frame their reasons for dismissal with care. It may now be possible to argue, on the basis of the Human Rights Act 1998, that prospective employees have no obligation to admit to previous union activity if questioned prior to their appointment where this is likely to lead to the employer failing to offer them a job on the ground that this would constitute an interference with their freedom of association or the right to respect for private life,[96] and that failure to disclose such activity should not prejudice a claim for unfair dismissal (or subjection to a detriment). The existing case law also needs to be considered in the context of recent provisions governing the use of 'blacklists' which we discuss in para 8.27 *et seq* below. Ultimately, however, this matter, in common with other cases where individuals are asked to reveal information at the recruitment stage which, if used to penalise

---

[92] *Fitzpatrick v British Railways Board* [1991] IRLR 376.

[93] [1991] IRLR 376.

[94] [1991] IRLR 376, 379 (Woolf LJ).

[95] *Fitzpatrick v British Railways Board* [1991] IRLR 376, affirming this aspect of *Birmingham District Council v Beyer* [1977] IRLR 211, EAT.

[96] In *NATFHE v UK* Application No 28910/95, the European Commission of Human Rights acknowledged that there may be circumstances where requiring an association to reveal the names of its members to a third party could constitute an unjustified interference with freedom of association; see also the DPA 1998, discussed in para 8.27. It is submitted that requiring an individual to reveal his or her associations may also be incompatible with Art 11, in addition to constituting an interference with the right to respect for private life under Art 8. In *Grande Oriente D'Italia di Palazzo Giustiniani v Italy*, judgment of 2 August 2001, the ECtHR held that a requirement for applicants for nomination and appointment to specified public offices to declare that they were not freemasons violated the Art 11 right of the applicant freemason association, which would suffer damage in terms of members and prestige, and that the interference could not be justified. See also *Grande Oriente D'Italia di Palazzo Giustiniani v Italy (No 2)*, judgment of 31 May 2007

them once in employment, would constitute a violation of their fundamental rights, would be better dealt with by specific legislative protection against subjection to such questions.[97]

(iii) Using trade union services at an appropriate time

8.11   Protection against dismissal for making use, or proposing to make use, of trade union services at an appropriate time was introduced by ERelA 2004 in response to the decision of the ECtHR in *Wilson and NUJ v UK, Palmer, Wyeth and RMT v UK* and *Doolan and others v UK*,[98] discussed in para 7.9 above. The same definition of 'appropriate time' applies in this context as in relation to union activities.[99] 'Trade union services' are broadly defined as 'services made available to the employee by an independent trade union by virtue of his membership of the union'.[100] This definition is clearly broad enough to cover raising grievances and queries with employers and negotiating terms and conditions of employment for an individual employee, and could also extend to services outside the field of employment, such as legal and financial services. It is expressly stated that an employee's 'making use' of services includes 'his consenting to the raising of a matter on his behalf by an independent trade union of which he is a member'.[101] In addition, where the reason for dismissal is that such a union (with or without the employee's consent) raised a matter on behalf of the employee as one of its members, this is deemed to fall within the scope of the protection.[102]

This provision is subject to the reservation that '[h]aving terms of employment determined by collective agreement' does not constitute 'making use of a trade union service' in this context.[103] This is designed to ensure that matters relating to collective agreements and personal contracts are considered exclusively under one provision of the Act, that is, that affording protection against inducements to give up representation or the possibility of representation by a union through collective bargaining (see para 8.17 *et seq* below).[104] However, it appears to leave open a 'spectacular lacuna in the structure of protection'.[105] In para 8.9 we discussed the implications of the Court of Appeal decision in *Therm A Stor Ltd v Atkins and Carrington*,[106] which held that employees dismissed in reaction to a letter from the union to the employer seeking recognition had not been taking part in the activities of the union. In that case the relevant provision was held 'not [to be] concerned with an employer's reactions to a trade union's activities, but with his reactions to an individual employee's activities in a trade union context'.[107] It is hard to see how employees in this situation would be protected under the new provisions. They would not have been dismissed for proposing to make use of trade union services because having terms of employment determined by collective agreement is specifically excluded from its scope. At the

---

[97] See further G Morris, 2001a.
[98] Judgment of 2 July 2002, [2003] IRLR 568.
[99] TULRCA 1992, s 152(2); see further para 8.10.
[100] TULRCA 1992, s 152(2A)(a).
[101] TULRCA 1992, s 152(2A)(b).
[102] TULRCA 1992, s 152(2B).
[103] TULRCA 1992, s 145B(4).
[104] TULRCA 1992, s 145B, s 152(1)(bb); *Explanatory Notes to Employment Relations Act 2004*, 2004, para 203.
[105] Bogg, 2005: p 74.
[106] [1983] IRLR 80.
[107] [1983] IRLR 78, 80 (Sir John Donaldson MR).

same time it would be difficult to argue that they had been made an 'offer' by the employer to avoid their terms of employment being so determined. On the basis of the authorities cited in para 8.9 above, it may be possible to argue that Article 11 of the ECHR requires the state to afford protection in this context.[108]

(iv) Failure to accept an offer made for an unlawful purpose relating to union membership, activities or services or collective bargaining

8.12   We discuss the circumstances in which an offer is deemed to be unlawful in paragraph 8.17 *et seq* below.

Protection against subjection to a detriment short of dismissal on grounds of trade union membership and activities

8.13   A 'worker'[109] has the right not to be subjected to any detriment as an individual by any act, or any deliberate failure to act, by his or her employer if the act or failure takes place for the sole or main purpose of preventing or deterring him or her from joining, or participating in the activities of, an independent trade union, or making use of the services of such a union, or penalising him or her for doing so.[110] In addition a worker has the right not to be subjected to any such detriment because he or she had failed to accept an offer made for an unlawful purpose relating to union membership, activities or services or collective bargaining.[111] In this context not conferring a benefit that, if the offer had been accepted by the worker, *would* have been conferred on him or her under the resulting agreement is taken to constitute subjection to a detriment and a deliberate failure to act.[112] This means that those who refuse such an offer should be no worse off than those who accept; the value of the offer should be reflected in the award of compensation.

In terms of the activities protected, this right parallels the protection afforded to employees against dismissal. Thus it is unlawful to take action against a worker for joining one union rather than another, for example, and in relation to 'activities' or 'services' of a union, identical criteria must be satisfied. Notably, however, protection now extends not only to 'employees' but to the wider category of 'workers'[113] as a result of ERelA 2004, a long-overdue reform. Where the

---

[108] See note 77 above. If a public authority (or at least a 'pure' public authority) interfered with the rights of its workers in this way they could bring a free-standing claim against the authority: HRA 1998, ss 6,7. See *Paloma Sanchez v Spain* judgment of 12 September 2011, [2011] IRLR 934, ECtHR for the positive obligations of the state.

[109] A 'worker' is an individual who works, or normally works, as mentioned in TULRCA 1992, s 296(1), s 151(1B); see further para 3.33 *et seq* above. A person who 'seeks to work' is not, therefore, covered, an exclusion that could create difficulties in the case of casual workers as they may lack the requisite mutuality of obligation. The same comments apply here as in relation to dismissal as regards the position under international treaties of those outside this definition: see para 8.5 above. The same groups are excluded from protection: see para 8.2 above. Once again there is no minimum period of employment or maximum age limit. However a 'worker' who is not an 'employee' is excluded where 'under his contract personally to do work or perform services [the] worker ... works outside Great Britain': TULRCA 1992, s 285(1A); see further para 2.47. Special provisions apply to employment on board a ship: s 285(2).

[110] TULRCA 1992, s 146, as amended by ERelA 1999 and ERelA 2004.

[111] TULRCA 1992, s 146, as amended; see further para 8.17 *et seq* below.

[112] TULRCA 1992, s 146(2D).

[113] TULRCA 1992, s 146.

detriment takes the form of dismissal and the worker is an 'employee', however, he or she must complain under the provisions discussed in para 8.5 *et seq* above.[114] As we indicate below, this can have the anomalous consequence that compensation in respect of dismissal may be lower for employees than for workers as there is no statutory limit on the amount that can be awarded in the context of subjection to a detriment and compensation can be awarded for injury to feelings. In addition 'employees' alone fall under the obligation to comply with the ACAS Code of Practice on Disciplinary and Grievance Procedures; should they fail to do so the tribunal has a discretion to reduce any award of compensation by up to 25%.[115] It may also be more difficult for an employee to win a dismissal claim where he or she lacks the qualifying period necessary to bring an ordinary unfair dismissal complaint because of the burden of proof and the absence of any express requirement for an employer to show the purpose for which it acted.[116] This may produce the unusual consequence of some 'workers' attempting to maintain that they are outside the category of 'employee' in this context.

8.14   A worker may be subjected to a detriment 'by any act or any deliberate failure to act'.[117] It is clear that it both acts and omissions, such as failing to award a pay increase or promote a worker, for example. However the meaning of 'deliberate' in this context is obscure; a Labour Government spokesman indicated that it covered both 'conscious and unconscious failures'[118] which, if correct, would leave the term with little meaning. The notion of subjection to a 'detriment' has been interpreted by the courts in the context of the equality legislation,[119] and it is likely that case law deriving from that context will be regarded as heavily persuasive in this. It is unclear whether workers who are *threatened* with deleterious consequences unless they cease their union membership or activities will be regarded as subjected to a detriment, but there are two grounds upon which it can be argued that it should be so regarded. First, threats of this nature have a serious psychological impact which can be deemed to constitute a detriment in itself.[120] Second, the HRA 1998 would also argue in favour of such an interpretation. The ECtHR has held in the context of the closed shop that the threat of dismissal involving loss of livelihood is a 'most serious form of compulsion',[121] and its other jurisprudence supports the view that the threat of lesser

---

[114] TULRCA 1992, s 146(5A). The definition of dismissal in ERA 1996, s 95 applies in this context: s 298. Note, however, the difficulties that may arise in drawing the line between damage caused by detriment short of dismissal, on the one hand, and dismissal on the other: see para 5.151 above and Bowers and Lewis, 2005: pp 86–89.

[115] TULRCA 1992, s 207A, Sch A2, inserted by EA 2008, s 3; see further para 2.21.

[116] See para 8.5 above. Cf the position under the 'blacklisting' provisions, discussed in para 8.27 *et seq* below.

[117] Prior to ERelA 1999, protection was afforded against 'action short of dismissal', which was held by the House of Lords in 1995 (controversially) not to include omissions: *Associated Newspapers Ltd v Wilson; Associated British Ports v Palmer* [1995] IRLR 258. This rendered the protection almost useless.

[118] Mr Michael Wills, Minister for Small Firms, Trade and Industry, Official Report of Standing Committee E, 18 March 1999, 2.30 pm (opposing an amendment to replace 'deliberate' with 'wilful').

[119] See para 6.51. Note, in particular, *Shamoon v Chief Constable of the Royal Ulster Constabulary* [2003] IRLR 285.

[120] Support for this view is provided by *Gloucester Working Men's Club and Institute v James* [1986] ICR 603, 606. Section 146(1) speaks of the act or failure to act *taking place* for the specified purposes. It is submitted that this is not inconsistent with a 'threat' constituting an act. In *Brassington v Cauldon Wholesale Ltd* [1978] ICR 405, the EAT left open the question whether 'action' included threats.

[121] *Young, James and Webster v UK* judgment of 13 August 1981, (1982) 4 EHRR 38, para 55.

forms of disciplinary action should also of itself constitute an interference with the exercise of Convention rights, including the rights to join a trade union and freedom of expression.[122]

The worker must be subjected to a detriment *as an individual*. As we indicated in para 8.2, protection against subjection to a detriment (in a different guise) was originally introduced in the Industrial Relations Act 1971. Although aimed at the protection of individuals, that Act did not exclude this protection being used as a vehicle for collective rights and, indeed, it was held by the House of Lords in *Post Office v Union of Post Office Workers*[123] that a disparity in the facilities accorded to one union as compared with another could give rise to a complaint by a member of the latter. In order to avoid this result the equivalent provision in the subsequent 'Social Contract' legislation inserted the qualification that the action must be taken against the employee 'as an individual'. This meant that adverse action taken against a union as an organisation, such as non-recognition or derecognition, could not be treated as action against individual workers even though it was likely to impact upon individual union members. However, action against members of a particular union as a group, such as failing to accord them a pay increase, could be protected provided that it affected them as individuals.[124] Moreover, in *FW Farnsworth Ltd v McCoid* the Court of Appeal affirmed that the legislation is not confined to the protection of a worker in his or her capacity as such; thus, the derecognition of an employee as a shop steward could constitute an act against him 'as an individual', although it was open to the employers to establish that they had taken the action in order to remove an unsuitable individual from that role rather than to prevent or deter him from taking part in union activities.[125]

8.15   The qualification at the end of the paragraph above is based on the last condition; that where prevention or deterrence of union membership or activities or use of union services, is alleged, the employer's act or failure to act must have taken place *for the sole or main purpose* of such prevention or deterrence. It is for the employer to show the sole or main purpose for which it acted or failed to act,[126] but it remains for the worker to show that the employer's purpose breached the statute. This may not be an easy task. In certain situations, such as a failure to promote, disclosure of information concerning other workers may be important and, if necessary, an order for further particulars and disclosure of documents can be sought from the employment tribunal.[127] However, even if such information is available, the worker may face considerable difficulty in the light of the restrictive judicial approach to the interpretation of 'purpose' exemplified by the Court of Appeal decision in *Gallacher v Department of Transport*.[128] In this case a promotions board had recommended that the employee should not be promoted because it was four years since he had held an official job and doubts as to his managerial ability and attitude remained. His career

---

[122] *Dudgeon v UK* judgment of 22 October 1981, (1982) 4 EHRR 149, paras 40, 41; *Ahmed v UK* judgment of 2 September 1998, [1999] IRLR 188.

[123] [1974] ICR 378.

[124] *Ridgway and Fairbrother v National Coal Board* [1987] IRLR 80. See also *Marshall v The Hampshire Probation Service* EAT 1440/98, 29 September 1999 (unreported); *Howle v GEC Power Engineering Ltd* [1974] ICR 13; *Cheall v Vauxhall Motors Ltd* [1979] IRLR 253.

[125] [1999] IRLR 626 (placing in context the dictum of Nicholls LJ in *Ridgway and Fairbrother*, above, at 88, that the action has to affect the employee other than merely *qua* member or officer of a union).

[126] TULRCA 1992, s 148(1). No account is to be taken of any pressure exercised on the employer to act or fail to act by calling, organising, procuring or financing industrial action or threatening to do so: s 148(2).

[127] Employment Tribunals (Constitution and Rules of Procedure) Regulations 2004, SI 2004/1861, Sch 1, para 10.

[128] [1994] IRLR 231. See also *Smyth-Britt v Chubb Security Personnel* UKEAT/0620/03/DA, 24 February 2004.

development officer advised him that to achieve promotion, he would need to acquire more line management experience. This would necessitate reducing his union activities (which took up 80% or 100% of his time). The employment tribunal held that these comments were intended to deter the employee from continuing with his union activities. The EAT and Court of Appeal upheld the employer's appeal, the Court of Appeal on the basis that the recommendation was not made 'for the purpose of' deterring him from continuing with his union activities, even if this was its likely effect. Neill LJ averred that 'purpose' denoted an object which the employer desired or sought to achieve which was, on these facts, ensuring that only those with sufficient managerial experience and skill were promoted. In *Associated Newspapers Ltd v Wilson; Associated British Ports v Palmer* the House of Lords confirmed that the fact that union membership may become less attractive as a result of an employer's act did not thereby mean that deterring union membership became its purpose.[129] On this basis it seems difficult to distinguish *Gallacher* even though the course of action recommended by the employer would inevitably mean that the worker ceases his or her union activities, provided that the employer puts in credible evidence of another purpose. In *Southwark London Borough Council v Whillier*[130] the employers failed to do this. Here, the employer offered the applicant, a union official, promotion to a higher grade on the basis that she would be paid at the higher rate of pay applicable to that grade only when she was able to undertake the duties of the post in question. The Court of Appeal held that the employment tribunal was entitled to conclude that the employer's purpose was to deter the applicant from taking part in the activities of her union, there being no evidence for holding that they had any other purpose than to oblige her to chose between promotion and retaining her union office.

Prior to ERelA 2004 it was sufficient that prevention or deterrence of union membership, etc, was the employer's 'purpose'; the legislation did not require it to be the 'sole or main' purpose. As we discuss in paras 8.18 and 8.19 below, the 'sole or main' purpose test is used in determining whether an employer's offer is unlawful and the Government claimed that the amendment to TULRCA 1992, s 146 was designed to ensure consistency between the relevant provisions and that, in any event, it reflected the approach that tribunals could be expected to adopt.[131] As we shall see, however, the use of that test in the context of inducements is highly controversial, and, arguably, has the result that UK law remains in breach of Article 11 of the ECHR. Clearly the change will not assist applicants who, as we have seen, as a result of *Gallacher* already face a difficult task. The problem may be compounded where the employer is a corporate body where decision-makers may not share a common motivation.[132] Where the complaint of subjection to a detriment is based on a worker's failure to accept an offer made for an unlawful purpose it is sufficient that the employer's act or failure to act was 'because of' this.[133] Here, it may be possible to argue that it is enough to show that the failure to accept the offer was one of a number of reasons for the employer's act or failure to act, rather than the predominant purpose, but the matter is not free from doubt.

---

[129] [1995] IRLR 258, Lord Lloyd at 267.

[130] [2001] ICR 1016, CA.

[131] Lord Triesman, HL Debs, GC 210, June 16 2004. In *Smyth-Britt v Chubb Security Personnel* UKEAT/0620/03/DA, 24 February 2004 the EAT considered that the legislation prior to the amendment invited 'consideration of the main or principal purpose of the employer' [25].

[132] *Smith v Hayle Town Council* [1978] ICR 996, discussed para 8.5 above. On the amendment to s 146 see Letter and Memorandum from Professor Lord Wedderburn of Charlton QC FBA, Joint Committee on Human Rights, Thirteenth Report, Session 2003–2004, Appendix 2c, paras 7.0–7.4.

[133] TULRCA 1992, s 146(2C).

8.16   A complaint of subjection to a detriment must be presented to an employment tribunal within three months beginning with the date of the act or failure to which the complaint relates or, where that act or failure is part of a series of similar acts or failures, the last of them.[134] A failure to act is treated as done when it was decided on;[135] in the absence of evidence to the contrary an employer is taken to have decided on a failure to act when it does an act inconsistent with such an act or, if no such inconsistent act was done, when the period expires when it might reasonably be expected to have done the failed act if it was to be done.[136] Where a complaint is upheld the tribunal makes a declaration to that effect and may also award such compensation as it considers 'just and equitable in all the circumstances having regard to the infringement complained of and to any loss sustained by the complainant which is attributable to the act or failure which infringed his [or her] right',[137] which may include non-pecuniary loss.[138] The EAT has indicated that there are no grounds for awarding lower levels of compensation for injury to feelings in this context than would be awarded in relation to other forms of discrimination, although the degree of distress caused in the instant case must be carefully examined.[139] Unlike the remedies for dismissal, there is no statutory limit on the amount of compensation, and unlike the equality legislation,[140] or, indeed, the provisions relating to refusal of employment on grounds of union membership discussed in para 8.21, tribunals have no power formally to recommend any course of action such as cessation of the unlawful treatment. The compensation awarded to 'employees' may be reduced by up to 25% if they have failed to comply with the ACAS Code of Practice on Disciplinary and Grievance Procedures 2009; equally it may be increased by up to 25% if the employer unreasonably fails to comply with the Code.[141]

Protection against inducements relating to union membership, activities or services and collective bargaining

8.17   Protection against inducements relating to union membership, activities or services, on the one hand, and to collective bargaining, on the other, was introduced by ERelA 2004 in response to

---

[134]   TULRCA 1992, s 147(1). Where the act extends over a period, the 'date of the act' refers to the last date of that period: s 147(2)(a): see also *Adlam v Salisbury and Wells Theological College* [1985] ICR 786 and *British Airways Board v Clark and Havill* [1982] IRLR 238. Where the tribunal is satisfied it was not 'reasonably practicable' for the complaint to be presented before the end of the three month period, it may be presented within such further period as it considers reasonable: see para 2.17 above.

[135]   TULRCA 1992, s 147(2)(b).

[136]   TULRCA 1992, s 147(3). In the event that the employer can show that it decided on a course earlier than it might reasonably be expected to do but that decision was not communicated to the worker, the tribunal may be inclined to extend the time limit if the worker could not be expected to have known of the decision. For consideration of the equivalent of s 147(3) in the context of disability discrimination, see *Matuszowicz v Kingston upon Hull City Council* [2009] EWCA Civ 22.

[137]   TULRCA 1992, s 149(2).

[138]   *Brassington v Cauldon Wholesale Ltd* [1978] ICR 405 (non-pecuniary loss could include injury to health or the frustration of a 'deep and sincere wish to join a union'); see also *Ridgway and Fairbrother v National Coal Board* [1987] IRLR 80, and *Cleveland Ambulance NHS Trust v Blane* [1997] IRLR 332. There is an obligation on complainants to mitigate loss and compensation may be reduced if the tribunal finds that they contributed to the action: TULRCA 1992, s 149(4), (6), although note also s 145E(6).

[139]   *London Borough of Hackney v Adams* [2003] IRLR 402, applied in *Saunders v Apcoa Parking UK Ltd* EAT/0526/02/ RN, 18 March 2003.

[140]   See ch 6.

[141]   TULRCA 1992, s 207A, Sch A2, inserted by EA 2008, s. 3; see further para 2.21.

the decision of the ECtHR in *Wilson and NUJ v UK*, *Palmer, Wyeth and RMT v UK* and *Doolan v UK*,[142] discussed in paras 7.9 and 8.3 above. These protections are available not only to 'employees' but to the wider category of 'workers' (both former and existing).[143] Complaints must be presented to an employment tribunal within three months beginning with the date when the offer was made by the employer or, where the offer is part of a series of similar offers to the complainant, the date when the last of them was made.[144] In either case, if the complaint is upheld, the tribunal must make a declaration to this effect and award the complainant the sum of £3,500;[145] at the time of writing it is not completely clear whether this may be reduced where an employee has failed to comply with the ACAS Code of Practice on Disciplinary and Grievance Procedures 2009.[146] If an offer unlawfully made is accepted, and this results in the worker agreeing to vary his or her terms of employment at a later date, the employer cannot enforce this agreement, nor can it recover any sum paid or other asset transferred under the agreement to vary.[147] If, however, the terms of employment have already been varied, the variation remains enforceable even though there has been a breach of the statutory provision.[148]

The respective rights in relation to inducements apply independently of the right to complain of subjection to a detriment discussed above,[149] and compensation for the latter right is not be reduced by any award in respect of an inducement found to have been unlawfully offered.[150] Not conferring a benefit that, had an offer been accepted by a worker, would have been conferred on him or her constitutes subjecting him or her to a detriment,[151] so allowing those who refuse an offer to be no worse off than those who accept it.

The scope of the protection against inducements relating to collective bargaining, with which *Wilson* and *Palmer* was most directly concerned, attracted greatest controversy during the legislation's parliamentary passage. We discuss this first, before considering inducements relating to union membership and activity, to which the same points, *mutatis mutandis*, apply.

(i) Inducements relating to collective bargaining

8.18   A worker who is a member of an independent trade union which is recognised, or seeking to be recognised, by his or her employer has the right not to have an offer made to him or her by the employer if (a) acceptance of the offer, together with other workers' acceptance of offers which the employer also makes to them, would have 'the prohibited result' and (b) the employer's sole

---

[142] Judgment of 2 July 2002, [2003] IRLR 568.

[143] TULRCA 1992, ss 145A(5), 145B(5), 145F(3); see further para 8.13 and para 3.33 *et seq* above.

[144] TULRCA 1992, s 145C. Where the tribunal is satisfied it was not 'reasonably practicable' for the complaint to be presented before the end of the three month period, it may be presented within such further period as it considers reasonable: see para 2.17 above.

[145] TULRCA 1992, s 145E(1)–(3); figure as of 1 February 2012 and at the time of writing. In determining whether the employer made the offer or the purpose for which it did so, no account is to be taken of any pressure by calling, organising, procuring or financing industrial action or threatening to do so: TULRCA 1992, s 145D(3).

[146] Although TULRCA 1992, s 207A and Sch A2 makes no provision for this there is no express provision in s 145E(3) corresponding to that introduced in relation to the now-repealed statutory grievance procedures.

[147] TULRCA 1992, s 145E(4)(a).

[148] TULRCA 1992, s 145E(4)(b).

[149] TULRCA 1992, s 145E(5).

[150] TULRCA 1992, s 145E(6).

[151] TULRCA 1992, s 146(2D).

or main purpose in making the offers is to achieve that result.[152] The 'prohibited result' is 'that the workers' terms of employment, or any of those terms, will not (or will no longer) be determined by collective agreement negotiated by or on behalf of the union'.[153] There is no requirement that the offers be made to the workers simultaneously.[154]

This provision is designed to make it unlawful for an employer to offer a worker an inducement to give up representation, or the possibility of representation, by a union in relation to the negotiation of terms and conditions of employment. Initially the government sought to confine the protection to members of recognised unions,[155] but it finally accepted the view of the Joint Committee on Human Rights ('JCHR')[156] and others that this would not give full effect to the decision in *Wilson and Palmer*. It is notable, however, that the union in question must still be 'seeking recognition'. On this basis it would be advisable for unions with members in a workplace to write to the employer to indicate their desire for recognition, even if the membership level is relatively low. The legislation envisages that the offer will be made to more than one worker, but not necessarily simultaneously. In this context the requirement to present a complaint to a tribunal within three months of the offer being made to the complainant could present a difficulty to the first recipient of an offer if no further offer is made within the three month period. Although *Wilson and Palmer* arose in the context of a concerted campaign by the respective employers, it is not clear why the requirement for offers to be made to other workers was thought appropriate or necessary in this context given that the right not to be treated less favourably for refusing to renounce union representation rests in the individual worker.

The employer must show what its sole or main purpose was in making the offers,[157] but it remains for the worker to show that this purpose was unlawful. As in the case of subjection to a detriment, this may not be easy where credible evidence of another purpose can be shown, particularly if tribunals and courts continue to distinguish between 'purpose' and 'effect'. In this context, however, tribunals are required to take into account any evidence relating to three specified matters. First, that when the offers were made, the employer had recently changed or sought to change, or did not wish to use, arrangements agreed with the union for collective bargaining. Second, that when the offers were made the employer did not wish to enter into arrangements proposed by the union for collective bargaining. Third, that the offers were made only to particular workers and were made with the sole or main purpose of rewarding those particular workers for their high level of performance or of retaining them because of their special value to the employer.[158]

8.19 It was strongly argued during the legislation's passage that the requirement that achievement of the 'prohibited result' must be the employer's 'sole or main' purpose in order for the offer to be unlawful, rather than merely its 'purpose', would fatally undermine the effectiveness of the protection and would fail to give effect to the judgment in *Wilson* and *Palmer*, where no such

---

[152] TULRCA 1992, s 145B(1).
[153] TULRCA 1992, s 145B(2).
[154] TULRCA 1992, s 145B(3).
[155] See Memorandum from the DTI in response to concerns raised by the Committee in its Third and Fourth Progress Reports of Session 2003–2004, JCHR, Thirteenth Report, Session 2003–2004, Appendix 2a, paras 40–48.
[156] JCHR, Tenth Report, Session 2003–2004, para 1.8.
[157] TULRCA 1992, s 145D(2).
[158] TULRCA 1992, s 145D(4).

requirement is envisaged.[159] The Labour Government resisted exhortations to amend this provision, concluding that:

> The words 'sole or main' are an essential component of the regime that we are seeking to construct. They are necessary to ensure that employers have some flexibility in setting their reward systems. We do not consider that employers should be prevented from making offers for justifiable business purposes just because a by-product or incidental consequence of making such offers would be to deter a person's involvement with a trade union.[160]

However it did undertake to keep the matter under review.[161] The difficulty of permitting employers to maintain that their primary purpose is to 'reward and retain key staff'[162] and that withdrawing adherence to terms that have been collectively agreed is only a subsidiary purpose, is that 'key staff' may come to be identified precisely by their willingness to transfer to personal contracts. In this context much may depend on the preparedness of tribunals to probe employers' evidence that particular individuals merited special treatment on the grounds of their performance or importance to the organisation.

A further criticism of the legislation is that it fails to accord a remedy to a union, as well as to the individual union member, despite the finding by the ECtHR in *Wilson and Palmer* that the rights of the applicant unions, as well as the individual applicants, had been violated[163] and the conclusion of the JCHR that the absence of such a remedy could leave the UK in continuing breach of Article 11.[164] The Labour Government's defence of its position can be divided into three lines of argument. The first rests on the interpretation of the ECtHR judgment. Here it maintained that 'the infringement of the rights of the applicant unions simply resulted from and was consequential upon the infringement of the rights of their members rather than an infringement of a free standing right of the unions.[165] Moreover, 'the Article 11 right of the applicant unions to strive for the protection of their members' interests is not a right separate from and independent of the Article 11 right of their members to freedom to belong to a union for the protection of their interests ... [T]rade unions are voluntary associations consisting of their members; if adequate remedies are given to the members the rights of the union are also protected'.[166] These views

---

[159] See, for example, Letter and Memorandum from Professor Lord Wedderburn of Charlton QC FBA, JCHR, Session 2003–2004, Appendix 2c, paras 6.0–7.4; Lord McCarthy HL Debs, GC 136, 15 June 2004. The JCHR at one stage recommended the omission of 'sole or main' (Tenth Report, Session 2003–2004, para 1.6) but accepted, in the light of a subsequent DTI Memorandum, that there was a case for retaining it and relying on tribunals sensibly to distinguish between cases where offers are made for the purpose, in effect, of achieving derecognition of a union and cases where they are made to retain or reward valuable staff, on the basis that amending legislation be introduced if the Art 11 right was not being protected in practice: JCHR, Thirteenth Report, Session 2003–2004, para 2.21.

[160] Lord Sainsbury, Parliamentary Under-Secretary of State, Department of Trade and Industry, HL Debs GC 139, 15 June 2004.

[161] Letter from Gerry Sutcliffe, JCHR, Seventeenth Report, Session 2003–2004, Appendix 2.

[162] Gerry Sutcliffe, HC Standing Committee D, col 104, 5 February 2004.

[163] Judgment of 2 July 2002, [2002] IRLR 568, para 48.

[164] Thirteenth Report, Session 2003–2004, para 2.19. As the Committee pointed out, if the employer were a 'public authority' for the purposes of HRA 1998, s 6 the union could bring proceedings under HRA 1998, s 7 in the event that its rights under Art 11 had been violated, but in relation to other employers it would be forced to seek redress before the ECtHR: Tenth Report, Session 2003–2004, para 1.4.

[165] Memorandum from the DTI in response to concerns raised by the Committee in its Third and Fourth Progress Reports of Session 2003–2004, Thirteenth Report, Session 2003–2004, Appendix 2a, para 25.

[166] Above, para 28.

were not accepted by the JCHR and, in our view, are not sustainable. Second, it asserted that '[w]hile the continuation of collective bargaining may be at issue, the objectionable conduct is done in relation to the individual members of the union.'[167] This fails to recognise the separate and legitimate interest of trade unions as collective organisations. Third, it argued that no other provisions in UK law that conferred individual rights in relation to union matters gave a separate means of redress to unions which could, in any event, actively support their members in making claims.[168] However this fails to accord adequate weight to the difficulties and risks that individuals may face in bringing a complaint, and, once again, overlooks the distinct position of unions as beneficiaries of freedom of association. We discuss this further in para 8.25 below.

Finally, the legislation extends protection only to those who are offered an inducement and not to those who are not recipients of such an offer. This means that if 'the employer accurately selects amongst the union members in his employ those who will succumb to the offer and he makes no offer of inducement to those who would refuse it ... there remain[s] no remedy for those subject to precisely the discrimination which the ... Court ... held was incompatible with Article 11'.[169] Initially the JCHR was sympathetic to this view,[170] but later accepted the Government's argument that the basis of the violation in *Wilson* and *Palmer* was that the offer *had* been made to union members to give up their rights and that there was currently no legal duty to change the law in relation to other possible violations, although it recommended that the issue be kept under review.[171]

(ii) Inducements relating to union membership or activities

8.20 The provision relating to union membership or activities is similarly structured to that relating to collective bargaining. A worker has the right not to have an offer made to him or her by his or her employer for the sole or main purpose of inducing the worker not to be or seek to become a member of an independent trade union; not to take part in the activities of such a union at an appropriate time; and not to make use, at an appropriate time, of union services.[172] 'Appropriate time', 'trade union services' and 'making use' of union services are defined in the same way as in the context of the protections against discrimination discussed above.[173] Once again the employer must show what its sole or main purpose was in making the offer,[174] although it remains for the worker to show that this purpose was unlawful. The comments that we made in para 8.19 above about this test apply equally in this context, as do our remarks about the failure to accord a remedy to unions as well as to individual applicants.

---

[167] Lord Sainsbury, HL Debs, GC 151, 15 June 2004.
[168] Lord Sainsbury, HC Debs, GC 151–152, 15 June 2004.
[169] Letter from John Hendy QC, JCHR, Session 2003–2004, Appendix 1.
[170] JCHR, Tenth Report, Session 2003–2004, para 17.
[171] JCHR, Thirteenth Report, Session 2003–2004, para 2.24. The JCHR also accepted the government's argument that the reference to an 'offer' did not enable an employer to circumvent the legislation by inviting employees themselves to make the offer on the ground that, at some stage, the employer is likely to have to make a counter offer: para 2.23. Cf Letter from John Hendy QC, JCHR, Tenth Report, Session 2003–2004, Appendix 1; Letter and Memorandum from Professor Lord Wedderburn of Charlton QC, FBA, JCHR, Session 2003–2004, Appendix 2c, paras 8.0–8.6.
[172] TULRCA 1992, s 145A.
[173] See paras 8.10 and 8.11.
[174] TULRCA 1992, s 145D(1).

Refusal of access to employment

8.21   It is unlawful to refuse a person employment under a contract of service or apprenticeship because he or she is a member of a trade union or a particular union or is unwilling to agree to leave, or not to join, a union.[175] It is also unlawful for an employment agency to refuse a person any of its services for such a reason.[176] Unlike protection against dismissal and subjection to a detriment, the union in question need not be 'independent' although clearly breaches of the statute are more likely to arise in practice where it is.[177] 'Refusal' goes beyond not offering a job; it also extends to refusing to process an application or inquiry (for example failing to respond to telephone calls); causing an individual to withdraw an application (for example saying there are no vacancies); offering the job on terms which no employer who wished to fill the post would offer and which the applicant does not accept (a test which, contemptuous offers apart, may be difficult to apply); and withdrawing an offer previously made.[178] Where employment is offered on condition that the applicant is not a union member, or leaves or agrees not to join a union, and the applicant does not accept the offer because he or she is unwilling to accept that requirement, this is treated as a refusal of employment for that reason.[179]

A person who is unlawfully refused employment on grounds of union membership may complain to an employment tribunal within three months of the conduct complained of or within such further period as the tribunal considers 'reasonable' where it is satisfied that compliance with the time limit was not 'reasonably practicable'.[180] The applicant must prove the reason for refusal; in doing so, as in the case of other forms of unlawful discrimination, discovery of information about successful candidates, if any, may be crucial (although there is no need to show that employment was offered to another person).[181] If an advertisement is published which might reasonably be understood as indicating that the employment is closed to those who do not satisfy the conditions relating to union membership (such as 'non-union members welcome') an applicant who does not satisfy such a condition is conclusively presumed to have been refused

---

[175] TULRCA 1992, ss 137(1), 143, 295. As in the case of dismissal and subjection to a detriment Crown employment is included unless s 275 applies but the armed forces and police are not. The protection does not apply where, under the contract, the employee would ordinarily work outside Great Britain: s 285; see further para 2.46. However ETA 1996, s 10(1) does not apply to s 137; cf para 8.2, note 2.

[176] TULRCA 1992, s 138. An 'employment agency' means a person who, for profit or not, provides services for the purpose of finding employment for workers or supplying employers with workers: s 143(1). The definition of employment (see ss 143, 295) means that services in relation to those other than employees are not covered. Unions are not regarded as employment agencies by reason of services provided by them only for, or in relation to, their members.

[177] Membership of a particular branch or section of a trade union is also covered: TULRCA 1992, s 143(3).

[178] TULRCA 1992, s 137(5). Section 138(4) defines refusal of service by an employment agency.

[179] TULRCA 1992, 137(6). Any pre-employment agreement not to join an independent trade union (or participate in its activities) would not, of course preclude access to protection against dismissal or subjection to a detriment if breached after the individual had been employed.

[180] TULRCA 1992, ss 137(2), 138(2), 139. See para 2.17 for the meaning of not 'reasonably practicable'. The 'date' of the conduct to which the complaint relates depends upon the nature of that conduct: s 139(2). It is submitted that this date should not be earlier than that on which the complainant becomes aware of the refusal (and see *Gisda Cyf v Barratt* [2010] IRLR 1073, SC, discussed in para 5.80 above). See ss 141 and 142 for provisions for joinder of another prospective respondent or third parties.

[181] On discovery of documents, see Employment Tribunals (Constitution and Rules of Procedure) Regulations 2004, SI 2004/1861 Sch 1, para 10. On a complaint by the TUC to the ILO that British law and practice failed to meet the requirements of Art 1 of Convention No 98 in relation to recruitment the Committee of Experts concluded that workers 'faced many practical difficulties in proving the real nature of their … denial of employment' and that in this respect the United Kingdom did not comply with the Convention: Case 1618, 287th Report, paras 224–267.

employment for that reason, regardless of his or her suitability for the job (although clear lack of suitability may affect compensation).[182] In the absence of such (improbable) evidence, asking questions about union membership should be sufficient to raise a *prima facie* case that this was relevant to the refusal, although it may be displaced by evidence to the contrary, for example that other members of the union are already employed by the employer. The remedies available are a declaration; financial compensation (subject to the limit of the compensatory award for unfair dismissal);[183] and/or a recommendation that the applicant takes, within a specified period, action to obviate or reduce the adverse effect on the complainant of the unlawful conduct.[184] As in the case of other grounds of discrimination, compensation may be awarded for injury to feelings,[185] and awards in those contexts may provide some guidance. Where it cannot be said that the complainant would have got the job but for the unlawful discrimination, for example if he or she was one of several rejected applicants, the difficulty of assessing loss does not mean that the award will thereby be purely nominal.[186] If the respondent fails without reasonable justification to comply with a recommendation, the tribunal may increase its award of compensation, subject to the overriding maximum limit or, if it has not made such an award, make one.[187]

8.22 The introduction of this protection against discriminatory hiring, which came only in 1990, was originally rooted in the Conservative Government's desire to prevent the lawful operation of pre-entry closed shops[188] where only union members could be considered for a job; this was the only aspect referred to in the Green Paper which preceded the legislation.[189] However, the legislation itself also covered discrimination against those wishing to be union members. Strikingly, by contrast to protection during employment, this protection does not cover participation in trade union activities. This was a deliberate omission; the government took the view that employers were entitled to protect themselves against 'troublemaker[s]'.[190] Currently, therefore, an employer may blatantly defend a claim before a tribunal by maintaining that employment was refused because of an applicant's record of union activities rather than his or her union membership (provided that this was not related to a 'blacklist': see para 8.27 below). This makes particularly important the concept of 'membership' in this context; as Townshend-Smith points out, 'in many cases the fact of membership will be less significant both for the individual and the prospective employer than what has been done with that membership'.[191] As we indicated in para 8.7 above, the concept of 'membership' was given a narrow meaning by the House of Lords

---

[182] TULRCA 1992, ss 137(3), 138(3).

[183] From 1 February 2012 and at the time of writing, £72,300.

[184] TULRCA 1992, s 140. Other analogies with equality law are limited, however. There is, for example, no concept of indirect discrimination in this context (although if a requirement were clearly a smokescreen for excluding union members, for example by limiting recruitment to those who had previously worked for a notorious non-union employer, this could be viewed as direct). See generally Townshend-Smith, 1991 and see further para 8.37 below.

[185] See para 6.66 above.

[186] See *Chaplin v Hicks* [1911] 2 KB 786, CA, where it was held that substantial damages could be claimed for loss of a contractual right to belong to a limited class of competitors for a prize; *Allied Maples Group Ltd v Simmons and Simmons (a firm)* [1995] 4 All ER 907; and see further para 6.66 above.

[187] TULRCA 1992, s 140(3).

[188] See *Removing Barriers to Employment*, Cm 655, 1989: ch 2; see also para 8.33 *et seq* below.

[189] *Removing Barriers to Employment*, Cm 655, 1989: ch 2.

[190] Patrick Nicholls, Parliamentary Under-Secretary of State for Employment, House of Commons, Official Report of Standing Committee D, col 27, 8 February 1990.

[191] Townshend-Smith, 1991: p 107.

in *Associated Newspapers Ltd v Wilson; Associated British Ports v Palmer*[192] in the context of detriment once in employment, although other cases took a broader view. This issue has become less pressing in relation to workers in employment because of the specific protection now accorded to making use of trade union services,[193] in addition to taking part in union activities. However, it remains important in this context. It may be possible to rely on the HRA 1998 to argue for a more expansive interpretation of TULRCA 1992, s 137, both for ordinary members[194] and those who have acted in capacities beyond that of the ordinary member. In *X v Ireland*[195] the European Commission of Human Rights considered that threats of dismissal or other actions intended to make an employee relinquish the office of shop steward could, in certain circumstances, seriously restrict or impede the lawful exercise of freedom of association under Article 11. More recently the ECtHR has held that the decision to transfer the applicant civil servant to another region on the ground of his union activities violated Article 11.[196] The EctHR has also held that action taken in relation to participation in the activities of a political party, including holding party office, may violate Article 10, which guarantees freedom of expression, as well as Article 11[197] and has emphasised the need for states to ensure that 'disproportionate penalties' do not dissuade union representatives from seeking to defend their members' interests.[198] It is conceivable that domestic courts and tribunals could be persuaded to interpret 'membership' in the light of these decisions. Alternatively, if the discriminatory employer is a 'public authority' (or at least if it is a 'pure' public authority) an individual may have a free-standing right of action, although this would depend upon acceptance of the argument that denial of employment constitutes an 'interference' with a Convention right.[199]

The confinement of the protection against discriminatory hiring to union membership is particularly anomalous in the light of the provisions relating to 'blacklisting', which we discuss in para 8.27 below, after our general review of the individual rights discussed in paras 8.5 *et seq* above.

The limits of protection

8.23   Analysis of the legislation upholding the rights to join, and participate in the activities of, trade unions reveals a number of deficiencies which raise doubts as to whether UK law affords adequate protection to comply with Article 11 of the ECHR even after the amendments made by ERelA 2004. In addition to these substantive deficiencies, there remain a number of other

---

[192] [1995] IRLR 258. In *Harrison v Kent County Council* [1995] ICR 434, discussed IRLB 519, 1995, p 6, the EAT held that if a person was refused employment because he or she was or had been a union activist it would be open to a tribunal to find that this was because of union membership. This reasoning cannot stand in the light of the House of Lords decision in *Associated Newspapers*.

[193] Although note the exclusion of having terms of employment determined by collective agreement from this protection; see further para 8.11 above.

[194] See *Wilson* and *Palmer*, discussed in para 7.9 above.

[195] (1971) Application No 4125/69.

[196] *Metin Turan v Turkey* judgment of 14 November 2006.

[197] *Vogt v Germany* judgment of 26 September 1995, (1996) 21 EHRR 205; see also *Ahmed v UK* judgment of 2 September 1998, [1999] IRLR 188.

[198] *Paloma Sanchez v Spain* judgment of 12 September 2011, [2011] IRLR 934.

[199] See G Morris 1999c: pp 497–501.

limitations relating to the procedures for the enforcement of these protections and the remedies available. In all these areas significant defects stem from the attempt artificially to separate individual and collective interests in a context in which the two are inextricably linked. We discuss these briefly and suggest some ways in which the problems which they present could be overcome.

8.24   In relation to the content of the rights, the difficulty of maintaining a boundary between individual and collective spheres is demonstrated by the volume of case law in which its location has been at issue. Its artificiality is perhaps most clearly exemplified in the requirement that a worker is only protected against subjection to a detriment 'as an individual'. As we have explained, this was inserted in 1975 into re-enacted provisions of the Industrial Relations Act 1971 which contained no such limitation and has been interpreted as excluding complaints relating to differential provision of trade union facilities of the kind which gave rise to a successful claim in *Post Office v Union of Post Office Workers*.[200] However, as Lord Reid explained in that case, 'discrimination against a man's [sic] trade union generally affects him personally'[201] and withdrawal of facilities such as notice boards, meeting rooms and office space has obvious implications for the individual member. One concern about removing the existing limitation on individual claims is that this would enable members to seek a remedy if their union, unlike another, was unrecognised. However, there would be nothing to prevent recognition being specifically excluded.[202] Moreover, the House of Lords in the *Post Office* case emphasised that its decision did not entail the provision of identical facilities for recognised and unrecognised unions; indeed, where a union was unrecognised the disparity in facilities as compared with a recognised union would need to be 'substantial'.[203] The line between 'organisational' and 'negotiating' activities which this approach implies is a much more logical and defensible line to draw than that between the individual and collective. A further exemplification of the anomalies which attempts to apply the existing divide have produced is the Court of Appeal decision in *Therm A Stor*, where the distinction drawn between an employer's reactions to the activities of individual members and those of their union again bears no relationship to industrial realities.

It is possible to frame legislation in a way which recognises the interplay between the individual and collective. In the United States, for example, the National Labor Relations Act 1935 provides that '[e]mployees shall have the right to self-organisation to form join or assist labor organisations to bargain collectively through representatives of their own choosing and to engage in other concerted activities for the purpose of collective bargaining or other mutual aid or protection'.[204] It is an unfair labour practice for employers to interfere with, restrain or coerce employees in the exercise of these rights.[205] This is not to imply that the US legislation does not have other

---

[200] [1974] ICR 378. See, for example, *Ridgway and Fairbrother v National Coal Board* [1987] IRLR 80 at 88 (Nicholls LJ), 94 (Bingham LJ).

[201] [1974] ICR 378, 399.

[202] Although cf Hendy and Walton, 1997, who argue that there should be an *individual* right to be represented by a union; see also Hendy, 1998.

[203] [1974] ICR 378, 412.

[204] Section 7.

[205] Section 8(a)(1).

defects[206] and, indeed, there is weighty evidence of employer opposition to trade unions in that country which the law in its existing form has been unable to counteract.[207] However, it remains the case that affirming general principles of the right to organise can provide a touchstone for a purposive interpretation of more specific provisions (those relating to discrimination against trade unionists, for example). In the British legislation, where no such general principles are enunciated, the courts have tended towards a narrow and technical approach, and decisions which attempt a more purposive interpretation by invoking the inferred policy of the legislation seem liable to be overturned.[208] Although the HRA 1998 may now encourage a purposive interpretation in some areas, it is no substitute for principles formulated specifically to apply to the employment context. The model of a statement affirming general principles followed by specified prohibited practices and remedies also communicates in a much clearer form the precise nature of both parties' respective rights and obligations. One example of where this would be particularly advantageous in British labour law would be an express prohibition on specifying non-membership of a union as a contractual term; although such a term is void,[209] it may nevertheless have an unwarranted deterrent effect upon an employee.

8.25   The second area where the legislation is deficient concerns the procedure for enforcement. Remedial action against an anti-union employer is entirely dependent upon an individual employee bringing a claim, with all its attendant difficulties and risks; there is no statutory acknowledgement that a union has a legitimate interest either on its own behalf or that of its members in pursuing such an action. To maintain that giving unions the right to seek redress where employers have induced their members to cease union membership or activities or surrender representational rights would be inconsistent with the general pattern of protection is to turn the argument on its head; the more appropriate course is to extend the capacity of unions to bring complaints to other areas. The provision for unions to bring an action for breach of statutory duty in the context of 'blacklisting', discussed in para 8.27 *et seq* below, makes the argument for extension to the wider context stronger (although the union's right of action in relation to blacklisting is confined to cases where the union itself has suffered loss; there is no provision currently for a representative action). Again an instructive comparison can be made with the United States, where anyone can report an unfair labour practice to the National Labor Relations Board which can then investigate and, if appropriate, issue an order which can be enforced through the courts. Although this is, in practice, a protracted process, the concept of admitting complaints by unions and others is a helpful one and, indeed, the powers of investigation and enforcement bestowed upon the EHRC in relation to the areas of discrimination for which it is responsible (discussed in chapter 6) could provide a model. A further current procedural difficulty is caused by the burden of proof lying upon the complainant

---

[206] For example the exclusion of supervisors and managers from the definition of employee. For a useful summary of the law see Gould, 2004; see also Towers, 1997; S Wood and J Godard, 1999 and references therein.

[207] Estimates of the proportion of union supporters dismissed by employers have ranged between one in twenty (Weiler, 1983) and one in sixty (LaLonde and Meltzer, 1991). Kochan states that 'in many organisations' a 'union avoidance ideology' is 'now a part of their publicly stated personnel policies': Kochan, 2003: p 169. In 2005 union density in the US was around 12.5%: Blanchflower, 2007: p 5.

[208] See, for example, the EAT's decision in *Therm A Stor*, discussed in para 8.9, and the Court of Appeal's decision in *Associated Newspapers Ltd v Wilson* [1994] ICR 97.

[209] TULRCA 1992, s 288.

(other than where he or she has been dismissed and would meet the general qualifications to claim unfair dismissal),[210] particularly where a union reason needs to be the 'principal' reason or there is a need to establish an employer's 'sole or main purpose' in acting or failing to act. Unlike in the case of the equality legislation, there is no questionnaire procedure which forces the employer to commit itself in writing to a reason for its action which is admissible in subsequent proceedings and from which adverse conclusions can be drawn in the event of evasion or equivocation. Last, in relation to procedure, the difficulties an applicant faces may be enhanced by the lack of any specific protection against victimisation for those who provide information or otherwise assist in supporting another worker's claim (although admittedly such provisions in other contexts are in need of strengthening). Such acts may possibly amount to protected participation in union activities, but this may depend upon whether the union encouraged them; it is unclear whether the requisite 'authorisation' could be implied within the principles set out in para 8.9. Failing that, protection against dismissal would require the applicant to meet the general qualifications for claiming unfair dismissal.

8.26 The final general criticism concerns the inadequacy of the remedies. The tribunals and courts have no capacity to issue an order which forces an employer to change its practices; the most which can be sought, in the context of discriminatory hiring only, is a non-enforceable recommendation relating specifically to the complainant. In the context of dismissal there is no automatic right to reinstatement or re-engagement and, even if ordered, the non-practicability of compliance is assessed in the light of the circumstances of the business rather than giving paramount weight to the employee's rights. In any case it is open ultimately to an employer to 'buy out' an employee (and possibly all union presence at the workplace) at a price which is most unlikely to constitute adequate compensation for an employee who may never work again.[211] In this context the lack of status quo provisions pending a ruling on the justification for dismissal, which, it may be argued, should apply across the board, is particularly damaging. In the case of a shop steward or other union official[212] the argument for a status quo procedure is even stronger as their removal from the workplace has an impact upon union organisation generally, not only on the individual.[213] The remedy of interim relief, which may be perceived as partly meeting this requirement, necessitates employees taking the initiative rapidly to seek it following termination, does not apply to unfair selection for redundancy and, unless the employer consents, does not secure continued access to the workplace.[214] The remedies for subjection to a detriment are even more inadequate; there is no mechanism for inhibiting such action from continuing, and the lack of any 'penal' element in the compensation, combined with the potential difficulties of demonstrating quantifiable loss, mean that it is unlikely to serve as a deterrent to a determined anti-union employer, who may escape with virtual impunity in financial terms from a successful claim against it. In relation to discriminatory hiring the ceiling upon compensation stands in

---

[210] See, however, our discussion of *Kuzel v Roche Products Ltd* [2008] IRLR 530 at para 8.5 above.

[211] Cf ILO, 2006: para 791.

[212] See Kersley *et al* 2006: pp 123–125 for the incidence of lay union representatives and ch 6 for the role and activities of employee representatives, including union representatives.

[213] And see ILO, 2006: para 799 *et seq*.

[214] *Quaere* whether, if a shop steward had a contractual right to be on the premises to exercise his or her functions (see *City and Hackney Health Authority v NUPE* [1985] IRLR 252) this would be covered by TULRCA 1992, s 164(1) (which includes 'any ... benefit derived from the employment ...'). In practice such circumstances are likely to be rare.

marked contrast to the lack of any limit on awards for other forms of discrimination, such as sex and race, and once again is unlikely to serve as a significant deterrent. In several respects, therefore, British legislation stands in need of reform if it is adequately to protect workers' rights of association and organisation in relation to employers.

Blacklists

8.27 ERelA 1999 empowered the Secretary of State to issue regulations prohibiting the compilation of lists of persons who have taken part in the activities of unions, as well as lists of union members, with a view to their being used by employers or employment agencies to discriminate in relation to recruitment or the treatment of workers.[215] However it was not until 2010 that this power was exercised; in 2003 the DTI circulated draft regulations for consultation but stated that, as there was no evidence of current blacklisting activity, it did not propose to implement them until there was evidence that the practice was returning.[216] In 2009 it became clear that the practice had not ceased, as previously believed. Under the Data Protection Act 1998 whether an individual is a union member constitutes 'sensitive personal data' which can be collected, held and disclosed to third parties only in a very limited range of circumstances.[217] In March 2009 the Information Commissioner's Office (ICO), which enforces the DPA 1998, uncovered a database operated by a private firm containing details on 3,213 construction workers, including their trade union activity, which was used by more than 40 construction companies, including major companies in the industry, to vet individuals for employment. The database appeared to have been operated for over 15 years. The ICO served an enforcement notice on the owner of the firm ordering him to cease trading. Having been prosecuted, he pleaded guilty and was fined £5,000 for failing to register as a data controller. The ICO also served enforcement notices on 14 companies which had paid for information on construction workers which instructed them to refrain from using or processing this information and to release all relevant information to the individuals concerned. Both the fine imposed against the owner and the limited number of companies subject to the ICO enforcement notices were subject to criticism.[218]

Following this case the Labour Government announced that it would issue regulations under ERelA 1999 and these eventually came into force on 2 March 2010.[219] In broad terms they prohibit the compilation or use of blacklists, which is actionable as a breach of statutory duty; and afford individuals protection against discriminatory hiring, dismissal or detriment in employment for a reason relating to a blacklist. We discuss the provisions in greater detail below.

---

[215] ERelA 1999, s 3. For further discussion of these provisions see Ewing, 1999: pp 284–286.

[216] *Draft Regulations to Prohibit the Blacklisting of Trade Unionists – A Consultation Document* DTI, URN 03/648, February 2003.

[217] DPA 1998, ss 2, 4(3), Sch 2 and 3. Although union activities are not explicitly included, it would not seem possible to disclose information about such activities without disclosing the fact of union membership. On the Act generally see further Jay, 2007, and para 4.120 above.

[218] See Ewing, 2009b, which explores the issues surrounding this case in greater detail.

[219] Employment Relations Act 1999 (Blacklists) Regulations (ERABR) 2010, SI 2010/493; see generally Barrow, 2010. BIS also issued non-statutory guidance on the Regulations: *The Blacklisting of Trade Unionists: BIS Guidance on Blacklisting*, March 2010.

(i) The general prohibition

8.28   Under the heading 'general prohibition', the Regulations provide that 'no person shall compile, use, sell or supply a prohibited list'. A 'prohibited list' is a list which -

(a)   contains details of persons who are or have been members of trade unions or persons who are taking part or have taken part in the activities of trade unions, and
(b)   is compiled with a view to being used by employers or employment agencies for the purpose of discrimination in relation to recruitment or in relation to the treatment of workers'. [220]

'Discrimination' means treating a person less favourably than another on grounds of trade union membership or trade union activities. There is no requirement for the union to be independent. We echo the title of the Regulations and the BIS Guidance relating to them in referring to the 'prohibited lists' as 'blacklists'. The Guidance suggests that 'details' in limb (a) of the definition could include names, addresses, national insurance numbers, occupations and work histories, photographs, newspaper cuttings and links to web-sites. It also makes clear that a 'mixed' list of members and non-members is intended to be covered.[221] Limb (b) means that lists compiled for non-discriminatory purposes (such as check-off of union subscriptions) will not be covered. The absence of a 'primary' or 'principal' purpose test means that it is sufficient if one of the purposes of compiling the list is discriminatory, although a list which was originally compiled for a non-discriminatory purpose and then used to discriminate may not be covered; this may require close scrutiny of whether there was any subsequent act which could constitute 'compilation'. Trade union membership and activities are not defined. The BIS Guidance suggests that 'activities' could 'encompass a range of a member's involvement with a trade union, such as attending union meetings at an appropriate time,[222] writing articles in a union journal, standing for office in a trade union or acting as a workplace representative of a trade union'.[223] It also states that participating in official (but not 'unofficial') industrial action would 'probably' be covered. As we saw in para 8.8 above, the courts have held (albeit, in our view, incorrectly) that participation in industrial action is not covered by TULRCA 1992, s 152(1)(b) and given that this is one ground on which employers may be tempted to discriminate, it is regrettable that this was not clarified in the legislation itself. The distinction between official and 'unofficial' industrial action in the Guidance has been criticised on the ground that it confuses the activity of a union with the act of a union[224] and it may not withstand scrutiny in the courts.

   A 'list' includes 'any index or other set of items whether recorded electronically or by any other means'.[225] The reference to 'persons' in (a) above suggests that information relating to a single individual would not be covered but the BIS Guidance suggests that if it were related to other records they could together be treated as a 'list'. It also emphasises that information on a list need not be held in one location, so that information in blogs or forums on social networking sites

---

[220]   ERABR 2010, reg 3. 'Employment agency' is defined in reg 2 in essentially the same terms as in TULRCA 1992, s 143(1): see note 176 above. Membership of particular branch or section of a trade union is included in the concept of trade union membership and activities. 'Worker' is defined in ERelA 1999 ss 3(5), 13.
[221]   Pages 3-4.
[222]   Note, however, that there is no requirement in ERABR 2010 that union activities should be at an 'appropriate time'.
[223]   Page 6.
[224]   Harvey, 1972, as updated, Division N1, paras 861.02-861.03.
[225]   ERelA 1999, s 3(5).

could be a list if it was organised systematically or linked by a search engine.[226] It is irrelevant that the list is compiled or held offshore; it is unlawful for a person in Britain to use information from a list outside Britain where the list would be prohibited if located within Britain.[227]

There are five specified exceptions to the general prohibition.[228] The broadest is where the person supplies a prohibited list but does not know that they are doing so and could not reasonably be expected to know it. This means that postal operators would not be liable, for example, provided that they satisfied these conditions. Other exceptions are designed, broadly speaking, to enable journalists, whistleblowers and others to draw attention to a breach of the Regulations; to comply with legal requirements; and in connection with legal proceedings or legal advice. There is also an exception where the principal purpose is to satisfy a requirement that an individual has experience or knowledge of trade union matters for an office or employment (where such a requirement is reasonable) or where being a member of a union is required for appointment or election to a union office.

(ii) Enforcement of the general prohibition in the County Court

8.29   A contravention of the general prohibition is actionable in the County Court (or Court of Session in Scotland) as a breach of statutory duty.[229] In accordance with general principles, the claimant will need to be a person or organisation which has suffered loss or may suffer a loss as a result of the alleged breach and will need to bring a claim within six years of that breach.[230] Thus, trade unions may bring proceedings on their own behalf if they would be liable to lose members, for example, but may not bring representative actions on behalf of members who have suffered loss.[231] If there are facts from which the court could conclude, in the absence of any other explanation, that the defendant has contravened or could contravene the general prohibition, the court must find in favour of the claimant unless the defendant proves otherwise.[232] The court may grant an order to restrain or prevent the defendant from contravening the general prohibition, such as requiring it to cease using a prohibited list; breach of such an order would constitute contempt of court.[233] It may also award damages, which may include damages for injured feelings.[234] There is no statutory limit on the damages which may be awarded.

As we indicate in (iii) and (iv) below, individuals may also complain to an employment tribunal on specified grounds. They may not complain to the court in respect of the same conduct, however, unless they wish to obtain an order to restrain or prevent a defendant contravening the general prohibition; in respect of financial compensation they will have to make a choice between the court and the tribunal route.[235] As well as the absence of a limit on damages, the longer time-

---

[226] Page 6.
[227] ERABR 2010, reg 2(2).
[228] ERABR 2010, reg 4.
[229] ERABR 2010, reg 13(1).
[230] See generally Clerk and Lindsell, 2010: ch 9.
[231] ERelA 1999 s 3(3)(d) empowered the Secretary of State to make provision for representative actions but no such provision was made in ERABR 2010.
[232] ERABR 2010, reg 4(2).
[233] See further para 11.51.
[234] ERABR 2010, reg 13(3).
[235] ERABR 2010, reg 13(4),(5).

limit for bringing claims in the County Court may be significant here; although employment tribunals have the discretion to extend their three-month time limit there will be an element of risk involved in relying on this. However, as we indicate in note 241 below, the preferable route may depend in some circumstances on when the three-month time limit starts to run.

(iii) Refusal of employment or employment agency services

8.30   It is unlawful for an employer to refuse to employ a person 'for a reason which relates to' a blacklist and either the employer (a) contravenes the general prohibition in relation to the list or (b) relies on information supplied by a person who contravenes the general prohibition in relation to the list and knows or ought reasonably to know that the information relied on is supplied in contravention of the general prohibition.[236] Limb (b) is intended to deal with indirect use of a blacklist via one or more intermediaries; the BIS Guidance advises employers and others using vetting agencies or other third parties in recruitment to scrutinise and understand how the organisation collects information and operates its listing practices.[237] Refusal of employment is defined in the same terms as in TULRCA 1992, s 137(5), discussed in para 8.21 above. It is also unlawful for an employment agency to refuse services to a person on these grounds.[238] In both cases, if there are facts from which the tribunal could conclude. in the absence of any other explanation, that the respondent contravened the general prohibition or relied on information supplied in contravention of it, the tribunal must find that such a contravention or reliance on information occurred unless the respondent shows that it did not. Thus, if a complainant shows that his or her name is on a blacklist to which the employer subscribes and he or she had been refused employment on a number of occasions despite being appropriately qualified, the tribunal should find that the employer had contravened the general prohibition if there is no other credible explanation.[239] 'Reason which relates to' a blacklist is not defined; the BIS Guidance states that this should cover a wide range of circumstances, including mistakenly believing that an individual is on a blacklist.[240] Claims must be presented within three months beginning with the date of the conduct to which the complaint relates, although a tribunal may consider a complaint which is otherwise out of time if, in all the circumstances of the case, it considers that it is just and equitable to do so.[241] Where a tribunal upholds a complaint, it must make a declaration to that effect and may, if it considers it just and equitable to do so, order the respondent to pay compensation and/or recommend that the respondent take within a specified period action appearing to the tribunal to be practicable for the purpose of obviating or reducing the adverse effect on the complainant

---

[236]   ERABR 2010, reg 5.
[237]   Page 7. In the case of intermediaries, this may require 'supplied' to be interpreted as 'supplied by another person' rather than 'supplied to the employer'.
[238]   ERABR 2010, reg 6; see further para 8.21 for when a service is refused.
[239]   BIS Guidance: p 8.
[240]   Page 7.
[241]   ERABR 2010, reg 7. The 'date' of the conduct to which the complaint relates depends upon the nature of that conduct: reg 7(3),(4). As in the context of TULRCA 1992, s 139(2) (see note 180 above) it is submitted that this date should not be earlier than that on which the complainant becomes aware of the refusal (and see *Gisda Cyf v Barratt* [2010] IRLR 1073, SC, discussed in para 5.80 above). See regs 14 and 15 for provision for joinder of another prospective respondent or third parties.

(only) of any conduct to which the complaint relates.[242] Compensation is to be assessed on the same basis as damages for breach of statutory duty and may include compensation for injury to feelings. If the respondent fails without reasonable justification to comply with a recommendation the tribunal may increase its award of compensation or, if it has not made such an award, make one. If the tribunal considers that any conduct of the complainant before the refusal to which the complaint relates was such as to make it just and equitable to reduce the award, it should make such a reduction and should also subtract from the award any compensation awarded under TULRCA 1992, s 140 (see para 8.21 above).[243] The comments we make in para 8.21 about assessing loss apply equally in this context. The minimum compensation to be awarded prior to any increase or reduction is £5,000; the total amount must not exceeed £65,300.[244]

(iv) Dismissal or other detriment

8.31   It is automatically unfair to dismiss an employee if the principal reason relates to a blacklist and either (a) or (b) as set out in in the first sentence of (iii) above (see para 8.30) applies. There is a similar provision relating to the burden of proof.[245] No qualifying period is required to bring a complaint.[246] Interim relief is available for dismissal on these grounds.[247] There is a minimum basic award of £5000 before any reductions.[248] It is also automatically unfair to select an employee for redundancy on these grounds.[249] Protection against subjection to a detriment 'by any act or deliberate failure to act' (see para 8.14 above) on these grounds is not confined to employees, but where the detriment in question takes the form of dismissal and the complainant is an employee, he or she must complain under the unfair dismissal provisions. The time limit for complaining both of unfair dismissal and of subjection to a detriment is three months, with the same provision for extension as in (iii) above.[250] Where the tribunal upholds a complaint of subjection to a detriment it must make a declaration to that effect and may also award such compensation as it considers 'just and equitable in all the circumstances having regard to the act or failure complained of and to any loss sustained by the complainant which is attributable to the respondent's act or failure.[251] 'Loss' includes any expenses which the complainant reasonably incurred in consequence of the act or failure and loss of any benefit

---

[242] See ERABR 2010, reg 8 for this and other provisions relating to remedies. Cf EqA 2010, s 124(3), which allows a recommendation to extend to 'any other person'.
[243] As Barrow, 2010 remarks at 310: '[a]rguably, the failure to recruit on grounds unrelated to trade union membership or activity is a separate issue entirely irrelevant to the use of a blacklist of trade unionists'.
[244] From 1 March 2010 and at the time of writing. There is no provision in ERelA 1999 s 34 for increasing compensation limits in respect of blacklists; a separate regulation would be required.
[245] ERA 1996, s 104F, inserted by ERABR 2010, reg 12.
[246] ERA 1996, s 108.
[247] ERA 1996, s 128(1)(b); see further para 8.5 above.
[248] ERA 1996, ss 120(1C), 122
[249] ERA 1996, s 105.
[250] ERA 1996, s 111(5); ERABR 2010, reg 10. See further para 8.16 for discussion of when time begins to run under reg 10, which is in substantially similar terms to TULRCA 1992, s 147. See reg 15 for provisions relating to joinder of third parties to proceedings.
[251] See generally ERABR 2010, reg 11. See also para 8.16 above.. In assessing compensation, no account is to be taken of any pressure exercised on the respondent by calling, organising, procuring or financing a strike or other industrial action or by threatening to do so. There is no specific provision for injury to feelings in reg 11 but the cases referred to in para 8.16 relating to TULRCA 1992, s 149 could be cited here.

which he or she might otherwise reasonably be expected to have had. There is a duty to mitigate loss. Where the conduct of the complainant before the act or failure complained of was such that it would be just and equitable to reduce the award, the tribunal should make such a reduction; it should also reduce the award if it finds the act or failure was caused or contributed to by the complainant, and should subtract from the award any compensation awarded under TULRCA 1992, s 149. The compensation awarded to 'employees' may also be reduced by up to 25% if they have failed to comply with the ACAS Code of Practice on Disciplinary and Grievance Procedures 2009; equally it may be increased by up to 25% if the employer unreasonably fails to comply with the Code [252] As with refusal of employment, the minimum compensation to be awarded prior to any increase or reduction is £5,000. However there is no maximum amount except where the complainant is a worker and the detriment consists of termination of the contract, when there is a maximum of £65,300.

(v) Concluding comments

8.32   The provisions of ERABR 2010, especially the enforcement mechanisms and remedies, were controversial. The failure of the Secretary of State to use the powers in ERelA 1999 to introduce criminal sanctions was a particular area of criticism.[253] At the time of writing it remains to be seen how effective the Regulations will be in practice; the absence of cases may mean that they are having the desired deterrent effect or merely that there are breaches which have not yet been discovered. In a number of respects, however, they mark an improvement on the pre-existing provisions relating to union membership and activities whose deficiencies we highlighted in paras 8.23-8.26 above.

Protection of the right not to join in relation to employers

8.33   It may appear anomalous that individuals should need to be protected against prejudicial action by employers for refusing union membership. The right not to join a union became significant in Britain because of the practice of the closed shop, 'a situation in which employees come to realise that a particular job is only to be obtained and retained if they become and remain members of one of a specified number of unions'.[254] Closed shops can, broadly speaking, take one of two forms: pre-entry, where an individual must be accepted into union membership before being considered for employment (historically important in the British merchant shipping, dockworking and printing industries, for example), and the more common post-entry closed shop (known in American parlance as the 'union shop') which requires employees to join a specified union shortly after taking up a job. By the early 1960s an estimated 3.75 million workers in Great Britain (16% of the total workforce) worked in a closed shop.[255] The common law placed no restriction

---

[252] TULRCA 1992, s 207A; see para 2.21 above.
[253] See Barrow, 2010: pp 310-311.
[254] McCarthy, 1964: p 9.
[255] McCarthy, 1964: p 9. Coal-mining, iron and steel, engineering, shipbuilding and printing accounted for two-thirds of this number.

on enforcing closed shops,[256] but legislative intervention came with the Industrial Relations Act 1971[257] and the closed shop has been subject to varying kinds of statutory regulation ever since.

Debate about whether closed shops should be permitted has been highly polarised and founded, from each side, upon both pragmatism and principle. Supporters have argued that closed shops strengthen unions' bargaining power, remove a source of alternative labour during strikes, and avoid 'free riders' who take the benefits of collective bargaining without contributing to union funds. Opponents have cited their allegedly harmful economic consequences and their unwarranted interference with individual liberty.[258] The former have been said to include restricted output; resistance to change; maintenance of outdated skills differentials; and damaging strikes, leading to escalating production costs, uncompetitive pricing, depressed profit margins and closures. In the light of this catalogue it may seem surprising that not all employers shared the antagonistic view. The reasons why any given closed shop was negotiated and accepted by respective employers depended upon a number of variables including the particular sector or workplace and industrial relations climate of the time.[259] However, research shows that in the late 1970s, at least, closed shops were regarded by many managers as bringing advantages, such as greater stability in bargaining arrangements; greater likelihood of compliance with unpopular negotiating decisions, reinforced by the possibility of union discipline against dissenters; and a method of warding off the danger of inter-union competition.[260]

8.34   At international level legal policy towards forms of the closed shop at one time varied widely: some countries proscribed them, others permitted them, others still permitted modified arrangements such as making union membership (but not that of any particular union) compulsory, or allowing 'agency shops' whereby the non-member was required to pay a sum to a specified union or to charity. Recent years have seen more widespread legislative prohibition of such arrangements, but international treaties remain inconsistent on this issue. Whether there should be a right not to join a union and, if so, whether it has equal weight to the right to join has been dubbed 'one of the oldest set of issues in trade union law in most industrial democracies'.[261] Its complexity is reflected

---

[256] Union action to enforce a closed shop was ultimately accepted by the courts as a legitimate interest for the purpose of the tort of conspiracy: *White v Riley* [1921] 1 Ch 1; *Reynolds v Shipping Federation Ltd* [1924] 1 Ch 28; *Crofter Hand Woven Harris Tweed Co Ltd v Veitch* [1942] AC 435. See generally von Prondzynski, 1987: ch 8. Industrial action to enforce union membership is now excluded from the statutory immunities: see para 11.30 below.

[257] Between 1927 and 1946 the Trade Disputes and Trade Unions Act 1927, s 6(1) made it unlawful for a local or other public authority to make it a condition of employment for any person that he or she should be a union member, or to impose any condition which subjected non-union members to any 'disability or disadvantage'.

[258] J Burton, 1979; Hanson *et al*, 1979; Robbins, 1978.

[259] See generally McCarthy, 1964; Dunn and Gennard, 1984; Dunn and Wright, 1993.

[260] See above. A survey of manufacturing industry found that three-quarters of employers with experience of closed shops saw advantages in the practice while only half saw disadvantages: M Hart, 1979. However, managers had few regrets that the law had changed: Dunn and Wright, 1993: p 22.

[261] Leader, 1992: p 123. Ultimately it is hard to separate consideration of the right not to join from broader industrial relations policy. This point is neatly illustrated by the Donovan Commission's conclusion that the right not to join is not the corollary of the right to join because inhibiting the latter is 'designed to frustrate the development of collective bargaining, which it is public policy to promote': *Royal Commission on Trade Unions and Employers' Associations 1965-1968*, Cmnd 3623, 1968: para 599. During the period of the 1979–1997 Conservative administration this issue would have been addressed from a very different public policy perspective.

in the terms of relevant international treaties. After considerable debate on this issue[262] the ILO adopted a neutral stance; the Conference specifically endorsed the view that Convention No 87, which grants workers the right to join organisations of their own choosing, neither authorised nor prohibited union security arrangements, such matters being for regulation by national practice.[263] However, the supervisory bodies have concluded that where such arrangements are imposed by law, rather than by voluntary agreement, this constitutes a breach of the Convention (a distinction which may appear illogical given that in the latter case the decision to permit such arrangements equally involves an exercise of state power).[264] By contrast the Universal Declaration of Human Rights 1948, article 20(2) provides that no one may be compelled to belong to an association, although proposals to give legal effect to this principle in the International Covenant on Civil and Political Rights were rejected. There was 'no real discussion' of the matter during the drafting of the International Covenant on Economic Social and Cultural Rights, but the UN supervisory committee, in common with the Committee of Independent Experts (now the ECSR) under the ESC, has inferred that the right to join a trade union implies the right not to join.[265]

8.35   The position under the ECHR is more opaque. In *Young, James and Webster v United Kingdom*[266] three British Rail employees complained that their dismissals for refusing to join a trade union pursuant to a closed shop agreement introduced after their employment had commenced breached Article 11 (see para 7.9 above). Two of the applicants had ideological objections to joining any of these unions; the third simply refused to join. Despite evidence from the *travaux préparatoires* that Article 11(1) did not incorporate a right not to join and that the closed shop was intended to be unaffected, the majority of the Court declined to rule directly on the question of whether it was included.[267] Rather the Court concluded that on the facts of the particular case the threat of dismissal directed against persons engaged before there was any obligation to join a particular trade union struck at the 'very substance of the freedom guaranteed by Article 11', although it did not then explain the content of such substance (which on this analysis would clearly need to include non-membership).[268] It also held that, in the light of the protection of personal opinion afforded by Articles 9 and 10, it was a breach of the Convention to exert pressure of this kind to compel individuals to join an association contrary to their convictions.

In a later decision the ECtHR – invoking the principle that the Convention is a 'living instrument which must be interpreted in the light of present-day conditions' – concluded that Article 11 does encompass a negative right, although it did not determine whether this should be

---

[262] Betten, 1993, records (at pp 76–77) that '[t]he question of whether or not the freedom of association includes also the freedom not to join, was one of the reasons why attempts failed in 1927 to get a freedom of association Convention adopted by the International Labour Conference …'.

[263] ILO, Record of Proceedings, ILC, 32nd Session, 1949, 468; ILO, 1994: para 205.

[264] For a critique of the neutral position see Leader, 1992: pp 152–158.

[265] Craven, 1998: pp 268–269.

[266] Judgment of 13 August 1981, [1981] IRLR 408.

[267] A number of members of the Court did record their views on this issue, however; see judgment above at 419 for the views of those who concurred with the majority judgement and above at 419-420 for the views of those who dissented.

[268] See Forde, 1982, for a trenchant critique of this decision. On the facts it was found that the restriction of the right was not 'necessary in a democratic society' within Art 11(2) because it could not be said that the railway unions would have been prevented from striving for the protection of their members' interests in the absence of legislation permitting the applicants' dismissal.

considered on an equal footing with the positive.[269] It is notable that the Court drew for support on ILO principles which, as we indicate above, affect only union security arrangements imposed by law; the Court here made no such distinction and, although the case at issue concerned such an arrangement, its judgment appears to extend more widely.[270] The Court also cited the Community Charter of the Fundamental Social Rights of Workers, adopted by eleven Member States (excluding the UK) in Strasbourg in 1989, which includes a right to join or not to join trade unions without suffering any 'personal or occupational damage'. In 2006 the majority of the Court, sitting as a Grand Chamber, stated that it did not 'in principle exclude that the negative and positive aspects of the Article 11 right should be afforded the same level of protection' but it was 'difficult to decide this issue in the abstract' since it could only be properly addressed in the circumstances of a given case.[271]

> In assessing whether a Contracting State has remained within its margin of appreciation in tolerating the existence of closed-shop agreements, particular weight must be attached to the justifications advanced by the authorities for them and, in any given case, the extent to which they impinge on the rights and interests protected by Article 11. Account must also be taken of changing perceptions of the relevance of closed-shop agreements for securing the effective enjoyment of trade union freedom.[272]

The Court affirmed that 'an individual cannot be considered to have renounced his negative right to freedom of association in situations where, in the knowledge that trade union membership is a precondition of securing a job, he accepts an offer of employment notwithstanding his opposition to the condition imposed'. On this basis a distinction between pre-entry and post-entry closed shops in terms of the protection guaranteed by Article 11 was 'not tenable'.[273] Applying these general principles to the facts, the Court observed that there was little support in the Contracting States for the maintenance of closed-shop agreements and the decisions of the ECSR and the Community Charter of 1989 referred to above clearly indicated that the use of such agreements in the labour market was 'not an indispensable tool for the effective enjoyment of trade union freedoms'.[274] In the instant case the State had 'failed to protect the applicants' negative right to trade union freedom'.[275]

This latest judgment of the ECtHR means that the scope of the protection accorded by Article 11 continues to remain uncertain. Although the Court appears to be moving closer to according equal protection to the negative right it has continued to hold open the possibility that 'the fair balance to be struck between the competing interests of the individual and of the community as

---

[269] *Sigurour A Sigurjonsson v Iceland* judgment of 30 June 1993, (1993) 16 EHRR 462: para 35. See also *Chassagnou v France* judgment of 29 April 1999, (2000) 29 EHRR 615, paras 103–117. Cf *Sibson v UK* judgment of 20 April 1993, (1994) 17 EHRR 193, where the relocation of the applicant to another depot, as permitted by his contract, was found by the ECtHR not to strike at the substance of the freedom.

[270] On this basis, individuals falling outside the definition of 'workers' who are subjected to a detriment for non-membership of a union would have a free-standing right of action under the HRA 1998 against a public authority (or at least a 'pure' public authority). In practice, this situation seems highly unlikely to arise.

[271] *Sorensen and Rasmussen v Denmark* judgment of 11 January 2006, para 56.

[272] Above, para 58.

[273] Above, para 56.

[274] Above, para 75.

[275] Above, para 76.

a whole' could still come down in favour of a state which failed to protect an applicant against the effect of a closed-shop agreement.[276]

8.36 Returning to the position under British legislation, the Industrial Relations Act 1971 attempted a concerted attack on the closed shop and created an individual right not to join a union. However, unions and employers co-operated to discourage individuals from exercising their new right and this provision had little impact on existing closed shops.[277] The succeeding Labour government's legislation, by contrast, marked a near-return to the previous non-interventionist position by removing restraints upon closed shops' enforcement; it was automatically fair for an employer to dismiss an employee who refused to join an independent trade union specified in a closed shop agreement except where the employee objected to the principle of union membership on grounds of religious belief.[278] Although the introduction of closed shops remained a matter of voluntary agreement it is notable that by mid-1978 at least 5.2 million workers in Great Britain (23%) were covered by such arrangements.[279]

The legal pendulum swung again with the election of the Thatcher government, whose hostility to union organisation we have described in chapter 7. Predictably the closed shop was regarded as complete anathema. Rather than attempting to outlaw the practice altogether, however, the government took incremental measures to reduce its effective operation. The first target was the post-entry closed shop, which became increasingly difficult to enforce; the range of exempted categories was expanded significantly and ballots requiring high majorities to start or continue closed shops were required. Finally, in 1988, the post-entry closed shop became completely unenforceable when the right of an individual not to join a union was given parallel protection to the right to join, with statutory protection against dismissal[280] and action short of dismissal for exercising that right.[281] This was followed by the death knell of the pre-entry closed shop in 1990, with the introduction of protection against refusal of employment for non-membership (and, as an afterthought, for membership as well).[282] The Labour Government which entered office in 1997 left the position unchanged in its essentials, beyond amendments that parallel those applicable to the right to join. Closed shops are not now illegal as such but they cannot be lawfully enforced and, although it seems that informal practices remained for a time in individual workplaces or among some types of employee, if they now exist at all they involve a fraction of those covered in 1978.[283] In practice, therefore, contentious issues arising in relation to the right not to join may

---

[276] Above, paras 58, 76. See also *Olafsson v Iceland* judgment of 27 April 2010. See Mantouvalou, 2010 for the argument that the ECtHR has not explored thoroughly the conditions under which union security clauses may be compatible with the ECHR.

[277] Weekes *et al*, 1975: ch 2.

[278] TULRA 1974, as amended by the Trade Union and Labour Relations (Amendment) Act 1976, para 6(5) of the Schedule.

[279] Dunn and Gennard, 1984: p 15.

[280] See now TULRCA 1992, s 152.

[281] See now TULRCA 1992, s 146.

[282] TULRCA 1992, s 137. In early 1989 the Department of Employment estimated that 1.3 million persons were in pre-entry closed shops: *Removing Barriers to Employment*, Cm 655 (1989), para 2.6–2.7, although others argued this figure was grossly exaggerated: see Lord McCarthy, HL Debs Vol 521, col 154, 10 July 1990; Dunn and Wright, 1993: pp 8–10.

[283] See generally Dunn and Wright, 1993 and Wright, 1996. The 1998 Workplace Employee Relations Survey found that in 2% of workplaces managers said employees had to be union members to get or keep their jobs, but did not probe further the basis of this compulsion: Cully *et al*, 1999: p 89; Millward *et al*, 2000: pp 146–149. The 2004 Survey did not ask a question in this form: Kersley *et al*, 2006: p 113.

be more likely to emerge from the consequences of a single-union recognition deal which accords differential treatment to members and non-members of that union rather than from the closed shop as such.[284] Because the entitlement, procedure and remedies for the right not to join are, in most respects, identical to those relating to the right to join we identify only the distinctive features of this right in para 8.37 below.

The scope of protection, entitlement and remedies

8.37   There is a statutory right not to join (or to refuse or propose to refuse to join) any, or a particular, union(s).[285] Enforcement of the 'agency shop', requiring a payment equalling the union subscription to the union or to charity to counter the free-rider charge, is also precluded; there is a right not to comply with a requirement to make a payment, or allow a deduction from remuneration, as an alternative to union membership.[286] In addition, it is automatically unfair to select an employee for redundancy on these grounds where the circumstances described in para 8.3 apply.[287] As in the case of the right to join, an employee who is dismissed need not meet the usual qualifications for claiming unfair dismissal (although, where they are not met, the applicant may need to prove the reason for dismissal), and identical remedies apply, including provision for the dismissed employee to seek interim relief, although if this is sought there is no requirement to obtain a certificate from a union official.[288] 'Workers' (not only 'employees') are protected against subjection to a detriment by any act or failure to act by the employer whose sole or main purpose is to compel the worker to be or become a member of a union or a particular union.[289] The procedure for complaining of subjection to a detriment on grounds of non-membership, and the remedies available, are identical to those available for infringement of the right to join (see para 8.13 *et seq*). In addition, workers have a right not to have an offer made by the employer for the sole or main purpose of inducing the worker to be or become a member of a union or a particular union,[290] and are protected against subjection to a detriment for failing to accept such an offer.[291]

The provisions covering refusal of employment specifically prevent employers relying on unions to supply labour; it is unlawful for an employer (or employment agency) to refuse to employ non-members pursuant to an arrangement or practice whereby employment is offered only to persons put forward or approved by a union where the union does this only in respect of its members (although an affected individual would need to complain for the practice to be

---

[284] See para 8.2 above for further discussion of single-union deals.

[285] TULRCA 1992, ss 137(1), 146(1)(c), 152(1)(c). This also includes membership of a particular branch or section of the union or one of a number of such branches or sections: ss 143(3), 151(1), 152(4). Note that this right is not confined to membership of an independent union.

[286] TULRCA 1992, ss 137(1)(b)(ii), 146(3), 152(3). See Benedictus, 1979: pp 162–163 for discussion of the use of such practices in the 1970s.

[287] TULRCA 1992, s 153. Note that where the terms of s 152 or s 153 are not satisfied, a dismissal for non-membership may still be unfair under the ordinary unfair dismissal provisions.

[288] TULRCA 1992, s 161(3). See para 8.5 above for discussion of the burden of proof.

[289] TULRCA 1992, s 146. 'Employees' must use s 152 in the event of dismissal; see further para 8.13 for the implications of this.

[290] TULRCA 1992, s 145A(1)(d); see further para 8.17.

[291] TULRCA 1992, s 146(2C). Once again 'employees' must use s 152 in the event of dismissal.

challenged).[292] In providing job-finding services, however, unions may legitimately discriminate between members and non-members; they are not regarded as 'employment agencies' by reason of services provided by them only for, or in relation to, their members.[293] Unions may also continue to demand that those applying for union office are members of that union[294] (but not of another union, even if that may be more appropriate to the job in question).

In relation to any proceedings relating to the right not to join, if either the complainant or respondent claims that the employer was induced to take the action in question by pressure from a union or other person calling, organising, procuring or organising a strike or other industrial action (or threatening to do so) because the complainant was not a union member, either party may request the tribunal to direct that such a person be joined as a party to the proceedings.[295] That third party may then be liable to pay all or a proportion of any compensation awarded to the complainant.[296]

Although the provisions governing the right not to join a union parallel those governing the right to join, in practice they are likely to be easier to enforce. An employer who takes prejudicial action against an employee for non-membership is likely to do so only against a background of universal or near-universal membership and it is, therefore, much more likely that an employee will be able to invoke circumstantial evidence to satisfy the employment tribunal that this was the reason for the action. To this extent, therefore, while the comments relating to the burden of proof in para 8.25 remain valid in formal terms, they are likely to present less of an obstacle to a successful claim. If one were to accept the principle of formal equality between these rights, the remarks made earlier as to the inadequacy of the remedies available are equally valid in this context. However, in practice it seems less likely that an employer will wish to buy its way into a closed shop than into a union-free environment; letting sleeping dogs lie or social sanctions by other workers are a more likely response to the presence of a non-member than dismissal.[297]

CONTRACT COMPLIANCE AND UNION MEMBERSHIP

8.38 We outlined contract compliance as a strategy for encouraging particular employment practices in chapter 2. In the context of union membership, as we indicated in para 8.2, the 1946 version of the House of Commons Fair Wages Resolution specified that government contracts with private employers should require contractors to recognise the freedom of their workers to be members of trade unions. Most local authorities also followed this example, although not required to do so, and some attempted to support trade unionism by requiring contractors to employ only union labour.[298] 1982 brought a complete reversal of policy when the Conservative Government gave notice to rescind the Fair Wages Resolution and introduced legislation proscribing the

---

[292] TULRCA 1992, s 137(4).
[293] TULRCA 1992, s 143(2).
[294] This covers 'officials' within s 119 or any other position to which the duty to hold elections applies: TULRCA 1992, s 137(7), (8).
[295] TULRCA 1992, ss 142, 150, 160.
[296] TULRCA 1992, ss 142, 150, 160.
[297] Dunn and Wright, 1993: p 4 *et seq*.
[298] In 1982 about one in eight imposed such requirements for manual workers: Ingham and Thompson, 1982: table 5A.

implementation of contract compliance policies in this area.[299] A term or condition of any contract for the supply of goods or services (including one entered by individual householders) which requires that the work, or any part, is done only by members of a union, or a particular union, or by non-union members, is void, and there is a statutory duty not to exclude persons from a list of approved suppliers, or to terminate or refuse to consider entering contracts with them, if one of the grounds is that such a requirement is unlikely to be met. This duty is owed both to the potential contractor and to 'any other person who may be adversely affected by its contravention'.[300] Unlike the Local Government Act 1988, which prohibits local authorities and several other public bodies from making decisions relating to public supply and works contracts by reference to 'non-commercial matters',[301] there is no requirement for persons awarding contracts to give reasons for their decisions. The ban on non-union labour clauses was inserted to demonstrate formal equality between the rights to join and not to join rather than because non-union clauses were perceived as presenting any problem in practice.[302]

FACILITIES FOR TRADE UNION REPRESENTATIVES AND TRADE UNION ACTIVITIES

8.39   As we saw in chapter 7, trade unions conduct a multiplicity of functions on behalf of their members. At workplace level these may include negotiation and consultation with employers, dealing with individual and collective grievances, and representing members at disciplinary hearings.[303] These functions are often performed by lay representatives (or 'shop stewards').[304] Lay representatives began to play an increasingly important role in British industrial relations after the Second World War. By 1961 there were estimated to be about 90,000 shop stewards; research for the Donovan Commission later in the decade put the number at 175,000 and by the late 1970s the figure had reached between 250,000 and 300,000.[305] In 2004, the DTI (now BIS) estimated that there were 322,000 representatives on-site at British workplaces, excluding representatives who deal exclusively with health and safety issues. However, in contrast to the position in the 1970s, this number is now divided equally between union and non-union representatives.[306]

Lay representatives can carry out their functions much more effectively if employers make available appropriate facilities at the workplace to assist them.[307] In many cases the most important single facility is likely to be time. In 1978 a survey estimated that in 12% of establishments with

---

[299] See now TULRCA 1992, s 145.

[300] TULRCA 1992, s 145(5).

[301] Local Government Act 1988, s 17(1). The Local Government Act 1999, s 19, empowers the Secretary of State to remove by order specified matters from the category of non-commercial matters in relation to 'best value' authorities, such as local authorities; see SI 2001/909, discussed at para 2.6, for the exercise of this power.

[302] See Evans and Lewis, 1988, for the background to these provisions.

[303] Note now the statutory right for workers to be accompanied by the companion of their choice, who may be a union official, at disciplinary and grievance hearings: see ERelA 1999, ss 10–15 and para 5.121 et seq.

[304] See para 8.9 above for discussion of this term.

[305] Various research findings summarised in P Edwards et al, 1992: p 22.

[306] DTI Consultation Document *Workplace representatives: a review of their facilities and facility time* January 2007, para 2.4. See also Kersley et al 2006: pp 123-125; Wynn and Pitt, 2010; Terry, 2010.

[307] For the range of functions performed by lay representatives, see the DTI Consultation Document, above; Kersley et al 2006: ch 6; *Reps in Action: How workplaces can gain from modern union representation*, BERR, May 2009.

manual stewards (and 2% of non-manual) at least one was full-time,[308] and even in 1990, 4% of workplaces with recognised unions had one or more full-time representatives (a higher proportion than in 1984).[309] In 1975 the Labour Government's 'Social Contract' legislation introduced a statutory obligation on employers to grant officials of *recognised* independent trade unions a reasonable amount of paid time off during working hours for industrial relations duties and training relevant to those duties. In addition, members of such unions were entitled to reasonable time off (which need not be paid) to participate in union activities or represent the union. Perhaps surprisingly, these rights survived the legislative changes of the 1980s, albeit with significant amendment in 1989 when the Employment Act narrowed the duties for which officials could claim time off to those concerned with negotiations on matters for which the union was specifically recognised. The Employment Act 2002 added an obligation to give paid time off to a newly-created class of 'union learning representatives'.

Time off has always been conditional on the employer granting permission, with a right to complain to an employment tribunal in the event of it being refused. Although time off rights apply to all employers without exception as to size and type of business or service, they have always been located within a framework which acknowledges the need to pay adequate regard both to the operational requirements of individual workplaces and to the difficulties of communicating with the specific workforce (for example, if part-time or shift work is common).

In 2006 the Labour Government launched a review of the facilities and facility time of workplace representatives; this was followed by a consultation exercise on possible reforms.[310] In the event the Government decided not to change the statutory framework[311] but it invited ACAS to revise its Code of Practice, drawing attention to a list of issues that ACAS may wish to consider, including the provision of cover when employees take time off; adjustment of representatives' workloads; advice to line managers; value of training and retraining representatives; access to e-learning; use of IT equipment; confidentiality of representatives' communications; and the position of representatives with atypical work patterns. It also asked ACAS to consider whether the Code should provide advice on non-union representation.[312] ACAS decided that the revised Code should remain confined to the statutory areas covered in the existing Code but that it should also issue non-statutory guidance covering the whole range of employee representation to complement the Code.[313] This non-statutory guidance covers both those with time off and facilities under specific statutory provisions, such as those discussed in chapter 9 below, and the position of non-statutory or 'voluntary' representatives.[314]

We examine below the scope of the statutory rights, and the remedies for their infringement, before commenting upon their adequacy. These rights currently apply only to employees rather

---

[308] W Brown, 1981: pp 63–67.

[309] Millward *et al*, 2000: p 153–154.

[310] DTI Consultation Document, above, note 306.

[311] BERR, *Workplace representatives: a review of their facilities and facility time: Government response to public consultation*, November 2007.

[312] ACAS, *Consultation on the Acas Code of Practice 3 on time off for trade union duties and activities and Draft guide on Developing effective employee representation: a guide to managing provisions for time off, training and facilities*, December 2008: foreword.

[313] Above.

[314] ACAS, *Trade Union Representation in the Workplace; Non-Union Representation in the Workplace*.

than the wider category of 'workers',[315] but require no minimum period of employment. The ACAS Code of Practice on Time Off for Trade Union Duties and Activities (Including Guidance on Time Off for Union Learning Representatives) 2010, like its predeccesors, strongly encourages agreements between employers and unions which can reflect their own situations.[316] Such agreements may be more generous than the legislation requires but only denial of the statutory entitlements can be the subject of complaint to a tribunal.

Time off rights of trade union officials

8.40   Union 'officials' (which include any lay representative elected or appointed in accordance with the union rules)[317] are entitled to paid time off for three purposes (although there is nothing to prevent the parties agreeing to such entitlement in a wider range of situations). The first is to carry out any of their duties, as such an official, concerned with negotiations with the employer related to or connected with any matters falling within the statutory definition of collective bargaining in relation to which the union is recognised by the employer.[318] To fall within this category, three conditions must be satisfied. First, the duties must relate to a matter for which the union is recognised by the employer in question; the fact that other employers in the same industry, or even an associated employer,[319] may have granted more extensive recognition is irrelevant. As we saw in para 7.27, recognition may be express or implied from conduct. Second, the matter must be listed in the Trade Union and Labour Relations (Consolidation) Act 1992, s 178(2), which specifies the matters constituting the subject-matter of 'collective bargaining'.[320] Last, the duties must be 'concerned with negotiations' with the employer. This condition was inserted by the Employment Act 1989 to require proximity to actual negotiations; attending meetings of bodies with no negotiating power to determine national union policies concerned with industrial relations matters, covered under previous legislation,[321] would no longer suffice.

Whether sufficient proximity exists will involve examining the facts in each case. In *Adlington v British Bakeries (Northern) Ltd*, decided during the legislative passage of the Employment Act 1989, branch officials of the Bakers, Food and Allied Workers' Union claimed paid time off to attend a union workshop concerning government proposals to repeal the Banking Industry (Hours of Work) Act 1954. The Court of Appeal upheld the claim on the basis that repeal would threaten the continued existence of the industry's National Working Agreement and was thus likely to lead to negotiations between the union and employers, Kerr LJ stressing the 'exceptionally close connection' between the repeal of the legislation and a specific bargaining matter that

---

[315]   Note, however, ERelA 1999, s 23, discussed at para 3.38. Special provision is made for attendance by a member of a police force at specified meetings of the Police Federation: Police Regulations 2003, SI 2003/527, reg 23. Note also provision for time off for a 'police friend' in SI 2008/2862, reg 5 and SI 2008/2864, reg 6.

[316]   Section 5. For a general discussion of the Code and the background to it, see Wynn and Pitt, 2010.

[317]   See TULRCA 1992, s 119. The ACAS Code uses the term 'union representative' to avoid confusion with an official who is employed by the union (referred to in the Code as a 'union full-time officer'): see Code, para 2. We retain the statutory language in our analysis of the legislation.

[318]   TULRCA 1992, s 168(1).

[319]   See para 3.65.

[320]   See para 7.27. See the Code of Practice, para 13, for examples under each heading.

[321]   *Beal v Beacham Group Ltd* [1982] IRLR 192.

existed.[322] In drafting the 1989 Act the Government sought explicitly to incorporate the concept of proximity propounded in this case. *London Ambulance Service v Charlton*[323] was decided under the new provision. Union officials sought paid time off to attend a union committee to coordinate the activities of its district committee within the London Ambulance Service. The EAT affirmed that meetings which were called actively to prepare for negotiations in connection with collective bargaining were covered provided that there was 'sufficient nexus between the collective bargaining and the duty involving preparation for that particular issue'.[324] Moreover, officials of a union which was a member of a multi-union Joint Consultative Committee (JCC) might wish to have their own meeting in the absence of other unions, although the frequency and timing of these separate meetings in relation to those of the JCC might be relevant in considering the issue of reasonableness (discussed below).

The second purpose for which an employer should grant paid time off is to carry out duties concerned with the performance on behalf of its employees of functions related to or connected with 'collective bargaining' matters which the employer has specifically agreed may be performed by the union.[325] Thus, officials should be given time off to represent individuals in grievance proceedings in circumstances beyond those required by statute,[326] for example, where the employer has agreed to this.

The ACAS Code of Practice emphasises that an official's duties must be connected with or related to negotiations or the performance of functions both in time and subject matter. It suggests that reasonable time off may be sought, for example, to prepare for negotiations, including relevant meetings; inform members of progress and outcomes; and prepare for meetings with the employer about matters for which the union has only representational rights,[327] although the latter is not, strictly speaking, within the terms of the legislation. Informing members about the outcome of industry-wide negotiations would seem not to be included,[328] although employers may wish to consider allowing time off for this purpose.

The third purpose for which time off should be granted is to carry out duties concerned with the receipt of information from and consultation with the employer in relation to collective redundancies and a transfer of the undertaking. We discuss those provisions in detail in chapter 9.

8.41   In addition to the conduct of these duties, officials are also entitled to paid time off for training relevant to them.[329] Training courses must be approved by the Trades Union Congress or by the official's own union.[330] The kind of training a particular official should have will depend upon the scope of any recognition or other agreement; the structure of the union; and the role

---

[322] [1989] IRLR 218, 222.

[323] [1992] IRLR 510.

[324] [1992] IRLR 510, 513.

[325] TULRCA 1992, s 168(1).

[326] See ERelA 1999, s 10; see further para 5.121 *et seq*.

[327] Para 14.

[328] Representation on regional or national bodies negotiating with a range of employers would also not be covered, although officials would be entitled to unpaid time off for this purpose: see para 8.45.

[329] TULRCA 1992, s 168(2).

[330] For the organisation and nature of training provided in practice see DTI Consultation Document, above note 306, para 4.10 *et seq*. The Code states that e-learning tools should be used where available and appropriate but that their best use is as an additional learning aid rather than to replace attendance at approved courses: para 27.

of the individual.[331] The relationship between training and the scope of recognition may put into question entitlement to attend courses which relate to several topics, not all of which may be covered by the individual recognition agreement.[332] However the EAT has indicated that the statute should not be given a narrow interpretation,[333] and many contemporary courses focus upon the development of skills required by officials, such as negotiating and representational skills, rather than substantive topics and so circumvent this problem. The Code of Practice recommends that employers should consider releasing officials for initial training in basic representational skills as soon as possible after their election or appointment, bearing in mind that suitable courses may be infrequent. It also recommends consideration of time off for further training, particularly where the official has special responsibilities; for training courses to develop representational, accompaniment; negotiating and consultation skills; to familiarise or update them on issues reflecting the developing needs of the workforce they represent; where there are proposals to change the scope or nature of collective bargaining at the workplace, where significant changes in the organisation of work are being contemplated, or where legislation may affect the conduct of employment relations at the place of work and may require the reconsideration of existing collective agreements.[334] The EAT relied upon the concept of 'special responsibilities' in holding that a union branch secretary who had been elected to the Management Committee of a pension scheme to represent his members and others, to report back to shop stewards and to advise members in connection with their pensions, was entitled to paid time off to attend a course on pensions.[335]

The 2004 Workplace Industrial Relations Survey found that almost three-quarters of union representatives had received some training for their role and around two-fifths had been trained in the previous 12 months.[336] From 1976 until 1996 the TUC and, latterly, non-affiliated independent unions also, received a government grant towards the cost of training lay and safety representatives, but this was withdrawn by the Conservative Government on the grounds that industrial relations had improved and the coverage of collective bargaining reduced, a step that overlooked the wide range of functions that representatives perform. In a reversal of its predecessor's policy, Labour Government provided support for TUC education, in addition to funding for 'partnership' projects, some of which included, *inter alia*, training union representatives.[337] The Union Modernisation Fund, discussed in para 7.30 above, was also used to support innovative training initiatives developed by unions.

---

[331] Code of Practice, para 24.
[332] *Menzies v Smith and McLaurin Ltd* [1980] IRLR 180. The identity of the personnel for whom the course is described as being designed may be a relevant factor: *Ministry of Defence v Crook and Irving* [1982] IRLR 488.
[333] *STC Submarine Systems v Piper* (11 March 1993, unreported), EAT.
[334] Para 26.
[335] *STC Submarine Systems v Piper*, above, note 333 Although the pension scheme was not directly negotiable, the EAT held that the employment tribunal was justified in concluding that pension rights were relevant to any negotiations over pay and conditions in general, and involved at least in the preparation of matters relevant to collective bargaining.
[336] Kersley *et al* 2006: p 157.
[337] DTI Consultation Document, above note 306, paras 4.15–4.16. A Partnership at Work Fund was established pursuant to a power granted to the Secretary of State by ERelA 1999, s 30 to provide money 'for the purpose of encouraging and helping employers (or their representatives) and employees (or their representatives) to improve the way they work together'. It was anomalous that this power was confined to 'employees', given that trade unions are organisations of 'workers': TULRCA 1992, s 1, discussed further para 7.20. The Fund closed in 2004.

8.42   The amount of time off which an employer should permit an official to take, and the purposes for which, occasions on which, and conditions subject to which it may be taken, are those which are 'reasonable in all the circumstances'.[338] In determining what it reasonable, which is pre-eminently a question for the employment tribunal as 'industrial jury' to decide,[339] regard is to be had to the ACAS Code of Practice. Where the employer and union have concluded their own time off agreement, as the Code strongly recommends,[340] its provisions are likely to influence a tribunal considerably in determining what is reasonable in the circumstances, although an agreement which is less favourable than the legislation ought not to prejudice an employee's position.[341] The Code states that each application for time off should be considered on its merits but the agreed time off already taken or in prospect will be relevant. It sets out in some detail the factors which each side should consider when seeking arrangements (for example, for unions, the operational requirements of the business; for employers, difficulties of representing workers such as shift workers and those at dispersed locations).[342] The Code also states that employers should ensure, where necessary, work cover and/or work load reductions are provided when time off is required.[343] As much notice as possible should be given to management when time off is sought, giving details of its purpose, the intended location, and its timing and duration.[344]

8.43   When time off is granted the employee should be paid as if he or she had worked.[345] The pre-Employment Act 1989 cases conflict on whether an employer can allow an official time off but argue that it was not reasonable for the official to be paid for that time.[346] Even then it was hard to reconcile such an argument with the statutory language[347] and the tighter definition of the duties for which paid time off is due would seem to diminish its chances of success. An employee who performs the relevant duties outside his or her own 'working hours'[348] has no statutory entitlement to compensating paid time off in lieu,[349] although the ACAS Code of Practice states that there is such an entitlement where the individual 'works flexible hours, such as night shift, but needs to perform representative duties during normal hours'.[350] This seems to go further than current

---

[338]   TULRCA 1992, s 168(3).
[339]   *Thomas Scott & Sons (Bakers) Ltd v Allen* [1983] IRLR 329; *Wignall v British Gas Corpn* [1984] IRLR 493.
[340]   Section 5.
[341]   TULRCA 1992, s 288 (cf the discussion in *Ashley v Ministry of Defence* [1984] IRLR 57, where the EAT distinguished between time off pursuant to an internal agreement, which may be in some respects more favourable and in others less favourable than the statute, and time off pursuant to the predecessor of s 168.)
[342]   Section 4. See also *Wignall v British Gas Corpn* above note 339.
[343]   Para 45.
[344]   Para 50.
[345]   TULRCA 1992, s 169. Where an employee's pay varies with the amount of work done, payment is to be calculated by reference to the average hourly earnings for the work the employee is employed to do. The Code of Practice emphasises the need to include, as appropriate, shift premia, performance related pay, bonuses and commission earnings and that where pay is linked to the achievement of performance targets it may be necessary to adjust such targets to take account of the reduced time the representative has to achieve the desired performance: para 18.
[346]   In *Beecham Group Ltd v Beal (No 2)* [1983] IRLR 317 the EAT held that the right to payment followed automatically; cf *Thomas Scott & Sons (Bakers) Ltd v Allen* [1983] IRLR 329, where the EAT took a different view but did not explain the basis for this conclusion.
[347]   See Fitzpatrick, 1983: p 260 for further comment.
[348]   The same definition as in the context of 'appropriate time' (see para 8.10) applies: TULRCA 1992, s 173.
[349]   See *Hairsine v Kingston upon Hull City Council* [1992] IRLR 211.
[350]   Para 19.

case law warrants.[351] In practice unions and employers should attempt to reach an agreement to cater for circumstances of this kind.[352] Problems may also arise for employees who do not work full-time who may thereby be disadvantaged if the time they spend on union duties exceeds their working hours. The ECJ has held that compensation received for loss of earnings due to attendance at training courses for staff committees in Germany falls within the definition of 'pay' for the purposes of Article 157 of the TFEU (ex Article 141 of the EC Treaty) and the Equal Pay Directive 75/117 because it constitutes a benefit paid by reason of the existence of an employment relationship. Since the members of such committees who are employed part-time are generally women, a legislative provision which results in part-time workers being paid less than full-time workers for attending courses whose length exceeds the number of hours they work constitutes indirect discrimination against women.[353] In *Manor Bakeries v Nazir*[354] the EAT held that this principle did not apply to attendance at a British union conference on the basis that this was not a species of 'work'. However in the later case of *Davies v Neath Port Talbot County Borough Council*[355] a differently-constituted EAT held that *Nazir* should not be followed, affirming that attendance at a union training course, like that of German staff committees, was by reason of the existence of the employment relationship. The ECJ had indicated that it was open to a Member State to justify legislation which limited part-time workers to compensation for their working hours by objective factors unrelated to any discrimination on grounds of sex.[356] In *Davies* the EAT took a robust approach to this issue, affirming that there could not be 'a justifiable policy or aim which maintains the inequality'.[357]

If an official is refused permission to take time off, the sole remedy is to complain to an employment tribunal;[358] there is a right to time off only with permission. (An employee who took time off without permission and was subsequently disciplined for doing so could not claim to have been taking part in a protected union activity because it would not have been at an appropriate time: see para 8.10.) An official can also complain if he or she was not paid in accordance with the legislation for time off which was granted.[359] Claims must be brought within three months of the failure to permit time off, or to make the requisite payment.[360] If it upholds the complaint, the tribunal must make a declaration and may award compensation, having regard to the employer's

---

[351] Wynn and Pitt, 2010: p 214.

[352] See Code of Practice, para 58

[353] C-360/90 *Arbeiterwohlfahrt der Stadt Berlin e V v Bötel* [1992] IRLR 423, ECJ; Case 457/93 *Kuratorium für Dialyse und Nierentransplantion eV v Lewark* [1996] IRLR 637.

[354] [1996] IRLR 604.

[355] [1999] IRLR 769.

[356] See *Lewark* note 353 above for consideration of the factors which may be relevant in this context.

[357] Above note 355 at 772.

[358] TULRCA 1992, ss 168(4), 173(2). Curiously, s 173(2) states that the sole remedy is by way of complaint to an employment tribunal under Part III of TULRCA 1992. However, ERA 1996 s 27(1)(e) includes payment for time off for union duties within the definition of 'wages', so allowing tribunals to treat non-payment as an unlawful deduction from 'wages' under ss 13–27 of that Act: see paras 4.71 *et seq*. Nothing would seem to turn on this in relation to a failure to pay on one occasion, but if the failure related to a series of non-payments the time limit under ERA 1996, s 23(3)(a) appears to be more generous.

[359] TULRCA 1992, s 169(5).

[360] TULRCA 1992, s 171. If the tribunal is satisfied that compliance with this time limit was not 'reasonably practicable' the complaint must be presented within such further period as the tribunal considers 'reasonable': see para 2.17. In *Young, Stewart and Morris v British Airways Board* unreported, EAT 175/83, it was held that the three-month period runs from the date when permission was refused.

default and any loss sustained by the employee because of the failure.[361] By analogy with the provisions relating to subjection to a detriment it seems likely that 'loss' can include non-pecuniary loss such as injury to health (see para 8.16). Where the complaint concerns a failure to pay the official, the tribunal will order payment by the employer of the amount due. Tribunals have no power to impose conditions on the parties as to how time off should be granted in the future.[362]

Time off for union learning representatives

8.44 'Union learning representatives' (ULR) are a relatively new type of lay union representative, whose main function is to advise union members about their training, educational and developmental needs. Their advice is usually provided direct to union members at their place of work. Prior to EA 2002 there were estimated to be around 3,000 ULRs in existence, but their activities were seen as being constrained by the limited abilities of unions to find, train and support suitable volunteers for this work.[363] Research conducted for the Labour Government suggested that ULRs had a significant impact in increasing motivation and enthusiasm for learning among both employers and employees,[364] and EA 2002 introduced a right to paid time off for ULRs to prepare for and conduct their activities. Although the CBI, like the TUC, agreed that ULRs could play a valuable role, the CBI considered that ULRs should be appointed only with the employer's agreement. The TUC opposed employers having any right of veto, and the government concluded that unions should be free to decide on the identity and number of ULRs at the workplace, although their entitlement to time off, like that of union officials, is subject to the requirement of 'reasonableness'.[365]

An employee who is a member of a recognised independent union and a 'learning representative' of that union is entitled to paid time off during working hours for specified activities in relation to fellow employees who are members of the ULR's union and for whom the ULR has the function of acting as such ('qualifying members' of the union).[366] ULRs are not therefore entitled to time off to provide services to non-union members or members of other unions. The activities for which time off should be permitted are to analyse learning or training needs; provide information and advice about learning or training matters; arrange learning or training; and promote the value of learning or training in relation to 'qualifying members'.[367]

---

[361] TULRCA 1992, s 172. To establish a right to compensation an employee must establish, on the balance of probabilities, that a request was made for time off, that it came to the notice of the employer's appropriate representative, and that they either refused it, ignored it or failed to respond to it: *Ryford Ltd v Drinkwater* [1996] IRLR 16. In *Skiggs v South West Trains Ltd* [2005] IRLR 459 the EAT held that 'compensation' could include the concept of a cash reparation to the individual for the fact that a wrong had been done to him, independently of any special consequential loss.

[362] *Corner v Buckinghamshire County Council* [1978] IRLR 320.

[363] *Regulatory Impact Assessment: Placing Union Learning Representatives (ULRs) on a Statutory Footing*, DTI. The Labour Government stated that about a third of ULRs did not receive paid time off for training, and about half did not receive paid time off to carry out their workplace duties: John Healey, Parliamentary Under-Secretary of State for Education and Skills, HC Standing Committee F, col 491, 17 January 2002.

[364] *Regulatory Impact Assessment: Placing Union Learning Representatives (ULRs) on a Statutory Footing*, DTI.

[365] The TUC estimated that there would be more than 22,000 ULRs after the legislation had been in force for an eight-year period: above. The TUC estimated that there around 18,000 ULRs in 2007: McIlroy, 2008: p 296. See Hollinrake *et al*, 2008 for discussion of the activities of ULRs.

[366] TULRCA 1992, s 168A(1),(2),(10).

[367] TULRCA 1992, s 168A(2)(a).

Time off should also be given for the ULR to consult the employer about carrying on any such activities[368] and to prepare for any of the specified matters.[369] An employee constitutes a ULR if he or she has been appointed as such in accordance with the union rules,[370] but is entitled to time off only if the union has notified the employer in writing that he or she is a ULR and has met the 'training condition'.[371] The 'training condition' requires the employee to have undergone sufficient training to enable him or her to carry out the role either at the start of the appointment or within six months of it; in the latter case, if the union does not confirm to the employer within the six month period that the requisite training has been completed, entitlement to time off lapses.[372] In deciding what constitutes sufficient training, regard is to be had to the ACAS Code of Practice.[373] The union cannot extend the appointment of a 'probationary' ULR by giving a second notice of future training,[374] although the Code of Practice states that in the interests of good practice the six-month period can be extended by agreement to take into account any significant unforeseen circumstances such as prolonged absence from work due to ill health, pregnancy or bereavement or unavoidable delays in arranging an appropriate training course.[375] Both 'probationary' and 'fully-fledged' ULRs are entitled to time off for training.[376]

Time off for ULRs, like that of union officials, is subject to a test of reasonableness and similar considerations to those indicated in para 8.42 apply. The remedies for wrongful refusal of time off are identical.

Time off for trade union activities

8.45   An employer must permit employees who are a members of an independent trade union which it recognises in respect of that description of employee to take reasonable time off during their working hours to take part in 'any activities' of the union and any other activities in relation to which they are acting as a representative of it.[377] The requirement of recognition for their description of employee means that if, for example, the employer recognises the X union exclusively for clerical staff, managerial grades who belong to the union will not be able to claim time off. There is no requirement that time off for these purposes should be paid, but employers and unions may nevertheless agree that it should be, and the Code of Practice suggests that employers should consider payment in certain circumstances, for example in order to ensure that

---

[368] The Code of Practice states that ULRs should liaise with their employers to ensure that their respective training activities complement each other and that the scope for duplication is minimised: para 17. It also states that employers may see it as in their interests to grant paid time off for ULRs to attend meetings with external partners concerned with the development and provision of workplace training: para 16.

[369] TULRCA 1992, s 168A(2)(b)(c).

[370] TULRCA 1992, s 168A(11).

[371] TULRCA 1992, s 168A(3).

[372] TULRCA 1992, s 168A(4).

[373] TULRCA 1992, s 168A(6). See the Code of Practice, paras 28-33.

[374] TULRCA 1992, s 168A(5).

[375] Para 29.

[376] TULRCA 1992, s 168A(6).

[377] TULRCA 1992, s 170.

workplace meetings are fully representative or to ensure that employees have access to services provided by Union Learning Representatives ('ULRs').[378]

The scope of union 'activities' is a question of fact for the employment tribunal. The Code of Practice gives as examples: attending workplace meetings to discuss and vote on the outcome of negotiations with the employer; meeting full-time officials to discuss issues relevant to the workplace; voting in union elections; and having access to services provided by a ULR.[379] It is arguable that the right should extend to any activities which the union may lawfully undertake, including those of a political, social or educational nature. However, the EAT has said that 'in a broad sense the activity should be one which is in some way linked to [the] ... employment relationship'.[380] On that basis it upheld the decision of the tribunal that a teacher was not entitled to time off to attend a TUC lobby of Parliament intended to convey political or ideological objections to proposed legislation, although it emphasised that not all lobbying would be outside the entitlement. The EAT contrasted lobbying consisting of 'the presentation of arguments intended to persuade a Member of Parliament to vote in a particular way on a particular issue' with 'an approach which is in essence based upon mere protest',[381] a distinction whose logic is hard to discern; even if (contrary to our view) one accepts such a limitation in principle, the subject-matter of the lobby would seem of greater relevance than the method of conducting it.

Activities where the employee is acting as a union 'representative' may include taking part in branch, area or regional meetings of the union, or meetings of official policy-making bodies such as the executive committee or annual conference, or meetings with full-time officials to discuss issues relevant to the workplace.[382] Thus union officials who are not entitled to paid time off for particular duties may qualify under this heading. The statute specifically excludes industrial action from the right to time off;[383] however, activities connected with its organisation or threat appear not to be excluded (although the matter is not free from doubt),[384] and the Code of Practice emphasises that officials should be given paid time off to represent members who are taking industrial action when they are not themselves so doing.[385] There is no definition of 'industrial action' in this context; the test of the purpose of the activity applied in the context of unfair dismissal (see para 11.74) would probably be applicable here.

---

[378] Para 41; see para 8.44 above. Initial uncertainty as to whether accessing the services of a ULR constituted taking part in union 'activities' was resolved by making specific provision for employees to have time off for this purpose: TULRCA 1992, s170(2A)-(2C). The right applies only if the ULR would be entitled himself or herself to time off to provide services to such members. The right does not extend to undergoing any consequent training.

[379] Para 37. Note that where union elections are governed by statute, at the time of writing voting must be fully postal: see para 10.16.

[380] *Luce v Bexley London Borough Council* [1990] IRLR 422, 425.

[381] *Luce v Bexley London Borough Council* [1990] IRLR 422, 425.

[382] Code of Practice, para 38. Representing individual members at employment tribunals would probably also fall within this category. Note that time off for workers (not just employees) to accompany individuals at disciplinary and grievance proceedings pursuant to the statutory right to be accompanied must be paid, regardless of whether the companion is a union official: ERelA 1999, s 10.

[383] TULRCA 1992, s 170(2).

[384] See *Midland Plastics v Till* [1983] IRLR 9, where for the purposes of TULRCA 1992, s 238, as amended, the threat of industrial action was held not to amount to 'industrial action', but cf *Lewis and Britton v E Mason and Sons* [1994] IRLR 4, where the EAT refused to characterise as perverse the tribunal's finding that the threat of industrial action itself constituted 'industrial action'.

[385] Para 62.

Time off for union activities is again subject to a test of reasonableness and similar considerations to those indicated in para 8.44 apply. The remedies for wrongful refusal of time off are identical, except that in this context there is no requirement that the time off should be paid.

Assessment

8.46   The provisions relating to the provision of facilities for trade union representatives and members are subject to a number of limitations. The first is their confinement to the provision of time off; there is no statutory requirement to provide other facilities which may assist union organisation, such as office space. ILO Convention No 135 provides that such facilities shall be afforded to workers' representatives 'as may be appropriate in order to enable them to carry out their functions promptly and efficiently'.[386] However, although the British legislation is restricted, interestingly the ACAS Code of Practice goes further in stating that employers 'should, where practical, make available to union representatives the facilities necessary for them to perform their duties efficiently and communicate effectively with their members, colleague union representatives and full-time officers'. Where resources permit, such facilities should include accommodation for meetings; access to a telephone and other communication media used or permitted in the workplace such as e-mail, intranet and internet; the use of notice boards; where the volume of the union representative's work justifies it, the use of dedicated office space; confidential space where an employee involved in a grievance or disciplinary matter can meet their representative or to discuss other confidential matters; access to members who work at a different location; and access to e-learning tools where computer facilities are available.[387] In practice a high proportion of employers with recognised unions do provide other facilities[388] and this is a matter which it would probably be difficult to enforce through legislation, particularly given the need to ensure that a union's independent status is not prejudiced by dependence on employer-provided facilities (see para 7.24).

A more fundamental objection is the limitation of all time off provisions to members of recognised unions. Lay representatives of all unions may have an important part to play in representing members in disciplinary and grievance proceedings; although they have a separate statutory right to time off for these activities, this applies only if specified conditions are met[389] and does not include time off for training for this role. There is also no reason why time off to participate in union activities should be dependent upon recognition, particularly given the part that unions may come to play in information and consultation roles short of recognition, discussed in chapter 9. The restriction of time off rights for ULRs to members of recognised unions is also a significant limitation. A further serious omission from the legislation is any right of access by paid officials of the union to the workplace to address meetings or investigate collective complaints, for

---

[386] Art 2(1). See also the more specific provisions of Recommendation No 143 concerning Protection and Facilities to be Afforded to Workers' Representatives in the Undertaking.

[387] Para 46. The Code also emphasises the need for agreed procedures in respect of the use of such facilities and of company information and the need for confidentiality of communications involving union representatives: paras 47-49.

[388] See Kersley *et al* 2006: pp 155–156.

[389] ERelA 1999, s 10; see further para 5.121 *et seq*.

example, which again we would argue should be independent of recognition.[390] In *Post Office v Union of Post Office Workers*[391] the House of Lords affirmed that employers should be required to accept minor infringements of their rights of property in relation to members' access to facilities on the premises, and in this context also employers' rights of property should be modified.

Turning to the more specific aspects of the existing time off provisions, the first limitation is that there is a right to time off only with permission. This would be unobjectionable if combined with a speedy method of redress where requests for time off were denied. Currently, however, the employee's only remedy is to complain to an employment tribunal which will hear the complaint long after the event for which time off was sought has passed. In this respect expedited access to a remedy along the lines of interim relief might be appropriate, with provision for a fuller hearing at a later date if one or other party wished to challenge the grounds of the decision. Furthermore, the remedies for a successful claim are totally inadequate. The tribunal has no power even to recommend a future course of conduct on the part of the employer, let alone enforce it. Financial compensation is not an adequate remedy particularly as, in many cases, any 'loss' suffered (which in any event may be very difficult to quantify) will be by the union or other members and not the individual concerned. It would be advantageous in appropriate cases for the tribunal to have the power to make recommendations for future conduct, if not enforceable orders.

UNION MEMBERSHIP AND DEDUCTIONS FROM WORKERS' PAY

8.47   An important method by which employers may show their support for union organisation is by facilitating the collection of union subscriptions. The practice of employers deducting subscriptions directly from workers' pay and passing them to the union concerned, known as the 'check-off', grew substantially from the 1960s onwards, although the practice became less common in the 1990s. Even so, in 2004 three-fifths of unionised workplaces were found to have a check-off system in place.[392] The introduction and maintenance of check-off is not necessarily a totally altruistic gesture by employers; as well as assisting good industrial relations, it enables them to keep track of the number and identities of union members and avoids the need for personal collection of subscriptions by union representatives who, in carrying out this function, have increased opportunity for contact with individual members.

The deduction of subscriptions was always subject to individual workers agreeing to this arrangement as a term of their contract with their employer, either directly or by virtue of a collective agreement incorporated into the contract.[393] In 1993, however, the Conservative

---

[390]   Cf the right of access which 'appropriate representatives' have to employees who are threatened with 'collective' redundancy, for example (see para 9.36) or rights of access to workers in the bargaining unit on the part of unions seeking recognition under the statutory procedure (see para 9.16).

[391]   [1974] IRLR 22, discussed in para 8.10 above. See para 9.16 for discussion of compatibility of access provisions with the HRA 1998 in the context of the statutory recognition procedure.

[392]   Kersley *et al* 2006: p 111.

[393]   *Williams v Butlers Ltd* [1974] IRLR 253 and [1975] IRLR 120. Provided the worker had consented in writing the restrictions on deductions from pay now contained in ERA 1996 (see para 4.71 *et seq* above) were not applicable: see ERA 1996, s 14(4).

Government introduced further restrictions requiring each worker[394] to provide specific written authorisation for a deduction and renewed written authorisation for such deduction at least every three years.[395] It also gave workers the right to withdraw authorisation for deductions at any time, and provided that where a deduction was made by an employer without due authorisation, or after the worker had given notice to withdraw it, the worker could complain to an employment tribunal which could order the employer to repay the amount deducted.[396] In addition, employers were also made responsible for giving workers written notification of any increase in the union subscription at least one month before making the deduction at the higher rate.

This procedure placed a considerable additional burden on employers and attracted considerable criticism from them, as well as, clearly, from trade unions. It was initially predicted that its effect on union membership and finances would be catastrophic. In the event this proved not to be the case on a general scale, although many unions reported difficulties contacting all their members, and in September 1994 it was estimated that between 600,000 and 1.2 million trade unionists who formerly had paid their subscriptions though the check-off had not signed new instructions by the beginning of the previous month.[397] Many unions had already transferred to a system of direct debit for the payment of subscriptions, some as a result of appreciating their vulnerability to interruption during industrial disputes; others encouraged their members to do this following the introduction of the new provisions. It was notable that trade union membership services packages frequently included discounted banking to encourage members to establish the requisite facilities for direct debit to operate.[398]

With effect from 23 June 1998 the requirements for employers to seek fresh authorisations from workers for the check-off every three years and to notify workers of increases in subscriptions were repealed, although the need to give an initial consent, the right to withdraw from the arrangement, and the right to seek redress in an employment tribunal for an unauthorised deduction, remained.[399] This reform was welcomed by both the TUC and the CBI, and removed at least one source of difficulty for unions which were struggling to maintain their levels of membership.

---

[394] See para 3.33 *et seq* above for the definition of this term.

[395] TULRCA 1992, s 68, as substituted by TURERA 1993, s 15 (now further substituted by SI 1998/1529; see note 399below).

[396] Where the deduction also infringed other statutory rights (ERA 1996, ss 13 *et seq* (see para 4.71), the right to an itemised pay statement (ERA 1996, s 8) and protection for non-contributors to a political fund (see para 10.19)) the amount ordered to be repaid could not exceed the greatest amount which could be awarded under any of them.

[397] Labour Research Department, reported *Financial Times*, 1 September 1994.

[398] Willman *et al*, 1993: p 209.

[399] The Deregulation (Deduction from Pay of Union Subscriptions) Order 1998, SI 1998/1529, made under the DCOA 1994.

9

COLLECTIVE REPRESENTATION AND THE LAW

INTRODUCTION

9.1 The distinctive voluntarist approach to the conduct of industrial relations in Britain has been emphasised at several points in this book. While this tradition still predominates, since 1971 legislation has played a role (albeit of diverse kinds) in regulating worker representation in relation to employers, and there is now a myriad of provisions in this area. Here, as in relation to freedom of association, the law is fragmented and incoherent and its distinctive features can properly be understood only in the light of the historical development of British legal policy outlined in chapter 7. During the 18 years of Conservative Government, beginning in 1979, the law in this area underwent radical transformation, reflecting government hostility towards collective organisation. Even at the end of that period, however, remnants of the previous order remained and obligations under EU law necessitated the retention of some measures which would undoubtedly otherwise have been repealed as incompatible with free market individualism. The entry into office of a Labour Government in 1997 heralded a more hospitable climate for worker representation and brought three important changes: the re-introduction of a statutory procedure for the mandatory recognition of trade unions by employers; the implementation of the EC Directive on European Works Councils following the UK 'opt-in' to the Agreement on Social Policy;[1] and the introduction of information and consultation obligations at national level following agreement to the Information and Consultation Directive. However, the importance of the voluntarist tradition was reflected by the continuing absence of a legal obligation upon the employer to apply terms and conditions which had been collectively agreed, even when recognition had been imposed by law. At the time of writing the Coalition Government has consulted on possible changes relating to collective redundancies and TUPE which we discuss later in the chapter and is considering its response.

We begin the chapter by considering the relationship between collective bargaining and the law. We first consider the nature and legal effect of voluntary recognition outside the statutory procedure. We then analyse the statutory procedure, under which employers of 21 or more workers may be required to recognise an independent trade union in relation to pay, hours and holidays, and the mechanism by which recognition is enforced. This is followed by a discussion of other legal consequences of recognition, irrespective of whether it is voluntary or mandatory in nature. We then examine the areas in which legislation requires all employers to provide information to, and consult, worker representatives. These arise in four important areas: in the event of a proposed dismissal for 'redundancy' (which in

---

[1] See para 2.37.

this context has a much broader meaning than that governing statutory redundancy payments); on a transfer of the undertaking; in relation to health and safety;[2] and pensions. The latter two categories lie beyond the scope of this work, although we refer to them in outline; the former are discussed in greater detail and assessed, where appropriate, against the requirements of the EU Directives which they are designed to implement. We then consider the obligation on some employers to consult on training. Finally we analyse the new obligations on larger employers to inform and consult on a wider range of matters,[3] with reference, once again, to the relevant Directive. This is followed by an overview of the regulations that implement the European Works Council Directive (recast in 2009), applicable to transnational 'Community-scale undertakings' or groups of undertakings, and a brief discussion of the requirements of the European Company statute and its accompanying Directive on Employee Involvement and other transnational provisions.

Until 1995 all the existing consultation requirements in Britain were vested exclusively in trade unions which were recognised by the employer in question. In the absence of a mandatory recognition procedure, they were thus dependent solely upon a voluntary act of the employer, a position which was held by the European Court of Justice to infringe obligations imposed by the respective directives relating to redundancies and transfer of undertakings.[4] As a consequence of this decision, the legislation was amended to require employers to consult, at their choice, *either* a recognised union or elected representatives of the affected employees. This marked a dramatic break with the traditional pattern of workers' representation in this country, which had been based upon 'single channel' union representation, and led Davies to warn that, in insisting upon Community-required consultation of a specific kind, national collective bargaining could be undermined and worker-representation ultimately down-graded.[5] This has proved a prescient prediction.[6] Although the legislation was further amended in 1999 to permit consultation of 'employee representatives' only if no independent union was recognised,[7] the concept of alternative-channel representation remains, and, indeed, has been radically extended: first, by the introduction of 'workforce agreements' in the context of working time, parental leave, and fixed-term contracts;[8] latterly and very significantly, by provision for informing and consulting non-union representatives on a much wider basis.[9] The TUC has taken these developments on board in its own policy formation, and has shown itself prepared to countenance non-union channels of representation operating alongside trade union-based collective bargaining.[10] We discuss the implications of these developments at the end of the chapter in the context of a broader consideration of the purposes of, and challenges faced by, worker representation in the contemporary labour market.

---

[2] In this area employers also have the option of providing information to, and consulting, employees directly, although it is unclear whether this complies with EU obligations: see further para 9.46 below.

[3] Here, again, it is open to employers to inform and consult directly in some circumstances: see further para 9.53.

[4] Case C-382/92 *EC Commission v United Kingdom* [1994] IRLR 392 and Case C-383/92 [1994] IRLR 412, ECJ.

[5] P Davies, 1994b: p 284. For a thoughtful analysis of the concept of 'single' and 'dual' channel. see Dukes, 2008a.

[6] See generally P Davies and C Kilpatrick, 2004.

[7] The Collective Redundancies and Transfer of Undertakings (Protection of Employment) (Amendment) Regulations 1999, SI 1999/1925.

[8] See paras 4.78, 4.90, 6.119, 3.52 and 5.75 respectively.

[9] See para 9.50 *et seq.*

[10] See the Joint Statement by the TUC and CBI on Statutory Trade Union Recognition, para 8, published 9 December 1997; *High Performing Workplaces – Informing and Consulting Employees: Consultation Document*, DTI, 2003: pp 5–23. See also Hall, 1996. On earlier TUC policy, see P Davies and M Freedland, 2007: pp 130–134.

We have used the term worker 'representation' in this chapter in preference to the term 'participation'. Although the latter is often used interchangeably with representation, the term participation is, in our view, more appropriate to signify direct forms of worker involvement in the enterprise. Such direct involvement may take different forms. It may revolve around the organisation of the working process; examples include quality circles, where employees meet regularly to discuss solutions to work-related problems, and delegation of work by management to self-organising teams. However, participation may also have a wholly different meaning of financial involvement in the enterprise. This type of participation, as described in para 4.74, may be constituted in a variety of arrangements, ranging from share option schemes to profit-related pay. Direct forms of participation are predicated upon, and are generally designed to promote, a more individualistic view of the employment relationship than a representational model, together with a close identification on the part of workers with the employer's objectives. While such schemes do not preclude the co-existence of collective representation they may sometimes be perceived by employers and/or workers as incompatible with it, although it is important to note that the two serve very different functions. Financial participation, in particular, does not bring with it access to decision-making at any level; even share ownership empowers workers ultimately only if they hold a sufficient proportion of the total share equity, an unlikely eventuality in practice. Moreover, financial participation is not required by law, although as we indicated in para 4.74, tax incentives have been given to encourage certain models. We do not consider these forms of participation further in this work, although our concluding discussion of the future of worker representation takes place against a backcloth of developments of this nature.

COLLECTIVE BARGAINING AND THE LAW

9.2   As we have indicated in earlier chapters, the essential feature of collective bargaining is the concept of joint regulation by the collective parties of the employment relationship, with the sanction of industrial action or recourse to some form of agreed dispute resolution procedure, such as arbitration, in the event of a failure to agree. As such it stands in contrast to consultation, where the employer retains the discretion to impose its views unilaterally although, as we discuss below, the two processes may sometimes be difficult to separate in practice. As we saw in chapter 7, the right to engage in collective bargaining is regarded by the ILO as an essential element of freedom of association and an undertaking on the part of contracting states to promote and encourage collective bargaining machinery is also contained in the European Social Charter. Moreover, in a landmark decision in 2008 the ECtHR decided that 'the right to bargain collectively with the employer has, in principle, become one of the essential elements' of the right to form and join trade unions under Article 11 of the ECHR.[11]

In chapters 2 and 4 we emphasised the important role of collective agreements as a source of labour law in Britain even though they lack contractual status and there is no legal obligation to treat them as a source of norms for individual contracts. This remains the case today even though the reach of collective bargaining narrowed considerably during the 1980s due cumulatively to a reduction in the proportion of workplaces where trade unions were recognised for at least some

---

[11] *Demir and Baykara v Turkey*, judgment of 12 November 2008, [2009] IRLR 766, para 154.

employees (from two-thirds in 1980[12] to just over half (53%) in 1990[13]) and in the proportion of employees covered by collective agreements (from 64% in 1984[14] to 47% in 1990[15]). It was estimated that in 1998 the number of employees covered by collective bargaining had fallen further, to 41% of all employees in workplaces with 25 or more employees.[16] Moreover,

> ... [t]he range of issues over which bargaining took place shrunk massively. By the end of the 1990s, in workplaces where 20 years earlier it would have been normal for managers to negotiate with union activists over questions of manning, overtime, recruitment, and working practices, it had become a rarity. For one-third of workplaces with union recognition there were no longer even annual pay negotiations.[17]

There was a growth in the number of recognition agreements in the period 1998–2004, possibly in response to the alternative prospect of unions applying for recognition under the statutory procedure, but no parallel increase in derecognition.[18] However 'the formal recognition of a union or unions does not necessarily imply that active negotiations take place over the full range of terms and conditions, or even at all'.[19] Collective bargaining coverage has not increased, and is concentrated in particular sectors. The 2004 Workplace Employment Relations Survey found in relation to pay determination that:

> ... [i]n the public sector, collective bargaining was the dominant form of pay setting - it was present in around four-fifths (83 per cent) of public sector workplaces and covered 82 per cent of public sector workers. In contrast, only 14 per cent of private sector workplaces used collective bargaining, with around one quarter (26 per cent) of private sector employees having their pay set through collective bargaining. Industry differences in the use and coverage of collective bargaining were very marked: it dominated Public administration and the Electricity, gas and water sector, but was almost non-existent in Hotels and restaurants where union recognition was also very low.[20]

These findings led Brown and Nash to conclude that in the private sector collective bargaining 'offers no more than a diminished, patchy and highly localised protection to a small and shrinking minority of workers'.[21]

---

[12] Daniel and Millward, 1983: p 20.

[13] Millward and Stevens, 1992: p 70.

[14] Millward and Stevens, 1986: p 94.

[15] Millward and Stevens, 1992: p 70.

[16] Cully et al, 1999: p 242; Kersley et al 2006: p 185.

[17] W Brown and S Oxenbridge, 2004: p 70.

[18] S Wood, S Moore and K Ewing, 2003; S Oxenbridge et al, 2003; Gall, 2004; Blanden, Machin and Van Reenan, 2006; W Brown and D Nash, 2008.

[19] Kersley et al 2006: p 118. On the content of new voluntary recognition agreements in the period 1998-2002, see Moore et al, 2004, 2005.

[20] Kersley et al 2006: pp 179–181. W Brown and D Nash, 2008: p 95 state that the WERS figures underestimate the coverage of collective bargaining in the public sector in relation to employees covered by the Pay Review Bodies, which they describe as 'in effect, a successful and highly institutionalised form of collective bargaining'. For more information about Pay Review Bodies, see www.ome.uk.com.

[21] W Brown and D Nash, 2008: p 102. See also Achur, 2011: ch 4.

We begin this section by exploring in greater detail the legal concept of 'recognition' outside the statutory procedure, and examine the legal implications of variation and withdrawal of recognition. We then analyse the statutory recognition procedure. This is followed by an account of the (limited) right of all recognised trade unions to information from employers for the purpose of collective bargaining; an examination of the statutory concept of a 'collective agreement'; and an analysis of the position as regards trade union recognition and existing collective agreements when an undertaking is transferred. Finally, we examine provisions which prohibit contract compliance strategies being used to promote collective bargaining and adherence to collectively-agreed terms.

Recognition and derecognition outside the statutory procedure

9.3   We outlined in para 7.27 when a trade union is 'recognised' for statutory purposes and the importance of this definition in terms of a union's access to a variety of statutory rights. It will be remembered that this means recognition by an employer, or two or more associated employers, 'to any extent, for the purposes of collective bargaining'.[22] In turn 'collective bargaining' is defined as 'negotiations relating to or connected with' one or more of the matters specified in TULRCA 1992, s 178(2).[23] We examine these matters, which are also material to the definition of a 'collective agreement' and of a 'trade dispute' for the purposes of immunity against liability for industrial action, more closely elsewhere.[24] Here, we are concerned primarily with the process of collective bargaining and, in particular, when the parties can be said to have engaged in 'negotiations', an issue which has been left to the tribunals and the courts to decide.

The case law on what constitutes 'recognition' has developed mainly in the context of redundancy dismissals where the union has argued that it has been recognised by the employer and should therefore have been consulted before the dismissals were implemented. The cases turn on their own facts but a number of general principles have emerged. First, there must have been an agreement between the employer and the union to negotiate on one or more of the specified matters, although such agreement may be express or implied. An express agreement which specifies the range of bargainable issues has advantages for both parties; it puts the fact and extent of recognition beyond doubt and will assist in determining the scope of the rights to disclosure of information and time off for union officials. However, in the absence of such agreement the conduct of the parties may allow recognition to be implied, although the courts have taken a cautious approach to this issue in the light of the legal obligations to which employers are then subject.

In the leading case of *NUGSAT v Albury Bros Ltd*[25] the Court of Appeal specified the requirements to be met. The union, NUGSAT, wrote to the employers stating that their rates of pay did not appear to accord with those specified in the collective agreement between the union and the employers' federation and asking for a meeting to discuss the matter. The employers tried to see the district secretary, who was busy, and then wrote to the union offering a meeting.

---

[22] TULRCA 1992, s 178(3).
[23] TULRCA 1992, s 178(1).
[24] See paras 7.27 above and 11.27 below.
[25] [1978] IRLR 504.

When the parties met they discussed whether the wages of one particular employee came within the general scale but did not come to any agreement. Later that day redundancy notices were issued to three employees. The employment tribunal and EAT both concluded that the contacts between the parties did not amount to recognition, and the Court of Appeal supported this conclusion. Eveleigh LJ emphasised the need for clear and distinct evidence that the employer had agreed to negotiate with a view to striking a bargain; a willingness merely to discuss would not suffice.[26] Sir David Cairns affirmed previous EAT decisions which had stressed that the acts relied upon 'must be clear and unequivocal and usually involve a course of conduct over a period of time'.[27] Here the matters relied upon were 'too limited in scope, too inconclusive in character, and of too brief a duration to have any such effect as would constitute recognition'.[28] Finally, the court affirmed that the fact that the employers' federation, of which the employer was a member, recognised the union did not constitute recognition by that employer.[29]

By contrast in the earlier decision of *Joshua Wilson & Bros Ltd v USDAW*[30] the EAT inferred recognition from the cumulative effect of contacts between the employer and the union over the period of a year: allowing the local union representative to put up a notice publicising an increase agreed by the joint industrial council for the industry; consulting him over changes to the allocation of duties; allowing him to collect union dues on the premises; and consulting with the area union organiser over security and discipline. 'Separately none [of these] might have been sufficient' but, taken together, they constituted 'clear and unequivocal evidence' of recognition.[31] By further contrast in *USDAW v Sketchley Ltd*[32] an agreement to provide 'recognition for representation' of members in grievance procedures, together with facilities for appointing shop stewards and collecting union subscriptions, did not amount to recognition for the purposes of negotiation.

One issue which remains unresolved is whether a disclaimer of recognition can prevent a union being 'recognised' in law. In *USDAW v Sketchley Ltd* the EAT, in assessing the implications of particular events, stated:

> ... [a]lthough during this period the union is plainly trying to gain wider recognition and the employers are getting very close to negotiating terms and conditions of employment with the union, the employers throughout make it clear by their express words that they have no intention of recognising the union. In such circumstances, it is impossible to draw any inference of a mutual intention contrary to Sketchley's expressed intention.[33]

However, this approach seems open to dispute; at the very least it could be argued that a concerted attempt by an employer to use the services of a union to secure agreements covering the workforce

---

[26] [1978] IRLR 504, 506.

[27] [1978] IRLR 504, 506.

[28] [1978] IRLR 504, 507.

[29] See also *Cleveland County Council v Springett* [1985] IRLR 131 where the EAT affirmed that appointment by the Secretary of State to a committee which at one time negotiated teachers' pay at national level did not bring recognition by an individual local education authority employer.

[30] [1978] IRLR 120.

[31] [1978] IRLR 120, 121.

[32] [1981] IRLR 291.

[33] [1981] IRLR 291, 295.

whilst disclaiming any intention to recognise could be challenged as an attempt to exclude entitlement to statutory rights.[34]

9.4 Where a union has been recognised outside the statutory procedure, there is no statutory constraint upon an employer varying the scope of recognition or withdrawing it altogether. A number of prominent employers derecognised trade unions during the 1990s,[35] although in numerical terms the incidence of wholesale derecognition, as opposed to an initial refusal to recognise, remained comparatively small.[36] Even where recognition is express a recognition agreement will constitute a 'collective agreement' in law and thus be covered by the statutory presumption of non-enforceability, displaceable only by a specific statement to the contrary of a kind which is rarely found. This is one area where the statutory imposition of legally enforceable collective agreements may have benefited trade unions in potentially requiring greater notice of intention to derecognise, although ultimately not preventing this development in the longer term. Moreover, it is most unlikely that a recognition agreement could be enforced through the individual contract; even if part of a wider collective agreement which is capable of incorporation into individual contracts of employment, terms relating to recognition will almost certainly be viewed by the courts as collective in their nature and thus not appropriate for such incorporation.[37] This does not mean that a decision to derecognise will never have legal implications, however. First, although a commitment to recognise a union is unlikely in itself to be a term of an individual contract, it is possible that some provisions which have been linked to recognition, such as time off rights for union members or individual representation in disciplinary and grievance proceedings which exceed the statutory rights, may have been incorporated into employees' contracts of employment. If so, any contractual term linked to recognition which the employer wishes to remove will require one of the procedures for contractual variation which we describe in para 4.35 *et seq* to be followed. Second, derecognition cannot be used to avoid statutory duties which have already become binding: thus once a union has requested specific information for collective bargaining purposes, for example, the duty to disclose such information survives subsequent derecognition.[38] Last, in the case of employers which are potentially susceptible to judicial review a decision to derecognise may be open to challenge by this means, at least as regards the procedure which is followed. In *R v Educational Services Committee of Bradford City Metropolitan Council, ex p PAT*[39] the (no-strike) Professional Association of Teachers successfully sought judicial review of the (Labour) Council's decision to rescind a resolution made three months earlier (by its Conservative predecessor) on the ground that it should have been afforded the opportunity to make representations to ensure that the deprivation of the valuable rights thereby occasioned was not unfair. Even this procedure does not ultimately constitute a substantive constraint on the employer's decision to derecognise, however. This position contrasts sharply with the restrictions

---

[34] TULRCA 1992, s 288. Cf, in the context of unfair dismissal, *Igbo v Johnson Matthey Chemicals Ltd* [1986] IRLR 215.

[35] See Taylor, 1994: pp 48–54; Claydon, 1996.

[36] Gall and McKay, 1994; Millward *et al*, 2000: pp 105, 232.

[37] See para 4.30 *et seq*. Withdrawal of recognition of one's union does not, *per se*, amount to subjection to a detriment on grounds of trade union membership or activities: see para 8.14 above.

[38] *Ackrill Newspapers Ltd v NUJ* (CAC 14 February 1992, unreported).

[39] (1986) Independent, 16 December.

on derecognition where recognition follows from a union having invoked the statutory procedure, which we describe in para 9.20.

A further, and less commented upon, consequence of the voluntary nature of trade union recognition is that there is no mechanism to control the employer's choice of union. Thus there is nothing to prevent an employer recognising a union which may have only minimal support among the workforce. Although workers who are members of other unions would remain protected against discriminatory action by the employer on grounds of their union membership and participation in union activities, and use of union services, at an appropriate time, there would be nothing to prevent an employer allowing only the recognised union access to facilities on its premises[40] and, by definition, members of unrecognised unions lack access to the decision-making process. The 1980s saw some highly-publicised incidents of single union deals, many on new sites in the 'high-tech' sectors, reached in some cases after a 'beauty contest' between unions before a single worker was employed.[41] The latter practice in particular makes a mockery of union recognition being the democratic representation of employee 'voice'. Moreover such deals have backfired on unions, many of which found that they 'do not guarantee high membership levels, because the employer selects the union, undermining employee choice, and the structures of bargaining are often restrictive rendering the union ineffectual'.[42]

These arrangements, which caused bitter inter-union conflict, were partially reinforced by the operation of the TUC's Bridlington Principles which, as we saw in para 2.13, were formulated in 1939 (with subsequent amendments) to minimise disputes between unions over membership by regulating their organisational and recruitment activities. Principle 3 of the current version, published in 2007, provides that:

> No union shall commence organising activities at any company or undertaking, in respect of any group of workers, where another union has the majority of workers employed in membership, and/or is recognised to negotiate terms and conditions, and/or is actively engaged in significant organising activity, unless by arrangement with that union. Neither, in such circumstances, shall a union make approaches to an employer or respond to an employer initiative, which would have the effect of, directly or indirectly, undermining the position of the established union, or the union currently engaged in that organising activity..... If agreement cannot be reached, then either union should refer the matter to the TUC.[43]

The Principles were supplemented by a code of conduct on recognition in 1988, which required prior notification of single union deals to the TUC for advice and guidance, a requirement extended by the current edition of the Principles to agreements sought under the statutory

---

[40] A worker must be subjected to a detriment 'as an individual': TULRCA 1992, s 146; see further para 8.14 above. Note, however, the right of workers to be accompanied by the companion of their choice, who may be a union official: ERelA 1999, s 10; see further para 5.121 et seq.

[41] Although highly-publicised, in numerical terms these deals were of negligible importance: Gall, 1993: p 72. The TUC's Bridlington Principles (see para 2.13) require affiliated unions to notify the TUC General Secretary at the initial stage of discussion if they are in the process of making a single union agreement and state that unions must not make any agreements that are designed to remove 'the basic democratic lawful rights of a trade union to take industrial action' in advance of recruiting members and without consulting them: notes on Principle 3.

[42] Gall, 1993: pp 73–74. On more recent use of 'constrained recognition agreements' see Gall and McKay, 2001; Gall, 2004; Dukes, 2008b: pp 258-260.

[43] TUC Disputes Principles and Procedures, TUC, 2007.

procedure.[44] However, the effectiveness of this code (now incorporated into the notes on Principle 3) is hard to judge.[45] In practice single union deals have undergone a sharp decline since the late 1980s, although the statutory procedure, which bars recognition applications when another union is recognised for any worker in the proposed bargaining unit, has the potential to encourage a revival.[46] Regardless of their numbers, they raise important issues in the wider debate as to the principles which should govern worker representation.

The statutory procedure for recognition and derecognition

9.5   The current statutory procedure enabling trade unions to obtain mandatory recognition by employers was introduced by ERelA 1999 and amended by ERelA 2004. It takes effect as TULRCA 1992, Schedule A1. As we saw in para 7.18, this was the most controversial aspect of the 1999 legislation, with employer representatives opposed to the very concept of mandatory recognition, and aspects of the procedure continue to remain contentious.[47] However, to date its operation, which is in the hands of the CAC,[48] has not been undermined by successful judicial review applications of the kind that paralysed its 'Social Contract' predecessor.[49] This may be due to the detailed statutory criteria that inform the CAC's decision-making, in contrast to the more open-ended discretion accorded to ACAS under the earlier provision.[50]

The procedure is complex and consists of several stages.[51] As we indicate below, there is generally a tight timetable for completion of each stage, although this can be extended by agreement of the parties and/or the CAC. There is a preference throughout for voluntary agreement between the parties (and the CAC is charged to assist this process at specified points), with a fall-back of determination by a tripartite panel in default of agreement, if necessary after a hearing at which the parties may (but need not be) legally represented. In addition to applying the specific tests applicable to a given stage of the procedure, the CAC has a general duty to 'have regard to the object of encouraging and promoting fair and efficient practices and arrangements in the workplace', in so far as that object is consistent with applying other provisions of the Schedule in the case concerned.[52] There is no general statutory requirement for the CAC to give reasons for its decisions in relation to the recognition procedure, but a failure to do so

---

[44]   *TUC Disputes Principles and Procedures*, TUC, 2007, notes on Principle 3.

[45]   Non-compliance with this code seems not to have been a decisive factor in disputes before the TUC Disputes Committee: Elgar and Simpson, 1994: pp 57–62.

[46]   For a notorious example, see the facts of *R (on the application of the NUJ) v CAC and MGN Ltd* [2006] IRLR 53. In this instance the union which concluded the recognition deal, the British Association of Journalists, although independent, is not a TUC-affiliate.

[47]   See Simpson, 2000; Ewing, Moore and Wood, 2003; *Review of the Employment Relations Act 1999: Government Response*, DTI, 2003: ch 2; Dukes, 2008b; Bogg,, 2009a; Gall, 2010a.

[48]   See further para 2.32.

[49]   See Simpson, 1979; L Dickens and G Bain, 1986; Simpson, 2007a.

[50]   See Simpson, 2007a: pp 309–14. For an analysis of CAC decision-making see Bogg, 2006, 2009a.

[51]   For a detailed technical analysis of the recognition and derecognition procedures prior to the ERelA 2004 amendments see G Morris and T Archer, 2000: paras 4.5–4.63; see also Simpson, 2000 and Bowers, Duggan and Reade, 2004. For comparison with, variously, earlier British legislation and with US and Canadian procedures, see S Wood and J Godard, 1999; McCarthy, 1999; Towers, 1999; Adams, 1999; Hepple 2000a, Dubinsky, 2000 and Dukes, 2008b. Guidance as to the practice of the CAC, information on applications for recognition, and decisions may be found at www.cac.gov.uk.

[52]   TULRCA 1992, Sch A1, para 171.

could be susceptible to challenge under general principles of judicial review and/or the HRA 1998,[53] and in practice reasons are provided. Recognition can be ordered only in relation to 'pay, hours and holidays', and the CAC may specify a 'method' of collective bargaining, enforceable by specific performance in the courts, only in relation to those matters, even if the parties, during the course of the statutory procedure, agree to recognition for a wider range of issues.[54] 'Pay, hours and holidays' are left undefined, and the meaning of 'pay', in particular, may prove contentious; although it probably covers pay systems, for example, it is less clear whether it extends to aspects of work organisation that affect pay, or job classification systems.[55] The issue has yet to come before the courts. The ERelA 2004 made clear that 'pay' does not include any matters relating to a person's membership or rights under an occupational or personal pensions scheme or an employer's contribution to such a scheme,[56] but it empowered the Secretary of State by order to add matters relating to pensions to the 'core' bargaining topic of pay, hours and holidays should he or she choose to do so at some future date.[57] The Labour Government indicated that it intended to exercise this power when there was evidence that pensions were typically included as an item for negotiation in voluntary agreements,[58] and in 2006 the DTI stated that pensions were becoming a more common subject for collective bargaining and that it was therefore appropriate for it to 'initiate, with the social partners, an examination of the evidence and case for extending the statutory procedure'.[59] No such extension was made before the Labour Government left office and there is no indication that the Coalition Government will change the current position.

(i) The recognition procedure: outline and analysis

9.6   *A valid request to the employer and the implications of the employer's response to that request.*   To invoke the statutory recognition procedure, a union[60] must first make a written request to the employer for recognition in respect of a specified group of workers (a 'bargaining unit'), making clear that the request is made under TULRCA 1992, Schedule A1. The union must have a certificate of independence, and on the day of the request the employer, together with any associated employer, must employ at least 21 workers, or have employed an average of at least 21 workers in the 13 weeks ending with that day,[61] although the proposed bargaining unit may

---

[53] See G Morris and T Archer, 2000: para 4.7.

[54] The CAC may specify a 'method' of collective bargaining at the request of either party where recognition has been agreed pursuant to a statutory request: see further para 9.18 below.

[55] Cf S Wood and J Godard, 1999: p 232.

[56] TULRCA 1992, Sch A1, para 171A(1), inserted by ERelA 2004, s 20; cf *Unifi and Union Bank of Nigeria plc* [2001] IRLR 712, CAC, discussed Rideout, 2002: pp 30–31.

[57] TULRCA 1992, Sch A1, para 171A(3)–(7).

[58] Lord Davies, HL Debs GC65, 9 June 2004.

[59] *Success at Work: Protecting Vulnerable Workers, Supporting Good Employers*, DTI, 2006: p 20.

[60] For simplicity we refer throughout to 'a union' applying for recognition, but unions may present a joint request, although the admissibility of such a request depends on compliance with specified conditions, discussed in para 9.9 below.

[61] See generally TULRCA 1992, Sch A1, paras 4–9. The request must be received by the employer. Para 7 stipulates how the average number of workers is to be calculated and the treatment of workers employed by associated companies outside Great Britain. Agency workers are to be treated as having a contract of employment with the temporary work agency (where they do not have such a contract) for the duration of the assignment with the employer: TULRCA 1992, Sch 1, para 7(5A), (5B).

be smaller. There is no requirement that workers should have worked a minimum number of hours to be counted for qualifying purposes, and the inclusion of 'associated employers'[62] means that employers cannot attempt to circumvent the application of the procedure by dividing their business into separate companies, each employing fewer than 21 workers. Even then, however, the 21 worker threshold was estimated by the Labour Government itself to exclude 31% of the workforce – located in small enterprises in which the incidence of recognition is generally low – from the recognition procedure.[63] This threshold has no place in ILO jurisprudence[64] and in 2007 the Committee of Experts on the Application of Conventions and Recommendations (CEACR) asked the Labour Government to indicate in its next report the measures taken or envisaged to further promote collective bargaining in small businesses.[65] CEACR reported in 2011 that the Coalition Government had stated that it believed UK recognition arrangements were fully compliant with the Convention and it had no plans to review the application of the procedure to small businesses.[66]

The next stage of the procedure depends upon the employer's response to the request. If the employer and union agree a bargaining unit and recognition within ten working days starting with the day after the employer receives the request (the 'first period') no further steps are taken in relation to the application; the same applies if, within that period, the employer indicates a willingness to negotiate and the parties reach agreement on these matters within 20 working days, starting with the day after the first period ends or such longer period as the parties may from time to time agree. The parties may request ACAS to assist in conducting the negotiations.[67] Any agreement reached during the first or second periods (or, indeed, at any stage prior to recognition being ordered or a recognition ballot being arranged) is capable of constituting an 'agreement for recognition',[68] and as such is protected against unilateral termination by the employer for a minimum three-year period unless the parties otherwise agree,[69] although it can be terminated after that time without the additional constraints, described below, that apply when recognition has been ordered by the CAC. In the event that the employer fails to respond to the union's request, or no agreement is reached between the parties, the union may apply to the CAC to determine whether the proposed bargaining unit is appropriate, and whether the union has the support of a majority of workers constituting the appropriate bargaining unit. The application

[62] See, for example, *GMB and Sussex Grange Furniture Ltd* TUR1/208, CAC. Note that bargaining units cannot be comprised of workers from two or more associated employers (see, for example, *Unite the Union and (1) MGN Ltd and (2) Trinity Mirror plc* TURI/681 (2009) and TURI/697, CAC) , although cf *GPMU v Derry Print Ltd* [2002] IRLR 380, CAC.

[63] Simpson, 2000: p 196; Cully *et al*, 1999: pp 264–266.

[64] Novitz, 2000: pp 388–389. Note now the possible relevance of *Demir and Baykara v Turkey*, judgment of 12 November 2008 [2009] IRLR 766, in this context; see further para 7.9 above. For a broader critique of the 'small employer' exclusion see Ewing and Hock, 2003; cf *Review of the Employment Relations Act 1999: Government Response*, DTI, 2003: paras 2.3–2.8.

[65] Individual Observation Concerning Right to Organise and Collective Bargaining Convention, 1949 (No 98), United Kingdom.

[66] As above,

[67] TULRCA 1992, Sch A1, para 10.

[68] Defined in TULRCA 1992, Sch A1, para 52. See *NUJ and Emap Healthcare* TUR2/1/02, CAC.

[69] TULRCA 1992, Sch A1, para 56. No sanction is prescribed if an employer sought to terminate an agreement for recognition prematurely but the statutory language suggests that such an attempt would be void, so that the union would still be 'recognised' for the purposes of rights dependent on recognition, such as consultation rights, and could seek the assistance of the CAC in specifying a bargaining method or specific performance of a method already specified by the CAC.

must be made in such form, and supported by such documents, as the CAC specifies.[70] The CAC must then decide, within ten working days starting with the day after that on which it receives the application, whether the application followed a valid request for recognition to the employer and whether it is admissible according to specified criteria.[71]

9.7   *Conditions of admissibility.*   There are four substantive grounds on which an application will be inadmissible.[72] The first is if the CAC is satisfied that there is already in force a collective agreement under which a union is recognised as entitled to conduct collective bargaining on behalf of *any* workers falling within the proposed bargaining unit.[73] This reflects the priority given to existing voluntary bargaining arrangements. This priority applies regardless of the level of membership that the incumbent union has within the bargaining unit; thus in *R (on the application of the NUJ) v CAC* the Court of Appeal confirmed that it was sufficient to bar an application by a union which claimed to have more than half the workers in the proposed bargaining unit in membership that a union with at most one member had been recognised by the employer.[74] However the collective agreement relied upon must be *in force*. In *R (on the application of the NUJ) v CAC* the Court of Appeal held that an agreement was 'in force' when it could 'be shown to be binding on the parties to it'.[75] This did not require 'evidence that any of its specific provisions had in fact been carried out'; 'an earnest desire to work within the agreement' would suffice. The Court recognised that 'there may come a time when failure to act or impossibility cause the agreement to collapse or force a tribunal to say that it has collapsed' but unless the possibility of an agreement operating was 'simply not believed in by the parties to it' it would be wrong to say that it did not come into 'present force simply on the basis of doubts about its future viability'.[76] It is notable that it is sufficient to bar an application that recognition is accorded in respect of a matter to which the recognition procedure itself does not apply, such as discipline or the allocation of duties.[77] Moreover, it would seem to be sufficient that a worker in the bargaining unit is covered by a national agreement so that a union is recognised to conduct collective bargaining on his or her

---

[70]   TULRCA 1992, Sch A1, paras 11, 12, 33. If the parties have agreed the bargaining unit, the union may apply to the CAC to decide solely the question of support. Note that the union will be barred from applying to the CAC if it has rejected the employer's proposal, made within a specified period, that ACAS should be asked to assist in the negotiations: para 12(5).

[71]   TULRCA 1992, Sch A1, para 15.

[72]   An application is also inadmissible if the union fails to give the employer notice, and a copy, of the application and any documents supporting it: TULRCA 1992, Sch A1, para 34.

[73]   TULRCA 1992, Sch A1, para 35. There is no requirement for a formal agreement: see, for example, *NUM and RJB Mining (UK) Ltd* TUR1/32, CAC; *UIU and University of Glasgow* TURI/684, CAC.

[74]   [2006] IRLR 53. The Court of Appeal rejected the argument that the rights of association of the National Union of Journalists, which had a greater number of members in the bargaining unit, under Art 11 of the ECHR had been subject to interference, nor could the failure of the state to take steps to prevent the use of para 35 of the Schedule in the way in which the employer had used it be characterised as an act of discrimination contrary to Art 14. Because the incumbent union, the British Association of Journalists, had a certificate of independence it was not open to the workers in the bargaining unit to apply for the union to be derecognised under the procedure we describe in para 9.20 below. For a more recent example where an application was barred where another union had only one member in the proposed bargaining unit see *IPA and Babcock Aerospace Ltd* TURI/742 (2011) and TURI/748, CAC.

[75]   [2006] IRLR 53, at [11] (Buxton LJ).

[76]   Above, [25], [21]. For examples of CAC decisions that a previous agreement did not block an application see *POA and Wackenhut (UK) Ltd Escort Services* TURI/108, CAC; *TSSA and Rail Europe Ltd* TUR1/154, CAC.

[77]   This is because 'collective bargaining' in this context is defined by TULRCA 1992, s 178 (see para 7.27): Sch A1, para 3(6); *TGWU and Asda* [2004] IRLR 836, CAC.

behalf, even if his or her own employer does not recognise the union.[78] However, the bar does not apply if the pre-existing recognition agreement is with the applicant union, and that union is not recognised in respect of all of the 'core topics' (pay, hours and holidays).[79] This means that independent unions can seek to extend the scope of their existing recognition if it does not cover all these topics. Perhaps surprisingly, although only independent unions can invoke the recognition procedure, there is no requirement for the pre-existing recognition agreement to be with an independent union, a position which, it can be argued, violates Articles 2 and 3 of ILO Convention No 98 in giving implicit encouragement to employers hostile to 'outside' union organisation to establish and recognise non-independent unions.[80] As we indicate in para 9.20 below, the legislation affords a mechanism for workers to obtain mandatory derecognition of such bodies, which has the effect of clearing the way for an application by an independent union for a three year period,[81] but despite the protection afforded against employers subjecting workers to any detriment for bringing and supporting such applications, described in para 9.21 below, workers may well feel fearful of pursuing such a course. An agreement with an organisation that does not satisfy the definition of a 'trade union' will not bar an application.[82]

As we saw in para 7.9, in 2008 the ECtHR 'reconsidered' its previous jurisprudence and decided that 'the right to bargain collectively with the employer has, in principle, become one of the essential elements' of the right to form and join trade unions under Article 11 of the ECHR, although states remain free to organise their system so as, if appropriate, to grant special status to representative trade unions.[83] The scope of this right, and the nature of the positive obligations that it may impose upon the state, await clarification. In particular in this context, whilst the special status of representative unions was acknowledged by the Court, nothing was said about an employer's freedom to choose an unrepresentative bargaining partner. However, it seems strongly arguable that, in permitting an application by a union with majority membership to be barred by recognition of a union with less support, the legislation may not now be in compliance with Article 11.[84]

9.8   The second ground of inadmissibility relates to the level of existing union membership and potential support for recognition. The CAC must find that members of the applicant union constitute a minimum of 10% of workers in the bargaining unit and that a majority of the workers

---

[78]   This follows from the definition of a 'collective agreement' in TULRCA 1992, s 178, which includes agreements made by or on behalf of one or more employers or employers' associations: see para 9.26; see also *Offshore Industry Liaison Committee and Wood Group Engineering (North Sea) Ltd* TUR1/282, CAC and *UIU and City of Edinburgh Council* TUR1/526/06, CAC; cf *UCATT and Swift Plant Hire* TUR1/537/06.

[79]   TULRCA 1992, Sch A1, para 35(2)(b), as amended by ERelA 2004, s 11.

[80]   In its 2007 Individual Observation, the ILO's CEACR asked the UK Government to reply to the TUC's concerns respecting this issue. See Ewing, 2000a and, for example, *POA and Securicor Custodial Services Ltd* TURI 5/00, CAC, *Unite – the Union and DSG Retail Ltd* TUR1/567/07, CAC. In 2003, the Labour Government was 'not attracted' to changing the position, and had seen 'no evidence of widespread recognition of non-independent unions ... as a device to avoid recognition claims by independent unions': *Review of the Employment Relations Act 1999: Government Response*, DTI, 2003: paras 2.95 and 2.98.

[81]   This is the effect of the tortuously-worded TULRCA 1992, Sch A1, para 35(4), which can also apply in a wider range of circumstances. In its comments to CEACR, above, the TUC stated that this procedure was not effective and pointed out that it had never been used successfully.

[82]   *TGWU and W Jordan (Cereals) Ltd* TUR1/258, CAC; *BECTU and City Screen Ltd* TUR1/309, CAC.

[83]   *Demir and Baykara v Turkey*, judgment of 12 November 2008 [2009] IRLR 766, paras 153, 154.

[84]   See also ILO, 2006, para 9.49 *et seq* on recognition of the most representative organisations.

in that unit would be 'likely' to favour recognition.[85] The first of these tests will be decided on the basis of factual evidence placed before the CAC. The admissibility requirement relating to potential support can often be particularly contentious. Evidence that a majority of workers in the bargaining unit are members of the applicant union is likely to be sufficient, in the absence of any evidence to the contrary; petitions from workers or surveys of the workforce, where available, may also be produced as evidence, as may statistics showing a growth in membership as a result of the recognition campaign. However, it cannot be assumed that workers who are not members of the union will not support recognition; indeed, the level of potential support may well be greater than actual membership. This is a matter for the CAC to decide in all the circumstances.

The CAC does not require the names and addresses of individuals to be disclosed, either in a union's application form or in supporting evidence. However, the union is required to specify the number of its members in the bargaining unit in its application, and if the employer challenges this there may be an independent check by CAC staff, subject to the agreement of both parties that the requisite information from each (petition evidence and membership and staff lists) may be provided in confidence for this purpose. If one or other party does not agree to such a course of action, the CAC may require an employer and union to provide information relating to workers or union members in the bargaining unit, as appropriate, together with information concerning the level of potential support for collective bargaining, to a CAC case manager, with power for the CAC to 'draw an inference' against a party who fails to comply with this requirement.[86] In practice there has been little need to rely on the statutory power.

9.9   Third, an application will be inadmissible where more than one union makes an application, unless the unions show that they will co-operate with each other 'in a manner likely to secure and maintain stable and effective collective bargaining arrangements' and that, if the employer wishes, they will enter into arrangements under which collective bargaining is conducted by the unions acting together on behalf of the workers in the bargaining unit.[87] This means that the applicant unions would need to agree to single-table bargaining, for example, if the employer wished to conduct collective bargaining on that basis. It also means that competing applications are ruled out. If an application is received in respect of a bargaining unit that overlaps to any extent with the unit specified in another application, and neither has been accepted, the CAC must apply the '10% membership' test to each (or all): if only one application passes the test, its admissibility may be further considered; otherwise all must be rejected.[88] Moreover, even if the CAC has accepted an application, if the appropriate bargaining unit in respect of that application remains undetermined, either by the parties or the CAC, and the 10% test is passed in respect of the competing application, the original application will be cancelled and treated as if it had never been admissible.[89] This reduces the possibility that a union which may have less support than the union presenting the competing application will be recognised under the statutory procedure. The fact that the application is treated as never having been admissible means that the union party

---

[85] TULRCA 1992, Sch A1, para 36.
[86] TULRCA 1992, s 170A, inserted by ERelA 2004, s 19.
[87] TULRCA 1992, Sch A1, para 37. See, for example, *UCATT and Unite the Union and Hillhouse Quarry Company* TUR1/735, CAC.
[88] TULRCA 1992, Sch A1, para 14. See, for example, *GMB and Faccenda Group Ltd* TUR1/209, CAC.
[89] TULRCA 1992, Sch A1, paras 38, 51.

to the original application will not be barred from presenting a fresh application by the 'three-year rule' described in para 9.10 below. Clearly, however, it would be desirable for the unions party to both the original and the competing applications to attempt to reach agreement on the appropriate demarcation line between their desired bargaining units or, if possible, present a joint application, as appropriate. The TUC provides assistance to unions applying to the CAC for recognition and will try to minimise inter-union problems and, where appropriate, facilitate joint applications. Unions preparing applications are required to notify the TUC General Secretary at least two weeks before they submit an application.[90]

9.10   Finally, an application will be inadmissible if the CAC had previously accepted an application relating to a bargaining unit and the application is made by a union or unions in respect of substantially the same unit within three years.[91] This provision is designed to deter premature applications. It does not prevent a different union making an application within three years; it is less clear whether, in the case of multi-union applications, the bar applies only if *all* such unions were party to the first application or if it is sufficient that any of them were. The three-year bar also applies where a union has been derecognised following a ballot of the workers in a bargaining unit (see para 9.20 below).[92]

9.11   ERelA 2004 introduced a new provision to afford a union (indirect) postal access to workers within the bargaining unit if its application for recognition has been accepted by the CAC.[93] A union that wishes to take advantage of this opportunity is likely to do so fairly quickly and, in any event, before the next stage of the statutory procedure, described in para 9.12 below. However, because it is easier to comprehend the details of the access provisions having understood that next stage, we discuss that first; we then examine the access provision in para 9.13 below.

9.12   *Determining the bargaining unit.*   Provided that the criteria of admissibility are met, the next question for the CAC will be to determine whether the bargaining unit proposed by the union is appropriate (unless this issue has already been agreed by the parties, in which case the CAC proceeds to determine whether recognition should be granted). The CAC must first try to 'help' the parties to reach within the 'appropriate period' (20 working days starting with the day after that on which notice of acceptance of the application is given or longer if the CAC so decides) an agreement as to what the appropriate bargaining unit is, although this period may be curtailed at the request of the parties or if the CAC considers that there is no reasonable prospect of agreement.[94] 'Help' in this context may include suggesting that the assistance of ACAS is sought. To facilitate this process, the employer must provide the union and the CAC with a list of the categories of worker in the proposed bargaining unit, a list of the workplaces at which they work, and the number of workers the employer reasonably believes to be in each category at each

---

[90] *TUC Disputes Principles and Procedures*, TUC, 2007: p 15.
[91] TULRCA 1992, Sch A1, para 39; see also para 40.
[92] TULRCA 1992, Sch A1, para 41.
[93] TULRCA 1992, Sch A1, para 19C–19F, inserted by ERelA 2004, s 5.
[94] TULRCA 1992, Sch A1, para 18, as amended by ERelA 2004, s 2.

workplace.[95] If the parties fail to reach agreement within the 'appropriate period' (or sooner, at the request of the union if the employer fails to supply the requisite information about workers in the bargaining unit)[96] the CAC itself will determine whether the proposed bargaining unit is appropriate.[97] If (and only if) it decides that the proposed bargaining unit is not appropriate, it must also decide a bargaining unit that is appropriate;[98] thus, the CAC 'cannot reject the union's request because it feels that a different unit would be more appropriate'.[99] In taking an employer's views into account for the purpose of deciding whether the proposed bargaining unit is appropriate, the CAC must take into account any view it has about any other bargaining unit that it considers would be appropriate.[100]

In deciding whether a bargaining unit is appropriate, the CAC must take into account 'the need for the unit to be compatible with effective management', together with five other matters 'so far as they do not conflict with that need'. These matters are the views of the employer and the union(s); existing national and local bargaining arrangements; the desirability of avoiding small fragmented bargaining units within an undertaking; the characteristics of workers falling within the bargaining unit under consideration and of any other employees (not workers) of the employer whom the CAC considers relevant; and the location of workers.[101] It is easy to imagine situations where these factors may not all point in one direction. If a plant, consists, say, of production, maintenance and managerial workers, each of which belong to separate unions, a 'worker characteristics' approach may suggest separate bargaining units for each group. However, this solution may conflict with the desirability of avoiding fragmented bargaining units, although much may depend upon the systems currently in place for determining the terms and conditions of employment for each group. In cases where the employer maintains that the bargaining unit should embrace more than one plant, the organisation of the personnel and finance functions may be significant; if, in practice, each plant operates autonomously in these respects it may be more difficult to sustain the argument that effective management requires a single unit. The parties are likely to argue tactically in this context; the union will wish to confine the bargaining unit to groups among which it has the greatest membership, employers will wish to broaden it to avoid the prospect of recognition being granted on the bases we describe below. The legislation does not prevent the CAC taking into consideration matters additional to those specified in the statute, although its decision could be challenged in judicial review proceedings if these matters were deemed to be irrelevant considerations or to further a purpose which was extraneous to that of the statute.[102]

---

[95] TULRCA 1992, Sch A1, para 18A, inserted by ERelA 2004, s 3. 'Workplace' is defined in the same way as in TULRCA 1992, s 228(4), discussed in para 11.35.

[96] TULRCA 1992, Sch A1, para 19A, inserted by ERelA 2004, s 4.

[97] TULRCA 1992, Sch A1, paras 19 and 19A, inserted by ERelA 2004. This formulation reflects the Court of Appeal decision in *R v CAC, ex p Kwik-Fit (GB) Ltd* [2002] IRLR 395.

[98] The amendment made by ERelA 2004 makes clear that the CAC cannot decide that there is *no* bargaining unit that is appropriate; cf *BECTU and BBC* TUR1/273, CAC.

[99] *R (on the application of Cable and Wireless Services UK Ltd) v CAC and CWU* [2008] IRLR 425, [9] (Collins J).

[100] TULRCA 1992, Sch A1, para 19B(4), inserted by ERelA 2004, s 4. For an example of a case where the CAC decided that neither the unions' nor the employer's proposed bargaining unit was appropriate, see *UCATT and Unite the Union and Hillhouse Quarry Company* TURI/735, CAC.

[101] TULRCA 1992, Sch A1, para 19. For consideration of the term 'small fragmented bargaining units' see *R (on the application of Cable and Wireless Services UK Ltd) v CAC and CWU* [2008] IRLR 425.

[102] *Associated Provincial Picture Houses v Wednesbury Corporation* [1948] 1 KB 223.

If the bargaining unit agreed by the parties during the appropriate period, or decided by the CAC, differs from that proposed in the original application, the CAC must decide whether the application is 'invalid' by reference to the same tests that govern admissibility, described above.[103] If the union considers that it is unlikely to win recognition in respect of the revised bargaining unit it would be prudent for it to withdraw its application at this stage as it will otherwise be subject to the three-year bar on any later application in relation to the revised, as well as the original, unit in the event that the application is not regarded as invalid.[104]

9.13   We referred in para 9.11 above to the right of access for a union to workers in the bargaining unit, introduced by ERelA 2004.[105] If the CAC accepts an application the union may apply to it to appoint a 'suitable independent person' to handle communications between the union and 'relevant workers' (those within the proposed bargaining unit, or appropriate bargaining unit once that has been agreed or determined) during the 'initial period'.[106] The 'initial period' starts when the CAC informs the parties of the name and date of the appointment of the 'appointed person', and ends when either the CAC informs the union of a declaration of recognition without a ballot or of the name of a person appointed to conduct a ballot;[107] the application is withdrawn; or the application is regarded as 'invalid' (see para 9.12 above). The employer then has a duty to give to the CAC, within ten working days starting with the day after that on which it is informed about the 'appointed person', the names and home addresses of the relevant workers, and to update this information if the relevant workers change as a result of an agreement or decision on the appropriate bargaining unit or if workers join or leave the bargaining unit for some other reason.[108] The CAC must pass any such information to the 'appointed person' as soon as reasonably practicable; he or she must then, at the union's request, send on to any relevant worker information supplied to him or her by the union.[109] The union is liable to pay the costs of the appointed person.[110] If the CAC is satisfied that the employer has failed to fulfil any of its duties and the initial period has not yet ended, it may order the employer to take specified steps within a specified time to remedy the failure.[111] If the employer then fails to comply with such an order, and the parties have agreed or the CAC has decided an appropriate bargaining unit, the CAC may declare the union recognised.[112] This means that recognition may be granted even if a majority of the workforce is not in fact in favour of this, although the CAC will need to have been satisfied that the majority would be *likely* to favour recognition in order for the application to have been ruled admissible. Where the employer's failure to comply with a remedial order occurs before the

---

[103]   TULRCA 1992, Sch A1, paras 20, 43–50.

[104]   TULRCA 1992, Sch A1, para 39.

[105]   ERelA 2004, s 5, inserting TULRCA 1992, Sch A1, para 19C–19F. Prior to this amendment the legislation afforded access only during the balloting period; see para 9.15 below.

[106]   TULRCA 1992, Sch A1, para 19C(1)–(4). A 'suitable independent person' is defined in the same way as a 'qualified independent person': para 19C(6) and para 9.15 below.

[107]   The union then has a separate right of communication during the balloting period under TULRCA 1992, Sch A1, para 26(6); see para 9.15 below.

[108]   TULRCA 1992, Sch A1, para 19D(1)–(3). The employer must comply with these duties 'so far as it reasonable to expect him to do so': para 19D(1).

[109]   TULRCA 1992, Sch A1, para 19D(4), 19E(1).

[110]   TULRCA 1992, Sch A1, para 19E(2)–(7). See also para 165A, inserted by ERelA 2004, s 14, for the right of appeal against a demand for costs.

[111]   TULRCA 1992, Sch A1, para 19F(1).

[112]   TULRCA 1992, Sch A1, para 19F(2)–(5).

agreement or decision on the appropriate bargaining unit, that will need to be agreed or decided prior to the CAC deciding whether recognition should be granted.

9.14   *The criteria and procedures for determining recognition.*   Assuming that the application is not invalid (or withdrawn) following an agreement or decision on the appropriate bargaining unit, the CAC must then determine whether the union should be recognised. If it is satisfied that a majority of the workers in the bargaining unit are members of the applicant union, it must declare the union recognised (unless the sentence which follows applies); otherwise it must notify the parties that it intends to arrange for the holding of a secret ballot. Controversially, the CAC may also order a ballot even if the union has a majority of the bargaining unit in membership if one of 'three qualifying conditions' is fulfilled.[113] The first is if the CAC is satisfied that this should be done in the interests of 'good industrial relations'.[114] The second is if the CAC has evidence, which it considers to be credible, from a significant number of the union members within the bargaining unit (not merely their employer) that they do not want the union to conduct collective bargaining on their behalf.[115] The reference to evidence that the CAC considers 'credible' gives the CAC discretion to examine the quality of the evidence, including whether workers were pressurised by the employer to write letters to the CAC that did not reflect their true views.[116] What constitutes a 'significant' number of union members will probably vary according to the context; the total number of workers in the bargaining unit and the percentage of union members may be relevant factors, for example.[117] The third is if 'membership evidence' is produced which leads the CAC to conclude that there are doubts whether a significant number of the union members within the bargaining unit want the union to conduct collective bargaining on their behalf. 'Membership evidence' is exhaustively defined for this purpose as evidence about the circumstances in which union members became members, or evidence about the length of time for which they have been members in circumstances where the CAC is satisfied that such evidence should be taken into account. The first of these limbs is presumably designed to take account of allegations of undue pressure being placed on individuals. In relation to the second, the fact that a substantial number of workers have recently joined the union may be indicative of enthusiasm for recognition, and it is for the CAC to decide on the facts whether it constitutes grounds for the holding of a ballot. In

---

[113] TULRCA 1992, Sch A1, paras 22, 23. Unusually, no time limit is laid down within which the CAC must decide if a ballot should be held. In *Fullerton Computer Industries Ltd v CAC* [2001] IRLR 752 the Court of Session held that since there was no obligation on the CAC Panel to give reasons for its decision under para 22(4), the fact that its reasoning was inadequate did not make its decision open to challenge given that there was no evidence of a flaw or irrationality in the reasoning.

[114] See, for example, *GPMU and Red Letter Bradford Ltd* TUR1/12/00, CAC; *TGWU and Economic Skips Ltd* TUR1/121/01, CAC; *Unite the Union and Gillette UK Ltd* TUR1/667, CAC.

[115] There is no definition of 'union' in the Schedule to confine the term to the union which has brought the request for recognition (cf the definition of 'employer' in TULRCA 1992, Sch A1, para 2(4)) but the reference to 'the' union suggests that this is intended in this context.

[116] TULRCA 1992, Sch A1 para 22(4)(b), inserted by ERelA 2004, s 6; Gerry Sutcliffe, Parliamentary Under-Secretary of State for Trade and Industry, HC Debs col 1471, 16 September 2004. In *R (on the application of Gatwick Express) v CAC* [2003] EWHC 2035 (Admin), decided prior to the amendment, the CAC had before it eight letters from union members of a bargaining unit of 38, all of which were in standard form, on company headed paper, and seven of which had been sent to the CAC by the employer's Human Resource Department. The court held that the CAC had erred in law in refusing to place evidential weight on the seven letters.

[117] See, for example, *UNIFI and Turkiye Is Bankasi* TUR1/90, CAC; *CWU and Cable and Wireless* TUR1/570/ 07, CAC; *Unite the Union and Eddie Stobart* TUR1/750, CAC.

this context, the terms on which workers joined – whether they were offered free or discounted membership, for example – may be material.[118]

Recognition through a ballot must be supported by a majority of the workers voting *and* at least 40% of the workers constituting the bargaining unit.[119] The second of these conditions, which 'represents a political compromise between employers' demands for a threshold of support by a majority of the ... bargaining unit ... and the trade union position that under normal principles applicable to ballots a majority of those voting should be sufficient',[120] is strongly opposed by the union movement. In 2007 the ILO's CEACR stated that:

> ... problems of conformity with ... Convention [No 98] may arise when the law stipulates that a trade union must receive the support of 50 per cent of the members of a bargaining unit to be recognised as a bargaining agent, as a majority union which fails to secure this absolute majority is thus denied the possibility of bargaining. The Committee considers that, under such a system, if no union covers more than 50 per cent of the workers, collective bargaining rights should be granted to all the unions in this unit, at least on behalf of their own members ... The Committee requests the Government to indicate the measures taken or envisaged to ensure that, in cases where no union has been able to obtain the required majority for bargaining, the organisations concerned should at least be able to conclude a collective agreement on behalf of their own members.[121]

At the time of writing there is no indication that the Coalition Government is intending to change the existing position.

9.15   Once the CAC has notified its intention to hold a ballot the union (or the parties jointly) may indicate within a specified period (the 'notification period') that it (or they) do not wish the ballot to take place.[122] The costs of the ballot are divided equally between the employer and union,[123] a provision justified by the Labour Government as an incentive to encouraging a party that knew its prospects of winning were remote to agree recognition or withdraw its application, as appropriate. The ballot must be conducted by a 'qualified independent person' ('QIP') appointed by the CAC, within 20 working days starting with the day after the 'QIP' is appointed or such longer period as the CAC decides, at a workplace or workplaces decided by the CAC; by post; or a combination of the two, depending upon the CAC's preference.[124] In reaching its decision the CAC must take into account the likelihood of the ballot being affected by unfairness or malpractice if it were conducted at a workplace; costs and practicality; and such other matters as it thinks appropriate (for example, which method is likely to secure a high participation rate). The CAC may not decide

---

[118] See, for example, *AEEU and Huntley Healthcare Ltd* TUR1/19/00, CAC but cf *ISTC and Mission Foods* TUR1/256/03, CAC.

[119] TULRCA 1992, Sch A1, para 29.

[120] Simpson, 2000: p 212.

[121] Individual Observation Concerning Right to Organise and Collective Bargaining Convention 1949, No 98.

[122] TULRCA 1992, Sch A1, para 24. The period may be extended by the CAC on joint application by the parties (for example, if they are discussing voluntary recognition): para 24(5)–(7), as amended by ERelA 2004, s 7.

[123] TULRCA 1992, Sch A1, para 28. See also para 165A, inserted by ERelA 2004, s 14, for the right of appeal against a demand for costs.

[124] TULRCA 1992, Sch A1, para 25. See the Recognition and Derecognition (Qualified Persons) Order 2000, SI 2000/1306, as amended.

upon a combination ballot unless there are 'special factors' making this appropriate; these include factors arising from the location of workers or the nature of their employment, and those put to it by either party, but other matters, such as the absence on leave of members of the bargaining unit, may also be considered. However, if the CAC decides that the ballot should (in whole or in part) be conducted at a workplace, it may require arrangements to be made for workers who would be unable, for reasons relating to them as individuals, to cast their vote in the ballot to be given the opportunity to vote by post if they request this far enough in advance of the ballot for this to be practicable.[125] This allows special arrangements to be made for workers who are absent because of sickness or otherwise on leave without the ballot thereby becoming (and needing to fulfil the conditions for) a combination ballot.

Once the employer has been notified of the arrangements for the ballot, it is subject to five duties.[126] The first, and overriding duty, is 'to co-operate generally, in connection with the ballot, with the union ... and the person appointed to conduct the ballot'. The wording of this provision was left deliberately vague to allow the CAC (which decides whether the duties have been breached) maximum flexibility. The second duty is to give the union 'such access to the workers constituting the bargaining unit as is reasonable to enable the union ... to inform the workers of the object of the ballot and to seek their support and their opinions on the issues involved'. This duty is expanded upon in a detailed Code of Practice, whose provisions we discuss in the paragraph below.[127] Third, the employer must give the CAC the names and home addresses of the workers constituting the bargaining unit, and update it on those who later join or leave the unit. This information is passed to the QIP, who is required to send to such workers, at the union's expense, any information the union requests. This enables the union to transmit information without workers' personal details being revealed.[128] Fourth, the employer must refrain from making any offer to any or all of the workers constituting the bargaining unit which has or is likely to have the effect of inducing any of them not to attend any 'relevant meeting' between the union and those workers and is not reasonable in the circumstances. This duty might be breached if, for example, the employer offered an additional payment to workers who failed to attend such a meeting or offered to allow them to go home early. Fifth, the employer must refrain from taking or threatening to take any action against a worker solely or mainly on the grounds that he or she attended or took part in any 'relevant meeting' between the union and workers in the bargaining unit or indicated his or her intention to attend or take part. A 'relevant meeting' for this purpose means a meeting that is organised in accordance with any agreement between the union and employer or as a result of a remedial order granted by the CAC and which the employer is required by such an agreement or order to permit the worker to attend.

---

[125] TULRCA 1992, Sch A1, para 25(6A), inserted by ERelA 2004, s 8.

[126] TULRCA 1992, Sch A1, para 26.

[127] ERelA 2004, s 9(3), (4D), inserting sub-para (4D) into TULRCA 1992 Sch A1, para 26, provides that an employer is taken to have failed to comply with the duty to give the union access if he refuses a request for a meeting between the union and all or any of the workers in the bargaining unit to be held without him or a representative of his (other than one who has been invited to attend) being present and it is not reasonable in the circumstances for him to do so; if he or a representative of his attends such a meeting without an invitation; or if he seeks to record or otherwise to be informed of the proceedings at any such meeting, or refuses to give an undertaking that he will not seek to do either of these things, where to do the thing in question is not reasonable.

[128] If the employer has already passed the relevant information to the CAC in relation to the union's communications with workers via an 'appointed person' (see para 9.13) it need not do this again: TULRCA 1992, Sch A1, para 26(4F), (4G).

If the CAC is satisfied that the employer has failed to fulfil any of these duties, and the ballot has not been held, it may order it to take specified steps to remedy the failure within a specified period.[129] If there is insufficient time for the request to be considered and any failure remedied prior to the ballot, the ballot may be rescheduled for a later date.[130] If the employer fails to comply with an order of the CAC, and the ballot has still not been held, the CAC has a discretion to declare the union recognised without a ballot.[131] This provision, like that we described in para 9.13 above, means that recognition may be granted even if a majority of the workforce is not in favour. However, it leaves a gap if the employer's non-compliance is not evident prior to the holding of the ballot or there is insufficient time before the ballot for a declaration to be issued; no account can be taken of any consequent disadvantage that the union may have suffered in the event that the result is opposed to recognition. This contrasts with the position where the employer has committed an 'unfair practice', introduced in relation to recognition ballots by ERelA 2004. We discuss these, and the consequences if one or other party is found to have used such a practice, in para 9.17 below.

9.16   Workers are likely to be subjected to intensive campaigning by their employer in the period prior to the ballot. The degree of access to them that the union can secure to put its case is therefore crucial. The Code of Practice on Access and Unfair Practices during Recognition or Derecognition Ballots,[132] which deals only with access at the workplace and/or during working time, aims in the first instance to help the parties agree their own arrangements which can take full account of individual circumstances, a process which should be started during the 'notification period'. It assumes that initial proposals should be made by the union which, if rejected by the employer, should be matched by timely counter-proposals. Where the parties fail to reach agreement, either party, acting separately or together, may ask ACAS to conciliate; if the process remains deadlocked, the CAC may be asked to assist and, ultimately, adjudicate and make an order.[133] The Code affirms that employers should be prepared to give access to full-time union officials, as well as nominated individuals from the proposed bargaining unit and other workplaces, in numbers proportionate to the scale and nature of the activities or events occurring within the agreed access programme.[134] The employer's typical methods of communicating with the workforce should be used as a benchmark of communication with the union.[135] Where practicable access should be granted at the workplace, and the employer should provide appropriate accommodation and ensure that the meeting is held in private.[136] Where security cameras or other security equipment

---

[129]   TULRCA 1992, Sch A1, para 27(1).

[130]   Code of Practice on Access and Unfair Practices during Recognition and Derecognition Ballots 2005, para 71. The power to reschedule could probably be derived from TULRCA 1992, Sch A1, para 25(3). See *R (on the application of Ultraframe) v CAC* [2005] IRLR 641 for the supervisory role of the CAC in relation to the conduct of ballots, including the power to order a re-run of a ballot which did not comply with the statutory requirements. On the powers of the CAC under ERelA 2004 where it finds an unfair practice has been committed , see para 9.17.

[131]   TULRCA 1992, Sch A1, para 27(2), (3).

[132]   The current edition of the Code came into force on 1 October 2005. See para 2.4 for the legal effect of Codes of Practice generally.

[133]   Code of Practice, paras 14–22. Note that the employer's statutory duty of co-operation and access take effect only when it has been informed that a ballot is to be arranged, ie, once the notification period has ended.

[134]   Para 26.

[135]   Para 28.

[136]   Paras 27, 45–47, 49.

are used, and could record meetings, the employer should inform the union accordingly unless key security considerations prevent such disclosure; the parties should then discuss ways to ensure the privacy of meetings.[137] A union should consider in advance whether it wishes to hold separate meetings for supervisors or managers who are part of the bargaining unit, and to exclude them from those with other workers, and inform those individuals accordingly.[138] 'In exceptional circumstances, due to the nature of the business or severe space limitations, access may need to be restricted to meetings away from the workplace premises … In these circumstances, the employer should give all reasonable assistance to the union in notifying workers in advance of where and when such off-site events are to take place.'[139]

On-site access should usually be during normal working hours but at times which minimise disruption to the employer's activities (once again, the employer's custom and practice in this regard will be material); off-site access will normally be outside such hours unless within easy walking distance of the workplace.[140] The Code proposes minimum standards for the frequency and duration of union activities, although what is reasonable for the union depends in part on the number of meetings held by the employer during working time.[141] Interestingly, it is suggested that where 'appropriate' there should be union 'surgeries' at the workplace during working hours at which each worker, without losing pay, would have the opportunity to meet a union representative for fifteen minutes on an individual basis or in small groups.[142] However whether this is appropriate depends in part on whether the employer is holding similar meetings and whether it would 'lead to an unacceptable increase in tension at the workplace'. Employers are urged 'where practicable' to provide a notice board for the union's use in a prominent location, and workers should be permitted access to the union's web-page and to the employer's e-mail and intranet systems where this is generally allowed for non-job-related purposes and in any event if the employer uses such systems to circulate information against the union's case.[143] The parties may also wish to consider the use of joint facilities and engaging in joint activities.[144] Finally, employers are urged to be receptive to suggestions from unions for securing access to 'non-typical' workers such as those who work from home or on a part-time basis.[145]

Although these provisions go some way to redressing the imbalance of power between unions and employers during a recognition campaign, unions remain disadvantaged in that employers are not prevented from organising 'captive audience' meetings during working hours, and they have direct access to individuals whose identities are known to them, whereas unions must hope that workers pick up literature made available to them at the workplace or via the

---

[137] Para 46.

[138] Para 44. Supervisors and line managers who are authorised by the employer to campaign against recognition on its behalf should make clear to workers when they undertake such activities that there are acting at the behest of the employer; equally union members who are authorised to represent the union in campaigning work should explain their role: para 57.

[139] Para 28.

[140] Para 29.

[141] Paras 30–33.

[142] Paras 31–33. There is no provision in the *statute* for workers to be paid: for the implications of this, see G Morris and T Archer, 2000: para 4.27.

[143] Paras 34–36.

[144] Para 41.

[145] Paras 38–39.

internet or QIP.[146] As we indicated above, complaints that the employer has failed in its duty to permit reasonable access may be taken to the CAC,[147] although the Code suggests that efforts should first be made to resolve minor complaints internally.[148] It has been argued that the access provisions are vulnerable to challenge by employers under the HRA 1998 as an interference with the employer's right to the peaceful enjoyment of its possessions, contrary to Article 1 of the First Protocol of the ECHR.[149] However the current Convention jurisprudence does not support this view. At one time it seemed that violation of the article required the economic value of a right or interest to be affected,[150] which clearly would not be the case here. However, in *Chassagnou v France*[151] the ECtHR found that the compulsory transfer of hunting rights over land belonging to landowners opposed to hunting constituted an interference with their rights as owners of the property, even though they were not deprived of their right to sell or use it and its market value did not seem to be reduced. It is submitted that the level of access required by the Code is of a very different nature and should be regarded as *de minimis* in this context; it may also be seen as relevant that the duty to afford it arises in the context of a process designed to establish the right of a union to be 'heard', an objective compatible with Article 11 of the ECHR.[152] Moreover, even if, contrary to this view, access were to be regarded as an 'interference', it would be open to the state to justify it as 'lawful' and striking a fair balance between the demands of the general interest of the community and the requirements of the protection of the individual's fundamental rights.[153]

9.17   *Unfair practices*   Once the parties have been informed by the CAC of the arrangements for the ballot they 'must refrain from using any unfair practice'.[154] Under the Act, a party uses an unfair practice if, with a view to influencing the result of the ballot, it:

(a)   offers to pay money or give 'money's worth' to a worker entitled to vote in the ballot in return for the worker's agreement to vote in a particular way or to abstain from voting. 'Money's

---

[146]   For a recent survey of the legal approach in eight other countries towards 'captive audience' meetings, see *Comparative Labor Law and Policy Journal* 29, (2007–2008) Winter 2008. On the union avoidance 'industry' in the United States, and its use in Britain, see Logan, 2006. The Code of Practice on Access and Unfair Practices during Recognition and Derecognition Ballots 2005 states that if a party hires a consultant to assist its campaign it is responsible for any unfair practice that consultant may commit. Such consultants should not present themselves as independent or impartial third parties when communicating with the workforce. See generally paras 57–60.

[147] Note that there is no mechanism by which employers can complain about a union's conduct, but the Code indicates that this may be a factor in determining whether the employer has acted unreasonably: para 73.

[148]   Paras 78–82.

[149]   D Brown and K Ewing, 2000: p 215.

[150]   *Rayner v UK* Application No 9310/81 47 DR 5 (1986); *S v France* Application No 13728/88 65 DR 250 (1990).

[151]   Judgment of 29 April 1999, (1999) 29 EHRR 615.

[152]   See *Van der Musselle v Belgium* judgment of 23 November 1983, (1984) 6 EHRR 163, para 49.

[153]   *James v UK* judgment of 21 February 1986, (1986) 8 EHRR 123; *Iatridis v Greece* judgment of March 25 1999 (1999) 30 EHRR 97; *Sporring and Lonnroth v Sweden* judgment of 23 September 1982, (1983) 5 EHRR 35, para 69.

[154]   ERelA 2004, s 10, inserting para 27A into TULRCA 1992, Sch A1. See Bogg, 2005, 2009b. The Code of Practice on Access and Unfair Practices during Recognition and Derecognition Ballots 2005 gives general guidance on standards of behaviour that are likely to prevent unfair practices from occurring, such as prior discussion between the parties as to the persons and organisations that are likely to campaign on their behalf. The ILO's CEACR has asked the Government to indicate the measures taken or envisaged to ensure protection against anti-union discrimination and interference in union affairs even before they have applied for recognition under the statutory procedure, the TUC having commented that an employer may commit acts of misconduct at a much earlier stage than the ballot period: Individual Observation Concerning Right to Organise and Collective Bargaining Convention 1949 (No 98). There is no indication that the Coalition Government will change the position.

worth' is not a term that is used in any other area of employment law, although it is used in a variety of other contexts such as property and family law. Despite a voluminous body of case law, there is no settled meaning of the term. Although it is tolerably clear that free goods or services, on which a monetary value can be put, would be covered, it is less clear whether some forms of benefit, such as an additional day's paid holiday, would be: it could be argued that a worker's salary remains unchanged but that he or she is effectively being offered an extra day's non-work time on which no material value may be able to be put. The Code of Practice on Access and Unfair Practices during Recognition and Derecognition Ballots does not resolve the difficulty, stating only that offers to provide additional paid holiday or other paid leave are *likely* to constitute 'money's worth'.[155]

(b) makes an 'outcome-specific offer' to a worker entitled to vote in the ballot. An 'outcome-specific offer' is an offer to pay money or give money's worth which is conditional on the CAC issuing a declaration that the union is, or is not, recognised, as the case may be, and is not conditional on anything which is done or occurs as a result of the declaration. 'Such offers are not explicitly linked to a person's agreement to vote in a particular way or not to vote at all. Instead, they represent more general offers to make payments to the workforce or give them money's worth provided the outcome of the ballot goes a particular way.'[156] Thus, as the Code of Practice states, an offer by one or other party to pay each worker £100 provided the ballot does, or does not, result in recognition would be categorised as an unfair practice. In contrast, an undertaking by a union to secure an increase of £1,000 in the annual pay of workers through the collective bargaining process following a vote for recognition would not be captured because the offer clearly depends on the negotiation of a collective agreement which is contingent on recognition being awarded.[157]

(c) coerces or attempts to coerce a worker entitled to vote in the ballot to disclose whether he or she intends to vote, or how he or she has voted or intends to vote;

(d) dismisses or threatens to dismiss a worker.[158] This provision may lead to difficulties where an employer intends to close or relocate its business, necessarily leading to dismissals, in the event of a vote in favour of recognition. The Code of Practice states that such statements 'should be avoided',[159] so suggesting that if an employer communicates such a message to the workforce this may lead to an adverse finding by the CAC. It is arguable that where a statement of this kind represents the employer's genuine intention, to impose a sanction for communicating it may be open to challenge under the HRA 1998 as an interference with the employer's freedom of expression which cannot be justified as 'necessary in a democratic society'.

(e) takes or threatens to take disciplinary action against a worker;

(f) subjects or threatens to subject a worker to any other detriment; or

(g) uses or attempts to use undue influence on a worker entitled to vote in the ballot. This term, borrowed from the Representation of the People Act 1983, is designed to be 'a general test

---

[155] Para 54.

[156] Gerry Sutcliffe, HC Debs, col 1472, 16 September 2004.

[157] Para 53.

[158] Note that this, in common with (e) and (f) below, is not restricted to a worker entitled to vote in the ballot; thus, disciplinary action against a union activist outside the bargaining unit could constitute an unfair practice: para 55.

[159] Para 67.

that will catch all possible cases of intimidatory or similar behaviour'.[160] The Code of Practice makes clear that 'undue influence' can take many forms, ranging from physical violence to more 'subtle' forms of behaviour such as the introduction of higher pay or better conditions in the ballot period if this is not the normal time for reviewing pay.[161] It also emphasises though that:

> Campaigning is inherently a partisan activity. Each party is therefore unlikely to put across a completely balanced message to the workforce, and some overstatement or exaggeration may well occur. In general, workers will expect such behaviour and can deal with it. Also, by listening to both sides, they will be able to question and evaluate the material presented to them.[162]

A party may complain to the CAC that the other has committed an unfair practice.[163] The complaint must be made on or before the first working day after the date of the ballot or, if votes may be cast on more than one day, the last of those days. The CAC must decide whether the complaint is well-founded within ten working days starting with the day after that on which the complaint was received or such longer period as the CAC may specify (the 'decision period'), and may postpone the ballot if it has not begun at the beginning of the decision period. A complaint is 'well-founded' for this purpose if the CAC finds that the party complained against used an unfair practice *and* the CAC is satisfied that the use of that practice changed or was likely to change the voting intentions (in terms of how, or whether, he or she would vote) or voting behaviour (how he or she voted) of a worker entitled to vote in the ballot. In the event that the CAC so finds, it may issue a remedial order requiring the party concerned to take specified action within a specified period to mitigate the effect of the unfair practice.[164] However, if the unfair practice consisted of or included the use of violence or the dismissal of a union official,[165] the CAC may declare at this stage that the union is, or is not, entitled to be recognised, depending on the party in default.[166] It may also issue such a declaration in the event that a second complaint is upheld against one of the parties or the party concerned fails to comply with a remedial order. There seems nothing in the legislation to exclude the CAC from requiring an employer to reinstate a dismissed worker under a remedial order, although such an order would not confer rights on the individual worker.[167]

Where the CAC finds an 'unfair practice' complaint to be well founded, it may also (or alternatively) cancel the initial ballot or annul a completed ballot without disclosing the result, and give notice to the parties that it intends to arrange for the holding of another ballot.[168] Where the CAC orders a fresh ballot to be held in these circumstances, that ballot is subject to the same principles as the original ballot, described in para 9.15 above, with three main exceptions.[169] First,

---

[160] Lord Triesman, HL Debs, GC 48–49, 7 June 2004.
[161] Para 56.
[162] Para 65.
[163] ERelA 2004, s 10, inserting para 27B into TULRCA 1992, Sch A1.
[164] ERelA 2004, s 10, inserting para 27C into TULRCA 1992, Sch A1.
[165] Defined TULRCA 1992, s 119.
[166] ERelA 2004, s 10, inserting para 27D into TULRCA 1992, Sch A1.
[167] TULRCA 1992, Sch A1, para 27A(4).
[168] TULRCA 1992, Sch A1, paras 27C(3)(b), 27E, 29(1A). This is at the CAC's discretion; it will not need to re-run a ballot if the victim of the unfair practice won the ballot: Gerry Sutcliffe, HC Debs col 472, 16 September 2004.
[169] TULRCA 1992, Sch A1, para 27F.

the notification period is five, not ten, working days; second, the employer need only inform the CAC of any changes in the names and home addresses of any workers in the bargaining unit rather than supplying a complete new list; and third, the costs of the ballot must be borne by such of the parties and in such proportions as the CAC may determine, rather than shared equally between them, so enabling the CAC, if it chooses, to require the party that committed the unfair practice to pay all or the majority of the costs. In addition, any remedial order made in relation to the holding of the original ballot, relating either to the breach of the employer's duties or an unfair practice, will have effect in relation to the fresh ballot to the extent the CAC specifies.

As of 18 March 2012 there had been seven complaints of unfair practices made to the CAC, none of which had been upheld.[170]

9.18   *Consequences of recognition.*   If the CAC declares a union recognised, the parties have 30 days (or longer if they so decide) in which to agree a 'method' by which they will conduct collective bargaining. If no agreement is made during this 'negotiation period' either party may apply to the CAC for assistance.[171] The CAC must first try to help the parties reach agreement, failing which it must itself specify a 'method', which has effect as if it were contained in a legally-enforceable contract unless the parties agree in writing otherwise. This does not prevent the parties replacing the method at a later stage; an agreement to effect such a replacement would also be legally enforceable but the replacement method itself, if appropriately drafted, need not be.[172] The term 'method' is not defined in the legislation; it is clear that it does not impose a substantive obligation to reach agreement, nor even to negotiate with a view to reaching an agreement (a requirement which is imposed on employers in order to fulfil their obligations to *consult* on collective redundancies); rather, it is a duty 'simply to meet and to talk'.[173] The government justified this limited obligation on the basis that statutory recognition should not deliver more than voluntary, where there are no constraints on bargaining conduct unless the parties otherwise agree. In specifying a 'method' the CAC must 'take ... into account' a detailed 'model' laid down by the Secretary of State, although it may depart from it as it thinks appropriate.[174] This model includes provision for a single Joint Negotiating Body, with exclusive bargaining rights over pay, hours and holidays; provision for paid time off for its union members employed by the employer to prepare the claim and attend the JNB, and access for other officials to the employer's premises for these purposes; the provision of accommodation and facilities for the union's private and exclusive use, where resources so permit; and a six-step bargaining procedure for dealing with the union's claims (presumptively presented annually), with specified actions and time limits attached to each stage. The employer is not permitted to vary the pay, hours, or holidays of workers in the bargaining unit unless it has first discussed its proposals with the union, although this restriction

---

[170] See Bogg, 2009b, for a critique of these decisions to the time of writing.

[171] TULRCA 1992, Sch A1, para 30. Either party may also apply for assistance in the event of non-compliance with an existing agreement: para 32, as amended by ERelA 2004, Sch 1, para 7; see *TGWU and GMB v Gala Casinos Ltd* TURI/206/02, CAC.

[172] TULRCA 1992, Sch A1, para 31. Note also the obligation on employers to consult on training matters if a 'method' of collective bargaining has been specified by the CAC and the parties have not varied its legal effect or content: see para 9.49 below.

[173] Lord McIntosh of Haringey, Deputy Chief Whip, HL Debs Vol 601, col 1275, 7 June 1999.

[174] TULRCA 1992, Sch A1, para 168; The Trade Union Recognition (Method of Collective Bargaining) Order 2000, SI 2000/1300.

does not apply where a worker has agreed that his or her terms may be varied by direct negotiation with the employer.[175]

Although the 'method' specified by the CAC has effect as a contract, the remedy for non-compliance is confined to one of specific performance,[176] an equitable and discretionary remedy which may be refused if applicants cannot show that they themselves have performed their contractual obligations and are ready and willing to perform future ones.[177] At one time the courts adopted the approach that there was no power to order specific performance of contracts which involved continuous or successive acts and which consequently required the continuous supervision of the court. In recent years, however, this position has been modified and greater emphasis has been placed on whether there is a sufficient definition of what is required to be done to comply with an order of the court.[178] The model procedure would seem capable of enforcement according to these criteria. Failure to comply with an order for specific performance constitutes contempt of court.[179] It remains uncertain whether an interim injunction could be available in this context;[180] in general, interim relief may be claimed in a specific performance action, and would be particularly useful to a union claimant in the event that an employer was attempting to vary terms and conditions of employment without going through the requisite procedure.

Both the nature of the obligation imposed on employers if recognition is ordered – the obligation merely to comply with a collective bargaining 'method' and the exclusive remedy of specific performance – have been heavily criticised by commentators, who contrast it unfavourably with the remedy of unilateral arbitration of substantive terms and conditions contained in the earlier procedure (and still applicable to claims for disclosure of information).[181] It is clear that the application of a 'method' does not of itself guarantee any material improvement for workers, and that even if collective agreements are reached, employers are not obliged to apply the norms they set to workers' individual contracts. However it is important not to overlook the collateral benefits, such as time off and consultation rights, that recognition brings, which we outline in para 7.26

The procedure came into operation on 6 June 2000. As of 1 March 2012, 783 applications had been presented to the CAC, 456 of which were accepted, 101 not accepted, and 210 withdrawn, with decisions pending on the remainder.[182] 128 were withdrawn at later stages of the procedure and 12 found to be invalid when the bargaining unit changed from that in the original application.

---

[175] Note, now, however, TULRCA 1992, s 145B, inserted by ERelA 2004, s 29, discussed in para 8.18 et seq. P Davies and M Freedland, 2007: p 161 note that the method is based on a model of 'episodic, not continuous interaction between an employer and trade union, ie, a rather distanced relationship which might be thought to be the opposite of a partnership'.

[176] TULRCA 1992, Sch A1, para 31(6). However failure to comply with the terms of the 'method' may also be relevant to the exercise of judicial discretion to grant an interim injunction to halt industrial action (see para 11.49) and to the length of time for which it is automatically unfair to dismiss an employee for taking 'protected industrial action' (see para 11.79 et seq).

[177] See generally Jones and Goodhart, 1996.

[178] *Posner v Scott-Lewis* [1987] Ch 25.

[179] See para 11.51 for the consequences of being found in contempt of court.

[180] The legislation, in stating that '[s]pecific performance shall be the only remedy available' would appear to exclude this, but the matter is not free from doubt. The government rejected an amendment to exclude interim proceedings in this context: see HL Debs Vol 601, cols 1234–1237, 7 June 1999. The government also rejected a proposed amendment to exclude liability in tort (in relation to trade disputes) in this context: see further Wedderburn, 2000: pp 40–41.

[181] See, for example, Wedderburn, 2000: pp 37–42; Simpson, 2000: pp 212–216; Dukes, 2008b. See para 9.22 et seq on disclosure of information.

[182] These figures, which are updated on a monthly basis, are available on the CAC's website www.cac.gov.uk

Recognition was ordered in 231 cases, 126 following a ballot and 105 without. Of those 231, a collective bargaining 'method' had been agreed between the parties in 204 cases and specified in 20; the issue was outstanding or the file had been closed[183] in the remainder. These figures may appear to suggest that relatively little use is being made of the procedure. However, this would fail to appreciate the impetus that its existence gives for employers to agree to recognition on a voluntary basis. Moreover, even if employers grant recognition once the statutory procedure has started, they retain greater flexibility in varying or terminating it (and may have a prospect of better relations with the union) than if it is ordered by the CAC. To that extent, therefore, the comparatively low number of recognition awards could be seen as a measure of success.[184]

(ii) Changes in the bargaining unit

9.19   As we have seen, recognition ordered by the CAC relates to a specific bargaining unit. It is possible, however, that a bargaining unit that was appropriate when recognition was being determined may cease to be so because of changes in the structure, organisation or nature of the business. In that event, the legislation makes provision for either party to apply to the CAC for the bargaining unit to be varied.[185] In order for the application to be admissible the CAC must decide that it is likely that the original unit is no longer appropriate by reference to statutory criteria. The parties then have the opportunity to agree a new bargaining unit, which will replace the old provided that it does not overlap with any pre-existing unit; in default of agreement, the CAC must decide upon the appropriate unit (which may turn out to be the existing one). An employer may also apply to the CAC for the bargaining arrangements to cease altogether if it believes that the unit covered by the declaration imposing recognition has ceased to exist, although this, too, may result in a revised bargaining unit (or maintenance of the old unit) if unsuccessful. There are complex provisions designed to ensure that there is no overlap between the new and any pre-existing bargaining unit. The CAC must then decide whether support for recognition in the new bargaining unit needs to be assessed; if so, it must determine whether there is the same level of actual and potential support required for an initial application to be admissible. If such support is found, whether recognition should be ordered is determined in an identical way to the initial application. As of 18 March 2012, there have been three applications to the CAC under this procedure.

(iii) Derecognition

9.20   As we saw in para 9.4, there is no statutory constraint on an employer which has recognised a union outside the statutory procedure varying the scope of recognition or withdrawing it altogether. The position is wholly different where recognition follows from the union having

---

[183] Due to company liquidation.

[184] For a more critical view, see Gall, 2010a.

[185] For a more detailed analysis of these highly complex provisions, which are contained in Part III of TULRCA 1992, Sch A1, see G Morris and T Archer, 2000: paras 4.35–4.42. See also *GMB and Ardengate Ltd* TUR3/2/03, CAC. Note that provisions relating to the collective bargaining method (whether derived from the parties' agreement or specified by the CAC) must apply in relation to the unit: para 64(1)(b).

invoked the statutory procedure. As we have already indicated, even if recognition is enshrined in an 'agreement for recognition' agreed voluntarily by the employer following a request under the statutory procedure, the employer may not terminate that agreement unilaterally within three years unless the parties have modified this restriction by consent.[186] However once that period (or any additional or lesser period that has been agreed) has passed, the employer is free to terminate recognition without union consent. By contrast, where recognition follows a declaration by the CAC it can be terminated by the CAC only in specified conditions, on application by the employer or worker a minimum of three years after the initial declaration.[187] The situations where recognition may be terminated mirror, in broad terms, those applicable to the granting of recognition. They are, in outline, as follows. The first is where the employer, together with any associated employer, employs an average of fewer than 21 workers in any period of 13 weeks ending on or after the 'relevant date' – the expiry of the period of three years starting with the date of the CAC's declaration awarding recognition. Derecognition on this basis is invoked by a notice served by the employer on the union and the CAC, and may be adjudicated upon by the CAC if challenged by the union.[188] Second, the employer may begin the derecognition process by making a request to the union to end the bargaining arrangements. Third, a worker in the bargaining unit may apply to the CAC. In the second and third cases, where recognition was ordered following a ballot, the CAC must first decide that at least 10% of the workers in the bargaining unit favour an end to the bargaining arrangements and that a majority of the workers constituting the unit would favour this.[189] It will then order derecognition, failing agreement between the parties, if the requisite support for the termination of the bargaining arrangements has been demonstrated in a ballot of the workers in the unit, conducted according to the principles that govern recognition ballots.[190] Where recognition was ordered without a ballot (on the basis of majority membership), however, and the application is made by an employer, it will be admissible if the CAC is satisfied that fewer than half the workers are members of the union.[191] In a parallel with the three-year bar on recognition applications, derecognition applications by employers and by workers may be considered only if there has been a three-year gap since the last application,[192] so ensuring an element of industrial relations stability.

It is conceivable that workers may wish their employer to change its bargaining partner from one union to another. For recognition agreements reached outside the statutory procedure there has traditionally been no legal mechanism for achieving this without the employer's consent.

---

[186] TULRCA 1992, Sch A1, para 56.

[187] There is an exception to the three-year rule if a union recognised pursuant to a request for recognition loses its certificate of independence; it is then immediately treated as being recognised on a voluntary basis unless there are other unions recognised for the unit that retain their certificates: TULRCA 1992, Sch A1, paras 149–154.

[188] TULRCA 1992, Sch A1, paras 96–103, as amended by ERelA 2004 and the Agency Workers Regulations 2010, SI 2010/93.

[189] See, for example, *Dr Robert Bradley and others and Unite and Honda of the UK Manufacturing Ltd* TUR4/005, CAC.

[190] TULRCA 1992 Sch A1, paras 104–121, as amended by ERelA 2004. Note the difference in sanction for a second unfair practice, breach of a CAC remedial order, dismissal of a union official or use of violence committed by an employer in relation to an application by a worker in para 119H (employer may be barred from further campaigning in relation to the ballot).

[191] TULRCA 1992, Sch A1, paras 122–133.

[192] In the case where the employer issues a notice stating that it employs fewer than 21 workers as above, the bar applies where the CAC accepts the earlier notice as complying with the requirements of TULRCA 1992, Sch A1, para 99(3): para 99A.

Moreover, even if a union has been the subject of a derecognition declaration, there is nothing to prevent an employer recognising it on a voluntary basis, so barring a claim for statutory recognition by another union. There is one exception to workers' inability to obtain recognition of a substitute union, which is where the employer recognises a union that lacks a certificate of independence. It is then open to any worker within the bargaining unit to apply to the CAC to have the bargaining arrangements ended, and the CAC will order this if it is supported in a ballot by a majority of the workers voting and at least 40% of the workers in the unit.[193] This is likely, in practice, to arise as the first step of an initiative by an independent union to gain recognition for the bargaining unit in question; even if the employer were to re-recognise the non-independent union, that recognition agreement, if made within three years of the previous recognition agreement ceasing, would not constitute a barrier to an application by an independent union to the CAC which, if successful, would mean that the bargaining arrangements with the non-independent union would cease.[194] Unlike other contexts in which derecognition may be sought, there is no requirement that the union should have been recognised for a minimum three-year period, nor is there any restriction on the frequency with which applications may be brought. However the efficacy of the procedure may be hindered in practice by the initial admissibility requirement that the CAC must find that at least 10% of the workers in the bargaining unit favour an end to the arrangements and that a majority of those in the bargaining unit would be likely to do so. Obtaining evidence of this may be difficult for workers in a situation where neither employer nor union are likely to co-operate

(iv) Protection of workers during recognition and derecognition campaigns

9.21   Workers are accorded protection against dismissal or subjection to other forms of detriment by their employer for specified acts relating to the recognition and derecognition procedures.[195] We discussed the concept of 'subjection to a detriment' in para 8.13 in relation to trade union membership and activities and the same comments apply, *mutatis mutandis*, in this context. Here, in particular, workers may be subject to threats of detrimental consequences if they lend their support to recognition; once again it is strongly arguable that workers have been 'subjected to a detriment' if they cease activities they wish to carry out because of intimidation. It is essential, however, that the employer's act can be attributed specifically to the action of the individual worker. Thus, a threat to the workforce in general that terms and conditions of employment will be less favourable, or that redundancies will follow, if a union is accorded recognition, whilst it may constitute an unfair practice,[196] will not suffice for the purpose of obtaining an individual remedy.[197] The grounds to which protection pertains are acting with a view to obtaining or preventing recognition of a union (or unions) by the employer under Schedule A1 of TULRCA 1992 or indicating support or lack of support for it; acting with a view to securing or preventing the ending of bargaining arrangements or indicating support or lack of support for this; voting in

---

[193] TULRCA 1992, Sch A1, paras 134–148.
[194] TULRCA 1992, Sch A1, paras 35(4), 148.
[195] TULRCA 1992, Sch A1, paras 156–165.
[196] See para 9.17 above.
[197] Under ERelA 2004, s 10, inserting para 27A(4) into TULRCA 1992, Sch A1, dismissal or the threat of dismissal can constitute an unfair practice; use of an unfair practice does not confer a right on an individual worker but does not affect any other right which he or she may have.

a ballot or influencing or seeking to influence other workers to vote or not to vote, or the way they cast their votes; or proposing, failing or proposing to decline to do any of these things. However an act is excluded from these grounds 'if it constitutes an unreasonable act or omission by the worker'.[198] Clearly there may be scope for argument as to when an act constitutes an 'unreasonable act or omission' – canvassing other workers during working hours rather than performing normal duties may be one example – so it may be prudent, where appropriate, to include an additional complaint in a tribunal application that the worker has been subjected to a detriment for taking part in union activities, where no such qualification applies.

A worker who is subjected to a detriment on one of the specified grounds may complain to an employment tribunal; in the event that he or she is an employee, and the detriment amounts to dismissal, a remedy must be sought under the unfair dismissal legislation, which has the additional advantage of the possibility of interim relief.[199] The time limit, procedure for complaining, and remedies available are identical to those applicable to detriments on grounds of union activities. Thus, there is no limit on the compensation that may be awarded, although if the detriment consisted of termination of the contract of a 'worker' who was not an 'employee', it is restricted to the total of the basic and compensatory awards for unfair dismissal.[200] In theory, therefore, a worker could be awarded more for suffering a detriment short of dismissal than for dismissal itself. Where an employee has been dismissed (or, in a 'redundancy case' selected for dismissal) on one of the specified grounds, the dismissal will be automatically unfair. There is no qualifying period applicable to such dismissals, although where the employee would not otherwise qualify to claim he or she may need to prove the reason for dismissal (see para 5.93 above). The remedy of interim relief may be particularly significant where the employer has dismissed employees prior to the ballot in the hope that they will thereby be excluded from participation in it.[201] It is a moot point, however, whether all the remedies available would secure participation. Reinstatement, which probably would, requires the consent of the employer, as does re-engagement (where the position is less clear). An order for continuation of the contract would allow participation only if it could be argued that this constitutes a 'benefit derived from the employment'. Even if this were to be the case, it may be otiose if the ballot had been held after the dismissal and prior to the tribunal's order. In these circumstances unions may wish to inform the CAC of any application for interim relief and request postponement of the ballot pending its outcome.

The conduct of collective bargaining: disclosure of information

9.22   As we saw in para 9.18, where a trade union is recognised pursuant to a statutory request for recognition, the CAC may specify, at the request of either party, the 'method' by which collective bargaining is to be conducted. Other than in these circumstances, the conduct of the collective bargaining process is left entirely to the discretion of the parties, with the exception of a limited statutory duty on employers to disclose certain information. Access to information

---

[198]   TULRCA 1992, Sch A1 paras 156(3), 161(3).
[199]   TULRCA 1992, Sch A1, paras 156(4), 161; ERA 1996, ss 128(1)(b) and 129(1), as amended by ERelA 1999, s 6. TULRCA 1992, s 207A, inserted by EA 2008, s 3(1),(2) applies to such claims.
[200]   TULRCA 1992, Sch A1, para 160.
[201]   See further para 5.153.

about an undertaking, particularly its financial position, is crucial to the conduct of collective bargaining; in Kahn-Freund's striking phrase, 'recognition does not deserve its name if one of the negotiating partners is kept in the dark about matters within the exclusive knowledge of the other which are relevant to an agreement'.[202] It may also be in an employer's interest that a union's case is not based upon false assumptions about the undertaking's state of health.[203] The need for adequate information is stressed in ILO Recommendation 163 concerning the Promotion of Collective Bargaining, Article 7 of which states that measures adapted to national conditions should be taken, if necessary, so that the parties have access to the information required for meaningful negotiations. Since 1977[204] employers have been required by legislation to disclose to representatives of recognised unions on request information about their undertaking for the purposes of all stages of collective bargaining about matters, and in relation to descriptions of workers, for which the union is recognised.[205] The information may be either in the employer's own possession or that of an associated employer. However, the utility of this requirement has been severely limited by its very restrictive scope.

9.23   The first restriction lies in the nature of the duty itself, which provides that the information must satisfy two tests. First, it must be information without which the union representatives would be to a 'material extent' impeded in carrying out collective bargaining with the employer. This test, in addressing the importance rather than the relevance of the information, 'focuses attention not on the nature of the bargaining that disclosure might facilitate but, rather, on whether bargaining can take place at all without disclosure'.[206] It may be difficult for a union to argue that bargaining is impossible if it has managed without such information in the past, and the difference which access to the information in question would have made can be a matter of speculation only. Research on the operation of the procedure has led to the conclusion that '[m]any employers have successfully objected that there was no impediment and unions are severely disadvantaged in arguing the need for information that they do not have'.[207] Second, it must be information which the employer should disclose in accordance with good industrial relations practice, on which regard should be had, *inter*

---

[202]   P Davies and M Freedland, 1983: p 110.

[203]   See L Dickens, 1980.

[204]   When this provision of the EPA 1975 came into force. Provision for disclosure was made in the IRA 1971 but it was never implemented.

[205]   See now TULRCA 1992, s 181(1). This may require the CAC to decide the scope of recognition: see, for example, *Unite the Union, the UCU, and Unison and University College, London*, D1/4/07 and *RMT and Carlisle Cleaning and Support Services Ltd* DI/6 (2010). 'Representative' means an official (defined TULRCA 1992, s 119) or other person authorised by the union to carry out such collective bargaining. For the definition of 'worker' see TULRCA 1992, s 296 and para 3.33 *et seq* above. Other rights of employee representatives to information are dealt with later in this chapter. Note that providing information which is confidential under the contract of employment to union representatives will be a breach of contract on the part of individual employees and seeking it may constitute the tort of inducing breach of contract: see *Bent's Brewery Co Ltd v Hogan* [1945] 2 All ER 570.

[206]   L Dickens and G Bain 1986: p 98. It is noteworthy, however, that the CAC has emphasised that 'collective bargaining must be looked at more widely than simply relating to a process in which two parties are clearly agreed that they are negotiating to reach a mutually acceptable solution. The term "collective bargaining" refers to the continuing relationship between an employer and a trade union, not simply the nature of the interaction on one particular occasion': *Annual Report*, 1995, para 2.17.

[207]   Gospel and Lockwood, 1999: p 244.

alia, to the ACAS Code of Practice.[208] The Code is not particularly helpful on this matter, however (possibly because of the difficulty of reconciling the views of the two sides of industry in preparing it).[209] It does not attempt to provide a 'checklist' of items which should be disclosed on the basis that this will vary according to factors such as the subject-matter and level of negotiations and the size of the company and business in which it is engaged.[210] Rather, it confines itself to giving examples of information which it suggests could be relevant in certain situations which it divides into five broad headings: pay and benefits; conditions of service; manpower (sic); performance (eg, productivity and efficiency data, savings from increased productivity and output, return on capital invested, sales and state of the order book) and financial matters (eg, profits; assets; loans to parent or subsidiary companies; and liabilities).[211] This rudimentary list does, at least, make clear that subjects which are not themselves within the statutory definition of 'collective bargaining' are nevertheless potentially within the duty. Two further aspects have emerged from decisions of the CAC, which adjudicates on complaints of failure to comply with the duty to disclose: that its application to 'all stages' of collective bargaining means that there is no need for negotiations to have started before disclosure is sought,[212] and information about workers who are outside the union's sphere of recognition may nevertheless be relevant to bargaining about those who are within it.[213] However, it is clear that the information need be disclosed only for the purpose of collective bargaining and, depending upon its nature, it is conceivable that an employer could restrain its use in any other context on the basis that this would constitute a breach of confidence.[214]

As well as being narrowly defined, the duty to disclose is also subject to additional limitations. First, there is a list of six specific categories of information which need not be disclosed.[215] The most wide-ranging are any information 'which has been communicated to ... [the employer] in confidence'[216] and information whose disclosure 'would cause substantial injury to ... [the employer's] undertaking for reasons other than its effect on collective bargaining'. For the latter the Code gives as examples cost information on individual products, detailed analysis of proposed investment, marketing or pricing policies, and price quotas or the make-up of tender prices;[217]

---

[208] ACAS Code No 2: *Disclosure of Information to Trade Unions for Collective Bargaining Purposes* (1997). This Code, which came into force on 5 February 1998, replaces the original version published in 1977. The CAC Annual Reports are a more useful source of guidance on good practice in this area. The CAC has emphasised that the 'information' to be disclosed may include the basis upon which subjective or professional judgments are made: *Annual Report*, 1995, paras 2.16 and 2.18.

[209] See Gospel, 1976.

[210] ACAS Code No 2, paras 11, 12.

[211] ACAS Code No 2, para 11.

[212] This approach was approved by Forbes J in *R v CAC, ex p BTP Tioxide Ltd* [1982] IRLR 60, 67.

[213] On the latter point see, for example, CAC *Annual Report* 1993, para 2.6, which recognises the interest of unions in knowing the level of pay increases, including those of senior managers, throughout a company.

[214] I Smith and A Baker, 2010: p 640. In *Unison and Midlothian Council* D1/1/06, CAC the CAC did not order full disclosure of information about a job evaluation scheme because it was not certain it would be used solely for collective bargaining purposes; rather, there was the issue of possible equal pay claims by employees. Cf *Lloyds Trade Union and Lloyds Banking Group* DI/2 (2011), para 43, where the CAC affirmed that if information was necessary for collective bargaining it was irrelevant that the union had an ulterior motive in seeking disclosure.

[215] TULRCA 1992, s 182(1).

[216] In *CSU v CAC* [1980] IRLR 274, it was held that the Ministry of Defence could rely on this defence in refusing to disclose to the Civil Service Union information as to the number of cleaners and their hours of work supplied in a tender from private contractors. Several cases before the CAC in recent years have concerned market-testing and contracting-out, including the information given to potential bidders. The CAC has urged upon those conducting the process the benefits of involving staff and their representatives at an early stage: see, for example, *Annual Report*, 1996, para 2.8.

[217] ACAS Code No 2, para 14.

substantial injury may occur if, for example, certain customers would be lost to competitors, or suppliers would refuse to supply necessary materials, or the ability to raise funds to finance the company would be seriously impaired as a result of disclosing certain information.[218] A further exempted category – information relating specifically to an individual without that individual's consent – has assumed greater practical significance with the spread of performance-related pay and management-only grading schemes. The CAC has acknowledged unions' interests in having the information necessary to monitor the operation of such schemes and has reconciled this with respect for individual confidentiality by awarding that particular breakdowns of annual salary increases should be provided, for example, by age groups, sex, and by functional area.[219] The second important limitation is that employers are not obliged to produce, or allow inspection of, any document,[220] a restriction which contrasts sharply with systems, most notably the Swedish,[221] which have allowed worker representatives, or their accountants, this right, and that requires a degree of trust on the part of unions which, if not present, risks merely fuelling cynicism and suspicion. Last, employers need not compile or assemble any information where this would involve an amount of work or expenditure 'out of reasonable proportion to the value of the information in the conduct of collective bargaining'.[222] This exception assumes both that the value of information can be objectively assessed and, moreover, that it can be assessed before disclosure. However, the Code goes beyond the statute in recommending that employers should present information in a form and style which recipients can reasonably be expected to understand,[223] and clearly it may be in the interests of employers to sustain any additional costs involved in doing this.

The general tenor of the Code is that the parties should try to reach their own understanding as to how the duty to disclose can best be fulfilled,[224] in contrast to the adversarial approach of the statute (which the CAC has attempted to minimise[225]) which seems to cast the employer in a role of 'reluctant divulger of secrets rather than active participant in information transmission'.[226] This is reinforced by the emphasis upon the confidentiality of information as a ground for withholding information. One method of circumventing this would be to allow privileged access to union representatives but to make this access subject to a duty of confidentiality: ILO Recommendation 163 states that 'where the disclosure of ... information could be prejudicial to the undertaking, its communication could be made conditional upon a commitment that it would be regarded as confidential to the extent required ...'.[227] This solution is adopted in ICER 2004 and TICER 1999.[228], however, it runs the risk of placing union representatives, as bearers of knowledge denied to members, in an invidious position.[229]

---

[218] ACAS Code No 2, para 15.
[219] See, for example, *Annual Reports* for 1991, 1992, and 1993.
[220] TULRCA 1992, s 182(2).
[221] Joint Regulation of Working Life Act 1976.
[222] TULRCA 1992, s 182(2).
[223] ACAS Code No 2, para 21.
[224] ACAS Code No 2, para 22.
[225] See, for example, *Annual Report*, 1993, para 3.4 and 1994, para 2.3.
[226] Gospel and Willman, 1981: p 22.
[227] Art 7(2)(a).
[228] See paras 9.56 and 9.63 below.
[229] In its *Annual Report*, 1996, para 2.7 the CAC referred rather cryptically to the possibility of an employer 'negotiating some understanding with a trade union officer over a wider release of confidential information' relating to a job evaluation exercise.

9.24   Where an employer fails to disclose information the union may complain to the CAC which may refer the complaint to ACAS for conciliation if it considers that this is reasonably likely to produce a settlement.[230] The CAC also seeks to encourage the parties to resolve their differences jointly, and generally holds an informal meeting involving a chairman, both parties and usually an ACAS conciliator as the first stage of the proceedings, although this may depend upon whether conciliation measures have already been attempted unsuccessfully prior to the presentation of the complaint. Failing a resolution of the complaint, the case proceeds to a full hearing, at which the parties are sometimes legally represented, following which the CAC makes a declaration on whether it finds the complaint well-founded, giving reasons. If the declaration requires the employer to disclose information and this is not done within the specified period, the union may present a further complaint to the CAC, and at the same time or subsequently present a claim that contracts of particular descriptions of employees should include specified terms and conditions.[231] The CAC, if it upholds the complaint, may, after hearing the parties, make an award (either in the terms sought by the union or otherwise) which takes effect as a term in the contracts of the employees affected, and may be superseded or varied only by a subsequent award under the same procedure, a collective agreement between the employer and the union representing those employees, or by express or implied agreement between the employer and individual employees if that agreement improves upon the terms specified in the award. This sanction thus constitutes a rare example of direct statutory intervention in the contract. However, as a remedy it contains significant weaknesses. First, it means that the duty to disclose cannot, ultimately, be enforced.[232] Second, although the duty is framed in terms of 'workers', only 'employees' may be the subject of a claim for improved terms and conditions. Third, although the duty covers information in the possession of an associated employer, there is no provision for a remedy against an associated employer who fails to comply. Fourth, there is no penal element allowed for in the award[233] and an employer whose terms and conditions compare favourably with those of others in the area may therefore have little to fear. Finally, the CAC is not empowered to prescribe the information which should be disclosed on future occasions,[234] although clearly the parties may be guided in their behaviour by the outcome of previous complaints. However, the fact that the CAC may adjudicate only upon a past failure to disclose means that 'the matter in dispute has to be capable of being pursued over a considerable length of time. Otherwise it will mean the employer can delay disclosure of the information until its usefulness is limited or has passed.'[235]

---

[230] TULRCA 1992, s 183.

[231] TULRCA 1992, ss 184, 185. Note that this remedy is not applicable to Crown employment or to House of Lords or House of Commons staff: TULRCA 1992, ss 273, 277, 278.

[232] *Quaere* whether the CAC could award any of the information sought as part of the contracts of employment. In *Holokrome Ltd v ASTMS* (CAC, 6 August 1979, unreported) the CAC did not accept the employer's argument that it could not award any of the information sought; the test was whether what was claimed was appropriate as a term or condition of an individual contract. In its decision the CAC thought that individual contracts could contain a term requiring information about salary ranges and increments within the grade in which an employee fell. However the actual award does not appear to mention 'information'; the CAC awarded that the salary ranges and increments should have effect as part of the contracts of employment.

[233] Another option would be a fixed sum payable to employees; cf, for example, the remedy for failure to provide an individual employee with a written statement of reasons for dismissal: see para 5.88 above.

[234] *R v CAC, ex p BTP Tioxide Ltd* [1981] ICR 843 at 859.

[235] Gospel and Lockwood, 1999: p 245.

9.25 In practice there has been only limited recourse to the enforcement provisions. Between February 1977 (when these provisions came into force) and the end of 2011, 573 complaints had been received of which only 13.26% resulted in a formal decision.[236] The majority of the remainder were withdrawn after a settlement had been reached, a tribute to the success of the CAC's procedure which favours the avoidance of 'win/lose scenarios'.[237] The highest number of complaints in any year was 62 (in 1978) and in many there have been considerably fewer.[238] This does not of itself indicate that the disclosure provisions have had little impact; their existence may have encouraged voluntary disclosure, a view endorsed by the CAC itself.[239] Moreover, from another angle, unions may think twice about pursuing complaints in a climate where, even if not in the instant claim,[240] recognition obtained outside the statutory procedure may be jeopardised by such a course of action. However, it seems to be generally accepted that the limited scope of the information of which disclosure may be ordered has contributed to the low level of recourse to this provision.[241] Its survival in a period of overt hostility to collective bargaining when the Conservative Government was in office could be regarded as a tribute to its ineffectual nature.[242] In its present form it perpetuates a view of workers as on 'the outside' of the enterprise, in comparison, for example, with shareholders, a view that ICER 2004, discussed in para 9.50 *et seq*, has the potential to ameliorate, although much will depend upon the nature of the agreements for information and consultation that employers reach and how these agreements operate in practice.

The legal effect of collective agreements

9.26 We discussed the role of collective agreements as a source of law in chapters 2 and 4. In those chapters we noted that collective agreements had become, and remained, an important source of norms despite their independence from the formal legal system. As we indicated, collective agreements are, in general, not legally enforceable between the collective parties nor do they automatically take effect as terms of individual employment contracts, the latter occurring only with the consent, express or implied, of the individual parties. We also noted the lack of

---

[236] Information supplied by the CAC.

[237] *Annual Report*, 1996, para 2.2. There have been only two cases to date where the CAC has had to issue a second award after an employer's failure to honour the first declaration.

[238] Information supplied by the CAC.

[239] *Annual Report* for 1993, para 3.4. On factors that influence whether employers disclose information to unions and to employees generally see Peccei *et al*, 2008.

[240] *Ackrill Newspapers Ltd v NUJ* (CAC, 14 February 1992, unreported): provided the union was recognised at the time of the request subsequent derecognition is irrelevant. See also *HM Prison Service v POA* (CAC, 27 March 1995, unreported) IRLB No 523, p 9: an employer cannot avoid the obligation to supply information by announcing in a given situation that it has decided not to negotiate.

[241] For an analysis of the matters in relation to which information has been sought, and CAC decisions up to the time of their respective publication, see Gospel and Willman, 1981; L Dickens and G Bain, 1986: pp 94–101; Gospel and Lockwood, 1999. In recent years information has been sought on a wide range of issues, including staffing, grading and pay distribution; pensions; financial information; market-testing and contracting-out; and redundancy plans and selection procedures.

[242] The Conservative Government's last White Paper in the area, *Industrial Action and Trade Unions*, Cm 3470, 1996, sought views on the abolition of the statutory procedure in favour of allowing disclosure of information to be the product of voluntary agreement between employers and unions: paras 3.4–3.5.

legal regulation of the content of collective agreements which, specific statutory exceptions aside, remains a matter for the negotiating parties. In this section we explore in greater detail the statutory concept of a 'collective agreement' and consider what is required if the collective parties wish to displace the statutory presumption of non-enforceability and to accord their agreements legal force.[243] We also discuss the status of those agreements which fall outside the statutory definition and are thereby not subject to the statutory presumption.

A 'collective agreement' generally means 'any agreement or arrangement made by or on behalf of one or more trade unions and one or more employers or employers' associations and relating to one or more of the matters specified' in TULRCA 1992, section 178(2).[244] These matters are, in brief, the terms and conditions of employment, or the physical conditions in which any workers are required to work; the engagement or non-engagement, or termination or suspension of employment or the duties of employment, of one or more workers; the allocation of work or duties as between workers; disciplinary matters; a worker's membership or non-membership of a trade union; facilities for union officials; and machinery for negotiation or consultation, and other procedures, relating to any of the above.[245] Such an agreement is conclusively presumed not to have been intended by the parties to be a legally enforceable contract unless the agreement is in writing and contains a provision which (however expressed) states that the parties intend the agreement to be a legally enforceable contract.[246] The courts have taken a strict approach to what is required to demonstrate this intention. A statement merely that the parties intend their agreement to be 'binding' will not suffice as this could equally mean 'binding in honour only'. In the words of Scott J, '[u]nless a collective agreement contains a statement in terms that show, at least, that the parties have directed their minds to the question of legal enforceability and have decided in favour of ... [it], there is, in my view, no sufficient statement of intention ...'.[247] However, while such a statement is a prerequisite to enforceability it does not follow that an agreement which includes it will necessarily constitute a contract; it may, for example, use language which is insufficiently clear to be judicially interpreted, or void as in restraint of trade, or for some other reason not a contract. In practice it is very rare for the collective parties to attempt to make their

---

[243] Note that agreements made between 1 December 1971 and 16 December 1974 were, under the IRA 1971, conclusively presumed to be legally enforceable unless they contained an express exclusion clause. It was almost universal practice for them to contain such a clause: see para 2.9 above.

[244] TULRCA 1992, s 178(1). For the purpose of excluding or modifying provisions of the WTR 1998, determining the terms upon which parental leave is taken, and modifying provisions relating to successive fixed-term contracts, however, the union parties are required to be 'independent': see paras 4.78, 4.90, 6.119, 3.52 and 5.75. For the purposes of s 178(1) it is irrelevant how an agreement was achieved, and the fact that it requires endorsement from another body makes no difference to its status: *Edinburgh Council v Brown* [1999] IRLR 208. In *Burke v Royal Liverpool University Hospital NHS Trust* [1997] ICR 730, the EAT, in holding that an exchange of letters between the employer and the union as to future terms of employment could constitute a 'collective agreement', stated at 738 that there needed to be 'a mutual intention on the part of employers and employees' bargaining agents to enter into a collective bargain, the effect of which will be to modify the contracts of employment between employer and employee'. The latter constitutes a gloss on the statute, and does not cater for procedural agreements or other agreements not dealing with substantive terms and conditions of employment. In *HM Prison Service v Bewley* [2004] ICR 422, the EAT held that where a collective agreement itself provides a mechanism for the final resolution of disputes (short of industrial action) in the form of binding pendulum arbitration, the arbitrator's award constitutes a 'collective agreement'.

[245] These matters, which are analysed in greater detail in para 11.27 below, also constitute the subject matter of 'collective bargaining': see para 7.27 above.

[246] TULRCA 1992, s 179(1), (2). Parts only of the agreement may be specified as intended to be enforceable; the presumption against enforceability will then apply to the remainder: s 179(3).

[247] *NCB v NUM* [1986] IRLR 439, 449. See also *Monterosso Shipping Co Ltd v ITWF* [1982] IRLR 468.

agreements legally enforceable[248] (although, as we saw in chapter 4, this does not prevent them being a source of enforceable terms of an individual employment contract).

Agreements may be made between employers and unions which fall outside the statutory definition of 'collective agreements'. Examples would include those concerning union involvement in future investment decisions or product development relating to the undertaking. These agreements are governed by the common law, which offers no clear guidance. It would be open to the parties to stipulate that they intended their agreement to constitute a contract and provided that the terms were sufficiently certain to be capable of enforcement by the courts, there would seem to be no barrier to this. If the agreement were silent on the question of intention it seems probable, in the light of *Ford Motor Co Ltd v AEU*,[249] that a court would conclude that the parties had not intended to create legal relations although it is conceivable (if unlikely) that the 'climate of opinion' may change so as to provide a different answer to that given in that case.

The effect of a transfer of the undertaking

9.27   As we discussed in chapter 3, when an undertaking is transferred within the meaning of these terms in TUPE 2006 a variety of consequences follow. There are two which relate specifically to collective bargaining.

First, regulation 6 states that where the transferor employer recognised an independent trade union to any extent in respect of the employees transferred then, after the transfer, the transferee is deemed to recognise the union to the same extent provided that after the transfer the transferred organised grouping of resources or employees 'maintains an identity distinct from the remainder of the transferee's undertaking'. This means that all rights which are dependent upon recognition will apply in the transferred undertaking. However, the requirement that a distinct identity is maintained may be difficult to show when the transferee already operates an undertaking of its own; it is common in such circumstances for trading methods, etc, as well as employee terms and conditions to be harmonised.[250] The practical effect of this provision is further weakened by the provision in the Regulations that after the transfer 'any agreement for recognition may be varied or rescinded accordingly'. Thus, where the transferor has recognised the union voluntarily the transferee is free to vary the scope of recognition or derecognise the union in the same way as the transferor could have done, subject to the existence of contractual obligations consequent upon recognition (see para 9.4) and any obligations relating to disclosure of information (see para 9.22 *et seq*) or consultation (see para 9.29) which may already have arisen.[251] However, if a transferor employer were to derecognise a union prior to the transfer at the insistence of the transferee it

---

[248] The collective agreement to ensure staff relations are conducted peacefully and without disruption to operations at GCHQ, 3 September 1997, and the Joint Industrial Relations Procedural Agreement in the prison service, 11 November 2004, which expired on 8 May 2008 after the POA gave notice to terminate it, were notable exceptions to this: see further para 11.12 below.

[249] [1969] 2 QB 303; see para 2.9 above.

[250] The precise meaning of 'distinct identity' has not, to date, been clarified: it could require a separate legal structure or merely a separate management structure.

[251] Wynn-Evans, 2006: p 97 suggests that the lack of protection for continued recognition 'raises the possibility of, in appropriate circumstances, the removal of recognition entitling an employee to resign and make a claim based on the ability established by reg 4(9) for a transferring employee to terminate his or her employment in response to a substantial change to his or her working conditions to his or her material detriment'.

may be possible to argue, by analogy with *Litster v Forth Dry Dock and Engineering Co Ltd*[252] that recognition should nevertheless continue to the point of transfer.

Where the transferor recognised the union pursuant to a CAC declaration or 'agreement for recognition' (see para 9.6), it would seem to be the case that the transferee employer will be bound by the same obligations as the transferor if the undertaking or part transferred maintains a distinct identity, given that the union is 'deemed to have been recognised by the transferee to the same extent' in respect of the employees for which it was recognised by the transferor.[253] If this is the case the transferee would be unable, for example, unilaterally to terminate an agreement for recognition before three years had expired from the date of the agreement. This interpretation would accord with Art 6(1) of the Acquired Rights Directive, which requires that '[i]f the undertaking, business or part of an undertaking or business [subject to a transfer] preserves its autonomy, the status and function of the representatives or of the representation of the employees affected by the transfer shall be preserved on the same terms and subject to the same conditions as existed before the date of the transfer *by virtue of law, regulation, administrative provision or agreement* (our italics), provided that the conditions necessary for the constitution of the employees' representation are fulfilled.'[254] However the matter is not free from doubt. Moreover, TUPE applies only to recognition in respect of 'employees', not, like the recognition procedure, 'workers'.[255] Thus, if the transferor's workers who comprised the bargaining unit were not employees, recognition would not transfer; if only some were employees and recognition were pursuant to a CAC declaration, the transferee employer would be able to invoke the statutory procedure applicable to changes in the bargaining unit outlined in para 9.19 above. ERelA 2004 empowered the Secretary of State to make provision by order for cases where, *inter alia*, an employer's identity has changed after a declaration of recognition, a power that is not limited to situations governed by TUPE.[256] Although the Labour Government indicated an intention to provide in regulations that, following a change of employer identity, responsibility for existing recognition awards 'can be reassigned from the original employers to their successors with the aim of ensuring continuity of treatment for the workers concerned',[257] no such regulations were issued.

Second, regulation 5 provides that any 'collective agreement'[258] made by or on behalf of the *transferor* with a union recognised in respect of any employee whose contract of employment is preserved by regulation 4(1) applies to that employee as if made by or on behalf of the *transferee*

---

[252] [1989] IRLR 161. See further para 5.185 above.

[253] If this argument is accepted, 'any' in reg 6(2)(b) would need to be interpreted as 'any agreement (if such exists)'. The BERR (now BIS) guide to TUPE *Employment Rights on the Transfer of an Undertaking*, 2007, states that 'different arrangements apply' to those set out in reg 6, referring to the 'position[ing]' of the statutory procedure in TULRCA 1992 and the intention to make separate regulations: p 12 and note 7. It is unclear to which element of reg 6 the statement about 'different arrangements' refers. The guide has no legal status.

[254] Council Directive 2001/23/EC. In a 2001 Consultation Document the Government stated that to 'make explicit' that UK legislation was fully in line with this requirement it proposed to 'provide expressly' that the effect of declarations by the CAC would be 'appropriately preserved across a transfer': *Transfer of Undertakings (Protection of Employment) Regulations 1981: Government Proposals for Reform: Detailed Background Paper*, September 2001, para 105.

[255] See further para 3.19 *et seq* and 3.33 *et seq* for analysis of these terms.

[256] TULRCA 1992, Sch A1, paras 169B, 169 C, inserted by ERelA 2004, s 18.

[257] *Review of the Employment Relations Act 1999: Government Response to the Public Consultation*, 2003, para 2.108. The BERR (now BIS) guide to TUPE, above n 253, states that Regulations 'are to be made, in due course ... to ensure that declarations made by the CAC, and applications made to the CAC, are appropriately preserved': p 12, n 7.

[258] Defined as in TULRCA 1992, 178(1): see para 9.26 above.

with that union.[259] This applies without prejudice to the statutory presumption that collective agreements are not intended by the parties to be legally enforceable contracts. However the fact that collective agreements are generally unenforceable means that regulation 5 is of limited significance, although it may be relevant in contexts where regard is paid to the terms of collective agreements in determining the scope of individual employees' rights, such as whether it was reasonable for a union official or member to claim time off for union duties or activities. Extra-contractual disciplinary and redundancy procedures may also be relevant to unfair dismissal claims. In addition, the Code of Practice on Industrial Action Ballots and Notice to Employers refers to completion of agreed procedures prior to conducting an industrial action ballot.[260]

Where the terms of a specific collective agreement have been incorporated into an employee's contract of employment, those terms will remain enforceable against the transferee by virtue of regulation 4(1).[261] What of the situation where employees have a contractual entitlement to have their terms and conditions of employment determined by reference to the collective agreement from time to time negotiated between the transferor employer and a specific union or unions? In *Whent v T Cartledge Ltd*[262] the applicant employees had been employed until 1994 by the London Borough of Brent, and their contracts specified that their terms of employment would be in accordance with the agreement made by a specific National Joint Council ('NJC'). In 1994 the activities of the Borough which the applicants were employed to fulfil were taken over by a private contractor which, after the transfer, wrote to their union withdrawing recognition and stating that any collective agreements which may have been in force covering the transferred employees no longer had effect. The applicants sued for the benefit of new pay rates subsequently agreed by the NJC, and the EAT held that their contracts of employment continued to provide that terms were determined by reference to the NJC agreement and it was irrelevant that their employer was not a party to that agreement.

At the time of writing a preliminary ruling from the CJEU is awaited on whether the 'dynamic' approach adopted in *Whent* is permitted by the Acquired Rights Directive. The issue has arisen following the ECJ decision in *Werhof v Freeway Traffic Systems GMBH and Co KG*.[263] Here the Court was asked whether it was compatible with Article 3(1) of the Directive for the transferee of a business to be bound only by the collective agreement in force at the time of the transfer but not by subsequent collective agreements made by the transferor in a situation where the transferred employee's contract with the transferor referred to the collective agreement in force at the material time negotiated between specified parties. Article 3(1) states that the transferor's rights and obligations arising from a contract of employment or from an employment relationship existing on the date of the transfer shall, by reason of such transfer, be transferred to the transferee. The ECJ held that Article 3(1) did not preclude the transferee not being bound by subsequent collective

---

[259] TUPE 2006, reg 5(a). Reg 5(b) provides that any order made in respect of such a collective agreement, in its application in relation to the employee, shall, after the transfer, have effect as if the transferee were a party to the agreement'.

[260] See para 11.45 below.

[261] See further para 3.75 *et seq* above.

[262] [1997] IRLR 153. Cf *William West and Sons (Ilkeston) Ltd v Fairgieve and EXEL/BRS Ltd*, (2000) IRLB January 2000, Vol 632, p 15, EAT: on the proper construction of the contract of employment the name of the transferee had been substituted for that of the transferor; *Ackinclose v Gateshead Metropolitan Borough Council* [2005] IRLR 79, EAT: contract of employment made reference only to a specific agreement; successor agreement not incorporated. See also *Ralton v Havering College of Further Education* [2001] IRLR 738.

[263] Case C-499/04, [2006] IRLR 400.

agreements made by the transferor. This conclusion was based on two lines of reasoning. The first referred to the terms of Article 3(3) of the Directive, which provides that:

> Following the transfer, the transferee shall continue to observe the terms and conditions agreed in any collective agreement on the same terms applicable to the transferor under that agreement, until the date of termination or expiry of the collective agreement or the entry into force or application of another collective agreement.
>
> Member States may limit the period for observing such terms and conditions with the proviso that it shall not be less than one year. [264]

The Court noted that, under Article 3(3), the terms and conditions under the collective agreement are to continue to be observed only until the date of the agreement's termination or expiry, or the entry into force or application of another collective agreement. It concluded that the legislature did not intend that the transferee should be bound by collective agreements other than the one in force at the time of the transfer. '[T]he Directive was not intended to protect mere expectations to rights and, therefore, hypothetical advantages flowing from future changes to collective agreements.'[265] The Court also held that the minimum one-year period referred to in the second paragraph of Article 3(3) was 'subsidiary', being applicable only if none of the situations mentioned in the first paragraph – termination or expiry of the existing collective agreement etc – arose within one year of the transfer.[266] The second line of reasoning in *Werhof* was based on the employer's freedom of association under Article 11 of the ECHR, which the Court has previously recognised as a fundamental right in EU law.[267] The application of a 'dynamic' interpretation of the reference in the individual contract to the collective agreement concluded in a particular sector[268] 'would mean that future collective agreements apply to a transferee who is not party to a collective agreement and that his fundamental right not to join an association could be affected', a situation which could be avoided by the 'static' interpretation.[269] The Court stated that '[i]n those circumstances, the claimant cannot maintain that a clause contained in an individual contract of employment and referring to collective agreements concluded in a particular sector must necessarily be "dynamic" and refers, by application of Article 3(1) of the Directive, to collective agreements concluded after the date of the transfer of the undertaking.'[270]

In *Parkwood Leisure Ltd v Alemo-Herron*[271] former employees of the London Borough of Lewisham were transferred first into the employment of CCL Ltd and then into that of the respondent employers. The employees' contracts of employment with Lewisham stated that their terms and conditions of employment would be in accordance with collective agreements

---

[264] *Werhof* was based on the interpretation of Art 3 of the predecessor Directive 98/50, in which the provision relating to collective agreements was Art 3(2). Art 3(3) is the same in all material respects.

[265] Para 29.

[266] Para 30.

[267] See para 2.39 above.

[268] In para 17 of the Opinion of Advocate General Ruiz-Jarabo Colomer it is stated that it was agreed that the employment relationship in question would be governed by the framework collective agreement and the wage agreement in force at the material time for workers in a specific sector.

[269] Paras 32–35. See also the Opinion of Advocate General Ruiz-Jarabo Colomer, who explained in para 49 that 'if the new owner wished to participate in agreements with the unions, it would have to join the negotiating employers' federation, which would undoubtedly curtail his freedom of association'.

[270] Para 36.

[271] [2011] IRLR 696.

negotiated from time to time by the NJC for Local Government Services. The issue was the same as *Whent*; were the employees entitled to the benefit of pay increases negotiated by the NJC after they were transferred to the respondent employers? The Supreme Court had no doubt that if the issue had been purely one of domestic law then they would be so entitled; there was no objection in principle to parties including a term in their contract that employees' pay would be determined by a third party of which the employer was not a member and on which it was not represented. The issue was whether EU law precluded this 'dynamic' interpretation in the light of *Werhof*. The Court considered the answer to this to be unclear and therefore referred the issue to the CJEU.

As we indicate above, Article 3(3) requires that the transferee should observe the terms and conditions agreed in any collective agreement until that agreement has expired or been replaced, subject to the right of Member States to limit the period. Neither Article 3(3) (nor its predecessor provision) have been transposed into TUPE. Some terms of a collective agreement may be incorporated into individual contracts of employment, and may thus be preserved under regulation 4. Others, however, may not be appropriate for incorporation and (subject to the points we make above about other contexts in which they may be relevant) there is nothing to prevent the transferee departing from them.[272] In 1989 the European Commission gave notice to the UK government that it had failed to comply with its obligations under the Directive in a number of respects which we outline in para 9.31. Among these was the complaint that the legislation did not require a transferee to continue to observe the terms and conditions agreed in any collective agreement on the same terms applicable to the transferor. The Commission did not, in the event, proceed with this complaint. At the time of writing the Coalition Government has consulted on whether it would be helpful to have a provision in TUPE limiting the future observance of terms and conditions derived from collective agreements and is considering its response.[273] This, presumably, is aimed at terms incorporated into individual contracts and may have been prompted by the ECJ ruling in *Scattolon v Ministero dell'Istruzione, dell'Universita e della Ricerca*.[274] The employee was a school cleaner who had been transferred from employment by a local authority to employment by the Italian state. Her terms of employment with the local authority were governed by the collective agreement for local authority employees. From the date of transfer her employment was governed by the collective agreement applicable to schools and she was therefore subject to the terms and conditions applicable to state employees. Relying on its decision in *Werhof* that the second paragraph of Article 3(3) was subject to the first, the Court said that it was 'lawful for the transferee to apply, from the date of the transfer, the working conditions laid down by the collective agreement in force with … [it], including those concerning remuneration.'[275] However, in line with the Directive's aim of preventing transferred workers being placed in a less favourable position solely because of the transfer, implementation of this option could not 'have the aim or effect of imposing on those workers conditions which are, overall, less favourable than those applicable before the transfer.'[276] It is

---

[272] In the case of employers whose decisions are potentially subject to judicial review, it is conceivable that a public law remedy may be sought but the circumstances would probably need to be unusual and this is not a remedy of general application.

[273] *Call for Evidence on the effectiveness of TUPE 2006*, BIS, November 2011, p 8, question 11.

[274] Case C-108/10, [2011] IRLR 1020.

[275] Para 74.

[276] Para 76.

hard to reconcile the capacity to have regard to the overall package with the approach of the Court in *Daddy's Dance Hall*.[277] Given that the UK has not to date transposed Article 3(3) into TUPE, it is also an open question whether and, if so, how the principle in *Scattolon* could be applied in British law.

Finally in this context, regulation 5 of TUPE 2006 states that 'anything done under or in connection with' the collective agreement by or in relation to the transferor before the transfer shall, after the transfer, be deemed to have been done by or in relation to the transferee. The meaning of this provision (which appeared in the 1981 Regulations) is obscure. It has been suggested that it includes commitments or offers made by the transferor during negotiations which have not yet been formalised in an agreement; if so, in the light of the opening words of the Regulation ('[w]here at the time of a relevant transfer there exists a collective agreement ...'), it can cover only changes to an existing agreement.[278]

Contract compliance and collective bargaining

9.28   As we saw in chapter 7, it was an important feature of the policy of successive governments from early in the twentieth century until 1979 that the government should act as a model employer which set an example in its employment practices to the private sector, a strategy which served, in some respects, as a substitute for legislation.[279] As we explained this policy was partly promoted by the strategy of contract compliance, whereby government departments undertook, in furtherance of a succession of House of Commons Fair Wages Resolutions, to include in contracts with private sector employers a term that contractors should pay their workers the 'going rate' for the job. This was defined in the 1946 Resolution specifically by reference to collective agreements for the trade or industry in the district made by substantially representative organisations. Although not covered by the Resolution, local authorities and other public employers were encouraged by successive governments to follow suit and did so regardless of their political hue: a 1982 survey of local authorities in Britain showed that over 87% inserted a fair wages clause in their outside contracts.[280]

The advent of the Thatcher Conservative Government in 1979 heralded a very different concept of the model state employer. As we described in para 8.38, the government not only rescinded the Fair Wages Resolution in 1983, itself a radical break with tradition; it went further and took steps to prevent the operation of contract compliance policies. The 1982 legislation, as well as covering union membership, also rendered void in contracts for the supply of goods or services any term or condition which required a party to recognise a union for its workers or any class of worker or negotiate with or consult a union official.[281] In addition it created a statutory duty not to exclude a person from a list of approved suppliers, or to terminate or refuse to consider entering contracts with them, if one of the grounds was that such a requirement was unlikely to be met.[282] As in the case

---

[277]   Case 324/86 [1988] IRLR 315 at para 15; see para 3.76 above.

[278]   Younson, 1989: p 115.

[279]   For a general discussion of this policy, and subsequent developments in the area, see Fredman and Morris, 1989: ch 12.

[280]   Ingham and Thomson, 1982: table 5A.

[281]   See now TULRCA 1992, s 186.

[282]   TULRCA 1992, s 187.

of union membership, this duty is owed both to the potential contractor and to 'any other person who may be adversely affected by its contravention'.[283] Organising or threatening industrial action to induce a person to include a term requiring recognition, etc, or to take a decision in relation to a contract with reference to one of these factors, also has no immunity in tort.[284] However, unlike the union membership provision, which covers insistence both on membership and non-membership, no reciprocal ban exists on taking decisions relating to contracts on the ground that a contractor recognises, rather than refuses to recognise, a union.

This legislation did not prevent the operation of fair wages clauses or insistence that contractors complied with the terms of collective agreements provided that this was not expressly linked to union recognition, and the practices of local authorities, for example, appear to have continued unchanged after it was introduced, despite government exhortations to follow its own example and abandon them. Such arrangements were finally prohibited altogether by the Local Government Act 1988 which forbids local authorities and several other public bodies from operating contracts by reference to 'non-commercial matters',[285] which, *inter alia*, cover fair wages clauses. The Act enables any person who has suffered loss or damage due to a breach of this provision to sue for damages and potential and former contractors are specifically empowered to bring judicial review proceedings.[286] The latter persons also have the right to written reasons for the decision in relation to a particular contract on request.[287] The advent of a Labour Government in 1997 brought no material change to this area. The Local Government Act 1999 empowers the Secretary of State to provide by order in relation to local authorities and other 'best value' bodies that any matter should cease to be a 'non-commercial' matter.[288] At the time of writing three matters, including the terms and conditions of employment of workers, are no longer to be treated as 'non-commercial', but only so far as necessary or expedient to permit or facilitate compliance with the best value requirements of the Act or where there is a transfer of staff to which TUPE may apply.[289] The general prohibition on prescribing recognition or consultation remained untouched. Recent decisions of the ECJ suggest that a requirement by the state, and, probably, an employers' association, for a contractor from another EU Member State to observe the terms of a British collective agreement when posting workers to Britain would be contrary to Article 56 TFEU given that the UK has not, to date, implemented either of the mechanisms contained in Directive 96/71/EC on posted workers (see para 2.49 above) which permit collective agreements to be a source of mandatory rules.[290] This is because the ECJ has held that host states cannot require posting employers to comply with standards that go beyond the terms of that Directive, such as wage

---

[283] TULRCA 1992, s 187(3).
[284] TULRCA 1992, s 225.
[285] LGA 1988, s 17.
[286] LGA 1988, s 19(7).
[287] LGA 1988, s 20.
[288] LGA 1999, s 19. 'Best value' authorities are defined in s 1; see also s 2.
[289] The Local Government Best Value (Exclusion of Non-Commercial Considerations) Order 2001, 2001/909; see further para 2.6 above.
[290] Case C-341/05 *Laval un Partneri Ltd v Svenska Byggnadsarbetareförbundet* [2008] IRLR 160; Case C-346/06 *Rüffert v Land Niedersachsen* [2008] IRLR 467.

rates that exceed the minimum laid down by law.[291] Overseas contractors may, however, decide to adhere to standards laid down in collective agreements of their own accord.[292]

STATUTORY RIGHTS OF INFORMATION AND CONSULTATION

Overview

9.29   There are four distinct contexts in which all employers have a statutory duty to consult employee representatives: in relation to dismissals for redundancy; where there is a transfer of the undertaking; on health and safety matters;[293] and in specified areas relating to pensions. In addition, employers must consult on training matters if they recognise a union in accordance with the statutory procedure and certain other conditions are met.[294] Finally, at domestic level, undertakings employing at least 50 employees in the UK may be required to inform and consult representatives (or, in certain circumstances, employees themselves) on a wider range of matters. A further (limited) class of employers is subject to transnational consultation obligations; these are discussed separately in para 9.59 *et seq* below.

Collective bargaining and the current statutory forms of consultation are both based upon collective representation. However, there is a crucial difference between them; whereas, as we explained above, bargaining connotes joint regulation of a particular area, in the case of consultation the right to decide remains ultimately with the employer.[295] However, this does not mean that the consultation process is a mere formality; serious consequences may ensue if an employer fails to meet its obligations. Moreover, in legal terms 'consultation' may mean different things in different contexts; thus, in relation to redundancies, for example, the employer must undertake consultation 'with a view to reaching agreement', a requirement which takes it close to negotiation.

In Britain legislation relating to consultation is of relatively recent origin. Historically the concept was not unknown but it was a purely voluntary practice. As Davies and Freedland explain:

> There has always been in the UK during this century a commitment amongst some employers
> and trade unions to the notion of consultation, even if it has been overshadowed by the

---

[291] In addition to the provisions in Arts 3(1),(8), and (10) of Directive 96/71/EC for collective agreements to be a source of mandatory rules , Art 3(10) allows Member States to require adherence to terms and conditions of employment not specified in Art 3(1) in the case of 'public policy provisions'. However this concept is narrowly defined (see Joined Cases C-369/96 and 376/96 *Arblade* [1999] ECR 1-8453, para 30 and Case C-319/06 *Commission v Luxembourg*, judgment of 19 June 2008, [2009] IRLR 388) and only national authorities, and not the private parties to a collective agreement, can rely upon this exception: *Laval*, above, para 84.

[292] *Laval*, above, note 290, para 81. See generally *Report of an Inquiry into the Circumstances Surrounding the Lindsey Oil Refinery Dispute*, ACAS, 16 February 2009 for the implications of the present position in Britain. This report concerned the construction sector.

[293] In this area, unlike the other three, employers also have the option of consulting employees individually: see further para 9.46 below.

[294] If a method of collective bargaining has been specified by the CAC and the parties have not varied its content or legal effect.

[295] See further Terry, 2010: p 280 *et seq.*

development of collective bargaining. In the inter-war period certain progressive employers … developed systems of consultation with their employees, generally through structures in which trade unions were accorded no role, the employee representatives being elected by and from the whole body of workers. Such forms of consultation can act as much to keep trade unions at bay as to involve employees in determining matters affecting their working lives. In the Second World War and the immediate post-war period there was a great development of Joint Production Committees, a tangible expression of the commitment of both unions and employers to the war effort, which committees the trade unions backed and were involved in. That joint commitment was dissipated in the 1950s and, with the growth of plant-level structures for bargaining with employers through shop stewards, the machinery for consultation, the lesser form of participation, naturally underwent a demise.[296]

During the 1970s, joint consultative committees once again became more common, and in 1980 they were reported in around a third of workplaces with 25 or more employees.[297] In 2004, 14% of establishments with 10 or more employees had a workplace-level consultative committee, although a further 25% had a multi-issue committee at a higher level in the organisation.[298] Among workplaces that recognised unions, the proportion with a workplace committee was higher (29%); workplace committees were also more common in workplaces with 100 or more employees (54%).[299] In 2004 the issues most commonly discussed by workplace committees were work organisation, future plans, health and safety, training, employment issues and welfare services and facilities.[300] It is notable that these issues clearly exceed the scope of matters traditionally viewed as suitable for collective bargaining. This research preceded the entry into force of legislation which may require information and consultation of employees and, as such, provides a 'benchmark' for considering the impact of that legislation.[301]

9.30   Legal obligations in Britain in the area of information and consultation derive almost entirely from EU law. From the early 1970s worker representation and participation was a central feature of European Community social policy proposals and the European Commission drafted a range of legislative measures in this area[302] designed to influence practices both within Member States and at transnational level. For many years little of this prodigious output was translated into practice; successive drafts of the European company statute, requiring European Companies or Societas Europeae (SE) to allow employees to participate in the supervision and strategic development of the company;[303] the fifth company law Directive; and the 'Vredeling' Directive on procedures for informing and consulting employees in multinational and multi-establishment enterprises via local management all failed to gain acceptance, and the only measures enacted by the Community were those requiring the provision of information to, and consultation with, worker representatives in the contexts of redundancies, transfers of undertakings and health

---

[296] P Davies and M Freedland, 1984: pp 230–231. See also Dukes, 2008a.
[297] Millward *et al*, 2000: p 108. See also MacInnes, 1985. This figure dropped to 29% in 1990, a figure which remained unchanged in 1998: Millward *et al*, 2000: p 108.
[298] See generally Kersley *et al* 2006: pp 125–130.
[299] Kersley *et al* 2006: pp 126–127.
[300] Kersley *et al* 2006: p 129.
[301] Kersley *et al* 2006: p 313.
[302] See Hall, 1992; Cressey, 1993; Wedderburn, 1997; and Weiss, 2004 for a discussion of these initiatives.
[303] See Wedderburn, 1990: ch 5.

and safety.[304] It will raise little surprise that the UK Conservative government was obdurately opposed to all these abortive initiatives although, in fairness, it was probably not alone in this; the Vredeling Directive, for example, attracted strong opposition from multinational business.[305] The difficulties of making any progress in this area were further compounded by the diversity of national systems of employee representation. However the Commission had greater success when, in the late 1980s, it focused more specifically upon the transnational dimension of employee information and consultation. This strategy was reflected in the Community Charter of the Fundamental Social Rights of Workers, concluded in 1989, which, in stating that '[i]nformation, consultation and participation for workers must be developed along appropriate lines, taking account of the practices in force in the various Member States',[306] affirmed that this was to apply especially in companies with establishments in several Member States. The Action Programme which accompanied the Charter eventually bore fruit in the shape of the European Works Council Directive, passed under the Agreement on Social Policy (from which the UK initially opted-out),[307] whose preamble stressed that national legislation was frequently not oriented to the transnational nature of the entity which takes decisions and emphasised the need to ensure that workers are informed and consulted about decisions taken in other Member States. Following the UK opt-in to the Agreement on Social Policy in 1997, the Directive was extended to the UK, with an implementation date of December 1999.[308] The Directive was recast in 2009, with an implementation date of June 2011;[309] we discuss the current regulations in para 9.60 *et seq* below.

In December 2000 another important breakthrough for the Commission came when, thirty years after its first proposal, the Council of Ministers reached political agreement on a Regulation to establish a European Company Statute, allowing companies to form an SE which can operate under EU law throughout the EU, together with a related Directive concerning employee involvement in such companies.[310] UK legislation to implement this provision came into force in October 2004.[311] Finally, in March 2002, agreement was reached on a Directive establishing an EU-wide framework of minimum standards of information and consultation at national level in undertakings where 50 or more employees are employed covering, *inter alia*, the development of employment within the undertaking and decisions likely to lead to substantial changes in work

---

[304] The Merger Control Regulation 4064/89 (see Anderman, 1993) gave a limited right to recognised representatives of workforces affected by a merger to be heard by the Commission as part of the process of deciding whether or not to approve that merger. This, however, is a right to be heard by a public authority rather than an employer. Regulation 4064/89 was replaced by Regulation 139/2004; see Barnard, 2006: pp 740–742.

[305] P Davies, 1992: p 333.

[306] Art 17.

[307] Council Directive 94/45 of 22 September 1994 on the establishment of a European Works Council or a procedure in Community-scale undertakings and Community-scale groups of undertakings for the purposes of informing and consulting employees. See Gold and Hall, 1994 for the background to this Directive; see also Colaianni, 1996. The Directive was extended to cover the three other Member States of the European Economic Area in June 1995.

[308] See Barnard, 1997, for the procedure adopted in relation to the extension directive.

[309] European Parliament and Council Directive 2009/38/EC of 6 May 2009 on the establishment of a European Works Council or a procedure in Community-scale undertakings and Community-scale groups of undertakings for the purpose of informing and consulting employees.

[310] Subsequently Regulation 1435/2003 provided for the establishment of a European Co-operative Society (SCE) and Directive 2003/72/EC for the involvement of employees in an SCE. Directive 2005/56 provides for employee involvement in the case of cross-border mergers of limited liability companies. See para 9.65 for UK implementation of these provisions.

[311] EPLLCR 2004; see further para 9.65.

organisation or in contractual relations.[312] This proposal was initially vehemently resisted by the UK Government, which preferred any such arrangements to be adopted on a purely voluntary basis, but after other countries previously opposed to it had indicated their willingness to compromise, the UK reluctantly agreed to it, having secured a longer transition period for its full implementation.[313] Thus, although Member States in general were required to implement the Directive by 23 March 2005, a state in which there was, at the date of the Directive's entry into force, no 'general, permanent and statutory system of information and consultation of employees', nor such a system of employee representation at the workplace, was permitted to limit the application of national provisions to undertakings employing at least 150 employees until 23 March 2007, and those employing at least 100 employees until the following year.[314] We discuss in greater detail the requirements of the Directive, and the extent to which UK law may fall short of its requirements, in para 9.50 *et seq* below.

9.31   It remains to be seen whether the UK legislation resulting from the 2002 Directive on information and consultation will lead to infringement proceedings before the CJEU. An earlier version of the legislation relating to redundancies and transfers of undertakings was subject to such proceedings, and it was subsequently amended in a number of respects, with significant implications for patterns of collective representation in general. The Directive on Collective Redundancies[315] and the Acquired Rights Directive[316] require the provision of information to, and consultation with, the 'worker' or 'employee' representatives respectively provided for by the law or practice of the Member States. The redundancy procedure was initially enacted as part of the Labour government's 'Social Contract' legislation in 1975 which it was likely would, in any event, have contained provisions on this subject although their shape was clearly influenced by the Directive.[317] By contrast, the transfer provisions were introduced in 1981 by the Conservative government only after the Commission had begun non-implementation proceedings in the ECJ, and even then it gave effect to the Directive with overt reluctance.[318] In both cases, the duty to consult arose only where the employer recognised a trade union for the category of employees affected.

From an early stage commentators had questioned whether either of the UK provisions in their initial form met the requirements of the respective Directives and in 1992 the European Commission instigated infringement proceedings citing a number of deficiencies.[319] Most of these had been admitted by the UK Government by the time the matter came before the ECJ, and

---

[312] Directive 2002/14/EC.

[313] See Bercusson, 2002 for the background to the Directive; also useful is P Lorber, 2003.

[314] Directive 2002/14/EC, Art 10. Alternatively, such states could limit the application of the Directive by reference to the number employed at establishments, but the UK chose the option in the text.

[315] Council Directive 75/129 on the approximation of the laws of the Member States relating to collective redundancies. The Directive was amended in 1992 by Council Directive 92/56, and both Directives were consolidated in Council Directive 98/59/EC.

[316] Council Directive 77/187 on the approximation of the laws of the Member States relating to the safeguarding of employees' rights in the event of transfers of undertakings, businesses or parts of businesses. The Directive was amended by Council Directive 98/50/EC, and both Directives were consolidated in Council Directive 2001/23/EC.

[317] P Davies, 1992: p 328. For a more detailed discussion of the background to the Directive and to the 1975 Act see Freedland, 1976a.

[318] P Davies and M Freedland, 1993: p 577.

[319] Case C-382/92 *EC Commission v United Kingdom* [1994] IRLR 392 (transfers) and Case C-383/92 [1994] IRLR 412 (collective redundancies).

important amendments were introduced in TURERA 1993 to correct them. (It is arguable, however, that other deficiencies, which were not grounds of complaint in those proceedings, still remain; we address these below.) The major outstanding issue from the infringement proceedings was the lack of any provision in UK law for the designation of worker representatives where the employer failed to recognise a union. The Commission argued that, for the obligations in the Directives to be effective, Member States must take all appropriate measures to ensure that representatives were designated; in UK law designation could be prevented where the employer was not in agreement. For its part, the UK contended that the Directives were not intended to amend existing laws or practices concerning designation. While accepting this argument the Court affirmed, on the basis of its previous decisions, that national legislation which made it possible to impede protection unconditionally guaranteed to workers was contrary to EC law.[320] The Directives left to Member States only the task of determining the arrangements for designating representatives; they could not be deprived of full effect by failing to have any system of designation whatsoever.

As a result of this decision, the Conservative Government introduced the Collective Redundancies and Transfer of Undertakings (Protection of Employment) (Amendment) Regulations 1995,[321] which required employers to consult, at their choice, *either* a recognised trade union or elected representatives of any of the employees who may be dismissed. The Regulations also made other significant amendments to the legislation.[322] Most notably, they provided that the duty to consult representatives on proposed redundancies arose only where the employer was proposing to dismiss 20 or more employees at one establishment within a period of 90 days or less. Although this threshold accords with the Directive,[323] prior to this the UK provisions had been more favourable, requiring consultation where only one employee was affected.[324] It was estimated by the Government that this amendment would remove the statutory obligation to consult from some 96% of UK businesses.[325]

---

[320] See Case 61/81 *EC Commission v United Kingdom* [1982] IRLR 333. See P Davies and M Freedland, 2007: p 147 for the argument that this decision constituted a 'misreading' of the Directive.

[321] SI 1995/2587.

[322] For an overview of the Regulations, see Hall, 1996 and Wedderburn, 1997 and on their operation in practice see J Smith *et al*, 1999 and Hall and Edwards, 1999. Hall and Edwards report that hardly any employers which recognised trade unions took the 'non-union' option: pp 306–308. Cf Cully *et al*,1999: p 97.

[323] Council Directive 75/129, Art 1(1)(a). The alternative threshold under the Directive is that the number of redundancies is, over a period of 30 days, at least 10 in establishments employing more than 20 and fewer than 100 workers; at least 10% of the number of workers in establishments normally employing at least 100 but fewer than 300; or at least 30 workers in establishments employing 300 or more.

[324] In *R v Secretary of State for Trade and Industry, ex p Unison* [1996] IRLR 438 the Divisional Court rejected the argument that by effecting this amendment of TULRCA 1992, s 188(1) by secondary legislation under the ECA 1972, s 2(2)(b), the Secretary of State was acting *ultra vires*, holding that 'the obligation to consult a trade union in regard to one redundancy' was 'related to a Community obligation, and not distinct, separate, or divorced from it' (per Otton LJ at 443). The Court also rejected the argument that because statistical evidence showed that one-third of women were employed in workplaces with fewer than 20 employees as compared with one-quarter of men, the change constituted unlawful discrimination contrary to Art 119 of the EC Treaty (now Art 157 TFEU) and the Equal Treatment Directive 76/207 because more women than men worked in workplaces where 20 or more employees could not be made redundant. The Court appears to have accepted the Government's argument that the impact of the measure could not be inferred from an analysis based on establishment size; it was necessary to look at the number of redundancies proposed at an establishment. Cf *R v Secretary of State for Employment, ex p Seymour-Smith and Perez (No 2)* [2000] IRLR 263, where the House of Lords was prepared to find prima facie indirect discrimination on the facts when presented with statistical evidence that women disproportionately had less than two years' service; it did not require evidence as to the incidence of dismissals relative to length of service: see further para 3.50 above.

[325] DTI press notice, 5 October 1995.

Although the Employment Department claimed that the 1995 Regulations brought UK law into compliance with the Directives it is debatable whether was so.[326] Further amending Regulations were introduced in 1999, following a fresh complaint by the European Commission to the UK Government that the Directives had not been properly implemented, questioning in particular the procedures for designating employee representatives and the effectiveness of the sanctions if employers failed to meet their obligations. Major changes introduced in 1999 included more detailed regulation of the election of employee representatives; the requirement that, if the employer recognised an independent trade union, its representatives should be consulted (so removing the employer's option to consult employee representatives in such circumstances); and, in relation to transfers, increased compensation for employees if an employer failed to meet its obligations. However, the 20-employee threshold introduced in 1995 remained, despite earlier indications that the Government was inclined to remove it.[327] Its maintenance does not mean that consultation becomes a purely voluntary act where fewer employees are dismissed, however; where those individuals qualify to claim unfair dismissal, employers must continue to comply with general principles of procedural fairness. [328] Moreover, recognised trade unions may have a right to information about prospective redundancies under the disclosure of information provisions, discussed in para 9.22 *et seq*, where no such qualifying threshold applies.[329] Finally, information and consultation representatives (or, in some circumstances, employees themselves) may have the right to be informed and consulted under ICER 2004 about 'decisions likely to lead to substantial changes in work organisation or in contractual relations' where fewer than 20 employees are involved.[330]

It is strongly arguable that, even after the amendments to the legislation governing collective redundancies and transfers of undertakings, the consultation provisions continue to fall short of the requirements of the respective Directives in important respects. If this is correct, it is conceivable that the *Francovich* principle could be invoked by those affected, although this requires proof that the Member State manifestly and gravely disregarded the limits on its discretion.[331] Moreover, in this context it may be difficult to prove that quantifiable loss was caused by the failure to comply. There has been no ruling as yet by the CJEU on whether the relevant provisions have direct effect, although in proceedings relating to redundancy consultation the High Court has held that, because the Collective Redundancies Directive gives the Member States such a wide

---

[326]   A judicial review application in which it was argued, *inter alia*, that the arrangements for selecting employee representatives meant that employers could still impede the protection guaranteed to employees by the Directives was unsuccessful: *R v Secretary of State for Trade and Industry, ex p Unison* [1996] IRLR 438, QBD. See Skidmore, 1996b for a critique of this decision.

[327]   *Employees' Information and Consultation Rights on Transfers of Undertakings and Collective Redundancies*, Department of Trade and Industry, URN 97/988, February 1998, paras 37–40.

[328]   See further para 5.119 *et seq*. *King v Eaton Ltd* [1996] IRLR 199 usefully illustrates the relationship between individual and collective consultation. In the light of the current Regulations consultation with non-union representatives should suffice where no union is recognised. Note that in *King* it was emphasised that fair consultation required consultation 'when the proposals are still at a formative stage': see further the discussion in para 9.33 below. The ACAS Code of Practice on Disciplinary and Grievance Procedures 2009 does not apply to redundancy dismissals.

[329]   See, for example, the CAC *Annual Report* 1994, para 2.8.

[330]   ICER 2004, reg 20(1). Although the DTI (now BIS) Guidance states that this provision does not apply where 'a small number of employees' is to be made redundant, no lower limit is specified; the Guidance states that this will depend on the circumstances of the case: *The Information and Consultation [of] Employees Regulations 2004: DTI Guidance*, January 2006: p 52. See further para 9.54

[331]   Cases C-46/93 and C-48/93: *Brasserie du Pecheur SA v Federal Republic of Germany* and *R v Secretary of State for Transport, ex p Factortame Ltd* [1996] ECR I-1029.

discretion in relation to the method of designating worker representatives, it is not unconditional and sufficiently precise to be directly effective.[332] We consider the compatibility of the current Regulations with EU law, as well as the desirability of other amendments, in greater detail in the analysis of the specific requirements of the current legislation which follows.

The duty to consult on redundancies

(i) Situations in which there is a duty to consult

9.32   An employer which is proposing to dismiss as redundant 20 or more employees at one establishment within a period of 90 days or less has a duty to consult about the dismissals 'all the persons who are appropriate representatives of any of the employees who may be affected by the proposed dismissals or may be affected by measures taken in connection with those dismissals'.[333] The duty applies regardless of whether the employees are entitled to a statutory redundancy payment (so can apply where they lack the requisite qualifying period of service or have waived the right to a payment, for example).[334] However the provisions do not apply to employment under a contract for a fixed term of three months or less, or under a contract made in contemplation of the performance of a specific task which is not expected to last for more than three months, provided that the employee has not, in fact, been continuously employed for a period for more than three months.[335] This means that, as well as being excluded from the duty, such employees do not count towards the number of employees that triggers the obligation to consult. The Directive excludes collective redundancies effected under contracts of employment concluded for limited periods of time or for specific tasks except where such redundancies take place prior to the date of expiry or the completion of such contracts.[336] The British exemption is wider in excluding contracts for three months or less even where the redundancies take place prior to the date of expiry or completion, but the Labour Government took the view that this exclusion was objectively justified on the ground that the contracts in question would generally have terminated prior to the end of the consultation periods.[337] However the British legislation is also broader in its application than

---

[332]   *Griffin v South West Water Services Ltd* [1995] IRLR 15; cf Skidmore, 1995b. Note that this Directive (unlike the Acquired Rights Directive) does not apply to 'public administrative bodies'. The court in *Griffin* did not accept that such bodies were coincident with those subject to the concept of direct effect but clearly this exclusion would narrow the application of direct effect were it to apply.

[333]   TULRCA 1992, s 188(1).

[334]   Note, however, that Crown servants, the armed forces, the police, Parliamentary staff, and share fishermen are excluded from these provisions: TULRCA 1992, ss 273, 274, 277, 278, 280, 284. However the provisions for disclosure for collective bargaining purposes, which may be relevant in the context of redundancies, (see para 9.22 *et seq*), extend to Crown employment, although they apply only where an independent union is recognised for the description of workers in question: see CAC *Annual Reports* for 1993 (paras 2.3–2.5), 1994 (para 2.8), 1996 (para 2.9), and 1997 (para 2.13) and note the restriction on remedy in note 232 above. See para 9.51 below for the application of ICER 2004 to public bodies. Note also TULRCA 1992, s 198, which enables the Secretary of State to modify or exclude the provisions by order on the application of all parties to a collective agreement provided specified conditions are met. At the time of writing no such orders have been made.

[335]   TULRCA 1992, s 282(1).

[336]   Council Directive 98/59/EC, Art 1(2)(a).

[337]   *Government Response to the Final Consultation on the Draft Fixed Term Employees' (Prevention of Less Favourable Treatment) Regulations 2002.*

the Directive in covering the termination of limited-term contracts of a longer duration than three months by virtue of the limiting event.[338]

In the context of the duty to consult, 'redundancy' goes beyond the definition applicable to statutory redundancy payments, extending to dismissal 'for a reason not related to the individual concerned or for a number of reasons all of which are not so related.'[339] It thus applies to dismissals arising from reorganisation or restructuring of a business as well as those arising from closure or slimming down the workforce, for example. Thus, if an employer dismisses employees and offers re-engagement on different terms and conditions it must comply with the duty to consult.[340] This extended definition was introduced in 1993 to comply with the perceived requirements of the Directive. However the definition of 'dismissal' in TULRCA 1992 means that UK law may still be unduly restrictive. In *EC Commission v Portuguese Republic* the ECJ held that the concept of 'redundancy' must' be given a uniform interpretation for the purposes of the Directive', and:

> ... has to be interpreted as including any termination of contract of employment not sought by the worker, and therefore without his consent. It is not necessary that the underlying reason should reflect the will of the employer.[341]

This interpretation was generally understood as bringing within the Directive 'involuntary' redundancies, such as those resulting from termination by operation of law; fire or other *force majeure*; or the death of the employer.[342] Such eventualities are treated as termination by the employer for the purposes of claiming individual statutory redundancy payments,[343] but under TULRCA 1992 they are not; here 'dismissal' 'unless the context otherwise requires' is to be construed in accordance with Part X of ERA 1996.[344] In *Rodriguez-Mayor v Herencia yacente de Rafael de las Heras Davila* the ECJ qualified its decision in *EC Commission v Portuguese Republic* by holding that termination following the death of an employer did not fall within the Directive. The Court held that the language of the Directive presupposed the existence 'both of an employer and of an act on his part' and of a legal person on whom obligations could be imposed.[345] As Kilpatrick notes, this approach leaves unclear the position of other circumstances at issue in

---

[338] 'Dismiss' is defined by reference to Part X of ERA 1996: TULRCA 1992, s 298. In *University of Stirling v UCU* [2012] IRLR 266 the EAT held that the employee's agreement at the outset that their employment would be finite amounted to a reason related to the individual concerned. This decision effectively negates the inclusion of limited-term contracts and it is open to question whether it is correct.

[339] TULRCA 1992, s 195. Cf ERA 1996, s 139(1), discussed at para 5155 *et seq*. See *University of Stirling v UCU* [2012] IRLR 266, above.

[340] See *GMB v Man Truck and Bus Ltd* [2000] IRLR 636; *Hardy v Tourism South East* [2005] IRLR 242 (applying *Hogg v Dover College* [1990] ICR 39 and *Alcan Extrusions v Yates* [1996] IRLR 327 in this context).

[341] Case C-55/02 [2004] ECR I-9387, paras 44, 50.

[342] The ECJ countered the argument that the full application of the Directive may be impossible in the case of 'involuntary' redundancies by pointing out that the purpose of consultation is not only to avoid redundancies but also to mitigate their consequences: paras 57–60.

[343] ERA 1996, s 136(5); see further para 5.163 above. Redundancies resulting from liquidation of the employer, which are a further example of 'involuntary' redundancies, may, depending on the circumstances, be classified as wrongful dismissal but the position is complex. See also note 345 below.

[344] TULRCA 1992, s 298. The definition in Part X is in ERA 1996, s 95.

[345] Case C-323/08 [2009] ECR I-11621.

Portuguese Republic, such as fire or other *force majeure*, where the employer is also unable to make a decision to terminate before the event triggering termination occurs.[346]

In relation to the collective redundancies procedures, as under ERA 1996, there may be a need to determine whether a contract is terminated by mutual consent or is, in reality, a dismissal; employees who have volunteered to be dismissed as part of a redundancy exercise are not, by virtue of being volunteers, excluded from the consultation requirements.[347]

A potential difficulty with the definition of redundancy in this context is that it requires 'all' the reasons for dismissal not to relate to the individual concerned. Taken literally, this could narrow the application of the duty considerably, given that selection for redundancy, in the sense used in relation to individual payments, is usually based upon factors relating to the individual such as performance, attendance or, at the very least, length of service. Such an interpretation would not accord with the intention of the government department that introduced the legislation,[348] and would be an appropriate occasion for recourse to the less ambiguous wording of the Directive ('dismissals ... for one or more reasons not related to the individual workers concerned') which the legislation is designed to implement.[349] There is a statutory presumption that a dismissal is for 'redundancy' unless the contrary is proved.[350]

In determining how many employees an employer is proposing to dismiss, no account is to be taken of any employees in respect of whom it has already begun consulting.[351] As Harvey points out, this can lead to apparently odd results:

> Suppose an employer proposes 30 redundancies. Obviously he has to consult about all 30. On the other hand, if he proposes 20 dismissals, begins consultations, and then decides that a further ten dismissals are necessary, there is no duty to consult ... about those additional ten; the original 20 are discounted. Conversely if he initially proposes ten redundancies (too few to attract the duty to consult) and subsequently adds 20 (within 90 days) then there is once more a duty to consult about all 30; the original ten are *not* discounted .[352]

Clearly employers may be tempted to try to avoid their statutory obligation by dividing a large group of redundancies into several successive small groups (although they would need to be aware of the implications of such a course of action as regards unfair dismissal claims by individuals).[353]

---

[346] Kilpatrick, 2010: p 298. In C-235/10 *Claes v Landsbank Luxembourg (in liquidation)* the ECJ held that Directive 98/59 EC covered collective redundancies arising from the termination of an establishment's activities as a result of a judicial decision and distinguished this from the situation at issue in *Rodriguez-Mayor*. Until the legal personality of the employer ceased to exist the obligations under the Directive must be carried out by the management, where it remained in place, or by the liquidator.

[347] *Optare Group Ltd v TGWU* [2007] IRLR 931; see also *Scotch Premier Meat Ltd v Burns* [2000] IRLR 639.

[348] At that time the Employment Department, which in its summary of TURERA (press notice 2 July 1993, p 19) stated that the definition 'is now widened'.

[349] Council Directive 98/59, Art 1(1)(a); on the principle of indirect effect see further Case C-14/83 *Von Colson and Kamann v Land Nordrhein-Westfalen* [1984] ECR 1891; Case C-106/89 *Marleasing SA v La Comercial Internacional de Alimentación SA* [1990] ECR I-4135; *Pickstone v Freemans plc* [1988] IRLR 357; *Litster v Forth Dry Dock and Engineering Co Ltd* [1989] IRLR 161. See also *University of Stirling v UCU* [2012] IRLR 266.

[350] TULRCA 1992, s 195(2).

[351] TULRCA 1992, s 188(3).

[352] Harvey, 1972 (as updated), Division E, para 2551.

[353] See further para 5.85 *et seq*.

In situations where this may have happened, employment tribunals can be expected to scrutinise the evidence carefully to ensure that the employer has behaved honestly.[354]

In calculating the number of employees the employer is proposing to dismiss, account is taken only of those working at one 'establishment'.[355] Oddly, given its importance, there is no definition of 'establishment', a concept which exists in a variety of statutory contexts, in TULRCA 1992. Prior to a 1995 ECJ decision the courts had taken a fairly wide view of its meaning; although there was no comprehensive test, '[a]mong the relevant factors in determining the scope of an establishment may be the geographical separation of the premises from other premises owned by the employer, the separation of financial accounting, the separation of services, and the separation of profits'.[356] In addition, an establishment was said to require some degree of permanence or stability.[357] Thus it was possible that a number of different sites could together constitute an 'establishment': for example 14 building sites administered from a company's headquarters were not treated as separate establishments,[358] nor were 28 retail shops, a factory and a bakery.[359] In 1995, however, the ECJ ruled that for the purposes of the Directive the term 'establishment' was a term of Community law which should:

> ... be interpreted as designating, depending on the circumstances, the unit to which the workers made redundant are assigned to carry out their duties. It is not essential in order for there to be an 'establishment' for the unit in question to be endowed with a management which can independently effect collective redundancies.[360]

In 2007 the ECJ further stated that an establishment:

> ... may consist of a distinct entity, having a certain degree of permanence and stability, which is assigned to perform one or more given tasks and which has a workforce, technical means and a certain organisational structure allowing for the accomplishment of those tasks... [T]he entity in question need not have any legal autonomy, nor need it have economic, financial, administrative or technological autonomy, in order to be regarded as an 'establishment'. [361]

The Court also affirmed that an 'establishment' need not be geographically separated from the other units and facilities of the undertaking.[362] In the context in which these decisions were given,

---

[354] Harvey, 1972 (as updated): Division E, para 2553, citing the tribunal decision in *TGWU v Nationwide Haulage Ltd* [1978] IRLR 143 as an example.

[355] In *MSF v Refuge Assurance plc* [2002] IRLR 324, 331 the EAT suggested that this limitation was not justified by Art 1(a)(ii) of Directive 98/59/EC.

[356] Hepple, 1981b: p 10. See generally *Barratt Developments (Bradford) Ltd v UCATT* [1978] ICR 319; *Bakers' Union v Clarks of Hove Ltd* [1977] IRLR 167 accepted on this point by the EAT [1977] IRLR 264 and CA [1978] IRLR 366.

[357] *May and Robertson v Ministry of Labour* (1967) 2 ITR 607.

[358] *Barratt Developments (Bradford) Ltd v UCATT* [1978] ICR 319; see also *Barley v Amey Roadstone Corpn Ltd (No 2)* [1978] ICR 190.

[359] *Bakers' Union v Clarks of Hove Ltd*; see note 356 above. See also *Mills and Allen Ltd v Bulwich* (2000) IRLB 648, 13.

[360] Case C-449/93 *Rockfon A/S v Specialarbejderforbundet i Danmark, acting for Nielsen* [1996] IRLR 168, 175, applied in *Mills and Allen Ltd v Bulwich* (2000) IRLB 648, 13; *MSF v Refuge Assurance plc* [2002] IRLR 324.

[361] *Athinaiki Chartopoiia AE v Panagiotidis* Case C-270/05 [2007] IRLR 284, paras 27 and 28.

[362] Para 29.

the ECJ expressly intended to maximise the application of the duty to consult.[363] However, when applied in the British context this interpretation may considerably reduce the occasions when the 20-employee threshold is crossed.[364] The scope of protection is further narrowed by the fact that the duty to consult is confined to a single employer; thus even if associated employers operate from the same establishment each set of redundancies must be considered separately.[365]

(ii) When consultation must begin

9.33 The duty to consult arises as soon as the employer is 'proposing' to dismiss for redundancy.[366] As we stated in para 9.32 above, the term 'dismiss' is to be construed in accordance with Part X of ERA 1996,[367] a provision which at one stage led the EAT to conclude that in the case of dismissal with notice, dismissal takes place on the expiry of that notice.[368] However in the context of collective redundancies subsequent EAT decisions have made clear that the legislation must now be interpreted in the light of the landmark European Court of Justice decision in *Junk v Kuhnel*.[369] Here the ECJ affirmed that 'the event constituting redundancy consists in the declaration by an employer of *his intention* to terminate the contract of employment', not the actual cessation of the employment relationship on the expiry of the period of notice.[370] Such an interpretation was confirmed by the purpose of the Directive, which is 'to avoid terminations of contracts of employment or to reduce the number of such terminations. The achievement of that purpose would be jeopardised if the consultation of workers' representatives were to be subsequent to the employer's decision'.[371] In addition the ECJ decided that a contract of employment could be terminated only after *the conclusion* of the consultation procedure.

> The effectiveness of ... an obligation [to negotiate] would be compromised if an employer was entitled to terminate contracts of employment during the course of the procedure or even at the beginning thereof. It would be significantly more difficult for workers' representatives to

---

[363] Both cases concerned Art 1(1)(a) of the Directive, which provides an alternative 'threshold' formulation for the obligation to consult which comes into play where, *inter alia*, redundancies affect at least 10% of workers in establishments employing at least 100 but fewer than 300 workers. According to this formulation, it benefits employees if 'establishment' is defined as extensively as possible.

[364] See, for example, *MSF v Refuge Assurance plc* [2002] IRLR 324. *Quaere* whether the words 'depending on the circumstances' in *Rockfon*, note 360, above, could be relied upon to justify a different approach where the effect is otherwise to narrow the application of the duty.

[365] *E Green & Son (Castings) Ltd; E Green & Son Ltd; E Green & Son (Site Services) Ltd v ASTMS* [1984] IRLR 135. *Quaere* whether the courts would ever 'lift the corporate veil' in this situation. Case law from the industrial action context suggests not (*Dimbleby and Sons Ltd v NUJ* [1984] IRLR 161) but cf the decision of the CAC in *GPMU v Derry Print Ltd* [2002] IRLR 380 in the context of the statutory recognition procedure.

[366] Note that there is no requirement for the individual(s) making the proposal to have the power to carry it out: *Dewhirst Group v GMB* [2003] All ER (D) 175 (Dec); see also *Leicestershire County Council v UNISON* [2005] IRLR 920, [28]–[30].

[367] TULRCA 1992, s 298; see ERA 1996, s 95.

[368] *Middlesbrough Borough Council v TGWU* [2002] IRLR 332, [38]–[44], disapproving the dictum of Philips J in *NUT v Avon County Council* [1978] ICR 626. See para 5.xx et seq.

[369] Case C-188/03 [2005] IRLR 310.

[370] Paras 39, 36.

[371] Para 38.

achieve the withdrawal of a decision that has been taken than to secure the abandonment of a decision that is being contemplated.[372]

Since *Junk*, the EAT has said that 'proposing to dismiss' should be construed as 'proposing to give notice of dismissal'[373] and confirmed that consultation should be completed before notices of dismissal are given to the workforce.[374]

The precise point at which the duty to consult first arises is still a contentious issue. Under TULRCA 1992, the duty to consult arises when the employer is 'proposing' to dismiss. By contrast, Art 2(1) of the Directive requires consultations to commence where an employer is 'contemplating' redundancies.[375] The British courts have held that 'proposing' goes beyond the mere contemplation of a possible event or 'the diagnosis of a problem and appreciation that at least one way of dealing with it would be by declaring redundancies';[376] rather, it involves laying before others 'something which one offers to do or wishes to be done'.[377] In *R v British Coal Corpn, ex p Vardy*[378] Glidewell LJ highlighted the implications of the difference in wording between TULRCA 1992 and the Directive, pointing out that:

> ... [t]he verb 'proposes' in its ordinary usage relates to a state of mind which is much more certain and further along the decision-making process than the verb 'contemplate'; in other words, the Directive envisages consultation at an early stage when the employer is first envisaging the possibility that he may have to make employees redundant.

The balance of opinion in British courts has been that 'contemplation' is referring to an earlier stage in the decision-making process than 'proposing',[379] and that domestic legislation cannot be made to accord with the Directive 'without distortion'.[380] However, in *UK Coal Mining Ltd v NUM (Northumberland) Ltd* the EAT held that the term 'proposed', when contrasted with 'contemplated', did not prevent the consultation obligations extending to consultation over closures leading to redundancies:

> In our judgment, in a closure context where it is recognised that dismissals will inevitably, or almost inevitably, result from the closure, dismissals are proposed at the point when the closure is proposed. The difference between proposed and contemplated will still impact on

---

[372] Para 44. The Directive imposes an obligation to consult 'with a view to reaching an agreement'. The ECJ, somewhat controversially, characterised this as 'an obligation to negotiate': para 43. This point was not directly at issue in the case.

[373] *Leicestershire County Council v Unison* [2005] IRLR 920, at [35].

[374] *UK Coal Mining Ltd v NUM (Northumberland Area)* [2008] IRLR 4, at [39].

[375] Directive 98/59, re-enacting Art 2(1) of Directive 75/129. Note that, for the purposes of the Directive, in the case of 'involuntary' redundancies the employer may be deemed to contemplate them after the event: see note 342 above.

[376] *Hough v Leyland DAF Ltd* [1991] IRLR 194, 198.

[377] *MSF v Refuge Assurance plc* [2002] IRLR 324 at [44] (Lindsay P).

[378] [1993] IRLR 104, 116; see also *MSF v Refuge Assurance Ltd* [2002] IRLR 324 at [42] (Lindsay P).

[379] *R v British Coal Corpn, ex p Vardy* [1993] IRLR 104, 116; see also *MSF v Refuge Assurance Ltd* [2002] IRLR 324, [42] (Lindsay P); cf *Griffin v South West Water Services Ltd* [1995] IRLR 15, 23 (Blackburn J).

[380] *MSF v Refuge Assurance Ltd* [2002] IRLR 324, at [42] (Lindsay P); *Scotch Premier Meat Ltd v Burns* [2000] IRLR 639 (*obiter*). Cf *UK Coal Mining v NUM (Northumberland Area)* [2008] IRLR 4 at [85] where the EAT expressed 'some reservations' about this conclusion.

the point at which the duty to consult arises - it will not be when the closure is mooted as a possibility but only when it is fixed as a clear, albeit provisional, intention.[381]

In *Akavan Erityisalojen Keskusliitto AEK ry v Fujitsu Siemens Computers Oy* the ECJ was asked what was meant by the term 'contemplating' in the Directive.[382] The ECJ said it was important that the duty was not triggered prematurely, accepting the UK Government's observation that this could lead to results contrary to the purpose of the Directive, such as restricting the flexibility available to undertakings undergoing restructuring and causing unnecessary concern to workers. 'Where a decision deemed likely to lead to collective redundancies is merely contemplated and where, accordingly, such collective redundancies are only a probability and the relevant factors for the consultations are not known' the objectives of the Directive could not be achieved.[383] Equally, however, beginning consultation only when a strategic or commercial decision which made collective redundancies necessary had already been taken would be too late as such consultations could not usefully involve any examination of alternatives to redundancy. The ECJ held that the consultation procedure must be started by the employer once a strategic or commercial decision compelling it to contemplate or plan for collective redundancies had been taken.[384] However confusingly, it also stated, in addressing another question, that 'a decision by [a] ... parent company which has the direct effect of compelling one of its subsidiaries to terminate the contracts of employees affected by the collective redundancies can be taken only on the conclusion of the consultation procedure within that subsidiary ....'[385]

In *USA v Nolan*[386] the employer submitted that *Akavan* was authority for a narrower interpretation of the Directive than that accorded to it by *Vardy* and *UK Coal*. The employer argued that the result of *Akavan* was that the consultation obligation was not triggered by a proposed business decision to effect the closure of a plant; rather it arose only at the later stage when the business decision had been made and the intention to make the employees redundant had been formed. The Court of Appeal held that the ECJ in *Akavan* had not given a clear answer to the question whether the consultation obligation arises (i) when the employer is proposing, but has not yet made, a strategic business or operational decision that will foreseeably or inevitably lead to collective redundancies or (ii) only when that decision has actually been made and the employer is then proposing consequential redundancies; it therefore referred these questions to the CJEU.[387] The Court of Appeal said that TULRCA 1992 was not purporting to impose a wider obligation to consult than that contained in the Directive and that *UK Coal* was merely applying the supposed meaning of the Directive so that if option (ii) above were correct, *UK Coal* would not have been correctly decided.

---

[381] [2008] IRLR 4 at [86].

[382] Case C-44/08, [2009] IRLR 944, ECJ.

[383] Para 46.

[384] See paras 45-49.

[385] Para 71.

[386] [2011] IRLR 40.

[387] The court made this reference despite the employer's express desire that no reference should be made on the basis that it was important both to the disposition of the case and to industrial relations practice generally. In March 2012 the Advocate General opined that neither of the Court of Appeal's options was correct, rather the obligation was triggered when a strategic or 'commercial decision that compels it to contemplate or plan for collective redundancies is made by a body or entity that controls the employers', Case C-583/10, para 53.

Regardless of the outcome of *USA v Nolan*, the principles of *Junk v Kuhnel* provide an incentive for employers to commence consultations at an early stage.[388] This will also be the case where dismissals arise in the context of reorganisation or restructuring, although this may work in opposition to the preferable course of attempting if possible to secure changes by agreement, with dismissals and re-employment only as a fall-back in the event that negotiations fail. However it may be difficult to determine when the duty starts if an employer, rather than dismissing, simply imposes changes to the contract and employees resign in response: constructive dismissal also constitutes 'dismissal' in this context.[389] Although, here, the employer may not have 'proposed' the dismissals it will have acted in a way which risks provoking them and thus, again, could be said at the least to have them within its contemplation.[390]

Once the employer is 'proposing to dismiss', consultation with 'appropriate representatives' must begin 'in good time'[391] and in any event at least 90 days before the first dismissal takes effect where the employer plans to dismiss 100 or more employees at one establishment within a period of 90 days or less; otherwise at least 30 days before the first dismissal takes effect.[392] The fact that these periods are calculated back from the date when the first dismissal 'takes effect' may appear problematic in that this date may not be known at the time when the dismissals are initially proposed and, indeed, it is one of the purposes of the consultation procedures to avoid dismissals. The better view is that this means the requisite period before the date on which the first dismissal would take effect if the employer's proposals were implemented.[393] Where employees are entitled to notice periods which exceed 30 or 90 days, employers may be tempted to issue notices before commencing consultation, but this would contravene the principles laid down in *Junk v Kuhnel*, which requires completion of the consultation process prior to issuing notices of dismissal. Once the consultation process has been completed, however, there is no requirement for the employer to wait until the end of the statutory minimum period before issuing dismissal notices in accordance with what has been agreed.

---

[388] Note also the rights of recognised independent trade unions under the disclosure of information provisions, discussed in para 9.22 *et seq*, to information at an early stage; the CAC has held that union may have a right to information relating to the decision to reduce a level of activity, close a site or restructure an organisation: CAC *Annual Report* 1993, paras 2.3–2.5; CAC *Annual Reports* for 1994, para 2.8 and 1996, para 2.9. See also ICER 2004, Reg 20(1), discussed in para 9.54 below.

[389] TULRCA 1992, s 298; see also *Pearl Assurance plc v MSF* 26.2.97, EAT 1162/96, IRLB 572.

[390] Constructive dismissal seems not to be covered by Directive 98/59: Art 1(1) refers to terminations of an employment contract which occur 'on the employer's initiative', but it is questionable whether this is wide enough to extend to such dismissals. Case C-284/83 *Dansk Metalarbejderforbund and Specialarbejder-forbundet i Danmark v H Nielsen & Son Maskinfabrik A/S (in liquidation)* [1985] ECR 553, in which the ECJ held that termination by workers of their contracts following an announcement by the employer that he was suspending payment of his debts did not constitute dismissal, was decided prior to the amendment of the Directive in 1992.

[391] Until the 1995 Regulations, this read 'at the earliest opportunity'. The new wording reflects Art 2(1) of the Directive. What constitutes 'in good time' may depend on all the circumstances: see *Amicus v Nissan Motor Manufacturing (UK) Ltd* UKEAT/184/05, EAT, [11].

[392] TULRCA 1992, s 188(1A). Although these periods fix the start, not the end, of consultation, s 188 does not provide an 'unlimited shelf-life' and it may be necessary to decide, where the process is protracted, whether a new round is required: *Vauxhall Motors Ltd v TGWU* [2006] IRLR 674 (consultation process lasting 22 months 'continued seamlessly'). At the time of writing the Coalition Government is considering its response to a call for evidence on the advantages and disadvantages of the 90-day time limit, which is not specified in the Directive: *Collective Redundancy Consultation Rules: Call for Evidence* , BIS, November 2011, paras 2.1-2.6.

[393] *E Green & Son (Castings) Ltd; E Green & Son Ltd; E Green & Son (Site Services) Ltd v ASTMS* [1984] IRLR 135; *TGWU v RA Lister & Co Ltd* (1986) IRLIB, 21 May 1989, p 11.

In circumstances where employee representatives need to be elected prior to the consultation process, it is sufficient for employers to comply with the statutory requirements as soon as reasonably practicable after the election provided that they have invited any of the affected employees to elect employee representatives long enough before consultation is required to begin to allow for an election to take place.[394] It is suggested in the BIS guidance on redundancy consultation that employers should also allow time for representatives to undertake appropriate training if necessary,[395] As we state in para 9.36, representatives have the right to be permitted by the employer to take reasonable time off for training but no statutory right to training itself, although training is strongly recommended by ACAS.

(iii) The persons who must be consulted

9.34   The employer must consult all 'appropriate representatives' of any of the employees who may be *affected* by the proposed dismissals or by measures taken in connection with those dismissals.[396] Before the 1999 amendments, the duty was confined to consultation with representatives of the employees whom it was proposed to dismiss. This wider formulation, which echoes the duty to consult in the event of a transfer of the undertaking,[397] would seem to cover all those whose terms and conditions of employment or working conditions may be affected by the proposed dismissals, which could mean much, if not all, of the workforce. The change makes it easier to find employees to stand for election as employee representatives, and they may be less demoralised than those representing only those whose jobs are at risk. However, it may not always benefit those whom it is proposed to dismiss; representatives who are answerable to a broader, and possibly much more numerous, constituency may be less willing to fight hard for the interests of the target group for redundancy if, in return, they are given assurances regarding the remainder of the workforce.

There are three possible sources from which 'appropriate representatives' may be drawn. First, if the employees are of a description in respect of which an independent trade union is recognised by the employer, the employer must consult representatives of that union, irrespective of whether the affected employees are union members.[398] Where more than one union is recognised for a particular description of employees, it follows from the obligation to consult *all* the appropriate representatives that all such unions must be consulted about the dismissals of all employees in that group.[399] If there is no independent recognised union the employer must consult 'employee representatives'. It must also do this in respect of any employees who lie outside the scope of

---

[394] TULRCA 1992, s 188(7A).

[395] *Redundancy consultation and notification: guidance* URN No 06/1965Y.

[396] TULRCA 1992, s 188(1).

[397] See para 9.43. It is not clear that this amendment was required by the Directive; whereas Art 6 of the Acquired Rights Directive specifies consultation of employees affected by a transfer, the Collective Redundancies Directive merely requires an employer who is contemplating collective redundancies to begin consultation with the workers' representatives: Art 2(1).

[398] TULRCA 1992, s 188(1B)(a). 'Representatives of a trade union' in this context means 'officials or other persons authorised by the trade union to carry on collective bargaining with the employer'. See TULRCA 1992, s 119 for the definition of 'official' and s 178(1), (2) for the definition of collective bargaining.

[399] This view, which seems clear from the wording of the legislation, was confirmed by the Northern Ireland Court of Appeal in *Governing Body of the Northern Ireland Hotel and Catering College and North Eastern Education and Library Board v NATFHE* [1995] IRLR 83.

recognition; it cannot choose to consult union representatives in respect of such a group. In such cases, the employer may choose either to consult persons elected specifically for the purpose of the consultation exercise in question or persons appointed or elected by the affected employees for another purpose who (having regard to the purposes for and the method by which they were appointed or elected) have authority from those employees to receive information and to be consulted about the proposed dismissals on their behalf.[400] In either situation such representatives must be employed by the employer when they are elected or appointed,[401] although not necessarily thereafter, so excluding external professional advisers. No guidance is given about a minimum (or maximum) number of representatives to be consulted, but the use of the plural in the legislation strongly suggests that there must be more than one.

9.35   Where an employer chooses to consult specifically elected representatives, it must invite affected employees to hold an election.[402] Candidates for election must themselves be affected employees, and no affected employee may be 'unreasonably excluded' from standing.[403] It is for the employer to determine the number of representatives, so that they are sufficient to represent the interests of all affected employees having regard to their number and classes.[404] The employer may also decide if employees should be represented by representatives of all affected employees or of particular classes; in this context no criteria are prescribed to inform the employer's choice and, as under the earlier provisions, 'it would be open to employers to determine numbers of representatives ... [and] ... constituencies in ways which they thought might produce a desirable outcome'.[405] If the reference to 'sufficient' representatives is taken to impose a purely numerical requirement, it is conceivable that where both managerial staff and those below them are 'affected employees', representatives may be elected by the workforce as a whole who are derived from the managerial group. The more appropriate view, however, where both managerial and non-managerial groups are affected, is that 'anyone holding a significant managerial role is not properly independent from management',[406] and so would could not sufficiently represent the interests of other employees, even if this is not expressly stipulated in the legislation. The employer must, prior to the election, prescribe the employee representatives' term of office, ensuring that it is of sufficient length to enable the consultative process to be completed.[407] All affected employees must be entitled to vote in the election, which must be conducted so as to secure that, so far as is reasonably practicable, those voting do so in secret and the votes are accurately counted.[408] Although, unlike elections to union office, there is no requirement that the ballot be conducted by the marking of

---

[400] TULRCA 1992, s 188(1B)(b). In Case C-382/92 *EC Commission v United Kingdom* [1994] IRLR 392 (transfers) and Case C-383/92 [1994] IRLR 412 (collective redundancies) the Advocate-General considered that the *ad hoc* designation of worker representatives would meet the requirements of the Directive. The ECJ was silent on the issue.

[401] TULRCA 1992, s 196(1).

[402] This is not directly stated in the legislation but is implicit from s 188(7A): see *Howard v Millrise Ltd t/a Colourflow (in liquidation)* [2005] IRLR 84 (on the equivalent provision in TUPE 1981, now TUPE 2006), applied *Hickling v Marshall* UKEAT/0217/10; see also *R v Secretary of State for Trade and Industry, ex p Unison* [1996] IRLR 438.

[403] TULRCA 1992, s 188A(1)(e) and (f). The decisions of the Certification Officer on 'unreasonable' exclusion in relation to standing for union office, although of no precedent value, may be a useful source of guidance: see para 10.15.

[404] TULRCA 1992, s 188A(1)(b).

[405] *Consultation about Collective Redundancies and Business Transfers: TUC Response to Legislative Proposals*, para 12.

[406] Hall and Edwards, 1999: p 310.

[407] TULRCA 1992, s 188A(1)(d).

[408] TULRCA 1992, s188A(1)(g),(h),(i).

a voting paper, this would seem the most effective way of satisfying the statutory conditions. The employer has a general duty to 'make such arrangements as are reasonably practical to ensure that the election is fair'.[409] A purposive construction of this duty would suggest that the employer should give appropriate publicity to the election. It may also suggest that the election should be held over a number of days if the workforce is peripatetic, or if shift and part-time workers are employed, although the reference in the statute to 'the date of the election' presents a difficulty in this respect.[410] In these circumstances, as where the workforce is not based at the workplace, a postal ballot may be the better option. Unlike elections for a special negotiating body under TICER 1999 or under the 'standard' information and consultation provisions of ICER 2004,[411] there is no requirement for employers to employ an independent person to conduct the election, although they may consider this a prudent course of action. In striking contrast to the provisions governing trade union elections and industrial action ballots,[412] the legislation does not prohibit the employer or third parties attempting to put pressure on employees to vote a certain way; it is questionable whether conduct of this nature would violate the duty to make 'arrangements' to ensure that the election is fair.[413] The statute does not expressly make compliance with the specific conditions relating to the ballot, such as voting entitlement and a secret ballot, the employer's direct responsibility. However, if the election does not satisfy all the statutory requirements listed, those elected will not be 'appropriate representatives' for consultation and it is therefore in an employer's interest to ensure compliance with them. The EAT has held that where the number of employee nominees or candidates matches the number of representatives to be elected and no further candidates are proposed there was deemed to have been an election for statutory purposes and there is no requirement to hold a ballot.[414] The EAT considered that the obligation on the employer to make arrangements to ensure that the election is fair constituted a safeguard against it 'rigging' the election by proposing the requisite number of 'yes men'.

If the employer invites affected employees to elect representatives and they fail to do so, it will be treated as having satisfied its statutory obligation to consult provided that the invitation was issued long enough before the time when consultations were required to begin to enable the election to take place.[415] However if, pursuant to an invitation, the employees fail to elect representatives (for example, because no candidate comes forward) the employer must give each employee individually the information it is required to give to appropriate representatives,[416] although there is no commensurate obligation to consult them. The Collective Redundancies Directive appears to envisage consultation (and the associated provision of information) only through the medium of

---

[409] TULRCA 1992, s 188A(1)(a).

[410] See TULRCA 1992, s 188(1A)(e) and (g). Cf TULRCA 1992, s 246, in relation to industrial action ballots and TICER 1999, reg 13(3)(b) and ICER 2004, reg 2. In this context there is no explicit requirement that those entitled to vote be given the opportunity to do so (cf TICER 1999, reg 14(2)(c)(i)), but this can probably be implied from the duty to make arrangements to ensure that the election is fair.

[411] See paras 9.61 and 9.54.

[412] See paras 10.16 and 11.37 below respectively.

[413] Note that the protection against dismissal or subjection to a detriment extends only to taking part in an election and not to the way the employee votes: see (iv) below.

[414] *Phillips v Xtera Communications Ltd* [2011] IRLR 724.

[415] That is the implication of TULRCA 1992, s 188(7A), which treats the employer as complying with the requirements to inform and consult if this is done as soon as reasonably practicable after the representatives are elected. If no representatives are elected, the employer cannot take these steps.

[416] TULRCA 1992, s 188(7B).

workers representatives,[417] and in *Mono Car Styling SA in liquidation v Odemis* the ECJ affirmed the collective nature of the rights.[418] If there are already potentially appropriate representatives in existence, such as a works council or other consultative body, it is strongly arguable that the employer should, in default of an election being held, consult those persons.

It is notable that although a union, in order to be consulted, must be independent of the employer, there is no explicit requirement that employee representatives should be; thus, they may be members of a body such as a staff council or consultative committee, which is dependent on the employer, financially or otherwise. In the consultation document that preceded the 1999 Regulations, the government claimed that independence would be secured if representatives were required to be properly elected, protected against dismissal or other detriment for acting as such, and with time off and the necessary training to fulfil their role (see para 9.36 below).[419] However this approach takes no account of other pressures, such as the threat to financial support of, or promise of future favours to, compliant representatives which may result from a relationship of dependence (and which also overlooks the fact that they may have obtained their position by appointment rather than election). The lack of any requirement for representatives to be independent would appear to allow employers even now to frustrate the protection for workers provided by the Directive.[420] A redundant or affected employee may complain to an employment tribunal that any one of the employee representatives consulted was not 'appropriate', or that there has been a failure in relation to the election.[421] On a complaint relating to 'appropriateness', it is for the employer to show that the representative had the authority to represent the affected employees; where it relates to the election, it must show that the statutory requirements have been satisfied.[422] Where the employer consults a pre-existing body, it may be possible to argue that dependence on the employer means that it lacks the requisite implied authority to be consulted about the proposed dismissals on their behalf. However this may be more difficult if the body concerned includes within its terms of reference consultation relating to matters which include redundancies.[423] Unless representatives lack authority, or there is a defect in the electoral process, employees would seem to have no remedy in the event that they think their interests will not be properly represented by those elected or appointed.[424]

---

[417] Cf Council Directive 89/391 on health and safety, discussed in para 9.46.

[418] Case 12/08 ECR 2009 I -06653. Cf *EC Commission v UK* where the ECJ, in rather ambiguous terms, affirmed that the Directive required Member States to take 'all measures necessary to ensure that workers are informed, consulted and in a position to intervene through their representatives in the event of collective redundancies': Case 383/92, [1994] IRLR 412, para 23

[419] *Employees' Information and Consultation Rights on Transfers of Undertakings and Collective Redundancies*, DTI, URN 97/988, February 1998.

[420] Case C-383/92 *EC Commission v UK* [1994] IRLR 412, paras 16–27.

[421] TULRCA 1992, s 189(1).

[422] TULRCA 1992, s 189(1A), (1B).

[423] In the case of representatives elected for another purpose, BIS suggests that where redundancies are to take place among sales staff, for example, it would not be sufficient to consult a committee of managers set up to consider the operation of a staff canteen, but it may be appropriate to consult a committee of employees, such as a works council or staff forum, that is regularly informed or consulted more generally about the business's financial position and/or personnel matters: *Redundancy consultation and notification: guidance* URN No 06/1965Y.

[424] *Northgate HR Ltd v Mercy* [2008] IRLR 222; see further para 9.38. In *R v Secretary of State for Trade and Industry, ex p Unison* [1996] IRLR 438, Otton LJ emphasised at 446 that the expression 'appropriate representatives' must be 'an objective obligation or test and not subjective at the whim of the employer'. In the event of employees having been elected, however, it would probably need to be argued that the arrangements made by the employer did not ensure that the election was fair: see *Phillips v Xtera Communications Ltd* [2011] IRLR 724., above note 414.

(iv) The rights of appropriate representatives

9.36   Employee representatives, and candidates for this position, are entitled to be permitted by the employer to take 'reasonable' paid time off during working hours to perform their functions and to undergo training to perform such functions (although the organisers of elections have no such right).[425] In its basic structure this provision is identical, *mutatis mutandis*, to that governing time off for union duties, discussed at para 8.40 *et seq*; thus, it is a right to time off only with the employer's permission, with recourse to an employment tribunal if time off or payment is unreasonably refused,[426] and payment need be made only for duties performed during working hours.[427] In contrast to time off for union duties, however, there is no reference to a Code of Practice to determine what is reasonable, although ACAS has issued a non-statutory guide to assist the parties.[428] The 'functions' for which time off must be permitted are not specified in the legislation. The right to time off for training was added in 1999, but notably there is no right to training itself,[429] so that representatives who are not members of or otherwise associated with an independent union may find it difficult to get access to the requisite assistance, particularly as time is of the essence. Moreover, they are likely to be financially dependent on the employer for any training that they do receive. The ACAS guide states that it is 'highly desirable' for representatives to receive training to enable them to learn quickly about their role and rights and to provide them with the knowledge and skills to evaluate the employer's decision.[430] Employers may consider it good industrial relations practice to pay for representatives to have access to external professional advice, but, although the Collective Redundancies Directive permits Member States to provide for such assistance, there is no obligation so to do.[431] Where representatives of recognised trade unions are being consulted, their rights to time off for this purpose and for relevant training are governed by the provisions relating to trade union duties.

Employers are required to allow appropriate representatives (union and 'employee') access to the affected employees and to afford them such accommodation and other facilities as may be appropriate; this would probably include meeting rooms, a telephone, and electronic communication media used or permitted in the workplace.[432] The amount and timing of such access is not spelt out, but would probably be viewed by tribunals as subject to a test of reasonableness. The union or employee representatives may complain to an employment tribunal if reasonable access or appropriate facilities are denied; the remedies if the complaint is upheld, which may include a protective award of compensation to the employees dismissed as redundant or whose dismissal was proposed, are discussed in para 9.38 *et seq* below. By contrast, if appropriate representatives are denied time off to perform their functions, which is potentially of equal, if not greater, significance for affected employees, the remedy is confined to a claim by individual representatives on their own behalf.

---

[425]   ERA 1996, s 61.

[426]   ERA 1996, s 63.

[427]   See ERA 1996, s 62 for the basis upon which payment is calculated. Note that these provisions are somewhat more detailed than those in TULRCA 1992, s 169 relating to payment for trade union duties.

[428]   *Non-Union Representation in the Workplace*, ACAS.

[429]   Cf the Health and Safety (Consultation with Employees) Regulations 1996, SI 1996/1513, reg 7; see para 9.46.

[430]   Above, note 428, p 17.

[431]   Council Directive 98/59, Art 2(2).

[432]   TULRCA 1992, s 188(5A). See ACAS Guide, above, note 428, p 19.

It is automatically unfair to dismiss, or to select for redundancy, an employee for performing or proposing to perform the functions or activities of an employee representative or of a candidate in an election for such a position, or for taking part in an election of employee representatives.[433] An employee who is dismissed on such a ground may apply for 'interim relief'.[434] The minimum basic award applicable to dismissals for 'trade union' reasons applies in this context:[435] see further para 8.5. Such employees also have the right not to be subjected to any 'detriment' by any 'act' or 'deliberate failure to act' by the employer on these grounds;[436] where this right is infringed, an employment tribunal may award such compensation as it considers just and equitable in the circumstances, having regard to the infringement of the right and any loss attributable to the employer's act or failure.[437] There is nothing specific in the legislation to prevent employers from according employee representatives more favourable treatment than those whom they represent and where dismissals are selective and representatives are members of the 'target group', employers may err on the side of caution by not dismissing them. However this must be read in the light of the general principles governing dismissal for redundancy. Thus, if an employer selected employees according to specified criteria such as their performance record and length of service, and did not apply those criteria to employee representatives, those dismissed in their stead may have a claim for unfair dismissal.

(v) The scope of the duty to consult

9.37   To comply with the duty to consult the employer must disclose in writing to the appropriate representatives a number of specified matters: the reasons for its proposals; the numbers and descriptions of employees it proposes to dismiss and the proposed method of selecting them; the total number of employees of such description(s) employed at the establishment in question; the proposed method of carrying out the dismissals, including the period over which they are to take effect; and the proposed method of calculating any redundancy payments, other than those required by statute. [438] As from 1 October 2011 the employer has also been required to disclose the number of agency workers working temporarily for and under the supervision and direction of the employer; the parts of the undertaking in which they are working; and the type of work they are carrying out.[439] In *Akavan Erityisalojen Keskusliitto AEK ry v Fujitsu Siemens Computers Oy* the ECJ confirmed that information can be provided during the course of the consultation

---

[433] ERA 1996, ss 103, 105(1), (6). Where the principal reason for dismissal is redundancy it must be shown that the circumstances constituting the redundancy applied equally to one or more employees in the same undertaking who held similar positions and who were not dismissed: s 105(1)(b). See further para 5.92 above for the concept of automatically unfair reasons. Employees who are being consulted in their capacity as union officials will be covered by the protections afforded to those dismissed, or subjected to a detriment short of dismissal, for 'trade union' reasons.

[434] ERA 1996, s 128; see further para 5.153.

[435] ERA 1996, s 120.

[436] ERA 1996, s.47. 'Detriment' does not include dismissal in this context; in that event, the provisions relating to compensation for unfair dismissal apply.

[437] TULRCA 1992, s 49; see further para 8.16. Loss includes any expenses reasonably incurred by the complainant in consequence of the act or failure to which the complaint relates and loss of any benefit which he or she may otherwise have had: s 49(3). There is a duty to mitigate loss (s 49(4)) and compensation may be reduced if the tribunal finds that the individual caused or contributed to the act or failure (s 49(5)).

[438] TULRCA 1992, s 188(4).

[439] Above.

process, so consultation need not be held up if information is not available at the start, and any new relevant information which becomes available to the employer during the consultations should be supplied to worker representatives up to the end of the process. [440] The consultation must include ways of avoiding the dismissals, reducing the number of employees to be dismissed and mitigating the consequences of dismissals. [441] The first two categories may include consideration, for example, of alternative strategies such as reallocating work, reducing overtime or giving employees the opportunity to work more flexible hours or to job share. Where appropriate the possibility of redeployment elsewhere in the organisation, possibly after training, should also be explored. Where dismissals are inevitable, mitigating action may include providing counselling and outplacements for employees, and information about retraining elsewhere. [442] At one time it had been assumed by the British courts that these provisions did not require consultation over the reasons for the redundancies. [443] However in *UK Coal Ltd v NUM (Northumberland Area)*, which concerned the closure of a coal mine, the EAT held that:

> .... the obligation to consult over avoiding the proposed redundancies inevitably involves engaging with the reasons for the dismissals, and that in turn requires consultation over the reasons for the closure. Strictly, of course, it is the proposed dismissals that are the subject of consultation, and not the closure itself. Accordingly, if an employer planned a closure but believed that redundancies would nonetheless be avoided, there would be no need to consult over the closure decision itself, at least not pursuant to the obligations under the 1992 Act. In the context of a closure, that is likely to be a very exceptional case. Where closure and dismissals are inextricably interlinked, the duty to consult over the reasons arises. [444]

This decision related specifically to a closure of the workplace and, as we discuss in para 9.33 above, whether the consultation obligation is triggered by a proposed decision to effect a closure (or other strategic or operational decision that will foreseeably or inevitably lead to redundancies) is currently the subject of a reference to the CJEU. The argument that the reasoning in *UK Coal* – that consultation over ways of avoiding redundancies requires engaging with the reasons underlying them – should apply in non-closure cases has not, at the time of writing, been the subject of a decision by the courts. [445]

The employer must undertake the consultation 'with a view to reaching agreement' with the appropriate representatives, [446] and must, therefore, be able to demonstrate that it took seriously the points which they put, and that it made reasonable efforts to reach an accommodation

---

[440] Case C-44/08 [2009] IRLR 944, paras 50-55. For earlier British decisions on this point see *MSF v GEC Ferranti (Defence Systems) Ltd (No 2)* [1994] IRLR 113, 116; *Securicor Omega Express Ltd v GMB* [2004] IRLR 9. Cf *E Green and Son (Casting) Ltd v ASTMS* [1984] IRLR 135, distinguished in *Securicor Omega Express*.

[441] TULRCA 1992, s 188(2). It is mandatory to consult on all these matters; an employer cannot argue that consultation would, in the circumstances, be futile: *Middlesbrough Borough Council v TGWU* [2002] IRLR 332, approved in *Susie Radin Ltd v GMB* [2004] IRLR 400, at [43].

[442] There is an obligation on employers to give employees who have been given notice of dismissal for redundancy time off work to look for new employment or to make arrangements for training for future employment: ERA 1996, ss 52–54.

[443] *R v British Coal Corpn, ex p Vardy* [1993] IRLR 104; *Middlesbrough Borough Council v TGWU* [2002] IRLR 332; *Securicor Omega Express Ltd v GMB* [2004] IRLR 9.

[444] [2008] IRLR 4 at [87] (Elias P).

[445] The EAT also noted the 'broad obligation to consult over all sorts of economic decisions' under ICER 2004 (see para 9.54 below), noting that it would be 'bizarre' if the duty under s 188 of TULRCA 1992 were more limited: above, [84].

[446] TULRCA 1992, s 188(2).

with them; the prudent employer will keep a written record of all meetings, with both parties signing them as accurate. While ultimately the employers retain the right to decide upon the implementation of redundancies, this procedure requires them to do more than go through the motions of listening to what representatives have to say. However its impact in practice may be limited where the employer is a subsidiary of another company and the proposals emanate from a policy decision that has been taken elsewhere within the group. In *Akavan* the ECJ confirmed that it is for the subsidiary employer itself to undertake the consultation even if decisions by the controlling company are binding on it.[447]

(vi) Remedies for failure to consult

9.38   If an employer fails to fulfil any of the statutory requirements a complaint may be made to an employment tribunal. If the failure relates to trade union or employee representatives, it may be made by the union or any of the employee representatives to whom the failure relates respectively; in any other case, including, specifically, a failure relating to the election of employee representatives, it may be made by any of the affected employees or any of the employees who have been dismissed as redundant.[448] However it seems that the scope for individual employees or ex-employees to complain about matters other than the conduct of an election may be confined to situations where the employer fails to issue an invitation to elect employee representatives; chooses to consult a body which does not have the authority of employees to consult on their behalf; or fails, in the event that there is no response to the invitation to elect employee representatives, to provide individual employees with the requisite information.[449] This is because, if appropriate representatives are in place, the employer's duty to provide information or engage in proper consultation is owed to them rather than to individual employees, and if such representatives are unwilling to complain to an employment tribunal there would seem nothing that individual employees could then do.[450]

The complaint to a tribunal must be presented before the date on which the last of the dismissals to which it relates takes effect or during the three-month period beginning with that date (with the usual exception where this was not 'reasonably practicable').[451]

9.39   The employer may defend the complaint by showing that there were 'special circumstances' which rendered it not reasonably practicable for it to comply with a particular requirement, and that it took all such steps to comply with that requirement as were reasonably practicable in the circumstances.[452] This defence has been construed narrowly by the courts: to be 'special', circumstances must be uncommon or out of the ordinary – a sudden and unexpected, rather

---

[447]   Above note 382 para 56-65.
[448]   TULRCA 1992, s 189(1).
[449]   See also para 9.34 *et seq* above.
[450]   *Northgate HR Ltd v Mercy* [2008] IRLR 222. In *Mono Car Styling SA (in liquidation) v Odemis* Case 12/08 ECR [2009] I-06653 the ECJ affirmed the collective nature of the right to information and consultation and held that the Directive does not preclude national rules which place limits on individual rights to secure compliance.
[451]   TULRCA 1992, s 189(5); see further para 2.17 above.
[452]   TULRCA 1992, ss 188(7), 189(6).

than a predictable, disaster.[453] The fact that dismissals were triggered by the employer becoming insolvent is not of itself a special circumstance. As Geoffrey Lane LJ explained in *Clarks of Hove Ltd v Bakers' Union*:[454]

> It will depend entirely on the cause of the insolvency whether the circumstances can be described as special or not. If, for example, sudden disaster strikes a company, making it necessary to close the concern, then plainly that would be a matter which is capable of being a special circumstance; and that is so whether the disaster is physical or financial. If the insolvency, however, was merely due to a gradual run-down of the company, as it was in this case, then those are facts on which the ... [Employment] ... Tribunal can come to the conclusion that the circumstances were not special ...

In a later case the EAT applied this test to hold that shedding workers to make the purchase of a business more attractive to a potential buyer, and the fact that the business had no orders and could not be sold, were not special circumstances but rather common incidents of insolvencies.[455] Nor does the fact that a company is in administration and the administrator proposes the dismissals constitute a special circumstance *per se*.[456] By contrast, where a bank suddenly withdrew further credit facilities and appointed a receiver, this was capable of constituting a special circumstance,[457] as was a situation where the employer had continued trading despite adverse economic pointers in the reasonable expectation of avoiding redundancies (although shutting its eyes to the obvious would not have been).[458] At one time it was thought that a failure to consult prior to the public announcement of a merger could be justified on the basis that this was necessitated by Stock Exchange rules.[459] This is not the case, however. The BIS guidance on consultation states that:

> Stock Exchange rules do *not* preclude employee representatives being informed and consulted in advance where collective redundancies are planned in connection with a restructuring (eg a plant closure or a takeover) which may involve price sensitive information. Provision can be made for employee representatives to be subject to confidentiality constraints for a specified period, but at the same time be sufficiently informed to hold meaningful consultations with the employer.[460]

It is notable, however that TULRCA 1992, unlike ICER 2004 and TICER 1999, does not provide for the transmission of information to union or employee representatives subject to such

---

[453] *Clarks of Hove Ltd v Bakers' Union* [1978] IRLR 366.

[454] [1978] IRLR 366, 369.

[455] *GMB v Rankin and Harrison (as joint administrators of Lawtex plc and Lawtex Babywear Ltd)* [1992] IRLR 514. In *Middlesbrough Borough Council v TGWU* [2002] IRLR 332, the EAT held that it could not conceive of circumstances that would be 'special' where an employer had sufficient time to consult on some matters but had entered into none on another.

[456] *Re Hartlebury Printers Ltd (in liquidation)* [1992] IRLR 516. Remuneration due under a protective award constitutes a preferential debt under the Insolvency Act 1986, Sch 6, para 13(2)(d).

[457] *USDAW v Leancut Bacon Ltd (in liquidation)* [1981] IRLR 295. See also *Hamish Armour v ASTMS* [1979] IRLR 24 (application for a further government loan pending).

[458] *Association of Pattern Makers and Allied Craftsmen v Kirvin Ltd* [1978] IRLR 318.

[459] This was argued before the employment tribunal *MSF v Refuge Assurance plc*: see [2002] IRLR 324, 331 (EAT).

[460] *Redundancy consultation and notification: guidance* URN No 06/1965Y.

confidentiality constraints[461] although this is what the Disclosure Rules and Transparency Rules of the Financial Services Authority may require.[462] The case law suggests that employers should, at least, offer to disclose information on confidential terms.[463] However there is a difficulty if no employee representatives are in place; the Disclosure Rules and Transparency Rules would almost certainly not permit disclosure to all affected employees,[464] which TULRCA requires in the event that they fail to respond to an invitation to elect employee representatives.[465] Finally, the statute provides that where the decision leading to the dismissals was taken by a person controlling the employer (directly or indirectly) rather than the employer itself, a failure by that person to provide information to the immediate employer cannot constitute the 'special circumstances' defence.[466] Thus a subsidiary of a transnational company, for example, cannot argue that it was unable to meet its obligations because its parent company, which took the decision to reduce the workforce, was unwilling to disclose the requisite information to it. However in considering the application of this provision it will be necessary to determine whether the duty to consult applies in the first place. In *Akavan Erityisalojen Keskusliitto AEK ry v Fujitsu Siemens Computers Oy* the ECJ held that:

> Where the parent company of a group of undertakings adopts decisions likely to have repercussions on the jobs of workers within that group, it is for the subsidiary whose employees may be affected by redundancies, in its capacity as their employer, to start consultations with the workers' representatives. It is therefore not possible to start such consultations until such time as that subsidiary has been identified… [Thus] the obligation to hold consultations … falls on the subsidiary … only once that subsidiary, within which collective redundancies may be made, has been identified.[467]

This decision suggests that the subsidiary itself must at the very least have been made aware of the contemplated redundancies for the duty to apply, even if the failure of the parent company to supply any further information cannot constitute a defence.

The 'special circumstances' defence does not appear on the fact of the Collective Redundancies Directive. It is, notable, however, that its presence in the legislation was not a ground of complaint by the European Commission in the infringement proceedings described in para 9.31. In *EC*

---

[461] See ICER 2004, reg 25 and TICER 1999, reg 23, discussed in paras 9.56 and 9.63 below.

[462] See DTR 2.5.6–2.5.9. See also Directive 2003/6/EC on insider dealing and market manipulation, Arts 3 and 6 and Case C-384/02 *Criminal Proceedings against Grongaard* [2006] IRLR 214, ECJ on a predecessor Directive.

[463] The EAT in *MSF v Refuge Assurance plc* above note 459 said *obiter* that it could not be assumed that disclosure to a senior union official on the like terms of confidence as would apply to the company's directors would necessarily be so restrictive that it would be completely useless to him or her and that it would therefore represent a step that need not be taken by the employer, or that such an official would necessarily decline to accept information on such terms. See also *Hamish Armour v ASTMS* [1979] IRLR 24, 25.

[464] DTR 2.5.7(2)(c) refers to 'employee representatives or trade unions acting on their behalf'. Although DTR 2.5.7(2) states that the categories of recipient are not limited to those specified, DTR 2.5.9 states that an issuer should bear in mind that the wider the group of recipients of inside information the greater the likelihood of a leak which will trigger full public disclosure.

[465] TULRCA 1992, s 188(7B); see para 9.35 above.

[466] TULRCA 1992, s 188(7). In *GMB and Amicus v Beloit Walmsley Ltd* [2004] IRLR 18, the EAT held that information in s 188(7) was not defined exclusively by the information required to be disclosed by s 188(4), and meant 'information about the decision leading to the proposed dismissals', a phrase which connotes both the causal effect of the decision (some dismissals for redundancy) and contemplation of its consequences.

[467] Case C-44/08 [2009] IRLR 944, paras 63 and 65.

v Portuguese Republic the ECJ acknowledged that the 'full application of the Directive' may be 'impossible in some circumstances in which the definitive termination of the undertaking's activity is not contingent upon the employer's will' but ruled that application of the Directive in its entirety should not be excluded for those circumstances.[468] In that case the Court appeared, therefore, to have implied into the Directive a specific version of the 'special circumstances' defence. By contrast, in the later case of *Rodriguez-Mayor v Herencia yacente de Rafael de las Heras Davila* the ECJ held that the very concept of 'collective redundancies' in the Directive implied 'a direct manifestation of the will of the employer',[469] so rendering any special defence in these circumstances unnecessary. As we discuss in para 9.32 the full implications of *Rodriguez-Mayor* remain to be determined.

9.40   If an employment tribunal upholds a complaint it must make a declaration and may also make a protective award in respect of employees in relation to whose dismissal or proposed dismissal the employer has failed to comply with a statutory requirement.[470] The award entitles the employees subject to it to receive their normal pay for the period of the award (the 'protected period').[471] If the employer fails to pay the requisite remuneration to an employee he or she may present an individual complaint to an employment tribunal.[472] The length of the protected period is at the discretion of the tribunal, but may not exceed 90 days.[473] Its length is such as the tribunal considers 'just and equitable in all the circumstances, having regard to the seriousness of the employer's default in complying with any [statutory] requirement …'[474] The interpretation of this provision – and, in particular, deciding whether the award was designed to compensate the employees affected, penalise the employer, or both – caused considerable controversy for many years. In 2004 the Court of Appeal resolved the matter by affirming that the purpose of the award was to provide a sanction for breach of the obligations to consult, not to compensate employees for loss that they had suffered as a result of the breach.[475] Tribunals should focus on the seriousness of the employer's default, which may vary from the technical to a complete failure to comply; the deliberateness of the failure may also be relevant, as may

[468] Case C-55/02 [2004] ECR I-9387, para 57.
[469] Case 323/08 [2009] ECR I-11621, para 40.
[470] TULRCA 1992 , s189(2), (3). In *TGWU v Brauer Coley Ltd* [2007] IRLR 207 the EAT held that, where a trade union had brought the complaint, a protective award could be made only in respect of employees for whom the union was recognised and in *Independent Insurance Co Ltd v Aspinall* [2011] IRLR 716 the EAT held that an individual claimant could obtain an award only for himself or herself, although acknowledging that a literal interpretation of the statutory language could suggest otherwise. In *Securicor Omega Express Ltd v GMB* [2004] IRLR 9 the EAT held, at [17], that 'proposed' dismissal in s189(3) referred to an 'anticipatory claim for a protective award' brought before redundancies had been announced and did not cover those who ultimately remained in the employer's employment.
[471] TULRCA 1992, ss 189(2), 190. The rate of remuneration is a week's pay (calculated according to ERA 1996, ss 220–229 (Chapter II of Part XIV): TULRCA 1992, s 190(5)) for each week of the award, with proportionate amounts for individual days. However the statutory maximum of a week's pay stipulated in s 227 does not appear to be applicable in this context: cf TULRCA 1992, s 70C(5B). In *Canadian Imperial Bank of Commerce v Beck* UKEAT/0141/10/RN the EAT held that a week's pay did not include a discretionary bonus where the date for considering whether to pay such a bonus had not yet occurred.
[472] TULRCA 1992, s 192. On the approach to the time limit for presenting a complaint where the protective award is made after the protected period ends, see *Howlett Marine Services Ltd v Bowlam* [2001] IRLR 201.
[473] TULRCA 1992, s 189(4).
[474] TULRCA 1992, s 189(4).
[475] *Susie Radin Ltd v GMB* [2004] IRLR 400, disapproving *Spillars-French (Holdings) Ltd v USDAW* [1979] IRLR 339.

the availability to the employer of legal advice about its obligations.[476] A proper approach to assessing the length of the protected period in a case where there had been no consultation was to start with the maximum period and reduce it only if there are mitigating circumstances justifying a reduction to the extent that the tribunal considers appropriate.[477] It is not open to an employer, in this context, to argue that consultation would have been futile.[478] The EAT has since confirmed that the effectiveness of the sanction should be judged at the time that the employer's failure to consult occurs, not at a later stage when redundancies are implemented or a complaint is presented to a tribunal; the fact that an employer may be insolvent by the time of the proceedings is irrelevant. [479]

Deciding when the protected period should begin has also been a source of difficulty for the courts. The statute states that it begins with the date on which the first of the dismissals to which the complaint relates 'takes effect' or the date of the award, whichever is the earlier.[480] There are conflicting decisions as to whether the date on which the first of the dismissals 'takes effect' means the date on which it was *originally proposed* that the first of the dismissals should take effect or the *actual* date.[481] The determination of this date was more significant before TURERA 1993 removed the provision requiring a protective award to be set off against payments under the contract of employment or damages for breach of contract.

The protective award is payable regardless of whether employees are working during the protected period. It is notable, however, that employees who are still employed during any part of the protected period will be entitled to payment under the protected award only if they would be entitled to payment under their contract of employment or under their statutory rights during a period of notice;[482] thus, employees who take unpaid leave, for example, will not be so entitled. Moreover, employees may lose the right to remuneration under a protective award if they are fairly dismissed for reasons other than redundancy[483] or unreasonably terminate the contract of employment when they would otherwise have been employed.[484] They also lose this right for the period when they would otherwise have been employed if, in circumstances where they are entitled to a statutory redundancy payment, they unreasonably refuse an offer of suitable employment from the employer (or new or renewed employment on the same terms), to take effect before or during the protective period.[485] If the purpose of the award is to provide a sanction for the failure to consult, it is not clear why any of these events should be relevant. Employees who

---

[476] See also *Amicus v GBS Tooling Ltd (in administration)* [2005] IRLR 683, where the EAT held that the fact that the employer had supplied some information prior to the date on which the proposal to dismiss was formulated could constitute mitigating circumstances; *Shanahan Engineering Ltd v Unite the Union* UKEAT/0411/09/DM, where the EAT held that a sudden and unexpected decision by a third party was potentially a mitigating circumstance.

[477] See also *UK Coal Mining Ltd v NUM* [2008] IRLR 4; *Hutchins v Permacell Finesse Ltd (in administration)*, UKEAT 0350/07; *Lancaster University v UCU* [2011] IRLR 4.

[478] *Susie Radin Ltd v GMB*, above, note 475, at [43], approving *Middlesbrough Borough Council v TGWU* [2002] IRLR 332. In *Amicus v GBS Tooling Ltd (in administration)* above, note 476, the EAT suggested that questions of futility, where there was no time for consultation, may be able to be addressed in the context of the 'special circumstances' defence.

[479] *Smith v Cherry Lewis Ltd* [2005] IRLR 86.

[480] TULRCA 1992, s 189(4).

[481] *TGWU v Ledbury Preserves (1928) Ltd* [1986] IRLR 492 adopts the former interpretation, following *E Green & Son (Castings) Ltd v ASTMS* [1984] IRLR 135 on this point in preference to *GKN Sankey Ltd v NSMM* [1980] IRLR 8.

[482] TULRCA 1992, s 190(4); see *Cranswick Country Foods plc v Beall* [2007] ICR 691.

[483] Note that in this context 'redundancy' has the wider meaning contained in TULRCA 1992, s 195(1).

[484] TULRCA 1992, s 191.

[485] TULRCA 1992, s 191. There is provision for a trial period where the terms and conditions of employment differ from the previous contract.

are unemployed and in receipt of a protective award may not claim a Jobseeker's Allowance for this period; if they have already done so and a protective award is subsequently made in respect of the period in question, the employer must deduct that amount from the award and pay it to the DWP.[486]

We return to the question of the adequacy of the sanction for failure to consult, stated in the legislation to be the exclusive remedy,[487] in para 9.42 below. At this stage, however, we merely contrast it with the remedy which may lie where the employer is a body whose decisions are susceptible to judicial review and there are consultation procedures particular to the industry or service in question. In 1992 decisions by British Coal and the Secretary of State to close collieries without any consultation, in breach of obligations under the Coal Industry Nationalisation Act 1946 and machinery established thereunder, were deemed to be a matter of public law and a declaration was granted that no decision should be made as to the closure of any collieries until the stipulated procedure had been followed.[488] Where, however, there is no special procedure and such an employer has failed to consult in accordance merely with the general law the statutory provision for exclusivity presents obstacles to a claim for any additional remedy.[489] Nevertheless, in principle, there seems no reason why, in an application for an interim injunction for breach of contract, the court cannot at least take into account an employer's breach of its statutory obligations to consult when exercising its discretion as to whether or not to make an order.[490] Equally, the fact that an employer has breached these obligations may render the dismissal unfair.

(vii) Notification requirements

9.41   In addition to the obligation to consult appropriate representatives, an employer proposing to dismiss for redundancy 20 or more employees at one establishment within a period of 90 days or less must notify BIS in writing of the proposal before giving notice to terminate an employee's contract of employment in respect of any of those dismissals and at least 30 days before the first dismissal takes effect. Where the employer proposes to dismiss 100 or more employees at one establishment within such a period, notification must be given at least 90 days before the first

---

[486]   The Employment Protection (Recoupment of Jobseeker's Allowance and Income Support) Regulations 1996, SI 1996/2349, reg 8, which also makes provision for recoupment of income support and the income-related employment and support allowance. Income support paid on incapacity grounds was replaced by the Employment and Support Allowance with effect from 27 October 2008.

[487]   TULRCA 1992, s 188(8).

[488]   See *R v British Coal Corpn and Secretary of State for Trade and Industry, ex p Vardy* [1993] IRLR 104. Note that the concept of consultation in this context may not be identical to the statutory formulation: in *R v British Coal Corpn and the Secretary of State for Trade and Industry, ex p Price* [1994] IRLR 72, Glidewell LJ suggested (at 75) that it involved 'giving the body consulted a fair and proper opportunity to understand fully the matters about which it is being consulted, and to express its views on those subjects, with the consultor thereafter considering those views properly and genuinely'.

[489]   See *Vardy*, above, at 116; *Griffin v South West Water Services Ltd* [1995] IRLR 15, where an application for an injunction restraining dismissals for redundancy pending conclusion of the consultation procedure was unsuccessful.

[490]   See further para 5.54 *et seq*.

dismissal takes effect.[491] The notification must, *inter alia*, identify the appropriate representatives and state when consultation with them began and the employer must give those representatives a copy of the notification[492] (although the duty to notify exists even if there were no 'appropriate representatives' because, for example, there were no candidates for an election). The employer must also supply any additional information which BIS requires.[493] It is implicit from the requirement to state when consultation began that such consultation should precede notification; this is clearer in Directive 98/59, which requires consultation when the employer is 'contemplating' collective redundancies and notification when they are 'projected'.[494] Employers who fail to comply with the obligation to notify the Secretary of State risk criminal prosecution and a fine of up to level 5 on the standard scale (at the time of writing, £5,000)[495] and, where the employer is a limited company, specified officers may incur personal liability.[496] The same 'special circumstances' defence as applies to the failure to consult applies also in this context.[497] Prosecutions may be instituted only by the Secretary of State or by an officer authorised for that purpose.[498] There is no record of any prosecutions for this offence;[499] in 2006 the DTI (BIS's predecessor) said that there was no evidence to suggest that employers do not comply with the notification requirements.[500]

The duty to notify collective dismissals also appears in Directive 98/59. The draft form of its predecessor (Directive 75/129) contained power for public authorities to postpone or prohibit dismissals in certain circumstances, a provision reflecting the position in some Member States at that time. The UK was 'in the vanguard of the opposition to that part of the proposals'[501] and a compromise was eventually reached where it was agreed that the provision of veto powers would remain optional. It seems that a legal duty on employers to seek prior approval by public authorities for dismissals is now 'highly unusual', recent trends being to reduce the level of formal regulation.[502] In France, for example, a requirement for prior authorisation by the labour inspectorate in respect of redundancies was abolished in 1986. The Directive states that the

---

[491]   TULRCA 1992, s 193, as amended in 2006 to take account of Case C-188/03 *Junk v Kuhnel* [2005] IRLR 310. discussed in para 9.33 above. In *Junk* the ECJ held that, in contrast to the consultation procedure, Directive 98/59 does not preclude termination of contracts of employment during the course of the notification procedure, provided that this occurs after the projected redundancies have been notified. Art 4(1) of Directive 98/59 requires that projected collective redundancies shall take effect not earlier than 30 days after notification, with a discretion for Member States to grant the competent public authority power to extend this to 60 days or longer in specified circumstances (Art 4(3)). The 90-day period is longer, therefore, than that required by the Directive. In November 2011 BIS stated that only 16% of notifications over the previous five years related to redundancies large enough to trigger the 90-day period: *Collective Redundancies Consultation Rules: Call for Evidence*, BIS, November 2011, para 2.3. There is no requirement to notify the Secretary of State where, under his or her contract of employment, an employee works outside Great Britain, although the duty to consult is not excluded: TULRCA 1992, s 285.

[492]   TULRCA 1992, s 193(4),(6).

[493]   TULRCA 1992, s 193(5).

[494]   Arts 2(1), 3(1).

[495]   Criminal Justice Act 1982, s 37(2), as substituted by the Criminal Justice Act 1991, s 17(1). There is no sanction for failure to give a copy of the notification to appropriate representatives.

[496]   TULRCA 1992, s 194.

[497]   TULRCA 1992, s 193(7).

[498]   TULRCA 1992, s 194(2).

[499]   Until EA 1989 a redundancy rebate was available from the Secretary of State and one sanction for breach of the notification requirements was that this rebate could be reduced. It seems that there may have been greater use of this sanction than that of prosecution: see *Secretary of State for Employment v Helitron Ltd* [1980] ICR 523.

[500]   *Collective Redundancies – Employer's Duty to Notify the Secretary of State*, DTI, September 2006, para 52.

[501]   Freedland, 1976a: p 27.

[502]   Hepple, 1998: paras 40, 39.

period after notification 'shall be used by the competent public authority to seek solutions to the problems raised by the projected collective redundancies'.[503] Although the DTI described the policy rationale for notification as being to alert and prepare the relevant agencies to take any appropriate measures to assist or retrain the employees in question,[504] this requirement is not reflected on the face of the British legislation.

Assessment of the redundancy consultation legislation

9.42   Any assessment of the adequacy of the redundancy consultation legislation requires first a consideration of its purpose. It was initially introduced as part of the 'Social Contract' legislation[505] and was, as such, part of a package of measures aimed at promoting security of employment and strengthening collective bargaining although, because of the European Community dimension, its background and history were distinct from the remainder of those provisions.[506] In 1994 the ECJ stated that '[b]y harmonising the rules applicable to collective redundancies, the Community legislature intended both to ensure comparable protection for workers' rights in the different Member States and to harmonise the costs which such protective rules entail for Community undertakings'[507]. However, as Paul Davies pointed out in 1992, it is notable that other costs, such as differing levels of severance or redundancy payments, were not addressed and given that Member States remained free to set more demanding standards than the Directive 'harmonisation' was not a wholly appropriate term.[508] In more recent case law the ECJ has described the Directivce as carrying out 'only a partial harmonisation of the rules for the protection of workers in the event of collective redundancies'.[509]

In the previous section we referred to the difficulties caused by the current provisions and, in particular, the issue as to whether the capacity for employers to consult non-independent employee representatives constitutes a continuing breach of the Directive. In this section we examine some more long-standing reasons which may account for the fact that, although the consultation process is potentially capable of averting redundancies (in the sense of job losses rather than reorganisation), it is far from clear that this has been achieved in practice.

First, the position of the representatives consulted may be undermined from the outset if employees volunteer for redundancy.[510] As we saw in chapter 5 the provision for statutory redundancy payments in the Redundancy Payments Act 1965 led to major changes in redundancy policies and practices including the introduction of voluntary severance schemes above the statutory minima. This had a dramatic impact upon the tactics which trade unions were able to deploy when redundancy dismissals were threatened. Whereas prior to this 'the characteristic

---

[503]   Art 4(2).

[504]   *Collective Redundancies – Employer's Duty to Notify the Secretary of State*, DTI, September 2006, para 5.

[505]   See para 7.16 above.

[506]   Freedland, 1976a: p 24.

[507]   See Case C-383/92 *EC Commission v United Kingdom* [1994] IRLR 412, 420.

[508]   P Davies 1992: p 330. Cf the notion of a 'floor of rights' in transnational labour law: see Deakin and Wilkinson, 1994.

[509]   *Akavan Erityisalojen Keskusliitto AEK ry v Fujitsu Siemens Computers Oy* Case C-44/08 [2009] IRLR 944.

[510]   In *R v British Coal Corpn and Secretary of State for Trade and Industry, ex p Price* [1994] IRLR 72, the court held that the payment of voluntary redundancy payments before the termination of the consultation process did not make that process a sham.

trade union response had been to oppose and resist the need for redundancies', as Daniel explains 'trade unions soon found themselves to be powerless in the face of the growth of voluntary redundancy schemes':[511]

> If they tried to challenge and oppose the need for redundancies, they were undermined by individual members eager to accept voluntary redundancy terms. In consequence, caught in a pincer movement between managerial strategy and individualist opportunism upon the part of members, trade union representatives had no alternative but to adopt two stances in relation to redundancy. The first was to insist upon 'No redundancy other than voluntary redundancy'. The second was to bargain over the inducements to volunteer and, in particular, to try to bid up the size of the employer's supplement to the statutory minimum payments.[512]

Daniel found that in the light of these developments the consultation procedures, when introduced in 1975, 'had little impact': in workplaces where unions were strong the opportunities for protecting jobs had already been compromised, in schemes which left intact the power of management to decide on the level and categories of job reduction; where unions were weak there was little scope for them to have an influence.[513] Having said that, it seemed that the presence of recognised unions may, at least, have afforded greater protection against compulsory, as compared with voluntary, redundancies, and that consultation may, in some circumstances influence the way in which redundancies are handled.[514]

Second, from its inception in 1975 it has been a duty only to consult, and not to bargain over, the implementation of redundancies.[515] It has been suggested that 'a major consideration [initially] in favour of a duty to consult rather than to bargain was that consultation … [did] … not commit the trade union to responsibility for approving the redundancy or selecting the employees to be made redundant to the degree that a joint agreement over these matters does'.[516] The duty which now exists to consult 'with a view to reaching agreement' with 'appropriate representatives' comes closer to the process of negotiation but ultimately leaves intact the managerial prerogative in this area.[517]

Third, the impact of the duty is likely to be limited when the employer is a subsidiary of another company and responsibility for the initial decision which underpins the proposed redundancies (such as the decision to close a workplace or outsource a particular area of operations) lies elsewhere. Such a situation may mean that, in practice, the discretion of the consulting employer

---

[511] Daniel, 1985: p 74.

[512] Daniel, 1985: p 74.

[513] Daniel, 1985, pp 78–79, 81.

[514] Millward et al 1992, pp 324–325; J Smith, P Edwards and M Hall, 1999; Kersley et al, 2006, pp 201–203.

[515] The information and consultation model is also laid down as a minimum standard in ILO Convention No 158 of 1982, Art 13, and ILO Recommendation 166 of 1982, Art 20.

[516] P Davies and M Freedland, 1984: p 237.

[517] In *Junk v Kuhnel* Case C-188/03 [2005] IRLR 310, para 43 the ECJ opined that the requirement in Art 2(1) of Directive 98/59 to consult 'with a view to reaching an agreement' imposed an obligation to negotiate. This point was not directly at issue in the case and the implications, if there is an obligation to negotiate, of a failure to agree were not discussed.

to reach an agreement with the representatives which constitutes any significant modification of its original proposals may be restricted.[518]

Fourth, the sanction available against an employer which fails to fulfil its duty to consult is wholly inadequate. When the Collective Redundancies Directive was being revised it was proposed that redundancies implemented in breach should be null and void. This proposal was ultimately dropped but there are strong arguments for saying that it is the only appropriate penalty in the circumstances. It is certainly the case that when large numbers of employees are involved, the redundancy consultation provisions can be an effective method of bringing employers to the bargaining table, particularly where job losses are associated with a transfer of the undertaking.[519] However, a financial penalty allows an employer ultimately to buy its way out of its legal obligations and fails to take account of the fact that consultation may have prevented the job loss altogether. It will be remembered that under the legislation the protective award is stated to be the exclusive remedy.[520] In *Griffin v South West Water Services Ltd*[521] Blackburne J refused an injunction restraining dismissals for redundancy pending conclusion of the consultation procedure for, *inter alia*, this reason. In doing so he opined that:

> Even if it were open to me in appropriate circumstances to disregard the exclusive sanction which Parliament has provided and grant injunctive relief of the kind sought I am not persuaded that I would have any sufficient grounds for doing so. It seems to me that an order restraining an employer from effecting any redundancies unless he has 'consulted with' his employees' representatives 'with a view to reaching agreement', which is what the ... [claimants] ... seek, is one which is fraught with practical difficulties not the least of which would be the difficulty faced by the employer in knowing just what he would be obliged to do and over what period in order to achieve compliance with the order and avoid proceedings for contempt.

However, in *R v British Coal Corpn and Secretary of State for Trade and Industry, ex p Vardy*,[522] where, as we indicated above, a judicial review application was successful, the court granted a declaration that no decision should be made as to the closure of any collieries until the specified procedure had been followed. The employer then returned to the court at a later date to determine whether it had done what was necessary to comply. This is obviously a cumbersome and expensive method of proceeding. In this case, however, failure to follow the procedure would have constituted a breach of an order of the court, a situation which the employers were no doubt anxious to avoid. If, by statute, dismissals implemented in breach of procedure were simply null and void the employer would be in no different a position from an employer which was implementing the procedure *ab initio*.

---

[518] See *Akavan Erityisalojen Keskusliitto AEK ry v Fujitsu Siemens Computers Oy* above note 509 for the operation of the Directive in relation to parent and subsidiary companies.

[519] See Armour and Deakin, 2000.

[520] TULRCA 1992, s 188(8). In response to the TUC's proposals in the context of the transfer of an undertaking that there should be a form of injunctive relief to prevent a transfer occurring until consultations with appropriate representatives had been completed, the Government expressed the view that the remedy (also financial) was adequate: *TUPE: Draft Revised Regulations: Government response to the public consultation*, DTI, February 2006, para 7.7.

[521] [1995] IRLR 15, 34–35.

[522] [1993] IRLR 104.

A final objection to the existing legislation of a rather different nature lies in the mechanism for enforcement of the duty. Although the sanction takes the form of a payment to the dismissed individual, once 'appropriate representatives' have been chosen he or she is dependent upon those representatives to take the matter to an employment tribunal in the first instance. Where the employer has voluntarily recognised a union it is possible to imagine circumstances where it may choose not to bring proceedings in order to safeguard its relationship with the employer, particularly if those dismissed are not union members. Even in the case of members there is no statutory mechanism by which an individual can force a union to bring proceedings on its behalf and it seems unlikely that this could be implied as a contractual term.[523] Where 'employee representatives' have the consultative role, they may lack the will, or the resources, to pursue a complaint on behalf of others.[524] There is a strong argument for saying that an individual should have the right to seek a remedy either independently or if the 'appropriate representative' fails within a specified period to take action on his or her behalf.[525]

Transfer of an undertaking

9.43   Where an undertaking is being transferred[526] both transferor and transferee employers have a duty to inform and consult 'appropriate representatives' of any 'affected employees'.[527] 'Affected employees' are defined as 'any employees[528] of the transferor or the transferee (whether or not assigned to the organised grouping of resources or employees that is the subject of a relevant transfer) who may be affected by the transfer or may be affected by measures taken in connection with it'.[529] They are not, therefore, confined to those to be transferred, and in many cases the majority, if not all, of the employees of both transferor and transferee employer may be 'affected'.[530] Employees of 'associated employers' of the transferor or transferee are not included

---

[523] See *Iwanuszezak v GMBATU* [1988] IRLR 219, where it was held that there was no implied duty on a union to bring its collective strength to bear to safeguard an individual member's existing conditions of employment. Lloyd LJ stated (at 220) that 'where the collective interests of the union conflict with the interests of an individual member it only makes sense … that the collective interests of the whole should prevail'.

[524] The dictum by the Court of Appeal in *Northgate HR Ltd v Mercy* [2008] IRLR 222 that there is no 'protection gap' in the legislation (Maurice Kay LJ, [15]) overlooks this point.

[525] The ECJ judgment in *Mono Car Styling SA (in liquidation) v Odemis* Case 12/08 [2009] ECR I-06653 affirmed the collective nature of the right to information and consultation but the Court said only that national rules limiting the right of individuals to bring complaints were not precluded by the Directive, not that they were mandatory.

[526] See para 3.66 *et seq* above. The substantive provisions of TUPE 2006 relating to information to and consultation of appropriate representatives are essentially unchanged from the preceding version of the Regulations with the exception of the changes we indicate below.

[527] TUPE 2006, regs 13–16.

[528] Note that in this context the definition of 'employee' is wider than usual, extending to 'any individual who works for another person whether under a contract of service or apprenticeship *or otherwise* (our italics) but does not include anyone who provides services under a contract for services …': reg 2(1).

[529] TUPE, 2006, reg 13(1). Although this provision could be read to require employers to inform and consult with representatives other than those of its own employees, it seems highly unlikely that this effect was intended: see Elias and Bowers: pp 96–97.

[530] In *Unison v Somerset County Council* [2010] IRLR 207 the EAT held at [21] that 'affected employees' were 'those who will be or may be transferred or whose jobs are in jeopardy by reason of the proposed transfer, or who have job applications within the organisation pending at the time of the transfer'. It did not extend to the whole workforce or to everyone in the workforce who might apply for a vacancy in the part transferred at some time in the future. *Quaere* whether this approach is unduly limited.

within the obligation, even though they may be affected by the transfer. However, unlike in the context of redundancies, there is no minimum number of employees who need to be affected by the transfer before the duty to inform and consult apply.

'Appropriate representatives' are defined in the same way as in the redundancy consultation provisions, analysed in para 9.34, and the same comments which were made there apply, *mutatis mutandis*, in this context. Thus, if an employer recognises an independent trade union in respect of the employees affected, representatives of that union must be informed and consulted; alternatively the employer must inform and consult 'employee representatives'.[531] Such representatives (and candidates for this position) also have identical rights to time off and protection against detrimental treatment by the employer; union representatives are likewise subject to the same general protections. Unlike the redundancy provisions, however, the duties of information and consultation relating to transfers are separate.[532] Whereas the duty to provide information applies in relation to representatives of any 'affected employees', the duty to consult applies only where the employer 'envisages that [it] will take measures in relation to an affected employee, in connection with the relevant transfer' and is technically, therefore, more restrictive in its application than the duty to inform.[533] In practice, however, it will probably be rare for no 'measures' to be envisaged. The word 'measures' is not defined, but it has been said to be 'a word of the widest import' including 'any action, step or arrangement',[534] and would certainly include changes in working practices and working conditions.

The prescribed information must be conveyed '[l]ong enough before a relevant transfer to enable the employer of any affected employees to consult the appropriate representatives of any affected employees'.[535] However, given that the duty to consult arises only where an employer envisages that it will 'take measures', this formulation of the time limit would appear to allow an employer who envisages taking no measures to comply with the duty to inform by advising representatives immediately before the transfer.[536] Although the EAT has held that the duty to consult applies to a proposed transfer which does not, in the event, take place,[537] this does not overcome the difficulty because of the specific link which is made between the time limit for the transmission of information and the consultation – a link which is additionally confusing

---

[531]   TUPE 2006, reg 13(3). Once again, if affected employees who have been invited to elect representatives fail to do so within a reasonable time, the employer must give specified information to each affected employee individually: TUPE 2006, reg 13(11). See TUPE 2006, reg 14 for the requirements for the election of employee representatives. On the employer's implied obligation to invite employees to elect representatives, see *Howard v Millrise Ltd t/a Colourflow* [2005] IRLR 84, applied *Hickling v Marshall* UKEAT/0217/10, discussed in para 9.35 above.

[532]   The EAT has confirmed that there is a duty to inform appropriate representatives even if there is no statutory duty to consult: *Todd v Strain* [2011] IRLR 11.

[533]   TUPE 2006, reg 13(1),(6).

[534]   *IPCS v Secretary of State for Defence* [1987] IRLR 373, at 376, Millett J, approved in *Todd v Strain* above, note 532, where the EAT emphasised at [20] that TUPE did not prescribe that the effect of any measures should be disadvantageous to employees to trigger the requirement to consult. In *IPCS* Millett J said that 'measures' did not include predictions which did not involve any positive steps being taken and that 'the desirability of the transfer itself or the sufficiency of the reasons for it' were 'matters of business policy for the transferring employer to decide'.

[535]   TUPE 2006, reg 13(2). In *Amicus v City Building (Glasgow) LLP* [2009] IRLR 253, the EAT held that neither TUPE 2006, reg 13 nor Art 7 of Directive 2001/23 required the transferee to consult after the transfer had taken place.

[536]   See Hepple, 1982: p 32.

[537]   *BIFU v Barclays Bank plc* [1987] ICR 495. Cf the view of Millett J in *IPCS v Secretary of State for Defence* [1987] IRLR 373, 377 that 'transfer' means the date of actual transfer.

because the duty to inform covers a much wider spectrum of matters than the duty to consult.[538] It has been suggested that an employer 'envisages' measures when it has 'formulated some definite plan or proposal which it has in mind to implement', so excluding mere hopes or possibilities.[539] Estimating the length of time to be allowed for consultation may be difficult given that this may vary greatly depending upon the number of employees affected and the nature and complexity of the measures envisaged; unlike the redundancy consultation procedures no minimum period is prescribed but employers will need to ensure that they allow sufficient time for the representatives to present their views, for a reasoned response to be made to them and, generally, for their agreement to the intended measures to be sought.[540] The position is further complicated where the employer has invited any of the affected employees to elect employee representatives. Here, provided that the employer issued the invitation long enough before the time when information must be transmitted to representatives to allow employees to elect them, it is treated as complying with the regulations if it complies with those requirements as soon as reasonably practicable after the election.[541] Where an employer wishes to keep the transfer secret for as long as possible it may be tempted not to create suspicions by inviting an election but, rather, to consult with persons already elected for some other purpose at the latest possible time. ICER, discussed in para 9.50 *et seq*, makes it more likely than in the past that such representatives will be in place.

9.44   The information to be provided by transferor and transferee employers falls into four categories: the fact that the transfer is to take place, the date or proposed date of the transfer and the reasons for it; its legal, economic and social implications for any affected employees;[542] the 'measures' which the employer 'envisages' it will, in connection with the transfer, take in relation to any affected employees (or, if no such measures, that fact); and, in the case of the transferor, the measures, in connection with the transfer, that it envisages the transferee will take in relation to any affected employees who will become its employees after the transfer by virtue of the regulations (or, if no such measures, that fact).[543] In relation to the fourth category, the transferee must give

---

[538] In *IPCS v Secretary of State for Defence*, above, Millett J (at 376) reconciled the apparent inconsistency by stating that the opening words of (the equivalent of) reg 13(2) were referring to voluntary consultations 'which the unions [at that stage the only consultees provided for in the legislation] may seek on any topic once they have the requisite information, but which the transferring employer is not compelled to grant if it chooses not to do so'. This approach was approved by the EAT in *Cable Realisations Ltd v GMB Northern* [2010] IRLR 42 and *Todd v Strain* above, note 532.

[539] *IPCS v Secretary of State for Defence*, above.

[540] See TUPE 2006, reg 13(6), (7).

[541] TUPE 2006, reg 13(10).

[542] This phrase appeared in Art 6 of EC Directive 77/187; see now Art 7 of EC Directive 2001/23. 'Legal' implications would seem to cover employees' contractual and statutory rights; 'economic and social implications' are delphic phrases which may cover matters such as the economic prospects of employees and job security implications, but this awaits clarification from the courts. In *Royal Mail Group Ltd v CWU* [2009] IRLR 1046 the Court of Appeal held that the employer was obliged to describe what it genuinely believed to be the legal implications having considered those implications but was not required to warrant the accuracy of the law.

[543] TUPE 2006, reg 13(3), and see reg 13(5) for specified modes of providing the information. Under TUPE 1981, the transferor was required to state the measures which the *transferee* envisaged it would take, not those the transferor envisaged the transferee would take. The rationale for this amendment was not explained by the Government. As Wynn-Evans comments, although calibrating the obligation by reference to the transferor may provide it with greater protection from claims, it seems possible that the reformulated provision requires greater consideration by the transferor of what it considers the transferee might do than reliance only on the transferee's notification by way of compliance with reg 13(4): Wynn-Evans 2006, p 154.

the transferor the requisite information 'at such a time as will enable' it to perform this duty.[544] The regulations do not lay down any means of enforcing this obligation directly but, as we discuss below, the transferor has the power to join the transferee to employment tribunal proceedings if it alleges that it is unable to fulfil its duty because of the transferee's default. Since 1 October 2011 there has also been an obligation on transferor and transferee employers to include specified information about their use of agency workers (if any): the number working temporarily for and under the supervision and direction of the employer; the parts of the undertaking in which they are working; and the type of work they are carrying out.

The duty to consult applies only to measures which the employer itself envisages taking; thus the transferor does not have to consult representatives about measures which the transferee may envisage, (although it must inform them of those measures). Consultation must be undertaken 'with a view to seeking their [ie. the representatives'] agreement to the intended measures', a formulation that echoes, but is arguable weaker than, the requirement to consult 'with a view to reaching agreement' in the redundancy consultation procedures[545] but one that still obliges the employer to approach the consultation process with an open mind. In the course of consultations the employer must consider any representations made by the representatives, reply to them, and give reasons if those representations are rejected.[546] Clearly there may be situations where, before or after the transfer of the undertaking, the transferor or transferee is proposing redundancy dismissals. In that situation the more extensive duty to consult on redundancies in relation to its own employees will apply contemporaneously. However the transferee will not be in a position to begin consulting about collective redundancies among transferred employees until after the transfer has taken place. At the time of writing the Coalition Government is considering its response to a consultation exercise on whether this causes difficulties for employers.[547]

As in the case of redundancy consultation the duty does not extend to measures which may be envisaged by an associated employer, thus excluding those of a parent company or another company in the same group. It is expressly provided that the duties to inform and consult under TUPE apply irrespective of whether the decision resulting in the relevant transfer is taken by the employer or a person controlling the employer[548] but where the latter is the case the latitude for the employer to modify its position in the course of consultations may be more limited.

9.45 If an employer fails to fulfil any of its statutory duties a complaint may be made to an employment tribunal.[549] If the failure relates to union or employee representatives, the complaint may be made by the union or employee representatives respectively; in any other case it may

---

[544] TUPE 2006, reg 13(4). Information may not be supplied under cover of commercial confidentiality so as to disable the transferor from complying with its duty: *IPCS v Secretary of State for Defence* [1987] IRLR 373, 375–376.

[545] TULRCA 1992, s 188(2).

[546] TUPE 2006, s 13(7). See also the definition of consultation propounded by Glidewell LJ in *R v British Coal Corpn and Secretary of State for Trade and Industry, ex p Price* [1994] IRLR 72, 75.

[547] *Collective Redundancy Consultation Rules: Call for Evidence*, BIS, November 2011, para 4.4.

[548] TUPE 2006, reg 13(12). See *Akavan Erityisalojen Keskusliitto AEK ry v Fujitsu Siemens Computers Oy* Case C-44/08 [2009] IRLR 944 for the operation of this principle in the context of collective redundancies.

[549] TUPE 2006, reg 15(1). The complaint must be presented before the end of the three-month period beginning with the date on which the relevant transfer was completed (with the usual exception where this was not 'reasonably practicable'): reg 15(12). This does not prevent a complaint being presented before the completion of the transfer: *BIFU v Barclays Bank plc* [1987] ICR 495; *South Durham Health Authority v UNISON* [1995] IRLR 407.

be made by any of the affected employees.[550] As in the context of redundancy consultation, the employer may defend the complaint by showing that there were 'special circumstances which rendered it not reasonably practicable' for it to perform the duty in question and that it took all such steps towards its performance as were reasonably practicable in the circumstances.[551] The case law developed in that context will be relevant here, although it is possible that the defence will be applied more readily in a transfer situation due to the speed with which a transfer can take place and because of the fact that, often, its occurrence is surrounded in secrecy.[552] Clearly, allowing secrecy *per se* as a defence could effectively nullify the duty. However, it is possible that if an exchange of contracts and completion took place on the same day, and a tribunal were persuaded that the sale would not otherwise have occurred, these may be regarded as 'special circumstances', although the defence is still subject to the requirement to take such steps as were reasonably practicable. As in the case of the redundancy consultation provisions the 'special circumstances' defence does not appear on the fact of the EC Directive.[553] If a transferor wishes to show that it was not reasonably practicable for it to perform its duty to inform appropriate representatives of the measures that it envisaged the transferee would take because the transferee failed to supply it with the requisite information at the requisite time, it must give the transferee notice of that fact, whereupon the transferee becomes a party to the proceedings.[554]

If the complaint is upheld the tribunal will make a declaration and may also order the employer to pay 'appropriate compensation' to such descriptions of affected employees as are specified in the award.[555] 'Appropriate compensation' means 'such sum not exceeding thirteen weeks' pay for the employee in question as the tribunal considers just and equitable having regard to the seriousness of the failure of the employer to comply with [its] duty'.[556] The EAT has held that, as in the context of the redundancy consultation procedure, the award is penal in nature, with the modification that a tribunal could have regard to any loss sustained by the employer's failure 'so long as it recognised that the focus of the award requires to be the penal nature which governs it and proof of loss is neither necessary nor determinative of the level at which to fix the award'.[557] Prior to the implementation of the 1999 amending regulations, compensation for breach of the duties in this context was limited to a maximum of four weeks' pay. It was strongly arguable that this did not meet the requirement under Community law for the penalty for infringements to be 'effective, proportionate and dissuasive'; it could still be argued, albeit with less force, that the revised figure

---

[550] TUPE 2006, reg 15(1). See *Nationwide Building Society v Benn* [2010] IRLR 922, Slade J at [59]-[60].

[551] TUPE 2006, reg 15(2). As in the case of the redundancy consultation procedures, a failure on the part of a person controlling (directly or indirectly) the employer to provide information to the employer does not constitute 'special circumstances': TUPE 2006, reg 15(6).

[552] Note, however, the Disclosure Rules and Transparency Rules of the Financial Services Authority, DTR 2.5.7, discussed in para 9.39 above. Rule 2.6(b) of the Takeover Rules provides that '[p]romptly after the publication of an announcement' of a firm intention to make an offer for a company, "both the offeror and the offeree company must make that announcement, or a circular summarising the terms and conditions of the offer, readily available to their employee representatives or, where there are no such representatives, to the employees themselves'.

[553] See the discussion in para 9.39.

[554] TUPE 2006, reg 15(5). If the transferor shows this was the case, the transferee may be ordered to pay compensation: TUPE 2006, reg 15(8)(b).

[555] TUPE 2006, reg 15(7),(8).

[556] TUPE 2006, reg 16(3). In *Zaman v Kozee Sleep Products Ltd (t/a Dorlux Beds UK)* [2011] IRLR 196 the EAT confirmed that the statutory maximum of a week's pay under ERA 1996, s 227 does not apply in this context.

[557] *Sweetin v Coral Racing* [2006] IRLR 252, [31] (Lady Smith).

fails to meet these conditions.[558] An employee who does not receive the compensation due to him or her under an award may complain to a tribunal, which will order the employer to pay the amount awarded.[559]

At one time there was concern that employees in a transfer situation could be at risk of awards being made against an insolvent transferor. Their position was safeguarded when the EAT held that liability for a failure to consult passed automatically, on a transfer, to the transferee.[560] However the Labour Government was concerned that this meant that 'there would arguably be little or no incentive for the transferor to comply with the relevant information and consultation requirements.'[561] TUPE 2006 provides that the transferee is jointly and severally liable with the transferor in respect of compensation payable under para 15(8)(a) (an order against the transferor for breaching its obligations to inform or consult or in relation to the election of employee representatives) or para 15(11) (an order against the transferor or transferee as applicable for failing to pay compensation it had previously been ordered to pay).[562] This will enable employees or their representatives to proceed against the employer which they consider can best meet the claim.[563] However the Government declined to introduce joint and several liability in relation to the protective award made in respect of collective redundancies under TULRCA 1992 due to the lack of consensus on this issue, a number of respondents having said that liability should rest with the culpable party and apply jointly only if both parties had been at fault.[564] As a consequence it seems that previous case law on this issue stands, on the basis of which liability for a protective award transfers to the transferee.[565]

A criticism relating to this procedure, which we also made in para 9.42, is that the decision to seek a remedy for non-compliance with the duties to inform and consult lies only with 'appropriate representatives' once they have been chosen. Where the representative is a union, then in relation to the transferee employer in particular it may not wish to risk prejudicing its future relationship and possibly voluntary recognition. Again it would seem desirable for an individual to have the right to seek a remedy either independently or if the union or employee representatives fail within

---

[558] In 2006 the Labour Government rejected the TUC proposal that a form of injunctive relief should be introduced to prevent a transfer occurring until consultations had been completed in accordance with the Regulations, stating that the existing remedy was adequate: *TUPE: Draft Revised Regulations: Government response to the public consultation*, DTI, February 2006, para 7.7. In *Marcroft v Heartland (Midlands) Ltd* [2011] IRLR 599 the Court of Appeal confirmed that compliance with reg 13 was not a condition precedent to an effective transfer of a contract of employment and that breach of the duty could not lead to an avoidance of the transfer.

[559] TUPE 2006, reg 15(10),(11). A complaint must be presented before the end of the three-month period beginning with the date of the tribunal's order (with the usual exception where this was not 'reasonably practicable'): reg 15(12). In *Dillon v Todd and Care Concern GB Ltd* UKEATS/0010/11/BI the EAT held that where the EAT made an order under reg 15(8) which was not made by the tribunal, or was in different terms, the time limit runs from the date of the EAT's order not that of the tribunal.

[560] *Kerry Foods Ltd v Creber* [2000] IRLR 10, *Alamo Group (Europe) Ltd v Tucker* [2003] IRLR 266; cf *TGWU v James McKinnon, JR (Haulage) Ltd* [2001] IRLR 597.

[561] *TUPE Draft Revised Regulations Public Consultation Document*, DTI, March 2005, at para 83; see generally paras 82–85.

[562] TUPE 2006, reg 15(9); see Directive 2001/23, Art 3(1).

[563] In *Amicus v Dynamex Friction Ltd* [2005] IRLR 724 a freezing order was made prohibiting transferee companies from disposing of any assets up to the value of £325,000 pending the conclusion of tribunal proceedings against them for failing to consult over redundancies in connection with a transfer of an undertaking in circumstances where the claimants had a good arguable case that there was a real risk that the assets would otherwise be dissipated.

[564] *TUPE: Draft Revised Regulations: Government response to the public consultation*, DTI, February 2006, para 7.8.

[565] *Kerry Foods Ltd v Creber* [2000] IRLR 10, *Alamo Group (Europe) Ltd v Tucker* [2003] IRLR 266; cf *TGWU v James McKinnon, JR (Haulage) Ltd* [2001] IRLR 597.

a specified period to take action on his or her behalf, although the less well-defined nature of the obligations in this case as compared with those applicable to redundancy may present formidable obstacles to assembling the evidence necessary to bring a claim in the absence of union co-operation and assistance.

Health and safety

9.46   A full examination of the law relating to health and safety lies beyond the scope of this work.[566] However, in this section we outline very briefly the provisions relating to worker representation in this context because of the interesting contrasts they provide to the other areas we discuss.

Health and safety has 'always had a reputation as being particularly suitable for consultation and unsuitable for bargaining'[567] although the basis of this assumption – that there is a 'greater natural identity of interests'[568] in this area than in most others – is highly contentious and seems not to stand up to empirical investigation.[569] However it is striking that the previous Conservative Government accepted proposals at European Community level furthering employee representation in health and safety, in marked contrast to its stance in other areas. The important provisions for information, consultation and worker participation contained in the Framework Directive on the working environment (Council Directive 89/391), which could have been adopted by a qualified majority under what is now Article 153 TFEU (then Article 118a of the EEC Treaty) were, in the event, approved unanimously.

Provision for employee representation in health and safety matters in domestic law was initially made in the Health and Safety at Work etc Act 1974. As originally formulated, this legislation envisaged the appointment of safety representatives either by trade union appointment or workforce election. However the latter option was quickly repealed by the 'Social Contract' legislation, partly on the ground that non-union representatives would lack the resources required to bring any effective pressure to bear on employers. Regulations were then promulgated under the Act giving recognised independent trade unions the right to appoint employees (who may, but need not be, union officials) as safety representatives, with the statutory functions, *inter alia*, of investigating potential hazards and employees' complaints and conducting regular inspections of the workplace.[570] Employers were also obliged to consult representatives on arrangements for co-operating with employees on promoting and developing health and safety measures and in checking their effectiveness[571] and to provide them with the information necessary to enable them to fulfil their functions (with specified exceptions).[572] Safety representatives were accorded the

---

[566] See further Ford, Clarke and Smart, 2010
[567] P Davies and M Freedland, 1983: p 231.
[568] *Report of the Committee on Safety and Health at Work*, Cmnd 5034, 1972.
[569] See P James, 1992, and P James and D Walters, 1997, and references therein.
[570] Safety Representatives and Safety Committee Regulations 1977, SI 1977/500; see also Health and Safety Commission Codes of Practice on Safety Representatives and Safety Committees (1978) and Time off for the Training of Safety Representatives (1978). The Police (Health and Safety) Regulations 1999, SI 1999/860 require police organisations to be treated as recognised unions in this context. In *Costain Building and Civil Engineering Ltd v Smith* [2000] ICR 215 the appointment of a safety representative was ineffective because at the time of the appointment he was not an employee.
[571] HSWA 1974, s 2(6).
[572] Safety Representatives and Safety Committees Regulations 1977, SI 1977/500, reg 7.

right to paid time off during working hours to perform their functions and to undergo reasonable training, with a right to complain to an employment tribunal if this was refused.[573] In addition, if at least two representatives so requested, employers were obliged to establish a 'safety committee' with the function of 'keeping under review the measures taken to ensure the health and safety at work of [the] employees and such other functions as may be prescribed'.[574] Beyond that their structure and remit was a matter for management and union(s) to decide.[575]

Following the entry into force of Council Directive 89/391, a number of measures were introduced into UK law to comply with EC requirements, including a specific duty to consult safety representatives 'in good time' on specified matters including the introduction of any measures which may substantially affect the health and safety of the employees they represent and the consequences of introducing new technologies.[576] However voluntary recognition by the employer of a union remained a pre-condition for the obligations to inform and consult to be triggered. The Directive requires that 'information, dialogue and balanced participation[577] on safety and health at work must be developed between employers and workers and/or their representatives by means of appropriate procedures and instruments, in accordance with national laws and/or practices.[578] In the light of the decisions of the ECJ in 1994 that the UK was in breach of its obligations in relation to redundancies and transfers of undertakings because of dependence upon the will of the employer[579] it seemed tolerably clear that similar principles applied in this context. In response to this concern the Health and Safety (Consultation with Employees) Regulations 1996[580] were introduced. Like the current legislation relating to redundancies and transfers, these operate by way of a back-up to the pre-existing provisions, requiring employers to consult employees only where they are not covered by safety representatives appointed by recognised trade unions.[581] However, they differ from those provisions in that in this context employers may choose to consult employees directly *or*, in respect of any group of employees, to consult one or more persons in that group (referred to as 'representatives of employee safety'), who were elected by employees in the group at the time of the election, to represent them for the purposes of such consultation.[582] No

---

[573] Safety Representatives and Safety Committees Regulations 1977, SI 1977/500, regs 4(2), 11 and Schedule. See also the Code of Practice issued by the Health and Safety Commission on Time Off for the Training of Safety Representatives (1978) and *Duthie v Bath and Somerset Council* [2003] ICR 1405.

[574] HSWA 1974, s 2(7); SI 1977/500, reg 9.

[575] It is automatically unfair for an employer to dismiss an employee in connection with being a safety representative or member of a safety committee (ERA 1996, s 100) and such employees have the right not to be subjected to 'any detriment': ERA 1996, s 44. There is no limit on the compensatory award for unfair dismissal if an employee is dismissed for health and safety reasons: s 124(1A). In *Shillito v Van Leer (UK) Ltd* [1997] IRLR 495, the EAT stated, *obiter*, that it was no defence to a complaint under s 44 that the safety representative intended to embarrass the employer in front of external safety authorities or that he performed these duties in an unreasonable way, unacceptable to the employer (see also *Bass Taverns Ltd v Burgess* [1995] IRLR 596, discussed at para 8.10).

[576] SI 1977/500, reg 4A, inserted by the Management of Health and Safety at Work Regulations 1992, SI 1992/2051, reg 17, Schedule. The 1992 Regulations have now been replaced by SI 1999/3242 but the amendments made by the 1992 Regulations remain in force subject to a minor amendment made by the 1999 Regulations.

[577] The meaning of 'balanced participation' is unclear: see Nielsen and Szyszczak, 1997: p 308; Neal, 1990: pp 97–98; Weiss, 1996: p 219.

[578] Preamble, para 12. Cf the wording of Art 1(2) which refers to 'workers *and* their representatives'.

[579] Case C-382/92 *EC Commission v United Kingdom* [1994] IRLR 392 (transfers) and Case C-383/92 [1994] IRLR 412 (collective redundancies); see further para 9.31 above.

[580] SI 1996/1513. For a critique of the Regulations and discussion of the wider issues raised by them, see P James and D Walters, 1997.

[581] SI 1996/1513, reg 3.

[582] SI 1996/1513, reg 4.

procedures are stipulated for the conduct of such elections.[583] Employers have a duty to ensure that representatives of employee safety receive reasonable training for the performance of their statutory functions (unlike safety representatives, at the employers' expense)[584] and representatives have a right to paid time off during working hours for training and to perform their functions, and may complain to an employment tribunal if time off is not granted.[585]

Employers are required to provide 'representatives of employee safety' with such information as is necessary to enable them to participate fully and effectively in consultations on the matters specified in the legislation and to carry out their functions of making representations on various health and safety matters.[586] However, the functions of 'representatives of employee safety' are less extensive than those of safety representatives; thus they do not have the right to conduct workplace inspections or the investigation of employee complaints, nor are they entitled to require the establishment of safety committees.

9.47   The 1996 Regulations appear to have led to an increase in consultation on health and safety. Prior to their introduction, although initially the legislation led to a significant growth in worker representation (with some research suggesting that around 80% of all employees were employed in workplaces with safety representatives), by 1987 the number of workplaces with representatives had declined,[587] and the 1990 Workplace Industrial Relations Survey found that in 37% of workplaces with 25 or more employees, management engaged in no consultation over health and safety matters.[588] By 2004, however, managers in workplaces with 10 or more employees reported that no steps were taken to consult in only 1% of workplaces, with 20% having single or multi-issue joint consultative committees dealing with health and safety, 22% consulting with safety representatives, and 57% consulting with employees directly. A striking feature of these figures is the number of workplaces engaging in direct consultation and the decline in the use of representative channels. Having a committee in place was more common in workplaces with union recognition, but even then there was a rise in direct consultation and decline in consultation through free-standing worker representatives.[589]

In the event that employers fail to comply with their duties to consult, health and safety inspectors are statutorily empowered to issue an 'improvement notice' which requires any person contravening the legislation to remedy the breach within a specified period; non-compliance with these regulations also constitutes a criminal offence. Initially the Health and Safety Commission resolved to try and avoid inspector involvement in industrial relations issues and stressed that enforcement action should not be considered unless inspectors were satisfied that all voluntary

---

[583] Cf the provisions governing redundancies and transfers of undertakings, discussed in para 9.35.

[584] Note, however, that the preface to the Code of Practice on Time Off for the Training of Safety Representatives suggests that the employer should provide training on hazards and arrangements specific to the workplace.

[585] Reg 7. Candidates for election also have a right to reasonable paid time off. It is automatically unfair to dismiss an employee for taking part or proposing to take part in consultations under the Regulations or in the election of representatives of employee safety (with no limit on the compensatory award): ERA 1996, ss 100(ba), 124(1A), and such employees have the right not to be subjected to 'any detriment': s 44(ba).

[586] SI 1996/1513, regs 5 and 6.

[587] Walters, 1990: p 11.

[588] Millward *et al*, 1992: pp 162–63 (and p 2).

[589] Kersley *et al* 2006, pp 203–205. As between 1998 and 2004 the evidence showed that the shift to direct communication was due to compositional change in the population of workplaces: p 204.

means of resolving a dispute, including resort to ACAS, had been exhausted.[590] Even in that eventuality the Commission suggested that the issuing of an improvement notice, rather than prosecution, would normally be the most appropriate first step. This reflects the emphasis of the Code of Practice which urges the employer, unions and safety representatives to make 'full and proper use of the existing agreed industrial relations machinery to reach the degree of agreement necessary to achieve the purpose of the Regulations and in order to resolve any differences'.[591] It was doubted by some commentators that a consensus-orientated approach of this nature could suffice,[592] and in 2000 the Commission consulted on a range of issues relating to employee consultation and involvement in health and safety, including how greater publicity can be given to the statutory obligations and the possibility of greater use of enforcement action by inspectors.[593] A further consultation exercise was undertaken in 2006.[594] At the time of writing, the HSE guidance for inspectors on worker consultation and involvement follows previous practice in emphasising that formal enforcement action should generally be a last resort but also states that where employers have failed to comply with legal duties on procedural matters, such as failing to comply with a request to create a safety committee or appointing representatives of employee safety rather than permitting elections, immediate enforcement action may be appropriate.[595] Moreover, failure to consult employees may be an aggravating factor in considering enforcement action under other regulations.[596] The guidance also states that 'w]hile employers have a free choice about the method of consultation, genuine consultation of every employee individually is likely to be impractical, except in small organisations (ie. those with less (sic) than 50 employees)'.[597]

Pensions

9.48   If an employer wishes its employees to be contracted out of the state earnings-related pensions scheme it must give written notice to the Commissioners for HMRC, having first consulted any independent trade union it recognises in respect of the earners concerned.[598] Where an employer has established a contracted-out scheme, unions also have the right to receive on request specified information relating to the scheme, including basic information about membership, contribution and benefits; the constitution of the scheme; and audited accounts and an actuarial statement.[599] Since April 2006 employers who wish to make certain changes to an occupational or personal pension scheme have been required to consult employees who are active or prospective members

---

[590]   HSC guidance issued October 1978. The Health and Safety Commission merged with the Health and Safety Executive in April 2008.

[591]   Safety Representatives and Safety Committee (1978), para 3.

[592]   See P James, 1992, for a discussion of possible reforms in this area; for discussion of the wider issues see P James and D Walters, 1997 ; Gunningham and Johnstone, 1999; Howes, 2007; for useful background, see Beck and Woolfson, 2000.

[593]   *Employee Consultation and Involvement in Health and Safety*, Health and Safety Discussion Document, 2000: para 64. See P James and D Walters 2002 and 2005 for a discussion of options for reform.

[594]   *Improving worker involvement – Improving health and safety: Consultative Document*, HSC, 2006.

[595]   HSE's Guidance for inspectors on worker consultation and involvement, July 2007, paras 44 and 45.

[596]   Para 50.

[597]   Para 43.

[598]   The Occupational Pension Schemes (Contracting Out) Regulations 1996, SI 1996/1172, regs 2- 4, as amended.

[599]   See generally the Occupational Pension Schemes (Disclosure of Information) Regulations, SI 1996/1655 as amended. Any dispute about whether a union is an independent union recognised by the employer, or whether the employer has complied with the consultation requirements, may be referred to an employment tribunal.

of the scheme to whom the change relates ('affected members') or their representatives before the change is made.[600] Where 'specified' arrangements for consultation already exist the employer must consult in accordance with such one or more of these arrangements as it may choose. 'Specified arrangements' are representation by an independent recognised union; by information or consultation representatives as defined in ICER 2004; or by representatives identified under a pre-existing agreement which satisfies the conditions in regulation 8 of ICER. The employer may consult employees directly if either a 'negotiated agreement' or pre-existing agreement under ICER provides for this. If any affected members are not covered by such arrangements the employer must consult representatives elected specifically for the purpose of such consultations or, there are none or there are affected members whose interests are not represented by such representatives, employees themselves. The remedy for failure to consult is by way of complaint to the Pensions Regulator who has the power to impose a fine of up to £50,000 for breach of the duty, and who may also issue an 'improvement notice' directing specified steps to be taken or not taken. In contrast to the provisions governing consultation on collective redundancies and transfers of undertakings, a complaint may be made either by a representative of affected members or by the affected members themselves. Consulted representatives are entitled to paid time off for performing their functions and are protected against dismissal and other detriment for activities as a representative or as a candidate in an election. These rights are enforced by complaint to an employment tribunal.

Training

9.49   An employer must consult an independent trade union about training matters where that union has been recognised in accordance with the statutory recognition procedure and a method for the conduct of collective bargaining has been specified by the CAC and neither its legal effect nor its content varied by the parties.[601] The employer must then 'from time to time' invite the union to send representatives to a meeting to consult on its training policy for workers within the bargaining unit and its training plans for the next six months, and to report on training since the previous meeting. The first meeting must be held within six months of the obligation coming into effect, with subsequent meetings at least every six months. Employers must provide the union with specified information, and must 'take account of any written representations about matters raised at a meeting' received from the union within four weeks of the meeting. It is unclear precisely what this duty entails; on one view it would suffice for the employer to take account of union views in its own mental deliberations, although a safer course would be to report its responses to the union in writing. If an employer fails to comply with its statutory obligations, a union may complain to an employment tribunal which, if it upholds the complaint, may award compensation of up to two weeks' pay to each member of the bargaining unit.[602]

---

[600]   Occupational and Personal Pension Schemes (Consultation by Employers and Miscellaneous Amendment) Regulations 2006, SI 2006/349.

[601]   TULRCA 1992, s 70B. See para 9.5 *et seq* for the statutory recognition procedure.

[602]   TULRCA 1992, s 70C. In this context the statutory maximum of a week's pay applies (£430 at 1 February 2012 and at the time of writing).

The Information and Consultation of Employees Regulations 2004

9.50   The Information and Consultation Directive, to which we referred in para 9.30, was implemented in Britain by ICER 2004,[603] which came into force on 6 April 2005. Initially only undertakings employing at least 150 employees in the UK were covered by the Regulations; those employing at least 100 were subject to them as from 6 April 2007, and those employing at least 50 as from 6 April 2008.[604] The Labour Government was determined from the outset to avoid a 'one size fits all' approach to information and consultation; rather, the aim was to 'build on UK experience and create room for the wide diversity of practices that have built over the years, combining both representative and direct forms of participation. Individual organisations should be able to develop their own arrangements tailored to the particular circumstances, through voluntary agreements'.[605] The basic framework of the Regulations was agreed between the Government and the TUC and CBI. Important features of that framework are provision for the establishment of an information and consultation ('I and C') procedure under the Regulations either at the initiative of the employer or at the request of employees (but no requirement to do so otherwise); a requirement for a 40% majority to trigger the procedure where there is a 'pre-existing agreement' for I and C; the option for a negotiated agreement under the statutory procedure to provide that the employer informs and consults employees directly rather than through their representatives; and the operation of a 'standard' procedure, reflecting the terms of Article 4(2) of the Directive, in the event of a failure to agree. The Regulations are, in general, enforced by the CAC (with provision for reference to ACAS if the CAC considers that ACAS could assist),[606] with a right of appeal to the EAT on a point of law.[607] However, if an employer has concluded an I and C agreement prior to an employee request, such an agreement is not subject to enforcement under ICER 2004 nor will it be subject to other ICER provisions such as those governing disclosure of information or the terms on which information is disclosed; rather, its content, application and legal status will be entirely a matter for the parties to determine.[608] There are strong incentives, therefore, for employers to attempt to conclude such agreements with their employees.[609] Unlike

---

[603]   SI 2004/3426. See generally Hall, 2005; Ewing and Truter, 2005; P Lorber, 2006; P Davies and M Freedland, 2007: pp 150–159. On the impact of ICER in practice, see Hall, 2006 and Hall *et al* 2007, 2008, 2009 and 2010; Deakin and Koukiadaki, 2012.

[604]   ICER 2004, reg 3, Sch 1. The Regulations apply where the registered or head office of the undertaking or its principal place of business is in Britain; there are separate Regulations governing Northern Ireland. Where the registered office is in Britain but the head office or principal place of business is in Northern Ireland or vice versa, they apply only where the majority of employees are employed to work in Britain: reg 3.

[605]   *High Performance Workplaces – Informing and Consulting Employees: Consultation Document*, DTI, 2003: p 5.

[606]   ICER 2004, reg 38.

[607]   ICER 2004, reg 35(6). In this context the CAC is expressly required to give reasons for its decisions: reg 35(5). In reaching its decisions, the CAC may draw an adverse inference from a party's failure to comply with any reasonable request to provide information or documents relevant to a complaint presented to it or an application made to it: reg 35(3).

[608]   Whether such an agreement constitutes a 'collective agreement' within TULRCA 1992, s 178, and is thereby governed by the statutory presumption in s 179 will depend upon its content, as well as whether a trade union is a party to it: see further para 9.26. Non-applicability of ICER 2004 is without prejudice to the separate provisions governing disclosure of information for collective bargaining purposes, discussed in para 9.22.

[609]   However, early research showed little sign of the widespread adoption of agreements meeting the statutory definition of a 'pre-existing agreement' : Hall, 2006: p 465. See Hall *et al*, 2010; Deakin and Koukiadaki, 2012a for later findings.

TICER 1999, which govern transnational I and C procedures, there is no requirement for such agreements to be concluded prior to the Regulations coming into force.[610] The Regulations, which are complex, are supplemented by Guidance from BIS (formerly the DTI) which aims to provide a 'plain explanation' of them together with 'recommended good practice',[611] although, unlike a Code of Practice, it has no legal force: those involved in CAC proceedings may bring the guidance to the attention of the CAC but the CAC is not bound to follow it.[612] At the time of writing only a relatively small number of cases have come before the CAC.[613] Space does not permit us to analyse in detail every aspect of ICER 2004. Rather, we examine below the general scheme prescribed by the Regulations before discussing those respects in which they may be regarded as falling short of the requirements of Directive 2002/14.

(i) Coverage

9.51   ICER 2004 apply to 'undertakings'. An 'undertaking' is defined as 'a public or private undertaking carrying out an economic activity' whether or not operating for gain'.[614] BIS considers that, in relation to companies, this term covers a separately incorporated legal, rather than an organisational, entity (establishment, division etc). It also covers all other employers, such as partnerships and individuals, as long as they carry out an economic activity.[615] Decisions on the application of the Acquired Rights Directive, which also refers to 'economic activities' and which we discuss in para 3.67 *et seq*, are likely to be relevant here. The application of ICER 2004 to some areas of the public sector may be difficult to determine, particularly where they carry out a range of activities, only some of which may be 'economic' in nature. However the Labour Government issued a Code of Practice which was intended to apply the general principles of ICER 2004 to central government departments and agencies which are not covered by the Regulations and which requires departments to encourage their non-departmental public bodies to do likewise.[616] At the time of writing this has not been amended or withdrawn. If followed, it may reduce the incidence of cases on the application of the Regulations.

In order to determine whether the undertaking has a sufficient number of employees to be covered by ICER 2004, it is necessary to calculate, according to specified criteria, the average number it has employed in the previous twelve months.[617] Employees on short-term contracts are included in this calculation, but certain part-time employees may be counted as half a

---

[610]   Under TICER 1999, however, the existence of an agreement removes the obligation to negotiate a new agreement entirely: Dukes, 2007, p 332; see para 9.64 below.

[611]   *The Information and Consultation of Employees Regulations 2004: DTI Guidance*, January 2006 (referred to below as 'DTI Guidance'): para 3.

[612]   DTI Guidance, para 4. In *Darnton v Bournemouth University* [2010] IRLR 294 the EAT pointed at [18] to a misstatement of the law in para 31 of the Guidance.

[613]   Guidance as to the practice of the CAC and decisions may be found at www.cac.gov.uk.

[614]   ICER 2004, reg 2, enacting the definition in Directive 2004/14, Art 2(a).

[615]   DTI Guidance, 2005: pp 4–5.

[616]   Cabinet Office Code of Practice on Informing and Consulting Employees in the Civil Service.

[617]   ICER 2004, reg 4(1), (2). If the undertaking has been in existence for less than twelve months, the number is to be calculated by reference to the number of months it has been in existence: reg 4(4). In this context agency workers who have a contract with a temporary work agency which is not a contract of employment are to be treated as employed by the temporary work agency for the duration of their assignment with the employer: ICER 2004, reg 3A.

person (in this context only) if the employer so decides.[618] Where an individual is employed in two or more undertakings he or she will be counted as an employee within each. There is no provision for adding the numbers employed by an 'associated employer' of the undertaking to determine whether the numerical threshold is met, in contrast to the statutory recognition procedure.[619] Whether an individual is an 'employee' of the undertaking, rather than being self-employed or working for an agency, for example, will be determined according to the principles that we discuss in chapter 3.

An employee or employees' representative (a term which under ICER 2004 is left undefined)[620] may request in writing data from an employer to determine the number of people employed by the undertaking.[621] This information may be required either to determine whether the undertaking is covered by ICER 2004; to calculate the number required to make a valid employee 'request', discussed below; or both. If, after a one-month period, the employer fails to provide this data, or it is false or incomplete in a material particular, the employee or representative who made the request may complain to the CAC, and if the complaint is upheld the CAC may order the employer to disclose specified data by a specified date.[622] Employers who do not consider that they are covered by ICER 2004 may themselves apply to the CAC for this to be determined, but only after an employee request has been made.[623]

(ii) Triggering the requirement to negotiate an information and consultation agreement

9.52   An employer is required to initiate negotiations with 'negotiating representatives' to reach a 'negotiated agreement' on I and C if it receives a 'valid employee request'.[624] A 'valid' request requires the support of at least 10% of employees in the undertaking, subject to a minimum of 15 and a maximum of 2,500 employees.[625] It may be made either in the form of a single request, or a number of separate requests, provided that these are made within a 'rolling' six-month period.[626] Requests (which must comply with certain formalities)[627] may be made directly to the employer or,

---

[618] ICER 2004, reg 4(3).
[619] See para 9.6 above.
[620] There seems to be no restriction on the person or body who may act in this capacity. The DTI Guidance, 2006: p 13, n 5 states that the provision is intended to allow employees to request data through a third party if, for example, they do not wish to identify themselves.
[621] ICER 2004, reg 5. See *Darnton and Bournemouth University* IC/14 (2007), CAC, 15 April 2008. In *Amicus (as Employees' Representative) and Macmillan Publishers* IC/4 (2005), CAC, the CAC held that the recipient of the information must himself or herself be put in a position to be enabled to make the calculation of the number of employees in the undertaking. This may go beyond disclosure of a bare number, and on the facts required disclosure of the establishments, sites and/or plants that the employer considered made up the undertaking and the number of employees in each.
[622] ICER 2004, reg 6. An order of the CAC may be relied on as if it were an order of the High Court: reg 35(4).
[623] ICER 2004, reg 13.
[624] An employer may also do this on its own initiative (ICER 2004, reg 11), but is much more likely to establish an agreement outside the statutory process where no prior request has been made (although note that where an employer has received a request in relation to one undertaking and wishes to negotiate an agreement covering both that undertaking and another undertaking where no request has been made it will need to notify the employees in the second undertaking of its intention to do this: reg 14(6), (7)). The same statutory framework applies where an employer initiates the statutory process *mutatis mutandis* as where it is initiated by employees. In this discussion we use the terminology applicable to the case in which the procedure has been initiated by employees.
[625] ICER 2004, reg 7(1)–(3).
[626] ICER 2004, reg 7(2).
[627] ICER 2004, reg 7(4).

alternatively, to the CAC, a route that employees may prefer to take if they do not wish to identify themselves to the employer. Where the CAC receives a request, it must notify the employer of this; request from the employer such information as it needs to verify the number and names of the employees who have made the request;[628] and, on the basis of this information inform the employer and the employees who have made the request how many employees have made it (but it will not name those employees).[629]

Special provision is made for the situation where a 'pre-existing agreement' ('PEA') is in place prior to the request being made. Here, if the request is made by fewer than 40% of the employees in the undertaking the employer has the option, instead of initiating negotiations, of holding a ballot of all employees in the undertaking to seek their endorsement of that request.[630] The employer must inform employees of its intention to hold such a ballot within one month of the employee request and arrange for the ballot to be held as soon as reasonably practicable thereafter (although not within 21 days of the ballot being announced).[631] A request is regarded as being 'endorsed' for this purpose if at least 40% of the employees employed in the undertaking *and* a majority of employees voting in the ballot have voted in favour: if this happens, the employer must then initiate negotiations;[632] otherwise a three-year 'moratorium' applies before another request can be made (subject to exceptions, discussed below).[633] The employer must make such arrangements as are reasonably practicable to ensure that the ballot is 'fair'; all employees must be given an entitlement to vote; and the ballot must be conducted so as to secure that votes are accurately counted and that, so far as is reasonably practicable, those voting do so in secret.[634] These conditions may best be achieved by employing an independent person to conduct the ballot, although this is not a statutory requirement. An employee or employees' representative may complain to the CAC if he or she considers that the statutory requirements governing such a ballot have not been met; if it upholds the complaint the CAC must then order the ballot to be re-run unless the employer has indicated, prior to this, that it would prefer to initiate negotiations.[635]

The high level of support required to trigger the obligation to negotiate an I and C agreement where there is a PEA means that voluntary arrangements cannot be easily disturbed. The nature of the arrangements that will act as such a barrier is clearly a crucial issue for employers and, possibly, in some cases for trade unions particularly where they are effectively operating a 'single-channel' form of workplace representation. Although the obligation to initiate negotiations under the statutory procedure does not of itself displace the PEA, that agreement will no longer of itself suffice to discharge the employer's statutory obligations. A requirement for a single PEA to cover all employees would have presented practical difficulties where collective agreements gave unions

---

[628] The employer must provide this information as soon as reasonably practicable: reg 7(6).

[629] ICER 2004, reg 7(5). In *Darnton v Bournemouth University* [2009] IRLR 4, para 47 the CAC held that the trigger for the date on which an employee request is made under reg 7(7)(b)(ii) is the date on which the CAC notifies the employer and the employees as to the number of employees who had made the request where the number of requests taken together satisfied the 10% threshold.

[630] ICER 2004, reg 8(1), (2).

[631] ICER 2004, reg 8(3). This gives an employee or employees' representative in the relevant undertaking the opportunity to complain to the CAC if he or she does not consider that there is a 'pre-existing agreement' complying with the statutory criteria in place: reg 10(1).

[632] ICER 2004, reg 8(6), (5).

[633] ICER 2004, reg 12(1)(c).

[634] ICER 2004, reg 8(4).

[635] ICER 2004, reg 10(2), (3). See also reg 8(7)–(9) for complaints relating to a failure to inform employees about the ballot or to hold the ballot.

consultation rights given that it is comparatively unusual for such agreements to extend to the entire workforce, including senior management. ICER 2004 deal with this by providing that the 40% barrier applies if, prior to the request being made, there are *one or more* PEAs which meet the specified criteria. Such agreements must: be in writing; cover all the employees of the undertaking; have been approved by the employees; and set out how the employer is to give information to the employees or their representatives and seek their views on such information.[636] This means that employers may, for example, have a collective agreement with a trade union or unions covering half the workforce and another agreement or set of agreements for the remainder. In *Stewart v Moray Council*[637] the EAT held that employees were 'covered' by an agreement made between a union and employer if they fell within the category or categories of employees intended to be regulated by it, regardless of whether they were union members. In that case the EAT also confirmed that, although the requirement to cover all employees may be met by a number of agreements read together, each of the other requirements has to be met by each individual agreement. Thus, where the employer submitted that there were three PEAs for the purposes of ICER, the finding that one such agreement did not set out how the employer was to give information to employees or their representatives and seek their views meant that the employer came under the statutory duty to initiate negotiations.

There are no restrictions on the method, frequency, timing or subject-matter of I and C arrangements established under pre-existing agreements.[638] Further flexibility is afforded by provision for the situation where a PEA in an undertaking also extends to employees in another undertaking or group of undertakings. Where a valid employee request is made by employees in an undertaking with a PEA covering more than one undertaking, employers may choose to ballot all the employees in all the undertakings together to determine whether they endorse the request[639] as an alternative to balloting only the employees in the undertaking making the request.[640] If a combined ballot is held and the request is endorsed, the employer will be required to initiate negotiations in all the undertakings covered by the ballot; if it is not endorsed, the three-year moratorium on a further request will apply to all those undertakings.[641]

If an employee or an employees' representative disputes whether any of the statutory criteria for a PEA in either a single undertaking or group of undertakings is met, he or she may complain to the CAC which, if it upholds the complaint, may order the employer to initiate negotiations.[642] Whether an agreement has been 'approved by the employees' may be particularly contentious. Although no method of securing approval is prescribed, it would be prudent for employers to obtain evidence of such support in writing and to retain such evidence in the event of a complaint to the CAC. The EAT has held that if an agreement was entered into by a union, it would usually be legitimate for the CAC to infer approval if, at the time the agreement was made, the majority of

---

[636] ICER 2004, reg 8(1). Seeking the views of employees does not correspond with the definition of 'consultation' in ICER 2004, reg 2, as 'the exchange of views and establishment of a dialogue': Ewing and Truter, 2005, p 631.

[637] [2006] IRLR 592; see Dukes, 2007.

[638] DTI Guidance, 2006: para 20. Annex 1 of the Guidance provides suggested contents. Where information about the employment situation is to be provided under a PEA, it must include specifed information relating to the use of any agency workers in that undertaking: ICER 2004, reg 8A.

[639] On the assumption that the request has been made by fewer than 40% of the employees in the undertakings covered by that agreement.

[640] ICER 2004, reg 9.

[641] ICER 2004, regs 9(2), 12(1)(c).

[642] ICER 2004, reg 10(1),(3).

the employees covered by it were members of the union or unions which are party to it, although the position may be different if there was evidence of a degree of opposition to the agreement from employees within the union. Conversely, if a minority of employees were union members, it would not be appropriate to infer approval and the employer would need to establish approval in some other way.[643] It is notable that the EAT focussed in this case on the position at the time when the agreement was made. In a context of high labour turnover, however, where a majority of union members has been replaced by a minority, or many of those who approved an agreement in a ballot have left the employer, there may be scope to argue that the agreement has not been approved by 'the employees.'[644]

There are three situations in which an employee request to initiate negotiations is restricted. The first is where a negotiated agreement already applies; no valid request can be made within a period of three years from the date of the agreement or, where the agreement is terminated within that period, before the date when the termination takes effect unless the agreement has ceased to cover all the employees in the undertaking.[645] The second is where the 'standard' I and C provisions apply; here there is a three-year bar from the date on which they started to apply.[646] The third is where a pre-existing agreement or set of agreements was in place and employees failed to endorse an employee request in a ballot; no further request can be made within a period of three years from the date of that request.[647] However, the three-year bar does not apply where there are 'material changes in the undertaking during the applicable period' having the result that the pre-existing agreement or agreements no longer cover all the employees of the undertaking or have not been approved by all the employees.[648] This could include situations where the undertaking has been involved in a merger or acquisition or there had been an expansion in the business which resulted in significant numbers of additional employees who would not be covered by the agreement(s).[649] Employers may apply to the CAC within one month of a request being made if they consider that the request is not valid because, for example, the requisite formalities were not observed; the requisite threshold has not been met; or it has been made during one of the restricted periods described above.[650]

(iii) Reaching a negotiated agreement

9.53   In order to initiate negotiations to reach an agreement, the employer must, as soon as reasonably practicable, make arrangements for the employees of the undertaking to elect or appoint negotiating representatives; inform employees in writing of their identity; and invite the

---

[643] *Stewart v Moray Council* [2006] IRLR 592.

[644] The argument that 'the employees' means 'employees at the date of the request' can be supported by reference to para 8(1)(b); it would seem not to be sufficient that all categories of employees were covered at the time of the agreement but not at the date of the request.

[645] ICER 2004, reg 12(1)(a), (2)(b).

[646] ICER 2004, reg 12(1)(b).

[647] ICER 2004, reg 12(1)(c).

[648] ICER 2004, reg 12(2)(a).

[649] DTI Guidance, 2006: para 29.

[650] ICER 2004, reg 13.

representatives to enter into negotiations.[651] The number of negotiating representatives is not prescribed, but their election or appointment must be arranged in such a way that all employees are represented by one or more representatives and all are entitled to take part in the election or appointment.[652] An employee or employees' representative who considers that these conditions have not been met may complain to the CAC, which must order the process to be re-run if it upholds the complaint.[653] Negotiations may last no longer than six months (starting at the end of the period of three months beginning with the date on which the employee request was made)[654] unless the employer and a majority of the negotiating representatives agree that the period should be extended.[655] There is a general duty on the parties to work in a spirit of co-operation and with due regard for their reciprocal rights and obligations, a duty that applies also to the implementation of an I and C procedure.[656]

There is considerable flexibility in the form and content of a 'negotiated agreement'. The agreement must cover all employees of the undertaking, but it may consist either of a single agreement or of different parts (for example, covering different establishments) which, taken together, cover all the employees. The agreement or each part must, *inter alia*, set out the circumstances in which the employer must inform and consult the employees to which it relates; be in writing and dated; and either provide for the appointment or election of I and C representatives, or provide that the employer must provide information directly to the employees to whom it relates and consult them directly.[657] Beyond this, the contents of the agreement are not prescribed; the parties may agree on the method, frequency, timing and subject matter of I and C best suited to their circumstances.[658] Where an agreement consists of different parts, these parts may differ as to the terms and nature of I and C and with whom it occurs.[659] Agreements are required to be approved in accordance with statutory criteria. Where there is a single agreement, it must be signed by all the negotiating representatives or, alternatively, by a majority of those representatives and either approved in writing by at least 50% of employees in the undertaking or approved in a ballot of those employees in which at least 50% of those voting voted in favour.[660] The ballot must

---

[651] ICER 2004, reg 14(1). In *Darnton v Bournemouth University* [2010] IRLR 294 the EAT held that there was no requirement to invite the negotiating representatives to enter into negotiations within three months of the employee request; the only requirement was to do so as soon as reasonably practicable. Reg 14(3) specifies an end and not a start date.

[652] ICER 2004, reg 14(2).

[653] ICER 2004, reg 15.

[654] Where there is a pre-existing agreement or agreements and the employer holds a ballot to determine whether the request is endorsed, the period between the employer notifying its employees of the decision to hold a ballot and the date of the ballot does not count toward the three-month period: reg 14(3)(a)(i). Provision is also made for other periods not to count where a complaint has been made to the CAC: reg 14(3)(a)(ii)–(iv), (b), (c).

[655] ICER 2004, reg 14(3), (5).

[656] ICER 2004, reg 21.

[657] ICER 2004, reg 16(1). 'Consultation' in this context means 'the exchange of views and establishment of a dialogue between' the I and C representatives or the employees and the employer, as appropriate: reg 2. See also *R v British Coal Corporation and the Secretary of State for Trade and Industry, ex p Price* [1994] IRLR 72, 75.

[658] Where an employer is to provide information about the employment situation, this must include specified information about any use of agency workers in the undertaking: ICER 2004, reg16(1)(g).

[659] ICER 2004, reg 16(2). It is also possible for agreements to cover more than one undertaking: see DTI Guidance, 2006: para 41 for further details. As we indicate in para 9.52 above, where an employer has received a request in relation to one undertaking and wishes to negotiate an agreement covering both that undertaking and another undertaking where no request has been made it will need to notify the employees in the second undertaking of its intention to do this: reg 14(6), (7).

[660] ICER 2004, reg 16(3).

comply with the same conditions applicable to ballots to endorse an employee request, discussed in para 9.52 above, although in this instance only a negotiating representative, not an individual employee, may complain to the CAC about the conduct of the ballot.[661] Where the negotiated agreement consists of different parts, each part must be separately approved either by all the negotiating representatives involved in negotiating it or by a majority of those representatives and at least 50% of the employees to whom the part relates either in writing or in a ballot.[662] There is no requirement for each part of the agreement to be approved at the same time or in an identical way. However if any part of the agreement is not approved in accordance with these principles, there will not be a 'negotiated agreement' for the purposes of ICER 2004 and the standard I and C provisions, which we discuss below, will apply. Negotiated agreements are enforceable through the CAC.

(iv) The standard I and C provisions

9.54   The 'standard' I and C provisions apply where an employer fails to initiate negotiations for an I and C agreement when required to do so, or where negotiations have failed to lead to an agreement.[663] These provisions apply at undertaking level only; arrangements may not cover more than one undertaking, nor can there be different arrangements in different parts of the undertaking.

Where negotiations have taken place but failed to lead to an agreement, the employer has a further six months after the expiry of the specified negotiating period to arrange for the election of I and C representatives; the employer will be liable to a penalty if the period expires and there are no I and C representatives in place (see para 9.55 below).[664] Where the employer fails to initiate any negotiations, the standard provisions apply six months after the employee request (or sooner, if the I and C representatives are elected before that date).[665] I and C representatives must be elected in a ballot, which it is the responsibility of the employer to arrange and pay for;[666] an employee or employee's representative may complain to the CAC if the employer fails to make the requisite arrangements and the CAC may order it to do so.[667] There must be one representative per 50 employees or part thereof, subject to a minimum of two and a maximum of 25.[668] There can be separate ballots for separate parts of the workforce if the employer considers that this would better reflect the interests of employees as a whole. There are detailed statutory conditions governing the conduct of the ballot: *inter alia*, all employees in the undertaking must have the opportunity to stand as candidates; so far as reasonably practicable employees' representatives or, if none, employees must be consulted on the proposed arrangements for the ballot; the final arrangements must be published at least 21 days before the ballot is held; an employee or employees' representative who considers that the arrangements are defective may complain to

---

[661] ICER 2004, regs 16(5), 17.
[662] ICER 2004, reg 16(4).
[663] ICER 2004, reg 18(1).
[664] ICER 2004, reg 18(2).
[665] ICER 2004, reg 18(1).
[666] ICER 2004, reg 19.
[667] ICER 2004, reg 19(4), (5). See *Amicus v Macmillan Publishers* [2007] IRLR 378, CAC.
[668] ICER 2004, reg 19(3).

the CAC; and the conduct of the ballot must be supervised by an 'independent ballot supervisor' who has a duty to ensure that all those who are entitled to vote have an opportunity to do so, an obligation which may require the ballot to be held over more than one day or take the form of a postal vote.[669] He or she must also ensure that those voting are able to do so in secret and that votes are fairly and accurately counted. If the independent ballot supervisor considers that any of the statutory requirements was not met, with the result that the outcome of the ballot would have been different, or that he or she could not form a proper judgment on this matter because of interference or lack of co-operation by management, an 'ineffective ballot report' must be issued which means that the ballot has no effect and another must be held.[670]

Where the standard I and C provisions apply, the employer must provide I and C representatives with information on the following matters:[671]

(a) the recent and probable development of the undertaking's activities and economic situation. The DTI Guidance suggests that this is information that will help I and C representatives understand the context in which decisions affecting employment, work organisation and contractual relations are made. It may include matters such as significant changes to products or services, takeovers and mergers, developments in production processes, reorganisations and changes in senior management.[672] Unlike TUPE 2006, takeovers and mergers by share transfer are not excluded.[673]

(b) the situation, structure and probable development of employment within the undertaking (including specified information on the use of any agency workers in the undertaking) and on any anticipatory measures envisaged, in particular, where there is a threat to employment within the undertaking. In relation to 'anticipatory measures' where there is a threat to employment, recital 8 to the Directive refers to employee training and skill development' with a view to increasing the 'employability and adaptability' of employees likely to be affected.

(c) decisions likely to lead to substantial changes in work organisation or in contractual relations. The DTI Guidance suggests that 'contractual relations' means 'employers' contractual relations with their employees, rather than a business's contracts with third parties', and would include a change of employer, a 'substantial change' in terms and conditions (excluding pay or benefits with a monetary value');[674] a change to the compulsory retiring age; changes to an occupational pension scheme where there is a contractual right to participate in the scheme; and changes in disciplinary or grievance procedures.[675] It considers that 'changes in work organisation' would include changes in the level or distribution of employment within the undertaking, including redundancies and relocation of posts; changes in policy on flexible working, part-time working and overtime; changes in work patterns; and the introduction of

---

[669] A person is an 'independent ballot supervisor' for this purpose if the employer reasonably believes that he or she will carry out functions relating to the ballot competently and has no reasonable grounds for believing that his or her independence might reasonably be called into question: ICER 2004, Sch 2, para 6.

[670] See generally ICER 2004, Sch 2.

[671] ICER 2004, reg 20(1). The wording reflects Art 2(2) of Directive 2002/14.

[672] DTI Guidance, 2005: pp 39–40.

[673] Welch, 2006: pp 24–25.

[674] BIS justifies this exclusion on the ground that Directive 2002/14 is based on Art 137 of the EC Treaty (now Article 153 TFEU), which excludes pay: DTI Guidance, 2006: para 55. We doubt whether exclusion on this basis is correct.

[675] DTI Guidance, 2006: para 55.

significant new technology or equipment and any training associated with it.[676]

Information must be given at such a time, in such fashion and with such content as are appropriate to enable, in particular, the I and C representatives to conduct an adequate study and, where necessary, to prepare for consultation.[677] The obligation to consult (defined as 'the exchange of views and establishment of a dialogue between' I and C representative and the employer[678]) applies only to categories (b) and (c) above.[679] Here, the employer must ensure that consultation is conducted: in such a way as to ensure that its timing, method and content are appropriate; on the basis of the information supplied by the employer to the I and C representatives and of any opinion which they express to the employer; and so as to enable the I and C representatives to meet the employer at the relevant level of management depending on the subject under discussion[680] and to obtain a reasoned response from the employer to any opinions they express.[681] Failure on the part of a person who controls the employer to provide information to it is not a valid reason for the employer failing to inform and consult.[682] Neither the Directive nor ICER 2004 is specific about the timing or frequency of I and C – in particular, it is not spelt out whether consultation must take prior to decisions being made by the employer or only in relation to the implementation of such decisions – although the recitals to the Directive indicate that its objective is to preclude decisions being taken without prior consultation.[683] However the DTI Guidance indicates that the 'requirement to provide information on the probable development of the undertaking's activities and economic situation, and of employment, clearly means that some information must be provided in advance of these developments'.[684] It also suggests that the definition of consultation, and the subjects to be covered, 'imply that ... [I and C] ... should be on-going and regular, and not simply a one-off event when a problem arises'.[685]

In relation to matters falling within category (c) above, the employer must consult 'with a view to reaching agreement on decisions falling within the scope of the employer's powers'.[686] The points we made in para 9.37 above about what that requires apply equally in this context. It is made clear in the Regulations that decisions within category (c) include decisions covered by sections 188–192 of TULRCA 1992 (collective redundancies); regulations 13–16 of TUPE 2006 (transfers of undertakings),[687] and, by implication, regulations 11–13 of the OPPSCER 2006 (occupational pensions)[688] which we discussed earlier in this chapter. However the duties to inform and consult under ICER 2004 cease to apply if the employer has become subject to one of these specific duties and has notified the I and C representatives in writing that it will be complying with it. This

---

[676] DTI Guidance, 2006: para 55.

[677] ICER 2004, reg 20(2).

[678] ICER 2004, reg 2. See also *R v British Coal Corpn and the Secretary of State for Trade and Industry, ex p Price* [1994] IRLR 72, 75. The duty of co-operation, referred to in para 9.53 above, also applies in this context: reg 21.

[679] ICER 2004, reg 20(3).

[680] The DTI Guidance, 2006: para 57 regards this as the 'level of management with the authority to change the decision being consulted about'.

[681] ICER 2004, reg 20(4)(a)–(c).

[682] ICER 2004, reg 20(6).

[683] See recitals 6 and 13 and the discussion in Bercusson, 2002: p 237–239.

[684] DTI Guidance, 2006: para 61.

[685] DTI Guidance, 2006: para 59.

[686] ICER 2004, reg 20(4)(d).

[687] ICER 2004, reg 20(5).

[688] ICER 2004, reg 20(5) refers to the Pension Scheme Regulations, defined in reg 2 as OPPSCER 2006.

notification must be given on each occasion that the employer has become or is about to become subject to the duty.[689] Employers will need to ensure that they are, objectively speaking, under the statutory duty in question before giving notice; if the number of proposed redundancies is below the 20-employee threshold, for example, they will not be subject to the duty under TULRCA 1992 so cannot avoid the duty under ICER 2004. The DTI Guidance states that there is no requirement under ICER 2004 to inform and consult where 'a small number of employees' is to be made redundant, but does not specify a lower limit; 'this will depend on the circumstances of the individual case', including the proportion of employees in the undertaking.[690] Employers may be best advised to err on the side of caution in this regard. Consulting under ICER 2004 does not relieve the employer of its duties under TULRCA 1992, TUPE 2006 or OPPSCER 2006. The obligation to consult under ICER 2004 applies at an earlier stage than the latter set of provisions, leaving open the possibility that in relation to TULRCA 1992 and TUPE 2006 the employer may need to consult more than one set of representatives. Unlike the redundancy consultation provisions ICER 2004 does not exclude contracts for three months or less[691] nor does it exclude Crown employment[692] (provided that the employer concerned constitutes an 'undertaking').

Where the standard provisions apply, it is open to the employer and elected representatives to come to a negotiated agreement. This must be a single agreement; cover all the employees in the undertaking; comply with other specified requirements relating to a 'negotiated agreement'; and be signed by a majority of the I and C representatives.[693] Although the three-year 'moratorium' on employee requests (or an employer notification) to initiate negotiations applies from the date of that agreement,[694] there seems no impediment to the parties mutually agreeing to terminate it before that date which they may wish to do if, for example, they agree it would be more desirable to have an agreement covering different parts of the undertaking.

(v) Compliance and enforcement

9.55   Where a negotiated agreement has been signed or the standard I and C provisions apply, a complaint may be presented to the CAC by a 'relevant applicant' (an I and C representative or, if none, an employee or employees' representative) that the employer has failed to comply with the terms of the agreement or of the standard provisions, as appropriate.[695] Where the CAC upholds the complaint it must make a declaration to that effect and may make an order requiring the employer to take specified steps within a specified period.[696] Where a 'relevant applicant' obtains such a declaration, or where a complaint that the employer has failed to arrange for the election of I and C representatives for the purposes of the 'standard procedure' is upheld, the applicant may

---

[689] ICER 2004, reg 20(5).
[690] DTI Guidance, 2006: para 55.
[691] Cf TULRCA 1992, s 282(1).
[692] Cf TULRCA 1992, s 273(2).
[693] ICER 2004, reg 18(2), (3).
[694] ICER 2004, regs 11, 12(1).
[695] ICER 2004, reg 22(1)–(3). The complaint must be made within three months of the date of the alleged failure: reg 22(2).
[696] ICER 2004, reg 22(4), (5).

apply to the EAT for a penalty notice to be issued.[697] The EAT must issue such a notice, requiring payment of a penalty to the Secretary of State, unless satisfied, on hearing representations from the employer, that the failure 'resulted from a reason beyond the employer's control or that he has some other reasonable excuse for his failure'.[698] The penalty may be up to a maximum of £75,000.[699] Matters to be taken account by the EAT when setting the amount include the gravity of the failure and the number of employees affected by it; the period of time over which it occurred and the reason for it; and the number of employees employed by the undertaking or undertakings concerned.[700] In *Amicus v Macmillan Publishers* the EAT fixed a penalty of £55,000, a sum which it considered would 'deter others from adopting what can only be described as the wholly cavalier attitude to their obligations that has been demonstrated by this company.' [701] In contrast to a failure to comply with the specific I and C requirements relating to collective redundancies and transfers of the undertaking (see paras 9.40 and 9.45), therefore, there is no provision for an award to the employees covered by the failure to inform and consult.[702] It is specifically provided that no CAC order can have the effect of suspending or altering the effect of any act done or agreement made by the employer, or of preventing or delaying any proposed act or agreement.[703]

(vi) Confidential information

9.56   The duties of employers under a negotiated agreement or the standard I and C procedure are subject to two significant qualifications.[704] First, they may require any information or document to be held in confidence, or on terms that restrict the extent of disclosure.[705] Employers may be obliged to impose an obligation of confidence on information that is price sensitive; the UK Disclosure Rules and Transparency Rules may allow employers to provide inside information to employee representatives or unions acting on their behalf, but only if such information is given in confidence.[706] Unauthorised disclosure constitutes a breach of statutory duty owed to the employer, except where the recipient reasonably believes this to be a 'protected disclosure' under

---

[697] ICER 2004, reg 22(6), 19(6). The application must be made within three months of the declaration under reg 22(4). The time limit applicable to a complaint under reg 19(4) is unclear; *quaere* whether it is within three months of an order under reg 19(5).

[698] ICER 2004, reg 22(7).

[699] ICER 2004, reg 23(2).

[700] ICER 2004, reg 23(3).

[701] [2007] IRLR 885 at [25] (Elias P).

[702] The legislation specifically provides that no other sanction can be imposed on the employer for infringement of the rights conferred by ICER 2004: reg 24. However as we explained in para 9.54 above, where there is a duty to consult under TULRCA 1992, ss 188–192, TUPE 2006, regs 13–16 or OPPSCER 2006, regs 11–13, such a duty is not removed by any co-extensive duty under ICER 2004.

[703] ICER 2004, reg 22(9). The Commission's original proposal that, in the case of a serious breach of the obligation to inform and consult employee representatives, a decision should have no legal effect on the contract of employment until adequate I and C had taken place was opposed by a number of countries, including the UK: see Bercusson, 2002: pp 239–240.

[704] These reflect Directive 2002/14, Art 6.

[705] ICER 2004, reg 25(1), (2).

[706] See DTR 2.5. Where a negotiated agreement provides for direct I and C, employers would not be able to share such information with the workforce as a whole. The DTI Guidance, 2006 encourages employers to take decisions that result in public announcements involving price-sensitive information during working hours so that details can be released to the stock market and to employees at the same time to avoid employees hearing about such developments in the media: see Annex 2.

the 'whistleblowing' provisions of ERA 1996.[707] This is without prejudice to any other form of liability, such as breach of confidence, which the recipient may incur.[708] This provision contrasts sharply with other provisions in domestic law relating to disclosure of information discussed earlier in this chapter, where no statutory provision is made for information to be disclosed on confidential terms, although there is a similar provision in TICER 1999. Welch points out that the duty of confidentiality 'may result in the weakening of information and consultation processes, as workplace representatives may feel unable to seek advice from external sources, such as their trade union full-time officials, or to seek the views of those they represent as to appropriate responses to the employer's proposals'.[709] However a failure to impose appropriate restrictions on the disclosure and dissemination of inside information would constitute a breach of EU law on market abuse.[710] A recipient to whom the employer has entrusted any information or document on a confidential basis may apply to the CAC to decide whether it was reasonable for the information to be impressed with confidence; if the CAC considers that disclosure would not, or would not be likely to, 'harm the legitimate interests of the undertaking' it will grant a declaration to that effect, whereupon the information is no longer subject to the confidentiality duty.[711] The second safeguard for employers is that there is no requirement to disclose any information or document where, 'according to objective criteria', this would 'seriously harm the functioning of, or would be prejudicial to, the undertaking'.[712] The fact that information is price sensitive would not, of itself, justify withholding information where there are I and C representatives to whom it can be disclosed on a confidential basis, but the DTI Guidance suggests that evidence of 'past leaks' may be relevant in assessing whether sensitive information should be disclosed.[713] A dispute between an employer and an I and C representative (if there is one) or an employee or employees' representative as to whether information falls within this category can be referred by either party to the CAC, which may order disclosure on specified terms if it does considers that disclosure would not be seriously harmful or prejudicial.[714]

(vii) Protection of individuals

9.57 Negotiating representatives and I and C representatives are entitled to be permitted to take reasonable paid time off during working hours in order to perform their functions, with recourse to an employment tribunal in the event that permission has been unreasonably refused or payment

---

[707] ICER 2004, reg 25(3), (5). See further para 4.117 on 'protected disclosures'. Technically an employer could still pursue other forms of action even if a disclosure were 'protected', but such an act would almost certainly fall within the public interest defence to breach of confidence (see generally Toulsen and Phipps, 2006: ch 6) ,and the standards set in ERA 1996 may themselves influence the courts in applying the public interest defence.

[708] ICER 2004, reg 25(4).

[709] Welch, 2006: p 27.

[710] Case C-384/02 *Criminal proceedings against Grongaard* [2006] IRLR 214, ECJ, on the predecessor of Directive 2003/6/EC.

[711] ICER 2004, reg 25(6)–(8).

[712] ICER 2004, reg 26. This reflects Art 6(2) of Directive 2002/14. 'It is not clear why, for some information to be banned, it must "seriously" harm functioning, but for other information it suffices to be merely "prejudicial" in order not to be disclosed': Bercusson, 2002: p 224.

[713] DTI Guidance, 2006: para 77.

[714] ICER 2004, reg 26(2)–(4).

withheld.[715] However, in contrast to time off rights of officials of recognised trade unions,[716] there is no entitlement to time off for training. Representatives who are not members of or otherwise associated with an independent union may find it difficult to obtain the expertise required to act as an effective I and C representative; although it is not required by the legislation, it would be good industrial relations practice to afford employees access to external training to perform their roles. Such persons, together with candidates for such positions and employees' representatives, are protected against unfair dismissal and subjection to a detriment for the performance of their functions, or for requesting time off to perform them,[717] and employees generally are protected against such acts for a range of reasons relating to ICER 2004.[718]

(viii) Compatibility with the Directive

9.58   ICER were introduced in order to implement the UK's obligations under Directive 2004/14.[719] However it is strongly arguable that they fail to do this. First, there is provision for a negotiated agreement to allow for direct I and C of employees. The Directive, by contrast, envisages consultation through employees' representatives;[720] although it is 'without prejudice to those systems which provide for the direct involvement of employees' this is 'so long as they are always free to exercise the right to be informed and consulted through their representatives'.[721] Second, it can be argued that the provision for a 'trigger' in the form of a minimum level of support before employers are required to establish I and C constitutes an impediment to the exercise of rights under the Directive, particularly where there is a PEA (which can also provide for direct I and C) and a 40% majority of employees in the undertaking is required before the employer must initiate negotiations.[722] The fact that these provisions were agreed by the TUC and CBI reduces the risk in practice of a domestic judicial review application, but would not prevent infringement proceedings by the Commission. Third, the lack of enforceability of PEAs may be a problem.[723] Fourth, concerns about the independence of I and C representatives which we articulated in the context of redundancies and transfers of the undertaking[724] apply equally in this context. Finally, it can be argued that the £75,000 penalty that can be imposed in the event of an employer's failure to meet its I and C obligations does not constitute an 'effective,

[715] ICER 2004, reg 27–29.
[716] TULRCA 1992, s 168(2); see para 8.41.
[717] Note, however, that there is no right to time off for candidates; cf ERA 1996, s 61 and TICER 1999, reg 25. The protections in ICER 2004 do not apply where the employee has disclosed confidential information in breach of a restriction imposed by the employer unless the employee reasonably believed the disclosure to be a 'protected disclosure': ICER 2004, regs 30(4), 32(4); see para 9.56 above.
[718] ICER 2004, regs 30–33.
[719] Note, however, that they were made under ERA 2004, s 42, not ECA 1972, s 2(2).
[720] Art 1(3).
[721] Recital 16.
[722] There is no provision for a trigger in the Directive. Recital 15 states that the Directive is 'without prejudice to national systems regarding the exercise of this right in practice where those entitled to exercise it are required to indicate their wishes collectively'. However, even if this permits some form of trigger, *quaere* whether the level of support required where there is a PEA is too high a hurdle. There have been few reported instances of the 'trigger mechanism' being used by employees, even where there is no PEA: Hall, 2006; Hall *et al*, 2007, 2008, 2010.
[723] Hall *et al* 2010: p 63, who base this point on *Commission Communication - Review of the application of Directive 2002/14 EC in the EU* COM (2008) 146.
[724] See paras 9.35 and 9.43.

proportionate and dissuasive' sanction,[725] particularly in the case of larger undertakings. At the time of writing it remains to be seen whether any action will be taken by the Commission in relation to any of these matters.

EMPLOYEE INVOLVEMENT AT TRANSNATIONAL LEVEL

9.59   As we indicated in para 9.30, there are four contexts in which European Union law requires employee involvement at transnational level: the European Works Council Directive; the Directive on Employee Involvement in the European Company (SE); the Directive on Employee Involvement in the European Co-operative Society (SCE); and the Cross-Border Mergers Directive. The European Works Council Directive was implemented in the UK by TICER 1999.[726] A revised form of the Directive came into force on 5 June 2011[727] and amendments to the UK regulations also came into force on that date.[728] We outline the main provisions of TICER 1999 as amended below, although, as we explain in para 9.64, whether the amended regulations apply in full will depend upon when and how the European Works Council was constituted. ICER 2004, which we discuss above, were modelled in certain respects on TICER 1999, although there are also significant differences between them. The Directive on Employee Involvement in the European Company was originally implemented by EPLLCR 2004,[729] which came into force on 8 October 2004; the provisions relating to employee involvement are now contained in EPLLCEIR 2009.[730] These Regulations can be properly understood only by reference to the European Company Statute, consideration of which lies beyond the scope of this work. We refer only briefly to the broad framework of the Statute and accompanying Directive in para 9.65 below, where we also specify the Regulations which implement the remaining transnational provisions.

European Works Councils

9.60   TICER 1999 provide for a European Works Council (EWC) or information and consultation procedure (ICP) to be established, either at the request of employees or their representatives or at the initiative of central management, in every 'Community-scale undertaking', defined as any undertaking with at least 1,000 employees (not 'workers') within the Member States and at least

---

[725] See Art 8(2) of Directive 2002/14.

[726] SI 1999/3323, issued under the ECA 1972, s 2(2).

[727] On 20 April 2004 the Commission initiated consultations with the EU-level cross-industry and sectoral social partners as part of a review of the original Directive: see *European Works Councils Bulletin* Issue 51, May/June 2004: pp 10–14. See also *Consultation on a Proposal to Amend the European Works Council Directive*, BERR, September 2008. For a critical analysis of the revised Directive see Laulom, 2010; Alaimo, 2010; see also J Waddington, 2011 and references therein. For a more positive view, see Jagodzinski, 2009.

[728] Amendments were made to TICER 1999 by SI 2010/1088. BIS issued non-statutory guidance on the amending regulations in April 2010. Amendments relating to agency workers came into force on 1 October 2011.

[729] SI 2004/2326 issued under the ECA 1972, s 2(2).

[730] As amended. EPLLCEIR 2009 came into force on 1 October 2009.

150 employees in each of at least two Member States,[731] and in every 'Community-scale group of undertakings.'[732] The rationale behind this dual threshold under the Directive was first, that small businesses should not be burdened with additional obligations which might be detrimental to their development, and second, that this proposal should have no effect on existing information and consultation procedures in Member States based on national legislation and practices. There is no definition of 'undertaking' in either TICER 1999 or the Directive,[733] but ECJ jurisprudence relating to Article 101 TFEU (formerly Article 81 EC), which prohibits anti-competitive behaviour, has made clear that the term covers any natural or legal person carrying on activities of an economic or commercial nature,[734] including, for example, limited companies, partnerships, trade associations, sole traders, and state corporations. The fact that the body is engaged in non-profit making activities does not, of itself, deprive its activities of their economic character.[735] The Directive requires the 'central management' of the undertaking to create the conditions and means necessary for establishing an EWC or ICP.[736] Reflecting the terms of the Directive, TICER 1999 impose this obligation on the central management where it is located in the UK or treated as such: that is, where it is located outside a Member State (in the USA, for example) but its 'representative agent' is situated in the UK or, if none, there are more employees employed in an establishment or group undertaking in the UK than are employed in any other establishment in a Member State.[737] It is notable that in the latter situation the crucial issue is not the total number of employees employed in the UK but the total number employed *in an establishment* in the UK. Thus, if a Japanese group of companies owns fifty establishments in the UK, each employing 100

---

[731] TICER 1999, reg 2(1); see reg 2(1) and para 3.19 *et seq* above for the definition of 'employee'. For UK employees, the number employed is determined by ascertaining the average number of employees employed during a two-year period, in accordance with specified criteria: reg 6. Certain part-time employees may be counted as half a person. The number of non-UK employees employed over a two-year period is to be calculated in accordance with the law and practice of the Member State in question. An employee or 'employees' representative' may request information from the management of an establishment or undertaking in the UK to determine whether it is part of a Community-scale undertaking or group of undertakings, with provision for complaint to the CAC if the recipient fails to obtain and provide accurate information as to the average number of employees employed by the undertaking or group in the UK and other Member States over the past two years and the structure of the undertaking or group and its workforce in the UK and each of the other Member States over the past two years, including specified information relating to any agency workers: regs 7 and 8. 'Member State' in this context extends to the European Economic Area and thus also includes Norway, Iceland and Liechtenstein. There is no definition of 'establishment'; see para 9.32 for the interpretation of this term in the context of collective redundancies. In Case C-62/99 *Betriebsrat der bofrost* Josef H Boquoi Deutschland West Gmbh & Co KG v bofrost* Josef H Boquoi Deutschland West Gmbh & Co KG* [2001] IRLR 403 the ECJ held that the communication of documents clarifying information provided for the purpose of determining whether employees or their representatives are entitled to request the opening of negotiations for establishing an EWC or ICP may be required. See also Case C-440/00 *Gesamtbetriebsrat der Kuhne & Nagel AG & Co KG v Kuhne & Nagel AG & Co KG* [2004] IRLR 332; Case C-349/01 *Betriebsrat dere Firma ADS Anker GmbH v ADS Anker GmbH* [2004] ECR I-6803. The obligation on the recipient of the request to 'obtain' information, introduced in 2011, reflects ECJ decisions that the recipient of a request need not be a controlling undertaking within a group of undertakings.

[732] A group of undertakings with at least 1,000 employees within the Member States; at least two group undertakings in different Member States; and at least one group undertaking with at least 150 employees in one Member State and at least one other group undertaking with at least 150 employees in another Member State: TICER 1999, reg 2(1). See TICER 1999, reg 2(1) for the meaning of 'group of undertakings'.

[733] Cf Directive 2002/14, art 2(1).

[734] Case 170/83 *Hydrotherm Geratebau GmbH v Compact del Dott. Ing. Mario Andreoli and CSAS* [1984] ECR 2999, paras 10–12.

[735] Case C-382/92 *Commission v UK* [1994] IRLR 392, 411. See further para 3.67 above for the meaning of 'undertaking' in the context of TUPE 2006 and the Acquired Rights Directive.

[736] Art 4(1).

[737] TICER 1999, regs 4 and 5.

employees, and a single establishment in France employing 300, the central management will not be treated as situated in the UK.

9.61   Negotiations for establishing an EWC or ICP may be initiated by central management. Alternatively, they must be initiated if at least 100 employees, or employees' representatives who represent at least that number, in at least two undertakings or establishments in at least two Member States so request.[738] 'Employees' representatives' under TICER 1999 fall into two distinct categories.[739] First, if the employees are of a description for which an independent trade union is recognised, they are representatives of the union who normally take part in the collective bargaining process. Second, the term covers 'any other employee representatives elected or appointed by employees to positions in which they are expected to receive, on behalf of the employees, information (i) which is relevant to the terms and conditions of employment of the employees, or (ii) about the activities of the undertaking which may significantly affect the interests of the employees'. However, representatives who are expected to receive information relevant only to a specific aspect of the terms and conditions or interests of employees, such as health and safety, are excluded.[740] It is notable that in this context, unlike that of collective redundancies, health and safety and transfers of the undertaking, a trade union, where recognised, is not the exclusive channel; even where there is such a union other employees' representatives may act.

The scope, composition, functions and term of office of a EWC or the arrangements for implementing an ICP are determined by a 'special negotiating body' (SNB) in conjunction with central management.[741] This means that the management cannot unilaterally foist a procedure on its workforce. The composition of the SNB where the central management is situated in the UK is tightly specified in TICER 1999. In each member State in which employees of the Community-scale undertaking or group of undertakings work, employees are to elect or appoint one member of the SNB for each 10% (or fraction of 10%) which they represent of the total number of employees in the undertaking or group;[742] thus, if employees in a Member State represent 38% of the total workforce, they will be entitled to four representatives. UK members of an SNB must be elected by a ballot of UK employees, supervised by an 'independent ballot supervisor', except where there is an elected 'consultative committee' representing the UK employees which may nominate SNB members from among its number.[743] These selection provisions apply regardless of whether the central management is in the UK. A 'consultative committee', broadly speaking, means a body whose normal functions include the carrying out of an information and consultation function in relation to all UK employees, which is able to carry out this function without interference from the UK management or from the central management, and which consists of persons elected by a

---

[738]   TICER 1999, reg 9. If the central management considers that the obligation to initiate negotiations did not apply to it on the relevant date it may apply to the CAC for a declaration: reg 10.

[739]   Cf ICER 2004, where the term 'employees' representative' is deliberately left undefined.

[740]   TICER 1999, reg 2. There is no definition of 'recognition' or collective bargaining in this context; cf TULRCA 1992, s 178. Note that, unlike a trade union, 'employees' representatives' are defined in terms of their relationships with 'employees' and not 'workers'.

[741]   TICER 1999, regs 16 and 17.

[742]   TICER 1999, reg 12. This provision reflects an amendment to the Directive which was designed to ensure fairer representation of employees.

[743]   TICER 1999, reg 13.

ballot in which all the then UK employees were entitled to vote.[744] An election may be mandatory, therefore, even where there is a recognised independent union; whether it will be needed where there are I and C representatives in place will depend upon whether they were elected and satisfy the other elements of the definition of a 'consultative committee'. The conditions that must be satisfied where a ballot to elect members of the SNB is required are, broadly speaking, the same as those applicable to the election of I and C representatives for the purposes of the 'standard' provisions under ICER 2004.[745]

The central management of the undertaking or group of undertakings must convene a meeting with the SNB to reach a written agreement on the detailed arrangements for the information and consultation of employees.[746] 'Consultation' means 'the exchange of views and establishment of dialogue' between members of an EWC, or ICP representatives, and central management or any more appropriate level of management.[747] For the purpose of its negotiations, the SNB may be assisted by experts of its choice, which may include representatives of European trade union organisations; such experts may, at the SNB's request, attend any meeeting in an advisory capacity. However, although the central management must pay for reasonable expenses incurred by the SNB that are necessary to enable it to carry out its functions, it is required to pay the expenses of one expert only.[748] SNB members are entitled to meet alone before and after meetings with the central management.

The parties may decide to establish an ICP instead of an EWC; if so, the resulting agreement must specify a method by which the representatives are to enjoy the right to meet to discuss the information conveyed to them.[749] If the parties decide to establish an EWC, their agreement must determine the undertakings or establishments covered by it; its composition, and the number and term of office of its members, and allocation of seats; the functions and procedure for informing and consulting it, including arrangements to link information and consultation of the EWC with information and consultation of national employee representation bodies;[750] the venue, frequency and duration of its meetings; provisions relating to a select committee where the parties decide to establish one; the financial and material resources to be allocated to it; the date of entry into

---

[744] TICER 1999, reg 15. There is provision for complaint to the CAC in the event that the UK management or an employee or employees' representative considers that the 'consultative committee' does not satisfy the statutory definition or any of the persons it nominates is not entitled to be nominated.

[745] See para 9.54 above; TICER 1999, regs 13 and 14. An 'independent ballot supervisor' is defined in reg 13(7).

[746] TICER 1999, reg 16(1).

[747] TICER 1999, reg 2. The timing and content of such consultation is explained in para 9.62 below.

[748] TICER 1999, reg 16(5), (6).

[749] TICER 1999, reg 17.

[750] 'National employee representation body' is defined in TICER reg 2 as (a) where the employees are of a description in respect of which an independent trade union is recognised by their employer for the purpose of collective bargaining, that trade union and (b) a body which has not been established with information and consultation on transnational matters as its main purpose, to which any employee representatives are elected or appointed by employees, as a result of which they hold positions in which they are expected to receive, on behalf of the employees, information (i) which is relevant to the terms and conditions of employment of the employees, or (ii) about the activities of the undertaking which may significantly affect the interests of the employees, (including information relevant only to a specific aspect of the terms and conditions or interests of the employees, such as health and safety or collective redundancies). Where no arrangements to link information and consultation of a EWC with that of national employee representation bodies have been made, and there are circumstances likely to lead to substantial changes in work organisation or contractual relations the management of every undertaking in the group; central management; or representative agent or management treated as the central management must ensure that the procedures for informing the EWC and national bodies are linked so as to begin within a reasonable time of each other. The national bodies referred to are those which are entitled, by law, agreement or custom and practice, to be informed and consulted on the matter in question: TICER 1999, reg 19E. For criticism that the recast Directive failed adequately to clarify the relationship between national and European procedures, see Laulom, 2010: 208.

force of the agreement and its duration; arrangements for amending or terminating it; and the circumstances in which it would be renegotiated and procedure for doing this.[751] These provisions allow the SNB to negotiate arrangements which are tailored to the individual enterprise, although in determining the allocation of seats an agreement must, so far as reasonably practicable, take into account the need for balanced representation of employees with regard to their role and gender and sector in which they work. The SNB is also free to decide, by a two-thirds majority, not to open, or to terminate such negotiations,[752] although it is difficult, prima facie, to imagine circumstances where it may wish to take this view.

9.62   As a fall-back to these provisions, the Regulations specify 'subsidiary requirements' which apply if the central management refuses to commence negotiations within six months of a valid request from employees or their representatives, or if the parties are unable to agree on information and consultation arrangements within three years of such a request.[753] In addition the parties may specifically decide to adopt all or any of the subsidiary requirements.[754] They provide, *inter alia*, for the composition of an EWC (to be determined according to the same formula applicable to an SNB); its competence; the appointment or election of its UK members; the frequency of its meetings; its procedures; and provision for the EWC to elect from among its members a select committee of up to five members to act on its behalf. [755] Notably, all UK members must be UK employees (in contrast to members of the SNB), so excluding union representatives who are not so employed.[756] Where all UK employees are represented by UK employees' representatives, those representatives choose the members of the EWC by whatever method they decide; otherwise UK members of the EWC must be elected by a ballot of employees which complies with the same conditions, *mutandis mutatis*, as apply to the election of members of the SNB, with identical provision for complaint to the CAC.[757] The competence of the EWC is limited to information and consultation on matters which concern the Community-scale undertaking or group of undertakings as a whole, or at least two of its establishments or group undertakings situated in different Member States.[758] Like an ICP, therefore, it cannot be used as a vehicle to deal with national or local concerns, although this is subject to the proviso that decisions taken in relation to employees in one Member State may impact on employees in another; in the area of redundancies, for example, job losses in one Member State may preserve jobs in another. The EWC has the right to meet with central management once a year to be informed and consulted, on the basis of a report drawn up by the

---

[751]   TICER 1999, reg 17. Where information disclosed under a EWC agreement or ICP includes information as to the employment situation in the undertaking or group, this should include specified information relating to the use of any agency workers. There is now a specific procedure in TICER 1999 which must be followed if the structure of an undertaking or group changes significantly and either the agreement does not specify how adaptation should take place or provisions in the agreement conflict with provisions in the agreement underpinning any other EWC involved.: TICER 1999, reg 19F.

[752]   TICER 1999, reg 16. If this happens, a new request to establish an EWC or ICP less than two years after that date must be disregarded unless the SNB and central management agree otherwise.

[753]   TICER 1999, reg 18.

[754]   TICER 1999, reg 17(6), 18. For information on the forms of agreements which have been adopted throughout the EEA, see the *European Works Councils Bulletin*.

[755]   See generally TICER 1999, Schedule.

[756]   TICER 1999, Schedule, para 3(1).

[757]   TICER 1999, Schedule, paras 3–5. See para 3(2) for the definition of 'represented by UK employees' representatives'.

[758]   TICER 1999, Schedule, para 6(1).

central management, on the progress and prospects of the undertaking or group. The information provided to the EWC for this purpose must relate in particular to the structure, economic and financial situation, probable development of the business and of production and sales of the undertaking or group. The meeting itself must relate in particular to:

> ... the situation and probable trend of employment, investments, and substantial changes concerning organisation, introduction of new working methods or production processes, transfers of production, mergers, cut-backs or closures of undertakings, establishments or important parts of such undertakings or establishments, and collective redundancies.[759]

In addition, whenever there are 'exceptional circumstances affecting the employees' interests to a considerable extent, particularly in the event of relocations, the closure of establishments or undertakings or collective redundancies', the select committee, or, where none exists, the EWC has the right to be informed and to meet, at its request, the central management or any other more appropriate level of management having its own power of decision, so as to be informed and consulted. If the meeting is held with the select committee, those EWC members elected or appointed by the establishments or undertakings directly concerned by the circumstances in question also have the right to participate in the meeting. However it is explicitly affirmed that an exceptional meeting of this nature does not affect the prerogatives of the central management.[760]

Subject to the duty of confidentiality, discussed below, EWC members must inform employees' representatives in the relevant establishment or undertakings, or, if none, employees themselves, of the content and outcome of the information and consultation procedure.[761] Before either a routine or exceptional meeting the EWC or select committee is entitled to meet without the management concerned being present. The operating expenses of the EWC must be borne by central management; in common with an SNB, the EWC or select committee may be assisted by experts of its choice, but central management need only pay for one such expert. In addition, the central management must provide members of the EWC and its select committee with the financial and material resources to enable them to perform their duties in an appropriate manner.[762] The employer must ensure that consultation is conducted in such a way that members of the EWC can, if they so request, meet with the central management and obtain a reasoned response from it to any opinion expressed by those representatives on the reports they receive.

Four years after its establishment, an EWC constituted by reference to the subsidiary requirements must examine whether it wishes to continue operating on these principles or whether it wishes to open negotiations with central management for different arrangements, in which case it then assumes the role taken by an SNB in relation to any subsequent negotiations.[763] Research published in June 2000 indicated that, at the time of writing, there had been no known case in which a company in any Member State had been required to establish an EWC according

---

[759] TICER 1999, Schedule, para 7. Art 12 of the Directive specifies that this obligation operates without prejudice to the information and consultation requirements of the directives on collective redundancies and transfers of undertakings, and this is reflected in domestic law.

[760] TICER 1999, Schedule, para 8. Where either these meetings or the annual meeting under para 7 includes information as to the employment situation, it should also include specified information about any use of agency workers.

[761] TICER 1999, Schedule, para 9.

[762] TICER 1999, Schedule, para 9.

[763] TICER 1999, Schedule, para 10.

to the subsidiary requirements, but that these provisions had strongly influenced arrangements introduced by agreement,[764] and this remained the case in 2005.[765] Regardless of whether the EWC has been agreed or imposed, it and central management must work in a 'spirit of cooperation with due regard to their reciprocal rights and obligations'.[766] In addition central management must provide EWC members 'with the means required to fulfil their duty to represent collectively the interests of the employees' of the group.[767] It is unclear precisely what this covers; time off for EWC duties or remuneration for such time off; the means required to undertake training; or time off for training or remuneration for such time off, covered elsewhere in the Regulations,[768] are specifically excluded. The BIS Guidance suggests that 'means' may include travel and accommodation costs of attending meetings; translation costs at meetings; facilities at the workplace (a computer, for example) for members to perform their EWC duties; and costs incurred when providing feedback to employees' representatives.[769]

EWC members or I and C representatives, as applicable, must be given information by the central management, or any more appropriate level of management, in such a time and manner as to enable them to acquaint themselves with and examine its subject-matter; undertake a detailed assessment of its possible impact; and, where appropriate, prepare for consultation.[770] The content of the consultation, time when, and manner in which it takes place must be such as to enable an EWC or I and C representative to express an opinion on the basis of the information provided to them. Any such opinion must be provided within a reasonable time after the information is supplied and 'having regard to the responsibilities of management to take decisions effectively' may be taken into account by management. Information and consultation is specifically limited to transational matters.

TICER 1999 now requires EWCs to inform employees' representatives in the relevant establishment or undertakings, or, if none, employees themselves, of the content and outcome of the information and consultation procedure (subject to the duty of confidentiality).[771] An employee or employees' representative may complain to the CAC if the EWC fails to do this or the information provided is false or incomplete, and if the CAC upholds the complaint it must order disclosure of specified information. The CAC must not uphold such a complaint if the central management was at fault.[772]

Enforcement of the majority of rights contained in TICER 1999 is by way of complaint to the CAC, with a right of appeal on a point of law to the EAT.[773] If the parties agreed to establish an EWC or ICP, or the subsidiary requirements became applicable, but, due to a failure of central management, no EWC or ICP has been established, the SNB or, where none exists, a former SNB member or an employee or employees' representative may complain to the CAC, which may order

---

[764] Carley and Hall, 2000: p 105.
[765] Hall, 2005: p 122.
[766] TICER 1999, reg 19. The same duty is placed on ICP representatives.
[767] TICER 1999, reg 19A.
[768] See TICER 1999, regs 19B; 25-27.
[769] *The Transational Information and Consultation of Employees (Amendment) Regulations 2010*, BIS, 2010: p 16.
[770] TICER 1999, reg 18A. Where information as to the employment situation in the undertaking or group is disclosed, this should include specified information relating to any use of agency workers.
[771] TICER 1999, reg 19C. Under the unamended regulations this duty applied only to EWCs governed by the subsidiary requirements.
[772] TICER 1999, reg 19D.
[773] TICER 1999, reg 38.

central management to take specified steps to establish the EWC or ICP.[774] Where an EWC or ICP has been established, the central management, EWC or any ICP representative may complain to the CAC that the terms of the parties' agreement, subsidiary requirements or statutory requirements for information and consultation have not been complied with because of the failure of the other party and the CAC may order that party to take specified steps.[775] Finally, there is provision for complaints to the CAC about failures by the relevant management to comply with specified duties relating to the SNB or EWC, including the provision of the means required for members of both bodies to undertake training and for members of the EWC to fulfil their duties, where again the CAC may order specified steps to be taken.[776] In none of these cases may a CAC order suspend or alter the effect of any act done or any agreement made by the central or local management. Where the CAC finds a complaint under one of these heads to be well-founded, the applicant may also apply to the EAT for an order requiring the central management to pay a penalty to the Secretary of State in respect of the failure. The statutory principles applicable to the notice and amount are the same, *mutatis mutandis*, as those applicable under ICER 2004, discussed in para 9.55 above, although from 5 June 2011 the statutory maximum under TICER 1999 was raised to £100,000.[777]

Employees have the right to paid time off to perform their functions in relation to membership of an SNB, EWC, or as an ICP representative, or as candidates for those positions, and members of an SNB or EWC have the right to paid time off for training necessary for the exercise of their representative duties.[778] Such persons also have protection against unfair dismissal and subjection to a detriment for the performance of their functions, or for requesting time off to perform them, and employees generally are protected against such acts for a range of reasons relating to the establishment or operation of an EWC or ICP.[779] These rights are enforceable by means of complaint to an employment tribunal.

9.63   Regardless of whether information and consultation procedures are agreed or imposed, they remain qualified by two very significant safeguards for management (which the Directive requires all Member States to put in place).[780] First, they provide that members of an SNB, EWC, ICP representatives or experts assisting them (collectively termed 'recipients') owe a permanent duty to the central management (UK or otherwise) not to disclose any information in their possession by virtue of their position as such which has been entrusted to them on confidential terms. As in the case of ICER 2004, disclosure constitutes a breach of a statutory duty, except where the recipient reasonably believes it to be a 'protected disclosure' under the 'whistleblowing'

---

[774]   TICER 1999, reg 20.

[775]   TICER 1999, reg 21.

[776]   TICER 1999, reg 21A. Complaints may also brought that members of the SNB were unable to meet without central management being present and that the duty under TICER 1999 reg 19E(2) applies and the EWC and national representative bodies have not been informed and consulted in accordance with that regulation (see note 749 above).

[777]   TICER 1999, reg 22. Prior to June 2011 the maximum was £75,000, which was chosen on the basis that the average estimated cost of holding an EWC was around £60,000: *Implementation in the UK of the European Works Council Directive*, URN 99/926, July 1999: p 37.The increase to £100,000 was partly to reflect the increase in RPI: BIS, *Implementation of the Recast EWC Directive: Impact Assesszment*, April 2010: p 21. The Directive merely requires Member States to 'provide for appropriate measures in the event of failure to comply with' the Directive, in particular adequate administrative or judicial procedures to enable the obligations deriving from it to be enforced: Art 11(2). It does not, therefore, specify the form of sanction.

[778]   TICER 1999, regs 25–27. These rights apply regardless of the location of central management.

[779]   TICER 1999, regs 28, 29, 31.

[780]   Art 8.

provisions of ERA 1996.[781] Again this is without prejudice to any other form of liability, such as breach of confidence, which the recipient may incur.[782] Where the central management is situated in the UK a recipient may apply to the CAC for a declaration as to whether it was reasonable for information to be impressed with confidence; if the CAC considers that disclosure would not be likely to prejudice or cause serious harm to the undertaking it grants a declaration to that effect, whereupon the information is no longer subject to the confidentiality duty.[783] Notably, however, the CAC will be powerless if the information reveals wrongdoing or a threat to the environment, for example, given that revelation of such information would almost certainly cause serious harm to the undertaking. In that event, the recipient would need to take the risk that he or she would be protected by ERA 1996 or the general 'public interest' defence, as appropriate, in the event of any ensuing detriment from the employer or legal action. The second safeguard for management is the exception from disclosure of any information where 'according to objective criteria' this would 'seriously harm the functioning of, or would be prejudicial to, the undertaking or group of undertakings concerned'. This applies only where central management is situated in the UK, but compliance with the Directive requires the same dispensation to be applied in other Member States. Again a dispute about whether information falls within the 'protected' category can be referred to the CAC, which may order disclosure on specified terms if it does not consider the criteria for protection to be met.[784] Logically, it would not seem reasonable for such terms to include a duty of confidentiality, given that the requisite criteria have not been satisfied, but the CAC could require information to be anonymised or particular sections to be removed from a document, for example.

9.64   The obligations laid down by the original Directive did not apply if, by the deadline for its implementation by states other than the UK (22 September 1996) there was already an agreement, covering the entire workforce, providing for the transnational information and consultation of employees (although in the event of non-renewal of such an agreement the Directive became applicable).[785] It was estimated that around 450 such agreements were concluded.[786] The Directive that extended the original Directive to the UK afforded a similar exemption to EWCs established by agreement before 16 December 1999.[787] The facility to establish EWCs outside the regime of

---

[781] TICER 1999, reg 23; see para 9.56.

[782] TICER 1999, reg 23(4).

[783] TICER 1999, reg 23(7). Cf ICER 2004, reg 25(7) where the test is whether disclosure would be likely to 'harm the legitimate interests of the undertaking'.

[784] TICER 1999, reg 24.

[785] Art 13.

[786] Carley and Hall, 2000: p 107. For a later study, which also discusses the content and impact of EWCs, see Hall and Marginson, 2004.

[787] Council Directive 97/74/EC, Art 3. Even during the period of the UK's opt-out from the Directive, where multinational companies based in the UK employed the threshold number of workers in two or more other Member States they fell within its terms. These companies appear to have extended EWC arrangements to their British operations, even though not legally obliged to do so: W Brown *et al*, 1997: p 74. Likewise, the vast majority of companies based elsewhere in the EU with an establishment in the UK decided to include UK workers in their consultation arrangements, even though such workers had no legal right to require this: see Weber *et al*, 2000. In 2008 it was estimated that 820 EWCs covering 14.5 million employees, representing about 36% of the companies within the Directive's scope, were operational; some 113 of those with EWCs were companies with headquarters in the UK (out of an estimated 265 companies with UK headquarters that could potentially fall within the scope of the Directive): *Consultation on a Proposal to Amend the European Works Council Directive*, BERR, September 2008, para 6. See further BIS, *Implementation of the Recast EWC Directive: Impact Assesszment*, April 2010 for data on EWCs in UK-based undertakings and www.worker-participation.eu for wider data.

the Directive meant that 'the specific framework of each EWC derived from a complex bargaining process reflecting the relative power of employee representatives and employers'.[788] These 'pre-existing' EWCs remain outside the obligations imposed under the revised Directive (and, indeed, outside the TICER 1999 regime altogether) with the exception of the provisions relating to the adaptation of an EWC or ICP where the structure of an undertaking or group changes significantly and either the agreement does not specify how adaptation should take place or provisions in the agreement conflict with provisions in the agreement underpinning any other EWC involved.[789] The legal position of other EWCs and ICPs is more complex. EWCs and ICPs established by agreement under TICER 1999 after 15 December 1999 and revised on or after 5 June 2009 and before 5 June 2011, or established by agreement under TICER 1999 on or after 5 June 2009 and before 5 June 2011, remain, in general, subject to TICER 1999 in their unamended form, the major exception again being the provisions relating to adaptation together with those relating to agency workers and some procedural changes.[790] EWCs established by agreement under TICER 1999 which were not revised in the period between 5 June 2009 and 5 June 2011, and those created on or after 5 June 2011 are subject to TICER 1999 in their amended form.

Employee Involvement in the European Company (Societas Europaea), European Co-operative Society (Societas Co-operativa Europaea) and Companies formed by Cross-Border Mergers

9.65   The European Company statute[791] allows a European Company (SE) to be established in four different ways: the merger of two or more existing public limited companies from at least two Member States; the formation of a holding company promoted by public or private limited companies from at least two Member States; the formation of a subsidiary of companies from at least two Member States; and the transformation of an existing public limited company which has, for at least two years, had a subsidiary in another Member State.[792] The initial intention was to 'offer a uniform set of rules, separate from any national system, which companies merging across national borders could adopt',[793] but as the statute requires reference to the national law of the Member State where the SE is registered in a number of important areas this goal has been only partially achieved. The accompanying Directive on Employee Involvement in the European Company[794] is complex and can be properly understood only in relation to the European Company statute, which lies beyond the scope of this work. Space permits us to highlight only three important features.[795] First, no SE may be registered unless one of three conditions relating

---

[788] Royle, 1999: p 330; see also Wedderburn, 1997: pp 21–26. Research has suggested widespread dissatisfaction amongst EWC representatives with the practices of EWCs, particularly regarding the quality of information and consultation: Villiers, 2000; J Waddington, 2003c; Hall and Marginson, 2004; J Waddington, 2011. It remains to be seen whether the recast Directive will eventually lead to an improvement.

[789] TICER 1999, regs 44, 45, 19F.

[790] TICER 1999, s 45A.

[791] Council Regulation (EC) No 2157/2001. We do not, in this very broad brush account, refer to numbered provisions of the Regulation or accompanying Directive.

[792] Keller, 2002: p 428.

[793] P Davies, 2003: p 77.

[794] Directive 2001/86.

[795] See P Davies, 2003: p 79 *et seq*; Villiers, 2006.

to employee involvement has been satisfied: management and employee representatives have reached an agreement on employee involvement; employee representatives have decided that they do not wish to negotiate special involvement arrangements for the SE; or the Standard Rules on employee involvement, set out in the Annex to the Directive, have been triggered. Second, the I and C provisions in the Directive are based on a similar structure to the European Works Councils Directive, although applicable regardless of the size of the Company. Finally, and ostensibly more radically, there is provision for board-level participation where this was previously required under the national law governing a substantial proportion of the workforce to be employed by the SE after it is formed. However, this was a 'defensive, not proactive' policy, designed to prevent the SE being used as a vehicle for undermining existing national provisions on board-level participation rather than positively to promote board-level participation.[796] The Directive was originaly implemented in the UK by the European Public Limited-Liability Company Regulations 2004;[797] the provisions on employee involvement are now contained in the European Public Limited-Liability Company (Employee Involvement) (Great Britain) Regulations 2009.[798] By February 2010 more than 500 SEs had been registered, but only around a quarter of these had both employees and a business purpose.[799]

The European Company statute was followed by legislation providing for the establishment of a European Co-operative Society (SCE),[800] with provisions for employee involvement that closely resemble those applicable to SEs.[801] These provisions have been implemented by the European Cooperative Society (Involvement of Employees) Regulations 2006.[802] The Cross-Border Mergers Directive,[803] which lays down complex principles relating to employee participation, has been implemented by the Companies (Cross-Border Mergers) Regulations 2007.[804]

COLLECTIVE REPRESENTATION: PROSPECTS FOR THE FUTURE

9.66   In this concluding section we discuss some of the broader issues raised by the subject-matter of this chapter.

The most basic question is whether, and on what ground, there should be *any* form of employee involvement, even consultation, in the decision-making processes of an enterprise. It could be argued that the employment relationship is purely a commercial one, based upon the exchange of wages for labour power, and that mutual satisfaction of that bargain is the sole legitimate interest of the worker. In reality, whatever their ideological stance, it is unlikely that many employers translate this view wholeheartedly into practice, although their channels of

---

[796] P Davies, 2003: p 84.
[797] SI 2004/2326, which came into force on 8 October 2004.
[798] SI 209/2401, as amended. EPLLCEIR 2009 came into force on 1 October 2009.
[799]   European Trade Union database: see www.worker-participation.eu. See also Keller and Werner, 2008; Gold and Schwimbersky, 2008.
[800] Council Regulation (EC) 1435/2003.
[801] Directive 2003/72. See I Smith, 2006.
[802] SI 2006/2059.
[803] Directive 2005/56.
[804] SI 2007/2974.

communication may be individualised rather than collective and information and consultative mechanisms may be merely cosmetic.

The arguments which proponents of worker involvement invoke divide broadly into three (overlapping) categories. The first can be labelled the 'democratic' argument – that workers have a right to participate in the decisions which affect their interests and working lives.[805] This may be viewed as an important element in a broader social consensus and cohesion; it is notable that the system of 'co-determination' introduced in Germany following the Second World War was seen as integral to the establishment of a democratic political order.[806] The second argument is economic: that although the representation of worker interests may delay the implementation of decisions, particularly in areas such as reorganisation and redundancies, ultimately it is likely to result in a much better reconciliation of interests between employers and workers which will be beneficial to the economic well-being of the enterprise. One commentator has concluded that in Germany, for example, co-determination 'has proven an effective mechanism to bring about an accommodation of interests at the level of the individual enterprise, resulting in a commitment of labour, in the form in which it is organised at the workplace, to competitiveness, productivity and profitability'.[807] The third argument relates to the well-being of the community. As Parkinson explains,[808] '[w]here employees have a say in investment or relocation decisions the economic well-being of the local community is likely to be better served than where these decisions are made entirely by distant boards or dispersed and remote investors. Similarly, employees might also be expected to show a greater sensitivity to the impact of commercial activity on the local physical environment, though there is no doubt scope here too for a conflict of interests between those who work in the enterprise and those who are otherwise affected by it'. The extent to which any of these three objectives underlying employee representation are ürealised in practice will depend upon a variety of factors including the form of worker involvement chosen and its relationship with other aspects of industrial relations, such as the structure of trade unions or other representative organisations, and with the broader political society.[809]

The second basic question posed is whether, and why, such representation should be collective rather than employees being informed and consulted by their employer on an individual basis. Recent years have seen a growing tendency by some employers to communicate directly with employees through methods such as meetings between senior managers and the workforce and newsletters.[810] Computer technology, in particular e-mail, has enhanced the possibility of interactive communications, sometimes to the top level of the organisation. In some cases this may be viewed and presented by management as a form of 'direct democracy' which circumvents the need for any collective representation. However, it is important to note that it is not a substitute. While individual employees may be well-informed about their own working environment and

---

[805] See, for example, Towers, 1997.

[806] Streeck, 1992. The concept of 'co-determination' in Germany refers both to co-determination at the workplace, exercised through works councils, and in the enterprise, exercised through worker representatives on company boards. In the UK the inclusion of worker representatives on company boards has never been wholeheartedly supported by the labour movement: Roderick Martin, 1992: p 71.

[807] Streeck, 1992: p 166. See also Rogers and Streeck, 1995. It should not be overlooked, however, that this co-determination operates within a framework in which collective bargaining of a more adversarial nature takes place at sectoral level between trade unions and employers' associations.

[808] Parkinson, 1993: p 398.

[809] See Hyman, 1997.

[810] Cully *et al*, 1999: pp 229–230; Kersley *et al* 2006: pp 134–143.

conditions they are unlikely to have the time, or possibly the resources and expertise, to be able to analyse from a broader perspective information about the enterprise as a whole. Moreover, their role in such procedures is likely ultimately to be a passive one of reacting to proposals emanating from management; even if they are invited to express their preferences the parameters of the discussion have been framed elsewhere. More fundamentally, the views of workers have considerably greater strength if they are presented as a collective voice rather than as a number of isolated individuals. Collectivism also minimises the possibility that individuals who challenge the status quo can be picked off silently as 'troublemakers': in this context solidarity (only) is power.

9.67   If one accepts the need for worker representation, this leads on to a question of its form. In accordance with the range of variables discussed above, there is no 'best' model of worker participation which can be readily transplanted between different societies and, indeed, there are wide discrepancies between individual countries. The problems of transplantation are compounded by the fact that classifications that appear to be similar such as 'works councils' are used to refer to different structures and even to completely divergent functions'.[811] Thus, while it may be beneficial to construct general criteria which it is desirable that a representative model should satisfy, which can then be incorporated into international standards, the precise structure needs to be considered in the light of national industrial relations culture and practice. Whether or not representation should continue to be channelled through trade unions has been, as we noted earlier in this chapter, an issue of debate in the UK in recent years in the light of reduced membership levels and of developments in EU law. Enterprise-level representation and trade unionism are not mutually exclusive and, indeed, in this country consultative committees have traditionally co-existed with union recognition.[812] In recent years the TUC has recognised that non-union channels of representation can exist alongside trade union collective bargaining,[813] and this may become an increasing pattern in the light of ICER 2004.[814] One fundamental principle is clear, however – regardless of its form effective worker representation requires independence from the employer, with adequate resources for the organisation to function in the face of managerial hostility. As compared with enterprise-based organisations, trade unions – whose membership in Britain will usually cover a range of employers – are more likely to be able to satisfy these tests, having a separate organisational base and senior officials who are employed by the union rather than the employer of the members they represent. Moreover, in covering a range of employers, trade unions are likely to acquire a broader knowledge base of terms and conditions in a particular sector which can enable them to represent their members more effectively. Whether they act as reliable conduits of their members' views clearly depends upon the internal structures of the union which enable these views to be transmitted. In the context of this discussion, the significance of extra-union forms of representation in varying

---

[811]   Biagi and Tiraboschi, 2010; see also Mückenberger, 2009.
[812]   See Cully, *et al*, 1999: p 100.
[813]   Statutory Trade Union Recognition Joint Statement by TUC and CBI, December 1997, para 8; *High Performing Workplaces – Informing and Consulting Employees: Consultation Document*, DTI, 2003: pp 5–23.
[814]   See Hall *et al*, 2007, 2008, 2009, 2010; Deakin and Koukiadaki, 2012a. On the failure to integrate the rules on consultation and on collective bargaining in ICER 2004 and the consequences of this, see P Davies and M Freedland 2007: pp 156–159. See Charlwood and Terry, 2007 for the argument that 'hybrid' forms of union and non-union representation are associated with the best outcomes in terms of lower wage dispersion and higher productivity.

or determining labour standards in the important areas of working time, parental leave and successive fixed-term contracts are particular causes for concern.[815]

9.68   A subsequent question is the function of worker representation in relation to employers and, in particular, whether it should take the form of joint regulation or, rather, be purely consultative. The standards in this area promulgated by the ILO strongly urge collective bargaining as the primary method of determining terms and conditions of employment. Thus Convention No 98 provides, in Article 4, that '[m]easures appropriate to national conditions shall be taken, where necessary, to encourage and promote the full development and utilisation of machinery for voluntary negotiation between employers or employers' organisations and workers' organisations, with a view to the regulation of terms and conditions of employment by means of collective agreements.'[816] The arguments for collective bargaining as compared with consultation again rest on several grounds. Once more the democracy argument is at the forefront. In the much-quoted words of the Donovan Commission: '[p]roperly conducted, collective bargaining is the most effective means of giving workers the right to representation in decisions affecting their working lives, a right which is or should be the prerogative of every worker in a democratic society'.[817] One may add to this the need to ensure that collective bargaining is backed up by appropriate sanctions available to workers, such as access to industrial action or voluntarily agreed alternative dispute mechanisms such as arbitration, should negotiations break down. The other arguments in favour of collective bargaining are primarily those which are capable of benefiting employers, although whether they are so perceived is another matter. First, in the case of all but small employers, it is likely to be a more efficient method of determining terms and conditions than negotiating with employees on an individual basis.[818] The transparency of collectively-agreed terms is also more likely to avoid suspicion and attempts at 'bidding up' by individual employees. On a more specific note it may also help to protect employers against equal pay claims – at least those brought by recognised trade unions. Second, collective bargaining can assist employers in 'selling' unpopular decisions to the workforce; if the union is party to a low wage settlement, for example, because of information about the undertaking's financial situation made available to it by the employer, this may be more likely to diffuse discontent, or at least the blame. Third, effective collective bargaining helps to ensure that employers do not seek to gain a competitive advantage by depressing terms and conditions of employment. Such a strategy, while it may benefit a firm in the short run, carries long-term costs in terms of worker demotivation and a loss of quality in performance. Where collective bargaining entrenches basic labour standards, therefore, it not only protects employees' rights but may also contribute to the greater productivity of both labour and capital.[819] However, the structural challenges to collective bargaining, which have not been confined to the UK,[820]

---

[815] See paras 4.78, 4.90, 6.119, 3.52 and 5.75 respectively.

[816] See also Convention No 154 concerning the Promotion of Collective Bargaining (1981) (which the UK has not ratified); Recommendation No 163 concerning the Promotion of Collective Bargaining (1981).

[817] *Royal Commission on Trade Unions and Employers' Associations 1965–1968*, Cmnd 3623, 1968: para 212.

[818] This is not to imply that collective bargaining is merely a collective version of individual bargaining, however. Such a view would overlook the rule-making function of collective agreements: see Flanders, 1970.

[819] Streeck, 1992; Deakin and Wilkinson, 1994; see also W Brown *et al*, 1997: p 80 *et seq* and references therein; Davidov, 2004.

[820] However, in no other western European country were there adverse changes in legal support for trade unionism of the type which occurred during the period of Conservative Government: see Terry, 1994: p 234; para 1.25 above.

should not be underestimated. Collective bargaining in its traditional form is predicated on the model of a more or less stable workforce which works on harmonised, or comparable, terms and conditions. This model is under threat both externally and internally. Changes in the labour market, which have brought greater flexibility of labour, and a growth in short-term, temporary work and in self-employment, have eroded the bargaining power of those who remain in the 'core'. Within organisations, there has been a growth in individualised work arrangements, such as personal contracts and performance- related pay, which, while they do not preclude collective bargaining in theory, are, in the case of the former in particular, likely to do so in practice.[821] In the UK, the decline in the coverage of collective bargaining did not of itself result in the development of alternative models of employee representation; on the contrary consultative committees tended to be confined to contexts where trade unions were recognised.[822] ICER 2004 gave employers a strong incentive to establish information and consultation arrangements in order to reduce the possibility of their employees initiating procedures which would then be governed by the more prescriptive provisions of the Regulations. Research to date indicates that some employers have given increased attention to informing and consulting their employees but unions have been cautious about the new provisions, fearing that they could further threaten their hegemony as worker representative bodies.[823] Perhaps surprisingly, unions have not, generally, used ICER 2004 as a method of 'getting a foot in the door' of employers where union membership is comparatively low and/or there is currently inadequate support to apply for statutory recognition.

The future shape of employee representation in Britain has been unpredictable for some years.[824] The statutory recognition procedure is having an impact, not least in encouraging some employers to reach voluntary agreements. Nevertheless this procedure applies only in workplaces employing 21 or more workers, can be obstructed (at least temporarily) by employers recognising a non-independent trade union, and the requirement for at least 40% of the workers in the bargaining unit, as well as a majority of those voting, to support recognition in a ballot may prove a difficult hurdle to surmount. Moreover the procedure does not, ultimately require employers to reach agreement with a trade union (nor, even if they do, to apply the terms agreed to individual workers). These factors, coupled with the defects of specific performance as a sanction, have led to the suggestion that consultation laws may ultimately be more effective in promoting collective bargaining and genuine 'partnership' with employers than mandatory recognition,[825] although much depends on the powers of the consultative bodies established and the training and experience of those who serve on them.[826] Despite recent legal developments, it is still the case that the future nature and extent of collective representation, and its implications for the trade union movement, remains uncertain.

---

[821] For an analysis which emphasises the variety of ways in which individualism and collectivism may relate in this context, however, see Kessler and Purcell, 1995.

[822] Cully *et al*, 1999: p 100.

[823] See Hall, 2006; Hall *et al*, 2007, 2008, 2009, 2010 for analysis of the impact of ICER 2008.

[824] See generally Hyman, 1997; Heery, 2009; W Brown, 2010.

[825] W Brown *et al*, 2001.

[826] See P Davies and C Kilpatrick, 2004.

10

TRADE UNIONS AND THEIR MEMBERS

INTRODUCTION

10.1   In the preceding chapters we have examined the law governing the relationship between trade unions and the state and between trade unions and employers. In this chapter we examine the law which governs the relationship between trade unions and their members.[1] This derives both from common law and from statute. A trade union is constituted by an association of individuals bound together by a contract of membership and the courts have jurisdiction to enforce this contract at the suit of union members.[2] Before 1971 the common law was the primary means of controlling the conduct of union affairs,[3] statutory regulation being confined to the areas of union political activities and mergers. The Trade Union Act 1871, which granted trade union purposes protection against the doctrine of restraint of trade,[4] specifically endorsed the principle that unions were autonomous bodies which should be free to determine their own constitutions.[5] This did not, in the event, mean that the law took a wholly non-interventionist approach to the area of trade union government; on the contrary the courts imposed considerable fetters in the guise of interpreting the contract of membership and through their powers to imply in, and strike out, terms. In particular they took the opportunity, through these mechanisms, to impose on unions the duty to comply with public law standards of procedural fairness in exercising their decision-making powers. Nevertheless the degree of external regulation emanating from the common law was modest in comparison with the extensive legislative intervention which now exists.

The first radical break with the abstentionist framework of the 1871 Act came with the Industrial Relations Act 1971, although even then its provisions were largely concerned with requiring unions to have rules on particular matters rather than requiring them to take a specific form.[6] With the return of the Labour government in 1974 the principle of union autonomy was to a large extent restored, the major exception being the application of the sex and race discrimination legislation to trade unions in their dealings with applicants and members. From 1980 onwards, however, the

---

[1] For a detailed analysis of this area up to the mid-1980s see Elias and Ewing, 1987. This text is particularly useful for the development of the common law which, in the light of the extensive scope of statutory intervention, we discuss only in outline in this chapter, although it still remains significant in some areas.

[2] Note also the jurisdiction of the Certification Officer in this area since 1999: see further para 2.33 and 10.6

[3] Initially the courts viewed property rights as the basis of jurisdiction, the contract basis of jurisdiction being established only in *Lee v Showmen's Guild of Great Britain* [1952] 2 QB 329; Elias and Ewing, 1987: pp 23–25.

[4] See para 7.12 above.

[5] This Act required unions to have rules on a limited range of matters but the substance of those rules was for the union to decide. Section 4 of that Act (now repealed), which precluded any of their agreements from being directly enforceable or subject to damages for breach, was designed to exclude union rules from the purview of the courts but due to tortuous drafting it achieved only partial success in this endeavour: see Elias and Ewing, 1987: pp 6–12.

[6] See Weekes *et al*, 1975, ch 3.

activities of unions were subjected to an increasing degree of statutory regulation. This process began slowly, starting with the introduction of protection for individuals against 'unreasonable' exclusion or expulsion from a union where a closed shop was in operation. The Trade Union Act 1984 brought much more extensive intervention with the introduction of statutory requirements to hold periodic elections for specified union offices, together with greater restrictions upon unions' political activities. In 1988 these requirements were extended and additional rights for union members were introduced, most notably restrictions on the type of conduct for which they could be disciplined by their unions. This Act also brought the creation of a Commissioner for the Rights of Trade Union Members (CROTUM), empowered to assist individuals wishing to bring proceedings against their unions. The Employment Act 1990 introduced additional restrictions on the conduct of ballots which were extended further in 1993. TURERA 1993 also prevented unions from excluding or expelling individuals except in circumstances permitted by the Act. In all cases the statutory provisions were deemed to prevail over anything to the contrary in the union rule book. The justifications for introducing individual statutory provisions varied. A central theme was the need for legislative imposition of democracy within trade unions, based on the assertion that union leaders did not adequately reflect the views of their members and that, in the light of the special 'privileges' and immunities which unions enjoyed, it was particularly important to ensure that the rights of individual members were adequately protected and that there was proper accountability for the use of union power.[7] We discuss the issues which are raised by these assumptions, and the approach to trade union government they exemplify, later in the chapter.

A number of the statutory constraints on union autonomy introduced by the Conservative Government (although not those pertaining to union elections) are regarded as incompatible with freedom of association principles by the ILO Committee of Experts on the Application of Conventions and Recommendations, and they have also attracted condemnation from the ECSR (formerly the CIE) of the European Social Charter. In 1985, the European Commission of Human Rights affirmed that the right to join a union guaranteed by Article 11 of the ECHR did not accord a general right to join the union of one's choice regardless of that union's rules,[8] and in 2007 the ECtHR upheld that view in a decision which we discuss in greater detail in para 10.10.[9] Despite the strong views expressed by these international bodies, the Labour Government did very little to alter the substantive framework regulating union conduct inherited from its predecessors,[10] although the CROTUM was abolished[11] and jurisdiction over specified contractual matters extended to the Certification Officer, providing an alternative (and speedier, cheaper and less

---

[7] See, variously, the Green Papers *Democracy in Trade Unions*, Cmnd 8778, 1983; *Trade Unions and their Members*, Cm 95, 1987; *Industrial Relations in the 1990s*, Cm 1602, 1991. For a more detailed analysis, and powerful critique, of the assumptions upon which these statements rest see Fredman, 1992a. On the background to, and impact of, the balloting provisions, see P Smith *et al*, 1993; Undy *et al*, 1996.

[8] *Cheall v UK* Application No 10550/83, (1986) EHRR 74.

[9] *ASLEF v Lee* judgment of 27 Feburary 2007, [2007] IRLR 361.

[10] ERelA 2004, s 33 allowed individuals to exclude or expel individuals as a result of their activities as a member of a political party; EA 2008, s 18 permits this on grounds of membership of a political party in specified circumstances: see further para 10.10.

[11] In 1998, the CROTUM absorbed a budget of £247,328, and dealt with 94 calls and two applications, calculated by Mr John Healey to cost £2,600 per call and £20,000 per application: House of Commons, Official Report of Standing Committee E, 4 March 1999, 4.15pm.

formal) route to seeking redress to that afforded by the High Court.[12] At the time of writing there is no indication that the Coalition Government plans to reform the law in this field. This is not an area in which the Human Rights Act 1998 is likely to be of great assistance to unions in view of the very detailed nature of the legislation, which leaves little room for argument that it should be interpreted in accordance with general freedom of association principles,[13] although the Act may have some part to play in relation to common law regulation.

We begin the chapter by examining the contract of membership and the criteria which have informed the judicial approach towards its construction. We then provide an overview of the statutory rights which union members and applicants for membership are now accorded in relation to trade unions. There follows a more detailed analysis of the principles, both common law and statutory, which govern union conduct in three important areas: access to membership and the exercise of disciplinary powers; access to union office; and union political activities. Our aim here is not to provide an exhaustive technical account of these provisions; the legislation, in particular, is in many places intricate and complex.[14] Rather we aim to highlight their most important features and, where appropriate, to compare the scope of the common law and legislation. In the concluding section we ask whether, in the light of the extent of external regulation which currently exists, unions can continue to be viewed as voluntary, autonomous bodies and assess the implications of the current legal framework applicable to them.

THE CONTRACT OF MEMBERSHIP

General principles

10.2   The contract of membership which individuals enter when they join a union[15] serves as the 'constitution' of the union. As such it generally covers a wide variety of matters including the rights and obligations of individual union members; the powers and composition of various bodies within the union; the purposes for which union funds can be expended; and the powers of union officers. It is open to any member to challenge the validity of union conduct on the ground that it is not

---

[12] See further para 2.33 for details of the Certification Officer's general jurisdiction, and para 10.5 below for a comparison of the remedies which may be sought from the respective avenues of redress for breach of union rules. Decisions of the Certification Officer since 2001 are available on www.certoffice.org.

[13] In *ASLEF v Lee* UKEAT/0625/03/RN it was argued that Art 11 of the ECHR was at issue but the matter was resolved on construction of the statute without reference to Art 11; see further para 10.10.

[14] For a more detailed technical analysis see G Morris and T Archer, 2000: ch 2.

[15] Before the IRA 1971 unregistered unions were incapable of contracting in their own right, while the judges were divided about whether registered unions had sufficient corporate status to contract or not. In *Bonsor v Musicians' Union* [1956] AC 104, the majority of the House of Lords considered that the contract of membership was a contract between the members *inter se* rather than between the member and the union. Under the IRA 1971 registered unions were incorporated bodies and so could contract; since that Act was repealed, all unions, listed and unlisted, can contract: see now TULRCA 1992, s 10(1)(a) and para 7.28 above. However, it does not necessarily follow from this that the contract is with the union. In practice, 'the courts may be tempted to adopt the view that every member is contractually bound to the union, unless there is a clear intention to the contrary. In order to reach this conclusion it would have to be agreed that not only were unions granted the capacity to contract, but in addition they have in fact exercised that power with those who were members when the capacity to contract was granted. However, even if the courts do not take this approach, *Bonsor* shows that the member will have no difficulty in enforcing the contract – even if it is with the members *inter se*': Elias and Ewing, 1987: p 46.

authorised by the union rules and thereby constitutes a breach of contract.[16] The primary source of this contract is the union rule book, which unions have a statutory obligation to supply to any person on request, either free or on payment of a reasonable charge.[17] The rule book is likely to be subject to amendment from time to time, either with the approval of the membership directly or that of their elected representatives, depending upon the procedure specified in the rules.

Rule books may vary considerably in the degree of detail they contain. Nevertheless, even if ostensibly comprehensive, they may also be supplemented by implied terms and by custom and practice within the union in question. The most notable judicial recognition of the role which custom and practice could play came from the House of Lords in *Heatons Transport (St Helens) Ltd v TGWU*[18] when Lord Wilberforce, giving the judgment of the court, affirmed that:

> ... it is not to be assumed, as in the case of a commercial contract which has been reduced into writing, that all the terms of the agreement are to be found in the rule book alone; particularly as regards the discretion conferred by the members upon committees or officials of the union as to the way in which they may act on the union's behalf. What the members understand as to the characteristics of the agreement into which they enter by joining a union is well stated in the section of the TUC handbook on the Industrial Relations Act which gives advice about the content and operation of unions' rules. Paragraph 99 reads as follows: 'Trade Union government does not ... rely solely on what is written down in the rule book. It also depends upon custom and practice, by (sic) procedures which have developed over the years and which, although well understood by those who operate them, are not formally set out in the rules. Custom and practice may operate either by modifying a union's rules as they operate in practice, or by compensating for the absence of formal rules. Furthermore, the procedures which custom and practice lays down very often vary from workplace to workplace within the same industry, and even within different branches of the same union.[19]

It is notable, however, that this statement was made in the context of industrial action proceedings where the court held the union liable for the acts of its shop stewards despite the lack of any authority for their actions in the rules. It has been observed that in other contexts the courts have shown much greater reluctance to take account of union practices, to the extent that 'the gap between the practical operation of the constitution and the way it works in theory, as reflected in the formal constitution, is effectively disregarded ...'.[20] Moreover, in accordance with general contractual principles, while custom and practice may moderate the operation of a rule it cannot entitle a union to act in conflict with it.[21]

---

[16] Occasionally the rule in *Foss v Harbottle* (1843) 2 Hare 461 will deny the member a remedy in cases where the action is not totally outside the powers of the union, but has not been taken by the properly-constituted body as the rules require. See Elias and Ewing, 1984, ch 4. On expenditure of union funds without the authority of the rules, see *YMA v Howden* [1903] 1 KB 308, CA, [1905] AC 256, HL; *Taylor v NUM (Derbyshire Area) (No 3)* [1985] IRLR 99.

[17] TULRCA 1992, s 27. Failure to supply a copy of the rules is a criminal offence, punishable by a fine not exceeding level 5 on the standard scale established by the Criminal Justice Act as substituted by the Criminal Justice Act 1991, s 17(1) (at the time of writing £5,000): s 45A.

[18] [1972] ICR 308.

[19] [1972] ICR 308, 393–394.

[20] Elias and Ewing, 1987: p 33. For consideration by the Certification Officer of custom and practice see *Scobie v TGWU (No 2)*, 25 April 2005, CO. The Certification Officer has interpreted 'rules' in TULRCA 1992 s 108A(1) as exceeding those in the rule book: see *Rawlins v BMA*, 2 February 2007, CO.

[21] *Porter v NUJ* [1980] IRLR 404, 410 (Viscount Dilhorne); *Taylor v NUM (Derbyshire Area)* [1985] IRLR 99.

Terms may also be implied into the contract of membership according to other general contractual principles.[22] However, the courts have shown that they are most unlikely to imply terms which extend the duties of members as against those of the union. Thus, in *Radford v NATSOPA*,[23] for example, Plowman J refused to accept the argument that the applicant was in breach of an implied obligation he was alleged to owe to the union given the very specific circumstances indicated in the rules as to when expulsion could be justified. Again, in *Leigh v NUR*[24] Goff J rejected the contention that qualifications for nomination to the office of president specified in the union rules were subject to additional qualifications as a matter of implication. *Iwanuszezak v GMBATU*[25] constituted an unusual attempt by a member to argue that his union had an implied duty to bring its collective strength to bear to safeguard an individual member's existing conditions of employment. This argument was rejected by the Court of Appeal. The brief judgment in this case was given pursuant to a striking out application by the union and did not explore in detail the interesting issues to which such a claim could give rise.[26]

10.3   The implied term is one important mechanism by which the courts can shape the contract of membership. Others are the power to interpret the scope and application of union rules and the power to strike out terms on public policy grounds. The dicta differ in emphasis as to the approach which should be adopted where the terms of the rule book are ambiguous. In *Heatons* Lord Wilberforce pointed out that:

> ... [t]rade union rule books are not drafted by parliamentary draftsmen. Courts of law must resist the temptation to construe them as if they were; for that is not how they would be understood by the members who are the parties to the agreement of which the terms, or some of them, are set out in the rule book ...[27]

However in *British Actors' Equity Association v Goring* Viscount Dilhorne affirmed that the same canons of construction should be applied to rule books as to any 'written documents. Our task is to construe them so as to give them a reasonable interpretation which accords with what in our opinion must have been intended'.[28] In *Jacques v AUEW (Engineering Section)* Warner J attempted to reconcile these approaches by stating that 'the rules of a trade union are not to be construed

---

[22]   See para 4.4 *et seq* for the nature of these tests; see also *AB v CD* [2001] IRLR 808.

[23]   [1972] ICR 484. See also *Spring v NASDS* [1956] 1 WLR 585. Cf, however, *McVitae v UNISON* [1996] IRLR 33, where Harrison J implied a power for the defendant union, created upon amalgamation of three existing unions, to discipline members for conduct prior to the amalgamation when such conduct was contrary to the rules both of the amalgamating union of which they were a member and of UNISON.

[24]   [1970] Ch 326.

[25]   [1988] IRLR 219.

[26]   Lloyd LJ opined at 220 that the [trial] 'judge put the matter well when he said that it is the primary function of a union to look after the collective interests of its members' ... and 'where the collective interests of the union conflict with the interests of an individual member it only makes sense ... that the collective interests of the members as a whole should prevail'. However, in view of the claimant's argument that this consideration was irrelevant it was put to one side by the court. There is authority to suggest that there may be scope to imply terms into the contract of membership requiring members' access to union services, particularly representation, to be decided in accordance with standards of substantive and procedural fairness: see further G Morris and T Archer, 2000: para 2.15. On union liability for sex discrimination in the context of collective bargaining see *Allen v GMB* [2008] IRLR 690 discussed at para 6.100 above.

[27]   [1972] ICR 308, 393.

[28]   [1978] ICR 791, HL at 794–795.

literally or like a statute, but so as to give them a reasonable interpretation which accords with what in the court's view they must have been intended to mean, bearing in mind their authorship, their purpose, and the readership to which they are addressed.'[29] This dictum has been cited frequently in subsequent cases. However, in the context of the exercise of disciplinary powers, where much of the case law has arisen, the courts have, in practice, tended towards an interpretation which protects the interests of the individual union member. In doing so, they have frequently referred to a dictum of Lord Denning MR that union rule books are:

> ... not so much a contract, ...but ... much more a legislative code laid down by some members of the union to be imposed on all members of the union. They are more like by-laws than a contract. In those circumstances the rules are to be construed not only against the makers of them, but further, if it should be found that if any of these rules is contrary to natural justice ... the courts would hold them to be invalid.[30]

This approach can be criticised as overlooking the role that members play in formulating and changing rules. It has nevertheless played an important part in shaping judicial attitudes towards unions as bodies against whom members are in need of protection. In an earlier judgment in *Lee v Showmen's Guild of Great Britain*, Denning LJ pointed out the differences between social clubs and those of certain other bodies of ostensibly identical legal status:

> In the case of social clubs the rules usually empower the committee to expel a member who, in their opinion, has been guilty of conduct detrimental to the club, and this is a matter of opinion and nothing else. The courts have no wish to sit on appeal from their decisions on such a matter any more than from the decisions of a family conference. They have nothing to do with social rights or social duties ... It is very different with domestic tribunals which sit in judgment on members of a trade or profession. They wield powers as great, if not greater, than any exercised by courts of law. They can deprive a man of his livelihood ... They are usually empowered to do this for any breach of their rules which ... are rules which they impose and which he has no real opportunity of accepting or rejecting. In theory their powers are based on contract. The man is supposed to have contracted to give them these great powers; but in practice he has no choice in the matter.[31]

This case also highlighted the degree to which unions could intervene in union decision-making through the mechanism of interpreting the contract of membership. Although a domestic union body may be regarded as the final arbiter of facts, Denning LJ pointed out that the application of the rules to the facts and the construction of the rules were often inextricably linked. Thus:

> ... the question whether the committee has acted within its jurisdiction depends ... on whether the facts adduced before them were reasonably capable of being held to be a breach of the rules. If they were, then the proper inference is that the committee correctly construed the rules and have acted within their jurisdiction. If, however, the facts were not capable of being

---

[29] [1986] ICR 683 at 692. This approach has been echoed by the Certification Officer: see, for example, *In the matter of complaints against BECTU*, 2 November 2000, CO; *Taylor v MU* 15 October 2002, CO.
[30] *Bonsor v Musicians' Union* [1954] Ch 479, 485–486.
[31] [1952] 2 QB 329, 343.

held to be a breach and yet the committee held them to be a breach, then the only inference is that the committee have misconstrued the rules and exceeded their jurisdiction.[32]

This approach has afforded the courts the opportunity to give their own interpretation of disciplinary offences such as conduct that renders an individual 'unfit for membership' or is 'detrimental to the interests of the union', so, effectively, pronouncing on what union interests require. One particularly striking example of this process, where the union did not even have the chance itself to consider whether the member's conduct breached a disciplinary rule, is *Esterman v NALGO*.[33] In pursuance of a dispute with local authority employers, NALGO instructed its members not to volunteer their assistance in forthcoming local elections and to withdraw any offers of assistance already made. The claimant refused to withdraw her offer of assistance, whereupon she was requested to attend a disciplinary meeting to consider whether her conduct merited expulsion from the union. The relevant disciplinary rule stated that '[a]ny member who disregards any regulation issued by the branch, or is guilty of conduct which, in the opinion of the executive committee, renders him unfit for membership, shall be liable to expulsion'. The claimant successfully sought an interim injunction against the union and members of the branch executive committee to restrain them from taking disciplinary action against her. Templeman J held that no committee, applying itself correctly to the law and obeying the principles of natural justice, could find that in these circumstances she had been guilty of conduct rendering her unfit to be a member of the union. It was not clear that the executive had the power to issue the order which they had and, even if they did, a member could well conclude that it was one to which it had no right to demand obedience and one which, as a loyal member of NALGO, acting in its best interests, he or she felt bound to disobey.[34]

The Human Rights Act 1998 has the capacity to serve as a brake on this form of interventionist approach to the interpretation of union rules. Article 11 of the ECHR guarantees the right to form and join trade unions.[35] In *ASLEF v UK*[36] the ECtHR took into account the terms of ILO Convention No 87,[37] which affirms the right of unions to draw up their own rules and to organise their administration and activities, in concluding that unions were free to establish their own rules concerning conditions of membership, subject to the obligation on the State to protect individuals against abuse of a dominant position, for example where rules were wholly unreasonable or arbitrary or where the consequences of exclusion or expulsion resulted in exceptional hardship. This decision reflects the approach by the European Commission of Human Rights in the earlier

---

[32] [1952] 2 QB 329, 345.

[33] [1974] ICR 625. In *Longley v NUJ* [1987] IRLR 109, the Court of Appeal emphasised that the courts should be slow to prevent domestic tribunals adjudicating upon a matter in the first instance and endorsed the view of the trial judge that this should be done only if there was persuasive evidence to suggest that the issues had been prejudged or that the prescribed procedures had not been complied with. However, cf *Porter v NUJ* [1980] IRLR 404, discussed in para 11.91 below.

[34] As P Davies and M Freedland, 1984: p 606, point out 'although formally the test applied by the court was whether no reasonable tribunal could have come to the conclusion that the plaintiff was unfit to be a member of the union (which apparently gives the domestic tribunal some scope in its interpretation of the union's rules), in practice the test applied seemed to be more like whether a reasonable member might consider the call for industrial action a breach of the union's rules or even simply unwise (a very different test)'.

[35] See further para 7.9.

[36] Judgment of 27 February 2007, [2007] IRLR 361. See also *RSPCA v A-G* [2001] 3 All ER 530, para 37(b) (Lightman J).

[37] Art 5 of the ESC was also cited by the ECtHR.

case of *Cheall v UK*.[38] At the time of writing it still remains to be seen whether the principle of union autonomy reflected in *ASLEF* informs the courts' (and Certification Officer's) approach towards the interpretation of union rules.

10.4   A further means by which the courts may control the conduct of union affairs is by striking out rules that conflict with public policy. One area where this power has proved significant is in relation to terms which attempt to exclude the jurisdiction of the courts; a rule which provides that the decision of an internal body shall be final will be void as contrary to public policy.[39] In theory a rule that members should exhaust internal remedies before resorting to the courts could also be construed as an attempt to oust their jurisdiction, albeit temporarily. In practice at common law the courts took the view that where such a rule did exist, it was for the claimant to show cause why the contractual position should not be adhered to,[40] the protection afforded to the member pending the exhaustion of internal procedures being material here.[41] The position in this context is now subject to statutory provisions which we discuss in para 10.5. Another important area where the courts have exercised their discretion to strike out rules, although the basis of doing so is more controversial,[42] is where they provide for union bodies to act in conflict with the principles of natural justice. In the context of disciplinary hearings these principles, broadly speaking, require members to be given notice of the charge against them, an opportunity to be heard, and a fair hearing by an unbiased judge. In the past the courts have also sought to circumvent union rules governing admission to the union where these conflicted with the 'right to work', although the basis for this was questioned both by judges and by commentators. We discuss the application of this and other forms of control over union government further in later sections of the chapter.

Remedies

10.5   A union member who alleges that the union has acted or threatened to act in breach of the contract of membership may seek a remedy in the High Court or, with some exceptions, apply to the Certification Officer.[43] The remedies which may potentially be sought from the High Court, depending upon the context, are a declaration, an injunction and damages.[44] Where time is of the essence – an impending election allegedly involving unlawful expenditure, or expulsion from the union, for example – a claimant may seek an interim injunction to restrain the union from carrying out or continuing an allegedly unlawful act.[45] We discuss the procedure for applying for

---

[38] Application No 10550/83, (1986) EHRR 74.

[39] *Lee v Showmen's Guild of Great Britain* [1952] 2 QB 329 at 342 (Denning LJ); *Lawlor v UPW* [1965] Ch 712.

[40] *Leigh v NUR* [1970] Ch 326 at 334; (cf *White v Kuzych* [1951] AC 585).

[41] *Leigh v NUR*, above; see also *Hiles v ASW* [1968] Ch 440 at 453.

[42] See Elias and Ewing, 1987: p 35–37.

[43] Note that a complainant must choose between these avenues of redress: TULRCA 1992, s 108A.

[44] For more detailed discussion of the issues raised by these remedies in relation to trade unions, and the basis on which unions may be liable for the acts of their officials, see Elias and Ewing, 1987: p 44–57.

[45] P Davies and M Freedland, 1984 highlight (at p 594) the contrast between the courts' willingness to grant injunctions to restrain unions from acting upon a member's unlawful expulsion and their reluctance to grant injunctions in the context of the contract of employment (see para 5.54 *et seq* above), the former not being viewed as a contract of personal service: see, for example, *Porter v NUJ* [1980] IRLR 404. In general the courts will not grant an interim declaration but for a rare example of such a case see *Clarke v Chadburn* [1984] IRLR 350, a case arising out of the 1984/85 miners' strike.

interim injunctions, the principles which govern the discretion to grant them, and the penalties for breaching them, in para 11.48 *et seq* below. Damages are most likely to be sought when a member is unlawfully expelled from a union. In practice there are very few reported cases dealing with this remedy,[46] and now that members cannot lawfully be deprived of their employment through loss of union membership,[47] quantifying such a claim may be difficult.[48]

As we discussed in para 10.4, where a union rule requires a member to exhaust internal remedies before resorting to the courts, the courts have considered that the claimant should show cause why the contractual position should not be followed. This rule is now subject to a statutory right not to be denied access to the courts.[49] Notwithstanding anything in the rules of the union or in the practice of any court, if a member or former member of a union brings proceedings in a court with respect to a matter to which this statutory right applies then, provided specified conditions are met, rules requiring or allowing the matter to be submitted for determination or conciliation, and the fact that any 'relevant steps'[50] remain to be taken under the rules, must be regarded as irrelevant to whether the legal proceedings should be dismissed or adjourned.[51] The right applies where:

> ... a matter is under the rules of a trade union required or allowed to be submitted for determination or conciliation in accordance with the rules of the union, but a provision of the rules purporting for that to be a person's only remedy has no effect (or would have no effect if there were one).[52]

The terms in which this right is framed are puzzling. The right clearly covers the situation where the rules attempt to oust the jurisdiction of the courts completely, and would also apply where the rules are silent; whether it applies where the rule merely provides for prior exhaustion of internal remedies is unclear, although it was the express intention of the Conservative Government that introduced the legislation that it should.[53] Two further conditions must be satisfied for the right to apply: the member or former member must have made a 'valid application' to the union for the matter to be submitted for determination or conciliation in accordance with the union's rules,[54] and the court proceedings must not have been commenced sooner than six months after the union received the application.[55] Once this period has expired, the court has no discretion to dismiss or adjourn the proceedings on the ground that internal remedies have not been exhausted (unless

---

[46] Elias and Ewing, 1987: p 55. The leading case is *Edwards v SOGAT* [1971] Ch 354, a case of expulsion in the context of a closed shop.

[47] See para 8.37.

[48] Note that the statutory limits on damages awards which apply to proceedings in tort do not apply in the context of contractual claims against unions: TULRCA 1992, s 22; see further para 11.47 below.

[49] TULRCA 1992, s 63.

[50] These include any steps falling to be taken in accordance with the rules for the purposes of, or in connection with, the determination or conciliation of the matter, or any appeal, review or reconsideration of any determination or award: TULRCA 1992, s 63(5)(b).

[51] TULRCA 1992, s 63.

[52] TULRCA 1992, s 63(1).

[53] See, for example, Mr Patrick Nicholls, House of Commons, Official Report of Standing Committee F, col 62, 17 November 1987.

[54] TULRCA 1992, s 63(2)(a). An application is deemed to be valid unless the union informs the applicant, within 28 days of receipt, of the respects in which the application contravened the requirement of the rules: s 63(3).

[55] TULRCA 1992, s 63(2)(b).

there has been delay in furthering the proceedings caused by the unreasonable conduct of the member),[56] although its discretion to do so on other grounds remains unaffected. The discretion of the court on general common law principles to grant a remedy before the statutory time limit has expired also remains unaffected,[57] although it is possible that the courts may be guided by the statutory period and refuse to intervene before that period has expired.

The right of a member to apply to the Certification Officer where he or she alleges a breach or threatened breach of union rules was introduced by the Employment Relations Act 1999.[58] It applies where the breach or threatened breach relates to[59] the appointment or election of a person to, or the removal of a person from, any office;[60] disciplinary proceedings (including expulsion); the balloting of members on any issue other than industrial action;[61] and the constitution or proceedings of any executive committee[62] or of any decision-making meeting.[63] The Secretary of State may add to this list by order.[64] There have been a number of cases where the issue of whether a rule relates to 'disciplinary proceedings' has arisen. In *Irving v GMB* the EAT held, in distinguishing between such proceedings and a grievance procedure, which lies outside the Certification Officer's jurisdiction, that it was 'a fundamental characteristic of any disciplinary proceedings that they include the conferring on one party to them of the power to impose a sanction on the other party'.[65] As well as industrial action ballots, dismissal and disciplinary proceedings against an employee of the union are excluded as are, by implication, allegations relating to the misuse of funds.[66] In contrast to High Court proceedings, which may normally be brought up to six years after the breach, a tight time limit applies to applications to the Certification Officer: the application must be brought within a six-month period starting with the day on which the breach or threatened breach is alleged to have taken place, or, if within that period any internal union complaints procedure is invoked to resolve the claim, within a six-month period starting with the day on which the procedure is

---

[56] TULRCA 1992, s 63(4).

[57] TULRCA 1992, s 63(6).

[58] TULRCA 1992, ss 108A, 108B. The Certification Officer has held that the 'rules' of a union are not always to be found exclusively in its rule book: *Rawlins v BMA* 2 February 2007, CO (Standing Orders in Council 'rules' for the purposes of s 108A). In *Heffernan v UNISON* 14 November 2011, CO, para 82, a Code of Good Branch Practice was held not to form part of the Union rules, On the broader jurisdiction of and procedure followed by the Certification Officer, see further para 2.33.

[59] The Certification Officer has held that this requires the connection between the rule allegedly breached and the matters set out in s 108A(2) to be 'clear and direct' (*Lynch v UNIFI* 7 October 2004, CO, para 49); it is not sufficient that a rule merely affects or impacts on one of the listed matters: *Dawes v RCN* 3 February 2011, CO.

[60] In *Finlay v Unite the Union (TGWU Section)* 30 October 2007, CO the Certification Officer held that his jurisdiction is not confined to rules which specifically mention appointments or elections; the decision as to whether rules are included depends on the rule book as a whole and custom and practice in the union.

[61] TULRCA 1992, s 108A(5). Industrial action ballots were excluded because they would draw the Certification Officer into deciding matters involving relations between unions and employers: Mr Michael Wills, Minister for Small Firms, Trade and Industry, Official Report of Standing Committee E, 4 March 1999, 4.15pm.

[62] Note that this goes beyond the 'principal committee' as defined in TULRCA 1992. s 119; see s 108A(10),(12).

[63] TULRCA 1992, s 108A(2), (11); see *Giles v GMB*, 15 June 2001, CO (limited to meetings which under the rules have power to made a decision that is final as regards the union or branch).

[64] TULRCA 1992, s 108A(2)(e), (13).

[65] [2008] IRLR 202, EAT, para 36. See also *Gallagher v UNISON* UKEAT/0280/05: decision to debar union members who had been debarred from holding office from attending the National Delegate Conference as members of the public not a disciplinary penalty; *Dennison v UNISON*, 15 April 2003, CO: Certification Officer's jurisdiction not confined to considering only breaches of rules that deal expressly with disciplinary proceedings where, in substance, a disciplinary penalty – here, suspension of legal assistance - has been imposed.

[66] Complaints relating to a failure to comply with political fund ballot rules must be brought under TULRCA 1992, s 80: s 108A(4).

concluded or the last day of the period of one year beginning with the day on which the procedure is invoked, whichever is the earlier.[67] Interestingly, the legislation reflects a preference for the use of internal complaints procedures where these exist; the Certification Officer may refuse to accept an application unless he or she is satisfied that the applicant has taken reasonable steps to resolve the claim by these means.[68] If the complaint is upheld, the Certification Officer must make, unless it is considered inappropriate, an enforcement order requiring the union to take specified steps to remedy the breach or withdraw the threat of a breach within a specified period and/or to abstain from specified acts with a view to securing that a breach of the same or a similar kind does not occur in future.[69] Recourse to the Certification Officer is likely to prove a much speedier and cheaper option than the High Court, unless the applicant seeks interim relief or damages, in which case he or she will have no alternative but to commence High Court proceedings (unless the complaint also relates to the statutory rights relating to expulsion or discipline, in which case the applicant has the option of complaining to an employment tribunal).[70] As the Certification Officer has remarked, the 'nature of many trade union rule books is such that there are clear advantages in their interpretation being given to a body conversant with the practicalities of running a union'.[71] Either party may appeal against a decision of the Certification Officer on a question of law to the EAT.

STATUTORY RIGHTS: AN OVERVIEW

10.6 The statutory rights which union members[72] may exercise in relation to their union, which apply regardless of the terms of union rules, can be divided into four broad categories. First, there are rights relating to union membership and discipline. Individuals who are excluded or expelled from a union other than in circumstances expressly permitted by the legislation,[73] or who are 'unjustifiably disciplined',[74] may seek a remedy from an employment tribunal and may be awarded substantial financial compensation. We examine these rights in greater detail in para 10.9 *et seq* below. In addition, the legislation implies into the contract of membership a right for members to terminate their membership on giving reasonable notice and complying with any reasonable conditions.[75] In

---

[67] TULRCA 1992, s 108A(6),(7). To rely on 108A(6)(b), the applicant must establish that the union has a complaints procedure: *Fradley v TSSA*, 23 October 2003, CO. In *Murphy v GMB* 29 November 2002, CO, the Certification Officer held that 'any' procedure should be given a wide interpretation, to include any procedure (not just written) generally known to the members as a way of raising and resolving complaints. See, however, *UNISON v Bakhsh* [2009] IRLR 418, EAT, emphasising the need for 'some recognisable formal procedure' (Underhill P at [14]).

[68] TULRCA 1992, s 108B(1).

[69] TULRCA 1992, s 108B(3),(4).

[70] See paras 10.9 and 10.12 below.

[71] Cockburn, 2006: p 100.

[72] It is not always easy to determine whether an individual is a union 'member', particularly where unions have different categories of membership, such as 'full', 'honorary', 'limited' and 'retired'. In *NUM (Yorkshire Area) v Millward* [1995] IRLR 411 the EAT affirmed that the provisions of the rule book may not always be determinative of membership for statutory purposes; in each case the relevant provision must be examined 'textually and contextually' (415).

[73] TULRCA 1992, ss 174–177.

[74] TULRCA 1992, ss 64–67.

[75] TULRCA 1992, s 69. It has been suggested that where subscriptions are collected monthly, at least one month's notice should be given: *Ashford v ASTMS* [1973] ICR 296 (decided under the comparable provision of the IRA 1971). However, *quaere* whether, if subscriptions are collected on an annual basis, reasonable notice may be less than a year, albeit without a refund of subscription: Kidner, 1983: p 26, n 96.

relation to the latter, it has been accepted that resignation may be postponed until the completion of any pending disciplinary action and that a member can be required to make up any arrears of subscription,[76] but a union cannot require the member to provide a reason for resigning.[77]

The second category covers rights not to be discriminated against in relation to membership and the benefits of membership. First, where a union has a political fund, contribution to the fund cannot be made a condition of admission to the union, nor may non-contributors be placed at any disadvantage as compared with other members except in relation to the control or management of the fund.[78] We discuss this and other rights relating to political funds further in para 10.19. Second, EU law requires that a worker who is a national of a Member State who is employed in the territory of another Member State shall enjoy equality of treatment as regards membership of unions and the exercise of rights attaching to membership, including the right to vote and eligibility for union administrative and management posts and the workers' representative bodies in the undertaking.[79] Last, the equality legislation makes it unlawful for any 'organisation of workers'[80] to discriminate against a person in specified ways, including membership and the arrangements for offering membership; the terms on which membership is offered; access to a benefit, facility or service; subjecting the member to 'any other detriment'; harassment; and victimisation.[81] There is also a duty to make reasonable adjustments.[82] Organisations may take positive action in relation to persons who share a protected characteristic under EqA 2010 (for example, in relation to holding office) where the tests for doing so, which we discuss in para 6.73 above, are satisfied.[83]

The third category concerns rights which may be exercised in the event of a union not complying with its statutory obligation to hold appropriately conducted ballots. These obligations arise in four situations: elections to specified offices; approval of the adoption by a union of 'political objects' and periodic reapproval of an existing political fund; industrial action; and union amalgamations and 'transfers of engagements'.[84] We discuss the first and second of these in paras 10.17 and 10.19; the third in para 11.92. We do not consider further

---

[76]   *Ashford v ASTMS* [1973] ICR 296.

[77]   *Ashford v ASTMS* [1973] ICR 296.

[78]   TULRCA 1992, s 82(1)(c).

[79]   European Parliament and Council Regulation (EU) 492/2011, Article 8. 'Worker' has a 'Community meaning' and includes part-time workers: Case 75/63 *Hoekstra (née Unger)* [1964] ECR 177; Case 53/81 *Levin v Secretary of State for Justice* [1982] ECR 1035; Case 66/85 *Lawrie Blum v Land Baden-Wurttemberg* [1986] ECR 2121. Note that the definition varies according to the context in which it is to be applied: see, for example, Case C-256/01 *Allonby v Accrington and Rossendale College* [2004] IRLR 224, para 63.

[80]   EqA 2010 re-enacts (with some amendments) previous prohibitions on discrimination by organisations of workers. This term is wider than that of a 'trade union', discussed in para 7.20; in particular, no specific purposes are stipulated; the organisation need not be permanent; and those with a professional/client relationship are not excluded: see *Sadek v Medical Protection Society* [2005] IRLR 57. On the liability of employers and principals, and of employees and agents, see EqA 2010, ss109, 110, discussed para 6.54 above.

[81]   EqA 2010, s 57. See generally ch 6. On the meaning of 'detriment' see now *Shamoon v Chief Constable of the Royal Ulster Constabulary* [2003] IRLR 285, discussed at para 6.51. See also *FTATU v Modgill* [1980 IRLR 142; *FBU v Fraser* [1998] IRLR 697; *Diakou v Islington Union 'A' Branch* [1997] ICR 121.

[82]   EqA 2010, s 57(6).

[83]   EqA 2010, s 158.

[84]   Under a transfer of engagements, the transferor union loses its legal identity while the organisation to which it transfers continues in being with its legal identity unchanged. An amalgamation produces a new organisation replacing the amalgamating bodies, which then cease to exist.

the highly specialist area of amalgamations and transfers of engagements which lies beyond the scope of this work.

Finally, members have a number of miscellaneous rights which enable them to supervise the conduct by unions of their statutory obligations. Unions are required to maintain a register of the names and addresses of their members and to secure, so far as possible, that the entries in that register are accurate and kept up-to-date.[85] Members are entitled to ascertain, free of charge and at any reasonable time, whether there is an entry on the register relating to them after giving the union reasonable notice.[86] Members also have the right to inspect, and take copies of, the union's accounting records or that of any of its branches or sections for the preceding six-year period within 28 days of so requesting.[87] They may be accompanied for this purpose by an accountant provided that he or she agrees to protect the confidentiality of the records.[88] A union member who claims that the union has failed to comply with its statutory duties relating to the register, or to comply with a request to inspect its records, may complain to the Certification Officer or the High Court (but not both).[89] A further set of provisions enables members to bring High Court proceedings on the union's behalf if the union unreasonably fails to recover payments unlawfully made to individuals who have committed, or may commit, an offence or contempt of court. They may also apply to the High Court for an order to prevent the union's trustees allowing unlawful application of its property or complying with an unlawful direction which has been given to them under the union rules. These rights are most likely to be exercised in the context of industrial action and we discuss them further in para 11.92 below.

RIGHTS RELATING TO UNION MEMBERSHIP AND DISCIPLINE

Common law

10.7   The power of a trade union to discipline its members is restricted by the Trade Union and Labour Relations (Consolidation) Act 1992, and the lawfulness of any disciplinary action should always be considered in the light of those restrictions, which we discuss in para 10.12 below. However these restrictions are in addition to, and not a substitute for, other rights,[90] and there may be situations where union action, although not contrary to the statute, constitutes a violation of its rules. Moreover, under statute the union cannot be required to halt disciplinary proceedings or to revoke a disciplinary penalty: the ultimate remedy is financial; by contrast, as we discuss in para 10.5, the courts and the Certification Officer may issue orders restraining a union from taking disciplinary action or from treating a disciplinary penalty as effective. The common law still remains important, therefore, in some contexts.

---

[85] TULRCA 1992, s 24(1).

[86] TULRCA 1992, s 24(3).

[87] TULRCA 1992, s 30. On the meaning of 'accounting records', see *Mortimer v Amicus*, 14 February 2003, CO; *Foster v MU*, 22 May 2003, CO, *Lee v NASUWT*, 13 January 2006, CO and *King and King v TGWU* 20 December 2006, CO.

[88] TULRCA 1992, s 30

[89] TULRCA 1992, ss 24A(6), 31.

[90] TULRCA 1992, s 64(5).

If members wish to challenge a decision to expel them from the union, or to subject them to some other disciplinary penalty, at common law the first question to consider will be what the rule book states. The power to discipline the member for the conduct in question must (usually) be present in the rules and the penalty which may be imposed for that offence must be clearly expressed.[91] As we saw in paras 10.3 and 10.4, although the union rules may make the domestic body the final arbiter of the facts, the courts can inquire into the application of the rules to the facts and this has, in practice, afforded them considerable scope to interpret union rules, even those which appear to give the union considerable discretion.[92]

As far as the procedure which is followed is concerned, any provision in the union rules must be followed to the letter.[93] In addition, regardless of the union rules, the courts will require the union to apply the rules of 'natural justice'.[94] These require a member to be given notice of the charge,[95] an opportunity to be heard, and a fair hearing by an unbiased judge.[96] If an initial hearing fails to comply with natural justice, it seems that this cannot be cured by a fair appeal within the union.[97]

10.8 The position of those who are refused entry to a union at common law is more complex given that they have no contractual relationship with the union; nor will the union have committed any tort against them provided that it is acting in what it perceives to be its own legitimate interests and no unlawful means are used.[98] In situations where membership of an organisation was necessary for access to, or retention of, employment the courts developed the concept of a 'right to work'[99] which meant that an application for membership should not be rejected arbitrarily or capriciously. In a departure from the existing principle,[100] in the landmark case of *Nagle v Feilden*[101] the Court of Appeal held that the claimant female trainer had an arguable case for a declaration that the

---

[91] See, for example, *Spring v NASDS* [1956] 1WLR 585. Cf, however, *McVitae v UNISON* [1996] IRLR 33, discussed in para 10.2, although the circumstances of that case – an amalgamation of three existing unions – were unusual, and the court implied a power to discipline for pre-amalgamation conduct only where the conduct contravened the rules both of the individual's pre-existing union and of the amalgamated union. On suspension, see *UNISON v Bakhsh* [2009] IRLR 418.

[92] See *Lee v Showmen's Guild of Great Britain* [1952] 2 QB 329; *Esterman v NALGO* [1974] ICR 625, discussed in para 10.3 above.

[93] See, for example, *Bonsor v MU* [1956] AC 104; *Santer v NGA* [1973] ICR 60.

[94] *Lee v Showmen's Guild of Great Britain* [1952] 2 QB 329; *Hiles v ASW* [1968] Ch 440; *Lawlor v UPW* [1965] Ch 712; *Roebuck v NUM* [1977] ICR 573. Cf *Maclean v Workers' Union* [1929] 1 Ch 602, 623–624.

[95] *Annamunthodo v Oilfield Workers' Trade Union* [1961] AC 945.

[96] *Maclean v WU* [1929] 1 Ch 602; *Taylor v NUS* [1967] 1 WLR 532; *Roebuck v NUM (Yorkshire Area)* [1977] ICR 573, and *Roebuck v NUM (Yorkshire Area) (No 2)* [1978] ICR 676. In *Thurbin v Prison Governors' Association*, 9 October 2008, CO the Certification Officer implied into the union's rules the right of a member to make oral representations prior to any decision to expel him or her.

[97] *Leary v NUVB* [1971] Ch 34, 49. A more liberal approach has been supported by the Privy Council in *Calvin v Carr* [1979] 2 All ER 440 but the court indicated that the approach in *Leary* was probably appropriate for trade union cases. In *McKenzie v NUPE* [1991] ICR 155, it was held that in the context of disciplinary proceedings against one of its members it was an implied term of the contract that a tribunal which had once heard a disciplinary matter should be entitled to reopen or rehear it whenever, in all the circumstances, justice required it.

[98] *Allen v Flood* [1898] AC 1. For liability in the economic torts see para 11.10 *et seq* below.

[99] The basis of the 'right to work' has been questioned both by judges and by commentators: see *McInnes v Onslow Fane* [1978] 3 All ER 211, 217 (Megarry J); *Forbes v New South Wales Trotting Club Ltd* (1979) 25 ALR 1, 17 (Barwick CJ); Hepple, 1981a: pp 78–81.

[100] Cf *Weinberger v Inglis (No 2)* [1919] AC 606.

[101] [1966] 2 QB 633.

unwritten rule of the Jockey Club, which controls horseracing on the flat, that women should not be granted licences was void as being in restraint of trade. This concept was later applied to a trade union when in *Edwards v SOGAT*[102] Lord Denning declared that all union rules which imposed an unwarranted encroachment on the right to work were *ultra vires* and void. This decision ran counter to an earlier House of Lords decision.[103] It also raised questions about the relationship between the 'right to work' and the doctrine of restraint of trade, against which trade unions are protected by statute,[104] although if the right to work is 'more than simply a positive reformulation of the negative doctrine of restraint of trade'[105] this would not be problematic.

In the light of the statutory restrictions upon closed shops, which we discuss in para 8.37 *et seq*, the concept of the 'right to work' is probably now otiose in the context of trade union membership. However, it is possible that, even in the absence of a closed shop, unions may continue to be subject to the administrative law concept of the 'duty to act fairly', which requires a decision to be made honestly and without caprice in considering applications for membership.[106] However, as this concept does not require an applicant to be given reasons if admission is refused, its use is likely to be limited unless the decision is patently arbitrary. In practice the introduction of the statutory right not to be excluded from a union other than in specified circumstances is much more likely to be invoked, although the common law principles may remain relevant where the exclusion falls within a category permitted by the statute.

Statutory rights to membership

(i) General principles

10.9 The extensive statutory right not to be excluded or expelled from a trade union was introduced by TURERA 1993.[107] There are now only four situations in which exclusion or expulsion is permitted.[108]

---

[102] [1971] Ch 354.

[103] *Faramas v Film Artistes Association* [1964] AC 925.

[104] See now TULRCA 1992, s 11. In *Faramas*, above, the court held that even if an arbitrary rule of exclusion was in restraint of trade at common law it would be protected by the statutory provision. The earlier statutory protection in the TUA 1871 only covered the 'purposes' of a trade union, and in *Edwards* Sachs LJ at 382 suggested that a rule which enabled 'capricious and despotic action' could not be proper to the 'purposes' of a union. This circumvention of the statutory protection was blocked by the inclusion of union rules as well as purposes in TULRA 1974 and subsequent legislation.

[105] Hepple, 1981b: p 111. This was suggested by Slade J in *Greig v Insole* [1978] 3 All ER 449, 510.

[106] See *McInnes v Onslow Fane* [1978] 3 All ER 211. In this case the application of the duty was based upon the fact that the body in question exercised monopoly control over boxing managers but it was suggested (at 216) that the duty may also apply to bodies which exercise control over activities which are important to many people both as a means of livelihood and for other reasons. *Quaere* whether the duty to act fairly could be extended to invalidate union rules themselves. For discussion of this case see Elias, 1979.

[107] This was inserted into TULRCA 1992, s 174, which has itself been amended by ERelA 2004, s 33 and ERelA 2008, s 19. See Simpson, 1993. Prior to this there was a right only not to be 'unreasonably' excluded or expelled from a union specified in a closed shop agreement: see K Miller, 1990.

[108] In *NACODS v Gluckowski* [1996] IRLR 252, Maurice Kay J held that 'exclusion' refers to a refusal to admit and not to expulsion. He thought it unlikely that constructive expulsion would be covered by the legislation (and see *McGhee v TGWU* [1985] IRLR 198). Note TULRCA 1992, s 177(2)(a), which governs the position where a union fails to respond to an application for membership.

(i)   If the individual does not satisfy, or no longer satisfies, an 'enforceable membership requirement' contained in the union rules. A requirement is 'enforceable' if it restricts membership solely by reference to one or more of three sets of criteria: employment in a specified trade, industry or profession; occupational description (including grade, level or category of appointment); or the possession of specified trade, industrial or professional qualifications or work experience.

(ii) If the individual does not qualify, or no longer qualifies, for membership of the union because it operates only in a particular part or parts of Great Britain.

(iii) In the case of a union whose purpose is the regulation of relations between its members and one particular employer or a number of associated employers, if the individual is not, or is no longer, employed by a relevant employer. This enables 'house' unions to confine their membership to a single employer.

(iv) If the exclusion or expulsion is entirely attributable to the conduct of the individual (which includes statements, acts and omissions[109]), provided that it is not 'excluded conduct' and the conduct to which it is wholly or mainly attributable is not 'protected conduct'. We discuss the concept of 'protected conduct', which relates to membership of a political party, in para 10.10 below. Conduct is 'excluded conduct' if it consists in the individual being or ceasing to be, or having been or ceased to be, a member of another trade union, or employed by a particular employer or at a particular place; or is conduct for which an individual has the statutory right not to be 'unjustifiably disciplined'.[110] Thus a union could not exclude an individual who expressed an intention never to take part in industrial action, for example.

A union cannot exclude an individual from membership purely on the ground that he or she has previously been expelled, but the EAT has held that exclusion does not breach the statute if it is entirely attributable to the conduct of the applicant which had led to the expulsion.[111] An individual is treated as expelled if under the union rules he or she ceases automatically to be a member on the occurrence of a specified event, such as non-payment of subscriptions.[112]

An individual who claims to have been excluded or expelled from a union in contravention of the legislation may complain to an employment tribunal.[113] Where the tribunal upholds the complaint it must make a declaration to this effect.[114] The applicant may then apply to a tribunal for an award of compensation from the union.[115] The award is to be such as the tribunal considers 'just and equitable in all the circumstances' subject to a maximum award of £85,200.[116] There is provision for a reduction of this award where the tribunal finds that the applicant has caused

---

[109] TULRCA 1992, s 177(1)(b).

[110] See further para 10.12 below. Where the disciplinary action which is 'unjustifiable' takes the form of expulsion the individual has a choice as to whether to pursue a remedy under TULRCA 1992, ss 64–65 or 174–177 but cannot proceed under both: ss 66(4), 177(4).

[111] *Potter v UNISON* UKEAT/0626/03, 1 March 2004.

[112] TULRCA 1992, s 177(2)(b). It seems likely that such a rule would now be seen as void at common law as being in breach of natural justice: see Elias and Ewing, 1987: pp 216–218.

[113] TULRCA 1992, s 174(5). The complaint must be presented within six months of the date of the exclusion or expulsion or within such further period as the tribunal considers 'reasonable' where it is satisfied that it was not 'reasonably practicable' for the complaint to be presented within six months: s 175; see further para 2.17.

[114] TULRCA 1992, s 176(1).

[115] TULRCA 1992, s 176(2), as amended by ERelA 2004, s 34(7)–(11). Prior to 31 December 2004 applications were made directly to the EAT if the applicant had not by then been admitted or re-admitted to the union.

[116] TULRCA 1992, s 176(4), (6). Figures as of 1 February 2012 and at the time of writing.

or contributed to the exclusion or expulsion.[117] However, if on the date of the application for compensation,[118] the applicant had not been admitted or re-admitted to the union, a minimum of £8,100 is to be awarded.[119] The statute does not, unlike the common law, afford a remedy that requires a union to retain the individual in membership, but he or she may bring proceedings for breach of contract, as well as a statutory complaint, if appropriate.[120]

We discuss the compatibility of these provisions with international standards in para 10.21 below.

(ii) Exclusion or expulsion for membership of a political party or activities as such a member

10.10 The right not to be excluded or expelled from a union, as introduced in TURERA 1993, expressly stated that an individual could not be excluded or expelled for being a member of a political party. It was unclear, however, whether a union could expel an individual for his or her political *activities*, an issue that became a pressing one for unions which discovered that they had in membership individuals who were active in the British National Party (BNP). The matter came before the courts in *ASLEF v Lee*,[121] where the union had expelled the complainant, who was an active member of the BNP, on the grounds that his membership of the BNP was incompatible with membership of ASLEF; that he was likely to bring the union into disrepute; and that he was against the objects of the union. The complainant alleged that his expulsion breached TULRCA 1992, s 174. The EAT held that the tribunal was required to consider whether the expulsion was because of his membership of the BNP or whether it was entirely attributable to his conduct (whether as such a member or otherwise), and remitted the case to a different tribunal to decide this question on the facts.

In response to the issues raised by this case, the Labour Government amended the legislation twice. The first amendment, contained in ERelA 2004, was designed to clarify the distinction between membership of a political party, on the one hand, and activities on the other, and to allow unions to expel or exclude individuals where membership of a political party was a relatively minor reason for their decision.[122] Exclusion or expulsion from a union was permitted if it was entirely attributable to the individual's conduct (other than 'excluded conduct': see para 10.9 above) and the conduct to which it was *wholly or mainly* attributable was not 'protected conduct'. 'Protected conduct' was defined as 'conduct which consists in the individual's being or ceasing to be, or having been or ceased to be, a member of a political party.[123] However conduct

---

[117] TULRCA 1992, s 176(5).

[118] Applications must be made no earlier than four weeks, and no later than six months, from the date of the declaration: s 176(3).

[119] TULRCA 1992, s 176(6A), inserted by ERelA 2004, s 33(6). Figure as of 1 February 2012 and at the time of writing. See s 176(6B) for circumstances where this does not apply.

[120] TULRCA 1992, s 177(5).

[121] UKEAT/0625/03/RN 24 February 2004. See D Mead, 2004.

[122] ERelA 2004, s 33. Prior to the ECtHR decision in *ASLEF v UK*, below, there were sharply differing views as to to whether this provision complied with human rights; see JCHR, Eighth Report, Session 2003–2004, paras 2.5–2.6; Thirteenth Report, Session 2003–2004, paras 2.15–2.17; Institute of Employment Rights Submission on TULRCA 1992, s 174, prepared by Professor Keith Ewing and John Hendy QC, JCHR Thirteenth Report, Session 2003–2004, App 2b; see also App 2d; Hendy and Ewing, 2005.

[123] TULRCA 1992, s 174(4A).

consisting of activities undertaken by an individual as a member of a political party was expressly excluded from this definition.[124] The Government said that on this basis a union would have 'acted lawfully if it expels a political activist principally on the grounds of their political activities where a subsidiary factor was the person's political party membership'.[125] More broadly, if a union excluded or expelled an individual from membership for a number of reasons, one of which was membership of a political party, the tribunal was required to decide what was the main reason for the union's action: if it was conduct other than membership of a political party, it would not breach section 174 (provided that it was not 'excluded conduct').

The law both prior to and following the EReIA 2004 amendment was found by the ECtHR to violate Article 11 of the ECHR. Applying the general principles which we outlined in para 7.9 above, the Court held that the UK had failed to strike the right balance between Mr Lee's rights and those of ASLEF.[126] The Court was not persuaded that expulsion impinged in any significant way on Mr Lee's exercise of freedom of expression or his lawful political activities, nor had he suffered any particular detriment save loss of membership in the union. There was no apparent prejudice in terms of his livelihood or in his conditions of employment given that ASLEF represented all workers in the collective bargaining context. Of more weight in the balance was:

> ... the applicant's right to choose its members. Historically, trade unions in the [UK], and elsewhere in Europe, were ... commonly affiliated to political parties or movements, particularly those on the left. They are not bodies solely devoted to politically-neutral aspects of the well-being of their members, but are often ideological, with strongly held views on social and political issues. There was no hint in the domestic proceedings that the applicant erred in its conclusion that Mr. Lee's political values and ideals clashed, fundamentally, with its own.[127]

Following this decision the Government undertook a consultation exercise on how TULRCA 1992 should be further amended. It took the (controversial) view that the judgment was 'rooted in the circumstances of this particular case' and that only those aspects of section 174 which referred to party political membership and activities needed to be changed, and it offered two options for effecting such a change.[128] The Government initially favoured the choice of the majority of the respondents in relation to this narrow question,[129] which was to remove the reference to a special category of 'protected conduct' relating to party political membership from section 174 on the ground that the law would then be clear and less complicated; it also agreed that there was no evidence of the arbitrary persecution of individuals by unions on the grounds of their political belief.[130] However, following concerns expressed during debates in the House of Lords and by the

---

[124] TULRCA 1992, s 174(4B).

[125] Gerry Sutcliffe, Under-Secretary of State, Department of Trade and Industry, HC Standing Committee D, col 228, 2 March 2004.

[126] *ASLEF v UK* judgment of 27 February 2007, [2007] IRLR 361, paras 49, 52.

[127] Above, para 50.

[128] DTI, *ECHR Judgment in ASLEF v UK Case – Implications for Trade Union Law: Consultation Document*, May 2007, paras 4.1–4.5.

[129] Most unions and several other respondents thought that neither of the two options would ensure that UK law did not breach the Convention but most indicated a preference between the two: above, para 3.3.

[130] BERR, *ECHR Judgment in ASLEF v UK Case – Implications for Trade Union Law: Government response to Public Consultation*, November 2007, paras 3.9–3.10.

Joint Committee on Human Rights (JCHR) that this approach did not offer sufficient safeguards to individuals to comply with the judgment in *ASLEF*,[131] the Government was persuaded, despite union opposition, to introduce a more complex provision. Following EA 2008, section 174 of TULRCA 1992 is even more labyrinthine. As before, it is first necessary to determine whether exclusion or expulsion from a union is *wholly or mainly attributable* to 'protected conduct',[132] that is 'conduct which consists in the individual's being or ceasing to be, or having been or ceased to be, a member of a political party',[133] in which case it is not permitted. 'Conduct which consists of activities undertaken by an individual as a member of a political party' remains excluded from the concept of 'protected conduct'.[134] Also now excluded by EA 2008 is '[c]onduct which consists in an individual's being or having been a member of a political party' if 'membership of that political party is contrary to (a) a rule of the trade union or (b) an objective of the union'.[135] In response to concerns that the reference to 'that' political party would enable individuals to evade exclusion or expulsion if the party of which they were a member changed its name, the Government said that the union would not be required to specify the party in question in its rule book; 'general rules or objectives about the union's political beliefs or attitudes, stating what it favours or what it dislikes, such as fascism or extreme xenophobic political parties, should suffice'.[136] The Labour Government also resisted Conservative calls to set a time limit on former membership of a party or to define the term 'political party', stating that the absence of a definition had not, since 1993, caused any difficulty.[137]

This new exclusion introduced by EA 2008 is itself subject to two broad qualifications:

(i)   An objective of the union is to be disregarded, in relation to an exclusion, if it is not reasonably practicable for the objective to be ascertained by a person working in the same trade, industry or profession as the individual and, in relation to an expulsion, if it is not reasonably practicable for the objective to be ascertained by a member of the union.[138]

(ii) The exclusion or expulsion is not within the category of conduct for which exclusion is permitted if any one or more of the following apply:

(a)   the decision to exclude or expel is taken otherwise than in accordance with the union's rules;

(b)   the decision to exclude or expel is taken unfairly. The decision is taken unfairly if (and only if) before the decision is taken the individual is not given notice of the proposal to exclude or expel him or her and the reasons for it, together with a fair opportunity to make representations in respect of that proposal, or representations made by the individual in respect of that proposal are not considered fairly;

(c)   the individual would lose his or her livelihood or suffer other 'exceptional hardship' by reason of not being, or ceasing to be, a member of the union. The term 'exceptional

---

[131] JCHR, Seventeenth Report, Session 2007–2008, HL 95/HC 501, 28 April 2008. Cf Ewing, 2009.
[132] TULRCA 1992, s 174(2)(d).
[133] TULRCA 1992, s 174(4A).
[134] TULRCA 1992, s 174(4B).
[135] TULRCA 1992, s 174(4C).
[136] Lord Bach, HL Debs Vol 702, col 28, 2 June 2008.
[137] Pat McFadden, Minister for Employment Relations and Postal Affairs, HC Debs, vol 479, col 83, 16 October 2008.
[138] TULRCA 1992, s 174(4D). Where the conduct consists of an individual *having been* a member of a political party, whether it was reasonably practicable for the objective to be ascertained is to be examined at the time of the conduct: s 174(4E).

hardship' derives from the judgment of the ECtHR in *ASLEF*.[139] In the Labour Government's view, the fact that enforcement of a closed shop is now unlawful[140] meant that 'exceptional hardship' would not be 'a real threat to most workers'.[141] It rejected a Conservative amendment to replace this term with 'material financial disadvantage' on the ground that this could include detriments such as loss of free or subsidised legal advice.[142]

If a tribunal upholds a complaint and decides that exclusion or expulsion was mainly attributable to 'protected conduct' it must make an additional declaration to that effect.[143] If it does so, and it also considers that the *other* conduct to which the exclusion or expulsion was attributable consisted wholly or mainly of conduct which was contrary to a union rule or objective it must so declare, in which case the minimum award applicable where a union has not admitted or re-admitted the complainant does not apply.[144] For conduct to be found to be contrary to a union objective the union must show that, at the time of the complainant's conduct, it was reasonably practicable for that objective to be ascertained by a person working in the same trade, industry or profession as the complainant (if the complainant was not then a member of the union) or by a member of the union (if he or she was a member).[145] These provisions date back to ERelA 2004 and reflected the concerns articulated at that time by the TUC that 'many unions do not refer to their equality or anti-racist policies in their rule books'.[146] It would seem to leave it open for a public sector union to argue, for example, that the minimum award should not apply in the event that it expels a member of a political party because he or she advocates privatisation of the health service.

It is strongly arguable that the judgment of the ECtHR in *ASLEF* requires more wide-ranging amendments to section 174 than those made by EA 2008.[147] We explore this argument further in para 10.21 below.

(iii) The 'Bridlington Principles'

10.11   The introduction of the right not to be excluded or expelled from a union necessitated revision of the TUC's Bridlington Principles, first promulgated in 1939 to minimise disputes between affiliated unions over membership issues. Although not intended to constitute a legally enforceable contract, they are 'accepted by all affiliated organisations as a binding commitment for their continued affiliation to the TUC'.[148] Before the 1993 revision these principles provided, *inter alia*, that the membership forms of all unions should inquire about the applicant's membership of other unions; that no union should accept as members applicants who were or had recently been members of any other affiliated union without inquiry of that union; that if that union

---

[139] Above, note 126, para 43.

[140] See para 8.37 *et seq*.

[141] Lord Bach, HL Debs Vol 702, col 15, 2 June 2008.

[142] Pat McFadden, above note 137, col 69.

[143] TULRCA 1992, s 176 (1A).

[144] TULRCA1992, s 176(1B), (6B); see para 10.9 above.

[145] TULRCA 1992, s 176(1D), as amended by EA 2008, s 19(3).

[146] Gerry Sutcliffe, HC Debs, col 1478, 16 September 2004.

[147] See Ewing, 2007 and, for a general critique, Ewing, 2009a.

[148] *TUC Disputes Principles and Procedures*, TUC, 2007; see further para 2.13 above for the status of these Principles.

objected, the applicant should not be accepted into membership; and that in the case of dispute the matter should be notified to the TUC and may be referred for adjudication by an internal Disputes Committee, composed of senior officials of affiliated unions. The Committee could award that individuals accepted into membership in breach of the Principles should be expelled, and advised to join or rejoin the appropriate union. Expulsions to give effect to decisions of the Disputes Committee were upheld at common law provided that the decision was properly one which fell under the terms of the Committee's remit under the procedures and the expulsion was authorised by the union rules.[149] In *Cheall v APEX*[150] the House of Lords rejected the argument that these arrangements contravened public policy in restricting the right of the individual to join and remain a member of the union of his or her choice. In giving the judgment of the court Lord Diplock affirmed that 'freedom of association can only be mutual; there can be no right of an individual to associate with other individuals who are not willing to associate with him'.[151] He continued:

> ... I know of no existing rule of public policy that would prevent trade unions from entering into arrangements with one another which they consider to be in the interests of their members in promoting order in industrial relations and enhancing their members' bargaining power with their employers; nor do I think it a permissible exercise of your Lordships' judicial power to create a new rule of public policy to that effect. If this is to be done at all it must be done by Parliament.[152]

The argument that the expulsion breached Article 11 of the ECHR also failed, the European Commission of Human Rights affirming that the right to join a union did not confer a general right to join the union of one's choice, regardless of the union rules, and that the complaint was, therefore, inadmissible.[153]

Revised Principles were drafted to accommodate the statutory restriction on exclusion and expulsion; initially promulgated in 1993, these now appear in the 2007 edition of the Principles.[154] They affirm that all TUC affiliates accept 'that they will not knowingly and actively seek to take into membership existing or "recent" members of another union by making recruitment approaches, either directly or indirectly, without the agreement of that organisation'. Unions must continue to include in their membership application form questions regarding past or present membership of another union, and if that other union has cause to object to the recruitment of a current or former member it should request a meeting with the prospective recruiting union. The effort at resolution will include a moral obligation on the part of the respondent union to 'offer compensation to the complainant union for any loss of income that it has suffered as a consequence of any knowing and

---

[149] Cf *Spring v NASDS* [1956] 1 WLR 585, which led to the TUC recommending unions to adopt a model rule permitting expulsions to comply with decisions of the Disputes Committee. See generally Simpson, 1993: pp 189–193 and Elgar and Simpson, 1994 for an evaluation of the operation of the Principles before revision.

[150] [1983] IRLR 215.

[151] [1983] IRLR 215, 218.

[152] [1983] IRLR 215, 218. The claimant's argument that the termination of his membership was void as being in breach of natural justice because he was not able to make representations to the Disputes Committee also failed.

[153] *Cheall v UK* Application No 10550/83, (1986) 8 EHRR 74. Although the state was required to protect an individual against a dominant position by unions, which could occur if there was a closed shop or the union rules were wholly unreasonable or arbitrary, this was not the case here.

[154] For an analysis of the 1993 changes to the Principles, see Simpson, 1994.

active recruitment of its members'. In case of continuing disagreement the issue will be referred to the TUC which, if other attempts at settlement fail, may refer it to the Disputes Committee. If it finds in its favour, the Committee may adjudicate on the financial compensation to be paid to the complainant union, up to a maximum of two years' loss of contributions, and/or may censure the respondent union and require it to print the censure in a prominent place in its journal. However, the Committee no longer has power to require the expulsion of those admitted to unions in breach of the Principles. When the new statutory rights were being proposed, several employers' groups expressed disquiet that they might destabilise existing arrangements, particularly single union deals, by encouraging unions to commence recruitment activities in an enterprise where other unions were stronger.[155] In practice, unions in present circumstances seem more likely to favour concentrating their efforts in areas where they are able to build a significant membership body rather than spreading their resources more thinly.[156]

In *ASLEF v UK*,[157] discussed in para 7.9 above, the ECtHR cited *Cheall* with approval and confirmed the freedom of trade unions to 'set up their own rules concerning conditions of membership, including administrative formalities and payment of fees, as well as other more substantive criteria …'[158] As we indicated in paragraph 10.10 above, it is strongly arguable that section 174 in its present form violates Article 11 of the ECHR. If the exclusion or expulsion of an individual to give effect to a decision of the TUC Disputes Committee was authorised by the union's rules, in the light of *Cheall* and *ASLEF* it would be difficult to argue that this could not be justified under Article 11(2) because it was 'wholly unreasonable or arbitrary'.[159]

Statutory rights in relation to union discipline

10.12   In addition to the protection against expulsion, members have the broader right not to be 'unjustifiably disciplined' by their union.[160] Discipline is 'unjustified' if the actual or supposed conduct which constitutes the reason, or one of the reasons, for it is a form of conduct listed in the legislation or something believed by the union to amount to such conduct.[161] This right is in addition to any other rights which may be available to an individual,[162] so if disciplinary action were to infringe the union rules as well as the statute the member could also bring proceedings for breach of contract.[163] A member may also wish to bring common law proceedings if the challenge is based upon the procedure followed rather than the substantive reason for the action.

---

[155] See Simpson, 1993: pp 187–189.

[156] Simpson, 1993: p 188; see also Brendan Barber, 2007 Principles, Introduction: 'The only way to re-build the movement is to recruit new members, not to re-cycle existing ones…'.

[157] Note 126 above.

[158] Above, para 38.

[159] See para 7.9 above and Ewing, 2007: pp 436–439.

[160] TULRCA 1992, s 64(1). See further para 10.21 for discussion of the compatibility of these provisions with Art 11 of the ECHR and other international standards. In *UNISON v Kelly* [2012] IRLR 442 the EAT held that s 65(2)(c) - (iii) below - did not violate Art 11, it being necessary in a democratic society to protect the right of union members to hold their unions to account for breaching their own rules where members act in good faith: Supperstone J at [43]-[44].

[161] TULRCA 1992, s 65(1).

[162] TULRCA 1992, s 64(5), although note s 66(4).

[163] Note, however, the difference in remedies: see para 10.5 above. Note also that the statutory right arises only when a disciplinary 'determination' has been made; it does not allow the individual to forestall the disciplinary process, although if *Longley v NUJ* [1987] IRLR 109, para 10.3 above, is followed this may not make any practical difference.

There are twelve types of conduct (which includes 'statements, acts and omissions')[164] for which disciplinary action is 'unjustified'.[165] Many relate to non-participation in, or opposition to, industrial action. In outline, they are as follows:

(i)   failing to participate in or support any strike or other industrial action[166] or indicating opposition to or lack of support for such action;

(ii) failing to contravene, for a purpose connected with such a strike or other industrial action, a requirement imposed on the individual by or under a contract of employment;[167]

(iii) asserting (or encouraging or assisting another to make such an assertion) that the union, any official[168] or representative[169] of it or trustee of its property contravened, or is proposing to contravene, a requirement which is, or is thought to be, imposed by the union rules or any other agreement or by any enactment or rule of law. The protection does not apply, however, if the assertion was false and the individual believed that or was otherwise acting in bad faith (although the member is not specifically required to have had reasonable grounds to believe that the assertion was true);

(iv) encouraging or assisting another to perform an obligation imposed by a contract of employment;[170]

(v)   contravening a requirement imposed by or in consequence of a determination which infringes the individual's or another individual's right not to be unjustifiably disciplined;

(vi) failing to agree, or withdrawing agreement to, the check-off;[171]

(vii) resigning or proposing to resign from the union or from another union, becoming or proposing to become a member of another union, refusing to become a member of another union or being a member of another union;

(viii) working with, or proposing to work with, individuals who are not members of the union or who are or are not members of another union;

(ix) working for, or proposing to work for, an employer who employs or has employed individuals who are not members of the union or who are or are not members of another union;

(x)   requiring the union to do an act which it is required under TULRCA 1992 to do at the requisition of a member;

---

[164] TURLCA 1992, s 65(7).

[165] TULRCA 1992, s 65(2)–(4). The statutory protection does not apply if it is shown that individuals would be disciplined by the union for such conduct irrespective of its connection with conduct for which discipline is unjustified: s 65(5). This provision was designed to protect unions, such as the Royal College of Nursing, which may discipline members in order to protect professional standards. In *UNISON v Kelly* [2012] IRLR 442 at [65] it was held that 'would be disciplined' meant 'would have been disciplined as the relevant individual was in fact disciplined'.

[166] In *Knowles v FBU* [1996] IRLR 617, the Court of Appeal held that 'the question of what is industrial action for the purposes of s 65 … is a mixed question of fact and law. In large measure it is a question of fact, but the facts have to be judged in the context of the Act which plainly contemplates that industrial action is a serious step'. It was 'necessary to look at all the circumstances … [which] will include the contracts of employment of the employees and whether any breach of or departure from the terms of the contract are involved, the effect on the employer of what is done or omitted, and the object which the union or the employees seek to achieve' (621, Neill LJ). See generally para 11.74.

[167] This includes any agreement between the individual and a person for whom he or she works or normally works: TULRCA 1992, s 65(7). Persons holding office or employment under the Crown are deemed to have contracts of employment for this purpose: TULRCA 1992, s 65(8).

[168] Defined TULRCA 1992, s 119. Note that this definition is wide enough to cover shop stewards.

[169] Defined TULRCA 1992, s 65(7).

[170] See note 167, above.

[171] See para 8.47 above for rights against employers.

(xi) consulting or asking advice from the Certification Officer on any matter or which involves consulting, or asking advice or assistance from, any other person with respect to a matter which forms, or might form, the subject of any assertion described in (iii) above;

(xii) proposing to engage in, or doing anything preparatory or incidental to, conduct falling within (i)-(xi) above.

A member is treated as 'disciplined' if a 'determination' is made, or purportedly made, under the union rules, or by a union official or persons including an official, that he or she should be expelled from the union or a branch or section of it; should make any payment or that subscriptions paid should be treated as unpaid or as paid for a different purpose; should be deprived to any extent of any benefits, services or facilities which would otherwise be available; that another union, or branch or section, should be encouraged not to accept him or her as a member; or that he or she should be subjected to 'some other detriment'.[172] In relation to the last 'catch-all' provision, the EAT has upheld the view that naming a member as a strike-breaker in a branch circular to cause her embarrassment could be described as a 'detriment'.[173] Banning a member from standing for, or holding, union office is included,[174] and preventing an individual from attending a branch meeting would almost certainly be covered.

An individual who claims to have been 'unjustifiably disciplined' may complain to an employment tribunal within three months of the date of the determination,[175] although this period may be extended, *inter alia*, where the tribunal is satisfied that any delay in making the complaint was due to a reasonable attempt to appeal against the determination or have it reconsidered or reviewed.[176] Where the tribunal upholds the complaint it must make a declaration to this effect, whereupon the applicant may apply for an award of compensation from the union.[177] The award is such as the tribunal considers 'just and equitable in all the circumstances', subject to a maximum award of £85,200.[178] An award may be reduced if the applicant has failed to mitigate his or her loss or where the tribunal finds that he or she has caused or contributed to the infringement.[179] However if, on the date of the application for compensation,[180] the determination infringing the

---

[172] TULRCA 1992, s 64(2). The provision for union officials to bind the union means that the union may be held responsible even if the determination is made by persons who have no express or implied authority to act on its behalf in this regard. The EAT has held that 'determination' means a decision which disposes of the issue, so does not cover a recommendation that requires affirmation by another body: *TGWU v Webber* [1990] IRLR 462. However, as the EAT recognised, there may be more than one 'determination' within the expulsion process, eg suspension leading to deprivation of benefits prior to the decision to expel; if so, there will be a need to keep a careful eye on time limits.

[173] *NALGO v Killorn* [1990] IRLR 464. In that case the EAT expressed the view (at 469) that 'whether or not a member suffered deprivation or detriment is the sort of question that … [Employment] … Tribunals, with their expertise on industrial matters, are peculiarly suited to answer'. See now *Shamoon v Chief Constable of the Royal Ulster Constabulary* [2003] IRLR 285, discussed at para 6.51, applied to s 64(2)(f) in *Unifi v Massey* UKEAT/0223/04/MAA 3 August 2004.

[174] See *UNISON v Kelly* [2012] IRLR 442.

[175] TULRCA 1992, s 66(1), (2)(a).

[176] TULRCA 1992, s 66(2)(b). An appeal need not be in any particular form and the EAT has said that tribunals should look at the reality and intention of a member's communication with the union rather than the use of specific wording: *NALGO v Killorn* [1990] IRLR 464. The period may also be extended where the tribunal is satisfied that it was not 'reasonably practicable' for the complaint to be presented in time: see para 2.17 above.

[177] TULRCA 1992, ss 67(1), as amended by ERelA 2004, s 34.

[178] TULRCA 1992, s 67(8) as amended; figure as of 1 February 2012 and at the time of writing. See generally *Massey v UNIFI* [2007] IRLR 902, where the Court of Appeal held that the existence of a cap on compensation did not justify construing the term 'just and equitable' differently in this context from its construction in relation to sex and race discrimination.

[179] TULRCA 1992, s 67(6), (7). Note that there is no duty to mitigate loss where the right not to be expelled or excluded from a union, discussed in para 10.9, has been infringed.

[180] Applications must be made no earlier than four weeks and no later than six months from the date of the declaration: TULRCA 1992, s 67(3).

applicant's right has not been revoked, or the union has failed to take all the steps necessary for securing the reversal of anything done for the purpose of giving effect to the determination,[181] a minimum of £8,100 is to be awarded.[182]

In common with the restriction on exclusion and expulsion from a union, this provision constitutes a considerable incursion on union autonomy. The provisions relevant to industrial action, which we discuss further in para 11.92, have been particularly controversial. It is a notable feature of these rights that they accord those who disagree with union policy a means of remaining in the union, enabling them, if they so choose, to bring legal proceedings in the event that the union does not comply with any element of the statutory requirements in their entirety. We return to a discussion of the compatibility of this situation with freedom of association principles later in the chapter.

TRADE UNION ELECTIONS

Common law

10.13 At common law the role of the courts has been largely confined to ensuring that the union rules are observed. Thus in *Leigh v NUR*,[183] for example, the claimant obtained an injunction to prevent an election taking place without his name being included on the list of candidates after he successfully argued that he met the qualifications for nomination specified in the rules. In two cases involving election to the office of shop steward, however, the concept of the duty to act fairly was successfully invoked by individuals who had been elected by their fellow workers but whose appointment was not given the requisite approval by higher bodies within the union.[184] As we describe in para 10.14, elections to the posts of union president, general secretary and member of the executive are now governed by detailed statutory procedures. However, if the rules impose restrictions which exceed, or do not conflict with, the statutory provisions, the common law will still be important. Thus in *Wise v USDAW*[185] for example, a decision by the executive council that a candidate for election to the office of general secretary must be nominated by not fewer than

---

[181] In *NALGO v Courteney-Dunn* [1992] IRLR 114, the EAT rejected the argument that 'necessary' meant 'requisite' or 'indispensable'; the union was required to put the member back into the same position he was in before the wrongful expulsion and the fact that the member himself could have done this (here, restored resumption of the check-off) was irrelevant. See also *Beaumont v Amicus MSF* UKEAT/0122/03/MAA, 12 February 2004.

[182] TULRCA 1992, s 67(8A), inserted by ERelA 2004, s 34(6); figure as of 1 February 2012 and at the time of writing. Prior to 31 December 2004 applications were made directly to the EAT in such circumstances. Compensation may be awarded for injury to feelings: *Bradley v NALGO* [1991] IRLR 159; *Beaumont v Amicus MSF* 29 November 2004 (revised judgment); *Massey v UNIFI* [2007] IRLR 902.

[183] [1970] Ch 326.

[184] *Breen v AEU* [1971] 2 QB 175; *Shotton v Hammond* (1976) 120 Sol Jo 780. Note the limitations of this doctrine, however: see para 10.8. In *Meacham v AEEU* [1994] IRLR 218, a union member who was not allowed for economic reasons to take up a full-time union post to which he had been elected was held to have only the same right to damages for breach of contract as any other prospective employee; the union was not obliged to act in accordance with natural justice in considering contracts of employment 'unless questions of vires arise, or the conduct or character of the member of the union was called into question' (at 226).

[185] [1996] IRLR 609. See also *Douglas v GMPU* [1995] IRLR 426: no power in the union rules for the executive council to cancel an election after the candidate with the highest number of votes had been declared elected, although cf *AB v CD* [2001] IRLR 808, 812 (Sir Andrew Morritt, VC).

25 union branches breached a rule that 'all branches shall have the right to make nominations' for the office of general secretary. Again in *Ecclestone v NUJ*[186] the union was found to have breached its rules in excluding the claimant from the shortlist for election to the post of deputy general secretary on the ground that he lacked the 'required qualifications' because he lacked the confidence of the union's national executive committee. Moreover, the common law will be the only avenue of redress in relation to offices not covered by the statutory provisions, such as that of shop steward. To date, however, there have been relatively few cases in the area of union elections pursued at common law.

The statutory requirements: the duty to conduct elections

10.14   Under statute, trade unions[187] must now ensure that their president,[188] general secretary[189] and every 'member of the executive'[190] hold office by virtue of an election conducted in accordance with complex statutory requirements.[191] These provisions apply notwithstanding anything to the contrary in the union's rules or practices,[192] although there is nothing to prevent a union adopting more stringent requirements in its rules. No officer who is subject to election may continue to hold office for more than five years without being re-elected.[193] Unless the election is uncontested the union must hold a fully postal ballot,[194] and in all cases[195] the election must be supervised by an independent 'scrutineer': either one of four specialist bodies specified in regulations or another appropriately qualified person (a solicitor or accountant qualified as an

---

[186] [1999] IRLR 166. See also *UNISON v Staunton* [2009] IRLR 418, EAT: a union rule giving power to suspend a member facing disciplinary charges from office did not exclude the individual from standing for election within the union.

[187] With the exception of unions of less than one year's standing, including those formed by amalgamation (TULRCA 1992, s 57), and those consisting wholly or mainly of constituent or affiliated organisations, or representatives of such organisations ('federated trade unions') and which either have no individual members, such as the TUC, or whose individual members are all merchant seamen and the majority are ordinarily resident outside the UK (s 118(6)), an exception asked for by the International Transport Workers' Federation. 'Special register bodies' need elect only voting members of their executive: ss 117(5), 46(5).

[188] Where there is no such office, the holder of the equivalent or nearest equivalent: TULRCA 1992, s 119. There is a limited exception in TULRCA 1992, s 46(4A), inserted by ERelA 2004, s 52.

[189] TULRCA 1992, s 119. Persons holding the position of president or general secretary on an honorary basis, with no voting rights, are not subject to election but this applies only where the holder changes on an annual basis and certain other conditions are satisfied: s 46(4),(5).

[190] TULRCA 1992, s 119; see further below.

[191] TULRCA 1992, ss 46–61. This requires direct elections to the office in question: *BECTU v Gates* EAT/1462/00 10 April 2001. On the principles governing the holding of office on an 'acting' basis, see *GMB v Corrigan* [2008] ICR 197. We aim here to describe the framework for union elections. For a more detailed account see G Morris and T Archer, 2000: paras 2.33–2.45.

[192] TULRCA 1992, s 46(6).

[193] TULRCA 1992, s 46(1)(b). There is an exception in relation to persons within five years of retirement provided that complex conditions are met: s 58. See *Beaumont v Amicus*, 14 May 2004, CO.

[194] TULRCA 1992, s 53.

[195] *In the matter of a complaint against the Offshore Industry Liaison Committee*, 25 November 1994, CO, the Certification Officer held that an independent scrutineer must be appointed even in an uncontested election. He or she is required to report whether there were reasonable grounds to believe that any statutory requirement had been contravened, including whether a candidate had been unreasonably excluded from standing, which could apply equally to a contested and an uncontested election. In *Hardman v Community*, 20 December 2006, CO, the Certification Officer held that the scrutineer must be appointed 'before the election is held'.

auditor, provided that their previous connections with the union do not disqualify them from this appointment).[196] These requirements alone mean that unions incur substantial costs in organising an election, particularly as the provision for refunding a proportion of the balloting costs, which was introduced in 1984, ceased for ballots after 31 March 1996.[197]

The term 'executive' means 'the principal executive committee of the union exercising executive functions, by whatever name it is called'.[198] This requires there to be one, but only one, such body;[199] other bodies which may exercise executive functions within the union which are subordinate to the 'executive' are not subject to the legislation. 'Members of the executive' clearly include those designated as such by the union's rules, either on an ordinary or an *ex officio* basis.[200] They also include:

> ... any person who, under the rules or practice of the union, may attend and speak at some or all of the meetings of the executive, otherwise than for the purpose of providing the committee with factual information or with technical or professional advice with respect to matters taken into account by the executive in carrying out its functions.[201]

This was intended to cover all those who 'act as though they are members of the ... [executive] and who participate in the decision-making process'.[202] This may not be an easy group to classify; it may vary according to the role of an individual office holder within a union and possibly the behaviour of an individual incumbent; thus one cannot state that all national or regional officers, for example, need, or need not, be elected. The position is further complicated by the ambiguities of the statutory language. There are four major problems: the meaning of 'may attend and speak', which could mean 'may attend by entitlement', 'is not prohibited from attending' or 'it is theoretically possible may attend'; the meaning of 'practice', whose longevity or consistency is unspecified; the number of meetings which an individual may attend without attracting the requirements for election;[203] and whether attendance at only part of a meeting is sufficient. The exception of those providing information or advice was intended to exclude individuals who offer merely 'supporting advice' to the committee rather than participating in 'decision-taking' but the line between the two activities may be easily crossed.[204] Union legal officers who advise on the legal consequences of a course of action, or research or regional officers who give merely

---

[196] TULRCA 1992, s 49; The Trade Union Ballots and Elections (Independent Scrutineer Qualifications) Order 1993, SI 1993/1909, as amended.

[197] TURERA 1993, s 7; the Funds for Trade Union Ballots Regulations (Revocation) Regulations 1993, SI 1993/233.

[198] TULRCA 1992, s 119.

[199] For a decision as to which of two union bodies should be designated the executive, see *Stone v NATFHE*, 30 June 1987, CO.

[200] TULRCA 1992, s 46(2)(b).

[201] TULRCA 1992, s 46(3).

[202] Lord Trefgarne, Joint-Under-Secretary of State for Employment, HL Debs, vol 486, cols 484–485, 28 March 1988.

[203] John Cope, Minister for Employment, considered that someone attending only occasionally was unlikely to require election (House of Commons, Official Report of Standing Committee F, col 366, 15 December 1987) but this is not made clear in the legislation.

[204] In *Re a complaint against the GPMU*, 11 March 1993, CO, the Certification Officer accepted the General Secretary's assurance that particular individuals fell within the exception in the absence of any evidence from the applicant to the contrary. This case shows the importance of ensuring that the union rules do not describe such individuals as members of the executive: cf *Re a complaint against SOGAT '82*, 31 July 1991, CO.

factual information, for example, would seem not to require election but their position may be jeopardised if they stray into a discussion of union policy based on their advice or report.

Individuals who fail to be re-elected can no longer continue to hold their positions, although the union may allow their membership of the committee to continue for a period of up to six months after the election in order to give effect to the result.[205] Any term or condition governing the official's employment with the union which conflicts with the obligation to leave office – for example, if or she is employed on a fixed term contract for a longer period – cannot affect this position.[206] This means that unions must ensure that the contracts of persons subject to election expire when the post falls due for election. It also means that unions are unable to offer any job security to individuals who may have been chosen for a particular office, in particular that of general secretary, for administrative rather than political skills.

The selection of candidates and election addresses

10.15   No union member may be 'unreasonably excluded' from standing as a candidate at an election.[207] Exclusion is not 'unreasonable' if it is because he or she belongs to a class all of whose members are excluded by the union rules.[208] This means that unions may require a minimum number of years' membership of the union, for example, although any such requirement must be stipulated in the rules; the legislation states that a rule which provides for a class to be determined by reference to whom the union chooses to exclude must be disregarded.[209] A further restriction is that no candidate may be required, directly or indirectly, to be a member of a political party.[210] Thus a union cannot require candidates to be a member of the Labour Party or to attend the Labour Party conference, which is open only to members. Notably, however, it does not prevent the exclusion of members of a particular party from standing; thus unions may lawfully exclude members of the Communist or the Conservative Party, for example. The Certification Officer has held that it is not unreasonable for a union to demand a certain level of support from fellow members as a pre-condition of standing, although the practical difficulties facing individuals

---

[205]   TULRCA 1992, s 59. Note also that if an individual who holds a specific post is permitted by the union rules to remain on the executive for a period after leaving office then there may be no need to hold an election to the second office if they can be regarded as having been elected to both offices at the time of the initial election: *Paul v NALGO* [1987] IRLR 43, CO (immediate past president allowed to retain a voting position on the union's council for one year after holding the presidency for a year).

[206]   TULRCA 1992, s 46(6).

[207]   TULRCA 1992, s 47(1). See generally *GMB v Stokes* UKEAT/0769/03/ILB 23 January 2004; *UNISON v Staunton* [2009] IRLR 418, EAT; *Scargill v NUM* 29 June 2009, CO; UKEAT/0407/09/RN. In *Bakhsh v UNISON (No 2)*, 16 May 2008, CO, the Certification Officer held that s 47 requires a person to have been excluded from a specific election in which he or she has sought to be a candidate.

[208]   TULRCA 1992, s 47(3). In *Beaumont and Smith v Unite the Union* 1 September 2011, CO, the Certification Officer held that although 'class' was to be given its ordinary literal meaning, the common attributes which qualify a person for membership of that class must be capable of objective determination.

[209]   TULRCA 1992, s 47(3). In *Ecclestone v NUJ* [1999] IRLR 166, Smith J held that the exclusion of those who did not have the confidence of the union's National Executive Council did not comply with s 47(3). In *Beaumont and Smith v Unite the Union*, above, the Certification Officer made clear that where a rule was disregarded under s 47(3), the exclusion must be decided on the basis of the general test of reasonableness.

[210]   TULRCA 1992, s 47(2). See para 10.20 for discussion of the meaning of 'political party'.

seeking nomination will be relevant here.[211] All candidates must be given the opportunity to prepare an election address in their own words and to submit it to the union, which must distribute it with the voting papers to the electorate.[212] Any facilities and restrictions regarding the preparation or modification of an address must be applied equally to each candidate and the same method of producing copies (which must be done free of charge) must be applied to each.[213] Unions may set a maximum limit for the length of an address, subject to a minimum of 100 words.[214] They have no power to reject an address, regardless of its contents. They are protected against liability for defamation in the event that an address contains material which is libellous,[215] although if a union continues with an election where one candidate argues that he or she has been prejudiced by the circulation of such material it may find itself in difficulties. While the statutory provisions are clearly designed to ensure equality of treatment between candidates, there seems nothing to prevent a union from distributing additional material indicating, for example, those candidates whom the executive supports, a view echoed by the Certification Officer on a number of occasions.[216]

The balloting constituency and the conduct of the election

10.16 As a general rule entitlement to vote should be accorded equally to all members of the union.[217] This rules out any system of branch, block or delegate voting, or election to a body which then selects representatives to sit on the executive.[218] However, a union may lawfully restrict the balloting constituency in certain specified respects if it so chooses. First, provided that the union rules so provide, it may exclude all those who are unemployed, in arrears with their subscriptions or contributions, and apprentices, trainees, students or new members.[219] It may also decide, it seems on an ad hoc basis, whether overseas members are included.[220] Second, it may restrict entitlement to members falling within a class determined by reference to a trade or occupation; a

---

[211] See *Paul v NALGO* [1987] IRLR 43, CO. Also relevant in this connection are *Re complaints against BETA*, 21 December 1990, CO; *Corti v TGWU*, 28 October 1986, CO; *Re a complaint against NATFHE*, 12 August 1988, CO; *Re complaints against ISTC*, 21 December 1990, CO; *In the matter of complaints against the MU*, 12 July 2000, CO.

[212] TULRCA 1992, s 48(1). See *Harrison v Unite the Union*, 4 June 2009, CO.

[213] TULRCA 1992, s 48(5)–(7). See generally *Beaumont v Amicus* 26 March 2003, CO. See also *POA v Darken* UKEAT/0380/06. The Certification Officer has held in a number of cases that s 48 does not require the union itself to be neutral in elections and does not prohibit or regulate the sending of other election material by or on behalf of any candidate: see *Lyons v Unite the Union (Amicus Section)* 23 October 2009, CO.

[214] TULRCA 1992, s 48(3). The union may also provide that addresses should incorporate only such matter as the union may determine as regards photographs and other matter not in words: s 48(3)(b). In *Re the matter of a complaint against the TGWU*, 19 June 1996, CO the Certification Officer held that the 'provision' did not need to be in writing; a long-established practice of not including photographs in addresses was sufficient, in the absence of any contrary indication.

[215] TULRCA 1992, s 48(8).

[216] See, for example, *Re a complaint against the CPSA*, 17 May 1995, CO.

[217] TULRCA 1992, s 50(1). See generally *Dooley v UCATT* 11 March 2011, CO. On the interpretation of 'member' see the EAT decision in *NUM (Yorkshire Area) v Millward* [1995] IRLR 411.

[218] *BECTU v Gates* EAT/1462/00 10 April 2001. On the variety of voting methods before the statutory provisions were introduced, see Undy and Martin, 1984.

[219] TULRCA 1992, s 50(2).

[220] TULRCA 1992, s 60(1). 'Overseas members' are those (other than merchant seamen or offshore workers) who are outside Great Britain throughout the period during which votes may be cast (s 60(2)), thus allowing the exclusion of those on holiday.

geographical area; or one which is, under the union rules, treated as a separate section within the union, or one determined by any combination of these factors.[221] However these restrictions must, again, be specified in the union rules,[222] and should not have the effect of excluding any individual member from voting in all elections.[223] It is notable that there is no provision for determining balloting constituencies based upon the employers of members.

At the time of writing,[224] election ballots must be conducted entirely by 'post', which is defined in terms which exclude delivery by hand, internal mail or private courier.[225] Although the legislation recognises that it is unrealistic to expect a union to guarantee delivery to every member who is entitled to vote,[226] it is not necessary to show that the number of members who were not supplied with a ballot paper was sufficiently great to have affected the result of the ballot in order for a remedy to be granted.[227] There are various provisions designed to ensure the secrecy and security of the ballot.[228] Members must be entitled to vote at no direct cost to themselves; this has been seen as requiring the union to pay the cost of return postage.[229] Voters must be allowed to vote without interference from, or constraint imposed by, the union or any of its members, officials or employees.[230] To date the Certification Officer has generally interpreted this as excluding conduct which would 'intimidate or put a member generally in fear of voting, or amount to physical interference',[231] but in 1996 an election was found to be inherently compromised because ballot papers before and after completion fell into the hands of union officials, even though there was no evidence of intimidation.[232] It is notable that the legislation does not prohibit employers or third parties from interfering with the conduct of the election or attempting to put pressure on individuals to vote in a particular way.

Votes must be fairly and accurately counted although any inaccuracy which is accidental and on a scale which could not affect the result of the ballot may be disregarded.[233] The union must ensure that the storage and distribution of voting papers, and the counting of votes cast, are undertaken by one or more independent persons appointed by the union.[234] This function may

---

[221] TULRCA 1992, s 50(3).

[222] TULRCA 1992, s 50(3). See *Ecclestone v NUJ* 2 July 2003, CO.

[223] TULRCA 1992, s 50(4).

[224] ERelA 2004, s 54 empowers the Secretary of State to make provision by order, in relation to any description of ballot or election authorised or required by TULRCA 1992, that it may be conducted by other means, subject to specified conditions, but at the time of writing no such orders have been made.

[225] TULRCA 1992, s 298. However, the Certification Officer has accepted that where an employer provides a delivery service to and from employees internally within a building, that would not normally infringe s 51(4): *Re complaints against the POA*, 9 August 1996, CO.

[226] See the concept of 'reasonable practicability' in TULRCA 1992, s 51(4).

[227] In this context the Certification Officer has regarded as highly material the efforts made by the union to maintain an accurate register of members' addresses and other efforts to publicise the election, to inform members of what to do if they fail to receive a ballot paper, and to enable members to vote: *Re complaints against COHSE*, 17 August 1990, CO. He indicated here that a stricter approach may be appropriate for elections than industrial action ballots; in this context, unlike the latter, an order could relate to the procedure for future elections.

[228] TULRCA 1992, s 51.

[229] *Paul v NALGO* [1987] IRLR 43, CO.

[230] TULRCA 1992, s 51(3)(a).

[231] *Paul v NALGO* [1987] IRLR 43, CO.

[232] *Re complaints against the POA*, 9 August 1996, CO. The Certification Officer has held that s 51(3)(a) does not prevent the Union campaigning for the person it considers best suited for the position: see, for example, *Higginbottom v URTU* 9 November 2006, CO.

[233] TULRCA 1992, s 51(5)(b).

[234] TULRCA 1992, s 51A(1).

be performed either by the independent scrutineer or by some other person whose appointment is made subject, *mutatis mutandis,* to the same conditions.[235] The independent scrutineer engaged to supervise the conduct of the ballot must issue a report stating, *inter alia*, whether he or she is satisfied that the security arrangements for handling voting papers and counting votes were such as to minimise the risk of unfairness or malpractice, as well as commenting more broadly on whether any of the statutory requirements were contravened.[236] The union has a duty to comply with all reasonable requests by the scrutineer connected with the performance of his or her functions;[237] this probably entails, for example, allowing the scrutineer to look at records, obtain relevant information, and visit premises as appropriate. The union must not publish the result of the election until it has received the scrutineer's report.[238] Its contents should be made known to union members and be made available to them on request, either free or on payment of a reasonable fee.[239] While a critical report will not of itself invalidate the ballot it may serve to draw the attention of members to possible grounds for challenging it.

The result of the election must be ascertained solely by counting the number of votes cast directly for each candidate by those voting (although the use of the single transferable vote is expressly permitted).[240] However in *R v Certification Officer for Trade Unions and Employers' Associations, ex p EPEA* it was held by the House of Lords that this does not necessarily mean that a 'first past the post' system must be uniformly applied. The union's rules allowed a maximum of four members of any one of its nine geographical divisions to serve on the national executive committee. Nine members of the committee were elected in divisional ballots, the remaining fifteen in a national ballot. The rule meant that if there were more than three candidates from any one division in the national ballot, only the three who polled the greatest number of votes as between themselves could be elected, even if the fourth candidate in that division polled more than a successful candidate in another division. The court held that the statutory provision was designed to secure that the only votes which would determine the outcome of an election were those directly cast by individuals; it did not mean that a bare count of votes determined the result of the election without recourse to the union rules. Any other construction would have been an 'unreasonable result which the legislature could not sensibly have intended'.[241]

Remedies for breach of the statutory requirements

10.17   A trade union member, or a candidate in the election, who alleges that the union has failed to comply with the statutory requirements may apply either to the Certification Officer or to the

---

[235] TULRCA 1992, s 51A(2)–(6).

[236] TULRCA 1992, s 49(3); s 52. In *Lyons v Unite the Union (Amicus Section)* 23 October 2009, CO, the Certification Officer confirmed that he had no jurisdiction to entertain complaints against the scrutineer.

[237] TULRCA 1992, s 49(7).

[238] TULRCA 1992, s 52(3). In *Douglas v GMPU* [1995] IRLR 426, Morison J thought it unlikely that a union could cancel a ballot once the scrutineer had expressed satisfaction under s 52, regardless of the terms of the union's rules. See also *Wise v USDAW* [1996] IRLR 609, but cf *AB v CD* [2001] IRLR 808, 812 (Sir Andrew Morritt, V-C).

[239] TULRCA 1992, s 52(4)–(6).

[240] TULRCA 1992, s 51(6), (7).

[241] [1990] IRLR 398, 400 (Lord Bridge).

High Court (but not both) for a declaration to that effect.[242] Where either grants a declaration, an enforcement order should also be granted, unless this is considered inappropriate.[243] This order should require the union to secure the holding of an election in accordance with the order; and/or to take any other specified steps to remedy the declared failure; and/or to abstain from specified acts with a view to securing that the same or a similar failure does not recur. The court may, additionally, grant interim relief,[244] which may be appropriate if the applicant wishes to halt an election before it is completed. In relation to an election which has taken place, non-compliance with the legislation does not affect the validity of anything done by a person improperly elected,[245] so any resolutions passed by the executive committee, for example, remain in force.

TRADE UNION EXPENDITURE FOR POLITICAL PURPOSES

The statutory framework

10.18   In this area, unlike the others we have examined in this chapter, statutory regulation dates back to early in the twentieth century.[246] As we saw in para 7.4, unions were involved in the political process during the nineteenth century and gave financial support to parliamentary candidates, initially to Liberals and Independents then, in the first decade of the twentieth century, to those belonging to the newly-formed Labour Party.[247] This practice was challenged in the famous case of *ASRS v Osborne*,[248] in which a branch secretary of the railwaymen's union sought a declaration that the compulsory political levy of his union was unlawful, and an injunction to restrain the union from raising and distributing money for political purposes. The House of Lords held that the definition of a trade union in the Trade Union Acts 1871–76, which made no reference to political action, was a limiting one and that it was therefore *ultra vires* the Act for the union to levy a contribution on members for this purpose.[249] This decision, which removed their only income from 16 Labour MPs,[250] put the whole future of the Labour Party at risk. The Liberal government of the day responded in two different ways. 'First, in 1911 public money was made available to provide salaries for the hitherto unpaid MPs ... Second, the government introduced a Bill to remove the legal restraints on trade union political spending, it being readily accepted that trade unions had a right to seek the realisation of their goals by representation in Parliament

---

[242]   TULRCA 1992, s 54(1), (2). See para 2.33 for the procedure followed by the Certification Officer and the effect of any orders made by him or her. Applications which relate to an election which has already been held must be made within one year of the union announcing the result: s 54(3). *Quaere* whether this precludes an application for breach of contract, which is not subject to this time limit, where the statutory requirements have been incorporated into the union rules: see *Veness and Chalkley v NUPE* [1991] IRLR 76.

[243]   TULRCA 1992, ss 55(5A), 56(4).

[244]   TULRCA 1992, s 56(7).

[245]   TULRCA 1992, s 61(2).

[246]   See Ewing 1982b, 1984 for further discussion of this area.

[247]   Wedderburn, 1986: p 759.

[248]   [1910] AC 87.

[249]   This decision involved the court treating the union as a corporate or, at least, a quasi-corporate entity, a highly questionable assumption: P Davies and M Freedland, 1984: p 685.

[250]   Wedderburn, 1986: p 760.

and that they should not be disabled from so doing by economic and legal barriers.[251] The Trade Union Act 1913 effectively overruled *Osborne* by permitting a union to have objects additional to its statutory objects.[252] It did not leave unions completely unfettered in this area, however. Rather it required that those which wished to spend money on 'political objects' must first ballot their members on whether such objects should be adopted. If the majority of those voting were in favour, the union could then adopt rules to establish a separate political fund which alone could be used for the purpose of financing those objects. The rules were required to provide that every member had a right to be exempt from the contribution to the fund. Other than the period 1927–1946, which altered the scheme from one of contracting-out to contracting-in to payment of the political levy,[253] the framework of the 1913 Act remained in place until the Trade Union Act 1984. This Act introduced a requirement for periodic ballots and extended radically the definition of political objects. Subsequent legislation brought further constraints on the conduct of the balloting process.

10.19   As well as holding a ballot initially to approve political objects unions must now hold a fresh ballot at least once every ten years in order to retain an existing fund.[254] The rules governing each ballot must be approved by the Certification Officer;[255] they must reflect the complex requirements of the legislation which are in most material respects identical to those governing elections which we described in para 10.16. Again the ballot must be fully postal[256] and supervised by an independent scrutineer, so imposing substantial costs upon the union. In this context, however, the union may not exclude any groups from the balloting constituency, with the exception of overseas members where the ballot is to continue an existing fund.[257] Political fund rules must be approved by the Certification Officer and must stipulate that any payments in furtherance of 'political objects' are made only from the fund.[258] Payments for purposes outside this definition may be made from the general fund provided that the union's rules so permit. Property may be added to the political fund only from members' contributions or those of persons other than the union, and that which accrues to the fund in the course of administering its assets, such as interest.[259] Thus unions cannot add to their political fund income generated by the investment of other funds and the Act may also prevent them borrowing money for political activities.[260] No liability of the fund may be discharged out of any other union fund;[261] thus a creditor will be unable to secure payment of a political fund debt out of the general fund.

---

[251] Elias and Ewing, 1987: p 168.
[252] See para 7.20 above for discussion of the current definition of a 'trade union' contained in TULRCA 1992, s 1.
[253] It seems that 'human apathy' plays a considerable role in this area; the contributions to political funds rose from 38% of members in TUC unions in 1945 to 60% in 1948: Wedderburn, 1986: p 762.
[254] TULRCA 1992, s 73(3). For the issues which arise if a political fund resolution expires without being replaced, see G Morris and T Archer, 2000: para 2.52.
[255] TULRCA 1992, s 74.
[256] At the time of writing; see para 10.16 above.
[257] TULRCA 1992, ss 76, 94.
[258] TULRCA 1992, s 82, as amended by ERelA 2004, Sch 1, para 6.
[259] TULRCA 1992, s 83(1).
[260] *ASTMS v Parkin* [1983] IRLR 448.
[261] TULRCA 1992, s 83(3).

Members must be notified by the union of their right of exemption from contributing to the fund in a form specified by statute.[262] Those who exercise this right must then be relieved from the political fund element of the normal periodical contribution to the union.[263] The rules must provide that contribution to the fund is not a condition of admission to the union and that exempted members are not excluded from any union benefits, or placed directly or indirectly at any disadvantage as compared with other members, except in relation to the control or management of the political fund.[264] A union cannot exclude a non-contributor from holding union office by failing to separate control of the fund from other union activities.[265] In 1984, in return for the government agreeing not to attempt to re-introduce 'contracting-in', the TUC issued a 'statement of guidance on political fund arrangements' designed to ensure that union members are informed about and able to exercise their right to contract out from contributing. It is unlawful for employers who operate the 'check-off' to deduct an amount from the wages of non-contributors which includes the political levy, nor may they avoid the administrative inconvenience of making deductions at differential rates by withdrawing the check-off facility for non-contributors alone.[266] However, it seems that this difficulty may be circumvented if unions invite non-contributors to consent to deduction of the full subscription but give them a rebate for the political fund contribution in advance.

There are four major categories of complaint that may arise in relation to expenditure for political objects, all but one of which can be pursued by a member before either the Certification Officer or the High Court.[267] The first is a complaint relating to a breach of the union's political fund rules. In this context, unusually, any order made by the Certification Officer may be enforced in the same way as an order of the county court rather than as an order of the High Court.[268] The second relates to a breach of the statutory provisions governing political funds, such as a complaint that money has been spent on 'political objects' without a political fund resolution being in force.[269] However it seems that if the political fund rules contain provisions that are permissible but not required by statute (the third category), complaints about breaches of those rules may be taken only to the High Court.[270] The final category is those relating to political resolution ballots.[271] In the case of a successful application, an 'enforcement order' requiring the union to remedy the defect will also normally be made.

---

[262] TULRCA 1992, s 84((1), (2). In the period 2009-2010, annual returns to the Certification Officer recorded more than 1.5 million members belonging to unions with a political fund who did not make a political fund contribution: *Annual Report of the Certification Officer for 2010–2011*, para 7.18.

[263] TULRCA 1992, s 85(1). Where a member gives an exemption notice within one month of members being notified of their right to do so, and at the time of the political resolution ballot no political resolution is in force, the exemption takes immediate effect; in all other cases it takes effect from 1 January after the notice is given: s 84(4).

[264] TULRCA 1992, s 82(1).

[265] *Birch v NUR* [1950] Ch 602.

[266] See TULRCA 1992, ss 86–88. On the regulation of the check-off, see para 8.47 above.

[267] See para 2.33 for the procedure followed by the Certification Officer and the effect of an order made by him or her. The Political Parties, Elections and Referendums Act 2000 also has implications for union spending on political objects, as part of a wider regulation of spending in this area: see Ewing, 2001.

[268] TULRCA 1992, s 82(4A)(4B), inserted by ERelA 2004, Sch 1, para 6.

[269] TULRCA 1992, s 72A. No specific provision is made in this context for the High Court to have jurisdiction, but s 72A(11) implies that it is intended to exist.

[270] TULRCA 1992, s 82(2) applies only to rules *made in pursuance of this section*, and breach of rules relating to political funds is not covered by s 108A.

[271] TULRCA 1992, s 79. Applications which relate to a ballot which has already been held must be made within one year of the union announcing the result: s 79(3).

The definition of 'political objects'

10.20   The 'political objects' which may be furthered exclusively by the expenditure of money from a union's political fund fall into six broad categories:[272]

(i)   Any contribution to the funds of a political party, or on the payment of expenses incurred directly or indirectly by it. 'Contribution' includes affiliation or membership fees and loans[273] and also extends to investments made on a commercial basis.[274] 'Expenses' would cover such matters as salaries, rents and administration. There is no statutory definition of a 'political party' and the issue has not, to date, arisen for decision in this context.[275]

(ii)   The provision of any service or property for use by or on behalf of any political party. 'Property' could include equipment, such as computers; 'service', the provision of staff.[276]

(iii)   Expenditure in connection with the registration of electors, the candidature of any person (including prospective candidature), the selection of any candidate or the holding of any ballot by the union in connection with any election to a political office. 'Political office' covers members of the UK and European Parliament and of a local authority and also includes any position within a political party.[277] It therefore covers internal party elections, such as the nomination of parliamentary candidates or prospective candidates.

(iv)   Expenditure on the maintenance of any holder of a political office. 'Maintenance' means the maintenance of a person as a politician and is not confined to expenses incurred to stay alive; it also covers expenses to facilitate the conduct of political functions, such as a grant for research, travel or secretarial expenses.[278]

(v)   Expenditure on the holding of any conference or meeting by or on behalf of a political party or of any other meeting the main purpose of which is the transaction of business in connection with a political party.[279]

---

[272]   TULRCA 1992, s 72(1), (2). In determining whether a union has incurred expenditure of this kind, no account is to be taken of the ordinary administrative expenses of the union: s 72(3). The union failed successfully to rely upon this exclusion in *Re a complaint against the ISTC*, 13 October 1994, CO.

[273]   TULRCA 1992, s 72(4).

[274]   *ASTMS v Parkin* [1983] IRLR 448.

[275]   The Political Parties, Elections and Referendums Act 2000 does not directly define a 'political party'; parties (which include 'any organisation or person': s 40) that intend to contest 'relevant elections' (parliamentary elections; elections to the European and Scottish Parliaments and the National Assembly for Wales and Northern Ireland Assembly; local government elections; and local elections in Northern Ireland) must register under the Act: ss 40; 22(5). EqA 2010, s 107 refers to a party registered under the Great Britain register of the Act. On the meaning of 'political purpose' in the context of charity law see *McGovern v A-G* [1981] 3 All ER 493, 509 (Slade J); see also *R v Radio Authority, ex p Bull* [1997] 2 All ER 561, CA. On the basis of these latter decisions, it is conceivable that Amnesty, the League Against Cruel Sports, and Friends of the Earth could be regarded as political parties, although this goes beyond what would seem to be intended in this context.

[276]   Elias and Ewing, 1987: p 170.

[277]   TULRCA 1992, s 72(4). 'Local authority' is defined in the Local Government Act 1972, s 270, as amended.

[278]   *ASTMS v Parkin* [1983] IRLR 448.

[279]   Where a person attends a conference or meeting as a delegate or otherwise as a participator in the proceedings, any expenditure incurred in connection with his or her attendance as such is taken to be expenditure incurred on the holding of the conference or meeting: TULRCA 1992, s 72(3). In *Bakhsh v UNISON (No 3)* 29 January 2010, CO, the Certification Officer held that 'participator' did not include attendance at meetings to provide information or lobbying, so that a union without a political fund could, for example, spend money for its General Secretary to attend a conference of a political party to make a speech. However expenditure to attend a political party rally or march to further the ends of that event would need to be made from a political fund.

(vi) Expenditure on the production, publication or distribution[280] of any literature, document, film, sound recording or advertisement, the main purpose of which is to persuade people to vote, or not to vote, for a political party or candidate.

The last category, first introduced by the TUA 1984, represented a particularly significant extension of the previous definition; under the TUA 1913, expenditure on political literature was required to be financed from a political fund only if it was directly and expressly in support of a political party.[281] In expanding the definition, the Conservative Government's primary target was 'the electoral expenditure of public sector unions concerned to protect their members' interests in the face of privatization and cuts'.[282] The government claimed that the 'main purpose' test would ensure that campaigns on matters such as jobs and other matters affecting members' interests could still be financed from unions' general funds; they would only need to be paid for out of political funds if their main purpose was to influence voting behaviour. The only case on this provision to date, *Paul v NALGO*,[283] lent some support to this view. NALGO, a public service union, issued leaflets during the run-up to local authority elections and in anticipation of a general election which drew attention to the impact of government cutbacks and privatisation policies on public services and pointed out that readers had a vote. The leaflets specifically disclaimed any intention of seeking or opposing the election of particular candidates but their distribution was concentrated in marginal Conservative constituencies. In finding that expenditure on the leaflets from the general fund was unlawful, the court dismissed the union's claim that this was a non-partisan campaign designed merely to persuade people that public services were a good thing; the only rational conclusion to be drawn from the literature was 'If you accept the message of this leaflet, vote against the Conservatives' and this being so the disclaimer was not effective to avoid liability. However, the court emphasised that it was the linkage of disapproval of Government policies in a biased way with the invitation to vote at the time of an election which had made the campaign a 'political object' and stressed that:

> ... nothing in th[e] judgment should be taken as suggesting that a publicity campaign ... at times other than an election and therefore at a time when neither directly nor indirectly can the union be inviting anybody to exercise a vote at the time, is unlawful, merely because it expresses disapproval of the Government's policy.[284]

Despite this limitation, however, the provision ensures that unions which lack a political fund cannot promote campaigns which criticise government policies at a time when they may be most effective, that is, before an election.

In the event many public service unions established political funds for the first time in order to fend off the possibility of their campaigns being susceptible to legal challenge including, much to the government's chagrin, unions in the civil service.[285] In addition, contrary to expectations,

---

[280] The Certification Officer has held that 'distribution' includes distribution to members and officials of the union, as well as to the general public, although limited circulation within a union office may not be covered: *McCarthy v APEX* [1980] IRLR 335.

[281] *Coleman v POEU* [1981] IRLR 427, CO.

[282] Elias and Ewing, 1987: p 172.

[283] [1987] IRLR 413.

[284] [1987] IRLR 413, at 421.

[285] See generally Fredman and Morris, 1989: pp 126–128.

all unions with existing political funds which were required to hold fresh ballots[286] returned a majority in favour of retaining them. The second wave of balloting in 1994/96 produced broadly similar results,[287] as did the third some ten years later, although on a lower turnout than the previous rounds.[288] At the end of March 2011 there were 28 political fund resolutions in force; returns received by the Certification Officer during the year ending 31 March 2011 showed that more than 4.4 million trade unionists contributed to such funds, which produced a combined total income of £22.01 million.[289]

ASSESSMENT

10.21   The law governing the relationship between trade unions and their members was transformed during the 1979-1997 Conservative Government from a relatively non-interventionist approach to one which is highly restrictive, limiting unions' scope for autonomous action. In analysing the significance of this development, it is important to note that the concept of trade union autonomy was not merely a product of the collective *laissez-faire* tradition in Britain; it is also regarded at international level as fundamental to the concept of freedom of association. Article 3 of ILO Convention No 87 concerning Freedom of Association and the Right to Organise (1948) declares that '[w]orkers' and employers' organisations shall have the right to draw up their constitutions and rules, to elect their representatives in full freedom, to organise their administration and activities and to formulate their programmes.[290] The public authorities shall refrain from any interference which would restrict this right or impede the lawful exercise thereof'.[291] The current scope of external regulation of union government makes it particularly pertinent to consider the extent to which the law can and should legitimately intrude upon the principle of trade union autonomy. This raises a complex set of issues, only a few of which are outlined here.[292]

The most rudimentary level of legal intervention would be merely to ensure that unions obey the rules which they themselves have determined, with members having recourse to the courts if they are breached. This would entail treating unions in the same way as other bodies founded upon a contract of membership. In Britain, achieving this approach would require a reining in of the judicial inclination to treat unions distinctively from other private law organisations, which has led them to superimpose on the contract of membership public law standards of procedural

---

[286] Unions which had adopted political funds more than nine years before the relevant part of the TUA 1984 came into effect were deemed to have passed them nine years earlier and were therefore required to re-ballot within a year.

[287] See Leopold, 1997.

[288] Leopold, 2006. In order to distance their campaigns from a likely general election in spring 2005 a number of unions held their third round ballots early: Leopold, 2006: p 199.

[289] *Annual Report of the Certification Officer for 2010–2011*, paras 7.11–7.17; App 9.

[290] Art 3(1).

[291] Art 3(2). The Committee of Experts has pointed out that legislative provisions which regulate in detail the internal functioning of workers' and employers' organisations pose a serious risk of interference by the public authorities. See the Report of the Committee of Experts on the Application of Conventions and Recommendations, Report III (Part 4A), ILO, Geneva, 1995: p 201.

[292] For a more detailed discussion of these issues see Elias and Ewing, 1987: ch 8; Fredman, 1992a; Leader 1992; Wedderburn, 1995; Undy *et al*, 1996; Estreicher *et al*, 2001.

fairness,[293] even, in some instances, at the cost of overriding substantive union rules. If the law is, on a principled and coherent basis, to take a more interventionist approach to union government than merely enforcing the contract of membership, the justifications for this need to be explored and clarified. In relation to access to union membership, in the past the closed shop has constituted the most powerful argument for constraining unions' capacity to act autonomously, given that denial of union membership could reduce or remove completely the access of the individual to the labour market. Now that the closed shop can no longer lawfully be enforced, the question arises as to whether other benefits of union membership justify constraining union discretion. It remains the case that, for most workers, union membership offers an important opportunity to participate in the regulation of their working life, particularly where their union is recognised. Other benefits of membership may include representation at disciplinary and grievance procedures[294] and legal representation. If one accepts the argument that these are benefits which should not be arbitrarily denied to workers, this leads to a discussion of the legitimate scope of any control. At a minimal level one may argue that the conditions of membership should be clearly articulated and that any discretionary powers which are left to unions should not be exercised in an arbitrary or capricious fashion. One may also wish to argue that fairness may demand that reasons should be given if membership is refused to an ostensibly qualified individual, as well as if an existing member is expelled. A further stage of interventionism is to exercise control over the substance of the rules themselves. If one is to exceed the principles which apply in other areas, such as those covered by the equality legislation,[295] this involves much more complex inquiry as to the legitimate reach of legal policy. In *Cheall v APEX* Lord Diplock affirmed that 'freedom of association can only be mutual; there can be no right of an individual to associate with other individuals who are not willing to associate with him'.[296] In *ASLEF v UK*, too, the ECtHR concluded that unions must remain free to decide, in accordance with their rules, questions concerning admission to and expulsion from the union, subject to safeguards against 'abuse of a dominant position'.[297] At present unions can only lawfully deny membership to, or expel from membership, individuals on grounds specified in statute; although, ultimately, they cannot be forced to admit or retain individuals the price of exclusion or expulsion can be a heavy one. The ILO Committee of Experts on the Application of Conventions and Recommendations considers that unions should have the right to determine whether or not it should be possible to discipline members who refuse to comply with democratic decisions to take lawful industrial action, and that the financial penalties imposed by the legislation infringe Article 3 of Convention No 87.[298] The ECSR, which supervises the ESC, has also concluded that the limitations on the right of unions to exclude or

---

[293] Although see D Oliver, 1997 for a justification of extending this approach to other bodies.

[294] See now ERelA 1999, ss 10–15, discussed para 5.121 *et seq.*

[295] See ch 6.

[296] [1983] IRLR 215, 218.

[297] Judgment of 27 February 2007, [2007] IRLR 361, paras 38, 39, 43; see further para 7.9.

[298] See Report of the Committee of Experts on the Application of Conventions and Recommendations, Report III (Part 4A), ILO, Geneva, 1999. In 2007 CEACR reiterated its request to the Government to consider 'taking measures as a matter of urgency' to amend TULRCA 1992, s 174 and to reply to the concern raised by the TUC over the obligation to pay compensation for each expulsion regardless of whether any loss has been suffered. See also para 11.92 below, where we discuss the ILO's condemnation of the response to the prohibition on unions indemnifying individuals for penalties for criminal offences or contempt of court.

expel individuals, or to discipline their members, are incompatible with the right to organise.[299] Despite these findings, the Labour Government refused to change the current legislation in this area.[300] It acknowledged that in the *ASLEF* case the ECtHR sought to apply general principles about freedom of association when assessing the issues raised but affirmed that 'those comments were made against the particular circumstances of the ... case' and that it did not follow that the Court would have reached the same conclusion in relation to other parts of TULRCA 1992, s 174.[301] We do not share the view that the implications of the *ASLEF* judgment are limited to its particular facts; rather, it requires the justification for all the restrictions on trade union autonomy to be carefully and individually considered.[302] Moreover, other parts of TULRCA 1992, s 174 have been specifically criticised by the ILO and ECSR.[303] To the extent, at least, that the law does not comply with international standards it is in urgent need of review.

10.22   The same issues as to the scope of union autonomy arise in relation to other aspects of union government, in particular the important area of access to union office. Is this an area where the role of the law, if any, should be confined to ensuring that unions comply with their own rules or is it one where a more interventionist approach is warranted: in short, should trade unions be obliged to behave according to some externally-imposed model of 'democracy'? One often-quoted answer to this question was given by VL Allen in 1954:

> Trade union organisation is not based on theoretical concepts prior to it, that is on some concept of democracy, but on the end it serves ... the end of trade union activity is to protect and improve the general living standards of its members and not to provide workers with an exercise in self-government.[304]

The current legislation is predicated on the premise that, before statutory controls were introduced, unions were not sufficiently representative of and accountable to their members, although, as has been pointed out by many commentators, no evidence for this was provided.[305] On the basis of these assumptions, a uniform model of elections was imposed on unions, which previously operated according to a wide variety of practices.[306] One notable characteristic of the

---

[299]   For a more detailed analysis of ILO and ECSR conclusions on this area see Institute of Employment Rights Submission on TULRCA 1992, s 174, prepared by Professor Keith Ewing and John Hendy QC, JCHR Thirteenth Report, Session 2003–2004, App 2b; see also App 2d and Hendy and Ewing, 2005; Ewing, 2007.

[300]   *Review of the Employment Relations Act 1999: Government Response*, DTI, 2003, para 6.17.

[301]   BERR, *ECHR Judgment in the ASLEF v UK Case: Implications for Trade Union Law: Government Response to Public Consultation*, November 2007, para 2.12; see also para 2.13–2.15.

[302]   See further Ewing, 2007. See also Leader, 1991: pp 42–59 (where it is argued that the protection against expulsion of those who refuse to strike cannot be justified as 'necessary in a democratic society' under Art 11(2)). A challenge to the legislation on this ground would seem to require an application to the ECtHR; it seems difficult to envisage a remedy being available under the HRA 1998.

[303]   Cf BERR, *ECHR Judgment in the ASLEF v UK Case – Implications for Trade Union Law: Government Response to Public Consultation*, November 2007, paras 4.10-4.12, where the Labour Government claimed that it was 'not unusual for member states of the ILO and Council of Europe to have differing views about the practical application of their treaty obligations' and that UK law complied with these obligations.

[304]   Allen 1954: p 122, quoted Wedderburn, 1995: p 180.

[305]   The issue of how 'democracy' in unions is to be measured is itself a highly complex one: see further Undy and Martin, 1984: p 189–210; Undy *et al*, 1996; Estreicher *et al*, 2001.

[306]   See generally Undy and Martin, 1984.

legislation is that it is based upon a model of union 'citizenship' which is highly individualistic. The introduction of these provisions led to substantial changes in union rules and practice.[307] To the extent that the Conservative Government's real agenda may have been not merely to change procedures but also to attempt to influence outcomes by creating the conditions in which a more 'moderate' leadership would prevail, the desired result did not materialise. Research has shown that, in its early years at least, the legislation 'singularly failed to initiate a transformation in the political complexion of union leadership or a reorientation of democracy in a 'moderate' direction ...'[308] Indeed, the suggestion has been made that in certain circumstances the need to ballot regularly can actively promote militancy.[309] Moreover, the Conservative Government's presumption that union members would display different political preferences when voting by secret ballot from when voting in a public forum was not borne out; voting patterns did not change in any consistent political direction.[310] This is not to suggest that compliance with these provisions has not had serious consequences for unions, including substantial financial costs. Given the additional obligation to employ an independent scrutineer, mandatory even in the case of uncontested elections, the price of the statutory concept of democracy for trade unions is now a very high one. Perhaps surprisingly, the regime of elections imposed upon unions has not been found by the ILO's Committee of Experts to breach Article 3, since it is seen as within the range of measures which are acceptable as 'intended to promote democratic principles within trade union organisations or to ensure that the electoral procedure is conducted in a normal manner and with due respect for the rights of members in order to avoid any dispute arising as to the result of the election'.[311]

10.23   A final major area of regulation which requires consideration is that of union political activities. It may be argued that the line between the industrial and political spheres of activity is impossible to draw and that unions should be entitled to decide whether, and to what extent, to use their resources to attempt to create a politically hospitable climate for their members. If one accepts that some limits should be imposed, it may be thought appropriate to view this question in the broader context of the funding of political parties and the constraints, if any, which are placed upon other organisations in this regard. Until recently, trade unions were treated wholly distinctively from other groups; companies, for example, were required to disclose their political donations but there was no equivalent form of shareholder control. The Companies Act 2006 now requires companies to obtain shareholders' approval at least every four years for a donation to a registered political party or to any other EU political organisation, or to incur 'any political expenditure' which exceeds £5,000 in aggregate over a 12 month period.[312] However, there are no equivalent rights to those of trade unionists for shareholders to contract out of such donations.

---

[307] P Smith *et al*, 1993; Undy *et al*, 1996: ch 5.

[308] P Smith *et al*, 1993: p 380.

[309] P Smith *et al*: p 379.

[310] Undy and Martin, 1996: ch 5. In unions which previously had used workplace ballots for the election of their executive committee, electoral participation declined: P Smith *et al*, 1993, p 179; thus, 'on the basis of the Conservatives' own limited model of representative democracy the introduction of postal ballots had the effect, in many unions, of reducing union democracy': p 242.

[311] Report of the Committee of Experts on the Application of Conventions and Recommendations, Report III (Part 4A), ILO, Geneva, 1985: p 197.

[312] Companies Act 2006, Part 14.

In 1984 Undy and Martin wrote that: '[t]o the extent that Conservative policy succeeds in reducing the unions to the status of other economic interest groups, the justification for external intervention in their internal decision-making procedures grows weaker'.[313] It is perhaps ironical that, during a period when the role of unions in the industrial and political spheres was marginalised, in relation to the regulation of internal union affairs it was government policy to accord unions a greatly enhanced 'public' status in legal terms. It may not be too cynical to suggest that, in the guise of individual rights, the Conservative Government promoted measures which were in reality 'highly restrictive of workers' rights and trade unionism'.[314] Acceptance of this view does not entail the argument that the interests of the individual, where these stand in opposition to those of the collective, should automatically be subordinate; rather that there is a need to construct a coherent framework which recognises the collective interest as legitimate and which attempts to give a principled justification for the appropriate balance to be struck between them. It also entails consideration of whether, if such a framework were to be formulated, it would be best operated by the courts or by some mechanism of self-regulation, possibly on the basis of a series of guidelines agreed between the government and the TUC, with these being embodied in a TUC Code of Practice and policed and enforced by the TUC. Proposals of this nature are far from new[315] and, indeed, a modest self-regulatory system was in operation to deal with admissions and expulsions for a number of years from 1976.[316] This may constitute a more appropriate method of resolving differences between trade unions and their members and prospective members than the highly adversarial means which is currently offered by the legal process.

[313] Undy and Martin, 1984: p 218.
[314] Fredman, 1992a: p 24.
[315] See Elias and Ewing, 1987: pp 279–287; and see, in particular, the proposals of the Donovan Commission for a review body consisting of two trade unionists chosen from a panel appointed by the Secretary of State after consultation with the TUC, and a legally-qualified chairman: *Royal Commission on Trade Unions and Employers' Associations 1965–1968*, Cmnd 3623, paras 648–669.
[316] In that year the TUC established an Independent Review Committee to consider appeals from individuals who had been dismissed or given notice of dismissal from their jobs as a result of being expelled from, or having been refused admission to, a union in a situation where union membership was a condition of employment. For an analysis of the work of the Committee, see Ewing and Rees, 1981.

11

INDUSTRIAL ACTION

INTRODUCTION

11.1 In this chapter we examine the legal implications of organising and participating in industrial action. The concept of 'industrial action' generally connotes restrictions imposed collectively by workers against employers and most of our discussion concerns this. Such restrictions can take a variety of forms, ranging from a strike, which involves a complete withdrawal of labour, to a work-to-rule, go-slow, overtime ban or ban on particular duties. However employers, too, may take measures which disrupt the normal operation of the employment relationship, most notably by a 'lock-out' of workers from the workplace.

The right of workers to withdraw their labour is guaranteed by a number of international treaties and we begin by examining the nature of this right and its rationale. We then outline the development of legal policy in this country towards industrial action, knowledge of which is vital for any understanding of the labyrinthine structure of the current law. There follows an analysis of the common law liabilities which those who organise industrial action may incur and of the criteria which govern whether a trade union will be legally liable for their activities. We then examine the protection which statute affords against these liabilities. Where trade unions are legally responsible for industrial action any statutory protection is conditional upon a prior ballot and provision of specified information to relevant employers in addition to the usual restrictions. We discuss these highly complex requirements in the subsequent section. We then explain the remedies available against those who organise industrial action. Having analysed the common law and domestic statutory provisions, we then consider in greater detail the implications of recent developments in EU law. This is followed by an overview of the liabilities, criminal as well as civil, which pickets may incur. Finally, in relation to the organisation of industrial action, we outline the restrictions on withdrawals of labour by particular categories of workers and indicate other methods, such as invoking emergency powers, by which the state may seek to lessen the impact of industrial disputes. The chapter then assesses the implications of industrial action for individual workers. It does so from three perspectives. The first, that of the employment relationship, involves analysing its impact both on contractual and on statutory rights, in particular protection against unfair dismissal. Second, we consider briefly the consequences of participation in industrial action for entitlement to a range of social security benefits. Although social security generally lies beyond the scope of this work it is particularly significant in this context because of its impact upon the financial capacity of workers to withstand disputes and, at a more theoretical level, as a product of the rhetoric of state neutrality. Lastly we indicate the rights which dissident union members can exercise against their unions when they wish to challenge the collective decision to take or support industrial action. In the concluding section we comment upon some of the major difficulties raised by the law in this area and outline those aspects which appear most in need of reform.

It will be rapidly apparent that the law in this area, even more than others which we examine in this work, is highly technical and even, at points, convoluted. For this reason we re-emphasise that our aim, as expressed in the preface, is not to provide an encyclopaedic knowledge of the substantive law, but rather to explore the underlying themes and issues.

INDUSTRIAL ACTION: ROLE, RATIONALE AND INTERNATIONAL STANDARDS

11.2   In 1972, Kahn-Freund and Hepple introduced a study of laws against strikes with the following question:

> Why is it that in all democratic countries the 'freedom to strike' or, as it is sometimes put, the 'right to strike' is considered to be a fundamental freedom, alongside the freedom to organise, to assemble peacefully, to express one's opinion? Why is the strike, or, better perhaps, the potentiality of a strike, that is, of an event which of necessity entails a waste of resources, and damage to the economy, nevertheless by general consent an indispensable element of a democratic society?[1]

The freedom of workers to withdraw their labour has been justified on a number of grounds. It can be seen as a fundamental human right.[2] Thus one leading commentator describes it as complementary to freedom from slavery and forced labour given that (at its extreme) denial of the freedom involves being forced to work against one's better judgement.[3] Related to this is the 'democratic' argument; that such a freedom is intrinsic to the notion of a democracy, a view reinforced by the fact that, conversely, it is often banned in totalitarian societies. From a narrower perspective it may be viewed specifically within the context of industrial relations. Here there are two major (again associated) justifications. The 'equilibrium' argument maintains that the concentrated power of capital, expressed in the capacity of employers to hire and fire workers and close down an enterprise, can only be matched by workers acting in concert. Within this framework the collective withholding of labour is a vital weapon in an economic conflict which imposes costs on both the parties: disrupted production, on the one hand, lost wages on the other.[4] The 'autonomous sanctions' argument sees the right to have recourse to industrial action as integral to the concept of collective bargaining as an autonomous norm-making system. Thus 'those who have made the autonomous rules should also wield the sanctions …',[5] a view acknowledged in 1942 by Lord Wright in describing the right to strike as 'an essential element in the principle of collective bargaining'.[6]

---

[1] Kahn-Freund and Hepple, 1972: p 4

[2] See Ben-Israel, 1988, ch 1; Ewing, 2004.

[3] See Ben-Israel, 1988: p 25. However, as Kahn-Freund and Hepple point out, it is possible effectively to undermine the freedom to strike by imposing sanctions against the organisers rather than forcing individuals to go to work.

[4] Ben-Israel, 1994: p 11.

[5] Kahn-Freund and Hepple, 1972: p 7.

[6] *Crofter Hand Woven Harris Tweed Co Ltd v Veitch* [1942] AC 435, 463.

The context in which one locates the right may have fundamental implications for its scope and nature.[7] If it is regarded as a human – or even constitutional – right, for example, this may suggest that it inheres in all workers, regardless of whether their union approves the action or, indeed, regardless of whether they are members of a union.[8] Conversely, if it is viewed within the context of collective bargaining this may imply that it should be subject to the exclusive control of the collective bargaining agent.

11.3   At international level the right to strike is guaranteed explicitly only in treaties covering socio-economic, rather than civil and political, rights. Thus the International Covenant on Economic, Social and Cultural Rights guarantees the right to strike, although, because it is subject to the proviso that 'it is exercised in conformity with the laws of the particular country',[9] the substantive content of the right is limited.[10] At European level the European Social Charter requires contracting states to recognise 'the right of workers and employers to collective action in cases of conflict of interest, including the right to strike, subject to obligations that might arise out of collective agreements previously entered into'.[11] Curiously, perhaps, there is no reference to the right to strike in ILO Conventions Nos 87 on Freedom of Association and Protection of the Right to Organise or 98 on the Right to Organise and Collective Bargaining. The reasons for this omission are not wholly clear; they have been summarised as 'procedural difficulties, political differences, the feeling that specific elaboration was unnecessary, and workers' fears that specifying a right to strike would also lead to its restriction'.[12] In practice, however, the right has been derived by the supervisory bodies from general freedom of association principles; the Committee of Experts on the Application of Conventions and Recommendations has consistently affirmed that this is one of the essential and legitimate means by which workers and their organisations may promote and defend their economic and social interests and, as such, it is an integral part of the free exercise of the rights guaranteed by Conventions 87 and 98.[13] On the basis of this view they have developed an extensive jurisprudence as to what this right entails. As we shall see, UK law falls short of these standards in a number of significant respects. In contrast to the ILO, the ECtHR until recently refused to imply a right to strike from the right to form and join trade unions in Article 11 of the ECHR, affirming that while the grant of such a right represents 'one of the most important' of the means by which the occupational interests of trade union members may be protected by

---

[7] See Novitz, 2003.

[8] Ewing, 2004: pp 48–50.

[9] Art 8. See generally Craven, 1998: ch 7.

[10] Ben-Israel, 1988: p 82. Cf Craven, 1998: p 281, where it is stated that it is 'arguably more appropriate to interpret the phrase "in conformity with the laws of the particular country" as legitimizing the imposition of certain procedural requirements, rather than allowing substantive limitations ...'. Note also that Art 8(3) affirms that for States that are party to ILO Convention No 87, Art 8 does not authorise measures that would prejudice the guarantees in that Convention (discussed below).

[11] Art 6 (in both the 1961 Charter and the Revised Charter of 1996). Note that states which ratify the treaty can, in the case of certain articles, including Art 6, choose whether to be bound by them: see para 2.43. The reference to 'conflicts of interest' – conflicts over the terms of new collectively-agreed provisions – is in contradistinction to 'conflicts of right' over the interpretation or application of existing agreements, terms which have little meaning in the British context. See further Kovaks, 2005; ECSR 2008: pp 53–58.

[12] Ben-Israel, 1988: pp 45–46; see generally pp 35–46.

[13] ILO, 2006, paras 520 et seq; Gernigon et al, 1998; Novitz, 2003: chs 5, 8, 11–15. In the case of public officials, however, recognition of the freedom to associate does not necessarily imply the right to strike: ILO, 2006: para 572.

trade union action, 'there are others'.[14] However, as we saw in para 7.9, in *UNISON v UK*,[15] the ECtHR, while reaffirming its traditional position, regarded restrictions on the right as falling within Article 11(1) in the case in question and in 2009 the Court held that a ban preventing public sector employees from taking part in a one-day national strike in support of the right to a collective-bargaining agreement violated Article 11.[16] In *ITWF v Viking Line*, the ECJ confirmed that 'the right to take collective action, including the right to strike, must ... be recognised as a fundamental right which forms an integral part of the general principles of Community law'.[17] However, it did so in a context where this right operated as a defence to employers' claims that their free movement rights under the EC Treaty (predecessor of the TFEU) had been infringed by trade unions and, as such, the Court required individual instances of collective action to be subject to forms of scrutiny which may severely limit the scope of the right in practice. As the right recognised by the ECJ is also subject to provisions of national law the Court's decision has the effect of adding new restrictions to those already present in relation to disputes with a cross-border dimension. The full implications of this decision can be properly appreciated only with an understanding of national law and for that reason we consider those implications later in the chapter.[18]

11.4   Developed legal systems vary considerably in how they treat the right to strike. This is the case even within the European Union. The Charter of Fundamental Rights of the European Union affirms the right of workers and employers, or their respective organisations, to take collective action, including strike action, in cases of conflicts of interest, but this is to be exercised 'in accordance with Community law and national law and practices.'[19] In practice there is no European standard,[20] let alone one on a more universal scale. Space does not permit us to describe the enormous diversity of provisions which can, in any case, be properly understood only within the broader framework of national legal and industrial relations systems.[21] We can, however, isolate some fundamental issues which all systems need to address. The first is the location of the right; does it lie with individuals (albeit exercised on a collective basis) – the 'individualist' right – or only with trade unions (the 'organic')? If it is to be found in a national constitution, as in France or Italy, then it is likely to be individualist, although even then one should beware of oversimplifying the position; in the French

---

[14] *Schmidt and Dahlstrom v Sweden* judgment of 6 February 1976, (1979–80) 1 EHRR 632, para 36.

[15] Admissibility decision of 10 January 2002, [2002] IRLR 497. See further para 11.9 for the implications of the HRA 1998 for the right to strike.

[16] *Enerji Yapi-Yol Sen v Turkey*, judgment of 21 April 2009. This decision, together with other case law of the ECtHR, has been widely interpreted (including judically) as supporting the conclusion that the right to strike is conferred by Article 11(1).•See *RMT v Serco Docklands*; *ASLEF v London Midland* [2011] IRLR 399, CA, Elias LJ at [8]; Ewing and Hendy, 2009b: pp 91–98; Ewing and Hendy 2010: pp 13-19; Ewing and Hendy, 2011 and Countouris and Freedland, 2010. For the effect of the ECHR jurisprudence in British courts, see para 11.9 below.

[17] Case C-438/05, para 44, [2008] IRLR 143. See also Case C-341/05 *Laval Un Partneri Ltd v Svenska Byggnadsarbetareforbundet* [2008] IRLR 160, para 91.

[18] See para 11.52 below. For the argument that accession by the EU to the ECHR may change the position see further para 11.52.

[19] Art 28. The right affirmed by the EC Social Charter of 1989 was similarly qualified, being 'subject to the obligations arising out of national regulations and collective agreements'. Note also provisions of the CFREU which could be read as supporting the interests of employers and non-strikers in the event of industrial action, including Art 15 (the right to engage in work), Art 16 (the freedom to conduct a business) and Art 17 (the right to property).

[20] See Wedderburn, 1991b; A Jacobs, 2009, 2010.

[21] See Ben-Israel, 1994; Goldman and Osborne, 2007.

public sector, for example, only a representative union can call a strike.[22] The second is the purpose for which the right exists. In general it is confined to 'industrial' or 'economic' matters and does not extend to the 'political' realm,[23] but systems can vary considerably in where they draw the line between the two, which can be a particularly fragile one where social and economic policies may have fundamental implications for wages and job security, for example. Whether the right is located solely within the framework of collective bargaining or whether it goes beyond it may be material here. A third issue is whether the right to strike can be restricted by agreement and, if so, by whom? In France, where it is an individual constitutional right it cannot be bargained away in relation to individual workers.[24] By contrast, in a number of systems where collective agreements are legally binding, industrial action over the terms of that agreement, or even over any issue during its currency ('relative' and 'absolute' peace obligations respectively) may be unlawful. This aspect is reflected in those international instruments which distinguish between conflicts of right, over the interpretation and application of existing collective agreements, and conflicts of interest over the terms of new collective rules. A fourth is the nature of the action which attracts the protection of the right. Some systems permit strikes but not certain lesser forms of action on the basis that the employer should not incur the expense of operating the enterprise if workers are in dispute. The fifth is the scope of the right: the legitimacy of secondary action by workers employed by other employers to further a dispute is also subject to wide discrepancies in treatment.[25] Sixth, some systems impose procedural limitations on the exercise of the right, requiring any withdrawal of labour to be preceded by the exhaustion of specified dispute settlement procedures, a ballot of the workers or the provision of a minimum period of notice to employers or the public authorities, for example. Seventh, there are a range of issues posed by the position of individual workers during disputes; should they be protected against dismissal or even temporary replacement, for example, and, if so, for how long? In many countries the contract of employment is suspended during a strike and workers are protected against discriminatory treatment due to their participation in it on resuming work.[26] Finally, a problem which every system faces is whether there are particular groups of workers which, because of the function they perform, should have no, or only limited, access to the right to strike. At one time it was common for all public servants to be denied this right on the ground that it was incompatible with their status as representatives of the sovereign power and, while comprehensive bans have generally been removed in western countries, it remains the case that the legal framework which governs public servants is usually more restrictive than for private sector workers,[27] although this is increasingly anachronistic in an environment in which identical tasks may be performed by workers in the public and the private sector. A more modern approach is to ask whether workers are performing an 'essential' service defined by reference to the function they perform rather than their legal status. The ILO, for example, considers that the right may be restricted in 'essential services', which it defines as those whose interruption 'would endanger the life, personal safety or health of

---

[22] The right is also guaranteed by the constitutions of Portugal, Spain, Greece and Sweden, for example, and by some Eastern European states: see A Jacobs, 2010: para 3.

[23] For an analysis of ILO principles see Ben-Israel, 1988, Pt III; see also ILO, 2006.

[24] Rojot, 1994: p 61.

[25] A Jacobs, 2010: para 25.

[26] A Jacobs, 2010: paras 57–63.

[27] See Ozaki, 1993; A Jacobs, 2010: paras 42–46. The ILO considers that the right may be restricted in the case of public servants exercising authority in the name of the State: ILO, 2006: paras 574–575; Gernigon et al, 1998: pp 448–449.

the whole or part of the population'[28] provided that any restrictions are accompanied by reciprocal guarantees to safeguard workers' interests.[29] Unfortunately in this area, as in relation to freedom of association more generally, international standards are divergent;[30] the European Social Charter, for example, allows restrictions which are 'necessary in a democratic society for the protection of the rights and freedoms of others or for the protection of the public interest, national security, public health or morals',[31] a much broader test than the ILO's.

In the area of industrial action, as in many others, labour law in Britain is unusual in comparison to other systems in not addressing the majority of these issues in a coherent and systematic fashion. There is no principled concept of 'lawful' or 'unlawful' industrial action; at collective level whether industrial action attracts legal liability depends upon a complex and not always predictable interaction between the common law and statute; in relation to the individual worker industrial action generally constitutes a breach of the employment contract, and there is only limited statutory protection against dismissal.[32] Similarly the use of the lock-out weapon by employers, which in some systems is permitted only as a defensive measure in response to industrial action by workers, is not subject to clear regulation. As we shall see the legal framework in this country has developed in a ramshackle, ad hoc manner which is all but incomprehensible to those coming from outside Britain and little more easily accessible to those who are more familiar with its legal system. The position has recently been further complicated in relation to disputes with a cross-border dimension by developments in EU law which we discuss in para 11.52 below.

LEGAL POLICY RELATING TO INDUSTRIAL ACTION: AN OVERVIEW[33]

11.5   In Britain those who organise industrial action have always been vulnerable to legal liability of some kind. Historically the most important source of constraint was the criminal law. Even when workers' combinations received limited protection against the doctrine of conspiracy this did not bring equivalent protection for industrial action; rather the 1825 Act specifically curtailed the freedom to strike and to picket against 'blacklegs' by creating vague offences of molestation, obstruction and intimidation. Moreover, it remained a criminal offence under the Master and Servant Acts to break a contract of employment. The Criminal Law Amendment Act 1871, in defining the offences laid down in the 1825 Act more precisely and adding those of 'persistently following a person' and 'watching and besetting premises', made virtually all picketing illegal and under this Act even posting-up a strike notice was held to constitute intimidation of employers.[34]

---

[28] ILO, 2006: paras 576, 581. The threat to 'life' etc must be 'clear and imminent'. See also Gernigon *et al*, 1998. Note that the police and armed forces are excluded altogether from the scope of these Conventions: see para 11.3 above.

[29] ILO, 2006 paras 595–603.

[30] See generally Novitz, 2003.

[31] Art 31 (Art G in the Revised Charter of 1996). The police and the armed forces are excluded under both these treaties.

[32] The law of unfair dismissal makes some distinction between 'unofficial' and other industrial action, but even in the case of action which is not unofficial the protection afforded is limited and often dependent upon whether that action is protected by the statutory immunities.

[33] In this section we aim merely to provide a framework for the more detailed analysis which follows. Full references are provided to the current law in later sections.

[34] A Jacobs, 1986: p 212. The 1871 Act repealed the Molestation of Workmen Act 1859 which had protected certain forms of peaceful picketing.

In addition to the statutory liabilities industrial action could also offend the common law; in the notorious case of *R v Bunn*[35] London gas workers who threatened a strike unless a colleague dismissed for union activities was reinstated were convicted of a common law conspiracy by threatening to break their contracts and by their 'unjustifiable annoyance and interference with the masters in the conduct of their business'.

The decision in *Bunn*, together with the 1871 Act, provoked considerable protest, a campaign which peaked during the 1874 general election 'when newly enfranchised working men supported opposition Conservative candidates who appeared more responsive to trade union pressure than the Liberal Government responsible for the 1871 Act'.[36] In 1875 the incoming Conservative Government led by Disraeli introduced the Conspiracy and Protection of Property Act. This Act repealed the Master and Servant Acts and the 1871 Act (although preserving some more specific offences) and also reversed the effect of *Bunn* in respect of acts 'in contemplation or furtherance of a trade dispute', the first appearance of the so-called 'golden formula'[37] protecting industrial action.

The 1875 Act marked the retreat of the criminal law from the area of industrial action. Since 1875, wartime apart, its role in this context has been largely confined to picketing.[38] For some groups of workers criminal liability remains potentially a threat. The 1875 Act made it an offence for a person 'wilfully and maliciously' to break a contract of service or of hiring, knowing or having reasonable cause to believe that the probable consequences, either alone or in combination with others, will be to endanger human life, cause serious bodily injury, or expose valuable property to destruction or serious injury. This offence is still on the statute book,[39] although there is no record of any prosecutions for it despite many disputes where there could have been. In addition, there are particular groups – the police, armed forces, merchant seamen and postal and, possibly, telecommunications workers – for whom industrial action is illegal.[40] However, with the possible exception of the police these provisions do not appear to have constituted a significant constraint (the armed forces not having threatened industrial action in recent times). Thus, even in essential services, the criminal law has not been invoked to restrict withdrawals of labour. Rather, unlike many countries, the traditional British strategy in these areas centred upon invoking emergency powers to lessen the impact of industrial action once it had been taken rather than attempting to forestall it in the first place. The Emergency Powers Act 1920 empowered the government, on proclaiming a state of emergency, to introduce measures to 'secure the essentials of life to the community' when the supply and distribution of specified commodities was interrupted or transport dislocated. It also legitimated the use of troops to replace striking workers, a practice which stretched back to the nineteenth century.[41] It did not, however, enable industrial action in essential services to be outlawed.

---

[35] (1872) 12 Cox CC 316.

[36] A Jacobs, 1986: p 213.

[37] A phrase coined by Lord Wedderburn (P Davies and M Freedland, 1983: p 314, n 8) which has become common currency.

[38] Note, however, its role in relation to incomes policies during the 1960s (P Davies and M Freedland, 1993: pp 177–181).

[39] TULRCA 1992, s 240.

[40] Criminal offences relating to industrial action in the gas and water industries, introduced in the 1875 Act, and extended to electricity in 1919, were repealed by the IRA 1971: see G Morris, 1986a: pp 21–22.

[41] See G Morris, 1986a: pp 97 *et seq*. The Emergency Powers Act 1920 has now been replaced by the Civil Contingencies Act 2004; see further para 11.62.

11.6   In the wake of the 1875 Act the legal focus in relation to industrial action shifted to the civil law. Between 1891 and 1906 the courts effectively outflanked the protections provided against the criminal law by expanding the scope of liability in tort. The new tort of conspiracy to injure was developed and the tort of inducing breach of contract applied to industrial action, for which the furtherance of union objectives was no defence. In 1901 the House of Lords decided, in the infamous *Taff Vale*[42] case, that a trade union registered under the Trade Union Act 1871, although not a corporate body, could nevertheless be sued for the torts of its officials, so exposing union funds to damages claims for losses caused by unlawful industrial action. This decision again provoked a powerful protest movement and, indeed, was one of the catalysts for the formation of the Labour Party. A Liberal government, having been elected with Labour support, pledged to change the law, and so the Trade Disputes Act 1906 was enacted. This Act accorded comprehensive immunity to trade unions against tortious liability. It also gave immunity to any person who 'in contemplation or furtherance of a trade dispute' committed the new tort of conspiracy, induced some other person to breach a contract of employment, or interfered with the trade, business or employment of another. In addition, it permitted peaceful picketing in trade disputes. A 'trade dispute' was defined as 'any dispute between employers and workmen, or between workmen and workmen, which is connected with the employment or non-employment, or the terms of the employment, or with the conditions of labour, of any person ...'[43]

The 1906 Act remained in force until 1971. With the exception of wartime restrictions on strikes and legislation passed in the wake of the General Strike, which were not in the event invoked,[44] it provided the bedrock of the freedom to organise industrial action for several decades.[45] It was also integral to the principle of collective *laissez-faire;* provided that the parties were acting peacefully and for 'industrial' objectives the law would not interfere in their disputes. This abstentionism was mirrored in the attitude of the state towards procedures for the settlement of industrial disputes.[46] Formal government responsibility in this area began with the Conciliation Act 1896 which gave the government the duty to encourage the development of joint machinery between employers and unions and powers to inquire into disputes and to initiate conciliation and arbitration. This process was strengthened in the aftermath of the Whitley Committee of 1916–1918; the Industrial Court (the forerunner of the CAC) was established as an arbitral body and the government itself was given power to inquire into trade disputes 'for the purpose of informing Parliament and the public of the facts' although it could not thereby impose a settlement. Crucially, therefore, dispute settlement within the private sector outside wartime[47] remained ultimately a matter for the collective parties who would be bound by the results of any procedures only if they so elected;

---

[42] *Taff Vale Rly Co v ASRS* [1901] AC 426.

[43] See para 11.25 below for the current definition. For a recent overview see contributions to Ewing, 2006.

[44] The Trade Disputes and Trade Union Act 1927 declared illegal strikes and lock-outs having any object other than or in addition to the furtherance of a trade dispute within the strikers' trade or industry and 'designed or calculated to coerce the Government either directly or by inflicting hardship upon the community'. The Act was repealed in 1946.

[45] See generally P Davies and M Freedland, 1993.

[46] For a valuable survey see Sir John Wood, 1992. See also Wedderburn and Davies, 1969; Mumford, 1996.

[47] During the two World Wars a system of compulsory arbitration was in force: see the Munitions of War Act 1915 and the Conditions of Employment and National Arbitration Order 1940 (SR&O 1940/1305). The latter continued in force until 1951, when it was replaced by the Industrial Disputes Order 1951, SI 1951/1376 which removed the ban on strikes contained in Order 1305: see further para 7.15 above. On developments in public services see Fredman and Morris, 1989: pp 417–422.

only in certain minimum wage-fixing machinery was arbitration compulsory[48] and even then it was not linked to a ban on industrial action. As we saw in our account of ACAS and the CAC in chapter 2 this voluntary approach to the settlement of industrial disputes has continued to prevail up to the present day.

11.7   Reliance upon an immunities approach to the legality of industrial action always carried risks, most notably that the courts would develop new forms of liability outside the scope of legislative protection, either in the context of industrial disputes or in other contexts where the 'economic torts' were at issue. As we shall see later in this chapter, judicial creativity in the industrial action forum was not wholly extinguished after 1906[49] but did not, in practice, threaten the basic framework of the law until the landmark House of Lords decision of *Rookes v Barnard*[50] in which the tort of 'intimidation' was applied to industrial action. At that time the Labour Government quickly introduced legislation in 1965 to extend immunity to this tort,[51] a response which has not been replicated in more recent years when new forms of liability have emerged. Individual dispute organisers also continued to remain vulnerable after 1906 because of the retention of the overriding discretion of the courts to grant injunctions to halt industrial action, the remedy which, in practice, is of most use to employers. Injunctions can be granted in interim proceedings, if necessary at short notice, to halt allegedly unlawful activity pending full trial of an action. Given that a case may take months or even years to come to trial, by which time the dispute is likely to have been settled, the interim proceedings effectively decide the issue in this context. The penalties for breaching an injunction, which constitutes a contempt of court, are severe: an unlimited fine; where appropriate, imprisonment; and possible sequestration of a defendant's assets. In impact, therefore, the ultimate penalties in civil law may differ little from those which may be imposed under the criminal law, with fewer procedural safeguards for respondents. Decisions made in interim proceedings have had fundamental consequences for the operation and development of industrial action law.

With certain well-publicised exceptions employers did not, before the 1980s, generally resort to the courts when faced with industrial action.[52] By the 1960s, however, there was growing concern about the number of unofficial strikes taking place in breach of (albeit unenforceable) procedures. The Donovan Commission which reported in 1968 emphasised the importance of attending to collective bargaining institutions and procedures rather than attempting to constrain industrial action by law.[53] The Heath Conservative Government thought differently and the Industrial Relations Act 1971 swept away the existing system of immunities and replaced it with a different framework which created new liabilities, dubbed 'unfair industrial practices', encouraged tighter control by unions of their shop stewards' activities and removed union immunity against liability in tort. In practice few employers relied on these provisions and research on the Act concluded

---

[48] The machinery of the Fair Wages Resolution provided for determination by the Industrial Court.
[49] See in particular *DC Thomson & Co Ltd v Deakin* [1952] Ch 646, where the Court of Appeal developed the indirect form of the tort of inducing breach of a commercial contract at a time when inducing contracts of employment only was protected by the statutory immunities. For the rest of the decade, however, 'employers seemed little interested in exploiting the possibilities for injunctive relief that the decision had created': P Davies and M Freedland, 1993: p 131.
[50] [1964] AC 1129.
[51] TDA 1965. This Act also countered the effect of *JT Stratford & Son Ltd v Lindley* [1965] AC 269.
[52] Evans, 1983: p 129.
[53] *Royal Commission on Trade Unions and Employers' Associations 1965–1968*: Report, Cmnd 3623, 1968, ch VII.

that they had had relatively little impact on the conduct of industrial relations.[54] Novel emergency powers were similarly unsuccessful; inspired by the American Taft-Hartley Act 1947, they enabled the executive, with judicial sanction, to interfere directly in the conduct of 'emergency' disputes by imposing a 'cooling-off period' or compulsory ballot of the workforce but were used only once.[55] Even before its defeat in the 1974 General Election the government had accepted the need for substantial amendment of the industrial action provisions.[56]

The incoming Labour Government restored the structure established by the 1906 Act but made it 'stronger and clearer'[57] by extending the scope of protection against liability in tort and extending the definition of a trade dispute.[58] Some members of the judiciary did not conceal their distaste for this legislation, in particular the protection it afforded to secondary industrial action, and Lord Denning MR led the Court of Appeal into a series of decisions which sought to restrict the scope of the 'golden formula' by, inter alia, superimposing upon the concept of 'furthering' a trade dispute a remoteness and an 'objective' test.[59] Even when the House of Lords reminded lower courts of the principle of Parliamentary supremacy and the rule of law a senior judge did not feel constrained from describing the legislation as 'intrinsically repugnant to anyone who has spent his life in the practice of the law or the administration of justice'.[60] Perhaps surprisingly, however, the Labour Government did not seek to extend the protection afforded to dispute organisers to those participating in disputes. No immunity was accorded against individual liability for breach of contract, which industrial action, even if preceded by notice, almost invariably constitutes. Moreover, in continuing the protection against unfair dismissal introduced by the Industrial Relations Act it maintained the position that only in the event of selectivity between those dismissed while taking part in industrial action would employment tribunals have jurisdiction over their dismissals. The same principle was also extended to those locked-out. Although this avoided employment tribunals assessing the merits of disputes it left those taking industrial action in a highly vulnerable position. They also stood to lose access to other statutory rights, most notably redundancy payments. The only measure which could be said to protect participation in industrial action, although not confined to this situation, was the re-enactment (again from the Industrial Relations Act) of a statutory prohibition against individual employees being ordered to work by an order for specific performance, or an injunction restraining a breach or threatened breach, of the contract of employment.

11.8   In 1979 the Conservative Government was returned to office in the wake of a 'winter of discontent' of high-profile strikes in both the public and the private sectors. In 1980 it began a process of restriction and regulation which, by degrees, confined lawful industrial action by reference to its protected purposes and scope and the procedures which must precede it.[61] Thus,

---

[54] Weekes *et al*, 1975: p 218.

[55] G Morris, 1986a: pp 82–87; Weekes *et al*, 1975: pp 213–216; Whelan, 1982.

[56] See Weekes *et al*, 1975: pp 218–219.

[57] *NWL Ltd v Woods* [1979] ICR 867, 886 (Lord Scarman).

[58] TULRA 1974, as amended in 1976.

[59] *Express Newspapers Ltd v McShane* [1979] ICR 210; *Associated Newspapers Group v Wade* [1979] ICR 664. See generally Ewing, 1979.

[60] *Duport Steels Ltd v Sirs* [1980] IRLR 112, 117 (Lord Diplock); see also Lord Edmund Davies and Lord Keith, 121 and also *McShane and Ashton v Express Newspapers Ltd* [1980] IRLR 35.

[61] For detailed analyses of the policy background to, and legislative history of, the relevant provisions up to their respective times of writing see Auerbach, 1990, and P Davies and M Freedland, 1993: ch 9 *et seq*.

immunity was removed for secondary industrial action and secondary picketing (a technical exception apart); the concept of a 'trade dispute' was confined to disputes between workers and their own employer which related 'wholly or mainly' to a protected purpose; increasingly prescriptive and complex balloting (and, latterly, notification) requirements were imposed where liability for industrial action was attributable to a union; and unions lost their comprehensive immunity against liability in tort. As well as thereby extending the remedies available to employers faced by industrial action the legislation also made available to union members and, latterly, the wider public, mechanisms for encouraging challenges to the organisation of such campaigns, with the facility for affected members of the public to seek assistance to bring proceedings against a union to halt industrial action from a Commissioner for Protection Against Unlawful Industrial Action. In addition the already limited protection against dismissal while taking part in industrial action was further narrowed, and removed altogether for participants in 'unofficial' industrial action, so enabling selective dismissal of union activists. Union members were also given the right not to be 'unjustifiably disciplined' by their union for refusing to participate in industrial action, or seeking to persuade others not to do so, albeit the action had been approved by a majority in a ballot. This process of restriction occurred incrementally – the Conservative Government had not forgotten the experience of the Industrial Relations Act – and one should beware of viewing these reforms as the product of a preconceived agenda.[62] Nevertheless the cumulative result of a series of statutes through the 1980s and early 1990s was a radical reversal of the collective *laissez-faire* tradition which brought in general terms a much greater willingness on the part of employers to resort to legal sanctions when faced with disputes.[63] By the end of the 1980s the ILO Committee of Experts on the Application of Conventions and Recommendations was expressing concern as to the volume and complexity of legislative changes in industrial action law;[64] the 1990s saw both compounded. As a consequence, the organisation of industrial action became a very expensive process for trade unions, particularly given the growing need for detailed legal advice and (for all but small disputes) mandatory postal ballots. Between 1983 and March 1996 there were 204 separate legal actions against trade unions, of which 169 were applications for an injunction; of those 169 applications, 137 were successful.[65] In 1998 it was estimated that the costs to unions of defending legal actions since 1983 had been nearly £4 million.[66]

11.9 The entry into office of the Labour Government in 1997 brought few changes to this area. The law governing the organisation of industrial action remained intact in its essentials, although some minor but important changes were made to the pre-action balloting and notification requirements and the (little-used) Commissioner for Protection Against Unlawful Industrial Action[67] was abolished. More significant are the changes to the position of employees who take

---

[62] See the texts referred to above.

[63] Note, however, that this pattern varied between sectors and between individual years, and disputes where employers resorted to litigation still remained comparatively rare. See Gall and McKay, 1996; McKay, 1996; Undy *et al*, 1996: ch 6; W Brown *et al*, 1997: pp 77–78; *Labour Research* October 1998: pp 15–16.

[64] See Report of the Committee of Experts on the Application of Conventions and Recommendations, Report III (Part 4A), ILO, Geneva, 1989: p 241.

[65] Gall and McKay, 1996: pp 567 and 573.

[66] *Labour Research*, October 1998, p 15.

[67] By 1998 the Commissioner had assisted only one applicant, which did not lead to a court case: *Fairness at Work* Cm 3968 (1998), para 4.31. In 1998 the Commissioner dealt with two applications, both of which were withdrawn, at a cost of £37,345 each: Ewing, 1999: p 296.

industrial action. The Employment Relations Act 1999 broke with the traditional position by making it automatically unfair to dismiss an employee for taking 'protected' industrial action within eight weeks of that employee commencing it, or at a later date if either the employee had stopped taking industrial action within the eight-week period or the employer had failed to take such procedural steps as would have been reasonable to resolve the dispute. However, the scope of 'protected' industrial action is limited, being confined to action that an employee is induced to take by an act which is not actionable by virtue of the statutory immunities that protect dispute organisers. The Employment Relations Act 2004 lengthened the 'protected period' and reduced (but did not remove) the vulnerability to dismissal of those locked-out, but the position of those taking industrial action still remains precarious. Moreover, the status of industrial action as (generally) a breach of contract remains untouched. The fact that the law continued to remain more restrictive than in comparable systems was not regarded as a matter for apology; rather the Labour Government explicitly reaffirmed its commitment to maintain the essential features of the pre-1997 law.[68] In 2010 the CBI called for the tighter regulation of strikes, including a requirement for unions to obtain the support of 40% of balloted members as well as a majority of those voting.[69] At the time of writing the Coalition Government has not indicated an intention to change the law in this area.

The HRA 1998 has the potential to affect the way in which the courts approach the liability of dispute organisers or individual strikers if, as we discuss in para 7.9 above, a right to strike is implied from the right to form and join trade unions.[70] In *Metrobus Ltd v Unite the Union* the Court of Appeal held that it would not be 'prudent' to proceed on the basis that the ECtHR decision in *Enerji Yapi-Yol Sen* had recognised a right to take industrial action as an essential element in the rights afforded by Article 11 of the ECHR.[71] It also refused to derive this right from the jurisprudence relating to other international treaties, such as the ESC and those promulgated by the ILO. Despite the significance accorded by the ECtHR to such jurisprudence in *Demir and Baykara v Turkey*,[72] the Court of Appeal held that such material merely provided 'part of the context for that decision' and was not directly relevant in the instant case.[73] The court considered that the current UK legislation, which was the product of both Conservative and Labour Governments, was 'an interesting example of the practical operation of a member state within the scope of the margin of appreciation'.[74] In the later case of *RMT v Serco Docklands; ASLEF v London Midland*[75] counsel for the union accepted that arguments that the detailed complexity of the balloting

---

[68] *Review of the Employment Relations Act 1999: Government Response*, DTI, 2003, para 3.19.

[69] CBI, 2010.

[70] See Ewing and Hendy, 2010 and see further para 11.53 *et seq* for the implications of the HRA 1998 for picketing. For a more sceptical approach to the argument that ECtHR jurisprudence can achieve an effective right to strike see Hepple, 2010.

[71] [2009] IRLR 851, Lloyd LJ at [35]. Lloyd LJ contrasted the 'full and explicit judgment of the Grand Chamber' in *Demir and Baykara v Turkey*, discussed at 7.9 above, with 'the more summary discussion of the point' in *Enerji Yapi-Yol Sen*. See Ewing and Hendy, 2010, pp 20-27; Dukes, 2010 for criticism of *Metrobus*. In *Ministry of Justice v POA* [2008] IRLR 380, QB the court held that Art 11 did not confer a right to strike.

[72] See para 7.9 above.

[73] Lloyd LJ at [50].

[74] Lloyd LJ at [56].

[75] *RMT v Serco Ltd t/a Serco Docklands; ASLEF v London and Birmingham Railway Ltd t/a London Midland* [2011] IRLR 399.

provisions interfered with the Article 11 right could not be raised again at Court of Appeal level.[76] However, importantly in that case the court emphasised that recognition of the right to strike in Article 11 meant that was no longer sustainable to say (as some courts had said in the past[77] and the employers in this case had argued) that because unions were seeking to take advantage of an immunity the law should be construed strictly against them. The effect of that approach was equivalent to a presumption that Parliament intended that the interests of employers should hold sway unless the legislation clearly dictated otherwise. Giving the judgment of the court, Elias LJ stated that '[t]he statutory immunities are simply the form which the law in this country takes to carve out the ability for unions to take lawful strike action'. The legislation should simply be construed in the normal way, without presumptions one way or the other.[78] This dictum, coupled with other aspects of the decision discussed in paras 11.32 *et seq*, should diminish the opportunity for employers to obtain an interim injunction on the basis of speculative arguments relating to the construction of the legislation itself. However, as we discuss in para 11.49 *et seq*, until the courts adopt a different test for deciding whether an interim injunction should be granted unions will remain vulnerable to industrial action being halted because of novel arguments raised on other grounds such as heads of civil liability outside the scope of the immunities. It should also be noted that, in some circumstances the HRA may add a further weapon to the armoury of employer claimants if industrial action interferes with the exercise of a Convention right such as freedom of expression or even, conceivably, the right to life.[79] As we stated in para 11.3 above the ECJ recognised the right to strike as a fundamental right in EU law, but in a context where, as we discuss in para 11.52 below, it has the potential further to restrict rather than to expand the scope of lawful industrial action.

The average number of disputes in the 1990s was 273, a sharp decline from the 1,129 average of the 1980s.[80] This trend has continued into the twenty-first century; there were 142 stoppages in 2007, 144 in 2008 and a mere 98 in 2009. [81] It is difficult to state precisely the role that the law, as opposed to other social and economic factors, has played in this; the changing structure and composition of the labour market and reduction in union membership are undoubtedly also relevant factors.[82] 'The safest conclusion is that the legal changes were part of a much wider range of developments affecting strike activity' but that they have made the use of industrial action 'a more considered move than it had been in the 1970s'.[83] As we indicate in para 11.42 below, there are considerably more ballots in support of strike action than eventual stoppages.

[76] At the time of writing the RMT has lodged a complaint with the ECtHR that specific statutory requirements relating to the notice unions organising industrial action must give employers and the absolute prohibition on solidarity action are incompatible with Art 11 of the ECHR. The decision of the Court of Appeal in *Serco* above may have lessened the force of some arguments relating to the fomer: see para 11.38 *et seq* below.

[77] For example *Express Newspapers Ltd v McShane* [1979] ICR 210, Lord Denning MR at 218.

[78] Above note 75 at [9].

[79] HRA 1998, Sch 1, Arts 2, 10.

[80] Monger, 2004: p 236.

[81] Data on stoppages are collected by the Office for National Statistics; see www.statistics.gov.uk. For a detailed analysis of 2009 disputes see Hale, 2010.

[82] See P Edwards, 1995: ch 14, esp pp 446–447; J Waddington, 2003b: pp 244–251; Godard, 2011. See also Ben-Israel, 1994: pp 28–29, and ch 1 above.

[83] Dickens and Hall, 2010: p 316.

LIABILITY IN TORT

11.10   As we indicated in para 11.6, those who organise industrial action are highly likely to commit at least one of the 'economic torts'. The purpose of these torts is to protect interests in trade, business or livelihood. The principles which shape them were laid down in a series of decisions dating from the turn of the last century. One fundamental principle, laid down by the House of Lords in *Allen v Flood*[84] is that an intention to harm another will not of itself give rise to liability without some additional element of unlawfulness. Such unlawfulness may take the form either of an interference with a pre-existing right of the claimant or the use of some independently unlawful means. There is one well-established exception to this principle: the tort of lawful means conspiracy, where the act of combination or association between the defendants, when coupled with an intention to harm the claimant, is sufficient for liability even though otherwise lawful means are used. In other respects the principle established by *Allen v Flood* remains essentially intact. Our framework for discussing these torts, which focuses in particular on their implications for industrial action,[85] reflects these principles in analysing first those torts which interfere with a pre-existing legal right; second, those which are based upon the use of unlawful means; and third, the torts of conspiracy. We also examine in this context the statutory right of individuals to seek an injunction to halt industrial action provided that certain conditions are met, a right which, in circumventing entirely the constraints upon the right to bring proceedings contained in the economic torts, expands considerably the range of potential claimants.

It is important to note at the outset that the elements and scope of the economic torts remain unclear in crucial areas, even in the aftermath of two recent decisions in the House of Lords.[86] What is the precise intention which the defendant is required to have in relation to the claimant to give rise to liability? What kinds of action can constitute 'unlawful means'? The responses to these questions by the House of Lords are not consistent as between one tort and another; in particular, the test of what can constitute 'unlawful means' for the purposes of the tort of unlawful means conspiracy is broader in its application than that favoured by the majority of their Lordships for the purposes of causing loss by unlawful means. Many pivotal decisions in this area have arisen out of applications for interim injunctions to prevent the commission or continuance of alleged torts when the court does not explore in detail the relevant legal principles and facts; it is sufficient for the claimant to show that there is a 'serious question to be tried'.[87] This has been a particular feature of industrial action cases because of the interest of employer claimants in arguing that wrongs have been committed which are outside the protection of the statutory immunities: inducing breach of statutory duty, for example. Convincing the court that such a wrong may exist can be sufficient, whereupon it can be added to the legal armoury of employers even though

---

[84] [1898] AC 1.

[85] For the most detailed consideration of the economic torts see Clerk and Lindsell, 2010, as updated, ch 24. See also Elias and Ewing, 1982; Wedderburn, 1986: ch 8; Carty, 1988; Weir, 1997; Deakin *et al*, 2008, ch 15; Carty, 2008, 2010; Deakin and Randall, 2009.

[86] *OBG v Allan; Douglas v Hello! Ltd (No 3)* and *Mainstream Properties Ltd v Young* [2008] 1 AC 1, [2007] IRLR 608 (henceforth 'OBG') and *Total Network SL v HMRC (suing as Commissioners of Customs and Excise)* [2008] 1 AC 1174 (henceforth '*Total Network*').

[87] *American Cyanamid Co v Ethicon Ltd* [1975] 1 All ER 504. Whether or not the injunction will be granted will then depend upon the 'balance of convenience': see further para 11.49 below.

questions may remain as to its elements. The uncertainties which remain following the House of Lords' decisions mean that this situation is likely to continue. The problems for dispute organisers are compounded by the fact that a decision in a wholly different context – litigation between two companies for example – may have fundamental (and unconsidered) implications for the scope of lawful industrial action. Thus labour lawyers must be constantly alert to developments in other areas. With these considerations in mind we now examine the current application of these torts to industrial action.

Torts based upon interference with the claimant's pre-existing rights

(i) Inducing breach of contract

11.11 The most important tort to fall within this heading for the purposes of industrial action is that of inducing breach of contract. The tort originated in the decision of *Lumley v Gye*,[88] in which the claimant successfully argued that the defendant had acted tortiously in persuading a Miss Wagner, who was under contract to sing exclusively at the claimant's theatre for three months, to sing instead at his theatre for a higher fee. The defendant was aware of the terms of the contract between the claimant and Miss Wagner. The tort was applied by the House of Lords in *South Wales Miners' Federation v Glamorgan Coal Co Ltd*[89] in which the Miners' Federation had ordered workers employed by the claimants not to work on certain days in order to maintain the price of coal to which wage levels were linked. In *OBG Ltd v Allan* the liability of the defendant under *Lumley v Gye* was described by the House of Lords as 'accessory to the liability of the contracting party', liability 'depending upon the contracting party having committed an actionable wrong'.[90] As such, it provides the claimant (such as an employer) with a cause of action in tort against the procurer (for example, a trade union) in addition to the contract claim available against the other party to the contract. A claim in tort is particularly valuable in this context because it allows an injunction to be sought against a dispute organiser to desist from specified conduct or to take positive steps to undo a wrong, whereas statute prevents an injunction being granted if it would have the effect of compelling an individual employee to do any work or attend at any place for the doing of any work.[91] In *OBG* the House of Lords affirmed the principle established in earlier cases that liability requires an intention to procure a breach of contract but (unlike the tort of causing loss by unlawful means) the defendant need not intend to cause the claimant harm.[92] 'If someone knowingly causes a breach of contract, it does not normally matter that it is the means by which he intends to achieve some further end or even that he would rather have been able to achieve

---

[88] (1853) 2 E & B 216. For a wide-ranging critique of this decision, see Howarth, 2005.

[89] [1905] AC 239.

[90] [2008] 1 AC 1; Lord Hoffmann at [5]; see also Lord Nicholls at [172]. For the reasons discussed by Deakin and Randall, 2009, the use of the term 'accessory' in this context is confusing and, in so far as it relies on an analogy with the criminal law concept of aiding and abetting a crime, liable to mislead.

[91] TULRCA 1992, s 236.

[92] *Smithies v NATSOPA* [1909] 1 KB 310, 316; *DC Thomson and Co v Deakin* [1952] Ch 646, Jenkins LJ at 696–697 and Morris LJ at 702; *Edwin Hill and Partners (a firm) v First National Finance Corporation Plc* [1988] 3 All ER 801. *Millar v Bassey* [1994] EMLR 44 (and Weir, 1997, App 1), criticised Weir, 1997: pp 18–19 and 38–39, was expressly overruled in *OBG*.

that end without causing a breach'.[93] In previous cases the precise nature of the knowledge of the contract and its terms that the courts had required a defendant to possess had varied. In *OBG* the House of Lords opined that '[i]t is not enough that you know that you are procuring an act which, as a matter of law or construction of the contract, is a breach. You must actually realize that it will have that effect. Nor does it matter that you ought reasonably to have done so.'[94] However this is subject to the 'blind eye' principle articulated by Lord Denning LJ in *Emerald Construction v Lowthian*, cited with approval in *OBG*,[95] that even if the union officials in question 'did not know the actual terms of the contract [between an employer and sub-contractor], but had the means of knowledge – which they deliberately disregarded – that would be enough. Like the man who turns a blind eye... For it is unlawful for a third person to procure a breach of contract knowingly, or recklessly, indifferent whether it is a breach or not'.[96] Given the emphasis in Lord Hoffmann's speech in *OBG* on the defendant's actual state of mind, liability based on recklessness appears to require subjective rather than objective recklessness, ie an inquiry into the defendant's own state of mind rather than that of a reasonable person,[97] an inquiry which could probably take place only at full trial. In *OBG* the House of Lords confirmed that bare interference with a contract which does not amount to a breach (where there is a *force majeure* clause in operation, for example) will not suffice for the purposes of this tort; this followed from the principle that there could be no secondary liability without primary liability.[98]

In the context of industrial action 'inducement' will normally consist of a direct approach but prior to *OMG* a broad interpretation was given to this concept, including 'direct prevention' of performance, such as hiding an employee's tools.[99] In *OBG* the House of Lords regarded direct prevention as more appropriately classified as a form of causing loss by unlawful means.[100] In *Union Traffic Ltd v TGWU*[101] the Court of Appeal held that the mere presence of pickets may be sufficient to constitute an inducement if it is clear that their presence is intended to, and is successful in its object of, inducing breach of a contract. Following *OBG*, establishing the liability of pickets for inducing breach of contract will require much closer analysis of the facts than the court conducted in *Union Traffic*.[102]

It is crucial that the persuasion is directed at one of the parties to the contract, a requirement which was emphasised by the Court of Appeal in *Middlebrook Mushrooms Ltd v TGWU*.[103] The claimant mushroom growers and the union failed to agree on the

---

[93] Lord Hoffmann, above note 86 at [42].

[94] Lord Hoffmann, above note 86 at [39]. On the basis of these principles the defendant in *Mainstream Properties Ltd v Young* was not liable for the tort. Cf *Metropolitan Borough of Solihull v NUT* [1985] IRLR 211, 213, where observations to the contrary were disapproved by Lord Nicholls at [202].

[95] Lord Hoffmann above note 86 at [40].

[96] [1966] 1 WLR 691, 700–701.

[97] Carty, 2008: p 652.

[98] Lord Hoffmann above note 86 at [44]; Lord Nicholls at [174] *et seq*. Cf *Torquay Hotel Co Ltd v Cousins* [1969] 2 Ch 106, 137–138; Lord Diplock in *Merkur Island Shipping Corpn v Laughton* [1983] 2 AC 570 607–608.

[99] *GWK Ltd v Dunlop Rubber Co Ltd* (1926) 42 TLR 376; DC *Thomson and Co v Deakin* above, Jenkins LJ at 696.

[100] Lord Hoffmann above note 86 at [22]–[25]; Lord Nicholls at [176]–[178].

[101] [1989] IRLR 127, 130 Cf the stricter approach to inducement to procure the infringement of copyright by Lord Templeman in *CBS Songs Ltd v Amstrad Consumer Electronics plc* [1988] 2 All ER 484, 496–497: '[g]enerally speaking, inducement, incitement or persuasion to infringe must be by a defendant to an individual infringer and must identifiably procure a particular infringement in order to make the defendant liable as a joint infringer'.

[102] This decision may also require reconsideration in the light of the HRA 1998: see paras 11.53 *et seq*.

[103] [1993] IRLR 232.

employer's proposal to alter overtime arrangements. This led to industrial action followed by the dismissal of 89 workers who participated in it. The union's regional officer announced that union members would attend at supermarkets supplied by the employers and distribute leaflets to prospective customers to inform them of the situation. The leaflet asked customers to support the dismissed strikers by refusing to buy the claimant's mushrooms when shopping at the store. The first instance judge granted an interim injunction restraining the union and three of its officials from organising picketing 'for the purpose of causing or procuring breach or breaches by customers of the ... [claimant] ... company of contracts made now or hereafter between the ... [claimant] ... company and such customers for the supply of mushrooms by the ... [claimant] ... or of interfering with the performance of any such contract'. On appeal, the Court of Appeal discharged the injunction. The leaflet in question was directed to the customers of the supermarket not to the managers and did not therefore fall within the principle of *Lumley v Gye* which required persuasion to be directed at one of the parties to the contract. In this case, by contrast, the suggested influence was exercised, if at all, through the actions or anticipated actions of third parties (the prospective customers) who were free to make up their own minds as to whether to buy the mushrooms.

Given that participation in industrial action, even when preceded by notice, will nearly always constitute a breach of contract (unless, unusually, notice of termination is given) dispute organisers will generally commit the tort of inducing breach of contract in persuading workers to take industrial action.[104] It may also be committed if, for example, a dispute organiser approaches a supplier of the employer in dispute and persuades it not to deliver supplies in breach of an existing contract.[105] There is a defence of justification available for this tort but it has been very narrowly construed. In the *South Wales Miners' Federation*[106] case the House of Lords rejected an argument to the effect that a union could be justified in organising industrial action where it was in the economic interests of its members. This means that the defence is virtually meaningless in the context of industrial action.[107] Indeed, it has succeeded only once in this context in highly unusual circumstances where it was argued that there was a duty to prevent the payment of insufficient wages to chorus girls because this led them to resort to prostitution.[108] It is strongly arguable that inducing employees to stop work for health and safety reasons should be covered by the defence given that there is a statutory right for individuals

---

[104] See para 11.65 *et seq*. TULRCA 1992, s 245 provides that where any person 'holds any office or employment under the Crown on terms which do not constitute a contract of employment', those terms shall nevertheless be deemed to constitute such a contract for the purposes of the torts based upon inducing breach of, or interference with, a contract.

[105] It remains lawful to persuade a person not to make a contract: *Midland Cold Storage Ltd v Steer* [1972] Ch 630. However, the courts have in the past been prepared to countenance granting injunctions (formerly known as *quia timet* injunctions) to prevent respondents from inducing breach of a future contract: see *JT Stratford & Son Ltd v Lindley* [1965] AC 269 at 339 (Lord Upjohn); *Union Traffic Ltd v TGWU* [1989] IRLR 127; see further para 11.48 below. *Quaere* whether this would be the case following *OBG*.

[106] [1905] AC 239. Cf the New Zealand case of *Pete's Towing Services v Northern Industrial Union of Workers* [1970] NZLR 32 where the defence was allowed when a union defendant was putting forward 'fair conditions' and the inducement was 'not being used as a sword to procure financial betterment but as a shield to avoid involvement in industrial discord' (Speight J at 51).

[107] It may be easier, however, to establish in other contexts: see *Edwin Hill & Partners (a firm) v First National Finance Corpn plc* [1989] 1 WLR 225, and for a useful discussion see O'Dair, 1991.

[108] *Brimelow v Casson* [1924] 1 Ch 302, approved in *Pritchard v Briggs* [1980] 1 All ER 294. See also *SOS Kinderdorf International v Bittaye* [1996] 1 WLR 987.

to stop work in these circumstances (see para 5.101)[109] but the caution of the courts in this area makes it difficult to predict whether this would be accepted. Ultimately one can say with confidence only that the application of the statutory immunity is the sole reliable basis upon which there is any defence against liability for this tort.

Prior to *OBG* there was a line of authority in support of an indirect form of the tort of inducing breach of contract, committed where, rather than directly inducing a breach of contract between B and C, A uses unlawful means which produce this result.[110] In *OBG* the House of Lords opined that this form of liability was more appropriately classified as an instance of causing loss by unlawful means and we therefore discuss it under that heading.

(ii) Liability for inducements other than to breach a contract

11.12   In *Lumley v Gye* Erle J stated that 'the procurement of the violation of a right is a cause of action in all instances where the violation is an actionable wrong'.[111] In recent years liability based on 'procurement of the violation of a right' has been extended beyond inducement to breach a contract to inducement to breach an equitable obligation[112] and inducement to breach a statutory duty. These were worrying developments for unions because neither of these wrongs is protected by the statutory immunities. Inducement to breach a statutory duty is a particular concern in public services, where many workers perform duties which their employer is obliged by statute to fulfil. The potential for this form of liability was first suggested by the Court of Appeal in *Meade v Haringey London Borough Council*.[113] Here the claimant parents argued that, by closing its schools during a strike by school caretakers, the authority was breaching its statutory duty to provide education. The majority of the court refused to decide this issue conclusively in interim proceedings but it was suggested that if the authority were in breach the unions, by calling on the employer to close the schools, could be inducing the authority to breach its statutory duty. The application of this tort was circumscribed by the general principle that, for the purposes of inducing breach of statutory duty, the statutory duty in question must be independently actionable at the suit of the claimant (a point not addressed in *Meade*).[114] Whether or not it will be independently actionable depends entirely upon the language and

---

[109] It may also be possible to argue that there is no breach of contract in these (or, indeed, a wider range of) circumstances if the approach in *Barber v RJB Mining (UK) Ltd* [1999] ICR 679 is applied (see A Edwards, 2000), although note also subsequent case law on this point: see further para 4.99.

[110] *DC Thomson & Co Ltd v Deakin* [1952] Ch 646. See also *JT Stratford and Son Ltd v Lindley* [1965] AC 269; *Dimbleby & Sons Ltd v NUJ* [1984] IRLR 67.

[111] (1853) 2 E & B 216, 232, cited with approval by Lords Hoffmann at [3] and Nicholls at [170] in *OBG*, above note 86.

[112] *Prudential Assurance Co Ltd v Lorenz* (1971) 11 KIR 78; *Boulting v ACTT* [1963] 2 QB 606, CA (breach of fiduciary duty); although cf *Metall und Rohstoff AG v Donaldson Lufkin Jenrette Inc* [1990] 1 QB 391. Whether there was a tort of procuring a breach of trust was left open in the Court of Appeal in *Crawley Borough Council v Ure* [1996] QB 13. In *Wilson v Housing Corpn* [1997] IRLR 346, Dyson J held that the tort of inducing unfair dismissal did not exist.

[113] [1979] ICR 494. See also *Associated Newspapers Group Ltd v Wade* [1979] IRLR 201; *Associated British Ports v TGWU* [1989] IRLR 305 (the Court of Appeal decision was reversed by the House of Lords at [1989] IRLR 399 on the point that there was no statutory duty in those circumstances).

[114] *Associated British Ports v TGWU* [1989] IRLR 305. In *X (Minors) v Bedfordshire County Council* [1995] 3 WLR 152, 200–201, Lord Browne-Wilkinson said that Lord Denning MR's dicta in *Meade* supporting a private law claim for breach of statutory duty under the Education Acts had 'no basis in authority'.

purpose of the statute in question; usually it involves showing that the duty was imposed for the benefit of a particular class of persons to which the claimant belongs[115] but whether this requirement will be met is often unpredictable.[116] In *OBG*, Lord Nicholls expressly left open the question of how far the *Lumley v Gye* principle applied to inducing a breach of actionable obligations other than breach of contract.[117]

Far from extending immunity to inducement to breach a statutory duty when the potential for this form of liability was initially shown, the Conservative Government specifically incorporated it in statute. This was first made explicit in the Telecommunications Act 1984,[118] now repealed and replaced by the Communications Act 2003.[119] It is also possible that such a right of action may, in certain circumstances, be available in the event of disruption to supply in the gas, electricity and water industries.[120] A prominent example of this form of liability is the Criminal Justice and Public Order Act 1994 which created a new statutory duty, owed to the Secretary of State, not to induce a prison officer (including a private sector 'prisoner custody officer' and 'custody officer'[121]) to withhold his services as such an officer or to commit a breach of discipline.[122] As well as being actionable by the Secretary of State, breach of this provision could also give rise to an application by a person exercising the statutory right to apply for an injunction to halt industrial action. In 2008 the statutory reference to inducing a prison officer to withhold his services was replaced by inducement to 'take (or continue to take) any industrial action'.[123] 'Industrial action' is defined as:

(a) the withholding of services as a prison officer; or
(b) any action that would be likely to put at risk the safety of any person (whether a prisoner, a person working at or visiting a prison, a person working with prisoners or a member of the public).[124]

---

[115] The other circumstance is where the statute creates a public right and a particular member of the public suffers special damage peculiar to himself or herself: see *Lonrho Ltd v Shell Petroleum Co Ltd (No 2)* [1981] 2 All ER 456, 461–462 (Lord Diplock).

[116] See generally Clerk and Lindsell, 2010, as updated: ch 9; Stanton *et al*, 2002. Note also in this context *Barratts & Baird (Wholesale) Ltd v IPCS* [1987] IRLR 3, discussed Fredman, 1987, Simpson, 1987, where the scope of the statutory duty was at issue.

[117] Above note 86, at [189].

[118] Section 18.

[119] See s 104 for the equivalent provision to s 18 of the 1984 Act.

[120] Gas Act 1986, s 30; Water Industry Act 1991, s 22; Electricity Act 1989, s 27.

[121] CJPOA 1994, s 127(4).

[122] CJPOA 1994, s 127(1), (2). See further G Morris, 1994b: pp 328–329. The pay of prison officers is determined by an independent Pay Review Body: see www.ome.uk.com. The Government has stated that Review Body awards will be departed from only in 'exceptional circumstances': see 336th Report of the ILO Committee on Freedom of Association, March 2005, paras 722–777; *Ministry of Justice v POA* [2008] IRLR 380,QBD. At the time of writing the POA has applied to the ECtHR challenging the prohibition on strikes by prison officers.

[123] CJPOA 1994, s 127(1), as amended by the Criminal Justice and Immigration Act 2008, s 138. The legally-enforceable Joint Industrial Relations Procedural Agreement between the Prison Service and the Prison Officers' Association, which led to the suspension of the statutory restriction, expired in May 2008.

[124] CJPOA 1994, s 127(1A), inserted by the Criminal Justice and Immigration Act 2008, s 138. In *POA v Iqbal* [2009] EWCA Civ 1312 the Court of Appeal held that the Prison Officers' Association was not liable for the tort of false imprisonment to a prisoner who was confined to his cell on a day when prison officers were on strike.

Causing loss by unlawful means

11.13   The tort of causing loss by unlawful means occurs where A uses unlawful means with the intention of causing loss to B.[125] In *OBG v Allan* Lord Hoffmann described the 'essence of the tort' as (a) a wrongful interference with the actions of a third party in which the claimant has an economic interest and (b) an intention thereby to cause loss to the claimant.[126] Unlike inducing breach of contract, this is a tort of 'primary liability' which does not require a wrongful act by anyone else; it is a tort of potentially very wide application. There are three crucial questions in relation to it: first, what acts are capable of constituting unlawful means; second, what is the nature of the intention that needs to be shown on the part of the defendant; and third, whether there is any defence available to this tort. We address these questions below. We also discuss the doctrine of economic duress in this context because of its relationship with facts that may constitute the tort of two-party intimidation.

(i) What acts may constitute unlawful means

11.14   In *OBG* the House of Lords classified the tort of intimidation – a tort based on the *threat* of unlawful acts – as an example of the tort of causing loss by unlawful means.[127] The tort of intimidation is particularly significant in the context of industrial action.[128] It is committed when A threatens B that he or she will commit an act or use means which are unlawful as against B with the intention of causing B to do or refrain from doing something which B is at liberty not to do or to do, so causing damage either to B (two-party intimidation) or C (three-party intimidation). In this context it has long been clear that the application of physical force or violence or the threat of such violence constitutes unlawful means;[129] thus, a threat of violence by a picket against a worker who crossed a picket-line would fall within this category, for example.[130] In the landmark case of *Rookes v Barnard*[131] the implications of this tort for industrial action were made apparent

---

[125] Prior to *OBG* this tort was alternatively styled 'interference with trade or business by unlawful means' , a name preferred by Lord Nicholls in *OBG*, above note 86 at [141]; as Simpson, 2007b: p 470 n 11 states, one of the merits of this name is that it 'points up the need for the interest which the tort is intended to protect to be identified'; see also Deakin and Randall, 2009. In *Nottingham City Council v Unison* [2004] EWHC 893 (QB) the claimant local authority failed to obtain an injunction against the defendant union in relation to industrial action by its Approved Social Worker members on the ground that, although some of the authority's activities could be described as a 'business', its powers and duties in relation to mental health provision could not. In practice it is exceptional for this point to be at issue and we do not explore it further here. As the majority of their Lordships in *OBG* and the court in *Total Network* used the term 'causing loss by unlawful means' we use that terminology here.

[126] Above note 86 at [47]. Lord Hoffmann made clear at [61] that in this analysis he was not referring to two-party intimidation: see further para 11.17 below.

[127] Lord Hoffmann, above note 86, at [47] and [49]; Baroness Hale, [302]; Lord Brown, [319]. Cf Clerk and Lindsell, 2010, as updated, para 24-58 which submits that *OBG* does not affect the separate existence and scope of the tort of intimidation although facts which may give rise to liability for intimidation may also satisfy the requirements of the wider tort, and the discussion in Deakin and Randall, 2009 on this point. See also Lord Neuberger in *Total Network* above note 86 at [216]. We discuss the implications of the possible existence of two separate torts, 'intimidation' and 'causing loss by unlawful means', with different requirements for the concept of unlawful means, in the text, below.

[128] See *Hadmor Productions Ltd v Hamilton* [1982] IRLR 102, 109 (Lord Diplock); *Merkur Island Shipping Corpn v Laughton* [1983] IRLR 218, 222–223 (Lord Diplock).

[129] *Tarleton v McGawley* (1793) Peake 270.

[130] See *Messenger Newspapers Group Ltd v NGA* [1984] ICR 345.

[131] [1964] AC 1129.

when the House of Lords accepted that a threat to break a contract could suffice. Here two shop stewards and a union official threatened an employer, BOAC, with a strike unless a non-unionist, Rookes, was dismissed. The employers terminated Rookes' contract lawfully and with due notice. Rookes then sued the union officers. It was conceded (most unusually) that a no-strike clause was incorporated as a term in the employees' contracts of employment.[132] The court held that, even though Rookes could not have sued BOAC for breach of contract this did not rule out his claim for the tort of intimidation given that BOAC had responded to pressure of an unlawful kind from the union officials who were intending to injure Rookes.[133] The threat to breach the contract of employment constituted intimidation; in Lord Reid's words, Rookes was suing for 'loss caused to him by the use of an unlawful weapon against him – intimidation of another person by unlawful means'.[134] In this respect a threat of a breach of contract was as much unlawful means as a threat of physical harm. As Lord Devlin put it, '[a]ll that matters to the ... [claimant] ... is that, metaphorically speaking, a club has been used. It does not matter to the ... [claimant] ... what the club is made of – whether it is a physical club or an economic club, a tortious club or an otherwise illegal club. If an intermediate party is improperly coerced, it does not matter to the ... [claimant] ... how he is coerced'.[135] The tort of intimidation is likely to be committed whenever industrial action is threatened provided that the action constitutes a breach of contract and it is therefore crucial for potential defendants to ensure that they are protected by the statutory immunities. Although it has been suggested that the breach of contract should be more than a minor one,[136] it is improbable, even if that argument were to be accepted, that in interim proceedings the nature of the breach would be investigated unless it were possible to argue that it may be too minor to cause damage.[137]

Prior to *OBG* the categories of unlawful means that could suffice for the purposes of the 'genus' tort of causing loss by unlawful means had become very wide[138] (although acts which were afforded immunity under the 'golden formula' could not constitute unlawful means).[139] The dividing line was said to be that between 'doing what you have a legal right to do and doing what you have no legal right to do ...'[140] Threats of unlawful action, as well as constituting the tort of intimidation, could also constitute 'unlawful means' for the purposes of the wider tort.[141] It seemed that the torts of *nuisance* (for example, blocking the entrance to an employer's premises) or *trespass*

---

[132] See para 11.67 for discussion of the current position.

[133] The basis of liability of one of the union officials has always been puzzling given that he was not employed by the employers and therefore had no contract he could threaten to break. In *Morgan v Fry* [1968] 2 QB 710 Lord Denning suggested that he not only threatened to induce a breach of contracts of employment (which would have been within the immunities as they then existed) but was also party to the conspiracy of the others to break contracts. However, as Kidner, 1983: p 133, n 85 states, '[t]his explanation is not entirely satisfactory as he would not have been directly liable for conspiracy to injure by unlawful means, but could only be liable for conspiring with others to use the unlawful means of the others'.

[134] [1964] AC 1129, 1168.

[135] [1964] AC 1129, 1209.

[136] *Morgan v Fry* [1968] 2 QB 710, 737–739.

[137] See Howarth and O'Sullivan, 2000: p 911 n 4.

[138] Here we mention only those most material to industrial action. For a wider discussion, see Sales and Stilitz, 1999; Deakin *et al*, 2008: pp 588–595; Carty, 2010: pp 84–98.

[139] *Hadmor Productions Ltd v Hamilton* [1982] IRLR 102.

[140] See *Rookes v Barnard* [1964] AC 1129, Lord Reid at 1168–1169; see also Lord Pearce at 1234; Lord Devlin at 1207, 1209; *DC Thomson and Co Ltd v Deakin* [1952] Ch 646, Lord Evershed MR at 679–682; *Torquay Hotel Co Ltd v Cousins* [1969] 2 Ch 106, Lord Denning MR at 139.

[141] [1982] IRLR 102.

may suffice.[142] In *Associated British Ports v TGWU* the majority of the Court of Appeal considered that inducing breach of a statutory duty may constitute unlawful means, regardless of whether the duty was independently actionable by the claimant.[143] This view had widespread implications for industrial action in public services whose provision was subject to statutory duties, and possibly also for situations where the unlawful means lay in breach of a penal statute.[144] Finally it had been suggested that breach of contract *per se* may constitute unlawful means for the purposes of the wider tort as it may for the tort of intimidation,[145] a view which would mean that individual participants in industrial action could be personally liable in tort to third parties whose businesses were interfered with by the action merely by breaching their own contracts of employment.[146] Moreover, there is no statutory immunity against breach of contract *simpliciter* so acceptance of this approach would have enabled claimants to claim damages from individual workers in circumstances where the dispute organisers were immune from liability, a consequence which would undermine entirely the already narrow freedom to withdraw labour.

In *OBG* the majority of the House of Lords concluded that acts against a third party could constitute unlawful means only if they were actionable by that third party, with the qualification that they would also be unlawful means if the only reason why they were not actionable was because the third party had suffered no loss. 'In the case of intimidation, for example, the threat will usually give rise to no cause of action by the third party because he will have suffered no loss. If he submits to the threat, then as the defendant intended, the claimant will have suffered loss instead. It is nevertheless unlawful means. But the threat must be to do something which *would* have been actionable if the third party had suffered loss.'[147] It was 'not for the courts to create a cause of action out of a regulatory or criminal statute which Parliament did not intend to be actionable in private law'.[148] On this basis, the possibility of liability for causing loss by unlawful means based purely on the commission of a crime would seem to be excluded, as would liability based on a breach of statutory duty where that breach is not independently actionable by the claimant.

---

[142] See *Norbrook Laboratories Ltd v King* [1984] IRLR 200; *Messenger Newspapers Group Ltd v NGA* [1984] IRLR 397.

[143] [1989] IRLR 305; Butler-Sloss LJ at 314; Stuart-Smith LJ at 316; cf the reservations expressed by Neill LJ at 311. Cf also *Michaels v Taylor Woodrow Developments Ltd* [2000] 4 All ER 645, Laddie J. The issue was also discussed (but not resolved) in *Nottingham City Council v Unison* [2004] EWHC 893, QB, [33]–[37]. The House of Lords reversed the Court of Appeal decision in *Associated British Ports* on the ground that the obligation of a registered dock worker to work for his employer was essentially a contractual obligation, and the statutory scheme did not impose a statutory obligation to work independent of, and additional to, this obligation. The case was therefore one of inducing dock workers to break their contracts of employment: [1989] IRLR 399.

[144] However there was weighty authority to the effect that breach of a penal statute should not amount to unlawful means for the purposes of this tort: *Lonrho Ltd v Shell Petroleum Co Ltd (No 2* [1981] 2 All ER 456; *RCA Corporation v Pollard* [1982] 3 All ER 771; *Lonrho Plc v Fayed* [1989] 2 All ER 65. Cf Sales and Stilitz 1999 p: 416, and authorities therein, where it is argued that this should not be a barrier if the requisite intention is shown.

[145] *Barratts & Baird (Wholesale) Ltd v IPCS* [1987] IRLR 3, 10. See further Fredman, 1987; Simpson, 1987: p 506

[146] Note that in view of TULRCA 1992, s 236, which prohibits a court from compelling an employee to do any work by way of an order for specific performance of the contract of employment or injunction restraining a breach or threatened breach, the claimant's remedy in such a case would probably be limited to damages.

[147] Lord Hoffmann, above, note 86, at [49]. Baroness Hale [302] and Lord Brown [319] agreed with this aspect of Lord Hoffmann's opinion. Lord Walker considered that neither the views of Lord Hoffmann or Lord Nicholls were likely to be the 'last word' on this 'difficult and important area' but leant towards those of Lord Hoffmann: [269]–[270].

[148] Lord Hoffmann, above note 86, at [57].

It is also unclear whether a breach of contract must be independently actionable in order to be unlawful means.[149] It would seem to follow from Lord Hoffmann's opinion, and in particular from the dictum that we have just cited, that it must be. However, this appears to contradict the *ratio decidendi* of the earlier House of Lords decision in *Rookes v Barnard*. There was no indication in *OBG* that the House of Lords was overruling *Rookes* (they would have had to invoke the 1966 Practice Statement in order to do so, but did not). As we have just seen, Lord Hoffmann attempted to reconcile his view of the law in *OBG* with the decision in *Rookes* by bringing within the category of unlawful means threats which would have become independently actionable had they been acted on and caused loss to the third party. This is a highly problematic test as it requires the court to consider what the effect of the defendant's conduct would have been in various hypothetical situations, the parameters of which may be ill-defined in certain contexts. One possible interpretation of Lord Hoffmann's opinion is that there are now two variants of the unlawful means tort: the tort of 'intimidation', in which the unlawful means, as they consist of threats, need not be independently actionable in themselves; and the tort of 'causing loss by unlawful means' properly so called, for which independent actionability, involving loss or damage to the third party (or conceivably to the claimant himself or herself, in the so-called 'two-person' version of the tort), is required. In the context of industrial action cases, most of which are decided on an application for an interim injunction and do not involve damages claims, threats are at issue rather than unlawful damage to the third party. Thus the apparently wider definition of unlawful means which may apply in intimidation cases could turn out to be of considerable significance for the scope of industrial action liabilities. A further feature of claims for interim injunctions is that obscure and difficult points of law (as this would appear to be) are sometimes decided in the claimant's favour by virtue of the application of the 'balance of convenience' principle.[150] For these reasons, it may be doubted whether Lord Hoffmann's narrowing the concept of unlawful means in *OBG* will make much difference in cases arising from industrial disputes, as opposed to the commercial claims which were at stake in *OBG*.

Lord Hoffmann placed a further restriction on the ambit of the tort in stating that:

> Unlawful means ... consists of acts intended to cause loss to the claimant by interfering with the freedom of a third party in a way which is unlawful as against that third party and which is intended to caused loss to the claimant. It does not in my opinion include acts which may be unlawful against a third party but which do not affect his freedom to deal with the claimant.[151]

Lord Nicholls, by contrast, considered that 'unlawful means' embraced 'all acts a defendant is not permitted to do, whether by the civil law or the criminal law' and that the approach of the majority represented 'an unjustified and unfortunate curtailment of the scope of this tort'.[152]

---

[149] Cf Lord Nicholls, above note 86, at [151], who assumed that even the 'restricted' view covered breaches of contract.

[150] See *Associated British Ports v TGWU* [1989] IRLR 305(CA) and, more generally on the 'balance of convenience' test, para 11.49, below.

[151] Above note 86 at [51]. Wedderburn, 2007: p 409 considers it no 'accident' that the limitation of liability in the economic torts was advanced in a case concerning commercial parties rather than trade unions.

[152] Above note 86 at [162], [155].

As we indicated in para 11.11 above, all members of the House agreed that what had previously been regarded as the 'indirect' form of the tort of inducing breach of contract[153] – where, rather than directly inducing a breach of contract between B and C, A uses unlawful means which produce this result – should be regarded as an example of causing loss by unlawful means. In relation to industrial disputes a common situation is where A persuades B's employees to take industrial action in breach of their contracts of employment and by these unlawful means produces the result that B is unable to fulfil a commercial contract with C. As Lord Hoffmann recognised in *OBG* the same facts could give rise to both accessory liability under *Lumley v Gye* and primary liability for using unlawful means:

> The areas of liability under the two torts may be intersecting circles which cover common ground. This often happened in 20th century industrial disputes, where, for example, a union would use unlawful means (inducing members to break their contracts of employment) to put pressure upon the employer to break his contract with someone else who was the union's real target. Leaving aside statutory defences, this would make the union liable both under *Lumley v Gye* as accessory to the employer's breach of contract and for causing loss to the target by unlawful means.[154]

However, this intersection did not make *Lumley v Gye* and causing loss by unlawful means the same tort.

(ii) The requisite intention for the tort

11.15   It is clear that the defendant must intend to cause loss to the claimant but the precise nature of that intention remains unclear even after *OBG*. Lord Hoffmann considered that it was 'necessary to distinguish between ends, means and consequences'. 'One intends to cause loss even though it is the means by which one achieved the end of enriching oneself. On the other hand, one is not liable for loss which is neither a desired end nor a means of attaining it but merely a foreseeable consequence of one's actions'.[155] Lord Nicholls, too, considered that a defendant may intend to harm the claimant either as an end in itself, such as where he or she had a grudge against the claimant, or as a means of promoting or protecting his or her own economic interests, but that foresight that the unlawful conduct may or will probably damage the claimant could not be equated with intention.[156] The line between foresight and intention may not always be easy to determine, particularly in the context of industrial disputes.

As Carty comments, the 'end or means to an end' test of itself (without a requirement – rejected by Lord Hoffmann – to 'target' the claimant[157]) has the potential to create a wide area of

---

[153] *DC Thomson & Co Ltd v Deakin [1952] Ch 646*; see also *JT Stratford and Son Ltd v Lindley* [1965] AC 269; *Dimbleby Sons Ltd v NUJ* [1984] IRLR 67.

[154] Lord Hoffmann, above note 86, at [21]. Cf Lord Neuberger in *Total Network v HMRC*, above, note 86, at [216], who stated that the 'so-called economic torts' included 'procuring a breach of contract, unlawful interference, causing loss by unlawful means, intimidation, and conspiracy to injure (or lawful means conspiracy)'.

[155] Above note 86, at [62].

[156] Above note 86, at [164]–[167].

[157] Above note 86, at [60].

liability in the absence of a narrow definition of 'unlawful means'[158]. Dicta in *Total Network* suggest that 'the *OBG* definition of intention for the economic torts may not prove the final word'.[159]

(iii) Defence

11.16 It seems unlikely that there is a defence of justification to this tort; if there is, the circumstances where it could apply would probably be rare.[160]

(iv) Two-party intimidation and economic duress

11.17 As we indicated in para 11.14 above, the tort of intimidation can take the form either of two party-intimidation – where A threatens B that he or she will commit an act or use means which are unlawful as against B with the intention of causing B to do or refrain from doing something which B is at liberty not to do or to do, so causing damage to B – or three-party intimidation, where the damage is caused to C. It has been argued that where a breach of contract constitutes the threat it would be inappropriate to extend the doctrine of *Rookes v Barnard* (a case of three-party intimidation) to two-party intimidation, where both claimant and defendant are parties to the same contract, on the ground that this would enable circumvention of rules of contract law, such as remoteness and mitigation, which limit the extent of contract damages in comparison with tort.[161] In *OBG* Lord Hoffmann expressly left open the question of whether a claimant who had been compelled by unlawful intimidation to act to his own detriment could sue for his loss on the ground that it raised 'altogether different issues'.[162] An alternative means of redress in this context has been presented by the development of the doctrine of *economic duress*[163] which, if found to apply, enables a party to a transaction to claim later that the transaction is invalid because he or she did not truly consent to it and to recover any money paid to the other party. To establish economic duress it must be shown that the victim has been placed in a situation where he or she is deemed to have no practical alternative to agreeing to the demand made by the other party by pressure which the law does not regard as legitimate. The form of the duress may constitute intimidation (or some other tort), but its scope may also go wider in that the action threatened

---

[158] 2008: p 654–655; see also pp 659 and Carty 2010: pp 79-84 for a critique of the rejection of the 'target' test.

[159] Carty, 2008: p 666, citing Lord Neuberger above note 86 at [221], Lord Hope at [44] and Lord Mance at [120].

[160] The possibility of a justification defence was rejected by the House of Lords in *Rookes v Barnard*, above note 131; see also Lord Denning in *Cory Lighterage Ltd v TGWU* [1973] ICR 339, 357 and the discussion in Carty, 2010: pp 100-101. Deakin *et al*, 2008 suggest that there may be a limited justification defence where the defendant was asserting a pre-existing legal right which was at least the equal of the right he or she was interfering with (p 595). See also the discussion of intention, 'targeting' and justification in Deakin and Randall, 2009.

[161] See the discussion in Carty, 2010: pp 159-160; cf Sales and Stilitz, 1999, pp 422–425.

[162] Above, note 86, at [61]. Cf Lord Nicholls at [161]. In *Total Network v HMRC*, however, the distinction raised by Lord Hoffmann was used to support a broader test of unlawful means in the context of unlawful means conspiracy and dicta in that case suggested that a broader test might also apply in the context of two-party causing loss by unlawful means more generally: see Carty, 2008: pp 664–665.

[163] For discussion of the doctrine see J Beatson, 1991: ch 5; Birks and Yin, 1995, and see generally G Jones, 2006, as updated. Note that the statutory limits which govern trade union liability in tort (see para 11.47) do not apply in this context.

need not always be unlawful.[164] The doctrine was applied to industrial disputes in *Universe Tankships Inc of Monrovia v ITWF*[165] where the owners of a ship flying a 'flag of convenience' were able to recover from the International Transport Workers' Federation payments of back pay to the crew and a contribution to the Seafarers' Welfare Fund which they had previously agreed to make under threat of blacking. On appeal to the House of Lords it was conceded by the ITWF that the consequences to the shipowners of the blacking continuing were sufficiently catastrophic to constitute economic duress. It was also conceded that guidance could be found as to the boundary between legitimate and illegitimate pressure from examining whether or not the action was within the statutory immunities as being 'in contemplation or furtherance of a trade dispute'. This meant that the court did not hear argument on either of these points, leaving open the possibility that a remedy based on 'economic duress' may be granted even if the action would be granted immunity in tort,[166] although there are highly persuasive dicta that such an approach would be contrary to legislative policy.[167]

Conspiracy

11.18   There are two forms of conspiracy: *lawful means conspiracy*, which does not require an element of independent unlawfulness, and *unlawful means conspiracy*.[168].

For the tort of *lawful means conspiracy*, the combination of two or more persons is the gist of the wrong, although damage is necessary to complete the cause of action.[169] Thus action which would not be unlawful if taken by one person can become so by virtue of the element of combination. However, it must be shown that the predominant purpose of the conspirators is to injure a third party rather than to serve their own bona fide and legitimate interests (itself an exception to the general principle that motive is irrelevant in relation to the lawful act of an individual).[170] This tort is now of little importance in the context of industrial disputes since the House of Lords decision in *Crofter Hand Woven Harris Tweed Co v Veitch* where the legitimacy of trade union interests (in this case to achieve 100% union membership) was recognised. Officials of the Transport and General Workers' Union and a group of employers with whom the union operated a 'closed shop' agreed to 'black' the supplies of the claimant and other employers on the island of Harris who were outside the closed-shop agreement. The union had members both in the mills and in the docks at Stornoway, the island's main port. The claimant's claim in conspiracy was rejected on the ground that the predominant purpose of the defendants was to protect their

---

[164] In *Universe Tankships Inc of Monrovia v ITWF* [1982] IRLR 200, 212, Lord Scarman seemed to suggest that economic duress could be actionable as a tort *per se*. If this were to be the case the principle of *Allen v Flood* requiring independent unlawfulness would be undermined.

[165] [1983] 1 AC 366. See also *Dimskal Shipping Co SA v ITWF* [1992] IRLR 78.

[166] [1982] IRLR 200, 205 (Lord Diplock), 214 (Lord Brandon). Cf Lord Scarman at 212 who considered that it would be 'inconsistent with legislative policy' to say that acts which were protected by statute from liability in tort could nevertheless amount to duress. See also *Dimskal Shipping Co SA v ITWF* [1992] IRLR 78, 82 (Lord Goff).

[167] See Lords Scarman and Goff, above.

[168] This is the terminology used by the House of Lords in *Total Network*; see also Lord Hoffmann in *OBG* above note 86 at [15].

[169] *Quinn v Leathem* [1901] AC 495.

[170] This requirement was emphasised in *Crofter Hand Woven Harris Tweed Co Ltd v Veitch* [1942] 1 All ER 142; *Lonrho Ltd v Shell Petroleum Ltd (No 2)* [1981] 2 All ER 456, *Lonrho plc v Fayed* [1991] 3 All ER 303.

own economic interests not to injure the claimant. Moreover, it was emphasised that the court would not make its own assessment of whether the action was, in objective terms, likely to achieve the combiners' goal. In the words of Lord Wright, 'The true contrast is … between the case where the object is the legitimate benefit of the combiners and the case where the object is deliberate damage without any such just cause. The courts have repudiated the idea that it is for them to determine whether the object of the combiners is reasonably calculated to achieve their benefit'.[171] In a later decision it was held that the 'lawful interest' of a union extended beyond those which could be exchanged for cash when a boycott by the Musicians' Union of the claimant's ballroom in protest against a 'colour bar' was found to be legitimate.[172] However, the concept does not extend to personal reasons, and members of a union district committee which treated the claimant as expelled from the union (although he was not) and prevented him from getting jobs was found to be based not on the interests of the union but on the 'ruffled dignity' of the defendants.[173]

The 'anomalous' nature of the tort has been acknowledged in a number of cases, particularly given the establishment of large corporations which, although legally single individuals, may wield extensive power.[174] Despite this the House of Lords has affirmed that it is 'too well-established' to be discarded.[175]

In the case of *unlawful means conspiracy* the precise nature of the intent required is not clear. In *Total Network v HMRC*[176] the requisite intention was framed in a variety of ways: the majority required the damage to be 'intentionally inflicted by persons who combine for that purpose'[177] or 'directed at' or 'targeted at' the claimant with an intention to harm him or her,[178] although Lord Neuberger suggested that it would be sufficient if loss to the claimant was 'the obvious and inevitable … result of the sole purpose of the conspiracy'.[179] This difference in emphasis – and the difference between these opinions and those in *OBG* in relation to intention[180] – means that the matter remains open to argument in future cases.

Prior to *Total Network* unlawful means conspiracy was significant because those who could not commit the tort of causing loss by unlawful means or intimidation individually could nevertheless be co-conspirators to the commission of the conspiracy tort.[181] Following that decision, and the decision in *OBG*, the importance of unlawful means conspiracy has been enhanced. As we saw in para 11.14 above, in *OBG* the majority of the House of Lords held that in order to constitute 'unlawful means' for the purposes of the tort of causing loss by unlawful means it was necessary for the act in question to be independently actionable by the claimant. In

[171] [1942] AC 435, 469.
[172] *Scala Ballroom (Wolverhampton) Ltd v Ratcliffe* [1958] 3 All ER 220.
[173] *Huntley v Thornton* [1957] 1 All ER 234, 249.
[174] *Crofter Hand Woven Harris Tweed Co Ltd v Veitch* [1942] 1 All ER 142, 161 (Lord Wright); *Lonrho Ltd v Shell Petroleum Ltd (No 2)* [1981] 2 All ER 456; *Lonrho plc v Fayed* [1991] 3 All ER 303. For more recent support for the tort, see *Total Network v HMRC*, above, note 86, Lord Mance at [122] and Lord Hope at [44].
[175] *Lonrho Ltd v Shell Petroleum Ltd (No 2)* [1981] 2 All ER 456, 464 (Lord Diplock).
[176] [2008] 2 WLR 711.
[177] Above, Lord Walker at [100].
[178] Above, note 176, Lord Hope at [44]; Lord Mance at [119]–[120].
[179] Above, note 176 at [221].
[180] In *Lonrho plc v Fayed* [1991] 3 All ER 303 the House of Lords affirmed that the two causes of action should stand or fall together. See also *Kuwait Oil Tanker Co Sak v Abdul Fattah Sulaiman Khalad Al Badar* [2001] 2 All ER (Comm) 271, para 118; *Michaels v Taylor Woodrow Developments Ltd* [2000] 4 All ER 645; *Meretz Investments NV v ACP Ltd* [2008] 2 WLR 904, Toulson LJ at [174].
[181] See *Rookes v Barnard* [1964] AC 1129, discussed in para 11.14 above.

Total Network a differently-composed House of Lords[182] unanimously held that for the purposes of unlawful means conspiracy this was not the case; crimes (although not all crimes) could constitute unlawful means. The court placed considerable emphasis on the distinction raised by Lord Hoffmann between two and three-party infliction of harm, ie whether the harm was inflicted on the claimant directly or indirectly (via a third-party intermediary) in support of the view that the test of unlawful means need not be the same in each context. Among the issues left unresolved by this decision, there a number of particular relevance to industrial action. First, which crimes will constitute unlawful means and which will not? Dicta in *Total Network* offer little assistance on this point. As we discuss elsewhere in this chapter, there are a range of criminal offences which particular groups of workers may commit in taking industrial action and whereas there may be a reluctance to prosecute in this context employers may be more willing to bring civil proceedings. The tort may also be significant in relation to the organisation of picketing. Second, can a non-actionable breach of statutory duty constitute unlawful means for this purpose?[183] If so, this could have implications for the lawfulness of industrial action in a range of public services. Third, can there be an actionable conspiracy to break contracts *simpliciter*?[184] If so, this would means that any two or more workers who agreed to take industrial action in breach of contract could be liable for conspiracy.

TULRCA 1992, section 219(2) provides that an agreement or combination by two or more persons to do or procure the doing of an act in contemplation or furtherance of a trade dispute is not actionable in tort if the act is one which, if done without any agreement or combination, would not be actionable in tort. Thus, to the extent that unlawful acts extend to non-tortious acts, the statutory immunities should provide protection.[185] However, as we shall see in paras 11.23 *et seq* below, careful navigation is required on the part of dispute organisers to fall within the statutory immunities and in interim proceedings a claimant has only to show that there is a 'serious question to be tried'.[186] Moreover, section 219(2) does not require the act, if done alone, to be actionable in tort *by the claimant*. This means that where it is alleged that organising industrial action involved the commission of a tort which was not actionable by the claimant, such as inducement to breach a statutory duty actionable by a third party, an action for conspiracy to commit that tort may still lie, even for action taken in contemplation or furtherance of a trade dispute.[187] As in the case of the causing loss by unlawful means, acts which are afforded statutory immunity cannot constitute the requisite 'unlawful means' for the purposes of the tort.[188]

---

[182] Lord Walker was the sole member to sit on both cases.

[183] See, for example, the cryptic dictum of Lord Walker in *Total Network* above note 176 at [96] that 'the sort of considerations relevant to determining whether a breach of statutory duty is actionable in a civil suit ... may well overlap, or even occasionally coincide with, the issue of unlawful means in the tort of conspiracy. But the range of possible breaches of statutory duty, and the range of possible conspiracies, are both so wide and varied that it would be unwise to attempt to lay down general rule'.

[184] This point was left open in *Rookes v Barnard* [1964] AC 1129, and in *Total Network* above note 176: see, for example, Lord Hope at [44] ('a conspiracy is tortious if an intention of the conspirators was to harm the claimant by using unlawful means to persuade him to act to his own detriment, even if those means were not in themselves tortious'); Lord Mance at [116] ('... the possibility that the wrongful means might consist of breach of contract').

[185] Simpson, 2007b: p 477.

[186] See further para 11.49 below.

[187] Simpson, 2007b: p 477.

[188] *Hadmor Productions Ltd v Hamilton* [1982] IRLR 102.

The statutory right of action

11.19   TURERA 1993 introduced a new statutory right of action which is notable in circumventing entirely the restrictions on the category of potential claimants erected by the courts at common law.[189] It enables any 'individual' who claims that a 'trade union or other person has done, or is likely to do, an unlawful act to induce any person to take part, or to continue to take part, in industrial action' where 'an effect, or a likely effect … is or will be to prevent or delay the supply of goods or services', or to reduce the quality of those supplied, to him or her to apply to the High Court for an order.[190] The right applies irrespective of whether the individual is entitled to be supplied with the goods or services in question; although, in theory, in the absence of a contract or other document specifying standards it may be hard to measure precisely the reduction in quality which may occur the courts will probably not scrutinise this question too closely.[191] There is no requirement to demonstrate that material loss or damage, or even inconvenience, has been, or would be, suffered as a result of the disruption so that non-collection of rubbish on a particular day, for example, would suffice.[192]

An act to induce any person to take part, or to continue to take part, in industrial action is 'unlawful' for this purpose in two contexts. The first is where it is actionable in tort *by any person*. Thus even if, at common law, the only claimant would be the employer in dispute, any 'individual' who meets the statutory test may apply; there is no requirement to show any intent towards him or her. Moreover, the individual is able to bring proceedings even if the protection of the statutory immunities in relation to the act in question is otherwise lost only in relation to the employer in dispute because the union has failed to comply with the requisite information and notification requirements.[193] The second context in which an act is 'unlawful' is if it is attributed by statute to a trade union and could form the basis of an application by a union member under TULRCA 1992, section 62 that he or she has been, or is likely to be, induced by the union to take part in industrial action which is not supported by a valid ballot. This second category will normally overlap with the first, but its inclusion means that there may be an individual right to bring proceedings in relation to industrial action which does not constitute a breach of contract by those participating in it and which may not, therefore, attract liability in tort. Where the argument is based upon a defect in the ballot this second category of unlawfulness will be the simplest line of argument as there will be no need to demonstrate that any tort has been committed.

Where the court finds the claim 'well-founded' it must make an order requiring the person committing the inducement to take steps to ensure that no (or no further) act is done by him or her to induce any persons to take (or continue to take) part in the industrial action and that no person takes industrial action as a result of any prior inducement. Interim relief may be granted for this purpose and in practice most applications will be dealt with in this way. Until 1999 where the actual or prospective defendant was a trade union, the individual could seek assistance to

---

[189] For a detailed discussion of this right see G Morris, 1993.
[190] TULRCA 1992, s 235A. The normal statutory principles apply in determining whether an act of inducement is done by a union.
[191] In *P v NAS/UWT* [2003] IRLR 307, discussed para 11.27 below, Morison J was willing to assume in favour of P that the industrial action was in breach of contract and that it reduced the quality of teaching that he received (Lord Hoffmann, at [18]).
[192] Baroness Denton, HL Debs Vol 543, col 494, 25 March 1993.
[193] See para 11.32.

bring proceedings from the Commissioner for Protection Against Unlawful Industrial Action, but this office was abolished by the ERelA 1999.[194]

This right of action dramatically extends the range of persons who may apply for an injunction to halt industrial action. In doing so it raises fundamental questions about the autonomy of the parties to the employment relationship (a factor which provoked widespread opposition by employers to its introduction[195]). Modern drafting practice treats 'individual' as excluding corporations, so a corporate claimant will need to rely upon the common law, as will any person seeking damages. However, there is nothing to prevent an individual member of an employer company, including a director, exercising the right *qua* individual. Perhaps surprisingly, at the time of writing little use has been made of this right.[196]

THE LIABILITY OF TRADE UNIONS IN TORT

11.20   As we explained in chapter 10, a trade union can act only through its members or officials. Whether and on what basis a union is fixed with legal liability for their tortious acts depends upon the tort in question. TULRCA 1992, section 20 governs union liability where proceedings in tort are brought against a union (a) on the ground that an act (i) induces another person to break a contract or interferes or induces another person to interfere with its performance, or (ii) consists in threatening that a contract (whether one to which the union is a party or not) will be broken or its performance interfered with, or that the union will induce another person to break a contract or interfere with its performance. It thus covers the torts of inducing breach of contract and intimidation. It also governs conspiracy to commit one of these torts and proceedings for failure to comply with an injunction imposed to restrain further commission of these torts. This form of drafting, in referring to interference with the performance of a contract, reflected the substance of the economic torts prior to the House of Lords decision in *OBG v Allan*[197] where, as we saw in para 11.11, it was held that this form of harm should be classified under the tort of causing loss by unlawful means. As in the case of the golden formula defence, where the same point arises, it is submitted that interference with the performance of a contract within the context of the wider tort should still be covered by this provision.

As we have seen in para 11.10 *et seq*, those who organise industrial action will generally commit at least one of these torts so the statutory formula is likely to apply in this context. It is important to know in advance of any dispute whether the union will be liable because in that event the action must be preceded by a ballot; if it is not, then statutory immunity will automatically be lost (unless the union takes advantage of the limited opportunity to repudiate the act in question). In the case of torts not within the statutory formula, such as nuisance, liability is determined by principles derived from the common law. Fixing liability to the union does not absolve individuals from personal liability,[198] but proceedings are likely to be brought against the union where this is possible, although individuals may be joined as co-defendants.

---

[194] Section 28. See further para 11.9.

[195] See G Morris, 1993.

[196] It was relied upon, however, in *P v NAS/UWT* [2003] UKHL 8, [2003] IRLR 307, discussed in para 11.27 below.

[197] [2008] 1 AC 1, [2007] IRLR 608.

[198] This is made explicit in TULRCA 1992, s 20(5).

(i) The statutory scheme of liability

11.21   TULRCA 1992 attributes liability to a union where an act was 'authorised' or 'endorsed' by one of three categories of persons.[199] The first is any person empowered by the union rules to do, authorise or endorse such acts. The term 'rules' is defined to mean both the written rules of the union and any other written provision forming part of the contract of membership.[200] Custom and practice in the union which has not been reduced to writing is therefore excluded in this context.[201] Second, regardless of the union rules, there is liability for the 'principal executive committee', president or general secretary of the union.[202] Last, again regardless of the rules, there is liability for any other 'committee' of the union[203] or any other official, whether employed by it or not. The definition of 'official' means that shop stewards and other lay officials fall within its scope provided that their election or appointment is in accordance with the union rules.[204] This means that the union is potentially liable for the acts of a very wide range of individuals irrespective of any limitations in its rules; action which would be viewed internally as 'unofficial' is nevertheless deemed to be its responsibility, the underlying purpose being to encourage greater control by unions over their officials' actions.[205] Moreover, the legislation attributes to an official any act done, authorised or endorsed by any 'group' (ad hoc or otherwise) of which he or she was at the material time a member whose purposes included organising or coordinating industrial action or an act by any member of such a group.[206] This means that the official need not personally have been involved in taking the decision to take industrial action – it is sufficient that he or she was a member of the group at the 'material time' – and, indeed, he or she may conceivably have participated in the activity of the 'group' in order to discourage this decision.[207]

In relation to an act by the third category of persons only, the union can avoid liability if the act in question is repudiated by the executive, president or general secretary as soon as reasonably practicable after coming to the knowledge of any of them.[208] Whether this happens 'as soon as reasonably practicable' will be a question of fact; in practice many disputes organised at local level begin and end very rapidly and may be over before repudiation has an opportunity to take place. 'Repudiation' involves an 'open disavowal and disowning of the acts of the officials concerned'.[209] The union must follow a rigid procedure to effect this. First, written notice of repudiation must

---

[199] TULRCA 1992, s 20(1)–(4). 'Authorised' and 'endorsed' are not defined in the statute; the term 'authorisation' is generally used when industrial action is approved before it commences; endorsement when it is authorised at a later stage. In *Gate Gourmet London Ltd v TGWU* [2005] IRLR 881, QBD, Fulford J concluded , in the context of an application for an interim injunction, that it was 'arguable', given their probable level of knowledge as to what was occurring, that specific officials had authorised tortious activities.

[200] TULRCA 1992, s 20(7).

[201] *British Railways Board v RMT* (QBD, 17 September 1992, unreported).

[202] See para 10.14 above for definitions of these terms.

[203] Any group of persons constituted in accordance with the union rules is a 'committee': TULRCA 1992, s 20(3).

[204] TULRCA 1992, s 119.

[205] Research showed that unions were exercising a greater degree of centralised control over members' actions even before EA 1990 widened the scope of potential liability: see Martin *et al*, 1991. See also Undy *et al*, 1996: ch 6.

[206] See *Gate Gourmet London Ltd v TGWU* [2005] IRLR 881, QBD.

[207] Although the Conservative Government denied that liability would attach in this situation (see Lord Strathclyde HL Debs, Vol 521, col 1250, 23 July 1990) this is not precluded by the statute.

[208] TULRCA 1992, s 21(1). Gall, 2006: p 336 states that unions 'have become expert in informally and secretly organising unofficial strikes while formally and visibly disavowing the actions though repudiation.' He reports that the overwhelming majority of unofficial strikes last for less than two days.

[209] *Express and Star Ltd v NGA* [1985] IRLR 455, 459.

be given 'without delay' to the committee or official whose act is attributable to the union.[210] Second, the union must 'do its best' to give individual written notice of the fact and date of repudiation, without delay, to every member who the union has reason to believe is taking part, or 'might' otherwise take part, in the action as a result of this act and to the employer of every such individual.[211] Trying to decide which individuals 'might' participate in the action, particularly where the call comes from a relatively junior or maverick official, may be highly problematic. The notice given to members must include the following words:

> Your union has repudiated the call (or calls) for industrial action to which this notice relates and will give no support to unofficial industrial action taken in response to it (or them). If you are dismissed while taking unofficial industrial action, you will have no right to complain of unfair dismissal.[212]

As well as ensuring that they comply with this initial procedure, unions must also be vigilant about their subsequent activities; repudiation may be rendered ineffective if, at any time in the future, the executive, president or general secretary behave in a manner inconsistent with the purported repudiation.[213] If this were to happen it seems that this would expose the union to liability at the instance of any person who would have had a claim against it had repudiation not occurred.

The effect of a union repudiating liability is to make the industrial action 'unofficial' as from the end of the next working day after the day on which repudiation takes place.[214] As we describe in para 11.85 below, employees participating in unofficial industrial action are denied the possibility of protection against even selective dismissals unless it is shown that they were dismissed for one of a narrow range of reasons. In any given situation, therefore, a union will have to consider carefully the consequences before embarking on repudiation which, while it may save union funds, puts members' jobs at risk and may create damaging splits among the membership, particularly if the grievance is thought justified or has implications for other workers. It is, of course, open to the union to repudiate but immediately call a ballot on the issue, although it would be advisable in that event for it to broaden the scope of the dispute, so rendering it a different dispute, to avoid the difficulty that immunity could be lost because it had 'called' the action before the date of the ballot, albeit that the call had subsequently been repudiated (see para 11.44). Where a purported repudiation by a union is deemed subsequently to be ineffective by a tribunal, it seems that the industrial action will remain 'non-unofficial' for unfair dismissal purposes and employees will retain the protection against selective dismissal.[215]

---

[210] TULRCA 1992, s 21(2)(a).

[211] TULRCA 1992, s 21(2)(b).

[212] TULRCA 1992, s 21(3).

[213] TULRCA 1992, s 21(5). They will be treated as so behaving if they fail to confirm the repudiation in writing 'forthwith' on a request made within three months of the purported repudiation by a party to a commercial contract whose performance was at risk of interference from the act in question who has not already received written notice of it: s 21(6).

[214] TULRCA 1992, s 237(4). In *Balfour Kilpatrick Ltd v Acheson* [2003] IRLR 683 the EAT held that 'the end of the next working day' meant midnight on the following working day, not the end of the period which constitutes the normal working hours for the day in question. That case also illustrates the fact that industrial action may be 'official' in relation to some employees but 'unofficial' in relation to others.

[215] *Balfour Kilpatrick Ltd v Acheson* [2003] IRLR 683.

(ii) Liability at common law

11.22   For torts not specified in the statute, such as nuisance, union liability is determined according to principles established by the common law. These dictate that the union is liable for the acts of individuals acting with its express or implied authorisation, regardless of whether they are its employees. The concept of authorisation in this context was interpreted broadly in the leading case of *Heatons Transport (St Helens) Ltd v TGWU*.[216] The defendant union had a policy that the loading and unloading of containers carried at sea should be reserved for dock workers registered under the statutory National Dock Labour Scheme then in operation and that lorries of firms refusing to honour this policy should be 'blacked'. Shop stewards at Liverpool and Hull established unofficial committees at their own initiative to direct the blacking although such committees were not provided for in the union rule book. The union argued that it could not be liable for the shop stewards' acts. The House of Lords rejected this argument on the ground that the stewards had general implied authority and discretion to act on the union's behalf in protecting members' wages and working conditions in the circumstances in question and they were promoting general union policy in doing this. The court emphasised that in determining the scope of the authority of an official to bind the union regard must be had both to the written rule book and to custom and practice, which could have the effect of modifying the union's rules as they operated in practice or compensating for the absence of formal rules. To avoid liability in this situation the union would have needed to withdraw the authority of the stewards to continue organising the industrial action 'in terms which would be reasonably understood by them as forbidding them to continue',[217] possibly by withdrawing their credentials and, if necessary, taking disciplinary action.

The approach to liability in *Heatons*, to the extent that it pays regard to the wider circumstances, and in particular whether officials are acting in accordance with union policy,[218] accords greater respect to internal union practices than the statutory approach. Nevertheless, it may require unions to go to extreme lengths to disassociate themselves from the actions of their members. The measures which the courts may require to avoid liability for the acts of members and officials who commit a tort in the course of picketing were considered by Stuart-Smith J in *News Group Newspapers Ltd v SOGAT '82 (No 2)*[219] where the liability of unions for, *inter alia*, the torts of public and private nuisance was at issue. Stuart-Smith J accepted that unions were not liable merely by organising a march or picketing during the course of which tortious acts are committed by third parties even though such acts can be foreseen. However, he held that unions may be taken to have authorised the commission of a nuisance or other tort or to have continued a nuisance[220] where they continue to organise events which in the light of experience constitute a tort, in the knowledge or presumed knowledge that such torts are being committed by those whom they organise. In this case the conduct of the pickets had been repeated regularly and must have been well known to the unions. The court rejected the argument that the union lacked sufficient control over its members to restrain commission of the torts in question; they

---

[216] [1972] ICR 308.
[217] [1972] ICR 308, 404 (Lord Wilberforce).
[218] On the importance of this element, see *General Aviation Services (UK) Ltd v TGWU* [1976] IRLR 224.
[219] [1986] IRLR 337.
[220] The concept of 'continuing' a nuisance, developed in the context of private nuisance in *Sedleigh-Denfield v O'Callaghan* [1940] AC 880, was applied by Stuart-Smith J also to public nuisance.

had failed to discipline or threaten to discipline those who persistently flouted union instructions that picketing was to be peaceful, nor had they forbidden them to act as official pickets. If the union could not exercise sufficient control they might have to desist from picketing altogether or organise it elsewhere. On the basis of this reasoning unions need to curtail or abandon picketing altogether to avoid liability for their members' acts.

THE SCOPE OF STATUTORY IMMUNITY

11.23   As we saw in para 11.10 *et seq*, the organisation of industrial action will almost invariably give rise to civil liability at common law. It then becomes necessary to ask whether that liability is removed because the tortious act in question is protected by the statutory immunities. This requires two elements to be satisfied. First, there must be statutory immunity for the tortious acts in question. We list the torts which are accorded immunity in para 11.24 below. Second, the act must fall within the formula which sets the perimeter of legitimate industrial action: it must have been done 'in contemplation or furtherance of a trade dispute'. We analyse this formula in para 11.25 *et seq*. Even if the act satisfies these two requirements, however, it may still be excluded from the statutory protection for one of several reasons. We examine these in para 11.30 *et seq*. They are, in outline: if the action constitutes unlawful secondary action or unlawful picketing; if its purpose is to enforce trade union membership or to require the employer to pursue a 'union-only' or 'recognition-only' practice in supply contracts; if it is related to the dismissal of employees in connection with unofficial industrial action; or, if a union is legally responsible for the action, if the statutory balloting requirements have not been followed. In addition, protection is excluded in relation to the employer in respect of whom the default occurs (and in relation to an individual exercising the statutory right of action) when a union fails to provide specified pre-ballot information, notify it of the ballot result, or give notice before industrial action starts. It is readily apparent from this list that unions have to steer a careful course in order to remain within the statutory protection.

Torts which are granted statutory immunity

11.24   The legislation states that an act done by a person in contemplation or furtherance of a trade dispute is not actionable in tort on the ground only (a) that it induces another person to break a contract or interferes or induces another person to interfere with its performance; or (b) that it consists in his or her threatening that a contract (whether one to which he or she is a party or not) will be broken or its performance interfered with, or that he or she will induce another person to break a contract or to interfere with its performance.[221] In addition, an agreement or combination by two or more persons to do or procure the doing of an act in contemplation or furtherance of a trade dispute is not actionable in tort if the act is one which, if done without any such agreement or combination, would not be actionable in tort.[222] This means

---

[221] TULRCA 1992, s 219(1).
[222] TULRCA 1992, s 219(2).

that there is statutory immunity for the torts of inducing breach of contract, intimidation based upon the threat to break a contract, lawful means conspiracy, and unlawful means conspiracy where the unlawful means are not themselves actionable in tort. In *Hadmor Productions Ltd v Hamilton*[223] the House of Lords affirmed that an act which was not actionable in itself by virtue of the legislation may not constitute the requisite 'unlawful' means for torts such as causing loss by unlawful means or unlawful means conspiracy.[224] The reference in the legislation to interference with the performance of a contract reflected the substance of the economic torts prior to the House of Lords decision in *OBG v Allan*[225] where, as we saw in para 11.11, it was held that this form of harm should be classified under the tort of causing loss by unlawful means. It is submitted that interference with the performance of a contract within the context of the wider tort should still be covered by this provision.

This method of listing torts, rather than of giving a comprehensive immunity against civil liability, means that those organising industrial action have always been vulnerable to new nominate torts being created. As we saw in para 11.10, it is a sufficient argument on an interim application that there is a serious issue to be tried; if the claimant can convince the court that a wrong has been committed which lies outside the scope of the immunity the issue shifts to the balance of convenience. Following *Rookes v Barnard*,[226] where, as we saw, the House of Lords accepted that a threat to breach a contract could be sufficient to constitute the tort of intimidation, the legislature extended protection to this tort.[227] Since 1979, however, an equivalent response to other extensions of the common law has not been forthcoming. Thus there is no statutory protection afforded against torts based upon breach of statutory duty, for example; nor is there any longer any immunity against breach of contract *simpliciter*,[228] an omission which would be highly significant if it were to be accepted as constituting the requisite unlawful means for the tort of causing loss by unlawful means.[229] We discuss the scope of any immunity which may apply to torts committed in the course of picketing, such as nuisance, in para 11.56 below.

The concept of a 'trade dispute'

11.25 A 'trade dispute' is defined as 'a dispute between workers and their employer which relates wholly or mainly' to one or more of the matters which now constitute the statutory subject-matter of 'collective bargaining'.[230] This definition requires consideration both of the parties to the dispute and its purpose.

---

[223] [1982] IRLR 102.

[224] Before 1980 this was specifically stated in the legislation (Trade Union and Labour Relations Act 1974, s 13(3), repealed by the Employment Act 1980).

[225] [2008] 1 AC 1, [2007] IRLR 608.

[226] [1964] AC 1129.

[227] TDA 1965.

[228] TULRA 1974, s 13(3) declared '[f]or the avoidance of doubt' that a breach of contract in contemplation or furtherance of a trade dispute shall not be regarded as the doing of an unlawful act or use of unlawful means for the purpose of establishing liability in tort. This provision was repealed by EA 1980.

[229] See *Barretts & Baird (Wholesale) Ltd v IPCS* [1987] IRLR 3, and the discussion in para 11.14 above. For the reasons we discuss para 11.14 we do not consider that breach of contract is capable of constituting unlawful means for the three-party version of the tort. On breach of contract and unlawful means conspiracy, see para 11.18 above.

[230] TULRCA 1992, s 244(1).

(i) The parties to a 'trade dispute'

11.26   It is consistent with the definition of a trade union that 'workers',[231] not merely 'employees', may be party to a trade dispute (although at the time of writing only employees have any chance of being protected against dismissal). Moreover, in this context the term 'worker' extends beyond those employed at the time of the dispute to former workers if their employment was terminated in connection with the dispute or where the termination was one of the circumstances giving rise to it.[232] At one time there was statutory provision that a dispute involving a union should be treated as one to which workers were a party; although now repealed it is probably the case that a union can be party to a dispute along with its members as long as it is representing them (but not if it is acting independently or has no members in that employment).[233]

The need for a dispute to be between 'workers and their employer' imposes five important limitations. First, it excludes cases where workers are employed through an intermediary company which is not their true 'employer'. To date the courts have refused to 'lift the corporate veil' and look at where power is centred in reality in the context of industrial action.[234] Second, it excludes situations where the employer's own workers are not in dispute with it, for example if picketing is organised at an employer's premises because it employs low-paid foreign workers who are not themselves objecting to their conditions.[235] Third, it excludes disputes between workers, such as demarcation or inter-union disputes, although circumstances where this does not spill into a dispute with the employer may be rare. Fourth, it excludes disputes which are characterised as being with an employer to whom workers may at some future date transfer. In *University College London NHS Trust v UNISON*[236] Trust employees threatened strike action because the Trust refused to guarantee that those of its employees transferred to a private sector consortium, and new employees engaged by the consortium, would have equivalent terms and conditions to those not transferred. The Court of Appeal rejected the argument that this could be regarded as a dispute between the employees and their current, rather than their so-far-unidentified new, employer. This conclusion was reached despite the fact that the current employer had the power to specify in a contract with the consortium the terms and conditions which would apply to the employees when employed by their new employer.[237] Last, it excludes industrial action against the government with three exceptions: where the government is the direct employer; if a settlement requires a minister to exercise a statutory power (such as the powers of the Secretary of State to

---

[231] See para 3.33 *et seq* above.

[232] TULRCA 1992, s 244(5).

[233] See *NALGO v Bolton Corpn* [1943] AC 166, (Lord Wright); *Associated British Ports v TGWU* [1989] IRLR 291, 300 (Millett J).

[234] *Dimbleby and Sons Ltd v NUJ* [1984] IRLR 161.

[235] Cf *NWL Ltd v Woods* [1979] IRLR 478. Before 1982 defendants could claim immunity in disputes between workers and any employer.

[236] [1999] IRLR 31. An application to the ECtHR that British law violated Art 11 of the ECHR was declared inadmissible; the prohibition on the union's ability to strike could in the circumstances regarded as 'necessary in a democratic society' for the protection of the rights of their current employer under Art 11(2).

[237] As R Davies, 2004 states at pp 101–102, UNISON achieved many of its objectives when the government introduced the 'Retention of Employment Model' (REM) in the NHS and the Code of Practice on Workplace Matters in Local Authority Service Contracts; see also G Morris, 2004a: pp 170–172. However the use of the REM has been greatly restricted since July 2009 and the Code of Practice referred to was withdrawn on 23 March 2011 with immediate effect in respect of future contracts.

make orders relating to teachers' pay and conditions of employment);[238] or the dispute relates to matters which have been referred to a joint body on which there is statutory provision for a minister to be represented.[239] These circumstances aside, in the light of the close relationship between the industry and the labour market, on the one hand, and government economic policies on the other, the line between action against the government and against an individual employer may sometimes be difficult to draw. As Kahn-Freund asked some years ago:

> Is it not true that, not only in publicly owned industries, governmental decisions on wages policies – whether statutory or not – on credits and on subsidies, on the distribution of industry ... and on a thousand other things, affect the terms and conditions of employment at least as much as the decisions of individual firms? Where is the line between a strike to induce an employer to raise, or not to reduce, wages and a strike to press the government for measures which would enable the employer to do so?[240]

To date the courts have not been faced with this argument in this form[241] although, as we indicate below, related problems may arise in determining a dispute's predominant purpose.

(ii) The purpose of a 'trade dispute'

11.27 The purposes of a 'trade dispute' are now co-extensive with the definition of the objects of 'collective bargaining' as statutorily defined (although originally no such link was made[242]). As we indicated in para 7.27, it is in the context of industrial action that the courts have been called upon to clarify the scope of some of these objects. They fall into seven categories:

(i) *Terms and conditions of employment, or the physical conditions in which any workers are required to work.* It has long been clear that the expression 'terms of employment' is not confined to contractual terms,[243] and in *P v NAS/UWT* the House of Lords affirmed that the 'composite' phrase 'terms and conditions of employment' ('chosen to avoid arguments as to whether something should properly be described' as a 'term' or 'condition') should be given a 'broad meaning'.[244] Here, the court held that a dispute about whether teachers should be required to comply with the head teacher's direction to teach P, an allegedly disruptive pupil, was about their 'terms and conditions of employment'. In reaching this conclusion the court rejected the claimant's argument that this was a dispute about the application of a rule rather than the rule itself and was not, therefore, about terms and conditions; Parliament could not have intended the immunities to turn upon such fine distinctions which were, in any event, impossible to make. 'A dispute about what the workers

---

[238] These powers are now contained in the Education Act 2002, s 122; see *Wandsworth London Borough Council v NAS/UWT* [1993] IRLR 344.

[239] TULRCA 1992, s 244(2).

[240] P Davies and M Freedland, 1983: p 317.

[241] However, see *Associated British Ports v TGWU* [1989] IRLR 291 for a related discussion.

[242] Auerbach, 1990.

[243] In *British Broadcasting Corpn v Hearn* [1977] IRLR 273 Lord Denning MR stated (at 275) that it could also cover those terms used and applied by the parties in practice or habitually or by common consent without ever being incorporated into the contract, and this was approved by Lord Diplock in *Hadmor Productions Ltd v Hamilton* [1982] IRLR 102, 108.

[244] [2003] IRLR 307, at [24] (Lord Hoffmann, with whose opinion Lords Hobhouse, Scott and Walker agreed).

are obliged to do or how the employer is obliged to remunerate them, at any level of generality or particularity, is about terms and conditions of employment.'[245] Moreover, the fact that not all of those taking action are personally affected by the subject-matter of the dispute does not take the dispute outside the immunities:[246] '... the representative function of trade unions would be set at nought if it were the case that employees could not take industrial action in relation to an attempt to change terms and conditions of employment of only some of them'.[247] However, 'terms and conditions of employment' does not cover terms which regulate a relationship between an employer and a third party acting as principal (rather than as agent for the employee) and for which no provision is made in the terms under which the employee works for the employer, such as the clauses of a collective agreement which relate solely to the relationship between a trade union and employer.[248] Moreover, in *University College London Hospital NHS Trust v UNISON*, discussed above, the Court of Appeal held that 'terms and conditions' were confined to those under which employees worked for their existing employer, and refused to characterise the dispute as one with the existing employer over future employment conditions; rather, it was with the new, to-date-unidentified, employer.[249]

(ii) *Engagement or non-engagement, or termination or suspension of employment or the duties of employment, of one or more workers.* As well as dismissals which have already taken place the courts have held that this includes fear of future dismissals, including redundancies; there is no need for dismissal notices to have been issued.[250]

(iii) *Allocation of work or the duties of employment as between workers or groups of workers.* This is limited to demarcation disputes between workers or groups of workers employed by the same employer.[251] Thus, if an employer's business is divided into separate companies, which may be operating on the same premises (a manufacturing and a distribution division, for example), a dispute over the allocation of work between those companies would not be a 'trade dispute'.

(iv) *Matters of discipline.*

(v) *A worker's membership or non-membership of a trade union* (although see now para 11.30 below).

---

[245] Lord Hoffmann above, at [28]
[246] *British Telecommunications plc v CMU* [2004] IRLR 58.
[247] Above, at [18] (Stanley Burnton J).
[248] *Universe Tankships Inc of Monrovia v ITWF* [1982] IRLR 200, 206 (Lord Diplock).
[249] [1999] IRLR 31; see also note 236 above. Hendy, 2000 argues (p 58) that this decision may require industrial action to be confined to existing terms and conditions, as well as being with an existing employer, so removing immunity from any worker seeking to change those terms, for example by pursuing a wage claim. However, it is far from clear that the decision does have this consequence, and in any event a dispute over higher wages could be regarded as a dispute over the unsatisfactory nature of the existing terms; the fact that it may lead to increased pay does not prevent the current pay level being the issue in dispute.
[250] *Hadmor Productions Ltd v Hamilton* [1982] IRLR 102; *General Aviation Services (UK) Ltd v TGWU* [1975] ICR 276; *Health Computing Ltd v Meek* [1980] IRLR 437.
[251] *Dimbleby & Sons Ltd v NUJ* [1984] IRLR 161.

(vi) *Facilities for officials*[252] *of trade unions.*

(vii) *Machinery for negotiation or consultation, and other procedures, relating to any of the above.* This includes the recognition by employers or employers' associations of the right of a trade union to represent workers in such negotiation or consultation or in the carrying out of such procedures.

11.28   The statute requires the dispute to relate 'wholly or mainly' to one of these matters. This requires a court to examine its predominant purpose.[253] Disputes which are judged to be furthering a 'political' or other non-industrial purpose, such as a personal feud or grudge,[254] will have no immunity. In this context, as in relation to determining the parties to a dispute, the line between the 'political' and the industrial may be difficult to draw. Particular problems may arise in public services; for example, disputes over matters such as wages or job cuts, which are clearly within the definition of a trade dispute, often involve challenging broader government policies, such as incomes policies, reductions in public spending or privatisation. At the time the predominant purpose test was introduced,[255] ministers maintained that they did not intend to jeopardise the lawfulness of public sector disputes concerning pay, conditions or jobs, even if they did challenge government policies. However, in interim proceedings, doubt about the predominant purpose of a dispute may be sufficient to persuade a court to grant an interim injunction. To date there have been five major decisions where the predominant purpose of a dispute has been at issue.[256]

Mercury Communications Ltd v Scott-Garner and the POEU[257] took place against the background of the breaking of the monopoly over the operation of telecommunications. The POEU instructed its members employed by the existing monopoly supplier, British Telecommunications (BT), not to connect Mercury, a private company, to the BT network. The union argued that it had issued this instruction in furtherance of a dispute with BT over employees' job security which, it claimed, would be put at risk if Mercury was connected. The Court of Appeal rejected this argument and held that the dispute was primarily concerned with the union's opposition to government policies of liberalisation and privatisation of the telecommunications industry. In reaching its decision the court was influenced heavily by evidence of a Job Security Agreement between the union and the employer which the union had not sought to invoke, a fact which pointed away from the union having a genuine concern about jobs.

The decision in *Mercury* does not mean that all industrial action relating to the consequences of privatisation will be unlawful, but unions need to be careful to ensure that it is linked sufficiently closely with one of the matters that characterise a trade dispute; had the union invoked the Job Security Agreement it might have been able to sustain the argument that, while the dispute took

---

[252] Defined TULRCA 1992, s 119.

[253] *Mercury Communications Ltd v Scott-Garner and the POEU* [1983] IRLR 494, CA.

[254] See, for example, *Huntley v Thornton* [1957] 1 WLR 321.

[255] EA 1982 amended TULRA 1974 (now repealed) which provided that the dispute had only to be 'connected with' a collective bargaining matter; a court had only to be satisfied that a collective bargaining matter was genuinely at issue: see *NWL Ltd v Woods* [1979] IRLR 478.

[256] In 1987 the Department of Employment secured an injunction against an officer of the Civil and Public Services Association who organised a strike in opposition to an ethnic monitoring exercise in unemployment benefit offices on the ground that this was a 'political' issue but no full judgment was given. For a recent discussion of the issues see Ewing and Hendy, 2011.

[257] [1983] IRLR 494.

place against the background of privatisation, its predominant purpose was concern about the risk to jobs. *Mercury* can be contrasted with *Associated British Ports v TGWU*,[258] where the union called a strike in furtherance of its demand from port employers for new national conditions in the docks after the government had announced the introduction of legislation to abolish the statutory National Dock Labour Scheme which provided that only registered dock workers could be employed in the docks, a measure which directly affected their terms and conditions of employment. Millett J rejected the employers' argument that this was not a 'trade dispute'; whereas in *Mercury* the matters of genuine industrial concern were only aspects of a 'wider political dispute', in this case 'the union's concern for the future employment conditions of former registered dock workers' could not be so characterised.[259] He also roundly rejected the contention that the dispute with the employers was manufactured as a spurious pretext for a dispute with the government; this was a 'serious calumny', 'wholly without substance'.[260] The link between legislation abolishing the scheme and dockers' terms and conditions of employment was inextricable, and given that the employers had made clear their intention to deprive dockers of valued features of their employment relationship which the scheme had bestowed, there was a genuine dispute between them. Although this case demonstrates that linkage with government policies need not preclude a 'trade dispute', it was pointed out by one commentator that the unions' success was 'secured only by very deliberate action' to ensure that there was the necessary evidence to substantiate its case.[261]

Third, in *Wandsworth London Borough Council v NAS/UWT* the union had instructed its members to boycott 'all the unreasonable and unnecessary elements of assessment connected with the national curriculum'. The Court of Appeal dismissed the employers' argument that this was a dispute about the content of work which the national curriculum required teachers to undertake; rather it was about teachers' working time, and therefore mainly related to terms and conditions of employment. In reaching this conclusion the court attached 'considerable importance' to the wording of the question put to members in the ballot which preceded the industrial action, which asked them whether they were willing to take action 'to protest against the excessive workload and unreasonable imposition made upon teachers, as a consequence of national curriculum assessment and testing'.[262]

Fourth, in *University College London Hospital NHS Trust v UNISON*[263] the employer sought to argue that the threatened industrial action over its refusal to guarantee that staff transferred to a private consortium, and those subsequently employed by the consortium, would be employed on terms at least as favourable as those applicable to staff it continued to employ, had a political objective. This argument was rejected by the Court of Appeal, although the more limited objective ascribed to the union of alleviating the consequences of the Private Finance Initiative was found, on the facts, not to fall within the terms of TULRCA 1992, section 244(1).

---

[258] [1989] IRLR 291, Ch D.
[259] [1989] IRLR 291, 301.
[260] [1989] IRLR 291, 299. The employers did not seek to raise this argument on appeal: [1989] IRLR 305, CA; revsd [1989] IRLR 399, HL.
[261] Simpson, 1989: p 237.
[262] [1993] IRLR 344, 350.
[263] [1999] IRLR 31.

Finally, in *The Lord Mayor and Citizens of Westminster City Council v UNISON*[264] the employer maintained (successfully at first instance) that a dispute over the compulsory transfer of staff to the employment of a private company was in reality a dispute about public policy. The Court of Appeal dismissed the argument, finding that the judge had drawn unwarranted inferences from the evidence, and that the dispute concerning the identity of the union members' employer related to their terms and conditions of employment.

Last in this context, a dispute relating to matters occurring outside the United Kingdom is capable of constituting a 'trade dispute', but only if the person(s) whose actions in the UK are said to be in contemplation or furtherance of a dispute relating to such matters are likely to be affected by the outcome of the dispute in respect of one or more of the matters specified in TULRCA 1992, section 244(1).[265] This prevents the organisation of any form of solidarity action with workers overseas where there is no immediate connection between the outcome of that dispute and UK workers. It also overlooks the fact that transnational companies may now be organised in such a way that decisions taken in relation to workers in another country (for example, in relation to working conditions or redundancies) may have significant repercussions in the UK.[266]

'In contemplation or furtherance of a trade dispute'

11.29   Once a 'trade dispute' has been established it is necessary to show that the defendant was acting 'in contemplation or furtherance' of it. Here both the *timing* of the action and its *purpose* are relevant. As far as *timing* is concerned:

> ... either a dispute is imminent and the act is done in expectation of and with a view to it, or
> ... the dispute is already existing and the act is done in support of one side to it.[267]

When a dispute is not in existence whether it is sufficiently imminent will be a question of degree. In *Bent's Brewery Co Ltd v Hogan*[268] the union sought certain information from its pub-manager members, including their takings, trade, and total wages bill, prior to formulating a wage claim. Giving the union this information would have involved these members breaking their contracts of employment. On an application for a declaration by the employers that their employees were not entitled to provide this information the court rejected the argument that the union was acting in contemplation of a trade dispute; such a dispute was neither in being nor imminent. No demand had been made for better conditions or increased wages by any of the managers or by the union on their behalf. The most that could be said was that the union had sent out documents which, after consideration of the information obtained, might lead to a request which, if not granted, might lead to a dispute. By contrast, in *Health Computing Ltd v Meek*[269] the union was held to be

---

[264] [2001] IRLR 524.

[265] TULRCA 1992, s 244(3).

[266] See Wedderburn, 2000: pp 28–33; Germanotta and Novitz, 2002.

[267] Lord Loreburn in *Conway v Wade* [1909] AC 506 at 512. See also *JT Stratford & Son Ltd v Lindley* [1965] AC 269 (emphasising the need for a 'live' dispute).

[268] [1945] 2 All ER 570.

[269] [1980] IRLR 437.

acting in contemplation of a trade dispute in sending out a circular instructing its members not to co-operate with the claimants, a private contractor which specialised in computer systems for medical services and which was seeking to do business with health authorities. The purpose of the circular, according to the union general secretary, was to pre-empt the disputes which would inevitably arise if the health authorities did do business with them. The evidence showed that some health authorities, at least, would be likely to say that they reserved the right to use the contractor's services and it was reasonable to foresee that the enforcement of the union's policy of banning the claimants from the NHS might lead to disputes with those authorities, the disputes being motivated by fear of future redundancies. Thus the court concluded that the circular had been distributed in contemplation of those disputes.

From the other end of the spectrum, there may be scope for argument as to whether a dispute has ended or still remains in being. This question is particularly significant because, where a union is organising the action, the requisite ballot must relate to the dispute it covers. Again, it will be a question of scrutinising the facts to establish whether the original dispute remains 'real or live'.[270]

Finally on this point, it is possible that a dispute may never come into existence at all if an employer submits to workers' demands under threat of industrial action. Such a threat, as we saw in para 11.16, can constitute the tort of intimidation. To cover such a situation the legislation provides that an act, threat or demand which, if resisted, would have led to a trade dispute shall be treated as having been done in contemplation of it even though no dispute arises because the other first submits.[271] It is essential, however, in this situation that the union ensures that the demand is sufficiently closely related to one of the matters listed in the statute. In *BBC v Hearn*[272] the union asked its members not to transmit the (football) Cup Final after the BBC refused to take steps to ensure that the broadcast would not be transmitted to South Africa where the policy of apartheid, to which the union was opposed, was still in force. The Court of Appeal held that there was no trade dispute in existence. However, Lord Denning MR suggested that it could have become one had the union asked the BBC to insert a clause in its members' contracts, or for a condition to be understood, that they would not be asked to participate in any broadcasts to South Africa while there was a policy of apartheid. This suggestion received support from Lord Diplock in a later case.[273] However its possibilities are not unlimited. In a subsequent decision Lord Cross emphasised that a union could not turn a dispute which in reality had no connection with terms and conditions of employment (in that case a demand that the employer made a payment to the union welfare fund) into a trade dispute merely by insisting that the employer inserted appropriate terms into contracts of employment.[274] This approach allows the courts discretion to decide whether the dispute has the appropriate connection.[275]

The test of the dispute organiser's *purpose* in acting is a subjective one; it is sufficient that he or she honestly thinks at the time that the action may help one of the parties to the trade

---

[270] See *Newham London Borough Council v NALGO* [1993] IRLR 83, 87. The suggestion made that for a dispute to continue it is sufficient if the side which still regards itself as being in dispute 'honestly and genuinely believes this is the position' is contrary to authority and indeed the court went on to affirm the need for the dispute to be 'real or live'. See also *Re South West Trains* (25 October 1999, Turner J), IRLB 647: pp 12–14.

[271] TULRCA 1992, s 244(4).

[272] [1977] IRLR 273, CA.

[273] *NWL Ltd v Woods* [1979] IRLR 478, 483, HL.

[274] *Universe Tankships Inc of Monrovia v ITWF* [1982] IRLR 200, 208.

[275] See, for example, Griffiths LJ at 71, Lord Donaldson MR at 73 in *Dimbleby & Sons Ltd v NUJ* [1984] IRLR 67 (decision affirmed [1984] IRLR 161, HL).

dispute to achieve its objective and it is done for that reason.[276] It is therefore immaterial that this belief may be unreasonable; that the action did not, in fact, assist the dispute, or that the action taken was disproportionate to the grievance to be settled. However, evidence that no reasonable person could have thought the action may have this result may be relevant to the credibility of the defendant's evidence that the belief was honestly held.[277] In practice, now that the legislation outlaws virtually all forms of secondary industrial action this issue is unlikely to be contentious other than in the context of picketing, where, as we describe in para 11.56 below, a narrow form of secondary action is permitted.[278]

Situations where the statutory protection does not apply

11.30   Having established that the tortious acts alleged are covered by the statutory immunities and that the defendant is acting in contemplation or furtherance of a trade dispute it is then necessary to examine whether protection is excluded for any reason. The grounds for exclusion can be divided into four main categories: where the requisite balloting and information procedures are not followed in relation to action organised by a union; where the action constitutes unlawful picketing; where the action is taken for a proscribed purpose; and where it constitutes unlawful 'secondary action'. The first and second are discussed in paras 11.32 *et seq* and 11.53 *et seq* respectively; the remainder we discuss below.

　　The 'forbidden' reasons for industrial action, which need not be the primary but only one motivating factor, fall into two categories. The first category concerns action relating to union membership and to recognition and collective consultation; initially introduced as a reflection of the Conservative Government's anti-collectivist stance, it survived unscathed under Labour. There is no protection for action motivated by the belief that an employer is employing, has employed, or might employ a non-union member (or a person who is not a member of a particular union) or may fail to accord more favourable treatment to union members or members of a particular union.[279] Thus, as well as preventing the imposition of a closed shop by these means, a union cannot take industrial action to enforce a demand that only union members should benefit from a wage increase secured by collective bargaining or that union members should be given preference when jobs are allocated. However, it would be open to a union to take action where an employer was favouring non-unionists provided that it was arguing only for equal treatment for its members. Acts to induce an employer to stipulate in a contract for the supply of goods or services that the work should be done only by union (or non-union) labour (or by members of a particular union) or to induce the employer to refuse to deal with another party who does not comply with these requirements are also unprotected. Any stipulation that the other party to a contract should recognise a union or consult with a union official is similarly treated. This means that industrial action cannot be used as a means of helping workers employed by another employer to gain recognition, or even consultation, rights from their employer. It is also unlawful

---

[276] *Express Newspapers Ltd v McShane and Ashton* [1980] IRLR 35. Note, however, that the 'trade dispute' itself must exist or be imminent as an objective fact: Lord Diplock at 39.

[277] *Express Newspapers*, above; see also *Duport Steels Ltd v Sirs* [1980] IRLR 116.

[278] TULRCA 1992, s 224(1), (4).

[279] TULRCA 1992, ss 219(4), 222.

for a union to organise industrial action by employees to persuade their employer's supplier to recognise the union. Second, industrial action is unprotected if one of the reasons for it is the fact or belief that an employer has dismissed one or more employees who have no right to complain of unfair dismissal because they were taking part in 'unofficial' industrial action at the time.[280] The fact that this need not be the primary reason means that if industrial action is taken for other reasons against an employer who has recently dismissed employees in such circumstances the union will have to ensure that the action is dissociated completely from the dismissal.

11.31   The exclusion of 'secondary action' from the statutory immunities is the culmination of the process of 'enterprise confinement';[281] the idea that collective organisation is legitimate, if at all, only at the level of the enterprise. 'Secondary action' occurs when there is inducement to breach, or interference with the performance of, a contract of employment (or the threat of such inducement or interference) and the employer under the contract is not party to the trade dispute.[282] By contrast, 'primary action' is where there is action of this nature and the employer under the contract is party to the trade dispute.[283] Exclusion of secondary action means, for example, that if employees of employer X are in dispute with X then if the union calls on employees of employer Y, who supplies goods to X, not to deliver those supplies, it will thereby have induced them to breach their contracts of employment, an act for which it will have no immunity in tort. An employer may not be treated as party to a dispute between another employer and its workers, and where more than one employer is in dispute with its workers each dispute is to be treated separately.[284] This means that it is impossible to organise national industrial action against more than one employer unless a dispute with each individual employer can be shown; a dispute with an employer as a member of an employers' association with which the union is in dispute, for example, will not suffice. However, an act in contemplation or furtherance of a trade dispute which is primary action in relation to that dispute may not be relied upon as secondary action in relation to another.[285] Thus, even if industrial action taken against one employer assists workers in dispute with another employer, it does not thereby constitute secondary action (unless it could not be said, in reality, to have been taken to further a dispute with the first employer). Thus, if a number of disputes are conducted contemporaneously and each reinforces the effectiveness of the other (in the National Health Service, for example, where individual locally-based trusts are autonomous employers) they are not thereby rendered unlawful.

The only exception to the ban on 'secondary action' is where there is an inducement, or threatened inducement, to breach a contract of an employee of another employer, such as a customer or supplier, in the course of otherwise lawful picketing. This means that if a picket peacefully persuades a lorry driver employed by a supplier not to cross the picket line and thereby induces a breach of his or her contract of employment immunity will not be lost on that ground. We explain this exception further in para 11.56.

---

[280] TULRCA 1992, ss 219(4), 223. In *British Railways Board v RMT* (17 September 1992, unreported, QBD) industrial action had no immunity on this basis.

[281] Wedderburn 1989: pp 27–30.

[282] TULRCA 1992, s 224(2).

[283] TULRCA 1992, s 224(5).

[284] TULRCA 1992, s 224(4).

[285] TULRCA 1992, s 224(5).

The withdrawal of immunity for secondary action applies even where the employers have parallel shareholdings; the courts refuse to 'lift the corporate veil' to take account of the financial realities of the situation and there is no exception for 'associated employers'.[286] This means that the scope of lawful industrial action is defined entirely by the legal scope of the employment unit; even if a dispute between one company and its employees in a group directly affects workers in another company in the same group, possibly operating from the same premises, the workers in the second company cannot take supportive industrial action.[287] The same point applies if workers are employed by a subsidiary company which is legally their employer but which lacks the decision-making power to resolve the issues in dispute.[288] Equally workers cannot organise industrial action against another employer to whom the manufacture or supply of goods or services have been diverted by the employer in dispute, even if that employer is 'associated' with the same employer. It is conceivable that workers employed by the second employer could take industrial action against their own employer as a result of the transfer of work if they could bring it within the scope of matters covered by a 'trade dispute', possibly by asking for a clause in their contract that they should not be required to handle such work (a 'hot cargo' clause).[289] However, such action, if official, would need to be supported by a ballot and the organisers would need to ensure that its predominant purpose was to further that dispute and not, in reality, the first.

The ban on secondary action represents a serious constraint on the organisation of industrial action. It is unclear whether employers would seek to structure their companies with the sole aim of circumventing disruption of this nature although it is unlikely that, in reorganising areas of the public sector, such as water, electricity and the NHS, into smaller employer units during the 1980s and 1990s the Conservative Government was unaware of these implications.[290] The restriction contravenes ILO standards on freedom of association; the Committee of Experts has repeatedly said that 'workers should be able to participate in sympathy strikes, provided the initial strike they are supporting is lawful, and to take industrial action in relation to matters that affect them, even though the direct employer may not be a party to the dispute ....'[291] The fact that unions cannot take action against a company which is the 'true' employer but which may hire workers through an intermediary company has also been criticised by the Committee of Independent Experts (now the European Committee of Social Rights) that supervises compliance with the

---

[286] *Dimbleby and Sons Ltd v NUJ* [1984] IRLR 161. See para 3.65 above.

[287] Harvey (1972, as updated) para 2052 argues that if an employer divides its enterprise into several subsidiaries, each having a different function, and all these companies are interdependent, any trade dispute should be treated as being with the group as a whole. This is an attractive argument but not one whose success could be confidently predicted.

[288] Although see *Porr v Shaw, Johnson and Holden (The Marabu Porr)* [1979] 2 Lloyd's Rep 331, CA (relationship between shipowners and service company employing the crew so close any dispute with the latter a dispute with the former).

[289] See further para 11.29 above.

[290] See G Morris, 1993: pp 91–93. Note also in relation to education the Education (Modification of Enactments Relating to Employment) (England) Order 2003, SI 2003/1964, Art 5, which renders industrial action by teachers in schools with delegated budgets in support of colleagues in other schools actionable in tort in certain circumstances, notwithstanding that those employees may share a common employer: see Freedland, 1989 on a predecessor of the current Order.

[291] CEACR: Individual Observation concerning Freedom of Association and Protection of the Right to Organise Convention 1948 (No 87) UK, 2007. This observation was reiterated most recently in 2011. For a critique of the ILO standards in this area see Germanotta, 2002.

ESC.[292] Nevertheless the Labour Government refused to change the position[293] and it is highly unlikely that the Coalition Government will contemplate doing so.

INDUSTRIAL ACTION BALLOTS AND NOTICE TO EMPLOYERS

11.32   Industrial action for which a trade union is legally liable is protected by the statutory immunities only if it has the support of a majority of those voting in a ballot. This applies both to industrial action by employees and those working under 'any contract under which one person personally does work or performs services for another', so covering contracts for services.[294] This requirement applies irrespective of whether the action constitutes a breach of contract on the part of those participating (although, as we have seen, it generally will).[295] Industrial action must generally start within four weeks of the ballot unless the parties agree to a longer period not exceeding eight weeks; once this period has expired a fresh ballot will be required.

The requirements governing the conduct of the ballot are extremely complex, technical and, in parts, ambiguous. In addition, unions are required to give employers of members covered by the ballot specified information both before and after the ballot takes place, and employers of proposed participants must receive a minimum of seven days' notice before it starts. The consequences of failing to comply with these requirements vary. In general, if industrial action lacks the support of a ballot the union has no immunity against liability in tort, regardless of the identity of the claimant. However, where the union fails to comply with its obligations to provide pre-ballot information, notify a relevant employer of the ballot result, or give notice before industrial action starts, protection is excluded only in relation to the employer in respect of whom the default occurs and, anomalously, individuals exercising the statutory right of action described in para 11.19. In addition, failure to comply with either the balloting or notification requirements means that an employment tribunal will be unable to determine a claim for unfair dismissal by any employee who is dismissed for taking part in the unprotected action, even during the first twelve weeks of his or her participation, unless that dismissal is 'selective' within the terms of the legislation.[296] The statutory requirements in this area are supplemented by a Code of Practice issued by the Secretary of State for Trade and Industry.[297] Its stated purpose is to provide 'practical guidance to trade unions and employers to promote the improvement of industrial relations and good practice in the conduct of

---

[292] See, for example, comments on the UK's compliance with Article 6(4) in the XIV-I supervision cycle.

[293] *Review of the Employment Relations Act 1999: Government Response*, DTI, 2003, para 3.19.

[294] TULRCA 1992, s 235, as amended. Ballots must also be held in respect of industrial action by civil servants and others holding 'any office or employment under the Crown': s 245.

[295] Where the action does not constitute a breach of contract, it may not attract liability in tort, but for applications by union members, and those exercising the statutory right to seek injunctive relief, 'industrial action' is defined as 'any strike or other industrial action by persons employed under contracts of employment' (in the extended sense applicable in this context): TULRCA 1992, s 62(6).

[296] See para 11.72 *et seq*. The definition of 'protected' industrial action in terms of an act 'which is not actionable in tort' (TULRCA 1992, s 238A(1)) suggests that action is outside the definition if immunity is lost in relation to only one of a number of employers involved in the dispute.

[297] Now titled the Secretary of State for Business, Innovation and Skills.

trade union industrial action ballots'.[298] As we discuss in para 11.45, it does not forbear from making recommendations which exceed the limits of the legislation. Although, like other Codes, its contents are not strictly speaking legally enforceable as such, non-compliance with its provisions may be influential when a court is deciding whether or not to grant an interim injunction to halt the action.

An exhaustive account of the intricacies of the balloting and notification requirements would occupy many more pages of this work than space permits. We have confined ourselves, therefore, to highlighting the essential elements and their implications. Even engaging in such a process at this level rapidly reveals the legal minefield which unions enter when embarking upon industrial action; despite greater clarity in some areas as a result of amendments made by the Employment Relations Acts of 1999[299] and 2004[300] many points of uncertainty remain (although the scope for legal challenge has recently been reduced by the Court of Appeal decision in *RMT v Serco Docklands; ASLEF v London Midland*, henceforth '*Serco*').[301] It is also a costly process: at the time of writing ballots must be fully postal,[302] and, since 1 April 1996 there has been no state subsidy for the costs of holding them.[303] In addition, even after *Serco*, unions may require expert legal advice to navigate the statutory channels. Moreover, where more than 50 people are balloted the union must appoint (and pay for) an 'independent scrutineer' to supervise the conduct of the ballot; this must be either one of six specialist bodies specified in regulations or another appropriately qualified person (a solicitor or accountant qualified as an auditor, provided that their previous connections with the union do not disqualify them from this appointment).[304] When consideration is given also to the possibility of challenge in the courts, with the attendant costs this brings, it is readily apparent that organising industrial action can be a very expensive undertaking for any union.

Determining the balloting constituency

11.33 The statutory principles governing the determination of the balloting constituency are in themselves extremely complex. They involve consideration of two interlocking questions: which union members should be given a vote, and how should the general scope of the balloting constituency be defined?

---

[298] Para 1.

[299] ERelA 1999, s 4; Sch 3.

[300] ERelA 2004, s 22–25; Schs 1 and 2. See Simpson, 2005.

[301] *RMT v Serco Ltd t/a Serco Docklands; ASLEF v London and Birmingham Railway Ltd t/a London Midland* [2011] IRLR 399. See generally Dukes, 2011. At the time of writing the RMT has lodged a complaint with the ECtHR that, *inter alia*, specific requirements relating to the notices to be supplied to employers breach Art 11 of the ECHR.

[302] ERelA 2004, s 54 empowers the Secretary of State to make provision by order, in relation to any description of ballot authorised or required by TULRCA 1992, that it may be conducted by other means, subject to specified conditions, but at the time of writing no such orders have been made.

[303] The Funds for Trade Union Ballots (Revocation) Regulations 1993, SI 1993/233. When mandatory balloting before industrial action was initially introduced the Certification Officer was empowered to refund certain costs associated with holding secret postal ballots.

[304] TULRCA 1992, s 226B; the Trade Union Ballots and Elections (Independent Scrutineer Qualifications) Order 1993, SI 1993/1909, as amended.

(i) Entitlement to vote

11.34   The legislation states that entitlement to vote in the ballot must be accorded equally to all union members whom it is reasonable 'at the time of the ballot' *for the union* to believe will be induced by the union to take part or to continue to take part in the industrial action in question, and to no others.[305] The words 'for the union' were inserted by ERelA 2004 to put beyond doubt that the union does not have to give such an entitlement to members who might take part even though not induced to do so by the union itself.[306] In addition, ERelA 1999 established by implication that industrial action is not regarded as failing to have the support of a ballot because individuals who take up employment or join the union after the ballot has been held participate in it, (giving statutory force to an earlier Court of Appeal decision[307] to this effect).[308] However, unions still need to ensure that if they call members out in rotation (for example, where there is a need to ensure a minimum level of service) all participants, and no non-participants, are included in the ballot.[309] In *P v NAS/UWT* the House of Lords held that an omission to send a ballot paper to a person entitled to vote did not of itself amount to a denial of entitlement to vote;[310] otherwise the requirement elsewhere in the legislation that 'so far as is reasonably practicable' every person who is entitled to vote must be sent a ballot paper[311]would be rendered otiose.

   An accidental failure to comply with the requirement relating to entitlement to vote which is on a scale which is unlikely to affect the ballot result can be disregarded.[312] This may be a particularly useful provision where some of those voting are workers under contracts for services, whose whereabouts may not always be known or who may be difficult to contact. In *Serco* the Court of Appeal rejected the employer's argument (accepted at first instance) that an error needed to be both unintentional and unavoidable to be 'accidental' and held that the erroneous inclusion of two members out of 600 in the ballot did not invalidate the process.[313] By contrast, in *British Airways plc v Unite the Union*[314] the union was unable to rely on this defence when it included several hundred members who were employed at the time of the ballot but who would have taken voluntary redundancy and left the employer by the time the industrial action could lawfully have started.

---

[305] TULRCA 1992, s 227(1), as amended by ERelA 2004, s 23. 'Time of the ballot' is not defined. In *P v NAS/UWT* [2003] IRLR 307 the House of Lords took the view that, in the light of its interpretation of the balloting provisions as a whole, it did not matter which particular time was meant; the question was whether 'looking at the balloting process as a whole' individuals had been denied entitlement to vote: [49] (Lord Hoffmann). In *London Underground Ltd v ASLEF* [2012] IRLR 196 the High Court held that the ballot was not required to be limited to those persons who will be induced to withdraw their labour in breach of contract but extends to all those who will be induced to take part in the industrial action in the sense described in *Bolton Roadways Ltd v Edwards* [1987] IRLR 392, discussed in para 11.75 below.

[306] Cf the approach to this issue in *RMT v Midland Mainline Ltd* [2001] IRLR 813 at [16] (Schiemann LJ).

[307] *London Underground Ltd v RMT* [1995] IRLR 636.

[308] TULRCA 1992, s 232A. This interpretation was approved by the House of Lords in *P v NAS/UWT* [2003] IRLR 307 at [47] (Lord Hoffmann).

[309] In *P v NAS/UWT* [2001] IRLR 532 the Court of Appeal held that workers can take part in industrial action by making it clear that they fully support it and would participate in it if asked, a dictum which assists unions with members in essential services. See para 11.75 below for discussion of this concept in the context of dismissal.

[310] [2003] IRLR 307 at [41] (Lord Hoffmann).

[311] TULRCA 1992, s 230(2).

[312] TULRCA 1992 s 232B, as amended by ERelA 2004, s 24(1), confirming the position reached by the House of Lords in *P v NAS/UWT* [2003] IRLR 307.

[313] Above, note 301, Elias LJ at [47]-[57]. The facts in the text above refer to the ASLEF ballot at issue in this decision. See also *Balfour Beatty Engineering Services Ltd v Unite the Union* [2012] IRLR 452.

[314] [2010] IRLR 423, QBD. See Prassl, 2011.

(ii) Geographical scope of the balloting constituency

11.35   In general the constituency for a ballot is a 'workplace'. Where intended participants have separate workplaces, there must be a separate ballot for each, and entitlement to vote must be accorded equally to, and restricted to, union members who have that workplace.[315] A separate majority must be obtained in each workplace and all the other statutory requirements must be satisfied for industrial action therein to be lawful.[316] 'Workplace' in relation to a person who is employed means '(a) if the person works at or from a single set of premises, those premises, and (b) in any other case, the premises with which the person's employment has the closest connection.'[317] The 'closest connection' means that everyone has a 'place of work'; for delivery drivers, for example, it will be the depot from which they set out, for homeworkers probably the administrative office of the employer with which they deal. 'Premises' are not defined.[318] It seems clear that different sites of the same undertaking would require a separate ballot; for a single site containing a number of buildings (such as a university) it is possible that a separate ballot may be required for each building: this would seem an undesirable consequence, but the matter is not free from doubt.[319] The 'workplace' of a worker who is employed to work in one place but temporarily moved to another is also unclear. However, the requirement to hold a separate ballot for each workplace does not apply if the union reasonably believes that the members accorded entitlement to vote have the same workplace,[320] so even if a court subsequently decides that the union was incorrect in its conclusion the ballot remains valid provided that the union's belief was 'reasonable'.

The restriction of ballots to a 'place of work' was originally designed to ensure that unions could not achieve a majority in favour of industrial action by aggregating votes at 'militant' and 'moderate' workplaces.[321] Votes could be aggregated in specified circumstances, but the statutory language governing these bordered on the incomprehensible. The Labour Government considered that there was little or no evidence that unions had attempted to obtain majorities by illegitimate means,[322] and the ERelA 1999 introduced a simplified (although still complex) provision which allows aggregate ballots instead of separate workplace ballots in three sets of circumstances, based, loosely speaking, on a common interest in the subject-matter of the dispute; common occupation(s); or a common employer or employers.[323] Aggregation is permitted on the basis of *common interest* where the workplace of each member of the union entitled to vote is the workplace of at least one member who is affected by the dispute. Those 'affected' fall into four categories, depending on the subject matter of the dispute. In relation to terms and conditions of employment, termination of employment, allocation of duties or matters of discipline, for example, 'affected' means members

---

[315] TULRCA 1992, s 228.
[316] TULRCA 1992, s 226(3).
[317] TULRCA 1992, s 228(4). Cf the position prior to ERelA 1999, when the equivalent definition required the premises to be 'occupied' by the employer.
[318] Cf the HSWA 1974, s 53.
[319] A government spokesman at the time of the original legislation's parliamentary passage considered that for the most part the term 'premises' implied a building: Patrick Nicholls, Parliamentary Under-Secretary of State for Employment, House of Commons, Official Report of Standing Committee F, col 523, 19 January 1988.
[320] TULRCA 1992, 228(2)
[321] Mr Patrick Nicholls, above, note 319, col 494, 14 January 1988.
[322] Lord McIntosh of Haringey, Deputy Chief Whip, HL Debs Vol 604, col 576, 15 July 1999.
[323] TULRCA 1992, s 228A(1).

whom the decision directly affects. The fact that only one member at each workplace needs to be affected reflects the recognition that '[w]here one or more workers are directly involved, it will normally be the case that others at the same workplace, sometimes many others, will rightly feel themselves to be indirectly involved by an employer's handling of an issue ... [which] may set a precedent in relation to other workers'.[324] It may not always be clear when workers are 'directly affected' however;[325] it is not sufficient that the union reasonably believes them to be so, and in cases where this is unclear unions may prefer to hold separate workplace ballots. Where a dispute relates to facilities for union officials, only those officials who would use the facilities concerned are 'affected members', so precluding aggregation in the case of full-time officials who are not attached to any particular workplace. Aggregation is permitted on the basis that members share a *common occupation or a number of specific kinds of occupation* provided that the union is not selective in according entitlement to vote. Here, aggregation may be across a number of employers with which the union is in dispute. The meaning of 'occupation' is unclear; it could be seen in terms of broad job specification of function, grade, qualifications, or a combination of those factors.[326] In this context it is sufficient that the union has a 'reasonable belief' that members have an occupation of a particular kind. Finally, aggregation is permitted where entitlement to vote is accorded, and limited, to all the members of the union who are employed by *a particular employer, or any number of employers*, with which the union is in dispute. Again it is crucial that the union is not selective in according entitlement to vote.

Of the three tests allowing aggregation, the 'common interest' test gives unions the greatest flexibility in that it does not require the inclusion of *all* workplaces at which the common interest applies. This means that a union may choose to exclude particular workplaces from the aggregated ballot, even if they are part of the same bargaining unit as those which are balloted together. Conversely, it means that if responsibility for industrial relations matters is devolved to regional management or regional centres of operation, those workplaces within the region may be balloted together. The need to ballot on a non-selective basis where a ballot is aggregated on the common occupation and common employer tests may create difficulties for unions which wish to maintain emergency cover during disputes. They may ballot only those whom they reasonably believe will be called upon to participate in the action, which suggests that members involved in maintaining emergency cover should not be balloted. However the union cannot exclude them if it wishes to aggregate the ballot (unless it is aggregated on the basis of a common occupation and all those furnishing emergency cover fall within a distinctive occupation). In this situation a union will probably have to try to ballot all the workers in dispute and then rotate those who provide emergency cover so that all those balloted are called upon at some stage to participate in the industrial action.[327]

[324] Lord McIntosh of Haringey, above, note 322.
[325] Cf the interpretation of 'directly interested' in TULRCA 1992, 238(3)(a) as those whose terms of employment are likely to be immediately and automatically affected by the outcome of the dispute: see para 11.76. This does not cater for forms of trade dispute, such as those motivated by fear of future redundancies, where employees are potentially, but not automatically, at risk.
[326] Cf TULRCA 1992, s 174(3)(b), where 'occupational description' is said to include 'grade, level or category of appointment'.
[327] The dictum in *P v NAS/UWT* [2001] IRLR 532 as to when workers are regarded as taking part in industrial action, discussed in para 11.34 above, may be useful to essential service unions here. The House of Lords did not refer to this point.

The content of the voting paper

11.36   The statute prescribes in detail the content of the voting paper for the ballot. It must state, *inter alia*, the name of the independent scrutineer, where applicable, and must specify, either individually or by description (members of the executive or regional officers for example), who in the event of a vote in favour of industrial action is authorised to call upon members to participate in it.[328] The member must be asked to indicate, by answering 'yes' or 'no', whether he or she is prepared to take part, or to continue to take part, in a strike or industrial action short of a strike, as the case may be. If the union wishes to obtain approval for both these forms of action the questions for each must be asked separately; it cannot be assumed that those who voted for a strike would necessarily approve of industrial action short of a strike.[329] However, it is sufficient for the union to obtain a majority on an individual question, and not the voting process as a whole, in order for that action to be approved.[330] Given the tendency by the courts to scrutinise voting papers closely, unions are best advised not to specify the form of industrial action they may take any more than the statute requires; otherwise they risk unnecessarily restricting the ballot mandate.[331] The need to obtain separate approval may necessitate the union holding more than one ballot during the course of a dispute; because the mandate provided by a ballot lapses after four weeks (unless extended by agreement between the union and the employer) a union cannot rely upon strike action as a 'fall-back' beyond that time if the more limited sanctions fail to produce a satisfactory settlement. Finally, it is mandatory for the voting paper to contain the statement:

> If you take part in a strike or other industrial action, you may be in breach of your contract of employment. However, if you are dismissed for taking part in strike (sic) or other industrial action which is called officially[332] and is otherwise lawful, the dismissal will be unfair if it takes place fewer than twelve weeks after you started taking part in the action, and depending on the circumstances may be unfair if it takes place later.[333]

This statement must not be 'qualified or commented upon by anything else on the voting paper'. Thus, even if industrial action, such as a ban on voluntary overtime,[334] is (probably) not a breach of contract, the union can indicate this only in a separate document, preferably, to be completely safe, to be sent out under separate cover.

---

[328] TULRCA 1992, s 229.

[329] *Post Office v UCW* [1990] IRLR 143. In the context of the balloting provisions in general, a 'strike' means 'any concerted stoppage of work': TULRCA 1992, s 246. ERelA 1999 amended this section to make clear that an overtime ban and call-out ban constitute industrial action short of a strike (see TULRCA 1992, s 229(2A)), to overrule *Connex South Eastern Ltd v RMT* [1999] IRLR 249. However, this continues to leave unclear the status of other forms of action which may involve stoppages for specific periods, such as a ban on lunch-time cover or on duties that take place only at specified times of day. In *British Telecommunications plc v CMU* [2004] IRLR 58 the court held that it was highly unlikely that the employers would succeed at trial in arguing that a strike was not supported by a ballot because of the outdated information given to members that a vote for strike action would also authorise industrial action short of a strike.

[330] *West Midlands Travel Ltd v TGWU* [1994] IRLR 578.

[331] *Blue Circle v TGWU* (7 July 1989, Alliott J, unreported) (support requested for one 24-hour strike per week did not permit action which went beyond that).

[332] Note than this term is not used elsewhere in the legislation: see para 11.72 *et seq.*

[333] TULRCA 1992, s 229(4), as amended by ERelA 2004, s 57(1), Sch 1, para 13.

[334] See para 11.66 below.

Despite the highly prescriptive nature of these provisions judicial creativity has still crept into this area. In *London Underground Ltd v NUR*[335] Simon Brown J suggested that the legislation would not be satisfied where the ballot posed a question which, either wholly or in part, asked whether members were prepared to participate in a strike by reference to matters which were not existing matters in dispute. In that case the ballot asked: '[d]o you agree to support the executive committee in their fight to maintain the current agreement on seniority and to resist the imposition of organisational changes [unsatisfactory attendance procedures and competitive tendering] by taking strike action?' The employers argued that, at the time of the ballot, there was no 'genuine, definite, substantial dispute' between the parties on any of the issues other than seniority, and the court considered that there were 'powerful arguments' to support this contention.[336] This approach has been criticised as confusing 'the conditions for a valid ballot with the need for a union to prove that it was acting in contemplation or furtherance of a trade dispute ... a separate prerequisite for the protection of the immunities.'[337] Nevertheless, the same approach was adopted by the Court of Appeal in *University College London Hospital NHS Trust v UNISON*.[338] Here the ballot asked members whether they were prepared to take strike action, *inter alia*, because the employer had failed to guarantee that staff who were employed by a private sector consortium in the future (and who had never been employed by the Trust) would receive the same terms and conditions of employment as those whom the Trust continued to employ. Having held that this demand could not constitute the subject-matter of a 'trade dispute', the court went on to hold that it was therefore 'an impermissible subject for the ballot' and, although it was only one of the issues identified on the ballot paper, nullified the ballot which had taken place.[339] A first instance court has held that there is no requirement for a union to define or describe every issue with which a dispute is concerned in the information supplied to members taking part in the ballot; it is sufficient that there was evidence to identify the strike which had been approved in the ballot.[340] Where there are a number of different issues, not all of which fall squarely within the 'trade dispute' definition, a union would be well advised not to detail those over which there is uncertainty. However, where there is some contention as to whether the central issue constitutes a 'trade dispute', spelling it out on the ballot paper in appropriately-drafted terms may help to substantiate the union's case.[341] In *London Borough of Wandsworth v NAS/UWT,*[342] where it was argued for the employers that the dispute in question was about the content of the work which the national curriculum required schoolteachers to undertake, the Court of Appeal attached 'considerable importance'[343] to the wording on the ballot paper which asked teachers whether they were willing to take action '[i]n order to protest against the excessive workload and unreasonable imposition made upon teachers, as a consequence of national curriculum assessment and testing ...'.[344]

---

[335] [1989] IRLR 341.
[336] [1989] IRLR 341, 342.
[337] Simpson, 1989: p 235.
[338] [1999] IRLR 31.
[339] [1999] IRLR 31, 35 (Lord Woolf MR).
[340] *Associated British Ports v TGWU* [1989] IRLR 291.
[341] *Wandsworth London Borough Council v NAS/UWT* [1993] IRLR 344.
[342] [1993] IRLR 344.
[343] [1993] IRLR 344, 350.
[344] [1993] IRLR 344, 348.

The conduct of the ballot

11.37   At the time of writing industrial action ballots must be conducted entirely by 'post',[345] which is defined in terms which exclude delivery by hand, internal mail or private courier.[346] 'So far as is reasonably practicable' every person who is entitled to vote in the ballot must have a voting paper sent to his or her home address[347] and be given a convenient opportunity to vote by post.[348] Members must be entitled to vote at no direct cost to themselves. The Code of Practice interprets this to mean that pre-paid reply envelopes should be included with the voting paper.[349] Ballots must be conducted so as to ensure that, so far as reasonably practicable, voting is in secret and there must be no interference from, or constraint imposed by, the union or any of its members, officials or employees.[350] However, in *Newham London Borough Council v NALGO*[351] the Court of Appeal affirmed that the union was 'perfectly entitled to be partisan'[352] and campaign for a 'yes' vote; when such campaigning will cross the line into unlawful interference is not readily apparent.[353] It is notable that no mention is made of interference by employers and, indeed, the requirement to give a pre-ballot notice to employers, which we describe in para 11.39, is designed, *inter alia*, to facilitate the case against industrial action being put to workers. Votes must be fairly and accurately counted although any inaccuracy which is accidental and on a scale which could not affect the result of the ballot may be disregarded.[354]

As soon as reasonably practicable after the holding of the ballot the union must take steps to ensure that voters are informed of the number of votes cast; the numbers voting "Yes" and "No" respectively to each question; and the number of spoiled ballot papers.[355] In *Network Rail Infrastructure v RMT*[356] the High Court held that the union had to take 'active steps' to bring this information to members' attention and that a text with a link to a website was insufficient. In *British Airways plc v Unite the Union (No 2)*, [357] however, the majority of the Court of Appeal held that

---

[345] TULRCA 1992, s 230(2). ERelA 2004, s 54 empowers the Secretary of State to make provision by order, in relation to any description of ballot authorised or required by TULRCA 1992, that it may be conducted by other means, subject to specified conditions, but at the time of writing no such orders have been made.

[346] TULRCA 1992, s 298.

[347] Or any other address he or she has requested the union in writing to treat as his or her postal address: s 230(2)(a). In *RMT v Midland Mainline Ltd* [2001] IRLR 813, the Court of Appeal considered that where a ballot paper was sent to an address from which a member had moved without informing the union, the union would probably have done all that was reasonably practicable if it had a system of reminding members of the need to notify a change of address and the member had not done this.

[348] See *P v NAS/UWT* [2003] IRLR 307. Note also TULRCA 1992, s 232B, considered in *RMT v Serco Docklands; ASLEF v London Midland*, above para 11.34; see also Balfour Beatty Engineerings Services Ltd v Unite the Union [2012] IRLR 452. The Code of Practice paras 27 and 28 gives guidance as to the period to be allowed for this process.

[349] Para 26. See also *Paul v NALGO* [1987] IRLR 43.

[350] TULRCA 1992, s 230(1)(a).

[351] [1993] IRLR 83.

[352] [1993] IRLR 83, 86.

[353] In relation to union elections the Certification Officer has held that this excludes 'such conduct as would intimidate or put a member in fear of voting, or amount to physical interference': *Rey v Film Artistes' Association* (11 April 1986, unreported). See also Code of Practice para 36 on communication with members.

[354] TULRCA 1992, s 230(4).

[355] TULRCA 1992, s 231.

[356] [2010] EWHC 1084 (QB).

[357] [2010] IRLR 809.

this was a gloss on the statute and that there was no requirement for a personal communication of these matters to members provided that the results were easily accessible to them.[358]

The independent scrutineer engaged to supervise the conduct of the ballot must issue a report within four weeks of the ballot, stating, *inter alia*, whether he or she is satisfied that the security arrangements for handling voting papers and counting votes were such as to minimise the risk of unfairness or malpractice as well as commenting more broadly on whether any of the statutory requirements were contravened.[359] The union has a duty to comply with all reasonable requests by the scrutineer connected with the performance of his or her functions;[360] this probably entails giving him or her access to look at records, obtain relevant information, and visit premises as appropriate. The scrutineer's report must be made available on request to any person entitled to vote in the ballot and the employer of any such person, either free or on payment of a reasonable fee. While a critical report will not of itself invalidate the ballot it may serve to draw the attention of employers and union members to possible grounds for challenging it.

Information and notice to employers

11.38   The information that unions must give to employers falls into three broad categories: information to be provided before the ballot; the result of the ballot; and information prior to the commencement of industrial action. The notification provisions contain no express 'saving' provision for accidental failures corresponding to that relating to entitlement to vote in the ballot, described in para 11.34 above. In *Serco*[361] it was argued that this was a deliberate omission that left no room for a *de minimis* defence which would allow trifling errors to be disregarded. In the light of its other findings it was unnecessary for the Court of Appeal to decide this point, but the court made clear its support for the *de minimis* principle and, indeed, the (possibly wider) doctrine of 'substantial compliance' with the statutory provisions enunciated by Smith LJ in *British Airways plc v Unite the Union (No 2)*.[362] Both judges pointed to the absurd position that would result if accidentally depriving someone of the opportunity to vote could be remedied but failing to include them in the relevant notice could not.

---

[358] The majority also considered that minor failures about the provision of results should not undermine the entire process. The Lord Chief Justice expressed surprise that employers could rely on a provision designed to protect the interests of union members in order to circumvent the latter's wishes: see [62].

[359] TULRCA 1992, ss 226B(1); 231B. Given that the ballot ceases to be effective at the end of a period of four weeks beginning with the date of the ballot (unless otherwise agreed between the union and employer) the industrial action may begin before the scrutineer's report has been received. To that extent the advice in the Code of Practice that unions may wish to delay any call until receiving the scrutineer's report (para 49) seems unrealistic.

[360] TULRCA 1992, s 226B(4).

[361] Above, note 301.

[362] See Elias LJ in *RMT v Serco Docklands; ASLEF v London Midland* above note 301 at [87]; Smith LJ in *British Airways plc v Unite the Union (No 2)* above note 357 at [149]–[153].

(i) Information to be provided before the ballot

11.39   The union must take such steps as are 'reasonably necessary' to ensure that, not later than the seventh day before the opening day of the ballot,[363] written notice of intent to hold it is received by all the employers of those to be balloted, and not later than the third day before the opening day of the ballot, a sample of the form of voting paper to be sent to its own employees is received.[364] This will enable the employer to learn whether a strike and/or industrial action short of a strike is contemplated. The pre-ballot notice must contain specified information, including detailed information about the employees of the employer concerned whom the union reasonably believes will be entitled to vote in the ballot.[365] First, it requires the notice to list the categories of employee to which the employees concerned belong and the workplaces at which they work, and to state the total number of employees concerned; the number in each category listed; and the number who work at each workplace listed.[366] 'Workplace' has the same definition as in the context of the balloting constituency,[367] and the comments we made in para 11.35 apply equally in this context. The Code of Practice suggests that unions should consider choosing a categorisation which relates to the nature of the employees' work, such as 'occupation, grade or pay band', although the availability of data to the union will be a 'legitimate factor' in determining the union's choice.[368] It is expressly provided that nothing requires a union to supply an employer with the names of the employees concerned.[369] Second, the union must supply an explanation of how those figures were arrived at.[370] If some or all of the employees concerned are employees in relation to whom the employer operates the 'check-off', the union may, alternatively, supply other information that will enable the employer readily to deduce the total number of employees concerned; the categories to which they belong and the number in each category; and the workplaces at which they work and the number who work at each.[371] In either case the lists and figures, or information, supplied must be as accurate as is reasonably practicable in the light of the information in the possession of the union at the time when it complies with the obligation to ensure it is received by the employer(s) concerned.[372] Information is 'in the possession of the union' for these purposes if it is held, for union purposes, in a document (whether in electronic or any other form) and 'in the possession or under the control of an officer or employee of the union'.[373] This means that information held only by branch officials or other lay representatives of the union is not in the union's possession for

---

[363] The first day when a voting paper is sent to any person entitled to vote: TULRCA 1992, s 226A(4).

[364] TULRCA 1992, s 226A, as amended by ERelA 2004, s 22. The ECSR considers that this requirement is excessive given the requirement to issue an additional strike notice before taking action: see, for example, Conclusions XVIII-I, Vol 2, Report No 25.

[365] TULRCA 1992, s 226A(2H). In *United Closures and Plastics Ltd (petitioner)* [2012] IRLR 29 the Court of Session emphasised that 'reasonably' qualifies the union's belief, not the employees' entitlement to vote (J Beckett QC at [51])

[366] TULRCA 1992, s 226A(2(c),(2A),(2B).

[367] TULRCA 1992, s 226A(2I).

[368] Para 15.

[369] TULRCA 1992, s 226A(2G).

[370] TULRCA 1992, s 226A(2)(c)(i).

[371] TULRCA 1992, s 226A(2)(c)(ii). In *Metrobus Ltd v Unite the Union* [2009] IRLR 851 the majority of the Court of Appeal held that where only some employees were covered by the check-off the requirement to provide an explanation of how the figures were arrived at for non-check off employees continued to apply.

[372] TULRCA 1992, s 226A(2D).

[373] TULRCA 1992, s 226A(2E). 'Officer' is defined in s 119 as including (a) any member of the governing body of the union, and (b) any trustee of any fund applicable for the purposes of the union.

this purpose.[374] In *Serco* the Court of Appeal emphasised that there is no obligation on the union to keep a record of workplaces or job categories for the specific purpose of organising industrial action;[375] its duty rather is to ' obtain any relevant documents from union officers and employees and to collate and analyse that information to enable it to supply the relevant lists and figures to the employer as accurately as it reasonably can'.[376]

The Code of Practice acknowledges that it is not reasonable to expect union records to be perfectly accurate and to contain detailed information on all members but (in a gloss on the statute) states that where the data are known to be incomplete or to contain other inaccuracies it is a desirable practice for unions to describe in the notice to the employer the main deficiencies.[377] In *Serco* the Court of Appeal held that the duty to supply an explanation is not an onerous one and need not go beyond the requirements of the Code of Practice;[378] it also stated that to invalidate a ballot the description of the process undertaken would need to be 'positively and materially misleading.'[379] On this basis, the union's statement that its database had been 'audited and updated' when it had in fact conducted a ballot-specific review did not breach its statutory duty; the term 'audit' was not so misleading as to defeat the statutory purpose.[380]

Prior to ERelA 2004, the union was required to provide 'such information in the union's possession as would help the employer to make plans and bring information to the attention of those of his employees' who it is reasonable for the union to believe would be entitled to vote in the ballot.[381] If the union possessed information as to the number, category or workplace of the employees concerned, the notice was required to contain that information (at least). It was also stated that it could not be a ground of non-compliance that the notice did not name any employees but it was arguable that, in some circumstances, it could necessitate the provision of information that was so specific that it was tantamount to naming individuals. The amended provisions may not afford employees greater protection than their predecessor in all cases. On the one hand, the courts have held that there is no requirement to use any particular category of jobs and that general job categories will suffice. In *Westminster City Council v Unison* the Court of Appeal rejected the employer's argument that it was insufficient for the union to refer to the

---

[374] Explanatory Notes to the ERelA 2004, para 149; Code of Practice para 14. Simpson, 2005: pp 335–336 criticises the inference in para 14 that there are circumstances in which lay officials might be union officers or employees. Cf the position before the amendment, as applied in *RMT v London Underground Ltd* [2001] IRLR 228 and *Willerby Holiday Homes Ltd v UCATT* [2003] EWHC 2608 (QB).

[375] See TULRCA 1992, s 24, discussed in para 10.6 above, for the duty to maintain a register of members' names and addresses.

[376] Above note 301, Elias LJ at [71]. Cf *EDF Energy Powerlink Ltd v RMT* [2010] IRLR 114, where Blake J considered that the fact that unions did not record information should not be decisive, otherwise they would be tempted to record minimal information to diminish the content of the duty. Elias LJ thought that this concern was exaggerated and that in practice it would be in unions' own interests to know how many members were employed, where and in what jobs: see [72]–[75].

[377] Para 16.

[378] Above note 301, Elias LJ at [95].

[379] Above at [103].

[380] Above at [104]. The court also pointed out that there was no duty to provide an audit and therefore no obligation to state whether one had been conducted: [105].

[381] Prior to ERelA 1999, a union was required to describe, so that the employer could 'readily ascertain them', the employees covered by the ballot, a requirement that the Court of Appeal held, on the facts, could be satisfied only if the union named individual staff: *Blackpool and Fylde College v NATFHE* [1994] IRLR 227. The Committee of Independent Experts (now the ECSR) that supervises the ESC considered that this was a threat to the right to organise as guaranteed by Art 5: Conclusions XIII-3, 109; Conclusions XIV-I. However, an application alleging that the requirement to reveal names violated Art 11 of the ECHR was ruled inadmissible by the European Commission of Human Rights: *NATFHE v UK* Application No 28910/95.

45 workers in the council's 'advice and assessment office' who paid their subscriptions by check-off; there was no requirement to distinguish between managers and other staff or to identify the various sub-units of the unit in question.[382] However even this broad-brush approach may not offer employees protection against identification by implication in small workplaces or where there are only a small number of individuals in a particular category. There is no specific protection against dismissal or other forms of detriment for taking part in an industrial action ballot (in contrast, for example, to ballots relating to recognition or derecognition).[383] It is arguable that were an employer to take measures, or, possibly, threaten them, this would infringe the protection against taking part in union activities at an appropriate time,[384] but it would be preferable for protection to be expressly accorded.

(ii) The result of the ballot

11.40   After the ballot, the union must take reasonable steps to ensure that every employer of persons entitled to vote in the ballot is informed of the number of votes cast; the numbers voting "Yes" and "No" respectively to each question; and the number of spoiled ballot papers.[385] In *Metrobus Ltd v Unite the Union* the Court of Appeal confirmed that this is a free-standing obligation which is independent of any decision to initiate industrial action.[386] In that case the court held that as soon as the union's regional industrial organiser had received the result from the scrutineer it was practicable for him to communicate it to the employer and it was no defence that he thought that he required authority from the union's general secretary to do so.

(iii) Information prior to the commencement of industrial action

11.41   The union must ensure that, before it induces any person to take part in industrial action, his or her employer receives a notice at least seven days before the action will begin (but this period cannot start before relevant employers have been informed about the ballot result). The notice must, *inter alia*, give information about the number and categories of 'affected employees', framed in similar terms, *mutatis mutandis*, to those discussed in para 11.39 above.[387] Employees are 'affected' if they are employees of the employer whom the union reasonably believes will be

---

[382] [2001] IRLR 524 at [57], [61]. See also Buxton LJ at [78]: 'Category' is 'a very broad word and not to be either exclusively or narrowly defined. It means no more than a reference to the general type of workers', and *RMT v Serco Docklands; ASLEF v London Midland*, above note 301,, Elias LJ at [124].

[383] See para 9.21 above.

[384] See para 8.8 *et seq* and 8.13 *et seq*.

[385] TULRCA 1992, s 231A. It would seem to be the case that where separate workplace ballots are required, results must be notified for each ballot; otherwise, employers should receive notification of the overall result. In *British Airways plc v Unite the Union (No 2)* [2010] IRLR 809 Judge LCJ suggested at [26] that different considerations may apply in considering the effect of failures in respect of notifying employers of the ballot result to those applicable to notifying union members but given that the statutory wording is the same in both it is not clear why this should be so (nor why Judge LCJ suggested that non-compliance with the obligation to supply information to the employer 'will almost inevitably be deliberate').

[386] [2009] IRLR 851, Lloyd LJ at [73].

[387] TULRCA 1992, s 234A, as amended by ERelA 2004, s 25.

induced by the union to take part in the industrial action.[388] It would be prudent for unions to review the lists that they provided to the employer prior to the ballot to take account of any new members or loss of members, changes in employment, or of any information provided by the employer in response to the pre-ballot notice, for example.

The comments that we made in para 11.39 about the continued risk that employees in some workplaces may be identified under these provisions apply equally in this context. There is a strong case for such individuals to be accorded specific protection against being put under pressure by their employers not to participate in the industrial action; although there is protection against dismissal in specified circumstances for those who take part in industrial action,[389] there is no protection for those threatened with a detriment were they to do so.[390]

The notice must also state whether the action is intended to be continuous or 'discontinuous'.[391] Industrial action is 'discontinuous' where the union intends it to take place only on some days where there is an opportunity to take it (for example, Mondays and Fridays); otherwise it is continuous. For continuous action the notice must specify when any of the affected employees will begin to take part in it; for discontinuous, the intended dates for any of the affected employees to take part. In *Milford Haven Port Authority v Unite*[392] the Court of Appeal held that notice of continuous and discontinuous action could be given in the same notice but left open the question whether notice could be given of both forms of action at the same time, so leaving the union's options open as to which form of action to take.

When continuous industrial action is called off or suspended, a fresh notice must be given if industrial action (whether continuous or discontinuous) is resumed at a later date. This is subject to two exceptions. The first is where the action is called off or suspended pursuant to a court order or undertaking to the court; this could occur if action were the subject of an interim injunction at first instance which was then lifted on appeal. The second (an exception introduced by ERelA 1999) is where the union agrees with the employer, prior to the action being suspended, that suspension will occur with effect from a specified date and that the action may be resumed from another specified date; this may encourage unions to allow a breathing space for negotiations. In the case of discontinuous industrial action there is no obligation for the union to take the action on any of the days it has previously notified, and the tactic of failing to take action on notified days could be highly effective (although an employer could probably refuse to pay for the days unexpectedly worked, or prevent workers from working, on the basis of an anticipatory breach of contract).[393]

11.42   As we indicated in para 11.32, in the event of a failure to comply with the obligations to give pre-ballot information, notify a relevant employer of the ballot result, or give notice before industrial action starts, the protection of the immunities is lost only in relation to the employer in respect of whom the default occurs and for the purposes of the statutory right of action. The general principles governing injunctions would suggest that it would be inappropriate to grant an

---

[388] TULRCA 1992, s 234A(5C). In *United Closures and Plastics Ltd (petitioner)* [2012] IRLR 29 the Court of Session emphasised that 'reasonably' qualifies the union's belief, not the inducing (J Beckett QC at [51]).

[389] See further para 11.72 *et seq.*

[390] See para 8.8 and 8.13.

[391] TULRCA 1992, s 234A.

[392] [2010] EWCA Civ 400.

[393] See further para 11.68 *et seq.*

injunction until, at the earliest, it is known that there is a majority in favour of industrial action on the basis that an unlawful act is not, before then, sufficiently likely.[394] However the courts have been willing to grant a remedy at an earlier stage. During a seafarers' dispute in 1988 the union was injuncted from conducting a ballot of the workforce (a lawful activity) on the basis that the proposed action would be unlawful secondary action,[395] and in *EDF Energy Powerlink Ltd v RMT* a failure in respect of the pre-ballot notice to the employer was held to justify an injunction to restrain the union from calling a strike on the basis of the ballot in question even though the ballot had not been concluded at the time of the employer's application to the court.[396] While it may be argued that, if action is to be injuncted, unions benefit from saving the costs involved in holding a ballot for action which never takes place, a majority in a ballot can be an important negotiating tactic for a union;[397] indeed, it was suggested early in the 1990s that balloting had been incorporated into bargaining processes by management and unions and that their results had often 'come to be seen as a useful indicator of the strength of employee feeling which clarifies positions, rather than one which commits parties to a definite course of action'.[398] Since then this has become an expensive method of ascertaining views, given that ballots must now be fully postal and supervised by an independent scrutineer, with no provision for recovery of costs. Despite this, over the period January 1995 to May 2003 nearly 9,000 ballots for industrial action were recorded,[399] and even in the period 2003-2009, when the incidence of stoppages fell to historic lows (see para 11.9 above), many more ballots than stoppages took place each year.[400] The Code of Practice states that unions should hold a ballot only if it is contemplating the organisation of industrial action.[401] However, it may be seen as objectionable that an organisation should be prevented from seeking the views of its members on any issue it chooses, regardless of whether it then puts those views fully into practice.

Call by a specified person

11.43 Industrial action may be validly called only by a person specified (either individually or by description) on the voting paper.[402] Curiously, such a person need not be authorised under the union rules to call industrial action; it is sufficient that he or she is within the range of persons for whose actions the union is responsible in the absence of any valid repudiation (see para 11.21). In *Tanks and Drums Ltd v TGWU*[403] the Court of Appeal allowed some flexibility in holding that it was

---

[394] See Spry, 2010: pp 377–382 and 468–470 on the principles governing injunctions formerly known as *quia timet* injunctions. As Auerbach (1988: p 229) points out, at the most there can only be a 'conditional' inducement of industrial action at the point when the ballot is proposed. For the statutory right of action an individual must claim that the unlawful act was, at the very least, 'likely': TULRCA 1992, s 235A(1).

[395] Auerbach, 1988.

[396] [2010] IRLR 114, QBD. Blake J thought it material in this context that the workers being balloted were technicians who worked in installations supplying power to the London Underground.

[397] See Martin *et al*, 1991; Elgar and Simpson, 1992 and 1996; Undy *et al*, 1996: ch 6.

[398] ACAS Annual Report 1993: p 16.

[399] Gall, 2006: p 335.

[400] Hale, 2008, 2010. In 2009 there were 98 stoppages and 458 ballots in favour of strike action: Hale, 2010: p 57.

[401] Para 6.

[402] TULRCA 1992, s 233.

[403] [1991] IRLR 372.

permissible for a specified person to authorise a subordinate union official to call a strike should further negotiations with the employer prove unsuccessful, although it emphasised that a very close link in time between the strike and the event precipitating the final action, such as an unsuccessful meeting, would be required, such closeness to be a question of fact and degree. The court also recognised in that case that it would be impractical to leave matters so that no discretion could be exercised by local officials as to how a call for industrial action was to be put into operation.

It is essential to the lawfulness of industrial action approved in a ballot that there should have been no call by the union to take part in it (or any authorisation or endorsement of such action) before the date of the ballot. The meaning of 'call' here is obscure, but appears to refer to a specific event rather than a prevailing attitude towards prospective action; in *Newham London Borough Council v NALGO*[404] the Court of Appeal affirmed that the union was not required to take a neutral stance before that time on whether industrial action should be taken; rather, it was 'perfectly entitled to be partisan'.[405] In the event that a 'call' for action is made before the date of the ballot the union will either need to repudiate it (where this is possible) or accept liability. The implications of a non-specified person whose actions are attributable to the union making a call depend upon the timing. A call made before the date of the ballot cannot be endorsed; the union will then have to choose between repudiation (where this is possible) or accepting liability. If a non-specified person makes a call after the date of the ballot it is possible that the union will not be liable provided that a specified person endorses it, although this is not free from doubt, nor is it clear whether the union can repudiate the unauthorised call (where it is open to it to do so) and still rely on the ballot to make a valid call thereafter, although the Code of Practice suggests that it can.[406] If an unauthorised call is made after a call by a specified person, the unauthorised call will be irrelevant.

The expiry date on the ballot mandate

11.44   A ballot in favour of industrial action ceases to be effective at the end of a period of four weeks beginning with the date of the ballot or a period 'of such longer duration not exceeding eight weeks as is agreed between the union and the members' employer'.[407] The provision for extension, introduced by ERelAct 1999, means that a union is not obliged to commence industrial action within the four-week period where, for example, the parties consider that a settlement could be achieved by negotiation. It is possible that industrial action may start and then be suspended for further negotiations to take place, only to be followed by the re-imposition of industrial action if these negotiations are not successful. As we indicated in para 11.41, the legislation now provides that where this is done by agreement between the parties no fresh notice need be issued in respect of resumed industrial action. However there is also the additional question whether or not a further ballot is required for the second period of industrial action. This depends upon whether it can be

---

[404] [1993] IRLR 383.

[405] [1993] IRLR 83, 86 (Woolf LJ).

[406] See footnote 11 in the Code.

[407] TULRCA 1992, s 234. The period of four weeks ends at the stroke of midnight on the last day of the fourth week, so where a ballot ceased to be effective on 12 June at the stroke of midnight, action called for 13 June was outside the period of the ballot mandate: *RJB Mining (UK) Ltd v NUM* [1995] IRLR 556.

viewed as sufficiently connected with the first to be regarded as a continuation of it, or whether the first was deemed to have terminated, in which case a fresh ballot will be required. In *Monsanto plc v TGWU*[408] union members voted in favour of industrial action 'in pursuit of a settlement of the dispute with Monsanto Ltd over the employment of Temporary Labour'. The company responded with counter-sanctions, including the suspension of sick pay, guaranteed week and early retirement schemes. The union suspended the industrial action pending further negotiations but re-imposed it two weeks later after negotiations broke down over these counter-sanctions. The Court of Appeal held that there was no need for a further ballot; the industrial action had not been discontinued but merely suspended temporarily for the purposes of negotiation with the intention that it would be resumed should negotiations fail. The court also rejected the employer's argument that the re-imposed action fell outside the terms of the ballot; these terms were sufficiently wide to encompass any matters within the scope of settlement of the original dispute.

This case was distinguished in *Post Office v UCW*.[409] In September 1988 postal officers and assistants voted in favour of industrial action in support of the union's opposition to the Post Office's plans to close up to 750 post offices, and between October and December there was a series of selective 24-hour strikes, culminating in a national one-day strike on 12 December. Between January and April 1989 there was no industrial action, although the union mounted a public relations campaign in opposition to the Post Office's policy, but in May the union's Assistant General Secretary told the annual conference that industrial action would continue. There were two brief local strikes in the autumn and in January 1990 the union gave instructions for a 24-hour strike in London and the South-East. The Post Office successfully applied for an interim injunction to halt this strike. The ground for the decision was that the form of question on the ballot paper did not meet the statutory requirements (having been presented in the rolled-up form 'are you willing to take industrial action up to and including strike action?'). However the Court of Appeal also held that the campaign of industrial action authorised by the ballot had terminated with the national strike in December 1988 and industrial action subsequent to that required the support of a fresh ballot. According to Lord Donaldson MR, it was implicit that industrial action, once begun, should continue without 'substantial interruption' if reliance were to continue to be placed upon the verdict of the initial ballot. This was a question of fact and degree but 'the question which the Court has to ask itself is whether the average reasonable trade union member, looking at the matter at or shortly after any interruption in the industrial action, would say to himself "the industrial action has now come to an end" even if he might also say "the union may want to call us out again if the dispute continues"'.[410]

For unions these cases contain two major lessons. First, where industrial action is suspended, they should make clear to their members that this suspension is contingent upon a successful outcome to negotiations, and they should not delay its resumption for an extended period.[411] Second, as *Monsanto* demonstrates, it is important to ensure that the terms of the questions on the ballot paper are sufficiently wide to cover any matters which might arise out of the dispute at issue (although bearing in mind the dangers of going beyond the central matter in dispute).

---

[408] [1986] IRLR 406.

[409] [1990] IRLR 143.

[410] [1990[IRLR 143, 147; see also Butler-Sloss LJ at 147–148. It is unclear why the test should depend on the views of a trade union member (or, indeed, an employer) rather than a court's objective assessment of the facts before it.

[411] See also *London Underground Ltd v RMT* (22 December 1998, unreported, QBD). In the case of continuous industrial action, due regard must also be paid to the provisions governing notice, discussed in para 11.41.

Originally the legislation made no provision for the situation where industrial action was halted temporarily by legal proceedings and during a docks dispute in 1989 the ballot mandate expired by the time that an interim injunction granted by the Court of Appeal was discharged by the House of Lords. The unfairness of this situation was appreciated by the Conservative Government. The legislation was amended to provide that where for any part of the four-week period the calling of industrial action was prohibited by a court order or by an undertaking to the court which subsequently ceases to apply, the union may apply to the court for an order that the period during which the prohibition took effect should not count towards the four-week limit, although no ballot may be regarded as effective more than twelve weeks after it took place.[412] Granting this extension is entirely at the discretion of the court, from which there is no appeal, but the extension must not be granted if the court considers that the ballot result no longer represents the views of the members concerned or that an event is likely to occur as a result of which those members would vote against industrial action were another ballot to be held. The speculative nature of this latter requirement, in particular, may present difficulties for a union, especially as one may argue that, given that most disputes end in compromise at some stage, such an 'event' will almost inevitably occur. Where an extension is refused a union will have to incur all the trouble and expense of a fresh ballot, even though its actions may have been fully vindicated in the legal proceedings which temporarily halted the industrial action.

The Code of Practice on Industrial Action Ballots and Notice to Employers

11.45   As we indicated in para 11.32, the Code of Practice, now in its fifth version, includes provisions which exceed the requirements of the legislation.[413] Particularly significant is the statement that a ballot should not take place until any agreed procedures, whether formal or otherwise, which might lead to a resolution of the dispute without the need for industrial action have been completed and consideration has been given to resolving the dispute by other means, including seeking assistance from ACAS.[414] This seems somewhat anomalous in the light of the fact that collective agreements are not, in general, legally enforceable and there is no equivalent exhortation where employers break agreements. There could also be scope for argument as to whether procedures have been exhausted in any given case. Another notable provision is that unions should consider delaying any call for industrial action following a ballot until the scrutineer's report has been received, which could create considerable difficulties given the tight time limits which apply.[415] A further example is the recommendation that unions should describe the main deficiencies in their data in the notices that they give to employers.[416] Although neither these nor other provisions of the Code are directly enforceable it is conceivable that non-observance

---

[412] TULRCA 1992, s 234. The period between the making of an application and its determination does not count towards the four-week period.

[413] This was also a feature of earlier Codes: see Simpson, 1995. On the 2005 Code, see Simpson, 2005. As Simpson, 2005: p 336 remarks, the Code does not include the additional requirements that have been read into the law by the courts so it cannot be seen as a complete statement of the law on all issues.

[414] Para 6.

[415] Para 49.

[416] Para 16.

of them, particularly the first, may be influential when a court is deciding whether to grant an interim injunction to halt the action.

CIVIL LAW REMEDIES

11.46   There are two primary remedies which those affected by unlawful industrial action may seek in the courts: an injunction and damages. As we discussed in para 11.17, claims in restitution for 'economic duress' are also possible, but as these claims can be brought only in limited circumstances we do not discuss them further here.

Damages

11.47   Damages are awarded according to the general principles applicable to the law of tort, aiming to put the claimant in the position he or she would have been in had the tort not been committed.[417] It is conceivable that exemplary or aggravated, as well as compensatory, damages may be awarded if the court considers that the defendant's conduct warrants this,[418] although the circumstances when exemplary (punitive) damages may be awarded have been restricted by the courts.[419] As usual it is necessary to prove that the defendant's act caused the damage in question, a requirement which may create difficulties where a defendant has committed various torts, all of which contributed to the claimant's loss but some of which are protected by the statutory immunities.[420] There have been no reported cases on this point as yet in English law, but the Northern Ireland Court of Appeal has held that damages must be limited to loss attributable to the non-protected torts.[421]

Before 1982 it was rare for employers to sue for damages, one reason doubtless being that such claims could be brought only against union officers and not against trade unions. This immunity was removed in 1982, although the implications for unions of unlimited liability were partially recognised in that the amount of damages which could be awarded in any proceedings in tort was subject to statutory maxima (with specified exceptions not relevant in the industrial action context).[422] The limit depends upon the size of the union: there is a maximum of £10,000 if the union has fewer than 5,000 members; £50,000 if it has between 5,000 and 24,999; £125,000 if it has between 25,000 and 99,999; and £250,000 if it has 100,000 or more.[423] However, this

---

[417] See generally McGregor, 2009, as updated.

[418] See *Messenger Newspapers Group Ltd v NGA* [1984] IRLR 397.

[419] See *Kuddus v Chief Constable of Leicestershire Constabulary* [2001] 3 All ER 193 and the discussion in Deakin *et al* 2008: pp 944-951.

[420] Wedderburn, 1986: p 682.

[421] *Norbrook Laboratories Ltd v King* [1984] IRLR 200.

[422] Damages for personal injury resulting from negligence, nuisance or breach of duty, or a breach of duty in connection with the ownership, occupation, possession, control or use of property or proceedings relating to product liability: TULRCA 1992, s 22(1).

[423] TULRCA 1992, s 22(2). The Secretary of State may vary these sums by order: ss 22(3), (4). As Wedderburn points out (1986: p 682) the relevant time for counting numbers is not specified: is it the date of the commission of the tort, the date of the claim form or the date of judgment?

protection is less extensive than it may appear; it does not include any interest which may be awarded on the damages, which may be substantial,[424] and it applies only in respect of a single set of proceedings, so that if there are multiple claimants suing in relation to a single act, each may claim to the limit, although if a single claimant issued several claim forms for different torts, or in respect of different acts, the union could ask for the proceedings to be consolidated. Moreover, the limits do not apply to actions outside the law of tort, such as restitution, nor to fines for contempt of court or to legal costs which unions may be required to pay.

The threat to sue for damages is a powerful weapon in the armoury of employers although it carries the disadvantage that the hearing is likely to take place long after the dispute is settled and proceedings are unlikely to promote good industrial relations.

Interim injunctions: introduction

11.48   Given the disadvantages of a damages claim referred to above, the remedy which is much more commonly sought in practice is an interim injunction to prevent the action starting or continuing, issued under the discretionary power of the High Court to make such orders pending the full trial of an action. Injunctions may order the defendant to desist from specified conduct, such as restraining a union from inducing breach of contract, or to take positive steps to undo a wrong, for example to withdraw instructions to take industrial action. It is also possible to grant an injunction (formerly known as a *quia timet* injunction) to prevent an apprehended legal wrong where an applicant can provide adequate evidence of the fear that a wrong is likely otherwise to be committed.[425] The courts have granted such an injunction to prevent a respondent from inducing the breach of a future contract,[426] and in 1988 such an order was even granted against the National Union of Seamen to prevent it from conducting a (lawful) ballot on the basis that the proposed industrial action would be unlawful.[427] However, injunctions cannot be used to force individual employees to return to work; by statute, no court may compel an employee to work or attend at any place to work by way of an injunction restraining a breach or threatened breach of a contract of employment.[428]

The normal purpose of an interim injunction is to preserve the status quo pending the full trial of an action. This may be necessary where, for example, the subject-matter may be destroyed without such an order. In the context of industrial action, however, the granting of an interim injunction effectively decides the matter. This makes the grounds upon which such injunctions may be granted particularly crucial; indeed, it may be said that the very freedom to take industrial action hinges upon this issue. For this reason we examine both the grounds and the procedure in some detail below.

---

[424] See *Boxfoldia Ltd v NGA* [1988] IRLR 383 (£90,000 interest awarded).

[425] See Spry, 2010: pp 377–382, 468–470 for the principles governing such injunctions.

[426] *JT Stratford & Son Ltd v Lindley* [1965] AC 269, 339 (Lord Upjohn); *Union Traffic Ltd v TGWU* [1989] IRLR 127. As Auerbach argues (1989: p 170), given that it remains lawful to persuade a person not to make a contract (*Midland Cold Storage Ltd v Steer* [1972] Ch 630) and if in fact the applicant has no long-term contract, this comes 'perilously close' to protecting the applicant's expectations, and not merely rights. *Quaere* whether a court would take the same approach after the House of Lords' decision in *OBG Ltd v Allan* [2008] 1 AC 1, [2007] IRLR 608, discussed at para 11.11 above.

[427] See Auerbach, 1988: p 229. See also *EDF Energy Powerlink Ltd v RMT* [2010] IRLR 114, QBD, discussed at para 11.42 above.

[428] TULRCA 1992, s 236.

Interim injunctions: the courts' approach

11.49   The granting of an interim injunction, which is an equitable remedy, is always at the discretion of the court.[429] In general, however, as a first step the court must be satisfied that there is a '*serious question to be tried*', a test which, in the House of Lords decision in *American Cyanamid Co v Ethicon Ltd*,[430] replaced the more stringent pre-existing requirement to show a *prima facie* case. To demonstrate a 'serious issue' may not be a difficult test to satisfy in industrial action cases, where the facts may be complex and disputed and the applicant may allege the commission of several torts, the boundaries and, indeed, the very existence of which may be debatable. If an applicant suggests a novel head of liability, the courts may be reluctant to dismiss the suggestion out of hand. In general the evidence before the court will be in written form – although there is power to cross-examine the deponent of a witness statement this is rarely done at interim stage [431] – and where the evidence before the court is insufficient to decide a disputed matter the court is likely to conclude that there is a 'serious question'.

Once a claimant has crossed this preliminary hurdle the court decides whether or not to grant an injunction according to the '*balance of convenience*' (although, as we indicate below, the statutory immunities, where applicable, will also need to be considered). This test requires the court to consider whether damages would be an adequate remedy for either side if its position were vindicated at the trial; if so, an injunction should be refused. Damages will rarely be viewed as adequate if the respondent is unable or unlikely to pay them and may not be sufficient if the alleged wrong is regarded by the court as irreparable, incapable of pecuniary compensation or if damages would be very difficult to assess.[432] If damages are not regarded as a sufficient remedy, the court will then consider whether more harm will be done by granting or refusing the injunction. As Lord Diplock expressed the position in *American Cyanamid*: [433]

> The object of the ... [interim] ... injunction is to protect the ... [applicant] ... against injury by violation of his right for which he could not be adequately compensated in damages recoverable in the action if the uncertainty were resolved in his favour at the trial; but the ... [applicant's] ... need for such protection must be weighed against the corresponding need of the ... [respondent] ... to be protected against injury resulting from his having been prevented from exercising his own legal rights for which he could not be adequately compensated under the ... [applicant's] ... undertaking in damages if the uncertainty were resolved in the ... [respondent's] ... favour at the trial. The court must weigh one need against another ...[434]

---

[429] For the statutory right of action an order to halt industrial action is the only form of relief available and, where a claim is well-founded, the statute states that the court 'shall' grant an order: TULRCA 1992, s 235A. However, it also indicates that interim relief may be granted for this purpose and we would argue that at the interim stage the decision as to whether to grant a remedy remains one for the discretion of the court.

[430] [1975] 1 All ER 504. Although some decisions in other contexts have shown a willingness to recognise the importance of a test of merits (*Lansing Linde Ltd v Kerr* [1991] 1 All ER 418; *Cambridge Nutrition Ltd v BBC* [1990] 3 All ER 523) this approach has yet to appear generally in the context of industrial action, although see *Viking Line ABP v ITWF* [2006] IRLR 58, CA at [62] (Waller LJ): employer had an 'uphill struggle'.

[431] For a rare example see the cross-examination of Ron Todd, General Secretary of the TGWU, and other TGWU officials in *Associated British Ports v TGWU* [1989] IRLR 291.

[432] *Merchant Adventurers Ltd v Grew and Co Ltd* [1972] Ch 242.

[433] [1975] 1 All ER 504.

[434] [1975] 1 All ER 504, 509.

In *American Cyanamid* the House of Lords warned against attempts to specify exhaustively the matters which the courts should take into account in assessing the 'balance of convenience'. With that warning in mind, some factors can be isolated which have proved influential in the industrial action context. One consistently weighty factor is the extent of the loss which the employer would suffer if the action went ahead. This was a particularly powerful argument before 1982, when trade unions could not themselves be sued in tort, leaving employers with a remedy only against individual dispute organisers who were unlikely to have the means to pay substantial damages and costs. In 1984 the House of Lords stated that the repeal of this immunity by EA 1982 meant that there was no reason for judges to assume that a case would never come to trial where the respondent was the union itself.[435] In practice, however, this change did not seem to have made judges less willing to grant interim injunctions, and at times it made employers more willing to apply for them.[436] Moreover, the statutory limit upon the amount which may be claimed in damages against a union, introduced to protect union funds, has been used against them in some cases, where the court has found that the losses which the employer would incur were the action not injuncted would exceed this sum.[437]

It has proved much more difficult for unions to persuade the courts that they and/or their members will suffer irrecoverable losses if an injunction is imposed; admittedly the losses which may arise from the inability lawfully to pursue industrial action are less tangible and less easy to quantify.[438] However the difficulty of qualifying loss, which on occasion has swayed the issue in favour of an employer,[439] has traditionally met with less success when used by unions, and the courts have tended not to accord great weight to the argument that industrial action, once postponed, may not be easily revived.[440] However, in the light of the statutory requirements for a postal ballot and (usually) independent scrutiny of industrial action ballots, both of which impose considerable costs on unions, the position may be different: these costs are quantifiable and, where claimed, will need to be taken into account by the court in exercising its discretion whether the injunction should be granted. Where an interim injunction has been granted, unions may be more inclined to take a case to full trial to recover these amounts. A further factor, whose weight remains untested, is that of damage to the 'public interest', which was propounded by the Court of Appeal as a factor for

---

[435] *Dimbleby & Sons Ltd v NUJ* [1984] IRLR 161.

[436] For an early survey see Evans, 1987; for later statistics see Gall and McKay, 1996; *Labour Research* October 1998: pp 15–16; TUC, *Focus on Balloting and Industrial Action: Trade Union Trends Survey*, 2001; Gall, 2006 (where it is reported that the frequency of applications declined in the period 1997–2005, although the threat or perceived threat of an application could have a considerable effect on union conduct: pp 337, 339).

[437] See, for example, *Mercury Communications Ltd v Scott-Garner* [1983] IRLR 494, CA; *News Group Newspapers Ltd v SOGAT '82 (No 2)* [1986] IRLR 337.

[438] For an example of judicial acknowledgement of this see *Barretts & Baird (Wholesale) Ltd v IPCS* [1987] IRLR 3, 11 (Henry J).

[439] See *News Group Newspapers Ltd v SOGAT '82 (No 2)* [1986] IRLR 337 (value of loss of key staff could not be quantified).

[440] See, for example, *Mercury Communications Ltd v Scott-Garner* [1983] IRLR 494, 504 (May LJ); *Associated British Ports v TGWU* [1989] IRLR 305. Cf recognition by Lord Diplock in *NWL v Woods* [1979] IRLR 478, 484 of the need for unions to 'strike while the iron is still hot'; *Cambridge Nutrition Ltd v BBC* [1990] 3 All ER 523: damages would not be an adequate remedy for the BBC if an action to restrain the broadcast of a TV programme failed at full trial because it would have been deprived of the opportunity to broadcast on a matter of public interest in the form and manner of its choice; *Viking Line ABP v ITWF* [2006] IRLR 58, CA, at [64]: to grant the injunction would be close to giving the employer the remedy which should only be available after full trial. See also the HRA 1998, s 12.

consideration during the 1989 docks dispute.[441] In 1998 a court took into account in granting an interim injunction to restrain strikes on the London underground the public disruption which the strikes would occasion, particularly if they were to take place on New Year's Eve, when large numbers of people wishing to travel into London would also raise questions of public safety.[442] The concept of the 'public interest' is undefined and malleable, and has the potential to justify injuncting industrial action in a wide variety of situations; indeed, '[i]n major disputes it could turn the balance of convenience into a mere formality'.[443] Another consideration of uncertain significance and scope is non-compliance with the extra-statutory requirements of the Code of Practice, such as those affirming that industrial action should be taken only after all other avenues have been explored.[444] Under the HRA 1998, the fact that industrial action will interfere with a 'Convention right', such as freedom of expression or, possibly, the right to life, may also influence a court in favour of granting an injunction and, indeed, in relation to some of the Convention rights at least, there may be a positive obligation on the court to grant the order. Finally, where the balance of convenience does not weigh decisively one way or the other, the court has regard to the desirability of preserving the status quo[445] which, where industrial action has not yet started, means preventing it occurring.[446]

Taken alone the criteria by which the courts decide whether or not to grant interim injunctions could undermine entirely the protection afforded by the statutory immunities. In an attempt to avoid this situation TULRCA 1992, s 221(2) (re-enacting a provision introduced shortly after the decision in *American Cyanamid*) states that where a respondent claims to have acted in contemplation or furtherance of a trade dispute:

> ... the court shall, in exercising its discretion whether or not to grant the injunction, have regard to the likelihood of that party's succeeding at the trial of the action in establishing any matter which would afford a defence to the action under section 219 (protection from certain tort liabilities) or section 220 (peaceful picketing).

In *NWL v Woods*[447] the House of Lords stated that this provision required the courts to put into the balance of convenience the degree of likelihood of the defence succeeding; the greater the degree of likelihood the greater the weight to be accorded to it. On this approach, where the immunities seem likely to apply the injunction should be refused. However, the impact of this provision is restricted in three different ways. First, it does not apply to situations where the applicant suggests heads of liability which are not within the scope of the immunities, such as breach of statutory duty; these will be decided on the basis of the *American Cyanamid* test alone. Second, as we have seen, there are several areas where the scope and/or application of the statutory immunities

[441] *Associated British Ports v TGWU* [1989] IRLR 305, above. The relevance and significance of this factor was not discussed by the House of Lords: [1989] IRLR 399.
[442] *London Underground Ltd v RMT* (22 December 1998, unreported, QBD). See also *British Airways plc v Unite the Union* [2010] IRLR 423, QB, Cox J at [83].
[443] Simpson, 1989: p 240.
[444] See para 11.45.
[445] *American Cyanamid Co v Ethicon Ltd* [1975] 1 All ER 504, 511.
[446] See, for example, *Associated British Ports v TGWU* [1989] IRLR 305; *London Underground Ltd v NUR* [1989] IRLR 341.
[447] [1979] IRLR 478.

defence may be uncertain. Until recently, where there has been doubt about the application of the immunities, the courts have generally seen granting the injunction as the more appropriate course. In *London Underground Ltd v NUR*[448] for example, Simon Brown J acknowledged that he was reaching a decision about whether the immunities applied 'after insufficient argument and certainly insufficient consideration'[449] but nevertheless granted the injunction. In *RMT v Serco Docklands; ASLEF v London Midland*, discussed in para 11.9 above, the Court of Appeal made clear that, following the recognition of the right to strike by the ECtHR, the immunities should not be construed against those seeking to rely on them.[450] This should make it harder for employers to obtain injunctions on the basis of speculative arguments that the immunities do not apply but where there are strong arguments either way the balance of convenience may still lead to an injunction being granted. Third, the courts have continued to affirm their residual discretion to grant an injunction irrespective of the likelihood of the immunities applying where the consequences of disruptive action for the employer or the public may be particularly 'disastrous'.[451] According to Lord Fraser, 'if the probable result of the threatened act would be to cause immediate serious danger to public safety or health and if no other means seemed to be available for averting the danger in time' then it would not be wrong to grant an injunction.[452] This position means that even industrial action which is clearly protected by the statutory immunities may nevertheless be enjoined by an injunction if the court considers that the circumstances warrant it. There have been no cases as yet where this has occurred.

Interim injunctions: procedure

11.50   The true significance of interim injunctions in the industrial action context can be appreciated only with knowledge of the procedure by which they may be sought. Normally applicants should serve on the respondent the application notice, together with evidence in support, not less than three days before the court is due to hear the application, and the hearing will then take place with all the parties to the proceedings being present before the court.[453] However, where a matter is sufficiently urgent the application may be made to the court even more speedily, even before a claim form is issued, without notice to the respondent. Due to the fact that imminent industrial action will generally be deemed sufficiently urgent to justify an application without notice, TULRCA 1992 attempts to provide some rudimentary protection for respondents. It states that when a party against whom an injunction without notice is sought claims, or in the opinion of the court would be likely to claim, that he or she acted in contemplation or furtherance of a trade dispute the court shall not grant the injunction unless satisfied that all steps which in the circumstances were reasonable have been taken with a view to securing that notice of the application and an opportunity of being heard with respect to it has been given to him or her.[454] There is an important obligation on an applicant to give full and frank disclosure of all material

---

[448] [1989] IRLR 341.
[449] [1989] IRLR 341, 342.
[450] [2011] IRLR 399, Elias LJ at [9].
[451] Lord Diplock in *NWL Ltd v Woods* [1979] IRLR 478 (as amended [1980] ICR 167).
[452] *Duport Steels Ltd v Sirs* [1980] ICR 161, 187.
[453] CPR Practice Direction 25A – Interim Injunctions.
[454] TULRCA 1992, s 221(1).

facts to the court, but nevertheless the absent respondent may still be at risk of losing the benefit afforded by the legislation since it will be for the applicant to explain to the court why better notice could not have been given, an explanation which, by definition, the respondent cannot challenge. It should be noted that only the steps, not the notice itself, need to be reasonable; the union which receives notice which is inadequate but nevertheless sufficient to enable it to appear in court, albeit unprepared, may be unable to rely on the statutory protection.[455] The requirement to take 'reasonable steps' to give the respondent notice has been liberally interpreted, covering telex, fax, or telegram and sometimes even a telephone call to the union headquarters (although there is a strong case for saying that with the extensive use of e-mail, an abortive communication by telephone should no longer be regarded as 'reasonable steps' save in exceptional circumstances). In *Barratts & Baird (Wholesale) Ltd v IPCS*[456] the applicants left a message on the union's answering machine after 5pm on a Friday afternoon. They then obtained an injunction without notice over the telephone the following Sunday afternoon. This decision seems at odds with the intention of the statute. The difficulties for unions are compounded by the fact that, once the injunction has been granted, it is very difficult to get it lifted. Although normally the terms of the injunction will grant the respondent the right to apply to the court to discharge or vary it on giving notice to the applicant of a specified number of hours or days (often 24 or 48 hours), such applications are not always afforded the expeditious treatment received by the original application and the court may be reluctant to disturb the status quo. In *Barratts & Baird*, for example, the hearing of the respondent's application for a discharge of the injunction made two days after it was granted was adjourned for a week because of pressure of business and a further two days passed before judgment was given and the injunction discharged. One may well imagine circumstances where these days may be vital to a union; indeed, delay of this length may mean that a union loses the protection provided by a ballot if the industrial action has not already started (see para 11.44).

An appeal can be made only with permission against the decision of a judge to grant or refuse an interim injunction.[457] Many appeals in the industrial action context proceed to the Court of Appeal and even to the Supreme Court very swiftly under an expedited procedure. An appeal court will only allow an appeal where the decision of the lower court was wrong, or where it was unjust because of a serious procedural or other irregularity in the proceedings.[458] Following the introduction of the Civil Procedure Rules in 1999, every appeal is now limited to a review of the decision of the lower court unless the Court considers that in the circumstances of an individual appeal it would be in the interests of justice to hold a re-hearing.[459] A decision of a lower court may, however, be set aside on the grounds that there has been a change of circumstances since the judge made the order that would have justified his or her acceding to an application to vary it.[460] There may be greater scope for appeal under the HRA 1998; failure to take appropriate account of the requirements of that Act will constitute a misunderstanding of the law.

---

[455] Although note the approach of Turner J in *Post Office v UCW* [1990] IRLR 143, who refused to grant an injunction on the ground, *inter alia*, that TULRCA 1992, s 221(1) had not been complied with, despite the attendance of the union, which had refused the offer of an adjournment, at the hearing.

[456] See [1987] IRLR 3 for the discharge of the injunction.

[457] CPR, r 52.3.

[458] CPR, r 52.11(3). See also *Tanfern Ltd v Cameron-MacDonald* [2000] 2 All ER 801.

[459] CPR, r 52.11(1). A Practice Direction may also make different provision for a particular category of appeal.

[460] See CPR, r 52.10 for the powers of an appeal court. For an example of important new evidence being introduced at the appeal stage see *Mercury Communications Ltd v Scott-Garner and the POEU* [1983] IRLR 494.

It has been persuasively argued by Countouris and Freedland that the approach of the British courts to interim injunctions in the context of industrial action fails to comply with the ECHR in two important respects.[461] The first is procedural. In *Micalef v Malta* the ECtHR, in a departure from its previous case law, held that Article 6 of the ECHR, which gives the right to a fair trial, applied to interim proceedings where civil rights and obligations were at issue provided that the interim measure could 'be considered effectively to determine the civil right or obligation at stake'.[462] As we have seen, in industrial action cases the interim stage effectively determines the outcome of the litigation and should, therefore, be presumed to be subject to the requirements of Article 6.[463] The second ground of non-compliance is substantive: if it is accepted that a right to strike can be derived from Article 11, injunctive relief should be based not on the *Cyanamid* test but on the principles of Article 11(2), so that any restriction should be no more than is necessary and proportionate in a democratic society.

The legal consequences of breaching an injunction

11.51   Breach of an interim injunction constitutes a contempt of court.[464] Where a union is a named respondent it will be liable for the acts of its members or officials according to the principles discussed in para 11.20 *et seq*. This means that where the injunction covers the torts specified in TULRCA 1992, s 20 the statutory principles will apply,[465] otherwise the situation is governed by common law principles of vicarious liability, so that the union will be liable for persons acting within the scope of their express or implied authority. If a union knows that breaches of the law are occurring it must take active steps to secure compliance;[466] in the case of union officers this may entail the union withdrawing their credentials.[467] Even if a union is not named in the interim order, it may be in contempt if it knowingly acts in breach of its terms or knowingly 'aids and abets' a respondent to commit a breach (as indeed may any third party).[468]

The penalties for contempt are designed to force the contemnors to purge their contempt and accept the authority of the court. This may mean imprisonment, although in the industrial

---

[461] Countouris and Freedland, 2010.

[462] Application No 17065/06, para 85.

[463] In *Micalef v Malta* above the Court said that there may be 'exceptional circumstances' in some cases where it may not be possible immediately to comply with all the requirements of Art 6: para 86. For the requirements of Art 6 see Clayton and Tomlinson, 2009: ch 11.

[464] Committal for a civil contempt is at the behest of the applicant, although it is possible that the court may also act of its own initiative: CPR Sch 1 RSC Ord 52, r 5; see also *Re Supply of Ready Mixed Concrete* [1992] ICR 229, 248 (Lord Donaldson MR); for a critique see Wedderburn, 1992b. For a detailed account of the law of contempt see Arlidge *et al*, 2007, as updated. For the operation of contempt during the 1984–1985 miners' strike see Lightman, 1987; also useful is O'Regan, 1991.

[465] TULRCA 1992, s 20(6).

[466] *UKAPE and Newall v AUEW (Technical and Supervisory Section)* [1972] ICR 151; *Heatons Transport (St Helens) Ltd v TGWU* [1972] IRLR 25; *Richard Read Transport Ltd v NUM (South Wales Area)* [1985] IRLR 67.

[467] *Heatons Transport (St Helens) Ltd v TGWU* [1972] IRLR 25; see also *Re Supply of Ready Mixed Concrete* [1992] ICR 229, 258 (Lord Donaldson MR).

[468] *Seaward v Paterson* [1897] 1 Ch 545. See also *A-G v Punch Ltd* [2002] UKHL 50, [2003] 1 All ER 289, discussed Devonshire, 2003 and Seymour, 2007. In *Gate Gourmet London Ltd v TGWU* [2005] IRLR 881, QBD, the court took the 'unusual' step of granting an injunction against unnamed, as well as named, defendants, and stipulated how the contents of the order should be circulated: para 33.

action context the courts are now unlikely to risk the martyrdom this can create; thus in 1984 when the president of the National Union of Mineworkers, Arthur Scargill, was judged guilty of 'wilful and repeated disobedience' of an order the penalty was a £1,000 fine. Where a union is in contempt the statutory limits applicable to awards of damages do not apply and in serious cases fines well in excess of these limits have been imposed; in 1983, for example, the NGA was fined over £525,000. However, the courts recognise that contempt may take various forms, ranging from 'flat defiance' at the top end of the scale to a 'half-hearted or perhaps colourable attempt' to comply with the court's order, down to a 'genuine whole-hearted' use of best endeavours to comply which has nevertheless been unsuccessful.[469] 'Flat defiance' is likely to attract a greater fine than a more minor or technical breach, when the penalty may be low or even waived altogether.[470] Where an individual union member or officer for whom the union is not legally liable is found to be in contempt, it is unlawful for union property to be used to pay the fine; if this were to happen it would be open to any union member, as well as the union itself, to recover from the individual the amount applied for this purpose.[471]

A further possible consequence of being found in contempt is sequestration of the union's assets, which will be returned only when the contemnor is released from the contempt, minus any fines, which may be deducted from the property, or costs incurred, which are likely to be large.[472] Third parties have a duty not to obstruct the sequestrators in carrying out their duties and a union's banks and auditors must co-operate in identifying the whereabouts of union property.[473] In *Clarke v Heathfield*,[474] the court even ordered the removal of the union's trustees and appointment of a receiver of its assets and income after 16 members brought an action claiming that the assets were in jeopardy since the union had already been fined for contempt and was likely to incur further fines. Thus a union may lose completely the ability to control its assets.[475] What is sufficient to purge contempt depends upon the attitude of the judge; in some cases rigorous action by the union to repudiate the unlawful action, coupled with an apology in open court, has been required; in others the judge has not insisted upon a formal apology if satisfied that the union has otherwise accepted the authority of the court.[476] The discretionary nature of this matter can make the process appear even more of a lottery.

---

[469] *Howitt Transport Ltd and Howitt Bros Ltd v TGWU* [1973] IRLR 25. On the requisite intention which needs to be shown, see *Re Supply of Ready Mixed Concrete* [1992] QB 213; *P v P* [1999] 3 FCR 547.

[470] In *Austin Rover Group Ltd v AUEW (Technical and Supervisory Section)* [1985] IRLR 162 no penalty was imposed because the contempt was not serious and the union might have taken sufficiently vigorous steps to dissociate itself from the industrial action had it taken legal advice at an early stage. Cf *Richard Read (Transport) Ltd v NUM (South Wales Area)* [1985] IRLR 67 (deliberate defiance); *Kent Free Press v NGA* [1987] IRLR 267 (union taking as long as possible to withdraw instructions).

[471] TULRCA 1992, s 15. This restriction does not cover payment of the expenses of defending the contempt proceedings. It is a moot point whether a union could organise a voluntary collection to indemnify a member who had been required to pay a fine; this would depend upon whether the money collected could be deemed to be the 'property' of the union.

[472] For the use of sequestration orders during the 1984–1985 miners' strike see Lightman, 1987. In a seafarers' dispute in 1988 the National Union of Seamen incurred sequestration costs of £0.5 million: Auerbach, 1990: p 99, n 118.

[473] *Eckman v Midland Bank Ltd* [1973] 1 All ER 609; *Messenger Newspapers Group Ltd v SOGAT '82* [1984] ICR 345.

[474] [1985] ICR 203; *Clarke v Heathfield (No 2)* [1985] ICR 606.

[475] There are now also extensive statutory provisions in this connection: see TULRCA 1992, s 16 and para 11.92 below.

[476] *Richard Read (Transport) Ltd v NUM (South Wales Area)* [1985] IRLR 67.

INDUSTRIAL ACTION AND EU LAW

11.52   As we indicated in para 7.7, the Social Policy provisions of the TFEU expressly exclude the right of association and the right to strike from the range of matters on which the EU organs are empowered to adopt directives or other relevant legal instruments.[477] However, as we discussed in para 7.11, this lack of competence has not prevented the recognition by the ECJ of freedom of association, including the right to strike, as a fundamental right. In two 2007 decisions the ECJ, referring to various international instruments including the ESC, ILO Convention No 87, and EU Charter of Fundamental Rights,[478] held that 'the right to take collective action, including the right to strike, must ... be recognised as a fundamental right which forms an integral part of the general principles of Community law'.[479] This is not the positive development for trade unions it may seem at first sight, however. The ECJ recognised the right to strike in a context where it served as a defence to employers' claims that their free movement rights under the EC Treaty (the predecessor of the TFEU) had been infringed by trade union action. As such a defence, the Court circumscribed the right by imposing tightly-defined conditions on its exercise, requiring individual campaigns of collective action to be closely scrutinised to assess whether they are justified. As the right recognised by the ECJ is also subject to provisions of national law, these decisions have the effect of adding new restrictions to those already present in British law in relation to disputes with a cross-border dimension. Space does not permit a full analysis of all the issues raised by the judgments of the Court.[480] Here we confine ourselves to giving a brief overview of the two cases followed by a discussion of the major implications of the judgments for British law.

ITWF v Viking Line arose out of the plan by a Finnish company to reflag a ferry, the Rosella, which operated between Estonia and Finland, under the Estonian flag so that it could staff the ferry with an Estonian crew which could be paid lower wages than the existing Finnish crew. A principal policy of the International Transport Workers' Federation (ITWF) is to oppose 'flags of convenience', under which a ship is registered in one country by a beneficial owner situated in another country. The Finnish Seamen's Union (FSU) planned industrial action against Viking and the ITWF told its affiliates not to enter into negotiations with Viking and to take other solidarity industrial action. Viking sought an injunction in the English courts to halt the boycott on the ground that it infringed Article 43 TEC (now Article 49 TFEU), the right to freedom of establishment.[481] A permanent injunction was granted at first instance but the Court of Appeal considered that the case raised a number of important issues relating to the interaction of the key provisions of the Treaty dealing with industrial action and the 'fundamental rights of workers to take industrial action'[482] which should be referred to the ECJ. The Court of Appeal set aside the injunction and, applying the balance of convenience test described in para 11.49 above, refused Viking interim relief.

---

[477] Art 153(5).

[478] Art 28.

[479] *ITWF v Viking Line* Case C-438/05, para 44, [2008] IRLR 143. See also Case C-341/05 *Laval Un Partneri Ltd v Svenska Byggnadsarbetareforbundet* [2008] IRLR 160, para 91. See further para 2.39 for the status of fundamental rights in EU law.

[480] For more detailed analyses, see A Davies, 2008; Syrpis and Novitz, 2008; Orlandini, 2008; Syrpis, 2008; Barnard, 2008a and 2008b; Dashwood, 2008; Novitz, 2008; Sciarra, 2008 and contributions to Ewing and Hendy, 2009a.

[481] Since the ITF's base is in London, jurisdiction was established pursuant to the Brussels Regulation (Regulation (EC) 44/2001); *Viking Line v ITWF* [2006] IRLR 58, CA, Waller LJ at [2].

[482] Waller LJ, above, at [1]. See A Davies, 2006 for a discussion of this decision.

The ECJ held that collective action initiated by a union in principle fell within the scope of Article 43 TEC and that Article 43 could confer rights on a private undertaking which may be relied on against a union or association of unions.[483] The Court recognised the right to take collective action in the terms we describe above, but went on to state that 'the exercise of that right may none the less be subject to certain restrictions. As is reaffirmed by Article 28 of the Charter of Fundamental Rights of the … [EU], those rights are to be protected in accordance with Community law and national law and practices'.[484] The Court rejected the unions' argument that the reasoning in *Albany* should be applied by analogy here to exclude the right to strike from the scope of the free movement provisions,[485] stating (without explanation) that 'it cannot be considered that it is inherent in the very exercise of trade union rights and the right to take collective action that … [the fundamental freedoms in Title III of the Treaty] … will be prejudiced to a certain degree'.[486] The Court held that collective action such as that at issue constituted a restriction on freedom of establishment within the meaning of Article 43 as it 'has the effect of making less attractive, or even pointless … Viking's exercise of its right to freedom of establishment' in that it prevented Viking from 'enjoying the same treatment in the host member state as other economic operators established in that state'.[487] The Court cited previous case law in support of the principle that a restriction on freedom of establishment could be accepted if it pursued a legitimate aim compatible with the Treaty and was justified by overriding reasons of public interest, but even then it would need to be 'suitable for securing the attainment of the objective pursued' and not go beyond what was necessary to attain it.[488] It stated that the right to take collective action for the protection of workers constituted a legitimate interest and the protection of workers was one of the overriding reasons of public interest recognised by the Court; the Community had 'not only an economic but also a social purpose', so the rights on the free movement must be 'balanced' against the objectives pursued by social policy.[489] It was for the national court to determine whether the collective action in question concerned the protection of workers; however, the ECJ stated that this could not be the case here if it were established that the jobs or conditions of employment of the workers concerned were not 'jeopardised or under serious threat'.[490] If such a threat were established, the national court would then need to consider whether the collective action in question was 'suitable for ensuring the achievement of the objective pursued and does not go beyond what is necessary to achieve that objective'. In doing so, it should examine in this case whether the FSU had 'other means at its disposal which were less restrictive of freedom of establishment in order to bring to a successful conclusion the collective negotiations entered into with Viking, and, on the other, whether that trade union had exhausted those means before initiating such action'.[491]

---

[483] See Syrpis and Novitz, 2008: pp 420–422 for a critique of this aspect of the decision.

[484] See note 479 above, para 44.

[485] See para 7.11 above.

[486] Above, note 479, para 52. Title III covered free movement of persons, services and capital; these are now contained in Title IV TFEU.

[487] Above, note 479, para 72.

[488] Above, note 479, para 75.

[489] Above, note 479, paras 77–79.

[490] Above, note 479, para 81. The Court considered that there would be no such threat if the employer undertook not to terminate the employment of the existing crew: para 82. As Davies points out, this ignores the broader context of the dispute: A Davies, 2008: p 144.

[491] Above, note 479, paras 84, 87. The ECJ considered it legitimate to 'provide guidance' on proportionality to 'enable the national court to give judgment on the particular case before it': para 85.

In the second case, *Laval*, a Latvian company had won a government contract to renovate school premises in Sweden. The company posted some Latvian workers to Sweden to work on the site who earned considerably less than their Swedish counterparts. The Swedish builders' union sought to persuade Laval to sign its collective agreement for the building sector, the terms of which went beyond those required by the Posted Workers' Directive and which contained a mechanism for pay determination which meant that Laval could not ascertain in advance what wages it would need to pay. Laval refused to sign, and the builders' union, supported by the electricians' union, began a blockade of Laval's building sites with the result that Laval was unable to carry out its activities in Sweden. Laval commenced proceedings in the Swedish courts arguing *inter alia* that the industrial action was a restriction on its freedom to provide services contrary to Article 49 EC (now Article 56 TFEU).[492] The Swedish court referred a number of questions to the ECJ. Part of the ECJ's judgment involved consideration of the Posted Workers' Directive; we discuss these aspects in para 2.49 above. In relation to the core principles governing the right to strike, the judgment essentially reflected that in *Viking*.[493] Here, the right of unions of a member state to take collective action by which undertakings established in other member states may be forced to sign the collective agreement for the building sector was 'liable to make it less attractive, or more difficult, for such undertakings to carry out construction work in Sweden' and as such consisted a restriction on the freedom to provide services.[494] Unlike in *Viking*, however, the ECJ itself gave a specific answer to the question of justification. Although the Court accepted that 'the right to take collective action for the protection of the workers of the host state against possible social dumping may constitute an overriding reason of public interest', in this case the action could not be justified since the negotiations on pay which the action sought to require Laval to enter formed part of a 'national context characterised by a lack of provisions ... which are sufficiently precise and accessible that they do not render it ... excessively difficult in practice for such an undertaking to determine the obligations with which it is required to comply as regards minimum pay.[495]

In *Viking* and *Laval* the ECJ said that the social and the economic must be 'balanced'. However in practice these judgments require the social to defend itself from the economic, not an easy task given the strict approach to justification and proportionality adopted by the Court, which essentially requires industrial action to be shown to be the last resort.[496] *Viking* was settled by the parties following the ruling by the ECJ and the English courts have not, at the time of writing, been required to apply the principles it establishes.[497] It is clear, however, that in cases with a cross-border dimension[498] a new set of restrictions has been added to those already in place in British law. As we saw in para 11.25 *et seq*, the application of the statutory

[492] See Eklund, 2006.

[493] See *Laval*, above, note 479, paras 86–111.

[494] Above, note 479, para 99.

[495] Above, note 479, paras 103 and 110. For responses to the judgment, see Eklund, 2008; Barnard, 2008a and 2008b, 2009; Rönnmar, 2008; Dashwood, 2008; Novitz, 2008; Sciarra, 2008; Deakin, 2008.

[496] Barnard, 2008a: p 264.

[497] In 2008 the British Airline Pilots' Association sought a ruling from the High Court on whether British Airways (BA) could rely on Art 43 EC (now Article 49 TFEU) in relation to a threatened strike by pilots over plans by BA to use lower paid pilots in its new subsidiary airline flying passengers from mainland European capitals to the USA. BALPA withdrew from the action after three days, fearing that, regardless of the outcome in the High Court, it would face the expense of appeals. See Ewing and Hendy, 2009c: pp 69–72 and CEACR : Individual Observation concerning Freedom of Association and Protection of the Right to Organise Convention 1948 (No 87) UK, 2011 (although note that the CEACR appeared to consider, erroneously, that an injunction had been granted in this case).

[498] See A Davies, 2008: p 146 for some examples.

immunities requires the courts to ask whether a dispute organiser has acted 'in contemplation or furtherance of a trade dispute'. A trade dispute must relate 'wholly or mainly' to one more of the matters which constitute the statutory subject-matter of 'collective bargaining', which may be some circumstances go beyond the 'protection of workers' as defined by the ECJ (for example, in relation to the fear of redundancies). The test of the dispute organiser's purpose in acting is subjective; it is sufficient that he or she honestly thinks that the action may help one of the parties to achieve its objective and it is done for that reason. The statutory immunities do not require the courts, in deciding whether industrial action is lawful, to assess its 'suitability' for achieving its objective and whether it is proportionate, let alone whether the dispute organiser has other 'less restrictive' means at its disposal and whether these have been exhausted, matters which, it is strongly arguable, go beyond the proper role of the courts.[499] As Davies states, the introduction of these questions has the potential to involve the courts in a much more politically sensitive set of issues which are particularly inappropriate given the courts' non-specialist nature.[500] Moreover, as we saw in para 11.48 *et seq*, the remedy most commonly sought by employers faced with industrial action or the threat of such action is an interim injunction, which requires the claimant to show only that there is a serious question to be tried whereupon the decision to grant the injunction turns upon the balance of convenience. The uncertainties surrounding the application of the questions which the ECJ requires the national court to address may well lead a court to find that there is a serious issue to be tried, particularly as answering these questions may require the facts to be closely scrutinised to an extent that can be done only at full trial. The partial protection provided to dispute organisers in interim proceedings by TULRCA 1992, section 221(2), which we discuss in paragraph 11.49, applies only to the likelihood of a defence under the statutory immunities succeeding, not to whether the additional hurdles erected by the ECJ are likely to be surmounted.[501] Finally, although the TUC derived some comfort in policy terms from the apparent recognition by the ECJ of some scope for secondary action,[502] the judgments equally have the potential to inspire employers to demand similar constraints on industrial action that interferes with 'free movement' within the UK; is there any reason to treat an employer which wishes to relocate from London to Liverpool in order to reduce its labour costs any differently to one which wishes to relocate from London to Latvia?[503] In this context, the recognition of the right to strike by the ECJ seems to be a very Pyrrhic victory.

---

[499] As we indicate in para 11.45, para 6 of the Code of Practice on Industrial Action Ballots and Notice to Employers 2005 states that an industrial action ballot should not take place until any agreed procedures which might lead to the resolution of the dispute without industrial action have been completed. However, although non-compliance with this provision may influence a court in favour of granting an interim injunction where there is otherwise a serious issue to be tried it is not incorporated in the test of lawfulness.

[500] A Davies, 2008: p 146.

[501] If industrial action does proceed, unions face the risk that the statutory cap on damages in TULRCA 1992, s 22, which we discuss in para 11.47, will be held not to apply where the action is found to interfere with a right which is protected in EU law. See Ewing and Hendy, 2009c: pp 71–72.

[502] See A Davies, 2008: pp 137–138.

[503] For discussion of exactly what constitutes an illegitimate interference with employer's free movement rights under Arts 43 and 49 of the EC Treaty (now Arts 49 and 56 TFEU), see Barnard, 2008b and Deakin, 2008. Although a transnational element to the dispute would have to be demonstrated in order to trigger rights under these Articles, there is generally no need to show discrimination on the grounds of nationality, simply a 'restriction' on freedom of movement, a somewhat narrower concept; nor is it necessary, in all cases, for the claimant to be an establishment domiciled in another member state in order to claim the protection of these articles.

As we indicate in para 2.39 above, Article 6(2) of the TEU provides for the EU to accede to the ECHR. At the time of writing negotiations for accession have yet to be concluded. If accession occurs, it may then be possible for those aggrieved by the Court of Justice's decisions in this area to complain that the Court has infringed Convention rights, thus requiring the EU to justify any restriction on the right to strike in order to uphold free movement as proportionate. As Novitz and Syrpis state, 'In EU law, the Court of Justice takes the economic goal of free movement as its starting point, and then assess the proportionality of any restrictions on free movement. Under the ECHR regime, the ... [ECtHR] ... takes Convention rights as its starting point, and assesses the proportionality of restrictions to those rights. The status of the economic and the social could thereby, in effect, be reversed'.[504] Much depends on whether the ECtHR seeks to avoid conflict with the CJEU in relation to the single market; Article 6(2) of the TEU also provides that accession to the ECHR 'shall not affect the Union's competencies as defined in the Treaties'. Even if it does, however, dialogue between the courts may lead the CJEU to align its own rulings more closely with those of the ECtHR and give greater weight to the human rights of workers.[505]

PICKETING

11.53   Workers who are involved in a dispute will generally wish to publicise, and mobilise support for, their campaign. One traditional way of doing this has been by picketing. This is not a legal 'term of art' but it is commonly understood to mean persons, either singly or in groups, attending at or near premises connected with an industrial dispute.[506] Pickets may have several objects; the most usual are to persuade non-strikers or substitute workers not to continue working or to persuade suppliers not to furnish goods or services to the employer in dispute. However, as Bercusson has pointed out a wide range of activities may be covered:

> The pickets may limit themselves to merely observing scabs; they may attempt to communicate information to them as to the existence of a strike; they may go beyond this and attempt to persuade them not to aid the employer by working for him (or in the case of customers, doing business with him) – using placards, speaking, shouting ... They may go beyond persuasion to where their behaviour amounts to a threat – through their mere presence, by physical violence, social ostracism or economic boycott; or they may engage in actual assaults, destruction of property or the physical blocking of entrances and interference with traffic. Picketing activity may range from one extreme to the other on this spectrum.[507]

---

[504] Novitz and Syrpis, 2010: p 482. See also Ewing and Hendy, 2010: pp 38-47, where the relationship between EU law and Article 11 of the ECHR is explored in greater detail, including the question whether EU accession to the ECHR would allow proceedings to be brought against the EU in the ECtHR on the ground that an action against a union for unlimited damages for breach of EU law, if upheld, (see note 501 above) violates Article 11.

[505] Novitz and Syrpis, above: p 483. At the time of writing the European Commission has proposed a Council Regulation on the exercise of the right to take collective action within the context of the freedom of establishment and the freedom to provide services: COM (2012) 130 final.

[506] Hepple, 1981b: para 89.

[507] Bercusson, 1977: pp 271–272.

Pickets have commonly been at risk of incurring civil liability; at the very least they may commit the tort of inducing breach of contract and possibly also other torts both within and beyond the statutory immunities. They may also incur criminal liability, even if acting peacefully. In addition to restrictions the general law imposes, guidance as to the conduct of picketing is provided by a Code of Practice, initially issued by the Secretary of State for Employment in 1980 and revised in 1992. Like its counterpart in the area of ballots this Code contains provisions which exceed the requirements of the legislation. One provision which has proved very influential is the statement that the number of pickets at any entrance to or exit from a workplace should not generally exceed six.[508] Prior to the HRA 1998 this figure was commonly reflected in the terms of injunctions ordered by the court to restrict the conduct of future picketing[509] and in the use of police discretion in this area. However this and other aspects of the legal framework governing picketing require reconsideration in the light of the HRA 1998. Both Article 11 of the ECHR, which guarantees the right to freedom of peaceful assembly, and Article 10, which guarantees the right to freedom of expression, are material in this context. The jurisprudence on this aspect of Article 11 is relatively meagre,[510] but the European Court of Human Rights has affirmed that Article 11 must be considered in the light of Article 10, given that '[t]he protection of personal opinions, secured by Article 10, is one of the objectives of freedom of peaceful assembly as enshrined in Article 11'.[511] In practice, therefore, the principles governing Article 10 are relevant in this context, even if the case appears more directly concerned with freedom of assembly. The concept of 'expression' has been interpreted widely by the Court, which has extended it to protests which take the form of impeding activities of which the demonstrators disapprove.[512] Cases therefore generally turn on whether an interference with the exercise of the right can be justified under Article 10(2), which provides that its exercise:

> ... since it carries with it duties and responsibilities, may be subject to such formalities, conditions, restrictions or penalties as are prescribed by law and are necessary in a democratic society, in the interests of national security, territorial integrity or public safety, for the prevention of disorder or crime, for the protection of health or morals, for the protection of the reputation or rights of others, for preventing the disclosure of information received in confidence, or for maintaining the authority and impartiality of the judiciary.

In this context, the scope of the margin of appreciation accorded to the state when the Court is deciding whether a restriction is 'necessary in a democratic society' has varied, with a wide

---

[508] Para 51.

[509] See *Thomas v NUM (South Wales Area)* [1985] IRLR 136 and *News Group Newspapers Ltd v SOGAT '82 (No 2)* [1986] IRLR 337.

[510] See D Mead, 2007, 2010.

[511] *Ezelin v France* judgment of 26 April 1991, (1992) 14 EHRR 362, para 37; for a recent iteration of the principle (which also refers to freedom of association) see *Paloma Sanchez v Spain* judgment of 12 September 2011, [2011] IRLR 934, para 52. For a discussion of the issues raised by Arts 10 and 11 in relation to the broader freedom to demonstrate, see Fenwick, 1999; see also Fenwick, 2009.

[512] *Steel v UK* judgment of 23 September 1998, (1999) 28 EHRR 603, para 92; *Hashman and Harrap v UK* judgment of 25 November 1999, (2000) 30 EHRR 241, para 28.

margin being accorded in relation to 'commercial' expression,[513] a much narrower margin to that which is regarded as contributing to the democratic process or 'public' or 'general' interest.[514] At the time of writing the Court has not been required to decide where picketing lies on this spectrum (which is, in any event, a controversial approach to classifying expression),[515] but where an interference with freedom of expression has taken the form of an injunction the categorisation approach appears, in any case, to be less prevalent.[516] It is strongly arguable that in the case of the provision of information, in particular, (for example, to other workers, or to customers) domestic courts should be 'exceedingly slow to make interim restraint orders where the applicant has not satisfied the court he [or she] will probably ... succeed at the trial.[517]

Regardless of the form that picketing takes, the principle of proportionality requires the courts to look more carefully at the terms in which interim injunctions are framed than pre-HRA 1998 to ensure that restrictions are not excessive in the light of individual circumstances, and to play closer attention to the exigencies of the situation rather than merely adopting the six-picket guideline in the Code of Practice (a provision which itself now requires amendment in the light of the HRA). This point was recognised by Fulford J in *Gate Gourmet London Ltd v TGWU*, where he stated that a 'consequence of limiting the number entitled to attend at ... site A or B to 10 (or some other small number) ... is that many who have not in any way breached the law will be denied an opportunity to express their point of view and concerns in this public way' [518] (although in the event he considered it appropriate to limit the picket numbers at site A to six). Indeed, the courts may also be required to consider the implications of Convention rights in deciding whether a tort has even been committed. We consider the implications of the HRA 1998 further in our discussion of the civil and criminal liabilities that pickets may incur.[519]

---

[513] *Markt Intern Verlag GmbH v FRG* judgment of 20 November 1989, (1990) 12 EHRR 161, although cf *Hertel v Switzerland* judgment of 25 August 1998, (1999) 28 EHRR 534.

[514] See, for example, *Lingens v Austria* judgment of 8 July 1986, (1986) 8 EHRR 103; *Castells v Spain* judgment of 23 April 1992, (1992) 14 EHRR 445; *Thorgeir Thorgeirson v Iceland* judgment of 25 June 1992, (1992) 14 EHRR 843.

[515] See Tierney, 1998; Lester, 1998a.

[516] *Observer and Guardian v UK* judgment of 26 November 1991, (1992) 14 EHRR 153; *Open Door Counselling and Well Women v Ireland* judgment of 29 October 1992, (1993) 15 EHRR 244; *Hertel v Switzerland*, above, note 513; cf *Markt Intern Verlag GmbH v Germany*, above, note 513. In the United States, picketing has been regarded as protected speech on the ground that discussion of conditions in industry and the causes of labour disputes is indispensable to popular government; however, it has been argued by Hogg, 1997 that it should best be regarded as commercial expression, 'since its main purpose is to encourage employees not to work and consumers not to buy': see Hepple, 2000b: p 191. The Canadian Supreme Court has held that picketing engages freedom of expression, benefitting not only individual workers and unions but society as a whole by bringing 'the debate on labour conditions into the public realm': *RWDSU, Local 558 v Pepsi-Cola Canada Beverages (West) Ltd* 2002 SCC 8 at para 35.

[517] *Cream Holdings Ltd v Banerjee* [2005] 1 AC 253, [22] (Lord Nicholls, giving the opinion of the Court). HRA s 12(3) provides that no relief which, if granted, might affect the exercise of the Convention right to freedom of expression, is to be granted so as to restrain publication before trial 'unless the court is satisfied that the applicant is likely to establish that publication should not be allowed'. In *Cream Holdings* the House of Lords affirmed that the degree of likelihood of success needed to satisfy s 12(3) must depend on the circumstances, but the statement in the text should be the 'general approach'.

[518] See *Gate Gourmet London Ltd v TGWU* [2005] IRLR 881, QBD, [26].

[519] Note also that state action which has an impact upon the free movement of goods when this process is disrupted by the activities of pickets may raise issues under EU law: see Case C-265/95 *Commission v France* [1997] ECR I-6959; *R v Chief Constable of Sussex, ex parte International Trader's Ferry Ltd* [1999] 1 All ER 129; Case C112/00 *Eugen Schmidberger Internationale Tranporte Planzuge v Austria* [2003] 2 CMLR 34. See generally Barnard and Hare, 2000; Facenna, 2004.

Civil liability

11.54   As with industrial action generally, the primary remedy sought by employers faced with picketing is an interim injunction to halt the action. The same general principles apply to the granting of injunctions in this context as those outlined in para 11.48 *et seq*. In the past, showing a serious issue to be tried has been unlikely to be difficult and the statutory immunities, which we discuss below, apply only when stringent conditions as to the conduct of the picketing are met. However, as we indicate in para 11.53 above, the courts will now additionally need to consider, in deciding whether an injunction should be granted (and possibly as a prior question, whether the defendant's action constitutes a tort), whether the interference with the respondents' rights to freedom of expression and/or freedom of assembly can be justified.

Pickets may commit any of the torts discussed in para 11.10 *et seq*. In particular they frequently commit the tort of inducing breach of contract, the contracts being the employment contracts of the workers they seek to persuade to stop working. However, it is important to note that persuasion must be directed at one of the parties to the contract. In *Middlebrook Mushrooms Ltd v TGWU*[520] the claimants failed to obtain an injunction to prevent union members handing out leaflets to customers of a supermarket to which they supplied their produce, one ground being that, even assuming the existence of a contract between the supermarket and the claimants, there was no direct pressure on the supermarket to breach it.

As we indicated in para 11.11, in *Union Traffic Ltd v TGWU*[521] the Court of Appeal held that the mere presence of pickets may be deemed sufficient to constitute an 'inducement' if it is clear that their presence is intended to induce breach of a contract and is successful in this object. This approach may require reconsideration in the light of the HRA 1998. Moreover following *OBG v Allan*,[522] establishing the liability of pickets for inducing breach of contract will require much closer analysis of the facts than the court conducted in *Union Traffic*. Prior to *OBG* pickets were commonly liable for the 'indirect' form of inducing breach of contract by preventing the performance of commercial contracts between an employer and its customers or suppliers. In *OBG* the House of Lords held that this form of action was more appropriately classified as causing loss by unlawful means (see further paras 11.11 and 11.13 *et seq*).

11.55   In addition to liability in the economic torts, there are four other forms of tortious liability to which picketing may give rise: trespass to the highway, private nuisance, public nuisance and liability under the Protection from Harassment Act 1997. Until relatively recently it appeared that trespass to the highway was committed by using the highway for purposes not reasonably incidental to passage.[523] However, in *Jones v DPP*[524] the House of Lords held that this view was unduly narrow, and that reasonable user of the highway could potentially extend to peaceful and non-obstructive assembly, although whether it did so would depend on the facts of the case. In practice this tort has been a dead letter in the context of industrial

---

[520] [1993] IRLR 232.
[521] [1989] IRLR 127.
[522] [2008] 1 AC 1, [2007] IRLR 608.
[523] *Harrison v Duke of Rutland* [1893] 1 QB 142, CA; *Hickman v Maisey* [1900] 1 QB 752, CA; *Hubbard v Pitt* [1975] ICR 77; 308.
[524] [1999] 2 All ER 257, 263, 265 (Lord Irvine LC), 287 (Lord Clyde), 297 (Lord Hutton).

action because only the owner of the subsoil – normally the highway authority – may sue for it; a highway authority is unlikely to seek an injunction and any damages it could obtain would almost certainly be nominal. More frequently invoked is the tort of private nuisance, which consists of an unlawful interference with a person's use or enjoyment of land, or some right over or in connection with it.[525] There has been judicial controversy as to whether picketing *per se* can constitute private nuisance. In 1899 the Court of Appeal considered that it could simply because of the attempt to persuade and regardless of any obstruction caused.[526] Seven years later, however, a different Court of Appeal reached the opposite conclusion[527] and this latter view was echoed by Lord Denning in a widely-quoted dissenting judgment in *Hubbard v Pitt* when he stated that:

> ... [p]icketing is not a nuisance in itself. Nor is it a nuisance for a group of people to attend at or near the ... [claimant's] ... premises in order to obtain or to communicate information or in order peacefully to persuade. It does not become a nuisance unless it is associated with obstruction, violence, intimidation, molestation or threats.[528]

In *Mersey Docks and Harbour Co v Verrinder*, however, the High Court held that putting what was perceived as improper pressure on employers could constitute a nuisance, thus relating liability to the motive for the pickets' action rather than the nature of that action. The aim of the pickets, who stood at the entrance to two container terminals, was to protest at the use of 'cowboy' haulage contractors who undercut established operators. They brought the terminals to a virtual standstill because drivers refused to cross the picket line but there was no allegation of violence. Judge McHugh found that the intention of the pickets was to ensure that only established operators were employed to the exclusion of others not acceptable to them, not merely to obtain or communicate information. 'In other words, the intention is to force the company to take some action against shipowners who employ "cowboys" or "scalliwags". It is tantamount ... to an attempt on the part of the defendants to regulate and control the container traffic to and from the company's terminals. If that is right, the conduct of the pickets is ... capable of constituting a private nuisance'.[529] This approach may now require reconsideration in the light of the HRA 1998; it is strongly arguable that conduct which does not obstruct others from crossing a picket line should not be regarded as a tort.[530]

In *Thomas v NUM (South Wales Area)* Scott J sought to extend the application of the tort of private nuisance in a number of respects. As well as affirming that mass picketing was in itself an actionable nuisance, a view supported by authority, he also considered that regular picketing outside the home of an individual non-striker would constitute the tort regardless of the number of those involved and however peaceful their conduct.[531] Even more controversially he also held

---

[525] In *Hunter v Canary Wharf Ltd* [1997] 2 All ER 426 the House of Lords affirmed the need for the claimant to have a right to the land affected. Ordinarily this requires a right to exclusive possession of the land. A mere licensee on the land has no right to sue.

[526] *J Lyons & Sons Ltd v Wilkins* [1899] 1 Ch 255.

[527] *Ward, Lock & Co Ltd v OPAS* (1906) 22 TLR 327.

[528] [1975] ICR 308, 318.

[529] [1982] IRLR 152, 155.

[530] See, *mutatis mutandis, Steel v UK* judgment of 23 September 1998, (1999) 28 EHRR 603.

[531] [1985] IRLR 136, 153, 149. See now the Protection from Harassment Act 1997, discussed below.

that unreasonable interference by way of harassment of workers who wished to use the highway to go to work could constitute a tort, which could be described as a species of private nuisance, despite the absence of any interference with the enjoyment of land. On this basis he held that the daily presence of between 50 and 70 men hurling abuse in circumstances requiring a police presence and the use of vehicles to transport the workers into work, was sufficient to constitute this wrong.

This decision provides a further instance of the judicial creativity which we saw to be a feature of the economic torts. In *News Group Newspapers Ltd v SOGAT '82 (No 2)*[532] Stuart-Smith J acknowledged the substance of the defendant's criticisms of such an extension of the tort, especially given that it did not appear that damage was a necessary ingredient. In the light of the House of Lords decision in *Hunter v Canary Wharf Ltd*[533] affirming the nature of private nuisance as a tort based upon the enjoyment of land, it would be difficult to argue that harassment *per se* can constitute a nuisance. However, the wider question whether there was a separate tort of harassment was not considered,[534] although this is now a less pressing question in the light of the Protection from Harassment Act 1997.

The tort of public nuisance is less commonly relied upon by claimants. A person is guilty of a public nuisance who (a) does an act not warranted by law, or (b) omits to discharge a legal duty, if the effect of the act or omission is to endanger the life, health, property or comfort of the public, or to obstruct the public in the exercise or enjoyment of rights common to all Her Majesty's subjects.[535] To sue for public nuisance an individual must show particular damage greater than that suffered by the public at large,[536] although this loss need not be of a pecuniary nature; inconvenience or delay may be sufficient.[537] Obstruction of the highway can constitute public nuisance provided that the defendant's use of the highway is 'unreasonable'.[538] In *News Group Newspapers Ltd v SOGAT '82*[539] the conduct of pickets and daily demonstrators was found by Stuart-Smith J to constitute unreasonable use, and various claimants were found to have suffered special damage, including the Times Newspaper which had lost journalists because of the demonstrations and an individual worker who could not leave the plant during the day and felt drained by the constant pressure of having to come to work through the picket line.

Finally, the Protection from Harassment Act 1997 also introduced a new statutory tort which, although aimed at stalkers, it is possible that pickets may commit.[540] The Act provides that a person must not pursue a 'course of conduct' (defined as involving conduct 'on at least two occasions'[541]) which: (a) amounts to harassment of another and which the defendant knows or ought to know amounts to harassment of the other or (b) involves harassment of two or more persons and which he or she knows or ought to know involves harassment of those persons and by which he or she intends to persuade any person (whether or not one of the aforementioned)

[532] [1986] IRLR 337, 348.
[533] [1997] 2 All ER 426.
[534] See *Khorasandjian v Bush* [1993] 3 All ER 669; Hepple, 2000b: p 180, n 22.
[535] Archbold, 2012: para 31-40.
[536] The meaning of particular damage in this context is obscure; see generally Spencer, 1989: especially pp 74–75.
[537] See for example *Halsey v Esso Petroleum Co Ltd* [1961] 2 All ER 145.
[538] See *DPP v Jones* [1999] 2 All ER 257, discussed above, on reasonable user.
[539] [1986] IRLR 337.
[540] See Finch, 2002; Ormerod, 2011: pp 695-705.
[541] Section 7(3).

not to do something that he or she is entitled or required to do or to do something that he or she is not under any obligation to do.[542] Whether a defendant ought to know that conduct involves harassment is tested by reference to whether a reasonable person in possession of the same information would think this.[543] 'Conduct' for the purposes of the Act includes speech.[544] A person who is or may be the victim of such conduct may seek an injunction to restrain it, and it is an offence, punishable by up to five years' imprisonment, to breach that injunction without reasonable excuse.[545] Damages may also be awarded in respect of harassment, including for any anxiety caused by it.[546] References to harassing a person include 'alarming the person or causing the person distress',[547] but the concept is not confined to this. Harassment may also constitute a criminal offence[548] and in *Majrowski v Guy's and St Thomas's NHS Trust* Lord Nicholls emphasised that, even in the context of civil proceedings, to 'cross the boundary from the regrettable to the unacceptable the gravity of the misconduct must be of an order which would sustain criminal liability....'[549] The complainant must be an individual and not a corporate body.[550] The wrong is not committed, *inter alia*, if the person who pursued the conduct shows that it was pursued under any enactment or rule of law or that 'in the particular circumstances the pursuit of the course of conduct was reasonable'.[551] Ormerod states that this protects the right of free speech and expression;[552] whether pickets will be able to rely on it may require close examination of the facts. It has been held that it is difficult, if not impossible, to imagine circumstances in which the pursuit of a course of conduct amounting to harassment in breach of an injunction could be 'reasonable', although an isolated act in exceptional circumstances, such as rescuing someone in danger, may be defended on that basis.[553]

---

[542] Section 1(1), (1A). Note also liability for aiding, abetting, counselling or procuring such conduct by any person: s 7(3A), which was enacted to deal with campaigns of collective harassment by two or more people: Ormerod, 2011: p 698. The knowledge and purpose of the aider, abetter, counsellor or procurer is judged at the time that the conduct was planned not when it is carried out.

[543] Section 1(2).

[544] Section 7(4).

[545] Section 3.

[546] Section 3(2); see *Majrowski v Guy's and St Thomas's NHS Trust* [2006] IRLR 695, HL.

[547] Section 7(2).

[548] Section 2; see further para 11.60. A person also commits an offence under the Act if he or she knows or ought to know that their course of conduct will cause another to fear, on at least two occasions, that violence will be used against them: s 4. In the case of both offences a court sentencing or otherwise dealing with a defendant may make an order prohibiting specified behaviour in order to protect the victim or any other person mentioned in the order from the offending conduct: s 5.

[549] [2006] IRLR 695, HL, [30], applied *Sunderland City Council v Conn* [2008] IRLR 324. Ormerod states that it cannot, however, ' be a requirement that each of the acts alleged to constitute part of the course of conduct is itself criminal' : *R (Jones) v Bedfordshire County Council* [2010] EWHC 523 (Admin) [27].

[550] Section 7(5). In *DPP v Dunn* [2001] 1 Cr App Rep 352, QBD, it was held that 'another' and 'the other' included the plural and that in certain circumstances charges could be brought in relation to harassment of a 'close knit definable group' even though only one might have been present during any one incident of harassment. In *DPP v Dziurzynski* [2002] EWHC 1380 (Admin) the court considered that 60 persons whose only common feature was that they worked for the same employer did not constitute a close-knit group but see also discussion of this principle in Seymour, 2005.

[551] Section 1(3)(c).

[552] Ormerod, 2011: p 702.

[553] *R v DPP, ex p Moseley*, (QBD, 9 June 1999, unreported).

The scope of statutory immunity

11.56   The scheme of statutory immunity applicable in the context of picketing is complex. First, there is a specific (but limited) immunity contained in TULRCA 1992, section 220. Second, the general immunities which we outlined in para 11.23 *et seq*, affording protection against certain of the economic torts, may also be applicable. However this itself depends upon two requirements being met. First the usual conditions for their application must be satisfied (if the action is attributable to a union a ballot must be held, and so on), and the general exclusions from their scope apply (see para 11.30). Second, the conduct of the pickets must stay within the boundaries of section 220; section 219(3) provides that nothing in section 219(1) or (2) prevents an act done in the course of picketing from being actionable in tort unless it is done in the course of attendance declared lawful by section 220.[554]

Section 220(1) provides that it is 'lawful for a person in contemplation or furtherance of a trade dispute' to attend at or near his own place of work 'for the purpose only of peacefully obtaining or communicating information, or peacefully persuading any person to work or abstain from working'. A union official may also attend for that purpose at or near the place of work of a member of that union whom he is accompanying and whom he represents. The term 'official' includes shop stewards, provided that their election or appointment is in accordance with the union rules, as well as branch and other union officers, but a person who has been elected or appointed to represent only a portion of the membership (eg those in an individual workplace or region) may attend to represent those particular members only.[555]

There is no statutory definition of 'place of work' for the purposes of section 220, in comparison with the provisions governing industrial action ballots where the equivalent term 'workplace' is defined.[556] The Code of Practice indicates that the 'place of work' restriction means that 'lawful picketing must be limited to attendance at, or near, an entrance to or exit from the factory, site or office at which the picket works'.[557] On this basis the immunity would not cover those picketing other premises of their own employer in a multi-plant group. If the picket works at an establishment composed of a large number of buildings on a single site (a university or a hospital, for example), on a narrow view this restriction could imply that the immunity extends only to the individual building in which the worker's office is located. However this would seem an unduly restrictive interpretation, which would not reflect the understanding of either the worker or the employer as to the location of the employment.

Union officials apart there are two further qualifications to the 'place of work' restriction. First, a worker who is 'not in employment' whose last employment was terminated in connection with a trade dispute, or the termination of whose employment was one of the circumstances giving rise to a trade dispute, can attend at or near his or her former place of work.[558] However, the exclusion of those 'not in employment' means that a worker who had found even a part-time job elsewhere would not qualify under this provision. Second, where a person does not normally work at any one place, or the location of the place makes it impracticable to attend there for the

[554] Note that the immunity is displaced *by an act done in the course of picketing*, not, for example, an act inducing a union to organise picketing in breach of its rules: see *Thomas v NUM (South Wales Area)* [1985] IRLR 136, 155.
[555] TULRCA 1992, ss 119, 220(4).
[556] See para 11.35.
[557] Para 17.
[558] TULRCA 1992, s 220(3).

protected purposes, the place of work is 'any premises of his employer from which he works or from which his work is administered'.[559] A lorry driver or a travelling service engineer would come into the first category, an oil-rig worker into the second. Notably, however, there is no express provision for picketing by dismissed workers whose former place of work has closed down. In *News Group Newspapers Ltd v SOGAT '82 (No 2)*[560] the court held that dismissed workers who had formerly worked in central London were outside the immunity when they picketed the employer's new premises in Wapping, given that they had never worked there. A similar result was reached in *Union Traffic Ltd v TGWU*[561] where the claimants had decided to close down one of their transport depots in Liverpool and make a number of drivers redundant. The drivers picketed another depot in Liverpool, where the employers carried on a container repair business, and a transport depot 13 miles away. The Court of Appeal found that, although these places had been ports of call, neither had been the 'base' from which the defendants worked and so could not be deemed their 'place of work'. This reasoning leaves workers in this situation with no premises which they can effectively picket.[562] It may be possible to argue that attendance at the empty site at which the pickets previously worked is 'impracticable' and that they should therefore be able to picket the new premises of the employer, but this approach has yet to be accepted by the courts.[563]

The Court of Appeal has interpreted the phrase 'at or near' in a more purposive fashion, however. In *Rayware Ltd v TGWU*[564] the claimant's factory was on a private trading estate on a private road some seven-tenths of a mile away from the entrance to the estate from the highway. The employees in dispute had established a picket at a gate leading from the highway on to the estate as being the nearest practicable point at which to picket without committing a trespass. The Court of Appeal held that they were within section 220. The court considered that the phrase 'at or near' had to be considered in a geographical sense in the light of the purpose of the legislation, which was to grant a freedom peacefully to persuade, and that 'near' should be seen as an 'expanding' word. Whether a particular spot will be deemed 'near' is a question of fact but two members of the court indicated that if their decision 'establish[ed] a precedent for other comparable industrial and commercial developments' they would 'not flinch from that result in an area of the law where it is especially desirable that rights and duties should be certain'.[565]

In other respects the ambit of section 220(1) and its predecessors[566] has been interpreted very restrictively by the courts. In particular the courts have been ready to infer that the conduct of

---

[559] TULRCA 1992, s 220(2). 'Any' in this context would appear not to limit the worker to one set of premises although cf Lloyd LJ in *Union Traffic Ltd v TGWU* [1989] IRLR 127, 133, who limited 'place of work' to the worker's 'principal place or work' or 'base'. By definition, however, this interpretation cannot apply in the case of those for whom picketing their place of work is impracticable.

[560] [1986] IRLR 337, 350.

[561] [1989] IRLR 127.

[562] Lloyd LJ assumed that a person could only have one 'place of work', his 'principal place of work' or 'base' (at 133) and Bingham LJ too spoke of the 'base' (at 131). However there is nothing in the section to prevent a person within s 220(2) having both a place 'at' which and a place 'from which' he works; the lorry drivers in *Union Traffic Ltd v TGWU*, above, n 559 may have come into this category.

[563] Auerbach 1989: pp 168–169. This involves arguing that s 220(2) and (3) may apply simultaneously, a proposition not ruled out by the statute. Lloyd LJ left the point open in *Union Traffic Ltd v TGWU* [1989] IRLR 127, above.

[564] [1989] IRLR 134.

[565] [1989] IRLR 134, 137.

[566] TDA 1906, s 2, continued in a modified form by the IRA 1971, s 134, substantially re-enacted by the TULRA 1974, s 15 and amended significantly by the EA 1980.

pickets has gone beyond that of communicating information or peacefully persuading. In *Tynan v Balmer*[567] the Divisional Court held that 40 pickets who were walking in a circle which spilt onto the public highway at the entrance to a factory had no immunity because one of their objects was to seal off the highway. In *Broome v DPP*[568] Lord Reid suggested that if pickets assembled in 'unreasonably large numbers' it would not be difficult to infer that they were doing this to prevent the passage of others. In later cases the courts were influenced by the six-picket limit suggested by the Code of Practice.[569] Thus, in *Thomas v NUM (South Wales Area)*[570] Scott J considered that the 50–70 pickets at the entrance to a workplace were outside the protection, suggesting that mere attendance in sufficient numbers could be sufficient to exceed its scope.

> It may be that the six persons who are selected to stand close to the gates could bring themselves within the provision, but the many others who are present cannot do so. What is their purpose in attending? It is obviously not to obtain or communicate information. Is it peacefully to persuade the working miners to abstain from working? If that is the case what is the need for vehicles to bring the working miners safely into the collieries?[571]

However the HRA 1998, whose application to picketing we explained in para 11.53, is now relevant in this context and courts need to pay much closer regard to the exigencies of the situation in question.[572]

Even if pickets manage to remain within section 220(1), the protection it affords is very limited. It does not give a right to picket, merely a limited immunity to attend for the specified purposes;[573] *a fortiori*, pickets have no right to require others to listen to their case.[574] This lack of any positive right has been particularly significant in the light of the broad discretionary powers of the police to control picketing, which we outline below, although once again the HRA 1998 is now material to the scope of these powers. Section 220 does not give any right to attend on land against the wishes of the owner (or the person to whom the owner has granted exclusive occupation), nor does it affect the operation of any byelaws by which the use and operation of land may be regulated.[575] It may afford protection against the torts of trespass to the highway and private nuisance,[576] but this is of little real importance; the former is irrelevant in practice, and where there is an actionable nuisance it is unlikely that the conduct will fall within the

---

[567] [1967] 1 QB 91.
[568] [1974] ICR 84, 90.
[569] Para 51.
[570] [1985] IRLR 136.
[571] [1985] IRLR 136, 148. See also *News Group Newspapers Ltd v SOGAT '82 (No 2)* [1986] IRLR 337.
[572] See *Gate Gourmet London Ltd v TGWU* [2005] IRLR 881, QBD.
[573] *Broome v DPP* [1974] ICR 84, HL; *Kavanagh v Hiscock* [1974] ICR 282, DC.
[574] [1974] ICR 84, 89–90 (Lord Reid).
[575] *British Airports Authority v Ashton* [1983] IRLR 287. On the issues posed by the use of 'quasi-public' spaces, see Gray and Gray, 1999 and the ECtHR decision in *Appleby v UK* judgment of 6 May 2003 (no breach of Arts 10 and 11 when applicants banned from distributing leaflets by a private company that owned a shopping centre although there may be circumstances, such as a 'corporate town', where a different approach may be taken). See Barendt, 2005: p 288 for a critique of *Appleby*. The Joint Committee on Human Rights (JCHR) has stated that where 'preventing protest on private land to which the public routinely has access would effectively deprive individuals of their right to peaceful protest, the Government should consider the position of quasi-public spaces to ensure that the right to protest is preserved': JCHR, Seventh Report, Session 2008-2009, HL 47-I/HC 320-I, para 68.
[576] The Code of Practice oversimplifies the position in para 5 by stating that the immunities afford no protection in relation to any civil wrong not specified in s 219; the examples given in para 27 of the Code are more appropriate.

section, particularly if nuisance is henceforth interpreted more restrictively in the picketing context. Its major significance is in relation to the application of section 219(1) of TULRCA 1992; as we indicated earlier, straying outside the terms of that section will of itself remove any protection against the torts it covers such as inducing breach of contract. Moreover, it is possible that liability for unlawful means conspiracy may arise if pickets who are 'lawfully' attending actively associate with others from whom the protection of the immunities has been removed.

The general withdrawal of immunity for secondary industrial action is particularly significant in this context.[577] It applies equally to pickets with one narrow exception: where secondary action occurs in the course of attendance which is lawful under section 220 by a worker employed[578] by the employer party to the dispute, or by a union official lawfully in attendance.[579] This means that protection will not automatically be lost if pickets interfere with the contract of employment of a worker employed by another employer, such as a lorry driver delivering goods from a supplier.

Picketing and the criminal law

11.57   Picketing is one area of industrial action where the criminal, as well as the civil, law may be important. There is a multiplicity of criminal offences which pickets may commit. In this section we merely outline the major ones in order to give an indication of the range of liabilities which pickets may incur.[580] It should be noted that, unlike liability under the civil law, criminal liability falls wholly on the individuals concerned. It is unlawful for union property to be used to pay a fine; nor may individuals be indemnified by the union for any liability they may incur,[581] although this restriction does not extend to the payment of the expenses of defending a prosecution if the union rules permit this.[582] The immunity afforded by TULRCA 1992, section 220 is negligible in this context.[583]

11.58   First, there is an offence specifically enacted to deal with picketing, originally contained in the Conspiracy and Protection of Property Act 1875 and now contained in an updated version in TULRCA 1992. Section 241 of that Act makes it an offence to do one of five acts 'wrongfully and without legal authority' 'with a view to compelling[584] another person 'to abstain from doing or to do any act which that person has a legal right to do or abstain from doing'. These acts are:

---

[577] In the USA restrictions on this type of industrial action have usually been regarded as legitimate in order to prevent the spread of action to so-called neutrals, and it seems unlikely that domestic courts will be inclined to take a different view under the HRA 1998: see Hepple, 2000b: pp 191–192. Cf the Canadian jurisprudence on secondary picketing, on which see Ewing and Hendy, 2011: p 49, n 89, and ILO jurisprudence on secondary action, discussed in para 11.31.

[578] In the case of a worker not in employment, last employed.

[579] TULRCA 1992, s 224(1), (3).

[580] For further details on the offences which pickets may commit see Ormerod, 2011: ch 32; JCHR Report , above, n 575; Card, 2000. For more detailed analyses of the policing of industrial disputes historically see Kahn *et al*, 1983; Geary, 1985; McCabe and Wallington, 1988.

[581] TULRCA 1992, s 15. At common law it was not unlawful for a union to authorise payment of fines for picketing offences by members after the offences were committed: *Drake v Morgan* [1978] ICR 56.

[582] TULRCA 1992, s 15.

[583] At most it may support the argument that picketing within its terms is not an 'unreasonable user' of the highway under the Highways Act 1980, nor without 'legal authority' for the purposes of TULRCA 1992, s 241.

[584] Persuasion is not compulsion for this purpose: *DPP v Fidler* [1992] 1 WLR 91.

(a) using violence to or intimidating that person or his wife (sic) or children or injuring his property;
(b) persistently following that person about from place to place;
(c) hiding any tools, clothes, or other property owned or used by that person, or depriving him of or hindering him in the use thereof;
(d) watching or besetting the house or other place where that person resides, works, carries on business or happens to be, or the approach to any such house or place; or
(e) following that person with two or more other persons in a disorderly manner in or through any street or road.

It seems now to be accepted that the term 'wrongfully and without legal authority' requires an activity to constitute at least a tort before it can give rise to liability under this section;[585] without this requirement many forms of picketing would immediately be illegal as involving 'watching and besetting'.[586] It is also arguable that picketing within the terms of section 220 is not 'without legal authority'. However, the protection afforded by the requirement that the activity should be tortious would be undermined almost entirely if the view of a Scottish court were accepted, to the effect that economic torts protected by the statutory immunities can nevertheless constitute the requisite 'wrongful' act because section 219 expressly applies only to proceedings in tort.[587] On the basis of this reasoning any picketing which involved an inducement to breach a contract could lead to a criminal charge, however few persons were involved. Given a maximum penalty of six months' imprisonment and a fine which currently stands at a maximum of £5,000[588] this would be an unfortunate result. However, it has been suggested that an interpretation of section 241 which means that peaceful picketing can become a criminal offence merely because it involves the torts of inducing breach of contract or nuisance would be incompatible with Articles 10 and 11 of the ECHR as it would not be proportionate to the aim of protecting the 'rights of others'.[589]

11.59 Other lesser charges to which pickets may be subject are obstruction of the highway under the Highways Act 1980, section 137 and obstruction of a constable in the execution of his duty under the Police Act 1996, section 89(2). The former makes it an offence 'in any way' to 'wilfully obstruct the free passage along a highway' without 'lawful authority or excuse'.[590] The requirement that the obstruction should be 'without lawful authority or excuse' allows consideration of whether the user was 'reasonable', which depends on factors such as the length of time the obstruction continues, its location, purpose, and whether there was an actual or only a potential obstruction.[591] It is arguable that picketing within the statutory immunity would be considered 'reasonable' but anything beyond that may not, although once again the HRA 1998

---

[585] *Ward, Lock & Co Ltd v OPAS* (1906) 22 TLR 327; *Thomas v NUM (South Wales Area)* [1985] IRLR 136; cf *J Lyons & Sons v Wilkins* [1896] 1 Ch 811.
[586] On harassment in the vicinity of a residence, see Criminal Justice and Police Act 2001, s 42A
[587] *Galt (Procurator Fiscal) v Philp* [1984] IRLR 156.
[588] Level 5 on the standard scale established by the Criminal Justice Act 1982, s 37(2), as substituted by the Criminal Justice Act 1991.
[589] Hepple, 2000b: p 191.
[590] There is a maximum fine of level 3 on the standard scale (at the time of writing £1,000).
[591] *Nagy v Weston* [1965] 1 All ER 78; see also *Hirst and Agu v Chief Constable of the West Yorkshire Police* (1986) 85 Cr App Rep 143. In *Jones v DPP* [1999] 2 All ER 257, Lord Irvine LC (at 266) and Lord Hutton (at 293) drew on these authorities in determining the boundaries of the tort of trespass to the highway.

will be material here. The offence of obstructing a constable most frequently arises in the picketing context if pickets refuse to obey police instructions designed to prevent a breach of the peace.[592] Every constable and, indeed, every citizen, has a common law power, and is subject to a duty, to seek to prevent any breach of the peace[593] occurring in his presence or any breach of the peace which is about to occur,[594] on either public or private property.[595] Preventative measures taken under this power may include restricting the number of pickets present, ordering them to move away or, where appropriate, arresting them,[596] although the specific measure taken should be reasonable and proportionate in the circumstances.[597] In the leading case of *R (on the application of Laporte) v Chief Constable of Gloucestershire*[598] the House of Lords confirmed that, in the case of a breach of the peace which has not yet occurred, the breach must be 'imminent'. Their Lordships also rejected the argument that action short of arrest may be taken when the breach of the peace is not so imminent as would be necessary to justify an arrest. Lords Rodger and Carswell recognised that the test of imminence has to be applied to contemporary conditions; modern communications may give officers good reason to anticipate that people are intending to take part in a breach of the peace, or become involved in one, a short time later or a short car ride away.[599] However all were insistent that, as an interference with fundamental rights, the test should be strictly construed. The Court of Appeal in *Laporte* had endorsed the controversial decision in *Moss v McLachlan*,[600] which arose out of the 1984 miners' strike during which the police used road blocks to prevent intending pickets assembling at working collieries, in some cases many miles away. The majority of their Lordships distinguished *Moss*, although Lords Bingham and Brown considered that it 'carried the notion of imminence to extreme limits'[601] and Lords Rodger and Mance thought that the court in that case may have materially misdirected itself.[602]

The power to prevent a breach of the peace has, in the past, accorded the police a broad discretion to control picketing behaviour. However, although the concept of a breach of the peace is centuries old, its precise definition has been the subject of judicial controversy,[603] focusing, in particular, on whether there must be a risk of violence[604] and whether, if so, that violence needs to be perpetrated by the defendant or whether it is sufficient that others may be provoked to violence.[605] In *Nicol v DPP* Simon Brown LJ affirmed that:

> ... the court would surely not find a [breach of the peace] proved if any violence likely to have been provoked on the part of others would be not merely unlawful but wholly unreasonable

[592] This carries a maximum penalty of 51 weeks' imprisonment and/or a maximum fine of level 3 on the standard scale.
[593] For consideration of this concept see *R v Howell* [1982] QB 416.
[594] *R (on the application of Laporte) v Chief Constable of Gloucestershire* [2007] 2 AC 105, Lord Bingham at [29].
[595] *Thomas v Sawkins* [1935] 2 KB 249; power preserved by the Police and Criminal Evidence Act 1984, s 17(6).
[596] *Albert v Lavin* [1982] AC 546 at 565.
[597] *R (on the application of Laporte) v Chief Constable of Gloucestershire* [2007] 2 AC 105, HL, Lord Mance at [152].
[598] Above.
[599] See Lord Rodger at [67]-[69], Lord Carswell at [102].
[600] [1985] IRLR 76. See G Morris, 1985a, and see also the Police and Criminal Evidence Act 1984, s 4.
[601] Lord Bingham at [51], Lord Brown at [118].
[602] Lord Rodger at [63], Lord Mance at [150].
[603] See Fenwick, 1999: pp 506–511.
[604] See *R v Howell* [1981] 3 All ER 383, 389 (Watkins LJ); cf *R v Chief Constable of Devon and Cornwall, ex p Central Electricity Board* [1982] QB 458, 471 (Lord Denning MR).
[605] See *Percy v DPP* [1995] 1 WLR 1382, where the latter view was adopted.

– as, of course, it would be if the defendant's conduct was not merely lawful but such as in no material way interfered with the other's rights. *A fortiori* if the defendant was properly exercising his own basic rights, whether of assembly, demonstration or free speech.[606]

Following *Laporte*, it could be said that where a breach of the peace is taking place, or is thought to be imminent, before the police can take any steps which interfere with or curtail the lawful exercise of rights by innocent third parties they must ensure that they have taken all other possible steps to ensure that the breach, or imminent breach, is obviated and that the rights of innocent third parties are protected.[607] In *Austin v Commissioner of Police of the Metropolis*,[608] however, the House of Lords accorded greater scope to police discretion. In the higher courts *Austin* turned on whether 'kettling' – detaining demonstrators and passers-by in a police cordon, in this case for seven hours – breached Article 5 of the ECHR. The House of Lords held (controversially) that Article 5 was not engaged. Analysis of *Austin* is outside the scope of this work, but its significance here lies in the suggestion that even peaceful pickets (or bystanders) can be detained or subject to other preventative measures on grounds of necessity for substantial periods when they are in the company of others who are causing or about to cause a breach of the peace.[609]

A constable who interfered with the exercise of freedom of expression or freedom of assembly which could not be justified would have acted unlawfully[610] and would not, therefore, be acting in the execution of his duty. The principles enunciated by the courts since the HRA 1998 add weight to the argument that the police should not rely on the six-picket guideline suggested by the Code of Practice where their apprehension of a breach of the peace is derived solely from the number present.

11.60   More specific preventive measures are laid down in the Public Order Act 1986, which gives the police extensive powers to control 'public processions' and 'public assemblies'[611] and makes it an offence to organise, take part in, or incite others to take part in, such assemblies or processions and knowingly fail to comply with conditions imposed by the police.[612] These conditions may be imposed either in advance or on the spot where the 'senior police officer' reasonably believes that an assembly or procession may result in serious public disorder, serious damage to property, or serious disruption to the life of the community, or that the purpose of the organisers is the intimidation of others with a view to compelling them not to do an act which

---

[606] *Nicol and Selvanayagam v DPP* [1996] JP 155, 163. See also *Redmond-Bate v DPP* [1999] 163 JP 789.

[607] *Austin v The Commissioner of Police of the Metropolis* [2008] 2 QB 660, CA, at [35] (Sir Anthony Clarke, MR); see also dicta in *Laporte*, above, note 597. Notably, the ECtHR has in the past shown less tolerance of peaceful direct action; in *Steel v UK* judgment of 23 September 1998, (1999) 28 EHRR 603 the Court required only an interference with the rights of others and the possibility of disorder in order to be satisfied that interference with the right to freedom of expression was proportionate; no added requirement to find that the defendant rather than the other party was acting unreasonably was proposed: see Fenwick, 1999: p 510. This decision sits uneasily with the judgment in *Plattform 'Ärzte für das Leben' v Austria* judgment of 21 June 1988, (1991) 13 EHRR 204, para 34. See now also *Ollinger v Austria*, judgment of 29 June 2006.

[608] [2009] 1 AC 564. See Fenwick, 2009 for a full analysis of *Laporte* and *Austin*.

[609] Fenwick, 2009: 754. See also the decision of the ECtHR in *Austin v UK* Application Nos 39692/09, 40713/09 and 41008/09, 15 March 2012; *R (Moos) v Commissioner of Police of the Metropolis* [2012] EWCA Civ 12.

[610] HRA 1998, s 6.

[611] Assemblies (which require a minimum of only two persons) or processions are 'public' where they are on the highway or any other place to which at the material time any section of the public has access as of right or by express or implied permission: Public Order Act 1986, s 16, as amended by the Anti-social Behaviour Act 2003, s 57.

[612] Public Order Act 1986, ss 12, 14.

they have a right to do or to do an act which they have a right not to do. Such conditions as to the place, size and maximum duration of the assembly or procession may then be imposed as appear to the officer to be necessary to prevent these consequences occurring. In the case of pickets this may involve moving them away from a workplace entrance to avoid contact with those going into it or restricting them to times when other workers are not using the entrance, as well as restricting their number,[613] although once again regard should now be had to the HRA 1998.[614] The Act also lays down a requirement to give the police advance notice of 'public processions'.[615] The Act introduced five new statutory offences which may be relevant to the conduct of picketing: in declining order of seriousness these are riot, violent disorder, affray, causing fear of violence or provoking it, and causing harassment, alarm or distress.[616] Subject to a narrow exception, all may be committed in both public and private places. In addition, the Criminal Justice and Public Order Act 1994 inserted into the Public Order Act 1986 a new offence of intentional harassment which, unlike the pre-existing offence, does not require a prior warning to cease the offending conduct.[617] Punishable by up to six months' imprisonment and a fine of £5,000, this may constitute a considerable threat to those who participate in picketing. Finally, the Protection from Harassment Act 1997 created the offences of harassment and putting another in fear of violence, which we described in para 11.55 in the context of the civil liability to which such conduct also may give rise. Harassment is punishable by a minimum of six months' imprisonment and/or a fine of up to level 5 on the standard scale; putting a person in fear of violence a maximum of five years' imprisonment, an unlimited fine, or both.[618]

'ESSENTIAL SERVICES' AND EMERGENCY POWERS[619]

11.61   In many countries workers in 'essential services', or in the public sector, have been subject to additional restrictions in relation to their capacity lawfully to take industrial action.[620] Restrictions on the former are determined by reference to the importance of the service to the community; the latter are based upon the notion of the state as 'sovereign employer'.[621] Labour law in Britain

---

[613] See also s 14A of the Public Order Act 1986, inserted by CJPOA 1994, which permits a chief officer of police to apply to the council of a district where he reasonably believes that an assembly is intended to be held on land to which the public has no, or only a limited, right of access and, *inter alia*, may result in serious disruption to the life of the community. The council may make an order with the consent of the Secretary of State. See *Jones v DPP* [1999] 2 All ER 257.

[614] See also the police powers of dispersal under the Anti-social Behaviour Act 2003, s 30, although directions to disperse may not be given in respect of persons who are engaged in conduct which is lawful under TULRCA 1992, s 220: s 30(5).

[615] Public Order Act 1986, s 11.

[616] Public Order Act 1986, ss 1–5.

[617] Public Order Act 1986, s 4A.

[618] Protection from Harassment Act 1997, ss 2, 4. See generally Ormerod, 2011: pp 695–705.

[619] For a detailed analysis of the law and practice in this area see G Morris, 1986a and 1991 from which the material in this section is drawn. As we indicated in para 11.4 above, there is no consensus as to the meaning of 'essential' in this context; here we adopt the ILO criterion of services whose disruption would threaten the life, personal safety or health of the whole or part of the population. For a summary of ILO standards in this area see Gernigon *et al*, 1998: pp 448–453 and ILO, 2006: paras 570 *et seq*; see also Novitz, ch 13.

[620] See Pankert, 1980; Cordova, 1985; Bernier, 1994; A Jacobs, 2010.

[621] For a useful discussion of the traditional position see Aaron and Wedderburn, 1972. For a critique of the 'sovereign employer' argument see G Morris and S Fredman, 1993; see also G Morris, 2000.

has never followed either of these approaches; there are particular groups of workers for whom distinctive restrictions apply but these restrictions were introduced at differing times for different reasons; they are not the product of an integrated strategy towards public or essential services. The only criminal offence affecting such groups[622] which was introduced with the specific purpose of curbing industrial action was the Police Act 1919, which also prohibited the police from joining trade unions.[623] Now contained in the Police Act 1996, it provides that:

> ... [a]ny person who causes, or attempts to cause, or does any act calculated to cause, disaffection amongst the members of any police force, or induces or attempts to induce, or does any act calculated to induce, any member of a police force to withhold his services

is liable to a maximum of two years' imprisonment, an unlimited fine, or both.[624] Those organising industrial action among the police would clearly commit this offence and it could probably be argued that participants would do so too by doing an act 'calculated to induce' other members of the force to do the same.[625] In fact no member of a police force has ever been charged with this offence.[626] An analogous provision relating to the armed forces, the Incitement to Disaffection Act 1934, also penalises the incitement of unrest, and could be applied to industrial action although it was enacted with wider purposes in mind.[627] For many years postal workers were subject to restrictions, derived from measures enacted in the early eighteenth century to deter individual acts of interference with the Royal Mail, although no charges were ever brought despite several campaigns of industrial action. The current legislation on postal services, unlike its predecessor,[628] exempts from the offence of intentionally delaying a postal packet in the course of its transmission delays as a result of industrial action in contemplation or furtherance of a trade dispute.[629] It is possible that postal workers could be prosecuted for intentionally intercepting a communication in the course of its transmission under the Regulation of Investigatory Powers Act 2000, which contains no such exemption, but this would require the consent of the DPP.[630] Telecommunications

---

[622] Industrial action by merchant seamen is also restricted but this is to protect the safety of ships and the interests of employers rather than the public at large: Merchant Shipping Act 1995, s 59. This provision (and its predecessor) has been condemned as violating the prohibition on forced labour in Art 1(2) of the European Social Charter by the Committee of Independent Experts (now the ECSR) that supervises the Charter: see, for example, Conclusions XIV-I. In Conclusions XVIII-1 Vol 2 Report No 25 the ECSR noted the report of the UK Government that s 59 must be read in conformity with the HRA 1998. In Conclusions XIX-3, UK, (2010), Article 6(4) it is stated that the UK Government intended to amend the legislation but at the time of writing no amendment has been made.

[623] Note also TULRCA 1992, s 240.

[624] Police Act 1996, s 91.

[625] Participation in industrial action would also contravene the Standards of Professional Behaviour contained in the Police (Conduct) Regulations 2008, SI 2008/2864.

[626] The only recorded prosecutions involved persons connected with the National Unemployed Workers' Movement between 1921 and 1932. The machinery for determining pay and other specified conditions in the police is summarised in *The Staff Side of the Police Negotiating Board v Secretary of State for the Home Department* [2008] EWHC 1173 (Admin).

[627] In 1931 the printer of the Daily Worker was convicted under the Incitement to Mutiny Act 1797 (now repealed) after the paper had exhorted sailors to join a fight against pay cuts: Young, 1976. Participation in industrial action would infringe military law.

[628] Post Office Act 1953, ss 58, 68.

[629] Postal Services Act 2000, s 83. 'Trade dispute' has the same meaning as in TULRCA 1992, s 244, and 'industrial action' is to be construed in accordance with that Act: s 83(5). As we discuss in para 11.74, the latter may not be a straightforward process.

[630] Section 1.

workers, too, could incur liability under that Act in certain circumstances.[631] As we discussed in para 11.12, in relation to certain groups of workers liability may lie for inducement to breach a statutory duty, a wrong against which there is no statutory immunity. As we have seen, it is not difficult for applicants to obtain an interim injunction to halt industrial action in any dispute, and in relation to disputes in essential services the nature of the disruption is likely to give them additional ammunition. Given the severe penalties for breaching an injunction, this may be a more powerful constraint than the criminal law.[632]

11.62   More important historically than restrictions on individual categories of workers have been the extensive powers available to the government to introduce alternative labour and take other emergency measures, such as rationing resources, when essential services and supplies are threatened by industrial action. Until recently these powers generally derived from the Emergency Powers Act 1920, which enabled the government, on proclaiming a state of emergency, to take extensive measures 'to secure the essentials of life to the community' when the supply and distribution of food, water, fuel or light, or the means of locomotion, were put at risk, although the Act could not be used to impose compulsory military service or to make it an offence to strike or peacefully persuade others to do so. There were twelve separate states of emergency under the Act, most recently in 1973–1974.[633] The enactment of this legislation was accompanied by administrative contingency planning to counter the impact of disruption, a process which became increasingly elaborate after the miners' strike of 1972. This Act was repealed by the Civil Contingencies Act 2004, which contains more extensive powers to prepare for and deal with disruption in a much wider range of circumstances, including industrial action, at both national and local level. Once again, however, emergency regulations may not impose compulsory military service or 'prohibit or enable the prohibition of participation in, or any activity in connection with, a strike or other industrial action.'[634]

Integral to contingency planning in the industrial sphere has been the use of troops to replace striking workers, a strategy dating back to the nineteenth century. Since 1939 the government has had a standing power, now contained in the Emergency Powers Act 1964, to deploy troops on 'urgent work of national importance' without a proclamation of emergency. Troops have been used to replace workers in dispute on over 30 occasions since 1945, most recently during a firefighters' dispute in 2002/2003. On some occasions (in 1979, 1981, 1982 and 1989–1990) the police have been used to replace ambulance workers in dispute, although their deployment for this purpose is of dubious legal and constitutional propriety.[635]

---

[631] Note, however, the restricted definition of 'intercept' in relation to communications in the course of transmission by means of a telecommunications system, which requires that the contents of the communication be made available to a person other than the sender or intended recipient of the communication: RIPA 2000, s 2(2). For potential liability for inducing a breach of statutory duty, discussed in para 11.12 above, see the Communications Act 2003, s 104(3).

[632] It is also conceivable that industrial action in essential services could fall within the definition of 'terrorism' under s 1 of the Terrorism Act 2000. The government denied that the definition was intended to cover lawfully organised industrial action in connection with a legitimate trade dispute, but refused to create an explicit exemption: see J Rowe, 2001: pp 531–532.

[633] See generally G Morris, 1986a: ch 3.

[634] Civil Contingencies Act 2004, s 23(3).

[635] See G Morris, 1980 and 1986a: pp 106–108. For a wider survey of current powers to use troops internally see Head, 2010.

As well as these general provisions there is also legislation of a more specific nature. When the electricity and water industries were privatised in 1989 government ministers were granted extensive powers to issue confidential directions, both general and specific, to relevant operators for purposes which include mitigating the effect of any 'civil emergency' which may occur, 'civil emergency' being defined in terms which are sufficiently wide to cover disruption caused by industrial action.[636] The powers under this legislation may be exercised without parliamentary approval or even knowledge.

11.63 The 'emergency powers' approach to disputes has limitations in relation to services that cannot be stored or rationed and where a workforce has special skills and cannot easily be replaced. These limitations were shown during the disputes of the 1970s when many public service workers, including health service staff, civil servants and local authority manual workers, took national industrial action for the first time and there were also forceful campaigns by other groups such as coalminers, electricity power workers and firefighters. In general during these disputes trade unions exercised self-restraint in their choice of sanctions and commonly formulated Codes of Conduct which indicated those services which members should seek always to maintain. This approach was formalised by the TUC in 1979 when it issued a Guide to Affiliated Unions on the Conduct of Industrial Disputes which advised unions to:

> ... make arrangements in advance and with due notice, in consultation and preferably by agreement with the employer, for the maintenance by their members of supplies and services essential to the health or safety of the community or otherwise required to avoid causing exceptional hardship or serious pollution.

This 'self-restraint' approach on the part of employees was usually expressly or impliedly conditional on employers exercising reciprocal self-restraint and not seeking to undermine the unions' campaign in ways which were considered unacceptable; reaching an 'understanding' that certain services should not be provided during the dispute, for example, or agreeing to pay workers who maintained emergency cover their full wages even though they were not performing all their duties.[637]

The 'winter of discontent' disputes of 1978–1979, which involved a number of public service groups, put on the political agenda the argument that industrial action in essential services should be restricted and the election manifesto of the incoming Conservative Government undertook to do this. In the event no specific legislation was introduced in this area, despite a further manifesto commitment in 1983. It is sometimes concluded from this that the Conservative Government did nothing about essential services.[638] However, it is strongly arguable that, on the contrary, it achieved the goal of inhibiting industrial action in this sector without having to pay either a political or financial price in the form of access to arbitration, index-linking or some other method of

---

[636] Electricity Act 1989, s 96; Water Industry Act 1991, s 208.

[637] For a case study of this approach in the NHS see G Morris with S Rydzkowski, 1984.

[638] In 1996 the Conservative Government issued proposals which included removing immunity for industrial action which would have 'disproportionate or excessive effects': *Industrial Action and Trade Unions* DTI, Cm 3470, 1996, The Stationery Office. This proposal was not well received even by employers, and no further steps were taken before the Conservatives left office in May 1997.

compensating those denied recourse to industrial action.[639] A number of these services, including electricity, water and the NHS, were divided into smaller employer units and this, combined with changes in the general law, particularly the removal of protection from secondary action, made the organisation of effective industrial action much more difficult. Wide-ranging competitive tendering programmes in the civil service, NHS and local government also reduced the scope for coordinated action. Moreover, confirmation by the courts of the legitimacy of making deductions from the pay of workers who do not perform their full range of duties, an area we explore in para 11.69 *et seq* below, placed a further significant weapon in the hands of employers. Combined with the availability of the statutory right of individuals to seek injunctions to halt industrial action, which undermines the autonomy of the parties to manage their dispute, there is now very little incentive for unions to co-operate with employers in minimising the damage which may be caused by industrial action in essential services.[640] At the time of writing there is no indication that the Coalition Government will reform the law in this area in any material way.

INDUSTRIAL ACTION AND CONTRACTUAL RIGHTS

11.64   In assessing the implications of taking industrial action on contractual rights the first question to consider is whether the action constitutes a breach of the contract of employment. If it does the employer has three remedies at its disposal: to sue individual workers in damages for the loss the industrial action causes; to withhold their pay; and, where the breach is sufficiently serious to repudiate the contract, to dismiss them without notice (although depending upon the circumstances, employees may then be able to claim unfair dismissal). These are powerful sanctions which, if threatened, may intimidate workers into abandoning their action. However, the employer cannot obtain a legal order to force employees back to normal work; by statute a court is prohibited from ordering an employee to work by way of an order for specific performance of the contract or an injunction restraining a breach or threatened breach.[641]

The common law does not recognise industrial action as any kind of 'special case' but in some circumstances the courts have sought to mitigate what they perceive to be the injustice for one or other party of applying contractual doctrines, on occasion leading to some fine distinctions and anomalous results. It is notable that, although the Labour Government accorded more extensive (albeit still heavily circumscribed) protection to participants in industrial action against unfair dismissal (see para 11.72 *et seq*), the Employment Relations Acts of 1999 and 2004 made no change to their contractual position. The HRA 1998 has not, to date, affected this situation but may do so in future now that the ECtHR has confirmed that the right to strike is formally protected by Article 11 (see further para 7.9 above).

---

[639] This argument is developed in G Morris, 1991.

[640] In 1997 a collective agreement between management and unions at Government Communications Headquarters (GCHQ) committed the unions not to induce or authorise any form of industrial action by GCHQ staff if this would disrupt GCHQ operations, such a question to be determined by the Secretary of State. This agreement, unusually, is contractually binding. Entry into an agreement of this nature was the price the unions paid for a restoration of staff rights to join national civil service unions: see further para 7.18 above.

[641] TULRCA 1992, s 236.

It is widely thought that the HRA 1998 requires the courts to interpret the employer's managerial prerogative and the corresponding duty on employees to obey lawful and reasonable orders in a way which is compatible with the 'Convention rights'.[642] This may be material in assessing whether employers are entitled to issue a particular instruction to their workers (to submit to intimate body searches, for example), and whether workers have a correlative obligation to obey; a collective refusal to comply may not be regarded as a breach of contract if the employer had no contractual authority to issue this instruction in the first place.[643] These circumstances apart, however, the position as set out below will apply unless and until the British courts are willing to consider whether specific employer responses to strike action by employees comply with Article 11.[644]

Strikes and the contract of employment

11.65 The courts have generally assumed that a strike, as a total cessation of work, will always constitute a breach of the contract of employment, regardless of the circumstances which provoked it.[645] Whether or not giving notice of a strike changes the position depends upon the terms of the notice given. The notice may explicitly evince an intention to break the contract, so enabling the employer to treat it as an anticipatory breach. Conversely, it may express an intention to terminate the contract. In that event, provided that a period of notice of sufficient length in relation to the individual participant has been given, and that notice has expired before strike action begins, there will be no breach because the contract will have ended (provided that there are no additional constraints on termination).[646] However, it is rare for this to happen and for good reason; collective resignation would be a very unwise course for workers to take, given that they would thereby forfeit even those limited statutory employment protection rights which they would otherwise have.

Commonly strike notices merely express an intention 'to strike', thereby leaving their legal effect for determination by the courts. In these circumstances there are powerful dicta to support the view that they should be interpreted as notices of intended breach of contract rather than of termination on the ground that strikers do not, in reality, wish to leave their employment but, rather, to remain on terms other than those on offer by the employer. Thus in *Rookes v Barnard* Lord Devlin stated that the object of the strike was to 'break the contract by withholding labour but keeping the contract alive for as long as the employers would tolerate the breach without

---

[642] See G Morris, 2001a.

[643] In the case of public authorities (or 'pure' public authorities at least), issuing an order to violate the Convention rights of others could be regarded as an unlawful act for the purposes of HRA 1998, s 6, and the order could be regarded as one which an employee is entitled not to obey: see *Gregory v Ford* [1951] 1 All ER 121; *Lister v Romford Ice and Cold Storage Co Ltd* [1957] AC 555 (Viscount Simonds); *Morrish v Henlys (Folkstone) Ltd* [1973] ICR 482.

[644] See Ewing and Hendy, 2010: 16-19 for the argument that the imposition of disciplinary sanctions, for example, may breach Article 11. The Court of Appeal decision in *Metrobus Ltd v Unite the Union*, [2009] IRLR 851, discussed in para 11.9 above, suggests that it may not be easy to persuade British courts readily to accept this line of argument. See also *Sehmi v Gate Gourmet Ltd* [2009] IRLR 807, Underhill P at [38].

[645] See, for example, Ewing, 1991. For a contrary argument, see Elias, 1994, summarised below.

[646] It is conceivable that a 'no-strike' agreement may restrict the right of workers collectively to terminate their contracts during a dispute but this restriction would need to have been incorporated into the contract of employment: see TULRCA 1992, s 180, discussed further below.

exercising their right of rescission'.[647] However, in *Boxfoldia Ltd v NGA*,[648] Saville J asserted that the meaning and effect of the words used in a strike notice should be examined in their context, with no preference for any particular construction. However, the details of his judgment indicate that even on this view the court is unlikely to find that notice of collective termination has been given without clear evidence of this. The union had given the employers by letter '14 days' notice of withdrawal of all NGA members' labour from the company'. The company claimed that the union had induced the employees to breach their contracts of employment and that, as this had not been preceded by a ballot, the union was liable in tort for damages. The union argued that the letter gave contractual notice of termination on behalf of all the NGA's members. Saville J was not persuaded that there was a rule of law that strike notices should be regarded as notice of intended breach, a view which presupposed 'that the party giving the notice wishes the contracts of employment to continue'. He developed this point by stating that:

> ... [t]o my mind this is not necessarily so, for in any given case the employees (or their union) may consider that by actually terminating the contracts on due notice, greater or more effective pressure can be put upon the employers, though, of course, by doing this the employees would ... lose certain unfair dismissal rights which would otherwise exist. Furthermore ... there is a distinction to be drawn between wanting to continue with the existing but improved contracts of employment and wanting to continue (but with new contracts) the relationship of employer and employee ... In addition there is something to be said for the proposition that it should not too readily be assumed that a party is acting unlawfully when his actions could equally well be construed as lawful'.[649]

In this case Saville J considered that 'withdrawal of labour' was capable of referring to notice of termination but on the facts found that this was not the case: the letter did not purport to be written by the union on behalf of or as agent for the employees, it did not communicate any decision by them to terminate their contracts, nor give on their behalf the appropriate termination notice stipulated in their contracts. This finding suggests that, despite his earlier remarks, Saville J too in practice required clear evidence in order to find that notice to terminate had been given. He also observed that there was nothing in the union's rules which gave it the requisite authority to terminate contracts on its members' behalf and he refused to imply such authority from the union's power to instruct members to take industrial action and to publicise that instruction.

   On the reasoning adopted in *Boxfoldia*, in the absence of express authority for a union to terminate its members' contracts, each striker would need to give notice of termination of employment on an individual basis or expressly authorise the union to give such notice on his or her behalf.[650] Where employees are required to give notice of differing lengths either of these procedures would be a complex organisational exercise. In view of the serious consequences for

---

[647] [1964] AC 1129, 1204. See also *JT Stratford & Son Ltd v Lindley* [1965] AC 269 at 285 (Lord Denning). To date the courts have not treated showing an intention to participate in a threatened or rolling strike if and when called upon to do so as a breach of contract: see *Ticehurst and Thompson v British Telecommunications plc* [1992] IRLR 219.

[648] [1988] IRLR 383.

[649] [1988] IRLR 383, 385.

[650] See also *Ideal Casements Ltd v Shamsi* [1972] ICR 408, where the need for authorisation by the rules for the giving of any form of strike notice by union officials was made clear. It is possible that custom and practice may also provide sufficient authority: *Heaton's Transport (St Helens) Ltd v TGWU* [1972] ICR 308, although it is suggested that the courts should require very clear evidence before finding this.

individuals of collective resignation, it is desirable that such obstacles exist to unions purporting to terminate their contracts of employment, especially given that, as *Boxfoldia* demonstrates, unions may be tempted to safeguard their own legal position by arguing that the form of the notice – one of termination – means that no tort has been committed.

In a number of systems industrial action suspends, rather than breaches, the contract of employment. In *Morgan v Fry*[651] Lord Denning made a preliminary attempt to introduce this concept into English law, stating that:

> The truth is that neither employer nor workmen wish to take the drastic action of termination if it can be avoided. The men do not wish to leave their work for ever. The employers do not wish to scatter their labour force to the four winds. Each side is, therefore, content to accept a 'strike notice' of proper length as lawful. It is an implication read into the contract by the modern law as to trade disputes. If a strike takes place, the contract of employment is not terminated. It is suspended during the strike: and revives again when the strike is over.[652]

As Ewing points out[653] Lord Denning's approach would not, itself, protect employees without employers being additionally constrained from terminating their contracts with due notice. In the event this approach was never taken further by the courts[654] and, as we discuss in para 11.93, could almost certainly take root only within a broader framework of reform of industrial action law. As the law now stands a strike would be viewed as suspensory only if there was a contractual term which specifically granted employees the right to suspend in these circumstances. It has been argued that if the terms of a collective agreement which forbids industrial action until a disputes procedure has been exhausted are incorporated into individual contracts then, on exhaustion of this procedure, a right to strike could be implied.[655] However, there is no authority to support this proposition and, in any event, incorporation of this kind of clause has been rare.[656]

It has been argued extra-judicially by Patrick Elias QC (now Elias LJ) that a defensive strike in response to a continuing repudiatory breach of contract by an employer should not be treated as a breach of contract by employees.[657] Elias justifies this contention on two separate grounds. The first is that employees can lawfully initiate the strike by 'concerted constructive dismissals' which, provided that it is made clear that they are resigning in response to the employer's repudiatory breach, need not require any period of notice.[658] He argues that this would then allow employees to claim wrongful dismissal if not subsequently reinstated and, more tentatively, that they would not at this point be 'taking part' in industrial action and so would not thereby jeopardise their unfair dismissal rights. As it stands, this argument is open to the objection which we discuss above as to the inadvisability of employees terminating their contracts of employment. However, it could

---

[651] [1968] 2 QB 710.
[652] [1968] 2 QB 710, 728.
[653] Ewing, 1991: pp 5–6.
[654] See *Simmons v Hoover Ltd* [1977] ICR 61.
[655] Hepple, 1981b: para 495.
[656] See para 11.67 below.
[657] Elias, 1994.
[658] Elias, 1994: p 259. In *Wilkins v Cantrell and Cochrane (GB) Ltd* [1978] IRLR 483, the EAT held that going on strike in response to a repudiatory breach of contract by the employer should not be regarded as a termination of the contract. To the extent that the judgment may be taken to imply that employees are not in law entitled as part of a concerted campaign to terminate their contracts in response to a repudiatory breach, Elias argues that it is erroneous.

be invoked for the purposes of unfair dismissal to support the argument that the employees have been constructively dismissed because their existing contracts of employment have terminated prior to the industrial action starting, even though they remain in the employment.[659] Elias's second argument is based upon the proposition that, by analogy with the position of employees, if the employer is not prepared to provide the whole of the consideration which is due to the employee under the contract of employment (for example, by cutting wages) the employee has the right to refuse to work.[660] At the time of writing there is no judicial authority which supports these arguments directly and, indeed, such authority as exists is to the contrary.[661]

Industrial action short of a strike and the contract of employment

11.66   The effect of industrial action short of a strike on the contract of employment depends upon its nature. In this area the implied duty of co-operation which employees owe to their employer, which, as we saw in para 4.98 *et seq* above has been given an extensive interpretation by the courts, has been particularly crucial. Sometimes a refusal to perform a particular duty, or to handle particular goods, as instructed by the employer will clearly constitute a breach. Where it is not apparent that it does constitute a breach, the duty of co-operation may lead the courts to conclude that the employee should nevertheless obey the instruction to perform the task, even if the task in question constitutes the very subject-matter of the dispute.[662] The same point applies to the operation of new working methods; provided that they can be viewed as different methods of performing the same task, rather than as a wholly different job, refusal to comply with the instruction to change will be a breach of contract.[663] The courts have leant towards an interpretation which favours flexibility and where workers dispute the employers' right to force the change upon them their only safe recourse is to the courts.[664] However, even then their chances of an interim injunction to restrain the alleged variation may not be great, and if the case went to full trial, which may be some years later, it is difficult to predict what damages, if any, could be obtained.

Where industrial action takes the form of a 'work-to-rule' this is likely to be viewed as a breach of the implied duty of co-operation or fidelity, at least where the rule book is construed as containing the lawful instructions of the employer to its workers as to how they are to work.

---

[659] See *Hogg v Dover College* [1990] ICR 39; *Alcan Extrusions v Yates* [1996] IRLR 327, discussed in paras 5.68 and 5.71.

[660] Authority for this is drawn from Lord Templeman's dictum in *Miles v Wakefield Metropolitan District Council* [1987] IRLR 193 at 198 that '[i]f the employer declines to pay, the worker need not work' which Elias extends to the whole of the consideration.

[661] In *Simmons v Hoover Ltd* [1977] ICR 61 it was suggested that strikes in opposition to changes imposed by the employer in breach of contract should not be treated as *repudiatory* breaches of the contract but other judges have refused to accept even this view: *Wilkins v Cantrell and Cochrane (GB) Ltd* [1978] IRLR 483; *Marsden v Fairey Stainless Ltd* [1979] IRLR 103.

[662] *Sim v Rotherham Metropolitan Borough Council* [1986] IRLR 391; see generally Fredman and Morris, 1987b. This approach was also followed in *Solihull Metropolitan Borough v NUT* [1985] IRLR 211, ChD, in deciding, in interim proceedings, that the defendants had committed the tort of inducing breach of contract. In *OBG v Allan* [2007] IRLR 608, HL Lord Nicholls specifically said at [202] that this decision should not be followed: see para 11.11 above.

[663] See, for example, *Cresswell v Board of Inland Revenue* [1984] IRLR 190.

[664] *MacPherson v London Borough of Lambeth* [1988] IRLR 470. Where an undertaking derives from a collective agreement, whether it is enforceable by an individual employee may also be an issue: see *Malone v British Airways plc* [2011] IRLR 32.

Authority for this view is provided by the Court of Appeal decision in *Secretary of State for Employment v ASLEF (No 2)*[665] which we discussed in para 4.101 above. It will be remembered that in this case a number of grounds were offered for the view that working to the letter of this rule book (which contained 239 rules) in the context of industrial action constituted a breach of contract.[666] For Lord Denning the breach consisted of taking steps wilfully to disrupt the undertaking, 'to produce chaos so that it will not run as it should'.[667] Thus it was the motive or object with which the act was done which rendered it unlawful. For Roskill LJ it lay in an implied term that the employee would not seek to obey lawful instructions in a wholly unreasonable way which 'has the effect of disrupting the system, the efficient running of which he is employed to ensure',[668] an approach which focuses upon the impact of the action. Buckley LJ based his decision upon an implied term that the employee would serve the employer faithfully with a view to promoting those commercial interests for which he is employed.[669] This decision does not mean that every work-to-rule will automatically be viewed as a breach of contract but the range of dicta in the case provide ample ammunition for the argument that it will. A 'go-slow' is likely to be similarly viewed; in *General Engineering Services Ltd v Kingston and St Andrew Corpn*[670] this form of action by firemen was classified by the Privy Council as a 'wrongful repudiation of an essential element of their contract of employment'.[671]

As we pointed out in para 4.103, Lord Denning's approach in *Secretary of State for Employment v Associated Society of Locomotive Engineers and Firemen (No 2)* conflicts with the general principle of English law that a bad motive does not render an otherwise lawful act unlawful.[672] Despite this the courts have invoked an analogous approach in relation to a withdrawal of 'goodwill' or 'co-operation'. In *Ticehurst and Thompson v British Telecommunications Ltd*[673] the employee, a manager in charge of 40 staff, had participated in her union's campaign of industrial action which consisted of a withdrawal of goodwill, followed by a series of one-day strikes. After participating in three of these strikes Mrs Ticehurst was asked by the employer to sign a document undertaking 'to work normally in accordance with the terms of my contract with BT from now on'. When she refused to sign she was asked to leave the premises and was not paid for the day in question. The same thing occurred on subsequent working days until the dispute was settled. The Court of Appeal found that the withdrawal of goodwill constituted a breach of the implied term of her contract identified by Buckley LJ in *ASLEF*; the duty to serve the employer faithfully within the requirements of the contract. The court rejected the argument that this term could not be breached unless the intended disruption of BT's undertaking was achieved in practice. Rather the term was breached 'when the employee does an act, or omits to do an act, which would be within her contract and the discretion allowed to her not to do, or to do, as the case may be, and the employee so acts or omits to do the act, not in honest exercise of choice

---

[665] [1972] 2 QB 455.
[666] See Napier, 1972, for a discussion of the principles underlying the judgment in this case.
[667] [1972] 2 QB 455, 492.
[668] [1972] 2 QB 455, 509.
[669] [1972] 2 QB 455, 498.
[670] [1988] 3 All ER 867.
[671] [1988] 3 All ER 867, 869 (Lord Ackner). The Privy Council concluded from this that the firemen were not acting in the course of their employment and the employer was not vicariously liable for the damage caused by their default.
[672] Cf Bogg, 2011: p 768.
[673] [1992] IRLR 219.

or discretion for the faithful performance of her work but in order to disrupt the employer's business or to cause the most inconvenience that can be caused'.[674]

Although *Ticehurst* concerned a managerial employee this dictum seems likely to be applied, *mutatis mutandis*, to all categories of worker. The court left open the position 'if the ill-intentioned course of conduct is shown to have had no significant consequences adverse to the employer and to be incapable of causing any such adverse consequences in future',[675] but the emphasis upon intent suggests that even this is likely to be regarded as a breach. The logic of this approach is that even a ban on voluntary overtime could constitute a breach of the contract of employment if employees' refusal to provide it was deliberately designed to cause disruption. In *Burgess v Stevedoring Services Ltd*, however, the Privy Council distinguished between employees performing duties in a deliberately obstructive way and 'refusing to do things altogether outside their contractual obligations (like going to work on Sunday) merely because they do not have a bona fide reason for refusal. They do not have to have any reason at all.'[676] In this case, employees were contractually obliged to report for overtime duty when so assigned by the union. The union, in breach of its obligations under the collective agreement with the employer, refused to make up overtime gangs. The Privy Council considered that had employees been assigned work and said that they were unavailable as part of a concerted action the *ASLEF* case might have had some relevance, but this was not the case here.

Finally, it should be noted that for industrial action short of a strike, giving notice cannot change its legal consequences; if the action itself breaches the contract, notice merely constitutes notice of intended breach, regardless of the circumstances.

The effect of 'no-strike agreements' on the contract of employment

11.67   In some areas of the private-sector collective agreements have been concluded which prohibit or restrict resort to industrial action.[677] Prominent examples were those agreed in the context of 'single-union' deals in high-tech industries. Although these agreements provoked considerable controversy within the union movement because of the symbolic significance of 'giving up' the freedom to take industrial action,[678] in reality their legal implications have been minimal. At collective level research showed that the parties had not inserted the explicit statement of enforceability which would be necessary to render them enforceable contracts.[679] In relation to the individual worker, given that industrial action is generally treated as a breach of contract, they would appear to add nothing to the general position. The only additional constraint which such

[674] [1992] IRLR 219, Ralph Gibson LJ at 225, with whom the other members of the court agreed.
[675] [1992] IRLR 219, 225.
[676] [2002] IRLR 810, at [27] (Lord Hoffmann).
[677] For an analysis of these 'deals' see R Lewis, 1990; Bassett, 1986. Note also the agreement concluded at GCHQ in 1997: see para 11.10 above.
[678] The notes on Principle 3 of the *TUC disputes principles and procedures* (2007) now state that '[u]nions must not make any agreements that remove, or are designed to remove, the basic democratic lawful rights of a trade union to take industrial action in advance of recruiting members and without consulting them'. See para 2.13 above for the status of these principles.
[679] R Lewis, 1990: p 38. Cf the agreement at GCHQ which, unusually, does provide for a legally enforceable contract.

an agreement might impose is if it were to restrict the right of workers collectively to terminate their contracts during a strike. However, there have been no test cases on this point.

If the parties were to attempt to incorporate a 'no-strike' agreement into individual contracts, possibly to serve as a 'reminder' of their obligations, a specific procedure must be followed. As we saw in para 4.30, not all the terms of a collective agreement are appropriate for incorporation into individual contracts and it would be necessary to ensure that the restriction was in a suitable form. A clause which merely stated, for example, 'there shall be no strikes or lock-outs until the procedure for the settlement of disputes has been exhausted' would seem not to be appropriate; it is unclear what the nature of the obligation on the individual would be and there is the additional problem that disputes procedures can usually only be invoked by the collective parties. More likely to be effective is a clause which attempts directly to translate the obligation into individual terms, for example a clause stating that:

> ... [t]here shall be expressly incorporated into the contract of each employee a provision
> that during the course of any negotiations, conciliation or arbitration, he [or she] will not
> participate in any strike or other forms of industrial action.[680]

However, by statute,[681] a clause which restricts the right of workers to engage in a strike or other industrial action may only form part of the individual contract if the collective agreement is in writing; contains a provision stating that the terms may be incorporated; is reasonably accessible at their place of work to the workers to whom it applies and available for them to consult during working hours; and each union party to the agreement is 'independent'. In practice it has been rare for the collective parties to attempt this.[682]

On occasion employers have attempted to require employees to sign undertakings that they will not participate, or take any further part in, existing disputes as a condition of being allowed to return to work. The courts have held that a refusal to give such an undertaking does not, of itself, constitute a breach of the contract of employment.[683]

Employer responses to industrial action in breach of contract

11.68   Where industrial action constitutes a breach of the contract of employment employers have a range of responses available to them. First, if the breach is sufficiently serious to constitute a repudiation of the contract the employer may decide summarily to dismiss the worker. Whether the breach will constitute a repudiation depends upon the facts. In general, strikes have been regarded as repudiatory.[684] It has been suggested that strikes in opposition to changes made by the employer which breach the contract would not be repudiatory,[685] but other judges have refused to

---

[680] R Lewis, 1990: p 51.
[681] TULRCA 1992, s 180(3).
[682] R Lewis, 1990: pp 37–38.
[683] See *Ticehurst and Thompson v British Telecommunications plc* [1992] IRLR 219, 228. *Chappell v Times Newspapers Ltd* [1975] ICR 145 also lends support to this view.
[684] See *Simmons v Hoover Ltd* [1977] ICR 61, 76.
[685] *Simmons v Hoover Ltd* [1977] ICR 61. See also *Thompson v Eaton Ltd* [1976] ICR 336, 342.

accept this view.[686] It is arguable that a strike of very short duration (for example, for a day or less) should not be seen as such, but such authority as there is on this point suggests the contrary.[687] For industrial action short of a strike a refusal to perform only a minor part of the employees' total duties should not, in principle, be seen as repudiatory but it is difficult to predict how a court will view such action. In *Wiluszynski v London Borough of Tower Hamlets* the claimant, an estates officer in the council's housing directorate, as part of a campaign of industrial action, refused to answer enquiries from council members as he was contractually obliged to do. When the campaign ended five weeks later it took him about three hours to deal with the backlog of inquiries. Despite the limited proportion of working time this occupied, two members of the Court of Appeal considered, obiter, that this was a repudiatory breach.[688]

Where a breach is not repudiatory an employer wishing to dismiss would need to give the contractual period of notice and comply with any other restrictions on termination contained in the contract. Where the employer fails to do this, however, the remedy would almost certainly be confined to damages; as we have seen the courts exercise their discretionary power to grant injunctive relief against dismissal only in exceptional circumstances and are unlikely to do so in a context where employees cannot show that they are ready and willing to perform their side of the contract[689] (see our discussion in para 5.54 *et seq*).

11.69   In theory employers who suffer loss as a result of industrial action in breach of contract could sue each individual worker for the damages flowing from that breach, regardless of whether the breach is repudiatory. However, each worker may be sued in contract only for the loss for which he is she was personally responsible.[690] In the case of assembly-line workers, for example, this would be the value of the lost production minus the costs which the employer would have had to incur as part of the process of production.[691] Where the worker is a supervisor or a managerial worker, on the other hand, it may be harder to establish direct loss; the most likely measure is the extra cost to the employer of providing a replacement if this was necessary.[692] This creates the somewhat paradoxical result that 'the damages assessed against a production worker will be greater than those assessed against a supervisory worker, even though the actual loss to the employers may ... be far greater where the industrial action is taken by members of the latter group because it causes a total closure of the enterprise'.[693] In practice it has been very rare for employers to sue

---

[686] *Wilkins v Cantrell and Cochrane (GB) Ltd* [1978] IRLR 483; *Marsden v Fairley Stainless Ltd* [1979] IRLR 103. Cf the position under the HRA 1998 where the employer's instruction interferes with the exercise of a Convention right, discussed at para 11.64.

[687] *Rasool v Hepworth Pipe Co Ltd* [1980] IRLR 88 (one-hour mass meeting during working hours without employer's consent a repudiatory breach of contract).

[688] [1989] IRLR 259; see Nicholls LJ at 264 with whom Mann LJ agreed.

[689] In *Chappell v Times Newspapers Ltd* [1975] ICR 145 the Court of Appeal refused to grant an injunction to restrain employers from treating workers as having terminated their contracts of employment where the workers had been instructed by their union to take industrial action, although they had not yet breached their contracts as individuals, on the basis, *inter alia*, that in the light of union instructions they would not undertake to perform their part of the contract.

[690] *National Coal Board v Galley* [1958] 1 WLR 16. However, proof of inducing fellow workers to break their contracts, or of conspiracy among workers to induce a breach, may give rise to liability in tort. *Quaere* whether breach of contract *per se* can constitute unlawful means for the purposes of the torts of causing loss by unlawful means (see para 11.14 above) and unlawful means conspiracy (see para 11.18 above).

[691] *Ebbw Vale Steel, Iron and Coal Co v Tew* (1935) 79 Sol Jo 593.

[692] *National Coal Board v Galley* [1958] 1 WLR 16.

[693] Ewing, 1991: p 19.

individual workers; in general they prefer to pursue a remedy in tort against those organising the industrial action. However, employers have become much more willing in recent years to invoke the 'self-help' remedy of making deductions from workers' wages and in this context the existence of a right to sue for damages, even if it is not exercised as such, is significant.

As we saw in para 4.62 *et seq*, the principles governing the right to payment, and the right of employers to make deductions, are complex. A number of the cases have been decided in the context of industrial action and the resulting principles are not completely clear. It is clear that workers who go on strike have no right to be paid for this period.[694] In addition, workers who refuse to perform their full range of contractual obligations may be sent home without pay unless the contract places some restriction on this.[695] It also seems that if partial working is imposed for only a proportion of the working week employers may state that they are not prepared to accept less than the full range of duties and 'send the worker home' without pay for that proportion of the week. This was the situation in the leading case of *Miles v Wakefield Metropolitan District Council*.[696] Mr Miles, a superintendent registrar of births, marriages and deaths, had refused to perform marriages on Saturday mornings for 14 months as part of a campaign for higher pay. He normally worked a 37-hour week, of which 3 hours were on Saturdays. The council told him that unless he was prepared to perform his full range of duties he would not be required to attend work on Saturdays and would not be paid for doing so. Mr Miles nevertheless continued to do other work on Saturday mornings and when the council withheld 3/37ths of his pay he sued for the unpaid salary. The House of Lords held that the council was entitled to refuse his offer of reduced working on Saturdays and his position was then the same as if he had withdrawn his labour completely for that period; he had no right to be paid for the work he had carried out on Saturdays.[697]

11.70 Where an employer allows workers to continue working on a restricted basis the legal position as regards the employee's right to payment is confused. In *Royle v Trafford Borough Council*[698] Park J refused to allow the council to deprive a teacher working restrictively of his entire wage; having accepted imperfect performance it could not then refuse to pay him anything for this. Another line of authority, however, holds that workers are not entitled under their contracts to any payment whatsoever. This view received support from Lords Templeman and Brightman, obiter, in *Miles*, although they considered that employees could claim payment on a *quantum*

---

[694] In *Cooper v Isle of Wight College* [2008] IRLR 124, Blake J held that the test of what can be deducted from an employee's wages is to determine what the employee could not sue for, and that for the purposes of this calculation the annual salary should be apportioned between the contractual working hours spread over 52 weeks, without discounting paid holidays.

[695] *Cresswell v Board of Inland Revenue* [1984] IRLR 190; see also *MacPherson v London Borough of Lambeth* [1988] IRLR 470; *Ticehurst and Thompson v British Telecommunications plc* [1992] IRLR 219 (although in *Ticehurst* it was stated that evincing an intention to respond to a strike call by the union, if and when made, would not have itself have entitled the employers to refuse to permit the employees to work in a situation where the value of the services received would not be reduced by the risk that at some future date the employee might refuse to perform her contract).

[696] [1987] IRLR 193. See also *Jakeman v South West Thames Regional Health Authority and London Ambulance Service* [1990] IRLR 62, QBD, where pay was withheld for periods for which the employer had refused to accept partial performance of duties. Mandatory interim relief was sought by the claimant employees and refused.

[697] On the issue of whether the pay period in question should properly have been treated as divisible, see para 4.69 above.

[698] [1984] IRLR 184.

meruit basis for the amount and value of the work they had performed,[699] a view which was contested by Lord Bridge who questioned whether entitlement to a *quantum meruit* could replace entitlement to remuneration at the contractual rate.[700] The view that there is no entitlement to payment also accords with the principle upheld by the Court of Appeal in *Henthorn and Taylor v Central Electricity Generating Board*.[701] Here the employers had refused to pay manual workers any wages for days when they were working to rule. A claim for unpaid wages by two employees was rejected by the courts on the basis that in order to claim money due under the contract they had first to prove that they themselves were willing to perform their contracts. Because they could not do this they had no remedy.[702] This view has been criticised on the ground, *inter alia*, that willingness to perform the contract is not relevant to a claim for money due in debt[703] (although it would not preclude an employer's counterclaim).

Argument may sometimes arise as to whether the employer has, indeed, accepted imperfect performance. This was the case in *Wiluszynski*.[704] The council responded to the employees' industrial action – refusing to answer council members' inquiries – by informing them that their presence on the premises was not required until they were prepared to resume normal working, and were they to attend for work and undertake limited working this would be regarded as unauthorised and voluntary in nature. Mr Wiluszynski continued to attend work during the five weeks the action lasted, performing all his other duties. On resuming his normal duties it took him about three hours to deal with the backlog of inquiries. When he sued for his unpaid salary the Court of Appeal rejected the argument that the council had acquiesced in his work and taken the benefit of it; it had not given him any directions to work so as to contradict the statement that it would regard any work as voluntary, and he could not have been misled as to the genuineness of the employer's pronouncement. The council could not be expected physically to prevent the relevant staff from entering the premises. Mr Wiluszynski had failed to discharge a material part of his contractual duties and the council was entitled to withhold his entire salary for the period.

The reasoning in this case is open to question. The court relied upon the principle that employees who sue for remuneration must show that they are ready and willing to discharge their own obligations, which it took to be the principle upheld in *Miles*. However, if this were to be the case there would seem to be nothing to prevent an employer accepting imperfect performance and still refusing to pay, making discussion of whether there had been acceptance of such performance irrelevant. The combined effect of *Miles* and *Wiluszynski* may suggest that those organising industrial action short of a strike would be best advised to restrict sanctions to limited quantifiable periods of time with full performance in between. If employers wish to maintain services, whilst also making some deduction, this may satisfy honour on both sides.[705] Even then, however, the reasoning in *Wiluszynski* indicates that employers may still be within their rights to withhold the entire salary on the basis that employees were not willing to perform the contract in its entirety. There is a fundamental and unresolved conflict here. *Wiluszynski*, in particular,

---

[699] [1987] IRLR 193, 199 (Lord Templeman), 195 (Lord Brightman).

[700] [1987] IRLR 193, 195. Lord Bridge's view that no claim could be brought on a *quantum meruit* basis was discussed and adopted in *Spackman v London Metropolitan University* [2007] IRLR 744, Cty Ct.

[701] [1980] IRLR 361.

[702] See also *MacPherson v London Borough of Lambeth* [1988] IRLR 470.

[703] See Napier, 1986.

[704] [1989] IRLR 259.

[705] See McLean, 1990.

presents considerable problems for unions with members in essential services who may wish to maintain an emergency service yet would be unwilling to do this for no remuneration whatsoever. One approach to this difficulty may be to argue that by accepting partial performance employers have thereby waived their right to claim non-performance of the contract, without prejudice to a claim in damages for loss caused by the employees' breach.

In *Royle*, as we have seen, the employee successfully challenged the employer's right to withhold the entire wage where it had accepted restricted working. There have been other cases where employees have challenged the employer's right to make even a partial deduction from wages. This argument has not met with success. However, the only attempt to provide a principled justification for deductions in this context has come from Scott J in *Sim v Rotherham Metropolitan Borough Council*.[706] Here the defendant education authority had deducted a sum from the claimant teacher's salary to represent her failure to provide cover for an absent colleague for a 35-minute period during a campaign of industrial action. She sued to recover this amount claiming, first, that she owed no contractual obligation to provide cover and, second, that even if she had, the employer's remedy lay only in damages. Scott J, having held that her failure to provide cover was a breach of contract,[707] affirmed that, given that she had been allowed to continue working, the contractual obligations on both sides remained on foot and she was entitled to her salary. However, her claim to payment in full was subject to the employer's cross-claim for damages for the loss flowing from the breach. Applying the doctrine of 'equitable set-off' Scott J held that it would be unjust to allow the claimant to proceed without taking account of the loss to the employer, which in this case it was agreed was no less than the sum the employers had deducted.

This decision allows employers to decide what sums reflect the damages to which they are entitled and puts the onus on employees to challenge this.[708] The reluctance of the courts to grant interim relief during disputes to order the employer to make withheld payments compounds the difficulties for employees who may suffer hardship as a result.[709] Moreover, because the restrictions on deductions imposed by the ERA 1996 do not apply to those made on account of industrial action,[710] employees who are dismissed for instituting legal proceedings on this matter who lack the requisite period of continuous employment will not qualify for protection against unfair dismissal (see para 5.98 above). The difficulties of quantifying loss in the case of clerical, managerial or professional workers[711] has not prevented this being a significant threat

---

[706] [1986] IRLR 391.

[707] See Fredman and Morris, 1987b, for a critique of this reasoning.

[708] See, however, *Cooper v Isle of Wight College* [2008] IRLR 124, where Blake J opined at [31] and [32] that equitable set off cannot be considered as a basis for *any* deduction by way of recoverable damages that the employer alleges flows from an admitted breach of contract and that *Sim* is of no assistance where the quantum of damages is disputed rather than agreed.

[709] See *Jakeman v South West Thames Regional Health Authority and London Ambulance Service* [1990] IRLR 62.

[710] Section 14(5). In *Gill v Ford Motor Company Ltd* [2004] IRLR 840, the EAT held that an employment tribunal must make a finding of fact as to whether a worker who has suffered a deduction has taken part in industrial action. However, if the worker has taken part in industrial action, a tribunal has no jurisdiction to examine whether the deduction was authorised by the contract: *Sunderland Polytechnic v Evans* [1993] IRLR 196; *Scott v Strathclyde Fire Board* EATS/0050/03 26 April 2004.

[711] In *Royle v Trafford Borough Council* [1984] IRLR 184, a teacher had refused to admit an additional five pupils into his class of 31. A reduction of 5/36ths was said to represent the 'notional value' of the services he had failed to perform. See also G Morris with S Rydzkowski, 1984: pp 160–161 on deductions in the NHS during the 1982 dispute. In *Jakeman v South West Thames Health Authority and London Ambulance Service* [1990] IRLR 62, the employer was seeking to rely on the losses it would otherwise incur in calling upon other agencies, such as the police and army, to help it out.

in the education sector and in white-collar areas of the civil service and local government where industrial action has traditionally taken the form of industrial action short of a strike.[712] It should be noted that all the time during which a worker is 'engaged in taking industrial action' is excluded in respect of the time for which the national minimum wage is payable.[713] Thus workers such as Wiluszynski would have had no minimum wage entitlement in relation to the work which they actually did.[714] There is no definition of 'industrial action' in this context, and on the basis of the interpretation of this concept in relation to unfair dismissal even a ban on non-contractual duties could fall within it (see para 11.74 below). By analogy with the unfair dismissal provisions, disputes may also arise as to when a worker is 'engaged in taking' industrial action; it would seem to be confined to times when the worker individually is working restrictively (going-slow, for example), but it could conceivably be argued to extend to any period during which the worker has evinced an intention to participate in industrial action (such as a programme of rolling strikes) if called upon to do so.

Lock-outs and the contract of employment

11.71   Unlike some systems, English law does not formally distinguish between 'offensive' and 'defensive' lock-outs of workers by employers.[715] However, as we have seen, where employees refuse to perform their full range of normal duties an employer is legally entitled to send them home without pay, the functional equivalent of one form of 'defensive' lock-out.[716] Where there is no preceding industrial action, or the threat of it, by employees a lock-out is likely to constitute a breach of contract on the part of the employer unless (exceptionally) there is provision for suspension of the contract during a lock-out or notice of appropriate length to terminate the contract is given. Merely giving notice to 'lock-out' may not be sufficient as this, like strike notice, can be seen as notice of intended breach.[717] Provided that employees can show that they were ready and willing to work during this period they would be able to sue for any losses to them resulting from the breach. Whether or not the breach will be serious enough to amount to repudiation of the contract will depend upon the facts;[718] the duration of the lock-out may be material here. Even if a lock-out is repudiatory, however, employees would be ill-advised to resign in response without careful consideration of the circumstances; although they would have a wrongful dismissal claim, there is no protection against unfair dismissal for employees dismissed during a lock-out unless the employer discriminates between those 'directly interested';[719] dismisses for a limited range of automatically unfair reasons; or dismisses the employee for taking protected industrial action once

---

[712] Elgar and Simpson, 1992: p 50.

[713] NMWR 1999, SI 1999/584, regs 15(6), 17(2), 18(2) and 21(4).

[714] Simpson, 1999a: pp 17–18; see also Simpson, 1999b.

[715] For a general comparative discussion see Briggs, 2005.

[716] 'Defensive' lock-outs take a variety of forms within different systems: see Ben-Israel, 1994: pp 14–19.

[717] In *Sanders v Ernest A Neale* [1974] ICR 565, the court assumed for the purposes of argument that a lock-out was a breach of contract by the employer; similarly in *Chappell v Times Newspapers Ltd* [1975] ICR 145. However, the Court of Appeal decision in *Express and Star Ltd v Bunday* [1987] IRLR 422, discussed in para 11.74 below, assumes that a lock-out will not necessarily constitute a breach.

[718] *Cummings v Charles Connell & Co (Shipbuilders) Ltd* 1969 SLT 25.

[719] TULRCA 1992, s 238.

the 'protected period' has commenced.[720] Moreover, for the purposes of a statutory redundancy payment, an employee who leaves during a lock-out cannot claim to have been constructively dismissed.[721] This leaves the extraordinary situation that an employer may be able to impose new terms and conditions upon its workforce and then lock out and dismiss with relative impunity those who do not accept them.[722] As we shall see in para 11.74 below, the position is further complicated by the fact that the line between a strike and a lock-out may, on occasion, be hard to draw.

Further difficulties arise if only a proportion of an employer's workforce is taking industrial action and it wishes to lock out the remainder. The limited authority which exists on this point suggests that, in the absence of a contractual right to suspend employees in these circumstances, the lock-out will constitute a breach of contract unless the employees have evinced a definite intention of participating in the action. In *Ticehurst v British Telecommunications plc*[723] the Court of Appeal rejected the employers' argument that the employee's evinced intention of future participation in a campaign of rolling strikes would alone be sufficient ground for them to refuse to allow her to work during the dispute unless it could be argued that the present value of her services would be reduced by such a risk. As Ralph Gibson LJ, giving the judgment of the court, explained:

> If in this case the only intention evinced by Mrs Ticehurst was to continue to respond to a strike call if and when called upon by her union to strike then … she would in effect have been saying to BT that she was intending … to perform the full range of her contractual duties until some time in the future, which might not happen at all, when she would break her contract by going on strike … If, during that time that her services would be rendered, BT would receive full value for those services, I can see no reason why BT should not perform their part of the contract which they had chosen to keep in existence.[724]

Similarly a refusal to give an undertaking not to participate in any further action will not, of itself, justify a lock-out.[725] However, the effectiveness of the remedy which may be available to an employee in this situation may be limited. In *Chappell v Times Newspapers Ltd*[726] the Court of Appeal refused to grant an injunction to restrain an employer from treating workers as having terminated their contracts of employment on the basis that they could be called upon to take industrial action, the grounds being that, even if the employers' action was not lawful, these workers could not affirm that they were ready and willing to perform their side of the contract. In such a case the employees' sole contractual remedy would be a claim for unpaid wages or damages for breach of contract.

If the contract of employment does permit an employer to lay off employees whose workload is reduced due to industrial action by other workers they may forfeit their right to a statutory guarantee payment. The legislation provides that this right is excluded where the failure to provide

---

[720] See para 11.72 *et seq* below.
[721] ERA 1996, s 136(1), (2).
[722] See K Miller and C Woolfson, 1994, for a description of the use of this tactic by Timex in 1993.
[723] [1992] IRLR 219.
[724] [1992] IRLR 219, 227.
[725] [1992] IRLR 219, 228.
[726] [1975] ICR 145.

work occurs in consequence of a strike, lock-out or other industrial action involving fellow employees or those of an associated employer.[727]

INDUSTRIAL ACTION AND STATUTORY RIGHTS

11.72   As the previous section makes clear the common law is ill-equipped to deal with the issues raised by industrial action. Perhaps more surprisingly, legislation, too, has not until recently accorded employees any additional protection; indeed, those taking industrial action have risked prejudicing a number of their statutory rights. In relation to unfair dismissal, the prevailing philosophy of all governments has been to exclude dismissals taking place during industrial disputes from the purview of employment tribunals. However, there has been a limited measure of protection against victimisation of particular employees in the case of 'non-unofficial' action only.[728] More recently, tribunals have been afforded jurisdiction where the employee was dismissed (or, in a redundancy case, selected for dismissal) for specified reasons, which render the dismissal automatically unfair. The most wide ranging of these reasons, introduced by the Employment Relations Act 1999, and applicable only to 'non-unofficial' action, is because the employee took industrial action (termed 'protected industrial action') that he or she was induced to take by an act which, by virtue of TULRCA 1992, s 219, is not actionable in tort; it is then automatically unfair to dismiss the employee during the first twelve weeks of his or her participation in the action,[729] or at a later date in specified circumstances. Although, as we discuss in para 11.79 *et seq*, this provision affords far from comprehensive protection to those who take industrial action, it marks a considerable extension of the previous position. Other statutory rights remain more vulnerable, however: participants in industrial action risk losing all or part of a statutory redundancy payment to which they may otherwise be entitled, and statutory rights to payment during statutory minimum notice periods are also put in jeopardy; if the employer gives notice but then terminates the contract in response to a repudiatory breach of contract by the employee (which can include industrial action) during the notice period, no payment will be due for the balance of the original notice period.[730] Furthermore, those who suffer financial loss against a background of industrial action may be denied access to payments to which they may be entitled in other contexts. We indicated the position in relation to statutory guarantee payments in para 11.71 above. Employees are also disqualified from receiving statutory sick pay if there is a stoppage of work due to a trade dispute at their place of employment unless they can prove no 'direct interest' in the dispute.[731] Entitlements to social security benefits, which we discuss in para 11.87 *et seq*, are also curtailed.

---

[727] ERA 1996, s 29(3). Note that there is no statutory definition of strike, industrial action or lock-out in this context; see further para 11.72 below.

[728] We use the inelegant term 'non-unofficial' for two reasons: first, because there is no statutory definition (or use in this context) of the term 'official' industrial action; and second, because 'unofficial' as defined in the Act does not correspond to the commonly understood meaning of that term. The ECSR has found that limiting protection against dismissal to official action is contrary to Art 6(4) of the ESC: Conclusions XVIII-I Vol 2, Report No 25.

[729] This period is lengthened if the employee is locked-out by the employer once he or she has started protected industrial action: TULRCA 1992, s 238A(7A)–(7D), inserted by ERelA 2004, s 26(3).

[730] ERA 1996, s 91(4). The right to payment is also excluded if the employee gives notice but participates in a strike as defined in s 235(5) before the notice expires: s 91(2).

[731] SSCBA 1992, 153(3), Sch 11.

Dismissal rights apart, only the continuity provisions provide a measure of protection to strikers. A week during any part of which an employee takes part in a 'strike', however short, does not count for the purpose of calculating his or her period of continuous employment but, in contrast to the usual position when a week cannot be credited, continuity remains unbroken so that the periods of employment before and after the strike can be aggregated.[732] This applies even if the employee is dismissed during the strike and subsequently re-employed.[733] Identical provision is made for weeks during any part of which the employee is locked-out from work where the contract does not remain in existence;[734] if it does so remain then the week of the lock-out counts for continuity purposes in the normal way.

The continuity provisions are unusual in being accorded a definition of 'strike' and 'lock-out'. 'Strike' in this context means:

(a) the cessation of work by a body of employed persons acting in combination, or
(b) a concerted refusal, or a refusal under a common understanding, of any number of
     employed persons to continue to work for an employer in consequence of a dispute,
done as a means of compelling their employer or any employed person or body of employed persons, or to aid other employees in compelling their employer or any employed person or body of employed persons, to accept or not to accept terms or conditions of or affecting employment.[735]

This definition covers strikes in support of other employees but does not extend to political or other stoppages whose purpose is not related to compelling acceptance of terms of or affecting employment. 'Lock-out' is defined in analogous terms and means:

(a) the closing of a place of employment, or
(b) the suspension of work, or
(c) the refusal by an employer to continue to employ any number of persons employed by
     him in consequence of a dispute,
done with a view to compelling persons employed by the employer, or to aid another employer in compelling persons employed by him, to accept terms or conditions of or affecting employment.[736]

These definitions apply also to the provisions governing notice rights and redundancy payments. They are not applied by statute to other contexts, however, although in the absence of any other definition, they may be seen as having some persuasive authority.[737] There is no meaningful definition of the term 'industrial action' in any part of the legislation.[738]

---

[732] ERA 1996, s 216(1), (2).
[733] *Hanson v Fashion Industries (Hartlepool) Ltd* [1980] IRLR 393.
[734] ERA 1996, s 216(3).
[735] ERA 1996, s 235(5).
[736] ERA 1996, s 235(4).
[737] Until TULRCA 1992 there was no definition of 'strike' or 'lock-out' for unfair dismissal purposes and the courts drew some guidance from these definitions. 'Strike' is now defined in this context (rather unhelpfully) as a 'concerted stoppage of work': s 246.
[738] The definition in TULRCA 1992, s 62(6) (rights of union members in relation to industrial action ballots) is tautologous.

We devote most of this section to a consideration of the rights under the unfair dismissal legislation of employees dismissed while taking industrial action or locked out, which is one of the most crucial areas in practice. In this context it is necessary to distinguish between 'unofficial' disputes, whose participants generally have no protection in any circumstances, and action which is not 'unofficial', where there is some protection. Because the distinction between the two was introduced only by the Employment Act 1990 the preponderance of the case law concerns non-unofficial disputes, and we therefore discuss these first, although much of the case law formulated in that context is relevant also to unofficial action. We then examine the effect of taking industrial action upon the right to a redundancy payment. It is notable that protection against dismissal during disputes is confined to 'employees' whereas the immunities against liability in tort apply where there is a 'trade dispute', defined as a dispute between 'workers' and their employer.[739] The obligation to hold a ballot also covers disputes involving those who work under contracts for services. In so restricting the protection, as in several other respects, the law falls short of the protection required by the freedom of association principles of the ILO.[740]

Unfair dismissal during 'non-unofficial' industrial action and lock-outs

11.73   Until recently, the fundamental policy of the unfair dismissal legislation has been to exclude dismissals during industrial disputes from the purview of employment tribunals. This also remains the starting-point of the current law, which affirms that tribunals have no jurisdiction to determine fairness where at the date of dismissal the complainant was taking part in a strike or other industrial action or the employer was conducting or instituting a lock-out.[741] However, in the case of industrial action which is not 'unofficial' within the meaning of the statute jurisdiction is restored in two broad sets of circumstances. The first is where it is shown that the employer discriminated between those defined as 'relevant employees' and a dismissed employee would otherwise qualify to claim;[742] the employer may then defend the claim in the normal way. The second applies where the employee was dismissed (or, in a redundancy case, selected for dismissal) on one of a number of specified grounds: taking 'protected industrial action' during the first twelve weeks of participation in that action (or longer in some circumstances); specified activities relating to health and safety; acting, or standing for election, as an employee representative or representative of the workforce; on the grounds of pregnancy or childbirth; reasons relating to leave for family reasons or flexible working; or reasons related to jury service. In these cases the dismissal is automatically unfair.[743]

The justification offered for excluding the jurisdiction of tribunals during industrial disputes was the desire to avoid them becoming embroiled in the merits of such disputes, although it has been argued that, in their initial form in the Industrial Relations Act 1971, the real purpose was to preserve the employer's sanction of dismissal.[744] This latter rationale was at the forefront of

---

[739] See para 11.25 above for the definition of a 'trade dispute' and paras 3.19 *et seq* and 3.33 *et seq* above for the definition of 'employee' and 'worker' respectively.

[740] See further para 11.93.

[741] TULRCA 1992, s 238(1).

[742] TULRCA 1992 s 238(2).

[743] TULRCA 1992, s 238(2A), (2B); s 238(2A); see further para 5.95 *et seq* above.

[744] See P Davies and M Freedland, 1993: pp 323–327; 375–376; Ewing, 1991: pp 41–44.

the judgment of the National Industrial Relations Court in *Heath and Hammersey v JF Longman (Meat Salesman) Ltd*[745] where it was held that in the context of the excluding provision 'date of dismissal' meant 'time', so preventing employers from dismissing employees who have indicated that their action is at an end.[746] Sir Hugh Griffiths stated:

> It appears to this court that the manifest overall purpose of ... [the section] ... is to give a measure of protection to an employer if his business is faced with ruin by a strike. It enables him in those circumstances, if he cannot carry on the business without a labour force, to dismiss the labour force on strike; to take on another labour force without the stigma of its being an unfair dismissal. That being the overall purpose it would appear to be manifestly wrong, when an employer has been told that strike action has been called off, that he should nevertheless still be free to dismiss those who took part in the strike, without any risk of a finding that he was acting unfairly.[747]

The continuation of this position in 1974 was a mark of the Labour Government's adherence in this area to the principle of collective *laissez-faire*; as Davies and Freedland point out, '[a] confident labour movement in 1975 may have felt few qualms about foregoing a protection it had never previously had – since before 1971 the issue could not have arisen'.[748] Even during the latter part of the 1970s, however, the weakness of this approach was highlighted by the sacking of strikers during the Grunwick dispute[749] and further emphasised by similar events in the Wapping dispute during the 1980s.[750] Although the protection afforded to participants in 'protected industrial action' ameliorates the position, the general principle of exclusion remains significant, not least because of the restricted scope of the new provision. Moreover, much of the case law which has developed in the context of the exclusionary principle is relevant to the discussion of 'protected industrial action'. For both these reasons, we discuss this principle first before considering 'protected industrial action'.

(i) The scope of the exclusion of jurisdiction

11.74   The language in which the general exclusion is drafted, as interpreted by the courts, has resulted in even narrower protection than might at first appear. First, jurisdiction is excluded if, judged objectively, employees were taking part in industrial action or locked out at the time of their dismissal; this need not be the reason for dismissal.[751] It follows that it is irrelevant whether the employers knew or acted properly in attempting to decide whether the dismissed employees

---

[745] [1973] IRLR 214.

[746] 'Date of dismissal' is defined in the statute as, where the employee's contract of employment was terminated by notice, the date on which the employer's notice was given and in any other case the effective date of termination: TULRCA 1992, s 238(5).

[747] [1973] IRLR 214, 215.

[748] P Davies and M Freedland, 1993: p 375.

[749] See Rogaly, 1977: pp 136–140.

[750] See Ewing and Napier, 1986.

[751] *Faust v Power Packing Casemakers Ltd* [1983] IRLR 117 at 121 (Stephenson LJ); *Bolton Roadways Ltd v Edwards* [1987] IRLR 392; *Manifold Industries Ltd v Sims* [1991] IRLR 242; *Jenkins v P & O European Ferries (Dover) Ltd* [1991] ICR 652.

were participating in a particular campaign at the time they were dismissed. Second, under current case law there is no room to argue that the action was engineered or provoked by the unreasonable or even the unlawful conduct of the employer. In *Wilkins v Cantrell and Cochrane (GB) Ltd*[752] there had been a number of occasions in which lorries had been sent out from the employers' depot in an overloaded condition. Ultimately the lorry drivers felt compelled to take strike action and were dismissed. It was argued for the three applicants that the employers were in breach of the law in sending out the lorries in this condition; that in requiring the drivers to go out with them they were putting the drivers at risk because they might find themselves charged with aiding and abetting the employers; and that in these circumstances the employers were in breach of the contract of employment. The employment tribunal concluded that at the worst these instances 'indicated negligence not amounting to deliberate breaches of the law' which did not constitute a fundamental breach of contract. The EAT, although expressing sympathy with the men, endorsed this view.[753] This approach may require modification in some circumstances in the light of the HRA 1998, which we discuss below.

Third, whether or not there is a 'strike', 'lock-out' or 'industrial action' taking place is a question of fact for the tribunal, acting as an industrial jury, to decide. Until TULRCA 1992 there was no statutory definition of 'strike' in this context; it is now (rather unhelpfully) defined as a 'concerted stoppage of work'.[754] For 'lock-out' and 'industrial action' there is no statutory definition whatsoever. The Court of Appeal has instructed tribunals to give the words 'industrial action' 'their natural and ordinary meaning'.[755] Thus one tribunal may decide that there is 'industrial action', another the opposite, on the same set of facts, with the scope for appeal being confined to the argument that the tribunal has given the term a meaning it could not reasonably bear (or that there is no evidence to support the finding of fact).[756]

In relation to a 'lock-out' and, before the 1992 Act, 'strike' the courts have had regard to the definitions provided for continuity purposes,[757] whilst emphasising that these definitions should not be applied exclusively and, indeed, it may be difficult to predict into which of these categories a particular situation falls. The difficulty in distinguishing between a strike and a lock-out is a particularly serious matter given that the definition of 'relevant employee' differs in each case and there is no protection afforded to employees who are dismissed while locked-out before 'protected industrial action' has started. In *Express and Star Ltd v Bunday*[758] the Court of Appeal rejected the argument that a lock-out required a breach of contract on the part of the employer; although in some cases this might be critical, its materiality would depend upon the facts. Thus if an employer unilaterally introduces new technology which employees refuse to use and they are then told not

---

[752] [1978] IRLR 483.

[753] See also *Marsden v Fairey Stainless Ltd* [1979] IRLR 103. The view expressed by Elias, 1994 (see para 11.65) would produce a different result but this has yet to be tested in the courts.

[754] TULRCA 1992, s 246. In *Connex South Eastern Ltd v RMT* [1999] IRLR 249, a ban on overtime and rest-day working was said to constitute a strike for the purposes of deciding whether the action was authorised in a ballot. This definition of 'strike' has been excluded for the purposes (only) of the question on the voting paper.

[755] *Faust v Power Packing Casemakers Ltd* [1983] IRLR 117 at 121 (Stephenson LJ). See also *Knowles v Fire Brigades Union* [1996] IRLR 617, discussed in para 10.12 above.

[756] *Express and Star Ltd v Bunday* [1987] IRLR 422; *Faust v Power Packing Casemakers Ltd* [1983] IRLR 117.

[757] See, for example, *Express and Star*, above. In relation to a strike some cases also refer to the definition offered by Lord Denning MR in *Tramp Shipping Corpn v Greenwich Marine Inc* [1975] ICR 261, 266.

[758] [1987] IRLR 422.

to return to work until they are so willing, this may equally be perceived as a strike or a lock-out. How it is perceived may be crucial for employees' rights.

It is perhaps even more anomalous that industrial action need not constitute a breach of the contract of employment. In *Faust v Power Packing Casemakers Ltd*[759] the Court of Appeal affirmed that a refusal to work overtime because of a wage dispute could constitute 'industrial action', notwithstanding that there was no contractual obligation for employees to do this work. This could be distinguished from a refusal to perform work for other reasons, such as personal reasons or the desire to attend a football match, by reference to its purpose – to put pressure on the employer. This emphasis on motive had been applied by the Court of Appeal in *Rasool v Hepworth Pipe Co Ltd (No 2)*[760] in finding that attendance at an unauthorised mass meeting convened to consider employees' views about impending wage negotiations was a union activity rather than industrial action because the intention was not that of putting pressure on the employer.[761]

The emphasis upon putting pressure on the employer as the hallmark may be appropriate in some cases but is probably unduly narrow in excluding disruptive action in protest at government policies or as a demonstration of solidarity which would almost certainly be viewed in practice as 'industrial action'. From another perspective, the interpretation of 'industrial action' may now require reconsideration in the light of the HRA 1998. As we discussed in para 11.64, the employer's managerial prerogative and the employee's correlative duty to obey lawful and reasonable orders must be interpreted by the courts and tribunals in the light of Convention rights. It is strongly arguable that the duty under HRA 1998, s 3 to give effect to legislation 'so far as it is possible to do so' in a way that is compatible with Convention rights requires courts and tribunals not to regard as 'industrial action' a refusal by workers to obey an order which interferes with the exercise of a Convention right and which will not as such constitute a breach of the contract of employment. The statutory exception where employees stop work for safety reasons should also be noted. As we indicated in para 5.101, it is automatically unfair to dismiss employees who leave, propose to leave or refuse to return to their place of work or any dangerous part thereof in circumstances of danger which they reasonably believe to be serious and imminent and which they could not reasonably have been expected to avert.[762] However, employees who stop work in order to exert pressure on an employer to improve safety conditions outside this specific situation,[763] or to support other workers whose safety is at risk, will not be protected by the statute and are likely to be viewed as taking part in industrial action. Moreover, the statute does not deal directly with the contractual position of the employee who stops work,[764] nor the position in tort of any individual who induces

---

[759] [1983] IRLR 117.

[760] [1980] IRLR 137. See also, however, *Knowles v Fire Brigades Union* [1996] IRLR 617, discussed in para 10.12 above, where Neill LJ, giving the judgment of the Court of Appeal in a case concerning TULRCA 1992, s 65, opined that in determining what was industrial action it was 'necessary to look at' all the circumstances, including the employees' contracts of employment and whether any breach of or departure from the terms of the contract are involved; the effect on the employer of what is done or omitted; and the object which the union or employees seek to achieve (at 621).

[761] Note that the EAT has held that TULRCA 1992, ss 146 and 152, on the one hand, and s 238 on the other are mutually exclusive: *Drew v St Edmundsbury Borough Council* [1980] IRLR 459.

[762] ERA 1996, s 100(1)(d).

[763] See *Balfour Kilpatrick Ltd v Acheson* [2003] IRLR 683, discussed in para 5.101; see also D Lewis, 2004.

[764] However see A Edwards, 2000, for the argument, based on *Barber v RJB Mining (UK) Ltd* [1999] ICR 679, that there may be a right for employees to refuse to comply with instructions which are harmful to their health, including circumstances beyond those within the terms of ERA 1996, s 100(1)(d). See now also para 4.10 above.

employees to stop work,[765] although these may now be regarded as subject to the employer's statutory duty to give effect to appropriate procedures to be followed in the event of serious and imminent danger to persons at work, including enabling them to stop work and to require them to be prevented from resuming work.[766]

At one time it was regarded as clear that 'industrial action' is a collective activity which cannot be taken by one employee alone, a view which corresponds both with the emphasis upon combination and concert in the statutory definitions of a strike and with industrial reality.[767] In *Lewis and Britton v E Mason & Sons*,[768] however, the EAT found that it was open to a tribunal to find that a single employee could be taking part in 'industrial action', thus potentially exposing an employee who refuses on one occasion to carry out an instruction by the employer to dismissal without statutory redress.[769] Although we would regard this decision as erroneous it demonstrates the serious implications of a non-interventionist approach by the legislature and judiciary to this matter. In that case also the EAT refused to characterise as perverse the tribunal's finding that the threat of industrial action itself was 'industrial action' on the basis that there was no further prospect of negotiation before the following day, despite earlier (and we would argue correct) authority to the contrary.[770]

11.75   The courts have held that the issue of whether an employee was 'taking part' in industrial action is also primarily a question for the tribunal, with scope to appeal only if the words are given a meaning of which they are not 'reasonably capable'.[771] With that reservation in mind, the cases offer guidance on some of the issues which this term raises. First, when do employees begin to 'take part' in industrial action? There is authority to suggest that this may be before the contractual obligation to work arises if they have made clear that they will withdraw their labour at that point. In *Winnett v Seamarks Bros Ltd*[772] the EAT upheld the decision of the employment tribunal that the applicant coach driver was 'taking part' in industrial action even though he was not due to work until the following morning given that he had intimated to the employers that he would not work then.[773] Second, when does participation cease? What if the employee falls sick, for example? In *Williams v Western Mail and Echo Ltd*[774] it was held that 'once men (sic) have stated that they will apply sanctions and do so they may be regarded as applying the sanctions either

---

[765] Note the emphasis in *OBG v Allan* [2007] IRLR 608, HL on the defendant's state of mind, however; see para 11.11 above.

[766] The Management of Health and Safety at Work Regulations 1999, SI 1999/3242, reg 8. Note also the implied term that employees will take reasonable care to safeguard the health and safety of their employees: see para 4.95. *Quaere* whether in relation to inducing breach of contract the defence of justification would be accepted: see para 11.11.

[767] *Bowater Containers Ltd v Blake* (27 May 1982, unreported); see also *Coates and Venables v Modern Methods and Materials Ltd* [1982] IRLR 318, 323 (Eveleigh LJ). Cf *McCormick v Horsepower Ltd* [1981] IRLR 217 (individual employee could be said to be on strike but not the same strike as other workers because community of purpose lacking).

[768] [1994] IRLR 4. See Dolding, 1994.

[769] This is highly unlikely to constitute 'protected industrial action'; see below.

[770] See *Midland Plastics v Till* [1983] IRLR 9.

[771] *Coates and Venables v Modern Methods and Materials Ltd* [1982] IRLR 318.

[772] [1978] IRLR 387.

[773] Cf *Naylor v Orton and Smith Ltd; Naylor v D Twedell Engineering Ltd* [1983] IRLR 233, where the EAT upheld the employment tribunal's decision that a resolution to impose an immediate overtime ban did not constitute industrial action; this decision presents the problem of defining when the action does begin (when the first employee refuses to work overtime?) and whether other employees are taking part in the action as from that moment or only when they in turn refuse such a request.

[774] [1980] IRLR 222, 224.

until they are discontinued or until they indicate an intention of stopping them'. However, there is no authority as to the position in relation to 'rolling strikes', whereby one group of employees comes out on one day, another the next. Should all employees who may be called upon to strike at some point be treated as 'taking part' from the outset? Conversely, should those who have already been on strike be treated as 'taking part' throughout because they intend to strike again should they be called upon to do so? Third, what of employees who fail to cross a picket line, perhaps for fear of abuse by strikers? In *Coates and Venables v Modern Methods and Materials Ltd*[775] the Court of Appeal supported an objective approach to this question; an employer is entitled to assume that any employee who does not come to work during a strike is taking part in it. Stephenson LJ appeared to consider that expressing disagreement with the strike may alter the position;[776] for Kerr LJ it was actions only which were material, although he suggested that if an employee was absent at the beginning of a strike for reasons unconnected with it, such as sickness or holidays, he would not be 'taking part'.[777] However, in *Bolton Roadways Ltd v Edwards*[778] the EAT held that employees who were lawfully absent when the action started would be capable of 'taking part' if they associated themselves with the strike, attended at the picket line, or took part in the other activities of the strikers with a view to furthering their aims; taking part in a strike did not require a breach of the contractual obligation to work.

(ii) Jurisdiction on the basis of victimisation

11.76   The employer's protection against unfair dismissal claims by employees dismissed while taking part in industrial action or locked out is lost in two situations (in addition to those where 'protected industrial action' or another specified reason is the reason for dismissal). The first is where it is shown that one or more 'relevant employees' of the same employer have not been dismissed.[779] The second is where it is shown that any 'relevant employee' has 'before the expiry of the period of three months beginning with the date of his dismissal been offered re-engagement and ... the complainant has not been offered re-engagement'.[780]

In relation to a strike or other industrial action, 'relevant employees' are 'those employees at the establishment of the employer at or from which the complainant works who at the date of his dismissal were taking part in the action'.[781] By analogy with the interpretation of this phrase in relation to the exclusion of jurisdiction,[782] 'date of dismissal' in this context is likely to be interpreted as 'time' of dismissal, so if a number of employees returned to work on the morning

---

[775] [1982] IRLR 318.

[776] [1982] IRLR 318, 323.

[777] [1982] IRLR 318, 325.

[778] [1987] IRLR 392. This approach is consistent with *Winnett v Seamarks Brothers Ltd*, above. See also *Rogers v Chloride Systems Ltd* [1992] ICR 198 where the EAT considered that had the applicant, who was on sick leave throughout the dispute, answered 'no' on being asked if she would have returned to work on a specific date had she not been sick, or whether she would have undertaken to work normally as soon as she was able, that would have been sufficient to constitute 'taking part'. Cf *Hindle Gears Ltd v McGinty* [1984] IRLR 477, 480.

[779] TULRCA 1992, s 238(2)(a).

[780] TULRCA 1992, s 238(2)(b).

[781] TULRCA 1992, s 238(3)(b). Where the action is 'unofficial' for some employees taking part in it but not others, the 'unofficial' participants remain 'relevant employees': s 238(3).

[782] See *Heath and Hammersey v JF Longman (Meat Salesman) Ltd* [1973] IRLR 214.

of a particular day the employer could probably safely dismiss those who had not done so later that day. There is no requirement that employees should receive any warning that they will be dismissed unless they return. There is no definition of 'establishment' nor has this issue to date arisen in the case law in this context; it is likely that the criteria applied by the British courts in relation to redundancy consultation, which we discussed in para 9.32 above, would be applied here as well.

For a lock-out, the concept of 'relevant employees' is more widely drawn to mean those who were 'directly interested in the dispute in contemplation or furtherance of which the lock-out occurred',[783] with no requirement that they should work at or from the complainant's establishment. 'Direct interest' is a concept borrowed from social security law and covers anyone whose terms of employment are likely to be immediately and automatically affected by the outcome of the dispute.[784] Whether or not employees were 'directly interested' is to be assessed on the date on which the lock-out occurred.[785] The scope of 'relevant employees' in the context of a lock-out was considered by the EAT in *Fisher v York Trailer Co Ltd*.[786] The employers were concerned that the employees who worked on the main container line at one of their factories were 'going slow'. They sent a letter to each of the 34 employees concerned which required them to give an undertaking that they would work at a normal incentive pace under the existing bonus scheme, failing which they would be suspended from the start of the next shift. On the next day no production occurred and the men held meetings. Subsequent to those meetings all but seven of the employees signed the document. The seven were eventually dismissed. The EAT upheld the tribunal's finding that they had been dismissed while the employer was conducting a lock-out. It also held that employees who are 'directly interested' in a dispute are not limited to those who remained locked out until the end of the dispute and, indeed, could extend to those who were not locked out at all. In this case all 34 employees were 'relevant employees'. This decision shows that an employer who wishes to retain the immunity may need to dismiss a much wider range of employees in a lock-out than a strike. In practice, a well-advised employer is more likely now to argue that employees were taking part in industrial action, thus enabling a smaller pool to be at issue, unless this would mean that the dismissals would then be automatically unfair because they were due to the employees taking part in 'protected industrial action' or for some other specified automatically unfair reason.

11.77   For the discriminatory treatment to take the form of offering re-engagement, this means:

> ... an offer (made either by the original employer or by a successor of that employer or an associated employer) to re-engage an employee, either in the job which he held immediately before the date of dismissal or in a different job which would be reasonably suitable in his case.[787]

---

[783] TULRCA 1992, s 238(3)(a).
[784] *Presho v Department of Health and Social Security (Insurance Officer)* [1984] IRLR 74.
[785] *H Campey & Sons Ltd v Bellwood* [1987] ICR 311.
[786] [1979] IRLR 385.
[787] TULRCA 1992, s 238(4). For a claim based on selective re-engagement the complainant must present the claim to an employment tribunal within six months of his or her own dismissal (with the usual provision for extension where the tribunal is satisfied that this was not 'reasonably practicable'): s 239(2).

The offer must be made specifically to the individual; a press advertisement inviting applications from the public at large constitutes merely an offer to treat for re-engagement,[788] in contrast to a communication which indicates that should individuals apply they will be re-engaged.[789] The offer need not be in writing and, indeed, may be constituted by tacit acceptance that the employment is continuing.[790] Although the employer must know about the first job from which the employee had been dismissed, this knowledge may be constructive (in the sense that it has the means of obtaining it) as well as actual, thus putting the onus on the employer to make adequate enquiries about the worker's position before re-engaging him or her.[791]

There is no definition of 'job' in TULRCA 1992 but under EPCA 1978, applicable before the entry into force of the 1992 Act, it was defined as 'the nature of the work which [the employee] ... is employed to do in accordance with his contract and the capacity and place in which he is so employed', and this definition, which now appears in ERA 1996, s 235(1), also applies in this context.[792] The term was examined by the Court of Appeal in *Williams v National Theatre Board Ltd*.[793] Thirty strikers were offered re-engagement on the basis that they were on second warning as regards their general conduct; one had an offer with no such conditions. The Court of Appeal held that if an employee was offered re-engagement in the same capacity as before there was no requirement that the terms and conditions should be identical, although Lord Denning MR opined that if the terms were unreasonable – half-pay or half-time, for example, to a former full-time worker – that might not constitute the same 'job'.[794] In this case, however, the condition of second warning did not prevent it being the same job. This decision means that employers may discriminate between employees to whom 're-engagement' is offered both in relation to their position under the disciplinary procedures and, at least in minor ways, substantive terms and conditions. Moreover, the terms offered to employees, on either a uniform or differential basis, may be the very ones which were the subject-matter of the original dispute.[795] Where an employee is offered a different job whether it is 'reasonably suitable' will probably depend, by analogy with cases relating to redundancy payments, upon factors such as status, use of skill, and pay and benefits.

11.78 The claim that the employer has selectively dismissed or offered re-engagement within the meaning of the legislation must be established before an employment tribunal has jurisdiction to hear the claim. The date upon which discrimination between 'relevant employees' must be shown is the time when the tribunal either determines the substantive issue (involving determination of the jurisdiction point as well) or the jurisdiction point on a preliminary hearing.[796] This means that an employer who dismisses selectively and then learns during the course of the hearing that one relevant employee was not dismissed can defeat the claim by

---

[788] *Crosville Wales Ltd v Tracey* [1993] IRLR 60.
[789] *Williams v National Theatre Board Ltd* [1982] IRLR 377.
[790] *Bolton Roadways Ltd v Edwards* [1987] IRLR 392.
[791] *Bigham and Keogh v GKN Kwikform Ltd* [1992] IRLR 4.
[792] TULRCA 1992, s 239(1) originally stated that s 238 shall be construed as one with Part v of EPCA 1978, and now states that it shall be construed as one with ERA 1996, Part X, to which the definition in ERA 1996, s 235(1) applies.
[793] [1982] IRLR 377.
[794] [1982] IRLR 377, 379.
[795] Ewing, 1991: p 59.
[796] *P & O European Ferries (Dover) Ltd v Byrne* [1989] IRLR 254.

dismissing that employee before the hearing ends. Even though the employee so dismissed may then have a claim for unfair dismissal, this may be the cheaper option for the employer. Moreover, in *P & O European Ferries (Dover) Ltd v Byrne*[797] the Court of Appeal held that where the identity of an alleged 'relevant employee' is unknown to the employers, the tribunal may order the name of that person to be disclosed by the complainant(s) either before or at the hearing in order to enable the employer to know the case it has to meet, even though this may enable the employer to take action which would defeat the claim. Less objectionably, an employer may defeat a claim based on selective re-engagement by offering the complainant 're-engagement' before the end of the tribunal hearing.[798]

It is important to emphasise that proving selectivity merely gives the tribunal jurisdiction to hear the unfair dismissal claim, which will be determined according to general principles. Thus, if the employee has been dismissed, or selected for dismissal, for reasons which constitute an automatically unfair dismissal, such as participation in union activities, the dismissal will be automatically unfair; otherwise it will be potentially fair if the employer can show that it is for a 'substantial' reason under section 98(1)(b) or 98(2) of ERA 1996.[799] In cases of selective re-engagement references to the principal reason for dismissal are to be read as references to the reason or principal reason for which he or she has not been offered re-engagement.[800] The relevant question then is 'not whether the initial dismissal was justified but whether the refusal to re-engage the applicants was justified when some employees have been taken back'.[801] Acts of gross misconduct during the dispute (such as damaging or stealing the employer's property) may justify selection for dismissal or failure to re-engage; an employee's conduct prior to the dispute may also be material. Thus in one case an employer implemented the next appropriate stage of the disciplinary code against employees who had participated in a strike and it was held that it was not unfair to dismiss those who were on final warning.[802] On the facts of *Sehmi v Gate Gourmet Ltd* the EAT held that the tribunal was entitled to find that it was within the range of reasonable responses for the employer to dismiss an employee for taking part in industrial action by absenting himself without leave for two (or three) consecutive shifts.[803] Participation in industrial action may also, in some circumstances, be a ground for selecting employees for redundancy. In *Cruikshank v Hobbs*[804] the EAT suggested three circumstances where this may be a fair ground for selection: if the strike had 'caused or aggravated the redundancy'; after a long strike, the difficulties of reintroducing strikers due to technical or administrative changes during their absence; and if the friction which would arise from dismissing non-strikers and replacing them with strikers would impair morale and efficiency.

[797] [1989] IRLR 254.

[798] See, for example, *Highlands Fabricators Ltd v McLaughlin* [1984] IRLR 482.

[799] See para 5.139 *et seq* above.

[800] TULRCA 1992, s 239(3).

[801] *Edwards v Cardiff City Council* [1979] IRLR 303, 305. In *Laffin and Callaghan v Fashion Industries (Hartlepool) Ltd* [1978] IRLR 448 it was held that if a reason would not justify dismissal, it would not justify a refusal to re-engage.

[802] *Bernard Matthews plc v Rowland* (24 May 1982, unreported).

[803] [2009] IRLR 807, Underhill P at [36].

[804] [1977] ICR 725. Cf *Laffin and Callaghan v Fashion Industries (Hartlepool) Ltd* [1978] IRLR 448, where it was held unfair to select on the basis solely of a 'loyalty' test.

(iii) 'Protected industrial action'

11.79 The Employment Relations Act 1999 accorded tribunals jurisdiction to examine whether an employee has been dismissed for taking 'protected industrial action'; if this is found to be the case, and specified conditions are met, the dismissal is automatically unfair.[805] No minimum period of employment is required.[806] However, the scope of this protection is heavily circumscribed. First, an employee takes 'protected industrial action' only if he or she commits an act which, *by virtue of section 219 of TULRCA 1992*, is not actionable in tort.[807] The restriction to acts not actionable by virtue of section 219 means that industrial action which is not actionable in tort at common law (for example, a ban on voluntary overtime, which may not constitute a breach of contract by those participating in it) is excluded. More importantly in practice, as we saw in para 11.24, section 219 does not afford protection against all the torts that those who induce employees to take part in industrial action may commit; thus, for example, it does not cover torts based upon a breach of a statutory duty. Finally protection under section 219 is conditional upon the union having met all the requirements relating to ballots and notices to employers (see para 11.32 *et seq*). The statutory language (an act 'which is not actionable in tort') suggests that it will be sufficient that immunity is lost in relation only to one of a number of employers involved in the dispute. Thus, if a union fails to give only one employer the requisite notice of the action to be taken, all employees who have been induced by a call made by the union to take industrial action will lose any protection against dismissal. Framing the definition of 'protected industrial action' in terms of immunity in tort also means that employment tribunals may be required, for the first time, to decide complex issues relating to the scope of the economic torts, a difficulty compounded by the fact that many of the decisions relating to the existence and ambit of these torts have been reached in interim proceedings only. Where proceedings in tort are being brought in the High Court against the union that organised the industrial action, it would seem sensible for tribunals to adjourn the unfair dismissal hearing pending judgment on that claim. Notably, however, tribunals are specifically empowered to adjourn unfair dismissal proceedings only until the conclusion of any *interim* proceedings,[808] although strictly speaking only a full trial on the merits would give an authoritative ruling on whether action was 'protected'. Where proceedings have not been brought in tort, there seems no basis on which a tribunal could refer the matter to the courts.

11.80 The second important limitation is that it is not sufficient to attract protection that the employee was dismissed while protected industrial action was being taken; the fact that the employee took such action must be the *reason* or principal reason for dismissal (or, in a 'redundancy case', for selection for dismissal).[809] Moreover, the burden to show the reason would seem to lie on the employee, given that the tribunal would not otherwise have jurisdiction. As cases in the context of 'trade union' dismissals show, this may not be an easy test to satisfy, particularly where the decision

---

[805] TULRCA 1992, s 238A. Note that this provision does not apply to 'unofficial' action, defined in s 237(2); see further para 11.85.
[806] TULRCA 1992 s 239(1). Note that ERA 1996, s 109 was repealed by EE(A)R 2006.
[807] TULRCA 1992, s 238A(1).
[808] The Employment Tribunals (Constitution and Rules of Procedure) Regulations 2004, SI 2004/1861, Sch 1, para 55.
[809] TULRCA 1992, s 238A(2); ERA 1996, s 105(7C). See ERA 1996, s 105(1),(9) for the definition of 'redundancy case'.

is taken by a group of persons.[810] Moreover, employers may well be tempted to use the occasion of the industrial action to dismiss those whom it has been wishing to dismiss for other reasons, such as their poor performance or absence records, without going through the requisite disciplinary or performance procedures. Provided that they do not displace their immunity by discriminating between 'relevant employees', or by dismissing for a limited range of other automatically unfair reasons, they will be able to do this with impunity. The restriction of protection to situations where the industrial action is the reason for dismissal stands in marked contrast to the general exclusion of jurisdiction, which applies where the employee is *taking part* in such action. It is also notable that the protection applies only if the employee 'took' such action; it does not appear to cover threatening to take it. Although participation in activities prior to a strike can constitute protected trade union activities,[811] it is unclear whether threatening to take industrial action would be covered by such protection in the light of the finding (in our view, mistaken) in *Lewis and Britton v E Mason and Sons*,[812] discussed above, that this could, of itself, constitute industrial action.

11.81   Third, the protection against dismissal for having taken protected industrial action applies only in three sets of circumstances. The first is where the date of dismissal[813] is 'within the protected period'.[814] Originally this was a period of eight weeks. ERelA 2004 amended TULRCA 1992 to provide that the 'protected period, in relation to the dismissal of an employee, is the sum of the basic period and any extension period in relation to that employee'.[815] The 'basic period' is twelve weeks 'beginning with the first day of protected industrial action', which is defined as 'the day on which the employee starts to take protected industrial action'.[816] Framing the protection in terms of the employee's own participation makes it crucial to determine when the employee individually started to take such action, a matter which, as we discussed above, may not be easy to determine, particularly in relation to rolling strikes and overtime bans. The initial legislation made no allowance for the situation where employees were locked-out by their employer, so allowing employers to 'sit-out' the period of automatic protection by preventing any return to work by employees taking industrial action (possibly also employing temporary workers in their stead). The Labour Government recognised that this was an undesirable position and ERelA 2004 introduced provision for an 'extension period', which is 'a period equal to the number of days falling on or after the first day of protected industrial action (but before the protected period ends) during the whole or any part of which the employee is locked out by his employer'.[817] Thus, if the

---

[810] *Smith v Hayle Town Council* [1978] ICR 996; see further para 8.5; see also the general discussion of the burden of identifying the reason for dismissal in para 5.94 above.

[811] *Britool Ltd v Roberts* [1993] IRLR 481. Industrial action itself has been held not to be within this protection: *Drew v St Edmundsbury Borough Council* [1980] IRLR 459.

[812] [1994] IRLR 4; cf *Midland Plastics v Till* [1983] IRLR 9.

[813] As defined in TULRCA 1992, s 238(5), s 238A(9). Under s 238(5) where notice of termination is given by the employer the 'date of dismissal' is the date when notice is given, not the date when it expires: see para 11.73 above.

[814] TULRCA 1992, s 238A, as amended by ERelA 2004, s 26(2).

[815] TULRCA 1992, s 238A(7A).

[816] TULRCA 1992, s 238A(7B),(7D), as inserted by ERelA 2004, s 26(3). The ECSR regards this time period as 'arbitrary' and not in conformity with Art 6(4) of the ESC: Conclusions XVIII-I Vol 2, Report No 25. See also CEACR: Individual Observation concerning Freedom of Association and Protection of the Right to Organise Convention 1948 (No 87) UK, 2011.

[817] TULRCA 1992, s 238A(7A),(7C), inserted by ERelA 2004, s 26(3). 'Lock-out' is not defined, the Government having decided that this should be left to courts and tribunals to decide on the facts: Lord Triesman, HL Debs GC 122, 9 June 2004.

employer locks out employees who are working-to-rule or banning specific duties, for example, for a ten-day period, those ten days will be added on to the twelve-week 'basic' period, and protection against dismissal for taking 'protected industrial action' during those ten days will continue to apply. In theory the period of protection could be extended indefinitely if workers remain locked out. However the protected period does not start until the employee himself or herself has started taking industrial action. Although this can be a day on which he or she is locked-out,[818] there is no unfair dismissal protection (other than for selective dismissals or the narrow range of other automatically unfair reasons) prior to that.

The second circumstance in which protection applies is if the dismissal takes place after the end of the protected period and the employee had stopped taking protected industrial action before the end of that period,[819] so preventing subsequent victimisation. Once again this is linked to the employee's own participation. An employee who wishes to cease to take protected industrial action and who is absent from work for other reasons, such as illness or holiday, would be well advised to ensure that he or she informs the employer in writing that his or her participation has ceased. The third is where the dismissal takes place after the end of the protected period; the employee had not stopped taking protected industrial action before the end of that period; and 'the employer had not taken such procedural steps as would have been reasonable for the purpose of resolving the dispute to which the protected industrial action relates'.[820] In determining whether an employer has taken such steps, tribunals are directed to have regard in particular to whether the employer or union complied with the procedures established by any applicable collective or other agreement; whether either party offered or agreed to commence or resume negotiations after the start of the protected industrial action; and whether either party unreasonably refused, after the start of the protected industrial action, a request that conciliation services be used, or mediation services be used in relation to procedures to be adopted for the purposes of resolving the dispute.[821] In addition, where there was agreement to use conciliation or mediation services, regard is to be had to the participation, co-operation and other specified conduct of the respective parties in the process,[822] a measure introduced by ERelA 2004 to give the parties a 'clearer indication' of their responsibilities 'to take reasonable procedural actions to resolve the dispute'.[823] However, no regard may be paid to the merits of the dispute.[824] Claims that rest upon this third ground are likely to be particularly contentious.

11.82   The extension of the protected period introduced by ERelA 2004, and provision for periods of lock-out, were welcome amendments to the original legislation.[825] However there remains no protection for those who are dismissed when locked-out by the employer (possibly in breach of contract) prior to 'protected industrial action' commencing, although the justification for a 'breathing space' for negotiations applies equally in this context. The Labour Government's

---

[818] TULRCA 1992, s 238A(7D), inserted by ERelA 2004, s 26(3).
[819] TULRCA 1992, s 238A(4), as amended by ERelA 2004, s 27.
[820] TULRCA 1992, s 238A(5), as amended by ERelA 2004, s 27.
[821] TULRCA 1992, s 238A(6)(a)–(d).
[822] TULRCA 1992, s 238A(6)(e), 238B, inserted by ERelA 2004, s 28.
[823] *Review of the Employment Relations Act 1999: Government Response*, DTI, 2003, para 3.39.
[824] TULRCA 1992, s 238A(7).
[825] That there is any time limit 'imposes a threshold not contemplated by international labour standards', however: Novitz, 2000: p 387. See also note 816, above.

justification for this was that lock-outs themselves were 'rare, and '[p]re-emptive lock-outs are much rarer still and there is less need to reshape the law to deal with this unlikely possibility'.[826] The fact that it is 'unlikely' does not mean that it may not occur, however, and indeed, the new provision for periods of lock-out in calculating the protected period may encourage such pre-emptive action. Moreover, as we discussed above, the dividing-line between a strike and a lock-out may be difficult to draw and the opportunities for appeal are limited. A further weakness of the legislation is that, in contrast to other automatically unfair reasons for dismissal, there is no accompanying protection against subjection to a detriment short of dismissal.[827] However, it may be possible to circumvent this gap if the detriment constitutes a fundamental breach of contract, such as a unilateral cut in wages or breach of the implied term of trust and confidence; in that event, the employee may be able to claim that he or she has been constructively dismissed, while remaining in the employer's employment.[828]

(iv) Other automatically unfair reasons for dismissal

11.83 There are other reasons, in addition to taking 'protected industrial action', that render the dismissal (or, in a 'redundancy case', selection for dismissal) of those taking part in industrial action automatically unfair. These reasons also extend to those dismissed while locked-out. The specified reasons are, in brief, specified activities relating to health and safety;[829] acting, or standing for election, as an employee representative or representative of the workforce; on the grounds of pregnancy or childbirth; reasons relating to leave for family reasons or flexible working; or reasons related to jury service.[830] Once again, there is no minimum period of employment required to qualify to claim, but the burden of proof would seem to lie on the applicant to show the reason for dismissal.[831] In practice, it may be difficult (but not impossible) to envisage circumstances where an individual would be able to show that he or she had been dismissed for any of the unfair reasons where all those participating in the action have been dismissed. It is notable that dismissal on grounds of trade union membership or participation in union activities is not specified as a reason that restores the tribunal's jurisdiction in this context.

(v) Remedies

11.84 Employees who are found to have been unfairly dismissed while taking industrial action have the usual remedies, discussed in para 5.138 *et seq*, available to them. The weakness of reinstatement, arguably the only satisfactory remedy to counter the absence of a doctrine

---

[826] *Review of the Employment Relations Act 1999: Government Response*, DTI, 2003, para 3.38.

[827] At the time of writing this is the subject of an application to the ECtHR by Unite in relation to the removal of travel benefits for British Airways cabin crew who took part in industrial action.

[828] *Hogg v Dover College* [1990] ICR 39; *Alcan Extrusions v Yates* [1996] IRLR 327. See further para 5.71.

[829] Note, however, the limited scope of the protection afforded to employees who stop work for health and safety reasons: see *Balfour Kilpatrick Ltd v Acheson* [2003] IRLR 683, discussed in para 5.101; see also para 11.74 above.

[830] TULRCA 1992, s 238(2A).

[831] ERA 1996, s 108. See para 5.94 for discussion of the burden of identifying the reason for dismissal.

of suspension of the contract during industrial action,[832] should be borne in mind here. If the employer has recruited replacement labour during the course of the dispute then, in reality, regardless of the circumstances, it may be impossible for dismissed workers to regain their jobs.[833] The position may be exacerbated when employees have been unfairly dismissed for taking 'protected industrial action', where no order for reinstatement or re-engagement may be made until *all* employees have ceased to take industrial action in relation to the relevant dispute, given that more time may then have passed since the applicant's dismissal.[834] Until relatively recently it was unclear whether participation in a strike or other industrial action could constitute contributory fault which can bring a reduction in the basic and/or compensatory award under ERA 1996, ss 122(2) and 123(6) (see paras 5.144 and 5.150). In *TNT Express (UK) Ltd v Downes*[835] the EAT held that employers should be able to invoke such arguments where the industrial action was wholly unmerited, an approach which conflicted with one objective of the legislation, to keep the merits of disputes away from employment tribunals. By contrast, in *Crosville Wales Ltd v Tracey (No 2)*[836] the House of Lords affirmed that any compensation due to the complainants in respect of their unfair dismissals, which arose from the employers' selective re-engagement of those dismissed while taking part in industrial action, did not fall to be reduced because of their conduct in participating in industrial action because of the difficulty of allocating blame for the industrial action to any individual complainant.[837] However, their Lordships stated obiter that individual blameworthy conduct additional to or separate from the mere act of participation in industrial action was in principle capable of amounting to contributory fault.[838] This means that individuals whose behaviour is perceived by a tribunal as 'over-hasty and inflammatory' may still be subject to a reduction in their compensation even if their dismissals are found to be unfair.[839]

Unfair dismissal and 'unofficial' industrial action

11.85 Where an employee is dismissed while taking part in 'unofficial' industrial action an employment tribunal has no jurisdiction to hear a claim for unfair dismissal,[840] the sole exceptions being where the reason for dismissal, or selection for redundancy, is one of those specified in para

---

[832] See para 11.65. On ILO standards in this area see Gernigon *et al* 1998: pp 461–467; ILO, 2006, paras 663 *et seq.*

[833] See *Port of London Authority v Payne* [1994] IRLR 9, discussed at para 5.141 above.

[834] TULRCA 1992, s 239(4)(a). This was justified by the Government on the dual grounds that it would 'make no sense' for tribunals to issue re-employment orders when 'the employees are unwilling to work', and that the terms of settlement of the dispute may include reinstatement of those dismissed: Mr Ian McCartney, Minister of State, Department of Trade and Industry, Official Report of Standing Committee E, 9 March 1999, 6.45 pm.

[835] [1993] IRLR 432, not following *Courtaulds Northern Spinning Co v Moosa* [1984] IRLR 43 on this point.

[836] [1997] IRLR 691.

[837] It was agreed between the parties that, even though the claim only came into existence because of the selective re-engagement, the wording of the legislation meant that the relevant question in the context of the compensation provisions was whether an employee had contributed to his or her dismissal, not to the failure to be re-engaged, following *Moosa* and *Downes* on this point.

[838] [1997] IRLR 691, 698.

[839] Lord Nolan expressly endorsed, at 698, the judgment of Waite LJ in this case relating to contributory fault: see [1996] IRLR 91, 98.

[840] TULRCA 1992, s 237(1). The exclusion applies when the employee was taking part in the action 'at the time of dismissal' (defined in (s237(5)), which makes it explicit that once an employer knows that industrial action has ended, it cannot dismiss employees later that day.

11.83 above or, additionally, that the employee made a 'protected disclosure' within the terms of ERA 1996, ss 43A-43L (see para 4.117).[841] Notably, once again, there is no protection for those chosen on grounds of their union activities, thus enabling employers to dismiss with impunity the 'ringleaders' behind industrial action. The same provision for stoppages in circumstances of serious and imminent danger applies in this context and, indeed, may be particularly significant here if the circumstances are such that no union official is involved and it may otherwise be deemed 'unofficial'. Our remarks relating to the HRA 1998 are also relevant.

As we stated in para 11.8, the policy which underlies this provision was to ensure that industrial action is either 'unofficial', or it is action for which a trade union is legally liable, in which case a ballot and prior notices to employers are required in order for immunity to be retained. There is a presumption that industrial action is 'unofficial' in relation to a particular employee[842] unless one of three conditions applies.[843] First, if he or she is a union member and the action is authorised or endorsed by that union. Second, if he or she is not a union member but participants in the action include members of a union which has authorised or endorsed the action.[844] Last, if none of the participants is a union member. Whether an employee is a member of a union is determined at the time he or she begins to take part in the action.[845] This means that employees cannot resign from the union after that point in order to protect their union against legal liability on the one hand and themselves against selective dismissal on the other.

Whether action has been authorised or endorsed by a union is determined according to the principles discussed in para 11.20 et seq. If the union is prima facie liable but is able, and elects, to repudiate the action, participants in the industrial action have a short period within which to end their action before being liable to selective dismissal; it is not to be treated as unofficial 'before the end of the next working day after the day on which the repudiation takes place'.[846] 'Working days' are days other than Saturdays, Sundays, Christmas Day, Good Friday and bank holidays.[847] The definition does not, therefore, allow for any variation according to the working patterns of the individual enterprise or individual employees. Thus, if a participant in unofficial action is not due to work the day following a repudiation by the union, or is unable to attend work due to illness, he or she will have to ensure that the employer is aware that his or her participation in the industrial action has come to an end; failure to do this will entitle the employer to assume continued participation and will therefore expose the employee to dismissal.[848] Employees who are unaware of the repudiation, whatever the reason, have no special protection; although unions are required to notify every member who they have reason to believe is taking part in the action

---

[841] TULRCA, s 237(1A); see further para 5.92 et seq.

[842] Action may be 'unofficial' in relation to some employees and not others; an individual may be a member of a union which has not authorised or endorsed the action even though another union has and thus not fall within either of the first two categories. See, for example, *Balfour Kilpatrick Ltd v Acheson* [2003] IRLR 683.

[843] TULRCA 1992, s 237(2).

[844] There is no requirement that these other participants should be 'employees' rather than 'workers'.

[845] TULRCA 1992, s 237(6). However, membership of a union 'for purposes unconnected with the employment in question' should be disregarded: ibid. This would cover, for example, a 'resting actor' who is a member of Equity, the actors' union, but temporarily engaged in different employment.

[846] TULRCA 1992, s 237(4). In *Balfour Kilpatrick Ltd v Acheson* [2003] IRLR 683 the EAT held that 'the end of the next working day' meant midnight on the following working day and not the end of the period which constitutes the normal working hours for the day in question.

[847] TULRCA 1992, s 237(5).

[848] See *Williams v Western Mail and Echo Ltd* [1980] IRLR 222, discussed in para 11.75. The case for individual notification is stronger for unofficial action because it may not be clear when the action has ended.

for a repudiation to be effective in removing liability from the union, there is no requirement for members to receive such notice before their protection against selective dismissal is removed.

In *Balfour Kilpatrick Ltd v Acheson*[849] the EAT indicated that a repudiation which is treated as ineffective for the purposes of union liability is also ineffective in the context of protection against unfair dismissal, thus rendering the action 'non-unofficial' and removing the employer's ability to dismiss selectively with impunity.[850] This case also shows the danger for the employer of dismissing an employee before the time when the action is treated as 'unofficial'.

Industrial action and redundancy

11.86   The effect of taking industrial action upon the right to receive a redundancy payment is complex. As we saw in para 5.170, section 140(1) of ERA 1996 deprives employees of a payment where the employer is entitled to terminate the contract without notice due to the employee's conduct provided that specified procedures are followed. This provision will apply to employees who take industrial action short of a strike provided that this constitutes a repudiatory breach of contract. In *Simmons v Hoover Ltd*[851] the EAT affirmed that this was the case both where there is a 'single' dismissal (ie a dismissal for redundancy, not explicitly for misconduct) as well as a 'double' dismissal (dismissal for redundancy followed by dismissal for misconduct); thus, an employer who gives insufficient notice of redundancy but then discovers misconduct on the part of the employee is relieved of liability.[852] Where the employer follows the section 140(1) procedure and the dismissal takes place within the 'obligatory period', the tribunal has discretion to award all or part of the redundancy payment if it thinks this just and equitable.[853] However, in *Simmons v Hoover* the court considered that this applied only where there are two dismissals, a view which benefits employers who act wrongfully by giving insufficient notice on a single dismissal.

Section 140(1) is modified in the case of strikes (for which the definition provided for continuity purposes applies).[854] An employee who has been dismissed who then takes part in a strike will retain the right to payment provided that the strike occurs during the obligatory period of the employer's notice.[855] In *Simmons* the EAT considered that this applied only where there was a 'double' dismissal and the strike followed the redundancy notice; where the redundancy followed the strike, section 140(1) remained the governing provision. Where an employee takes strike action following notice of redundancy, the employer can serve written notice requesting the employee to agree to extend the contract by the number of days the strike lasts.[856] Employees who refuse to agree to this lose the right to a redundancy payment unless they can show that they were unable to comply or it was reasonable not to, in which case the tribunal has a discretion

---

[849] [2003] IRLR 683.
[850] Note also TULRCA 1992, s 237(4) which states that the question whether industrial action is taken to have been authorised or endorsed by a union is to be determined by reference to the facts at the time of dismissal.
[851] [1976] IRLR 266.
[852] *X v Y Ltd* (1969) 4 ITR 204.
[853] ERA 1996, s 140(5), (3). See s 136(4) for the definition of 'obligatory period'.
[854] ERA 1996, s 235(5).
[855] ERA 1996, s 140(2), (5).
[856] ERA 1996, ss 143, 144. The notice must contain specified information.

to award some or all of the payment.[857] Finally, if an employee terminates his or her contract of employment without notice in response to a lock-out which constitutes a repudiatory breach of contract by the employer, this is excluded from the definition of 'constructive dismissal',[858] so denying the employee any form of statutory redundancy payment. There is a clear danger that employees who lack appropriate advice may be manipulated into resigning by employers who may initiate a lock-out by proposing terms which they can predict will be unacceptable to the workforce, knowing that redundancies would in any case be imminent. It is difficult to understand the policy justification for this position.

INDUSTRIAL ACTION AND SOCIAL SECURITY BENEFITS

11.87   An individual who participates in or who, in certain circumstances, is affected by a strike or industrial action, thereby loses the right to receive the jobseeker's allowance for the period while he or she is out of work as a consequence of the relevant stoppage.[859] A claim may be made for income support in respect of other members of the claimant's family for the relevant period, but any such payment will be subject to a number of deductions, including an amount in respect of strike pay from the claimant's trade union whether or not such strike pay is actually received. These rules go back to the beginnings of the modern social security system. The National Insurance Act 1911 excluded the right to unemployment benefit where the claimant was out of work 'by reason of a stoppage which was due to a trade dispute at the factory, workshop or other premises at which he was employed'.[860] This was justified, above all, by the principle of state neutrality. In evidence given to the Royal Commission on Unemployment Insurance in 1931,[861] the Ministry of Labour argued that it would have been inappropriate for the national insurance fund to be seen to support either side to the dispute. As a general justification, the argument of neutrality is very flimsy. In *Lascaris v Wyman* the New York Court of Appeal referred to the same argument as a 'fiction' in the context of a constitutional challenge to the state's practice of paying social assistance to destitute strikers: 'although, on the one hand, the State may not be acting in a strictly neutral fashion if it allows strikers to obtain public assistance, it may not, on the other hand, be seriously maintained that the State adopts a neutral policy if it renders strikers helpless by denying them public assistance or welfare benefits to which they would otherwise be entitled'.[862] A more specific reason for the approach taken in the UK, which is consistent with general attitudes towards the role of the courts in this area, is that social security tribunals and officials should not be drawn into judging the merits of particular industrial disputes. In addition, concern has been expressed at various times that the payment of benefits prolongs disputes,[863] and that the potentially large number of claims arising out of industrial action would disrupt the administration of the social security system.

---

[857] ERA 1996, s 143(5).
[858] ERA 1996, s 136(2).
[859] Jobseekers Act 1995, s 14. The Jobseekers Act 1995 replaced earlier measures with broadly equivalent provisions. See P Wood *et al*: 2011 for a fuller treatment of this subject; see also Ewing, 1991: chs 5–8; and Mesher and Sutcliffe, 1986.
[860] NIA 1911, s 87(1).
[861] Royal Commission on Unemployment Insurance, Minutes of Evidence 10.7.31, Q 9779, cited in Ewing, 1991: p 65.
[862] 292 NE 2d 667 (1972), discussed by Ewing, 1991: p 160.
[863] For discussion, see Durcan and McCarthy, 1974; Gennard and Lasko, 1974.

The exclusionary rule in respect of means-tested benefits may be traced to the decision of the Court of Appeal in *A-G v Merthyr Tydfil Union*[864] in 1900. There the court held that the Poor Law Guardians had no power to make payments to the strikers themselves, but that it was not necessarily unlawful for them to give outdoor relief to members of their families, nor to other workers laid off as a result of the dispute. In this last respect, the position under the poor law was more favourable than that taken by the National Insurance Acts, which excluded both those taking part in a strike and others who were the incidental victims of the stoppage. However, later legislation in the area of social assistance adopted the wider exclusion contained in the national insurance legislation, ostensibly on the same ground of state neutrality.[865]

Unemployment-related benefits and the trade dispute disqualification

11.88 Under section 14 of the Jobseekers Act 1995, a person is not entitled to a jobseeker's allowance for any week which includes a day where there is a stoppage of work which is due to a trade dispute at his or her place of work and which causes them not to be employed on that day, unless they can show that they were 'not directly interested in the dispute'. For this purpose, the legislation retains the substance of the definition of trade dispute taken from the Trade Disputes Act 1906, namely 'any dispute between employers and employees, or between employees and employees, which is connected with the employment or non-employment or the terms of employment or the conditions of employment of any persons, whether employees in the employment of the employer with whom the dispute arises, or not'.[866] It is significant that the narrowing of the trade dispute formula for collective purposes[867] after 1982 did not take place as well in the area of social security, so that the jobseeker's allowance may be lost in a much wider range of circumstances than dispute organisers are protected from liability in tort. Moreover, the social security exclusion applies even if there are good grounds, objectively speaking, for the stoppage: claimants have been disqualified for taking part in strikes over their employer's infringement of health and safety regulations[868] and after being dismissed for refusing to accept cuts in pay.[869]

The disqualification applies even to those affected by a stoppage in which they are not directly participating if it occurs at their 'place of work'. This means, 'in relation to any person, ... the premises or place at which he was employed'.[870] This is limited by the important proviso that the claimant must have been 'directly interested' in the dispute (the claimant is required to prove that he or she was not 'directly interested'). At one stage the claimant also had to show that he or she was neither participating in nor financing the dispute, *and* that he or she was not a member of a 'grade or class' whose members were either participating in, financing or directly interested in the dispute. The Donovan Commission[871] recommended the removal of these provisions on the

---

[864] [1900] 1 Ch 516; Ewing, 1991: pp 91–94.
[865] Ewing, 1991: pp 97–98.
[866] Jobseekers Act 1995, s 35(1).
[867] TULRCA 1992, s 244; see above, para 11.25 *et seq.*
[868] *R v National Insurance Comr, ex p Thompson*, appendix to *R(U) 5/77*; *R(U) 4/65*; *R(U) 3/71.*
[869] *R(U) 27/56*. See generally P Wood *et al* 2011: pp 76–82.
[870] Jobseekers Act 1995, s 14(4).
[871] *Royal Commission on Trade Unions and Employers' Associations 1965–1968* Cmnd 3623, 1968, paras 975–976.

grounds that there need be no necessary assumption of a common interest from the membership of a 'group or class'; the reference to finance, in particular, was capable of producing unfairness since it would exclude many individuals simply on the grounds that their trade union was paying strike pay to those immediately involved. This recommendation was implemented in the SSA 1975.

The meaning of 'directly interested' was considered by the House of Lords in *Presho v Insurance Officer*.[872] Their Lordships rejected an argument that only those whose own pay and conditions of employment were in dispute could be 'directly interested', in favour of a two-stage test formulated by Lord Brandon. First, it had to be shown that the result of the dispute would be applied to groups of employees other than those participating in the strike or industrial action and, second, that this wider application would take place automatically by virtue either of a collective agreement (whether legally binding or not) or custom and practice in the workplace concerned.

The denial of unemployment benefit to those directly involved in the dispute can be seen as putting pressure on them to break the strike, notwithstanding the official claims that state neutrality is the basis for the rule; the employees' need for income will often be much more immediately pressing than the employer's need for their services.[873] But even if the trade dispute disqualification could be justified on the slightly different ground that it is important to avoid placing social security officers and tribunals in a position of adjudicating on the rights and wrongs of industrial action, this would hardly justify the disqualification of those who are not taking part but may in some way be affected by the outcome of the dispute. As Ewing has pointed out, claimants disqualified under this heading could include those who might be *prejudiced* by the outcome of the dispute.[874] This group in particular might be expected to respond to disqualification by putting extra pressure on the strikers to end their dispute.

The second category of disqualification relates to claimants who withdraw their labour in furtherance of a trade dispute.[875] This provision, which was introduced by the SSA 1986, catches those who take part in a trade dispute which is not connected with a stoppage at their own place of work.

The loss of entitlement may continue as long as the stoppage or the withdrawal of labour, as the case may be. However, it comes to an end if the claimant has, in the meantime, become bona fide employed elsewhere (the assumption being that he or she then lost this second employment while the original stoppage was still continuing); is dismissed by reason of redundancy; or bona fide resumes his or her employment with the employer and then leaves for a reason unconnected with the dispute.[876]

---

[872] [1984] AC 310, followed in *Cartlidge v Adjudication Officer* [1986] 2 All ER 1, CA.

[873] The supply of agency labour by an employment business in substitution for workers taking part in industrial action is prohibited by the Conduct of Employment Agencies and Employment Businesses Regulations 2003, SI 2003/3319, reg 7; see also the Gangmasters (Licensing Conditions) Rules 2009, SI 2009/307, reg 4; Sch, para 10. However these prohibitions do not apply if the industrial action in question is 'unofficial' for the purposes of TULRCA 1992, s 237.

[874] Ewing, 1991: p 87.

[875] Jobseekers Act 1995, s 14(2). In addition, where the partner of a person in receipt of the jobseeker's allowance becomes involved in a trade dispute, a deduction from the allowance may be made in respect of the partner: s 15.

[876] Jobseekers Act 1995, s 14(3); see P Wood *et al*, 2011: p 82, where it is asked whether resumption means that the employment was terminated and re-employment offered, or merely that the claimant returned to work during the trade dispute, or both. Note also that the claimant's loss of entitlement may affect a claim for the jobseeker's allowance by his or her partner, even where the latter is not involved in any trade dispute. See Jobseekers Allowance Regulations 1996, SI 1996/207, reg 52(2).

Loss of income support

11.89   An individual who would be disqualified from the jobseeker's allowance under the provisions which we have just considered is also disqualified from claiming income support unless, during the same period, he or she is incapable of work by reason of disease or disablement, or she is pregnant, in which case a claim may be made for the 'maternity period' either side of the expected week of confinement.[877] In other cases, after a period of seven days the claimant is able to make a claim in respect of other members of his or her family. The benefit payable is calculated by reference to the normal allowances, or their equivalents, for dependent members of the claimant's family. The sums payable are subject, however, to a deduction in respect of any strike pay received from the claimant's trade union, or any sum of strike pay which the claimant was entitled to receive, but did not, up to a maximum sum which from 9 April 2012 and at the time of writing is £38.[878] This provision was introduced in 1980 on the grounds that the full payment of social assistance amounted to subsidising strikes and prolonging their duration.[879] It is arguable that in addition to being a potential cause of hardship for families, it contradicts the official position of state neutrality in industrial disputes.

INDUSTRIAL ACTION AND THE RIGHTS OF UNION MEMBERS

11.90   As we saw in chapter 10, union members have rights against their union which may derive either (or concurrently) from the common law or statute. In this section we summarise the rights which are most relevant to industrial action, although some also have a wider application. In doing so we shall assume that readers are familiar with the general principles of union government outlined in chapter 10.

Rights at common law

11.91   Union members may challenge the decision of their union to support industrial action in three major ways.[880] First, they may wish to restrain the union from organising the industrial action in question. Second, they may seek to restrain the unauthorised expenditure of money, such as strike pay, in support of it. Last, they may refuse to participate in the action and attempt to forestall or challenge disciplinary action against them for this refusal. In the context of industrial action, where time is of the essence, claimants commonly seek an interim injunction to halt the allegedly unlawful activity. In deciding applications the criteria set out in para 11.49 *et seq*, *mutatis mutandis*, will be applied by the court and the penalties described in para 11.51 will be relevant

---

[877] SSCBA 1992, s 126.

[878] This is the effect of SSCBA 1992, s 126(5)–(7) and the Income Support (General) Regulations 1987, SI 1987/1967, Sch 9, para 34. Certain other special rules apply: see P Wood *et al*, 2011: pp 10-13.

[879] SSA 1980, s 6(1); see Mesher, 1985, for a discussion of its impact in the 1985 miners' strike.

[880] Elias and Ewing, 1987: p 236. The case law concerning the 1984–1985 miners' strike illustrates all three of these processes in operation: see Ewing, 1985. For a more detailed analysis, see G Morris and T Archer, 2000: paras 6.109–6.117.

if an order is granted and breached. In this context the power to order sequestration of a union's assets in the event that it acts in contempt of court, or to appoint a receiver to manage and control its assets, may be particularly important.[881]

The grounds for challenging the union's actions are various. Most straightforward are the arguments that the union's rules do not permit industrial action in the circumstances in question or, more likely, that the procedure stipulated in the rules has not been followed. Despite the comprehensive statutory procedures the common law may remain relevant here if, for example, the rules require the support of a two-thirds majority in a ballot, rather than a simple majority, before industrial action can be called. Even if the rules do ostensibly permit the action, there is some authority that it is beyond the powers of a union deliberately to embark upon activities, including industrial action, which would be bound to involve offences against the criminal law; this could be relevant to certain kinds of picketing and also industrial action by specific groups of workers.[882] It has also been argued on occasion, with less success, that union rules cannot authorise industrial action which would lead to a commission of a tort.[883] Clearly if this argument were ever to be accepted if would expose a very high proportion of campaigns to challenge. However, a direct instruction to commit a tort would probably be unlawful; this would be the situation, for example, if the union were to instruct its members to 'sit-in', so committing a trespass. Other grounds upon which it may arguably be unlawful to discipline a member, although they rest on only tenuous authority, are failure to strike in breach of a procedure agreement[884] and where the member was justified in concluding that the order was one to which the union had no right to demand obedience.[885] However, neither of these have been applied other than in the particular case in which they were suggested.

Disciplinary action against members is, in practice, most likely to be challenged under the statutory protection against 'unjustifiable discipline' outlined below. The common law, however, may remain relevant for two reasons: first, because, it offers the possibility of injunctive relief, whereas the statute provides only for financial compensation; and second, because the statute requires a disciplinary 'determination' to have been made, whereas on occasion the courts have been prepared to grant a remedy at an earlier stage, sometimes restraining the union from holding even an initial inquiry as to whether there has been a breach of the union rules. Thus in *Esterman v NALGO*[886] Templeman J considered that no reasonable tribunal could *bona fide* conclude that disobedience to the strike call in question demonstrated unfitness to be a member of the union as charged and granted an interim injunction to restrain any disciplinary action (although emphasising that this should be done only in 'exceptional circumstances'[887]). In *Porter v NUJ*[888] the House of Lords also took a highly interventionist approach, holding that since there were

---

[881] See *Clarke v Heathfield* [1985] ICR 203.

[882] See *Thomas v NUM (South Wales Area)* [1985] IRLR 136, 153. See Ewing, 1985: pp 164–165; 174–175; Elias and Ewing, 1987: pp 237–240. On picketing see para 11.53 *et seq* above; on special groups para 11.61 above.

[883] See *Thomas v NUM* 1985] IRLR 136, 153- 154. See also *Sherard v AUEW* [1973] ICR 421, 433 (Lord Denning MR). Cf *National Sailors' and Fireman's Union of Great Britain and Northern Ireland v Reed* [1926] Ch 536, 539–540, where it was held unlawful for a union to call a strike where there was no trade dispute.

[884] *Partington v NALGO* [1981] IRLR 537, 542 (Lord Allanbridge); see also *Porter v NUJ* [1979] IRLR 404, 407 (Lord Denning MR) (decision upheld by the House of Lords [1980] IRLR 404 without reference to this point).

[885] *Esterman v NALGO* [1974] ICR 625.

[886] [1974] ICR 625.

[887] [1974] ICR 625, 632.

[888] [1980] IRLR 404; see Lord Diplock at 406.

serious issues of disputed fact as to the lawfulness of the strike call and as to whether the union was entitled to take disciplinary proceedings against the claimants the balance of convenience lay in favour of maintaining the status quo, by which the claimants remained members of the union, until the trial. However, in the later case of *Longley v NUJ*[889] the Court of Appeal emphasised that the courts should be slow to prevent domestic tribunals adjudicating upon a matter in the first instance and endorsed the view of the trial judge that this should be done only if there was persuasive evidence to suggest that the issues had been prejudged or that the prescribed procedures would not be complied with. This latter approach accords with that of the legislation and, if followed, would make it more difficult for claimants to forestall the disciplinary process. In view of the fact that an interim injunction forces the union to undertake potentially lengthy litigation if it wishes to proceed with a disciplinary matter it seems the preferable approach to take, particularly now that with the demise of the closed shop, loss of union membership no longer carries the threat of exclusion from employment.

Statutory rights

11.92   The statutory rights most relevant to industrial action can be divided into four broad categories. The first is the right to a ballot. A member who claims that members of the union (of which he or she is one) are likely to be, or have been, induced by the union to take part in industrial action which lacks the support of a properly-conducted ballot may apply to the High Court for an injunction restraining such inducement.[890] The second is the highly controversial right not to be 'unjustifiably disciplined', with substantial financial compensation available if this right is infringed.[891] Debate about this right, which we discussed in para 10.12, focused in particular upon its relevance to industrial action. It accords absolute supremacy to the individual over the collective by providing that an individual may not be disciplined for failing to participate in or support any industrial action, notwithstanding that it is lawful and may have achieved a high level of support in a ballot. The introduction of this provision attracted considerable criticism from the right, as well as the left, of the political spectrum, one argument from the former being that it would undermine the representativity of the ballot by discouraging those opposed to the action from expressing their views at that stage if they knew they would be protected against retaliatory action for non-participation.[892] It has been found by the ILO Committee of Experts to infringe Article 3 of Convention 87 on the ground that this requires that union members should be permitted when drawing up their constitutions and rules to determine whether or not it should be possible to discipline members who refuse to participate in lawful strikes or other industrial action. It has also been regarded by the Committee of Independent Experts (now the European Committee of Social Rights) as incompatible with the right to organise guaranteed

---

[889] [1987] IRLR 109.

[890] TULRCA 1992, s 62. The 'inducement' need not be effective: s 62(6). A member may also apply if the union has called on its members to take part in the action before the date of the ballot or if the call is made by someone other than a specified person: s 62(2).

[891] TULRCA 1992, ss 64–67.

[892] See Leader, 1991, where it is also argued that the measure impinges on trade unionists' right to freedom of association under Art 11(1) of the ECHR in forcing them to keep within their ranks individuals who refuse to take part in industrial action.

by Article 5 of the European Social Charter.[893] However, despite these findings, the Labour Government took no steps to remove these restrictions; rather it specifically defended them as providing 'necessary protections for individual workers in their relationship with their unions'.[894] There is no indication that the Coalition Government will change the position. The Conservative Government's justification for their introduction was that 'every union member should be free to decide for himself whether or not he wishes to break his contract of employment and run the risk of dismissal without compensation',[895] although this was inadequate to explain the extension of protection to those who attempted to persuade others to continue working. Their retention now that there is at least limited protection against dismissal for participating in 'protected industrial action' is even more difficult to justify.

The third statutory intervention in this area is the prohibition upon unions indemnifying individuals for penalties for criminal offences or for contempt of court.[896] At one time several unions made provision in their rules for indemnifying members, in particular officials, for specified unlawful acts. At common law, provided that their rules so permitted, unions were free to resolve to make payments in respect of offences already committed, but not future offences.[897] This practice is now prohibited and any payments made are recoverable from the recipient at the suit of the union or an individual member on behalf of the union where he or she claims the union's failure to act is 'unreasonable'.[898] This, too, was condemned by the ILO Committee of Experts in its 1989 report in the following terms:

> The Committee has consistently taken the view that legislative provisions which are intended to ensure sound administration and the honest and efficient management of union funds and other funds and assets are not incompatible with the Convention ... However such provisions should not be of such a character as to deprive unions of the right to draw up their constitutions or rules and to organise their administration and activities free of interference by the public authorities – nor should they deny trade unions the right to utilise their funds as they wish for normal and lawful trade union purposes. [This provision] appears to do both of these things ...[899]

In more recent reports, however, the Committee took a less confident tone, appearing to acknowledge the Conservative Government's case which included the argument that where penalties were imposed on an individual, rather than a union, this would 'imply a clear finding of wilful and unlawful action by that individual'.[900] However, it has maintained the view that indemnification in respect of legal liabilities incurred on behalf of the union should be possible.

---

[893] See, for example, Conclusions XIV-I.

[894] See, for example, the 2002 Report of the ILO Committee of Experts on the Application of Conventions and Recommendations on the UK's compliance with ILO Convention No 87.

[895] *Trade Unions and their Members* Cm 95, 1987: pp 7–8.

[896] TULRCA 1992, s 15. The Secretary of State may by order designate offences in relation to which the section does not apply (s 15(5)) but at the time of writing no such order has been made.

[897] *Drake v Morgan* [1978] ICR 56; cf *Thomas v NUM (South Wales Area)* [1985] IRLR 136.

[898] TULRCA 1992, s 15(2), (3).

[899] Report of the Committee of Experts on the Application of Conventions and Recommendations, Report III (Part 4A), ILO, Geneva 1989: p 237.

[900] Report of the Committee of Experts on the Application of Conventions and Recommendations, Report III (Part 4A), ILO, Geneva, 1992: p 245.

The European Committee of Social Rights also takes the view that in principle unions should be free to use their property as they consider appropriate.

The final statutory right allows members to apply to the High Court if they claim that the union's trustees are carrying out, or proposing to carry out, their functions so as to 'cause or permit' any unlawful application of the union's property, or that they have complied or are proposing to comply with an unlawful direction which has or may be given under the union rules.[901] The latter provision means that even if the trustees are specifically empowered by the rules or trust instrument to act in a particular way, or are obliged to obey the instructions of the union's executive, the member may have a remedy.[902] If the court upholds the complaint it may make such order as it considers appropriate including requiring the trustees to take specified steps to protect or recover union property; to appoint a receiver; and to remove one or more trustees.[903] If union property has been applied in contravention of a court order, or the trustees were proposing such action, all the trustees must be removed except any who can convince the court there is 'good reason' to allow him or her to remain.[904] This may lead to the appointment of new trustees by the court[905] or the appointment of a receiver. The power of members to intervene when they claim that trustees are 'proposing' to act in one of these ways gives them a wide preventative power, particularly as the court is empowered to grant relief on an interim basis. They are protected against being disciplined for exercising this right.[906] The existence of powers of this nature may throw greater light on the legislative strategy of the former Conservative Government of making it prohibitively expensive for unions to remove dissident members, who may be opposed to every aspect of union policy, from their midst.

ASSESSMENT

11.93   Our analysis of the law relating to industrial action reveals that it is fragmented, complex, often unpredictable and sometimes unprincipled in nature. These characteristics alone are cause for concern. In substance it breaches international standards in a number of important respects, in particular those determined by the ILO. This is the case both in relation to the position of individual workers and that of their organisations. The judgments of the ECJ in *Viking* and *Laval*, which we discuss in para 11.52 above, have added an additional layer of uncertainty when there is a cross-border dimension to disputes.

These conclusions are not difficult to reach. Much more contentious is the direction which any reform of the law should take. In para 11.4 we outlined some fundamental questions which any legal system needs to address in relation to industrial action. We do not attempt to address all

---

[901] TULRCA 1992, s 16(1). As union property is held on trust for the union, members would seem not to be direct beneficiaries of the trust so their *locus standi* to bring an action for breach of trust, other than where there has been a breach of the union rule book, is uncertain: cf *Hughes v TGWU* [1985] IRLR 382.
[902] Under the general law trustees are bound to obey only the lawful instructions of the union's executive committee: *Clarke v Heathfield (No 2)* [1985] ICR 606, 614.
[903] TULRCA 1992, s 16(3).
[904] TULRCA 1992, s 16(4).
[905] Trustee Act 1925, s 41.
[906] TULRCA 1992, s 65(2)(c).

those issues here but merely isolate those areas which in our view are most in need of scrutiny by policy makers.[907]

(i) One issue which is often raised is whether withdrawing labour should be expressed as a freedom or a right. If one accepts the view that it is necessary to define the scope of the capacity of workers lawfully to withdraw their labour, and the conditions under which this may be done, the existence of a positive right has advantages. It accords the withdrawal of labour a status among competing rights, such as rights of property and, once established, may make it more difficult to curtail than an immunity, which carries the danger of being presented as a 'privilege'. As we saw in para 11.9 above. in *RMT v Serco Docklands; ASLEF v London Midland*[908] the Court of Appeal stated that '[t]he statutory immunities are simply the form which the law in this country takes to carve out the ability for unions to take lawful strike action' and that Article 11 of the ECHR meant that it was no longer sustainable to say that because unions were seeking to take advantage of an immunity the law should be construed against them. However, even a positive right is not immune from creative interpretation by the courts[909] and may, indeed, be as vulnerable to circumvention as an immunity in the hands of an adjudicating body which is attuned more to the individualistic tradition of the common law rather than collective values. Thus, of itself, there is no guarantee that a system of positive rights would confer greater legal freedom to strike.[910] The crucial question is the substance of the 'right' or 'freedom', not its form.[911]

(ii) UK law has traditionally focused upon protecting the organisers of industrial action from legal liability, overlooking the vulnerability of the individual worker for whom there is no regime of 'statutory immunity', however rudimentary. However, the freedom to take industrial action is undermined completely if individual workers thereby jeopardise the continuation of their employment or are otherwise vulnerable to discriminatory treatment. Despite the introduction of protection for employees (only) against dismissal for taking 'protected industrial action', a welcome but still unduly limited reform, there remain a number of features of the present law which require reconsideration here. One is the position whereby industrial action generally constitutes a breach of the contract of employment. In 1968 the Donovan Commission pointed to the technical problems raised by the introduction of a doctrine of suspension of the contract. These included how to define the forms of industrial action to which it would apply; whether an employer would be able to dismiss an employee for gross misconduct during the course of the dispute; whether strikers would be free to take up other employment while the contract of employment was suspended; and if efforts to end the strike failed, upon what event would the suspension of the contract cease and be replaced by termination?[912] None of these difficulties is insuperable, however, and indeed the legal systems of many other European countries, including France, Italy

---

[907] For more detailed discussions see Ewing, 1991; Wedderburn, 1991b and Ewing, 2006; for a useful international perspective see Ben-Israel, 1994 and for a study of international standards, Novitz, 2003.

[908] *RMT v Serco Ltd t/a Serco Docklands; ASLEF v London and Birmingham Railway Ltd t/a London Midland* [2011] IRLR 399, Elias LJ (giving the judgment of the court) at [9].

[909] See Wedderburn, 1991b: pp 314–316.

[910] P Davies and M Freedland, 1984: pp 786–787.

[911] As shown by *Viking* and *Laval*: see para 11.52 above. On the merits of recognising a right to strike as a human right, see Ewing, 2004.

[912] *Royal Commission on Trade Unions and Employers' Associations 1965–1968*, Cmnd 3623, 1968, para 943.

and Germany, incorporate a doctrine of suspension, albeit that the conditions under which it operates may vary.[913] A further question is the issue of effective protection for workers (not just employees) participating in lawful disputes against dismissal and other prejudicial action, which suspension of the contract alone would not achieve. The requirement that protection be effective leads in turn to the issue of remedies for infringing workers' rights. Should there be automatic reinstatement for dismissed employees regardless of the circumstances, for example? What of the position of any replacement labour which the employer may have hired during the dispute? Should such persons be subject to a statutory presumption that their dismissal is for a fair reason, by analogy with replacements for those on maternity leave, on the basis that they were aware of the position when they took the job? A final important issue in relation to the rights of individual workers is that of payment if the employer accepts partial performance of contractual duties. Although this form of industrial action is not protected in some legal systems it has advantages, particularly in essential services where a total withdrawal of labour can present serious difficulties. If it is to be permitted, consideration should be given as to whether there should be prior approval of any deduction from wages by an external body rather than maintaining the current position which allows the employer unilaterally to set the level of wages to be paid, with the onus upon workers to challenge this amount.

(iii) At the collective level a fundamental question is whether a new framework of protected action, with corresponding liabilities for action beyond it, should be enacted. If the organisation of industrial action could be insulated against the common law this would avoid it being prey to developments which can radically affect its lawfulness, such as the application of the wrong of inducing breach of a statutory duty and that of economic duress. If the doctrine of suspension of the contract of employment, which would remove liability for inducing breach of such a contract, were to be accepted this would necessitate constructing a new framework. Consideration would also need to be given to the permissible limits of secondary action, particularly in view of the lack of limitation on employers transferring work between companies and the reluctance of the courts to 'lift the corporate veil'. Pre-industrial action procedures also require attention, albeit that the Employment Relations Acts 1999 and 2004 made some reforms; thought should be given to reducing the complexity and cost to unions of holding ballots with a view to the creation of a climate more conducive to a settlement of the underlying issues rather than focusing attention upon complying with the technicalities of the legal process.[914] Any reform would also need to consider whether it would be possible to minimise the possibility of the statutory framework being undermined by the availability of interim injunctions. In Ireland once the requisite pre-strike procedures have been followed the employer is prohibited from obtaining an injunction without the respondent being present before the court, and the court 'shall not grant an injunction restraining the strike or other industrial action where the respondent establishes a fair case that he was acting in contemplation or furtherance of a trade dispute'.[915] Although this provision (which operates within a continued system of immunities) has been criticised as inadequate (it does not extend to applications by third parties, for example) it provides one example of how the present

---

[913] See A Jacobs, 2010: paras 57–63.
[914] See further Elgar and Simpson, 1996.
[915] Irish Industrial Relations Act 1990, s 19.

position could be modified.[916] A more radical solution might be possible if the area of industrial action was removed from the purview of the common law courts altogether.

(iv) In line with the review of industrial action by workers there is a need to examine the circumstances in which an employer may lawfully institute a lock-out and the impact of such action upon the employment relationship, including protecting affected workers against dismissal.

(v) In relation to trade unions the restrictions on discipline of members who seek to retain their membership whilst refusing to accept collective decisions should be subject to review, as should restrictions on expenditure to indemnify members who incur penalties in the course of complying with union policy.

(vi) Consideration should be given as to whether there should be separate provision for industrial action in 'essential services' and if so, of what nature and subject to what conditions.[917] In this context the 'statutory right of action' available to consumers of goods of services is particularly pertinent in threatening to remove control over the management of disputes from the parties.[918]

In reforming the law, the overriding aim should be to construct a coherent legal framework which incorporates ILO standards and makes a genuine attempt to balance the legitimate interests of the parties and, where appropriate, of the wider public. British law still has some considerable way to go before this aim can be said to have been achieved.

---

[916] For a trenchant critique of this Act see B Wilkinson, 1991; see also Hepple, 2010.
[917] See further G Morris, 1991.
[918] See further G Morris, 1993.

BIBLIOGRAPHY

Aaron, Benjamin and KW Wedderburn (1972) *Industrial Conflict: a comparative legal survey* (Longman, Harlow).

Achur, James (2011) *Trade Union Membership 2010* (Department of Business, Innovation and Skills, London)

Adams, Lorna, Ashley Moore, Katie Gore and Joni Browne (2009): *Research into enforcement of employment tribunal awards in England and Wales*. Ministry of Justice, London.

Adams, Roy J (1999) Why Statutory Recognition is Bad Labour Policy: the North American Experience *Industrial Relations Journal* 30, 96-100.

Addison, John T (1986) Job Security in the United States: Law, Collective Bargaining, Policy and Practice *British Journal of Industrial Relations* 24, 381-418.

Addison, John T and Alberto Castro (1987) The Importance of Life-Time Jobs: Differences between Union and Non-Union Workers *Industrial and Labor Relations Review* 40, 393-405.

Addison, John T and W Stanley Siebert (1991) The Social Charter of the European Community: Evolution and Controversies *Industrial and Labor Relations Review* 44, 597-625.

Addison, John T and W Stanley Siebert (1992) The Social Charter: Whatever Next? *British Journal of Industrial Relations* 30, 495-513.

Alaimo, Anna (2010) The New Directive on European Works Councils: Innovations and Omissions *International Journal of Comparative Labour Law and Industrial Relations* 26, 217-230.

Albin, Einat (2011) A Worker-Employer-Customer Triangle: The Case of Tips *Industrial Law Journal* 40, 181-206.

Alcock, A (1971) *History of the International Labour Organisation* (Macmillan, London).

Allen, V L (1954) *Power in Trade Unions: a study of their organisation in Great Britain* (Longman, London).

Anderman, Steven D (1986) Unfair Dismissal and Redundancy, in *Labour Law in Britain* ed Roy Lewis (Basil Blackwell, Oxford).

Anderman, Steven D (1993) European Community Merger and Social Policy *Industrial Law Journal* 22, 318-321.

Anderman, Steven D (2000) The Interpretation of Protective Employment Statutes and Contracts of Employment *Industrial Law Journal* 29, 223-242.

Anderman, Steven D (2004) Termination of Employment: Whose Property Rights? in *The Future of Labour Law: Liber Amicorum Sir Bob Hepple* QC ed Catherine Barnard, Simon Deakin and Gillian S Morris (Hart Publishing, Oxford).

Anderson, Gordon (1991) The Employment Contracts Act 1991: An Employer's Charter? *New Zealand Journal of Industrial Relations* 16, 147-162.

Anderson, Lucy (2003) Sound Bite Legislation: The Employment Act 2002 and New Flexible Working 'Rights' for Parents *Industrial Law Journal* 32, 37-42.

Antcliff, Valerie and Richard Saundry (2009) Accompaniment, Workplace Representation and Disciplinary Outcomes in British Workplaces - Just a Formality? *British Journal of Industrial Relations* 47, 100-121.

Archbold (2012) *Criminal Pleading Evidence and Practice* (Sweet and Maxwell, London)

Arlidge, Anthony, David Eady and ATH Smith (2007) *Arlidge, Eady and Smith on Contempt* 3rd edn (Sweet and Maxwell, London).

Armour, John and Simon Deakin (2000) The Rover Case (2): Bargaining in the Shadow of TUPE *Industrial Law Journal,* 29: 395-402.

Armour, John and Simon Deakin (2003) Insolvency and employment protection: the mixed effects of the Acquired Rights Directive *International Review of Law and Economics* 23, 1-23.

Armour, John and Sandra Frisby (2001) Rethinking Receivership *Oxford Journal of Legal Studies* 21, 73-102.

Arrowsmith, S (1995) Public Procurement as an Instrument of Policy and the Impact of Market Liberalisation *Law Quarterly Review* 111, 235-284.

Arrowsmith, Sue (2005) *The Law of Public and Utilities Procurement* 2nd edn (Sweet and Maxwell, London).

Arrowsmith, Sue and Peter Kunzlik (eds) (2009) *Social and Environmental Policies in EC Procurement Law: New Directives and New Directions* (Cambridge University Press, Cambridge).

Arthurs, Harry (2002) Private Ordering and Workers' Rights, in the Global Economy: Corporate Codes of Conduct as a Regime of Labour Market Regulation in *Labour Law in an Era of Globalization: Transformative Practices and Possibilities* ed Joanne Conaghan, Richard Michael Fischl and Karl Klare (Oxford University Press, Oxford).

Ashburner, Walter (1933) *Principles of Equity* 2nd edn by Dennis Browne (Butterworths, London).

Ashcroft, John, Juan Yermo and Fiona Stewart (2011) Regulatory and Supervisory Context for Occupational Pension Provision, in *Good Governance of Pension Schemes* eds. Paul Thornton and Donald Fleming (CUP, Cambridge).

Ashiagbor, Diamond (2000) Flexibility and Adaptability in the EU Employment Strategy in *Legal Regulation of the Employment Relation* eds Hugh Collins, Paul Davies and Roger Rideout (Kluwer, Deventer).

Atkinson, John (1985) *Flexibility, Uncertainty and Manpower Management* IMS Report No 89 (Institute of Manpower Studies, Brighton).

Atleson, James B (1983) *Values and Assumptions in American Labor Law* (University of Massachusetts Press, Amherst).

Auerbach, Simon (1988) Injunction Procedure in the Seafarers' Dispute *Industrial Law Journal* 17, 227-238.

Auerbach, Simon (1989) Injunctions against Picketing *Industrial Law Journal* 18, 166-170.

Auerbach, Simon (1990) *Legislating for Conflict* (Clarendon Press, Oxford).

Auerbach, Simon (1993) *Derecognition and Personal Contracts: Fighting Tactics and the Law* (Institute of Employment Rights, London).

Auvergnon, Philippe and José-Luis Gil y Gil (1994) La Réforme du Droit du Travail en Espagne *Droit Social,* 199-208.

Ayres, Ian and Robert Gertner (1989) Filling Gaps in Incomplete Contracts: a Theory of Default Rules (1989) *Yale Law Journal* 99, 87-130.

Bacon, Nicholas and John Storey (2000) New Employee Relations Strategies in Britain: Towards Individualism or Partnership? *British Journal of Industrial Relations* 38, 404-427.

Bailey, Ruth, and John Kelly (1990) An Index Measure of British Trade Union Density *British Journal of Industrial Relations* 28, 267-270.

Bailey, S.H. (2007) Judicial Review of Contracting Decisions *Public Law* 444-463.

Bailey, Suzanne (1989) Equal Treatment/Special Treatment: the Dilemma of the Dismissed Pregnant Employee *Journal of Social Welfare Law* 85-100.

Bain, George Sayers (1970) *The Growth of White-Collar Unionism* (Clarendon Press, Oxford).

Bain, George Sayers and Robert Price (1983) Union Growth: Dimensions, Determinants, and Destiny, in *Industrial Relations in Britain* ed George Sayers Bain (Basil Blackwell, Oxford).

Bainbridge, D (1990) *Computers and the Law* (Pitman, London).

Baker, Aaron (2008) Proportionality and Employment Discrimination in the UK *Industrial Law Journal* 37, 305-328.

Bamber, Greg J, Peter Sheldon and Bernard Gan (2010) Collective Bargaining: An International Analysis in *Comparative Labour Law and Industrial Relations in Industrialized Market Economies* 10th edn, ed Roger Blanpain (Wolters Kluwer, The Netherlands).

Bamforth, Nicholas (1994) Sexual Orientation and Dismissal *New Law Journal* 144, 1402-1419.

Bamforth, Nicholas (1997) *Sexuality, Morals and Justice: A Theory of Lesbian and Gay Rights Law* (Cassell, London).

Bamforth, Nicholas (1999) The Application of the Human Rights Act 1998 to Public Authorities and Private Bodies *Cambridge Law Journal* 58, 159-170.

Bamforth, Nicholas (2000) Sexual Orientation Discrimination after *Grant v South West Trains* *Modern Law Review* 63, 694-720.

Barbagelata, H (1986) Categories of Workers and Labour Contracts, in *Comparative Labour Law and Industrial Relations in Industrialised Market Economies Vol 1* ed R Blanpain (Kluwer, Deventer-Boston).

Barendt, Eric (2005) *Freedom of Speech* 2nd edn (Oxford University Press, Oxford).

Barmes, Lizzie (2003) Promoting Diversity and the Definition of Direct Discrimination *Industrial Law Journal* 32, 200-213.

Barmes, Lizzie (2004) The Continuing Conceptual Crisis in the Common Law of the Contract of Employment *Modern Law Review* 67, 435-464.

Barmes, Lizzie (2007) Constitutional and Conceptual Complexities in UK Implementation of the EU Harassment Provisions *Industrial Law Journal* 36, 446-447.

Barnard, Catherine (1992) A Social Policy for Europe: Politicians 1, Lawyers 0 *International Journal of Comparative Labour Law and Industrial Relations* 8, 15-31.

Barnard, Catherine (1994) Sunday Trading: a Drama in Five Acts *Modern Law Review* 57, 449-60.

Barnard, Catherine (1997a) The United Kingdom, the 'Social Chapter' and the Amsterdam Treaty *Industrial Law Journal* 26, 275-282.

Barnard, Catherine (1997b) *P v S*: Kite Flying or a New Constitutional Approach? in eds A Dashwood and S O'Leary *The Principle of Equal Treatment in EC Law* (Sweet and Maxwell, London).

Barnard, Catherine (1998) The Principle of Equality in the Community Context: *P, Grant, Kalanke* and *Marschall*: Four Uneasy Bedfellows? *Cambridge Law Journal* 57, 352-373.

Barnard, Catherine (1999) The Working Time Regulations 1998 *Industrial Law Journal* 28, 61-75.

Barnard, Catherine (2000) The Working Time Regulations 1999 *Industrial Law Journal* 29, 167-171.

Barnard, Catherine (2006) *EC Employment Law* 3rd edn (Oxford University Press, Oxford).

Barnard, Catherine (2008a) Social Dumping or Dumping Socialism? *Cambridge Law Journal* 67, 262-264.

Barnard, Catherine (2008b) *Viking* and *Laval*: An Introduction *Cambridge Yearbook of European Legal Studies* 10, 463-92.

Barnard, Catherine (2009a) The UK and Posted Workers: The Effect of Commission v Luxembourg on the Territorial Application of British Labour Law *Industrial Law Journal* 38, 122-132.

Barnard, Catherine (2009b) 'British Jobs for British Workers': The Lindsey Oil Refinery Dispute and the Future of Local Labour Clauses in an Integrated EU Market *Industrial Law Journal* 38, 245-277.

Barnard, Catherine (2012) The Financial Crisis and the Euro Plus Pact: A Labour Lawyer's Perspective *Industrial Law Journal* 41, 98-114.

Barnard, Catherine and Simon Deakin (2000) In Search of Coherence: Social Policy, the Single Market and Fundamental Rights *Industrial Relations Journal* 31, 331-345.

Barnard, Catherine and Simon Deakin (2008) Una ridefinizione del rapporto di lavoro dipendente: flessibilità o sicurezza? *Lavoro e Diritto*, 287-304.

Barnard, Catherine and Simon Deakin (2012) Social Policy and Labour Market Regulation, in *Oxford Handbook of the European Union* eds Erik Jones, Anand Menon and Stephen Weatherill (OUP, Oxford).

Barnard, Catherine and Ivan Hare (2000) Police Discretion and the Rule of Law: Economic Community Rights versus Civil Rights *Modern Law Review* 63, 581-595.

Barnard, Catherine, and Bob Hepple (1999) Indirect Discrimination: Interpreting *Seymour-Smith*, *Cambridge Law Journal* 58, 399-412.

Barnard, Catherine, and Bob Hepple (2000) Substantive Equality *Cambridge Law Journal* 59, 562-585.

Barnard, Catherine, and Tamara Hervey (1998) European Union Employment and Social Policy Survey 1996 and 1997 *Yearbook of European Law*, 18, 613-657.

Barrett, Brenda (1995) Work-induced Stress *Industrial Law Journal* 24, 343-352.

Barrett, Brenda (1996) Stress and the Public Liability of Employers *Industrial Law Journal* 25, 45-55.

Barrett, Brenda (1997) Employers' Criminal Liability Under HSWA 1974 *Industrial Law Journal* 26, 149-158.

Barrett, Brenda (1998) Renaissance of Civil Liability for Breach of Statutory Duty? *Industrial Law Journal* 27, 59-63.

Barrett, Brenda (1999) Compensation for Psychiatric Injury: Have their Lordships Righted a Wrong? *Industrial Law Journal* 28, 263-268.

Barrett, Brenda (2000) Harassment at Work: A Matter of Health and Safety *Journal of Business Law* 214-231.

Barrett, Brenda (2001) Policy Issues Concerning Compensation for Psychiatric Injury *Industrial Law Journal* 30, 110-115.

Barrett, Brenda (2004) Employers' Liability for Stress at the Work Place: Neither Tort nor Breach of Contract? *Industrial Law Journal* 33, 343-349.

Barrett, Brenda (2005) Employers' Liability after *Hatton v Sutherland, Industrial Law Journal* 34, 182-189.

Barrett, Brenda (2008) Liability for Safety Offences: Is the Law Still Fatally Flawed? *Industrial Law Journal* 37, 100-118.

Barrett, Brenda (2009) The Health and Safety (Offences) Act 2009 *Industrial Law Journal* 38, 73-79.

Barrow, Charles (2010) The Employment Relations Act 1999 (Blacklists) Regulations 2010: SI 2010 No 493 *Industrial Law Journal* 39, 300-311.

Bartolomei de to Cruz, Hector G, Geraldo von Potobsky, and Lee Swepston (1996) *The International Labour Organisation: The International Standards System and Basic Human Rights* (Westview Press, Boulder).

Bassett, Philip (1986) *Strike Free: New Industrial Relations in Britain* (Macmillan, London).

Bayliss, F J (1962) *British Wages Councils* (Basil Blackwell, Oxford).

Beatson, J (1991) *The Use and Abuse of Unjust Enrichment: Essays on the Law of Restitution* (Clarendon Press, Oxford).

Beatson, J (1997) Has the Common Law a Future? *Cambridge Law Journal* 56, 291-314.

Beatson, Mark (1995) Progress towards a Flexible Labour Market *Employment Gazette* 103, 55-66.

Beaumont, PB and RID Harris (1991) Trade Union Recognition and Employment Contraction in Britain 1980-84 *British Journal of Industrial Relations* 29, 49-73.

Beck, Matthias and Charles Woolfson (2000) The Regulation of Health and Safety in Britain: from Old Labour to New Labour, *Industrial Relations Journal* 31, 35-49.

Becker, Gary S (1971) *The Economics of Discrimination* 2nd edn (University of Chicago Press, Chicago).

Becker, Gary S (1975) *Human Capital: A Theoretical and Empirical Analysis, with Special Reference to Education* 2nd edn (University of Chicago Press, Chicago).

Belcher, Alice (1997) *Corporate Rescue* (Sweet & Maxwell, London).

Bell, Derrick (1992) An Allegorical Critique of the United States Civil Rights Model, in *Discrimination: the Limits of the Law* eds B A Hepple and Erika Szyszczak (Mansell, London).

Bell, DW and CG Hanson (1987) *Profit-Sharing and Profitability* (Kogan Page, London).

Bell, Mark (2000) Article 13 EC: The European Commission's Anti-discrimination Proposals *Industrial Law Journal* 29, 79-84.

Bell, Mark (2011) Achieving the Objectives of the Part-Time Work Directive? Revisiting the Part-Time Workers Regulations *Industrial Law Journal* 40, 254-279.

Bellace, Janice R (2001) The ILO Declaration of Fundamental Principles and Rights at Work *The International Journal of Comparative Labor Law and Industrial Relations* 17, 269-287.

Benedictus, Roger (1979) Closed Shop Exemptions and Their Wording *Industrial Law Journal* 8, 160-171.

Ben-Israel, Ruth (1988) *International Labour Standards: The Case of Freedom to Strike* (Kluwer, Deventer).

Ben-Israel, Ruth (ed) (1994) *Strikes and Lock-outs in Industrialized Market Economies* (Kluwer, Deventer-Boston).

Bennett, Michael (1994) Practicability of Reinstatement and Re-engagement Orders *Industrial Law Journal* 23, 164-166.

Bercusson, Brian (1976) The New Fair Wages Policy: Schedule 11 to the Employment Protection Act *Industrial Law Journal* 5, 129-147.

Bercusson, Brian (1977) One Hundred Years of Conspiracy and Protection of Property: Time for a Change *Modern Law Review* 40, 268-292.

Bercusson, Brian (1978) *Fair Wages Resolutions* (Mansell, London).

Bercusson, Brian (1986) Workers, Corporate Enterprise and the Law, in *Labour Law in Britain* ed Roy Lewis (Basil Blackwell, Oxford).

Bercusson, Brian (1990) The European Community's Charter of Fundamental Social Rights *Modern Law Review* 53, 624-642.

Bercusson, Brian (1992) Maastricht: a Fundamental Change in European Labour Law *Industrial Relations Journal* 23, 177-191.

Bercusson, Brian (1994a) The Dynamic of European Labour Law after Maastricht *Industrial Law Journal* 23, 1-31.

Bercusson, Brian (1994b) *Working Time in Britain: Towards a European Model Part I: The European Union Directive* (Institute of Employment Rights, London).

Bercusson, Brian (1994c) *Working Time in Britain: Towards a European Model Part II: Collective Bargaining in Europe and the UK* (Institute of Employment Rights, London).

Bercusson, Brian (1994d) Collective Bargaining and the Protection of Social Rights in Europe, in *Human Rights and Labour Law* eds KD Ewing, CA Gearty and BA Hepple (Mansell, London).

Bercusson, Brian (2009) *European Labour Law* 2nd edn (Cambridge University Press, Cambridge).

Bercusson, Brian (2000) Transnational Trade Union Rights, in *Legal Regulation of the Employment Relation* eds Hugh Collins, Paul Davies and Roger Rideout (Kluwer, London).

Bercusson, Brian (2001) A European Agenda?, in *Employment Rights at Work* ed KD Ewing (Institute of Employment Rights, London).

Bercusson, Brian (2002) The European Social Model Comes to Britain *Industrial Law Journal* 31, 209-244.

Bercusson, Brian (2004) Episodes on the Path Towards the European Social Model: The EU Charter of Fundamental Rights and the Convention on the Future of Europe in *The Future of Labour Law: Liber Amicorum Sir Bob Hepple QC* ed Catherine Barnard, Simon Deakin and Gillian S Morris (Hart Publishing, Oxford).

Bercusson, Brian (2007) The Trade Union and the European Union: Judgment Day *European Law Journal* 13, 278-308.

Bercusson, Brian, Ulrich Mückenberger and Alain Supiot (1992) *Application du Droit du Travail et Diversité Culturelle en Europe* Etude réalisée pour le Ministère du Travail, de l'Emploi et de la Formation Professionelle (Nantes, ARSH).

Bercusson, Brian, Mike Clancy, Keith Ewing, John Foster, Sandy Fredman, Aileen McColgan, Rod Robertson and Stephen Wood (1998) *Need to be Heard at Work?: Recognition Laws – Lessons From Abroad* (Institute of Employment Rights, London).

Bercusson, Brian, Simon Deakin, Pertti Koistinen, Yota Kravaritou, Ulrich Mückenberger, Alain Supiot and Bruno Veneziani (1997) *A Manifesto for Social Europe* (European Trade Union Institute, Brussels).

Bernier, Jean (1994) *Strikes and Essential Services* (Les Presses de l'Université Laval, Quebec).

Betten, Lammy (1993) *International Labour Law* (Kluwer, Deventer-Boston).

Betten, Lammy, and Vivienne Shrubshall (1998) The Concept of Positive Sex Discrimination in Community Law – Before and After the Treaty of Amsterdam *International Journal of Comparative Labour Law and Industrial Relations* 14, 65-80.

Biagi, Marco (1998b) The Implementation of the Amsterdam Treaty with regard to Employment: Co-ordination or Convergence? *International Journal of Comparative Labour Law and Industrial Relations* 14, 325-337.

Biagi, M and M Tiraboschi (2010) Forms of Employee Representational Participation, in *Comparative Labour Law and Industrial Relations in Industrialised Market Economies* 10th edn ed R Blanpain (Kluwer Law International, The Hague).

Bird, D (1991) Industrial Stoppages in 1990 *Employment Gazette* 99, 379-390.

Bird, D, M Stevens and A Yates (1991) Membership of Trade Unions in 1989 *Employment Gazette* 99, 347-353.

Birks, Peter and Chin Nyuk Yin (1995) On the Nature of Undue Influence in Good Faith and Fault in Contract Law in *Good Faith and Fault in Contract Law*, ed Jack Beatson and Daniel Friedmann (Clarendon Press, Oxford).

Bishop, William, and John Kay (1987) Taxation and the Rule in *Gourley's* Case *Law Quarterly Review* 193, 211-233.

Black, Ole, Ian Richardson and Rhys Herbert (2004) Jobs in the Public Sector mid-2003 *Labour Market Trends* (July), 271-281.

Blackburn, Sheila C (2009) Curse or Cure? Why Was the Enactment of Britain's 1909 Trade Boards Act so Controversial? *British Journal of Industrial Relations* 47, 214-239.

Blair, Tony (1998) *The Third Way: New Politics for a New Century* (Fabian Society, London).

Blake, Leslie (1991) 'Compensation for Child Care Costs' *New Law Journal* 141, 1734-1743.

Blake, Nicholas and Raza Husain (2003) *Immigration, Asylum and Human Rights* (OUP, Oxford).

Blanchflower, David G (2007) International Patterns of Union Membership *British Journal of Industrial Relations* 45, 1-28.

Blanchflower, David, Neil Millward and Andrew Oswald (1988) *Unionisation and Employment Behaviour* Centre for Labour Economics Discussion Paper 339 (London School of Economics, London).

Blandon, Jo, Stephen Machin and John Van Reenan (2006) Have Unions Turned the Corner? New Evidence on Recent Trends in Union Recognition in UK Firms *British Journal of Industrial Relations* 44, 169-190.

Blank, Rebecca (1994) Does a Larger Social Safety Net Mean Less Economic Flexibility?, in *Working Under Different Rules* ed Richard B Freeman (Russell Sage Foundation, New York).

Blanpain, Roger (ed) (1988) *Legal and Contractual Limitations on Working Time in the European Community* European Foundation for the Improvement of Living and Working Conditions (OOPEC, Luxembourg).

Blanpain, Roger (ed) (1999) *Private Employment Agencies* Bulletin of Comparative Labour Relations No 36 (Kluwer, The Hague).

Blanpain, Roger (ed) (2001) *The Council of Europe and the Social Challenges of the XX1st Century* (Kluwer, The Hague).

Blanpain, Roger (2010) Multinational Enterprises and Codes of Conduct in *Comparative Labour Law and Industrial Relations in Industrialized Market Economies* 10th edn, ed Roger Blanpain (Wolters Kluwer, The Netherlands).

Blanpain, Roger, and Chris Engels (1993) *European Labour Law* (Kluwer, Deventer-Boston).

Blanpain, Roger and Ronnie Graham (eds) (2004) *Temporary Agency Work and the Information Society* (Kluwer Law International, The Hague).

Blom-Cooper, Sir Louis and Richard Drabble (2010) GCHQ revisited *Public Law* 18-24.

Bogg, Alan L (2005) Employment Relations Act 2004: Another False Dawn for Collectivism? *Industrial Law Journal* 34, 72-82.

Bogg, Alan (2006) Politics, Community, Democracy: Appraising CAC Decision-Making in the First Five Years of Schedule A1 *Industrial Law Journal* 35, 245-271.

Bogg, Alan (2009a) *The Democratic Aspects of Trade Union Recognition* (Hart Publishing, Oxford).

Bogg, Alan (2009b) The Mouse that Never Roared: Unfair Practices and Union Recognition *Industrial Law Journal* 38, 390-402.

Bogg, Alan (2010a) Sham Self-employment in the Court of Appeal *Law Quarterly Review* 126, 166-171.

Bogg, Alan (2010b) *Bournemouth University Higher Education Corpn v Buckland*: Re-establishing Orthodoxy at the Expense of Coherence? *Industrial Law Journal* 39, 408-419.

Bogg, Alan L (2011) Good Faith in the Contract of Employment: A Case of the English Reserve *Comparative Labor Law and Policy Journal*, 32, 729-772.

Bond, Abigail (1995) The Young Persons Directive *Industrial Law Journal* 24, 377-382.

Boon, Andrew, Peter Urwin and Valeriya Karuk (2011) What Difference Does it Make? Facilitative Judicial Mediation of Discrimination Cases in Employment Tribunals *Industrial Law Journal* 40, 45-81.

Bourn, Colin (1992) *Sex Discrimination Law: A Review* (Institute of Employment Rights, London).

Bowers, John, and Andrew Clarke (1981) Unfair Dismissal and Managerial Prerogative: a study of 'Some other Substantial Reason' *Industrial Law Journal* 10, 34-44.

Bowers, John and Jeremy Lewis (2005) Non-Economic Damage in Unfair Dismissal Cases: What's Left after *Dunnachie*? in *Industrial Law Journal* 34, 83-95.

Bowers, John, and Elena Moran (2002) Justification in Direct Sex Discrimination: Breaking the Taboo *Industrial Law Journal* 31, 307-320.

Bowers, John, Michael Duggan and David Reade (2004) *The Law of Industrial Action and Trade Union Recognition* (Oxford University Press, Oxford).

Bowers, John, Jack Mitchell and Jeremy Lewis (1999) *Whistleblowing: The New Law* (Sweet & Maxwell, London).

Bowers, John, Elena Moran and Simon Honeyball (2003) Justification in Direct Sex Discrimination: A Reply *Industrial Law Journal* 32, 185-187.

Braverman, Harry (1974) *Labour and Monopoly Capital* (Monthly Review Press, New York).

Briggs, Chris (2005) Lockout Law in a Comparative Perspective: Corporatism, Pluralism and Neo-Liberalism *International Journal of Comparative Labour Law and Industrial Relations* 21, 481-502.

Brillat, Regis (1996) A New Protocol to the European Social Charter Providing for Collective Complaints *European Human Rights Law Review*, 52-62.

Brodie, Douglas (1996) The Heart of the Matter: Mutual Trust and Confidence *Industrial Law Journal* 25, 121-136.

Brodie, Douglas (1998a) Specific Performance and Employment Contracts *Industrial Law Journal* 27, 37-48.

Brodie, Douglas (1998b) Beyond Exchange: the New Contract of Employment *Industrial Law Journal*, 27, 79-102.

Brodie, Douglas (1999a) A Fair Deal at Work *Oxford Journal of Legal Studies* 19, 83-98.

Brodie, Douglas (1999b) Wrongful Dismissal and Mutual Trust *Industrial Law Journal* 28, 260-262.

Brodie, Douglas (2001a) Mutual Trust and the Values of the Employment Contract *Industrial Law Journal* 30, 84-100.

Brodie, Douglas, (2001b) Legal Coherence and the Employment Revolution *Law Quarterly Review* 117, 604- 625.

Brodie, Douglas (2002) Fair Dealing and the Disciplinary Process *Industrial Law Journal* 31, 294-297.

Brodie, Douglas (2003) *A History of British Labour Law 1867-1945* (Hart Publishing, Oxford).

Brodie, Douglas (2004) Protecting Dignity in the Workplace: the Vitality of Mutual Trust and Confidence *Industrial Law Journal* 33, 349-354.

Brodie, Douglas (2008) Mutual Trust and Confidence: Catalysts, Constraints and Commonality *Industrial Law Journal* 37, 329-346.

Brodie, Douglas (2011) How Relational is the Employment Contract? *Industrial Law Journal* 40, 232-253.

Brodin, Emma (1996) The Employment Status of Ministers of Religion *Industrial Law Journal* 25, 211-224.

Brodin, Emma (1997) *Sex Discrimination in Employment within the Church of England*, Ph D, University of Huddersfield, 1997.

Brown, Damian (1994) Remedies for Breach of Employment Contracts *Industrial Law Journal* 23, 331-333.

Brown, Damien and Keith Ewing (2000) Human Rights at Work: Possibilities and Problems, in *Human Rights at Work* ed Keith Ewing (Institute of Employment Rights, London).

Brown, Damian and Aileen McColgan (1992) UK Employment Law and the International Labour Organisation: The Spirit of Cooperation? *Industrial Law Journal*, 21, 265-279.

Brown, William (1972) A Consideration of Custom and Practice *British Journal of Industrial Relations* 10, 42-61.

Brown, William (1973) *Piecework Bargaining* (Basil Blackwell, Oxford).

Brown, William (ed) (1981) *The Changing Contours of British Industrial Relations: A Survey of Manufacturing Industry* (Blackwell, Oxford).

Brown, William (1992) Bargaining Structure and the Impact of Law, in *Legal Intervention in Industrial Relations: Gains and Losses* ed William McCarthy (Blackwell, Oxford).

Brown, William (1993) The Contraction of Collective Bargaining in Britain *British Journal of Industrial Relations* 31, 189-200.

Brown, William (2000) Putting Partnership into Practice in Britain *British Journal of Industrial Relations* 38, 299-316.

Brown, William (2008) Review of P Davies and M Freedland *Towards a More Flexible Labour Market* (2007) *Industrial Law Journal* 37, 188-189.

Brown, William (2009) The Process of Fixing the British National Minimum Wage 1997-2007 *British Journal of Industrial Relations* 47, 429-443.

Brown, William (2010) Negotiation and Collective Bargaining in *Industrial Relations: Theory and Practice* 3rd edn ed Trevor Colling and Michael Terry (Wiley, Chichester).

Brown, William and David Nash (2008) What has been happening to collective bargaining under New Labour? Interpreting WERS 2004 *Industrial Relations Journal* 39, 91-103.

Brown, William and Sarah Oxenbridge (2004) Trade Unions and Collective Bargaining: Law and the Future of Collectivism, in *The Future of Labour Law: Liber Amicorum Sir Bob Hepple QC* ed Catherine Barnard, Simon Deakin and Gillian S Morris (Hart Publishing, Oxford).

Brown, William, and Sushil Wadwhani (1990) The Economic Effects of Industrial Relations Legislation since 1979 *National Institute Economic Review*, 57-70.

Brown, William, and Janet Walsh (1990) Pay Determination in Britain in the 1980s: the Anatomy of Decentralisation *Oxford Review of Economic Policy* 7, 44-59.

Brown, William, Simon Deakin and Paul Ryan (1997) The Effects of British Industrial Relations Legislation 1979-1997 *National Institute Economic Review* 161, 69-83.

Brown, William, Paul Marginson and Janet Walsh (2003) The Management of Pay as the Influence of Collective Bargaining Diminishes in *Industrial Relations: Theory and Practice* 2nd edn ed Paul Edwards (Blackwell Publishing, Oxford).

Brown, William, Simon Deakin, Maria Hudson and Cliff Pratten (2001) The Limits of Statutory Trade Union Recognition *Industrial Relations Journal* 32, 180-194.

Brown, William, Simon Deakin, David Nash, and Sarah Oxenbridge (2000) The Employment Contract: from Collective Procedures to Individual Rights *British Journal of Industrial Relations* 38, 611-629.

Browne-Wilkinson, The Hon Mr Justice (1982) The Role of the Employment Appeal Tribunal in the 1980s *Industrial Law Journal* 11, 69-77.

Brudney, James J (2007) Recrafting a Trojan Horse: Thoughts on Workplace Governance in Light of Recent British Labor Law Developments *Comparative Labor Law and Policy Journal* 28, 193-212.

Bruun, Niklas, Klaus Lörcher and Isabelle Schömann (eds) (2012) *The Lisbon Treaty and Social Europe* (Hart, Oxford).

Bryson, Alex and Rafael Gomez (2005) Why Have Workers Stopped Joining Unions? The Rise in Never-Membership in Britain *British Journal of Industrial Relations* 43, 67-92.

Buchanan, John and Simon Deakin (2012) Pension Fund Governance: Evolution of the Trust Model CBR Working Paper, September (Cambridge, Centre for Business Research).

Büchtemann, Christoph (1990) More Jobs through Less Employment Protection? Evidence for West Germany *Labour* 3, 23-56.

Büchtemann, Christoph (1993) Introduction: Employment Security and Labor Markets, in *Employment Security and Labor Market Behavior. Inter-Disciplinary Approaches and International Evidence* ed Christoph Büchtemann (Cornell University Press, Ithaca NY).

Büchtemann, Christoph, and Sigrid Quack (1989) 'Bridges' or 'traps'? Non-standard Employment, in the Federal Republic of Germany, in *Precarious Jobs in Labour Market Regulation* eds Gerry and Janine Rodgers (International Institute for Labour Studies, Geneva).

Burchell, Brendan, Simon Deakin and Sheila Honey (1999) *The Employment Status of Workers in Non-standard Employment*. EMAR research series 6 (Department of Trade and Industry, London).

Burton, J (1979) *The Trojan Horse: Union Power in British Politics* (Adam Smith Institute, London).

Burton, Sir Michael (2005) The Employment Appeal Tribunal: October 2002 - July 2005 *Industrial Law Journal* 34, 273-283.

Buxton, Richard (2011) The Limited Freedom of Local Authorities: a Note on Shoesmith *Public Law*, 698-702.

Cabrelli, David (2011) The Hierarchy of Differing Behavioural Standards of Review in Labour Law *Industrial Law Journal* 40, 146-180.

Caraciollo di Tirella, Eugenia (1999) Recent Developments in Pregnancy and Maternity Rights *Industrial Law Journal* 28, 276-282.

Card, Richard (2000) *Public Order Law* (Jordans, Bristol).

Carley, M (2008) *Industrial Relations Developments in 2007: Collective bargaining Developments* (European Industrial Relations Observatory Online: www.eurofound.europa.eu/eiro).

Carley, Mark and Mark Hall (2000) The Implementation of the European Works Councils Directive *Industrial Law Journal* 29, 103-124.

Carty, Hazel (1988) Intentional Violation of Economic Interests: The Limits of Common Law Liability *Law Quarterly Review* 104, 250-285.

Carty, Hazel (2008) The Economic Torts in the 21st Century *Law Quarterly Review* 124, 641-674.

Carty, Hazel (2010) *An Analysis of the Economic Torts* 2nd edn (Oxford University Press, Oxford).

Casey, Bernard (1988) *Temporary Employment in Britain* (Policy Studies Institute, London).

Casey, Bernard, Hilary Metcalf and Neil Millward (1997) *Employers' Use of Flexible Labour* (Policy Studies Institute, London).

Cavalier, Stephen and Richard Arthur (2006) *Providing a Service? The New TUPE Regulations 2006* (Institute of Employment Rights, Liverpool)

Cella, GP and T Treu (2007) National Trade Union Movements in *Comparative Labour Law and Industrial Relations in Industrialized Market Economies* 9th edn, ed Roger Blanpain (Wolters Kluwer, The Netherlands).

Charlwood, Andy (2003) Willingness to unionize amongst non-union workers in *Representing Workers: Trade Union Recognition and Membership in Britain* ed Howard Gospel and Stephen Wood (Routledge, London).

Charlwood, Andy (2004a) Influences on Trade Union Organising Effectiveness in Britain *British Journal of Industrial Relations* 42, 69-93.

Charlwood, Andy (2004b) The New Generation of Trade Union Leaders and Prospects for Union Revitalization *British Journal of Industrial Relations* 42, 379-397.

Charlwood, Andy and Mike Terry (2007) 21st-century models of employee representation: structures, processes and outcomes *Industrial Relations Journal* 38, 320-337.

Cheetham, Simon (2006) *Age Discrimination: The New Law* (Jordans, Bristol).

Christian, TJ and KD Ewing (1987) Labouring under the Canadian Constitution *Industrial Law Journal* 17, 73-91.

Churchill, Robin R and Urfan Khaliq (2004) The Collective Complaints System of the European Social Charter: An Effective Mechanism for Ensuring Compliance with Economic and Social Rights? *European Journal of International Law* 15, 417-456.

Clancy, Mike and Roger Seifert (2000) *Fairness at Work? The Disciplinary and Grievance Provisions of the 1999 Employment Relations Act* (Institute of Employment Rights, London).

Clark, Jon (1999) Adversarial and Investigative Approaches to the Arbitral Resolution of Dismissal Disputes: A Comparison of South Africa and the UK *Industrial Law Journal* 28, 319-335.

Clark, Jon and Mark Hall (1992) The Cinderella Directive? Employee Rights to Information about Conditions applicable to their Contract or Employment Relationship *Industrial Law Journal* 21, 106-118.

Clark, Jon, and Lord Wedderburn (1983) Modern Labour Law: Problems, Functions and Policies, in *Labour Law and Industrial Relations: Building on Kahn-Freund* eds Lord Wedderburn, Roy Lewis and Jonathan Clark (Clarendon Press, Oxford).

Clark, Jon, and Lord Wedderburn (1987) Juridification – A Universal Trend?, in *Juridification of Social Spheres* ed Gunther Teubner (Walter de Gruyter, Berlin).

Clarke, Linda (1999) Mutual Trust and Confidence, Fiduciary Relationships and the Duty of Disclosure *Industrial Law Journal* 28, 348-360.

Claydon, Tim (1996) Union De-Recognition: a Re-Examination in *Contemporary Industrial Relations*, ed Ian J. Beardwell (Oxford University Press, Oxford).

Clayton, Gina (2004) *Textbook on Immigration and Asylum Law* (OUP, Oxford).

Clayton, Richard and Hugh Tomlinson (2009) *The Law of Human Rights, Vol 1*, 2nd edn (OUP, Oxford).

Clegg, Hugh (1985) *A History of British Trade Unions since 1889 Volume II: 1911-1933* (Clarendon Press, Oxford).

Clerk and Lindsell (2010) *Clerk and Lindsell on Torts*, 20th edn (Sweet and Maxwell, London).

Cockburn, David (1995) Changes to the Industrial Relations System *Industrial Law Journal* 24, 285-291.

Cockburn, David (2006) The Certification Officer in *The Changing Institutional Face of British Employment Relations* ed Linda Dickens and Alan C Neal (Kluwer Law International, The Netherlands).

Colaianni, Tia (1996) *European Works Councils* (Sweet and Maxwell, London).

Collard, R and B Dale (1989) Quality Circles, in *Personnel Management in Britain* ed Keith Sisson (Basil Blackwell, Oxford).

Colling, Trevor (2006) What Space for Unions on the Floor of Rights? Trade Unions and the Enforcement of Statutory Individual Employment Rights *Industrial Law Journal* 35, 140-160.

Collins, Hugh (1982) Capitalist Discipline and Corporatist Law *Industrial Law Journal* 11, 78-93, 170-177.

Collins, Hugh (1986) Market Power, Bureaucratic Power and the Contract of Employment *Industrial Law Journal* 15, 1-15.

Collins, Hugh (1989a) Employee Share Option Schemes *Industrial Law Journal* 18, 54-59.

Collins, Hugh (1989b) Transfer of Undertakings and Insolvency *Industrial Law Journal* 18, 144-158.

Collins, Hugh (1989c) Labour Law as a Vocation *Law Quarterly Review* 105, 468-484.

Collins, Hugh (1990a) Ascription of Legal Responsibility to Groups in Complex Patterns of Economic Integration *Modern Law Review* 53, 731-744.

Collins, Hugh (1990b) Independent Contractors and the Challenge of Vertical Disintegration to Employment Protection Laws *Oxford Journal of Legal Studies* 10, 353-380.

Collins, Hugh (1993) *Justice in Dismissal* (Clarendon Press, Oxford).

Collins, Hugh (1994) CCT, Equal Pay and Market Forces *Industrial Law Journal* 23, 341-345.

Collins, Hugh (1997) The Productive Disintegration of Labour Law *Industrial Law Journal* 26, 295-309.

Collins, Hugh (2000a) Justifications and Techniques of Legal Regulation of the Employment Relation, in *Legal Regulation of the Employment Relation* eds Hugh Collins, Paul Davies and Roger Rideout (Kluwer, London).

Collins, Hugh (2000b) Employment Rights of Casual Workers *Industrial Law Journal* 29, 73-78.

Collins, Hugh (2000c) Finding the Right Direction for the 'Industrial Jury' *Industrial Law Journal* 29, 293-296.

Collins, Hugh (2001a) Is There a Third Way in Labour Law?, in *Labour Law in an Era of Globalisation: Transformative Practices and Possibilities* eds. Joanne Conaghan, Michael Fischl and Karl Klare (OUP, Oxford).

Collins, Hugh (2001b) Regulating the Employment Relation for Competitiveness *Industrial Law Journal* 30, 1-31.

Collins, Hugh (2001c) Claim for Unfair Dismissal *Industrial Law Journal* 30, 305-309.

Collins, Hugh (2003) *Employment Law* (OUP, Oxford).

Collins, Hugh (2004) *Nine Proposals for the Reform of the Law on Unfair Dismissal* (Institute of Employment Rights, London).

Collins, Hugh (2006) The Protection of Civil Liberties in the Workplace *Modern Law Review* 69, 619-643.

Collins, Hugh (2007) Legal Responses to the Standard Form Contract of Employment *Industrial Law Journal* 36, 2-18.

Collins, Hugh, Paul Davies and Roger Rideout (eds) (2000) *Legal Regulation of the Employment Relation* (Kluwer, London).

Collins, Lawrence, CGJ Morse, David McClean, Adrian Briggs, Jonathan Harris and Campbell McLaghlan (2008) *Dicey, Morris and Collins on the Conflict of Laws* 14th edn (Sweet and Maxwell, London).

Conaghan, Joanne (1996) Gendered Harms and the Law of Tort: Remedying Sexual Harassment *Oxford Journal of Legal Studies* 16, 407-431.

Conaghan, Joanne, and Louise Chudleigh (1987) Women in Confinement: Can Labour Law Deliver the Goods? *Journal of Law and Society* 14, 133-147.

Connolly, Michael (1998) Discrimination Law: Requirements and Preferences *Industrial Law Journal* 27, 133-142.

Connolly, Michael (2000) Discrimination Law: Victimisation *Industrial Law Journal* 29, 305-311.

Coppel, Jason (1997) Horizontal Effect of Directives *Industrial Law Journal* 26, 69-73.

Coppel, Jason (1998) *The Human Rights Act 1998: Enforcing the European Convention in the Domestic Courts* (Wiley, Chichester).

Corby, Susan (2002) On Parole: Prison Service Industrial Relations *Industrial Relations Journal* 33, 286-297.

Corby, Susan and Paul L. Latreille (2011) *The role of lay members in employment rights cases – survey evidence* (available on University of Greenwich website).

Corby, Susan and Paul Latreille (2012) Tripartite adjudication – an endangered species *Industrial Relations Journal* 43, 94-109.

Cordova, Efren (1985) Strikes in the Public Service: Some Determinants and Trends *International Labour Review* 124, 163-179.

Cornford, Tom and Maurice Sunkin (2001) The Bowman Report, Access and the Recent Reforms of the Judicial Review Procedure *Public Law*, 11-20.

Countouris, Nicola and Mark Freedland (2010) Injunctions, *Cyanamid*, and the Corrosion of the Right to Strike in the UK *European Labour Law Journal* 1, 489-507.

Countouris, Nicola and Rachel Horton (2009) The Temporary Agency Work Directive: Another Broken Promise? *Industrial Law Journal* 38, 329-338.

Cousins, Christine (1994) A Comparison of the Labour Market Position of Women in Spain and the UK with Reference to the 'Flexible' Labour Debate *Work, Employment and Society* 8, 45-67.

Coutts, Ken, and Robert Rowthorn (1995) *Employment in the United Kingdom: Trends and Prospects* ESRC Centre for Business Research, University of Cambridge, Working Paper No 3.

Couturier, Gérard (1988) *Droit du Travail I: Les Relations Individuels de Travail* (PUF, Paris).

Craig, Christine, Jill Rubery, Roger Tarling and Frank Wilkinson (1982) *Labour Market Structure, Industrial Organisation and Low Pay* (CUP, Cambridge).

Craig, Christine, Jill Rubery, Roger Tarling and Frank Wilkinson (1985) Economic, Social and Political Factors in the Operation of the Labour Market in *New Approaches to Economic Life* eds Bryan Roberts, Ruth Finnegan and Duncan Gallie (MUP, Manchester).

Craig, John DR and Hazel D Oliver (1998) The Right to Privacy in the Workplace: Should the Private Sector be Concerned? *Industrial Law Journal* 27, 49-59.

Craig, PP (1996) Proceeding Outside Order 53: A Modified Test? *Law Quarterly Review* 112, 531-535.

Craven, Matthew (1998) *The International Covenant on Economic, Social and Cultural Rights* (Clarendon Press, Oxford).

Creigh, Stephen, Ceridwen Roberts, Andrea Gorman and Paul Sawyer (1986) Self-employment in Britain. Results from the Labour Force Surveys 1981-1984 *Employment Gazette* 94, 193-194.

Creighton, Breen (1994) The ILO and Protection of Freedom of Association in the United Kingdom, in *Human Rights and Labour Law: Essays for Paul O'Higgins* eds KD Ewing, CA Gearty and BA Hepple (Mansell, London).

Creighton, Breen (2004b) The Future of Labour Law: Is there a Role for International Labour Standards? in *The Future of Labour Law: Liber Amicorum Sir Bob Hepple* QC ed Catherine Barnard, Simon Deakin and Gillian S Morris (Hart Publishing, Oxford).

Creighton, B (2010) Freedom of Association in *Comparative Labour Law and Industrial Relations in Industrialized Market Economies* 10th edn, ed Roger Blanpain (Wolters Kluwer, The Netherlands).

Cressy, P (1993) Employee Participation in *The Social Dimension: Employment Policy in the United Kingdom* ed M Gold (Macmillan, London).

Cripps, Yvonne (1995) *The Legal Implications of Disclosure in the Public Interest* 2nd edn (Sweet and Maxwell, London).

Cripps, Yvonne (2000) The Public Interest Disclosure Act 1998, in *Freedom of Expression and Freedom of Information* ed Jack Beatson and Yvonne Cripps (Oxford University Press, Oxford).

Crouch, Colin (2000) The Snakes and Ladders of Twenty-First-Century Trade Unionism *Oxford Review of Economic Policy* 16, 70-83.

Cullen, Holly (2000a) The Collective Complaints Mechanism of the European Social Charter *European Law Review* 25, HR 18-29.

Cullen , Holly (2000b) The Interaction of Forms of Regulation in International Labour Law, in *Legal Regulation of the Employment Relation* ed Hugh Collins, Paul Davies and Roger Rideout (Kluwer, London).

Cully, Mark and Stephen Woodland (1997) Trade Union Membership and Recognition *Labour Market Trends*, June, 231-239.

Cully, Mark, Stephen Woodland, Andrew O'Reilly and Gill Dix (1999) *Britain at Work. As depicted by the 1998 Workplace Employment Relations Survey* (Routledge, London).

Cunningham, Naomi (1995) Sex Discrimination: Equal but Different? *Industrial Law Journal* 24, 177-181.

Curran, Simon (1994) Unfairly Dismissed though still Employed? *Hogg v Dover College* Revisited *Industrial Law Journal* 23, 166-169.

Curtin, Deirdre (1992) State Liability under Community Law: A New Remedy for Private Parties *Industrial Law Journal* 21, 74-81.

Daniel, WW (1985) United Kingdom, in *Managing Workforce Reduction* ed M Cross (Croom Helm, London).

Daniel, WW (1987) *Workplace Industrial Relations and Technical Change* (Frances Pinter/PSI, London).

Daniel, WW (1990) *The Unemployed Flow* (Policy Studies Institute, London).

Daniel, WW and Neil Millward (1983) *Workplace Industrial Relations in Britain: The DE/PSI/SSRC Survey* (Heinemann Educational Books, London).

Daniel, WW and Elizabeth Stilgoe (1978) *The Impact of Employment Protection Laws* (Policy Studies Institute, London).

Dashwood, Alan (2008) *Viking* and *Laval*: Issues of Horizontal Direct Effect *Cambridge Yearbook of European Legal Studies* 10, 525-540.

Daübler, Wolfgang (1991) *Das Arbeitsrecht* (Rowohlt, Reinbek).

Daübler, Wolfgang, and Martine le Friant (1985) Un récent exemple de flexibilisation législative: la loi allemande pour la promotion de l'emploi du 26 avril 1986 *Droit Social*, 715-720.

Davidov, Guy (2004) Collective Bargaining Laws: Purpose and Scope *International Journal of Comparative Labour Law and Industrial Relations* 20, 81-106.

Davidov, Guy (2005) Who is a Worker? *Industrial Law Journal* 34, 57-71.

Davies, Anne CL (2004) *Perspectives on Labour Law* (CUP, Cambridge).

Davies, ACL (2006a) The Right to Strike Versus Freedom of Establishment in EC Law: The Battle Commences *Industrial Law Journal* 35, 75-86

Davies, ACL (2006b) Casual Workers and Continuity of Employment *Industrial Law Journal* 35, 196-201.

Davies, ACL (2007) The Contract for Intermittent Employment *Industrial Law Journal* 36, 102-118.

Davies, ACL (2008) One Step Forward, Two Steps Back? The Viking and Laval Cases in the ECJ *Industrial Law Journal* 37, 126-148.

Davies, A.C.L. (2009) Sensible Thinking About Sham Transactions: *Protectacoat Firthglow Ltd v Szilagyi, Industrial Law Journal* 38, 318-328.

Davies, A.C.L. (2010) The Implementation of the Directive on Temporary Agency Work in the UK: A Missed Opportunity *European Labour Law Journal* 1, 303-327

Davies, Paul (1989) Acquired Rights, Creditors' Rights, Freedom of Contract, and Industrial Democracy *Yearbook of European Law* 9, 21-53.

Davies, Paul (1992) The Emergence of European Labour Law, in *Legal Intervention in Industrial Relations: Gains and Losses* ed William McCarthy (Blackwell, Oxford).

Davies, Paul (1994a) Employee Claims in Insolvency: Corporate Rescues and Preferential Claims *Industrial Law Journal* 23, 141-151.

Davies, Paul (1994b) A Challenge to Single Channel *Industrial Law Journal* 23, 272-285.

Davies, Paul (1995) Market Integration and Social Policy in the Court of Justice *Industrial Law Journal* 24, 49-77.

Davies, Paul (1996) The European Court of Justice, National Courts and the Member States, in *European Community Labour Law: Principles and Perspectives. Liber Amicorum Lord Wedderburn* eds Paul Davies, Antoine Lyon-Caen, Silvana Sciarra and Spiros Simitis (Clarendon Press, Oxford).

Davies, Paul (1997) Posted Workers: Single Market or Protection of National Labour Law Systems? *Common Market Law Review* 34, 571-602.

Davies, Paul (1998) Amendments to the Acquired Rights Directive *Industrial Law Journal* 27, 365-375.

Davies, Paul (2001) Transfers – the UK Will Have to Make Up Its Own Mind *Industrial Law Journal* 30, 231-235.

Davies, Paul (2003) Workers on the Board of the European Company? *Industrial Law Journal* 32, 75-96.

Davies, Paul and Mark Freedland (1983) *Kahn-Freund's Labour and the Law* (Stevens and Sons, London).

Davies, Paul and Mark Freedland (1984) *Labour Law: Text and Materials* 2nd edn (Weidenfeld and Nicolson, London).

Davies, Paul and Mark Freedland (1993) *Labour Legislation and Public Policy* (Clarendon Press, Oxford).

Davies, Paul and Mark Freedland (1997) The Impact of Public Law on Labour Law 1972-1997 *Industrial Law Journal*, 26, 311-335.

Davies, Paul and Mark Freedland (2000) Employees, Workers and the Autonomy of Labour Law, in *Legal Regulation of the Employment Relation* eds Hugh Collins, Paul Davies and Roger Rideout (Kluwer, London).

Davies, Paul and Mark Freedland (2004) Changing Perspectives on the Employment Relationship in British Labour Law, in *The Future of Labour Law: Liber Amicorum Sir Bob Hepple QC* eds Catherine Barnard, Simon Deakin and Gillian S Morris (Hart Publishing, Oxford).

Davies, Paul and Mark Freedland (2007) *Towards a More Flexible Labour Market. Labour Legislation and Regulation since the 1990s* (Oxford University Press, Oxford).

Davies, Paul and Claire Kilpatrick (2004) UK Worker Representation After Single Channel *Industrial Law Journal* 33, 121-151.

Davies, Paul, Antoine Lyon-Caen, Silvana Sciarra and Spiros Simitis (eds) (1996) *European Community Labour Law: Principles and Perspectives. Liber Amicorum Lord Wedderburn* (Clarendon Press, Oxford).

Davies, Robert (2004) Contracting Out and the Retention of Employment Model in the National Health Service *Industrial Law Journal* 33, 95-120.

Davis, JE (1868) *The Master and Servant Act 1867* (Butterworths, London).

Dawe, Alex and Fiona Neathey (2008) *ACAS Conciliation in Collective Employment Disputes* (ACAS, London).

Dawson, Sandra, Paul Willman, Alan Clinton and Martin Bamford (1988) *Safety at Work: the limits of self-regulation* (Cambridge University Press, Cambridge).

De Búrca, Gráinne (2001 The Drafting of the European Union Charter of Human Rights *European Law Review* 26, 126-138.

De Schutter, Olivier and Simon Deakin (2005) *Social Rights and Market Forces: Is Open Coordination the Future for European Employment and Social Policy?* (Bruylant, Brussels).

Deakin, Simon (1986) Labour Law and the Developing Employment Relation-ship in the UK *Cambridge Journal of Economics* 10, 225-246.

Deakin, Simon (1989) *Contract, Labour Law and the Developing Employment Relationship* PhD Thesis, University of Cambridge.

Deakin, Simon (1990a) Equality under a Market Order: the Employment Act 1989 *Industrial Law Journal* 19, 1-23.

Deakin, Simon (1990b) The Floor of Rights in European Labour Law *New Zealand Journal of Industrial Relations* 15, 219-240.

Deakin, Simon (1991) Legal Change and Labour Market Restructuring in Western Europe and the US *New Zealand Journal of Industrial Relations* 16, 109-125.

Deakin, Simon (1992) Logical Deductions? Wages Law before and after *Delaney v Staples Modern Law Review* 55, 848-857.

Deakin, Simon (1994a) Part-time Employment, Qualifying Thresholds and Economic Justification *Industrial Law Journal* 23, 151-155.

Deakin, Simon (1994b) Open for Business *Industrial Law Journal* 23, 333-337.

Deakin, Simon (1995) Levelling Down Employee Benefits *Cambridge Law Journal* 54, 35-37.

Deakin, Simon (1996a) The Utility of Rights Talk: Employees' Personal Rights, in *Understanding Human Rights* eds Conor Gearty and Adam Tomkins (Mansell, London).

Deakin, Simon (1996b) Labour Law as Market Regulation, in *European Community Labour Law: Principles and Perspectives. Liber Amicorum Lord Wedderburn* eds. Paul Davies, Antoine Lyon-Caen, Silvana Sciarra and Spiros Simitis (Clarendon Press, Oxford).

Deakin, Simon (1996c) Law and Economics, in *Legal Frontiers* ed Philip A Thomas (Dartmouth, Aldershot).

Deakin, Simon (1998) The Evolution of the Contract of Employment 1900-1950: the Influence of the Welfare State, in *Governance, Industry and Labour Markets in Britain and France. The modernising state in the mid-twentieth century* eds Noel Whiteside and Robert Salais (Routledge, London).

Deakin, Simon (1999) Organisational Change, Labour Flexibility and the Contract of Employment in Great Britain, in *Employment Relations, Individualisation and Union Exclusion. An International Study* eds. Stephen Deery and Richard Mitchell (Federation Press, Annandale, NSW).

Deakin, Simon (2000) Legal Origins of Wage Labour: the Evolution of the Contract of Employment from Industrialisation to the Welfare State in *The Dynamics of Wage Relations in the New Europe* eds Linda Clarke, Peter de Gijsel and Jörn Janssen (Kluwer, Deventer).

Deakin, Simon (2001a) The Changing Concept of the Employer in Labour Law *Industrial Law Journal* 30, 72-84.

Deakin, Simon (2001b) Employment Protection and the Employment Relationship: Adapting the Traditional Model?, in *Employment Rights at Work: Reviewing the Employment Relations Act 1999* ed Keith Ewing (Institute of Employment Rights, London).

Deakin, Simon (2001c) The Many Futures of the Contract of Employment, in *Labour Law in an Era of Globalisation: Transformative Practices and Possibilities* eds Joanne Conaghan, Michael Fischl and Karl Klare (OUP, Oxford).

Deakin, Simon (2002) Equality, Non-Discrimination, and the Labour Market: a Commentary on Richard Epstein's Critique of Anti-Discrimination laws, in *Equal Opportunity or More Opportunity? The Good Thing about Discrimination* ed. Richard Esptein (Institute for the Study of Civil Society, London).

Deakin, Simon (2003) Interpreting Employment Contracts: Judges, Employers and Workers, in *Commercial Law and Commercial Practice* ed Sarah Worthington (Hart Publishing, Oxford).

Deakin, Simon (2004) Workers, Finance and Democracy, in *The Future of Labour Law: Liber Amicorum Sir Bob Hepple QC* eds Catherine Barnard, Simon Deakin and Gillian S. Morris (Hart Publishing, Oxford).

Deakin, Simon (2007) Does the 'Personal Employment Contract' Provide a Basis for the Reunification of Labour Law? *Industrial Law Journal* 36, 68-83.

Deakin, Simon (2008) Regulatory Competition after *Laval Cambridge Yearbook of European Legal Studies* 10, 581-609.

Deakin, Simon (2011) Inside Pension Fund Governance, in *Good Governance of Pension Schemes* eds. Paul Thornton and Donald Fleming (CUP, Cambridge).

Deakin, Simon (2012) The Lisbon Treaty, the *Viking* and *Laval* Judgments, and the Financial Crisis: In Search of New Foundations for Europe's 'Social Market Economy', in *The Lisbon Treaty and Social Europe* eds Niklas Bruun, Klaus Lörcher and Isabelle Schömann (Hart, Oxford).

Deakin, Simon, Dominic Chai and Colm McLaughlin (2012) Gender Equality and Reflexive Law: The Potential of Different Regulatory Régimes for Making Employment Rights Effective, in *Making Employment Rights Effective: Issues of Compliance and Enforcement* ed. Linda Dickens (Hart, Oxford).

Deakin, Simon and Francis Green (2009) One Hundred Years of British Minimum Wage Legislation *British Journal of Industrial Relations* 47, 205-213.

Deakin, Simon and Alan Hughes (1999) Economic Efficiency and the Proceduralisation of Company Law *Company, Financial and Insolvency Law Review* 3, 169-189.

Deakin, Simon and Aristea Koukiadaki (2012a) Capability Theory, Employee Voice and Corporate Restructuring: Evidence from UK Case Studies *Comparative Labor Law and Policy Journal* 33, forthcoming.

Deakin, Simon and Aristea Koukiadaki (2012b) Deliberative Democracy and Capability for Voice: Legal Strategies for the Implementation of Social Rights in the European Union, in *Deliberative Democracy and Situated Capability for Voice* eds Ota De Leonardis and Serafino Negrelli (Policy Press, Bristol).

Deakin, Simon and Colm McLaughlin (2008) The Regulation of Women's Pay: from Individual Rights to Reflexive Law?', in Jackie Scott, Shirley Dex and Heather Joshi (ed) *Women and Employment: Changing Lives and New Challenges* (Edward Elgar, Cheltenham).

Deakin, Simon and John Randall (2009) Rethinking the Economic Torts *Modern Law Review* 72, 519-553.

Deakin, Simon and Hannah Reed (2000a) The Contested Meaning of Labour Market Flexibility: Economic Theory and the Discourse of European Integration in *Social Law and Policy in an Evolving European Union* ed Jo Shaw (Hart Publishing, Oxford).

Deakin, Simon and Hannah Reed (2000b) River Crossing or Cold Bath? Deregulation and Employment in Britain in the 1980s and 1990s in *Why Deregulate Labour Markets?* eds Gosta Esping-Andersen and Marino Regini (OUP, Oxford).

Deakin, Simon, and Prabirjit Sarkar (2008) Assessing the Long-Run Economic Impact of Labour Law Systems: A theoretical Reappraisal and Analysis of New Time series Data *Industrial Relations Journal* 39, 453-487.

Deakin, Simon, and Frank Wilkinson (1991) Labour Law, Social Security and Economic Inequality *Cambridge Journal of Economics* 15, 125-148.

Deakin, Simon, and Frank Wilkinson (1992) The Law and Economics of the Minimum Wage *Journal of Law and Society*, 19, 279-392.

Deakin, Simon, and Frank Wilkinson (1994) Rights vs Efficiency? The Economic Case for Transnational Labour Standards *Industrial Law Journal* 23, 289-310.

Deakin, Simon, and Frank Wilkinson (1996) Contracts, Cooperation and Trust: the Role of the Institutional Framework, in *Contract and Economic Organisation: Socio-Legal Initiatives* eds David Campbell and Peter Vincent-Jones (Dartmouth, Aldershot).

Deakin, Simon and Frank Wilkinson (1999) The Management of Redundancies in Europe – the Case of Great Britain *Labour* 13, 41-89.

Deakin, Simon and Frank Wilkinson (2000a) Labour Law and Economic Theory: A Reappraisal, *Legal Regulation of the Employment Relation* eds Hugh Collins, Paul Davies and Roger Rideout (Kluwer, London).

Deakin, Simon and Frank Wilkinson (2000b) 'Capabilities', ordineo spontaneo del mercato e diritti sociali *Il diritto del mercato del lavoro*, 2, 313-344; also published in English as ESRC Centre for Business Research Working Paper No. 174.

Deakin, Simon and Frank Wilkinson (2005) *The Law of the Labour Market: Industrialization, Employment and Legal Evolution* (OUP, Oxford).

Deakin, Simon, Sara Horrell and Jill Rubery (1989) *Working Time and Plant Operating Times in the EEC Internal Market: the UK Report,* Report for the European Commission (Department of Applied Economics, University of Cambridge).

Deakin, Simon, Angus Johnston and Basil Markesinis (2003) *Markesinis and Deakin's Tort Law,* 5th edn (Clarendon Press, Oxford).

Deakin, Simon, Angus Johnston and Basil Markesinis (2008) *Markesinis and Deakin's Tort Law* 6th edn (Clarendon Press, Oxford)

Deakin, Simon, Jonathan Michie and Frank Wilkinson (1992) *Inflation, Employment, Wage-bargaining and the Law* (Institute of Employment Rights, London).

Del Rey Guanter, Salvador (1992) Contrato de Trabajo y Derechos Fundamentales en la Doctrina Constitucional, in *Constitucion y Derecho del Trabajo: 1981-1991 Análisis de Diez Años de Jurisprudencia Constitucional* ed RM Alarcón Caracuel (Marcial Pons, Madrid).

Denning, AT (1939) Wages during Sickness *Law Quarterly Review* 54, 353-357.

Derbyshire, Wyn, Stephen Hardy and David Wilman (2011) The Pension Scheme in the Employment Package, in *Good Governance of Pension Schemes* eds. Paul Thornton and Donald Fleming (CUP, Cambridge).

Desmond, Helen (2000) Research and Reports, *Winning the Generation Game* etc. *Industrial Law Journal* 29, 403-406.

Desmond, Helen (2003) The Generation Game: Pensions and Retirement *Industrial Law Journal* 32, 218-222.

Devonshire, Peter (2003) *Spycatcher* Returns to the House of Lords *Law Quarterly Review* 119, 384-387.

Diamond, Paul (1991) Dishonourable Defences: the Use of Injunctions and the EEC Treaty – Case Study of the Shops Act 1950 *Modern Law Review* 54, 72-87.

Dicey, AV [1908] (1979) *An Introduction to the Study of the Law of the Constitution* 7th edn reprinted with an introduction by ECS Wade (Macmillan, London).

Dickens, Linda (1980) What are Companies Disclosing for the 1980s? *Personnel Management*, April, 28-30, 48.

Dickens, Linda (1988) Justice in the Industrial Tribunal System *Industrial Law Journal* 17, 58-61.

Dickens, Linda (1992a) *Whose Flexibility?* (Institute of Employment Rights, London).

Dickens, Linda (1992b) Maintaining a Collective Interest *Industrial Law Journal* 21, 305-6.

Dickens, Linda (2000) Doing More with Less, in *Employment Relations in Britain: 25 Years of the Advisory Conciliation and Arbitration Service* ed Brian Towers and William Brown (Blackwell, Oxford)

Dickens, Linda and George Sayers Bain (1986) A Duty to Bargain? Union Recognition and Information Disclosure, in *Labour Law in Britain*, ed Roy Lewis (Blackwell, Oxford).

Dickens, Linda and Mark Hall (2003) Labour Law and Industrial Relations: A New Settlement? in *Industrial Relations: Theory and Practice* 2nd edn ed Paul Edwards (Blackwell Publishing, Oxford).

Dickens, Linda and Mark Hall (2010) The Changing Legal Framework of Employment Relations in *Industrial Relations: Theory and Practice* 3rd edn ed Trevor Colling and Michael Terry (Wiley, Chichester).

Dickens, Linda, Michael Jones, Brian Weekes and Moira Hart (1985) *Dismissed: A Study of Unfair Dismissal and the Industrial Tribunal System* (Blackwell, Oxford).

Dickens, Richard and Alan Manning (2003) Minimum Wage, Minimum Impact, in *The Labour Market under New Labour: The State of Working Britain 2003* eds Richard Dickens, Paul Gregg and Jonathan Wadsworth (Palgrave, Basingstoke).

Dickens, Richard, Paul Gregg, Stephen Machin, Alan Manning and Jonathan Wadsworth (1993) Wages Councils: Was There a Case for Abolition? *British Journal of Industrial Relations* 31, 516-529.

Dicks, M and N Hatch (1989) *The Relationship between Employment and Unemployment*, Bank of England Working Paper (London).

Dilnot, Andrew and Richard Disney (1989) Pension Schemes after the 1989 Budget *Fiscal Studies*, 10/3, 34-49.

Disney, Richard (1990) Explanations of the Decline in Trade Union Density in Britain: an Appraisal *British Journal of Industrial Relations* 28, 165-177.

Disney, Richard, and Erika Szyszczak (1984) Part-Time Employment and Sex Discrimination in Great Britain *British Journal of Industrial Relations* 22, 78-100.

Disney, Richard, and Erika Szyszczak (1989) Reply to Catherine Hakim *Industrial Law Journal* 18, 223-228.

Dix, Gill (2000) Operating with Style: the Work of the ACAS Conciliator in Individual Employment Rights Cases in *Employment Relations in Britain: 25 Years of the Advisory Conciliation and Arbitration Service* ed Brian Towers and William Brown (Blackwell, Oxford)

Dix, Gill and Sarah Oxenbridge (2004) *Coming to the Table: The role of Acas in collective disputes and improving workplace relations* (ACAS, London).

Dolding, Lesley (1994) Unfair Dismissal and Industrial Action *Industrial Law Journal* 23, 243-246.

Donaldson, Sir John (1975) The Role of Labour Courts *Industrial Law Journal* 4, 63-68.

Dore, Ronald (1987) *Taking Japan Seriously: A Confucian Perspective on Leading Economic Issues* (Stanford University Press, Stanford).

Dorssemont, Filip (2012) Values and Objectives, in *The Lisbon Treaty and Social Europe* eds Niklas Bruun, Klaus Lörcher and Isabelle Schömann (Hart, Oxford).

Douglas Scott, Sionaidh (1998) In Search of Union Citizenship *Yearbook of European Law* 18, 29-65.

Doyle, Brian (1994) *New Directions Towards Disabled Workers' Rights* (Institute of Employment Rights, London).

Doyle, Brian (1995) *Disability, Discrimination and Equal Opportunities* (Mansell, London).

Doyle, Brian (1997) Enabling Legislation or Dissembling Law? The Disability Discrimination Act 1995 *Modern Law Review*, 60, 64-78.

Doyle, Brian (2008) *Disability Discrimination: Law and Practice* 6th edn (Jordans, Bristol)

Drouin, Renee-Claude (2010) Labor Rights through International Framework Agreements: Practical Outcomes and Recent Challenges *Comparative Labor Law and Policy Journal* 31, 591-636.

Dubinsky, Laura (2000) *Resisting Union-Busting Techniques: Lessons from Quebec* (Institute of Employment Rights, London).

Dukes, Ruth (2007) The ICE Regulations: Pre-Existing Agreements and Standard Provisions: a Warning to Employers *Industrial Law Journal* 36, 329-340.

Dukes, Ruth (2008a) Voluntarism and the Single Channel: the Development of Single-Channel Worker Representation in the UK *International Journal of Comparative Labour Law and Industrial Relations* 24, 87-121.

Dukes, Ruth (2008b) The Statutory Recognition Procedure 1999: No Bias in Favour of Recognition *Industrial Law Journal* 37, 236-267.

Dukes, Ruth (2010) The Right to Strike under UK Law: Not Much More than a Slogan? *Industrial Law Journal* 39, 82-91.

Dukes, Ruth (2011) The Right to Strike under UK Law: Something More Than a Slogan? *Industrial Law Journal* 40, 302- 311.

Dunn, Stephen and John Gennard (1984) *The Closed Shop in British Industry* (Macmillan, London).

Dunn, Stephen and Martyn Wright (1993) *Managing Without the Closed Shop* (Centre for Economic Performance Discussion Paper No 118, London School of Economics).

Durcan, JW and WE J McCarthy (1974) The State Subsidy Theory of Strikes: An Examination of Statistical Data for the Period 1956-1970 *British Journal of Industrial Relations*, 12, 26-47.

Eady, Jennifer (1994) Collective Dismissals, Consultation and Remedies *Industrial Law Journal* 23, 350-354.

Earnshaw, Jill and Stephen Hardy (2001) Assessing an Arbitral Route for Unfair Dismissal *Industrial Law Journal* 30, 289-304.

Earnshaw, Jill, and David Pace (1991) Homosexuals and Transsexuals at Work: Legal Issues, in *Vulnerable Workers: Psychosocial and Legal Issues* eds Marilyn J Davidson and Jill Earnshaw (Wiley, Chichester).

Earnshaw, Jill, John Goodman, Robin Harrison and Mick Marchington (1998) *Industrial Tribunals, Workplace Disciplinary Procedures and Employment Practice* EMAR Research Paper No 2 (Department of Trade and Industry, London).

Edwards, Anna (2000) *Barber v RJB Mining* in the Wider Context of Health and Safety *Industrial Law Journal* 29, 280-287.

Edwards, Paul (1995) Strikes and Industrial Conflict in *Industrial Relations: Theory and Practice in Britain*, ed Paul Edwards (Blackwell, Oxford).

Edwards, Paul, Mark Hall, Richard Hyman, Paul Marginson, Keith Sisson, Jeremy Waddington and David Winchester (1992) Great Britain: Still Muddling Through, in *Industrial Relations in the New Europe* eds Anthony Ferner and Richard Hyman (Blackwell, Oxford).

Edwards, Paul, Mark Hall, Richard Hyman, Paul Marginson, Keith Sisson, Jeremy Waddington and David Winchester (1998) Great Britain: From Partial Collectivism to Neo-liberalism to Where?, in *Changing Industrial Relations in Europe* ed Anthony Ferner and Richard Hyman, 2nd edn (Blackwell, Oxford).

Eklund, Ronnie (2006) The *Laval* Case *Industrial Law Journal* 35, 202-208

Eklund, Ronnie (2008) Swedish Perspective on Laval *Comparative Labor Law and Policy Journal* 29, 551-571

Elgar, Jane and Bob Simpson (1992) *The Impact of the Law on Industrial Disputes in the 1980s* (Centre for Economic Performance, London School of Economics).

Elgar, Jane and Bob Simpson (1994) A Final Appraisal of 'Bridlington'? An Evaluation of TUC Disputes Committee Decisions 1974-1991 *British Journal of Industrial Relations* 32, 47-66.

Elgar, Jane and Bob Simpson (1996) *Industrial Action Ballots and the Law* (Institute of Employment Rights, London).

Elias, Patrick (1978) Unravelling the Concept of Dismissal *Industrial Law Journal* 7, 16-29.

Elias, Patrick (1979) Admission to Trade Unions *Industrial Law Journal* 8, 111-113.

Elias, Patrick (1981) Fairness in Unfair Dismissal: Trends and Tensions *Industrial Law Journal* 10, 201-217.

Elias, Patrick (1982) The Structure of the Employment Contract *Current Legal Problems* 35, 95-116.

Elias, Patrick (1994) The Strike and Breach of Contract: A Reassessment in *Human Rights and Labour Law: Essays for Paul O'Higgins* eds KD Ewing, CA Gearty and BA Hepple (Mansell, London).

Elias, Patrick and John Bowers (no date given) *Transfer of Undertakings: The Legal Pitfalls* (FT Law and Tax, London).

Elias, Patrick and Keith Ewing (1987) *Trade Union Democracy, Members' Rights and the Law* (Mansell, London).

Elias, Patrick, Brian Napier and Peter Wallington (1980) *Labour Law: Cases and Materials* (Butterworths, London).

Ellis, Evelyn (1991) *European Community Sex Equality Law* (Clarendon Press, Oxford).

Ellis, Evelyn (1994) The Definition of Discrimination in European Sex Equality Law *European Law Review* 19, 563-580.

Ellison, Robin (1987 as updated) *Pensions Law and Practice* (Longman, London).

Elvin, Jesse (2003) Can an Employer be under a Duty to Dismiss an Employee for his Own Good in Order to Protect his Health? *Cambridge Law Journal* 62, 20-23.

Emerson, Michael (1988) Regulation or Deregulation of the Labour Market: Policy Regimes for the Recruitment and Dismissal of Employees in Industrialised Countries *European Economic Review* 32, 775-817.

Enonchong, Nelson (1996) Contract Damages for Injury to Reputation *Modern Law Review* 59, 592.

Epstein, Richard (1983) A Common Law for Labour Relations: a Critique of the New Deal Labor Legislation *Yale Law Journal* 92, 1357-1408.

Epstein, Richard (1984) In Defense of the Contract at Will *University of Chicago Law Review* 51, 947-982.

Epstein, Richard (ed) (2002) *Equal Opportunity or More Opportunity? The Good Thing About Discrimination* (Institute for the Study of Civil Society, London).

Estlund, Cynthia L (2002) An American Perspective on Fundamental Labour Rights in *Social and Labour Rights in a Global Context* ed Bob Hepple (Cambridge University Press, Cambridge).

Estreicher, Samuel, Harry C Katz and Bruce E Kaufman eds (2001) *The Internal Governance and Organisational Effectiveness of Labor Unions: Essays in Honor of George Brooks* (Kluwer Law International, New York).

European Committee on Social Rights (2008) *Digest of the Case Law of the European Committee on Social Rights* (Council of Europe).

Evans, Stephen (1983) The Labour Injunction Revisited: Picketing, Employers and the Employment Act 1980 *Industrial Law Journal* 12, 129-147.

Evans, Stephen (1987) The Use of Injunctions in Industrial Disputes *British Journal of Industrial Relations* 25, 419-435.

Evans, Stephen (1990) Free Labour Markets and Economic Performance: Evidence from the Construction Industry *Work, Employment and Society*, 4, 239-252.

Evans, Stephen and Roy Lewis (1987) Anti-Union Discrimination: Practice, Law and Policy *Industrial Law Journal* 16, 88-106.

Evans, Stephen and Roy Lewis (1988) Labour Clauses: From Voluntarism to Regulation *Industrial Law Journal*, 17, 209-226.

Evans, Stephen, John Goodman and Leslie Hargreaves (1985) *Unfair Dismissal Law and Employment Practice in the 1980s* Research Paper No 53 (Department of Employment, London).

Evju, Stein (2001a) The European Social Charter in *The Council of Europe and the Social Challenges of the XX1st Century* ed R Blanpain (Kluwer, The Hague).

Evju, Stein (2001b) Collective Agreements and Competition Law: The *Albany* Puzzle and *van der Woude International Journal of Comparative Labour Law and Industrial Relations* 17, 165-184.

Ewing, Keith (1979) The Golden Formula: Some Recent Developments *Industrial Law Journal* 8, 133-146.

Ewing, Keith (1982a) Homeworking: A Framework for Reform *Industrial Law Journal* 11, 94-110.

Ewing, Keith (1982b) *Trade Unions, the Labour Party and the Law. A Study of the Trade Union Act 1913* (Edinburgh University Press, Edinburgh).

Ewing, Keith (1984) Trade Union Political Funds: The 1913 Act Revisited *Industrial Law Journal* 13, 227-242.

Ewing, Keith (1985) The Strike, the Courts and the Rule-Books *Industrial Law Journal*, 14, 160-175.

Ewing, Keith (1986) The Right to Strike *Industrial Law Journal* 15, 143-160.

Ewing, Keith (1988) Il diritto del lavoro negli anni '20: l'esperienza inglese, in *Diritto del lavoro e corporativismi in Europa: ieri e oggi* ed G Vardaro (Franco Angeli, Milan).

Ewing, Keith (1989) Job Security and the Contract of Employment *Industrial Law Journal* 18, 217-222.

Ewing, Keith (1990a) Trade Union Recognition – A Framework for Discussion *Industrial Law Journal*, 19, 209-227.

Ewing, Keith (1990b) Economics and Labour Law in Britain: Thatcher's Radical Experiment *Alberta Law Review* 28, 632-651.

Ewing, Keith (1991) *The Right to Strike* (Clarendon Press, Oxford).

Ewing, Keith (1993a) Swimming with the Tide: Employment Protection and the Implementation of European Labour Law *Industrial Law Journal* 22, 165-180.

Ewing, Keith (1993b) Remedies for Breach of the Contract of Employment *Cambridge Law Journal* 52, 405-436.

Ewing, Keith (1994a) *Britain and the ILO*, 2nd edn (Institute of Employment Rights, London).

Ewing, Keith (1994b) The Bill of Rights Debate: Democracy or Juristocracy in Britain? in *Human Rights and Labour Law: Essays for Paul O'Higgins* eds KD Ewing, CA Gearty and BA Hepple (Mansell, London).

Ewing, Keith (ed)(1996) *Working Life: A New Perspective of Labour Law* (The Institute of Employment Rights, Lawrence and Wishart, London).

Ewing, Keith (1998a) Australian and British Labour Law: Differences of Form or Substance? *Australian Journal of Labour Law* 11, 44-68.

Ewing, Keith (1998b) The Human Rights Act and Labour Law *Industrial Law Journal* 27, 275-292.

Ewing, Keith (1999) Freedom of Association and the Employment Relations Act *Industrial Law Journal* 28, 283-298.

Ewing, Keith (2000a) Trade Union Recognition and Staff Associations – A Breach of International Labour Standards? *Industrial Law Journal* 29, 267-273.

Ewing, Keith (ed) (2000b) *Human Rights at Work* (Institute of Employment Rights, London).

Ewing, Keith (2001) The Political Parties, Elections and Referendums Act 2000 – Implications for Trade Unions *Industrial Law Journal* 30, 199-205.

Ewing, Keith (2003) The Implications of *Wilson and Palmer Industrial Law Journal* 32, 1-22.

Ewing, Keith (2004) Laws Against Strikes Revisited, in *The Future of Labour Law: Liber Amicorum Sir Bob Hepple QC* ed Catherine Barnard, Simon Deakin and Gillian S Morris (Hart Publishing, Oxford).

Ewing, Keith (2005) The Function of Trade Unions *Industrial Law Journal* 34, 1-22.

Ewing, KD (ed) (2006) *The Right to Strike: From the Trade Disputes Act 1906 to a Trade Union Freedom Bill 2006* (Institute of Employment Rights, Liverpool).

Ewing, Keith (2007) The Implications of the *ASLEF* case *Industrial Law Journal* 36, 425-445.

Ewing, KD (2009a) Implementing the *ASLEF* Decision - A Victory for the BNP? *Industrial Law Journal* 38, 50-57.

Ewing, Keith (2009b) *Ruined Lives: Blacklisting in the UK Construction Industry* (Institute of Employment Rights, Liverpool).

Ewing, Keith and Andrew Grubb (1987) The Emergence of a New Labour Injunction *Industrial Law Journal* 16, 145-163.

Ewing, KD and John Hendy (eds) (2009a) *The New Spectre Haunting Europe* (Institute of Employment Rights, Liverpool).

Ewing KD and John Hendy (2009b) The Legal Accountability of the ECJ: the ILO, the Social Charter and the ECHR in *The New Spectre Haunting Europe* (Institute of Employment Rights, Liverpool).

Ewing KD and John Hendy (2009c) The ECJ Decisions and the Trade Union Freedom:Lessons from the United Kingdom in *The New Spectre Haunting Europe* (Institute of Employment Rights, Liverpool).

Ewing, KD and John Hendy (2010) The Dramatic Implications of *Demir and Baykara Industrial Law Journal* 39, 2-51.

Ewing, KD and John Hendy (2011) *Days of Action: The legality of protest strikes against government cuts* (Institute of Employment Rights, Liverpool).

Ewing, Keith and John Hendy (2012) Unfair Dismissal Law Changes – Unfair? *Industrial Law Journal*, 41, 115-121.

Ewing, Keith and Anne Hock (2003) Trade Union Recognition in Small Enterprises (Popularis Ltd, Kingston upon Thames).

Ewing, Keith and Gillian Morris (2000) Labour Law, in *Law's Future(s)* ed David Hayton (Hart Publishing, Oxford).

Ewing, Keith and Brian Napier (1986) The Wapping Dispute and Labour Law *Cambridge Law Journal* 45, 285-304.

Ewing, Keith and William Rees (1981) The TUC Independent Review Committee and the Closed Shop *Industrial Law Journal* 10, 84-100.

Ewing, Keith and Tom Sibley (2000) *International Trade Union Rights for the New Millenium* (Institute of Employment Rights, London).

Ewing, KD and GM Truter (2005) The Information and Consultation of Employees Regulations: Voluntarism's Bitter Legacy *Modern Law Review* 68, 626-641.

Ewing, Keith, CA Gearty and BA Hepple (eds) (1994) *Human Rights and Labour Law: Essays for Paul O'Higgins* (Mansell, London).

Facenna, Gerry (2004) *Eugen Schmidberger Internationale Transporte Planzuge v Austria*: Freedom of Expression and Association versus Free Movement of Goods *European Human Rights Law Review* 73-80.

Fairbrother, Peter (2000) *Trade Unions at the Crossroads* (Mansell, London).

Fairgrieve, Duncan (2001) The Human Rights Act 1998, Damages and Tort Law *Public Law*, 695-716.

Farrington, Dennis and David Palfreyman (eds) (2006) *The Law of Higher Education* (Oxford University Press, Oxford)

Felstead, Alan and Nick Jewson (1995) Working at Home: Estimates from the 1991 Census *Employment Gazette* 104, 95-99.

Fenwick, Helen (1999) The Right to Protest, the Human Rights Act and the Margin of Appreciation *Modern Law Review* 62, 491-514.

Fenwick, Helen (2009) Marginalising Human Rights: Breach of the Peace, 'Kettling', the Human Rights Act and Public Protest *Public Law* 737-765.

Finch, Emily (2002) Stalking the Perfect Stalking Law: An Evaluation of the Efficacy of the Protection from Harassment Act 1997 *Criminal Law Review* 703-718.

Findlay, Patricia and Chris Warhurst (2011) Union Learning Funds and Trade Union Revitalization: A New Tool in the Toolkit? *British Journal of Industrial Relations* 49, s115-s134.

Finkin, Matthew W (ed) (1994) *The Legal Future of Employee Representation* (ILR Press, Ithaca, NY).

Finkin, Matthew W (2008) Privatization of Wrongful Dismissal Protection in Comparative Perspective *Industrial Law Journal* 37, 149-168.

Finley, Lucinda (1986) Transcending Equality Theory: A Way Out of the Maternity and the Workplace Debate *Columbia Law Review* 86, 1118-1182.

Fischel, Daniel and Edward Lazear (1986) Comparable Worth and Discrimination in Labor Markets *University of Chicago Law Review* 53, 901-909.

Fitzpatrick, Barry (1983) Time Off: Recent Developments in the Court of Appeal *Industrial Law Journal* 12, 258-61.

Fitzpatrick, Barry (1992) Community Social Law after Maastricht *Industrial Law Journal* 21, 199-213.

Fitzpatrick, Barry (1994) Equality in Occupational Pension Schemes: Still Waiting for *Coloroll, Industrial Law Journal* 23, 155-163.

Fitzpatrick, Barry (1997) Straining the Definition of Health and Safety *Industrial Law Journal*, 26, 115-135.

Fitzpatrick, Barry (1999) The Fair Employment and Equal Treatment (Northern Ireland) Order 1998 *Industrial Law Journal* 28, 336-347.

Flanders, Allan (1970) *Management and Unions: The Theory and Reform of Industrial Relations* (Faber and Faber, London).

Flynn, Leo (1995) Gender Equality Law and Employers' Dress Codes *Industrial Law Journal* 24, 255-272.

Fodder, Martin and Gary Freer (2001) The Effect of Contractual Provision for Payment in Lieu of Notice *Industrial Law Journal* 30, 215-224.

Ford, Michael (1998a) Rethinking the Notice Rule *Industrial Law Journal* 27, 220-233.

Ford, Michael (1998b) *Surveillance and Privacy at Work* (Institute of Employment Rights, London)

Ford, Michael (1999) The Data Protection Act 1998 *Industrial Law Journal* 28, 57-60.

Ford, Michael (2000) Article 8 and the Right to Privacy at the Workplace, in *Human Rights at Work*, ed Keith Ewing (Institute of Employment Rights, London).

Ford, Michael (2002) Two Conceptions of Worker Privacy *Industrial Law Journal* 31,135-155.

Ford, Michael and Jonathan Clarke (2010), *Redgrave's Health and Safety* 7th edn (LexisNexis, London)

Forde, Michael (1982) The 'Closed Shop' Case *Industrial Law Journal*, 11, 1-15.

Fordham, Michael (2001) Judicial Review: the New Rules *Public Law*, 4-10.

Forshaw, Simon and Marcus Pilgerstorfer (2005) Illegally Formed Contracts of Employment and Equal Treatment at Work *Industrial Law Journal* 34, 158-177.

Foster, Ken (1983) The Legal Form of Work in the Nineteenth Century: The Myth of Contract? Paper presented to the conference on *The History of Law, Labour and Crime*, University of Warwick.

Fox, Alan (1974) *Beyond Contract: Work, Power and Trust Relations* (Faber, London).

Fox, Alan (1985) *History and Heritage* (Allen & Unwin, London).

Fraser, Sarah and Adam Sher (2006) The National Minimum Wage: Under Threat From an Unlikely Source? *Industrial Law Journal* 35, 289-301.

Fraser Butlin, Sarah (2011) The UN Convention on the Rights of Persons with Disabilities: Does the UK Measure Up to UK International Commitments? *Industrial Law Journal* 40, 428-438.

Fredman, Sandra (1985) Crown Employment, Prerogative Powers, Consultation and National Security *Industrial Law Journal* 14, 42-46.

Fredman, Sandra (1987) The Right to Strike: Policy and Principle *Law Quarterly Review* 103, 176-182.

Fredman, Sandra (1992a) The New Rights: Labour Law and Ideology in the Thatcher Years *Oxford Journal of Legal Studies*, 12, 24-44.

Fredman, Sandra (1992b) European Community Sex Discrimination Law: A Critique *Industrial Law Journal* 21, 119-134.

Fredman, Sandra (1994a) Equal Pay and Justification *Industrial Law Journal* 23, 37-41.

Fredman, Sandra (1994b) A Difference with Distinction: Pregnancy and Parenthood Reassessed *Law Quarterly Review* 110, 106-123.

Fredman, Sandra (1997a) Reversing Discrimination *Law Quarterly Review* 113, 575-600.

Fredman, Sandra (1997b) Labour Law in Flux: The Changing Composition of the Workforce *Industrial Law Journal* 26, 337-352.

Fredman, Sandra (1997c) *Women and the Law* (Clarendon Press, Oxford).

Fredman, Sandra (2001) Equality: A New Generation? *Industrial Law Journal* 30, 145-168.

Fredman, Sandra (2004a) The Ideology of New Labour Law, in *The Future of Labour Law: Liber Amicorum Sir Bob Hepple* QC eds Catherine Barnard, Simon Deakin and Gillian S. Morris (Hart Publishing, Oxford).

Fredman, Sandra (2004b) Women at Work: The Broken Promise of Flexicurity *Industrial Law Journal* 33, 299-313.

Fredman, Sandra (2004c) Marginalising Equal Pay Laws *Industrial Law Journal* 33, 281-285.

Fredman, Sandra (2008) Reforming Equal Pay Laws *Industrial Law Journal* 37, 193-218.

Fredman, Sandra (2011) The Public Sector Equality Duty *Industrial Law Journal* 40, 405-427.

Fredman, Sandra, and Simon Lee (1987) Natural Justice for Employees: the Unacceptable Face of Proceduralism *Industrial Law Journal* 25, 15-31.

Fredman, Sandra and Gillian S Morris (1987a) Teachers' Pay and Conditions Act *Industrial Law Journal* 16, 107-110.

Fredman, Sandra and Gillian S Morris (1987b) The Teachers' Lesson: Collective Bargaining and the Courts *Industrial Law Journal* 16, 215-226.

Fredman, Sandra and Gillian S Morris (1988) Union Membership at GCHQ *Industrial Law Journal* 17, 105-108.

Fredman, Sandra and Gillian S Morris (1989) *The State as Employer: Labour Law in the Public Services* (Mansell, London).

Fredman, Sandra and Gillian S Morris (1991a) Public or Private? State Employees and Judicial Review *Law Quarterly Review* 107, 298-316.

Fredman, Sandra and Gillian S Morris (1991b) Judicial Review and Civil Servants: Contracts of Employment Declared to Exist *Public Law*, 485-490.

Fredman, Sandra and Gillian S Morris (1992) School Teachers' Pay and Conditions Act 1991 *Industrial Law Journal* 21, 44-47.

Fredman Sandra and Gillian S Morris (1994) The Costs of Exclusivity: Public and Private Re-examined *Public Law*, 69-85.

Fredman, Sandra and Sarah Spencer (eds) (2003) *Age as an Equality Issue: Legal and Policy Perspectives* (Hart Publishing, Oxford).

Freedland, Mark (1976a) Employment Protection: Redundancy Procedures and the EEC *Industrial Law Journal* 5, 24-34.

Freedland, Mark (1976b) *The Contract of Employment* (Clarendon Press, Oxford).

Freedland, Mark (1980) Leaflet Law: the Temporary Short-Time Working Compensation Scheme *Industrial Law Journal* 9, 254-258.

Freedland, Mark (1983) Labour Law and Leaflet Law: the Youth Training Scheme of 1983 *Industrial Law Journal* 12, 220-235.

Freedland, Mark (1984) High Trust, Pensions and the Contract of Employment *Industrial Law Journal* 13, 25-39.

Freedland, Mark (1989) The Education (Modification of Enactments Relating to Employment) Order 1989 *Industrial Law Journal* 18, 231-234.

Freedland, Mark (1992) The Role of the Department of Employment – Twenty Years of Institutional Change in *Legal Intervention in Industrial Relations: Gains and Losses* ed William McCarthy (Blackwell, Oxford).

Freedland, Mark (1994) Equal Treatment, Judicial Review and Delegated Legislation *Industrial Law Journal* 23, 338-341.

Freedland, Mark (1995) Contracting the Employment of Civil Servants – A Transparent Exercise? *Public Law*, 224-233.

Freedland, Mark (1996a) Employment Policy, in *European Community Labour Law: Principles and Perspectives: Liber Amicorum Lord Wedderburn* eds Paul Davies, Antoine Lyon-Caen, Silvana Sciarra and Spiros Simitis (Clarendon Press, Oxford).

Freedland, Mark (1996b) The Rule against Delegation and the *Carltona* Doctrine in an Agency Context *Public Law* 19-30.

Freedland, Mark (1999) Deductions, Red Herrings and the Wage-Work Bargain *Industrial Law Journal* 28, 255-259.

Freedland, Mark (2000) Finding the Right Direction for the 'Industrial Jury' *Industrial Law Journal* 29, 288-293.

Freedland, Mark (2001) Claim for Unfair Dismissal *Industrial Law Journal* 30, 309-311.

Freedland, Mark (2003) *The Personal Employment Contract* (Oxford University Press, Oxford).

Freedland, Mark (2006) From the Contract of Employment to the Personal Work Nexus *Industrial Law Journal* 35, 1-29.

Freedland, Mark (2007) Privacy, Employment and the Human Rights Act 1998 in *Human Rights and Private Law* ed Katja S. Ziegler (Hart Publishing, Oxford)

Freedland, Mark and Nicola Countouris (2008) Towards a Comparative Theory of the Contractual Construction of Personal Work Relations in Europe *Industrial Law Journal* 37, 49-74.

Freedland, Mark and Nicola Kountouris (2011) *The Legal Construction of Personal Work Relations* (OUP, Oxford).

Freedland, Mark and Nicola Kountouris (2012) Employment Equality and Personal Work Relations – A Critique of *Jivraj v Hashwani*, *Industrial Law Journal* 41, 56-66.

Freeman, Richard and Wayne Diamond (2003) Young Workers and Trade Unions in *Representing Workers: Trade Union Recognition and Membership in Britain* ed Howard Gospel and Stephen Wood (Routledge, London).

Freeman, Richard B and Jeremy Pelletier (1990) The Impact of Industrial Relations Legislation on British Union Density *British Journal of Industrial Relations* 28, 141-164.

Frisby, Sandra (2000) TUPE or not TUPE? Employee Protection, Corporate Rescue and 'One Unholy Mess' *Company, Financial and Insolvency Law Review* 4, 249-271.

Fryer, Robert (1973) The Myths of the Redundancy Payments Act *Industrial Law Journal* 2, 1-16.

Fudge, July (2008) The Supreme Court of Canada and the Right to Bargain Collectively: The Implications of the *Health Services and Support* case in Canada and Beyond *Industrial Law Journal* 37, 25-48.

Fudge, Judy (2012) Constitutional Rights, Collective Bargaining and the Supreme Court of Canada: Retreat and Reversal in the *Fraser* Case *Industrial Law Journal* 41, 1-29.

Gall, Gregor (1993) What Happened to Single Union Deals? – a Research Note *Industrial Relations Journal* 24, 71-75.

Gall, Gregor (2004) Trade Union recognition in Britain 1995-2002: turning a corner? *Industrial Relations Journal* 35, 249-270.

Gall, Gregor (2006) Research Note: Injunctions as a Legal Weapon in Industrial Disputes in Britain 1995-2005 *British Journal of Industrial Relations* 44, 327-349.

Gall, Gregor (2010a) The First Ten Years of the Third Statutory Union Recognition Procedure in Britain *Industrial Law Journal* 39, 444-448.

Gall, Gregor (2010b) *'Union Organising' and the Health of the Union Movement in Britain* (Institute of Employment Rights, Liverpool).

Gall, Gregor and Sonia McKay (1994) Trade Union Derecognition in Britain *British Journal of Industrial Relations* 32, 433-448.

Gall, Gregor and Sonia McKay (1996) Research Note: Injunctions as a Legal Weapon in Industrial Disputes *British Journal of Industrial Relations* 34, 567-582.

Gall, Gregor and Sonia McKay (1999) Developments in Union Recognition and Derecognition in Britain 1994-1998 *British Journal of Industrial Relations* 37, 601-614.

Gaymer, Janet (2006) The Employment Tribunal System Taskforce in *The Changing Institutional Face of British Employment Relations* ed Linda Dickens and Alan C Neal (Kluwer Law International, The Netherlands).

Geary, Roger (1985) *Policing Industrial Disputes: 1893-1985* (Cambridge University Press, Cambridge).

Genn, Hazel and Yvette Genn (1989) *The Effectiveness of Representation at Tribunals* (Faculty of Law, Queen Mary College, University of London).

Gennard, J and R Lasko (1974) Supplementary Benefits and Strikers *British Journal of Industrial Relations* 12, 1-25.

Gennard, John (2009) Voluntary Arbitration: the Unsung Hero *Industrial Relations Journal* 40, 309-323.

Germanotta, Paul (2002) *Protecting Worker Solidarity Action: A Critique of International Labour Law* (Institute of Employment Rights, London).

Germanotta, Paul and Tonia Novitz (2002) Globalisation and the Right to Strike: The Case for European-Level Protection of Secondary Action *International Journal of Comparative Labour Law and Industrial Relations* 18, 67-82.

Gernigon, Bernard, Alberto Odero and Horacio Guido (1998) ILO Principles Concerning the Right to Strike *International Labour Review* 137, 441-481.

Gernigon, Bernard, Alberto Odero and Horacio Guido (2000) ILO Principles concerning Collective Bargaining *International Labour Review* 139, 33-55.

Ghosheh, Najati (2008) *Age Discrimination and Older Workers: Theory and Legislation in Comparative Context*, Conditions of Work and Employment Series No 20 (ILO, Geneva).

Gibbons, Steve (2004) *Decoding Some New Developments in Labour Standards Enforcement* (Institute of Employment Rights, London).

Giddens, Anthony (1998) *The Third Way: The Renewal of Social Democracy* (Polity Press, Cambridge)

Gilbert, Kay (2012) Promises and Practices: Job Evaluation and Equal Pay Forty Years On *Industrial Relations Journal* 43, 137-151.

Gill, Tess and Karon Monaghan (2003) Justification in Direct Sex Discrimination Law: Taboo Upheld *Industrial Law Journal* 32, 115-122.

Gladstone, A (2010) Settlement of Disputes over Rights in *Comparative Labour Law and Industrial Relations in Industrialised Market Economies* 10th edn, ed Roger Blanpain (Kluwer Law International, The Hague).

Glasbeek, Harry (1984) The Utility of Model Building: Collins' Capitalist Discipline and Corporatist Law *Industrial Law Journal* 13, 133-152.

Gobert, James and Maurice Punch (2000) Whistleblowers, the Public Interest, and the Public Interest Disclosure Act 1998 *Modern Law Review* 63, 25-54.

Godard, John (2011) What has Happened to Strikes? *British Journal of Industrial Relations* 49, 282-305.

Gold, Michael and Mark Hall (1994) Statutory European Works Councils: the Final Countdown? *Industrial Relations Journal* 25, 177-186.

Gold, Michael and Sandra Schwimbersky (2008) The European Company Statute: Implications for Industrial Relations in the European Union *European Journal of Industrial Relations* 14, 46-64.

Goldman, Alvin L and Amy Beckham Osborne (2007) Comparative Analysis of Labor Law: Learning from the Work Products of A Model Collaborative Design *Comparative Labor Law and Policy Journal* 28, 423-441.

Gooding, Caroline (1996) *Disability Discrimination Act 1995* (Blackstone Press, London).

Goodman, Alissa and Steven Webb (1994) For Richer, for Poorer: the Changing Distribution of Income in the UK, 1961-1991 *Fiscal Studies* 15/4, 28-62.

Goodman, John (2000) Building Bridges and Settling Differences: Collective Conciliation and Arbitration under ACAS, in *Employment Relations in Britain: 25 Years of the Advisory Conciliation and Arbitration Service* ed Brian Towers and William Brown (Blackwell, Oxford)

Goodman, Michael J (ed) (1978 as updated) *Encyclopaedia of Health and Safety at Work, Law and Practice* (Sweet & Maxwell, London).

Gordon, A (1984) *Redundancy in the 1980s* (Institute of Manpower Studies, Brighton).

Gosling, Amanda and Stephen Machin (1995) Trade Unions and the Dispersion of Earnings in British Establishments, 1980-1990 *Oxford Bulletin of Economics and Statistics* 57, 167-84.

Gospel, Howard (1976) Disclosure of Information to Trade Unions *Industrial Law Journal*, 5, 223-236.

Gospel, Howard and Graeme Lockwood (1999) Disclosure of Information for Collective Bargaining: The CAC Approach Revisited *Industrial Law Journal* 28, 233-248.

Gospel, Howard and Paul Willman (1981) Disclosure of Information: the CAC Approach *Industrial Law Journal* 10, 10-22.

Gospel, Howard and Stephen Wood (2003) Representing Workers in Modern Britain in *Representing Workers: Trade Union Recognition and Membership in Britain* eds Howard Gospel and Stephen Wood (Routledge, London).

Gould, William B IV (2004) *A Primer on American Labor Law*, 4th edn (MIT Press, Cambridge, Mass).

Goulding, Paul (ed) (2007) *Employee Competition: Covenants, Confidentiality and Garden Leave* (Oxford University Press, Oxford).

Gouldstone, Simon and Gillian Morris (2006) The Central Arbitration Committee in *The Changing Institutional Face of British Employment Relations* ed Linda Dickens and Alan C Neal (Kluwer Law International, The Netherlands).

Gouldner, Alvin W (1954) *Wildcat Strike* (Antioch Press, New York).

Graham, Cosmo and Norman Lewis (1985) *The Role of ACAS Conciliation in Equal Pay and Sex Discrimination Cases* (Equal Opportunities Commission, Manchester).

Grahl, John, and Paul Teague (1992) Integration Theory and European Labour Markets *British Journal of Industrial Relations* 30, 515-529.

Gray, Kevin and Susan Francis Gray (1999) Civil Rights, Civil Wrongs and Quasi-Public Space *European Human Rights Law Review*, 46-102.

Grief, Nicholas (1991) The Domestic Impact of the European Community on Human Rights as Mediated through Community Law *Public Law* 555-567.

Griffith, JAG and Michael Ryle (1989) *Parliament: Functions, Practice and Procedures* (Sweet and Maxwell, London).

Grosz, Stephen, Jack Beatson and Peter Duffy (2000) *Human Rights: the 1998 Act and the European Convention* (Sweet and Maxwell, London).

Guest, David (1990) Personnel Management: the End of Orthodoxy? *British Journal of Industrial Relations* 29, 149-175.

Guest, David E and Riccardo Peccei (2001) Partnership at Work: Mutuality and the Balance of Advantage *British Journal of Industrial Relations* 39, 207-236.

Guest, David, William Brown, Riccardo Peccei and Katy Huxley (2008) Does Partnership at Work Increase Trust? An Analysis Based on the 2004 Workplace Employment Relations Survey (2008) *Industrial Relations Journal* 39, 124-152.

Gunningham, Neil, and Richard Johnstone (1999) *Regulating Workplace Safety: Systems and Sanctions* (Oxford University Press, Oxford).

Hakim, Catherine (1985) *Employers' Use of Outwork* Research Paper 44 (Department of Employment, London).

Hakim, Catherine (1987) Trends in the Flexible Workforce *Employment Gazette* 95, 594-560.

Hakim, Catherine (1989a) Employment Rights: a Comparison of Full-Time and Part-Time Employees *Industrial Law Journal* 18, 69-83.

Hakim, Catherine (1989b) Workforce Restructuring, Social Insurance Coverage and the Black Economy *Journal of Social Policy* 18, 471-583.

Hakim, Catherine (1990) Core and Periphery in Employers' Workforce Strategies: Evidence from the 1987 ELUS Survey *Work, Employment and Society* 4, 157-188.

Hakim, Catherine (1993) The Myth of Rising Female Employment *Work, Employment and Society* 7, 97-120.

Hale, Dominic (2008) Labour disputes in 2007 *Economic and Labour Market Review* 2, 18-29 (Office for National Statistics, London).

Hale, Dominic (2010) Labour disputes in 2009 *Economic and Labour Market Review* 6, 47-59 (Office for National Statistics, London).

Hall, M (1992) Behind the European Works Council Directive: The European Commission's Legislative Strategy *British Journal of Industrial Relations*, 30, 547-566.

Hall, Mark (1996) Beyond Recognition? Employee Representation and EU Law *Industrial Law Journal* 25, 15-27.

Hall, Mark (2005) Assessing the Information and Consultation of Employees Regulations *Industrial Law Journal* 34, 103-126.

Hall, Mark (2006) A Cool Response to the ICE Regulations? Employer and Trade Union Approaches to the New Legal Framework for Information and Consultation *Industrial Relations Journal* 37, 456-472.

Hall, Mark and Paul Edwards (1999) Reforming the Statutory Redundancy Consultation Procedure *Industrial Law Journal* 28, 299-318.

Hall, Mark and Sue Hutchinson, Jane Parker, John Purcell and Michael Terry (2007) *Implementing information and consultation: early experience under the ICE Regulations*, DTI Employment Relations Research Series No 88.

Hall, Mark and Sue Hutchinson, Jane Parker, John Purcell and Michael Terry (2008) *Implementing information and consultation in medium-sized organisations*, DTI Employment Relations Research Series No 97.

Hall, Mark and Sue Hutchinson, John Purcell, Michael Terry and Jane Parker (2009) *Implementing information and consultation: developments in medium-sized organisations* (BIS Employment Relations Research Series No 106).

Hall, Mark and Sue Hutchinson, John Purcell, Michael Terry and Jane Parker (2010) *Information and consultation under the ICE regulations: evidence from longitudinal case studies* (BIS Employment Relations Research Series No 117).

Hall, Mark and Paul Marginson (2004) *Developments in European Works Councils* (European Foundation for the Improvement of Living and Working Conditions, Dublin)

Hanson, Charles and Graham Mather (1988) *Striking Out Strikes* (Institute of Economic Affairs, London).

Hanson, CS, S Jackson and D Miller (1979) *The Closed Shop* (Gower Press, Aldershot).

Hardy, Stephen, and Richard Painter (1999) The New Acquired Rights Directive and its Implications for European Employee Relations in the Twenty-First Century *Employee Relations* 21, 378-388.

Hare, Ivan (1991) Pregnancy and Sex Discrimination *Industrial Law Journal* 20, 124-130.

Harpum, Charles (1986) The Stranger as Constructive Trustee *Law Quarterly Review* 102, 114-162, 267-291.

Harpum, Charles (1994) Knowing Assistance and Receipt as the Basis of Equitable Liability, in *The Frontiers of Liability* ed PBH Birks (Clarendon Press, Oxford).

Harris, DJ (1984) *The European Social Charter* (University Press of Virginia, Charlottesville).

Harris, DJ, M O'Boyle and C Warbrick (1995) *Law of the European Convention on Human Rights* (Butterworths, London).

Harris, Neville (2000) *Social Security Law in Context* (OUP, Oxford).

Hart, Moira (1979) Why Bosses Love the Closed Shop *New Society*, 15 February.

Hart, Oliver (1989) Incomplete Contracts, in *Allocation, Information and Markets* eds John Eatwell, Murray Milgate and Gianfranco de Vivo (Macmillan, London).

Hartley, Trevor (1998) *The Foundations of European Community Law,* 4th edn (Clarendon Press, Oxford).

Harvey (1972 as updated) *Harvey on Industrial Relations and Employment Law* (Butterworths, London).

Harvey, Mark (1995) *The Tax Trap of Self-Employment: Towards the Insecurity Society* (Institute of Employment Rights, London).

Hay, Douglas and Paul Craven (eds) (2004) *Masters, Servants and Magistrates in Britain and the Empire, 1562-1955* (University of North Carolina Press, Chapel Hill and London).

Hayek, FA (1960) *The Constitution of Liberty* (Routledge, London).

Hayek, FA (1973) *Law, Legislation and Liberty Volume 1: Rules and Order* (Routledge, London).

Hayek, FA (1980) *1980s Unemployment and the Unions* (Institute of Economic Affairs, London).

Hayes, Jason and Helen Rainbird (2011) Mobilising Resources for Union Learning: a Strategy for Revitalisation? *Industrial Relations Journal* 42, 565-579.

Hayward, Bruce, Mark Peters, Nicola Rousseau and Ken Seeds (2004) *Findings from the Survey of Employment Tribunal Applications 2003*, Employment Relations Research Series No 33 (DTI, London)

Head, Michael (2010) Calling out the Troops and the Civil Contingencies Act: Some Questions of Concern *Public Law* 340-361.

Heather, Pauline, Jo Rick, John Atkinson and Stephen Morris (1996) Employers' Use of Temporary Workers *Labour Market Trends* September 1996, 403-411.

Heery, Edmund (1996) The New New Unionism in *Contemporary Industrial Relations: A Critical Analysis*, ed. Ian J. Beardwell (Oxford University Press, Oxford).

Heery, Edmund (2002) Partnership versus Organising: Alternative Futures for British Trade Unionism *Industrial Relations Journal* 33, 20-35.

Heery, Edmund and Melanie Simms (2008) Constraints on Union Organising in the United Kingdom *Industrial Relations Journal* 39, 24-42.

Heery, Edmund, John Kelly and Jeremy Waddington (2003) Union Revitalization in Britain *European Journal of Industrial Relations* 9, 79-97.

Heery, Edmund (2009) The Representation Gap and the Future of Worker Representation *Industrial Relations Journal* 40, 324-336.

Heidenreich, Martin and Jonathan Zeitlin (eds) (2009) *Changing European Employment and Welfare Régimes: The Influence of the Open Method of Coordination on National Reforms* (Routledge, London).

Heldman, D, J Bennett and M Johnson (1981) *Deregulating Labor Relations* (Fisher Institute, Dallas).

Hendrickx, Frank (2001) Privacy and Employment Law: General Principles and Application to Electronic Monitoring, in *On-line Rights for Employees in the Information Society* ed Roger Blanpain (Kluwer Law International, The Hague).

Hendy, John (1998) *Every Worker Shall Have the Right to be Represented by a Trade Union* (Institute of Employment Rights, London).

Hendy, John (2000) Caught in a Fork, *Industrial Law Journal* 29, 53-60.

Hendy, John and K.D. Ewing (2005) Trade Unions, Human Rights and the BNP *Industrial Law Society* 34, 197-216.

Hendy, John, and Jeremy McMullen (1987) Injunctions in Contracts of Employment: the New Growth (Part 1) *Law Society Gazette*, 3568-3576.

Hendy, John, and Jeremy McMullen (1988) Injunctions in Contracts of Employment: the New Growth (Part 2) *Law Society Gazette*, 28-31.

Hendy, John and Michael Walton (1997) An Individual Right to Union Representation in International Law *Industrial Law Journal* 26, 205-223.

Henty, Paul (2011) The Equality Act 2010 and the Public Sector Equality Duty: Implications for Public Pocurement *Public Procurement Law Review* 3, NA 108-114.

Hepple, Bob (1968) *Race, Jobs and the Law* (Penguin, Harmondsworth).

Hepple, Bob (1974) Conflicting Collective Agreements; Effect of Signed Receipt of Employment Terms *Industrial Law Journal* 3, 164-166.

Hepple, Bob (1978) Conflict of Laws on Employment Relationships in the EEC, in *Harmonisation of Private International Law by the EEC* ed K Lipstein (Institute of Advanced Legal Studies, London).

Hepple, Bob (1981a) A Right to Work? *Industrial Law Journal* 10, 65-83.

Hepple, Bob (1981b) *Hepple and O'Higgins: Employment Law* 4th edn (Sweet and Maxwell, London).

Hepple, Bob (1982) The Transfer of Undertakings (Protection of Employment) Regulations *Industrial Law Journal* 10, 29-40.

Hepple, Bob (1983) Individual Labour Law, in *Industrial Relations in Britain* ed George Sayers Bain (Basil Blackwell, Oxford).

Hepple, Bob (1986a) Introduction, in *The Making of Labour Law in Europe* ed BA Hepple (Mansell, London).

Hepple, Bob (1986b) Restructuring Employment Rights *Industrial Law Journal* 15, 69-89.

Hepple, Bob (1987) The Crisis in EEC Labour Law *Industrial Law Journal* 16, 77-87.

Hepple, Bob (1990a) *Working Time A New Legal Framework?* Employment Paper No 3 (Institute for Public Policy Research, London).

Hepple, Bob (1990b) The Implementation of the Community Charter of Fundamental Social Rights *Modern Law Review* 53, 643-654.

Hepple, Bob (1992a) The Fall and Rise of Unfair Dismissal in *Legal Intervention in Industrial Relations: Gains and Losses*, ed William McCarthy (Blackwell, Oxford).

Hepple, Bob (1992b) Have Twenty-Five Years of the Race Relations Acts in Britain been a Failure?, in *Discrimination: the Limits of the Law* eds BA Hepple and Erika Szyszczak (Mansell, London).

Hepple, Bob (1993) *European Social Dialogue – Alibi or Opportunity?* (Institute of Employment Rights, London).

Hepple, Bob (1995) The Future of Labour Law *Industrial Law Journal* 24, 303-322.

Hepple, Bob (1996) Equality and Discrimination, in *European Community Labour Law: Principles and Perspectives Liber Amicorum Lord Wedderburn* eds. Paul Davies, Antoine Lyon-Caen, Silvana Sciarra and Spiros Simitis (Clarendon Press, Oxford).

Hepple, Bob (1997a) New Approaches to International Labour Regulation *Industrial Law Journal*, 26, 353-366.

Hepple, Bob (1997b) European Rules on Dismissal Law *Comparative Labor Law* 18, 204-228.

Hepple, Bob (1998a) Flexibility and Security of Employment, in *Comparative Labour Law and Industrial Relations in Industrialized Market Economies* 6th edn, eds R Blanpain and C Engels (Kluwer, Deventer-Boston).

Hepple, Bob (1998b) The Impact on Labour Law in *The Impact of the Human Rights Bill on English Law,* ed B Markesinis (Oxford University Press, Oxford).

Hepple, Bob (1999a) Employee Loyalty in English Law *Comparative Labor Law and Policy Journal* 20, 204-224.

Hepple, Bob (1999b) A Race to the Top? International Investment Guidelines and Corporate Codes of Conduct *Comparative Labor Law and Policy Journal* 20, 347-363.

Hepple, Bob (1999c) UK in *Private Employment Agencies* Bulletin of Comparative Labour Relations No 36 ed Roger Blanpain (Kluwer, The Hague).

Hepple, Bob (2000a) Supporting Collective Bargaining: Some Comparative Reflections, in *Employment Relations in Britain: 25 Years of the Advisory Conciliation and Arbitration Service* ed Brian Towers and William Brown (Blackwell, Oxford)

Hepple, Bob (2000b) Freedom of Expression and the Problem of Harassment, in *Freedom of Expression and Freedom of Information* ed Jack Beatson and Yvonne Cripps (OUP, Oxford).

Hepple, Bob (2001a) *Human Rights and the Contract of Employment* (Employment Lawyers' Association, London).

Hepple, Bob (2001b) The EU Charter of Fundamental Rights *Industrial Law Journal* 30, 225-231.

Hepple, Sir Bob (2005a) *Rights at Work: Global, European and British Perspectives* (Sweet and Maxwell, London).

Hepple, Sir Bob (2005b) *Labour Laws and Global Trade* (Hart Publishing, Oxford).

Hepple, Bob (2006) The Equality Commissions and the Future Commission for Equality and Human Rights in *The Changing Institutional Face of British Employment Relations* ed Linda Dickens and Alan C Neal (Kluwer Law International, The Netherlands).

Hepple, Bob (2008) The Aims of Equality Law *Current Legal Problems* 61, 1-22

Hepple, Bob (2010) Rethinking Laws against Strikes *The Industrial Relations Act 1990: 20 Years On* ed Anthony Kerr (Round Hall, Dublin).

Hepple, Bob (2011a) *Equality: The New Legal Framework* (Hart Publishing, Oxford).

Hepple, Bob (2011b) Enforcing Equality Law: Two Steps Forward and Two Steps Backwards for Reflexive Regulation *Industrial Law Journal* 40, 315-335.

Hepple, Bob (2012) Agency Enforcement of Workplace Equality in *Making Employment Rights Effective: Issues of Compliance and Enforcement* ed Linda Dickens (Hart Publishing, Oxford).

Hepple, Bob and Angela Byre (1989) EEC Labour Law in the United Kingdom – A New Approach *Industrial Law Journal* 18, 129-143.

Hepple, Bob and Sandra Fredman (1992) *Labour Law and Industrial Relations in Great Britain,* 2nd edn (Kluwer, Deventer-Boston).

Hepple, Bob and Gillian S Morris (2002) The Employment Act 2002 and the Crisis of Individual Employment Rights *Industrial Law Journal* 31, 245-269.

Hepple, Bob and Karen Mumgaard (1998) Pension Rights in Business Transfers *Industrial Law Journal* 27, 309-324.

Hepple, Bob and Brian Napier (1978) Temporary Workers and the Law *Industrial Law Journal* 7, 84-99.

Hepple, Bob and Paul O'Higgins (1971) *Public Employee Trade Unionism in the United Kingdom: The Legal Framework* (Institute of Labor and Industrial Relations, The University of Michigan – Wayne State University, Ann Arbor).

Hepple, Bob and Erika Szyszczak (eds) (1992) *Discrimination: the Limits of the Law* (Mansell, London).

Hepple, Bob, Mary Coussey and Toufyal Choudhury (2000) *Equality: A New Framework. Report of the Independent Review of the Enforcement of UK Anti-Discrimination Legislation* (Hart Publishing, Oxford).

Hepple, Bob, TM Partington and Bob Simpson (1977) The Employment Protection Act and Unemployment Benefit: Protection for Whom? *Industrial Law Journal* 6, 54-58.

Hervey, Tamara (1997) *Francovich* Liability Simplified *Industrial Law Journal* 26, 74-79.

Hervey, Tamara (1998) *European Social Law and Policy* (Longmans, London).

Hervey, Tamara and Jeff Kenner (eds) (2003) *Economic and Social Rights under the European Charter of Fundamental Rights: A Legal Perspective* (Hart Publishing, Oxford).

Hervey, Tamara and David O'Keeffe (1996) *Sex Equality Law in the European Union* (John Wiley and Sons, Chichester).

Hills, John (1988) *Changing Tax* (Child Poverty Action Group, London).

Hills, John (1993) *The Future of Welfare. A Guide to the Debate* (Joseph Rowntree Foundation, York).

Hills, John (2009) *Towards a More Equal Society? Poverty, Inequality and Policy since 1997* (Policy Press, Bristol).

Hobbs, Richard and Wanjiru Njoya (2005) Regulating the European Labour Market: Recent Developments *British Journal of Industrial Relations* 43, 297-319.

Hodges-Aeberhard J and A Odero de Dios (1987) Principles of the Committee on Freedom of Association concerning Strikes *International Labour Review* 126, 543-563.

Hogg, Peter W (1997) *Constitutional Law of Canada* 4th edn (Carswell, Scarborough, Ontario).

Holland, James and Adrian Chandler (1988) Implied Mobility Clauses *Industrial Law Journal* 17, 253-256.

Hollingsworth, Mark and Charles Tremayne (1989) *The Economic League: The Silent McCarthyism* (National Council for Civil Liberties, London).

Hollinrake, Alison, Valerie Antcliff and Richard Saundry (2008) Explaining activity and exploring experience - findings from a survey of union learning representatives *Industrial Relations Journal* 39, 392-410.

Honeyball, Simon (1988) Employment Law and the Primacy of Contract *Industrial Law Journal* 17, 97-108.

Honeyball, Simon (2000) Pregnancy and Sex Discrimination *Industrial Law Journal* 29, 43-52.

Horrell, Sara and Jill Rubery (1991a) *Employers' Working Time Policies and Women's Employment* EOC Research Series (HMSO, London).

Horrell, Sara and Jill Rubery (1991b) Gender and Working Time: an Analysis of Employers' Working Time Policies *Cambridge Journal of Economics* 15, 373-391.

Horrell, Sara, Jill Rubery and Brendan Burchell (1989) Unequal Jobs or Unequal Pay? *Industrial Relations Journal* 20, 176-191.

Horton, Rachel (2008) The End of Disability-Related Discrimination in Employment? *Industrial Law Journal* 37, 376-83.

Howarth, David (1988) The Autonomy of Labour Law: A Response to Professor Wedderburn *Industrial Law Journal* 17, 11-25.

Howarth, David (2005) Against *Lumley* v *Gye Modern Law Review* 68, 195-232.

Howarth, David and Janet O'Sullivan (2000) *Hepple, Howarth and Matthews' Tort: Cases and Materials* 5th edn (Butterworths, London).

Howe, John and Richard Mitchell (1999) The Evolution of the Contract of Employment in Australia: a Discussion *Australian Journal of Labour Law* 12, 113-130.

Howes, Victoria (2007) Workers' Involvement in Health and Safety Management and Beyond: the UK Case *International Journal of Comparative Labour Law and Industrial Relations* 23, 245-265.

Hughes, Kirsty (2009) Horizontal privacy *Law Quarterly Review* 125, 244-247.

Hunt, Chris (2011) Strasbourg and Privacy Injunctions *Cambridge Law Journal* 70, 489-491.

Hunt, Jo (1999) Success at Last? The Amendment of the Acquired Rights Directive *European Law Review* 24, 215-230.

Hunt, Murray (1997) *Using Human Rights Law in English Courts* (Hart Publishing, Oxford).

Hunt, Murray (1998) The 'Horizontal' Effect of the Human Rights Act *Public Law*, 423-443.

Hutchins, B and A Harrison (1926) *The History of Factory Legislation* (Routledge, London).

Hydén, Haken (1992) Working Environment, in *The Nordic Labour Relations Model* eds Niklas Bruun, Boel Flodgren, Marit Halverson, Haken Hydén and Ruth Nielsen (Dartmouth, Aldershot).

Hyman, Richard (1994) Changing Trade Union Identities and Strategies, in *New Frontiers in European Industrial Relations* eds Richard Hyman and Anthony Ferner (Blackwell, Oxford).

Hyman, Richard (1997) The Future of Employee Representation *British Journal of Industrial Relations* 35, 309-331.

IER (2009) *Twenty Years of Progress. A Report on IER's Contribution to Advancing Workers' Rights* (Institute of Employment Rights, London).

IFS (1995) *Pensions Policy in the UK: An Economic Analysis* (Institute of Fiscal Studies, London).

Ingham, Mike and Andrew Thomson (1982) *Dimensions of Industrial Relations in Local Authorities* (University of Glasgow, Glasgow).

Inglis-Jones, Nigel (1989 as updated) *The Law of Occupational Pension Schemes* (Sweet & Maxwell, London).

Ingram, Peter (1991) Changes in Working Practices in British Manufacturing Industry in the 1980s: a Study of Employee Concessions Made during Wage Negotiations *British Journal of Industrial Relations* 29, 1-13.

Institute of Personnel Management (1987) *Contract Compliance: The UK Experience* (IPM, London).

International Labour Office (ILO) (1956) Social Aspects of European Economic Cooperation *International Labour Review* 74, 99-123.

International Labour Office (ILO) (1994) *Freedom of Association and Collective Bargaining: General Survey by the Committee of Experts on the Application of Conventions and Recommendations* (International Labour Office, Geneva).

International Labour Office (ILO) (2006) *Freedom of Association: Digest of decisions and principles of the Freedom of Association Committee of the Governing Body of the ILO* 5th (revised) edn (International Labour Office, Geneva).

Jackson, David (1999) *Immigration: Law and Practice* (Sweet & Maxwell, London).

Jackson, David and George Warr (2001) *Immigration Law and Practice* (Sweet and Maxwell, London).

Jacobs, Antoine (1986) Collective Self-Regulation, in *The Making of Labour Law in Europe* ed Bob Hepple (Mansell, London).

Jacobs, Antoine (2009) Collective Labour Relations in *The Transformation of Labour Law in Europe* ed Bob Hepple and Bruno Veneziani (Hart Publishing, Oxford).

Jacobs, ATJM (2010) The Law of Strikes and Lockouts in *Comparative Labour Law and Industrial Relations in Industrialized Market Economies* 10th edn, ed Roger Blanpain (Wolters Kluwer, The Netherlands).

Jacobs, Francis G and Robin CA White (1996) *The European Convention on Human Rights,* 2nd edn (Clarendon, Oxford).

Jacoby, Sanford M (1982) The Duration of Indefinite Employment Contracts in the United States and England: an Historical Analysis *Comparative Labor Law,* 85-128.

Jagodzinski, Romuald (2009) Recast directive on European works councils: cosmetic surgery or substantial progress? *Industrial Relations Journal* 40, 534-545.

James, Grace (2006) The Work and Families Act 2006: Legislation to Improve Choice and Flexibility? *Industrial Law Journal* 35, 272-278.

James, Phil (1992) Reforming British Health and Safety Law: A Framework for Discussion *Industrial Law Journal* 21, 83-105.

James, Phil (1993) *The European Community: A Positive Force in UK Health and Safety Law?* (Institute of Employment Rights, London).

James, Phil and David Lewis (1986) Health and Safety at Work, in *Labour Law in Britain* ed Roy Lewis (Basil Blackwell, Oxford).

James, Philip and David Walters (1997) Non-Union Rights of Involvement: The Case of Health and Safety at Work *Industrial Law Journal* 26, 35-50.

James, Phil and David Walters (2002) Worker Representation in Health and Safety: Options for Regulatory Reform *Industrial Relations Journal* 33, 141-156.

James, Phil and David Walters (2005) *Regulating Health and Safety at Work: An Agenda for Change?* (Institute of Employment Rights, London).

Jay, Rosemary (2007) *Data Protection Law and Practice* 3rd edn (Sweet and Maxwell, London).

Jefferson, Michael (1997) Restraint of Trade: Dismissal and Drafting *Industrial Law Journal* 26, 62-68.

Jenkins, G and M Poole (1990) *New Forms of Ownership* (Routledge, London).

Jenkins, Richard (1988) Discrimination and Equal Opportunity in Employment: Ethnicity and 'Race' in the United Kingdom, in *Employment in Britain* ed Duncan Gallie (Basil Blackwell, Oxford).

Joerges, Christian and Florian Rödl (2004) 'Social market economy' as Europe's social model?' EUI Working Paper LAW No. 2004/8, European University Institute, Florence.

Johansen, Atle Sonsteli (2004) The '*Albany*-Test' Compared with the 'EFTA Guidelines' *Industrial Law Journal* 33, 73-80.

Jones, Gareth (2006) *Goff and Jones: The Law of Restitution* 6th edn (Sweet and Maxwell, London)

Jones, Gareth and William Goodhart (1996) *Specific Performance* 2nd edn (Butterworths, London).

Joseph, Philip A (2010) Parliament's attenuated privilege of freedom of speech *Law Quarterly Review* 126, 568-592.

Joseph, Sarah (2010) UN Covenants and Labour Rights in *Human Rights at Work: Perspectives on Law and Regulation* ed Colin Fenwick and Tonia Novitz (Hart Publishing, Oxford).

Justice (1987) *Industrial Tribunals* (Justice, London).

Kahn, Peggy, Norman Lewis, Rowland Livock and Paul Wiles (1983) *Picketing: Industrial Disputes, Tactics and the Law* (Routledge and Kegan Paul, London).

Kahn-Freund, Otto (1949) The Tangle of the Truck Acts *Industrial Law Review* 4, 2-9.

Kahn-Freund, Otto (1951) Servants and Independent Contractors, *Modern Law Review* 14, 504-509.

Kahn-Freund, Otto (1954a) Intergroup Conflicts and their Settlement *British Journal of Sociology* 5, 193-227.

Kahn-Freund, Otto (1954b) Legal Framework, in *The System of Industrial Relations in Britain* eds Allan Flanders and Hugh Clegg (Basil Blackwell, Oxford).

Kahn-Freund, Otto (1959) Labour Law, in *Law and Public Opinion in Britain in the Twentieth Century* ed M Ginsberg (Stevens, London).

Kahn-Freund, Otto (1967) A Note on Status and Contract in Modern Labour Law *Modern Law Review* 30, 635-644.

Kahn-Freund, Otto (1972) On Uses and Misuses of Comparative Law *Modern Law Review* 37, 1-27.

Kahn-Freund, Otto (1978a) Notes on the Conflict of Laws in Relation to Employment Contracts in English and Scottish courts, in *Selected Writings* (Stevens, London).

Kahn-Freund, Otto (1978b) Blackstone's Neglected Child: the Contract of Employment *Law Quarterly Review* 93, 508-528.

Kahn-Freund, Otto and BA Hepple (1972) *Laws Against Strikes* (Fabian Research Series 302, London).

Keep, Ewart (1990) Training for the Low Paid, in *Improving Incentives for the Low-Paid* eds Alex Bowen and Ken Mayhew (Macmillan/NEDO, London).

Keller, Berndt (2002) The European Company Statute: Employee Involvement – and Beyond *Industrial Relations Journal* 33, 424-445.

Keller, Berndt and Frank Werner (2008) The Establishment of the European Company: The First Cases from an Industrial Relations Perspective *European Journal of Industrial Relations* 14, 153-175.

Kelly, John (1990) British Trade Unionism 1979-1989: Changes, Continuity and Contradictions *Work, Employment and Society*, Special Issue May 1990, 35-45.

Kelly, John, and Rachel Bailey (1989) British Trade Union Membership, Density and Decline in the 1980s *Industrial Relations Journal* 20, 54-61.

Kenner, Jeff (1999a) The EC Employment Title and the Third Way: Making Soft Law Work? *International Journal of Comparative Labour Law and Industrial Relations* 15, 33-60.

Kenner, Jeff (1999b) Statement or Contract? – Some Reflections on the EC Employee Information (Contract or Employment Relationship) Directive after *Kampelmann Industrial Law Journal* 28, 205-231.

Kenner, Jeff (2003) *EU Employment Law* (Hart Publishing, Oxford)

Kerr, Tony (1984) Contract Doesn't Live Here Any More? *Modern Law Review* 47, 30-47.

Kersley, Barbara, Carmen Alpin, John Forth, Alex Bryson, Helen Bewley, Gill Dix and Sarah Oxenbridge (2005) *Inside the Workplace: First Findings from the 2004 Workplace Employment Relations Survey* (DTI, London).

Kersley, Barbara, Carmen Alpin, John Forth, Alex Bryson, Helen Bewley, Gill Dix and Sarah Oxenbridge (2006) *Inside the Workplace: Findings from the 2004 Workplace Employment Relations Survey* (Routledge, Abingdon).

Kessler, Ian and John Purcell (1995) Individualism and Collectivism in Theory and Practice: Management Style and the Design of Pay Systems, in *Industrial Relations: Theory and Practice in Britain*, ed. Paul Edwards (Blackwell Business, Oxford).

Kidner, Richard (1983) *Trade Union Law* 2nd edn (Stevens, London).

Kidner, Richard (1991) Unjustified Discipline by a Trade Union *Industrial Law Journal*, 20, 284-291.

Kidner, Richard (1998) Jurisdiction in European Contracts of Employment *Industrial Law Journal* 27, 103-120.

Kilpatrick, Claire (1994) Deciding When Jobs of Equal Value Can be Paid Unequally: an Examination of s 1(3) of the Equal Pay Act 1970 *Industrial Law Journal* 23, 311-325.

Kilpatrick, Claire (2004) Has New Labour Reconfigured Employment Legislation? *Industrial Law Journal* 32, 135-163.

Kilpatrick, Claire (2010) The European Court of Justice and Labour Law in 2009 *Industrial Law Journal* 39, 287-299.

Knight, KG and Paul L Latreille (2000) Discipline, Dismissals and Complaints to Employment Tribunals *British Journal of Industrial Relations* 38, 533-555.

Kochan, Thomas A (2003) A US Perspective on the Future of Trade Unions in Britain, in *Representing Workers: Trade Union Recognition and Membership in Britain* eds Howard Gospel and Stephen Wood (Routledge, London).

Kollonay-Lehoczky, Csilla, Klaus Lörcher and Isabelle Schömann (2012) The Lisbon Treaty and the Charter of Fundamental Rights of the European Union, in *The Lisbon Treaty and Social Europe* eds Niklas Bruun, Klaus Lörcher and Isabelle Schömann (Hart, Oxford).

Koukiadaki, Aristea (2009) Case Law Developments in the Area of Fixed-Term Work *Industrial Law Journal* 38, 89-100.

Kovaks, Erika (2005) The Right to Strike in the European Social Charter *Comparative Labor Law and Policy Journal* 26, 445-476.

Labour Research Department (1986) The Growing Army of the Self-Employed *Labour Research* February.

Lacey, Nicola (1986) Dismissed by Reason of Pregnancy *Industrial Law Journal* 15, 43-46.

Lacey, Nicola (1992) From Individual to Group?, in *Discrimination: the Limits of the Law* eds BA Hepple and Erika Szyszczak (Mansell, London).

LaLonde, Robert J and Bernard D Meltzer (1991) Hard Times for Unions: Another Look at the Significance of Employer Illegalities *University of Chicago Law Review*, 58, 1006-1014.

Langille, Brian and Guy Davidov (eds) (2006) *Boundaries and Frontiers of Labour Law* (Hart Publishing, Oxford).

Langrish, Sally (1998) The Treaty of Amsterdam: Selected Highlights *European Law Review* 23, 3-19.

Larkin, Philip (2000) Compensation for Repetitive Strain Injury *Industrial Law Journal* 29, 88-95

Latreille, Paul L, JA Latreille and KG Knight (2005) Making a Difference? Legal Representation in Employment Tribunal Cases: Evidence from a Survey of Representatives *Industrial Law Journal* 34, 308-330.

Laulom, Sylvaine (2010) The Flawed Revision of the European Works Council Directive *Industrial Law Journal* 39, 202-208.

Laws, The Hon Sir John (1993) Is the High Court the Guardian of Fundamental Constitutional Rights? *Public Law*, 59-79.

Laws, The Hon, Sir John (1997) Public Law and Employment Law: Abuse of Power *Public Law*, 455-466.

Lawson, Anna (2011) Disability and Employment in the Equality Act 2010: Opportunities Seized, Lost and Generated *Industrial Law Journal* 40, 359-383.

Le Sueur, Andrew (2005) The Rise and Rise of Unreasonableness? *Judicial Review* 10, 32-51.

Leader, Sheldon (1991) The European Convention on Human Rights, The Employment Act 1988 and the Right to Refuse to Strike *Industrial Law Journal* 20, 39-59.

Leader, Sheldon (1992) *Freedom of Association* (Yale University Press, New Haven and London).

Leigh, Ian (1999) Horizontal Rights: The Human Rights Act and Privacy: Lessons from the Commonwealth *International and Comparative Law Quarterly* 48, 57-87.

Leigh, Ian and Laurence Lustgarten (1991) Employment, Justice and Detente: the Reform of Vetting *Modern Law Review* 54, 613-642.

Leigh, Ian and Laurence Lustgarten (1999) Making Rights Real: The Courts, Remedies and the Human Rights Act *Cambridge Law Journal* 58, 509-543.

Leighton, Patricia (1982) Employment Status and the 'Casual' Worker *Industrial Law Journal* 13, 62-66.

Leighton, Patricia (1986) Marginal Workers, in *Labour Law in Britain* ed Roy Lewis (Basil Blackwell, Oxford).

Leighton, Patricia, and Stephen Dunville (1977) From Statement to Contract: Some Effects of the Contracts of Employment Act 1972 *Industrial Law Journal* 16, 133-148.

Leighton, Patricia, and Michael Wynn (2011) Classifying Employment Relationships—More Sliding Doors or a Better Regulatory Framework? *Industrial Law Journal* 40, 5-44.

Lenaerts, Koen (2000) Fundamental Rights in the European Union *European Law Review* 25, 575-600.

Lenaerts, Koen and Eddy Eddy de Smijter (2001) A 'Bill of Rights' for the European Union *Common Market Law Review* 38, 273-300.

Leonard, Alice (1986) *The First Eight Years: a profile of applications to the industrial tribunals under the Sex Discrimination Act 1975 and the Equal Pay Act 1970* (Equal Opportunities Commission, Manchester).

Leonard, Alice (1987) *Pyrrhic Victories: Winning Sex Discrimination and Equal Pay Cases in the Industrial Tribunals 1980-1984* EOC Research Series (HMSO, London).

Leopold, John W (1997) Trade Unions, Political Fund Ballots and the Labour Party *British Journal of Industrial Relations* 35, 23-38.

Leopold, John W (2006) Trade unions and the third round of political fund review balloting *Industrial Relations Journal* 37, 190-208.

Lester, Lord (1994) Discrimination: What can Lawyers Learn from History? *Public Law*, 224-237.

Lester, Lord (1998a) Universality versus Subsidiarity: A Reply, *European Human Rights Law Review*, 73-81.

Lester, Lord (1998b) Opinion: The Art of the Possible – Interpreting Statutes under the Human Rights Act *European Human Rights Law Review*, 665-675.

Lester, Lord and David Pannick (2000) The Impact of the Human Rights Act on Private Law: The Knight's Move *Law Quarterly Review* 116, 380-385.

Levie, H, D Gregory and C Callender (1984) Redundancy Pay: Trick or Treat? in *Fighting Closures* eds H Levie, D Gregory and N Lorentzen (Spokesman, Nottingham).

Lewis, Clive (2008) *Judicial Remedies in Public Law* 4th edn (Sweet and Maxwell, London).

Lewis, Clive and Sarah Moore (1993) Duties, Directives and Damages in European Community Law *Public Law*, 151-170.

Lewis, David (1995) Whistleblowers and Job Security *Modern Law Review* 58, 208-221.

Lewis, David (1998) The Public Interest Disclosure Act 1998 *Industrial law Journal* 27, 325-330.

Lewis, David (1999) Re-Employment as a Remedy for Unfair Dismissal: How Can the Culture be Changed? *Industrial Law Journal* 28, 183-185.

Lewis, David (2001) Whistleblowing at Work: On what Principles Should Legislation be Based? *Industrial Law Journal* 30, 169-193.

Lewis, David (2004) How Should Safety Concerns be Handled? *Industrial Law Journal* 33, 42-45.

Lewis, David (2006) Whistleblowers, Reasonable Belief and Data Protection Issues *Industrial Law Journal* 35, 324-328.

Lewis, David (2007) Personal and Vicarious Liability for the Victimisation of Whistleblowers *Industrial Law Journal* 36, 224-227.

Lewis, Paul (2000) Pregnant Workers and Sex Discrimination: the Limits of Purposive, Non-comparative Methodology *International Journal of Comparative Labour Law and Industrial Relations* 16, 55-69.

Lewis, Roy (1979) Collective Agreements: The Kahn-Freund Legacy *Modern Law Review* 42, 613-622.

Lewis, Roy (1986) The Role of the Law in Employment Relations, in *Labour Law in Britain* ed Roy Lewis (Basil Blackwell, Oxford).

Lewis, Roy (1990) Strike-free Deals and Pendulum Arbitration *British Journal of Industrial Relations*, 28, 32-56.

Lewis, Roy (1998) The Employment Rights (Dispute Resolution) Act 1998 *Industrial Law Journal* 27, 214-219.

Lewis, Roy and Jon Clark (1993) *Employment Rights, Industrial Tribunals and Arbitration: The Case for Alternative Dispute Resolution* (Institute of Employment Rights, London).

Lightman, Gavin (1987) A Trade Union in Chains: Scargill Unbound - The Legal Constraints of Receivership and Sequestration *Current Legal Problems* 40, 25-54.

Lightman, Sir Gavin and John Bowers (1998) Incorporation of the ECHR and its Impact on Employment Law *European Human Rights Law Review* 560-581.

Lindbeck, Assar, and Dennis J Snower (1989) *The Insider-Outsider Theory of Employment and Unemployment* (MIT Press, Boston).

Linden, Tom (2006) Employment Protection for Employees Working Abroad *Industrial Law Journal* 35, 186-195.

Lindley, RM (1983) Active Employment Policy, in *Industrial Relations in Britain* ed George Sayers Bain (Basil Blackwell, Oxford).

Lindsay, Craig and Claire Macauley (2004) Growth in Self-Employment in the UK *Labour Market Trends* 112, 399-404.

Lindsay, Hon Mr Justice (2001) The Implied Term of Trust and Confidence *Industrial Law Journal* 30, 1-16.

Lock, GF (1983) Labour Law, Parliamentary Staff and Parliamentary Privilege *Industrial Law Journal* 12, 28-37.

Lockwood, Graeme (2006) The administration of union business: the role of the Certification Officer *Industrial Relations Journal* 37, 209-221.

Logan, John (2006) The Union Avoidance Industry in the United States *British Journal of Industrial Relations* 44, 651-675.

Lorber, Pascale (1999) Regulating Fixed-Term Work in the United Kingdom: A Positive Step towards Workers' Protection? *International Journal of Comparative Labour Law and Industrial Relations* 15, 121-135.

Lorber, Pascale (2003) National Works Councils: Opening the Door on a Whole New Era in United Kingdom Employment Relations? *International Journal of Comparative Labour Law and Industrial Relations* 19, 297- 319.

Lorber, Pascale (2004) Reviewing the European Works Council Directive: European Progress and United Kingdom Perspective *Industrial Law Journal* 33,191-199.

Lorber, Pascale (2006) Implementing the Information and Consultation Directive in Great Britain: A New Voice at Work *International Journal of Comparative Labour Law and Industrial Relations* 22, 231-258.

Lorber, Stephen (2004) Data Protection and Subject Access Requests *Industrial Law Journal* 33, 179-190.

Lörcher, Klaus (2012) Social Competences, in *The Lisbon Treaty and Social Europe* eds Niklas Bruun, Klaus Lörcher and Isabelle Schömann (Hart, Oxford).

Low Pay Unit (1988) Escaping the Clutches of the Poverty Trap *Low Pay Review*, Spring.

Low Pay Unit (1992) NES 1991: Pay-Gap Yawns as Low-Paid Left Behind *New Review of the Low Pay Unit*, 13, 8-12.

Lupton, T and A Bowey (1974) *Wages and Salaries* (Penguin, Harmondsworth).

Lustgarten, Laurence (1986) *The Governance of Police* (Sweet and Maxwell, London).

Lyon-Caen, Gérard, Jean Pélissier and Alain Supiot (1996) *Droit du Travail* 18th edn (Dalloz, Paris).

MacDonald, Elizabeth (1992) Exclusion Clauses: the ambit of s 13(1) of the Unfair Contract Terms Act *Legal Studies* 12, 277-301.

Macdonald, Ian and Nicholas Blake (1995) *Immigration Law and Practice in the United Kingdom* (Butterworths, London).

Machin, Stephen (1996) Wage Inequality in the UK *Oxford Review of Economic Policy* 12, 47-64

Machin, Stephen (2000) Union Decline in Britain *British Journal of Industrial Relations* 38, 631-645

Machin, Stephen (2003) Trade Union Decline, New Workplaces and New Workers, in *Representing Workers: Trade Union Recognition and Membership in Britain* ed Howard Gospel and Stephen Wood (Routledge, London).

Machin, Stephen, and Andrew Manning (1992) *Minimum Wages, Wage Dispersion and Employment: Evidence from UK Wages Councils* Discussion Paper 80 Centre for Economic Performance (London School of Economics).

MacInnes, John (1985) Conjuring Up Consultation: The Role and Extent of Joint Consultation in Post-War Private Manufacturing Industry *British Journal of Industrial Relations* 23, 93-113.

MacMillan, John K (1999) Employment Tribunals: Philosophies and Practicalities *Industrial Law Journal* 28, 33-56.

Maine, Sir Henry [1861] (1927) *Ancient Law: its connection with the early history of society, and its relation to modern ideas* ed Sir Frederick Pollock (Murray, London).

Mantouvalou, Virginia (2008) Human Rights and Unfair Dismissal: Private Acts in Public Spaces *Modern Law Review* 71, 912-939.

Mantouvalou, Virginia and Hugh Collins (2009) Private Life and Dismissal *Industrial Law Journal* 38, 133-138.

Mantouvalou, Virginia (2010) Is There a Human Right Not to Be a Trade Union Member? Labour Rights under the European Convention on Human Rights in *Human Rights at Work: Perspectives on Law and Regulation* ed Colin Fenwick and Tonia Novitz (Hart Publishing, Oxford).

Marchington, Mick (1992) *New Developments in Employee Involvement* Employment Department Research Series No 2 (Employment Department, London).

Marginson, Paul, Mark Gilman, Otto Jacobi and Hubert Kreiger (1998) *Negotiating European Works Councils: an Analysis of Agreements under Article 13* (European Foundation for the Improvement of Living and Working Conditions).

Marginson, Paul, PK Edwards, Rod Martin, John Purcell and Keith Sisson (1988) *Beyond the Workplace: Managing industrial relations in the multi-establishment enterprise* (Basil Blackwell, Oxford).

Markesinis, Basil S (1990) Our Patchy Law of Privacy – Time to Do Something About It *Modern Law Review* 53, 802-809.

Markesinis, Basil S (1994) A Matter of Style *Law Quarterly Review* 110, 607-627.

Markesinis, Basil (1999) Privacy, Freedom of Expression and the Human Rights Bill: Lessons from Germany *Law Quarterly Review* 115, 47-88.

Marsden, David, and Marc Thompson (1990) Flexibility Agreements in Practice *Work, Employment and Society* 4, 83-104.

Marsh, Catherine (1991) *Hours of Work of Women and Men in Great Britain.*

Marsh, Catherine, Rosemary McAuley and Sian Penlington (1990) The Road to Recovery? Some Evidence from Vacancies in One Labour Market *Work, Employment and Society* 4, 31-58.

Martin, Roderick (1992) *Bargaining Power* (Clarendon Press, Oxford).

Martin, Roderick, Patricia Fosh, Huw Morris, Paul Smith and Roger Undy (1991) The Decollectivisation of Trade Unions? Ballots and Collective Bargaining in the 1980s *Industrial Relations Journal* 22, 197-208.

Martin, Ross M (1980) *TUC: The Growth of a Pressure Group 1868-1976* (Clarendon Press, Oxford).

Marx, Irene (1999) Low Pay and Poverty in OECD Countries *Employment Audit* 10, 17-21.

Matthews, Paul (1982) Salaries in the Apportionment Act 1870 *Legal Studies* 2, 302-312.

Mayhew, Ken and John T Addison (1983) Discrimination in the Labour Market, in *Industrial Relations in Britain* ed George Sayers Bain (Basil Blackwell, Oxford).

McCabe, Sarah and Peter Wallington (1988) *The Police, Public Order and Civil Liberties* (Routledge, London).

McCallum, Ronald (1989) Exploring the Common Law: Lay-off, Suspension and the Contract of Employment *Australian Journal of Labour Law* 2, 211-233.

McCarthy, Lord (1999) *Fairness at Work and Trade Union Recognition: Past Comparisons and Future Problems* (Institute of Employment Rights, London).

McCarthy, WEJ (1964) *The Closed Shop in Britain* (University of California Press, Berkeley and Los Angeles).

McCarthy, WEJ (1992) The Rise and Fall of Collective Laissez-Faire in *Legal Intervention in Industrial Relations: Gains and Losses* ed WEJ McCarthy (Basil Blackwell, Oxford).

McCarthy, WEJ (2000) Representative Consultations with Specified Employees – or the Future of Rung Two, in *Legal Regulation of the Employment Relation* eds Hugh Collins, Paul Davies and Roger Rideout (Kluwer, London).

McColgan, Aileen (1994) *Pay Equity – Just Wages for Women?* (Institute of Employment Rights, London).

McColgan, Aileen (1997) *Just Wages for Women* (Clarendon Press, Oxford).

McColgan, Aileen (2000a) Missing the Point? The Part-time Workers (Prevention of Less Favourable Treatment) Regulations 2000 (SI 2000, No 1551) *Industrial Law Journal* 29, 260-267.

McColgan, Aileen (2000b) Family Friendly Frolics? The Maternity and Parental Leave etc. Regulations 1999 *Industrial Law Journal* 29, 125-144.

McColgan, Aileen (2000c) *Discrimination Law. Text, Cases and Materials* (Hart Publishing, Oxford).

McColgan, Aileen (2000d) Article 10 and the Right to Freedom of Expression: Workers Ungagged? in *Human Rights at Work* ed Keith Ewing (Institute of Employment Rights, London).

McColgan, Aileen (2009) Class Wars? Religion and (In)equality in the Workplace *Industrial Law Journal* 38, 1-29.

McCrudden, Christopher (1983) Equal Pay for Work of Equal Value: the Equal Pay (Amendment) Regulations 1983 *Industrial Law Journal* 12, 197-219.

McCrudden, Christopher (1985) Institutional Discrimination *Oxford Journal of Legal Studies* 4, 303-367.

McCrudden, Christopher (1988) The Northern Ireland Fair Employment White Paper: a Critical Assessment *Industrial Law Journal* 17, 162-181.

McCrudden, Christopher (1996) Third Time Lucky? The Pensions Act 1995 and Equal Treatment in Occupational Pensions *Industrial Law Journal* 25, 28-42.

McCrudden, Christopher (2007a) *Buying Social Justice* (Oxford University Press, Oxford).

McCrudden, Christopher (2007b) Buying Social Justice: Equality and Public Procurement *Current Legal Problems* 60, 121-147.

McCrudden, Christopher (2007c) Equality Legislation and Reflexive Regulation: a Response to the Discrimination Law Review's Consultative Paper *Industrial Law Journal* 36, 255-266.

McCrudden, Christopher (2012a) Two Views of Subordination: The Personal Scope of Employment Discrimination Law in *Jivraj v Hashwani Industrial Law Journal* 41, 30-55.

McCrudden, Christopher (2012b) Procurement and Fairness in the Workplace, in *Making Employment Rights Effective: Issues of Compliance and Enforcement* ed Linda Dickens (Hart, Oxford).

McCrudden, Christopher, David Smith, Colin Brown and Jim Knox (1991) *Racial Justice at Work* (Policy Studies Institute, London).

McGregor, Harvey (2011) *McGregor on Damages* 19th edn (Sweet and Maxwell, London).

McHale, Jean (1992) Whistleblowing in the NHS *Journal of Social Welfare Law*, 363-371.

McHale, Jean (1993) Whistleblowing in the NHS Revisited *Journal of Social Welfare and Family Law*, 52-57.

McIlroy, John (2008) Ten Years of New Labour: Workplace Learning, Social Partnership and Union Revitalization in Britain *British Journal of Industrial Relations* 46, 283-313.

McIlroy, John (2009) A Brief History of Bristol Trade Unions and Neoliberalism in the Age of New Labour in ed Gary Daniels and John McIlroy *Trade Unions in a Neoliberal World* (Routledge, London).

McIlroy, John and Gary Daniels (2009) Introduction: Trade Unions in a Neoliberal World in ed Gary Daniels and John McIlroy *Trade Unions in a Neoliberal World* (Routledge, London).

McKay, Sonia (1996) *The Law on Industrial Action under the Conservatives* (Institute of Employment Rights, London).

McKay, Sir William (ed) (2004) *Erskine May's Treatise on the Law, Privileges, Proceedings and Usage of Parliament* 23rd edn (LexisNexis UK, London).

McKendrick, Ewan (1988) The Rights of Trade Union Members – Part I of the Employment Act 1988 *Industrial Law Journal* 17, 141-161.

McKendrick, Ewan (1990) Vicarious Liability and Independent Contractors – a Reassessment *Modern Law Review* 53, 770-784.

McKinnon, Catherine (1979) *Sexual Harassment of Working Women* (Yale UP, New Haven).

McLaughlin, Eithne, Jane Millar and Kenneth Cooke (1989) *Work and Welfare Benefits* (Avebury, Aldershot).

McLean, Hazel (1990) Contract of Employment - Negative Covenants and No Work, No Pay *Cambridge Law Journal*, 49, 28-31.

McLean, Hazel (1992) An Employer's Right to be Unreasonable *Cambridge Law Journal* 51, 23-26.

McLean, Hazel (1994) *Fair Shares – The Future of Employee Financial Participation in the UK* (Institute of Employment Rights, London).

McMullen, Jeremy, and Philippa Kaufman (1991) *Labour Law Review* (Institute of Employment Rights, London).

McMullen, John (1982) A Synthesis of the Mode of Termination of Contracts of Employment *Cambridge Law Journal* 41, 110-141.

McMullen, John (1992) *Business Transfers and Employee Rights* 2nd edn (Butterworths, London).

McMullen, John (1994) Contracting-out and Market Testing – the Uncertainty Ends? *Industrial Law Journal* 23, 230-240.

McMullen, John (1995) Enforcing Contracts of Employment – 'Going Back to Basics' in the Resolution of Employment Disputes *Industrial Law Journal* 24, 353-363.

McMullen, John (1996) Enforcing Contracts of Employment – A Postscript *Industrial Law Journal* 25, 140-144.

McMullen John (1997) Extending Remedies for Breach of the Employment Contract *Industrial Law Journal* 26, 245-247.

McMullen, John (1999a) TUPE: Waiver of Employment Rights & Contract Changes after *Wilson Industrial Law Journal* 28, 76-84.

McMullen, John (1999b) TUPE – Sidestepping *Süzen, Industrial Law Journal* 28, 360-364.

McMullen, John (2006) An Analysis of the Transfer of Undertakings (Protection of Employment) Regulations 2006 *Industrial Law Journal* 35, 113-139.

Mead, David (2004) To BNP or Not to BNP: Union Exclusion on Ground of Political Activity – A Commentary on *ASLEF* v *Lee, Industrial Law Journal* 33, 267-277.

Mead, David (2007) The right to peaceful protest under the European Convention on Human Rights – a content study of Strasbourg case law *European Human Rights Law Review* 4, 345-384.

Mead, David (2010) *The New Law of Peaceful Protest* (Hart Publishing, Oxford).

Mead, Geoffrey (1990) The Role of Intention in Direct Discrimination *Industrial Law Journal* 19, 250-252.

Mead, Geoffrey (1991) Restitution within Contract? *Legal Studies* 11, 172-188.

Meager, Nigel (1986) Temporary Work in Britain *Employment Gazette* 94, 7-15.

Meehan, Elizabeth (1985) *Rights at Work: Campaigns and Policy in Britain and the United States* (Macmillan, Basingstoke).

Meeran, Goolam (2006) The Employment Tribunals in *The Changing Institutional Face of British Employment Relations* ed Linda Dickens and Alan C Neal (Kluwer Law International, The Netherlands).

Merrett, Louise (2010) The Extra-Territorial Reach of Employment Legislation *Industrial Law Journal* 39, 355-381.

Merritt, Adrian (1982a) 'Control' v 'Economic Reality': Defining the Contract of Employment *Australian Business Law Review*, 105-124.

Merritt, Adrian (1982b) The Historical Role of the Law in the Regulation of Employment – Abstentionist or Interventionist? *Australian Journal of Law and Society* 1, 56-86.

Mesher, John (1985) Social Security in the Coal Dispute *Industrial Law Journal* 14, 191-202.

Mesher, John (1993) Social Security for Occupational Pensions: Is the Law of Trusts Superannuated? *Current Legal Problems* 46, 96-112.

Mesher, John and Frank Sutcliffe (1986) Industrial Action and the Individual, in *Labour Law in Britain* ed Roy Lewis (Blackwell, Oxford).

Metcalf, David (1986) *Labour Market Flexibility and Jobs: a survey of evidence from OECD countries with special reference to Great Britain and Europe* Discussion paper No 254 (Centre for Labour Economics, London School of Economics).

Metcalf, David (1989) Water Notes Dry Up: the Impact of the Donovan Reform Proposals and Thatcherism at Work on Labour Productivity in British Manufacturing *British Journal of Industrial Relations* 27, 1-31.

Metcalf, David (1993) Industrial Relations and Economic Performance *British Journal of Industrial Relations* 31, 255-284.

Metcalf, David (1999) The British National Minimum Wage *British Journal of Industrial Relations* 37, 171-201.

Metcalf, David (2004) British Unions: Resurgence or Perdition? http://cep.lse.ac.uk/people/cv/david_metcalf.pdf.

Metcalf, David (2008) Why Has the British National Minimum Wage had Little or No Impact on Employment? *Journal of Industrial Relatoins* 50, 489-511.

Meyers, Frederic (1964) *Ownership of Jobs: A Comparative Study* (University of California Press, Los Angeles).

Middlemiss, Sam (2004) The Truth and Nothing but the Truth: The Legal Liability of Employers for Employee References *Industrial Law Journal* 33, 59-67.

Miller, Kenneth (1990) Reasonableness and Section 4 of the Employment Act 1980 *British Journal of Industrial Relations* 28, 69-83.

Miller, Kenneth and Charles Woolfson (1994) Timex: Industrial Relations and the Use of the Law in the 1990s *Industrial Law Journal* 23, 209-225.

Mills, Shaun (1997) The International Labour Organisation, the United Kingdom and Freedom of Association: An Annual Cycle of Condemnation *European Human Rights Law Review* 1, 35-53.

Millward, Neil and Mark Stevens (1986) *British Workplace Industrial Relations 1980-1984: the DE/ESRC/PSI/ACAS Surveys* (Gower, Aldershot).

Millward, Neil, Alex Bryson and John Forth (2000) *All Change at Work?* (Routledge, London).

Millward, Neil, Mark Stevens, David Smart and WR Hawes (1992) *Workplace Industrial Relations in Transition: The ED/ESRC/PSI/ACAS Surveys* (Dartmouth, Aldershot).

Minford, Patrick, with Paul Ashton, Michael Peel, David Davies and Alison Sprague (1986) *Unemployment: Cause and Cure* (Basil Blackwell, Oxford).

Mirza, Qudsia (1994) *Race Relations in the Workplace* (Institute of Employment Rights, London).

Mitchell, Richard (ed.) (1995) *Redefining Labour Law* (Centre for Employment and Labour Relations Law, University of Melbourne).

Moffat, Graham and Sue Ward (1986) Occupational Pensions, in *Labour Law in Britain* ed Roy Lewis (Basil Blackwell, Oxford).

Mogridge, Christine (1981) Illegal Contracts of Employment: Loss of Statutory Protection *Industrial Law Journal* 20, 23-33.

Moher, Jim (1989) *The London Millwrights and Engineers 1755-1825* PhD Thesis, University of London.

Moher, Jim (1995) *Trade Unions and the Law – The Politics of Change* (Institute of Employment Rights, London).

Monaghan, Karon (2000) *Challenging Race Discrimination at Work* (Institute of Employment Rights, London)

Monger, Joanne (2004) Labour Disputes in 2003 *Labour Market Trends* (June).

Moore, Sian, Sonia McKay and Helen Bewley (2004) *The Content of New Voluntary Trade Union Recognition Agreements, 1998-2002: Volume One – An Analysis of New Agreements and Case Studies* (Employment Relations Research Series No 26, BERR (formerly DTI) London).

Moore, Sian, Sonia McKay and Helen Bewley (2005) *The Content of New Voluntary Trade Union Recognition Agreements 1998-2002: Volume Two - Findings from the Survey of Employers* (Employment Relations Research Series No 43, BERR (formerly DTI) London).

Moore, Sian, Stephen Wood, and Paul Davies (2000) Recognition of Trade Unions – Consultation over the Access Code and Method of Bargaining *Industrial Law Journal* 29, 406-415.

Moreham, NA (2005) Privacy in the Common Law: a doctrinal and theoretical analysis *Law Quarterly Review* 121, 628-56.

Moreham, NA (2008) The Right to Respect for Private Life in the European Convention on Human Rights: A Re-examination *European Human Rights Law Review*, 44-79.

Morris, Debra (1993a) The Commissioner for the Rights of Trade Union Members – A Framework for the Future? *Industrial Law Journal* 22, 104-118.

Morris, Debra (1993b) 'Trade Union Members Are My Prime Concern' *Industrial Law Journal*, 22, 307-309.

Morris, Debra (1999) Volunteering and Employment Status *Industrial Law Journal* 28, 249-255.

Morris, Gillian S (1980) The Police and Industrial Emergencies *Industrial Law Journal* 9, 1-12.

Morris, Gillian S (1985a) Road Blocks and Bail Conditions *Industrial Law Journal* 14, 109-111.

Morris, Gillian S (1985b) The Ban on Trade Unions at Government Communications Headquarters *Public Law*, 177-186.

Morris, Gillian S (1986a) *Strikes in Essential Services* (Mansell, London).

Morris, Gillian S (1986b) Employment Rights and Public Law Remedies *Industrial Law Journal*, 15, 194-196.

Morris, Gillian S (1991) Industrial Action in Essential Services: The New Law *Industrial Law Journal* 20, 89-101.

Morris, Gillian S (1993) Industrial Action: Public and Private Interests *Industrial Law Journal* 22, 194-210.

Morris, Gillian S (1994a) Freedom of Association and the Interests of the State, in *Human Rights and Labour Law: Essays for Paul O'Higgins*, eds KD Ewing, CA Gearty and BA Hepple (Mansell, London).

Morris, Gillian S (1994b) Employment in the Prison Service: Whither Public Service Regulation? *Public Law*, 535-39.

Morris, Gillian S (1994c) The New Legal Regime for Prison Officers *Industrial Law Journal* 23, 326-331.

Morris, Gillian S (1998a) Local government workers and rights of political participation: time for a change *Public Law*, 25-33.

Morris, Gillian S (1998b) Political Activities of Public Servants and Freedom of Expression in *Importing the First Amendment*, ed Ian Loveland (Hart Publishing, Oxford).

Morris, Gillian S (1998c) The Human Rights Act and the Public/Private Divide in Employment Law *Industrial Law Journal* 27, 293-308.

Morris, Gillian S (1999a) Fragmenting the State: Implications for Accountability for Employment Practices in Public Services *Public Law*, 64-83.

Morris, Gillian S (1999b) The Political Activities of Local Government Workers and the European Convention on Human Rights *Public Law*, 211-218

Morris, Gillian S (1999c) The European Convention on Human Rights and Employment: To Which Acts Does it Apply? *European Human Rights Law Review*, 496-511.

Morris, Gillian S (1999d) The Role of Local Education Authorities as Employers *Journal of Local Government Law* 2, 54-57.

Morris, Gillian S (2000) Employment in Public Services: The Case for Special Treatment *Oxford Journal of Legal Studies* 20, 167-183.

Morris, Gillian S (2001a) Fundamental Rights: Exclusion by Agreement? *Industrial Law Journal* 30, 49-71.

Morris, Gillian S (2001b) The Employment Relations Act 1999 and Collective Labour Standards *International Journal of Comparative Labour Law and Industrial Relations* 17, 63-77.

Morris, Gillian S (2002a) The Use of E-Mail and the Internet at Work in English Law in *Online Rights of Employees* ed R Blanpain (Kluwer, The Hague).

Morris, Gillian S (2002b) Extending the Police Family: Issues and Anomalies *Public Law* 670-677.

Morris, Gillian S (2004a) The Future of the Public/Private Labour Law Divide, in *The Future of Labour Law: Liber Amicorum Sir Bob Hepple QC* ed Catherine Barnard, Simon Deakin and Gillian S Morris (Hart Publishing, Oxford).

Morris, Gillian S (2004b) England, in *Temporary Agency Work and the Information Society* ed Roger Blanpain and Ronnie Graham (Kluwer Law International, The Hague).

Morris, Gillian S (2005) Britain's New Statutory Procedures; Routes to Resolution or Barriers to Justice? *Comparative Labor Law and Policy Journal* 25, 477-486.

Morris, Gillian S (2012) The Development of Statutory Employment Rights in Britain and Enforcement Mechanisms in *Making Employment Rights Effective: Issues of Compliance and Enforcement* ed Linda Dickens (Hart Publishing, Oxford).

Morris, Gillian S and Timothy J Archer (2000) *Collective Labour Law* (Hart Publishing, Oxford).

Morris, Gillian S and Sandra Fredman (1993) Is there a Public/Private Labour Law Divide? *Comparative Labor Law Journal* 14, 115-137.

Morris, Gillian S with Stephen Rydzkowski (1984) Approaches to Industrial Action in the National Health Service *Industrial Law Journal* 13, 153-164.

Morris, Jenny (1985) *Women Workers and the Sweated Trades* (Gower, Aldershot).

Morse, CJG (1982) Contracts of Employment and the EEC Contractual Obligations Convention, in *Contract Conflicts* ed PM North (North Holland, Amsterdam).

Mosley, Hugh (1990) The Social Dimension of European Integration *International Labour Review* 129, 147-163.

Mowbray, Alastair (1997) The European Court of Human Rights' Approach to Just Satisfaction *Public Law*, 647-659.

Mückenberger, Ulrich, and Simon Deakin (1989) From Deregulation to a European Floor of Rights: Labour Law, Flexibilisation and the European Single Market *Zeitschrift für ausländisches und internationales Arbeits- und Sozialrecht* 3, 157-206.

Mückenberger, Ulrich (2009) Workers' Representation at the Plant and Enterprise Level in *The Transformation of Labour Law in Europe* ed Bob Hepple and Bruno Veneziani (Hart Publishing, Oxford).

Mumford, Karen (1996) Arbitration and ACAS in Britain: a Historical Perspective *British Journal of Industrial Relations*, 34, 287-305.

Munday, Roderick (1981) Tribunal Lore: Legalism and the Industrial Tribunals *Industrial Law Journal* 10, 146-159.

Murray, Jill (1999) Normalising Temporary Work *Industrial Law Journal* 28, 269-275.

Murray, Jill (2001) A New Phase in the Regulation of Multinational Enterprises: The Role of the OECD *Industrial Law Journal* 30, 255-270.

NACAB (1990) *Hard Labour* (National Association of Citizens' Advice Bureaux, London).

Napier, Brian (1972) Working to Rule – A Breach of the Contract of Employment? *Industrial Law Journal*, 1, 125-134.

Napier, Brian (1983) Dismissals: the New ILO Standards *Industrial Law Journal* 12, 17-27.

Napier, Brian (1986) The Contract of Employment, in *Labour Law in Britain* ed Roy Lewis (Basil Blackwell, Oxford).

Napier, Brian (1987) Breach of Statutory Duty and Unlawful Means in Strike Law *Cambridge Law Journal* 46, 222-224.

Napier, Brian (1989) AIDS, Discrimination and Employment Law *Industrial Law Journal*, 18, 84-96.

Napier, Brian (1992) Computerisation and Employment Rights *Industrial Law Journal* 21, 1-14.

Napier, Brian (1993) *CCT, Market Testing and Employment Rights. The effects of TUPE and the Acquired Rights Directive* (Institute of Employment Rights, London).

Naylor, Kate (1994) Part-time Working in Britain: an Historical Analysis *Employment Gazette*, 102, 473-484.

Neal, Alan C (1990) The European Framework Directive on the Health and Safety of Workers: Challenges for the United Kingdom? *International Journal of Comparative Labour Law and Industrial Relations* 6, 80-117.

Neal, Alan C (1998) Regulating Health and Safety at Work: Developing European Union Policy for the Millenium *International Journal of Comparative Labour Law and Industrial Relations* 14, 217-236.

Nicholls, Paul and David Bradley (2000) It's Good to Talk: The Eighth Annual Industrial Relations Survey (Gee Publishing, London).

Nickell, Stephen (1997) Unemployment and Labour Market Rigidities: Europe versus North America *Journal of Economic Perspectives* 11, 55-74.

Nickell, Stephen (1999) Unemployment in Britain, in Paul Gregg and Jonathan Wadsworth (eds) *The State of Working Britain* (Manchester University Press, Manchester).

Nielsen, Ruth and Erica Szyszczak (1997) *The Social Dimension of the European Community*, 3rd edn (Handelshojskolens Forlag, Copenhagen).

Njoya, Wanjiru (2004) Employee Ownership and Efficiency: An Evolutionary Perspective *Industrial Law Journal* 30, 211-241.

Njoya, Wanjiru (2007) *Property in Work: The Employment Relationship in the Anglo-American Firm* (Ashgate, Aldershot).

Nobles, Richard (1986) Pensions: the New Framework *Modern Law Review* 49, 42-67.

Nobles, Richard (1993) *Pensions, Employment and the Law* (Clarendon Press, Oxford).

Nobles, Richard (1996) Pensions Act 1995 *Modern Law Review* 59, 241-260.

Nobles, Richard (1998) The Death of Deferred Pay? *Industrial Law Journal* 27, 142-146.

Nobles, Richard (2000a) Access to the Law of Pensions: the Lessons from *National Grid v Laws*, *Industrial Law Journal* 29, 172-175.

Nobles, Richard (2000b) Enforcing Employees' Pension Rights – the Courts' Hostility to the Pensions Ombudsman *Industrial Law Journal* 29, 243-259.

Nobles, Richard (2001) Pension Scheme Surpluses: *National Grid* in the House of Lords *Industrial Law Journal* 30, 318-324.

Nolan, Donal (1995) Recovering Damages for Psychiatric Injury at Work *Industrial Law Journal* 24, 280-284.

Nolan, Peter (1989) Walking on Water? Economic Performance and Industrial Relations under Thatcher *Industrial Relations Journal* 20, 81-92.

Nolan, Peter, and Paul Marginson (1990) Skating on Thin Ice? David Metcalf on Trade Unions and Productivity *British Journal of Industrial Relations* 28, 227-247.

Novitz, Tonia (1997) Negative Freedom of Association *Industrial Law Journal* 26, 79-87.

Novitz, Tonia (1998) Freedom of Association and "Fairness at Work" – An Assessment of the Impact and Relevance of ILO Convention No 87 on its Fiftieth Anniversary *Industrial Law Journal* 27, 169-191.

Novitz, Tonia (2000) International Promises and Domestic Pragmatism: To What Extent will the Employment Relations Act 1999 Implement International Labour Standards Relating to Freedom of Association *Modern Law Review* 63, 379-393.

Novitz, Tonia (2003) *International and European Protection of the Right to Strike* (OUP, Oxford).

Novitz, Tonia (2008) A Human Rights Analysis of the Viking and Laval Judgments *Cambridge Yearbook of European Legal Studies* 10, 541-561.

Novitz, Tonia and Paul Skidmore (2001) *Fairness at Work. A Critical Analysis of the Employment Relations Act 1999 and its Treatment of Collective Rights* (Hart Publishing, Oxford).

Novitz, Tonia and Phil Syrpis (2006) Assessing Legitimate Structures for the Making of Transational Labour Law: The Durability of Corporatism *Industrial Law Journal* 35, 367-394.

Novitz, Tonia and Phil Syrpis (2010) Giving with the One Hand and Taking with the Other: Protection of Workers' Human Rights in the European Union in *Human Rights at Work: Perspectives on Law and Regulation* ed Colin Fenwick and Tonia Novitz (Hart Publishing, Oxford).

O'Cinneide, Colm (2001) The Race Relations (Amendment) Act 2000 *Public Law*, 220-232.

O'Cinneide, Colm (2007) The Commission for Equality and Human Rights: A New Institution for New and Uncertain Times *Industrial Law Journal* 36, 141-162.

O'Dair, Richard (1991) Justifying an Interference with Contractual Rights *Oxford Journal of Legal Studies* 11, 227-246.

O'Higgins, Paul (1991) The European Social Charter in *Human Rights for the 1990s* eds Robert Blackburn and John Taylor (Mansell, London).

O'Higgins, Paul (2002) The interaction of the ILO, the Council of Europe and European Union Labour Standards in *Social and Labour Rights in a Global Context* ed Bob Hepple (Cambridge University Press, Cambridge).

O'Neill, Aidan (2011) *EU Law for UK Lawyers* 2nd edn (Hart Publishing, Oxford).

O'Regan, Catherine (1991) Contempt of Court and the Enforcement of Labour Injunctions *Modern Law Review*, 53, 385-407.

Oakley, Ann (1972) *Sex, Gender and Society* (Temple Smith, London).

OECD (1986a) *Labour Market Flexibility: a report by a high level group of experts to the Secretary-General* (Organisation for Economic Cooperation and Development, Paris).

OECD (1986b) *Flexibility in the Labour Market* (Organisation for Economic Cooperation and Development, Paris).

OECD (1991) *Employment Outlook* (Organisation for Economic Cooperation and Development, Paris).

OECD (1994) *Employment Outlook* (Organisation for Economic Cooperation and Development, Paris).

Oliver, Dawn (1993) *Pepper v Hart*: a Suitable Case for Reference to *Hansard*? *Public Law*, 5-13.

Oliver, Dawn (1997) Common Values in Public and Private Law and the Public/Private Divide *Public Law* 630-646.

Oliver, Hazel (2002) Email and Internet Monitoring in the Workplace: Information, Privacy and Contracting-Out *Industrial Law Journal* 31, 321-352.

Oliver, Hazel (2004) Sexual Orientation Discrimination: Perceptions, Definitions and Genuine Occupational Requirements *Industrial Law Journal* 33, 1-21.

Orlandini, Giovanni (2008) Trade Union Rights and Market Freedoms: The European Court of Justice Sets the Rules *Comparative Labor Law and Policy Journal* 29, 573-603.

Ormerod, David (2011) *Smith and Hogan's Criminal Law*, 13th edn (Oxford University Press, Oxford).

Orth, John V (1991) *Combination and Conspiracy: A Legal History of Trade Unionism 1721-1906* (Clarendon Press, Oxford).

Oxenbridge, Sarah and William Brown (2004) Achieving a New Equilibrium? The stability of cooperative employer-union relationships *Industrial Relations Journal* 35, 388-402.

Oxenbridge, Sarah, William Brown, Simon Deakin and Cliff Pratten (2003) Initial Reponses to the Statutory Recognition Provisions of the Employment Relations Act 1999 *British Journal of Industrial Relations* 41, 315-334.

Ozaki, M (1993) Labour Relations in the Public Service, in *Comparative Labour Law and Industrial Relations in Industrialised Market Economies* 5th edn, eds R Blanpain and C Engels (Kluwer, Deventer-Boston).

Palmer, Stephanie (2000) Human Rights: Implications for Labour Law *Cambridge Law Journal* 59, 168-200.

Panitch, Leo (1976) *Social Democracy and Industrial Militancy* (CUP, Cambridge).

Pankert, A (1980) Settlement of Labour Disputes in Essential Services *Inter-national Labour Review*, 119, 723-37.

Pankhurst, Kate (1988) Work Effort under the Incomplete Contract of Employment (Mimeo, New Hall, Cambridge).

Pannick, David (1985) *Sex Discrimination Law* (Clarendon Press, Oxford).

Pannick, David (1998) Principles of Interpretation of Convention Rights under the Human Rights Act and the Discretionary Area of Judgment *Public Law*, 545-551.

Parker, Kenneth (1992) State Liability in Damages for Breach of Community Law *Law Quarterly Review* 108, 181-6.

Parker, S, C Thomas, N Ellis and WEJ McCarthy (1971) *Effects of the Redundancy Payments Act* (HMSO, London).

Parkinson, JE (1993) *Corporate Power and Responsibility: Issues in the Theory of Company Law* (Clarendon Press, Oxford).

Peccei, Riccardo, Helen Bewley, Howard Gospel and Paul Willman (2008) Look Who's Talking: Sources of Variation in Information Disclosure in the UK *British Journal of Industrial Relations* 46, 340-366.

Pedrazzoli, Marcello (ed) (1989) *Lavoro Subordinato e Dintorni: Comparazione e Prospettive* (Il Mulino, Bologna).

Peel, Edwin (2007) *Treitel on the Law of Contract* 12th edn (Sweet and Maxwell, London).

Peers, Steve (2010) Non-regression Clauses: The Fig Leaf Has Fallen *Industrial Law Journal* 39, 436-443.

Pélissier, Jean, Alain Supiot and Antoine Jeammaud (2008) *Droit du travail* 24th edn (Dalloz, Paris).

Pendleton, Andrew, Nicholas Wilson and Mike Wright (1998) The Perception and Effects of Share Ownership: Empirical Evidence from Employee Buy-Outs *British Journal of Industrial Relations* 36, 99-123.

Peters, Mark, Ken Seeds, Carrie Harding and Erica Garnett 2010: *Findings from the Survey of Employment Tribunal Applications 2008* EMAR No 107 (BIS, London).

Peters, Nancy (2004) The UK Calibreates the US National Labor Relations Act: Possible Lessons for the US? *Comparative Labor Law and Policy Journal* 25, 227-256.

Phillips, The Hon Mr Justice (1978) Some Notes on the Employment Appeal Tribunal *Industrial Law Journal* 7, 137-142.

Pilgerstorfer, Marcus and Simon Forshaw (2008) A Dog's Dinner? Reconsidering Contractual Illegality in the Employment Sphere *Industrial Law Journal* 37, 268-278.

Pilgerstorfer, Marcus and Simon Forshaw (2008) Transferred Discrimination in European Law *Industrial Law Journal* 37, 384-393.

Pitt, Gwyneth (1989) Dismissal at Common Law: the Relevance in Britain of American Developments *Modern Law Review* 52, 22-41.

Pitt, Gwyneth (1992) Can Reverse Discrimination be Justified?, in *Discrimination: the Limits of the Law* eds BA Hepple and Erika Szyszczak (Mansell, London).

Pitt, Gwyneth (1993) Justice in Dismissal: a Reply to Hugh Collins *Industrial Law Journal* 22, 251-268.

Pitt, Gwyneth (2011) Keeping the Faith: Trends and Tensions in Religion or Belief Discrimination *Industrial Law Journal* 40, 384-404.

Pollard, David (1996) Insolvent Companies and TUPE *Industrial Law Journal*, 25, 191-210.

Pollard, David (2005) Pensions and TUPE *Industrial Law Journal* 34, 127-157.

Pollert, Anna (1991) *Farewell to Flexibility?* (Basil Blackwell, Oxford).

Pollert, Anna (2005) The Unorganised Worker: The Decline in Collectivism and New Hurdles to Individual Employment Rights *Industrial Law Journal* 34, 217-238.

Pollert, Anna (2007) *The Unorganised Vulnerable Worker: The Case for Union Organising* (Institute of Employment Rights, London).

Pollock, Sir Frederick (1908) *Law of Torts* 8th edn (Stevens & Sons, London).

Pond, Chris, and Anna Searl (1991) *The Hidden Army: Children at Work in the 1990s* (Low Pay Unit, London).

Poole, Michael (1989) *The Origins of Economic Democracy* (Routledge, London).

Poole, Thomas (2000) Judicial Review and Public Employment: Decision-Making on the Public-Private Divide *Industrial Law Journal* 29, 61-67.

Popplewell, Sir Oliver (1987) Random Thoughts from the President's Chair *Industrial Law Journal* 16, 209-214.

Prassl, Jeremiah (2011) To Strike, to Serve? Industrial Action at British Airways. *British Airways plc v Unite the Union (Nos 1 and 2) Industrial Law Journal* 40, 82-91.

Prechal, S (1996) Case note on Case C-450/93 *Kalanke* v. *Freie Hansestadt Bremen* [1995] ECR I-3051 *Common Market Law Review* 33, 1245-1259.

Price, Robert and George Sayers Bain (1976) Union Growth Revisited: 1948-1974 in Perspective *British Journal of Industrial Relations* 14, 339-355.

Puttick, Keith (1999) 2020: A Welfare Odyssey – A Commentary on Principles into Practice and the Reform Programme *Industrial Law Journal* 28, 190-196.

Raday, Frances (1997) Trials and Tribulations of *Associated Newspapers* in Foreign Forums *Industrial Law Journal* 26, 235-245.

Raday, Frances (2002) The Decline of Union Power – Structural Inevitability or Policy Choice? in *Labour Law in an Era of Glabalization: Transformative Practices and Possibilities* ed Joanne Conaghan, Richard Michael Fischl, and Karl Klare (Oxford University Press, Oxford).

Reid, Karen (2012) *A Practitioner's Guide to the European Convention on Human Rights* 4th edn (Sweet and Maxwell, London)

Reynold, Frederic and John Hendy (2012) Reserving the Right to Change Terms and Conditions: How far Can the Employer Go? *Industrial Law Journal* 41, 79-92.

Reynold, Frederic and Anya Palmer (2005) Proving Constructive Dismissal: Should One be Concerned With What Was in the Employer's Mind? *Industrial Law Journal* 34, 96-102.

Richardson, JH (1938) *Industrial Relations in Great Britain* 3rd edn (PS King, London).

Rideout, RW (2002) What shall we do with the CAC? *Industrial Law Journal* 31, 1-34.

Robbins, L (ed) (1978) *Trade Unions: Public Goods or Public 'Bads'* (Institute of Economic Affairs, London).

Rodgers, Gerry, and Janine Rodgers (eds) (1989) *Precarious Jobs in Labour Market Regulation The growth of atypical employment in Western Europe* (International Institute for Labour Studies, Geneva).

Rodgers, Lisa (2009) The Notion of Working Time *Industrial Law Journal*, 38, 80-88.

Rogaly, Joe (1977) *Grunwick* (Penguin, Harmondsworth).

Rogers, Joel, and Wolfgang Streeck (eds) (1995) *Works Councils: Consultation, Representation, and Cooperation in Industrial Relations* (University of Chicago Press, Chicago).

Rogowski, Ralf (1994) Industrial Relations, Labour Conflict Resolution and Reflexive Labour Law, in *Reflexive Labour Law* eds Ralf Rogowski and Ton Wilthagen (Kluwer, Deventer-Boston).

Rogowski, Ralf and Ton Wilthagen (1994) Reflexive Labour Law An Introduction, in *Reflexive Labour Law* eds Ralf Rogowski and Ton Wilthagen (Kluwer, Deventer-Boston).

Rojot, Jacques (1994) France, in *Strikes and Lock-outs in Industrialised Market Economies*, ed Ruth Ben-Israel (Kluwer, Deventer-Boston).

Rojot, Jacques (2010) Security of Employment and Employability in *Comparative Labour Law and Industrial Relations in Industrialized Market Economies* 10th edn, ed Roger Blanpain (Wolters Kluwer, The Netherlands).

Rönnmar, Mia (2008) Free Movement of Services versus National Labour Law and Industrial Relations Systems: Understanding the Laval Case from a Nordic Perspective *Cambridge Yearbook of European Legal Studies*, 10: 493-523.

Rowbottom, David (2010) Justifying Service-Related Pay in the Context of Sex Discrimination Law *Industrial Law Journal* 39, 382-407.

Rowe, JJ (2001) The Terrorism Act 2000 *Criminal Law Review* 527- 542.

Rowe, Nicola and Volker Schlette (1998) The Protection of Human Rights in Europe after the Eleventh Protocol to the ECHR *European Law Review* 23 HR, 3-16.

Royle, Tony (1999) Where's the Beef? McDonald's and its European Works Council *European Journal of Industrial Relations* 5, 327-347.

Royston, Tom (2011) Agency Workers and Discrimination Law: *Muschett v HM Prison Service*, *Industrial Law Journal* 40, 92-102.

Rubery, Jill (1989) Precarious Forms of Work in the United Kingdom, in *Precarious Jobs in Labour Market Regulation* eds Gerry and Janine Rodgers (International Institute for Labour Studies, Geneva).

Rubery, Jill and Frank Wilkinson (1981) Outwork and Segmented Labour Markets, in *The Dynamics of Labour Market Segmentation* ed Frank Wilkinson (Academic Press, London).

Rubery, Jill, Simon Deakin and Sara Horrell (1994) United Kingdom, in *Times are Changing: Working Time in 14 Industrialised Countries* eds Gerhard Bosch, Peter Dawkins and Francois Michon (International Institute for Labour Studies, Geneva).

Rubery Jill, Roger Tarling and Frank Wilkinson (1987) Flexibility, Marketing and the Organisation of Production *Labour and Society* 12, 131-151.

Rubin, Gerry (1987) *War, Law and Labour* (Clarendon Press, Oxford).

Rubin, Gerry R (2000) The Historical Development of Collective Labour Law: The United Kingdom in *The Rise and Development of Collective Labour Law* ed Marcel van der Linden and Richard Price (Peter Lang, Bern).

Rubinstein, Michael (1988) *The Dignity of Women at Work* (Commmission of the European Communities, Brussels).

Rutherford, Ian and James Achur (2010) *Survey of Pay and Work Rights Helpline callers*. EMAR No 113 (BIS, London).

Ryan, Bernard (1997) Employer Enforcement of Immigration Law after Section Eight of the Asylum and Immigration Act *Industrial Law Journal*, 26, 136-148.

Ryan, Bernard (2008) The Accession (Immigration and Worker Authorisation) Regulations 2006 *Industrial Law Journal* 37, 75-88.

Sales, Philip (1990) Covenants Restricting Recruitment of Employees and the Doctrine of Restraint of Trade *Law Quarterly Review* 104, 600-616.

Sales, Philip (2006) *Pepper v Hart*: A Footnote to Professor Vogenauer's Reply to Lord Steyn *Oxford Journal of Legal Studies* 26, 585-592.

Sales, Philip and Daniel Stilitz (1999) Intentional Infliction of Harm by Unlawful Means *Law Quarterly Review* 115, 411-437.

Samuel, Lenia (1997) *Fundamental Social Rights: Case Law of the European Social Charter* (Council of Europe Publishing, Strasbourg).

Sandberg, Russell (2006) A Whitehall farce? Defining and conceptualising the British Civil Service *Public Law,* 653-663.

Sanders, Astrid (2009) Part One of the Employment Act 2008: 'Better' Dispute Resolution? *Industrial Law Journal* 38, 30-49.

Sargeant, Malcolm (1999) *Age Discrimination in Employment* (Institute of Employment Rights, London).

Sargeant, Malcolm (2003) Protecting Employees with Insolvent Employers *Industrial Law Journal* 32, 53-59.

Sargeant, Malcolm (2006) The Employment Equality (Age) Regulations 2006: A Legitimisation of Age Discrimination in Employment *Industrial Law Journal* 35, 209-227.

Saundry, Richard, Carol Jones and Valerie Antcliff (2011) Discipline, representation and dispute resolution – exploring the role of trade unions and employee companions in workplace discipline *Industrial Relations Journal* 42, 195-211.

Schiek, Dagmar (1996) Positive Action in Community Law *Industrial Law Journal* 25, 239-246.

Schiek, Dagmar (2000) Positive Action before the European Court of Justice – New Conceptions of Equality in Community Law? From *Kalanke* and *Marschall* to *Badeck, International Journal of Comparative Labour Law and Industrial Relations* 16, 251-275.

Schiek, Dagmar (2006) The ECJ Decision in *Mangold*: A Further Twist on Effects of Directives and Constitutional Relevance of Community Equality Legislation *Industrial Law Journal* 35, 329-341.

Schoer, Karl (1987) Part-time Employment: Britain and West Germany *Cambridge Journal of Economics* 11, 83-94.

Schumacher, Robert (1994) Business Transfers and Insolvency. Case-law of the German Federal Labour Court *Industrial Law Journal* 22, 101-107.

Sciarra, Silvana (2008) Viking and Laval: Collective Labour Rights and Market Freedoms in the Enlarged EU *Cambridge Yearbook of European Legal Studies* 10, 563-580.

Scrutton, TE (1923) The Work of the Commercial Courts *Cambridge Law Journal* 1, 6-20.

Sedley, Stephen (1994) Public Law and Contractual Employment *Industrial Law Journal* 23, 201-208.

Selznick, Philip (1980) *Law, Society and Industrial Justice* (Transaction Books, New Brunswick).

Sengenberger, Werner (1994) Labour Standards: an Institutional Framework for Restructuring and Development, in *Creating Economic Opportunities: The Role of Labour Standards in Industrial Restructuring* eds Werner Sengenberger and Duncan Campbell (International Institute for Labour Studies, Geneva).

Sewerynski, Michal (ed) (2003) *Collective Agreements and Individual Contracts of Employment* (Kluwer Law International, The Hague)

Seymour, Jillaine (2005) Who can be harassed? Claims against animal rights protesters under section 3 of the Protection from Harassment Ac 1997 *Cambridge Law Journal* 64, 57-65.

Seymour, Jillaine (2007) Injunctions Enjoining Non-Parties: Distinction Without Difference? *Cambridge Law Journal* 66, 605-624

Shaw, Jo (ed) (2000) *Social Law and Policy in an Evolving European Union* (Hart Publishing, Oxford).

Simester, AP and Winnie Chan (2004) Inducing Breach of Contract: One Tort or Two? *Cambridge Law Journal* 63, 132-165.

Simitis, Spiros (1987) Juridification of Labor Relations, in *Juridification of Social Spheres* ed Gunther Teubner (Walter de Gruyter, Berlin).

Simitis, Spiros (1991) Developments in the Protection of Workers' Personal Data *ILO Conditions of Work Digest* 10/2, 7-24.

Simitis, Spiros (1994) The Rediscovery of the Individual in Labour Law, in *Reflexive Labour Law* eds Ralf Rogowski and Ton Wilthagen (Kluwer, Deventer-Boston).

Simitis, Spiros (1998) From the General Rules on Data Protection to a Specific Regulation of the Use of Employee Data: Policies and Constraints of the European Union *Comparative Labor Law and Policy Journal* 19, 351-371.

Simms, Melanie and Andy Charlwood (2010) Trade Unions: Power and Influence in a Changed Context in *Industrial Relations: Theory and Practice* 3rd edn ed Trevor Colling and Michael Terry (Wiley, Chichester).

Simon, Daphne (1954) Master and Servant, in *Democracy and the Labour Movement* ed J Saville (Lawrence and Wishart, London).

Simpson, Bob (1979) Judicial Review of ACAS *Industrial Law Journal* 8, 420-426.

Simpson, Bob (1987) The Labour Injunction, Unlawful Means and the Right to Strike *Modern Law Review* 50, 506-516.

Simpson, Bob (1989) The Summer of Discontent and the Law *Industrial Law Journal* 18, 234-241.

Simpson, Bob (1990) Code of Practice on Trade Union Ballots on Industrial Action *Industrial Law Journal* 19, 29-32.

Simpson, Bob (1991) *Trade Union Recognition and the Law* (Institute of Employment Rights, London).

Simpson, Bob (1993) Individualism versus Collectivism: an Evaluation of Section 14 of the Trade Union Reform and Employment Rights Act 1993 *Industrial Law Journal* 22, 181-193.

Simpson, Bob (1994) Bridlington '2' *Industrial Law Journal* 23, 170-174.

Simpson, Bob (1995) Code of Practice on Industrial Action Ballots and Notice to Employers *Industrial Law Journal* 24, 337-342.

Simpson, Bob (1999a) A Milestone in the Legal Regulation of Pay: The National Minimum Wage Act 1998 *Industrial Law Journal* 28, 1-32.

Simpson, Bob (1999b) Implementing the National Minimum Wage – The 1999 Regulations *Industrial Law Journal* 28, 171-182.

Simpson, Bob (2000) Trade Union Recognition and the Law, a New Approach – Parts I and II of Schedule A1 to the Trade Union and Labour Relations (Consolidation) Act 1992, *Industrial Law Journal* 29, 193-222.

Simpson, Bob (2001) Code of Practice on Industrial Action Ballots and Notice to Employers 2000 *Industrial Law Journal* 30, 194-198.

Simpson, Bob (2004) The National Minimum Wage Five Years On: Reflections on Some General Issues *Industrial Law Journal* 33, 22-41.

Simpson, Bob (2005) Strike Ballots and the Law: Round Six *Industrial Law Journal* 34, 331-337.

Simpson, Bob (2007a) Judicial Control of the CAC *Industrial Law Journal* 36, 287-314.

Simpson, Bob (2007b) Economic Tort Liability in Labour Disputes: The Potential Impact of the House of Lords' Decision in *OBG* v *Allen Industrial Law Journal* 36, 468-479.

Simpson, Bob (2009) The Employment Act 2008's Amendments to the National Minimum Wage Legislation *Industrial Law Journal* 38, 57-64.

Sims, Vanessa (2001) Is Employment a Fiduciary Relationship? *Industrial Law Journal* 30, 101-110.

Singh, Rabinder, Murray Hunt and Marie Demetriou (1999) Is there a Role for the "Margin of Appreciation" in National Law after the Human Rights Act? *European Human Rights Law Review*, 15-22.

Sinzheimer, Hugo (1910-11) Die Fortentwicklung des Arbeitsrechts und die Aufgabe der Rechtslehre *Soziale Praxis* 20, 1237.

Sisson, Keith and John Taylor (2006) The Advisory, Conciliation and Arbitration Service in *The Changing Institutional Face of British Employment Relations* ed Linda Dickens and Alan C Neal (Kluwer Law International, The Netherlands).

Skidmore, Paul (1995a) No Gays in the Military – Lawrence of Arabia Need Not Apply *Industrial Law Journal* 24, 363-368.

Skidmore, Paul (1995b) Enforcement of Rights to Worker Representation in Community Law *Modern Law Review* 58, 744-751.

Skidmore, Paul (1996a) Homosexuals have Human Rights Too *Industrial Law Journal* 25, 63-65.

Skidmore, Paul (1996b) Worker Rights – A Euro-litigation Strategy? *Industrial Law Journal* 25, 225-230.

Skidmore, Paul (1999) Dress to Impress: Employer Regulation of Gay and Lesbian Appearance *Social and Legal Studies* 8, 509-29.

Skidmore, Paul (2001) EC Framework Directive on Equal Treatment in Employment: Toward a Comprehensive Community Anti-Discrimination Policy? *Industrial Law Journal* 30, 126-32.

Sly, Frances and Darren Stillwell (1997) Temporary Workers in Great Britain *Labour Market Trends* September, 347-354.

Smith, Adam [1776] (1886) *An Inquiry into the Nature and Causes of the Wealth of Nations* With an Introductory Essay and Notes by Joseph S Nicholson (Nelson, London).

Smith, ATH (1987) *The Offences against Public Order* (Sweet and Maxwell, London).

Smith, Graham (1989) Part Work, No Pay? The Obligation to Pay Wages for Part Performance of Contracts of Employment *Australian Journal of Labour Law* 2, 91-106.

Smith, Ian (2006) Employee Involvement in the European Cooperative Society: A Range of Stakeholders? *International Journal of Comparative Labour Law and Industrial Relations* 22, 213-230.

Smith, Ian and Aaron Baker (2010) *Smith and Wood's Employment Law*, 10th edn (Oxford University Press, Oxford).

Smith, J, P Edwards and M Hall (1999) *Redundancy Consultation: A Study of Current Practice and the Effects of the 1999 Regulations* (DTI, Employment Relations Research Series No 5, London).

Smith, Paul and Gary Morton (2001) New Labour's Reform of Britain's Employment Law: The Devil's Not Only in the Detail but in the Values and Policy Too *British Journal of Industrial Relations* 39, 119-138.

Smith, Paul and Gary Morton (2006) Nine Years of New Labour: Neoliberalism and Workers' Rights *British Journal of Industrial Relations* 44, 401-420.

Smith, Paul, Patricia Fosh, Roderick Martin, Huw Morris and Roger Undy (1993) Ballots and Union Government in the 1980s *British Journal of Industrial Relations* 31, 365-382.

Smith, Raymond, and Valerie Cromack (1993) International Employment Contracts – the Applicable Law *Industrial Law Journal* 22, 1-13.

Smith, Stephen (1986) *Britain's Shadow Economy* (Clarendon Press, Oxford).

Solanke, Iyiola (2011) Infusing the Silos in the Equality Act with Synergy *Industrial Law Journal* 40, 336-358.

Sooben, Philip A (1990) *The Origins of the Race Relations Act 1976* Research Papers in Ethnic Relations No 12 (Centre for Research in Ethnic Studies, University of Warwick).

Spaak (1956) *Rapport des chefs de délégation aux ministres des affaires étrangères* (Comité Intergouvernmental créé par la Conférence de Messine, Brussels).

Spain, Jonathan (1991) Trade Unionists, Gladstonian Liberals, and the Labour Law Reforms of 1875, in *Currents of Radicalism Popular Radicalism, Organised Labour and Party Politics in Britain 1850-1914* eds Eugenio F Biagini and Alistair J Reid (CUP, Cambridge).

Spencer, John (1973) Signature, Consent and the Rule in *L'Estrange v Graucob, Cambridge Law Journal* 32, 104-122.

Spencer, JR (1989) Public Nuisance – A Critical Examination *Cambridge Law Journal* 48, 55-84.

Spry, ICF (2010) *The Principles of Equitable Remedies* 8th edn (Sweet and Maxwell, London).

Stacey, Mary, and Andrew Short (2000) *Challenging Disability Discrimination at Work* (Institute of Employment Rights, London)

Stanton, Keith, Paul Skidmore and Michael Harris (2002) *Statutory Torts* (Sweet and Maxwell, London).

Stanworth, J and Stanworth, C (1989) Hometruths about Teleworking *Personnel Management*, November.

Steele, Iain (2005) Tracing the Single Source: Choice of Comparators in Equal Pay Claims *Industrial Law Journal* 34, 338-344

Steinfeld, Robert (2001) *Coercion, Contract and Free Labor in the Nineteenth Century* (CUP, Cambridge).

Stewart, Margaret (1969) *Britain and the ILO: The Story of Fifty Years* (HMSO, London).

Stone, Katherine VW (2007) Revisiting the At-Will Employment Doctrine: Imposed Terms, Implied Terms and the Normative World of the Workplace *Industrial Law Journal* 36, 84-101.

Streeck, Wolfgang (1988) Comment on 'Rigidities in the Labour Market' *Government and Opposition* 23, 413-23.

Streeck, Wolfgang (1992) *Social Institutions and Economic Performance: Studies of Industrial Relations in Advanced Capitalist Economies* (Sage, London).

Streeck, Wolfgang (1995) Neo-Voluntarism: A New European Social Policy Régime *European Law Journal* 1, 31-59.

Street, Harry, Geoffrey Howe and Geoffrey Bindman (1967) *Report on Anti-Discrimination Legislation* (Political and Economic Planning, London).

Streit, Manfred, and Werner Mussler (1995) The Economic Constitution of the European Community: From 'Rome' to 'Maastricht' *European Law Journal* 1, 5-30.

Stuart, Mark and Miguel Martinez-Lucio (eds) (2005) *Partnership and Modernisation in Employment Relations* (Routledge, London).

Stuart, Mark, Andy Charlwood, Miguel Martinez Lucio and Emma Wallis (2006) *Union Modernisation Fund: Interim Evaluation of First Round* ((Employment Relations Research Series No 68, BERR (formerly DTI) London).

Stuart, Mark, Miguel Martinez Lucio and Andy Charlwood (2009) *Union Modernisation Fund: Round One: Final Evaluation Report* (BIS Employment Relations Research Series No 104)

Stuart, Mark, Miguel Martinez Lucio, Jennifer Tomlinson and Robert Perrett (2010) *Union Modernisation Fund: Round Two: Final Evaluation Report* (BIS Employment Relations Research Series No 111).

Summers, Clyde (1969) Collective Agreements and the Law of Contracts *Yale Law Journal* 90, 537-575.

Supiot, Alain (1994) *Critique du Droit du Travail* (PUF, Paris).

Supiot, Alain (ed) (1999) *Au-delà de l'emploi: Transformations du travail et l'avenir du droit du travail en Europe. Rapport pour la Commission Europeénne* (Flammarion, Paris).

Supiot, Alain (2001) The Dogmatic Foundations of the Market *Industrial Law Journal* 29, 321-345.

Supiot, Alain (2005) *Homo juridicus: Essai sur la fonction anthropologique du droit* (Seuil, Paris).

Supperstone, Michael (1997) The Ambit of Judicial Review, in *Judicial Review* ed Michael Supperstone and James Goudie, 2nd edn (Butterworths, London).

Sweeney, Kate (1997) Labour disputes in 1996 *Labour Market Trends* June, 217-229.

Sweet and Maxwell's Encyclopaedia of Employment Law, 1992, as updated (Sweet and Maxwell, London).

Swepston, Lee (1997) Supervision of ILO Standards *International Journal of Comparative Labour Law and Industrial Relations* 13, 327-344.

Swepston, L (2007) International Labour Law in *Comparative Labour Law and Industrial Relations in Industrialized Market Economies* 9th edn, ed Roger Blanpain (Wolters Kluwer, The Netherlands).

Swepston, L (2010) International Labour Law in *Comparative Labour Law and Industrial Relations in Industrialized Market Economies* 10th edn, ed Roger Blanpain (Wolters Kluwer, The Netherlands).

Swift, Jonathan (2006) Justifying Age Discrimination *Industrial Law Journal* 35, 228-244.

Sypris, Phil (2007) *European Union Intervention in Domestic Labour Law* (Oxford University Press, Oxford).

Syrpis, Phil (2008) The Treaty of Lisbon: Much Ado ... But About What? *Industrial Law Journal* 37, 219-235.

Syrpis, Phil (2011) Reconciling Economic Freedoms and Social Rights - The Potential of *Commission v Germany* (Case C-271/08, Judgment of 15 July 2010) *Industrial Law Journal* 40, 222-229.

Syrpis, Phil and Tonia Novitz (2008) Economic and social rights in conflict: political and judicial approaches to their reconciliation *European Law Review* 33, 411-426

Szyszczak, Erika (1985) Pay Inequalities and Equal Value Claims *Modern Law Review* 48, 139-157.

Szyszczak, Erika (1986) Employment Protection and Social Security, in *Labour Law in Britain* (Basil Blackwell, Oxford).

Szyszczak, Erika (1990) *Partial Unemployment The Regulation of Short-Time Working in Britain* (Mansell, London).

Szyszczak, Erika (1999) The Working Environment v. Internal Market *European Law Review* 24, 196-201.

Szyszczak, Erika (2000a) *EC Labour Law* (Longman, Harlow).

Szyszczak, Erika (2000b) The Evolving European Employment Strategy, in *Social Law and Policy in an Evolving European Union* ed Jo Shaw (Oxford, Hart).

Tarling, Roger, and Frank Wilkinson (1977) The Social Contract: Post-war Incomes Policies and their Inflationary Impact *Cambridge Journal of Economics* 1, 395-414.

Tarling, Roger, and Frank Wilkinson (1982) The Movement of Real Wages and the Development of Collective Bargaining in the UK: 1855-1920 *Contributions to Political Economy* 1, 1-35.

Taylor, Robert (1994) *The Future of the Trade Unions* (Andre Deutsch, London).

Taylor, Robert (2000) *The TUC: From the General Strike to New Unionism* (Palgrave, Basingstoke).

Taylor, Robert (no date given) *Britain's World of Work – Myths and Realities* (ESRC, Swindon).

Taylor, Robert (2004) *Partnerships at Work: The Way to Corporate Renewal?* (ESRC, Swindon).

Terry, Michael (1994) Workplace Unionism: Redefining Structures and Objectives, in *New Frontiers in European Industrial Relations*, eds Richard Hyman and Anthony Ferner (Blackwell, Oxford).

Terry, Michael (2010) Employee Representation in *Industrial Relations: Theory and Practice* 3rd edn ed Trevor Colling and Michael Terry (Wiley, Chichester).

Tether, Melanie (1995) Sex Equality and Occupational Pension Schemes *Industrial Law Journal* 24, 194-203.

Thomas, Melanie (2000) Equal Pay and Redundancy Schemes *Industrial Law Journal* 29, 68-72.

Thurman, J and G Trah (1990) Part-time Work in International Perspective *International Labour Review* 129, 23-40.

Tierney, Stephen (1998) Press Freedom and Public Interest *European Human Rights Law Review*, 419-429.

Tillyard, FW (1928) *Industrial Law* 2nd edn (A & C Black, London).

Tiraboschi, Michele (1999) Glancing at the Past: An Agreement for the Markets of the XXIst Century *International Journal of Comparative Labour Law and Industrial Relations* 15, 105-119.

TNS (2008) *Service User Perceptions of ACAS' Conciliation in Employment Tribunal Cases 2007* (ACAS, London).

Todd, Paul (2000) Action Short of Dismissal, in *Legal Regulation of the Employment Relation* eds Hugh Collins, Paul Davies and Roger Rideout (Kluwer, London).

Tolley (2012) *Tolley's Health and Safety at Work Handbook* 24th. ed. (Tolley, London).

Tomlins, Christopher L (1993) *Law, Labour and Ideology in the Early American Republic* (CUP, Cambridge).

Toulson, RG and CM Phipps (2006) *Confidentiality* 2nd edn (Sweet and Maxwell, London).

Towers, Brian (1997) *The Representation Gap: Change and Reform in the British and American Workplace* (Oxford University Press, Oxford).

Towers, Brian (1999) *Developing Recognition and Representation in the UK: How Useful is the US Model?* (Institute of Employment Rights, London).

Towers, Brian and William Brown (2000) *Employment Relations in Britain: 25 Years of the Advisory, Conciliation and Arbitration Service* (Blackwell, Oxford).

Townley, Barbara (1987) Union Recognition: A Comparative Analysis of the Pros and Cons of a Legal Procedure *British Journal of Industrial Relations* 25, 177-199.

Townshend-Smith, Richard (1991) Refusal of Employment on Grounds of Trade Union Membership or Non-Membership: The Employment Act 1990 *Industrial Law Journal*, 20, 102-112.

Townshend-Smith, Richard (2000) Seymour-Smith: the Closing Stages *Industrial Law Journal* 29, 296-304.

Trades Union Congress (1993) *TUC Disputes: Principles and Procedures* (TUC, London).

Trades Union Congress (1995) *Your Voice at Work* (TUC, London).

Trebilcock, Anne (2010) Putting the record straight about International Labor Standard Setting *Comparative Labor Law and Policy Journal* 31, 553-570.

Tsogas, George (2000) Labour Standards in the Generalised Systems of Preferences of the European Union & the United States *European Journal of Industrial Relations* 6, 349-370.

Turnbull, Peter (1991) Labour Market Deregulation and Economic Performance: the Case of Britain's Docks *Work, Employment and Society* 5, 17-35.

Turner, Adair (2001) *Just Capital* (Macmillan, London).

Turner, HA (1962) *Trade Union Growth, Structure and Policy* (Allen and Unwin, London).

Undy, Roger (1999) The British Merger Movement: the Importance of the "Aggressive" Unions *Industrial Relations Journal* 30, 464-481.

Undy, Roger and Roderick Martin (1984) *Ballots and Trade Union Democracy* (Basil Blackwell, Oxford).

Undy, Roger, Patricia Fosh, Huw Morris, Paul Smith and Roderick Martin (1996) *Managing the Unions: The Impact of Legislation on Trade Unions' Behaviour* (Clarendon Press, Oxford).

Upex, Robert (1999) The Acquired Rights Directive and its Effect Upon Consensual Variation of Employees Contracts *European Law Review* 24, 293-299.

Upex, Robert (2001) *The Law of Termination of Employment* 6th edn (Sweet and Maxwell, London).

Valticos, Nicolas and Geraldo von Potobsky (1995) *International Labour Law* (Kluwer, Deventer-Boston).

Van Dijk, Pieter and GJH Van Hoof (1998) *Theory and Practice of the European Convention on Human Rights*, 3rd edn (Kluwer, The Hague).

Vickers, Lucy (1995) *Protecting Whistleblowers at Work* (Institute of Employment Rights, London).

Vickers, Lucy (2002) *Freedom of Speech and Employment* (OUP, Oxford).

Vickers, Lucy (2003) The Employment Equality (Religion or Belief) Regulations 2003 *Industrial Law Journal* 32, 188-193.

Vickers, Lucy (2008) *Religious Freedom, Religious Discrimination and the Wokplace* (Hart Publishing, Oxford).

Villiers, Charlotte (2000) The Rover Case (1) – The Sale of Rover Cars by BMW – The Role of the Works Council *Industrial Law Journal* 29, 386-394.

Villiers, Charlotte (2006) The Directive on Employee Involvement in the European Company: Its Role in European Corporate Governance and Industrial Relations *International Journal of Comparative Labour Law and Industrial Relations* 22, 183-211.

Vogel-Polsky, Eliane (1986) The Problem of Unemployment, in *The Making of Labour Law in Europe* ed BA Hepple (Mansell, London).

Vogel-Polsky, Eliane (1990) What Future is there for a Social Europe following the Strasbourg Summit? *Industrial Law Journal* 19, 65-80.

Vogenauer, Stefan (2005) A Retreat from *Pepper v Hart*? A Reply to Lord Steyn *Oxford Journal of Legal Studies* 25, 629-674.

Von Prondzynski, Ferdinand (1987) *Freedom of Association and Industrial Relations: A Comparative Study* (Mansell, London).

Vousden, Stephen (2000) *Albany*, Market Law and Social Exclusion *Industrial Law Journal* 29, 181-191.

Waddington, Jeremy (2003a) Heightening Tension in Relations between Trade Unions and the Labour Government in 2002 *British Journal of Industrial Relations* 41, 335-358.

Waddington, Jeremy (2003b) Trade Union Organization, in *Industrial Relations: Theory and Practice* 2nd edn ed Paul Edwards (Blackwell Publishing, Oxford).

Waddington, Jeremy (2003c) What do Representatives Think of the Practices of European Works Councils? Views from Six Countries *European Journal of Industrial Relations* 9, 303-325.

Waddington, Jeremy (2006) The trade union merger process in Europe: defensive adjustment or strategic reform? *Industrial Relations Journal* 37, 630-651.

Waddington, Jeremy (2011) European Works Councils: the challenge for labour *Industrial Relations Journal* 42, 508-529.

Waddington, Jeremy and Colin Whitson (1995) Trade Unions: Growth, Structure and Policy in *Industrial Relations: Theory and Practice in Britain*, ed. Paul Edwards (Blackwell Business, Oxford).

Waddington, Lisa (1999) Testing the Limits of the EC Treaty Article on Non-Discrimination *Industrial Law Journal* 28, 133-151.

Waddington, Lisa (2000) Article 13 EC: Setting Priorities in the Proposal for a Horizontal Employment Directive *Industrial Law Journal* 29, 176-181.

Wade, HWR (1993) Visitors and Errors of Law *Law Quarterly Review* 109, 155-159.

Wade, HWR (2000) Horizons of Horizontality *Law Quarterly Review* 116, 217-224.

Wade, HWR, and Christopher Forsyth (2009) *Administrative Law* 10th edn (Clarendon Press, Oxford).

Waite, Sir John (1986) Lawyers and Laymen as Judges in Industry *Industrial Law Journal* 15, 32-41.

Walsh, Janet and William Brown (1990) *Regional Earnings and Pay Flexibility* Department of Applied Economics Working Paper 9008 (University of Cambridge).

Walters, David R (1990) *Worker Participation in Health and Safety: A European Comparison* (Institute of Employment Rights, London).

Wareing, M (1992) Working Arrangements and Patterns of Working Hours in Britain *Employment Gazette* 100, 88-100.

Watson, Loraine (1995) Employees and the Unfair Contract Terms Act *Industrial Law Journal* 24, 323-336.

Watt, Robert A (1992) HIV, Discrimination, Unfair Dismissal and Pressure to Dismiss *Industrial Law Journal* 23, 280-292.

Watt, Robert A (1998) Goodbye 'But-for', Hello 'But-Why?' *Industrial Law Journal* 27, 121-132.

Weatherill, Stephen (2001) Breach of Directives and Breach of Contract *European Law Review* 26, 177-186.

Webb, Sidney and Beatrice Webb (1920) *The History of Trade Unionism* New edition (Longmans, Green and Co, London).

Webb, Sidney and Beatrice Webb [1898] (1920) *Industrial Democracy* (Longmans, Green and Co, London).

Weber, Tina, Peter Foster, and Kursat Levent Egriboz (2000) *Costs and Benefits of the European Works Councils Directive* (DTI Employment Relations Research Series No 9, London).

Wedderburn, Lord (1980) Industrial Relations and the Courts *Industrial Law Journal* 9, 65-94.

Wedderburn, Lord (1983) Otto Kahn-Freund and British Labour Law, in *Labour Law and Industrial Relations: Building on Kahn-Freund* eds Lord Wedderburn, Roy Lewis and Jonathan Clark (Basil Blackwell, Oxford).

Wedderburn, Lord (1984) Labour Law Now – a Hold and a Nudge *Industrial Law Journal* 13, 73-85.

Wedderburn, Lord (1985) The New Politics of Labour Law, in *Trade Unions* 2nd edn, ed WEJ McCarthy (Penguin, Harmondsworth).

Wedderburn, Lord (1986) *The Worker and the Law* 3rd edn (Penguin, Harmondsworth).

Wedderburn, Lord (1987a) Labour Law: From Here to Autonomy? *Industrial Law Journal* 16, 1-29.

Wedderburn, Lord (1987b) Freedom of Association or Right to Organise? *Industrial Relations Journal* 18, 244-254.

Wedderburn, Lord (1989) Freedom of Association and Philosophies of Labour Law *Industrial Law Journal* 18, 1-38.

Wedderburn, Lord (1990) *The Social Charter, European Company and employment rights: An outline agenda* (Institute of Employment Rights, London).

Wedderburn, Lord (1991a) The Social Charter in Britain – Labour Law and Labour Courts *Modern Law Review* 54, 1-47.

Wedderburn, Lord (1991b) *Employment Rights in Britain and Europe: Selected Papers in Labour Law* (Lawrence and Wishart, London).

Wedderburn, Lord (1992a) European Community Law and Workers' Rights after 1992: Fact or Fake? *Dublin University Law Journal* 13, 1-25.

Wedderburn, Lord (1992b) Contempt of Court: Vicarious Liability of Companies and Unions *Industrial Law Journal* 21, 51-58.

Wedderburn, Lord (1992c) Inderogability, Collective Agreements, and Community Law *Industrial Law Journal* 21, 245-264.

Wedderburn, Lord (1993) Companies and Employees: Common Law or Social Dimension? *Law Quarterly Review* 109, 220-262.

Wedderburn Lord (1995) *Labour Law and Freedom: Further Essays in Labour Law*, (Lawrence and Wishart, London).

Wedderburn, Lord (1997) Consultation and Collective Bargaining in Europe: Success or Ideology? *Industrial Law Journal* 26, 1-34.

Wedderburn, Lord (2000) Collective Bargaining or Legal Enactment? The 1999 Act and Union Recognition *Industrial Law Journal* 29, 1-42

Wedderburn, Lord (2001) Underground Labour Injunctions *Industrial Law Journal* 30, 206-214.

Wedderburn, Lord (2004) *The Future of Company Law: Fat Cats, Corporate Governance and Workers* (Institute of Employment Rights, London)

Wedderburn, Lord (2007) Labour Law 2008: 40 Years On *Industrial Law Journal* 36, 397-424.

Wedderburn, KW (Lord) and PL Davies (1969) *Employment Grievances and Disputes Procedures in Britain* (University of California Press, Berkeley and Los Angeles).

Wedderburn, Lord, and Silvana Sciarra (1988) Collective Bargaining as Agreement and as Law: Neo-Contractualist and Neo-Corporative Tendencies of our Age, in *Law in the Making* ed A Pizzorusso (Springer, Berlin).

Weekes, Brian, Michael Mellish, Linda Dickens and John Lloyd (1975) *Industrial Relations and the Limits of Law; The Industrial Effects of the Industrial Relations Act 1971* (Blackwell, Oxford).

Weiler, Paul (1983) Promises to Keep: Securing Workers' Rights to Self-Organization under the NLRA *Harvard Law Review* 96, 1769-1827.

Weir, Tony (1991) Physician – Kill Thyself! *Cambridge Law Journal* 50, 397-399.

Weir, Tony (1997) *Economic Torts* (Clarendon Press, Oxford).

Weiss, Manfred (1992) *European Employment and Industrial Relations Glossary – Germany* European Foundation for the Improvement of Living and Working Conditions (Sweet & Maxwell, London/OOPEC, Luxembourg).

Weiss, Manfred (1994) Germany, in *Strikes and Lock-outs in Industrialised Market Economies* ed R Ben Israel (Kluwer, Deventer-Boston).

Weiss, Manfred (2004) The Future of Workers' Participation in the EU, in *The Future of Labour Law: Liber Amicorum Sir Bob Hepple QC* ed Catherine Barnard, Simon Deakin and Gillian S Morris (Hart Publishing, Oxford).

Weitzman, Martin (1983) *The Share Economy. Conquering Stagflation* (Harvard University Press, Cambridge MA).

Welch, Roger (2006) *The Information and Consultation Regulations - Whither Statutory Works Councils?* (Institute of Employment Rights, London).

Wheeler, Sally (1997) Works Council: Towards Stakeholding? *Journal of Law and Society* 24, 44-64.

Whelan, Christopher J (1982) On Uses and Misuses of Comparative Labour Law: A Case Study *Modern Law Review* 45, 285-300.

White, M and J Lakey (1992) *The Restart Effect: Does Active Labour Market Policy Reduce Unemployment?* (Policy Studies Institute, London).

White, Richard (1997) Repudiatory Breach and the Definition of Dismissal *Industrial Law Journal* 26, 252-258.

White, Richard (1998) Waiver of Statutory Rights in Fixed Term Contracts *Industrial Law Journal*, 27, 238-244.

White, Richard (2008) Working Under Protest and Variation of Employment Terms *Industrial Law Journal* 37, 365-370.

White, Stuart (1999) Rights and Responsibilities: A Social Democratic Perspective, *Political Quarterly* 70, 166-186.

Whiteford, Elaine (1993) Social Policy after Maastricht *European Law Review*, 202-222.

Wikeley, NJ (1989a) Migrant Workers and Unemployment Benefit in the European Community *Journal of Social Welfare Law*, 300-315.

Wikeley, NJ (1989b) Unemployment Benefit, the State and the Labour Market *Journal of Law and Society* 16, 291-309.

Wikeley, NJ (1990) Training for Employment in the 1990s *Modern Law Review* 53, 354-368.

Wikeley, NJ (2002) *Wikeley, Ogus and Barendt's The Law of Social Security* 5th edn (Butterworths, London).

Wilkinson, Brian (1991) The Irish Industrial Relations Act 1990 – Corporatism and Conflict Control *Industrial Law Journal* 20, 21-37.

Wilkinson, Frank (1987) Deregulation, Structured Labour Markets and Unemployment, in *Unemployment: Theory, Policy and Structure* eds P Pedersen and R Lund (Walter de Gruyter, Berlin).

Wilkinson, Frank (1991) *Why Britain Needs a Minimum Wage* (Institute of Public Policy Research, London).

Wilkinson, Frank (1995) Changing Notions of Unemployment and what they Mean for the Poor. Paper presented to the Annual Conference of the International Working Party on Labour Market Segmentation, University of Siena.

Williams, David W (1982) *Social Security Taxation* (Sweet and Maxwell, London).

Williams, Glanville (1941) Partial Performance of Entire Contracts *Law Quarterly Review*, 57, 373-389, 490-511.

Williams, Glanville (1960) The Effect of Penal Legislation in the Law of Tort *Modern Law Review*, 23, 233-259.

Williams, Kevin (1983) Unfair Dismissal: Myths and Statistics *Industrial Law Journal* 12, 157-165.

Williams, Kevin and David Lewis (1981) The Aftermath of Tribunal Reinstatement and Re-engagement, Department of Employment Research Paper No 23.

Willman, Paul, Tim Morris, and Beverly Aston (1993) *Union Business* (Cambridge University Press, Cambridge).

Wintemute, Robert (1997a) Recognising New Kinds of Direct Sex Discrimination: Transsexualism, Sexual Orientation and Dress Codes *Modern Law Review* 60, 334-359.

Wintemute, Robert (1997b) *Sexual Orientation and Human Rights: the United States Constitution, the European Convention and the Canadian Charter* (Clarendon Press, Oxford).

Wintemute, Robert (1998) When is Pregnancy Discrimination Indirect Discrimination? *Industrial Law Journal* 27, 23-36.

Wood, Penny (1978) The Central Arbitration Committee's Approach to Schedule 11 to the Employment Protection Act 1975 and the Fair Wages Resolution 1946 *Industrial Law Journal* 7, 65-83.

Wood, Penny, Richard Poynter, Nick Wikeley, and David Bonner (2011): *Social Security Legislation 2011/12 Vol II: Income Support, Jobseeker's Allowance, State Pension Credit and the Social Fund* (Sweet and Maxwell, London).

Wood, Sir John (1990) The Employment Appeal Tribunal as it Enters the 1990s *Industrial Law Journal* 19, 133-141.

Wood, Sir John (1992) Dispute Resolution – Conciliation, Mediation and Arbitration in *Legal Intervention in Industrial Relations: Gains and Losses*, ed William McCarthy (Blackwell, Oxford).

Wood, Stephen and John Godard (1999) The Statutory Union Recognition Procedure in the Employment Relations Bill: A Comparative Analysis *British Journal of Industrial Relations* 37, 203-244.

Wood, Stephen, Sian Moore and Keith Ewing (2003) The impact of the trade union recognition procedure under the Employment Relations Act, 2000-2 in *Representing Workers: Trade Union Recognition and Membership in Britain* ed Howard Gospel and Stephen Wood (Routledge, London).

Wood, Stephen, Sian Moore and Paul Willman (2002) Third Time Lucky for Statutory Union Recognition in the UK? *Industrial Relations Journal* 33, 215-233.

Woods, DC (1982) The Operation of the Master and Servant Acts in the Black Country *Midland History* 7, 93-115.

Woolf, The Rt Hon Lord Justice (1986) Public Law – Private Law: Why the Divide? A Personal View *Public Law*, 220-238.

Woolf, The Rt Hon Lord Woolf of Barnes (1995) Droit Public – English Style *Public Law*, 57-71.

Woolf, Harry, Jeffrey Jowell, Andrew Le Sueur and Catherine M Donnelly (2009) *De Smith's Judicial Review: Mainwork and Supplement* 6th edn (Sweet and Maxwell, London).

Wright, Martyn (1996) The Collapse of Compulsory Unionism? Collective Organisation in Highly Unionised British Companies 1979-1991 *British Journal of Industrial Relations* 34, 497-513.

Wynn, Michael (1999) Pregnancy Discrimination: Equality, Protection or Reconciliation? *Modern Law Review* 62, 435-447.

Wynn, Michael 2009: Regulating Rogues? Employment Agency Enforcement and Sections 15-18 of the Employment Act 2008 *Industrial Law Journal* 38, 64-72.

Wynn, Michael and Patricia Leighton (2006) Will the Real Employer Please Stand Up? Agencies, Client Companies and the Employment Status of the Temporary Agency Worker *Industrial Law Journal* 35, 301-320.

Wynn, Michael and Gwyneth Pitt (2010) The Revised Acas Code of Practice 2010 on Time Off for Trade Union Duties and Activities: Another Missed Opportunity? *Industrial Law Journal* 39, 209-217.

Wynn-Evans, Charles (2005) Self Incrimination in English Employment Law *Industrial Law Journal* 178-182.

Wynn-Evans, Charles (2006) *Blackstone's Guide to the New Transfer of Undertakings Legislation* (Oxford University Press, Oxford).

Wynn-Evans, Charles (2008) Service Provision Fragmentation and the Limits of TUPE Protection *Industrial Law Journal* 37, 371-376.

Wynn-Evans, Charles (2009) Age Discrimination and Redundancy *Industrial Law Journal* 38, 113-121.

Young, Thom (1976) *Incitement to Disaffection* (The Cobden Trust, London).

Younson, F (1989) *Employment Law and Business Transfers A Practical Guide* (Sweet and Maxwell, London).

Zabalza, A and Z Tzannatos (1985) Women and Equal Pay. The effects of legislation on female employment and wages in Britain (CUP, Cambridge).

Zappala, Loredana (2006) Abuse of Fixed-Term Employment Contracts and sanctions in the recent ECJ's Jurisprudence *Industrial Law Journal* 35, 439-444.

INDEX